CHASERS &
HURDLERS
2006/07

Price £70.00

A TIMEFORM PUBLICATION

A Timeform Publication

Compiled and produced by

G. Greetham (Director), P. A. Muncaster, P. E. Turner (Editors), M. S. Rigg, M. J. Taylor (Handicappers), J. Ingles (Essays & Editor for pedigrees and 'Top Horses In France'), H. W. J. Bowles, D. P. Cleary, E. K. Wilkinson (Essays), G. L. Taylor (Short Commentaries), S. T. Heath (additional essays), G. Crowther, G. Johnstone (proof checking), H. Brewer, M. Hall, D. Holdsworth, W. Muncaster, A-M. Stevens and R. Todd (Production).

© **Portway Press Limited 2007**

ISBN 978 1 901570 66 3

CONTENTS

The age, weight and distance table, for use in applying the ratings in races involving horses of different ages, appears on the end paper at the front of the book

Kauto Star became the first winner of the Betfair Million, earning connections a £1m bonus for winning the Betfair Chase (registered as the Lancashire Chase) at Haydock (top left), the Stan James King George VI Chase (top right) and the totesport Cheltenham Gold Cup (bottom picture, with Exotic Dancer right). Kauto Star ended the season with a Timeform rating of 184+, the joint highest (with Moscow Flyer) achieved by a jumper since Desert Orchid who died peacefully at the age of twenty-seven in the latest season

Chasers & Hurdlers 2006/07

Introduction

Thankfully, jumping looks healthy enough to fend off the immediate threat posed by another extension of all-weather Flat racing over the next winter. The new Gambling Act allows longer opening hours for betting shops from September. An extra raft of floodlit meetings, running to the middle of April, will focus more attention on the Flat. Introduced mainly to cover for jumping abandonments and to maintain an even flow of fixtures for betting, all-weather Flat racing is firmly established and now accounts for over a third of all fixtures on the Flat. The emergence of the Dubai Carnival as a winter attraction has led the Flat Race Committee to look at ways of lifting the quality of Britain's winter all-weather programme. The success of the polytrack surface has also encouraged more leading Flat trainers to become involved, and the introduction of six new listed races for the winter programme indicates that the days when the all-weather could be dismissed as a bottom-of-the-heap 'irritant', rather than a competitor to jumping, may soon be consigned to history.

There is no room for complacency. All-weather races have forty-eight-hour declarations, as do all Flat fixtures in Britain, which gives the Flat a big advantage over jumping which still has twenty-four-hour declarations except for its Grade 1 non-novice events and Grade 3 handicaps. The sooner the system is universally adopted the better. With racing's share of the domestic betting market in decline and little prospect of additional revenue from global exposure (unlike the Flat), jumping can't afford to miss the chance to promote itself to full effect. The prosperity of jumping is now directly linked to the prosperity of the betting industry (levy payments based on bookmakers' gross profits on racing provide two thirds of the prize money), and forty-eight-hour declarations have the potential to play an important role in stimulating betting turnover through better promotion of the sport. The current final declarations for jumps meetings are published too late for the deadline for most evening newspapers which show forty-eight-hour runners in full for the all-weather meetings. Although the majority of trainers are opposed to forty-eight-hour declarations, jumping is missing out on valuable promotion and the opportunity to widen interest in the sport, which has much to offer at the moment.

The need to make jumping commercially appealing for betting was acknowledged in a thought-provoking blueprint published in November 2003 by Racecourse Holdings Trust, which (now renamed Jockey Club Racecourses) runs a large group of tracks including Cheltenham and Aintree. A BHB Review Group, at around the same time, also acknowledged that problems of small fields in jumping had to be addressed if the betting industry's push for more all-weather fixtures, at the expense of jumping fixtures, was to be resisted. Jumping has done much in the interim to put its house in order, particularly in delivering more competitive racing by increasing the average number of runners in a race (through more thoughtful race-programming and ensuring racecourses provide going that is 'at least good to firm'). As long ago as 1997, the BHB's Off-Course Betting Development Group, which also emphasised the need to produce races attractive to punters, included, along with a number of other good ideas not adopted, a call for forty-eight-hour declarations for all Saturday

TV meetings, for which entries should be available a week in advance to enable broadcasters and Sunday papers to publicise them more fully.

Jumping is now doing more to market itself, the Order of Merit series born out of the suggestion in the Racecourse Holdings Trust blueprint for a '£500,000 Grand Prix series' for the top hurdlers and chasers who would earn points on a sliding scale based on performances in designated races. The points-based Racing UK Order of Merit lived up to its name in the latest season when its first prize of £200,000 went to the best chaser around, **Kauto Star**, with the second prize of £175,000 collected by the horse who finished runner-up to him in both the King George VI Chase and the Cheltenham Gold Cup, **Exotic Dancer**. Encouraging the leading jumpers to run more often was one of the aims of the Order of Merit initiative (won by Inglis Drever and Royal Shakespeare in its first two years). Kauto Star made six appearances, winning all six, and Exotic Dancer made seven, winning four major races in addition to his two seconds to Kauto Star. Kauto Star's Timeform rating of 184+ is the joint highest (with Moscow Flyer) achieved by a jumper since Desert Orchid. Only three-times Gold Cup winner Best Mate has consistently earned wider recognition outside the confines of the sport in the period since Desert Orchid but Kauto Star could be on the way to making a similarly big name for himself. In the latest season, he put up the best performances at two miles, two and a half and at around three miles, versatility almost on a par with that shown by Desert Orchid (whose stamina stretched to win a Whitbread and an Irish Grand National). Kauto Star's prize-money earnings of £607,263 were a record seasonal total for a jumper trained in Britain and Ireland. He also became the first horse to land the Betfair Million, a bonus of £1m put up by the Lancashire Chase sponsors if the winner goes on to success in the King George (or the Lexus at Leopardstown) and the Cheltenham Gold Cup.

For too long, jumping tended to survive on the two big spring meetings, the Cheltenham Festival and the Grand National meeting. The inauguration

One of the founders of Betfair, Andrew Black (left) presents the £1m bonus to connections of Kauto Star, jockey Ruby Walsh, owner Clive Smith and trainer Paul Nicholls

The longest continuous commercial sponsorship in racing celebrates its golden jubilee as State of Play wins the fiftieth Hennessy Gold Cup

of the Betfair at Haydock, the continued development of Cheltenham's two big pre-Christmas meetings, now known as the Open and the International, and the return of extensively-redeveloped Ascot has contributed to making a vibrant programme in the first half of the jumping season, one which for so long hinged on Cheltenham's two traditional pre-Christmas handicaps and on the Hennessy Cognac Gold Cup which celebrated its fiftieth running in the latest season (its rich history dealt with fully on the winner **State of Play**). Nearly £1.4m was on offer at Ascot's six jumps meetings before the turn of the year, as the 'new' Ascot set its stall out to advance the general profile of jumping in the first half of the season, its strategy discussed in the essay on **Hardy Eustace**. There was a mixed reaction at first to the new surface at Ascot amid fears that it would come up too firm. They proved largely unfounded and, in one of the wettest winters of recent years, there was much more for other courses to worry about, including Cheltenham whose watered ground for the Open meeting was widely criticised. A host of winter meetings across the country were staged on soft or heavy going—it was surprising some were allowed to go ahead (a subject discussed in **New Little Bric**)—and just over a week before the Cheltenham Festival the going was 'heavy, soft in places'. Further predicted rain did not materialise, however, and the ground dried out. Conditions on the opening day were firmer than the official 'soft, good to soft', a description amended later in the afternoon to 'good to soft, soft in places'—too late, however, for those who had supported the heavily-backed favourite for the Supreme Novices' Hurdle, **Amaretto Rose**, who was proven on very testing

Twelve months on from victory in the Arkle, Voy Por Ustedes takes the Queen Mother Champion Chase at the Cheltenham Festival, overcoming this mistake at the second last as he challenges between Dempsey (No.2) and Ashley Brook

ground and whose essay examines the responsibilities of the clerks of the course to punters for returning accurate going descriptions. Inaccurate assessments have a damaging effect on the confidence of punters. Dolling out, or realignment of courses, which frequently casts doubts over the accuracy of advertised race distances, is another on-going issue, along with decisions taken at short notice to reduce the number of jumps on safety grounds. Clerks of the course have a duty to provide the best possible ground, and to safeguard the horses, but they must ensure that rail movement and omitting obstacles does not change the distance and the nature of a particular race. If distances are affected, the public must be provided with that information.

The Cheltenham Festival—where the average value of the twenty-four races was £132,000 (greater than the Royal Ascot average)—was largely dominated by home-trained runners. Irish-trained horses had won the three principal championship races two years in a row, including a one, two, three in the Gold Cup and a one, two, three, four in the Champion Hurdle in 2006. Ireland's Gold Cup challenge was weakened by the late defection of the 2006 winner **War of Attrition** and **In Compliance**, but Irish-trained runners dominated the Champion Hurdle again, though the particular dominance of the familiar Irish quartet **Brave Inca** (second), Hardy Eustace (fourth), Macs Joy and Harchibald (neither a runner in the latest edition but both Champion Hurdle runners-up) was brought to an end by the victory of **Sublimity**, a smart performer on the Flat having only his sixth start over hurdles. Harchibald was well below his best in the latest season, though his stable still had two good-class hurdlers in **Iktitaf**, successful in the Morgiana Hurdle, and **Jazz Messenger** who won the Christmas Hurdle at Kempton. The latter's essay examines the history of international racing over jumps. British-trained favourite for the Champion **Detroit City** was disappointing after eight successive victories, which included the 'Bula' whose change of name caused controversy. Sublimity was ridden by Philip Carberry, brother of twice Irish champion Paul and of Nina who won the Cross Country Handicap on Heads Onthe Ground. There are now five Carberry siblings riding, a subject for the essay on Irish-trained County Hurdle winner **Pedrobob**.

Ireland's total of five victories at the Festival—half as many as the previous year—included two other Grade 1s, the first of them the Supreme Novices' won by 40/1-shot **Ebaziyan**, a second win in the race for his trainer who would have won a third but for the last-flight fall in 2002 of **Adamant Approach**, at the veteran stage in the latest season and still going strongly. **Cork All Star** maintained the tremendous Irish record in the Champion Bumper. **Voy Por Ustedes**, the previous year's Arkle winner, succeeded **Newmill** (Ireland's other principal hope, soft-ground specialist **Nickname**, was withdrawn on the day) as the winner of the Queen Mother Champion Chase. Voy Por Ustedes was the second leg of a Grade 1 treble for the stable of Alan King, which also won the Arkle with most exciting prospect **My Way de Solzen** (in which King's former boss David Nicholson is remembered) and the Triumph with **Katchit** who followed Detroit City when completing the Triumph/Anniversary double to put himself firmly in the number-one spot among an above-average crop of juveniles.

The leading Irish two-mile chaser **Schindlers Hunt** was robbed of a place in the Arkle field by a clerical error, but he won two Grade 1s in Ireland, including the Arkle at Leopardstown, and had every chance when blundering two out in the Swordlestown Cup at the Punchestown Festival. That race was one of four Grade 1s at the meeting won by British-trained challengers, **Another Promise** providing an important win for the Ferdy Murphy stable which also completed the Scottish National/Betfred Gold Cup double with **Hot Weld** and had a double for the second year running at the Cheltenham Festival, **Joes Edge** (whose essay examines some puzzling remarks by the BHB's senior handicapper) prevailing in the closest finish at the Festival for many years in the William Hill Trophy (formerly the National Hunt Handicap) and **L'Antartique**

Hot Weld jumps the last in front in the Betfred Gold Cup and becomes the first horse to win the Scottish Grand National and Sandown's big end-of-season staying chase; the two were just a week apart and were the most valuable handicap chases in the latest season, after the Grand National

landing one of the newer races, the Jewson. The latter was added to the programme when Cheltenham introduced a fourth day, which, following a review after the third year, is to become permanent. Timeform's views on the four-day Festival are dealt with principally in the essay on **Wichita Lineman**, though the subject is also touched on in the extended entries on **Butler's Cabin** (National Hunt Chase), **United** (discussion of the merits of the new mares race for 2008), **Inglis Drever**, who became only the fourth horse to win the staying hurdlers' championship at Cheltenham more than once, and **Taranis** (whose write-up also takes a look at good horses who have successfully mixed chasing and hurdling).

A number of the Cheltenham Festival winners were not seen out again, principally among them Kauto Star and his stable-companion **Denman** who annihilated his field in the Royal & SunAlliance. My Way de Solzen, Voy Por Ustedes, Sublimity and **Idole First**, who joined a select band who have won more than one handicap at the Festival, were others retired for the season. Eleven Cheltenham Festival winners (though only three of the ten Grade 1 winners) and ten runners-up went on to Aintree—there was a four-week gap between the two meetings—and the runners-up fared better, Katchit the only winner to follow up while Exotic Dancer (Betfair Bowl), **Mighty Man** (who turned the tables on Inglis Drever in the Long Distance Hurdle but then suffered a near-certain, career-ending injury at Punchestown), **Tidal Bay** and **Silver Birch** all went one better at Aintree.

By the time Aintree came around, Britain was, in sharp contrast to the winter, enjoying its driest and warmest April on record, with some areas not receiving a drop of rain. Aintree deserved the praise it received for producing a good racing surface. The essay on Mersey Novices' Hurdle winner Tidal Bay examines the returns his owners, Andrea and Graham Wylie, who had eighty

Leading owner in Britain and Ireland, J. P. McManus, receives the Timeform Personality of the Year award from Timeform chairman Reg Griffin at the annual charity dinner in June

Gaspara gives the Pipe family a memorable day at the Cheltenham Festival;
carrying the colours of Martin Pipe, she is a first Festival winner for son David (right) as a trainer

horses running in their colours in the latest season, have had from their spending on jumpers. Graham Wylie, whose personal wealth was put at £200m in the latest *Sunday Times* Rich List, says he does not expect 'to get back a penny . . . I am in it for the love of the sport.' Jumping is a financial non-starter for an owner, the overall rewards, compared to the Flat, slight in comparison to the costs. The sport is fortunate to have the patronage of some very rich owners who, like Graham Wylie, are 'in it for the love of the sport'. J. P. McManus (worth £561m according to the Rich List) had around two hundred and fifty horses in training in the latest season when he topped the owners' table in Britain for the third time and was leading owner over jumps in Ireland for the twelfth consecutive season. Nearly sixty per cent of the runners sent out by Jonjo O'Neill, runner-up in the British trainers' championship, carried the McManus colours, including the stable's three Cheltenham Festival winners (four winners in all took McManus's total at jumping's showpiece to twenty-seven). More background can be found in the entry on Butler's Cabin, who also won McManus a second Irish Grand National. Second, third and fourth (the Wylies were fifth) in the list of leading owners in Britain were Sir Robert Ogden (£135m), David Johnson and Trevor Hemmings (£980m).

David Johnson, who has never appeared in the *Sunday Times* Rich List but reportedly sold igroup for £216m in 2002, has been leading owner five times and is the principal patron of Pond House stables. David Pipe took over from his father Martin there in the latest season and was the leading trainer numerically with one hundred and thirty-four wins. A third of the runners from Pond House, and seven of its twelve highest earners, were owned by Johnson whose three most successful horses were **Acambo** (essay discusses the 'war' between major bookmakers and Turf TV over betting shop pictures), **Our Vic** and the returning **Well Chief**, the last of the 'golden trio' of two-mile chasers from 2004/5 still in training. The Johnson horses at the stable had something of an up-and-down season, including a near two-month drought that included Cheltenham and Aintree, the only winner for the Pipe yard at the two meetings being the Martin Pipe-owned juvenile **Gaspara** who landed the £75,000 bonus for adding a Cheltenham Festival victory to her win the previous weekend in the Imperial Cup.

The champion trainer Paul Nicholls, whose £2,882,752 in 1,2,3 prize money in Britain broke the record set by Martin Pipe in 2004/5, has a much wider network of owners than some of his main rivals. Manor Farm Stables' top thirteen earners, which also included the yard's only runner in Ireland, Punchestown Gold Cup winner **Neptune Collonges**, and the Maghull Chase winner **Twist Magic** (whose entry discusses the reduction of weight allowances for four- and five-year-old chasers), were divided between eleven different owners or syndicates. The Grand National winner **Silver Birch** had been with Nicholls until May when he was sold for 20,000 guineas at Doncaster and sent to young Irish trainer Gordon Elliott who, like Sublimity's trainer John Carr, was virtually unheard of in his own country, let alone in Britain. The starting of big fields over jumps sometimes leaves something to be desired and there was another false start to the National, following the previous year's recall (there is more on starts in the essay on **Fair Along**). It was the fortieth anniversary of Foinavon's Grand National win which is recalled in the essay on Silver Birch, complete with the transcript of Michael O'Hehir's commentary at the infamous twenty-third fence (Tony O'Hehir, who followed in his father's footsteps, vividly captured the excitement of the durable **Beef Or Salmon**'s last-gasp victory over **The Listener** in the latest Hennessy at Leopardstown).

Forty years on and Foinavon's National is recalled in the essay on Silver Birch. Foinavon is pictured (top right, light braces) after finding his way through the chaos at the twenty-third fence. Runner-up Honey End (light sleeves) is being turned in front of the fence on the right, and third Red Alligator (winner in 1968) is facing the camera in the centre of the picture

April 7th, and a sad day as Turgeonev (David O'Meara) is the last winner over Haydock's distinctive steeplechase course, with its drop fences. The creation of a second flat course means chases will now be run on the hurdles track using portable fences. 'A disgrace', 'utterly disgusting', 'horrific' and 'completely wrong' were among the reactions of some jumps trainers, while the Levy Board's chief executive praised the course for an 'excellent example of strategic thinking'

Another of the races over Aintree's Grand National fences, the Topham Trophy, was made into an open handicap with the BHB handicapper given dispensation to depart from existing marks in framing the weights. The winner **Dunbrody Millar** also held a National entry but, oddly, was treated differently in the two races. His essay highlights the fact that the 'Aintree factor' is as important as ever when it comes to races over the big, unusual fences. The entry on Aintree Hurdle winner **Al Eile** examines the validity of a similar theory when it comes to the Mildmay course.

Apart from Aintree's National course, no other track's fences had the individual nature of Haydock's traditional steeplechase course which, sadly, is no more after the course executive's decision—probably initiated by the Jockey Club Racecourses grouping of which Haydock is part—to increase its more remunerative portfolio of Flat fixtures. Steeplechases at Haydock will now be contested, using portable fences, on what was the hurdles course inside the old chase course, the much tighter circuit changing the nature of the test. The decision drew a predictably angry response from some quarters, as touched on in the essay on **Heltornic**, the last big-race winner over the traditional fences in the Red Square Vodka Gold Cup. Heltornic's victory contributed to a very good season for fillies and mares generally, in Britain and Ireland, and over both hurdles and fences. More can be found in the write-up on **Labelthou**. The owners of some of the good mares around will be hoping they will go on to emulate the achievements at stud of such as Be My Hope (three runners at the Cheltenham Festival), Polly Puttens and Park Breeze, whose records are recounted in the entries on **Cane Brake**, **Silverburn** and **Offshore Account** respectively.

13

Offshore Account won the new Grade 1 Champion Novices' Chase over an extended three miles at the Punchestown Festival, a race that would probably have gone to British challenger **Aces Four** but for his horrific fall when in front at the last. Punchestown, which is to be needlessly extended from four to five days in the next season (the latest attendences were 17,974, 20,153, 19,858 and 32,883), seemed to feature more than its share of major championship contenders who ran too badly to be true, a subject touched on in the entry on **Silent Oscar**, surprise winner of the ACCBank Champion Hurdle. The lateness in the season, coupled with the shorter than usual gap between Aintree and Punchestown, were put forward as reasons, though two of the British-trained winners **Punjabi** (Champion Four Year Old Hurdle) and **Refinement** (Champion Stayers') had both run well in defeat at Aintree having also contested races at Cheltenham. J. P. McManus had two winners at Aintree, Reveillez and Two Miles West, the latter one of three saddled by Jonjo O'Neill whose others were for Sir Robert Ogden (Exotic Dancer) and Trevor Hemmings (**Albertas Run**). The only winner in the McManus colours at Punchestown was the veteran cross country performer Spot Thedifference who won an eventful renewal of the La Touche Cup to provide his trainer Enda Bolger with a tenth successive winner of the race.

Over half of the McManus winners in Britain were ridden by Tony McCoy who was champion jockey for the twelfth time with 184 wins, thirty in front of perennial runner-up Richard Johnson despite missing virtually the whole of August and September with a broken wrist. Neither Johnson, nor eventual third Tom O'Brien, the season's record-breaking, leading conditional (about whom more can be found on **McKelvey**), managed to get in front of McCoy during his enforced absence. McCoy reached the milestone of 2,500 victories in Britain on **Kanpai** in October, but in the latest season he rode only seven winners in Ireland (just four in the McManus colours) from fifty-seven rides in that country. If there had been a jockeys' championship based on performances in Britain and Ireland combined, the winner would have been McCoy's great rival

It's not all plain sailing when you're at the top. Twist Magic and Don't Push It,
the mounts of jumping's two leading riders Ruby Walsh (nearest camera) and Tony McCoy,
fall independently at the second last in the Arkle Trophy

Tom O'Brien was the season's leading conditional with a record one hundred and seven winners which also put him third behind McCoy and Johnson in the jockeys' championship itself; tough, northern veteran Russ Garritty retired after a twenty-three-year career in which he rode five hundred and thirty winners, his last ride coming when third on Lease Lend in Aintree's championship bumper which had to be rearranged for shortly after the end of the season

Ruby Walsh, about whom more can be found in the essay on **Snowy Morning**. Nicky Henderson's partnership with Mick Fitzgerald will continue for another season after the rider reversed his decision to retire from the saddle, but the ranks of the northern jockeys will be without the tough Russ Garritty who has given up to become assistant to Tim Easterby. Garritty played down his career, which included a Cheltenham Festival winner on Hussard Collonges, by saying that 'the game isn't about jockeys, it's about horses.'

The pick of the Irish-trained chasers, hurdlers and bumper performers not seen out in Britain are, as usual, covered in this edition of *Chasers & Hurdlers* in which the number of individual entries tops 10,000 for the first time. The leading French-trained jumpers are dealt with in Timeform 'Top Horses In France' which appears at the back of this edition, along with the complete results for reference of over 200 important or significant races in the three countries. The British season ran from April 30th 2006-April 28th 2007. Some performances after the end of the season are referred to in the essays where appropriate but please note that, for technical reasons, the form figures relating to those performances do not appear at the start of the commentary. The horses highlighted in bold in this introduction are among those which have extended entries or essays in the A to Z section.

September 2007

Kauto Star (Ruby Walsh) after the Gold Cup

CHAMPION JUMPER, BEST STAYING CHASER &
BEST TWO-MILE CHASER – RATED AT 184+

KAUTO STAR

7 b.g. Village Star – Kauto Relka (Port Etienne)
Owner Clive D. Smith   Trainer P. F. Nicholls

BEST TWO-MILE HURDLER – RATED AT 164
SUBLIMITY
7 b.g. Selkirk – Fig Tree Drive (Miswaki)
Owner Mr W. Hennessy   Trainer J. G. Carr

BEST STAYING HURDLER — RATED AT 172
MIGHTY MAN
7 b.g. Sir Harry Lewis – Vanina II (Italic)
Owner Mr E. R. Hanbury   Trainer H. D. Daly

BEST NOVICE CHASER — RATED AT 161p
DENMAN
7 ch.g. Presenting – Polly Puttens (Pollerton)
Owner Mrs M. Findlay & P. K. Barber   Trainer P. F. Nicholls

BEST PERFORMANCE IN A HUNTER CHASE – RATED AT 131
DROMBEAG
9 b.g. Presenting – Bula Beag (Brush Aside)
Owner Mr John P. McManus   Trainer Jonjo O'Neill

BEST NOVICE HURDLER – RATED AT 152p
WICHITA LINEMAN
6 b.g. King's Theatre – Monumental Gesture (Head For Heights)
Owner Mr John P. McManus   Trainer Jonjo O'Neill

BEST JUVENILE HURDLER – RATED AT 151
KATCHIT
4 b.g. Kalanisi – Miracle (Ezzoud)
Owner DSJP Syndicate   Trainer A. King

BEST BUMPER PERFORMER – RATED AT 124
THEATRICAL MOMENT
4 b.g. Royal Anthem – Given Moment (Diesis)
Owner Elsa Crankshaw & G. Allan II   Trainer G. A. Swinbank

THE TIMEFORM 'TOP 100' CHASERS AND HURDLERS

Hurdlers

172	Mighty Man
166	Inglis Drever
164	Sublimity
162	Iktitaf
161+	Black Jack Ketchum
161	Hardy Eustace
160	Blazing Bailey
160	Brave Inca
160	Detroit City
159	Afsoun
159	Al Eile
157	Newmill
157	Silent Oscar
156	Asian Maze
156	Desert Quest
156	Macs Joy
156	Zaiyad
155	Jazz Messenger
155	Millenium Royal
155	Straw Bear
154	Arcalis
154	Kasbah Bliss
154	Mid Dancer
153	Powerstation
152p	Wichita Lineman
152§	Westender
152	Noble Request
152	Rosaker
151	Adamant Approach
150	Essex
150	Refinement
148	Celestial Wave
148	Flight Leader
148	Irish Wolf
148	Kawagino
148	Tidal Bay
147+	My Way de Solzen
147	Lord Sam
147	Massini's Maguire
147	Mister Hight
147	Oscar Park
146p	Glencove Marina
146	Material World
146	Overstrand
145+	Ashley Brook
145+	Ebaziyan
145	Callow Lake
145	Catch Me
145	Crow Wood
145	Dom d'Orgeval
145	Rhinestone Cowboy
145	United
145	Wins Now
144p	Aran Concerto
144p	Blythe Knight
144§	Redemption
144	Chief Dan George
144	Laetitia
143p	Black Harry
143+	Kazal
143	Acambo
143	Halcon Genelardais
143	Strangely Brown
143	The French Furze
142+	Labelthou
142+	Star de Mohaison
142§	Harchibald
142	Granit Jack
142	Silverburn
142	Special Envoy
141+	Amaretto Rose
141+	Osana
141§	Ouninpohja
141	De Soto
141	Emmpat
141	Fair Along
141	Orcadian
141	Royal Shakespeare
141	Studmaster
141	Sweet Wake
141	Whispered Promises
140	Chilling Place
140	Emotional Moment
140	Faasel
140	Johnnie Dillinger
140	Lough Derg
140	Pedrobob
140	Southern Vic
140	Taranis (FR)
139+	Spring The Que
139x	No Refuge
139§	Temoin
139	Bob Justice
139	Burntoakboy
139	Bywell Beau
139	Caracciola
139	Jazz d'Estruval
139	Penzance
139	Premier Dane
139	Royals Darling
139	Self Defense

Chasers

184+	Kauto Star
175+	Exotic Dancer
168§	Our Vic
168	The Listener
167+	Well Chief
167x	Beef Or Salmon
166	Impek
166	Racing Demon
165	War of Attrition
164	Nickname
163?	Hedgehunter
163	Voy Por Ustedes
162	Ashley Brook
162	Dempsey
162	Halcon Genelardais
161p	Denman
161§	Turpin Green
161	Neptune Collonges
160	Eurotrek
160	Monet's Garden
160	My Will
160	State of Play
159	Nil Desperandum
159	Taranis (FR)
158+	Star de Mohaison
158§	Kingscliff
157p	My Way de Solzen
157	Andreas
157	L'Ami
157	Monkerhostin
157	Nozic
156	Billyvoddan
156	Cane Brake
156	Ollie Magern
155	Foreman
154p	Aces Four
154p	Twist Magic
154	Armaturk
154	Juveigneur
154	Reveillez
153x	Sporazene
153	Don't Push It
153	Forget The Past
153	Mister McGoldrick
153	River City
152p	In Compliance
152+	Cailin Alainn
152	Ansar
152	Justified
152	Little Brick
152	Oneway
152	Too Forward
151	Central House
151	Cerium
151	Hi Cloy
151	Mid Dancer
151	Newmill
151	Thisthatandtother
150§	Faasel
150§	Watson Lake
150	Lacdoudal
150	Madison du Berlais
149	Crossbow Creek
149	Fair Along
149	Idle Talk
149	Mansony
149	Offshore Account

148x	Ladalko	147	Silver Birch	145	Baron Windrush
148	Commercial Flyer	147	Southern Vic	145	ChillinG Place
148	Sir OJ	146p	Briareus	145	Euro Leader
148	Slim Pickings	146	Alderburn	145	McKelvey
148	Snowy Morning	146	Jack The Giant	145	Mon Mome
148	Yes Sir	146	Kill Devil Hill	145	One Cool Cookie
147§	Sir Rembrandt	146	Laetitia	145	Strong Project
147	Alexander Taipan	146	Le Volfoni	145	Supreme Prince
147	Bob Bob Bobbin	146	Natal	145	Ungaro
147	D'Argent	146	Simon	145	Zabenz
147	Gungadu	146	Tumbling Dice		
147	Parsons Legacy	145	According To John		

THE TIMEFORM TOP JUVENILES, NOVICES, HUNTER CHASERS AND NH FLAT HORSES

Juvenile Hurdlers
151	Katchit
149+	Gaspara
145	Punjabi
142?	Lounaos
142	Liberate
140	Mobaasher
139	Zilcash
135	Degas Art
135	Parrain
133	Altilhar
132+	Good Bye Simon
132	Raslan
131p	Grand Bleu
131	Is It Me
130	Laustra Bad
130	Tritonix
129	Financial Reward
129	Poquelin
128+	Pauillac
127	Duty
127	Predateur

Novice Hurdlers
152p	Wichita Lineman
148	Flight Leader
148	Tidal Bay
147	Massini's Maguire
146p	Glencove Marina
145+	Ebaziyan
145	Catch Me
145	Wins Now
144p	Aran Concerto
144p	Blythe Knight
144	Chief Dan George
143p	Black Harry
143+	Kazal
142+	Labelthou
142	Granit Jack
142	Silverburn
142	Special Envoy
141+	Amaretto Rose
141+	Osana
141§	Ouninpohja
141	De Soto

Novice Chasers
161p	Denman
157p	My Way De Solzen
154p	Aces Four
154p	Twist Magic
153	Don't Push It
152+	Cailin Alainn
150§	Faasel
149	Fair Along
149	Offshore Account
148	Snowy Morning
148	Yes Sir
147	Alexander Taipan
147	Gungadu
146p	Briareus
146	Jack The Giant
146	Laetitia
146	Natal
145	According To John
145	One Cool Cookie
145	Ungaro

National Hunt Flat Horses
124	Theatrical Moment
122	Cork All Star
120	Kealshore Boy
119	Aranleigh
119	Sizing Africa
119	Sophocles
118+	Fiveforthree
118	Crocodiles Rock
118	Den of Iniquity
118	Turbo Linn
117p	Aux Le Bahnn
117	Lease Lend
117	Mick The Man
116	Abstinence
116	Cooldine
115p	Master Overseer
115	Jass
115	Mad Fish
115	Mendo
115	Skippers Brig
115	Swaythe

Hunter Chasers
136	Bothar Na*
131	Drombeag
131	Kerstino Two*
131	Whyso Mayo
127	General Striker
126	Ned Kelly
126	Pak Jack
126	Scots Grey
123§	Sonevafushi
123	Joe Blake
123	Patricksnineteenth*
122p	It's Like That
122	Old Scew Bald
121	Beau Supreme*
121	Bica
121	Bosham Mill*
121	Don't Be Daft
121	Which Pocket*
120	Honourable Spider
120	Lord Nellerie

*NB * indicates best performance achieved in a race other than hunter chase*

2006/07 STATISTICS

The following tables show the leading owners, trainers, jockeys, sires of winners and horses over jumps in Britain during 2006/07. The prize-money statistics, compiled by *Timeform*, relate to win-money and to first-three prize money. Win money has traditionally been used to decide the trainers' championship, though since 1994 the BHB and the National Trainers' Federation have recognised championships decided by total prize money as determined by the *Racing Post*. The jockeys' championship has traditionally been decided by the number of winners.

	OWNERS (1,2,3 earnings)	Horses	Indiv'l Wnrs	Races Won	Runs	%	Stakes £
1	Mr John P McManus	163	63	93	632	14.7	1,307,276
2	Sir Robert Ogden	34	14	27	97	27.8	928,750
3	Mr D A Johnson	74	30	59	316	18.6	795,861
4	Mr Trevor Hemmings	77	29	42	287	14.6	716,933
5	Andrea & Graham Wylie	80	31	45	242	18.5	625,924
6	Mr Clive D Smith	4	1	6	21	28.5	616,299
7	Mr Brian Walsh	3	2	3	11	27.2	435,239
8	The Stewart Family	18	12	18	84	21.4	381,231
9	Mrs M Findlay & P K Barber	4	4	10	18	55.5	254,233
10	Mr Alan Peterson	5	2	6	22	27.2	213,136

	OWNERS (by win-money)	Horses	Indiv'l Wnrs	Races Won	Runs	%	Stakes £
1	Mr John P McManus	163	63	93	632	14.7	784,786
2	Sir Robert Ogden	34	14	27	97	27.8	695,519
3	Mr Clive D Smith	4	1	6	21	28.5	607,263
4	Mr D A Johnson	74	30	59	316	18.6	546,277
5	Andrea & Graham Wylie	80	31	45	242	18.5	440,181
6	Mr Brian Walsh	3	2	3	11	27.2	408,981
7	Mr Trevor Hemmings	77	29	42	287	14.6	394,986
8	Mrs M Findlay & P K Barber	4	4	10	18	55.5	241,252
9	The Stewart Family	18	12	18	84	21.4	208,674
10	Mr W Hennessy	1	1	1	1	100.0	205,272

	TRAINERS (1,2,3 earnings)	Horses	Indiv'l Wnrs	Races Won	Runs	%	Stakes £
1	P F Nicholls	148	78	124	539	23.0	2,882,752
2	Jonjo O'Neill	193	82	126	821	15.3	1,619,583
3	A King	122	59	92	417	22.0	1,543,850
4	D E Pipe	178	75	134	767	17.4	1,496,169
5	P J Hobbs	159	64	111	609	18.2	1,386,117
6	N J Henderson	104	48	74	320	23.1	905,886
7	P Bowen	71	37	74	354	20.6	886,973
8	Miss Venetia Williams	100	47	76	417	18.2	872,007
9	Ferdy Murphy	103	33	61	439	13.8	858,914
10	N G Richards	97	48	64	320	20.0	728,829
11	J Howard Johnson	126	37	54	399	13.5	712,927
12	Evan Williams	140	45	66	505	13.2	575,737

TRAINERS (by win-money)	Horses	Indiv'l Wnrs	Races Won	Runs	%	Stakes £
1 P F Nicholls	148	78	124	539	23.0	2,123,229
2 A King	122	59	92	417	22.0	1,208,542
3 Jonjo O'Neill	193	82	126	821	15.3	1,107,415
4 D E Pipe	178	75	134	767	17.4	1,044,380
5 P J Hobbs	159	64	111	609	18.2	941,045
6 Miss Venetia Williams	100	47	76	417	18.2	628,904

TRAINERS (with 100+ winners)	Horses	Indiv'l Wnrs	Races Won	2nd	3rd	Runs	%
1 D E Pipe	178	75	134	90	76	767	17.4
2 Jonjo O'Neill	193	82	126	112	94	821	15.3
3 P F Nicholls	148	78	124	101	68	539	23.0
4 P J Hobbs	159	64	111	93	66	609	18.2

JOCKEYS (by winners)	1st	2nd	3rd	Unpl	Total Mts	%
1 A P McCoy	184	117	97	359	757	24.3
2 Richard Johnson	154	138	108	448	848	18.1
3 T J O'Brien	107	82	67	300	556	19.2
4 Robert Thornton	99	77	66	308	550	18.0
5 Timmy Murphy	98	71	53	320	542	18.0
6 G Lee	89	98	65	425	677	13.1
7 P J Brennan	80	60	62	311	512	15.4
8 Noel Fehily	75	65	64	270	474	15.8
9 Sam Thomas	73	68	40	281	462	15.8
10 R Walsh	73	55	40	123	291	25.0
11 Tony Dobbin	69	60	42	229	400	17.2
12 Mick Fitzgerald	60	42	47	220	369	16.2

JOCKEYS (1,2,3 earnings)	Races Won	Rides	%	Stakes £
1 A P McCoy	184	757	24.3	2,259,552
2 R Walsh	73	291	25.0	2,249,981
3 Richard Johnson	154	848	18.1	1,866,634
4 Robert Thornton	99	550	18.0	1,604,526
5 Timmy Murphy	98	542	18.0	1,382,373
6 G Lee	89	677	13.1	969,167
7 Mick Fitzgerald	60	369	16.2	933,706
8 T J O'Brien	107	556	19.2	911,294
9 P J Brennan	80	512	15.4	871,661
10 Tony Dobbin	69	400	17.2	813,409
11 Noel Fehily	75	474	15.8	786,752
12 Sam Thomas	73	462	15.8	723,310

JOCKEYS (by win-money)	Races Won	Rides	%	Stakes £
1 R Walsh	73	291	25.0	1,671,722
2 A P McCoy	184	757	24.3	1,539,323
3 Robert Thornton	99	550	18.0	1,250,590
4 Richard Johnson	154	848	18.1	1,210,254
5 Timmy Murphy	98	542	18.0	1,032,992
6 G Lee	89	677	13.1	661,901
7 P J Brennan	80	512	15.4	602,161
8 Tony Dobbin	69	400	17.2	584,741

CONDITIONAL JOCKEYS

		1st	2nd	3rd	Unpl	Total Mts	%
1	T J O'Brien	107	82	67	300	556	19.2
2	Phil Kinsella	46	40	45	286	417	11.0
3	Daryl Jacob	40	45	46	250	381	10.4

AMATEUR RIDERS

		1st	2nd	3rd	Unpl	Total Mts	%
1	Mr T Greenall	31	29	29	174	263	11.7
2	M. D England	22	12	12	96	142	15.4
3	Mr J Snowden	13	7	5	33	58	22.4

SIRES OF WINNERS
(1,2,3 earnings)

		Races Won	Runs	%	Stakes £
1	Roselier (by Misti IV)	48	399	12.2	744,513
2	Presenting (by Mtoto)	69	491	14.0	649,070
3	Supreme Leader (by Bustino)	92	638	14.4	646,527
4	Village Star (by Moulin)	6	6	100.0	607,263
5	Lord America (by Lord Gayle)	41	355	11.5	605,661
6	Turgeon (by Caro)	16	67	23.8	557,762
7	In The Wings (by Sadler's Wells)	27	146	18.4	501,860
8	Accordion (by Sadler's Wells)	40	289	13.8	444,621
9	Clearly Bust (by Busted)	5	12	41.6	422,383
10	Old Vic (by Sadler's Wells)	27	287	9.4	405,595
11	Anshan (by Persian Bold)	27	339	7.9	399,803
12	Alderbrook (by Ardross)	41	226	18.1	376,119
13	Sir Harry Lewis (by Alleged)	22	165	13.3	369,343
14	Villez (by Lyphard's Wish)	11	81	13.5	312,317
15	Zaffaran (by Assert)	36	291	12.3	310,190

SIRES OF WINNERS (by win-money)

		Horses	Indiv'l Wnrs	Races Won	Stakes £
1	Village Star (by Moulin)	1	1	6	607,263
2	Roselier (by Misti IV)	108	31	48	590,571
3	Supreme Leader (by Bustino)	182	64	92	477,153
4	Presenting (by Mtoto)	145	43	69	475,019
5	Clearly Bust (by Busted)	2	2	5	413,103
6	Lord America (by Lord Gayle)	92	27	41	403,167

LEADING HORSES (1,2,3 earnings)

		Races Won	Runs	Stakes £
1	Kauto Star 7 b.g Village Star–Kauto Relka	6	6	607,263
2	Exotic Dancer 7 b.g Turgeon–Northine	4	7	429,383
3	Silver Birch 10 b.g Clearly Bust–All Gone	1	3	407,465
4	Voy Por Ustedes 6 b.g. Villez–Nuit d'Ecajeul	2	4	247,091
5	Taranis 6 ch.g Mansonnien–Vikosa	3	6	212,799
6	Katchit 4 b.g Kalanisi–Miracle	7	8	206,578
7	Sublimity 7 b.g Selkirk–Fig Tree Drive	1	1	205,272
8	Monet's Garden 9 gr.g Roselier–Royal Remainder	3	5	205,221
9	McKelvey 8 b.g Anshan–Chatty Actress	2	6	203,910
10	Inglis Drever 8 b.g In The Wings–Cormorant Creek	2	4	192,870

EXPLANATORY NOTES

'Chasers & Hurdlers 2006/07' deals individually, in alphabetical sequence, with every horse that ran over the sticks or in National Hunt Flat races in Britain during the 2006/7 season, plus a number of foreign-trained horses that did not race here. For each of these horses is given (1) its age, colour and sex, (2) its breeding and, where this information has not been given in a previous Chasers & Hurdlers or Racehorses Annual, a family outline (3) a form summary giving its Timeform rating—or ratings—at the end of the previous season, followed by the details of all its performances during the past season, (4) a Timeform rating—or ratings—of its merit (which appears in the margin), (5) a Timeform commentary on its racing or general characteristics as a racehorse, with some suggestions, perhaps, regarding its prospects for 2007/8 and (6) the name of the trainer in whose charge it was on the last occasion it ran.

The book is published with a twofold purpose. Firstly, it is intended to have permanent value as a review of the exploits and achievements of the more notable of our chasers and hurdlers in the 2006/7 season. Thus, while the commentaries upon the vast majority of the horses are, of necessity, in note form, the best horses are more critically examined. The text is illustrated by half-tone portraits of the most notable horses (where these are available) and photographs of the major races. Secondly, the book is designed to help the punter to analyse races, and the notes which follow contain instructions for using the data.

TIMEFORM RATINGS

The Timeform Rating of a horse is simply the merit of the horse expressed in pounds and is arrived at by careful examination of its running against other horses using a scale of weight for distance beaten. Timeform maintains a 'running' handicap of all horses in training throughout the season.

THE LEVEL OF THE RATINGS

At the close of each season the ratings of all the horses that have raced are re-examined, and, if necessary, the general level of the handicap is adjusted so that all the ratings are kept at the same standard level from year to year. Some of the ratings may, therefore, be different from those in the final issue of the 2006/7 Timeform Chasing Black Book series.

RATINGS AND WEIGHT-FOR-AGE

The reader has, in the ratings in this book, a universal handicap embracing all the horses in training it is possible to weigh up, ranging from tip-top performers, with ratings from 170 upwards, down to the meanest platers, rated around the 60 mark. All the ratings are at weight-for-age, so that equal ratings mean horses of equal merit. In using Timeform to assess the prospects of various runners, allowance should be made for any difference specified by the Age, Weight and Distance Table at the front.

Steeplechase ratings, preceded by c, should not be confused with hurdle ratings, preceded by h. Where a horse has raced over fences and also over hurdles its ratings as a chaser and hurdler are printed one above the other, the steeplechase rating (c) being placed above the hurdle rating (h).

Thus with REGALITY c157
h143

the top figure, 157, is the rating to be used in steeplechases, and the one below, 143, is for use only in hurdle races. Where a horse has a rating based on its performance in a National Hunt Flat race (usually referred to in the text as a bumper) it is preceded by 'F'. The procedure for making age and weight adjustments to the ratings (i.e. for the calculation of Race Ratings) is as follows:

A. Horses of the Same Age

If the horses all carry the same weight there are no adjustments to be made, and the horses with the highest ratings have the best chances. If the horses carry different weights, jot down their ratings, and to the rating of each horse add one point for every pound the horse is set to carry less than 12st 7lb, or subtract one point for every pound it has to carry more than 12st 7lb. When the ratings have been adjusted in this way the highest resultant figure indicates the horse with the best chance at the weights.

Example (any month of the season)

Teucer	5 yrs (11-0) ..	Rating 140 ..	add 21	161
Kiowa	5 yrs (10-7) ..	Rating 125 ..	add 28	153
Golden Age	5 yrs (10-4) ..	Rating 120 ..	add 31	151

Teucer has the best chance, and Golden Age the worst

B. Horses of Different Ages

In this case, reference must be made to the Age, Weight and Distance Table at the front. Use the Table for steeplechasers and hurdlers alike. Treat each horse separately, and compare the weight it has to carry with the weight prescribed for it in the table, according to the age of the horse, the distance of the race and the month of the year. Then, add one point to the rating for each pound the horse has to carry less than the weight given in the table: or, subtract one point from the rating for every pound it has to carry more than the weight prescribed by the table. The highest resultant figure indicates the horse most favoured by the weights.

Example (2¾m steeplechase in January)

(Table Weights: 8-y-o 12-7; 7-y-o 12-7; 5-y-o 12-6)

Black Book	8 yrs (12-8) ..	Rating 140 ..	subtract 1 ..	139
Pressman	7 yrs (12-3) ..	Rating 132 ..	add 4	136
Copyright	5 yrs (12-7) ..	Rating 150 ..	subtract 1 ..	149

Copyright has the best chance, and Pressman the worst

Example (3m hurdle race in March)

(Table Weights: 9-y-o 12-7; 5-y-o 12-7; 4-y-o 11-11)

Oxer	9 yrs (10-12) ..	Rating 110 ..	add 23 ..	133
Clairval	5 yrs (10-7) ..	Rating 119 ..	add 28	147
Gallette	4 yrs (10-7) ..	Rating 128 ..	add 18 ..	146

Clairval has the best chance, and Oxer the worst

C. Horses in National Hunt Flat races

The procedure for calculating Race Ratings in National Hunt Flat races is precisely the same as in (A) or (B).

Example (2m N.H. Flat in February)

(Table Weights: 6-y-o 12-7; 5-y-o 12-7; 4-y-o 12-1)

Squall	6 yrs (10-12) ..	Rating 88 ..	add 23	111
Lupin	5 yrs (11-3) ..	Rating 97 ..	add 18	115
Chariot	4 yrs (10-9) ..	Rating 84 ..	add 20	104

Lupin has the best chance, and Chariot the worst

The National Hunt Flat ratings are on a scale comparable with that used for hurdlers and chasers. The ratings can therefore be used not only within the context of National Hunt Flat races themselves, but also as an indication of the potential form of such horses in their first few starts over jumps.

JOCKEYSHIP AND RIDERS' ALLOWANCES

For the purposes of rating calculations it should, in general, be assumed that the allowance the rider is able to claim (3 lb, 5 lb, or 7 lb) is nullified by his or her inexperience. Therefore, the *weight adjustments to the ratings should be calculated on the weight allotted by the handicapper, or determined by the conditions of the race,* and no extra addition should be made to a rating because the horse's rider claims an allowance. This is the general routine procedure; but, of course, after the usual adjustments have been made the quality of jockeyship is still an important factor to be considered when deciding between horses with similar chances.

WEIGHING UP A RACE

The ratings tell which horses in a particular race are most favoured by the weights; but complete analysis demands that the racing character of each horse is also studied carefully to see if there is any reason why the horse might be expected not to run up to its rating. It counts for little that a horse is thrown in at the weights if it has no pretensions whatever to staying the distance, or is unable to act on the prevailing going. Suitability of distance and going are no doubt the most important points to be considered, but there are others. For example, the ability of a horse to accommodate itself to the conformation of the track. There is also the matter of a horse's ability and dependability as a jumper and of its temperament: nobody would be in a hurry to take a short price about a horse with whom it is always an even chance whether it will get round or not, or whether it will consent to race.

A few minutes spent checking up on these matters in the commentaries upon the horses concerned will sometimes put a very different complexion on a race from that which is put upon it by the ratings alone. We repeat, therefore, that the correct way to use Timeform, or this annual volume, in the analysis of individual races is, first to use the ratings to discover which horses are most favoured by the weights, and second, to check through the comments on the horse to see what factors other than weight might also affect the outcome of the race.

THE FORM SUMMARIES

The form summaries enclosed in the brackets list each horse's performances in the last season in sequence, showing, for each race, its distance in furlongs, the state of the going and the horse's placing at the finish. Steeplechase form figures are prefixed by the letter 'c' and N.H. Flat race (bumper) form figures by the letter 'F', the others relating to form over hurdles.

The going is symbolised as follows: f–firm, m–good to firm, g–good, d–good to soft/dead, s–soft, v–heavy.

Placings are indicated up to sixth place, by superior figures, an asterisk denoting a win; and superior letters are used to convey what happened to the horse during the race: F–fell (F^3 denotes remounted and finished third); pu–pulled up; ur–unseated rider; bd–brought down; R–refused; rtr–refused to race; su–slipped up; ro–ran out; co–carried out; wd–withdrawn; dis–disqualified.

Thus, [2006/7 h82, F80: 16g 16s* c18g^{pu} 16f^2 c20v^F Apr 10] states that the horse was rated 82 over hurdles and 80 in bumpers at the end of the previous season. In the 2006/7 jumping season the horse ran five times; unplaced in a 2m hurdle race on good going, winning a 2m hurdle race on soft going, being pulled up in a 2¼m steeplechase on good going, running second in a 2m hurdle race on firm going and falling in a 2½m steeplechase on heavy going. Its last race was on April 10th.

Where sale prices are given they are in guineas unless otherwise stated. The prefix IR denotes Irish guineas, IR £ denotes Irish punts, $ refers to American dollars, francs refers to French francs and € indicates the euro. Any other currencies are converted into pounds sterling at the prevailing exchange rate.

THE RATING SYMBOLS

The following symbols, attached to the ratings, are to be interpreted as stated:-

p   likely to improve.

P   capable of *much* better form.

+   the horse may be better than we have rated it.

d   the horse appears to have deteriorated, and might no longer be capable of running to the rating given.

§   unreliable (for temperamental or other reasons).

§§   so temperamentally unsatisfactory as to be not worth a rating.

x   poor jumper.

xx   a very bad jumper, so bad as to be not worth a rating.

?   the horse's rating is suspect or, used without a rating, the horse can't be assessed with confidence or, if used in the in-season Timeform publications, that the horse is out of form.

CHASERS & HURDLERS 2006/07

Horse	Commentary	Rating

ABA GOLD (IRE) 7 b.m. Darnay – Abadila (IRE) (Shernazar) [2006/7 h–: 16s 17d **h–**
20g Jun 27] no form: tried blinkered. *James Clements, Ireland*

ABBEY DAYS (IRE) 10 ch.g. Be My Native (USA) – Abbey Emerald (Baptism) **c113**
[2006/7 c103+, h–: c24g* c19m* c26s² Feb 18] lengthy gelding: poor form completed **h–**
outing over hurdles: winning pointer, including in January: useful hunter chaser: won
novice events at Bangor and Exeter within 5 days in May: stays 3¼m: acts on soft and
good to firm ground. *S. Flook*

ABBONDANZA (IRE) 4 b.g. Cape Cross (IRE) – Ninth Wonder (USA) (Forty Niner **h–**
(USA)) [2006/7 16gᵖᵘ Oct 14] fairly useful 1¼m winner at 3 yrs, ran poorly both
subsequent starts on Flat: shaped as if amiss on hurdling debut. *J. Howard Johnson*

ABERDEEN PARK 5 gr.m. Environment Friend – Michelee (Merdon Melody) **h79**
[2006/7 h65: 16g* 16s⁶ 20vᵖᵘ Feb 17] small mare: modest on Flat (stays 1¼m): poor
form over hurdles: won seller at Towcester (sold from Mrs H. Sweeting 9,800 gns) in
November: raced mainly at 2m. *Heather Dalton*

ABERLADY BAY (IRE) 4 ch.f. Selkirk (USA) – Desert Serenade (USA) (Green **h–**
Desert (USA)) [2006/7 16g⁴ Nov 18] smallish filly: maiden on Flat: soon behind in
juvenile on hurdling debut. *T. T. Clement*

ABIGAIL ADAMS 6 ch.m. Kris – Rose Vibert (Caerleon (USA)) [2006/7 16g⁶ Dec **h–**
30] half-sister to fair hurdler Serbelloni (by Spectrum), stayed 21f: well held in 2 maidens
on Flat at 3 yrs for P. Harris: soon tailed off in novice on hurdling debut. *R. Johnson*

ABIT IRISH (NZ) 6 ch.g. Oregon (USA) – Irish Talk (NZ) (Omnicorp (NZ)) [2006/7 **h87**
17s⁴ 17s 16s 19g 22mᶠ Apr 22] in frame twice from 3 starts over 7f on Flat in New
Zealand in autumn 2005: best effort over hurdles (modest form) on debut: likely to prove
best at easy 2m: takes strong hold. *J. L. Spearing*

A BIT OF FUN 6 ch.g. Unfuwain (USA) – Horseshoe Reef (Mill Reef (USA)) [2006/7 **h–**
h110: 17gᵖᵘ May 5] workmanlike gelding: fair handicap hurdler: stays 2½m: acts on any
going: has found cheekpieces/swished tail. *J. T. Stimpson*

ABLE DARA 4 b.g. Lahib (USA) – Nishara (Nishapour (FR)) [2006/7 F14s² Oct 29] **F82**
rather leggy gelding: half-brother to 1m winner Dara Mac (by Presidium): dam of little
account: 13 lengths second to Turbo Linn in 3-y-o bumper at Carlisle on debut. *N. Bycroft*

ABLE KING (NZ) 7 b.g. King's Theatre (IRE) – Edsa (NZ) (Grosvenor (NZ)) [2006/7 **h115**
20fᶠ 19m² 20m² 20f* 19m* Aug 24] in frame 6 times from 12 starts up to 11f on Flat in
New Zealand: winning maiden: won handicap at Uttoxeter in July and claimer at Stratford
(claimed £12,000) in August: will stay beyond 2½m: raced on good to firm/firm going:
front runner. *Miss S. West*

ABOVE GROUND (IRE) 5 b.g. Presenting – What A Topper (IRE) (Petoski) [2006/7 **h–**
F16m 20g Sep 17] €39,000 3-y-o: second foal: dam, ran twice in bumpers, half-sister **F73**
to fairly useful hurdler/smart chaser Tipping Tim, stayed 25f: mid-field in bumper at
Stratford on debut: tailed off in novice hurdle 2 weeks later: sold 5,400 gns Doncaster
November Sales, unseated both starts in points. *Jonjo O'Neill*

A BOY NAMED SIOUX (IRE) 9 b.g. Little Bighorn – Gayable (Gay Fandango **c78 +**
(USA)) [2006/7 c?: c25f² May 10] fairly useful pointer: 24 lengths second of 4 to Finest
of Men on completed start in hunters at Kelso. *Mrs E. J. Reed*

ABOYNE (IRE) 4 b.g. Mull of Kintyre (USA) – Never End (Alzao (USA)) [2006/7 **h–**
16d⁵ Oct 30] fair on Flat (stays 1¼m), sold out of M. Quinlan's stable 5,500 gns
Newmarket July Sales: no show in juvenile on hurdling debut. *K. F. Clutterbuck*

ABRAGANTE (IRE) 6 b.g. Saddlers' Hall (IRE) – Joli's Girl (Mansingh (USA)) **c125 p**
[2006/7 h112§: c20gᶠ c20g* c24dᵘʳ c23s* c23s* 22s² 23s³ 24g⁴ 24g* Apr 19] **h135 +**
lengthy, good-topped gelding: useful handicap hurdler: won at Exeter in December and
Cheltenham in April: blinkered, best effort when beating Beau Michel easily by 7 lengths
at latter, leading on bridle last: fairly useful novice chaser: successful both completed

27

starts (would have won but for falling last on debut), in handicaps at Haydock in November and Taunton in December: stays 3m: raced on good ground or softer (acts on soft): usually wears cheekpieces: not straightforward, but probably hasn't finished progressing. *D. E. Pipe*

ABRAHAM SMITH 7 b.g. Lord Americo – Alice Smith (Alias Smith (USA)) [2006/7 h109: c20g c24v^F c24s^pu c19s^pu c20v^F c21s^4 c23m^4 Apr 15] sturdy gelding: fair handicap hurdler: modest over fences: looked likely winner when fell 2 out in novice handicap at Bangor fifth start: stays easy 23f: acts on good to firm going, probably on heavy. *A. M. Hales* **c93** **h–**

ABSOLUTELYTHEBEST (IRE) 6 b.g. Anabaa (USA) – Recherchee (Rainbow Quest (USA)) [2006/7 h97: 19g^4 19m^2 16m^2 17g* 19m* 21m^5 c19m^3 c20d^5 17g Apr 11] good-topped gelding: fair hurdler: won novice handicap at Market Rasen (flashed tail) in July and novice at Hereford in September: better effort over fences when third to Borora in maiden at Hereford: stays 2½m: acts on good to firm going, possibly unsuited by heavy: tried in cheekpieces: jumps none too fluently. *J. G. M. O'Shea* **c99** **h100**

ABSOLUT POWER (GER) 6 ch.g. Acatenango (GER) – All Our Dreams (Caerleon (USA)) [2006/7 h116: 22d^6 20g^3 20g* 24s 22s^4 19d^4 19s^2 22s^5 21g^3 20g 20f^6 Apr 28] lengthy gelding: fairly useful handicap hurdler: won at Chepstow in October by short head from Businessmoney Jake: failed to convince with attitude most starts after: stays 2¾m: unraced on heavy ground, acts on any other: wears cheekpieces: temperament under suspicion. *J. A. Geake* **h120**

ABSTINENCE (IRE) 4 b.g. Spectrum (IRE) – Ballerina Gold (USA) (Slew O' Gold (USA)) [2006/7 F16g* Apr 3] second foal: dam, fairly useful maiden in France, stayed 1¼m: looked above-average prospect when winning 17-runner bumper at Wetherby on debut by 3½ lengths from Nodforms Paula (easy winner later in month), merely kept up to work after leading early in straight. *P. D. Niven* **F116**

ABSTRACT FOLLY (IRE) 5 b.g. Rossini (USA) – Cochiti (Kris) [2006/7 16g 16g^2 16g^2 Apr 15] fair on Flat (stays 1¾m), successful twice in 2006: progressive form over hurdles, second to easy winner Gringo (pair clear) in novice at Kelso final start: will be suited by further than 2m. *J. D. Bethell* **h95**

ABUTILON 4 ch.g. Desert Prince (IRE) – Ardisia (USA) (Affirmed (USA)) [2006/7 F14g^6 F14s^2 18s 16d 16s^5 16g Apr 14] 11,000 2-y-o: workmanlike gelding: half-brother to ungenuine winning hurdler/chaser Ashgar (by Bien Bien), stayed 3¼m, and several winners on Flat: dam, winner around 1¼m, half-sister to Oaks winner Ramrama: unraced on Flat for L. Cumani: fair form both starts in 3-y-o bumpers: modest form over hurdles, left with plenty to do last 2 starts: possibly capable of better. *B. G. Powell* **h86 +** **F90**

ABZUSON 10 b.g. Abzu – Mellouise (Handsome Sailor) [2006/7 c90x, h95: c20s^5 c24s^pu 27s 20s^pu Jan 31] big, strong gelding: fair hurdler at best: maiden chaser: no form in 2006/7: stays 3m: acts on heavy going: tried in visor/cheekpieces. *J. R. Norton* **c– x** **h–**

ACACIA AVENUE (IRE) 7 b.g. Shardari – Ennel Lady (IRE) (Erin's Hope) [2006/7 h–: 22g^4 c22f Jun 6] close-coupled, good-topped gelding: point winner: poor form over hurdles: well beaten on chasing debut. *Ian Williams* **c–** **h76**

ACAMBO (GER) 6 ro.g. Acambaro (GER) – Artic Lady (FR) (No Pass No Sale) [2006/7 h126: 16f* 16d* 16d^pu 20g^6 Apr 12] **h143**

'If we poured as much energy into working together as we do into damaging each other, the results would be amazing.' The words of Ladbrokes chief executive Chris Bell as the major bookmakers and the top racecourses slugged it out in a 'war' over the televising of racing in betting shops. Turf TV, set up by Britain's Racing UK-aligned racecourses (in a joint venture with Alphameric), has broken the twenty-year monopoly held over the provision of shop pictures by Satellite Information Services whose main shareholders include Ladbrokes (23%) and William Hill (20%). The first manifestation of the changes (which will be felt in full from January 2008) came in April when all live, non-terrestrial pictures from Ascot, Bangor, Chester, Goodwood, Newbury and York (whose SIS contracts had expired) became exclusive to Turf TV. The screens in SIS shops, such as those run by Hills, Ladbrokes, Coral (not a shareholder in SIS), Betfred and—until they eventually signed up in early-June (at a substantial discount)—the Tote, were left with relatively slim pickings from those meetings to show on their screens, though they continued to provide data to enable customers to bet on the non-terrestrial races at the six courses involved. The first major meeting to be affected was Royal

Ascot, where six races were absent from screens in betting shops not signed up to Turf TV. The announcement about establishing Turf TV came after the Government had finally agreed to the request from racing's governing body and the bookmakers to retain the Levy Board, which yields around £90m a year for racing (through a 10% levy on bookmakers' profits on the sport). The bookmakers estimate the cost of Turf TV would amount to another £50m on top of their current expenditure and point out they would expect levy payments to be balanced accordingly, were they to pay.

Another consequence of the dispute will be a review by bookmakers of their extensive big-race sponsorship. Coral, Ladbrokes and Hills all sponsor at the Festival at Cheltenham, for example, which will be aligned with Turf TV in 2008, when the number of non-SIS courses will rise to thirty-one—others include Aintree, Haydock, Kempton and Sandown (where Hills and Betfred have pulled out of the Tingle Creek and Gold Cup Chase respectively as a result of this dispute). Acambo's two wins in the latest season came in well-endowed, bookmaker-sponsored handicaps, the Betfred Swinton at Haydock very early in the season and The Ladbroke at Ascot in December. There were twenty-one runners in the Swinton, in which the emphasis on speed and fluency of jumping suited 16/1-shot Acambo who was well on top at the line, giving the impression there was better still to come. Incidentally, that Haydock victory will go down in the record books as the final winner for Martin Pipe, who was still registered as the licence-holder at Pond House due to a slight official delay in approving the handover to son David following the legendary trainer's retirement on the final day of 2005/6.

After missing the Greatwood Hurdle at Cheltenham with a minor injury, Acambo improved again when next seen in the Ladbroke Handicap Hurdle in December off a BHB mark 8 lb higher than in the Swinton. An excellent renewal of the Ladbroke attracted a field of twenty and three of the progressive sorts came to the fore, the well-backed Acambo winning from Tarlac (fresh from an easy course-and-distance win) and Victram (a stone higher than when winning the previous season's Imperial Cup). Acambo carried 11-9 in the Ladbroke, giving David Pipe (who landed a treble on the card) his biggest win since taking over and providing the stable with its third successive win in the race, Pipe senior having landed both renewals staged at Sandown while major reconstruction was going on at Ascot. The totesport Trophy at Newbury in February was next for Acambo who had top weight of 11-12 in the twenty-strong line-up for Britain's richest handicap hurdle (though worth only slightly more than the Ladbroke). Britain has had a dearth of top two-

Betfred Swinton Handicap Hurdle, Haydock—stand-in jockey Andrew Glassonbury
swoops on the grey Acambo to beat Callow Lake (noseband) and Saif Sareea

Ladbroke Handicap Hurdle, Ascot—Timmy Murphy sits tight after a last-flight blunder to hold off Tarlac

mile hurdlers in recent seasons but any idea that Acambo might develop into a leading Champion Hurdle contender was scotched when he was pulled up after dropping away tamely at Newbury. As it turned out, a bruised foot caused Acambo to miss Cheltenham, where he'd been declared for the Champion, and he was seen out only once more, finishing a fairly creditable sixth under top weight in the John Smith's Handicap Hurdle over two and a half miles at Aintree. His future will almost certainly be over fences, though, and he could well develop into a live candidate for the next Arkle, a race his owner has won four times, with Or Royal in 1997, Champleve in 1998, Well Chief in 2004 and Contraband in 2005. Indeed, Acambo featured quite prominently in the ante-post betting for the latest Arkle at various stages of the season, despite reportedly having never been schooled over fences.

Acambo (GER) (ro.g. 2001)	Acambaro (GER) (gr 1996)	Goofalik (b 1987)	Lyphard
			Alik
		Astica (gr 1989)	Surumu
			Auenliebe
	Artic Lady (FR) (ch 1988)	No Pass No Sale (b 1982)	Northfields
			No Disgrace
		Landlady (ch 1982)	Arctic Tern
			Dame Paque

Like Well Chief, the smallish Acambo began his racing career in Germany on the Flat, where he was successful four times at up to around nine furlongs before joining the Pipe stable as a four-year-old. Acambo's sire Acambaro was a smart performer, runner-up in the 1999 Deutsches Derby. He is a half-brother to Auetaler, another ex-German Flat performer who became a very smart hurdler for the Pipe stable. Acambo's dam Artic Lady, a daughter of Poule d'Essai des Poulains winner No Pass No Sale, won over six furlongs as a two-year-old in France and is a half-sister to the useful but ill-fated Lady Normandy, who died after breaking a leg in the 1991 Prix Marcel Boussac. The grandam Landlady also raced at pattern level in France and was a listed winner at a mile and a quarter. Acambo probably stays two and a half miles, but he has a good turn of foot and may well turn out to be best at the minimum trip. He acts on firm and good to soft going and is usually held up to make most effective use of his finishing speed. He ran poorly once when tried in a visor but his stable was out of form at the time. *D. E. Pipe*

ACCA LARENTIA (IRE) 6 gr.m. Titus Livius (FR) – Daisy Grey (Nordance (USA)) **h–**
[2006/7 h–: 18f⁴ 16g May 24] little impact over hurdles. *Mrs H. O. Graham*

ACCELERATION (IRE) 7 b.g. Groom Dancer (USA) – Overdrive (Shirley Heights) **c– §**
[2006/7 h87§: 16vᵖᵘ 16m² 16m c17dᵖᵘ 20s³ Dec 5] tall gelding: modest handicap hurdler: **h87 §**
left R. Allan, no show in maiden on chasing debut (for J. Haldane): stays 2½m: acts on
firm and soft going: has worn headgear: often tongue tied nowadays: ungenuine (reluctant to race last 2 starts). *Karen McLintock*

ACCENT (IRE) 4 b.g. Beckett (IRE) – Umlaut (Zafonic (USA)) [2006/7 17gᵖᵘ Mar 25] **h–**
lightly-raced maiden on Flat, sold out of Sir Mark Prescott's stable 8,500 gns Newmarket
Autumn Sales: no show in juvenile maiden on hurdling debut. *Miss Tor Sturgis*

ACCEPTING 10 b.g. Mtoto – D'Azy (Persian Bold) [2006/7 h–: 24v³ 26d² 26d⁵ 24m **h92**
Jul 11] compact gelding: modest handicap hurdler: stays 27f: acts on good to firm and
good to soft going: usually wears headgear (didn't in 2006/7, looked hard ride last 2
starts). *Mrs S. J. Smith*

ACCORDELLO (IRE) 6 b.m. Accordion – Marello (Supreme Leader) [2006/7 **h121 p**
h108p: 20s* 20g* 24d³ 22d Feb 3] neat mare: fair maiden on Flat: fairly useful form over
hurdles: won maiden at Wetherby and handicap at Aintree (by 1¼ lengths from Ostfanni,
pair clear) in November: unsuited by steady pace last 2 starts: stays 3m: raced on good
ground or softer: remains open to improvement. *K. G. Reveley*

ACCORDING TO JOHN (IRE) 7 br.g. Accordion – Cabin Glory (The Parson) **c145**
[2006/7 h136p: c20v* c22v* c24d⁴ c24d⁴ c24g³ Mar 14] well-made gelding: unbeaten in **h–**
4 novice hurdles in 2005/6: smart novice chaser: won at Carlisle in November and Kelso
in December: easily best effort when 13½ lengths third of 14 finishers to Denman in
Royal & SunAlliance Chase at Cheltenham: likely to stay beyond 25f: raced on good
going or softer (acts on heavy). *N. G. Richards*

ACCORDING TO PETE 6 b.g. Accordion – Magic Bloom (Full of Hope) [2006/7 **h122**
h107p, F110: 22g* 19dᵖᵘ 20s* 21d² 20v³ 16v³ Feb 24] leggy gelding: fairly useful
handicap hurdler: won at Kelso in May and Wetherby (beat Totally Scottish 4 lengths) in
October: better form still when placed 3 starts after: will stay 3m: raced on good ground
or softer (acts on heavy): hung badly left second start (only run on right-handed course).
J. M. Jefferson

ACCORDION ETOILE (IRE) 8 b.g. Accordion – Royal Thimble (IRE) (Prince **c?**
Rupert (FR)) [2006/7 c152, h149+: c17mᵘʳ Apr 10] strong, lengthy, good sort: high-class **h–**
hurdler: smart novice chaser in 2006/7: off 11½ months (reported in October to have met
with setback), never dangerous and unseated 2 out in valuable handicap won by Gemini
Lucy at Fairyhouse: has form at 2½m and on soft/heavy going, better at 2m under less
testing conditions: patiently ridden, and has a turn of foot. *Paul Nolan, Ireland*

ACCORDION OPERA (IRE) 7 ch.m. Accordion – Sparkling Opera (Orchestra) **h70**
[2006/7 20s 16v 16g 16s³ 16v⁶ 16d Jan 14] half-sister to several winners, including fairly
useful hurdler/fair chaser Ciara's Prince (by Good Thyne), stayed 3m: dam unraced: poor
maiden hurdler: raced mainly at 2m: acts on heavy going. *G. Keane, Ireland*

ACCUMULATE 4 b.g. Second Empire (IRE) – Bee-Bee-Gee (IRE) (Lake Coniston **h94**
(IRE)) [2006/7 17g 17m² Sep 28] no show in 2 maidens at 2 yrs for R. Fahey: much
better effort in juvenile hurdles (modest form) when second to Wise Choice at Hereford.
C. W. Moore

ACCUMULUS 7 b.g. Cloudings (IRE) – Norstock (Norwick (USA)) [2006/7 F84: **h105**
16m² 17g* 16g⁵ 16d⁵ Nov 19] fair form over hurdles: confirmed promise of debut when
winning novice at Hereford in October by 1¼ lengths from Prince Vector: bred to stay
beyond 17f: ridden by 10-lb claimer in 2006/7. *Noel T. Chance*

ACE BABY 4 b.g. First Trump – Mise En Scene (Lugana Beach) [2006/7 16d² 16s⁵ 17s **h83**
16s Dec 27] sturdy gelding: fair 5f/6f performer at 2 yrs for Mrs L. Stubbs, very lightly
raced on Flat since: form in juvenile hurdles only when second to easy winner Marodima
at Chepstow: raced around 2m on good to soft/soft ground: tongue tied last 2 starts.
K. J. Burke

ACE OF CLUBS (IRE) 5 b.g. Supreme Leader – Gain Control (IRE) (Mandalus) [2006/7 F16s³ F16d² 22d 19d 22sᵖᵘ Feb 3] £15,000 3-y-o: second foal: dam maiden jumper: fair form when placed both starts in bumpers at Worcester: mid-field at best in novice hurdles: should stay 2½m+. *N. A. Twiston-Davies*   **h79** **F95**

ACERTACK (IRE) 10 b.g. Supreme Leader – Ask The Madam (Strong Gale) [2006/7 c98d, h–: c20g² c22mᵖᵘ c23m⁶ c20g⁵ c16d⁴ c20vᵖᵘ 16v c20m⁴ Apr 8] lengthy gelding: modest handicap chaser, badly out of sorts after reappearance: stays 2½m: acts on heavy going: sometimes blinkered in 2006/7. *R. Rowe*   **c86 d** **h–**

ACES FOUR (IRE) 8 ch.g. Fourstars Allstar (USA) – Special Trix (IRE) (Peacock (FR)) [2006/7 h122: c21dᶠ c20g* c24s* c25s² c24g⁴ c25g* c25mᶠ Apr 24]   **c154 p** **h–**

'The best news of the week is that Aces Four is all right.' That was Ferdy Murphy's reaction in the aftermath of another big-race win for his Hot Weld in the Betfred Gold Cup at Sandown. This upbeat bulletin came just four days after Aces Four, one of the season's most progressive novice chasers, had fallen very heavily at the last in the Ellier Developments Hanover Quay Champion Novices' Chase at Punchestown. There'd been widespread relief at the time when the eight-year-old eventually got to his feet and was able to be led away, albeit slowly. Aces Four looked very sorry for himself, his crashing fall when two lengths up having left him concussed. The incident was a virtual carbon-copy of the one that befell the smart Aidan O'Brien-trained novice Corket, who suffered a horrific last-fence fall himself when holding every chance in the equivalent race back in 1997. Corket lay prostrate for some ten minutes as screens were erected around him, whilst jockey Trevor Horgan was so badly injured it proved to be his final ride. Unfortunately, the incident also seemed to leave its mark on Corket, who never fulfilled his promise and managed just one win from twenty-nine subsequent starts under Rules.

It's possible the confidence of the normally sound-jumping Aces Four may also be affected in the longer term but, equally, many others have bounced back from similar or even worse mishaps. Ballycassidy, for instance, was also concussed when falling in the 2006 Grand National but returned within three weeks to win a good prize at Perth. One of the most remarkable recoveries was made by Moorcroft Boy. In 1994 he damaged his neck so badly in a fall in Aintree's Becher Chase that he needed six weeks treatment at the University of Liverpool Veterinary Hospital followed by three months box rest. Yet seventeen months later Moorcroft Boy, at the age of eleven, produced a lifetime's best to win the Scottish National. Here's

John Smith's Mildmay Novices' Chase, Aintree—a bold display from the front-running Aces Four, who is followed over this early fence by eventual third Dom d'Orgeval

The DPRP Aces Partnership's "Aces Four"

hoping that Aces Four makes a complete recovery and returns to build on what he achieved in his first season over fences, as he has the potential to develop into a high-class staying chaser when he goes into open company.

Aces Four began his career in bumpers, showing plenty of ability without winning, trained at that time by Billy McKeown who was also in charge when Aces Four finished in the frame in novice hurdles on his first four outings in 2005/6. Joining Murphy after being sold for 20,000 guineas midway through that season, Aces Four was soon showing much improved form and made up into a fairly useful hurdler, winning at Ludlow, Ayr and Perth. Aces Four's first race over fences came in a novice event at Fakenham in October and, like his last, it ended in a fall at the final fence, although on this occasion he was held in third having shaped as if the outing was needed. In between those falls Aces Four often impressed with his jumping and never stopped improving. After winning a maiden (beating Character Building) and a novice at Newcastle in November, Aces Four finished in the frame twice at Cheltenham, undergoing a wind operation after the first of those and returning to take fourth place at 25/1 in the Royal & SunAlliance Chase over three months later, beaten around fourteen lengths by Denman. Aces Four looked the second-best horse in the Royal & SunAlliance, paying the price for taking on the winner for the lead on the second circuit and also for a bad stumble three out. The performance looked to give him a leading chance on his next appearance, in the John Smith's Mildmay Novices' Chase at Aintree, and Aces Four was sent off favourite to account for nine rivals in a good renewal of this long-established Grade 2 contest. They included Ungaro, Dom d'Orgeval and Turko, all of whom had been out of the frame in the Royal & SunAlliance, and Faasel, fourth in the Arkle Trophy at the Cheltenham Festival. Aces Four had finished distressed at Cheltenham and didn't take the eye particularly at Aintree. However, any thoughts that his hard race might have taken the edge off him were soon dispelled. He put up a cracking performance, one as good as has been seen in this particular race in the past fifteen years. Soon racing in second as Yes Sir set a sound pace, Aces Four was sent on six out and won unchallenged from Faasel, fourteen lengths clear at the last but eased towards the finish, the winning margin down to eight lengths as a result. Aces Four was sweating slightly when he reappeared eleven days later at Punchestown, but his paddock appearance again proved no guide as to how he would perform once racing. Taking over after five out, Aces Four had shaken off all bar Offshore Account turning for home and was just beginning to get the better of that rival when he came down.

Aces Four (IRE) (ch.g. 1999)	Fourstars Allstar (USA) (b 1988)	Compliance (b 1978)	Northern Dancer / Sex Appeal
		Broadway Joan (ch 1979)	Bold Arian / Courtneys Doll
	Special Trix (IRE) (ch 1993)	Peacock (gr 1968)	Devon / Peace Rose
		Forgello (ch 1969)	Bargello / Four Aces

Bought as an unraced four-year-old for €39,000, Aces Four is the second foal of Special Trix, an unraced sister to the 1994 Ladbroke Hurdle/Irish Arkle Chase winner Atone and half-sister to the useful chaser at up to two and a half miles Music Be Magic. Special Trix's only other winner to date is her first foal Ocras Mor (by Old Vic), a fairly useful Irish hurdler at up to two and a half miles who won twice in 2004/5, but died without producing a live foal once retired to stud. Her fifth foal, the Broken Hearted gelding Back On The Road, fetched €85,000 as an unraced four-year-old at the 2006 Derby Sale. As that price tag might suggest, this pedigree has proved a fruitful source for jumping talent down the years, with winners including Aces Four's grandam Forgello, who was successful three times over hurdles in Ireland. Great grandam Four Aces was even better, showing useful form over both hurdles and fences, finishing third when a hot favourite for the 1961 Gloucestershire Hurdle at Cheltenham. Aces Four, who will stay beyond twenty-five furlongs, acts on soft and good to firm ground, and he finished second in a bumper on his debut on the only occasion he has encountered heavy going. *Ferdy Murphy*

ACES OR BETTER (IRE) 6 b.g. Saddlers' Hall (IRE) – Aon Dochas (IRE) (Strong Gale) [2006/7 F18m* F20d² 20v² 24v* 24v 20m Apr 8] €175,000 3-y-o: fourth foal: half-brother to fairly useful hurdler Thames (by Over The River), stays 3m: dam, won 2m chase, half-sister to smart chaser up to 21f Native Charm and useful 2½m chaser Sir Dante: placed in points: fairly useful form both starts in bumpers at Galway, winning 20-runner event in August: fair form over hurdles: won maiden at Listowel in September: stays 3m: acts on heavy ground (bumper win on good to firm): front runner: sold 65,000 gns Doncaster May Sales. *Ms M. Mullins, Ireland*   **h114 F101**

ACKHURST (IRE) 8 br.g. Anshan – Sassy Sally (IRE) (Callernish) [2006/7 19d⁴ 21d 20s⁴ c19v³ c20s⁴ c19v³ c19g⁴ Mar 21] 4,000 5-y-o: strong gelding: second foal: dam, maiden hurdler, out of half-sister to Midlands Grand National winner Another Excuse: winning pointer: fourth in novice hurdles: better form (modest) over fences: should stay beyond 2½m: acts on heavy going. *G. F. Edwards*   **c96 h82**

ACKNOWLEDGEMENT (IRE) 5 b.g. Josr Algarhoud (IRE) – On Request (IRE) (Be My Guest (USA)) [2006/7 16s 16d 26v 16s^pu 23d^pu Mar 21] rather leggy gelding: half-brother to 2¾m hurdle winner Jay Bee Ell (by Pursuit of Love): fair maiden on Flat (stays 1¾m), sold out of D. Elsworth's stable 40,000 gns Newmarket Autumn Sales: no form over hurdles: blinkered final start. *Carl Llewellyn*   **h–**

ACROPOLIS (IRE) 6 b.g. Sadler's Wells (USA) – Dedicated Lady (IRE) (Pennine Walk) [2006/7 h99p: 16v⁴ 20s^pu Jan 31] compact gelding: formerly very smart on Flat for A. O'Brien: modest form at best in novice hurdles: carries head awkwardly: joined I. Semple. *J. Howard Johnson*   **h87**

ACT GOLD (GER) 5 b.g. Slip Anchor – Alisa (GER) (Daun (GER)) [2006/7 F16v F16s⁴ 21g 16g Mar 29] tall gelding: fifth foal: half-brother to several winners on Flat   **h80 F80**

in Germany: dam German 1m winner: modest form on second start in bumpers: never dangerous both outings over hurdles. *Ian Williams*

ACTION STRASSE (IRE) 5 b.g. Old Vic – Platin Run (IRE) (Strong Gale) [2006/7 **h93** F86+: F17d² 19v⁴ 16d⁶ 20g⁵ 20g³ Dec 30] in frame both starts in bumpers: modest form **F92** in novice hurdles: stays 2½m: raced on good ground or softer. *J. Howard Johnson*

ACUZIO 6 b.g. Mon Tresor – Veni Vici (IRE) (Namaqualand (USA)) [2006/7 16g 17g⁶ **h94 ?** 17d³ 20g Apr 21] fair up to 13.4f on Flat, successful twice in 2006: modest form over hurdles: raced mainly around 2m. *W. M. Brisbourne*

ADALPOUR (IRE) 9 b.g. Kahyasi – Adalya (IRE) (Darshaan) [2006/7 16v Feb 18] **h–** maiden hurdler: stays 3m: acts on soft and good to firm going: tried in cheekpieces/ tongue tied. *M. F. Harris*

ADAMANT APPROACH (IRE) 13 b.g. Mandalus – Crash Approach (Crash **c140** Course) [2006/7 c–, h137: 17s² 20v* 16fF 16m⁶ 22m 17g⁵ 20d* 20f² c19v* c20g⁵ **h151** 16s c20v⁴ 20v* 24d* 24g³ 24m* 24m⁵ Apr 26]

    Racing at Leopardstown on February 6th 2000 provided some memorable sport: Florida Pearl won a second Irish Hennessy, defeating Dorans Pride; Native Upmanship beat Commanche Court in the Dr P. J. Moriarty Novices' Chase; Youlneverwalkalone landed the odds in the Deloitte & Touche Novices' Hurdle; and the hunter chase saw a shock defeat for Sheltering, who could finish only third behind Dan's Your Man and Spot Thedifference. The Weatherbys Ireland INH Flat Race which closed the card proved a contest of lasting significance too, with four of the field still in action now. The runner-up Risk Accessor, after a career as a smart if wayward chaser, has found a new lease of life in hunter chases (won twice shortly after the end of the 2006/7 season), while the third I'vehadit, who was useful at his best, was third in a point early in the year before running in the hunter chase on the same Leopardstown card seven years on. Last home that winter's day back in 2000 was Native Commander, who took his career tally to five wins with handicap successes at Taunton over hurdles and at Fontwell in a selling chase in the spring. That trio, however, are clearly veterans in the twilight of their career but Adamant Approach, who won the bumper, is only just getting going, enjoying a good season by any standards and a remarkable one for a horse of his age. He won more races in 2006/7 than he had in seven previous seasons put together, showing his best form over both fences and, at the age of thirteen, over hurdles.

    Adamant Approach had looked one to follow in landing that bumper but those that took the advice were ill rewarded initially. He finished runner-up three times in five starts over hurdles in 2000/1 before winning a maiden hurdle on his reappearance the following season. However, only one further success followed in eight more starts that campaign, albeit in the Pierse Hurdle at Leopardstown, though Adamant Approach would also have won the Supreme Novices' at Cheltenham but for falling at the last. At eight, he would have been old for a winner of that race, though, coincidentally, his fall let in another of that age in Like-A-Butterfly. A fall also robbed Adamant Approach of a Grade 1 victory over fences in 2002/3, as he had the race at his mercy when departing two out in the Powers Gold Cup at Fairyhouse. As it was, he ended the season with two wins in lesser company. Three seasons of honest endeavour followed, mostly at two miles over hurdles, and he continued to be competitive in big handicaps without getting his head in front. He finished fourth in the 2005 Pierse, third in the 2006 County Hurdle (behind two at least half his age) and second in a listed handicap at Punchestown on his final start in 2005/6.

    Adamant Approach was kept on the go after that and eleven runs, including his first two starts on the Flat, before the end of September brought three wins, in minor hurdles at Navan and Tipperary and quite a valuable handicap chase at Listowel. Adamant Approach needed to be nowhere near his best for the hurdle wins and there were only three finishers at Listowel, though runner-up Waltons Mountain would have won the Denny Gold Medal at Tralee the time before but for falling and Adamant Approach showed just about his best form over fences. Two more successes came in five further starts before the end of the year, in a qualified riders' race over a mile and three quarters on the Flat at Galway and in a two-and-a-half-mile handicap hurdle at Punchestown (his second win of the campaign under conditional Richard Kiely) on New Year's Eve.

Racing Post In Ireland Hurdle, Fairyhouse—
the sixth win of a memorable campaign for the veteran Adamant Approach

A fourth attempt at the Pierse was on the cards but, after seeing out the race at Punchestown really well in testing conditions, Adamant Approach was stepped up to three miles for the first time and won the Pertemps qualifier on the same Leopardstown card, scoring under trainer Willie Mullins' son Patrick (who'd also been on board for that Flat win at Galway). Patiently ridden by the young amateur —who is just four years the gelding's senior—Adamant Approach was brought with a well-timed run to beat Artiste Bay by a head, giving weight to all but one of his twenty-six rivals. Despite a fairly stout pedigree, Adamant Approach had been reported by his riders as not seeing out the trip when tried beyond two miles in his younger days, but at the fiftieth attempt over jumps Adamant Approach now seemed to have found his optimum distance.

All three of his later races were at three miles and he ran really well each time, having little trouble landing a minor event at the Fairyhouse Irish National meeting under Ruby Walsh. He put up even better performances on the starts either side, with Patrick Mullins again in the saddle. Adamant Approach finished third to Oscar Park in the Pertemps Final at Cheltenham and, with his rider unable to claim, fifth to Refinement in the Champion Stayers' Hurdle at Punchestown. At Cheltenham he was giving weight to all but two of his rivals and, judged on form, his display would have been good enough to earn him fifth in the World Hurdle earlier in the afternoon. The oldest runner in the World Hurdle was eight but it is not especially unusual for a teenager like Adamant Approach to run at Cheltenham—there have been twenty-nine at the last six Festivals—nor even to be placed. Earthmover won the 2004 Foxhunter and Lord of The River, Banker Count and Spot Thedifference have all finished second in handicap chases since then. However, as a hurdler, Adamant Approach is a rarity, the first of his age to appear in that sphere at the Festival since 2000 and even more of a rarity for a horse of his ability in showing improvement.

The only hurdler of recent times at Cheltenham that bears much comparison to Adamant Approach is Mole Board who was thirteen when he finished eighth to Alderbrook in the 1995 Champion Hurdle and went on to show smart form the following season, winning a conditions race at Ascot and starting at 14/1 for the Stayers' Hurdle, only to be pulled up lame. No hurdler as old as thirteen has won at the Cheltenham Festival since the remarkable Willie Wumpkins completed his hat-trick of wins in the Coral Golden Hurdle Final in 1981. Willie Wumpkins won four Festival races in all, the other the 1973 Aldsworth Hurdle (now the Ballymore Properties Baring Bingham Hurdle), and was retired after his third Final triumph. Adamant Approach wasn't the only durable veteran to make a mark in 2006/7 either. The French Furze was placed in both the 'Fighting Fifth' at Newcastle and the Champion Hurdle Trial at Haydock and fourteen-year-old Spot Thedifference, another survivor from that Leopardstown card long ago, landed three more prizes over cross-country fences.

Sometimes, of course, things don't go so well. There was much criticism of Michael Hourigan after the fourteen-year-old Dorans Pride was injured with fatal consequences in the 2003 Foxhunter, and Native Commander's Fontwell victory came from Wot No Cash, a fifteen-year-old having his first run in a year who collapsed and died after the race. And there's the rub. Everyone loves gallant veterans, defying the years, but when something unfortunate happens the clamour for something to be done can be deafening—'Wot No Cash shouldn't have been allowed to run' and 'the BHB/HRA should have prevented the tragedy' formed the basis of most complaints afterwards. As it happened, the HRA vet in attendance at Fontwell had examined Wot No Cash before the race and found him 'in good

Greenstar Syndicate's "Adamant Approach"

condition and fit to race'. It was reported, however, that the HRA is looking at making it mandatory for horses of a certain age to be examined before they are allowed to run. Of course, horses should be fit to race, though a move to retire horses at a set age, as happens in trotting, would meet with little support. After all, the remarkable Mac Vidi, who like Wot No Cash was handled by a permit holder, belied his years to be placed in the 1980 Cheltenham Gold Cup at the age of fifteen. Youth, by the way, is no guarantee against a horse dropping dead from its exertions, as the connections of the promising five-year-old War General will attest.

	Mandalus	Mandamus	Petition
	(b 1974)	(br 1960)	Great Fun
Adamant Approach (IRE)		Laminate	Abernant
(b.g. 1994)		(gr 1957)	Lamri
	Crash Approach	Crash Course	Busted
	(ch 1985)	(b 1971)	Lucky Stream
		Farm Hill	Coxcomb
		(ch 1962)	Flotation

Adamant Approach is set to carry on in 2007/8, when a mix of hurdling and chasing is again likely to be on the agenda. His trainer attributes his fine 2006/7 campaign, in part, to regular racing on good ground. Adamant Approach certainly handles that sort of going well, though he also acts on heavy and ran creditably at the time on his only start on firm. The sturdy Adamant Approach was tried tongue tied several times in 2004/5. It goes almost without saying that he is tough and most genuine and reliable. *W. P. Mullins, Ireland*

ADARE (GER) 4 b.g. Saddlers' Hall (IRE) – Aughamore Beauty (IRE) (Dara Monarch) [2006/7 F13v³ Jan 20] half-brother to several winners on Flat, including useful performer up to 1½m Albany Hall (by Turtle Island): dam unraced: favourite, 11 lengths third of 6 to Lease Lend in 4-y-o bumper at Haydock on debut: will stay at least 2m. *T. P. Tate*   **F94**

ADARE PRINCE (IRE) 6 b.g. Supreme Leader – Legal Challenge (IRE) (Strong Gale) [2006/7 F16d² 17d 16d⁴ 17s 17s⁴ c16rpu Jan 12] 27,000 3-y-o: lengthy gelding: first foal: dam, fair hurdler, stayed 3m: runner-up in bumper on debut: modest form over hurdles: bled on chasing debut: will be suited by 2¼m+: raced on ground softer than good. *P. J. Hobbs*   **c–** **h87** **F80**

ADDICTED (IRE) 4 b.g. Machiavellian (USA) – Peneia (USA) (Nureyev (USA)) [2006/7 16d⁴ 16d 16s⁶ 16g Mar 31] rather leggy gelding: lightly raced on Flat, fairly useful form when winning 1m maiden in July, sold out of M. Halford's stable 52,000 gns Newmarket Sales later in month: best effort over hurdles (fair form) on debut: bled final start: likely to prove best at 2m with emphasis on speed. *N. J. Henderson*   **h105**

ADECCO (IRE) 8 b.g. Eagle Eyed (USA) – Kharaliya (FR) (Doyoun) [2006/7 c96, h90: c16s³ c18g⁶ c16d⁴ c16s³ c16s³ c16d³ Jan 30] useful-looking gelding: modest hurdler/chaser: stays 19f: acts on firm and soft going: tried blinkered: flashes tail under pressure: often let down by jumping over fences. *G. L. Moore*   **c93 x** **h–**

ADELPHI BOY (IRE) 11 ch.g. Ballad Rock – Toda (Absalom) [2006/7 20m⁶ 21m Sep 26] lengthy gelding: lightly-raced winning hurdler: off 2 years, no show in 2006/7: should stay beyond 2m. *M. Todhunter*   **h–**

ADELPHI THEATRE (USA) 10 b.g. Sadler's Wells (USA) – Truly Bound (USA) (In Reality) [2006/7 c105, h100: c20g³ c20spu c24g⁶ Nov 7] useful-looking gelding: winning hurdler: fair novice chaser: breathing problem last 2 starts: stays easy 2¾m: acts on good to soft going, probably on good to firm: none too consistent. *R. Rowe*   **c102 §** **h–**

ADJAMI (IRE) 6 b.g. Entrepreneur – Adjriyna (Top Ville) [2006/7 h111: 16sF 17d³ 16s⁶ 16m² Apr 10] compact gelding: fairly useful hurdler, off 15 months prior to return: stays 19f: acts on soft and good to firm going: has jumped none too fluently. *A. King*   **h114**

ADLESTROP 7 ch.m. Alderbrook – Lady Buck (Pollerton) [2006/7 h88, F92: 19m⁵ 20d² 20d 21s c19g⁶ Apr 11] modest maiden hurdler: well held in novice handicap on chasing debut: should stay beyond 2½m: acts on heavy going. *R. T. Phillips*   **c–** **h93**

ADMIRAL COMPTON 6 ch.g. Compton Place – Sunfleet (Red Sunset) [2006/7 16f 16m³ 16f⁵ 16m⁴ Oct 16] half-brother to fair 2m hurdler No Pattern (by Rock City): fair on Flat (stays 1¼m): modest novice hurdler: likely to prove best at 2m with emphasis on speed: sold 9,000 gns Newmarket Autumn Sales. *J. R. Boyle*   **h91**

ADMIRAL PEARY (IRE) 11 b. or br.g. Lord Americo – Arctic Brief (Buckskin (FR)) [2006/7 c116, h113: c23s^F c24s^3 c24g^3 c31s^pu Apr 27] smallish, close-coupled gelding: winning hurdler: maiden chaser, below best in 2006/7: stays 3¾m: acts on heavy and good to firm going: not a fluent jumper: tricky ride. *C. R. Egerton* **c106 x h–**

AD MURUM (IRE) 8 ch.g. Hubbly Bubbly (USA) – Cailin Cainnteach (Le Bavard (FR)) [2006/7 h94, F–: 23g^2 24g^5 20f* 22d^4 21m c20d c20s c23m^5 c25g^ur Nov 29] lengthy, well-made gelding: fair hurdler: won handicap at Sedgefield in August: never dangerous 3 completed starts over fences: should stay 3m: acts on firm going. *G. M. Moore* **c– h104**

ADOLPHUS (IRE) 10 b.g. Tidaro (USA) – Coxtown Queen (IRE) (Corvaro (USA)) [2006/7 c88, h–: c16f^5 c25d^F Oct 21] good-topped gelding: maiden hurdler: winning chaser: well beaten completed outing in handicaps in 2006/7: best form around 2½m: acts on firm and soft going: tried in headgear: tongue tied once. *Miss S. E. Forster* **c– h–**

ADOPTED HERO (IRE) 7 b.g. Sadler's Wells (USA) – Lady Liberty (NZ) (Noble Bijou (USA)) [2006/7 h130d: 16m^3 c17g^6 16g^6 16m 16g^5 16g* Apr 7] smallish, good-topped gelding: useful handicap hurdler: left J. Howard Johnson, back to best when winning at Haydock by 11 lengths from Sunday City, hanging left: tailed off in maiden at Ascot on chasing debut: raced around 2m: acts on soft and good to firm going: tried visored/in cheekpieces. *G. L. Moore* **c– h131**

ADORABELLA (IRE) 4 b.f. Revoque (IRE) – Febrile (USA) (Trempolino (USA)) [2006/7 aF13g^4 F12s^5 aF16g^5 Mar 9] angular filly: first foal: dam unraced half-sister to Ribblesdale Stakes winner Spanish Sun: modest form in bumpers. *A. King* **F80**

ADORABLY ADORABLE (IRE) 5 b.m. Florida Son – Tootsie (Hotfoot) [2006/7 F16g F16s Jan 25] plain, very light-framed mare: second foal: dam unraced half-sister to fairly useful chaser The Kew Tour, stays 3¼m: no show in bumpers. *P. R. Rodford* **F–**

A DOUBLE EWE BEE 6 b.m. Kingsinger (IRE) – Some Dream (Vitiges (FR)) [2006/7 17s^pu 16s^2 16s 17s^2 17g^F 17g^2 17g^2 Apr 27] modest hurdler: likely to stay 2½m: acts on soft going. *W. G. M. Turner* **h86**

ADVENTINO 12 gr.g. Neltino – My Miss Adventure (New Member) [2006/7 c–, h–: 20s c19m^5 c16m^pu Jul 5] no longer of any account: walked over in point in April. *P. R. Johnson* **c– h–**

ADVENTURIST 7 ch.g. Entrepreneur – Alik (FR) (Targowice (USA)) [2006/7 h111: 22v^5 Jan 25] strong gelding: fair hurdler: tongue tied, well held in handicap only outing in 2006/7: stays easy 3m: possibly unsuited by going softer than good: wore cheekpieces last 4 starts. *P. Bowen* **h–**

AEGEAN 13 b.g. Rock Hopper – Sayulita (Habitat) [2006/7 c103, h–: c20d c22g^5 c24g^2 c24s^ur c25d^4 c30s^pu c24g^4 c23m^3 Apr 15] tall gelding: modest handicap chaser: stays 25f: acts on good to firm and good to soft going. *Mrs S. J. Smith* **c93 h–**

AEGEAN PIRATE (IRE) 10 b.g. Polykratis – Rusheen Na Corra (IRE) (Burslem) [2006/7 c16g^pu 18d^pu Nov 12] angular gelding: no form: tried tongue tied/in cheekpieces. *K. J. Burke* **c– h–**

AELRED 14 b.g. Ovac (ITY) – Sponsorship (Sparkler) [2006/7 c–, h82: c25m^pu c25g Apr 2] sturdy gelding: maiden hurdler: winning chaser: in frame in points in 2007: stays 3m: acts on heavy and good to firm going: has worn cheekpieces: tried tongue tied: won or placed in 13 of 17 races at Newcastle: usually races prominently. *Mrs Sarah E. Murray* **c– h–**

AERODROME (IRE) 5 b.g. Presenting – Two Will Do (IRE) (Air Display (USA)) [2006/7 F16d 20v^pu Dec 15] good-bodied gelding: first foal: dam unraced: no show in bumper or maiden hurdle. *Heather Dalton* **h– F–**

AFAIR PROMISE (NZ) 7 br.g. Vain Promise (AUS) – Diamond Fair (NZ) (Diamante D) [2006/7 16v^pu 20g^6 Apr 11] tall, leggy gelding: sixth in Grade 2 bumper on debut in 2004/5: looked difficult ride both starts over hurdles. *A. King* **h73 +**

A FEW KIND WORDS (IRE) 6 b.g. Darazari (IRE) – Aussieannie (IRE) (Arapahos (FR)) [2006/7 h97, F89: 24s^5 May 14] placed in bumpers/over hurdles: lame only outing in 2006/7: should stay at least 2½m. *Mrs K. Waldron* **h93**

AFRAD (FR) 6 gr.g. Linamix (FR) – Afragha (IRE) (Darshaan) [2006/7 h133: c20g^F c17v^2 c19s* 21s^3 23s^2 c26g^3 Apr 1] leggy gelding: useful hurdler: good placed efforts in valuable handicap at Kempton and Grade 2 at Haydock (8 lengths second to Labelthou) fourth/fifth starts: fairly useful form over fences: fortunate to win maiden at Chepstow in December: less than fluent throughout and typically none too keen under pressure when **c124 § h137**

running poorly final outing: stays 23f: raced on good going or softer (acts on heavy): carries head high: one to be wary of over fences. *N. J. Henderson*

AFRICA BLAZE (IRE) 4 b.f. Imperial Ballet (IRE) – Renata's Ring (IRE) (Auction Ring (USA)) [2006/7 aF16g Mar 9] €12,000 3-y-o: half-sister to 3 winners, including fair 2m hurdler The Ring (by Definite Article): dam placed at 7f in Ireland: raced freely when tailed off in bumper on debut. *M. Scudamore*   **F—**

AFSOUN (FR) 5 b.g. Kahyasi – Afragha (IRE) (Darshaan) [2006/7 h135: 16s* 16dF 16v* 16s² 16d³ 20g³ Apr 14]   **h159**

Plans to send the smart juvenile hurdler Afsoun chasing after he was bought for 270,000 guineas at the Doncaster May Sales didn't materialise. However, had he been sent back through the sale-ring at the end of 2006/7 he would surely have made considerably more than even that sizeable sum. He enhanced his reputation, kept over hurdles, with wins in the Gerry Feilden at Newbury and the Champion Hurdle Trial at Haydock, and a highly creditable third in the Champion Hurdle itself at Cheltenham. With fences beckoning at last in 2007/8, Afsoun will have the chance to make his mark and may well return to the Cheltenham Festival a major contender for the Arkle, or possibly even the Royal & SunAlliance Chase.

Afsoun was impressive in both his wins, beating Craven by eight lengths under top weight in the Gerry Feilden (known as the Stan James Intermediate Handicap) and The French Furze by nine in the bonusprint.com-sponsored Trial at Haydock. It's not inconceivable that Afsoun would have won his start in between, too, as he was going strongly in front when falling at the fifth in the Christmas Hurdle at Kempton. His one disappointing run (reportedly subdued afterwards) came in the Kingwell Hurdle at Wincanton where he was a below-par second to Straw Bear. Afsoun started 28/1 at Cheltenham but showed himself a good deal better than those odds indicated, staying on well to take third near the line, just over three lengths behind the winner Sublimity. Afsoun ran respectably when also filling third, behind Al Eile in the Aintree Hurdle, on his final start and is certainly worth another try over two and a half miles or further.

The well-made Afsoun is yet another fine National Hunt prospect from the Aga Khan's studs, a subject dealt with in detail in the essay on Ebaziyan, from a family which has already produced a handful of above-average jumpers. His half-brothers include stable-companion Afrad (by Linamix), who is a useful hurdler and ungenuine winning chaser, while his dam Afragha is closely related to the useful hurdler at up to two and a half miles Afarad. Afragha won at a mile and a quarter for

bonusprint.com Champion Hurdle Trial, Haydock—the first leg of a Grade 2 double for Messrs Henderson and Fitzgerald as Afsoun proves far too strong for eventual third Overstrand (No.4)

Mr Trevor Hemmings' "Afsoun"

		Ile de Bourbon (br 1975)	Nijinsky
	Kahyasi (b 1985)		Roseliere
		Kadissya (b 1979)	Blushing Groom
Afsoun (FR) (b.g. 2002)			Kalkeen
		Darshaan (br 1981)	Shirley Heights
	Afragha (IRE) (br 1994)		Delsy
		Afasara (br 1988)	Shardari
			Afeefa

John Oxx on her only start, and three of her four offspring to race have won on the Flat too, including Afrad, who won the Goodwood Stakes in 2005, and Afsoun himself, who showed fairly useful form at up to fifteen furlongs for Alain de Royer Dupre. Incidentally, Afsoun's trainer Nicky Henderson does very well with his occasional Flat runners and Afsoun wouldn't be a forlorn prospect were he to be trained for the Cesarewitch. Afsoun has sometimes got very stirred up in the preliminaries (has worn ear plugs), though he was relatively calm at Cheltenham and very relaxed at Aintree. He acts well on soft/heavy going. *N. J. Henderson*

AFTER EIGHT (GER) 7 b.g. Sir Felix (FR) – Amrei (Ardross) [2006/7 h127: 21g⁶ 22s³ 24s⁵ Dec 23] small, compact gelding: fairly useful handicap hurdler: stays 2¾m: acts on any going. *Miss Venetia Williams*   **h122**

AFTER GALWAY (IRE) 11 b.g. Camden Town – Money For Honey (New Brig) [2006/7 c16vᵖᵘ Dec 6] lightly raced: winning hurdler for Miss V. Scott: off 20 months, no show in maiden on chasing debut: should stay 2½m. *Ferdy Murphy*   **c–** **h–**

41

AFTER LENT (IRE) 6 b.g. Desert Style (IRE) – Yashville (Top Ville) [2006/7 h87: **h92**
17g* May 16] compact gelding: modest hurdler: won claimer at Newton Abbot in May:
likely to have proved best around 2m: not straightforward: dead. *D. E. Pipe*

AFTER MIDNIGHT (IRE) 5 b.g. In The Wings – Medway (IRE) (Shernazar) **c89 p**
[2006/7 16m* 18f² 16g 17s* 21d* c17v⁵ c17s c18v 16g 24m³ Apr 26] leggy, narrow **h107**
gelding: half-brother to fairly useful 2¼m hurdle Settlement Craic (by Ela-Mana-Mou):
lightly raced on Flat: generally progressive over hurdles in 2006/7, winning handicaps in
large fields at Listowel in June, Tralee in October and Cheltenham (conditional jockeys)
in November: best effort in maiden chases when fifth to Alexander Taipan at Fairyhouse,
not knocked about: stays 3m: acts on firm and soft ground: held up: should still do better
over fences. *A. J. Martin, Ireland*

AFTER THE BALL (SAF) 8 ch.m. Rocky Marriage (USA) – Aerial Dancer (SAF) **h–**
(Dancing Champ (USA)) [2006/7 16gᵖᵘ 16vᵖᵘ Jan 17] half-sister to winner in South
Africa by Kefaah: dam won in South Africa: disappointing maiden on Flat: sold out of
S. Seemar's stable 1,000 gns Newmarket Autumn (2005) Sales: no show in maiden
hurdles. *R. M. Clark*

A GLASS IN THYNE (IRE) 9 br.g. Glacial Storm (USA) – River Thyne (IRE) **c119**
(Good Thyne (USA)) [2006/7 c133, h–: c24g⁴ c24s Nov 25] leggy gelding: runner-up on **h–**
second of 2 outings in novice hurdles: lightly-raced chaser, useful winner in 2005/6:
below form both starts after 8-month absence, lame second one: should stay beyond 3m:
acts on heavy ground. *B. N. Pollock*

AGNESE 7 ch.m. Abou Zouz (USA) – Efizia (Efisio) [2006/7 h77: 23g⁵ 19d⁴ 20s³ 24gᵖᵘ **h73**
22m³ 22g⁵ Sep 17] sturdy mare: poor maiden hurdler: stays 3¼m: acts on firm and soft
going: tried in cheekpieces, blinkered in 2006/7. *M. Dods*

AGUS A VIC (IRE) 6 b.g. Old Vic – Marovia (IRE) (Montelimar (USA)) [2006/7 **c118**
c23s² c20d* c25m² Apr 10] second foal: dam unraced: won points late in 2006: useful
form in hunters, won at Down Royal (by 9 lengths from Howryafeelin) in March: 1¼
lengths second to Beautiful Sound (pair clear) at Fairyhouse following month: stays 25f.
Patrick Martin, Ireland

AHAZ 5 b.g. Zaha (CAN) – Classic Faster (IRE) (Running Steps (USA)) [2006/7 16sᵖᵘ **h–**
17d 17g 17d Dec 26] strong gelding: poor maiden on Flat: no form over hurdles.
J. F. Coupland

AHEADOFHISTIME (IRE) 8 b.g. Supreme Leader – Timely Run (IRE) (Deep Run) **c86**
[2006/7 20s⁵ c21s² c23dᵖᵘ c26gᵖᵘ c24g⁵ Apr 27] rangy, good sort: maiden hurdler/chaser, **h–**
lightly raced: winning pointer, including in 2007: left D. Rees after fourth start (visored):
stays 21f: acts on soft going: tongue tied last 4 outings. *Marc Barber*

AHMEDY (IRE) 4 b.g. Polish Precedent (USA) – Nawaji (USA) (Trempolino (USA)) **h118**
[2006/7 16g² 16g* 16g³ 16s³ 17m* Apr 15] leggy gelding: fairly useful on Flat (should
stay 1½m), successful in September, sold out of M. Channon's stable 42,000 gns Newmarket Autumn Sales: fairly useful juvenile hurdler: landed odds at Musselburgh (by 3
lengths from Folk Tune) in December and Market Rasen (very easily) in April: raced
around 2m: best form on good/good to firm ground. *J. J. Quinn*

AIMIGAYLE 4 b.f. Midnight Legend – Cherrygayle (IRE) (Strong Gale) [2006/7 **F87**
F18g* F17g Apr 19] tall filly: third foal: dam winning pointer: won maiden humper at
Plumpton on debut in March: failed to settle when well held next time. *Miss Suzy Smith*

AINTNECESSARILYSO 9 ch.g. So Factual (USA) – Ovideo (Domynsky) [2006/7 **h–**
16d 17g Apr 11] half-brother to bumper winner Gay Gladys (by Ridgewood Ben): modest
on Flat (effective at 5f to 7f): showed nothing in 2 runs over hurdles. *J. M. Bradley*

AINTNONANCY 5 b.m. Rakaposhi King – Threads (Bedford (USA)) [2006/7 F16g⁵ **F70**
Apr 8] half-sister to 25f chase winner Optimistic Alfie (by Afzal): dam placed twice in
bumpers: 7¼ lengths fifth to Aya in weak bumper at Towcester on debut. *C. P. Morlock*

AIN'T NO SUNSHINE (IRE) 7 b.g. Rainbows For Life (CAN) – Landa's Counsel **h–**
(Pragmatic) [2006/7 F16v 24mᵖᵘ Apr 15] rangy gelding: second foal: dam placed in **F–**
bumpers: no show in bumper and novice hurdle (bled). *R. T. Phillips*

AIRBOUND (USA) 4 ch.g. Fusaichi Pegasus (USA) – Secrettame (USA) (Secretariat **h–**
(USA)) [2006/7 16sᵖᵘ 17g Mar 25] angular gelding: fair on Flat (stays 12.2f), successful in August, sold out of M. Johnston's stable 10,000 gns Newmarket Autumn Sales:
possibly amiss both starts over hurdles. *H. J. L. Dunlop*

AIREDALE LAD (IRE) 6 b.g. Charnwood Forest (IRE) – Tamarsiya (USA) (Shah- **h84**
rastani (USA)) [2006/7 16sᵖᵘ 16g 17m² Apr 28] workmanlike gelding: modest maiden

on Flat (stays 10.5f): best effort over hurdles when second in seller at Market Rasen. *R. M. Whitaker*

AIRES ROCK (IRE) 7 b.g. Courtship – Newgate Music (IRE) (Accordion) [2006/7 F–: 20s³ 20g⁶ 24s⁶ Sep 21] no form, including in point. *Miss J. E. Foster*   **h–**

AIR FORCE ONE (GER) 5 ch.h. Lando (GER) – Ame Soeur (FR) (Siberian Express (USA)) [2006/7 24s⁵ 20d* 21m* 24g² Mar 16] well-made horse: successful twice up to 13f on Flat at 3 yrs: progressive novice hurdler: ran out early in juvenile at Munich: left M. Hofer, won at Leicester in December and Ludlow in January: excellent effort (useful form) in Grade 2 Spa Novices' Hurdle at Cheltenham, staying on well and left second at last when beaten 12 lengths by Wichita Lineman: stays 3m: open to further improvement. *C. J. Mann*   **h137 p**

AIR GUITAR (IRE) 7 b.g. Blues Traveller (IRE) – Money Talks (IRE) (Lord Chancellor (USA)) [2006/7 h108, F85: 22sᵖᵘ 20m³ 16m⁵ 18m³ 20g⁶ 17v⁴ 19g 16s 21m⁵ Apr 9] workmanlike gelding: fair hurdler at best: largely disappointing in 2006/7 for 4 different trainers: stays 2¾m: acts on soft and firm going: tried in cheekpieces: weak finisher. *J. Ryan*   **h95 §**

AIRGUSTA (IRE) 6 b.g. Danehill Dancer (IRE) – Ministerial Model (IRE) (Shalford (IRE)) [2006/7 h96: 16d³ 18m⁴ 17m* 20d* 20m⁶ 19d⁴ 22d⁶ Nov 16] modest hurdler: won seller at Hereford in June and handicap at Southwell in August: lame final outing: should stay beyond 2½m: unraced on extremes of going over hurdles. *C. P. Morlock*   **h97**

AIRMAN (IRE) 4 b.g. Danehill (USA) – Jiving (Generous (IRE)) [2006/7 F12v Jan 1] 2,200 3-y-o: third foal: half-brother to smart 6f/7f winner Excusez Moi (by Fusaichi Pegasus): dam, ran twice, half-sister to excellent broodmare Hasili: never a factor in listed 4-y-o bumper on debut. *W. M. Brisbourne*   **F–**

Mr Brian Walsh's "Air Force One"

AIROSKI 11 b.g. Petoski – Thames Air (Crash Course) [2006/7 c23v⁴ Feb 27] work-manlike gelding: fairly useful pointer at best: last of 4 finishers in maiden hunter at Leicester on chasing debut. *Mrs C. J. Robinson* c– h–

AISJEM (IRE) 8 ch.m. Anshan – Emma's Way (IRE) (Le Bavard (FR)) [2006/7 c84x, h–: 23d* c26dᵖᵘ 24g⁵ 26m Sep 24] modest hurdler: won novice handicap at Fakenham in May: maiden chaser, usually let down by jumping: stays 25f: acts on good to soft going: usually wears headgear. *Evan Williams* c– x h85

AITCH DOUBLEYOU (IRE) 7 ch.g. Classic Memory – Bucksreward (IRE) (Buckskin (FR)) [2006/7 F16d² F16s* 20v⁴ 20v* 20v² 20v² 20g 20s⁶ Apr 27] strong gelding: fairly useful form in bumpers, won at Uttoxeter in May: confirmed promise of hurdling debut when winning maiden at same course in December: left E. McMahon after next outing, well held in handicaps last 2: will stay beyond 2½m: acts on heavy going. *H. P. Hogarth* h106 F96

AITMATOV (GER) 6 b.g. Lomitas – Atoka (GER) (Kaiseradler) [2006/7 16g³ 16s² 16v* 16s² 20v* 20d² 23v² 20m* 20m⁴ Apr 27] strong, good sort: type to make a chaser: useful on Flat, successful 4 times up to 15f for E. Libaud: useful novice hurdler: won at Galway in October, Navan (never off bridle) in December and Fairyhouse (Grade 2 Rathbarry & Glenview Studs Festival Novices' Hurdle, beat Davorin by 5½ lengths) in April: also ran well when head second to Kazal in Grade 3 at Leopardstown seventh start: stays 23f: unraced on firm going, acts on any other: usually tongue tied (has won when not): held up. *N. Meade, Ireland* h132

AJAY (IRE) 6 ch.g. Posidonas – Gothic Shadow (IRE) (Mandalus) [2006/7 F88: 20s Jan 31] tall, workmanlike gelding: fair form on second of 2 outings in bumpers for T. Walford: never-dangerous seventh to Imperial Commander in novice hurdle at New-castle. *Ferdy Murphy* h94

AKASH (IRE) 7 b.g. Dr Devious (IRE) – Akilara (IRE) (Kahyasi) [2006/7 h97: 16m³ 17s² 16s 17vᵖᵘ 21sᵖᵘ 20g⁵ 16m⁴ Apr 24] compact gelding: modest form when placed over hurdles: should be suited by 2¼m+: tongue tied last 3 outings. *Miss J. Feilden* h94 d

AKHTARI (IRE) 7 b.g. In The Wings – Akishka (Nishapour (FR)) [2006/7 c20d* c16s⁵ c20m³ c25d³ c21s* c20d* c28dᵖᵘ 20m⁶ Apr 9] rangy gelding: successful 3 times over hurdles, well below form in listed event final start after 5-month absence: fairly useful chaser: won maiden at Kilbeggan in May and handicaps at Roscommon and Punchestown (by 1½ lengths from Allez Petit Luis) in October: stays 21f: acts on heavy and good to firm going. *D. T. Hughes, Ireland* c125 h94

AKILAK (IRE) 6 br.g. Charnwood Forest (IRE) – Akilara (IRE) (Kahyasi) [2006/7 h134: c16s² c20d² c21v⁴ c20v² c20v³ Mar 18] well-made gelding: usually impresses in appearance: useful hurdler on his day: fairly useful form over fences, placed 4 of 5 starts in maidens: stays 2½m: acts on heavy going. *J. Howard Johnson* c116 h–

ALAGON (IRE) 7 b.g. Alzao (USA) – Forest Lair (Habitat) [2006/7 h93+: 24s 24d 24g c23m² Apr 15] good-topped gelding: modest on Flat, successful in January: winning hurdler, largely disappointing since 2004/5: ½-length second to Square Mile in maiden at Worcester on chasing debut: stays easy 3m: acts on soft and good to firm going: usually wears headgear: open to improvement over fences: sold 14,000 gns Doncaster May Sales. *Ian Williams* c91 p h–

ALAKDAR (CAN) 13 ch.g. Green Dancer (USA) – Population (General Assembly (USA)) [2006/7 c–, h–: c16v c22f c21g⁴ c26dᵖᵘ c26d⁶ Aug 15] good-topped gelding: winning chaser, no form in 2006/7: stays 3m: acts on firm and soft going: tried in head-gear. *Jane Southcombe* c– h–

ALAMBIQUE (IRE) 8 b.g. Alderbrook – Calora (USA) (Private Account (USA)) [2006/7 c21g¹* c21gᵖᵘ Apr 27] €40,000 3-y-o: ex-Irish gelding: half-brother to winning pointer by Arzanni: dam, won on Flat/over jumps (up to 19f) in France, half-sister to high-class chaser Chatam: lightly raced in bumpers/over hurdles for N. Meade: success-ful twice in points in Britain, including in February: won novice hunter at Newton Abbot in April on chasing debut: amiss next time: stays 21f: tried blinkered. *T. W. Dennis* c101 h–

ALAMKHAN (IRE) 5 ch.g. Ashkalani (IRE) – Alaiyda (USA) (Shahrastani (USA)) [2006/7 F16d³ Oct 18] half-brother to Irish Derby/King George VI & Queen Elizabeth Diamond Stakes winner Alamshar (by Key of Luck) and 1½m winner Alaya (by Ela-Mana-Mou): dam 1¼m winner who stayed 2m: tongue tied, travelled best long way when 7¼ lengths third to Golden Child in bumper at Worcester on debut. *D. R. Gandolfo* F94 +

ALAM (USA) 8 b.g. Silver Hawk (USA) – Ghashtah (USA) (Nijinsky (CAN)) [2006/7 c–x, h–: c20d c16g² c18s* c21s³ c20g c16g Apr 19] sturdy gelding: fair handicap c105 x h–

chaser: refound some form in 2006/7 after change of stable, winning at Market Rasen in March: stays 2¾m: acts on heavy going: races prominently: often let down by jumping. *Dr R. D. P. Newland*

ALAN THE AUSSIE 4 b.g. Rossini (USA) – In Ernest (IRE) (Forest Wind (USA)) [2006/7 16s^pu 16g^3 Apr 23] no form on Flat: little impact both starts over hurdles (saddle slipped on debut). *G. Prodromou*   **h–**

ALARM CALL 4 b.f. Mind Games – Warning Bell (Bustino) [2006/7 17d^pu 17d 16g^pu Nov 29] lengthy, angular filly: little show on Flat or in juvenile hurdles: tried in cheek-pieces. *I. A. Brown*   **h–**

ALASAO 4 b.g. Inchinor – Daisy May (In The Wings) [2006/7 17g Mar 25] little show in maiden at 2 yrs or juvenile maiden hurdle. *C. J. Gray*   **h–**

ALASIL (USA) 7 b.g. Swain (IRE) – Asl (USA) (Caro) [2006/7 h–: 16s Feb 16] strong, compact gelding: maiden hurdler, lightly raced and no form since 2004/5: usually wears cheekpieces/blinkers. *R. J. Price*   **h–**

ALASKAN FIZZ 6 ch.m. Efisio – Anchorage (IRE) (Slip Anchor) [2006/7 h–p, F86: 19g^4 20m^3 22g^4 24d 22f^4 Oct 5] bumper winner: poor over hurdles: stays easy 2½m: acts on good to firm going: tongue tied final outing: sold 3,800 gns Doncaster November Sales. *R. T. Phillips*   **h79**

ALBANOV (IRE) 7 b.g. Sadler's Wells (USA) – Love For Ever (IRE) (Darshaan) [2006/7 16s 16v^4 16v^3 16v^* 16s^5 20v^5 16m Apr 9] close-coupled gelding: useful on Flat (stays 15.5f), left M. Rolland in France after final start in 2005: fairly useful novice hurdler: won at Naas in January by 1½ lengths from Charlie Yardbird: best form when fifth in Grade 2 events at Punchestown and Naas (beaten 22¼ lengths by Kazal): stays 2½m: acts on heavy ground. *Mrs J. Harrington, Ireland*   **h118**

ALBARINO (IRE) 8 ch.g. Royal Abjar (USA) – Miss Lee Ann (Tumble Wind) [2006/7 h125: c16g^3 c19m^4 17m^3 17d 16d c16g^F c17s^pu c16d^4 c16d^5 c16v^4 c16g^6 Mar 19] stocky gelding: fairly useful hurdler/fair fencer after final start in 2006/7: disappointing in 2006/7 after third outing: raced mainly around 2m: acts on soft and good to firm going: tried tongue tied. *M. Scudamore*   **c100 d**
  h115 d

ALBATROS (FR) 9 b. or br.g. Shining Steel – Abalvina (FR) (Abdos) [2006/7 c98, h–: c25g c25g Apr 15] angular gelding: formerly fairly useful hurdler/chaser: winning pointer, including in February: well beaten in hunters in 2006/7: stays easy 3m: acts on any going: tried tongue tied. *A. R. Trotter*   **c–**
  h–

ALBERTAS RUN (IRE) 6 b.g. Accordion – Holly Grove Lass (Le Moss) [2006/7 F103: 16s^* 20s^4 21s^* 20s^* 24g^* Apr 14]   **h136 p**

    Jonjo O'Neill has enjoyed something of a purple patch over the past two seasons when it comes to staying novice hurdlers. Black Jack Ketchum carried all before him in 2005/6 and Wichita Lineman emerged as the leading staying novice

European Breeders' Fund Sunderlands 'National Hunt' Novices' Handicap Hurdle Final, Sandown—Tony McCoy gets a fine leap from Albertas Run at the last to see off outsider Double Eagle (noseband)

John Smith's Extra Cold Handicap Hurdle, Aintree—Noel Fehily is able to do 10-4 as the progressive novice lands this valuable prize from the grey Lyes Green

in 2006/7. The presence of the last-named at Jackdaws Castle no doubt played a role in the decision to send the promising Albertas Run into battle against more experienced handicappers in the John Smith's Extra Cold Handicap Hurdle over three miles on Grand National day, rather than take on his stable companion in the Grade 1 staying novices' event, the Sefton Hurdle, on the previous afternoon. In the event, it was the star turn who fluffed his lines (Wichita Lineman suffering a shock defeat) whilst the understudy flourished on the big stage. Albertas Run produced further improvement to hold Lyes Green by half a length, with a further length and a quarter back to stable-companion Refinement, who'd won this listed event twelve months earlier when side-stepping Black Jack Ketchum in similar fashion. This valuable prize capped another lucrative three days on Merseyside for O'Neill, who has now saddled fifteen winners at the last six Aintree Festivals. His only blank year during this period, 2005, featured Clan Royal's luckless exit when leading in the Grand National. Meanwhile it was also a good week for another understudy in Noel Fehily, who has thrived in his role as second jockey at Jackdaws Castle (posted a career-best tally in 2006/7) and partnered two of O'Neill's three winners at the latest Aintree Festival, standing in for Tony McCoy at 10-4 on Albertas Run presumably because the champion jockey would have had difficulty doing the weight.

Two hard-fought victories in Haydock bumpers and a tilt at the Champion Bumper at Cheltenham (no danger from halfway) was Albertas Run's introduction to racing in the 2005/6 season. He always looked as though he would make a jumper and made a winning start over hurdles in a two-mile novice at Uttoxeter in October, kept right up to his work after fluffing the last. His hurdling rather let him down when pitched straight into handicap company at Haydock next time, but he got his career back on track with a victory over two miles five furlongs at Huntingdon. That stamina was Albertas Run's strong suit was again apparent in the

46

European Breeders' Fund Sunderlands 'National Hunt' Novices' Handicap Hurdle Final at Sandown in March. In a race that fulfilled its purpose of attracting purpose-bred National Hunt horses, Albertas Run impressed as one of the best chasing types in a field full of such animals. Quickening well with runner-up Double Eagle, he created an excellent impression, winning in a style that suggested at the time that he might even be worth trying in the Sefton at Aintree.

Albertas Run (IRE) (b.g. 2001)	Accordion (b 1986)	Sadler's Wells (b 1981)	Northern Dancer / Fairy Bridge
		Sound of Success (ch 1969)	Successor / Belle Musique
	Holly Grove Lass (br 1986)	Le Moss (ch 1975)	Le Levanstell / Feemoss
		Girseach (br 1980)	Furry Glen / Happy Lass

A brother to his stable's fair but temperamental staying hurdler/chaser High Gear, Albertas Run boasts a fine jumping pedigree. Though his dam, Holly Grove Lass, showed little in five starts in Irish bumpers/hurdles, she is a half-sister to the top-class hurdler Mister Morose (winner of the 2000 Aintree Hurdle), the useful two-and-a-half-mile chaser Southolt and the smart staying hurdler The Proms. Albertas Run is by some way the best of Holly Grove Lass's progeny. Fetching IR 11,000 guineas as a foal before realising €20,000 as a three-year-old, Albertas Run is by Accordion, who died in 2006 after a progressive stud career which has seen him register successive top ten finishes in the National Hunt stallion statistics for the past two seasons. Initially, Accordion was an influence for speed, his best representatives including the top-class two-milers Dato Star and Flagship

Mr Trevor Hemmings' "Albertas Run"

Uberalles. However, that was before National Hunt breeders became fully aware of his prowess and started to send him more stoutly-bred mares. The useful-looking Albertas Run, who has plenty of scope, has shown a good attitude to racing in most of his outings to date, and he stays three miles well, as emphasised by his Aintree victory. He has been raced only on good going or softer so far, and acts on soft. He looks one of the most exciting novice chase prospects for 2007/8. *Jonjo O'Neill*

ALBERT MOONEY (IRE) 7 b.g. Dr Massini (IRE) – Prudent Rose (IRE) (Strong Gale) [2006/7 h116p: c16s⁵ c17dF Nov 17] tall gelding: useful bumper performer: successful on first of 2 outings over hurdles in 2005/6: left D. Wachman and off 9½ months, fair form on completed start over fences, none too fluent: will stay beyond 2m: raced on good to soft/soft ground over jumps: open to improvement over fences. *Jonjo O'Neill* — c106 + h–

ALBERT PARK (IRE) 6 ch.g. Presenting – Victoria Belle (IRE) (Black Minstrel) [2006/7 aF16g Mar 9] €8,000 4-y-o: second foal: dam unraced half-sister to 2 winning pointers: tailed off in bumper on debut. *John R. Upson* — F–

ALBINUS 6 gr.g. Selkirk (USA) – Alouette (Darshaan) [2006/7 16s³ 16d⁴ 20d³ 17v Jan 27] good-topped gelding: useful on Flat (will stay 1¾m), suffered tendon injury after final start at 4 yrs: fair novice hurdler: stays 2½m: raced on ground softer than good. *A. M. Balding* — h108

ALCATRAS (IRE) 10 b. or br.g. Corrouge (USA) – Kisco (IRE) (Henbit (USA)) [2006/7 c88§, h78§: c22s³ c23s* c23v⁴ c20g⁶ c21g⁵ c23m Apr 15] workmanlike gelding: modest handicap chaser: won at Taunton in December: stays 3m: acts on soft and good to firm going: tried in headgear: has refused to race/taken little interest: often let down by jumping. *B. J. M. Ryall* — c94 § h– §

ALCHIMISTE (FR) 6 gr.m. Linamix (FR) – Alcove (USA) (Valdez (USA)) [2006/7 c–, h–: 16m May 16] leggy mare: maiden chaser: winning hurdler: no form in Britain: tried blinkered. *Mrs E. Langley* — c– h–

ALDEA (FR) 6 b.g. Pistolet Bleu (IRE) – Heleda (FR) (Zino) [2006/7 F91: 20s 20s⁵ 16dᵖᵘ 20v 27v 20s² 24m⁴ Apr 15] good sort, unfurnished at present: modest novice hurdler: likely to prove suited by 3m+: acts on soft and good to firm ground. *Mrs S. J. Smith* — h98

ALDERBROOK GIRL (IRE) 7 b. or br.m. Alderbrook – Trassey Bridge (Strong Gale) [2006/7 h79: 25d* 26sᵖᵘ c20v² c24s* c23mᵖᵘ Apr 15] lengthy, angular mare: poor hurdler: made all in novice handicap at Plumpton in November: better form over fences, won novice handicap at Huntingdon in January: should stay beyond 25f: acts on heavy ground: usually wears headgear. *R. Curtis* — c89 h73

ALDERBURN 8 b.g. Alderbrook – Threewaygirl (Orange Bay) [2006/7 c131+, h–: c25mᵖᵘ c24d³ c24g⁴ Mar 24] tall, good-topped gelding: winning hurdler: smart handicap chaser: won at Kempton (by length from Yardbird) in December and Newbury in March), improved effort when beating Alexanderthegreat by 3 lengths in strongly-run event at latter: should stay beyond 3m: acts on heavy and good to firm going: usually patiently ridden. *H. D. Daly* — c146 h–

ALDERMAN ROSE 7 b.g. Alderbrook – Rose Ravine (Deep Run) [2006/7 h–: 22sᵖᵘ 22g* Apr 7] compact gelding: much improved over hurdles (fair form) when winning novice handicap at Newton Abbot in April: stays 2¾m. *R. T. Phillips* — h106 +

ALDHAHER BEEBERS (IRE) 5 b. or br.g. City Honours (USA) – Bint Shruhoon (IRE) (Be My Native (USA)) [2006/7 F16d⁵ F16f² F17m² F16m* F17g* Aug 27] sturdy gelding: second foal: brother to winning pointer: dam, poor/ungenuine hurdler, stayed 2¾m: useful bumper performer: won at Cork and Ballinrobe in August, by 10 lengths from Golden Aran at latter. *M. Phelan, Ireland* — F107

ALDIRUOS (IRE) 7 ch.g. Bigstone (IRE) – Ball Cat (FR) (Cricket Ball (USA)) [2006/7 h103: 21f⁶ 20g* 20mᵘʳ 24m⁴ 20g² 20g⁶ 20g 20gᵖᵘ 20f Apr 28] rather sparely-made gelding: fair handicap hurdler: won at Wetherby in June: poor efforts last 3 outings: stays easy 3m: acts on heavy and good to firm going: tried blinkered/tongue tied, not for long time. *A. W. Carroll* — h112

ALEEMDAR (IRE) 10 b.g. Doyoun – Aleema (Red God) [2006/7 h77: 16fᵖᵘ 17vᵖᵘ 20dᵖᵘ Nov 11] winning hurdler: no form in 2006/7: best around 2m: acts on good to firm going, formerly on soft: usually wears headgear: tried tongue tied. *A. E. Jones* — h–

ALE HOUSE (IRE) 5 b.g. Taipan (IRE) – Vultang Lady (Le Bavard (FR)) [2006/7 F16g⁴ Mar 29] 25,000 3-y-o: half-brother to 3 winners, including fairly useful hurdler — F94

Snapper Creek (by Castle Keep), stays 2½m: dam unraced sister to dam of high-class staying chaser Couldnt Be Better and half-sister to smart chaser up to 3m Kilkilowen: 9 lengths fourth to Gypsy Scholar in bumper at Towcester on debut, nearest finish. *P. Winkworth*

AL EILE (IRE) 7 b.g. Alzao (USA) – Kilcsem Eile (IRE) (Commanche Run)   **h159**
[2006/7 h159: 20s 20v⁵ 16v⁴ 20g* Apr 14]
    The 'Aintree factor' is an oft-used term to describe the much improved form that some horses regularly show over the famous Grand National fences compared to their achievements on conventional tracks. The vast majority of races at Aintree, of course, actually take place on the easier Mildmay course, which has also thrown up its fair share of course specialists down the years. A major feature of the Mildmay course is its sharpness and, as a result, it presents a very different test to most other Grade 1 tracks, notably Cheltenham. The Henrietta Knight-trained Stompin could manage only a tired eighteenth place in the 1995 Triumph Hurdle, yet proved a different proposition when winning the Anniversary Hurdle at Aintree three weeks later (Cheltenham winner Kissair was pulled up). As can sometimes be the case with leading juveniles, Stompin never really fulfilled his potential and managed just one more win from seventeen starts over jumps, but that victory came in the valuable two-mile handicap hurdle on Grand National day back at Aintree in 1996. Runner-up in both races, incidentally, was Clifton Beat who made the frame on all his five appearances at the meeting. Quirky staying hurdler Carlovent also reserved his best for the Merseyside air, returning to form from out of the blue to win the meeting's listed three-mile handicap hurdle in 2001 (25/1) and 2003 (16/1), his only two wins from his last thirty-four starts. Going further back, useful chaser King Or Country was gaining only his second win in four years when defying his veteran status to land the Tim Brookshaw Memorial Handicap Chase

Baltika Beer Aintree Hurdle—Timmy Murphy and Al Eile repeat their 2005 win, chased home by the gallant juvenile Gaspara (centre)

there in 1983, in the process recording his third victory in the race. Multiple victories at Aintree aren't confined to handicappers who've slipped down the weights, either. Top-notch chaser Direct Route always came up just short at Cheltenham but could boast an impressive record of three wins (plus two placed efforts) from five consecutive appearances at the Aintree Festival, whilst Mighty Man is unbeaten in three visits there, showing himself to be the top staying hurdler around when comprehensively reversing Cheltenham form for those last two wins. The meeting's other prolific hurdler in recent times has been Al Eile, who for the third time in four years improved markedly on the form he had been showing elsewhere to cause something of a shock at Aintree. Al Eile was below form in three runs over hurdles before the latest Aintree Hurdle, beating two home after blundering his chance away in the Lismullen Hurdle at Navan in November, finishing a remote last of five to Brave Inca in the Hatton's Grace at Fairyhouse the following month and finishing eleven and a quarter lengths behind the same rival in the four-runner December Festival Hurdle at Leopardstown, again last to complete.

However, Al Eile has gone well fresh before, on the Flat as well as over jumps, and in the three and a half months he was off the track after Leopardstown he made a full recovery from whatever had been ailing him in the first half of the season. Al Eile's two previous wins at Aintree came in the Anniversary Hurdle in 2004, as a 25/1-shot, and in the following season's Aintree Hurdle at 11/1 (when beating Inglis Drever and Exotic Dancer in a three-way finish). He had been a 100/30-shot in 2006 when putting up a disappointing effort in the Aintree Hurdle, a shoulder injury subsequently found to be a mitigating factor. Al Eile was sent off at 12/1 for the latest running of the Aintree Hurdle. With doubts surrounding the well-being of Detroit City and 2006 winner Asian Maze, not to mention Al Eile

Mr M. A. Ryan's "Al Eile"

himself, the race looked by no means a vintage renewal beforehand, though the third, fifth, sixth and seventh from the Champion Hurdle were turned out. In the event, the four-year-old filly Gaspara gave Al Eile the most to do. Gaspara was the only member of the eleven-strong field to have won on her latest outing, having completed the Imperial Cup and Fred Winter Juvenile Handicap Hurdle double within four days in March. In a truly-run race at Aintree, Al Eile tracked the leaders before taking over from Gaspara two out and keeping on to win by a length and a half. Al Eile followed Daring Run, Aonoch and Danoli as dual winners (Monksfield won the race on three occasions, Morley Street on four), Al Eile, the first to regain the title. Al Eile clearly goes well at Aintree, but another factor seems to be the rapport with Timmy Murphy who has now ridden Al Eile to his four most recent victories over jumps, and is well suited to the patient tactics that seem to suit Al Eile. Not for the first time, Al Eile left the impression that he will prove effective at beyond two and a half miles, and he would have made an interesting opponent for the established three-milers at Punchestown, finishing fourth in the Northumberland Plate on his return. As it was, Al Eile bypassed Punchestown in favour of a summer Flat campaign. Though lightly raced in that sphere, he has made up into a useful handicapper. After finishing in the frame in a listed event and the Queen Alexandra Stakes in 2005, Al Eile ran well to finish runner-up in handicaps at Navan and Leopardstown (the November) in 2006, on the latter occasion—just seven days before making his reappearance over hurdles in the Lismullen Hurdle—finishing three lengths behind Lounaos, who subsequently showed herself a smart juvenile hurdler.

Al Eile (IRE) (b.g. 2000)	Alzao (USA) (b 1980)	Lyphard (b 1969)	Northern Dancer
			Goofed
		Lady Rebecca (b 1971)	Sir Ivor
			Pocahontas II
	Kilcsem Eile (IRE) (b 1989)	Commanche Run (b 1981)	Run The Gantlet
			Volley
		Senane (ch 1981)	Vitiges
			Formulate

The pedigree of the rather leggy Al Eile was covered fully in *Chasers & Hurdlers 2004/05* and there is nothing to add to what was stated there. Al Eile requires a good test at two miles, stays two and a half miles, and shapes as if worth a try over further. He acts on heavy and good to firm going (has Flat form on firm). *John Queally, Ireland*

ALERON (IRE) 9 b.g. Sadler's Wells (USA) – High Hawk (Shirley Heights) [2006/7 c119, h–: 17d 17g² 19g* 16d² 16d⁴ c16v⁴ c17d⁵ c21vᵘʳ c20s 16m⁶ Apr 21] leggy, quite good-topped gelding: fair on Flat: useful handicap hurdler: won valuable event at Market Rasen in September by 1¼ lengths from Ball O Malt: not quite so good over fences: stays 19f: acts on good to soft and good to firm going: wears cheekpieces: usually races prominently. *J. J. Quinn*   **c125 h130**

ALETHEA GEE 9 b.m. Sure Blade (USA) – Star Flower (Star Appeal) [2006/7 h73§: 16mʳᵒ 17dᵖᵘ 16m 16mᵘʳ 16fᵖᵘ Jul 19] lengthy mare: poor maiden hurdler: best efforts around 2m: acts on firm and good to soft going: unreliable (ran out on reappearance). *K. G. Reveley*   **h– §**

ALEXANDER EXCHANGE (IRE) 6 ch.g. Alderbrook – Had Enough (Hadeer) [2006/7 17sᵘʳ 16m* 20g⁵ 21s⁵ Nov 29] 20,000 3-y-o: half-brother to 2 winners by Treasure Hunter, including fairly useful hurdler/useful chaser I'vehadit, stays 29f: dam unraced half-sister to smart 2m to 2½m hurdler Path of Peace: fair novice hurdler: sold out of D. Hughes's stable 9,000 gns Doncaster May Sales: easily won maiden at Worcester in September: lame final start: probably stays 2½m: acts on heavy and good to firm going: tried tongue tied. *Evan Williams*   **h103**

ALEXANDER MUSICAL (IRE) 9 b. or br.g. Accordion – Love For Lydia (IRE) (Law Society (USA)) [2006/7 c62, h–: c16m c19g³ 19d 16vᵖᵘ Nov 23] tall, angular gelding: maiden hurdler/chaser, no form in 2006/7: best up to 19f: often blinkered/visored. *S. T. Lewis*   **c– h–**

ALEXANDER SAPPHIRE (IRE) 6 gr.m. Pennekamp (USA) – Beautiful France (IRE) (Sadler's Wells (USA)) [2006/7 h84: 16g 21g 23vᵖᵘ c21gᵖᵘ Apr 9] poor maiden hurdler: left N. King, no show in novice hunter on chasing debut: probably stays 21f: tried in cheekpieces/visor (has suspect attitude): often tongue tied. *Mrs Fleur Hawes*   **c– h73 +**

ALEXANDER TAIPAN (IRE) 7 b.g. Taipan (IRE) – Fayafi (Top Ville) [2006/7   **c147**
h123, F102: c16v² c20v² c20vᵘʳ c17v* c21vᶠ c21m* Apr 27]   **h–**

'At last he got his jumping together. I think that trip was too short and he wants better ground so he'll hopefully improve into the spring.' That was the view of trainer Willie Mullins after Alexander Taipan had got off the mark over fences at the fourth attempt, in a maiden over seventeen furlongs on heavy ground at Fairyhouse in January. Mullins proved spot on. Three months later, Alexander Taipan showed himself one of Ireland's leading novice chasers when defying top weight in the betfair.com Novices' Handicap Chase, run over twenty-one furlongs on good to firm going at the Punchestown Festival. It looked a good renewal of this valuable event, run previously over a distance half a mile further, with a sizeable proportion of the fourteen runners stepping out of graded company, including Alexander Taipan himself. His only outing between Fairyhouse and Punchestown had come in the Grade 1 Dr P. J. Moriarty Novices' Chase at Leopardstown, in which he was in the process of showing improved form when falling at the last, involved in a battle with the eventual seven-length winner Mister Top Notch at the time. Alexander Taipan was sent off favourite for the betfair.com Chase, and his supporters had some anxious moments before they collected. Patiently ridden, Alexander Taipan still had nine of his rivals ahead of him going to four out but he responded well when shaken up at the next and delivered his challenge two out, wandering as he took the lead off Washington Lad approaching the last before knuckling down to repel the strong challenge of Anothercoppercoast by a neck, the pair pulling clear. Mullins then decided Alexander Taipan should follow the same route as another leading novice chaser Rule Supreme had done back in 2004, sending the gelding back over hurdles to tackle France's two main hurdling prizes of the spring/summer, the Prix La Barka and the Grande Course de Haies, both at Auteuil. Rule Supreme richly rewarded Mullins for this enterprising approach, finishing third and first respectively in the two races. Unfortunately, Alexander Taipan never looked like emulating those achievements, managing only eleventh in the Prix La Barka (when one of three Mullins-trained runners) and seventh in the Grande Course de Haies (albeit not disgraced), which both took place shortly after the end of the British and Irish seasons.

Over fences, there could be better still to come from Alexander Taipan, as he is still only seven with not many races under his belt. He started off in bumpers, winning a maiden at Punchestown (by a neck from future Galway Hurdle winner Cuan Na Grai) on the second of two runs in that sphere. Later in the 2005/6 season Alexander Taipan gained his only win over hurdles in a maiden on the same course, showing fairly useful form. He is the seventh foal of Fayafi who has also produced a trio of winning pointers. This is a notable jumping family, however, as Fayafi (a

betfair.com Novices' Handicap Chase, Punchestown—top weight Alexander Taipan confirms himself a smart novice in beating Anothercoppercoast (No.7) and Washington Lad (almost hidden)

winning two-mile hurdler in Ireland) is a half-sister to two high-class hurdlers in Anzum and Jazilah, the former a stayer and the latter raced only at two miles. In addition, Fayafi's half-brothers also include the smart staying hurdler Sh Boom and the useful two-mile hurdler Nahar. Alexander Taipan himself is likely to stay three miles. A good sort in appearance, he acts on heavy and good to firm going. *W. P. Mullins, Ireland*

ALEXANDERTHEGREAT (IRE) 9 b.g. Supreme Leader – Sandy Jayne (IRE) (Royal Fountain) [2006/7 c–, h–: c20d c22g* c32s^{pu} c25v⁶ c24s^{ur} c26v^{pu} c24g² c25g* Apr 18] lengthy gelding: winning hurdler: fairly useful handicap chaser: won at Kelso in November and Cheltenham (left Heather Dalton, beat Kenzo III by ½ length) in April: stays 25f: acts on soft going: wore cheekpieces fourth start (final one for Ferdy Murphy): tried tongue tied: usually waited with. *Miss Venetia Williams*   **c123 h–**

ALFABET SOUK 6 b.g. Alflora (IRE) – Levantine Rose (Levanter) [2006/7 F17v F13s² 16s 20v⁴ 20g Mar 27] 25,000 4-y-o: rangy gelding: has scope: brother to fair hurdler up to 2½m Fragrant Rose and half-brother to fair hunter chaser Derryrose (by Derrylin): dam, winning hurdler, stayed 25f: modest form in bumpers: well held over hurdles: will be suited by 3m+. *Mrs S. J. Smith*   **h– F81**

ALFADORA 7 ch.g. Alflora (IRE) – Dorazine (Kalaglow) [2006/7 h–: 20d⁵ 22d 22v³ 20s⁵ c16d³ c20v³ c24s² c24v* c20v* c24s* c21s^{pu} c19g³ c31s^{pu} Apr 27] tall gelding: poor maiden hurdler: modest handicap chaser: won at Kempton, Fontwell and Warwick within 9 days in March: stays 3m: acts on heavy going: usually tongue tied. *M. F. Harris*   **c89 h68**

AL FALCON 5 ch.g. Alflora (IRE) – Northern Falcon (Polar Falcon (USA)) [2006/7 F91: F17v F14d⁴ 16g Mar 17] fair form at best in bumpers: little impact in novice on hurdling debut: tongue tied in 2006/7. *M. W. Easterby*   **h– F79**

ALFANO (IRE) 9 b.g. Priolo (USA) – Sartigila (Efisio) [2006/7 20s 24v⁵ 20g^{pu} Mar 27] strong gelding: modest form at best over hurdles, very lightly raced: would probably have proved best short of 3m: tried tongue tied: dead. *Miss P. Robson*   **h78**

ALFASONIC 7 b.g. Alflora (IRE) – Lady Solstice (Vital Season) [2006/7 h113: 24v^{pu} 23v* 25v⁴ Jan 25] strong gelding: fairly useful hurdler: won handicap at Lingfield in January by 5 lengths from Mylo: improved again in similar event later in month: thorough stayer: raced on going softer than good (acts on heavy). *A. King*   **h122**

ALFA SUNRISE 10 b.g. Alflora (IRE) – Gipsy Dawn (Lighter) [2006/7 c–x, h105: 24d⁵ 25d⁴ 24v⁴ 26s c24d⁵ 26s⁵ 22s c25v* Feb 28] angular gelding: fair hurdler/chaser at best: has deteriorated, though won handicap chase at Folkestone (in cheekpieces) in February: stays 25f well: acts on heavy going: tried blinkered: often let down by jumping over fences. *R. H. Buckler*   **c74 x h94**

ALFIE BOE 4 b.g. Shambo – Love Potion (Neltino) [2006/7 F12v F16g 20g Apr 14] sturdy gelding: first foal: dam poor 2m maiden hurdler: well held in bumpers/novice hurdle. *J. W. Mullins*   **h– F—**

ALFIE'S SUN 8 b.g. Alflora (IRE) – Sun Dante (IRE) (Phardante (FR)) [2006/7 c121, h–: c24s⁵ c20g* c21f* Apr 5] big, rangy gelding: winning hurdler: fairly useful form at best over fences, off 15 months prior to return: won novices at Huntingdon in March and Wincanton (odds on in 4-runner race) in April: stays 3m: acts on firm and good to soft going. *D. E. Cantillon*   **c106 h–**

ALFIE TWOFOURTWO (IRE) 11 b.g. Jolly Jake (NZ) – Spin N'Win (Cardinal Flower) [2006/7 c25m⁴ c25v^{pu} c25g⁵ Apr 15] good-topped gelding: winning pointer: poor maiden hurdler/chaser: probably stays 25f: tried in cheekpieces/visor (refused to race). *Miss J. Hutchinson*   **c83 § h– §**

ALFLORAMOOR 5 b.g. Alflora (IRE) – Diamond Wind (USA) (Wind And Wuthering (USA)) [2006/7 F17g F17g Apr 27] third foal: brother to a winning pointer: dam winning pointer: fell both starts in points: well held in bumper. *J. A. T. de Giles*   **F—**

ALFONSO 6 ch.g. Efisio – Winnebago (Kris) [2006/7 16s 16v 16v 16d⁵ 16v Mar 9] brother to modest 2m hurdler San Antonio: fair on Flat (should stay 1¼m), sold out of I. Semple's stable 11,000 gns Newmarket Autumn Sales: form (poor) over hurdles only when fifth in novice at Musselburgh: likely to need emphasis on speed at 2m. *P. Monteith*   **h82**

ALFRED THE GREY 10 gr.g. Environment Friend – Ranyah (USA) (Our Native (USA)) [2006/7 c72§, h–: c26m³ c26g⁶ Jun 4] leggy gelding: poor chaser: stays 3½m: acts on soft and good to firm going: tried blinkered, usually wears cheekpieces: ungenuine. *Miss Suzy Smith*   **c68 § h–**

ALF'S SPINNEY 7 ch.g. Anshan – Netherdrom (Netherkelly) [2006/7 h94: 21s 26s^{pu} 19g Mar 28] maiden hurdler, no form in 2006/7: should stay beyond 19f: acts on soft ground. *Ian Williams*   **h–**

ALFY RICH 11 b.g. Alflora (IRE) – Weareagrandmother (Prince Tenderfoot (USA)) [2006/7 c105, h–: c24s^{pu} c21m c16d⁵ c20d² c20v⁴ c20s³ c20v^{pu} c24g Apr 7] tall gelding: winning hurdler: fair handicap chaser: stays 25f, effective at much shorter: acts on heavy and good to firm going: tried visored, usually wears cheekpieces: tried tongue tied: often makes running: not one to rely on. *M. Todhunter*   **c101 §** **h–**

ALGARVE 10 b.g. Alflora (IRE) – Garvenish (Balinger) [2006/7 c94, h–: c21g Apr 12] rangy, useful-looking gelding: modest hurdler/novice chaser: successful twice in Irish points in November: stays 25f: acts on soft going: wore cheekpieces in Fox Hunters' at Aintree (stiff task). *N. Nevin, Ireland*   **c–** **h–**

ALGENON (DEN) 7 br.g. Asaasy (USA) – La Natte (FR) (Native Guile (USA)) [2006/7 16v 16s⁴ Apr 27] placed in bumper on debut: poor form over hurdles, left Ferdy Murphy and off 32 months prior to return. *P. J. Hobbs*   **h80**

ALHERI 16 gr.g. Puget (USA) – Miss Haddon (Free Boy) [2006/7 c25g^F c26d^{pu} Jun 12] workmanlike gelding: winning pointer: maiden hurdler/chaser: tried tongue tied: makes mistakes. *J. A. T. de Giles*   **c–** **h–**

ALIBY (IRE) 7 ch.g. Ali-Royal (IRE) – Byliny (IRE) (Archway (IRE)) [2006/7 17g^{pu} 20f^{pu} 19g³ 24g³ 19d 22g 22m⁶ 20s⁴ Oct 11] ex-Irish gelding: no form on Flat/in points: poor maiden hurdler: stays 3m: tried tongue tied: has hung left. *D. A. Rees*   **h77**

ALICE'S OLD ROSE 10 b.m. Broadsword (USA) – Rosie Marchioness (Neltino) [2006/7 h–: 22f 24s^{pu} May 17] maiden hurdler: tried in cheekpieces. *Mrs H. O. Graham*   **h–**

ALIKAT (IRE) 6 b.m. Alhaarth (IRE) – Be Crafty (USA) (Crafty Prospector (USA)) [2006/7 h130: c22d* c24f² c26d* c23m c24g Feb 21] leggy mare: useful handicap hurdler: just modest form over fences, landed odds in maiden at Market Rasen in June and novice at Newton Abbot (farcical 3-runner event, left well clear before attempting to pull herself up) in August: stays 3m: acts on firm and soft going: often wears headgear: one to treat with caution over fences. *D. E. Pipe*   **c96 §** **h–**

ALINA RHEINBERG (GER) 5 ch.m. Waky Nao – Auenfeuer (GER) (Big Shuffle (USA)) [2006/7 16g⁴ 16d⁶ 17s⁵ 17d⁵ 16v⁵ 16f² 19m² 19m⁵ Apr 22] sparely-made mare: won around 1¼m at Frankfurt in June for Dirk Baltromei: modest hurdler: won mares novice at Hexham in October: stays 19f: acts on firm going, well below form on soft/heavy: visored fifth start (has shaped as if worth another try). *M. F. Harris*   **h91**

ALISONS TREASURE (IRE) 8 b.g. Treasure Hunter – The Long Bill (IRE) (Phardante (FR)) [2006/7 h–, F–: 25s 20d 22s c24d^{pu} Dec 10] no form. *Karen McLintock*   **c–** **h–**

ALITTLEBITOPOWER 10 ch.g. Alflora (IRE) – What A Moppet (IRE) (Torus) [2006/7 c–: c25g^{pu} May 24] winning pointer: maiden hunter chaser: tried tongue tied: has been let down by jumping. *C. Storey*   **c–**

ALLABOVEBOARD (IRE) 8 ch.m. Alphabatim (USA) – Always Proud (IRE) (Supreme Leader) [2006/7 h99: 21g 20m* 20m² 20m⁶ 20m* 20g* 16s* 20d⁶ 18d² 23s* 23d⁶ c20d c20s^{ur} Mar 11] sturdy mare: winning pointer: modest hurdler: won 5 claimers in 2006/7, at Fontwell (3), Perth (easily landed odds) and Wetherby: let down by jumping both starts over fences: stays 23f: acts on heavy and good to firm ground: usually front runner. *P. Bowen*   **c–** **h99**

ALLBORN LAD (IRE) 7 b.g. Fourstars Allstar (USA) – Billeragh Girl (Normandy) [2006/7 h80: 26g^{pu} 21m⁴ May 18] close-coupled gelding: poor form in novice hurdles: tried blinkered: sold 8,000 gns Doncaster May (2006) Sales, won point in April. *C. J. Mann*   **h75**

ALLEGEDLY SO (IRE) 6 b.g. Flemensfirth (USA) – Celtic Lace (Celtic Cone) [2006/7 h87, F82: 24v⁶ 20g 21v 24v* 20s⁶ 24v^{pu} 24s³ 27s Apr 27] fair hurdler: won novice at Newcastle in January: should stay beyond 3m: raced mainly on ground softer than good (acts on heavy): tongue tied last 5 outings. *D. W. Whillans*   **h100**

ALLEGIANCE 12 b.g. Rock Hopper – So Precise (FR) (Balidar) [2006/7 h–: 16g 20d Nov 11] leggy gelding: one-time modest hurdler around 2m: lightly raced and no form since 2000/1: blinkered/visored earlier in career. *P. Wegmann*   **h–**

ALLEZ MELINA 6 b.m. Cloudings (IRE) – Theme Arena (Tragic Role (USA)) [2006/7 h–, F84: c18m³ c16m⁵ c16d^{pu} 18g³ 17g 19d 18g⁶ 21g^{pu} Apr 23] poor novice hurdler: no solid form over fences: tried tongue tied. *Mouse Hamilton-Fairley*   **c–** **h69**

ALLEZ PETIT LUIS (FR) 9 br.g. Grand Tresor (FR) – Galissima (FR) (Sicyos (USA)) [2006/7 c16s⁴ c20d² c19d² c17v⁴ 20g⁴ Apr 4] fair handicap hurdler, good fourth to Golden Empire at Gowran final start: fairly useful chaser: won maiden at Limerick in 2005/6: in frame in handicaps, best effort when 4-length second to Well Tutored at Naas third outing: stays 2½m: acts on heavy going. *Colm A. Murphy, Ireland* — c121 h112

ALL FOR JAKE (IRE) 12 ch.g. Sirsan (IRE) – Kelly's Gift (Santa's Sleigh) [2006/7 c21sᵖᵘ May 29] ex-Irish gelding: winning pointer in Ireland: no form in 3 other events. *Cooper Wilson* — c– h–

ALL FOR LUCK (IRE) 6 b.g. Heron Island (IRE) – Castle Graigue (IRE) (Aylesfield) [2006/7 20g⁶ 20v² 23v* 25s⁶ Feb 3] fourth foal: half-brother to fair hurdler Billy Bush (by Lord Americo), stays 2¾m: dam maiden in bumpers/over hurdles: won maiden Irish point in 2006: fairly useful form over hurdles: best effort when winning maiden at Wetherby in January by 15 lengths from Unowatimeen: should stay 3m+: acts on heavy going. *N. G. Richards* — h125

ALL FUN AND GAMES (IRE) 6 b.g. Duky – Congress Lass (IRE) (Boreen (FR)) [2006/7 F– 21v 24mᵖᵘ Mar 31] sturdy gelding: no form in bumpers/over hurdles. *John R. Upson* — h–

ALL IN THE STARS 9 ch.g. Fourstars Allstar (USA) – Luton Flyer (Condorcet (FR)) [2006/7 c136, h–: c25s c29sᵖᵘ c25s⁴ c24g c29mᵖᵘ Apr 9] smallish, sturdy gelding: useful handicap chaser at best, little impact in 2006/7: should stay beyond 3½m: acts on soft going: tried visored (not for long time)/blinkered. *D. P. Keane* — c121 h–

ALLISTATHEBARRISTA (IRE) 8 b.g. Leading Counsel (USA) – Rechime (Prince Regent (FR)) [2006/7 20v* 20v³ 23v² 23v* 23s 24gᵖᵘ Mar 24] 6,200 4-y-o: big, workmanlike gelding: eighth foal: half-brother to useful hunter Prince Buck (by Buckskin), stayed 4m: dam unraced: progressive over hurdles first 4 starts: won novice at Uttoxeter in May and handicap at Wetherby (fairly useful form, by 3 lengths from Darina's Boy) in December: lost both front shoes fifth outing: should stay 3m+: acts on heavy going. *Mrs S. J. Smith* — h122

ALLOW DANCER (IRE) 7 ch.g. Humbel (USA) – Curraleigh Queen (IRE) (Balinger) [2006/7 c21g³ c26d² Aug 7] winning pointer: visored, placed both starts in chases, extremely flattered in novice second time. *R. H. York* — c86 ?

ALL SONSILVER (FR) 10 b.g. Son of Silver – All Licette (FR) (Native Guile (USA)) [2006/7 c–, h–: c16d c21v c24vᵖᵘ c24v² c26vᵖᵘ c25dᵖᵘ c16v* Feb 15] useful-looking gelding: poor handicap chaser: ended long losing run at Chepstow: effective at 2m (given stiff test) to 25f: acts on heavy going: tried in headgear/tongue tied: unreliable. *P. Kelsall* — c80 § h–

ALL SQUARE (IRE) 7 ch.g. Bahhare (USA) – Intricacy (Formidable (USA)) [2006/7 h84: 22m 16m 20fᵖᵘ Jul 19] maiden on Flat: poor hurdler: no form in 2006/7: stays 2½m: acts on firm ground: tried in cheekpieces: effective tongue tied or not. *R. A. Farrant* — h–

ALL STAR (GER) 7 b.g. Lomitas – Alte Garde (FR) (Garde Royale) [2006/7 h128: c17g* c20g³ c16s⁴ 21g c20g⁵ Apr 25] angular gelding: fairly useful handicap hurdler: similar form over fences: won maiden at Ascot in November by 1¾ lengths from Flying Enterprise: 14 lengths third of 4 to New Little Bric in Grade 1 novice at Sandown next time: stays 2½m, at least when conditions aren't testing: acts on heavy and good to firm going. *N. J. Henderson* — c125 h–

ALL THAT JAZZ 8 b.g. Bandmaster (USA) – Miss Corinthian (Cardinal Flower) [2006/7 20d 22sᵖᵘ Oct 26] tall, angular gelding: no form in points in 2005 or in maiden hurdles. *Mrs S. M. Johnson* — h–

ALLTHEWAYINTIME (IRE) 5 b.g. Pistolet Bleu (IRE) – Tinogloria (FR) (Al Nasr (FR)) [2006/7 F17s Dec 23] 10,000 4-y-o: second foal: dam 13f winner in France: well backed, breathing problem in bumper on debut. *Miss Suzy Smith* — F–

ALLUMEE 8 ch.g. Alflora (IRE) – Coire Vannich (Celtic Cone) [2006/7 c106p, h110: c18g² c18sᵖᵘ c17g* c16gᵖᵘ Apr 19] sturdy gelding: fair hurdler: better form over fences: improved when winning handicap at Newbury in March by length from Glengarra: amiss next time: raced mainly around 2m: acts on good to firm and good to soft going (probably unsuited by softer). *A. King* — c122 h–

ALLY SHRIMP 6 b.g. Tamure (IRE) – Minigale (Strong Gale) [2006/7 h106p: 24g* May 5] strong gelding: fairly useful form in novice hurdles, won at Bangor in May by 8 lengths from Corrib Eclipse: stays 3m: raced on good/good to soft ground: looked open to further improvement, but not seen out again. *T. P. Tate* — h121 +

AL MABROOK (IRE) 12 b.g. Rainbows For Life (CAN) – Sky Lover (Ela-Mana-Mou) [2006/7 h–: 20s⁶ 20g⁵ 22m⁴ 22g* Sep 17] close-coupled gelding: poor handicap hurdler: won seller at Uttoxeter in September: stays 2¾m: acts on any going: tried in cheekpieces/visor. *Miss P. Robson* **h73**

ALMANSHOOD (USA) 5 b.g. Bahri (USA) – Lahan (Unfuwain (USA)) [2006/7 16m⁵ 16m* 16dᵖᵘ Nov 11] close-coupled gelding: fairly useful on all-weather on Flat (stays 1¼m): best effort over hurdles (fair form) when winning maiden at Plumpton in October: likely to prove best around 2m: acts on good to firm going. *P. L. Gilligan* **h102**

ALMAVARA (USA) 5 b. or br.g. Fusaichi Pegasus (USA) – Name of Love (IRE) (Petardia) [2006/7 h100?: 20v⁴ 18m⁴ 16d⁵ 22v⁵ 16v 25v 24v 20g Apr 11] compact gelding: fair on Flat (stays 1½m): modest hurdler: likely to prove best at 2m for time being: acts on heavy ground. *C. P. Morlock* **h85**

ALMAYDAN 9 b.g. Marju (IRE) – Cunning (Bustino) [2006/7 c136§, h–: 16m c21d³ c19d⁴ c16v² c22v⁶ c21g⁴ Apr 18] strong gelding: winning hurdler: useful handicap chaser: creditable efforts in 2006/7 when in frame, never-dangerous fourth of 6 to Nycteos in Grade 2 at Cheltenham final start: stays 21f: acts on any going: usually blinkered: usually races prominently: sometimes takes little interest. *R. Lee* **c130 §** **h–**

ALMIER (IRE) 9 gr.g. Phardante (FR) – Stepfaster (Step Together (USA)) [2006/7 c101p, h112: 16d 17m⁵ c17f³ 17f³ 20d⁵ c16s Sep 20] small gelding: fair hurdler/chaser: stays 19f: acts on firm and soft going: in cheekpieces last 3 starts: often races prominently. *M. Hourigan, Ireland* **c100** **h108**

ALMIRE DU LIA (FR) 9 ch.g. Beyssac (FR) – Lita (FR) (Big John (FR)) [2006/7 c101, h–: c25dᵖᵘ c29sᵖᵘ c28sᵖᵘ c24s⁴ c25v* c29vᵖᵘ c28gᵖᵘ Apr 7] big, good-topped gelding: winning hurdler: fair handicap chaser: won at Ayr in March: stays 29f: acts on any going: has won in cheekpieces, usually visored: races prominently: runs as if amiss. *Mrs S. C. Bradburne* **c101** **h–**

ALMIZAN (IRE) 7 b.g. Darshaan – Bint Albaadiya (USA) (Woodman (USA)) [2006/7 h103: 18g³ 20g* 20g 21g³ Apr 23] angular gelding: fair hurdler: won handicap at Fontwell in November: stays 21f: raced on good/good to soft going: tried blinkered. *G. L. Moore* **h108**

ALMNADIA (IRE) 8 b.m. Alhaarth (IRE) – Mnaafa (IRE) (Darshaan) [2006/7 h118: 20gᵇᵈ 16s 19d 22g 22d⁶ 19mᶠ 22d⁴ Aug 19] smallish mare: fairly useful handicap hurdler at best: little impact in 2006/7: stays 3m: acts on firm and good to soft going: blinkered penultimate outing, in cheekpieces previous 6. *S. Gollings* **h90 §**

ALMOST BROKE 10 ch.g. Nearly A Hand – Teletex (Pollerton) [2006/7 c136, h96+: 22d² 21v⁴ c24v c25s⁵ c24g c21gᵘʳ Apr 13] tall gelding: reportedly had breathing operation prior to return: fair maiden hurdler: useful handicap chaser at best: below that in 2006/7, left P. Nicholls after fourth start: effective at 2½m to 3¼m: acts on heavy ground: has fallen/unseated all 3 outings over National fences. *G. Brown* **c116** **h106**

ALMOST FAMOUS (IRE) 8 ch.g. Grand Lodge (USA) – Smouldering (IRE) (Caerleon (USA)) [2006/7 18g² 16m² 16f³ 16m³ 18g⁶ 16g⁵ 16g 19dᶠ Mar 26] smallish gelding: useful at one time on Flat (stayed 1¼m), little show after 2003: modest novice hurdler: left P. Nolan in Ireland before final outing: raced mainly around 2m: acted on firm ground: tried blinkered/tongue tied: dead. *M. Keighley* **h89**

AL MOULATHAM 8 b.g. Rainbow Quest (USA) – High Standard (Kris) [2006/7 16dᵖᵘ Jan 5] half-brother to poor hurdler Comfortable Call (by Nashwan), stays 21f: one-time smart performer on Flat, sold out of E. Charpy's stable 1,800 gns Doncaster October Sales, successful in March: no show in seller on hurdling debut. *R. Ford* **h–**

ALMUTASADER 7 b.h. Sadler's Wells (USA) – Dreamawhile (Known Fact (USA)) [2006/7 h96p: 16d³ 22s³ Nov 17] sturdy, angular horse: modest form over hurdles: will stay 3m. *J. A. B. Old* **h98**

ALPH 10 b.g. Alflora (IRE) – Royal Birthday (St Paddy) [2006/7 h134: c17vᵖᵘ c17vᶠ c17sᵖᵘ 16gᶠ 16m³ Apr 27] tall, lengthy, rather sparely-made gelding: useful form over hurdles, though none of it solid, 7 lengths third to dead-heaters Arcalis and Penzance in valuable minor event at Sandown: failed to complete all 4 starts over fences, running best race when falling last in novice won by Phar Bleu at Plumpton second time: raced around 2m: acts on heavy going, seemingly on good to firm. *B. R. Johnson* **c113** **h132 ?**

ALPHABETICAL (IRE) 8 b. or br.g. Alphabatim (USA) – Sheeghee (IRE) (Noalto) [2006/7 c115, h94+: 21d c20s³ c21g* c19s⁶ c21s³ Mar 8] good-topped gelding: maiden hurdler: fairly useful handicap chaser: won at Wincanton in December by 2½ lengths **c118** **h–**

from Englishtown: stays 21f: acts on soft ground: in cheekpieces last 3 starts: none too consistent. *C. J. Mann*

ALPHAGRAN (IRE) 7 b.g. Alphabatim (USA) – Grannie No (Brave Invader (USA)) [2006/7 18s 22s[6] 22v[4] 23d 27m Apr 26] rather leggy gelding: little sign of ability. *Miss A. M. Newton-Smith* h–

ALPHA IMAGE (IRE) 8 b.g. Alphabatim (USA) – Happy Image (Le Moss) [2006/7 c–, h–: c21v[pu] c20s[pu] c16v[3] Nov 28] rather leggy gelding: little form: has worn cheekpieces/blinkers. *Mrs L. Williamson* c–
h–

ALPHA JULIET (IRE) 6 b.m. Victory Note (USA) – Zara's Birthday (IRE) (Waajib) [2006/7 h78: 17m 17m 21m[4] 20m Apr 9] leggy mare: maiden hurdler, well beaten in 2006/7: stays 21f: acts on soft and good to firm going. *C. J. Teague* h–

ALPHAZAR (IRE) 12 br.g. Alphabatim (USA) – Ravaleen (IRE) (Executive Perk) [2006/7 c21g Apr 12] lengthy gelding: fair hurdler/chaser at best: won point in January: stays 2¾m: acts on heavy going: often wears headgear. *W. P. Mullins, Ireland* c–
h–

ALPHA ZULA (IRE) 9 b.g. Alphabatim (USA) – Sweet Castlehyde (IRE) (King's Ride) [2006/7 c23m[pu] Apr 15] fair form in bumper in 2004 (for Mrs J. Harrington): won maiden point in March: tailed off on chasing debut. *G. Elliott, Ireland* c–

ALPHEUS (IRE) 12 b. or br.g. Alphabatim (USA) – Cold Evening (IRE) (Strong Gale) [2006/7 c23m[6] Apr 22] winning hurdler/pointer: sixth in hunter on chase debut: will stay 3m. *A. J. Mason* c85
h–

ALPINE HIDEAWAY (IRE) 14 b.g. Tirol – Arbour (USA) (Graustark) [2006/7 c–, h80: 19s[6] 16d 17s 19g[6] 19s[6] Nov 16] angular gelding: fair hurdler at best: no show in 2006/7: stays 19f: acts on any going: often wears headgear. *J. S. Wainwright* c–
h–

ALPINE WARRIOR 6 ch.g. Karinga Bay – Redelva (Fidel) [2006/7 F16d Oct 21] third foal: dam winning pointer: well beaten in bumper on debut: won twice in points in April. *Miss Lucinda V. Russell* F–

ALQAAB (USA) 4 b.g. Silver Hawk (USA) – Guerre Et Paix (USA) (Soviet Star (USA)) [2006/7 16v[2] 16v[4] 16v* 17g Mar 16] strong gelding: fairly useful on Flat (should have stayed 1½m), sold out of M. Tregoning's stable 80,000 gns Newmarket Autumn Sales and gelded after final start: fairly useful juvenile hurdler: won maiden at Navan (by 28 lengths) in March: stiff task, mid-division in 23-runner Grade 1 at Cheltenham later in month: raced around 2m: acted on heavy ground: dead. *N. Meade, Ireland* h119

ALRAFID (IRE) 8 ch.g. Halling (USA) – Ginger Tree (USA) (Dayjur (USA)) [2006/7 c108, h115: c16g c16g[3] c16m[2] c16m[3] c16d[3] c18m* 16f[3] 16g[3] 16s[4] c16d* c21g[5] Apr 19] medium-sized gelding: fair handicap hurdler: fairly useful form over fences, won maiden at Fontwell in August and handicap at Lingfield (beat Cossack Dancer 1¼ lengths) in November: best up to 2¼m: acts on soft and good to firm going: takes good hold. *G. L. Moore* c118
h112

ALRAUNE (GER) 4 b. or br.f. Platini (GER) – Avanti Adda (GER) (Law Society (USA)) [2006/7 16m* 16m[6] 17g[2] Oct 1] well held over 1¼m on Flat: won juvenile at Bad Harzburg on hurdling debut in August: runner-up at Hanover, well beaten at Stratford in between. *C. von der Recke, Germany* h–

ALRIGHT NOW M'LAD (IRE) 7 b.g. Supreme Leader – Chattering (Le Bavard (FR)) [2006/7 h127: c23s* c23s[4] c25s[4] c25v[3] c20s* c24g[pu] Mar 14] useful-looking gelding: fairly useful hurdler: similar form over fences: won maiden at Wetherby in October and novice handicap at Haydock (left in lead 2 out, beat Go For One 2 lengths) in February: stays 25f: acts on heavy going. *Jonjo O'Neill* c128
h–

ALROYAL (GER) 8 ch.g. Royal Solo (IRE) – Alamel (USA) (Shadeed (USA)) [2006/7 c16f[2] Aug 22] rangy, useful-looking gelding: fair hurdler: off nearly 2 years, neck dropped out of 4 finishers in handicap at Worcester on chasing debut: likely to prove best around 2m: acts on firm and good to soft going: presumably difficult to train. *C. J. Mann* c112 +
h–

ALSTEDA (IRE) 7 ch.m. Executive Perk – Fair Experience (IRE) (Tale Quale) [2006/7 F17d Oct 7] €1,300 3-y-o: fourth foal: dam lightly raced in points: tailed off in mares bumper on debut. *Mrs V. J. Makin* F–

ALTAY 10 b.g. Erins Isle – Aliuska (IRE) (Fijar Tango (FR)) [2006/7 c16d[3] c16s[2] c17s[2] c16d[3] Dec 4] big, leggy gelding: as good as ever when winning both starts on Flat in 2006: fairly useful handicap hurdler: similar form over fences, in frame all 4 starts in 2006/7: best around 2m: acted on firm and soft going: has reportedly been retired. *R. A. Fahey* c119
h–

ALTENBURG (FR) 5 b.g. Sadler's Wells (USA) – Anna of Saxony (Ela-Mana-Mou) **h85 §**
[2006/7 h–§: 16s⁴ Jan 15] fairly useful maiden on Flat (stays 1¾m): form (modest) over
hurdles only when fourth in novice only outing in 2006/7: not one to trust. *Mrs N. Smith*

ALTERNATOR (IRE) 5 ch.g. Pistolet Bleu (IRE) – Marello (Supreme Leader) **h105 p**
[2006/7 F17s² F16v* 20v⁴ 19d² Feb 19] 17,000 3-y-o: leggy, useful-looking gelding: **F102**
second foal: half-brother to fairly useful 2½m hurdle winner Accordello (by Accordion):
dam high-class hurdler up to 25f: won bumper at Warwick in December: better effort over
hurdles when 9 lengths second to Valiant Shadow in maiden at Market Rasen: will prove
suited by 2½m+: capable of better again over hurdles. *Jonjo O'Neill*

ALTILHAR (USA) 4 b.g. Dynaformer (USA) – Al Desima (Emperor Jones (USA)) **h133**
[2006/7 16d* 16d⁶ 16d* 16d² 16g* 16m⁴ Apr 21] sturdy gelding: fairly useful on Flat
(stays 11.5f), successful twice in 2006: useful juvenile hurdler: progressive form when
winning at Fakenham in November, Ludlow in January and Ascot (handicap, beat
stable-companion Mon Michel by ½ length) in March: will be suited by further than 2m:
unraced on extremes of going: blinkered. *G. L. Moore*

ALTITUDE DANCER (IRE) 7 b.g. Sadler's Wells (USA) – Height of Passion (Shir- **h101**
ley Heights) [2006/7 h103d: 24g 24mF Jul 11] smallish gelding: fair handicap hurdler:
left A. Crook after first outing: stayed 27f: acted on good to firm going: tried blinkered:
moody: dead. *J. L. Flint*

ALTO VERTIGO 4 b.g. Averti (IRE) – Singer On The Roof (Chief Singer) [2006/7 **F–**
F14s Dec 16] strong gelding: seventh foal: half-brother to 2¼m chase winner in Germany
by Slip Anchor and 6f winner Pink Bay (by Forzando): dam, 1m winner, half-sister to
Prix Saint-Alary winner Air de Rien: well held in 3-y-o bumper on debut. *P. C. Haslam*

ALVA GLEN (USA) 10 b.g. Gulch (USA) – Domludge (USA) (Lyphard (USA)) **h– §**
[2006/7 h98§: 21f Apr 30] sturdy gelding: modest handicap hurdler: effective at 2¾m, at
least when conditions aren't testing: acts on good to firm and good to soft going: tried in
cheekpieces/tongue tied: temperamental. *B. J. Llewellyn*

ALVAREZ 10 b.g. Gran Alba (USA) – Glorious Jane (Hittite Glory) [2006/7 c20s⁴ **c–**
c20m c20mF Jun 22] modest form in bumpers: off 4 years, no form over fences: dead.
P. C. Haslam

ALWAYS 8 b.g. Dynaformer (USA) – Love And Affection (USA) (Exclusive Era **c124 §**
(USA)) [2006/7 c120§, h–: 16mrtr c17m⁴ c22g 16d c21grtr Apr 13] leggy gelding: win- **h– §**
ning hurdler, left N. Meade prior to fourth start: fairly useful chaser: probably stays 2¾m:
acts on good and good to firm going: often wore blinkers nowadays: has had tongue tied:
untrustworthy (refused to race 3 of last 6 outings). *John Long, Ireland*

ALWAYS BAILEYS (IRE) 4 ch.g. Mister Baileys – Dubiously (USA) (Jolie Jo **h91**
(USA)) [2006/7 16s 16g⁶ 20g⁴ Apr 1] fair on Flat (stays 1½m): modest form in novice
hurdles: stays 2½m: acts on good ground. *T. Wall*

ALWAYS WAINING (IRE) 6 b.g. Unfuwain (USA) – Glenarff (USA) (Irish River **c134**
(FR)) [2006/7 h117: 20g² 24s⁴ c22vpu c24s⁴ c19s* c22g* c21g³ c25m* Apr 21] close- **h118**
coupled gelding: fairly useful handicap hurdler, good efforts first 2 starts in 2006/7:
useful novice chaser: won maiden at Taunton in January and, after leaving R. Stronge,
handicaps at Newbury in March and Ayr (beat Get My Drift by 6 lengths) in April:
failed post-race test) in April: stays 25f: unraced on firm going, acts on any other.
P. Bowen

ALYSSIA MIA 6 br.m. Bob's Return (IRE) – Amazon (IRE) (Petorius) [2006/7 16m **h–**
Jun 28] no show in bumper (for M. Bosley) and novice hurdle 16 months apart. *Andrew
Turnell*

AMADEUS (AUS) 10 ch.g. Brief Truce (USA) – Amazaan (NZ) (Zamazaan (FR)) **c102**
[2006/7 c102, h76: c16m³ 21g⁴ 21d⁴ c21s* 20g⁴ 24dpu 17s⁶ c20v⁶ c24s⁶ Mar 10] **h81**
angular gelding: poor hurdler: fair handicap chaser: won at Newton Abbot in June: left
M. Scudamore after eighth start: stays 21f: acts on soft and good to firm going. *Ms
Caroline Walker*

AMALFI STORM 6 b.m. Slip Anchor – Mayroni (Bustino) [2006/7 h75, F80: 20d³ **c71**
16s³ 16g² 16g³ 16f⁴ 16d³ c16d⁵ c17gpu c17vF Dec 3] poor maiden handicap hurdler: **h84**
beaten fair way only completed start in novice handicap chases: likely to prove best at
2m: acts on soft going: blinkered final outing. *M. W. Easterby*

AMALFITANO (IRE) 7 br.g. Semillon – Tipsy Miss (IRE) (Orchestra) [2006/7 20v* **h117**
21d* 24dpu 24d³ Jan 14] first foal: dam unraced half-sister to useful staying hurdler Now
Your Talkin: bumper winner: fairly useful hurdler: won maiden at Listowel in September
and listed novice at Limerick in October: good third of 27 to Adamant Approach in

Pertemps Qualifier at Leopardstown on handicap debut: stays 3m: raced on going softer than good (acts on heavy). *A. K. Wyse, Ireland*

AMANPURI (GER) 9 br.g. Fairy King (USA) – Aratika (FR) (Zino) [2006/7 h105: 17d c23d³ c23d³ Oct 26] workmanlike gelding: fair handicap hurdler: similar form in maiden on chasing debut, badly let down by jumping next time: stays 23f: best form on going softer than good (acts on heavy): usually races prominently. *Mrs A. M. Thorpe*

c105 h–

AMARETTO ROSE 6 b.m. Alflora (IRE) – Teenero (Teenoso (USA)) [2006/7 F95: F16g* 16d* 16v* 16d³ Mar 13]

h141 + F109 +

Although the Timeform Race Card no longer states, as it once did, that the most important factor affecting the performance of a horse is the ground, there is no doubting that the state of the going is materially relevant when assessing the outcome of a race. In broad terms, the more extreme the going, the more effect it has on the result. So, the prospect of heavy ground at Cheltenham was widely discussed in the media and much mulled over by those pontificating at preview evenings in the build-up to the latest Festival. Five days before the meeting opened, 'heavy' looked set to figure in the official going description for the first time in eighteen years. In the ten days up to the Tuesday before the Festival, 55mm of rain was reported as falling. With further rainfall predicted, gruelling conditions were on the cards, among those likely to be most inconvenienced being Black Jack Ketchum, long-time favourite for the World Hurdle, who was reportedly friendless in the ante-post markets. By that stage, however, the weather had begun to change and over the following few days dry, warm conditions, very different from those initially predicted by the weather forecasters, led to the official description on the opening day, staged on the Old Course, being 'soft, good to soft in places'. Even so, conditions were still widely anticipated to be a good deal more testing than usual.

Not for the first time, the clock told a different story. The time for the Supreme Novices', the opening race of the meeting, indicated that the going was on the border between good and good to soft. Taking the times for all races that day into account, along with the opinion of one of our on-course representatives who walked the course beforehand, *Timeform* struck a balance and described the ground as good on the chase course and good to soft on the hurdles. The times can occasionally be misleading, and the view of the representative who walked the course for *Timeform*

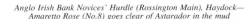

Anglo Irish Bank Novices' Hurdle (Rossington Main), Haydock—
Amaretto Rose (No.8) goes clear of Astarador in the mud

was that the going was essentially good to soft. That said, in most years the times for races such as the Supreme Novices' and the two that follow it, the Arkle and Champion Hurdle, which are contested by a similar standard of horse and usually run in a similar fashion, are usually a fairly reliable and objective means of determining the ground. Even allowing for alterations to the course or excessive dolling out to save fresh ground for the next day, it seems clear that the official going description turned out to be both inaccurate and misleading. Clerks of the course have a difficult and wide-ranging job, particularly at a Grade 1 track such as Cheltenham, so it is understandable that punters' interests aren't necessarily always their top priority. They don't have the benefit of hindsight either, after studying the opening races. However, the need for accurate going descriptions really should be afforded greater importance by racing's officials, whatever the level of meeting.

As it was, punters had to contend with the official going description being changed—to 'good to soft, soft in places'—midway through the opening day of the 2007 Festival. That was too late for those who'd wagered on the meeting's curtain-raiser, the Supreme Novices', a traditionally strong betting race which again proved popular in 2007—£3,744,519.86 was traded on Betfair alone.

Partly in expectation of soft or heavy going, the mare Amaretto Rose started a heavily-backed favourite for the Supreme Novices'. She had won twice from three starts in bumpers, all against her own sex, at Towcester on her debut in 2005/6 and at Warwick on her reappearance in October, when she showed useful form in beating ordinary opposition by ten lengths or more. Amaretto Rose then had two outings in novice hurdles. At Ascot in December on good to soft going, she was most impressive, travelling strongly throughout and quickening away in the

Weatherbys Racing Club's "Amaretto Rose"

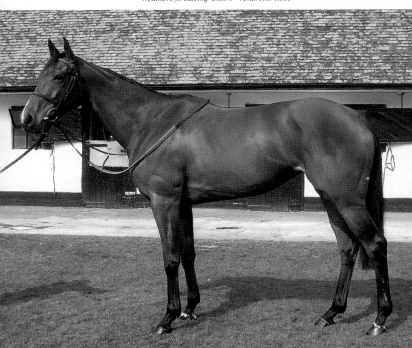

straight to win with plenty in hand, beating the useful Hobbs Hill by thirteen lengths with the rest of a sizeable field well strung out behind. A month later, Amaretto Rose was stepped up to graded company, in the Rossington Main Novices' Hurdle at Haydock, which, like the Supreme Novices', was sponsored by Anglo Irish Bank. On particularly testing ground, she faced seven opponents, all at least fairly useful. Starting odds on, she produced a scintillating performance, one of the best by a novice hurdler all season, not extended to draw away after the last and beat Astarador, who conceded 10 lb, by eighteen lengths. Even without the mares allowance, Amaretto Rose would have had a leading chance at Cheltenham on that run—only Hide The Evidence, on the form he showed in the AIG Europe Champion Hurdle, would have figured ahead of her on Timeform ratings had the race been run at level weights. Three mares had won the Supreme since the introduction of the mares allowance, Tourist Attraction in 1995, French Ballerina in 1998 and Like-A-Butterfly, somewhat fortuitously, in 2002. They received 5 lb from the colts and geldings. In receipt of 7 lb, Amaretto Rose had an outstanding chance and fully deserved to be 2/1 favourite. As it turned out, she wasn't quite able to match her Haydock effort, though she held every chance despite being done no favours at the delayed start. Again travelling well through the race, she was perfectly placed entering the straight but couldn't reproduce the turn of foot which had marked her previous performances, going down by three lengths and a neck to Ebaziyan and Granit Jack. It wasn't so much that the ground beat Amaretto Rose, more that soft or heavy ground would have played to her strengths more over the two-mile trip.

Amaretto Rose wasn't seen out after Cheltenham. She cut her leg there and the cut became infected, so much so that she wasn't even able to make a date at the Cheltenham Sales in April, where she looked set to be the star lot. She had appeared there two years previously, when she made £10,000, bought on behalf of David and Anne Hockenhull, who later leased her to the Weatherbys Racing Club, in whose colours she ran. That lease came to an end after Cheltenham. At the time of writing, Amaretto Rose's future is unclear, though hopefully she will be back on the racecourse in the coming season, as she has the potential to improve a fair bit further as a hurdler.

		Niniski	Nijinsky
	Alflora (IRE)	(b 1976)	Virginia Hills
	(b 1989)	Adrana	Bold Lad
Amaretto Rose		(ch 1980)	Le Melody
(b.m. 2001)		Teenoso	Youth
	Teenero	(b 1980)	Furioso
	(b 1993)	Miss Nero	Crozier
		(br 1981)	Romany Miss

The Hockenhulls established the Shade Oak Stud in Shropshire, home of Amaretto Rose's sire Alflora, who is now firmly established as a leading British-based National Hunt stallion. Alflora's three best offspring over jumps, Central House, Hand Inn Hand and Farmer Jack, have shown their best form over fences but it remains to be seen whether Amaretto Rose will follow that route. She lacks the size for chasing, being rather leggy in appearance, and the new programme of races for mares over hurdles may well prove tempting in 2007/8. That said, it is possible she could progress enough, once stepped up in trip, to emulate her grandam Miss Nero, who was twice placed in the Stayers' Hurdle, finishing second to the previous year's winner Galmoy in 1988 and third behind Rustle and Galmoy in 1989. Miss Nero hasn't passed on much of her ability to her immediate offspring and it wasn't until 2006/7 that she finally had a jumping winner outside of points, her son The Hardy Boy being successful four times over fences. Miss Nero's only other winner under Rules has been dual bumper scorer Latin Mistress. Meanwhile, her two winning pointers include the Irish gelding Kildoire (by Alflora), who made just 1,400 gns at the latest Doncaster May Sales after reaching the frame only once from eleven starts outside points. Amaretto Rose's dam Teenero was well beaten in a bumper on her only start. Amaretto Rose is Teenero's second foal, the first One Wild Night, who is by another Shade Oak stallion Rakaposhi King, was placed twice over hurdles. Her third foal is a five-year-old brother to Amaretto Rose called At Your Peril, who was pulled up in a maiden Irish point on his debut in April.

Teenero has since produced three fillies to Shropshire-based stallions, namely Terimon in 2004, the now-deceased Karinga Bay in 2005 and Alflora again in 2007. One of the more notable performers in this family tree is Miss Nero's half-brother Dunkirk, though it must be stressed he wasn't *the* Dunkirk. This one showed useful form over fences at up to two and a half miles in the 'eighties for Merrick Francis. Amaretto Rose will stay at least two and a half miles and has raced only on going softer than good over hurdles. She clearly acts well on heavy. *N. J. Henderson*

AMARULA RIDGE (IRE) 6 b.g. Indian Ridge – Mail Boat (Formidable (USA)) [2006/7 c101, h86: 16m* c16mpu 17g4 Sep 8] rather leggy gelding: winning chaser: fair hurdler: won amateur novice at Huntingdon in May: likely to prove best around 2m: acts on soft and good to firm going. *P. J. Hobbs*
c–
h113

AMAZING PROPOSAL (IRE) 7 b.g. Oscar (IRE) – Parsonage (The Parson) [2006/7 17d Oct 17] ex-Irish gelding: half-brother to winning pointer by Spanish Place: dam unraced: little impact in bumpers: modest form at best over hurdles: won point in April 2006: sold 20,000 gns Doncaster Sales following month: will be suited by 2½m+. *J. G. Portman*
h80

AMAZING VALOUR (IRE) 5 b.g. Sinndar (IRE) – Flabbergasted (IRE) (Sadler's Wells (USA)) [2006/7 h99: 20m6 24f2 24f* Jul 6] compact gelding: modest hurdler: landed odds by wide margin in maiden at Perth in July: stays 3m: acts on soft and firm going: usually blinkered/visored: hard ride. *P. Bowen*
h97

AMBER BROOK (IRE) 6 ch.m. Alderbrook – Me Grannys Endoors (IRE) (Tremblant) [2006/7 F17g4 Apr 27] €2,000 3-y-o, €3,500 4-y-o: first foal: dam unraced: failed to complete in 3 points in 2006: 7¾ lengths fourth to Covert Mission in bumper at Newton Abbot, always well placed. *N. J. Hawke*
F82 ?

AMBER DAWN 8 ch.m. Weld – Scrambird (Dubassoff (USA)) [2006/7 c89, h68: 27d6 27d6 c21g6 c23dur c23spu Dec 1] angular mare: maiden hurdler/chaser: no form in 2006/7: best form at 2m: acts on firm going: tried in headgear. *N. J. Dawe*
c–
h–

AMBER LIGHT (IRE) 7 ch.m. Anshan – Ebony Jane (Roselier (FR)) [2006/7 c24g c24d4 c27dur 26s6 c27v3 24spu c23s3 c25vpu Feb 28] sister to bumper winner Gansey and half-sister to poor/ungenuine staying chaser Ebony Jack and fair 2½m hurdle winner Bolt Action (both by Phardante): dam won Irish Grand National: won mares maiden point in 2006: poor maiden hurdler/chaser: left David Kiely after first outing: barely stays testing 27f: acts on heavy going: in headgear last 6 starts. *Evan Williams*
c74
h–

AMBERSONG 9 ch.g. Hernando (FR) – Stygian (USA) (Irish River (FR)) [2006/7 h95: 16f4 17g4 17d2 Aug 7] modest hurdler: raced around 2m: acts on soft going. *A. W. Carroll*
h88

AMBER WARRIOR (IRE) 7 b. or br.g. College Chapel – Book Choice (North Summit) [2006/7 19spu 16g2 Mar 29] half-brother to 2m hurdle winner Quill Project (by Project Manager): dam unraced: well beaten in bumper: won maiden Irish point later in 2004: much improved over hurdles (off over 2 years before return) when second to Inherent in novice at Towcester. *J. J. Quinn*
h104

AMBITION ROYAL (FR) 7 ch.g. Cyborg (FR) – Before Royale (FR) (Dauphin du Bourg (FR)) [2006/7 c89, h93: c16g4 c24d3 c26s4 c24g5 c21vpu Dec 11] strong, stocky gelding: maiden hurdler/chaser, poor form over fences in 2006/7: stays 3¼m: acts on heavy going (possibly unsuited by good to firm): tried visored/in cheekpieces: temperamental. *Miss Lucinda V. Russell*
c81 §
h–

AMBLE FORGE (IRE) 5 b.g. Needle Gun (IRE) – La Mode Lady (Mandalus) [2006/7 F18s2 F16g Dec 26] €18,000 4-y-o: fourth foal: half-brother to winning pointer by Glacial Storm: dam winning chaser around 2m: 1½ lengths second to Deep Reflection at Plumpton, better effort in bumpers. *C. L. Tizzard*
F91

AMEEQ (USA) 5 b. or br.g. Silver Hawk (USA) – Haniya (IRE) (Caerleon (USA)) [2006/7 h84p: 16m* 16m* 16g2 16d2 17g 16g Apr 14] leggy gelding: fairly useful on Flat (stays 1½m): similar standard over hurdles: easily won novices at Wincanton in May and Huntingdon in September: contested valuable handicaps after, second to Mahogany Blaze at Chepstow and Detroit City at Cheltenham: likely to prove best around 2m: acts on good to firm and good to soft going (well held only outing on heavy). *G. L. Moore*
h123

AMERAS (IRE) 9 b.m. Hamas (IRE) – Amerindian (Commanche Run) [2006/7 c71, h–: 16f c16mur Aug 22] angular mare: winning pointer: poor novice hurdler/chaser: barely stays 3m: acts on heavy going: tried tongue tied. *Miss S. E. Forster*
c–
h–

Barrack Homes Pat Taaffe Handicap Chase, Punchestown—
the mare American Jennie (noseband) thwarts British raider Noir Et Vert

AMERICANCONNECTION (IRE) 11 b.g. Lord Americo – Ballyea Jacki (Straight Lad) [2006/7 c97, h–: c23g⁵ May 14] tall gelding: lightly-raced winning hurdler/maiden chaser (makes mistakes): stays 25f: acts on firm going. *D. McCain* — c– x / h–

AMERICAN CRICKET (IRE) 6 b. or br.g. Lord Americo – Dixons Dutchess (IRE) (Over The River (FR)) [2006/7 F17s* Jan 26] €12,000 3-y-o: brother/half-brother to winning pointers: dam unraced: runner-up on completed start in Irish points in 2006: bought £42,000 Cheltenham April Sales: won 16-runner bumper at Hereford by short head from Quarry Town, pair clear. *Carl Llewellyn* — F108 +

AMERICAN DUKE (USA) 6 b.g. Cryptoclearance (USA) – Prologue (USA) (Theatrical) [2006/7 17m³ 17m Aug 2] fairly useful on Flat (stays 1¼m) at 3 yrs for B. Meehan: pulled hard and well beaten both starts over hurdles. *P. J. Hobbs* — h–

AMERICAN IDOL (IRE) 7 ch.g. Good Thyne (USA) – Beatrice Allegro (IRE) (Phardante (FR)) [2006/7 22mᵖᵘ Jun 8] first foal: dam, ran twice in bumpers, half-sister to useful staying hurdler Garruth (by Good Thyne): won maiden point in 2006: no show on hurdling debut. *Evan Williams* — h–

AMERICAN JENNIE (IRE) 9 br.m. Lord Americo – Cathy's Girl (Sheer Grit) [2006/7 c125+, h104: 16v⁶ c24d⁶ c24vᵖᵘ 19v c29m³ c25m* Apr 26] useful-looking mare: fair handicap hurdler: useful chaser: improved form last 2 outings, 2¾ lengths third of 29 to Butler's Cabin in Irish Grand National (in frame in race for second time) at Fairyhouse, then won valuable handicap at Punchestown gamely by short head from Noir Et Vert: will stay beyond 29f: acts on heavy and good to firm going: patiently ridden. *Michael Cullen, Ireland* — c138 / h107 +

AMERICAN PRESIDENT (IRE) 11 br.g. Lord Americo – Deceptive Response (Furry Glen) [2006/7 h–: 16g* c16g³ c16mᶠ c17g³ c18d³ Dec 26] sturdy gelding: fair hurdler at best, won novice at Hexham in May: modest form over fences: stays 19f: acts on heavy and good to firm going: front runner. *J. J. Quinn* — c98 / h88

AMHAIRGHIN (IRE) 7 ch.g. Accordion – North Gale (Oats) [2006/7 F93: F17v⁶ 19g² 20g² Dec 30] rangy gelding: fair form in bumpers: runner-up in maiden hurdles at Catterick and Musselburgh: stays 2½m. *G. A. Harker* — h96 / F92

AMICELLI (GER) 8 b.g. Goofalik (USA) – Arratonia (GER) (Arratos (FR)) [2006/7 c113
c124, h124: 27d² c26d² c20m* c22g* c27d^F 24s 24g Mar 24] useful-looking gelding: h122
fairly useful hurdler: similar form at about over fences, landed odds in novices at Bangor
and Market Rasen in September: stays 27f: acts on good to firm and good to soft going:
usually races prominently: reliable in main, though well held last 2 outings. *P. J. Hobbs*

AMID THE CHAOS (IRE) 7 ch.g. Nashwan (USA) – Celebrity Style (USA) (Seek- c97
ing The Gold (USA)) [2006/7 c93, h–: 21f^pu c19m^pu c20m⁴ c17m⁵ Jul 20] well-made h–
gelding: winning hurdler, no form in 2 handicaps in Britain: modest maiden chaser: stays
2¾m: acts on heavy and good to firm going: often blinkered, visored final outing: tongue
tied last 2. *C. J. Mann*

AMIGRA (IRE) 5 b.m. Grand Lodge (USA) – Beaming (Mtoto) [2006/7 16m 16d 16d h–
Nov 20] half-sister to winning 2m hurdler in France by Sri Pekan: poor maiden on Flat
(stays 1m), sold out of Ms J. Doyle's stable £1,950 Ascot June (2005) Sales: well beaten
over hurdles. *Miss J. S. Davis*

AMIR EL JABAL (FR) 4 b.g. Enrique – Premonitory Dream (FR) (Exit To Nowhere h106
(USA)) [2006/7 18s* 16v⁶ 16s 16d⁴ 16s Mar 3] leggy gelding: half-brother to winning 2m
hurdler around 2m Allez Cash (by Marignan): fair on Flat (stays 10.5f): won juvenile at
Auteuil in November on hurdling debut: left Mme L. Audon, well below that form in
Britain, though shaped as if capable of better fourth outing: stays 2¼m. *D. E. Pipe*

AMJAD 10 ch.g. Cadeaux Genereux – Babita (Habitat) [2006/7 c–x, h–x: 17d⁴ 21m 17f⁴ c– x
17m³ 16f⁴ 17s³ 17s⁴ 19v⁵ Feb 27] leggy gelding: maiden chaser: poor hurdler: best h63 x
around 2m: acts on firm and good to soft going: tried in cheekpieces: pulls hard: not a
fluent jumper. *Miss Kate Milligan*

AMMUNITION (IRE) 7 b.g. Needle Gun (IRE) – Flapping Freda (IRE) (Carlingford h102
Castle) [2006/7 h81p, F94: 19d² 20s⁶ 22d³ 20g^pu Apr 27] useful-looking gelding: fair
novice hurdler: stays 2¾m: raced on good going or softer. *Carl Llewellyn*

AMNESTY 8 ch.g. Salse (USA) – Amaranthus (Shirley Heights) [2006/7 h90§: 16g⁴ h71 §
May 14] angular gelding: modest maiden hurdler: raced around 2m: acts on soft going:
blinkered: untrustworthy. *G. L. Moore*

AMORE MIO (IRE) 7 b.g. Anshan – Dalua Leader (IRE) (Supreme Leader) [2006/7 h–
20m^pu 16m 16g^su 16g⁶ Apr 27] well held in bumper: sold out of A. Mullins' stable 6,200
gns Doncaster November (2005) Sales: in frame in points: little impact over hurdles.
M. Scudamore

AMORIST (IRE) 5 b.g. Anabaa (USA) – Moivouloirtoi (USA) (Bering) [2006/7 16g^pu h–
16d^pu Dec 28] useful-looking gelding: fairly useful on Flat (stays 1¼m), sold out of Sir
Mark Prescott's stable 80,000 gns Newmarket February (2006) Sales: little aptitude for
hurdling: headstrong. *J. Howard Johnson*

AMOUR DARIA (FR) 4 b.g. Nikos – Ecluse (FR) (Morespeed) [2006/7 16d⁶ 16v^pu h–
16s 16d Feb 14] brother to 2 winning hurdlers around 2m in France: dam maiden: once-
raced on Flat: no form over hurdles, left T. Trapenard after third start: tried blinkered.
S. H. Shirley-Beavan

AMOUR MULTIPLE (IRE) 8 b.g. Poliglote – Onereuse (Sanglamore (USA)) c–
[2006/7 c119, h117: 19d³ 16m⁵ 16s⁵ 17s* 16s* 19s Feb 3] sturdy gelding: twice-raced h127
over fences in France: fairly useful handicap hurdler: ridden more prominently than
usual, won at Hereford in December and Wincanton (beat Magic Sky by ¾ length) in
January: stays 19f: acts on heavy and good to firm going: consistent. *S. Lycett*

AMRON HILL 4 b.g. Polar Prince (IRE) – Maradata (IRE) (Shardari) [2006/7 17m⁶ h80 p
Mar 29] brother to 2m hurdle winner Viper and half-brother to 2m hurdle winner
Itcanbedone Again (by Sri Pekan): modest maiden on Flat (stays 9.5f): never better than
mid-field when sixth to Classic Dream in juvenile at Hereford on hurdling debut: should
benefit from experience. *R. Hollinshead*

AMSTECOS (IRE) 7 b.g. Presenting – Mrs Doeskin (IRE) (Buckskin (FR)) [2006/7 h131 p
F114+: F16v* F16v* 20v* Mar 22] useful form in bumpers, won at Perth in May: unbeaten F114 +
in 2 starts over hurdles, in maiden at Fairyhouse in February and novice at Ayr in March:
useful form when beating Ossmoses by neck at latter, 5 lengths clear at last before idling:
will stay beyond 2½m: raced mainly on going softer than good: type to do better again.
B. R. Hamilton, Ireland

AN ACCORDION (IRE) 6 b.g. Accordion – Jennie's First (Idiot's Delight) [2006/7 c135
F16d² c23g* c22s* c21v³ Jan 27] well-made gelding: half-brother to 2 winners, notably F108
smart chaser Horus (by Teenoso), stayed 3¼m: dam unraced half-sister to useful staying

chaser You're Agoodun: successful all 3 starts in points in 2006: 4 lengths second to Cork All Star in listed bumper at Cheltenham: good start to chasing career, landing odds in maiden at Leicester (hanging left) in November and novice at Fontwell in January: useful form when 9¼ lengths third to Flying Enterprise in novice handicap at Cheltenham, held when mistake last: stays 23f: raced on good going or softer. *D. E. Pipe*

ANATAR (IRE) 9 b.g. Caerleon (USA) – Anaza (Darshaan) [2006/7 c–, h108: 20m^2 21m^4 c19m^{pu} 19s^4 24m Jul 4] leggy gelding: fairly useful at best over hurdles, has deteriorated considerably: lightly-raced maiden chaser: stays 2¾m: acts on heavy and good to firm going: wears headgear: ungenuine: sold 2,400 gns Doncaster August Sales, third in point in April. *D. E. Pipe*   c– §   h91 §

AN CAPALL DUBH (IRE) 11 b. or br.g. Air Display (USA) – Lady of Wales (Welsh Pageant) [2006/7 c105, h–: c24s^4 May 20] tall gelding: fairly useful hunter chaser: below best in points in 2007: stays 25f: acts on firm and soft going: tongue tied early in career. *Mrs Edward Crow*   c90   h–

ANCHORS AWAY 5 b.g. Slip Anchor – Qurrat Al Ain (Wolver Hollow) [2006/7 F101: F17d^4 20s^4 16d^4 20s^6 17s^4 20v 20s^4 17m Apr 9] tall, leggy, close-coupled gelding: bumper winner: modest novice hurdler: bred to stay beyond 2½m: acts on soft ground: blinkered last 2 starts. *T. D. Easterby*   h89   F84

AND ALL THAT JAZZ 5 b.m. Morpeth – Kindly Lady (Kind of Hush) [2006/7 F17g^6 F14s 17g Apr 7] medium-sized mare: third foal: half-sister to winning pointer by Pontevecchio Notte: dam winning pointer: well held in bumpers and maiden hurdle. *J. D. Frost*   h–   F–

ANDIJAN (IRE) 6 b.g. Marju (IRE) – Anazeem (IRE) (Irish River (FR)) [2006/7 16d 16m 20s^6 Sep 21] second foal: dam, third at 7f from 2 starts, half-sister to very smart performer up to 1½m in France/USA Astarabad: poor maiden hurdler: left N. Glynn prior to final start: raced mainly around 2m. *J. J. Lambe, Ireland*   h–

ANDORRAN (GER) 4 b.g. Lando (GER) – Adora (GER) (Danehill (USA)) [2006/7 16s^{pu} 16m 17m^{pu} 17g Apr 23] maiden on Flat, well held in handicaps in 2006: no form in juvenile hurdles: tried in cheekpieces/tongue tied. *A. Dickman*   h–

ANDREA GALE (IRE) 6 b. or br.m. Presenting – Pegus Gold (Strong Gale) [2006/7 F16s F17g^2 24m^5 16d^6 16d^4 20d* 22d 21s^3 c24d^6 Feb 2] ex-Irish mare: sixth foal: half-sister to bumper winner Triple Rum (by Be My Native) and fairly useful pointer by Anshan: dam placed in bumpers: left D. Berry, best effort in bumpers when second to True Dove at Newton Abbot: poor hurdler: won mares handicap at Sedgefield in November: not knocked about when well held in handicap on chasing debut: stays 21f: acts on soft going. *Evan Williams*   c–   h81   F80

ANDREAS (FR) 7 b.g. Marchand de Sable (USA) – Muscova Dancer (FR) (Muscovite (USA)) [2006/7 c145, h137+: c17m^3 c17d^3 c16g^3 c16g* c16g^F Apr 12]   c157   h–

    Those who supported the well-backed favourite Andreas in the 2006 running of the Grand Annual at the Cheltenham Festival didn't get much of a run for their money. A fourth-fence faller that day, Andreas made amends in the latest edition of the Festival's feature two-mile handicap chase, galvanised by first-time partner Robert Thornton and showing unexpected resolution when the chips were down to snatch victory in the last seventy-five yards after seemingly handing the race to Hasty Prince with a mistake two out. Thornton had a splendid Cheltenham, riding with skill and tenacity over the four days, his four winners making him leading rider at the Festival. Andreas, who started at 12/1, was matched at 25/1 and 23/1 on Betfair straight after his mistake but he rallied splendidly for Thornton and, after being switched to the stands' side, produced a fine leap at the last before forging ahead to beat Hasty Prince by three lengths. Ironically, Andreas' trainer Paul Nicholls, who also ended the meeting with four winners and the title of leading Festival trainer, was responsible for the hot favourite in the Grand Annual, sixth-placed Saintsaire (the mount of stable jockey Ruby Walsh), whom he had nominated as the stable's 'Festival handicap banker', just as he had Andreas the previous year. Andreas's pre-Cheltenham reputation this time around as a weak finisher was well-founded and he had flattered to deceive when third on each of his previous starts in the season, in handicaps at Ascot in October and November and at Sandown in February, finishing a place behind Hasty Prince in the last two. The pair met again in the Red Rum Handicap at Aintree in April, a race in which Andreas had been a weak-finishing third twelve months earlier. The race was won

*Johnny Henderson Grand Annual Chase Challenge Cup (Handicap), Cheltenham—
fourth winner of the meeting for Robert Thornton, who conjures an unusually strong rally from Andreas
to overhaul perennial rival Hasty Prince (hoops)*

by the Grand Annual fifth Bambi de l'Orme but Andreas (with Walsh back on
board) was running well—his mark having been raised 11 lb—until falling two
out after typically moving smoothly into contention. Whether Andreas really is a
reformed character, or not, is a question that will now have to wait until the next
season.

    The useful-looking Andreas, who invariably impresses in appearance, ran
twice on the Flat and was successful twice from five starts over hurdles as a juvenile
in France for Marc Boudot before joining his present stable. He made an ignominious start to his career in Britain, finishing last of ten in a juvenile hurdle at Ayr, but
then made a very promising beginning over fences until concerns over his limited
response under pressure led to his reportedly having an operation in the first part
of the 2005/6 season to cure a suspected wind problem. Andreas is the second foal
of the maiden Muscova Dancer, who has also produced two winning jumpers in
France, namely cross-country chaser Art of Figthing (by Marignan) and two-mile/
two-and-a-quarter-mile hurdler Miss Cozzene (by Solid Illusion). Andreas travels
strongly in his races and is always likely to prove most effective at around two
miles, although Nicholls is reportedly keen to try him over further. He has won on
going ranging from good to firm to good to soft. He has worn a tongue strap since
his early days in Britain. *P. F. Nicholls*

ANDRE CHENIER (IRE) 6 b.g. Perugino (USA) – Almada (GER) (Lombard   **c109**
(GER)) [2006/7 h115: 16m⁶ 16g³ 16m* 16v c16d 16v c16v² 17s⁶ c17v³ c16v³ c16g* c16s⁶   **h109**
Apr 27] leggy, useful-looking gelding: fair hurdler: won claimer at Perth in August:
looked quirky seventh outing: similar form over fences, won maiden at Sedgefield in
March: raced around 2m: unraced on firm going, acts on any other. *P. Monteith*

ANDSOSAYALLOFUS (IRE) 6 b.g. Luso – Glenamena Glory (IRE) (Glad Dancer)   **h–**
[2006/7 F16vᵖᵘ 20mᵘʳ Apr 9] €34,000 3-y-o: fourth foal: dam unraced: runner-up in   **F–**
points in 2005: fair form when placed in bumpers: unseated second on hurdling debut.
S. Donohoe, Ireland

ANDURIL 6 ch.g. Kris – Attribute (Warning) [2006/7 17m Jun 4] half-brother to   **h–**
winning French jumper up to around 19f King of Revolution (by Hernando): fair on Flat
(stays 1¼m, tends to find little), won in August: breathing problem on hurdling debut.
Miss M. E. Rowland

ANDY GIN (FR) 8 b.g. Ski Chief (USA) – Love Love Kate (FR) (Saint Andrews   **h92 §**
(FR)) [2006/7 h105§: 20v 16s⁵ 16gᶠ Mar 28] leggy gelding: fair handicap hurdler on
his day: raced mainly around 2m: acts on heavy going: visored once: unreliable. *Miss
E. M. England*

ANEMIX (FR) 6 gr.g. Linamix (FR) – Sallivera (IRE) (Sillery (USA)) [2006/7 h123: **h108**
16s 16d Feb 1] leggy gelding: fairly useful over hurdles, below best both starts in 2006/7:
best at 2m with emphasis on speed. *L. Corcoran*

A NEW STORY (IRE) 9 b.g. Fourstars Allstar (USA) – Diyala (FR) (Direct Flight) **c128**
[2006/7 c125, h99+: 20s 23v³ c24v⁵ c24d² 24s⁴ 22v⁴ c29mᵘʳ c32m Apr 21] close-coupled **h106**
gelding: fair handicap hurdler: fairly useful handicap chaser: best effort when ¾-length
second to Point Barrow in Pierse Chase (Handicap) at Leopardstown: ran poorly in Irish/
Scottish National last 2 starts: stays 29f: acts on heavy going: in cheekpieces last 6 starts:
patiently ridden. *M. Hourigan, Ireland*

ANFLORA 10 b.m. Alflora (IRE) – Ancella (Tycoon II) [2006/7 c75, h62: 24d⁴ c26v **c63**
c19d² c25dᵖᵘ c20sᵖᵘ Dec 5] lengthy mare: poor maiden hurdler/handicap chaser: **h61**
lame final start: stays 3¼m: acts on heavy and good to firm going: tried in cheekpieces.
B. J. Llewellyn

ANGE DE VILLEZ (FR) 6 b.g. Villez (USA) – La Mesange (FR) (Olmeto) [2006/7 **c113 x**
c16sᵖᵘ c23sᶠ c23sᵖᵘ c20m* c20mᵘʳ Apr 20] leggy, useful-looking gelding: **h–**
half-brother to several winners, including useful French jumper up to 2¾m Mister Ange
(by Mister Jack): dam maiden hurdler/chaser around 2m: fair hurdler: won twice at
Auteuil in 2004/5, including when blinkered: similar form over fences, left J. Bertran de
Balanda prior to reappearance: usually let down by jumping in Britain, though won
maiden at Uttoxeter in March: should stay beyond 2½m: unraced on firm ground, acts on
any other. *P. F. Nicholls*

ANGELLO (FR) 6 gr.g. Kaldounevees (FR) – Mount Gable (Head For Heights) **c– §**
[2006/7 h93: c23d⁵ c20mᵖᵘ c19vᶠ c23sᵖᵘ c21v⁵ 24vʳᵗʳ 24m Apr 15] novice hurdler: no **h82 §**
form over fences: should stay beyond 2½m: acts on soft going: tried in blinkers/
cheekpieces: refused to race sixth start. *N. J. Hawke*

ANGLICISME (FR) 5 b.g. Kahyasi – Anglaise (IRE) (Darshaan) [2006/7 c17s⁵ c20s⁶ **c96**
20s* 20v⁵ 25v⁵ 20g Apr 7] leggy, close-coupled gelding: second foal: half-brother to **h108**
fairly useful French 2¼m chase winner Anglican (by Starborough): dam unraced: thrice-
raced on Flat: maiden hurdler/chaser for G. Cherel in France: 33/1, improved form when
winning steadily-run novice hurdle at Haydock in December on British debut by 1¼
lengths from Hills of Aran: stays 2½m: acts on heavy going: tried blinkered in France.
Ian Williams

A NICE SORT 7 b.m. Bandmaster (USA) – Precis (Pitpan) [2006/7 F17g Jul 23] half- **F–**
sister to 2¾m hurdle winner First Thought (by Primitive Rising): dam, won around 2m
over hurdles, out of smart staying chaser Ottery News: soundly beaten in bumper on
debut. *O. J. Carter*

ANILLUSION 6 b.g. Dreams End – Cinderosa (IRE) (Kings Lake (USA)) [2006/7 **h–**
F16g 17dᵖᵘ 17d Nov 16] first foal: dam, poor maiden, stayed 1m: no form in bumper/over **F–**
hurdles. *B. J. Llewellyn*

ANKLES BACK (IRE) 10 b.g. Seclude (USA) – Pedalo (Legal Tender) [2006/7 c–§, **c– §**
h–: c25gᵖᵘ c24mᵘʳ Jun 8] close-coupled, workmanlike gelding: winning chaser around **h–**
3m, though usually shapes as if amiss and no form since 2004/5: tried tongue tied: one to
leave alone. *T. Wall*

ANNALS 5 b.m. Lujain (USA) – Anna of Brunswick (Rainbow Quest (USA)) [2006/7 **h–**
h–: 16g³ Jul 31] sparely-made mare: poor on Flat in 2006: no form over hurdles: has worn
headgear: sold €11,000 Goffs February Sales. *R. C. Guest*

ANNA PANNA 6 b.m. Piccolo – Miss Laetitia (IRE) (Entitled) [2006/7 h93: 16m **h–**
Oct 16] modest maiden hurdler: stays 19f: acts on heavy going. *R. H. Alner*

ANNE SIAN (IRE) 4 b.f. Anshan – Celts Dawn (Celtic Swing) [2006/7 F14s F14v **F–**
Dec 2] leggy, close-coupled filly: first foal: dam maiden half-sister to smart sprinter
Repertory: soundly beaten in 3-y-o bumpers. *H. Alexander*

ANNIBALE CARO 5 b.g. Mtoto – Isabella Gonzaga (Rock Hopper) [2006/7 16g 16g⁶ **c89**
16d⁶ c16g³ c17gᶠ Apr 2] fairly useful 11f/1½m winner at 3 yrs but well held all 3 starts on **h87**
Flat since, sold out of Sir Mark Prescott's stable 12,500 gns Doncaster August Sales:
modest form over hurdles/on completed outing over fences: raced around 2m on good/
good to soft ground. *Grant Tuer*

ANNIE DIPPER 12 ch.m. Weld – Honey Dipper (Golden Dipper) [2006/7 c21g⁴ **c–**
Apr 27] maiden chaser/pointer: stays 3m. *P. F. Popham*

ANNIE FLEETWOOD 9 ch.m. Anshan – Gold Luck (USA) (Slew O' Gold (USA)) **h97**
[2006/7 h89: 22m* 22d³ 17d³ 22d 24s Dec 7] tall mare: modest hurdler: won handicap at
Wincanton in May: stays 2¾m: acts on good to firm and good to soft going. *R. H. Alner*

ANNIE'S ANSWER (IRE) 7 b.m. Flemensfirth (USA) – As An Sli (IRE) (Buckskin **h111 +**
(FR)) [2006/7 F81: F16s* F16g* 20s⁴ 16s* 17g* 21g Apr 19] rather leggy mare: winning **F103**
pointer: fairly useful form in bumpers, winning at Uttoxeter in May and June: confirmed
promise of hurdling debut when winning mares maiden at Huntingdon in February and
novice at Bangor (beat Mag Num 7 lengths) in March: effort best forgiven final outing:
should prove at least as effective at 2½m as 2m: raced on good ground or softer: front
runner/races prominently. *Mrs V. J. Makin*

ANNIES CASTLE 6 ch.m. Carlingford Castle – Jasilu (Faustus (USA)) [2006/7 F16s **F—**
F16g F17g Apr 27] £1,300 4-y-o: second foal: dam, fair chaser, stayed 3m: well beaten in
bumpers: blinkered final outing. *F. E. Sutherland*

ANN'S DREAM 7 ch.m. You My Chief – Lady Verdi (USA) (Monteverdi) [2006/7 **h—**
16gᵖᵘ Apr 27] half-sister to winning pointer by Current Edition: dam, 1½m winner on
Flat/no form over hurdles, half-sister to fair staying hurdler Alphasonic: no show in
maiden hurdle on debut. *B. J. Llewellyn*

ANOTHER BIGDIAMOND 6 b.g. Botanic (USA) – Tenpenny (Hadeer) [2006/7 **F—**
F16s F16m⁵ Apr 9] 7,200 4-y-o: workmanlike gelding: second foal: dam ran twice: little
encouragement in 2 bumpers 11 months apart, trained on debut by T. Keddy. *T. Keddy*

ANOTHER BOTTLE (IRE) 6 b.g. Cape Cross (IRE) – Aster Aweke (IRE) (Alzao **h103 p**
(USA)) [2006/7 17s³ 16g 16g Apr 27] good-topped gelding: half-brother to fairly useful
2m hurdler Say What You See (by Charnwood Forest): useful on Flat (stays 1¼m): left
R. Charlton, encouraging hurdling debut when 6½ lengths third to Lead On in novice at
Taunton: not at all knocked about both starts after (tongue tied final one): likely to prove
best at 2m with emphasis on speed: probably remains capable of better. *P. F. Nicholls*

ANOTHER BURDEN 6 b.m. Alflora (IRE) – Dalbeattie (Phardante (FR)) [2006/7 **h94**
h83+, F—: 16m 16d 16s⁵ 22sᵖᵘ 21s⁶ 16g* Mar 28] lengthy, rather unfurnished mare:
modest hurdler: won handicap at Towcester in March: should stay beyond 2m. *H. D. Daly*

ANOTHER CHAT (IRE) 7 ch.g. Executive Perk – Lucky Fiver (Tumble Gold) **h—**
[2006/7 h—, F67: 23sᵖᵘ 22d Nov 30] sturdy gelding: winning pointer: no form over
hurdles: tried tongue tied. *R. T. Phillips*

ANOTHER CLIENT (IRE) 11 ch.g. Denel (FR) – Proverbs Girl (Proverb) [2006/7 **c68**
c76, h—: c21g May 3] ex-Irish gelding: winning pointer, placed in 2007: maiden hurdler/ **h—**
chaser: stays 2¾m: acts on heavy going: tried in cheekpieces: not a fluent jumper.
Mrs A. R. Hewitt

ANOTHER CLUB ROYAL 8 b.g. Overbury (IRE) – Miss Club Royal (Avocat) **c100**
[2006/7 c100, h—: c25d³ c26mᵖᵘ 24dᵖᵘ c24m c24g⁴ Feb 21] workmanlike gelding: **h—**
winning hurdler: fair handicap chaser: form in 2006/7 only on final start: stays 3½m: acts
on good to firm and good to soft going, probably on soft: usually blinkered/tongue tied.
D. McCain Jnr

ANOTHER CON (IRE) 6 b.m. Lake Coniston (IRE) – Sweet Unison (USA) (One For **h—**
All (USA)) [2006/7 17fᶠ Aug 11] half-sister to 2 winning hurdlers: modest on Flat (stayed
2m), successful 3 times in 2006: fell fatally on hurdling debut. *P. A. Blockley*

ANOTHER CONKER 6 b.g. El Conquistador – Perrinpit Annapolis VII (Damsire **F—**
Unregistered) [2006/7 F16g F16m Jun 11] second foal: half-brother to winning pointer
by Henbit: dam unraced: tailed off in 2 bumpers. *Mrs Tracey Barfoot-Saunt*

ANOTHER CONQUEST 8 b.m. El Conquistador – Kellys Special (Netherkelly) **c96 x**
[2006/7 c94x, h—: c25sᵖᵘ c26v c24s* c19v⁵ Feb 18] workmanlike mare: maiden hurdler: **h—**
modest handicap chaser: won at Towcester in February: thorough stayer: acts on heavy
going: in cheekpieces last 2 starts: sketchy jumper. *J. W. Mullins*

ANOTHERCOPPERCOAST (IRE) 7 ch.g. Presenting – Parsee (IRE) (Persian **c137**
Mews) [2006/7 20g³ c20d* c20v c24v³ c21v⁶ c20m³ c20m c21m² Apr 27] rather leggy gelding: **h107**
fair maiden hurdler: useful novice chaser: won at Cork (beat idling Mossbank by short
head) in November: much better form after, notably on handicap debut when neck second
to Alexander Taipan in betfair.com Novices' Chase at Punchestown: stays 3m: acts on
heavy and good to firm going: held up. *Paul A. Roche, Ireland*

ANOTHER DECKIE (IRE) 9 b.g. Naheez (USA) – Merry Friends (King's Ride) **h97**
[2006/7 h105: 16g 20m Feb 4] good-topped gelding: fair handicap hurdler at best: left
L. Lungo and off 16 months, little impact in 2006/7: stayed 2½m: acted on soft and good
to firm going: dead. *D. J. P. Barry, Ireland*

ANOTHER FLINT (IRE) 7 ch.g. Accordion – Island Run (Deep Run) [2006/7 h–, **h69**
F–: 22m⁵ May 11] lengthy, angular gelding: poor maiden hurdler: tongue tied last 3
outings. *R. Flint*

ANOTHER GALE (IRE) 8 b.g. Supreme Leader – Gale Eight (IRE) (Strong Gale) **c–**
[2006/7 19d⁴ 18mᵖᵘ c21vᶠ 21s 17s⁵ 17d⁶ 22g⁴ Apr 7] smallish, angular ex-Irish gelding: **h87**
first foal: dam maiden sister to useful chaser up to 25f Force Seven: fair form in bumpers:
modest maiden hurdler: sold out of T. Mullins' stable 6,200 gns Doncaster August Sales:
fell heavily on chasing debut next time: stays 2¾m: acts on good to soft ground: often
tongue tied, also in cheekpieces sixth start. *Evan Williams*

ANOTHER GRADUATE (IRE) 9 ch.g. Naheez (USA) – Another Daisy (Major **h–**
Point) [2006/7 24dᵖᵘ 25dᵖᵘ 22vᵖᵘ Jan 2] smallish gelding: no sign of ability: tried in
cheekpieces/blinkered. *John R. Upson*

ANOTHER JAMESON (IRE) 7 b.m. Good Thyne (USA) – Another Grouse (Prag- **h83**
matic) [2006/7 h83, F–: 24g² 24g⁴ 20f² 25s⁵ 20g² 22v⁵ 16g⁴ Apr 23] poor hurdler: should
stay beyond 3m: probably acts on any going. *J. M. Jefferson*

ANOTHER JOKER 12 b.g. Commanche Run – Just For A Laugh (Idiot's Delight) **c126**
[2006/7 c115, h–: c17v² c20m⁴ c23m* c22gᵖᵘ c19g⁶ c16sᵖᵘ c20mᵖᵘ Apr 22] lengthy, **h–**
workmanlike gelding: fairly useful handicap chaser: won at Stratford in September by
9 lengths from He's The Biz: ran poorly after (breathing problem final outing): stays 23f:
acts on any going: bold-jumping front runner. *J. L. Needham*

ANOTHER LORD (IRE) 8 b. or br.g. Mister Lord (USA) – Queen Ofthe Island **h–**
(IRE) (Carlingford Castle) [2006/7 F88: 20gᵖᵘ 24sᵖᵘ Sep 21] winning pointer: second in
bumper: off 11 months, no show in novice hurdles: sold 3,000 gns Doncaster October
Sales. *Mrs B. K. Thomson*

ANOTHER MISK 5 ch.g. Storm Boot (USA) – Pure Misk (Rainbow Quest (USA)) **h–**
[2006/7 h74: 16m Jun 8] sturdy gelding: poor maiden hurdler: raced mainly around 2m:
tried in cheekpieces. *M. E. Sowersby*

ANOTHER NATIVE (IRE) 9 b.g. Be My Native (USA) – Lancastrians Wine (IRE) **c103 +**
(Lancastrian) [2006/7 c108+, h–: c20d⁴ Oct 18] well-made gelding: maiden hurdler: **h–**
fair chaser: left with plenty to do only start in 2006/7: stays 2¾m: acts on heavy going.
C. J. Mann

ANOTHER PENNY 7 b.m. Petoski – Penlea Lady (Leading Man) [2006/7 h–, F–: **c–**
c16s⁶ c20sᵖᵘ May 21] no solid form. *R. Dickin* **h–**

ANOTHER PROMISE (IRE) 8 b.g. Presenting – Snape (IRE) (Strong Gale) **c144 p**
[2006/7 h91: c25f* c25d* c24gᶠ c24s² c20s* c16s* c16g⁵ c16m* Apr 26] **h–**
'Geoff always used to say to me that he liked his horses big and black.'
Ferdy Murphy on the late Geoff Hubbard, whose green and white silks were carried
with distinction in the latest season by the 'dark brown'—though officially bay
—gelding Another Promise, a rangy, imposing, bold-jumping individual who made
giant strides over fences. Hubbard and Murphy enjoyed considerable success
together from the mid-'eighties through to the early-'nineties, with the likes of
Sibton Abbey, Cuddy Dale and Gee-A, though the best horse to run for Hubbard
arrived after Murphy had relocated to North Yorkshire in 1994. Strong Promise was
trained initially by Hubbard himself and then by Chris Kinane and, like Another
Promise, enjoyed spectacular success in his first season over fences—namely six
wins, including a defeat of One Man in the Grade 1 Comet Chase at Ascot. He
went on to be placed twice in the Cheltenham Gold Cup, doing so on the second
occasion—when third to Looks Like Trouble in 2000—just a week after his
owner's death. Unfortunately, Strong Promise lived for only three weeks longer
himself, suffering a fatal fall in the Martell Cup at Aintree, an incident which
reportedly prompted the Hubbard estate to name this sizeable son of Presenting,
then a yearling, in honour of his illustrious near-lookalike.
The Hubbard silks are still seen on the occasional chasing type trained by
Murphy, although few can have imagined, when Another Promise made his chasing
debut in a 0-95 handicap at Hexham in September, that they would be on parade at

Swordlestown Cup Novices' Chase, Punchestown—a 1,2 for British raiders in this Grade 1, with the prolific Another Promise too good for Royal Shakespeare

the Cheltenham and Punchestown Festivals later in the campaign. The progress made by Another Promise reached its zenith at the latter course on his final start of the season in the seven-runner Grade 1 Swordlestown Cup Novices' Chase. In a competitive renewal, Another Promise's excellent jumping stood him in good stead while the pick of Ireland's two-mile novices were let down by theirs, Gemini Lucy unseating at the first, Blueberry Boy falling four from home and Schindlers Hunt blundering away his chance two out to leave Another Promise with the advantage, one that he held to beat fellow British-trained challenger Royal Shakespeare by three and a half lengths. Given that Another Promise had begun the season winning twenty-five-furlong handicap chases at Hexham and Kelso, it is a tribute to his versatility that he proved so highly effective over two miles. Having shown just modest form in nine starts over hurdles for John Supple, winning a novice handicap at Warwick in December 2004, Another Promise was well backed at Hexham on his first start for seventeen months and made a good impression. He defied a 10 lb rise in the weights when following up at Kelso by nine lengths from Hugo de Grez without coming off the bridle. After disappointing slightly in a good-quality event at Bangor in November (held only place prospects when unlucky faller two out), Another Promise resumed his progress with two good efforts at Newcastle. Ridden more patiently than previously, he ran well when two lengths second to another future Punchestown winner in Neptune Collonges (who was conceding 26 lb) in the Rehearsal Chase. Meanwhile, a shorter trip didn't prevent Another Promise resuming winning ways in fine style with a nine-length handicap win back at Gosforth Park in December.

Another Promise (IRE) (b.g. 1999)	Presenting (br 1992)	Mtoto (b 1983)	Busted
			Amazer
		D'Azy (b 1984)	Persian Bold
			Belle Viking
	Snape (IRE) (b 1989)	Strong Gale (br 1975)	Lord Gayle
			Sterntau
		Scotsman Ice (b 1980)	Deep Run
			Khalketta

Given Another Promise's stamina, it came as something of a surprise when he finished the season dropped back even further in trip with three runs over two miles. The HBLB Lightning Novices' Chase, run at Huntingdon in January, after

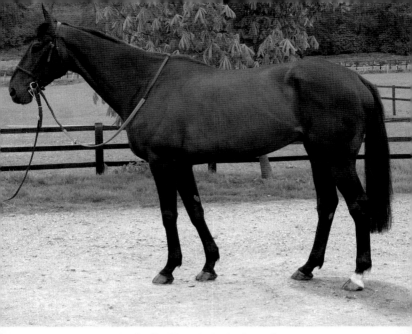

Geoff Hubbard Racing's "Another Promise"

being transferred from an abandoned meeting at Ascot, was a slowly-run affair and Another Promise had to work quite hard to land the odds by a length from fellow northern raider Rasharrow. In the Arkle at Cheltenham, Another Promise showed further improvement, his effort particularly noteworthy as he was held up, in the end finishing twelve and three quarter lengths fifth of the ten finishers. Coincidentally, he produced a similar level of form and shaped in almost identical fashion to Truckers Tavern, also trained by Murphy, in the 2002 renewal. That horse, who died during the latest season, proved best at three miles and beyond and went on to finish runner-up in the Cheltenham Gold Cup in 2003. Whilst the Gold Cup division looks considerably stronger now than it did a few years ago, Another Promise is the type to progress further in 2007/8, his fine jumping always likely to stand him in good stead. Another Promise, who is another feather in the cap for the top National Hunt sire of 2006/7 Presenting, is the third foal out of Snape, an unraced sister to winning two-and-a-half-mile chaser Ambrosia and half-sister to fair winning hurdler Merilena, who both raced for Hubbard. The grandam Scotsman Ice, a lightly-raced winning hurdler, was actually a half-sister to a couple of notable Flat animals, the dual Group 2-winning mile-and-a-half performer Head For Heights and the 1982 Cambridgeshire winner Majestic Star. Like Another Promise, Snape's first two foals Little Saxtead (by Anshan) and Faith And Fortune (by Mtoto) joined Ferdy Murphy and raced in the ownership of Geoff Hubbard Racing in the latest season, the former brought down at the first on his only outing, the latter seemingly in need of the experience when fifth of fourteen in a mares bumper at Sedgefield. Another Promise is effective at two miles and has won over twenty-five furlongs. He acts on any going. *Ferdy Murphy*

71

ANOTHER RALEAGH (IRE) 13 b.g. Be My Native (USA) – Caffra Mills (Pitpan) [2006/7 c121, h–: c21g³ May 3] tall gelding: one-time useful chaser: successful in points/hunter in 2006: stayed 23f: acted on heavy going: reportedly retired. *Graeme P. McPherson* — **c105 h–**

ANOTHER RUM (IRE) 9 b.g. Zaffaran (USA) – Sharp Fashion VII (Damsire Unregistered) [2006/7 c131, h114: c24s⁵ c26gᵘʳ c29s c24v c26d³ c32m Apr 21] good-topped gelding: winning hurdler: useful chaser on his day, not at best in 2006/7: thorough stayer: acts on heavy and good to firm going: tried blinkered (including last 3 starts). *I. A. Duncan, Ireland* — **c121 h–**

ANOTHER STORM 5 gr.m. Shambo – Stormswift (Neltino) [2006/7 F16d F16s Nov 22] small, strong mare: second foal: half-sister to bumper winner Rising Tempest (by Primitive Rising): dam maiden pointer: well held in bumpers. *B. I. Case* — **F–**

ANOTHER SUPERMAN (IRE) 8 b.g. Beneficial – Royal Broderick (IRE) (Lancastrian) [2006/7 h83: 16s⁶ 20s* 20s 19v⁵ Jan 11] sturdy gelding: modest hurdler: won novice handicap at Perth in September: stays 2¾m: acts on heavy going, probably on good to firm: usually in headgear. *Lindsay Woods, Ireland* — **h91**

ANOTHER TAIPAN (IRE) 7 b.g. Taipan (IRE) – Sheeghee (IRE) (Noalto) [2006/7 c–, h–: 20v² 21d⁵ 26d 20s c25d³ Oct 21] poor maiden hurdler: similar form on completed start in handicap chases: stays 25f: acts on heavy going: sold 9,500 gns Doncaster November Sales, won maiden point in February. *A. C. Whillans* — **c79 h79**

ANSAR (IRE) 11 b.g. Kahyasi – Anaza (Darshaan) [2006/7 c143+, h135: c22g² 20d⁶ Sep 3] leggy gelding: smart chaser: good 3½ lengths second of 22 to Far From Trouble when attempting to complete hat-trick in Galway Plate in August: useful hurdler: odds on, found to have mucus on lungs final start: effective at 2m to 25f: acts on soft and good to firm going: blinkered twice: has won 7 times on Flat/over jumps at Galway. *D. K. Weld, Ireland* — **c152 h–**

ANSA THE QUESTION 6 b.m. Overbury (IRE) – Olive Branch (Le Moss) [2006/7 F71: 24m 20sᵖᵘ 20v⁴ 21s 24vᵖᵘ c20s c25sᵖᵘ Feb 27] good-topped mare: signs of only a little ability: tried blinkered. *A. H. Mactaggart* — **c– h73**

ANSHABIL (IRE) 8 br.g. Anshan – Billeragh Thyne (IRE) (Good Thyne (USA)) [2006/7 c93, h–: c20dᶠ c21d² c19s* c23dᵖᵘ Mar 20] useful-looking gelding: maiden hurdler: fair handicap chaser: won at Hereford in December: should stay beyond 21f: acts on soft going. *A. King* — **c103 h–**

ANSHAMPSHIRE (IRE) 8 br.m. Anshan – Hamshire Gale (IRE) (Strong Gale) [2006/7 c24sᵖᵘ May 20] winning pointer, placed in 2007: didn't see race out in hunter on chase debut. *P. Jones* — **c–**

ANSHAN SPIRIT (IRE) 9 ch.m. Anshan – Saffron Spirit (Town And Country) [2006/7 c81: c25m³ c20v⁴ c25g* c25sᵘʳ c25g² Apr 15] winning pointer, including in 2007: fair hunter chaser: won at Kelso in May: stays 25f: acts on good to firm going (well beaten only start on heavy). *R. W. Green* — **c98**

ANTICIPATING 7 b.g. Polish Precedent (USA) – D'Azy (Persian Bold) [2006/7 h113: 16g Mar 23] rather leggy gelding: fair hurdler: favourite but off 12 months, well held in handicap only start in 2006/7: should stay beyond 2m: acts on firm and good to soft going. *G. L. Moore* — **h–**

ANTIGIOTTO (IRE) 6 ch.g. Desert Story (IRE) – Rofool (IRE) (Fools Holme (USA)) [2006/7 h97§: 20s⁶ 17m⁵ 16m⁵ 21g⁴ 17vᶠ Nov 28] sturdy gelding: maiden hurdler: left P. Bowen and off 9 months, poor form in 2006/7: barely stayed 19f: tried blinkered/in cheekpieces: tongue tied last 4 starts: ungenuine: dead. *Mrs D. A. Hamer* — **h83 §**

ANTY WREN 5 gr.g. Tragic Role (USA) – Granny Nix (Zambrano) [2006/7 F–: F17d⁶ F18v¹⁹ 19d 21gᵖᵘ Mar 20] rather leggy gelding: little sign of ability. *Mary Meek* — **h– F–**

APACHE BRAVE (IRE) 4 ch.g. Kahtan – Glenstal Forest (IRE) (Glenstal (USA)) [2006/7 F17s³ F17g* Mar 24] third foal: half-brother to 21f hurdle winner My Good Lord (by Mister Lord): dam maiden half-sister to useful 2m hurdler Joking Aside: confirmed promise of debut when winning maiden bumper at Bangor in March by head from Oneforsaturday. *H. P. Hogarth* — **F101**

APADI (USA) 11 ch.g. Diesis – Ixtapa (USA) (Chief's Crown (USA)) [2006/7 c80§, h82§: c16m⁴ c16m⁵ 17d⁴ c16f Sep 29] sturdy gelding: poor handicap hurdler/chaser: barely stays 19f: acts on any going: tried in cheekpieces: headstrong: has refused/been very reluctant to race: not one to trust. *R. C. Guest* — **c80 § h– §**

APATURA DIK 6 b.g. Deltic (USA) – Apatura Hati (Senang Hati) [2006/7 F79: F16d[5] 24s[pu] 19v[3] 19v[2] Jan 17] tall, workmanlike gelding: mid-field both starts in bumpers: seemingly improved markedly over hurdles when second to Oceanos des Obeaux in novice at Newbury: bred to stay beyond 19f: acts on heavy going. *N. R. Mitchell* **h112 ?** **F81**

APOCALOZZO (IRE) 5 ch.g. Michelozzo (USA) – Supremely Deep (IRE) (Supreme Leader) [2006/7 16s 16v 16v 22m Apr 28] neat gelding: first foal: dam unraced: well held over hurdles (jumped poorly when well backed on handicap debut). *R. C. Guest* **h–**

APOLLO LADY 6 b.m. Alflora (IRE) – Stac-Pollaidh (Tina's Pet) [2006/7 F105: 16d[4] 16g[4] 16g[*] 20s[2] 21g[6] Mar 24] unfurnished mare: useful bumper performer: fair novice hurdler: won mares races at Worcester in October and Wincanton in December: will prove better around 2½m than shorter: acts on soft going. *A. King* **h112**

APOLLO THEATRE 9 b.g. Sadler's Wells (USA) – Threatening (Warning) [2006/7 h–: 24d[pu] Nov 21] useful-looking gelding: fair hurdler at best: very lightly raced and amiss last 2 seasons: stays 2¾m: raced on good going or softer: effective tongue tied or not. *R. Rowe* **h–**

A POUND DOWN (IRE) 10 b.g. Treasure Hunter – Ann's Queen (IRE) (Rhoman Rule (USA)) [2006/7 c–, h–: c23m[ur] c26d[pu] c21s[pu] Jun 27] tall gelding: little form over hurdles/fences: dead. *N. G. Ayliffe* **c–** **h–**

APPACH (FR) 8 gr.g. Riche Mare (FR) – Simply Red (FR) (R B Chesne) [2006/7 c109, h–: c16g[2] c16m[*] c16d[F] c20m[6] c16d[2] Sep 22] ex-French gelding: maiden hurdler: fair handicap chaser: won at Huntingdon in June: best around 2m: acts on good to firm going, probably on soft. *J. W. Mullins* **c111** **h–**

APPLEADAY (IRE) 6 gr.g. Beneficial – Hello Aris (IRE) (Aristocracy) [2006/7 F16d[*] F16d[4] 16g Mar 24] tall gelding: fairly useful form in bumpers: off 21 months after debut, won at Ludlow in December by 6 lengths from Blue Teal: eighth of 18 to Special Envoy in novice at Newbury on hurdling debut: likely to be suited by 2¼m+: should do better. *P. R. Webber* **h98 p** **F102**

APPLE JOE 11 b.g. Sula Bula – Hazelwain (Hard Fact) [2006/7 c–, h–: c26v[5] c24s[*] c24v[3] c26s[4] c24v[4] c24s[4] c23s c26v Mar 10] lengthy gelding: poor handicap chaser: won at Towcester in November: stays 29f: acts on heavy going: sometimes wears cheekpieces. *A. J. Whiting* **c73** **h–**

APRIL ATTRACTION (FR) 5 b.m. Mark of Esteem (IRE) – April Lee (USA) (Lyphard (USA)) [2006/7 17m 16d 16g[6] Oct 17] ex-French mare: half-sister to fairly useful hurdler April Allegro (by Doyoun), stays 3m: dam won at around 2m over hurdles in France: successful at 10.5f/1½m on Flat in Provinces at 3 yrs for H-A. Pantall, well beaten both starts in Britain: poor form in novice hurdles: tongue tied last 2 starts. *C. J. Down* **h76**

APRIL SAN 4 b.c. Nashwan (USA) – April Lee (USA) (Lyphard (USA)) [2006/7 16v[2] 16v[4] Feb 5] half-brother to fairly useful hurdler April Allegro (by Doyoun), stays 3m: dam won at around 2m over hurdles in France: useful on Flat (stays 11f), successful 3 times, including twice in 2006, sold out of P. Khozian's stable €80,000 Goffs Arc Sale: modest form when in frame both starts in juvenile hurdles. *Ferdy Murphy* **h89**

APRIL SPIRIT 12 b.m. Nomination – Seraphim (FR) (Lashkari) [2006/7 c25m[4] c30m[*] May 16] leggy, sparely-made mare: modest chaser: better effort in hunters when winning at Huntingdon in May, 5 lengths second when left clear last: winning pointer, including in 2007: stays 3¾m: acts on any going. *S. J. Wiles* **c77 +** **h–**

APT TO RUN (USA) 4 b. or br.g. Aptitude (USA) – Tufa (Warning) [2006/7 16v[3] 16s 16s[4] 16g[*] 16m Apr 25] well-made gelding: seventh foal: half-brother to French 18.5f hurdle winner Mount Etna (by Affirmed): dam 2-y-o 7f winner on only start: fairly useful on Flat (stays 11f), trained by E. Dunlop at 3 yrs, successful in March 2007: easily best effort in juvenile hurdles when winning 19-runner maiden at Tipperary in April by 15 lengths from Merveilles: raced at 2m: best effort on good ground: blinkered last 2 starts: tongue tied after debut. *M. D. Murphy, Ireland* **h111**

AQUA PURA (GER) 8 b.g. Acatenango (GER) – Actraphane (Shareef Dancer (USA)) [2006/7 17v[*] c24v[pu] 22v[2] c20v[pu] c22s[pu] 23d[4] Mar 21] lengthy gelding: poor hurdler: favourite, much improved when readily winning selling handicap at Folkestone in December: failed to complete all 3 starts over fences, though has shaped as if capable of better: stays 2¾m: acts on heavy ground: blinkered final outing. *B. J. Curley* **c– p** **h83**

AQUILINE 9 ch.g. Sanglamore (USA) – Fantasy Flyer (USA) (Lear Fan (USA)) [2006/7 17d[pu] May 24] good-bodied gelding: modest form when runner-up twice **h–**

73

over hurdles in 2002: no form otherwise, including in points: should stay beyond 2m. *John A. Harris*

ARABIAN MOON (IRE) 11 ch.g. Barathea (IRE) – Excellent Alibi (USA) (Exceller (USA)) [2006/7 19m³ 24g 21g⁵ 19g* Nov 5] compact gelding: winning chaser: modest hurdler nowadays: won conditional jockeys seller at Hereford in November: stays 3m: has won on good to soft going, best form on good or firmer: tried in headgear: has looked unenthusiastic. *R. Brotherton*   **c– §**
  h93 §

ARABIE 9 b.g. Polish Precedent (USA) – Always Friendly (High Line) [2006/7 16s 16s 16m⁴ 16m² Apr 24] lengthy, angular gelding: fairly useful on Flat (stays 1¼m) at 7 yrs, has become thoroughly temperamental (refused to race 4 of last 5 starts in 2006, left Peter Grayson after final one): poor hurdler: raced at 2m: acts on good to firm ground: tends to run in snatches. *B. R. Summers*   **h74 §**

ARADNAK (IRE) 7 b.m. Son of Sharp Shot (IRE) – Kandara (FR) (Dalsaan) [2006/7 F16sᵖᵘ Nov 22] strong mare: tailed off on completed start in bumpers: saddle slipped when next seen 2½ years later. *K. J. Burke*   **F–**

ARAGLIN 8 b.g. Sadler's Wells (USA) – River Cara (USA) (Irish River (FR)) [2006/7 16g 16g 16m Apr 24] small, sturdy gelding: handicap hurdler: sold out of Miss S. Wilton's stable £2,000 Ascot April (2006) Sales and off 20 months, poor form in 2006/7: stays 2¾m: acts on good to firm and good to soft going: tried blinkered. *B. D. Leavy*   **h82**

ARAN CONCERTO (IRE) 6 b.g. Zaffaran (USA) – Frizzball (IRE) (Orchestra) [2006/7 F19d* 19d⁶ 16s* 20v* 18v* 21g⁵ Mar 14]   **h144 p**
  F106

National Hunt racing is littered with horses who've failed to live up to huge home reputations once tackling serious competition on the track. Leading Irish trainer Noel Meade has predicted far more gems than duds down the years when it comes to assessing his stable stars, top performers including the likes of Cockney Lad, Sausalito Bay, Harbour Pilot, Harchibald, Nicanor and Iktitaf. However, the stable has endured a frustrating time with the highly-touted Sweet Wake, whom Meade rated as his top novice of 2005/6 even after coming up some way short at both the Cheltenham and Punchestown Festivals. Sweet Wake was a smart performer in Germany during his Flat days so it's not hard to imagine his creating a very favourable impression on the Meade gallops, yet he flattered to deceive when unplaced on all three starts in top handicap company in the last season (well supported each time) before finishing only seventh of eight in the ACCBank Champion Hurdle at Punchestown in late-April. One would imagine Meade felt reluctant to make big predictions of his younger charges in 2006/7, so it is particularly noteworthy that his verdict on the imposing six-year-old Aran Concerto last winter was: 'I probably shouldn't say it, but this horse could be the best I've had. I think he has the potential to be a Gold Cup horse one day.' The fact Aran Concerto is bred for jumping, in contrast to above-average Flat recruits such as Sausalito Bay and Sweet Wake, suggests his prowess on the home gallops is even more significant and Meade's words could well be vindicated yet, despite another expensive reverse for Irish punters at the latest Cheltenham Festival.

Sent off favourite for a bumper at Naas in October, Aran Concerto went some way to demonstrating why his trainer held such a high opinion of him, cruising into contention turning into the straight and coasting home for a nine-length win. Travelling in similarly smooth style on his hurdling debut, back at Naas, Aran Concerto looked all over the winner when nearly brought down in an ugly melee two out (he was sent crashing through the inside rail). Jockey Paul Carberry wisely left his mount to come home in his own time, but the duo still passed a few horses on the run-in to claim an eye-catching sixth. Two victories at Navan made up for that unfortunate incident, Aran Concerto treating his rivals with contempt in a maiden hurdle in November before winning the Barry and Sandra Kelly Memorial Hurdle in December, easily beating Footy Facts by seven lengths, with fourth-placed Kazal suffering his only defeat of the campaign. A second Grade 1 success came in the Deloitte Novices' Hurdle at Leopardstown two months later, which Aran Concerto won by three lengths from stable-companion Leading Run, after main rival Catch Me had been knocked out of the race two out.

A possible tilt at the Supreme Novices' was mooted after this latest win, but connections opted to stick with their original plan and follow the same path as Nicanor twelve months earlier. Aran Concerto really took the eye at Cheltenham

Deloitte Novices' Hurdle, Leopardstown—
Paul Carberry steers Aran Concerto to his second Grade 1 success

before the Ballymore Properties-sponsored Baring Bingham Hurdle, but inexperience told in the jumping department. Despite a number of errors, Aran Concerto still moved up to the leaders two out in typically impressive fashion until seeming to get a foreleg tangled with eventual runner-up Tidal Bay. The resulting stumble took its toll and Aran Concerto managed only fifth behind Massini's Maguire, after which he was not seen out again. Aran Concerto was without his regular jockey for that Cheltenham date, with Tony McCoy taking over in the saddle. Paul Carberry was absent from the four-day Festival, with a foot in plaster as a result of being trodden on by one of his hunters—though, typically, Cheltenham was rife with fanciful rumours as to the exact cause of injury. It wasn't the first time Carberry had been forced to sit out rides at the Festival, with hunting accidents providing their fair share of injury scares down the years. He was restricted to just three rides in 2000, aggravating a back injury (caused by a hunting fall) when winning the Supreme Novices' Hurdle on Sausalito Bay, and then again when runner-up in the Gold Cup on Florida Pearl. Five years later, there was an anxious wait for Carberry to be passed fit to ride Harchibald and Beef Or Salmon, in the Champion Hurdle and Gold Cup respectively, which was the legacy of another back injury sustained when his mount turned a somersault leaping a five-barred gate. An earlier hunting skirmish is reputed to have seen Carberry gored in the stomach by a stag. Meanwhile, there was a self-inflicted setback when Carberry's frustration at attending the Velka Pardubicka as a mere spectator (he was out with an arm injury) led to a longer spell on the sidelines after reportedly attempting to jump one of the famously daunting water jumps without an equine partner. Carberry's reputation earned him some unwanted publicity after he was found guilty of setting fire to a newspaper on an Air Lingus aeroplane—a two-month jail sentence was reduced on appeal to community service the day after Aran Concerto had made his winning debut (when ridden by Carberry's sister Nina). Perhaps the prospect of linking up with such an exciting prospect as Aran Concerto will have a calming influence on someone widely regarded as the most naturally gifted jockey around, though Carberry reportedly says he would miss hunting more than racing if he were to give up one of the two.

Aran Concerto (IRE) (b.g. 2001)	Zaffaran (USA) (b 1985)	Assert (b 1979)	Be My Guest Irish Bird
		Sweet Alliance (b 1974)	Sir Ivor Mrs Peterkin
	Frizzball (IRE) (br 1992)	Orchestra (ch 1974)	Tudor Music Golden Moss
		Credit Card (b 1971)	Current Coin Tarkita

The tall Aran Concerto, who has considerable physical scope, suffers from stringhalt. At €60,000 as a yearling, he was easily the most expensive of Zaffaran's progeny offered at public auction in 2002, before being sold on to Noel Meade as a four-year-old for €40,000—his year-younger brother Browns Baily made €100,000 at the same sale and showed some promise when mid-division in a Cork maiden hurdle for Mouse Morris in the latest season. That Aran Concerto impresses as a chasing type is hardly surprising given his pedigree, the now-deceased Zaffaran having Cheltenham Gold Cup winner Looks Like Trouble and Whitbread winner Beau among his best offspring. Aran Concerto's dam, Frizzball, showed little in two bumpers for Charlie Brooks, but she is a half-sister to the high-class hurdler/chaser Run For Free, who won both the Welsh and Scottish National in 1992/3, and the smart Irish staying jumper Bankers Benefit, who was runner-up in the 1987 Irish Grand National as a novice. Grandam Credit Card was useful and was also placed in the Fairyhouse showpiece, finishing third to Tied Cottage in 1979. With connections keen on pursuing a chasing career (decided as early as his debut victory), Aran Concerto, who has raced only on good ground or softer and acts on heavy, looks a most exciting prospect who will stay a lot further than twenty-one furlongs, the longest trip he has tackled so far. All being well, he will have every chance of living up to his trainer's high hopes for him. *N. Meade, Ireland*

ARANLEIGH (IRE) 5 b.g. Insan (USA) – Lexy Lady (IRE) (Strong Gale) [2006/7   **F119** F16v* F16g³ Mar 14] €30,000 3-y-o: strong gelding: fourth foal: dam, placed in bumper, out of half-sister to very smart hurdler/useful chaser Gala's Image: won bumper at Fairyhouse in January on debut by 5 lengths from Mad Fish, pair well clear: similar form when 2¾ lengths third of 24 to Cork All Star in Champion Bumper at Cheltenham, not clearest of runs and staying on well: will stay at least 2½m: good prospect. *Anthony Mullins, Ireland*

AR AN SHRON 7 b.g. Alderbrook – Charlotte's Festival (Gala Performance) [2006/7   **c–** 24m² 20m* 22d 22m² c23mᵖᵘ Apr 25] 26,000 3-y-o: half-brother to several winners,   **h99** useful 2½m chaser Thoseweredays (by Past Glories) and fairly useful staying jumpers Ceilidh Boy (by Oats) and Stan's Your Man (by Young Man): dam unraced: modest form over hurdles: won novice at Worcester in August: off 5½ months, little impact in novice handicap on chasing debut: stays 3m: acts on good to firm going. *Jonjo O'Neill*

ARCALIS 7 gr.g. Lear Fan (USA) – Aristocratique (Cadeaux Genereux) [2006/7 h155:   **h154** 16s⁴ 17s⁴ 16v⁶ 16d⁵ 17g⁵ 20g⁴ 16m* Apr 27] close-coupled gelding: smart hurdler: back to best in spring, dead-heated with Penzance in valuable minor event at Sandown, running on well after left with fair bit to do: beaten just 2 lengths when fifth of 28 to Pedrobob in County Hurdle (Handicap) at Cheltenham fifth start: barely stays 2½m (stamina stretched when fourth in Aintree Hurdle): acts on soft and good to firm going (seemingly not on heavy): tried tongue tied: held up. *J. Howard Johnson*

ARCANGELA 4 b.f. Galileo (IRE) – Crafty Buzz (USA) (Crafty Prospector (USA))   **h–** [2006/7 16g 18sꟳ 16v Feb 24] long-backed, angular filly: poor maiden on Flat, sold out of J. Given's stable 3,000 gns Doncaster November Sales: no form over hurdles. *Miss Tracy Waggott*

ARC EN CIEL (GER) 7 b.g. Daun (GER) – Amarna (GER) (Nebos (GER)) [2006/7   **c109** h121: 17s³ 19f³ 16m⁴ 20m⁵ 16m 18s⁵ 18v⁵ 16v⁴ 23s 16s⁴ c20g² c22m² Apr 15] fairly   **h124**

useful hurdler: second in minor events over fences last 2 starts, left with plenty to do final one: stays 2¾m: acts on any going: held up. *Gerard Cully, Ireland*

ARCH 4 ch.g. Arkadian Hero (USA) – Loriner's Lass (Saddlers' Hall (IRE)) [2006/7 F16v³ F17s Feb 19] third foal: dam maiden who stayed 1¾m: better effort in bumpers (modest form) when third to Kealshore Boy at Kelso. *A. M. Crow*   **F84**

ARCHBISHOP 10 ch.g. Minster Son – Elitist (Keren) [2006/7 c25g^{pu} May 3] tall, quite good-topped gelding: successful twice in points, little form in other events: tried in cheekpieces: dead. *Mrs H. M. Kemp*   **c–**
h–

ARCHDUKE FERDINAND (FR) 9 ch.g. Dernier Empereur (USA) – Lady Norcliffe (USA) (Norcliffe (CAN)) [2006/7 h103: 20g^{pu} 21s⁴ 22g² Apr 7] close-coupled gelding: fairly useful on Flat (best at 2m+) nowadays: fair maiden hurdler: stays 2¾m: acts on soft ground: often takes good hold. *A. King*   **h108**

ARCH FOLLY 5 b.g. Silver Patriarch (IRE) – Folly Fox (Alhijaz) [2006/7 19m⁶ Sep 28] fair on Flat (stays 2¼m), successful in July (claimed from J. Portman £10,000): no show in novice on hurdling debut: joined R. Price. *Ian Williams*   **h–**

ARCHIE BABE (IRE) 11 ch.g. Archway (IRE) – Frensham Manor (Le Johnstan) [2006/7 h–: 17s³ 16d* 16g 16s⁴ c16v* c16v² c20s⁶ c16v⁵ Mar 15] workmanlike gelding: fair handicap hurdler: won at Wetherby in October: similar form when winning maiden at Hexham in December on chasing debut: went with little zest when well beaten 3 starts after: should stay beyond 2m: acts on heavy going: one to treat with caution over fences. *J. J. Quinn*   **c111 §**
h111

ARCHIE GUNN 5 b.g. Silver Patriarch (IRE) – Persistent Gunner (Gunner B) [2006/7 F16s⁴ F16g⁵ Mar 19] tall gelding: chasing type: fourth foal: half-brother to winning hurdler La Marette (by Karinga Bay), stays 25f: dam, poor hurdler who stayed 19f, half-sister to useful 2m hurdler Teletrader: modest form 2 starts in bumpers. *R. J. Hodges*   **F84**

ARCHIMBOLDO (USA) 4 ch.g. Woodman (USA) – Awesome Strike (USA) (Theatrical) [2006/7 17m⁶ 17s⁴ 17g² 17g* 17m³ 16s⁴ 16g* 16d⁵ 16s³ 16g 16m⁵ 20g³ Apr 20] lengthy, angular gelding: fair but ungenuine on Flat (stays 2m): fair juvenile hurdler: won at Bangor in September and Haydock (by 7 lengths from Touch of Ivory) in November: good efforts in handicaps last 2 starts: stays 2½m: acts on soft and good to firm ground: usually blinkered: ridden by conditional: pulls hard/carries head high. *T. Wall*   **h109**

Betfredcasino Hurdle, Sandown—
the grey Arcalis leaves it late to claim a share of the spoils with Penzance (blinkered first time)

ARCHIRONDEL 9 b.g. Bin Ajwaad (IRE) – Penang Rose (NZ) (Kingdom Bay (NZ)) **h85**
[2006/7 17d² 17m² 19g⁴ Nov 5] smallish gelding: modest novice hurdler: sold out of
N. Wilson's stable £2,200 Ascot August Sales after second start: best around 2m: acts on
good to firm going. *B. P. J. Baugh*

ARCHWAY COPSE 7 ch.m. Anshan – Finkin (Fine Blue) [2006/7 F16s⁶ 16s 16s³ **c89**
16v³ 19s c19gᵖᵘ c24m² Apr 14] sturdy mare: seventh foal: dam winning pointer: sixth in **h78**
bumper: poor form over hurdles: much better effort in handicap chases (breathing **F64**
problem on first occasion) when runner-up at Chepstow: better suited by 3m than shorter:
acts on heavy and good to firm going. *Ian Williams*

ARC LEMANIQUE (GER) 7 b.g. Hernando (FR) – Arkona (GER) (Aspros (GER)) **h122 +**
[2006/7 20g³ 16d* 20m* Aug 3] ex-German gelding: 1¼m/11f winner on Flat in native
country: fairly useful novice hurdler: left G. Cully prior to return: much improved last 2
starts, winning twice within 3 days at Galway in August, maiden on first occasion: stays
2½m: probably acts on any going. *P. A. Fahy, Ireland*

ARC OF STONE (IRE) 7 ch.g. Arc Bright (IRE) – Stoney Broke (Pauper) [2006/7 **h76**
h71: 22m May 11] maiden pointer: poor form in novice hurdles: will stay 3m. *D. J. Wintle*

ARCTIC CHERRY (IRE) 9 b.g. Arctic Lord – Cherry Avenue (King's Ride) [2006/7 **c78**
c76, h–: 16dᵖᵘ c16mᵘʳ c19m² c20m⁴ Apr 25] winning pointer: poor maiden hurdler/ **h–**
handicap chaser: sold out of R. Ford's stable £5,000 Ascot August Sales prior to reappearance: stays 19f: acts on soft and good to firm going. *A. J. Whitehead*

ARCTIC COVE 6 b.g. Vettori (IRE) – Sundae Girl (USA) (Green Dancer (USA)) **h75**
[2006/7 h78+: 17dᵖᵘ 17m 17m 24sᵖᵘ 20vᵇᵈ 19s⁴ 16sᶠ 16s⁴ 20g Apr 3] good-topped
gelding: one-time fair performer on Flat (stays 1¾m): poor maiden hurdler: stays 19f:
acts on soft and good to firm going. *Micky Hammond*

ARCTIC ECHO 8 b.g. Alderbrook – Arctic Oats (Oats) [2006/7 h106: 20g* 21s* 25s* **h129**
25s⁴ 20v³ 24g Apr 14] sturdy gelding: fairly useful hurdler: won maiden at Hexham in
May and novices at Sedgefield in December and Catterick (4 ran, easily by 13 lengths
from Ellerslie George) in January: good third to Bedlam Boy in novice handicap at
Newcastle: stays 25f: acts on heavy and good to firm going. *G. A. Swinbank*

ARCTIC EMPEROR (IRE) 6 b.g. Arctic Lord – Madness In Motion (IRE) (Le **h–**
Johnston) [2006/7 F17v⁶ 16v⁶ 19v Feb 20] €9,000 3-y-o, 10,000 4-y-o: half-brother to fair **F–**
chaser Clearly In Motion (by Clearly Bust), stays 2½m, and winning pointer by Yashgan:
dam unraced: little impact in bumper/2 starts over hurdles. *A. Bateman*

ARCTIC GHOST 7 gr.g. Environment Friend – Saxon Gift (Saxon Farm) [2006/7 **c107 p**
F101: F16g* 22s³ 20g⁴ c25s⁴ c20s* c20gᵖ Apr 3] big gelding: fair form in bumpers, won **h97**
at Uttoxeter in May: in frame in maiden hurdles: successful 2 of 3 outings over fences, in **F94**
maiden at Sedgefield in March and novice at Wetherby following month: stays 2¾m: acts
on soft ground: front runner/races prominently: capable of better over fences. *N. Wilson*

ARCTIC GLOW 8 ch.m. Weld – Arctic Mission (The Parson) [2006/7 h63: 24v² 19g **h81**
Mar 25] tailed off in point: poor handicap hurdler: stays 25f: acts on heavy going.
Mrs H. Pudd

ARCTIC KING 14 b.g. Arctic Lord – Dunsilly Bell (London Bells (CAN)) [2006/7 **c– x**
25gᵖᵘ 22dᵖᵘ Nov 12] rangy gelding: winning pointer: maiden chaser: no form over **h–**
hurdles: stays 23f: acts on soft going: tried blinkered: sketchy jumper. *Mrs P. N. Dutfield*

ARCTIC LAGOON (IRE) 8 ch.g. Bering – Lake Pleasant (IRE) (Elegant Air) **c–**
[2006/7 c80, h85: 24s 25m⁶ 23d 27sᵖᵘ Nov 26] good-topped gelding: modest hurdler/ **h–**
chaser at best: little sign of retaining ability in 2006/7: stays 3m: acts on soft and good to
firm going: tried visored: usually tongue tied. *R. M. Stronge*

ARCTIC MAGIC (IRE) 7 b.m. Saddlers' Hall (IRE) – Arctic Verb (Proverb) [2006/7 **F103**
F16d* F16s³ Mar 10] €44,000 4-y-o: good-topped mare: half-sister to useful chaser
Certainly Strong, stayed 2½m, and high-class chaser up to 25f Speaker Weatherell (both
by Strong Gale), and fair hurdler/chaser Eskimo Pie (by Glacial Storm), stays 3m: dam
winning Irish pointer: created good impression when winning mares bumper at Chepstow
in February on debut by 13 lengths from New Mill Moll: 5½ lengths third to Swaythe in
listed event at Sandown. *W. S. Kittow*

ARCTIC PLAYBOY 11 b.g. Petoski – Arctic Oats (Oats) [2006/7 17dᵖᵘ 16vᶠ Nov 23] **h–**
angular gelding: no form over hurdles, left I. Williams and off nearly 3 years prior to
return. *B. R. Summers*

ARCTIC RAINBOW (IRE) 9 b.g. King's Ride – Arctic Chatter (Le Bavard (FR)) [2006/7 c21s^pu Jan 30] workmanlike gelding: modest form over hurdles: off nearly 3 years, lame on chasing debut: should have stayed 3m: dead. *G. L. Moore*   c– h–

ARCTIC SHADOW 5 b.g. Bonny Scot (IRE) – Dickies Girl (Saxon Farm) [2006/7 F16s^5 Feb 3] 5,000 4-y-o: half-brother to fair 2m chaser Arctic Spirit (by Arctic Lord) and modest 2m hurdler Bill Brown (by North Briton): dam poor maiden hurdler: poor form when fifth in bumper on debut. *R. Dickin*   **F68**

ARCTIC SKY (IRE) 10 b.g. Arctic Lord – Lake Garden Park (Comedy Star (USA)) [2006/7 c–, h–: c25m^pu Apr 15] one-time fair hurdler/chaser: placed in points in 2007: let down by jumping in hunters: should stay beyond 21f: acts on good to firm going. *Nick Kent*   c– h–

ARCTIC SPIRIT 12 b.g. Arctic Lord – Dickies Girl (Saxon Farm) [2006/7 c–, h–: c17m^2 c19m^pu 21m^pu c16d^ur c16g^5 c23d^F c19g c16m* Apr 24] close-coupled gelding: maiden hurdler: handicap chaser: dropped in weights, won at Towcester in April: barely stays 19f: probably acts on any going: tried visored. *R. Dickin*   **c94 d** h–

ARCTIC TIMES (IRE) 11 ch.g. Montelimar (USA) – Miss Penguin (General Assembly (USA)) [2006/7 c110, h–: c20d^3 c24s^3 c26g^6 c21g^4 c25g^4 Apr 25] good-topped gelding: prolific winning pointer: useful hunter chaser: good sixth to Drombeag in Foxhunter at Cheltenham third start: stays 3¼m: acts on heavy and good to firm going: usually wears cheekpieces: has been let down by jumping/looked none too keen. *Eugene M. O'Sullivan, Ireland*   **c113** h–

ARCTIC TOUR (IRE) 7 b.g. Doubletour (USA) – Arctic Kate (Sandalay) [2006/7 F16v^6 F16s* F16m^2 Apr 26] 5,000 4-y-o: good-topped gelding: second foal: dam, fairly useful hurdler, stayed 3m: dead-heated in maiden point in 2006: useful form in bumpers: won at Down Royal in February: best effort when head second to Meadow Vale in 24-runner event at Punchestown. *P. F. Cashman, Ireland*   **F106**

ARDAGHEY (IRE) 8 b. or br.g. Lord Americo – Mrs Pepper (Lancastrian) [2006/7 c125, h–: c24s* c26s^pu c25s c24d^6 c24v^2 Jan 27] workmanlike gelding: winning hurdler: useful handicap chaser: won amateur event at Cheltenham in October by 12 lengths from Xellance: beaten 9 lengths second to Simon in valuable race at Southwell: will stay beyond 3¼m: acts on heavy going: usually tongue tied nowadays: probably best on galloping track: sometimes let down by jumping. *N. A. Twiston-Davies*   **c143 x** h–

ARDAGH LORD (IRE) 6 b.g. Mister Lord (USA) – Artanagh Rosa (IRE) (Roselier (FR)) [2006/7 F17v Nov 28] second foal: dam unraced: well beaten in maiden Irish points/bumper. *P. Bowen*   **F–**

ARDENTE SAUVAGE (FR) 7 b.m. Feu Ardent (FR) – L'Eau Sauvage (Saumarez) [2006/7 F14g^4 F16d^5 20s Dec 5] second foal: half-sister to one-time useful hurdler/fairly useful chaser Do L'Enfant d'Eau (by Minds Music), stays 21f: dam ran once: poor form in bumpers: tailed off in maiden on hurdling debut. *C. J. Gray*   h– **F69**

ARDENT WAY 8 b.m. Bob's Return (IRE) – Beringa Bee (Sunley Builds) [2006/7 17d^pu May 31] half-sister to 21f hurdle winner Cap In Hand (by Nearly A Hand): dam unraced: fell in point in 2006: jumped badly in seller on hurdling debut (bled). *D. McCain*   h– x

ARDGLASS (IRE) 5 b.g. Danehill Dancer (IRE) – Leggagh Lady (IRE) (Doubletour (USA)) [2006/7 h99: 20d 16v 16s^6 Jan 15] novice hurdler, no form in 2006/7: tried in headgear/tongue tied: often let down by jumping. *Mrs P. Townsley*   h–

ARDMORE LAD (IRE) 5 b.g. Anshan – Chelsea Native (Be My Native (USA)) [2006/7 F16d F16g Mar 19] €46,000 4-y-o: useful-looking gelding: fourth foal: half-brother to bumper winner Long Road Home (by Supreme Leader): dam, fairly useful hurdler who stayed 3m, out of half-sister to dam of very smart 2m chaser Feroda: well held in bumpers, though travelled easily under restraint long way second start. *Miss E. C. Lavelle*   **F–**

ARD SOLUS (IRE) 10 b.g. Supreme Leader – Red Bit (IRE) (Henbit (USA)) [2006/7 c16g^4 May 24] strong gelding: lightly raced: winning hurdler: maiden chaser/pointer: raced around 2m: acts on heavy going: difficult to train. *Mrs D. Schilling*   c– h–

ARE YOU THERE 6 b.m. Presidium – Scoffera (Scottish Reel) [2006/7 16d^3 17m Nov 7] 5f winner on Flat at 2 yrs: poor form in novice hurdles, third in claimer: blinkered next time. *C. L. Tizzard*   **h70**

ARFARF 4 b.f. Turtle Island (IRE) – Macklette (IRE) (Buckskin (FR)) [2006/7 F16s F17g Apr 19] smallish filly: third foal: dam winning Irish pointer: no show in bumpers. *H. J. Evans*   **F–**

ARGENTO 10 b.g. Weldnaas (USA) – Four M'S (Majestic Maharaj) [2006/7 c105, h103: 16g⁵ c17m⁴ 16g 21d Nov 10] leggy gelding: fair hurdler/fairly useful handicap chaser at best: left G. M. Moore, no form last 3 starts: raced mainly around 2m: acts on any going: jumps boldly, but is prone to mistakes over fences. *Dr P. Pritchard*
    c– x
    h95

ARGONAUT 7 ch.g. Rainbow Quest (USA) – Chief Bee (Chief's Crown (USA)) [2006/7 h93: 20vᴿ 21mᴿ Jun 8] modest form when fourth in maiden on hurdling debut: badly let down by jumping/attitude both starts since: sold 1,200 gns Doncaster October Sales. *P. Bowen*
    h– §

ARIMERO (GER) 7 b.g. Monsun (GER) – Averna (Heraldiste (USA)) [2006/7 h–: 16f⁵ 16d² 17d Oct 26] leggy, useful-looking gelding: modest maiden hurdler, off 17 months prior to return: raced around 2m: acts on good to firm and good to soft going: in headgear last 6 starts: tried tongue tied: none too consistent. *J. G. Portman*
    h87

ARISEA (IRE) 4 b.f. Cape Cross (IRE) – Castelfranca (IRE) (Scenic) [2006/7 17sᵘʳ 16m² 16g⁴ 17s³ 16s* 16g² 16v* 16d⁴ 16g Mar 31] sturdy filly: well beaten on Flat: fair juvenile hurdler: won seller at Wetherby in November and, claimed from R. C. Guest £8,000 next start, mares novice at Uttoxeter in January: raced around 2m: acts on heavy ground. *B. G. Powell*
    h100

ARISTI (IRE) 6 b.m. Dr Fong (USA) – Edessa (IRE) (Tirol) [2006/7 16d³ 18s⁴ 19v⁴ 21g Mar 20] one-time fair stayer on Flat (usually wears headgear), seemingly on down-grade in 2006 for M. Quinn: regressive form over hurdles, failing to impress with attitude: should be suited by 2½m+: tried in cheekpieces. *R. M. Stronge*
    h84

ARISTOCRATIC YANK (IRE) 8 b. or br.g. Lord Americo – Dixons Dutchess (IRE) (Over The River (FR)) [2006/7 c–: 26mᵖᵘ 22m⁶ 24sᵖᵘ Apr 1] winning pointer: no form over hurdles/in chases: tried in cheekpieces. *S. G. Chadwick*
    c–
    h–

ARISTOXENE (FR) 7 b.g. Start Fast (FR) – Petite Folie (Salmon Leap (USA)) [2006/7 c133x, h–: c24d⁴ c24sᵖᵘ 22s⁴ 24g⁶ Mar 24] good-topped gelding: useful handicap chaser at best, better effort in 2006/7 when 6½ lengths fourth to Darby Wall in amateur event at Cheltenham: fair form over hurdles: stays 25f: acts on heavy going: tried blink-ered/in cheekpieces: usually let down by jumping: sold 19,000 gns Doncaster May Sales. *N. J. Henderson*
    c123 x
    h102 x

ARJAY 9 b.g. Shaamit (IRE) – Jenny's Call (Petong) [2006/7 h74: 19dᶠ 16m 17m 20g⁶ 17m 16dᵖᵘ 16g c20d c18dᵘʳ c16sᵖᵘ Jan 24] workmanlike gelding: poor hurdler: no form over fences: best around 2m: acts on soft and good to firm going: usually wears headgear. *S. B. Clark*
    c–
    h72

ARMAGH SOUTH (IRE) 8 ch.g. Topanoora – Mogen (Adonijah) [2006/7 h–: 17m 16m 22d⁵ 21s* 21m* Apr 9] modest hurdler: back in form last 2 starts, winning handicaps at Plumpton in November (novice) and April: stays 3m: acts on soft and good to firm going. *J. C. Tuck*
    h91

ARMAGUEDON (FR) 9 b.g. Garde Royale – Miss Dundee (FR) (Esprit du Nord (USA)) [2006/7 c105, h–: c16s* c16vᵖᵘ Dec 27] good-topped gelding: lightly raced: winning hurdler: successful both completed starts over fences, fairly useful form when beating Stormy Beech by 13 lengths in handicap at Ayr in November: bled following month: raced mainly around 2m: acts on heavy going. *L. Lungo*
    c129
    h–

ARM AND A LEG (IRE) 12 ch.g. Petardia – Ikala (Lashkari) [2006/7 c–, h107: c20f² c21mᵖᵘ Sep 2] leggy gelding: fair handicap hurdler: similar form when runner-up on completed start over fences: should stay 3m: acts on any going: tried in cheekpieces. *Mrs D. A. Hamer*
    c104
    h–

ARMARIVER (FR) 7 ch.g. River Mist (USA) – Armalita (FR) (Goodland (FR)) [2006/7 h113: 16g³ 16s³ 19m* 21d 19s* 19s⁶ Feb 3] tall, lengthy gelding: fairly useful hurdler: won novices at Ascot (handicap) in October and Taunton (beat Lincoln's Inn by 6 lengths) in December: stays 19f: acts on soft and good to firm going: held up: consistent. *P. F. Nicholls*
    h120 +

ARMATURK (FR) 10 ch.g. Baby Turk – Armalita (FR) (Goodland (FR)) [2006/7 c155, h–: c20s² c16d² c16dᵘʳ c17d³ c21g c21gᵇᵈ Apr 13] tall, angular gelding: has report-edly had breathing operation: smart chaser: as good as ever in 2006/7, placed first 3 completed starts, 19 lengths third of 5 finishers to impressive Well Chief in Grade 2 at Newbury: brought down third in Topham Chase at Aintree: effective at 2m to 21f: acts on heavy and good to firm going: tried tongue tied, not since 2004/5: genuine. *P. F. Nicholls*
    c154
    h–

ARMENTIERES 6 b.m. Robellino (USA) – Perfect Poppy (Shareef Dancer (USA))   **h80 §**
[2006/7 h84§: 20g 20d⁵ 20d² 16g³ 17vᵖᵘ 16v 25vᵖᵘ 23g 16g Apr 23] close-coupled mare:
poor hurdler: left Mrs E. Slack, no form last 5 starts: stays 2½m: acts on heavy going:
wears headgear: ungenuine. *James Moffatt*

ARMOURY HOUSE 6 ch.g. Gunner B – Coire Vannich (Celtic Cone) [2006/7 F–: 16s   **c–**
16s 16d 16s c16s⁶ c23mᵖᵘ Apr 25] sturdy gelding: poor form over hurdles: no show in   **h84**
handicap chases: tried tongue tied. *T. R. George*

ARNO RIVER 5 ch.g. Halling (USA) – Moonlight Saunter (USA) (Woodman (USA))   **h–**
[2006/7 h–: 16d Oct 14] well held over hurdles: runner-up in maiden point in April.
D. Brace

AR NOS NA GAOITHE (IRE) 8 b.m. Toulon – Sidhe Gaoth (Le Moss) [2006/7   **h97**
F82: 20g 21m* 16d² Oct 22] failed to complete in 2 points: placed in bumpers: modest
form in novice hurdles, made all in mares event at Ludlow in October: will stay beyond
21f: unraced on extremes of going. *Mrs A. M. Thorpe*

AROUND BEFORE (IRE) 10 ch.g. Be My Native (USA) – Glynn Cross (IRE)   **c115**
(Mister Lord (USA)) [2006/7 c119, h96: c28s³ c26g⁴ c32mᵖᵘ Jul 2] winning hurdler: **h–**
fairly useful handicap chaser: stays 3½m: acts on firm and soft going: tried in cheekpieces: usually tongue tied. *Jonjo O'Neill*

AROUND NASSAU TOWN 7 b.m. Bahamian Bounty – Sarouel (IRE) (Kendor   **F–**
(FR)) [2006/7 F–: F17s F17g F16m Sep 10] no form in bumpers. *C. J. Gray*

ARPEGGIO MAJOR (IRE) 5 b.g. Beauchamp King – Bucks Slave (Buckskin (IRE))   **h80**
[2006/7 F18s 24s⁵ 24s 20v⁶ 26g Mar 14] half-brother to bumper/2½m hurdle winner   **F–**
Scarvagh Diamond (by Zaffaran) and fair hurdler/fairly useful chaser Toulouse-Lautrec
(by Toulon): stayed 33f: dam winning pointer: well held in bumper: poor form over hurdles: may prove best around 2½m for time being: tried in cheekpieces. *Heather Dalton*

ARPETCHEEO (USA) 5 b. or br.h. Deputy Minister (CAN) – Lizanne (USA) (Theat-   **h86**
rical) [2006/7 16g³ 20m⁶ 16s 16v 24dᵖᵘ 16g Apr 5] modest maiden on Flat (stays 9.5f):
likewise over hurdles, left D. Carroll after second start: should stay beyond 2m: tried
tongue tied. *J. P. Broderick, Ireland*

ARRAYOU (FR) 6 b.g. Valanjou (FR) – Cavatine (FR) (Spud (FR)) [2006/7 h128§:   **c107 §**
c19d⁴ c21g²* c23m³ c20gᴲ 21g³ c19s² c24d⁶ 22d 24g 24g Apr 19] smallish, close-coupled   **h124 §**
gelding: fair chaser: won maiden at Southwell in June: fairly useful handicap hurdler:
stays 23f: acts on soft and good to firm going: blinkered/visored: held up: irresolute.
O. Sherwood

ARRESTING 7 b.g. Hector Protector (USA) – Misbelief (Shirley Heights) [2006/7   **c99**
16s* 16m* 17s* 20g c16m* c16g³ c20s³ 16g 18s Oct 21] fairly useful at best on Flat   **h103**
(stays 1½m): left B. Galvin and off a year, much improved when winning handicap
hurdles at Perth (2, first occasion sole outing for G. Cromwell) and Newton Abbot in
May/June: fair form over fences: won maiden at Perth in August: likely to prove best
around 2m: acts on soft and good to firm going. *G. Elliott, Ireland*

ARRIVE SIR CLIVE (IRE) 6 b.g. Un Desperado (FR) – Greek Melody (IRE)   **h131 p**
(Trojan Fort) [2006/7 20v⁴ 18v² 20v* 18v³ Feb 10] €35,000 3-y-o: strong gelding: will
make a chaser: fourth foal: half-brother to fair 2m hurdler Best Wait (by Insan): dam,
bumper winner, half-sister to useful hurdler up to 2½m Kiora: successful in point/
bumper: useful form over hurdles: won maiden at Leopardstown in December by 9
lengths from Judge Deed: 6 lengths last of 3 finishers to Aran Concerto in Grade 1 novice
at same course: will be suited by further than 2½m: raced on heavy going over hurdles
(won bumper on good): remains open to improvement. *Philip Fenton, Ireland*

ARROWS GOLD 9 b.g. Sure Blade (USA) – Gamefull Gold (Mummy's Game)   **h–**
[2006/7 21sᵖᵘ 26v 26g Apr 20] winning pointer: no form over hurdles. *M. A. Doyle*

ARRY DASH 7 b.g. Fraam – Miletrian Cares (IRE) (Hamas (IRE)) [2006/7 h108: 16d⁵   **h108**
Nov 30] smallish gelding: fair on Flat (stays 1¼m): fair hurdler: respectable effort in
handicap only start in 2006/7: raced at 2m: acts on soft going. *M. J. Wallace*

ARSHAN BEIGH (IRE) 5 b.g. Exit To Nowhere (USA) – Cyrano Imperial (IRE)   **F–**
(Cyrano de Bergerac) [2006/7 F16g Mar 24] €30,000 3-y-o, resold 40,000 3-y-o: tall
gelding: fourth foal: half-brother to bumper/2m hurdle winner Beyond The Pale (by Be
My Native): dam unraced: tailed off in bumper on debut. *C. R. Egerton*

ARTADI (FR) 4 b.g. Cadoudal (FR) – Vol Sauvage (FR) (Always Fair (USA)) [2006/7   **h119 +**
18s⁴ 18s³ 18s 17vᵖᵘ 16v³ 17g* 16g 16f* Apr 22] leggy gelding: sixth foal: half-brother

to several winners, notably smart hurdler/chaser Vol Solitaire (by Loup Solitaire), stayed 2½m: dam unraced: maiden on Flat: fairly useful juvenile hurdler, left J. Bertran de Balanda prior to fifth start: won maiden at Taunton in March and novice at Wincanton (by 4 lengths from Prince Ary) in April: likely to prove best around 2m: acts on firm going: tongue tied last 3 starts. *P. F. Nicholls*

ARTANE BOYS 10 b.g. Saddlers' Hall (IRE) – Belleminette (IRE) (Simply Great (FR)) [2006/7 c–, h103: c20m^{pu} 16m^3 19m^5 Jul 17] lengthy gelding: fair hurdler, well below best in sellers in 2006/7: little show over fences: stays 2½m: acts on any going: has won in cheekpieces: tried tongue tied: ungenuine: sold 4,000 gns Doncaster August Sales. *Jonjo O'Neill*

c– §
h73 §

ART BANK 4 b.g. Saddlers' Hall (IRE) – Langton Lass (Nearly A Hand) [2006/7 F17s^4 Mar 13] 10,000 3-y-o: half-brother to useful staying chaser Bosuns Mate (by Yachtsman) and winning 2m hurdler/chaser Ovahandy Man (by Ovac): dam unraced half-sister to high-class chaser up to 27f Young Hustler: 9 lengths fourth of 5 to Theatrical Moment in bumper at Sedgefield on debut. *J. Howard Johnson*

F90

ARTEEA (IRE) 8 b.g. Oscar (IRE) – Merric (IRE) (Electric) [2006/7 c142, h–: c17d^3 Oct 8] close-coupled, deep-girthed gelding: winning hurdler: useful chaser: possibly in need of race only start in 2006/7: stays 2½m: acts on heavy going: usually patiently ridden. *M. Hourigan, Ireland*

c133
h–

ART HISTORIAN (IRE) 4 b.g. Barathea (IRE) – Radhwa (FR) (Shining Steel) [2006/7 16v^{ur} 16d^5 16v^4 16v^4 Feb 15] leggy gelding: modest maiden on Flat (stays 1½m): fair juvenile hurdler: would have been more successful debut but for unseating 2 out at Wetherby: didn't progress: raced at 2m on ground softer than good. *T. J. Pitt*

h100

ARTHUR PARKER 6 b.g. Cloudings (IRE) – Black H'Penny (Town And Country) [2006/7 F17s F13m^6 Mar 29] fifth foal: half-brother to winning pointer by Rakaposhi King: dam, fair winning 2¾m hurdler, half-sister to very smart staying hurdler Simpson and useful hurdler/fairly useful staying chaser Three Farthings: tongue tied, better effort in bumpers when sixth in maiden at Hereford. *J. A. B. Old*

F74 ?

ARTHURS DREAM (IRE) 5 b.g. Desert Prince (IRE) – Blueprint (USA) (Shadeed (USA)) [2006/7 h–: 16v^5 17s^3 17g* 16m Apr 22] leggy gelding: maiden on Flat: modest hurdler: improved to win novice seller at Hereford in April: raced around 2m: acts on soft going. *A. W. Carroll*

h92

ARTHUR SYMONS 9 b.g. River Falls – Anchor Inn (Be My Guest (USA)) [2006/7 16m^3 Jul 2] very lightly raced: first form over hurdles when third in novice at Uttoxeter: pulled up in point. *Ian Williams*

h94

ARTIC BLISS 5 ch.m. Fraam – Eskimo Nel (IRE) (Shy Groom (USA)) [2006/7 16g Mar 14] half-sister to fairly useful 2m hurdler Mexican Pete (by Atraf): poor maiden on Flat: well held in mares maiden on hurdling debut. *G. F. Bridgwater*

h–

ARTIC DREAM (IRE) 4 b.f. Lord Americo – Nurse Maid (IRE) (Hatim (USA)) [2006/7 F16m^5 Apr 21] smallish, sturdy filly: fifth foal: dam, 2m hurdle winner, half-sister to usefuljumper up to 2½m Arctic Weather: green, 3½ lengths fifth to Evelith Echo in bumper at Ayr on debut, hanging left. *Liam Lennon, Ireland*

F85

ARTIC JACK (FR) 11 b.g. Cadoudal (FR) – Si Jamais (FR) (Arctic Tern (USA)) [2006/7 c120, h–: c22v^{pu} Feb 22] big, rangy gelding: smart chaser at best: left Mrs S. Smith, won point in February: stays 3½m: acts on heavy and good to firm going. *R. Ford*

c–
h–

ARTIC JOHN (IRE) 6 b.g. Arctic Lord – King's Penny (IRE) (King's Ride) [2006/7 F16s 16s 20d 17v Feb 20] tall, unfurnished gelding: fourth foal: dam unraced out of half-sister to smart 2m hurdler Carobee: well beaten in bumper/novice hurdles. *R. C. Guest*

h–
F–

ARTIC REASON (IRE) 8 b.g. Perugino (USA) – Vendetta Valentino (USA) (Bering) [2006/7 c20d^F c16m^3 Apr 24] lengthy, rather sparely-made gelding: maiden hurdler: poor form on completed start in handicap chases: raced mainly around 2m: acts on soft and good to firm ground: tried blinkered. *Andrew Turnell*

c75 +
h–

ARTICULATION 6 b.g. Machiavellian (USA) – Stiletta (Dancing Brave (USA)) [2006/7 c16g^2 c16g^2 c16s c16m^2 16m Apr 9] good-topped gelding: 11f winner on Flat: fairly useful hurdler, below form in minor event at Fairyhouse final start: fair form when runner-up 3 of 4 starts over fences: raced around 2m: acts on good to firm and good to soft ground: usually in blinkers/cheekpieces. *Charles Byrnes, Ireland*

c108
h–

ARTIPREUIL (FR) 5 gr.g. Saint Preuil (FR) – Artilute (FR) (Arctic Tern (USA)) **c94**
[2006/7 16s⁴ 19d³ 17s³ c19s³ 21s³ 24g Mar 25] rather leggy ex-French gelding: first foal: **h106**
dam placed on Flat and over hurdles: fair maiden hurdler, left J-P. Totain prior to return:
modest form when third in handicap at Hereford on chasing debut: stays 21f: acts on soft
going. *P. J. Hobbs*

ARTIST'S MUSE (IRE) 5 b.m. Cape Cross (IRE) – Naked Poser (IRE) (Night Shift **h121**
(USA)) [2006/7 h123: 16d³ 16s² 16d³ 16d Jan 14] fairly useful hurdler: placed first
3 starts in 2006/7, creditable second of 24 to Lenrey in handicap at Fairyhouse: likely
to prove best around 2m: acts on soft going, ran poorly on heavy (blinkered): held up.
T. M. Walsh, Ireland

ART MODERN (IRE) 5 ch.g. Giant's Causeway (USA) – Sinead (USA) (Irish River **h95**
(FR)) [2006/7 16gᵖᵘ 18m⁴ 16f² 16m⁴ 16mᵇᵈ 16g⁵ Nov 7] fairly useful on Flat (stays
1½m), sold out of Mrs A. Perrett's stable 58,000 gns Newmarket Autumn (2005) Sales,
successful in March/April: modest novice hurdler (reportedly distressed on debut for
C. Egerton): likely to prove best at 2m with emphasis on speed: acts on firm ground.
G. L. Moore

ART POINT (GER) 8 b.g. Dashing Blade – A Real Work of Art (IRE) (Keen) [2006/7 **h–**
20d 21sᵖᵘ Jan 24] angular gelding: fair form over hurdles: off over 2 years, little impact in
handicaps in 2006/7: stays 19f. *Mrs L. Wadham*

ART VIRGINIA (FR) 8 b.g. Art Bleu – Sweet Jaune (FR) (Le Nain Jaune (FR)) **c125**
[2006/7 h108, F92: 21d³ 25m⁵ c24dᵖᵘ c20d* c22gᵘʳ c20m² Apr 27] useful-looking **h108**
gelding: fair maiden hurdler: better form both completed starts in chases, won novice
handicap at Ludlow in December by 3 lengths from Dearson: stays 2¾m: acts on good to
firm and good to soft going: blinkered last 3 outings: tried tongue tied. *N. J. Henderson*

ARUMUN (IRE) 6 b.g. Posidonas – Adwoa (IRE) (Eurobus) [2006/7 h100, F–: c20g* **c114**
c18sᶠ c16v³ c24d³ c16s² c17g 21gᵖᵘ Apr 18] tall gelding: maiden hurdler: fair chaser: **h–**
won handicap at Haydock in October by 3 lengths from Shannon's Pride: generally
disappointing after: stays 2½m: acts on soft going: tried tongue tied: often front runner
over hurdles. *M. Scudamore*

ASAATEEL (IRE) 5 br.g. Unfuwain (USA) – Alabaq (USA) (Riverman (USA)) **h78**
[2006/7 h–: 16d 16s³ 17v³ 16v² 16s⁴ 16s Feb 12] useful-looking gelding: fair but unreliable 1¼m winner on Flat: poor novice hurdler: raced around 2m: acts on heavy going:
blinkered/in cheekpieces in 2006/7: has found little: sold £8,000 Ascot February Sales.
G. L. Moore

ASABACHE (IRE) 12 b.g. Alphabatim (USA) – Inga Murphy (IRE) (Buckskin (FR)) **c–**
[2006/7 c–: c22sᵖᵘ May 21] ex-Irish gelding: tubed: winning pointer: maiden chaser: no
sign of retaining ability in 2006: tried blinkered/visored. *Sean Regan*

ASBURY PARK 4 b.g. Primo Valentino (IRE) – Ocean Grove (IRE) (Fairy King **h–**
(USA)) [2006/7 16g Mar 24] compact gelding: fair maiden on Flat (stays 11f), left
E. McMahon before final start at 3 yrs: raced too freely on hurdling debut. *M. R. Bosley*

ASCOOLASICE 9 b.g. Thethingaboutitis (USA) – Frozen Pipe (Majestic Maharaj) **c–**
[2006/7 c26sᵖᵘ c25sᵖᵘ c20v c24vᵖᵘ Jan 21] of little account: sold £1,500 Ascot February
Sales. *L. A. Dace*

A SEA COMMANDER (GER) 5 b.g. Winged Love (IRE) – As Tu As (USA) (Irish **h–**
River (FR)) [2006/7 F78?: F16m⁶ 17s 16sᴿ 18s⁵ 16g 20gᵖᵘ Apr 14] workmanlike gelding: **F–**
little impact in bumpers/over hurdles. *J. W. Mullins*

ASHFORD COMMON LAD (IRE) 7 b.g. Lord Americo – Fair View (IRE) (Castle **c–**
Keep) [2006/7 F18m aF16g⁴ 22v⁶ 22s 27v c24s³ c24gᵖᵘ c24gᶠ Mar 28] €9,300 3-y-o, **h–**
€13,000 4-y-o: first foal: dam ran once: no solid form: tried visored/in cheekpieces. **F–**
A. Ennis

ASHGAN (IRE) 14 br.g. Yashgan – Nicky's Dilemma (Kambalda) [2006/7 c61, h73: **c–**
21f 20s 19m 24m 22m c16d c19d⁴ c25d⁶ 19v 20v 24s c24sᵖᵘ c19m c24gᵖᵘ Apr 27] **h–**
lengthy gelding: veteran jumper: best form around 2½m: acts on firm and soft going: tried
blinkered/visored, not for long time. *Dr P. Pritchard*

ASHGREEN 10 b.g. Afzal – Space Kate (Space King) [2006/7 c104, h–: c26s⁵ c23v⁵ **c–**
Feb 27] workmanlike gelding: fair handicap chaser at best: no show 2 starts in 2006/7: **h–**
stays 25f: acts on any going: tried blinkered/in cheekpieces. *Miss Venetia Williams*

ASHLEYBANK HOUSE (IRE) 10 b.g. Lord Americo – Deep Perk (IRE) (Deep Run) [2006/7 c75?, h–: c23g⁵ c25g⁶ c20d⁵ c24g^pu 24m^pu 26m^pu c27d^pu c24g^pu Apr 21] well-made gelding: winning hurdler/maiden chaser: little form since 2003/4: usually in headgear/tongue tied: ungenuine. *D. Pearson*

c– §
h– §

ASHLEY BROOK (IRE) 9 ch.g. Magical Wonder (USA) – Seamill (IRE) (Lafontaine (USA)) [2006/7 c163, h–: 17v* c17d² c16g^F Mar 14]
The old adage 'they never come back' describes the rarity with which top sporting performers return to their peak after recovering from serious injury. It looked like being disproven in the latest season by two of the leading two-mile chasers of recent years, Well Chief and Ashley Brook. For the moment, however, it is still a case of wait and see for those two. Ashley Brook returned from fourteen months on the sidelines to win impressively over hurdles at Cheltenham in January, taking advantage of what was a lenient mark relative to his chasing one—some 34 lb lower than that from which he had competed in the Haldon Gold Cup at Exeter in November 2005. Ashley Brook was sent off at 11/2 in the thirteen-runner Michael Doocey Memorial Handicap Hurdle and made a mockery of his mark, typically racing with plenty of zest, looking sure to win from a long way out and finishing twenty lengths clear of French Saulaie. The performance is easily the best Ashley Brook has put up over hurdles and seemed convincing evidence that he had returned from his lay-off with all of his old ability.
Ashley Brook was 9/4 favourite for a cracking renewal of the Game Spirit Chase at Newbury a fortnight later when he faced Well Chief, next best at 5/2, who was making his return from an absence of almost two years. Also in the line-up was Voy Por Ustedes, conceding 10 lb to the aforementioned pair. With the latter losing Robert Thornton at the fifth, the first two in the betting soon had the race to themselves. Ashley Brook forced a strong pace as usual but had no answer when Well Chief took over on the bridle three out, and was eventually beaten eleven lengths by a horse who—like Ashley Brook at Cheltenham—put up a performance of such authority that it appeared he had returned to his top-class best. The Queen Mother Champion Chase at Cheltenham went to Voy Por Ustedes, however, with neither Ashley Brook nor Well Chief completing the course. Whereas the latter fell early on in the contest, Ashley Brook looked certain to be placed at worst when coming to grief at the last. Just over a length behind in third, but rallying at the time, he is rated as finishing second, slightly ahead of runner-up Dempsey. It must be a source of frustration to connections that Ashley Brook, a strong individual, has seen the racecourse just five times since his impressive sixteen-length rout of War of Attrition in the Maghull Novices' Chase at Aintree in April 2005 (with Dempsey nine lengths further back in third on that occasion). It is to be hoped that Ashley Brook manages to complete a full campaign in 2007/8, although it looks as if that may be at distances beyond two miles, with the King George VI Chase a target. A bold jumper (he'd been splendidly fluent prior to his Cheltenham tumble), Ashley Brook may yet illustrate that sometimes they can come back. He is most game and reliable, acts on heavy going and goes particularly well for Paddy Brennan. *K. Bishop*

c162
h145 +

ASHSTANZA 6 gr.g. Ashkalani (IRE) – Poetry In Motion (IRE) (Ballad Rock) [2006/7 17s 16g⁴ Mar 17] modest maiden on Flat (stays 1½m) for R. Woodhouse: better effort in novice hurdles when fourth at Newcastle, dictating. *J. Hetherton*

h91 ?

ASHWELL LAD (IRE) 5 gr.g. Sea Raven (IRE) – Irene's Call (IRE) (Cardinal Flower) [2006/7 F18g⁴ F16d² F16d² F16s⁵ 17s² Feb 26] £15,000 3-y-o: stocky gelding: fourth foal: half-brother to winning pointer by Presenting: dam winning pointer: fair form in bumpers: encouraging hurdling debut when 5 lengths second to ready winner Tisseman in maiden at Hereford: likely to improve when faced with stiffer test of stamina. *R. T. Phillips*

h89 p
F91

ASHWELL ROSE 5 b.m. Anabaa (USA) – Finicia (USA) (Miswaki (USA)) [2006/7 16s^pu 19d Mar 26] good-topped mare: poor maiden on Flat, left R. Phillips after tailed off in July: no promise in maiden hurdles. *C. J. Drewe*

h–

ASIAN MAZE (IRE) 8 ch.m. Anshan – Mazuma (IRE) (Mazaad) [2006/7 h162: 21s 16s² 20v⁴ 16d⁶ 16d 20g⁶ Apr 14] rather leggy, close-coupled mare: very smart hurdler: 1¼ lengths second of 4 to Iktitaf in Grade 1 at Punchestown in November, but below form

h156

otherwise in 2006/7: stayed 3m: acted on heavy going: usually raced prominently: retired: in foal to Presenting. *Thomas Mullins, Ireland*

ASK BOBBY 8 b.g. Primitive Rising (USA) – Ask Jean (Ascertain (USA)) [2006/7 c25^{ur} Mar 7] fair pointer, successful in January/February: odds on, going well when unseating fourteenth in novice hunter at Catterick on chase debut. *Mrs M. Sowersby*   **c105 +**

ASKHAM LAD (IRE) 6 b.g. Courtship – Raymylettes Niece (IRE) (Dock Leaf) [2006/7 F–: 16d Oct 21] little impact in bumpers/maiden hurdle. *M. Todhunter*   **h–**

ASK ME WHAT (IRE) 10 b.m. Shernazar – Laffan's Bridge (IRE) (Mandalus) [2006/7 20m^{pu} Apr 25] lengthy mare: modest handicap hurdler at best: maiden chaser, usually makes mistakes: stays 3m: acts on heavy and good to firm going: tried blinkered. *Miss Paula Hearn*   **c– x**   **h–**

ASKTHEMASTER (IRE) 7 b.g. Oscar (IRE) – Nicola Mac (IRE) (King's Ride) [2006/7 20d* 16v^6 Dec 3] rangy gelding: second foal: dam unraced: fairly useful bumper winner: impressive start over hurdles when winning 24-runner maiden at Cork in November, beating Corrigeenroe easily by 8 lengths: stiff task in Grade 1 novice following month: likely to stay beyond 2½m: raced on going softer than good. *Robert Tyner, Ireland*   **h122**

ASK THE UMPIRE (IRE) 12 b.g. Boyne Valley – Ask Breda (Ya Zaman (USA)) [2006/7 c77, h95: c24s^3 21v^4 20s^4 21d c19s^2 c19v^4 24s c19s c20v^3 Mar 9] leggy gelding: fair handicap chaser: won at Towcester (3 ran) in May: poor chaser: stays 21f: acts on heavy going (bumper winner on firm): wears headgear: tried tongue tied: tends to make mistakes over fences. *N. E. Berry*   **c79 x**   **h103**

ASLEEP AT THE BACK (IRE) 4 b.g. Halling (USA) – Molomo (Barathea (IRE)) [2006/7 17d Mar 19] modest maiden on Flat (stays 2m): no show in juvenile on hurdling debut. *J. G. Given*   **h–**

ASPARAGUS WINGNUT (IRE) 5 ch.g. In The Wings – Damiana (IRE) (Thatching) [2006/7 F16d^4 F17g^3 Mar 25] £1,600 4-y-o: second foal: half-brother to fairly useful 7f to 1¼m winner Desert Cristal (by Desert King): dam French maiden who stayed 1m: better effort in bumpers when around length third to Team Chaser at Taunton: tongue tied on debut. *V. R. A. Dartnall*   **F90**

ASPENDOS (GER) 4 ch.g. Kornado – Amrei (Ardross) [2006/7 aF16g^F Mar 9] fifth foal: half-brother to fairly useful hurdler After Eight (by Sir Felix), stays 2¾m: dam 7f/ 1¼m winner in Germany: running to fair level when breaking down over 1f out in bumper on debut: dead. *M. F. Harris*   **F87**

ASPHARASYOUSEE (IRE) 9 b.g. Phardante (FR) – Brave Express (Brave Invader (USA)) [2006/7 16v^{pu} May 18] maiden hurdler: tried blinkered/tongue tied: dead. *J. G. Cosgrave, Ireland*   **h–**

ASRAR 5 b.m. King's Theatre (IRE) – Zandaka (FR) (Doyoun) [2006/7 F79: F16g^3 17v^6 16s 16s Jan 17] in frame in bumpers: poor form over hurdles: tongue tied in 2006/7. *Miss Lucinda V. Russell*   **h77**   **F77**

ASSIGNATION 7 b.g. Compton Place – Hug Me (Shareef Dancer (USA)) [2006/7 h–: 17m^5 17g^5 16f Jun 21] close-coupled gelding: maiden hurdler: won points in March/ April: usually wears cheekpieces. *Miss M. Bragg*   **h–**

ASSUMETHEPOSITION (FR) 7 gr.g. Cyborg (FR) – Jeanne Grey (FR) (Fast Topaze (USA)) [2006/7 c93, h91: 21m 20v^4 20v^3 c17d^5 c20m^{pu} c25s^{pu} c20m c20g^2 c20g* c20m^F c25g^6 c20s^3 20d* 19g^2 c25v^{pu} c19d^{pu} c16s c22s* c20m^4 Apr 15] lengthy gelding: modest hurdler: won seller at Sedgefield in November: modest but error-prone chaser: won handicaps at Market Rasen in August and March (novice): stays 2¾m: acts on heavy and good to firm ground: wears headgear: front runner/races prominently. *R. C. Guest*   **c95 x**   **h99**

ASSUMPTALINA 7 b.m. Primitive Rising (USA) – New Broom (IRE) (Brush Aside (USA)) [2006/7 h–: 20m^6 16d^6 17d Nov 8] no solid form: tried tongue tied. *R. T. Phillips*   **h–**

ASSURING WAYS (IRE) 8 b.m. Erins Isle – Treasure (IRE) (Treasure Kay) [2006/7 22d^6 16f^{pu} 18g^5 17m^4 Aug 29] half-sister to winning hurdler/chaser Kerry's Blade (by Daggers Drawn), stays 21f: little form on Flat/in points: beaten when fell 2 out in mares maiden on chase debut: poor maiden hurdler: raced mainly around 2m: tried in cheekpieces. *J. J. Lambe, Ireland*   **c–**   **h74**

ASTARADOR (FR) 5 b.g. Astarabad (USA) – Touques (FR) (Tip Moss (FR)) [2006/7 F103: 16s* 16s* 16v^3 16v^2 Jan 20] lengthy, useful-looking gelding: will make a chaser: bumper winner: useful form in novice hurdles: odds on, won easily at Wetherby in October and Ayr in November: placed in graded events after, 18 lengths second to   **h130**

impressive Amaretto Rose in Grade 2 at Haydock: bred to stay 2½m: acts on heavy ground: front runner. *J. Howard Johnson*

ASTHEFELLOWSSAID (IRE) 10 ch.g. Glacial Storm (USA) – Celias Fancy (IRE) (Mandalus) [2006/7 c21v* Feb 28] first foal: dam unraced: successful 4 times in points in Britain: blinkered, also won maiden hunter at Folkestone on chase debut: will stay 3m. *Mrs S. J. Hickman*   c95

ASTON LAD 6 b.g. Bijou d'Inde – Fishki (Niniski (USA)) [2006/7 h120: 20v⁵ 23v 20s³ Apr 26] rather leggy gelding: fairly useful handicap hurdler, creditable efforts first and final starts: should stay 3m: acts on heavy going: patiently ridden. *Micky Hammond*   h118

ASTON (USA) 7 b.g. Bahri (USA) – Halholah (USA) (Secreto (USA)) [2006/7 c94, h94: c28dᵖᵘ c23g³ c27m⁶ c23m² c23f² c24g⁴ c23m³ c27m⁴ c24g⁶ c24dᶠ c24g⁴ c29s⁶ 27d c24g² c25m² Apr 28] rather leggy gelding: winning hurdler: modest handicap chaser: stays easy 25f: acts on firm going: usually wears headgear: sketchy jumper *R. C. Guest*   c94 x / h82

ASTORVALE (IRE) 6 ch.g. Fourstars Allstar (USA) – Carrignaveen Lady (IRE) (Hardboy) [2006/7 F17s F16d F17s 16v 20m 20g⁵ Apr 16] €10,000 3-y-o: strong gelding: second foal: dam unraced out of sister to Captain Christy: no form in bumpers/novice hurdles. *Mrs S. J. Smith*   h– / F–

ASTRAL AFFAIR (IRE) 8 br.m. Norwich – Jupiters Jill (Jupiter Pluvius) [2006/7 h64: 22mᶠ 24sᵖᵘ Dec 29] placed in point: poor form over hurdles: stays 3m: best efforts on good/good to firm going. *P. A. Pritchard*   h71

ASTRONAUT 10 b.g. Sri Pekan (USA) – Wild Abandon (USA) (Graustark) [2006/7 h86§: c20g Mar 27] good-topped gelding: winning pointer: modest hurdler: left R. C. Guest, tailed off in hunter on chasing debut: stays easy 3m: acts on good to firm and good to soft going: tried blinkered/in cheekpieces/tongue tied: ungenuine. *George R. Moscrop*   c– § / h– §

ASTRONOMIC 7 b.g. Zafonic (USA) – Sky Love (USA) (Nijinsky (CAN)) [2006/7 c–, h–: 16d 16v⁶ 16g Mar 17] strong, close-coupled gelding: poor walker: successful first 2 outings over hurdles in 2004/5: little impact since, including over fences: raced around 2m on good going or softer (well held on heavy): has shaped as if amiss more than once. *J. Howard Johnson*   c– / h116 d

ASTURION (GER) 4 ch.c. Sternkoenig (IRE) – Astica (GER) (Surumu (GER)) [2006/7 F16v Jan 27] lengthy, angular colt: half-brother to several winners, notably one-time very smart hurdler/winning chaser Auetaler (by Niniski), stays 2¾m: dam German 7f/1m winner: well held in 4-y-o bumper on debut. *M. Hofer, Germany*   F–

ASTYANAX (IRE) 7 b.g. Hector Protector (USA) – Craigmill (Slip Anchor) [2006/7 h107: 21g 22mᵘʳ 20m* 20g Oct 7] sturdy gelding: fair hurdler: won handicap at Huntingdon in September: should stay beyond 21f: acts on good to firm going, possibly unsuited by soft: usually makes running/races prominently: sometimes let down by jumping: sold 3,000 gns Doncaster May Sales. *N. J. Henderson*   h109

ASUDO (IRE) 6 ch.g. Flemensfirth (USA) – Nugget Moss (Le Moss) [2006/7 F97: 24d* 25d² 26s 20d² Feb 3] workmanlike gelding: bumper winner: fairly useful form over hurdles: won novice at Towcester in October: runner-up in handicaps after, beaten 5 lengths by Or Jaune in 17-runner novice event at Sandown second occasion: will stay beyond 25f: raced on going softer than good: front runner. *N. A. Twiston-Davies*   h120 +

ATAHUELPA 7 b.g. Hernando (FR) – Certain Story (Known Fact (USA)) [2006/7 h–: 17g⁶ 20d⁴ 19d⁶ 16g⁶ 16s³ 16s³ 16v⁴ Feb 22] leggy gelding: modest handicap hurdler nowadays, sold out of Jennie Candlish's stable 2,500 gns Doncaster August Sales after first outing: raced mainly around 2m: acts on soft going, probably on good to firm: tried tongue tied. *Miss L. V. Davis*   h95

ATARAXIA 5 b.m. Kayf Tara – Page of Gold (Goldhill) [2006/7 F16g Mar 21] 5,000 4-y-o: half-sister to winning hurdler/chaser New Leaf (by Brush Aside), stayed 25f: dam, winning staying chaser, half-sister to dam of top-class staying chaser/very smart hurdler Rule Supreme: well held in bumper on debut. *C. L. Popham*   F–

ATHOLLBROSE (USA) 6 b.g. Mister Baileys – Knightly Cut Up (USA) (Gold Crest (USA)) [2006/7 c25fⁿ Feb 28 h– May 10] leggy gelding: maiden hurdler: last in point: no show in hunter on chase debut: raced mainly around 2m. *Mrs C. J. Kerr*   c– / h–

ATLANTIC CROSSING (IRE) 10 b.g. Roselier (FR) – Ocean Mist (IRE) (Crash Course) [2006/7 c–x, h–: c22sᵖᵘ May 21] leggy, quite good-topped gelding: winning hurdler/maiden chaser, little form since 2003: runner-up in points: should stay beyond   c– x / h–

2½m: acts on soft going: tried blinkered/in cheekpieces: often makes mistakes over fences. *David Horton*

ATLANTIC JANE 7 b.m. Tamure (IRE) – Atlantic View (Crash Course) [2006/7 h112: c20g^{pu} Nov 8] fair winning hurdler: left Mrs S. Smith, no show in maiden on chasing debut (mistakes): stays 3m: raced on good/soft ground. *F. Jordan*   c– h–

ATLANTIC RHAPSODY (FR) 10 b.g. Machiavellian (USA) – First Waltz (FR) (Green Dancer (USA)) [2006/7 20s^4 16d^6 c23d^{bd} c24s^6 22v c20v^6 c22v^{pu} c16v 18g* 16m 20g^5 Apr 27] leggy gelding: modest hurdler/maiden chaser nowadays: sold out of T. Walsh's stable 6,200 gns Doncaster January Sales: won seller at Fontwell in March: best around 2m: acts on heavy going, probably on good to firm: has worn blinkers/cheekpieces: successful only outing in tongue strap: patiently ridden: ungenuine. *B. J. Llewellyn*   c98 § h99 §

ATLANTIC STORY (USA) 5 b. or br.g. Stormy Atlantic (USA) – Story Book Girl (USA) (Siberian Express (USA)) [2006/7 16s^{pu} May 14] fairly useful on Flat (stays 1¼m): showed little in novice on hurdling debut. *M. W. Easterby*   h–

ATLANTIS (HOL) 8 ch.g. No Ski – File Moon (HOL) (Man In The Moon (USA)) [2006/7 h87§: c20m^{pu} 16d^4 c21d^6 c20s^3 c21d^{pu} c20v^4 c22s^{pu} 17v^2 c18g Mar 18] good-topped gelding: poor maiden hurdler/chaser: stays 2½m: acts on heavy and good to firm going: usually wears blinkers/cheekpieces: ungenuine. *G. L. Moore*   c81 § h77 §

A TOI A MOI (FR) 7 ch.g. Cyborg (FR) – Peperonelle (FR) (Dom Pasquini (FR)) [2006/7 h–: c23d^{pu} c20s^3 c23v* c20m^F Mar 25] tall, lengthy gelding: winning hurdler: fairly useful novice chaser (reportedly had breathing operation after debut), finished alone in maiden at Taunton in March: close third when fell 2 out at Southwell: likely to prove as effective at 3m as 2½m: acts on heavy going, probably on good to firm. *C. E. Longsdon*   c121 h–

ATOMIC BREEZE (IRE) 13 b. or br.g. Strong Gale – Atomic Lady (Over The River (FR)) [2006/7 c–§, h–: c25m^6 c27m^{ur} Jun 7] plain gelding: veteran jumper: stays 3½m: acts on firm and good to soft going: unreliable. *R. E. Barr*   c– § h–

ATOMICSTORM (IRE) 7 br.g. Glacial Storm (USA) – Mightyatom (Black Minstrel) [2006/7 24g^{pu} May 13] runner-up in point: no other sign of ability: dead. *Roy Wilson, Ireland*   h–

ATOUCHBETWEENACARA (IRE) 6 b. or br.g. Lord Americo – Rosie Lil (IRE) (Roselier (FR)) [2006/7 F16v^2 22d^4 19d^6 Mar 26] €16,000 4-y-o: tall, useful-looking gelding: first foal: dam, fair hurdler, stayed 3m: fell in maiden Irish point: 5 lengths second of 18 to West End King in maiden bumper at Huntingdon: modest form 2 outings over hurdles: bred to stay well, but races freely. *Miss Suzy Smith*   h97 F100

AT THE MONEY 4 b.g. Robellino (USA) – Coh Sho No (Old Vic) [2006/7 16v* Feb 23] dam 21f hurdle winner: fair on Flat (stays 2m), won twice in 2006: successful on hurdling debut in juvenile at Warwick by 21 lengths from Billy Murphy: will stay beyond 2m: likely to improve. *J. M. P. Eustace*   h108 p

ATTORNEY GENERAL (IRE) 8 b.g. Sadler's Wells (USA) – Her Ladyship (Polish Precedent (USA)) [2006/7 h144§: 20s 25d^{pu} 25v 24g Mar 15] workmanlike gelding: useful handicap hurdler at best, below that in 2006/7: should stay beyond 3m: raced on good going or softer: wore cheekpieces/tongue strap final start: hard ride (carries head awkwardly). *J. A. B. Old*   h121 §

ATURA GATTI 8 b.g. Teenoso (USA) – Five And Four (IRE) (Green Desert (USA)) [2006/7 20s c20d* c21v^{pu} c16s^{pu} Apr 1] long-backed gelding: third foal: dam, no sign of ability, half-sister to very smart staying hurdler Burgoyne and useful hurdler up to 3m Errand Boy: winning pointer: well held in bumper/novice hurdle, sold out of M. Hourigan's stable 5,000 gns Doncaster May Sales in November: enterprisingly ridden when winning maiden at Sedgefield in November, only completed start in chases: stays 2½m: raced on ground softer than good. *Mrs S. J. Smith*   c100 ? h–

AUBIGNY (FR) 5 b.g. Tel Quel (FR) – La Beaumont (FR) (Hellios (USA)) [2006/7 F83: 22s 17s 16g 21s^{pu} Feb 9] good-topped gelding: runner-up in bumper: form (poor) in novice hurdles only on third start: likely to prove best short of 21f. *A. King*   h84

AUBURNDALE 5 b.g. Mind Games – Primitive Gift (Primitive Rising (USA)) [2006/7 16g^{pu} 20m^{pu} Mar 25] well beaten on Flat: no show over hurdles (breathing problem on debut). *A. Crook*   h–

AUBURN DUKE 7 ch.g. Inchinor – Dakota Girl (Northern State (USA)) [2006/7 F16d 20v^{pu} c24g^5 c24m^4 Apr 10] big gelding: poor form in bumpers, off 2 years before return: no promise in maiden hurdle/chases: tried blinkered (looked ungenuine). *Carl Llewellyn*   c– §
h–
F74

AUBURN GREY 5 gr.g. Environment Friend – Odyn Dancer (Minshaanshu Amad (USA)) [2006/7 F71: 19d^{pu} 16s 19s 16v^5 18v^6 Jan 25] big, rather leggy gelding: no solid form over hurdles. *M. D. I. Usher*   h–

AUCHTERARDER 5 gr.g. I'm Supposin (IRE) – Misty View (Absalom) [2006/7 F16v 16v 20v^6 16d Mar 21] rather leggy gelding: fifth foal: half-brother to bumper winner Just Classic (by Classic Cliche): dam 7f (at 2 yrs) and 1¼m winner: well held in bumper/maiden hurdles: needs to improve jumping. *D. E. Pipe*   h–
F–

AUDITOR 8 b.g. Polish Precedent (USA) – Annaba (IRE) (In The Wings) [2006/7 c74§, h–: c16m c19m c19m^3 c23m^{pu} c20m^{pu} c20g c18g^2 c16m^5 c24m^{ur} c19g^6 c23g^6 c16s^6 c19g^6 c24m^5 Apr 14] rather sparely-made gelding: poor handicap chaser: stays 19f: acts on firm and good to soft going: wears headgear: ungenuine. *S. T. Lewis*   c72 §
h–

AUENMOON (GER) 6 ch.g. Monsun (GER) – Auenlady (GER) (Big Shuffle (USA)) [2006/7 h124: 16g^{pu} Oct 21] tall, leggy, lengthy gelding: rather plain on Flat (stays 1¼m): fairly useful hurdler: ran as if amiss only start in 2006/7: raced at 2m: acts on good to firm and heavy going: front runner/races prominently: fluent jumper. *P. Monteith*   h–

AUGUSTINO (FR) 4 b.g. Kayf Tara – Akilinda (FR) (Monsun (GER)) [2006/7 F14s Dec 16] first foal: dam German 1¼m winner: mid-field in 3-y-o bumper on debut: dead. *P. Monteith*   F71

AUGUST ROSE (IRE) 7 b. or br.m. Accordion – Lockersleybay (IRE) (Orchestra) [2006/7 h91: 20v^2 20v^5 20g^4 Apr 16] fair maiden hurdler: off 10 months, best effort on return: should stay 3m: acts on heavy ground, probably on good to firm. *Miss Lucinda V. Russell*   h105

AUGUSTUS LIVIUS (IRE) 4 b.g. Titus Livius (FR) – Regal Fanfare (IRE) (Taufan (USA)) [2006/7 16m 16s^4 17d^5 16g^{pu} 16s Dec 16] close-coupled, leggy gelding: poor maiden on Flat (stays 9.8f): no solid form in juvenile hurdles: blinkered last 2 starts. *W. Storey*   h–

AUNTIE KATHLEEN 8 gr.m. Terimon – Lady High Sheriff (IRE) (Lancastrian) [2006/7 h89: c27s^{pu} c20s^4 c19s^6 c22v* Feb 22] good-topped mare: twice-raced over hurdles: modest form over fences, off 13 months prior to return: improved to win novice handicap at Haydock in February, idling after left in front last: should stay beyond 2¾m: raced on ground softer than good (acts on heavy). *J. J. Quinn*   c99
h–

AUNT MILLY 5 b.m. Paris House – Ramilie (Rambah) [2006/7 F16m^5 Jul 27] half-sister to fair hurdler around 2m Familie Footsteps (by Primitive Rising): dam, fair hurdler, stayed 2¾m: favourite, fifth of 7 in bumper at Uttoxeter on debut. *G. A. Swinbank*   F82

AURORAS ENCORE (IRE) 5 b.g. Second Empire (IRE) – Sama Veda (IRE) (Rainbow Quest (USA)) [2006/7 F17d^2 F17s^2 Mar 13] 9,500 3-y-o: fifth foal: half-brother to 3 winners on Flat, including 1¼m winner Veda's Rainbow (by Petardia): dam raced once: runner-up to Theatrical Moment in bumpers at Market Rasen and Sedgefield. *Mrs S. J. Smith*   F98

AUSONE 5 b.m. Singspiel (IRE) – Aristocratique (Cadeaux Genereux) [2006/7 h88, F73: 16d^3 20g^3 22s^{pu} 16g Apr 8] modest novice hurdler: stays 2½m: raced on good ground or softer. *Miss J. R. Gibney*   h90

AUTOGRAPH 6 b.m. Polar Prince (IRE) – Seraphim (FR) (Lashkari) [2006/7 F91: 17s^4 19v^2 20s^3 23g^2 Apr 3] tall, useful-looking mare: bumper winner: modest form in frame over hurdles: will stay 3m: acts on heavy going. *Mrs S. J. Smith*   h97

AUTOMATION 4 b.f. Tamure (IRE) – Anatomic (Deerhound (USA)) [2006/7 16g^{pu} Nov 1] rather leggy filly: sister to 17f hurdle winner Deer Dancer: well beaten on Flat: pulled very hard on hurdling debut. *C. W. Thornton*   h–

AUTUMN MIST (IRE) 12 br.g. Phardante (FR) – Sprinkling Star (Strong Gale) [2006/7 c93, h–: c33g^{pu} May 3] winning hurdler: modest chaser: stays 3¼m: acts on any going: blinkered/visored: formerly tongue tied: front runner. *M. Scudamore*   c–
h–

AUTUMN PROMISE (IRE) 4 b.g. Montjeu (IRE) – Seasonal Pleasure (USA) (Graustark) [2006/7 16g 16d^6 17d Nov 8] half-brother to fairly useful hurdler/chaser up to 19f Jaboune (by Johann Quatz): successful once from 4 starts up to 12.5f on Flat (fairly useful form), sold out of A. Fabre's stable 125,000 gns Newmarket July Sales: last in juvenile hurdles. *Jonjo O'Neill*   h–

AUX LE BAHNN (IRE) 6 b.g. Beneficial – Helvick Lass (IRE) (Mandalus) [2006/7 **F117 p** F115p: aF16g* Mar 21] won maiden on last of 3 starts in Irish points: created good impression when successful both starts in bumpers 15 months apart, beating Popcorn Rosie by 6 lengths at Lingfield in March, moving through effortlessly from rear and merely shaken up briefly to draw clear: smart prospect. *Noel T. Chance*

AVADI (IRE) 9 b.g. Un Desperado (FR) – Flamewood (Touching Wood (USA)) [2006/7 **c73** c85, h–: c19s5 c19sur c24vpu c20vpu c23vpu Mar 9] useful-looking gelding: maiden **h–** hurdler: poor chaser, failed to complete after reappearance: stays 3m: acts on heavy going: tried in cheekpieces. *P. T. Dalton*

AVALON 5 b.g. Kingmambo (USA) – Lady Carla (Caerleon (USA)) [2006/7 h96p: 20s **h101** 20g3 23d4 Dec 4] angular, close-coupled gelding: fair novice hurdler: stays 2½m: raced on good going or softer: blinkered last 2 starts, also tongue tied final one. *Jonjo O'Neill*

AVAS DELIGHT (IRE) 9 b.g. Ajraas (USA) – Whothatis (Creative Plan (USA)) **c–** [2006/7 c77p, h–: c17d3 c19spu c16g Apr 7] winning hurdler/chaser, no solid form over **h–** fences after 13-month absence: stays 2½m: acts on good to soft and good to firm ground. *R. H. Alner*

AVESOMEOFTHAT (IRE) 6 b.g. Lahib (USA) – Lacinia (Groom Dancer (USA)) **h111** [2006/7 h94: 16g4 17m* 17g2 17m4 18mF 16mpu 16f* 16s3 22g Apr 27] lengthy gelding: fair handicap hurdler: won at Newton Abbot in June and Wincanton in October: best around 2m: acts on firm and good to soft going, probably on soft: tried tongue tied: usually makes running/races prominently. *J. W. Mullins*

AVIATION 5 b.g. Averti (IRE) – Roufontaine (Rousillon (USA)) [2006/7 h104: 20g **c104** c16s4 c16vF c16d5 c16s2 c16g* c16v c16v6 16g 20g5 Apr 16] smallish, sturdy gelding: **h105** fair hurdler/chaser: won handicap over fences at Catterick in February: stays 2½m: acts on soft and good to firm going: effective blinkered or not. *G. M. Moore*

AVICIA 5 ch.m. Vettori (IRE) – Amarice (Suave Dancer (USA)) [2006/7 20g Apr 11] **h–** maiden on Flat, well held in 2006, sold out of C. Horgan's stable £800 Ascot October Sales: well beaten in maiden on hurdling debut. *K. M. Prendergast*

AVITTA (IRE) 8 b.m. Pennekamp (USA) – Alinova (USA) (Alleged (USA)) [2006/7 **c123 §** c104§, h–§: c19d* c20s* c19d* c24vpu 16v6 c23v4 c24gpu Mar 24] rangy mare: winning **h– §** hurdler: fairly useful handicap chaser: won at Hereford and Plumpton in November and Exeter (beat Bishop's Bridge 1½ lengths) in December: stays 2¾m: probably acts on any going: tried tongue tied: sometimes let down by jumping: irresolute. *Miss Venetia Williams*

AXINIT (GER) 7 gr.g. Linamix (FR) – Assia (IRE) (Royal Academy (USA)) [2006/7 **h89** 18g4 20mpu 17d6 Nov 16] successful 3 times on Flat, twice in Germany at 3 yrs and once in Ireland in 2006: modest hurdler: stays 19f: acts on soft going: tried blinkered, wears cheekpieces nowadays: tongue tied. *T. Hogan, Ireland*

AYA 5 b.m. Double Trigger (IRE) – Upper Mount Street (IRE) (Strong Gale) [2006/7 **F86** F16g* F17g Apr 19] lengthy mare: fourth foal: dam Irish bumper winner: won bumper at Towcester on debut: ninth of 18 at Cheltenham 11 days later. *R. H. York*

AYALA COVE (USA) 4 ch.f. Mt Livermore (USA) – Kitra (USA) (Woodman (USA)) **h–** [2006/7 16gF 17f4 17m Aug 26] no form on Flat or juvenile hurdles: tongue tied. *P. C. Haslam*

AYMARD DES FIEFFES (FR) 5 ch.g. Lute Antique (FR) – Margot Des Fieffes **h–** (FR) (Magistros (FR)) [2006/7 F71: F16v aF16g6 16mpu Apr 10] leggy gelding: poor **F71** form in bumpers: failed to settle and made mistakes in maiden on hurdling debut. *R. A. Harris*

AYURVEDA 6 b.g. Classic Cliche (IRE) – Herballistic (Rolfe (USA)) [2006/7 F16s4 **h–** F16s 24s 20vpu Dec 15] 5,800 3-y-o, 25,000 4-y-o: good-bodied gelding: fourth foal: **F75** half-brother to modest hurdler up to 2¾m Miniballist (by Tragic Role): dam, unplaced in 2 bumpers, half-sister to top-class staying chaser Go Ballistic: modest form in bumpers: no show over hurdles. *Mrs K. Waldron*

AZAHARA 5 b.m. Vettori (IRE) – Branston Express (Bay Express) [2006/7 h71: 17d6 **h–** 16mpu Sep 26] poor maiden hurdler, left K. Reveley prior to final outing: dead. *G. M. Moore*

AZIONE 4 b.f. Exit To Nowhere (USA) – Little Feat (Terimon) [2006/7 F12s F17s6 **F85** F16d3 F18v3 Mar 7] rather leggy filly: first foal: dam dual bumper winner: best effort in bumpers (fair form) on third start: free-going sort. *R. A. Farrant*

AZKABAN WINGS (IRE) 6 ch.g. In The Wings – Isabella R (IRE) (Indian Ridge)   h–
[2006/7 21s^{pu} Feb 9] good-topped gelding: first foal: dam maiden half-sister to smart
chaser up to 2½m Hill Society: fair form in bumpers: well beaten 2 starts over hurdles 11
months apart, left D. Wachman after first. *M. J. McGrath*

AZTEC PRINCE (IRE) 7 ch.g. King Persian – China Doll (IRE) (West China)   c96
[2006/7 h–: 16g c17v² c16d⁴ c17v* c16s³ c16v⁶ c17g^{pu} Apr 2] tall gelding: no form   h–
over hurdles: modest chaser: 8 lb out of weights, won handicap at Kelso in January:
keen-going sort, may prove best around 2m: acts on heavy going: tongue tied over fences.
Miss S. E. Forster

AZTEC WARRIOR (IRE) 6 b.g. Taipan (IRE) – Eurocurrency (IRE) (Brush Aside   c130
(USA)) [2006/7 h117, F98: 16g⁵ c21m^{pu} c21g* c21s⁴ c21s* c20g² c21g c22g* Apr 10]   h117
tall, good sort: winning hurdler: useful novice chaser: won at Folkestone in November,
Wincanton (left clear 3 out) in January and Fontwell (4 ran, didn't need to be at best) in
April: ran well when 8 lengths second of 4 to ready winner New Little Bric in Grade 1 at
Sandown: stays 2¾m: acts on heavy going. *Miss H. C. Knight*

AZTURK (FR) 5 b.m. Baby Turk – Pocahontas (FR) (Nikos) [2006/7 16d Oct 21]   h–
68,000 3-y-o: first foal: dam, winning hurdler/chaser up to 21f in France, half-sister to
top-class 2m chaser Azertyuiop (by Baby Turk) and very smart staying chaser Bipbap:
well beaten in maiden hurdle on debut. *J. P. L. Ewart*

B

BAAWRAH 6 ch.g. Cadeaux Genereux – Kronengold (USA) (Golden Act (USA))   c83 ?
[2006/7 h77: 21m 24g c20d⁴ c24g^F Dec 20] strong gelding: poor handicap hurdler: fourth   h65
in maiden at Musselburgh on completed start over fences, possibly flattered: stays 2½m:
acts on soft and good to firm going: tried in cheekpieces. *M. Todhunter*

BABE HEFFRON (IRE) 6 ch.g. Topanoora – Yellow Ochre (IRE) (Ore) [2006/7   h77
19d^{pu} 19g⁴ Mar 25] first foal: dam unraced: won maiden Irish point in 2006: first form
(poor) over hurdles on final start. *D. G. Bridgwater*

BABY BONNETT (IRE) 5 b.m. City Honours (USA) – Daddy's Hat (IRE) (Dancing   F69
Dissident (USA)) [2006/7 F16s⁶ F16m Mar 31] second foal: dam 6.5f winner: poor form
in mares bumpers. *T. R. George*

BABY RUN (FR) 7 b.g. Baby Turk – Run For Laborie (FR) (Lesotho (USA)) [2006/7   c142
c132p, h–: c16s³ Dec 9] good-topped gelding: winning hurdler: useful form over fences: h–
won listed novice at Aintree sole 2005/6 start: off over 13 months, good 8 lengths third to
Kalca Mome in handicap at Cheltenham (broke down): raced around 2m over jumps: acts
on heavy going: free-going soft. *N. A. Twiston-Davies*

BABY SISTER 8 ch.m. King Among Kings – Market Blues (Porto Bello) [2006/7 h–:   h69
16g⁴ 16g⁶ 16v 20v³ 24v⁵ Mar 9] smallish, leggy mare: poor handicap hurdler: stays 3m:
acts on heavy going. *D. W. Whillans*

BACK AMONG FRIENDS 8 b.g. Bob Back (USA) – Betty's Girl (Menelek)   h113
[2006/7 h87+: 19s⁶ 16v* Feb 15] close-coupled gelding: bumper winner: easily best
effort over hurdles (fair form) when making all in maiden at Chepstow in February: bred
to be suited by further than 2m, but races freely: raced on going softer than good (acts on
heavy): seems best when dominating. *J. A. B. Old*

BACKBEAT (IRE) 10 ch.g. Bob Back (USA) – Pinata (Deep Run) [2006/7 c135, h–:   c–
c24d Dec 16] sturdy gelding: winning hurdler: useful chaser: well held in listed handicap   h–
only start in 2006/7: stays 3m: raced on good ground or softer: blinkered (jumped badly
right) on chasing debut: tends to sweat. *J. Howard Johnson*

BACKBORD (GER) 5 b.g. Platini (GER) – Bukowina (GER) (Windwurf (GER))   h118
[2006/7 h112: 21d 21d* 22d 19g² 24m* 24m⁴ Apr 26] sturdy gelding: fairly useful novice
hurdler: didn't need to be at best to land odds at Ludlow in November and Worcester (beat
River Indus easily by 13 lengths) in April: good fourth of 24 to Sonnyanjoe in handicap at
Punchestown: stays easy 3m: acts on good to firm and good to soft going: tongue tied last
5 outings. *Mrs L. Wadham*

BACK DE BAY (IRE) 7 b.g. Bob Back (USA) – Baybush (Boreen (FR)) [2006/7 c–,   c–
h–: c21m^{pu} Sep 26] no sign of ability. *J. R. Cornwall*   h–

BACK FOR THE CRAIC (IRE) 8 ch.g. Bob Back (USA) – Alice Brennan (IRE) **c101**
(Good Thyne (USA)) [2006/7 h–p: c24d^pu c23s^2 c24d^2 c23s* Jan 31] well-made gelding: **h–**
breathing problem on hurdling debut: fair form in chases, won maiden at Leicester in
January: stays 3m: raced on good to soft/soft ground: sold 2,000 gns Doncaster May
Sales. *N. J. Henderson*

BACK IN BUSINESS (IRE) 7 b. or br.g. Bob Back (USA) – Rose of Burnett (IRE) **c107**
(Be My Native (USA)) [2006/7 c24s^3 c24s^3 c24s^pu c23s^3 c23s^2 c25m* c26m^2 c31s* **h–**
Apr 27] first foal: dam lightly-raced half-sister to fairly useful 3m chase winner The
Duckpond: pulled up in point: winning hurdler: sold out of D. Hassett's stable 10,000 gns
Doncaster May (2006) Sales: fair chaser: won handicaps at Hereford (by 24 lengths) in
March and Perth in April: stays 31f: acts on soft and good to firm going: has been tongue
tied. *Evan Williams*

BACK IN FRONT (IRE) 10 br.g. Bob Back (USA) – Storm Front (IRE) (Strong **c133 +**
Gale) [2006/7 c152, h157: c20d^F c24v* c24v^6 Dec 28] workmanlike gelding: high-class **h–**
hurdler/smart chaser at best: won minor event at Thurles (beat Romek 6 lengths, idling)
in November: mistakes when tailed off in Grade 1 at Leopardstown: stays 3m: acts on
heavy going (won bumper on good to firm). *E. J. O'Grady, Ireland*

BACK IN VOGUE 6 ch.m. Bob Back (USA) – Cooks Lawn (The Parson) [2006/7 **h–**
F69: 20g 19d 22s^pu 22g^5 Mar 31] tall, unfurnished mare: little form in bumpers/over
hurdles: tried blinkered. *J. G. Portman*

BACK NINE (IRE) 10 b.g. Bob Back (USA) – Sylvia Fox (Deep Run) [2006/7 c125+, **c113**
h–: c25d^2 c24s* c25d^2 Mar 20] strong gelding: winning hurdler: useful hunter chaser: **h–**
won Royal Artillery Gold Cup at Sandown in February by 21 lengths from Whitenzo:
stays 25f: acts on heavy going: tried tongue tied. *Miss J. Western*

BACK ON LINE (IRE) 7 br.m. Bob Back (USA) – Ballyvooney (Salluceva) [2006/7 **h106**
19v^2 16v^2 20v^su 20v* 21g^pu Mar 24] good-topped ex-Irish mare: fourth foal: dam,
winning hurdler/chaser who stayed 3m: well held in bumper: won mares maiden point
in 2006: easily best effort over hurdles (fair form) when winning maiden at Fontwell in
March: should stay beyond 2½m: acts on heavy going. *Miss Venetia Williams*

BACKSTAGE (FR) 5 b.g. Passing Sale (FR) – Madame Nathalie (FR) (Dreams To **c114**
Reality (USA)) [2006/7 17s^6 17s^4 c18d^3 c16g* c16g^3 Nov 19] leggy, close-coupled **h92**
gelding: fifth foal: half-brother to 3 winning hurdlers in France, including around 2½m
The Mack and Marchand de Dames (both by Marchand de Sable): dam maiden: modest
novice hurdler: left J. Bertran de Balanda, better form when winning novice chase at
Cheltenham in October by 16 lengths from Carthys Cross, making all: raced around 2m:
acts on heavy ground. *Evan Williams*

BACKSTREET LAD 5 b.g. Fraam – Forest Fantasy (Rambo Dancer (CAN)) [2006/7 **h–**
h94: 24v^pu Dec 15] rather leggy gelding: maiden hurdler: no show only start in 2006/7:
tried in headgear/tongue tied. *Evan Williams*

BACK THE MUSIC (IRE) 6 br.m. Bob Back (USA) – Bagatelle (IRE) (Strong Gale) **F75**
[2006/7 F16s F16m^4 F16m F16m Apr 15] €21,000 4-y-o: third foal: dam unraced out of
half-sister to Buck House: modest form in bumpers: likely to be suited by further.
C. E. Longsdon

BACK TO BEN ALDER (IRE) 10 b. or br.g. Bob Back (USA) – Winter Fox (Mart- **h–**
inmas) [2006/7 h125: 23f^F May 6] good sort: fairly useful handicap hurdler, lightly-raced:
weakening when fell 2 out only start in 2006/7: stays 2½m: acts on soft going: room for
improvement in jumping. *N. J. Henderson*

BACK TOO BEDLAM 4 b.g. Petoski – Lutine Royal (Formidable (USA)) [2006/7 **h80**
16m 17f^pu 17s^pu 20m^4 Apr 9] good-topped gelding: half-brother to selling hurdler Zesti
(by Charmer), stayed 2¼m: well held sole Flat outing: first form (poor) over hurdles on
final start. *Mrs S. A. Watt*

BACK WITH A BANG (IRE) 8 b.g. Oscar (IRE) – Trapper Jean (Orchestra) [2006/7 **h–**
h–, F84: 26g^pu May 4] placed first 2 starts in bumpers: no form since, including over
hurdles: should stay beyond 2m: tried blinkered. *Mrs N. S. Evans*

BADGER KENNEDY (IRE) 7 b.g. Perugino (USA) – Peace Dividend (IRE) (Alzao **h–**
(USA)) [2006/7 20g 20g^6 16g 16s Sep 2] stocky gelding: fair 6.5f to 1m winner on Flat (often
blinkered): no solid form over hurdles: has had tongue tied. *V. P. Donoghue, Ireland*

BADLY BRUISED (IRE) 6 b.g. Tiraaz (USA) – Krissykiss (Gildoran) [2006/7 F16s **F82**
Oct 25] rather leggy gelding: first foal: dam, well held in bumper, out of half-sister to
Celtic Ryde and Noddy's Ryde and the dam of Teeton Mill: won maiden Irish point on

debut in 2006: bought 10,000 gns Doncaster August Sales: mid-field in bumper at Cheltenham. *M. Keighley*

BAFANA BOY 7 br.g. Presenting – Lorna's Choice (Oats) [2006/7 c84+, h–: c24s* c27m* c25s^{pu} 24g^5 24d* 24m* 22g^6 Apr 2] progressive hurdler/chaser since switched to handicap company: won over fences at Perth (novice) in May and Sedgefield in June, and over hurdles at Musselburgh in January and February (novice): stays 27f: acts on soft and good to firm going: prone to mistakes but probably capable of better still. *N. G. Richards*   **c105 p** **h104 p**

BAFFLING SECRET (FR) 7 gr.g. Kizitca (FR) – Kadroulienne (FR) (Kadrou (FR)) [2006/7 h83§: 16s 16s* 16v^3 16v^4 Jan 17] lengthy gelding: modest hurdler: won handicap at Newcastle in December: raced around 2m on soft/heavy ground over jumps: has refused to race. *L. Lungo*   **h93**

BAGGER VANCE (IRE) 9 ch.g. Spectrum (IRE) – Shabarana (FR) (Nishapour (FR)) [2006/7 17s Nov 17] soundly beaten in various events, left C. Roche before sole outing in 2006/7. *D. J. Wintle*   **h–**

BAGWELL BEN 10 ch.g. Karinga Bay – Nine Hans (Prince Hansel) [2006/7 h–: 21s^{pu} 19d^{pu} Jun 12] no form over hurdles. *M. J. Coombe*   **h–**

BAHRAIN STORM (IRE) 4 b.g. Bahhare (USA) – Dance Up A Storm (USA) (Storm Bird (CAN)) [2006/7 16g^3 16d^3 16d 16v* 16v^3 16m* 16m^3 Apr 26] good-topped gelding: fairly useful on Flat (stays 1½m): useful juvenile hurdler: won maiden at Limerick (easily by 15 lengths) in March and minor event at Fairyhouse (beat Financial Reward by ¾ length) in April: good 8¾ lengths third to Punjabi in Champion Four Year Old Hurdle at Punchestown final start, though not entirely convincing with jumping/attitude: raced at 2m: acts on heavy and good to firm going: blinkered after debut. *P. J. Flynn, Ireland*   **h125**

BAIE DES FLAMANDS (USA) 5 b.g. Kingmambo (USA) – Isle de France (USA) (Nureyev (USA)) [2006/7 h108d: 19g^{pu} 16d 16m 21d^{pu} Mar 22] close-coupled gelding: won juvenile maiden on hurdling debut: no form since: tried in cheekpieces, blinkered in 2006/7: tongue tied last 3 starts. *Miss S. J. Wilton*   **h–**

BAIKAL 7 b.g. Singspiel (IRE) – Siberian Habit (Siberian Express (USA)) [2006/7 20g* 18s 20g Apr 7] smallish, stocky ex-Irish gelding: fair 2m winner on Flat: modest handicap hurdler: won at Roscommon in July: left N. Madden and off over 5 months, tailed off on British debut: stays 2½m: probably acts on firm ground, well held on soft: form over hurdles only when blinkered. *Jonjo O'Neill*   **h92 +**

BAIKALINE (FR) 8 b.m. Cadoudal – Advantage (FR) (Antheus (USA)) [2006/7 c–, h97: 24d May 19] leggy mare: modest chaser/maiden hurdler: well held only start in 2006/7: stays 3m: raced on good going or softer. *Ian Williams*   **c–** **h–**

BAILEYS BEST 5 b.g. Mister Baileys – Miss Rimex (IRE) (Ezzoud (IRE)) [2006/7 18m^3 16m^3 20s^4 20s^2 22m^5 16s 20d^5 24d^4 26s 26g Apr 20] neat gelding: fair up to 1¼m on Flat: modest novice hurdler: stays 3m: acts on soft and good to firm going: tried visored/in cheekpieces. *J. G. M. O'Shea*   **h86**

BAILEYS PRIZE (USA) 10 ch.g. Mister Baileys – Mar Mar (USA) (Forever Casting (USA)) [2006/7 c–§, h–§: 19m c18m May 28] medium-sized gelding: maiden hurdler: no form over fences: tried in headgear: ungenuine. *P. R. Rodford*   **c– §** **h– §**

BAINY 5 ch.g. Genuine Gift (CAN) – Royal Mixture (Rakaposhi King) [2006/7 F16m 20g^{pu} 25s Jan 24] workmanlike gelding: first foal: dam unraced: no sign of ability in bumper/over hurdles. *F. P. Murtagh*   **h–** **F–**

BAJAN SUNSHINE (IRE) 6 b.g. Presenting – Tina's Charm (IRE) (Hatim (USA)) [2006/7 F17g* F16d* 20d* 19d Nov 8] €56,000 4-y-o: fourth foal: half-brother to 1¼m winner Tina's Indian (by Indian Ridge): dam winning 2m hurdler/9f winner on Flat: successful both starts in bumpers, at Newton Abbot in August and Worcester in September: better effort in novice hurdles when winning at Fakenham on debut in October: stays 2½m. *Jonjo O'Neill*   **h94 +** **F94**

BAKER OF OZ 6 b.g. Pursuit of Love – Moorish Idol (Aragon) [2006/7 h62: 21d^{pu} 19v Mar 1] angular, plain gelding: maiden hurdler: has worn cheekpieces. *M. A. Doyle*   **h–**

BAKER'S GIRL (IRE) 4 gr.f. Silver Patriarch (IRE) – Bewitch (Idiot's Delight) [2006/7 F13s^6 Dec 1] fifth foal: dam, second in bumper, half-sister to fairly useful hurdler/chasers up to 3m First Love and Shining Strand, out of half-sister to high-class staying chaser Spanish Steps: mid-field in 3-y-o bumper on debut: likely to be suited by stiffer test of stamina. *Mrs Norma Pook*   **F–**

BAK ON BOARD 11 b.g. Sula Bula – Kirstins Pride (Silly Prices) [2006/7 c23v³ c21g⁵ Apr 27] workmanlike gelding: winning pointer: maiden hurdler/chaser: stays 3¼m: acts on any going: tried blinkered. *A. J. Tizzard*   **c68** **h–**

BAK TO BILL 12 b.g. Nicholas Bill – Kirstins Pride (Silly Prices) [2006/7 c–, h110: c20fᵖᵘ 22g Mar 19] lengthy gelding: fair hurdler/chaser at best: no show in 2006/7: stays 3¼m, effective at 19f when conditions are testing: acts on any going: tried in cheekpieces: ridden by Miss L. Gardner. *Mrs S. Gardner*   **c–** **h–**

BALAKAN (IRE) 6 b.g. Selkirk (USA) – Balanka (IRE) (Alzao (USA)) [2006/7 16m² 16d² 17d³ Aug 30] €28,000 3-y-o: fifth foal: half-brother to very smart 1m to 1½m winner Balakheri (by Theatrical): dam, French 1m/1¼m winner, half-sister to high-class French staying chaser Bannkipour: bumper winner: fair on Flat (stays 13f): fairly useful form in maiden hurdles, won 20-runner event at Tralee in August by 1½ lengths from Mister Farmer (pair clear): will stay beyond 17f: unraced on extremes of going. *M. Halford, Ireland*   **h119**

BALAMORY DAN (IRE) 6 b.g. Fort Morgan (USA) – Musical Horn (Music Boy) [2006/7 F101: F17s³ Oct 22] good-topped gelding: fairly useful form in bumpers: off 11 months, creditable third to Super Nick at Aintree. *G. A. Harker*   **F98**

BAL BIRNIE 4 ch.g. Bal Harbour – Kalymnia (GER) (Mondrian (GER)) [2006/7 F14v F17m³ Apr 28] fifth foal: half-brother to winner abroad by Highest Honor: dam, German 1½m winner, half-sister to Derby Italiano winner Kallisto: much better effort in bumpers when third to Georgian King at Market Rasen. *M. W. Easterby*   **F85**

BALEARIC STAR (IRE) 6 b.g. Night Shift (USA) – La Menorquina (USA) (Woodman (USA)) [2006/7 16g³ 17s 17s Dec 29] modest on Flat (best around 1m): best effort over hurdles (modest form) on debut: possibly unsuited by soft ground.   **h86**

BALIGRUNDLE 7 b.g. Moshaajir (USA) – Masirah (Dunphy) [2006/7 F16d⁶ 16gᵖᵘ 17vᵖᵘ 16v⁶ 16dᵖᵘ 20v³ c20s* c25sꟑ c20vᵘʳ c21v⁴ c17g c20g³ Apr 23] sixth in bumpers: little form over hurdles: poor handicap chaser: won at Newcastle in January: seems barely to stay 21f: acts on heavy ground. *W. S. Coltherd*   **c72** **h58 +** **F–**

BALINOVA (IRE) 10 b.g. Lord Americo – Shuil Comeragh (Laurence O) [2006/7 c20s* Feb 16] compact gelding: winning pointer: successful 2 of 3 starts in hunters, including at Sandown in February: will stay beyond 25f: raced on soft going. *C. J. Bennett*   **c111**

BALLABRIGGS (IRE) 6 b.g. Presenting – Papoose (IRE) (Little Bighorn) [2006/7 F16s⁵ 20v 20s² 20v² 20g Apr 7] tall, good-topped gelding: chasing type: second foal: brother to fairly useful hurdler/chaser Letterman, stays 2¾m: dam, winning pointer, half-sister to very smart chaser Hi Cloy, out of half-sister to Champion Hurdle winner For Auction: fifth in bumper: fair form over hurdles: best efforts when runner-up in novices at Newcastle and Ayr: will be suited by further than 2½m: acts on heavy going. *D. McCain Jnr*   **h104** **F81**

BALLABROOK (IRE) 5 b.g. Alderbrook – Summer Holiday (IRE) (Kambalda) [2006/7 F16s⁴ Jan 24] unfurnished gelding: second foal: dam unraced half-sister to useful chaser Torduff Boy, stays 29f: modest form when fourth in maiden bumper at Catterick on debut. *D. McCain Jnr*   **F82**

BALLADEER (IRE) 9 b.g. King's Theatre (IRE) – Carousel Music (On Your Mark) [2006/7 c111, h–: c22m² c22f⁵ c22g* c26m³ c24g* c24dᵖᵘ Nov 24] close-coupled gelding: winning hurdler: fairly useful handicap chaser: won at Fontwell in September and Kempton in November: probably stays 3¼m: acts on any going: prone to mistakes. *Mrs T. J. Hill*   **c116** **h–**

BALLAMUSIC (IRE) 5 b.g. Accordion – Hazy Fiddler (IRE) (Orchestra) [2006/7 F14s³ F16d⁴ 20g* Apr 27] good-topped gelding: half-brother to 3¼m chase winner Trovaio (by Un Desperado): dam unraced: fair form when in frame in bumpers: successful hurdling debut when beating Templer by head (pair clear) in novice at Chepstow: will stay beyond 2½m: likely to improve. *A. King*   **h109 p** **F87**

BALLAROYALE (IRE) 5 b.g. Supreme Leader – Royal Fluff (IRE) (King's Ride) [2006/7 F16v³ Jan 25] well-made gelding: first foal: dam unraced half-sister to useful chaser up to 25f Ashwell Boy: favourite, 7½ lengths third of 19 to Freddie The Third in bumper at Warwick on debut, fading final 1f. *Jonjo O'Neill*   **F97 +**

BALL BOY 5 b.g. Xaar – Tanz (IRE) (Sadler's Wells (USA)) [2006/7 h–: 16m 16mᵘʳ 16d 16g⁵ Apr 9] medium-sized gelding: no form over hurdles: usually tongue tied. *G. Haine*   **h–**

BALLERINA GIRL 6 b.m. Overbury (IRE) – Flakey Dove (Oats) [2006/7 F18s F14s **h–**
16g 18g Apr 10] 32,000 4-y-o: fourth foal: half-sister to winning pointer by Environment **F–**
Friend: dam, top-class hurdler up to 21f, won 1994 Champion Hurdle: well beaten in
bumpers/over hurdles. *N. J. Gifford*

BALL GAMES 9 b.g. Mind Games – Deb's Ball (Glenstal (USA)) [2006/7 h91: 16m³ **h91 §**
17d⁵ 17m³ 24mᵖᵘ Jul 11] close-coupled, leggy gelding: modest hurdler: barely stays
2½m: acts on soft and good to firm going: has worn visor/cheekpieces: tends to get
behind. *James Moffatt*

BALLINRUANE (IRE) 8 br.g. Norwich – Katie Dick (IRE) (Roselier (FR)) [2006/7 **c94 ?**
h–: c16g⁴ c16s⁴ Mar 7] tall gelding: maiden hurdler: modest and better effort over fences **h–**
when fourth in maiden at Catterick, possibly flattered. *B. S. Rothwell*

BALLISTRAW (IRE) 8 ch.g. Carroll House – Well Over (Over The River (FR)) **c134**
[2006/7 c127: c19d c18v⁴ c20v* c24v² Dec 27] good-topped gelding: former smart
hunter chaser: useful form in handicaps in 2006/7: won at Punchestown in December by
neck from Vedelle (pair clear): good ½-length second to Cane Brake in valuable event at
Leopardstown later in month: will stay at least 3¼m: acts on heavy going. *M. W. Hickey,
Ireland*

BALLITO (IRE) 8 ch.g. Flying Legend (USA) – Whatt Ya Doin (IRE) (Duky) [2006/7 **c85 x**
c–p, h90: 24d c23g c25fʳᵒ c20f³ c20f³ c21m² c25fᵖᵘ 21g* 21d c24g⁶ Dec 20] angular **h99**
gelding: modest hurdler: won seller at Ludlow in October: poor maiden chaser: stays 3m:
acts on firm and good to soft going: tried blinkered, best efforts in cheekpieces: ran out
third outing: often let down by jumping over fences. *J. G. Carr, Ireland*

BALL O MALT (IRE) 11 b.g. Star Quest – Vera Dodd (IRE) (Riot Helmet) [2006/7 **c129**
c120, h116: 20m² c20f* c22gᶠ 19g² 20gᵖᵘ Nov 19] big, lengthy gelding: fairly useful **h122**
handicap hurdler/chaser: won quite valuable event over fences at Perth in July by 2
lengths from Bohemian Spirit: good efforts when runner-up over hurdles in 2006/7, sold
out of R. Fahey's stable 25,000 gns Doncaster October Sales before final outing: stayed
3m, at least as effective as shorter: acted on heavy and good to firm going: consistent:
dead. *R. M. Whitaker*

BALLYAAHBUTT (IRE) 8 b.g. Good Thyne (USA) – Lady Henbit (IRE) (Henbit **c79**
(USA)) [2006/7 c–, h–: c25s⁶ c24d⁶ c25d³ c26s⁴ c20v² c22s² c20v² c20d* c19g⁴ c20mᵖᵘ **h–**
Apr 25] poor handicap chaser: won at Lingfield in March: stays 2¾m: acts on heavy
going: blinkered/visored after reappearance: often makes running/races prominently.
B. G. Powell

BALLY ABBIE 6 b.m. Weldnaas (USA) – Bally Small (Sunyboy) [2006/7 h–, F–: 20g **h–**
Apr 30] good-topped mare: no impact over hurdles: pulled up in point. *P. Beaumont*

BALLYAGRAN (IRE) 7 b.g. Pierre – Promalady (IRE) (Homo Sapien) [2006/7 20mʳᵒ **c121**
16m² 16m⁵ c19v* c16s* c18d⁴ Oct 18] lengthy, useful-looking gelding: fair hurdler: **h109**
fairly useful form over fences, winning maiden at Listowel in September and Grade 3
novice at Roscommon (by 7 lengths from Some Timbering) in October: just respectable
fourth to Gemini Lucy in listed novice at Punchestown: should stay beyond 19f: acts on
heavy going, probably on good to firm: tried blinkered over hurdles (ran out once).
N. Meade, Ireland

BALLYALBANY (IRE) 9 b.g. Lord Americo – Raisin Turf (IRE) (Phardante (FR)) **c79**
[2006/7 c20s c17gᵖᵘ c16g⁵ Mar 2] rangy gelding: fair maiden hurdler: off 19 months, **h–**
poor form in maiden chases: stays 21f: raced on good going or softer. *Mrs Susan Nock*

BALLYBEAN (IRE) 7 b.g. Simply Great (FR) – Youthful Capitana (Hardboy) [2006/7 **c–**
c–, h–: c17m⁴ c16dᵖᵘ Nov 22] won Irish point in 2004: no form otherwise. *K. C. Bailey* **h–**

BALLYBEG (IRE) 8 b.g. Top of The World – Commanche Glen (IRE) **h99**
(Commanche Run) [2006/7 21m³ 24v⁴ 21sˢᵘ 16s Jan 31] ex-Irish gelding: second foal:
half-brother to 19f hurdle winner L'Orage Lady (by Glacial Storm) and bumper winner
Wee Bertie (by Sea Raven): dam unraced half-sister to Grand National winner Papillon:
bumper winner: modest maiden hurdler, sold out of P. Rothwell's stable 5,000 gns
Doncaster August Sales and off over a year prior to return: stays 21f: acts on good to firm
going, probably on heavy: in cheekpieces/blinkers last 3 outings. *Evan Williams*

BALLYBOE BOY (IRE) 8 b.g. Flying Spur (AUS) – Born To Fly (IRE) (Last **c–**
Tycoon) [2006/7 c76, h86: c17vᵖᵘ c20vᵖᵘ 20g c16m³ c20gᵖᵘ Apr 23] lengthy gelding: **h–**
winning hurdler/maiden chaser, no form in 2006/7 after 17-month absence: best around
2m: usually blinkered. *R. C. Guest*

BALLYBOLEY (IRE) 9 b.g. Roselier (FR) – Benbradagh Vard (IRE) (Le Bavard (FR)) [2006/7 h102: 25s² c25v² c26vᵖᵘ 24m² Mar 31] lengthy gelding: lightly raced: fair form over hurdles, placed all 4 starts: remote second of 5 to Fair Question in maiden at Hereford on completed start over fences/final outing for R. Phillips: should stay beyond 25f: acts on heavy going, below best on good to firm. *D. J. Wintle* — **c100 h105**

BALLY BOLSHOI (IRE) 7 b.m. Bob Back (USA) – Moscow Money (IRE) (Moscow Society (USA)) [2006/7 h105: c19vᵖᵘ c22sᵖᵘ Dec 5] useful-looking mare: fair hurdler: failed to convince with jumping both starts over fences: should stay beyond 19f: best efforts on heavy going. *Mrs S. D. Williams* — **c– h–**

BALLYBOUGH BILLY (IRE) 6 b.g. Taipan (IRE) – Bramblehill Fairy (IRE) (Toulon) [2006/7 F16f⁴ F16m⁴ 19mᵘʳ 24m Jul 4] first foal: dam unraced out of half-sister to Whitbread Gold Cup winner Harwell Lad: well beaten in maiden Irish points in 2005: poor form in bumpers: no show on completed start over hurdles: sold £5,000 Ascot February Sales, won point in April. *Carl Llewellyn* — **h– F73**

BALLYBOUGH JACK (IRE) 7 b.g. Shernazar – Lunar Approach (IRE) (Mandalus) [2006/7 c25sᶠ c19s² c20v³ c22sᵖᵘ Feb 18] strong gelding: winning pointer: runner-up both starts in bumpers: off 20 months, failed to see race out all outings in chases, beaten in strides final one: joined Mrs T. Hill. *B. G. Powell* — **c93**

BALLYBOUGH RASHER (IRE) 12 b.g. Broken Hearted – Chat Her Up (Proverb) [2006/7 c–x, h–: c25sᵖᵘ Jan 20] sturdy gelding: winning hurdler: smart chaser at best: failed to complete last 5 outings, left J. Howard Johnson and off over a year prior to only one in 2006/7: stays 4m: acts on soft and good to firm going: usually let down by jumping over fences. *A. King* — **c– x h–**

BALLYBRAKES (IRE) 7 ch.g. Moonax (IRE) – Deep Solare (Deep Run) [2006/7 h93, F90: 16g⁵ 24f³ Jul 6] modest form in 2½m novice (fell last) on first of 3 outings over hurdles: walked over in point in April. *N. G. Richards* — **h80**

BALLYCASSIDY (IRE) 11 br.g. Insan (USA) – Bitofabreeze (IRE) (Callernish) [2006/7 c149, h130: c24g⁴ c32mᵘʳ c22g² c24m c25mᵖᵘ c25v⁵ c24dᵖᵘ c24g c36gᵘʳ c32m⁶ Apr 21] strong, lengthy gelding: useful hurdler: smart handicap chaser: creditable second to stable-companion Yes Sir in valuable event at Market Rasen: largely disappointing after, though signs of return to form last 2 outings, again prominent until departing well onto second circuit in Grand National at Aintree: stays 27f: acts on firm and good to soft going, probably on soft: blinkered once, also tried in cheekpieces: sometimes let down by jumping: usually races prominently. *P. Bowen* — **c144 h–**

BALLYCLARE (IRE) 6 b.g. Shaamit – Jinglers Court (Jamesmead) [2006/7 F17g F18d Oct 30] 5,000 4-y-o: second foal: dam unraced half-sister to dam of smart hurdler up to 21f Urubande: successful in maiden point in 2006: showed little in bumpers, tongue tied second time. *W. S. Kittow* — **F–**

BALLY CONN (IRE) 5 br.g. Supreme Leader – Gladtogetit (Green Shoon) [2006/7 F16v* 26s⁵ 20v⁶ 22s⁴ Feb 3] half-brother to several winners, including fairly useful chaser Free Gift (by Presenting), best form around 2½m: dam, modest chaser, stayed 3m: won maiden Irish point in 2006: successful also in bumper at Towcester in November by ½ length from What A Buzz: well held 3 starts in novice hurdles: looks a thorough stayer. *Miss H. C. Knight* — **h89 F93**

BALLYDAY (IRE) 5 b.g. Oscar (IRE) – Malbay Sunrise (IRE) (Religiously (USA)) [2006/7 F17d⁶ 17dᵖᵘ 19g Nov 5] €21,000 3-y-o: first foal: dam unraced half-sister to useful bumper winner/winning chaser Ballytrim, out of useful hurdler up to 2½m Helynsar: pulled up in Irish point in 2006: bought 20,000 gns Doncaster May Sales: sixth of 11 in bumper at Market Rasen: no show in 2 novice hurdles. *E. A. Elliott* — **h– F71**

BALLYFIN (IRE) 9 b.g. Lord Americo – Scar Stream (Paddy's Stream) [2006/7 c80, h–: c26g³ Oct 30] winning Irish hunter chaser: poor form in handicaps: stays 3¼m: acts on good to soft going. *J. A. Geake* — **c80 h–**

BALLYFINNEY (IRE) 6 ch.g. Good Thyne (USA) – Sounds Confident (IRE) (Orchestra) [2006/7 c16s c17d⁵ c18s* c22v³ c25v⁴ c22s² c20v⁶ c24g² Mar 30] 26,000 4-y-o: lengthy, workmanlike gelding: second foal: dam winning pointer: winning hurdler/pointer: fair chaser: won maiden at Downpatrick in November: better form in handicaps after, neck second to Inaro at Ascot final outing: will stay beyond 25f: raced on good ground or softer (acts on heavy). *D. T. Hughes, Ireland* — **c111 h–**

BALLYFITZ 7 b.g. Overbury (IRE) – Running For Gold (Rymer) [2006/7 h114p: c24sᵘʳ Oct 25] close-coupled gelding: unbeaten in 2 starts over hurdles in 2005/6: off — **c– h–**

nearly a year, several mistakes and behind when all but refusing and unseating sixteenth in novice at Cheltenham on chasing debut: stays 3m: presumably not easy to train. *N. A. Twiston-Davies*

BALLYFOY (IRE) 6 b. or br.g. Alderbrook – Okanagan Valley (IRE) (Decent Fellow) [2006/7 21d^{pu} c20v^3 c25v^{wo} c21g* c25g^2 Apr 18] rangy gelding: third foal: dam unraced: runner-up 3 times from 5 starts in maiden Irish points: bled on hurdling debut: useful novice chaser: walked over at Exeter in February prior to winning 4-runner event at Ascot following month by length from Boychuk: neck second of 5 to idling Classified at Cheltenham, again jumping soundly: stays 25f. *T. R. George* **c130 h–**

BALLYGALLEY BOB (IRE) 6 br.g. Bob Back (USA) – Follow The Guide (IRE) (Strong Gale) [2006/7 F16v^4 22v^{pu} 26v^6 Jan 11] €25,000 3-y-o: first foal: dam well held in bumper: won maiden Irish point in 2006: bought 38,000 gns Doncaster May Sales: favourite, staying-on fourth to Private Note in bumper at Chepstow: little show both starts over hurdles. *O. Sherwood* **h– F84**

BALLYGOREY 6 b.g. Komaite (USA) – Chasmarella (Yukon Eric (CAN)) [2006/7 F16v^6 F16g Mar 29] second foal: dam modest staying hurdler: well beaten in bumpers. *Miss Z. C. Davison* **F–**

BALLYHALE (IRE) 9 br.g. Mister Lord (USA) – Deep Inagh (Deep Run) [2006/7 h93: 21m^4 26d 19d^2 20d^{pu} 20g Apr 3] useful-looking gelding: winning Irish pointer: modest novice hurdler: stays 21f: unraced on extremes of going: tried in cheekpieces. *P. D. Niven* **h93**

BALLYHOO (IRE) 7 b.m. Supreme Leader – Ballyhouraprincess (IRE) (Mulhollande (USA)) [2006/7 h91, F80: 24g^6 24d^4 25m^2 24d^5 24d^6 24s^5 21m^F 27m^6 Apr 26] compact mare: modest handicap hurdler: stays 27f: acts on soft and good to firm going: usually visored. *J. W. Mullins* **h97**

BALLYHURRY (USA) 10 b.g. Rubiano (USA) – Balakhna (FR) (Tyrant (USA)) [2006/7 h98: 16g^5 16m 16f* 16m^3 16m^3 16m^4 16g 16s Apr 25] fair hurdler: won maiden at Perth in July: best at 2m with emphasis on speed (acts on firm going): tried in cheekpieces: consistent. *J. S. Goldie* **h99**

BALLYJOHNBOY LORD (IRE) 8 b.g. Arctic Lord – Mount Sackville (Whistling Deer) [2006/7 c85, h114: c19s^4 c24v^2 c16g^4 c23m Apr 25] leggy, rather lightly-made gelding: fair hurdler: just poor form over fences, often let down by jumping: stays 27f: acts on heavy going. *M. Scudamore* **c85 x h–**

BALLYKELLY (IRE) 6 b.g. Insan (USA) – Lady Oakwell (IRE) (King's Ride) [2006/7 F98: 21m Oct 16] Irish point winner: fairly useful form in bumpers: mistakes and finished lame on hurdling debut. *R. T. Phillips* **h–**

BALLYKILN (IRE) 6 br.g. Petoski – Hunt The Thimble (FR) (Relkino) [2006/7 h–: 22d^6 22d^6 c24s^{bd} c22s^2 c24g^{pu} Mar 14] well-made gelding: some promise in novice hurdles: head second to Superrollercoaster at Fontwell, completed outing in handicap chases: lame next time: should stay 3m. *Miss H. C. Knight* **c95 h89**

BALLYLIFFEN BOY (IRE) 10 br.g. Executive Perk – Through The Roof (IRE) (Orchestra) [2006/7 c23v^{pu} May 27] maiden pointer: no show in hunter chase. *Lady Susan Brooke* **c–**

BALLYLUSKY (IRE) 10 b.g. Lord Americo – Blackbushe Place (IRE) (Buckskin (FR)) [2006/7 c25d^{pu} May 19] medium-sized, well-made gelding: useful handicap hurdler/fair chaser at best: successful 6 times in points, mostly in 2007: stays 25f: acts on heavy and good to firm ground: usually front runner over hurdles: poor jumper of fences. *Evan Williams* **c– x h–**

BALLYMAN (IRE) 6 b.g. Accordion – Sliabhin Rose (Roselier (FR)) [2006/7 F16d F17s 16s^5 c23s^F c23s^4 c20d^2 c24m^3 Apr 10] good-bodied gelding: first foal: dam unraced from family of smart staying chasers Earthstopper and Ebony Jane: won maiden Irish point in 2005: mid-field in bumpers: modest form when placed in maiden chases: stays 3m: acts on soft and good to firm ground. *J. A. Geake* **c84 F83**

BALLY MAYQUEEN (IRE) 5 br.m. Gothland (FR) – Aotearoa (IRE) (Flash of Steel) [2006/7 F16s 19d^{pu} 19g^{pu} Feb 2] 2,000 3-y-o: leggy mare: sister to 2m hurdle winner Mossland and half-sister to fairly useful 6f performer Russian Romeo (by Soviet Lad): dam unraced: no show in bumper/novice hurdles: blinkered final outing. *T. D. Walford* **h– F–**

BALLYMENA 6 b.m. Saddlers' Hall (IRE) – Ace Gunner (Gunner B) [2006/7 h74, F86: 20d^5 22f^5 Oct 5] bumper winner: little form over hurdles. *R. A. Harris* **h–**

BALLYNATTIN BUCK (IRE) 11 b.g. Buckskin (FR) – Dikler Gale (IRE) (Strong Gale) [2006/7 c–, h97: c24g^{pu} Apr 8] rangy gelding: maiden hurdler: fairly useful chaser at best: no form over fences since 2004/5, including in point: stays 3m: probably acts on any going: usually tongue tied. *S. Lloyd*   **c–** **h–**

BALLYNURE (IRE) 9 b. or br.g. Roselier (FR) – Fresh Partner (IRE) (Yashgan) [2006/7 c–, h94: 25g^6 c20m^4 c20g^4 c24g^{pu} c20g^8 c20g c21m^6 c20s^4 c22m^5 c25g^6 c28s^5 c24s^5 c20g^8 c23g^{pu} c20s^5 Apr 27] sturdy gelding: novice hurdler: modest chaser: won novice handicaps at Perth in August and Carlisle in April: best efforts around 2½m: acts on soft going: visored. *Miss Lucinda V. Russell*   **c85** **h–**

BALLYRAINEY (IRE) 8 b. or br.g. Carroll House – Foxborough Lady (Crash Course) [2006/7 c78?, h–, F83: c21m^{pu} c20d c16d^F c16s* c16d^5 c16s^4 c16v^2 c17v* c20m^2 Apr 8] workmanlike gelding: modest chaser: won handicaps at Folkestone (novice) in December and Plumpton (4 ran) in March: stays easy 2½m: acts on heavy and good to firm going: in cheekpieces last 6 outings. *Mrs L. C. Jewell*   **c85** **h–**

BALLYROBERT (IRE) 10 b. or br.g. Bob's Return (IRE) – Line Abreast (High Line) [2006/7 c104x, h88: 20d^5 Oct 18] good-bodied gelding: fair chaser/novice hurdler: stays 2¾m: acts on good to soft and good to firm going: sketchy jumper of fences. *A. M. Hales*   **c– x** **h100**

BALLY'S BRO (IRE) 8 ch.g. Zaffaran (USA) – Dalaray (Dalesa) [2006/7 h106p, F95: 20d^2 21g^{pu} Nov 15] lengthy, sparely-made gelding: lightly raced: placed in bumper/ novice hurdles: will stay 3m: raced on good/good to soft ground: presumably difficult to train. *N. A. Twiston-Davies*   **h97**

BALLYSHAN (IRE) 9 b.g. Synefos (USA) – Bramble Leader (IRE) (Supreme Leader) [2006/7 h114: c23s^{pu} 24s 20d^6 24v* 27s Apr 27] tall, angular gelding: fairly useful hurdler: back to best when winning 5-runner handicap at Kempton (by ½ length from Knighton Lad, making all) in March: stays 3m: acts on heavy going: not a fluent jumper (numerous mistakes on chasing debut). *N. A. Twiston-Davies*   **c–** **h116**

BALLYSHEEDY (IRE) 9 b.g. Moscow Society (USA) – Goforroad (IRE) (Mister Lord (USA)) [2006/7 24g 19d c17g^2 20f^5 24f^{ur} c22m c23d* c25g^5 c25s^{pu} c20v^6 c24v c22m^5 Apr 15] maiden hurdler: poor chaser: won handicap at Downpatrick in September: stays 23f: acts on any going: tried in headgear. *A. J. McNamara, Ireland*   **c78** **h74**

BALLYTRIM (IRE) 6 b.g. Luso – Helynsar (Fidel) [2006/7 F107: c22g^6 c18v c24v^4 c24v^3 c17d^2 c24v^2 c18v^3 c20v* c33g Mar 15] strong gelding: useful bumper winner: fair chaser: won maiden at Navan in March: none too fluent when below form in National Hunt Chase at Cheltenham next time: should stay beyond 3m: raced on good going or softer (acts on heavy): often races prominently. *W. P. Mullins, Ireland*   **c110**

BALLYVERANE OSCAR (IRE) 6 b.g. Oscar (IRE) – Nighty Bless (IRE) (Executive Perk) [2006/7 F16s^2 F16v^2 Feb 24] second foal: dam unraced: maiden pointer: runner-up in bumpers, second and better effort (fairly useful form) when beaten neck by Cooldine at Fairyhouse. *Eoghan O'Grady, Ireland*   **F102**

BALLYVOGE (IRE) 6 b.g. Presenting – Ardnurcher (IRE) (King's Ride) [2006/7 24s* 24s^4 20g^2 Mar 27] good-topped gelding: first foal: dam unraced: won both starts in Irish points: won maiden at Newcastle in November by 4 lengths from Fastaffaran: odds on, possibly pressed too far out when 4 lengths second to That's Rhythm in novice at Sedgefield, again hanging under pressure. *N. G. Richards*   **h110**

BALMORAL QUEEN 7 br.m. Wizard King – Balmoral Princess (Thethingaboutitis (USA)) [2006/7 h77: 20g 20g^p 20v^2 21d^3 24m^F 24m 22m* 20m^{pu} 22g^F 24g^{su} 22d^{ur} 20d 20v 16v^{pu} 22g 22m Apr 28] stocky mare: poor hurdler: won selling handicaps at Uttoxeter (made all) in May and Cartmel (conditional jockeys, sold from D. McCain Jnr 6,400 gns) in August: out of sorts after, sold to B. Storey after twelfth start: stays 2¾m: acts on heavy and good to firm going. *M. A. Barnes*   **h80**

BALMORAL STAR 6 b.m. Wizard King – Balmoral Princess (Thethingaboutitis (USA)) [2006/7 F–: F16s F16m Apr 15] no form in bumpers. *R. E. Peacock*   **F–**

BALOO 11 b.g. Morpeth – Moorland Nell (Neltino) [2006/7 c99, h99: 24m c21s^2 c26d^2 c21d^6 18g Mar 18] small gelding: modest handicap hurdler/chaser: stays 27f: probably acts on any going: tried tongue tied. *J. D. Frost*   **c92** **h–**

BALYAN (IRE) 6 b.g. Bahhare (USA) – Balaniya (USA) (Diesis) [2006/7 h108p: 20m^2 16g^2 18v Mar 3] smallish gelding: fairly useful on Flat: fair maiden hurdler: stays 2½m: acts on good to firm going: tried in cheekpieces. *J. Howard Johnson*   **h106**

BAMALAM 4 br.f. Hunting Lion (IRE) – Dragons Daughter (Mandrake Major) [2006/7 16g Apr 15] no form on Flat at 3 yrs or in novice hurdle. *C. R. Wilson*   **h–**

John Smith's Red Rum Handicap Chase, Aintree—
the grey Bambi de L'Orme goes two places better than in 2005 as he holds off Marshall Hall

BAMBI DE L'ORME (FR) 8 gr.g. True Brave (USA) – Princesse Ira (FR) (Less Ice) **c138**
[2006/7 c138, h–: c16d⁵ c17s² c17dᵖᵘ c16v³ c16g c16g⁵ c16g* c16m* Apr 21] big, **h–**
close-coupled gelding: useful handicap chaser: back to best when winning at Aintree
(Grade 3 John Smith's Red Rum Handicap, responded generously to beat Marshall Hall
by 1½ lengths) and Ayr (by 2 lengths from Calatagan in 4-runner event after runner-up's
mistake at last) in April: likely to stay 2½m: acts on firm and soft going: free-going sort,
usually waited with. *Ian Williams*

BAMBINO ROSSI 6 ch.m. Classic Cliche (IRE) – Leading Note (USA) (Blushing **F64**
John (USA)) [2006/7 F17m⁵ Aug 6] first foal: dam, modest hurdler, stayed 21f: shaped
like a stayer when under 25 lengths fifth to Major Comet in bumper at Market Rasen on
debut. *E. W. Tuer*

BAMBY (IRE) 7 b.m. Glacial Storm (USA) – Ardfallon (IRE) (Supreme Leader) **h–**
[2006/7 h–, F–: 19g 17s⁶ May 20] no form since debut in bumper. *R. Ford*

BANBROOK HILL (IRE) 8 b.g. Sharp Charter – Crook Lady (Croghan Hill) **c–**
[2006/7 c–: c24dᵖᵘ c20sᵖᵘ Dec 5] no form in chases: tried in cheekpieces. *G. Brown*

BANDALONE 7 ch.g. Band On The Run – Remalone (Remezzo) [2006/7 F17g Sep 23] **F–**
first foal: dam poor maiden pointer: no form in bumper or points. *R. J. Armson*

BANDEAU CHARMER 4 b.f. Band On The Run – Fair Enchantress (Enchantment) **F–**
[2006/7 F17m Apr 15] third foal: dam, 5f winner, also winning pointer: well held in
bumper on debut. *C. N. Kellett*

BAN DUBH 8 b.m. Syrtos – Hatherley (Deep Run) [2006/7 c21d^{pu} 21v^6 21s^{pu} 21d^3 21m^6 16s 21s^4 20m 21f^3 21g^4 Apr 18] sturdy mare: winning pointer: modest maiden hurdler: no show on chasing debut: stays 21f: acts on soft and firm going: inconsistent. *M. Sheppard*
c–
h87

BANG AND BLAME (IRE) 11 b.g. Be My Native (USA) – Miss Lucille (Fine Blade (USA)) [2006/7 c108, h–: c23s^{pu} c25d* c30s* c28s^4 c32v^{pu} Mar 3] tall, workmanlike gelding: fair handicap chaser: won at Catterick in December and January: stays 3¾m: acts on heavy going: makes running/races prominently: game. *M. W. Easterby*
c113
h–

BANNISTER LANE 7 b.g. Overbury (IRE) – Miss Club Royal (Avocat) [2006/7 c107, h90: c25m^4 c24g^5 c20g c23s^3 c28s^{pu} c26v* c29s* c30g Mar 31] sturdy gelding: winning hurdler: fairly useful handicap chaser: won at Uttoxeter (2-finisher event) in February and Warwick (beat Like A Bee by 4 lengths) in March: stays 29f: acts on heavy going: blinkered/in cheekpieces last 4 starts: inconsistent. *D. McCain Jnr*
c115 §
h–

BANNOW BEACH (IRE) 6 b.m. Saddlers' Hall (IRE) – Mullaghcloga (IRE) (Glacial Storm (USA)) [2006/7 F–: 19g^{pu} May 4] no form in bumpers/novice hurdle. *J. Mackie*
h–

BANNOW STRAND (IRE) 7 b.g. Luso – Bid For Fun (IRE) (Auction Ring (USA)) [2006/7 c132, h–: c21s^{pu} 24v Jan 17] big gelding: maiden hurdler: useful chaser at best: ran as if amiss last 4 outings: bred to be suited by further than 2½m: acts on soft going. *D. E. Pipe*
c–
h–

BANOGE (IRE) 5 b.g. Flemensfirth (USA) – Prove It (IRE) (Black Monday) [2006/7 F16v^3 F17v^2 Mar 18] €11,000 3-y-o: smallish gelding: third foal: dam unraced: placed both starts in bumpers, better effort when 9 lengths second to Harry Wood at Carlisle, well suited by emphasis on stamina. *L. Lungo*
F95

BANOO (IRE) 4 b.f. Hernando (FR) – Toi Toi (IRE) (In The Wings) [2006/7 aF16g^6 aF16g^4 F17g^5 Apr 19] leggy filly: fourth foal: half-sister to 2 Flat winners, including 2m winner Alani (by Benny The Dip): dam 1¾m winner who stayed 2m: fair form in bumpers. *D. W. P. Arbuthnot*
F87

BAODAI (FR) 5 b.g. Cadoudal (FR) – Royale Aube (FR) (Garde Royale) [2006/7 16g c20d c19d^3 c18v^4 c16g c20g^2 c20g* c20s Apr 25] sturdy gelding: fourth foal: half-brother to 5f to 1m winner Satchmo Bay (by Alamo Bay): dam, 14.5f winner on Flat, won at 15f over hurdles: successful in 4 juvenile events for G. Macaire in French Provinces in 2005/6, 3 over hurdles and one over fences: well held in 4-y-o handicap hurdle on British debut: fair form in handicap chases after, won at Fontwell in April: stays 2½m: raced on good ground or softer. *P. J. Hobbs*
c106
h101

BARANOOK (IRE) 6 b.g. Barathea (IRE) – Gull Nook (Mill Reef (USA)) [2006/7 h–: 19m^4 20f^{pu} Jun 3] sturdy gelding: modest maiden hurdler: tongue tied last 3 starts: dead. *B. J. Llewellyn*
h90

BARATHEA BLUE 6 ch.g. Barathea (IRE) – Empty Purse (Pennine Walk) [2006/7 h95: 19g^2 c22d^2 c22m^3 c21f^4 Jul 19] modest maiden hurdler/chaser: stays 2¾m: acts on firm and good to soft going: tongue tied. *D. E. Pipe*
c95
h95

BARBERS SHOP 5 b.g. Saddlers' Hall (IRE) – Close Harmony (Bustino) [2006/7 F101p: 16d^3 22d* 24s^2 22d^2 17g^{ur} Mar 24] tall, good-topped gelding: chasing type: bumper winner: useful form over hurdles: easily won maiden at Ascot in December: best effort when beaten ½ length by Secret Ploy in novice at Kempton next time: let down by jumping last 2 starts: stays 3m: acts on soft going. *N. J. Henderson*
h132

BARCELONA 10 b.g. Barathea (IRE) – Pipitina (Bustino) [2006/7 c–, h–: c25m^6 c20m^{ur} c23m^{pu} c21m^4 24m^{pu} c23m^{pu} Apr 22] compact gelding: winning hurdler/maiden chaser, no solid form for long time: often blinkered/in cheekpieces: tongue tied. *Lady Susan Brooke*
c–
h–

BARCHAM AGAIN (IRE) 10 b.g. Aristocracy – Dante's Thatch (IRE) (Phardante (FR)) [2006/7 c–, h–: c25f^F c24s^{ur} 22s^{pu} 22v c20d^{pu} 24d Jan 19] good-topped gelding: maiden hurdler: winning chaser around 3m: no form since 2004: wears headgear. *Mrs C. J. Kerr*
c–
h–

BARCLAY BOY 8 b.g. Terimon – Nothings Forever (Oats) [2006/7 h101: 21m^2 21d^F 21m c24s^{pu} c22s^{pu} 22g^{pu} Mar 19] good-topped gelding: maiden hurdler: disappointing in 2006/7, including over fences: stays 21f: acts on heavy and good to firm going. *R. M. Stronge*
c–
h86

BARELLA (IRE) 8 b.g. Barathea (IRE) – Daniella Drive (USA) (Shelter Half (USA)) [2006/7 c?, h93: 20s 17d* 17g^{pu} Apr 7] modest hurdler: won seller at Newton Abbot in
c–
h78

June: bled when next seen 10 months later: fell both starts over fences: raced mainly around 2m: acts on good to soft ground: often wears headgear (cheekpieces for both wins). *L. Corcoran*

BAREME (FR) 8 b.g. Homme de Loi (IRE) – Roxa (FR) (Kenmare (FR)) [2006/7 c22vF c20vpu c16v c20vF c24spu Apr 25] rangy, useful-looking gelding: lightly-raced winning 2m hurdler for N. Henderson: bought 600 gns Doncaster August Sales: completed only once from 5 starts over fences, third when falling 2 out in maiden at Ayr won by First Look fourth one: raced on going softer than good. *W. S. Coltherd* **c98 h–**

BARFLEUR (IRE) 7 b.m. Anshan – Lulu Buck (Buckskin (FR)) [2006/7 h–, F–: 22g* 22d4 22m3 22m3 19m3 Apr 22] medium-sized mare: modest hurdler: won novice at Uttoxeter in May: stays 2¾m: acts on good to soft and good to firm going. *P. Bowen* **h92**

BARGAIN HUNT (IRE) 6 b.g. Foxhound (USA) – Atisayin (USA) (Al Nasr (FR)) [2006/7 h86§: 16g 16g* 16g6 17d4 20gur 20f3 20f3 17m3 18mF Oct 1] smallish gelding: poor hurdler: won selling handicap at Hexham in May: stays 2½m, at least when emphasis is on speed: acts on firm and soft going: ran out once. *W. Storey* **h84**

BAR GAYNE (IRE) 8 ch.g. Good Thyne (USA) – Annie's Alkali (Strong Gale) [2006/7 c89, h91: c21dur May 21] modest hurdler: similar form over fences, though makes mistakes and completed only once from 4 starts: stays 3¼m: raced on good going or softer: sold 9,000 gns Doncaster May (2006) Sales. *T. R. George* **c– x h–**

BARILOCHE 4 b.c. Benny The Dip (USA) – Bella Lambada (Lammtarra (USA)) [2006/7 Aug 26] fair 1½m winner on Flat, has become temperamental: visored, never travelling/jumping with much fluency on hurdling debut. *J. R. Boyle* **h–**

BARMAN (USA) 8 ch.g. Atticus (USA) – Blue Tip (FR) (Tip Moss (FR)) [2006/7 16g 17s4 18s5 16d4 16v3 16v5 Jan 11] workmanlike gelding: modest maiden hurdler: will probably stay 2½m: raced on good going or softer: tried tongue tied. *Eric McNamara, Ireland* **h99**

BARNARDS GREEN (IRE) 9 ch.g. Florida Son – Pearly Castle (IRE) (Carlingford Castle) [2006/7 c–§, h–§: 22mpu May 5] lengthy gelding: maiden hurdler: poor chaser: stays 2½m: acts on good to soft and good to firm going: often wears headgear: ungenuine. *M. Madgwick* **c– § h– §**

BARNBROOK EMPIRE (IRE) 5 b.m. Second Empire (IRE) – Home Comforts (Most Welcome) [2006/7 h88: 19d* 24spu 22m6 Sep 10] rather sparely-made mare: modest at best over hurdles: won seller at Newton Abbot in August: let down by jumping after: stays 19f: acts on good to soft going. *L. A. Dace* **h78 x**

BARNEY (IRE) 6 b.g. Basanta (IRE) – Double Or Nothing (IRE) (Doubletour (USA)) [2006/7 c–, h–, F–: 21d* 16m 17m* 17g 17m 18mpu 16d2 20s 18v 17s5 17m4 c16g2 Apr 23] tall gelding: modest handicap hurdler: won at Sedgefield in May (novice) and June: poor form on second of 2 outings over fences: stays 21f: acts on good to firm and good to soft going, below form on softer: has had tongue tied, including when successful. *Mrs E. Slack* **c73 h84**

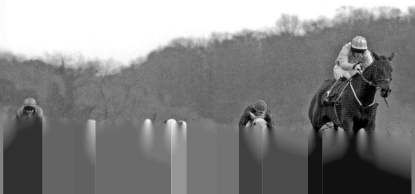

John Smith's Midlands Grand National Chase (Handicap), Uttoxeter—
Baron Windrush and new jockey Jason Maguire have the measure of outsider D'Argent (grey) two out

BARNEY'S DREAM (IRE) 4 b.g. Orpen (USA) – Guama Lass (IRE) (Krayyan) **h96 +**
[2006/7 16v⁴ 16v⁴ 16v⁴ 16v* Mar 22] strong gelding: brother to fair hurdler Orpen
Guama, stays 2½m: fair on Flat (stays 9f), successful in October: modest form over
hurdles: left M. Halford, won 5-runner novice at Ayr by 7 lengths from Idarah: raced at
2m on heavy going: wore cheekpieces third start. *Grant Tuer*

BARNEYS JOY 8 ch.g. Keen – Tullow Lady (IRE) (Mazaad) [2006/7 F–: 20sᵖᵘ 17v **h–**
Feb 20] good-topped gelding: no sign of ability. *C. W. Thornton*

BARNEYS LUCK (IRE) 6 b.g. Pasternak – Half Irish (Carlingford Castle) [2006/7 **c–**
F16m 17d⁵ 17d 20s⁶ c16sᵖᵘ 20g Mar 17] sturdy gelding: second foal: half-brother to fairly **h69 +**
useful hurdler What A Scientist (by Karinga Bay), stays 3m: dam unraced out of **F–**
half-sister to Desert Orchid: well beaten in bumper: poor form over hurdles: never
dangerous on chasing debut: bred to stay 3m. *R. C. Guest*

BARNEYS LYRIC 7 ch.g. Hector Protector (USA) – Anchorage (IRE) (Slip Anchor) **c– §**
[2006/7 24g⁴ 16g 20s Apr 26] strong gelding: fairly useful hurdler: fit from points (in **h117 §**
frame all 4 completed starts), easily best effort in 2006/7 when fourth to Ice Tea in
handicap at Newcastle: downed tools final outing: stays 3m: acts on heavy going: one to
treat with caution. *M. W. Easterby*

BARNEYS MATE 7 ch.g. Sir Harry Lewis (USA) – Welsh Clover (Cruise Missile) **h–**
[2006/7 22vᵖᵘ 26gᵖᵘ Apr 11] tall, close-coupled gelding: winning pointer: no form over
hurdles: tried blinkered. *S. Donohoe, Ireland*

BARNEYS REFLECTION 7 b.g. Petoski – Annaberg (IRE) (Tirol) [2006/7 c75d, **c–**
h–: c20gᵘʳ 16gᵖᵘ 24m 17gᵖᵘ 18m 26gᵖᵘ 17d Oct 26] close-coupled gelding: winning **h–**
hurdler: maiden chaser: no form since 2005, left A. Crook after third start: finished alone
in point in February: wears headgear. *J. L. Flint*

BARODINE 4 ch.g. Barathea (IRE) – Granted (FR) (Cadeaux Genereux) [2006/7 17s **h91**
17g 16f³ Apr 22] fairly useful on Flat (stays 1½m), successful in May, sold out of
H. Cecil's stable 38,000 gns Newmarket Autumn Sales and gelded: best effort (modest
form) over hurdles when third to Artadi in novice at Wincanton. *R. J. Hodges*

BARON BLITZKRIEG 9 b.g. Sir Harry Lewis (USA) – Steel Typhoon (General **c86 §**
Ironside) [2006/7 c76, h72: c21mᵖᵘ c19sᶠ c19d⁵ c21d² c19s c20v² c20s⁶ c24s⁴ Feb 16] **h– §**
workmanlike gelding: maiden hurdler: modest handicap chaser: stays 2¾m: acts on
heavy going: unreliable. *D. J. Wintle*

BARON DE FEYPO (IRE) 9 b.g. Simply Great (FR) – Fete Champetre (Welsh **c118**
Pageant) [2006/7 c123, h124: c20s⁴ 20s c23s⁶ c17v⁴ c20v⁵ 20v⁶ c17s 16v³ c19v* 16dᵇᵈ **h132**
19v³ c19s⁵ c16s³ 20v² c20v³ 21g³ 17g Mar 16] angular gelding: useful hurdler: improved
form when 8 lengths third of 28 to Burntoakboy in Coral Cup (Handicap) at Cheltenham
penultimate start: again ridden more prominently than usual and far from discredited
when twelfth of 28 to Pedrobob in County Hurdle (Handicap) there 2 days later: fairly
useful chaser: won novice at Naas in January by 3 lengths from Snowy Morning:
mistakes next 2 starts over fences: stays 21f: acts on heavy going: tried in cheekpieces/
blinkers. *Patrick O. Brady, Ireland*

BARON MONTY (IRE) 9 b.g. Supreme Leader – Lady Shoco (Montekin) [2006/7 **c114**
c–, h–: c25sᵖᵘ c21v² c20v² c20s c25s² c25v* Mar 9] workmanlike gelding: traces of stringhalt: **h–**
fairly useful hurdler in 2004/5: fair form over fences: didn't need to be at best to win
maiden at Ayr by length from Theboyfrombulawayo: stays 25f: raced on good ground or
softer (acts on heavy): in cheekpieces last 2 starts: often races prominently. *C. Grant*

BARON ROMEO (IRE) 7 gr.g. Baron Blakeney – Langretta (IRE) (Lancastrian) **h89**
[2006/7 h86, F107: 25s⁴ Oct 15] big, lengthy gelding: point/bumper winner: modest form
over hurdles: will prove suited by test of stamina: jumps none too fluently. *R. T. Phillips*

BARONS KNIGHT 6 ch.g. Lahib (USA) – Red Barons Lady (IRE) (Electric) [2006/7 **h–**
h–, F–: 16f 17d May 24] tall gelding: no form in bumpers/over hurdles: tongue tied in
2006/7. *M. A. Barnes*

BARON WINDRUSH 9 b.g. Alderbrook – Dame Scarlet (Blakeney) [2006/7 c140, **c145**
h–: c27dᵖᵘ c24sᵖᵘ c29s⁵ c32sᵖᵘ c29v* c33s* Mar 17] tall, strong gelding: useful handicap **h–**
chaser: back to best last 2 starts, winning 6-runner event at Warwick (easily) in February
and 18-runner John Smith's Midlands Grand National at Uttoxeter following month:
travelled and jumped with zest when beating D'Argent by 12 lengths at latter, leading 5
out and clear from next: stays 33f: acts on heavy going: tried blinkered: often makes
mistakes. *N. A. Twiston-Davies*

BARRACAT (IRE) 10 b.g. Good Thyne (USA) – Helens Fashion (IRE) (Over The River (FR)) [2006/7 20d 17s⁴ c20g* c20dF c24d* c20dᵖᵘ 20g* 20g³ Apr 3] smallish gelding: modest chaser/hurdler: won novice handicaps over fences at Musselburgh in November and December, and similar event over hurdles at Newcastle in March: stays 3m: best efforts on good/good to soft ground: tends to jump left over fences. *W. T. Reed* **c90 x h85**

BARRANCO (IRE) 6 b.g. Sadler's Wells (USA) – Belize Tropical (IRE) (Baillamont (USA)) [2006/7 h79: 21g 18v 19d⁶ Mar 21] compact gelding: poor hurdler: well held in handicaps in 2006/7: stays 2½m: acts on soft and good to firm going: usually blinkered. *G. L. Moore* **h–**

BARREN LANDS 12 b.g. Green Desert (USA) – Current Raiser (Filiberto (USA)) [2006/7 c108, h–: c18m² c22f² c24m² c20m* c23g⁶ c23f* Aug 22] compact gelding: fair handicap chaser: back in form early in season, winning at Fontwell and Worcester (twice): stays 3m: acts on any going: often makes running. *K. Bishop* **c110 h–**

BARRONS PIKE 8 ch.g. Jumbo Hirt (USA) – Bromley Rose (Rubor) [2006/7 c84, h–: c25f⁵ c25g⁵ c27sᵖᵘ c24g c25v³ c25vᵘʳ c20vᵘʳ c20vᵖᵘ Mar 15] lengthy gelding: maiden chaser, no form in 2006/7: tried in cheekpieces/blinkers: sold 2,800 gns Doncaster May Sales. *B. Storey* **c– h–**

BARROW DRIVE 11 b.g. Gunner B – Fille de Soleil (Sunyboy) [2006/7 c141, h117: c19vᵘʳ c24dᵖᵘ c22s³ 22s³ c27dᵖᵘ Nov 11] sturdy gelding: winning hurdler: useful chaser: not at best in first half of season: stays 25f, effective at much shorter: probably acts on any going: effective in cheekpieces or without: usually tongue tied: often races prominently. *Anthony Mullins, Ireland* **c126 h124**

BARRSHAN (IRE) 8 b.g. Anshan – Bula Beag (IRE) (Brush Aside (USA)) [2006/7 c–: 16d⁴ 16g 16g 20m 16d 18s Mar 25] good-topped gelding: failed to complete all 3 starts in chases: no solid form over hurdles: wore cheekpieces/blinkers last 5 starts: tongue tied. *J. K. Magee, Ireland* **c– h–**

BARRY THE CRACKER 4 gr.g. Baryshnikov (AUS) – Kins Token (Relkino) [2006/7 F16s 17vᵖᵘ Feb 20] unfurnished gelding: half-brother to 3 winning chasers, including fairly useful but unreliable Kings Brook (by Alderbrook), stays 2¾m: dam unraced: no show in bumper and novice hurdle. *J. Howard Johnson* **h– F–**

BARTERCARD (USA) 6 b.g. Sir Cat (USA) – Pure Misk (Rainbow Quest (USA)) [2006/7 F77: F18g* 16m³ 16vᵖᵘ Jan 7] medium-sized gelding: fair form in bumpers, won at Plumpton in May by 1¼ lengths from Or Sing About: 7¾ lengths third to The Rocking Dock in novice at Stratford on completed outing over hurdles: likely to need emphasis on speed around 2m. *C. J. Mann* **h91 F92**

BARTON BANDIT 11 ch.g. Sula Bula – Yamrah (Milford) [2006/7 c–, h–: c16g c20m c17sᵖᵘ May 26] medium-sized gelding: no longer of any account: tried in cheekpieces/blinkers: often tongue tied. *Miss Sarah Kent* **c– h–**

BARTON BEAU (IRE) 8 b.g. Kylian (USA) – Hetty Green (Bay Express) [2006/7 22sᵖᵘ 16v Feb 12] sturdy gelding: winning 2m hurdler: off 2 years, no show both starts in 2006/7: usually blinkered. *Miss A. M. Newton-Smith* **h–**

BARTON BELLE 5 b.m. Barathea (IRE) – Veronica (Persian Bold) [2006/7 F100: F16v² F17d* 16s⁶ 16g⁶ 16m⁵ Apr 24] big, lengthy mare: fairly useful form in bumpers, winning at Southwell in June by 12 lengths from Red Scally: sold out of G. A. Swinbank's stable 28,000 gns Doncaster October Sales: little impact in 3 starts over hurdles. *C. N. Kellett* **h– F104**

BARTON DREAM (IRE) 11 b.g. Le Bavard (FR) – Tax Dream (IRE) (Electric) [2006/7 24m⁶ 20f⁴ 24m⁴ Aug 1] winning pointer: poor maiden hurdler: stays 3m: acts on firm going: wore cheekpieces in 2006/7. *Tim Vaughan* **h79**

BARTON FLOWER 6 br.m. Danzero (AUS) – Iota (Niniski (USA)) [2006/7 h104: c19g* c17f² 17s* 16g* Aug 26] workmanlike mare: fair hurdler: won mares novice at Market Rasen in August: better form over fences, winning novice handicap at Hereford in May and novice at Newton Abbot (beat Cream Cracker 1¾ lengths with something in hand) in August: will stay 2½m: raced mainly on good ground or softer: reliable. *D. P. Keane* **c115 + h104**

BARTON GATE 9 b.g. Rock Hopper – Ruth's River (Young Man (FR)) [2006/7 c–, h96: 18s Dec 5] tall, close-coupled gelding: modest hurdler, well held only start in 2006/7: similar form on first of 2 completed outings over fences: best efforts at 2m: acts on heavy going: blinkered/visored. *D. P. Keane* **c– h–**

BARTON HILL 10 b.g. Nicholas Bill – Home From The Hill (IRE) (Jareer (USA)) [2006/7 c101, h–: c16g⁵ May 6] leggy gelding: fair chaser at best: won point in April: stays 21f: acts on heavy going: blinkered: held up. *D. P. Keane*   c– h81

BARTON LEGEND 7 b.g. Midnight Legend – Home From The Hill (IRE) (Jareer (USA)) [2006/7 h117: c21v⁵ c18sᵖᵘ c22sᵘʳ 24s c22vᵖᵘ c20gᵖᵘ Mar 14] tall, close-coupled, good-topped gelding: fair form over hurdles, folded tamely fourth start: similar form on chasing debut, failed to complete all 4 outings over fences after: stays 21f: acts on heavy going: blinkered last 4 starts. *D. P. Keane*   c107 d h–

BARTON NIC 14 b.g. Nicholas Bill – Dutch Majesty (Homing) [2006/7 h119, h–: c19sᵖᵘ c24sᵖᵘ c19sᵖᵘ Dec 27] workmanlike gelding: fairly useful hurdler/chaser at best: badly out of sorts in 2006/7: best form at 2m to 2½m: acts on heavy going: wears head-gear. *D. P. Keane*   c– h–

BARTON PARK 7 b.g. Most Welcome – William's Bird (USA) (Master Willie) [2006/7 c95, h92: c17m³ c19mᵖᵘ c16gᵖᵘ c16m* c16g³ Jul 21] tall gelding: winning hurdler: better form over fences, winning handicap at Uttoxeter in July: fortunate to follow up at Southwell 10 days later, held in third when left clear 2 out: raced mainly at 2m: acts on good to firm going: tongue tied nowadays: held up (has pulled hard). *D. P. Keane*   c107 h–

BARTON SUN (IRE) 8 b.g. Indian Ridge – Sun Screen (Caerleon) (USA) [2006/7 h75: 16v⁶ c25d³ c20v² c16s* c16s⁴ c16gᵘʳ c16s⁶ Apr 1] good-topped gelding: maiden hurdler: modest chaser: won novice handicap at Newcastle in January: likely to prove best up to 2½m: raced on good going or softer. *Ferdy Murphy*   c88 h–

BARUM BELLE 7 b.m. Thowra (FR) – La Belle Shyanne (Shy Groom (USA)) [2006/7 h–: 20dᵖᵘ 19m 16m 17g Nov 9] no form: wore headgear last 3 starts: tongue tied. *R. A. Farrant*   h–

BASIC FACT (IRE) 5 b.g. Rudimentary (USA) – Native Emma (IRE) (Be My Native (USA)) [2006/7 F86: F14g³ 16m² 17d² 17g c20sᵖᵘ 21s³ 20s* 16d² 21sᵖᵘ 22d Mar 26] tall, unfurnished gelding: in frame in bumpers: fair hurdler, won novice handicap at Huntingdon in January: jumped poorly on chasing debut: stays 21f: acts on soft and good to firm ground: blinkered last 4 starts. *Jonjo O'Neill*   c– h104 F90

BASINET 9 b.g. Alzao (USA) – Valiancy (Grundy) [2006/7 h82+: 16f² 16d³ 16d³ 16g⁵ Dec 10] compact gelding: modest handicap hurdler: best around 2m: acts on firm and good to soft going: tried in cheekpieces (successful in headgear on Flat): takes good hold. *J. J. Quinn*   h97

BATCHELOR BOYS (IRE) 11 b.g. Accordion – Polly Fort (Pollerton) [2006/7 c20v² c21s⁴ May 29] ex-Irish gelding: winning pointer: easily best effort in hunters when second to Spring Margot over 2½m at Perth. *W. F. Kerr*   c99

BATCHWORTH BEAU 6 ch.g. Bluegrass Prince (IRE) – Batchworth Belle (Interrex (CAN)) [2006/7 16f 16d 16m⁶ 16d* 17g³ 17vᵖᵘ Nov 27] no form on Flat: poor over hurdles: won novice claimer at Plumpton in October: raced around 2m: acts on good to soft ground. *A. M. Hales*   h78

BATCHWORTH LOCK 9 b.g. Beveled (USA) – Treasurebound (Beldale Flutter (USA)) [2006/7 c25d⁵ c24g³ Apr 27] winning pointer, placed in 2007: better effort in hunters when third to Kilbreena in novice at Chepstow. *Paul Williams*   c78

BATHWICK EMMA (IRE) 4 ch.f. Raise A Grand (IRE) – Lindas Delight (Bats-hoof) [2006/7 17mᵖ Sep 28] fair at best on Flat (stays 1m), successful in January: well held in juvenile on hurdling debut: joined M. Doyle. *P. D. Evans*   h–

BATHWICK LUCY (IRE) 7 b.m. Oscar (IRE) – Protrial (Proverb) [2006/7 F17v⁵ 22v⁴ 24d Mar 22] half-sister to fairly useful hunter chaser Glacial Trial and modest hurdler up to 3m Lizzie Bathwick (both by Glacial Storm) and fair staying chaser Nativetrial (by Be My Native): dam winning pointer: in frame both completed starts in maiden Irish points in 2006: well held in mares bumper/novice hurdles: tried tongue tied. *J. G. Portman*   h– F–

BATHWICK ROX (IRE) 4 b.g. Carrowkeel (IRE) – Byproxy (IRE) (Mujtahid (USA)) [2006/7 16m⁶ 16g 16d⁴ 16d³ 16sᵖᵘ 16dᵖᵘ Mar 22] modest maiden at best on Flat, lightly raced since 2 yrs: poor form over hurdles: lame final outing: wore cheekpieces after debut. *P. D. Evans*   h72

BATHWICK SHANNON (IRE) 6 ch.m. Anshan – Glacier Lilly (IRE) (Glacial Storm (USA)) [2006/7 F16g 16gᵖᵘ 19d 19s 24vᵖᵘ 26gᵖᵘ Apr 20] €7,500 4-y-o: first foal: dam unraced half-sister to fairly useful staying hurdlers Ask The Gatherer and Jeremy Cuddle Duck: no form in bumper or over hurdles. *J. G. Portman*   h– F–

BATOKA (UAE) 6 b.g. Hennessy (USA) – Zambezi (USA) (Rahy (USA)) [2006/7 h–
17f⁵ 20sᵖᵘ Aug 19] poor form in bumper on debut: left G. Harker and off 20 months, no
show in 2 starts over hurdles. *J. M. Saville*

BATSWING 12 b.g. Batshoof – Magic Milly (Simply Great (FR)) [2006/7 c–§, h–§: c– §
16d⁴ 18m⁵ 18m³ Jun 6] lengthy gelding: fairly useful chaser at best: winning hurdler, just h88 §
modest form early in 2006/7: barely stays 21f: acts on heavy and good to firm going: tried
in cheekpieces/blinkers: has had tongue tied: ungenuine. *G. L. Moore*

BATTLECRY 6 b. or br.g. Accordion – Miss Orchestra (IRE) (Orchestra) [2006/7 h123
F16d* F16d³ 17sꟳ 21dᵖᵘ 21s² 21g 24gᵖᵘ Apr 13] 20,000 3-y-o, €1,200 4-y-o: good- F106
topped gelding: first foal: dam fairly useful staying chaser (won Midlands Grand
National): made virtually all in bumper at Worcester on debut in October, winning by 22
lengths from Adare Prince, despite hanging left: creditable 10 lengths third to Cork All
Star in listed event at Cheltenham next time: fairly useful form in novice hurdles: 4
lengths second of 15 to Duc de Regniere at Kempton: very stiff tasks last 2 starts: stays
21f: raced on good ground or softer. *N. A. Twiston-Davies*

BATTLEFIELD 7 b.g. Overbury (IRE) – Tapua Taranata (IRE) (Mandalus) [2006/7 c78 x
20g c22vᵖᵘ c20s⁶ c19s⁶ c16m c16v⁶ c20d³ c24m⁶ Apr 14] 34,000 4-y-o: tall, good-topped h–
gelding: half-brother to winning 3m chaser Co Optimist and winning 2m hurdler Gentle
Beau (both by Homo Sapien): dam unraced: fell both starts in Irish points: well held in
maiden/novice hurdles: maiden chaser: sold out of M. Morris' stable 7,000 gns Doncaster
May Sales, just poor form in 2006/7: seems barely to stay 3m: acts on soft and good to
firm going: tried in cheekpieces: poor jumper. *R. Lee*

BATTLE STATIONS 6 ch.g. Classic Cliche (IRE) – Lady Padivor (IRE) (Zaffaran F89 ?
(USA)) [2006/7 F16d⁵ Nov 11] first foal: dam dual bumper winner: 6¼ lengths fifth
to Johnny Bissett in slowly-run bumper at Uttoxeter on debut, making lot of running.
R. Ford

BATTO 7 b.g. Slip Anchor – Frog (Akarad (FR)) [2006/7 c–, h–: c25gᵖᵘ May 13] poor c–
form at best over hurdles: failed to complete both starts over fences. *G. M. Moore* h–

BAUHAUS (IRE) 6 b.g. Second Empire (IRE) – Hi Bettina (Henbit (USA)) [2006/7 h97
h97: 16g² 16f² 16v⁶ 21s 16g² Apr 27] lengthy gelding: fairly useful 1½m winner on Flat:
modest maiden hurdler: raced mainly around 2m: acts on firm and soft going: tried in
cheekpieces. *R. T. Phillips*

BAWN BOY (NZ) 8 gr.g. Haayil (AUS) – Lissom (NZ) (Bellissimo (FR)) [2006/7 16d h99
16g 17s⁶ 16g² Mar 14] lengthy gelding: ran 5 times in maidens on Flat in New Zealand:
best effort over hurdles (modest form) when second at Huntingdon on handicap debut:
raced around 2m: acts on soft going. *Andrew Turnell*

BAYADERE (GER) 7 b.m. Lavirco (GER) – Brangane (IRE) (Anita's Prince) [2006/7 c–
c93, h78: 20mᵖᵘ Apr 25] poor hurdler, off 12 months prior to return: successful on h–
completed outing over fences: stays 2½m: acts on good to firm and good to soft going.
K. F. Clutterbuck

BAYAZID (IRE) 5 b.g. Grand Lodge (USA) – Bayrika (IRE) (Kahyasi) [2006/7 c– x
h91x: c16vᵖᵘ Nov 22] good-topped gelding: let down by jumping over hurdles (for h– x
N. Henderson) and on chasing debut (breathing problem): tried blinkered: dead. *Evan
Williams*

BAYCLIFFE ROSE 8 b.m. Karinga Bay – Bolt Hole (Laggards Lane) [2006/7 24s³ h82 p
May 20] fourth foal: dam, winning hurdler/chaser, stayed 3¼m: left with too much to do
when 14 lengths third to Corrib Eclipse in novice hurdle at Worcester on debut: looked
sure to improve, but not seen out again. *C. J. Mann*

BAYFORD BOY 7 b.g. Miner's Lamp – Emma's Vision (IRE) (Vision (USA)) [2006/7 h–
h–: 16s Jan 20] no form over hurdles, left K. Bishop prior to only outing in 2006/7: tried
tongue tied. *P. R. Rodford*

BAY HAWK 5 b.g. Alhaarth (IRE) – Fleeting Vision (IRE) (Vision (USA)) [2006/7 h75: h95
16m⁶ 18g³ 19m² 21gᵖᵘ Oct 19] fair on Flat (should be suited by 1¾m+), successful in
November: modest maiden hurdler: stays 19f: acts on good to firm ground: has reportedly
had breathing problems. *B. G. Powell*

BAY ISLAND (IRE) 11 b. or br.g. Treasure Hunter – Wild Deer (Royal Buck) [2006/7 c101
c101, h–: c22gᵖᵘ c22v⁴ c20d⁵ Dec 28] tall gelding: has had breathing operation: fair h–
handicap chaser: won at Towcester in November: stays 3¼m: acts on heavy and good to
firm going: in cheekpieces last 7 starts: usually tongue tied: often front runner: tends to
jump right. *Carl Llewellyn*

BAYLOCK BOY (IRE) 6 b. or br.g. Accordion – She Insists (IRE) (Executive Perk) **h84**
[2006/7 20d⁶ 19g⁴ 22sᵖᵘ 22g⁴ Mar 18] first foal: dam, winning pointer, out of half-sister
to smart chaser up to 25f Sparky Gayle: well held in maiden Irish point: poor form over
hurdles: stays 2¾m. *John R. Upson*

BAY OF KINSALE (IRE) 7 b.g. Anshan – Gale Spring (IRE) (Strong Gale) [2006/7 **c–**
c23m⁶ Apr 22] pulled up in point in 2005: tongue tied, possibly amiss on chasing debut.
C. E. Longsdon

BAYSIDE 6 ch.g. Docksider (USA) – Sister Sophie (USA) (Effervescing (USA)) **h82**
[2006/7 16s 16sᵘʳ 19g 16v⁴ 20d 16s² 19g⁴ Feb 2] compact gelding: bumper winner: poor
hurdler, off nearly 20 months prior to return: stays 19f: raced on good ground or softer:
tried tongue tied: sold 4,000 gns Doncaster March Sales. *K. G. Reveley*

BAY SOLITAIRE 6 b.g. Charnwood Forest (IRE) – Golden Wings (USA) (Devil's **h88 ?**
Bag (USA)) [2006/7 20s³ 20sᵖᵘ Nov 6] lengthy, useful-looking gelding: modest maiden
hurdler, off nearly 2 years prior to return. *T. D. Easterby*

BAY SWIFT (IRE) 7 b.g. Norwich – Arrogant Miss (King's Ride) [2006/7 16fᶠ 17d⁶ **h–**
20mᵖᵘ Nov 24] seventh foal: dam unraced: travelling strongly when falling 3 out in
maiden hurdle at Kelso on debut: no show 2 starts after: dead. *N. G. Richards*

BAYTOWN LULU 4 b.f. Timeless Times (USA) – Judys Girl (IRE) (Simply Great **h–**
(FR)) [2006/7 16mᵖᵘ Sep 2] modest on Flat (stays 6f), well held in 2006: no show in
juvenile on hurdling debut. *H. S. Howe*

BDELLIUM 9 b.m. Royal Vulcan – Kelly's Logic (Netherkelly) [2006/7 c–, h–: 24s² **c–**
27s⁶ 26sᵖᵘ 25v 24vᵖᵘ c24g⁶ c26g⁶ Mar 26] sturdy mare: maiden chaser: poor hurdler: no **h77 d**
form after reappearance: stays 3¼m: acts on soft and good to firm going: tried visored.
B. I. Case

BEACHCOMBER BAY (IRE) 12 ch.g. Un Desperado (FR) – Beachcomber Lass **c114**
(Day Is Done) [2006/7 c114, h–: c24v² c21g Apr 12] lengthy gelding: useful hunter **h–**
chaser: better effort in 2006/7 when length second to Don't Be Daft at Gowran in March
(would have won if asked for effort earlier): stays 25f: acts on heavy going: tried
blinkered: often let down by jumping. *I. J. Keeling, Ireland*

BEACON RAMBLER 5 ch.g. Cayman Kai (IRE) – Bunty's Friend (Highlands) **h–**
[2006/7 17m Sep 26] no sign of ability on Flat or on hurdling debut. *F. Watson*

BEACON WHITE 10 b.g. Homo Sapien – Sally Ho (Gildoran) [2006/7 c21gᵖᵘ **c–**
May 24] poor maiden pointer: tongue tied on chase debut. *Mrs Z. E. Pennells*

BEAMISH PRINCE 8 ch.g. Bijou d'Inde – Unconditional Love (Polish Patriot **c–**
(USA)) [2006/7 c–, h–: c16s c20d⁴ c16v⁵ c20sᶠ 16s* 20g c16s⁵ Apr 1] leggy gelding: **h96 +**
maiden chaser: modest hurdler nowadays: won seller at Catterick in March: left
G. M. Moore after next start: best around 2m: acts on heavy and good to firm going: has
bled from nose. *Mrs S. A. Watt*

BEARAWAY (IRE) 10 b.g. Fourstars Allstar (USA) – Cruiseaway (Torus) [2006/7 **c115**
c101§, h–: c16g* c17g c16m* c16f² c16mᵖᵘ Jul 2] useful-looking gelding: winning **h–**
hurdler: fairly useful handicap chaser: left Heather Dalton and off 6 months, improved
form when winning at Uttoxeter in May and Newton Abbot (beat Kings Brook by 7
lengths) in June: stays 19f: acts on firm and good to soft going: tried in cheekpieces:
several tongue tied: has shaped as if amiss on several occasions. *D. McCain Jnr*

BEARE NECESSITIES (IRE) 8 ch.g. Presenting – Lady Laburnum (Carlingford **h105**
Castle) [2006/7 h103: 20g 22s³ 24v³ 24d⁴ 24v⁴ Mar 3] medium-sized gelding: fair
hurdler: generally good efforts in frame in handicaps in 2006/7: stays 3m: acts on heavy
going: tried in cheekpieces. *M. J. Hogan*

BEAT THE BANDITS 4 ch.g. Double Trigger (IRE) – Juno Beach (Jupiter Island) **F–**
[2006/7 F13d Oct 17] first foal: dam successful in 13.5f bumper and over 1¾m on Flat:
well held in 3-y-o bumper on debut. *G. R. I. Smyly*

BEAT THE BOYS (IRE) 6 gr.g. Portrait Gallery (IRE) – Portia's Delight (IRE) (The **h97**
Parson) [2006/7 F90: 21g⁴ 20v 24g 21d Mar 22] workmanlike gelding: chasing type:
modest form over hurdles: should stay 3m. *N. A. Twiston-Davies*

BEAT THE HEAT (IRE) 9 b.g. Salse (USA) – Summer Trysting (USA) (Alleged **c105**
(USA)) [2006/7 c107, h–: c20g³ c24mᵖᵘ 22mᵖᵘ Jul 27] angular gelding: winning hurdler: **h–**
fair handicap chaser: stays 2¾m: acts on heavy and good to firm going: usually blinkered/
in cheekpieces: tried tongue tied: held up. *Jedd O'Keeffe*

BEAU ARTISTE 7 ch.g. Peintre Celebre (USA) – Belle Esprit (Warning) [2006/7 20g⁴ **h–** Sep 6] fair novice hurdler in 2004/5 for J. Howard Johnson: off 14 months, well held only start in 2006/7: raced mainly around 2m: tried in blinkers/cheekpieces. *W. B. Stone*

BEAUCHAMP ORACLE 10 gr.g. Mystiko (USA) – Beauchamp Cactus (Niniski **c109** (USA)) [2006/7 c96: c25g* c24m* c26gᵘʳ c24gᵖᵘ c26g³ c24g³ Apr 21] lengthy gelding: fairly useful hunter chaser: won at Cheltenham and Huntingdon (nearly ran out flat) in early-2006/7: stays 25f: acts on firm and soft going. *S. Flook*

BEAUCHAMP PRINCE (IRE) 6 gr.g. Beauchamp King – Katie Baggage (IRE) **c100 x** (Brush Aside (USA)) [2006/7 c110, h–: c25dᶠ c28sᵖᵘ c24g c24v⁴ c24dᵖᵘ c24vᶠ **h–** c24d c23m* Apr 15] tall gelding: fair handicap chaser: back to form when winning at Worcester in April: stays 3m: acts on heavy and good to firm going: tried tongue tied: often let down by jumping. *M. Scudamore*

BEAUCHAMP QUEST 8 b.g. Pharly (FR) – Beauchamp Kate (Petoski) [2006/7 **h–** 16mᵖᵘ Aug 22] smallish gelding: no sign of ability: tried tongue tied/blinkered (hung badly): sold 800 gns Doncaster October Sales. *Mike Lurcock*

BEAUCHAMP STAR 6 ch.m. Pharly (FR) – Beauchamp Cactus (Niniski (USA)) **h100** [2006/7 h94: 16s² 16s 20d⁴ 18s² 20d⁵ 18v 16g* 16g⁴ 18g² Apr 10] compact mare: fair hurdler: won ladies handicap at Huntingdon in March: likely to prove best around 2m: acts on soft and good to firm ground: has been let down by jumping. *N. B. King*

BEAUCHAMP TRUMP 5 b.g. Pharly (FR) – Beauchamp Kate (Petoski) [2006/7 h–: **h–** 19dᵖᵘ 16s⁴ 16s Dec 8] smallish gelding: fair on Flat (stays 2¼m), left G. Butler after final start in June: no form over hurdles: tried tongue tied/blinkered. *Tim Vaughan*

BEAUCHAMP TWIST 5 b.m. Pharly (FR) – Beauchamp Cactus (Niniski (USA)) **h–** [2006/7 h–: 16d 20dᵇᵈ 19v⁵ 16v 21g⁵ Apr 23] rather leggy mare: no solid form over hurdles: tried blinkered. *M. R. Hoad*

BEAUCHAMP UNIQUE 4 b.f. Compton Admiral – Beauchamp Jade (Kalaglow) **h–** [2006/7 17m⁶ 17gᵖᵘ Sep 8] fair on Flat (stays 1¼m), claimed from G. Butler £6,000 in July: no show in juvenile hurdles: tried in eyeshields: joined R. Simpson. *James Moffatt*

BEAUCHAMP UNITED 4 b.g. Compton Admiral – Beauchamp Kate (Petoski) **h–** [2006/7 17mᵖᵘ 17d³ 16fᶠ 17dᶠ Nov 23] disappointing maiden on Flat for G. Butler/ B. Palling: well beaten on completed outing in juvenile hurdles: blinkered after debut: also usually tongue tied: sold 600 gns Doncaster January Sales. *Tim Vaughan*

BEAU COUP 10 b.g. Toulon – Energance (IRE) (Salmon Leap (USA)) [2006/7 c–, h–: **c–** 22m 24g 24d⁴ Mar 19] modest hurdler: ran as if almost only outing over fences: stays 3m: **h87** acts on soft going, below form on good to firm: none too consistent. *John R. Upson*

BEAUFORT COUNTY (IRE) 10 b.g. Torus – Afternoon Tea (IRE) (Decent Fellow) **c86** [2006/7 c–, h–: c23mᵖᵘ c24mᶠ c17f³ c16m⁵ Aug 28] good-topped gelding: maiden **h–** hurdler/chaser: running best race over fences when falling last in handicap at Hunting-don: stays 3m: acts on heavy and good to firm going: tongue tied last 2 starts: has finished weakly. *Evan Williams*

BEAU LARGESSE 5 b.g. Largesse – Just Visiting (Superlative) [2006/7 F79: 17d³ **c–** 16s⁶ 16g⁶ 17v⁵ 17s c16s 17m⁴ Apr 28] angular gelding: fourth in bumper: modest novice **h91** hurdler: well beaten in novice handicap on chasing debut: not sure to stay much beyond 2m: acts on heavy going: tried blinkered. *J. Howard Johnson*

BEAU MICHEL (FR) 5 b.g. Saint Preuil (FR) – Rosacotte (FR) (Rose Laurel) **h123** [2006/7 F16s* 17d* 20d⁴ 17v 22s* 24g² Apr 19] €88,000 3-y-o: tall, rather leggy geld- **F105** ing: brother to winning hurdler/useful chaser Marcus du Berlais, stays 29f, and fairly useful French hurdler/chaser up to 2¾m Psychee du Berlais: dam winning hurdler/chaser up to 21f: won bumper at Worcester (impressively) in May: fairly useful hurdler: won novice at Exeter in October and handicap at Wincanton (beat Nathos by 2 lengths) in February: will stay beyond 3m: acts on soft going: blinkered final start (ran creditably): often soon off bridle. *P. F. Nicholls*

BEAUMONT GIRL (IRE) 5 ch.m. Trans Island – Persian Danser (IRE) (Persian **h–** Bold) [2006/7 h–: 19g⁵ 20m 19d Feb 19] leggy, close-coupled mare: modest on Flat (stays 13.8f): no solid form over hurdles: tongue tied in 2006/7. *Miss M. E. Rowland*

BEAU NASH (USA) 4 b.g. Barathea (IRE) – Style N' Elegance (USA) (Alysheba **h104** (USA)) [2006/7 17s³ 17v 16s 16f³ 17m² Apr 17] sturdy gelding: useful on Flat (should stay 1½m) for P. Chapple-Hyam: fair novice hurdler: placed in handicaps final 2 starts: raced around 2m: acts on firm and soft going: tried in cheekpieces: tongue tied. *D. E. Pipe*

BEAU PEAK 8 ch.m. Meadowbrook – Peak A Boo (Le Coq d'Or) [2006/7 h–: 18v^{bd}   **h–**
20v⁵ 24s Jan 31] leggy mare: no form over hurdles. *D. W. Whillans*

BEAU REGARD (IRE) 5 b.g. Beau Sher – Paico Ana (Paico) [2006/7 F17v² F16m⁵   **F89**
Apr 10] €5,500 3-y-o, €24,000 4-y-o: half-brother to winning staying hurdler Bally-
edward (by Roselier) and 3¼m chase winner Nick Junior (by Norwich): dam unraced
half-sister to smart chaser at 2½m+ Givus A Buck: better effort in bumpers when
runner-up to Stripe Me Blue in maiden at Exeter: probably unsuited by lesser test of
stamina 3 months later: sold 17,000 gns Doncaster May Sales. *C. L. Tizzard*

BEAU SADDLER 6 b.g. Accondy (IRE) – Wand of Youth (Mandamus) [2006/7 F–:   **h–**
24f⁶ Jun 21] no sign of ability. *A. M. Crow*

BEAU SUPREME (IRE) 10 b.g. Supreme Leader – Miss Sabreur (Avocat) [2006/7   **c121**
c121, h95: c25g² c20g³ c19f* Apr 11] useful-looking gelding: maiden hurdler: fairly   **h–**
useful chaser, left C. Down after first outing: won hunter at Exeter by 1½ lengths from
Innocent Rebel: will stay beyond 25f: acts on firm and soft going: tried in cheekpieces,
blinkered in 2006/7. *L. Jefford*

BEAUTIFUL NIGHT (FR) 5 b.m. Sleeping Car (FR) – Doll Night (FR) (Karkour   **c–**
(FR)) [2006/7 c92, h87: 16g 16f² Oct 5] modest form over hurdles/fences, left Micky   **h87**
Hammond after first outing: raced around 2m: acts on soft and firm ground. *P. F. Nicholls*

BEAUTIFUL SOUTH 4 b.f. Forzando – Fly South (Polar Falcon (USA)) [2006/7 17d   **h–**
Jul 22] modest maiden on Flat (should stay 6f), well held in 2006: no show in juvenile on
hurdling debut. *N. Wilson*

BEAUTIFUL VISION (IRE) 7 ch.g. Moscow Society (USA) – Rumi (Nishapour   **c115**
(FR)) [2006/7 h125: c17d^F c16s c16s⁴ c17d³ c17d^{bd} c17s³ c16v³ c20m² c25m³ Apr 26]   **h–**
good-topped gelding: fairly useful hurdler/novice chaser: best efforts over fences last 2
starts: stays 25f: acts on heavy and good to firm going: tried in cheekpieces: effective
tongue tied or not. *T. J. Taaffe, Ireland*

BEAU TORERO (FR) 9 gr.g. True Brave (USA) – Brave Lola (FR) (Dom Pasquini   **c96**
(FR)) [2006/7 c–, h94: 16m^{pu} 17s^{pu} c16d² c16d* Jan 15] lengthy, useful-looking gelding: **h–**
placed on Flat in 2006: winning hurdler: modest form over fences: won novice handicap
at Fakenham in January, despite tack breaking: stays easy 19f: acts on good to firm and
good to soft going. *B. N. Pollock*

BEAUTY ONE 4 b.g. Josr Algarhoud (IRE) – Beauty (IRE) (Alzao (USA)) [2006/7   **h–**
F14g⁴ F14s* 17v³ 20d^{ur} 16g Mar 20] strong gelding: first foal: dam maiden who stayed   **F90**
1¼m: won 3-y-o bumpers at Ayr in November: well held on completed starts over
hurdles. *P. C. Haslam*

BEAVER (AUS) 8 b.g. Bite The Bullet (USA) – Mahenge (AUS) (Twig Moss (FR))   **h98**
[2006/7 h86: 16m² May 18] angular gelding: left R. C. Guest and off 7 months, best effort
over hurdles when second in novice handicap at Ludlow in May: raced mainly around 2m
on good going or firmer: has worn cheekpieces/tongue strap: weak finisher. *Miss Suzy
Smith*

BEBEDASH 6 b.m. Lord Americo – Elleena Rose (IRE) (Roselier (FR)) [2006/7 F17g   **F92**
aF16g* F16s³ F16s³ Dec 27] small, stocky mare: first foal: dam unraced out of half-
sister to Scottish National winner Moorcroft Boy: unseated in maiden point: fair form in
bumpers: won on polytrack at Lingfield in November: wore cheekpieces after debut:
front runner. *K. J. Burke*

BE BE KING (IRE) 8 b.g. Bob Back (USA) – Trimar Gold (Goldhill) [2006/7 h132:   **c116 p**
23d⁶ c23s^F Feb 8] lengthy gelding: useful hurdler: not discredited when sixth in well-   **h125 +**
contested handicap at Haydock on reappearance: would probably have made successful
chasing debut in maiden at Taunton when beaten by Rowlands Dream but for falling 3 out:
stays 3m: raced on good going or softer: remains type to do well over fences. *P. F. Nicholls*

BECKY MO (IRE) 4 b.f. Beckett (IRE) – Mo Ceri (Kampala) [2006/7 17m 16m Oct 1]   **h–**
half-sister to several winners, including modest 2m hurdler Mazilla (by Mazilier): dam,
1½m winner, stayed 1¾m: well beaten in juvenile hurdles. *Micky Hammond*

BEDLAM BOY (IRE) 6 br.g. Broken Hearted – Evening Fashion (IRE) (Strong Gale)   **h138**
[2006/7 F96: 16f⁴ 20d² 19g^F 16v* 20v⁶ 20g³ Apr 12] unfurnished, close-coupled gelding: in frame in bumpers: developed into useful hurdler, won maiden at Hexham (odds
on) and novice handicap at Newcastle (beat Storymaker 8 lengths) in February: further
improvement when 11½ lengths third to Tidal Bay in Grade 2 novice at Aintree: likely to
stay beyond 2½m: acts on heavy going. *N. G. Richards*

BED

BEDOUIN BLUE (IRE) 4 b.g. Desert Style (IRE) – Society Fair (FR) (Always Fair (USA)) [2006/7 16g⁴ 16d² Feb 14] fair on Flat (stays 1½m), successful twice in 2006: in frame both starts over hurdles, better effort (fair form) when second to Sharp Reply in novice at Musselburgh, again racing freely and carrying head awkwardly: may do better again. *P. C. Haslam* **h104 +**

BEDTIME BOYS 10 gr.g. Gran Alba (USA) – Path's Sister (Warpath) [2006/7 c113: c24g⁵ c23vᶠ Mar 9] sturdy gelding: successful in January: useful hunter chaser, below form 2 outings in 2006/7: stays 3¼m: acts on soft and good to firm going. *Miss H. Campbell* **c88**

BEE AN BEE (IRE) 10 b.g. Phardante (FR) – Portia's Delight (IRE) (The Parson) [2006/7 c126§, h–: c20g³ c20g⁵ May 14] well-made gelding: winning hurdler: fairly useful handicap chaser: creditable third to Bronzesmith at Bangor: will stay beyond 25f: acts on heavy and good to firm going: wears headgear: ungenuine. *T. R. George* **c122 § h–**

BEECHWOOD 9 b.g. Fraam – Standard Rose (Ile de Bourbon (USA)) [2006/7 h94: 17d³ 16d³ 17g* Apr 7] lengthy, good sort: fair hurdler, lightly raced: improved form when easily winning seller at Newton Abbot in April: needs emphasis on speed around 2m: raced mainly on good/good to soft going. *P. R. Rodford* **h110**

BEEF OR SALMON (IRE) 11 ch.g. Cajetano (USA) – Farinella (IRE) (Salmon Leap (USA)) [2006/7 c174x, h123: 16s² c24s* c24d² 18v* c24v² c24v* c26g c25g Apr 25] **c167 x h123 +**

Michael O'Hehir's epic description of the chaos at the twenty-third fence in Foinavon's Grand National—reproduced in the essay on Silver Birch—has been one of the most often played pieces of sporting commentary down the years. Tony O'Hehir, who stood with his legendary father that day as he rattled off the names, has followed very ably in his footsteps and, forty years after Foinavon, provided the commentary on a notably famous occasion for Irish jumping. Beef Or Salmon's third success in the Hennessy Cognac Gold Cup at Leopardstown in February was achieved in amazing fashion as he overturned a seven-length deficit at the last to catch The Listener who had beaten him in the Lexus Chase over the course and distance a little over six weeks earlier. The Hennessy commentary will not be replayed so often as that of Foinavon's National, but it captured the excitement as well as providing an admirable sense of history. 'As they come down now towards the final fence, The Listener is out in front. Beef Or Salmon is trying hard to cut down the deficit and over the last it's The Listener from Beef Or Salmon, who is still trying to make ground and is closing with every stride as they race into the last 200 yards. It's The Listener, Beef Or Salmon still cutting down the lead but The Listener has 150 yards to go. Beef Or Salmon putting in a tremendous late bid on the inside, and Beef Or Salmon is going to get up. Beef Or Salmon is going to win his tenth Grade 1 and his third Hennessy. He has got his revenge over The Listener.'

Beef Or Salmon's third Hennessy gave him his sixth Grade 1 success at Leopardstown where he has also won three runnings of another of Ireland's most significant chases, the Lexus (formerly Ericsson), in one of which he inflicted a seven-length defeat on Best Mate, Beef Or Salmon's rider on that occasion, Paul Carberry, getting into hot water for gesturing to Best Mate's jockey on the run-in to 'hurry up'. Beef Or Salmon has also taken the scalps of two other Cheltenham Gold Cup winners in another of Ireland's Grade 1 chases, the James Nicholson Wine Merchant Champion Chase at Down Royal. He beat Kicking King by three and a half lengths in the 2004/5 edition and his meeting with War of Attrition in the latest one in early-November was the subject of much discussion beforehand. The decision to rate Beef Or Salmon the best chaser of the 2005/6 season—ahead of Kingscliff and War of Attrition—earned Timeform plenty of criticism at the time. 'Beef Or Salmon the top-rated chaser? I'm not swallowing that one. If War of Attrition is not better than Beef Or Salmon, I'll take up morris dancing,' wrote Claude Duval in *The Sun*. Since Beef Or Salmon beat War of Attrition on both occasions that they met in the latest season, Duval should have developed into an accomplished performer with the traditional handkerchiefs and sticks. Mind you, it was a closely-run thing in Down Royal's Champion Chase, Beef Or Salmon putting in one of his better rounds of jumping and staying on well under pressure to challenge War of Attrition at the last and get up close home. The margin was a neck, Beef Or Salmon winning on merit, though the modest pace at which the race was

James Nicholson Wine Merchant Champion Chase, Down Royal—
a second win in the race for Beef Or Salmon (noseband), who stages a grandstand finish
to get the better of Cheltenham Gold Cup winner War of Attrition

run meant that the first two weren't able to show their true superiority over the rest (the smart second-season chaser Justified finished thirteen lengths back in third). Beef Or Salmon reappeared a fortnight after Down Royal in the Lancashire Chase at Haydock, the Betfair-sponsored Grade 1 again carrying a £1m bonus if the winner went on to add the King George VI Chase (or the Lexus) and the Cheltenham Gold Cup. Beef Or Salmon had finished a good second to Kingscliff in the inaugural running and he was runner-up again, though he was some way below his best this time in being beaten seventeen lengths by Kauto Star who went on to land the Betfair Million. L'Ami, in the frame in the previous season's King George and Gold Cup, filled third spot, a length behind the strong-finishing Beef Or Salmon who got up for second only after the last (Kingscliff was a tailed-off last of six). L'Ami was also in the line-up the following month for the Lexus Chase, starting third favourite behind Beef Or Salmon (a winner over hurdles at Fairyhouse in between) and War of Attrition, with the only challenger from Britain, The Listener, next in the betting. Beef Or Salmon finished five lengths ahead of War of Attrition and a further five and a half in front of L'Ami, but he never looked like getting in a blow at the bold-jumping The Listener who dictated the pace with L'Ami. Beef Or Salmon finished eight lengths behind The Listener, bringing his record in the race to three wins, a second and a third in five runnings. When Beef Or Salmon turned the tables on The Listener in the Hennessy a little over six weeks later, his record in that race read three wins and a second in four appearances.

Contrast Beef Of Salmon's record in Leopardstown's two biggest three-mile chases with his record in the Cheltenham Gold Cup and it is easier to see why many British racegoers still remain puzzled by the admiration their Irish counter-parts have for him. Beef Or Salmon has contested five Gold Cups at Cheltenham and has only once reached the frame, when a staying-on fourth (beaten three and a half lengths) to Best Mate when that horse won his third Gold Cup in the 2003/4 season. Beef Or Salmon's latest effort—in which he was ridden much more prominently than usual—saw him manage only thirteenth of fourteen finishers after

Hennessy Cognac Gold Cup, Leopardstown—Daryl Jacob looks to have matters under control on The Listener before the last, but Beef Or Salmon stays on for a memorable last-gasp win

dropping away from six out. Beef Or Salmon ran another lacklustre race—under conditions not really ideal for him—in the Punchestown Gold Cup in April on his only subsequent outing. He was toiling from a long way out, losing a good early position through some indifferent jumping, which has been a feature of his career over fences. There must be considerable doubt whether Beef Or Salmon was quite so good in the latest season as he was in his prime, notwithstanding his top-class performance in the Hennessy. Even that almost certainly owed a good deal to The Listener's faltering in the closing stages, which accentuated the impression created by Beef Or Salmon's late rally. The Listener forced a very strong pace and Beef Or Salmon was seemingly flat out to keep up some way from home. In mitigation, Beef Or Salmon's achievements in the latest season came against a background of a miserable winter for Michael Hourigan's yard which, except for Beef Or Salmon, had a campaign to forget. The victories for Beef Or Salmon over hurdles at Fairyhouse and in the Hennessy were the only ones for the County Limerick yard during the final four and a half months of 2006/7, with Hourigan's other stable stars Hi Cloy and Church Island both drawing a blank from busy campaigns. Beef Or Salmon's victories were some consolation for Hourigan's new stable jockey Andrew McNamara whose sterling, never-say-die effort on Beef Or Salmon in the Hennessy, when some might have accepted defeat, richly earned its reward on the day.

		Run The Gantlet	Tom Rolfe
	Cajetano (USA)	(b 1968)	First Feather
	(b 1986)	Intensive	Sir Wiggle
Beef Or Salmon (IRE)		(1979)	Flying Legs
(ch.g. 1996)		Salmon Leap	Northern Dancer
	Farinella (IRE)	(ch 1980)	Fish-Bar
	(ch 1988)	Boldella	Bold Lad
		(b 1977)	Ardelle

    This is the fifth essay to appear on Beef Or Salmon whose pedigree has been fully covered in previous Annuals. He is by the little-known Cajetano and is the only winner out of the once-raced Farinella who died in 2000. However, most of her other offspring were mares and three of them—Ballyvelig Lady (by Project Manager), Smoked Salmon (by Bonnie Prince) and Dining Hall (by Saddlers' Hall)—have been fast-tracked into broodmare careers on the back of their half-brother's exploits. The usually patiently-ridden Beef Or Salmon, a strong gelding, will stay beyond three and a quarter miles, but he has a good turn of foot for a staying chaser and doesn't need a thorough test of stamina (his Grade 1 wins include the Punchestown Chase over two and a half miles and he has twice won the

Hilly Way Chase over two). In an attempt to improve Beef Or Salmon's sometimes haphazard and sluggish jumping, he has been tried in cheekpieces latterly and was blinkered ('to try to wake him up a bit', according to his trainer) for the first time in the latest Hennessy, something repeated on his two subsequent outings. Given this increasing tendency towards laziness, it wouldn't be a surprise to see Beef Or Salmon tried over long distances as he approaches his twelfth birthday. His best efforts have been on going softer than good, and he acts on heavy. *M. Hourigan, Ireland*

BEEHAWK 8 b.g. Gunner B – Cupids Bower (Owen Dudley) [2006/7 h105: c19^{sur} c23d^{pu} Mar 26] strong gelding: fair hurdler in early-2005/6: left P. Nicholls and off 20 months, failed to complete in handicap chases: stays 3¼m: acts on good to firm and good to soft going: has had tongue tied. *K. Bishop*   c– h–

BEEN HERE BEFORE 7 ch.g. Fearless Action (USA) – Mistral Magic (Crofter (USA)) [2006/7 c85+: c20v² c20v^{pu} c25s⁴ c22d^{pu} c23g^{pu} Apr 16] winning pointer: novice chaser, no form in 2006/7: tried in cheekpieces. *Mrs Marjorie Fife*   c–

BE FAIR 9 br.g. Blushing Flame (USA) – Tokyo (Mtoto) [2006/7 c21g³ c24g* c25g^F Apr 25] well-made gelding: useful bumper winner: won all 3 starts over hurdles in 2003/4: off 2½ years, fairly useful form in hunter chases, winning easily at Fakenham in April by 12 lengths from Cantarinho: still travelling well when fell 5 out in Champion Hunter at Punchestown: stays 3m: acts on good to firm and good to soft going: has awkward head carriage. *D. E. Cantillon*   c108 + h–

BEFORE DARK (IRE) 9 b.g. Phardante (FR) – Menebeans (IRE) (Duky) [2006/7 h108: 26s* Dec 22] sturdy gelding: fairly useful hurdler: better than ever when winning handicap at Hereford by 3½ lengths from Jug of Punch, only start in 2006/7: stays 27f: acts on heavy going. *Heather Dalton*   h117

BEFORE THE MAST (IRE) 10 br.g. Broken Hearted – Kings Reserve (King's Ride) [2006/7 c92, h80: 17g⁴ 16d⁵ 19s^{pu} 18m² 20d² c17d³ c21v² c16d^F c21d* c20d^{ur} c19v² c24v^{pu} Jan 4] rangy gelding: poor hurdler: modest chaser, won handicap at Fakenham in November: stayed 21f: acted on heavy and good to firm going: often let down by jumping over fences: dead. *M. F. Harris*   c88 x h84

BEFORE TIME 5 ch.g. Giant's Causeway (USA) – Original Spin (IRE) (Machiavellian (USA)) [2006/7 h91: 16f 20g May 6] tall gelding: maiden hurdler: raced mainly around 2m: tried blinkered. *Mrs A. M. Thorpe*   h–

BEGGARS CAP (IRE) 5 ch.g. Lord of Appeal – Ann's Cap (IRE) (Cardinal Flower) [2006/7 16v 20v^{pu} 16v⁶ Mar 2] compact gelding: half-brother to 2 winners by Roselier, notably smart chaser Alcapone, stays 3m: dam unraced half-sister to dam of top-class staying chaser Carvill's Hill: first form (poor) over hurdles when sixth in novice at Ayr, not knocked about. *Ferdy Murphy*   h82 +

BEGUILING (IRE) 6 ch.m. Dr Massini (IRE) – Belle Dame (IRE) (Executive Perk) [2006/7 F16s Dec 7] €27,000 4-y-o: fourth foal: closely related to bumper winner In House Appraisal (by Accordion): dam unraced half-sister to smart 2m hurdler Spirit Leader: soundly beaten in mares bumper on debut. *P. R. Webber*   F–

BEHAVINGBADLY (IRE) 12 b.g. Lord Americo – Audrey's Turn (Strong Gale) [2006/7 c90x, h–: c30d² c24d^{pu} c28s⁶ c24s⁶ c25d^{ur} c28v^{ur} 27v c29v² c26g Apr 7] good-topped gelding: winning hurdler: modest handicap chaser: stays 31f: acts on heavy going: wore cheekpieces last 3 starts: usually let down by jumping over fences. *A. Parker*   c90 x h–

BEHERAYN 4 b.g. Dansili – Behera (Mill Reef (USA)) [2006/7 F16v³ F12g⁴ Mar 23] good-bodied gelding: half-brother to several winners, notably very smart hurdler/top-class chaser Behrajan (by Arazi), stayed 3¼m: dam won Prix Saint-Alary and second in Arc: better effort in bumpers (fairly useful form) when fourth of 18 to Whiteoak in 4-y-o event at Newbury. *H. D. Daly*   F96

BEIJING BREEZE (IRE) 6 br.g. Taipan (IRE) – Windyhouse Way (IRE) (Roselier (FR)) [2006/7 22d^{pu} Oct 1] €16,000 3-y-o, 44,000 4-y-o: fourth foal: dam poor form over hurdles: no show in novice hurdle on debut: sold 2,800 gns Doncaster November Sales, well held completed outings in points. *P. J. Hobbs*   h–

BEING THERE 4 b.g. Bien Bien (USA) – Segsbury Belle (Petoski) [2006/7 16g Apr 27] modest maiden on Flat (seems to stay 1½m), left P. Cole after final start in August: well held in maiden on hurdling debut. *C. P. Morlock*   h–

BEKSTAR 12 b.m. Nicholas Bill – Murex (Royalty) [2006/7 h80: 20g³ May 5] lengthy, rather sparely-made mare: poor hurdler: probably best short of 3m: acts on firm and soft going. *J. C. Tuck*   **h81**

BELLA COSA (IRE) 5 b.m. Darnay – Adjamiya (USA) (Shahrastani (USA)) [2006/7 F–: 16sᵖᵘ 16s 16v Dec 3] lengthy mare: no form in bumpers (for Mrs L. Normile)/over hurdles. *James Clements, Ireland*   **h–**

BELLA LIANA (IRE) 7 b.m. Sesaro (USA) – Bella Galiana (ITY) (Don Roberto (USA)) [2006/7 c–, h79, F63: 16s 22d⁴ 22d⁴ 22s⁴ 18vᵖᵘ 18s Mar 25] poor maiden hurdler: no form over fences: stays 3m: acts on good to soft going: blinkered last 3 starts. *James Clements, Ireland*   **c–** **h73**

BELLANEY JEWEL (IRE) 8 gr.m. Roselier (FR) – Sister of Gold (The Parson) [2006/7 c97+, h100: c28dᵖᵘ c25d² c30sᵘʳ c28s² c32v* Mar 3] leggy mare: fair hurdler/chaser: best effort when winning Ashleybank Investments Scottish Borders National (Handicap) at Kelso in March by 1¼ lengths from Keepatem: stays 4m: acts on heavy going. *J. J. Quinn*   **c114** **h–**

BELLASSINI 7 b.m. Dr Massini (IRE) – Carlingford Belle (Carlingford Castle) [2006/7 F16m F13s⁶ 21dᵖᵘ Jan 8] small mare: third foal: dam, poor winning chaser who stayed 3m, out of half-sister to useful staying chasers Rambling Artist and The Langholm Dyer: hinted at ability in bumpers: little impact in maiden on hurdling debut: tongue tied last 2 starts. *J. L. Needham*   **h–** **F64**

BELLATORIA 4 b.f. Bello Carattere – Miss Tabitha (Infantry) [2006/7 F14g Apr 10] third foal: dam 3-day eventer: no show in bumper on debut. *M. Madgwick*   **F–**

BELLEDESARO (IRE) 7 br.m. Un Desperado (FR) – Cedarbelle (IRE) (Regular Guy) [2006/7 h–: 24s⁵ 16d⁵ 19d³ Nov 16] poor maiden hurdler: should stay beyond 19f: raced on good to soft/soft ground. *Heather Dalton*   **h77**

BELL ROCK 9 ch.g. Charmer – Sule Skerry (Scottish Rifle) [2006/7 c87, h–: c18fᵖᵘ 20m 18mᵖᵘ Sep 21] maiden hurdler/winning chaser: fairly useful pointer nowadays, successful all 3 starts in 2007: should stay beyond 21f: raced on good going or firmer: tried blinkered. *Mrs T. J. Hill*   **c–** **h–**

BEL OMBRE (FR) 7 b.g. Nikos – Danse du Soleil (FR) (Morespeed) [2006/7 c89, h–: c16v⁴ May 20] good-topped gelding: novice hurdler: modest chaser: raced around 2m on good going or softer: sold 5,200 gns Doncaster May Sales, walked over in point in April. *O. Sherwood*   **c– §** **h–**

BELORD (GER) 4 ch.g. Lord of Men – Belmoda (GER) (Jalmood (USA)) [2006/7 16d² 16s³ 16s² 16v² 16d 16g² Apr 5] won 11f maiden in Germany: fair juvenile hurdler: placed 5 times in maidens: raced at 2m: acts on heavy going: in headgear last 4 starts: refused to race intended seventh outing. *E. J. O'Grady, Ireland*   **h105 §**

BELTER 7 b.g. Terimon – Bellinote (FR) (Noir Et Or) [2006/7 h–: 20g Apr 30] compact gelding: little impact in novice hurdles. *S. P. Griffiths*   **h–**

BELTON 5 b.g. Lujain (USA) – Efficacious (IRE) (Efisio) [2006/7 h–: 16sᵖᵘ 17m 16d 17m Aug 29] tall gelding: no form over hurdles: tried blinkered/tongue tied. *Ronald Thompson*   **h–**

BE LUCKY LADY (GER) 5 br.m. Law Society (USA) – Ballata (GER) (Platini (GER)) [2006/7 h–: 17d c19s⁵ Dec 14] lengthy mare: no form over hurdles/in novice chase: tried blinkered. *N. J. Dawe*   **c–** **h–**

BELUGA (IRE) 8 gr.g. John French – Mesena (Pals Passage) [2006/7 c–, h–: c24gᵘʳ c20d³ c20d* c19sᵖᵘ c24g³ Mar 28] good-topped gelding: maiden hurdler: much improved over fences in 2006/7, modest form when winning minor event at Leicester in November, idling: stays 2½m: raced on good going or softer. *Carl Llewellyn*   **c91** **h–**

BELVOIR BEEVER (IRE) 5 b.m. Turtle Island (IRE) – Wamdha (IRE) (Thatching) [2006/7 F16s 16d 16sᵖᵘ Jan 24] smallish mare: second foal: dam fair 2m hurdler: no show in bumper/novice hurdles. *C. R. Dore*   **h–** **F–**

BE MY BETTER HALF (IRE) 12 b.g. Be My Native (USA) – The Mrs (Mandalus) [2006/7 c124, h–: c24g c21g c20d⁴ c19d Feb 2] big, workmanlike gelding: fairly useful handicap chaser at best, no form in 2006/7: stays 3m: acts on heavy going: tried blinkered: let down by jumping 4 starts over National fences at Aintree. *Jonjo O'Neill*   **c–** **h–**

BE MY DREAM (IRE) 12 b.g. Be My Native (USA) – Dream Toi (Carlburg) [2006/7 c100, h–: c25d² c24gᵖᵘ Apr 8] tall gelding: hunter chaser, runner-up at Hereford in May: **c88** **h–**

stays 25f: acts on heavy and good to firm going: wore visor/cheekpieces in 2003/4. *Mrs C. Wilesmith*

BE MY MANAGER (IRE) 12 b.g. Be My Native (USA) – Fahy Quay (Quayside) [2006/7 c25s^F c31s⁴ Apr 26] tall gelding: one-time useful chaser: well beaten in hunter completed start in 2006/7: stays 3m: acts on any going: tried in cheekpieces/blinkers: reportedly difficult to train. *P. Kirby* **c–**
h–

BEN BELLESHOT 8 gr.g. Vague Shot – Ballygriffin Belle (Another Realm) [2006/7 h–: 22m^{pu} 16f^{ur} 16m⁴ Sep 3] sturdy gelding: little sign of ability. *D. G. Bridgwater* **h–**

BENBOW 10 ch.g. Gunner B – Juno Away (Strong Gale) [2006/7 c24g^{pu} May 5] maiden jumper: tried blinkered. *G. L. Edwards* **c–**
h–

BENBRIDGE 6 b.g. Overbury (IRE) – Celtic Bridge (Celtic Cone) [2006/7 F–: 17m^F 17m 19m⁵ 20m Jul 12] sturdy gelding: no show in bumper/over hurdles. *Mrs S. M. Johnson* **h–**

BEN BRITTEN 8 ch.g. Sabrehill (USA) – Golden Panda (Music Boy) [2006/7 h97: c24d² c22s⁵ c20g* Dec 20] workmanlike gelding: winning hurdler: fair form in handicap chases: much improved when winning at Musselburgh in December, tying up run-in: has won over 3m, may prove better at shorter: acts on firm and good to soft going. *N. G. Richards* **c107 +**
h–

BENDARSHAAN 7 b.g. Darshaan – Calypso Run (Lycius (USA)) [2006/7 17d⁵ 19m Aug 3] fairly useful on Flat (stays 2m), well below form in 2006, sold out of R. Hannon's stable 9,000 gns Newmarket February Sales: little impact over hurdles. *C. A. Dwyer* **h–**

BENEDICT BAY 5 b.g. In The Wings – Persia (IRE) (Persian Bold) [2006/7 h89: 19v^{pu} 16s 16v 22s 22s² 23d⁶ Mar 21] good-bodied gelding: maiden hurdler: stays 2¾m: raced mainly on soft/heavy ground: visored. *J. A. Geake* **h82**

BENEFICIAL BUD (IRE) 7 ch.g. Beneficial – Lady Shalom (IRE) (Aylesfield) [2006/7 F16f* 21d^{pu} 21s^{pu} 16s 22m^{pu} Apr 26] second foal: half-brother to fair/unreliable hurdler/chaser Yes My Lord (by Mister Lord), stays 3½m: dam ran twice: fair form in bumpers, won at Clonmel in June: sold out of Ms M. Mullins' stable 20,000 gns Doncaster August Sales, no show over hurdles: bred to stay well: tongue tied last 2 starts: has raced freely. *Miss Tor Sturgis* **h–**
F91

BENEFICIAL GUEST (IRE) 6 b.g. Beneficial – Kyle Lark (Miner's Lamp) [2006/7 F16d⁶ 20s 16d* c17v Jan 21] sixth foal: brother to 2 winners, including fairly useful hurdler/chaser up to 2¾m Washington Lad: dam unraced half-sister to useful hurdler/chaser up to 25f Lake Teereen: placed in bumper: easily better effort in maiden hurdles when winning at Ballinrobe in May: tailed off in maiden on chasing debut: likely to do better over fences. *A. J. Martin, Ireland* **c– p**
h105
F77

BENEFIT 13 b.g. Primitive Rising (USA) – Sobriquet (Roan Rocket) [2006/7 c84d, h–: 26m^{pu} c25d⁴ c23g^{pu} c27m Jun 7] small, lengthy gelding: winning hurdler: handicap chaser, on the downgrade: stays 25f: acts on good to firm and heavy going: tried in cheekpieces. *Miss L. C. Siddall* **c–**
h–

BENEFIT FUND (IRE) 7 b.g. Beneficial – Pampered Sally (Paddy's Stream) [2006/7 h81: 16d 19m⁴ c16s^{ur} 16d⁵ 20g^{pu} Apr 14] pulled up both starts in Irish points: poor hurdler: unseated fourth on chase debut. *D. J. Wintle* **c–**
h78

BENEFIT NIGHT (IRE) 7 b.g. Beneficial – Broomhill Star (IRE) (Deep Society) [2006/7 c20s c24v² c24v* c24v^{ur} c19v* c20v* c20v* Feb 25] first foal: dam unraced: won 2 points early in 2006: progressed very well in chases, successful last 4 completed starts, in handicaps at Thurles in December, Naas (novice) in January and Navan in February, and Grade 2 novice at Naas (by 1¼ lengths from Letterman, fairly useful form) later in February: stays 3m: raced mainly on heavy going. *Daniel William O'Sullivan, Ireland* **c124**

BENE LAD (IRE) 5 b. or br.g. Beneficial – Sandwell Old Rose (IRE) (Roselier (FR)) [2006/7 16v⁵ 18v 16s Jan 31] €26,000 3-y-o: tall, good-topped gelding: third foal: dam unraced: poor form in maiden/novice hurdles: will be suited by 2½m+. *J. S. Goldie* **h74**

BENELLINO 4 b.g. Robellino (USA) – Benjarong (Sharpo) [2006/7 F14s Nov 26] £900 3-y-o: fourth foal: half-brother to 6f winner Ben Lomand (by Inchinor): dam 5f (at 2 yrs) and 1m winner: no promise in 3-y-o bumper on debut. *R. M. Stronge* **F–**

BENETWOOD (IRE) 6 b.g. Beneficial – Donegal Thyne (IRE) (Good Thyne (USA)) [2006/7 F94: 16s² 18s⁸ 18s² 16g* Mar 28] lengthy, good sort: will make a chaser: bumper winner: fairly useful form over hurdles: won maiden at Fontwell in January and novice at **h116**

Kempton (beat Petrovka comfortably by 4 lengths) in March: likely to stay 2½m: raced on good/soft going. *V. R. A. Dartnall*

BEN FROM KETTON 12 b.g. Cruise Missile – Saucy Girl (Saucy Kit) [2006/7 c20dpu c20m c27s⁴ Mar 13] form in hunter chases only when successful in May 2004: stays 27f. *S. J. Robinson* — c—

BENGAL BULLET 10 b.g. Infantry – Indian Cruise (Cruise Missile) [2006/7 c98: c26m* c26m³ 22d⁵ Oct 17] one-time fair chaser: didn't have to be near best to win hunter at Newton Abbot in May: well held in amateurs novice on hurdling debut: stays 3¼m: acts on heavy and good to firm going: sometimes let down by jumping. *C. F. Blank* — c89 + h—

BENGO (IRE) 7 b.g. Beneficial – Goforroad (IRE) (Mister Lord (USA)) [2006/7 c115, h115: c24g² c24v⁵ c24d² c24s² c33gur c24g⁴ c31spu Apr 27] rangy gelding: winning hurdler: fair chaser: runner-up in handicaps 3 of 5 completed starts in 2006/7: stays 3m: acts on heavy and good to firm going: tried blinkered: not a fluent jumper. *B. De Haan* — c110 x h—

BENMORE BOY (IRE) 4 b.g. Old Vic – Proudstown Lady (IRE) (Ashford (USA)) [2006/7 F16g Apr 7] good-topped gelding: second foal: dam maiden: well held in bumper on debut. *Miss H. C. Knight* — F—

BEN NELLY (IRE) 6 b.g. Taipan (IRE) – Cothu Na Slaine (IRE) (Roselier (FR)) [2006/7 h73: 20g⁴ 20dpu 20vpu Dec 11] poor form over hurdles: should stay 2¾m. *M. Todhunter* — h73

BENNETT (IRE) 7 b. or br.g. Grand Plaisir (IRE) – Ozone River (IRE) (Over The River (FR)) [2006/7 F18d² c24d³ c25s 24gpu Mar 23] €11,500 4-y-o: useful-looking gelding: third foal: dam won point in Ireland: won maiden point in Ireland in 2006: runner-up in bumper at Plumpton: disappointing after. *Noel T. Chance* — c— h— F94

BENNY BOY (IRE) 7 b.g. Beneficial – Seefin Lass (IRE) (Mandalus) [2006/7 c—: c25m May 6] winning pointer: well beaten completed start in hunter chases. *S. G. Waugh* — c—

BENNYNTHEJETS (IRE) 5 b.g. Beneficial – Lucky Adventure (IRE) (Hymns On High) [2006/7 F17d³ F17d³ Mar 19] €5,000 4-y-o: good-topped gelding: fourth foal: dam unraced out of half-sister to Arkle winner Denys Adventure: fair form when third in bumpers at Market Rasen, racing freely: bred to be suited by further. *C. C. Bealby* — F94

BENNY THE PILER (IRE) 7 b. or br.g. Beneficial – An Charraig Mhor (IRE) (Tremblant) [2006/7 h—, F86: 22m* 22d³ 24m⁴ Apr 20] good-topped gelding: fair form over hurdles: left N. Richards and off 7 months, won novice at Kelso in October: should stay 3m: acts on soft and good to firm ground. *M. Todhunter* — h101

BENRAJAH (IRE) 10 b.g. Lord Americo – Andy's Fancy (IRE) (Andretti) [2006/7 c114, h—: c20g⁶ c21gF Apr 12] well-made gelding: fairly useful chaser at best: left M. Todhunter, runner-up in point then sixth of 7 finishers on completed outing in hunters: stays 3¼m: second in bumper on soft going, raced mainly under less testing conditions (simple task on firm): often races up with pace. *P. Kirby* — c91 h—

BEN'S TURN (IRE) 6 b.m. Saddlers' Hall (IRE) – Christines Gale (IRE) (Strong Gale) [2006/7 h109, F106: 22s* 24d⁴ 22s³ 21g Apr 19] rangy mare: fair hurdler: won handicap at Sandown in December: stays 3m: acts on soft going: has raced freely. *A. King* — h111

BEN TALLY HO 6 ch.g. Classic Cliche (IRE) – Poussetiere Deux (FR) (Garde Royale) [2006/7 h85: 20s 20vpu c24g³ c23dpu Mar 20] useful-looking gelding, unfurnished at present: maiden hurdler: modest form on completed outing in handicap chases (breathing problem final start): stays 3m. *Ian Williams* — c92 h—

BENTINCK (IRE) 5 b.g. In The Wings – Bareilly (USA) (Lyphard (USA)) [2006/7 F—: F16g² 16m² 22g Jul 23] in frame in bumper: better effort over hurdles (lame final start) when second in novice at Worcester: should stay beyond 2m. *M. Scudamore* — h90 F91

BENTLEY BROOK (IRE) 5 ch.g. Singspiel (IRE) – Gay Bentley (USA) (Riverman (USA)) [2006/7 17d³ Aug 15] closely related to fair hurdler Vintage Port (by In The Wings), stays 2¾m: fairly useful at best on Flat (stays 1¼m), has deteriorated: not fluent when third of 4 finishers in maiden on hurdling debut. *P. A. Blockley* — h—

BENTYHEATH LANE 10 b.g. Puissance – Eye Sight (Roscoe Blake) [2006/7 c—, h—: 24dpu c17g⁶ c16gpu c20f⁵ Jul 25] lengthy, angular gelding: no longer of any account: tried in headgear. *M. Mullineaux* — c— h—

BE POSITIVE 7 b.g. Petoski – Go Positive (Profilic) [2006/7 F81: 17s 17v⁶ 19v³ 16d 20g Apr 11] poor maiden hurdler, flattered third outing: headstrong. *C. J. Down* — h77

BERENGARIO (IRE) 7 b.g. Mark of Esteem (IRE) – Ivrea (Sadler's Wells (USA)) [2006/7 c111, h109?: 20g* 20d³ 24g⁴ Apr 21] fair handicap hurdler: left S. Burrough — c— h114

114

and off nearly a year, well-backed winner at Huntingdon in November: similar form when placed over fences: stays 3m: acts on soft going: tried blinkered: has carried head awkwardly (none too keen second start). *A. King*

BERIGA (GER) 6 ch.m. Devil River Peek (USA) – Belena (GER) (Assert) [2006/7 16m⁶ 16s⁶ 16gᶠ 16s 16d Jan 5] trained by P. Vovcenko in Germany at 3 yrs (raced only at 7f/1m), won maiden at Dresden: no form in novice hurdles. *P. Monteith* **h–**

BERING DE LAURIERE (FR) 4 ch.g. Evening World (FR) – Shenedova (FR) (Hellios (USA)) [2006/7 F12v F18m² Apr 26] tall, angular gelding: third foal: closely-related to winning hurdler/chaser up to 19f Belle Divine (by Signe Divine): dam unraced: much better effort in bumpers when runner-up to Hills of Home at Fontwell. *Jean-Rene Auvray* **F88**

BERINGS EXPRESS (FR) 4 b.g. Bering – Ess Express (FR) (Subotica (FR)) [2006/7 F14g* F16g Mar 14] tall, good-topped gelding: first foal: dam 1m to 1½m winner, including Swedish 1000 Guineas and Swedish Oaks: well backed, useful form when winning 17-runner 3-y-o bumper at Warwick in November by 1½ lengths from Helens Vision: well held in Grade 1 at Cheltenham 4 months later: joined Jonjo O'Neill. *N. Clement, France* **F109**

BERKELEY COURT 6 b.g. Croco Rouge (IRE) – Penultimate (USA) (Roberto (USA)) [2006/7 h–, F67: 16g c16d³ Nov 23] no show over hurdles and, after sold out of G. L. Moore's stable £1,100 Ascot July Sales, in maiden on chasing debut (tongue tied). *C. L. Popham* **c– h–**

BERKELEY HOUSE (IRE) 7 b.m. Beneficial – Danny's Charm (IRE) (Arapahos (FR)) [2006/7 20v⁶ 22sᶠ 20v 21d⁶ 20vᶠ 24v 22g⁴ Apr 2] €20,000 4-y-o: half-sister to fairly useful hurdler/useful chaser The Bunny Boiler (by Tremblant), stayed 4¼m, and fair hurdler Tandys Bridge (by Mister Lord), stayed 2¾m: dam unraced: bumper winner: modest maiden hurdler: should stay 3m: raced mainly on ground softer than good. *C. F. Swan, Ireland* **h92**

BERKHAMSTED (IRE) 5 b.g. Desert Sun – Accounting (Sillery (USA)) [2006/7 h–: c16f⁴ Apr 5] fairly useful on Flat (stays 1½m), sold out of T. Dascombe's stable 12,000 gns Doncaster January Sales: let down by jumping in juvenile hurdles for M. Harris: fourth of 5 in novice at Ludlow on chasing debut. *Evan Williams* **c99 h–**

BERLIN BUNKER (IRE) 6 b.g. Right Win (IRE) – Venture To Heaven (IRE) (The Parson) [2006/7 c20v⁴ 24v* 20g³ Mar 27] fourth foal: half-brother to winning pointers by Moscow Society and Mandalus: dam twice-raced half-sister to fairly useful hurdler/chaser up to 21f Regal Venture: placed in maiden Irish points: mistakes when fourth of 5 finishers in maiden at Sedgefield on chase debut: modest form over hurdles, won novice at Hexham in March: stays 3m: acts on heavy going: joined L. Dace. *B. Ellison* **c88 h92**

BERMUDA POINTE (IRE) 5 ch.g. Lahib (USA) – Milain (IRE) (Unfuwain (USA)) [2006/7 F101: 22s³ 19s 20v Jan 11] bumper winner: shaped as if having a problem all 3 starts over hurdles. *N. A. Twiston-Davies* **h?**

BERNARD 7 b.g. Nashwan (USA) – Tabyan (USA) (Topsider (USA)) [2006/7 21s 17s 16s c20dᵘʳ Mar 26] workmanlike gelding: fair maiden on Flat (stays 1¾m) at 3 yrs, sold out of R. Charlton's stable £4,500 Ascot December (2003) Sales: no form over hurdles/on chasing debut. *K. Bishop* **c– h–**

BERNINI (IRE) 7 b.g. Grand Lodge (USA) – Alsahah (IRE) (Unfuwain (USA)) [2006/7 c24dᵖᵘ Oct 1] good-topped gelding: disappointing maiden hurdler/chaser, left N. Henderson and off 19 months before sole 2006/7 outing: should have stayed beyond 2m: acted on soft going: tried blinkered: dead. *R. Ford* **c– h–**

BERNIX 5 gr.g. Linamix (FR) – Bernique (USA) (Affirmed (USA)) [2006/7 F17s F16d 16s 16s⁴ 17v⁴ Feb 20] lengthy gelding: chasing type: brother to smart performers Berni-mixa (stayed 13.5f) and Miraculous (stayed 15.5f), and half-brother to 3 Flat winners: dam won in USA and runner-up in 9f Grade 3 event: well held in bumpers: best effort over hurdles (modest form) in novice fourth start: tongue tied after debut (usually shapes as if amiss): third in maiden on Flat in April. *T. D. Easterby* **h89 F–**

BERTIE MAY 5 gr.g. Terimon – Kalogy (Kalaglow) [2006/7 F16d* F16d* Mar 17] 6,500 4-y-o: tall, useful-looking gelding: fourth foal: dam, maiden hurdler, stayed 21f: looked a good prospect when winning bumpers at Wincanton (very green) in February and Uttoxeter (beating Rightway Star by neck) in March. *K. Bishop* **F114**

BERWICK LAW (IRE) 5 ch.g. Snurge – Cruby Hill (IRE) (Prince Rupert (FR)) [2006/7 F16v* F16v* Mar 10] 15,500 3-y-o: half-brother to winner abroad by Simply **F111 p**

Great: dam unraced: impressive winner of bumpers at Ayr in December and March, beating Mey Clouds easily by 15 lengths on latter occasion: will stay beyond 2m: good prospect. *L. Lungo*

BESEIGED (USA) 10 ch.g. Cadeaux Genereux – Munnaya (USA) (Nijinsky (CAN)) [2006/7 h124?: c19m^F Jun 4] workmanlike gelding: fairly useful handicap hurdler: weakening when fell 2 out in maiden on chasing debut: stays 19f, at least when conditions aren't testing: acts on good to firm and good to soft going: pulled up in point in February. *J. L. Spearing*   c–
h–

BEST ACCOLADE 8 b.g. Oscar (IRE) – Made of Talent (Supreme Leader) [2006/7 h88p: 23v^{pu} Dec 2] strong, useful-looking gelding: third in bumper/novice hurdle, very lightly raced. *J. Howard Johnson*   h–

BEST ACTOR (IRE) 8 b.g. Oscar (IRE) – Supreme Princess (IRE) (Supreme Leader) [2006/7 h97, F96: 22s* 19d⁴ 25s² Mar 11] good-topped gelding: chasing type: bumper winner: fairly useful hurdler: made all in maiden at Fontwell in December, barely off bridle to beat Burren Legend by 22 lengths: let down by jumping next 2 starts: stays 25f: raced on ground softer than good. *Carl Llewellyn*   h118

BEST DEAL 6 gr.g. Presenting – Miss Drury (Baron Blakeney) [2006/7 F85: 20d Oct 20] shaped like a stayer in bumpers: offered nothing in novice on hurdling debut. *B. I. Case*   h–

BESTOFTHEBROWNIES (IRE) 6 b.g. Bob Back (USA) – Just A Brownie (IRE) (Orchestra) [2006/7 h–p, F88: 20g² c20d² c16v^{pu} c16v³ c16g³ c20m* Apr 9] strong, stocky gelding: runner-up in novice at Wetherby completed outing over hurdles: fair chaser: didn't need to be at best to win maiden at Sedgefield in April: should stay 3m: acts on heavy and good to firm going. *J. Howard Johnson*   c106 +
h99

BEST PROFILE (IRE) 7 b.g. Flemensfirth (USA) – Lincoln Green (IRE) (Ela-Mana-Mou) [2006/7 h120: c23d* c21s^{pu} Dec 9] lengthy gelding: fairly useful hurdler: promising chasing debut when winning novice at Stratford in October by 7 lengths from Wild Is The Wind: ran as if amiss 2 months later: will stay beyond 3m: raced on going softer than good (acts on heavy): effective tongue tied or not. *N. A. Twiston-Davies*   c118 +
h–

BE TELLING (IRE) 8 b.g. Oscar (IRE) – Manhattan King (IRE) (King's Ride) [2006/7 c69, h81: c20s² 20f² 24m³ 22m² c26g² c24s^F Feb 16] leggy gelding: modest novice hurdler: sold out of B. Curley's stable 13,500 gns Doncaster August Sales prior to fourth start: fairly useful chaser: much improved in handicaps last 2 starts, winning at Fakenham by 30 lengths from Alfadora: stays 3¼m: acts on firm and soft going: reliable. *Miss Tor Sturgis*   c121
h89 +

BETHANYS BOY (IRE) 6 ch.g. Docksider (USA) – Daymoon (USA) (Dayjur (USA)) [2006/7 16m^{pu} Jul 11] fairly useful at best over flat (stays 1¾m), successful in seller in March for P. Blockley: not knocked about once beaten in novice on hurdling debut. *A. M. Hales*   h–

BETHEBESTYOUCANBE 6 b.g. Morpeth – Anagmor's Daughter (Funny Man) [2006/7 F17d⁵ 16s 17d 19s Dec 29] lengthy gelding: fifth foal: dam, modest hurdler/ chaser, suited by test of stamina: well held in bumper/novice hurdles. *J. D. Frost*   h–
F–

BE THE TOPS (IRE) 9 br.g. Topanoora – Be The One (IRE) (Supreme Leader) [2006/7 c108§, h–§: c26s^{pu} c24d^{pu} c22d⁴ c24m^{pu} c26m* Jul 20] lengthy gelding: fair handicap chaser: back to form when winning at Cartmel in July, getting back up under strong ride on line (jockey on runner-up stopped riding final few strides): stays 3¼m: acts on heavy and good to firm going: wears headgear: hard ride (all 4 chase wins for A. McCoy). *Jonjo O'Neill*   c99 §
h– §

BETHS CHOICE 6 b.h. Midnight Legend – Clare's Choice (Pragmatic) [2006/7 h–, F83?: 17v 16d^F 17g⁶ Apr 20] close-coupled horse: runner-up in weak bumper on debut: no form since, mainly over hurdles. *J. M. Bradley*   h–

BETTERAS BERTIE 4 gr.g. Paris House – Suffolk Girl (Statoblest) [2006/7 F16g Mar 17] third foal: brother to 7f winner Suffolk House: dam won bumper: well held in bumper/maidens on Flat. *M. Brittain*   F–

BETTER MOMENT (IRE) 10 b.g. Turtle Island (IRE) – Snoozeandyoulose (IRE) (Scenic) [2006/7 c94§, h93§: c18f² 20m² 19d³ 24d⁵ 19d² 17d 17v⁴ c19s* 19s⁶ 19v 16g 17g⁶ 21m* Apr 8] smallish gelding: modest handicap hurdler: won conditional jockeys selling event at Plumpton (sold 5,100 gns) in April: won 2 of 4 completed starts over fences, including conditional jockeys handicap at Taunton in December: stays easy   c104 §
h94 §

21f: probably acts on any going: usually visored, wore cheekpieces last 3 starts: tried tongue tied: unreliable. *D. E. Pipe*

BETTER TOGETHER 5 ch.g. Spadoun (FR) – Persian Jewel (Lord Bud) [2006/7 F16d 16d Feb 2] 19,500 3-y-o: strong gelding: chasing type: second foal: dam unraced: mid-field (not knocked about) in bumper at Newbury on debut: behind in novice hurdle. *N. J. Gifford* **h–** **F–**

BEWLEYS BERRY (IRE) 9 ch.g. Shernazar – Approach The Dawn (IRE) (Orchestra) [2006/7 c141, h–: c24m⁴ c26g² c28s c36gᶠ Apr 14] lengthy, workmanlike gelding: winning hurdler: useful chaser: ran well when 8 lengths second to Eurotrek in Becher Chase at Aintree: going really well in front when falling at second Becher's in Grand National: should stay beyond 3¼m: acts on heavy and good to firm going: races prominently. *J. Howard Johnson* **c141** **h–**

BEWLEYS GUEST (IRE) 8 b.g. Presenting – Pedigree Corner (Pollerton) [2006/7 c69, h–: c20g⁴ c16f⁶ Aug 22] tubed: Irish point winner: no form over hurdles: poor handicap chaser: should stay beyond 2½m. *Miss Venetia Williams* **c62** **h–**

BEYOND CONTROL (IRE) 12 b.g. Supreme Leader – Bucktina (Buckskin (FR)) [2006/7 22sᵖᵘ 22dᵖᵘ 24vᵖᵘ Jan 8] strong, useful-looking gelding: completed only once in 4 chases: fairly useful hurdler at best: no sign of retaining ability in 2006/7, trained first 2 starts by P. Rodford: stays 3¼m: acts on heavy going. *Miss Sarah Robinson* **c–** **h–**

BEYONDTHEREALM 9 b.g. Morpeth – Workamiracle (Teamwork) [2006/7 h96: 24d³ 23d² 20v⁴ c19s⁴ c23dᵖᵘ Mar 20] medium-sized gelding: winning pointer: modest handicap hurdler, lightly raced: similar form on completed outing in chases: lame next time: stays 3m: acts on heavy going. *J. D. Frost* **c86** **h89**

BIBLE LORD (IRE) 6 ch.g. Mister Lord (USA) – Pharisee (IRE) (Phardante (FR)) [2006/7 c23d⁶ 17s c20s² c20v* c20d* Mar 21] rangy gelding: brother to fairly useful chaser up to 3m Kew Jumper and half-brother to smart/unreliable hunter chaser Caught At Dawn (by Supreme Leader), stays 4m: dam unraced: won second of 2 starts in maiden Irish points in 2006: well held on hurdling debut: progressive chaser: won novices at Kempton (by 15 lengths from Il Duce) and Lingfield in March: bordering on useful form when beating Dunsfold Dunce 6 lengths in handicap at latter, dictating and not extended to assert: should stay beyond 2½m: raced on going softer than good: open to further improvement. *Andrew Turnell* **c128 p** **h–**

BICA (FR) 7 b.g. Cadoudal (FR) – Libertina (FR) (Balsamo (FR)) [2006/7 c89+, h–: c25s* c25s* c26g⁵ Mar 16] useful-looking gelding: fairly useful hurdler/chaser when trained in France: won at Wetherby and Kelso in February on first 2 starts in hunters: better form when around 17 lengths fifth to Drombeag in Foxhunter at Cheltenham, up with pace until 3 out: stays 3¼m: acts on heavy ground: sound jumper. *R. Waley-Cohen* **c121** **h–**

BIDOSKI 5 b.g. Petoski – No Bid (High Line) [2006/7 F17d F17v 16g 16sᵖᵘ Mar 1] reportedly tubed: fifth foal: dam unraced out of half-sister to smart 2m hurdler Sailor's Dance: no form in bumpers or over hurdles. *M. Sheppard* **h–** **F–**

BIEN BRONZE 6 b.g. Florida Son – Solazzi (FR) (Saint Cyrien (FR)) [2006/7 F17s* 16s⁶ 18v³ 18s³ 16v* 16m² Apr 25] €18,000 3-y-o: strong gelding: first foal: dam won 2¾m hurdle: winning pointer: successful only start in bumpers, at Killarney in May: fairly useful hurdler: won maiden at Fairyhouse in February by short head from Alabama Banjo: best effort when 3 lengths second of 22 to Bobs Pride in valuable handicap at Punchestown, though not for first time raced less than seemed likely: will stay 2½m: unraced on firm going, acts on any other. *A. L. T. Moore, Ireland* **h121** **F102**

BIG-AND-BOLD (IRE) 11 gr.g. Legal Circles (USA) – Kodak Lady (IRE) (Entre Nous) [2006/7 c111, h99+: c24sᵘʳ May 18] big, strong, lengthy gelding: winning hurdler: one-time useful chaser: has finished weakly all completed starts since near 4-year absence: should stay beyond 2½m: acts on good to firm ground, won bumper on heavy: usually tongue tied. *N. G. Richards* **c–** **h–**

BIG BERTHA 9 ch.m. Dancing Spree (USA) – Bertrade (Homeboy) [2006/7 h79: 20g Nov 13] good-bodied mare: poor form in novice hurdles, very lightly raced. *Micky Hammond* **h72**

BIG BOOTS (IRE) 4 b.g. Turtle Island (IRE) – Straight 'n Furry (Furry Glen) [2006/7 F16d⁴ F16v³ Mar 2] fourth foal: dam bumper winner: fair form in frame in bumpers at Leopardstown and Ayr, making running. *Lindsay Woods, Ireland* **F90**

BIG BUSINESS 7 b.g. Slip Anchor – Absalom's Lady (Absalom) [2006/7 22m* c23dᵖᵘ Oct 5] second foal: half-brother to useful hurdler/smart chaser Bob Bob Bobbin (by Bob **c–** **h98**

117

Back), stays 3¼m, and useful hurdler War General (by Classic Cliche), stayed 2½m: dam, very smart hurdler/chaser, stayed 3m: modest form over hurdles: sold out of T. Taaffe's stable 8,000 gns Doncaster May Sales and off 9 months, made all in maiden at Fontwell in August: ran as if amiss on chasing debut: should stay 3m: acts on soft and good to firm ground: wore tongue strap all starts in Ireland. *Evan Williams*

BIG JOHN MACARTY (IRE) 6 b.g. Accordion – Sprinkling Star (Strong Gale) [2006/7 F16s⁵ F16d 20v 24m² 24m³ Apr 15] workmanlike gelding: sixth foal: half-brother to modest chaser Autumn Mist (by Phardante), stays 3¼m: dam, placed over hurdles, half-sister to smart chaser up to 3m Super Furrow: twice-raced in bumpers: poor form in maiden/novice hurdles: looks a thorough stayer: sold 15,000 gns Doncaster May Sales. *M. Scudamore*   **h80**
                                                                                              F—

BIG MAX 12 b.g. Rakaposhi King – Edwina's Dawn (Space King) [2006/7 c–x, h79: 20m³ 20mᵖᵘ Aug 11] well-made gelding: maiden chaser: winning hurdler, poor nowadays: stays 3m: unraced on firm going, acts on any other: has been let down by jumping over fences. *Karen George*   **c– x**
                                                                                              h77

BIG MOMENT 9 ch.g. Be My Guest (USA) – Petralona (USA) (Alleged (USA)) [2006/7 c118, h120: 20s⁵ 21s 24d Feb 10] smallish gelding: one-time smart hurdler, soundly beaten in handicaps last 2 starts: winning chaser, generally let down by jumping: should stay 3m: raced on good going or softer (acts on heavy). *Mrs A. J. Perrett*   **c—**
                                                                                              h124

BIG PALOOKA 5 ch.g. Great Palm (USA) – Penniless (IRE) (Common Grounds) [2006/7 F—: 20sᵖᵘ Oct 11] workmanlike gelding: no show in bumper/novice hurdle. *B. S. Rothwell*   **h—**

BIG QUICK (IRE) 12 ch.g. Glacial Storm (USA) – Furryvale (Furry Glen) [2006/7 c–, h82: 22m 27dᵖᵘ 21fᵖᵘ 26mᵖᵘ Sep 24] once-raced over fences: handicap hurdler, no form at 3m+: unraced on heavy going, acts on any other: blinkered final outing. *L. Wells*   **c—**
                                                                                              h—

BIG RALPH 4 ch.g. Mark of Esteem (IRE) – Wish Me Luck (IRE) (Lycius (USA)) [2006/7 aF13g Nov 22] half-brother to 2-y-o 6f winners by Alhaarth and Green Desert: dam, Irish 2-y-o 6f winner: ninth of 14 in 3-y-o bumper at Lingfield: poor form on Flat. *M. Wigham*   **F—**

BIG ROB (IRE) 8 b.g. Bob Back (USA) – Native Shore (IRE) (Be My Native (USA)) [2006/7 c128, h91: c20g* c20dᵖᵘ c20sᵖᵘ c21gᵖᵘ c24g c20m⁴ Apr 27] tall, good-topped gelding: novice hurdler: fairly useful chaser on his day: off 7 months, didn't need to be at best to win handicap at Huntingdon in November: generally let down by jumping/shaped as if amiss after, in cheekpieces last 2 starts: stays 2¾m: acts on heavy going. *B. G. Powell*   **c120**
                                                                                              h—

BIG SECRET 4 b.g. Zilzal (USA) – Phylian (Glint of Gold) [2006/7 F13d* Oct 17] half-brother to 2 winners, including 2m chaser Mr Smithers Jones (by Emperor Jones): dam 1¼m/11f winner: 7/1 from 33/1, won 3-y-o bumper at Exeter on debut by 5 lengths from Kayf Keel, travelling strongly and soon clear after leading 2f out. *G. C. Bravery*   **F95**

BIG STAR (IRE) 10 ro.g. Fourstars Allstar (USA) – Dame Blakeney (IRE) (Blakeney) [2006/7 c26vᵘʳ May 20] winning pointer in 2006, little sign of ability otherwise: tried tongue tied. *Miss J. Froggatt*   **c—**
                                                                                              h—

BIG TREE (FR) 9 ch.g. Apple Tree (FR) – Maria Cara (FR) (Trepan (FR)) [2006/7 c25s⁵ c25sᵖᵘ Feb 15] tall gelding: no form over hurdles/fences, very lightly raced: trained by N. Gifford on reappearance. *B. Storey*   **c—**
                                                                                              h—

BIG WHEEL 12 ch.g. Mujtahid (USA) – Numuthej (USA) (Nureyev (USA)) [2006/7 c–, h93: 20gᵖᵘ Mar 27] angular gelding: lightly raced over fences (fell twice): fair hurdler at best: reportedly lost action only outing in 2006/7: barely stays 21f: acts on firm and soft going: tried blinkered early in career: sometimes finishes weakly. *N. G. Richards*   **c—**
                                                                                              h—

BIG ZEB (IRE) 6 b.g. Oscar (IRE) – Our Siveen (Deep Run) [2006/7 F16s³ 16v* 16g² Apr 27] €34,000 3-y-o: half-brother to fair chaser Herbert Buchanan (by Henbit), stayed 3m: dam winning Irish hurdler: placed in maiden bumpers: created good impression when winning maiden at Fairyhouse on hurdling debut in March, going clear on bridle after 2 out and beating Best Malt 12 lengths: better form (fairly useful) when 3½ lengths second of 24 to Sizing Europe in novice at Punchestown, tending to hang under pressure: will stay 2½m: acts on heavy ground: useful prospect. *Colm A. Murphy, Ireland*   **h117 p**
                                                                                              F90

BIG ZOOMO (IRE) 13 ch.g. Broken Hearted – Crest Bavard (Le Bavard (FR)) [2006/7 c22v² c26g c25mᵖᵘ Apr 10] big gelding: useful hunter chaser: won at Down Royal in 2006: much improved when 5 lengths second to Don't Be Daft at Fairyhouse in   **c119**

February: made mistakes when well held in Foxhunter at Cheltenham next time: probably stays 25f: acts on heavy going: front runner. *Sean McParlan, Ireland*

BILKIE (IRE) 5 ch.g. Polish Precedent (USA) – Lesgor (USA) (Irish River (FR)) [2006/7 h80: 21g May 14] lightly-raced maiden on Flat: poor form over hurdles. *John Berry*   **h83 +**

BILL BENNETT (FR) 6 b.g. Bishop of Cashel – Concert (Polar Falcon (USA)) [2006/7 20d Mar 17] smallish gelding: fair but inconsistent on Flat (seemingly effective at 1¼m to 2m): eighth of 14 finishers in novice on hurdling debut, dropped out and not given hard time. *J. Jay*   **h–**

BILL BROWN 9 b.g. North Briton – Dickies Girl (Saxon Farm) [2006/7 c86, h–: 16s 16s 17d⁴ 16g⁴ Mar 28] leggy gelding: winning hurdler, modest at best: similar form only outing over fences (unseated last): raced mainly around 2m: acted on heavy going: dead. *R. Dickin*   **c–** **h79**

BILLESEY (IRE) 9 b.g. King's Ride – Rose Runner (IRE) (Roselier (FR)) [2006/7 c–, h101+: c24dᵖᵘ Nov 21] well-made gelding: won bumper on debut: failed to complete 2 starts over fences: fair form on completed outing over hurdles: should stay 3m. *S. E. H. Sherwood*   **c–** **h–**

BILLIE JOHN (IRE) 12 ch.g. Boyne Valley – Lovestream (Sandy Creek) [2006/7 c103, h–: 16gᵘʳ c17g⁶ c20f⁶ c20g³ c21f³ c21m⁶ c20g⁴ 16g Oct 19] winning hurdler: handicap chaser, modest in first half of 2006/7: barely stays 21f: raced mainly on good going or firmer (acts on firm): tried in cheekpieces. *Mrs K. Walton*   **c89** **h–**

BILL OWEN 11 ch.g. Nicholas Bill – Pollys Owen (Master Owen) [2006/7 c–: c19mᵘʳ c19dᵖᵘ Nov 16] medium-sized gelding: modest chaser at best: failed to complete both outings in 2006/7, unseated at start on reappearance: stays 19f: acts on firm going: wears headgear: front runner. *D. P. Keane*   **c–**

BILL'S ECHO 8 br.g. Double Eclipse (IRE) – Bit On Edge (Henbit (USA)) [2006/7 c120, h97: c19s⁴ c17g⁵ c20m* Mar 31] leggy gelding: maiden hurdler: fairly useful handicap chaser, off 15 months and left R. C. Guest prior to reappearance: blinkered, improved form when winning 5-runner event at Uttoxeter in March by 8 lengths from Dead Mans Dante: stays 2½m: acts on firm and good to soft going: held up: has found little. *P. F. Nicholls*   **c127 +** **h–**

BILLSGREY (IRE) 5 gr.g. Pistolet Bleu (IRE) – Grouse-N-Heather (Grey Desire) [2006/7 F–: 17d 16d 22g 20sᵖᵘ 17vᶠ Feb 20] no sign of ability. *J. S. Haldane*   **h–**

BILLSLEGACY (IRE) 5 ch.g. Commanche Run – Nickys Peril (Nicholas Bill) [2006/7 F16v May 18] first foal: dam well beaten in bumpers: tailed off in bumper on debut. *J. S. Haldane*   **F–**

BILLYANDI (IRE) 7 ch.g. Zaffaran (USA) – Top Dart (Whistling Top) [2006/7 h109: 16s* 17d c16vᵖᵘ c16d⁴ c20g c16g⁶ Apr 7] workmanlike gelding: fair hurdler: won handicap at Perth in September: form over fences only when fourth to Jarro in handicap at Ludlow: seems best at 2m: acts on heavy going: tongue tied final outing: usually front runner. *N. A. Twiston-Davies*   **c111** **h111**

BILLY BRAY 7 b.g. Alflora (IRE) – Chacewater (Electric) [2006/7 h–: 17d c16s* c21d³ c23s c16d c20s⁵ c20s⁴ Apr 27] workmanlike gelding: no form over hurdles: 33/1, won conditional jockeys handicap at Towcester in November on chasing debut: disappointing after, not impressing with attitude/jumping: should stay beyond 17f: acts on soft going: blinkered final outing. *Miss Venetia Williams*   **c95** **h–**

BILLY BUSH (IRE) 8 b.g. Lord Americo – Castle Graigue (IRE) (Aylesfield) [2006/7 c–, h–: 22g* 23v⁵ 20v⁴ Jan 27] strong, lengthy gelding: fairly useful hurdler: off 9 months, improved form when winning handicap at Kelso in November by 6 lengths from Totally Scottish: let down by jumping in maiden chases: stays 2¾m: acts on heavy going. *Ferdy Murphy*   **c–** **h116**

BILLY MURPHY 4 gr.g. Silver Patriarch (IRE) – Sperrin View (Fidel) [2006/7 F13s 16s⁴ 16v² 21g Mar 20] third foal: dam, winning chaser, stayed 2½m: tailed off in bumper: modest form when in frame over hurdles: bred to stay beyond 2m: needs to learn to settle. *P. E. Cowley*   **h85** **F–**

BILLY ROW 6 b.g. Keen – Arasong (Aragon) [2006/7 F–: 17dᵖᵘ c16vᵖᵘ Dec 15] strong gelding: seems of no account: left James Moffatt prior to chasing debut: sold 1,000 gns Doncaster January Sales. *R. F. Fisher*   **c–** **h–**

BGC Silver Cup Handicap Chase, Ascot—
Billyvoddan is transformed by first-time blinkers as he claims a wide-margin win under Leighton Aspell

BILLYVODDAN (IRE) 8 b.g. Accordion – Derryclare (Pollerton) [2006/7 c138, h–: **c156**
c19d⁵ c24d* c21g³ c36gᵖᵘ Apr 14] strong, lengthy gelding: winning hurdler: very smart **h–**
chaser: blinkered last 3 outings, improved form when winning listed BGC Silver Cup
Handicap Chase at Ascot in December by 12 lengths from Zabenz, then close third to
Taranis (FR) in Grade 2 Festival Trophy at Cheltenham (hampered 4 out and keeping on
strongly): didn't take to fences after hampered badly Canal Turn in Grand National at
Aintree: probably stays 25f: raced on good going or softer: has run well when sweating
and edgy. *H. D. Daly*

BILLYWILL (IRE) 13 b. or br.g. Topanoora – Sandy Maid (Sandy Creek) [2006/7 **c–**
c21gᵘʳ May 3] lengthy gelding: winning chaser, well held when unseating on hunter **h–**
debut: successful in point earlier in 2006: stays 21f: acts on heavy going: tried in cheekpieces: tongue tied last 6 starts. *Mrs K. Smyly*

BINT SESARO (IRE) 6 b.m. Sesaro (USA) – Crazed Rainbow (USA) (Graustark) **h–**
[2006/7 h–, F–: 16g 20dᵖᵘ 20m⁶ Feb 4] no form. *Mrs L. B. Normile*

BIRCHALL (IRE) 8 b.g. Priolo (USA) – Ballycuirke (Taufan (USA)) [2006/7 c–, h–: **c–**
20g 22m⁵ 24m⁵ Jul 12] good-topped gelding: poor maiden hurdler: well beaten only **h77**
outing over fences: probably stays easy 3m: tongue tied last 4 starts: sold 1,500 gns
Doncaster May Sales. *Ian Williams*

BIRDWATCH 9 b.g. Minshaanshu Amad (USA) – Eider (Niniski (USA)) [2006/7 **c89 §**
h103: c17s⁵ c22v⁴ c16vᶠ c16v² c16s⁴ c20d⁴ c16v c22d⁴ c25m Apr 28] sturdy gelding: fair **h–**
hurdler: modest novice chaser: effective at 2m (given testing conditions) to 3m: acts on
heavy going: often wears blinkers, in cheekpieces last 2 outings: temperamental: sold
7,500 gns Doncaster May Sales. *K. G. Reveley*

BIRKSIDE 4 ch.g. Spinning World (USA) – Bright Hope (IRE) (Danehill (USA)) **h–**
[2006/7 16vᵖᵘ 16mᵖᵘ Apr 9] fairly useful maiden on Flat (stays 1¼m) at 3 yrs for
W. Swinburn, below form in 2007: no show both starts over hurdles: wears headgear: also
tried tongue tied. *B. G. Powell*

120

BIRKWOOD 8 b.g. Presidium – Wire Lass (New Brig) [2006/7 c100: c25v^F Mar 2] fairly useful pointer: won maiden hunter in 2006: narrow lead when falling fatally 3 out at Ayr: stayed 25f. *Ian Stark* **c104**

BISCAR TWO (IRE) 6 b.g. Daggers Drawn (USA) – Thoughtful Kate (Rock Hopper) [2006/7 h101§: 17s 24v 16g^F Mar 21] small, leggy, angular gelding: fair hurdler in 2005/6, lightly raced since: dropped markedly in class, upsides winner when falling last in seller at Chepstow: stays 2½m: raced on good going or softer (acts on heavy): wears blinkers/cheekpieces: ungenuine. *A. E. Jones* **h89 §**

BISCAY WIND (IRE) 7 ch.m. Anshan – La Bise (Callernish) [2006/7 h–: 25d^pu c20s^pu c26s^pu Dec 23] rather sparely-made mare: no form: tried blinkered: sold 900 gns Doncaster January Sales. *T. R. George* **c–** **h–**

BISHOP'S BRIDGE (IRE) 9 b.g. Norwich – River Swell (IRE) (Over The River (FR)) [2006/7 c112§, h108§: c17m^6 19d* c18g* c19g* c19d^2 c19g^2 Mar 31] tall gelding: fairly useful hurdler: left Andrew Turnell and off 5 months, improved form when winning handicap at Exeter in October by 2½ lengths from Double Dizzy: also progressed well back over fences: won handicaps at Fontwell and Ascot (beat Turgeonev by ½ length) in November: runner-up 2 starts after, useful form when 1¼ lengths behind Misty Dancer in quite valuable handicap at Ascot final one: stays 2½m: acts on soft and good to firm going: effective with or without headgear: idles in front, sometimes markedly. *Miss E. C. Lavelle* **c130** **h121**

BISHY BARNABY (IRE) 6 b.g. Flemensfirth (USA) – Brief Gaiety (IRE) (Be My Native (USA)) [2006/7 F16v Jan 12] €5,000 3-y-o: rangy gelding: third foal: dam unraced: backward, well held in bumper on debut. *H. B. Hodge* **F–**

Mr Trevor Hemmings' "Billyvoddan"

BITE UN FIGHT 4 ch.f. Classic Cliche (IRE) – Ginger Rogers (Gildoran) [2006/7 **h89**
16m 17m⁴ 16d⁵ 20g⁶ 19s³ 21v³ 22v 22s 24m* 24m³ Apr 25] smallish, lengthy filly: first
foal: dam fair 1¾m to 17f winner: modest hurdler: won conditional jockeys handicap at
Exeter in April: stays 3m: acts on heavy and good to firm going: in cheekpieces last 2
starts: tried tongue tied. *Miss J. S. Davis*

BLACK AND TAN (IRE) 7 b. or br.g. Presenting – Bold Glen (Bold Owl) [2006/7 **h–**
h102, F88: 16s 20v Feb 16] good-topped gelding: fair form at best over hurdles: well held
both starts in 2006/7, left P. Hobbs after first: will stay 3m. *Carl Llewellyn*

BLACK APALACHI (IRE) 8 b.g. Old Vic – Hattons Dream (IRE) (Be My Native **c120**
(USA)) [2006/7 c128, h–: c29s c24vᵖᵘ c24d c24v⁵ 20v Feb 21] leggy, angular gelding: **h94**
fairly useful chaser: not at best in handicaps in 2006/7: well held in minor event back over
hurdles final start: stays 3½m: raced on good going or softer: wore cheekpieces fourth
start. *P. J. Rothwell, Ireland*

BLACKBRIERY THYNE (IRE) 8 br.m. Good Thyne (USA) – Briery Gale (Strong **h109**
Gale) [2006/7 h77, F88: 16g* 21v³ 22s 21g⁴ 21g Apr 19] leggy, good-topped mare: fair
novice hurdler: won mares race at Towcester in November: best effort when fourth to
Karello Bay in listed mares handicap at Newbury: likely to stay 3m: raced on good
ground or softer (acts on heavy). *H. D. Daly*

BLACKBURY 5 b.m. Overbury (IRE) – Fenian Court (IRE) (John French) [2006/7 F–: **h–**
16f 17m 16m⁶ Jun 11] no sign of ability. *J. W. Unett*

BLACK CHALK (IRE) 9 br.g. Roselier (FR) – Ann's Cap (IRE) (Cardinal Flower) **c83**
[2006/7 c20dᶠ c24g⁴ c20dᶠ Dec 30] no form over hurdles for B. Jones: failed to complete **h–**
in 2 points in 2006: poor form in chases: made all in amateur handicap at Musselburgh in
December: barely stays 3m. *D. J. P. Barry, Ireland*

BLACK CLOUD 4 b.g. Cloudings (IRE) – Dutch Czarina (Prince Sabo) [2006/7 16s **h73 +**
18g Mar 18] rangy gelding: half-brother to 2 winners on Flat, including fairly useful
sprinter Czar Wars (by Warrshan): dam 1¼m winner: little impact in 2 starts over hurdles,
though signs of ability second time. *A. Ennis*

BLACK COLLAR 8 br.m. Bob's Return (IRE) – Rosemoss (Le Moss) [2006/7 h71: **c100**
c25d³ c25s* c24sᵖᵘ Jan 24] tall mare: poor novice hurdler: quickly better over fences, **h–**
winning handicap at Folkestone in January: bled next time: stays 25f: raced on going
softer than good over jumps. *K. C. Bailey*

BLACKCOMB MOUNTAIN (USA) 5 b. or br.m. Royal Anthem (USA) – Ski **h79**
Racer (FR) (Ski Chief (USA)) [2006/7 h–: 16g 16m⁵ 20m² 23d³ 17d³ 19mᵖᵘ 22m⁴ 20m³
24m³ 17s⁵ 22m³ 22m⁵ Sep 2] poor novice hurdler: runner-up in points in 2007: stays 3m:
acts on good to firm and good to soft going: usually wears headgear nowadays.
M. F. Harris

BLACKCURRANT (FR) 7 br.g. Cadoudal (FR) – Double Spring (FR) (Double Bed **c–**
(FR)) [2006/7 20g 22v 19sᵖᵘ 16v 17dᵖᵘ c20gᵖᵘ 16g Apr 9] lengthy gelding: first foal: dam **h–**
won at around 1¾m over hurdles in France: sixth in bumper: no form over jumps: tried
visored: sold 1,500 gns Doncaster May Sales. *J. R. Turner*

BLACK DE BESSY (FR) 9 b.g. Perrault – Emerald City (Top Ville) [2006/7 c126, **c120**
h115+: c24g⁶ Oct 14] sturdy gelding: successful only start over hurdles in Britain: fairly **h–**
useful handicap chaser: left D. Elsworth, respectable effort only outing in 2006/7: stays
25f: acts on soft and good to firm going. *R. H. Alner*

BLACKERGREEN 8 b.g. Zaffaran (USA) – Ballinderry Moss (Le Moss) [2006/7 **c90 x**
c94x, h116: c25s c25dᵘʳ c22v⁶ c24v² c25g⁶ 24g⁶ Apr 21] useful-looking gelding: fairly **h107**
useful hurdler, respectable effort final outing: usually let down by jumping and modest
form at best over fences: stays 27f: acts on soft and good to firm going, probably on
heavy: wore cheekpieces once. *Mrs S. J. Smith*

BLACK FROST (IRE) 11 ch.g. Glacial Storm (USA) – Black Tulip (Pals Passage) **c–**
[2006/7 c–, h–: c24m⁴ May 10] sturdy gelding: useful handicap chaser at one time: in **h–**
frame all completed starts in points, including in 2007: stays 2¾m: acts on heavy and
good to firm going: has been let down by jumping. *J. M. Turner*

BLACK HARRY (IRE) 7 b. or br.g. Flemensfirth (USA) – Raise An Ace (Buck- **h143 p**
skin (FR)) [2006/7 F111p: 20s 16s⁵ 20v³ 19v* 24v* 24gᶠ Mar 16]
    Twelve months on from recommending a smart Irish novice hurdler by
Flemensfirth as one to follow over fences, *Chasers & Hurdlers* has no hesitation in
doing so again. That despite being wide of the mark last time, with Mounthenry

returned to hurdling, unsuccessfully, after failing to win any of the three chases he contested, largely let down by his jumping. It will be disappointing if Black Harry, a rangy individual who looks every inch a chaser, doesn't fare a great deal better. Indeed, he looks capable of making his presence felt in the top staying novice events.

Black Harry, now seven, has had relatively little racing, not making his debut until December 2005 then off the course for eleven months before his hurdling career got under way. It was clear from his debut that Black Harry had plenty of ability—in winning a seven-runner bumper at Leopardstown he had subsequent Champion Bumper winner Hairy Molly two lengths behind in second—though it took a little while for him to reproduce that sort of form over hurdles, not getting off the mark until his fourth start. That was in a twenty-five-runner maiden over nineteen furlongs at Naas in January, Black Harry justifying favouritism by six lengths from Head Held High. Two weeks later, Black Harry started favourite for a novice event at Fairyhouse, where he was up against two other winning hurdlers in Offaly and Wickford. The latter failed by a long way to give his running, but Offaly made a race of it with Black Harry until his stamina gave out. Black Harry, on the other hand, showed that he had stamina in abundance, making most of the running on his first attempt at three miles and already well in command when Offaly was eased on the run-in, keeping on strongly to draw a distance clear. Raced only on soft or heavy ground thus far, Black Harry had much less testing conditions to contend with on his next start, in the Spa Novices' Hurdle at Cheltenham, though he faced much more testing opposition. One of four Irish challengers in the twenty-runner field, Black Harry was the shortest-priced of that quartet, just ahead of Hairy Molly in the betting, and proved easily the best of them, the only horse in the field to give supporters of hot favourite Wichita Lineman any cause for concern in the latter

Sean O'Driscoll's "Black Harry"

stages. After travelling strongly, racing close to the pace, Black Harry led going best three out, and Wichita Lineman pulled away from the remainder soon after jumping two out. Gradually giving way on the long run to the last, Black Harry was a length behind and held when he made his first mistake and took a heavy fall, but for which he would have finished a clear second. Not surprisingly, Black Harry, who had quite a hard race and lay winded for a little while after his fall, wasn't asked to do any more in the latest season. Nevertheless, the fact that old rivals Hairy Molly and Head Held High could manage only eleventh and fifteenth respectively at Cheltenham is a clear illustration of the rapid progress Black Harry had made.

Black Harry (IRE) (b. or br.g. 2000)	Flemensfirth (USA) (b 1992)	Alleged (b 1974)	Hoist The Flag
			Princess Pout
		Etheldreda (ch 1985)	Diesis
			Royal Bond
	Raise An Ace (b 1987)	Buckskin (b 1973)	Yelapa
			Bete A Bon Dieu
		Rent A Card (b 1977)	Raise You Ten
			Doone Valley

Flemensfirth, whose other notable produce include Cheltenham Festival winners Total Enjoyment (2004 Champion Bumper) and Idole First (2005 Coral Cup and 2007 Racing Post Plate), was lightly raced himself. He had just nine starts in four seasons' racing for John Gosden, showing very smart form at up to around a mile and a quarter, winning five races including the Prix Dollar as both a three- and four-year-old, and he also finished a creditable fifth to Celtic Swing in the Prix du Jockey Club on his only outing over a mile and a half. Black Harry's dam Raise An Ace was lightly raced as well, though her brief spell over hurdles and in Irish points (runner-up once in each sphere) came during a break from her broodmare duties—she produced her first foal aged just four. Her only other winner to date is Executive Ace (by Executive Perk), who looked an exciting prospect when beating future Grand National hero Silver Birch to win a maiden Irish point in 2002 but never raced again. Raise An Ace has visited Flemensfirth no less than eight times since 1998, Black Harry one of seven foals she's returned during this period, with fillies accounting for all bar one of the six others. These include Black Harry's unraced sisters Scotch Ace (2001) and Grancore Girl (2003), the latter making €18,000 at the 2006 Goffs Land Rover Sales. Meanwhile, Raise An Ace's unnamed 2005 gelding fetched €60,000 later in the year, which was the highest price paid for any of the forty-six Flemensfirth yearlings sold at public auction in 2006. Raise An Ace, a half-sister to four winning jumpers including the fairly useful staying chaser Yorkshire Edition, is out of the unraced Rent A Card, herself a half-sister to the top-class hurdler/very smart chaser at up to two and a half miles Dramatist. It would be a surprise if Black Harry doesn't further enhance this family's reputation in 2007/8. *W. P. Mullins, Ireland*

BLACK HILLS 8 b.g. Dilum (USA) – Dakota Girl (Northern State (USA)) [2006/7 h114: c17d³ c17m² c18s³ c20d² c21s* c21s² c22g² c21g² c20m* Apr 27] big gelding: winning hurdler: useful chaser: won handicaps at Wincanton in January and Sandown (by 4 lengths from Mr Boo in 5-runner event) in April: good second in similar events all starts in between: stays 2¾m: acts on soft and good to firm going: usually tongue tied, also wears cheekpieces nowadays: consistent. *J. A. Geake*   **c133 h–**

BLACKIES ALL (USA) 9 b.g. Hazaam (USA) – Allijess (USA) (Tom Rolfe) [2006/7 h–: 20s^F 20s² 24g 20m Jul 25] modest handicap hurdler: off 2 years, form in 2006/7 only on second outing: lame final one: stays 3m: acts on soft going: tried blinkered. *W. M. Brisbourne*   **h89**

BLACK JACK KETCHUM (IRE) 8 b.g. Oscar (IRE) – Cailin Supreme (IRE) (Supreme Leader) [2006/7 h159p: 21s* 24v⁵ 24gᶠ 24g² Apr 12]   **h161 +**
That Jackdaws Castle would win a Grade 1 staying hurdle with one of its offspring of Oscar seemed almost a given at the start of the season; that the stable did so with Refinement at Punchestown, rather than with Black Jack Ketchum at Cheltenham, was the source of surprise and, for connections of the latter at least, some disappointment. After his unbeaten novice season, which included impressive wins in both the Spa Hurdle at Cheltenham and the Sefton at Aintree, Black

Jack Ketchum was made ante-post favourite for the World Hurdle in 2007, a position he maintained until the race itself. But, come the day, he was an early casualty. Black Jack Ketchum's campaign was otherwise restricted to three runs, and on only one of them was he successful. His second season over hurdles provided more questions than answers, raising doubts about his well-being, his stamina, his ability to handle testing ground and even whether he was quite so good as he had looked as a novice.

Black Jack Ketchum's season, when it eventually got under way, started well enough. Looking in the pink of condition, he landed the odds in the Mears Group "Relkeel" Hurdle at Cheltenham in December with considerable ease, by three lengths from Blazing Bailey (who was receiving 6 lb), his one serious opponent in a field of five for what was hardly a race befitting its Grade 2 status—though, in mitigation, potential rivals were probably scared off by Black Jack Ketchum's presence. Sound jumping, an ability to travel strongly and a good turn of foot, features of his wins the previous season, were all in evidence over an extended two miles five furlongs on soft ground. As a novice, Black Jack Ketchum had raced on ground no softer than good to soft—he won on good to firm in the Spa—and the prospect of very soft ground had led to his missing his intended first outing of the season, in the West Yorkshire Hurdle at Wetherby in late-October. The testing ground was also given as an explanation for his absence from a minor event at Cheltenham on New Year's Day, when he would have faced another straightforward task. However, with the wet winter showing no sign of letting up, Black Jack Ketchum took his chance in the Cleeve Hurdle, again at Cheltenham, at the end of January, despite the ground being heavy, as heavy as has been seen at the track in recent times. He started odds on, despite fears about the ground and despite the opposition including the 2005 Stayers' Hurdle winner Inglis Drever. Again travelling well, Black Jack Ketchum looked poised for victory turning for home before he stopped quickly, his rider Tony McCoy accepting the situation very quickly and allowing him to come home in his own time, crossing the line thirty-five lengths fifth behind Blazing Bailey, whom he had beaten so easily less than

Mears Group "Relkeel" Hurdle, Cheltenham—a sparkling start to an anti-climactic campaign for Black Jack Ketchum, who gives weight and a comprehensive beating to Blazing Bailey (white face)

two months previously. The verdict of both trainer and rider was that the ground was to blame.

Another explanation offered itself, however: that something was not right with Black Jack Ketchum. After all, the ground appeared no handicap until approaching the last, where he was beaten in a stride. He also appeared to be not striding out properly near the finish. A low blood count had resulted in Black Jack Ketchum's missing outings in the Betfair Handicap Hurdle at Haydock and the Long Distance Hurdle at Newbury in November and, even before his reappearance, there had been speculation as to his well-being. However, O'Neill reported that no physical problem came to light with Black Jack Ketchum after the Cleeve. Odds on for the World Hurdle prior to the Cleeve, Black Jack Ketchum was available at 3/1 for that race after his defeat, the prospect of testing ground at the Festival meaning that he remained at around those odds up to the week before. As the ground dried, however, so his odds shortened and Black Jack Ketchum started 2/1 favourite, only to fall heavily at the third after a rare jumping lapse.

The Liverpool Hurdle offered Black Jack Ketchum the chance to redeem himself, taking on the first three at Cheltenham, Inglis Drever, Mighty Man and Blazing Bailey. Black Jack Ketchum just shaded favouritism ahead of Mighty Man and the pair had the race between them into the straight, with Black Jack Ketchum looking to be travelling the better before finding no extra after two out. In form terms, Black Jack Ketchum ran as well as he ever has, going down by thirteen lengths to a top-class opponent, and his performance may be as good as he is. That is a view which is still rather hard to swallow, however, as there is certainly nothing wrong with the form of his visually most impressive Sefton win—third-placed Neptune Collonges and fifth-placed Ungaro both landed Grade 1 events over fences during the latest season, whilst the fourth Powerstation (beaten seventeen and a half lengths at Aintree) rounded off his 2006/7 campaign with a close second to Refinement in the aforementioned Punchestown race. It could simply be that, against the very best opposition, three miles stretches Black Jack Ketchum's stamina and he may well prove at least as effective over shorter. So far as championship races are concerned that would effectively mean dropping to two miles prior to the Aintree Hurdle (the Hatton's Grace at Fairyhouse is over two and a half but usually run on testing ground) That said, Black Jack Ketchum has yet to race over two miles over hurdles, regarded by connections as a stayer for all that he shows plenty of speed at longer distances. A run at two miles would certainly be worth the experiment, though it looks unlikely given that the unfortunate absence of Mighty Man leaves the staying division that bit weaker in the coming season and Black Jack Ketchum, on form, must be a leading contender for the stayers' crown again. It seems unlikely that he will be switched to fences, as he is an unprepossessing sort, smallish and close coupled.

Black Jack Ketchum (IRE) (b.g. 1999)	Oscar (IRE) (b 1994)	Sadler's Wells (b 1981)	Northern Dancer
			Fairy Bridge
		Snow Day (b 1978)	Reliance II
			Vindaria
	Cailin Supreme (IRE) (b 1991)	Supreme Leader (b 1982)	Bustino
			Princess Zena
		Cailin Donn (ch 1978)	London Gazette
			Sunny Gal

Black Jack Ketchum's family was covered in detail in *Chasers & Hurdlers 2005/06* and there is little to add about his immediate relations. He is the first foal of his dam Cailin Supreme, a useful hurdler herself at up to two and a half miles in Ireland. Her second foal Castlekelly (by Bob Back), altogether a much more imposing sort, made his debut for his owner/breeder in the Grade 1 bumper at the Punchestown Festival in April but, looking far from wound up and lacking experience, finished tailed off. Cailin Supreme's third foal Saddleeruppat (by Saddlers' Hall), winner of two bumpers in 2005/6, wasn't seen out in the latest season.

As stated, Black Jack Ketchum is by Oscar and his failures at Cheltenham and Aintree looked likely to make it a modest season in pattern events for his sire, particularly given how many foals he had running for him. This was redeemed to some extent at Punchestown, where Refinement was one of three Grade 1 winners for the 1997 Prix du Jockey Club runner-up. Silent Oscar and Offshore Account were the others, the latter Oscar's best chaser to date. Like Black Jack Ketchum, Refinement and Silent Oscar seem likely to prove best over hurdles and Oscar's record doesn't compare favourably as a potential sire of chasers with, say, Presenting's. The 1995 Derby third Presenting, who has been at stud a year longer, also had three Grade 1 winners in 2006/7, Denman, Another Promise and Silverburn, and already has a Cheltenham Gold Cup winner, War of Attrition, and third, Turpin Green.

Black Jack Ketchum spoilt his appearance by sweating before the World Hurdle and didn't take the eye so much as his rivals in the paddock at Aintree, though his somewhat uninspiring appearance at the latter track wasn't pronounced enough to have been a factor in his performance. He was given a thorough veterinary examination in the weeks after that performance and was operated on for a soft palate. *Jonjo O'Neill*

BLACKMAIL (USA) 9 b.g. Twining (USA) – Black Penny (USA) (Private Account (USA)) [2006/7 16mᵖᵘ Apr 8] fair on Flat (stays 1¾m), successful twice in 2006: never a factor in maiden on belated hurdling debut. *P. Mitchell*   h–

BLACK OPTIMIST (IRE) 13 br.g. Roselier (FR) – Borys Glen (Furry Glen) [2006/7 c–: c25gᵖᵘ May 3] workmanlike gelding: winning pointer: lightly-raced chaser, second in novice in 2002 only completed outing: tried blinkered. *Mrs S. J. Maiden*   c–

BLACKOUT (IRE) 12 b.g. Black Monday – Fine Bess (Fine Blade (USA)) [2006/7 c–, h–: c25gᶠ Nov 4] of little account. *J. Barclay*   c–
h–

BLACK RAINBOW (IRE) 9 br.m. Definite Article – Inonder (Belfort (FR)) [2006/7 24g⁶ 17s² 19s* 20s 16s Jan 31] sturdy mare: winning pointer: modest hurdler: won handicap at Market Rasen in August: stays 19f: acts on soft going: trainer ridden. *Miss T. Jackson*   h92

BLACK SHAN (IRE) 7 br.g. Anshan – Singing Forever (Chief Singer) [2006/7 h–: c21s⁶ c20g⁴ c23m Apr 25] lengthy gelding: tubed: no solid form over jumps: visored last 2 starts. *A. Ennis*   c–
h–

BLACK SMOKE (IRE) 10 gr.g. Ala Hounak – Korean Citizen (IRE) (Mister Lord (USA)) [2006/7 c20v c25vᵖᵘ c28v⁵ c29vᵖᵘ c28g⁵ Apr 7] good-topped gelding: modest handicap chaser in 2004/5 for R. C. Guest: off 21 months, well below best in 2006/7: stays 3¾m: raced on good going or softer. *K. G. Reveley*   c75
h–

BLACKTHORN 8 ch.g. Deploy – Balliasta (USA) (Lyphard (USA)) [2006/7 h81: 16s* 16d² 16d 16s⁵ 20vᵖᵘ 19g⁴ 16m Apr 24] modest hurdler: won seller at Leicester in November: stays 19f: acts on heavy and good to firm going: races prominently. *M. Appleby*   h86

BLACKTHORN BOY (IRE) 5 b.g. Zaffaran (USA) – First And Foremost (IRE) (Boreen (FR)) [2006/7 aF16g³ aF16g³ F14g* F18m Apr 26] first foal: dam unraced out of half-sister to smart staying chaser Glyde Court: fair form in bumpers: won at Fontwell in April by 7 lengths from Taipan's Promise: possibly amiss there next time. *G. L. Moore*   F91

BLACK VEN (IRE) 6 b.g. Presenting – Mini Minor (IRE) (Black Minstrel) [2006/7 F16g May 6] fourth foal: dam unraced half-sister to fairly useful staying hurdler/chaser Menebuck: never dangerous in bumper on debut. *O. Sherwood*   F–

BLAEBERRY 6 b.m. Kirkwall – Top Berry (High Top) [2006/7 h108: 24d* 24d 24d⁶ 16s³ 21d² 21g⁴ Apr 19] good-topped mare: fairly useful handicap hurdler: won at Exeter in October: best efforts last 2 starts, including when fourth of 18 to Silver Charmer in listed mares event at Cheltenham: stays 3m: raced on good going or softer: reliable. *Miss E. C. Lavelle*   h122

BLAIRGOWRIE (IRE) 8 b.g. Supreme Leader – Parsons Term (IRE) (The Parson) [2006/7 c114p, h113: c16dᵖᵘ c22vᶠ Nov 30] fair winning hurdler/chaser: should have stayed beyond 21f: acted on heavy going: tongue tied in 2006/7: front runner/raced prominently: dead. *C. J. Mann*   c–
h–

BLAKE HALL LAD (IRE) 6 b.g. Cape Cross (IRE) – Queen of Art (IRE) (Royal Academy (USA)) [2006/7 h–: 20fᶠ 24mᵖᵘ Sep 3] angular gelding: no form in novice hurdles. *S. T. Lewis*   h–

BLAKENEY COAST (IRE) 10 b.g. Satco (FR) – Up To More Trix (IRE) (Torus) [2006/7 c106, h–: c20sᵖᵘ c20f c16d³ Jun 12] good sort: fair handicap chaser, won 3 times in early-2005/6: little impact since: stays 2½m: best efforts on good/good to firm ground: tried in cheekpieces/visor: tongue tied. *C. L. Tizzard*   c–
h–

BLAKENEY RUN 7 gr.g. Commanche Run – Lady Blakeney (Baron Blakeney) **h89 ?**
[2006/7 F70: 19m^{pu} 22d^{pu} 20s^3 24v 20v 22d Mar 20] workmanlike gelding: third to
Supreme Huntress in falsely-run novice at Chepstow, only form over hurdles: prone to
mistakes. *Miss M. Bragg*

BLANDFORD FLYER 4 b.g. Soviet Star (USA) – Vento Del Oreno (FR) (Lando **h84**
(GER)) [2006/7 16v^6 16m^6 16m^6 16v 17g^3 17m^3 17m Apr 28] maiden on Flat, sold out of
W. Swinburn's stable 3,200 gns Doncaster November Sales: poor hurdler, third in sellers:
raced around 2m: acts on good to firm ground: tried tongue tied. *M. Appleby*

BLANDINGS CASTLE 6 b.g. Cloudings (IRE) – Country House (Town And **h73**
Country) [2006/7 h–: 20m 22g 17g* 16d 19d^3 17s^6 Nov 17] poor hurdler: won conditional jockeys handicap at Newton Abbot in August: stays 19f: acts on good to soft going:
tried visored. *Nick Williams*

BLANK CANVAS (IRE) 9 b.g. Presenting – Strong Cloth (IRE) (Strong Gale) **c–**
[2006/7 c79?, h–: c25d^{pu} c19d^{pu} Jun 2] useful-looking gelding: lightly raced: modest **h–**
form over hurdles: never dangerous only completed outing over fences: stays 3m: tried
tongue tied. *K. C. Bailey*

BLAST THE PAST 5 b.m. Past Glories – Yours Or Mine (IRE) (Exhibitioner) [2006/7 **h93 +**
F–: 20d 19d 20s^{ur} 17m* Apr 9] leggy, lengthy mare: much improved (modest form) when
winning novice handicap hurdle at Sedgefield: will prove best around 2m with emphasis
on speed. *T. D. Walford*

BLAZE AHEAD (IRE) 7 ch.g. Mohaajir (USA) – Flaxen Queen (Peacock (FR)) **c98**
[2006/7 22d 21s^3 22v^5 21s* c25s^3 c22s c24m^2 Apr 9] sturdy gelding: half-brother to 3m **h88**
chase winner Brunker Buoy (by Glacial Storm): dam maiden: runner-up 3 times in Irish
points in 2006: bought 14,000 gns Doncaster May Sales: improved effort over hurdles
(modest form) when winning novice handicap at Towcester in December: better form
again when placed 2 of 3 starts in chases: stays 25f: acts on soft and good to firm ground.
B. G. Powell

BLAZE ON 8 ch.g. Minster Son – Clova (Move Off) [2006/7 c92x, h–: 19v 16v^6 16d **c– x**
Mar 21] leggy gelding: winning pointer: maiden hurdler/chaser, inclined to make **h–**
mistakes in hunters: should stay 3m. *R. H. York*

BLAZING BAILEY 5 b.g. Mister Baileys – Wannaplantatree (Niniski (USA)) **h160**
[2006/7 h144: 16f 16d* 21s^2 25d^4 24v* 24g^3 24g^F Apr 12]
      Widely expected to be a race which would serve to strengthen the World
Hurdle claims of ante-post favourite Black Jack Ketchum, the Grade 2 Byrne Bros
Cleeve Hurdle, run over three miles at Cheltenham in January, proved anything but
as the form-book was turned on its head. When odds-on Black Jack Ketchum cried
enough on the run to the last, it was 14/1-shot Blazing Bailey who took command,
in stark contrast to the occasion when the pair had met over an extended twenty-one
furlongs at the same venue the previous month. That time, Blazing Bailey had
played the supporting role, with Black Jack Ketchum (who was conceding 6 lb)
shrugging him aside on the run-in. While Black Jack Ketchum clearly wasn't at his
best in the Cleeve Hurdle, there was no doubt that the longer trip played more to
Blazing Bailey's strengths and that he was deserving of far more credit than he
received at the time, his improved performance tending to be overshadowed by the
disappointment with Black Jack Ketchum's. What couldn't be overlooked was the
fact that Blazing Bailey himself had staked his claim to be regarded as a serious
contender for the World Hurdle.
      Blazing Bailey had become another of the principals from the 2006
Triumph Hurdle, in which he finished six lengths third to Detroit City, to boost the
form of that event, though in his case it had required a step up from two miles to do
so. Although Blazing Bailey had defied top weight to win a four-year-old handicap
at the minimum trip at Haydock in November, following a six-month break, the
race was, overall, by no means a strong one—though subsequent totesport Trophy
winner Heathcote was beaten just over two lengths into third when in receipt of
20 lb. Blazing Bailey's battling qualities were clearly intact, however, and he duly
built on that form when stepped up in trip subsequently. He didn't do himself justice
when first tried at three miles, when fourth to Mighty Man in the Long Walk Hurdle
at Ascot, although interference after five out arguably proved costly in a muddling
affair. He proved a different proposition in the Cleeve Hurdle, on heavy going,
however, which also ended up a tactical contest. The gelding's trainer and rider

reportedly walked the course independently beforehand to identify the best ground, and Blazing Bailey raced apart from the others after he was switched to the inside turning into the straight. Running on strongly under pressure after hitting the front, Blazing Bailey pulled away to win by four lengths from the 2005 World Hurdle winner Inglis Drever, from whom he received 8 lb. Blazing Bailey couldn't confirm the placings when the pair met at level weights in the World Hurdle, run under much less testing conditions over the same course and distance in March, but, in finishing third behind Inglis Drever and Mighty Man, Blazing Bailey showed further improvement. Waited with, travelling well, he looked to be going best when making a mistake two out, following it with another error at the last when still holding every chance. Unable to quicken, he finished four and three quarter lengths behind the winner, high-class form which might have been improved on but for those errors, though it is unlikely he would have been any closer than third. Blazing Bailey's jumping was to let him down to a much greater degree on his only subsequent outing, when he fell at the fourth last in the Liverpool Hurdle at Aintree, too far out to say how he would have fared. He was niggled at at the time, but close up in third behind the winner Mighty Man and runner-up Black Jack Ketchum. Despite appearances to the contrary on his last two starts, Blazing Bailey's jumping isn't a cause for too much concern, and he remains one who is going to be a force to reckon with in the good staying races.

Blazing Bailey (b.g. 2002)	Mister Baileys (b 1991)	Robellino (b 1978)	Roberto
			Isobelline
		Thimblerigger (ch 1976)	Sharpen Up
			Tender Annie
	Wannaplantatree (b 1991)	Niniski (b 1976)	Nijinsky
			Virginia Hills
		Cataclysmic (br 1985)	Ela-Mana-Mou
			Hardirondo

A fair handicapper on the Flat for Stuart Williams, successful over a mile and three quarters at Nottingham, Blazing Bailey was sold for 27,000 guineas at the 2005 Newmarket Autumn Sales and quickly made his mark over hurdles for his

Byrne Bros Cleeve Hurdle, Cheltenham—Blazing Bailey (white face) knuckles down in typically game fashion to lower the colours of Inglis Drever (jumping) and a below-par Black Jack Ketchum

new connections. Blazing Bailey won juvenile events at Fontwell on his first two starts, and, as well as finishing third in the Triumph, he was runner-up in both the Adonis Hurdle (beaten by the World Hurdle fifth Kasbah Bliss) and the Mersey Novices' Hurdle in his first season. By the 1994 Two Thousand Guineas winner Mister Baileys, Blazing Bailey gets his stamina from his dam Wannaplantatree, who was also a fair handicapper on the Flat for Norman Babbage. Wannaplantatree also got off the mark in a mile-and-three-quarter event at Nottingham. That was as a four-year-old, and the following season she sprang a 25/1 surprise in the Queen's Prize over two miles at Kempton. Retired after reportedly breaking a blood vessel on her next outing, Wannaplantatree produced two foals before Blazing Bailey, both of whom were successful on the Flat for Alan Jarvis. Aker Wood (by Bin Ajwaad) was a fairly useful winner at up to a mile and a half, while Armada Grove (by Fleetwood) was a fair seven-furlong winner at two. Blazing Bailey's grandam Cataclysmic, a daughter of the fairly useful and game stayer Hardirondo, won twice over a mile and a half as a three-year-old. A game performer, like his great grandam, Blazing Bailey has run well on ground ranging from heavy to good to firm over hurdles. He won on firm on the Flat, and wasn't disgraced on the only occasion he has encountered such a surface as a hurdler, tenth of eighteen finishers (under top weight) when faced with an insufficient test of stamina in the Swinton Handicap at Haydock on his first start in the latest season. *A. King*

BLAZING BATMAN 14 ch.g. Shaab – Cottage Blaze (Sunyboy) [2006/7 c81§, h–§: c26d^R c23f^6 c18g^6 22d c26v 21s^3 c19d^5 21d c31s 17v c16v^5 c24d 16v Feb 18] sturdy gelding: maiden hurdler: winning chaser: no solid form in 2006/7: blinkered once: unenthusiastic. *Dr P. Pritchard* c– §
h– §

BLAZING GUNS (IRE) 8 ch.g. Un Desperado (FR) – Quefort (Quayside) [2006/7 19d 16s 17s^6 c20d^6 Mar 26] very tall gelding: fair form in 2 bumpers in 2003/4: well held over hurdles/on chasing debut. *Miss H. C. Knight* c–
h–

BLAZING HILLS 11 ch.g. Shaab – Cottage Blaze (Sunyboy) [2006/7 c92, h–: c24s c26s^{pu} c26g^2 c24m* c23g^{ur} c23g^4 c24g^{pu} c23m^5 24d^{pu} c24m c22g^2 c23m^{ur} Nov 13] good-bodied gelding: maiden hurdler: fair handicap chaser on his day: won at Southwell in June: stays 3¼m: acts on firm and good to soft going: has worn blinkers, in cheekpieces last 2 starts: usually races prominently: unreliable. *P. T. Dalton* c101 §
h–

BLAZING SKY (IRE) 7 b.m. Beneficial – Blazing Comet (Deroulede) [2006/7 18s* 16v^5 20v^2 20d^5 18v* 20m 18m^3 Apr 25] €19,000 4-y-o: rather leggy mare: fourth foal: half-sister to winning hurdlers Blazing Missile (by Durgam), at 2½m, and Halley's Comet (by Roselier), stayed 3m: dam, winning 2m chaser, from family of useful 2m to 2½m hurdler/chaser: bumper winner: fairly useful novice hurdler: reportedly injured knee and off 17 months prior to reappearance: won mares events at Punchestown (listed race, easily by 9 lengths from Brogella) in October and Downpatrick (made most to beat Candy Girl 5½ lengths) in February: creditable 3 lengths third to Grangeclare Lark in Grade 3 mares race at Punchestown: stays 2½m: acts on heavy and good to firm going: has folded tamely. *F. F. McGuinness, Ireland* h125

BLEAK HOUSE (IRE) 5 b.g. Rudimentary (USA) – Dannkalia (IRE) (Shernazar) [2006/7 F104: 16g* 16d^3 19g^3 Feb 2] lengthy gelding: has scope: bumper winner for T. Tate: winning hurdling debut in 17-runner maiden at Aintree in October: mistakes both starts after, better effort when third of 5 to Kicks For Free in listed novice at Haydock next time: should stay beyond 2m. *J. Howard Johnson* h113

BLENDON BOY (IRE) 5 b.g. Brave Act – Negria (IRE) (Al Hareb (USA)) [2006/7 16v 20m^{pu} Mar 29] leggy gelding: no form on Flat or over hurdles. *D. W. Thompson* h–

BLEU POIS (IRE) 5 ch.g. Pistolet Bleu (IRE) – Peas (IRE) (Little Wolf) [2006/7 F91: F16v^3 F17s^2 19d^6 16v 17m 19m Apr 28] useful-looking gelding: fair form when placed in bumpers: little show over hurdles. *J. Howard Johnson* h74
F88

BLIZZARD BEACH (IRE) 6 gr.m. Saddlers' Hall (IRE) – Stepfaster (Step Together (USA)) [2006/7 F–: 17s 20m 20g 24v^{pu} 16v Feb 27] smallish, good-topped mare: no form: left J. Parkes after reappearance. *A. Parker* h–

BLOOMFIELD STORM (IRE) 14 b.g. Glacial Storm (USA) – Mylie's Response (Moyrath Response) [2006/7 c24m^{pu} May 16] medium-sized gelding: fairly useful chaser at best, usually let down by jumping: no show only start outside points since 2001/2. *Mrs S. Mollett* c– x

BLUE AMERICO (IRE) 9 br.g. Lord Americo – Princess Menelek (Menelek) **c92 x**
[2006/7 c92x, h–x: c21m^F Jun 8] tall, useful-looking gelding: fairly useful handicap **h– x**
hurdler at best: modest form over fences: likely winner when falling fatally last in maiden
at Newton Abbot: should have stayed 3m: acted on soft and good to firm going: held up,
and took good hold: made mistakes. *P. F. Nicholls*

BLUEBERRY BOY (IRE) 8 b.g. Old Vic – Glenair Lady (Golden Love) [2006/7 **c143**
h133: c16s* c20v^4 c17s^3 c16v^6 c16m^F Apr 26] strong gelding: useful hurdler: at least as **h–**
good over fences: won Grade 2 Volkswagen Craddockstown Novices' Chase at Punchestown in November by 2½ lengths from Gemini Lucy, idling markedly: in frame in
Grade 1 novices at Fairyhouse (forced good pace when 13 lengths fourth to Cailin
Alainn) and Leopardstown (11 lengths third to Schindlers Hunt) next 2 starts: stays 2½m:
acts on heavy going: races prominently: often hangs left: usually sound jumper (fell 4 out
in Grade 1 at Punchestown final start when still in contention). *Paul Stafford, Ireland*

BLUE BUSTER 7 b.g. Young Buster (IRE) – Lazybird Blue (IRE) (Bluebird (USA)) **h96**
[2006/7 h105: 16v^5 16d^3 Dec 28] tall, good sort: dual bumper winner: fair form at best
over hurdles: stays 19f: acts on soft going. *M. W. Easterby*

BLUEBYYOU (IRE) 6 b.g. Lake Coniston (IRE) – Stony View (IRE) (Tirol) [2006/7 **h91 p**
F20d* F16v* F16v^6 Jan 20] €16,000 3-y-o: third foal: closely related to 17f hurdle winner **F108**
Dolphins View (by Dolphin Street): dam unraced half-sister to smart 2m to 2½m hurdler
Bank View: useful form in bumpers: won at Sligo on debut in 2005, and at Galway and
Listowel (by ¾ length from Conor's Secret) in September: well-held fifth of 9 to Albanov
in novice at Naas on hurdling debut: tongue tied: should improve over hurdles. *T. Hogan,
Ireland*

BLUE CASCADE (IRE) 8 b.g. Royal Academy (USA) – Blaine (USA) (Lyphard's **h–**
Wish (FR)) [2006/7 16f^pu Jun 21] no show in selling/claiming hurdles: tongue tied.
G. E. Jones

BLUECOAT (USA) 7 b.g. Majestic Twoeleven (USA) – Elusive Peace (USA) (Proud **h81**
Truth (USA)) [2006/7 h–, F94: 16g 16v^5 16v^F 17s^5 20g^5 17m Apr 9] workmanlike
gelding: poor maiden hurdler: stays 2½m: acts on heavy going (won bumper on firm):
sold 1,200 gns Doncaster May Sales. *M. W. Easterby*

BLUE DOVE 4 gr.g. Silver Patriarch (IRE) – Pasja (IRE) (Posen (USA)) [2006/7 F17m **F–**
Apr 28] fifth foal: half-brother to bumper winner True Dove (by Kayf Tara) and 15f
winner Ambitious Annie (by Most Welcome): dam winning 21f hurdler: tailed off in
bumper on debut. *M. E. Sowersby*

BLUE EYED ELOISE 5 b.m. Overbury (IRE) – Galix (FR) (Sissoo) [2006/7 F16g^6 **h–**
F16v 16m Apr 8] 3,000 4-y-o: second foal: dam won twice around 2m over fences in **F83**
France: modest form on first of 2 outings in bumpers: jumped badly on hurdling debut.
B. R. Johnson

BLUE FLIGHT (IRE) 6 b.g. Fayruz – Iva's Flyer (IRE) (Imperial Frontier (USA)) **F–**
[2006/7 F17s F16d Mar 22] sixth foal: half-brother to fairly useful 5f/6f winner Reptar
(by Elbio): dam 2-y-o 5f winner: tailed off in bumpers. *Mrs P. Ford*

BLUE HILLS 6 br.g. Vettori (IRE) – Slow Jazz (USA) (Chief's Crown (USA)) [2006/7 **h–**
h85: 16m 20m 22m^pu Jul 16] rather leggy gelding: fair on Flat (stays 2m), successful 3
times on all-weather in 2007: maiden hurdler: tried in cheekpieces. *P. W. Hiatt*

BLUELAND (IRE) 8 b.m. Bigstone (IRE) – Legally Delicious (Law Society (USA)) **h91**
[2006/7 h85: 24g^5 26d^6 16v 21v^4 22g 25m* Apr 9] modest hurdler: left Noel Chance after
third outing: won handicap at Plumpton in April: stays 25f: acts on heavy and good to
firm going: wore headgear last 3 starts. *Jim Best*

BLUE LEADER (IRE) 8 b.g. Cadeaux Genereux – Blue Duster (USA) (Danzig **c– §**
(USA)) [2006/7 c–§, h95§: 17g^pu Nov 9] tall gelding: let down by jumping all 3 starts **h– §**
over fences: modest handicap hurdler: off 13 months, lame again only outing in 2006/7:
best around 2m: acts on soft going: often wears headgear/tongue strap: unreliable.
M. B. Shears

BLUE NUN 6 b.m. Bishop of Cashel – Matisse (Shareef Dancer (USA)) [2006/7 h–: **c–**
16m c19d^ur 19g^pu Jun 20] close-coupled mare: no form over hurdles: unseated sixth on **h–**
chasing debut: tried in cheekpieces/blinkers. *C. L. Popham*

BLUE PATRICK 7 gr.g. Wizard King – Great Intent (Aragon) [2006/7 16s 17g^pu **h–**
Nov 5] lengthy gelding: fair on Flat (stays 1¼m), successful in early-2006, claimed from
K. Ryan £8,000 in April: no promise in maiden hurdles. *P. A. Blockley*

BLUE REBEL (IRE) 5 gr.g. Ala Hounak – Country Melody (IRE) (Orchestra) **F–**
[2006/7 F16s Mar 3] 27,000 4-y-o: rangy gelding: half-brother to poor hurdler/chaser
Southerndown (by Montelimar), stays 3¼m, and winning 2m hurdler Little Ora (by Black
Monday): dam unraced half-sister to Sun Alliance Novices' Hurdle winner Rebel Song:
green, well held in bumper on debut. *B. I. Case*

BLUE RISING 6 gr.g. Primitive Rising (USA) – Pollytickle (Politico (USA)) [2006/7 **c–**
h86: c24s^{pu} Dec 2] sturdy gelding: modest maiden hurdler: no show in handicap on **h–**
chasing debut: stays 3m: raced on going softer than good over jumps: joined Ferdy
Murphy. *D. P. Keane*

BLUE SOVEREIGN 7 gr.g. Sovereign Water (FR) – Slack Alice (Derring Rose) **c94 §**
[2006/7 c–: c23s^4 c26d^{ro} c23m^3 c24g^{ur} c23m^F c23m^2 c23g^{ur} Nov 30] leggy gelding:
winning pointer: modest maiden chaser: would have won at Exeter fifth start but for
falling 2 out: stays 23f: acts on good to firm going: usually wears headgear: has run out/
looked less than keen. *J. L. Spearing*

BLUE SPLASH (FR) 7 b.g. Epervier Bleu – Harpyes (FR) (Quart de Vin (FR)) **c135 p**
[2006/7 h100, F83: 24g^4 24v^2 26s^2 c25v* c25s^4 c24v* Feb 24] strong gelding: fairly **h119**
useful hurdler, rejoined former trainer (from Evan Williams) prior to winning handicap at
Aintree in October by 14 lengths from Le Joyeux: quickly showed himself better still
over fences, winning novices at Exeter in January and Newcastle (jumped better, beat
More Likely easily by 14 lengths) in February: stayed last of 4 finishers to Heltornic
in Grade 2 novice at Wetherby in between: will stay beyond 3¼m: acts on heavy going:
races prominently: open to further improvement over fences. *P. Bowen*

BLUES STORY (FR) 9 b.g. Pistolet Bleu (IRE) – Herbe Sucree (FR) (Tiffauges) **c–**
[2006/7 c–, h82d: 16s^4 19g 17d Aug 7] lengthy gelding: maiden hurdler: no form either **h–**
start over fences: stays 2½m: tongue tied. *N. G. Ayliffe*

BLUE TEAL (IRE) 5 b.g. Pistolet Bleu (IRE) – Boreen Brook (IRE) (Boreen (FR)) **h87 p**
[2006/7 F16s F16d^2 F16d^4 16g^5 Mar 30] tall, good-bodied gelding: third foal: dam **F97**
maiden jumper: fairly useful form in bumpers, in frame at Ludlow and Wincanton: not
knocked about when 24 lengths fifth to Mendo in novice at Ascot on hurdling debut:
likely to do better. *Miss H. C. Knight*

BLUE TRAIN (IRE) 5 b.g. Sadler's Wells (USA) – Igreja (ARG) (Southern Halo **h95**
(USA)) [2006/7 16m^5 16d^3 16d^6 16m^4 21f^F 19m Sep 28] brother to 19f hurdle winner
Duke's View: fairly useful on Flat (stays 1¼m), successful at 3 yrs for Sir Michael Stoute:
modest novice hurdler: stays 21f: acts on firm and good to soft going: tongue tied last 4
starts, also blinkered final one. *Jonjo O'Neill*

BLUNHAM HILL (IRE) 9 ch.g. Over The River (FR) – Bronach (Beau Charmeur **c99**
(FR)) [2006/7 c105, h–: c22v^{pu} c26v^2 c24v^4 c23v^4 c23v^4 Feb 27] quite good-topped **h–**
gelding: maiden hurdler: fair handicap chaser: form in 2006/7 only on second start: stays
29f: acts on heavy going: can take plenty of driving. *John R. Upson*

BLUSHING PRINCE (IRE) 9 b.g. Priolo (USA) – Eliade (IRE) (Flash of Steel) **h90**
[2006/7 16d* 16d^6 17m^5 Apr 9] modest on Flat (stays 1¼m) nowadays, successful in
February: modest handicap hurdler: won at Fakenham in October: best at 2m: acts on
firm and good to soft going: tongue tied. *R. C. Guest*

BLU TEEN (FR) 7 ch.g. Epervier Bleu – Teene Hawk (FR) (Matahawk) [2006/7 h114: **c115 +**
c16d^4 c16s^4 c24m* Apr 10] tall, good-topped gelding: winning hurdler: fairly useful form **h–**
over fences: off 4 months and upped markedly in trip, won maiden at Chepstow in April
by 6 lengths from Lawyer des Ormeaux: stays 3m: acts on soft and good to firm ground:
tried tongue tied. *P. F. Nicholls*

BLYTHE KNIGHT (IRE) 7 ch.g. Selkirk (USA) – Blushing Barada (USA) **h144 p**
(Blushing Groom (FR)) [2006/7 17d* 16v^3 16d^2 16g* Apr 13]
          There's no need to look any further than Blythe Knight for a good example
of the skill and versatility of his trainer John Quinn, who for some time has been
making a name for himself on the Flat and is now beginning to do the same over
jumps. From sprinters to long-distance chasers, Quinn has the knack of getting the
best out of his charges. While Blythe Knight fits into neither of the aforementioned
categories, he's proved a money-spinner both on the Flat and over hurdles since
joining Quinn after being bought out of Ed Dunlop's stable for 90,000 guineas at
the Autumn Sales in 2005. Some might have questioned the wisdom of laying out
such a sum on a horse who, though undoubtedly possessing ability, sometimes
found less off the bridle than expected. It took just five months for Blythe Knight,

gelded in the interim, to recoup a hefty chunk of his purchase price when winning the William Hill Lincoln with a resolute display. More success followed when Blythe Knight was switched to hurdling towards the end of 2006. So well did he take to this new discipline that he ended up as the season's highest-rated British-trained two-mile novice hurdler, with his trainer already making plans for the 2008 Champion Hurdle.

Blythe Knight was started off in low grade company over hurdles, an eleven-runner novice event at Bangor in November the race in which he made his debut. While the term 'journeyman' might best describe Quinn during his days as a jump jockey—his seasonal tallies broke into double figures on only a few occasions and the highlight was probably his third place on 150/1-shot Past Glories in the 1990 Champion Hurdle—he pitched at a much higher level when it came to choosing a rider for Blythe Knight. The champion jockey, no less, was booked, even though Tony McCoy's leading patrons J. P. McManus and Jonjo O'Neill had representatives in the race. The partnership got off to a flying start, McCoy enjoying an armchair ride as Blythe Knight, who jumped soundly apart from at the last, landed the odds in impressive fashion, taking over two out and not needing to come off the bridle to score by three lengths. McCoy was also on board in each of Blythe Knight's three subsequent races, the first of them a novice event at Uttoxeter for which Blythe Knight again started at odds on. This time he finished only third but shaped far better than that suggests faced with extremely heavy ground, travelling like the best horse in the race until two out but outstayed by Little Rocker and Here's Johnny. Blythe Knight was also beaten on his next start, when five lengths second to De Soto, a long way clear of the remainder, on good to soft going at Kempton on Boxing Day. It was mid-April before Blythe Knight was seen out again over hurdles, by which time he'd had a couple of outings on the Flat, including finishing ninth (from a poor draw) when going for a repeat in the Lincoln. The race chosen for his return to jumping was a Grade 2 contest, the John Smith's Imagine Appeal Top Novices' Hurdle at Aintree, won twelve months earlier by Straw Bear with the best performance by a two-mile novice hurdler in 2005/6. On ground less testing than he had encountered previously over hurdles, Blythe Knight emulated Straw Bear without reaching quite the same level of form in what was still an above-average renewal. Blythe Knight was sent off a well-supported 14/1 shot in

John Smith's Imagine Appeal Top Novices' Hurdle, Aintree—smart Flat recruit Blythe Knight (white face) proves too strong for Osana (centre) and the irresolute Ouninpohja

an eight-runner field, the market leaders including the favourite Ouninpohja and Osana, second and tenth respectively in the County Hurdle on their previous start, and De Soto who had also been in action at the Cheltenham Festival, finishing fourth in the Supreme Novices'. The strong pace forced by 12/1-shot Bywell Beau and Osana set the race up for those patiently ridden, Blythe Knight and Ouninpohja among them, and the latter pair were poised in the straight to challenge Osana, the race now concerning only these three. With Ouninpohja once again failing to go through with his effort and Osana finding his exertions beginning to tell, it was Blythe Knight who came to the fore. After travelling strongly from the off, he quickened when asked for his effort and needed only to be pushed out to win by two and a half lengths from Osana, with Ouninpohja a further five lengths back in third. Straw Bear found competing against the best a bit beyond him in his second season, and Blythe Knight clearly still has some way to go to reach the top level, though there is almost certainly better to come from him and he won't be one to be dismissed lightly in good races over two miles when the emphasis is on speed. He wasn't seen out again over hurdles after Aintree but did go on to show himself better than ever on the Flat, winning a listed handicap at York in May and the Group 3 Diomed Stakes at Epsom in June. Following the second victory, one firm cut Blythe Knight's Champion Hurdle odds from 33/1 to 16/1.

			Sharpen Up	Atan
Blythe Knight (IRE)	Selkirk (USA)		(ch 1969)	Rocchetta
(ch.g. 2000)	(ch 1988)		Annie Edge	Nebbiolo
			(ch 1980)	Friendly Court
	Blushing Barada (USA)		Blushing Groom	Red God
	(br 1990)		(ch 1974)	Runaway Bride
			Galletto	Nijinsky
			(b 1974)	Gaia

Maxilead Limited's "Blythe Knight"

Blythe Knight raced in the colours of the late Maktoum Al Maktoum during his first four seasons, showing smart form at up to a mile and a quarter and not that far below his best on the only occasion he tackled as far as a mile and a half, while effective on ground ranging from firm to soft and also on polytrack. He was also tried in a variety of headgear during this period, though without success. Bred by his then owner's Gainsborough Stud, Blythe Knight is the fourth foal of the lightly-raced maiden Blushing Barada, whose other successful produce include a couple of fairly useful winners at up to two miles on the Flat, Bid Me Welcome (by Alzao) and High Topper (by Wolfhound). Blushing Barada herself is a half-sister to the 1986 Irish St Leger winner Authaal, their dam the Galtres Stakes winner Galletto, a daughter of the 1969 Irish Oaks winner Gaia. Blythe Knight, a lengthy gelding, hasn't raced on ground firmer than good over hurdles, though he has plenty of form on the Flat under those conditions. *J. J. Quinn*

BOARDWALK KNIGHT (IRE) 10 b.g. Shardari – Takhyira (Vayrann) [2006/7 20g 24g[pu] Jun 15] one-time modest 2m hurdler: no show in 2006/7 after lengthy absence: well held only outing over fences. *Miss L. Harrison* — c– h–

BOB AR AGHAIDH (IRE) 11 b.g. Bob Back (USA) – Shuil Ar Aghaidh (The Parson) [2006/7 c115, h–x: 26m[pu] c24g[6] Apr 9] sturdy gelding: winning hurdler: fairly useful chaser at best, left C. Tinkler after first outing: placed in points in 2007: stays 3½m: acts on heavy and good to firm going. *Mrs M. Harvey* — c– h– x

BOBATIM (IRE) 6 gr.m. Alphabatim (USA) – Rose Wood (Derring Rose) [2006/7 20v[4] Jan 9] second foal: dam unraced half-sister to dam of high-class 2m hurdler Relkeel: signs of ability in mares novice hurdle on debut, shaping like a stayer. *Ferdy Murphy* — h70 +

BOB BAILEYS 5 b.g. Mister Baileys – Bob's Princess (Bob's Return (IRE)) [2006/7 16g Apr 23] modest on Flat (stays 8.6f), successful once in 2006: well held in maiden on hurdling debut. *P. R. Chamings* — h–

BOBBIE'S QUEST (IRE) 5 b.m. Bob's Return (IRE) – Lauristown Cross (IRE) (Mandalus) [2006/7 F16d F16v[6] F16v Jan 27] £3,800 4-y-o: good-topped mare: first foal: dam, lightly raced in points, out of half-sister to high-class chaser up to 3¼m Another Coral: well beaten in bumpers. *L. P. Grassick* — F–

BOBBING COVE 8 b.g. Bob's Return (IRE) – Candlebright (Lighter) [2006/7 h83: 20s[5] 22d 20s[5] 17d[3] 20s 20g[4] 24d 24m c20g[pu] c20s[F] Apr 27] modest maiden hurdler: stays 2½m: acts on soft going: sometimes let down by jumping, including 2 starts over fences. *Mrs L. B. Normile* — c– h90

BOB BITES BACK (IRE) 5 br.g. Bob Back (USA) – Philips River (IRE) (Over The River (FR)) [2006/7 F16s[4] 21d[*dis] c21g[3] c21d[3] c24m[ur] c20g[2] Apr 23] fifth foal: half-brother to winning pointer by Lord Americo: dam unraced half-sister to useful chaser up to 25f On The Other Hand: placed in maiden Irish points: fourth of 6 in bumper: won maiden at Ludlow in January on hurdling debut, idling (later disqualified on technical grounds): modest form over fences: stays 21f: acts on good to soft going: blinkered/visored last 2 starts. *Evan Williams* — c94 h97 + F87

BOBBLE WONDER 6 b.m. Classic Cliche (IRE) – Wonderfall (FR) (The Wonder (FR)) [2006/7 F–: 19d Mar 26] leggy mare: no form in bumpers (for J. O'Shea) or maiden hurdle after 15-month absence. *N. E. Berry* — h–

BOB BOB BOBBIN 8 gr.g. Bob Back (USA) – Absalom's Lady (Absalom) [2006/7 c136, h136: c24g[*] c24s[4] c26g[pu] Mar 16] tall, leggy gelding: useful hurdler: smart chaser: improved form when winning handicap at Bangor in November by 2 lengths from Distant Thunder (pair long way clear): creditable fourth to Neptune Collonges in valuable similar event at Newcastle 17 days later, despite jumping none too fluently: very stiff task final start (lame): will stay beyond 3¼m: acts on heavy going: races prominently. *C. L. Tizzard* — c147 h–

BOBBY BROWN (IRE) 7 b.g. Insan (USA) – Miss Sally Knox (IRE) (Erdelistan (FR)) [2006/7 c–, h–: c21g May 6] deep-girthed gelding: no sign of ability: tried tongue tied/in blinkers: sold 8,000 gns Doncaster May Sales. *P. C. Haslam* — c– h–

BOBBY BULLOCK (IRE) 5 b.g. Old Vic – Miss Chickabee (IRE) (Jolly Jake (NZ)) [2006/7 F18v[5] Mar 7] €11,000 3-y-o: strong, workmanlike gelding: fourth foal: dam unraced: fifth of 11 in bumper on debut. *M. Scudamore* — F–

BOBBY DONALD (IRE) 5 b.g. Lord Americo – River Rescue (Over The River (FR)) [2006/7 F17v 19g[5] 20s[5] 19s[5] 24g Apr 21] €16,000 3-y-o: neat gelding: brother to poor chaser Harem Scarem, stayed 21f, and half-brother to bumper winner Stylish Linda (by — h81 F–

Insan): dam unraced half-sister to fairly useful staying chaser Corner Boy: won maiden
Irish point in 2006: well beaten in bumper: poor form over hurdles: stays 2½m: acts on
soft going. *R. T. Phillips*

BOBBY GEE 6 ch.g. Bob's Return (IRE) – Country Orchid (Town And Country) **h100 +**
[2006/7 F17s⁴ F16g F16v⁵ 20s³ 20d³ Mar 17] good-bodied gelding: first foal: dam fairly **F91**
useful hurdler around 2m: fair form in bumpers, left K. Reveley after second start, and
when third in novice hurdles: will stay beyond 2½m: acts on soft going. *Mrs P. Robeson*

BOBDAMAN (IRE) 7 b. or br.g. Supreme Leader – Mary Kate Finn (Saher) [2006/7 **h–**
F16gᵖᵘ 16g Mar 17] 4,500 5-y-o: brother to smart hurdler/very smart chaser Fota Island, **F–**
stays 2½m: dam, maiden on Flat/over hurdles, half-sister to useful hurdlers Castle-
kellyleader and Cailin Supreme (both by Supreme Leader), latter also dam of high-class
hurdler Black Jack Ketchum: lost action in bumper: well held in maiden on hurdling
debut. *Mrs S. J. Smith*

BOB HALL (IRE) 6 b.g. Sadler's Wells (USA) – Be My Hope (IRE) (Be My Native **c138**
(USA)) [2006/7 h117p: c20g³ c20d* c16d⁵ c21g² c20g² Apr 14] useful-looking gelding: **h–**
fairly useful form over hurdles in 2005/6 for D. Wachman: useful chaser: won maiden at
Leicester in December: improved form when runner-up in novice handicaps, beaten 3
lengths by Private Be in conditional/amateur event at Aintree: likely to be suited by
further than 21f: acts on heavy going: tongue tied last 4 outings. *Jonjo O'Neill*

BOB JUSTICE (IRE) 11 b.g. Bob Back (USA) – Bramdean (Niniski (USA)) [2006/7 **c–**
c–, h130: 16d* c24gᵖᵘ Apr 9] rather leggy gelding: winning chaser: useful handicap **h139**
hurdler: won at Aintree (beat Jack The Giant 6 lengths) in May: sold out of J. Howard
Johnson's stable 26,000 gns Doncaster Sales later in month, pulled up in point/hunter:
effective at 2m to easy 3m: acts on heavy and good to firm going: tried blinkered.
S. J. Stearn

Mr John P. McManus' "Bob Hall"

BOB MOUNTAIN (IRE) 6 b. or br.g. Bob Back (USA) – Honey Mountain (Royal **h108**
Match) [2006/7 F68: F16m⁵ F17d² 20g* 20s⁴ 20g 16g⁴ 20g* Apr 27] angular gelding: **F91**
best effort in bumpers when runner-up at Newton Abbot: fair hurdler: won novice at
Uttoxeter in September and, having left C. Tinkler after fifth outing, handicap at Chepstow in April: will stay beyond 2½m: tongue tied in 2006/7. *D. W. P. Arbuthnot*

BOB'S BUSTER 11 b.g. Bob's Return (IRE) – Saltina (Bustino) [2006/7 c99, h88: **c105 +**
c20g c17g* c16m⁴ c16f⁶ c16m⁶ c16f⁶ c24g² c20m² c22m⁴ c20d c25s* c28s Nov 17] **h–**
sturdy gelding: winning hurdler: fair handicap chaser: won at Southwell in June and
Wetherby in October: stayed 25f: acted on heavy and good to firm going: tried blinkered,
usually wore cheekpieces: tongue tied once: held up: sometimes found little: dead.
R. Johnson

BOB SCOTTON (IRE) 8 b.g. Bob Back (USA) – Zephyrelle (IRE) (Celio Rufo) **h–**
[2006/7 23gᵖᵘ Apr 30] €55,000 3-y-o: ex-Irish gelding: second foal: brother to bumper
winner Boberelle: dam, fair form in bumpers, sister to useful 2m hurdler Winter Squall
and half-sister to smart 2m hurdler Carobee: runner-up on second of 2 starts in Irish points
in 2004: fair form when third in bumper: left M. Flavin, no show in maiden on hurdling
debut. *K. A. Ryan*

BOB'S DREAM (IRE) 5 b.g. Bob's Return (IRE) – Back In Kansas (IRE) (Mister **h97 ?**
Lord (USA)) [2006/7 F16g⁵ 20g 20m² 17v⁵ 20g 22g 16g⁶ Apr 15] 7,200 3-y-o: first foal: **F83**
dam unraced: fifth in bumper: modest maiden hurdler: easily best effort at Musselburgh
third start, possibly flattered: should stay beyond 2½m: acts on good to firm ground: not a
fluent jumper. *W. Amos*

BOBSLEIGH 8 b.g. Robellino (USA) – Do Run Run (Commanche Run) [2006/7 h–: **c96 ?**
19g³ 25d⁵ 24s c25v⁴ c21g⁴ c26g³ Apr 7] angular gelding: fair stayer on Flat in 2006: **h91**
modest hurdler nowadays: failed with jumping whilst showing similar form
over fences: probably stays 3¼m: acts on heavy going: tried blinkered. *H. S. Howe*

BOBSOUROWN (IRE) 8 b.g. Parthian Springs – Suir Queen (Deep Run) [2006/7 c–, **c65**
h68: c21g⁵ c25m⁵ Jun 3] winning pointer: poor maiden hurdler/chaser: should be suited **h–**
by further than 2m. *D. McCain Jnr*

BOBS PRIDE (IRE) 5 b.g. Marju (IRE) – Vyatka (Lion Cavern (USA)) [2006/7 **h135 p**
h109: 16s* 16s² 18s*ᵈⁱˢ 16v⁴ 16m* 16m* Apr 25]
      Away from the testing conditions which he'd encountered on his first six
starts, Bobs Pride finally began to produce the useful form he'd shown at up to a
mile and quarter on the Flat, at the same time shaping as if capable of reaching an
even higher level as a hurdler. His trainer Dermot Weld certainly has great hopes
for him. After Bobs Pride won a handicap at Punchestown on his final start of the
season, Weld was unrestrained in his praise, saying: 'He was a very classy horse on
the Flat and I wouldn't be surprised to see him go to the top over hurdles.' Weld has
a decent track record of spotting above-average performers within his small
National Hunt sideline, with the likes of Fortune And Fame, General Idea and Stage
Affair all competing with distinction at the highest level—even his Melbourne Cup
hero Vintage Crop had a brief flirtation with hurdling, winning twice in novice
company before finishing an honourable sixth in the 1993 Champion Hurdle (seven
and a half months before that historic Australian triumph).
      Weld is also likely to have harboured hopes that Bobs Pride would go to the
very top on the Flat after winning two of his first three starts in that sphere, notably
the Grade 3 Ballysax Stakes at Leopardstown (his victims including future above-
average hurdlers Mister Hight and Premier Dane) when following in the footsteps
of Derby winners Galileo and High Chaparral. Bobs Pride wasn't in that sort of
league, though, and his limitations were quickly exposed, his season ending with a
seventh-of-eight finish behind Dubawi in the Irish Two Thousand Guineas. Given a
couple of runs over hurdles early in 2006, finishing runner-up in a Grade 3 juvenile
at Fairyhouse on the second occasion, Bobs Pride had an unsuccessful spell on the
Flat (tried blinkered) before making a successful return to jumping in a maiden at
Listowel in September (with subsequent Grade 2 winner Orbit O'Gold back in
third). Two outings later he passed the post first in a novice at Fairyhouse, only to
be disqualified some time later after it was discovered that a prohibited substance
had been administered unknowingly. So it wasn't until April, when he encountered
ground on the firm side of good for the first time over hurdles, that Bobs Pride
gained win number two. It came in a twenty-four-runner novice handicap at Fairy-

Oberstown Developments Handicap Hurdle, Punchestown—Ruby Walsh has hit the front on the progressive Bobs Pride, who easily justifies favouritism in this 22-runner event

house, where the amateur-ridden Bobs Pride showed much improved form in winning by three lengths from Top The Charts, still going well when produced to lead at the last and just pushed clear. When Bobs Pride reappeared at Punchestown just over two weeks later it was off a mark 10 lb higher in an open handicap, but the outcome was the same. Reunited with Ruby Walsh and a well-backed favourite, Bobs Pride accounted for his twenty-one rivals in impressive fashion, travelling very smoothly indeed as he tracked the leaders before taking over soon after two out. Although doing little once in front, Bobs Pride still had three lengths to spare over nearest pursuer Bien Bronze at the line, showing that he was still very much on the upgrade. Bobs Pride, the first foal of the well-bred unraced mare Vyatka, will prove best at around two miles. While he has won on soft ground, easily his two best performances were put up on good to firm. *D. K. Weld, Ireland*

BOB'S TEMPTATION 8 br.g. Bob's Return (IRE) – Temptation (IRE) (Clearly Bust) [2006/7 h–, F–: c17g⁶ c20f⁶ c17d⁵ Oct 14] good-topped gelding: maiden hurdler: poor form over fences: usually tongue tied. *A. J. Wilson* **c70 h–**

BOB'S YOUR UNCLE 4 br.g. Zilzal (USA) – Bob's Princess (Bob's Return (IRE)) [2006/7 17d⁴ Nov 16] fair on Flat (stays 11.6f), successful 3 times in 2006: modest form when fourth in juvenile maiden on hurdling debut. *J. G. Portman* **h87**

BOB THE BUILDER 8 b.g. Terimon – True Clown (True Song) [2006/7 c130, h–: 24s⁵ c20g c21g c21g⁶ c25gF Apr 18] big, good-topped gelding: maiden hurdler: useful chaser at best: most disappointing in 2006/7: stays 3m: acts on good to soft going: tends to jump left: front runner/races prominently. *N. A. Twiston-Davies* **c– h–**

BODELL (IRE) 5 b.g. Turtle Island (IRE) – Reddish Creek (USA) (Mt Livermore (USA)) [2006/7 F–: F16g Nov 10] unfurnished gelding: shaped like a non-stayer in bumpers. *Mark Campion* **F–**

BODFARI SIGNET 11 ch.g. King's Signet (USA) – Darakah (Doulab (USA)) [2006/7 c–, h108d: 20m 16m⁴ 16f 20f² 24f⁴ 24g 20m 16s² Sep 20] leggy, angular gelding: modest hurdler: effective at 2m to easy 3m: acts on firm and soft going, below form on heavy: occasionally wears headgear: usually waited with: hard ride. *Mrs S. C. Bradburne* **c– h92 §**

BODKIN BOY (IRE) 7 b.g. Darnay – Kristar (Kris) [2006/7 h–: c17g⁴ c17s⁶ c21vᵖᵘ c25vᵘʳ Jan 12] no solid form over jumps: in cheekpieces last 2 starts. *Mrs S. C. Bradburne* **c– h–**

138

BOG OAK (IRE) 7 b.g. Accordion – Miss Amy (IRE) (Supreme Leader) [2006/7 c20d c22s c19v c20s c20v⁴ c25g² Apr 2] €30,000 3-y-o: rather leggy gelding: first foal: dam unraced out of half-sister to dam of One Man: fair hurdler: modest maiden chaser: stays 25f: raced on good ground or softer (bumper winner on heavy). *C. F. Swan, Ireland*   **c88 h–**

BOGSIDE DANCER 5 b.g. Groom Dancer (USA) – Madame Crecy (USA) (Al Nasr (FR)) [2006/7 17s 16m 16m 17s Oct 4] fairly useful on Flat (stays 1¼m) at 3 yrs for A. Oliver: no form over hurdles. *A. J. Martin, Ireland*   **h–**

BOGUS DREAMS (IRE) 10 ch.g. Lahib (USA) – Dreams Are Free (IRE) (Caerleon (USA)) [2006/7 c104, h106: 16g³ 16m⁴ 16d* Feb 14] strong, well-made gelding: has reportedly had wind operation: winning chaser: useful handicap hurdler: much improved in 2006/7, winning at Musselburgh in December and February (beat Double Vodka by neck, idling run-in): should stay beyond 2m: acts on soft and good to firm going. *D. J. P. Barry, Ireland*   **c– h130**

BOHEMIAN BOY (IRE) 9 gr.g. Roselier (FR) – Right Hand (Oats) [2006/7 c103, h115: c19d² c24d⁴ c23vᵖᵘ 26g² Mar 14] compact gelding: fair handicap hurdler: has regressed over fences, badly let down by jumping when blinkered third outing: stays 3¼m: acts on soft going. *Carl Llewellyn*   **c95 h113**

BOHEMIAN SPIRIT (IRE) 9 b.g. Eagle Eyed (USA) – Tuesday Morning (Sadler's Wells (USA)) [2006/7 c124, h118: 20g² c20f² c22g⁵ c16s² c16s* c16gF c16s⁴ c19g⁴ Mar 31] lengthy gelding: fairly useful handicap hurdler: useful handicap chaser: sweating and on toes, improved form when winning at Sandown in January by 18 lengths from Charlton Kings: has was over 25f, best form up to 2½m: acts on any going: takes keen hold, and usually makes running/races prominently: usually sound jumper: genuine and reliable. *N. G. Richards*   **c139 h121**

BOLD BISHOP (IRE) 10 b.g. Religiously (USA) – Ladybojangles (IRE) (Buckskin (FR)) [2006/7 c145, h–: c17s³ c25sᵖᵘ c20s c21g Mar 15] angular gelding: winning hurdler: smart chaser at best, well below form in 2006/7: effective at 2m to 2½m: acts on soft and good to firm going: tried blinkered/in cheekpieces: not straightforward (hasn't always impressed with finishing effort). *Jonjo O'Neill*   **c127 h–**

BOLD EYDIA (IRE) 4 ch.g. Bold Fact (USA) – Aneydia (IRE) (Kenmare (FR)) [2006/7 F14s Oct 29] workmanlike gelding: third foal: half-brother to 7f/1m winner Stedfast McStaunch (by Desert Style): dam second over 10.5f in France: no show in 3-y-o bumper on debut. *J. K. Magee, Ireland*   **F–**

BOLD FINCH (FR) 5 b.g. Valanour (IRE) – Eagle's Nest (FR) (King of Macedon) [2006/7 16sᵖᵘ 17gF 20s 26v Jan 11] good-topped gelding: lightly raced on Flat in France, well held in Britain for K. Cunningham-Brown: no form over hurdles. *S. G. Griffiths*   **h–**

BOLD FIRE 5 b.m. Bold Edge – Kirkby Belle (Bay Express) [2006/7 h125: 16g 22m* c20s* c24dᵖᵘ c20vᵘʳ c22g⁴ c16sᵇᵈ Apr 27] leggy, lengthy mare: useful hurdler: improved form when winning valuable mares handicap at Wincanton in November by 5 lengths from United: odds on, wide-margin winner of mares novice at Huntingdon in December on chasing debut: completed only once after, knocked over by loose horse final start: stays easy 2¾m: acts on soft and good to firm going: takes good hold. *P. F. Nicholls*   **c122 + h133 +**

BOLD NAVIGATOR 17 b.g. Lighter – Drummond Lass (Peacock (FR)) [2006/7 c26vᵖᵘ May 20] veteran chaser: winning pointer, including in February: stays 27f: acts on soft going. *A. M. Crow*   **c–**

BOLD 'N' BRAVE 8 ch.g. Fearless Action (USA) – Quenby Girl (IRE) (Remainder Man) [2006/7 c–: c23dᵖᵘ Oct 11] strong gelding: winning pointer: no show in maiden chases. *C. C. Bealby*   **c–**

BOLD PIONEER (USA) 4 b.g. Pioneering (USA) – Uber Alyce (USA) (Bold Forbes (USA)) [2006/7 16s 16s 16v 17g Mar 25] good-topped gelding: lightly-raced maiden on Flat, modest form at best: poor form over juvenile hurdles. *C. P. Morlock*   **h73**

BOLD POLICY (IRE) 4 b.g. Shernazar – Lady Vic (IRE) (Old Vic) [2006/7 F16s² Apr 27] €36,000 3-y-o: first foal: dam unraced: encouraging 3 lengths second to Silver By Nature in bumper at Perth on debut: likely to improve. *P. F. Nicholls*   **F101 p**

BOLD PURSUIT (IRE) 5 br.g. Bold Fact (USA) – Lyphard Belle (Noble Patriarch) [2006/7 h86d: 16m 16g 17mᵖᵘ Aug 6] smallish, sturdy gelding: maiden hurdler: left Mrs A. Duffield, no form in 2006/7. *S. B. Clark*   **h–**

BOLD RANSOM (IRE) 5 b.g. Lord of Appeal – Bodalmore Rose (IRE) (Roselier (FR)) [2006/7 F16v³ 25g³ Apr 16] €14,000 4-y-o: fourth foal: half-brother to fair chaser Giolla An Bhaird (by Supreme Leader), stays 3m: dam unraced: third in bumper (green)   **h73 p F73**

and maiden hurdle, poor form behind Hilly Gale at Wetherby in latter: should improve.
K. G. Reveley

BOLD TIGER (IRE) 4 b.g. Bold Fact (USA) – Heart of The Ocean (IRE) (Soviet Lad   **h—**
(USA)) [2006/7 17f^{pu} Aug 11] poor maiden on Flat: no show in juvenile on hurdling
debut. *Miss Tracy Waggott*

BOLD TRUMP 6 b.g. First Trump – Blue Nile (IRE) (Bluebird (USA)) [2006/7 h72+:   **h88**
22m 17g^2 Apr 11] modest on Flat (stays 1½m): modest maiden hurdler, runner-up in
sellers: should stay beyond 17f: tried tongue tied. *Mrs N. S. Evans*

BOLLIN RUTH 5 gr.m. Silver Patriarch (IRE) – Bollin Roberta (Bob's Return (IRE))   **h104**
[2006/7 16s^2 16g 16v^3 18s^5 16v* Mar 15] never dangerous in maidens on Flat, sold out of
T. Easterby's stable 5,000 gns Doncaster August (2005) Sales: fair novice hurdler: further
improvement to win conditional jockeys mares handicap at Hexham in March: should
stay beyond 2m: acts on heavy going. *D. W. Whillans*

BOLLIN THOMAS 9 b.g. Alhijaz – Bollin Magdalene (Teenoso (USA)) [2006/7   **h103 d**
h100: 17d* 17d^2 16s^3 16f^5 16s 16s^{ur} Feb 15] sturdy gelding: fair hurdler: won handicap
at Sedgefield in May: stays 2½m: acts on heavy going: tried blinkered/in cheekpieces.
R. Allan

BOLLITREE BOB 6 b.g. Bob's Return (IRE) – Lady Prunella (IRE) (Supreme   **c92**
Leader) [2006/7 h85: c16m^{F}c16m^5 c16s^{ur} 17d c16m* c16g^2 Apr 20] tall gelding: maiden   **h—**
hurdler: modest handicap chaser: won 5-runner novice handicap at Huntingdon (by 18
lengths) in April: raced around 2m: acts on good to firm and good to soft going: headstrong. *M. Scudamore*

BOLSHOI BALLET 9 b.g. Dancing Spree (USA) – Broom Isle (Damister (USA))   **c—**
[2006/7 c—, h91: 17d 16g^5 16f^6 20m 17m^6 22d 16g c16g^{pu} Apr 23] quite good-topped   **h92 d**
gelding: modest handicap hurdler: largely well held in 2006/7, left R. Fahey before fourth
start: well held completed outing over fences: should stay 2½m: acts on heavy and good
to firm going: wears headgear. *Miss J. E. Foster*

BOLSHOI BOY (IRE) 5 ch.g. Moscow Society (USA) – Theatre Sister (IRE) (Duky)   **F77**
[2006/7 F16g Mar 24] €33,000 4-y-o: smallish, angular gelding: fourth foal: dam lightly
raced out of half-sister to Night Nurse: troublesome at start, mid-field in bumper at
Newbury on debut. *Mrs L. Wadham*

BONCHESTER BRIDGE 6 b.m. Shambo – Cabriole Legs (Handsome Sailor)   **h107**
[2006/7 h83, F94: 16g* 16d^2 17s* 21v^2 21g 20s Apr 26] sturdy mare: bumper winner:
fair hurdler: won handicaps at Huntingdon and Folkestone (mares event) in November:
stays 21f, effective over shorter: acts on heavy going: has carried head high/found little.
N. J. Henderson

BOND MILLENNIUM 9 ch.g. Piccolo – Farmer's Pet (Sharrood (USA)) [2006/7 h–:   **h—**
16g 16d 16g^{pu} Jun 15] strong gelding: no form over hurdles: tongue tied final outing:
dead. *B. N. Pollock*

BON ENFANT (IRE) 9 gr.m. Roselier (FR) – Small Slam (Buckskin (FR)) [2006/7   **h—**
24m Jul 5] fourth foal: dam unraced: last in novice hurdle on belated debut. *N. A. Twiston-
Davies*

BONGO FURY (FR) 8 b.m. Sillery (USA) – Nativelee (FR) (Giboulee (CAN))   **c124**
[2006/7 h127: c16d^3 c16s* c16v^2 c16s^{pu} 16d Feb 10] sparely-made mare: fairly useful   **h—**
handicap hurdler: similar form over fences, won maiden at Chepstow in December by 7
lengths from Hashid: best effort when second to Transit in handicap at Sedgefield: ran
poorly last 2 starts: stays 19f: has won on firm going, best form on good or softer (acts on
heavy): visored since debut: has idled. *D. E. Pipe*

BONNET'S PIECES 8 b.m. Alderbrook – Chichell's Hurst (Oats) [2006/7 c90, h86:   **c—**
16d^2 16g 16v^2 21s^5 16s^2 16v^2 16g Mar 28] medium-sized mare: modest maiden chaser/   **h90**
hurdler: runner-up 4 times at Towcester in 2006/7: stays 2½m: acts on heavy going: free-
going front runner. *Mrs P. Sly*

BONNEY FLAME 7 ch.m. Bonny Scot (IRE) – Fountain of Fire (IRE) (Lafontaine   **h—**
(USA)) [2006/7 F–: 16v^4 16m 24m^{pu} Jul 4] no show in bumper/over hurdles.
J. L. Spearing

BONNY BOY (IRE) 12 b.g. Bustino – Dingle Bay (Petingo) [2006/7 c81, h81: 20g^{pu} **c— §**
24s^4 27m^{pu} 24m^{pu} c19d^4 c19d^{pu} Nov 1] sturdy gelding: winning pointer: poor hurdler/   **h67 §**
maiden chaser: stays 3m: acts on soft going: wears headgear/tongue tied: ungenuine.
D. A. Rees

BONNY GREY 9 gr.m. Seymour Hicks (FR) – Sky Wave (Idiot's Delight) [2006/7 **h–**
h106: 17g^F May 5] leggy mare: fair handicap hurdler: stayed 2½m: acted on soft and
good to firm going: dead. *D. Burchell*

BONNY GROVE 7 b.g. Bonny Scot (IRE) – Binny Grove (Sunyboy) [2006/7 h–, F–: **h–**
26g^{pu} 26d^{pu} May 17] lengthy gelding: no form in bumpers/over hurdles. *H. J. Evans*

BONNY JAGO 6 ch.g. Bonny Scot (IRE) – Bold Honey (IRE) (Nearly A Nose (USA)) **F–**
[2006/7 F–: F16g Jun 8] leggy gelding: little impact in bumpers. *R. Brotherton*

BONNYKINO 5 ch.m. Meadowbrook – Jukino (Relkino) [2006/7 F–: F17d May 17] **F–**
no promise in bumpers. *S. C. Burrough*

BONUS BRIDGE (IRE) 12 b.g. Executive Perk – Corivia (Over The River (FR)) **c117 x**
[2006/7 c130x, h–: c17m^{pu} c20g^5 c17d c17g Mar 24] tall gelding: winning hurdler: useful **h–**
chaser, below form in handicaps in 2006/7: stays 2½m: acts on soft and good to firm
going: usually races prominently: has wandered under pressure/finished weakly: sketchy
jumper. *H. D. Daly*

BON VIVEUR 4 b.g. Mozart (IRE) – Fantazia (Zafonic (USA)) [2006/7 17s^4 17v^6 16s **h100**
16g^6 Mar 31] rather leggy gelding: fair up to 1¼m on Flat (often wears cheekpieces),
successful twice in 2006, sold out of R. Hannon's stable 45,000 gns Newmarket Autumn
Sales: fair form over hurdles, seemingly best effort on handicap debut final outing: likely
to prove best at sharp 2m: breathing problem third outing. *P. J. Hobbs*

BOOMERANG BUD 4 b.g. Kayf Tara – Blossoming (Vague Shot) [2006/7 F16m **F79**
Apr 24] second foal: dam unraced: green, mid-field in maiden bumper on debut.
B. R. Summers

BOOMERANG (IRE) 5 b.g. Needle Gun (IRE) – Garden County (Ragapan) [2006/7 **F73**
F16s^4 F17s Jan 26] 8,000 4-y-o: half-brother to fairly useful hurdler/winning chaser Joe
Luke (by Satco), stayed 27f: dam unraced out of fairly useful staying chaser Kylogue
Lady, herself half-sister to Foxhunter winner Three Counties: poor form in bumpers.
H. D. Daly

BOOM OR BUST (IRE) 8 ch.g. Entrepreneur – Classic Affair (USA) (Trempolino **c–**
(USA)) [2006/7 17g^4 17m 16m 17g^4 17g 24s^{pu} 19v^6 17s^4 17g Apr 1] angular gelding: **h81 d**
error-prone maiden hurdler, little form in 2006/7: no show on chasing debut: best at
2m: acts on soft and good to firm going: tried blinkered, often wears cheekpieces. *Karen
George*

BOOMSHAKALAKA (IRE) 7 ch.g. Anshan – Fairy Gale (IRE) (Strong Gale) **h102**
[2006/7 F94: F16d^5 16v^2 21g Mar 23] lengthy, well-made gelding: bumper winner: better **F95**
effort in maiden hurdles when 12 lengths second to Back Among Friends at Chepstow.
N. J. Henderson

BOOSTER DIVIN (FR) 5 b.g. Signe Divin (USA) – Shenedova (FR) (Hellios (USA)) **h–**
[2006/7 F–: 16m 16d 16m 16m^{pu} Jul 2] no sign of ability. *M. J. Gingell*

BOOTLEGGER (IRE) 5 b.g. Pistolet Bleu (IRE) – Mullaun (Deep Run) [2006/7 **F107**
F16v^5 F16s F16v^2 F19v* F16m Apr 25] lengthy gelding: half-brother to useful hurdler/
chaser up to 21f Native Endurance (by Be My Native), fairly useful hurdler/chaser around
2m Total Success (by King's Ride) and useful bumper winner/hurdler Master Albert (by
Supreme Leader): dam placed in bumpers: useful form in bumpers: upped in trip, won at
Naas in February: mid-field in Grade 1 event at Punchestown next time. *Thomas Mullins,
Ireland*

BOOZIN BORIS (IRE) 6 b.g. Entrepreneur – Atlantic Dream (USA) (Muscovite **h–**
(USA)) [2006/7 17s^{pu} 16g Mar 21] half-brother to fair hurdler/chaser Latin Queen (by
Desert Prince), stayed 19f: dam Irish 2-y-o 6f winner: failed to complete in points: no
show in selling hurdles: tried in cheekpieces/tongue tied. *B. J. Llewellyn*

BORA SHAAMIT (IRE) 5 b.m. Shaamit (IRE) – Bora Bora (Bairn (USA)) [2006/7 **h–**
F–: F16d 21s^{pu} 22d 17s^{pu} Feb 26] no sign of ability. *M. Scudamore* **F–**

BORDER CASTLE 6 b.g. Grand Lodge (USA) – Tempting Prospect (Shirley Heights) **h124**
[2006/7 h116: 17s* 20s^{pu} 16s^5 Mar 10] tall gelding: fairly useful handicap hurdler:
improved when winning 16-runner event at Cheltenham in December by 3 lengths
from Pilca: off 2½ months and blinkered, creditable fifth to Gaspara in Imperial Cup at
Sandown: though not for first time didn't convince with attitude: stays 19f: raced on good
to soft/soft going. *Miss Venetia Williams*

BORDER FOX 4 b.g. Foxhound (USA) – Vado Via (Ardross) [2006/7 F14s^3 F14s^3 **F100**
F14d* Feb 14] sturdy gelding: half-brother to one-time useful performer up to 1½m

Mi Odds (by (by Sure Blade), also won over hurdles: dam fairly useful staying hurdler: fairly useful form in bumpers, winning at Musselburgh in February by 5 lengths from New Lodge: takes strong hold. *L. Lungo*

BORDER FUSION 8 b.g. Weld – Monteviot (Scallywag) [2006/7 c24g³ c24s² c26d² May 31] third foal: dam modest 2m novice hurdler: fairly useful winning pointer: fairly useful form when placed all starts in hunters: stays 3¼m: acts on soft going. *G. D. Hanmer* **c100**

BORDER SOVEREIGN 7 b.g. Sovereign Water (FR) – Skelton (Derrylin) [2006/7 F–: 16s^pu 16s Apr 27] no show in bumper and maiden hurdles. *J. S. Haldane* **h–**

BORDER STAR (IRE) 10 b.g. Parthian Springs – Tengello (Bargello) [2006/7 c–, h–: 22m 20s 24s^pu May 28] lengthy gelding: no show only start over fences: poor hurdler, lightly raced and no form since 2004: usually wears cheekpieces/blinkers: tried tongue tied. *B. G. Powell* **c– h–**

BORDER TALE 7 b.g. Selkirk (USA) – Likely Story (IRE) (Night Shift (USA)) [2006/7 h110d: c21m³ c16g⁵ c25g^pu c20g^pu Nov 24] sturdy gelding: fair handicap hurdler at one time: best effort in novice chases (modest form) on reappearance: best form around 2m: acts on good to firm going, possibly not on soft/heavy: tried in cheekpieces (raced moodily)/tongue tied. *James Moffatt* **c87 h–**

BOREHILL JOKER 11 ch.g. Pure Melody (USA) – Queen Matilda (Castle Keep) [2006/7 c90, h95: 16s* c16v* c16d² c20m* 22m* c21d³ c21f² c24d 16g^pu 22g⁵ Apr 27] sparely-made gelding: fair handicap hurdler/chaser: better than ever in early-2006/7, winning over hurdles at Towcester and Uttoxeter and over fences at Towcester and Southwell: stays 2¾m: acts on any going: tried blinkered: usually tongue tied: tough. *V. R. A. Dartnall* **c104 h104**

BORING GORING (IRE) 13 b.g. Aristocracy – Coolrusk (IRE) (Millfontaine) [2006/7 c–x, h–: 21g 20m^pu 22g^pu 26m^pu Sep 24] rangy gelding: winning hurdler/maiden chaser, little form for long time: tried blinkered: formerly tongue tied: poor jumper of fences. *E. J. Farrant* **c– x h–**

BORIS THE BLADE 5 gr.g. Cloudings (IRE) – Cherry Lane (Buckley) [2006/7 F16g³ Apr 23] 14,000 4-y-o: second foal: dam unraced: 26 lengths third to Laborec in maiden bumper at Hexham on debut: likely to be suited by further than 2m. *Miss T. Jackson* **F80**

BORIS THE SPIDER 6 b.g. Makbul – Try Vickers (USA) (Fuzzbuster (USA)) [2006/7 h96: 16m 16d⁴ 16s⁵ 16g^pu Apr 2] angular gelding: modest handicap hurdler: should stay beyond 17f: acts on heavy going: has had breathing problem. *Micky Hammond* **h94**

BORITA (IRE) 4 ch.f. Lahib (USA) – Bora Bora (Bairn (USA)) [2006/7 F12s F16d Feb 2] unfurnished filly: second foal: dam, dual bumper winner/fairly useful hurdler, half-sister to fairly useful hurdler/chaser up to 3¼m Mariners Mirror: no show in bumpers. *M. Scudamore* **F–**

BORORA 8 gr.g. Shareef Dancer (USA) – Bustling Nelly (Bustino) [2006/7 h125: 17m⁶ 17g 20g c19m* c19s³ c16s⁴ c16g c21g Apr 19] close-coupled gelding: fairly useful handicap hurdler: won maiden at Hereford in November on chasing debut by 4 lengths from Flying Enterprise: better form in frame in novices next 2 starts: stays 19f: acts on soft and good to firm going: usually patiently ridden: consistent. *R. Lee* **c115 h115**

BOSCALL HILL (IRE) 8 ch.g. Teamster – Annabella (Habitat) [2006/7 20v 18v 18v 20v c20v^F c24g⁶ 23g⁶ Apr 3] placed in points: has shown little otherwise, left M. Daly in Ireland after fourth outing. *M. J. Gingell* **c– h–**

BOSHAM MILL 9 ch.g. Nashwan (USA) – Mill On The Floss (Mill Reef (USA)) [2006/7 c114+, h–: c33g* c28v⁴ c23g³ c26m* Jul 17] leggy gelding: winning hurdler: fairly useful chaser: won hunter at Cheltenham (by 25 lengths) in May and handicap at Newton Abbot (beat Comanche War Paint by 11 lengths) in July: stays 33f: acts on good to firm going (reportedly lost action on soft): tried blinkered (didn't impress with finishing effort). *P. J. Hobbs* **c121 h–**

BOSS IMPERIAL (FR) 4 b.g. Raintrap – L'Imperialis (FR) (Apeldoorn (FR)) [2006/7 15s* 17s* 18s² 18s c17s⁶ 16s 17d^ur 16g 16m⁵ Apr 25] close-coupled gelding: third foal: half-brother to French winner up to 1½m Nijinskha (by Baroud d'Honneur): dam 1m/1¼m winner: twice-raced on Flat: won twice over hurdles at Dieppe in summer 2006: left C. Cardenne, seemingly best effort in 4 starts in Britain when mid-field in handicap won by Adopted Hero at Haydock penultimate outing: raced mainly around 2m: acts on soft going. *Mrs L. Wadham* **c97 h116 ?**

BOSS MAK (IRE)   4 ch.g. Shinko Forest (IRE) – Lucky Achievement (USA) (St Jovite (USA)) [2006/7 16m⁴ 18gᵖᵘ 16m Oct 12] modest maiden on Flat (should be suited by 1m+): form in juvenile hurdles only on debut: tried visored: sold 7,500 gns Newmarket Autumn Sales. *V. Smith*   **h82**

BOSTON FLYER   5 ch.g. Alflora (IRE) – Kkalipto Girl (Final Straw) [2006/7 F16d Dec 14] neat gelding: second foal: dam unraced: tailed off in bumper on debut. *C. A. Mulhall*   **F–**

BOSTON MATE   5 b.g. Bal Harbour – Grindalythe (Bustino) [2006/7 F17d 19d 19sᵖᵘ 20s 19vᵖᵘ Feb 27] sparely-made gelding: third foal: dam unraced half-sister to fairly useful staying chasers River Don and Mister Muddypaws: well held in bumper: poor form in novice hurdles. *R. D. E. Woodhouse*   **h68** / **F–**

BOSTON MONDAIN (FR)   6 b.g. Le Pommier d'Or – Armalita (FR) (Goodland (FR)) [2006/7 F13s F17v Jan 11] £30,000 4-y-o: leggy, close-coupled gelding: fifth foal: half-brother to very smart chaser Armaturk (by Baby Turk), stays 21f, and fairly useful hurdler Armariver (by River Mist), stays 2½m: dam winning hurdler/chaser up to 19f: well held in bumpers. *Sir John Barlow Bt*   **F–**

BOSUNS MATE   14 ch.g. Yachtsman (USA) – Langton Lass (Nearly A Hand) [2006/7 20dᵖᵘ c24sᶠ c24vᵖᵘ Jan 4] useful-looking gelding: veteran chaser: often wears headgear: poor jumper. *M. Keighley*   **c– x** / **h–**

BOSWORTH GYPSY (IRE)   9 b.m. Aahsaylad – Googly (Sunley Builds) [2006/7 c–, h76: 22v⁶ 20dᶠ 26s 21v⁶ 19v Jan 5] angular mare: little form over hurdles: pulled up on chasing debut (in cheekpieces). *Miss J. S. Davis*   **c–** / **h–**

BOTALDOR (FR)   5 ch.h. Indian River (FR) – Fast Green (FR) (Carwhite) [2006/7 F16v F16m⁴ Apr 10] £6,000 3-y-o: angular horse: sixth foal: half-brother to several winners in France, including winning chaser up to 2¾m Fastdor (by Saint Preuil): dam, 11f winner on Flat, successful up to around 2¾m over jumps: better effort in bumpers when fourth to Oberon Moon at Chepstow, taking good hold. *A. King*   **F82**

BOTHAR NA (IRE)   8 ch.g. Mister Lord (USA) – Country Course (IRE) (Crash Course) [2006/7 c120: c20d⁵ c22g⁵ c20d* c24s* c24d⁵ c24sᵘʳ c26sᵖᵘ c36gᵖᵘ c25m Apr 26] strong, lengthy gelding: useful handicap chaser: won Denny Gold Medal Chase at Tralee in August and Kerry National at Listowel (beat Pearly Jack comfortably by 2 lengths) in September: should stay beyond 3¼m: acts on soft and good to firm going: tried tongue tied. *W. P. Mullins, Ireland*   **c136**

BOTTOM DRAWER   7 b.g. My Best Valentine – Little Egret (Carwhite) [2006/7 h79: 16g 16m 17gᵖᵘ Aug 26] good-topped gelding: novice hurdler, no form in 2006/7: tried in cheekpieces. *Mrs D. A. Hamer*   **h–**

BOTTOMLESS WALLET   6 ch.m. Titus Livius (FR) – Furry Dance (USA) (Nureyev (USA)) [2006/7 17m⁵ 17m⁶ 16g Mar 17] half-sister to fairly useful 2m hurdler Nuvellino (by Robellino) and fairly useful hurdler/useful chaser Green Tango (by Greensmith), stayed 19f: poor and inconsistent maiden on Flat: no form over hurdles, though not knocked about first 2 starts. *F. Watson*   **h–**

BOUGOURE (IRE)   8 b.g. Oscar (IRE) – Jasmine Melody (Jasmine Star) [2006/7 h120: c20g⁵ c20d² c19sᶠ c19s³ c20sᶠ c20v² c20g Apr 14] sturdy gelding: fairly useful hurdler/maiden chaser: running best race over fences when falling 2 out in novice handicap at Haydock won by Alright Now M'Lad fifth start: likely to stay beyond 2½m: acts on heavy going. *Mrs S. J. Smith*   **c119** / **h–**

BOULAVOGUE (IRE)   4 b.g. Turtle Island (IRE) – Nilousha (Darshaan) [2006/7 16d* 18s Nov 5] half-brother to bumper/2½m hurdle winner Makeabreak (by Anshan): dam winning hurdler/chaser up to 2¼m: fairly useful performer on Flat (stays 1½m): evens, won 24-runner juvenile maiden at Punchestown on hurdling debut by 1¾ lengths from Victoria Night: tenth of 14 in Group 1 juvenile at Auteuil following month. *C. F. Swan, Ireland*   **h114**

BOULEVIN (IRE)   7 b. or br.g. Perugino (USA) – Samika (IRE) (Bikala) [2006/7 h94: 17g² 16d 16gᵖᵘ c16mᵖᵘ 17s 16v Jan 12] leggy gelding: modest on Flat (stays 1½m): modest novice hurdler: form in 2006/7 only on first outing: no show in novice on chasing debut: raced around 2m. *R. J. Price*   **c–** / **h97 d**

BOUNCING BOB   6 ch.g. Florida Son – Dancing Dove (IRE) (Denel (FR)) [2006/7 F16d Dec 29] chunky gelding: third foal: half-brother to fair hurdler Muckle Flugga (by Karinga Bay), stays 3m: dam, fairly useful hurdler at 2m to 2¾m, half-sister to smart staying chaser Niki Dee: well held in bumper on debut. *John Allen*   **F–**

BOUNCING KING 5 b.g. Kayf Tara – Springfield Girl (Royal Vulcan) [2006/7 F16d³ 21s² 20s³ 16v³ 20v³ 20g² Apr 21] fifth foal: half-brother to useful chaser General Striker (by Classic Cliche): dam tailed off all 3 starts on Flat: third in bumper: fair novice hurdler, placed all 5 starts: stays 21f: acts on heavy going. *D. McCain Jnr* **h102 F91**

BOUNCY CASTLE (IRE) 6 b.g. Rock Hopper – Time To Smile (IRE) (Good Thyne (USA)) [2006/7 F16m³ F17m* 20dᵖᵘ Dec 4] €32,000 3-y-o: third foal: dam placed in point: won bumper at Hereford in September: lame on hurdling debut. *Jonjo O'Neill* **h– F95**

BOUND 9 b.g. Kris – Tender Moment (IRE) (Caerleon (USA)) [2006/7 c–, h127: 16d 16s 17mᵖᵘ Jun 30] big, lengthy gelding: winning chaser: fairly useful handicap hurdler at best: no form in 2006/7 (lame final start): best around 2m: acts on soft and good to firm going: often tongue tied: races freely: has found little. *Mrs L. Wadham* **c– h–**

BOUND TO BE LIGHT 7 b.g. Mistertopogigo (IRE) – St Kitts (Tragic Role (USA)) [2006/7 c16gᵖᵘ May 24] second foal: dam 1¼m seller winner/poor novice hurdler: failed to complete in points/hunter. *C. White* **c–**

BOURNEAGAINKRISTEN 9 ch.m. Afzal – Miss Lawn (FR) (Lashkari) [2006/7 c–, h–: 23m⁴ May 10] no sign of ability. *C. C. Bealby* **c– h–**

BOWDLANE BARB 6 b.m. Commanche Run – Foxs Shadow (Neltino) [2006/7 F–: 24sᵖᵘ 16s* 17dᵖᵘ 16d 20g 16d 16s³ 16v² 21g² Mar 14] lengthy mare: poor novice hurdler: won mares event at Uttoxeter in May: stays 21f: acts on heavy going: in cheekpieces last 3 starts. *John A. Harris* **h72**

BOWLEAZE (IRE) 8 br.g. Right Win (IRE) – Mrs Cullen (Over The River (FR)) [2006/7 c116p, h102+: 24mᵖᵘ c23m² c23d* c21mᶠ c23d³ c25g⁶ c19d⁵ Mar 20] rangy gelding: winning chaser: fairly useful chaser: landed odds in 3-runner maiden at Exeter in October, idling: stays 3m: acts on soft and good to firm going. *R. H. Alner* **c115 h–**

BOW SCHOOL (IRE) 6 b.g. New Frontier (IRE) – Sallaghan (IRE) (Hays) [2006/7 F93: 20d 20s 16s⁵ Mar 7] fifth in bumper on debut: first form (poor) in novice hurdles on final start, not knocked about. *J. Howard Johnson* **h81 +**

BOXCLEVER 6 b.g. Accordion – Pugilistic (Hard Fought) [2006/7 h88, F73: 16g 20g Apr 3] modest maiden hurdler, off 11 months after first outing: will be suited by further than 2½m. *J. M. Jefferson* **h85**

BOYASTARA (FR) 4 b.g. Astarabad (USA) – Boya Girl (FR) (Boyatino (FR)) [2006/7 15g³ 15v* 17v³ 16d 24g⁴ Apr 18] compact gelding: fourth foal: half-brother to 21f chase winner Take Girl (by Take Risks): dam winning hurdler around 2m, also successful up to 15.5f on Flat: once-raced on Flat: twice-raced in juvenile hurdles in Provinces, winning at Saint-Brieuc in October: left Y. Fertillet, fair form when in frame in novices in Britain, though looked none too keen final start: stays 3m: usually blinkered. *P. F. Nicholls* **h110**

BOYCHUK (IRE) 6 b.g. Insan (USA) – Golden Flower (GER) (Highland Chieftain) [2006/7 h129, F91: 23f³ c23m* c21m² c24d* c24d² c21g² c25g⁵ c25g³ Apr 18] close-coupled, rather unfurnished gelding: useful hurdler/novice chaser: successful over fences in maiden at Exeter in October and Grade 2 event at Newbury (5 ran, by 1½ lengths from Gungadu) in November: generally ran well in defeat other starts: stays 25f: acts on firm and good to soft going: often races lazily. *P. J. Hobbs* **c137 h135**

BOY'S HURRAH (IRE) 11 b.g. Phardante (FR) – Gorryelm (Arctic Slave) [2006/7 c–: c26vᵖᵘ Feb 26] strong gelding: one-time fair handicap chaser: no form since 2004/5, left J. Howard Johnson before return: stays 25f: acts on any going: bold jumper: often front runner. *R. Gurney* **c–**

BOYSTEROUS (IRE) 7 b.g. Lord Americo – Hells Angel (IRE) (Kambalda) [2006/7 F75: 21d⁶ 19d⁶ 24m⁶ Mar 31] tall, close-coupled gelding: modest form in bumpers: won maiden point in 2006: mid-field in maiden hurdles: sold 3,000 gns Doncaster May Sales. *Heather Dalton* **h75**

BOYTJIE (IRE) 7 b.g. Un Desperado (FR) – Miss Cali (Young Man (FR)) [2006/7 h–: 19vᵖᵘ c24mᵖᵘ Apr 10] rangy gelding: little show over hurdles, left Miss H. Knight and off 14 months before return: mistakes in rear in handicap on chasing debut. *Nick Williams* **c– h–**

BRABINGER (IRE) 4 b.g. Xaar – Particular Friend (Cadeaux Genereux) [2006/7 16mᵖᵘ 18gᵖᵘ 16gᵖᵘ Oct 7] no sign of ability on Flat or in juvenile hurdles: ungenuine. *B. G. Powell* **h– §**

BRACKNEY BOY (IRE) 13 b.g. Zaffaran (USA) – Donard Lily (Master Buck) [2006/7 c–x, h83: c20d c23g⁴ c26dᵖᵘ May 27] poor handicap hurdler: little aptitude for **c71 x h–**

chasing: stays 3¼m: acts on soft and good to firm going: tried blinkered. *I. A. Duncan, Ireland*

BRADDERS 5 b.g. Silver Patriarch (IRE) – Lolita (FR) (Hellios (USA)) [2006/7 h–, F–: 16s^{pu} 16m^{ro} Jun 11] compact gelding: more temperament than ability: tried visored/tongue tied. *J. R. Jenkins* — h– §

BRADLEY BOY (IRE) 6 ch.g. Presenting – Mistric (Buckley) [2006/7 F102: 20d* 20g* 25s³ Feb 3] sturdy gelding: progressive form over hurdles, won maiden at Worcester in October and novice at Huntingdon (easily landed odds) in November: off 11 weeks, fairly useful form when around 7 lengths third to Chief Dan George in Grade 2 novice at Wetherby: stays 25f: raced on good ground or softer: may do better still. *Carl Llewellyn* — h129 +

BRADS HOUSE (IRE) 5 b.g. Rossini (USA) – Gold Stamp (Golden Act (USA)) [2006/7 h109: 21d² 18m* 17m² 16g³ 20s⁴ 20g⁴ 20s³ 21s 20d^F Feb 2] small, angular gelding: fairly useful hurdler: won novice at Fontwell in May: generally ran creditably in defeat otherwise: stays 21f: acts on soft and good to firm going. *J. G. M. O'Shea* — h115

BRADY BOYS (USA) 10 b.g. Cozzene (USA) – Elvia (USA) (Roberto (USA)) [2006/7 c–, h–: 20s 16f Jun 21] lengthy gelding: no longer of any account: often visored/in cheekpieces. *R. Lee* — c– h–

BRAEBURN 12 b.g. Petoski – Great Granny Smith (Fine Blue) [2006/7 c21s⁵ May 29] useful-looking gelding: winning pointer: maiden chaser: probably stays 23f. *J. S. Swindells* — c66

BRAHMS AND MIST (FR) 7 b.g. River Mist (USA) – Strabit (Stradavinsky) [2006/7 F18s F16s 16g 19g 21m^{pu} Apr 9] 28,000 4-y-o: workmanlike gelding: sixth foal: brother to winning jumper in Italy and 3 Flat winners in France: dam, placed at 1¼m on Flat, half-sister to useful French hurdler Bitwood: no form in bumpers/maiden hurdles. *Miss Suzy Smith* — h– F–

Mrs D. L. Whateley's "Boychuk"

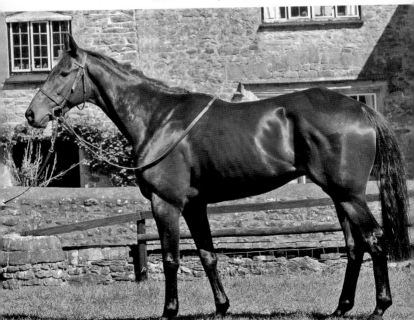

BRAMANTINO (IRE) 7 b.g. Perugino (USA) – Headrest (Habitat) [2006/7 h77: **h70** 16d^{pu} 17m^6 Apr 9] workmanlike gelding: poor maiden hurdler: raced around 2m: acts on heavy going: often in cheekpieces/blinkers. *T. A. K. Cuthbert*

BRANDY HOUSE (IRE) 8 b.m. Carroll House – Brandy's Sister (IRE) (Strong State- **c–** ment (USA)) [2006/7 22g 17g^6 20d^2 c19m^F Apr 10] poor maiden hurdler: behind when **h72** fell 4 out on chasing debut: stayed 2½m: acted on soft going: dead. *N. A. Twiston-Davies*

BRANDY WINE (IRE) 9 b.g. Roselier (FR) – Sakonnet (IRE) (Mandalus) [2006/7 **c101** c109, h95: c28s^4 c25v^2 Dec 11] rangy gelding: winning hurdler: fair handicap chaser: **h–** thorough stayer: acts on heavy going: in cheekpieces/blinkers last 7 outings. *L. Lungo*

BRANKLEY BOY 9 ch.g. Afzal – Needwood Fortune (Tycoon II) [2006/7 h127: **h126** 23d^{pu} 21v^{pu} 22d^3 Mar 17] tall gelding: chasing type: fairly useful handicap hurdler: went as if amiss first 2 starts: stays 25f: acts on heavy going. *N. J. Henderson*

BRASILIA PRINCE 8 ch.g. Karinga Bay – Cappuccino Girl (Broadsword (USA)) **h84** [2006/7 h70: 22m^{pu} 25g^3 24f^6 26m^4 26m^4 Sep 24] poor maiden hurdler: stays 3¼m: acts on good to firm going: tried in visor/cheekpieces. *G. P. Enright*

BRASTAR JELOIS (FR) 4 b.f. Vive True Brave (USA) – Star Angels (FR) (Ski Chief **h–** (USA)) [2006/7 16s 16d^4 16d 17s^4 17v 17g Apr 7] smallish filly: second foal: half-sister to French winner up to 11f Star Jelois (by Marchand de Sable): dam 1¼m/1½m winner: successful 7 times up to 1¼m on Flat, including 5 in 2006, left A. de Royer Dupre after final start: little form over hurdles: races freely. *D. E. Pipe*

BRAVE BENEFACTOR (IRE) 7 b.g. Beneficial – Brown Forest (Brave Invader **h84** (USA)) [2006/7 h–: 19d^3 22m^2 24d^5 24d Oct 31] lengthy gelding: poor form over hurdles: will stay beyond 3m: raced on good to firm and good to soft ground: has flashed tail. *B. G. Powell*

BRAVE BRIGADIER 4 b.g. Shambo – Fardella (ITY) (Molvedo) [2006/7 F14s F14v^2 **F76** F16s^4 Feb 3] leggy gelding: half-brother to fairly useful chasers up to 3m Dunston Bill (by Sizzling Melody) and Lord of The Sky (by Lord Bud) and winning hurdler up to 2½m Solitary Reaper (by Valiyar): dam 11f winner in France: modest form in frame in bumpers, making running. *Mrs S. Lamyman*

BRAVE BRONCHO (IRE) 5 b.g. Taipan (IRE) – Bro Ella (IRE) (Cataldi) [2006/7 **h83 p** 20v^4 16d Mar 26] tall gelding: second foal: dam unraced half-sister to very smart staying hurdler/chaser Royal Emperor and useful staying chaser A Piece of Cake: in need of run when fourth to Back On Line in maiden hurdle at Fontwell on debut, not knocked about: insufficient emphasis on stamina next time: likely to prove capable of better, particularly once qualified for handicaps. *D. E. Pipe*

BRAVE DANE (IRE) 9 b.g. Danehill (USA) – Nuriva (USA) (Woodman (USA)) **h§§** [2006/7 h86§: 16d^4 16m^{pu} 16g^{pu} Mar 14] long-backed gelding: fair on Flat (stays 1¼m), successful twice in 2006: modest hurdler: left A. Carroll after second start: raced around 2m: acts on good to firm and good to soft going: in cheekpieces final outing: has refused/ been reluctant to race (including all 3 starts in 2006/7): one to leave alone. *K. J. Burke*

BRAVE HIAWATHA (FR) 5 b.g. Dansili – Alexandrie (USA) (Val de L'Orne (FR)) **h–** [2006/7 h86p: 17d 20m^{pu} Apr 25] sturdy gelding: poor form at best over hurdles: left J. Old after reappearance (lame). *G. J. Smith*

BRAVE INCA (IRE) 9 b.g. Good Thyne (USA) – Wigwam Mam (IRE) (Com- **h160** manche Run) [2006/7 h167: 16s^3 20v* 16v* 16d^2 16d^2 24m^6 Apr 26]
  'We didn't make many mistakes with Night Nurse but we should have gone over fences with him sooner than we did.' So says Night Nurse's trainer, Peter Easterby, about the dual Champion Hurdle winner who adapted splendidly to jumping fences and would have won a Gold Cup had his stable not also saddled Little Owl for the race in 1981. The brilliant mare Dawn Run was successful in both the Champion Hurdle and the Gold Cup, but no other winner of hurdling's championship has come closer to adding the Gold Cup than Night Nurse who went down by a length and a half to his stable-companion, with Silver Buck, who won the race the following year, ten lengths away in third. The transition from top-class hurdler to top-class chaser can be difficult—plenty have failed—and it is always understandable when the connections of a horse like Brave Inca, for example, post-pone a career over fences. Night Nurse set out on his chasing career as a seven-year old, winning seven of his ten starts in his first season over fences, one of his defeats coming at the hands of Silver Buck in an epic ding-dong battle for the Embassy

*Ballymore Properties Hatton's Grace Hurdle, Fairyhouse—
it's very hard work for Brave Inca and Tony McCoy in this rescheduled race*

Final at Haydock and another in the Cheltenham Gold Cup, in which he was unplaced soon afterwards, probably feeling the effects of his race in the Embassy. Like Night Nurse, a big, strong sort who was practically everyone's nomination to make the grade over fences at the time, the reliable Brave Inca has always had the physique to suggest he could become a very good chaser one day. Before he got his head in front in the Emo Oil Champion Hurdle just after the end of the 2004/5 campaign, after a succession of placed efforts in good races, it seemed likely that Brave Inca—then a seven-year-old—would be sent over fences. He had gone down by a short head in the AIG Europe Champion Hurdle at Leopardstown and by a neck and the same in the Champion Hurdle itself at Cheltenham but, after his win at Punchestown, connections became persuaded to keep him over hurdles—he was 6/1 ante-post favourite for the 2006 Arkle Trophy when the announcement was made in September 2005 that his proposed switch to fences had been postponed for 'twelve months'. This decision was rewarded handsomely when Brave Inca won four more top races after his return from a summer break, including both those two championship events at Leopardstown and Cheltenham.

Though there hasn't been much to choose between the top two-milers in recent seasons, Brave Inca's gameness and consistency seemed sure to earn him more big-race victories over hurdles in the latest season and consideration of a change to steeplechasing was postponed again. At the age of nine, time is now running out for Brave Inca to make a successful switch and it seems likely that an impressive record in the top races over hurdles, coupled with a well-earned reputation for toughness, will be his legacy. If he is kept over hurdles again, he may well find it hard to add significantly to his nine Grade 1 victories. He was the second-oldest runner in the latest Champion Hurdle (behind old rival Hardy Eustace) and, though he finished in the first three for the third year running, he was swamped for

bewleyshotels.com December Festival Hurdle, Leopardstown—a winning first ride on Brave Inca for Ruby Walsh as the Morgiana form is reversed with Iktitaf; Silent Oscar (checked cap) takes third

finishing speed by the two-years-younger Sublimity, going down by three lengths and just holding off Afsoun and Hardy Eustace for second.

The balance of Brave Inca's form in the latest season suggests that he has passed his absolute peak. It seemed significant that, even though Sublimity missed the ACCBank Champion Hurdle at Punchestown in late-April, Brave Inca was aimed instead at the Champion Stayers' Hurdle the day before in the hope that the much longer distance—it was the first time he had been tried beyond two and a half miles—would bring him back to his very best form. In the event, he ran a rare poor race, off the bridle a long way out and gradually losing his position, beaten before stamina became an issue (possibly past his best after another tough campaign). Brave Inca's season had also begun disappointingly when he was decisively beaten by Iktitaf and Asian Maze in the Morgiana Hurdle, a race he had won the previous year. Brave Inca had odds-on Asian Maze back in fourth when winning the Bally-more Properties Hatton's Grace Hurdle on his second start, a race rescheduled (the same five runners lined up) after gale force winds forced the abandonment of the original fixture three days earlier after just two races had taken place. The going at Fairyhouse was very heavy and Brave Inca needed reminders with a circuit to go before making hard work of beating Rosaker, idling markedly after leading before three out and almost pulling himself up after being three lengths clear on the run-in. In the end he had just three quarters of a length to spare, with 66/1 outsider Brogella only a further two lengths back in third. Brave Inca could hardly have looked less like a reigning champion that day, but he travelled much better when winning his second successive bewleyshotels.com December Festival Hurdle at Leopardstown. Ruby Walsh replaced Tony McCoy who had ridden Brave Inca in eight of his nine previous races (Barry Geraghty was on board in the latest Morgiana) but was claimed to ride at Newbury. In typical style, Brave Inca responded well under pressure, aided by a fine jump at the last, to hold on by a length and a quarter from the odds-on Iktitaf who was poised on the bridle at the last, looking as if he could pass Brave Inca at any time. Brave Inca didn't win again but he showed similar form when runner-up (under McCoy) to Hardy Eustace in the AIG Europe

Champion Hurdle at Leopardstown, typically niggled along from a good way out, and also when losing his English crown to Sublimity, when Walsh rode him (as he did at Punchestown).

Brave Inca (IRE) (b.g. 1998)	Good Thyne (USA) (br 1977)	Herbager (b 1956)	Vandale II Flagette
		Foreseer (b or br 1969)	Round Table Regal Gleam
	Wigwam Mam (IRE) (ch 1993)	Commanche Run (b 1981)	Run The Gantlet Volley
		Rozifer (ch 1978)	Lucifer Rozeen

The strong, good-bodied Brave Inca is bred to stay well, his now-deceased sire the 1980 Irish St Leger runner-up Good Thyne being an influence for stamina and his dam the unraced Wigwam Mam, whose only runner he is to date, being by St Leger winner Commanche Run (sire of two Irish Grand National winners) out of winning hurdler/chaser Rozifer who won at up to two and three quarter miles. Rozifer is a half-sister to the dam of the top-class chaser Merry Gale out of the unraced Rozeen who is also the great grandam of Racing Demon. Brave Inca has often shaped as if he would be suited by further than two miles, the distance over which most of the top prizes over hurdles are run, and he is definitely worth another chance at three. It might also be worth giving blinkers or a visor a try. The suggestion of headgear might seem an affront to such a splendidly tough gelding but it must be stressed that Brave Inca, who has traditionally made his jockeys work hard for their fees, did seem to become even lazier in the latest season ('He's minding himself more than he used to, he's got cuter' was McCoy's verdict after the Hatton's Grace). Brave Inca has been raced mainly on good going or softer, and he acts on heavy. *Colm A. Murphy, Ireland*

BRAVE JO (FR) 6 ch.g. Villez (USA) – Eau de Nuit (Kings Lake (USA)) [2006/7 h–, F68: 19dF 16d² 17m⁶ 16m³ 19d⁵ 17s⁴ 17v³ 18s³ 19v* 19g 22g⁵ 24m² Apr 25] angular gelding: poor hurdler: well-backed favourite, made all in handicap at Exeter in January: stays 3m: acts on heavy and good to firm going. *N. J. Hawke* **h84**

BRAVE LAD (IRE) 6 b.g. Acting Brave – Carolin Lass (IRE) (Carlingford Castle) [2006/7 F16m⁶ 24fpu 24mpu Sep 3] fifth foal: half-brother to winning pointer by Shiel Hill: dam unraced: no form in bumper/over hurdles: tried blinkered: won point in March. *Mrs N. S. Evans* **h–** **F–**

BRAVE PADDY (IRE) 5 b.g. Brave Act – So Kind (Kind of Hush) [2006/7 24spu Jan 30] half-brother to several winners, including hurdler/chaser around 2m Knight's Emperor (by Grand Lodge): dam 6f winner: showed nothing in novice hurdle on debut. *A. J. Honeyball* **h–**

BRAVE REBELLION 8 b.g. Primitive Rising (USA) – Grand Queen (Grand Conde (FR)) [2006/7 c–p, h116, F95: 20gF 20m⁴ 19s² 20g* 20g* Apr 16] sturdy gelding: fairly useful novice hurdler: successful twice at Wetherby in April, beating Ice Tea a head in conditional jockeys event on first occasion: should stay beyond 2½m: acts on soft going (won bumper on good to firm). *K. G. Reveley* **c–** **h115**

BRAVERY (IRE) 8 b.g. Zaffaran (USA) – Carrick Shannon (Green Shoon) [2006/7 c20d² c20m⁶ c20f² c20m⁵ c22m⁴ c22g² c22g² c21d⁵ c31d c20m² c24fsu Apr 27] big, rangy gelding: winning hurdler: fairly useful handicap chaser, runner-up 5 times in 2006/7: stays 2¾m: acts on firm and good to soft ground: ran well both starts in cheekpieces (made running). *C. F. Swan, Ireland* **c118** **h–**

BRAVE THOUGHT (IRE) 12 b.g. Commanche Run – Bristol Fairy (Smartset) [2006/7 c111, h–: 17s c16s⁴ 20s c16v² c16v* c16s⁶ Apr 26] strong, lengthy gelding: fair handicap chaser: won at Ayr in March, but is inconsistent nowadays: stays 2½m: raced mainly on going softer than good (acts on heavy). *P. Monteith* **c111** **h–**

BRAVE VILLA (FR) 8 b.g. Villez (USA) – Brave Lola (FR) (Dom Pasquini (FR)) [2006/7 16g c16d³ c17g² c16dt c16v* c18s⁴ c16v* Feb 20] lengthy gelding: second foal: half-brother to modest 2m hurdler Beau Torero (by True Brave): dam once-raced half-sister to dam of smart French hurdler Kidder: winning hurdler: left A. Moore after first outing: improved form over fences after, won novice handicaps at Hereford and Chepstow in November and Taunton in February: best at 2m: acts on heavy going: tongue tied last 5 outings: front runner/races prominently. *M. Sheppard* **c103** **h–**

BRAVE VISION 11 b.g. Clantime – Kinlet Vision (IRE) (Vision (USA)) [2006/7 **h104** h104: 16g^{pu} 20s^4 16v* 17s^4 16v^4 16s Apr 25] sturdy gelding: fair handicap hurdler: won at Kelso in January: effective at 2m to 2½m: acts on heavy and good to firm going. *A. C. Whillans*

BREAKING SILENCE (IRE) 6 b.g. Simply Great (FR) – Lady of Tara (Deep Run) **h124** [2006/7 F16g^3 F16m* 18s* 19g^4 16m^3 20m^3 Apr 27] useful-looking gelding: type to **F101** make a chaser: half-brother to bumper winner Lady Accord (by Accordion): dam won 3m hurdle: better effort in bumpers when winning at Cork in June: progressive over hurdles, won maiden at Sligo in September: fairly useful form in minor event at Fairyhouse (6 lengths third to Scotsirish) and Champion Novices' Hurdle at Punchestown (20 lengths third to Glencove Marina) last 2 starts: stays 2½m: acts on soft and good to firm going. *T. J. Taaffe, Ireland*

BREAK THE ICE 6 b.m. North Col – Frozen Pipe (Majestic Maharaj) [2006/7 h–, **h–** F78: 20g 21m^6 Oct 16] fourth in bumper on debut, looking a stayer: no form over hurdles. *L. A. Dace*

BREAKWATER HOUSE (IRE) 5 b.g. Supreme Leader – Millicent Bridge (IRE) **F93 +** (Over The River (FR)) [2006/7 F16s^3 Jan 31] tall gelding: second foal: dam unraced out of half-sister to Cheltenham Gold Cup winner Imperial Call: won bumper at Newcastle on debut by short head from Robbie Dye: will stay beyond 2m. *Miss Lucinda V. Russell*

BREATHING FIRE 5 b.g. Pivotal – Pearl Venture (Salse (USA)) [2006/7 h134: 17s^2 **h122** 16m 17g* 16g 16s^2 16d^2 18s^2 19d^2 16d^F Jan 14] leggy gelding: fairly useful hurdler on balance: easily landed odds in maiden at Tralee in August: runner-up last 4 completed starts, beaten 3½ lengths by Ringaroses in novice at Ascot final time: stayed 19f: acted on good to firm going, possibly not at best on soft: tried in cheekpieces/tongue tied: sometimes found little: dead. *Mrs J. Harrington, Ireland*

BREDON HILL 7 b.m. Rakaposhi King – Society News (Law Society (USA)) [2006/7 **F–** F–: F17s May 20] well beaten in points/bumpers: sold 1,800 gns Doncaster May (2006) Sales. *R. T. Phillips*

BREEDSBREEZE (IRE) 5 b.g. Fresh Breeze (USA) – Godfreys Cross (IRE) (Fine **h106** Blade (USA)) [2006/7 22d^3 16s^3 Jan 20] €8,200 3-y-o: lengthy, rather unfurnished gelding: half-brother to 21f hurdle winner Safe Enough (by Safety Catch): dam winning Irish pointer: won maiden Irish point in October: better effort over hurdles when 3¼ lengths third to Barbers Shop in 2¾m maiden at Ascot. *P. F. Nicholls*

BREEZER 7 b.g. Forzando – Lady Lacey (Kampala) [2006/7 h78§: 21g^6 19s 19v 20g **h67 §** Apr 14] angular gelding: poor handicap hurdler: stays 2½m: acts on good to firm going: tried visored, usually in cheekpieces in 2005/6: ungenuine. *J. A. Geake*

BREEZY WARRIOR (IRE) 8 b.g. Commanche Run – Another Crash (Crash **h–** Course) [2006/7 h–: 21s^{pu} 17d May 29] useful-looking gelding: no form over hurdles: tried in cheekpieces. *J. M. Saville*

BREMHILL GIRL 4 b.f. Petoski – Balula's Girl (Gildoran) [2006/7 F16g F16m^6 **F70** Apr 15] second foal: dam unraced sister to fair 2½m chaser L'Orphelin: never dangerous in bumpers, looking in need of experience: likely to be suited by further than 2m. *C. L. Tizzard*

BRENDAN'S SURPRISE 5 b.g. Faustus (USA) – Primrose Way (Young Generation) **h82** [2006/7 h–: 18m^5 19m^3 22m Jul 16] leggy gelding: poor maiden hurdler: should stay 2½m: acts on good to firm going: sold 4,200 gns Doncaster August Sales, won point in January. *K. J. Burke*

BRENDAR (IRE) 10 b.g. Step Together (USA) – Willabelle (Will Somers) [2006/7 c–, **c–** h101: 20s^4 21s* Jan 15] lengthy gelding: failed to complete 2 starts over fences: fair **h108** handicap hurdler: won at Plumpton in January: stays 2¾m: acts on heavy and good to firm ground: tried blinkered. *Jim Best*

BRENIN CWMTUDU 4 b.g. Saddlers' Hall (IRE) – Keel Row (Relkino) [2006/7 **F83** F16v^6 F16s^{pu} F16m^2 Apr 10] 9,000 3-y-o: tall gelding: fourth foal: dam, modest 2m hurdler, half-sister to useful hurdler/fairly useful chaser up to 2½m Easter Ross: modest form 2 completed starts in bumpers (saddle slipped in between). *Evan Williams*

BRER BEAR 8 b.g. Perpendicular – Nessfield (Tumble Wind) [2006/7 c104: c25g^{pu} **c–** May 3] fairly useful pointer/hunter chaser: should stay beyond 3m: acts on soft going. *Mrs E. Insley*

BRESSBEE 9 ch.g. Twining (USA) – Bressay (USA) (Nureyev (USA)) [2006/7 **h83** h83: 20f^{pu} Jun 3] smallish, leggy gelding: poor form in maiden hurdles (broke down only outing in 2006/7): stays 2½m: raced on good to firm/firm going: visored on debut. *J. W. Unett*

BRETTON WOODS (IRE) 5 b.g. Supreme Leader – Bella Velutina (Coquelin (USA)) [2006/7 F17s³ Feb 19] half-brother to modest hurdler/fair chaser Martinstown (by Old Vic), stays 23f: dam half-sister to dual Stayers' Hurdle winner Galmoy and high-class hurdler/smart chaser who stayed 3m Youlneverwalkalone, and to dam of top-class chaser up to 2½m Direct Route: needed experience (barely ever on bridle) when staying-on third to Harry Wood in bumper at Carlisle on debut: will be suited by 2½m+. *N. G. Richards* **F88 +**

BREWSTER (IRE) 10 b.g. Roselier (FR) – Aelia Paetina (Buckskin (FR)) [2006/7 h129: 25dᵖᵘ c26s³ Dec 3] rather leggy gelding: smart novice hurdler in 2004/5: largely disappointing since, including on chasing debut (jumped slowly): stays 3m: acts on heavy and good to firm going. *Ian Williams* **c–ʰ–**

BRIAN (IRE) 5 b.g. Darnay – Sayulita (Habitat) [2006/7 F17d F16g Oct 7] €2,000 3-y-o: half-brother to several winners, including fair chaser Aegean (by Rock Hopper), stays 25f: dam, modest maiden, stayed 1½m: well held in bumpers: pulled up in point: sold 2,000 gns Doncaster May Sales. *N. A. Twiston-Davies* **F–**

BRIANNIE (IRE) 5 b.m. Xaar – Annieirwin (IRE) (Perugino (USA)) [2006/7 h68: 23dᵖᵘ May 21] sparely-made mare: little form over hurdles (lame only outing in 2006/7): wears cheekpieces. *P. Butler* **h–**

BRIAREUS 7 ch.g. Halling (USA) – Lower The Tone (IRE) (Phone Trick (USA)) [2006/7 h151: c17d² c19d* Dec 15] tall, good-topped gelding: smart hurdler, won Grade 2 at Wincanton in 2005/6: promising start over fences, winning 5-runner Grade 2 Scanmoor Noel Novices' Chase at Ascot in December by 3 lengths from Knight Legend: reported in mid-February to have suffered a ligament strain and missed rest of season: effective from 2m to 19f: has won on soft going, possibly best under less testing conditions: should still do better over fences. *A. M. Balding* **c146 pʰ–**

BRICKETSTOWN KING (IRE) 11 br.g. Mandalus – Laurel Walk (Buckskin (FR)) [2006/7 c21mᵖᵘ Jul 27] winning pointer: little form in chases. *Mark Campion* **c–**

BRICKIES MATE (IRE) 6 ch.g. Double Trigger (IRE) – Avena (Oats) [2006/7 F16s⁶ 16d⁵ 20m⁴ 20v⁴ 20s* Apr 25] 16,000 3-y-o: fourth foal: dam, 2m hurdle winner, half-sister to useful hurdler/chaser up to 21f Major Rumpus: mid-field in bumpers: fair form over hurdles: improved effort when winning maiden at Perth in April: will stay beyond 2½m: acts on soft going, probably on good to firm. *I. R. Ferguson, Ireland* **h102 F67**

BRIDGE FLIGHT (IRE) 9 ch.g. Air Display (USA) – Classic Travel (Deep Run) [2006/7 c20m c20g c23d³ c22s⁴ c25sᵖᵘ c24sᵖᵘ c24dᵖᵘ Jan 8] winning pointer: poor chaser: won amateur handicap at Hereford (final start for W. Burke, Ireland) in November: no form after: stays 25f: probably acts on heavy going: sometimes wears blinkers/cheekpieces. *Heather Dalton* **c80**

BRIDGE RUN (IRE) 6 b.g. Flemensfirth (USA) – Sweet Run (Deep Run) [2006/7 F16v* 20v* 20v Feb 25] half-brother to winning pointer Help Yourself and winning staying chaser Silverlight Lad (both by Roselier): dam once-raced half-sister to useful staying chaser Sommelier: won second of 2 starts in maiden Irish points in 2006: justified favouritism in bumper at Galway in October and maiden hurdle at Gowran (beat Clarkey easily by 5 lengths) in December: ran as if amiss in Grade 2 novice at Naas: will stay beyond 2½m: raced on heavy going. *N. Meade, Ireland* **h121 F107**

BRIERY BREEZE (IRE) 5 ch.m. Anshan – Briery Gale (Strong Gale) [2006/7 F16s F16v F16m Mar 25] half-sister to winning 2m hurdler Blackbriery Thyne (by Good Thyne) and useful chaser up to 3m Briery Fox (by Phardante): dam poor novice hurdler: well held in bumpers (badly hampered final start). *Mrs K. Walton* **F–**

BRIERY FOX (IRE) 9 ch.g. Phardante (FR) – Briery Gale (Strong Gale) [2006/7 c120, h–: c20d* c24g c21d⁴ c24g³ c21gᵘʳ Apr 13] sturdy, lengthy gelding: winning hurdler: useful chaser: improved to win handicap at Worcester in October, coming from unpromising position to beat Nayodabayo 1½ lengths: back to form when 6¾ lengths third of 18 to Rambling Minster in valuable handicap at Sandown: stays 3m: raced mainly on good/good to soft going. *H. D. Daly* **c130 h–**

BRIGADIER DU BOIS (FR) 8 gr.g. Apeldoorn (FR) – Artic Night (FR) (Kaldoun (FR)) [2006/7 c88, h85: c20sᵖᵘ 16v⁴ c19s c19s³ c20vᵖᵘ Jan 25] lengthy gelding: modest hurdler/chaser: not at best in 2006/7: stays 2½m: acts on heavy going: tried blinkered/in cheekpieces/tongue tied: joined N. King. *Mrs L. Wadham* **c72 h70**

BRIGHT 4 ch.g. Mister Baileys – Razzle Dazzle (IRE) (Caerleon (USA)) [2006/7 16d 16vᵖᵘ Feb 5] no form on Flat or in juvenile hurdles. *Robert Gray* **h–**

BRIGHT APPROACH (IRE) 14 gr.g. Roselier (FR) – Dysart Lady (King's Ride) **c95**
[2006/7 c116: c33g³ c30m³ c31g* May 24] smallish gelding: veteran chaser: won hunter
at Folkestone in May: suited by thorough test of stamina: best efforts on good going or
firmer (acts on firm). *J. G. Cann*

BRIGHT EAGLE (IRE) 7 ch.g. Eagle Eyed (USA) – Lumiere (USA) (Northjet) **c99**
[2006/7 c16s² c16dᵖᵘ c16v³ c17s³ c17vᵘʳ c17gᶠ Mar 24] small, leggy gelding: placed in **h–**
novice hurdles: modest maiden chaser, off 2 years before reappearance: raced around 2m:
acted on soft and good to firm going: dead. *R. Lee*

BRIGHT PRESENT (IRE) 9 b. or br.g. Presenting – Bright Rose (Skyliner) [2006/7 **c–**
c63, h–: c25dᵖᵘ May 17] winning pointer, placed in Britain in 2007: little form in other **h–**
events: tried in cheekpieces/blinkers, also tongue tied last 4 outings. *B. N. Pollock*

BRIGHT SPARKY (GER) 4 ch.g. Dashing Blade – Braissim (Dancing Brave **h105**
(USA)) [2006/7 17g⁴ 17g⁴ 16d 17d⁵ 16d⁴ 16d⁴ 19s* 20g² 20g Apr 16] poor maiden on
Flat (should stay beyond 6f): fair juvenile hurdler: won handicaps at Musselburgh in
January and Catterick in March: stays 2½m: acts on soft going: usually tongue tied.
M. W. Easterby

BRIGHT STEEL (IRE) 10 gr.g. Roselier (FR) – Ikeathy (Be Friendly) [2006/7 c72§, **c– §**
h–: 20d 24d May 19] rather leggy gelding: maiden hurdler: poor form only completed **h–**
outing in chases: probably stays 25f: acts on heavy ground: tried in cheekpieces/blinkers.
M. Todhunter

BRIGHTWELL 6 b.g. Charnwood Forest (IRE) – Ski Blade (Niniski (USA)) [2006/7 **F–**
F16v⁶ F17d⁶ Jun 4] £1,500 4-y-o: fourth live foal: dam tailed off both starts: modest
pointer, successful in 2006: well beaten in bumpers: sold £9,000 Ascot June Sales.
R. D. E. Woodhouse

BRILLIANT CUT 7 gr.g. Terimon – Always Shining (Tug of War) [2006/7 F83: 16d **h–**
24g⁶ Mar 23] rangy gelding: chasing type: modest form when fourth in bumper: off 18
months, no show in novice hurdles. *N. J. Henderson*

BRILLIANT (GER) 4 ch.c. Risk Me (FR) – Belle Orfana (GER) (Orfano (GER)) **h70**
[2006/7 18gᵖᵘ 17v⁴ 16v 17v³ 16gᵖᵘ Apr 9] won 1¼m handicap at Dusseldorf in August
from 6 starts on Flat in Germany in 2006 for C. von der Recke: poor juvenile hurdler:
should prove suited by test of speed at 2m: blinkered/visored after debut. *M. F. Harris*

BRINGEWOOD FOX 5 gr.g. Cloudings (IRE) – Leinthall Fox (Deep Run) [2006/7 **F86**
F–: F17d⁴ F16d⁶ Dec 21] easily best effort in bumpers when sixth of 14 at Ludlow.
J. L. Needham

BRING ME SUNSHINE (IRE) 6 ch.g. Alderbrook – Hilarys Pet (Bonne Noel) **c114**
[2006/7 h110, F96: 21g* 22dᵖᵘ 23vᵖᵘ c16s* c19dᵖᵘ Mar 20] tall gelding: fairly useful **h115**
hurdler: won handicap at Towcester in November: created good impression when winning maiden at Taunton on chasing debut by 6 lengths from Spidam: third poor run of
season 8 days later: should stay beyond 21f: acts on heavy going. *C. L. Tizzard*

BRING ON THE BLING (IRE) 4 b.f. Fruits of Love (USA) – Genetta (Green **h66**
Desert (USA)) [2006/7 16v⁴ 16v 16g 19v⁶ 20m 24m² Apr 17] smallish filly: modest
maiden on Flat (stays 1½m) for M. Halford: first form over hurdles (poor) on final start:
stays 3m with emphasis on speed. *D. McCain Jnr*

BRINKMANSHIP (USA) 5 b.g. Red Ransom (USA) – Whist (Mr Prospector (USA)) **h83**
[2006/7 F86: F16m³ F17v 17d Oct 31] leggy gelding: fair form in bumpers, sold out **F82**
of G. A. Swinbank's stable 10,000 gns Doncaster August Sales after first outing: little
impact in novice on hurdling debut, carrying head awkwardly. *Tim Vaughan*

BRISCOE PLACE (IRE) 7 b.g. Dr Massini (IRE) – Laridissa (IRE) (Shardari) **c125**
[2006/7 h105, F100: 22gᵖᵘ 22m³ c23f* c20m* c20dᵘʳ c17m⁴ c19g³ c21d Dec 4] medium- **h94**
sized gelding: winning hurdler: fairly useful chaser: won maiden at Worcester and novice
at Market Rasen (easily) in June: improved effort when third to Bishop's Bridge in handicap at Ascot: stays 23f: acts on firm going: sound jumper: usually races prominently.
Jonjo O'Neill

BRISTOL BRIDGE 10 b.g. Shannon Cottage (USA) – Plassey Bridge (Pitpan) **c–**
[2006/7 c–: c19gᵖᵘ May 4] of no account. *Ms M. L. Byrom*

BRITANNIC 4 ch.g. Rainbow Quest (USA) – Anka Britannia (USA) (Irish River (FR)) **h– p**
[2006/7 16g Apr 15] useful on Flat (stays 1½m) at 3 yrs, sold out of A. Fabre's stable
43,000 gns Doncaster November Sales, and gelded: took strong hold when well held in
novice on hurdling debut: joined T. Tate: should do better. *R. C. Guest*

BRIYATHA 5 ch.m. Montjoy (USA) – Just One Way VII (Damsire Unregistered) **F–**
[2006/7 F–: F16f\ :sup:pu F16v May 20] no form in bumpers: tried tongue tied. *C. N. Kellett*

BROAD TOWN GIRL 4 b.f. Woodborough (USA) – Fortunes Course (IRE) (Crash **F– §**
Course) [2006/7 F13d\ :sup:ro F14g F14s Jan 4] rather leggy filly: second foal: half-sister to
bumper/21f hurdle winner Mountain Approach (by Kayf Tara): dam 2¼m winner on Flat
and fair staying hurdler/chaser: more temperament than ability in bumpers: well beaten
on Flat. *Mrs H. Sweeting*

BROADWAY CALLING 4 ch.g. Dr Fong (USA) – Manhattan Sunset (USA) (El **h–**
Gran Senor (USA)) [2006/7 17s\ :sup:pu Aug 26] modest maiden on Flat (bred to stay 1¼m+),
sold out of A. Balding's stable 2,500 gns Doncaster May Sales: no show in juvenile on
hurdling debut. *M. E. Sowersby*

BROCHRUA (IRE) 7 b.m. Hernando (FR) – Severine (USA) (Trempolino (USA)) **h94**
[2006/7 h94: 22g⁶ 17g³ 19m⁵ 19v⁴ 20v⁵ 21g* Mar 26] modest hurdler: claimed from
J. Frost £5,600, back to best when winning conditional jockeys handicap at Plumpton in
March: stays 21f: acts on good to firm and good to soft going (below form on soft/heavy):
tried blinkered (saddle slipped). *A. M. Hales*

BROGELLA (IRE) 7 b.m. King's Theatre (IRE) – Metroella (IRE) (Entitled) [2006/7 **h130**
h123+: 17s⁸ 18s² 20s³ 20v³ 20v Dec 17] close-coupled mare: useful hurdler: won handicap at Killarney (beat Adamant Approach easily by 6 lengths) in May: appeared to excel
herself in face of very stiff task when 2¾ lengths third of 5 to Brave Inca in Grade 1 at
Fairyhouse fourth start, possibly not over that very hard race when rare below-par effort
next time: stays 2½m: acts on heavy going: effective blinkered or not. *Ms F. M. Crowley,
Ireland*

BROKEN REED (IRE) 8 b.g. Broken Hearted – Kings Reserve (King's Ride) **c100**
[2006/7 h96p: 24v* c20g c24s⁴ c23d* c24v⁵ Jan 12] deep-girthed gelding: successful **h102**
both starts over hurdles, including in minor event at Perth in May: also fair form over
fences: won novice at Leicester in December, held when left clear last: stays 3m: acts on
any going. *T. R. George*

BROKEN SEA (IRE) 5 b.m. Gothland (FR) – Pelm (IRE) (John French) [2006/7 **h–**
16d\ :sup:pu Mar 22] fourth foal: dam unraced: no show in claiming hurdle on debut. *Sean
Osborne, Ireland*

BROKE ROAD (IRE) 11 b.g. Deploy – Shamaka (Kris) [2006/7 c–, h109: c16v³ **c93**
c19m³ c16m 16d⁶ Aug 14] leggy gelding: fair hurdler/modest chaser: raced mainly **h99**
around 2m: acts on soft and good to firm going, probably on heavy: visored once: usually
tongue tied: inconsistent. *Heather Dalton*

BROMLEY ABBEY 9 ch.m. Minster Son – Little Bromley (Riberetto) [2006/7 c–, **c–**
h83: 22f\ :sup:pu 16d 20d 20s c16v\ :sup:pu c24d Jan 19] lengthy mare: novice hurdler, out of sorts in **h–**
2006/7: no form over fences: stays 3m: wears cheekpieces. *Miss S. E. Forster*

BROMLEY MOSS 8 ch.g. Le Moss – Little Bromley (Riberetto) [2006/7 h–: c20v\ :sup:pu **c–**
c22v c21v\ :sup:pu c20s\ :sup:pu Dec 26] workmanlike gelding: won maiden point in 2006, no other **h–**
form: tried tongue tied: joined R. Ford. *M. A. Barnes*

BRONSON F'SURE 8 b.g. Overbury (IRE) – T'Be Sure (IRE) (Doubletour (USA)) **c105 +**
[2006/7 c21s⁴ c23d⁵ c20d c20v⁵ c24v² c20v⁴ c23v\ :sup:ur c24g* c24m* c24m* Apr 9] quite
good-topped gelding: first foal: dam, ran once in point, out of sister to dam of high-class
chaser up to 3m Farmer Jack: successful twice in points: bought 6,000 gns Doncaster
August Sales: fair chaser: improved form faced with less testing ground, making all in
handicaps at Huntingdon and Southwell in March and novice at Huntingdon in April:
stays 3m: best form on good/good to firm going: may do better still. *C. T. Pogson*

BRONX GIRL (IRE) 5 ch.m. Quws – Mill Lane Lady (IRE) (Un Desperado (FR)) **h111**
[2006/7 F16s³ F18v* F16s* 16v* 16v³ Mar 18] €24,000 3-y-o: first foal: dam, fair hurd- **F95**
ler/chaser who stayed 2½m, half-sister to fairly useful hurdler/chaser Storm Damage:
fairly useful form in bumpers, winning at Punchestown and Navan in December:
successful in 30-runner maiden at Navan following month on hurdling debut: better form
when 11 lengths third to Chomba Womba in listed mares novice at Limerick: will stay
2½m: raced on good going or softer. *F. Flood, Ireland*

BRONZE KING 7 b.g. Rakaposhi King – Bronze Sunset (Netherkelly) [2006/7 h–, F–: **c–**
17s 22d c20v\ :sup:co Feb 27] quite good-topped gelding: no sign of ability: tried tongue tied. **h–**
J. A. B. Old

BRONZESMITH 11 b.g. Greensmith – Bronze Age (Celtic Cone) [2006/7 c128, h–: **c130**
c20g* c23m\ :sup:F c21d\ :sup:pu c24g\ :sup:pu c24g² Apr 21] lengthy gelding: useful handicap chaser: won **h–**

153

at Bangor in May by 2 lengths from Christopher: off 6½ months, back to form when ½-length second to Out The Black there: stays 3m: acts on soft and good to firm going (bumper form on heavy): tried tongue tied. *B. J. M. Ryall*

BROOKBY (NZ) 7 b.g. Groom Dancer (USA) – Kappadios (NZ) (Great Charmer (USA)) [2006/7 16gpu Nov 7] successful twice up to 1m from 20 starts on Flat in New Zealand for S. Curtis, fair form in handicaps in Britain: no show in novice on hurdling debut. *Miss S. West*   h–

BROOKING (IRE) 9 b.g. Roselier (FR) – Kilkil Pin (Bowling Pin) [2006/7 h–: 20d 24vpu Nov 23] no form over hurdles. *R. T. Phillips*   h–

BROOKLYN BREEZE (IRE) 10 b. or br.g. Be My Native (USA) – Moss Gale (Strong Gale) [2006/7 c143, h123+: 20s 24g² c21g Apr 13] rangy, useful-looking gelding: has had wind operation: useful handicap chaser at best: fairly useful hurdler: off 14 months, easily better effort in handicaps in 2006/7 when 1¾ lengths second to Ice Tea at Newcastle: effective at 2m (given a test) to 3m: acts on good to firm and good to soft going. *L. Lungo*   c119 + h124 +

BROOKLYN BROWNIE (IRE) 8 b.g. Presenting – In The Brownies (IRE) (Lafontaine (USA)) [2006/7 h117: c16g* c20m³ c20s² c21d⁴ 19s⁵ c20g² c25mpu Apr 21] strong, lengthy gelding: fairly useful hurdler/chaser: won maiden at Hexham on chasing debut in May: improved form when runner-up to Nice Try in handicap at Bangor sixth start: went as if amiss next time: should stay at least 2¾m: acts on good to firm and good to soft going. *J. M. Jefferson*   c123 h108

BROOKLYN'S GOLD (USA) 12 b.g. Seeking The Gold (USA) – Brooklyn's Dance (FR) (Shirley Heights) [2006/7 c105, h92: c19g May 4] close-coupled gelding: one-time fairly useful handicap hurdler: fair maiden chaser: best form around 2m: has won on soft going, best form on good/good to firm: usually races prominently: none too keen nowadays. *Ian Williams*   c– § h–

BROOK NO ARGUMENT 5 ch.m. Alderbrook – Gloriana (Formidable (USA)) [2006/7 F16v² F16v² F17d* F17g Apr 13] sturdy mare: fifth foal: half-sister to 7f/1m winner Thunderclap (by Royal Applause): dam, 1m/9f winner on Flat, also successful at 2¼m over hurdles: fair form in bumpers, won at Market Rasen in March: well held in listed event at Aintree. *J. J. Quinn*   F91

BROOMERS HILL (IRE) 7 b.g. Sadler's Wells (USA) – Bella Vitessa (IRE) (Thatching) [2006/7 h–: 22m³ 24vpu 21m c26mF Apr 8] sturdy gelding: little form over hurdles: disputing lead when falling heavily 4 out in novice handicap at Plumpton on chasing debut: usually wears headgear: tried tongue tied. *L. A. Dace*   c? h66

BROOMLEY MAX 11 b.g. Green Adventure (USA) – Little Hut (Royal Palace) [2006/7 c20m⁵ c20s⁶ Jun 25] winning pointer: no form in chases. *W. T. Reed*   c76

BRORA SUTHERLAND (IRE) 8 b.g. Synefos (USA) – Downtotheswallows (IRE) (Boreen (FR)) [2006/7 c–, h–: c16m May 6] big, good-topped gelding: little form: tried in cheekpieces: sold 1,600 gns Doncaster May (2006) Sales, no show in points. *Miss Lucinda V. Russell*   c– h–

BROTHER OSCAR 6 b.g. Oscar (IRE) – Sister Stephanie (IRE) (Phardante (FR)) [2006/7 F17s* Feb 26] 5,800 3-y-o: third foal: dam, useful chaser who stayed 4¼m, became reluctant: won maiden on second of 2 starts in points in 2006: bought £40,000 Ascot December Sales: fairly useful form when successful in bumper at Hereford by 3 lengths from Team Chaser (pair clear). *R. S. Brookhouse*   F100

BROTHER TED 10 b.g. Henbit (USA) – Will Be Wanton (Palm Track) [2006/7 c–, h–: 16mpu Nov 9] leggy gelding: once-raced over fences: little form over hurdles: sometimes tongue tied. *J. K. Cresswell*   c– h–

BROWNEYES BLUE (IRE) 9 b.g. Satco (FR) – Bawnard Lady (Ragapan) [2006/7 h–: 24m⁶ 20m⁵ 22g⁵ 25dpu Dec 28] little form over hurdles, left D. MacLeod before third start: tried tongue tied/in cheekpieces. *James Moffatt*   h78 ?

BROWN FOX (FR) 6 b.m. Polar Falcon (USA) – Garmeria (FR) (Kadrou (FR)) [2006/7 h73: 16g² 19g 17d⁵ 17v* 16s⁴ 16g 17m⁴ Apr 17] good-topped mare: poor hurdler: won amateur novice handicap at Hereford in November: possibly best around 2m: acts on any ground: tongue tied. *C. J. Down*   h83

BROWN TEDDY 10 b.g. Afzal – Quadrapol (Pollerton) [2006/7 c108, h–: c17g* Mar 24] lengthy gelding: winning hurdler: fair chaser: off 16 months, won handicap at Bangor in March: stays 2½m: acts on heavy going, probably on good to firm. *R. Ford*   c113 h–

BRUMOUS (IRE) 7 b.g. Glacial Storm (USA) – Ath Leathan (Royal Vulcan) [2006/7   **c120** h122: c19s⁵ c23v* c24g Mar 24] good-topped gelding: fairly useful form over hurdles/   **h–** fences: won 5-runner novice chase at Leicester (by short head from Esprit Saint, idling close home) in February: should stay beyond 23f: acts on heavy going. *O. Sherwood*

BRUNATE 8 b.g. Chaddleworth (IRE) – Dawn Call (Rymer) [2006/7 h–: 17m 22mᵖᵘ   **h–** Jun 18] no show in bumper/over hurdles. *J. A. Danahar*

BRUNDEANLAWS 6 b.m. Endoli (USA) – The Respondant (Respect) [2006/7 c–,   **c?** h85, F–: c25f³ c26dᵖᵘ c22mᵘʳ c25dᵖᵘ Oct 21] leggy mare: little solid form over hurdles/   **h–** fences. *Mrs H. O. Graham*

BRUNSTON CASTLE 7 b.g. Hector Protector (USA) – Villella (Sadler's Wells   **c–** (USA)) [2006/7 h–: 16v c21gᵖᵘ Mar 16] of little account: sold out of A. Carroll's stable   **h–** 3,200 gns Ascot August Sales after first outing: tried visored/tongue tied. *Henry Kinchin*

BRUTTO FACIE (IRE) 8 b.g. Old Vic – Elas Image (IRE) (Ela-Mana-Mou) [2006/7   **c117** c126, h–: c20s* c22gᵖᵘ c20dᵖᵘ Aug 31] tall, useful-looking gelding: fairly useful chaser: **h–** won minor event at Killarney in May: ran poorly both starts after: probably stays 21f: acts on soft and firm ground. *Mrs J. Harrington, Ireland*

BUACHAILL EILE (IRE) 7 b.g. Lord Americo – Suilvaun (Lafontaine (USA))   **h119** [2006/7 h104: 24v 24g⁶ 22v 21d⁴ 22v² 24d⁵ 22d³ Jan 28] lengthy, rather sparely-made gelding: fairly useful hurdler: mostly creditable efforts in handicaps in 2006/7: stayed 3m: acted on heavy going: dead. *Eric McNamara, Ireland*

BUACHAILL ON EIRNE (IRE) 4 b.g. Desert Sun – Peig Sayers (IRE) (Royal   **F–** Academy (USA)) [2006/7 F16g Apr 23] fifth foal: half-brother to modest performer up to 2m Tharua (by Indian Danehill): dam, Irish maiden (best at 1m at 2 yrs), closely related to very smart stayer Assessor: well held in maiden bumper on debut. *R. C. Guest*

BUAILTES AND FADAS (IRE) 12 b. or br.g. Be My Native (USA) – Ballyline   **c117** Dancer (Giolla Mear) [2006/7 c116: c16g⁶ c31d³ Nov 10] workmanlike gelding: fairly useful chaser: successful twice in cross-country events at Punchestown in 2002/3, and ran as well as ever when third to Spot Thedifference at Cheltenham final start: stayed 33f, effective at much shorter: acted on heavy going: dead. *Enda Bolger, Ireland*

BUALA BOS (IRE) 6 b.g. Oscar (IRE) – Cathy Dee (IRE) (Cataldi) [2006/7 F17s   **F76** F16g Mar 28] £46,000 4-y-o: lengthy gelding: first foal: dam unraced half-sister to useful hunter Kilbready Boy: little impact in bumpers. *Carl Llewellyn*

BU ALI (USA) 4 b.f. Silver Hawk (USA) – Mantua (Mtoto) [2006/7 16m⁶ 16g⁴ 16mᵖᵘ   **h–** Sep 2] little show on Flat or in juvenile hurdles: tried blinkered. *B. W. Duke*

BUBBLE BOY (IRE) 8 ch.g. Hubbly Bubbly (USA) – Cool Charm (Beau Charmeur   **c122** (FR)) [2006/7 c115: c25g³ c25mᵖᵘ c24g² c27d³ c24s* c25g⁴ c24v c24m* Apr 9] lengthy gelding: fairly useful handicap chaser: shaped as if amiss on occasions in 2006/7 (has reportedly suffered breathing problem), though made most when winning 4-runner events at Sandown (by distance) in December and Huntingdon (beat Mister Apple's by 1¼ lengths) in April: probably stays 3¼m: acts on heavy and good to firm going: claimer ridden: races prominently. *B. G. Powell*

BUBBLING FUN 6 b.m. Marju (IRE) – Blushing Barada (USA) (Blushing Groom   **h–** (FR)) [2006/7 h–: 16m Sep 24] medium-sized mare: modest on Flat (seems to stay easy 1¾m): no show over hurdles: sold 10,000 gns Doncaster January Sales. *T. Wall*

BUBBLING UNDER (IRE) 7 b.g. Presenting – Millies Luck (Al Sirat) [2006/7 20s⁴   **h84** 22s 22s 26gᵖᵘ Apr 11] €30,000 4-y-o: useful-looking gelding: half-brother to fair hurdler/ chaser Hunting Lore (by Lafontaine), stayed 3m, and winning pointer by Be My Native: dam unraced: pulled up in 2 maiden Irish points in 2005: form (poor) over hurdles only on debut: tried in cheekpieces. *Miss E. C. Lavelle*

BUBBS 5 b.m. Robellino (USA) – Llancillo Lady (IRE) (Be My Native (USA)) [2006/7   **h82** F17d³ F14g³ 17s 22m* Apr 17] first foal: dam unraced out of half-sister to smart 2m   **F85** hurdler/useful chaser Native Mission, useful hurdler/chaser up to 3¼m Joss Naylor and useful chaser around 2½m Jack Doyle: fair form on first of 2 starts in bumpers for C. Egerton: 33/1-winner of 5-runner novice hurdle at Exeter in April: stays 2¾m: acts on good to firm going. *N. G. Ayliffe*

BUCK COMPTON (IRE) 5 b.g. Safety Catch (USA) – Tempestuous Girl (Tumble   **h–** Wind) [2006/7 20sᵖᵘ 21s⁵ 20vᵖᵘ 20g Apr 23] £30,000 4-y-o: strong gelding: half-brother to winning 2m hurdler Layham Low (by Mandalus) and winning pointer/hunter chaser Red Square Lad (by Toulon), stays 23f: dam placed over 2m on Flat in Ireland: no show in 2 Irish points and novice hurdles. *M. Todhunter*

BUCKINGHAM BOYS 5 b.g. Terimon – No Bloomers (Gildoran) [2006/7 F16s 16g 25g⁵ Apr 16] 19,000 4-y-o: lengthy gelding: second foal: dam unraced half-sister to fairly useful hurdler/chaser up to 25f Aussie Bob: no form in various events. *P. R. Webber* **h–** **F–**

BUCKLAND GOLD (IRE) 7 b.g. Lord Americo – Beann Ard (IRE) (Mandalus) [2006/7 c–, h90: 17s² 17v² c16sᶠ 18s 18s⁵ Feb 18] compact gelding: fair novice hurdler: let down by jumping over fences: stays 2¾m: acts on heavy going: has bled from nose. *D. M. Grissell* **c85** **h100**

BUCKS 10 b.g. Slip Anchor – Alligram (USA) (Alysheba (USA)) [2006/7 h79: 19m May 9] fair on Flat (stays 2m) nowadays: poor form over hurdles: will stay beyond 2½m. *Ian Williams* **h–**

BUCKSTRUTHER (IRE) 5 ch.g. Anshan – Immediate Action (Roselier (FR)) [2006/7 F16s F16v⁶ 16g⁶ 16g⁴ Apr 15] good-topped gelding: chasing type: second foal: dam winning pointer: tailed off in bumpers: poor form in novice hurdles at Kelso: likely to be suited by further than 2m. *Mrs H. O. Graham* **h80 +** **F–**

BUCK THE LEGEND (IRE) 5 b. or br.g. Anshan – Patience of Angels (IRE) (Distinctly North (USA)) [2006/7 F16s⁶ F16s³ F16d 24sᶠ Mar 3] tall, useful-looking gelding: will make a chaser: third foal: half-brother to fair hurdler/maiden chaser Newtown Dancer (by Danehill Dancer), stayed 21f: dam, maiden hurdler, stayed 2½m: fair form in bumpers: weakening when failing last in novice at Newbury on hurdling debut: looks a stayer: raced on good to soft/soft ground: likely to do better. *N. A. Twiston-Davies* **h89 p** **F88**

BUDDYS LOOKOUT (IRE) 5 ch.g. Buddy's Friend (IRE) – Grey Lookout (IRE) (Roselier (FR)) [2006/7 F16g F16g Mar 24] 4,600 3-y-o: unfurnished, close-coupled gelding: first foal: dam unraced out of half-sister to useful staying hurdler/chaser Gola Cher: little encouragement in bumpers. *A. King* **F72**

BUENA VISTA (IRE) 6 b.g. In The Wings – Park Special (Relkino) [2006/7 h140: c19s* c16v* c16g⁶ c20mᶠ Apr 21] leggy gelding: useful hurdler: similar form over fences, won novices at Exeter in December and Hereford (by short head from unlucky Chief Yeoman) in January: below form when sixth to My Way de Solzen in Arkle Trophy at Cheltenham: stays 2½m: has won on heavy going, possibly ideally suited by less testing conditions (acts on good to firm): often in cheekpieces: front runner/races prominently: tends to idle but is reliable. *D. E. Pipe* **c136** **h–**

BUFFERS LANE (IRE) 8 b.g. Fourstars Allstar (USA) – River of Wine (River Knight (FR)) [2006/7 h96, F84: 19v³ c20sᵖᵘ c16dᴿ 16d Jan 8] compact gelding: winning Irish pointer: disappointing over hurdles since debut: let down by jumping in novice handicap chases: should stay beyond 21f. *N. A. Twiston-Davies* **c–** **h78**

BUFFY 7 b.m. Classic Cliche (IRE) – Annie Kelly (Oats) [2006/7 h82: 22fᶠ 20s 22g³ 24g 20d³ 20m⁵ Feb 4] poor novice hurdler: stays 2¾m: acts on soft and good to firm going. *B. Mactaggart* **h77**

BULDAAN (FR) 5 ch.g. Muhtathir – Fee Eria (FR) (Always Fair (USA)) [2006/7 h–: 17m⁴ 17s 16g⁴ Nov 29] poor maiden hurdler: raced around 2m: acts on good to firm and good to soft ground. *W. Amos* **h75**

BULLHILL FLYER (IRE) 6 ch.g. Flemensfirth (USA) – Chatter Bug (Le Bavard (FR)) [2006/7 16m 20g* 19d* 20g² 18s* 24vᵖᵘ Dec 28] €23,000 3-y-o: neat gelding: half-brother to 2m hurdle winner Us And Mary (by Buckskin): dam unplaced only outing in bumper and over hurdles: once-raced on Flat: fairly useful hurdler: progressed well in 2006/7, won handicaps at Roscommon in August and Kilbeggan in September and minor event at Fairyhouse (beat Breathing Fire by length) in December: stays 2½m: acts on soft ground: usually held up. *Sabrina Joan Harty, Ireland* **h124**

BULLIES ACRE (IRE) 7 b.g. Arctic Cider (USA) – Clonminch Lady (Le Bavard (FR)) [2006/7 c–, h–: 20d 20d⁶ 20d⁶ Nov 7] no sign of ability: tried tongue tied. *F. P. Murtagh* **c–** **h–**

BULLSEYE 5 b.g. Polish Precedent (USA) – Native Flair (Be My Native (USA)) [2006/7 17fᵘʳ 16mᵖᵘ 20gᵖᵘ Sep 17] modest maiden at best on Flat (stays 1¼m), largely out of form in 2006 for A. Jarvis/J. Boyle: no form over hurdles (let down by jumping): tried visored. *M. J. Gingell* **h– x**

BUMPER (FR) 6 b.g. Cadoudal (FR) – Dame Blonde (FR) (Pampabird) [2006/7 h115: 24sᵖᵘ c24dᵘʳ 21s 22dᵖᵘ 18g⁴ Apr 10] unfurnished gelding: bumper winner: fairly useful hurdler at best: no form in 2006/7, unseated fifth on chasing debut: should stay 3m: acts on heavy going: tried visored: sold 1,800 gns Doncaster May Sales. *D. E. Pipe* **c–** **h–**

BUNMAHON (IRE) 7 b. or br.g. Broken Hearted – Glenpatrick Peach (IRE) (Lafon-taine (USA)) [2006/7 18f⁵ 17fᵖᵘ 18m⁵ c16g⁶ c18d c16g c17dᵖᵘ c18mᵖᵘ Apr 28] workmanlike gelding: fourth foal: half-brother to fair 2m hurdler Prescetto Lady (by Toulon): dam, thrice-raced in bumpers, half-sister to very smart 2m hurdler/smart chaser Space Trucker: once-raced on Flat: modest hurdler/maiden chaser: raced mainly around 2m: acts on good to firm going: tried tongue tied: none too consistent. *Mrs J. Harrington, Ireland*   **c92 h92**

BUREAUCRAT 5 b.g. Machiavellian (USA) – Lajna (Be My Guest (USA)) [2006/7 h131: 16g⁴ 16m c16d* c19sᶠ 16m Apr 12] sturdy gelding: fairly useful hurdler: easily best effort in 2006/7 when fourth to Mahogany Blaze in 4-y-o handicap at Chepstow: odds on, made all in 3-runner maiden at Taunton in November on chasing debut: reluctant to race and fell tenth next time: raced mainly around 2m: acts on good to firm and good to soft going: sometimes jumps left (particularly in latter stages): usually front runner: remains with potential over fences. *P. J. Hobbs*   **c101 p h128**

BURN BROOK 7 br.m. Alderbrook – One of Those Days (Soviet Lad (USA)) [2006/7 F–: 22g 20m 21s 22d⁶ 25v² 21g⁵ 26g Apr 20] rather leggy mare: well bred but no solid form. *R. J. Armson*   **h–**

BURNING DESIRE 5 b.g. Pursuit of Love – Shimmer (Bustino) [2006/7 F16m⁵ Sep 10] half-brother to 2001 2-y-o 5f/6f winner Young Lion (by Lion Cavern): dam maiden: fifth in bumper on debut: dead. *M. W. Easterby*   **F82**

BURNLEY (IRE) 4 b.g. Distant Music (USA) – Dance Ahead (Shareef Dancer (USA)) [2006/7 F14g Nov 15] 5,200 2-y-o: close-coupled gelding: half-brother to several win-ners, including useful 6f (at 2 yrs) to 9f (in USA) winner Dance Clear (by Marju): dam, 2-y-o 7f winner, out of half-sister to Yorkshire Oaks winners Untold and Sally Brown: unraced on Flat for M. Tregoning: ninth of 17 in 3-y-o bumper on debut. *Mrs A. L. M. King*   **F–**

BURNT EMBER (IRE) 6 b.g. Fourstars Allstar (USA) – Everdancing (Dance In Time (CAN)) [2006/7 F16v F16s Apr 1] half-brother to winning hurdler in US by Oscar: dam, prolific winner in Italy, half-sister to smart stayer Buckley: well beaten in bumpers: tried tongue tied. *G. A. Charlton*   **F–**

BURNTOAKBOY 9 b.g. Sir Harry Lewis (USA) – Sainte Martine (Martinmas) [2006/7 22d 21d 24s² 22d³ 16s⁵ 20v² 20s* 21g* 20g Apr 12] leggy gelding: modest form only outing over fences: useful handicap hurdler: left M. Cunningham after second start and much improved after, winning at Leicester in January and 28-runner Coral Cup at Cheltenham (by 3 lengths from Powerstation) in March: plenty to do after mistake 5 out when creditable seventh to Two Miles West in listed event at Aintree: stays 3m: acts on heavy going: blinkered once: a credit to connections. *Dr R. D. P. Newland*   **c– h139**

Coral Cup (Handicap Hurdle), Cheltenham—a first Festival win for rookies Dr Richard Newland and Sam Jones as Burntoakboy pulls clear of Powerstation (left) and Baron de Feypo (right)

BURREN LEGEND (IRE) 6 b.g. Flying Legend (USA) – Burren View (IRE) **h99**
(Mazaad) [2006/7 21d⁶ 22s² 18s³ 20vᵖᵘ 22g 21g* Apr 23] useful-looking gelding: first
foal: dam lightly-raced maiden hurdler: well beaten on completed start in Irish points
in 2006: modest hurdler: won handicap at Plumpton in April: stays 2¾m: raced on good
ground or softer (acts on soft). *R. Rowe*

BURREN MOONSHINE (IRE) 8 ch.m. Moonax (IRE) – Burren Beauty (IRE) **c102**
(Phardante (FR)) [2006/7 h99: 24m³ 26d³ 27m* 24m² c21m³ c24g² c21mᶠ c24m³ Apr **h117**
10] winning pointer: fairly useful handicap hurdler: won at Stratford (much improved
form, beat Solway Minstrel by 18 lengths) in June: placed all 3 completed starts over
fences: stays 27f: best on good going or firmer (acts on firm): tried in cheekpieces.
P. Bowen

BURWOOD BREEZE (IRE) 11 b.g. Fresh Breeze (USA) – Shuil Le Cheile (Quay- **c118 +**
side) [2006/7 c95+, h–: c24s* c32mᵖᵘ c21gᵘʳ Nov 19] workmanlike gelding: fairly useful **h–**
handicap chaser: back to best when winning at Perth in May by 9 lengths from Very Very
Noble: unfortunate when failing to complete both starts over National fences at Aintree,
again went with zest when hampered and unseated 4 out (still in touch) in Grand Sefton:
stays 3m: acts on heavy and good to firm going: tried blinkered (made mistakes):
patiently ridden: has hung left and often finds little. *T. R. George*

BUSHIDO (IRE) 8 br.g. Brief Truce (USA) – Pheopotstown (Henbit (USA)) [2006/7 **c–**
c123, h–: 24m c22m² Jun 30] small gelding: fairly useful hurdler/chaser at best, well **h–**
below form both starts in 2006/7: effective around 2½m to 3¼m: acts on soft and firm
going: hasn't always looked easy ride. *Mrs S. J. Smith*

BUSH PARK (IRE) 12 b.g. Be My Native (USA) – By All Means (Pitpan) [2006/7 **c82 §**
c82§, h–: c21g⁶ May 24] strong, lengthy gelding: winning hurdler: modest hunter chaser **h–**
nowadays: in frame in points in 2007: stays 25f: acts on any going: tried blinkered/
visored: has had tongue tied: lazy. *Mrs Monica Tory*

BUSINESSMONEY JAKE 6 b.g. Petoski – Cloverjay (Lir) [2006/7 h114+: 20g² **h116**
Oct 7] fairly useful handicap hurdler: good effort only start in 2006/7: stays 3m: raced on
good going or softer. *V. R. A. Dartnall*

BUSINESS TRAVELLER (IRE) 7 ch.g. Titus Livius (FR) – Dancing Venus **c– §**
(Pursuit of Love) [2006/7 c–§, h89§: 26m⁵ 24m* 20g 26g Oct 15] smallish gelding: **h99 §**
modest handicap hurdler: went with more zest than usual when winning at Ludlow in
May: tailed off when refused fourth only outing over fences: stays 3m: acts on soft and
good to firm going: usually blinkered/visored/tongue tied: held up. *R. J. Price*

BUSKER ROYAL 4 ch.g. Shahrastani (USA) – Close Harmony (Bustino) [2006/7 **F99**
F16d² F16g⁶ Apr 7] smallish, angular gelding: third foal: half-brother to bumper/useful
2¾m hurdle winner Barbers Shop (by Saddlers' Hall): dam, maiden 2m hurdler, sister to
fairly useful 2m hurdler Bella Macrae: better effort in bumpers when 3½ lengths second
to Sir Harry Ormesher at Ascot. *W. J. Musson*

BUSTAN (IRE) 8 b.g. Darshaan – Dazzlingly Radiant (Try My Best (USA)) [2006/7 **h–**
16gᵖᵘ Nov 17] sturdy gelding: useful on Flat (stays 1½m), successful in April: not fluent
and soon beaten in novice on hurdling debut. *G. C. Bravery*

BUSTER COLLINS (IRE) 7 b. or br.g. Alderbrook – Carmen (IRE) (Meneval **c–**
(USA)) [2006/7 h110+: c23dᶠ 22sᵖᵘ Jan 20] useful-looking gelding: winning Irish point- **h–**
er: fair hurdler at best: tenderly handled both starts in 2006/7, adrift when fell heavily 5
out in handicap on chasing debut: bled next time: stays 21f: acts on heavy and good to
firm going. *Miss E. C. Lavelle*

BUSTER HYVONEN (IRE) 5 b.g. Dansili – Serotina (IRE) (Mtoto) [2006/7 16g* **h121**
16d⁴ 16s* 16vᵖᵘ 16g Apr 14] good-topped gelding: fairly useful on Flat (stays 1½m):
ran to similar level when winning 18-runner novice hurdles at Huntingdon in November
(readily) and January (beat I'm So Lucky by 1½ lengths): disappointing last 2 starts:
raced at 2m: acts on soft going. *J. R. Fanshawe*

BUSTER MAI 7 gr.g. Terimon – Just Maisy (Broadsword (USA)) [2006/7 21dᶠ 20s **h–**
Dec 5] third foal: dam placed in points: runner-up all 3 starts in maiden points in 2006:
tailed off on completed outing over hurdles: dead. *D. M. Grissell*

BUSY BAY 5 b.m. Busy Flight – Killala Bay (IRE) (Executive Perk) [2006/7 F16v F16g **h–**
20m Apr 15] first foal: dam no form over fences: well held in bumpers and maiden hurdle **F–**
(carried badly right after first). *B. I. Case*

BUSY ISIT 7 br.g. Busy Flight – Eatons (Daring March) [2006/7 F17d* 21d* 22s⁶   **h108** Jan 20] second foal: dam signs of only a little ability: won maiden point in 2006: success-   **F87** ful also in bumper at Exeter in May for M. Coombe and maiden hurdle at Ludow (idled) in January: well held on handicap debut. *P. J. Hobbs*

BUTCHER BAYES (IRE) 9 b.g. Mandalus – Dunmanway (Le Bavard (FR)) [2006/7   **c83** c31g⁴ May 24] winning pointer: fourth in hunter on chase debut: sold £7,200 Ascot June Sales. *Mrs A. A. Hawkins*

BUTLER'S CABIN (FR) 7 b.g. Poliglote – Strictly Cool (USA) (Bering) [2006/7   **c144 +** h99, F90: c20f³ c19g* c20g* c20g* c20d⁴ c20s³ c21s c33g* c29m* Apr 9]   **h–**
    'One hundred and forty-eight years and all of a sudden the race is a problem.' Just one of the two thousand or so postings that have appeared on the Betfair forum about the National Hunt Chase. The race was first run in 1860 at Market Harborough and, having initially been staged at different venues from year to year, has had a permanent home at Cheltenham since 1911. Its future first came under serious threat when three horses were killed in the race in 2006. The general view, in the long-running forum thread which has been going for well over a year, seems to be that the National Hunt Chase was initially made a scapegoat after a spate of deaths at the four-day Cheltenham Festival in 2006. Cheltenham responded by making a change to the fence at the top of the hill (the fourth last) on the New Course, moving it back nearer the bend to give a straighter landing. The safety limit for the National Hunt Chase, a four-mile-one-furlong novice chase for amateur riders, was trimmed from twenty-four to twenty. However, the RSPCA called for a further review of the race after another fatality in the latest running, in which nine of the nineteen runners fell or unseated, whilst the winner Butler's Cabin finished distressed and could not be returned to the winner's circle because he was being given oxygen. The death of Swift Thyne at the twentieth of the twenty-seven fences was the eighth fatality in the race since it was opened up in 2002 to better quality runners (i.e. those that had won over hurdles in previous seasons) after traditionally being the preserve of horses who had not won a race of any description—except certain types of hunter chases—before the start of the current season. Most of the deaths have been of a type that could have happened anywhere and they should not be used specifically as an argument against the National Hunt Chase which, for the most part, has had more finishers since the quality of runners was raised. Though it is a better race than it used to be, however, it is still weaker than most others at the Festival (where the cross country chase is the crowning insult) and is not worth its place in the Festival programme, nor would it be in the amended form that it is set to take in 2008. Its distance looks set to be reduced to three miles six and a half furlongs, there will be stricter entry conditions for runners and their amateur riders (with the possibility of opening the race to conditionals) over four miles or more and the race will be returned to the Old Course, swapping places with the Fulke Walwyn Kim Muir and being run on Wednesday's programme.
    Until around the middle of the twentieth century, the National Hunt Chase was the most prestigious event at what was then known as the National Hunt meeting at Cheltenham. Those who have labelled it, in recent times, 'a needless appendage to an elite meeting' are, however, pretty close to the mark, especially as tradition could no longer be a justification for keeping it once its previously distinc-tive conditions were changed. Those who defend the race tend to do so nowadays on the grounds that it is 'an academy for future winners of the top staying chases'. But the Festival is about ultra-competitive races, many of them championships in their own right, and is not about races that are mere stepping stones to the top races. The best way to restore the National Hunt Chase to something approaching its former glories—and to justify its place at the Festival—would be to turn it into a really valuable open handicap (for professional riders) over four miles or more. Established out-and-out staying handicappers have no suitable Festival target at the moment and a big field with wide-open betting would be assured, especially if Uttoxeter moved back the Midlands National from the Saturday after Cheltenham to the February slot previously occupied by the Singer & Friedlander National Trial. The proposal would go a long way to addressing the fears of those Festival regulars who view the four-day meeting as a 'watered-down' version of its pre-decessor, particularly if the new race, for example, was given top billing along with

*National Hunt Chase Challenge Cup (Amateur Riders' Novices' Chase), Cheltenham—
33/1-shot Butler's Cabin gamely gets the better of the erratic Character Building (grey)*

the World Hurdle on the Thursday, thereby giving that day's programme a much-needed boost. If promoted correctly, it could quickly be regarded as the first leg of a new Spring Double with the Grand National—especially if a lucrative bonus was on offer to win both races—and would hopefully attract a healthy quota of leading Aintree contenders, whose campaigns have become increasingly sparse in recent years due to connections protecting their big-race handicap marks. In addition, it would provide an overdue alternative to those top-notch stayers who are regularly forced to take their chance in the Gold Cup even though conditions are never likely to place a sufficient emphasis on stamina—Run For Free (best Gold Cup finish eighth), Suny Bay (fifth) and Grey Abbey (fifth) just three such examples from the past fifteen years.

Timeform argued for the creation of a big long-distance handicap in a paper submitted to Cheltenham when it sought views in 2002 on expanding the Festival from three to four days. Timeform suggested at the time that perhaps the Kim Muir (for amateurs) and the National Hunt Handicap (now the William Hill), which cater for the same type of horses, might have to be amalgamated to create an opening for the proposed new long-distance open handicap. However, both those races have been attracting big fields in recent seasons and were oversubscribed in 2006 (also a common occurrence for the Grand National nowadays), ten eliminated from the Kim Muir and three from the William Hill at the overnight stage (both races have a safety limit of twenty-four). Butler's Cabin was one of those who did not make the cut in the Kim Muir and he was turned out instead in the National Hunt Chase, for which he was sent off at 33/1 (his connections were also represented by 12/1-shot Garde Champetre), having previously not raced at beyond twenty-one furlongs and looking unlikely to get the extreme trip. Butler's Cabin would have qualified for the National Hunt Chase under its old conditions, having started the season as a maiden after being brought along steadily in bumpers (in the frame all three starts) and showing fair form on his first two starts in novice hurdles before being well beaten

160

in a tongue strap on his final outing in that sphere, after which he was operated on for a wind infirmity. Butler's Cabin developed into a useful chaser in the first part of the latest season, completing a quickfire hat-trick when winning handicaps at Hereford, Aintree and Cheltenham (when left clear by Abragante's last-fence fall) in October, after which he acquitted himself well when fourth to stable-companion Exotic Dancer in the Paddy Power Gold Cup at Cheltenham's Open meeting. He did, however, look somewhat unenthusiastic when in the frame in a handicap at Newbury later in November before finishing only tenth in the boylesports.com Gold Cup back at Cheltenham in December on his next start (tried in first-time cheekpieces).

Another of the criticisms of the National Hunt Chase in its present form is that it can take runners away from the staying novices' championship, the Royal & SunAlliance Chase. Among those in the latest edition of the National Hunt Chase were Gungadu, hot favourite after winning one of the traditional trials for the Royal & SunAlliance, the Reynoldstown at Ascot, and the Towton Chase runner-up Miko de Beauchene. Neither of those got round, Gungadu holding every chance when falling at the second last and Miko de Beauchene also looking likely to be involved in the finish when unseating his rider just behind the leaders as part of an ugly melee three out. Butler's Cabin, under a well-judged ride by stable amateur Alan Berry, moved into contention fairly late in the race and kept a straighter line on the run-in than the eventual second Character Building to prevail by three quarters of a length, the pair ten lengths clear of rank outsider Countess Trifaldi in third. Butler's Cabin was the fourth winner of the National Hunt Chase for his trainer Jonjo O'Neill in the six years since the conditions were changed, and his fifth in all, Front Line having won for O'Neill in the days when he trained in Cumbria (where he had fifteen seasons) before moving to Jackdaws Castle in Gloucestershire for the 2001/2 season. O'Neill had built up connections from his riding days with Irish owner J. P. McManus, who bought Jackdaws Castle in 2000, and Front Line was one of three Cheltenham Festival winners—Danny Connors and Master Tern were the others—saddled for McManus while O'Neill trained in Cumbria. O'Neill's Festival record has since been considerably enhanced (his score stands at fourteen) and all three of his winners at the latest Festival carried the McManus colours, Wichita Lineman and Drombeag providing a last-day double after the success of Butler's Cabin and bringing the total number of Festival winners for their owner to twenty-seven. McManus has had a couple of costly failures in the National Hunt Chase—Jack of Trumps at 11/8-on in 1978 and Deep Gale at 11/10 in 1979 (both fell)—but, in a race which he has always prized, Butler's Cabin is the third winner he has had trained by O'Neill, Rith Dubh in 2002 following Front Line. Until the

Powers Whiskey Irish Grand National Chase (Handicap), Fairyhouse—British-trained novices Butler's Cabin and Nine de Sivola (No.25) dominate the latter stages; Church Island (noseband) fades into fourth

latest Festival, however, the 50/1-winner of the 2004 Pertemps Handicap Hurdle Final, Creon, was the only McManus-owned Festival winner saddled by O'Neill since Rith Dubh, that victory little consolation for the rare defeat inflicted on the French-trained, McManus-owned Baracouda by the O'Neill-trained Iris's Gift in that year's Stayers' Hurdle (O'Neill also saddled three McManus-owned runners in that year's National Hunt Chase, which he won with his fourth runner Native Emperor).

Apart from his O'Neill-trained winners of the National Hunt Chase, J. P. McManus also won it in 1983 with Bit of A Skite (he has also had High Peak, Spot Thedifference, Drombeag and Far From Trouble placed). Bit of A Skite followed up in the Irish Grand National on his first race over fences outside novice, hunter or point-to-point company. Like Butler's Cabin, Bit of A Skite was raced at much shorter distances before the National Hunt Chase, finishing a staying-on fifth in the Arkle at Leopardstown on his last outing before Cheltenham. McManus is still waiting for his first Grand National winner but he has now won the Irish version twice, Butler's Cabin following in the footsteps of Bit of A Skite and, with Tony McCoy in the saddle, showing further improvement under another patient ride to win the twenty-nine-runner Powers Whiskey Irish Grand National at 14/1, again finishing distressed and revived this time by water, with the required oxygen down at the third-last where Cheeky Lady was a fatality in a pile-up involving beaten horses. The result at Fairyhouse, incidentally, provided the defenders of the under-fire National Hunt Chase with a publicity opportunity since the runner-up Nine de Sivola, beaten a length by Butler's Cabin, had looked sure to play a big part in the Cheltenham race before becoming another casualty in the aforementioned melee three out. Grist was added to the mill when Silver Birch, who was fourth in the 2004 edition of the National Hunt Chase, won the Grand National, and the 2006 National Hunt Chase winner Hot Weld landed the Scottish Grand National/Betfred Gold Cup double. In addition, Timbera (runner-up in 2002) and Point Barrow (fifth in 2003) are two other recent Irish National winners to have figured prominently in the National Hunt Chase, whilst the likes of Hedgehunter (unlucky tenth in 2003), Celestial Gold (runner-up in 2004) and Far From Trouble (third in 2006) are other big-race winners to have emerged from this contest since its conditions were changed. As well as yielding the second biggest prize in Irish jumping (behind only the Punchestown Gold Cup), Butler's Cabin's Irish Grand National victory also earned connections a bonus of €100,000 offered by the sponsors to any British-trained horse successful in the race after winning at the same year's Cheltenham Festival (a feat not achieved since the Pipe-trained Kim Muir winner Omerta in 1991).

		Sadler's Wells (b 1981)	Northern Dancer / Fairy Bridge
	Poliglote (b 1992)	Alexandrie (b or br 1980)	Val de L'Orne / Apachee
Butler's Cabin (FR) (b.g. 2000)		Bering (ch 1983)	Arctic Tern / Beaune
	Strictly Cool (USA) (ch 1992)	Strictly Raised (ch 1980)	Raise A Native / A Wind Is Rising

Butler's Cabin's victory crowned a magnificent season for his owner who had over two hundred and fifty horses in training and topped the owners' table in Ireland (where he had horses with thirty-three trainers) for the twelfth consecutive time. He was also leading owner in Britain for a third time, following his success in 1998/9 (helped by the achievements of Istabraq) and in 2005/6 (when Francois and Thierry Doumen supplied two of his leading three earners). Though he has branched out in recent seasons in Britain and had some horses trained away from Jackdaws Castle (he had horses with eight other British-based trainers in 2006/7), McManus enjoyed his biggest successes in the latest season with horses based at Jackdaws Castle, where Jonjo O'Neill enjoyed his best season to date with one hundred and twenty-six winners, his 1,2,3 earnings of £1,619,583 bringing second place in the trainers' championship. O'Neill had a day to remember after Butler's Cabin won at Hereford, where he had a three-timer to go with three winners the same afternoon at Carlisle, four of the six winners carrying the McManus colours. O'Neill rode five winners in a day at Perth in April, 1978, scoring on all his rides on the card which were saddled by four different trainers; he had started the day needing two to break Ron Barry's record for the number of winners by a jump jockey in a single season, and went on to ride one hundred and forty-nine winners to take the jockeys' title by a margin of sixty-six, recording a strike rate of winners to mounts over the season in excess of 27%.

French-bred Butler's Cabin, a useful-looking gelding who was picked up as a yearling for 25,000 guineas at Tattersalls, is a half-brother to the useful two-mile hurdler and error-prone winning chaser Heezapistol (by Pistolet Bleu) and to the fair two-mile hurdler Jaamid (by Desert Prince), both of whom won on the Flat (the former was useful at up to a mile and a half). His half-sister Highest Cool (by Highest Honor) was also a useful miler on the Flat in France. The dam Strictly Cool, who won over nine furlongs in France as a two-year-old, is from a well-known Flat family, being out of Strictly Raised, a winning half-sister to It's In The Air, a champion three-year-old filly in the United States who won sixteen races in her career, five of them at Grade 1. Another half-sister to Butler's Cabin's grandam Strictly Raised is Morning Has Broken, grandam of the 1994 Oaks and Irish Derby winner Balanchine and the 1997 Derby third Romanov, among others. It's In The Air is herself the grandam of 2002 Champion Stakes winner Storming Home and 2003 Poule d'Essai des Pouliches winner Musical Chimes. That the family should now boast a winner of the Irish Grand National illustrates the vagaries of thoroughbred breeding. The sire of Butler's Cabin, Poliglote, was second in Celtic Swing's Prix du Jockey Club, but he was a hard puller and has not been a significant influence for stamina at stud. Butler's Cabin stays extreme distances and probably acts on any going. He was tongue tied on his final outing in 2005/6 and ran in cheekpieces on his last three starts in the latest season. The Grand National is likely to be his main target in the next season. *Jonjo O'Neill*

BUTLER SERVICES (IRE) 7 b.g. Muroto – Toevarro (Raga Navarro (ITY)) [2006/7 h–, F78: 16m⁶ 16g 24gᵖᵘ Jul 21] no form over hurdles: bred to be suited by 2½m+: tried blinkered: sold 4,200 gns Doncaster August Sales, won point in April: resold 4,500 gns Doncaster May Sales. *Jonjo O'Neill* — **h–**

BUTTERFLY ROSE 6 b.m. Tragic Role (USA) – Rosemoss (Le Moss) [2006/7 F16m F16g F17g⁴ Apr 19] long-backed mare: sixth foal: half-sister to 25f chase winner Black Collar (by Bob's Return): dam placed in bumpers/novice hurdle: best effort in bumpers when fourth to I'm Delilah at Cheltenham. *Miss H. C. Knight* — **F88**

BUTTRESS 8 b.g. Zamindar (USA) – Furnish (Green Desert (USA)) [2006/7 h93: c16m c17fᶠ c16g⁶ c16v⁵ 16g c17gᶠ Mar 24] strong gelding: modest form at best over hurdles: running easily best race over fences when falling last in handicap at Bangor second start: will prove best at sharp 2m: acts on firm going: weak finisher. *Heather Dalton* — **c91 h–**

BUY ONLING (IRE) 6 b.g. Fourstars Allstar (USA) – Meadow Lane (IRE) (Over The River (FR)) [2006/7 h84, F83: 22s 24gᵘʳ 22dᵖᵘ 22g Apr 7] leggy gelding: pulled up in points: fourth in bumper: poor form at best over hurdles. *C. J. Mann* — **h–**

BUZYBAKSON (IRE) 10 b. or br.g. Bob Back (USA) – Middle Verde (USA) (Sham (USA)) [2006/7 c–x, h–: c26g⁶ c24vᵖᵘ c24vᵖᵘ 16s Jan 31] workmanlike gelding: winning hurdler/chaser, no longer of any account: tried in headgear/tongue tied. *J. R. Cornwall* — **c– x h–**

BY GEORGE (IRE) 5 b.g. New Frontier (IRE) – Ann's Fort (Crash Course) [2006/7 F16s⁶ F16g Mar 24] useful-looking gelding: half-brother to winning pointer by Jolly Jake: dam winning pointer: better effort in bumpers when 22¼ lengths seventh of 22 to Helens Vision at Newbury. *N. J. Gifford* — **F84**

BYNACK MHOR (IRE) 6 b.g. Taipan (IRE) – Pride of Poznan (IRE) (Buzzards Bay) [2006/7 F80: 19s 18s Jan 4] rangy gelding: chasing type: mid-division in bumper on debut: behind in maiden hurdles: bred to stay well. *Miss H. C. Knight* — **h–**

BYTHEHOKEY (IRE) 6 b.g. Barathea (IRE) – Regal Portrait (IRE) (Royal Academy (USA)) [2006/7 h90d: 20gᵖᵘ Jun 8] winning pointer: novice hurdler, poor on balance of form. *B. P. J. Baugh* — **h–**

BYWAYS BOY 4 ch.g. Groom Dancer (USA) – Fuwala (Unfuwain (USA)) [2006/7 F18v⁶ 16v Mar 12] second foal: dam no form: well held in bumper/novice hurdle: races freely. *P. A. Blockley* — **h– F–**

totepool Premier Kelso Hurdle (Novices'), Kelso—another wide-margin win for front-running Bywell Beau, who is steered round the last (omitted because of low sun) by Jan Faltejsek

BYWELL BEAU (IRE) 8 b.g. Lord Americo – Early Dalus (IRE) (Mandalus) **h139** [2006/7 h102: 16g² 16m 20s³ 16v* 16v² 16s* 18v* 16g⁴ 16m Apr 24] strong gelding: developed into useful novice hurdler in 2006/7, winning at Kelso in December (maiden), February and March (beat Mohayer by 23 lengths in Grade 2 totepool Premier Kelso Hurdle, despite jumping markedly right): ran well when around 16 lengths fourth of 8 to Blythe Knight in Grade 2 at Aintree: best form at 2m/2¼m: acts on heavy going, below form on good to firm: usually tongue tied: headstrong, best allowed to stride on. *G. A. Charlton*

C

CABBYL DOO 4 b.c. Killer Instinct – Chipewyas (FR) (Bering) [2006/7 F16g Apr 3] **F–** half-brother to 1¼m winner Daggers Canyon (by Daggers Drawn): dam unraced: well held in bumper on debut. *James Moffatt*

CABER (IRE) 7 b.g. Celtic Swing – Arusha (IRE) (Dance of Life (USA)) [2006/7 **c– x** c19m 26m c25m^{ur} c23d^{pu} Oct 17] point winner: form in other events only on hurdling **h–** debut in 2003/4: tried visored: sold £6,100 Ascot November Sales. *R. H. Alner*

CADEAUX ROUGE (IRE) 6 ch.m. Croco Rouge (IRE) – Gift of Glory (FR) (Niniski **h–** (USA)) [2006/7 h73: 17d^{pu} 21m 16d^{F} 16g 23d^{pu} Jan 15] maiden hurdler, no form in 2006/7: usually tongue tied. *D. W. Thompson*

CADOGAN (FR) 7 gr.g. Cadoudal (FR) – The Exception (FR) (Melyno) [2006/7 16v* **h119 +** 16s 18v³ 16v⁴ 16v² 17g Mar 16] rangy gelding: half-brother to several winning jumpers, notably useful staying chaser Mely Moss (by Tip Moss): dam won up to 1½m in France: fifth in bumper at Down Royal: fairly useful hurdler: won maiden at Gowran in 2004/5 and minor event at Punchestown (off 21 months, beat Militant easily by 4½ lengths) in November: well held in County Hurdle (Handicap) at Cheltenham final outing: stays 2¼m: raced mainly on soft/heavy going. *J. T. R. Dreaper, Ireland*

CADOUDALAS (FR) 4 b.g. Cadoudal (FR) – Popie d'Ecorcei (FR) (Balsamo (FR)) **F81 +** [2006/7 F16g F16m⁵ Apr 25] half-brother to several winners, notably very smart chaser Poliantas (by Rasi Brasak), stayed 2½m: dam, winning hurdler/chaser, stayed 25f:

modest form in bumpers, still seeming green when fifth to Hello You at Worcester. *P. F. Nicholls*

CADOULITIQUE (FR) 4 b.g. Antarctique (IRE) – Cadoulie Wood (FR) (Cadoudal (FR)) [2006/7 c17s c17s² 16d^ur Mar 21] first foal: dam 15f hurdle winner: maiden on Flat: once-raced over hurdles in France: better effort in 3-y-o chases at Enghien when second to Mille Et Une: sold from T. Trapenard €47,000, unseated second in maiden hurdle on British debut. *D. E. Pipe* **c102 h–**

CAESAREAN HUNTER (USA) 8 ch.g. Jade Hunter (USA) – Grey Fay (USA) (Grey Dawn II) [2006/7 c–§, h111d: c23s^pu c20d⁵ Mar 26] lengthy gelding: winning hurdler: little form since 2005, mainly over fences (has looked unwilling): best short of 2¾m: acts on heavy going: tried tongue tied/in cheekpieces. *R. T. Phillips* **c– § h–**

CAESAR'S PALACE (GER) 10 ch.g. Lomitas – Caraveine (FR) (Nikos) [2006/7 h100§: 24g 24g 24s² 23g⁶ 24s⁵ 24v⁶ 24s³ 24v⁴ 24v² 22m⁴ 24s⁶ Apr 25] workmanlike gelding: modest handicap hurdler: stays 27f: probably acts on any going: wears headgear: ungenuine (often gets behind). *Miss Lucinda V. Russell* **h88 §**

CAILIN ALAINN (IRE) 8 br.m. Mister Lord (USA) – Royal Toombeola (IRE) (Royal Fountain) [2006/7 h127: c20g* c20v* c20v* c24v* c25v^F c24g^F Mar 14] **c152 + h–**

Cailin Alainn travelled a long way in a very short time. Not seen on a racecourse until February 2006, she opened her account two months later in a mares maiden hurdle at Tramore and within a year had gained five more wins and shown form that made her a worthy second favourite, behind Denman, for the Royal & SunAlliance Chase. Unfortunately, Cailin Alainn got no further than the ninth at Cheltenham, and, having also fallen there on her previous outing, it looks to be a case of back to the drawing board with a mare who had been shaping up into a high-class chaser in the making. Her jumping problems do need to be sorted out if she's to reach her full potential, though however she fares from now on she has already done her owners proud. So far as the Dewdrop Racing Syndicate is concerned Cailin Alainn, Gaelic for 'beautiful girl', has more than lived up to her name.

After following up her Tramore victory just seven days later, when beating Celestial Wave (who was conceding 6 lb) by two lengths in a Grade 3 mares' novice final at Fairyhouse, Cailin Alainn was off for six months, switched to fences on her return and continuing to stretch her winning run. Not particularly impressive when justifing favouritism in a novice event at Cork on her chasing debut, jumping hesitantly, Cailin Alainn showed the benefit of that experience when running out an eight-length winner of a mares listed race at Clonmel next time. Further marked

Ballymore Properties Drinmore Novices' Chase, Fairyhouse—
Davy Russell loses an iron but Cailin Alainn (noseband) rallies to beat Schindlers Hunt

Powers Whiskey Novices' Chase, Leopardstown—
Cailin Alainn confirms herself as Ireland's leading novice chaser

improvement followed when she was stepped up again in class. At Fairyhouse in December she was one of ten runners, all of them previous winners over fences, who lined up for the first Grade 1 novice of the season in Ireland. It was an up-to-scratch renewal of the Ballymore Properties Drinmore Novices' Chase, and, with the ground heavy and Blueberry Boy and O'Muircheartaigh forcing a sound pace, the emphasis was firmly on stamina at the two-and-a-half-mile trip, which wasn't a problem for Cailin Alainn. She did hand the initiative to Schindlers Hunt when not so fluent as that rival two out, but responded well to pressure to wear him down close home and win by three quarters of a length, with a further eleven lengths back to fellow mare Gazza's Girl in third. The manner of Cailin Alainn's victory suggested she wouldn't fail through lack of stamina when stepped up to three miles in another Grade 1 contest later in the month, the Powers Whiskey Novices' Chase run at Leopardstown. It was another strong field (including four of her rivals from the Drinmore), although the betting did suggest that the race lay between Cailin Alainn, who went off favourite, and Patsy Hall, the latter having readily accounted for Aces Four at Cheltenham on his previous appearance. And that is how it turned out. The ground was again very testing, although this time the pace was only fair and several were still well bunched two out, where Cailin Alainn made a mistake for the second start running. Recovering quickly, Cailin Alainn was still travelling well when taking it up turning into the straight and ran on strongly to win by four and a half lengths, driven right out as she and Patsy Hall pulled a long way clear of the remainder. The option of going for another novice chase in Ireland before the Royal & SunAlliance was eschewed in favour of a crack at the Letheby & Christopher-sponsored Cotswold Chase at Cheltenham at the end of January. The race long known as the Pillar Chase, in which Cailin Alainn took on a high quality field of seasoned chasers, was chosen to provide experience of the Cheltenham track. Cailin Alainn blundered at the fifteenth and fell heavily three out, but, by then, she had more than underlined the impression made in Ireland that she was one of the best novice chasers around. At the time of her departure Cailin Alainn was a close third behind Neptune Collonges and Our Vic, just ahead of eventual winner Exotic Dancer, and still to be asked fully for her effort. Cailin Alainn was clearly in the process of showing further improvement, though just how much is hard to say. Unfortunately that was the last opportunity to assess her in 2006/7. Just over three weeks after the Royal & SunAlliance, Cailin Alainn was declared for the Powers Gold Cup at Fairyhouse but had to be withdrawn at the eleventh hour after bruising a foot.

Cailin Alainn (IRE) (br.m. 1999)	Mister Lord (USA) (b 1979)	Sir Ivor (b 1965)	Sir Gaylord Attica
		Forest Friend (bl 1966)	Linacre Belle Sauvage
	Royal Toombeola (IRE) (b or br 1989)	Royal Fountain (br 1977)	Royalty Fountain
		Toombeola (br 1971)	Raise You Ten Sorrento

Cailin Alainn is the fourth foal and only winner to date produced by Royal Toombeola, whose three-year-old Bach gelding made €20,000 at the latest Goffs Land Rover Sale. Royal Toombeola is an unraced half-sister to several winning jumpers, however, notably the useful chaser at up to three miles Kentish Piper —Cailin Alainn's tendency to hit two out seems to run in the family as Kentish Piper would have claimed his biggest career win but for a bad mistake at that obstacle in the 1994 John Hughes Memorial (Topham) at Aintree, failing by just a neck to peg back the winner Indian Tonic. Cailin Alainn's grandam Toombeola was a fairly useful juvenile hurdler in Ireland, also successful at up to thirteen furlongs on the Flat there. The lengthy, angular Cailin Alainn should stay beyond three miles. She has raced only on good ground or softer and goes very well on heavy. *Charles Byrnes, Ireland*

CAISLEAN NA DEIRGE (IRE) 9 b.g. Boyne Valley – Bramble Lane (Boreen (FR)) [2006/7 c20g 20m 16g⁵ 20m 24g⁴ c22s c16s⁴ c20s⁶ c16v³ c16v³ Feb 28] winning hurdler: modest maiden chaser: left Peter McCreery after eighth outing: effective at 2m, probably stays 3m: acts on heavy and good to firm going: wore cheekpieces final start. *Evan Williams* **c87 h81**

CALARA HILLS 6 ch.m. Bluegrass Prince (IRE) – Atlantic Line (Capricorn Line) [2006/7 17gᵖᵘ 24gᵖᵘ Mar 26] leggy mare: sister to bumper winner Rupert Blues and useful hurdler up to 2½m Thrower: dam unraced half-sister to useful 2m to 3m chaser Baluchi: poor maiden on Flat: no form over hurdles: tongue tied last 2 outings. *Mrs S. E. Handley* **h–**

CALATAGAN (IRE) 8 ch.g. Danzig Connection (USA) – Calachuchi (Martinmas) [2006/7 c127, h124: c20g⁴ c22g c16s* c20d c17d c16v* c16s² c16g c16m² Apr 21] good-topped gelding: fairly useful chaser: won at Wetherby in October and December (beat Coat of Honour by 2 lengths in quite valuable event): creditable second 2 of last 3 starts, every chance when mistake last in race won by Bambi de L'Orme at Ayr final one: stays 2½m with emphasis on speed: acts on heavy and good to firm going: free-going sort: races prominently/makes running. *J. M. Jefferson* **c138 h–**

CALCOT FLYER 9 br.g. Anshan – Lady Catcher (Free Boy) [2006/7 c97, h–: c24g* c24dᵖᵘ Jan 15] rather leggy gelding: modest handicap chaser: won at Huntingdon in May, not looking keen when left clear last: ran poorly when next seen 8 months later: stays 3¼m: raced on good going or softer. *A. King* **c97 § h– §**

CALCULAITE 6 b.g. Komaite (USA) – Miss Calculate (Mummy's Game) [2006/7 h89p: 16d² 16gᶠ 16g³ 17m* Apr 9] good-topped gelding: progressive form in handicap hurdles in 2006/7, winning at Sedgefield by head from English City: suited by emphasis on speed at 2m: acts on good to soft and good to firm ground: may do better again. *M. Todhunter* **h112**

CALCUTTA CUP (UAE) 4 br.g. Jade Robbery (USA) – Six Nations (USA) (Danzig (USA)) [2006/7 16m² 16g⁴ Dec 30] fair maiden on Flat (stays 1½m): in frame in 2 juvenile hurdles at Musselburgh, headed on line by Stainley on first occasion. *Karen McLintock* **h100**

CALFRAZ 5 b. or br.g. Tamure (IRE) – Pas de Chat (Relko) [2006/7 h102: 20s⁴ 20v⁶ **h98**
Dec 12] close-coupled gelding: fair hurdler: lame on second of 2 outings in 2006/7: will
stay beyond 2½m: raced on good going or softer (acts on heavy). *Micky Hammond*

CALIBAN (IRE) 9 ch.g. Rainbows For Life (CAN) – Amour Toujours (IRE) (Law **c– §**
Society (USA)) [2006/7 c82, h103§: 16s 20v⁵ Mar 4] neat gelding: fair hurdler at best, **h– §**
well beaten both starts in 2006/7: poor form only outing over fences: best efforts around
2m: acts on soft and good to firm going: wears headgear: carries head high. *Ian Williams*

CALIMAN (FR) 4 gr.g. Mansonnien (FR) – Dona Cali (FR) (Dom Pasquini (FR)) **h102**
[2006/7 F13d 17d² 16dᵘʳ 16v 21f 27m* Apr 26] €40,000 3-y-o: neat gelding: third foal: **F–**
brother to French 21f chase winner Calisson and half-brother to French 2m hurdle winner
Calideo (by Video Rock): dam winning hurdler/chaser in France around 2m: well held in
bumper: upped further in trip, easily best effort over hurdles (fair form) when winning
handicap at Fontwell: stays 27f: acts on good to firm going. *D. E. Pipe*

CALKE PARK 10 gr.g. Neltino – Karena Park (Hot Spark) [2006/7 c16m Jul 12] pulled **c–**
up all 4 starts in points in 2006: reportedly lame on chasing debut. *R. J. Armson*

CALL BUTTERFLY (IRE) 5 br.g. Bob's Return (IRE) – Strong Swimmer (IRE) **h–**
(Black Minstrel) [2006/7 22sᶠ 20sᵖᵘ 21s Feb 9] €13,000 3-y-o, resold £10,000 3-y-o:
good-topped gelding: sixth foal: half-brother to winning pointers by Riberubto and Eurobus: dam unraced half-sister to useful hurdler/smart chaser up to 3m The Illywhacker: no
show over hurdles. *P. J. Hobbs*

CALLED TO THE BAR 14 b.g. Legal Bwana – Miss Gaylord (Cavo Doro) [2006/7 **c– x**
c–, h–: c19vᵘʳ c25sᵖᵘ 20v Jan 11] workmanlike gelding: winning hurdler, lightly raced: **h–**
failed to complete all 4 starts over fences: stays 3½m: acts on soft and good to firm going:
tried in headgear/tongue tied. *R. Lee*

CALLHERWHATULIKE 6 b.m. Old Vic – Fleece Alley (IRE) (Brush Aside **h131**
(USA)) [2006/7 F98: 20s⁴ 20v² F18v² 22d² 23v* 20v² Feb 25] point/bumper winner: **F98**
useful hurdler: won maiden at Navan in January: easily best effort when 1¼ lengths
second to Kazal (pair clear) in Grade 2 novice at Naas following month: stays 23f: raced
on good ground or softer (acts on heavy). *Robert Tyner, Ireland*

CALLINGWOOD (IRE) 7 ch.g. Pierre – Clonroche Artic (Pauper) [2006/7 h–, F–: **c–**
c20mᵖᵘ Apr 9] lengthy gelding: no form in various events. *Paul Murphy* **h–**

CALLITQUITS (IRE) 5 b.g. Desert Story (USA) – Quits (IRE) (Brief Truce (USA)) **h–**
[2006/7 h–: 17mᵖᵘ 16f 17mᵖᵘ Aug 29] no form over hurdles. *Jennie Candlish*

CALLITWHATYALIKE 5 b.m. Tamure (IRE) – Studio Venture (Camden Town) **F86**
[2006/7 F16s² aF16g Mar 21] £5,000 4-y-o: third foal: dam unraced half-sister to very
smart chaser up to 2¾m Idiot's Venture, out of sister to Grand National winner Maori
Venture: better effort in bumpers when neck second to Diavoleria in mares event at
Ludlow. *K. J. Burke*

CALL ME CAPTAIN (IRE) 7 b.g. Bob Back (USA) – Imminent Approach (IRE) **F–**
(Lord Americo) [2006/7 F16sᵖᵘ Oct 27] fourth foal: dam unraced half-sister to Irish
Grand National winner Feathered Gale: 15/2 from 25/1, one of first beaten in bumper on
debut. *C. P. Morlock*

CALLMECOZMO (IRE) 9 ch.g. Zaffaran (USA) – Call Me Connie (IRE) (Combine **c?**
Harvester) [2006/7 c24mᶠ Apr 10] lengthy gelding: bumper/chase winner: left P. Webber,
off 2 years and favourite, several mistakes prior to falling 6 out in handicap at Chepstow:
stays 3m: possibly unsuited by soft/heavy ground. *P. J. Hobbs*

CALL ME DAVE 6 b.g. Bin Ajwaad (IRE) – Heckle (In The Wings) [2006/7 F16v⁵ **F–**
Mar 3] first foal: dam German 7f winner: well beaten in bumper on debut. *Miss
Z. C. Davison*

CALL ME EDWARD (IRE) 6 b.g. Safety Catch (USA) – Smith's Cross (IRE) **c93**
(Crash Course) [2006/7 h86: 24m c16m* c16s⁶ c16g⁵ Oct 19] modest form when **h–**
successful in handicap at Huntingdon in August on chasing debut: disappointing after, as
he became over hurdles: stays 2½m: acts on soft and good to firm going. *N. A. Twiston-
Davies*

CALL ME MAX 5 b.g. Vettori (IRE) – Always Vigilant (USA) (Lear Fan (USA)) **h87**
[2006/7 16d 18s 18v 16g⁶ Dec 20] fairly useful on Flat (stays 1¼m), sold out of
E. Dunlop's stable 18,000 gns Newmarket July Sales: mid-division in maiden/novice
hurdles. *Eoin Doyle, Ireland*

CALL ME SIR (IRE) 5 br.g. Lord Americo – Crash Call (Crash Course) [2006/7 **F69**
F16d⁶ F17v² F17g Apr 27] €14,000 4-y-o: unfurnished gelding: half-brother to fairly
useful chaser Datito (by Over The River), stays 3¼m: dam, winning chaser, stayed 25f:
poor form in bumpers: tends to hang. *Mrs S. Gardner*

CALL OUT (IRE) 7 br.g. Dr Massini (IRE) – Parsons Storm (IRE) (Glacial Storm **h–**
(USA)) [2006/7 h82?: 22d⁶ Jun 12] point winner: no solid form over hurdles.
Mrs S. Gardner

CALLOW LAKE (IRE) 7 b.g. Bahhare (USA) – Sharayif (IRE) (Green Desert **c120**
(USA)) [2006/7 h138: 16f² 16f² c16g* c16dᵘʳ c16s⁴ 17g 16m 16m⁴ Apr 27] smallish, **h145**
strong gelding: smart hurdler: good efforts first and final outings, second to Acambo in
Swinton Handicap Hurdle at Haydock and fourth to Silent Oscar in Grade 1 at Punchestown: fairly useful form over fences: successful in maiden at Tralee in August: let down
by jumping after: placed on soft going, raced mainly under less testing
conditions (acts on firm): blinkered last 6 starts over hurdles. *Mrs J. Harrington, Ireland*

CALOMERIA 6 b.m. Groom Dancer (USA) – Calendula (Be My Guest (USA)) **c–**
[2006/7 c–, h96: 20d 16v* 16d² Jun 2] close-coupled mare: modest handicap hurdler: **h98**
won 5-runner conditional jockeys mares event at Towcester in May: offered nothing
only outing over fences: barely stays 3m: acts on heavy going: tried blinkered, wore
cheekpieces last 2 starts: flashes tail. *D. McCain*

CALON LAN (IRE) 16 b.g. Bustineto – Cherish (Bargello) [2006/7 c92§, h–: c21sᵖᵘ **c– §**
Jun 27] strong gelding: veteran handicap chaser: stays 21f: acts on any going: tried **h–**
blinkered: has bled from nose: unreliable. *N. E. Berry*

CALUSA CALDERA (IRE) 5 b.g. Presenting – Stormy Sea (IRE) (Strong Gale) **h91**
[2006/7 F16m F16s 21g 20g Apr 27] 55,000 3-y-o: sturdy gelding: fifth foal: half-brother **F79**
to useful winner Murrosie (by Anshan): dam unraced: mid-division at best in bumpers/
novice hurdles. *B. G. Powell*

CALUSA CHARLIE (IRE) 8 b.g. Old Vic – Star Cream (Star Appeal) [2006/7 h117: **h117**
25d³ Nov 11] compact gelding: fairly useful hurdler: good third to Star de Mohaison
in handicap at Cheltenham, only outing in 2006/7: stays 25f: acts on heavy going.
B. G. Powell

CALUSA CRYSTAL (FR) 4 b.f. Double Bed (FR) – Mahogany River (Irish River **F–**
(FR)) [2006/7 F17g Apr 19] 30,000 3-y-o: useful-looking filly: fifth foal: half-sister to
fairly useful hurdler Mahogany Blaze (by Kahyasi), probably stays 3m, and 1½m winner
Red Lion (by Lion Cavern): dam 1¼m winner: favourite, well held in mares bumper at
Cheltenham on debut. *P. J. Hobbs*

CALVER'S CONQUEST 5 b.g. El Conquistador – Spinayab (King of Spain) [2006/7 **h–**
F–: 16v⁵ Feb 16] no show in bumper/novice hurdle. *J. A. B. Old*

CALVIC (IRE) 9 ch.g. Old Vic – Calishee (IRE) (Callernish) [2006/7 c129, h–: c32mᵖᵘ **c110**
23v⁴ c32s⁵ c33v⁵ Feb 24] small, leggy gelding: winning hurdler: fairly useful handicap **h–**
chaser, below best in 2006/7: thorough stayer: acts on heavy going: tried blinkered
(jumped poorly). *T. R. George*

CAMBO (FR) 6 b. or br.g. Mansonnien (FR) – Royal Lie (FR) (Garde Royale) [2006/7 **h82**
h101?: 21g⁴ 25gᵖᵘ 20m⁶ 20gᵘʳ 18m⁴ 22g³ 21f⁵ 22d⁴ Nov 12] poor maiden hurdler on
balance: stays 2¾m: acts on good to firm going. *Miss S. West*

CAMDEN BELLA 7 b.m. Sir Harry Lewis (USA) – Camden Grove (Uncle Pokey) **h112**
[2006/7 h101, F92: 25d 22v³ 20s* 24g⁶ Mar 17] bumper winner: fair hurdler: best effort
when winning handicap at Carlisle in February: lame next time: should stay 3m: raced on
good ground or softer (acts on heavy). *N. G. Richards*

CAMDEN CARRIG (IRE) 12 b. or br.g. Camden Town – Tinnecarrig Grove (Boreen **c72**
(FR)) [2006/7 c101: c22d⁴ c29g Mar 21] tall gelding: fairly useful hunter chaser: well
below best both starts in 2007: stays 3¼m: acts on soft and good to firm going. *Simon
Bloss*

CAMDEN GEORGE (IRE) 6 b.g. Pasternak – Triple Town Lass (IRE) (Camden **h117 p**
Town) [2006/7 F99: F17s* 17v² 19d² 20s² 20g² 20g⁵ Apr 7] lengthy, raw-boned gelding: **F102**
won bumper at Market Rasen in May: progressed steadily when runner-up first 4 starts
over hurdles, fairly useful form when beaten 1¾ lengths by Ring The Boss in handicap at
Wetherby on final occasion: not at all discredited in similar event 3 weeks later: stays
2½m: raced on good ground or softer: remains capable of better yet and of winning races
over hurdles. *Mrs S. J. Smith*

CAMDEN TANNER (IRE) 11 b.g. Camden Town – Poor Elsie (Crash Course) **c130**
[2006/7 c130, h115: c19s³ 19v² Mar 11] good-topped gelding: useful handicap chaser: **h121**
fairly useful handicap hurdler, neck second to Wheresben at Naas: effective at 19f to 3m:
raced on good going or softer (acts on heavy): patiently ridden: tends to find little. *Robert
Tyner, Ireland*

CAMERON BRIDGE (IRE) 11 b.g. Camden Town – Arctic Raheen (Over The **c123**
River (FR)) [2006/7 c121, h–: c20g c20f* c20g* 20m c21dᵖᵘ c20mᶠ c20gᵖᵘ c25g* **h–**
Apr 20] useful-looking gelding: winning hurdler: fairly useful handicap chaser: dropped
in weights, back to near best when winning at Worcester and Uttoxeter (beat Rob The
Five a length) in June: first completed outing over fences after when easily making
successful hunter debut at Hereford: stays 25f: unraced on heavy going, acts on any other:
usually held up: sometimes let down by jumping. *P. J. Hobbs*

CAMERONS FUTURE (IRE) 5 b.g. Indian Danehill (IRE) – Wicken Wonder (IRE) **h74 ?**
(Distant Relative) [2006/7 h–, F–: 18m 16m⁵ 19g 18g⁶ Nov 3] little show over hurdles:
sold £3,000 Ascot November Sales. *J. A. Geake*

CAMEROONEY 4 b.g. Sugarfoot – Enkindle (Relkino) [2006/7 F13g⁴ F14g F14s **F77**
F16d⁶ Jan 19] useful-looking gelding: second live foal: half-brother to bumper/25f hunter
chase winner Vital Spark (by Primitive Rising): dam, poor novice hurdler, half-sister to
high-class stayer Recupere: modest form in bumpers. *A. D. Brown*

CAMINO REAL 4 ch.f. Benny The Dip (USA) – Kingdom Ruby (IRE) (Bluebird **F94**
(USA)) [2006/7 F16m² Mar 25] second foal: half-sister to fairly useful 1¼m/1½m winner
Estepona (by Polar Falcon), also winning 2m hurdler: dam 7f winner: 1½ lengths second
to Turbo Linn in bumper at Southwell on debut: sold 42,000 gns Doncaster May Sales.
Miss J. A. Camacho

CAMPAIGN TRAIL (IRE) 9 b.g. Sadler's Wells (USA) – Campestral (USA) **c– §**
(Alleged (USA)) [2006/7 c–, h131d: 20gᵖᵘ 22g 20g⁵ 20m⁴ c24sᵖᵘ 21g 24s⁵ 25v Jan 13] **h116 §**
good-topped gelding: winning chaser, usually let down by jumping/attitude: fairly useful handicap hurdler nowadays: should stay beyond 3¼m: acts on soft going: tried in
blinkers/cheekpieces: edgy sort (tends to sweat): patiently ridden: temperamental. *Jonjo
O'Neill*

CAMPLI (IRE) 5 b.g. Zafonic (USA) – Sept A Neuf (Be My Guest (USA)) [2006/7 **h88**
F93: F17m* F17g⁴ 17f² 17f 16d⁵ 20s Nov 11] tall, good-topped gelding: fair in bumpers, won **F94**
at Sedgefield in June: modest form over hurdles: likely to prove best around 2m:
runner-up in maiden on Flat debut in April. *Micky Hammond*

CANADA STREET (IRE) 6 b.g. Old Vic – Saucy Sprite (Balliol) [2006/7 h97+: **c114**
23g* c22sᶠ c21v² c20v² c25s* c22g⁴ Apr 7] tall gelding: fair form over hurdles, won **h106**
maiden at Wetherby very early in season: improved further over fences: runner-up 2 starts
prior to winning maiden at Kelso in February by neck from Baron Monty: will stay
beyond 25f: acts on heavy going. *J. Howard Johnson*

CANADIAN STORM 6 gr.g. With Approval (CAN) – Sheer Gold (USA) (Cutlass **h95 §**
(USA)) [2006/7 h94§: 16f* 16f³ 17g 16mᶠ Sep 10] neat gelding: modest hurdler: won
claimer at Ludlow in April 2006: fell fatally at Stratford: raced around 2m: acted on firm
and good to soft going (unraced on softer): wore cheekpieces: headstrong: ungenuine.
A. G. Juckes

CANADIAN SUNSET (IRE) 8 b.m. Flemensfirth (USA) – Parish Parade (The **h76 +**
Parson) [2006/7 16s⁴ 22dᵘʳ May 29] runner-up in maiden point in 2004: upped in trip,
travelling comfortably in lead and running better race over hurdles when unseating 3 out
in mares maiden at Cartmel. *J. J. Lambe, Ireland*

CANATRICE (IRE) 7 gr.m. Brief Truce (USA) – Cantata (IRE) (Saddlers' Hall **h74**
(IRE)) [2006/7 16dᵖᵘ 18s⁵ Nov 26] good-topped mare: poor maiden hurdler, off 2 years
before reappearance: usually wears cheekpieces. *T. D. McCarthy*

CA NA TRONA (IRE) 8 b.g. Accordion – Sterna Star (Corvaro (USA)) [2006/7 c24d² **c115**
c24dᵖᵘ c23dᶠ c24g* c26g* Apr 7] good-topped gelding: winning hurdler: off 2 years, **h–**
generally progressive over fences in 2006/7: successful in handicaps at Ludlow (slowly
away/went in snatches in conditional jockeys event) in February and Newton Abbot
(fairly useful form, by length from Yes My Lord) in April: stays 3¼m: acts on soft and
good to firm going: blinkered last 3 starts: sold 23,000 gns Doncaster May Sales.
C. J. Mann

CAN CAN FLYER (IRE) 6 ch.g. In The Wings – Can Can Lady (Anshan) [2006/7 **h91**
h87: 19m 19d 17g* Apr 27] leggy gelding: won sellers at Chepstow in 2005/6 and

Newton Abbot in April: no other form over hurdles: should stay beyond 17f: acts on good to soft going. *J. C. Tuck*

CANDARLI (IRE) 11 ch.g. Polish Precedent (USA) – Calounia (IRE) (Pharly (FR)) **h109**
[2006/7 h109: 19m³ 16m² 16s Jan 13] rather sparely-made gelding: fair handicap hurdler: stays 19f: acts on soft and good to firm going: has run as if amiss more than once: front runner/races prominently. *D. R. Gandolfo*

CANDY GIRL (IRE) 8 b.m. Un Desperado (FR) – Dynamic Venture (IRE) (King's **h123**
Ride) [2006/7 18v² 16v* 18v² 16v² 19d* Apr 1] strong mare: first foal: dam fair hurdler who stayed 3m: fairly useful hurdler: won maiden at Leopardstown in December and mares event at Limerick (landed odds by 2 lengths from Massini Magic) in April: best efforts when runner-up in mares novices in between, beaten length by Chomba Womba in listed race at Limerick fourth start: probably stays 2½m: acts on heavy ground: held up. *W. P. Mullins, Ireland*

CANE BRAKE (IRE) 8 b.g. Sadler's Wells (USA) – Be My Hope (IRE) (Be My **c156**
Native (USA)) [2006/7 c127x, h113: c17v² c24s* c24v* c26g⁵ c29mᵖᵘ Apr 9] **h–**
The broodmare Be My Hope was well represented at the latest Cheltenham Festival. Three of her offspring ran at the meeting, which was noteworthy enough, but, in addition, all were full brothers by multiple champion Flat sire Sadler's Wells. The youngest brother, four-year-old Judge Roy Bean, finished down the field in the Champion Bumper but there will be other opportunities for him. Six-year-old Bob Hall came closest of the three to winning, finishing second in the Jewson Novices' Handicap Chase. But it was the oldest brother Cane Brake who excelled himself when taking fifth place in the Gold Cup. More used to much softer conditions, 20/1-shot Cane Brake was initially outpaced when the race began in earnest, but was running on again at the finish and was beaten less than eleven lengths behind the winner Kauto Star. At the start of the campaign, Cane Brake would have looked a most unlikely Gold Cup representative for his stable, which had the 2005 winner Kicking King still on the sidelines in the latest season. Cane Brake had been a useful novice chaser in 2004/5, winning his first four completed starts over fences, including a defeat of future Irish and English Grand National winner Numbersixvalverde plus a Grade 2 victory at Limerick. But, barring a fourth place in the Cork Grand National, his second season over fences had proved disappointing, with his jumping often letting him down. With his former trainer, David Wachman, now concentrating on his expanding Flat string, Cane Brake began the latest season with Tom Taaffe who wasted little time in exploiting his potentially well-handicapped new arrival.

Paddy Power Chase (Handicap), Leopardstown—Troytown winner Cane Brake (cheekpieces)
completes a notable double, beating Ballistraw (left) and Cheeky Lady (No.22)

After shaping encouragingly when second over an inadequate trip at Galway on his reappearance, Cane Brake landed two of Ireland's most valuable staying handicap chases, the Troytown at Navan in November and the Paddy Power at Leopardstown a month later—in the process becoming just the fourth horse to win both races in the same season after Loving Record (1961), Fort Leney (1966) and King of The Gales (1993). Facing fifteen rivals at Navan in the williamhill.ie-sponsored Troytown, Cane Brake proved well suited by the step back up to three miles and won in very good style by four lengths and seven from Kerryhead Windfarm and On The Net, making steady headway to take the lead three out from the top weight and short-priced favourite Southern Vic and soon in complete control. A 13 lb rise in Cane Brake's mark for the Paddy Power took him close to the ceiling for the race restricted to horses rated 0-145. Cane Brake carried top weight of 11-10, less the 7 lb claimed by his conditional rider Adrian Joyce. With nearly £75,000 on offer to the winner, the Paddy Power produced a typically competitive renewal, though little more than half of the twenty-eight runners ended up completing the course. The first three in the betting, Sher Beau, Newbay Prop and Sound Witness, were among those who came to grief, with 2006 Irish National winner Point Barrow (brought down) also among the casualties. Showing no sign of his previous jumping frailties, Cane Brake kept out of trouble on the outside and gradually crept into the race, joining issue round the home turn and taking over from the bold-jumping front-runner Cheeky Lady at the last. Knuckling down really well on the run-in, Cane Brake fended off the strong challenge of Ballistraw to win by half a length, with Cheeky Lady third and Well Tutored completing the frame, the first four clear of the remainder.

Mount Temple Racing Syndicate's "Cane Brake"

Like Kicking King two years earlier, Cane Brake was given a rest between Christmas and the Gold Cup. His combined efforts at Leopardstown and Cheltenham understandably resulted in a further hike in the weights (another 17 lb), resulting in top weight again for his final 2006/7 outing in the Irish Grand National in which he was allotted 12-0, Adrian Joyce again taking 7 lb off. Cane Brake's presence at Fairyhouse put more than half the field out of the weights but enabled his own stable-companion, Kings Advocate, who started favourite, to race from his correct mark of 10-0. Racing on ground firmer than good for the first time, Cane Brake was dropped out and never figured before being pulled up before four out.

Cane Brake (IRE) (b.g. 1999)	Sadler's Wells (USA) (b 1981)	Northern Dancer (b 1961)	Nearctic
			Natalma
		Fairy Bridge (b 1975)	Bold Reason
			Special
	Be My Hope (IRE) (b 1989)	Be My Native (br 1979)	Our Native
			Witchy Woman
		Diamond Gig (b 1963)	Pitskelly
			Gem of Gems

Be My Hope, who has produced fillies in Commander Collins in 2004 and Saddlers' Hall in 2005, has had four runners to date and her sons by Sadler's Wells account for her three winners. Whilst Sadler's Wells has had plenty of runners over jumps, the majority of them have been hurdlers who began their careers on the Flat, Istabraq being the best example. Few of his sons have shown much aptitude for fences (as already implied, Cane Brake was hardly a natural himself to begin with), or been given the opportunity for that matter, so Cane Brake, Sadler's Wells' best chaser and, like his brothers, unraced on the Flat, is hardly typical of his sire. Then again, Be My Hope, by leading jumps sire Be My Native, would not be typical of the mares Sadler's Wells has covered in his now lengthy stud career. Although she was a useful winner on the Flat in Ireland at a mile and nine furlongs and second in a listed race at the Curragh over a mile and a quarter, Be My Hope proved at least as good over hurdles for Noel Meade in the colours of Judge Roy Bean's owner Mrs John Magnier. Her two wins in that sphere included a defeat of subsequent Irish Champion Hurdle winner Cockney Lad in a valuable handicap at the Punchestown Festival over two and a quarter miles. Be My Hope is a sister to two modest Flat winners and also a half-sister to Cullian, a modest two-and-a-half-mile chaser who won twice for John O'Shea in 2006/7. Grandam Diamond Gig is a maiden half-sister to Amyndas, who was high-class at his best on the Flat, winning the Magnet Cup and finishing third in the Champion Stakes as a three-year-old.

Cane Brake will be obliged to take on the top staying chasers more regularly from now on, and, if he appears again in handicap company, it could be in the Grand National—a race in which Tom Taaffe has now finished third as both a jockey (Monanore in 1988) and trainer (Slim Pickings in 2007). Cane Brake is proven over at least three and a half miles. His run in the Gold Cup shows he doesn't require soft or heavy ground to show his best, and he is a more accomplished jumper these days, so he'd be worth his place in the National line-up. Cane Brake has worn blinkers (once) and cheekpieces in the past and his best races in the latest season (his two wins and the Gold Cup) came when the cheekpieces were re-applied. *T. J. Taaffe, Ireland*

CANNI THINKAAR (IRE) 6 b.g. Alhaarth (IRE) – Cannikin (IRE) (Lahib (USA)) **h77 §**
[2006/7 h–§: 20m⁶ 21g* 18m 16m² 19gᵖᵘ 18mᵖᵘ 20g⁴ 16f³ 20d 17v⁵ 22v⁵ Jan 2] small gelding: poor hurdler: won amateur handicap at Plumpton in May: stays 21f: acts on soft and firm going: wears headgear: temperamental. *P. Butler*

CANNON BRIDGE (IRE) 9 ch.g. Definite Article – Hit For Six (Tap On Wood) **c84 +**
[2006/7 c104+: c28s³ May 26] useful pointer, successful on all 15 completed starts, including in March: also won novice hunter on chasing debut in 2005/6, didn't seem to stay three miles in valuable event at Stratford month later: stays 3m: acts on good to firm going. *Evan Williams*

CANNON FIRE (FR) 6 ch.h. Grand Lodge (USA) – Muirfield (FR) (Crystal Glitters **c97**
(USA)) [2006/7 h108: 21f² 22m* c20g³ c24d⁴ 24s⁴ 20d* 21s Mar 2] angular horse: fair **h113**
handicap hurdler: won at Newton Abbot in May and Chepstow in February: modest

form both starts over fences: stays 3m: acts on firm and soft going: tried visored/in cheekpieces. *Evan Williams*

CANNY BAY 4 b.g. Lahib (USA) – Calachuchi (Martinmas) [2006/7 F16v F16g Mar 17] big, strong gelding: half-brother to fairly useful hurdler/useful chaser Calatagan (by Danzig Connection), stays 2½m: dam prolific winner from 7.5f to 12.4f: better effort in bumpers when 10½ lengths eighth to Tazbar at Wetherby, still looking in need of experience. *Miss J. A. Camacho* **F88**

CANOPUS 4 b.g. Giant's Causeway (USA) – Brightest Star (Unfuwain (USA)) [2006/7 17m² 17d⁴ 17m 16m 17s² 22s² Jan 10] 250,000Y: leggy gelding: second foal: half-brother to Italian winner up to 11f Strepadent (by Diesis): dam, placed all 3 starts in maidens up to 1½m, half-sister to Oaks winner Lady Carla: fair juvenile hurdler: won at Newton Abbot in August: best effort upped in trip final start when second to Celtic Major in handicap at Wincanton: stays 2¾m: acts on soft and good to firm ground: blinkered/in cheekpieces after debut: tends to find little. *Jonjo O'Neill* **h105 §**

CANSALRUN (IRE) 8 b.m. Anshan – Monamandy (IRE) (Mandalus) [2006/7 c96, h97: c20f⁵ c20f* Sep 3] modest novice hurdler: similar form over fences: won novice handicap at Worcester in September: stays 2¾m: acts on firm and soft going: tried tongue tied: consistent. *R. H. Alner* **c97 h–**

CANTABILLY (IRE) 4 b.g. Distant Music (USA) – Cantaloupe (Priolo (USA)) [2006/7 17s⁴ 17s* 17v⁴ 16g² Mar 26] fairly useful on Flat (stays 17f), successful 3 times in 2006, sold out of M. Channon's stable 30,000 gns Newmarket Autumn Sales: fair form over hurdles: won maiden at Taunton in February: best effort when ½-length second of 5 to Lester Leaps In in juvenile at Plumpton: raced around 2m. *R. J. Hodges* **h110**

CANTARINHO 9 b.g. Alderbrook – Hot Hostess (Silly Season) [2006/7 c98: c21s² c24g⁶ c24g² c23m³ Apr 22] useful-looking gelding: fair hunter chaser: effective at 2½m to 3½m: acts on soft and good to firm going: in cheekpieces last 3 starts: tried tongue tied: front runner/races prominently. *D. J. Kemp* **c98**

CANTGETON (IRE) 7 b.g. Germany (USA) – Lahana (IRE) (Rising) [2006/7 h124: 16d 19d 20v⁴ Mar 4] tall, leggy gelding: fairly useful handicap hurdler at best: off a year, well held in 2006/7: stays 21f: acts on soft going. *D. E. Pipe* **h105**

CANTRIP 7 b.m. Celtic Swing – Circe (Main Reef) [2006/7 16mᶠ Oct 16] half-sister to winning hurdlers Grasp (by Kayf Tara) and Odyssey (by Slip Anchor): fair form (stays 1¾m) for Miss B. Sanders, not at best in 2006: fell first on hurdling debut. *S. Dow* **h–**

CAN'T WACK IT 5 b. or br.g. Relief Pitcher – Lonicera (Sulaafah (USA)) [2006/7 F78: F18g⁶ 20g 22fᵖᵘ Apr 22] failed to complete in 2 points in 2006: modest form in bumpers: jumped poorly both starts in novice hurdles. *R. H. Alner* **h– F75**

CAPER 7 b.g. Salse (USA) – Spinning Mouse (Bustino) [2006/7 c76, h81: c24d c24m⁴ c24fᶠᵒ c25m⁴ c23f⁴ c24m c24mᵖᵘ 26g Oct 15] poor hurdler/maiden chaser: stays 3¼m: acts on soft and firm going: blinkered once, often wears cheekpieces: has looked none too keen (ran out third start): sold £7,800 Ascot November Sales, placed in points in 2007. *R. Hollinshead* **c67 h–**

CAPE TEAL (IRE) 8 b.g. Sharifabad (IRE) – Careful Minstrel (Black Minstrel) [2006/7 c–, h–: c24f 20m 24m⁶ 22m Sep 10] point winner: well beaten on completed start in chases: little solid form over hurdles. *D. Brace* **c– h–**

CAPISTRANO 4 b.g. Efisio – Washita (Valiyar) [2006/7 17d 16s 16v Jan 4] stocky gelding: brother to fair hurdler Gustavo, stays 19f, and half-brother to modest hurdler Izzykeen (by Keen), stays 21f: fair on Flat (stays 1¼m), sold out of B. Hills's stable 30,000 gns Newmarket July Sales: well held in juvenile hurdles. *Mrs P. Sly* **h–**

CAPITALISE (IRE) 4 b.g. City On A Hill (USA) – Prime Interest (IRE) (Kings Lake (USA)) [2006/7 16g² 17g* 16d⁴ 16dᶠ 19g Mar 24] compact gelding: modest maiden on Flat (stays 2¼m): fair juvenile hurdler: won maiden at Market Rasen in November: running best race when falling last in handicap at Musselburgh: should stay beyond 17f: raced on good/good to soft going. *V. Smith* **h104**

CAPITANA (GER) 6 ch.m. Lando (GER) – Capitolina (FR) (Empery (USA)) [2006/7 h121: 17m⁶ 16g Apr 7] small, sparely-made mare: fairly useful hurdler, below best in 2 starts in 2006/7 10 months apart: probably best with emphasis on speed around 2m: acts on good to soft and good to firm going. *N. J. Henderson* **h108 +**

CAPPANRUSH (IRE) 7 gr.g. Medaaly – Introvert (USA) (Exbourne (USA)) [2006/7 h90: 18s⁶ 18v Mar 7] angular gelding: modest hurdler at best: below form in 2 handicaps in 2006/7: raced mainly around 2m: acts on good to firm going (bumper form on soft). *A. Ennis* **h76**

CAPRICORN RED 7 ch.m. Rashik – Bella Maggio (Rakaposhi King) [2006/7 16m[pu] **h–**
Apr 24] no show on Flat at 2 yrs or on hurdling debut. *G. J. Smith*

CAPTAIN AUBREY (IRE) 8 b.g. Supreme Leader – Hamers Girl (IRE) (Strong **c88**
Gale) [2006/7 h–: c20s[pu] c23d[6] c21s[pu] c23d[3] Mar 20] strong gelding: fair at best in **h–**
bumpers: fell only outing over hurdles, and hasn't impressed with jumping over fences,
first form when third in novice handicap at Exeter: stays 23f. *J. A. B. Old*

CAPTAIN BOLSH 4 b.g. Tagula (IRE) – Bolshoi Star (Soviet Star (USA)) [2006/7 **h77**
16m[5] 16s 17g Nov 5] modest maiden on Flat (stays easy 1½m): looks to have stamina
limitations over hurdles. *J. Pearce*

CAPTAIN DO INS (UAE) 5 b.g. Timber Country (USA) – Sandova (IRE) (Green **h–**
Desert (USA)) [2006/7 16s[pu] 20d[pu] Dec 28] tall, workmanlike gelding: no form on Flat at
3 yrs for J. Bridger or over hurdles (tried blinkered). *A. M. Hales*

CAPTAIN FLINDERS (IRE) 10 b.g. Satco (FR) – Auburn Queen (Kinglet) [2006/7 **c94 §**
h79: 22s[3] 22s[5] c20d c24v[2] c24s[6] c25s[pu] Mar 8] rangy, good sort: modest maiden hurdler/ **h88 §**
chaser: stays 3m: raced on good ground or softer: wore cheekpieces final outing:
ungenuine. *Miss H. C. Knight*

CAPTAIN MACHELL (IRE) 9 b. or br.g. King's Ride – Flying Silver (Master **c85**
Buck) [2006/7 c86, h–: c25s[6] 22s[pu] c26g[pu] c24g[3] Apr 27] good sort: twice-raced over **h–**
hurdles: modest maiden chaser: stays 3m: raced on good going or softer: visored final
outing: has looked reluctant. *Miss E. C. Lavelle*

CAPTAIN MARLON (IRE) 6 b.g. Supreme Leader – Marlonette (IRE) (Jareer **h109**
(USA)) [2006/7 F97: 20s[5] 20d[pu] 16s[4] 20s[6] 16s[2] 18v[5] 16s[4] Mar 3] tall, useful-looking
gelding: chasing type: fair novice hurdler, in-and-out form in 2006/7: bred to be suited by
2½m+: raced on good ground or softer. *C. L. Tizzard*

CAPTAIN MURPHY (IRE) 9 b.g. Executive Perk – Laura Daisy (Buckskin (FR)) **c–**
[2006/7 21v[6] c25v[F] c16s[pu] c16g Apr 7] tall gelding: fairly useful in bumpers in 2003/4: **h–**
well beaten on completed starts over hurdles/fences after lengthy absence: bred to stay at
least 2½m. *G. A. Charlton*

CAPTAIN O'NEILL 13 b.g. Welsh Captain – The Last Tune (Gunner B) [2006/7 **c57 x**
c20g[6] c19d[2] c20d[5] Nov 26] lengthy, angular gelding: tubed: winning hurdler/pointer: **h– §**
maiden chaser, retains little ability: stays 3m: acts on any going: tried visored/tongue tied:
sketchy jumper: not one to trust. *B. R. Summers*

CAPTAIN'S LEGACY 6 b.g. Bob's Return (IRE) – Tuppence In Clover (Petoski) **h97**
[2006/7 h96: 19d[4] 21v[2] 22s[F] 20v[2] 23d Mar 21] rather unfurnished gelding: modest novice
hurdler: will stay 3m: raced on going softer than good (acts on heavy). *D. M. Grissell*

CAPTAIN SMOOTHY 7 b.g. Charmer – The Lady Captain (Neltino) [2006/7 h–: **h86**
20d[2] 20g 23d Dec 4] novice hurdler, modest form on occasions: stays 2½m: probably acts
on soft going. *M. J. Gingell*

CAPTAINS TABLE 14 b.g. Welsh Captain – Wensum Girl (Ballymoss) [2006/7 c–: **c79**
c20g[5] c17d[3] c19d[3] Oct 26] workmanlike gelding: veteran handicap chaser: stays 2½m:
acts on soft and good to firm going. *S. J. Gilmore*

CAPTAIN TIMELESS 4 b.g. Timeless Times (USA) – The Lady Captain (Neltino) **F–**
[2006/7 F14g Nov 1] plain gelding: third foal: dam bumper winner: tailed off in bumper
on debut. *M. J. Gingell*

CAPTAIN WILLOUGHBY (IRE) 6 b.g. Good Thyne (USA) – Wadablast (IRE) **F–**
(Milk of The Barley) [2006/7 F17d Mar 19] second foal: dam won 2m hurdle in Ireland:
well held in bumper on debut. *Mrs L. C. Jewell*

CAPTAIN WINDSOR (IRE) 6 ch.g. Windsor Castle – Change The Pace (IRE) **c113 d**
(Lancastrian) [2006/7 h–p: c21d[2] c25d[5] c26g[4] Apr 1] well-made gelding: Irish point **h–**
winner: fair form when 5 lengths second to Flying Enterprise in maiden at Wincanton on
chasing debut: has failed to see other races out, including only outing over hurdles: should
stay 3m. *P. F. Nicholls*

CAPTAIN ZINZAN (NZ) 12 b.g. Zabeel (NZ) – Lady Springfield (NZ) (Sharivari **c–**
(USA)) [2006/7 c–, h–: 21f 20f 20m[4] 24m Jun 28] leggy gelding: maiden chaser: **h104**
handicap hurdler, fairly useful at best in early-2003/4, off nearly 3 years after: stays 2¾m
with emphasis on speed: acts on good to firm going: held up. *L. A. Dace*

CAPTIVATE 4 ch.f. Hernando (FR) – Catch (USA) (Blushing Groom (FR)) [2006/7 **h–**
18m[bd] Apr 26] modest on Flat (stays 1¾m), sold out of A. McCabe's stable 8,000 gns
Doncaster January Sales: behind until brought down bend after fifth in mares maiden at
Fontwell on hurdling debut. *Mrs L. C. Jewell*

CAPT JACK (IRE) 8 b.g. Houmayoun (FR) – Pride of The West (IRE) (Be My Native (USA)) [2006/7 23v⁶ 20m³ 20f⁴ 20s* 20g* 22d⁴ 23vᵖᵘ Dec 2] fair pointer, successful twice (including walkover) in 2006: fair hurdler: won maiden at Bangor in August and novice at Uttoxeter in September: lame final outing: stays 2¾m: acts on soft going. *J. Mackie* **h107**

CARACCIOLA (GER) 10 b.g. Lando (GER) – Capitolina (FR) (Empery (USA)) [2006/7 c139, h136: 16f 16m² 16s 16d⁴ 17g⁶ 16m⁵ Apr 21] leggy gelding: useful handicap hurdler/chaser: raced only over hurdles in 2006/7, good efforts when in frame in valuable events at Ascot (second to Desert Air) and Newbury (fourth to Heathcote), and when sixth of 28 to Pedrobob in similar contest at Cheltenham: best at 2m: acts on good to firm and good to soft going, below form all starts on softer. *N. J. Henderson* **c–** **h139**

CARAMAN (IRE) 9 ch.h. Grand Lodge (USA) – Caraiyma (IRE) (Shahrastani (USA)) [2006/7 h116: 17d* 19d 16d³ 17g⁴ 16g² Dec 30] smallish, workmanlike horse: fair on Flat: fairly useful handicap hurdler: won at Bangor in October: good efforts last 3 starts, especially when 4 lengths second to Double Vodka at Musselburgh: best around 2m: acts on good to soft going (yet to race on firmer than good): tried in headgear/tongue tied: free-going sort. *J. J. Quinn* **h128**

CARAPUCE (FR) 8 ch.g. Bigstone (IRE) – Treasure City (FR) (Moulin) [2006/7 c–, h119: 20s⁵ 20v³ 25vᵖᵘ Mar 18] good-topped gelding: fairly useful handicap hurdler: back to best when winning at Carlisle by 4 lengths from Great Approach: winning chaser, but usually makes mistakes: stays 25f: raced on good going or softer (acts on heavy): tried in cheekpieces: sold 5,000 gns Doncaster May Sales. *A. C. Whillans* **c–** **h124**

CARA SPOSA (IRE) 5 b.g. Lend A Hand – Charlton Spring (IRE) (Masterclass (USA)) [2006/7 17v 16g² 16g² Apr 15] tailed off in 6f race at 2 yrs for Stef Liddiard: last of 4 finishers in maiden Irish point in 2006: fair form when runner-up in novice events over hurdles: takes keen hold. *R. C. Guest* **h102**

CARDENAS (GER) 8 b. or br.g. Acatenango (GER) – Cocorna (Night Shift (USA)) [2006/7 21g Oct 24] leggy gelding: useful form over hurdles in 2003/4, won Group 1 in Italy: left C. Egerton and off 2½ years: well beaten in handicap at Cheltenham: stays 2½m: usually races prominently: has hung left. *J. A. Geake* **h–**

CARDIFF GATE (IRE) 4 b.g. Great Palm (USA) – Nervous Kate (IRE) (Over The River (FR)) [2006/7 F12g Mar 23] useful-looking gelding: third foal: half-brother to winning pointer by Supreme Leader: dam 2½m chase winner: looked green and not unduly punished when mid-field in 4-y-o bumper won by Whiteoak at Newbury: likely to improve. *Miss H. Lewis* **F84 p**

CARDINAL SINN (UAE) 6 ch.g. Gulch (USA) – Ines Bloom (IRE) (Sadler's Wells (USA)) [2006/7 F79: 16m 21g⁴ 16d Nov 21] compact gelding: modest form at best in bumpers: let down by jumping 3 starts over hurdles. *Carl Llewellyn* **h79 x**

CARDINAL SPIRIT 5 b.g. Selkirk (USA) – Answered Prayer (Green Desert (USA)) [2006/7 F17s⁶ 16g⁴ c20d³ 21d⁵ 16v⁶ Dec 3] fifth foal: half-brother to 3 winners on Flat, including French 1m/10.5f winner Grateful Thanks (by Bering): dam, ran once in France, out of Oaks winner Jet Ski Lady: well beaten in bumper: poor form over hurdles/on chasing debut. *Ferdy Murphy* **c81** **h84** **F–**

CARDINGTON 8 b.g. Saddlers' Hall (IRE) – Passionelle (Nashwan (USA)) [2006/7 21mᶠ 20g⁶ 16g² c20m³ c17m* Aug 4] lengthy gelding: fair maiden hurdler, off 2 years before reappearance: similar form when winning 3-runner novice chase at Bangor: stays 2½m: unraced on extremes of going. *Mrs S. J. Smith* **c108** **h102**

CAREW LAD 11 b.g. Arzanni – Miss Skindles (Taufan (USA)) [2006/7 h107: 24s c24vᵘʳ c24vᶠ Mar 10] workmanlike gelding: fair hurdler, very lightly raced: let down by jumping both starts over fences: should stay beyond 3m: acts on soft going. *Mrs D. A. Hamer* **c–** **h–**

CARIBBEAN COVE (IRE) 9 gr.g. Norwich – Peaceful Rose (Roselier (FR)) [2006/7 c99x, h–: c19m⁴ c23f* Jul 19] close-coupled gelding: winning hurdler: modest handicap chaser: won 4-runner event at Worcester in July: stays 23f, at least when emphasis is on speed: acts on any going: usually wears cheekpieces/blinkers nowadays: often makes mistakes. *Miss Venetia Williams* **c97 x** **h–**

CARIBBEAN NIGHTS (IRE) 4 b.g. Night Shift (USA) – Caribbean Knockout (IRE) (Halling (USA)) [2006/7 16mᵖᵘ 17m 16m 17m Apr 17] modest maiden on Flat (stays 1m), sold out of T. Easterby's stable 2,500 gns Doncaster August Sales: no form over hurdles: wore cheekpieces/tongue strap final outing. *V. J. Hughes* **h–**

CARIBOU (FR) 5 b.g. Epervier Bleu – Cardoudalle (FR) (Cadoudal (FR)) [2006/7 h118+: c20d³ c16g² c20d² c18v⁴ c16v* c24s* Apr 25] big, lengthy gelding: has plenty of scope: progressive juvenile hurdler in 2005/6: also fairly useful form over fences: improved efforts last 2 starts, winning 4-runner maiden at Leicester in February and novice at Perth (by 3½ lengths from Lankawi, pair clear) in April: stays 3m: acts on heavy going: has tended to jump right. *O. Sherwood* **c126 h—**

CARINA BAY (IRE) 14 b.g. Jurado (USA) – Lecale Lady (Torus) [2006/7 c18g³ c17fᵖᵘ c20s⁵ Aug 19] sturdy ex-Irish gelding: modest handicap chaser nowadays, left M. Kenirons before reappearance: stays 2½m: acts on firm and soft going: blinkered second outing. *Miss Venetia Williams* **c88 h—**

CARLBURG (IRE) 6 b.g. Barathea (IRE) – Ichnusa (Bay Express) [2006/7 16g Mar 16] maiden on Flat, fair at best at 2 yrs: well beaten after racing freely in maiden on hurdling debut. *Mrs C. A. Dunnett* **h—**

CARLITOS 5 br.g. Hernando (FR) – Queen of Spades (IRE) (Strong Gale) [2006/7 F16d* 16d² 16d³ 20v⁶ 21g⁸ 20g Apr 12] lengthy, angular gelding: second foal: dam, fairly useful hurdler/useful chaser around 2m, out of sister to very smart staying chaser Garamycin: won bumper at Sandown on debut in November: fairly useful novice hurdler: won maiden at Newbury in March by 5 lengths from Gauvain, ridden more patiently: went in snatches when disappointing in Grade 2 at Aintree 3 weeks later: likely to stay beyond 21f: acts on good to soft going. *N. A. Twiston-Davies* **h119 F105**

CARLTON SCROOP (FR) 4 ch.g. Priolo (USA) – Elms Schooldays (Emarati (USA)) [2006/7 16m⁴ 16f³ 18g⁴ 17g⁵ 16d 16s Dec 3] fair on Flat (stays 1¾m), successful in March: modest juvenile hurdler: will probably stay 2½m: acts on firm going (possibly unsuited by softer than good): tried blinkered. *J. Jay* **h84**

CARLY BAY 9 b.m. Carlton (GER) – Polly Minor (Sunley Builds) [2006/7 h94: 16v³ c17v² c18v⁶ c17vᵖᵘ 21v⁶ Feb 26] useful-looking mare: modest handicap hurdler: no form over fences: stays 21f: raced on good going or softer (acts on heavy): has worn cheekpieces, including all outings in 2006/7. *G. P. Enright* **c— h89 d**

CARLYS QUEST 13 ch.g. Primo Dominie – Tuppy (USA) (Sharpen Up) [2006/7 h138§: 25s⁶ 25d 23d 20v⁶ 24s 24s³ 23v³ 23s⁴ 23s⁴ 24v⁵ 24mᵖᵘ Apr 26] leggy gelding: fairly useful handicap hurdler nowadays: stays 25f: acts on heavy and good to firm going: often blinkered/visored: has had tongue tied: usually gets behind: temperamental. *Ferdy Murphy* **h122 §**

CARMENS BOY (IRE) 6 br.g. Simply Great (FR) – Rathbawn Realm (Doulab (USA)) [2006/7 20s 18d 20vᵖᵘ 17s 16d⁴ 16s 19g 18v 20m Apr 15] sturdy gelding: 1m winner on Flat: modest handicap hurdler: stays 2½m: acts on soft and good to firm ground: tongue tied: has found little. *D. Loughnane, Ireland* **h87**

CARNANEY HILL (IRE) 7 b.m. Arzanni – Gale Day (IRE) (Jurado (USA)) [2006/7 F16d 17d May 24] first foal: dam unraced: well beaten in bumper/novice hurdle: fell both starts in points later in 2006. *J. K. Magee, Ireland* **h— F—**

CARNEYS CROSS (IRE) 9 b.g. Kahyasi – Cityjet (IRE) (Orchestra) [2006/7 17s Oct 15] stocky ex-Irish gelding: fair hurdler: off 9 months and left S. Treacy, seventh of 12 in handicap at Carlisle: fairly useful handicap chaser: won twice at Naas in 2004/5: effective at 19f, will stay beyond 3m: raced on good going or softer (acts on heavy). *J. M. Saville* **c— h94**

CARNIVAL TOWN 6 b.g. Classic Cliche (IRE) – One of Those Days (Soviet Lad (USA)) [2006/7 h—, F92: 17d² 20d⁴ 20v² 19s⁶ Feb 23] tall, useful-looking gelding: fairly useful over hurdles: won maiden at Chepstow in November by head from Leading Contender: possibly amiss last 2 starts: will stay 3m: acts on heavy going. *Jonjo O'Neill* **h118**

CARNT SPELL 6 b.g. Wizard King – Forever Shineing (Glint of Gold) [2006/7 h77?: 16mᵖᵘ 20sᵖᵘ 24g c23dᵘʳ c21s³ c23d³ c23s⁵ 21m² c19s* c20s⁴ c19s⁴ c24vᵘʳ c23s c24m² c20m⁵ Apr 25] good-bodied gelding: poor chaser/maiden hurdler: won minor event at Towcester in November: barely stays 3m: acts on soft and good to firm going, probably on heavy. *J. T. Stimpson* **c76 h80**

CARPE MOMENTUM (USA) 8 b.g. Marlin (USA) – Carsona (USA) (Carson City (USA)) [2006/7 h—: c17g c20g⁶ Aug 14] no form over hurdles/fences: tongue tied in 2005/6. *R. C. Guest* **c— h—**

CARPET RIDE 5 ch.g. Unfuwain (USA) – Fragrant Oasis (USA) (Rahy (USA)) [2006/7 h64: 16mᵘ 16mᵖᵘ c20s³ c21v⁵ c18g⁵ c20g³ c17m³ Apr 8] strong, good-bodied gelding: little form over hurdles, sold out of B. Powell's stable £1,700 Ascot October **c83 h—**

Sales after second outing: poor novice chaser, left K. Tork after fourth start: stays 2½m: acts on soft and good to firm going: tried tongue tied/in cheekpieces. *B. R. Johnson*

CARRAIG (IRE) 5 b.m. Orpen (USA) – Rose of Mooncoin (IRE) (Brief Truce (USA)) [2006/7 h83: 16m May 6] novice hurdler: failed to complete in points in 2007: likely to prove best at easy 2m: tried in cheekpieces/visor. *Evan Williams*   **h–**

CARR HALL (IRE) 4 b.g. Rossini (USA) – Pidgeon Bay (IRE) (Perugino (USA)) [2006/7 17d⁴ 17fᶠ Aug 11] half-brother to 2m chase winner High Calibre (by Definite Article): modest maiden on Flat (stays 1¼m): poor form on completed outing over hurdles: sold to race in Jersey 6,000 gns Doncaster October Sales. *T. D. Easterby*   **h76**

CARRIAGE RIDE (IRE) 9 b.g. Tidaro (USA) – Casakurali (Gleason (USA)) [2006/7 c97, h–: c25m⁵ c24m c25sᵖᵘ c24m² c26g⁴ Oct 30] angular gelding: poor novice chaser: left N. Richards after first outing: stays 3¼m: acts on heavy and good to firm going: usually wears headgear nowadays. *W. B. Stone*   **c85** **h–**

CARRICK DHU (IRE) 5 b.g. Lend A Hand – Simply A Dream (IRE) (Simply Great (FR)) [2006/7 F16s F16m⁴ F16v⁴ F16s⁵ Apr 27] half-brother to 11f winner in Spain by Hamas: dam won at around 2m over hurdles in France: runner-up once from 3 starts in maiden points in 2006: modest form in bumpers. *I. R. Ferguson, Ireland*   **F79**

CARRICKLEE BOY (IRE) 10 b. or br.g. Jurado (USA) – Garland (Night Star) [2006/7 c–, h–: c26gᵖᵘ c23s⁶ c24m* c22g⁴ c25mᵖᵘ c24m c24mᵖᵘ Oct 4] ex-Irish gelding: 50/1 and 11 lb out of weights, form outside points only when winning very weak 3m handicap chase at Huntingdon in June: in cheekpieces last 2 starts: formerly tongue tied. *Mrs L. C. Jewell*   **c69** **h–**

CARRICK OSCAR (IRE) 7 b.g. Oscar (IRE) – Regents Prancer (Prince Regent (FR)) [2006/7 19s* Feb 1] €35,000 4-y-o: sixth foal: half-brother to bumper/2¾m hurdle winner Supreme Hill (by Supreme Leader): dam lightly raced in bumpers/points: created good impression when winning novice hurdle at Towcester on debut by 12 lengths from Mark The Book, challenging going well 3 out and soon clear from next: potentially smart, but presumably difficult to train. *Carl Llewellyn*   **h132 p**

CARRIETAU 4 b.g. Key of Luck (USA) – Carreamia (Weldnaas (USA)) [2006/7 16s⁵ 16m² 16d² 16g² 17d* 17d² 16s² 16d² 16v³ 16g 16s Apr 1] rangy gelding: modest maiden on Flat (stays 1¼m), claimed from J. Given £6,000 in August: fair juvenile hurdler: won at Sedgefield in November: raced around 2m: acts on soft and good to firm ground: edgy sort: consistent. *F. P. Murtagh*   **h110**

CARRIGEEN KALMIA (IRE) 8 b.m. Norwich – Carrigeen Kerria (IRE) (Kemal (FR)) [2006/7 c20d⁶ c21s⁶ c18s* c19s* 22v³ c20g² Apr 25] second foal: half-sister to fairly useful chaser Carrigeen Victor (by Old Vic), stays 21f: dam, fairly useful chaser, stayed 25f: lightly raced over hurdles, stamina seemingly stretched when third in handicap at Thurles fifth outing: useful chaser: won listed event at Thurles and handicap at Leopardstown (by head from In The High Grass) in January: further improvement when ¾-length second to Royal County Star in valuable handicap at Punchestown: stays 2½m: acts on heavy ground: amateur ridden: remains open to improvement over hurdles. *R. H. Lalor, Ireland*   **c133** **h95 p**

CARRIGEEN VICTOR (IRE) 9 b.g. Old Vic – Carrigeen Kerria (IRE) (Kemal (FR)) [2006/7 22v⁶ c16v c21dᵖᵘ Dec 16] well-made gelding: has reportedly been hob-dayed: excellent start over fences in 2004/5, winning novice at Gowran and Grade 1 Dr P. J. Moriarty Novices' Chase at Leopardstown: off 20 months, nowhere near best in 2006/7, including hurdling debut: should stay beyond 21f: raced on ground softer than good. *Mrs J. Harrington, Ireland*   **c–** **h–**

CARROLL'S O'TULLY (IRE) 7 b.m. Carroll House – Miss O'Tully (IRE) (Fidel) [2006/7 h67, F–: 26g 24d c23d⁴ c26v⁴ c26gᵘʳ c24d c26s³ c26s⁵ c20v⁵ c22s³ c20s³ Feb 18] smallish mare: winning pointer: poor novice hurdler/chaser: stays 3¼m: acts on heavy going: tried tongue tied. *L. A. Dace*   **c69** **h–**

CARRYDUFF 6 b.g. Deploy – Pink Brief (IRE) (Ela-Mana-Mou) [2006/7 h–: 24m⁴ 20sᵖᵘ Oct 27] lengthy gelding: Irish point winner: poor form in novice hurdles: bled final start. *Ferdy Murphy*   **h74**

CARRYONHARRY (IRE) 13 gr.g. Roselier (FR) – Bluebell Avenue (Boreen Beag) [2006/7 c24m* c23v* c26g Mar 16] leggy gelding: useful pointer/hunter chaser nowa-days: won at Huntingdon and Stratford (ladies event) in May: successful 6 times in points in 2007, when well held in Foxhunter at Cheltenham: stays 25f: acts on heavy and good to firm going: formerly visored, wears cheekpieces nowadays: has been let down by jumping. *Miss E. Leppard*   **c115** **h–**

CARTHAGO (IRE) 10 b.g. Roselier (FR) – Hi Cousin (Condorcet (FR)) [2006/7 c–, h91: c25d^pu May 17] leggy gelding: modest handicap hurdler in 2005/6: maiden chaser: winning pointer, including in 2007: stays 3¼m: acts on heavy going: often blinkered in France. *Miss T. McCurrich*   c– h–

CARTHALAWN (IRE) 6 ch.g. Foxhound (USA) – Pohutakawa (FR) (Affirmed (USA)) [2006/7 20d^5 c17d^3 c19v^F c17g* c17v c17v^3 c16v^F c16s* c16g^F c16m^3 Apr 26] rather leggy gelding: fair hurdler: useful novice chaser: won maiden at Gowran in October and handicap at Naas in February: much improved when 6½ lengths third to Another Promise in Grade 1 Swordlestown Cup Novices' Chase at Punchestown final outing: still travelling well off pace when falling 3 out in Grand Annual Chase (Handicap) at Cheltenham time before: best form at 2m: acts on heavy and good to firm ground: has won when making running or held up. *Charles Byrnes, Ireland*   c138 h107

CARTHYS CROSS (IRE) 8 ch.g. Moscow Society (USA) – Sweet Tarquin (Lucifer (USA)) [2006/7 c114, h–: c16g^2 c21g^4 c16g^2 c17g^3 c16s^3 c16g^6 Dec 26] well-made gelding: fair hurdler/maiden chaser: stays 2½m: raced on good going or softer (yet to race on heavy): wore cheekpieces final outing. *T. R. George*   c112 h–

CARTOONIST (IRE) 4 ch.g. Fruits of Love (USA) – Verusa (IRE) (Petorius) [2006/7 16g^5 Oct 21] tall, good-topped gelding: half-brother to winning hurdler Niciara (by Soviet Lad), stays 19f: modest maiden on Flat (should stay beyond 10.5f), left A. King after well beaten last 3 starts: well held in juvenile hurdle. *Evan Williams*   h–

CASADEI (IRE) 8 ch.g. Great Commotion (USA) – Inishmot (IRE) (Glenstal (USA)) [2006/7 c94, h–: c20m^4 c20f^5 20g^5 20m^2 20g^5 c24m^2 c24m^3 c20g^5 Dec 20] modest handicap hurdler/chaser: stays 3m: best on good going or firmer: tried in cheekpieces: tongue tied. *T. G. McCourt, Ireland*   c96 h94

CASALANI (IRE) 8 br.m. Fourstars Allstar (USA) – Brandy Hill Girl (Green Shoon) [2006/7 c–, h72: 19m 24g^4 26m^pu 20d^pu c24s^pu c24d^3 c24v* c23s* c29g^6 Mar 20] leggy, workmanlike mare: poor maiden hurdler: slightly better form over fences, winning handicaps at Southwell in January and Leicester in February: stays 3m: acts on heavy going: held up. *Jennie Candlish*   c84 h81

CASALESE 5 ch.g. Wolfhound (USA) – Little Redwing (Be My Chief (USA)) [2006/7 h–: 18m^6 Oct 1] sturdy gelding: poor form over hurdles. *Micky Hammond*   h75

CASCADE LAKES 5 ch.m. Fraam – Spring Flyer (IRE) (Waajib) [2006/7 22d 19d 17m 20d^pu Nov 30] half-sister to fairly useful hurdler up to 3m Miss Tango (by Bats-hoof) and useful hurdler/temperamental chaser up to 3m Roveretto (by Robellino): poor maiden on Flat at 2 yrs for W. M. Brisbourne: no form over hurdles: wore cheekpieces/tongue strap final outing. *D. E. Pipe*   h–

CASEWICK MIST 7 ch.m. Primitive Rising (USA) – Buckmist Blue (IRE) (Buckskin (FR)) [2006/7 F86: F16g^su F17m^2 Jun 7] fair form in bumpers, won at Market Rasen on debut in late-2005/6: will be suited by further. *J. M. Jefferson*   F92

CASEY JONES 6 b.g. Oscar (IRE) – Arborfield Brook (Over The River (FR)) [2006/7 16s^5 22d* 20s^2 16v^2 20v^3 20v^5 20m^3 24m* Apr 28] €35,000 3-y-o: fifth living foal: half-brother to fair staying chaser The Rebel Lady (by Mister Lord) and modest 2m chaser Dante's Brook (by Phardante): dam unraced: won maiden bumper at Gowran in late-2005/6: fairly useful novice hurdler: won at Down Royal (maiden) in November and Punchestown in April: better form when placed most starts in between, in graded events 3 times, 6¼ lengths third to Aitmatov at Fairyhouse penultimate outing: stays 3m: unraced on firm going, acts on any other. *N. Meade, Ireland*   h119

CASH AND CARRY (IRE) 9 b.g. Norwich – Little And Often (IRE) (Roselier (FR)) [2006/7 16m^6 19m^pu Aug 24] useful-looking gelding: bumper winner: fair chaser/maiden hurdler: refused/reluctant to race last 3 starts, sold out of E. O'Grady's stable 3,000 gns Doncaster May Sales after first occasion: bred to stay beyond 17f: acts on any going: tried blinkered: one to leave alone. *Evan Williams*   c§§ h§§

CASH AND NEW (IRE) 8 b.m. Supreme Leader – Shannon Lough (IRE) (Deep Run) [2006/7 h105: c25d^5 c19s^pu Dec 14] good-topped mare: fair hurdler: no show both starts over fences: stays 3m: raced mainly on going softer than good: wore cheekpieces final start: not a fluent jumper. *R. T. Phillips*   c– h–

CASHARI (IRE) 9 b.g. Shardari – Somewhat Better (Rheingold) [2006/7 c20s^5 Feb 14] winning pointer: blinkered, well held in novice hunter on chasing debut: has report-edly broken blood vessels. *W. J. Warner*   c–

CASH BACK 7 b.g. Bob's Return (IRE) – Connie's Pet (National Trust) [2006/7 F75?: 17m³ 17g 19m² 17m⁶ c16gᶠ Oct 15] maiden hurdler, runner-up in seller: no show on chasing debut: stays 19f: acts on good to firm going. *J. D. Frost* c– h86

CASHBACK ROSE (IRE) 6 b. or br.m. Alflora (IRE) – Grayrose Fleur (Henbit (USA)) [2006/7 F16m* 20d 17g 20m Apr 9] €6,000 3-y-o: plain mare: first foal: dam bumper winner: placed once in points in 2006: won bumper at Cork in June: sold out of P. Cashman's stable 35,000 gns Doncaster August Sales: well held in novice hurdles: bred to stay 3m. *N. G. Richards* h– F88

CASH BONANZA (IRE) 7 ch.g. Beneficial – Vulcash (IRE) (Callernish) [2006/7 c82, h–: c25vᵘʳ c21v² c28vᵖᵘ c25v³ Mar 2] novice hurdler: fair form when placed in handicap chases, in cheekpieces final outing: stays 25f: raced on going softer than good (acts on heavy). *N. G. Richards* c102 h–

CASHEL DANCER 8 b.m. Bishop of Cashel – Dancing Debut (Polar Falcon (USA)) [2006/7 h87: c20d⁶ c20sᵖᵘ 21d c19gᵖᵘ 20g Apr 11] lengthy, angular mare: modest handicap hurdler at one time: no form in 2006/7, including over fences: stays 2½m: acts on good to firm and good to soft going. *S. A. Brookshaw* c– h–

CASHEMA (IRE) 6 b.m. Cape Cross (IRE) – Miss Shema (USA) (Gulch (USA)) [2006/7 h–: 16g 20d 16v⁵ 16d⁴ 16g⁶ Apr 15] lengthy, sparely-made mare: has little ability: left D. MacLeod after first outing: tried in cheekpieces: often tongue tied. *James Moffatt* h–

CASH FLOW 4 b.f. Mtoto – Little Change (Grundy) [2006/7 17d 17m 17f⁵ 17s³ 16mʳᵒ 16m³ 16g³ 17g⁶ Apr 23] half-sister to winning French hurdler around 2m Summer Chance (by Robellino): well held in maiden at 2 yrs for D. Barker: poor maiden hurdler: ran out early fifth outing. *Mrs S. A. Watt* h67 §

CASH FOR HONOURS 4 b.g. City Honours (USA) – Copper Breeze (IRE) (Strong Gale) [2006/7 F16g Apr 3] €54,000 3-y-o: half-brother to poor hurdler Just For Fun (by Kahyasi), stays 27f, and winning pointer by Erins Isle: dam unraced half-sister to useful staying chaser Sir Leonard: mid-field in bumper won by Abstinence at Wetherby on debut: bred to stay well. *Mrs S. J. Smith* F69

CASH IN HAND (IRE) 7 b.g. Charente River (IRE) – Fern Fields (IRE) (Be My Native (USA)) [2006/7 c20s³ c23v² c20g⁶ c19mᵖᵘ Apr 24] good-topped gelding: well held both starts over hurdles: successful twice in Irish points: bought 15,000 gns Doncaster May Sales: best effort in hunters when second to Irilut in maiden at Leicester: stays 23f: acts on heavy going. *R. Harvey* c92 h–

CASH MAN (IRE) 6 b.g. Flemensfirth (USA) – Bollero (IRE) (Topanoora) [2006/7 F–: F17d³ F16s 16f 17d⁴ 20d³ 20v² 24v³ 20g³ 16s⁶ Mar 7] easily best effort in bumpers when third to Riodan at Sedgefield: fair novice hurdler: may prove best short of 3m when conditions are testing: acts on heavy going. *Mrs E. Slack* h100 F89

CASH 'N CARROTS 8 b.g. Missed Flight – Rhiannon (Welsh Pageant) [2006/7 h–: c21g⁶ c21gᵖᵘ c19d Oct 26] leggy gelding: of no account. *R. C. Harper* c– h–

CASH ON FRIDAY 6 b.g. Bishop of Cashel – Til Friday (Scottish Reel) [2006/7 h85: 20g³ 20s 20g 20g 24v³ 20v 24d⁴ 24v⁶ 20v 23g⁴ c25gᵖᵘ Apr 23] tall gelding, unfurnished at present: poor novice hurdler: seemed to lose confidence after mistake first on chasing debut (returned distressed): stays 3m: acts on heavy going (bumper form on good to firm). *R. C. Guest* c– h78

CASH ON (IRE) 5 ch.g. Spectrum (IRE) – Lady Lucre (IRE) (Last Tycoon) [2006/7 h79§: 17g³ 16f 16m³ 16m* 20f² 16d³ 17m⁴ Oct 4] modest hurdler: won maiden at Worcester in August: best form around 2m: acts on good to firm and good to soft going: tried blinkered/in cheekpieces: has looked unwilling. *Karen George* h99 §

CASH RETURN 8 b.m. Bob's Return (IRE) – We're In The Money (Billion (USA)) [2006/7 h74: 20m Jun 28] lengthy mare: poor maiden hurdler: form only around 2m: wears cheekpieces: has had tongue tied. *Miss M. E. Rowland* h–

CASONOVA (IRE) 4 b.g. Trans Island – Sherna Girl (IRE) (Desert Story (IRE)) [2006/7 17d 17fᵖᵘ Aug 11] poor maiden on Flat (should be suited by 7f/1m): no show in 2 juvenile hurdles: sold 1,200 gns Doncaster October Sales. *T. D. Easterby* h–

CASSIA HEIGHTS 12 b.g. Montelimar (USA) – Cloncoose (IRE) (Remainder Man) [2006/7 c110, h–: c20g c25d² c30dᵖᵘ c24m⁵ c24g⁶ c20g⁵ c21g⁴ c21d³ c24sᵖᵘ c29g c24g c28gᵖᵘ c21g Apr 13] tall gelding: handicap chaser, on the downgrade: stays 31f: acts on soft and firm going: tongue tied. *S. A. Brookshaw* c106 d h–

CASSIUS DIO (IRE) 5 ch.g. Anshan – Roisin Beag (IRE) (Cardinal Flower) [2006/7 **h–**
F–: 17d 20m Apr 9] strong gelding: no show in bumper/novice hurdles. *J. Wade*

CASSIUS (IRE) 5 b.g. Pistolet Bleu (IRE) – L'Enfant Unique (IRE) (Phardante (FR)) **F76**
[2006/7 F16g Apr 3] fourth foal: half-brother to 2m hurdle winner Open Range (by
Saddlers' Hall) and winning pointer by Presenting: dam unraced half-sister to dam of
high-class chaser around 3m Strong Flow: mid-field in bumper won by Abstinence at
Wetherby on debut. *B. Mactaggart*

CASTERFLO 8 b.m. Primitive Rising (USA) – Celtic Sands (Celtic Cone) [2006/7 **c70**
h75: c16d³ Nov 3] sturdy mare: poor hurdler: similar form on chasing debut after 17- **h–**
month absence: stays 2½m: acts on any going: tried tongue tied. *W. S. Coltherd*

CAST IRON CASEY (IRE) 5 ch.g. Carroll House – Ashie's Friend (IRE) (Over The **F95**
River (FR)) [2006/7 F16s* F17v⁶ Mar 18] third foal: dam winning pointer: won bumper
at Wetherby on debut in February by 4 lengths from Thenford Snipe with something in
hand: tied up badly under even more testing conditions next time. *J. Howard Johnson*

CASTLE ARROW (IRE) 14 b.g. Mansooj – Soulful (So Blessed) [2006/7 c–, h–: **c–**
c26g^pu May 24] compact gelding: winning pointer: maiden hurdler/chaser: has been **h–**
blinkered. *Miss R. Williams*

CASTLECOMER (IRE) 6 ch.g. Presenting – Miss Mylette (IRE) (Torus) [2006/7 **c86**
21d^pu c24d³ c23s² c24s² Feb 16] first foal: dam, no sign of ability, out of half-sister to **h–**
high-class chaser up to 3¼m Another Coral: won maiden Irish point in 2006: no show on
hurdling debut: modest form in maiden chases: stays 3m. *A. Ennis*

CASTLE CRAIGS (IRE) 5 b.g. Bob's Return (IRE) – Graigue Glen (Glen Quaich) **F–**
[2006/7 F16v⁵ Mar 2] €20,000 3-y-o: fourth foal: half-brother to 2m hurdle winner
Kilcash Native (by Be My Native): dam, lightly raced in points, half-sister to Whitbread
Gold Cup winner Shady Deal: well beaten in bumper on debut. *N. G. Richards*

CASTLECROSSINGS (IRE) 4 br.f. Broken Hearted – Peacefull River (IRE) (Over **F90**
The River (FR)) [2006/7 F16d² F16v² F16s Mar 10] unfurnished ex-Irish filly: half-sister
to 3m chase winner Bracken Boy (by Phardante): dam, won over 2½m over hurdles,
half-sister to dam of smart chaser Go Roger Go: fair form when runner-up first 2 starts in
bumpers (left Patrick Hughes in between), beaten 14 lengths by impressive One Gulp in
mares event at Haydock on second occasion: will be suited by further than 2m. *Jonjo
O'Neill*

CASTLEFORD (IRE) 9 b.g. Be My Native (USA) – Commanche Bay (IRE) (Com- **c70**
manche Run) [2006/7 c–, h–: c24g^pu c25s⁴ Feb 3] medium-sized gelding: fair pointer: **h–**
maiden hurdler/chaser, no form in hunters: should stay beyond 3¼m: acts on soft ground.
W. Kinsey

CASTLE FROME (IRE) 8 b.g. Spectrum (IRE) – Vendimia (Dominion) [2006/7 **c83**
c86?, h–: c17g⁵ c17g⁶ c16v³ c20s² c16s³ c19s^F Dec 29] point winner: no form over **h–**
hurdles: poor maiden chaser: stays 2½m: acts on soft ground: tried visored, in cheekpieces last 4 starts. *A. E. Price*

CASTLE GUNNER 7 b.g. Gunner B – Castle Tyrant (Idiot's Delight) [2006/7 F16v **F–**
F17d Jun 14] first foal: dam fair pointer: well held in 2 bumpers: third in maiden point in
March. *G. A. Harker*

CASTLEMAINEVILLAGE (IRE) 7 b.g. Supreme Leader – Jennys Castle (Carl- **h85 p**
ingford Castle) [2006/7 F91: 19s 17s 17s⁴ 16g⁴ Mar 19] workmanlike gelding: bumper
winner: progressive over hurdles, modest form when fourth to Tytheknot in handicap at
Wincanton final start: bred to stay well: likely to improve further granted more of an
emphasis on stamina. *M. R. Bosley*

CASTLEMORE (IRE) 9 b.g. Be My Native (USA) – Parsonetta (The Parson) **c95 x**
[2006/7 c102x, h–: c24g* Apr 8] fair hurdler/chaser: left P. Hobbs and fit from points, **h–**
fortunate to win hunter at Towcester, length down and very tired when left clear last: stays
25f: acts on firm and good to soft ground, unraced on softer. *Michael Blake*

CASTLESHANE (IRE) 10 b.g. Kris – Ahbab (IRE) (Ajdal (USA)) [2006/7 c–p, **c–p**
h117: 16f² 16g⁶ 16g³ 16d⁶ 16g 16m 16s³ Feb 14] tall, quite good-topped gelding: one- **h104**
time useful hurdler, has deteriorated considerably: badly let down by jumping both starts
over fences: best around 2m: acts on firm and soft going: tried in headgear: front runner.
S. Gollings

CASTLETOWN BOY (IRE) 5 b.g. Shernazar – Glenelly Valley (IRE) (Presenting) **F95**
[2006/7 F16m³ Apr 21] €15,500 3-y-o, resold €26,000 3-y-o: strong gelding: chasing

type: first foal: dam unraced: half-sister to useful stayer Clara Allen: 2 lengths third to Evelith Echo in bumper at Ayr on debut: likely to be suited by further than 2m. *G. A. Charlton*

CASTLE VIC (IRE) 5 b.g. Old Vic – Celtic Gale (Strong Gale) [2006/7 F16v* Dec 16] brother to fair chaser Itsuptoharry, stays 2½m, and half-brother to modest hurdler/chaser Paddy The Duke (by Phardante), stays 2½m: dam fair hurdler: fairly useful form when winning bumper at Fairyhouse on debut by head from Baltiman. *W. P. Mullins, Ireland* **F97**

CATALAN GIRL 8 ch.m. Lancastrian – Miss Vagabond (Scallywag) [2006/7 c–: c20m^{pu} May 18] of no account. *Miss E. J. Murray* **c–**

CATCH ME (GER) 5 b.g. Law Society (USA) – Calcida (GER) (Konigsstuhl (GER)) [2006/7 16s* 16d* 16v² 18v^{ur} 21g³ 20m^F Apr 27] **h145**

While Well Chief and Fair Along were the best known of the handful of German-breds racing over jumps in Britain and Ireland in the latest season, a couple of Irish-trained novice hurdlers with the (GER) suffix were shaping as though they, too, could be making names for themselves before too long. Aitmatov and Catch Me, both useful performers on the Flat, took well to hurdling, the former winning three races including a Grade 2 novice at Fairyhouse, and the latter successful twice before finishing third in the Baring Bingham Novices' Hurdle (sponsored by Ballymore Properties) at the Cheltenham Festival. The five-year-old Catch Me, the better of the pair, is likely to be kept to hurdling in the next season, when he should be up to winning graded events; the chances are that the year-older Aitmatov will be tried over fences, being much more of a chasing type. Catch Me had one season's racing in Germany before joining Edward O'Grady, winning a maiden over eleven furlongs on his second start then going on to show better form, including when fourth in the German St Leger on his final one. He made an immediate impact for his new connections. Successful in a couple of minor events in April 2006, over two miles at the Curragh (when beating future Coral Cup winner Burntoakboy into second) and a mile and three quarters at Tipperary, Catch Me stretched his winning run to four when he had his attentions turned to hurdling over six months later, picking up a maiden and a minor event at Naas, which were both confined to four-year-olds. Catch Me started odds on both times at Naas and gave his supporters little cause for concern in either race, beating Sigma Digital by two lengths with plenty to spare in the maiden, then Breathing Fire by seven lengths after dictating the pace in the minor event.

Subsequently moved up in class, Catch Me failed to add to those victories but did show much improved form. After finishing a neck second to another above-average novice, De Valira, in a Grade 2 race at Leopardstown, Catch Me raced only in Grade 1 events. He was still in with every chance when hampered and unseating Barry Geraghty two out in the Deloitte Novices' Hurdle at Leopardstown won by Aran Concerto in February. Stepped up again in trip, Catch Me had that rival two places behind him when they reopposed in the Baring Bingham, leading briefly two out at Cheltenham but then finding Massini's Maguire and Tidal Bay just too strong, going down by a neck and a length and a half. Catch Me was let down by his jumping on his only subsequent start, in the Land Rover Champion Novices' Hurdle at Punchestown, but he still ran right up to his best. Although far from fluent, Catch Me led from three out until headed by fellow joint-favourite Glencove Marina going to the last where Catch Me fell, rallying at the time and giving the impression he would have run the eventual five-length winner close had he completed. Incidentally, that fall handed second place to another useful German-bred Flat recruit in Kalderon (Aitmatov was a below-par fourth). Catch Me, an angular gelding, is the first foal of Calcida, a prolific winner at up to eleven furlongs in Germany. He acts on heavy and good to firm going. *E. J. O'Grady, Ireland*

CATCHTHEBUG (IRE) 8 b.g. Lord Americo – Just A Maid (Rarity) [2006/7 c–p, h109p: 22m² 22g⁴ 22d^{pu} 20g³ 24s 26s⁵ 22m Apr 15] sturdy gelding: fair handicap hurdler: fell only start over fences: stays 2¾m: acts on heavy and good to firm going: has shaped as if amiss more than once. *Jonjo O'Neill* **c–**
h112

CATCH THE PERK (IRE) 10 b.g. Executive Perk – Kilbally Quilty (IRE) (Monte-limar (USA)) [2006/7 c116, h109: 24s⁶ c24m c24m⁴ c26m⁵ c24g* c24s³ c24s* 24d⁶ c32s c20m⁴ c32m Apr 21] medium-sized gelding: fairly useful handicap chaser: won at Perth in August and September: fair handicap hurdler: probably stays 31f, effective at much shorter: acts on soft and good to firm going: usually wears cheekpieces: races prominently. *Miss Lucinda V. Russell* — **c117 h97**

CATEGORICAL 4 b.g. Diktat – Zibet (Kris) [2006/7 16m⁵ 16g² 16s* 16s⁴ 16v⁶ 16g² 20g⁶ 16g⁶ Apr 16] fairly useful on Flat (stays 1m), left J. Toller after third 3-y-o start: fair juvenile hurdler: won at Wetherby in November by 10 lengths from Special Order: creditable efforts most starts after: stays easy 2½m: acts on soft going: takes good hold, and ridden patiently. *K. G. Reveley* — **h102**

CATHEDRAL ROCK (IRE) 5 b.g. New Frontier (IRE) – Cathadubh (IRE) (Naheez (USA)) [2006/7 F89: 16v³ 17s³ 16v* 20s Mar 10] fourth in bumper on debut: fair form over hurdles: won novice at Kempton in March by 1¾ lengths from Duelling Banjos, idling markedly/hanging left: should stay at least 2½m: raced on going softer than good. *N. J. Gifford* — **h106**

CATHERINE'S RUN (IRE) 5 b. or br.m. Kotashaan (FR) – Satco Street (IRE) (Satco (FR)) [2006/7 F16m* F14g* F16m³ Oct 28] rather unfurnished mare: second foal: dam unraced sister to smart staying chaser Sackville: fair form in bumpers, winning at Worcester in July and Fontwell (beat Sirnando a neck) in September. *V. Smith* — **F92**

CATHERINES VERSE (IRE) 6 b.m. Old Vic – Simply Lucky (IRE) (Simply Great (FR)) [2006/7 F17g Apr 23] fourth foal: half-sister to 3m hunter chase winner Kilbreena (by Carroll House): dam lightly-raced maiden: twice-raced in points in 2006, winning maiden on completed start: well held in bumper at Sedgefield. *J. J. Lambe, Ireland* — **F—**

CATHY'S IDOL (IRE) 8 br.g. Lord Americo – Cathy's Girl (Sheer Grit) [2006/7 19mᵖᵘ Jun 4] brother to fair hurdler/useful chaser American Jennie, stays 29f: dam won 25f chase: no form in points/selling hurdle. *D. A. Rees* — **h—**

CATILINE (IRE) 6 b.g. Nashwan (USA) – Mild Intrigue (USA) (Sir Ivor (USA)) [2006/7 16g 16v 20s 19s Dec 1] useful-looking gelding: poor novice hurdler: in cheek-pieces final start. *Eoin Doyle, Ireland* — **h81**

CATZYBABY (IRE) 6 b.m. Darazari (IRE) – Try Le Reste (IRE) (Le Moss) [2006/7 21v 26v Jan 11] sturdy, good-topped mare: half-sister to ungenuine winning hurdler/chaser Secret Drinker (by Husyan), stays 29f: dam lightly raced in points: no form in points/novice hurdles: tried visored. *Miss Tor Sturgis* — **h—**

CAUGHT AT DAWN (IRE) 13 b.g. Supreme Leader – Pharisee (IRE) (Phardante (FR)) [2006/7 c122⁵: c33g⁴ c30dᵖᵘ May 27] workmanlike gelding: prolific winning pointer: fairly useful chaser at one time, well below best in 2006: stays 4m: acts on soft and good to firm going: unreliable. *M. H. Weston* — **c83 §**

CAULKLEYS BANK 7 b.g. Slip Anchor – Mayroni (Bustino) [2006/7 h89+: 16g² 16g* Nov 29] good-topped gelding: useful form in bumpers in 2004/5: improved effort over hurdles when easily winning selling handicap at Catterick in November: best form at 2m. *M. W. Easterby* — **h109**

CAVA BIEN 5 b.g. Bien Bien (USA) – Bebe de Cham (Tragic Role (USA)) [2006/7 h107§: 18m² 20s² 20f* 22s* 22m² Jul 27] leggy gelding: fair hurdler: won maiden at Worcester and novice at Newton Abbot in June: stays 2¾m: acts on any going. *B. J. Llewellyn* — **h112**

CAVALLINI (USA) 5 b. or br.g. Bianconi (USA) – Taylor Park (USA) (Sir Gaylord) [2006/7 16v⁴ Feb 24] sturdy gelding: half-brother to 2½m hurdle winner Howjal (by Conquistador Cielo): fairly useful on Flat (stays 11.6f): tailed-off last of 4 finishers to Shatabdi in Grade 2 novice at Kempton on hurdling debut, jumping slowly after hampered third: should do better. *G. L. Moore* — **h– p**

CAVE HILL (IRE) 5 b.g. Dr Massini (IRE) – Eurogal (IRE) (Strong Gale) [2006/7 F17v* Nov 28] third foal: dam well beaten in bumper: successful in maiden Irish point in 2006: useful form when also winning bumper at Hereford by head from Greenbridge, pair clear. *Miss H. C. Knight* — **F109**

CAVEMAN 7 b.g. Primitive Rising (USA) – Ferneyhill Lady (Menelek) [2006/7 c81, h86: c16g⁴ c19d* c20m³ c22mᵖᵘ c24g³ Apr 9] tall, angular gelding: modest form in novice hurdles: similar form over fences, won maiden at Towcester in June: sold out of O. Brennan's stable 7,200 gns Doncaster August Sales after fourth outing: won point in March: should stay beyond 2½m: acts on good to soft going. *N. M. Bloom* — **c88 h–**

CAVE OF THE GIANT (IRE) 5 b.g. Giant's Causeway (USA) – Maroussie (FR) **h111**
(Saumarez) [2006/7 h111: 19d⁴ Mar 26] leggy gelding: lightly raced on Flat: fair maiden
hurdler: shaped as if in need of race only outing in 2006/7: stays 21f: raced on good going
or softer (acts on heavy): consistent. *T. D. McCarthy*

CAVERS GLEN 5 b.g. Overbury (IRE) – Thorterdykes Lass (IRE) (Zaffaran (USA)) **h97**
[2006/7 F83: 25s⁵ 21v⁵ 16v⁵ 18v² 18s⁶ 22v³ 20v 20sᵖᵘ Apr 25] small, leggy gelding:
modest maiden hurdler: stays 2¾m: raced only on soft/heavy going over hurdles: hard
ride (tends to hang left). *A. C. Whillans*

CAWKWELL MEG 7 ch.m. Afif – Cawkwell Patricia (Boco (USA)) [2006/7 20mᵖᵘ **h–**
Jun 31] failed to complete in points/novice hurdles. *F. Jestin*

CAYMAN CALYPSO (IRE) 6 ro.g. Danehill Dancer (IRE) – Warthill Whispers **h94**
(Grey Desire) [2006/7 h81: 16g² 16g⁴ 16m² Jun 22] modest novice hurdler: should stay
at least 2½m. *Mrs P. Sly*

CAYMANS GIFT 7 ch.g. Cayman Kai (IRE) – Gymcrak Cyrano (IRE) (Cyrano de **h–**
Bergerac) [2006/7 h–: 17sᵖᵘ Oct 6] modest maiden on Flat (stays 15f): no form over
hurdles: tried in cheekpieces: sold 800 gns Doncaster October Sales. *A. C. Whillans*

CEARAN (CZE) 4 b.g. Rainbows For Life (CAN) – Ceara (CZE) (Corvaro (USA)) **h–**
[2006/7 17m⁶ Apr 15] Czech-bred gelding: successful over 9f (at 3 yrs) on Flat in
Switzerland: left M. Weiss, well beaten in juvenile on hurdling debut. *F. Jordan*

CECCHETTI (IRE) 4 b.f. Imperial Ballet (IRE) – Quiver Tree (Lion Cavern (USA)) **h–**
[2006/7 17dᵖᵘ Aug 21] half-sister to fairly useful hurdler Harrycat (by Bahhare), stays
2¾m: poor maiden on Flat (stays 1m): left Mrs H. Sweeting, pulled too hard on hurdling
debut. *M. F. Harris*

CEDAR CHIEF 10 b.g. Saddlers' Hall (IRE) – Dame Ashfield (Grundy) [2006/7 c80§, **c86 §**
h–§: c24dᵖᵘ c24s⁴ c24s² c21gᶠ Apr 12] stocky gelding: winning pointer: poor maiden/ **h– §**
maiden chaser: trained first start by B. Johnson: stays 3m: acts on any going: tried in
cheekpieces, usually wears blinkers: sketchy jumper: hard ride. *K. Tork*

CEDAR RAPIDS (IRE) 7 b. or br.g. Lord Americo – Amys Girl (IRE) (Pauper) **c–**
[2006/7 c92, h80+: c20f Jun 17] useful-looking gelding: maiden hurdler: modest chaser **h–**
at best: bred to stay beyond 2m: headstrong. *H. P. Hogarth*

CEDRUS LIBANI (IRE) 6 b.g. Beneficial – Cedar Castle (IRE) (Castle Keep) **h124**
[2006/7 h79p: 16s* 21v³ 16s* 16d Mar 13] tall gelding: has scope: won novice hurdles at
Hexham in November and Newcastle in January: very stiff task, seemingly much better
form when mid-field in 22-runner Supreme Novices' Hurdle at Cheltenham: bred to stay
2½m+ (possibly amiss second start): raced on going softer than good. *J. Howard Johnson*

CEEAWAYHOME 8 b.g. Nomadic Way (USA) – Dame Scarlet (Blakeney) [2006/7 **h122**
h122, F95: 16s³ Oct 1] fairly useful hurdler: good third to Scarthy Lad in Grade 2 at
Tipperary, only outing in 2006/7: will stay 3m: raced on going softer than good. *John
E. Kiely, Ireland*

CEEBEE 5 b.g. Petoski – Two Shares (The Parson) [2006/7 F16g Apr 23] half-brother **F–**
to winning hurdler/chaser Knockaulin (by Buckley), stayed 2½m: dam won 17f hurdle in
Ireland: well beaten in bumper on debut. *J. M. Saville*

CEE CEE RIDER 5 b.m. Classic Cliche (IRE) – Rachel C (IRE) (Phardante (FR)) **F74**
[2006/7 F17v³ F17s F16s Mar 3] 13,000 4-y-o: lengthy, rather unfurnished mare: fourth
foal: half-sister to fair hurdler Smart Mover (by Supreme Leader), stays 3m: dam unraced
half-sister to useful Irish chaser Master Aristocrat VI and to dam of top-class staying
chaser Lord Noelie: 14 lengths third to Maggie Mathias at Folkestone on debut, only form
in 3 bumpers. *A. King*

CELEBRITY CALL (IRE) 6 ch.g. Fourstars Allstar (USA) – Callerbann (Caller- **h99**
nish) [2006/7 F18s 21d² 21s 21v³ 23g² Apr 9] sturdy gelding: half-brother to 2m hurdle **F75**
winner King Tiger (by Flemensfirth): dam placed in point: won maiden Irish point in
2006: bought 16,000 gns Doncaster May Sales: seventh in bumper at Plumpton: modest
form over hurdles, best effort when second to Kidithou in handicap at Fakenham on final
start: will stay 3m: raced on good ground or softer. *O. Sherwood*

CELESTIAL WAVE (IRE) 7 b.m. Taipan (IRE) – Blossom World (IRE) (The **h148**
Parson) [2006/7 h131: 18s³ 20v* 24v* 24v* Jan 25]
In the aftermath of Tony McCoy's record-breaking achievements, it is all
too easy to overlook the impact Adrian Maguire made on the National Hunt scene
during the early-'nineties, his rapid rise to the top very similar to the one McCoy

undertook a few years later (both riders, coincidentally, began their British careers with Toby Balding). Maguire ended his riding career with a total of 1,024 wins on British soil, placing him ninth in the all-time list, and holds strong claims to be regarded as the best never to win the jockeys' championship—he fell just three wins short of the title in 1993/4 (led by forty-two wins at one stage) and then suffered a broken arm late the following season when level with arch rival Richard Dunwoody. Unfortunately, such ill-luck became the unwanted hallmark of Maguire's later years in the saddle, particularly with regard to the Cheltenham Festival. Initially the meeting was a happy hunting ground for the Irishman and he made his mark there in breathtaking fashion, winning the 1991 Kim Muir on Omerta (his first-ever ride in Britain) before producing a virtuoso performance on 25/1-shot Cool Ground to come out on top in a three-way finish to the following year's Gold Cup. By 1994 Maguire had notched up a further four Festival wins, including memorable successes on Viking Flagship (Champion Chase) and Mysilv (Triumph Hurdle) at that year's meeting. However, he missed four of the next seven Festivals through injury or family bereavement (his mother died in 1995) and didn't ride another winner at jumping's showpiece event prior to his retirement, on medical grounds, in October 2002.

The front-running Celestial Wave looked the ideal mare to put Maguire on the map in his fledgling career as a trainer. A bumper winner in March 2005, Celestial Wave won her first three starts over hurdles in 2005/6, on the last two winning listed mares' events at Leopardstown and Limerick. She ended that campaign with a good second to Cailin Alainn in a valuable Grade 3 mares' novice at Fairyhouse, an effort that looks even better in hindsight than it may have done at the time. Maguire's yard was in poor form when Celestial Wave made a rather disappointing reappearance in another listed mares event, this time at Punchestown in October. Given a two-month break after that defeat, Celestial Wave improved markedly when stepped up in trip for her first hurdling venture outside mares company, winning the Giltspur Scientific Tara Hurdle at Navan under Timmy Murphy in December by a length and a half from Southern Vic. Well backed, she was joined in the lead four out and battled on under pressure to give Maguire his

Giltspur Scientific Tara Hurdle, Navan—
Timmy Murphy steers Celestial Wave to the biggest win of her short, ill-fated career

first winner since June. The victory in the woodiesdiy.com Christmas Hurdle at Leopardstown eleven days later represented further improvement and saw her odds halve in the World Hurdle ante-post betting. Celestial Wave ran out an impressive winner in a field that included the likes of Rosaker and Emotional Moment—the two most recent winners of the Christmas Hurdle—and Strangely Brown, a Group 1 winner in France. Again allowed to bowl along in front, Celestial Wave was clearly travelling the best three out and came home ten lengths clear of fellow mare Sweet Kiln. Celestial Wave completed her hat-trick when landing the odds in the Alo Duffin Memorial Galmoy Hurdle at Gowran the following month by five lengths from Studmaster, with several of her Christmas Hurdle rivals again down the field. Despite that, Celestial Wave was not so impressive as at Leopardstown, giving the impression that she was idling when not particularly fluent at the last two flights. It was further proof, however, of her prowess on heavy ground and Maguire stated that she would be heading to Cheltenham only if conditions came up testing. In the event, bad luck once again struck Maguire in the lead-up to a Festival, with Celestial Wave found cast in her box a week before the opening day, meaning she would miss the race regardless of conditions (her odds had dropped to 8/1 by that stage). Connections hoped to get her back for the Champion Stayers' Hurdle at Punchestown, but she had to be retired to the paddocks where, unfortunately, she suffered a rupture and had to be put down in April.

Celestial Wave (IRE) (b.m. 2000)	Taipan (IRE) (b 1992)	Last Tycoon (b 1983)	Try My Best
			Mill Princess
		Alidiva (b 1987)	Chief Singer
			Alligatrix
	Blossom World (IRE) (b 1989)	The Parson (b 1968)	Aureole
			Bracey Bridge
		Stormy Wave (b 1981)	Gulf Pearl
			Stormy Breeze

The leggy Celestial Wave was a half-sister to a winning pointer by Posen called Odeeka, who is now a broodmare. The dam Blossom World, who won and was placed twice in points, finished well held in a bumper at Tramore on her only start outside of that sphere. The bottom half of this pedigree is a largely undistinguished family, though grandam Stormy Wave is a half-sister to a Grade 2-winning jumper in Foodbroker Star, who took advantage of his rivals' jumping frailties to spring a 33/1 surprise in a four-finisher renewal of the December Novices' Chase at Lingfield in 1996. Celestial Wave is the best hurdler produced by Taipan (who died in 2002), though Alexander Taipan was in the same crop as Celestial Wave and has shown smart form over fences, notably when winning a competitive novices' handicap at Punchestown in April. Taipan was a very smart performer, who won four times at Group 1 level for John Dunlop in the mid- to late-'nineties. He was the first offspring of the remarkable broodmare Alidiva, who produced other Group 1 winners Ali-Royal and Sleepytime in the two years after Taipan. All three won at the highest level on the Flat in 1997. Celestial Wave was raced only on going softer than good, and acted well on heavy. She was a game front runner who stayed three miles. *Adrian Maguire, Ireland*

CELIAN (FR) 4 b.g. Indian River (FR) – Celinda (FR) (Bering) [2006/7 F16g Apr 7] £11,000 3-y-o: good-topped gelding: second foal: dam in frame up to 1½m in France: seventh of 16 to Marleybow in bumper at Haydock on debut. *N. B. King*   **F75**

CELIA'S HIGH (IRE) 8 br.g. Hymns On High – Celia's Fountain (IRE) (Royal Fountain) [2006/7 c69x, h–: 27mᵖᵘ Jun 8] lengthy gelding: Irish point winner: no form over hurdles: poor maiden chaser: stays 27f: tried in cheekpieces: tongue tied: prone to mistakes. *D. McCain Jnr*   **c– x** **h–**

CELIOSO (IRE) 10 b.g. Celio Rufo – Bettons Rose (Roselier (FR)) [2006/7 c115x, h–: 21m⁴ 24g 26g Jun 4] lengthy gelding: one-time fairly useful handicap chaser, usually let down by attitude/jumping nowadays: below best over hurdles first 2 starts in 2006/7: best form at 3½m+: acts on good to firm and good to soft going. *Mrs S. J. Smith*   **c– x** **h85**

CELTIC BLAZE (IRE) 8 b.m. Charente River (IRE) – Firdaunt (Tanfirion) [2006/7 c93§, h93§: 20v² c24mᵖᵘ 20m⁵ 24f⁴ Jul 19] small, sturdy mare: modest hurdler/chaser at best, below that in early-2006/7: stays 23f: acts on heavy and good to firm going: visored once, usually wears cheekpieces: tongue tied: unreliable. *B. S. Rothwell*   **c– §** **h83 §**

CELTIC BOY (IRE) 9 b.g. Arctic Lord – Laugh Away (Furry Glen) [2006/7 c127x, h127: c25g* c24m³ c23m* c20f⁵ c22g c24s² 24s c25m⁶ c24dᵖᵘ Nov 17] quite good-topped gelding: fairly useful hurdler, went as if amiss seventh outing: useful chaser: further improvement in 2006/7, winning intermediate at Kelso in May and handicap at Stratford (by 9 lengths from Totheroadyouvegone) in June: effective at 2½m to 25f: probably acts on any going: often let down by jumping: joined Miss H. Lewis. *P. Bowen*   **c136 x**
h–

CELTIC CARISMA 5 b.m. Celtic Swing – Kathryn's Pet (Blakeney) [2006/7 16s⁴ 20g³ 20g² 20g⁵ 22g³ Mar 31] sturdy mare: fair on Flat (stays 2m): modest form over hurdles: stays 2¾m: raced mainly on good ground over hurdles. *K. G. Reveley*   **h96**

CELTICELLO (IRE) 5 b. or br.g. Celtic Swing – Viola Royale (IRE) (Royal Academy (USA)) [2006/7 16d 17d 17d 16d² 16d⁶ 16g³ 16m 16fᵘʳ Apr 5] leggy gelding: fairly useful up to 1m at 3 yrs for M. Jarvis, very lightly raced on Flat since: modest novice hurdler: raced around 2m: acts on firm and good to soft going (unraced on softer over hurdles): tried in cheekpieces. *Heather Dalton*   **h91**

CELTIC EMPIRE (IRE) 4 b.g. Second Empire (IRE) – Celtic Guest (IRE) (Be My Guest (USA)) [2006/7 16s 17v 20s 20vᵖᵘ 16v⁴ Mar 9] poor maiden on Flat (stays 1¾m): little impact over hurdles. *Jedd O'Keeffe*   **h84 ?**

CELTIC FLAME 8 ch.m. Bold Fox – Annie Bee (Rusticaro (FR)) [2006/7 h–, F–: 16g 16d² 20m⁵ 24v⁵ 16d⁵ 21s³ 23vᶠ 25g⁵ 16g Mar 29] smallish mare: poor maiden hurdler: probably stays 25f: acts on soft ground. *O. Brennan*   **h75**

CELTIC FLOW 9 b.m. Primitive Rising (USA) – Celtic Lane (Welsh Captain) [2006/7 c69, h–: c25s³ c29s* c27dᵖᵘ c28vᶠ c32vᵖᵘ Mar 15] leggy mare: maiden hurdler: poor handicap chaser: upped in trip, won easily at Wetherby in November: stays 29f: acts on soft going. *C. R. Wilson*   **c79**
h–

CELTIC GLADIATOR 5 ch.g. Alflora (IRE) – Queenford Belle (Celtic Cone) [2006/7 F16v³ F16v⁶ F16v 25gᵖᵘ 22gᵖᵘ Apr 15] 25,000 3-y-o: sturdy, workmanlike gelding: fifth foal: dam, 2½m hurdle winner, half-sister to high-class staying chaser Couldnt Be Better: modest form in bumpers: looked reluctant both starts over hurdles: one to treat with caution. *T. P. Tate*   **h– §**
F81

CELTIC HEATHER (IRE) 6 b.m. Darazari (IRE) – Kirsten (FR) (New Chapter) [2006/7 F16gᵇᵈ F13s⁴ F17v³ Feb 13] workmanlike mare: half-sister to fairly useful hurdler Chaprassi (by Tropular), stayed 19f, and Irish 2½m bumper winner Stormy (by Glacial Storm): dam placed on Flat at 2 yrs: modest form in bumpers. *Carl Llewellyn*   **F76**

CELTIC LEGEND (FR) 8 br.g. Celtic Swing – Another Legend (USA) (Lyphard's Wish (FR)) [2006/7 c98, h91: 16g³ Nov 2] tall, leggy gelding: modest handicap hurdler/chaser: effective at 2m to 21f: acts on firm and soft going: tried tongue tied: patiently ridden: has carried head high/hung right. *K. G. Reveley*   **c–**
h90

CELTIC MAJOR (IRE) 9 gr.g. Roselier (FR) – Dun Oengus (IRE) (Strong Gale) [2006/7 c–, h–: 22s* 22s* 24gᵖᵘ 24gʳᵒ Mar 25] sturdy gelding: fairly useful hurdler: left P. Bowen, much improved first 2 starts in 2006/7, winning handicaps at Wincanton (beat Abragante a length on second occasion) in January: stiff task next time, ran out first final outing: well beaten completed start over fences: stays 2¾m: acts on soft going: front runner. *Miss H. Lewis*   **c–**
h116

CELTIC PRIDE (IRE) 12 gr.g. Roselier (FR) – Grannie No (Brave Invader (USA)) [2006/7 c–, h–: c26gᵖᵘ Oct 30] tall gelding: winning hurdler/chaser: lightly raced and no form since 2004/5 (went lame at Warwick in October): should stay beyond 3m: used to act well on soft/heavy going: visored. *Jennie Candlish*   **c–**
h–

CELTIC ROMANCE 8 b.m. Celtic Swing – Southern Sky (Comedy Star (USA)) [2006/7 h75: 16g 16m 16d 17d 17s⁵ 17d 16gᵖᵘ Apr 8] leggy mare: poor maiden hurdler: raced mainly around 2m: acts on soft going. *Ms Sue Smith*   **h71**

CELTIC SOCIETY (IRE) 6 ch.g. Moscow Society (USA) – Final Peace (IRE) (Satco (FR)) [2006/7 F78: 20d 21g 20s 22v⁶ 24v⁶ 19d⁴ 26gᵖᵘ Apr 20] sparely-made gelding: no solid form over hurdles. *P. C. Ritchens*   **h–**

CELTIC SON (FR) 8 b.g. Celtic Arms (FR) – For Kicks (FR) (Top Ville) [2006/7 c142§, h–: c24vᵖᵘ c36gᵖᵘ Apr 14] sturdy gelding: winning hurdler: impressive chasing debut when winning Grade 2 at Wincanton in November 2005: has shaped as if amiss/found little all starts since: stays 25f: acts on heavy going: tried in cheekpieces: tongue tied: one to treat with caution. *D. E. Pipe*   **c– §**
h–

CELTIC STAR (IRE) 9 b.g. Celtic Swing – Recherchee (Rainbow Quest (USA)) [2006/7 c81§, h–§: c22m 24g Jun 15] lengthy gelding: poor handicap hurdler/chaser: **c68 §**
h– §

barely stays 3¼m: acts on firm and soft going: usually wears headgear: unreliable. *Mrs L. Williamson*

CELTIC STARLIGHT 8 gr.m. Arzanni – Celtic Berry (Celtic Cone) [2006/7 h–: 24s 24v⁴ Jan 21] tailed off 3 starts over hurdles. *S. M. Jacobs*   **h–**

CELTIC VISION (IRE) 11 b.g. Be My Native (USA) – Dream Run (Deep Run) [2006/7 c–x, h–: c17g^{pu} 23v⁶ 22m^{pu} 20g 20d^{pu} 19v^{pu} Feb 27] rather leggy gelding: winning hurdler/maiden chaser: no form since 2003, left P. Haslam after second start, F. Jordan after fifth: tried in headgear: sometimes tongue tied. *K. J. Burke*   **c– x**   **h–**

CELTIC WARRIOR (IRE) 4 b.g. Celtic Swing – Notable Dear (ITY) (Last Tycoon) [2006/7 16v* 16s⁴ 16s⁵ 16s² 17v⁶ 16v 16d Mar 13] angular gelding: fairly useful on Flat at up to 1½m: similar standard in juvenile hurdles: won maiden at Thurles in November: stiff task, ran to best when ninth of 24 to Gaspara in listed 4-y-o handicap at Cheltenham final outing: raced around 2m: acts on heavy ground: well beaten only try in blinkers. *Liam Roche, Ireland*   **h112**

CEMGRAFT 6 b.m. In The Wings – Soviet Maid (IRE) (Soviet Star (USA)) [2006/7 h91: 19v² May 23] modest on Flat (probably stays 2m), successful in July: ran to similar level first 2 starts over hurdles, in 2005/6: stays 2½m: acts on heavy going: tried in cheekpieces: tongue tied. *A. J. Lidderdale*   **h74**

CENTRAL HOUSE 10 b.g. Alflora (IRE) – Fantasy World (Kemal (FR)) [2006/7 c155, h–: c16s² c16s⁴ c17v² c17v³ c16s² c19d⁶ c20v² c17m⁵ c16m Apr 24] tall gelding: smart chaser: no match for Nickname when runner-up on 4 occasions in 2006/7, in Fortria Chase at Navan and Tied Cottage Chase at Punchestown first/fifth outings: well held in valuable handicap at Fairyhouse and Grade 1 at Punchestown (sweating) last 2 starts: barely stays 2½m: acts on heavy and good to firm going: visored once (ran too freely), has won with blinkers or without: sometimes tongue tied: usually jumps well/makes running. *D. T. Hughes, Ireland*   **c151**   **h–**

CEOPERK (IRE) 8 ch.m. Executive Perk – Golden Mela (Golden Love) [2006/7 h93: 19g^{ur} 21v³ 22v 17d 22s⁴ 21m⁴ 16s* 21g³ Mar 20] modest handicap hurdler: fortunate to win conditional jockeys event at Warwick in March, left in lead 2 out: stays 21f: unraced on firm ground, acts on any other. *D. J. Wintle*   **h98**

CERIUM (FR) 6 b.g. Vaguely Pleasant (FR) – Tantatura (FR) (Akarad (FR)) [2006/7 c132, h–: c19d* c21s c19d^{pu} Feb 17] leggy gelding: smart chaser: off 7 months (had breathing operation), much improved when beating Knowhere 3½ lengths in Grade 2 Amlin 1965 Chase (Limited Handicap) at Ascot in November: disappointing both outings after (bled final one): stays 19f: acts on soft going: blinkered once: tongue tied 2 of last 4 starts. *P. F. Nicholls*   **c151**   **h–**

Amlin 1965 Chase (Limited Intermediate Handicap), Ascot—Sam Thomas celebrates his new role as Paul Nicholls' second jockey with victory on Cerium (centre) over Knowhere (right); last-fence faller Chilling Place is also pictured

CERVINIA TWO 6 b.g. Zaffaran (USA) – A Regular Perk (IRE) (Executive Perk) **c61** [2006/7 25g⁶ 20s 21vᵖᵘ c25v³ Feb 13] sturdy gelding: second foal: dam unraced: not **h–** fluent and no form over hurdles: in cheekpieces, poor form on chasing debut (finished distressed). *Jonjo O'Neill*

C'EST LA VIE 5 ch.m. Bering – Action de Grace (USA) (Riverman (USA)) [2006/7 **c– p** h–: 17d 16m 16m⁴ 16m 17m⁴ 16m² c16m⁵ Nov 5] useful-looking mare: poor novice **h78** hurdler: some promise on chasing debut: raced around 2m: acts on good to firm going: tried tongue tied. *Miss J. E. Foster*

CETSHWAYO 5 ch.g. Pursuit of Love – Induna (Grand Lodge (USA)) [2006/7 h–: **h–** 16sᵖᵘ Dec 8] fair on Flat (stays 1¼m), won seller in September: no form in 3 starts over hurdles: sold 800 gns Newmarket February Sales. *J. M. P. Eustace*

CETTI'S WARBLER 9 gr.m. Sir Harry Lewis (USA) – Sedge Warbler (Scallywag) **c110** [2006/7 c96, h–: c22v² c23s⁵ c21s* Mar 17] tall mare: fair handicap chaser: off 14 months **h–** prior to reappearance: better than ever when winning at Uttoxeter in March: should stay 3m: acts on heavy going: tongue tied last 4 outings. *Mrs P. Robeson*

CHABRIMAL MINSTER 10 b.g. Minster Son – Bromley Rose (Rubor) [2006/7 **c110** c104, h–: c28s* c25d⁴ c29v c33v³ c31sᵘʳ Apr 27] leggy gelding: fair handicap chaser: **h–** won easily at Kelso in November: good efforts when in frame after, third to Nil Desperandum in Eider at Newcastle: stays 33f: acts on heavy going: makes the odd mistake. *R. Ford*

CHA CHA CHA DANCER 7 ch.g. Groom Dancer (USA) – Amber Fizz (USA) **c–** (Effervescing (USA)) [2006/7 c–, h–: 21vᵖᵘ 20v⁴ 20v* 21s³ 22g Apr 2] strong gelding: **h107** fair hurdler: first form since 2004/5 when easily winning conditional jockeys selling handicap at Newcastle in March: failed to complete both starts over fences: probably stays easy 3m: acts on heavy going: wore cheekpieces second outing. *G. A. Swinbank*

CHAIM (IRE) 5 b. or br.g. Lord Americo – Furry Gran (Furry Glen) [2006/7 F99: **h95** F16s* 16d 17v³ 16sᶠ 21v⁴ 16d⁵ Mar 17] tall, lengthy, unfurnished gelding: fairly useful **F99** bumper winner, including at Uttoxeter in October: modest form over hurdles: should stay beyond 17f. *Mrs L. Wadham*

CHAIN 10 b.g. Last Tycoon – Trampship (High Line) [2006/7 c77, h–: c21m³ c24m⁶ **c71 x** c22dᵖᵘ c20gᵖᵘ 20d Nov 14] ex-Irish gelding: winning hurdler: poor maiden chaser: stays **h–** 25f: best form on good going or firmer (acts on firm): tried in blinkers/cheekpieces: usually tongue tied: makes mistakes. *O. Brennan*

CHAMACCO (FR) 7 b.g. Cadoudal (FR) – Awentina (FR) (Caerwent) [2006/7 h94: **c–** 24v³ 20d 22m* 24v* 20s⁵ 23v c23dᵖᵘ Mar 20] leggy gelding: fair hurdler: won handicaps **h104** at Exeter and Chepstow in November: always behind on chasing debut: stays 3m: acts on heavy and good to firm going. *M. F. Harris*

CHAMOSS ROYALE (FR) 7 ch.m. Garde Royale – Chamoss (FR) (Tip Moss (FR)) **c134** [2006/7 c25d* c19s* 20v² c26v² c22g² Mar 24] angular mare: has reportedly been **h134** fired: useful handicap hurdler: good second to United in mares event at Sandown third outing: similar form over fences: landed odds in mares maiden at Folkestone (first outing for 19 months) in November and mares novice at Exeter (beat Inch Pride 12 lengths) in December: good 8 lengths second to Penneyrose Bay in listed mares handicap at Newbury final start: will stay beyond 3¼m: raced on good going or softer (acts on heavy). *P. F. Nicholls*

CHAMPAGNE FLOOZIE 4 ch.f. Fleetwood (IRE) – On Request (IRE) (Be My **F–** Guest (USA)) [2006/7 F12g Mar 23] leggy filly: half-sister to 3 winners, including modest hurdler Jay Bee Ell (by Pursuit of Love), stays 2¾m: dam, lightly raced at 2 yrs, sister to smart winner up to 1¼m Invited Guest: well held in bumper on debut. *J. C. Fox*

CHAMPAGNE HARRY 9 b.g. Sir Harry Lewis (USA) – Sparkling Cinders (Nether- **c– x** kelly) [2006/7 c–, h124: 21g 21d 24g⁴ Mar 24] workmanlike gelding: fairly useful **h115** hurdler, off 14 months before reappearance: placed in maiden chases in 2004/5, but often let down by jumping over fences: stays 3m: acts on any going: has had tongue tied. *N. A. Twiston-Davies*

CHAMPAGNE ONLY (IRE) 6 b.m. Un Desperado (FR) – Rainbow Native (IRE) **h–** (Be My Native (USA)) [2006/7 F16f² F16f⁶ F16v 16s 19vᵖᵘ 20gᵖᵘ Apr 3] leggy mare: **F78** first foal: dam unplaced in 2 bumpers in Ireland: won maiden point in Ireland in 2006: second in bumper at Perth: no form after, including over hurdles (bled final outing). *Mrs L. B. Normile*

CHAMPAGNE ROSSINI (IRE) 5 b.g. Rossini (USA) – Alpencrocus (IRE) **h70**
(Waajib) [2006/7 h53: 16m^F 16m^6 16m^F 17m^2 16d^ur 16g^3 16d^pu 16d^6 16g 16g 16g^3 Apr 9]
poor maiden hurdler: raced around 2m: acts on good to firm going: blinkered final start.
M. C. Chapman

CHAMPAGNE SUNDAE (IRE) 9 b.g. Supreme Leader – Partners In Crime (Croft- **c–**
hall) [2006/7 c81?, h–: 22v^pu Jan 1] novice hurdler: running better race over fences when **h–**
falling last (remounted) in novice at Exeter: stays 19f: tongue tied last 3 starts (has shaped
as if amiss more than once). *B. R. Millman*

CHAMPION DE SOU (FR) 5 ch.g. Adnaan (IRE) – Tamilda (FR) (Rose Laurel) **h–**
[2006/7 16s 20v^pu Feb 13] workmanlike gelding: half-brother to several winners, including fairly useful chasers up to 2¾m and 3m Tacolino and Tiraldo (both by Royal Charter):
dam unraced half-sister to smart French chaser Talego: no show both starts over hurdles.
C. R. Egerton

CHANCELLOR (IRE) 9 ch.h. Halling (USA) – Isticanna (USA) (Far North (CAN)) **h90**
[2006/7 16g^6 16d Dec 29] good-topped horse: half-brother to winning 2m hurdler Ragged
Jack (by Cape Cross): one-time smart 1¼m performer on Flat, unreliable nowadays,
though won in 2006 for Ernst Oertel: modest form when sixth to Spear Thistle in novice
at Leicester on hurdling debut: bled next time (raced freely in visor): tongue tied. *Mrs
Caroline Bailey*

CHANCERS DANTE (IRE) 11 b.g. Phardante (FR) – Own Acre (Linacre) [2006/7 **c70 §**
c71§, h–§: c26d^pu c27m^5 24f Jul 16] angular gelding: winning hurdler: poor chaser: stays **h– §**
27f: has form on heavy going, possibly better on good/good to firm: usually blinkered:
unreliable. *Ferdy Murphy*

CHANCERY LAD (IRE) 6 b.g. Leading Counsel (USA) – Carrigbuck (IRE) **h–**
(Buckskin (FR)) [2006/7 19v^pu Feb 23] €22,000 3-y-o: third foal: dam unraced sister to
useful hurdler/fairly useful chaser Yellow Spring, best up to 21f: fell in maiden Irish point
in 2005: showed nothing in novice on hurdling debut. *R. T. Phillips*

CHANDLERS CROSS (IRE) 5 ch.g. Rakaposhi King – Tullow Lady (IRE) **h95 ?**
(Mazaad) [2006/7 F16s F16d 16m^F 16m^4 Apr 25] close-coupled, workmanlike gelding: **F–**
third foal: dam, poor maiden hurdler up to 21f, half-sister to grandam of War of Attrition:
well held in 2 bumpers: 10¼ lengths fourth to Kanad in steadily-run novice at Worcester,
completed outing over hurdles. *M. Scudamore*

CHANGE AGENT 11 br.g. Royal Fountain – Flashy Looks (Impecunious) [2006/7 **c78**
c25d c23s^4 c20v^6 Jan 12] big gelding: modest winner over fences: best effort in handicaps
after 21-month absence when fourth to Alcatras at Taunton: stays 3m: acts on soft going.
J. B. Groucott

CHANGING GEAR (IRE) 8 b.g. Gothland (FR) – Wondering Lady (IRE) (Kemal **c–**
(FR)) [2006/7 16m^5 16s^2 20g 19g^6 16m* c16g^pu 19g^2 Aug 26] modest hurdler: won weak **h93**
maiden at Worcester in August: never a threat on chasing debut: stays 19f: acts on soft
and good to firm going: blinkered last 3 outings: none too resolute. *Jonjo O'Neill*

CHANGIZ 4 b.g. Foxhound (USA) – Persia (IRE) (Persian Bold) [2006/7 17s^5 18s^6 16d **h77**
16s 16s^2 22s 17d Mar 19] compact gelding: modest maiden on Flat (stays 1¼m): poor
form over hurdles: in cheekpieces last 3 outings. *J. A. Geake*

CHANINBAR (FR) 4 b.g. Milford Track (IRE) – Logicia (FR) (Homme de Loi (IRE)) **h117**
[2006/7 16g^2 16s^4 16d^3 Dec 4] tall, rather leggy gelding: sixth foal: half-brother to French
2m hurdle winner Logicmoon de Bessy (by Arctic Tern) and winner on Flat in France
by River Bay: dam unraced: in frame twice (at 6f/7f) from 4 starts at 2 yrs in French
Provinces for J-L. Pelletan: shaped most encouragingly when 1½ lengths second to
Katchit in juvenile at Chepstow on hurdling debut: found little on softer ground both
subsequent starts: free-going sort. *P. F. Nicholls*

CHANNAHRLIE (IRE) 13 gr.g. Celio Rufo – Derravarragh Lady (IRE) (Radical) **c–**
[2006/7 c87, h–: c25g c24m^6 c26g^4 Nov 15] tall, angular gelding: veteran handicap **h–**
chaser: stays 3½m: acts on soft and firm going: wears headgear: usually races prominently. *R. Dickin*

CHANTICLIER 10 b.g. Roselier (FR) – Cherry Crest (Pollerton) [2006/7 c85, h95: **c91**
c24s^4 May 8] well-made gelding: maiden hurdler/chaser, modest form on completed **h–**
starts over fences: stays 25f: raced on good going or softer (acts on soft): ran poorly in
cheekpieces: tongue tied nowadays: sold 12,000 gns Doncaster May (2006) Sales, won
point in December. *R. T. Phillips*

CHANTILLY PASSION (FR) 6 b.g. Double Trigger (IRE) – Chantilly Fashion (FR) **F71**
(Northern Fashion (USA)) [2006/7 F–: F16g⁴ Apr 23] raced 3 times in bumpers, poor
form on return from near 2-year absence. *B. Storey*

CHAPEL FLOWERS (IRE) 5 b.g. Pistolet Bleu (IRE) – Stormweather Girl (IRE) **h– p**
(Strong Gale) [2006/7 F16g 18v Jan 12] €52,000 3-y-o: good-topped gelding: fourth foal: **F69 +**
half-brother to winning pointers by Fourstars Allstar and Bob's Return: dam once-raced
half-sister to useful staying hurdler Miracle Man: some promise when well held in
bumper and novice hurdle: should do better. *N. G. Richards*

CHAPEL TIMES (IRE) 8 b.g. Supreme Leader – Dippers Daughter (Strong Gale) **h–**
[2006/7 h84: 20v 22dᵖᵘ 26sᵖᵘ Dec 23] tall gelding: bumper winner: maiden hurdler, no
form in 2006/7. *H. D. Daly*

CHAPEL WOOD LADY (IRE) 6 b.m. Zaffaran (USA) – Pharrambling (IRE) **h86**
(Phardante (FR)) [2006/7 20d⁴ 17s⁵ 16v Jan 12] €60,000 4-y-o: lengthy mare: second
foal: half-sister to winning pointer by Roselier: dam, fair hurdler who stayed 25f,
half-sister to smart staying chaser Seven Towers: left Mrs J. Harrington and off 8 months,
best effort over hurdles (modest form) when fourth to The Entomologist in novice at
Fakenham: bred to be suited by 3m+: mulish at start second outing, blinkered next time.
M. G. Quinlan

CHAPLIN 6 b.g. Groom Dancer (USA) – Princess Borghese (USA) (Nijinsky (CAN)) **h–**
[2006/7 h–: 17s Feb 8] well-made gelding: no form over hurdles: tried visored: usually
tongue tied. *Evan Williams*

CHARACTER BUILDING (IRE) 7 gr.g. Accordion – Mrs Jones (IRE) (Roselier **c139**
(FR)) [2006/7 h106, F100: c20g² c26s* c21v⁴ c20d* c33g² c32mᵖᵘ Apr 21] lengthy geld- **h–**
ing: winning hurdler: much better over fences, won maiden at Warwick in December and

Mrs E. Wright's "Character Building"

novice handicap at Market Rasen (by 3½ lengths from Ice Melted) in February: ran well when ¾-length second to Butler's Cabin in National Hunt Chase (Amateurs) at Cheltenham fifth outing, drifting right when challenging after last: stays 33f: raced largely on good going or softer (ran poorly on good to firm in Scottish National): not straightforward (tends to idle) but is consistent: fluent jumper. *J. J. Quinn*

CHARANGO STAR 9 b.g. Petoski – Pejawi (Strong Gale) [2006/7 c109, h103: c32mᵖᵘ Jul 2] fair hurdler/chaser: stays 31f: acts on any going: blinkered/visored last 6 starts in 2005/6: has been let down by jumping over fences: tends to race lazily. *W. K. Goldsworthy*
c—
h—

CHARIOT (IRE) 6 ch.g. Titus Livius (FR) – Battle Queen (Kind of Hush) [2006/7 h72: 16g* 17d² Jun 12] sturdy gelding: poor hurdler: won selling handicap at Fakenham in May: will prove best at 2m: acts on soft and good to firm going: tongue tied last 5 outings. *M. R. Bosley*
h82

CHARIOTS OF BLUE 6 ch.g. Bluebird (USA) – Boadicea's Chariot (Commanche Run) [2006/7 16g 19dᵖᵘ Oct 26] half-brother to fair 2m hurdler Green Icini (by Greensmith): dam winning 2m hurdler: no form in 2 starts on Flat at 2 yrs or in novice hurdles. *W. G. M. Turner*
h—

CHARIZARD (IRE) 10 ch.g. Montelimar (USA) – Running Line (Deep Run) [2006/7 20mᵖᵘ Jun 11] poor maiden hurdler: pulled up all 4 starts in points in autumn: stays 2¾m: acts on firm going. *Noel C. Kelly, Ireland*
h—

CHARLENE (IRE) 6 b.m. King's Theatre (IRE) – Kayradja (IRE) (Last Tycoon) [2006/7 16s 16f⁵ 16mᶠ Nov 9] fair maiden on Flat: little form over hurdles. *Peter Casey, Ireland*
h65

CHARLES STREET 5 gr.g. Cois Na Tine (IRE) – Yemaail (IRE) (Shaadi (USA)) [2006/7 F16v F16d 16s 16s 20g⁵ Mar 27] half-brother to useful chaser Ross Comm, seems to stay 4m, and 2½m hurdle winner Shady Grey (both by Minster Son): dam unraced: little sign of ability. *C. Grant*
h—
F—

CHARLIE BAND 6 b.g. I'm Supposin (IRE) – Stubbs Daughter (Stubbs Gazette) [2006/7 F16d Dec 14] tall, quite good-topped gelding: seventh foal: dam fair/untrustworthy 2m chaser: last in bumper on debut. *C. A. Mulhall*
F—

CHARLIE BLUE 4 b.g. Shahrastani (USA) – Lady Blue (Puissance) [2006/7 F17d Feb 19] unfurnished gelding: first foal: dam well held on Flat: last in bumper on debut. *Mrs C. J. Ikin*
F—

CHARLIE GEORGE 6 ch.g. Idris (IRE) – Faithful Beauty (IRE) (Last Tycoon) [2006/7 h—: 20m c17m⁴ Aug 26] poor maiden on Flat (stays 9f): well held all starts over jumps: headstrong. *P. Monteith*
c—
h—

CHARLIES DOUBLE 8 b.g. Double Eclipse (IRE) – Pendil's Niece (Roscoe Blake) [2006/7 h100: 21g c16d⁵ c24pᵘ c16s⁴ c16sᵖᵘ Feb 9] sturdy, lengthy gelding: modest hurdler at best: no form since 2005, though out of depth most starts over fences: stays 3¼m: acts on good to firm and good to soft going: blinkered once. *J. R. Best*
c—
h—

CHARLIES FUTURE 9 b.g. Democratic (USA) – Faustelerie (Faustus (USA)) [2006/7 c110, h—: c23d* c25d⁶ c23v² c24sᵖᵘ c23v² Feb 25] tall gelding: fair handicap chaser: very fortunate to win at Exeter in October: ran well when second there twice after: should stay beyond 3m: acts on heavy going: often races prominently. *R. H. Alner*
c114
h—

CHARLIE STRONG (IRE) 14 b.g. Strong Gale – The Village Vixen (Buckskin (FR)) [2006/7 c21sᶠ Jun 27] strong gelding: fairly useful hunter chaser at one time: winning pointer, placed in 2006: should have stayed beyond 23f: acted on firm and soft going: dead. *J. A. T. de Giles*
c—

CHARLIE TANGO (IRE) 6 b.g. Desert Prince (IRE) – Precedence (IRE) (Polish Precedent (USA)) [2006/7 h93: 17m⁶ 17f* 17m 16dᵖᵘ 17mᵖᵘ Apr 9] quite good-topped gelding: modest hurdler: won selling handicap at Sedgefield in August: raced around 2m: acts on firm and soft going: blinkered/tongue tied final outing (lost action): inconsistent: sold 2,500 gns Doncaster May Sales. *D. W. Thompson*
h91

CHARLIE YARDBIRD 6 ch.g. Accordion – Reine Berengere (FR) (Esprit du Nord (USA)) [2006/7 F16s² F16g⁴ F16v* 20s 18s* 16v² 20s³ 16g2 20mᶠ Apr 28] €30,000 3-y-o: third foal: dam unraced half-sister to Grande Course de Haies d'Auteuil winner Le Roi Thibault: won bumper at Wexford in October: fairly useful hurdler: won 26-runner maiden at Leopardstown in December by 3 lengths from Deep Thinker: runner-up in
h117
F98

novices at Naas and Gowran, beaten ¾ length by Shanghide at latter: should stay 2½m: acts on heavy going: usually tongue tied over hurdles. *N. Meade, Ireland*

CHARLOTTE STREET (IRE) 5 b.g. Sassanian (USA) – Street Peddler (Boreen (FR)) [2006/7 F17d³ Nov 16] fourth foal: dam unraced half-sister to smart 2m/3m chaser Anabatic: 17 lengths third to Platin Grounds in maiden bumper at Hereford on debut, racing wide. *Carl Llewellyn*   **F74**

CHARLOTTE VALE 6 ch.m. Pivotal – Drying Grass Moon (Be My Chief (USA)) [2006/7 h104: 16s 16s² 16v³ 17s 16s² Apr 25] workmanlike mare: fair handicapper on Flat: likewise over hurdles: will stay beyond 17f: raced on going softer than good (acts on heavy): consistent. *Micky Hammond*   **h111**

CHARLTON KINGS (IRE) 9 b.g. King's Ride – Grove Gale (IRE) (Strong Gale) [2006/7 c–, h102: 22g⁵ 19sᵖᵘ c20m⁵ c16m² c17dᵘʳ c16m² c19d³ c20s³ c17d* c16s² Jan 6] strong, lengthy gelding: fair hurdler: at least as good over fences: made all in novice handicap at Ascot in December: stays 2¾m, effective at much shorter: acts on heavy and good to firm going. *R. J. Hodges*   **c111** **h99**

CHARMAHAL (IRE) 6 b.g. Charnwood Forest (IRE) – Final Contract (IRE) (Shaadi (USA)) [2006/7 F16d³ F16g⁴ 16g⁵ 16d⁶ 17g⁵ c16dᵖᵘ Dec 28] big gelding: sixth foal: brother to French 17f chase winner Maracaibo and half-brother to several winners, including modest 2m hurdler Tribal Princess (by Namaqualand): dam 9f winner: fair form in bumpers, won at Ballinrobe in May: left W. Lanigan and off 5 months, poor form over hurdles: mistakes and never dangerous on chasing debut. *Jonjo O'Neill*   **c–** **h79 +** **F91**

CHARMATIC (IRE) 6 br.m. Charnwood Forest (IRE) – Instamatic (Night Shift (USA)) [2006/7 h104: 16s³ 16s* 16v Nov 26] angular mare: fair hurdler: landed odds in mares novice at Uttoxeter in May: won on Flat nearly year later: raced around 2m on good going or softer (acts on soft): tongue tied once. *Andrew Turnell*   **h105**

CHARM INDEED 7 b.g. Charmer – House Deed (Presidium) [2006/7 h–, F–: 16s 16dᵖᵘ Mar 21] lengthy, angular gelding: no form in bumpers/over hurdles: tried tongue tied. *N. J. Henderson*   **h–**

CHARMING FELLOW (IRE) 7 b.g. Taipan (IRE) – Latest Tangle (Ragapan) [2006/7 h98p: 16d⁵ c20s⁶ c24d² c26g* Nov 15] tall, useful-looking gelding: modest form over hurdles: progressive in handicap chases, winning at Warwick by 5 lengths from Be Telling, well in control when blundering last: stays 3¼m: raced on good going or softer. *P. A. Blockley*   **c110 +** **h94 +**

CHARMING OSCAR (IRE) 5 b.g. Oscar Schindler (IRE) – Lady of The West (IRE) (Mister Lord (USA)) [2006/7 F16d F17s F16g³ F16m⁵ Apr 10] 22,800 (privately) 3-y-o: rangy gelding: has scope: second foal: half-brother to modest hurdler/chaser Wenceslas (by Un Desperado), stays 2½m: dam once-raced sister to useful staying chaser Lord of The West: seemingly best effort in bumpers when 4¾ lengths third to I'msingingtheblues in maiden at Wincanton, probably flattered. *R. H. Buckler*   **F81**

CHARMING ROGUE 5 gr.g. Robellino (USA) – Silver Charm (Dashing Blade) [2006/7 20vᵖᵘ 16vᵖᵘ Feb 22] sturdy gelding: little form on Flat at 3 yrs, sold out of S. Kirk's stable 11,000 gns Newmarket Autumn (2005) Sales: no show in novice hurdles. *M. Mullineaux*   **h–**

CHARM OFFENSIVE 9 b.m. Zieten (USA) – Shoag (USA) (Affirmed (USA)) [2006/7 c–, h66: 27dᵖᵘ Aug 15] poor hurdler: no show in 2 maiden chases: stays 27f: acts on firm and soft going: has worn cheekpieces/visor: tried tongue tied. *C. J. Gray*   **c–** **h–**

CHARNWOOD STREET (IRE) 8 b.g. Charnwood Forest (IRE) – La Vigie (King of Clubs) [2006/7 h–§: 16s 20sᵖᵘ Apr 28] close-coupled gelding: maiden hurdler: stays 3m: acts on soft and good to firm going: visored: ungenuine. *D. Shaw*   **h– §**

CHARTER ROYAL (FR) 12 gr.g. Royal Charter (FR) – Tadjmine (FR) (Tadj (FR)) [2006/7 c21dᵖᵘ Aug 28] compact gelding: maiden hurdler: winning chaser: no sign of retaining ability in 2006/7, including in point: blinkered once. *A. M. Crow*   **c– §** **h–**

CHASE THE SUNSET (IRE) 9 ch.g. Un Desperado (FR) – Cherry Chase (IRE) (Red Sunset) [2006/7 c108, h109: 21g May 4] useful-looking gelding: fair hurdler/maiden chaser: stays 3m: acts on firm and soft going: tried blinkered: often finds little: sold 13,000 gns Doncaster May (2006) Sales, resold 5,500 gns Doncaster August Sales. *Miss H. C. Knight*   **c–** **h–**

CHASING CARS (IRE) 5 b.g. Supreme Leader – Great Outlook (IRE) (Simply Great (FR)) [2006/7 F16v³ F16s³ F16mˢᵘ Apr 26] useful-looking gelding: third foal: dam   **F101**

unraced half-sister to fairly useful hurdler/winning chaser at 2¾m Whattabob: third in bumpers at Fairyhouse and Leopardstown, fairly useful form when beaten 6 lengths by Townabrack at latter: in touch when slipped up on home bend at Punchestown 4 months later. *Mrs J. Harrington, Ireland*

CHATEAU BURF 11 ch.g. Cruise Missile – Headstrong Miss (Le Bavard (FR)) c–
[2006/7 c33gᵖᵘ May 3] winning but ungenuine pointer: jumped poorly on chasing debut. *Mrs K. Smyly*

CHATEAU (IRE) 5 ch.g. Grand Lodge (USA) – Miniver (IRE) (Mujtahid (USA)) h–
[2006/7 F–: 17g⁴ 16s 19s 19d 16s Mar 7] strong, compact gelding: won 7f seller on Flat in 2006: sold out of G. A. Swinbank's stable 5,500 gns Doncaster October Sales: no solid form over hurdles: has had tongue tied, including last 3 starts. *M. E. Sowersby*

CHATEAU ROUGE (IRE) 6 b.g. Tiraaz (USA) – Carolina Rua (USA) (L'Emigrant h88
(USA)) [2006/7 h94, F94: 20s² 20sᵖᵘ 20vᵖᵘ Dec 26] leggy, quite good-topped gelding: fair form in bumpers: placed first 2 starts over hurdles 9 months apart, 6 lengths second to Lord Rosskit in novice at Wetherby on second occasion: ran poorly after: stays 2½m: acts on soft going. *Micky Hammond*

CHAUVINIST (IRE) 12 b.g. Roselier (FR) – Sacajawea (Tanfirion) [2006/7 c130, h–: c–
c20gᵖᵘ May 5] compact gelding: useful hurdler/chaser at best: distressed only outing in h–
2006/7: stayed 2½m: raced on good going or softer (acted on heavy): usually sweated/on toes: reportedly retired. *N. J. Henderson*

CHEATING CHANCE (IRE) 6 b.g. Oscar (IRE) – Clochban Clonroche (IRE) (The h–
Noble Player (USA)) [2006/7 20sᵖᵘ Nov 25] good-topped gelding: second foal: dam maiden half-sister to useful chaser up to 27f Glemot: won maiden Irish point in 2006: went as if amiss on hurdling debut. *N. G. Richards*

CHECKED SHIRT 4 b.g. Beat All (USA) – Nice 'n Easy (IRE) (Perugino (USA)) F–
[2006/7 F17m Apr 28] third foal: dam showed little on Flat: always behind in bumper on debut. *Mrs F. Kehoe*

CHECKERBOARD (IRE) 4 b.g. Alderbrook – Jamie's Lady (Ashmore (FR)) F95
[2006/7 F16g* Apr 7] €85,000 3-y-o: useful-looking gelding: half-brother to useful 2m hurdler Major Jamie (by Welsh Term) and fair chaser Red Man (by Toulon), stays 2¾m: dam won up to 1¾m on Flat: won steadily-run 17-runner bumper at Haydock on debut by 3½ lengths from Glenary. *J. Howard Johnson*

CHECK UP (IRE) 6 b.g. Frimaire – Melons Lady (IRE) (The Noble Player (USA)) h84
[2006/7 F13m F16g³ F16mᵖᵘ F17g² 21m⁴⁴ 22d 22s Dec 23] unfurnished gelding: second F84
foal: dam ran 3 times: improved form in bumpers when second to Keepitsecret at Hereford: best effort in maiden hurdles when fourth to Zonic Boom at Ludlow: stays 21f: acts on good to firm going: took fierce hold/hung badly right at Worcester third outing. *B. W. Duke*

CHEEKY LAD 7 b.g. Bering – Cheeky Charm (USA) (Nureyev (USA)) [2006/7 c–§, c106
h–§: c16mᵖᵘ c18m⁵ c17g⁵ c17g⁴ c16m⁴ 16m⁶ c16f* c17m* c16d* c16g c20sᶠ c19d⁶ h63 +
Nov 16] heavy-bodied gelding: winning pointer: left R. C. Harper, first form over hurdles when sixth in selling handicap at Worcester (very slowly away and ran in snatches): much improved over fences after, won handicaps at Worcester (2) and Stratford in August/September: best efforts around 2m: acts on firm and good to soft going: usually front runner: has his quirks. *M. Sheppard*

CHEEKY LADY (IRE) 10 b.m. Roselier (FR) – Railstown Cheeky (IRE) (Strong c126
Gale) [2006/7 20v⁵ c24v³ c24vᵖᵘ c24g³ c29mᶠ Apr 9] IR 7,500 4-y-o: sparely-made h104
mare: second foal: sister to fair hurdler/modest chaser Rosetown, stays 3¼m: dam unraced: winning pointer: fair handicap hurdler: fairly useful chaser: successful in mares maiden at Thurles, only outing in 2005/6: best effort when 2¾ lengths third of 24 to Cloudy Lane in Kim Muir Handicap Chase (Amateurs) at Cheltenham penultimate start: weakening when fell 3 out in Irish National at Fairyhouse: stayed 3m: acted on heavy and good to firm going: dead. *Colm A. Murphy, Ireland*

CHEEKY TRUCKER 6 ch.m. Atraf – Cheeky Monkey (USA) (Beau Genius (CAN)) h–
[2006/7 F17m F16g 17s Dec 23] first foal: dam 10.5f winner: no form in bumpers/maiden F–
hurdle. *R. T. Phillips*

CHEER US ON 5 b.g. Bahhare (USA) – Markapen (IRE) (Classic Music (USA)) h100
[2006/7 F98: F16f* F16g* 16s 17v³ 19d³ 21s⁵ 16g 16g Apr 16] fairly useful in bumpers, F100
winning at Ludlow and Worcester (by 1¼ lengths from Treasury Counsel) early in

season: fair novice hurdler: likely to prove best short of 21f: raced on good ground or softer over jumps (won bumper on firm). *M. W. Easterby*

CHEF DE CAMP (FR) 4 gr.g. Smadoun (FR) – Jolie Cheftaine (FR) (Chef de Clan II (FR)) [2006/7 F13g Nov 2] €8,000 2-y-o: second foal: dam won both starts up to around 1½m on Flat in France: last in bumper on debut: sixth in non-thoroughbred event on Flat for G. Macaire in April. *M. R. Hoad* — **F–**

CHEF TARTARE (FR) 7 b.g. Nikos – Rive Tartare (FR) (Riverquest (FR)) [2006/7 c93§, h–§: 20s^{pu} 21s 20v 20v^{pu} Feb 17] big, useful-looking gelding: fair chaser/maiden hurdler at best, never dangerous all 4 starts in 2006/7: stays 2½m: acts on heavy going: usually tongue tied: ungenuine. *Mrs K. Waldron* — **c– §** **h– §**

CHELSEA HARBOUR (IRE) 7 b.g. Old Vic – Jennyellen (IRE) (Phardante (FR)) [2006/7 h112, F82: 20s* c16s c16d c20s^F c20v⁴ c20v* c24v* c21v⁴ c24g^{ur} c29m Apr 9] workmanlike gelding: fair hurdler: easily won minor event at Punchestown in May: fairly useful novice chaser: won handicap and Grade 2 Woodlands Park 100 Club Novices' Chase at Naas in January, beating O'Muircheartaigh by 5½ lengths in latter: creditable efforts after in Grade 1 at Leopardstown (9¼ lengths fourth to Mister Top Notch) and Irish National at Fairyhouse (tenth of 29 to Butler's Cabin): stays 29f: acts on any going. *Thomas Mullins, Ireland* — **c129** **h112**

CHERINGTON 4 b.g. Dancing Spree (USA) – Watcha (USA) (Blushing Stage (USA)) [2006/7 aF16g F14g^{ur} Apr 10] first foal: dam, won in USA at 3 yrs, raced mainly around 1m: little show on completed outing in bumpers (well adrift when running off course and unseating home turn at Fontwell next time). *Andrew Turnell* — **F–**

CHERISHED NUMBER 8 b.g. King's Signet (USA) – Pretty Average (Skyliner) [2006/7 16d* 17d* 16m⁵ 16g⁵ 16d^{pu} Dec 27] rather leggy gelding: ran on Flat (stays 1¼m): ran to similar level first 3 starts over hurdles, winning novice at Fakenham in May and intermediate at Southwell in June: poor efforts in handicaps 5 months apart last 2 outings: likely to prove best around 2m: tried blinkered. *A. M. Hales* — **h106**

CHERNIK (IRE) 6 b.g. Norwich – Sue Pickering (IRE) (Tremblant) [2006/7 F16g⁵ F16g³ Apr 23] second foal: dam well beaten in bumper: fair form in bumpers, 17½ lengths third to Nodforms Paula in maiden at Hexham. *Micky Hammond* — **F90**

CHEROKEE INDIAN 6 b.g. Commanche Run – Adventurous Lady (Roman Warrior) [2006/7 F16m⁶ Sep 10] fourth foal: dam never ran: well held in bumper on debut. *D. G. Bridgwater* — **F–**

CHERRY PYE 5 gr.m. Environment Friend – Dayamen (Rudimentary (USA)) [2006/7 F17s F17d 17s 16s^{pu} Feb 22] lengthy mare: first foal: dam, ran twice over hurdles, out of half-sister to top-class staying hurdler/useful chaser Paddy's Return: no form in bumpers/maiden hurdles: tongue tied final outing. *J. Mackie* — **h–** **F–**

CHERRY'S ECHO 7 gr.m. Keen – Distant Cherry (General Ironside) [2006/7 F–: 17d 16f Jun 17] no show in bumper or over hurdles. *H. P. Hogarth* — **h–**

CHERUB (GER) 7 b.g. Winged Love (IRE) – Chalkidiki (GER) (Nebos (GER)) [2006/7 h135: c16f³ c16m* c16g³ c20g³ c18s⁶ Nov 25] compact gelding: useful hurdler: fair form over fences: won maiden at Towcester in October by neck from Charlton Kings: stays easy 2½m: acts on heavy and good to firm ground: blinkered last 4 starts: usually tongue tied prior to then: has worn crossed noseband. *Jonjo O'Neill* — **c112** **h–**

CHERY D'OR (FR) 6 b.g. Kizitca (FR) – Robe de Gala (FR) (Gairloch) [2006/7 19s³ 20d^{pu} 16s* 18s c16m⁶ Apr 14] ex-French gelding: first foal: dam won at 15f and 19f over fences in France: fairly useful chaser: won 6-runner event at Nimes in 2005/6 for J. Ortet and, switched back to fences, handicap at Chepstow (by 8 lengths from Syroco) in April: fair form over hurdles, successful in steadily-run novice at Wincanton in January by 1¼ lengths from Captain Marlon: best form at 2m: ran as if amiss second/fourth starts. *A. King* — **c117** **h110**

CHESNUT ANNIE (IRE) 6 ch.m. Weld – Leaden Sky (IRE) (Roselier (FR)) [2006/7 F–: F16f³ F17d³ 20m 24f⁴ 22g⁵ 24m^{ur} 27d⁵ c24g^{pu} Apr 27] winning pointer, including in February/April: placed twice from 3 starts in bumpers: poor form over hurdles: no show in hunter on chasing debut: should stay beyond 3m. *Miss H. E. Roberts* — **c–** **h68** **F75**

CHESS BOARD 4 b.c. Vettori (IRE) – Cruinn A Bhord (Inchinor) [2006/7 17m^{ur} 18g* 18m² 16g* Oct 19] dam, useful 7f winner, half-sister to high-class 1¼m/1½m performer Ouija Board and useful hurdler/fairly useful chaser up to 2¾m Spectrometer: easily best effort on Flat when winning 1½m handicap in June: sold out of Sir Mark Prescott's stable — **h117 +**

30,000 gns Newmarket July Sales: fairly useful form in juvenile hurdles: clear when jinking and unseating 2 out at Newton Abbot on debut: went on to win at Fontwell (by 23 lengths) in September and Ludlow (by 4 lengths from Capitalise) in October: stays 2¼m: raced on good/good to firm ground. *P. J. Hobbs*

CHESTNUT CHARLIE (IRE) 5 ch.g. Desert King (IRE) – Sea Wedding (Groom Dancer (USA)) [2006/7 F16v² F18v*dis F19v*dis Mar 18] fourth foal: half-brother to fairly useful 1m and (at 2 yrs) 9.4f winner Shakakhan (by Night Shift): dam, ran twice, closely related to St Leger second High And Low and smart stayer Corradini: useful form in bumpers: won at Downpatrick (by 26 lengths in maiden) in February and Limerick (beat Cailin Vic Mo Cri 5½ lengths) in March, but subsequently disqualified from both after being found to have run in flapping races under name of The Boxer: wore blinkers on debut. *Lindsay Woods, Ireland*
F108 +

CHEVALIER BAYARD (IRE) 14 br.g. Strong Gale – Flying Pegus (Beau Chapeau) [2006/7 c17gᵖᵘ c18g Jul 9] rangy gelding: modest handicap chaser at best: effective from 2m to 21f: acted on soft and good to firm going: usually wore headgear: dead. *J. R. Adam*
c–
h–

CHEVALIER ERRANT (IRE) 14 b. or br.g. Strong Gale – Luminous Run (Deep Run) [2006/7 c21dᵇᵈ c22g c20m⁴ c23m⁵ c24s⁴ c20g⁴ c27d³ c24d* Dec 10] tall, good sort: one-time fairly useful handicap chaser: left M. Todhunter and off 25 months prior to reappearance, trained first 5 starts by J. Adam: dropped long way in weights before gaining first success for 4½ years at Musselburgh in December, making most: stays 3m: acts on heavy and good to firm going. *B. Storey*
c90
h–

CHEVAUX LOCO (IRE) 8 br.g. Jolly Jake (NZ) – Kilbane Lass (IRE) (Strong Gale) [2006/7 c25d⁴ 17g 16g⁶ c19v⁵ c24s² c16s³ c24s² 21v⁶ c20s Feb 4] lightly-raced hurdler: modest maiden chaser: stays 3m, effective at much shorter: acts on soft and good to firm going: wore cheekpieces last 5 outings. *M. Hourigan, Ireland*
c99
h83

CHEVELEY FLYER 4 ch.g. Forzando – Cavern Breeze (Lion Cavern (USA)) [2006/7 16f⁵ 16m* 16g* 16d³ 17s 20s⁴ 16g 21g⁵ Apr 18] close-coupled gelding: modest maiden at best on Flat (stays 1m): fair juvenile hurdler: won at Ludlow (maiden) and Warwick in October: may prove best short of 2½m: signs of temperament. *J. Pearce*
h110

CHEVY TO THE LEVY (IRE) 5 b.g. Saddlers' Hall (IRE) – Be The One (IRE) (Supreme Leader) [2006/7 F16g² Mar 21] €20,000 4-y-o: third foal: half-brother to modest hurdler/fair chaser Be The Tops (by Topanoora), stays 3¼m: dam poor half-sister to fairly useful hurdler up to 2½m More of It: 10/1 from 9/2, short-head second to Hillridge in bumper at Chepstow on debut, finishing best: will be suited by further: sold £60,000 Cheltenham April Sales. *C. L. Tizzard*
F89

CHEZ BLEU 6 b. or br.g. Pistolet Bleu (IRE) – Tourbelaine (FR) (Cadoudal (FR)) [2006/7 F81: F16m May 6] third in Irish point on debut: best effort in bumpers when fifth at Newbury in 2005/6. *P. J. Hobbs*
F73

CHICAGO ALLEY 6 br.m. Bob Back (USA) – Winnetka Gal (IRE) (Phardante (FR)) [2006/7 F16s F17s⁴ F16d⁵ 19s⁶ 21v 16s⁵ 16g⁶ Mar 30] rangy mare: third foal: dam, lightly raced, showed some temperament: best effort in bumpers when fifth to Golden Child in falsely-run race at Ascot: poor form over hurdles. *D. J. Wintle*
h80
F83

CHICAGO BULLS (IRE) 9 b.g. Darshaan – Celestial Melody (USA) (The Minstrel (CAN)) [2006/7 c–, h119: 24s 24v⁴ 24s⁶ 24s⁴ c23m² Apr 22] compact gelding: fairly useful handicap hurdler at best, has deteriorated: modest form over fences (often let down by jumping), left A. King prior to final outing: stays 25f: best form on good ground or softer (acts on heavy): tried blinkered: has raced lazily. *Miss E. C. Lavelle*
c93
h111

CHICAGO JAZZ (IRE) 6 b. or br.g. Erins Isle – Just Jazzy (Prince Tenderfoot (USA)) [2006/7 F16d F13s 17s⁶ 19d Mar 26] €17,000 3-y-o, £12,000 4-y-o: lengthy gelding: brother to Sondheim, fair 2m winner on Flat/winning 3¼m hurdler: dam unraced: mid-field in slowly-run bumper on debut: no show after, over hurdles last 2 outings. *R. T. Phillips*
h–
F–

CHICAGO VIC (IRE) 8 b.m. Old Vic – Clearwater Glen (Furry Glen) [2006/7 16m* 23f² 16f³ 16m c16g² 20f³ c19v² c21s* c20v² c17v² c20d³ c20s³ Jan 23] fairly useful hurdler: won maiden event at Listowel in June: creditable efforts next 3 starts: similar standard as a chaser: won mares maiden at Fairyhouse in November: placed all other starts over fences in 2006/7, third to One Cool Cookie in Grade 2 novice at Limerick and Gazza's Girl in Grade 3 mares novice at Thurles last 2: stays 23f: acts on any going: wore cheekpieces last 6 starts: consistent. *Eric McNamara, Ireland*
c118
h124

CHICHEROVA (IRE) 4 b.f. Soviet Star (USA) – Ruby Rose (Red Ransom (USA)) **h–**
[2006/7 16f 16g^{pu} 17d Nov 23] sturdy filly: modest maiden on Flat (stays 1m), sold out of
T. D. Barron's stable 1,400 gns Doncaster August Sales: no form in juvenile hurdles:
tongue tied final outing: sold to join W. M. Brisbourne £1,200 Ascot December Sales.
R. Fielder

CHICKAPEAKRAY 6 b.m. Overbury (IRE) – Nevermind Hey (Teenoso (USA)) **c112**
[2006/7 h93: 24g 21m^6 20d* 24s* 20v^3 23v* 20v^5 20s^5 c20s* c22g^2 Apr 7] leggy, **h114**
close-coupled, smallish mare: fair handicap hurdler: won at Worcester and Uttoxeter in
October (both mares events) and Haydock (best effort when beating Clemax 8 lengths)
in December: similar form both outings over fences, winning mares novice at Carlisle (by
3 lengths from Cloudless Dawn) in February: stays 3m: best efforts on good ground or
softer (acts on heavy): tough. *D. McCain Jnr*

CHIDDINGFOLD CHICK 6 ch.m. Zaffaran (USA) – Cindie Girl (Orchestra) **F80**
[2006/7 F16g^4 F16g^4 Apr 9] half-sister to several winners, including fairly useful chaser
Dorans Gold (by Gildoran), stayed 3m, and fair hurdler Barton Dante (by Phardante),
stayed 21f: dam fairly useful hurdler who stayed 21f: fourth in bumpers at Wincanton
(better effort, 7¼ lengths behind I'msingingtheblues) and Fakenham. *P. Winkworth*

CHIEF CONFIDANT (IRE) 5 b.m. Oscar (IRE) – Royal Greenwood (IRE) (Radi- **h–**
cal) [2006/7 F16v 20s Mar 13] €8,500 3-y-o, 50,000 4-y-o: seventh foal: half-sister to **F–**
winning pointers by Roselier and Supreme Leader: dam, won bumper/point, half-sister to
useful chaser up to 3m Greenwood Lad: well beaten in mares bumper/novice hurdle.
J. Howard Johnson

CHIEF DAN GEORGE (IRE) 7 b.g. Lord Americo – Colleen Donn (Le Moss) **h144**
[2006/7 h106, F85: 22f^3 24s^3 22g^3 27m^4 17d^F 24v* 21v* 25s* 23s* 24g 24g*
Apr 13]
    Chief Dan George's name lives on, and not only through his books and
films. The native American, who died in 1981, is perhaps best known for his roles
in Little Big Man, for which he received an Oscar nomination, and The Outlaw
Josey Wales. Now Chief Dan George the horse is making the headlines, never more
so than on his final outing of 2006/7 when he sprang a surprise in the Citroen C6
Sefton Novices' Hurdle at Aintree. Chief Dan George, starting at 20/1, came late on
the scene to overhaul hot favourite Wichita Lineman and win by four lengths.
Given that midway through the season Chief Dan George was still a maiden after
seventeen outings, four of those in bumpers, it was remarkable that he should end
up as one of the season's leading novices, with five wins under his belt by then.
    The Aintree victory came almost two years after Chief Dan George had
made an inauspicious debut in an eighteen-runner bumper at Perth, where he beat
only one home. He did make the frame in bumpers on his next three starts, but the
form he showed was only modest, as it was during the early stages of his hurdling
career. A step up in distance brought about some improvement, with Chief Dan
George running one of his best races while still a maiden when fourth in a handicap
over three miles three furlongs at Stratford in June, after which he left David
MacLeod's stable upon the Scot's decision to end his own training operation and
join the all-powerful Flat team run by his compatriot Mark Johnston. Well held
when falling at the last over an inadequate trip at Sedgefield on his first appearance
for his current trainer, Chief Dan George was then returned to further and fitted
with cheekpieces, and his transformation began. He finally opened his account in a
maiden at Hexham in December and quickly followed up in a novice at Ayr, beating
the well-regarded Nicky Richards' inmate Double Default on both occasions, the
pair a distance clear each time. The winning run continued following a short break,
with Chief Dan George picking up Grade 2 events at Wetherby and Haydock in
February. Chief Dan George beat Fastaffaran a head in a muddling renewal of the
River Don Novices' Hurdle (sponsored by Brit Insurance), always prominent in a
steadily-run race and holding on determinedly after being sent on early in the
straight: on the second occasion, he had fifteen lengths to spare over Itsa Legend in
the Brit Insurance Prestige Novices' Hurdle, drawing well clear after two out. Chief
Dan George managed only a remote eighth behind Wichita Lineman in the Spa
Hurdle at Cheltenham, but, according to his trainer, there was a good reason for his
disappointing display, the horse having tweaked a muscle in his quarters when
kicking a plastic rail on the way to the start.

Citroen C6 Sefton Novices' Hurdle, Aintree—Wichita Lineman's exertions are beginning to tell and he's unable to hold off the staying-on Chief Dan George (left)

Four weeks later Chief Dan George took on Wichita Lineman again in the Sefton Novices', the latter odds on and the betting suggesting that Massini's Maguire and Silverburn, first and fourth respectively in the Baring Bingham Novices' at Cheltenham, were the only real threats to him. Chief Dan George's trainer was reported on the morning of the race as saying that if the gallop was strong he would ask Mick Fitzgerald, deputising for the injured Alan Dempsey, to drop Chief Dan George in a bit. Fitzgerald did just that, and those tactics played a major part in the race's outcome. It developed into a battle between old rivals Massini's Maguire and Wichita Lineman, with the pace stepping up considerably going out on the final circuit, the pair looking to be going too fast for their own good too far from home. Chief Dan George gradually pegged them back. A remote fourth three out, he moved into second when Massini's Maguire cracked approaching the last, still with a few lengths to make up on Wichita Lineman at that point. However, Wichita Lineman's exertions were also beginning to take their toll, and Chief Dan George, continuing to stay on strongly, collared him early on the run-in. Chief Dan George was flattered by the result, with Wichita Lineman the best horse in the race by some way, but the result has been taken at face value by the BHB's handicappers, and in the Anglo-Irish National Hunt Classifications, published after the end of the season, Chief Dan George is rated the leading staying novice. Whichever way the form is viewed, Chief Dan George confirmed himself a smart novice. He had done his stable proud yet again, being responsible for all but one of its six wins in 2006/7. James Moffatt, a former jockey who as a claimer won the 1995 County Hurdle on Home Counties, trained by his father Dudley, was quick to praise Dempsey for the part he had played in Chief Dan George's success, saying 'Chief Dan George was a swine of a horse when he arrived and his jumping was erratic, but Alan found the key to him and gave him confidence.' Missing Aintree was very tough on Dempsey who has suffered more than his share of misfortune in his career. Towards the end of 2004, he had eight plates inserted in his face after a fall at Ayr, and the latest season ended for him in March when his mount in a

198

handicap chase at Newcastle was brought down. He didn't need surgery this time, despite fracturing his skull and suffering facial injuries, including multiple fractures of the left eye socket and a broken cheekbone.'I must have a concrete head. I have got a few breaks but nothing that needs an operation,' said Dempsey, underlining the toughness and resilience of jump jockeys.

Chief Dan George (IRE) (b.g. 2000)	Lord Americo (b 1984)	Lord Gayle (b 1965)	Sir Gaylord
			Sticky Case
		Hynictus (b 1968)	Val de Loir
			Hypavia
	Colleen Donn (ch 1986)	Le Moss (ch 1975)	Le Levanstell
			Feemoss
		Rievaulx Abbey (ch 1974)	Double Jump
			Gold Pin

Chief Dan George, bought as a yearling for IR 17,000 guineas, is the seventh foal of the unraced Colleen Donn. Three of her earlier produce, all by Mandalus, were also successful. They were the fair hurdler/chaser at up to three miles Macnance, No Upside, a poor winner at twenty-one furlongs over fences in Ireland and, far and away the best of them, Macgeorge. Macgeorge was a smart staying chaser, one whose most important victory also came at Aintree's Grand National meeting, when springing a surprise in the 1999 Martell Cup. Colleen Donn's eighth foal, a full brother to Chief Dan George named Port of Mogan, won a maiden hurdle over two and three quarter miles at Stratford in October for Steve Brookshaw. Colleen Donn is a half-sister to the top-class hurdler Deep Idol who won the 1987 Irish Champion before finishing fourth to See You Then in the Champion Hurdle itself. Their dam Rievaulx Abbey didn't show much on the Flat but was a half-sister to several winners, including the useful Golden Jet who won the 1972 Aurelius Hurdle at Ascot. Chief Dan George's first two wins were gained on heavy going but, as he demonstrated at Aintree, he doesn't need the mud, with a distance of three miles and a strong gallop sufficient to bring out the best of him on good ground there. Kept to hurdling, the quite good-topped Chief Dan George could struggle to make an impact against the leading stayers, and there must be a chance he will be sent chasing in the next season, though he wasn't one of the more obvious chasing types on view at Cheltenham and Aintree. *James Moffatt*

CHIEF SCOUT 5 br.g. Tomba – Princess Zara (Reprimand) [2006/7 16v⁴ 16v³ 16s⁶ Jan 31] close-coupled, good-bodied gelding: fairly useful on Flat (stays 1¼m), successful twice in 2006 for I. Semple: modest form in novice hurdles: raced at 2m on soft/heavy going. *Mrs S. C. Bradburne*   **h96**

CHIEF YEOMAN 7 b.g. Machiavellian (USA) – Step Aloft (Shirley Heights) [2006/7 h137: 16d⁶ c16v² c19s² c16s* c16s* c21gᶠ c20g⁴ c16s² Apr 27] close-coupled gelding: useful handicap hurdler: several creditable efforts in good company despite no wins since juvenile campaign, including when sixth of 20 to Acambo in Ladbroke at Ascot on reappearance: fairly useful over fences: won maiden at Leicester (very simple task) and novice at Huntingdon (beat Garde Champetre by 3 lengths) in February: creditable efforts last 2 starts, in cheekpieces when 8 lengths second to Echo Point in novice at Perth: stays 2½m: acts on heavy and good to firm going: has made mistakes over fences. *Miss Venetia Williams*   **c127 h132**

CHIGORIN 6 b.g. Pivotal – Belle Vue (Petong) [2006/7 h81: 19vᵖᵘ 16v 16s⁶ 17d 24m Mar 31] leggy gelding: poor maiden hurdler: likely to prove best at 2m with emphasis on speed: tongue tied last 4 starts. *Miss S. J. Wilton*   **h66 +**

CHILLING PLACE (IRE) 8 ch.g. Moscow Society (USA) – Ethel's Dream (Relkino) [2006/7 c140, h–: c17dᵘʳ c19dᶠ c16g 19g 21g² 20f² Apr 28] lengthy gelding: useful hurdler: good efforts when runner-up in handicaps last 2 starts, made most when beaten 1¼ lengths by Oslot at Sandown final one: smart chaser (sometimes let down by jumping), running well 4 lengths behind winner Impek when baulked and rider unseated 4 out in William Hill Gold Cup (Handicap) at Exeter on reappearance: stays 21f: acts on soft and firm going: usually races prominently: genuine. *P. J. Hobbs*   **c145 h140**

CHILLY MILLY 6 b.m. Shambo – Phrase'n Cold (IRE) (Strong Statement (USA)) [2006/7 h86: 21d* 21vᵖᵘ 21sᶠ 21m² Jan 29] angular mare: modest hurdler: left V. Smith,   **h92**

won conditional jockeys handicap at Plumpton in October: should stay 3m: acts on good to firm and good to soft ground (no form on softer). *A. M. Hales*

CHIMICHURRI (FR) 5 ch.g. Nikos – Wackie (USA) (Spectacular Bid (USA)) [2006/7 F91: 16d 16s⁶ 21g Mar 23] lengthy gelding: some promise in bumper on debut: never dangerous 3 starts over hurdles: claimer ridden. *M. Bradstock*   **h74**

CHIP N RUN (IRE) 5 b.g. Cardinal Flower – Buckfast Lass (Buckskin (FR)) [2006/7 F16g F16d F16m Apr 21] €600 3-y-o: half-brother to stayers Mister Pickwick (hurdler, by Commanche Run) and Buckshot (chaser, by Le Moss): dam unraced: well beaten in bumpers: tried in cheekpieces/blinkers. *J. K. Magee, Ireland*   **F—**

CHIRAPATRE 5 b.m. Alflora (IRE) – Tenella's Last (Broadsword (USA)) [2006/7 20vᵖᵘ 24vᵖᵘ Jan 17] 5,500 4-y-o: second foal: dam winning pointer: showed nothing in 2 novice hurdles. *W. Amos*   **h—**

CHISEL 6 ch.g. Hector Protector (USA) – Not Before Time (IRE) (Polish Precedent (USA)) [2006/7 h–: 16vᵖᵘ 16s 21g 16g⁶ Mar 26] strong gelding: no form over hurdles: tried tongue tied. *M. Wigham*   **h—**

CHISOM 4 b.g. Averti (IRE) – Cinder Hills (Deploy) [2006/7 17dᵖᵘ Aug 15] lightly-raced maiden on Flat, sold out of M. Easterby's stable £1,300 Ascot July Sales: showed nothing in juvenile on hurdling debut. *Mrs L. J. Young*   **h—**

CHITA'S FLIGHT 7 gr.m. Busy Flight – Chita's Cone (Celtic Cone) [2006/7 c84?, h–: c20s* c21g² c21g⁶ Apr 27] maiden hurdler: winning pointer, including in 2007: successful also in novice hunter at Leicester in February: should stay beyond 2½m: acts on soft going: tried tongue tied. *R. M. Treloggen*   **c93** **h—**

CHIVALRY 8 b.g. Mark of Esteem (IRE) – Gai Bulga (Kris) [2006/7 20g Nov 19] lengthy, well-made gelding: useful hurdler at best: left J. Howard Johnson and off 19 months, eighth of 20 to Accordello in handicap at Aintree, leading 3 out only to tire from next: last in novice at same course only outing over fences: probably best around 2m: raced on good going or softer: often blinkered for former stable: not a fluent jumper: signs of temperament. *Miss Venetia Williams*   **c—** **h124**

CHOCKDEE (FR) 7 b.g. King's Theatre (IRE) – Chagrin d'Amour (IRE) (Last Tycoon) [2006/7 c103+, h118§: c16gᵘʳ 20f⁵ 16m⁵ 24m* c21m⁵ Jul 17] useful-looking gelding: fair hurdler: won claimer at Southwell (claimed from P. Nicholls £10,000) in July: third in maiden at Taunton, better completed effort over fences: stays 3m: probably acts on any going: tongue tied last 3 starts: weak finisher. *M. J. McGrath*   **c— §** **h113 §**

CHOCOLATE BOY (IRE) 8 b.g. Dolphin Street (FR) – Kawther (Tap On Wood) [2006/7 h91: 20g⁶ Sep 3] leggy gelding: modest on Flat (stays easy 2m): fourth in maiden at Cheltenham, only form in 3 starts over hurdles. *G. L. Moore*   **h—**

CHOMBA WOMBA (IRE) 6 b.m. Fourstars Allstar (USA) – Miss Muppet (IRE) (Supreme Leader) [2006/7 F95: F16g⁸ F16g⁶ 16g F16v³ 19d⁴ 18v* 20v⁴ 20v² 16v* 20m³ Apr 8] leggy mare: successful twice from 7 starts in bumpers, including at Gowran very early in season: fairly useful over hurdles: won maiden at Limerick in December and mares novices at Cork in January and Limerick (beat Candy Girl a length in listed event) in March: good 2½ lengths third to Grangeclare Lark in Grade 3 mares novice at Fairyhouse: effective at 2m given testing conditions, and will stay beyond 2½m: acts on heavy and good to firm going: tough and consistent: sold £160,000 Cheltenham April Sales. *Ms M. Mullins, Ireland*   **h128** **F98**

CHOOKIE WINDSOR 4 b.g. Lake Coniston (IRE) – Lady of Windsor (IRE) (Woods of Windsor (USA)) [2006/7 17gᵖᵘ 16mᵖᵘ Sep 2] modest on Flat (stays 1¼m): no show in juvenile hurdles: visored second outing (showed temperament on debut): sold £1,200 Ascot October Sales. *R. M. Stronge*   **h—**

CHOPNEYEV (FR) 9 b.g. Goldneyev (USA) – Pierre de Soleil (FR) (Jefferson) [2006/7 c94, h–: c24dᵖᵘ c25s* c24s² c23v³ c24vᵛ c22v⁴ Feb 22] close-coupled gelding: useful hurdler in 2002/3, subsequently off 3 years: fair chaser: won handicap at Hereford (by 27 lengths) in December and novice at Huntingdon in January: stays 3¼m: acts well on soft/heavy going: blinkered last 6 outings: usually races prominently nowadays. *R. T. Phillips*   **c103** **h—**

CHORIZO (IRE) 6 b.g. Kahyasi – Bayariyka (IRE) (Slip Anchor) [2006/7 F97: 22d 19v⁴ 22g⁶ Mar 19] runner-up both starts in bumpers: modest form in novice hurdles: will stay 3m: sold 20,000 gns Doncaster May Sales. *P. F. Nicholls*   **h97**

CHOSEN (IRE) 7 b.m. Glacial Storm (USA) – Liddy's Choice (IRE) (Buckskin (FR)) [2006/7 F16m* Jun 11] £1,200 4-y-o, £2,100 5-y-o: second foal: dam unraced half-sister   **F85 +**

to 2 winning 3m chasers: successful twice in points in 2006: also won maiden at Stratford on bumper debut by 12 lengths from Musique En Tete, making all virtually unchallenged. *R. H. York*

CHOUMAKEUR (FR) 5 ch.g. Mansonnien (FR) – Feuille de Chou (FR) (Faucon Noir (FR)) [2006/7 F18v* F16g Mar 14] €80,000 4-y-o: rather leggy gelding: second foal: half-brother to 2m hurdle winner Valanchou (by Valanjou): dam, 1¼m winner in France, half-sister to useful hurdler/fairly useful gelding Garde Champetre, stays 3m: favourite, won maiden bumper at Plumpton on debut easily by 8 lengths from Quintessentially: always towards rear in Grade 1 at Cheltenham following month. *D. E. Pipe* **F99**

CHOUXDAMOUR (FR) 4 ch.g. Murmure (FR) – Choucouli (FR) (Homme Fathal (FR)) [2006/7 F12g Mar 23] rather leggy gelding: second foal: dam unraced half-sister to useful hurdler/fairly useful chaser Garde Champetre, stays 3m: well held in bumper on debut. *N. J. Henderson* **F—**

CHRISTDALO (IRE) 7 ch.m. Glacial Storm (USA) – Benbradagh Vard (IRE) (Le Bavard (FR)) [2006/7 25gpu 24s* 24s⁴ 26s³ 23s⁶ 22v* 24g² 21g² Apr 19] leggy mare: third foal: dam in frame both starts in Irish bumpers: won 3 of 5 starts in points prior to winning mares point-to-point bumper at Tipperary for J. Brassil in early-2005/6: useful novice hurdler: landed odds at Chepstow (maiden) in December and Folkestone (very simple task) in February: further improvement when second in handicaps last 2 starts, beaten 6 lengths by Silver Charmer in listed mares event at Cheltenham final one: stays 3m: raced on good ground or softer (acts on heavy): has carried head awkwardly. *D. E. Pipe* **h130**

CHRISTON CANE 9 b.g. El Conquistador – Dancing Barefoot (Scallywag) [2006/7 h—: 26v c26vpu Feb 12] lightly raced: no form in novice hurdles/chase. *Dr J. R. J. Naylor* **c—
h—**

CHRISTOPHER 10 gr.g. Arzanni – Forest Nymph (NZ) (Oak Ridge (FR)) [2006/7 c120, h—: c20g² May 5] close-coupled gelding: fairly useful handicap hurdler/chaser: probably stays 3m: acts on any going: went wrong way temperamentally in points in 2007. *P. J. Hobbs* **c120
h—**

CHRISTY BEAMISH (IRE) 10 b. or br.g. Jolly Jake (NZ) – Ballinatona Bridge (Black Minstrel) [2006/7 c127: c28sF c26gpu Mar 16] workmanlike gelding: smart hunter chaser, second in Fox Hunters' at Aintree in 2006: off 10 months, never a factor in Foxhunter at Cheltenham: possibly best short of 3m when conditions are testing. *P. Jones* **c—**

CHRYSAOR (FR) 5 ch.g. Bachir (USA) – Daroura (USA) (Forli (ARG)) [2006/7 F17g⁶ F17s Oct 25] half-brother to 3 winners on Flat, including French 15f Daryapour (by Kahyasi) winner: dam unraced: well beaten in bumpers. *Mrs S. J. Smith* **F—**

CHUKCHI COUNTRY (IRE) 9 b.g. Arctic Lord – Ann's Queen (IRE) (Rhoman Rule (USA)) [2006/7 19dpu 16s 18spu 16s⁵ c20vpu c16g* Apr 23] workmanlike gelding: maiden hurdler: modest handicap chaser: first form in 2006/7 when winning at Sedgefield after 3½-month absence, clear most of way: stays easy 3m, effective over much shorter: probably acts on any going: often blinkered: tried tongue tied. *J. J. Lambe, Ireland* **c87
h—**

CHUNKY LAD 7 ch.g. Karinga Bay – Madam's Choice (New Member) [2006/7 h83, F79: 16f Jun 21] poor form over hurdles: bred to stay at least 2½m, but pulls hard: ran out once. *W. G. M. Turner* **h81**

CHURCHILL FLYER 9 b. or br.g. Sulaafah (USA) – Sally's Song (True Song) [2006/7 c25gur May 3] won maiden point in 2006, only completed start over jumps. *Mrs S. Greathead* **c—**

CHURCH ISLAND (IRE) 8 ch.g. Erins Isle – Just Possible (Kalaglow) [2006/7 c134, h—: c25s c25s 24v 19s c28s c29m⁴ Apr 9] tall, good-bodied gelding: winning hurdler, well held in handicap third start: useful chaser: back to best when fourth of 29 to Butler's Cabin in Irish National at Fairyhouse: stays 29f: acts on any going. *M. Hourigan, Ireland* **c136
h—**

CIARANS LASS 8 b.m. Factual (USA) – Tradespark (Vital Season) [2006/7 h—, F—: 24spu May 14] no sign of ability. *C. Roberts* **h—
F—**

CILLA BLACK 5 br.m. Overbury (IRE) – Camillas Legacy (Newski (USA)) [2006/7 F17v Jan 8] second foal: dam, poor maiden hurdler/chaser, out of half-sister to Cheltenham Gold Cup runner-up Dubacilla: tailed off in bumper on debut. *Miss Sarah Inglis* **F—**

CINDERS OF ERIN 5 b.m. Midnight Legend – Derry Blue (Derrylin) [2006/7 F16d⁶ Mar 22] first foal: dam, runner-up in point, showed little otherwise: well held in bumper on debut. *C. Roberts* **F—**

CINEMA (FR) 7 b.m. Bering – Laquifan (USA) (Lear Fan (USA)) [2006/7 h106d: **h96**
16s* 16f⁶ 18s Oct 21] sturdy mare: modest hurdler: won mares intermediate event at
Perth in May: stays 2½m: acts on heavy going. *B. R. Hamilton, Ireland*

CINNAMON GIRL 4 ch.f. Erhaab – Distant Cheers (USA) (Distant View **F—**
(USA)) [2006/7 aF16g Mar 9] £550 3-y-o: first foal: dam 1m winner: soundly beaten in
bumper/maiden on Flat. *A. M. Hales*

CINNAMON LINE 11 ch.g. Derrylin – Cinnamon Run (Deep Run) [2006/7 c102x, **c105**
h–: c22g⁴ c24s⁶ c24v* c26v* c29s⁴ Mar 11] tall, good sort: fair handicap chaser: won at **h—**
Uttoxeter in December and Warwick in January: stayed 3¼m: raced on good going or
softer (acted on heavy): dead. *R. Lee*

CIONN MHALANNA (IRE) 9 b.g. Corrouge (USA) – Pennyland (Le Bavard (FR)) **c—**
[2006/7 c25dᵖᵘ c24vᵘʳ c23v⁴ c25sᵘʳ c27m Apr 9] strong gelding: modest chaser at best: **h—**
off 21 months, no form in 2006/7: stays 25f: acts on good ground: has worn cheekpieces/
blinkers: sold 1,100 gns Doncaster May Sales. *P. Beaumont*

CIRCASSIAN (IRE) 6 b.g. Groom Dancer (USA) – Daraliya (IRE) (Kahyasi) [2006/7 **h125**
h123: 18f² 16s⁴ 20sᵖᵘ 20v⁵ 16v⁵ 18g² Apr 15] leggy gelding: fairly useful hurdler: best
efforts in handicaps in 2006/7 on second/final starts, second to Saif Sareea at Kelso on
latter: should be suited by 2½m+: winner on soft ground, best efforts under less testing
conditions: not a fluent jumper. *J. Howard Johnson*

CIRCUMSPECT (IRE) 5 b.g. Spectrum (IRE) – Newala (Royal Academy (USA)) **h—**
[2006/7 h96: 16m 17g Jul 9] lengthy gelding: modest form at best over hurdles, well
beaten both starts in 2006/7: sold 6,500 gns Doncaster October Sales. *P. C. Haslam*

CIRCUS ROSE 5 ch.m. Most Welcome – Rosie Cone (Celtic Cone) [2006/7 F73+: **h74**
16d⁶ 16s⁴ 16s 16g Mar 29] plain mare: poor form over hurdles: raced at 2m. *Mrs P. Sly*

CIRRIOUS 6 gr.m. Cloudings (IRE) – Westfield Mist (Scallywag) [2006/7 h96+: 17g⁴ **h101**
May 4] lightly raced over hurdles, won mares maiden in April 2006: better form only
subsequent outing: raced around 2m. *P. J. Hobbs*

CISTERCIAN (IRE) 8 b.m. Anshan – Monks Lass (IRE) (Monksfield) [2006/7 18gᶠ **h—**
16m 21mᵖᵘ Oct 12] fifth in bumper on debut: fell in mares point in Ireland: well held
completed start in novice hurdles (lame next time). *Miss H. C. Knight*

CITY AFFAIR 6 b.g. Inchinor – Aldevonie (Green Desert (USA)) [2006/7 h71§: 19mᶠ **h86 §**
16g⁴ 19g⁵ 19vᵖᵘ 19g² 20g³ 20m³ Apr 25] well-made gelding: modest maiden hurdler:
left C. Down after reappearance, sold out of J. O'Shea's stable £1,500 Ascot December
Sales after third start: stays 2½m: acts on soft and good to firm going: tried visored/in
cheekpieces: has been mulish at start. *P. S. Payne*

CITY BREEZE (IRE) 6 b.g. City Honours (USA) – Orchard Lass (On Your Mark) **h79**
[2006/7 F16d⁴ F17s³ 19s 19g Apr 8] rather unfurnished gelding: half-brother to 2m **F80**
hurdle winner Insan Magic (by Insan) and bumper winners That's Magic (by Lord
Americo) and Lady Toulon (by Toulon): dam unraced half-sister to smart staying hurdler
Kristenson: modest form in frame in bumpers: little impact in 2 starts over hurdles 4
months apart, trained first one by A. King. *J. A. T. de Giles*

CITY GENERAL (IRE) 6 ch.g. General Monash (USA) – Astra (IRE) (Glenstal **h—**
(USA)) [2006/7 h–: 16m 18g⁵ 22d 19d 19g Nov 9] no form over hurdles. *B. Scriven*

CITY MUSIC (IRE) 6 b.g. City Honours (USA) – Rahanine Melody (IRE) (Orches- **h91**
tra) [2006/7 F73: F16m³ 21mᵖᵘ 24f* 20s⁵ 27s Dec 5] strong gelding: third at Worcester **F76**
on second start in bumpers: modest novice hurdler: upped further in trip, won at Hexham
in September: stays 3m: acts on firm and soft going. *Mrs S. J. Smith*

CITY OF MANCHESTER (IRE) 5 b.g. Desert Style (IRE) – Nomadic Dancer **h98**
(IRE) (Nabeel Dancer (USA)) [2006/7 h86, F–: 16sᵖᵘ 19m⁵ 17m⁵ 16d² 16m⁶ 17v* 16v²
16d⁵ 16dᵖᵘ 20vᵖᵘ 16s⁴ 16v⁶ 16s 16g³ 16m Apr 24] strong, compact gelding: modest
hurdler: won seller at Hereford (sold from B. Leavy 8,000 gns) in November: raced
mainly around 2m: acts on heavy and good to firm ground: tried visored/in cheekpieces:
inconsistent. *M. A. Allen*

CITY PALACE 6 ch.g. Grand Lodge (USA) – Ajuga (USA) (The Minstrel (CAN)) **h—**
[2006/7 h83: 16gᵖᵘ 16f Jun 21] sturdy gelding: maiden hurdler, no show in sellers in
2006/7: tried in cheekpieces/tongue tied. *Evan Williams*

CITY STREETS 5 b.g. Overbury (IRE) – Snowdon Lily (Town And Country) [2006/7 **c— p**
19s* 20gᵖᵘ c16mᵖᵘ Mar 29] 20,000 3-y-o: second foal: dam, poor handicap chaser, stayed **h104**
3¼m: 10/1 from 20/1, won novice hurdle at Taunton in December on debut readily by 4

lengths from Just Supposin: situation soon accepted after mistakes both starts after, including on chasing debut: bred to be suited by 2½m+: remains open to improvement. *Jonjo O'Neill*

CIVIL GENT (IRE) 8 ch.g. Flying Spur (AUS) – Calamity Kate (IRE) (Fairy King (USA)) [2006/7 c–, h–: c20m³ c20m⁴ c20f* c25s⁵ c22g⁴ c22g* c25m³ c25d⁶ c22g³ c24mᵖᵘ c22v⁵ Oct 1] compact gelding: poor chaser: won handicaps at Hexham in June and Market Rasen in July: stays easy 25f: acts on firm going, probably on soft: in cheekpieces/blinkers last 3 starts: tongue tied. *M. E. Sowersby*   **c79 h–**

CLAIM TO FAME 6 b.g. Selkirk (USA) – Loving Claim (USA) (Hansel (USA)) [2006/7 h–: c21gᵖᵘ May 24] well-made gelding: third in point in 2006, has shown little otherwise. *Ms Grace Muir*   **c– h–**

CLANDE BOYE (IRE) 6 b.g. Lord Americo – Over The Sands (IRE) (Over The River (FR)) [2006/7 F16s 20gᶠ Apr 27] €15,000 4-y-o: first foal: dam, winning Irish pointer, sister to useful chaser up to 3m Over The Furze: pulled up in maiden Irish point in 2006: bought 2,500 gns Doncaster May Sales: no show in bumper/novice hurdle. *S. J. Gilmore*   **h– F–**

CLAN ROYAL (FR) 12 b.g. Chef de Clan II (FR) – Allee du Roy (FR) (Rex Magna (FR)) [2006/7 c146, h113: 20s⁶ c26gᶠ c24dᵖᵘ c36g Apr 14] tall gelding: winning hurdler: smart handicap chaser: won Topham Chase and Becher Chase at Aintree in 2003, and did nearly all his racing over fences after over National course, placed in Grand National in 2004 and 2006, and clear when carried out by loose horse year in between: retired after down the field in 2007 renewal: stayed 4½m: acted on heavy and good to firm going: took good hold, and was held up: sometimes swished tail under pressure but was game. *Jonjo O'Neill*   **c– h–**

CLANRYE (IRE) 6 b. or br.g. Insan (USA) – Lake Majestic (IRE) (Mister Majestic) [2006/7 h–: 24sᵖᵘ 18s Jan 4] won maiden on last of 5 starts in Irish points in 2005: no form over hurdles (bled final outing). *P. G. Murphy*   **h–**

CLARNAZAR (IRE) 5 b.g. Shernazar – Legal Countess (IRE) (Legal Circles (USA)) [2006/7 F18v* 22d* Dec 26] first foal: dam little form in juvenile hurdles: won maiden on completed start in Irish points in 2006: successful also in maiden bumper at Downpatrick (by 6 lengths from So Many Questions) and maiden hurdle at Limerick (beat Callherwhatulike ½ length despite saddle slipping long way out), both in December: promising. *N. Meade, Ireland*   **h132 F101**

CLASSIC ACT 5 b.g. Classic Cliche (IRE) – Katoski (Petoski) [2006/7 F16v F17s⁶ Feb 19] €6,000 4-y-o: first foal: dam unraced out of half-sister to smart hurdler/useful chaser up to 3m Forest Sun: little show in 2 bumpers. *T. Butt*   **F–**

CLASSICAL LOVE 7 b.m. Classic Cliche (IRE) – Hard Love (Rambo Dancer (CAN)) [2006/7 h78: 22sᵖᵘ Nov 17] poor maiden hurdler: stays 2¾m: acts on soft going: has worn cheekpieces/visor. *Jane Southcombe*   **h–**

CLASSIC CALVADOS (FR) 8 b.g. Thatching – Mountain Stage (IRE) (Pennine Walk) [2006/7 c–, h88: 17d² 16m 16s 16g c20m³ c20gᵖᵘ c20dᵖᵘ 17m Apr 9] strong gelding: maiden hurdler/chaser, only poor form in 2006/7: stays 2½m: acts on good to firm and good to soft going: tried in cheekpieces/blinkers: tongue tied. *Mrs S. A. Watt*   **c68 h76**

CLASSIC CAPERS 8 ch.g. Classic Cliche (IRE) – Jobiska (Dunbeath (USA)) [2006/7 c128?, h–: c20g⁶ c20d c20g⁶ c22s² c22v² c25d* c30s² c20v³ c32mᵘʳ c24s Apr 26] tall, good-topped gelding: useful handicap chaser: back to best in winter, winning at Catterick in December and placed there and at Newcastle next 2 outings: effective at testing 2½m to 3¾m: raced largely on good going or softer (acts on heavy): blinkered on reappearance, wore cheekpieces last 3 starts: often takes plenty of driving. *J. M. Jefferson*   **c130 h–**

CLASSIC CLOVER 7 ch.g. Classic Cliche (IRE) – National Clover (National Trust) [2006/7 h68: c23s⁵ c25s⁶ c23sᶠ Dec 29] well-made gelding: little form over hurdles/fences: visored final outing. *C. L. Tizzard*   **c– h–**

CLASSIC CROCO (GER) 6 gr.g. Croco Rouge (IRE) – Classic Light (IRE) (Classic Secret (USA)) [2006/7 h93: 16f* 18g³ 16g⁵ 16d* 16g³ 16d³ 16g³ 18s 16d 16m 16g Apr 14] workmanlike gelding: fair hurdler: won novice claimer at Worcester (claimed from P. Nicholls £10,000) in June and novice at Wexford in August: best effort when third to Bogus Dreams in handicap at Musselburgh seventh outing: best form at 2m: acts on firm and good to soft ground: usually wears cheekpieces (blinkers final outing): tongue tied last 3 starts: often races prominently. *T. Hogan, Ireland*   **h115**

Mrs E. Roberts' "Classic Fiddle"

CLASSIC DREAM (GER) 4 b.g. Grape Tree Road – Classic Queen (GER) (Greinton) [2006/7 17g² 16v* 16d³ 16m 17m* Mar 29] successful twice up to around 1¼m on Flat in Germany in 2006, left P. Schiergen after final start in May: fairly useful juvenile hurdler: won at Plumpton in December and Hereford (beat Mister Benedictine by 3½ lengths) in March: best effort when third to Altilhar at Ludlow: successful on heavy going, but likely to prove best around 2m with emphasis more on speed: front runner. *B. G. Powell*   **h118 +**

CLASSIC EVENT (IRE) 6 ch.g. Croco Rouge (IRE) – Delta Town (USA) (Sanglamore (USA)) [2006/7 h–: 17d⁵ 17s³ 19d 16d* 16g⁴ c20d⁵ c16v³ c16d⁴ Dec 28] well-made gelding: fair handicap hurdler: won at Kelso in October: modest form over fences: stays 19f: acts on heavy and good to firm going. *T. D. Easterby*   **c94 h108**

CLASSIC FAIR 6 b.m. Classic Cliche (IRE) – Bay Fair (Arctic Lord) [2006/7 F16m 21v⁴ 24s* 24vᵖᵘ Feb 18] rangy mare: first foal: dam, modest hurdler/chaser, stayed 3¼m: well held in bumper: modest form over hurdles, winning mares maiden at Taunton in December: ran poorly on handicap debut: will prove best at 3m+: acts on soft going: tongue tied last 2 outings. *A. J. Honeyball*   **h89 F—**

CLASSIC FIDDLE 5 ch.m. Classic Cliche (IRE) – Fiddling The Facts (IRE) (Orchestra) [2006/7 F112: 20v* 20d² 17v* Mar 4] useful bumper winner: made good start over hurdles, landing odds in novices at Hereford in January and Bangor (didn't need to come off bridle to beat Gunnasayso 23 lengths in 5-runner mares event) in March: second to Gaspara at Chepstow in between: will stay beyond 2½m: acts on heavy going: remains capable of better. *N. J. Henderson*   **h125 p**

CLASSIC GOLD (GER) 6 br.g. Gold And Ivory (USA) – Classic Woman (IRE) (Classic Secret (USA)) [2006/7 16d 16dᵖᵘ 16vᵖᵘ Mar 3] useful-looking gelding: successful 4 times on Flat (stays 1¼m) in Germany in 2005, sold out of W. Giedt's stable 42,000 gns Newmarket Autumn (2005) Sales: no form in 3 novice hurdles: tongue tied final outing. *B. De Haan*   **h– p**

CLASSIC HARRY 6 b.g. Classic Cliche (IRE) – Always Shining (Tug of War) **h–**
[2006/7 F91: 20s^{pu} 21s⁶ 20s 20s^{pu} 20s^{pu} Apr 25] big, strong gelding: chasing type: placed 3 of 4 starts in bumpers: no solid form over hurdles (has had breathing problems): bred to stay well: tried in cheekpieces. *P. Beaumont*

CLASSIC LASH (IRE) 11 b.g. Classic Cheer (IRE) – Khaiylasha (IRE) (Kahyasi) **c–**
[2006/7 c76, h71: c20g⁶ c21d 20s^{pu} Jun 25] winning hurdler/chaser, no longer of much **h–**
account: tried blinkered/in cheekpieces. *P. Needham*

CLASSIC QUART (IRE) 6 b.m. Classic Cliche (IRE) – Ganpati (IRE) (Over The **h89 +**
River (FR)) [2006/7 h82p: 16d³ 16d^F Nov 8] leggy mare: bumper winner: modest form in novice hurdles: in narrow lead when falling 2 out at Lingfield: should be suited by further than 2m. *M. Scudamore*

CLASSIC RARITY 5 b.g. Classic Cliche (IRE) – Gently Ridden (IRE) (King's Ride) **F–**
[2006/7 F–: F17d⁵ F16m Apr 15] well held in bumpers, left R. Baker and off 11 months before final start. *K. Bishop*

CLASSIC ROCK 8 b.g. Classic Cliche (IRE) – Ruby Vision (IRE) (Vision (USA)) **c97**
[2006/7 c93, h69: c23m* c23m^{pu} 20d* 20s c20m c24m³ c23m² c23m² Apr 25] leggy, **h77**
lengthy gelding: poor hurdler: won 20-runner handicap at Uttoxeter in November: better over fences, won novice handicap at Worcester in May: ran well when placed last 3 starts: stays 3m: acts on good to firm and good to soft going: reportedly had fibrillating heart second outing. *J. W. Unett*

CLASSIC ROLE 8 b.g. Tragic Role (USA) – Clare Island (Connaught) [2006/7 h113: **h101**
17v 16d 16d³ 16f⁶ 16m⁵ 16g⁴ Nov 23] leggy gelding: fair hurdler: not at best in 2006/7, but did win maiden at Plumpton by 3½ lengths from Count Kristo, tending to idle: raced around 2m: acts on soft going, probably on firm: blinkered once, in cheekpieces/visor last 4 starts. *L. Wells*

CLASSIC ROSE (IRE) 8 gr.g. Roselier (FR) – Carrigkem (IRE) (Kemal (FR)) **h–**
[2006/7 22g^{pu} 24s 23v^{ur} 26v^{pu} Jan 11] fourth foal: dam, fair hurdler, stayed 2½m, half-sister to useful hurdler/fairly useful chaser Yellow Spring, stayed 21f: no form in Irish points/over hurdles: wore headgear last 3 starts. *Mrs L. Williamson*

CLASSIFIED (IRE) 11 b.g. Roselier (FR) – Treidlia (Mandalus) [2006/7 h142: 23f^{ur} **c135**
c23s* c22s* c22v^F c20v^{pu} c24g² c25g* Apr 18] rather leggy, quite good-topped gelding: **h–**
very smart hurdler in 2002/3, subsequently off 3 years: useful novice chaser: won at Taunton (maiden) and Fontwell in December and Cheltenham in April: best effort when beating Ballyfoy a neck in 5-runner event at last-named, idling markedly: stays 25f: acts on soft going (won bumper on heavy): in cheekpieces last 2 starts. *D. E. Pipe*

CLASSI MAUREEN 7 ch.m. Among Men (USA) – Hi-Hannah (Red Sunset) [2006/7 **c84**
c81, h–: c20m* c20m⁴ c20m⁴ 24d^{pu} Nov 20] no form over hurdles: fairly useful pointer, success- **h–**
ful 5 times in 2006: took advantage of lowly mark in novice handicap chase at Plumpton in September, winning unchallenged: well beaten in similar event 4 days later: barely stays 3m: acts on good to firm going: front runner. *Evan Williams*

CLASS KING (USA) 6 b.g. Royal Academy (USA) – Krissante (USA) (Kris) [2006/7 **h84**
17s 17s^F 18s⁵ 18s 17d⁵ 17g⁴ 17s^F 16d Nov 11] modest 9.5f winner on Flat: poor form over hurdles: tongue tied, last in seller at Uttoxeter final outing. *Mrs Savinja Braem, Belgium*

CLASSY CHAV (IRE) 5 b.g. Classic Cliche (IRE) – Gavotte du Cochet (FR) (Urbain **h82**
Minotiere (FR)) [2006/7 F82: F16d⁵ 17v 16v⁵ 16v³ 16v⁴ 18s Feb 15] modest form in **F82**
bumpers: poor form over hurdles: will be well suited by 2½m+: raced on ground softer than good. *P. Monteith*

CLAUDIA MAY 6 gr.m. Cloudings (IRE) – Princess Maxine (IRE) (Horage) [2006/7 **h–**
h–, F–: 17m Aug 29] no sign of ability. *Miss Lucinda V. Russell*

CLAY HOLLISTER 4 ch.g. Monsun (GER) – Polish Palace (IRE) (Polish Precedent **F97**
(USA)) [2006/7 F14s* F16v Feb 24] small, plain gelding: first foal: dam unraced half-sister to 2¾m hurdle winner Salt Cellar: won bumper at Fontwell on debut, beating Snakecharm by 1½ lengths without hardly coming off bridle: again odds on, soundly beaten in similar event at Kempton 6 days later. *N. J. Henderson*

CLAYMORE (IRE) 11 b.g. Broadsword (USA) – Mazza (Mazilier (USA)) [2006/7 **c–**
c136, h124: c20s^F Nov 25] leggy, lengthy gelding: useful hurdler/chaser: disputing lead **h–**
when falling fatally 3 out in handicap chase at Newbury won by Gallant Approach: stayed 3m: acted on heavy and good to firm going: prone to odd mistake over fences but was reliable. *O. Sherwood*

CLEARLY IN MOTION (IRE) 10 b.g. Clearly Bust – Madness In Motion (IRE) **c98**
(Le Johnstan) [2006/7 c21m c20g⁶ c16d c19d* c18d² c24s⁵ c24sᵘʳ c24sᵘʳ c18g* c20m*
c20g* c22m⁴ Apr 26] modest chaser: won handicaps at Taunton (seller, final outing for
G. Kelleher) in October and Fontwell, Southwell and Plumpton within 9 days in March:
best form up to 2½m: unraced on firm ground, acts on any other: tried blinkered, wears
cheekpieces nowadays: sometimes let down by jumping. *C. J. Mann*

CLEARLY OSCAR (IRE) 8 b.g. Oscar (IRE) – Clear Bid (IRE) (Executive Perk) **c–**
[2006/7 h–, F85: 18s⁴ 16f⁵ 20m 18d c20dᵖᵘ Nov 11] sturdy gelding: modest maiden **h87**
hurdler: left Michael J. Fitzgerald, soon detached and blundered sixth in novice at
Cheltenham on chasing debut: stays 2½m: acts on firm and soft going: tried tongue tied.
Seamus O'Farrell, Ireland

CLEAR RIPOSTE (IRE) 5 b.m. King's Theatre (IRE) – Niamh Cinn Oir (IRE) (King **h121**
of Clubs) [2006/7 h122: 19s⁵ 19s² 16s Dec 2] fairly useful hurdler, lightly raced in
2006/7: stays 19f: acts on soft going. *W. P. Mullins, Ireland*

CLEMAX (IRE) 6 gr.g. Linamix (FR) – Chauncy Lane (IRE) (Sadler's Wells (USA)) **c104**
[2006/7 c104, h104: c24d³ c26s c26vᵖᵘ 23v² 24v⁵ 24v* 24s⁵ Apr 25] angular gelding: fair **h107**
hurdler/chaser: took advantage of slipping mark when winning novice handicap hurdle
at Ayr in March: stays 27f: raced on going softer than good (acts on heavy): wore
cheekpieces last 2 starts (tried blinkered when trained in France). *Ferdy Murphy*

CLENI BOY (FR) 5 b.g. Panoramic – Kailasa (FR) (R B Chesne) [2006/7 F102+: 16g* **h119**
16g³ 16g³ 16v⁵ 22s* Jan 23] lengthy gelding: fairly useful novice hurdler: won at Galway
(20-runner maiden) in September and Thurles (not hard ridden to beat Pontium ½ length,
pair clear) in January: best effort when just over 6 lengths third to Hide The Evidence
in Grade 1 at Fairyhouse third start: stays 2¾m: raced on good going or softer (acts on
heavy). *N. Meade, Ireland*

CLEOPATRAS THERAPY (IRE) 10 b.g. Gone Fishin – Nec Precario (Krayyan) **c–**
[2006/7 c–, h–: 24sᵖᵘ 20v³ 19d* 20g⁶ Apr 21] good-topped gelding: modest hurdler on **h93**
his day: won handicap at Lingfield in March by 17 lengths: pulled up only outing over
fences: stays 2½m: acts on heavy going. *T. H. Caldwell*

CLEVERALITY (IRE) 7 b.g. John French – Apple Betty (Runnett) [2006/7 h–, **c–**
c23mᵖᵘ May 9] tall gelding: no show over hurdles/on chasing debut: sold £1,100 Ascot **h–**
June Sales, won twice in points in 2007. *Evan Williams*

CLEVER DICKIE 12 b.g. Rakaposhi King – Whew (Ginger Boy) [2006/7 c19mᵖᵘ **c–**
Apr 24] modest pointer: no show in maiden hunter. *G. C. Evans*

CLEVERMANSAM 5 b.g. Tragic Role (USA) – Flower of Tintern (Free State) **h–**
[2006/7 F16g F16g F16g 16g Mar 16] half-brother to winning 2m chaser Arceye (by Weld): **F–**
dam, fairly useful up to 1¼m on Flat, winning 2m hurdler: well beaten in bumpers/
maiden hurdle. *M. J. Gingell*

CLEYMOR HOUSE (IRE) 9 ch.g. Duky – Deise Lady (Le Bavard (FR)) [2006/7 c–, **c–**
h68: 21s⁵ 24g 26mᵘʳ 21m c19d⁶ Nov 1] lengthy gelding: little form over hurdles or **h62**
fences: tried blinkered (has looked hard ride): claimed £6,000 final start. *John R. Upson*

CLICHY 7 b.m. Classic Cliche (IRE) – Kentucky Tears (USA) (Cougar (CHI)) [2006/7 **h–**
h–: 17s Dec 5] leggy mare: no solid form over hurdles. *Mrs S. J. Smith*

CLIFDEN BOY (IRE) 5 br.g. Anshan – Pharandom (IRE) (Phardante (FR)) [2006/7 **F–**
F14v⁵ F16s Feb 9] €28,000 4-y-o: rather unfurnished gelding: first foal: dam placed in
bumper: no show in bumpers. *C. L. Tizzard*

CLIFFORDS GIRL 5 b.m. Overbury (IRE) – Arctic Revel (Arctic Lord) [2006/7 **h–**
F17d F16d² F14g⁵ 18sᶠ 17s Jan 26] second foal: dam winning pointer: modest form in **F67**
bumpers: tailed off completed outing over hurdles. *W. K. Goldsworthy*

CLIFFORDS LADY 7 b.m. Petoski – Four M'S (Majestic Maharaj) [2006/7 19sᵖᵘ **h–**
22vᵖᵘ Dec 12] £1,205 6-y-o, resold £1,400 6-y-o: half-sister to fair hurdler/fairly useful
chaser around 2m Argento (by Weldnaas) and winning hurdler/chaser Minioso (by
Teenoso), stayed 2¾m: dam winning pointer: no show both starts over hurdles. *L. A. Dace*

CLIFFORD T WARD 7 b.g. Silver Wizard (USA) – Moonduster (Sparkler) [2006/7 **h–**
h–, F–: 16g⁵ May 13] sturdy gelding: no form over hurdles: sold £1,500 Ascot June Sales,
in frame in points in 2007. *D. McCain*

CLIFTON 5 b.m. Bal Harbour – Contradictory (Reprimand) [2006/7 F80: F16v 16s **h68**
19d⁵ 16s⁵ Mar 7] tall mare: second in bumper on debut: little show since, including over **F–**
hurdles (in seller final outing). *M. W. Easterby*

CLIMATE CHANGE (USA) 5 ch.g. Langfuhr (CAN) – Summer Mist (USA) (Miswaki (USA)) [2006/7 16s⁵ 16s* 16v⁴ 16d 16sᵖᵘ Apr 25] sturdy, workmanlike gelding: useful on Flat (stays 1¼m), sold out of J. Gosden's stable 46,000 gns Newmarket Autumn (2005) Sales: fair form over hurdles when winning 21-runner maiden at Newbury in December by 4 lengths from Magical Quest: very disappointing after: raced at 2m on ground softer than good: carries head awkwardly. *Miss Venetia Williams* **h108**

CLIMATE CONTROL (IRE) 11 b.g. Montelimar (USA) – Fraoch Ban (Deep Run) [2006/7 c127p: c22v⁵ c26g Mar 16] big, rangy gelding: multiple point winner: useful hunter chaser: well below best at Fairyhouse and Cheltenham (Foxhunter, made mistakes) in 2007: should stay beyond 3m: acts on soft going: tongue tied. *John Paul Brennan, Ireland* **c105**

CLOCKERS CORNER (IRE) 10 b.g. Eurobus – Pampered Finch VII (Damsire Unregistered) [2006/7 c22g³ c20d⁴ c24sᵖᵘ c19s³ c24s⁵ c24vᵖᵘ c19s⁶ Dec 26] lengthy gelding: successful 3 times in points in Ireland: bought 12,000 gns Doncaster May Sales: poor maiden chaser: lame final outing: probably stays 3m. *J. R. Cornwall* **c71**

CLOCK HOUSE (IRE) 7 b.g. Mohaajir (USA) – Risk-A-Dinge (IRE) (King's Ride) [2006/7 16g 16v* 20vᵖᵘ c19gᶠ Mar 21] good-topped gelding: first foal: dam lightly-raced maiden (including in points): modest handicap hurdler on his day: sold out of M. Hourigan's stable 1,500 gns Doncaster May Sales after first outing: back to best when making all in conditional/amateur event at Wetherby in January: fell both starts over fences: raced mainly around 2m: acts on heavy going. *T. R. George* **c–**
h94

CLODAGH VALLEY (IRE) 12 b.g. Doubletour (USA) – Raise A Princess (USA) (Raise A Native) [2006/7 c–, h–: c20vᵖᵘ Mar 4] winning pointer: no form in other events over jumps: tried blinkered. *R. J. Hewitt* **c–**
h–

CLOONAVERY (IRE) 5 b.g. Xaar – Hero's Pride (FR) (Hero's Honor (USA)) [2006/7 h67: 16gᵖᵘ 16d 16m⁵ 16m 16f³ Jul 19] good-topped gelding: poor maiden hurdler. *B. Llewellyn* **h75 ?**

CLOONE ROCKET (IRE) 5 b.g. Pistolet Bleu (IRE) – Site-Leader (IRE) (Supreme Leader) [2006/7 F16s⁴ F16v³ F16m³ F18m* Apr 28] first foal: dam, fairly useful hurdler who stayed 2½m, half-sister to useful hurdler/chaser over 2½m+ Cloone Bridge: fairly useful form in bumpers: favourite, won 25-runner event at Punchestown by 2 lengths from Sir Moko. *C. F. Swan, Ireland* **F98**

CLOPF (IRE) 6 b.g. Dr Massini (IRE) – Chroma (IRE) (Supreme Leader) [2006/7 F108: 16s* 16s* 16v² 16m* Apr 24] **h137**

Patience is a quality the vast majority of newcomers to racehorse ownership need in abundance while they dream of having their first winner and, possibly one day, a horse good enough to compete successfully in the best races. It wasn't something Bernard Heffernan required, though, when he decided to try his luck with an unraced gelding he named Clopf. Heffernan hit the jackpot straight away, and on both counts. Clopf, carrying his owner's white and purple colours for the first time, won a maiden bumper at Limerick in February 2006, and just over a year later, with five more wins under his belt, was even being touted as a future Champion Hurdle winner.

Clopf followed up his Limerick maiden bumper win at the same course six weeks later (with a narrow defeat of Woodbine Willie), then finished sixth to Leading Run in the Champion Bumper at Punchestown. He made an immediate impact when sent hurdling in the latest season, jumping soundly both times when landing the odds in novice events at Clonmel and Navan on his first two appearances, beating the useful Aitmatov into second on each occasion. After his impressive twelve-length victory in the Grade 3 Bar-One Racing "For Auction" Novices' Hurdle on the latter course in November, Clopf was installed as favourite for Cheltenham's Supreme Novices', though he didn't hold that position for long. Three weeks to be exact, until he contested the Grade 1 Royal Bond Novices' Hurdle at Fairyhouse. Once again Clopf was odds on, although he didn't have quite the chance the betting suggested, and he ran perfectly respectably in finishing six lengths second to Hide The Evidence, who himself had won all three of his previous starts over hurdles. The race, the second on the card, was run in gale force winds which forced the remainder of the meeting to be abandoned, so it was possibly significant that the waited-with winner was covered up for longer than Clopf. Held up by minor leg problems, Clopf was next seen in April although he had been left in

vcbet.com Champion Novices' Hurdle, Punchestown—Clopf (right) gains compensation for missing Cheltenham by defeating the Dusty Sheehy-trained pair Rindoon (left) and Holly Tree (noseband)

the Supreme Novices' until the overnight stage. The race chosen for his comeback took place on the Flat, a minor event over a mile and three quarters at Tipperary, and Clopf showed his well-being, as well as fairly useful form, when easily accounting for sixteen rivals. The Supreme Novices' winner Ebaziyan was one of eight others in the field when Clopf was returned to hurdling later in the month in the vcbet.com Champion Novices' Hurdle at Punchestown, though even the presence of Ebaziyan wasn't enough to stop Clopf going off favourite again. In the event, Ebaziyan ran no sort of race, while third favourite De Valira failed to complete. Clopf managed to win, but he made hard work of doing so, showing form way below the usual standard for the race. Held up as 25/1-shot Rindoon set a strong gallop, Clopf initially made little impression when asked for his effort, but he had worked his way into third turning into the straight, where Rindoon's stable-companion Holly Tree, who started at 20/1, was badly hampered as he tried to challenge on the leader's inside, forced to switch. Clopf finally got his head in front after the last as Rindoon's exertions took their toll, and he went on to beat that horse by a length and a quarter, with the rallying Holly Tree just a neck further behind in third. Holly Tree, who would have gone close to winning with a clear run, was subsequently placed second, with Rindoon demoted to third. It was hardly a performance to set the pulse racing with the 2008 Champion Hurdle in mind, and quotes as low as 16/1 about Clopf's winning that race were frankly ridiculous. Having said that, the gelding is clearly well regarded by his trainer—whose yard has produced top performers such as Jack of Trumps, Golden Cygnet, Sound Man, Back In Front, Nick Dundee and Ned Kelly down the years—so it's not out of the question he'll go on to better things.

Clopf (IRE) (b.g. 2001)	Dr Massini (IRE) (b 1993)	Sadler's Wells (b 1981)	Northern Dancer
			Fairy Bridge
		Argon Laser (b 1983)	Bold Reason
			Special
	Chroma (IRE) (b 1991)	Supreme Leader (b 1982)	Bustino
			Princess Zena
		Raby (br 1979)	Pongee
			Sherry

Clopf, who gets his name from a brand of polypropylene fibres used to maintain the quality of sand gallops, is the second live foal out of Chroma whose first, an unraced sister to Clopf named Dame O'Neill, was sold for €30,000 at

Fairyhouse in February. Chroma, who died in 2001, was also unraced but she was a half-sister to three winners, the pick of them the fairly useful hurdler/chaser Shiny Bay, who won at up to two and a half miles but showed her best form at two. Their dam Raby was a fair hurdler who stayed three miles. Clopf's sire Dr Massini, a smart winner at up to a mile and a quarter who later turned temperamental (refused to race twice), is also the sire of Massini's Maguire, winner of the twenty-one-furlong Baring Bingham Novices' Hurdle at the latest Cheltenham Festival. Clopf has raced only at two miles over hurdles so far, but he won a bumper over nineteen furlongs and seems sure to stay two and a half. A sturdy gelding, he acts on heavy and good to firm going. *E. J. O'Grady, Ireland*

CLOSED ORDERS (IRE) 10 b.g. Phardante (FR) – Monks Lass (IRE) (Monksfield) [2006/7 c87, h–: c18m^pu c18f Jun 6] ex-Irish gelding: winning chaser: no form in Britain: raced mainly around 2m: acts on firm ground: tried in cheekpieces. *B. J. Llewellyn* c–, h–

CLOSED SHOP (IRE) 6 b.g. Saddlers' Hall (IRE) – Roses Niece (IRE) (Jeu de Paille (FR)) [2006/7 h101: 22s² 22s⁶ 20s^F Apr 25] workmanlike gelding: point/bumper winner: short-head second to Cruising River in novice at Wincanton on hurdling debut: disappointing both starts after: stays 2¾m: raced on soft ground. *P. J. Hobbs* h106

CLOUDIER 6 b.m. Cloudings (IRE) – Hutcel Loch (Lochnager) [2006/7 F16s⁵ F17g⁴ Mar 24] second foal: half-sister to winning pointer by Primitive Rising: dam modest winning 2m hurdler: better effort in bumpers (fair form) when 5½ lengths fourth to Apache Brave in maiden at Bangor, racing freely. *T. D. Walford* F89

CLOUDINA 6 b.m. Cloudings (IRE) – Lucia Forte (Neltino) [2006/7 F79: 21s^pu 16s 16g Mar 14] smallish, compact mare: modest form when runner-up in bumpers: little show over hurdles: has had breathing problem. *P. T. Dalton* h–

CLOUDING OVER 7 gr.m. Cloudings (IRE) – Wellwotdouthink (Rymer) [2006/7 c113, h–: c16m² c20f 16g⁴ c20g⁵ 16s³ 16d⁵ 16v* 16d Feb 14] rather leggy mare: fair handicap hurdler/chaser: won mares hurdle at Southwell in January, ridden more prominently than usual: stays 2½m: probably acts on any going. *K. G. Reveley* c112 h106

CLOUDLAND (IRE) 10 ch.g. Eurobus – Turbulence (FR) (Targowice (USA)) [2006/7 c24g² Mar 16] lightly-raced maiden hurdler/chaser: left Ms F. Crowley, won maiden point in February, then close second to Hibernian in maiden chase at Fakenham: stays 3m: wore blinkers/cheekpieces last 2 starts: joined A. Jones. *N. F. Glynn, Ireland* c96 h–

CLOUDLESS DAWN 7 b.m. Cloudings (IRE) – Charlotte's Emma (Oats) [2006/7 h107: c22s* c20s⁴ c20s² c22g⁵ Mar 24] tall mare: good sort: fair hurdler: fairly useful novice chaser: won handicap at Kelso in November by 9 lengths from Three Mirrors: best effort after when second to Chickapeakray in mares event at Carlisle: stays 2¾m: acts on soft and good to firm going. *P. Beaumont* c115 h–

CLOUDMOR (IRE) 6 b.g. Cloudings (IRE) – Glen Morvern (Carlingford Castle) [2006/7 h87, F–: c16d⁶ c20s² 20s* 20s* c20v* c20s² c20s^ur c16s² 24s Apr 25] big, lengthy gelding: has scope: fair hurdler/chaser: won minor event and conditional jockeys handicap (dead-heated with Nobody's Perfect) over hurdles in December and handicap over fences in January, all at Sedgefield: good second to Honest Endeavour in novice handicap chase at Hexham penultimate start: should stay beyond 2½m: raced on good ground or softer (acts on heavy). *L. Lungo* c110 h104

CLOUDY BAYS (IRE) 10 ch.g. Hubbly Bubbly (USA) – Bellteen (Beau Charmeur (FR)) [2006/7 24g c24s^F c16v^pu c22v* 24d 24g^F c36g^R c25g Apr 25] rather leggy gelding: smart chaser at best: missed 2005/6: won listed event at Tramore in January by length from Mossy Green: last in Grade 1 only other completed outing over fences in 2006/7, very slowly away and rear until refusing Chair in Grand National at Aintree: fairly useful handicap hurdler: stays 3m: acts on any going: tried blinkered, usually wears cheekpieces: tried tongue tied, not since 2002/3: races prominently. *Charles Byrnes, Ireland* c133 h117

CLOUDY GREY (IRE) 10 gr.g. Roselier – Dear Limousin (Pollerton) [2006/7 h135: c19m⁴ Oct 28] big, lengthy gelding: useful hurdler, lightly raced: last of 4 to Time To Shine in maiden at Ascot on chasing debut, only outing in 2006/7: should be suited by further than 2m: acts on heavy going. *Miss E. C. Lavelle* c108 p h–

CLOUDY LANE 7 b.g. Cloudings (IRE) – Celtic Cygnet (Celtic Cone) [2006/7 h134, F100+: c20d³ c20g⁶ c24s* c24d² c28s c24g* c29m^ur Apr 9] useful hurdler: soon progressed to same level over fences, winning maiden at Newcastle in December and 24-runner Fulke Walwyn Kim Muir Challenge Cup (Amateurs) at Cheltenham in March, c142 h–

*Fulke Walwyn Kim Muir Challenge Cup Handicap Chase (Amateur Riders), Cheltenham—
Cloudy Lane helps Richard Burton repeat his 2005 win in the same colours;
Ponmeoath (centre) and Darby Wall (white face) fade into fourth and fifth respectively*

in latter travelling/jumping well and leading from 5 out when beating Parsons Legacy by
¾ length: would also have won novice at Newcastle fourth outing but for blundering last:
badly hampered and unseated 3 out (weakening at time) in Irish National at Fairyhouse:
stays 3m: acts on soft going (won bumper on good to firm): genuine. *D. McCain Jnr*

CLOVA STAR (IRE) 7 b.g. Fourstars Allstar (USA) – Push On Polly (IRE) (Salluceva) [2006/7 F16m⁶ F17g³ F16m⁵ 21g^F Mar 20] first foal: dam little worthwhile form:
fair form first 2 starts in bumpers, sold out of P. Niven's stable 5,000 gns Doncaster
August Sales in between: no show on hurdling debut. *N. E. Berry*   h–
F87

CLOVELLA 6 b.m. Missed Flight – Royella (Royal Fountain) [2006/7 F–: F16m 19g^pu
20s Mar 13] no form in bumpers/novice hurdles. *R. Allan*   h–
F–

CLOVER GREEN (IRE) 5 b.m. Presenting – Coolshamrock (IRE) (Buckskin (FR))
[2006/7 21v⁶ 24s Jan 30] €90,000 3-y-o: useful-looking mare: fourth foal: sister to high-
class but moody chaser Turpin Green, stays 3¼m: dam winning pointer: well beaten in
novice hurdles. *B. I. Case*   h–

CLUB ROYAL 10 b.g. Alflora (IRE) – Miss Club Royal (Avocat) [2006/7 c–, h74:
c23g³ c21m^pu c23f Jun 21] good-topped gelding: winning pointer: poor hurdler/maiden
chaser: stays 23f: acts on soft going: tried blinkered/in cheekpieces. *L. J. Williams*   c75
h–

CLUELESS 5 b.g. Royal Applause – Pure (Slip Anchor) [2006/7 h85p: 16s 16v 16s 16g
Apr 2] sturdy gelding: modest form over hurdles, never dangerous all 4 starts in 2006/7:
likely to prove best at 2m with emphasis on speed. *N. G. Richards*   h85

COACH LANE 6 b.g. Barathea (IRE) – Emplane (USA) (Irish River (FR)) [2006/7
h105: c16d^ur c16d² c16d* c16v* c19v⁴ c16v* c20d c20s Apr 25] useful-looking gelding:
winning hurdler: took well to chasing, winning at Lingfield (handicap) in November, Ayr
(novice) in December and Kempton (novice handicap, fairly useful form when beating
Original Fly 1¾ lengths) in March: shaped as if possibly amiss last 2 outings: best around
2m: raced on going softer than good (acts on heavy). *Miss Venetia Williams*   c117
h–

210

COAL QUEEN 8 b.m. Dajitus – Crown Royale (Some Hand) [2006/7 c23v^{ur} c24g^{pu} Apr 27] modest pointer, successful in March: failed to complete in 2 hunters: tongue tied. *N. Tamplin* **c–**

COAT OF HONOUR (USA) 7 gr.g. Mark of Esteem (IRE) – Ballymac Girl (Niniski (USA)) [2006/7 c124, h140: c16g c16v* c16v^2 c20s^2 c16g Mar 16] close-coupled, quite good-topped gelding: useful hurdler/chaser, raced in handicaps over fences in 2006/7: won at Wetherby in December by 2½ lengths from Jurado Express: good second in quite valuable events there next 2 starts: stays 2½m: acts on heavy and good to firm going: successful only outing in blinkers. *J. Howard Johnson* **c133 h–**

COBBET (CZE) 11 b.g. Favoured Nations (IRE) – Creace (CZE) (Sirano (CZE)) [2006/7 c120d, h–: c16g^4 c20f^2 c20m^3 c20m^2 c20m^4 Aug 6] leggy gelding: fairly useful handicap chaser: barely stays 21f: acts on firm and good to soft going: sold to join N. King 15,000 gns Doncaster August Sales. *T. R. George* **c115 h–**

COBHAM 7 ch.g. Rakaposhi King – Faint Praise (Lepanto (GER)) [2006/7 F16g^2 F16s* F16f^2 F20f^2 F17f* F16f^4 F16g^5 18v^4 18s^6 16v^F 16d^2 Jan 28] half-brother to modest staying hurdler Laudamus (by Anshan) and winning pointer by Lochnager: dam unraced out of half-sister to very smart staying chaser Special Cargo: fairly useful in bumpers, won at Clonmel (maiden) in May and Bellewstown in July: in frame twice from 3 completed starts in maiden hurdles (looked likely winner when falling last at Cork), 3½ lengths second of 24 to stable-companion Scotsirish at Leopardstown: bred to be suited by 2½m+: probably acts on any going. *W. P. Mullins, Ireland* **h118 F104**

COBRECES 9 b.g. Environment Friend – Oleada (IRE) (Tirol) [2006/7 c115, h–: c25f^3 c22v* c26g Mar 16] tall, useful-looking gelding: useful hunter chaser: won at Haydock (beat Natiain by 8 lengths) in February for second year running: again struggled in Foxhunter at Cheltenham following month: stays 25f: acts on heavy and good to firm going: tried blinkered/tongue tied in 2004. *Mrs L. Borradaile* **c115 h–**

Mr Trevor Hemmings' "Cloudy Lane"

COCIEMBE (IRE) 8 ch.g. Anshan – Lady Suntan (Over The River (FR)) [2006/7 c17s **c99** c20m⁵ c26dˢᵘ c24m⁵ c25m* c23d⁴ c24g⁵ c27d³ Nov 23] ex-Irish gelding: poor maiden **h–** hurdler: modest chaser: left J. A. Berry after reappearance: subsequently improved, winning handicap at Exeter in October, though form tailed off: stays 3¼m: acts on good to firm and good to soft going: tongue tied last 6 outings: front runner. *D. E. Pipe*

COCKATOO RIDGE 10 ch.g. Riverwise (USA) – Came Cottage (Nearly A Hand) **h– §** [2006/7 h99§: 19dᵖᵘ 22sᵖᵘ Feb 17] sturdy gelding: modest maiden handicap hurdler: lame final outing: stays 3m: acts on soft going (won bumper on firm): inconsistent. *N. R. Mitchell*

COCKATOO (USA) 4 b.g. Dynaformer (USA) – Enticed (USA) (Stage Door Johnny **h96** (USA)) [2006/7 16d⁵ 16d⁶ 16s³ 17g⁵ 16m³ 16g* Apr 23] compact gelding: lightly-raced maiden on Flat: fair juvenile hurdler: odds on, won 4-runner event at Plumpton, needing firm driving: raced around 2m: acts on soft and good to firm going: blinkered last 2 starts. *G. L. Moore*

COCKSPUR (IRE) 6 b.g. Darazari (IRE) – Melarka (Dara Monarch) [2006/7 F93: **c82** 20d⁴ 16d³ 16d 16g c16g 21v c25s³ c25sᵖᵘ Jan 16] medium-sized gelding: bumper winner: **h90** placed up to 25f but largely disappointing over hurdles/fences: blinkered final outing. *Jonjo O'Neill*

CODE (IRE) 6 b.g. Danehill (USA) – Hidden Meaning (USA) (Gulch (USA)) [2006/7 **h–** h–, F–: 19d⁴ 22gᵖᵘ Jul 23] fair form in bumpers: no show 3 starts over hurdles: tried tongue tied/in cheekpieces. *Miss Z. C. Davison*

CODY 8 ch.g. Zilzal (USA) – Ibtihaj (USA) (Raja Baba (USA)) [2006/7 c–, h72: 20dᵖᵘ **c– §** 24s⁴ 24g 24gᵖᵘ Nov 10] close-coupled gelding: poor hurdler: no show only outing over **h67 §** fences: stays 27f: acts on heavy going: wears headgear: often tongue tied: unenthusiastic. *James Moffatt*

COE (IRE) 5 br.g. Presenting – Dante's Skip (IRE) (Phardante (FR)) [2006/7 F13s⁵ **F76** F16v⁴ F17v⁴ Mar 18] strong gelding: third foal: half-brother to winning pointer by Anshan: dam, lightly raced in points, half-sister to top-class staying chaser Run And Skip: modest form in bumpers: bred to stay well. *Mrs S. J. Smith*

COEUR D'ALENE 6 gr.g. Hernando (FR) – Chambre Separee (USA) (Cozzene **h84** (USA)) [2006/7 h86, F86: 21d⁴ 25d² 23d³ 24s⁶ 25s³ 22d 27m⁴ Apr 26] smallish gelding: modest maiden hurdler: barely stays 27f: acts on soft and good to firm going: blinkered sixth outing (ran poorly). *Dr J. R. J. Naylor*

COF UP THE CASH 6 b.g. Celtic Swing – Laylee (Deploy) [2006/7 F16s F16s 16gᵖᵘ **h–** Mar 17] lengthy gelding: first foal: dam placed twice around 1½m in France: no form in **F–** bumpers/maiden hurdle. *Lady Susan Watson*

COGANS LAKE (IRE) 5 b.g. Even Top (IRE) – Imperial Comet (IRE) (Imperial **h119** Frontier (USA)) [2006/7 h123+: 16d⁴ 16d 17v* 20v⁶ Feb 24] workmanlike gelding: fairly useful hurdler: won 20-runner handicap at Gowran in January by length from Molly Massini: below form starts either side: raced mainly around 2m on going softer than good (acts on heavy). *Kieran Purcell, Ireland*

COIN MAN (IRE) 8 ch.g. Presenting – Dark Friend (IRE) (Mandalus) [2006/7 20s **c–** 16m⁴ 22f* 20m² 20g* 24f* 22g* 24g 21d⁴ 25g⁴ 24mᵖᵘ Apr 26] €5,000 3-y-o: lengthy, **h112** workmanlike gelding: third foal: dam once-raced pointer out of half-sister to high-class staying chaser Drumlargan: point/bumper winner: fair hurdler: much improved and successful 4 times in 2006/7, in maiden at Kilbeggan in July, and novices at Sligo and Tralee and handicap at Bellewstown (in between) in August: last only outing in chase (should do better): stays 3m: acts on firm and good to soft going: tried blinkered/in cheekpieces: formerly tongue tied: usually front runner/races prominently. *Eoin Doyle, Ireland*

COIS NA TINE EILE 5 br.m. Cois Na Tine (IRE) – Water Pixie (IRE) (Dance of Life **h100** (USA)) [2006/7 h85: 16g⁵ 24g³ 24f* Jun 3] small, close-coupled mare: fair hurdler: upped markedly in trip and improved efforts last 2 starts, winning novice handicap at Worcester: stays 3m: acts on firm going, probably on soft. *N. A. Twiston-Davies*

COLD MOUNTAIN (IRE) 5 b.g. Inchinor – Streak of Silver (USA) (Dynaformer **h105** (USA)) [2006/7 h103: 16f⁵ 16d⁴ 16g⁶ 16s⁴ 16d⁶ 19d³ 16d⁵ 17d³ 22g⁵ Apr 7] smallish, close-coupled gelding: fair handicap hurdler: probably stays 2¾m: acts on soft going (possibly not on firm): consistent. *J. W. Mullins*

COLEMANSTOWN 7 b.g. Charnwood Forest (IRE) – Arme Fatale (IRE) (Trem- **h–** polino (USA)) [2006/7 17m 16m 16m 16d 16s⁵ 16m⁵ Apr 9] sturdy gelding: fair on Flat (stays 8.6f), sold out of B. Ellison's stable £1,800 Ascot April (2006) Sales: no form over hurdles. *Miss C. J. E. Caroe*

COLERAINE (IRE) 7 b.g. Supreme Leader – Ring Mam (IRE) (King's Ride) [2006/7 **h–**
h75, F73: 25g^{pu} May 14] poor maiden hurdler: lame only outing in 2006/7: should be
suited by 3m+. *O. Sherwood*

COLJON (IRE) 9 br.g. Roselier (FR) – Native Ocean (IRE) (Be My Native (USA)) **c128 §**
[2006/7 c129: c20d^2 c24s c22v^{pu} c24v* c24m^5 Apr 7] fairly useful chaser: won handicap
at Limerick (beat Vicars Way by 2½ lengths) in March: should stay beyond 3m: acts on
heavy going (well beaten on good to firm): tried in blinkers, often wears cheekpieces:
front runner: has been let down by jumping: temperamental. *Paul Nolan, Ireland*

COLLEGE ACE (IRE) 6 b.g. Taipan (IRE) – Frantesa (Red Sunset) [2006/7 h112: **c115**
c20g^3 c20g* c24d^{pu} c21g^{pu} c24m^3 24m^2 Apr 17] tall gelding: fair hurdler: slightly better **h112**
form in handicap chases: won at Huntingdon (by head from Miss Shakira) in Novem-
ber: stays 3m: acts on soft and good to firm ground: probably needs strong handling.
P. J. Hobbs

COLLEGE CITY (IRE) 8 b.g. College Chapel – Polish Crack (IRE) (Polish Patriot **c103**
(USA)) [2006/7 c106, h89: c17m^{pu} 16m 16g c17f^2 20f 22m^2 16f^4 16f^5 22d* 17s^2 18g^4 **h84**
c21d^2 c16d 16s 20s^{ur} c17v^4 20v^2 19g^3 18s 22v^4 c18s^2 c16g^4 Apr 7] good-topped gelding:
fair chaser: poor handicap hurdler: won at Kelso in October: effective at 17f to easy 2¾m:
acts on heavy and good to firm going: tried blinkered/visored, usually wears cheekpieces.
R. C. Guest

COLLEGE REBEL 6 b.m. Defacto (USA) – Eccentric Dancer (Rambo Dancer **h–**
(CAN)) [2006/7 17g^{pu} 16v^{pu} Jan 3] good-topped mare: maiden on Flat, has lost her form:
no show in novice hurdles. *J. F. Coupland*

COLLIERS COURT 10 b.g. Puget (USA) – Rag Time Belle (Raga Navarro (ITY)) **c–**
[2006/7 19g^{pu} 16g c16g^5 Apr 7] lengthy gelding: missed 2005/6: no form over hurdles: **h–**
fairly useful chaser at best, well held final start: best around 2m: acts on soft and good to
firm going: headstrong front runner. *Mrs L. Williamson*

COLLINE DE FLEURS 7 b.m. Alflora (IRE) – B Greenhill (Gunner B) [2006/7 **h103**
h119, F98: 21d 26s^4 20g^6 Mar 21] sturdy mare: bumper winner: fair hurdler: should stay
beyond 21f: acts well on heavy going. *J. A. B. Old*

COLMCILLE (IRE) 7 ch.g. Desert Story (IRE) – Lasting Peace (IRE) (Pennine **c–**
Walk) [2006/7 c–, h–: c18f c19m^6 c19m Jun 19] compact gelding: winning hurdler/ **h–**
chaser: no form in 2006/7: stays 2¾m: acts on firm and soft going: tried blinkered/in
cheekpieces: sometimes tongue tied. *Evan Williams*

COLOMBE D'OR 10 gr.g. Petong – Deep Divide (Nashwan (USA)) [2006/7 c–§, h–§: **c– §**
c24m^{pu} Oct 4] maiden hurdler: no form in points/chases: tried blinkered/in cheekpieces: **h– §**
ungenuine. *M. F. Harris*

COLONEL HAYES (IRE) 7 b.g. Flemensfirth (USA) – Laura Daisy (Buckskin **h–**
(FR)) [2006/7 F85: 23g Apr 30] big, lengthy gelding: modest form in bumpers: tailed off
in maiden on hurdling debut. *J. I. A. Charlton*

COLONEL JAMES (IRE) 7 br.g. Invited (USA) – Carrignaveen Queen (IRE) (Tore- **c– x**
naga) [2006/7 h–: 16g 16g 16s^5 16v^{pu} c16s^5 c16g^F c20g^F Apr 7] good-topped gelding: **h81**
poor maiden hurdler: badly let down by jumping over fences: raced mainly around 2m on
good ground or softer (acts on soft). *R. Johnson*

COLONEL POTTER 6 ch.g. Pursuit of Love – Constant Delight (Never So Bold) **F79**
[2006/7 F16g^4 Apr 8] half-brother to 2¾m chase winner Father Mulcahy (by Safawan):
dam 9f winner: modest form when fourth to Aya in bumper at Towcester on debut.
D. McCain Jnr

COLONY HILL (IRE) 9 ch.g. Broken Hearted – Arctic Raheen (Over The River **c–**
(FR)) [2006/7 h90: 19d^{pu} 22s^{pu} c22s^4 c26s^{pu} 18s c16v^4 Feb 28] angular gelding: lightly **h–**
raced: runner-up in novice hurdle: off 16 months, no form in 2006/7, including over
fences. *R. H. Buckler*

COLOPHONY (USA) 7 ch.g. Distant View (USA) – Private Line (USA) (Private **h103**
Account (USA)) [2006/7 h97: 20g^3 Apr 7] close-coupled gelding: fair handicap hurdler:
fit from Flat, ran well only start in 2006/7: stays 21f: acts on soft going, probably on good
to firm: has had tongue tied. *K. A. Morgan*

COLORADO PEARL (IRE) 6 br.m. Anshan – Flying Silver (Master Buck) [2006/7 **h105 p**
h96p: 22m* Jul 17] rather unfurnished mare: fair form over hurdles: won mares novice at
Newton Abbot (beat Gotta Get On by 16 lengths, left clear 2 out) in July: will probably
stay 3m: tongue tied last 3 starts: looked open to further improvement. *P. F. Nicholls*

COLOURFUL LIFE (IRE) 11 ch.g. Rainbows For Life (CAN) – Rasmara (Kala- **c– x**
glow) [2006/7 c142x, h–: 24m⁴ 24m⁶ 20f 22d 22m³ 23g 22g⁴ 23s² 25d 23vᵖᵘ Dec 26] **h99**
big, lengthy gelding: one-time fairly useful hurdler/useful chaser, has deteriorated
considerably: stays 3¼m: acts on heavy and good to firm going: tried in cheekpieces:
usually held up, and tends to carry head awkwardly under pressure: prone to mistakes
over fences. K. G. Reveley

COLTSCROFT 7 b.g. Teenoso (USA) – Marquesa Juana (Lepanto (GER)) [2006/7 **h106 §**
h73: 22m³ 20s* 22d² 20f³ 27m² Aug 2] useful-looking gelding: fair hurdler: won
handicap at Worcester in May: better form when placed all starts after: stays 27f: unraced
on heavy going, acts on any other: has pulled hard: hung badly left only start on right-
handed track: irresolute. J. C. Fox

COLUMBUS (IRE) 10 b.g. Sadler's Wells (USA) – Northern Script (USA) (Arts And **c– §**
Letters (USA)) [2006/7 c–§, h113§: c27dᵖᵘ 24s⁶ 26s 25v⁶ 27v⁶ 24v Mar 10] angular **h96 §**
gelding: one-time fairly useful handicap hurdler, largely disappointing since early-2004/5
(including over fences): stays 27f: acts on firm and soft going: blinkered/visored: usually
gets behind: ungenuine. Jennie Candlish

COLWAY RITZ 13 b.g. Rudimentary (USA) – Million Heiress (Auction Ring (USA)) **h78**
[2006/7 h69: 16g³ 16s May 17] lengthy, angular gelding: poor hurdler: stays 2½m: tried in
cheekpieces 3 of last 4 starts. W. Storey

COMANCHE WAR PAINT (IRE) 10 b.g. Commanche Run – Galeshula (Strong **c125**
Gale) [2006/7 c125, h–: 27mᵖᵘ c26m² Jul 17] useful-looking gelding: has reportedly been **h–**
pin-fired and had breathing operation: fair hurdler: fairly useful chaser: stayed 3¾m:
probably acted on any going: sold 28,000 gns Doncaster August Sales, died after third in
point. P. F. Nicholls

COMBAT DRINKER (IRE) 9 b.g. Mandalus – Auburn Park (Sonnen Gold) [2006/7 **c–**
c90, h90: c20g⁶ Nov 24] tall, useful-looking gelding: modest hurdler: similar form on **h–**
chasing debut: left D. McCain and off a year prior to only start in 2006/7: stays 3¼m: acts
on soft and good to firm going: usually tongue tied (has run as if amiss more than once).
M. Todhunter

COMBER (IRE) 5 b.g. Luso – Charleys Lane (IRE) (Remainder Man) [2006/7 20s⁴ **c–**
21g⁵ 19v⁴ c19sᵖᵘ 22d⁴ 20g Apr 21] chunky gelding: eighth foal: dam unraced: in frame **h94**
all 3 starts in Irish points in 2006: modest maiden hurdler: not fluent when never
dangerous on chase debut: will stay 3m: acts on heavy going. Miss H. C. Knight

COME BYE (IRE) 11 b.g. Star Quest – Boreen Dubh (Boreen (FR)) [2006/7 c–, h107: **c–**
18g 19d 20g⁶ 21s² 22s* 23sᵖᵘ 22v* 21g⁴ Apr 23] medium-sized gelding: no form in 2 **h107**
chases: fair hurdler on his day: won seller (easily) in January and handicap in February,
both at Folkestone: stays 2¾m: acts on heavy going: used to wear headgear: tongue tied:
front runner: has won 4 times at Fontwell. Miss A. M. Newton-Smith

COME ON JIM (IRE) 6 b.g. Goldmark (USA) – Galapagos (Pitskelly) [2006/7 F–: **F–**
F16s Nov 19] tailed off in 2 bumpers 11 months apart. A. J. Whiting

COME ON JONNY (IRE) 5 b.g. Desert King (IRE) – Idle Fancy (Mujtahid (USA)) **h–**
[2006/7 16vᵖᵘ Dec 15] smallish, close-coupled gelding: smart on Flat (stays 1½m),
successful 3 times as 3-y-o, below form in 2006: favourite, raced too freely and none too
fluent in maiden on hurdling debut. R. M. Beckett

COME ON POPS (IRE) 4 ch.g. Sonus (IRE) – Arctic Flora (Arctic Lord) [2006/7 **h–**
F14d⁶ 20g Apr 3] third foal: dam no form over hurdles: little impact in bumper and novice **F–**
hurdle. J. Howard Johnson

COME OUT FIRING (IRE) 5 b.g. Supreme Leader – Thegirlfromslane (IRE) **h100**
(Mandalus) [2006/7 20dᵖᵘ 21d³ 16v 20vᵖᵘ 18v³ 22v⁵ Feb 28] €65,000 3-y-o: fifth foal:
dam unraced half-sister to fairly useful hurdler/chaser up to 2¾m Moonshine Bay: fair
novice hurdler: folded tamely final start: should stay beyond 21f. Jonjo O'Neill

COME TO THE BAR (IRE) 8 b.g. Witness Box (USA) – Copper Hill (IRE) (Zaffa- **h–**
ran (USA)) [2006/7 h–: 24f Jun 21] winning pointer: soundly beaten over hurdles.
W. W. Dennis

COME WHAT AUGUSTUS 5 b.g. Mujahid (USA) – Sky Red (Night Shift (USA)) **h87**
[2006/7 h87: 22m⁶ 19g⁴ Nov 15] close-coupled gelding: modest maiden on Flat (stays
2m): modest novice hurdler: stays 2¾m: acts on soft ground: tried in cheekpieces.
R. M. Stronge

COMFORTABLE CALL 9 ch.g. Nashwan (USA) – High Standard (Kris) [2006/7 **h–**
h70: 20vᵖᵘ 21m Jun 7] lengthy gelding: winning hurdler, little form since 2004/5: stays
21f: acts on soft and good to firm going: tongue tied. H. Alexander

COMICAL ERRORS (USA) 5 b.g. Distorted Humor (USA) – Fallibility (USA) **h88**
(Tom Rolfe) [2006/7 h97: 17g³ 17s⁶ 17m³ Jun 7] modest maiden on Flat (stays 2m):
winning hurdler, below best in 2006/7: raced around 2m: acts on good to firm going,
probably on soft: in cheekpieces final start: sold 4,000 gns Doncaster October Sales.
P. C. Haslam

COMING AGAIN (IRE) 6 b.g. Rainbow Quest (USA) – Hagwah (USA) (Dancing **h77**
Brave (USA)) [2006/7 h83: 17g⁶ 16d⁶ May 19] sparely-made gelding: poor novice
hurdler: raced around 2m: acts on good to soft ground: tried in blinkers: tongue tied.
D. McCain

COMMANCHE DAWN 5 b.m. Commanche Run – Charlycia (Good Times (ITY)) **h–**
[2006/7 F–: F14g⁴ 16d 16d Nov 19] no form in bumpers and novice hurdles. *G. P. Enright* **F–**

COMMANCHE HERO (IRE) 14 ch.g. Cardinal Flower – Fair Bavard (Le Bavard **c97 §**
(FR)) [2006/7 c24m May 16] workmanlike gelding: maiden hurdler: fair chaser at best: **h– §**
successful 6 times in points, including twice in 2007: stays 3¾m: acts on heavy and good
to firm going: not one to trust. *Mrs J. Dawson*

COMMANDER VIC (IRE) 5 b.g. Old Vic – Miss Agarbie (IRE) (Tremblant) **h98 p**
[2006/7 16s⁶ 17g⁴ 20g³ Apr 14] tall, good-topped gelding: second foal: dam, winning
pointer, half-sister to useful hurdler/chaser around 2m Premier Cru: encouraging efforts
3 starts over hurdles, again left with plenty to do when third to Inherit in novice at
Chepstow: will stay beyond 2½m: remains open to improvement, and type to make his
mark in handicaps. *D. E. Pipe*

COMMEMORATION DAY (IRE) 6 b.g. Daylami (USA) – Bequeath (USA) (Lyp- **c?**
hard (USA)) [2006/7 h–§: c18g⁴ 17g* 16d² 16v² 16d⁴ 21f* 20g² 22g² Apr 27] good- **h105**
topped gelding: successful 4 times up to 1½m on Flat in Germany in 2006: fourth start
over fences: fair hurdler: won at Bad Harzburg (for C. von der Recke) in July and
Ludlow in April: stays 2¾m: probably acts on any ground: formerly often blinkered/
visored: tongue tied 3 of last 4 starts: edgy sort. *M. F. Harris*

COMMERCIAL EXPRESS (IRE) 6 b.g. Oscar (IRE) – Biddy Earley (IRE) (Black **c93 +**
Minstrel) [2006/7 22m 24v⁴ 20s c24s² c24dᵖᵘ 24m 24d* 22g² Apr 2] €15,000 3-y-o: first **h99**
foal: dam placed in points: won maiden hurdle: left D. Pipe
prior to sixth start: won ladies handicap at Musselburgh in February: similar form on
completed outing in chases: stays easy 3m: acts on good to firm going, probably on
heavy: tried in cheekpieces: not straightforward. *P. Monteith*

COMMERCIAL FLYER (IRE) 8 ch.g. Carroll House – Shabra Princess (Buckskin **c148**
(FR)) [2006/7 c123, h–: c25sᶠ c24dᵖᵘ c24gᵖᵘ Mar 13] lengthy, angular gelding: useful **h–**
hurdler: highly promising chasing debut when winning maiden in February 2006: has
failed to complete since, though still on bridle behind leaders when falling 3 out in listed
handicap at Cheltenham won by D'Argent on return: stays 27f: acts on heavy and good to
firm going: tongue tied: patiently ridden. *D. E. Pipe*

COMMONCHERO (IRE) 10 b.g. Desert of Wind (USA) – Douala (GER) **c131**
(Pentathlon) [2006/7 c134, h118: c17m c20f* c22d³ c17m⁴ c24sᶠ 16s 16s 16v⁶ c16g **h109**
c16m 22g Apr 24] good-topped gelding: winning hurdler: useful chaser: won handicap at
Tipperary in July by 8 lengths from Laragh House: largely below form after: stays 2½m:
acts on firm and soft going: effective with or without tongue strap: usually held up.
M. J. P. O'Brien, Ireland

COMMON GIRL (IRE) 9 gr.m. Roselier (FR) – Rumups Debut (IRE) (Good Thyne **c–**
(USA)) [2006/7 h101: c24g c24mᵖᵘ Apr 9] lengthy, workmanlike mare: fair hurdler: off **h–**
over 10 months, no show 2 starts over fences: stays 23f: acts on heavy and good to firm
going: usually races prominently. *O. Brennan*

COMPLETE OUTSIDER 9 b.g. Opera Ghost – Alice Passthorn (Rapid Pass) **h114**
[2006/7 h108: 22g³ 22m* 22dᵘʳ Aug 20] stocky gelding: fair hurdler: won handicap in
May and novice (by ½ length from Lucifer du Montceau) in June, both at Newton Abbot:
running well when unseating 2 out in valuable handicap there won by Rushneeyriver:
stays 3m: acts on soft and good to firm going (won bumper on firm): has given trouble in
preliminaries. *Nick Williams*

COMPTON COMMANDER 9 ch.g. Barathea (IRE) – Triode (USA) (Sharpen Up) **h84**
[2006/7 h–: 24g² 22dᵖᵘ Oct 21] quite good-topped gelding: poor maiden hurdler: stays
3m: acts on good to firm and good to soft going: tried visored/in cheekpieces: not a
straightforward type. *E. W. Tuer*

COMPTON DRAGON (USA) 8 ch.g. Woodman (USA) – Vilikaia (USA) (Nureyev **h85**
(USA)) [2006/7 h76: 16s⁴ 16g⁵ 16m² 17g³ 20m 16g⁵ 18m Oct 1] close-coupled gelding:
modest maiden hurdler: best around 2m: acts on soft and good to firm going: ran

poorly both outings in cheekpieces (effective in them on Flat): joined W. M. Brisbourne. *R. Johnson*

COMPTON EARL 7 ch.g. Efisio – Bay Bay (Bay Express) [2006/7 h–: 17m^F Jun 7] no show over hurdles: tried in tongue strap/cheekpieces: dead. *J. J. Lambe, Ireland* — **h–**

COMPTON ECLAIRE (IRE) 7 ch.m. Lycius (USA) – Baylands Sunshine (IRE) (Classic Secret (USA)) [2006/7 20g 20d^4 24g^2 25d^4 24d Jan 19] smallish, good-bodied mare: modest on Flat (stays 2m), successful in June, sold out of B. Ellison's stable 1,500 gns Doncaster October Sales: poor novice hurdler: barely stays 25f: raced on good/good to soft ground: tried blinkered. *N. Wilson* — **h84**

COMPTON ECLIPSE 7 ch.g. Singspiel (IRE) – Fatah Flare (USA) (Alydar (USA)) [2006/7 17m^3 Jun 7] half-brother to fair hurdler Protagonist (by In The Wings), stays 21f: fair up to around 1m on Flat nowadays: poor novice hurdler: raced mainly around 2m: tried tongue tied. *J. J. Lambe, Ireland* — **h78**

COMPTON FLYER 4 ch.c. Compton Admiral – Elegantissima (Polish Precedent (USA)) [2006/7 17m^{pu} 17d^R 17m^{ur} Sep 28] little form on Flat: failed to complete in juvenile hurdles. *J. M. Bradley* — **h–**

COMPTON STAR 7 ch.g. Compton Place – Darakah (Doulab (USA)) [2006/7 h73: 19g^6 17d^4 21m^6 16g^2 19s^3 17v^6 17s^3 16g^5 Mar 19] modest handicap hurdler: won at Taunton in October: likely to prove best around 2m: acts on soft and good to firm going, ran poorly both starts on heavy. *R. J. Hodges* — **h85**

CONBENO (IRE) 5 b.g. Scribano – Lucy's Light (IRE) (Miner's Lamp) [2006/7 F16m^4 F16g Apr 7] third foal: dam unraced: poor form on first of 2 starts in bumpers. *A. M. Crow* — **F74**

CONEMARA BREEZE 9 b.g. Old Vic – Belle Perk (IRE) (Executive Perk) [2006/7 h–: 20g 21s^4 21d 24v^{pu} Nov 23] little form in novice hurdles, including seller. *Miss L. C. Siddall* — **h60**

CONKERING (USA) 4 ch.g. Horse Chestnut (SAF) – Nunbridled (USA) (Unbridled (USA)) [2006/7 16d^4 Nov 30] fairly useful on Flat (stays 1¼m), successful in April 2006, changed hands 105,000 gns Newmarket Autumn Sales: jumped none too fluently when fourth in juvenile on hurdling debut: likely to improve. *J. R. Fanshawe* — **h86 p**

CONNA CASTLE (IRE) 8 b.g. Germany (USA) – Mrs Hegarty (Decent Fellow) [2006/7 h138p: 17s* c17v^2 c16s^F 16v^4 19v 20g Apr 12] big, good sort: useful hurdler: won minor event at Killarney (long odds on) in May: well below form in handicaps last 2 starts: twice-raced in graded company over fences, running to useful level when falling 2 out in race won by Blueberry Boy at Punchestown: stays 19f: acts on heavy going: keen sort. *James Joseph Mangan, Ireland* — **c132 h138**

CONROY 8 b.g. Greensmith – Highland Spirit (Scottish Reel) [2006/7 c101, h106: c16f^F c16g^5 16m^{pu} Jun 18] leggy gelding: fair handicap hurdler: similar form at best over fences: raced around 2m: acted on good to firm and good to soft going, ran poorly on soft: dead. *F. Jordan* — **c92 h–**

CONSERVATION (FR) 4 b.g. Green Desert (USA) – Lightly Dancing (FR) (Groom Dancer (USA)) [2006/7 16s Jan 10] good-topped gelding: fair maiden on Flat (stays 11.6f), sold out of P. Chapple-Hyam's stable 48,000 gns Newmarket Autumn Sales: raced freely and mistakes in juvenile on hurdling debut. *N. J. Gifford* — **h– p**

CONSIDINE (USA) 6 b.g. Romanov (IRE) – Libeccio (NZ) (Danzatore (CAN)) [2006/7 h–: 22g 21d^5 19m^F 19m^{*dis} 19s 21s^5 19m* 20m^6 20m^5 Apr 28] sturdy, close-coupled gelding: fair hurdler: first past post in maiden at Stratford (subsequently disqualified due to prohibited substance) in August, then sold out of C. Mann's stable 6,500 gns Doncaster October Sales: won 21-runner maiden at Cork in April: stays 21f: acts on soft and good to firm going. *Eric McNamara, Ireland* — **h106**

CONSTABLE BURTON 6 b.g. Foxhound (USA) – Actress (Known Fact (USA)) [2006/7 h98: 16s 17g^4 Apr 11] workmanlike gelding: fair on Flat (stays 1¼m), well held both starts in 2006, sold out of Mrs A. Duffield's stable 17,000 gns Doncaster October Sales: fair hurdler: will prove best around 2m: acts on good to soft and good to firm ground: front runner. *D. C. O'Brien* — **h103**

CONSTANTIUS 6 b.g. Halling (USA) – Premier Night (Old Vic) [2006/7 F91: 16d 16v 17s Feb 8] tall gelding: chasing type: fair form in bumper on debut: off 14 months, well held over hurdles. *K. C. Bailey* — **h–**

CONTACT DANCER (IRE) 8 b.g. Sadler's Wells (USA) – Rain Queen (Rainbow Quest (USA)) [2006/7 h112: 20v^F c19f^3 Apr 11] rangy gelding: fair hurdler in 2005/6 for C. Swan: staying on well until blundering last when third to Phar Bleu in novice at Exeter — **c92 p h–**

on chasing debut: stays 3m: acts on heavy going: in cheekpieces in 2006/7: should do better over fences. *P. Bowen*

CONTENDO 6 ch.g. Classic Cliche (IRE) – Madam Ross (Ardross) [2006/7 F74: 22g^{pu} 16v^6 21v^{pu} 16v^6 Feb 22] big gelding: little sign of ability: bred to stay well: tried in cheekpieces. *N. W. Alexander*   **h–**

CONTRABAND 9 b.g. Red Ransom (USA) – Shortfall (Last Tycoon) [2006/7 c150, h–: c16g^2 c17d^{pu} c21s 16d^4 16s^5 19g Mar 31] good-topped gelding: smart novice chaser in 2004/5, won Arkle Challenge Trophy at Cheltenham: lightly raced since, looking ungenuine and shadow of former self most starts in 2006/7, including back over hurdles 3 outings after leaving D. Pipe: best around 2m: acts on heavy and good to firm going: tried in headgear/tongue tied: free-going sort: sold 14,500 gns Doncaster May Sales. *S. Gollings*   **c133 §**   **h133 §**

CONTRACT SCOTLAND (IRE) 12 br.g. Religiously (USA) – Stroked Again (On Your Mark) [2006/7 c96, h–: c20g* May 30] deep-girthed gelding: modest handicap hurdler/chaser: won over fences at Hexham only start in 2006/7: effective at 2½m to 27f: acts on soft and good to firm going: tried in cheekpieces. *L. Lungo*   **c99**   **h–**

CONTROL MAN (IRE) 9 ch.g. Glacial Storm (USA) – Got To Fly (IRE) (Kemal (FR)) [2006/7 c129x, h–: c26g Mar 16] angular, sparely-made gelding: winning hurdler: one-time useful chaser: left M. Pipe, successful 3 times in points in 2007: well beaten in Foxhunter at Cheltenham: should stay beyond 29f: acts on heavy going: visored: hard ride: jumping usually lacks fluency. *Miss Gina Weare*   **c– x**   **h–**

CONVINCING 4 b.c. Selkirk (USA) – Hot Thong (BRZ) (Jarraar (USA)) [2006/7 16v* 16s 16v* 16v* 17g Mar 16] rather leggy colt, unfurnished at present: fairly useful juvenile hurdler: won up to 1¼m on Flat, successful twice in 2006: fairly useful juvenile hurdler: won at Fairyhouse (maiden) in December, Punchestown (Grade 3) in January and Leopardstown (Grade 2 Cashmans Juvenile Hurdle, beat Financial Reward by neck) in February: mid-division in Triumph Hurdle at Cheltenham: raced around 2m: acts on heavy ground: reportedly found to be running temperature after running poorly second start. *John Joseph Murphy, Ireland*   **h117**

COOK O'HAWICK (IRE) 10 b.g. King's Ride – Miners Yank (Miner's Lamp) [2006/7 c19m^{ro} May 9] good-topped gelding: maiden hurdler: poor completion record in points (ran out in hunter). *Mrs S. J. Batchelor*   **c– §**   **h–**

COOL ALICE 5 ch.m. Cool Jazz – Dominion's Dream (Dominion) [2006/7 F13m^2 F16d^5 16d 17g 17g^5 Apr 20] fourth foal: half-sister to 13f bumper winner Regal Angel (by Roi de Rome): dam, modest hurdler who stayed 2½m, also 7f winner on Flat: poor form in bumpers: never dangerous 3 starts over hurdles. *Jean-Rene Auvray*   **h72 ?**   **F72**

COOLAW (IRE) 4 b.f. Priolo (USA) – Cool Gales (Lord Gayle (USA)) [2006/7 16v^{pu} 17s Jan 16] half-sister to 2½m hurdle winner Bartra Rock (by Persian Bold): little form on Flat (usually wears headgear): no show in juvenile hurdles. *G. G. Margarson*   **h–**

COOLCASHIN (IRE) 6 b.g. Taipan (IRE) – Daisy A Day (IRE) (Asir) [2006/7 F16s* F16v* Oct 30] second foal: half-brother to 2½m bumper winner Veedon Fleece (by Eurobus): dam fairly useful hurdler up to 2½m: successful in bumpers at Tramore (maiden) and Galway in October, useful form when beating Druids Castle by 10 lengths in 6-runner event at latter. *James Bowe, Ireland*   **F110 +**

COOL CHILLI 9 gr.g. Gran Alba (USA) – Miss Flossa (FR) (Big John (FR)) [2006/7 c–, h–: c16g c16m 16m c18g^{pu} c16g^2 c16m^F c16g Oct 19] workmanlike gelding: modest chaser in 2004/5: no form since, including in point: raced mainly at 2m: tongue tied. *N. J. Pomfret*   **c–**   **h–**

COOL CLICHE 5 b.g. Classic Cliche (IRE) – Ardent Love (IRE) (Ardross) [2006/7 F17s^3 F16s Mar 3] 30,000 4-y-o: workmanlike gelding: fourth foal: brother to untrustworthy 2¾m hurdle winner Love of Classics and half-brother to untrustworthy 2¾m hurdle winner Wimbledonian (by Sir Harry Lewis): dam, modest staying hurdler, sister to very smart but temperamental staying hurdler Burgoyne: fair form in bumpers, 1½ lengths third of 17 to Kavatcha in maiden at Taunton: will be suited by further. *Evan Williams*   **F95**

COOL COSSACK (IRE) 10 ch.g. Moscow Society (USA) – Knockacool Breeze (Buckskin (FR)) [2006/7 c112, h–: 24v^4 24s^4 25v^2 Feb 27] strong, lengthy gelding: fair chaser/maiden hurdler: off 20 months prior to return: stays 25f: unraced on firm going, acts on any other. *Mrs S. J. Smith*   **c–**   **h104**

COOLDINE (IRE) 5 b.g. Beneficial – Shean Alainn (IRE) (Le Moss) [2006/7 F16v* F16g F16m Apr 25] €10,000 3-y-o: workmanlike gelding: sixth foal: dam, winning 21f   **F116**

hurdler, sister to useful staying chaser Brackenfield: favourite, won bumper at Fairyhouse in February on debut by neck from Ballyverane Oscar: much better form (smart) when 5¾ lengths seventh of 24 to Cork All Star in Grade 1 at Cheltenham next time. *W. P. Mullins, Ireland*

COOLDINE LAD (IRE) 7 b.g. Flemensfirth (USA) – Lotto Lady (Le Moss) [2006/7 h85: 24g^pu Oct 21] lengthy, workmanlike gelding: Irish point winner: poor form once in 4 starts over hurdles. *J. Howard Johnson*   **h–**

COOLEFIND (IRE) 9 b.g. Phardante (FR) – Greavesfind (The Parson) [2006/7 c104: c22d* c24g⁴ Mar 23] tall gelding: useful hunter chaser: improved form when winning 5-runner event at Newbury in March by 11 lengths from Spring Grove: stays 3m: acts on good to soft and good to firm going. *W. J. Warner*   **c113**

COOLE GLEN (IRE) 11 b.g. Executive Perk – Cailin Liath (Peacock (FR)) [2006/7 c92: c16g* c17s² c20g⁵ Mar 28] sturdy gelding: fair hunter chaser: won at Cheltenham in May: stays 21f, effective over shorter: best efforts on good ground. *W. J. Warner*   **c97**

COOLE VENTURE (IRE) 13 b.g. Satco (FR) – Mandavard (IRE) (Mandalus) [2006/7 c24m⁴ c23v⁶ May 27] winning pointer, including in 2007: fair hunter chaser: stays 3½m: acts on good to soft and good to firm going: tried blinkered. *Mrs C. Banks*   **c96**

COOL HUNTER 6 ch.g. Polar Falcon (USA) – Seabound (Prince Sabo) [2006/7 16g^pu 19d 16v 20g Dec 30] workmanlike gelding: fairly useful on Flat (stays 1½m), sold out of W. Swinburn's stable 16,000 gns Newmarket Autumn Sales: no form over hurdles. *R. C. Guest*   **h–**

COOL LINNETT 6 br.g. Cool Jazz – Dowdency (Dowsing (USA)) [2006/7 h–: 16s^pu May 20] no show both starts over hurdles. *B. N. Pollock*   **h–**

COOL ROXY 10 b.g. Environment Friend – Roxy River (Ardross) [2006/7 h124: 20g³ c16g* 16g c21d² c24d* c21d⁴ c20s² 19d c21g* 24g³ c20m³ Apr 22] stocky gelding: fairly useful chaser/handicap hurdler: won over fences at Fakenham in May (maiden) and November (novice), and handicap there (again beat Herecomestanley) in March: stays 3m, effective at much shorter: acts on soft and good to firm going: wore cheekpieces once (ran creditably): races prominently: has gained 8 of 9 wins at Fakenham: tough and reliable. *A. G. Blackmore*   **c121** **h121**

COOL SOCIETY 5 b.g. Atraf – Cool Run (Deep Run) [2006/7 h–, F–: 16d⁶ 22s 19g⁵ 16f 22m^F Apr 17] leggy gelding: poor novice hurdler. *R. H. Alner*   **h70**

COOL SONG 11 ch.g. Michelozzo (USA) – Vi's Delight (New Member) [2006/7 c77, h–: c26g³ c24s⁴ Dec 26] big, strong gelding: maiden hurdler: poor handicap chaser: should stay beyond 3¼m: raced on good going or softer: sold 3,000 gns Doncaster May Sales. *Miss Suzy Smith*   **c74** **h–**

COOMAKISTA 10 b.m. Primitive Rising (USA) – Miss Eros (Royal Fountain) [2006/7 c87+: c28s* c25s^F c25g⁵ Apr 2] fairly useful pointer/hunter chaser: won at Stratford (beat Moonoki by 4 lengths) in May: stays 31f: acts on soft and good to firm going. *Mrs E. J. Reed*   **c97**

COOPERSTOWN 4 ch.g. Dr Fong (USA) – Heckle (In The Wings) [2006/7 16g Nov 29] strong gelding: fairly useful form when placed in 1m maidens on Flat: jumped poorly when well beaten in juvenile on hurdling debut: should prove capable of better. *J. Howard Johnson*   **h– p**

COORBAWN VIC (IRE) 6 ch.g. Old Vic – Double Harmony (IRE) (Orchestra) [2006/7 h75, F76: 21m⁶ 19g 20v⁴ 20v³ 24v³ 26s² 24s 24v^F 26g Mar 14] smallish gelding: modest maiden hurdler: stays 3¼m: acts on heavy ground: tried in cheekpieces. *S. A. Brookshaw*   **h91**

COPPER BAY (IRE) 5 b.g. Revoque (IRE) – Bahia Laura (FR) (Bellypha) [2006/7 h96: c17s^pu c17g³ c16g² c16d* c16d* c16s^F Jan 10] lengthy, good-topped gelding: maiden hurdler: fair handicap chaser: won novice events at Leicester (2) in December: raced around 2m on good going or softer: tends to sweat: has had 2 handlers in paddock: has finished weakly. *A. King*   **c106** **h–**

COPPERMALT (USA) 9 b.g. Affirmed (USA) – Poppy Carew (IRE) (Danehill (USA)) [2006/7 c–x, h69: 22m⁵ 22m⁵ 20m 16f* 18g 16d⁵ 19g² 16d* 19s 16g Mar 28] leggy gelding: modest handicap hurdler: won at Plumpton in September (seller) and November: little form over fences, often let down by jumping: effective at 2m to easy 3¼m: acts on firm and good to soft going: visored last 7 starts. *R. Curtis*   **c– x** **h97**

COPPLESTONE (IRE) 11 b.g. Second Set (IRE) – Queen of The Brush (Averof) [2006/7 c20g^F c17m* c16s⁴ c20g² c20g³ c25g^F Apr 23] compact gelding: modest handicap hurdler for W. Storey: missed 2005/6: poor form over fences: won novice handicap   **c83** **h–**

at Cartmel in August: stays 2¾m: acts on heavy and good to firm going: usually wears cheekpieces (visored final 2004/5 start). *A. C. Whillans*

COPSALE LAD 10 ch.g. Karinga Bay – Squeaky Cottage (True Song) [2006/7 c148, h–: c20d^{pu} c24d^{pu} 24d* 21g c25g^5 Apr 13] big, strong, lengthy gelding: smart chaser: hampered in valuable handicaps first 2 starts, at third on second occasion and jumping badly after: useful hurdler: won handicap at Newbury in February easily by 5 lengths from Minella Tipperary: well-backed favourite, only mid-field in Coral Cup at Cheltenham next time: stays 25f: acts on soft and good to firm going. *N. J. Henderson* **c138 + h136**

CORALBROOK 7 b.g. Alderbrook – Coral Delight (Idiot's Delight) [2006/7 h93: c20f^{pu} c20m^F c20d^{pu} c20m^{pu} 22m^F Apr 28] tall gelding: modest hurdler: failed to complete all 4 starts over fences, falling last in maiden won by Predator at Huntingdon second time, 15 lengths second at time: stayed 21f: wore headgear after 2005: dead. *Mrs P. Robeson* **c69 h–**

CORAL ISLAND 13 b.g. Charmer – Misowni (Niniski (USA)) [2006/7 c95, h–: c18m May 28] useful-looking gelding: fair handicap chaser at best, little form for long time: placed in points in 2007: stays 2¾m: acts on firm and soft going: tried blinkered early in career. *R. M. Stronge* **c– h–**

CORALS LAUREL (IRE) 8 b.g. Accordion – Bold Tipperary (IRE) (Orchestra) [2006/7 h98: 21s 16v^5 20s Jan 24] lengthy gelding: bumper winner: maiden hurdler, well below best in 2006/7: stays 2½m: acts on heavy going: tongue tied 4 of last 5 starts, also in cheekpieces last 2. *R. T. Phillips* **h79**

CORBIE LYNN 10 ch.m. Jumbo Hirt (USA) – Kilkenny Gorge (Deep Run) [2006/7 h–: 24g^{bd} 24g^2 c20v c25v^2 c24s^F 22v^{pu} c22s c24v^{pu} c32v^{pu} c26g c25g^6 Apr 23] smallish mare: modest hurdler: maiden chaser, lost her way after fourth outing: stays 25f: acts on heavy going. *W. S. Coltherd* **c98 d h98 d**

CORBLE (IRE) 7 b.g. Broken Hearted – Itaparica (FR) (Mistigri) [2006/7 h91: 21d^{pu} May 15] lightly raced over hurdles, modest form at best: dead. *P. J. Hobbs* **h–**

CORDIER 5 b.g. Desert Style (IRE) – Slipper (Suave Dancer (USA)) [2006/7 16g^{pu} 16g^2 16s Dec 8] tall gelding: fairly useful on Flat (stays 1½m), lightly raced and no form on turf: easily best effort over hurdles (saddle slipped on debut) when 1¾ lengths second of 19 to Eleazar in novice at Haydock, making most. *J. Mackie* **h99**

CORDILLA (IRE) 9 b.g. Accordion – Tumble Heather (Tumble Wind) [2006/7 c116x, h–: c20g^{pu} c20g^{pu} Mar 22] big gelding: winning hurdler: fairly useful chaser on his day for N. Richards: no show in hunters in 2007, whipped round at start on first occasion: stays 25f: raced mainly on soft/heavy going: often let down by jumping over fences: has carried head awkwardly. *P. H. Hogarth* **c– x h–**

CORK ALL STAR (IRE) 5 b.g. Fasliyev (USA) – Lucky State (USA) (State Dinner (USA)) [2006/7 F16f* F16g* F16d* F16g* F16m5 Apr 25] **F122**

Ireland's firm grip on the Champion Bumper at Cheltenham shows no sign of being weakened. Far from it, with Irish stables filling seven of the first eight places in 2007, from a team of just eleven, with Crocodiles Rock, from Jonjo O'Neill's yard, in sixth, the only British runner to get in on the act. Victory went to Cork All Star, the second favourite, who had won his three previous races, summer bumpers at Cork and Galway (not the first Champion Bumper winner to have been campaigned at that time of year) and the listed Open Bumper at Cheltenham in November, in which he beat the subsequently useful novice chaser An Accordion by four lengths. Since it was inaugurated in 1992, the Champion Bumper (known initially as the Festival Bumper) has fallen to a British-trained runner only three times, notably two subsequently very good hurdlers in Dato Star (1995) and Monsignor (1999), and also Liberman, who was trained by Paddy Mullins in Ireland prior to joining Martin Pipe for his final run before the 2003 renewal. British bumpers are open to professional riders, whereas in Ireland they are nearly all for amateurs (some are open to the equivalent of conditional riders). However, though they are a fair bit more competitive than they used to be, the steady pace at which the vast majority of bumpers in Britain are run probably does not provide the experience required for a truly-run race at the highest level.

Having a professional in the saddle is an advantage in the Champion Bumper itself, those riders who have won it twice including Richard Dunwoody, Charlie Swan, Paul Carberry and Ruby Walsh (the first success as an amateur),

Weatherbys Champion Bumper, Cheltenham—Barry Geraghty is seen to particularly good effect as Cork All Star (left) maintains his unbeaten record in a race dominated by Irish-trained runners

while three other champions have been victorious once, Tony McCoy, Jamie Spencer (on a rare National Hunt ride) and now Barry Geraghty. The only amateur, apart from Ruby Walsh, to score was Willie Mullins on board Wither Or Which in 1996, the first of five Champion Bumper winners he has saddled. The benefit of professional handling, particularly now that riders (including amateurs) are unable to claim allowances in the Champion Bumper, was all too apparent in the latest renewal, with Cork All Star getting a much better ride than two of his amateur-ridden rivals. While he travelled smoothly behind the leaders and was sent on in the straight, responding well to pressure despite drifting right, the amateur-ridden runner-up Sophocles and fifth Fiveforthree were asked to make up a lot of ground in the straight, neither given as much help from the saddle as they might have been, Sophocles in particular spoiling his chance by hanging badly left, something his rider Pauline Ryan was unable to correct. Fiveforthree, meanwhile, fared best of Mullins' three-strong team (which included disappointing favourite Mad Fish) but also shaped as if he'd have benefited from professional handling, his jockey picking up a suspension along with Ryan for excessive use of the whip, the latter also receiving a further ban for careless riding in allowing her mount to drift away from the whip all the way up the straight. Fran Berry, now a full-time Flat jockey, also picked up a careless riding ban after allowing his mount, Crocodiles Rock, to interfere with Fiveforthree on the bend.

On paper, it looked a strong renewal of the Champion Bumper, which merited taking a positive view of the form, but by the time Cork All Star and Sophocles (as well as the fourth Shirley Caspar and seventh Cooldine) turned up at Punchestown for the Grade 1 bumper there the Cheltenham race had taken a couple of knocks, including when Fiveforthree was a beaten favourite at Fairyhouse's Irish National meeting. Still, Cork All Star looked to hold a good chance of becoming the first to complete the Cheltenham-Punchestown bumper double—the penalised Montelado in 1992 and Hairy Molly in 2006 had both finished second, from four to try previously—but the Champion Bumper form met with further setbacks. None of those that ran in both matched their Cheltenham form, Shirley Caspar doing best in third behind Mick The Man, who had won just one of his five previous starts and had finished only narrowly ahead of Fiveforthree when they were second and third at Fairyhouse. Cork All Star took fifth, failing to quicken after being well placed into the straight, and even ran below his earlier Open meeting form. Sophocles was back in ninth. Cork All Star was far from being alone at Punchestown in failing to show his Cheltenham form, a topic discussed in the essay on Silent Oscar, but the Champion Bumper form had to be viewed quite a bit differently six weeks down the line.

Cork All Star is very unusual among Champion Bumper winners in that he is bred for the Flat. His sire Fasliyev was raced only at two, when he was unbeaten in five starts, including the Phoenix Stakes and the Prix Morny. His forte at stud so far has been sprinting two-year-olds and he has had few winners over much more than a mile. He has had a handful of hurdles winners at around two miles, the best of them River Logic (who won three juveniles for Alan Brown in 2006/7), as well as the modest winning chasers Straycat Strut and Insurgent, the latter having form at up to two and a half miles. Cork All Star's dam Lucky State won over a mile in

France for Criquette Head-Maarek and is a half-sister to that stable's 1988 One Thousand Guineas winner Ravinella. Her previous foals include the fair mile-and-a-half winner and fair hurdler Glencoyle, but he was by In The Wings, much more of an influence for stamina than Fasliyev. Among her other winners are Gold Lance (by Seeking The Gold) and In For The Craic (by Our Emblem), successful at a mile and at a mile and a quarter on the Flat respectively. Lucky State has also produced a Grade 3 winner in Brazil by Thunder Gulch. Grandam Really Lucky was smart in France, despite the handicap of being blind in one eye, her two wins including a listed race over a mile. Meanwhile, the third dam Realty was all about speed, being a high-class French sprinter in the 'seventies who was placed in both the King's Stand Stakes and the July Cup.

	Fasliyev (USA) (b 1997)	Nureyev (b 1977)	Northern Dancer Special
Cork All Star (IRE) (b.g. 2002)		Mr P'S Princess (b 1993)	Mr Prospector Anne Campbell
	Lucky State (USA) (ch 1988)	State Dinner (b 1975)	Buckpasser Silver Bright
		Really Lucky (ch 1978)	Northern Dancer Realty

Cork All Star has been through the sale-ring twice, making €24,000 as a yearling (one of his sire's lowest prices of that year) and being bought back by his vendor for 10,000 guineas at the Newmarket Breeze-Up Sales in April 2004. Surprisingly, given that it is often run on ground near good, horses bred for the Flat have made relatively little impact in the Champion Bumper—Alan Swinbank, interestingly, has yet to saddle a runner in the Cheltenham showpiece from his powerful team of largely Flat-bred bumper horses—and those that have succeeded in doing so have not always done as well as might be expected once sent jumping. In the first fourteen runnings, only about a dozen who were bred for the Flat made

Mr Cathal M. Ryan's "Cork All Star"

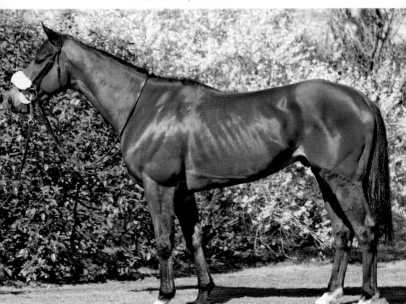

the frame (the exact number is debatable). Just two previous winners have a Flat background, Rhythm Section and, less categorically, Liberman, neither of whom made the impact expected over jumps, showing no better than fairly useful form. Four runners-up have fared better, with Tiananmen Square (smart but fragile), Aries Girl (runner-up in the 1995 AIG Europe), Alzulu (useful before going wrong) and De Soto (useful at best in the latest season) all showing ability well above average over hurdles. Rhythm Section had Flat-breds in third (the useful jumper Winter Belle) and fourth (fairly useful hurdler Aslan) when winning a below-par renewal in 1993, whilst Liberman's was also a substandard one. Cork All Star's early appearances over hurdles should give a clear indication of how much of an impact he will make as a jumper. In his favour, he is an athletic sort, useful-looking in appearance. He has already shown a good deal more stamina than might be expected from his pedigree, but it would be no surprise if he proved best at around two miles and on ground other than soft or heavy. *Mrs J. Harrington, Ireland*

CORKER 5 ch.g. Grand Lodge (USA) – Immortelle (Arazi (USA)) [2006/7 h98: 20d^{ro} 16s⁵ 17v⁴ 17v² 16v³ 20v^{bd} 20v³ 21g² 24g³ Apr 18] smallish gelding: fair maiden hurdler: stays 3m, at least when conditions aren't testing: raced on good ground or softer (acts on heavy): ungenuine (ran out on reappearance). *D. M. Grissell* **h107 §**

CORLANDE (IRE) 7 br.g. Teamster – Vaguely Deesse (USA) (Vaguely Noble) [2006/7 h120: c20d⁶ c23d c20d⁵ c25v³ c24v³ c24v² c22v^F c22s⁴ Mar 11] sturdy, lengthy gelding: fairly useful hurdler for Mrs S. Smith: modest novice chaser: again made running and still in front when fell last in handicap at Haydock: likely to stay beyond 3m: acts on heavy going: wore cheekpieces last 2 outings. *J. M. Saville* **c96 h—**

CORNELIA 4 gr.f. Silver Patriarch (IRE) – Ludoviciana (Oats) [2006/7 F14g Nov 1] leggy filly: half-sister to 2m chase winner Terivic (by Terimon) and winning hurdler/chaser Viciana (by Sir Harry Lewis), stays 2½m: dam winning pointer: mid-field in 3-y-o bumper won by Fintan at Huntingdon on debut: will be suited by stiffer test of stamina. *C. F. Wall* **F75**

CORNISH CONNECTION (IRE) 5 b.g. Secral (USA) – Bryan's Call (IRE) (Shernazar) [2006/7 h: 17s 16g⁶ 21m^{pu} Apr 8] third foal: brother to a winning pointer and half-brother to 1¼m winner in Italy by Great Commotion: dam unraced: no form over hurdles: tried in cheekpieces. *R. C. Harper* **h—**

CORNISH GALE (IRE) 13 br.g. Strong Gale – Seanaphobal Lady (Kambalda) [2006/7 c102, h—: c26d* May 31] well-made gelding: fairly useful hunter chaser: won at Cartmel in May: multiple point winner, including in 2007: stays 3¼m: acts on good to firm and good to soft going: has had tongue tied. *D. McCain Jnr* **c96 h—**

CORNISH JACK 7 b.g. Thowra (FR) – Melody Mine (Torus) [2006/7 h—, F—: 19d⁶ 19d^{pu} Aug 21] no form in bumper/over hurdles: tried blinkered. *J. D. Frost* **h—**

CORNISH ORCHID (IRE) 6 ch.g. Be My Guest (USA) – Nilousha (Darshaan) [2006/7 h—: 19m³ 19g 17d⁵ 20d 19s^{ro} 22s 25m² 24m^{pu} Apr 17] tall, unfurnished gelding: poor novice hurdler: sold out of C. Down's stable £1,200 Ascot December Sales after fifth outing: lame final one: stays easy 25f: acts on soft and good to firm going: has worn headgear. *M. Appleby* **h71**

CORNISH REBEL (IRE) 10 br.g. Un Desperado (FR) – Katday (FR) (Miller's Mate) [2006/7 c163, h—: c26s^{pu} c25s c26v* c28s⁵ c24g c32m^{pu} Apr 21] rangy, good-topped gelding: has reportedly had breathing operation: very smart handicap chaser at best: increasingly temperamental and well below that in 2006/7 (usually blinkered), though did win 4-runner event at Cheltenham in January by 1¾ lengths from The Bajan Bandit: stays 33f: acts on heavy going: patiently ridden: one to treat with caution. *P. F. Nicholls* **c139 § h—**

CORNISH SETT (IRE) 8 b.g. Accordion – Hue 'n' Cry (IRE) (Denel (FR)) [2006/7 c143, h—: 21g c24d* c24d c24v² c29f⁶ Apr 28] lengthy, useful-looking gelding: winning hurdler: useful chaser: won 4-runner minor event at Cheltenham in November by neck from Fundamentalist: creditable efforts in handicaps next 2 starts, never-nearer 10 lengths second to Simon in Grade 3 Racing Post Chase at Kempton: stays 3m: acts on heavy and good to firm ground: blinkered nowadays. *P. F. Nicholls* **c140 h—**

CORONADO FOREST (USA) 8 b.g. Spinning World (USA) – Desert Jewel (USA) (Caerleon (USA)) [2006/7 16g^{pu} May 14] poor on Flat nowadays, raced mainly on all-weather: no show both starts over hurdles. *M. R. Hoad* **h—**

CORPORATE PLAYER (IRE) 9 b.g. Zaffaran (USA) – Khazna (Stanford) [2006/7 c109, h—: c19d^{ur} c20s⁴ c19d^{pu} Feb 2] rangy, useful-looking gelding: lightly raced: **c92 h—**

winning hurdler: fair chaser, below best only completed outing in 2006/7: stays 2½m: acts on soft and good to firm going: often tongue tied. *Noel T. Chance*

CORRAN ARD (IRE) 6 b.g. Imperial Ballet (IRE) – Beeper The Great (USA) (Whadjathink (USA)) [2006/7 17d² 16s* Dec 8] useful on Flat (stays 1¼m), off nearly 2 years prior to unbeaten in 3 starts in 2006: promising hurdling debut when second to Ouninpohja in maiden at Taunton, and didn't need to repeat that form to win steadily-run similar event at Southwell by neck from Pevensey: likely to prove best around 2m: remains open to improvement. *Evan Williams* **h122 p**

CORRIB DRIFT (USA) 7 ch.g. Sandpit (BRZ) – Bygones (USA) (Lyphard (USA)) [2006/7 c81, h81: c18m² c21m³ c16m* c20m* c20m³ Aug 6] poor novice hurdler: better over fences, winning novice handicaps at Worcester and Stratford in July: stays 2½m: acts on soft and good to firm going. *Jamie Poulton* **c100** **h–**

CORRIB ECLIPSE 8 b.g. Double Eclipse (IRE) – Last Night's Fun (IRE) (Law Society (USA)) [2006/7 24g² 24s* May 20] compact gelding: bumper winner: useful on Flat (successful twice up to 2¾m) for Jamie Poulton: encouraging start in novice hurdles, second to Ally Shrimp at Bangor then won at Worcester comfortably by 8 lengths from Original Thought, again making much of running: will prove best again, but ran as if amiss final outing on Flat in 2006. *Ian Williams* **h120**

CORRIB LAD (IRE) 9 b.g. Supreme Leader – Nun So Game (The Parson) [2006/7 c110, h92+: 17s² c20v* 20v⁶ c20s* Jan 5] well-made gelding: modest handicap hurdler: better over fences and won both starts in 2006/7, handicaps at Carlisle in November and Musselburgh (made all) in January: possibly best up to 21f: raced on good going or softer (acts on heavy). *L. Lungo* **c110** **h94**

CORROBOREE (IRE) 10 b.g. Corrouge (USA) – Laura's Toi (Quayside) [2006/7 c85, h–: c20v⁸ Apr 27] leggy gelding: signs of stringhalt: lightly raced: winning hurdler: poor form over fences: left N. Twiston-Davies and off 14 months, showed nothing only outing in 2006/7: should stay beyond 2m: acts on heavy going. *F. P. Murtagh* **c–** **h–**

CORSO PALLADIO (IRE) 5 b.g. Montjeu (IRE) – Falafil (FR) (Fabulous Dancer (USA)) [2006/7 17d 16g⁶ 17g 17s 16v Jan 12] quite good-topped gelding: half-brother to 3 winning jumpers abroad: fairly useful on Flat (stays 1½m), successful in France at 3 yrs, runner-up once from 3 starts in 2006: left J. E. Hammond, poor form in novice hurdles: raced around 2m on good ground or softer. *Jonjo O'Neill* **h79**

CORTINAS (GER) 5 b.g. Lomitas – Cocorna (Night Shift (USA)) [2006/7 16g² 17v⁴ Jan 8] good-topped gelding: half-brother to useful hurdler Cardenas (by Acatenango), stays 2½m: fairly useful on Flat, successful twice around 1¼m, including at Krefeld in 2006 for A. Wohler: fair form in frame both starts over hurdles, 12½ lengths fourth to impressive Predateur in novice at Taunton, no extra run-in after taking keen hold: may do better under less testing conditions. *C. J. Mann* **h105**

Jersey Graduation Chase, Cheltenham—
the blinkered Cornish Sett pips Fundamentalist in a typically small field for one of these new contests

CORUM (IRE) 4 b.c. Galileo (IRE) – Vallee Des Reves (USA) (Kingmambo (USA)) **h98**
[2006/7 16v 17v 17m⁴ 19g⁴ Apr 8] lengthy colt: useful on Flat (stays 1½m), successful in
June, sold out of J. Gosden's stable 32,000 gns Doncaster November Sales: fair form over
hurdles when fourth in juvenile at Hereford and maiden at Towcester. *Mrs K. Waldron*

COSMIC SKY 10 ch.g. Charmer – Silver Cirrus (General Ironside) [2006/7 c–: c24sᶠ **c–**
Feb 22] strong gelding: fair pointer, successful 6 times, including in January: failed to
complete in 2 hunters. *Robert Abrey*

COSMOLOGIST (USA) 4 b.g. Galileo (IRE) – Fontemar (ARG) (Babor (ARG)) **h103**
[2006/7 aF13g² 16d 17s² Jan 16] €150,000Y: close-coupled gelding: half-brother to **F89**
several winners abroad, including Argentinian Group 1 winner First One (by Southern
Halo): dam won 3 Group 1s in Argentina, including 1000 Guineas: second to Turbo Linn
in 3-y-o bumper at Lingfield on debut: better effort over hurdles when ¾-length second to
Gracechurch (pair clear) in juvenile maiden at Folkestone: makes running. *C. R. Egerton*

COSSACK DANCER (IRE) 9 b.g. Moscow Society (USA) – Merry Lesa (Dalesa) **c121**
[2006/7 c114, h102+: c17m c16g² c16d² c17d² Dec 15] leggy gelding: winning hurdler: **h–**
fairly useful chaser: runner-up in handicaps last 3 starts, beaten neck by Jericho III at
Ascot final one, blundering seventh and wandering run-in: effective from 2m to 2½m:
acts on firm and good to soft going, probably on soft: wears cheekpieces: front
runner: consistent. *M. Bradstock*

COSTA COURTA (FR) 5 b.g. Marly River (FR) – Tosca de Bellouet (FR) (Olmeto) **F94**
[2006/7 F16s² May 20] sixth foal: half-brother to smart hurdler/chaser Toto Toscato,
stayed 25f, and winning 2m hurdler Comedie Divine (both by Lesotho): dam 9.5f to 12.5f
winner: 6 lengths second to impressive Beau Michel in bumper at Worcester on debut.
C. P. Morlock

COST ANALYSIS (IRE) 5 ch.g. Grand Lodge (USA) – Flower Girl (Pharly (FR)) **h–**
[2006/7 16m 16gᵖᵘ Nov 1] stocky gelding: half-brother to winning hurdlers Water Flower
(by Environment Friend) and King's Chambers (by Sabrehill), both of whom stayed 19f:
fair maiden on Flat (should stay 1¼m) at 3 yrs for M. Jarvis: no show both starts over
hurdles, looked temperamental in blinkers second time: sold £1,200 Ascot December
Sales. *N. J. Gifford*

COTSWOLD ROSE 7 b.m. Sovereign Water (FR) – Rosehall (Ardross) [2006/7 h73: **c–**
27dᵖᵘ c23sᵖᵘ Dec 29] poor novice hurdler: off 11 months, no show in 2 handicaps (second **h–**
one over fences) in 2006/7: stays 3¼m. *N. M. Babbage*

COTTAM ECLIPSE 6 b.g. Environment Friend – Che Gambe (USA) (Lyphard **h–**
(USA)) [2006/7 h–, F–: 19gᵖᵘ 16sᵖᵘ Nov 22] no sign of ability. *J. S. Wainwright*

COTTAM GRANGE 7 b.g. River Falls – Karminski (Pitskelly) [2006/7 h114: 21s⁶ **h–**
22m⁶ Apr 15] medium-sized gelding: fair handicap hurdler: left M. Easterby and off 16
months, well below best both outings in 2006/7: stays 3m: acts on heavy and good to firm
going. *I. W. McInnes*

COTTINGHAM (IRE) 6 b.g. Perugino (USA) – Stately Princess (Robellino (USA)) **c–**
[2006/7 c–, h84: 16d² 17g² 16s² 17s² 16d 16m⁴ Apr 10] compact gelding: fair on Flat **h112**
(stays 1¼m), won 4 times in 2006, sold out of T. D. Barron's stable 26,000 gns Doncaster
August Sales: fair maiden hurdler, runner-up first 4 starts in 2006/7: well behind when
falling only outing over fences: raced around 2m: acts on soft and good to firm ground:
held up (has raced freely). *R. Lee*

COUGAR (IRE) 7 b.g. Sadler's Wells (USA) – Pieds de Plume (FR) (Seattle Slew **h72**
(USA)) [2006/7 h–: 21d⁶ 25d⁵ 22v⁴ 23d 25m³ Apr 9] well-made gelding: novice hurdler,
only poor form in 2006/7: probably stays easy 25f: acts on good to firm going, probably
on heavy: tried tongue tied/in cheekpieces. *R. Rowe*

COULDBETHEONE (IRE) 6 ch.m. Carroll House – Dell Raven (USA) (Salute The **h76**
Brave) [2006/7 19m⁵ 20m 18g 20f 21s 19sᵖᵘ Dec 7] half-sister to winning pointer by
Spicy Story: dam ran in USA: poor maiden hurdler: probably stays 2½m: tried in cheek-
pieces/blinkers. *Michael Butler, Ireland*

COULD HAPPEN (IRE) 6 b.m. Dr Massini (IRE) – Supreme Alliance (IRE) **F–**
(Supreme Leader) [2006/7 F17v Oct 1] €4,000 4-y-o: third foal: dam, bumper winner,
half-sister to useful staying chasers Unholy Alliance and Jolly Green Giant: tailed off in
bumper on debut. *Mrs P. Sly*

COULD IT BE LEGAL 10 b.g. Roviris – Miss Gaylord (Cavo Doro) [2006/7 h–: **h–**
17gᵖᵘ Apr 7] workmanlike gelding: no sign of ability. *R. Lee*

COUNT BORIS 6 b.g. Groom Dancer (USA) – Bu Hagab (IRE) (Royal Academy **h101**
(USA)) [2006/7 h101: 22s² 22v³ 21s⁴ 24v 26g⁵ 22d⁵ Mar 20] rather leggy gelding: fair
novice hurdler: stays 3¼m: acts on heavy going: visored last 2 starts. *J. A. Geake*

COUNTESS POINT 9 ch.m. Karinga Bay – Rempstone (Coronash) [2006/7 c19s⁴ **c88 p**
Dec 14] tall mare: bumper winner: fair form over hurdles: off 2 years, 27 lengths fourth to **h–**
Chamoss Royale in mares novice at Exeter on chasing debut: should be suited by further
than 19f: raced on good to soft/soft going over jumps: should improve over fences.
C. L. Tizzard

COUNTESS TRIFALDI (IRE) 7 b.m. Flemensfirth (USA) – Course Royal (Crash **c111**
Course) [2006/7 c20gᵖᵘ c22v⁵ c24s c22sᵖᵘ c33g³ c24m⁴ c30m⁶ Apr 27] lengthy mare:
won Irish point in 2005: fair form in chases: 100/1, best effort when 10¾ lengths third to
Butler's Cabin in National Hunt Chase (Amateurs) at Cheltenham: stays 33f: acts on soft
going. *M. Phillips, Ireland*

COUNT FOSCO 9 b.g. Alflora (IRE) – Carrikins (Buckskin (FR)) [2006/7 c–, h–: **c98**
c21m⁵ c16d⁴ c21dᶠ c25gᴿ Nov 29] rather leggy gelding: winning hurdler: easily best **h–**
effort over fences (modest form) when fourth in novice at Carlisle: should stay 3m: acts
on soft and good to firm going. *M. Todhunter*

COUNTING HOUSE (IRE) 4 ch.g. King's Best (USA) – Inforapenny (Deploy) **h107 +**
[2006/7 16d² 17g Mar 16] close-coupled gelding: fairly useful maiden on Flat (should
stay 1¾m), sold out of R. Charlton's stable 55,000 gns Newmarket Autumn Sales, and
gelded: promising second to Mountain in juvenile at Sandown on hurdling debut: well
beaten in Grade 1 at Cheltenham following month, again taking good hold: may yet
improve. *J. A. B. Old*

COUNT KRISTO 5 br.g. Dr Fong (USA) – Aryadne (Rainbow Quest (USA)) [2006/7 **h95**
16s 16g⁵ 17g⁵ 16g² Apr 23] tall gelding: fair on Flat (stays 1½m), successful in 2006, sold
out of C. Cox's stable 20,000 gns Newmarket Autumn Sales: modest form over hurdles:
raced around 2m: takes strong hold. *B. G. Powell*

COUNTRY ESCAPE 4 b.g. Zafonic (USA) – Midnight Allure (Aragon) [2006/7 16s **h91 p**
17s 16s Feb 17] compact gelding: fairly useful on Flat (stays 1m), successful twice in
2006 for C. Wall: modest form over hurdles, progressing with each run: needs to brush up
jumping but likely to do better again. *Jonjo O'Neill*

COUNTRYWIDE BELLE 4 b.f. Josr Algarhoud (IRE) – Dancing Bluebell (IRE) **h78**
(Bluebird (USA)) [2006/7 17mᵘʳ 16m³ 17m³ 18m⁴ Sep 21] modest on Flat (stays 8.6f),
successful in February 2006, claimed from K. Ryan £6,000 following month: poor form
in juvenile hurdles: tried in cheekpieces. *J. L. Flint*

COUNTRYWIDE LUCK 6 b.g. Inchinor – Thelma (Blakeney) [2006/7 16g Oct 7] **h– p**
fairly useful on Flat (stays 1½m), successful in early-2006: well held in novice on
hurdling debut: likely to do better. *N. P. Littmoden*

COUNTRYWIDE SUN 5 b.g. Benny The Dip (USA) – Sundae Girl (USA) (Green **h93**
Dancer (USA)) [2006/7 h78: 22f⁴ 24d 20gᵘʳ 20m* 18s 20g 20s 20s Apr 27] close-coupled
gelding: modest hurdler: improved to win novice at Perth in June: no form after: stays
2¾m: best efforts on good going or firmer. *A. C. Whillans*

COUNT THE COST (IRE) 8 ch.g. Old Vic – Roseaustin (IRE) (Roselier (FR)) **h101 d**
[2006/7 24s² 26d⁵ 27dᶠ 27sᶠ 27vᵖᵘ Feb 20] workmanlike gelding: fair handicap hurdler:
failed to complete last 3 starts: suited by good test of stamina: raced on good going or
softer: wears cheekpieces. *J. Wade*

COUNT THE TREES 4 ch.f. Woodborough (USA) – Numerate (Bishop of Cashel) **h–**
[2006/7 16d⁶ 16s⁶ 17s⁴ 18g 16f Apr 5] modest maiden on Flat (stays 1¼m): no form over
hurdles. *W. G. M. Turner*

COUNT TIROL (IRE) 10 b.g. Tirol – Bid High (IRE) (High Estate) [2006/7 c19mᵖᵘ **c–**
Sep 28] no form over jumps: tried blinkered. *N. J. Dawe* **h–**

COUNTY DERRY 14 b.g. Derrylin – Colonial Princess (Roscoe Blake) [2006/7 **c–**
c33gᵖᵘ May 3] strong gelding: smart hunter chaser at best: suited by more testing
conditions (acted on heavy): often wore
cheekpieces, visored final start: sometimes made mistakes: dead. *J. Scott*

COUNTY FINAL (IRE) 8 b.g. Norwich – Soul Lucy (Lucifer (USA)) [2006/7 c17d² **c104 d**
c17dᵖᵘ c22m c21m² c24gᵖᵘ c24dᵖᵘ Oct 20] useful-looking ex-Irish gelding: half-brother **h–**
to several winners, including useful hurdler/chaser up to 3m The Carrig Rua and useful
but temperamental staying chaser Sister Stephanie (both by Phardante): dam winning 2m
hurdler: fair hurdler: disappointing over fences after debut: left N. Meade before fourth

outing: stays 2½m: acts on heavy going: tried tongue tied: has hung/jumped left. *Jonjo O'Neill*

COUNTY ZEN (FR) 4 b. or br.g. Lost World (IRE) – Fair County (FR) (Armos) [2006/7 F12v³ F17s³ F16d⁵ Mar 17] €18,000 3-y-o: unfurnished gelding: seventh foal: half-brother to 3 winning jumpers in France around 2m: dam winning hurdler around 2m: fairly useful form when third in bumpers, beaten 10 lengths by American Cricket at Hereford on second occasion. *P. J. Hobbs*   **F95**

COURSING RUN (IRE) 11 ch.g. Glacial Storm (USA) – Let The Hare Run (IRE) (Tale Quale) [2006/7 c114§, h–§: c24v⁵ c29s⁵ Mar 11] smallish, angular gelding: fairly useful handicap chaser at best: soundly beaten in 2006/7: stays 29f: acts on heavy going: tried visored (badly let down by jumping), in cheekpieces 4 of last 5 starts: unreliable. *H. D. Daly*   **c– §** / **h– §**

COURT ALLIANCE 8 ch.g. Alhijaz – Fairfields Cone (Celtic Cone) [2006/7 h72: 16s 22s² 22v² 19d⁴ Mar 26] small, angular gelding: modest novice hurdler, lightly raced: should prove better at 2¾m+ than shorter: acts on soft going. *Evan Williams*   **h93**

COURT AWARD (IRE) 10 b.g. Montelimar (USA) – Derring Lass (Derring Rose) [2006/7 c–, h–: c21gᵖᵘ May 24] modest pointer, runner-up 3 times in 2007: no form in other events: tried blinkered. *Mrs Alison Hickman*   **c–** / **h–**

COURT EMPEROR 7 b.g. Mtoto – Fairfields Cone (Celtic Cone) [2006/7 h69: 16m 20g⁶ 24m² Jul 12] modest novice hurdler: stays 3m: raced on good/good to firm going over jumps. *Evan Williams*   **h89**

COURT ONE 9 b.g. Shareef Dancer (USA) – Fairfields Cone (Celtic Cone) [2006/7 h94: 20m³ 22d* 16s⁶ 22m 25g 18s 21s⁵ 20g 20g Apr 16] small, sparely-made gelding: fair hurdler: won handicap at Cartmel in May: well held last 6 starts: stays 3m: acts on good to firm and good to soft ground (ran poorly on heavy): tried in cheekpieces. *R. E. Barr*   **h100 d**

COURT RULER 5 b.g. Kayf Tara – Fairfields Cone (Celtic Cone) [2006/7 19dᶠ 16g* 16d Dec 15] useful-looking gelding: sixth foal: half-brother to useful hurdler up to 21f Court Shareef and fair staying hurdler Court One (both by Shareef Dancer): dam useful hurdler up to 2¾m: no sign of ability on Flat for R. Price: 50/1, won novice hurdle at Ascot by 5 lengths from Hawridge Star: virtually lost all chance with blunder third in Grade 2 month later: will stay at least 2½m: should still progress. *Evan Williams*   **h114 p**

COUSIN NICKY 6 ch.g. Bob Back (USA) – Little Red Spider (Bustino) [2006/7 c106+, h–: 21v* 22s⁴ c19d³ c20s³ c21v⁵ c24sᵘʳ 24d² Mar 19] workmanlike gelding: fairly useful handicap hurdler/chaser: made all in novice event over hurdles at Newbury in November: would probably also have won 5-runner handicap chase at Sandown but for unseating last, around length ahead of Reflected Glory at time: stays 3m: acts on heavy going: front runner/races prominently. *P. J. Hobbs*   **c121** / **h119**

COUSTOU (IRE) 7 b.g. In Command (IRE) – Carranza (IRE) (Lead On Time (USA)) [2006/7 h91: 19d³ 19m 19v 20sᵖᵘ 19sᵖᵘ 20gᵖᵘ Apr 21] medium-sized gelding: modest maiden hurdler: form in 2006/7 only on reappearance: stays 2¾m: acts on soft going: blinkered once (found little), usually wears cheekpieces: patiently ridden: has bled from nose. *R. M. Stronge*   **h93 d**

COVENT GARDEN 9 b.g. Sadler's Wells (USA) – Temple Row (Ardross) [2006/7 h128: 20v Dec 2] sturdy gelding: fairly useful handicap hurdler, lightly raced: off a year, never dangerous (jumped right) at Wetherby: stays easy 3m: acts on firm and good to soft going: sometimes soon off bridle. *J. Howard Johnson*   **h114**

COVERDALE LADY 5 b.m. Prince Daniel (USA) – Lisband Lady (IRE) (Orchestra) [2006/7 F16g F16g 16v⁶ 17gᵖᵘ 20g⁶ Apr 16] unfurnished mare: second foal: dam of little account: no form in bumpers/over hurdles. *J. M. Saville*   **h–** / **F–**

COVERT MISSION 4 b.f. Overbury (IRE) – Peg's Permission (Ra Nova) [2006/7 F12v⁵ F16mʳᵒ F17g* Apr 27] unfurnished filly: second foal: dam unraced: won bumper at Newton Abbot by ¾ length from Felinious, though again looked wayward: close up when running very wide and unseating time before. *P. D. Evans*   **F98**

COWBOYBOOTS (IRE) 9 b.g. Lord Americo – Little Welly (Little Buskins) [2006/7 c119§, h–§: c28s³ c28d* c26s³ c29v⁶ c25sᵇᵈ c24s² c32s² c33v c25gᵖᵘ c29fᵖᵘ Apr 28] sturdy, good-bodied gelding: winning hurdler: fairly useful handicap chaser: won at Fontwell (fourth course success) in November by 1¼ lengths from Sungates: good efforts when runner-up sixth/seventh starts, let down by attitude all outings after (blinkered final one): stays 4m: acts on heavy going: temperamental. *L. Wells*   **c128 §** / **h– §**

COWBOYS CRUNCH (IRE) 7 ch.g. Moonax (IRE) – Tiffany Downs (Green Shoon) [2006/7 20v^pu Mar 6] half-brother to winning pointer by Good Thyne: dam unraced: no sign of ability, mainly in points. *W. Storey* — h—

COXWELL COSSACK 14 ch.g. Gildoran – Stepout (Sagaro) [2006/7 c–, h80: 19d^F 20f Jul 19] sturdy gelding: winning hurdler, lightly raced nowadays: tried in cheekpieces. *Mark Campion* — c— h—

COY LAD (IRE) 10 ch.g. Be My Native (USA) – Don't Tutch Me (The Parson) [2006/7 c82, h–: c20g 20s^4 Jun 25] useful-looking gelding: winning pointer, including in 2007: poor maiden hurdler/chaser: likely to stay 3m: tried in cheekpieces: sold 3,000 gns Doncaster August Sales. *Miss P. Robson* — c71 + h—

CRACBOUMWIZ (FR) 7 b.g. Baby Turk – Ellapampa (FR) (Pampabird) [2006/7 h98p: 19v^2 Feb 20] tall gelding: won bumper on debut: better effort in novice hurdles (fair form) over 14 months apart when second to Pur de Sivola at Taunton, taking good hold. *Heather Dalton* — h104

CRACKADEE 8 b. or br.g. Alflora (IRE) – Carnetto (Le Coq d'Or) [2006/7 c–, h–: c22v^2 c24s^4 c24v* c24v^pu Mar 6] no show in novice hurdle: fair chaser: won maiden at Newcastle in January: will stay beyond 3m: raced on soft/heavy going. *Miss R. Brewis* — c102 h—

CRACKING CLICHE 5 ch.m. Classic Cliche (IRE) – Calametta (Oats) [2006/7 F14s^2 F16s^4 F17g^F Apr 13] workmanlike mare: half-sister to several winners, including fairly useful staying chaser Skillwise (by Buckley) and fairly useful 2m hurdler Beechcourt (by Son Pardo): dam Irish maiden: fair form in frame in bumpers: travelling well when hampered and fell over 5f out in listed race at Aintree: bred to be suited by further. *Miss Venetia Williams* — F94

CRACKINGTON (FR) 7 gr.g. Linamix (FR) – Ta Awun (USA) (Housebuster (USA)) [2006/7 h–, F–: 16s^pu 19d^pu Feb 19] of no account. *H. Alexander* — h— F—

CRACKLEANDO 6 ch.g. Forzando – Crackling (Electric) [2006/7 h100d: 24s^F 17s 22s^3 24m 20v^3 24d^6 27v^2 27v 24v 20g^3 Mar 27] close-coupled gelding: modest handicap hurdler, left Mrs J. McGregor after seventh outing: stays 27f: acts on heavy going: sometimes takes plenty of driving. *A. D. Brown* — h92 §

CRACK ON (IRE) 5 b.g. Flemensfirth (USA) – Carols Cracker (IRE) (Persian Mews) [2006/7 19s 16d^6 19s c25v^pu 21m^3 Apr 9] €20,000 3-y-o: rather unfurnished gelding: fourth foal: half-brother to winning pointer by Glacial Storm: dam unraced half-sister to useful staying chaser King Lucifer: won maiden Irish point in 2006: no form over hurdles: not fluent on chasing debut: tried tongue tied. *D. E. Pipe* — c— h—

CRAFTY LADY (IRE) 8 b. or br.m. Warcraft (USA) – Kilmana (IRE) (Castle Keep) [2006/7 F73: 20g 18g^3 Apr 10] runner-up in bumper: poor form over hurdles. *Miss Suzy Smith* — h64

CRAGG PRINCE (IRE) 8 b.g. Roselier (FR) – Ivory Queen (Teenoso (USA)) [2006/7 c–, h83: 22g^pu 25g^pu 24v^pu May 20] no longer of any account. *Mrs C. J. Ikin* — c— h—

CRASHTOWN HALL 6 b.h. Saddlers' Hall (IRE) – Crashtown Lucy (Crash Course) [2006/7 F84: F16s* F16m^5 Jan 29] good-topped horse: fair form in bumpers: off 9 months, won at Huntingdon in December (final start for C. Tinkler). *D. W. P. Arbuthnot* — F88

CRASHTOWN LEADER (IRE) 8 b.g. Supreme Leader – Crashtown Lucy (Crash Course) [2006/7 h–: 22d^6 24v^5 Oct 21] well-made gelding: chasing type: bumper winner: fair form when third over hurdles in 2004/5: lightly raced and disappointing since: should stay 3m: sold 1,800 gns Doncaster May Sales. *C. Tinkler* — h—

CRATHORNE (IRE) 7 b.g. Alzao (USA) – Shirley Blue (IRE) (Shirley Heights) [2006/7 h118: 20m* 17d 22d 16d^6 16g^3 16g^2 Nov 2] rather leggy gelding: fair on Flat (stays 2m): fairly useful handicap hurdler: won at Southwell in June by 2½ lengths from Ball O Malt: good efforts final 2 starts: stays 2½m: acts on good to firm and good to soft going. *M. Todhunter* — h124

CRAVEN (IRE) 7 b.g. Accordion – Glen Dieu (Furry Glen) [2006/7 h123, F105: 16s^2 c20d^pu c16m^2 c23g* Mar 25] tall gelding: impresses in appearance: fairly useful hurdler: left N. Henderson, creditable second to Afsoun in limited handicap at Newbury on return: fair form over fences: landed odds in 5-runner maiden at Taunton in March: stays 23f: acts on soft going: blinkered last 2 outings: ungenuine: sold 30,000 gns Doncaster May Sales. *P. F. Nicholls* — c102 § h123 §

CREAM CRACKER 9 b.m. Sir Harry Lewis (USA) – Cream By Post (Torus) [2006/7 h104: 17m 16m^3 17m^2 c16d^4 16d* 16g^2 16g^2 18g^6 c20g^2 c16d^4 Nov 21] lengthy mare: — c113 h114 fair handicap hurdler: won at Southwell in August: similar form over fences, won maiden at Newton Abbot previous month by 18 lengths from Kings Brook: stays 2½m: acts on firm and good to soft going: waited with: reliable. *R. H. Alner*

CREATE A STORM (IRE) 7 b. or br.m. Elag (Strong Gale) – Elag (Strong Gale) **h—** [2006/7 h–, F–: 16g^{pu} Oct 7] workmanlike mare: no solid form in bumpers/novice hurdles: sold €3,200 Fairyhouse February Sales. *J. G. Portman*

CREDENTIAL 5 b.h. Dansili – Sabria (USA) (Miswaki (USA)) [2006/7 16d 16v^{pu} **h—** Dec 15] smallish horse: fair on Flat (stays 1½m), successful in January: not fluent and no form over hurdles. *John A. Harris*

CREDIT (IRE) 6 b.g. Intikhab (USA) – Tycooness (IRE) (Last Tycoon) [2006/7 h100: **h—** 16m^{pu} 20m 20d Oct 18] good-topped gelding: fairly useful juvenile hurdler in 2004/5: disappointing in handicaps since: tried blinkered/in cheekpieces. *Jennie Candlish*

CREGG HOUSE (IRE) 12 ch.g. King Persian – Loyal River (Over The River (FR)) **c— §** [2006/7 c123§, h–§: c17m^5 16g c20v^{pu} Feb 24] tall gelding: fairly useful handicap chaser **h— §** on his day: no form in 2006/7, including over hurdles: effective at 2m to 25f (refused both starts over further): acts on heavy going: tried blinkered/in cheekpieces: has had tongue tied: temperamental. *S. Donohoe, Ireland*

CREGG LORD (IRE) 8 b.g. Lord Americo – Philips River (IRE) (Over The River **h— x** (FR)) [2006/7 20s^{pu} May 17] ex-Irish gelding: brother to a winning pointer: dam unraced half-sister to useful staying chaser On The Other Hand: runner-up on first of 2 starts in Irish points in 2004, pulled up in Britain in 2006: jumped poorly on hurdling debut. *Mrs L. B. Normile*

CREINCH 6 b.g. Overbury (IRE) – Kingsfold Blaze (Mazilier (USA)) [2006/7 h95: **h102** 20d^4 19m^2 16d* 16s^{ur} 16m^4 16f* 19g 16s 16d 16s^5 Nov 22] lengthy gelding: will make a chaser: fair hurdler: won novice at Fakenham in May and handicap at Plumpton in September: looked none too straightforward last 2 starts: stays 2½m: acts on firm and good to soft going. *M. F. Harris*

CRIMOND (IRE) 5 b.m. Zaffaran (USA) – Bayalika (FR) (Kashtan (FR)) [2006/7 **h91** F67+: F16g F17d^5 24s^3 22d^4 Feb 1] leggy, unfurnished mare: mid-field in bumpers: **F79** upped in trip, modest form in frame in maiden/novice hurdles: stays 3m. *G. R. I. Smyly*

CRIMSON PIRATE (IRE) 10 b.g. Phardante (FR) – Stroked Again (On Your Mark) **c—** [2006/7 c114+, h–: c16s^{pu} Apr 26] strong gelding: very lightly raced: winning hurdler: **h—** off almost 3 years, won novice handicap at Wincanton in 2005/6 on chasing debut: ran as if amiss when next seen 16 months later: will be suited by 2½m. *B. De Haan*

CRISTAL LILY 4 ch.f. River Falls – Broad Appeal (Star Appeal) [2006/7 F14s Jan 4] **F—** narrow, angular filly: fourth foal: dam untrustworthy 1m winner: well beaten in mares bumper on debut. *Mrs Norma Pook*

CRISTOPHE 9 b.g. Kris – Our Shirley (Shirley Heights) [2006/7 c91, h–: c23m^5 **c94** c25m^{pu} 24m 22g^2 24g^2 c23m* c26d^3 c24m^3 c24m^4 Sep 24] lengthy gelding: modest **h96** handicap hurdler/chaser, left P. Bowen after second start: won over fences at Worcester in August: stays 3¼m: acts on good to firm and good to soft going: tried in headgear (not since early-2003/4): 4 of 5 wins for Wayne Hutchinson. *Mrs A. M. Thorpe*

CRITICAL STAGE (IRE) 8 b.g. King's Theatre (IRE) – Zandaka (FR) (Doyoun) **c—** [2006/7 h104: 17g^{su} 16f^3 17d^4 17s^3 c17d^5 c16m^{pu} 16d^{pu} 19s* Dec 7] compact gelding: **h104** fair on Flat (stays 1½m): fair hurdler: won claimer at Newton Abbot in August and seller at Taunton in December: well held on completed start over fences (stiff task): stays 19f: acts on soft and good to firm going: tried tongue tied: has shaped as if amiss more than once. *J. D. Frost*

CROCODILE BAY (IRE) 4 b.g. Spectrum (IRE) – Shenkara (IRE) (Night Shift **h82** (USA)) [2006/7 16m^5 16g^3 17d^6 Nov 8] fairly useful on Flat, successful twice at 2 yrs, sold out of J. Osborne's stable 70,000 gns Newmarket Autumn Sales, well held in 2006: best effort in juvenile hurdles when third to Katies Tuitor at Kempton, not easy for 3yr ride: joined B. Meehan. *Carl Llewellyn*

CROCODILE DUNDEE (IRE) 6 b.g. Croco Rouge (IRE) – Miss Salsa Dancer **h118** (Salse (USA)) [2006/7 16g^2 16v* 16d^3 16g^6 Apr 13] good-topped gelding: smart on Flat (stays 1½m), successful in August, sold out of L. Cumani's stable 190,000 gns Newmarket Autumn Sales: fairly useful form in novice hurdles: landed odds at Kelso in January by 2½ lengths from Storm Prospect: 25/1, well-held sixth of 7 finishers in Grade 2 event at Aintree: raced at 2m: acts on heavy going. *J. Howard Johnson*

CROCODILES ROCK (IRE) 5 b.g. Heron Island (IRE) – That's The Bonus (IRE) **F118**
(Executive Perk) [2006/7 F17s⁵ F16d* F16d* F16g⁶ Mar 14] £15,000 3-y-o: good-
topped gelding: fifth foal: brother to a winning pointer and half-brother to 2m hurdle
winner He's My Man (by Be My Native): dam unraced half-sister to useful 2m hurdlers
Thats My Man and Spirit Leader: smart form in bumpers: won at Newbury in December
and February, beating Just A Thought by length in Grade 2 event in latter: creditable 4¾
lengths sixth of 24 to Cork All Star in Champion Bumper at Cheltenham (hampered in
straight). *Jonjo O'Neill*

CROFTING (IRE) 7 b.m. Naheez (USA) – Crofter's Law (Furry Glen) [2006/7 16sᵖᵘ **h–**
19s Mar 12] pulled up in 2 Irish points prior to successful on completed start in Britain in
2006: little show in mares maiden hurdles: tried in cheekpieces. *Mrs H. R. J. Nelmes*

CROFT (IRE) 4 b.g. Mull of Kintyre (USA) – Home Comforts (Most Welcome) **h–**
[2006/7 17g 18m⁶ Sep 21] half-brother to winning hurdler Barnbrook Empire (by Second
Empire), stays 19f: modest maiden on Flat (stays 1m): little impact in juvenile hurdles.
R. M. Stronge

CROFTON ARCH 7 b.g. Jumbo Hirt (USA) – Joyful Imp (Import) [2006/7 h–: 16gᶠ **c–**
22vᵖᵘ c16vᵘʳ c16g Apr 7] no form over hurdles/in maiden chases: tried tongue tied/in **h–**
cheekpieces. *J. E. Dixon*

CROFTON (IRE) 5 b.g. Bob's Return (IRE) – Star of The Orient (IRE) (Moscow **h86**
Society (USA)) [2006/7 16s⁶ 16s 16d⁶ 22v 20gᵖᵘ Mar 17] big, leggy gelding: second
foal: dam Irish bumper winner: modest novice hurdler: should stay at least 2½m. *Ferdy
Murphy*

CROIX DE GUERRE (IRE) 7 gr.g. Highest Honor (FR) – Esclava (USA) (Nureyev **c129 §**
(USA)) [2006/7 c121, h127: c16gᶠ c20gᶠ 17g⁶ c17d³ c16g c19gᵘʳ 20fᵈ Apr 28] tall **h127**
gelding: fairly useful handicap hurdler/chaser: good fourth to Oslot in quite valuable
event over hurdles at Sandown: largely let down by temperament/jumping over fences in
2006/7: stays 21f: acts on soft and firm going: blinkered. *P. J. Hobbs*

CROMWELL COURT 6 b.g. Overbury (IRE) – Slip A Coin (Slip Anchor) [2006/7 **h98**
F16v⁵ 16v⁴ 16s⁴ 16v* 16v⁴ 20vᵖᵘ Mar 22] good-topped gelding: fourth foal: dam 9.4f **F69**
seller winner: fifth in bumper: modest hurdler: made all in maiden at Hexham in February: bled final start: raced mainly at 2m, only on soft/heavy ground. *D. McCain Jnr*

CROOKHAVEN 4 b.g. Dansili – My Mariam (Salse (USA)) [2006/7 16s 16v 16v⁶ 17g **h126**
16mᶠ Apr 10] smallish gelding: useful up to 1¼m on Flat, successful in June: seemingly
easily best effort in juvenile hurdles when seventh to Katchit in Triumph at Cheltenham
fourth outing: raced around 2m: dead. *John Joseph Murphy, Ireland*

CROON 5 b.g. Sinndar (IRE) – Shy Minstrel (USA) (The Minstrel (CAN)) [2006/7 19g⁴ **h93**
16s 16d⁶ Dec 30] leggy, sparely-made gelding: fairly useful on Flat (stays 1¾m),
successful twice in 2006 for H. Morrison: modest form in novice hurdles: joined T. Pitt.
Mrs Caroline Bailey

CROP WALKER (IRE) 5 b. or br.g. Kotashaan (FR) – Miss Mutley (Pitpan) [2006/7 **F88**
F16g⁵ F16m Apr 21] rather leggy gelding: fifth foal: half-brother to useful staying chaser
Model Son (by Leading Counsel): dam unraced: fair form in bumpers: will stay further.
Mrs K. Walton

CROSBY DANCER 8 b.g. Glory of Dancer – Mary Macblain (Damister (USA)) **h81**
[2006/7 h–: 17d³ 21m² 20s 24g⁶ 16m⁵ 18m 17s Oct 25] poor hurdler: won conditional
jockeys selling handicap at Sedgefield in May: well held last 5 starts: stays 21f: acts on
good to firm and good to soft going. *W. S. Coltherd*

CROSSBARRY BOY (IRE) 8 b.g. Fresh Breeze (USA) – Santamore (Buckskin **c101**
(FR)) [2006/7 c16m⁴ c22m² c24d⁵ c24vᶠ c22d³ Mar 29] rangy gelding: maiden hurdler: **h–**
fair chaser: stays 2¾m: acts on good to firm going. *John Joseph Murphy, Ireland*

CROSSBOW CREEK 9 b.g. Lugana Beach – Roxy River (Ardross) [2006/7 c109+, **c149**
h135: 16m 17g³ c16g* c17m* c16gᵖᵘ Apr 12] rangy gelding: won maiden on Flat in **h134**
August: useful handicap hurdler, third to Ellerslie Tom at Bangor following month: smart
chaser: much improved when winning handicaps at Kempton and Ascot (listed event,
beat Demi Beau by 1¼ lengths) in October: off 5½ months, lost all chance with blunder
seventh in Grade 3 event at Aintree: raced around 2m: runner-up on heavy going, best
form under less testing conditions: held up. *M. G. Rimell*

CROSSGUARD (USA) 4 b.g. Royal Anthem (USA) – Foible (USA) (Riverman **F73 +**
(USA)) [2006/7 F16m⁶ Jan 29] 9,000 3-y-o: third foal: half-brother to winner in Austria
by Belong To Me: dam, French 1m (at 2 yrs) and 1½m winner, half-sister to dam of 1000

Guineas winner Wince: unraced on Flat for J. Gosden: soon plenty to do when sixth of 16 in bumper at Ludlow on debut. *D. J. Wintle*

CROSS MY SHADOW (IRE) 5 b.g. Cape Cross (IRE) – Shadowglow (Shaadi (USA)) [2006/7 h–: 16s⁶ 16s⁶ Dec 7] no form over hurdles, including in seller: tongue tied. *M. F. Harris*   **h–**

CROSS THE HIGHMAN (IRE) 9 b.g. Un Desperado (FR) – Adabiya (IRE) (Akarad (FR)) [2006/7 20g³ c23m² c22g² c23m² c22g² c24m⁵ c20gᵖᵘ Oct 3] ex-Irish gelding: fair hurdler/maiden chaser, off over 21 months prior to return: stays 3m: acts on good to firm and good to soft ground: tried blinkered: temperamental: sold 6,000 gns Doncaster October Sales, placed in points. *Jonjo O'Neill*   **c103 §**   **h103 §**

CROSS THE PALM (IRE) 4 gr.f. Great Palm (USA) – Smooth Leader (IRE) (Supreme Leader) [2006/7 F16v Jan 28] €17,000 3-y-o: fifth foal: half-sister to bumper/ 17f hurdle winner Young Albert (by Taipan): dam unraced: no show in maiden bumper on debut. *S. J. Marshall*   **F–**

CROUCH END FLYER 5 b.m. Overbury (IRE) – Edithmead (IRE) (Shardari) [2006/7 F16s⁴ F17v⁴ 19s⁶ Mar 12] fifth foal: dam modest maiden hurdler up to 2¾m: poor form in bumpers: well held in mares maiden on hurdling debut, though travelled strongly long way: should do better. *Carl Llewellyn*   **h– p**   **F69**

CROWNFIELD 8 b.g. Blushing Flame (USA) – Chief Island (Be My Chief (USA)) [2006/7 16d⁵ 17vˢᵘ 16dᵖᵘ Oct 20] workmanlike gelding: fair hurdler at best: left K. Reveley, no form in 2006/7: should have stayed beyond 2m: tried tongue tied: dead. *B. N. Pollock*   **h–**

CROWN GAMBLE 5 b. or br.g. Silver Patriarch (IRE) – Gemma's Wager (IRE) (Phardante (FR)) [2006/7 F17s F16v 21g³ Mar 26] third foal: half-brother to 2m chase winner Green Gamble (by Environment Friend): dam won 21f chase: signs of ability in novice on hurdling debut (finished lame). *D. M. Grissell*   **h71**   **F–**

CROW WOOD 8 b.g. Halling (USA) – Play With Me (IRE) (Alzao (USA)) [2006/7 h135: 17s² 16m* 16s⁶ 17s³ 17g Mar 16] useful-looking gelding: smart hurdler: further improvement in 2006/7, winning 6-runner £1 Million totetofollow Elite Hurdle (Limited Handicap) at Wincanton in November by ½ length from Desert Quest, making all later well-judged ride: ran well at Cheltenham last 2 starts, on final one ridden less prominently than usual when 4 lengths eighth of 28 to Pedrobob in County Hurdle (Handicap): likely to prove best at 2m: has form on soft going, probably ideally suited by less testing conditions (acts on good to firm). *J. J. Quinn*   **h145**

CROZAN (FR) 7 b.g. Sassanian (USA) – La Guyonniere (FR) (Silver Rainbow) [2006/7 c141d, h–: c21d² c22vᵖᵘ c21gᶠ c20g⁴ Apr 13] tall, rather leggy gelding: maiden hurdler: useful chaser: creditable efforts on completed starts in 2006/7, around 20 lengths fourth of 6 to Monet's Garden in Grade 1 at Aintree on final one: likely to prove best short of 3m: acts on soft going: blinkered last 2 starts: has shaped as if amiss more than once. *N. J. Henderson*   **c142**   **h–**

CRUISE DIRECTOR 7 b.g. Zilzal (USA) – Briggsmaid (Elegant Air) [2006/7 h95: 16d³ Nov 19] good-topped gelding: fairly useful on Flat (stays 1½m): modest maiden hurdler: raced around 2m on good ground or softer. *Ian Williams*   **h92**

CRUISING RIVER (IRE) 8 b.g. Over The River (FR) – Jellaride (IRE) (King's Ride) [2006/7 c121, h–: c26g³ 22d* 22s* 24sᵖᵘ c24g Apr 21] sturdy gelding: fair hurdler: won novices at Uttoxeter and Wincanton in October: fairly useful chaser at best, no show either start in 2006/7: stays 3m: acts on soft going. *Miss H. C. Knight*   **c–**   **h113**

CRUSOE (IRE) 10 b.g. Turtle Island (IRE) – Self Reliance (Never So Bold) [2006/7 h–: c16sᵖᵘ c16vᶠ Jan 27] small gelding: poor on Flat (stays 11f), successful twice in 2006: no form over hurdles/fences: tried blinkered/tongue tied. *A. Sadik*   **c–**   **h–**

CRUSSET (IRE) 9 b.g. Petardia – Go Flightline (IRE) (Common Grounds) [2006/7 16gᵖᵘ Mar 26] good-topped gelding: fairly useful hurdler at best: off 2½ years, in third when broke down after last in seller at Plumpton: raced mainly around 2m: acted on heavy ground: tried blinkered: often tongue tied prior to 2004/5: dead. *W. G. M. Turner*   **h–**

CRY ALOT BOY 4 ch.g. Spinning World (USA) – Intellectuelle (Caerleon (USA)) [2006/7 aF16g* Mar 9] £2,600 3-y-o: fourth foal: closely related to French 6f winner Fastidia (by Fasliyev): dam, 1m winner, half-sister to smart French performer up to 10.5f Audacieuse and useful stayer Lord Jim: allowed to build long lead when winning bumper at Lingfield on debut by 5 lengths from Easement. *K. A. Morgan*   **F94**

CRY OF THE BANSHEE (IRE) 12 b.g. Yashgan – Cry Before Dawn (IRE) (Rose-lier (FR)) [2006/7 20f c24fpu c20f6 Jul 21] won maiden point in 2002, placed on several occasions since: no form in maiden hurdle or in chases: tongue tied. *J. Woods, Ireland*   c–
h–

CRYSTAL DANCE (FR) 7 gr.g. Loup Solitaire (USA) – Somptueuse (FR) (Crystal Palace (FR)) [2006/7 c–, h–: c21g2 c19m4 Apr 24] leggy gelding: maiden hurdler/chaser: fit from points (won in 2006), in frame in hunters in 2006/7: stays 2¾m: raced mainly on good ground or softer. *D. J. Kemp*   c91
h–

CRYSTAL HOLLOW 7 b.g. Riverwise (USA) – Pallanda (Pablond) [2006/7 h–, F–: c16gF May 16] no sign of ability. *N. R. Mitchell*   c–
h–

CRYSTAL KA (FR) 5 b.g. Northern Crystal – Kahuna Magic (FR) (Dancing Spree (USA)) [2006/7 h–: 16g6 16d 17v Dec 12] ex-French gelding: no form over hurdles. *M. R. Hoad*   h–

CUAN NA GRAI (IRE) 6 b.g. Erins Isle – Volnost (USA) (Lyphard (USA)) [2006/7 16g3 20s* 16f* 16m* 16m* 16d6 16m2 20mpu Apr 27]   h133
      It was very much a case of being in the right place at the right time for the riders of the winners of the two feature races at the Galway Festival in August. The day after Roger Loughran had successfully deputised for the injured Tony McCoy on Far From Trouble in the Galway Plate, another 'supersub' was in action in the Guinness Galway Hurdle. Barry Geraghty had been due to partner one of the favourites for this competitive handicap, Cuan Na Grai, but he suffered a broken nose and jaw in a fall earlier in the afternoon. In stepped Paddy Flood to ride a race of which Geraghty himself would have been proud. On a relatively-inexperienced novice making his first appearance in a handicap, Flood (claiming his biggest win to date) adopted the front-running tactics which had served Cuan Na Grai so well on his three previous starts, when successful at Wexford (twice) and Limerick, and the combination was never headed. Cuan Na Grain, jumping fluently, had all nineteen of his rivals in trouble once kicked clear two out and kept up the gallop to win by four lengths from Shandon Star, with several of those held up, including fourth-placed Emmpat, almost certainly at a disadvantage. It represented further improvement from Cuan Na Grai, whose first win had been gained over two and a half miles on soft going before he rapidly made up into a useful hurdler given the chance to race over two miles on ground firmer than good. Cuan Na Grai's victory was a third in the race in five years for trainer Paul Nolan, also successful with Say Again in 2002 and Cloone River in 2004. Cuan Na Grai was unable to match the form he showed at Galway in three subsequent appearances, although he wasn't that far below it when, reappearing after a five-month break, he finished a neck second to De Valira in a Grade 2 novice at Fairyhouse in April. The ground had been on the soft side when Cuan Na Grai had finished a well-beaten sixth in a similar event at Cheltenham in November; and on his final outing he ran as though all was not well in the Champion Novices' Hurdle at Punchestown (won by Fairyhouse third Glencove Marina), beaten before stamina became an issue given

Guinness Galway Hurdle (Handicap)—novice Cuan Na Grai provides Paul Nolan with his third win in the last five renewals; Shandon Star, The Last Hurrah (blinkers) and Emmpat (spots) fill the places

another try at two and a half miles. Cuan Na Grai is a brother to the useful middle-distance performer Arellano and a half-brother to several other Flat winners, but has never raced on the Flat himself, placed on both starts in bumpers (beaten a neck by Alexander Taipan on his debut) before being sent hurdling. A lengthy individual, Cuan Na Grai looks the sort who will also do well over fences when the time comes. *Paul Nolan, Ireland*

CUCCINELLO (IRE) 4 b.f. Makbul – Costa Verde (King of Spain) [2006/7 17s^{ur} 16g 16v^5 16v^6 Feb 27] big, leggy filly: half-sister to winning hurdler around 2m Troodos Jet (by Atraf): no form on Flat, trained at 3 yrs by K. Hogg: poor form over hurdles: likely to prove best at 2m. *I. McMath* — **h66**

CUCHULAINS SON (IRE) 5 b.g. Bob Back (USA) – Gallic Approach (IRE) (Toulon) [2006/7 F16s F16m^2 F16m^4 Apr 25] sturdy gelding: first foal: dam unraced half-sister to Irish Grand National winner Feathered Gale: progressive in bumpers, useful form when 4½ lengths fourth of 19 to Mick The Man in Grade 1 at Punchestown, again racing prominently. *W. P. Mullins, Ireland* — **F107**

CULCABOCK (IRE) 7 b.g. Unfuwain (USA) – Evidently (IRE) (Slip Anchor) [2006/7 h105: 16d^5 22d 16m^6 16g^3 16g^3 16s^5 18s^3 18s 16v^2 20g^4 18g^3 Apr 15] close-coupled gelding: poor form on Flat in 2006: fair handicap hurdler: mostly creditable efforts in 2006/7: stays 2¾m: acts on heavy and good to firm going: consistent. *Miss Lucinda V. Russell* — **h105**

CUL LA BALLA (IRE) 7 b.g. Hubbly Bubbly (USA) – Belon Breeze (IRE) (Strong Gale) [2006/7 c25d^4 c27s^F c27v^{pu} c25g^4 c25g^{pu} Apr 23] €8,000 4-y-o: third foal: brother to fairly useful hurdler/smart chaser Idle Talk, stays 33f: dam ran once: won maiden Irish point in 2006: no show in chases. *M. Todhunter* — **c–**

CULLIAN 10 b.m. Missed Flight – Diamond Gig (Pitskelly) [2006/7 c87, h79: c21g* c20f^3 c20m* c22m^5 Jun 30] good-topped mare: winning hurdler: modest handicap chaser: won novice events at Uttoxeter in May and Worcester in June: stays 3m: acts on firm going: tried blinkered/tongue tied, usually wears cheekpieces: sold 4,800 gns Doncaster August Sales. *J. G. M. O'Shea* — **c93 x** / **h–**

CULTURED 6 b.m. Danzero (AUS) – Seek The Pearl (Rainbow Quest (USA)) [2006/7 h–: 16m^{pu} Aug 28] no form over hurdles: tried blinkered. *Mrs A. J. Bowlby* — **h–**

CUMBO KID (IRE) 5 b.g. Supreme Leader – Palette (IRE) (Scenic) [2006/7 F16d F16d 16s 17v 16v Mar 6] 10,000 2-y-o, 24,000 3-y-o: rangy gelding, unfurnished at present: first foal: dam, useful hurdler/chaser up to 3m, out of half-sister to dam of smart 2m hurdler Destriero: mid-division at best in bumpers: no show in novice hurdles: tongue tied after debut. *C. Grant* — **h–** / **F73**

CUMBRIAN KNIGHT (IRE) 9 b.g. Presenting – Crashrun (Crash Course) [2006/7 c96, h97: 20g^2 20g^{pu} 16m^4 16s^3 c16d^3 c19g^2 c16v^3 c20s^{pu} c20m^{pu} Apr 9] good-topped gelding: modest handicap hurdler/chaser: effective at 2m to 2½m: has form on soft going, very best efforts under less testing conditions (acts on firm): tried blinkered/in cheek-pieces. *J. M. Jefferson* — **c97** / **h94**

CUNNING PURSUIT 6 b.g. Pursuit of Love – Mistitled (USA) (Miswaki (USA)) [2006/7 h106: 17s^2 c20m^2 c20m^3 c21d^{pu} Oct 20] tall gelding: fair hurdler: modest form in novice chases: should prove as effective at 2½m as 2m: acts on soft and good to firm going: tongue tied in 2006/7. *R. Ford* — **c88** / **h108**

CUPID'S MISSION (IRE) 7 b.m. Afflora (IRE) – Poppea (IRE) (Strong Gale) [2006/7 19g 16d 22g^3 Apr 15] €34,000 4-y-o: strong, workmanlike mare: first foal: dam, fair hurdler/chaser, stayed 3m, half-sister to useful 3m chaser Killusty: first form (poor) over hurdles on final start. *A. H. Mactaggart* — **h70**

CUPLA CAIRDE 7 b.h. Double Eclipse (IRE) – Four-Legged Friend (Aragon) [2006/7 c72x, h–: c21m^5 c16v^2 May 23] compact horse: winning hurdler: poor maiden chaser, usually let down by jumping: best form at 2m: acts on heavy going, probably on good to firm: often blinkered. *O. Brennan* — **c72 x** / **h–**

CURLY SPENCER (IRE) 13 br.g. Yashgan – Tim's Brief (Avocat) [2006/7 c75, h–: c20s^5 c23d* c29s^5 Dec 3] leggy, quite good-topped gelding: winning hurdler: modest chaser: won handicap at Leicester in November: stays 25f: best efforts on going softer than good (acts on heavy). *R. J. Hewitt* — **c97** / **h–**

CURRADOON (IRE) 6 b.g. Lord Americo – Clara Petal (IRE) (Castle Keep) [2006/7 22d 19d Mar 26] sturdy gelding: second foal: dam unraced: third both starts in maiden — **h–**

Irish points in 2006: bought 19,000 gns Doncaster August Sales: well held in maiden hurdles. *Mrs A. Barclay*

CURRAGH GOLD (IRE) 7 b.m. Flying Spur (AUS) – Go Indigo (IRE) (Cyrano de Bergerac) [2006/7 c–, h–: 17g⁶ 20m Jun 6] maiden hurdler: no form over fences: tried in headgear. *Mrs P. N. Dutfield*
c–
h–

CURRAGH VIEW (IRE) 7 b.g. Moonax (IRE) – Musicara (Black Minstrel) [2006/7 F17d² 24d* c24sF 21dᵖᵘ Nov 10] strong gelding: fifth foal: half-brother to winning pointer by Royal Fountain: dam, maiden Irish pointer, sister to fairly useful winning 2m jumper Blacksburg: won maiden Irish point in 2006: runner-up in bumper for J. Wainwright: fair form when winning novice at Worcester in October on hurdling debut: fell on chasing debut, and jumped with no confidence back over hurdles final start: stays 3m: raced on good to soft/soft going. *Evan Williams*
c–
h100 +
F87

CURRAHEEN CHIEF (IRE) 12 b.g. Little Bighorn – Sprightly's Last (Random Shot) [2006/7 h–: c19d² c19dF c20d⁴ c20vᵖᵘ c19vᵖᵘ Feb 18] very lightly raced: bumper winner: no show in novice hurdle: easily best effort over fences when runner-up in maiden at Hereford: stays 2½m: tongue tied once: sold £700 Ascot February Sales. *J. L. Spearing*
c102 d
h–

CURRAN (IRE) 5 b.g. Good Thyne (USA) – Weather Along (Strong Gale) [2006/7 F16g 22d 24s⁵ Apr 1] good-topped gelding: third foal: dam ran once: third in maiden Irish point: well held in bumper/novice hurdles. *P. Beaumont*
h–
F–

CURROW KATE 10 br.m. Anshan – Dereks Daughter (Derek H) [2006/7 16m⁴ May 16] winning pointer: poor form when fourth in amateur novice on hurdling debut. *John Berry*
h74

CURVED AIR (IRE) 5 gr.m. Turtle Island (IRE) – Poetry (IRE) (Treasure Kay) [2006/7 F16s² F16g⁴ F17s⁴ F17g³ 17m 17g 16d 18m Apr 26] fourth foal: dam 7f winner: modest form when in frame in bumpers for Stef Liddiard: well beaten in novice hurdles. *B. G. Powell*
h–
F76

CUSHTY 4 gr.f. Baryshnikov (AUS) – Craberi Flash Foot (Lighter) [2006/7 F14s F14s 16v 16f Apr 22] angular filly: third foal: dam unraced: no sign of ability in bumpers/over hurdles. *C. L. Tizzard*
h–
F–

CUSP 7 b.m. Pivotal – Bambolona (Bustino) [2006/7 c84, h–: 16v 20v³ 21v* 19s* 21g Mar 28] tall mare: maiden chaser: fair handicap hurdler: won mares events at Plumpton in February and Market Rasen in March: stays 21f: acts on heavy going. *Mrs A. M. Thorpe*
c–
h102

CUSTOM DESIGN 6 ch.g. Minster Son – Scotto's Regret (Celtic Cone) [2006/7 h89, F104: 19g³ 19v* 19d 20s 17v⁴ 17m 20sᵖᵘ Apr 26] leggy gelding: fair handicap hurdler: won at Market Rasen in November: bred to stay 3m: acts on heavy going: tried visored: temperament under suspicion. *G. A. Harker*
h102

CUTE N YOU KNOW IT 4 b.f. Tamure (IRE) – Clodaigh Gale (Strong Gale) [2006/7 F14v³ F16v⁵ F16s² Mar 7] 6,000 3-y-o: sturdy filly: sister to 25f hurdle winner Hilly Gale and half-sister to staying chasers Hurricane Bay (by Karineja Bay) and Gumley Gale (by Greensmith), latter fairly useful: dam, placed once in bumpers, sister to useful chasers Full Strength and Wind Force: poor form in bumpers. *A. Crook*
F74

CUT 'N' RUN (IRE) 5 b. or br.m. Mister Mat (FR) – Hue 'n' Cry (IRE) (Denel (FR)) [2006/7 F16m⁴ F16m Jul 26] half-sister to 3 winners, including fairly useful hurdler/smart chaser Cornish Sett (by Accordion), stays 3m, and useful hurdler/chaser Major Sponsor (by Strong Gale), stayed 21f: dam unraced half-sister to Rhyme 'N' Reason out of half-sister to Hallo Dandy: modest form on first (when trained by G. Harker) of 2 starts in bumpers. *J. F. C. Maxwell, Ireland*
F77

CYBORG DE SOU (FR) 9 b.g. Cyborg (FR) – Moomaw (Akarad (FR)) [2006/7 c110, h–: c16vF c16m Jun 11] tall gelding: winning hurdler: fair chaser: effective at 2m, should stay 3m: acts on heavy going: in cheekpieces in 2006/7: sometimes let down by jumping over fences. *G. A. Harker*
c110 x
h–

CYD CHARISSE 5 b.m. Kayf Tara – Silk Stockings (FR) (Trempolino (USA)) [2006/7 F16g⁴ 19d 20s 21s⁵ 18m² Apr 26] leggy mare: first foal: dam little form on Flat: fourth in mares bumper: best effort over hurdles (modest form) when second to Sandymac in mares maiden at Fontwell: should prove suited by 2½m+: acts on good to firm going: tongue tied first 4 starts. *Mrs P. Robeson*
h99
F85

CYRIUM (IRE) 8 b.g. Woodborough (USA) – Jarmar Moon (Unfuwain (USA)) [2006/7 c25gᵖᵘ Apr 23] big, rangy gelding: novice hurdler: successful twice in points in March: no show in maiden hunter on chase debut: stays 2¾m. *P. J. Millington*
c–
h–

233

D

DABARATSA (FR) 4 b.f. Astarabad (USA) – Miss Reddy (FR) (Agent Bleu (FR)) **F–**
[2006/7 F17m⁶ Apr 15] €20,000 3-y-o: third foal: half-sister to winning hurdler/chaser up to 19f Star d'Avril (by Phantom Breeze): dam 2m hurdle winner: well beaten in mares bumper on debut. *Miss Tor Sturgis*

DADA CUP (FR) 4 b.g. Dadarissime (FR) – Colonial Cup (FR) (Air du Nord (USA)) **h85 +**
[2006/7 17s³ 19v 16s⁵ Mar 8] has scope: fourth foal: dam unraced: best effort over hurdles (modest form) when third in maiden at Taunton: possibly amiss next time, then not knocked about final outing: may yet do better. *D. E. Pipe*

DAD SAYS HEAZLE 7 ch.g. Midnight Legend – Blackdown Court (Pharly (FR)) **h83**
[2006/7 19v⁵ 17v 17s³ 21sᵖᵘ 18g 20g⁵ 17g⁴ Apr 27] rather leggy gelding: first foal: dam no sign of ability: won maiden point in 2006: poor novice hurdler: should be suited by 2½m+: acts on heavy going: tried blinkered. *J. D. Frost*

DADS LAD (IRE) 13 b.g. Supreme Leader – Furryvale (Furry Glen) [2006/7 c28v⁵ **c82**
c26vᵘʳ c24v⁵ c26sʳᵒ Jan 15] veteran handicap chaser, off almost 2 years before reappearance: every chance when ran out last final outing: thorough stayer: acts on heavy going: blinkered. *Miss Suzy Smith*

DAFARABAD (IRE) 5 b.g. Cape Cross (IRE) – Daftara (IRE) (Caerleon (USA)) **c–**
[2006/7 16m⁴ 16s⁴ 17s⁴ Jan 30] compact gelding: fair novice hurdler: no show on **h101**
chasing debut: raced around 2m on good to soft/soft going, may prove suited by less testing conditions. *Jonjo O'Neill*

DAFFI (IRE) 7 b.m. Zaffaran (USA) – Bdoore (IRE) (Petoski) [2006/7 c–: c24gᶠ c21v² **c84**
Mar 9] won mares maiden Irish point in February: second of 3 finishers at Ayr on completed outing in hunters: should stay 3m. *F. Jestin*

DAGENHAM YANK 7 b.g. Classic Cliche (IRE) – Loving Legacy (Caerleon (USA)) **c–**
[2006/7 c24gᵖᵘ Apr 27] ex-Irish gelding: fourth dam disappointing maiden: runner-up **h–**
in bumper: poor form over hurdles: sold out of T. Walsh's stable 14,000 gns Doncaster October Sales, won maiden point in April: no show in hunter on chase debut (got loose beforehand): tried blinkered. *Mrs C. M. Marles*

DAGGY BOY (NZ) 7 ch.g. Daggers Drawn (USA) – La Berceuse (NZ) (Kings Island) **c–**
[2006/7 h–: 22v⁶ c20vᵖᵘ Mar 7] sturdy gelding: no form over hurdles, left R. C. Guest and **h–**
off 12 months prior to return: badly let down by jumping on chasing debut. *Miss Venetia Williams*

DAGOLA (IRE) 6 b.g. Daggers Drawn (USA) – Diabola (USA) (Devil's Bag (USA)) **h78**
[2006/7 16g 16m⁴ 16m² Aug 3] modest on Flat (stays 1½m), successful in May: poor form over hurdles, probably flattered second start. *C. A. Dwyer*

DAISYDELL (IRE) 6 b.m. Sharifabad (IRE) – Daisy Mutlar (IRE) (Lafontaine **h83**
(USA)) [2006/7 24g⁴ 20v⁶ 20s Feb 22] left M. Butler, won mares maiden Irish point in November: poor maiden hurdler: stays easy 3m: tried in cheekpieces. *Eoin Doyle, Ireland*

DAISYPLANT 7 b.m. Faustus (USA) – Rosieplant (Queen's Soldier (USA)) [2006/7 **h–**
F17s F16s 20dᵖᵘ Feb 2] first foal: dam modest pointer: no show in bumpers/novice **F–**
hurdle: tongue tied. *Mrs D. A. Hamer*

DALARAM (IRE) 7 b.g. Sadler's Wells (USA) – Dalara (IRE) (Doyoun) [2006/7 c87, **c101**
h134: c20d² 21sᵖᵘ 17v 16v 16s 22d Mar 17] rather leggy gelding: in frame in novice **h114**
chases: one-time useful hurdler for J. Howard Johnson: little impact in handicaps in 2006/7: stays 21f: acts on good to firm and good to soft going: tongue tied. *D. J. Wintle*

DALAWAN 8 b.g. Nashwan (USA) – Magdala (IRE) (Sadler's Wells (USA)) [2006/7 **h82**
h79, F93: 24v³ 20g⁶ 24s⁵ 20s⁵ 20s⁶ 21v³ 24m 24v* 24sᵖᵘ Apr 26] poor hurdler: won conditional jockeys handicap at Ayr in March: stays 3m: acts on heavy going: inconsistent. *Mrs J. C. McGregor*

DALCASSIAN BUCK (IRE) 13 ch.g. Buckskin (FR) – Menebeans (IRE) (Duky) **c– x**
[2006/7 c–x, h–: 24s⁶ May 28] workmanlike gelding: winning hurdler/maiden chaser: **h–**
stays 3m: often let down by jumping over fences. *Mrs L. J. Young*

DALDINI 5 b.g. Josr Algarhoud (IRE) – Arianna Aldini (Habitat) [2006/7 h96: 16g⁶ **h106**
16v⁴ 16g* 16s Apr 25] leggy gelding: fair hurdler: improved to win maiden at Wetherby in March: free-going sort, will prove best around 2m: acts on good to firm going, well below best on soft/heavy. *Mrs S. J. Smith*

DALKEYS LAD 7 b.g. Supreme Leader – Dalkey Sound (Crash Course) [2006/7 16s⁶ **h81**
17d* 16s 16v 20sᵖᵘ Apr 27] sturdy gelding: poor hurdler: won maiden at Cartmel in May:
stays 2½m: raced on going softer than good. *Mrs L. B. Normile*

DALRIATH 8 b.m. Fraam – Alsiba (Northfields (USA)) [2006/7 c86, h78: c16fᵘʳ 20m* **c96 x**
17s² c17d² c21s* c20m⁴ c20mᵘʳ c20m⁵ c16gᶠ c16g⁵ c17m⁵ c17m³ c16g³ c16gᵘʳ **h93**
c21d⁴ c16g⁵ c20g⁵ c16d⁵ c16d² c16g⁶ c17d³ c21v³ c16v² c21vᵘʳ c16s² 19s³ c20m⁵ c21g²
c20m⁵ c20m⁴ Apr 28] lengthy mare: modest hurdler/chaser on her day, ran 30 times in
2006/7: won mares handicap hurdle at Fakenham and maiden chase at Cartmel in May:
stays 21f: acts on heavy and good to firm going: often let down by jumping over fences.
M. C. Chapman

DALUCCI (IRE) 4 gr.g. Daylami (IRE) – Coigach (Niniski (USA)) [2006/7 16s 16v **h103 +**
16v 16s⁵ 16g² 16m* 16m* Apr 28] half-brother to modest hurdler Aston Mara (by
Bering), stays 21f: fairly useful on Flat (stays 1½m), successful in September: fair
hurdler: won handicaps at Cork and Punchestown in April: raced at 2m: acts on good to
firm ground, little form on soft/heavy. *C. F. Swan, Ireland*

DAMARISCO (FR) 7 b.g. Scribe (IRE) – Blanche Dame (FR) (Saint Cyrien (FR)) **c99**
[2006/7 h83: 17g² 16d⁴ c16d* c16g³ c20mᶠ 17gᶠ Aug 26] angular gelding: modest **h94**
hurdler/chaser: won handicap over fences at Newton Abbot in June: best form around
2m: unraced on firm going, acted on any other: dead. *P. J. Hobbs*

DAME EDNA (FR) 7 b.m. Octagonal (NZ) – Mohave Desert (USA) (Diesis) [2006/7 **h–**
19mᵇᵈ 19s Jun 27] lightly raced and no sign of ability: visored/tongue tied in 2006/7.
M. B. Shears

DAME MAGGIE 6 b.m. Karinga Bay – Rempstone (Coronash) [2006/7 F16v⁵ 16g **h–**
17gᵖᵘ Apr 17] compact mare: fourth foal: sister to fairly useful staying chaser Earl's **F78**
Kitchen and bumper/17f winner Countess Point: dam poor pointer: shaped like a
stayer when fifth in bumper: no show over hurdles: likely to need 2½m+: tried tongue
tied. *V. R. A. Dartnall*

DANAHILL LAD (USA) 6 b.g. Danehill (USA) – Carmen Trial (USA) (Skip Trial **h–**
(USA)) [2006/7 F–: F16dᵖᵘ 21d 26vᵖᵘ Jan 11] no sign of ability in bumpers/novice **F–**
hurdles: tried tongue tied. *J. A. Danahar*

DANARAMA 8 b.m. Rock City – Ballyannagh (Rugantino) [2006/7 c22v³ c23v³ Mar **c–**
9] fourth foal: dam maiden hurdler/chaser: remote third in maiden chases. *D. P. Keane*

DANCEBACK (IRE) 6 b. or br.m. Bob Back (USA) – Grafton Girl (IRE) (Carmelite **h–**
House (USA)) [2006/7 F17s⁶ F16m⁵ 20v 20dᵖᵘ Jan 19] third foal: dam, in frame 3 of 4 **F–**
starts in bumpers, half-sister to dam of useful staying hurdler Spirit Dancer: no form in
bumpers/mares novice hurdles. *Grant Tuer*

DANCE HALL DIVA 5 b.m. Zaha (CAN) – Eastwell Star (Saddlers' Hall (IRE)) **h75**
[2006/7 h76: 19m 16v² 20m⁴ Jun 6] poor maiden hurdler: stays 2½m: acts on heavy and
good to firm going. *M. D. I. Usher*

DANCER LIFE (POL) 8 b.g. Professional (IRE) – Dyktatorka (POL) (Kastet (POL)) **c118**
[2006/7 c120, h–: c25m⁴ c24m⁴ 17s⁶ 20v 24s Jan 30] angular gelding: winning hurdler, **h–**
well beaten in handicaps in 2006/7: fairly useful chaser: stays 3m: acts on soft and good
to firm going: tried blinkered/visored (below form). *Evan Williams*

DANCER'S SERENADE (IRE) 5 b.g. Almutawakel – Dance Serenade (IRE) **h112**
(Marju (IRE)) [2006/7 20s⁴ 25s⁴ 20g² 20g Apr 23] good-bodied gelding: fairly useful on
Flat (stays 2m), successful in August: fair form in novice hurdles: favourite, won at Newcastle
in January by neck from Ballabriggs: should stay beyond 2½m: acts on soft going: sold
42,000 gns Doncaster May Sales. *T. P. Tate*

DANCE THE MAMBO 5 b.m. Benny The Dip (USA) – Debutante Days (Dominion) **h94**
[2006/7 h79, F79: 16g 17s 20d³ 24vᵖᵘ 16v* 16s 16v³ 19s⁵ Mar 11] good-topped
mare: modest hurdler: won mares races at Newcastle (maiden) in January and Catterick
(novice handicap) in February: stays 2½m: acts on heavy going: blinkered last 4 starts.
M. W. Easterby

DANCEWITHTHEDEVIL (IRE) 6 b. or br.g. Dr Massini (IRE) – Hibba (IRE) **c– p**
(Doubletour (USA)) [2006/7 F100: 20gᵖᵘ 16d 16s³ c16vᵖᵘ 17gᶠ Apr 27] workmanlike **h89 p**
gelding: bumper winner: modest form over hurdles: every chance when badly hampered
4 out in novice handicap on chasing debut: should be suited by further than 2m: possibly
not straightforward (tried blinkered), but remains open to improvement. *Jonjo O'Neill*

DANCE WITH WOLVES (FR) 7 ch.g. Tel Quel (FR) – La Florian (FR) (River Mist **h95**
(USA)) [2006/7 h91: 16g⁵ 16d³ 16v* 17v⁴ 16v* 21vᵖᵘ 18s Feb 18] leggy gelding: modest

handicap hurdler: won at Plumpton in December and January: raced mainly around 2m: acts on heavy going: usually wears blinkers/cheekpieces: has hinted at temperament. *Jim Best*

DANCE WORLD 7 b.g. Spectrum (IRE) – Dansara (Dancing Brave (USA)) [2006/7 h102: 17s^pu c17s^4 Feb 3] rather leggy gelding: fairly useful at best on Flat (stays 1¾m): fair hurdler: well held in maiden on chasing debut (should do better): raced mainly around 2m on good to soft/soft ground: free-going sort. *Miss J. Feilden*   **c– p** **h–**

DANCING AT DAWN (IRE) 6 b.m. Accordion – Lakshmi Dawn (IRE) (Lashkari) [2006/7 F17g Mar 25] third foal: dam unraced daughter of National Hunt Chase winner Hazy Dawn: seventh of 9 in bumper on debut. *C. J. Down*   **F74**

DANCING BAY 10 b.g. Suave Dancer (USA) – Kabayil (Dancing Brave (USA)) [2006/7 h139: c18v^2 c24s* c20v^pu Mar 3] sturdy gelding: smart stayer on Flat: useful hurdler: fair form over fences, fortunate winner of 4-runner maiden at Fakenham in February (left clear at last): stays 3m: acts on heavy and good to firm going: held up: temperament under suspicion. *N. J. Henderson*   **c114** **h–**

DANCING DASI (IRE) 8 b.m. Supreme Leader – Little Dasi (IRE) (Mandalus) [2006/7 19d^2 19v^5 16d^5 Feb 17] 10,000 4-y-o: medium-sized mare: third foal: dam, poor novice hurdler, sister to dam of smart hurdler up to 3m Powerstation: unplaced in maiden points in 2004: best effort in novice hurdles (fair form) when beaten head by Here's Johnny at Exeter: bred to stay 2½m+: possibly unsuited by heavy ground. *Mrs S. Gardner*   **h107**

DANCING HILL 8 b.m. Piccolo – Ryewater Dream (Touching Wood (USA)) [2006/7 h80: 22g 20f* 20m* 20m* Aug 4] fair hurdler: won seller at Worcester in July and handicaps there later in month and Bangor in August: stays 2½m: acts on firm going: tried tongue tied. *K. Bishop*   **h104**

DANCING LYRA 6 b.g. Alzao (USA) – Badaayer (USA) (Silver Hawk (USA)) [2006/7 16d^3 16d^3 16g* 16m 16g 16g^3 Apr 14] small gelding: fairly useful on Flat (stays 13f), successful twice in 2006: fairly useful hurdler: won maiden at Musselburgh in December readily by 5 lengths from Balyan: improved form when third of 22 to Kings Quay in valuable handicap at Aintree final start: may prove best with emphasis on speed at 2m: unraced on extremes of going. *R. A. Fahey*   **h117 +**

DANCING MELODY 4 b.f. Dr Fong (USA) – Spring Mood (FR) (Nashwan (USA)) [2006/7 16g^bd 18s 17d Mar 20] lengthy filly: modest maiden on Flat (stays 1m): little impact over hurdles: tried in cheekpieces. *J. A. Geake*   **h–**

DANCING ROCK 9 b.g. Dancing High – Liblet (Liberated) [2006/7 h96: 22s^5 24s c24d^pu c22s^3 c23v^3 Feb 25] tall, angular gelding: fair hurdler/novice chaser (distressed on debut): will stay beyond 3m: acts on heavy going. *P. J. Hobbs*   **c106** **h104**

DANCING SHIRLEY 9 b.m. Dancing Spree (USA) – High Heather (Shirley Heights) [2006/7 h–: 21s 22m c23m^F Jun 18] little form over hurdles: fell third on chasing debut. *Miss A. M. Newton-Smith*   **c–** **h–**

DANCING TORNADO (IRE) 6 ch.g. Golden Tornado (IRE) – Lady Dante (IRE) (Phardante (FR)) [2006/7 F16g F16v^6 F16v* F16v* F16v* 16v^4 Feb 3] first foal: dam unraced: progressive form in bumpers for M. Keane: won at Cork in December (maiden) and January (useful form when beating Baltiman by 1¾ lengths): fourth of 16 in maiden on hurdling debut: likely to do better. *M. Hourigan, Ireland*   **h92 p** **F110**

DAND NEE (USA) 5 b.m. Kabool – Zobaida (IRE) (Green Desert (USA)) [2006/7 F93: F16g^2 F16g^2 F17g Apr 13] leggy mare: fair bumper performer, runner-up at Musselburgh and Catterick in 2006/7. *G. A. Swinbank*   **F94**

DANDYGREY RUSSETT (IRE) 6 gr.m. Singspiel (IRE) – Christian Church (IRE) (Linamix (FR)) [2006/7 h88: 16d 17d^2 17s* 16v Jan 12] leggy mare: modest hurdler: won mares maiden at Bangor in December: may prove best around 2m: raced on going softer than good: front runner. *B. D. Leavy*   **h88**

DANEBANK (IRE) 7 b.g. Danehill (USA) – Snow Bank (IRE) (Law Society (USA)) [2006/7 h94: 16m 16g Sep 17] compact gelding: modest on Flat (stays 1¾m): maiden hurdler, well held in 2006/7: stays 19f: in cheekpieces last 4 starts: sold 5,500 gns Doncaster January Sales. *J. Mackie*   **h–**

DANEHILL DAZZLER (IRE) 5 b.m. Danehill Dancer (IRE) – Finnegans Dilemma (IRE) (Marktingo) [2006/7 16g 17d^4 Aug 15] fairly useful on Flat (stays 1m), successful twice in 2005 for A. Jarvis: has looked non-stayer over hurdles: sent to race in Jersey. *Ian Williams*   **h–**

DANEHILL WILLY (IRE) 5 b.g. Danehill Dancer (IRE) – Lowtown (Camden Town) [2006/7 16s^4 Mar 1] half-brother to 2m hurdle winner Beebeep (by Distinctly   **h90 p**

North): useful on Flat (stays 1½m): left N. Callaghan, promising fourth of 16 to I'm So Lucky in novice at Ludlow on hurdling debut: sure to improve. *Evan Williams*

DANGER BIRD (IRE) 7 ch.m. Eagle Eyed (USA) – Danger Ahead (Mill Reef (USA)) [2006/7 h–: 17m 19m^F 17d^3 Nov 16] poor maiden hurdler, often let down by jumping. *R. Hollinshead* **h82 x**

DANGEROUSLY GOOD 9 b.g. Shareef Dancer (USA) – Ecologically Kind (Alleged (USA)) [2006/7 20g 21g Mar 14] leggy gelding: fair on Flat (stays 1¾m): useful hurdler at best: left G. L. Moore, always behind in valuable handicap at Cheltenham final start: stays 2¾m: acts on good to firm and good to soft going: usually wears headgear: held up: rejoined former stable. *J. Howard Johnson* **h–**

DANIEL'S DREAM 7 b.g. Prince Daniel (USA) – Amber Holly (Import) [2006/7 h–, F–: 16f^3 17d^6 18v 16v 16g^4 Apr 15] smallish, sturdy gelding: seemingly much improved over hurdles when never-nearer fourth in novice at Kelso, possibly flattered: raced around 2m: acts on firm going. *J. E. Dixon* **h91 ?**

DANISH MONARCH 6 b.g. Great Dane (IRE) – Moly (Inchinor) [2006/7 16d^6 17d Nov 23] modest on Flat (stays 1¼m), successful in May and September: some promise in maiden hurdles (breathing problem second start): likely to prove capable of better. *David Pinder* **h74 p**

DANNYMOLONE (IRE) 8 b.g. Anshan – Moy Farina (Derrylin) [2006/7 c–: c19m^4 c21m^{pu} c23m^2 c25m^2 Apr 15] poor chaser: sold out of Micky Hammond's stable 5,200 gns Doncaster August Sales, won point in April: stays 25f: form only on good to firm ground. *C. C. Pimlott* **c78**

DANS BLARNEY (IRE) 10 b.g. Teenoso (USA) – Easby Mandrina (Mandalus) [2006/7 c–: c21g^{pu} c24g^{pu} Apr 27] poor pointer: successful twice, including in March: no show in chases. *B. R. Hughes* **c–**

DANS EDGE (IRE) 7 b.g. Fourstars Allstar (USA) – Collopy's Cross (Pragmatic) [2006/7 h–: 21g^6 26g^{pu} Nov 5] workmanlike gelding: no form over hurdles: tried blinkered (raced freely). *Heather Dalton* **h–**

DANSE MACABRE (IRE) 8 b.g. Flemensfirth (USA) – My Romance (Green Shoon) [2006/7 h108: 16d c20s^4 c20v^5 19v^3 c20v^4 Mar 12] sturdy gelding: fair handicap hurdler: best effort over fences (modest form) when third in maiden at Towcester: effective at 2m (won at 2m when conditions are testing) to 3m: acts on heavy going (well beaten on firm). *A. W. Carroll* **c91 h–**

DAN'S HEIR 5 b.g. Dansili – Million Heiress (Auction Ring (USA)) [2006/7 h110: 21d 16d c20g^4 Apr 16] small gelding: fair on Flat (stays 2m), successful in October: successful 2 of first 3 starts over hurdles in 2005/6, most disappointing since, including on chasing debut: stays 2½m: acts on soft going: in cheekpieces last 2 outings: has looked none too keen. *P. C. Haslam* **c– h–**

DAN'S MAN 6 ch.g. Zaffaran (USA) – Solo Girl (IRE) (Le Bavard (FR)) [2006/7 h91d, F91: c17d^4 c21v^{pu} c19m^{pu} Nov 7] big gelding: maiden hurdler: modest form when winning handicap at Bangor in October on chasing debut: shaped as if amiss next 2 starts (blinkered final one): bred to be suited by further than 21f: acts on soft ground: has raced freely. *N. A. Twiston-Davies* **c91 h–**

DANTE CITIZEN (IRE) 9 ch.g. Phardante (FR) – Boreen Citizen (Boreen (FR)) [2006/7 c108, h–: c25g^3 c26g^6 Apr 19] sturdy gelding: fair pointer, successful 3 times in 2007: fair chaser, left T. George after first start: stays 25f: acts on soft going, probably on good to firm. *Mrs K. Smyly* **c108 h–**

DANTECO 12 gr.g. Phardante (FR) – Up Cooke (Deep Run) [2006/7 c70x, h–: c21d^5 c21m^{pu} 20g Mar 27] big gelding: winning hurdler: poor handicap chaser: stays 27f: acts on firm and good to soft going: tried in cheekpieces: headstrong, and often makes running: sketchy jumper of fences. *Miss Kate Milligan* **c73 x h–**

DANTE'S BACK (IRE) 9 b.g. Phardante (FR) – Jordans Pet (IRE) (Vision (USA)) [2006/7 c91x, h–: c26g c20m^4 Jun 13] tall gelding: maiden hurdler: novice chaser, modest at best: thorough stayer: tongue tied last 2 starts: sold £1,700 Ascot November Sales, successful 4 times in points in 2007. *N. A. Twiston-Davies* **c– x h–**

DANTE'S BROOK (IRE) 13 ch.g. Phardante (FR) – Arborfield Brook (Over The River (FR)) [2006/7 c–, h–: c16f c16f c17f^5 Jul 25] strong, lengthy gelding: has been hobdayed: winning chaser, no form since 2004/5: often tongue tied. *B. Mactaggart* **c– h–**

DANTE'S PROMISE (IRE) 11 b.g. Phardante (FR) – Let's Compromise (No Argument) [2006/7 c80, h–: c23m c26d^{pu} Jun 12] winning pointer: maiden chaser: well held only outing over hurdles: stayed 23f: wore cheekpieces final 4 starts: dead. *C. J. Down* **c– h–**

boylepoker.com Chase (Handicap), Cheltenham—
the grey D'Argent holds on by two short heads from New Alco (left) and top weight My Will

DANTES REEF (IRE) 11 b.g. Phardante (FR) – Thousand Flowers (Take A Reef) **c132 x**
[2006/7 c118x, h–: 19v c20s* c29m⁵ Apr 9] winning hurdler: useful chaser: won minor **h94 +**
event at Clonmel (by 4½ lengths from Lost Time) in March: best effort when fifth of 29
to Butler's Cabin in Irish National at Fairyhouse: effective at 2½m to 29f: acts on heavy
and good to firm going: held up: often makes mistakes over fences. *A. J. Martin, Ireland*

DANTES VENTURE (IRE) 10 b.g. Phardante (FR) – Fast Adventure (Deep Run) **c–**
[2006/7 c–, h–: 24d 26gᵖᵘ 24m Apr 15] sturdy gelding: fair hurdler in 2004/5: lightly **h–**
raced and little form since, left Miss I. Craig and off 14 months before reappearance: let
down by jumping over fences: stays 3¼m: acts on heavy and good to firm going: often
visored, blinkered last 2 starts: has won when tongue tied: sold 1,000 gns Doncaster May
Sales. *Miss Suzy Smith*

DANTOR 5 b.g. Dansili – Shallop (Salse (USA)) [2006/7 h–: 23g 20g 17d⁶ 20m³ 20f **c–**
16fᵖᵘ 20g c17sᶠ 16g⁵ 17s 16g⁵ 21v² Jan 2] modest maiden hurdler: fell heavily first on **h87**
chasing debut: stays 21f: acts on heavy and good to firm going: tongue tied. *M. A. Barnes*

DANZARE 5 b.m. Dansili – Shot of Redemption (Shirley Heights) [2006/7 h–: 16s **h– p**
Feb 22] angular mare: modest on Flat (stays 1¼m), successful in January: no form 3 starts
over hurdles (first 2 for Mouse Hamilton-Fairley), not knocked about only one in 2006/7:
likely to do better now qualified for handicaps. *J. L. Spearing*

DANZIG CONQUEST 7 ch.g. Danzig Connection (USA) – Seren Quest (Rainbow **h84**
Quest (USA)) [2006/7 17d 20v 20g Apr 27] sturdy gelding: fair form in bumpers: off 18
months, poor form on first of 3 starts in novice hurdles. *Mrs A. T. Cave*

DARAB (POL) 7 ch.g. Alywar (USA) – Damara (POL) (Pyjama Hunt) [2006/7 h–: **h104**
21d* 22d⁵ 24mᵖᵘ Jul 11] sparely-made gelding: fair hurdler: left Mrs S. Smith, improved
to win conditional jockeys handicap at Southwell (by 21 lengths) in June: stays 25f: acts
on good to firm and good to soft going: has worn cheekpieces: sold 1,800 gns Doncaster
August Sales. *T. R. George*

DARA MAC 8 b.g. Presidium – Nishara (Nishapour (FR)) [2006/7 16d⁶ Oct 30] modest **h–**
on Flat (stays 9.5f), well beaten in 2006: left L. Grassick, well held in novice claimer on
hurdling debut. *M. Scudamore*

DARAYBAD (FR) 5 b.g. Octagonal (NZ) – Daraydala (IRE) (Royal Academy (USA)) **h109**
[2006/7 h98+: 16m³ 16s² 17s⁴ Dec 22] lengthy, good sort: fair maiden hurdler: raced
around 2m: acts on soft and good to firm going. *N. J. Henderson*

DARAZARI BAY (IRE) 6 b.g. Darazari (IRE) – Conna Dodger (IRE) (Kemal (FR)) **F–**
[2006/7 F–: F17s F16g Nov 10] big, strong gelding: no form in bumpers. *K. G. Reveley*

DARBY WALL (IRE) 9 ch.g. Beveled (USA) – Nikkis Pet (Le Moss) [2006/7 c119, **c132**
h–: 16g⁶ c24s⁵ c24sᶠ c24d* c16s⁵ 20v c24g⁵ c24fᵖᵘ Apr 27] leggy gelding: winning **h102**
hurdler: useful chaser: won amateur handicap at Cheltenham in November by neck from
No Guarantees: sweating, improved form when fifth of 24 to Cloudy Lane in similar
valuable event there on penultimate outing: reportedly broke blood vessel next time: best
around 3m: acts on any going. *Enda Bolger, Ireland*

DARCY WELLS 6 b.g. Saddlers' Hall (IRE) – Qurrat Al Ain (Wolver Hollow) **h–**
[2006/7 F–: 17dᵖᵘ Oct 25] quite good-topped gelding: little show in bumpers/novice
hurdle: sold £4,000 Ascot December Sales. *T. D. Easterby*

DARE 12 b.g. Beveled (USA) – Run Amber Run (Run The Gantlet (USA)) [2006/7 **c– §**
c24sᵖᵘ May 20] leggy gelding: winning hurdler: modest pointer, successful twice in 2006: **h– §**
no form in chases: tried in headgear: usually tongue tied: weak finisher. *J. A. Lee*

DARE TOO DREAM 8 b.g. Thowra (FR) – Dubacilla (Dubassoff (USA)) [2006/7 c–, **c– §**
h100: c21sᵖᵘ c21sᵖᵘ 21s Mar 2] big, rangy, good sort: winning hurdler/maiden chaser: **h– §**
no form in 2006/7, left Miss Sarah Inglis before final start: tried visored: unreliable.
C. L. Tizzard

D'ARGENT (IRE) 10 gr.g. Roselier (FR) – Money Galore (IRE) (Monksfield) [2006/7 **c147**
c25s* c29sᵖᵘ c24gᵖᵘ c33s² Mar 17] leggy, useful-looking gelding: smart handicap chaser: **h–**
off 20 months, won listed event at Cheltenham in December by short head from New
Alco: back to form when 12 lengths second of 18 to Baron Windrush in Midlands Grand
National at Uttoxeter: stays 33f: acts on soft and good to firm going: often let down by
jumping: best form over fences on left-handed tracks. *A. King*

DARIAK (FR) 4 gr.g. Highest Honor (FR) – Darakiyla (IRE) (Last Tycoon) [2006/7 **h96**
16s 16sᵖᵘ 16gᵘʳ Mar 16] maiden on Flat, placed up to 1¼m in France at 3 yrs, sold out of
A. de Royer Dupre's stable €115,000 Goffs July Sale: modest form on completed outing
over hurdles: left S. Mahon in Ireland, saddle slipped final start. *P. R. Webber*

DARIALANN (IRE) 12 b.g. Kahyasi – Delsy (FR) (Abdos) [2006/7 c75, h81: c23g* **c82**
c20gᶠ May 11] compact gelding: winning hurdler: poor chaser: won maiden at Wetherby **h–**
on first day of season: stays 23f: acts on soft and good to firm going: tried blinkered:
tongue tied once: hard ride. *O. Brennan*

DARINA'S BOY 11 b.g. Sula Bula – Glebelands Girl (Burslem) [2006/7 c111, h–: **c121**
c25gᵘʳ c20g⁶ c25d* 24m⁵ c22gᶠ c25vᵇᵈ c26s⁶ 23v² 23s Feb 17] workmanlike gelding: fair **h110**
hurdler: fairly useful handicap chaser: improved form when winning at Aintree in May
by 2½ lengths from Cassia Heights (pair clear): stays 27f: acts on heavy and good to firm
going: usually races prominently. *Mrs S. J. Smith*

DARIZAN (IRE) 6 b.g. Darazari (IRE) – Casaurina (IRE) (Le Moss) [2006/7 17s 20s **h100 +**
17s³ 17s* Feb 26] eighth foal: dam unraced half-sister to several winning jumpers: fair
form over hurdles: won maiden at Hereford by 4 lengths from Jaunty Flight: should stay
2½m: raced on soft going. *V. R. A. Dartnall*

DARJEELING (IRE) 8 b.m. Presenting – Afternoon Tea (IRE) (Decent Fellow) **c–**
[2006/7 c–, h99: 24mᵘʳ 19g² 24m² 27d⁴ 24m³ Apr 17] angular mare: fair handicap **h103**
hurdler: fell first only outing over fences: stays 3m: acts on soft and good to firm going:
tried in cheekpieces: has looked tricky ride. *Mrs S. Gardner*

DARK ATHLETE (IRE) 8 b.g. Accordion – Joyau (IRE) (Roselier (FR)) [2006/7 17s **h–**
26v⁴ 20vᵖᵘ Feb 17] €10,000 4-y-o: third foal: half-brother to winning pointer by Be My
Native: dam unraced sister to Grand National winner Royal Athlete: completed once in 3
starts in points: no form over hurdles. *Evan Williams*

DARK BEN (FR) 7 b.g. Solar One (FR) – Le Vrai Mc Coy (FR) (Cap Martin (FR)) **c108**
[2006/7 c105, h108: c28d² May 1] winning hurdler: fair chaser: stays 3½m: acts on heavy **h–**
going: genuine. *Miss Kate Milligan*

DARK CHARACTER 8 b.g. Reprimand – Poyle Jezebelle (Sharpo) [2006/7 h93: **c–**
c16vᵖᵘ Dec 11] tall gelding: lightly raced: bumper winner: modest form at best over **h–**
hurdles for G. A. Swinbank: off a year, ran as if amiss on chasing debut. *Miss S. E. Forster*

DARK CORNER 5 b.g. Supreme Leader – Made For A King (Roselier (FR)) [2006/7 **h118**
F97: 20s 20s 26s³ 25v* 20v⁶ 24s² Mar 11] useful-looking gelding: chasing type: bumper
winner: fairly useful hurdler: won handicap at Warwick in January by 2 lengths from Ile
de Paris: good second to Gidam Gidam in similar event at Market Rasen: stays 3¼m: acts
on heavy going. *N. A. Twiston-Davies*

DARK DIVA 9 b.m. Royal Fountain – Little Greyside (Nearly A Hand) [2006/7 c–, **c92**
h64: c22v³ c20sᵖᵘ Dec 26] workmanlike mare: winning pointer: fourth in maiden hurdle: **h–**
modest form on completed start in chases. *Mrs S. J. Smith*

DARK MANDATE (IRE) 9 b. or br.m. Mandalus – Ceoltoir Dubh (Black Minstrel) **c–**
[2006/7 c25s⁵ Mar 7] no form outside points. *J. S. Haldane* **h–**

DARK PLANET 4 ch.g. Singspiel (IRE) – Warning Shadows (IRE) (Cadeaux Gener- **h–**
eux) [2006/7 16dᵘʳ Jan 8] fair on Flat (stays 1½m), successful in July, sold out of
C. Brittain's stable 12,000 gns Newmarket Autumn Sales: unseated first on hurdling
debut. *D. Burchell*

DARK PLEASURE 9 b.g. Castle Keep – Dark Trix (Peacock (FR)) [2006/7 20g 16gᵖᵘ **h–**
Jun 15] refused to race in point on debut in 2006: no show in maiden hurdles.
M. Mullineaux

DARK ROSALINA 6 b.m. Defacto (USA) – Zihuatanejo (Efisio) [2006/7 h–, F–: 20m **h–**
Jul 12] compact mare: no form in bumpers/novice hurdles. *C. W. Moore*

DARK SHADOWS 12 b.g. Machiavellian (USA) – Instant Desire (USA) (Northern **c–**
Dancer) [2006/7 c–, h–: 20vᵖᵘ Mar 2] smallish gelding: maiden hurdler: no show in **h–**
chases/points: tried in cheekpieces. *W. G. Young*

DARKSHAPE 7 b.g. Zamindar (USA) – Shapely (USA) (Alleged (USA)) [2006/7 h85: **h85**
16s⁴ 16d³ 20v 17gᵖᵘ Apr 11] leggy gelding: modest handicap hurdler: likely to prove best
at 2m: acts on soft going, probably on good to firm: has hinted at temperament. *Miss
Venetia Williams*

DARKSIDEOFTHEMOON (IRE) 5 b.g. Accordion – Supreme Valentine (IRE) **F86**
(Supreme Leader) [2006/7 F17s⁴ F14s Feb 18] €12,000 3-y-o, resold £25,000 3-y-o:
good sort: first foal: dam unraced out of half-sister to high-class 2m to 2½m chaser Travado: better effort in bumpers when fourth to Wise Men Say at Folkestone. *N. J. Gifford*

DARK SOCIETY 9 b.g. Imp Society (USA) – No Candles Tonight (Star Appeal) **h–**
[2006/7 h84: 16m Sep 2] modest handicap hurdler at best, largely well held since 2004/5:
raced mainly around 2m: acts on heavy going: held up. *A. W. Carroll*

DARK THUNDER (IRE) 10 br.g. Religiously (USA) – Culkeern (Master Buck) **c74**
[2006/7 c82, h75: c27d² c27sᶠ Mar 13] poor hurdler/chaser, left Ferdy Murphy after **h–**
first outing: little impact in points: stays 27f: acts on heavy going: tried visored, usually
blinkered. *Mrs K. J. Tutty*

DARNAYSON (IRE) 7 b.g. Darnay – Nakuru (IRE) (Mandalus) [2006/7 c87d, h–: **c– §**
c24dᶠ May 15] tall gelding: modest form over hurdles: little show over fences since **h–**
debut: stays 3m: raced on ground softer than good: tried blinkered: temperamental.
N. A. Twiston-Davies

DARN GOOD 6 ch.g. Bien Bien (USA) – Thimbalina (Salmon Leap (USA)) [2006/7 **h103 §**
h103: 26d* 27m Jun 11] reportedly tubed: fair hurdler: made very hard work of landing
odds in maiden at Hereford in May: stays 3¼m: unraced on extremes of going: tried
visored/tongue tied: unreliable. *A. King*

DARN HIM (IRE) 5 b.g. Darnay – Wyckoff Queen (IRE) (Carefree Dancer (USA)) **h73**
[2006/7 F16s F16d⁶ 16d Mar 22] €9,000 3-y-o: good-topped gelding: chasing type: third **F73**
foal: half-brother to 2¼m hurdle winner Killeen Queen (by Beneficial): dam unraced
half-sister to fairly useful staying chaser Celioso: poor form in bumpers/claiming hurdle:
will be suited by greater test of stamina. *N. A. Twiston-Davies*

DARNIL (IRE) 9 b. or br.g. Grand Plaisir (IRE) – Art Lover (IRE) (Over The River **c91**
(FR)) [2006/7 c24dᵖᵘ c26d⁴ May 31] winning pointer: fourth at Cartmel on completed
start in hunter chases. *Mrs Edward Crow*

DARNLEY 10 b. or br.g. Henbit (USA) – Reeling (Relkino) [2006/7 24sᵖᵘ c16v⁵ c20vᵖᵘ **c80**
c16gᶠ c17g³ 24sᵖᵘ Apr 25] tall gelding: winning hurdler: poor chaser nowadays: raced **h–**
mainly around 2m: acts on soft and good to firm going. *J. N. R. Billinge*

DARSHARP 5 b.m. Josr Algarhoud (IRE) – Dizzydaisy (Sharpo) [2006/7 16f 19g **h–**
17mᵘʳ 17m⁶ 24f 20vᵖᵘ 21mᵖᵘ Apr 8] poor maiden on Flat (stays 1m), sold out of Gay
Kelleway's stable £2,600 Ascot August (2005) Sales: no form over hurdles. *Miss Jane
Mathias*

DARUSSO 4 ch.g. Daylami (IRE) – Rifada (Ela-Mana-Mou) [2006/7 16s³ 16s⁶ 16s³ **h98**
16v² 17g Mar 16] workmanlike gelding: half-brother to smart French hurdler Tiger
Groom (by Arazi) and useful hurdler Rifawan (by Cox's Ridge), both stayed 2½m: fair
maiden on Flat (should stay at least 1¼m): fair juvenile hurdler: out of depth final outing:
should stay beyond 2m: acts on heavy ground. *J. S. Moore*

DARWAZ (IRE) 5 ch.g. Grand Lodge (USA) – Dawala (IRE) (Lashkari) [2006/7 h88: **h90**
16m⁵ 20d Oct 18] lengthy gelding: modest form over hurdles: best at 2m: acts on good to
firm ground. *D. R. Gandolfo*

DARYAL (IRE) 6 b.g. Night Shift (USA) – Darata (IRE) (Vayrann) [2006/7 h123: 16s* **h121**
17s⁶ 21s⁶ 22sᵖᵘ 16g⁴ Mar 23] good-topped gelding: fairly useful handicap hurdler: off a
year, won at Lingfield in November by 1¾ lengths from Guru: back to form when fourth
to Fleet Street at Newbury, jumping markedly left last: probably stays 21f: acts on heavy
going: blinkered last 2 starts. *A. King*

DASHING CHARM 8 b.g. Charmer – New Cruiser (Le Solaret (FR)) [2006/7 17d⁶ **c56**
c24s³ c26v⁴ c19s c20s⁴ Jan 31] stocky gelding: no form in bumpers/over hurdles: bad **h–**
maiden chaser: joined B. Ellison. *Robert Gray*

DASHING GEORGE (IRE) 5 ch.g. Beneficial – Here It Is (Stanford) [2006/7 F16s **h98**
16v 20s 18v⁴ 16v³ 16s³ 19s² 19m Apr 7] £15,000 4-y-o: angular gelding: fifth foal: **F–**
half-brother to winning pointer by Phardante: dam bumper/hurdle winner: well held in
bumper: modest maiden hurdler: tried to run out final start: should stay at least 2½m:
raced mainly on soft/heavy ground. *Eric McNamara, Ireland*

DATBANDITO (IRE) 8 gr.g. Un Desperado (FR) – Most of All (Absalom) [2006/7 **h–**
h–: 20gᵖᵘ May 5] good-topped gelding: fair form in bumpers: no show over hurdles:
should be suited by further than 2m: sold 1,500 gns Doncaster May (2006) Sales, well
held in points. *L. Lungo*

DATITO (IRE) 12 b.g. Over The River (FR) – Crash Call (Crash Course) [2006/7 c106, **c109**
h–: c26v* c28s c33vᵖᵘ 25v⁴ c31s⁵ Apr 27] tall gelding, lightly raced: modest maiden **h99**
hurdler: fair handicap chaser: left R. Phillips, second successive winning reappearance at
Carlisle in November: stays 3¼m: acts on heavy going. *Mrs K. Walton*

DAUNTSEY BAY 6 b.g. Primitive Rising (USA) – Penny Falls (Push On) [2006/7 **h74**
20d⁶ 16v⁵ 22g⁴ Apr 15] 6,200 4-y-o: seventh foal: half-brother to winning pointers by
Heighten and Jula Bula: dam winning hunter chaser: first form in novice hurdles when
fourth to Harry Flashman at Kelso. *A. Parker*

DAUPHIN DES CARRES (FR) 9 ch.g. Dauphin du Bourg (FR) – Hypne (FR) **c?**
(Carmarthen (FR)) [2006/7 c20d c23gᶠ c20sᴿ 17s 18v c21d³ c21d² c23dᵖᵘ c21gᵖᵘ Mar 19] **h?**
winning hurdler: one-time fairly useful chaser: placed twice in Provinces but no other
form in 2006/7, left R. Chotard and off 4 months before final start: stays 25f: acts on
heavy ground: sold 3,800 gns Doncaster March Sales. *D. E. Pipe*

DAVENPORT DEMOCRAT (IRE) 9 ch.g. Fourstars Allstar (USA) – Storm Court **c123**
(IRE) (Glacial Storm (USA)) [2006/7 c142, h–: c24d⁴ 18m² 20g* 20m⁴ 17m* 16g⁶ **h124**
c19v* 21d² 18d² 16d² 16v Dec 31] tall, lengthy gelding: useful chaser: didn't need to be at
best to win minor event at Listowel in September: fairly useful hurdler: won novices at
Roscommon in July and September and minor event at Bellewstown in August: no match
for very easy winner Iktitaf when runner-up in 4-runner events at Punchestown (listed)
and Down Royal (Grade 3) ninth/tenth starts: stays 21f: probably acts on any going: often
front runner. *W. P. Mullins, Ireland*

DAVID'S SYMPHONY (IRE) 5 ch.g. Almutawakel – Habemus (FR) (Bluebird **h79 §**
(USA)) [2006/7 h82: 16sᵖᵘ 17s 22s 20v⁴ 16g² 20g Apr 14] neat gelding: poor maiden
hurdler: stays 2½m: acts on heavy going: tried visored, including last 3 starts: inconsistent. *A. W. Carroll*

DAVNIC 7 ch.m. Weld – Lahtico VII (Damsire Unregistered) [2006/7 h–, F–: 16f Apr **h–**
30] lengthy mare: no form in bumpers/over hurdles. *T. Wall*

DAVORIN (JPN) 6 br.h. Warning – Arvola (Sadler's Wells (USA)) [2006/7 16s* 18s* **h120**
16v⁴ 16s 20m² 20m⁵ Apr 27] stocky horse: useful on Flat (stays 1½m): fairly useful
novice hurdler: won at Punchestown (maiden) in October and Fairyhouse (awarded race
after beaten ¾ length by Bobs Pride) in November: easily best effort when 5½ lengths
second to Aitmatov in Grade 2 at Fairyhouse: stays 2½m: acts on heavy and good to firm
ground. *R. P. Burns, Ireland*

DAVOSKI 13 b.g. Niniski (USA) – Pamela Peach (Habitat) [2006/7 c–§, h–: 20m⁶ **c– §**
Aug 11] angular gelding: 50/1-winner of handicap chase at Cheltenham in 2004/5: little **h–**
form since: stays 21f: acts on heavy and good to firm going: tried blinkered/in cheekpieces: often jumps poorly: ungenuine. *Dr P. Pritchard*

DAVY JACK (IRE) 9 br.g. Camden Town – Tops O'Crush (Menelek) [2006/7 20m⁵ **c–**
20f⁴ c20gᵖᵘ Nov 1] sturdy gelding: brother to fairly useful hurdler Shean Town, stayed **h–**
2½m, and half-brother to very smart chaser Opera Hat (by Strong Gale), stayed 3m: dam
maiden: won maiden Irish point in 2005: little show in novice hurdles/chase. *J. R. Jenkins*

DAVY'S BOY 4 b.g. Zahran (IRE) – So We Know (Daring March) [2006/7 F17v 16vᵖᵘ **h–**
Feb 23] fifth foal: half-brother to 3m hunter winner Martin Ossie (by Bonny Scot): dam **F–**
bad novice hurdler: no show in bumper/juvenile hurdle. *J. M. Bradley*

DAVY'S LUCK 7 ch.m. Zahran (IRE) – Cursneh Decone (Celtic Cone) [2006/7 h75:   **h–**
17m Jun 19] poor hurdler: likely to prove best around 2m: acts on good to firm going.
J. M. Bradley

DAWESVILLE 6 ch.g. Karinga Bay – Le Belle Avril (IRE) (Le Moss) [2006/7 F17g⁴   **h–**
F17m 20g Sep 17] first foal: dam unraced: poor form in bumpers: tailed off in novice on   **F78**
hurdling debut: bred to be suited by 2½m+. *P. Bowen*

DAWN AT SEA 5 b.m. Slip Anchor – Finger of Light (Green Desert (USA)) [2006/7   **h75**
16d 16d³ 21s⁵ 16sᵖᵘ 19vᵖᵘ 24mᵖᵘ Apr 17] good-topped mare: half-sister to fairly useful
2m hurdler/chaser The Local (by Selkirk): fair maiden on Flat (stays 1½m), claimed from
J. Fanshawe £12,000 final start at 3 yrs: best effort over hurdles (poor form) on second
outing (claimed from A. E. Jones £6,000). *Mrs K. Waldron*

DAWN FOR THE STARS (IRE) 7 b.m. Fourstars Allstar (USA) – Spanish Slave   **h–**
(IRE) (Spanish Place (USA)) [2006/7 F–: 16mᵖᵘ Jun 11] no show in various events.
J. A. Danahar

DAWN FROLICS 6 gr.m. Silver Patriarch (IRE) – Mighty Frolic (Oats) [2006/7 c–,   **c–**
h–: c18m⁴ c21dᵘʳ c16s⁶ c16dᵖᵘ c24vᶠ 20v 16v 22v 23d Jan 15] sturdy, workmanlike mare: **h–**
no form: signs of temperament. *M. J. Gingell*

DAWN RIDE (IRE) 6 b.g. New Frontier (IRE) – Atlantic Dawn (IRE) (Radical)   **h77**
[2006/7 F16s⁵ 16v⁶ 16v³ 20g Apr 3] unfurnished gelding: first foal: dam unraced: fifth in   **F77**
bumper: poor form on second outing over hurdles: finished distressed next time. *Micky
Hammond*

DAWN WAGER 5 b.m. Silver Patriarch (IRE) – Gemma's Wager (IRE) (Phardante   **h81**
(FR)) [2006/7 h–, F75: 22m² 23d Nov 8] poor form over hurdles: left D. Feek, lame final
outing: will stay 3m: acts on good to firm ground. *D. M. Grissell*

DAYDREAMER (USA) 14 b.g. Alleged (USA) – Stardusk (USA) (Stage Door   **c–**
Johnny (USA)) [2006/7 c21g May 24] angular gelding: modest novice hurdler in 1998/9:   **h–**
very lightly raced in points since, winner in 2002: well beaten in maiden hunter on chase
debut. *Mrs S. J. Hickman*

DAY DU ROY (FR) 9 b.g. Ajdayt (USA) – Rose Pomme (FR) (Rose Laurel) [2006/7   **c85 §**
c97§, h94§: c16g 20g c20s⁵ c19sᶠ c20s³ c24sᵖᵘ c21g* Apr 9] rather leggy gelding: **h– §**
winning hurdler: modest handicap chaser: ended long losing sequence at Fakenham in
April: stays 21f: acts on soft and good to firm going: tried blinkered: tongue tied once:
usually finds little. *Miss L. C. Siddall*

DAY OF CLAIES (FR) 6 b.g. Passing Sale (FR) – Dayoula (Mouktar) [2006/7 h115:   **c112**
c20gᶠ c20d* c20v³ c22v³ c20g* c20gᵖᵘ Apr 14] useful-looking gelding: winning hurdler   **h–**
for N. Twiston-Davies: fair novice chaser: won at Sedgefield (maiden) in November and
Wetherby in March: stays 3m: acts on heavy going: tried blinkered. *H. P. Hogarth*

DAY ONE 6 ch.h. Daylami (IRE) – Myself (Nashwan (USA)) [2006/7 24g 22mᶠ Apr 22]   **h–**
fairly useful maiden on Flat (stays 1½m) at 3 yrs, has deteriorated markedly: tailed off on
completed start over hurdles. *R. J. Price*

DAYTIME ARRIVAL (IRE) 9 ch.g. Lucky Guest – Daymer Bay (Lomond (USA))   **c– x**
[2006/7 c20fᵖᵘ Jul 16] angular gelding: no form outside points: tried blinkered.   **h–**
K. S. Thomas

DAY TO REMEMBER 6 gr.g. Daylami (IRE) – Miss Universe (IRE) (Warning)   **h118 +**
[2006/7 17g* 16v Dec 26] compact gelding: useful on Flat (stays 1½m), successful in
May, sold out of E. Vaughan's stable 42,000 gns Newmarket Autumn Sales: successful
hurdling debut when beating Westgate by 12 lengths in novice at Market Rasen in
December, eased right down: probably unsuited by heavy ground next time: may be
capable of better back under less testing conditions. *J. J. Quinn*

DAZZLING JIM 7 b.g. Bob's Return (IRE) – Pytchley Dawn (Welsh Captain) [2006/7   **h95**
F16s⁴ F17d⁴ F16m* F13m⁵ 16m⁴ 20m² 19m* 19d⁴ 18m² 22m² Sep 10] first foal: dam   **F88**
poor maiden: maiden pointer: won maiden bumper at Stratford in June: modest novice
hurdler: awarded maiden at same course in August: stays 2¾m: acts on good to firm
going: has shown signs of temperament/looked difficult ride. *S. Lycett*

DEAD-EYED DICK (IRE) 11 b.g. Un Desperado (FR) – Glendale Charmer (Down   **c125 d**
The Hatch) [2006/7 c130, h–: c32m³ c21dᵖᵘ c22g c27sᶠ c23d⁵ c29sᶠ Dec 2] tall, quite   **h–**
good-topped gelding: fairly useful handicap chaser: below form in 2006/7 after third to
McKelvey in valuable event at Uttoxeter: stays 4m: acts on heavy and good to firm going:
has run as if amiss more than once, and seems best fresh. *Nick Williams*

DEAD MANS DANTE (IRE) 9 ch.g. Montelimar (USA) – Great Dante (IRE) (Phardante (FR)) [2006/7 c116, h89+: c24s^pu c24g^F c20g^6 c16s^5 c16v c20s^3 c20m^2 c20m* Apr 9] leggy gelding: maiden hurdler: fair handicap chaser: won at Sedgefield in April: probably stays 3m: acts on any going: free-going sort, usually held up: tends to find little. *Ferdy Murphy*   **c108 §**   **h–**

DEALER'S CHOICE (IRE) 13 gr.g. Roselier (FR) – Cam Flower VII (Damsire Unregistered) [2006/7 c101§, h–§: c25g^pu c26s^pu May 14] quite good-topped gelding: winning hurdler: fair handicap chaser at best: no show both starts early in 2006/7: stays 27f: acts on soft going: tried blinkered/in cheekpieces: usually let down by jumping/temperament. *Miss Victoria Roberts*   **c– §**   **h– §**

DEARSHA (FR) 5 b.g. Dear Doctor (FR) – Doushama (FR) (Nashamaa) [2006/7 F16g 19s 20v 16m 16m^5 Apr 24] close-coupled gelding: first foal: dam raced only up to 13f on Flat in France: no solid form in bumper/over hurdles: tried blinkered. *G. R. I. Smyly*   **h–**   **F–**

DEAR SIR (IRE) 7 ch.g. Among Men (USA) – Deerussa (IRE) (Jareer (USA)) [2006/7 16g 20g^5 22s^pu 19g 20g^F Apr 11] tall gelding: poor handicap hurdler: failed to complete in maiden chases: probably stays 2½m: acts on firm going. *Mrs P. N. Dutfield*   **c–**   **h76**

DEARSON (IRE) 6 b.g. Definite Article – Petite Maxine (Sharpo) [2006/7 h111: c20d^2 c20d^5 16m^3 Apr 10] lengthy gelding: fair hurdler: sold out of C. Mann's stable 17,000 gns Doncaster October Sales and off 8½ months, much better effort (fairly useful form) over fences at Ludlow when 3 lengths second to Art Virginia in novice handicap: stays 21f: acts on soft and good to firm going. *Evan Williams*   **c117**   **h111**

DEASUN (IRE) 9 b.g. Shernazar – Bettyhill (Ardross) [2006/7 16v 20s^pu c17v c20s c25v^pu Mar 9] half-brother to useful hurdlers/chasers Mr Pointment (by Old Vic), stays 3m, and Ground Ball (by Bob's Return), stays 2½m: winning pointer: no form in other events: tried blinkered. *Stephen McConville, Ireland*   **c–**   **h–**

DEBAUCHERY (IRE) 5 b.g. Old Vic – Bring It With You (Callernish) [2006/7 F16d^5 F17v^3 F18v* F16v* Feb 17] seventh foal: dam winning pointer: useful form in bumpers: won at Plumpton in January and Uttoxeter (suited by thorough test of stamina, beat Garleton by 6 lengths) in February: will be suited by 2½m+. *Carl Llewellyn*   **F112**

DEBOMAR (IRE) 8 b.g. Taos (IRE) – Crimson Mary (Lucifer (USA)) [2006/7 16s^pu 20m^pu Feb 4] no show in 2 starts over hurdles (reportedly broke blood vessel on debut): tried in cheekpieces. *D. J. P. Barry, Ireland*   **h–**

DEBUT (IRE) 5 b.m. Presenting – Kings Rose (IRE) (King's Ride) [2006/7 F14s* F16s Mar 10] sturdy mare: second foal: dam unraced half-sister to useful bumper winner No Shenanigans: won mares bumper at Fontwell on debut in December: tailed off in similar listed event 2½ months later. *N. J. Henderson*   **F93**

DECENT BOND (IRE) 10 b.g. Witness Box (USA) – Decent Skin (IRE) (Buckskin (FR)) [2006/7 c27s^3 c25g^pu Apr 2] winning pointer: in cheekpieces, well held on completed start in hunter chases. *V. Thompson*   **c60**

DECKIE (IRE) 12 b.g. Be My Native (USA) – Shannon Spray (Le Bavard (FR)) [2006/7 c92+, h–: c24d^4 c26s* c22g* Mar 28] angular gelding: prolific winning pointer: useful hunter chaser: better than ever when winning at Fontwell in February and Towcester (not fully extended to beat My Best Buddy by 12 lengths) in March: stays 3¼m: acts on firm and soft going: effective tongue tied or not: reluctant to race once. *D. J. Kemp*   **c116 +**   **h–**

DECLANS CHOICE (IRE) 7 b.g. Lord of Appeal – Hurricane Ceva (IRE) (Salluceva) [2006/7 24s^4 22s^pu c23d c25s^pu c26s^ur c24v^ur c24d^pu 22s 27m^pu Apr 26] €3,200 3-y-o: workmanlike ex-Irish gelding: second foal: dam unraced: runner-up in point in 2004: maiden hurdler/chaser: left K. Purcell, no form in 2006/7: usually wears headgear. *N. R. Mitchell*   **c–**   **h–**

DECREE NISI 4 ch.g. Compton Place – Palisandra (USA) (Chief's Crown (USA)) [2006/7 16f^3 17g^2 16d^6 16d^6 18s^4 17s^pu 16s^6 16s 16s^5 16m^3 16f^3 17g^3 Apr 27] leggy gelding: fair on Flat (stays 1m), claimed from Mrs A. Duffield £6,000 in September: modest juvenile hurdler, left L. Corcoran after fifth start: likely to prove best around 2m: acts on firm and good to soft going: effective visored or not. *M. F. Harris*   **h91**

DEDRUNKNMUNKY (IRE) 8 b. or br.m. Rashar (USA) – Rostoonstown Lass (IRE) (Decent Fellow) [2006/7 c94, h–: c22s^pu 22s c22s^pu Jan 4] angular mare: modest hurdler/chaser at best: no show in 2006/7: should prove suited by 3m+: acts on soft and good to firm going. *Miss Tor Sturgis*   **c–**   **h–**

DEEDAYBOOTS 4 b.g. Allied Forces (USA) – Dusty Shoes (Shareef Dancer (USA)) **h–**
[2006/7 16s⁶ 17d⁴ 17v Dec 12] tall gelding: little show in 3 runs on Flat at 2 yrs: no solid
form in juvenile hurdles: tried in cheekpieces/blinkers. *G. M. Moore*

DEEP KING (IRE) 12 b. or br.g. King's Ride – Splendid Run (Deep Run) [2006/7 **c–**
c111d: c19gᵖᵘ c20mᶠ c20f c25g⁶ Apr 20] lengthy gelding: fair chaser in 2005/6: no show
in points/hunters since: best efforts at 2m to 2½m: acts on firm and soft going: has had
tongue tied. *Col R. I. Webb-Bowen*

DEEP MOON (IRE) 7 b.g. Moonax (IRE) – Mrs Hegarty (Decent Fellow) [2006/7 h–, **c–**
F99: 17d 22sᵖᵘ 19vᵖᵘ c24vᵖᵘ Jan 27] tall, angular gelding: runner-up in bumper on debut: **h–**
no form over hurdles/in handicap chase: tried in cheekpieces/blinkered/tongue tied: sold
£1,600 Ascot February Sales. *C. J. Down*

DEEP POCKETS (IRE) 8 b.g. Fourstars Allstar (USA) – Pocket Price (IRE) **c–**
(Moscow Society (USA)) [2006/7 c103: c26gᵖᵘ c24dᵖᵘ May 15] winning pointer/hunter
chaser: let down by jumping in 2006/7: stays 25f. *Mrs Caroline Keevil*

DEEP QUEST 8 b.g. El Conquistador – Ten Deep (Deep Run) [2006/7 16s 22dᵖᵘ **h–**
Nov 16] big, good-topped gelding: chasing type: no form in novice hurdles, off almost 3
years before return. *D. P. Keane*

DEEP REFLECTION 7 b.g. Cloudings (IRE) – Tudor Thyne (IRE) (Good Thyne **h92 x**
(USA)) [2006/7 F90: F18s* 20vᵖᵘ 17s⁵ 16d⁵ 22dᵖᵘ 19g⁵ Apr 8] useful-looking gelding: **F104**
fairly useful bumper winner, including at Plumpton (first start after leaving J. Supple)
in November: modest maiden hurdler: should stay 2½m: acts on soft ground: tried in
cheekpieces: not a fluent jumper. *B. I. Case*

DEEP RETURN (IRE) 10 b.g. Bob's Return (IRE) – Parsons Honour (IRE) (The **c120**
Parson) [2006/7 c20d⁵ c22m c20f³ c25g* c25d* c22g² c20s⁵ c24s³ c28d c25m Apr 26] **h–**
well-made gelding: fairly useful hurdler: similar standard over fences in 2006/7, winning
maiden in August and handicap (by 3½ lengths from Kings Orchard) in September, both
at Kilbeggan: good efforts in novices over fences when placed behind Oodachee at Galway and
Mossbank at Clonmel: stays 25f: acts on any going. *N. Meade, Ireland*

DEER PARK COUNTESS 6 ch.m. Shaddad (USA) – Logani (Domynsky) [2006/7 **h–**
F17dᵖᵘ 19vᵖᵘ 16gᵖᵘ Dec 10] first foal: dam, no sign of ability, half-sister to useful staying **F–**
chaser Ardent Scout: no form, including on Flat: tongue tied last 2 starts. *D. A. Nolan*

DEFERLANT (FR) 10 ch.g. Bering – Sail Storm (USA) (Topsider (USA)) [2006/7 **c126**
c–§, h–§: c26g* c26s* c29vᵖᵘ Jan 7] close-coupled gelding: winning hurdler: left K. Bell **h–**
and off 16 months, improved over fences in 2006/7: won 2 handicaps at Fontwell in
November, fairly useful form when beating He's The Gaffer by 7 lengths on second
occasion, left clear 2 out (going best at time): lame final start: stays 3¼m: acts on soft and
good to firm going: formerly visored/in cheekpieces/tongue tied, not for present stable:
has looked moody. *Carl Llewellyn*

DEFINITE APPROACH (IRE) 9 b.g. Presenting – Crash Approach (Crash Course) **c– §**
[2006/7 c–, h–: c24dᶠ c21dᴿ c20vᵖᵘ Jan 25] useful-looking gelding: modest form in **h–**
novice hurdles: tongue tied, failed to complete all 5 starts over fences (refused to race
penultimate outing): should stay beyond 3m: blinkered last 2 outings. *R. T. Phillips*

DEFINITE DANCER (IRE) 5 b.g. Definite Article – Greeba (Fairy King (USA)) **F87**
[2006/7 F16s³ Mar 8] rather leggy gelding: second foal: dam, sprint maiden, out of
half-sister to Cadeaux Genereux: around 14 lengths third in maiden bumper won by
Gansey at Wincanton on debut. *Mrs S. D. Williams*

DEFINITE EDGE (IRE) 5 ch.g. Definite Article – Itkan (IRE) (Marju (IRE)) [2006/7 **F–**
F16d⁶ Feb 10] workmanlike gelding: fourth foal: half-brother to useful Irish 6f/7f winner
Exceptional Paddy (by Common Grounds): dam lightly-raced maiden: well held in
Grade 2 bumper on debut. *W. J. Musson*

DEFINITE LYNN (IRE) 4 bl.f. Definite Article – Gavotte du Cochet (FR) (Urbain **F–**
Minotiere (FR)) [2006/7 F16s Mar 1] 32,000 3-y-o: second foal: dam maiden half-sister
to high-class hurdler/top-class chaser Jair du Cochet, who stayed 25f: green, well held in
mares bumper on debut: sold 6,000 gns Doncaster May Sales. *N. J. Henderson*

DEGAS ART (IRE) 4 b.g. Danehill Dancer (IRE) – Answer (Warning) [2006/7 16s* **h135**
16g* 16m* 17g 16g³ Apr 12] strong, good-bodied gelding: smart on Flat (stays 1½m),
won twice in 2006 for D. Elsworth: useful juvenile hurdler: won at Wetherby (listed
event, by 1½ lengths from Katchit, rec. 8 lb) in October, Aintree in November and
Musselburgh in February: behind Katchit in Grade 1s at Cheltenham and Aintree after,
much better effort when 12 lengths third in Anniversary 4-y-o Novices' Hurdle at latter:

Constant Security Wensleydale Juvenile Novices' Hurdle, Wetherby—
smart Flat recruit Degas Art inflicts the only defeat on top juvenile Katchit

likely to stay beyond 2m: acts on soft and good to firm going: not a fluent jumper: carries head awkwardly but is genuine. *J. Howard Johnson*

DEJA VU (IRE) 8 b.g. Lord Americo – Khalkeys Shoon (Green Shoon) [2006/7 c108, **c–**
h–: c21^{vpu} c24s^{pu} c22v^{pu} c20g^{pu} Apr 7] sturdy gelding: fair hurdler/chaser at best: off a **h–**
year and left J. Howard Johnson, shaped as if amiss/let down by jumping in 2006/7: stays 21f: acts on heavy and good to firm ground. *Ferdy Murphy*

DELAMEAD (IRE) 4 b.g. King of Kings (IRE) – Al Saqiya (USA) (Woodman **h–**
(USA)) [2006/7 17d Nov 21] well held in 3 maidens on Flat in 2006: well beaten in juvenile on hurdling debut. *B. Ellison*

DELANEYS TRIUMPH (IRE) 7 b. or br.g. Taipan (IRE) – Hoodsgrove Lady (IRE) **c–**
(Over The River (FR)) [2006/7 22g 23f^4 24m 27v^5 c24d 22v c26m^{ur} c26m^5 Apr 26] **h–**
no solid form over hurdles, left Patrick Martin, Ireland after third start: well held in completed outings over fences: tried blinkered/tongue tied. *J. W. Mullins*

DELAWARE (FR) 11 b.g. Garde Royale – L'Indienne (FR) (Le Nain Jaune (FR)) **c– §**
[2006/7 c–§, h82§: 19s^3 19m^4 19g^4 19d^4 22m^F 20g^5 19m^4 26g Oct 15] leggy, angular **h85 §**
gelding: winning chaser (sketchy jumper): modest hurdler nowadays: probably stays 27f,

effective at much shorter: acts on heavy and good to firm going: has worn headgear (not in 2006/7): ungenuine. *H. S. Howe*

DELAWARE TRAIL 8 b.g. Catrail (USA) – Dilwara (IRE) (Lashkari) [2006/7 c–: 17s 17d⁶ 16m⁴ 16g⁶ 16d² c17m³ 22m c16d c17g^F c20v⁶ c20g⁴ c17v⁶ c24g^pu 16d 16s 19s 20g⁶ c16g⁴ Apr 23] big, workmanlike gelding: poor maiden hurdler/chaser: tried in cheekpieces: usually tongue tied. *R. Johnson* **c73 +** **h82**

DELCOMBE 6 b.g. Deltic (USA) – Nellie's Joy VII (Damsire Unregistered) [2006/7 F–: 17s⁶ 19v⁵ Feb 20] poor form over hurdles. *N. R. Mitchell* **h70**

DELENA 6 b.m. Classic Cliche (IRE) – Formal Affair (Rousillon (USA)) [2006/7 F87: 21d² 19s² 22g⁴ Apr 1] bumper winner: runner-up in mares events over hurdles at Ludlow (novice) and Taunton (maiden): should stay beyond 21f: acts on soft going. *P. F. Nicholls* **h100**

DELFINIA 6 b.m. Kingsinger (IRE) – Delvecchia (Glint of Gold) [2006/7 c20d^pu c16d^pu 17s c25s^pu Mar 7] sturdy mare: won maiden point in February: little sign of ability otherwise, left Miss Tracy Waggott after third start. *M. V. Coglan* **c–** **h–**

DELICEO (IRE) 14 b.g. Roselier (FR) – Grey's Delight (Decent Fellow) [2006/7 c98§, h–§: c25d^pu May 17] leggy gelding: winning handicap chaser: modest handicap chaser: stays 25f: acts on any going: has worn cheekpieces: ungenuine. *M. Sheppard* **c– §** **h– §**

DELIGHTFUL CLICHE 6 b.g. Classic Cliche (IRE) – Ima Delight (Idiot's Delight) [2006/7 h91, F82: 21g⁶ 24d² 24f* 24m 23s⁶ 26g* 24s 23s⁶ 24g* 24g Apr 18] sturdy gelding: fair hurdler: won maiden at Worcester in June and handicaps at Huntingdon in November and Towcester in March: stays 3¼m when conditions aren't testing: has form on soft going, seems best nowadays under less testing conditions. *Mrs P. Sly* **h105**

DELIGHTFULLY 6 b.m. Definite Article – Kingpin Delight (Emarati (USA)) [2006/7 16v⁵ 16g 16g^pu Apr 8] angular mare: 1½m winner on Flat: poor novice hurdler: tried blinkered. *Jean-Rene Auvray* **h82**

DELORAIN (IRE) 4 b.g. Kalanisi (IRE) – Lady Nasrana (FR) (Al Nasr (FR)) [2006/7 20d 16g 22m⁶ Apr 26] modest maiden on Flat (stays 2m), sold out of J. Toller's stable 12,000 gns Newmarket Autumn Sales: tailed off over hurdles: blinkered/visored: ungenuine. *W. B. Stone* **h– §**

DELRAY BEACH (FR) 5 b.m. Saint Preuil (FR) – Icone (FR) (Nikos) [2006/7 17s* 20f* 25g⁶ 22v 27s² c20s² c22v² c20s⁴ c29v* Mar 10] unfurnished mare: second foal: dam, 15f hurdle winner, half-sister to useful 2m hurdler/chaser Santenay: modest chaser: won 5-runner handicap at Ayr in March: fair hurdler: won claimer at Auteuil (claimed from J. Bertran de Balanda €12,500) in May and mares novice at Hexham in September: stays well: acts on any going. *Ferdy Murphy* **c90 +** **h107**

DELTA FORCE 8 b.g. High Kicker (USA) – Maedaley (Charmer) [2006/7 19d⁵ Aug 21] modest on Flat (stays 17f), missed 2005 because of leg injury: well beaten in maiden on hurdling debut. *P. A. Blockley* **h–**

DELTA LADY 6 b.m. River Falls – Compton Lady (USA) (Sovereign Dancer (USA)) [2006/7 16v^pu 16s 16g⁴ Mar 17] half-sister to winning hurdler/chaser Seef (by Slip Anchor), stayed 3¼m: poor maiden on Flat (stays 1m) at 2/3 yrs for R. Bastiman: first form (poor) over hurdles on final start. *Miss L. C. Siddall* **h80 ?**

DELTIC ARROW 9 b.g. Deltic (USA) – Jolly Girl (Jolly Me) [2006/7 c–, h–: c25v^pu c26v⁴ c24g⁵ Mar 28] lengthy gelding: winning pointer: well held in novice hurdle: no solid form in chases. *G. Brown* **c–** **h–**

Carey Group Handicap Chase, Ascot—
front-runner Demi Beau (noseband) lands this very valuable prize; Andreas fades into third

Cunningham Racing's "Demi Beau"

DEMI BEAU 9 b.g. Dr Devious (IRE) – Charming Life (NZ) (Sir Tristram) [2006/7   **c142** c136, h–: c17m² c17d* c16gᵖᵘ c16g c16f⁴ Apr 28] tall, good-topped gelding: winning   **h–** hurdler: useful chaser: won Carey Group Handicap at Ascot in November by 2 lengths from Hasty Prince: respectable fourth behind Dempsey in Grade 2 event at Sandown: will probably stay 2½m: acts on firm and good to soft going (yet to race on soft/heavy): sometimes used to shape as if amiss: has been let down by jumping. *Evan Williams*

DEMPSEY (IRE) 9 b.g. Lord Americo – Kyle Cailin (Over The River (FR))   **c162** [2006/7 c155, h–: c17dᵘʳ c20g⁴ c16sᵘʳ c16g* c16g² c16f* Apr 28]   **h–**
It wasn't quite third time lucky for Dempsey at the Cheltenham Festival, but his latest visit had a far better outcome than his first two ventures there. He'd been pulled up in the Champion Bumper as a five-year-old and then had the misfortune to be brought down by Kauto Star's third-fence fall in the Queen Mother Champion Chase three years later. In the latest season, he was in the Champion Chase field again, leading narrowly from two out where Voy Por Ustedes made a mistake, but unable to hold that rival when he renewed his challenge from the last. Dempsey passed the post a length and a half down in second, though Ashley Brook might have taken that place from him up the hill had he not come down at the final fence when rallying in a close third.

Dempsey's fine effort at Cheltenham laid to rest any notion that he needed a right-handed track to perform to his best; he may have done all his winning going that way round, but that's only because he's done the vast majority of his racing on right-handed tracks, a handful of runs at Cheltenham and Aintree the only exceptions. That said, Dempsey has an excellent record around Sandown, which by the end of the season stood at four wins and a second from five completed starts there. A horse with that kind of record on a track which puts a premium on jumping cannot be labelled a poor jumper, but Dempsey can make the odd bad mistake, and when he unseated his rider at the first of the railway fences (six out) when leading in the Tingle Creek Chase in December, it was a continuation of an uninspiring start to 2006/7. He had also unseated early on in the Haldon Gold Cup at Exeter on his reappearance and, between those two non-completions, on a rare outing at beyond two miles, he was a remote last of four finishers in the Peterborough Chase at Huntingdon.

The second half of Dempsey's campaign took a marked turn for the better, however, and he won at Sandown on either side of his second place at Cheltenham. In 2006, Dempsey had finished second in the Victor Chandler Chase which had been transferred to Sandown after falling victim to the weather. The same fate befell the race in the latest season, and again Sandown filled the gap by boosting the value of its two-mile handicap chase at their early-February meeting, run this time as the Fraser Steele HBLB Handicap Chase. As well as runner-up Dempsey, Tysou (first), Kalca Mome (third) and Bambi de L'Orme (fourth) re-opposed from the Victor Chandler the year before, while Oneway, third in the last two Tingle Creeks, was the only one in the field of twelve above Dempsey in the weights. With Timmy Murphy replacing his then-regular jockey Andrew Tinkler following those two unseated (Murphy had ridden him to wins early in his career in a bumper and three novice hurdles), Dempsey this time put in an error-free round to record a career-best effort, making the running as usual and being given a breather at the end of the back straight before readily seeing off his pursuers, who were headed by Hasty Prince, beaten five lengths in second, with favourite Andreas another length and a half away in third and Tysou fourth.

With Murphy back in the saddle again (Noel Fehily had deputised at Cheltenham when he'd been claimed to ride early faller Well Chief), Dempsey made the most of a good opportunity at Sandown on the final day of the season in the Betfred Celebration Chase where, at level weights, he had much the best form on offer. River City, third in the Champion Chase, looked his main rival but a hard race at Punchestown earlier in the week seemed to leave its mark on the previous year's winner. The front-running Dempsey was well on top from the Pond fence and ran out a seven-length winner from another with a good course record, Hoo La Baloo, with Tysou third. As a point of interest, Dempsey broke News King's twenty-five-year-old track record, though, as invariably in such instances, that was more a reflection of the exceptionally firm conditions (despite overnight watering)

Fraser Steele HBLB Handicap Chase, Sandown—a sparkling display from Dempsey reunited with Timmy Murphy in a race whose value was boosted as a result of the abandonment of the Victor Chandler

*Betfred Celebration Chase, Sandown—the course record is lowered
as Dempsey registers a fourth win at Sandown; Hoo La Baloo and Tysou (white face) give chase*

rather than an outstanding effort on the part of the winner, who, on form, didn't need to run up to his best. Although his times have been bettered since, Tingle Creek in the 'seventies remains the supreme exponent of jumping at speed around Sandown's two-mile chase course; he lowered the course record in each of his three wins in the Sandown Pattern Chase, the last of them (on 'hard' ground) at the age of twelve on his final start before retirement. Also a course-record holder at several other tracks and particularly effective round Sandown (but not Cheltenham), Tingle Creek was described by *Chasers & Hurdlers 1978/79* as 'one of the most skilful jumpers we have seen; his jumping was consistently brilliant and he never fell in the course of his seven seasons in England.' Indeed it was this breathtaking style of racing, coupled with his longevity, that made the gelding such a hit with racegoers, though he often had his limitations somewhat exposed at the very top level. For example, leading performers of the era such as Bula and Pendil both comprehensively defeated him, even around Sandown.

Despite his racing record, Dempsey has a pedigree that suggests stamina rather than speed. In the latest season alone, his sire Lord Americo was represented by the Irish National third American Jennie, one of the leading staying novices over hurdles, Chief Dan George, and the Topham winner Dunbrody Millar. His earlier offspring include a Royal & SunAlliance Chase winner, Lord Noelie, and a runner-up in the same race, Lord of The River, who, like Dempsey, was out of an Over The River mare, that sire normally a byword for stamina in pedigrees. Dempsey's dam Kyle Cailin has visited Lord Americo several times, though Dempsey is only her second winner to date after Puget Blue, a useful chaser at up to three miles for Mouse Morris. Another brother, Murphy, had a couple of runs in bumpers in the latest season for Dempsey's stable, showing some promise on his debut. Kyle Cailin, who won a mares maiden Irish point, has since produced sons to Carroll House and Great Palm in 2004 and 2006 respectively. She is a sister to unbeaten hunter Overheard and a half-sister to the chasers Ballystone and Mr Pickpocket, all of whom won at up to at least three miles. Grandam Gusserane Princess, who was lightly raced, was out of a half-sister to the dam of crack hunter chaser Eliogarty.

Dempsey (IRE) (b.g. 1998)	Lord Americo (b 1984)	Lord Gayle (b 1965)	Sir Gaylord
			Sticky Case
		Hynictus (b 1968)	Val de Loir
			Hypavia
	Kyle Cailin (ch 1985)	Over The River (ch 1974)	Luthier
			Medenine
		Gusserane Princess (ch 1979)	Paddy's Stream
			Stalino's Artist

According to his trainer, Dempsey may be given another chance at beyond two miles. He is up against strong competition at the minimum trip from the likes of Voy Por Ustedes, Well Chief and Twist Magic, not to mention Kauto Star who

Mrs T. Brown's "Dempsey"

seems likely to bid for a third Tingle Creek. Most of those names will probably also be leading contenders for the Victor Chandler Chase, which will switch from a handicap to a level-weights conditions race next winter upon its promotion to Grade 1 status. Given his free-going nature, if Dempsey is given an extended run over further he is likely to need conditions and a track that put the emphasis on speed. He has won on all types of ground, though, heavy included. Dempsey played an important part in a successful first full season with a trainer's licence for Carl Llewellyn, who had previously assisted Dempsey's former trainer Mark Pitman. *Carl Llewellyn*

DENADA 11 ch.g. Bob Back (USA) – Alavie (FR) (Quart de Vin (FR)) [2006/7 c100x: c24d³ c24s² c24v^{ur} c24s^{pu} Jan 24] lengthy gelding: modest maiden chaser: likely to stay beyond 3¼m: acts on soft going: often let down by jumping. *Mrs Susan Nock*   **c92 x**

DENARIUS SECUNDUS 10 ch.g. Barathea (IRE) – Penny Drops (Sharpo) [2006/7 c71, h67: c16s⁵ c19d^{pu} c20s^{pu} 22v^{pu} c20v c22s 17d c18m³ Apr 26] rather leggy gelding: poor maiden hurdler/winning chaser: little form in 2006/7: stays 2½m: acts on heavy and good to firm going: tried in cheekpieces, usually blinkered nowadays. *N. R. Mitchell*   **c59 h–**

DENISE'S DIP 4 b. or gr.g. Benny The Dip (USA) – Kembla (Known Fact (USA)) [2006/7 F13g F13s F16g⁶ Mar 14] sixth foal: half-brother to 3 winners abroad, including useful French performer up to 1¼m Quit Rent (by Fairy King): dam, 2-y-o 5.7f winner who later won in Italy, half-sister to very smart performer up to 1½m Urgent Request: mid-division at best in bumpers. *Ian Williams*   **F87 ?**

DENMAN (IRE) 7 ch.g. Presenting – Polly Puttens (Pollerton) [2006/7 h155: c17d* c20d* c20v* c24d* c24g* Mar 14]

'You don't see great horses all that often. I've only known one so far and I don't expect to see his like again.' Tom Dreaper, who trained some of the finest steeplechasers in British and Irish jumping history, was talking about Prince Regent who won the first Cheltenham Gold Cup after the Second World War (aged eleven), a performance he followed by finishing third under 12-5 when 3/1 favourite in the 1946 Grand National, retrospectively earning a Timeform equivalent rating of 183. Wartime restrictions meant Prince Regent was confined to racing in Ireland during his peak years, which included a win in the Irish National under 12-7. Dreaper wasn't to know that exactly twenty years later his Greenogue stables would house—concurrently—the two steeplechasers who now head the historical list of Timeform ratings, Arkle (rated 212) and Flyingbolt (rated 210), the former winning his third successive Cheltenham Gold Cup (by thirty lengths), his fifth win of the 1965/6 season in as many starts, and the latter, who had put up a scintillating display to win the Massey-Ferguson under 12-6 at Cheltenham in December, romping home in the Two-Mile Champion Chase (by fifteen lengths) before finishing third in the Champion Hurdle the next day. Flyingbolt crowned a fine season, in which he won all six of his races over fences, by winning the Irish Grand National under 12-7, a performance that showed the seven-year-old was almost as good as Arkle at his best. The second and third, the top-class mare Height o' Fashion and the previous year's Irish National winner Splash, received 42 lb and 53 lb beatings respectively from Flyingbolt; when filling the same places behind Arkle in the Leopardstown Handicap Chase the previous month, they had come out 43 lb and 55 lb inferior at the weights. Very few contemporaries of Arkle and Flyingbolt could be set to carry 10-0 against their 12-7 in handicaps. Height o' Fashion carried 9-7 in the Leopardstown and 9-9 in the Irish National, Splash (who had won his Irish National with 10-13) carried 9-7 in both.

Arkle and Flyingbolt (whose career was subsequently dogged by illness and injury) never met in racecourse competition, but their regular rider Pat Taaffe recounted an occasion when they 'staged their own private race during what was supposed to be a normal session of morning schooling.' The pair were hacking alongside when Flyingbolt suddenly took off, Arkle, ridden by Taaffe, taking an equally strong hold to get back upsides. 'They took the next four fences, neck and neck, flat out as though their lives depended upon the outcome, while Paddy [Woods] and I held on to them for dear life and waited for the fires to die down.' According to Taaffe, Tom Dreaper never allowed the pair to be schooled together again. Arkle and the two-years-younger Flyingbolt lit up the 1965/6 season but, as so often happens in jumping, both were hit by injuries in the next season, Arkle breaking a bone in his foot during the King George VI Chase, which turned out to be the final race of his career, and Flyingbolt not seen out after a disappointing third in the National Hunt Centenary Chase at Cheltenham in the autumn. Woodland Venture won the Cheltenham Gold Cup narrowly from Stalbridge Colonist who had

Jim Brown Memorial Novices' Chase, Cheltenham—Denman (left) is given a good race by Don't Push It

inflicted a rare defeat on Arkle, from whom he received 35 lb, in the Hennessy Gold Cup at Newbury in November (What A Myth, who went on to win the Gold Cup in 1969, was third at Newbury in receipt of 33 lb).

Flyingbolt was still a novice when Arkle won his second Cheltenham Gold Cup and he went through his first season over fences unbeaten, winning four novice chases—reportedly doped when unimpressive in the Cotswold Chase (now the Arkle!) at Cheltenham—and a handicap, all at around two miles. In the same way as Flyingbolt looked destined for the top after his novice season, so too does the strapping Denman who is also housed in the same yard as a reigning Gold Cup winner, Kauto Star. Denman's winning record in his novice season was also five out of five and, though he started out at around two miles, staying is very much his game and he demolished a good field in the Royal & SunAlliance Chase at the Festival. Incidentally, he mostly exercises alone and has never worked with Kauto Star ('Denman would be too slow,' according to his trainer). All being well, however, the pair are set to meet in the 2008 Cheltenham Gold Cup. That is a long way off but Denman looks a very exciting prospect, his second season over fences something to look forward to with relish. Denman's form was well above average for the season's leading novice and his performances in novice company—as opposed to open company—have been bettered only by Florida Pearl, Escartefigue, Looks Like Trouble, Nick Dundee and Carvill's Hill since *Chasers & Hurdlers* began. The first quartet earned their ratings in successive editions of the Royal & SunAlliance Chase in the late-'nineties, Florida Pearl and Escartefigue in 1998 and Looks Like Trouble and Nick Dundee (a late faller) in 1999, whilst Carvill's Hill won the 1989 Tattersalls Gold Cup, a very valuable novice handicap at Punchestown, by a distance, conceding between 19 lb and 28 lb to ten rivals.

Denman has had a lofty reputation from the day he made his debut under Rules in a two-and-three-quarter-mile novice hurdle at Wincanton in October, 2005. He landed the odds that day with a bit to spare and followed up—on the only occasion in his career he has not started favourite—by beating the previous season's top bumper performer Karanja in a similar contest over the same course. The Grade 1 Challow Hurdle and a win at Bangor at 12/1-on followed before Denman suffered the only defeat of his eleven-race career to date (including a point) when beaten by Nicanor in the Royal & SunAlliance Novices' Hurdle at Cheltenham, Denman probably undone by a combination of resilient underfoot

toteplacepot Novices' Chase, Newbury—
much easier this time as Denman records his second successive wide-margin win at the Berkshire track

*Royal & SunAlliance Chase, Cheltenham—one of the performances of the week;
the game Aces Four (left) has no more to give two out*

conditions and the lack of a strong gallop. He made his eagerly-awaited first
appearance over fences over an extended two miles, a trip way short of his best, at
Exeter in late-October. Jumping well overall, though there was plenty of focus on a
bad blunder four out, Denman won by ten lengths from Penzance. Denman had to
work pretty hard to supplement that success against the promising Don't Push It at
Cheltenham the following month, not earning top marks for his jumping on this
occasion but getting home by three quarters of a length, the first two well clear. That
race and Denman's next, in the Grade 2 Berkshire Novices' Chase at Newbury's
Hennessy meeting, were both over two and a half miles. He won the Berkshire by
twelve lengths from his only serious rival, Snakebite, jumping more assuredly than
at Cheltenham and scoring in a style which suggested there was still plenty of
improvement to come. Denman was returned to Newbury in February for his final
outing before the Royal & SunAlliance, his first appearance in a three-mile novice
chase, the conditions of which had been changed since the *Programme Book*, amid
some controversy. The toteplacepot Novices' Chase was originally advertised as
for novices 'which have not won more than two steeplechases' and rival trainers
were understandably miffed that three-times winner Denman had been accommo-
dated in such a manner. The racecourse justified the decision to upgrade the
conditions by saying that the race strengthened the card. Denman's presence
certainly did that and he could hardly have been more impressive, making all,
jumping really well and thrashing his two rivals, the useful pair Mr Pointment and
Standin Obligation, winning by a distance.

The latest edition of the Royal & SunAlliance Chase would have been up
to scratch even without Denman. The Feltham Novices' Chase winner Ungaro,
unbeaten in three starts over fences, and Denman's stable-companion Turko,
successful in three of his four steeplechases, both had good credentials, while smart
hurdler Dom d'Orgeval had won his two chases in novice company with plenty to
spare. A strong Irish challenge included the Drinmore Novices' Chase and Powers
Whiskey Novices' Chase winner Cailin Alainn, the Powers Whiskey runner-up
Patsy Hall and the first two in the Ten Up Novices' Chase, Snowy Morning and
Gazza's Girl. Denman started 6/5 favourite, with Cailin Alainn at 13/2, Dom
d'Orgeval at 8/1, Turko at 9/1, Snowy Morning at 10/1, Ungaro at 11/1 and 20/1 bar
in a field of seventeen, the largest since 2002. The race was run at a good gallop
with Denman and 25/1-shot Aces Four (second to Patsy Hall at Cheltenham in
December) really stepping it up after halfway. The pair were clear from early on
the final circuit and Denman was just beginning to assert himself when Aces Four
stumbled badly at the third last. Staying on well and never in danger afterwards,
Denman came home ten lengths clear of Snowy Morning, with 66/1-shot According To John a further three and a half lengths away in third, just ahead of Aces Four.
Gazza's Girl, Ungaro and Turko were the only others to finish within twenty-eight
lengths of the winner. Patsy Hall and Dom d'Orgeval came ninth and tenth
respectively, while Cailin Alainn fell.

Denman is a big, strong, good sort who strengthened further over his
summer break before beginning his career over fences. He is not the best of walkers
and sometimes fails to impress in appearance, though he was in superb shape at

Mrs M. Findlay & P. K. Barber's "Denman"

		Mtoto (b 1983)	Busted Amazer
	Presenting (br 1992)	D'Azy (b 1984)	Persian Bold Belle Viking
Denman (IRE) (ch.g. 2000)		Pollerton (b 1974)	Rarity Nilie
	Polly Puttens (b 1982)	My Puttens (b 1972)	David Jack Railstown

Cheltenham in November and certainly looked better at the Festival than he had the previous year (he is an unusual, liver-coloured chestnut which his trainer thinks contributes to his not always filling the eye). Denman's sire the 1995 Derby third Presenting was champion sire over jumps—in a close finish with Old Vic—for the first time, judged on total prize money won in Britain and Ireland, a notable achievement considering that his oldest progeny are only nine (he was the second-youngest sire in the top ten, after third-placed Oscar). Presenting operates under the Rathbarry Stud banner and he looks like proving a worthy successor in time to that stud's flagship National Hunt stallion Strong Gale who died in 1994. Presenting was marketed as a National Hunt stallion from the outset, starting off at a fee of IR £850 which has risen steadily to €9,000 which is the highest advertised fee of the specialist jumps stallions still active. Strong Gale never sired a Cheltenham Gold Cup winner (one of his best sons Strong Promise was placed twice) but Presenting has already had one—War of Attrition—and could well have another with Denman. Denman's dam, the poor maiden hurdler Polly Puttens, was sold, in foal to Strong Gale, as a six-year-old and has done exceptionally well for her owner, Irish hobby breeder Colman O'Flynn. Full details of this burgeoning jumping family are covered in the essay on Denman's year-younger brother Silverburn, who was also a Grade 1 winner during the latest season. Polly Puttens bred ten foals during her first ten years at stud, largely patronising Rathbarry Stud stallions during this period. After an early abortion (a term used for a mishap within the first five months after covering) of her planned 1999 foal by Presenting, Polly Puttens was returned to Presenting and produced Denman the following year. Denman failed a wind test when sent to the Derby Sale as a four-year-old and had to be withdrawn. He was hobdayed before winning a maiden Irish point as a five-year-old from the Adrian Maguire yard, starting favourite and trotting up by eight lengths, after which he was purchased by Paul Barber and transferred to Paul Nicholls. Nicholls also acquired Silverburn from the Maguire yard for another of his patrons Paul Green after Denman won the Challow Hurdle. Denman is a strong-galloping stayer who will get further than three miles. He has been raced only on good going or softer, and he acts on heavy. His Christmas target is said to be the Lexus Chase at Leopardstown, thereby avoiding a clash with Kauto Star in the King George VI Chase at Kempton. *P. F. Nicholls*

DENNICK 5 b.g. Nicolotte – Branston Dancer (Rudimentary (USA)) [2006/7 h98: 19g 16g 19d 17m⁶ Apr 28] sturdy gelding: modest hurdler for P. Haslam: well held in 2006/7, including in seller: probably best around 2m: acts on heavy going: tongue tied for both wins: takes strong hold. *S. B. Clark*   **h–**

DENNIS THE LEGEND 6 b.g. Midnight Legend – Fly The Wind (Windjammer (USA)) [2006/7 F16m⁶ Jun 13] third foal: half-brother to winning pointer by Dilum: dam winning staying hurdler/chaser: winning pointer, including in 2007: sixth of 8 in bumper. *J. G. Cann*   **F80**

DEN OF INIQUITY 6 b.g. Supreme Leader – Divine Comedy (IRE) (Phardante (FR)) [2006/7 F16s* F16v* F16g Mar 14] strong, stocky gelding: sixth foal: brother to fair   **F118**

Mr Malcolm C. Denmark's "Den of Iniquity"

hurdler Overserved, stays 3m: dam, poor form in bumper, half-sister to useful staying chaser Dakyns Boy: created excellent impression when winning bumpers at Warwick in December and January (listed event, landed odds readily by 6 lengths from Edgbriar): well held in Grade 1 at Cheltenham under less testing conditions. *Carl Llewellyn*

DENVALE (IRE) 9 b.g. Denel (FR) – Brackenvale (IRE) (Strong Gale) [2006/7 c110§: c26g³ c24spu c22d² c24g* Mar 29] tall, angular gelding: has reportedly had soft-palate operation: fair chaser: won handicap at Towcester in March: stays 3¼m: acts on soft going. *Mrs Caroline Bailey* — **c107**

DEO GRATIAS (POL) 7 b.g. Enjoy Plan (USA) – Dea (POL) (Canadian Winter (CAN)) [2006/7 h82: 26g² 22m c24m⁴ c26d⁵ 26m⁴ 26m² 26g² 26g Oct 15] angular gelding: maiden handicap hurdler: much better effort in handicap chases when fourth at Southwell: stays 3¼m: acts on good to firm going: has worn cheekpieces, visored last 4 starts: tried tongue tied. *Carl Llewellyn* — **c79 h87**

DEPRAUX (IRE) 4 br.g. Generous (IRE) – Happy Memories (IRE) (Thatching) [2006/7 16m Jan 29] fair maiden on Flat (stays 1½m), claimed from W. Haggas £8,000 in December: well held in juvenile hurdle. *D. McCain Jnr* — **h–**

DEPUTY CONSORT (USA) 4 b.g. Stravinsky (USA) – Possible Consort (USA) (Deputy Minister (CAN)) [2006/7 16d³ 16s³ 16v⁶ 16d 16m Apr 26] tall gelding: fair up to 1¼m on Flat, improved to win maiden at the Curragh in October on first start after leaving J. Gosden: fairly useful juvenile hurdler: won maiden at Down Royal in November: better form when third to Lounaos in Grade 2 at Leopardstown and midfield behind Gaspara in 24-runner listed 4-y-o handicap at Cheltenham (tongue tied) penultimate outing: raced at 2m: acts on soft ground, well held on heavy. *M. J. P. O'Brien, Ireland* — **h112**

DEPUTY MAYOR (IRE) 7 b.g. Saddlers' Hall (IRE) – Nora's Charm (IRE) (King's Ride) [2006/7 17s⁶ 20g³ 24g 19g Nov 5] seventh in bumper: fourth in Irish maiden point in November 2005: best effort over hurdles (modest form) when third to Sultan Fontenaille at Uttoxeter on handicap debut: seemingly reluctant to race final outing: stays 2½m. *P. D. Nolan* — **h91 §**

DERAINEY (IRE) 8 b.g. Farhaan – Hurricane Hazel (Lorenzaccio) [2006/7 c–, h–: c16g⁵ c20m 24mpu 20g Aug 1] lengthy gelding: little form: tried in headgear/tongue tied: sold 3,000 gns Doncaster August Sales. *R. Johnson* — **c– h–**

DERAMORE RYTHM (IRE) 8 b. or br.g. Norwich – Those Brown Eyes (IRE) (Strong Gale) [2006/7 17d³ 20m 16s Sep 2] maiden hurdler, modest form at best: stays 2¾m. *I. A. Duncan, Ireland* — **h78**

DERE LYN 9 b.g. Awesome – Our Resolution (Caerleon (USA)) [2006/7 c95, h91: c19d⁵ May 17] smallish, rather leggy gelding: modest handicap hurdler: similar form on first of 2 outings over fences: needs testing conditions around 2m and stays 3m: acts on heavy going: often wears headgear: tried tongue tied. *D. Burchell* — **c– h–**

DERE STREET 13 b.g. Derring Rose – Jed Again (Cagirama) [2006/7 c25s³ Mar 7] modest pointer, won match in April: achieved little in 2 hunters. *S. J. Leadbetter* — **c–**

DEROSA 10 br.g. Little Wolf – Easter Carnival (Pardigras) [2006/7 c81: c26m⁵ May 11] modest pointer: runner-up in novice at Newton Abbot on first of 2 starts in hunters in 2006. *Mrs E. Scott* — **c–**

DERRAVARRA EAGLE (IRE) 7 br.g. Flemensfirth (USA) – Rathcolman Queen (IRE) (Radical) [2006/7 16g 16s* 20s³ 16v 18v* 16m⁶ Apr 10] lengthy gelding: third foal: half-brother to winning hurdlers Derravarra Breeze (stays 2½m) and Derravarra Sunset (at 2m), both by Supreme Leader: dam unraced half-sister to useful chaser up to 3m Greenwood Lad: bumper winner for N. Meade: fairly useful novice hurdler: won at Punchestown (despite swerving left) in November and Fairyhouse in March, beating Sweet Kiln 1¼ lengths in minor event at latter: should stay 2½m: acts on heavy going, below form on good to firm. *Mark Leslie Fagan, Ireland* — **h124**

DERREEN BOY (IRE) 10 ch.g. Tanaos – Lancana (IRE) (Lancastrian) [2006/7 20f⁵ 24gpu 20m 22mpu 24g³ 26m⁶ 24d³ 25g Oct 24] good-bodied ex-Irish gelding: second foal: half-brother to bumper winner Niamh's Leader (by Supreme Leader): dam lightly-raced hurdler: bumper winner: poor maiden hurdler: off 3 years and left P. Nolan prior to reappearance: stays 3m: acts on good to soft and good to firm ground. *S. Lycett* — **h77**

DERRING DOVE 15 b.g. Derring Rose – Shadey Dove (Deadly Nightshade) [2006/7 c24gur Apr 27] angular gelding: maiden chaser: winning pointer, including in 2007: stays 3¼m: acts on heavy and good to firm going: tried visored: unreliable. *Marc Barber* — **c– § h–**

DERRINTOGHER YANK (IRE) 13 b.g. Lord Americo – Glenmalur (Black Minstrel) [2006/7 c106, h–: c21g* c21g⁴ c20gᶠ Mar 28] rangy gelding: fairly useful hunter chaser nowadays: won at Cheltenham in May: stays 3m: raced mainly on good going or softer: front runner. *Miss R. S. Reynolds* **c102 h–**

DESAILLY 13 ch.g. Teamster – G W Superstar (Rymer) [2006/7 c127, h–: c24d c24s³ c24v c23s⁴ c21s Mar 8] strong, lengthy gelding: one-time useful handicap chaser, just fair nowadays: best at 2¾m+: raced on good going or softer (acts on soft): sound jumper: tends to finish weakly. *J. A. Geake* **c102 h–**

DESERT AIR (JPN) 8 ch.g. Desert King (IRE) – Greek Air (IRE) (Ela-Mana-Mou) [2006/7 h136: 16d c18v³ c17v* c16s³ c21gᵖᵘ 20g 20f Apr 28] angular gelding: useful handicap hurdler, well held last 2 starts: easily best effort over fences when winning maiden at Plumpton in February by 5 lengths from Spidam, making virtually all: stays 19f: acts on heavy going: effective with or without headgear: tongue tied: hard ride. *D. E. Pipe* **c125 § h128 §**

DESERT INFERNO (FR) 5 b.g. Simon du Desert (FR) – Dora Dante (IRE) (Phardante (FR)) [2006/7 F16s² aF16g 16g³ Mar 29] second foal: dam unraced half-sister to dam of Triumph Hurdle winner Snow Drop: better effort in bumpers when 17 lengths second to Helens Vision at Stratford: 6¾ lengths third of 16 to Inherent in novice at Towcester on hurdling debut: likely to be suited by further than 2m: should do better. *Mrs L. Wadham* **h96 p F94**

DESERTMORE CHIEF (IRE) 8 b.g. Broken Hearted – Mangan Lane (Le Moss) [2006/7 c–, h84?: c16gᵖᵘ May 4] lengthy gelding: little form: usually wears headgear. *G. J. Smith* **c– h–**

DESERT NOVA (IRE) 5 ch.g. Desert King (IRE) – Assafiyah (IRE) (Kris) [2006/7 16s 16v⁵ 16g⁵ Mar 17] neat gelding: lightly-raced maiden on Flat in Ireland: poor form on last of 3 outings over hurdles. *Mark Campion* **h79 ?**

DESERT QUEST (IRE) 7 b.g. Rainbow Quest (USA) – Jumilla (USA) (El Gran Senor (USA)) [2006/7 h149: 16m* 16m² 16s 16d³ 17g Mar 16] leggy, rather sparely-made gelding: very smart hurdler: won valuable handicap at Ascot in October, beating **h156**

William Hill Handicap Hurdle, Ascot—a sparkling return by top weight Desert Quest

Caracciola easily by 3 lengths: good ½-length second of 6 to Crow Wood in Elite Hurdle (Limited Handicap) at Wincanton 7 days later: below best after, looking none too hearty fourth outing: best form around 2m: has won on good to soft going, best under less testing conditions: patiently ridden, and usually travels strongly. *P. F. Nicholls*

DESERT SECRETS (IRE) 5 b.m. Almutawakel – Shaping Up (USA) (Storm Bird (CAN)) [2006/7 h92: 16g c16d* c16d² 21g^pu Apr 19] tall, leggy mare: modest hurdler: won mares novice at Leicester in November on chasing debut: better form but again made mistakes there next time: stays 2¼m: best form on good/good to soft going: tried in cheekpieces: none too consistent. *J. G. Portman* `c89` `h98`

DESERT SPA (USA) 12 b.g. Sheikh Albadou – Healing Waters (USA) (Temperence Hill (USA)) [2006/7 h91: 16f³ 17g* 17s 17m 16d Mar 22] lengthy gelding: fair hurdler: won selling handicap at Hereford in May: no form after: barely stays 2½m: acts on soft and good to firm going: tried tongue tied. *G. E. Jones* `h101`

DESERT STORM (DEN) 5 br.g. Desert Prince (IRE) – Boss Lady (IRE) (Last Tycoon) [2006/7 17g^pu 17g⁶ Apr 1] half-brother to fair 2m hurdler High Priestess (by Priolo) and 2½m hurdle winner Pirates Punch (by Croco Rouge): fair on Flat (stays 2m), successful twice in 2006, sold out of Rae Guest's stable 56,000 gns Newmarket Autumn Sales: well held on completed outing in novice hurdles: will be suited by greater test of stamina. *P. J. Hobbs* `h– p`

DESERT TOMMY 6 b.g. Desert King (IRE) – Flambera (FR) (Akarad (FR)) [2006/7 h117: 24s* 23d 24d^pu 23v² 25v 24g⁶ Mar 15] small, rather leggy gelding: fairly useful handicap hurdler: won at Chepstow in October by 7 lengths from Jockser: creditable efforts after only when second to Huka Lodge at Haydock (cheekpieces) and sixth to Oscar Park at Cheltenham (visored): stays 3m: unraced on firm going, acts on any other: often races prominently. *Evan Williams* `h124`

DE SOTO 6 b.g. Hernando – Vanessa Bell (IRE) (Lahib (USA)) [2006/7 h103p: 16g 17s* 16d* 16v⁴ 16d⁴ 16g⁵ Apr 13] smallish, lengthy gelding: useful novice hurdler: off 10½ months after debut in 2005/6 due to hairline fracture of shin: won at Taunton and Kempton (by 5 lengths from Blythe Knight) in December: ran well when 4 lengths fourth to Ebaziyan in 22-runner Supreme Novices' Hurdle at Cheltenham fifth start: possibly amiss at Aintree month later: raced around 2m on good ground or softer (possibly unsuited by heavy): tongue tied last 5 starts: sold 360,000 gns Doncaster May Sales: joined Jonjo O'Neill. *P. R. Webber* `h141`

DESPERADO QUEEN (IRE) 9 b.m. Un Desperado (FR) – Auburn Queen (Kinglet) [2006/7 c20d* 18s c20s³ c29s c24v⁴ Jan 1] leggy mare: fair hurdler: fairly useful chaser: successful in mares races first 3 starts over fences, including at Cork (by ¾ length from Greenhill Rambler) in May: probably flattered when third of 4 to In Compliance in Grade 3 at Down Royal, dictating: should stay beyond 2½m: acts on heavy and good to firm going: jumps well: often makes running. *L. W. Doran, Ireland* `c129` `h–`

DESPERATE BOB (IRE) 5 b.g. Bob's Return (IRE) – Desperate Dame (IRE) (Un Desperado (FR)) [2006/7 c17v^pu c24v^pu c24g^pu Apr 7] €8,000 3-y-o: lengthy, workmanlike gelding: first foal: dam, unraced, out of sister to useful 2m hurdler Hidebound: well held in maiden Irish points in 2006: no show in novice chases. *R. Johnson* `c–`

DESPERATE DEX (IRE) 7 b.g. Un Desperado (FR) – Too Sharp (True Song) [2006/7 h–, F–: 24g‡ 24v* 24s^pu 21s^pu 22d Feb 19] tall, good-bodied gelding: 50/1, won novice hurdle at Uttoxeter in November by 5 lengths from Joyryder, only form: stays 3m: acts on heavy going: wore cheekpieces final outing. *G. J. Smith* `h102`

stanjamesuk.com Novices' Hurdle, Kempton—De Soto catches the eye of prospective bidders at the Doncaster May Sales with a convincing victory over Blythe Knight

DESTINO 8 ch.g. Keen – Hanajir (IRE) (Cadeaux Genereux) [2006/7 h–: 19g 20m c–
c20gᵖᵘ c26d Aug 28] maiden hurdler: no form since 2004, including over fences. *Mrs* h–
S. J. Smith

DETROIT CITY (USA) 5 gr. or ro.g. Kingmambo (USA) – Seattle Victory h160
(USA) (Seattle Song (USA)) [2006/7 h146p: 16d* 17s* 16d* 16d⁶ 20g Apr 14]
    A season which promised so much ended in disappointment. After a run of
eight successive victories, including a notable one on the Flat, Detroit City was
beaten favourite in both the Champion Hurdle and Aintree Hurdle, raising serious
questions, above all about his attitude. He may yet bounce back but his performance
in finishing last of the ten to complete at Aintree, which *Timeform Perspective*
described as 'indolent and disappointing', indicated that there is a lot of work to be
done before Detroit City can be seriously supported again at the highest level.
    Until the Champion Hurdle, things had looked altogether more rosy. Detroit
City had won his last four races as a juvenile in 2005/6, including the top two events
for his age group in Britain, the JCB Triumph Hurdle at Cheltenham and the Sportsman Anniversary Hurdle at Aintree (as it turned out the Anniversary Hurdle was
an unfortunate race for *The Sportsman* to sponsor, the short-lived daily folding in
October, barely six months after its launch). Detroit City had been the first to
complete the Triumph/Anniversary Hurdle double since Pollardstown in 1979,
though the feat wasn't quite so outstanding as that makes it sound as, until 2005, the
winner of the Triumph had to carry a penalty at Aintree. Both Spectroscope in 2003
and Made In Japan in 2004 were narrowly beaten, with a 4-lb penalty making the
difference to the result. The 1999 winner Hors La Loi III carried a penalty for his
win in the Supreme Novices' at Cheltenham.
    Still, Detroit City showed smart form to record those two wins—subsequent
events suggest it was even better form than it appeared at the time—and had to be
considered as a Champion Hurdle contender. Indeed, he figured as second favourite
behind the 2006 winner Brave Inca in the ante-post lists at the end of October. By
then he had gained his most valuable win, one worth considerably more than either
the Triumph (£57,020) or the Anniversary (£68,424), as he returned to the Flat to
land the Cesarewitch (£93,480 to the winner) at Newmarket. Wearing blinkers in
place of the visor worn for his two big hurdle wins (plus his only previous success
on the Flat), Detroit City raced in what had become his customary lazy fashion
before staying on strongly to beat Inchnadamph by a length, putting up a smart
performance.
    Detroit City was clearly a highly progressive young hurdler, but opposition
to him as a Champion Hurdle candidate was rooted in history, specifically in the
record of five-year-olds in the Champion Hurdle. Only two had been successful
since Persian War, the last Triumph Hurdle winner to win the following season's
Champion in 1968. They were the multiple champions Night Nurse and See You
Then. Since See You Then in 1985, seventy-one five-year-olds had run in the
Champion without success. In the intervening twenty renewals, twelve Triumph
Hurdle winners had contested the following season's Champion, the five most
recent to try, Kissair (66/1), Upgrade (66/1), Katarino (25/1), Scolardy (66/1) and
Penzance (40/1) making little impact. The last contender with strong claims had
been Mysilv, a 15/2-chance when fifth to Alderbrook in the 1995 Champion. Prior
to her, Shawiya (16/1), Duke of Monmouth (25/1), Rare Holiday (50/1) and First
Bout (16/1) had managed no better than seventh between them, though 20/1-shot
Oh So Risky had finished half a length second to Royal Gait in 1992 and Kribensis
had started 11/8 favourite in 1989 when seventh to Beech Road. Oh So Risky was
second again in 1994, while Kribensis beat the five-year-old Nomadic Way when
claiming the championship in 1990.
    There was another historical quirk to overcome: no Triumph winner had
made a winning return over hurdles since 1989, when Ikdam landed odds of 10/1-
on in the three-runner Inkberrow Hurdle at Worcester (runner-up Martinsmoon won
just one of her twenty-four starts over hurdles, the other runner, 33/1-chance Sibton
Abbey, went on to win a Hennessy Gold Cup). Races such as the Inkberrow and the
four-year-old conditions hurdle at Newbury's October meeting (a race Kribensis
won on his return in 1988/9) no longer exist. The only two hurdle races confined to
four-year-olds during the autumn of 2006/7, both run at around two miles, were

Greatwood Handicap Hurdle, Cheltenham—
an impressive return to hurdling by the recent Cesarewitch winner Detroit City

Chepstow's long-standing Bet At Blue Square Handicap Hurdle (formerly known as the Free Handicap) in October and the second running of a limited handicap staged on Haydock's Lancashire Chase card in November (latest renewal won by Blazing Bailey). As it was, Philip Hobbs entered Detroit City for a minor event at Kempton in October that he'd won twice with the same owner's Rooster Booster (including when the race was staged at Huntingdon in 2005), but the lure of a big pay-day at Newmarket prompted connections to opt for the Cesarewitch on the same afternoon, Detroit City having confirmed his well-being when winning a charity Flat race at Chepstow earlier in the month. Detroit City was returned to hurdling in the Greatwood Handicap at Cheltenham's Open meeting in November. A change to front-running tactics in a race with no obvious pacemaker—a move suggested by Jamie Spencer after he had ridden the horse in the Cesarewitch —resulted in a most impressive return, Detroit City (again in blinkers) quickening right away after three out to beat Ameeq by fourteen lengths. Just nine went to post, though, after the withdrawal of three significant contenders in Acambo (eleventh-hour setback), Crow Wood and Caracciola (both due to softer-than-expected ground). As valuable handicap hurdles go, there were stronger races than the Greatwood. However, there was no denying the style of the performance and Detroit City was cut to 4/1 or shorter in the Champion Hurdle ante-post books.

Next up was the Grade 2 boylesports.com International back at Cheltenham the following month. This was a new name for an old race, the Bula, a familiar title evoking memories, even to those that are much too young to recall Bula himself. The course claimed a desire to build the profile of the December meeting as a justification for the change, one which the British Horseracing Board accepted, though a significant increase in the amount of money put up by the sponsors played its part. In addition to the massive first prize of £114,040 that Detroit City netted, Boylesports also stumped up a £200,000 bonus if he went on to land the Champion Hurdle itself. Justifying the change of name, Cheltenham's director of sponsorship Peter McNeile said: 'The Bula title has had its day. There will be a large number of today's generation of racegoers who would not even have seen Bula run.' On those grounds, the 'Arkle' Trophy should have gone first. Ironically, the "Relkeel"

Hurdle took place just three races earlier on the same Cheltenham December card, a Grade 2 event honouring the popular David Nicholson-trained grey who won three successive 'Bula Hurdles' in the late-'nineties but couldn't really be considered in the same league as Bula himself. Sponsors, obviously, want their money's worth and it was no surprise that Nigel Payne, who as chief executive of the Horseracing Sponsors' Association might be said to have a vested interest, was on hand to 'warmly congratulate' Cheltenham and the BHB on their 'enlightened attitude' in dropping the Bula tag. It must irritate sponsors when their races are constantly referred to by a permanent title. But, at the same time, those who follow the sport and value its history and traditions deserve consideration too. Had the Anniversary Hurdle been just the Sportsman Hurdle it would have required a new tag for 2007. Turnover of sponsors does not help continuity.

Cheltenham is building quite a record for accommodating name changes, presumably requested by sponsors. The National Hunt Handicap no longer exists, the Stayers' Hurdle now has a permanent name every bit as nebulous as the International and the Cathcart's replacement, the Festival Trophy which is already on to its second sponsor, now carries that title in parentheses. The latter fate has also befallen the sport's only five-times Cheltenham Gold Cup winner, as only those with a jeweller's eyepiece are probably aware that the (bracketed) Golden Miller Trophy is still staged at the course's two-day April meeting. Meanwhile, Mildmay of Flete was consigned to history, the victim of a bidding war between newspapers, and the end of one long-standing sponsorship, for a race once known as the Aldsworth Hurdle, has introduced the name Baring Bingham (a former owner of Cheltenham) to the Festival programme. It will be interesting to see whether the cross country chase, for which a new sponsor is required in 2007/8, finds a new handle to try to counteract the habit of referring to it as simply the cross country.

boylesports.com International (Hurdle), Cheltenham—
the grey gets the better of Hardy Eustace in a muddling race for what was previously the Bula Hurdle

Agfa UK Hurdle, Sandown—a seventh straight win over hurdles for Detroit City, who survives a last-flight blunder to beat Straw Bear (hoops)

For the enlightenment of Peter McNeile and younger readers, Bula's achievements place him among the very best jumpers of the last forty years, as a hurdler/chaser behind only Night Nurse, Captain Christy, Desert Orchid and Moscow Flyer (though the three last-named all had lower hurdles ratings). Bula was top class over fences, with a best Timeform rating of 174, but it was as a hurdler that he was truly outstanding, twice voted Horse of the Year and among the top ten of all-time in Timeform's view. He won twenty-one of his twenty-six starts in four seasons over hurdles and was unbeaten in his first thirteen races. *Chasers & Hurdlers 1976/77* commented: 'Bula had excellent finishing speed and was usually saved for a late run; spectacular victories gained by picking off the opposition in contemptuous style on the flat became the hallmark of his career.' The Fred Winter-trained Bula twice won the Champion Hurdle, defeating the triple winner Persian War (whose name is remembered in a Grade 2 novice hurdle at Chepstow) by four lengths in the 1971 running and following up in breathtaking fashion a year later. Bula came closer than any Champion Hurdle winner, up to that time, to landing the Cheltenham Gold Cup as well when third in the 1975 renewal, unseasonably heavy ground arguably costing him victory that day. Since then only 1981 runner-up Night Nurse (grievously neglected so far as the naming of races is concerned) and 1986 winner Dawn Run have bettered that achievement. Bula's final race also came at Cheltenham when, at the age of twelve, he fell at the fifth in the Two-Mile Champion Chase (sent off a short-priced favourite) and injured a shoulder so seriously that he was eventually put down two months later—after which the course honoured him by renaming the Cheltenham Trial Hurdle as the 'Bula'. If the sponsors of the International make half the contribution that Bula made to the sport, they will be doing very well indeed.

The sponsors and Cheltenham must have hoped that their largesse would attract more than the four runners that went to post for the first running of the International. Detroit City was opposed by the dual Champion Hurdle winner Hardy Eustace, the useful handicapper Crow Wood and the former Supreme Novices' winner Arcalis. Of the trio, only Hardy Eustace, conceding Detroit City 4 lb, was considered a serious threat but Detroit City had to work to beat him, ridden out after the last in a steadily-run affair, winning by a length with ten lengths back to the tenderly-handled Crow Wood. The performance hardly warranted any shortening in Detroit City's odds for the Champion Hurdle, particularly as Detroit City's jumping left plenty to be desired. The *Racing Post* headline 'Detroit masters Hardy in giant step on path to Champion' seemed an exaggerated assessment of his performance and odds of 5/2 about his Champion Hurdle prospects looked decidedly short. However, Detroit City was even shorter after his next race, the Agfa Hurdle at Sandown (Rooster Booster's final prep-run prior to his 2003 Champion win). Six went to post this time, but again there was just one serious opponent, the 'Fighting Fifth' winner Straw Bear, and Detroit City was again odds on. Meeting at level weights, Detroit City held Straw Bear by a length and three quarters after a blunder at the last. Otherwise Detroit City's jumping was rather more accomplished than in the International, but the performance was no better than his two earlier ones and he continued to represent poor value for the Champion itself, for all that he appealed as one who'd be suited back in a more truly-run race.

Support for Detroit City remained solid, however, and he was sent off at 6/4 favourite for the Champion Hurdle. Those who backed him knew their fate very early in the race. Detroit City was off the bridle before the field passed the stands with a circuit to go and, jumping less than adequately, he lost his position before three out and finished sixth of the eight to complete, just under nineteen lengths behind Sublimity. His rider Richard Johnson reported the horse was beaten by the first. While Detroit City could be excused one off-day, his performance at Aintree, where he wore a tongue strap rather than blinkers or a visor, pointed to temperament as a possible cause for his poor display in the Champion. No physical problem reportedly came to light after Aintree. Detroit City figures behind only Sublimity and the latest Triumph Hurdle winner Katchit in the ante-post lists for the 2008 Champion Hurdle at the time of writing, but he has a considerable amount to prove.

Detroit City (USA) (gr. or ro.g. 2002)	Kingmambo (USA) (b 1990)	Mr Prospector (b 1970)	Raise A Native Gold Digger
		Miesque (b 1984)	Nureyev Pasadoble
	Seattle Victory (USA) (ro 1990)	Seattle Song (b or br 1981)	Seattle Slew Incantation
		Will of Victory (gr 1978)	Dancer's Image Warsaw

The big, strong Detroit City has the physique to make a chaser, though he seems likely to continue over hurdles in the coming season. He was bred in North America, though both his sire and dam made their mark in Europe. His sire Kingmambo, who has done very well with his offspring in Europe, was a high-class miler while Detroit City's dam Seattle Victory was a mile- and mile-and-a-quarter winner in France, winning a listed event at the shorter trip, before going on to win over a mile in the States. Detroit City is a half-brother to the fairly useful six-furlong winner Clotted Cream (by Eagle Eyed), as well as a winner in Mexico. Both the grandam Will of Victory and third dam Warsaw were well above average on the Flat and have been successful at stud. Warsaw is the dam of the 1985 Prix Vermeille winner Walensee and the 1982 Grande Course de Haies d'Auteuil winner World Citizen. Walensee's best offspring Westerner, who finished second in the Prix de l'Arc de Triomphe and won the Gold Cup at Ascot, is now at stud as a National Hunt stallion and covered over two hundred mares in 2006. Detroit City should stay beyond two miles. He acts on soft and good to firm going. *P. J. Hobbs*

DEUTERONOMY (IRE) 6 b.g. Beneficial – Good Heavens (IRE) (Heavenly **h–** Manna) [2006/7 F–: 22g 24s⁶ 25g Apr 16] big, strong, workmanlike gelding: well held in bumper/novice hurdles, left E. Elliott after second start. *J. Wade*

DEUTSCHLAND (USA) 4 b.g. Red Ransom (USA) – Rhine Valley (USA) (Danzig **h118** (USA)) [2006/7 16v* 16x² 16m Apr 10] fairly useful on Flat (stays 1½m), sold out of M. Jarvis' stable 70,000 gns Newmarket July Sales: successful in juvenile maiden at Punchestown on hurdling debut in December, beating Shazand easily by 5 lengths: fairly useful form when 4 lengths second to stable-companion J'Y Vole in juvenile at Fairyhouse: well held in valuable handicap on much firmer ground: will stay beyond 2m. *W. P. Mullins, Ireland*

DE VALIRA (IRE) 5 ch.g. Shantou (USA) – Valira (USA) (Nijinsky (CAN))   **h138 +**
[2006/7 F16s² 18v* 16v* 16s² 16d 16m* 16m^ur Apr 24]   **F110**

    On pedigree alone De Valira, a half-brother to the top-class two-mile
hurdler Valiramix (by Linamix), looked a particularly interesting contender when
he appeared for the first time, in a bumper at Leopardstown in March 2006. He
justified good support on that occasion to win by five lengths, seeming destined for
better things. He wasn't raced again in bumpers after being beaten at odds on at
Punchestown in November but, once switched to hurdles, he began to fulfil his
potential. He was tried in a tongue strap and looked none too keen that day (hanging
left), but raced without that particular piece of equipment subsequently, his manner
giving no cause for any concern. De Valira was successful on three of his six
outings over hurdles, including on his first two in a maiden at Fairyhouse (beating
the useful Arrive Sir Clive) and the Grade 2 paddypower.com Future Champions
Novices' Hurdle at Leopardstown, both in December. In the latter, De Valira had a
neck to spare over Catch Me, the winner of both his previous races over hurdles,
moving through smoothly to dispute the lead at the last and edging ahead after
jumping it more fluently than the runner-up. Two defeats followed, though De
Valira ran at least creditably each time. He didn't enjoy the run of things in a falsely-
run race when second to 50/1-shot Orbit O'Gold in a Grade 2 at Punchestown, then
performed better than his position suggests when tenth of twenty-two to Ebaziyan
in the Supreme Novices' at Cheltenham, still fifth but unable to quicken when
losing his back legs at the last. Regular jockey Andrew Lynch, who was just pipped
to the 2006/7 Irish conditional crown by Andrew Leigh, had been replaced by
Andrew McNamara at Cheltenham (possibly as a result of that Punchestown
defeat) but was back in the saddle for De Valira's next outing in the Grade 2
Dunboyne Castle Hotel & Spa Novices' Hurdle at Fairyhouse in April. Conceding
weight to all seven of his rivals, De Valira travelled better than at Cheltenham
(despite firmer conditions) but didn't improve on the form he had shown there in
winning by a neck from Galway Hurdle winner Cuan Na Grai. Joining the latter in
the lead turning in, De Valira looked set for a comfortable victory when quickly
going a length up approaching the last but was all out to hang on as the runner-up
rallied. On his only subsequent outing, De Valira had still to be asked for his effort

Dunboyne Castle Hotel & Spa Novices' Hurdle, Fairyhouse—
a second Grade 2 success for De Valira (noseband), who just hangs on from Cuan Na Grai

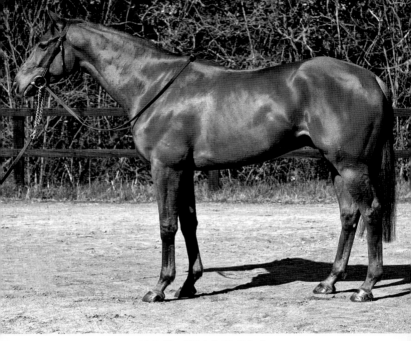

Mr D. Mac A'Bhaird's "De Valira"

when blundering and unseating his rider at the sixth in the Champion Novices' Hurdle at Punchestown, too far out to say where he might have finished. De Valira, by 1996 St Leger winner Shantou, is out of the winning miler Valira, herself a daughter of 1981 Yorkshire Oaks winner Condessa. He is likely to stay beyond two and a quarter miles, the longest trip he has been asked to tackle so far, and he acts on heavy and good to firm going. *M. J. P. O'Brien, Ireland*

DEVILS AND DUST (IRE) 6 b.g. Needle Gun (IRE) – Tartan Trouble (Warpath) [2006/7 F80: F17s⁶ 20v 17v 16v 25sᵖᵘ 24v⁶ 19g² Mar 28] sparely-made gelding: modest form in bumpers: in cheekpieces, much improved over hurdles when second to Go Harvey Go in conditional jockeys handicap at Towcester, making most: should stay beyond 19f. *D. McCain Jnr*   **h88 F80**

DEVILS DELIGHT (IRE) 5 b.m. Desert King (IRE) – Devil's Crown (USA) (Chief's Crown (USA)) [2006/7 h78: 20sᵖᵘ 17d 17dᵖᵘ 17m⁴ 20mF 17m 17s 20d⁵ Nov 7] poor maiden hurdler, has been reluctant to race: visored/tongue tied final outing: one to leave alone. *James Moffatt*   **h73 §**

DEVIL'S DISGUISE 5 b.g. Atraf – Dunloe (IRE) (Shaadi (USA)) [2006/7 F90: 20s³ 20d⁴ 20s⁵ 22vᵖᵘ 24mᵖᵘ Mar 25] compact gelding: poor form over hurdles, went as if amiss last 2 outings: should stay beyond 2½m: acts on soft going. *Ferdy Murphy*   **h84**

DEVIL'S PERK (IRE) 9 b.g. Executive Perk – She Devil (Le Moss) [2006/7 c20dᵖᵘ Nov 7] won maiden point in 2004: no show in maiden hurdle/chase: dead. *J. Wade*   **c– h–**

DEVILS RIVER (IRE) 5 b.g. Anabaa (USA) – Riviere du Diable (USA) (Irish River (FR)) [2006/7 h91: 16gᵖᵘ 16s⁴ 16dᵖᵘ 16f Apr 5] workmanlike gelding: modest form over hurdles: raced at 2m. *Mrs A. E. Brooks*   **h89**

DEVIL'S RUN (IRE) 11 b.g. Commanche Run – She Devil (Le Moss) [2006/7 c108, **c118** h–: c28d* c26s c25v* c25v⁴ c30sᵖᵘ c33v c24g Apr 7] good-topped gelding: fairly useful **h–** handicap chaser: won at Sedgefield in May and Ayr (beat Brandy Wine 13 lengths) in December: no form last 3 outings: stays 4m: raced on good going or softer (acts on heavy). *J. Wade*

DEVITO (FR) 6 ch.g. Trempolino (USA) – Snowy (FR) (Wollow) [2006/7 h109: 20gᶠ **h104** 20g 19d 19g⁶ 19d² 19s⁶ 17s⁵ 19v² Jan 1] fair handicap hurdler: needs further than 2m and stays 2¾m: acts on heavy and good to firm going: tried visored. *G. F. Edwards*

DEVON BLUE (IRE) 8 ch.m. Hubbly Bubbly (USA) – Tuney Blade (Fine Blade **h86 ?** (USA)) [2006/7 F–: 24mᵖᵘ Apr 15] sturdy mare: lightly raced: in frame in bumpers: off 17 months, mid-field in mares novice won by Hendre Hotshot at Newton Abbot on hurdling debut: possibly found next race coming too soon. *C. J. Down*

DEVONDALE (IRE) 11 b.g. Be My Native (USA) – Lancastrian Rose (IRE) **c–** (Lancastrian) [2006/7 c93, h–: c20gᵖᵘ Oct 7] maiden hurdler: modest handicap chaser: **h–** reportedly struck into only outing in 2006/7: stays 3m: acts on any going: has had tongue tied. *Ferdy Murphy*

DEVON RUBY 4 ch.f. Zilzal (USA) – Last Result (Northern Park (USA)) [2006/7 **h–** 17mᵖᵘ 17dᵖᵘ 16f⁴ 17dᵖᵘ Nov 23] poor maiden on Flat (stays 1m): showed nothing in juvenile hurdles (including seller): tried in cheekpieces/tongue tied: sold £700 Ascot February Sales. *C. L. Popham*

DHEHDAAH 6 b.g. Alhaarth (IRE) – Carina Clare (Slip Anchor) [2006/7 h115: 16m **h121** 16s* 17s⁴ 16d² 19s⁴ 16s⁴ 16g⁵ Apr 7] angular gelding: fair on Flat (stays 2m), successful in late-April: fairly useful handicap hurdler: won quite valuable event at Cheltenham in October by 5 lengths from Glingerbank: good efforts last 4 starts, including when fourth to Gaspara in Imperial Cup at Sandown: stays 19f: acts on soft going: reliable. *Mrs P. Sly*

DIAFA (USA) 5 b.m. Swain (IRE) – I'm Unapproachable (USA) (Distinctive Pro **h71** (USA)) [2006/7 h–: 16g 16s⁴ 17s⁶ 17g² 20m 17gᵘʳ Apr 11] poor maiden on Flat: likewise over hurdles: visored last 3 starts. *J. G. M. O'Shea*

DIAMOND CUTTER (NZ) 8 br.g. Strike Diamonds (NZ) – Lough Allen (NZ) **h–** (Omnicorp (NZ)) [2006/7 h100: 17m Jun 8] leggy gelding: fair hurdler: well held in handicaps last 3 starts, left R. C. Guest after second one: probably best short of 2½m: unraced on extremes of going. *R. T. Phillips*

DIAMOND DAN (IRE) 5 b.g. Foxhound (USA) – Kawther (Tap On Wood) [2006/7 **h75** 16m⁴ Sep 3] half-brother to 2m hurdle winner Diamond Maxine (by Turtle Island): modest on Flat (stays 1¼m), successful 3 times in 2006: 20 lengths fourth to Alexander Exchange in maiden at Worcester on hurdling debut. *P. D. Evans*

Jewson Handicap Hurdle Race Final, Cheltenham—16/1-shot Dhehdaah copes well with the rain-softened ground, beating market leaders Glingerbank (hoops) and Armariver

DIAMOND DESTINY (IRE) 4 ch.f. Carrowkeel (IRE) – Papal (Selkirk (USA)) **F79**
[2006/7 F14v⁵ F16v⁵ Feb 22] lengthy filly: third foal: half-sister to fairly useful 2m
hurdler Prize Fighter (by Desert Sun): dam unraced: second and better effort in bumpers
when around 23 lengths fifth to One Gulp in mares event at Haydock. *D. Carroll*

DIAMOND DEW 7 b.m. Double Trigger (IRE) – Scarlet Dymond (Rymer) [2006/7 **h–**
19s 22g 20m Apr 15] half-sister to 3 winners, including fairly useful hurdler Rowley Hill
(by Karinga Bay), stays 3¼m: dam, poor novice hurdler/winning chaser, stayed 25f: well
held 3 starts over hurdles. *Mrs H. Pudd*

DIAMOND HARRY 4 b.g. Sir Harry Lewis (USA) – Swift Conveyance (IRE) (Strong **F110**
Gale) [2006/7 F16s* Mar 3] 11,000 3-y-o: rangy gelding: has scope: sixth living foal:
dam, modest 2m hurdler, out of half-sister to dam of high-class staying chaser Drumlargan: 33/1, useful form when winning 21-runner bumper at Newbury on debut by ½
length from Procas de Thaix. *Nick Williams*

DIAMOND JACK (IRE) 9 gr.g. Sexton Blake – Dockmaid (IRE) (Dock Leaf) **c–**
[2006/7 h79: 16sᵖᵘ c16m 16f 18g 17dᵖᵘ Aug 28] rather leggy gelding: poor hurdler: no **h–**
form in 2006/7 (not fluent on chasing debut): raced mainly around 2m: acts on good to
firm and good to soft going: usually wears headgear. *J. J. Lambe, Ireland*

DIAMOND MAGNOLIA 5 b.m. Banker Mason (USA) – Diamante VII (Damsire **F–**
Unregistered) [2006/7 F17mᵖᵘ Aug 6] first foal: dam unraced: showed nothing in bumper
on debut. *Jedd O'Keeffe*

DIAMONDS AND DUST 5 b.g. Mister Baileys – Dusty Shoes (Shareef Dancer **h82**
(USA)) [2006/7 16d 16g⁵ 16g³ Apr 15] fairly useful on Flat (stays 13f), sold out of
M. Tompkins' stable 10,000 gns Newmarket Autumn Sales, claimed from N. Littmoden
£11,000 after successful in January, from S. Dow £13,000 in February: progressive form
over hurdles, third to Gringo in novice at Kelso. *F. P. Murtagh*

DIAMOND SUPREME (IRE) 5 b.g. Supreme Leader – Castlemartin (IRE) (Carl- **F–**
ingford Castle) [2006/7 F16g Mar 24] sturdy gelding: half-brother to 21f hurdle winner
Mandys Native (by Be My Native): dam unraced half-sister to top-class 2½m to 3m
chaser Beau Ranger and high-class staying chaser Beau: backward, well held in bumper
at Newbury on debut. *Miss H. C. Knight*

DIAMOND VEIN 8 b.g. Green Dancer (USA) – Blushing Sunrise (USA) (Cox's Ridge **h80**
(USA)) [2006/7 h–: 19dᵖᵘ 16vᵖᵘ 16v 16s* 19s 17d 16g Apr 16] quite good-topped gelding: poor hurdler: won selling handicap at Wetherby in February, only form in 2006/7:
probably stays 2½m: acts on heavy going: blinkered/in cheekpieces after reappearance:
tried tongue tied. *S. P. Griffiths*

DIAMOND WINNIE 4 b.f. Komaite (USA) – Winsome Wooster (Primo Dominie) **h–**
[2006/7 16mᵖᵘ Sep 2] lightly raced on Flat, form only on debut: no show in juvenile
hurdle. *Mrs N. S. Evans*

DIANA BISCOE 4 b.f. Riverwise (USA) – Cut Above The Rest (Indiaro) [2006/7 F14s **F—**
F16d F17g Apr 19] sturdy filly: sister to fair staying hurdler/chaser Kittenkat: dam
second in points: no form in bumpers. *N. R. Mitchell*

DIARIUS (GER) 4 br.g. Ungaro (GER) – Diavolessa (GER) (Subotica (FR)) [2006/7 **h110**
18s 20d 16s⁶ 16g² 19s⁴ 19g* Mar 24] good-topped gelding: successful once over 9f from
3 starts in Italy at 2 yrs, left H. Blume after runner-up over 11f at Cologne in mid-October:
improved form over hurdles when winning juvenile handicap at Newbury by 1¾ lengths
from Impress, hanging badly right after leading last: stays 19f: raced on good ground or
softer: blinkered on debut. *Mrs L. Wadham*

DIAVOLERIA 4 b.f. Slip Anchor – Markapen (IRE) (Classic Music (USA)) [2006/7 **F83**
F16v³ F16s* F17g Apr 13] rather leggy filly: third foal: half-sister to bumper winner
Cheer Us On (by Bahhare) and 6f to 1m winner in Italy by Vettori: dam no sign of ability:
confirmed promise of debut when winning mares bumper at Ludlow in March by neck
from Callitwhatyalike: behind when hampered over 5f out in listed race at Aintree.
M. W. Easterby

DIBBLY DOBBLER (IRE) 5 gr.m. Beauchamp King – Long Room Lady (IRE) **F—**
(Brush Aside (USA)) [2006/7 F14s Jan 4] lengthy, plain, unfurnished mare: first foal:
dam, fair hurdler, stayed 3¼m: tailed off in mares bumper on debut. *M. Scudamore*

DICEMAN (IRE) 12 b.g. Supreme Leader – Henry's Gamble (IRE) (Carlingford **c80**
Castle) [2006/7 c20g⁶ Apr 16] lengthy gelding: one-time fairly useful handicap chaser for **h—**
Mrs S. Smith: fit from points, well held in hunter at Wetherby: should stay beyond 2½m:
acts on soft going. *Mrs C. A. Coward*

DICKENSBURY LAD (FR) 7 b.g. Luchiroverte (IRE) – Voltige de Cotte (FR) **c113** (Saumon (FR)) [2006/7 c113, h–: c21d² Oct 14] workmanlike gelding: winning hurdler: **h–** fair chaser: creditable effort only outing in 2006/7: stays 3m: acts on soft going: usually races prominently. *J. L. Spearing*

DICKIE LEWIS 9 b.g. Well Beloved – Moneyacre (Veloski) [2006/7 c–x, h97: c24d **c82 +** c24v⁶ 24v⁵ 20v⁵ c23v* Mar 9] good-bodied gelding: modest handicap hurdler, well held **h83** third/fourth outings: jumped better and first form (poor) over fences when easily winning handicap at Leicester, making virtually all: should stay beyond 3m: acts on heavy going. *D. McCain Jnr*

DICKINSBURY LASS 7 b.m. Mazaad – Energance (IRE) (Salmon Leap (USA)) **c–** [2006/7 24s c20gᵖᵘ c26gᵖᵘ c23mᵘʳ Apr 22] half-sister to 2¾m hurdle winner Beau Coup **h–** (by Toulon) and winning pointer by Cataldi: dam, Irish bumper/2m hurdle winner, half-sister to fairly useful 2m jumper Nordic Thorn: won maiden point in 2006: no form on hurdling debut/in chases: blinkered final outing. *J. L. Spearing*

DICTAMIX (FR) 4 gr.g. Sagamix (FR) – Dictania (FR) (Iron Duke (FR)) [2006/7 **F79** F13v⁶ F16v³ Feb 5] 6,000 3-y-o: half-brother to several winners in France, including hurdler around 2m Diableret (by Akarad): dam successful 3 times up to 10.5f on Flat: modest form in bumpers: dead. *C. W. Fairhurst*

DICTATOR (IRE) 6 ch.g. Machiavellian (USA) – Obsessed (Storm Bird (CAN)) **c–** [2006/7 c86, h86: c16vᵖᵘ 19sᵖᵘ 21g⁵ Apr 23] tall, good-topped gelding: modest form over **h–** hurdles/fences, little impact in 2006/7, in cheekpieces last 2 outings: stays 2½m: raced on good going or softer: tongue tied: not a fluent jumper. *D. R. Gandolfo*

DICTUM (GER) 9 ch.g. Secret 'n Classy (CAN) – Doretta (GER) (Aspros (GER)) **c126** [2006/7 c–, h–: c17d⁵ c16v* c20v* c21g Mar 15] good-topped gelding: fairly useful **h–** hurdler, lightly raced: similar form over fences: won maiden at Uttoxeter in December and novice at Haydock (beat Baron Monty easily by 19 lengths) in January: sweating and not take eye, only tenth of 19 to L'Antartique in listed novice handicap at Cheltenham final start: should stay beyond 2½m: acts on heavy going: often not fluent over hurdles. *Mrs Susan Nock*

DIDBROOK 5 b.m. Alzao (USA) – Nedaarah (Reference Point) [2006/7 F–: F16m³ **F83** F16m* Jun 28] modest form in bumpers, winning maiden at Worcester in June. *Mrs Mary Hambro*

DIDCOT 8 ch.g. Roselier (FR) – Astromis (IRE) (Torus) [2006/7 16vᵖᵘ Dec 19] modest **h–** form in bumpers: no show in 2 starts over hurdles 2½ years apart. *S. Wilson, Ireland*

DIEGO CAO (IRE) 6 b.g. Cape Cross (IRE) – Lady Moranbon (USA) (Trempolino **h134** (USA)) [2006/7 h–: 16v⁶ 16g² 16g² Apr 14] sturdy gelding: useful hurdler: trained on reappearance only by Mrs N. Smith: subsequently had breathing operation: back to best when runner-up in handicaps at Fakenham and Aintree, under pressure long way out when beaten length by Kings Quay in valuable 22-runner event at latter: raced mainly around 2m on good/good to soft going. *N. J. Gifford*

DIEGO EL GRECO (FR) 5 b. or bl.g. Cadoudal (FR) – Boya Girl (FR) (Boyatino **c?** (FR)) [2006/7 19dᵖᵘ c17d³ 20vᵖᵘ Mar 2] third foal: half-brother to 21f chase winner Take **h–** Girl (by Take Risks) and 15f hurdle winner Boyastara (by Astarabad): dam, won around 2m over hurdles, also successful up to 16.5f on Flat: third in 4-y-o event at La-Roche-Posay on chasing debut: little form over hurdles, leaving G. Macaire before final start. *M. Todhunter*

DIEGO GARCIA (IRE) 7 b.g. Sri Pekan (USA) – Chapel Lawn (Generous (IRE)) **h121 p** [2006/7 22m* Aug 5] rangy gelding: fairly useful on Flat, successful 3 of 4 starts in 2006: similar standard over hurdles, won handicap at Galway (by ¾ length from Tasman) in August: stays 2¾m: acts on soft and good to firm ground. *W. P. Mullins, Ireland*

DIFFERENT CLASS (IRE) 8 b.g. Shardari – Hollygrove Cezanne (IRE) (King's **h111** Ride) [2006/7 h–, F80: 16s* 19m* 20m⁴ 22m* Aug 24] fair novice hurdler: won at Towcester, Hereford (by 3 lengths from Absolutelythebest) and Stratford in first part of season: well suited by test of stamina: acts on soft and good to firm going. *Jonjo O'Neill*

DIGGER BOY 4 b.g. King's Best (USA) – Chameleon (Green Desert (USA)) [2006/7 **h74** 17dᵘʳ 16s 17d⁴ 17g⁵ 21gᵘʳ Apr 23] compact gelding: fair maiden on Flat (may prove best short of 1½m), left M. Jarvis and well beaten in 2007: poor form over hurdles, trained on debut only by C. Egerton. *J. Gallagher*

DIGGER JAKE 5 b.g. Miner's Lamp – Sister Seven (IRE) (Henbit (USA)) [2006/7 **F–** F16g Apr 23] third foal: dam winning pointer: well beaten in bumper on debut. *G. A. Charlton*

DIGITAL FORTRESS (IRE) 7 b.g. Dr Massini (IRE) – Evergreen Lady (Smartset) [2006/7 19v² 25s⁶ 24d⁴ c16d² c25d² Dec 26] half-brother to 23f hurdle winner Bassey (by Be My Native): dam, lightly raced in points, half-sister to useful Irish 2½m chaser The Lady's Master: won maiden point in 2005: fourth in maiden bumper at Navan for Michael Aherne: off 17 months, modest form when second in novice hurdle/handicap chases: stays 25f: acts on heavy going. *Jonjo O'Neill*   **c98 h95**

DIGITAL MEDIA (IRE) 5 b.g. Taipan (IRE) – Cats Concert (IRE) (Montelimar (USA)) [2006/7 F16s* F16d³ 20s 16v⁵ 16v⁴ Mar 6] €25,000 3-y-o, resold £35,000 3-y-o: good-topped gelding: second foal: half-brother to bumper winner Sorrentina (by Muroto): dam unraced: fairly useful form in bumpers, winning at Wetherby on debut in November by 1¾ lengths from Jemez (pair clear): best effort over hurdles when fourth to King Mac in novice at Newcastle: should stay 2½m. *J. Howard Johnson*   **h82 F96**

DIK DIK 4 b.g. Diktat – Totom (Mtoto) [2006/7 16vᵇᵈ 25sᵖᵘ 17s Mar 12] modest maiden on Flat (should stay 2m): no form over hurdles: wears cheekpieces. *J. S. Moore*   **h–**

DIKTATIT 5 b.m. Diktat – Mystique Smile (Music Boy) [2006/7 h77: 16f 16f⁴ 17m⁴ 16m⁵ Jul 27] small, angular mare: poor novice hurdler: likely to prove best at 2m. *R. C. Guest*   **h81**

DIKTATORIAL 5 br.g. Diktat – Reason To Dance (Damister (USA)) [2006/7 16m Feb 4] Group 3 winner on Flat at 2 yrs for A. Balding, without a win since but still fairly useful up to 1½m in 2006 (usually tongue tied): sold out of G. Butler's stable 85,000 gns Newmarket Autumn Sales: not fluent and never a danger in maiden at Musselburgh on hurdling debut. *J. Howard Johnson*   **h79**

DIKTATORSHIP (IRE) 4 b.g. Diktat – Polka Dancer (Dancing Brave (USA)) [2006/7 16d Nov 14] modest on Flat (stays 1½m), successful in January: soundly beaten in juvenile on hurdling debut: joined G. A. Swinbank. *Ernst Oertel*   **h–**

DILLAY BROOK (IRE) 7 b.m. Supreme Leader – Anns Run (Deep Run) [2006/7 h92, F83: 24g² 22d⁵ 24s⁴ Dec 18] modest novice hurdler: stays 3m: raced on good going or softer (acts on heavy). *T. R. George*   **h93**

DING DANG DO 4 br.g. Diktat – Twilight Sonnet (Exit To Nowhere (USA)) [2006/7 F14d⁵ F16m⁵ Apr 15] first foal: dam, 5f winner (ran only at 2 yrs), half-sister to Queen's Vase winner Shanty Star: modest form in bumpers. *N. Tinkler*   **F79**

DINNIE FLANAGAN (IRE) 7 b.g. Windsor Castle – Princess Diga (IRE) (Black Minstrel) [2006/7 h95: 26g⁵ 24v* 24v⁶ Jan 17] tall gelding: modest form over hurdles: left P. Haslam and off 6 months, made all in handicap at Towcester in November, only outing for F. Jordan: suited by 3m+: raced on good going or softer (acts on heavy). *J. G. M. O'Shea*   **h97**

DIP ANCHOR 4 b.g. Slip Anchor – Streccia (Old Vic) [2006/7 F12v F16s Feb 9] useful-looking gelding: first foal: dam, well beaten on Flat, half-sister to useful stayer Saltrio (by Slip Anchor): well held both outings in bumpers. *Mouse Hamilton-Fairley*   **F–**

DIPLOMATIC DAISY (IRE) 8 b.m. Alflora (IRE) – Landa's Counsel (Pragmatic) [2006/7 h82p: 16d⁵ 16v³ 17d³ 16vᵖᵘ Jan 12] tall mare: poor novice hurdler: lame final outing (visored): raced around 2m on ground softer than good. *D. R. Gandolfo*   **h81**

DIRECT ACCESS (IRE) 12 ch.g. Roselier (FR) – Spanish Flame (IRE) (Spanish Place (USA)) [2006/7 c132, h–: c24s c20vᵖᵘ Jan 2] tall, rangy, angular gelding: useful handicap chaser on his day: should stay beyond 25f: acts on heavy going, probably on good to firm: blinkered once: has shaped as if amiss several times, including both starts in 2006/7. *N. G. Richards*   **c– h–**

DIRECT FLIGHT (IRE) 9 ch.g. Dry Dock – Midnight Mistress (Midsummer Night II) [2006/7 c131, h116: c24g Mar 14] tall, useful-looking gelding: fairly useful hurdler: useful handicap chaser: left Noel Chance, well beaten only outing in 2006/7: stays 2¾m: acts on soft going: has had tongue tied (including last 4 starts). *C. R. Egerton*   **c– h–**

DIRTY DEN (IRE) 5 b.g. Heron Island (IRE) – Fleeting Arrow (IRE) (Commanche Run) [2006/7 F17s⁶ F17v⁴ Jan 11] €15,000 3-y-o, €31,000 4-y-o: fourth foal: half-brother to useful hurdler/chaser up to 21f Rasharrow (by Rashar): dam unraced: well held in bumpers at Hereford. *Miss H. Lewis*   **F–**

DISCOMANIA 5 b.g. Pursuit of Love – Discomatic (USA) (Roberto (USA)) [2006/7 h–: 16m⁶ 18g 16d⁵ 16dᵖᵘ 16d 16s³ c16dᵘʳ c16dᵖᵘ 16g² c16gᵘʳ Apr 20] smallish gelding: poor maiden hurdler: should stay beyond 2m: tried visored/blinkered. *K. F. Clutterbuck*   **c– h74**

DISCORD 6 b.g. Desert King (IRE) – Lead Note (USA) (Nijinsky (CAN)) [2006/7 F–: **h–**
16g May 11] good-topped gelding: well held in bumpers/novice hurdle: fair maiden on
Flat. *T. H. Caldwell*

DI'S DILEMMA 9 b.m. Teenoso (USA) – Reve En Rose (Revlow) [2006/7 h91: 21g^F **h80**
16v^5 20m^6 Sep 24] small mare: modest maiden hurdler, below best in 2006/7 (lame final
outing): stays 23f, effective at much shorter: acts on heavy and good to firm going:
consistent, but hard to win with. *C. C. Bealby*

DISHDASHA (IRE) 5 b.g. Desert Prince (IRE) – Counterplot (IRE) (Last Tycoon) **h104 +**
[2006/7 h83: 16s 16m^6 17m 18g^2 16d* 16g* 18d^2 16s^4 Dec 7] fair hurdler: sold out of
C. Dore's stable £2,000 Ascot August Sales after third start: much improved after,
winning handicaps at Stratford (ladies) in October and Kempton (conditional jockeys) in
November: best at 2m: acts on soft and good to firm going. *Mrs A. M. Thorpe*

DISPOL PETO 7 gr.g. Petong – Plie (Superlative) [2006/7 h–: 16s^4 16v^6 Mar 22] **h67**
modest on Flat (stays 1½m): poor form over hurdles: likely to prove best around 2m: tried
in cheekpieces. *R. Johnson*

DISPOL SAMURAI 4 gr.g. Shinko Forest (IRE) – Natural Pearl (Petong) [2006/7 **h–**
17g^{pu} Apr 23] little form at 2 yrs for T. D. Barron: no show on hurdling debut. *T. Butt*

D'ISSAN (IRE) 9 br.g. Commanche Run – Loch Phar (IRE) (Phardante (FR)) [2006/7 **h–**
22v^{pu} Feb 25] no show in bumper and maiden hurdle nearly 4 years apart. *M. B. Shears*

DISTANT THUNDER (IRE) 9 b.g. Phardante (FR) – Park Breeze (IRE) (Strong **c142**
Gale) [2006/7 c128, h–: c24g^2 c24g^3 c29m Apr 9] lengthy gelding: has reportedly had **h–**
breathing operation: useful handicap chaser: left R. Alner, back to best in 2006/7, 2
lengths second to Bob Bob Bobbin at Bangor, then third (beaten 2 short heads) to Joes
Edge in William Hill Trophy at Cheltenham (sweating and on toes) 4 months later:
seemed not to stay when eighth of 29 to Butler's Cabin in Irish National at Fairyhouse:
stays 3m: acts on good going, probably on soft. *Noel T. Chance*

DIVET HILL 13 b.g. Milieu – Bargello's Lady (Bargello) [2006/7 c–, h97: c28d^{pu} **c–**
May 1] good-topped gelding: fair hurdler: fairly useful handicap chaser at best: stays 25f: **h–**
acts on good and good to soft going: front runner. *Mrs A. Hamilton*

DIVEX (IRE) 6 b.g. Taipan (IRE) – Ebony Countess (IRE) (Phardante (FR)) [2006/7 **h91**
h93, F98: 17s 20s^3 20g^6 20g^3 20g Apr 7] tall gelding: modest maiden hurdler: will stay
beyond 2½m: acts on soft and good to firm going. *Micky Hammond*

DIVIDING LINE 4 ch.g. Zafonic (USA) – Division Bell (Warning) [2006/7 F14g 17v **h–**
16v^{pu} 18s Feb 15] stocky gelding: third foal: half-brother to 2 winners on Flat, including **F–**
7.5f/1¼m winner Mount Usher (by Polar Falcon): dam useful 1m winner in France: no
form in bumper/juvenile hurdles: tongue tied 3 of 4 starts: dead. *M. W. Easterby*

DIVINE GIFT 6 b.g. Groom Dancer (USA) – Child's Play (USA) (Sharpen Up) **h110 p**
[2006/7 16m* Aug 22] half-brother to modest and temperamental hurdler around 2m
Montessori Mio (by Robellino): useful on Flat (stays 1¼m), successful in May: landed
odds comfortably by 4 lengths from Pearson Glen in 6-runner novice at Perth on hurdling
debut: looked sure to progress, but not seen out again: joined Noel Chance. *K. A. Ryan*

DIVINE WISDOM 6 ch.m. Silver Patriarch (IRE) – Ardent Bride (Ardross) [2006/7 **h80 +**
21g^2 Mar 28] second foal: half-sister to bumper winner The Package (by Kayf Tara):
dam, showed little in bumper/novice hurdles, half-sister to useful 2m chaser Shamana:
looked in need of experience when 2 lengths second to Heavenly Pleasure in mares
novice hurdle at Towcester on debut, tending to hang left off bridle before keeping on
well: may do better. *Mrs L. Wadham*

DIVVYS DREAM 5 gr.g. Environment Friend – Oriel Dream (Oats) [2006/7 F16s **F–**
Dec 26] fourth foal: half-brother to one-time fairly useful hurdler/chaser Lazy But Lively
(by Supreme Leader), stays 4m: dam fair staying hurdler: well held in bumper on debut.
P. Beaumont

DIX HUIT CYBORG (FR) 6 ch.g. Cyborg (FR) – Dix Huit Brumaire (FR) (General **F71**
Assembly (USA)) [2006/7 F16g F16s May 14] tall gelding: form in bumpers only on
debut in 2004/5 when trained by J. Howard Johnson: won maiden point in April.
J. R. Norton

DIXIE'S GIRL 6 gr.m. Revoque (IRE) – Chickamauga (USA) (Wild Again (USA)) **F–**
[2006/7 aF16g Mar 21] third foal: dam ran once: tailed off in bumper on debut. *Mrs
Norma Pook*

DIX VILLEZ (FR) 8 b.g. Villez (USA) – Dix Huit Brumaire (FR) (General Assembly   **c124**
(USA)) [2006/7 c110, h104: c24m* c22g³ c22gᶠ c24d³ c28d³ 22v c29mᵇᵈ c25m Apr 26]   **h105**
lengthy, useful-looking gelding: fair hurdler: fairly useful chaser: improved effort when
winning minor event at Cork in June by length from Shining Lights: good efforts in
competitive handicaps next 4 outings: should stay beyond 3½m: acts on heavy and good
to firm going: usually front runner/races prominently. *Paul Nolan, Ireland*

DIZZY FUTURE 5 b.g. Fraam – Kara Sea (USA) (River Special (USA)) [2006/7 h–:   **h97**
16f 21s² 20v⁵ 16m 20f³ 22m* 26m³ 21s⁵ 22s 19g 26g* Apr 20] neat gelding: maiden
on Flat: modest hurdler, left B. Llewellyn after third start: won handicaps at Stratford
(conditional jockeys) in September and Hereford in April: stays 3¼m: best form on good/
good to firm going: has worn cheekpieces. *M. R. Bosley*

DJESS 7 b.m. Alderbrook – Poussetiere Deux (FR) (Garde Royale) [2006/7 F16m⁶ 16f⁶   **h–**
20g 22g Sep 15] first foal: dam, French 19f hurdle winner (also won on Flat), half-sister   **F–**
to Grand Steeple-Chase de Paris winner Vieux Beaufai: well beaten, including in points.
Dermot Day, Ireland

D J FLIPPANCE (IRE) 12 b.g. Orchestra – Jane Bond (Good Bond) [2006/7 c99,   **c–**
h98: c25sᵖᵘ Feb 3] rangy gelding: modest hurdler/chaser: left A. Parker, failed to   **h–**
complete in point/hunter in 2007: stayed 3¾m: acted on heavy going: tried in cheekpieces: dead. *G. L. Edwards*

DOCKBRIDGE (IRE) 5 br.g. Presenting – Rahan Bridge (IRE) (The Parson) [2006/7   **F–**
F17s Feb 19] second foal: dam bumper winner: favourite, tailed off in bumper at Carlisle
on debut. *N. G. Richards*

DOC ROW (IRE) 7 b.g. Dr Massini (IRE) – Roberto Moss (Le Moss) [2006/7 h112:   **c117 +**
c23dᶠ 21d⁵ c32s² 24s Dec 27] good-topped gelding: fair hurdler, ran poorly final outing: **h112**
fairly useful form both starts in handicap chases at Exeter, every chance when falling last
on first occasion and made mistakes when second of 5 to Ranelagh Grey: stays 4m: raced
on good to soft/soft going. *D. E. Pipe*

DOCTOR DAVID 4 gr.g. Zilzal (USA) – Arantxa (Sharpo) [2006/7 16d² 16d⁵ 16g*   **h112**
16g Apr 12] close-coupled gelding: half-brother to fairly useful hurdler/winning chaser
Vicario (by Vettori), probably stays 2¾m: modest maiden on Flat (best efforts at 1m,
raced only on polytrack), left Ernst Oertel after final 3-y-o start: fairly useful juvenile
hurdler: won conditional jockeys maiden at Fakenham in March readily by 14 lengths
from Impostor: stiff task, eighth to Katchit in Grade 1 at Aintree, forcing pace until 3 out:
raced at 2m on good/good to soft ground: may still do better. *Mrs Caroline Bailey*

DOCTORED 6 ch.g. Dr Devious (IRE) – Polygueza (FR) (Be My Guest (USA))   **h–**
[2006/7 h–: 16vᵘʳ Jan 4] well beaten on completed outing over hurdles, subsequently off
a year. *D. C. O'Brien*

DOCTOR GRAF 6 b.g. Goofalik (USA) – Auenlust (GER) (Surumu (GER)) [2006/7   **h–**
F16d³ F17m⁵ 22fᵖᵘ Apr 22] half-brother to several winners on Flat, including stayer Irish   **F80**
Ballad (by Singspiel): dam German 1m winner: modest form in maiden bumpers: left
D. Wintle and off nearly 11 months, lame on hurdling debut: dead. *S. C. Burrough*

DOCTOR KILBRIDE (IRE) 4 ch.g. Fruits of Love (USA) – Kilbride Lass (IRE)   **F87**
(Lahib) [2006/7 F17m² Apr 17] half-brother to 3 winners on Flat, including fairly
useful 2m winner Boumahou (by Desert Story): dam unraced half-sister to very smart
1½m performer Phoenix Reach: 2 lengths second of 4 finishers to Lit Up in bumper at
Exeter on debut: sold 7,500 gns Doncaster May Sales. *P. Winkworth*

DOCTOR SUPREMO (IRE) 6 b.g. Dr Massini (IRE) – Supreme View (Supreme   **h–**
Leader) [2006/7 h–, F–: 21m 21dᵖᵘ Oct 30] no form, including in points. *D. M. Grissell*

DOLANS BAY (IRE) 6 b.g. Old Vic – Kyle House VII (Damsire Unregistered)   **h82**
[2006/7 h–: 20s* 20vᵘʳ 21s⁴ 21v 25v⁵ 20v⁴ Mar 18] workmanlike gelding: poor novice
hurdler: well backed, won handicap at Carlisle in November: stays 21f: raced on ground
softer than good (acts on heavy): tried in cheekpieces. *G. M. Moore*

DO L'ENFANT D'EAU (FR) 8 ch.g. Minds Music (USA) – L'Eau Sauvage   **c106**
(Saumarez) [2006/7 c115, h–: c16vᵖᵘ c20vᵖᵘ c16vᵖᵘ c16g c20s⁴ Apr 25] compact gelding: **h–**
one-time useful hurdler: fairly useful handicap chaser, disappointing in 2006/7: stays 21f:
acts on heavy going, below form on good to firm: in cheekpieces last 2 starts. *B. Storey*

DOLLY 5 b.m. Thowra (FR) – Sweet Symphony (IRE) (Orchestra) [2006/7 18sᵖᵘ Nov   **h–**
26] poor maiden up to 1¼m on Flat (tried in cheekpieces): no show in mares maiden on
hurdling debut. *Tom Dascombe*

DOLMUR (IRE) 7 b. or br.g. Charnwood Forest (IRE) – Kawanin (Generous (IRE)) **c108**
[2006/7 c110, h–: c25m² c24mᵖᵘ c24sᵖᵘ c24d⁴ c25g⁴ c23g² Apr 16] angular gelding: **h–**
winning hurdler: fair chaser: stays 3¼m: acts on soft and good to firm going: tried in
cheekpieces. *Ferdy Murphy*

DOM D'ORGEVAL (FR) 7 b.g. Belmez (USA) – Marie d'Orgeval (FR) (Bourbon **c142**
(FR)) [2006/7 h145: 21s³ 25s⁴ 24s³ c24d* c25v* c24g c25g³ Apr 13] workmanlike **h145**
gelding: smart hurdler: off 5 months and sweating, 5 lengths third of 5 to Inglis Drever in
Grade 2 Long Distance Hurdle at Newbury, third start/final one for N. Williams: landed
odds with plenty to spare first 2 outings over fences, in maiden at Fakenham in January
and novice at Hexham (beat L'Antartique by 2 lengths) in February: better form (useful)
when 8½ lengths third to ready winner Aces Four in Grade 2 novice at Aintree: likely to
stay beyond 25f: has won on good to firm going, goes particularly well on soft/heavy:
visored once: patiently ridden: reliable. *D. E. Pipe*

DOME 9 b.g. Be My Chief (USA) – Round Tower (High Top) [2006/7 c59, h–: c24m⁵ **c56**
c20gᵖᵘ Aug 14] useful-looking gelding: lightly-raced novice hurdler, little solid form: has **h–**
had tongue tied. *Carl Llewellyn*

DOMENICO (IRE) 9 b.g. Sadler's Wells (USA) – Russian Ballet (USA) (Nijinsky **c– §**
(CAN)) [2006/7 c–§, h95§: 16f⁴ 16d⁴ 16m⁶ 6d* Apr 8] good-topped gelding: poor handicap **h82 §**
hurdler: pulled up only outing over fences: should stay 2½m: acts on any going: tried in
headgear/tongue tied: ungenuine. *J. R. Jenkins*

DOMESTIC FLIGHT 4 b.f. Missed Flight – Lady Manello (Mandrake Major) **F–**
[2006/7 F16v F16v⁶ Feb 5] half-sister to 3 winners, including modest chaser Miss
Royello (by Royal Fountain), stays 27f, and bumper winner Having A Party (by Dancing
High): dam, placed over hurdles, half-sister to fairly useful chasers up to 25f Sword
Beach and Divet Hill: soundly beaten in mares bumpers. *Mrs A. Hamilton*

DOMINICAN MONK (IRE) 8 b.g. Lord Americo – Ballybeg Katie (IRE) (Roselier **h108**
(FR)) [2006/7 h118: 19d 17s⁴ Dec 29] smallish gelding: fairly useful hurdler:
off 16 months, below best both starts in 2006/7: bred to stay well beyond 17f: acts on soft
and good to firm going: joined D. Arbuthnot. *C. Tinkler*

DONALD (POL) 7 b.g. Enjoy Plan (USA) – Dahira (POL) (Dakota) [2006/7 22dᵖᵘ **h–**
21sᵖᵘ 22sᵖᵘ Feb 17] leggy gelding: fair hurdler for M. Pitman: off 2 years, no form
in 2006/7, left Miss E. Lavelle prior to final start: stays 2¾m: acts on soft going.
B. G. Powell

DON AND GERRY (IRE) 6 ch.m. Vestris Abu – She's No Tourist (IRE) (Doubletour **h99**
(USA)) [2006/7 h100, F89: 19g* 16d³ 19m⁴ 22mᵖᵘ Jul 17] smallish, angular mare:
modest novice hurdler: won mares event at Hereford in May: went amiss after being
hampered final outing: should stay 2¾m: acts on firm and good to soft going (won
bumper on soft). *P. D. Evans*

DONATESSA (GER) 4 b.f. Sternkoenig (IRE) – Donadea (GER) (Dashing Blade) **h78 p**
[2006/7 18m⁴ Apr 26] useful on Flat (stays 11f), successful twice in Germany, including
at Bremen in November: left M. Hofer, not fluent when never-nearer fourth in mares
maiden at Fontwell on hurdling debut: should do better. *C. J. Mann*

DON CASTILLE (USA) 5 ch.g. Royal Anthem (USA) – Suzie Sparkle (USA) (High **c–**
Brite (USA)) [2006/7 F90: c16g⁴ 20vᵖᵘ Jan 27] lengthy gelding: fair form in bumpers in **h–**
2005/6: no show in maiden chase or Grade 2 novice hurdle. *P. R. Webber*

DONEGAL SHORE (IRE) 8 b.g. Mujadil (USA) – Distant Shore (IRE) (Jareer **h–**
(USA)) [2006/7 16dᵖᵘ Oct 1] maiden hurdler: has had tongue tied. *P. L. Clinton*

DON FERNANDO 8 b.g. Zilzal (USA) – Teulada (USA) (Riverman (USA)) [2006/7 **c–**
c–, h117+: 20m⁵ c16mᵘʳ 17d 19d⁵ 19sᶠ Dec 7] leggy gelding: winning hurdler, has become **h114 d**
useful hurdler, has become disappointing: probably best short of 3m: acts on soft and
good to firm going: wore headgear in 2006/7, also tongue tied last 2 starts. *D. E. Pipe*

DONIE DOOLEY (IRE) 9 ch.g. Be My Native (USA) – Bridgeofallen (IRE) (Torus) **c91**
[2006/7 h–: 16s* c21g³ c16gᵖᵘ c23m⁶ Jun 28] workmanlike gelding: modest handicap **h94**
hurdler: back to best to win at Uttoxeter in May: similar form on chasing debut, bled next
time: stays 21f: acts on soft and good to firm going. *P. T. Dalton*

DONNA'S DOUBLE 12 ch.g. Weldnaas (USA) – Shadha (Shirley Heights) [2006/7 **h76**
h88: 16d 16m⁶ 16g 20d 16s⁴ 16g Mar 16] smallish, rather leggy gelding: modest on Flat
(stays 1½m), twice successful in 2006: poor maiden hurdler: stays easy 2½m: acts on soft
ground. *Karen McLintock*

DONNYBROOK TRAVEL (IRE) 8 b.g. Ballinvella Boy – Run Rose (IRE) (Rose-lier (FR)) [2006/7 16f Apr 5] won maiden Irish point in 2005: poor form over hurdles: left A. Kennedy, soon tailed off on British debut. *P. Henderson*   **h–**

DONOVAN (NZ) 8 b.g. Stark South (USA) – Agent Jane (NZ) (Sound Reason (CAN)) [2006/7 c93, h103: c16g³ c17sᶠ c20g³ c19d⁴ c19s⁴ c24gᵖᵘ c20m⁴ c23m⁵ Apr 15] close-coupled gelding: winning hurdler: modest handicap chaser: failed to impress with attitude final 3 starts: stays easy 23f: acts on heavy and good to firm going: used to wear headgear: held up. *Ian Williams*   **c93** **h–**

DON PASQUALE 5 br.g. Zafonic (USA) – Bedazzling (IRE) (Darshaan) [2006/7 h–: 16g 17v Nov 28] lengthy gelding: no form over hurdles: tried tongue tied. *J. T. Stimpson*   **h–**

DON'T ASK ME (IRE) 6 b.g. Spectrum (IRE) – Ediyrna (IRE) (Doyoun) [2006/7 h99: 20s* 18m 20mᵖᵘ 24f⁵ 19d 21s⁵ 17v² 22s* Feb 1] quite good-topped gelding: modest hurdler: won sellers at Uttoxeter (handicap) in May and Fontwell in February: stays 2¾m, at least as effective at 2m: acts on good to firm and heavy going: has worn visor/cheek-pieces: tongue tied. *D. E. Pipe*   **h92**

DON'T BE BITIN (IRE) 6 b.g. Turtle Island (IRE) – Shonara's Way (Slip Anchor) [2006/7 h133: c20s³ c18v* c17s⁵ c20v⁴ c16s* c16v⁵ c16v⁴ c16mᶠ Apr 24] leggy, angular gelding: useful hurdler: fairly useful novice chaser: won at Thurles (maiden) in November and Naas (beat Dunguaire Lad by 1½ lengths, taken wide most of way) in February: best short of 2½m when conditions are testing: acts on heavy going: consistent. *Eoin Griffin, Ireland*   **c124** **h–**

DON'T BE DAFT (IRE) 7 b.g. Tidaro (USA) – Langtry Bay (Pollerton) [2006/7 c24v⁵ c22v* c24v* Mar 19] strong, lengthy gelding: winning pointer: useful form in hunter chases: won at Fairyhouse (beat Big Zoomo 5 lengths) in February and Gowran (by length from Beachcomber Bay) in March: stays 3m: raced on heavy going. *John Joseph Murphy, Ireland*   **c121**

DON'T KEEP ON (IRE) 6 b.g. Arctic Lord – Pirolina (IRE) (Tirol) [2006/7 F16m⁴ Jun 11] €4,200 4-y-o: second foal: dam little sign of ability: poor form when fourth in maiden bumper on debut. *J. W. Mullins*   **F70**

DON'T MATTER 7 b.m. Petong – Cool Run (Deep Run) [2006/7 c–, h–: 16s 16gᵖᵘ 16mᵖᵘ 16fᵘʳ 17dᵖᵘ Oct 6] no form over hurdles/in maiden chases: tongue tied in 2006/7. *M. A. Barnes*   **c–** **h–**

DON'T PUSH IT (IRE) 7 b.g. Old Vic – She's No Laugh Ben (USA) (Alleged (USA)) [2006/7 h127p, F93+: c20s* c20d² c21s* c16d* c16gᶠ c16g⁵ Apr 14]   **c153** **h–**

> The only horse to run the season's leading novice chaser Denman close in 2006/7 didn't get the opportunity to take him on again. In a novice event over an

boylecasino.com Novices' Chase, Cheltenham—Don't Push It (centre) gets the better of a good duel with Mr Pointment (right); also pictured is third-placed Heez A Dreamer

extended two and a half miles at Cheltenham in November, Don't Push It gave those who had laid the odds on Denman a fright before going down by three quarters of a length, flying the last and briefly looking as though he might get the better of the favourite. The performance was all the more meritorious as Don't Push It didn't really enjoy the run of things, losing his back legs when hampered three out and then intimidated by Denman when that rival hung left on the run-in. At that stage, there was a possibility the pair could meet again at the same venue in March, in the Royal & SunAlliance Chase, but, whereas Denman went on to maintain his unbeaten record in that race, Don't Push It lined up for the mile-shorter Arkle Trophy instead. Whether Don't Push It would have been able to trouble an improved Denman to the same extent must have been doubtful, though that isn't to say he won't prove effective over so far as three miles—we certainly think he will. What his performance in the Arkle demonstrated, though, is that Don't Push It clearly has the speed to be effective at two miles, as he was still very much in with a shout (albeit niggled) when falling two out. Unlike Denman and other good novice chasers such as My Way de Solzen, Aces Four and Twist Magic, Don't Push It hasn't a big-race win to his name, but it won't be too long before he does. A lightly-raced seven-year-old who has come a long way in a short time, Don't Push It looks the sort to do well in open company in the next season.

Don't Push It had only three runs under his belt when he made his chasing debut in a maiden at Stratford in October. A promising third in a bumper at Warwick in December 2004, he won a similar event at Market Rasen over nine months later and a two-and-a-half-mile novice hurdle at Haydock at the end of 2005. Very much the type to make a chaser, the well-made Don't Push It had no

Mr John P. McManus' "Don't Push It"

difficulty at Stratford, jumping fluently in the main, making smooth headway from the rear on the final circuit and stretching clear from two out. Following his good effort against Denman, Don't Push It was quickly back on the winning trail. Returned to Cheltenham in December for a cracking novice event over twenty-one furlongs, Don't Push It landed the odds by a length and three quarters from the useful Mr Pointment, doing well to recover from a bad mistake at the tenth and battling on well to edge ahead on the run-in. The race was run at a steady pace, but the ground was testing and Don't Push It's finishing effort suggested that he was likely to stay further. With the Arkle in mind, Don't Push It had his final outing before the Cheltenham Festival over two miles, in a four-runner novice event at Chepstow. Beforehand the race looked a match between him and the Paul Nicholls-trained Phar Bleu, but it turned out to be a very one-sided contest. Although Don't Push It's jumping was far from convincing in the early stages, it became more assured as the race wore on and he drew well clear from three out. Don't Push It started at 4/1 for the Arkle, with only My Way de Solzen and Fair Along at shorter, and he was still close up, behind Jack The Giant and eventual winner My Way de Solzen, when he fell two out along with Twist Magic, who also held every chance at the time. Don't Push It renewed rivalry with Twist Magic and others in the Maghull Novices' Chase at Aintree, but any clues as to where he might have finished had he completed at Cheltenham weren't forthcoming. The seven-year-old had looked hard trained in the paddock before the Arkle and, again light in condition, certainly shaped as if past his best for the season at Aintree, jumping deliberately on occasions faced with an even sharper test and finishing a well-held fifth of six behind Twist Magic.

		Sadler's Wells	Northern Dancer
	Old Vic	(b 1981)	Fairy Bridge
	(b 1986)	Cockade	Derring-Do
Don't Push It (IRE)		(b 1973)	Camenae
(b.g. 2000)		Alleged	Hoist The Flag
	She's No Laugh Ben (USA)	(b 1974)	Princess Pout
	(b 1987)	Swirlaway	Sir Ivor
		(b 1977)	Flo's Pleasure

Don't Push It is the sixth foal of She's No Laugh Ben, whose only other successful produce to date is her third foal Larifaari (by Lashkari), a fair winner at up to a mile and a mile and a quarter in Ireland. She has produced two more foals since Don't Push It, including his 2002 half-brother by Perpendicular who is also under the care of Jonjo O'Neill having been bought for €15,000 in 2006. She's No Laugh Ben, who showed no sign of ability in five runs on the Flat in Ireland, is a daughter of Swirlaway, a winner four times in the States including in a stakes race; and a granddaughter of Flo's Pleasure, whose twelve victories there also included two in stakes races. Don't Push It has raced only on good ground or softer to date, and he acts well on soft. *Jonjo O'Neill*

DON'T SIOUX ME (IRE) 9 b.g. Sadler's Wells (USA) – Commanche Belle (Shirley Heights) [2006/7 16m^{ur} Jul 11] lengthy, angular gelding: fair hurdler at best: off a year, unseated third in seller: stays 19f: acts on soft and good to firm going: often tongue tied: front runner. *K. A. Morgan*   **h–**

DONT TOUCH ME (IRE) 7 b. or br.m. Key of Luck (USA) – Figini (Glint of Gold) [2006/7 17f^5 16f^5 18f^{ur} 17m^{pu} Aug 29] half-sister to fairly useful hurdler Mimosa (by Midyan), stayed 21f: twice-raced on Flat: poor maiden hurdler: form only around 2m: acts on firm going: has had tongue tied, including last 6 starts. *J. G. Carr, Ireland*   **h79**

DON VALENTINO (POL) 8 ch.g. Duke Valentino – Dona (POL) (Dakota) [2006/7 c97, h–: c20m^{pu} Jun 13] tall, close-coupled gelding: winning hurdler: modest novice chaser: ran as if amiss only start in 2006/7: stays 2½m: acts on soft and good to firm going: tried blinkered/visored/tongue tied. *T. R. George*   **c–**   **h–**

DOOF (IRE) 7 b.g. Old Vic – Ashpark Rose (IRE) (Roselier (FR)) [2006/7 h–: c26s^4 c21g^3 c19f^6 Apr 11] sparely-made gelding: winning hurdler: left M. Pipe, won point in February: modest form at best in hunter chases: stays 2¾m: acts on heavy going: head-strong front runner. *Ms Sarah Townrow*   **c83 x**   **h–**

DOOLEY 9 b.g. Alflora (IRE) – Lady Phyl (Northiam (USA)) [2006/7 20v^F May 20] ex-Irish gelding: runner-up in bumper: well beaten completed start over hurdles, left N. Meade prior to only outing in 2006/7. *Jonjo O'Neill*   **h–**

DOONEYS GATE (IRE) 6 b.g. Oscar (IRE) – Park Breeze (IRE) (Strong Gale) [2006/7 F16s* 16v⁶ 18v* Dec 6] €45,000 3-y-o: brother to smart chaser Offshore Account and half-brother to several winners, including top-class chaser The Listener and useful chasers Fork Lightning (both by Roselier) and Distant Thunder (by Phardante), all best at 3m+: dam unraced sister to useful staying chaser Risk of Thunder: successful in bumper at Wexford on debut in May: much better effort in maiden hurdles when winning 22-runner event at Fairyhouse by short head from Kendor Dine, always close up: will be suited by 2½m+: raced on soft/heavy ground: useful prospect. *W. P. Mullins, Ireland*   **h117 p**   **F93 +**

DORAN'S EXPRESS (IRE) 5 b.g. Supreme Leader – Tullahought (Jaazeiro (USA)) [2006/7 F16s⁶ Dec 26] €22,000 3-y-o: brother to 3m chase winner Hibernian and half-brother to useful 2m hurdler Frances Street (by Be My Native): dam fair 2m to 2½m hurdler: sixth of 10 in bumper on debut. *O. Sherwood*   **F–**

DORANS LANE 9 b.m. Gildoran – Snitton Lane (Cruise Missile) [2006/7 h70, F–: 17dᵖᵘ 20gᵖᵘ Apr 14] lengthy mare: poor maiden hurdler. *W. M. Brisbourne*   **h–**

DORIS'S GIFT 6 gr.g. Environment Friend – Saxon Gift (Saxon Farm) [2006/7 h–: 24mᵖᵘ 25g⁴ 23sᵖᵘ Nov 22] big, strong gelding: little show in novice hurdles: poor form on completed start over fences: looks a stayer: tried in cheekpieces. *J. Howard Johnson*   **c71**   **h–**

DORMY TWO (IRE) 7 b.m. Eagle Eyed (USA) – Tartan Lady (IRE) (Taufan (USA)) [2006/7 h–§: 20g⁴ 20s⁵ May 14] leggy mare: poor maiden hurdler: stayed 21f: acted on soft and good to firm going: often wore cheekpieces: refused to race final 2005/6 start: dead. *J. S. Wainwright*   **h75 §**

DORNEYS WELL (IRE) 7 b. or br.g. Supreme Leader – Princess Millicent (Proverb) [2006/7 h103: c19d⁵ c16dᵖᵘ c16vᵖᵘ Jan 9] fair handicap hurdler: no show over fences: should stay 2½m: acts on heavy going. *Evan Williams*   **c–**   **h–**

DOSCO (IRE) 8 b. or br.g. Oscar (IRE) – Broken Rein (IRE) (Orchestra) [2006/7 c25d⁶ c20m c20g⁵ c23d³ c24sᵇᵈ c21s* c24d² c24v* 20s* 24v* 24d⁶ 22m c25m⁶ Apr 26] tall, good-topped gelding: first foal: dam lightly-raced half-sister to smart 2m/2½m chaser Light The Wad: fair hurdler/fairly useful chaser: much improved in handicaps in 2006/7, winning over fences at Punchestown and Thurles (beat Benefit Night by 6 lengths) in November and over hurdles at Navan and Leopardstown in December: stays 3m: acts well on soft/heavy ground: tried tongue tied. *D. T. Hughes, Ireland*   **c125**   **h106 +**

DO THE TRICK (AUS) 6 b.g. Favorite Trick (USA) – Verscay (AUS) (Marscay (AUS)) [2006/7 16g² 16d* 16s³ 16m⁴ Apr 8] fairly useful form on Flat: likewise over hurdles: won maiden at Sligo in August: best effort when fourth of 24 to Bobs Pride in handicap at Fairyhouse: raced at 2m. *M. Halford, Ireland*   **h119 +**

DOTSNEW DAWN 6 b.m. Lord Americo – Dawn O'Er Kells (IRE) (Pitskelly) [2006/7 F–: F17d⁶ F17m F16m Jun 13] tailed off in bumpers. *N. E. Berry*   **F–**

DOUBLE ANGE (FR) 9 b.g. Double Bed (FR) – La Mesange (FR) (Olmeto) [2006/7 c88, h–: c25d⁶ c17s³ May 26] good-topped gelding: placed in hunter chases in Britain: stays 3m: tried blinkered. *Mrs Katie Baimbridge*   **c72**   **h–**

DOUBLE BLADE 12 b.g. Kris – Sesame (Derrylin) [2006/7 16m⁶ c17gᵘʳ c16m Jun 11] strong, lengthy gelding: winning hurdler/chaser, no form in 2006/7: best at 2m: acts on firm and good to soft going: has won 5 times at Sedgefield: finds little. *N. Wilson*   **c– §**   **h– §**

DOUBLE CENTENARY (IRE) 4 b.g. Lahib (USA) – Sutton Centenary (IRE) (Godswalk (USA)) [2006/7 F14s F14g⁶ Apr 10] 10,000 3-y-o: fifth foal: dam 7f winner: no show in bumpers. *Miss Tor Sturgis*   **F–**

DOUBLE DATE (FR) 6 b. or br.g. Double Bed (FR) – Gay Native (FR) (Gay Minstrel (FR)) [2006/7 h–: 21dᵖᵘ 22vᵖᵘ Jan 2] tall, workmanlike gelding: more signs of temperament than ability in novice hurdles: tongue tied last 2 starts. *C. P. Morlock*   **h–**

DOUBLE DEFAULT (IRE) 6 ch.g. Beneficial – Over The Risc (IRE) (Over The River (FR)) [2006/7 24v² 21v² 20v* 24s* Apr 1] €11,500 3-y-o: first foal: dam unraced: won maiden point in Ireland in 2006: fairly useful form when runner-up to Chief Dan George first 2 starts over hurdles: didn't need to repeat that to land odds in maiden at Ayr in March and novice at Hexham in April: stays 3m: raced on soft/heavy ground: probably capable of better. *N. G. Richards*   **h124 p**

DOUBLE DEPUTY (IRE) 6 b.h. Sadler's Wells (USA) – Janaat (Kris) [2006/7 16f⁴ 16d⁵ 20d 17s² 20d⁵ 25sᶠ 20s⁵ Apr 1] close-coupled horse: fairly useful on Flat (stays 1¾m), sold out of Saeed bin Suroor's stable 60,000 gns Newmarket Autumn (2005) Sales, well beaten 2 starts in 2006: modest novice hurdler: should be suited by 2½m+: acts on soft ground: tried visored/tongue tied. *J. J. Quinn*   **h96**

DOUBLE DIZZY 6 b.g. Double Trigger (IRE) – Miss Diskin (IRE) (Sexton Blake) **h112**
[2006/7 h108: 19d² 22m* 24d² 24d⁵ 24g² 21g⁶ Apr 18] angular, leggy gelding: fair novice
hurdler: didn't need to be at best to win amateur event at Exeter in November: stays 3m:
acts on soft and good to firm going: tongue tied last 3 starts: often front runner.
R. H. Buckler

DOUBLE EAGLE 5 b.g. Silver Patriarch (IRE) – Grayrose Double (Celtic Cone) **h120**
[2006/7 F17s* F16d 21s⁴ 24s³ 20v³ 20s* 20s² Mar 10] stocky gelding: ninth foal: **F103**
half-brother to bumper winners Grayrose Fleur (by Henbit) and The Muratti (by Alflora):
dam, winning hurdler who stayed 3m, out of half-sister to smart 2m to 3m chaser Clear
Cut: impressive debut when winning bumper at Carlisle in October by 23 lengths: fairly
useful novice hurdler: won at same course (by 4 lengths from Camden George) in
February: sweating and on toes, improved again when 4 lengths second of 16 to Albertas
Run in valuable handicap at Sandown: probably stays 3m: raced on ground softer than
good. *D. McCain Jnr*

DOUBLE ELLS 5 b.m. Yaheeb (USA) – Knayton Lass (Presidium) [2006/7 h–: 16g **h80**
21m 20s² 23sᵖᵘ 19v⁶ 24sᵖᵘ 20vᵖᵘ Mar 2] good-topped mare: traces of stringhalt: form
(poor) over hurdles only on third outing: should stay beyond 2½m: acts on soft ground:
tongue tied last 2 starts. *J. M. Jefferson*

DOUBLE GEM (IRE) 8 ch.g. Grand Plaisir (IRE) – Thatilldofornow (IRE) (Lord **h95**
Americo) [2006/7 h95: 16v³ Dec 3] sturdy gelding: modest novice hurdler, off 13 months
prior to only start in 2006/7: bred to stay beyond 2m: probably acts on heavy and good to
firm going. *J. I. A. Charlton*

DOUBLE GIN 7 gr.g. Double Trigger (IRE) – Belmore Cloud (Baron Blakeney) **h95**
[2006/7 h87p: 20g³ May 11] leggy gelding: third in novice hurdles, better effort (modest
form) behind Panzer at Wetherby in May: stays 2½m. *W. Amos*

DOUBLE HONOUR (FR) 9 gr.g. Highest Honor (FR) – Silver Cobra (USA) (Silver **c–**
Hawk (USA)) [2006/7 c136, h–: 23f May 6] close-coupled gelding: winning hurdler: **h136**
useful handicap chaser: successful in points in December/April: stays 33f: acts on soft
and good to firm going: blinkered: often jumps less than fluently/needs plenty of driving.
P. J. Hobbs

DOUBLE INTRUDER (IRE) 6 ch.g. Alderbrook – Aunty Dawn (IRE) (Strong **h83 +**
Gale) [2006/7 16s 19d 16m Apr 10] well-made gelding: fifth foal: half-brother to 2½m
chase winner Phar City (by Phardante) and winning pointer by Fourstars Allstar: dam
unraced from family of Dawn Run: most encouraging run in maiden/novice hurdles on
debut: reportedly distressed next time. *N. J. Gifford*

DOUBLE KEEN 6 ch.m. Keen – Thirkleby Skeena (Marching On) [2006/7 F17s F17d **h–**
16fᵖᵘ Jun 17] dam little sign of ability: no form in bumpers/mares novice hurdle. **F–**
P. Beaumont

DOUBLE LAW 7 ch.g. Double Trigger (IRE) – Sister-In-Law (Legal Tender) [2006/7 **h109**
h103, F–: 19m⁴ 21v² Nov 26] rather leggy gelding: fair novice hurdler: will be suited by
3m: acts on heavy going. *Miss E. C. Lavelle*

DOUBLE MAGNUM 7 b.g. Double Trigger (IRE) – Raise The Dawn (Rymer) **h–**
[2006/7 26sᵖᵘ 16vᵖᵘ Jan 21] fair form in bumpers: no show in points/novice hurdles: tried
in cheekpieces. *P. E. Cowley*

DOUBLE MEAD 5 b.m. Double Trigger (IRE) – Normead Lass (Norwick (USA)) **F85**
[2006/7 F16m³ F16g⁶ Oct 7] third foal: brother to a winning pointer: dam winning
pointer: better effort in bumpers when third to Sirnando at Stratford: won twice in points
in 2007: sold 25,000 gns Doncaster May Sales. *C. J. Down*

DOUBLE MEASURE 7 b.g. Double Eclipse (IRE) – Double Resolve (Gildoran) **h–**
[2006/7 h–, F77: 17mᵖᵘ Jun 7] no show in novice hurdles: tried tongue tied: runner-up in
maiden point in April. *J. K. Magee, Ireland*

DOUBLE MYSTERY (FR) 7 ch.g. Starborough – Chene de Coeur (FR) (Comrade **c82**
In Arms) [2006/7 c20m³ c20gᵖᵘ Apr 10] fair on Flat (stays 13f), successful in 2006, left **h–**
E. Griffin and well beaten in Britain: maiden hurdler: tongue tied over fences, poor form
on completed outing: probably stays 2½m: acts on good to firm and good to soft ground.
K. J. Burke

DOUBLE OBSESSION 7 b.g. Sadler's Wells (USA) – Obsessive (USA) (Seeking **h114 +**
The Gold (USA)) [2006/7 16d⁶ 16g³ 20g Apr 12] compact gelding: half-brother to
temperamental 2m hurdler Medallist (by Danehill): fairly useful on Flat (stays 2½m), left

D. Nicholls after final 2006 outing: fair form in novice hurdles, stiff task final outing: has been bandaged behind: may do better now qualified for handicaps. *A. M. Balding*

DOUBLE PAST 5 b.g. Yaheeb (USA) – Gale Blazer (Strong Gale) [2006/7 24s^pu 23v^pu 16v^4 c16v^pu c17g c16g^6 Apr 23] strong gelding: first foal: dam well beaten in bumper: form (poor) in maiden hurdles only on third start: no show over fences. *P. Beaumont*　c–　h66

DOUBLE RUNNER 5 b.m. Doubletour (USA) – Running Frau (Deep Run) [2006/7 F17d F16m 20m Apr 9] good-topped mare: half-sister to winning pointer by Mister Lord: dam unraced: no show in bumpers for K. Thomas and novice hurdle. *F. P. Murtagh*　h–　F–

DOUBLE'S DAUGHTER 5 b.m. Double Trigger (IRE) – Flexwing (Electric) [2006/7 F17g Apr 19] 3,000 5-y-o: stocky mare: fourth foal: half-sister to winning hurdler/chaser Snipe (by Anshan), stays 3m: dam placed in bumpers: soundly beaten in mares bumper on debut. *H. S. Howe*　F–

DOUBLE SPECTRE (IRE) 5 b.g. Spectrum (IRE) – Phantom Ring (Magic Ring (IRE)) [2006/7 h92: c16g^4 16s Dec 13] sturdy gelding: fair on Flat (stays 1½m), successful in April: maiden hurdler: well held in novice on chasing debut: tried tongue tied: free-going front runner. *Jean-Rene Auvray*　c–　h–

DOUBLE SPREAD 8 b.g. Alflora (IRE) – Flora Louisa (Rymer) [2006/7 h–, F–: 22g^pu May 6] no form in bumpers/novice hurdles. *M. Mullineaux*　h–

DOUBLE THE TROUBLE 6 b.g. Double Trigger (IRE) – Upton Lass (IRE) (Crash Course) [2006/7 F–: 16d 21s^pu 17s^pu Feb 26] lengthy gelding: no show in bumpers/over hurdles. *R. H. Buckler*　h–

DOUBLE VODKA (IRE) 6 b. or br.g. Russian Revival (USA) – Silius (Junius (USA)) [2006/7 h121: 16d* 17d 16s 16s^pu 16g^4 16g* 16m^5 16d^2 16g* Mar 17] workmanlike gelding: useful hurdler: won novice at Aintree in May and handicaps at Musselburgh in December and Newcastle (further progress to beat Locksmith by 1½ lengths) in March: raced around 2m: acts on soft and good to firm going. *C. Grant*　h131

DOUBLY SHARP (USA) 4 ch.g. Diesis – La Soberbia (ARG) (Octante (ARG)) [2006/7 F12g^5 Mar 23] good-topped gelding: second foal: dam champion older mare in Argentina: 8/1 from 22/1, 5¾ lengths fifth of 18 to Whiteoak in 4-y-o bumper at Newbury on debut: sold 30,000 gns Doncaster May Sales. *C. J. Mann*　F96

DOVEDALE 7 b.m. Groom Dancer (USA) – Peetsie (IRE) (Fairy King (USA)) [2006/7 17m^6 Nov 7] lengthy mare: fair on Flat (stays 1¾m), successful at 5 yrs for Mrs M. Hambro: little impact in bumpers/mares novice hurdle. *H. S. Howe*　h69

DOVEDON LANE (IRE) 4 b.f. Exit To Nowhere (USA) – Katherine Kath (Merdon Melody) [2006/7 F16s 16g^4 18g^F 18m^6 Apr 26] third foal: dam showed little in Irish bumpers: always behind in bumper: poor form over hurdles. *N. B. King*　h77　F–

DOWNING STREET (IRE) 6 b.g. Sadler's Wells (USA) – Photographie (USA) (Trempolino (USA)) [2006/7 h116: 26m^4 20f^3 c23f^F Jun 21] fairly useful handicap hurdler: back to best when strong-finishing third to Moon Catcher at Worcester: fell sixth in maiden on chasing debut: stays 3¼m: acts on firm and good to soft going: blinkered: patiently ridden. *Jennie Candlish*　c–　h121

DOWN'S FOLLY (IRE) 7 b.g. Darnay – Pils Invader (IRE) (Carlingford Castle) [2006/7 h117+: c20g^3 c20d^2 Nov 20] useful-looking gelding: fairly useful handicap hurdler: off 8 months, fair form when placed over fences: stays 2½m: acts on soft and good to firm going. *H. D. Daly*　c113　h–

DOWN THE STRETCH 7 b.g. Rakaposhi King – Si-Gaoith (Strong Gale) [2006/7 c87, h–: c16g^pu c21m^F c17d^4 c20s^4 c23m* c23d^F c19d^4 c19d^4 Mar 20] neat gelding: twice-raced over hurdles: fair chaser: fortunate to win maiden at Exeter in November, looked held when left clear 2 out: stays 23f: acts on soft and good to firm ground: tried in cheekpieces. *J. R. Payne*　c108 ?　h–

DRAGON EYE (IRE) 5 b.g. Saddlers' Hall (IRE) – Bint Alsarab (Rainbow Quest (USA)) [2006/7 F16v^3 Mar 3] fourth foal: half-brother to fair hurdler/chaser Allstar (by Fourstars Allstar), effective at 2m to 3m: dam, 1m winner, sister to Derby runner-up Blue Judge and half-sister to smart chaser up to 21f Stately Home: shaped quite well when 9 lengths third to Ruairi in maiden bumper at Kempton on debut, not knocked about after taking keen hold: likely to improve. *A. King*　F95 p

DRAMATIC QUEST 10 b.g. Zafonic (USA) – Ultra Finesse (USA) (Rahy (USA)) [2006/7 c87§, h–: 16s^6 19m^6 Jun 4] good-topped gelding: winning hurdler/maiden　c– §　h71 §

chaser: no show in points: stays easy 2¾m: acts on soft going: wears headgear: moody.
A. G. Juckes

DRAMATIC REVIEW (IRE) 5 b.g. Indian Lodge (IRE) – Dramatic Shift (IRE) **h—**
(Night Shift (USA)) [2006/7 h90: 17m 16f⁶ 16g^pu 16v⁶ 16v^pu Mar 22] modest maiden on
Flat (stays 1¼m): maiden hurdler, no form in 2006/7, left P. Haslam after second outing:
tried in cheekpieces/blinkers: usually tongue tied. *J. Barclay*

DRAT 8 b.g. Faustus (USA) – Heresy (IRE) (Black Minstrel) [2006/7 c90: 17m 16f⁶ 16g^pu 20v **c—**
c24v^pu c21s^pu c22g⁴ c24m^pu Apr 10] sturdy gelding: novice hurdler/chaser, no form in **h—**
2006/7: stays 2½m: acts on heavy going: tried blinkered/visored. *R. Mathew*

DRAWN OUT (IRE) 4 ch.g. Daggers Drawn (USA) – Fastnet (Forzando) [2006/7 **h70**
17m 17m⁴ Aug 26] maiden on Flat, well beaten in 2006: in cheekpieces, better effort in
juvenile hurdles when fourth at Cartmel. *P. C. Haslam*

DR CERULLO 6 b.g. Dr Fong (USA) – Precocious Miss (USA) (Diesis) [2006/7 h101: **h104**
22g³ 22g³ 24s² 20d⁵ 20g Nov 3] medium-sized gelding: fair handicap hurdler: stays 3m:
acts on soft and good to firm going: tried blinkered. *C. Tinkler*

DR CHARLIE 9 ch.g. Dr Devious (IRE) – Miss Toot (Ardross) [2006/7 h—: 22s^pu 22s **h—**
Feb 17] angular gelding: winning hurdler, lightly raced and no form since 2004/5: stays
2¾m: acts on heavy and good to firm going: blinkered once. *Miss C. Dyson*

DREAM ALIVE 6 b.g. Unfuwain (USA) – Petite Sonnerie (Persian Bold) [2006/7 **h72**
17m⁵ 17g 16m 16m⁵ Aug 3] modest maiden on Flat (probably stays 1¼m): poor form
over hurdles, sold out of P. Hobbs's stable £2,400 Ascot July Sales after third outing:
joined C. Cox. *S. Curran*

DREAM ALLIANCE 6 ch.g. Bien Bien (USA) – Rewbell (Andy Rew) [2006/7 h127, **c137**
F94: 24s⁵ c23d* c25v² c24s⁴ c24g³ c24g⁶ c24s* Apr 26] lengthy gelding: fairly useful **h127**
hurdler: useful chaser: won novice at Exeter in November and handicap at Perth
(improved to beat Lothian Falcon by 8 lengths) in April: stays 25f: acts on heavy and
good to firm going. *P. J. Hobbs*

DREAM CASTLE (IRE) 13 b.g. Poet's Dream (IRE) – Kerry's Castle (Deep Run) **h106**
[2006/7 h108: 16g* Apr 16] good-topped gelding: fair handicap hurdler: off 16 months
and 33/1, won at Wetherby by 2½ lengths from Macchiato: stays 2½m: acts on firm and
soft going: tried in cheekpieces: front runner. *Barry Potts, Ireland*

DREAM FALCON 7 br.g. Polar Falcon (USA) – Pip's Dream (Glint of Gold) [2006/7 **c112**
h121: c23d³ c23m² c23d² c19s⁵ Dec 1] lengthy gelding: fairly useful handicap hurdler: **h—**
easily best effort over fences (fair form) when runner-up to Dream Alliance in novice at
Exeter: stays 25f: acts on soft going. *R. J. Hodges*

DREAM GARDEN 4 b.g. Kayf Tara – Arcady (Slip Anchor) [2006/7 F17m⁵ Apr 28] **F81**
fourth foal: dam, 13f to 2m winner, half-sister to smart performer up to 1m Atavus:
modest form when fifth in bumper on debut. *C. C. Bealby*

DREAM OF LOVE 5 b.m. Pursuit of Love – Affaire de Coeur (Imperial Fling (USA)) **F—**
[2006/7 F16m Jun 11] sixth foal: half-sister to 1m winner Prince Valentine (by My Best
Valentine): dam, 1m winner, also 2m winner over hurdles: tailed off in bumper on debut.
D. B. Feek

DREAM ON MAGGIE 7 ch.m. Dreams End – Alto Bella (High Line) [2006/7 h87?, **c—**
F—: 16s^pu 16m^F 16m 17g⁴ 17g⁴ c16m⁶ Jul 12] medium-sized mare: modest hurdler: won **h88**
selling handicap at Hereford in June: little impact in maiden on chasing debut (jumped
right): raced mainly around 2m: acts on good to firm going: tongue tied last 4 starts.
P. Bowen

DREAMS JEWEL 7 b.g. Dreams End – Jewel of The Nile (Glenstal (USA)) [2006/7 **h101**
h84, F—: 16g 17m⁵ 17m⁵ Jul 17] lengthy, angular gelding: fair handicap hurdler: raced
around 2m: acts on good to firm going (bumper win on good to soft): has made mistakes.
C. Roberts

DREAM WITNESS (FR) 4 gr.f. Sagamix (FR) – Dial Dream (Gay Mecene (USA)) **h96**
[2006/7 17g³ 16f² 18g* 16g⁵ Oct 24] angular filly: modest maiden on Flat (seems to stay
1½m): claimed from W. Muir £6,000 in August: easily best effort in juvenile hurdles
when winning maiden at Fontwell in September: raced around 2m on good and firm
going. *B. W. Duke*

DR FLIGHT 5 b.g. Dr Fong (USA) – Bustling Nelly (Bustino) [2006/7 F92: 22s 24s **c—**
22g c24m c26g³ Apr 23] rather leggy gelding: well held in novice hurdles/handicap **h76**
chases: tried visored. *B. G. Powell*

DRINK LIGHT (IRE) 7 ch.m. Anshan – Mid Day Chaser (IRE) (Homo Sapien) **h–**
[2006/7 F–: F16m⁴ 20sᶠ Dec 7] little impact in bumpers 12 months apart: fell fifth in **F–**
mares novice on hurdling debut: sold 1,000 gns Doncaster January Sales. *P. R. Webber*

DR MANN (IRE) 9 b. or br.g. Phardante (FR) – Shuil Le Laoi (IRE) (Lancastrian) **c81 §**
[2006/7 c77, h–: c23m⁴ c24v² c24d³ c24v² c25s² c24v c25s⁴ c24g² Mar 28] sturdy **h–**
gelding: novice hurdler: poor maiden handicap chaser: stays 25f: acts on good to firm and
heavy going: tried blinkered: temperamental. *Miss Tor Sturgis*

DROMBEAG (IRE) 9 b.g. Presenting – Bula Beag (IRE) (Brush Aside (USA)) **c131**
[2006/7 c115: c26g* c21g⁶ Apr 12]
    Amid the plethora of success in good staying chases for graduates of
Cheltenham's four-mile National Hunt Chase this spring, the Christie's Foxhunter
Chase victory of Drombeag at the Festival shouldn't be overlooked. It was the best
performance of the season in a hunter chase, a useful effort from a still relatively
lightly-raced performer who could make an impact in some of the big long-distance
events if switched to handicaps.
    Drombeag was still a maiden over fences when third behind stable-
companion Native Emperor and Celestial Gold in the 2004 National Hunt Chase, a
place ahead of subsequent Grand National winner Silver Birch, looking a promising stayer who might well have been a leading contender for the race the following
year. However, Drombeag wasn't seen again until 2006, when he was aimed instead
at the Foxhunter (his owner had another leading candidate for the National Hunt
Chase in Far From Trouble), starting second favourite after winning novice hunters
at Huntingdon and Sedgefield but managing only ninth after a far from trouble-free
run. Drombeag went on to contest the big hunters at Aintree and Punchestown, as at
Cheltenham wearing blinkers. He was still going well when falling five out in the
Fox Hunters' but then failed to give his running in Ireland.
    Drombeag was returned to Cheltenham in 2007 without a preparatory run
and was something of a forgotten horse. With cheekpieces replacing blinkers, he
started at 20/1 this time, with the 2006 winner Whyso Mayo favourite at 2/1 ahead
of Patches and Bica, formerly above-average performers for Paul Nicholls and
Guillaume Macaire respectively but now in the care of Richard Barber and Robert
Waley-Cohen. Other significant runners included a quartet of relative veterans

Christie's Foxhunter Chase Challenge Cup, Cheltenham—
jumping wins the day for Drombeag over last year's winner Whyso Mayo (white face)

Mr John P. McManus' "Drombeag"

who had been even better in their prime: Ned Kelly, Sonevafushi, Telemoss and Drombeag's stable-companion Knife Edge, all still in training in top professional yards. Grumblings about the farming of hunter chases by professional yards have grown louder in recent seasons, with champion trainer Paul Nicholls coming in for much of the criticism from some sections of the point-to-point fraternity due to his rerouting of useful handicappers to the hunter ranks. In truth, however, these sort of complaints have been around for at least thirty years. Fred Winter had notable victories in this sphere with Rolls Rambler, Venture To Cognac and Observe in the 'eighties; before him, both Arthur Stephenson and Bob Turnell enjoyed success in both the Foxhunter and Fox Hunters'. Unless the rules are changed to exclude such horses, there isn't much that can be done. Whether anything should be done is, in any case, a moot point. Richard Barber is no less a professional trainer, in a general sense, than many of those who hold a full licence, and he has strong links to the top jumping yard in the country. The 2003 Foxhunter winner Kingscliff was trained by Sally Alner before making the short journey to husband Robert's yard to be campaigned in handicaps. Hardly a winner in the last dozen years has not, in some sense, been professionally handled. That is as it should be, even in a branch of the sport that is supposedly amateur in the non-pejorative sense of the word. With Patches an early casualty in the latest running of the Foxhunter, Drombeag and Whyso Mayo eventually fought out the finish. Through some excellent jumping, Drombeag held the lead or shared it for most of the way, and rallied splendidly after being headed before two out, a mistake at the last by the error-prone Whyso Mayo handing him the initiative again. Drombeag held on gamely under pressure to win by half a length, with fifteen lengths back to Ned Kelly in third.

Drombeag was not his owner J. P. McManus's first winner of the Foxhunter, as he scored with Elegant Lord in 1996, trained and ridden by Enda Bolger. Elegant Lord was a top-class hunter who would have made an impact in open company. All his twenty starts under Rules were in hunter chases. He defeated the subsequent Cheltenham Gold Cup winner Cool Dawn when successful in 1996 and ran four times in all in the Foxhunter (starting a short-priced favourite on each occasion), finishing third in 1995 and second to the ill-fated Castle Mane in 1999. Elegant Lord also finished second in the 1998 Fox Hunters' at Aintree and made his final appearance when winning that race a year later, beating the subsequent Grand National runner-up Mely Moss. Cavalero, like Elegant Lord, won both of the top British hunter chases, adding a Foxhunter to his tally in 2000, and Drombeag tried to emulate them at Aintree four weeks on from Cheltenham. Had he won he would have been the first to complete the double in the same season since Double Silk in 1993. As it was, the greater emphasis on speed told against Drombeag, particularly after he'd been done no favours by the starter, and he could manage only sixth, nearly thirty-three lengths behind the Nicky Henderson-trained Scots Grey. Neither Cavalero, who was pulled up after a slipped saddle, nor Double Silk, injured whilst loose after a fall at the thirteenth, had the best of fortune in their Grand National attempts but Drombeag, despite falling in 2006 and being well held in the latest season, has shown an aptitude for Aintree's big, unusual fences and might well be worth aiming at that race in 2008.

Drombeag (IRE) (b.g. 1998)	Presenting (br 1992)	Mtoto (b 1983)	Busted
			Amazer
		D'Azy (b 1984)	Persian Bold
			Belle Viking
	Bula Beag (IRE) (b 1993)	Brush Aside (b 1986)	Alleged
			Top Twig
		Bulabos (b 1978)	Proverb
			Clonmel

The big, rangy Drombeag is an old-fashioned chaser in appearance by Presenting, responsible also for War of Attrition and Denman. Drombeag's family is undistinguished. His dam Bula Beag was unraced. Drombeag is her first foal. Her second, Barrshan (by Anshan), has won in points but shown little otherwise, while her third, Drombeag's sister Knotted Midge, won a mares' maiden point in November under Drombeag's regular rider, John Thomas McNamara, but failed to make an impact in three steeplechases subsequently (including a cross-country event). Her 2001 foal Barreenagh Beag (by Darazari) also ran in points in the latest season, though without success. Bula Beag has since produced two more sons to Presenting, in 2003 and 2005. Drombeag will stay very long distances and has raced mainly on good going or softer, winning on heavy at Sedgefield. *Jonjo O'Neill*

DROPPY'S (IRE) 6 br.g. Houmayoun (FR) – Whizaway (IRE) (Archway (IRE)) [2006/7 F16s⁶ F16s 19s⁴ 20v⁵ 19v c26vᵖᵘ Feb 23] sturdy, useful-looking gelding: first foal: dam no form on Flat or over hurdles: won maiden Irish point in 2006: bought 15,000 gns Doncaster May Sales: better effort in bumpers when sixth at Cheltenham: poor form in novice hurdles: no show on chasing debut. *J. A. B. Old* c– h81 F87

DRUIDS CASTLE (IRE) 6 b.g. Oscar (IRE) – Portphelia (Torus) [2006/7 F16g* F16v² F16d³ 20s 16v 16v² 19v* 24s 20v⁴ 20dᵖᵘ Apr 1] ninth foal: dam unraced: won bumper at Cork on debut in October: fairly useful hurdler: won maiden at Naas in January and minor event at Punchestown (by ¾ length from Powerstation) in February: good 6¾ lengths fourth to Kazal in Grade 2 novice at Thurles: reportedly broke blood vessel final outing: stays 2½m: acts on heavy going. *Joseph Crowley, Ireland* h120 F102

DRUMAVISH LASS (IRE) 8 b. or br.m. Oscar (IRE) – Fraulein Koln (IRE) (Mandalus) [2006/7 16m* 19g⁶ 16f 18d c16mᶠ 16s⁶ 16d Dec 21] third foal: half-sister to winning hurdlers up to 2¾m Bowling Green (by Bowling Pin) and Koln Stars (by Fourstars Allstar): dam lightly raced: dual bumper winner: modest hurdler: won mares maiden at Cork in June: left P. Lenihan, fell fifth in novice handicap on chasing debut: stays 2½m: acts on good to firm ground: in cheekpieces last 2 starts (out of form). *Evan Williams* c– h89

DRUMDERRY (IRE) 5 b.m. Shernazar – Karlybelle (FR) (Sandhurst Prince) [2006/7   **F94**
F16m* F17g⁶ F16f* F16s F17g F16m Apr 25] smallish, angular mare: second foal: dam,
placed once (over 1¼m) on Flat in France/once-raced over hurdles, out of half-sister to
dam of top-class 2m chasers Viking Flagship and Flagship Uberalles: fair bumper
performer: won at Galway in August and Cork (mares event) in September. *W. P. Mullins,
Ireland*

DRUMDOWNEY LAD (IRE) 8 b.g. Darnay – Alpencrocus (IRE) (Waajib) [2006/7   **c–**
c19sᵖᵘ c19mᵖᵘ c17v Jan 27] winning pointer: no form in chases, left N. Henderson after
second start: tried tongue tied. *Patrick O. Brady, Ireland*

DRUMINTINE (IRE) 6 b.m. Mister Mat (FR) – Ballytrustan Maid (IRE) (Orchestra)   **c– x**
[2006/7 c–; c21s⁴ c25v⁴ c25s⁶ Apr 1] winning pointer: no form in chases: poor jumper.
Liam Lennon, Ireland

DRUMMER FIRST (IRE) 7 ch.g. Grand Plaisir (IRE) – Second Fiddle (IRE)   **c114**
(Orchestra) [2006/7 c22v⁴ c17g c20s 22v³ 24v⁵ 22v 16v² c22s c20v³ c20g⁵ Apr 4] first   **h122**
foal: dam, modest novice hurdler, stayed 3m: fairly useful hurdler, ran well 3 of 4 starts in
2006/7: fair novice chaser: best effort when 2 lengths third to Farmer Grant in handicap at
Naas: effective at 2m when conditions are testing and stays 3m: acts on good to firm and
heavy going: not a fluent jumper of fences. *John E. Kiely, Ireland*

DRUMOSSIE (AUS) 7 ch.g. Strategic (AUS) – Migvie (NZ) (Sir Tristram) [2006/7   **c85**
c82, h68+: c16m c16g³ 16gᵖᵘ c20gᵖᵘ c20m⁵ c20m Apr 25] angular gelding: maiden   **h–**
hurdler: modest handicap chaser, left R. C. Guest after second start: stays 2½m: acts on
good to firm going: usually wears headgear. *Ian Williams*

DRUMROLL (IRE) 5 b.g. Diktat – Mystic Tempo (USA) (El Gran Senor (USA))   **h–**
[2006/7 16gᵖᵘ Jul 23] fair maiden on Flat (stays 9.5f): no show in seller on hurdling debut:
sold £2,000 Ascot August Sales. *Miss J. Feilden*

DR WILLIE MARTIN (IRE) 7 b. or br.g. Dr Massini (IRE) – Patchouli's Pet   **h115**
(Mummy's Pet) [2006/7 20d 20m³ 18s² 18v 20vᵖᵘ 18v⁵ 16s* 16d⁵ Apr 1] banker winner:
fairly useful hurdler: won minor event at Thurles (by 9 lengths from Middlemarch) in
January: good fifth to Wishwillow Lord in similar event at Limerick final outing: stays
2½m: acts on heavy going: blinkered last 2 starts. *W. J. Austin, Ireland*

DRYLINER 7 gr.g. Terimon – Take The Veil (Monksfield) [2006/7 h–, F–: 24gᵖᵘ 22vᵖᵘ   **c–**
c25dᵖᵘ c19sᵖᵘ Jan 26] no sign of ability. *A. E. Price*   **h–**

DUAL STAR (IRE) 12 b.g. Warning – Sizes Vary (Be My Guest (USA)) [2006/7 c–,   **c–**
h–: c16gᵖᵘ Jun 20] sparely-made gelding: winning hurdler/chaser, no form after 2003/4:   **h–**
tried blinkered/visored: usually tongue tied: dead. *L. Waring*

DUBAI ACE (USA) 6 b.g. Lear Fan (USA) – Arsaan (USA) (Nureyev (USA)) [2006/7   **c95**
h105: c20m² c20g³ c20m³ Aug 11] smallish gelding: fair hurdler: modest form over   **h–**
fences: stays 21f: acts on soft and good to firm going (well beaten on heavy): in
cheekpieces last 2 starts: formerly tongue tied: tail flasher. *Miss S. West*

DUBAI AROUND (IRE) 4 ch.g. Zinaad – Triple Transe (USA) (Trempolino (USA))   **h111**
[2006/7 16m* Oct 1] modest maiden on Flat (stays 12.4f): better form when winning
juvenile at Kelso on hurdling debut by 5 lengths from Carrietau, tending to hang right.
Micky Hammond

DUBAI BOUND (USA) 8 ch.g. Foxhound (USA) – Bound Forever (USA) (Timeless   **c109**
Moment (USA)) [2006/7 c16m⁵ c17f* c16d Nov 10] lengthy gelding: 1¼m winner on   **h–**
Flat: winning hurdler: fair chaser: won 4-runner minor event at Tipperary in July: seems
best around 2m: acts on firm ground: has worn blinkers, including when successful.
Andrew Lee, Ireland

DUBAI DREAMS 7 b.g. Marju (IRE) – Arndilly (Robellino (USA)) [2006/7 h80: 17g   **h69**
16m⁴ 17m⁴ 16g³ 19g 20m⁴ 16f⁵ Aug 22] close-coupled gelding: poor maiden hurdler:
likely to prove best around 2m: acts on firm going, probably on soft: blinkered/in cheekpieces since debut, also tongue tied last 4 starts: free-going front runner. *M. Sheppard*

DUBAI SUNDAY (JPN) 6 b.g. Sunday Silence (USA) – Lotta Lace (USA) (Nureyev   **c–**
(USA)) [2006/7 F95: 16d⁶ c20m³ 22m Sep 10] leggy gelding: modest on Flat (stays   **h–**
13f): successful in March: bumper winner: no show over hurdles/in maiden chase.
P. S. McEntee

DUBLIN HUNTER (IRE) 11 br.g. Treasure Hunter – Cutty Sark (Strong Gale)   **c123**
[2006/7 c121, h–: 22s⁶ c24s⁶ c24s c24vᵖᵘ c28s² c20v c30g⁶ c30m³ Apr 27] good-topped   **h109**
gelding: winning hurdler: fairly useful handicap chaser: below form in 2006/7 except

when placed, length third to Kings Glen in amateur event at Punchestown: stays 4m: acts on heavy and good to firm ground: probably best in blinkers. *D. T. Hughes, Ireland*

DUCAL MISS PETUNIA 5 ch.m. Classic – Miss Primrose (Primitive Rising (USA)) [2006/7 F17m Aug 6] fifth foal: sister to winning 23f hurdler/pointer Lady Misprint: dam unraced: no promise in bumper on debut. *C. J. Teague*   **F–**

DUC DE REGNIERE (FR) 5 b.g. Rajpoute (FR) – Gladys de Richerie (FR) (Le Pontet (FR)) [2006/7 17s³ 16d* 21s* 21g Mar 14] tall gelding: sixth foal: half-brother to winning hurdler/chaser up to 21f Gladys des Essarts (by Chamberlin): dam ran twice: off 7 months and left G. Cherel after debut, created good impression first 2 starts over hurdles in Britain, winning novices at Newbury (by 2½ lengths from Osana, pair clear) in December and Kempton (beat Battle Cry by 4 lengths with something to spare) in February: mistakes when running poorly in Grade 1 event at Cheltenham: stays 21f: raced on good ground or softer: remains good prospect. *N. J. Henderson*   **h138 +**

DUCKWORTH LEWIS (IRE) 6 b.g. Moonax (IRE) – Dromin Hill (IRE) (Supreme Leader) [2006/7 F16d 21v^{pu} Nov 25] £11,000 5-y-o: first foal: dam maiden: little impact in bumper (joint favourite) and novice hurdle. *N. A. Twiston-Davies*   **h–**   **F75**

DUELING B'ANJIZ (USA) 8 b.g. Anjiz (USA) – Stirling Gal (USA) (Huckster (USA)) [2006/7 16d⁶ 19g c20s^{ur} c19s^{pu} c20v c22s Feb 4] poor maiden on Flat: maiden hurdler: no form over fences: tried in blinkers/cheekpieces/tongue tied. *E. J. Creighton*   **c–**   **h–**

Sir Peter & Lady Gibbings' "Duc de Regniere"

DUELLING BANJOS 8 ch.g. Most Welcome – Khadino (Relkino) [2006/7 17v 16v² **h92** 16d⁶ Mar 21] smallish gelding: fair up to 13f on Flat: modest form over hurdles. *J. Akehurst*

DUETTO (IRE) 4 b.f. Exit To Nowhere (USA) – Chopins Revolution (Rakaposhi **F–** King) [2006/7 F14g⁶ F14v F16v Feb 22] smallish filly: first foal: dam, modest hurdler up to 2¾m, half-sister to fairly useful hurdler Bora Bora (would have stayed 3m) and fairly useful chaser Mariners Mirror (stays 3¼m): well held in bumpers. *M. Scudamore*

DUKE OF BUCKINGHAM (IRE) 11 b.g. Phardante (FR) – Deselby's Choice **c134** (Crash Course) [2006/7 c141, h–: c20f³ Jul 6] lengthy, good sort: winning hurdler: useful **h–** handicap chaser: not discredited when 6 lengths third to Ball O Malt at Perth only start in 2006/7: stays 21f: acts on firm going: formerly front runner, held up nowadays: usually sound jumper. *P. R. Webber*

DUKE OF KENTFORD 5 b.g. Shambo – Kentford Duchess (Jupiter Island) [2006/7 **h–** F71: 17s 19s 22s 26g 24m Apr 25] useful-looking gelding: little impact in bumpers/over hurdles: sold 2,000 gns Doncaster May Sales. *P. R. Webber*

DUKE OF MALFI 4 b.g. Alflora (IRE) – Princess Maxine (IRE) (Horage) [2006/7 **F86** F14s² F16v Feb 24] quite good-topped gelding: fourth foal: dam, 2m novice hurdler, fair up to 1m on Flat: much better effort in bumpers when second to Beauty One in 3-y-o event at Ayr. *Miss Lucinda V. Russell*

DUKE OF STRADONE (IRE) 7 b.g. Beneficial – Thethingtodo (Kambalda) **c99** [2006/7 h–, F85: c23f⁵ c17m c24f* c21g² c22g c25dᶠ Sep 8] leggy gelding: no show in **h–** novice hurdle: modest novice chaser: won 3-finisher event at Perth in July: stays 3m: acts on firm going: has worn blinkers. *S. Donohoe, Ireland*

DUKE ORSINO (IRE) 7 b.g. Old Vic – Deselby's Choice (Crash Course) [2006/7 c–, **c98** h101: c16d⁵ c16s⁴ c20s³ c21v⁶ c20v³ c20g² c20gᶠ Apr 16] tall, lengthy gelding: **h–** maiden novice hurdler: modest novice chaser: likely to prove best up in 2½m: acts on heavy going: reliable. *Miss Lucinda V. Russell*

DUKES BOND 4 gr.g. Paris House – Glowing Lake (IRE) (Lake Coniston (IRE)) **h–** [2006/7 17gᵘʳ 17gᵖᵘ Sep 23] well beaten in 1m maiden on Flat: failed to complete in juvenile hurdles. *M. E. Sowersby*

DUKE'S VIEW (IRE) 6 b.g. Sadler's Wells (USA) – Igreja (ARG) (Southern Halo **h74** (USA)) [2006/7 h–: 22g 19m* 19d² Aug 7] poor hurdler: most fortunate to win conditional jockeys handicap at Newton Abbot in August, left in front 2 out: stays 19f: acts on soft and good to firm going: in cheekpieces last 5 starts. *D. C. Turner*

DULY NOTED (IRE) 6 b.m. Flemensfirth (USA) – Lancastrian Height (IRE) **F64** (Lancastrian) [2006/7 F16g Dec 26] €5,000 3-y-o: half-sister to bumper winner Atlantic Run (by Commanche Run) and 2 winning pointers: dam unraced: won mares maiden Irish point in 2006: bought 20,000 gns Doncaster May Sales: tongue tied, well held in bumper. *C. J. Mann*

DUMADIC 10 b.g. Nomadic Way (USA) – Duright (Dubassoff (USA)) [2006/7 c102, **c119** h–: c28d⁴ c21d² c23g* c24mᵖᵘ c24m⁶ c20s* c20g² c20m⁴ Apr 20] tall gelding: fairly **h–** useful handicap chaser: won at Wetherby in June and Sedgefield (readily, by 7 lengths from Reasonably Sure) in March: creditable efforts in frame behind Three Mirrors final 2 starts: stays 25f: acts on heavy and good to firm going: has found little/shaped as if amiss. *R. E. Barr*

DUMARAN (IRE) 9 b.g. Be My Chief (USA) – Pine Needle (Kris) [2006/7 h101: **h95** 16m⁶ 16s⁵ 17s 16sᵇᵈ Feb 22] leggy gelding: fair on Flat (stays 10.4f): modest handicap hurdler, lightly raced: raced around 2m: acts on soft and good to firm going. *W. J. Musson*

DUN AENGUS 11 b.g. Lighter – Bantel Bouquet (Red Regent) [2006/7 c26d⁴ c24gᵖᵘ **c–** c23dᵖᵘ c27d⁴ Oct 25] maiden pointer: tongue tied, no form in chases. *K. J. Burke*

DUN AN DORAS (IRE) 11 b.g. Glacial Storm (USA) – Doorslammer (Avocat) **c111** [2006/7 c105, h–: c21g* c21d⁴ c18g³ c25s⁶ c22s² c20s c19vᵖᵘ c21g⁶ Apr 1] leggy **h–** gelding: winning hurdler: fair chaser: won handicap hunter at Newton Abbot in May: stays 2¾m: acts on any going. *J. D. Frost*

DUNASKIN (IRE) 7 b.g. Bahhare (USA) – Mirwara (IRE) (Darshaan) [2006/7 h97: **h95** 16g² Mar 16] useful on Flat (stays 1½m), in-and-out form in 2006: modest form when runner-up in maidens at Fakenham on completed starts over hurdles a year apart. *Karen McLintock*

DUNBRODY MILLAR (IRE) 9 b. or br.g. Lord Americo – Salt Mills (Proverb) **c133**
[2006/7 c128, h–: 27m^{pu} c32m^{pu} c24g^{su} c24g^3 c26g^3 c24d^4 c29v^4 c24s^4 c24g c25g^2 **h–**
c21g* Apr 13]

    The Topham Trophy, run over a circuit and a bit of the Grand National course, was instituted by Mirabel Topham in 1949 after Lord Sefton's sale of Aintree racecourse to Tophams Limited, making the family company outright owners of the track. The family had already been associated with the racecourse for well over a century by that time. Edward William Topham, known as the 'The Wizard', was responsible, among other things, for framing the weights for the very first running of the Grand National as a handicap in 1843. The Topham Trophy continued to be run under that name until 1982, but from 1983 the Topham element was dropped in favour of a succession of sponsors' prefixes which came and went. More continuity was restored when the race was renamed the John Hughes Trophy in 1989 (with a lowest-ever field of just seven) to honour Aintree's former clerk of the course who had died the year before. The traditional Topham name was brought back in 2002, and since then the race has gone from strength to strength, attracting maximum or near-maximum fields, with the winner's prize money almost doubling in that short period. The latest winner of the John Smith's-sponsored race, Dunbrody Millar, earned £62,630, putting the race among the top ten most valuable handicap chases run in Britain in the latest season—ahead of the likes of the Welsh National and the Racing Post Chase. Recent Grand National winners Bindaree, Monty's Pass and Amberleigh House all gained Aintree experience in the Topham before their big wins (Monty's Pass finishing second in 2002, a year before winning the big one), though, surprisingly, no Topham winner has ever gone on to win the National itself. Clan Royal came closest among recent winners when runner-up in the 2004 National, and back in 1977 Churchtown Boy ran second to Red Rum in the National just two days after winning the Topham (something which the rules would now disallow these days).

    Another important development in the history of the race took place in the latest season when it was made an open handicap. Most recently, it had been restricted to horses rated up to 150. In addition, on an experimental basis, it was made an early-closing race (the weights were published in late-March), with the BHB handicappers given the freedom to depart from official marks in framing the weights, as is now the practice in the Grand National, partly to take into account the seemingly resurgent 'Aintree factor'. Four horses were entered in the Topham who would have been rated too highly to qualify for the race the year before and one of that quartet, Armaturk, duly took his chance on the day, heading the weights from a BHB mark of 155. His presence resulted in no fewer than sixteen horses running from out of the handicap (compared to just seven the year before when the top weight's BHB mark was 145). Oddly, despite the handicappers' scope to treat horses with form over the big fences as special cases in both the National and the Topham, Dunbrody Millar, who was among several horses entered in both, was given vastly different weight assessments in the two races. With National top weight Hedgehunter on a BHB mark of 158, just 3 lb higher than Armaturk in the Topham, there should have been little more than a few pounds difference at most in the weights allotted to horses entered in both races, assuming of course that a horse had not shown considerable improvement between the closing dates of the National in mid-February and the Topham in late-March. Dunbrody Millar's stable-companion McKelvey, for example, was assigned 10-5 in the Topham and 10-4 in the National. But, bizarrely, Dunbrody Millar was set to carry just 8-9 in the long handicap for the Topham but 10-1 in the National! Either he merited an inflated rating to take into account his good record over the National fences in both races, or he didn't. Ironically, his higher weight in the National handicap was still not high enough to ensure he made the final field of forty, though he was third on the list of four reserves. From 17 lb out of the handicap, Dunbrody Millar only just scraped into the Topham field (twenty-sixth of the thirty declared).

    Dunbrody Millar had finished a good fourth to Liberthine in the Topham the year before when in the handicap proper, also having failed to make the cut for the National. Having joined Peter Bowen's stable from Ireland (when trained by Michael Cullen) at the start of that season, still a maiden over fences with just fair form at best, he made rapid progress in handicaps, with wins in the Sussex National at Plumpton and the Agfa Diamond at Sandown the highlights of his 2005/6 campaign. However, Dunbrody Millar seemed to have paid for that success in the latest season and, whilst his form-figures looked respectable enough going into the Topham, they masked a steady decline in his form which had seen him drop nearly a stone in the weights. Even his second place at Wetherby, when refitted with cheekpieces (which he often wore in Ireland), ten days before the Topham, did not really indicate a revival in fortunes. Significantly, the exception to his slump in form had come in the Becher Chase at Aintree's November meeting. Racing over the big fences seemed to rekindle his zest and, always at the head of affairs despite a few minor errors, Dunbrody Millar rallied in the straight to take third behind Eurotrek and Bewleys Berry, finishing half a length in front of Aintree regular Nil Desperandum.

Dunbrody Millar started at 25/1 for his second attempt at the Topham, his weight and recent form seemingly outweighing his good record over the fences and the excellent form of his stable at the time. Le Volfoni, with only stable-companion Armaturk above him in the weights, was sent off the 13/2 favourite. The twenty-nine-runner field was soon reduced to twenty-eight when 100/1-shot Always refused to jump off in what was a ragged start, whilst that number dropped further when Dunbrody Millar's stable-companion Iron Man (the choice of Tom O'Brien) unseated at the first. Another change to the Topham in recent years was its reduction in distance by half a furlong in 2001 to two miles five and a half furlongs, reducing the run to the first fence which had claimed several victims the previous year (including two fatalities). It was the Chair, jumped as the third fence, which caused the most trouble this time. Coming much earlier in the Topham than it does in the National, the largest but narrowest fence is reached before the field has been either thinned out or become strung out, and, while Dunbrody Millar kept clear of trouble jumping it at the head of affairs with the previous year's runner-up Hakim, a number of those behind were caught in a melee caused by Kasthari coming down at the head of the main body of the field. One of the favourites Briery Fox was among those put out of the race, as were Armaturk and Lord Rodney, the last-named fatally injured. It usually pays to race handily in shorter races over the National course (Scots Grey had made most in the Fox Hunters' the day before), not just to avoid trouble, but because front runners taking a cut at their fences can prove difficult to peg back. Although Dunbrody Millar forfeited the lead to Hakim running down to Becher's, he remained handy, though a mistake four out briefly looked to have him in trouble. Responding tenaciously coming back on to the racecourse, Dunbrody Millar regained the lead from another of the better-fancied runners Irish Raptor, who had taken it up at halfway. Kept up to his work in front, Dunbrody Millar drew clear on the run-in to win by six lengths from Theatre Knight, with the fast-finishing Latimer's Place and Ground Ball also making the frame among fifteen finishers. This lucrative success proved a welcome change of luck for Jamie Moore, who'd been forced to miss the Cheltenham Festival due to an eight-day 'improper riding' ban, particularly as his association with Dunbrody

John Smith's Topham Chase (Handicap), Aintree—outsider Dunbrody Millar again shows his aptitude for the National fences as he improves three places from 2006

Dundon Else Partnership's "Dunbrody Millar"

		Lord Gayle	Sir Gaylord
	Lord America	(b 1965)	Sticky Case
	(b 1984)	Hynictus	Val de Loir
Dunbrody Millar (IRE)		(b 1968)	Hypavia
(b. or br.g. 1998)		Proverb	Reliance II
	Salt Mills	(ch 1970)	Causerie
	(ch 1984)	Ballymacarett	Menelek
		(ch 1977)	Lilquin

Millar is a chance one—Moore's first ride on the gelding had been as an eleventh-hour replacement for Tony Dobbin (stood down with dehydration) in the 2006 Topham, whilst Bowen regular Seamus Durack turned down the ride this time around in favour of ninth-placed Hakim. Incidentally, the latest Topham result gave further fuel to the theory that the 'Aintree factor' is very much on the increase since modifications to the National fences in 2001. In common with Dunbrody Millar, runner-up Theatre Knight showed form far in advance of any of his recent efforts over conventional fences—the 66/1-shot, who was 20 lb wrong in the Topham, had previously coped well with the Aintree course when third in the Grand Sefton back in the autumn. It was a similar story in the Grand National itself just over twenty-four hours later, with 2004 Becher Chase winner Silver Birch just holding off the late surge of McKelvey (who'd shaped well in the latest renewal of that race). In addition, Aintree specialists accounted for six of the ten other finishers, including previous winners in fifth-placed Liberthine (2006 Topham), sixth-placed Numbersixvalverde (2006 National), ninth-placed Hedgehunter (2005 National) and eleventh-placed Clan Royal (2003 Topham and Becher Chases).

Dunbrody Millar is much the best of three winners out of his dam Salt Mills who finished well beaten over hurdles on her only start. Her two other winners are also by Lord Americo: Annameadle, who won a two-and-a-half-mile mares' handicap at Ballinrobe in the latest season for Timothy Doyle, and Spring To Life, a winner over jumps in Switzerland. Salt Mills is a half-sister to two winners, notably the useful two-mile chaser Town Crier who was killed in a fall over hurdles at Aintree in the autumn. Grandam Ballymacarett won at around two miles over both hurdles and fences in Ireland and was a half-sister to The Proclamation, potentially much the best member of this family. He won the BMW Champion Novices' Hurdle at Punchestown in 1989 on the last of just three starts over hurdles and made an impressive start to his chasing career at Ascot the following season with Nicky Henderson, though had to be put down following a fall at the same track on his next outing. Dunbrody Millar therefore stays better than most in his family; the Topham was his first success at short of three miles, and he was won at up to twenty-nine furlongs. He has, though, been well beaten in two outings over four miles, including in the Summer National at Uttoxeter at the start of the latest season. Even so, with his record over the big fences, Dunbrody Millar deserves a crack at the Grand National, though whether he'll get the opportunity will again depend largely on how the handicapper treats him. In the meantime, the Becher Chase would seem the obvious race for him in the autumn. He's a game and bold-jumping front runner who acts on soft and good to firm ground. *P. Bowen*

DUNCAIRN 6 b.g. Samraan (USA) – Tiny Feet (Music Maestro) [2006/7 F16g 16d Jan 5] ninth foal: dam ran once at 2 yrs: well beaten in various events. *I. A. Duncan, Ireland*   h– F–

DUNCLIFFE 10 b.g. Executive Perk – Ida Melba (Idiot's Delight) [2006/7 c–, h106: 24d* 20s³ c24dᵖᵘ c20s c21gᵖᵘ Mar 19] well-made gelding: useful chaser at best, poor efforts last 3 starts: fair form in novice hurdles, winning at Ascot in November by 4 lengths from Double Dizzy: stays 3m: acts on soft going: front runner/races prominently. *R. H. Alner*   c– h109

DUNDICLOU 4 b.g. Benny The Dip (USA) – Balleta (USA) (Lyphard (USA)) [2006/7 F14v Dec 2] 3,500 2-y-o: strong, workmanlike gelding: half-brother to several winners, including fair hurdlers War Cabinet (at 17f, by Rainbow Quest) and Gala Evening (at 21f, by Daylami): dam, 1m to 1¼m, sister to Dancing Brave and Jolypha: favourite, looked temperamental when mid-field in bumper at Wetherby on debut. *G. A. Swinbank*   F–

DUN DISTINCTLY (IRE) 10 b.g. Distinctly North (USA) – Dunbally (Dunphy) [2006/7 c25mᵖᵘ May 6] leggy gelding: winning 2m hurdler: no form in chases: maiden pointer: tried blinkered. *Miss G. T. Lee*   c– h–

DUNDOCK 6 gr.g. Cloudings (IRE) – Rakajack (Rakaposhi King) [2006/7 F89: F16d⁴ F16m² 16g 16s³ Apr 27] fair form when in frame in bumpers: considerably handled on hurdling debut, then third to Midnight Chase in maiden at Perth: bred to be suited by further than 2m. *A. C. Whillans*   h81 F90

DUN DOIRE (IRE) 8 b.g. Leading Counsel (USA) – Yes Boss (IRE) (Carlingford Castle) [2006/7 c138, h94p: 20d c26gᶠ 22v² 24s⁵ c26d* c36gᵖᵘ Apr 14] strong gelding: fair hurdler: made remarkable improvement over fences in 2005/6, winning 6 handicaps, including William Hill Trophy at Cheltenham: didn't have to run near best to justify favouritism in 3-finisher minor event at Down Royal in March: had earlier fallen at Chair in Becher Chase at Aintree, and didn't take to fences at all in Grand National (soon tailed off): should stay beyond 3¼m: raced on good going or softer (acts on heavy): held up. *A. J. Martin, Ireland*   c122 + h109 +

DUNDONALD 8 ch.g. Magic Ring (IRE) – Cal Norma's Lady (IRE) (Lyphard's Special (USA)) [2006/7 c16fᵖᵘ Apr 30] strong, workmanlike gelding: no form over jumps: tried in headgear: usually tongue tied. *M. Appleby*   c– h–

DUNDRIDGE NATIVE 9 b.m. Be My Native (USA) – Fra Mau (Wolver Hollow) [2006/7 h80: 18s 24sᵖᵘ 25v⁶ 27v³ 24s 22v³ c20g⁵ Mar 26] angular mare: poor maiden hurdler: stays 27f: acts on heavy going: in cheekpieces/blinkers last 5 starts. *M. Madgwick*   c– h70

DUNDRY 6 b.g. Bin Ajwaad (IRE) – China's Pearl (Shirley Heights) [2006/7 16s^{pu} h–
Nov 25] fairly useful on Flat (stays 2m), successful twice in 2007: took good hold and
behind when pulled up in novice at Newbury on hurdling debut. *G. L. Moore*

DUNE RAIDER (USA) 6 b.g. Kingmambo (USA) – Glowing Honor (USA) (Seattle   h115 p
Slew (USA)) [2006/7 16m* 17m* 16g* 17d^5 Jul 22] fairly useful on Flat (stays 17.5f) at
4 yrs for K. Ryan: made excellent start to hurdling career, winning maiden at Worcester
and novices at Exeter and Uttoxeter (by 1¼ lengths from Cardington) in little over a
month: progressed a bit more when fifth to Tycoon Hall in valuable handicap at Market
Rasen: likely to do better again faced with stiffer test of stamina: joined C. Llewellyn.
T. R. George

DUNGUAIRE LAD (IRE) 7 b. or br.g. Heron Island (IRE) – Time In Life (Bishop of   c119
Orange) [2006/7 c22s c21v^2 c17v* c16s^2 c20g^{pu} Apr 25] €16,000 3-y-o: half-brother to
winning 3¼m chaser Royal Corrouge (by Corrouge) and winning 21f hurdler Bucktime
(by Buckskin): dam unraced half-sister to fairly useful staying chaser Sounds Fyne:
placed in points: fairly useful form in chases: won maiden at Navan in January by 4½
lengths from Washington Lad: creditable second to Don't Be Bitin in novice at Naas,
easily beaten subsequent effort: stays 21f: acts on heavy ground: front runner. *Patrick
Hughes, Ireland*

DUNGUAIRE LADY (IRE) 8 ch.m. Toulon – Why Me Linda (IRE) (Nashamaa)   c89
[2006/7 h84: 20d^3 21d^4 16f^2 20s* 20m 22d^3 c20z1v^4 c12s^{pu} c20s^3 c20v^5 c20g^2 c25g   h91
Apr 23] good-topped mare: modest hurdler: won novice at Hexham in June sold out of
Mrs K. Walton's stable 2,100 gns Doncaster October Sales after sixth start: modest maid-
en chaser: should stay beyond 2½m: acts on any going: often tongue tied. *P. Needham*

DUNKERRON 10 b.g. Pursuit of Love – Top Berry (High Top) [2006/7 c–, h73: 22m^F c–
22g 18g 20g^4 Apr 14] compact gelding: winning chaser: poor handicap hurdler: trained   h63
by J. Joseph until after third outing: stays easy 21f: acts on firm and good to soft going:
tried blinkered. *J. D. Frost*

DUNLEA DANCER 6 b.g. Groom Dancer (USA) – Be My Lass (IRE) (Be My Guest   h–
(USA)) [2006/7 16d^F Dec 27] rather leggy gelding: fair form over hurdles: off 21 months,
weakening out of contention when falling heavily 2 out in handicap won by Princelet at
Kempton: raced at 2m: tried tongue tied: takes good hold. *P. J. Hobbs*

DUN LOCHA CASTLE (IRE) 12 b.g. Cataldi – Decent Preacher (Decent Fellow)   c–
[2006/7 c79, h–: c26m^{pu} c25d^{pu} Mar 20] workmanlike gelding: poor chaser: little form in   h–
points in 2007: stays 3½m: acts on heavy and good to firm ground: tried in blinkers/
cheekpieces. *Mrs E. Mitchell*

DUNMAGLASS (USA) 5 ch.g. Cat Thief (USA) – Indian Fashion (USA) (General   h–
Holme (USA)) [2006/7 16m 22g 16m 22m Sep 2] lightly raced on Flat, sold out of
P. Cole's stable 4,500 gns Doncaster May (2005) Sales: tailed off all starts over hurdles,
including in sellers: tried blinkered. *Evan Williams*

DUNMANUS BAY (IRE) 10 gr.g. Mandalus – Baby Fane (IRE) (Buckskin (FR))   c– x
[2006/7 c–x, h–: c24d^{ur} May 15] winning chaser/pointer: no form in hunters: stays 3¼m: h–
usually visored/blinkered: bad jumper: not one to trust. *Mrs Julie Read*

DUNSEMORE 7 b.m. Prince Daniel (USA) – Admire-A-More (Le Coq d'Or) [2006/7   h–
h–: 16v^{pu} 20s^{pu} Apr 25] modest form on hurdling debut: no show in 3 starts since.
Mrs A. F. Tullie

DUNSFOLD DUKE 7 b.g. Cloudings (IRE) – Rositary (FR) (Trenel) [2006/7 h114:   c124
c20v* c20v^R c20d^2 c21g^6 Apr 19] tall, useful-looking gelding: fair hurdler: fairly useful   h–
form over fences: won maiden at Lingfield in January by 7 lengths from Esprit Saint:
good second to Bible Lord in novice handicap at same course: will stay beyond 21f: raced
on good going or softer (acts on heavy): none too reliable. *P. Winkworth*

DUNSHAUGHLIN (IRE) 10 b.g. Supreme Leader – Russian Gale (IRE) (Strong   h–
Gale) [2006/7 h–: 21d^{pu} May 15] useful-looking gelding: lightly-raced maiden hurdler,
no form in 2 starts since 2004/5: should be suited by 2½m+: tried tongue tied. *J. A. B. Old*

DUNSTON DURGAM (IRE) 13 b.g. Durgam (USA) – Blazing Sunset (Blazing   c–
Saddles (AUS)) [2006/7 h–: 24m c20f^6 c23f^{pu} Sep 3] angular gelding: of little account.   h–
Ms Sue Smith

DURANTE (IRE) 9 ch.g. Shernazar – Sweet Tune (Welsh Chanter) [2006/7 h103: 23v^5 c113
c26v^2 c23v^F Mar 9] good-bodied gelding: fair maiden hurdler: better form on completed   h90 +
outing over fences when ½-length second to Cinnamon Line in handicap at Warwick:
stays 3¼m: acts on heavy going: tongue tied in 2006/7. *J. A. B. Old*

DURBA (AUS) 7 ch.g. Desert Prince (IRE) – Placate (AUS) (Brief Truce (USA)) [2006/7 h–: 16m⁴ May 10] angular gelding: bad maiden hurdler: lame only outing in 2006/7: tried in eyeshield/tongue strap. *R. C. Guest*   **h59**

DURLSTON BAY 10 b.g. Welsh Captain – Nelliellamay (Super Splash (USA)) [2006/7 c105d, h–: c24g² c24dᵖᵘ May 15] sturdy gelding: winning hurdler/chaser: modest pointer nowadays: stays 2¾m: acts on firm and good to soft going. *S. Dow*   **c86** **h–**

DUSKY LORD 8 b.g. Lord Americo – Red Dusk (Deep Run) [2006/7 h130p: 19d⁵ 16d* 18sᶠ 21g 20f Apr 28] sturdy gelding: useful handicap hurdler: won at Sandown (beat Slew Charm ½ length) in November: off 3½ months, eighth of 28 to Burntoakboy in Coral Cup at Cheltenham fourth start, poorly placed before finishing best: will stay beyond 21f: acts on soft going, below form on firm. *N. J. Gifford*   **h130**

DUSKY WARBLER 8 br.g. Ezzoud (IRE) – Bronzewing (Beldale Flutter (USA)) [2006/7 h136: 21g 20g Apr 12] lengthy gelding: useful handicap hurdler: not discredited when ninth to Burntoakboy in Coral Cup at Cheltenham on reappearance: stays 21f: acts on heavy going: in cheekpieces 4 of last 5 starts: carries head awkwardly: moody. *G. L. Moore*   **h137 §**

DUSTY DANE (IRE) 5 b.g. Indian Danehill (IRE) – Teer On Eer (IRE) (Persian Heights) [2006/7 h105: 18m* 19d³ 16s⁴ 17s⁶ 17d⁵ 16d⁸ 18g³ 16f⁵ Apr 5] compact gelding: fair hurdler: won intermediate at Fontwell in May: at least creditable efforts most starts after: stays 19f: acts on firm and soft going: usually tongue tied. *W. G. M. Turner*   **h110**

DUTCH STAR 8 b.m. Alflora (IRE) – Double Dutch (Nicholas Bill) [2006/7 h–, F64: 16dᵖᵘ Jun 2] strong mare: no form in novice hurdles. *G. P. Enright*   **h–**

DUTY (IRE) 4 b.g. Rainbow Quest (USA) – Wendylina (IRE) (In The Wings) [2006/7 16v² 16v* 16v* 17g 16m⁵ Apr 26] lengthy, sparely-made gelding: useful up to 14.8f on Flat, sold out of Sir Michael Stoute's stable 58,000 gns Newmarket Autumn Sales: useful juvenile hurdler: won maiden at Gowran (swished tail as ridden clear) and Grade 3 Aramark Winning Fair Juvenile Hurdle at Fairyhouse (beat J'Y Vole by 6 lengths) in February: below form in Grade 1 events after, looking reluctant final outing: will be suited by further than 2m: acts on heavy going. *K. F. O'Brien, Ireland*   **h127**

DYNAMIC BEMMY 5 ch.m. Fleetwood (IRE) – Wigit (Safawan) [2006/7 F16fᵖᵘ Apr 30] £400 3-y-o, resold £1,000 3-y-o: fourth foal: half-sister to 1¼m winner Sayit (by Sayaarr) and a winning pointer by Wolfhound: dam unraced: challenging when going wrong in bumper on debut. *N. M. Babbage*   **F–**

DYNAMIC LEAP 4 b.g. Turtle Island (IRE) – Caramello (Supreme Leader) [2006/7 F16g Apr 7] €80,000 3-y-o: well-made gelding: third foal: half-brother to useful hurdler Karello Bay (by Kahyasi), stays 2¾m: dam unraced sister to high-class hurdler up to 3m Marello: joint favourite, well held in bumper at Haydock on debut, forced wide turning in and soon weakening: should prove capable of better. *Jonjo O'Neill*   **F– p**

DYNAMIC RHYTHM (USA) 4 b.g. Kingmambo (USA) – Palme d'Or (IRE) (Sadler's Wells (USA)) [2006/7 16v³ 16d⁵ 16v⁴ 19g Mar 30] small, good-bodied gelding: fairly useful maiden on Flat (will stay 1¼m), sold out of J. Noseda's stable 22,000 gns Newmarket Autumn Sales: fair form in juvenile hurdles. *G. Brown*   **h95 ?**

DYNEBURG (POL) 7 ch.h. Alywar (USA) – Dora Baltea (POL) (Beauvallon (FR)) [2006/7 h98: 16m² 16m³ 16m³ 16g⁵ Nov 7] leggy horse: fair hurdler, placed in handicaps first 3 starts in 2006/7: raced around 2m: acts on firm going. *T. R. George*   **h108**

DZESMIN (POL) 5 b.g. Professional (IRE) – Dzakarta (POL) (Aprizzo (IRE)) [2006/7 16dᶠ Oct 14] won 2000 Guineas, Derby and St Leger in Poland at 3 yrs, fairly useful form on Flat in Britain: none too fluent and fading in fourth when falling 2 out in maiden at Stratford on hurdling debut. *R. C. Guest*   **h88**

E

EALAND JASPER 7 ch.g. Country Classic – Final Action (Nicholas Bill) [2006/7 F17gᵖᵘ Sep 23] second foal: dam little form on Flat: tailed off when pulled up in bumper on debut. *R. F. Marvin*   **F–**

EARCOMESANNIE (IRE) 7 ch.m. Anshan – Play It By Ear (IRE) (Be My Native (USA)) [2006/7 h72: c26gᶠ c23d³ c24gᶠ c24g³ c24m³ Apr 14] leggy mare: poor novice   **c82** **h–**

hurdler/chaser: probably stays 3¼m: acts on good to firm and good to soft going: not a fluent jumper. *P. A. Pritchard*

EARCOMESTHEDREAM (IRE) 4 b.g. Marignan (USA) – Play It By Ear (IRE) **F91** (Be My Native (USA)) [2006/7 F16m⁴ Apr 24] fourth foal: dam thrice-raced out of half-sister to dam of very smart 2m to 3m chaser Opera Hat: around 10 lengths fourth to The Package in maiden bumper at Towcester on debut. *P. A. Pritchard*

EARL KRAUL (IRE) 4 b.g. Imperial Ballet (IRE) – Bu Hagab (IRE) (Royal Aca- **h– p** demy (USA)) [2006/7 16v⁴ Feb 12] half-brother to fairly useful hurdler Take A Mile (by Inchinor), stays 2½m: modest on Flat (stays 1¼m), first past post twice in January (demoted second occasion): well beaten but not knocked about on juvenile at Plumpton on hurdling debut: likely to prove capable of better. *G. L. Moore*

EARL OF BUCKINGHAM 9 b.g. Alderbrook – Arctic Oats (Oats) [2006/7 **c–** c25gᵖᵘ May 3] workmanlike gelding: fair pointer: offered nothing in hunter chase. *Mrs C. Wilesmith*

EARL OF SPECTRUM (GER) 6 b.g. Spectrum (IRE) – Evry (GER) (Torgos) **h101** [2006/7 h87: 16g 16m² 16f* 17m³ 17s 16d 17g 16g⁴ 16g⁵ 19d⁵ Nov 16] sturdy gelding: fair hurdler: won conditional jockeys selling handicap at Uttoxeter (sold from J. Spearing 6,800 gns) in July: likely to prove best around 2m: best form on good going or firmer. *Mrs L. Williamson*

EARL'S KITCHEN 10 ch.g. Karinga Bay – Rempstone (Coronash) [2006/7 c115§, **c– §** h–: c29sᵖᵘ c26vᵖᵘ c29sᵖᵘ Mar 11] deep-girthed gelding: lightly raced over hurdles: fairly **h–** useful handicap chaser on his day, no form in 2006/7: thorough stayer: raced on good going or softer (acts on heavy): wore cheekpieces last 5 outings: effective tongue tied or not: inconsistent: joined V. Dartnall. *C. L. Tizzard*

EARLY EDITION 11 b.g. Primitive Rising (USA) – Ottery News (Pony Express) **c82** [2006/7 c23v⁴ May 27] tall gelding: winning hurdler/chaser: successful also in points, **h–** including in 2007: stays 3¼m: acts on good to soft going: tried tongue tied: often makes mistakes. *A. W. G. Geering*

EARLY WINGS (GER) 5 b.g. Winged Love (IRE) – Emy Coasting (USA) (El Gran **h87** Senor (USA)) [2006/7 16d² 17s⁶ Dec 18] useful on Flat (stays 1¼m), successful at 3 yrs for A. Wohler, well beaten sole start in 2006: runner-up in 4-y-o event at Baden-Baden on hurdling debut: left M. Hofer, around 18 lengths sixth to South O'The Border in maiden at Taunton. *R. T. Phillips*

EARMARK 4 b.g. Halling (USA) – Earlene (IRE) (In The Wings) [2006/7 16g⁵ 16v² **h106** 16s* 16m⁵ 16m Apr 25] €16,000 3-y-o: smallish, angular gelding: first foal: dam, 1m to 12.5f winner, closely related to smart 1¼m to 1½m winner Foyer: fair juvenile hurdler: won maiden at Wexford in March by 2½ lengths from Alltrap: better form when 14 lengths fifth to Bahrain Storm in minor event at Fairyhouse following month, final start for T. Arnold: will stay beyond 2m: acts on heavy and good to firm ground. *James McAuley, Ireland*

EARN A BUCK 6 b.m. Young Ern – Buck Comtess (USA) (Spend A Buck (USA)) **F–** [2006/7 F–: F16gᵖᵘ F14g⁶ Nov 3] tall, angular mare: no form in bumpers. *B. I. Case*

EARNEST 7 b.g. Oscar (IRE) – Unassisted (IRE) (Digamist (USA)) [2006/7 h–: **h96** 24gᵘʳ 17m³ 20m² 24sᵖᶜ 24g⁵ Mar 23] rather leggy gelding: modest novice hurdler: stays 2½m: acts on good to firm going, possibly unsuited by soft. *Ian Williams*

EARTH MAGIC (IRE) 7 b.g. Taipan (IRE) – Miss Pollerton (IRE) (Pollerton) **h117** [2006/7 16s⁴ 16m² 16g* 16s 20v⁵ 18v⁴ 20v² 20v² 20d⁶ 20v⁴ 16v² 23v⁵ 16g⁴ 20m³ Apr 28] third foal: half-brother to useful hurdler up to 3m Sweet Kiln (by Beneficial): dam, unplaced in bumpers/maiden hurdle, half-sister to dam of top-class 2m/3m hurdler Limestone Lad: bumper winner: fairly useful hurdler: won 20-runner maiden at Galway in September: best efforts after when runner-up 3 times in novices, including when beaten 1¾ lengths by Kazal in Grade 2 at Naas eighth outing: stays 23f: acts on good to firm and heavy going: usually front runner: not a fluent jumper. *Michael J. Bowe, Ireland*

EARTH MAN (IRE) 8 b.g. Hamas (IRE) – Rajaura (IRE) (Storm Bird (CAN)) **h117** [2006/7 h111: 16d 19g⁴ Mar 31] good-topped, attractive gelding: fairly useful hurdler, lightly raced (has had breathing problem): barely stays 19f: unraced on extremes of going. *P. F. Nicholls*

EARTH MOVING (IRE) 7 ch.g. Anshan – Jacks Sister (IRE) (Entitled) [2006/7 **c–** h75+, F95: c17vᵖᵘ Feb 12] tall, angular gelding: fair form in bumpers: went as if amiss on **h–**

hurdling debut: left P. Nicholls and off over a year, bled on chasing debut (raced freely). *C. L. Tizzard*

EARTH PLANET (IRE) 5 b.g. Kayf Tara – Arctic Rose (IRE) (Jamesmead) [2006/7 F16g* F16d² F16d³ Feb 10] rangy gelding: first foal: dam unraced out of half-sister to top-class 2m/2½m hurdler Mighty Mogul: useful form in bumpers, won at Chepstow on debut in October by short head from Truckers Delight: placed after in Grade 2 events, 10 lengths third to Crocodiles Rock at Newbury, tending to hang left. *P. F. Nicholls* **F107**

EARTH WORLD (IRE) 6 b.g. Fourstars Allstar (USA) – Hillside Flame (IRE) (Lancastrian) [2006/7 19s 22s 24vᵖᵘ Feb 20] €7,000 4-y-o: sturdy gelding: second foal: dam never ran: no form over hurdles: tongue tied. *D. P. Keane* **h–**

EASBY MANDARIN 6 b.g. Emperor Fountain – Beijing (USA) (Northjet) [2006/7 h90, F–: 16g⁴ 20sᵖᵘ c19dᵘʳ c18d² c19g Feb 2] well-made gelding: modest novice hurdler: similar form when 1½ lengths second to Eborarry in novice at Market Rasen, better completed outing over fences: should stay beyond 2¼m: raced mainly on good going or softer. *C. W. Thornton* **c97 h92**

EASBY PARK 4 b.g. Tamure (IRE) – Mossfield (Le Moss) [2006/7 F16v Feb 27] leggy, unfurnished gelding: half-brother to winning pointers by Mandalus and Buckskin: dam unraced: green, never a factor in bumper on debut. *G. M. Moore* **F–**

EASEMENT 4 b.g. Kayf Tara – Raspberry Sauce (Niniski (USA)) [2006/7 aF16g² F16g² F18m³ Apr 26] sturdy gelding: third foal: half-brother to fairly useful performer Boot 'N Toot (by Mtoto), stays 1½m: dam 1m to 11.6f winner: fair form when runner-up in bumpers, beaten 5 lengths by Theft at Kempton second time. *C. A. Cyzer* **F93**

EASE THE WAY 6 b.g. Nashwan (USA) – Desert Ease (IRE) (Green Desert (USA)) [2006/7 20m² 20g c17d⁵ c23dᶠ c16s* c19s⁵ c16v c16f³ c16s³ Apr 27] rather leggy gelding: fair hurdler, won minor event at Bellewstown in 2005/6: fairly useful chaser: sold out of D. Weld's stable 15,000 gns Doncaster October Sales after fourth outing: won novice at Ludlow in December: stays easy 2½m: acts on any ground: usually blinkered over hurdles, in cheekpieces over fences. *Evan Williams* **c117 h114**

EASIBET DOT NET 7 gr.g. Atraf – Silvery (Petong) [2006/7 h86: 16f⁴ 20g³ 16g Dec 20] fair but irresolute on Flat (stays 2m): best effort (modest form) over hurdles when fourth in novice at Musselburgh on debut in 2005/6: left I. Semple after second start (cheekpieces) in 2006/7: tried tongue tied. *Miss Lucinda V. Russell* **h79**

EASIBROOK JANE 9 b.m. Alderbrook – Relatively Easy (Relkino) [2006/7 c98x, h–: c16vᵖᵘ 22sᵇᵈ c19s c20s³ c19d* Feb 2] tall mare: winning hurdler: modest chaser: won handicap at Chepstow in February: stays 21f: acts on heavy and good to firm going: tried in cheekpieces/tongue tied: often let down by jumping over fences. *C. L. Tizzard* **c97 x h–**

EASTERN ACCORD (IRE) 7 ch.g. Accordion – Muscovy Duck (IRE) (Moscow Society (USA)) [2006/7 24g² 24d² 24m⁴ 23fᵖᵘ Jun 16] modest maiden hurdler: stayed 3m: acted on good to firm and good to soft going: dead. *M. Hourigan, Ireland* **h93**

EASTERN CANAL (IRE) 6 b.g. Son of Sharp Shot (IRE) – Suez Canal (FR) (Exit To Nowhere (USA)) [2006/7 F16v³ F16v⁵ 19g Mar 30] big, lengthy, good-topped gelding: third foal: dam ran twice on Flat in France: best effort in bumpers when 9½ lengths to Gem Daly at Leopardstown: raced freely when well held in maiden at Ascot on hurdling debut. *Mrs J. Harrington, Ireland* **h– F94**

EASTERN DAGGER 7 b.g. Kris – Shehana (USA) (The Minstrel (CAN)) [2006/7 h–: 16g⁶ 20d 16d⁵ 17s* 17d Feb 19] heavy-bodied gelding: poor hurdler: easily best effort when winning handicap at Bangor in December: likely to prove best around 2m: acts on soft going. *Miss L. V. Davis* **h81**

EASTERN LEADER (IRE) 8 b.g. Supreme Leader – Noreaster (IRE) (Nordance (USA)) [2006/7 16sᵖᵘ 16g Mar 20] ex-Irish gelding: second foal: brother to smart chaser Euro Leader, stays 5f: dam winning 2m hurdler: maiden hurdler: sold out of T. Mullins' stable 1,000 gns Doncaster November (2005) Sales, failed to complete in 3 points in Britain in 2006. *G. P. Mcpherson* **h–**

EASTERN POINT 13 b.m. Buckskin (FR) – Deep Creek (Deep Run) [2006/7 c–, h–: 25g⁴ 26g⁵ 22v* c24s⁴ c21s² c25v³ c24gᵖᵘ Mar 28] lengthy mare: poor chaser: modest hurdler: won novice handicap at Folkestone in December: stays 25f: acts on heavy going: often gets behind. *R. H. York* **c75 h86**

EASTER PRESENT (IRE) 8 br.g. Presenting – Spring Fiddler (IRE) (Fidel) [2006/7   **c–** c–, h91+: c20s^pu c21g^pu Apr 19] lengthy, useful-looking gelding: has reportedly had   **h–** breathing operation: bumper winner: fair maiden hurdler at best: failed to complete all 3 starts over fences (bled final one): should stay at least 2½m: acts on soft going. *Miss H. C. Knight*

EAST LAWYER (FR) 8 b.g. Homme de Loi (IRE) – East Riding (FR) (Fabulous   **c115 x** Dancer (USA)) [2006/7 c116x, h–: c21gpu c31d^6 Nov 10] good-topped gelding: has   **h–** reportedly had breathing operation: fairly useful chaser: left P. Nicholls, creditable sixth to Spot Thedifference in cross-country event at Cheltenham: stays 31f, effective at much shorter: acts on heavy going: tried blinkered/tongue tied: usually sketchy jumper. *C. R. Egerton*

EAST TYCOON (IRE) 8 ch.g. Bigstone (IRE) – Princesse Sharpo (USA) (Trempo-   **c125** lino (USA)) [2006/7 c134, h–: c21v^3 c23mpu 16m* 17d 16m c16s c16g^4 c20m* Apr 22]   **h130** tall, angular gelding: fairly useful handicap hurdler/chaser: won over hurdles in July (beat Estate by 7 lengths) and over fences in April (by 8 lengths from Smart Cavalier), both at Stratford: stays 21f: acts on good to firm and good to soft going, below form on softer: has worn blinkers/cheekpieces, in eyeshields 4 of last 6 starts: has been let down by jumping over fences: inconsistent. *Jonjo O'Neill*

EASTVIEW PRINCESS 5 ch.m. J B Quick – Staggering (IRE) (Daring March)   **F–** [2006/7 F17m F17g F17m Apr 15] third foal: sister to bumper winner Jay Be Junior: dam, poor novice hurdler who stayed 2½m, half-sister to useful hurdler up to 25f Sip of Orange: no show in bumpers: left C. Thornton before final start. *K. G. Reveley*

EASY LAUGHTER (IRE) 6 b.g. Danehill (USA) – All To Easy (Alzao (USA))   **h91** [2006/7 h93: 16d^4 16d^3 19g^6 16f Apr 5] stocky gelding: modest novice hurdler: finished sore final start: likely to prove best around 2m: acts on good to soft going. *A. King*

EAU PURE (FR) 10 b.m. Epervier Bleu – Eau de Nuit (Kings Lake (USA)) [2006/7   **c88** c94, h86: c22m^3 May 5] angular mare: modest handicap hurdler/chaser: stays 23f: acts on   **h–** soft and good to firm going: tried in cheekpieces, effective with or without blinkers: has had tongue tied. *G. L. Moore*

EBAC (IRE) 6 b.g. Accordion – Higher Again (IRE) (Strong Gale) [2006/7 h84: 20g^pu   **c88 x** 17m c20s^pu c20g^3 c24d^pu Dec 10] maiden hurdler: modest form on completed outing over   **h–** fences (has failed to impress with jumping): stays 2½m: tongue tied. *J. Howard Johnson*

EBAZIYAN (IRE) 6 gr.g. Daylami (IRE) – Ebadiya (IRE) (Sadler's Wells   **h145 +** (USA)) [2006/7 16v^2 16s* 16d* 16m Apr 24]

Defying the old adage that it is better to travel hopefully than to arrive, 40/1-chance Ebaziyan surpassed the expectations of his trainer Willie Mullins ('Just hopeful of a good run') when landing the opening race of the Cheltenham Festival, the Anglo-Irish Bank Supreme Novices' Hurdle, by three lengths and a neck from the second favourite Granit Jack and the short-priced favourite Amaretto Rose. After travelling strongly held up, Ebaziyan was improving in eye-catching fashion when pecking two out but soon recovered to challenge then lead on the run-in, his turn of foot decisive against jumping-bred rivals on ground that was a good deal more resilient than anticipated. The Supreme has tended in recent times to go the way of the market, with seven of the nine previous winners starting at 10/1 or shorter. Neither of the others in that period, Sausalito Bay and Arcalis, 14/1 and 20/1 respectively, were exactly outsiders either—particularly if judged on their Flat form. Ebaziyan was the longest-priced winner of the Supreme since fellow grey Arctic Kinsman at 50/1 in 1994, as well as being a second winner in the race for his trainer who scored with another largely unconsidered runner Tourist Attraction at 25/1 in 1995. Mullins would also probably have won with 12/1-shot Adamant Approach in 2002 had he not fallen at the last.

Unlike Tourist Attraction and Adamant Approach, and many of the other good horses from this stable with such a good record in bumpers, Ebaziyan raced on the Flat before going jumping, winning twice at a mile and a half for John Oxx as a four-year-old. In all, Ebaziyan had six starts on the Flat, three as a three-year-old, and then had two over hurdles before his win at Cheltenham. He is the eighth Flat recruit to win the Supreme Novices' since 1991, excluding Montelado, who won his only start on the Flat after contesting bumpers before his 1993 victory. Of the seven others, three were similar to Ebaziyan in that they were having their third run over hurdles when successful at Cheltenham, Shadow Leader in 1997, French Ballerina in 1998 and the aforementioned Sausalito Bay. Indefence in 1996 and Hors La Loi III in 1999 were having their fourth start, while Arcalis was making his fifth appearance over jumps. Flown, in 1992, had run just once previously. Ebaziyan's performance is probably all the more meritorious in that he was a good deal less experienced on the Flat than all of the others mentioned except for Hors La Loi III, who had just four starts on the Flat in France prior to being sent hurdling. French Ballerina, with eleven runs, was the least experienced of the remaining sextet when sent over hurdles. Indefence, Flown and Arcalis had totals in the teens, while Sausalito Bay and Shadow Leader mustered well over twenty each. Apart from French Ballerina, they all had experience in the hustle and bustle of handicaps with big fields, though she had won a sixteen-runner conditions race. Ebaziyan's wins on the Flat came in fields of eighteen and fifteen.

Ebaziyan had also faced a host of opponents in his two previous hurdle races, twenty-four taking part when he went down by a short head to another useful Flat recruit, the Noel Meade-trained Academy Reward, in a maiden at Cork in January and eighteen when he defeated the dead-heaters Dancing Hero and Jumeirah Scarer by a length in a six-year-old maiden at Thurles early the following month. He won comfortably on soft ground that day but his Cheltenham performance, when less testing conditions and a good gallop looked to bring out the best in him, was clearly of a much higher order. By way of a postscript to Ebaziyan's victory, the Supreme Novices' is a Festival race which illustrates the difficult balance between the needs of sponsors and the traditions of the sport, a subject covered in depth on Detroit City. Since Waterford Crystal ended their long-running sponsorship of the race in 1990, the Supreme has had no fewer than six sponsors. For those struggling to recall the five that preceded Anglo Irish Bank, they were Trafalgar House, Citroen, Capel Cure Sharp, Gerrard and Letheby & Christopher.

Ebaziyan's Cheltenham win represents just about the best two-mile novice hurdle form of 2006/7 but, unfortunately, he failed badly to repeat the form when running no sort of race on his only start after Cheltenham. In the two-mile Champion Novices' at Punchestown, starting second favourite behind the Cheltenham absentee Clopf, he was soon well adrift after jumping hesitantly early on and was tailed off well before the climb towards the straight. Nothing untoward came to light afterwards and connections were inclined to blame the ground, which was good to firm.

Anglo Irish Bank Supreme Novices' Hurdle, Cheltenham—a bleak start for punters as Davy Condon forces through 40/1-shot Ebaziyan between the other grey Granit Jack and hot favourite Amaretto Rose (No.21)

The Aga Khan's studs produce stock with more stamina than many of their more commercially-minded rivals and have thrown up a goodly number of above-average jumpers among their cast-offs over the years. Perhaps best of all was Behrajan, a top-class staying jumper out of the 1989 Arc runner-up Behera. The mating of the Aga Khan's 1988 Derby winner Kahyasi with Bayazida produced the 1996 Triumph Hurdle winner and high-class staying hurdler Paddy's Return (he sold the mare when she was in foal with Paddy's Return). Shawiya, whose sire and dam were both bred by the Aga Khan, was another Triumph Hurdle winner (in 1993), while the 1994 Stayers' Hurdle winner Balasani and Afsoun, third in the latest Champion Hurdle, are other notable products of the Aga Khan's studs. Another Aga Khan-bred jumper of particular note in the latest season was Karasi who won the Nakayama Grand Jump in Japan, the world's most valuable jumps race, for the third year running in April (for further details see the essay on Jazz Messenger).

Ebaziyan isn't the first jumper from his family, as the third dam Ezana has produced two winning hurdlers, including the useful stayer Erzadjan, a son of Kahyasi. Ezana, whose latest foal is a two-year-old called It's My Day in training with Jane Chapple-Hyam, has had three other winners to date, the most notable of which is Ebaziya, Ebaziyan's grandam. Ebaziya was a smart middle-distance filly and has produced three Group 1 winners on the Flat, the high-class stayer Enzeli (winner of the 1999 Gold Cup at Ascot and 2000 Doncaster Cup), the 1998 Moyglare Stud Stakes winner Edabiya and Ebaziyan's dam Ebadiyla, who won both the Irish Oaks and Prix Royal Oak in 1997. Ebaziya's other winners include Ebaraya, like Ebadiyla by Sadler's Wells, who won at a mile and a half and was sold for broodmare purposes in a private deal for €925,000 in 2002—she made 500,000 gns when sold again two years later to dissolve a partnership. Ebaraya is not, though, the most expensive member of this family. Expensive in more than one sense of the word. After Ezana left the Aga Khan's studs, she produced a Darshaan colt that made 600,000 guineas as a yearling in 2002. Named King Kasyapa, he actually managed to be placed in a Derby at Epsom. Unfortunately, that was the Jump Jockeys Derby, a 0-80 handicap, in which he finished third as a four-year-old, after he had been sold for just 11,500 guineas to join Peter Bowen after just two runs in France under the Gainsborough Stud banner. He is still a maiden after five starts.

Ebaziyan (IRE) (gr.g. 2001)	Daylami (IRE) (gr 1994)	Doyoun (b 1985)	Mill Reef
			Dumka
		Daltawa (gr 1989)	Miswaki
			Damana
	Ebadiyla (IRE) (b 1994)	Sadler's Wells (b 1981)	Northern Dancer
			Fairy Bridge
		Ebaziya (b 1989)	Darshaan
			Ezana

Ebaziyan is Ebadiyla's second foal. Her next foal Ehsan (by Sinndar) won a mile-and-a-quarter maiden on the first of two starts (useful form) at three years and, after being sold out of John Oxx's stable for €54,000 in the autumn of 2006, won a two-and-a-half-mile maiden hurdle at Tramore (on firm ground) for James McAuley shortly after the end of the latest season. Ebadiyla has since produced the three-year-old colt Eyshal (by Green Desert), who has shown useful form at up to a mile and a quarter, and the two-year-old filly Ebalista (by Selkirk), who was unraced at the time of writing. In common with virtually all of the members of this family owned by the Aga Khan, this pair have started their career with John Oxx.

The lengthy Ebaziyan himself went through the sale-ring at the end of his four-year-old season, making €150,000 at the Goffs October Sales to join Ian Williams, only to be failed by the vet. He joined Willie Mullins soon afterwards but fractured his pelvis, which put back his debut over hurdles for a season. Ebaziyan will stay beyond two miles, though a campaign aimed at the 2008 Champion Hurdle, for which he was quoted at 14/1 after his Supreme Novices' win, is on the cards. He drifted to more than double those odds in several places after Punchestown and has a fair amount of improvement to make if he is to put in a strong challenge at the top level, though he certainly has the potential to do so. He wore a tongue strap in his three starts on the Flat at four but has not yet required any such equipment in his career over hurdles. *W. P. Mullins, Ireland*

EBONY JACK (IRE) 10 b. or br.g. Phardante (FR) – Ebony Jane (Roselier (FR)) **c81 §**
[2006/7 c88§: c26g³ c26s² c26s⁵ c24v c26s³ c26v² c24g⁴ c26g⁴ c24mᶠ c26m* Apr 26]
poor handicap chaser: won at Fontwell in April: stays 3¼m: acts on heavy and good to
firm going: usually wears headgear: has had tongue tied, including last 2 starts: seems
best when able to dominate: ungenuine. *C. L. Tizzard*

EBONY LADY 4 br.f. Vettori (IRE) – Keen Melody (USA) (Sharpen Up) [2006/7 17g³ **h83**
17d 16d 18vᶠ Feb 12] half-sister to fair chaser War Tune (by Warrshan), stayed 2¾m:
modest maiden on Flat (stays 1½m), sold out of R. Whitaker's stable £3,200 Ascot
August Sales: easily best effort over hurdles on debut: tongue tied last 2 starts. *P. Bowen*

EBONY LIGHT (IRE) 11 br.g. Buckskin (FR) – Amelioras Daughter (General **c115 §**
Ironside) [2006/7 c128, h–: c27s⁵ c26vᵖᵘ c24s c25vᵂ c24vᵖᵘ c24s⁵ Mar 10] tall gelding: **h–**
fairly useful handicap chaser: typically in-and-out form in 2006/7, despite jumping
markedly right latter stages: thorough stayer: acts on heavy and good to firm going: tried blinkered, usually in
cheekpieces: usually front runner: moody. *D. McCain Jnr*

EBONY QUEEN 6 br.m. Classic Cliche (IRE) – Queen of Spades (IRE) (Strong Gale) **h–**
[2006/7 F76: F18g⁵ 16d 16s Jan 20] modest form at best in bumpers: well beaten in **F70**
novice hurdles: tongue tied since debut. *Miss H. C. Knight*

EBORARRY (IRE) 5 b.g. Desert Sun – Aztec Princess (Indian King (USA)) [2006/7 **c95**
h103: c20gᵖᵘ c16vᵖᵘ c18d* c16v² c16v³ c16s³ c16v⁶ c16g Apr 7] sturdy gelding: winning **h–**
hurdler: modest novice chaser: won at Market Rasen in December: raced mainly around
2m: acts on heavy going: has finished weakly. *T. D. Easterby*

ECCLESWALL LADY (IRE) 5 ch.m. Poltarf (USA) – Down The Yard (Batshoof) **F–**
[2006/7 F16s F17s May 20] first foal: dam, modest 2m hurdler, won over 1m on Flat:
little impact in mares bumpers: third in point in January. *M. Scudamore*

ECHO BLU (IRE) 9 b.g. Sharifabad (IRE) – Muchsorrylady (IRE) (Boreen (FR)) **c–**
[2006/7 c–, h–: 24sᵖᵘ May 14] winning pointer: no form over hurdles/in chases: tried in **h–**
cheekpieces. *Miss Joanne Priest*

ECHO CRAG (IRE) 6 b.m. Zaffaran (USA) – Roll It Rosin (IRE) (Gorytus (USA)) **F63**
[2006/7 F16f⁶ Jul 6] €2,000 3-y-o: sixth foal: dam lightly raced on Flat: tongue tied, sixth
in bumper on debut: dead. *J. I. A. Charlton*

ECHO POINT (IRE) 7 b.g. Luso – Lady Desart (IRE) (Buckskin (FR)) [2006/7 h120: **c131 §**
c16s⁴ c20s* c16vᵘʳ c16s³ c16v⁴ c16s* Apr 27] useful-looking gelding: twice-raced over **h–**
hurdles, easy winner of novice: useful chaser, off a year prior to return: won maiden at
Sedgefield (by 22 lengths) in December and novice at Perth in April, improved effort
when beating Chief Yeoman by 8 lengths (pair clear) at latter: stays 2½m: raced on going
softer than good: often front runner: unreliable. *N. G. Richards*

ECHO SOUND 5 b.m. Forzando – Grey Blade (Dashing Blade) [2006/7 F17s F13m **F–**
Jun 19] second known foal: dam no form on Flat or over hurdles: well beaten in bumpers.
P. R. Webber

ECLIPSE PARK 4 ch.g. Rainbow Quest (USA) – Gino's Spirits (Perugino (USA)) **h–**
[2006/7 17sᵖᵘ 18sᵖᵘ Dec 5] workmanlike gelding: fair maiden at best on Flat (stays 1¼m),
has lost his way: no show in juvenile hurdles: tried blinkered/tongue tied: sold 2,500 gns
Doncaster January Sales to race in Sweden. *M. J. McGrath*

EDDIES JEWEL 7 b.g. Presidium – Superstream (Superpower) [2006/7 17mᵖᵘ **h–**
Sep 26] poor on Flat (effective from 7f to 1½m): no show in novice in hurdling debut.
I. W. McInnes

EDEN CRACKET 4 gr.f. Silver Patriarch (IRE) – Meltonby (Sayf El Arab (USA)) **h–**
[2006/7 16mᵖᵘ Oct 1] fifth foal: half-sister to winning 2m hurdler/chaser Meltonian (by
Past Glories): dam 6f to 1m winner: no show in juvenile hurdle on debut. *W. Storey*

EDEN LINTY 6 b.m. Zaffaran (USA) – Rio Dancer (IRE) (Where To Dance (USA)) **h111 p**
[2006/7 F96: 20s³ 19vᵖᵘ 19s* Mar 12] well-made mare: bumper winner for W. Storey:
better completed effort over hurdles when winning mares maiden at Taunton by length
from Delena: will stay beyond 2½m: raced on soft/heavy going over hurdles: remains
capable of better. *P. J. Hobbs*

EDEN SAMAS 5 b.m. Kayf Tara – Girlzone (IRE) (Orchestra) [2006/7 F17g Apr 23] **F–**
1,500 4-y-o: first foal: dam bumper winner: well beaten in mares bumper on debut.
W. Storey

EDE'S 7 ch.g. Bijou d'Inde – Ballagarrow Girl (North Stoke) [2006/7 c16s⁵ c20vᵘʳ c20d⁵ **c74** Mar 21] sturdy gelding: winning hurdler: off 2 years, poor form on first of 2 completed **h–** outings over fences: should stay beyond 2m: acts on soft and good to firm going. *P. M. Phelan*

EDGAR WILDE (IRE) 9 b.g. Invited (USA) – Ou La La (IRE) (Be My Native **c–** (USA)) [2006/7 h91: 22vᵖᵘ 20s³ 21s c20gᵘʳ Mar 14] good-topped gelding: placed in **h86** maiden Irish points: modest novice hurdler, off a year before return: let down by jumping in novice on chasing debut: stays 2½m: acts on soft going. *R. Rowe*

EDGBRIAR (FR) 5 b.g. Brier Creek (USA) – Harmonie de Valtat (FR) (Video Rock **h102 p** (FR)) [2006/7 F16v F16v² F16v² 16d² Mar 21] 22,000 3-y-o: tall, useful-looking gelding: **F102** second foal: dam unraced half-sister to useful French chaser around 2¾m Dom Halma de Valta: fairly useful form in bumpers, still green when second to Den of Iniquity in listed event at Warwick third start: encouraging second to Lindop in maiden at Lingfield on hurdling debut: likely to improve, particularly over further. *P. R. Webber*

EDGEHILL (IRE) 6 b.g. Ali-Royal (IRE) – Elfin Queen (IRE) (Fairy King (USA)) **h99** [2006/7 h99: 20s³ 20g* 20d 20g 24d⁴ 24m Feb 4] unfurnished gelding: modest hurdler: won maiden at Hexham in October: stays easy 3m: acts on soft going: tried blinkered (failed to settle). *R. Ford*

EDGEOVER 5 br.g. Overbury (IRE) – Dusky Dante (IRE) (Phardante (FR)) [2006/7 **F107** F16s³ F16g⁶ Mar 24] 34,000 4-y-o: strong, sturdy gelding: first foal: dam, poor 2m novice hurdler/chaser, out of sister to high-class 2m/2½m chaser Deep Sensation: much better effort (useful form) in bumpers at Newbury when 2¼ lengths third of 21 to Diamond Harry on debut. *P. R. Webber*

EFFUSION 4 b.g. Efisio – Polmara (IRE) (Polish Precedent (USA)) [2006/7 aF16g **F–** F16g Mar 29] second foal: dam ran once: tongue tied, well held in bumpers. *M. F. Harris*

EGYPT POINT (IRE) 10 b.g. Jurado (USA) – Cherry Jubilee (Le Bavard (FR)) **c105** [2006/7 c25g² May 3] lengthy gelding: well held in bumper/novice hurdles for D. Bridg- **h–** water: fair pointer nowadays, successful in 2006: 9 lengths second to Beauchamp Oracle in hunter at Cheltenham on chasing debut: stays 25f. *Miss S. Waugh*

EHAB (IRE) 8 b.g. Cadeaux Genereux – Dernier Cri (Slip Anchor) [2006/7 c76, h–: **c–** c24gᶠ c23d⁶ c23g⁵ Nov 9] tall gelding: maiden hurdler/chaser, no form in 2006/7: tried **h–** blinkered: tongue tied. *Miss A. M. Newton-Smith*

EIDSFOSS (IRE) 5 b.g. Danehill Dancer (IRE) – Alca Egeria (ITY) (Shareef Dancer **h–** (USA)) [2006/7 h–: 16d 16mᶠ Jul 2] no show over hurdles. *T. T. Clement*

EIGHTY DAYS (IRE) 8 b.g. Air Quest – Valley Hope (IRE) (Altountash) [2006/7 **c–** c25gᵖᵘ May 24] fairly useful pointer: tongue tied, no show in hunter on chase debut. *Mrs R. L. Elliot*

EILA 4 b.f. Turtle Island (IRE) – Brambly Hedge (Teenoso (USA)) [2006/7 F16d F16s **F–** Mar 1] first foal: dam, modest hurdler/chaser, stayed 3½m, sister to useful chaser up to 2½m Rubberdubber: soundly beaten in bumpers. *N. A. Twiston-Davies*

ELA JAY 8 b.m. Double Eclipse (IRE) – Papirusa (IRE) (Pennine Walk) [2006/7 22gᵖᵘ **h–** Jul 9] medium-sized mare: fair hurdler: amiss only start in 2006/7: should have been suited by 2½m+: acted on good to firm going: dead. *M. G. Rimell*

EL ANDALUZ (FR) 7 b.g. Baby Turk – Elise L'Ermitage (FR) (Quart de Vin (FR)) **c–** [2006/7 c86, h–: 20dᵖᵘ 23s² 24g² 24s* 23s Feb 17] good-topped gelding: winning chaser: **h112** fair handicap hurdler: improved to win conditional jockeys event with ease at Newcastle in January: will stay beyond 25f: acts on soft and firm going. *B. Ellison*

ELA RE 8 ch.g. Sabrehill (USA) – Lucia Tarditi (FR) (Crystal Glitters (USA)) [2006/7 **c112** c75+, h106: 16s* 17d c16d² c16s³ c16s⁶ c16v³ c16vᶠ c16vᶠ 16g c17g* Apr 21] **h118** raw-boned gelding: fairly useful handicap hurdler: won at Hexham (by 7 lengths from Megaton) in June: fair novice chaser: won in small fields at Wetherby (maiden) in December and Bangor in April: stays 2½m: acts on heavy and good to firm going: headstrong: usually gives plenty of trouble at start (has bolted), and has been attended by trainer/work rider on way to start and jockey put up late. *Mrs S. J. Smith*

EL BANDINDALE (IRE) 6 b.g. Darazari (IRE) – Supreme Weasel (IRE) (Supreme **h93 p** Leader) [2006/7 F88: 16g⁴ 16m² Apr 10] compact gelding: fifth in bumper: off 17 months, modest form in frame in novice/maiden hurdles, second to Gentle John at Chepstow: open to improvement granted stiffer test of stamina. *D. E. Pipe*

ELBDOUBLEU 7 ch.m. Classic Cliche (IRE) – Bowling Fort (Bowling Pin) [2006/7 h–: 22d^{pu} 19s 22s^3 24s^2 24v^5 22g 24m^6 Apr 15] workmanlike mare: bumper winner: modest maiden hurdler: stays 3m: raced mainly on ground softer than good. *C. J. Down* **h91**

ELBOW LANE (IRE) 7 b.g. Oscar (IRE) – Ah Donna (Don) [2006/7 F16v 21s^5 26s 26v^2 26s^{pu} 26g Mar 14] half-brother to winning pointers by Supreme Leader and Commanche Run: dam won 2m bumper and 17f hurdle: successful twice in Irish points: well beaten in 2 bumpers, left W. J. Burke in between: poor novice hurdler: stays 3¼m: acts on heavy going: tried tongue tied. *Mrs Tracey Barfoot-Saunt* **h79 F–**

EL CHAPARRAL (IRE) 7 b.g. Bigstone (IRE) – Low Line (High Line) [2006/7 17d^3 17m^4 16d^3 16g 20m^3 17m^{pu} Apr 9] medium-sized gelding: half-brother to temperamental hurdler Top Trees (by Charnwood Forest), stays 19f: fair but quirky on Flat (stays 1½m), successful twice at 5 yrs for D. Ivory: modest novice hurdler: lost action final start: should stay beyond 17f. *F. P. Murtagh* **h96**

EL CORREDOR (IRE) 8 b.g. Sadler's Wells (USA) – Meteor Stage (USA) (Stage Door Johnny (USA)) [2006/7 h86: 22m* 22m^3 26m* 27m^5 22g^6 26g 16d 26g 25d^{pu} Dec 28] sturdy gelding: modest hurdler: won handicaps at Fontwell in May and Hereford in June: left D. Pipe after fifth outing: stays 3¼m: acts on good to firm and good to soft going: tried in headgear: often tongue tied: ungenuine. *M. F. Harris* **h99 §**

EL COTO 7 b.g. Forzando – Thatcherella (Thatching) [2006/7 16g^F Oct 19] useful on Flat (effective at 7f to 1¼m), in-and-out form for current stable in 2006: no extra when fell last in novice on hurdling debut. *K. A. Ryan* **h– p**

EL DEE (IRE) 4 br.g. Brave Act – Go Flightline (IRE) (Common Grounds) [2006/7 17m^6 16m^3 16m^2 17s^2 16s^2 16v Jan 6] smallish gelding: half-brother to 2m hurdle winner Crusset (by Petardia): modest maiden on Flat (stays 1½m): modest juvenile hurdler: raced around 2m: acts on soft and good to firm ground. *D. Carroll* **h88**

ELDORADO 6 b.g. Hernando (FR) – Catch (USA) (Blushing Groom (FR)) [2006/7 16g Mar 24] compact gelding: fair on Flat (stays 1¾m), successful in 2006, sold out of S. Kirk's stable 16,000 gns Newmarket Autumn Sales: no show in novice on hurdling debut. *G. L. Moore* **h–**

ELEAZAR (GER) 6 b.g. Alkalde (GER) – Eicidora (GER) (Surumu (GER)) [2006/7 h107: 16g* 16d^{pu} c16d^3 c16d^4 c18s^5 20g* Apr 7] tall, useful-looking gelding: fairly useful hurdler: won novice at Haydock in November and handicap there (17 ran, beat Loulou Nivernais by 11 lengths) in April: let down by jumping all starts over fences: stays 2½m: raced on good going or softer: free-going sort. *Mrs L. Wadham* **c100 x h121**

ELECTRIQUE (IRE) 7 b.g. Elmaamul (USA) – Majmu (USA) (Al Nasr (FR)) [2006/7 16g c20g^F c16g^4 Aug 14] leggy gelding: running easily best race over hurdles when falling last on debut in 2003/4, off 18 months prior to return: well held in handicap completed start over fences: likely to prove best with emphasis on speed around 2m: sold 2,200 gns Doncaster January Sales. *Mrs S. J. Smith* **c– h–**

ELEGANT CLUTTER (IRE) 9 b.g. Petorius – Mountain Hop (IRE) (Tirol) [2006/7 h106: 17s^5 16s* 16g^4 16s 20d^5 16v^5 16v c19s^2 c16s^F Mar 12] fair handicap hurdler: won at Uttoxeter in May (final start for R. Bevis): similar form on completed outing over fences: stays 19f: acts on heavy going: tried blinkered/tongue tied. *N. A. Twiston-Davies* **c108 h107**

ELEGANT ESKIMO 8 b.m. Elegant Monarch – Eskimo Slave (New Member) [2006/7 h92, h83: c26g^2 c24g^{pu} c23d^2 Mar 20] angular mare: winning pointer: maiden hurdler: modest novice chaser: looked likely winner until faltering run-in final start, 6 lengths clear at last: stays 3¼m: raced on good going or softer: free-going sort, possibly needs to dominate. *S. E. H. Sherwood* **c96 h–**

ELENAS RIVER (IRE) 11 br.g. Over The River (FR) – Elenas Beauty (Tarqogan) [2006/7 c116, h–: c25g^8 c26g^2 Jun 8] rather sparely-made gelding: winning hurdler: fairly useful handicap chaser: won at Wincanton in May: further improvement when 4 lengths second to Omni Cosmo Touch (pair well clear) at Uttoxeter: stays 3½m when conditions aren't testing: acts on firm and soft going: usually sound jumper: effective ridden from front or not. *P. J. Hobbs* **c122 h–**

EL FARO (FR) 4 b.g. Fantastic Light (USA) – Pagoda (FR) (Sadler's Wells (USA)) [2006/7 16d^5 16v 16d^5 16v 16d^6 20g^{pu} Apr 27] lightly-raced maiden on Flat: modest juvenile hurdler: tried tongue tied. *A. Fleming, Ireland* **h84**

ELFEET BAY (IRE) 12 b.g. Yashgan – Marjoram (Warpath) [2006/7 20g^5 May 5] maiden hurdler/chaser: should stay beyond 17f: acts on soft going: tried blinkered/in cheekpieces. *Mrs P. A. Rigby* **c– h–**

ELFSTONE 4 ch.f. Magic Ring (IRE) – Lyssage (Lycius (USA)) [2006/7 F16g Apr 9] F–
second foal: dam unraced: well beaten in mares bumper on debut. *G. Haine*

ELGAR 10 ch.g. Alflora (IRE) – School Run (Deep Run) [2006/7 c86, h–: c19d* c16s* **c114**
c19s3 c16v* c16s* c16s6 Mar 10] big, strong gelding: maiden hurdler: fair handicap **h–**
chaser: better than ever in 2006/7, winning at Chepstow (seller) in November, Huntingdon in December (conditional jockeys, left clear last) and January and Leicester in
February: stays 2¾m, at least as effective at shorter: acts on heavy going: usually tongue
tied. *Mike Hammond*

EL HOMBRE DEL RIO (IRE) 10 ch.g. Over The River (FR) – Hug In A Fog (IRE) **c– §**
(Strong Gale) [2006/7 c–§, h105§: c23dpu Oct 31] rangy gelding: fair handicap chaser/ **h– §**
novice hurdler: lame only start in 2006/7: stays 3½m: acts on heavy and good to firm
going: tried visored/blinkered: ungenuine. *V. G. Greenway*

ELITE LAND 4 b.g. Namaqualand (USA) – Petite Elite (Anfield) [2006/7 16g 17g6 **h–**
17d Nov 16] modest maiden up to 11f on Flat (tried blinkered): no form in juvenile
hurdles: joined N. Bycroft. *B. Llewellyn*

ELJAY'S BOY 9 b.g. Sir Harry Lewis (USA) – Woodland Flower (Furry Glen) [2006/7 **c120**
c98, h–: c21m2 c20f* c20f3 c21d2 c17m2 c20m* c21f* c21g3 Mar 30] tall, useful-looking **h–**
gelding: maiden hurdler: fairly useful handicap chaser: won at Worcester (novice) in
June, Fontwell in September and Wincanton (improved effort, comfortably by 9 lengths
from Terrible Tenant) in October: off 6 months, good 6 lengths third to Stern at Ascot:
stays 2¾m, effective at much shorter: acts on firm going, probably on good to soft: tried
blinkered/tongue tied. *C. L. Tizzard*

ELJUTAN (IRE) 9 b.g. Namaqualand (USA) – Camarat (Ahonoora) [2006/7 h95: 23d4 **h86**
Nov 8] workmanlike gelding: modest handicap hurdler: stays 23f: acts on heavy and good
to firm going: tried in cheekpieces/blinkers. *J. Joseph*

ELLA MACCADELLA 5 b.m. Endoli (USA) – Leighten Lass (IRE) (Henbit (USA)) F–
[2006/7 F16m F16d Jan 5] fourth foal: half-sister to bumper winner The Hollow Bottom
(by Kadeed): dam, little sign of ability, out of sister to useful but ungenuine staying chaser
Attitude Adjuster: well held in bumpers. *Mrs H. O. Graham*

ELLANDSHE (IRE) 7 b. or br.g. Topanoora – Fox Glen (Furry Glen) [2006/7 h89: **c–**
c16g Oct 15] workmanlike gelding: form (modest) in novice hurdles only on debut: no **h–**
show in novice chase: should stay beyond 2½m: sold 1,000 gns Doncaster November
Sales, runner-up in points. *P. R. Webber*

ELLA ROYALE (IRE) 5 b.m. Raise A Grand (IRE) – Ella-Mou (IRE) (Ela-Mana- F–
Mou) [2006/7 F13m Jun 19] second foal: dam unraced: no show in bumper on debut.
Mrs P. N. Dutfield

ELLE EST SI BONNE 7 b.m. Gold Dust – Anshegee (Strong Gale) [2006/7 F14g **h–**
16gpu 19vpu 16spu Feb 1] second foal: dam poor/ungenuine novice hurdler: no sign of **F–**
ability in bumper/over hurdles. *M. Scudamore*

ELLE ROSE 4 b.f. Emperor Fountain – Elle Flavador (El Conquistador) [2006/7 18gpu **h–**
Sep 30] second foal: dam unraced: showed nothing in juvenile on hurdling debut.
W. G. M. Turner

ELLERSLIE ALI (IRE) 5 b.m. Zaffaran (USA) – Garrisker (IRE) (King's Ride) **F77**
[2006/7 F16m5 Apr 24] €25,000 4-y-o: second foal: dam unraced sister to smart staying
hurdler Merry Masquerade and useful hurdler Over The Bar: 9½ lengths fifth to The
Package in maiden bumper at Towcester on debut: will be suited by further. *O. Brennan*

ELLERSLIE GEORGE (IRE) 7 br.g. Presenting – Proud Polly (IRE) (Pollerton) **h108**
[2006/7 F99: 20g* 20s3 25s2 20g Apr 7] tall, good-topped gelding: third in bumpers: fair
form over hurdles: won maiden at Newcastle in November: stays 25f: acts on soft ground:
races prominently. *T. P. Tate*

ELLERSLIE JACK (IRE) 5 b.g. Danetime (IRE) – White Jasmin (Jalmood (USA)) **h–**
[2006/7 19g Nov 5] half-brother to moody hurdler Ludere (by Desse Zenny), stays 3m:
poor maiden on Flat at 3 yrs for T. Tate: well held in novice on hurdling debut. *O. Brennan*

ELLERSLIE LISA 5 b.m. Kayf Tara – Vax Rapide (Sharpo) [2006/7 F17g4 F16d **F67**
Nov 20] second foal: half-sister to 1m winner Grand Rapide (by Grand Lodge): dam
2-y-o 5f winner: little impact in bumpers. *O. Brennan*

ELLERSLIE TOM 5 br.g. Octagonal (NZ) – Tetravella (IRE) (Groom Dancer (USA)) **h134**
[2006/7 h104x: 16f2 18f* 17m 16m3 17m* 17d* 16m* 17g* 19g4 16g3 16g Apr 7] leggy
gelding: useful hurdler: improved considerably in 2006/7, winning handicap at Kelso in

May, novices at Bangor, Newton Abbot and Stratford in August, and handicap at Bangor (by 6 lengths from Aleron) in September: off 6 months, creditable third to Fleet Street in handicap at Newbury penultimate outing: likely to prove best around 2m: acts on firm and good to soft going: front runner. *P. Bowen*

ELLI LEWTIA 4 ch.f. Tomba – Troia (IRE) (Last Tycoon) [2006/7 18m Sep 21] little form on Flat: no show in juvenile in hurdling debut. *J. Jay*   **h–**

ELLIOTT 5 b.g. I'm Supposin (IRE) – Kiloran Bay (Lyphento (USA)) [2006/7 F16g⁴ Mar 28] lengthy, angular gelding: first foal: dam well beaten: tongue tied, around 8 lengths fourth to Theft in bumper at Kempton on debut. *R. Rowe*   **F89**

ELLO LUCKY (IRE) 5 b.m. Key of Luck (USA) – Ellopassoff (Librate) [2006/7 17g⁶ 17d⁵ 16v³ 19vᵖᵘ Dec 31] small, sturdy mare: no form on Flat: poor form over hurdles. *C. Roberts*   **h66**

ELLWAY PROSPECT 7 ch.m. Pivotal – Littlemisstrouble (USA) (My Gallant (USA)) [2006/7 h98: 19g² 19d* 16s 16v³ 21g Apr 19] lengthy mare: fair handicap hurdler: won at Taunton in November: stays 21f: acts on heavy going: tried in cheek-pieces. *M. G. Rimell*   **h112**

ELRAAWY (USA) 5 b. or br.g. Red Ransom (USA) – Fatina (Nashwan (USA)) [2006/7 20dᵖᵘ Dec 4] fairly useful up to 1½m on Flat, sold out of E. Dunlop's stable 25,000 gns Newmarket Autumn (2005) Sales: always behind in novice on hurdling debut. *C. J. Mann*   **h–**

ELSIE'S PRIDE (IRE) 5 gr.g. Turgeon (USA) – Magnissima (FR) (Rex Magna (FR)) [2006/7 F17d F16v⁴ 16v⁵ 19d Mar 28] €21,000 3-y-o: very tall gelding: has plenty of scope: half-brother to several winners abroad, notably useful French hurdler/chaser Grand Souvenir (by Legend of France), stayed 3m: dam won around 11f in France: signs of ability in bumpers/over hurdles: should stay beyond 2m. *Miss Venetia Williams*   **h80 F80**

EL SUENO (IRE) 7 b.g. Anshan – Dont Rough It (Pragmatic) [2006/7 F16sᵖᵘ Dec 27] half-brother to 2 winning hurdlers, including at 2½m Missrepresenting (by Presenting): dam, winning hurdler up to 2½m, half-sister to useful chaser Thyne Will Tell, stayed 2¾m: tongue tied, no show in bumper on debut. *K. J. Burke*   **F–**

ELUVAPARTY 7 b.g. El Conquistador – Ruby Celebration (New Member) [2006/7 F80: 25sᵖᵘ Mar 11] tall, useful-looking gelding: modest form in bumpers (looked a stayer): left D. P. Keane and off over 16 months, no show in novice on hurdling debut. *Simon Earle*   **h–**

ELVERYS (IRE) 8 b.g. Lord Americo – Paddy's Babs (Little Buskins) [2006/7 h100p: c20gᶠ c19dᵖᵘ Dec 28] good-topped gelding: fair form over hurdles: off 8 months, set to make successful chasing debut in novice handicap at Musselburgh when falling 4 out: bled next time: should stay beyond 19f: raced on good ground or softer. *R. A. Fahey*   **c114 h–**

EL VIEJO (IRE) 10 b.g. Norwich – Shuil Na Gale (Strong Gale) [2006/7 c98, h–: c22mᵖᵘ c20g⁵ c21dᵖᵘ c21s c20vᵖᵘ Jan 25] rangy, useful-looking gelding: winning hurdler: maiden chaser, no form in 2006/7: should stay 3m: acts on soft and good to firm going: often blinkered: ungenuine. *L. Wells*   **c– § h– §**

ELVIS RETURNS 9 b.g. Alhaatmi – Buckmist Blue (IRE) (Buckskin (FR)) [2006/7 c108, h108: c26s* c28s* c26s c32s⁵ c25vᵖᵘ c32s c23d⁶ c24g* Apr 7] big gelding: novice hurdler: fairly useful handicap chaser: won at Uttoxeter and Stratford (idled both times) in May and Carlisle (dropped in weights, beat Shannon's Pride by 5 lengths) in April: stays 3½m: acts on heavy going. *J. M. Jefferson*   **c120 h–**

EMBER DANCER 5 b.g. Emarati (USA) – Bella Coola (Northern State (USA)) [2006/7 h97?, F77: 17sᵖᵘ 16d 17s 16v² 16sᶠ 17v 17sᶠ 16gᶠ 16m³ Apr 24] medium-sized gelding: modest maiden hurdler: raced mainly around 2m: unraced on firm ground, acts on any other: often let down by jumping. *Ian Williams*   **h86 x**

EMERALD DESTINY (IRE) 5 b.g. Key of Luck (USA) – Green Belt (FR) (Tirol) [2006/7 h86: 21mᵖᵘ c17gᵖᵘ c19d* c20d² c20s⁴ c20m² Apr 9] tall, shallow-girthed gelding: maiden hurdler: poor handicap chaser: won at Catterick in December: stays 2½m: unraced on extremes of going: in cheekpieces last 4 starts. *Jedd O'Keeffe*   **c84 h–**

EMILY 7 ch.m. Moshaajir (USA) – Gaelic Empress (Regular Guy) [2006/7 F16d 21vᵖᵘ 21vᵖᵘ 22gᵖᵘ Apr 15] fifth foal: half-sister to 3m hurdle winner Em's Royalty (by Royal Fountain): dam winning pointer: no sign of ability. *A. Parker*   **h– F–**

EMILY ABBY (IRE) 7 br.m. Presenting – Mountcatherinerose VII (Damsire Unregistered) [2006/7 22m⁶ c23m c26vᵖᵘ c26g³ c24dᵖᵘ c20vʳᵗʳ Dec 28] sister to winning chaser   **c68 §**

up to 25f Premount: dam unraced: won point in 2005: poor maiden hurdler/chaser: left Miss E. Lavelle, refused to race final outing: stays 3¼m: acts on soft going: tried in cheekpieces/blinkers. *P. J. F. Hassett, Ireland*

EMILY'S FLORA 4 ch.f. Alflora (IRE) – Emilymoore (Primitive Rising (USA)) [2006/7 F14v F16s F17d Mar 19] tall, angular filly: chasing type: fifth foal: dam, modest novice hurdler, probably stayed 25f: little impact in bumpers: tried tongue tied. *P. Beaumont* **F—**

EMMA GEE 5 ch.m. Sure Blade (USA) – Elusive Star (Ardross) [2006/7 F16d Dec 29] lengthy, angular mare: on weak side at present: second foal: dam 1½m winner on Flat/2m winner over hurdles: well held in bumper, and claimer/seller on Flat. *J. Akehurst* **F—**

EMMA JANE (IRE) 7 b.m. Lord Americo – Excitable Lady (Buckskin (FR)) [2006/7 22v* 24v* 24v⁶ 20s⁵ 20d⁴ 24m² Apr 28] half-sister to fair hurdler/chaser Woodfield Gale (by Strong Gale), stayed 25f: dam won bumper/2½m chase: won point in 2005: runner-up in bumpers: fair form over hurdles: won novices at Thurles in November and Cork (Grade 3, by 1½ lengths from Another Nation) following month: in cheekpieces, creditable efforts last 2 starts, ½-length second of 24 to Casey Jones in novice at Punchestown: stays 3m: acts on heavy and good to firm going. *D. P. Berry, Ireland* **h110**

EMMASFLORA 9 b.m. Alflora (IRE) – Charlotte's Emma (Oats) [2006/7 c83+, h110: 22s² 20g⁵ 20d⁵ c16gᶠ 24s⁵ 21gᵖᵘ 16g³ 21m² Apr 9] good-topped mare: twice-raced over fences: fair handicap hurdler: needs good test around 2m, probably stays 3m: acts on heavy going: usually races prominently. *C. T. Pogson* **c— h108**

EMMPAT (IRE) 9 b.g. Bigstone (IRE) – Nordic Abu (IRE) (Nordico (USA)) [2006/7 16fᴰ 16m⁴ 16m* 16m* Apr 21] **h141**

Keeping their powder dry paid off for the connections of Emmpat for whom top-of-the-ground conditions seem to hold the key. When he lined up for the very valuable Menolly Homes Handicap Hurdle at Fairyhouse in April, it was his first start over hurdles since finishing a never-nearer fourth in the Galway Hurdle at the beginning of August, not enjoying the run of things in that race for the second year running (brought down in 2005). Emmpat mixes Flat racing with hurdling but he hadn't been seen on the Flat either for over six months. 'We've been praying for this type of ground [good to firm] for months,' said his trainer Charlie Swan after Emmpat beat a typically-competitive field to land a second big win in three days for his stable at the Fairyhouse Easter Festival following One Cool Cookie's in the Powers Gold Cup. Both Emmpat and One Cool Cookie showed improved form to win their respective races, well ridden by David Casey whose victory on Emmpat was his fifth in the handicap now known as the Menolly Homes. He had won the equivalent race on Mystical City in 1996, She's Our Mare in 1999, Killultagh Storm in 2000 and the Swan-trained Anxious Moments in 2002—a fall from Emotional Article in the 2005 renewal, however, left Casey sidelined for five and a half months due to a broken bone in his neck (he also suffered a dislocated hip in the incident). Emmpat took over in the lead before the last and, though not fluent at that

Menolly Homes Handicap Hurdle, Fairyhouse—Emmpat (spots) returns better than ever after a winter break to land this valuable prize; New Field (hoops) finishes second

Samsung Electronics Scottish Champion Hurdle (Limited Handicap), Ayr—further improvement 11 days later as Emmpat shows far more resolution than novice Ouninpohja (almost hidden)

obstacle, he rallied well when the Pierse Hurdle third New Field came at him and was well on top at the end, winning by three lengths from New Field who did best of those who had run in the County Hurdle at the Cheltenham Festival (the County winner Pedrobob managed only nineteenth at Fairyhouse, whilst Cheltenham seventh Sweet Wake was a disappointing unplaced favourite).

Emmpat had taken up his engagement in the Menolly Homes in preference to an alternative at Aintree, ground conditions deciding the issue, but he was in action in Britain later in April. He defied a mark 14 lb higher than at Fairyhouse to take the Samsung Electronics Scottish Champion Hurdle, a valuable limited handicap at Ayr, in the process becoming the first Irish-trained winner of this race (and only second ever) since Captain Christy in 1973. Ground conditions placed the emphasis firmly on speed again and, travelling smoothly throughout, Emmpat won readily by four lengths and a length and a quarter from Ouninpohja (conceding 6 lb) and Premier Dane (conceding 5 lb) respectively, that duo having also finished second and third in the County Hurdle. A measure of Emmpat's progress is that when he ran next in the Swinton Hurdle at Haydock (reinstated after a mix-up led to his being put in the wrong race), at the start of the 2007/8 season, he raced off a BHB mark 22 lb higher than that from which he had run fourth in the same race twelve months earlier. Emmpat ran as if something seemingly went amiss in the latest edition, travelling really well for a long way but finishing fourteenth after seeming to lost his action. Emmpat is well suited by good ground and firmer, all four of his wins over hurdles (two of them as a novice when trained by Anthony Mullins) having come on good to firm, as have his three wins on the Flat, in which sphere he is a useful handicapper, successful at nine furlongs to a mile and a half.

303

Mr Michael D. Mee's "Emmpat"

Emmpat (IRE) (b.g. 1998)	Bigstone (IRE) (b 1990)	Last Tycoon (b 1983)	Try My Best
			Mill Princess
		Batave (ch 1982)	Posse
			Bon Appetit
	Nordic Abu (IRE) (b 1990)	Nordico (b 1981)	Northern Dancer
			Kennelot
		Noora Abu (b 1982)	Ahonoora
			Ishtar Abu

The good-topped Emmpat is by the miler Bigstone (now in Australia) who is probably best known to followers of British jumping as the sire of the one-time very smart two-mile chaser Kadarann. Emmpat's dam Nordic Abu was a lightly-raced maiden on the Flat but was out of the smart Noora Abu, a very tough and genuine Jim Bolger-trained mare who was successful at up to a mile and a quarter. Nordic Abu has bred three other winners apart from Emmpat, the pick of them Dudley Docker (by Victory Note), a fairly useful performer at around a mile. The family is Flat-oriented but has had a couple of notable jumpers in Noora Abu's half-brothers Condor Pan and Vestris Abu. *C. F. Swan, Ireland*

EMOTIONAL ARTICLE (IRE) 7 ch.g. Definite Article – Cairo Lady (IRE) (Persian Bold) [2006/7 h108x: 20m² 22d* 24g³ 21g² 20m Apr 24] useful-looking gelding: fairly useful handicap hurdler: improved form in 2006/7, won at Tralee in August by length from Mouftari: good placed efforts next 2 starts, beaten ½ length when second to Monolith in 19-runner event at Cheltenham: stays 3m: acts on heavy and good to firm going: has been let down by jumping. *T. J. Taaffe, Ireland* **h125**

304

EMOTIONAL MOMENT (IRE) 10 b.g. Religiously (USA) – Rosceen Bui (IRE) (Phardante (FR)) [2006/7 c–, h154: 20d^{pu} 20s 20s^2 c24v^3 24v^5 24v^4 21v^3 21g Mar 14] leggy gelding: smart hurdler at best, below form in 2006/7: winning chaser, often let down by jumping: stays 3m: acts on heavy going: wore cheekpieces last 3 starts, also tongue tied final one: usually front runner/races prominently. *T. J. Taaffe, Ireland*   **c120 x** **h140**

EMOTIVE 4 b.g. Pursuit of Love – Ruby Julie (Clantime) [2006/7 16g 16g 16d Feb 14] sparely-made gelding: fair on Flat (stays 8.3f), successful in May/June, sold out of I. Wood's stable 7,600 gns Doncaster October Sales: soundly beaten over hurdles. *F. P. Murtagh*   **h–**

EMPEROR CAT (IRE) 6 b.g. Desert Story (IRE) – Catfoot Lane (Batshoof) [2006/7 17m^{pu} Jun 19] modest on Flat (stays 1¼m): no show in seller on hurdling debut. *Mrs N. S. Evans*   **h–**

EMPEROR ROSS (IRE) 12 b. or br.g. Roselier (FR) – Gilded Empress (Menelek) [2006/7 c108, h–: c22m^{ur} c24g^F Oct 19] useful-looking gelding: has reportedly had breathing operations: fair chaser, let down by jumping in 2006/7: stays 27f: acts on firm and good to soft going, probably not at best on soft/heavy: formerly tongue tied: joined M. Todhunter. *N. G. Richards*   **c– x** **h–**

EMPERORS GUEST 9 b.g. Emperor Jones (USA) – Intimate Guest (Be My Guest (USA)) [2006/7 c–, h–: 16s^6 16s 16s Feb 22] tall gelding: one-time useful handicap chaser: winning hurdler: lightly raced and no form since 2004/5: raced mainly around 2m: acts on heavy going: tried in cheekpieces, has won in blinkers. *Miss C. Dyson*   **c–** **h–**

EMPEROR'S MONARCH 8 ch.g. Emperor Fountain – Shalta (FR) (Targowice (USA)) [2006/7 h82: 17d 20v^5 17m^4 16g c20g 20s^2 19s^5 19g^6 20g^4 24s^3 Apr 25] leggy gelding: poor handicap hurdler: well held on chasing debut: stays 3m, effective at much shorter: acts on heavy going: in cheekpieces last 5 starts. *J. Wade*   **c–** **h82**

EM'S GUY 9 b.g. Royal Fountain – Gaelic Empress (Regular Guy) [2006/7 c–, h–: c25m^{pu} May 6] lengthy gelding: no sign of ability: tried in cheekpieces/tongue tied. *W. Amos*   **c–** **h–**

EMSKI 6 b.m. Gunner B – Moheli (Ardross) [2006/7 F–: 16g 22d^{pu} 25g^{pu} Jun 1] little impact in bumpers/over hurdles: sold 2,200 gns Doncaster August Sales, no show in points. *P. Beaumont*   **h–**

EMS MELODY 6 ch.m. Moshaajir (USA) – Gaelic Empress (Regular Guy) [2006/7 c25v^{pu} Mar 9] sixth foal: half-sister to 3m hurdle winner Em's Royalty (by Royal Fountain): dam winning pointer: no show in maiden chase on debut. *W. Amos*   **c–**

EM'S ROYALTY 10 b.g. Royal Fountain – Gaelic Empress (Regular Guy) [2006/7 c–, h93: 24s^{pu} 24v^4 24v 27v 24v^4 24s^5 Apr 25] fair hurdler: won handicap at Ayr in January: well held after: failed to complete over fences: stays 3m: acts on heavy going. *A. Parker*   **c–** **h102**

ENCORE CADOUDAL (FR) 9 b.g. Cadoudal (FR) – Maousse (FR) (Labus (FR)) [2006/7 c113d, h–: 17d c22v c21v* c21g Apr 12] leggy gelding: winning hurdler: fair chaser: left H. Hogarth, confirmed promise of hunter debut when winning at Ayr in March: stays 21f: acts on heavy going: tried in cheekpieces/tongue tied: seems best held up. *Miss T. Jackson*   **c102** **h–**

ENDLESS POWER (IRE) 7 b.g. Perugino (USA) – Charroux (IRE) (Darshaan) [2006/7 h–: 20s 20v^4 20v^6 16v^4 16v^2 20v^4 20s^3 Apr 1] tall gelding: fairly useful handicap hurdler: much improved in 2006/7, won at Ayr in January and March (beat Tell Henry by 10 lengths): stays 2½m: raced on going softer than good (acts well on heavy). *J. S. Goldie*   **h119**

END OF AN ERROR 8 b.m. Charmer – Needwood Poppy (Rolfe (USA)) [2006/7 h85+: 20m^F Apr 25] small, leggy mare: modest handicap hurdler: left A. Carroll and off 17 months, fell first only start in 2006/7: stays 27f: acts on firm and soft going: gets behind. *G. F. Bridgwater*   **h–**

ENERGY BOY 5 ch.g. Doubletour (USA) – Morcat (Morston (FR)) [2006/7 F16d 19d 16s 20m Mar 31] strong gelding: first foal: dam poor maiden jumper: no sign of ability. *T. D. Walford*   **h–** **F–**

ENFORCE (USA) 4 b. or br.f. Kalanisi (IRE) – Kinetic Force (USA) (Holy Bull (USA)) [2006/7 16g* 16g Apr 13] smallish filly: useful on Flat up to 1¼m, won minor events at Longchamp and Saint-Cloud in 2006: sold out of Mme C. Head-Maarek's stable 105,000 gns Newmarket December Sales: successful hurdling debut in 18-runner mares maiden at Huntingdon: well beaten in Grade 2 novice at Aintree following month: joined E. Dunlop: remains open to improvement. *Mrs L. Wadham*   **h103 p**

ENGLISH CITY (IRE) 4 ch.c. City On A Hill (USA) – Toledana (IRE) (Sure Blade   **h99 +**
(USA)) [2006/7 16m⁶ 16d⁵ 16s⁶ 16m⁶ 16g 16d 16v⁶ 18s* 17m² 16m² Apr 21] smallish
colt: half-brother to modest 2m hurdler South West Nine (by Oscar): modest on Flat
(stays 10.3f), left B. Smart after final 3-y-o start: fair juvenile hurdler: won at Kelso in
February: probably flattered final start: stays 2¼m: acts on soft and good to firm going.
Mrs L. B. Normile

ENGLISH JIM (IRE) 6 b.g. Saddlers' Hall (IRE) – Royal Folly (IRE) (King's Ride)   **h96**
[2006/7 h80: 21d² 27s* 22sᶠ 23v³ 24vᵖᵘ 21v² 26g 21g⁴ 27mᵖᵘ Apr 26] sturdy gelding:
modest handicap hurdler: won at Fontwell in November, idling: stays 27f: acts on heavy
going (below form on good/good to firm last 3 starts). *Miss A. M. Newton-Smith*

ENGLISHTOWN (FR) 7 b.g. Mark of Esteem (IRE) – English Spring (USA) (Grey   **c109**
Dawn II) [2006/7 c–, h119: 24d c21g² c20s* c21sᵘʳ c23d² c24g⁴ Apr 21] leggy,   **h–**
close-coupled gelding: fairly useful handicap hurdler: fair chaser: won handicap at
Leicester in January: stays 3m: acts on firm and soft going: tried blinkered: effective
tongue tied or not: often makes mistakes over fences. *Jonjo O'Neill*

ENHANCER 9 b.g. Zafonic (USA) – Ypha (USA) (Lyphard (USA)) [2006/7 h122:   **c119**
26m* 24m c16g² c19m² Oct 28] good-topped gelding: fairly useful handicap hurdler: **h119**
won at Southwell in May by ¾ length from Rosarian: off 4 months, similar form when
runner-up in maiden chases, beaten 4 lengths by Time To Shine at Ascot final start: stays
3¼m, effective at much shorter: acts on good to firm and good to soft going: held up.
M. J. McGrath

ENITSAG (FR) 8 ch.g. Pistolet Bleu (IRE) – Rosala (FR) (Lashkari) [2006/7 c101x,   **c103 x**
h–§: c16g² c21g⁵ c20m* c22m³ c20f⁴ c20gᵖᵘ Feb 21] leggy gelding: winning pointer: fair   **h– §**
chaser: won hunter at Ludlow in May: trained fourth/fifth starts by R. Price: stays 21f:
acts on soft and good to firm going, probably on firm: has worn headgear: sketchy jumper.
S. Flook

ENLIGHTENMENT (IRE) 7 b.g. Presenting – Shaiybaniyda (He Loves Me)   **h129**
[2006/7 20s⁵ 24m⁴ 16d* 20s⁴ 16v* 16g⁵ Mar 28] rangy gelding: half-brother to several
winners, including 1¼m winner Hopesville (by Top Ville): dam, 1m winner, half-sister to
Triumph Hurdle winner Shawiya: fairly useful novice hurdler: sold out of D. Hughes's
stable 13,500 gns Doncaster August Sales, improved to win at Worcester (maiden) in
October and Plumpton (off 4½ months, beat Mon Michel by 10 lengths) in March: lame
final start: should prove as effective beyond 2m: acts on good to firm and heavy ground.
Evan Williams

ENQUIRING MIND (IRE) 5 b.g. Definite Article – Zuhal (Busted) [2006/7 F16s*   **F111**
F16gᵖᵘ Mar 14] sturdy gelding: half-brother to 7f/1m winner Common Thought (by
Common Grounds) and winning hurdler Grain Storm (by Marju): dam 1½m winner:
second outing in bumpers, won at Punchestown in November by 4 lengths from hanging
De Valira: seemingly amiss in Grade 1 at Cheltenham 4 months later. *E. J. O'Grady,
Ireland*

ENROBLIM TROP (IRE) 5 b.g. Supreme Leader – Crafty Women (IRE) (Warcraft   **F91**
(USA)) [2006/7 F16s² F14v³ F16s Mar 3] 18,000 4-y-o: lengthy gelding: first foal: dam
unraced out of half-sister to top-class 2m chaser Badsworth Boy: best effort in bumpers
when second to Mountain Oscar at Towcester on debut. *C. L. Tizzard*

ENTAILMENT 5 b.g. Kris – Entail (USA) (Riverman (USA)) [2006/7 17s 17s 16s 17g   **h80**
Apr 27] fair at one time on Flat (stays 13f) for Gay Kelleway: poor form in novice
hurdles. *Miss M. Bragg*

ENTHUSIUS 4 b.g. Generous (IRE) – Edouna (FR) (Doyoun) [2006/7 16g Mar 24]   **h93 p**
leggy gelding: modest on Flat (stays 1½m), successful in February: not knocked about
when seventh of 18 in novice at Newbury on hurdling debut, carrying head awkwardly:
likely to do better. *G. L. Moore*

ENTRELECHAMBRE 5 b.g. Entrepreneur – Cambronne (Darshaan) [2006/7 F85:   **h81 +**
20f⁶ 20g⁴ 16s⁵ 20s Oct 27] leggy gelding: poor form in novice hurdles. *M. J. Gingell*

ENVIOUS 8 ch.g. Hernando (FR) – Prima Verde (Leading Counsel (USA)) [2006/7   **h81**
h81: 21m⁴ May 16] good-topped gelding: poor handicap hurdler, very lightly raced
nowadays: stays 21f: acts on firm and good to soft ground: has worn cheekpieces.
Miss J. Feilden

EQUILIBRIA (USA) 5 b.g. Gulch (USA) – Julie La Rousse (IRE) (Lomond (USA))   **h102**
[2006/7 h96: 18m* 16g⁵ 16d⁵ 16d⁴ 16d Dec 28] rather leggy gelding: modest on Flat
(barely stays 16.4f), successful in August: fair handicap hurdler: won at Fontwell later in

month: stays 2¼m: acts on soft and good to firm going: possibly not straightforward but is largely consistent. *G. L. Moore*

EQUIVOCATE 5 br.m. Karinga Bay – Heresy (IRE) (Black Minstrel) [2006/7 F–: 21vᵖᵘ 22dᵖᵘ Feb 1] medium-sized mare: no sign of ability. *R. Mathew*   **h–**

ERICAS CHARM 7 b.m. Alderbrook – Springaleak (Lafontaine (USA)) [2006/7 h81, F77: 19d⁶ 16g³ 17m* c16m* c16v⁴ c17d⁵ Dec 15] good-topped mare: fair novice hurdler/ chaser: won handicaps over hurdles at Hereford in September and over fences at Ludlow in November: should stay beyond 2m: acts on good to firm going: has shaped as if amiss more than once. *P. Bowen*   **c107 h103**

ERINS LASS (IRE) 10 b.m. Erins Isle – Amative (Beau Charmeur (FR)) [2006/7 c86§, h79: 22s⁶ 22g* 22dᵖᵘ 19s³ Aug 26] workmanlike mare: winning chaser: poor handicap hurdler: won conditional jockeys event at Market Rasen in July: stays 2¾m: acts on firm and soft going: has worn headgear, including all starts in 2006/7: has been let down by jumping/temperament, particularly over fences: sold €15,000 Fairyhouse December Sales. *R. Dickin*   **c– § h82 §**

ERISKAY (IRE) 11 b.g. Montelimar (USA) – Little Peach (Ragapan) [2006/7 c–, h–: 24g 24g* c16s⁵ c25vᵖᵘ c20d³ c24s³ c21vᶠ Mar 22] strong gelding: fair handicap hurdler/ chaser: won over hurdles at Hexham in May: stays 3m when conditions aren't testing: raced on good going or softer (acts on soft): tried blinkered. *L. Lungo*   **c105 h103**

ERNIE'S MAITE 8 b.g. Komaite (USA) – Jarin Rose (IRE) (Jareer (USA)) [2006/7 16m 16f Jul 19] third foal: dam little sign of ability: well held over hurdles. *J. W. Unett*   **h–**

ERROL 8 ch.g. Dancing Spree (USA) – Primo Panache (Primo Dominie) [2006/7 h91: 17v 16d⁵ 16g⁶ 19g 17m⁵ Apr 15] compact gelding: poor handicap hurdler nowadays: raced mainly around 2m: acts on soft going. *J. F. Coupland*   **h74**

ERTE 6 ch.g. Vettori (USA) – Cragreen (Green Desert (USA)) [2006/7 16v 16d c20gᵖᵘ Apr 23] successful both completed starts in points in 2006: no form over hurdles or on chasing debut. *W. Storey*   **c– h–**

ESCAYOLA (IRE) 7 b.g. Revoque (IRE) – First Fling (IRE) (Last Tycoon) [2006/7 20m* 20g² 20m* Apr 9] strong gelding: useful on Flat (stayed 2¼m), sold out of W. Haggas' stable 14,000 gns Newmarket Autumn Sales prior to successful in November: won twice over hurdles, maiden at Musselburgh in November and novice at Sedgefield (hung left) in April: raced around 2½m on good/good to firm ground: tried tongue tied: dead. *Grant Tuer*   **h113**

ESCOBAR (POL) 6 b.g. Royal Court (IRE) – Escola (POL) (Dixieland (POL)) [2006/7 h77: 16d 18m 16d* 16d⁴ 16d c17vᵘʳ c16d⁴ 16g Mar 19] close-coupled gelding: modest hurdler: won conditional jockeys selling handicap at Fakenham in October: no show over fences: likely to prove best around 2m: acts on good to soft going: tried in cheekpieces. *Mrs P. Townsley*   **c– h86**

ESCOMPTEUR (FR) 7 b.g. Poliglote – Escopette (FR) (Tourangeau (FR)) [2006/7 c120, h–: c17f⁴ c21d⁴ c18mᶠ Aug 24] sturdy gelding: winning hurdler: fairly useful maiden chaser, below best in 2006/7 (tongue tied): stays 21f: acts on heavy and good to firm going: visored final start: free-going sort: has looked none too genuine. *D. E. Pipe*   **c108 h–**

ESENDI 12 b.g. Buckley – Cagaleena (Cagirama) [2006/7 c20m Apr 15] tall, leggy gelding: lightly raced: maiden hurdler/chaser: winning pointer: stays 3m: acts on soft going. *Mrs A. E. Brooks*   **c– h–**

ESHBRAN LAD 10 b.g. Golden Lahab (USA) – Lansdowne Lady (Orange Bay) [2006/7 17dᵖᵘ Jun 4] leggy gelding: third in novice for N. Henderson on completed outing over hurdles: dead. *D. W. Thompson*   **h–**

ESKIMO JACK (IRE) 11 ch.g. Glacial Storm (USA) – Covette (Master Owen) [2006/7 c120§, h–: c21g Apr 12] useful-looking gelding: useful chaser at one time: has deteriorated considerably, though successful twice in points in 2007: stays 3m: acts on heavy going: refused to race once in 2005/6. *T. R. George*   **c? h–**

ESKIMO PIE (IRE) 8 ch.g. Glacial Storm (USA) – Arctic Verb (Proverb) [2006/7 c116, h–: c24d⁴ c25s⁴ c21g c31sʳᵒ c31sᵖᵘ Apr 27] tall, rather leggy gelding: winning hurdler: fairly useful chaser at best, disappointing in handicaps in 2006/7: stays 3m: acts on heavy going: blinkered 4 of last 7 starts (including when running out in cross-country event). *C. C. Bealby*   **c106 h–**

ESPOIR DU BOCAGE (FR) 12 b.g. Epervier Bleu – Skay (FR) (Sicyos (USA)) [2006/7 18s³ 18d³ 18d³ 21vᵖᵘ c16g² c16gᵖᵘ c21gᵘʳ Apr 13] strong, sturdy gelding: **c112 h–**

successful up to 1½m on Flat: fairly useful hurdler/chaser in France, claimed from F. Cottin €10,000 third outing: form after only when second to Roznic in handicap chase at Kempton: stays 21f: acts on heavy ground. *M. Scudamore*

ESPRESSO FORTE (IRE) 8 ch.g. Anshan – Symphony Express (IRE) (Orchestra) [2006/7 c94, h–: c23mᵖᵘ May 9] useful-looking gelding: winning hurdler: let down by jumping all 3 starts in chases: will stay beyond 3¼m: acts on soft going: tried tongue tied: sold £5,800 Ascot June Sales, won point in April. *Miss H. C. Knight* c– h–

ESPRIT SAINT (FR) 6 b.g. Mansonnien (FR) – Escopette (FR) (Tourangeau (FR)) [2006/7 c22s⁴ c20v² c19v² c23v² Feb 27] ex-French gelding: half-brother to several winners, including fairly useful hurdler Escompteur (by Poliglote), stays 21f, and fairly useful chaser around 2½m Escorteur (by Roi de Rome): dam middle-distance winner: thrice-raced over hurdles in Provinces, off 18 months prior to winning 5-y-o event at Pau: left G. Macaire, fairly useful form over fences (favourite all 4 starts), jumping none too fluently: stays 23f: raced on going softer than good: sold 62,000 gns Doncaster May Sales. *A. King* c115 h–

ESSEX (IRE) 7 b.g. Sadler's Wells (USA) – Knights Baroness (Rainbow Quest (USA)) [2006/7 h157: 16s⁵ 20m* 24m⁴ Apr 26] leggy, angular gelding: smart hurdler: off 11 months, won listed contest at Fairyhouse in April by 3 lengths from Sweet Kiln: back near best when under 6 lengths fourth to Refinement in Champion Stayers' Hurdle at Punchestown: barely stays 3m: unraced on going softer than good, acts on any other: effective with or without cheekpieces. *M. J. P. O'Brien, Ireland* h150

ESSIFER (IRE) 6 b.g. Lord Americo – Coral Cluster (Jasmine Star) [2006/7 F16d F16d 16s 20g⁵ 24v⁵ 24d² 24sᵖᵘ Apr 25] seventh foal: half-brother to disqualified 2¼m hurdle winner Equivocal (by Roselier): dam bumper winner: won maiden Irish point in 2006: well held in bumpers: modest form over hurdles: stays 3m: acts on good to soft going. *C. A. McBratney, Ireland* h93 F–

ESTANCIA 5 b.m. Grand Lodge (USA) – Donostia (Unfuwain (USA)) [2006/7 20d 22s 16g 20g Apr 11] angular mare: modest maiden on Flat (should be suited by 1¼m) at 3 yrs for H. Morrison: poor form over hurdles. *Miss Tor Sturgis* h75

ESTATE 5 b.g. Montjeu (IRE) – Fig Tree Drive (USA) (Miswaki (USA)) [2006/7 h96: 16g* 16d² 17m⁵ 16m² 16m² 17s* Aug 19] useful-looking gelding: fairly useful hurdler: won novice at Huntingdon in May and handicap at Bangor (further progress when beating Crow Wood 1½ lengths) in August: raced around 2m: acts on soft and good to firm going: patiently ridden. *R. S. Brookhouse* h121

ESTEBAN 7 b.g. Groom Dancer (USA) – Ellie Ardensky (Slip Anchor) [2006/7 h–: c17dᶠ c17s 16m c22m⁶ c16m⁴ c17m⁵ c16m c20g³ c16dᶠ 16f⁶ c16d² Sep 29] tall gelding: maiden hurdler: modest novice chaser: clear when fell 2 out in handicap at Tralee ninth start: best form around 2m: acted on good to firm and good to soft going: dead. *Eugene M. O'Sullivan, Ireland* c86 h65

ESTEPONA 6 ch.g. Polar Falcon (USA) – Kingdom Ruby (IRE) (Bluebird (USA)) [2006/7 h106+: 16fᶠ May 6] successful on second of 2 outings over hurdles in 2005/6: fell fatally in valuable handicap at Haydock. *J. Howard Johnson* h–

ESTERS BOY 9 b.g. Sure Blade (USA) – Moheli (Ardross) [2006/7 h99: 22g⁵ Jul 23] workmanlike gelding: modest handicap hurdler: stays 3¼m: acts on good to firm going: jumping has lacked fluency: sold £1,000 Ascot August Sales, pulled up in point. *P. G. Murphy* h94

ETENDARD INDIEN (FR) 6 b.g. Selkirk (USA) – Danseuse Indienne (IRE) (Danehill (USA)) [2006/7 h96§: 16m 26g 24dᵖᵘ 19g⁶ Mar 28] angular gelding: very disappointing since winning on hurdling debut in 2004/5, often finding little: tried blinkered. *Simon Earle* h73 §

ETERNA 7 b.m. Terimon – Nothings Forever (Oats) [2006/7 F16g⁵ F16m* Jul 5] second foal: dam unraced: modest form when winning bumper at Worcester: sold 22,000 gns Doncaster August Sales. *Karen George* F78

ETHAN SNOWFLAKE 8 b.g. Weld – Snow Child (Mandrake Major) [2006/7 h83: 16m c21d⁵ c18f 16m² c16m Jul 5] leggy gelding: modest hurdler: little impact in 3 starts over fences: raced mainly around 2m: acts on soft and good to firm going: blinkered 6 of last 7 outings. *N. B. King* c78 h87

ETIJAHAAT (IRE) 5 b.g. King's Best (USA) – Dance Ahead (Shareef Dancer (USA)) [2006/7 16s⁵ 17d 16fᵖᵘ Sep 29] fairly useful at best on Flat in Ireland for D. Weld: no form in Britain, including over hurdles. *C. W. Fairhurst* h–

ET MAINTENANT (FR) 5 ch.g. Johann Quatz (FR) – Dunlora (Sagaro) [2006/7 **h105** 16s³ 17v³ 19d^pu Mar 26] strong gelding: successful over 11.5f on Flat, sold out of J-M. Beguigne's stable €50,000 Goffs (France) July Sale: fair form when 6½ lengths third to Buster Hyvonen in novice at Huntingdon on hurdling debut: let down by jumping both starts after (raced freely second time). *N. J. Henderson*

ETOILEROUGE 6 b.m. Singspiel (IRE) – Bayrouge (IRE) (Gorytus (USA)) [2006/7 **F70** F80: F16g⁵ May 14] modest form at best in bumpers, not looking straightforward. *P. F. Nicholls*

ETOILE RUSSE (IRE) 5 b.g. Soviet Star (USA) – To The Skies (USA) (Sky Classic **h113 x** (CAN)) [2006/7 h104: 16g* 16s⁴ 16v⁵ 16v Jan 13] tall, narrow gelding: fair on Flat: similar standard over hurdles: won handicap at Wetherby in May, clear almost through-out: mistakes when running poorly last 2 starts (in cheekpieces final one): best short of 2½m: acts on soft going: tongue tied: front runner. *P. C. Haslam*

ETTRBEE (IRE) 5 b. or br.m. Lujain (USA) – Chief Ornament (USA) (Chief's Crown **F—** (USA)) [2006/7 F17d F16g Nov 29] 5,000 2-y-o: unfurnished mare: half-sister to 3 winners abroad, including UAE 7f winner Takteek (by Machiavellian): dam, 8.5f/1¼m winner, out of half-sister to champion US filly Althea and to dam of Green Desert: tailed off in bumpers/seller on Flat. *H. Alexander*

EUMENE (IRE) 4 ch.g. Grand Lodge (USA) – Pelagic (Rainbow Quest (USA)) **h91** [2006/7 17s⁶ 16s Mar 1] rather leggy gelding: useful up to around 1½m on Flat in France, successful twice in Provinces, sold out of J-C. Rouget's stable €125,000 Goffs Arc Sale: modest form on first of 2 outings in novice hurdles (mucus in lungs next time). *C. C. Bealby*

EURO AMERICAN (GER) 7 b.g. Snurge – Egyptale (Crystal Glitters (USA)) **c125** [2006/7 h134: 20g 20v c24d³ c19s² c25s^F c20v³ c20v* Mar 18] sturdy gelding: useful **h119 +** handicap hurdler, possibly needed race first 2 outings in 2006/7: fairly useful form over fences, winning maiden at Carlisle by ½ length from Bougoure, idling: should stay beyond 2¾m: acts well on soft/heavy going: usually waited with. *E. W. Tuer*

EURO BLEU (FR) 9 b.g. Franc Bleu Argent (USA) – Princess Card (FR) (Gift Card **c75** (FR)) [2006/7 c84, h–: c20g Mar 22] useful-looking gelding: maiden jumper: stays 2½m: **h—** acts on heavy going: has worn blinkers/cheekpieces: tried tongue tied. *Miss E. J. Lucas*

EUROCELT (IRE) 9 b.g. Eurobus – Seklo Lady (IRE) (Selko) [2006/7 c25s⁴ c24d **c—** c22s^pu 24v² 24v² 24g Mar 29] ex-Irish gelding: winning pointer: fair maiden hurdler, left **h107** G. Hayes before fourth outing: modest form at best over fences: stays 25f: acts on heavy ground: has worn blinkers/cheekpieces. *P. G. Murphy*

EUROCHANCER (IRE) 8 b.g. Eurobus – Woodfield Lass (IRE) (Bustineto) [2006/7 **c131** c24s³ c17s² c16s* c24g^pu Mar 14] workmanlike gelding: fair winning hurdler: useful **h—** novice chaser: much improved when winning maiden at Navan in November by 3½ lengths from Justpourit: out of contention when blundered fourteenth and pulled up in Grade 1 at Cheltenham: effective at 2m to 2¾m: acts on heavy ground: races prominently. *J. G. Fox, Ireland*

EUROCOMACH (IRE) 6 b.g. Saddlers' Hall (IRE) – Boro Penny (Normandy) **h75 +** [2006/7 F17m² F17m⁵ 17v⁶ 16v⁵ 18s Jan 4] €25,000 4-y-o: useful-looking gelding: **F88** brother to fair chaser Penny Hall, stays 3½m, and half-brother to 3 winners, including useful chaser up to 3m Sir Leonard (by Strong Gale): dam, poor bumper performer/maiden on Flat, sister to Galway Plate winner Boro Quarter and half-sister to smart 2m to 2½m hurdler Boro Eight: better effort in bumpers when runner-up at Bellewstown on debut: left A. Mullins, poor form on much softer ground over hurdles: likely to be suited by 2½m+: may yet do better now qualified for handicaps. *D. E. Pipe*

EURO DILEMMA (IRE) 6 b.m. Flying Spur (AUS) – Sandy Maid (Sandy Creek) **c—** [2006/7 26m² 24f^pu c23m^R Aug 1] bumper winner: maiden hurdler, left E. Sheehy before **h74 +** reappearance: well beaten when refusing last in maiden at Worcester on chasing debut: barely stays 3¾m: acts on good to soft and good to firm ground. *Evan Williams*

EUROFIDDLE (IRE) 8 b.g. Eurobus – Wrecktress (IRE) (The Parson) [2006/7 24g **h—** Feb 21] won maiden in November 2005 on completed start in Irish points: well held in maiden on hurdling debut. *Miss F. Slevin, Ireland*

EURO LEADER (IRE) 9 b.g. Supreme Leader – Noreaster (IRE) (Nordance (USA)) **c145** [2006/7 c142, h142: 25s⁵ c17m* 17g² 20f* 16v⁶ c20g⁶ Oct 7] good-topped gelding: **h131** smart chaser: won handicap at Galway in August: reportedly lame final outing: useful hurdler: won minor event at Cork in September by 3½ lengths from Adamant Approach:

stays 25f: acts on heavy and good to firm going: effective making running or held up.
W. P. Mullins, Ireland

EUROPEAN DREAM (IRE) 4 br.g. Kalanisi (IRE) – Tereed Elhawa (Cadeaux   **h111 p**
Genereux) [2006/7 17g^2 16d* 16s^3 16g* 16s^5 16g Dec 30] neat gelding: useful on Flat
(stays 1m), successful in March: fairly useful juvenile hurdler: won at Wetherby (maiden)
in October and Newcastle (comfortably by 1¾ lengths from Categorical) in November:
likely to prove best around 2m: raced on good going or softer: has worn cheekpieces,
including when successful: takes good hold: likely to do better in 2007/8. *R. C. Guest*

EUROTREK (IRE) 11 ch.g. Eurobus – Orient Jewel (Pollerton) [2006/7 c140, h–:   **c160**
c26g* c36g^{pu} Apr 14] tall gelding: very lightly raced: winning hurdler: progressive handi-   **h–**
cap chaser: 25/1, high-class form when winning 21-runner listed totesport.com Becher
Chase at Aintree in November, travelling strongly throughout and beating Bewleys
Berry 8 lengths despite jockey nearly taking wrong course on run-in: soon behind after
hampered badly first Valentine's in Grand National 5 months later: stays 29f: raced on
good going or softer over jumps: tried tongue tied: difficult to train. *P. F. Nicholls*

EURYALUS (IRE) 9 ch.g. Presenting – New Talent (The Parson) [2006/7 c20s^F Feb   **c–**
14] sturdy gelding: no form in novice hurdles: fair pointer, successful in April: fell in   **h–**
hunter chase: headstrong. *A. G. Hobbs*

EVANLY MISS 10 b.m. Michelozzo (USA) – Snitton (Rymer) [2006/7 19m 16m^5 16f   **h–**
Jun 21] won maiden in 2005, has failed to complete all starts in points since: no form over
hurdles. *R. Hollinshead*

EVELITH ABBEY (IRE) 5 br.m. Presenting – Papoose (IRE) (Little Bighorn)   **F76 +**
[2006/7 F16s^5 Mar 1] €105,000 4-y-o: third foal: sister to fairly useful hurdler/chaser
Letterman, stays 2¾m: dam, winning pointer, half-sister to very smart chaser up to 25f
Hi Cloy, out of half-sister to Champion Hurdle winner For Auction: 9¼ lengths fifth to
Diavoleria in mares bumper at Ludlow on debut, considerably handled having moved
smoothly in mid-field long way. *P. J. Hobbs*

EVELITH ECHO 4 b.g. Overbury (IRE) – Sunday News'n'echo (USA) (Trempolino   **F103**
(USA)) [2006/7 F12v^5 F13v^2 F16v* F16m* Apr 21] £18,000 3-y-o: smallish gelding:
half-brother to 2 winners on Flat by Wizard King and winning pointer by Classic Cliche:
dam, fair 2m hurdle winner, also 1¼m/1½m winner on Flat: fairly useful in bumpers: won
at Kempton (sweating/edgy) in February and Ayr in April, beating Quws Law by neck
after leader tied up at latter: bred to be suited by further than 2m. *A. King*

EVELITH FORREST 7 b.g. Overbury (IRE) – Forest Nymph (NZ) (Oak Ridge (FR))   **h117**
[2006/7 19v^2 22v* 24v^2 26s^3 24g Mar 24] half-brother to fairly useful hurdler/chaser up
to 2¾m Christopher and useful staying hurdler Toby Brown (both by Arzanni): dam 1m
winner: won maiden Irish point in 2005, placed both completed starts in 2006: best effort
(fairly useful form) over hurdles when winning maiden at Folkestone in December easily
by 9 lengths from Leading Authority: should be as effective at 3m+: acts on heavy
ground. *P. J. Hobbs*

totesport.com Becher Handicap Chase, Aintree—
top weight Eurotrek (right) takes the final ditch alongside runner-up Bewleys Berry

Mr Paul Green's "Eurotrek"

EVELITH PRINCESS 5 b.m. Overbury (IRE) – Forest-Nymph (NZ) (Oak Ridge (FR)) [2006/7 F16s 21v 20d⁵ 19v⁶ Feb 20] close-coupled mare: sister to winning pointer/2¾m hurdler Evelith Forrest and half-sister to useful staying hurdler Toby Brown and fairly useful hurdler/chaser up to 2¾m Christopher (both by Arzanni): dam 1m winner: mid-field in bumper: soundly beaten over hurdles. *Heather Dalton* **h–** **F66**

EVEN FLO 6 b.m. River Falls – Re-Spin (Gildoran) [2006/7 F89: 16gᵖᵘ 19d 21d⁶ 24s⁶ 22g 17m Apr 17] leggy mare: in frame in bumpers: sold out of Jean-Rene Auvray's stable 20,000 gns Doncaster August Sales: no form over hurdles: blinkered final start. *K. C. Bailey* **h–**

EVEN MORE (IRE) 12 b.g. Husyan (USA) – Milan Moss (Le Moss) [2006/7 c113§: c24v⁵ c23d⁶ c27dᵘʳ c25d³ c23d⁴ c25gᵘʳ c23v* c25d² c23s* c33s⁶ c27f⁵ Apr 5] workmanlike gelding: fair handicap chaser: won at Taunton in January and February (by 2½ lengths from Wizard of Edge): stays 33f: acts on heavy and good to firm going: sometimes let down by jumping: unreliable. *R. H. Alner* **c112 §**

EVEN SMARTER 5 b.g. Entrepreneur – College Night (IRE) (Night Shift (USA)) [2006/7 F16m⁴ F16f⁴ F16s Apr 27] 600 2-y-o: third living foal: dam, 6f winner, half-sister to dam of Prix Vermeille and Arc runner-up Leggera: poor form in bumpers. *Mrs J. C. McGregor* **F70**

EVEON (IRE) 7 b.m. Synefos (USA) – Lovely Grand (Le Bavard (FR)) [2006/7 c–, h–: c23m* c25mᵖᵘ Jun 4] well-made mare: won novice handicap chase at Exeter in May, only form. *Ian Williams* **c76** **h–**

EVEREST (IRE) 10 ch.g. Indian Ridge – Reine d'Beaute (Caerleon (USA)) [2006/7   **h102 ?**
17s⁴ Aug 26] fairly useful on Flat (stays 9.5f), successful in August: 8½ lengths fourth of
6 to Kings Quay in maiden at Market Rasen on belated hurdling debut, travelling well but
rather let down by jumping. *B. Ellison*

EVER PRESENT (IRE) 9 ch.g. Presenting – My Grand Rose (IRE) (Executive Perk)   **c136**
[2006/7 c116, h115: c20s* c25v* c24vᵖᵘ Jan 27] well-made gelding: fairly useful   **h–**
handicap hurdler: most progressive first 4 starts over fences, winning handicaps at
Carlisle in November and Kelso (beating Rambling Minster by length, hanging right
close home) in December: clearly amiss when pulled up early final outing: stays 25f: acts
on heavy going: front runner/races prominently. *N. G. Richards*

EVER SO SLIGHTLY (IRE) 6 b.g. Good Thyne (USA) – Loch Lomond (IRE) (Dry   **h100**
Dock) [2006/7 F90: 20v² 20g 20v⁶ 20v* 20s² 24m³ Apr 20] lengthy, well-made gelding:
fair hurdler: won novice handicap at Wetherby in December: should be suited by 3m: acts
on heavy going. *Mrs S. J. Smith*

EVER SPECIAL (IRE) 4 b.g. Fruits of Love (USA) – El Corazon (IRE) (Mujadil   **h103**
(USA)) [2006/7 17m³ 17d* 17m⁵ 16g* 16s* 20d* 19g⁵ 19d 16s⁶ Feb 1] poor form up to
around 1¼m on Flat: fair hurdler: won juvenile at Market Rasen in July, sellers at
Leicester (sweating) and Towcester (sold from P. Haslam 9,100 gns) in November and
handicap at Leicester (improved to beat Vicario 6 lengths) in December: below form last
2 starts: stays 2½m: acts on soft and good to firm ground: usually makes running.
J. T. Stimpson

EVOLVE BABY (IRE) 5 b.m. Sea Raven (IRE) – Supreme Baloo (IRE) (Supreme   **h–**
Leader) [2006/7 22m 19m Oct 4] little form on Flat: modest juvenile hurdler in 2005/6:
left C. Swan and off 4 months, well held both starts in Britain, tongue tied in seller second
one: best form around 2m: acts on soft and good to firm ground. *D. J. Wintle*

EWAR FINCH (FR) 5 b.m. Kayf Tara – Ewar Empress (IRE) (Persian Bold) [2006/7   **h–**
h–: 21sᵖᵘ 17d⁶ Jun 12] no form in 3 selling hurdles. *C. L. Popham*

EWE BEAUTY (FR) 7 b.m. Phantom Breeze – Baie de Chalamont (FR) (Balsamo   **h–**
(FR)) [2006/7 h–: 16g⁶ 22dᵖᵘ May 27] leggy mare: little solid form: lame final outing.
Ferdy Murphy

EXECUTIVE DECISION (IRE) 13 ch.g. Classic Music (USA) – Bengala (FR)   **c95 §**
(Hard To Beat) [2006/7 c114§, h–§: c16d⁴ c16s⁶ 16v⁴ Jan 13] rangy gelding: fair   **h99 §**
handicap hurdler/chaser, respectable effort final outing: best around 2m: acts on heavy
and good to firm going: blinkered/visored: usually finds little, and not one to trust.
Mrs L. Wadham

EXECUTIVE PADDY (IRE) 8 b.g. Executive Perk – Illbethereforyou (IRE)   **h97**
(Supreme Leader) [2006/7 19g³ 19d 16d³ 18g* 17g* 20d* 21dᵖᵘ 18s⁵ 16f 17m² 16f⁶
Apr 22] sturdy gelding: modest hurdler: much improved when winning selling handicaps
at Fontwell, Taunton and Fakenham (sold from Eoin Doyle 12,000 gns) within 2 weeks
in November: stays 2½m: acts on firm and good to soft going: tried tongue tied: has raced
freely. *I. A. Wood*

EXECUTIVE SPORT (IRE) 8 b.m. Executive Perk – Laura Daisy (Buckskin (FR))   **h–**
[2006/7 17m Oct 4] €2,500 4-y-o: third foal: half-sister to winning hurdler/chaser
Iceberg (by Glacial Storm), stays 3¼m: dam, placed in point, half-sister to dam of
Champion Bumper winner Hairy Molly: fell both starts in maiden points: also jumped
poorly on hurdling debut. *N. J. Hawke*

EXIT FAST (USA) 6 ch.g. Announce (USA) – Distinct Beauty (USA) (Phone Trick   **c–**
(USA)) [2006/7 c20g⁴ Apr 23] workmanlike gelding: well held in selling hurdle/maiden   **h–**
chase: placed on completed start in points/in seller on Flat. *P. T. Midgley*

EXIT RED (IRE) 4 ch.f. Exit To Nowhere (USA) – Unknown Quality (Sabrehill   **F–**
(USA)) [2006/7 F17v F17m Apr 15] first foal: dam unraced sister to useful 2m hurdler
Bring Sweets: showed nothing in 2 bumpers. *F. Jestin*

EXIT SWINGER (FR) 12 b.g. Exit To Nowhere (USA) – Morganella (FR) (D'Arras   **c99 d**
(FR)) [2006/7 c–, h–: c26s³ c27sᵖᵘ c24gᵖᵘ c28gᵖᵘ Apr 7] angular gelding: one-time smart   **h–**
chaser: third in hunter on reappearance, only form since 2003/4: best form up to 25f: acts
on heavy and good to firm going: wore cheekpieces second outing. *R. Ford*

EXMOOR RANGER (IRE) 5 ch.g. Grand Plaisir (IRE) – Slyguff Torus (IRE)   **F78**
(Torus) [2006/7 F16g⁶ Mar 21] first foal: dam unraced: sixth of 13 in bumper at Chepstow
on debut. *V. R. A. Dartnall*

EXOTIC DANCER (FR) 7 b.g. Turgeon (USA) – Northine (FR) (Northern Treat (USA)) [2006/7 c136, h–: c20s^2 c20d* c21s* c24d^2 c25v* c26g^2 c25g* Apr 12]   **c175 + h–**

After Neptune Collonges won the Punchestown Gold Cup at the end of April, some bookmakers were reportedly contemplating opening a market on his trainer Paul Nicholls emulating Michael Dickinson's achievement of saddling the first five in the Cheltenham Gold Cup. Dickinson's feat, achieved in 1983, will probably never be equalled and it is a measure of the strength in depth of the staying chasers in the Nicholls string that the idea could be considered without being met with derision. Nicholls had six entries in the 2007 Gold Cup: Kauto Star, who won, Neptune Collonges, who finished eighth before going on to success at Punchestown, My Will, who came twelfth, and Cornish Rebel, Eurotrek and Sleeping Night, none of whom met the engagement in the end. The outstanding Royal & SunAlliance Chase winner Denman, Festival Trophy winner Taranis and Star de Mohaison (out with a tendon strain in the second half of 2006/7) are among others who could enter the Nicholls stable's Gold Cup calculations in 2008. However, the Nicholls stable doesn't hold all the aces. The Jonjo O'Neill-trained Exotic Dancer stands head and shoulders above most of the potential Gold Cup candidates at Manor Farm Stables, with the obvious exception of Kauto Star who was in a different league to everything else in the latest season. Exotic Dancer enjoyed a tremendous season himself, winning four major races and coming second to Kauto Star in the two most prestigious championship events for the staying chasers, the King George VI Chase at Kempton and the Cheltenham Gold Cup. Exotic Dancer may not be able to hold a candle to Kauto Star but he is a top-class chaser, clearly

Paddy Power Gold Cup Chase (Handicap), Cheltenham—
Exotic Dancer (cheekpieces) makes his move two out as Taranis falls;
also pictured (from left to right) are New Alco (third), Tamarinbleu (sixth) and Graphic Approach (fifth)

superior to the rest of the established chasers who ran at around three miles in the latest season.

Exotic Dancer's two defeats by Kauto Star were not, however, the only ones he suffered. His campaign got off to an ignominious start in a three-runner graduation chase at Carlisle in November. Having his first outing since fracturing his pelvis in a fall at Sandown over ten months earlier, Exotic Dancer was beaten twenty-eight lengths by odds-on Turpin Green, pulling far too hard for his own good in a farcical affair in which the runners stood still for nearly twenty seconds after the tapes went up before setting off at a crawl, the race developing into a virtual sprint from four out. Exotic Dancer had managed four races over fences in his novice season, showing useful form when winning a four-runner event at Cheltenham (by a length and a quarter from Bewleys Berry) before his fall at Sandown. As a hurdler, he had shown very smart form when a close third (at 50/1) to Al Eile and Inglis Drever in the Aintree Hurdle after coming seventh in the World Hurdle at Cheltenham (where he was still second turning in). Nonetheless, his BHB mark over fences of 139 seemed plenty high enough at the time and, furthermore, his jumping wasn't fluent at Carlisle, even when the pace was slow. The transformation in Exotic Dancer five days later in the Paddy Power Gold Cup at Cheltenham was remarkable. Exotic Dancer was refitted with cheekpieces, which he had worn when showing improved form on those last two starts over hurdles. Starting at 16/1 in a sixteen-runner renewal of the Open meeting's feature handicap, Exotic Dancer again pulled hard under restraint. Held up and still last three out, but travelling strongly, Exotic Dancer made rapid progress to lead at the final fence. He soon drew clear to win by three lengths, kept up to his work. Second was the Pipe-trained favourite Vodka Bleu, attempting to become the eighth winner in eleven runnings of the race for his stable, and third was northern raider New Alco. It is a measure of Exotic Dancer's progress after the Paddy Power that Vodka Bleu and New Alco, who received 5 lb and 9 lb respectively at Cheltenham, would both have received around two stone if they had met Exotic Dancer in handicap company at the end of the season.

The boylesports.com Gold Cup, which had its fourth name change in as many years, fits in well for those who have contested the Paddy Power. The races are a month apart, the distances over which they are run are almost the same and

boylesports.com Gold Cup (Handicap Chase), Cheltenham—Tony Dobbin proves an able deputy for the unavailable Tony McCoy as Exotic Dancer (right) overhauls the blundering Knowhere; Taranis (left) takes third

Letheby And Christopher Chase (Cotswold), Cheltenham—jumping errors two out by Our Vic (left) and the grey Neptune Collonges (about to fall) present Exotic Dancer with a wide-margin success

both are run at Cheltenham, the first of them on the Old Course and the second on the New. Fondmort, who was forced into retirement after fracturing a pelvis on the gallops in November during preparations for another tilt at the Paddy Power, had a very good record at Cheltenham and won both races, though not in the same season. However, the feat was achieved by Exotic Dancer who followed up after being raised 10 lb for his Paddy Power win. If anything, he was even more impressive, cruising into contention three out under Tony Dobbin (standing in for Tony McCoy who was claimed to ride the McManus-owned Reveillez). Exotic Dancer won in good style by a length and a half and three and a half lengths from two who had fallen in the Paddy Power, the novice Knowhere and Taranis. Reveillez came eighth of the eleven finishers. Only Pegwell Bay and Senor El Betrutti had previously completed the double in the same season in the two traditional Cheltenham handicaps that started life as the Mackeson Gold Cup and the Massey-Ferguson Gold Cup in the early-'sixties. Pegwell Bay won both in the 1988/9 season and Senor El Betrutti emulated him in 1997/8, while Fifty Dollars More, Another Coral and Dublin Flyer won the two races a year apart, and Beau Ranger won the Mackeson three years after winning the Kennedy Construction (as the Massey-Ferguson became in the early-'eighties).

Exotic Dancer hadn't seen out the three miles thoroughly when tried at the trip for the first time in the World Hurdle but, nearly two years on, though still rather leggy, he had matured and looked stronger. In a rapid turn of events, no sooner had he become widely regarded as a two-and-a-half-miler than he went on to show further improvement campaigned for the rest of the season at three miles or more. Kauto Star understandably dominated the media build-up to the King George VI Chase at Kempton on Boxing Day, with Exotic Dancer sent off at 9/1 fourth favourite in the field of nine despite his big Cheltenham double. Exotic Dancer put up a top-class effort, patiently ridden as became typical and still travelling smoothly when making a bad mistake at the second last. Kauto Star, who had belted the fourth last, blundered at the final fence but was in control by then and Exotic Dancer followed him home at a distance of eight lengths, with a further length and a quarter back to Racing Demon. Exotic Dancer's owner also had the previous year's Royal & SunAlliance Chase winner Star de Mohaison (in Kauto Star's stable) but, with that horse on the sidelines, Exotic Dancer was now aimed at the Cheltenham Gold Cup. He was seen next at the end of January in the Cotswold Chase, a race long

Betfair Bowl Chase, Aintree—a fine end to a lucrative campaign;
My Will (right) will be 13 lengths adrift come the line

known as the Pillar which is now sponsored by Letheby & Christopher. The race provided Exotic Dancer with his third big-race win of the season at Cheltenham and ended any lingering doubts over his stamina. He beat the Charlie Hall winner Our Vic and the Welsh National winner Halcon Genelardais by eighteen lengths and seven in heavy ground. Neptune Collonges was in third when falling at the second last where Our Vic also blundered, but Exotic Dancer was already poised to take over at that point and kept on strongly up the steep final climb to the line.

Horses kept on the boil after showing good early-season form can be difficult to produce at their peak again for the major Festivals in the spring. But there was no tapering of Exotic Dancer's performances. Far from it. Starting 9/2 second favourite in the Cheltenham Gold Cup, Exotic Dancer was moving well, waited with by McCoy, until Kauto Star put his stamp on the race as the field turned for home. Exotic Dancer was never able to land a blow after being momentarily held in by Kauto Star as the pair challenged wide and then being further inconvenienced by the attentions of a loose horse. That said, Exotic Dancer wasn't cutting into Kauto Star's lead significantly on the run-in and went down by two and a half lengths. Turpin Green finished the same distance behind Exotic Dancer in third but the muddling pace of the Gold Cup—a third of the field was still bunched turning for home—meant that Kauto Star and Exotic Dancer were unable to show their true superiority over the rest on the day. While Kauto Star was put away for the season, Exotic Dancer met Turpin Green, the Gold Cup sixth State of Play and My Will in the Betfair Bowl at Aintree, a field of five completed by Our Vic, runner-up to Taranis in the Festival Trophy at Cheltenham. Meeting his three Gold Cup rivals on terms 4 lb worse than at Cheltenham, Exotic Dancer put them firmly in their place. Looking in great shape and showing no signs of his lengthy season, Exotic Dancer made a couple of significant mistakes in the first part of the race before drawing clear with My Will after four out. Exotic Dancer quickened impressively at the second last and won by thirteen lengths and twelve from My Will and Our Vic. The blinkers didn't work a second time on Turpin Green, who turned in a sour performance, trailing in last. The Betfair Bowl was, incidentally, Exotic Dancer's first success in Britain away from Cheltenham. He had also been entered in the Grand National at Aintree (sharing top weight on 11-12 with Hedgehunter) but connections confirmed that the entry was 'precautionary' in case Exotic Dancer missed the Cheltenham Festival. Exotic Dancer's mark in the National was effectively 158, as opposed to the 170 he'd have been allotted in other handicaps at that time. Victory in the Betfair Bowl also secured for Exotic Dancer's connections the

£75,000 prize for the runner-up in the BHB's Order of Merit, finishing twenty-eight points adrift of Kauto Star in a clear second. This lucrative bonus haul came about due to the BHB tweaking the Order of Merit rules for 2006/7, with the previously-used categories for top hurdler and top chaser (plus novices) scrapped in favour of cash prizes for just the top three point-scorers overall. Immediately after the Betfair Bowl there was talk of Exotic Dancer's going on to carry top weight in the Betfred Gold Cup at Sandown but, in the end, nothing came of it and he was retired for the season, the winner of four of his seven races with total first-three prize money of £429,383, again putting him second behind Kauto Star in Britain. If Kauto Star hadn't been around, Exotic Dancer would have had the stage to himself and would have been a worthy winner of the award for the season's Best Staying Chaser. He is rated more highly than quite a few who have lifted the award since *Chasers & Hurdlers* began in 1975/6, including, in the last decade, Cool Dawn (173 in 1997/8), Best Mate and Florida Pearl (both 173 in 2001/2) and Beef Or Salmon (174x in 2005/6).

Exotic Dancer (FR) (b.g. 2000)	Turgeon (USA) (gr 1986)	Caro (gr 1967)	Fortino II
			Chamboro
		Reiko (b 1979)	Targowice
			Beronaire
	Northine (FR) (ch 1985)	Northern Treat (b 1976)	Northern Dancer
			Exotic Treat
		Lepine (ch 1976)	Philemon
			Hermouke

Exotic Dancer is French-bred, like Kauto Star and an increasing number of important jumping winners these days. At the top level, French-breds again won more graded races over jumps in Britain and Ireland than those who were British-

Sir Robert Ogden's "Exotic Dancer"

bred, finishing clear second behind the Irish-breds. The French-bred chasers did particularly well, winning thirty of the seventy-four Grade 1 and Grade 2 races over fences in Britain and Ireland (Irish-breds won thirty-eight, with British-breds and German-breds sharing the six others equally). All twenty-seven Grade 1 chases, incidentally, were won by Irish- or French-breds. Village Star, the sire of Kauto Star, was the highest-placed French stallion in the combined table covering Britain and Ireland, Kauto Star being his only representative and putting him in fourteenth place. In fifteenth was Exotic Dancer's sire Turgeon whose other representatives included the useful novice chaser Turko, the useful handicap chaser Turgeonev and the prolific staying handicap chaser Zimbabwe. Turgeon, a smart stayer who completed the Irish St Leger/Prix Royal-Oak double at the age of five in 1991 and was also placed in two Gold Cups at Ascot, has done well as a jumps stallion, his winners in France including the 2004 Prix La Haye Jousselin winner Turgot, and he stands at Haras du Mesnil with a fee of €6,000. Exotic Dancer's dam Northine was a winning hurdler at around two miles and is out of a half-sister to Moncourt, a good French chaser at around two and three quarter miles. Northine has bred several other winners apart from Exotic Dancer, the pick of them Pasquane (by Dom Pasquini), a smart chaser at up to two and three quarter miles. Northine's two-year-old colt Exotic Man (by the Pistolet Bleu stallion Arvico) was bought on behalf of Exotic Dancer's owner Sir Robert Ogden for €180,000 at Saint-Cloud in July. Exotic Dancer was runner-up over a mile and a half on his only outing on the Flat in France, and won on both his starts in juvenile hurdles at Auteuil for Marcel Rolland (beating 2007 Fox Hunters' runner-up Pak Jack on each occasion) before joining his present stable as a four-year-old. Exotic Dancer stays three and a quarter miles, though is equally as effective over shorter, and has done his racing on good going or softer (he acts on heavy). As well as being equipped with cheekpieces nowadays, he also wears ear plugs. He takes a good hold and is best held up. His jumping isn't always fluent, but that doesn't seem a major issue nowadays. *Jonjo O'Neill*

EXPECTED BONUS (USA) 8 b. or br.g. Kris S (USA) – Nidd (USA) (Known Fact (USA)) [2006/7 17m Aug 6] poor on Flat (stays 1¼m) nowadays: well beaten in novice on hurdling debut. *Jamie Poulton*   **h–**

EXPERIMENTAL (IRE) 13 b.g. Top of The World – Brun's Toy (FR) (Bruni) [2006/7 16g 16g Apr 8] sparely-made gelding: maiden chaser: one-time useful handicap hurdler: fit from Flat, well beaten both starts in 2006/7: raced around 2m: acts on good to firm and heavy going: tried in headgear/tongue tied. *John A. Harris*   **c–** **h89**

EXPLODE 10 b.g. Zafonic (USA) – Didicoy (USA) (Danzig (USA)) [2006/7 h–: 16s^pu 16g^pu 19d 20d^pu 16g^F 16d^3 16s 16s^pu 16s^2 16g Apr 9] medium-sized gelding: modest on Flat: bad 2m maiden hurdler: blinkered nowadays: unreliable. *Miss L. C. Siddall*   **h57 §**

EXPLOSIVE FOX (IRE) 6 ch.g. Foxhound (USA) – Grise Mine (FR) (Crystal Palace (FR)) [2006/7 h103: 22m² c23m⁴ c26d³ c23f⁴ c25s c23g^ur c25g^pu Apr 11] leggy gelding: fairly useful hurdler: improved form when second to El Corredor in handicap at Fontwell on reappearance: modest form over fences: stays 2¾m: acts on firm going: tried in blinkers, usually wears cheekpieces: often front runner over hurdles. *S. Curran*   **c95** **h115**

EXSTOTO 10 b.g. Mtoto – Stoproveritate (Scorpio (FR)) [2006/7 20d* c24d³ c25d³ Dec 9] angular gelding: fair handicap hurdler: off over 2 years, won at Uttoxeter in October by short head from Before The Mast: fairly useful chaser: respectable efforts in handicaps last 2 starts: stays 4m: acts on firm and soft going (pulled up only run on heavy): genuine. *R. A. Fahey*   **c115** **h107**

EXTRA BOLD 5 b.g. Overbury (IRE) – Tellicherry (Strong Gale) [2006/7 h–, F76: 16s⁵ 22s 20s⁶ 16v 22g⁶ Apr 7] lengthy gelding: little form. *R. Lee*   **h73**

EXTRA CACHE (NZ) 14 br.g. Cache of Gold (USA) – Gizmo (NZ) (Jubilee Wine (USA)) [2006/7 c74, h–: c20g² Apr 30] leggy gelding: veteran jumper: stays 21f: acts on any going: tried in headgear. *O. Brennan*   **c73** **h–**

EXTRA SMOOTH 6 br.g. Cloudings (IRE) – Miss Ondee (FR) (Dress Parade) [2006/7 h107: c20s* Oct 28] fair hurdler: off 7 months, better form when making successful chasing debut in 3-finisher novice handicap at Wetherby, jumping soundly and keeping on strongly after leading 4 out to beat Ice Melted by distance: will stay 3m: raced   **c120 p** **h–**

mainly on going softer than good: presumably met with setback, but remains open to improvement over fences. *C. C. Bealby*

EXUBERANCE (IRE) 5 b.g. Exit To Nowhere (USA) – Hook's Close (Kemal (FR)) **h96**
[2006/7 F16s³ F17v⁴ 19s³ 20v⁴ 22d⁵ 19s Mar 2] rangy gelding: half-brother to 2½m chase **F92**
winner Tailored (by King's Ride) and a winning pointer by Montelimar: dam, placed in bumper, out of sister to very useful chaser Cancello: in frame both starts in bumpers: modest form over hurdles, made bad mistake last 2 outings: stays 2¾m: raced on ground softer than good. *Miss H. C. Knight*

EYES TO THE RIGHT (IRE) 8 ch.g. Eagle Eyed (USA) – Capable Kate (IRE) **c–**
(Alzao (USA)) [2006/7 c–, h–: 17d⁵ 17d⁴ 16f³ 16m 16f⁴ 16m c16f c16gᵖᵘ 16dᵖᵘ 16d **h64**
c16v⁴ c16v⁴ Nov 28] leggy gelding: poor hurdler: left D. Burchell after tenth outing: no form over fences: best around 2m: acts on soft and firm going. *M. A. Doyle*

EYZE (IRE) 11 b.g. Lord Americo – Another Raheen (IRE) (Sandalay) [2006/7 c–, **c75**
h–: c20g⁶ c20fᵖᵘ Jun 17] maiden hurdler: winning chaser: lightly raced and little form **h–**
since 2003, often shaping as if amiss: stays 25f: acts on firm and good to soft going. *B. Mactaggart*

F

FAASEL (IRE) 6 b.g. Unfuwain (USA) – Waqood (USA) (Riverman (USA)) [2006/7 **c150 §**
h150: 16m⁵ 16s⁵ c19s* c16g⁴ c25g² c20m³ Apr 21] strong, close-coupled gelding: smart **h140**
hurdler, below best first 2 starts in 2006/7: smart novice chaser: won maiden at Catterick in January on debut over fences: better form next 2 starts, 6¾ lengths fourth to My Way de Solzen in Arkle Trophy at Cheltenham and 8 lengths second to ready winner Aces Four in Mildmay Novices' Chase at Aintree: stays 25f: unraced on firm going, acts on any other: wears headgear: held up: irresolute. *N. G. Richards*

FABLE (USA) 11 b.g. Hansel (USA) – Aragon (USA) (Raconteur) [2006/7 c21g c25g **c92**
Apr 25] strong gelding: carries condition: one-time fairly useful handicap chaser: left **h–**
N. Meade, won point in March: mid-division in Fox Hunters' at Aintree and Champion Hunters' at Punchestown: stays 21f: acts on firm and soft going: has worn headgear: often tongue tied. *G. Elliott, Ireland*

FABREZAN (FR) 6 gr.m. Nikos – Fabulous Secret (FR) (Fabulous Dancer (USA)) **h–**
[2006/7 c–, h–: 24vᵖᵘ 24s 23g⁶ Apr 9] smallish gelding: one-time fair hurdler, no form in 2006/7 after lengthy absence: has worn blinkers/cheekpieces. *C. N. Kellett*

FAD AMACH (IRE) 6 gr.m. Flemensfirth (USA) – Fortina's Angle (Buckskin (FR)) **h–**
[2006/7 F–: F16d⁵ 16dᵖᵘ 22s^F 20d 16v 22sᵖᵘ Feb 3] good-topped mare: signs of ability **F73**
final start in bumpers: no form over hurdles. *G. R. I. Smyly*

FADANSIL (IRE) 4 b.g. Dansili – Fatah Flare (USA) (Alydar (USA)) [2006/7 17fᵖᵘ Aug 11] **h–**
half-brother to winning hurdler Protagonist (by In The Wings), stays 2¾m: modest maiden on Flat (stays 1¼m): pulled too hard on hurdling debut. *J. Wade*

FADDAD (USA) 11 b.g. Irish River (FR) – Miss Mistletoes (IRE) (The Minstrel **c85**
(CAN)) [2006/7 c80, h88: c21m² c21d² c18f c26d⁴ c23f⁴ 24f² c23m* c23m⁴ Aug 3] **h85**
angular gelding: modest hurdler/chaser: won strongly-run handicap chase at Worcester in July: stays 3m: probably best on good going or firmer: tongue tied. *Mrs A. M. Thorpe*

FADING MEMORY 5 ro. or gr.m. Environment Friend – Lasting Memory (Ardross) **F–**
[2006/7 F16g May 14] sixth foal: dam fair staying hurdler: well beaten in bumper on debut. *C. J. Down*

FAIR ALONG (GER) 5 b.g. Alkalde (GER) – Fairy Tango (FR) (Acatenango **c149**
(GER)) [2006/7 h135: 17d 21g³ c16d* c16s* c18s* c16g² 17g c16g² Apr 14] **h141**
        The starting of big fields, in particular at the Cheltenham Festival, continues to leave something to be desired. New procedures at the spring festivals (Cheltenham and Aintree) included having the starter on his rostrum as soon as the runners arrived and having a loudspeaker in the collecting or 'girthing-up' area off the track near the start so that instructions could be heard clearly. The measures were successfully rehearsed at the Cheltenham Open meeting in November but, come the Festival, there were again a number of starts which gave cause for embarrassment and complaint, particularly on the first two days when only four of the twelve could be said to have been executed smoothly. The problems began in

the very first race, the Supreme Novices', the start of which was delayed after the tape was broken at the first attempt. Hot favourite Amaretto Rose wasn't ideally placed when the tape eventually went up for the Supreme, but worse befell Fair Along, the favourite for the second race, the Arkle Trophy, after a false start that saw Lennon taking his jockey through the tape and bolting. When the re-formed field got away, it was in ragged fashion, Fair Along one of those flat-footed and also affected by scrimmaging among those lined up near the inside rail. Ironically, Lennon was among those who made a quick start on the outside. Lennon took the start at the canter, which would normally have resulted in the starter refusing to let the field go.

Horses are expected to move out, when first called on to the course from the collecting area, in an orderly fashion, those jockeys set on disputing the lead or wanting to be prominent encouraged to make their way out first. The runners are permitted only to walk or jog until the starter releases the tape. The starter's job is to achieve a fair start, thankfully nowadays without the runners having to be at a virtual standstill with their noses almost on the tape. 'Walk-in' starts, after the runners have lined up away from the tape, are now permitted and, when they work first time, seem the most effective way of achieving a level break. Part of the problem at a meeting as important as the Cheltenham Festival is the over-eagerness of some jockeys to secure a good position. Another new measure introduced at the Cheltenham Festival was a camera recording what happens at the start, the film available immediately after the runners have been despatched so that the starter can quickly report jockeys who have disobeyed his instructions. Conditional jockeys Andrew Glassonbury and Tjade Collier were stood down for a day after being reported by the starter following a delay to the fourth race on the opening day, the William Hill Trophy. These problems at Cheltenham arguably planted the seeds for the shambolic scenes witnessed at Aintree four weeks later, with the Grand

Independent Newspaper Novices' Chase (November), Cheltenham—a sparkling start over fences by four-year-old Fair Along, who comprehensively outpoints Natal (left) and Penzance

Sodexho Prestige Henry VIII Novices' Chase, Sandown—Fair Along is promoted to ante-post favourite for the Arkle as he lowers the colours of My Way de Solzen (right)

National start delayed by some ten minutes after the tape was broken at the first attempt. Senior starter Peter Haynes placed the blame firmly on the jockeys for disobeying his instructions on the numerous attempted re-starts, a claim that was firmly rebuffed by the Jockeys' Associations on both sides of the Irish Sea, with Irish riders' chief Andrew Coonan taking great exception to Haynes' comment that 'a lot of the trouble is with those Irish lads who come over and don't ride here regularly.' Haynes, a former jockey best known for his association with the globe-trotting hurdler/chaser Grand Canyon, appears to have possibly lost the confidence of some riders when it comes to the big occasion. The Horseracing Regulatory Authority was only prepared to back him verbally after the Aintree meeting—which had also featured a false start in the Fox Hunters', plus a ragged getaway in the Topham twenty-four hours afterwards. Explaining the lack of punishment for Grand National jockeys, HRA spokesman Paul Struthers said: 'We couldn't find anywhere between twenty to forty of them in breach on the day because it would look silly.' That wasn't the case back in 2004, when all twenty-five amateurs were fined for disobeying Haynes' instructions before that year's Fox Hunters'. In addition, Haynes' predecessor Simon Morant oversaw the 2003 Champion Hurdle, where sixteen of the seventeen riders (Tony Dobbin escaped censure on the reluctant-to-race Hors La Loi III) were cautioned after breaking through the tape.

Fair Along's trainer Philip Hobbs was one of several who complained about their horses' chances being affected by incidents at the start during the latest Festival. 'If the starter had let them go first time, the horse might have been all right. He got a bump when they lined up and lost his position,' Hobbs said after the Arkle (Nicky Richards, the trainer of eventual fourth Faasel—'he was always three lengths further back because of the ground he lost'—also felt the Arkle field should have been allowed to go first time). Fair Along was a worthy favourite for the Arkle. In receipt of the over-generous age allowance for four-year-olds (the change to which is discussed in Twist Magic's essay), he won all three of his outings over fences before the turn of the year, after which he was given a fairly

321

lengthy break before the Festival, as in the previous season when he had returned to finish a good second to his stable-companion Detroit City in the Triumph Hurdle.

Fair Along started life in handicap hurdles at the beginning of the latest season, giving weight away all round under 11-12 when down the field in the Summer Hurdle at Market Rasen in July and again when finishing an excellent third in useful company at Cheltenham in October, on both occasions also being the only four-year-old in the line-up. Fair Along showed much improved form when winning two handicaps on the Flat at Salisbury in between Market Rasen and Cheltenham and, after his third to Monolith at the latter track, it was all change again as he began a new career over fences. Fair Along made a fine impression in the Independent Newspaper (November) Novices' Chase at Cheltenham, soon in front, jumping with speed and agility, and winning by nine lengths and the same from odds-on Natal and Penzance. Fair Along followed up in equally good style in the Sodexho Prestige Henry VIII Novices' Chase at Sandown in December, beating My Way de Solzen by ten lengths, inflicting on him and third-placed New Little Bric their only defeats in four races over fences before the Cheltenham Festival. Fair Along's third steeplechase win came at long odds-on at Newbury just after Christmas when he was left clear to win by a distance after his two main rivals blundered five out. Given the presence of several other front runners in the field, it was hardly surprising that Fair Along wasn't ridden prominently at Cheltenham after failing to get away cleanly. He did well to get up for second in the circumstances, even though fourth place is probably the best he could have hoped for had Twist Magic and Don't Push It not fallen two out. A mistake four out just as the race was taking shape didn't help, whilst Fair Along was also hampered in the aforementioned incident at the second last. Fair Along kept on well on the run-in, finishing five lengths behind My Way de Solzen. Fair Along was seen out twice at

Mr Alan Peterson's "Fair Along"

the Cheltenham Festival but ran a long way below his best when a well-backed favourite in the last race of the meeting, the County Hurdle. His performances seem sure to prompt the racing quiz question: 'Which horse started favourite for two races at the 2007 Cheltenham Festival, and won neither?' It was back over fences at Aintree where Fair Along, again more patiently ridden than usual, went down by five lengths to Twist Magic, shaping as if he might be worth another try over further than two miles (his smart performance over hurdles at Cheltenham in October came over two miles five furlongs).

		Konigsstuhl	Dschingis Khan
	Alkalde (GER)	(b or br 1976)	Konigskronung
	(b or br 1985)	Astra	Kaiseradler
Fair Along (GER)		(b 1978)	Anekdote
(b.g. 2002)		Acatenango	Surumu
	Fairy Tango (FR)	(ch 1982)	Aggravate
	(ch 1994)	Fairy Bluebird	Be My Guest
		(b 1981)	Fair Filly

Fair Along has changed hands several times in his career. He made €10,000 as a yearling in Germany where his sire Alkalde (a leading miler who died in 2007) and dam Fairy Tango were both successful. Full details of Fair Along's family appeared in last year's Annual, the most notable member being the 1994 Irish Two Thousand Guineas winner Turtle Island, whose grandam was a half-sister to Fair Along's great grandam Fair Filly. Fair Along won a seller at Wolverhampton as a two-year-old (trained by William Jarvis) on New Year's Eve in 2004 and a handicap at Southwell early on as a three-year-old (for Paul Blockley) before being claimed for £6,000 by Welsh permit holder John Flint for whom he won twice over hurdles at Bangor (by a distance and then by twenty-five lengths) before joining his present stable. Sent to the Doncaster Spring Sales at the end of his juvenile campaign, Fair Along failed to meet a reserve of 62,000 guineas. A deal to sell him to go jumping in North America also reportedly fell through in the summer. There is not a lot of substance to Fair Along—he is smallish and rather leggy—which has almost certainly played its part in his somewhat itinerant existence up to now. What he lacks in stature, however, he more than makes up for in enthusiasm for racing. Genuine and reliable, he is a fast and fluent jumper of fences who should continue to pay his way, particularly as he is versatile with regard to the ground (effective on soft and good to firm). He is best known as a front runner but isn't ridden so forcibly nowadays (including when making most at both Sandown and Newbury), while he also performed well with more patient tactics when a good second in the Chester Cup back on the Flat in May. *P. J. Hobbs*

FAIR DUAL (IRE) 6 b.g. Shardari – Cons Dual Sale (IRE) (Tidaro (USA)) [2006/7 F20f⁵ F18m 24m 20v 18s 16v⁴ 25mᵖᵘ c20gᶠ Apr 23] ex-Irish gelding: little sign of ability (including in points), left J. Motherway after fourth start: tried tongue tied/in cheekpieces. *G. Brown*   **c– h– F–**

FAIRFIELD 6 b.m. Alflora (IRE) – April City (Lidhame) [2006/7 F–: 22fᵖᵘ 19d 18v Jan 12] tall mare: no form. *B. Storey*   **h–**

FAIRLIGHT EXPRESS (IRE) 7 ch.g. Carroll House – Marble Fontaine (Lafontaine (USA)) [2006/7 F74: 20g* 22sᵖᵘ 22gᵖᵘ Mar 19] rather leggy gelding: fair maiden on Flat: won novice at Fontwell in September, only form over hurdles: stays 2½m: tongue tied final outing. *B. G. Powell*   **h91**

FAIRLIGHT SHADOW (IRE) 6 b.g. Good Thyne (USA) – Marble Fontaine (Lafontaine (USA)) [2006/7 21m⁴ 22dᵖᵘ Nov 16] half-brother to smart chaser El Vaquero (by Un Desperado), stayed 3m, and winning hurdlers at 2½m/2¾m Alota Baby (by Satco) and Fairlight Express (by Carroll House): dam placed in 2m hurdle: 26 lengths fourth to Paulo Dancer in maiden hurdle at Plumpton on debut: never dangerous but not knocked about next time: should still do better. *D. P. Keane*   **h78 p**

FAIRLY HIGH (IRE) 7 b.m. Sri Pekan (USA) – Ecco Mi (IRE) (Priolo (USA)) [2006/7 h74: 16sᶠ 17s 17d 22g Apr 27] poor 2m hurdler: off 19 months, no form in 2006/7: often wears cheekpieces. *N. G. Ayliffe*   **h–**

FAIR PROSPECT 11 b.g. Sir Harry Lewis (USA) – Fair Sara (McIndoe) [2006/7 c130, h–: c20vᵖᵘ Mar 6] useful-looking gelding: lightly-raced winning hurdler/chaser for   **c– h–**

P. Nicholls, useful form at best over fences: stays 3m: raced mainly on good/good to soft ground: sold 2,000 gns Doncaster March Sales. *Miss Lucinda V. Russell*

FAIR QUESTION (IRE) 9 b.g. Rainbow Quest (USA) – Fair of The Furze (Ela-Mana-Mou) [2006/7 h128: c25v* c20v^F c26v* c33g^F Mar 15] leggy, useful-looking gelding: useful handicap hurdler: similar form when successful both completed starts over fences, in maiden at Hereford (by distance) in November and novice at Plumpton (3 ran, made all to beat Chamoss Royale 11 lengths) in February: disputed lead until fell seventeenth in National Hunt Chase (Amateurs) at Cheltenham: stays 3¼m: has won on firm going, best form on soft/heavy: front runner. *Miss Venetia Williams*   **c132 +** **h–**

FAIR SHAKE (IRE) 7 b.g. Sheikh Albadou – Shamrock Fair (IRE) (Shavian) [2006/7 h88: 16g⁴ 16s⁶ 16g 17s⁴ 16g 16g⁶ Apr 2] sturdy, compact gelding: fair miler on Flat (wears headgear): modest novice hurdler: best at 2m with emphasis on speed: in cheekpieces/visor last 4 starts. *Karen McLintock*   **h95**

FAIR SPIN 7 ch.g. Pivotal – Frankie Fair (IRE) (Red Sunset) [2006/7 h–: 17d⁶ 16d* 17v 19g 16v 16v Jan 13] angular gelding: modest on Flat (stays 2m): fair handicap hurdler on his day: won at Hexham in November: should stay beyond 2m: raced on good going or softer (acts on heavy): wears headgear: not one to rely on. *Micky Hammond*   **h101 §**

FAIR TOUCH (IRE) 8 b.g. Air Display (USA) – Anns Touch (IRE) (Ragapan) [2006/7 h–: 18m 20m Aug 11] failed to complete in 2 Irish points: no form over hurdles: usually tongue tied. *C. P. Morlock*   **h–**

FAIR VIEW (GER) 6 b.m. Dashing Blade – Fairy Tango (FR) (Acatenango (GER)) [2006/7 c–, h–§: 16d 16g Jun 8] ex-German mare: placed over fences: refused on hurdling debut, no solid form in Britain. *Dr P. Pritchard*   **c–** **h– §**

FAIRY VIC (IRE) 6 b.m. Old Vic – Youngandfair (IRE) (Phardante (FR)) [2006/7 22d 22s 22v^{pu} Dec 3] €3,500 4-y-o: third foal: dam lightly-raced hurdler/pointer: little sign of ability. *Frederick John Bowles, Ireland*   **h–**

FAITH AND FORTUNE 5 b.m. Mtoto – Snape (IRE) (Strong Gale) [2006/7 F17g⁵ Apr 23] sixth foal: closely related to winning hurdler/smart chaser up to 25f Another Promise (by Presenting): dam unraced: looked in need of experience when 22¾ lengths fifth to One Rose in mares bumper at Sedgefield on debut. *Ferdy Murphy*   **F72**

FAITH AND REASON (USA) 4 b.g. Sunday Silence (USA) – Sheer Reason (USA) (Danzig (USA)) [2006/7 16v^{pu} 16s⁵ 17v 16v⁶ 17s Mar 11] leggy gelding: fairly useful on Flat (probably stays 11.6f), sold out of Saeed bin Suroor's stable 32,000 gns Newmarket Autumn Sales, and gelded: poor form over hurdles: likely to benefit from less testing conditions: wore cheekpieces final outing. *B. J. Curley*   **h80 +**

FAITHISFLYING 5 ch.g. Wolfhound (USA) – Niggle (Night Shift (USA)) [2006/7 16s 16g 20g Mar 27] modest on all-weather on Flat (stays 1m): left D. Chapman, well held over hurdles. *Mrs Marjorie Fife*   **h–**

FAIT LE JOJO (FR) 10 b.g. Pistolet Bleu (IRE) – Pretty Davis (USA) (Trempolino (USA)) [2006/7 c–, h135: c20d⁶ 16d² 18s³ 17s⁵ c19s⁶ 19s 21g Apr 18] rather leggy gelding: winning chaser (often let down by jumping): useful handicap hurdler: poor efforts last 2 outings: stays 19f: acts on firm and soft going: visored fifth start: ridden by 5-lb claimer: front runner/races prominently. *L. Corcoran*   **c102** **h136**

FAKIMA (IRE) 9 b.g. Commanche Run – El Scarsdale (Furry Glen) [2006/7 h91d: 22d 24f^{pu} 16v 18s Mar 25] good-topped gelding: failed to complete in points: maiden hurdler, modest at best: left J. G. Carr and off over 6 months, inadequate trip last 2 starts: will stay beyond 3m: acts on heavy going: tried in cheekpieces/blinkers. *A. J. Martin, Ireland*   **h86**

FALCHION 12 b.g. Broadsword (USA) – Fastlass (Celtic Cone) [2006/7 c–, h–: 24s^{pu} Nov 29] quite good-topped gelding: winning hurdler/chaser: little show since 2004/5: stays 25f: acts on heavy going: tried blinkered: tongue tied. *J. R. Bewley*   **c–** **h–**

FALCON BENEFICIAL (IRE) 5 br.m. Beneficial – Winnie Wumpkins (IRE) (Roselier) [2006/7 h–, F79: 17v⁵ Jan 2] leggy mare: little form in bumpers/over hurdles: temperament under suspicion. *G. L. Moore*   **h–**

FALCON QUEEN (GER) 6 ch.m. Kornado – Felicienne (FR) (Policeman (FR)) [2006/7 16s^F 16s 16s 16v^{pu} Feb 18] maiden hurdler, poor at best. *Gerard Cully, Ireland*   **h–**

FALCON'S CLICHE 6 b.m. Classic Cliche (IRE) – Guinda (Corvaro (USA)) [2006/7 h87, F–: 24g^{pu} 22d 20s^{pu} 20d^{pu} 20d 16v Feb 27] close-coupled mare: fifth in novice on hurdling debut in 2005/6: no form since: in headgear last 2 starts: has had tongue tied. *P. Beaumont*   **h–**

FALCONS GIFT (IRE) 5 b.m. Zaffaran (USA) – Falcon Crest (FR) (Cadoudal (FR)) **h78 p**
[2006/7 F16v⁴ F16s 17g⁴ Apr 7] rather unfurnished mare: half-sister to several winners, **F81**
including useful French hurdler Seven (by Passing Sale) and fairly useful hurdler around
2m Sobers (by Epervier Bleu): dam, useful juvenile hurdler, sister to high-class French
hurdler Tenerific: 16½ lengths fourth to Evelith Echo at Kempton, better effort in
bumpers: 16 lengths fourth to High Life in mares maiden at Newton Abbot on hurdling
debut: likely to be suited by further than 17f: should improve. *R. H. Alner*

FALCON'S GUNNER 5 ch.m. Gunner B – Broadcast (Broadsword (USA)) [2006/7 **F85**
F16s³ F16d³ Feb 14] 5,200 4-y-o: good-topped mare: chasing type: first foal: dam, poor
and temperamental maiden jumper, out of useful chaser Olympian Princess, herself
half-sister to smart staying chaser Bob Tisdall: modest form when third in bumpers at
Catterick and Musselburgh. *P. Beaumont*

FALCON'S TRIBUTE (IRE) 5 b.m. Beneficial – Early Storm (IRE) (Glacial Storm **h–**
(USA)) [2006/7 F–: 16g 17d 17d 17sᵖᵘ Dec 5] no sign of ability. *P. Beaumont*

FALKENAUGE (GER) 6 ch.g. Platini (GER) – Fleurie (GER) (Dashing Blade) **c–**
[2006/7 24d³ 16s⁴ c16vᵖᵘ Jan 11] lengthy, angular ex-Irish gelding: half-brother to very **h83**
smart hurdler/chaser Foreman (by Monsun), effective at 2m to 21f, and 2m hurdle winner
Fantastic Fleur (by Winged Love): dam German 2-y-o 6f/7f winner: poor maiden hurdler:
left M. Morris, not fluent when pulled up in handicap on chasing debut: stays 3m: raced
on ground softer than good: tried tongue tied. *Jonjo O'Neill*

FALL IN LINE 7 gr.g. Linamix (FR) – Shortfall (Last Tycoon) [2006/7 c27sᵖᵘ Dec 5] **c–**
half-brother to one-time smart chaser around 2m Contraband (by Red Ransom): fairly
useful on Flat (will stay 1¾m), successful 6 times in 2 weeks early in 2004, tailed off only
start in 2005, sold out of Sir Mark Prescott's stable 42,000 gns Newmarket Autumn
(2005) Sales: ran as if amiss in maiden chase on jumps debut. *J. Howard Johnson*

FALLOUT (IRE) 6 b.m. Goldmark (USA) – Tearful Reunion (Pas de Seul) [2006/7 **c–**
c85, h85: c21m³ c21m³ c20g⁴ c21dᵘʳ c25d⁴ Nov 27] lengthy mare: modest hurdler: **h–**
similar form on chasing debut in 2005/6, little show since: probably stays 21f: acts on
heavy going: in cheekpieces last 2 starts. *J. W. Mullins*

FALPIASE (IRE) 5 b.g. Montjeu (IRE) – Gift of The Night (USA) (Slewpy (USA)) **h116 p**
[2006/7 16s³ 20g³ Apr 3] fairly useful form on Flat (stays 1½m), sold out of L. Cumani's
stable 65,000 gns Newmarket Autumn Sales: third both starts over hurdles, beaten around
½ length by Brave Rebellion in conditional jockeys novice at Wetherby over 2½m,
pulling hard long way and narrow lead when blundering last: open to further improvement and well up to winning a race. *J. Howard Johnson*

FAMCRED 4 b.f. Inchinor – Sumingasefa (Danehill (USA)) [2006/7 16d Dec 27] **h–**
lengthy, angular filly: fairly useful on Flat (stays 1m), sold out of L. Cumani's stable
12,000 gns Newmarket Autumn Sales: soundly beaten in keenly-contested juvenile at
Kempton on hurdling debut. *P. M. Phelan*

FAMILY BUSINESS (IRE) 11 ch.g. Over The River (FR) – Morego (Way Up North) **c115**
[2006/7 c29g* Mar 21] lengthy gelding: fairly useful chaser at best: fit from points, won **h–**
hunter at Chepstow by 3½ lengths from Paddy For Paddy, making virtually all: stays 29f:
acts on soft and good to firm going, probably on heavy: wore headgear last 4 starts: has
worn near-side pricker: often let down by jumping. *Mrs Debby Ewing*

FANEUIL HALL (IRE) 5 b.g. Saddlers' Hall (IRE) – Romany Rose (IRE) (Monte- **F–**
limar (USA)) [2006/7 F17s⁴ Feb 26] €40,000 3-y-o: second foal: dam unraced sister
to useful staying chaser Southern Star: well-held fourth of 9 in bumper on debut.
Mrs A. L. M. King

FANMAIL (IRE) 5 b.g. Luso – Ms Mellini (Duky) [2006/7 F17s⁵ Feb 26] €38,000 **F–**
3-y-o: eighth foal: dam unraced half-sister to dam of smart hurdler up to 21f Monsignor:
favourite, well-held fifth of 9 in bumper on debut. *Carl Llewellyn*

FANTASMIC 11 ch.g. Broadsword (USA) – Squeaky Cottage (True Song) [2006/7 **c–**
c102, h–: c16dᵖᵘ Nov 11] good-topped gelding: winning hurdler: fair handicap chaser: **h–**
lame only outing in 2006/7: stays 21f: acts on soft and good to firm going: takes good
hold. *M. J. M. Evans*

FANTASTIC ARTS (FR) 7 b.g. Royal Applause – Magic Arts (IRE) (Fairy King **c– §**
(USA)) [2006/7 c92§, h–§: 16m⁵ 17g* 19s⁵ Dec 7] rather leggy, close-coupled gelding: **h107 §**
fair hurdler: improved form when winning maiden at Hereford in November by 4 lengths
from Cottingham, making all: largely let down by jumping/attitude over fences: best
around 2m with emphasis on speed: inconsistent. *Miss Venetia Williams*

FANTASTIC CHAMPION (IRE) 8 b.g. Entrepreneur – Reine Mathilde (USA) **c70 §**
(Vaguely Noble) [2006/7 c–§, h–§: 26m^{pu} c24s^6 Feb 22] strong, close-coupled gelding: **h– §**
winning hurdler: little form in chases: sold out of J. Cornwall's stable £2,000 Ascot June
Sales after first outing: won twice in points in April: tried blinkered: moody. *S. Flook*

FANTASTISCH (IRE) 4 b.f. Fantastic Light (USA) – Alexandra S (IRE) (Sadler's **h88**
Wells (USA)) [2006/7 17g^3 Mar 25] fairly useful on Flat (best form at 1m) at 3 yrs for
H. Cecil: 13¾ lengths third to Artadi in juvenile maiden at Taunton on hurdling debut.
A. King

FARADAY (IRE) 4 b.g. Montjeu (IRE) – Fureau (GER) (Ferdinand (USA)) [2006/7 **h–**
16v^6 16d 16s Apr 1] maiden on Flat: no form in 3 starts over hurdles. *B. J. Curley*

FARAWAY ECHO 6 gr.m. Second Empire (IRE) – Salalah (Lion Cavern (USA)) **c–**
[2006/7 h71d: 17m^3 16g^3 17s 16v^6 c16s Apr 1] leggy, sparely-made mare: poor hurdler: **h72**
last on chasing debut: form only around 2m: acts on soft and good to firm going: tried
visored. *James Moffatt*

FARD DU MOULIN MAS (FR) 14 b. or br.g. Morespeed – Soiree d'Ex (FR) **c–**
(Kashtan (FR)) [2006/7 c–, h100: 20f^{pu} Jun 21] good-topped gelding: winning chaser: **h–**
fair handicap hurdler: stays 3m: acts on soft and good to firm going. *M. E. D. Francis*

FAREWELL GIFT 6 b.g. Cadeaux Genereux – Daring Ditty (Daring March) [2006/7 **h89 p**
16s^5 Jan 10] strong gelding: fairly useful on Flat (stays 1m, usually blinkered): left
R. Hannon, 13½ lengths fifth of 17 to Le Burf in maiden at Wincanton on hurdling debut,
weakening: likely to do better, especially with less emphasis on stamina. *Carl Llewellyn*

FAR FROM TROUBLE (IRE) 8 b.g. Good Thyne (USA) – Derry Girl (Rarity) **c136**
[2006/7 c130+, h–: c22g* 20s* Feb 7] good sort: lightly raced over hurdles, impressive **h135**
when winning minor event at Down Royal in February by 13 lengths from Powerstation:
also most progressive over fences: useful form when winning 22-runner William Hill
Plate (Handicap) at Galway in August, beating Ansar by 3½ lengths with something in
hand: stayed 33f, effective at much shorter: acted on heavy going (won bumper on good
to firm): among ante-post market leaders for Grand National before having to be put
down after picking up leg infection. *C. Roche, Ireland*

FARINGTON LODGE (IRE) 9 b.g. Simply Great (FR) – Lodge Party (IRE) (Strong **c89 x**
Gale) [2006/7 c98, h78: 20s^3 c26d^5 c24g^3 c24s^2 c24s^F c24v^{su} c24v^{pu} c27v^{pu} c24m^4 c25s^3 **h78**
Apr 1] tall, leggy gelding: maiden hurdler: modest handicap chaser: stays 3¼m: acts on
good to firm and heavy going: sketchy jumper. *J. M. Saville*

FAR LILY (IRE) 6 b.m. Avarice – Amy Just (IRE) (Bustomi) [2006/7 F16v F16m **F–**
Jun 11] fourth foal: sister to fairly useful hurdler Up Above, stays 2½m, and half-sister to
poor chaser up to 3¼m Just Anvil (by Baron Blakeney): dam unraced: soundly beaten in
bumpers/point: has had tongue tied. *J. R. Bewley*

FARLINGTON 10 b.g. Alflora (IRE) – Annapuma (Rakaposhi King) [2006/7 c–: **c–**
c26s^{pu} May 14] tall gelding: one-time fair chaser: well below best since 2004, though
successful in points in March/April: stays 3m: acts on soft going: has been let down by
jumping (including when blinkered). *P. Bowen*

FARMER BRENT (IRE) 7 b. or br.g. Lord Americo – Highland Party (Deep Run) **h78**
[2006/7 F86: F16d 20s^3 24s^5 19v Jan 1] fair form on first of 2 starts in bumpers: poor **F73**
form over hurdles (bled final outing). *C. J. Down*

William Hill Plate (Handicap Chase), Galway—a chance ride for Roger Loughran
as the ill-fated Far From Trouble comes between Ansar (noseband) and a third successive win in the race

FARMER BROWN (IRE) 6 b.g. Bob Back (USA) – Magic Moonbeam (IRE) **h128**
(Decent Fellow) [2006/7 F103: 16s² 16v² 16v² 16v* 16s 16mᶠ 16m³ Apr 25] leggy,
angular gelding: fairly useful hurdler: won handicap at Leopardstown in February by
head from Well Mounted, despite jumping none too fluently: further progress last 2 starts,
4 lengths third to Bobs Pride in 22-runner handicap at Punchestown, left with lot to do
and nearest finish: raced at 2m: acts on heavy and good to firm going: patiently ridden.
Patrick Hughes, Ireland

FARMER'S LAD (IRE) 5 b.g. Leading Counsel (USA) – Lucky Dante (IRE) **h89**
(Phardante (FR)) [2006/7 F16s² F16d³ 19d⁶ 16s⁴ 17s⁵ 21d Mar 22] €17,000 3-y-o: third **F95**
foal: dam bumper winner: placed in bumpers at Uttoxeter and Chepstow: only modest
form over hurdles: should be suited by further than 2m: room for improvement in
jumping. *P. J. Hobbs*

FARMER TOM (IRE) 7 br.g. Lord Americo – Churchtown Mist (Modern Dancer) **h77**
[2006/7 F16d⁶ 20s 24m⁵ Mar 31] poor form in bumpers/over hurdles, off nearly 2 years **F75**
after debut. *M. C. Pipe*

FARNE ISLE 8 ch.m. Midnight Legend – Biloela (Nicholas Bill) [2006/7 h110: 20dᵘʳ **h93**
16m 18g 19g Nov 29] smallish mare: fair handicap hurdler at best, has lost her way: stays
21f: acts on heavy going: wears cheekpieces nowadays: tried tongue tied. *G. A. Harker*

FARSCAPE 6 ch.m. Silver Patriarch (IRE) – Lon Isa (Grey Desire) [2006/7 F18v⁴ **F–**
F16mᵖᵘ Apr 10] unfurnished mare: fourth foal: half-sister to fairly useful sprinter
Matsunosuke (by Magic Ring): dam maiden who stayed 1½m: well beaten on completed
outing in bumpers. *R. A. Harris*

FASHION SHOOT 6 b.m. Double Trigger (IRE) – Paris Fashion (FR) (Northern **h–**
Fashion (USA)) [2006/7 h–, F–: 16d 21vᵖᵘ 21dᵖᵘ Dec 21] of no account: tried tongue tied/
blinkered. *P. Kelsall*

FASSAROE 5 b.g. Kayf Tara – Kosheen (IRE) (Supreme Leader) [2006/7 F17g³ **F101**
Mar 24] 13,000 4-y-o: second foal: dam, placed in bumpers/over hurdles, daughter of
useful hurdler Koshear, stayed 2¾m: encouraging debut when under length third of 15 to
Apache Brave in maiden bumper at Bangor, impeded by winner final 1f: sold £32,000
Cheltenham April Sales. *O. Sherwood*

FASTAFFARAN (IRE) 6 b.g. Zaffaran (USA) – Break Fast (Prince Tenderfoot **h129**
(USA)) [2006/7 h94: 20dᵖᵘ 24s² 24v² 25s² 24gᵖᵘ Apr 14] big gelding: fairly useful
maiden hurdler: in cheekpieces, much improved when head second to Chief Dan George
in Grade 2 novice at Wetherby fourth outing: left I. McMath, disappointing in listed
handicap at Aintree (tongue tied) over 2 months later, ridden more prominently: stays
25f: raced on good going or softer: has hung left under pressure. *Miss Lucinda V. Russell*

FAST AND FIERY (IRE) 7 ch.m. Zaffaran (USA) – Shawiba (IRE) (Rainbows For **h–**
Life (CAN)) [2006/7 h79: 16m 16f 20f Jul 7] angular mare: maiden hurdler: well beaten
on completed outing in Irish points: best efforts around 2m: acts on soft going: tried
tongue tied/in cheekpieces. *I. A. Duncan, Ireland*

FAST FORWARD (NZ) 7 gr.g. Grosvenor (NZ) – Abachi (NZ) (Three Legs) [2006/7 **c128**
h110, F110: 22s⁵ c19d* c24v* c20v² c24s² c24s⁴ Apr 25] compact gelding: fair form over **h85 +**
hurdles: better over fences: won handicap at Ascot (despite mistakes) in December and
3-finisher novice at Chepstow (idled) in February: ran well when ¾-length second to
Nenuphar Collonges in handicap at Uttoxeter fifth outing: stays 3m: raced on ground
softer than good. *Miss Venetia Williams*

FAST MIX (FR) 8 gr.g. Linamix (FR) – Fascinating Hill (FR) (Danehill (USA)) **h– §**
[2006/7 21g 21g Apr 7] angular gelding: fairly useful hurdler at one time: off almost 2
years, well beaten both starts in 2006/7, including in seller: stays 19f: probably acts on
any going: usually wears visor/cheekpieces: sketchy jumper: unreliable. *D. E. Pipe*

FATHER JIM 12 b.g. Seymour Hicks (FR) – Deaconess (The Parson) [2006/7 c84, **c91**
h–: c21g⁶ c21g³ c25mᵖᵘ c23m Jul 12] fair pointer/maiden hunter chaser: stays 21f: tried **h–**
blinkered. *J. A. T. de Giles*

FATHER MANSFIELD (IRE) 13 b.g. Phardante (FR) – Lena's Reign (Quayside) **c–**
[2006/7 c33g⁶ c29gᵖᵘ Mar 21] rangy gelding: fair pointer, won in February: little form in **h–**
hunter chases. *Mrs S. Prouse*

FATHER PAT 4 br.g. Chaddleworth (IRE) – Lady Crusty (Golden Dipper) [2006/7 **F–**
F12g Mar 23] leggy gelding: half-brother to modest hurdler Mike Simmons (by Ballacashtal), stays 21f: dam selling hurdler who stayed 25f: soundly beaten in bumper on
debut. *L. P. Grassick*

FATHER REID (IRE) 7 b.g. Carroll House – Macamore Rose (Torus) [2006/7 16s^{pu} **c–**
Jan 24] lengthy gelding: won maiden Irish point in 2005: no form in 2 starts over hurdles/ **h–**
maiden chase. *O. Sherwood*

FATHER TOM (IRE) 13 b.g. Mazaad – Pride's Imp (Imperius) [2006/7 c20m^{2d} **c74**
c23m^3 c16f^4 c23f^6 c24g^4 Oct 19] ex-Irish gelding: maiden hurdler/chaser: fairly useful **h–**
pointer: successful 12 times in Britain, including on 4 occasions in 2006: stays 3m: acts
on heavy and good to firm going: tried blinkered/tongue tied. *M. Sheppard*

FAUCON BLEU (FR) 4 gr.g. Cadoudal (FR) – Label Bleu (FR) (Pistolet Bleu (IRE)) **h115**
[2006/7 16s* 16g^3 Nov 19] tall, good-topped gelding: first foal: dam lightly-raced
maiden: fairly useful juvenile hurdler: placed twice at Enghien for P. Peltier: off 6 months,
justified favouritism at Uttoxeter in October on British debut, beating Risk Runner 8
lengths with plenty to spare: better form when 12½ lengths third of 5 to Degas Art at
Aintree, mistake 2 out and eased final 75 yds. *Miss H. C. Knight*

FAYRZ PLEASE (IRE) 6 ch.g. Fayruz – Castlelue (IRE) (Tremblant) [2006/7 16m^{pu} **h–**
May 10] no longer of much account on Flat: no show in selling hurdle. *M. C. Chapman*

FEANOR 9 b.m. Presidium – Nouvelle Cuisine (Yawa) [2006/7 c–, h100: 16g 16m^3 **c–**
16s^{pu} 16g^4 16d 16m^4 17v 16d c20s c16g^5 c16g^5 16g Apr 23] leggy mare: little form over **h90 d**
fences: one-time fair handicap hurdler, on downgrade: best around 2m: acts on soft and
good to firm going: tongue tied: held up. *Mrs S. A. Watt*

FEARLESS FOURSOME 8 b.g. Perpendicular – Harrietfield (Nicholas Bill) **c106**
[2006/7 c–, h94: 16v^2 c16d c25g^{pu} c22s^6 c17v* c21v* c16v* c20v* c17v^2 Jan 12] modest **h92**
maiden hurdler: progressed into fair chaser: won handicaps at Kelso, Ayr (2) and
Wetherby, all in December, all bar one a novice event: effective at 2m and should have
stayed 3m: raced on good ground or softer (acted well on heavy): usually tongue tied:
dead. *N. W. Alexander*

FEARLESS MEL (IRE) 13 b.g. Mandalus – Milan Pride (Northern Guest (USA)) **c89 §**
[2006/7 c104§: c23s^6 Dec 29] lengthy gelding: fair handicap chaser: left Heather Dalton,
well held only outing in 2006/7: stays 3m: acts on good to firm and good to soft going:
effective in cheekpieces or without: tried tongue tied (fell both times): unreliable. *Miss
Joanne Priest*

FEARMORE 4 b.g. Fasliyev (USA) – Flower O'Cannie (IRE) (Mujadil (USA)) **F79**
[2006/7 F14s^4 F16v^3 Jan 28] big gelding: second foal: dam, fairly useful 6f (at 2 yrs) to
1½m winner, sister to useful hurdler up to 3¼m Barba Papa: modest form in frame in
bumpers. *M. W. Easterby*

FEARNOUGHT 5 b.g. Kayf Tara – Cavina (Ardross) [2006/7 F16m 16d Dec 29] **h–**
useful-looking gelding: third foal: half-brother to fairly useful hurdler Tomina (by **F77**
Deploy), stayed 3¼m, and fair hurdler Marjina (by Classic Cliche), stays 3m: dam, fair
2¾m hurdler, half-sister to dam of top-class staying chaser Bacchanal: eighth of 9 in
bumper at Ascot, not knocked about once outpaced: jumped poorly on hurdling debut.
Miss E. C. Lavelle

FEAR SIUIL (IRE) 14 b.g. Strong Gale – Astral River (Over The River (FR)) [2006/7 **c78**
c95d, h–: c25f^5 c23v^3 c21g^5 c21s^4 c23m^{pu} Jul 12] lengthy gelding: veteran chaser: left **h–**
Michael Blake after second outing: stays 3m: acts on good to firm and good to soft going,
probably on firm: tongue tied. *C. J. Gray*

FEEL THE PRIDE (IRE) 9 b.m. Persian Bold – Nordic Pride (Horage) [2006/7 **c121**
c126, h–: c17v^4 c17m^5 Jun 11] leggy mare: fairly useful hurdler/chaser: raced mainly **h–**
around 2m: acts on firm and good to soft going, below best on softer: effective blinkered
or not: possibly best on left-handed tracks. *Jonjo O'Neill*

FELINIOUS 4 b.f. Kayf Tara – Lucia Forte (Neltino) [2006/7 F12s^4 F17g^2 Apr 27] **F96**
€95,000 3-y-o: rather unfurnished filly: fourth foal: dam, useful hurdler who stayed 3m,
sister to top-class staying chaser Teeton Mill: better effort in bumpers when ¾-length
second to Covert Mission at Newton Abbot, finishing strongly. *Jonjo O'Neill*

FELIX REX (GER) 7 ch.g. Tempeltanz (GER) – Figlia d'Oro (GER) (Luigi (GER)) **h–**
[2006/7 h102: 16g Mar 28] tall, leggy gelding: lightly-raced novice hurdler, fair form at
best: probably stays 21f. *J. Pearce*

FELLOW SHIP 7 b.g. Elmaamul (USA) – Genoa (Zafonic (USA)) [2006/7 17v^4 19d^{pu} **h–**
16m^{pu} Apr 8] leggy gelding: poor and ungenuine on Flat nowadays: no form over hurdles:
tried in headgear: usually tongue tied. *P. Butler*

FEMME D'AVRIL (FR) 5 b.m. Homme de Loi (IRE) – Free Demo (FR) (Hero's **c88**
Honor (USA)) [2006/7 h–: 16d^4 16g* c16v^2 c16s* c20v^4 c16g^5 c20m^3 Apr 8] lengthy **h75**
mare: poor hurdler: won novice handicap at Wincanton in December: better over fences,

winning handicap at Hereford in February: possibly best around 2m: acts on heavy going. *D. E. Pipe*

FENCOTE GOLD 7 ch.g. Bob's Return (IRE) – Goldaw (Gala Performance) [2006/7 h77: c16s Apr 27] good-topped gelding: well held in novice hurdles/chase, latter after 17-month absence: bred to be suited by test of stamina. *P. Beaumont*   c–
h–

FENCOTE MYSTERY 5 b.g. Classic Cliche (IRE) – Soupinette (FR) (Noblequest (FR)) [2006/7 F16s F16d 16s Apr 27] 26,000 4-y-o: first foal: dam useful hurdler/chaser at around 2m in France: well held in bumpers/maiden hurdle. *P. Beaumont*   h–
F–

FENIX (GER) 8 b.g. Lavirco (GER) – Frille (FR) (Shareef Dancer (USA)) [2006/7 h127: 16g⁶ 18s* 16s 20s² Dec 23] good-topped gelding: useful handicap hurdler: won at Fontwell in November by 7 lengths from Gods Token: stays 2¾m: raced on good ground or softer (acts on soft): blinkered/visored: reliable. *Mrs L. Wadham*   h130

FENNY LANE 6 b.g. Safawan – Alipampa (IRE) (Glenstal (USA)) [2006/7 F16s⁶ F14s Feb 18] 3,600 3-y-o: leggy, rather unfurnished gelding: half-brother to useful hurdler/chaser Olney Lad (by Democratic), stayed 25f, and fair 2m hurdler Petuntse (by Phountzi): dam unraced: little sign of ability in point/bumpers. *Mrs F. Kehoe*   F–

FERIMON 8 br.g. Terimon – Rhyming Moppet (Rymer) [2006/7 c97p, h–: c23d c24d² c24s* c24v⁶ c24sᵖᵘ Jan 13] sturdy, good sort: winning hurdler: improved effort (fair form) over fences when winning novice handicap at Huntingdon in December, making all: disappointing both starts after: should stay beyond 3m: raced on going softer than good: none too consistent. *H. D. Daly*   c113
h–

FERMAT (FR) 5 gr.g. Great Palm (USA) – Five Rivers (FR) (Cadoudal (FR)) [2006/7 F16s³ F17v² F16s 16g⁶ Mar 29] 40,000 3-y-o: good-topped gelding: second foal: dam, placed over hurdles around 2m, sister to very smart French staying hurdler Gilder: fair form when placed in bumpers: around 15 lengths sixth to Inherent in novice at Towcester on hurdling debut: tongue tied: likely to improve. *P. R. Webber*   h88 p
F95

FERRANDO 5 b.g. Hernando (FR) – Oh So Misty (Teenoso (USA)) [2006/7 16s² 20g² 20v⁵ Mar 2] fair maiden on Flat (stays 1¼m): best effort over hurdles (fair form) when 9 lengths second to easy winner Key Time in 2½m novice at Musselburgh: stamina stretched under more testing conditions next time. *G. A. Swinbank*   h104

FESTIVAL FLYER 12 b.g. Alhijaz – Odilese (Mummy's Pet) [2006/7 h95: 22s 24s⁵ 22s⁵ 22gᵖᵘ Apr 27] compact gelding: modest handicap hurdler: well below form in 2006/7: probably stays 3¼m: acts on soft going. *Miss M. Bragg*   h79

FESTIVAL KING (IRE) 5 br.g. King's Theatre (IRE) – Mary Linda (Grand Lodge (USA)) [2006/7 F16g F16g⁶ 16v³ 16v⁶ 19g 22gᵖᵘ Apr 2] 27,000 3-y-o: close-coupled gelding: second foal: half-brother to useful French winner around 7f Indian Beauty (by Mujadil): dam 1¼m winner in France: poor form in bumpers/over hurdles. *L. Lungo*   h79
F76

FESTIVE CHIMES (IRE) 6 b.m. Efisio – Delightful Chime (IRE) (Alzao (USA)) [2006/7 h111: 16g* 16g 16d³ 19d⁶ 16g* 16g² 16mᵘʳ Apr 20] small mare: fairly useful handicap hurdler: improved further in 2006/7, winning at Huntingdon in October and Fakenham (by 1¼ lengths from Diego Cao) in March: good fourth to Adopted Hero at Haydock: best efforts around 2m: acts on soft and good to firm going: tough and reliable. *N. B. King*   h122

FIBRE OPTICS (IRE) 7 b.g. Presenting – Hooch (Warpath) [2006/7 h83+: c16m⁶ c21g⁴ c20m c24gᶠ c25m* c25d³ c24mᵖᵘ Sep 8] bumper winner: poor form over hurdles: modest chaser: won handicap at Market Rasen in August: stays 25f: acts on good to firm and good to soft going: effective with or without cheekpieces: sold 20,000 gns Doncaster October Sales. *Jonjo O'Neill*   c86
h–

FIDDLE 4 gr.f. Silver Patriarch (IRE) – Swindle (Sir Harry Lewis (USA)) [2006/7 F12s⁵ F16v³ F16s* Mar 11] good-topped filly: first foal: dam, bumper/19f hurdle winner, half-sister to useful hurdler/staying chaser Heist, herself out of half-sister to Stayers' Hurdle winner Rustle: fair form in bumpers, won mares event at Warwick by ¾ length from Izita Star. *R. Waley-Cohen*   F87

FIDDLERS CREEK (IRE) 8 b.g. Danehill (USA) – Mythical Creek (USA) (Pleasant Tap (USA)) [2006/7 h81: 16s 16g* 16m⁶ 16f⁴ 16g 18m c16g 16g 17m Apr 9] sturdy gelding: modest hurdler: won novice handicap at Kelso in May: largely well below form after (last on chasing debut): raced around 2m: acts on firm and soft going: often wears headgear/tongue tied: unreliable. *R. Allan*   c– §
h85 §

FIDDLING AGAIN 4 b.f. Hernando (FR) – Fiddling The Facts (IRE) (Orchestra) [2006/7 F12s* F16s* F16g F17gᵖᵘ Apr 13] leggy, close-coupled filly: second foal: F109 half-sister to fairly useful hurdler Classic Fiddle (by Classic Cliche), stays 2½m: dam, fairly useful hurdler/smart chaser, stayed 29f: won bumpers at Newbury (3-y-o event) in December and Fakenham (beat Swaythe by 3 lengths) in February: disappointing when upped in class, already off bridle when hampered over 5f out at Aintree final outing. *N. J. Henderson*

FIELDINGS SOCIETY (IRE) 8 ch.g. Moscow Society (USA) – Lone Trail (IRE) (Strong Gale) [2006/7 h–: 26g^{pu} 26d^2 24s^2 27m^5 Jun 11] workmanlike gelding: modest form over hurdles, left Jennie Candlish after second outing: stays 27f: acts on soft and good to firm going: best form in headgear: sold £1,500 Ascot November Sales. *Mrs A. M. Thorpe*   **h86**

FIELD MASTER (IRE) 10 ch.g. Foxhound (USA) – Bold Avril (IRE) (Persian Bold) [2006/7 h77: 20s^{pu} 20f^3 Jul 19] medium-sized gelding: poor handicap hurdler: stays 3m: acts on firm and soft going: sold £1,600 Ascot August Sales, unplaced in points in 2007. *C. J. Gray*   **h71**

FIELD OF BLUE 8 b.g. Shambo – Flashing Silks (Kind of Hush) [2006/7 16d Nov 21] leggy gelding: little sign of ability: tried visored/tongue tied. *Jim Best*   **c–**   **h–**

FIELD ROLLER 7 ch.g. High Roller (IRE) – Cathedral Road (Hardboy) [2006/7 c99, h–: c16s^4 c17g c20m* c20f^2 c20g^2 Aug 1] winning hurdler: modest chaser: won novice at Hexham in June: stays 2½m: acts on soft and firm going. *P. Monteith*   **c99**   **h–**

FIELDSOFCLOVER (IRE) 10 b.g. Montelimar (USA) – Power Point (Pollerton) [2006/7 c88, h90: c19g^2 c19m* c20m^2 c21g^{pu} 21f^2 18g c20m* Apr 25] rather leggy gelding: modest hurdler: fair handicap chaser: won at Hereford in June and Worcester in April, improved form when beating Presenting Alf comfortably by 14 lengths at latter on return from 7-month absence: barely stays 3m: acts on firm ground: visored sixth outing (shaped as if amiss): has had tongue tied, including last 6 starts. *Miss E. C. Lavelle*   **c110**   **h92**

FIER NORMAND (FR) 8 b.g. Cyborg (FR) – Moomaw (Akarad (FR)) [2006/7 h115: c20g* Oct 19] angular gelding: fairly useful hurdler: 5/4-on and upped in trip, won 6-runner maiden at Ludlow on chasing debut by length from Keepthedreamalive, jumping soundly and leading close home: stays 2½m: raced on good going or softer: presumably met with setback, but remains open to improvement over fences. *Jonjo O'Neill*   **c109 p**   **h–**

FIERY DIPPER 8 b.g. Rock Hopper – Blazing Pearl (Blazing Saddles (AUS)) [2006/7 16m Apr 25] maiden pointer: tailed off on hurdling debut. *S. J. Gilmore*   **h–**

FIESTY FROSTY (IRE) 9 b.m. Glacial Storm (USA) – Smashed Free (IRE) (Carlingford Castle) [2006/7 c23d^{pu} May 17] fair pointer: successful 5 times, including on 4 occasions in 2006: no show in hunter chase. *Mrs Marilyn Scudamore*   **c–**

FIESTY MADAM 6 ch.m. Bien Bien (USA) – Riverine (Risk Me (FR)) [2006/7 20v^F Feb 15] workmanlike mare: no sign of ability. *M. S. Sweetland*   **h–**

FIFTH COLUMN (USA) 6 b.g. Allied Forces (USA) – Miff (USA) (Beau Genius (CAN)) [2006/7 c–: 17f^3 21m^6 c21v^3 c21g^{ur} c20g Mar 27] twice-raced over hurdles (for Miss Tracy Waggott): modest form in hunter chases: won point in April. *M. V. Coglan*   **c77**   **h–**

FIGARO DU ROCHER (FR) 7 ch.g. Beyssac (FR) – Fabinou (FR) (Cavan) [2006/7 c126, h108: c16f^4 c16d* 16g^2 19g* 16d c19d^6 c16g c16g Apr 19] smallish gelding: fairly useful handicap chaser: back to best when winning at Carlisle in October by 9 lengths from Gone Too Far: fair handicap hurdler: made all in amateur event at Taunton in November: best up to 19f: acts on any going: formerly visored: tongue tied: usually front runner/races prominently. *D. E. Pipe*   **c125**   **h111 +**

FIGHTER PILOT 8 ch.g. Alflora (IRE) – Gunna Be Precious (Gunner B) [2006/7 c–, h–: 20m^5 May 5] ex-Irish gelding: fair hurdler at best, little show in 2 starts in Britain: better effort in maiden chases when third at Down Royal: stays 21f: acts on heavy ground. *Jim Best*   **c–**   **h–**

FIGHTING CHANCE (IRE) 7 b.g. Germany (USA) – Una Juna (IRE) (Good Thyne (USA)) [2006/7 20s^{pu} Dec 2] rangy gelding: trained by R. Alner, third in bumper at Newbury on debut in 2004: successful both completed starts in points following year: ran as if amiss on hurdling debut. *P. J. Hobbs*   **h–**

FIGHT THE FEELING 9 ch.g. Beveled (USA) – Alvecote Lady (Touching Wood (USA)) [2006/7 c82, h85: c21g^3 24d c20f^4 c19m^6 c21g^5 c20s* c20d^5 c20v^3 c24g c24m^{pu} c24g^5 c20m 24m^5 Apr 25] medium-sized gelding: maiden hurdler: poor chaser: won strongly-run novice handicap at Ludlow in December: stays 3m: acts on any going: tried visored/blinkered (fell). *J. W. Unett*   **c85**   **h–**

FILEY BUOY 5 b.g. Factual (USA) – Tugra (FR) (Baby Turk) [2006/7 16d^{pu} 17m^{pu} Apr 28] dam winning pointer: poor on Flat (best efforts at 7f/1m): no show both starts over hurdles. *R. M. Whitaker*   **h–**

FILEY FLYER 7 ch.m. Weldnaas (USA) – Chasers' Bar (Oats) [2006/7 h86, F–: 16g³ **c88**
16g 17d³ 16g⁴ c16d³ c16sᶠ c16s³ c16gᵖᵘ c16g Apr 7] big, close-coupled mare: poor maid- **h84**
en hurdler: modest maiden chaser: should stay beyond 2m: acts on soft going. *J. R. Turner*

FILLIEMOU (IRE) 6 gr.m. Goldmark (USA) – St Louis Lady (Absalom) [2006/7 16g **h–**
Oct 7] half-sister to 2m chase winner Twentytwosilver (by Emarati): maiden on Flat: well
beaten in novice on hurdling debut. *A. W. Carroll*

FILL THE BUNKER (IRE) 7 b.g. Detroit Sam (FR) – Midland Queen (Midland **c108**
Gayle) [2006/7 h–: c22v* c22s² c24gᶠ c24dᵘʳ c22v³ c24d³ c24m² c24s² c23dᶠ Mar 26] **h–**
well beaten over hurdles: fair novice chaser: won handicap at Market Rasen in October:
fell fatally 2 out at Stratford: stayed 3m: unraced on firm ground, acted on any other:
raced prominently. *N. A. Twiston-Davies*

FILLYOFTHEVALLEY 4 b.f. Wizard King – Slipmatic (Pragmatic) [2006/7 F16g **F–**
Mar 24] workmanlike filly: third foal: half-sister to bumper winners Lady Bling Bling
(by Midnight Legend) and Stripe Me Blue (by Miner's Lamp): dam, fair hurdler, stayed
2¾m: well held in bumper at Newbury on debut. *P. J. Jones*

FILLY SO FICKLE 5 b.m. Kayf Tara – Mavourneen (IRE) (Strong Gale) [2006/7 **F–**
F16m Apr 24] first foal: dam poor maiden hurdler: green, well held in bumper on debut.
J. L. Spearing

FINAL BID (IRE) 4 b.g. Mujadil (USA) – Dusky Virgin (Missed Flight) [2006/7 16d* **h112 +**
16d³ 16s* 19gᶠ Mar 24] leggy gelding: modest maiden on Flat (probably stays 1½m):
progressive over hurdles, winning juvenile seller at Ludlow in December and 20-runner
handicap at Huntingdon (beating Diarius by 2½ lengths) in February: raced mainly at 2m.
M. G. Quinlan

FINALLY SORTED 10 b.g. Sure Blade (USA) – Romantic Run (Deep Run) [2006/7 **c–**
c21gᵖᵘ Apr 27] of no account in points and temperamental to boot. *Ms Sarah Townrow*

FINAL OVER 7 br.m. Overbury (IRE) – Final Pride (Push On) [2006/7 h–, F–: 21dᵖᵘ **c–**
17s c20s⁶ Mar 1] no sign of ability. *W. K. Goldsworthy* **h–**

FINAL PROMISE 5 b.g. Lujain (USA) – Unerring (Unfuwain (USA)) [2006/7 16s **h80**
16gᶠ 16d 17g⁶ Apr 27] tall, close-coupled gelding: half-brother to 2¼m hurdle winner
Kick And Prance (by Groom Dancer): fair 1m winner at 3 yrs, well held on Flat in 2006:
poor form over hurdles: has had tongue tied. *J. A. Geake*

FINAL VETO 4 ch.g. Vettori (IRE) – Robin Lane (Tenby) [2006/7 F14g⁴ F14v² F12v⁶ **F97**
F16g Mar 17] sturdy gelding: third foal: half-brother to fair 2m hurdle winner Hearthstead Dream (by Dr Fong): dam 9f to 1½m winner: fairly useful form when in frame in
bumpers, disappointing last 2 outings. *T. P. Tate*

FINANCIAL REWARD (IRE) 4 b.c. Fruits of Love (USA) – Lamp of Phoebus **h129**
(USA) (Sunshine Forever (USA)) [2006/7 16s* 16s² 16s⁴ 16s* 16v² 16v³ 17g 16m² 16m²
Apr 26] tall colt: fairly useful up to 1½m on Flat: useful juvenile hurdler: won at Limerick
(maiden) in November and Thurles in January: ran best races when second to Punjabi
in Champion Four Year Old Hurdle at Punchestown in late-April and stable-companion
J'Y Vole in Group 3 at Auteuil after end of British season: stays 19f: acts on good to firm
and heavy ground: tried in cheekpieces (eighth in Triumph): effective tongue tied or not.
W. P. Mullins, Ireland

FINBAR'S LAW 10 b.g. Contract Law (USA) – De Valera (Faustus (USA)) [2006/7 **c– x**
16v⁵ 16d 16v c16vᵖᵘ c20sᵖᵘ Apr 27] winning hurdler: off over 2 years, no form in 2006/7: **h–**
has failed to complete over fences: stays at least 2½m: acts on good to soft going,
probably on good to firm: tried in cheekpieces: tongue tied. *R. Johnson*

FINBAR'S PI (IRE) 5 b.g. Moscow Society (USA) – Blue Rinse (Bluerullah) [2006/7 **F86**
F18m⁴ Apr 26] 15,000 4-y-o: half-brother to smart staying chaser Blue Charm (by Duky):
dam poor maiden Irish jumper: needed experience when 25½ lengths fourth of 9 to Hills
of Home in bumper at Fontwell on debut, off bridle in rear from early stage. *B. G. Powell*

FIN BEC (FR) 14 b.g. Tip Moss (FR) – Tourbrune (FR) (Pamponi (FR)) [2006/7 c106x, **c– x**
h–: c25m⁴ Apr 15] strong, lengthy gelding: fair chaser: probably needed race in hunter **h–**
only outing in 2006/7: stays 3½m: acts on any going: tried in cheekpieces, usually
blinkered: front runner: often let down by jumping. *R. Curtis*

FIND IT OUT (USA) 4 b.g. Luhuk (USA) – Ursula (VEN) (Phone Trick (USA)) **h67**
[2006/7 17d 16d 16s³ 21g 16v³ 16g⁴ Mar 26] disappointing maiden on Flat, sold out
of T. D. Barron's stable 4,000 gns Doncaster October Sales: poor form over hurdles:
raced mainly around 2m: acts on heavy going: in cheekpieces/blinkers last 4 outings.
B. J. Llewellyn

FIND ME ANOTHER (IRE) 11 b.g. Shardari – Naujwan Too (Kafu) [2006/7 c104: c24m⁵ May 16] fairly useful pointer/hunter chaser, gained eleventh win in points in 2007: stays 3m: acts on good to firm and good to soft going. *Mrs Caroline Bailey* — **c93**

FIND THE KING (IRE) 9 b.g. King's Theatre (IRE) – Undiscovered (Tap On Wood) [2006/7 16m⁴ 24g 22d⁶ 22g⁵ 22g Apr 7] good-topped ex-Irish gelding: one-time fairly useful hurdler/chaser, off 2 years after final outing in 2003/4: fair form over hurdles in 2006/7, left E. O'Grady after third start: stays 2¾m: acts on soft and firm going: tried blinkered: usually tongue tied: has been led in (started slowly final outing). *D. W. P. Arbuthnot* — **c–**, **h108**

FIND THE WAY (IRE) 9 br.g. Arctic Lord – Cash Chase (IRE) (Sexton Blake) [2006/7 20v 22v 23v c20g⁴ c16f⁵ c20m Apr 15] ex-Irish gelding: maiden hurdler: placed in points, no form in chases: sold out of Mrs Denise Foster's stable €4,000 Fairyhouse February Sales after third outing: stays 2½m: acts on heavy ground: has had tongue tied. *Miss J. E. Foster* — **c–**, **h–**

FINE BY ME (IRE) 8 b.g. Accordion – Girseach (Furry Glen) [2006/7 20s* 24g³ 20s⁴ 24s³ c20s⁵ 20v⁴ 24g* 24s⁴ Apr 25] ex-Irish gelding: fair hurdler: won novice handicaps at Bangor (first start after leaving C. Roche) in May and Taunton in March: never dangerous on chasing debut: stays 3m: acts on soft going: wore cheekpieces last 2 starts. *J. S. Smith* — **c70**, **h107**

FINE DEED 6 b.g. Kadeed (IRE) – Kristis Girl (Ballacashtal (CAN)) [2006/7 F17d F17m 16m Apr 25] second foal: half-brother to 9.4f/11f winner Heathers Girl (by Superlative): dam 5f (including at 2 yrs) and 1m winner: well beaten in bumpers/novice hurdle. *Ian Williams* — **h–**, **F–**

FINE EDGE 6 ch.m. Keen – Cap That (Derek H) [2006/7 F70: F18g May 14] poor form in bumpers. *H. E. Haynes* — **F67**

FINEST OF MEN 11 b.g. Tina's Pet – Merry Missus (Bargello) [2006/7 c82: c25f* c25g c25sᵖᵘ c20m⁴ c22m³ c25d⁴ c24g⁴ Apr 7] poor chaser: won 4-runner hunter at Kelso in May: stays 25f: acts on firm ground: tried in cheekpieces. *J. B. Walton* — **c81**

FINGERMOUSE 5 ch.m. Peter Quince – Universal Didgit (Cosmonaut) [2006/7 F17v F16gᵖᵘ Nov 29] smallish mare: first foal: dam unraced: no show in bumpers. *M. E. Sowersby* — **F–**

FINGER ONTHE PULSE (IRE) 6 b.g. Accordion – Quinnsboro Ice (IRE) (Glacial Storm (USA)) [2006/7 h123: 20d* 20s* 21s 21gᵘʳ 20mᶠ Apr 9] angular gelding: useful hurdler: improved efforts when winning handicaps at Naas in October, beating Pacolet a length in 19-runner event on second occasion: failed to complete at Cheltenham (stumbled and unseated early) and Fairyhouse (running well in listed race won by Essex when falling 2 out) last 2 starts: should stay beyond 2½m: unraced on firm going, acts on any other. *T. J. Taaffe, Ireland* — **h135**

FINGERSTHUMBSNGUMS (IRE) 6 br.g. Oscar (IRE) – Smart Fashion (Carlburg) [2006/7 F–: 16vᵖᵘ 26sᵖᵘ 19s 24m⁵ 20gᶠ Apr 16] angular gelding: poor form over hurdles: blinkered last 3 outings. *C. C. Bealby* — **h70**

FINIANS IVY (IRE) 12 b.g. Orchestra – Rambling Ivy (Mandalus) [2006/7 c20d 20mᵖᵘ Aug 4] deep-girthed gelding: fairly useful chaser/fair hurdler at best: stayed 25f: acted on heavy going: tongue tied: dead. *A. J. Martin, Ireland* — **c–**, **h–**

FINNEGANS RAINBOW 5 ch.g. Spectrum (IRE) – Fairy Story (IRE) (Persian Bold) [2006/7 h82?: 17dᵖᵘ 17d⁵ 17d³ 17g⁶ 17m 17m³ 19s 22m⁶ 20g³ 17g 17s⁶ 16v 16s⁴ 19d⁴ 17dᶠ Mar 19] workmanlike gelding: maiden on Flat: likewise over hurdles: best efforts around 2m: acts on soft and good to firm going. *M. C. Chapman* — **h90 d**

FINTAN 4 ch.g. Generous (IRE) – Seeker (Rainbow Quest (USA)) [2006/7 F14g* F12v aF16g³ Mar 9] tall, lengthy, good-topped gelding: second foal: dam, 1½m winner, out of half-sister to Kris and Diesis: 40/1, showed good attitude to win 3-y-o bumper at Huntingdon on debut in November by head from Helens Vision: better effort after when equal-third to Cry Alot Boy at Lingfield, hampered start. *Mrs A. L. M. King* — **F99**

FINZI (IRE) 9 b.g. Zaffaran (USA) – Sporting Talent (IRE) (Seymour Hicks (FR)) [2006/7 c98, h73: c26sᵘʳ c25vᵖᵘ c26g⁴ c29s⁴ 26g⁵ c26v³ c26v² c26v* c29g⁴ 24m Apr 25] good-topped gelding: maiden hurdler: modest handicap chaser: won at Chepstow in March: thorough stayer: acts on heavy and good to firm going: tongue tied final outing: usually races prominently: tough. *M. Scudamore* — **c97**, **h–**

FIORI 11 b.g. Anshan – Fen Princess (IRE) (Trojan Fen) [2006/7 c111, h–: 16m⁴ 24g Sep 6] close-coupled gelding: impresses in appearance: fair handicap chaser: winning — **c–**, **h–**

hurdler, little form last 3 starts: successful both outings in points in 2007: stays 21f: acts on good to firm and heavy going: tried in cheekpieces: usually races prominently/jumps soundly. *P. C. Haslam*

FIREAWAY 13 b.g. Infantry – Handymouse (Nearly A Hand) [2006/7 c96, h–: c21g⁵ c20m Apr 15] lengthy gelding: winning hurdler: modest chaser: off 14 months, last both starts in 2006/7: stays 3m: acts on firm and soft going: has hung/jumped left under pressure. *O. Brennan*　　**c–**　**h–**

FIRE DRAGON (IRE) 6 b.g. Sadler's Wells (USA) – Cattermole (USA) (Roberto (USA)) [2006/7 h157: 19d⁶ 25d 24vᵖᵘ 24g 24gᵖᵘ Apr 12] close-coupled, useful-looking gelding: has reportedly had breathing operation: very smart hurdler at best: badly out of sorts in 2006/7: stays 3m: acts on good to firm and good to soft going: usually blinkered: tried tongue tied: has sweated/got on edge: temperament under suspicion. *Jonjo O'Neill*　　**h–**

FIRE RANGER 11 ch.m. Presidium – Regal Flame (Royalty) [2006/7 h102: 19d² 22g² 19d Oct 17] fair hurdler at best, runner-up in sellers first 2 starts after 10-month absence: stays 2¾m: acts on soft and firm going. *J. D. Frost*　　**h96**

FIRESIDE LEGEND (IRE) 8 b.g. College Chapel – Miss Sandman (Manacle) [2006/7 h–§: 21g 22vᵖᵘ 18vᵘʳ Mar 7] leggy gelding: poor winning hurdler: no form since 2004/5: usually wears headgear: has had tongue tied: temperamental. *Miss M. P. Bryant*　　**h– §**

FIRION KING (IRE) 7 b.g. Earl of Barking (IRE) – Miss Tan A Dee (Tanfirion) [2006/7 c–, F–: c16g c16g c20m³ c20gᵖᵘ c20mᵖᵘ c20m³ c20s² c17m⁶ Aug 26] poor maiden chaser: sold out of W. Coltherd's stable 800 gns Doncaster May Sales after second outing: won point in April: stays in cheekpieces last 3 starts. *P. T. Dalton*　　**c73**

FIRST AUTHOR (IRE) 6 b.g. Orpen (USA) – Welsh Brook (Caerleon (USA)) [2006/7 F101: F16d² Nov 3] unfurnished gelding: won 21-runner bumper at Fairyhouse on debut in 2005/6: useful form when 1½ lengths second to Powerberry at Down Royal. *G. O'Leary, Ireland*　　**F105**

FIRST BLUE (IRE) 4 b.g. Supreme Leader – Bilberry (Nicholas Bill) [2006/7 F16s F13m² Mar 29] 20,000 3-y-o, resold £26,000 3-y-o: rather unfurnished gelding: half-brother to fairly useful hurdler Pedina (by Toulon), stays 3m, and bumper winners by Toulon and Shernazar: dam, 1¾m winner, half-sister to high-class 2m hurdler Past Glories: fair form in bumpers, 2½ lengths second to Regal Angel in maiden at Hereford. *P. R. Webber*　　**F85**

FIRST CENTURION 6 b.g. Peintre Celebre (USA) – Valley of Hope (USA) (Riverman (USA)) [2006/7 h75: 16g Oct 30] poor form over hurdles: tried visored/blinkered. *Ian Williams*　　**h–**

FIRST CRY (IRE) 7 b.g. Topanoora – Open Cry (IRE) (Montelimar (USA)) [2006/7 h–, F96: 16s² 16f³ 17fᵘʳ 21m* 17m³ 22d² 20gᵖᵘ Nov 19] well-made gelding: fair hurdler: landed odds in maiden at Sedgefield in August: ran as if amiss final outing: stays 2¾m: acts on firm and soft going. *N. G. Richards*　　**h104**

FIRST DOWN JETS (IRE) 10 b.g. Arctic Lord – Kentish Town (Camden Town) [2006/7 c122, h–: c28vᵘʳ c22v³ c26g c25m⁴ c25g Apr 25] sturdy gelding: useful hunter chaser: let down by jumping in Foxhunter at Cheltenham third outing (best effort when runner-up in race previous year): stays 3¼m: acts on good to firm and heavy going: tried blinkered/in cheekpieces. *W. J. Burke, Ireland*　　**c112**　**h–**

FIRST FEERIE (FR) 4 b.f. Turgeon (USA) – Funny Feerie (FR) (Sillery (USA)) [2006/7 16g² 16g⁵ 16d* 17s⁴ 19g Mar 24] tall, useful-looking filly: half-sister to 2¼m hurdle winner Frejus (by Mansonnien): placed once over 1½m from 3 starts on Flat in Provinces, left Mme C. Head-Maarek after final one: fair hurdler: won mares novice at Ascot in February by 7 lengths from Inherent: should stay beyond 2m: raced on good ground or softer. *Noel T. Chance*　　**h99**

FIRSTFLOR 8 b.m. Alflora (IRE) – First Crack (Scallywag) [2006/7 h61x: 20m⁶ 20m³ 22f³ 26g⁴ 26g Apr 20] rather leggy mare: bumper winner: poor maiden hurdler: stays 2¾m: acts on soft and firm going: often jumps none too fluently. *F. Jordan*　　**h64 x**

FIRST FOUGHT (IRE) 5 b.g. Germany (USA) – Royal Flame (IRE) (Royal Academy (USA)) [2006/7 h106: 16d⁶ 17d³ 16m 16s⁴ 16m c16g c16g⁵ c16g⁴ Apr 20] close-coupled gelding: fair hurdler: creditable effort in 2006/7 only second start: poor form over fences: raced around 2m: acts on soft going: tongue tied. *D. McCain Jnr*　　**c83**　**h103 d**

FIRST LOOK (FR) 7 b.g. Acatenango (GER) – First Class (GER) (Bustino) [2006/7 h126: c20v³ c20v* c24s³ Apr 25] workmanlike gelding: fairly useful hurdler: landed odds in maiden chase at Ayr in March comfortably by 8 lengths from Lethem Air: better form　　**c117 +**　**h–**

when third to According To John in novice at Carlisle 4 months earlier: stays 2½m (finished tired over 3m): raced on going softer than good (acts on heavy). *P. Monteith*

FIRST LOVE 11 br.g. Bustino – First Romance (Royalty) [2006/7 c123, h–: c20s⁴ Feb 16] good sort: winning hurdler: fairly useful chaser: off another 10½ months, below-par fourth of 6 to Balinova in hunter at Sandown (won race previous year): stays 3m: raced on good going or softer (acts on heavy): usually sound jumper: free-going sort, best allowed to stride on. *N. J. Henderson* **c112 h–**

FIRST PARTNER (IRE) 8 b.m. Accordion – Fresh Partner (IRE) (Yashgan) [2006/7 c20mᵖᵘ Jun 22] poor pointer: pulled up in maiden chase (tongue tied): sold £4,000 Ascot August Sales. *J. L. Needham* **c–**

FIRST ROW (IRE) 5 b.g. Daylami (IRE) – Ballet Society (FR) (Sadler's Wells (USA)) [2006/7 h124: 16d⁶ 20v 16v* 16d 16v 19g⁶ 16m Apr 25] workmanlike gelding: fairly useful handicap hurdler: won at Leopardstown in December by neck from Woodhouse: little impact after: best form at 2m: acts on heavy going: wore cheekpieces 2 of last 5 starts (including when successful): often races prominently. *D. T. Hughes, Ireland* **h118**

FIRST SILVER 5 b.g. Silver Patriarch (IRE) – Native Valley (IRE) (Be My Native (USA)) [2006/7 F18d Oct 30] second foal: dam, of little account, out of half-sister to smart hurdler upto 21f Urubande: last in bumper on debut. *Mrs Caroline Bailey* **F–**

FIRST SLIP 4 b.g. Slip Anchor – Nanouche (Dayjur (USA)) [2006/7 16d 16v⁵ 16v⁴ 16s Mar 11] good-topped gelding: fair maiden on Flat (stays 1½m), sold out of Mrs A. Perrett's stable 12,000 gns Newmarket Autumn Sales: well held 4 starts over hurdles. *Jonjo O'Neill* **h82**

FIRST STOP 4 b.g. Chocolat de Meguro (USA) – One Stop (Silly Prices) [2006/7 F16v⁶ F16g Apr 23] first foal: dam modest hurdler around 2m: well beaten in bumpers. *M. A. Barnes* **F–**

FIRST TEE (IRE) 8 ch.g. Un Desperado (FR) – Bright Future (IRE) (Satco (FR)) [2006/7 h–: c21sᵖᵘ Oct 1] never a factor in novice hurdle/maiden chase 10 months apart: dead. *Jonjo O'Neill* **c– h–**

FIRST THOUGHT 9 b.m. Primitive Rising (USA) – Precis (Pitpan) [2006/7 17s² 22g* 27m³ 19d³ Aug 20] successful both completed outings in points in 2006: improved on return to hurdles winning maiden at Newton Abbot in July: left C. Down before final start: should be suited by further than 2¾m: acts on soft going. *O. J. Carter* **h89**

FISBY 6 ch.g. Efisio – Trilby (In The Wings) [2006/7 h–: 17s 16g 16sᵖᵘ 22m* Apr 15] modest hurdler: improved effort when winning handicap at Market Rasen in April: stays 2¾m: best effort on good to firm ground. *K. J. Burke* **h91**

FISHERMAN JACK 12 b.g. Carlingford Castle – Troublewithjack (Sulaafah (USA)) [2006/7 c69: c24v⁴ 24s³ 23s⁵ c26s³ c24v* c24v⁴ c23s² c23v³ Mar 9] stocky gelding: poor handicap chaser: won at Towcester in January despite trying to run out run-in: achieved little in 2 starts over hurdles: stays 3¼m: acts on heavy going: wears cheekpieces. *G. J. Smith* **c74 h62**

FISHER STREET 12 gr.g. Tigani – Pricket Walk (Amboise) [2006/7 c–, h–: c20vᵘʳ May 18] leggy gelding: winning chaser, lightly raced and no form since 2002: tried in headgear. *Mrs C. J. Kerr* **c– h–**

FITASABUCKSTOAT (IRE) 4 b.g. Fayruz – Bardia (Jalmood (USA)) [2006/7 17mᵖᵘ Apr 28] little form, raced mostly on Flat: dead. *K. W. Hogg, Isle of Man* **h–**

FIT TO FLY (IRE) 6 b.g. Lahib (USA) – Maid of Mourne (Fairy King (USA)) [2006/7 16g 16d Dec 28] modest on Flat (stays 1m), sold out of R. C. Guest's stable 3,200 gns Doncaster August Sales: no show both starts over hurdles: wore cheekpieces. *C. A. Mulhall* **h–**

FIVE ALLEY (IRE) 10 gr.g. Roselier (FR) – Panel Pin (Menelek) [2006/7 c91, h101: 24m c25gᵖᵘ Oct 15] sturdy gelding: fair maiden hurdler: modest chaser: lame final outing: should stay extreme distances: acts on heavy going: has looked hard ride, including in blinkers. *R. H. Buckler* **c– h–**

FIVE COLOURS (IRE) 7 b. or br.g. Lord Americo – Thousand Springs (IRE) (King's Ride) [2006/7 h122: c20s³ Oct 26] close-coupled gelding: fairly useful hurdler: off 7 months (suffered hairline fracture to hind leg), looked and ran as if in need of race when 11 lengths third to Don't Push It in maiden at Stratford on chasing debut: should stay 3m+: acts on soft going, below form on good to firm: seemed sure to improve over fences, but not seen out again. *A. King* **c95 p h–**

FIVEFORTHREE (IRE) 5 gr.g. Arzanni – What A Queen (King's Ride) [2006/7 F16v* F16g5 F16m3 Apr 8] rangy, rather unfurnished gelding: half-brother to 2 winners, notably top-class chaser Celestial Gold (by Persian Mews), stays 4m: dam unraced out of half-sister to top-class staying chaser L'Escargot: favourite, won 20-runner maiden bumper at Punchestown on debut in February by 7 lengths from I Hear A Symphony, always going well: smart form when 3¾ lengths fifth of 24 to Cork All Star in Champion Bumper at Cheltenham, rapid progress from rear then staying on after meeting trouble in straight: not at best with less emphasis on stamina when third to Sizing Africa at Fairyhouse: will be suited by 2½m+: promising. *W. P. Mullins, Ireland* **F118 +**

FIVE O'S (IRE) 7 ch.g. Accordion – Tarte Cannelle (Keen) [2006/7 20s6 Aug 19] first foal: dam unraced: winning Irish pointer: fair form in bumpers: modest form on first of 3 starts over hurdles, sold out of P. Fenton's stable 1,800 gns Doncaster May Sales before reappearance (wore cheekpieces): dead. *Evan Williams* **h–**

FIVE YEARS ON (IRE) 6 b.g. Desert Sun – Snowspin (Carwhite) [2006/7 16fpu 16f2 16fbd 17f2 16d 16vpu 16m Apr 16] workmanlike gelding: fair maiden at best on Flat for R. Beckett, well held in 2005: modest maiden hurdler, left S. Mahon after fifth start: raced around 2m: acts on firm ground. *T. J. Arnold, Ireland* **h87**

FIXATEUR 5 b.g. Anabaa (USA) – Fabulous Account (USA) (Private Account (USA)) [2006/7 h95+: c16d3 c20g 19v 16s 17s Jan 30] strong, close-coupled gelding: modest maiden hurdler at best, well beaten in handicaps last 2 outings: poor form in handicap chases: likely to prove best around 2m: acts on soft going: tried blinkered: joined J. Given. *C. C. Bealby* **c75 h–**

FIXED INTEREST (IRE) 5 b.g. Taipan (IRE) – Fixed Assets (Rare One) [2006/7 F89: F16g F18m 16mF Nov 4] unfurnished gelding: modest form in bumpers, sold out of H. Daly's stable 40,000 gns Doncaster May Sales, after first outing: led (set steady pace) until falling 2 out in novice won by Kicks For Free at Wincanton on hurdling debut. *R. H. Buckler* **h– p F80**

FIZANNI (IRE) 7 ch.m. Arzanni – Lady Isaac (IRE) (Le Bavard (FR)) [2006/7 20s 21s3 Dec 5] second foal: half-sister to winning pointer by Jurado: dam unraced: won maiden point in 2006: seemingly poor form on second of 2 outings over hurdles. *Miss F. Slevin, Ireland* **h81 ?**

FLAGMOUNT KING (IRE) 6 b.g. Lord Americo – Dessie's Error (IRE) (King's Ride) [2006/7 F16vsu Feb 27] 12,000 4-y-o: fourth foal: dam unraced: failed to complete in 2 points in 2006: held when slipped up over 1f out in maiden bumper. *W. Storey* **F–**

FLAHIVE'S FIRST 13 ch.g. Interrex (CAN) – Striking Image (IRE) (Flash of Steel) [2006/7 c103, h–: c16g c21d c17m4 c20f6 c16m2 c20m3 c23m c22d6 c20g5 c21f3 c21g4 c21s6 c19g Oct 15] sparely-made gelding: winning hurdler: modest handicap chaser nowadays, typically in-and-out form in 2006/7, left D. Burchell before final start: stays 21f: acts on soft and firm going: held up: has won 6 times at Cartmel: hard ride. *M. A. Doyle* **c94 § h– §**

FLAKE 7 ch.g. Zilzal (USA) – Impatiente (USA) (Vaguely Noble) [2006/7 c105, h100: 16m c20m3 c16g2 16g* c16d* c16g* c16s5 16v* c16gur Apr 7] smallish, close-coupled gelding: fair handicap hurdler/chaser: won over hurdles at Haydock (conditional/amateur event) in October and Newcastle in March, and over fences at Sedgefield (easily) and Catterick in November: stays 21f: acts on heavy going, probably on good to firm: usually races prominently (headstrong). *Mrs S. J. Smith* **c113 h106**

FLAMAND (FR) 6 b.g. Double Bed (FR) – Rays Honor (Ahonoora) [2006/7 h79: 16gpu 17mpu 16g 16m* 16g2 Nov 13] fair handicap hurdler: reportedly had breathing operation after third start, and much improved to win at Stratford in September: raced around 2m: acts on good to firm going: tongue tied last 3 starts. *C. P. Morlock* **h103**

FLAME CREEK (IRE) 11 b.g. Shardari – Sheila's Pet (IRE) (Welsh Term) [2006/7 c–x, h–: 16mur 17g Mar 16] tall, leggy gelding: fairly useful on Flat, successful twice in December: one-time smart hurdler, well beaten in valuable handicap final outing: unbeaten but failed to convince with jumping first 3 starts over fences, and fell only outing in 2005/6: should be as effective at 2½m as 2m: successful on firm going, raced mainly on good or softer (acts on heavy). *E. J. Creighton* **c– x h–**

FLAME PHOENIX (USA) 8 b.g. Quest For Fame – Kingscote (Kings Lake (USA)) [2006/7 c91§, h107§: 17gpu May 5] sturdy gelding: fair handicap hurdler: maiden chaser: stayed 2½m: acted on soft and good to firm going: tried in cheekpieces/blinkers: tongue tied: moody. *D. McCain* **c– § h– §**

FLAMETHROWER (IRE) 7 b.g. Warcraft (USA) – Gallic Flame (Cyrano de Bergerac) [2006/7 F–: 20vpu 20spu Nov 25] workmanlike gelding: no show in maiden bumper/novice hurdles. *E. A. Elliott* **h–**

FLAMING CHEEK 9 b.g. Blushing Flame (USA) – Rueful Lady (Streetfighter) **h94**
[2006/7 h–: 21g⁵ 19s³ 16d 21s⁴ Nov 19] good-topped gelding: modest handicap hurdler:
stays 21f: acts on soft and good to firm going. *A. G. Blackmore*

FLAMING HECK 10 b.g. Dancing High – Heckley Spark (Electric) [2006/7 c94§, **c95**
h87§: c16s³ 17s² 17s³ 17s⁶ c16s⁴ c16v² c16s⁶ c16vᵖᵘ c17g⁵ Apr 2] rangy gelding: modest **h92**
handicap chaser/maiden hurdler: stays 2½m: acts on heavy going: usually makes
running/races prominently. *Mrs L. B. Normile*

FLAMING WEAPON 5 b.g. Unfuwain (USA) – Flame Valley (USA) (Gulch (USA)) **h116**
[2006/7 h114: 16sᵖᵘ 16v⁶ 18s⁴ 17d* Mar 20] lengthy gelding: maiden on Flat: fairly
useful hurdler: back to best to win handicap at Exeter in March by 4 lengths from Ma
Yahab: likely to prove best around 2m: raced on going softer than good: wore cheekpieces
second outing. *G. L. Moore*

FLASH CUMMINS (IRE) 7 b. or br.g. Corrouge (USA) – Corshanna River (IRE) **c115**
(Over The River (FR)) [2006/7 c–p, h91+: c20s* c20g* c24v³ Dec 31] sturdy gelding: **h–**
novice hurdler: fairly useful form over fences: won novice at Sedgefield in October and
handicap at Leicester (by ½ length from Tom Fruit, idling) in November: stays 2½m: acts
on soft ground: tongue tied in 2006/7. *D. E. Pipe*

FLASHER (IRE) 7 b.g. Presenting – Lady Slavey (Furry Glen) [2006/7 F16g⁵ F17g* **h69**
21d Jan 8] €3,000 4-y-o: half-brother to winning pointer by Tremblant: dam unraced: **F79**
won bumper at Hereford in November: well beaten in maiden on hurdling debut.
N. A. Twiston-Davies

FLASH POINT (IRE) 8 b. or br.g. Executive Perk – Shine Your Light (Kemal (FR)) **c–**
[2006/7 24dᵖᵘ c20dᵖᵘ c23s⁶ c19v⁶ c19sᶠ Jan 30] half-brother to fair staying chaser High- **h–**
Spec (by Strong Gale) and bumper winner Dantes Sun (by Phardante): dam fair winning
hurdler up to 2¾m: won maiden point in 2004: no solid form in novice hurdle/maiden
chases (mistakes): dead. *J. G. Cann*

FLASHY FILLY 7 b.m. Puissance – Tempted (IRE) (Invited (USA)) [2006/7 h–: 16s **c–**
17d 22dᵖᵘ 20fᵖᵘ 20dᵖᵘ c16g Apr 23] of little account: has worn cheekpieces/eyeshields. **h–**
J. C. Haynes

FLAT STANLEY 8 b.g. Celtic Swing – Cool Grey (Absalom) [2006/7 c23gᵖᵘ c24sᵖᵘ **c–**
May 20] winning pointer: maiden hunter, no show in 2006/7: tried in cheekpieces. **h–**
P. Grindrod

FLEET ADMIRAL 6 ch.g. Fleetwood (IRE) – Dame du Moulin (Shiny Tenth) **h–**
[2006/7 20sᵖᵘ Sep 20] half-brother to several winners, including fair hurdler Cinder Hills
(by Deploy), stayed 2¾m: dam 2-y-o 7f winner: no show in maiden hurdle on debut.
J. Wade

FLEETFOOT MAC 6 b.g. Fleetwood (IRE) – Desert Flower (Green Desert (USA)) **c85**
[2006/7 c–, h–: 16m⁴ 17d³ 21m³ c25s* 22g⁶ c25sᵖᵘ c25s c25v⁴ c27s c24d⁵ c28v⁴ c32v* **h92**
c26gᵖᵘ Apr 7] medium-sized gelding: modest handicap hurdler/chaser: won over fences
at Hexham (novice) in June and March: stays 4m: acts on heavy going: tried in headgear.
B. Storey

FLEET STREET 8 ch.g. Wolfhound (USA) – Farmer's Pet (Sharrood (USA)) [2006/7 **c–**
c111p, h–: 16g* 20m 16m Apr 25] leggy gelding: useful hurdler: off another 15 months, **h132**
won handicap at Newbury in March by 2½ lengths from Swing Bill: well held after in
valuable handicaps at Punchestown on consecutive days: fourth to Voy Por Ustedes in
novice in 2005/6, only start over fences (should do better): should stay beyond 2m: acts
on soft and good to firm going. *N. J. Henderson*

FLEETWOOD FOREST 7 b.g. Fleetwood (IRE) – Louise Moillon (Mansingh **h102**
(USA)) [2006/7 21s* Dec 7] close-coupled gelding: fair hurdler: off 21 months, won
18-runner handicap at Huntingdon in December: stays 21f: acts on soft going. *A. King*

FLEMENSBARR (IRE) 6 b.g. Flemensfirth (USA) – Soft Talk (Goldhill) [2006/7 **h–**
16v 16sᵖᵘ 16v 18s⁴ 24sᵖᵘ Apr 25] €12,000 4-y-o, resold £36,000 4-y-o: half-brother to
winning staying chasers No Problem and There Tis For Ya (both by Le Moss): dam
winning pointer: won maiden point in October: no form over hurdles: tongue tied last 3
starts. *C. A. McBratney, Ireland*

FLEMENSGOLD (IRE) 7 ch.m. Flemensfirth (USA) – Nugget Moss (Le Moss) **h–**
[2006/7 21sᵖᵘ 24fᵖᵘ Jun 21] no show over hurdles or in points. *G. J. Smith*

FLEMINGSTONE (IRE) 7 b.m. Flemensfirth (USA) – Philly Athletic (Sit In The **h72 ?**
Corner (USA)) [2006/7 h72, F–: 21s 20v⁴ 21m 20f 22mᶠ 20m⁶ 20s² 25sᵖᵘ Oct 29] small
mare: poor novice hurdler: stays 2½m: acts on heavy going. *M. J. Gingell*

FLEUR BABE 4 b.f. Alflora (IRE) – Tui (Tina's Pet) [2006/7 17m 19v 16v[6] Feb 15]   **h–**
first foal: dam, modest winning hurdler, effective at 2m to 3m: no form over hurdles.
P. Bowen

FLEUR D'ECOSSE (FR) 6 b.m. Villez (USA) – Polly Verry (Politico (USA))   **h–**
[2006/7 20v[pu] Jan 9] sixth foal: dam winning pointer: no show in novice hurdle on debut.
B. Storey

FLEUR DES PRES (FR) 5 gr.m. Robin Des Pres (FR) – Divine Rodney (FR) (Kendor   **h56**
(FR)) [2006/7 h–, F69: 16g 16g 22m[F] 17g[F] Nov 9] in cheekpieces and well backed, first
form over hurdles (held in fifth) when falling last in selling handicap on final start.
A. E. Jones

FLEURETTE 7 b.m. Alflora (IRE) – Miss Wrensborough (Buckskin (FR)) [2006/7   **c91**
h104: c19g[5] c16s[4] c19s[4] 19v[3] 21s[2] Mar 11] long-backed mare: fair hurdler: modest form   **h102**
over fences: will stay beyond 21f: acts on heavy going: in cheekpieces last 2 outings.
D. R. Gandolfo

FLIGHT COMMAND 9 ch.g. Gunner B – Wing On (Quayside) [2006/7 c113, h–:   **c114 §**
c20g[5] c22s[2] c20g[3] c20m[2] c20f[3] c20g[2] c19g[4] c16v[2] c17g[6] c16g[5] c21g Apr 13] good-   **h– §**
topped gelding: fair handicap chaser: stays 25f, effective at much shorter: acts on any
going: often in cheekpieces: usually sound jumper: weak finisher. *P. Beaumont*

FLIGHT LEADER (IRE) 7 b.g. Supreme Leader – Stormy Petrel (IRE) (Strong   **h148**
Gale) [2006/7 F92: 24v* 22d[2] 24s* 20v* 24v[3] 24g[4] Mar 16]
    The final day of the Cheltenham Festival will not hold fond memories for
trainer Colin Tizzard, who was represented by Flight Leader and Bob Bob Bobbin,
the two best horses in his yard. Not too much could have been expected of Bob Bob
Bobbin, a 100/1-shot for the Gold Cup. However, he was ruled out for the remainder of the season after returning lame, which only added to the disappointment of
Flight Leader's defeat in the Spa Hurdle, the preceding race on the card (in which
Bob Bob Bobbin had finished a good fourth in 2005). Flight Leader started second
favourite for the Brit Insurance-sponsored novices' hurdle, but the ground was
much less testing than when he had put up his best performances and he failed to do
himself justice. Flight Leader was outpaced down the hill before staying on all too
late to take fourth, twenty lengths behind the winning favourite Wichita Lineman.
Flight Leader, like his stablemate, wasn't seen out again, and when he returns it will
be to embark on a career over fences. It didn't take Flight Leader long to show
himself a smart novice in his first season over hurdles, and there is every reason
to expect that he will prove at least as effective over fences when stamina is at a
premium.
    Flight Leader was a late starter, not seen out until turned six, then having
three runs in bumpers in a little more than a month. He showed a fair amount of
ability in that sphere, runner-up at Plumpton on the second occasion, though hardly
enough to make it obvious that he was going to reach the heights he did in his first
season over hurdles. Flight Leader changed that as early as his hurdling debut,
when stepped up markedly in trip for a maiden at Chepstow in October. That race,
run over three miles on heavy ground, provided Flight Leader with the sort of test
that suits him ideally, and he didn't go unbacked in upsetting the Paul Nicholls-
trained favourite Get My Drift at 18/1, staying on strongly on the extended run-in
to win by five lengths. A creditable second to another Nicholls inmate Leading
Attraction (not seen out again) over a slightly shorter trip at Wincanton next time,
Flight Leader resumed winning ways returned to three miles in the Bristol Novices'
Hurdle, sponsored by Brit Insurance, at Cheltenham in December. It was a
competitive renewal of this Grade 2 event, a race won in recent years by such as
Iris's Gift and Black Jack Ketchum, and Flight Leader took it in very good style by
nine lengths from Labelthou, travelling strongly in a well-run contest, clearly going
best when leading two out and still pulling away from his pursuers at the line—Air
Force One, who went on to finish runner-up in the Spa, was a distant fifth, making
his hurdling debut. Flight Leader had two more outings before the Spa, both at
Cheltenham in January, and he ran very well in each of them. The heavy ground and
strong gallop played to Flight Leader's strengths when he was dropped in trip in a
quite valuable four-runner minor event on New Year's Day, as did the fact that his
two main rivals Temoin and The French Furze, to whom he was conceding weight,

probably weren't at their best. Flight Leader again took it up at the second last and was all out to hold off the strong-finishing Temoin, three quarters of a length the winning margin. Richard Johnson was in the saddle for this win as regular jockey, Tizzard's son Joe, opted for a full book of rides on the same afternoon's card at Exeter, where he rode a short-priced double for the stable. The light was very poor for Flight Leader's two victories at Cheltenham—both at or near the end of the programme—which explains the absence of photographs in his essay. Back at three miles in the Grade 2 Cleeve Hurdle, Flight Leader put up another smart performance for a novice to finish ten lengths third to Blazing Bailey (who received 4 lb), the pair split by subsequent World Hurdle winner Inglis Drever, Flight Leader showing in front under pressure turning into the straight but then unable to quicken.

Flight Leader (IRE) (b.g. 2000)	Supreme Leader (b 1982)	Bustino (b 1971)	Busted
			Ship Yard
		Princess Zena (b 1975)	Habitat
			Guiding Light
	Stormy Petrel (IRE) (br 1989)	Strong Gale (br 1975)	Lord Gayle
			Sterntau
		Gorryelm (ch 1973)	Arctic Slave
			Dippity Do

Bought for €31,000 at the 2004 Derby Sale, Flight Leader is the second foal of Stormy Petrel and her only runner under Rules to date, though his two-years-younger sister Downsouth was last of five finishers in a mares maiden Irish point on her debut in November. The dam has since produced a 2005 colt and a 2006 filly, both by Old Vic. They made €27,000 and €16,000 respectively as foals. Stormy Petrel was one of very few jumpers to represent Derby-winning trainer Peter Walwyn and, although just a poor performer, she did win a mares novice event over two and a half miles at Huntingdon on her chasing debut, ridden by Philip Hide. Hide was still riding winners in the latest season though it probably isn't one he will want to remember. Returning to the saddle in February after suffering a triple fracture to his pelvis in a fall three months earlier, Hide was back on the sidelines a few weeks later after aggravating an old shoulder injury, causing him to miss the remainder of the campaign. Stormy Petrel is a sister to the fairly useful chaser at up to three miles Strong Deel and to the fair Irish hurdler/chaser Strong Hurricane, who also stayed three miles. Their dam, the lightly-raced maiden Gorryelm, has produced several other winning jumpers, the most recent the fair staying chaser Boy's Hurrah. The next dam Dippity Do won a bumper and a maiden hurdle in Ireland. The useful-looking Flight Leader, who will stay very long distances, has raced only on good ground or softer to date. *C. L. Tizzard*

FLIGHT OF EARLS (IRE) 6 b.g. Dr Devious (IRE) – Eleanor Antoinette (IRE) (Double Schwartz) [2006/7 16s c24v^{ur} c20v^{pu} Mar 4] workmanlike gelding: form on Flat only when second in 9f handicap at 4 yrs: no form over hurdles/fences, left C. O'Brien, Ireland before reappearance: tongue tied last 2 starts. *P. C. Haslam*   c– h–

FLINDERS BAY (IRE) 7 b. or br.g. Luso – McMufins Princess (Decent Fellow) [2006/7 16s^4 16d 17s c20d^6 16g Mar 19] strong, lengthy, good sort: bumper winner: modest form over hurdles: last in novice handicap chases: should be suited by further than 2m: acts on soft going. *Miss H. C. Knight*   c– h89

FLINTOFF (USA) 6 ch.g. Diesis – Sahibah (USA) (Deputy Minister (CAN)) [2006/7 h110+: c16v^2 c22s^2 c20v^3 c20v* c24v* c24g Feb 3] rather leggy gelding: successful on 3 of 4 starts over hurdles: left R. C. Guest and off a year prior to return: improved form (useful) over fences when winning maiden at Wetherby (by 26 lengths) and handicap at Newbury within 5 days in January, beating Ice Melted by 14 lengths at latter: let down by jumping in valuable handicap at Sandown next time: stays 3m: acts on heavy going: blinkered last 3 starts. *Miss Venetia Williams*   c137 h–

FLIRTY JILL 6 b.m. I'm Supposin (IRE) – Gaye Mercy (Petoski) [2006/7 h85, F68: c20g^6 22m^5 Apr 22] rangy mare: winning pointer: modest novice hurdler at best, left P. Webber and off 5 months prior to final start: no show on chase debut: stays 2¾m: tongue tied. *P. E. Cowley*   c– h–

FLOODLIGHT FANTASY 4 b.g. Fantastic Light (USA) – Glamadour (IRE) (Sanglamore (USA)) [2006/7 16g 16v 16v Jan 28] smallish, sturdy gelding: fair on Flat (stays 1¼m), successful in October, sold out of E. McMahon's stable 20,000 gns Newmarket Autumn Sales: no promise in juvenile hurdles. *Jedd O'Keeffe*   h–

FLORA BUNDY 7 ch.m. Genuine Gift (CAN) – Pharly Rose (Pharly (FR)) [2006/7   **F–**
F17d F16m⁶ F16g Dec 10] third foal: dam unraced: well beaten in bumpers. *Miss Lucinda
V. Russell*

FLORADORADO 5 b.m. Alflora (IRE) – Cream By Post (Torus) [2006/7 F14s⁵ F17g⁵   **F80**
Apr 27] seventh foal: half-sister to 3 winners, including temperamental 2m chase winner
Post It (by Thowra) and fair hurdler/chaser Cream Cracker (by Sir Harry Lewis), stays
2½m: dam, winning hurdler/pointer, out of half-sister to useful hurdler/chaser up to 25f
Gallaher: modest form in bumpers: will be suited by stiffer test of stamina. *P. F. Nicholls*

FLORAL FUTURE 7 b.m. Alflora (IRE) – Political Prospect (Politico (USA))   **h–**
[2006/7 h–, F–: 20d Nov 3] no show in bumper/novice hurdles. *A. C. Whillans*

FLORAL GIFT 7 b.m. Gunner B – Kings Athlete (IRE) (King's Ride) [2006/7 F16d   **h–**
F16d 20mᵖᵘ 24sᵖᵘ 22gᶠ 20sᵖᵘ Apr 25] 1,500 5-y-o: second foal: dam, well held in 2 novice   **F–**
hurdles, out of half-sister to Grand National winner Royal Athlete: no form in bumpers/
over hurdles. *E. J. Jamieson*

FLORA MAY 6 b.m. Alflora (IRE) – Kings Athlete (IRE) (King's Ride) [2006/7 F16d³   **F97**
F16v* Jan 17] third foal: dam, well held in 2 novice hurdles, out of half-sister to Grand
National winner Royal Athlete: bettered debut effort when winning mares bumper at
Newcastle in January by 3 lengths from Brook No Argument: sold 25,000 gns Doncaster
May Sales. *Mrs S. J. Smith*

FLORA THE EXPLORA 6 gr.m. Alflora (IRE) – The Whirlie Weevil (Scallywag)   **h–**
[2006/7 F–: F16d 16vᵖᵘ 20sᵖᵘ Apr 25] unfurnished mare: no form in bumpers/maiden   **F–**
hurdles: tried tongue tied. *Mrs L. B. Normile*

FLORAZINE (IRE) 6 gr.m. Alflora (IRE) – Dorazine (Kalaglow) [2006/7 h65, F–:   **h80**
16d 16m 16f 22g 24g⁶ 20v² 22v⁶ 16v² 20v³ 18s⁶ 16s² 20vᵖᵘ 20g 20vᵖᵘ 16g² Apr 23]
angular, sparely-made mare: poor maiden handicap hurdler: stays 2½m: acts on heavy
going: tried in cheekpieces/tongue tied. *Frederick John Bowles, Ireland*

FLOREANA (GER) 6 b.m. Acatenango (GER) – Frille (FR) (Shareef Dancer (USA))   **c86 p**
[2006/7 h108: c26g* May 14] leggy mare: fair hurdler: favourite, won maiden at   **h–**
Plumpton on chasing debut in May: stays 3¼m: acts on soft going: seemed likely to
improve but not seen out again. *C. J. Mann*

FLORIDA DREAM (IRE) 8 b.g. Florida Son – Ice Pearl (Flatbush) [2006/7 c117x,   **c117 x**
h–: c24d c24v* c24g c31d c20s Apr 25] well-made gelding: winning hurdler: fairly   **h–**
useful handicap chaser: won at Warwick (jumped right) in December by 12 lengths from
All Sonsilver: disappointing otherwise in 2006/7: stays 25f: acts on heavy going:
blinkered: front runner/races prominently: often let down by jumping: temperament
under suspicion. *N. A. Twiston-Davies*

FLORITCHEL (FR) 10 b.g. Dark Stone (FR) – Aktia (FR) (Lyphard's Special   **c–**
(USA)) [2006/7 c–, h–: c25g⁵ Apr 23] winning pointer: no form in 2 chases. *G. F. White*

FLOWER HAVEN 5 b.m. Dr Fong (USA) – Daisy May (In The Wings) [2006/7 h86:   **h76**
16v 17d⁶ 16m⁵ 19m Apr 22] leggy mare: lightly-raced maiden on Flat: poor novice
hurdler: may prove best around 2m: acts on soft going, probably on good to firm: tried in
cheekpieces. *M. J. Gingell*

FLOWERPOTMAN 5 b.g. Zaffaran (USA) – Calabria (Neltino) [2006/7 F73: F16v⁶   **h68**
20d⁵ 17sᵖᵘ 20g Apr 16] tall gelding: modest form in bumpers: little impact in novice   **F77**
hurdles, lost action after third start. *M. W. Easterby*

FLUFF 'N' PUFF 13 ch.g. Nicholas Bill – Puff Puff (All Systems Go) [2006/7 c21f⁵   **c90**
c23d* c23g² c20d³ c26sᵖᵘ c24gᵘʳ c24g³ c24m⁶ c24g Apr 27] strong gelding: modest   **h–**
handicap chaser: left D. P. Keane and off 18 months prior to return: won at Taunton in
October, idling markedly: effective at testing 2m to 25f: acts on good to firm and heavy
going: often wears headgear: not straightforward (tends to find little). *Andrew Turnell*

FLYING DANCER 5 b.m. Danzero (AUS) – Alzianah (Alzao (USA)) [2006/7 16m⁴   **h70**
Oct 12] poor maiden on Flat (probably stays 7f): fourth in seller on hurdling debut (none
too fluent): sold 5,000 gns Doncaster October Sales. *R. A. Harris*

FLYING DICK 8 b.g. Thowra (FR) – Birbrook Girl (Henricus (ATA)) [2006/7 h–: 24d   **h–**
Oct 5] no form over hurdles. *A. G. Newcombe*

FLYING DOCTOR 4 b.g. Mark of Esteem (IRE) – Vice Vixen (CAN) (Vice Regent   **h95**
(CAN)) [2006/7 16g 16m⁵ 17v³ 16v² 16d² 16v² 16v⁵ Mar 2] tall, close-coupled gelding:
half-brother to winning hurdler/chaser up to 3¼m Commanche Creek (by Commanche
Run) and modest hurdler around 2m Mount Benger (by Selkirk): modest form on Flat at
2 yrs, sold out of G. M. Moore's stable 4,000 gns Doncaster May (2006) Sales: fair juvenile hurdler: likely to be suited by further than 2m: acts on heavy ground. *N. G. Richards*

Sixty Years of Timeform Novices' Handicap Chase, Cheltenham—the sponsor's top-rated Flying Enterprise (No.3) already has the measure of Good Citizen (about to fall) at the last

FLYING ENTERPRISE (IRE) 7 b.g. Darshaan – Flying Kiss (IRE) (Sadler's Wells (USA)) [2006/7 h128: c19m² c17g² c21d* c16s² c21d* c21v* c16d² c20s c21g Mar 15] angular gelding: fairly useful hurdler: took well to chasing, winning maiden at Wincanton in November and novices at Ascot (beat below-par Pole Star 19 lengths) in December and Cheltenham (useful form when beating Ofarel d'Airy by 8 lengths in Sixty Years of Timeform Novices' Handicap Chase) in January: respectable ninth of 19 to L'Antartique in similar event back at Cheltenham final outing: stays 21f: acts on heavy going, probably on good to firm: tried blinkered. *Miss Venetia Williams*   **c133 h–**

FLYING FALCON 8 b.g. Polar Falcon (USA) – Lemon Balm (High Top) [2006/7 h119p: 19d³ 16s² 20g Apr 12] good-topped gelding: fairly useful hurdler: good efforts in valuable handicaps first 2 starts, 6 lengths second of 17 to Gaspara in Imperial Cup at Sandown: should stay beyond 19f: acts on heavy going (bumper winner on good to firm). *Miss Venetia Williams*   **h123**

FLYING FORME (IRE) 7 b.g. Muroto – Coolavanny Queen (Furry Glen) [2006/7 16s 17v⁵ 19d 22s 21s³ 26gᵖᵘ c23m⁴ Apr 25] workmanlike gelding: first foal: half-brother to fair 2m hurdler Mission Possible (by Beneficial): dam, placed over fences, half-sister to smart 2m/2½m hurdler Tom Sharp: won maiden Irish point in 2006: poor form over hurdles/on chasing debut: stays 23f. *P. J. Hobbs*   **c83 h80**

FLYING HIGH (IRE) 12 b.g. Fayruz – Shayista (Tap On Wood) [2006/7 17m Jun 7] compact gelding: winning chaser/maiden hurdler: tried in blinkers/visor, often wears cheekpieces. *A. M. Crow*   **c– h–**

FLYING JODY (IRE) 8 b.g. Frimaire – Flying Flo Jo (USA) (Aloma's Ruler (USA)) [2006/7 h88: 20g 20g Apr 21] lengthy ex-Irish gelding: winning pointer/hurdler, off 17 months prior to return: raced at 2½m over hurdles: acts on good to firm ground: in cheekpieces in 2006/7. *Sir John Barlow Bt*   **h80**

FLYING PASS 5 b.g. Alzao (USA) – Complimentary Pass (Danehill (USA)) [2006/7 18m² 16m⁵ Jul 26] fair maiden on Flat (barely stays 1½m): poor form over hurdles, claimed from D. ffrench Davis £6,000 on debut. *R. J. Price*   **h83**

FLYING PENNE 4 b.f. Pennekamp (USA) – Flying Wind (Forzando) [2006/7 17dᵖᵘ 16gᵖᵘ Nov 1] neat filly: maiden on Flat, well held in 2006: no form in juvenile hurdles: sold £900 Ascot November Sales. *R. Curtis*   **h–**

FLYING SPIRIT (IRE) 8 b.g. Flying Spur (AUS) – All Laughter (Vision (USA)) [2006/7 c129, h–: 18g c16g c20g⁵ c19sᵘʳ c19g c16g Apr 19] medium-sized gelding: fairly useful hurdler/chaser at best, below form in 2006/7, failing to impress with attitude final start: stays easy 2½m: acts on firm and good to soft going: usually wears cheekpieces/blinkers. *G. L. Moore*   **c118 h104**

340

FLYING SPUR (IRE) 6 b.g. Norwich – Moorstown Rose (IRE) (Roselier (FR))   **c94**
[2006/7 h86, F87: c20f^F c20m⁶ 22s c24v c20v^{pu} 21g Feb 21] tall gelding: bumper winner: **h82**
modest form at best over hurdles/fences, disappointing after reappearance: stays 19f:
probably acts on any going: in cheekpieces last 4 starts: tried tongue tied. *D. E. Pipe*

FLYING TRIX (IRE) 11 b.g. Lord Americo – Bannow Drive (IRE) (Miner's Lamp)   **c–**
[2006/7 c97, h–: 24g c26g⁶ Sep 30] sturdy gelding: fair handicap hurdler/chaser at best: **h–**
no show in 2006/7, including in point: should stay beyond 3¼m: acts on good to firm and
heavy going: blinkered last 3 starts: not a straightforward ride. *P. J. Hobbs*

FLY KICKER 10 ch.g. High Kicker (USA) – Double Birthday (Cavo Doro) [2006/7   **c85**
16m 16g 20m³ 20g⁵ c16g⁶ Apr 7] modest handicap hurdler: similar form in maiden on   **h85**
chasing debut: stays easy 2½m: acts on firm and good to soft going: effective with or
without cheekpieces. *W. Storey*

FLY ME TO DUNOON (IRE) 5 b.m. Rossini (USA) – Toledana (IRE) (Sure Blade   **h–**
(USA)) [2006/7 17g⁶ Mar 24] half-sister to winning hurdlers around 2m English City (by
City On A Hill) and South West Nine (by Oscar): little show in maidens on Flat at 2 yrs
for K. Burke or in mares claimer on hurdling debut. *H. P. Hogarth*

FLYOFF (IRE) 10 b.g. Mtoto – Flyleaf (FR) (Persian Bold) [2006/7 21g 16g⁶ Apr 9]   **h–**
smallish gelding: maiden hurdler, no show in 2006/7: wears headgear. *Mrs N. Macauley*

FLY TIPPER 7 ch.g. Environment Friend – Double Birthday (Cavo Doro) [2006/7 h66,   **h81 x**
F–: 20g 16s 17d 16f³ 17m⁶ 20g² 20m³ 22m⁵ 24g⁴ Oct 7] compact gelding: poor maiden
hurdler: probably stays 2¾m: acts on firm going: tried in cheekpieces: usually makes
running: not a fluent jumper. *W. Storey*

FLY TO DUBAI (IRE) 5 b.g. Fly To The Stars – Morna's Fan (FR) (Lear Fan (USA))   **h100**
[2006/7 16f* 16d 16d³ 16g³ 21m⁴ Oct 12] fairly useful on Flat (stays 1¼m), successful 4
times in 2005 for E. O'Neill, below best in 2006: fair hurdler: won maiden at Sligo on
debut in July: may prove best around 2m: acts on firm and good to soft ground.
T. G. McCourt, Ireland

FOCUS POINT (IRE) 7 b. or br.g. Presenting – Merry Madness (Raise You Ten)   **c86**
[2006/7 16v 22v c27g² Apr 23] litttle impact over hurdles: left E. O'Grady, Ireland and   **h–**
easy to back, modest form when runner-up in novice handicap on chasing debut: stays
27f: sold 12,500 gns Doncaster May Sales. *P. C. Haslam*

FOLIE A DEUX (IRE) 5 b.g. Anshan – Flynn's Girl (IRE) (Mandalus) [2006/7 F16s   **h77**
F17g⁴ 20s 19s⁶ 20s⁶ 21f⁶ Apr 5] €24,000 3-y-o: good-topped gelding: fourth foal: dam,   **F83**
poor maiden jumper, half-sister to dam of useful 2m hurdler Spirit Leader: mid-field at
best in bumpers/over hurdles. *Miss H. C. Knight*

FOLIE DANCER 4 b.f. Exit To Nowhere (USA) – Kirov Royale (Rambo Dancer   **F82**
(CAN)) [2006/7 F12s³ Dec 13] useful-looking filly: third foal: dam lightly-raced maiden
who stayed 1m: 17/2 from 33/1, 2½ lengths third of 18 to Fiddling Again in 3-y-o bumper
at Newbury on debut: will stay 2m. *Miss E. C. Lavelle*

FOLIGOLD (FR) 5 b.g. Gold Away (IRE) – Folidalways (FR) (Always Fair (USA))   **h119**
[2006/7 16d 16g² 18d* 20v* 20s⁶ 22v² 20d³ 21g Mar 14] rather leggy, close-coupled
gelding: first foal: dam, lightly raced on Flat in France, closely related to Prix Saint-Alary
runner-up Folie Danse: runner-up once at 1½m from 4 starts on Flat in France for Y. de
Nicolay: fairly useful novice hurdler: won at Limerick (minor event) and Galway (beat
Callherwhatyoulike by 1¼ lengths) in October: better form when placed behind Kazal in
Grade 3 events sixth/seventh starts: stays 2¾m: acts on heavy going: tried visored (stiff
task, raced freely). *Mrs J. Harrington, Ireland*

FOLK TUNE (IRE) 4 b.c. Danehill (USA) – Musk Lime (USA) (Private Account   **h115**
(USA)) [2006/7 17v² 16g² 16g² 16d⁶ 16g* 16s² Apr 1] useful on Flat (stays 1m),
successful 3 times in 2006, sold out of J-C. Rouget's stable €32,000 Goffs Arc Sale: fairly
useful juvenile hurdler: landed odds in maiden at Wetherby by 2½ lengths from
Abstract Folly: ran well when 5 lengths second to Idarah at Hexham final outing: likely
to prove best around 2m: acts on soft going. *Ferdy Murphy*

FOLLINGWORTH (IRE) 4 ch.f. Midhish – Pennine Way (IRE) (Waajib) [2006/7   **h–**
19d^{ur} 16s^{ur} Mar 7] tall filly: no form on Flat: unseated both starts over hurdles.
A. D. Brown

FOLLOW THE BEAR 9 ch.g. Weld – Run Lady Run (General Ironside) [2006/7   **c–**
h85§: 21s² 16s c20v^F c20s⁶ Jan 15] tall gelding: maiden hurdler: well held completed   **h92 §**
outing over fences: stayed 3m: blinkered/visored: temperamental: dead. *D. R. Gandolfo*

FOLLOW THE COLOURS (IRE) 4 b.g. Rainbow Quest (USA) – Gardenia (IRE) **h78**
(Sadler's Wells (USA)) [2006/7 17d 17g⁶ 16g Apr 14] fair on Flat (stays 1¼m) for
J. Hills, successful in July: poor form in novice hurdles. *M. Scudamore*

FOLLOW THE FLOW (IRE) 11 ch.g. Over The River (FR) – October Lady **c– §**
(Lucifer (USA)) [2006/7 c104: c25sᵖᵘ c24sᵖᵘ c29g Mar 20] lengthy gelding: fair handicap
chaser at best, no show in 2006/7: suited by 3m+: acts on heavy and good to firm going:
has worn cheekpieces: races prominently: unenthusiastic. *P. A. Pritchard*

FOLLOW YOUR HEART (IRE) 7 b. or br.g. Broken Hearted – Souled Out (IRE) **c–**
(Noalto) [2006/7 c–, h96: 17v c24vᵖᵘ Mar 3] useful-looking gelding: novice hurdler: **h–**
ran as if amiss on reappearance: no form in handicap chases: probably stays 2½m.
N. J. Gifford

FOLY PLEASANT (FR) 13 ch.g. Vaguely Pleasant (FR) – Jeffologie (FR) (Jefferson) **c99**
[2006/7 c107, h–: c22vᵖᵘ c25s* c26gᶠ c24g Apr 21] sturdy gelding: winning hurdler: **h–**
fairly useful hunter chaser nowadays: won 3-finisher event at Ludlow in March: stays
3¼m: acts on heavy and good to firm going: tongue tied. *Mrs K. Waldron*

FOND OF A DROP 6 br.g. Overbury (IRE) – Pearl's Choice (IRE) (Deep Run) **h– p**
[2006/7 F18v* 19v F16s³ F19v⁴ Feb 25] €40,000 4-y-o: first foal: dam, modest chaser, **F107**
stayed 3m: useful form in bumpers: won maiden at Thurles in December by 16 lengths
from The Ex Townie: well held in maiden on hurdling debut: likely to do better.
D. T. Hughes, Ireland

FONTANESI (IRE) 7 b.g. Sadler's Wells (USA) – Northern Script (USA) (Arts And **c– §**
Letters (USA)) [2006/7 c123§, h120§: 22g³ 21d 20g 19gᶠ Mar 29] smallish, sparely- **h113 §**
made gelding: winning chaser: one-time useful handicap hurdler, won County Hurdle at
Cheltenham in 2004/5: well below best since, claimed £6,000 final outing: stays 21f: acts
on soft and good to firm going: has worn cheekpieces/visor: unenthusiastic. *D. E. Pipe*

FOODBROKER FOUNDER 7 ch.g. Groom Dancer (USA) – Nemea (USA) (The **h111**
Minstrel (CAN)) [2006/7 h115: 16m* 16d Nov 4] fair hurdler, lightly raced: won
handicap at Stratford in June: raced around 2m: acts on soft and good to firm going.
D. R. C. Elsworth

FOOLISH GROOM 6 ch.g. Groom Dancer (USA) – Scared (Royal Academy (USA)) **h–**
[2006/7 16m 16d Oct 1] fair on Flat (stays 1¼m): soundly beaten in novice hurdles: tried
tongue tied/visored. *R. Hollinshead*

FOOLISH MYTH 5 b.g. Midnight Legend – Xylotymbou (Town And Country) **h–**
[2006/7 20s⁵ 16v 22gᵖᵘ Mar 19] second foal: dam poor maiden: no form over hurdles.
D. P. Keane

FOOL ON THE HILL 10 b.g. Reprimand – Stock Hill Lass (Air Trooper) [2006/7 **c134 d**
c116, h–: c21v* c22g⁴ c21d c24gᵇᵈ c24d⁵ c22v⁴ c24d⁵ c24v³ c24s⁵ c24s⁵ Mar 3] rather **h–**
leggy gelding: winning hurdler: useful handicap chaser: won at Stratford in May by 14
lengths from Ticket To Ride: generally well below best: stays 2¾m: acts on heavy
and good to firm going: has had jumping problems. *P. J. Hobbs*

FOOTBALL CRAZY (IRE) 8 b.g. Mujadil (USA) – Schonbein (IRE) (Persian **h–**
Heights) [2006/7 h128: 20m⁴ Jul 5] lengthy, lengthy gelding: fairly useful handicap
hurdler: well held only outing in 2006/7: effective at 19f to 25f: acts on good to firm and
good to soft going (below best on soft): tried in headgear (not when successful). *P. Bowen*

FOOTY FACTS (IRE) 7 b.g. Oscar (IRE) – Princess Henry (IRE) (Callernish) **h136**
[2006/7 F115: 16s³ 24d⁴ 20s* 20v² Dec 17] point/bumper winner: took well to hurdling,
won listed novice at Cork and Grade 3 Bank of Ireland "Monksfield" Novices' Hurdle at
Navan (useful form, beat Casey Jones by 9 lengths) in November: 7 lengths second of 6
to very impressive Aran Concerto in Grade 1 at Navan: stays 3m: acts on heavy going.
Robert Tyner, Ireland

FORAFEWDOLLARSMORE (IRE) 5 b.g. Saddlers' Hall (IRE) – Gentle Leader **F111**
(IRE) (Supreme Leader) [2006/7 F18m* Jul 13] 32,000 3-y-o: brother to winning pointer
and half-brother to another by Fourstars Allstar: dam placed in points: favourite, won
bumper at Gowran on debut by 3 lengths from The Black Lion (pair well clear): looked
sure to go on to better things, but not seen out again. *N. Meade, Ireland*

FORAGER 8 ch.g. Faustus (USA) – Jolimo (Fortissimo) [2006/7 h–: c20d c24g⁴ **c94**
Mar 16] angular gelding: useful hurdler at best, no form in handicaps in 2005/6: modest **h–**
form over fences, lame final start: probably stays 3m: acts on soft going. *J. Ryan*

FOR ALL MANKIND 6 b.g. Zaffaran (USA) – Gilston Lass (Majestic Streak) **h116**
[2006/7 F92: 19s⁴ 21v⁵ 25v³ 21gᵘʳ Apr 18] well-made gelding: fairly useful form over

hurdles: won novice at Lingfield in November by 2½ lengths from Otto des Pictons: much better completed effort after when 2 lengths third to Supreme Cara at Warwick, not impressing with attitude: stays 25f: acts on heavy going: blinkered last 2 starts. *Carl Llewellyn*

FORBEARING (IRE) 10 b.g. Bering – For Example (USA) (Northern Baby (CAN)) **h72 §**
[2006/7 h–§: 16f 16s⁴ 16s⁵ 16m⁴ 16dᶠ Oct 22] angular gelding: poor hurdler nowadays: best around 2m: acts on soft going: formerly wore headgear: tongue tied last 2 outings: ungenuine. *K. G. Wingrove*

FORDHAM GLORY 9 b.g. Past Glories – Celtic Express (Pony Express) [2006/7 **c–**
c24s Mar 10] tall gelding: winning pointer: visored, well held in amateur event on chase debut. *Miss L. A. Blackford*

FORDINGBRIDGE (USA) 7 b.g. Diesis – Souffle (Zafonic (USA)) [2006/7 20d⁶ **h93**
24d Nov 21] lengthy gelding: fair hurdler at best: off 19 months, below form in 2006/7: should be suited by 2½m+: acts on soft ground: tried blinkered. *P. J. Hobbs*

FOREMAN (GER) 9 ch.g. Monsun (GER) – Fleurie (GER) (Dashing Blade) [2006/7 **c155**
c155, h128+: 19s² c16d³ c17dᵖᵘ Feb 10] lengthy, angular gelding: usually impresses in **h130 +**
appearance: very smart hurdler at best, second to Malcom in Grade 3 at Enghien on return: very smart chaser: ran creditably when 6½ lengths third of 5 to Voy Por Ustedes in steadily-run Grade 2 at Kempton (not helped by loose horse): rare poor effort next time (distressed): effective from 2m to 21f: acts on heavy and good to firm going: tried blinkered: sound jumper: reliable. *T. Doumen, France*

FOREST DANTE (IRE) 14 ch.g. Phardante (FR) – Mossy Mistress (IRE) (Le Moss) **c–**
[2006/7 c96, h83: c24mᵖᵘ c20gᵖᵘ Apr 23] big, lengthy gelding: twice-raced over hurdles: **h–**
modest handicap chaser: no show in 2006/7: effective at 19f to 3¼m: acts on good to firm and heavy going: blinkered once, usually wears cheekpieces: tends to idle. *F. Kirby*

FOREST EMERALD (IRE) 5 b.m. Desert Sun – Moonbi Range (IRE) (Nordico **h76**
(USA)) [2006/7 F79: 19gᵖᵘ 20mᵘʳ 16s⁶ 16g⁵ 16sᵖᵘ 19g 17g⁶ 16m⁴ 16f⁵ Apr 22] compact mare: poor novice hurdler: best around 2m: acts on firm going: visored last 7 starts. *J. W. Mullins*

FOREST GREEN (FR) 5 b.g. Green Tune (USA) – Farama (USA) (Seattle Song **h114**
(USA)) [2006/7 16s³ 16g³ 20s³ 16d⁶ 16s 20g Apr 12] tall, leggy gelding: has had breathing operation: brother to 11f winner/2¼m hurdle winner Faragreen and half-brother to 2m hurdle winner Le Farceur (by Zayyani): dam placed at 1¼m in France: fairly useful hurdler on his day, won 4-y-o event at Enghien in late-2005/6 for P. Sobry: placed in novices in Britain: likely to prove best around 2m: acts on soft going: tongue tied last 2 starts: tends to finish weakly. *P. F. Nicholls*

FOREST GUNNER 13 ch.g. Gunner B – Gouly Duff (Party Mink) [2006/7 c–, h–: **c–**
c26gᵘʳ Nov 19] leggy gelding: winning hurdler: useful chaser: twice successful over **h–**
National fences at Aintree, in Fox Hunters' and Grand Sefton in 2004, and fifth in Grand National following year: probably best short of 4½m: raced mainly on good going or softer (acted on soft): front runner/raced prominently: reportedly retired. *R. Ford*

FOREST LEAVES (IRE) 7 bl.g. Charnwood Forest (IRE) – Premier Code (IRE) **c110 §**
(Kefaah (USA)) [2006/7 22d* c17g c16s c20d c22s c24vᵘʳ c24v² c24s² c21vᶠ c21g⁴ c25m **h100 §**
Apr 28] compact gelding: fair novice hurdler/chaser: won maiden over hurdles at Down Royal in May: in lead when fell last in handicap chase at Fairyhouse won by The Flying Dustman: stays 3m: acts on heavy going: tried blinkered: ungenuine. *D. T. Hughes, Ireland*

FOREST MILLER 8 b.g. Classic Cliche (IRE) – Its My Turn (Palm Track) [2006/7 **c82**
h96, F85: 24s² c25s⁵ c26v³ c25s⁶ Jan 16] modest maiden hurdler: well beaten in maiden/ **h93**
handicap chases: should stay beyond 3m: raced on going softer than good. *R. T. Phillips*

FOREST PENNANT (IRE) 5 b.g. Accordion – Prudent View (IRE) (Supreme **F106 +**
Leader) [2006/7 F16s⁴ F16v⁶ F16s* Feb 9] tall, unfurnished gelding: fourth foal: half-brother to winning pointer by Shardari: dam unraced half-sister to useful staying hurdler/chaser Mr Gossip: improved form (useful) in bumpers when winning maiden at Kempton in February by 10 lengths from Ocean du Moulin: will stay beyond 2m. *P. F. Nicholls*

FOREST SILVER 5 gr.g. Silver Patriarch (IRE) – Miss Orphan (FR) (Round **F87**
Sovereign (FR)) [2006/7 F18d⁴ F17s³ F18v² F18v Mar 7] workmanlike gelding: second foal: dam fairly useful hurdler around 2m: fair form in bumpers. *J. W. Mullins*

FOREVER DREAM 9 b.g. Afzal – Quadrapol (Pollerton) [2006/7 c96§, h–: 21f 20f⁶ **c– §**
Jun 3] useful-looking gelding: winning chaser: fairly useful handicap hurdler at best, **h106 §**

below form early in 2006/7: successful over 23f, best form around 2m: acts on firm and soft going: has worn blinkers: held up: temperamental. *P. J. Hobbs*

FOREVER EYESOFBLUE 10 b.g. Leading Counsel (USA) – Forever Silver (IRE) (Roselier (FR)) [2006/7 c91x, h105: c24s⁴ c24mᵖᵘ c25s⁴ c25s² 27g² c24g² c28g² Apr 15] lengthy gelding: fair handicap hurdler: not as good over fences (often let down by jumping): stays 27f: acts on soft and good to firm ground. *A. Parker*   c93 x h102

FOREVER ROCKY 4 b.g. Kayf Tara – Song For Jess (IRE) (Accordion) [2006/7 16mᴿ Jul 16] of no account on Flat: behind when refused fifth in juvenile on hurdling debut. *F. Jordan*   h–

FORFEITER (USA) 5 ch.g. Petionville (USA) – Picabo (USA) (Wild Again (USA)) [2006/7 h–: 16g 16d⁵ 20s Apr 1] fair on Flat (stays 9f): modest form over hurdles: will prove best around 2m. *R. Ford*   h87

FORGET THE PAST 9 b.g. Past Glories – Worth Matravers (National Trust) [2006/7 c161, h–: 20v⁴ c20s* c24v⁴ c26g 24m³ 24m Apr 26] tall, strong gelding: lightly raced over hurdles, won minor event at Punchestown in January by ½ length from You Sir: very smart chaser at best, third to War of Attrition in 2006 Cheltenham Gold Cup: not quite so good in 2006/7, though won Grade 2 Kinloch Brae Chase at Thurles in January by 2 lengths from Hi Cloy: well held in latest renewal of Gold Cup: stays 3¼m: unraced on firm going, acts on any other: tongue tied in 2006/7. *M. J. P. O'Brien, Ireland*   c153 h122

FORGOTTEN FLOWERS (IRE) 6 b.m. Zaffaran (USA) – Mille Fleurs (FR) (Mister Mat (FR)) [2006/7 F17d⁶ Nov 7] first foal: dam, placed over 13f on Flat, out of half-sister to top-class hurdler/useful chaser Mister Banjo: in bumper on debut. *C. Grant*   F–

FORK LIGHTNING (IRE) 11 gr.g. Roselier (FR) – Park Breeze (IRE) (Strong Gale) [2006/7 c136, h–: c25mᶠ c24dᵘʳ c26v³ c24g c20vᶠ c19gᵖᵘ Mar 31] workmanlike gelding: useful handicap chaser at best: below form in 2006/7, possibly set too strong a pace fourth/fifth starts: would have been suited by further than 3¼m: acted on heavy and good to firm going: often jumped right over fences: reportedly retired. *A. King*   c122 x h–

FORMAL CLICHE 8 b.g. Classic Cliche (IRE) – Formal Affair (Rousillon (USA)) [2006/7 20s 24gᵘʳ 19v³ 24vᵖᵘ 20v² 21g* Mar 14] useful-looking gelding: poor hurdler: won selling handicap at Huntingdon in March: stays 3m: acts on heavy going: tried tongue tied. *K. G. Reveley*   h71

FORTHRIGHT 6 b.g. Cadeaux Genereux – Forthwith (Midyan (USA)) [2006/7 h103: 17s² 16m* 16g Apr 14] tall, strong gelding: fairly useful on Flat (stays 1½m), successful twice in 2006: fairly useful hurdler: improved form switched to handicap company when winning quite valuable event at Musselburgh in February by 1¾ lengths from Kings Quay, not always fluent: likely to prove suited by truly-run 2m: acts on soft and good to firm going: waited with: joined D. Loughnane in Ireland. *A. W. Carroll*   h121

FORTO (GER) 11 ch.g. Acatenango (GER) – Flunder (Nebos (GER)) [2006/7 c23mᵖᵘ Jun 28] medium-sized gelding: winning hurdler: runner-up in maiden on completed outing over fences, subsequently off 2 years: stays 3m: acts on soft and good to firm going. *Ian Williams*   c– h–

FORT ORD (IRE) 8 br.g. Norwich – Newtown Rose (IRE) (Roselier (FR)) [2006/7 16f 16m c20sᵖᵘ 18g⁵ 26g² 20d* 26g² 21s⁵ Dec 7] €16,000 4-y-o: leggy ex-Irish gelding: first foal: dam unraced: fair handicap hurdler, left N. Madden after second start: won conditional jockeys event at Sandown in November: none too fluent in handicap on chasing debut (finished distressed): stays 3¼m: acts on soft going (won bumper on firm). *Jonjo O'Neill*   c– h110

FORTUNATE DAVE (USA) 8 b.g. Lear Fan (USA) – Lady Ameriflora (USA) (Lord Avie (USA)) [2006/7 h–: 16g 22m* Apr 28] angular gelding: winning pointer: fair hurdler at best: in cheekpieces, won conditional jockeys handicap at Market Rasen in April: stays 2¾m: acts on soft and good to firm going: tried visored. *M. Smith*   h89 +

FORTUNATE ISLE (USA) 5 ch.g. Swain (IRE) – Isla Del Rey (USA) (Nureyev (USA)) [2006/7 16d³ 16m³ Feb 4] half-brother to fair hurdler Island Light (by Woodman), stays 21f: useful on Flat (stays 1¼m), sold out of B. Hills's stable 30,000 gns Newmarket Autumn Sales: third in maiden hurdles at Catterick (mistakes latter stages) and Musselburgh. *R. A. Fahey*   h99

FORTUNE POINT (IRE) 9 ch.g. Cadeaux Genereux – Mountains of Mist (IRE) (Shirley Heights) [2006/7 c–, h89: c16f³ c17g³ c16f* c17dᵖᵘ Oct 14] angular gelding: fair on Flat, successful in June: winning hurdler: modest chaser: won maiden at Worcester in September: raced around 2m: acts on soft and firm going: tried visored: moody. *A. W. Carroll*   c95 § h– §

FORTUNE'S FOOL 8 b.g. Zilzal (USA) – Peryllys (Warning) [2006/7 h69: 20d^{pu} 16g 19g c20m^{pu} c20g^{pu} Apr 23] rather leggy gelding: poor handicap hurdler: no show in maiden chases: stays 21f: acts on firm going. *I. A. Brown*   **c–**
h–

FORTY SHAKES (IRE) 8 ch.g. Moonax (IRE) – Forty Quid (IRE) (Exhibitioner) [2006/7 F–: c25s* c27s* c20g^3 Mar 27] strong gelding: won twice in points in 2005: successful first 2 starts in hunters, at Catterick (novice) and Sedgefield (fairly useful form, readily by 6 lengths from Rebel Army) in March: stays 27f, effective over shorter: acts on soft going. *Miss Maria D. Myco*   **c103**

FORZACURITY 8 ch.g. Forzando – Nice Lady (Connaught) [2006/7 h101d: 16m^4 19d^4 17m 17d 16m 20m 17m 20m 20g 16d^6 16d^{pu} 16d^5 16d^5 17v^4 16d 17s^5 Dec 23] leggy gelding: fair handicap hurdler at best: little form in 2006/7, left D. Burchell after tenth start: raced mainly around 2m: acts on good to firm and heavy going: tried in cheekpieces/tongue tied. *M. A. Doyle*   **h85 d**

FORZAISLE 5 b.g. Forzando – Broom Isle (Damister (USA)) [2006/7 F16m Jun 11] fourth foal: half-brother to fair 2m hurdler Bolshoi Ballet (by Dancing Spree): dam, winning hurdler up to 2½m, also successful up to 15f on Flat: joint favourite, well beaten in maiden bumper on debut. *J. R. Best*   **F–**

FOSROC (USA) 5 ch.g. Royal Anthem (USA) – Stellar Blush (USA) (Blushing John (USA)) [2006/7 16g^3 16f^6 19m Oct 4] maiden on Flat, sold out of J. S. Moore's stable £350 Ascot October Sales: best effort over hurdles when sixth in novice at Plumpton: tongue tied last 2 outings. *B. R. Johnson*   **h85**

FOTA ISLAND (IRE) 11 b.g. Supreme Leader – Mary Kate Finn (Saher) [2006/7 c156, h–: c16s^5 c16s^6 c19d^5 Feb 17] big, good sort: smart chaser: below best in 2006/7, helped force good pace when fifth of 7 to Monet's Garden in Grade 1 at Ascot final start: stays 2½m: acts on heavy going. *M. F. Morris, Ireland*   **c144 +**
h–

FOUNTAIN CRUMBLE 6 b.m. Dr Massini (IRE) – My Lisa Too (K-Battery) [2006/7 h81+, F90: 22g* 20m^5 24m^4 22m^3 21m^2 24d* 24g* 24s* 24d^2 25v^4 22g^2 21g Apr 19] small mare: developed into fairly useful hurdler in 2006/7, winning novices at Newton Abbot (handicap) in May, Exeter (amateur event) in October and Taunton in November, and handicap at Taunton (by 7 lengths from Lyes Green) in December: good efforts in handicaps 3 of last 4 starts: stays 25f: acts on heavy and good to firm going (bumper winner on firm): sometimes let down by jumping: consistent. *P. F. Nicholls*   **h121**

FOUNTAIN FORTUNE 5 b.g. Kayf Tara – My Lisa Too (K-Battery) [2006/7 F16g^4 F16d F17g^2 F17s 19v 21g Mar 23] lengthy gelding: closely related to fairly useful hurdler Fountain Crumble (by Dr Massini), stays 25f: dam lightly-raced novice hurdler: fair form in frame in bumpers: well held over hurdles. *A. J. Honeyball*   **h–**
F85

FOUNTAIN HILL (IRE) 8 b.g. King's Theatre (IRE) – Highest Land (FR) (Highest Honor (FR)) [2006/7 c19s^2 c21v^3 c23g^3 Mar 25] good-topped gelding: useful hurdler in 2004/5: fair form first 2 starts in maiden chases, third to Moncadou at Folkestone: should prove as effective at 3m+ as shorter: acts on heavy ground (bumper winner on good to firm). *P. F. Nicholls*   **c114**
h–

FOURBOYSTOY (IRE) 8 ch.g. Roselier (FR) – Little Twig (IRE) (Good Thyne (USA)) [2006/7 c–, h–: c19g^{ur} c20d^{pu} 24s^{pu} Mar 11] lengthy gelding: won maiden hurdle in 2004: no other form (has had pelvis problem). *C. C. Bealby*   **c–**
h–

FOUR CANDLES 7 b.m. Perpendicular – Skyers Tryer (Lugana Beach) [2006/7 16v^{pu} 16v^{pu} Feb 17] of no account. *B. P. J. Baugh*   **h–**

FOUR FOR A LAUGH (IRE) 8 b.g. Fourstars Allstar (USA) – She's No Laugh Ben (USA) (Alleged (USA)) [2006/7 h95p, F–: 20s^F 20d^5 Dec 28] modest form at best in novice hurdles, reportedly fractured pelvis in mid 2005/6 outing. *A. King*   **h85**

FOUR IN HAND 9 b.m. Supreme Leader – Relkissimo (Relkino) [2006/7 h77?: 22m May 11] lightly-raced maiden pointer: poor form over hurdles. *Mrs K. M. Sanderson*   **h–**

FOUR KISSES (IRE) 7 b.m. Supreme Leader – Danjo's Lady (IRE) (Carlingford Castle) [2006/7 F–: F16f F17m F16s Dec 26] sturdy mare: well held in bumpers. *Ms Sue Smith*   **F–**

FOUR OPINIONS 11 b.g. Cruise Missile – Stockton Slave (Bivouac) [2006/7 c23f^3 c25d^4 c16s^3 c25g^2 Apr 11] fair pointer, successful twice in 2006: maiden chaser: stays 25f: let down by jumping second outing. *Miss Joanne Priest*   **c90**

FOURPOINTONE 6 b.g. Overbury (IRE) – Praise The Lord (Lord Gayle (USA)) [2006/7 24g^5 22m^2 22m 24f 20g^3 24d^2 20v^4 26g^4 24d^5 22v^4 21v^6 Dec 28] close-coupled   **h79**

gelding: poor maiden handicap hurdler: stays 3¼m: acts on heavy and good to firm going: wears cheekpieces: consistent. *Eric McNamara, Ireland*

FOUR SCHOOLS (IRE) 5 b.g. Raise A Grand (IRE) – Haanem (Mtoto) [2006/7   **c107** h110: 17s^pu 16m^4 16g 16g^6 c20s^4 c16s c16d^2 c19d^ur c21s^ur Jan 20] leggy gelding: fairly   **h117** useful hurdler: fair form over fences, let down by jumping last 2 starts: probably stays 2½m: acts on soft and good to firm going: has worn blinkers, including last 3 outings. *Jonjo O'Neill*

FOURTH PRESENCE 5 b.g. Overbury (IRE) – East Rose (Keen) [2006/7 F17s^5   **F77** Jun 27] first foal: dam ran once: fifth of 11 in bumper at Newton Abbot on debut, pulling hard. *M. D. I. Usher*

FOURTY ACERS (IRE) 7 ch.g. Bob Back (USA) – Guest Cailin (IRE) (Be My Guest   **c117 x** (USA)) [2006/7 h116p, F104: c20d* c21v^pu c20g^ur c23f* c21g^3 Apr 27] bumper winner: **h–** fairly useful form over hurdles: likewise over fences, winning maiden at Ludlow in November and 3-runner handicap at Exeter in April: shaped as if amiss/let down by jumping all other starts: will stay 3m: acts on soft and firm going: tongue tied in 2006/7. *D. E. Pipe*

FOX JOHN 8 b.g. Ballet Royal (USA) – Muskerry Miss (IRE) (Bishop of Orange)   **c–** [2006/7 c25g^pu c23f^pu Jun 3] in frame in bumpers: no form over hurdles/in chases (lame   **h–** final outing), though successful twice in points in 2006: should stay at least 2½m. *H. J. Manners*

FOXMEADE DANCER 9 b.g. Lyphento (USA) – Georgian Quickstep (Dubassoff   **c–** (USA)) [2006/7 c77, h79: c16v^pu Jan 11] good-topped gelding: poor hurdler/chaser: stays   **h–** 2¾m: acts on heavy going: tends to find little. *P. C. Ritchens*

FOX 'N' GOOSE (IRE) 7 ch.g. Ashmolean (USA) – Creative Flight (IRE) (Creative   **h–** Plan (USA)) [2006/7 h96: 20s^pu 17s 18s 16s 19g Mar 25] good-topped gelding: second in novice hurdle on debut in 2005: no form since: tongue tied last 4 starts. *P. C. Ritchens*

FOX POINT (USA) 7 b.g. Foxhound (USA) – Linklee (USA) (Linkage (USA))   **h105** [2006/7 h105: 21g^2 21m^2 May 16] good-topped gelding: fair hurdler: stays 21f: acts on heavy and good to firm ground: tried in cheekpieces: sold 5,000 gns Doncaster October Sales. *P. C. Haslam*

FOXTON BROOK (IRE) 8 br.g. Presenting – Martins Times (IRE) (Bulldozer)   **h–** [2006/7 16s Oct 25] well-made gelding: modest form on first of 3 outings over hurdles: placed 4 times in maiden points in 2006: should stay beyond 21f. *K. C. Bailey*

FOXTROT YANKEE (IRE) 8 b.g. Lord Americo – Derby Fox (IRE) (King's Ride)   **h98** [2006/7 h81: 21m^pu 16m^5 17s^2 Nov 17] angular gelding: modest maiden hurdler: keen-going sort, likely to have proved best around 2m: dead. *Andrew Turnell*

FRANCESCAS BOY (IRE) 4 b.g. Titus Livius (FR) – Mica Male (ITY) (Law   **h–** Society (USA)) [2006/7 17g^pu Sep 23] no form on Flat or hurdling debut. *P. D. Niven*

FRANCESCHIELLA (ITY) 6 gr.m. Beat of Drums – Filicaia (Sallust) [2006/7 F70:   **h–** F17d 16d 16s 16g 20g^pu 16g Apr 9] workmanlike mare: little sign of ability: tried   **F–** blinkered. *Lady Susan Watson*

FRANCINES-BOY (IRE) 11 b.g. Namaqualand (USA) – Nancy Drew (Sexton   **c99** Blake) [2006/7 c20s^3 c20g^4 c24g* c24s^5 Sep 20] sturdy gelding: one-time fair handicap   **h–** chaser: left C. Roche and off over 2 years, best effort in 2006/7 when winning at Uttoxeter in July: stays 3m: acts on good to firm and heavy going: tried blinkered. *J. S. Smith*

FRANCIS DUNSTAN (IRE) 5 b.g. Shernazar – Audrey's Turn (Strong Gale)   **F–** [2006/7 F16m F16m Apr 10] big, lengthy gelding: half-brother to winning hurdler/chaser Behavingbadly (by Lord Americo), stays 31f, and to 2 winning pointers: dam unraced half-sister to useful staying chaser Deep South: well held in bumpers. *A. W. Carroll*

FRANCO (IRE) 9 b.g. Rashar (USA) – Market Thyne (IRE) (Good Thyne (USA))   **c– x** [2006/7 c–x, h106: 19d* Dec 26] tall, lengthy gelding: winning pointer: let down by   **h125** jumping both starts in hunter chases (bled second time): improved form (fairly useful) over hurdles when winning handicap at Market Rasen (making all to beat Kingsbury by 3½ lengths) in December, only outing in 2006/7: stays 2¾m: acts on soft going: ran out once in 2005/6. *Mrs A. E. Brooks*

FRANK CARTWRIGHT (IRE) 4 b.g. Mull of Kintyre (USA) – Punta Gorda (IRE)   **h–** (Roi Danzig (USA)) [2006/7 17m^pu Aug 26] no show on Flat or hurdling debut. *A. Berry*

FRANKIE DORI (IRE) 8 b.g. Key of Luck (USA) – Kitty's Sister (Bustino) [2006/7   **c–** c100, h–: c27m^F Jun 7] lengthy gelding: fair handicap chaser: fell fatally at Sedgefield: **h–** stayed 25f: acted on heavy going: tried blinkered: inconsistent. *S. Donohoe, Ireland*

FRANKIE FIGG (IRE) 5 b.g. Portrait Gallery (IRE) – Ardnataggle (IRE) (Aristo-   **h97**
cracy) [2006/7 20d⁴ 24v⁴ 16v² 25g² Apr 16] €30,000 3-y-o: first foal: dam, modest
staying chaser, sister to smart staying hurdler/chaser Lord Transcend: modest form over
hurdles: found little when second to Hilly Gale in maiden at Wetherby final outing.
J. Howard Johnson

FRANKINCENSE (IRE) 11 gr.g. Paris House – Mistral Wood (USA) (Far North   **h79**
(CAN)) [2006/7 h–: 20d 20v⁶ 19s⁶ 19g⁵ 17d 19v² 20g* 23gᵘʳ Apr 3] close-coupled
gelding: poor handicap hurdler: won selling event at Sedgefield in March: barely stays
testing 27f: acts on heavy going: has worn cheekpieces: usually races prominently.
A. J. Lockwood

FRANKLINS TRAIL (IRE) 6 b.g. Imperial Ballet (IRE) – Nettle (Kris) [2006/7   **h123**
18v⁴ 16v* 18v² Jan 6] lightly-raced 9f winner on Flat: confirmed promise of hurdling
debut when winning 20-runner maiden at Gowran in December by head from Druids
Castle, having been left with bit to do: better form again when 2 lengths second to Wins
Now in minor event at Cork: stays 2¼m: raced on heavy going. *W. P. Mullins, Ireland*

FRED BOJANGALS (IRE) 5 b.g. Scribano – Southern Princess (Black Minstrel)   **h–**
[2006/7 16s Jan 31] big gelding: chasing type: third foal: half-brother to 2m hurdle
winner Soundz of Muzic (by Supreme Leader): dam winning Irish pointer: well beaten in
novice hurdle on debut: joined Mrs A. Hamilton. *J. Howard Johnson*

FREDDIES RETURN (IRE) 5 b.g. Flemensfirth (USA) – Rachael's Dawn   **h92 +**
(Rakaposhi King) [2006/7 F16d F16v 19v² Feb 23] €45,000 4-y-o: strong gelding: **F85**
second foal: dam bumper winner: mid-field in bumpers: 50/1, 15 lengths second to
Pancake in novice at Warwick on hurdling debut, keeping on well having still been in rear
leaving back straight: will be suited by 2½m+. *J. A. B. Old*

FREDDIE THE THIRD (IRE) 5 b.g. Good Thyne (USA) – Actress Mandy (IRE)   **F105**
(Mandalus) [2006/7 F16v³ F16v* F16d F16s Apr 27] €9,000 3-y-o: big, strong gelding:
ninth foal: half-brother to 2 winning pointers by Montelimar: dam unraced: confirmed
promise of debut when winning 19-runner bumper at Warwick in January by 6 lengths
from Spud: lost all chance when running very wide on first bend in Grade 2 at Newbury
next time: bred to stay 2½m+: front runner. *N. A. Twiston-Davies*

FREDDY'S STAR (IRE) 5 ch.g. Kris – Kutaisi (IRE) (Soviet Star (USA)) [2006/7   **F89**
F16v F16v⁶ F16g³ Mar 21] 4,000 4-y-o: leggy gelding: fourth foal: half-brother to bumper winner Rachel's Choice (by Ela-Mana-Mou): dam unraced out of smart performer up
to 1¼m Mamouna: best effort in bumpers (raced on heavy going previously) when third
to Hillridge at Chepstow, making running and collared only on line. *L. Corcoran*

FREDENSBORG (NZ) 6 b.g. Danske (NZ) – Showplace (AUS) (Palace Music   **h114**
(USA)) [2006/7 F94: 16d⁴ 17s³ 16s* Jan 10] tall, useful-looking gelding: best effort over
hurdles (raced freely first 2 outings) when winning 18-runner maiden at Wincanton by 4
lengths from Habanero, around ½ length down when left in lead last: raced around 2m on
ground softer than good. *Miss Venetia Williams*

FREEDOM FLYING 4 b.f. Kalanisi (IRE) – Free Spirit (IRE) (Caerleon (USA))   **h73**
[2006/7 F14v F14v⁴ 16v² 17v³ 20s⁶ Mar 13] smallish, sparely-made filly: fourth foal: **F73**
half-sister to fairly useful 1m winner (including at 2 yrs) Arkholme (by Robellino) and
6f winner Perfect Love (by Pursuit of Love), both fairly useful: dam unraced half-
sister to smart 1m/1¼m performer Gold Academy: poor form in bumpers/over hurdles.
P. C. Haslam

FREEDOM FRIX 5 b.g. Bandmaster (USA) – Almary (Almoojid) [2006/7 F16g F16g   **F–**
Mar 19] second foal: dam well beaten in bumpers: towards rear in bumpers. *R. H. Buckler*

FREEDOM NOW (IRE) 9 b.g. Sadler's Wells (USA) – Free At Last (Shirley   **h–**
Heights) [2006/7 h102: 17v 24s 23gᵘʳ Apr 3] close-coupled gelding: fair handicap hurdler
on his day: left R. Alner, well held on completed outings in 2006/7 for P. Rodford: sold
£1,000 Ascot February Sales: effective at 2m to 3m: acts on good to firm and good to soft
going. *W. M. Brisbourne*

FREE FROM MAGEE (IRE) 7 ch.g. Denel (FR) – Arctic Gem (Rakaposhi King)   **h–**
[2006/7 16gᵖᵘ 24sᵖᵘ 20gᵖᵘ Apr 16] €1,400 6-y-o: second foal: dam, lightly raced in
points, out of half-sister to dam of top-class 2m chaser Pearlyman: no form over hurdles.
J. R. Norton

FREE GIFT 9 b.g. Presenting – Gladtogetit (Green Shoon) [2006/7 c120+: c20m²   **c116**
c21m² c20d⁴ c23s⁵ c21g² c21g Mar 30] lengthy gelding: fairly useful handicap chaser:
best form around 2½m: acts on soft and good to firm going: usually races prominently:
sound jumper. *R. H. Alner*

FREELOADER (IRE) 7 b.g. Revoque (IRE) – Indian Sand (Indian King (USA)) **h108 +**
[2006/7 17g* 16g⁴ 16d Nov 11] sturdy gelding: fairly useful on Flat (stays 1¼m), successful in September: won novice at Market Rasen on hurdling debut week later, jumping fluently and beating Mr Shambles 9 lengths with something to spare: much stiffer task next time/possibly unsuited by softer ground final outing: may still do better at 2m with emphasis on speed. *R. A. Fahey*

FREE STRIKE (NZ) 10 ch.g. Straight Strike (USA) – Ansellia (NZ) (Nassipour **c–**
(USA)) [2006/7 24fᵖᵘ Jun 3] leggy, plain gelding: novice hurdler/chaser, very lightly **h–**
raced. *P. Mitchell*

FREE TO AIR 4 b.g. Generous (IRE) – Petonica (IRE) (Petoski) [2006/7 16d Nov 24] **h–**
tall, angular gelding: fairly useful on Flat (stays 1½m), successful twice in 2006: well held in juvenile at Newbury on hurdling debut. *A. M. Balding*

FREETOWN (IRE) 11 b.g. Shirley Heights – Pageantry (Welsh Pageant) [2006/7 c–, **c–**
h123: 24s² 24v⁶ 24g 24g Apr 14] leggy gelding: winning chaser but failed to complete **h132 d**
last 2 starts over fences: useful handicap hurdler: neck second to Material World at Cheltenham on reappearance, hanging right: well below that form after: suited by 3m+: raced mainly on good going or softer (acts on heavy), probably unsuited by firm: won only start in cheekpieces, usually blinkered nowadays. *L. Lungo*

FREE WORLD (IRE) 5 b.g. Luso – Paddy's Dancer (Paddy's Stream) [2006/7 F16v **F– p**
Nov 26] big, rangy gelding: half-brother to winning pointer by Over The River: dam placed in points: shaped better than result suggested when tenth of 18 to Schiehallion in bumper at Newbury on debut, still travelling well entering straight and not at all knocked about once beaten: sure to improve. *Carl Llewellyn*

FREEZE THE DREAM 5 b.m. North Col – Frozen Pipe (Majestic Maharaj) [2006/7 **F–**
F16s Dec 3] fourth foal: dam winning pointer: soundly beaten in bumper on debut. *L. A. Dace*

FREEZE THE FLAME (GER) 4 b.g. In The Wings – Fantastic Flame (IRE) (Gene- **h124**
rous (IRE)) [2006/7 17m³ 17g* 16s* 16g* 16d² 16d² 17g Mar 16] compact gelding: modest maiden up to 1½m on Flat: fairly useful juvenile hurdler: won at Bangor in September and Uttoxeter in October: ran well when twice runner-up after, including when beaten neck by Katchit in Grade 2 at Cheltenham: off 4 months, well held in Triumph Hurdle: will stay beyond 2m: acts on soft ground: races prominently. *C. R. Egerton*

FREEZE UP (IRE) 5 b.g. Presenting – Ballymacoda Lady (IRE) (Lord Ha Ha) **F86**
[2006/7 F17v⁴ F16g⁶ Mar 6] rather unfurnished gelding: fourth foal: dam, fair hurdler, stayed 3m: better effort in bumpers when around 10 lengths sixth to Theft at Kempton: will be suited by 2½m+. *V. R. A. Dartnall*

FRENCH BOY (IRE) 14 b.g. John French – Whiteroom (Bulldozer) [2006/7 c21gᵘʳ **c–**
May 3] workmanlike ex-Irish gelding: modest pointer, finally got off mark in 2006: little **h–**
form in other events: has worn blinkers. *Mrs S. S. Harbour*

FRENCH DIRECTION 8 ch.g. John French – Shelikesitstraight (IRE) **c80 x**
(Rising) [2006/7 c98§, h–x: 18m⁶ c18f⁴ Jun 6] maiden hurdler: winning chaser, poor on **h75 x**
balance of form: raced mainly around 2m: acts on firm and good to soft going: usually front runner/races prominently: makes mistakes: not one to rely on. *R. Rowe*

FRENCHGATE 6 br.g. Paris House – Let's Hang On (IRE) (Petorius) [2006/7 h–: 16s⁶ **h–**
16v 16d Dec 28] sparely-made gelding: poor maiden around 1m on Flat: no form over hurdles. *I. W. McInnes*

FRENCH OPERA 4 b.g. Bering – On Fair Stage (IRE) (Sadler's Wells (USA)) **h114 p**
[2006/7 17g* Mar 25] modest form on Flat (should be suited by 1½m): left J. Osborne and favourite, won juvenile maiden at Taunton on hurdling debut by 3½ lengths from Sabre Hongrois, recovering from stumble turning in and forging away run-in: should progress. *N. J. Henderson*

FRENCH SAULAIE (FR) 6 b.g. French Glory – Parade Royale (FR) (Garde Royale) **h130 +**
[2006/7 16s* 17s⁵ 16v⁴ 16v* 17v² 19d 16s² 21g* Apr 18] leggy, useful-looking gelding: second foal: half-brother to winning 2¼m/2½m French chaser by Signe Divin: dam 1½m winner/winning 2m hurdler in France: useful hurdler: in frame both completed starts in 5-y-o events at Pau for Mlle S. Losch: successful in novices at Worcester in May and Huntingdon in January, and handicap at Cheltenham in April: upped in trip, further progress when beating stable-companion Chilling Place 5 lengths at last-named, shaken up to assert run-in: stays 21f: raced on good ground or softer: races freely. *P. J. Hobbs*

FRESH AIR AND FUN (IRE) 4 b. or br.g. Trans Island – Executive Ellie (IRE) **F101**
(Executive Perk) [2006/7 F12g² Mar 23] €33,000 3-y-o, resold £38,000 3-y-o:
good-topped, attractive gelding: third foal: half-brother to fairly useful 19f hurdle winner
Malachy's Attic (by Old Vic): dam unraced: encouraging debut when length second of 18
to Whiteoak in 4-y-o bumper at Newbury. *Jonjo O'Neill*

FRESH WINTER 5 br.g. Overbury (IRE) – Olnistar (FR) (Balsamo (FR)) [2006/7 **F90**
F16v³ F17d⁶ Mar 19] 11,000 3-y-o: good-bodied gelding: half-brother to winning
hurdler/chaser Petolinski (by Petoski), stayed 3m, and modest staying hurdler Ardent
Lover (by Ardross): dam, fairly useful hurdler up to 25f, half-sister to high-class hurdler/
chaser Sabin du Loir: better effort in bumpers when 6½ lengths third to Massasoit in
maiden at Catterick: will be suited by 2½m+. *J. Mackie*

FRETEVAL (FR) 10 b.g. Valanjou (FR) – La Beaumont (FR) (Hellios (USA)) [2006/7 **c– x**
c77x, h–: c21s Jan 2] good-bodied gelding: poor handicap chaser: well beaten only **h–**
completed start since 2003/4: stays 3m: acts on soft going. *S. J. Gilmore*

FRIEDHELMO (GER) 11 ch.g. Dashing Blade – Fox For Gold (Glint of Gold) **c– §**
[2006/7 c–§, h–§: 16s³ 17d 16g⁵ 16f⁴ 17f³ 16fᵖᵈ 17m² 17m 17v⁵ 16d Oct 22] strong, **h62 §**
lengthy gelding: winning chaser: poor hurdler nowadays: raced mainly around 2m: acts
on firm and soft going: tried in cheekpieces: tongue tied: unreliable. *S. B. Clark*

FRIENDLY GIRL (IRE) 8 b.m. King's Ride – Royal Patrol (IRE) (Phardante (FR)) **h–**
[2006/7 24d Oct 5] little sign of ability: sold 1,500 gns Doncaster January Sales.
N. J. Hawke

FRIENDLY REQUEST 8 b.m. Environment Friend – Who Tells Jan (Royal Foun- **h81**
tain) [2006/7 h85: 24gᵖᵘ 22d 24g⁶ 22g⁶ 22m⁵ 27m⁴ 24g 21f 22s⁴ 22s 20s⁵ 19dᶠ 22m
Apr 28] angular mare: poor handicap hurdler: stays 3m: acts on soft going. *N. J. Hawke*

FRISKY JOHN 4 gr.g. My Best Valentine – Risky Girl (Risk Me (FR)) [2006/7 F16m **F80**
F16m⁶ Apr 24] first foal: dam, 6f winner, successful over hurdles around 2m: better effort
in bumpers when sixth to The Package in maiden at Towcester. *H. J. Manners*

FROGHOLE FLYER 8 ch.g. Presenting – Peptic Lady (IRE) (Royal Fountain) **c–**
[2006/7 h85: 16s⁶ 22m 20mᵖᵘ Jun 8] rather plain gelding: won selling handicap hurdle **h–**
at Plumpton in 2005/6, virtually only form: tried blinkered. *G. L. Moore*

FROGS' GIFT (IRE) 5 gr.m. Danehill Dancer (IRE) – Warthill Whispers (Grey **h–**
Desire) [2006/7 17m 16g Oct 7] poor maiden on Flat: well beaten in novice hurdles.
G. M. Moore

FROM DAWN TO DUSK 8 b.g. Afzal – Herald The Dawn (Dubassoff (USA)) **c130**
[2006/7 h100p: 21g* 20dⁿ 21d² 21d⁴ c24s⁴ c20d³ c19d* c22g* c25m³ Apr 21] good- **h118 +**
topped, workmanlike gelding: fairly useful hurdler: won handicaps at Huntingdon
(easily) in May and Worcester in October: twice in frame in 3 days at Cheltenham next 2
starts, including when second to After Midnight in conditional jockeys handicap:
progressive form in novice chases: won at Exeter in March and Haydock in April, useful
form when beating Chickapeakray by 5 lengths at latter: ran as if amiss final outing: stays
2¾m: acts on good to firm and good to soft going. *P. J. Hobbs*

FROM LITTLE ACORNS (IRE) 11 b.g. Denel (FR) – Mount Gawn (Harwell) **c–**
[2006/7 16g 17d² 21m c25sᵖᵘ Jun 25] small gelding: winning pointer, off 4 years before **h92**
return in 2006: modest hurdler: pulled up on chasing debut: should stay 2¾m: acts on
good to firm and good to soft going. *Ferdy Murphy*

FRONTENAC (IRE) 11 ch.g. Mister Lord (USA) – Daffydown Dolly (IRE) (The **c84**
Parson) [2006/7 c–: c26m⁴ c26v² May 20] fair pointer, successful in April: best effort in
hunters when second to Knife Edge at Uttoxeter: will stay extreme distances: acts on
heavy going. *Mrs Mandy Hand*

FRONT RANK (IRE) 7 b.g. Sadler's Wells (USA) – Alignment (IRE) (Alzao (USA)) **h124 §**
[2006/7 h114§: 16mᶠ 16g⁵ 16s³ 16m* 17s* 16m 16gᵖᵘ 16v⁵ 20vᵖᵘ 20s Apr 26] sturdy
gelding: fairly useful handicap hurdler: won at Kelso and Carlisle (best effort, beat Time
Marches On 6 lengths) in October: ran poorly after: best form around 2m: unraced on
firm going, acts on any other: has worn blinkers (including when successful)/cheek-
pieces: tried tongue tied: inconsistent. *Mrs Dianne Sayer*

FROSTY JAK 9 b.g. Morpeth – Allied Newcastle (Crooner) [2006/7 h73: c20m⁴ 27m⁶ **c107**
c21g² c24s* c24d* c24dᶠ c23vᵖᵘ Jan 1] leggy gelding: poor hurdler: much better over **h–**
fences: won handicaps at Uttoxeter in October and Chepstow (novice) in November, and
novice at Fakenham (beat only other finisher Lord of The Road 2½ lengths) in December:
went as if amiss final outing: stays 3m: acts on soft going: tried blinkered. *J. D. Frost*

FROSTY RUN (IRE) 9 b.g. Commanche Run – Here To-Day (King's Equity) [2006/7   **c91 x**
c91, h–: c25m³ c24sᵖᵘ 26m 24mᵖᵘ Apr 15] sturdy gelding: lightly raced: winning hurdler: **h– x**
modest form both completed starts over fences: stays 3¼m: acts on good to firm and good
to soft going: usually let down by jumping: sold 1,000 gns Doncaster May Sales. *Heather
Dalton*

FUERO REAL (FR) 12 b.g. Highest Honor (FR) – Highest Pleasure (USA) (Foolish   **c–**
Pleasure (USA)) [2006/7 27dᵖᵘ Aug 21] sturdy gelding: of no account nowadays: tried in **h–**
headgear. *R. Brotherton*

FU FIGHTER 6 b.g. Unfuwain (USA) – Runelia (Runnett) [2006/7 h100: c26mᶠ   **c§§**
c20mᴿ 19gᴿ Jul 23] sturdy gelding: fair handicap hurdler: held in third when fell 4 out in **h§§**
maiden at Southwell on chasing debut: reluctant to race/refused early both starts after:
stays 3¼m: acts on good to firm and good to soft going: tried in cheekpieces: has had
tongue tied: one to avoid. *Evan Williams*

FULLARDS 9 b.g. Alderbrook – Milly Kelly (Murrayfield) [2006/7 c105, h98: 23d*   **c98**
c24sᵘʳ c28d³ c24sᵖᵘ c24sᵖᵘ 24sᶠ Mar 11] sturdy gelding: fair chaser/handicap hurdler: **h113**
better than ever when winning at Lingfield in November: failed to complete most starts
after: stays 3¼m: raced on good going or softer (acts on heavy): successful with or
without tongue strap: sometimes let down by jumping over fences. *Mrs P. Sly*

FULL AS A ROCKET (IRE) 6 b.g. Foxhound (USA) – Taysala (IRE) (Akarad (FR))   **h91**
[2006/7 16d* 19d 20v* Dec 27] useful-looking gelding: runner-up in bumper: modest
maiden on Flat, well beaten both starts in 2006: similar standard over hurdles, won sellers
at Uttoxeter in November and Wetherby (in cheekpieces, by 24 lengths) in December:
stays 2½m: acts on heavy ground: has raced freely. *R. Ford*

FULL HOUSE (IRE) 8 br.g. King's Theatre (IRE) – Nirvavita (FR) (Highest Honor   **c135**
(FR)) [2006/7 c144, h–: c22gᵖᵘ c20gᶠ c16f⁶ Apr 28] leggy, close-coupled gelding: **h–**
winning hurdler: useful chaser: lightly raced in 2006/7, possibly amiss on return (fit from
Flat, won in June), then stiff tasks in Grade 2 events: stays 2¾m: acts on good to soft and
good to firm going. *P. R. Webber*

FULL OF ZEST 5 ch.m. Pivotal – Tangerine (Primo Dominie) [2006/7 16f 20g⁴ 20g⁴   **h81**
19v⁴ 20m Mar 25] fair maiden at best on Flat: poor novice hurdler: stays 2½m, at least
when conditions aren't testing: blinkered last 2 starts. *Mrs L. J. Mongan*

FULL ON 10 b.g. Le Moss – Flighty Dove (Cruise Missile) [2006/7 c96, h91: c20mᶠ   **c75**
c22g c24v c24v² c23s⁶ c25v⁵ c26g² c23m⁵ Apr 25] useful-looking gelding: maiden **h–**
hurdler/chaser, just poor form in 2006/7: stays 3¼m: acts on heavy going, probably on
good to firm: blinkered (folded tamely) once, in cheekpieces last 2 starts. *A. M. Hales*

FU MANCHU 5 b.g. Desert Style (IRE) – Robsart (IRE) (Robellino (USA)) [2006/7   **h103 §**
h95§: 17g* 17m⁶ 20m² 20d³ Aug 14] compact gelding: fair hurdler: off 7 months, won
novice handicap at Newton Abbot in June: stays 2½m: acts on good to firm and good to
soft going: tried blinkered: temperamental. *Jonjo O'Neill*

FUNDAMENTALIST (IRE) 9 b.g. Supreme Leader – Run For Shelter (Strong Gale)   **c137 x**
[2006/7 c151, h–: c24d² c24s c25v⁵ c20s⁶ c25gᵖᵘ Apr 13] strong, well-made gelding: **h–**
one of best novice hurdlers of 2003/4, won Royal & SunAlliance at Cheltenham: also
made very promising start over fences, but largely let down by jumping since and useful
form at best in 2006/7: stays 3m: raced on good going or softer: tried tongue tied.
N. A. Twiston-Davies

FUNNY FELLOW 5 b.g. Defacto (USA) – Royal Comedian (Jester) [2006/7 F–: F18s   **h–**
F14v 21g⁴ 19g Apr 8] well beaten in bumpers: dropped out and not given hard time over **F–**
hurdles: tried blinkered. *R. Rowe*

FUNNY TIMES 6 b.m. Silver Patriarch (IRE) – Elegant City (Scallywag) [2006/7   **h– x**
h107p: 20s⁵ Oct 11] workmanlike mare: dual bumper winner: showed promise first
2 starts in novice hurdles: off 8 months, tended to jump right when well held only outing
in 2006/7: likely to stay beyond 2½m: sold 34,000 gns Doncaster January Sales.
N. G. Richards

FUTOO (IRE) 6 b.g. Foxhound (USA) – Nicola Wynn (Nicholas Bill) [2006/7 h84:   **h–**
16g 16d⁵ 17m Apr 15] tall, rather leggy gelding: modest on Flat (best short of 1½m)
nowadays: maiden hurdler, little show in 2006/7: in cheekpieces/blinkers 3 of last 4 starts.
D. W. Chapman

FUTURE LEGEND 6 ch.g. Lomitas – Proudy (IRE) (Night Shift (USA)) [2006/7 h94:   **h85**
24d⁵ 20gᵖᵘ 20m⁵ Jul 12] modest maiden hurdler: stays 2½m: acts on good to firm going:
tongue tied last 4 outings. *J. A. B. Old*

G

GABIER 4 b.c. Galileo (IRE) – Contare (Shirley Heights) [2006/7 16d⁶ 16v³ 20v* 21g* **h116 p**
20g* Apr 20] strong, close-coupled colt: closely-related to smart performer Montare
(by Montjeu), stays 15.5f: fairly useful on Flat (stays 12.5f), successful in October for
J. Pease: progressive over hurdles, won maiden at Folkestone in February, novice at
Plumpton (by 25 lengths) in March and novice handicap at Hereford (fairly useful form
when beating Commemoration Day by ¾ length) in April: stays 21f: acts on heavy going:
open to further improvement. *G. L. Moore*

GABLA (NZ) 11 b.g. Prince of Praise (NZ) – Dynataine (NZ) (Centaine (AUS)) **c–**
[2006/7 c–, h–: c20gᵖᵘ Mar 27] leggy gelding: winning hurdler/chaser: no solid form **h–**
since 2004/5, left R. C. Guest before return: successful in point in April: raced mainly
around 2m: acts on good to firm going, probably on firm: usually wears headgear. *Mrs
Lynne Ward*

GABOR 8 b.g. Danzig Connection (USA) – Kiomi (Niniski (USA)) [2006/7 c–§, h88§: **c– §**
17gᵖᵘ 16f* 20m³ 22d* 22g³ 21d³ 27d⁶ Nov 21] good-topped gelding: maiden chaser: fair **h107 §**
handicap hurdler: left D. Thompson after first outing, back near best when winning at
Hexham in June and Cartmel in August: stays 2¾m: acts on firm and soft going: has worn
headgear: races lazily. *Mrs S. J. Smith*

GAELIC FLIGHT (IRE) 9 b. or br.g. Norwich – Ash Dame (IRE) (Strong Gale) **c101**
[2006/7 c106+, h104x: c21m⁵ c24d* c24d³ c21d³ Dec 30] rangy gelding: fair hurdler/ **h– x**
chaser: won handicap over fences at Fakenham in October: jumped badly left final
outing: stays 3m: acts on soft and good to firm going: tongue tied last 5 starts, also
blinkered last 3: often makes mistakes. *C. R. Egerton*

GAELIC GIFT (IRE) 5 b.m. Presenting – Gaelic Leader (IRE) (Supreme Leader) **h89**
[2006/7 F87: F16d⁵ 16d³ 16s* 20s⁴ 20d 20v 21v 27m³ Apr 26] rather unfurnished mare: **F79**
runner-up in bumpers: modest novice hurdler: won mares event at Lingfield (easily) in
November: stays 27f: acts on soft and good to firm going. *B. G. Powell*

GAELIC MUSIC (IRE) 8 b.g. Accordion – Cuilin Bui (IRE) (Kemal (FR)) [2006/7 **c–**
c23mᵖᵘ c23g³ c23s⁶ Dec 18] sturdy, workmanlike gelding: bumper winner: fairly useful **h–**
form when runner-up in novice hurdle in 2004/5: off 20 months, little impact over fences:
stays 3m. *M. Bradstock*

GAELIC ROULETTE (IRE) 7 b.m. Turtle Island (IRE) – Money Spinner (USA) **h104 §**
(Teenoso (USA)) [2006/7 h92: 24g 20m* 22g 20m* 22m 19g 22vᵖᵘ Nov 23] lengthy
mare: fair handicap hurdler: won at Huntingdon in June and Bangor in July: stays 2¾m:
acts on soft and good to firm going (possibly unsuited by heavy): inconsistent. *J. Jay*

GAELSBOB 10 ch.g. Bob Back (USA) – Gaelstrom (Strong Gale) [2006/7 c26gᶠ **c–**
Apr 19] sturdy gelding: fair pointer, won in March: hampered and fell seventh in hunter
on chase debut. *Miss E. J. Baker*

GAGARIN (FR) 7 b.g. Quest For Fame – Good To Dance (IRE) (Groom Dancer **h–**
(USA)) [2006/7 16s 20vᵖᵘ Mar 6] smallish gelding: lightly raced on Flat: no show in
novice hurdles. *Miss L. C. Siddall*

GAIAC (FR) 13 b.g. Passing Sale (FR) – Ustitine (FR) (Moshi (GER)) [2006/7 c106, **c–**
h–: 20sᵖᵘ Feb 22] fairly useful hunter chaser: maiden hurdler, no show in handicap only **h–**
start in 2006/7: stays 3m: acts on any going: usually blinkered. *Ms N. M. Hugo*

GAINING GROUND (IRE) 7 ch.g. Presenting – Lorglane Lady (IRE) (Lancastrian) **h–**
[2006/7 h–: 24g⁵ Apr 21] strong, compact gelding: no sign of ability. *John R. Upson*

GALA DU MOULIN MAS (FR) 13 b.g. Le Riverain (FR) – Soiree d'Ex (FR) (Kash- **c–**
tan (FR)) [2006/7 19mᵖᵘ Aug 24] rangy gelding: maiden hurdler/winning chaser, very **h–**
lightly raced and no form since 2002/3: tried in cheekpieces/blinkers. *M. E. D. Francis*

GALA EVENING 5 b.g. Daylami (IRE) – Balleta (USA) (Alzao (USA)) [2006/7 **h107**
h–p: 17s⁵ 20v² 20d³ 21s* Mar 2] stocky gelding: fair hurdler: won handicap at
Newbury in March: likely to stay beyond 21f: acts on heavy going. *J. A. B. Old*

GALAHAD (FR) 6 b.g. Apple Tree (FR) – Reine Elodie (FR) (Cadoudal (FR)) [2006/7 **c–**
h–: c22mᶠ c16dᵖᵘ 24gᵖᵘ Nov 10] lengthy, good sort: no sign of ability. *B. Storey* **h–**

GALANDORA 7 b.m. Bijou d'Inde – Jelabna (Jalmood (USA)) [2006/7 h–: 20d Dec 4] **h–**
no show in novice hurdles. *Dr J. R. J. Naylor*

ladbrokes.com Handicap Chase, Newbury—
Gallant Approach (No.4) and Jimmy McCarthy just get the better of No Full

GALANT EYE (IRE) 8 ch.g. Eagle Eyed (USA) – Galandria (Sharpo) [2006/7 h–: 17m² 19s* 16m⁶ Jul 12] compact gelding: modest hurdler: won seller at Newton Abbot in June: stays 19f: acts on soft and good to firm going: tried in cheekpieces/blinkers. *R. J. Baker* **h92**

GALANTOS (GER) 6 b.g. Winged Love (IRE) – Grey Metal (GER) (Secret 'n Classy (CAN)) [2006/7 19v³ May 23] successful 5 times on Flat (stays 2m), twice in Germany in 2005 for C. von der Recke and 3 times in Britain in 2006: bad mistake last when distant third to Irish Guard in maiden at Towcester on hurdling debut. *G. L. Moore* **h74 +**

GALAPIAT DU MESNIL (FR) 13 b.g. Sarpedon (FR) – Polka de Montrin (FR) (Danoso) [2006/7 c82, h–: c21m* c21s³ Feb 16] leggy, angular gelding: winning hurdler: poor chaser nowadays: won handicap at Fakenham in May: successful in point in 2007: stays 31f: acts on good to firm and heavy going: tried in cheekpieces: sound jumper. *R. Gurney* **c82 h–**

GALA QUEEN 7 gr.m. Accondy (IRE) – Miss Jedd (Scallywag) [2006/7 F–: 21vᵖᵘ 20v 16v 20v⁶ Mar 2] good-bodied mare: no sign of ability. *W. G. Young* **h–**

GALA SUNDAY (USA) 7 b.g. Lear Fan (USA) – Sunday Bazaar (USA) (Nureyev (USA)) [2006/7 h–: 17v Dec 12] fair on Flat nowadays (best around 1¼m), successful 5 times in 2006: well beaten over hurdles: tongue tied in 2005/6. *M. W. Easterby* **h–**

GALAXIA (IRE) 5 b. or br.g. Fourstars Allstar (USA) – Cool N Calm (Arctic Lord) [2006/7 h–: 16m⁶ 21d 20d Dec 4] tall, useful-looking gelding: no solid form in novice hurdles. *K. C. Bailey* **h–**

GALEAWAY (IRE) 13 b.g. Strong Gale – Geeaway (Gala Performance) [2006/7 c21gᵖᵘ c20sᵖᵘ Feb 4] tall, angular gelding: winning pointer/chaser, no show in hunters in 2006/7: tried blinkered/tongue tied. *Mrs D. M. Grissell* **c– h–**

GALE DANCER 5 b.m. Saddlers' Hall (IRE) – Barton Gale (IRE) (Strong Gale) [2006/7 F–: F16f⁴ F17g Apr 23] no form in bumpers. *D. W. Whillans* **F–**

GALERO 8 b.g. Overbury (IRE) – Rare Luck (Rare One) [2006/7 c111, h–: c19g Feb 2] useful-looking gelding: fair hurdler/chaser: off 9 months, well beaten only start in 2006/7: should stay beyond 2½m: raced on good ground or softer. *J. Howard Johnson* **c– h–**

GALE STAR (IRE) 14 b.g. Strong Gale – Fairly Deep (Deep Run) [2006/7 c87, h–: c21dᵖᵘ c22gᵖᵘ c16gᵖᵘ Jul 21] winning hurdler/chaser, no form in 2006/7: stays 25f: probably acts on any going: has won with/without blinkers: usually tongue tied. *Ó. Brennan* **c– h–**

GALIBARD (IRE) 4 b.g. Montjeu (IRE) – His Lady (IRE) (Selkirk (USA)) [2006/7 16m^{pu} 16g 17d^{pu} 20m Mar 29] twice-raced on Flat for A. Balding: more temperament than ability over hurdles: blinkered last 2 starts. *J. Rudge* **h– §**

GALLANT APPROACH (IRE) 8 ch.g. Roselier (FR) – Nicks Approach (IRE) (Dry Dock) [2006/7 c131+, h111p: c20s* c24s^3 c24g c36g Apr 14] rangy gelding: twice-raced over hurdles, successful on second occasion: useful handicap chaser: off 7 months, won at Newbury in November by ½ length from No Full: good efforts next 2 starts, seventh of 23 to Joes Edge in valuable event at Cheltenham: mistakes and always in rear when last of 12 finishers in Grand National at Aintree: should stay beyond 3m: raced on good ground or softer (acts on soft). *C. R. Egerton* **c137 h–**

GALLANT GIRL 6 ch.m. Topanoora – High 'b' (Gunner B) [2006/7 F16s^4 F16v 20s^{pu} 20d^{pu} 20v^{ro} 20s^{pu} Mar 13] €11,000 4-y-o: sturdy, lengthy mare: fourth foal: dam unraced daughter of useful staying chaser Highfrith: form (including over hurdles) only in maiden bumper on debut. *W. Amos* **h– F80**

GALLEY LAW 7 ch.g. Most Welcome – Miss Blitz (Formidable (USA)) [2006/7 17m^3 16s Mar 1] modest on Flat (stays 1½m), sold out of R. Craggs's stable 7,500 gns Doncaster November Sales: much better effort in novice hurdles 9 months apart when third at Sedgefield. *W. M. Brisbourne* **h80**

GALLIK DAWN 9 ch.g. Anshan – Sticky Money (Relkino) [2006/7 c110d, h–: c26s^{pu} c25s^3 c26g^2 Apr 19] sturdy gelding: maiden hurdler: fair chaser, left A. Hollingsworth after first outing: stays 3½m: acts on soft and good to firm going. *Ms Sharan Smith* **c105 h–**

GALLOPING HOME (IRE) 9 ch.g. Rashar (USA) – Gort Na Lynn (IRE) (Strong Statement (USA)) [2006/7 c19g^{pu} May 4] ex-Irish gelding: maiden pointer: tongue tied, no form in 2 chases: sold £900 Ascot June Sales. *Richard Mathias* **c–**

GALLOP RHYTHM (IRE) 11 ch.g. Mister Lord (USA) – Kiltannon (Dalsaan) [2006/7 c26g^{pu} Apr 19] big, angular gelding: runner-up in novice hurdle in 2001/2, only form. *Ms Caroline Walker* **c– h–**

GALOSHES 5 b.g. Kayf Tara – Seymourswift (Seymour Hicks (FR)) [2006/7 F17v* Jan 11] second foal: half-brother to fair hurdler/fairly useful chaser Mercuric (by Silver Patriarch), stays 3m: dam, fair hurdler/chaser, stayed 25f: green, won maiden bumper at Hereford on debut by 1¾ lengths from Fermat. *D. R. Gandolfo* **F97**

GALTEE VIEW (IRE) 9 b.g. Namaqualand (USA) – Miss Dolly (IRE) (Alzao (USA)) [2006/7 c98, h–: c25g* c21m^3 c25m* c32m^6 c26g^3 c27s^6 c28d^4 c25s c23v^{pu} Jan 8] useful-looking gelding: winning hurdler: fair handicap chaser: won at Hereford in May and June: largely below form after: stays 25f: suited by good going or firmer: usually wears headgear (not last 3 outings): tongue tied once: held up. *Evan Williams* **c111 h–**

GALWAY BREEZE (IRE) 12 b.g. Broussard (USA) – Furena (Furry Glen) [2006/7 c106, h–: c21s^{pu} c24g^4 Apr 9] big gelding: pointer/hunter chaser nowadays, no show in 2006/7: tried tongue tied. *Mrs Julie Read* **c– h–**

GALWAY (IRE) 14 b.g. Jurado (USA) – Solanum (Green Shoon) [2006/7 c96, h–: c19m^3 Mar 29] lengthy gelding: fairly useful pointer/hunter chaser: nearly as good as ever when winning at Hereford in March by 6 lengths from Viscount Bankes: effective at 2m to 25f: acts on heavy and good to firm going: often forces pace. *Mrs Marilyn Scudamore* **c106 h–**

GAME ON (IRE) 11 b.g. Terimon – Nun So Game (The Parson) [2006/7 c93, h–: c19g c16g^{ur} Oct 30] maiden hurdler: winning chaser: off 8 months, no show in handicaps in 2006/7: stays 2½m: acts on soft and good to firm going: tongue tied once. *B. N. Pollock* **c– h–**

GAMESET'N'MATCH 6 b.g. Hector Protector (USA) – Tanasie (Cadeaux Genereux) [2006/7 h–: 16g^{pu} May 14] maiden on Flat: no form over hurdles. *Miss M. P. Bryant* **h–**

GANACHE (IRE) 5 ch.g. Halling (USA) – Granted (FR) (Cadeaux Genereux) [2006/7 F76: F16s F14s^6 Feb 18] smallish, sparely-made gelding: modest form in bumpers: fair form in maidens on Flat. *P. R. Chamings* **F81**

GANGSTERS R US (IRE) 11 br.g. Treasure Hunter – Our Mare Mick (Choral Society) [2006/7 c93, h–: c25m^F c20g* c21g Apr 12] tall gelding: modest chaser: off 10 months, won hunter at Sedgefield in March: stays 25f: acts on any going: sometimes hangs/runs as if amiss. *A. Parker* **c98 h–**

GANSEY (IRE) 5 br.g. Anshan – Ebony Jane (Roselier (FR)) [2006/7 F16d^3 F16s* Mar 8] 46,000 3-y-o: good-topped gelding: half-brother to poor staying chaser Ebony Jack and fair 2½m hurdle winner Bolt Action (both by Phardante): dam won Irish Grand **F106**

National: odds on, won maiden bumper at Wincanton in March by 14 lengths from Imperial Silver: will stay beyond 2m. *P. F. Nicholls*

GANYMEDE 6 gr.g. Daylami (IRE) – Germane (Distant Relative) [2006/7 h–: 17s May 20] fair on Flat (stays 2m), successful in October/November for Mrs L. Mongan: little impact over hurdles: tried in cheekpieces. *J. G. M. O'Shea* **h–**

GAORA GALE (IRE) 7 b.g. Anshan – Dancing Gale (Strong Gale) [2006/7 24s⁴ Dec 2] rangy gelding: runner-up in maiden Irish point: poor form in novice hurdles 20 months apart: tried tongue tied. *P. F. Nicholls* **h83**

GAPPERSONNELDOTCOM (IRE) 6 b. or br.g. Topanoora – Four Oaks (IRE) (Yashgan) [2006/7 F16m² F16g 16m 17m⁴ 17g⁶ 21g 16mᶠ 17d⁴ 17v⁴ 16s Jan 24] 6,000 3-y-o: good-topped gelding: second foal: dam little sign of ability: second of 5 in bumper at Ludlow: little form over hurdles. *D. McCain Jnr* **h64 ? F83**

GARDASEE (GER) 5 gr.g. Dashing Blade – Gladstone Street (IRE) (Waajib) [2006/7 h121: 20vᵖᵘ 24gᵖᵘ 20g Apr 12] tall, good-topped gelding: fairly useful juvenile hurdler: off a year, no show in handicaps in 2006/7: should stay 2½m: raced on good going or softer (acts well on heavy): front runner/races prominently: has made mistakes. *T. P. Tate* **h–**

GARDE BIEN 10 br.g. Afzal – May Lady (Deep Run) [2006/7 c–: c22s* c24mᵖᵘ Jun 22] lengthy gelding: fair handicap chaser: off 6½ months, back to best to win at Market Rasen in May: effective at 2m to 2¾m: acts on firm and soft going. *Mrs S. J. Smith* **c101**

GARDE CHAMPETRE (FR) 8 b.g. Garde Royale – Clementine Fleurie (FR) (Lionel (FR)) [2006/7 c131, h–: c16d* c21g² c24s² c16s² c33g Mar 15] tall, close-coupled gelding: usually impresses in appearance: useful novice hurdler in 2003/4 for P. Nicholls: fairly useful novice chaser: landed odds at Carlisle in October by 3½ lengths from Ela Re: stays 3m, effective over much shorter: raced on good going or softer (acts on heavy): tried in cheekpieces: sketchy jumper. *Jonjo O'Neill* **c126 x h–**

GARDEN FEATURE 9 b.m. Minster Son – Super Fountain (Royal Fountain) [2006/7 c24dᶠ May 15] workmanlike mare: winning hunter: fairly useful pointer, won in March/April: 4 lengths third when fell 2 out in hunter at Towcester on chase debut: should stay at least 3m. *J. B. Walton* **c94 h–**

GARDEN SHED REBEL 7 b.g. Tragic Role (USA) – Clare Island (Connaught) [2006/7 F16vᵖᵘ 16d⁵ 16s 20s 24m Mar 25] lengthy, sparely-made gelding: no sign of ability. *K. F. Clutterbuck* **h– x F–**

GARDOR (FR) 9 b.g. Kendor (FR) – Garboesque (Priolo (USA)) [2006/7 17d⁵ May 31] leggy gelding: maiden hurdler: in frame in points: raced mainly around 2m on good going or softer: tried tongue tied. *Miss J. E. Foster* **c– h–**

GARIBALDI (GER) 5 ch.g. Acatenango (GER) – Guanhumara (Caerleon (USA)) [2006/7 h98: 16m Jun 18] good-topped gelding: fair on Flat (stays easy 16.5f): easily best effort in 3 starts over hurdles when fifth in juvenile on debut. *D. R. C. Elsworth* **h–**

GARLETON (IRE) 5 b.g. Anshan – Another Grouse (Pragmatic) [2006/7 F16v² Feb 17] £52,000 4-y-o: third foal: dam fairly useful staying chaser: tongue tied, shaped like a stayer when 6 lengths second to Debauchery in bumper at Uttoxeter on debut. *K. Bishop* **F99**

GARNETT (IRE) 6 b.g. Desert Story (IRE) – In Behind (IRE) (Entitled) [2006/7 h103: c21g* Apr 9] good-topped gelding: fair hurdler: fit from Flat (fair winner up to 2m), won novice hunter at Fakenham in April on chase debut, despite tending to jump low: stays 23f: acts on firm ground: wears cheekpieces. *D. E. Cantillon* **c98 h–**

GARPLE BURN 5 b.g. Zaha (CAN) – Skedaddle (Formidable (USA)) [2006/7 18m May 28] poor maiden on Flat (should stay 1½m): well beaten in 4-y-o novice on hurdling debut. *Jim Best* **h–**

GARRULOUS (UAE) 4 b.g. Lomitas – Friendly (USA) (Lear Fan (USA)) [2006/7 16g³ 16d⁵ 16d⁵ 18v² Jan 25] compact gelding: modest form on Flat (stays 1¼m), sold out of M. Johnston's stable 6,000 gns Newmarket July Sales: fair form over hurdles: stays 2¼m: acts on heavy going: wandered final outing. *G. L. Moore* **h104 +**

GARRYVOE (IRE) 9 b.g. Lord Americo – Cottage Theme (Brave Invader (USA)) [2006/7 c112, h–: 26s⁵ c25vᵖᵘ c32s* c33sᵖᵘ c30g² Mar 31] strong gelding: lightly raced: novice hurdler: fairly useful handicap chaser: won at Stratford in February by neck from Cowboyboots: good second to Martha's Kinsman at Ascot: stays 4m: acts on heavy going. *T. R. George* **c127 h–**

GARSTON STAR 6 ch.g. Fleetwood (IRE) – Conquista (Aragon) [2006/7 19v⁵ 22s⁶ 16s 20v⁶ 18v³ Mar 7] compact gelding: modest on Flat (stays 1½m), generally below best **h94 +**

in 2006 for J. S. Moore: modest maiden hurdler: stays 19f: raced on soft/heavy going. *P. G. Murphy*

GARVIVONNIAN (IRE) 12 b.g. Spanish Place (USA) – Garvivonne (Belfalas) [2006/7 c138, h92: c22v⁵ c28s c25vᶠ c19v² Mar 11] rather leggy gelding: winning hurdler: useful chaser: won Becher Chase at Aintree in 2005/6: easily best effort in 2006/7 when 12 lengths second of 5 to easy winner Mansony in minor event at Naas: stays 3½m: acts on heavy and good to firm going. *Edward P. Mitchell, Ireland*

c135
h–

GASPARA (FR) 4 b.f. Astarabad (USA) – Gaspaisie (FR) (Beyssac (FR)) [2006/7 15s⁵ 17s* 18s³ 18s c17sᶠ 18s⁶ c17s² c17s² 19v* 20d* 16s* 16d* 20g² Apr 14]

c108 p
h149 +

Fifteen trainers' championships, two hundred wins in a season eight times, thirty-four Cheltenham Festival wins and 4,182 victories in total Flat and jumps: Martin Pipe was always going to be a hard act to follow, but son David made a very good fist of things in his first season in charge at Pond House. The stable regained its position as the leading yard by number of wins, a tally of 134 placing it ahead of Jonjo O'Neill (126) and returning champion Paul Nicholls (124) and bettering the disappointing 2005/6 total, including in terms of strike rate. Win prize money was slightly down, though again topped the million-pound mark and would have bettered the 2005/6 figure had wins by Acambo, in the Swinton Hurdle, and Westender, also at Haydock, at the very start of the 2006/7 season, been credited to David rather than Martin, following delays in granting David the licence.

David Pipe's first season is certainly a good platform on which to build, though the yard's reliance on leading owner David Johnson could be a concern. His horses accounted for nearly a third of the yard's runners and seven of the twelve highest earners in the stable. Paul Nicholls, on the other hand, has a far wider spread of owners, with the stable's top thirteen earners split between eleven different owners or syndicates. Jonjo O'Neill is, of course, heavily reliant on the backing of J.P. McManus, whose colours were carried by nearly sixty per cent of the yard's runners, though McManus operates on a different plane to any other jumping owner (nearly 1,100 runners—more than were sent out by Alan King and Philip Hobbs combined—ran in his colours in Britain and Ireland in 2006/7, running for forty-four different stables). Unlike his leading rivals, Pipe doesn't enjoy the patronage of any of the major owners apart from Johnson—Trevor Hemmings and Sir Robert Ogden both have horses with Nicholls, King, O'Neill and Nicky Henderson, whilst McManus has horses with Hobbs and Henderson.

Several big wins came the Pipe yard's way during the season, Acambo, Madison du Berlais and Whispered Secret landing big sponsored handicaps and Our Vic and Well Chief gaining pattern victories. Luck didn't go the way of the last-named pair when it came to the Cheltenham Festival, but David Pipe still got off the mark there in his first year thanks to the four-year-old filly Gaspara who landed the Fred Winter Juvenile Novices' Handicap Hurdle by five lengths from Altilhar. Not only that, but her victory, following on from her success in the

Sunderlands Imperial Cup Handicap Hurdle, Sandown—
Tony McCoy dons the colours of his old boss Martin Pipe as Gaspara (hooped sleeves)
justifies favouritism from Flying Falcon (left) and outsider Magnesium (centre)

Fred Winter Juvenile Novices' Handicap Hurdle, Cheltenham—the bonus is landed just three days later under an enterprising ride from 5-lb claimer Andrew Glassonbury

Sunderlands Imperial Cup at Sandown three days previously, netted the £75,000 bonus offered to the connections of any horse which wins the Imperial Cup and follows up in a race at the Cheltenham Festival. The owner of Gaspara just happens to be Martin Pipe, who twice successfully landed the Imperial Cup/Festival double bonus as a trainer, with Olympian in 1993 and Blowing Wind in 1998. Like father, like son indeed.

Like so many juveniles imported from France over the years by the Pipe team, Gaspara is nothing on looks—she is small and leggy—and there wasn't a lot in her form with Thomas Trapenard to indicate she would be up to landing prizes of the stature that she did, nor that she would end the season rated behind only Katchit among her age group. Gaspara won just once from ten starts in France, a three-year-old fillies hurdle at Auteuil in June, and ran her best race there when sixth in a Group 3 for fillies in November. She was also runner-up on both completed starts (faller on chasing debut) over fences at Enghien, the second Parisian track where the obstacles are a good deal less demanding than those at Auteuil. The likelihood of better to come was soon manifested when she joined David Pipe, having been bought for €52,000 at Deauville in December on the dispersal of Trapenard's entire stable. On her British debut in January, Gaspara won a mares novice hurdle at Taunton with something in hand and followed up with a comprehensive defeat of odds-on shot Classic Fiddle in a similar event at Chepstow a month later. The Chepstow form wasn't the easiest to assess but a BHB mark of 126 could hardly be termed harsh and, with Tony McCoy released by J. P. McManus to team up with his old boss, Gaspara was well supported before going off 11/4 favourite in the Imperial Cup, faced with sixteen opponents in an ordinary renewal. Dropped back from two and a half miles, Gaspara benefited from the testing conditions at Sandown and stayed on strongly to defeat Flying Falcon by six lengths.

There was a choice of targets at Cheltenham, but the Fred Winter, under just a 4-lb penalty, looked an easier option than the Baring Bingham against the top staying novices, even if the latter was over a more suitable trip. Stable conditional Andrew Glassonbury took the ride this time, complete with his handy 5-lb claim,

356

and sensibly made plenty of use of Gaspara, who produced a most willing display to complete the double and lift the mood of her stable, which had endured the loss of the highly-regarded Little Brick (also ridden by Glassonbury) earlier on the card. Gaspara was in little danger after being sent on in earnest at the fourth and she produced a useful performance, one on which she might have been expected to build when returned to further. Just how much improvement she had in her soon became apparent. Stepping up to Grade 1 level from handicaps, Gaspara beat all but Al Eile in the Aintree Hurdle. Had she jumped more fluently, she might even have won but, as it was, she went down by a length and a half, nevertheless finishing three lengths in front of Champion Hurdle third Afsoun. Gaspara had another new partner at Aintree in Tom Scudamore, who was promoted to stable jockey at Pond House in the latter stages of 2006/7 after several big-race weekend wins (including on Madison du Berlais) and is another following in the footsteps of a famous father—Peter Scudamore enjoyed the most successful period of his (then) record-breaking career when riding for Pipe senior.

Gaspara (FR) (b.f. 2003)	Astarabad (USA) (b 1994)	Alleged (b 1974)	Hoist The Flag Princess Pout
		Anaza (b 1986)	Darshaan Azaarika
	Gaspaisie (FR) (b 1994)	Beyssac (ch 1978)	Paris Jour Dori
		Alizane (b 1988)	Mourtazam Kermaline

Gaspara is a daughter of Astarabad, a son of Alleged and a very smart performer at up to a mile and a half. As well as Gaspara, his first two crops include

Mr M. C. Pipe's "Gaspara"

the useful Howard Johnson-trained novice hurdler Astarador and Gaspara's stable-companion and old rival, the useful ex-French juvenile Laustra Bad (a €75,000 purchase at the same sale), who beat her once over fences at Enghien and finished third in the Fred Winter. Astarabad has had a couple of Group 3 winners at Auteuil but Gaspara's success may well mean he eventually makes as much impact in Britain. Presumably the sire of Gaspara's dam Gaspaisie, Beyssac, was part of the appeal of Gaspara for the Pipes. Beyssac is the sire of Iris Bleu and Banjo, two big-race winners for the yard, as well as the Nicholls-trained Royal & SunAlliance Chase winner Star de Mohaison. Gaspara is the fourth foal out of Gaspaisie, who won over hurdles and fences at Auteuil and had form at up to two and a half miles. The first three have all shown ability over jumps, with the second Gaspaie (by Cyborg) and third Gaspaisienne (by Mansonnien) both prolific winners over hurdles and fences at up to two and a half miles. Gaspaie also won on the Flat, while Gaspaisienne was in good form in the spring, completing a hat-trick at Lyon-Parilly. Gaspara's grandam Alizane was next to useless, managing just one fourth place from no fewer than twenty-three starts on the Flat, but she bred two other winners apart from Gaspaisie, the bumper winner Kimono Royal and the fairly useful chaser at up to twenty-one furlongs Imprevue (also by Beyssac). Gaspara has raced on good going or softer and has shown her effectiveness on very testing ground more than once, though her best performances have come on good to soft and good at Cheltenham and Aintree. Despite her lack of stature, there may well be more to come when Gaspara tackles three miles. Indeed, she seems set to be one of David Pipe's standard bearers as he bids to build on his very promising first season. *D. E. Pipe*

GASTORNIS 9 ch.g. Primitive Rising (USA) – Meggies Dene (Apollo Eight) [2006/7 c20dpu c20d* c20sur c20m² Apr 28] lengthy, angular gelding: winning hurdler: fair novice chaser: won handicap at Musselburgh in January: should stay beyond 2½m: acts on good to firm and good to soft going (seemingly not on soft/heavy): blinkered final outing: usually tongue tied. *M. W. Easterby*   **c107 h–**

GATORADE (NZ) 15 ch.g. Dahar (USA) – Ribena (NZ) (Battle-Waggon) [2006/7 c113, h–: 16m May 6] leggy gelding: winning hurdler: fair handicap chaser, usually made frame: stayed 25f: acted on any going: wore cheekpieces: held up: reliable: has reportedly been retired. *R. C. Guest*   **c– h–**

GATSBY (IRE) 11 gr.g. Roselier (FR) – Burren Gale (IRE) (Strong Gale) [2006/7 c117, h–: c24dpu c28vpu c32spu Nov 15] workmanlike gelding: useful hunter chaser at best, no form in 2006/7 (including in handicap): stays 3¼m: acts on heavy and good to firm going. *J. B. Groucott*   **c– h–**

GAUCHO 10 b.g. Rambo Dancer (CAN) – Sioux Be It (Warpath) [2006/7 c73, h–: c20g⁴ c21spu c23g Jun 1] strong, compact gelding: winning pointer: maiden chaser: probably stays 2½m: acts on heavy going: tried blinkered, usually wears cheekpieces: sold 2,800 gns Doncaster October Sales. *Miss T. Jackson*   **c– h–**

GAUVAIN (GER) 5 b.g. Sternkoenig (IRE) – Gamina (GER) (Dominion) [2006/7 16d³ 16s² 21g² Mar 23] good-topped gelding: successful twice up to around 1¼m on Flat in Germany, including at Cologne in July, left P. Rau after third in September: fair form over hurdles, 5 lengths second of 16 to Carlitos in maiden at Newbury final start: stays 21f. *C. J. Mann*   **h110 +**

GAVANELLO 4 br.g. Diktat – Possessive Artiste (Shareef Dancer (USA)) [2006/7 17g 16s² 20d 17d 17mpu Apr 15] no form on Flat: poor form over hurdles: tried tongue tied. *M. C. Chapman*   **h73**

GAVIOLI (IRE) 5 b.g. Namid – Pamina (IRE) (Perugino (USA)) [2006/7 20gF Sep 6] modest on Flat (best form at 6f): weakening when falling fell sixth in novice on hurdling debut. *J. M. Bradley*   **h–**

GAVZ BOY (IRE) 5 b.g. Executive Perk – Waltznis Comma (IRE) (Commanche Run) [2006/7 F71: F17s 16s Feb 15] poor form on first of 2 starts in bumpers: breathing problem on hurdling debut: sold 5,000 gns Doncaster May Sales. *Miss Lucinda V. Russell*   **h– F–**

GAWROSZ (POL) 8 ch.g. Saphir (GER) – Galarda (POL) (Parysow) [2006/7 16dpu 24mpu Mar 31] successful 11 times on Flat in Poland, poor form in Britain: wearing eyecover, no show over hurdles (looked ungenuine on debut). *G. J. Smith*   **h–**

GAYE SOPHIE 5 gr.m. Environment Friend – Gaye Memory (Buckskin (FR)) [2006/7 F17v⁶ Jan 11] half-sister to 3 winners, including fairly useful hurdler/smart chaser Simon   **F–**

(by Overbury), stays 29f, and fairly useful 2½m hurdle winner Taking My Cut (by Classic Cliche): dam, dual bumper winner and runner-up only outing over hurdles, sister to very smart staying chaser Black Humour, and half-sister to top-class 2m to 3m hurdler Gaye Brief and very smart staying jumper Gaye Chance: well backed, well held in bumper on debut. *J. L. Spearing*

GAY OSCAR (IRE) 8 b. or br.g. Oscar (IRE) – Deep Inthought (IRE) (Warcraft (USA)) [2006/7 20g Nov 10] good-topped gelding: bumper winner: well held in maiden hurdles 2 years apart: should stay 2½m. *Mrs K. Walton*   **h–**

GAZUMP (FR) 9 b.g. Iris Noir (FR) – Viva Sacree (FR) (Maiymad) [2006/7 c114, h–: c20f⁴ c20s² c20gᵖᵘ Feb 21] rangy gelding: winning hurdler: fairly useful chaser at best, sold out of N. Twiston-Davies' stable 7,400 gns Doncaster May Sales after first outing: fit from points, better effort in hunters when runner-up at Fontwell: stays 21f: acts on good to soft going, probably on good to firm: tried blinkered/tongue tied: usually makes running/races prominently: inconsistent. *Mrs Marilyn Scudamore*   **c89**   **h–**

GAZZA'S GIRL (IRE) 7 b. or br.m. Norwich – Miss Ranova (Giacometti) [2006/7 c20s³ c22v* c20vᵘʳ c20v³ c24vᶠ c20s* c24vⁱ c24g⁵ c29m Apr 9] smallish, close-coupled mare: eighth living foal: sister to winning hurdler Square Ball, stays 2½m, and half-sister to 2m hurdle winner Thistlekicker (by Mandalus): dam lightly-raced half-sister to very smart 2m hurdler Ra Nova: winning hurdler: useful novice chaser: successful at Galway (maiden) in October and Thurles (beat Sabina Park easily by 4 lengths in Grade 3 mares event) in January: best efforts seventh/eighth starts, second to Snowy Morning in Grade 2 at Navan and fifth to Denman in Royal & SunAlliance at Cheltenham: well beaten in Irish National at Fairyhouse: stays 3m: acts on heavy going: patiently ridden. *Mrs J. Harrington, Ireland*   **c136**   **h–**

Mr Patrick McCooey's "Gazza's Girl"

G'DAY MATE (IRE) 7 b.g. Taipan (IRE) – The Long Bill (IRE) (Phardante (FR)) **h118**
[2006/7 F16f* F16s* 18s² 16s^F 16g* Apr 4] tall, good sort: third foal: dam unraced: **F110**
useful form in bumpers, won at Tipperary in June and October: confirmed earlier promise
in maiden hurdles when winning at Gowran comfortably by 3 lengths from Dancing
Hero: likely to have proved best around 2m: put down after breaking a bone above his
hock. *John E. Kiely, Ireland*

GEE AKER MALAYO (IRE) 11 b.g. Phardante (FR) – Flying Silver (Master Buck) **c75**
[2006/7 c–§, h–§: c21v⁵ c26g³ c20g* Apr 23] strong, lengthy gelding: poor handicap **h–**
chaser: won at Hexham in April: stays 3¼m, effective at shorter: acts on soft going: tried
blinkered: formerly temperamental. *Miss Lucinda V. Russell*

GEE ARE THREE (IRE) 4 b.f. Deploy – Wingfield Lady (IRE) (Erdelistan (FR)) **F67**
[2006/7 F16m⁶ Mar 31] second foal: dam unraced half-sister to useful staying chaser
Kinburn: faded when sixth in mares bumper at Uttoxeter on debut. *N. B. King*

GEE DEE NEN 4 b.g. Mister Baileys – Special Beat (Bustino) [2006/7 17d⁶ Mar 19] **h83 p**
half-brother to modest 2m hurdle winner Queen's Dancer (by Groom Dancer): fairly
useful on Flat (should stay 2m), in frame 9 of 10 starts in 2006: sixth of 13 finishers in
juvenile on hurdling debut: likely to do better, especially granted increased test of
stamina. *M. H. Tompkins*

GEEVEEM (IRE) 7 b.g. Supreme Leader – Glacial Field (IRE) (Glacial Storm (USA)) **c124**
[2006/7 h118: c26d* c29v³ c24s³ Mar 17] good-topped gelding: fairly useful form over **h–**
hurdles/fences: won novice at Plumpton in November on chase debut: better efforts when
third in handicaps at same course and Uttoxeter (novice, blinkered): will stay long
distances: raced on going softer than good (acts on heavy). *P. F. Nicholls*

GEM DALY (FR) 6 b.g. Nikos – Tinopasa (FR) (No Pass No Sale) [2006/7 F16v* **F103 p**
Dec 28] tall, lengthy, good sort: has scope: brother to fair winning chaser at 21f in France
Nikotina and half-brother to 2 winners in France, including fair hurdler/fairly useful
chaser Tinobruno (by Arctic Tern), stays 2¾m: dam winning hurdler/chaser at 15f to
2¼m: pulled up in point in 2006: won maiden bumper at Leopardstown comfortably by 6
lengths from Oscar Time: likely to improve. *N. Meade, Ireland*

GEMGABALLOU (IRE) 4 b.f. Luso – Time To Kill (IRE) (Millfontaine) [2006/7 **F74**
F13s⁴ F16g Mar 21] sixth foal: dam unraced out of half-sister to Champion Hurdle winner
For Auction: poor form in bumpers: hung right on debut. *Mrs S. Gardner*

GEMINI LUCY (IRE) 7 ch.m. Glacial Storm (USA) – Jodi (IRE) (Phardante (FR)) **c140**
[2006/7 c16m* c20m* c17m* c17d^F c18d* c16s² c16v² c16g c17m* c16m^{ur} Apr 26] **h–**
€20,000 3-y-o: long-backed mare: first foal: dam, bumper winner, out of sister t top-class
chaser Jodami: winning hurdler: useful novice chaser: won at Punchestown (maiden),
Killarney, Galway and Punchestown again (listed event) in first half of 2006/7, and
valuable handicap at Fairyhouse (best effort when beating Old Flame by 17 lengths) in
April: stays 2½m: acts on heavy and good to firm going: bold-jumping front runner (has
jumped right). *Mrs J. Harrington, Ireland*

GEMINI STORM 7 br.g. Jendali (USA) – Fanny Adams (Nicholas Bill) [2006/7 F–: **c81**
19d⁶ 16g c24g⁵ c22g² c23m^F c22m² Apr 24] workmanlike gelding: well held in bumpers/ **h–**
novice hurdles: upped markedly in trip, poor form in maiden chases: probably stays 3m:
acts on good to firm going. *O. Brennan*

GEM MILL (IRE) 5 b.g. Exit To Nowhere (USA) – Cara Gail (IRE) (Strong Gale) **h–**
[2006/7 F16v F14s 16g Mar 29] lengthy, good-topped gelding: third foal: dam poor **F–**
maiden hurdler: well held in bumpers/novice hurdle. *Miss H. C. Knight*

GEMSTER 9 b.m. Alflora (IRE) – Gemmabel (True Song) [2006/7 c25g⁴ May 3] angu- **c88**
lar mare: maiden hurdler: fair fourth in hunter on chase debut: stays 25f. *Miss A. Dare* **h–**

GENAU (IRE) 4 ch.g. Grand Lodge (USA) – Intizaa (USA) (Mr Prospector (USA)) **h–**
[2006/7 16g⁵ 17m^{pu} 17d⁴ 17g Nov 5] fair maiden on Flat (should stay 1¼m), sold out of
Mrs L. Stubbs's stable 5,500 gns Doncaster May Sales: no form in juvenile hurdles: tried
tongue tied. *Evan Williams*

GENERAL ALARM 10 b.g. Warning – Reprocolor (Jimmy Reppin) [2006/7 c16m⁴ **c119**
c20m^{rtr} c16m² c17m² c16f² c21m* c24g* 21d² Nov 7] ex-Irish gelding: fair hurdler: **h110**
fairly useful novice chaser, sold out of T. Taaffe's stable 8,000 gns Doncaster May Sales:
won at Sedgefield in September and Huntingdon (5 ran, beat Herecomestanley by 26
lengths) in October: stays 3m: acts on any going: has worn headgear: has twice refused to
race (including in visor): front runner. *R. Ford*

GENERAL CLONEY (IRE) 11 ch.g. Simply Great (FR) – Kitty's Sister (Bustino) [2006/7 c89, h–: c20d⁴ May 1] sturdy gelding: one-time useful hurdler: modest maiden chaser: stays easy 2¾m: acts on any going: blinkered nowadays. *S. Donohoe, Ireland*   **c90 ?**
h–

GENERAL DUROC (IRE) 11 ch.g. Un Desperado (FR) – Satula (Deep Run) [2006/7 c–, h115: 22vᵖᵘ 20vᵖᵘ 27v 25vᵖᵘ Mar 18] well-made gelding: fair handicap hurdler at best: off 10 months, no form in 2006/7: jumped poorly only outing over fences: stays 27f: acts on heavy going: tried blinkered, usually wears cheekpieces: has had tongue tied: front runner. *B. Storey*   **c–**
h–

GENERAL GREY (IRE) 7 gr.g. Fourstars Allstar (USA) – Tara The Grey (IRE) (Supreme Leader) [2006/7 c100, h–: c23g* c23mᵖᵘ 22g² 22m² 26g Oct 3] good-topped gelding: fair chaser/hurdler: won novice over fences at Exeter in May: stays 23f: acts on good to firm and good to soft going: inconsistent: sold 4,200 gns Doncaster May Sales. *Miss H. C. Knight*   **c102**
h102

GENERAL HARDI 6 b.g. In Command (IRE) – Hardiprincess (Keen) [2006/7 h94, F–: 16d³ 20v⁵ 19s⁵ 20m 20g Mar 17] sturdy gelding: modest novice hurdler: should stay beyond 2½m: acts on heavy going. *J. Wade*   **h88**

GENERAL HOPKINS (IRE) 12 b.g. Cataldi – Kewanee (Kafu) [2006/7 c–, h–: 21m⁵ c20m⁵ c20g⁶ c20g⁶ c21d³ c21d⁵ c16s 16g Apr 9] tall gelding: maiden hurdler: no form over fences: tried blinkered/visored: headstrong. *G. R. Pewter*   **c–**
h–

GENERAL KNOWLEDGE (USA) 4 ch.g. Diesis – Reams of Verse (USA) (Nureyev (USA)) [2006/7 16d Dec 29] small, leggy gelding: useful at best on Flat (should stay 1¼m), successful in July, sold out of A. Fabre's stable 32,000 gns Newmarket Autumn Sales: not at all knocked about in juvenile on hurdling debut: likely to improve. *B. G. Powell*   **h– p**

Queens Prices Syndicate's "Gemini Lucy"

GENERAL LEDGER (IRE) 5 b.g. Alderbrook – Las-Cancellas (Monksfield) **F96**
[2006/7 F16v⁵ F16v* Feb 5] €100,000 4-y-o: useful-looking gelding, unfurnished at
present: half-brother to 3 winners, including top-class chaser Harbour Pilot (by Be My
Native), stayed 3¼m, and unreliable winning hurdler/fair chaser Metal Detector (by
Treasure Hunter), stays 25f: dam, 1¼m/1½m winner on Flat/2m winner over hurdles,
sister to dam of Grand National winner Monty's Pass: much better effort in bumpers when
winning 6-runner maiden at Hexham by ¾ length from Brook No Argument: likely to be
suited by 2½m+. *J. Howard Johnson*

GENERAL O'KEEFFE 10 b.g. Alflora (IRE) – Rosie O'Keeffe (IRE) (Royal **c88**
Fountain) [2006/7 c–, h–: c27d* Nov 23] modest chaser: left Mrs S. Old, off 8 months **h–**
and attracted support, first win outside points in handicap at Taunton in November: stays
27f: raced on good going or softer (acts on soft). *L. Corcoran*

GENERALS LASTSTAND (IRE) 9 b.g. Little Bighorn – Our Dorcet (Condorcet **c–**
(FR)) [2006/7 h70: 20dpu c20dpu Nov 21] useful-looking gelding: lightly raced: bumper **h–**
winner: little form over hurdles: no show in maiden chase: tried blinkered/in cheekpieces.
Mrs L. B. Normile

GENERAL SMITH 8 b.g. Greensmith – Second Call (Kind of Hush) [2006/7 h87: **h98**
16m* 19d³ 16m⁴ 16m⁴ 16g 19d⁶ 16g⁶ 17g⁵ Apr 11] compact gelding: modest handicap
hurdler: won at Worcester in May: best around 2m with emphasis on speed: acts on good
to firm going. *H. J. Evans*

GENERAL STRIKER 7 ch.g. Classic Cliche (IRE) – Springfield Girl (Royal Vulcan) **c127**
[2006/7 c123: c23s* Dec 26] useful hunter chaser: successful in 20-runner event at Down
Royal by neck from Agus A Vic, only outing in 2006/7: will stay beyond 25f: raced on
good going or softer: wore cheekpieces last 4 starts in 2005/6. *Enda Bolger, Ireland*

GENEROUS LAD (IRE) 4 b.g. Generous (IRE) – Tudor Loom (Sallust) [2006/7 **h–**
17dpu Aug 21] fair on Flat (stays 1½m), successful in December for A. Haynes: no show
in juvenile maiden on hurdling debut. *Miss J. S. Davis*

GENEROUS STAR 4 ch.g. Generous (IRE) – Elegant Dance (Statoblest) [2006/7 **F78 +**
F14g F16s F16m² Apr 9] tall gelding: second foal: dam, 6f winner, half-sister to fairly
useful hurdler/useful chaser Green Tango (stayed 19f): modest form in bumpers.
J. Pearce

GENEROUSTOAFAULT 4 ch.g. Generous (IRE) – Inflation (Primo Dominie) **F96**
[2006/7 F14g⁵ Nov 1] good-topped gelding: third foal: half-brother to 5f/6f winner
Global Achiever (by Key of Luck): dam sprint maiden: around 3 lengths fifth to Fintan in
3-y-o bumper at Huntingdon on debut (tended to edge left). *Noel T. Chance*

GENGHIS (IRE) 8 br.g. Persian Bold – Cindy's Baby (Bairn (USA)) [2006/7 h145: **c102**
c20d² c16d⁵ c16v³ Jan 11] rather leggy gelding: smart hurdler: off a year, fair form when **h–**
second in maiden on chasing debut, making mistakes: ran as if amiss next 2 starts:
effective at 2m to 2½m: acts on heavy going: makes running. *P. Bowen*

GENTIAN 4 ch.f. Generous (IRE) – French Spice (Cadeaux Genereux) [2006/7 16m⁵ **h103**
17m² 17s* 17m* 16m³ Oct 1] modest on Flat (stays 1½m), sold out of Sir Mark Prescott's
stable 10,000 gns after successful in June: fair juvenile hurdler: won at Bangor and
Cartmel in August: raced around 2m. *D. McCain Jnr*

GENTLE JOHN (FR) 5 b.g. Le Balafre (FR) – Perky (FR) (Kendor (FR)) [2006/7 **h102 p**
F72: 19d 16m* Apr 10] mid-field in bumpers: left R. Stronge, easily better effort over
hurdles when winning maiden at Chepstow by 2½ lengths from El Bandindos: should
stay beyond 2m: acts on good to firm ground: open to further improvement. *P. J. Hobbs*

GENTLEMAN JIMMY 7 b.g. Alderbrook – Irish Orchid (Free State) [2006/7 h111, **c120**
F94: c16d² c17v⁴ c20d c17d² c20d³ c21g⁴ Mar 31] good-topped gelding: winning **h–**
hurdler: fairly useful novice chaser: good efforts when placed, including when 6 lengths
third to Bible Lord in handicap at Lingfield: should stay beyond 2½m: raced on good
ground or softer (acts on soft). *H. Morrison*

GENTLE RIVAGE (FR) 13 b.g. Rose Laurel – Silverado Trail (USA) (Greinton) **c92**
[2006/7 c26s² Mar 11] useful-looking gelding: one-time useful hurdler: maiden chaser: **h–**
fair pointer, successful in February: stays 3¼m: acts on good to firm and heavy going:
often forces pace. *F. M. O'Brien*

GENTLE WARNING 7 b.m. Parthian Springs – Manx Princess (Roscoe Blake) **h–**
[2006/7 h68²: 16dpu 22s⁴ 24vpu 20s Nov 26] small, sparely-made mare: maiden hurdler,
no form in 2006/7. *Mrs Barbara Waring*

GEOGRAPHY (IRE) 7 ch.g. Definite Article – Classic Ring (IRE) (Auction Ring (USA)) [2006/7 c–§, h78§: 22m⁶ 21d 23dᵖᵘ 22v³ 22s⁴ Dec 14] good-topped gelding: no form over fences: poor handicap hurdler: stays 25f: acts on any going: tried visored, usually wears cheekpieces: tried tongue tied: inconsistent. *P. Butler*   c– § / h77 §

GEORDIE PEACOCK (IRE) 8 b.g. Roselier (FR) – Cotton Call (IRE) (Callernish) [2006/7 h95, F74: 24d² Oct 22] medium-sized gelding: fair novice hurdler: will stay extreme distances: acts on heavy going. *Miss Venetia Williams*   h103

GEORGEDOUBLEYOU (IRE) 6 b.g. Lord Americo – Ballybeg Rose (IRE) (Roselier (FR)) [2006/7 F–: F16s F16v⁵ F16s⁴ Jan 31] unfurnished gelding: poor form in bumpers. *Miss T. Jackson*   F72

GEORGES BOY (IRE) 9 b.g. Toulon – Glebelands Girl (Burslem) [2006/7 c–, h85: 22s⁶ 22v² 25sꟳ 20v 22v⁴ 24v³ 23d* Mar 21] quite good-topped gelding: fell only outing over fences: modest hurdler: won novice handicap at Lingfield in March: stays 3m: acts on heavy going: visored/blinkered nowadays: often races prominently. *P. J. Jones*   c– / h91

GEORGE THE GREY 6 gr.g. Silver Patriarch (IRE) – Miss Firecracker (Relkino) [2006/7 F–: F16d 20s⁶ 19d⁵ 20vᵖᵘ 20dꟳ Feb 14] well held in bumpers: poor form in novice hurdles: hung violently left fourth outing: sold 21,000 gns Doncaster May Sales. *S. Gollings*   h75 / F–

GEORGIAN KING 4 b.g. Overbury (IRE) – Roslin (Roscoe Blake) [2006/7 F17m* Apr 28] second foal: dam unraced from family of top-class staying chaser Brown Chamberlin: won bumper at Market Rasen on debut by length from Issaquah, *A. King*   F103 +

GEORGIE'S LASS (IRE) 8 gr.m. Flemensfirth (USA) – Rongai (IRE) (Commanche Run) [2006/7 h–, F–: 16dᵖᵘ Oct 18] no form (refused early both starts in points). *R. J. Price*   h–

GERALDINE 6 br. or b.m. Minster Son – Church Leap (Pollerton) [2006/7 h67, F78: 19g³ 17v⁵ 19dᵘʳ 23v 23d⁴ Jan 15] close-coupled mare: poor maiden hurdler. *Mrs S. Lamyman*   h77

GERMANY PARK (IRE) 9 ch.g. Germany (USA) – Lohunda Park (Malinowski (USA)) [2006/7 c–, h–: c21mᵖᵘ 20sᵖᵘ Jun 25] winning pointer: no form in other events: tried visored. *W. B. Stone*   c– / h–

GERRARD (IRE) 9 b.g. Jurado (USA) – Vienna Waltz (IRE) (Orchestra) [2006/7 c77, h–: c23mᵖᵘ c21d* c21s³ c21d⁵ c20d* c20mᵖᵘ Apr 25] lengthy gelding: no form over hurdles: modest handicap chaser: won novice events at Folkestone in November and Stratford in March: stays 23f: acts on heavy ground, possibly unsuited by good to firm: visored/blinkered. *Mrs A. Barclay*   c92 / h–

GERRY SUR (IRE) 8 b. or br.g. Presenting – Inquisitive Lady (Quisling) [2006/7 c21vᵖᵘ c20gᵖᵘ Mar 27] winning pointer: no form otherwise: tried blinkered. *W. Storey*   c– / h–

GETAWAY GIRL 9 b.m. Perpendicular – Viowen (IRE) (Denel (FR)) [2006/7 h–: 16m 19d³ 20dᵖᵘ Nov 14] little sign of ability. *O. Brennan*   h–

GETINBYBUTONLYJUST 8 b.g. King's Ride – Madame President (IRE) (Supreme Leader) [2006/7 c95, h90: c24dꟳ c25v* c25v* c22s² Feb 15] winning hurdler: fairly useful novice chaser: won handicaps at Hexham in December and Ayr (beat Lucky Nellerie by 8 lengths in 3-finisher event, left clear 4 out) in January: stays 27f: acts on heavy and good to firm going: usually races prominently. *Mrs Dianne Sayer*   c116 / h–

GET MY DRIFT (IRE) 8 b.g. Beneficial – Boreen Bro (Boreen (FR)) [2006/7 24v² c23d⁴ c26s² c25m² Apr 21] tall gelding: has reportedly had breathing operation: winning pointer: runner-up 2 starts over hurdles, off 19 months in between: fairly useful novice chaser: best effort when 6 lengths second of 5 to Always Waining in handicap at Ayr final start: stays 3¼m: unraced on firm going, acts on any other: tongue tied 5 of last 6 outings, also blinkered last 2: sold 18,000 gns Doncaster May Sales. *P. F. Nicholls*   c124 / h113

GETON (IRE) 7 b.g. Glacial Storm (USA) – Monavale (IRE) (Strong Gale) [2006/7 c? , h–: 16s⁵ c16g² c20dᵖᵘ Dec 10] winning hurdler: fair form when runner-up in novice at Hexham, only completed outing over fences: should stay beyond 17f: acts on good to soft going: has shaped as if amiss more than once. *P. Monteith*   c104 / h–

GET SMART (IRE) 10 ch.g. Nucleon (USA) – Dark Colleen (Kambalda) [2006/7 c81d: c16v³ c20gᵖᵘ Feb 21] lengthy gelding: poor chaser: sold out of F. Murphy's stable 3,500 gns Doncaster May Sales after first outing, won point in April: stays 21f: acts on any going: tried tongue tied. *Miss L. A. Blackford*   c69

GETTYSBURG (IRE) 4 b.g. Imperial Ballet (IRE) – Two Magpies (Doulab (USA)) **h84**
[2006/7 16d^{ro} 16g^{pu} 16v 16v 16m 17g^3 Apr 23] sturdy, close-coupled gelding: half-
brother to winning 2m hurdler Dangerman (by Pips Pride): modest maiden on Flat
(stays 13.8f): modest juvenile hurdler, sold out of J. Howard Johnson's stable 3,500 gns
Doncaster November Sales after second start: raced around 2m: acts on good to firm
ground: hasn't looked straightforward (ran out on debut). *J. J. Lambe, Ireland*

GHADAMES (FR) 13 b.g. Synefos (USA) – Ouargla (FR) (Armos) [2006/7 c125, **c106**
h88+: c21v^{pu} c20g^4 c21g^5 Apr 12] lengthy gelding: winning hunter: fairly useful hunter **h–**
nowadays, fifth of 27 to Scots Grey in Fox Hunters' at Aintree: stays 21f: acts on any
going: has worn cheekpieces: has broken blood vessels. *A. Kirtley*

GHAILL FORCE 5 b.g. Piccolo – Coir 'a' Ghaill (Jalmood (USA)) [2006/7 h85: 16m **h–**
16m 16m 16m^{pu} Apr 8] rather leggy gelding: maiden hurdler, no show in 2006/7: raced
around 2m: tried in cheekpieces: usually tongue tied. *P. Butler*

GIANT EAGLE (USA) 5 b.g. Giant's Causeway (USA) – Alaskan Idol (USA) **F104**
(Carson City (USA)) [2006/7 F16g* F16s^2 F16m Apr 25] tall, good-topped gelding: first
foal: dam once-raced half-sister to Breeders' Cup Classic winner Arcangues: fairly useful
form in bumpers: won 19-runner event at Gowran (beat Well Saved by length) on debut in
October: best effort when eighth of 19 to Mick The Man in Grade 1 event at Punchestown.
Thomas Foley, Ireland

GIDAM GIDAM (IRE) 5 b.g. King's Best (USA) – Flamands (IRE) (Sadler's Wells **h130**
(USA)) [2006/7 h114: 23g* 21d^{pu} 22d^5 24d^6 24s* 24d* 24g Apr 14] workmanlike
gelding: useful handicap hurdler: won at Haydock in October and twice at Market Rasen
(beat Cousin Nicky easily by 5 lengths on second occasion) in March: stays 3m: acts
on soft and good to firm going: wears cheekpieces: often races prominently: consistent.
J. Mackie

GIELGUD 10 b.g. Faustus (USA) – Shirl (Shirley Heights) [2006/7 c103, h–: c21g* **c93**
c23m c21f^5 c21s^5 c24g c23m^5 Apr 22] strong, sturdy gelding: modest chaser: won hunter **h–**
at Folkestone in May: stays 3m: acts on soft and good to firm going: visored final start:
tried tongue tied. *B. G. Powell*

GIFTED GLORI 4 ch.g. Vettori (IRE) – Azira (Arazi (USA)) [2006/7 17g^5 16m^4 17s^6 **h72**
16g Feb 2] modest maiden on Flat (stays 7f): poor form in juvenile hurdles, left J. J. Quinn
before final start: will prove best at 2m with emphasis on speed: joined T. D. Barron.
Micky Hammond

GIFT OF LIFE (FR) 7 b.m. Android (USA) – Teardrops Fall (FR) (Law Society **h–**
(USA)) [2006/7 22v^{pu} Feb 25] third on completed start in points in 2006, only sign of
ability. *Miss Sarah Robinson*

GIFT VOUCHER (IRE) 6 ch.g. Cadeaux Genereux – Highland Gift (IRE) (Generous **c92**
(IRE)) [2006/7 h–: c16g^5 c20g^2 Jul 9] tall gelding: winning hurdler: modest form 2 starts **h–**
over fences: barely stayed 2½m: acted on soft going: tongue tied last 3 starts: dead.
P. R. Webber

GIGANTES 6 b.g. Nashwan (USA) – Mahasin (USA) (Danzig (USA)) [2006/7 F17d^{pu} **F–**
May 17] brother to smart 1¼m and 1½m winner Elhayq, and half-brother to several other
Flat winners: dam 7f/1m winner: went as if amiss in bumper on debut: dead. *O. Sherwood*

GIGS BOUNTY 9 ch.g. Weld – City's Sister (Maystreak) [2006/7 c–, h–: c17d^6 c20s^3 **c93**
c24d^{ur} 25d Dec 14] fair form over hurdles in 2003/4 for M. Pitman: lightly raced and little **h–**
form since, mainly over fences: stays 21f: acts on soft going: sold 500 gns Doncaster
January Sales. *C. C. Bealby*

GILO 6 b.g. Overbury (IRE) – Caithness Dawn (Deep Run) [2006/7 16g^F F19m^6 16m^3 **h99**
16m^2 20m^4 18s^{pu} 16s* 16v^5 17s 22v^{pu} 16s^{pu} Feb 1] sturdy gelding: half-brother to win- **F84**
ning hurdler/chaser The Hen Hut (by Henbit), stays 21f: dam, no sign of ability, out of
half-sister to dam of useful staying chaser Dakyns Boy: placed in points: sixth in bumper:
modest hurdler: won maiden at Tramore in October: left Mrs Maureen Danagher, below
form 3 starts in Britain: best at 2m: acts on heavy and good to firm going: has worn
cheekpieces, including at Tramore. *D. J. Wintle*

GILZINE 11 b.g. Gildoran – Sherzine (Gorytus (USA)) [2006/7 c96, h–: c19m^2 May 9] **c96**
maiden hurdler: fairly useful pointer, successful in February: runner-up both starts in **h–**
novice chases: stays 3m: acts on good to firm going. *E. Parry*

GIMMEABREAK (IRE) 7 b.g. Beneficial – Gentle Eyre (IRE) (Aristocracy) **c– p**
[2006/7 h89p: 22g^6 c20d^{pu} Nov 8] tall gelding: winning Irish pointer: poor form over **h– p**
hurdles: though has left impression capable of better: off 6 months, not knocked about
again once beaten in handicap on chasing debut: should still improve. *Miss E. C. Lavelle*

GINGERSLOOKINGREAT (IRE) 8 ch.g. Ashkalani (IRE) – Just An Illusion **h71**
(IRE) (Shernazar) [2006/7 h–: 16g Nov 1] lengthy gelding: tongue tied, fourth in bumper
in 2003: poor form on second of only 2 starts over hurdles since. *O. Brennan*

GIN PALACE (IRE) 9 gr.g. King's Theatre (IRE) – Ikala (Lashkari) [2006/7 16g⁵ **h– §**
18dᵖᵘ 26sᵖᵘ 20v⁴ 20vᵖᵘ 16gᵇᵈ 20m Apr 25] good-topped gelding: one-time fairly useful
handicap hurdler: off 2½ years, shaped as if having physical/mental problems in 2006/7,
left G. L. Moore after second start: stays 21f: acts on soft and good to firm going: tried
blinkered/tongue tied: one to leave alone. *W. Davies*

GIOVANNA 6 b.m. Orpen (USA) – Red Leggings (Shareef Dancer (USA)) [2006/7 **h110**
h101: 20mᶠ 20m² 20m* 22m⁸ Sep 21] small mare: bumper winner: fair hurdler: won
mares novice at Bangor in July and handicap at Fontwell in September: stays 2¾m: acts
on soft and good to firm going: reliable. *R. T. Phillips*

GIPSY CRICKETER 11 b.g. Anshan – Tinkers Fairy (Myjinski (USA)) [2006/7 c77, **c87 x**
h57: c16m⁵ c17g² c19m c16m² c16mᵘʳ c17mᶠ c16f² c16m³ c16g⁴ c16f³ c17d² c16g* **h– §**
c16g³ c16m³ c16g⁴ c16d* c16s⁵ Dec 7] leggy, sparely-made gelding: maiden hurdler:
modest handicap chaser: won at Ludlow in October and Fakenham in November:
effective at 2m to 2½m: acts on firm and soft going: tried tongue tied: has been reluctant
at start/often finds little: sketchy jumper. *M. Scudamore*

GIPSY WOOD 11 gr.m. Rakaposhi King – Silva Linda (Precipice Wood) [2006/7 **c– §**
c20mʳᵗʳ Jun 22] winning pointer: no form in other events, refused to race on chase debut: **h– §**
sold 1,200 gns Doncaster January Sales. *P. Beaumont*

GIRARDII 4 ch.g. Sinndar (IRE) – Armeria (USA) (Northern Dancer) [2006/7 16g⁶ **h80**
16g⁴ 16d³ 19g⁵ 26g³ Apr 11] stocky gelding: half-brother to fairly useful hurdler up
to 19f Migration (by Rainbow Quest): fair maiden up to 1½m on Flat, sold out of
R. Charlton's stable 22,000 gns Newmarket July Sales: modest juvenile hurdler: stays
3¼m: raced on good to soft ground: has worn cheekpieces/blinkers. *K. C. Bailey*

GIULIANI 7 b.g. Sadler's Wells (USA) – Anka Germania (Malinowski (USA)) [2006/7 **c92**
c18d c20dᵘʳ c20d² c20s c25s⁴ Feb 27] useful-looking gelding: winning hurdler: runner-up **h–**
at Musselburgh, only form in maiden chases: stays 23f: acts on good to firm and good to
soft going. *I. R. Ferguson, Ireland*

GIUST IN TEMP (IRE) 8 b.g. Polish Precedent (USA) – Blue Stricks (Bluebird **c86**
(USA)) [2006/7 h92: 17m⁵ 17d³ 19s⁵ 16m⁴ 16m⁴ 17d⁶ c16d³ c16g⁵ 19m⁶ c16gᵖᵘ Apr 20] **h92**
sparely-made gelding: modest hurdler: similar form on first of 3 starts over fences: best at
2m with emphasis on speed: acts on firm and good to soft going. *Mrs K. M. Sanderson*

GIVE ME A DIME (IRE) 5 b.g. Beneficial – Miss Di (IRE) (Phardante (FR)) [2006/7 **h101 p**
F16d 19g* Apr 8] lengthy gelding: second foal: dam unraced half-sister to useful hunter **F85**
Coolefind: in need of race when mid-field in bumper: still green, won maiden at
Towcester on hurdling debut by short head from Waltham Abbey: sure to improve.
N. J. Gifford

GIVE ME LOVE (FR) 7 ch.g. Bering – Cout Contact (USA) (Septieme Ciel (USA)) **c102 §**
[2006/7 c115, h115: c20mᵖᵘ c20d c19sᵘʳ c19s⁵ c20s² c20v² c18s⁴ Mar 11] leggy gelding: **h–**
winning hurdler: fair chaser nowadays: stays 21f: acts on heavy going: tried in cheekpieces, usually blinkered: tongue tied: finds little. *A. G. Juckes*

GIVEN A CHANCE 6 b.g. Defacto (USA) – Milly Molly Mango (Mango Express) **h–**
[2006/7 h86: 19gᵖᵘ Jul 23] good-topped gelding: modest maiden hurdler, off 11 months
and left Mrs S. Lamyman before only start in 2006/7: tailed off on Flat week later: raced
mainly around 2m. *T. J. Pitt*

GIVEUSACLUE (IRE) 6 b. or br.g. Presenting – Branscombe (IRE) (Buckskin (FR)) **h100 +**
[2006/7 F17v³ F17s* 17d² 17g⁶ Mar 12] €64,000 4-y-o: compact gelding: first foal: dam, **F99**
poor form over hurdles, half-sister to useful staying chaser G V A Ireland and useful but
untrustworthy 2m chaser Dines: won bumper at Carlisle in October: much better effort in
novice hurdles when beaten 6 lengths second to Beau Michel at Exeter: should be suited by
2½m+: raced on ground softer than good. *Jonjo O'Neill*

GIVEUSAWAVE (IRE) 6 b.g. Presenting – Sea Scare (IRE) (Glacial Storm (USA)) **h–**
[2006/7 16m⁶ 20d 24d Oct 5] €3,000 4-y-o: second foal: dam ran twice in bumpers: poor
maiden pointer: well beaten over hurdles. *M. Sheppard*

GLACIAL DELIGHT (IRE) 8 b.g. Glacial Storm (USA) – Annagh Delight (Saint **c–**
Denys) [2006/7 c124, h95+: c24g Oct 14] big gelding: winning hurdler: fairly useful **h–**
handicap chaser: won 3 times at Taunton in 2005/6: no form over fences away from there,
left Miss E. Lavelle prior to only start in 2006/7: should stay 3m+: acts on firm and good
to soft going. *Ferdy Murphy*

GLACIAL GILLETTE (IRE) 8 ch.m. Glacial Storm (USA) – Brown Gillette **c85**
(Callernish) [2006/7 c23f c24g² c25m^pu Aug 6] ex-Irish mare: second foal: dam maiden
pointer: won mares maiden point in 2006: modest chaser: left M. Cotter, second in
weak maiden at Southwell: stays 3m: sold €11,000 Tattersalls Ireland November Sale.
K. G. Reveley

GLACIAL RAMBLER (IRE) 8 b.g. Glacial Storm (USA) – Rambling Ivy (Manda- **c—**
lus) [2006/7 c25g^ur Apr 15] maiden chaser: left T. Doyle in Ireland, won maiden point in
March. *J. F. W. Muir*

GLACIAL SUNSET (IRE) 12 ch.g. Glacial Storm (USA) – Twinkle Sunset (Deep **h128**
Run) [2006/7 h131: 19g⁶ 20g³ 21g* 22g 21g⁴ Apr 18] workmanlike gelding: fairly
useful handicap hurdler: won at Kempton in November by 5 lengths from Wee Dinns:
left C. Tinkler before final start: effective around 2½m and stays 3¼m: acts on firm
and good to soft going: often makes running: has shaped as if amiss more than once.
D. W. P. Arbuthnot

GLAD BIG (GER) 5 b.g. Big Shuffle (USA) – Glady Sum (GER) (Surumu (GER)) **h92**
[2006/7 16m³ 16g 17d⁵ Nov 23] lengthy, workmanlike gelding: fairly useful on Flat
(stays 8.6f), successful 3 times in 2006, sold out of J. Osborne's stable 28,000 gns Newmarket July Sales: looks to have stamina limitations over hurdles. *R. T. Phillips*

GLADS IMAGE 5 ch.m. Handsome Ridge – Secret So And So (So Factual (USA)) **h—**
[2006/7 16g Nov 1] lengthy, angular mare: little form on Flat: tailed off in novice on
hurdling debut. *S. W. Hall*

GLADYS GERTRUDE 6 ch.m. Double Trigger (IRE) – Nour El Sahar (USA) **h—**
(Sagace (FR)) [2006/7 20m Jun 13] soundly beaten in mares bumper/maiden hurdle.
M. J. Gingell

GLASHEDY ROCK (IRE) 10 b.g. Shernazar – Classical Lady (IRE) (Orchestra) **c—**
[2006/7 c87, h—: c24g^bd c21m^pu c19m^bd c24m c24g⁶ Apr 27] lengthy gelding: winning **h—**
pointer: maiden hurdler/chaser, no form in 2006/7: blinkered last 3 starts. *M. F. Harris*

GLASKER MILL (IRE) 7 b.g. Old Vic – Lucey Allen (Strong Gale) [2006/7 h132: **c117**
c18v* c20s^F c19v^F 22d Mar 17] sturdy, good sort: useful hurdler, well beaten in handicap **h—**
final start: fairly useful form when winning maiden at Fontwell on chasing debut in
January by 3½ lengths from Dancing Bay, only completed outing over fences: should be
suited by 3m+: acts on heavy going. *Miss H. C. Knight*

GLENARY (IRE) 5 ch.g. Presenting – My Native Glen (IRE) (Be My Native (USA)) **F93**
[2006/7 F16g³ F16g² Apr 7] €62,000 3-y-o: good-topped gelding: third foal: brother to
bumper winner Nelson's Spice: dam unraced half-sister to useful chaser up to 3m
Montana Glen, became unreliable: fair form when placed in bumpers at Huntingdon and
Haydock: will stay beyond 2m. *H. D. Daly*

GLENCOVE MARINA (IRE) 5 b.g. Spectrum (IRE) – Specifiedrisk (IRE) **h146 p**
(Turtle Island (IRE)) [2006/7 F107p: 16v* 16m³ 20m* Apr 27]
The traditionally strong bumper team of Willie Mullins wasn't up to quite
its usual standard in 2006/7, with no placed runners from a total of seven representatives in the three valuable events at both the Cheltenham and Punchestown
Festivals. Fortunately, the trainer's novice hurdlers more than held their own in the
latest campaign. Ebaziyan achieved the most notable win, in the Supreme Novices'
at Cheltenham, which took the stable's Festival tally of wins into double figures. In
addition, Black Harry, who would have finished second in the Spa but for falling at
the last, and the promising Fairyhouse winner Scotsirish (unplaced at Cheltenham)
have the look of leading novice chasers for 2007/8. The stable's 2006 Goffs Land
Rover Bumper winner Glencove Marina didn't make it to Cheltenham but he also
looks to have a very bright future. Glencove Marina was kept off the course in the
latest season until March, but he soon made up for lost time, finishing third in a
Grade 2 novice at Fairyhouse and showing smart form in landing the Grade 1 Land
Rover Champion Novices' Hurdle at Punchestown.
In truth, the field for the two-and-a-half-mile Champion Novices' was a
little short of Grade 1 standard. In an all-Irish field of ten, Glencove Marina started
11/4 joint favourite with Catch Me, third to Massini's Maguire in the Baring
Bingham at Cheltenham. Aitmatov, who had won the Grade 2 Festival Novices'
over the trip at Fairyhouse, was next in at 4/1, with the Galway Hurdle winner Cuan
Na Grai a 5/1-chance. Cuan Na Grai had finished a place in front of Glencove
Marina in the two-mile Grade 2 at Fairyhouse, the pair finishing behind De Valira,

and was now 3 lb better off, though the longer trip was expected to suit Glencove Marina and he was also the more likely to improve. Glencove Marina was sent to Fairyhouse with just a win in a maiden at Thurles in March under his belt, his lack of experience over hurdles showing in a tendency to jump too big.

Both the longer distance and the benefit of experience contributed to a much improved effort from Glencove Marina in the Champion Novices', and coming to the last the race lay between him and Catch Me. Glencove Marina had been going the better when nodding two out but had recovered to take a narrow lead when Catch Me fell at the last. It would have been a close-run thing but, as it was, Glencove Marina was left to come home five lengths ahead of Kalderon, the pair well clear. Aitmatov made little impact and Cuan Na Grai was pulled up before the last, dropping out as if he had gone wrong. It seems reasonable to assess Glencove Marina as of about the same merit as Catch Me, even if Kalderon, who had finished sixth in the Supreme Novices', is not regarded as showing improved form on his first outing at two and a half miles. That is the view reflected in the ratings in this Annual, though the Anglo-Irish Jumps Classification assesses Glencove Marina as 5 lb inferior to Catch Me, reputedly partly because Edward O'Grady, the trainer of Catch Me, convinced the Turf Club handicapper that his horse was below form. Should Catch Me have to give 5 lb to Glencove Marina in a handicap, O'Grady may wish he'd kept quiet, though, as it is, the pair may not meet again over hurdles. Glencove Marina, who would have the makings of a candidate for good races over hurdles at two and a half miles or further, seems likely to be sent over fences instead, with the Arkle at Cheltenham the reported long-term aim. Glencove Marina is useful looking in appearance and has the physical scope for fences, though his background is essentially a Flat one (even though the third dam Lancette produced winning hurdlers by the unlikely trio of Tirol, Glow and Thatching).

Glencove Marina's sire Spectrum, who now stands in South Africa, has produced a few notable hurdlers, including the 2003 Triumph Hurdle winner Spectroscope and the 2003 Finale Hurdle winner Sunray. Glencove Marina's unraced dam Specifiedrisk, who is by the now jumps-oriented Turtle Island, is a half-sister to six

Land Rover Champion Novices' Hurdle, Punchestown—
Glencove Marina is left clear by Catch Me's heavy fall at the last

			Rainbow Quest	Blushing Groom
	Spectrum (IRE)		(b 1981)	I Will Follow
	(b 1992)		River Dancer	Irish River
Glencove Marina (IRE)			(b 1983)	Dancing Shadow
(b.g. 2002)			Turtle Island	Fairy King
	Specifiedrisk (IRE)		(b 1991)	Sisania
	(b 1996)		Spear Dance	Gay Fandango
			(b 1982)	Lancette

winners, including the very smart stayer Mr Dinos, who won the Gold Cup at Ascot in 2003, and the smart seven-furlong to mile-and-a-quarter winner Risk Material. Risk Material was a winner over hurdles as well (though he refused to race on the last of his three starts in that sphere), and so too is another half-brother Masai Warrior, who showed fairly useful form at up to nineteen furlongs. Specifiedrisk was out of a sister to the 1981 Jersey Stakes winner Rasa Penang. Glencove Marina is her second foal. The third Crazy Bear (by King Charlemagne) was placed on the all-weather for Kevin Ryan and has since joined Tom George. Glencove Marina's only appearance at three came in the Goffs sale-ring, where he fetched €48,000 at the Land Rover Sale. He won both his starts in bumpers in 2005/6, the second of them the Land Rover Bumper itself, which was run at Punchestown for the second time. The race had a chequered heritage at its former home, Fairyhouse, where it was inaugurated in 1997, Hardy Eustace and Newmill two notable victors, while only Arteea and the ill-fated Tuco of the others managed so much as a graded win over jumps. Central House and Beef Or Salmon were placed in it, though. The Champion Novices' wasn't quite the end of Glencove Marina's season, as he ran in the Prix La Barka at Auteuil at the end of May, bidding to add to his trainer's successful record at the track. He fared best of the three Mullins-trained runners but, in truth, never made any impact on very testing ground after a mixed round of jumping, finishing eighth of eleven finishers. *W. P. Mullins, Ireland*

GLENFARCLAS BOY (IRE) 11 b.g. Montelimar (USA) – Fairy Blaze (IRE) (Good Thyne (USA)) [2006/7 c92§, h–§: c24s^4 c20d^{pu} c20v c20v^5 c20s^6 c21v^2 c26g^6 Apr 7] good-topped gelding: maiden chaser: poor handicap chaser nowadays: stays 21f: acts on heavy going: usually wears cheekpieces: has been let down by jumping: inconsistent. *Miss Lucinda V. Russell*   **c76 §** **h– §**

GLENFIELD HEIGHTS 12 b.g. Golden Heights – Cleeveland Lady (Turn Back The Time (USA)) [2006/7 h87: 22m^{pu} 18m 20f^2 20m^3 Jul 4] angular gelding: modest hurdler nowadays, off another 10 months before return: stays 25f: acts on firm and soft going: tried tongue tied. *W. G. M. Turner*   **h94**

GLENFINN CAPTAIN (IRE) 8 br.g. Alderbrook – Glenfinn Princess (Ginger Boy) [2006/7 h135p: c16s* c17s^F Dec 26] bumper winner: useful hurdler: created good impression when winning maiden at Fairyhouse on chasing debut in October by 8 lengths from Khetaam: again favourite, going strongly in front when fell 4 out in Grade 1 novice at Leopardstown next time: reported in mid-January to have suffered bout of colic which required surgery: bred to stay at least 2½m: raced on going softer than good (acts on heavy): sure to progress over fences provided he makes full recovery. *T. J. Taaffe, Ireland*   **c138 p** **h–**

GLENFOLAN (IRE) 9 ch.g. Montelimar (USA) – Donegal Thyne (IRE) (Good Thyne (USA)) [2006/7 c92, h–p: c24m^5 c22s^2 c22s^3 c21s^3 c20s^6 c20m^3 c25m^3 Apr 28] lengthy gelding: once-raced over hurdles: modest handicap chaser: jumped right at Cheltenham fourth start. *A. J. Martin, Ireland*   **c95** **h–**

GLENGARRA (IRE) 10 ch.g. Phardante (FR) – Glengarra Princess (Cardinal Flower) [2006/7 c117, h–: 18g^{pu} c16s^2 c16d^3 c21g^{ur} c21s^{pu} c17g^2 c16g^2 c16g* Apr 19] deep-girthed gelding: maiden hurdler: fairly useful handicap chaser: better than ever when winning at Cheltenham in April by ½ length from Rapide Plaisir: stays 2½m: acts on soft going: tried tongue tied: front runner/races prominently. *D. R. Gandolfo*   **c120** **h–**

GLEN HARLEY (IRE) 7 br.m. Presenting – Asidewager (IRE) (Brush Aside (USA)) [2006/7 c–, h75: c20d^4 24g^4 20g^3 16m^3 20s^5 20g^6 20d^4 c20s* c18v* c17v^2 Mar 24] modest hurdler: won mares novice at Hexham in June: fair novice chaser: won maiden at Down Royal and mares event at Downpatrick in February: stays 2½m: unraced on firm going, acts on any other: tongue tied: refused to race final 2005/6 start: often amateur ridden. *Roy Wilson, Ireland*   **c111** **h89**

GLENKILL (IRE) 9 b.m. Beneficial – Parsons Choice (IRE) (The Parson) [2006/7 c–, h–: 16g^bd 17v^5 21s^ur 17s^pu 19v 19v^pu Mar 1] ex-Irish mare: no form outside points: tried in cheekpieces. *S. M. Jacobs* **c– h–**

GLENMORE BOY (IRE) 7 b.g. Titus Livius (FR) – Requena (Dom Racine (FR)) [2006/7 c20f^pu 16g^4d Jul 31] angular ex-Irish gelding: maiden hurdler/chaser, left S. Mahon prior to return (bled): best around 2m: acts on soft ground: tried in cheekpieces/blinkers: usually tongue tied: sold 500 gns Doncaster October Sales. *K. J. Burke* **c– h–**

GLEN OMEN (IRE) 7 b.g. Flying Legend (USA) – Miners Own (IRE) (Miner's Lamp) [2006/7 h96, F90: 19v 20s 26s^3 Jan 26] lengthy gelding: third in bumper: modest form over hurdles: stays 3¼m: acts on soft ground. *Jennie Candlish* **h92**

GLEN OSCAR (IRE) 8 b.g. Oscar (IRE) – Lady Ara (IRE) (Jurado (USA)) [2006/7 h–: 20d 16g May 13] no form in points/over hurdles: tried blinkered/in cheekpieces. *Miss S. E. Forster* **h–**

GLENQUIN CASTLE (IRE) 7 b.g. Dabali (IRE) – Polls Joy (Pollerton) [2006/7 F106: F16v^3 F16s Oct 1] progressive form first 4 starts in bumpers, winning at Listowel (maiden) and Galway in 2005/6, after 11 months off, third to Bluebyyou at Listowel: well below best at Tipperary 10 days later: will stay at least 2½m. *A. J. McNamara, Ireland* **F106**

GLEN ROUGE (IRE) 6 ch.g. Fourstars Allstar (USA) – Charcol (Nicholas Bill) [2006/7 F16m^4 24s^pu Sep 21] €14,000 3-y-o: second foal: dam, poor maiden hurdler, sister to useful stayer Double Dutch: shaped like a stayer when fourth in bumper: no show in novice on hurdling debut. *N. G. Richards* **h– F75**

GLENS BAIRN 4 ch.g. Sir Harry Lewis (USA) – Bairn Glen (Bairn (USA)) [2006/7 F14v F16s Jan 24] leggy, close-coupled gelding: fourth foal: dam no sign of ability: no impact in bumpers: tried in cheekpieces. *B. Ellison* **F–**

GLEN TANAR (IRE) 6 ch.g. Zaffaran (USA) – Mandyslady (IRE) (Husyan (USA)) [2006/7 F16m Apr 9] €10,500 3-y-o: big gelding: first foal: dam unraced out of half-sister to dam of top-class 2m to 2½m chaser Sound Man: in need of experience when behind in bumper on debut. *H. B. Hodge* **F–**

GLEN THYNE (IRE) 7 b.g. Good Thyne (USA) – Glen Laura (Kambalda) [2006/7 c83, h–: c16v^4 19s^3 c20g^3 c16s^2 c22s^pu c16s* c20s^3 c20v^2 c20d^2 c24g^4 c16m^5 Apr 24] rangy gelding: maiden hurdler: modest handicap chaser, sold out of K. Bailey's stable 29,000 gns Doncaster May Sales after first outing: won at Towcester in February: possibly best up to 2½m: acts on heavy ground: blinkered. *Mrs Caroline Bailey* **c93 h–**

GLEN TULLOCH (IRE) 8 b.m. Hushang (IRE) – Glenamal (Kemal (FR)) [2006/7 c22d c17d^pu c20v c20s^F c22v c25v^4 c25s Apr 1] poor maiden chaser: stays 25f: acts on heavy going. *A. J. Martin, Ireland* **c74**

GLEN WARRIOR 11 b.g. Michelozzo (USA) – Mascara VII (Damsire Unregistered) [2006/7 c122, h–: c30d^pu c26s^pu c29s^2 c33s^F Mar 17] tall, lengthy gelding: winning hurdler: fairly useful handicap chaser: respectable second of 5 to Mr Dow Jones at Warwick (tended to run in snatches), only completed outing in 2006/7: best at 3m+: acts on heavy ground: tried in cheekpieces. *J. S. Smith* **c118 h–**

GLIDE 6 ch.g. In The Wings – Ash Glade (Nashwan (USA)) [2006/7 h77: 16s^4 24f^3 Jun 3] poor novice hurdler: stays 3m: acts on firm and soft going. *J. A. B. Old* **h81**

GLIMMER OF LIGHT (IRE) 7 b.g. Marju (IRE) – Church Light (Caerleon (USA)) [2006/7 h113: 16f^6 16m^pu 17s^pu c16s c16v^3 c20d^pu c16g* c18s^ur c20g^2 c17g^pu c16g c20m^pu Apr 28] medium-sized gelding: fair hurdler: first form (modest) over fences when winning handicap at Ludlow in February: stays easy 2½m: acts on firm and good to soft going: tried in cheekpieces: tongue tied last 6 outings. *S. A. Brookshaw* **c97 h114**

GLINGERBANK (IRE) 7 b.g. Supreme Leader – Mauradante (IRE) (Phardante (FR)) [2006/7 h105p: 20s* 16s* 16s^2 Oct 25] strong gelding: fair form over hurdles: won maiden in May and novice (beat Mister Jungle by 3½ lengths) in September, both at Perth: ran well when 5 lengths second to Dhehdaah at Cheltenham on handicap debut: will stay beyond 2½m: raced on good to soft/soft going: may do better still. *N. G. Richards* **h113 +**

GLINGER (IRE) 14 b.g. Remainder Man – Harilla (Sir Herbert) [2006/7 c–, h–: c24g^pu Aug 1] workmanlike gelding: maiden hurdler: fairly useful handicap chaser at best, very lightly raced nowadays: stays 2¾m: acts on good to firm and good to soft going: sound jumper. *N. G. Richards* **c– h–**

GLINTON 5 ch.g. Most Welcome – Chichell's Hurst (Oats) [2006/7 F93: 16s⁶ 20g⁴ **h115**
17v* 16s* 16v* 20s 16g Mar 23] workmanlike gelding: fairly useful novice hurdler: won
at Market Rasen in November and Towcester in December and January (beat Warne's
Way by ½ length): should stay beyond 2m: acts on heavy ground: takes good hold.
Mrs P. Sly

GLITTER ICE 6 b.m. Intikhab (USA) – Golden Circle (USA) (Theatrical) [2006/7 h–: **c–**
20mᵖᵘ 17vᵖᵘ c20g⁵ c16dᵇᵈ c16d⁵ Jan 16] rather unfurnished mare: no form over hurdles/ **h–**
fences. *G. Haine*

GLOBAL CHALLENGE (IRE) 8 b.g. Sadler's Wells (USA) – Middle Prospect **h105 §**
(USA) (Mr Prospector (USA)) [2006/7 h121§: 25m⁴ 25d⁶ Nov 18] sturdy gelding: fairly
useful hurdler at best: stayed 3m: acted on any going: usually wore headgear: tried tongue
tied: ungenuine: dead. *P. G. Murphy*

GLOBEL TRUCKER (IRE) 5 b.g. Anshan – Seat of Learning (Balliol) [2006/7 16g **h108**
F16g F16s⁶ 16v⁴ 16s⁴ 16g³ 16g³ Apr 27] tall gelding: half-brother to smart hurdler/useful **F83**
chaser around 2m Space Trucker (by Kambalda): dam ran 3 times: mid-field in bumpers:
fair maiden hurdler: raced at 2m: acts on heavy ground. *Mrs J. Harrington, Ireland*

GLORY BE 7 ch.m. Gunner B – Geoffreys Bird (Master Willie) [2006/7 h99: 17sᵖᵘ **c95**
c16s⁵ c20s⁴ c16g* Mar 22] good-topped mare: modest form over hurdles, lightly raced: **h–**
similar form over fences, winning maiden at Ludlow in March: likely to prove best
around 2m: acts on heavy going: has raced freely. *Miss Venetia Williams*

GLORY TRAIL (IRE) 13 b.g. Supreme Leader – Death Or Glory (Hasdrubal) **c–**
[2006/7 c–, h–: c21vᵖᵘ Feb 28] winning pointer: little form otherwise (has been let down **h–**
by jumping). *Mrs D. M. Grissell*

GOBAVINA (IRE) 11 ch.g. Ashmolean (USA) – Biddy Parson (The Parson) [2006/7 **c–**
c23fᵖᵘ c23dᵖᵘ Oct 14] little sign of ability. *Miss C. J. E. Caroe*

GOBEJOLLY 4 b.f. Exit To Nowhere (USA) – Ollejess (Scallywag) [2006/7 F16s⁴ **F87**
F16s Mar 10] €31,000 3-y-o, resold £36,000 3-y-o: has scope: first foal: dam, well beaten
in novice hurdle, sister to smart hurdler/useful chaser Better Times Ahead, stayed 3¾m:
fourth in mares bumper at Fakenham on debut: much stiffer task next time. *B. I. Case*

GOBLET OF FIRE (USA) 8 b.g. Green Desert (USA) – Laurentine (USA) (Private **c– §**
Account (USA)) [2006/7 c120, h134: c23m⁶ Jun 18] good-topped gelding: useful **h–**
handicap hurdler: fairly useful chaser, well held in handicap only start in 2006/7: stays
3m: acts on soft and good to firm going: blinkered: tried tongue tied: not a straightforward
ride. *P. F. Nicholls*

GOBLIN 6 b.g. Atraf – Forest Fantasy (Rambo Dancer (CAN)) [2006/7 c89, h–: c16g³ **c119**
c20m* c20f* c22m* Jun 30] leggy gelding: winning hurdler: fairly useful chaser: **h–**
progressed well when winning novice at Huntingdon and handicaps at Worcester and
Market Rasen (by 29 lengths from Bushido, left clear 3 out), all in June: stays 2¾m: acts
on firm and good to soft going. *D. E. Cantillon*

GO COMMERCIAL (IRE) 6 b.g. Supreme Leader – Mullaun (Deep Run) [2006/7 **h–**
h–, F83: 20s 23vᵖᵘ 16vᵘʳ 16s Dec 16] sturdy, useful-looking gelding: no form over
hurdles, banned 40 days under non-triers rule on return. *P. Monteith*

GODS TOKEN 9 gr.g. Gods Solution – Pro-Token (Proverb) [2006/7 h126: 18s² 17g **h135**
20g² Apr 12] smallish, sturdy gelding: useful handicap hurdler: good efforts when
runner-up twice from 3 starts in 2006/7, beaten only a head by Two Miles West despite
mistakes in listed event at Aintree final one: stays 2½m: acts on soft going: tried tongue
tied: races prominently: reliable. *Miss Venetia Williams*

GO FIGURE (IRE) 4 ch.g. Desert Prince (IRE) – Interpose (Indian Ridge) [2006/7 **h– p**
17g⁵ Apr 23] fairly useful on Flat (stays 1¼m), successful in October, sold out of
B. Meehan's stable 27,000 gns Doncaster November Sales: tongue tied, shaped as if in
need of run in juvenile maiden on hurdling debut: likely to do better. *J. Wade*

GO FOR BUST 8 b.g. Sabrehill (USA) – Butsova (Formidable (USA)) [2006/7 c–, **c100**
h121: c20g⁴ c20g² Mar 22] compact gelding: fairly useful handicap hurdler for N. Hend- **h–**
erson: successful twice in points in 2007: fair form when in frame in hunters in between:
effective at 2m to easy 3m: acts on soft and good to firm going. *Mrs Edward Crow*

GO FOR ONE (IRE) 8 b.g. Muroto – Barntown (Belfalas) [2006/7 h79+: 24gᵖᵘ 16d⁵ **c114**
c19d* c20v* c21s³ c20s² c22d³ Mar 2] tall, sparely-made gelding: thrice-raced over **h99**
hurdles: fair chaser: won maiden at Catterick and novice handicap at Haydock in December: good efforts last 2 outings: should stay 3m: acts on heavy going. *D. J. Wintle*

GOFORTHEGAP (IRE) 8 ch.g. Broken Hearted – Gender Gap (USA) (Shecky Greene (USA)) [2006/7 c20d c25d² 24g 24vᵖᵘ c19g Mar 21] sixth foal: dam won 4 races in North America: won maiden Irish point in 2006: bought 10,000 gns Doncaster November Sales: runner-up in maiden chase at Hereford: no show next 3 outings, including over hurdles. *R. Lee* **c90**
h–

GO FREE 6 b.g. Easycall – Miss Traxdata (Absalom) [2006/7 17m⁴ 17m⁴ 19d⁶ 16f* 16g⁴ 16s⁵ 16d Nov 11] modest on Flat (stays 13f): fair novice hurdler: left C. Down, won maiden at Worcester in July: best around 2m: acts on firm and soft going: front runner/races prominently. *J. G. M. O'Shea* **h100**

GO GO 7 ch.m. Alderbrook – Go Mary (Raga Navarro (ITY)) [2006/7 20m⁴ Apr 15] first foal: dam fair hurdler, stayed 21f: poor form when fourth in mares maiden hurdle on debut (tended to jump right): likely to do better. *Mrs S. M. Johnson* **h73 p**

GO GUNNER (IRE) 5 b.g. Needle Gun (IRE) – Highland Spirit (Scottish Reel) [2006/7 F17g Apr 27] seventh foal: half-brother to 3 winning 2m hurdlers, including fair Langkawi Island (by Never So Bold) and Conroy (by Greensmith): dam, fairly useful 2m to 2½m hurdler, also won at 6f and 7f at 2 yrs: well beaten in bumper on debut. *John Allen* **F–**

GO HARVEY GO (IRE) 8 b.g. Supreme Leader – Python Wolf (IRE) (Jolly Jake (NZ)) [2006/7 h–: 22s⁴ 25d⁴ 22v⁵ 19g* 20g⁵ Apr 21] modest hurdler: won conditional jockeys handicap at Towcester in March: probably stays 2¾m: best form on good going: travels strongly. *R. T. Phillips* **h98**

GO JOHNNY GO (IRE) 5 b.g. Moonax (IRE) – The Helmet (IRE) (Riot Helmet) [2006/7 F13s³ F17v⁶ Jan 8] 13,500 4-y-o: unfurnished gelding: fourth foal: half-brother to ungenuine 3m chase winner Ironside (by Mister Lord): dam unraced sister to Hennessy Gold Cup winner Coome Hill: modest form in bumpers: bred to stay well. *C. L. Tizzard* **F77**

The Silver Cod Partnership's "Gods Token"

GO JOHNNY (IRE) 7 b.g. Taipan (IRE) – Glenmore Memories (IRE) (Strong Gale) **h83**
[2006/7 F72+: 17s 18s⁴ 16s 24s⁵ 20s⁵ Apr 27] good-topped gelding: poor maiden hurdler:
bred to be suited by 2½m+: raced mainly on soft ground: needs to brush up jumping.
V. R. A. Dartnall

GOLA CHER (IRE) 13 b.g. Beau Sher – Owen Money (Master Owen) [2006/7 c26g⁵ **c77**
Apr 19] rangy gelding: useful hurdler/chaser at best for A. King: winning pointer: well **h–**
held on hunter debut: will stay beyond 3½m: acts on heavy going: tried blinkered/in
cheekpieces: lazy. *Miss V. Collins*

GOLA SUPREME (IRE) 12 gr.g. Supreme Leader – Coal Burn (King Sitric) [2006/7 **c– §**
c92§, h–§: 24mᵖᵘ c24vᵖᵘ May 23] workmanlike gelding: winning hurdler: novice chaser: **h– §**
no show in 2006/7: should stay beyond 3m: acts on heavy going: tried tongue tied:
unreliable. *R. Lee*

GOLD AGAIN (IRE) 9 b.g. Old Vic – Thomastown Girl (Tekoah) [2006/7 16s⁴ 17s **h85**
19s⁵ 19g⁵ 20m⁴ Apr 25] lengthy gelding: bumper winner: modest novice hurdler, off 22
months prior to return: stays 2½m: acts on soft and good to firm going: often blinkered.
Noel T. Chance

GOLD BEACH (IRE) 7 b.g. Jurado (USA) – Grange Park (IRE) (Warcraft (USA)) **h–**
[2006/7 F97: F17d 19gᵖᵘ Jul 9] runner-up in bumper on debut: has regressed, and no show **F–**
in novice on hurdling debut: joined R. Dickin. *M. G. Rimell*

GOLDBROOK 9 b.g. Alderbrook – Miss Marigold (Norwich (USA)) [2006/7 c102+, **c110 §**
h124§: c16g⁴ c16m⁴ c16s² c16m³ c21d⁵ c22gᵘʳ c16m⁴ c16g⁵ Oct 15] good-topped **h– §**
gelding: winning hurdler: fair chaser: below form last 4 starts: stays 2½m: acts on any
going: has finished weakly/run as if amiss more than once. *R. J. Hodges*

GOLDEN ALASKA 5 ch.m. Washington State (USA) – Arctic River (FR) (Arctic **h–**
Tern (USA)) [2006/7 F16d 16g Feb 21] half-sister to several winners, including 1¼m **F–**
winner Baajil (by Marju): dam, French 1¼m winner, out of sister to Arc winner Gold
River: no form in bumper/maiden hurdle (mistakes). *J. M. Bradley*

GOLDEN ALCHEMIST 4 ch.g. Woodborough (USA) – Pure Gold (Dilum (USA)) **h103 +**
[2006/7 16v⁵ 17g³ Apr 18] compact gelding: fair maiden on Flat (form up to 7f):
much better effort in juvenile hurdles when third to Laustra Bad at Cheltenham, settling
better: likely to prove best at sharp 2m. *M. D. I. Usher*

GOLDEN AMBER (IRE) 8 ch.g. Glacial Storm (USA) – Rigton Angle (Sit In The **c–**
Corner (USA)) [2006/7 23g 21dᵖᵘ c20m c24dᵖᵘ c24v⁴ c25sᵖᵘ Dec 12] no sign of ability: **h–**
blinkered last 2 starts. *John R. Upson*

GOLDEN BAY 8 ch.m. Karinga Bay – Goldenswift (IRE) (Meneval (USA)) [2006/7 **h131**
h115: 24d⁶ 21d² 22d 22s⁴ 21g Mar 14] medium-sized mare: useful handicap hurdler:
better than ever in 2006/7, would have won but for falling heavily 2 out at Wincanton:
insufficient test of stamina in Coral Cup at Cheltenham next time: should stay 3m: acts on
soft ground: genuine and reliable. *Miss Suzy Smith*

GOLDEN BOOT 8 ch.g. Unfuwain (USA) – Sports Delight (Star Appeal) [2006/7 **h85**
19g² 17d⁶ Nov 8] half-brother to winning selling hurdler around 2m I Wish You Love (by
Risk Me): fair at best up to 2m on Flat, on downgrade in 2006: poor form in novice
hurdles 3 days apart: dead. *A. Bailey*

GOLDEN CHILD (IRE) 5 b.g. Supreme Leader – Native Singer (IRE) (Be My **h111**
Native (USA)) [2006/7 F16d* F16d* 19d 21vᵛ* 20m³ Mar 25] €14,000 3-y-o: third foal: **F101**
dam unraced sister to high-class hurdler/smart chaser up to 2½m Ned Kelly and half-
sister to very smart staying chaser Nick Dundee: made all in bumpers at Worcester in
October and Ascot in November: easily best effort in novice hurdles when winning
5-runner event at Kempton in March by 11 lengths from Greenhill Bramble, wandering
into several flights: will stay beyond 21f: acts on heavy going. *N. A. Twiston-Davies*

GOLDEN CREST 7 ch.g. Rakaposhi King – Golden Aureole (Gildoran) [2006/7 h–: **c–**
25gᵖᵘ c20sᵘʳ 25s Jan 24] leggy, angular gelding: no show over hurdles and in maiden **h–**
chase. *W. Amos*

GOLDEN CRUSADER 10 b.g. Gildoran – Pusey Street (Native Bazaar) [2006/7 c–, **c114**
h–: 18m c16g* c16mᵖᵘ Aug 2] tall gelding: maiden hurdler, off 12 months prior to return: **h–**
fair chaser: better than ever when winning handicap at Newton Abbot in June: lame
next time: best at 2m: acts on soft and good to firm going: only blinkered: headstrong front runner.
J. W. Mullins

GOLDEN DUCK (IRE) 7 b.g. Turtle Island (IRE) – Mazeeka (IRE) (Glow (USA)) **c103**
[2006/7 c18v² c17d* c16g* c19s² c16g² Feb 2] strong gelding: maiden hurdler: fair **h–**
chaser: won handicaps at Stratford in October and Warwick in November: stays 2¾m:
acts on heavy going. *N. A. Twiston-Davies*

GOLDEN EMPIRE (FR) 6 b.g. Dernier Empereur (USA) – Freccia (IRE) (Caerleon (USA)) [2006/7 20s 16m³ 20s² 21v³ 18s* 20g* 20m Apr 24] good-topped gelding: half-brother to 1m winner Filelfo (by Exit To Nowhere) and 1½m winner in Belgium by Bigstone: dam French 9f winner: won point in 2006: fairly useful hurdler: won maiden at Downpatrick in March and handicap at Gowran (beat Pagan Magic comfortably by 1½ lengths) in April: respectable seventh of 25 to Charlies First in valuable handicap at Punchestown final start: stays 21f: acts on heavy and good to firm going. *Andrew Heffernan, Ireland* **h116**

GOLDEN FEATHER 5 ch.g. Dr Fong (USA) – Idolize (Polish Precedent (USA)) [2006/7 h93: 16g⁵ 17d 23d 20s² 21d 20g² Apr 27] rather leggy gelding: modest handicap hurdler: effective from 2m to 21f: acts on soft going: blinkered/in cheekpieces last 4 starts. *Miss Venetia Williams* **h99**

GOLDEN GUN (IRE) 6 b. or br.g. Accordion – Kennycourt Lady (IRE) (Persian Mews) [2006/7 16d⁵ Oct 1] €50,000 4-y-o: first foal: dam unraced half-sister to useful 2m chaser Dines and Midlands Grand National winner G V A Ireland: fifth in novice hurdle on debut: dead. *Jonjo O'Neill* **h89**

GOLDEN HARMONY (IRE) 5 ch.g. Anshan – Dream of Money (IRE) (Good Thyne (USA)) [2006/7 F16s Apr 27] sixth foal: half-brother to 2¼m chase winner Maid of Dreams (by Mandalus): dam unraced half-sister to smart staying chasers Ten of Spades and Maid of Money: no show in bumper on debut. *W. T. Reed* **F–**

GOLDEN HAWK (USA) 12 ch.g. Silver Hawk (USA) – Crockadore (USA) (Nijinsky (CAN)) [2006/7 h–: 18sᵖᵘ 24mᶠ Nov 24] winning hurdler, lightly raced and no show nowadays: tried blinkered. *R. M. Clark* **h–**

GOLDENHAY IMPOSTER 8 b.g. Man Among Men (IRE) – Golden Affair (Golden Shields) [2006/7 24sᵖᵘ Jan 30] second foal: dam tailed off in bumper: no promise in novice hurdle on debut. *C. J. Down* **h–**

GOLDEN JACK (FR) 13 b.g. Matahawk – Union Jack III (FR) (Mister Jack (FR)) [2006/7 c?, h–: c33gᶠ May 3] winning cross-country chaser in France and pointer in Britain: blinkered, failed to complete in hunters: stays long distances: acts on soft and firm going. *Mrs A. L. Tory* **c–** **h–**

GOLDEN OAK (IRE) 7 b.g. Goldmark (USA) – Embroidery (Lords (USA)) [2006/7 16v 17s⁵ 16d c16v* c20s³ c31sᵖᵘ Apr 27] compact gelding: second in bumper in 2003/4 for R. Fahey: not knocked about over hurdles: modest form in handicap chases: won 4-runner event at Folkestone in February: stays 2½m: raced on going softer than good (acts on heavy). *Jonjo O'Neill* **c97** **h80**

GOLDEN ODYSSEY (IRE) 7 ch.m. Barathea (IRE) – Opus One (Slip Anchor) [2006/7 h–§: 18fⁿ May 10] fair hurdler at best: off a year, well held last 2 starts: stays 21f: acts on good to soft ground: temperamental. *K. G. Reveley* **h– §**

GOLDEN PARACHUTE (IRE) 6 b.g. Executive Perk – Ardfallon (IRE) (Supreme Leader) [2006/7 F100: 20gᵖᵘ 24g 24m* Mar 31] good-topped gelding: bumper winner: first form over hurdles when winning maiden at Uttoxeter by 6 lengths from Ballyboley, jumping better: will stay beyond 3m. *C. C. Bealby* **h110**

GOLDEN SNOOPY (IRE) 10 ch.g. Insan (USA) – Lovely Snoopy (IRE) (Phardante (FR)) [2006/7 16vᵖᵘ 25g Apr 16] workmanlike gelding: fifth in bumper in 2003/4: left H. Daly and off 3½ years, no show over hurdles. *J. M. Saville* **h–**

GOLDEN SQUARE 5 ch.g. Tomba – Cherish Me (Polar Falcon (USA)) [2006/7 h92: 16m³ 16g 16g 16s⁶ Dec 2] angular gelding: fair on Flat (stays 8.6f), successful twice in 2006: modest novice hurdler: likely to prove best around 2m with emphasis on speed. *A. W. Carroll* **h92**

GOLDEN SQUAW 5 ch.m. Grand Lodge (USA) – Wig Wam (IRE) (Indian Ridge) [2006/7 h–: 16m Jun 18] no show over hurdles and in points. *Miss C. J. E. Caroe* **h–**

GOLDEN STREAK (IRE) 5 b.g. Indian Lodge (IRE) – Final Contract (IRE) (Shaadi (USA)) [2006/7 F95: F16m* F16g² 19g 16s 19d⁴ 25s 25vᵖᵘ 22m Apr 28] sturdy gelding: fairly useful in bumpers, won maiden at Worcester in May: sold out of C. Egerton's stable 13,000 gns Doncaster May Sales before next start: form over hurdles only when fourth in novice at Market Rasen: stays 19f. *S. B. Clark* **h90** **F95**

GOLD GUEST 8 ch.g. Vettori (IRE) – Cassilis (IRE) (Persian Bold) [2006/7 h95: 19mᵖᵘ 16f⁵ 16s² 19g⁶ 16mᵘʳ 16d² 16vᵖᵘ 16d Dec 21] tall, good-topped gelding: modest hurdler: best at 2m: acted on firm and soft going: tried visored: usually tongue tied: dead. *P. D. Evans* **h85**

Goffs Land Rover Bumper I.N.H. Flat, Punchestown—
Gonebeyondrecall lives up to his name as he lands a gamble

GOLD GUN (USA) 5 b.g. Seeking The Gold (USA) – Possessive Dancer (Shareef **h95**
Dancer (USA)) [2006/7 16d⁴ 16gᵖᵘ Mar 17] useful at one time on Flat (stays 1½m) for
M. Jarvis, reportedly suffered hairline fracture of cannon bone in 2005, well held since:
modest form when fourth in novice on hurdling debut: possibly amiss following month:
joined Mrs A. Thorpe. *K. A. Ryan*

GOLDING HOP 7 b.g. Alflora (IRE) – Rainbow Fountain (Royal Fountain) [2006/7 **h–**
F–: 18sᶠ 17s Jan 30] useful-looking gelding: no show in bumper/over hurdles.
P. Winkworth

GOLD RING 7 ch.g. Groom Dancer (USA) – Indubitable (Sharpo) [2006/7 16d⁶ **h105**
Nov 4] leggy gelding: useful on Flat (stays 1¾m) for G. Balding, well held in 2006:
fairly useful form at best over hurdles: will stay 2½m: room for improvement in jumping.
J. A. Geake

GOLDSMEADOW 8 b.g. Thowra (FR) – Fanny Adams (Nicholas Bill) [2006/7 F75: **h–**
17g 24vᵖᵘ Oct 1] poor form in bumpers: no show in novice hurdles. *O. Brennan*

GOLD THREAD (IRE) 6 b.g. Oscar (IRE) – Queen Boadicea (IRE) (Farhaan) **h92 +**
[2006/7 F99: F16m⁶ 17v⁴ 20d* Feb 14] lengthy gelding: bumper winner: modest form in **F86**
novice hurdles, won at Musselburgh in February by 1½ lengths from The Gleaner (pair
clear): likely to prove suited by 2½m+. *J. Howard Johnson*

GOLLINGER 11 b.g. St Ninian – Edith Rose (Cheval) [2006/7 c84: c20dᵘʳ c20g c20d⁴ **c56**
c24d⁵ Dec 30] winning pointer: maiden chaser, left R. Tierney after first outing: seems to
stay 3m. *P. D. Niven*

GOLO GAL 5 b.g. Mark of Esteem (IRE) – Western Sal (Salse (USA)) [2006/7 16sᵖᵘ **h–**
Nov 29] fair form on Flat at 3 yrs, well held in 2006: hampered third and never dangerous
in novice on hurdling debut. *Mrs L. J. Mongan*

GONDOLIN (IRE) 7 b.g. Marju (IRE) – Galletina (IRE) (Persian Heights) [2006/7 **c– §**
h82§: 19s² c20sᵖᵘ c18d⁴ 24dᵖᵘ 17v⁶ 20d c20gᵖᵘ Mar 27] tall gelding: modest maiden **h87 §**
hurdler: no show in handicap chases: stays 2¾m: acts on heavy going: tried in cheek-
pieces/blinkers: not one to trust. *G. Brown*

GONEBEYONDRECALL (IRE) 4 b.g. Dr Massini (IRE) – Green Walk (Green **F100 p**
Shoon) [2006/7 F16m* Apr 24] €50,000 3-y-o: has scope: fourth foal: dam, poor winning
chaser who stayed 25f, from family of Irish Grand National winner Ebony Jane: third in
maiden point in February: 3/1 favourite, won 22-runner Goffs Land Rover Bumper at
Punchestown in April by 9 lengths from Lifes Star, leading entering straight and merely
nudged clear: open to improvement. *N. F. Glynn, Ireland*

GONE MISSING 8 b.g. Early Edition – Tom's Little Bet (Scallywag) [2006/7 19m⁴ **c–**
22s⁴ 22g⁴ Jul 23] workmanlike gelding: modest form over hurdles: winning pointer, **h89**
including in March: will be suited by 3m+. *C. J. Down*

GONE TO LUNCH (IRE) 7 ch.g. Mohaajir (USA) – Jayells Dream (Space King) **c?**
[2006/7 c26gᶠ Mar 16] €14,000 4-y-o: rangy gelding: sixth foal: half-brother to winning
pointer by Jolly Jake: dam, modest hurdler up to 2¾m, half-sister to useful staying chaser
Sam Wrekin: fair pointer, successful in February: plenty to do when fell 4 out in Foxhunter at Cheltenham on chase debut. *J. Scott*

GONE TOMORROW (IRE) 5 b.g. Flemensfirth (USA) – Here To-Day (King's **F85**
Equity) [2006/7 F16s Mar 3] 8,000 4-y-o: strong gelding: ninth foal: half-brother to 2¾m

hurdle winner Frosty Run (by Commanche Run): dam, behind in bumpers/novice hurdles, half-sister to fairly useful staying chaser Shoon Wind: won maiden point in February: mid-field in bumper at Newbury, looking in need of further. *T. D. Walford*

GONE TOO FAR 9 b.g. Reprimand – Blue Nile (IRE) (Bluebird (USA)) [2006/7 c118, h115: c17f^{pu} c17g^2 16f^2 c18g^4 c16s^4 16m c16d^2 c16s^{pu} 18s c16v^5 c20d^4 16d^2 Jan 5] lengthy, angular gelding: fairly useful hurdler/handicap chaser: below best last 5 starts: stays 2½m: acts on firm and good to soft going: wears headgear: usually races prominently: moody. *P. Monteith*
   c116 d
   h118 d

GO NOMADIC 13 br.g. Nomadic Way (USA) – Dreamago (Sir Mago) [2006/7 c84: c25v^2 c28v^2 c27v^{pu} c26g^{pu} Apr 7] lengthy gelding: poor handicap chaser: stays 31f: acts on heavy going: has worn cheekpieces: tongue tied. *P. G. Atkinson*
   c83

GOODBADINDIFERENT (IRE) 11 b. or br.g. Mandalus – Stay As You Are (Buckskin (FR)) [2006/7 c80x: c24s^3 c20m^6 c24g^F c20v^6 c24s^{pu} c20d^F c20s^5 c20g^5 Apr 23] sturdy, compact gelding: poor handicap chaser: out of sorts in 2006/7: stays 25f: acts on good to firm going: sketchy jumper. *Mrs J. C. McGregor*
   c– x

GOOD BONE (FR) 10 b.g. Perrault – Bone Crasher (FR) (Cadoudal (FR)) [2006/7 c98: c25f^2 c25d* c26d c25s^2 c22g^3 Mar 28] tall gelding: fair hunter chaser: won at Hereford in May: stays 25f: acts on soft and good to firm going: tried tongue tied. *S. Flook*
   c98

GOOD BOOK (IRE) 9 b.g. Good Thyne (USA) – Book of Rules (IRE) (Phardante (FR)) [2006/7 25g* c23s^{pu} 26s^{pu} c29g* Mar 20] useful-looking gelding: winning pointer: form over hurdles only when winning novice at Warwick in October: visored, much better effort in handicap chases when winning at same course by 7 lengths from Grenfell, making virtually all: stays 29f: form only on good ground: tried in cheekpieces: has wandered under pressure. *A. Bateman*
   c101
   h89

GOOD BYE SIMON (FR) 4 gr.g. Simon du Desert (FR) – Marie de Pharis (FR) (Pas de Seul) [2006/7 18s^2 18s* 18s^2 16s* 17v^2 18s^4 Apr 13]
   h132 +

    The French connection was maintained for the latest running of the Finale Juvenile Hurdle at Chepstow in December. Four of the eight most recent winners, Mister Banjo, Nas Na Riogh, Phar Bleu and Blue Shark, were French bred and/or

Coral Future Champion Finale Juvenile Hurdle, Chepstow—
French raider Good Bye Simon lands the spoils

Prix Alain du Breil-Course de Haies d'Ete des Quatre Ans Hurdle, Auteuil—Good Bye Simon knuckles down well to beat Big Buck's (noseband); between the pair is fourth-placed Gaelic Ocean

had begun their careers across the Channel, and Thierry Doumen's Good Bye Simon became the third winner in that same period trained in France, following Guillaume Macaire's pair, Jair du Cochet and Tempo d'Or, successful in 2000 and 2001 respectively. The Grade 1 race for juveniles was run as the Coral Future Champion Finale Juvenile Hurdle in the latest season, though, at that time, only the ill-fated Jair du Cochet could have been considered a future champion among those recent winners and the field for the latest renewal was not a strong one. Good Bye Simon did not have to improve significantly on his French form at Chepstow to win his second race over hurdles, quickening smartly in a modestly-run race to lead before three out and not having to be fully extended to account for Ned Ludd by four lengths. Underlining the relatively modest nature of the contest, the next three home contested the Fred Winter at the Cheltenham Festival, rather than the Triumph, and all were well beaten at long odds. Good Bye Simon's other outing in Britain ended in defeat, though he actually enhanced his reputation and stepped up on his Chepstow form when taking on the season's top juvenile Katchit in the Finesse Hurdle at Cheltenham in late-January. Good Bye Simon got closer to the winner than most horses did all season, responding to pressure to put in a challenge at the last, only to prove unable to quicken on the run-in before going down by a length and three quarters. Rather than returning to Cheltenham for the Triumph Hurdle, Good Bye Simon was given a two-and-a-half-month break before reappearing at Auteuil in April in the Group 3 Prix de Pepinvast, finishing a creditable fourth behind Gaelic Ocean. That set him up nicely for a Group 1 success in the Prix Alain du Breil at the same course in June, where he had Gaelic Ocean back in fourth, with the Willie Mullins-trained pair Financial Reward and J'Y Vole back in sixth and seventh respectively. Good Bye Simon's form there represented further progress on his good efforts at Auteuil in the autumn. Beaten by the Francois Doumen-trained Parrain (a gelding he beat twice subsequently) on his hurdling debut, he won next time out before going down by half a length to Royal Honor in the Group 1 Prix Cambaceres in November, going one better than his dam Marie de Pharis who was third in the race in 1990. Good Bye Simon was bred by Robert Collet, who trained both his sire (a smart miler) and dam, and he was named after his sire who died of a heart attack aged only ten just weeks before Good Bye Simon was foaled. The dam's two other winning jumpers, Giant Jumper and Rebelote (the latter a full brother to Good Bye Simon), were both successful for Collet over hurdles at Auteuil as three-year-olds over fifteen furlongs. The good-topped Good Bye Simon stays nineteen furlongs and has so far raced only on soft or heavy ground. *T. Doumen, France*

GOOD CAUSE (IRE) 6 b.g. Simply Great (FR) – Smashing Pet (Mummy's Pet)   **h–** [2006/7 F16g 20s Nov 19] half-brother to useful hurdler/winning chaser Comex Flyer   **F–** (by Prince of Birds), stayed 2¾m: dam lightly-raced half-sister to very smart 1m/

1¼m performer Broken Hearted: little impact in bumpers/maiden hurdle: joined Mrs S. Lamyman, probably flattered in maidens on Flat. *E. U. Hales, Ireland*

GOOD CITIZEN (IRE) 7 b.g. Good Thyne (USA) – Citizen Levee (Monksfield) [2006/7 h111: c16v³ c21v* c24v^F c21v^F c22v^pu Feb 17] good-topped gelding: maiden hurdler: fairly useful novice chaser: won handicap at Sedgefield in December by ¾ length from Canada Street (pair clear): fell next 2 starts, would have finished good second to Flying Enterprise but for departing last in similar event at Cheltenham on second occasion: should stay 3m: acts on heavy going: best form on left-handed tracks. *T. R. George*
   c126
   h–

GOOD COMPANY (IRE) 7 b.g. Among Men (USA) – Khatiynza (Nishapour (FR)) [2006/7 F16v⁴ F16g 16s⁵ 18v* Feb 28] half-brother to 3 winners, including fair hurdler around 2m Your Cheatin Heart (by Broken Hearted): dam placed in bumpers: fair form on first of 2 starts in bumpers: confirmed promise of previous run (banned for 60 days under non-triers rule) over hurdles when winning maiden at Downpatrick by ½ length from Tailor's Hall: will stay 2½m: acts on heavy going: open to further improvement. *C. Roche, Ireland*
   h118 p
   F90

GOOD EVENING (IRE) 5 b.g. Even Top (IRE) – Our Next Rose (IRE) (Be My Native (USA)) [2006/7 F17v Mar 18] first foal: dam unraced out of half-sister to National Hunt Chase winner Loving Around and useful hurdler up to 21f Verrazano Bridge: twice-raced in maiden points in 2006, runner-up on completed start: well beaten in bumper, not knocked about. *C. Grant*
   F–

GOOD INVESTMENT 5 b.g. Silver Patriarch (IRE) – Bundled Up (USA) (Sharpen Up) [2006/7 h86: 16m 16f 17m⁴ c20d^ur 20d 20d⁴ 22s 27s 24v^pu 24v^pu Jan 2] rather sparely-made gelding: poor hurdler, left P. Haslam after third start: unseated early on chasing debut: stays 2½m: acts on good to firm going, well below form on soft/heavy: wears headgear: unreliable. *Miss Tracy Waggott*
   c– §
   h79 §

GOOD JUDGEMENT (IRE) 9 b.g. Good Thyne (USA) – Loch Na Mona (IRE) (King's Ride) [2006/7 c102d, h–: c23m^pu May 6] tall, good sort: twice-raced over hurdles, successful on debut: maiden chaser, has usually run as if amiss: stays 25f. *Jonjo O'Neill*
   c–
   h–

GOODLEIGH GENERAL 5 b.g. Prince of Peace – Blue-Bird Express (Pony Express) [2006/7 F16d⁶ F17d Nov 16] third foal: dam winning pointer: better effort in bumpers (modest form) on debut. *W. S. Kittow*
   F78

GOOD LINE (IRE) 6 b.g. Saddlers' Hall (IRE) – Chattering (Le Bavard (FR)) [2006/7 F16s^pu Dec 26] sixth foal: half-brother to fairly useful hurdler/chaser Alright Now M'Lad (by Supreme Leader), should stay beyond 25f, and winning 2½m chaser Bandon Valley (by Montelimar): dam, modest hurdler/chaser who stayed 3m, sister to dam of high-class staying hurdler Marello: favourite, went as if amiss in bumper on debut. *Noel T. Chance*
   F–

GOOD MAN AGAIN (IRE) 9 b.g. Arctic Lord – Amari Queen (Nicholas Bill) [2006/7 c95d, h94d: 23m⁵ 24f^pu 26m⁴ 22m^pu c23m⁴ c23m² c26d⁵ c24s^pu c23d⁶ c19v^pu c25s^pu c20m^pu Apr 25] tall gelding: maiden hurdler: winning chaser: form in handicaps in 2006/7 only when second at Worcester: stays 3¼m: acts on good to firm and heavy going: tried in headgear: often tongue tied: sketchy jumper. *A. Sadik*
   c82 x
   h–

GOOD MUSIC (IRE) 5 b.g. Good Thyne (USA) – Global Diamond (IRE) (Classic Music (USA)) [2006/7 F16m Feb 4] €3,500 4-y-o: first foal: dam, 13f winner on Flat, successful at 2m over hurdles: tailed off in bumper on debut. *T. Butt*
   F–

GOODNIGHT TOM 8 b.g. Midnight Legend – Rosealeena (Derring Rose) [2006/7 16d³ 26m³ 24f* Jul 19] second foal: dam unraced: half-sister to useful staying chaser Celtic Abbey: error-prone maiden hurdler: improved form (modest) over hurdles when winning maiden at Worcester by 4 lengths from Shining Joy: stays 3m. *M. Scudamore*
   h97

GOOD OUTLOOK (IRE) 8 b.g. Lord Americo – I'll Say She Is (Ashmore (FR)) [2006/7 c104x, h–: c20g May 14] sturdy gelding: lightly raced over hurdles: fair handicap chaser: effective at 2m to 3m: acts on good to firm and good to soft going, probably on heavy: takes good hold and usually makes running: often let down by jumping over fences. *R. C. Guest*
   c– x
   h–

GOOD POTENTIAL (IRE) 11 b.g. Petardia – Steel Duchess (IRE) (Yashgan) [2006/7 c–§, h83§: 20m 24g 24d² 24d⁶ 24d⁵ 22v⁴ 23s^pu Feb 16] workmanlike gelding: modest handicap hurdler: no form over fences: stays 3¼m: acts on any going: tried blinkered/in cheekpieces: usually tongue tied: ungenuine. *D. J. Wintle*
   c– §
   h89 §

Million In Mind Partnership's "Good Spirit"

GOOD SPIRIT (FR) 5 b.g. Smadoun (FR) – Haute Tension (FR) (Garde Royale)   **c132**
[2006/7 18s^F c16g^3 c17s* c20v^2 c16g Mar 13] sparely-made gelding: third foal: half- **h?**
brother to useful hurdler/fairly useful chaser Hautclan (by Chef de Clan II), probably
stays 3½m, and fairly useful hurdler/chaser Positive Thinking (by Nikos), stays 2½m:
dam, 2¼m hurdles winner on only start, sister to dam of useful hurdler/Flat stayer Heros
Fatal: 11.5f winner at 3 yrs, only start on Flat: successful in juvenile hurdles at Vichy and
Toulouse: left G. Macaire, progressive form first 3 starts over fences in Britain, easily
winning maiden at Stratford in February: 3 lengths second to stable-companion Natal in
Grade 2 novice at Kempton: stiff task final outing: stays 2½m: raced on good ground and
softer (acts on heavy): sold 200,000 gns Doncaster May Sales. *P. F. Nicholls*

GOOD TIME WILLIE (IRE) 5 br.g. Good Thyne (USA) – Hazel Sylph (IRE)   **h88**
(Executive Perk) [2006/7 F17d 17d^5 16g^3 16m 24s^{pu} Apr 25] unfurnished gelding: first **F–**
foal: dam unraced out of sister to very smart 2m chaser Young Snugfit: seventh of 13 in
bumper on debut: modest form over hurdles: should be suited by further than 2m.
P. Bowen

GOOD TO TRAVEL (IRE) 4 b.f. Night Shift (USA) – Harir (Kris) [2006/7 16g^{bd} **h–**
17g 16s 16v Dec 7] half-sister to useful 2m hurdler In The Forge (by Zilzal) and modest
2½m hurdle winner Mama Jaffa (by In The Wings): modest on Flat (stays 1¼m) for
K. Prendergast, successful at 2 yrs: no form in juvenile hurdles: tried blinkered. *G. Elliott,
Ireland*

GOOD VINTAGE (IRE) 12 b.g. Lashkari – Furry Hope (Furry Glen) [2006/7 c87,   **c85**
h–: c31g^3 May 24] workmanlike gelding: fair pointer/hunter chaser: stays 31f: acts on **h–**
any going: hasn't always impressed with attitude (tried in headgear). *S. R. Andrews*

GO ON AHEAD (IRE) 7 b.g. Namaqualand (USA) – Charm The Stars (Roi Danzig   **h–**
(USA)) [2006/7 F97+: F16d 20d^{pu} Jan 15] tall, good-topped gelding: best effort in **F69**

378

bumpers when winning at Worcester in late-2005/6: mistakes and dropped right away in maiden at Fakenham on hurdling debut: free-going sort, may prove best at 2m. *M. J. Coombe*

GO ON LINE 5 b.g. Overbury (IRE) – Lamper's Light (Idiot's Delight) [2006/7 F16g 21g^{pu} Mar 23] 28,000 3-y-o: good-topped gelding: fifth foal: half-brother to fairly useful hurdlers Sea The Light (by Blue Ocean), stays 19f, and Trigger The Light (by Double Trigger), stays 3m: dam, well beaten in bumper, half-sister to very smart 2m chaser Martin's Lamp and useful 2m to 3¼m chaser Hurricane Lamp: offered little in bumper/maiden hurdle nearly 6 months apart. *Jonjo O'Neill* — h– F–

GOOSE CHASE 5 b.g. Inchinor – Bronzewing (Beldale Flutter (USA)) [2006/7 h–: 16m⁶ 17g⁵ Nov 9] rather leggy gelding: fair on Flat (stays 1m), well below best in 2007: no form over hurdles: tried blinkered: headstrong: sold 7,000 gns Doncaster January Sales. *A. M. Hales* — h–

GO PETE (NZ) 8 ch.g. Senor Pete (USA) – Lillibet (NZ) (First Norman (USA)) [2006/7 25d^{pu} 17s^{pu} c18g⁴ Mar 18] no show over hurdles: achieved little on chasing debut. *Miss Venetia Williams* — c– h–

GOSCAR ROCK (IRE) 6 b.g. Synefos (USA) – Almost Regal (IRE) (Jurado (USA)) [2006/7 F99: 17s 20s⁶ 19v 19s⁶ 22d^{pu} Mar 20] tall gelding: placed in bumpers: disappointing over hurdles. *P. J. Hobbs* — h87

GO SOLO 6 b.g. Primo Dominie – Taza (Persian Bold) [2006/7 16s 16d⁴ 16s 19g 17m* 20m² Apr 20] good-topped gelding: half-brother to useful hurdler/fairly useful chaser Il Capitano (by Be My Chief), stayed 27f: useful on Flat (stays 1½m), successful 3 times in 2006, sold out of G. A. Swinbank's stable 52,000 gns Newmarket Autumn Sales: fair hurdler: won 3-runner handicap at Exeter in April: stays 2½m: acts on good to firm and good to soft going. *D. E. Pipe* — h112

GOSPEL SONG 15 ch.g. King Among Kings – Market Blues (Porto Bello) [2006/7 h90d: 16s⁵ 17d May 24] small gelding: veteran hurdler: best up to easy 2½m: acts on heavy going: tried tongue tied: free-going sort. *A. C. Whillans* — h79

GOSPEL TRUTH (FR) 4 ch.g. Sendawar (IRE) – Take My Hand (GER) (Dashing Blade) [2006/7 F13d⁶ F14s⁴ Nov 26] second foal: dam, German 1m winner, half-sister to high-class hurdler Muse: favourite, failed to see race out both starts in 3-y-o bumpers. *Carl Llewellyn* — F76

GOSS 10 gr.g. Linamix (FR) – Guillem (USA) (Nijinsky (CAN)) [2006/7 c–, h107§: 16s⁴ 16m⁴ 20m⁵ 19m 19m⁵ c17d^{pu} Oct 7] tall gelding: winning chaser (lame final outing): fair handicap hurdler on his day: best around 2m: acts on good to firm and heavy going: wore headgear last 2 starts: has had tongue tied: unreliable. *Jonjo O'Neill* — c– § h107 §

GOTHEBUG 7 b.m. Gothenberg (IRE) – Midge (Reformed Character) [2006/7 16m^{pu} 16s^{pu} Feb 15] first foal: dam winning pointer: more signs of temperament than ability in 2 starts over hurdles: tongue tied on debut. *Mrs H. O. Graham* — h–

GOTTA GET ON 6 b.rm. Emperor Fountain – Lonicera (Sulaafah (USA)) [2006/7 h75?: 16m 20m³ 20m⁶ 22m² 20g 24s 22s^{pu} Jan 10] lengthy mare: poor novice hurdler: stays 2¾m: acts on good to firm going, possibly not on soft. *R. H. Alner* — h73

GOURANGA 4 b.f. Robellino (USA) – Hymne d'Amour (USA) (Dixieland Band (USA)) [2006/7 16s⁴ 16s 16v³ 17s Mar 12] smallish, close-coupled filly: half-sister to one-time fairly useful hurdler/fair chaser Guard Duty (by Alderbrook), stayed 25f: fair maiden on Flat (stays 1½m), sold out of H. Candy's stable 6,000 gns Newmarket Autumn Sales: well held over hurdles. *A. W. Carroll* — h–

GOVERNMENT (IRE) 6 b.g. Great Dane (IRE) – Hidden Agenda (FR) (Machiavellian (USA)) [2006/7 c–, h–: 17g 17v³ 17s⁵ 19v c16s^F Dec 8] leggy gelding: modest on Flat (stays 7f), successful in March: bad 2m maiden hurdler: let down by jumping both starts over fences: headstrong. *M. C. Chapman* — c– x h53

GO WHITE LIGHTNING (IRE) 12 gr.g. Zaffaran (USA) – Rosy Posy (IRE) (Roselier (FR)) [2006/7 c–, h–: c29g^{pu} Mar 21] leggy gelding: maiden chaser: stays 33f: acts on soft going (won bumpers on good to firm and heavy): free-going front runner: often shapes as if amiss. *Mrs H. Wintle* — c– h–

GOWNA'S HOPE (IRE) 4 b.g. Distant Music (USA) – Embolden (Warning) [2006/7 18s 16s 16v^{pu} 16g Apr 14] no form on Flat in Ireland or over hurdles. *J. W. Mullins* — h–

GRACECHURCH (IRE) 4 b.g. Marju (IRE) – Saffron Crocus (Shareef Dancer (USA)) [2006/7 18s^F 17v² 17s* 16v⁴ 16d 17g³ Apr 1] smallish, leggy gelding: fairly useful on Flat (stays 10.5f), successful twice in 2006, sold out of M. Channon's stable — h118

379

32,000 gns Newmarket Autumn Sales: fairly useful juvenile hurdler: won maiden at Folkestone in January: best effort when third to Ingratitude in novice at Newton Abbot: raced around 2m: acts on heavy going. *R. J. Hodges*

GRACEFUL DANCER 10 b.m. Old Vic – Its My Turn (Palm Track) [2006/7 c101, h96: 24v^{pu} 23v Jan 4] good-topped mare: fair chaser/handicap hurdler, poor efforts in 2006/7: stays 29f: raced on good going or softer (acts on heavy): tried in blinkers, often visored. *B. G. Powell*   c– h–

GRACEFUL EXIT (IRE) 4 ch.g. Hussonet (USA) – La Sencilla (ARG) (Lookinfor-thebigone (USA)) [2006/7 aF13g Nov 22] fourth foal: half-brother to 3 winners in Chile: dam unraced: well held in bumper on debut. *C. E. Longsdon*   F–

GRACIALINA (GER) 4 ch.f. Kornado – Giovanella (IRE) (Common Grounds) [2006/7 16g^5 16d Nov 4] successful twice around 1½m on Flat at 3 yrs, claimed from M. Rosseel €16,400 after runner-up at Clairefontaine in August: well held in juvenile hurdles. *J. C. Fox*   h–

GRACIE BEACH 5 b.m. Alflora (IRE) – Ur Only Young Once (Pitpan) [2006/7 F16g F16s^{pu} F16s Dec 7] £2,500 4-y-o: first foal: dam bumper winner: no form in bumpers. *H. E. Haynes*   F–

GRAFFITI TONGUE (IRE) 14 b.g. Be My Native (USA) – Lantern Line (The Parson) [2006/7 c–, h102§: 27m^{pu} Jun 11] fair hurdler: stays 27f: acts on any going: has worn headgear, including cheekpieces last 5 starts: tried tongue tied: hard ride. *Evan Williams*   c– h– §

GRAFTY GREEN (IRE) 4 b.g. Green Desert (USA) – Banafsajee (USA) (Pleasant Colony (USA)) [2006/7 F13g F14v 20v^{pu} Jan 6] 8,000 3-y-o: rather leggy, lengthy gelding: fourth foal: half-brother to 1 winner on Flat, including useful 1m winner Banksia (by Marju): dam French 1m to 10.5f winner: no sign of ability. *T. H. Caldwell*   h– F–

GRAN AMOR 4 ch.f. Piccolo – Sunfleet (Red Sunset) [2006/7 17m^{pu} Jun 30] half-sister to fair 2m hurdler No Pattern (by Rock City): no form in Flat maiden/juvenile hurdle. *P. D. Cundell*   h–

GRAND AFFAIR 10 ch.g. Karinga Bay – Levant Row (Levanter) [2006/7 c20f^{pu} Apr 5] maiden pointer: jumped violently left on chasing debut. *Mrs A. L. Tory*   c–

GRAN DANA (IRE) 7 b.g. Grand Lodge – Olean (Sadler's Wells (USA)) [2006/7 h–: 20g^6 May 6] angular gelding: no show over hurdles: poor form when placed in points in 2007: tried tongue tied. *G. Prodromou*   h–

GRAND BLEU (IRE) 4 b.g. Great Palm (USA) – Blue Pool (Saddlers' Hall (IRE)) [2006/7 17s* 16s* 16g^4 Apr 12] €35,000 3-y-o: big, lengthy gelding: has scope: first foal: dam lightly-raced half-sister to smart stayer Orchestra Stall and fairly useful hurdler/chaser Berlin Blue, stayed 4m: useful form in juvenile hurdles: won at Fontainebleau on debut in December and quite valuable 5-runner event at Haydock (beat King's Revenge readily by 15 lengths) in February: not discredited under less testing conditions when fourth to Katchit in Grade 1 at Aintree: remains type to progress further. *F. Doumen, France*   h131 p

GRAND DAUM (FR) 6 b. or br.g. Double Bed (FR) – Maousse (FR) (Labus (FR)) [2006/7 h–, F84: 20g^2 24g 20g^6 Apr 3] quite good-topped gelding: poor form over hurdles: sold out of T. Tate's stable 7,000 gns Doncaster May Sales and off 6 months after first outing: stays 2½m. *Micky Hammond*   h77

GRAND DISPLAY (IRE) 6 b. or br.g. Grand Lodge (USA) – Special Display (Welsh Pageant) [2006/7 20m^3 22m^5 20d^3 16m 16s^{pu} 20g^3 Nov 3] brother to fairly useful 2m hurdler Berengarius and modest hurdler Houseparty, stayed 2½m: modest maiden on Flat (stays 2m), sold out of J. Bolger's stable 9,000 gns Newmarket July Sales: modest novice hurdler: stays 2½m: tried tongue tied. *B. W. Duke*   h96

GRANDE CREOLE (FR) 8 b.g. Byzantium (FR) – Sclos (FR) (Direct Flight) [2006/7 c–, h100: 22g Apr 27] fair hurdler when with P. Nicholls: has failed to complete over fences (including point): should stay beyond 3m. *A. J. Honeyball*   c– h–

GRAND IDEAS 8 br.g. Grand Lodge (USA) – Afrafa (IRE) (Lashkari) [2006/7 h–: 16s^{pu} May 14] maiden on Flat: no show both starts over hurdles. *G. J. Smith*   h–

GRAND MANNER (IRE) 7 b.g. Desert Style (IRE) – Reacted (IRE) (Entitled) [2006/7 h–: c20m* Apr 28] leggy gelding: poor over hurdles: off 2 years, won conditional jockeys handicap at Market Rasen on chasing debut by ¾ length from Insurgent: stays 2½m: acts on soft and good to firm going: open to improvement over fences. *K. G. Reveley*   c77 p h–

GRANDMA'S GIRL 5 b.m. Desert Style (IRE) – Sakura Queen (IRE) (Woodman (USA)) [2006/7 h66: 16m^pu Jun 17] smallish mare: maiden on Flat: poor form over hurdles. *Robert Gray* **h–**

GRANDOS (IRE) 5 b.g. Cadeaux Genereux – No Reservations (IRE) (Commanche Run) [2006/7 17g Apr 1] modest maiden on Flat (stays 7.5f), sold out of T. Easterby's stable £2,600 Ascot June Sales and no form subsequently: well held in novice on hurdling debut. *Karen George* **h–**

GRANDPOPS JOY (IRE) 6 ro.g. Clerkenwell (USA) – Silver Bay Lady (IRE) (Zaffaran (USA)) [2006/7 F16g aF16g^3 F16v c16d^5 c16s^ur c21s^5 Jan 30] leggy gelding: first foal: dam unraced: little sign of ability. *K. J. Burke* **c–** **F–**

GRAND SLAM HERO (IRE) 6 ch.g. Anshan – Tidal Princess (IRE) (Good Thyne (USA)) [2006/7 h92, F68: 26d^3 20f* 20m^2 24m 20m^2 19d* 19d^2 20d^2 Sep 22] fair hurdler: won maiden at Worcester in June and novice at Newton Abbot in August: stays 2½m: acts on firm and good to soft going: usually tongue tied. *P. Bowen* **h105**

GRAND WELCOME (IRE) 5 b.g. Indian Lodge (IRE) – Chocolate Box (Most Welcome) [2006/7 17s Mar 12] poor on Flat (stays 11f) nowadays, has won in Spain: tongue tied, well beaten in seller on hurdling debut. *E. J. Creighton* **h–**

GRANGECLARE FLIGHT (IRE) 5 b.m. Old Vic – Grangeclare Rose (IRE) (Gianchi) [2006/7 F16d* Feb 14] €52,000 3-y-o: sister to useful hurdler Grangeclare Lark, will stay 3m, and 2m hurdle winner Classic Vic, and half-sister to useful hurdler/chaser Scarthy Lad (by Magical Wonder), effective at 2m to 3m: dam unraced half-sister to fairly useful staying chaser Thinking Cap: won mares bumper at Musselburgh on debut by 4 lengths from Mary Pat, under pressure soon after halfway: will be suited by greater test of stamina: likely to improve. *N. G. Richards* **F94 p**

GRANGECLARE LARK (IRE) 6 b.m. Old Vic – Grangeclare Rose (IRE) (Gianchi) [2006/7 F16s* 16d* 16s* 20v* 18v^6 20m* 18m* Apr 25] **h134** **F90 +**
The Dessie Hughes-trained six-year-old Grangeclare Lark enjoyed a tremendous campaign, winning six of her seven starts and making up into a useful hurdler in the process. Her exploits, plus those of Celestial Wave and Cailin Alainn in recent seasons, give a further illustration as to the rewards currently on offer for above-average mares on Irish soil, with those six wins—all bar one of which came in mares company—netting connections £103,094. Despite showing promise, notably when third to Brogella in a Grade 3 mares novice at the Punchestown

Irish Stallions Farms European Breeders Fund (Mares) Novices' Hurdle, Fairyhouse—Grangeclare Lark resumes winning ways after a rare flop;
also pictured are third Chomba Womba and fourth Lounaos (white cap)

*Bewleys Hotels Irish Stallion Farms European Breeders Fund Mares Hurdle, Punchestown—
Grangeclare Lark (No.1) shows her battling qualities to defeat old rivals Shuil Aris (right)
and Blazing Sky (No.2)*

Festival, Grangeclare Lark had failed to get off the mark in two starts in bumpers
and over hurdles in the previous season, but wasted no time shedding that maiden
tag when winning a bumper at Fairyhouse in October on her reappearance.
Returned to hurdling, Grangeclare Lark justified favouritism twice the following
month, in a Grade 3 mares novice at Down Royal, by three and a half lengths from
Strike An Ark, before narrowly landing the odds from Mickataine in a five-year-old
minor event at Cork sixteen days later. Stepped up to two and a half miles for a
ten-runner mares listed event at Leopardstown's four-day Christmas meeting,
Grangeclare Lark showed marked improvement when winning in good style by
five and a half lengths from Blazing Sky. Given an eleven-week break after
disappointing in a novice at Cork in January, Grangeclare Lark returned at the top
of her game, winning the fourteen-runner Irish Stallion Farms EBF (Mares)
Novices' Hurdle at Fairyhouse on her return. She led at the second last but was all
out after being steadied into the last, beating Shuil Aris by a short head, with her
Cork conqueror Chomba Womba and leading juvenile Lounaos filling third and
fourth respectively. At Punchestown later in the month, Grangeclare Lark repeated
the form with the runner-up back at two and a quarter miles, coping better than
Shuil Aris with the lesser test of stamina to win the even more valuable Grade 3
Bewleys Hotels Irish Stallion Farms European Breeders Fund Mares Hurdle by two
and a half lengths, her battling qualities once again standing her in good stead as
she eventually won going away after looking in trouble turning for home. Whilst
Grangeclare Lark will stay three miles, her final performance supports the view that
she is not going to prove purely a stayer.

Grangeclare Lark (IRE) (b.m. 2001)	Old Vic (b 1986)	Sadler's Wells (b 1981)	Northern Dancer / Fairy Bridge
		Cockade (b 1973)	Derring-Do / Camenae
	Grangeclare Rose (IRE) (b 1990)	Gianchi (br 1982)	Niniski / Honey Bridge
		Grangeclare Lady (ch 1972)	Menelek / Loquacious

The sturdy Grangeclare Lark is the sixth foal of an unraced half-sister to the
1987 Troytown Chase winner Thinking Cap. Grangeclare Lark is a sister to the
Jessica Harrington-trained Classic Vic, a bumper winner who has since shown fair
form over hurdles, in the latest season awarded a two-mile maiden at Fairyhouse.
Another full sister, Grangeclare Flight, made a winning start to her career when
winning a mares bumper at Musselburgh for Nicky Richards in the latest season,
shaping very much like a stayer. Grangeclare Lark is also a half-sister to her stable's
useful hurdler and chaser Scarthy Lad (by Magical Wonder) who is effective at two
miles to three miles. Dessie Hughes also won the bidding for the dam's 2004 Lord
Americo gelding, who fetched €32,000 at the latest Derby Sale. *D. T. Hughes,
Ireland*

GRANGETOWN (IRE) 7 ch.g. Idris (IRE) – Marqueterie (USA) (Well Decorated (USA)) [2006/7 20s^{pu} 17m^6 16g^6 18g^{pu} c21m^{pu} Aug 29] well beaten both starts on Flat: poor maiden hurdler: left N. Meade prior to reappearance: no encouragement on chasing debut: raced mainly around 2m: tried blinkered. *J. J. Lambe, Ireland*   c–
h80

GRANITE MAN (IRE) 7 b.g. Glacial Storm (USA) – Silkaway (IRE) (Buckskin (FR)) [2006/7 c–p, h–p, F92: 22m^3 24f^2 20m* 22m* 24s* 22g^5 Sep 23] lengthy gelding: upped in trip and much improved over hurdles in 2006/7, winning handicaps at Newton Abbot, Worcester (both novices), Cartmel and Market Rasen before end of August: tailed off in 2m handicap only outing over fences: will stay beyond 3m: acts on firm and soft going. *Jonjo O'Neill*   c–
h107 +

GRANIT JACK (FR) 5 gr.g. Glaieul (USA) – Line Grey (FR) (Le Nain Jaune (FR)) [2006/7 20s^3 20s^2 19v* 16d^2 Mar 13]   c?
h142

He came good in the end, but Granit Jack's first couple of starts in Britain seemed to show that, for all the apparent similarities between himself and stable-companion Neptune Collonges, ability wasn't something they had in equal measure. In 2005/6, the one-year older Neptune Collonges had won four of his seven starts over hurdles for owner John Hales and trainer Paul Nicholls, finishing second in the Long Walk Hurdle against the top stayers and proving himself one of the best novices over hurdles. The same connections appeared to have a similar type on their hands for the latest season in Granit Jack, right down to sharing the same coat colour. Granit Jack had come from the same trainer as Neptune Collonges, Jacques Ortet in south-west France, and had run in the same colours there too (when owned by Madame Georges Vuillard) as they followed very similar campaigns. Granit Jack had won his last four chases at Pau as a juvenile (only one of them by less than eight lengths), a year after Neptune Collonges had run up a four-timer at the same course. Both horses had completed their four-timer in the same listed event and, by all accounts, Granit Jack would have gone on to contest some of the top chases for four-year-olds at Auteuil, as Neptune Collonges had done, had his sale not gone through. In an interview in *Paris-Turf* in May, Ortet explained how the market for French jumpers has changed in recent years, making it difficult for French owners to turn down offers from Britain. A few years earlier, a young French horse might be capable of winning twice as much in prize money in France as the sum offered for him, whereas nowadays the prices being commanded by young French jumpers can be anything from two and five times what the horse might reasonably be expected to earn. Ortet added that if his best chaser, the Vuillard-owned Or Jack, had been around nowadays, he would almost certainly have been unable to keep him in his stable.

Granit Jack's reputation preceded him when he made his British debut at Chepstow (where Neptune Collonges had also started off) and he started odds on for the Persian War Novices' Hurdle. When he managed only a remote third to Kanpai and Massini's Maguire, it looked as though lack of fitness, rather than stamina, was the more plausible explanation for his defeat, even though the stable's runners are rarely lacking in that regard. When Granit Jack was beaten at odds on again next time out, finishing a remote second to the mare Labelthou, in another Grade 2 event, the Winter Novices' Hurdle at Sandown (won by Neptune Collonges the year before), it was beginning to look as though temperament might have become an issue, Granit Jack not finding nearly so much as the winner when shaken up.

In the event, however, a physical problem was found to be behind Granit Jack's disappointing start to his career in Britain. After a break of nearly three months, he reappeared in a maiden hurdle at Taunton in February, tongue tied and reportedly having been treated for stomach ulcers since his last outing. Even allowing for the ordinary opposition he faced on this occasion, Granit Jack looked a different horse and ran out an impressive winner, setting quite a searching gallop in the heavy ground and coming home a distance clear of the eased-down runner-up Missis Potts. Raced at around two and a half miles thus far in Britain (as he had been latterly in France), Granit Jack was dropped to two miles for the Supreme Novices' Hurdle at Cheltenham, despite seeming unlikely to improve over the shorter trip against some rivals with above-average Flat form. One of those, Ebaziyan, proved too good for him, but, starting second favourite and looking in good trim (also tongue tied again) the well-ridden Granit Jack, who was up there all the way, finished three lengths behind him, battling on to retake second after being hard ridden into the straight and lacking the winner's pace.

		Lear Fan	Roberto
	Glaieul (USA)	(b 1981)	Wac
	(b or br 1989)	Gracious Lassie	Kalamoun
Granit Jack (FR)		(br 1977)	Gracious
(gr.g. 2002)		Le Nain Jaune	Pharly
	Line Grey (FR)	(ch 1979)	Lady Berry
	(gr 1995)	Cackle	Crow
		(ro 1982)	Gracious Sakes

Granit Jack is by the 1991 Criterium de Saint-Cloud winner Glaieul who has had only a handful of runners in Britain and Ireland, the best of them Jim, a smart Irish chaser at up to around two and a half miles. On the distaff side, Granit Jack's family stems from America, his grandam Cackle (by St Leger winner Crow and half-sister to numerous winners out of a minor stakes winner) bought there for 200,000 dollars as a yearling. Raced first in Britain, she showed little in four starts for Gavin Pritchard-Gordon but, sent to France, won a small race over a mile and a half in the Provinces. Cackle has proved much more successful at stud than on the racecourse, and while Granit Jack's dam Line Grey never ran (Granit Jack is her second foal), she has numerous winning siblings. Cackle's first winner, Crystal Jack was a fairly useful sprinter in Britain who later became a prolific winner at up to a mile in Italy. However, he turned out to be anything but typical of his dam's future progeny. Best of them was another Vuillard-Ortet representative, the smart chaser Grey Jack, whose sixteen wins over jumps included Italy's top chase in

Mr J. Hales' "Granit Jack"

2000, the Gran Premio Merano—a race Or Jack won three times in the 'nineties. Cackle's other winners include the one-time useful chaser in Britain, Mondial Jack, who stays an easy three miles. Whilst less of a stayer than Neptune Collonges, Granit Jack will be suited by a return to further than two miles and certainly looks worth another chance back at two and a half. Ineligible for novice chases, he'll have to take on more seasoned rivals back over fences from now on, something which proved no handicap to Neptune Collonges who was in the same position at the start of the latest season. A good-topped gelding, Granit Jack was worth a rating of 130p on his form over fences as a juvenile in France and looks set to prove a better chaser than a hurdler. He has raced only on good going or softer and acts on heavy. *P. F. Nicholls*

GRANNY'S FOOTSTEPS (IRE) 5 b.m. Dushyantor (USA) – Just A Second (Jimsun) [2006/7 F18d³ F16s F16v 24dᵖᵘ Mar 22] half-sister to fair hurdler/chaser Sorry Al (by Anshan), stays 3m: dam, maiden hurdler/chaser, suited by test of stamina: third in bumper at Plumpton (carried head awkwardly) on debut: no form after, over hurdles final start. *D. R. Gandolfo*   h– F80

GRANOSKI GALA 8 b.m. Petoski – Great Granny Smith (Fine Blue) [2006/7 c25g² Apr 23] fair pointer, won twice in 2007: favourite, 4 lengths second to Thorsgill in maiden hunter at Hexham on chasing debut. *Mrs Morag Herdman*   c86

GRAPEVINE SALLY (IRE) 6 b.m. Saddlers' Hall (IRE) – Mrs Battleaxe (IRE) (Supreme Leader) [2006/7 F16d² 16d* 19s* 20v⁴ 20mᵖᵘ Apr 24] rather unfurnished mare: first foal: dam once-raced half-sister to useful staying hurdler What A Question: fairly useful in bumpers, won at Wexford in 2005/6: fair hurdler: won maiden at Clonmel and mares minor event at Limerick (by 2½ lengths from Midnight Gift) in November: good fourth to Grangeclare Lark in listed mares event at Leopardstown: reportedly bled final start: stays 2½m: acts on heavy going. *E. J. O'Grady, Ireland*   h108 F98

GRAPHEX 5 b. or br.g. Inchinor – Allegra (Niniski (USA)) [2006/7 F85: 16d 17vᵖᵘ 16v 16d 19g Feb 21] small, workmanlike gelding: modest in bumpers for A. King: no form over hurdles: tried visored. *B. Storey*   h–

GRAPHIC APPROACH (IRE) 9 b.g. King's Ride – Sharp Approach (Crash Course) [2006/7 c138, h–: c20d⁵ c24d³ c21gᵘʳ c36gᵘʳ Apr 14] strong, lengthy gelding: winning hurdler: useful handicap chaser: creditable efforts first 2 starts, 14 lengths third of 18 to Billyvoddan in listed event at Ascot: jumped well in rear until departing at second Becher's in Grand National at Aintree final start (collapsed with heat stress after running loose and later had to be put down): stayed 3m: raced on good ground or softer (acted on soft): blinkered third outing (made mistakes). *C. R. Egerton*   c137 h–

GRASP 5 b.g. Kayf Tara – Circe (Main Reef) [2006/7 h121: 16g 16s 17sᵖᵘ 16d Dec 27] close-coupled gelding: fair on Flat (stays 17f), successful in November: fairly useful hurdler at best, little impact in handicaps in 2006/7: will stay 2½m: acts on heavy going: usually blinkered/visored: tongue tied prior to last 3 starts: often front runner. *G. L. Moore*   h113

GRATTAN LODGE (IRE) 10 gr.g. Roselier (FR) – Shallow Run (Deep Run) [2006/7 c–, h105: c26s³ c26vᵖᵘ c25v⁵ c24vᵖᵘ 25v³ 27s Apr 27] lengthy gelding: fair hurdler: one-time useful handicap chaser: little show since 2004 except when third to Twelve Paces at Carlisle on reappearance: should stay beyond 27f: acts on heavy going: tried blinkered. *J. Howard Johnson*   c124 h102

GRAVE DOUBTS 11 ch.g. Karinga Bay – Redgrave Girl (Deep Run) [2006/7 h128: 17m⁴ 20m³ 24m* 20mᶠ 24mᵖᵘ 22d 19g 19m* 24dᵖᵘ 22mᵖᵘ Apr 11] good-topped gelding: fairly useful handicap hurdler: won at Worcester in June and Exeter (by 1¼ lengths from Bay Hawk) in October: stays 3m, effective at much shorter: acts on firm and good to soft going: tongue tied: inconsistent. *K. Bishop*   h119

GRAY'S EULOGY 9 b.g. Presenting – Gray's Ellergy (Oats) [2006/7 c95, h–: c25d⁴ c24sᶠ c26vᵖᵘ Mar 7] sturdy gelding: modest handicap chaser, possibly needed run only completed outing in 2006/7: best at 3m+: raced on good going or softer (acts on soft): wears blinkers/cheekpieces nowadays. *D. R. Gandolfo*   c83 h–

GREAT APPROACH (IRE) 6 b.g. Simply Great (FR) – Gayles Approach (Strong Gale) [2006/7 h96p: c20sᵖᵘ 25g* 22v² 25v² Mar 18] tall gelding: progressive over hurdles, won handicap at Catterick in February by neck from Im A Witness: runner-up in similar events both outings after, fairly useful form when beaten 4 lengths by Carapuce at Carlisle final one: mistakes when pulled up in handicap on chasing debut: stays 25f: raced on good ground or softer (acts on heavy). *N. G. Richards*   c– h120

GREAT AS GOLD (IRE) 8 b.g. Goldmark (USA) – Great Land (USA) (Friend's **c115** Choice (USA)) [2006/7 c110, h–: 24v³ c20s² 23v⁶ Jan 6] leggy, close-coupled gelding: **h107** fair handicap hurdler/chaser: won on Flat in April: should stay beyond 3m: acts on heavy and good to firm going: wears headgear: sometimes races lazily. *B. Ellison*

GREAT BENEFIT (IRE) 8 ch.g. Beneficial – That's Lucy (IRE) (Henbit (USA)) **c–** [2006/7 c–, h–: 26m c26d⁵ c20g Aug 14] no form: wore cheekpieces in 2006/7. *Evan* **h–** *Williams*

GREAT COMPTON 7 b.g. Compton Place – Thundercloud (Electric) [2006/7 h70: **h–** 22m 20mᵘʳ Jun 6] medium-sized gelding: poor novice hurdler: stays 2¾m: tried blinkered/in cheekpieces. *B. J. Llewellyn*

GREAT JANE (FR) 5 b.m. Great Palm (USA) – Gaelic Jane (FR) (Hero's Honor **c93** (USA)) [2006/7 24f⁴ 20g⁵ 16m⁵ c20d⁵ c16sᶠ c24g³ c21v* c20s² Apr 27] close-coupled, **h–** sparely-made ex-French mare: second foal: dam maiden: maiden hurdler: left J. Bertran de Balanda after 2005/6: modest form over fences: jumped well and improved last 2 starts, winning handicap at Ayr in March: stays easy 3m: acts on heavy going. *Mrs S. C. Bradburne*

GREAT MAN (FR) 6 b.g. Bering – Great Connection (USA) (Dayjur (USA)) [2006/7 **h–** 16d Feb 2] fair on Flat (stays 1½m): well beaten on completed outing in novice hurdles: sold 1,600 gns Doncaster May Sales. *Noel T. Chance*

GREAT MEMORIES 8 b.g. Alflora (IRE) – Four Thyme (Idiot's Delight) [2006/7 **c–** h88, F85: c17gᶠ May 5] modest form over hurdles: fell on chasing debut: would have **h–** stayed beyond 2m: dead. *Jonjo O'Neill*

GREAT QUEST (IRE) 5 b.m. Montjeu (IRE) – Paparazzi (IRE) (Shernazar) [2006/7 **h76 p** 19vᵛᵖᵘ 16g⁶ Mar 17] fair on Flat (stays 17f), successful in 2006 for T. Stack: better effort over hurdles when sixth to Daldini in maiden at Wetherby, left with plenty to do and not unduly punished: likely to improve further. *James Moffatt*

GRECIAN GROOM (IRE) 5 b.g. Groom Dancer (USA) – Danse Grecque (IRE) **h101** (Sadler's Wells (USA)) [2006/7 F115p: F16g* F16d 19d 16s 16v* 16s 22gᵖᵘ 20g⁶ Apr 27] **F100** leggy gelding: won first 2 starts in bumpers, at Huntingdon in late-2005/6 (most impressive, for P. Niven) and October: 33/1-winner of 2m novice at Lingfield in January: very disappointing over hurdles otherwise: tried tongue tied. *Jonjo O'Neill*

GREEK STAR 6 b.g. Soviet Star (USA) – Graecia Magna (USA) (Private Account **h–** (USA)) [2006/7 h91: 21dᵖᵘ 20d Jan 5] workmanlike gelding: maiden hurdler, modest at best: stays easy 3m: acts on heavy and good to firm ground. *K. A. Morgan*

GREEN ADMIRAL 8 b.g. Slip Anchor – Jade Mistress (Damister (USA)) [2006/7 **c–** c25m Aug 6] smallish gelding: maiden hurdler: won both starts in points in 2006: **h–** reportedly suffered fatal heart attack on chasing debut: probably stayed 19f. *P. D. Niven*

GREENASH GOLF 7 b.g. Afzal – Space Kate (Space King) [2006/7 22d 22sᵖᵘ 20d **c–** c25dᵘʳ c24vᴿ Nov 23] big, rangy gelding: brother to fair chaser Ashgreen, stays 25f: dam, **h–** won 3¼m hurdle, sister to useful 2m chaser Space Fair: no form, including in points. *M. Scudamore*

GREEN BELT FLYER (IRE) 9 b.g. Leading Counsel (USA) – Current Liability **c135** (Caribo) [2006/7 c137, h–: c17s c16s c16s⁵ c24s* c25gᵖᵘ Apr 13] useful-looking gelding: **h–** winning hurdler: useful handicap chaser: upped in trip, won at Newbury in March by 9 lengths from Harrycone Lewis, only form in 2006/7: stays 3m: acts on heavy and good to firm going: effective blinkered or not: inconsistent. *Miss Venetia Williams*

GREENBRIDGE (IRE) 5 b.g. Luso – Green Divot (Green Desert (USA)) [2006/7 **F108** F17v² F17v* F16d Feb 10] €32,000 3-y-o: useful-looking gelding: fourth foal: half-brother to fair 2m hurdler/chaser Wages (by Lake Coniston): dam lightly-raced half-sister to smart hurdler/top-class chaser Tiutchev, effective at 2m to 25f: useful form in bumper on debut: didn't have to run near that to land odds at Taunton in January by 1½ lengths from Merlin's Magic, hanging left final 1f: well held in Grade 2 at Newbury. *A. King*

GREENCARD GOLF 6 b.g. Foxhound (USA) – Reticent Bride (IRE) (Shy Groom **c– §** (USA)) [2006/7 h85§: 20g⁴ 20sᵖᵘ 19m c19mᵖᵘ c25mᵘʳ c24gᶠ 19m 20s⁵ 16d Nov 11] **h– §** good-topped gelding: poor hurdler, little form in 2006/7: let down by jumping all 3 starts over fences (left Jennie Candlish after first): probably stays 3m: acts on soft going: tried in headgear. *P. L. Clinton*

GREENFIELD (IRE) 9 ch.g. Pleasant Tap (USA) – No Review (USA) (Nodouble **h85 §** (USA)) [2006/7 h113: 19g 24d 22d 21s⁴ 22d 20g Apr 16] good-topped gelding: one-time fair handicap hurdler, little form since 2005: stays 2¾m: acts on heavy going: usually wears headgear: tried tongue tied: often shapes as if amiss. *R. T. Phillips*

GREEN FINGER 9 b.g. Environment Friend – Hunt The Thimble (FR) (Relkino) [2006/7 c111, h–: c16m² c20g⁴ c16f* 20s² c18g* 17m² c21d² c23m⁶ c22g⁵ c21d³ Oct 14] workmanlike gelding: modest form over hurdles: fairly useful handicap chaser: won at Hexham in June and Market Rasen in July: sold out of J. Quinn's stable 20,000 gns Doncaster August Sales: good efforts 3 of 4 starts after: stays 2¾m: acts on firm and good to soft going: tried in cheekpieces. *P. Bowen*　　**c118 h95**

GREENFORT BRAVE (IRE) 9 b.g. Bravefoot – Greenfort Belle (IRE) (Beyssac (FR)) [2006/7 h74: 20f⁴ 20m⁶ 22m³ 24g* 22g² 21m³ 24s³ 24g⁵ 20s Nov 4] leggy gelding: modest handicap hurdler: won at Perth in August: stays 3m: acts on firm and soft going: best efforts in cheekpieces: no easy ride (has carried head awkwardly). *J. J. Lambe, Ireland*　　**h94**

GREEN GAMBLE 7 gr.g. Environment Friend – Gemma's Wager (IRE) (Phardante (FR)) [2006/7 c94, h–: 17m 16mᵖᵘ c19g⁵ Apr 27] good-topped gelding: modest chaser/maiden hurdler, below best since 2005, trained until after reappearance by D. Feek: best around 2m: acts on good to soft and good to firm going: tried blinkered. *D. M. Grissell*　　**c– h–**

GREEN GO (GER) 9 ch.g. Secret 'n Classy (CAN) – Green Fee (GER) (Windwurf (GER)) [2006/7 c21d⁴ c21f* c24sᵖᵘ c21s⁴ Oct 1] angular gelding: winning hurdler: modest handicap chaser, off 2 years before reappearance: won at Stratford in September: stays 3¼m: acts on firm and good to soft going: has shaped as if amiss more than once: front runner. *A. Sadik*　　**c85 h–**

GREENHILL BRAMBLE (IRE) 7 b.g. Supreme Leader – Green Thorn (IRE) (Ovac (ITY)) [2006/7 F16g² 19d² 17s² 19d⁵ 20d 19dᵇᵈ 21v² 19g⁶ Mar 30] well-made gelding: useful form in bumpers, won at Newton Abbot in 2004/5 for P. Hobbs: fair novice hurdler: probably stays 21f: raced on good going or softer (acts on heavy): has been let down by jumping. *N. J. Hawke*　　**h106 F110**

GREENHOPE (IRE) 9 b.g. Definite Article – Unbidden Melody (USA) (Chieftain) [2006/7 c137, h117: 17s c16g c16g⁴ Apr 12] good-topped gelding: fairly useful handicap hurdler, needed run on reappearance: useful handicap chaser: good fourth of 15 to Bambi de L'Orme in Grade 3 at Aintree: will stay 2½m: acts on soft and good to firm going: tongue tied last 2 starts: usually races up with pace (ridden more patiently at Aintree). *N. J. Henderson*　　**c139 h–**

GREEN IDEAL 9 b.g. Mark of Esteem (IRE) – Emerald (USA) (El Gran Senor (USA)) [2006/7 c113, h–: c20s c25sᵖᵘ c20s⁵ c20v² c20v⁴ c20sᵖᵘ Apr 25] leggy, close-coupled gelding: fair but unreliable handicap chaser: form in 2006/7 only when second at Newcastle: best efforts around 2½m: acts on heavy going: tried in cheekpieces, usually blinkered: tongue tied once. *Ferdy Murphy*　　**c111 § h–**

GREENLOUGH (IRE) 6 b.m. Zaffaran (USA) – Bright Princess (IRE) (Deep Run) [2006/7 F17d* Oct 7] sixth foal: half-sister to winning pointer by Phardante: dam, ran once in bumper, half-sister to dam of high-class staying chaser Keen Leader: won mares maiden Irish point in 2006: also successful in mares bumper at Bangor by 11 lengths from Single Handed: will stay at least 2½m. *N. A. Twiston-Davies*　　**F98**

GREEN 'N' GOLD 7 b.m. Cloudings (IRE) – Fishki (Niniski (USA)) [2006/7 c–, h94: 20gᵖᵘ 20v* 20s* 17s⁴ 22v⁵ 20s³ 21v 16s³ c22v² c20v² c20m² Mar 31] smallish mare: fair handicap hurdler: won twice at Uttoxeter in May (seller first occasion, sold from Micky Hammond 6,000 gns): modest form over fences when runner-up last 3 starts: stays 23f: acts on heavy and good to firm going. *D. McCain Jnr*　　**c89 h99**

GREENOCK 6 b.g. Silver Patriarch (IRE) – Merilena (IRE) (Roselier (FR)) [2006/7 16s⁵ 21s³ 20v Dec 30] 20,000 3-y-o, €52,000 4-y-o: workmanlike gelding: first foal: dam, fair hurdler who stayed 2¾m, half-sister to dam of smart chaser up to 25f Another Promise: form in novice hurdles only when third at Sedgefield: likely to stay 3m: sold 4,000 gns Doncaster May Sales. *Ferdy Murphy*　　**h83**

GREEN PROSPECT (FR) 7 b.g. Green Tune (USA) – City Prospect (FR) (Diamond Prospect (USA)) [2006/7 c–, h106: 22s³ 20m⁴ 22sᵖᵘ 24vᵖᵘ 19s⁶ 18g 21g³ Mar 26] winning chaser in France: modest handicap hurdler nowadays: stays 21f: acts on soft and good to firm going: in headgear last 6 outings: has found little. *M. J. McGrath*　　**c– h94**

GREEN TANGO 8 br.g. Greensmith – Furry Dance (USA) (Nureyev (USA)) [2006/7 c140, h–: c17dᶠ c17dᵘʳ Nov 18] good-topped gelding: winning hurdler: useful chaser: let down by jumping in 2006/7, unseating 3 out in handicap at Ascot won by Demi Beau: stayed 19f: acted on soft and good to firm going: consistent: dead. *H. D. Daly*　　**c– h–**

GREGORY PECKORY (IRE) 9 b. or br.g. Teamster – Vill Alba (IRE) (Cataldi) [2006/7 c23d^{pu} May 17] close-coupled gelding: in frame in bumper/novice hurdle for N. Twiston-Davies in 2003: fair pointer, successful 3 times in 2007: no show in hunter on chase debut (none too fluent). *Mrs Jelly O'Brien*   c–
h–

GRENFELL (IRE) 8 br.m. Presenting – Arumah (Arapaho) [2006/7 h87: 16d^4 20g^4 21s^4 24v^4 c24d c29g^2 c28g^2 Apr 7] good-topped mare: modest novice hurdler: similar form when runner-up in handicap chases: stays 29f: acts on heavy going. *N. A. Twiston-Davies*   c96
h87

GREY BROTHER 9 gr.g. Morpeth – Pigeon Loft (IRE) (Bellypha) [2006/7 c–, h112: 22m^3 22g^2 19g^F Jul 23] sturdy gelding: fairly useful handicap hurdler, lightly raced: ran well when placed at Newton Abbot on completed starts early in 2006/7: failed to complete in 2 runs over fences: stays 2¾m: acts on good to firm and good to soft ground. *Nick Williams*   c–
h117

GREY FINALE 5 b.m. Grey Desire – Tanoda (Tyrnavos) [2006/7 F17s F16s Nov 22] good-topped mare: sixth foal: dam 5f (at 2 yrs) to 1½m winner: well beaten in bumpers and Flat maiden. *M. Brittain*   F–

GREY KID (IRE) 9 gr.g. Roselier (FR) – Gala's Pride (Gala Performance) [2006/7 c–, h–: c25d^3 c24g^6 Apr 27] well beaten over hurdles: modest pointer/hunter chaser: stays 25f. *E. W. Morris*   c79
h–

GREY KITE 5 gr.g. Silver Patriarch (IRE) – Flemings Delight (Idiot's Delight) [2006/7 F–: F16s 20d Jan 15] workmanlike gelding: no sign of ability: tried tongue tied. *A. E. Jessop*   h–
F–

GREY MAGGIE (IRE) 6 gr.m. Anshan – Bere Science (IRE) (Roselier (FR)) [2006/7 F16v F16s^6 Feb 3] second foal: half-sister to bumper winner Laborec (by Oscar): dam ran twice in bumpers: little impact in bumpers. *D. Carroll*   F–

GREY PAINT (USA) 4 gr. or ro.g. El Prado (IRE) – Devil's Art (USA) (Devil's Bag (USA)) [2006/7 18g^2 16m^4 Oct 12] fair on Flat (may prove best short of 2m) for R. Hannon: modest form in frame in juvenile maiden hurdles: likely to prove best around 2m with emphasis on speed: visored/tongue tied. *D. E. Pipe*   h89

GREY SAMURAI 7 gr.g. Gothenberg (IRE) – Royal Rebeka (Grey Desire) [2006/7 17g 16g 16g^4 16v^3 16g^2 16s* Dec 8] lengthy gelding: modest novice hurdler: won handicap at Southwell in December: raced around 2m on good going or softer (acts on heavy). *B. Ellison*   h96

GREY SHARK (IRE) 8 gr.g. Roselier (FR) – Sharkezan (IRE) (Double Schwartz) [2006/7 20d 20v 24v^{pu} 19v^{pu} 19v^5 Jan 21] angular gelding: novice hurdler, left D. P. Keane and off 22 months prior to return: should stay beyond 2¾m: raced on ground softer than good: tried in cheekpieces/tongue tied. *D. Burchell*   h78

GREYSIDE (USA) 4 gr.g. Tactical Cat (USA) – Amber Gold (USA) (Mr Prospector (USA)) [2006/7 16m* 16g^4 17s^{pu} 16d^6 Jan 19] strong, lengthy gelding: fair maiden on Flat: modest form over hurdles: won juvenile at Kelso in October: no show last 2 starts, blinkered final one: joined C. Mulhall. *J. Howard Johnson*   h83

GREY TORNADO 6 gr.g. My Best Valentine – Grey Baroness (Baron Blakeney) [2006/7 F–: F16d Dec 16] lengthy, useful-looking gelding: soundly beaten in bumpers 9 months apart: sold 1,200 gns Doncaster January Sales. *C. G. Cox*   F–

GRIFFIN'S LEGACY 8 b.g. Wace (USA) – Griffin's Girl (Bairn (USA)) [2006/7 h78§: 17g^6 19s^6 19d 22g^{su} 19m^6 17g 24s^{pu} Dec 29] medium-sized gelding: bumper winner: poor maiden hurdler: stays 2¾m: acts on soft going: tried blinkered/in cheekpieces: irresolute. *N. G. Ayliffe*   h69 §

GRINGO 5 gr.g. Alzao (USA) – Glen Falls (Commanche Run) [2006/7 16g^4 16s^4 16g* 16d^4 16m 16g* Apr 15] brother to fair hurdler Gulf Raider, stays 2½m: fairly useful on Flat (stays 1½m), successful in June/July for B. Hills: fairly useful novice hurdler: won at Musselburgh in December and Kelso (easily by 2 lengths from Abstract Folly) in April: likely to prove best at 2m with emphasis on speed. *J. Howard Johnson*   h115

GRIPIT N TIPIT (IRE) 6 b.g. Saddlers' Hall (IRE) – Savanagh (IRE) (Brush Aside (USA)) [2006/7 F88: F16d^2 F16g* 16s^3 16v^2 16v* 19s^2 20v^6 20v 16g^3 20m^F Apr 24] good-topped gelding: won bumper at Galway in September: fairly useful hurdler: won maiden at Navan in December easily by 9 lengths from My Auld Man: good ¾-length second to You Sir in minor event at Limerick next time: should stay 2½m: acts on heavy going (bumper form on good to firm): often makes running. *C. F. Swan, Ireland*   h117
F92

GRITTI PALACE (IRE) 7 b.g. Duky – Glittering Grit (IRE) (Sheer Grit) [2006/7 **c98 p**
h118: 24s c25s⁵ Nov 22] lengthy gelding: fairly useful hurdler, shaped as if in need of **h–**
race on return: bit deliberate when fifth of 8 in maiden at Wetherby on chasing debut:
needs thorough test of stamina: raced on going softer than good (acts on heavy): likely to
improve over fences. *John R. Upson*

GROOM COTTAGE 7 ch.g. Master Willie – Kingky's Cottage (Kinglet) [2006/7 **F70**
F17m Aug 6] third foal: dam unraced out of half-sister to very smart staying chaser Tied
Cottage: seventh of 14 in bumper on debut. *C. Grant*

GROUND BALL (IRE) 10 b. or br.g. Bob's Return (IRE) – Bettyhill (Ardross) **c140**
[2006/7 c142, h139: c16g⁴ c17d² c22gᵖᵘ c16v c17s⁶ 20v³ 19v⁴ c16g c16g³ c21g⁴ Apr 13] **h130**
well-made gelding: useful hurdler/chaser: ran well in race for third time when 7 lengths
third of 23 to Andreas in Grade 3 Grand Annual Chase (Handicap) at Cheltenham
penultimate start: stamina stretched when 10¼ lengths fourth of 29 to Dunbrody Millar in
Topham Chase at Aintree: stays 2½m: acts on heavy and good to firm going: jumped
markedly right when asked to lead fifth outing. *C. F. Swan, Ireland*

GROUND BREAKER 7 b.g. Emperor Jones (USA) – Startino (Bustino) [2006/7 c97, **c93**
h90: c16gᵖᵘ c16g 16gᵖᵘ c16m⁴ c16d⁴ c16s* c16d⁴ Jan 8] workmanlike gelding: maiden **h–**
hurdler: modest chaser, sold out of M. Easterby's stable 6,600 gns Doncaster May Sales
after second start: won handicap at Huntingdon in December: should stay beyond 17f:
acts on soft and good to firm going: tried tongue tied. *G. J. Smith*

GROUND PATROL 6 b.g. Ashkalani (IRE) – Good Grounds (USA) (Alleged (USA)) **h–**
[2006/7 16sᵖᵘ Jan 10] fair on Flat (stays 1½m), successful in 2006, left G. L. Moore after
final outing: breathing problem on hurdling debut. *N. R. Mitchell*

GROUSE MOOR (USA) 8 b.g. Distant View (USA) – Caithness (USA) (Roberto **c90 +**
(USA)) [2006/7 c–, h–: c19v³ c17m² c20gᵖᵘ Apr 23] sturdy gelding: has had breathing **h–**
operation: winning hurdler: modest chaser, lightly raced: easily landed odds in maiden at
Plumpton in April: stays 2½m: acts on heavy going, probably on good to firm: tried
tongue tied. *P. Winkworth*

GUDASMUM 9 b.m. Primitive Rising (USA) – Comarch (Ancient Monro) [2006/7 **c–**
c89: c20mᵖᵘ Jun 3] fair pointer: runner-up on completed outings in hunter chases: stays
3m. *J. P. Elliot*

GUE AU LOUP (FR) 13 gr.g. Royal Charter (FR) – Arche d'Alliance (FR) (Pamponi **c– x**
(FR)) [2006/7 c–x, h–: c17s⁴ May 26] tall gelding: winning chaser: no form since 2003/4, **h–**
including in points. *J. Groucott*

GUERILLA (AUS) 8 b. or br.g. Octagonal (NZ) – Partisan (AUS) (Canny Lad (AUS)) **h99**
[2006/7 h–p: 20g* 17d 20m⁶ 16f⁶ 20f³ 16g 17m² 16d 16g 16g Nov 13] lengthy gelding:
modest hurdler: won novice at Wetherby on first day of season: stays 2½m: acts on good
to soft and good to firm going: tried tongue tied. *R. C. Guest*

GUESS WHAT 7 b.g. Warcraft (USA) – Double Talk (Dublin Taxi) [2006/7 F–: 20dᵖᵘ **h–**
May 1] sturdy gelding: little sign of ability: sold 1,200 gns Doncaster August Sales.
Mrs S. J. Smith

GUIGNOL DU COCHET (FR) 13 ch.g. Secret of Success – Pasquita (FR) (Bour- **c–**
bon (FR)) [2006/7 c89d, h–: c21gᵖᵘ c24mᵖᵘ May 16] tall gelding: modest pointer nowad- **h–**
ays: stays easy 3m: has worn blinkers/visor: tried tongue tied. *S. Flook*

GUILT 7 b.g. Mark of Esteem (IRE) – Guillem (USA) (Nijinsky (CAN)) [2006/7 c20s⁵ **c102 §**
c16m⁶ c20f⁵ c20g⁴ c21s³ c19s c20s³ c16s⁵ c21g Apr 1] tall, leggy ex-Irish gelding: fair **h–**
handicap chaser, left D. Hughes after fifth start: barely stays 2½m: acts on heavy ground,
probably on good to firm: often in headgear/tongue tied: unreliable. *K. J. Burke*

GUMLAYLOY 8 ch.g. Indian Ridge – Candide (USA) (Miswaki (USA)) [2006/7 c–: **c–**
19m⁶ Jun 19] winning pointer: no show in hunter chase/novice hurdle. *M. Scudamore* **h–**

GUMLEY GALE 12 b.g. Greensmith – Clodaigh Gale (Strong Gale) [2006/7 c120, **c119 d**
h–: c24g³ c28s^F c26g⁵ c32m c26s⁶ Aug 19] sturdy gelding: fairly useful handicap chaser: **h–**
form in 2006/7 only on first outing: stays 4m: acts on heavy and good to firm going: tried
blinkered: tongue tied. *K. Bishop*

GUNADOIR (IRE) 5 b.m. Needle Gun (IRE) – Rent Day (Town And Country) **h91**
[2006/7 F71: F16d 16s² 16v² 20v² 17s 21v² 24s⁶ Apr 25] mid-field in bumpers: modest **F70**
novice hurdler: well held last 3 starts: should stay beyond 2½m: acts on heavy going.
N. G. Richards

GUNFIGHTER (IRE) 4 ch.c. Machiavellian (USA) – Reunion (IRE) (Be My Guest **F—**
(USA)) [2006/7 F17g Mar 24] fourth foal: dam 6f (at 2 yrs) and 7f (Nell Gwyn) winner:
no show in maiden bumper on debut: third in maiden on Flat debut. *J. S. Wainwright*

GUNGADU 7 ch.g. Beneficial – Tsarella (Mummy's Pet) [2006/7 h140: c24s* **c147**
c24d² c24s* c24d* c33gF Mar 15] **h—**
       After two years at Lingfield the Reynoldstown Novices' Chase was
returned to its traditional home, Ascot, where it was first run in 1971. A Grade 2
event, the John Smith's Reynoldstown (named after the dual Grand National
winner of the 'thirties) has been won down the years by jumping luminaries such
as Brown Lad, Lanzarote, Little Owl, Royal Athlete, Mr Mulligan and One Man.
It tends to be regarded as a stepping stone to the Royal & SunAlliance Chase, even
though the ill-fated Killiney in 1973 remains the only horse to have completed
the double. Ordinarily the winner of the latest edition, Gungadu, would have been
looked upon as a strong contender for the Cheltenham race. The only way Gungadu
was going to compete in the Royal & SunAlliance, though, was if anything untoward happened to the hot favourite for that race Denman, in the same ownership as
Gungadu and also trained by Paul Nicholls. Thankfully for connections, Denman
was able to take up his intended engagement, and when Gungadu turned up at
the Cheltenham Festival it was to contest the National Hunt Chase, for which he,
too, started a short-priced favourite—2/1 in a field of nineteen. Unlike Denman,
Gungadu let his supporters down, putting in a mixed round of jumping for amateur
Jamie Snowdon and eventually making one mistake too many when falling two
out. He still had every chance at the time, holding a narrow advantage having led or
disputed the lead from the off, although he wouldn't necessarily have beaten
Butler's Cabin or Character Building had he completed, nor run up to his best for
that matter. It's the only time Gungadu has failed to complete in fifteen appearances, the first four of which came in Irish points, Gungadu successful in the last
three of those. He quickly developed into a useful novice hurdler after joining his
present yard for the 2005/6 season, winning at Chepstow and Wincanton, and it

*John Smith's Reynoldstown Novices' Chase, Ascot—
odds-on Gungadu is pushed closest by outsider Wee Robbie*

took him even less time to reach a similar level when switched to fences. Gungadu made the running when landing the odds in novice events at Cheltenham in October by eleven lengths from Openide and Warwick in January by twenty-five lengths from In Accord. In between, when also odds on, he finished a length and a half second to Boychuk in a Grade 2 novice at Newbury, leading until just after the last. His jumping wasn't without blemish in those events, with his tendency to go to the right evident on the left-handed tracks. That was less of a problem when going right-handed in the Reynoldstown, though Gungadu did make one notable error at Ascot, at the fourteenth, Ruby Walsh (who was in the saddle for all three wins) putting it down to his mount being distracted by the BBC mobile camera on the inside of the course. Gungadu, once again at odds on, quickly recovered from his mistake, continuing in the lead and in command turning into the straight, idling thereafter but still having four lengths to spare over nearest pursuer Wee Robbie. Gungadu's jumping should improve as he gains experience, and he'll make up into a smart chaser, one who could well win a valuable handicap in the next season when stamina is at a premium. A sturdy gelding, he has raced only on good going or softer to date. *P. F. Nicholls*

GUNNABELIL 5 b.m. Gunner B – Young Tess (Teenoso (USA)) [2006/7 F17s 16v 17s 17s Mar 11] fourth foal: dam, poor hurdler, stayed 3¼m: well held in bumper/over hurdles. *P. Bowen* — **h–** **F–**

GUNNASAYSO 6 b.m. Gunner B – Sayshar (Sayfar) [2006/7 F83: F17s³ 21v 20d⁴ 16v² 17v² Mar 4] quite good-topped mare: placed in bumper: poor form in novice hurdles: bred to be suited by 2½m+: raced on going softer than good (acts on heavy). *J. A. B. Old* — **h79 +** **F76**

GUNNER JACK 6 b.g. Gunner B – Wayuphill (Furry Glen) [2006/7 F102+: 20s* Oct 29] good-bodied gelding: type to make a chaser: won bumper at Ayr on debut in 2005/6: favourite, successful also on hurdling debut when beating Mr Preacher Man readily by 10 lengths in 16-runner novice at Carlisle: will stay beyond 2½m: looked capable of better, but not seen out again. *N. G. Richards* — **h114 p**

GUNNER ROYAL 9 b.g. Gunner B – Loadplan Lass (Nicholas Bill) [2006/7 c25g⁵ Nov 29] good-topped gelding: fair pointer, won 3 times in 2006, bought 12,000 gns Doncaster May Sales: maiden hurdler/chaser, off 7 months before only outing in 2006/7: stays 25f: tried in cheekpieces. *J. Howard Johnson* — **c87** **h–**

GUNS AND BUTTER (IRE) 5 b.g. Definite Article – Clairification (IRE) (Shernazar) [2006/7 F16g³ F16d² Jan 5] 22,000 2-y-o, €26,000 3-y-o: sixth foal: half-brother to several winners on Flat, including sprinter The Jobber (by Foxhound): dam 7f/1m winner: runner-up in maiden Irish point in 2006: fairly useful form when placed in bumpers at Musselburgh, 3 lengths second of 15 to Sir Boreas Hawk. *N. G. Richards* — **F99**

GUNSHIP (IRE) 8 b.g. Needle Gun (IRE) – Teejay's Future (IRE) (Buckskin (FR)) [2006/7 c66, h73, F74: c23s⁶ c24d⁴ c24d* c23vᵘʳ c20dᵖᵘ Mar 21] lengthy gelding: maiden hurdler: modest handicap chaser: easily best effort when winning at Chepstow in February: stays 3m: raced on good ground or softer: blinkered last 4 outings: sold 6,200 gns Doncaster May Sales. *P. J. Hobbs* — **c87** **h–**

GUN SMITH 5 b.g. Pistolet Bleu (IRE) – Bayariyka (IRE) (Slip Anchor) [2006/7 F16m* F16s Mar 3] 135,000, 4-y-o: lengthy, rather unfurnished gelding: fourth foal: half-brother to fair hurdler around 2m Polly Anthus (by Kahyasi): dam, fair hurdler up to 2½m/fairly useful up to 1¾m on Flat, half-sister to top-class staying hurdler Paddy's Return: favourite, won bumper at Ludlow on debut by head from Marsh Court: tailed off on soft ground just over month later. *Jonjo O'Neill* — **F92**

GUNSMOKE 9 gr.g. Thethingaboutitis (USA) – Fairy Princess (IRE) (Fairy King (USA)) [2006/7 c–, h–: c16m c17gᶠ Jul 5] no form outside points (has run out). *Mrs P. Ford* — **c– §** **h–**

GUNS OF LOVE (IRE) 5 b.g. Lord of Appeal – Golden Seekers (Manado) [2006/7 F17g 16d 16v 16vᵖᵘ c20mᵖᵘ c16m⁴ Apr 14] £16,000 3-y-o, £5,000 4-y-o: lengthy gelding: half-brother to several winners, including fair hurdler/chaser Goldenswift (by Meneval), stayed 3m: dam ran once: no sign of ability: tried tongue tied. *R. Dickin* — **c–** **h–** **F–**

GUNSON HIGHT 10 b.g. Be My Chief (USA) – Glas Y Dorlan (Sexton Blake) [2006/7 c–§, h–§: 20sᵖᵘ c16m⁴ c21m³ c16f⁴ c23dᵖᵘ c20sᵖᵘ c16g² c20d⁶ c19d Dec 28] deep-girthed, workmanlike gelding: tubed: winning hurdler: poor chaser: stays 21f: tried in headgear: usually tongue tied: has refused to race. *W. Amos* — **c72 §** **h– §**

GUNVILLE 8 ch.g. Infantry – Emily's Niece (Balinger) [2006/7 c20d^{pu} c23d^5 c18s^{pu} Nov 26] modest pointer, won maiden in 2006: no form in chases: tried in cheekpieces. *A. J. Whiting* **c–**

GURTEENOONA (IRE) 5 b.g. Insan (USA) – Copper Hill (IRE) (Zaffaran (USA)) [2006/7 F85: F17d^4 22d 19s Dec 29] rather unfurnished gelding: modest form in frame in maiden bumpers: no impact over hurdles. *Ian Williams* **h–**
F78

GURU 9 b.g. Slip Anchor – Ower (IRE) (Lomond (USA)) [2006/7 c106+, h117: 16s* 16s^2 16s c20v^4 c19d^{pu} Feb 2] leggy gelding: fairly useful handicap hurdler: well-backed favourite, back to best when winning at Stratford in May by 1¼ lengths from Neveesou: off 6 months, good second to Daryal at Lingfield next time: form over fences only on debut in 2005/6 (looked most ungenuine last 2 starts): should stay beyond 2¼m: acts on soft and good to firm going: tried in cheekpieces: one to avoid over fences. *G. L. Moore* **c– §**
h117

GUS 4 b.g. Dr Fong (USA) – Tender Moment (IRE) (Caerleon (USA)) [2006/7 16g^4 Apr 8] half-brother to fairly useful 2m hurdler/winning chaser Bound (by Kris) and modest hurdler Summer Bounty (by Lugana Beach), stays 19f: fair maiden on Flat (stays 1¼m), sold out of B. Hills's stable 7,500 gns Doncaster November Sales: took keen hold when fourth in juvenile at Towcester on hurdling debut. *C. C. Bealby* **h72**

GUSTAVO 8 b.g. Efisio – Washita (Valiyar) [2006/7 h97: 17s* 19s* 21v^3 Feb 24] smallish gelding: fair handicap hurdler: successful first 2 starts after 12-month absence, at Folkestone in January and Taunton in February: should stay 21f: raced on good going or softer (acts on soft). *Miss Venetia Williams* **h112**

GUSTY LAW 7 b.g. Feelings (FR) – Royal Fern VII (Damsire Unregistered) [2006/7 c25g^{ur} c25g^3 Apr 15] successful twice in points: tongue tied, third at Kelso on completed start in hunter chases. *A. Crozier* **c77**

GUTHRIE (IRE) 9 ch.g. Mister Lord (USA) – Nephin Far (IRE) (Phardante (FR)) [2006/7 22m^4 22g 21m c23d^{pu} Oct 18] lengthy gelding: little form over hurdles: maiden chaser: modest pointer, successful in February: stays 3m: hasn't always impressed with jumping/attitude. *S. J. Gilmore* **c–**
h–

GUYMUR (FR) 7 ch.g. Murmure (FR) – Meggy (FR) (Master Thatch) [2006/7 h–: 16s^6 16g^4 16g^3 c16g* c16s^3 Apr 26] angular gelding: lightly raced: has reportedly had breathing operation: fair novice hurdler: similar form in handicap chases, successful at Newton Abbot in April: will prove best at 2m with emphasis on speed. *P. J. Hobbs* **c107**
h101

G V A IRELAND (IRE) 9 b.g. Beneficial – Dippers Daughter (Strong Gale) [2006/7 c133, h–: c20v c24v c24d c28s c33s^{pu} c29m c30m Apr 27] good-topped gelding: useful handicap chaser, won Midlands Grand National at Uttoxeter in 2005/6: below best since: suited by thorough test of stamina: acts on heavy going. *F. Flood, Ireland* **c125**
h–

GWYN'S CHOICE 6 b.g. Faustus (USA) – Shalholme (Fools Holme (USA)) [2006/7 h–, F–: 20v 24s^{pu} c25d^{pu} Dec 23] no form. *C. Roberts* **c–**
h–

GYPSY SCHOLAR 4 b.g. Bal Harbour – Gypsy Race (IRE) (Good Thyne (USA)) [2006/7 F16g* Mar 29] third foal: half-brother to modest hurdler Miss Cospector (by Emperor Fountain), stays 3m: dam modest novice hurdler/chaser: 33/1, won 16-runner bumper at Towcester on debut by 2½ lengths from Soixante, merely nudged clear: sold 70,000 gns Doncaster May Sales. *H. D. Daly* **F101 +**

GYPSY'S KISS 4 b.g. Cyrano de Bergerac – Reina (Homeboy) [2006/7 17s^{pu} Aug 19] half-brother to winning hurdler around 2m Cynara (by Imp Society): well beaten on Flat: no show in novice on hurdling debut. *B. P. J. Baugh* **h–**

H

HAAFEL (USA) 10 ch.g. Diesis – Dish Dash (Bustino) [2006/7 c109§, h–: c20g^F May 4] angular gelding: fair handicap chaser: stays 21f: acts on firm and soft going: effective blinkered or not: unreliable. *G. L. Moore* **c– §**
h–

HABANERO 6 b.g. Cadeaux Genereux – Queen of Dance (IRE) (Sadler's Wells (USA)) [2006/7 h–: 16s^2 16s^6 17d^6 16m^2 Apr 22] angular gelding: fair novice hurdler, left Miss S. Wilton before final start: likely to prove best around 2m with emphasis on speed. *A. King* **h109**

HABITUAL DANCER 6 b.g. Groom Dancer (USA) – Pomorie (IRE) (Be My Guest (USA)) [2006/7 h124: c25v^{ur} c21v^3 c24d^{pu} 25v 20s^{pu} 24g 27s^{pu} Apr 27] compact gelding: **c108 ?**
h–

fairly useful handicap hurdler at best: has lost his form: little aptitude for chasing: should stay beyond 3m: acts on heavy going: tried blinkered: usually front runner/races prominently. *Jedd O'Keeffe*

HABITUAL (IRE) 6 b.g. Kahyasi – Kick The Habit (Habitat) [2006/7 c–x, h109: 20g 24f 22m^{pu} Sep 10] fair hurdler at best, below form in 2006/7: no form over fences (often let down by jumping): stays 3¼m: acts on firm ground: tried tongue tied. *John A. Quinn, Ireland*
`c– x`
`h–`

HACKLERS ROW (IRE) 8 ch.g. Gone Fishin – Mirella Parsons (Mirror Boy) [2006/7 c24f^{pu} Jul 6] maiden pointer: no show in novice on chase debut. *James Clements, Ireland*
`c–`

HADDAAF (USA) 5 b.g. Kingmambo (USA) – Bint Salsabil (USA) (Nashwan (USA)) [2006/7 17m^4 Aug 2] easily best effort (fairly useful form) on Flat on debut at 3 yrs, sold out of J. Dunlop's stable 12,000 gns Newmarket Autumn Sales: tongue tied, modest form when fourth in maiden on hurdling debut: seemed likely to improve, but not seen out again. *C. J. Mann*
`h85 p`

HADEQA 11 ch.g. Hadeer – Heavenly Queen (Scottish Reel) [2006/7 c–§, h–: c25f c24m^{ur} May 16] compact gelding: fair pointer: no impact in hunter chases: has had tongue tied. *M. J. Brown*
`c– §`
`h–`

HADES DE SIENNE (FR) 12 b.g. Concorde Jr (USA) – Aube de Sienne (FR) (Cupids Dew) [2006/7 c81, h–: c33g^{pu} May 3] workmanlike gelding: winning chaser: maiden pointer: stays 4m: acts on heavy going: tried visored/in cheekpieces: tongue tied last 3 starts. *Miss Tracey Watkins*
`c–`
`h–`

HADITOVSKI 11 b.g. Hatim (USA) – Grand Occasion (Great Nephew) [2006/7 c–, h98: 16d^6 16v^3 16s^2 17d^5 16d* Nov 30] compact gelding: winning chaser: fair handicap hurdler: won at Leicester in November: best around 2m: acts on heavy going: visored: usually ridden up with pace. *J. Mackie*
`c–`
`h102`

HAGGLE TWINS (IRE) 7 b.g. Thowra (FR) – Orwell Gaye (IRE) (Strong Gale) [2006/7 c22d^3 c20d^2 c24s^5 21s^2 20v* 22s^3 c24v^3 c20s^2 Mar 11] €24,000 3-y-o: strong gelding: third foal: dam unraced half-sister to high-class staying chaser Kingsmark, out of half-sister to top-class 2m to 3m hurdler Gaye Brief and very smart staying jumper Gaye Chance: bumper winner: fairly useful handicap hurdler/chaser, sold out of Ms F. Crowley's stable €35,000 Goffs October Sales after reappearance: won over hurdles at Southwell in January by length from Burntoakboy: stays 2¾m: acts on heavy ground: in cheekpieces last 3 starts. *C. J. Mann*
`c120 +`
`h128`

HAILE SELASSIE 7 b.g. Awesome – Lady of The Realm (Prince Daniel (USA)) [2006/7 c95, h–: c20s^R c17g^4 c16m^5 c20m^{pu} Apr 25] close-coupled gelding: maiden hurdler: modest handicap chaser: below form in 2006/7, off 10 months after first outing: stays 2½m: acts on soft and good to firm ground: tried blinkered. *W. Jenks*
`c77`
`h–`

HAIL THE KING (USA) 7 gr.g. Allied Forces (USA) – Hail Kris (USA) (Kris S (USA)) [2006/7 h101: 18m* 16s^6 18d^6 c19s^3 16v^3 16s^F 18g c16m^6 Mar 29] leggy gelding: fair handicap hurdler: won at Fontwell in May: mostly below form after: well held in novice chases: will stay 2½m: acts on heavy and good to firm going: held up. *R. M. Carson*
`c–`
`h103`

HAIRY MOLLY (IRE) 7 b.g. Shernazar – Ballilaurenka (IRE) (Buckskin (FR)) [2006/7 F121: 16d^3 19s* 24g Mar 16] lengthy gelding: will make a chaser: smart bumper performer in 2005/6, won Champion Bumper at Cheltenham: progressive form over hurdles, won maiden at Naas in February: better than bare result (eleventh to Wichita Lineman) in Grade 2 novice at Cheltenham, still close up before 2 out: may prove best short of 3m: raced on good ground or softer: open to further improvement. *Joseph Crowley, Ireland*
`h127 p`

HAKIM (NZ) 13 ch.g. Half Iced (USA) – Topitup (NZ) (Little Brown Jug (NZ)) [2006/7 c133, h–: c21g^F c19v^5 c21g c21g Apr 13] sturdy gelding: maiden hurdler: much improved handicap chaser in 2005/6, successful 4 times, including in Grand Sefton at Aintree: below that form in 2006/7: stays 21f: acts on soft and good to firm going: free-going sort, makes running/races prominently. *J. L. Spearing*
`c124`
`h–`

HALCON GENELARDAIS (FR) 7 ch.g. Halcon – Francetphile (FR) (Farabi) [2006/7 c142p, h132: 23d* c29s* c25v^3 c26g^{pu} Mar 16]
    For the second successive year the Coral Welsh National was dominated by French-breds. They had provided the winner L'Aventure as well as the second and fourth in 2005, while the latest edition saw them go one better with Halcon
`c162`
`h143`

Genelardais leading home Mon Mome and Juveigneur. Also linking L'Aventure (seventh in the latest renewal) and Halcon Genelardais is the fact that they are the youngest winners, both aged six, since the race moved to Chepstow in 1949. The Welsh National began life at Cardiff's Ely racecourse, which staged the race from 1895 until its closure in 1939, and Newport's Caerleon racecourse was also home to the race once in 1948 (the planned 1947 renewal there was abandoned due to waterlogging), though that track was closed down itself shortly afterwards. The story of both courses—among ninety or so that closed in Britain in the twentieth century—can be found in the fully revised edition of *A Long Time Gone* by Chris Pitt, which was published by Portway Press in 2006. There were several young winners during this period, including the six-year-olds Legal Tender (1897), Succubus (1914) and Miss Gaynus (1932), whilst there was also a trio of five-year-olds in Nat Gould (1899), Razorbill (1908) and Jacobus (1912). Each of this sextet was actually younger than both L'Aventure and Halcon Genelardais as all of their wins took place in March or April rather than December. It is safe to say, however, that the most distinguished period of the race's long history has come since the switch to Chepstow and the Festive marathon is usually the preserve of more established chasers nowadays, particularly as it is often regarded as a stepping stone to the Grand National itself. Earth Summit, successful in 1997 aged nine, was the last Welsh National winner to achieve glory at Aintree in the same season (Rag Trade and Corbiere completed the same double), although since then his stable-companion Bindaree has won the Welsh National after winning at Aintree, while the latest National winner Silver Birch had been successful in the Welsh equivalent over two years earlier. It's a double Halcon Genelardais had no chance of achieving in the latest season, as he wasn't even entered for the National. Perhaps his age and lack of experience—he was running for only the fifth time over fences at Chepstow—had something to do with that decision, but it's also possible the National will never figure on his agenda. Immediately after the Welsh National, Halcon Genelardais' trainer Alan King was reported as saying that 'He's not a natural National horse, and I doubt the owners would let me put him in the race anyway.'

The Welsh National had been the target for Halcon Genelardais ever since he'd finished fifth in the Scottish equivalent. That particular performance brought to a close a very good first season over fences for Halcon Genelardais, who was successful in all three of his starts in novice chases including the Grade 2 Towton Novices' at Wetherby. In order to preserve his handicap mark, the only outing he had between Ayr and Chepstow was over hurdles, in the valuable and well-

Betfair Handicap Hurdle, Haydock—Halcon Genelardais (left) takes advantage of a significantly lower mark over hurdles to beat Irish Wolf (cheekpieces)

Coral Welsh National (Handicap Chase), Chepstow—Wayne Hutchinson records his biggest win to date as Halcon Genelardais pulls away from Mon Mome (left) and Juveigneur (white face)

contested Betfair Handicap at Haydock in November. The winner of novice hurdles at Fontwell and Uttoxeter in 2004/5, Halcon Genelardais took advantage of his lower mark back in this sphere but still showed useful form in accounting for sixteen rivals at Haydock, wearing down Irish Wolf near the finish. The first part of the plan had been successfully accomplished—'He had the ideal prep race and fortunately the handicapper couldn't put him up for it,' said King—and Halcon Genelardais was initially installed as favourite for the Welsh National, although, by the off, both Simon and L'Aventure were shorter in an open-looking renewal. As usual, the contest provided a thorough test of stamina and Halcon Genelardais, conceding weight to all but two of his seventeen rivals, proved extremely well suited by it. Making steady headway from mid-division to lead three out, Halcon Genelardais typically found plenty under pressure and stayed on strongly to win by four lengths, in the process making it three wins from as many starts for King's number-two jockey Wayne Hutchinson (regular rider Robert Thornton completed a big-race double for the yard aboard Voy Por Ustedes at Kempton less than half an hour later). The performance of Halcon Genelardais was a high-class one and the best in the Welsh National since Master Oats won it in 1994 (when staged in England, at Newbury, after bad weather had ruled out Chepstow). Master Oats went on to win the Cheltenham Gold Cup less than three months later, and Halcon Genelardais was given the opportunity to emulate him despite having his limitations exposed in the Cotswold Chase at Cheltenham at the end of January. Halcon Genelardais finished a remote third to Exotic Dancer that day, and would have managed only fifth but for the departures of two others in the later stages. Tried blinkered in the Gold Cup, Halcon Genelardais found a steadily-run race on good ground all against him and he was tailed off when pulled up three out.

		Rainbow Quest (b 1981)	Blushing Groom
Halcon Genelardais (FR) (ch.g. 2000)	Halcon (b 1993)		I Will Follow
		Teresa (b 1984)	Rheffissimo
			Takala
	Francetphile (FR) (b 1982)	Farabi (ch 1964)	Net
			Fangoli
		Ablette (b 1976)	Trenel
			Abonette

Halcon Genelardais' pedigree was dealt with fully in *Chasers & Hurdlers 2005/06*. Suffice to say here that he is the seventh and final foal of Francetphile, who was well beaten in three starts on the Flat in France, and her only winner. He also remains the only winner of his little-used sire Halcon, whose own sire Rainbow Quest died at the age of twenty-six in July after a far longer, and very successful, career at stud. A workmanlike individual, Halcon Genelardais has raced only on good going or softer and acts on heavy, with his effectiveness increasing the more emphasis the ground places on stamina. The major long-distance handicaps are the races around which his programme will probably continue to be geared, though, with a bit more improvement possible, given that he is still relatively inexperienced, Halcon Genelardais could yet make an impact in graded non-handicaps when stamina is at a premium. *A. King*

HALCYON EXPRESS (IRE) 5 b.g. Mujadil (USA) – Hakkaniyah (Machiavellian (USA)) [2006/7 h–: 17v^{pu} 16g 21m 18s^{pu} Dec 5] angular gelding: no solid form over hurdles: tongue tied. *Mary Meek*   h–

HALEXY (FR) 12 b.g. Iron Duke (FR) – Tartifume II (FR) (Mistigri) [2006/7 c123d, h–: c28d^{pu} c22v^{pu} c20g^6 Mar 28] tall, good sort: winning hurdler: one-time fairly useful handicap chaser, has deteriorated considerably: sold out of M. Todhunter's stable 6,000 gns Doncaster May Sales after first outing: runner-up in points in 2007: has won at 3m, best form over shorter: raced mainly on good going or softer: tried blinkered. *Mrs S. M. McPherson*   c– h–

HALF AN HOUR 10 b.g. Alflora (IRE) – Country Mistress (Town And Country) [2006/7 c108d, h–: c20m^{pu} c23m^{pu} Jul 26] well-made gelding: fair handicap chaser at best, no form since reappearance in 2005/6: effective from 2m to 2¾m: acts on firm and good to soft going (won bumper on soft): often in headgear. *P. Bowen*   c– h–

HALFWAY CUT 5 b.g. Definite Article – Forest of Arden (Tap On Wood) [2006/7 F16g F16v^3 F16v^5 Jan 7] half-brother to several winners, including useful 6f (at 2 yrs)/7f winner Forest Cat (by Petorius): dam 7f winner: easily best effort in bumpers when third to Pompeius Magnus at Navan. *E. U. Hales, Ireland*   F88

HALIGREEN (IRE) 5 b.m. Saddlers' Hall (IRE) – Always Greener (IRE) (Vision (USA)) [2006/7 F18m* F16s F17g Apr 13] sturdy mare: third foal: dam, poor hurdler, stayed 2½m: fair form in bumpers: won maiden at Plumpton on debut in October: hung badly right next time. *J. W. Mullins*   F91

HALLAND 9 ch.g. Halling (USA) – Northshiel (Northfields (USA)) [2006/7 20s^{pu} Apr 27] workmanlike gelding: fair on Flat (probably stays 2¼m) nowadays: novice hurdler: reluctant to line up only outing in 2006/7. *T. J. Fitzgerald*   h–

HAMADEENAH 9 ch.m. Alhijaz – Mahbob Dancer (FR) (Groom Dancer (USA)) [2006/7 h–: 22g 19m^5 Jun 4] leggy mare: fair handicap hurdler, very lightly raced nowadays: stays 19f with emphasis on speed: acts on soft and good to firm going: tried tongue tied. *C. J. Down*   h95

HAMBAPHAMBILI 7 b.g. Cloudings (IRE) – Sun Dante (IRE) (Phardante (FR)) [2006/7 h96, F81: c24d^3 c25s c24s^F 21s Jan 24] big, sturdy gelding: winning pointer: modest novice hurdler: no show in chases: will stay beyond 25f: acts on heavy going: tried tongue tied. *O. Sherwood*   c– h–

HAMBURG SPRINGER (IRE) 5 b.g. Charnwood Forest (IRE) – Kyra Crown (IRE) (Astronef) [2006/7 h87§: 17d Mar 19] smallish, close-coupled gelding: little form over hurdles: tried blinkered/in cheekpieces/tongue tied: temperamental. *C. J. Teague*   h– §

HAM JAMMER (IRE) 6 b.g. Rashar (USA) – Rostoonstown Lass (IRE) (Decent Fellow) [2006/7 25s^{su} 20g 24s^3 Nov 25] €5,000 4-y-o: brother to 2½m chase winner Dedrunknmunky: dam unraced: won maiden Irish point in 2006: bought 20,000 gns Doncaster May Sales: poor form in maiden hurdles: dead. *Ferdy Murphy*   h75

HAMMER TIME (IRE) 4 br.g. Rudimentary (USA) – Miss Franco (IRE) (Lanfranco) [2006/7 F12v F16v^5 Jan 27] €26,000 3-y-o: good sort: first foal: dam, point/3m hurdle winner, out of sister to Hennessy Gold Cup winner Broadheath: modest form in 4-y-o bumpers: withdrawn after bolting intended third outing: tongue tied. *Heather Dalton*   F84

HAMNOTEAR 11 b.g. Batshoof – Topcliffe (Top Ville) [2006/7 20g^{pu} Dec 10] second foal: dam, 1½m winner, stayed 17f: breathing problem on very belated debut. *E. M. Caine*   h–

HANAZAKARI 6 b.g. Danzero (AUS) – Russian Rose (IRE) (Soviet Lad (USA)) [2006/7 19g^{pu} Nov 5] poor maiden on Flat: left J. Toller, no show in novice on hurdling debut. *Mrs A. V. Roberts*   h–

HAND INN HAND 11 b.g. Alflora (IRE) – Deep Line (Deep Run) [2006/7 c148, h–: **c–**
25d^pu c20s^pu Nov 25] close-coupled, workmanlike gelding: has reportedly had breathing **h–**
operation: winning hurdler: one-time very smart chaser: finished lame second outing in
2006/7: stays 25f: unraced on firm going, acts on any other: weak finisher. *H. D. Daly*

HANDY BEN (IRE) 6 ch.g. Ridgewood Ben – Regal Destiny (IRE) (Silver Kite **h80**
(USA)) [2006/7 16f⁴ 16f 20m 16f 24m Apr 25] third foal: dam, Irish maiden, half-sister
to useful performer up to 1m Nashcash: poor form over hurdles: left M. Hourigan and off
9 months, well held last 2 starts. *T. R. George*

HANDYMAN (IRE) 13 b.g. Hollow Hand – Shady Ahan (Mon Capitaine) [2006/7 **c–**
c84, h–: c25d^pu Mar 20] leggy gelding: winning chaser: fair pointer nowadays: stays **h–**
3¼m: acts on heavy and good to firm going. *Michael M. Watson*

HANDY MONEY 10 b.g. Imperial Frontier (USA) – Cryptic Gold (Glint of Gold) **c128**
[2006/7 c116, h131: c16g* c20g^F c21g³ c17d c16g c20f* c20m³ Apr 27] workmanlike **h–**
gelding: useful hurdler: fairly useful chaser: won maiden at Huntingdon in May and
handicap at Ludlow (beat High Calibre by 3½ lengths) in April: stays 21f: acts on any
ground: bled fifth start. *A. King*

HANKO (GER) 11 b.g. Surumu (GER) – Hankaretta (USA) (Pirate's Bounty (USA)) **c96**
[2006/7 c–, h–: c16g⁴ c20m^pu 16d³ 22g⁴ Aug 26] modest chaser/maiden hurdler **h88**
nowadays: stays 2¾m: acts on soft and good to firm ground: blinkered in eyeshields last
2 starts: has shaped as if amiss/looked ungenuine. *Jonjo O'Neill*

HANNAH'S JOY (IRE) 7 b.m. Rock Hopper – Any Offers (Paddy's Stream) [2006/7 **h–**
20m 22m 26m^pu Aug 28] half-sister to fair hurdler/fairly useful chaser Malek (by
Tremblant), stayed 4m, and bumper winner by Phardante: dam of little account: little sign
of ability, including in points, left P. Rothwell, Ireland prior to final outing. *Miss Joanne
Priest*

HANNAH'S TRIBE (IRE) 5 b.m. Daggers Drawn (USA) – Cala-Holme (IRE) **h–**
(Fools Holme (USA)) [2006/7 h–: 19m^pu Jun 19] smallish mare: no form over hurdles:
tried in eyeshields. *C. W. Moore*

HAOYUNMA (IRE) 5 ch.m. Old Vic – A Bit of Luck (IRE) (Good Thyne (USA)) **F68**
[2006/7 F16m Jan 29] €11,000 3-y-o, 15,000 4-y-o: sixth foal: half-sister to fair chaser
Monty's Quest (by Montelimar), stays 25f: dam unraced: shaped as if needing greater test
of stamina in bumper (tenth of 16) on debut. *D. J. Wintle*

HAPENEY (IRE) 4 b.f. Saddlers' Hall (IRE) – Pennys Pride (IRE) (Pips Pride) **F86 p**
[2006/7 F17g⁶ Apr 19] 20,000 3-y-o: lengthy, rather unfurnished filly: first foal: dam,
bumper winner/fair up to 1¼m on Flat, half-sister to top-class chaser up to 2½m Direct
Route and smart 2m hurdler Joe Mac: bit backward, encouraging sixth of 18 to I'm
Delilah in mares bumper at Cheltenham on debut: should do better. *K. G. Reveley*

HAPPILY EVER AFTER 7 b.m. Contract Law (USA) – Nibelunga (Miami Springs) **F68**
[2006/7 F16f⁵ F16m⁵ Aug 1] half-sister to several winners, including fair staying jumper
Hurricane Blake (by Blakeney), became ungenuine: dam won up to 9f: poor form in
bumpers. *J. M. Saville*

HAPPY HUSSAR (IRE) 14 b.g. Balinger – Merry Mirth (Menelek) [2006/7 c88x, h–: **c88 x**
c24d² c24d⁴ 20g² c24s⁵ c31d 27s⁴ 22s 19v⁵ 24v⁴ c24s Mar 10] workmanlike gelding: has **h81**
stringhalt: winning hurdler/chaser: modest nowadays: stays 29f: acts on any going: has
broken blood vessels: sketchy jumper: tends to get behind. *Dr P. Pritchard*

HAPPY SHOPPER (IRE) 7 b.g. Presenting – Reach Down (IRE) (Cheval) [2006/7 **c98**
c99, h80+: c24d³ c24v^pu c24s^pu c26g⁵ c24g² Apr 27] novice hurdler: modest handicap **h–**
chaser: form in 2006/7 only on final start: should stay beyond 3m: acts on soft going:
visored/in cheekpieces last 4 starts: hard ride. *D. E. Pipe*

HAPTHOR 8 ch.m. Zaffaran (USA) – My Goddess (Palm Track) [2006/7 h76, h–: 24g³ **c–**
22g⁶ 20m² 20f 20f⁵ c25s^F Feb 15] poor maiden hurdler: fell in hunter on chase debut: won **h83**
point in March: stays 3m: acts on firm going. *F. Jestin*

HARBOUR BREEZE (IRE) 5 b.g. Slip Anchor – New Wind (GER) (Windwurf **h92**
(GER)) [2006/7 F91: F18s⁶ 20s⁴ 20v^pu 20m² Apr 25] bumper winner: modest form over **F91**
hurdles: will stay beyond 2½m. *Jennie Candlish*

HARBOUR BUOY 6 ch.g. Bal Harbour – Elissa (Tap On Wood) [2006/7 F–: F17d **F–**
May 1] leggy gelding: soundly beaten in bumpers. *J. Wade*

HARCHIBALD (FR) 8 b.g. Perugino (USA) – Dame d'Harvard (USA) (Quest For **h142 §**
Fame) [2006/7 h166§: 16s⁴ 16v⁵ 16m⁵ Apr 27] lengthy, useful-looking gelding: has

reportedly had wind operation: top-class hurdler at best, well below form all 3 starts in 2006/7: raced around 2m: best form on good/good to soft ground: tongue tied earlier in career: held up, and well served by good gallop: finds little and not one to trust. *N. Meade, Ireland*

HARCOURT (USA) 7 b.g. Cozzene (USA) – Ballinamallard (USA) (Tom Rolfe) **h95** [2006/7 h85: 16d* 17v 18v⁴ 16v⁵ Feb 26] modest hurdler: won novice at Plumpton (by 16 lengths) in November: raced around 2m on going softer than good. *M. Madgwick*

HARD ACT TO FOLLOW (IRE) 8 ch.g. Shernazar – Lauren's Gem (Over The **c128 P** River (FR)) [2006/7 h119: c23d* Oct 11] big, rangy, angular gelding: fairly useful form **h–** when successful first 2 outings in novice hurdles in 2005/6: off 6 months, very promising chasing debut when landing odds in maiden at Wetherby in October by distance from King of Confusion, easily going clear from 3 out: stays 25f: raced on ground softer than good (acts on heavy): open to significant improvement and looked sure to make mark at higher level over fences, but presumably met with setback. *J. Howard Johnson*

HARDKNOTT (IRE) 5 ch.g. Intikhab (USA) – Danita (Roi Danzig (USA)) **F83** [2006/7 F83: F16m⁵ Jul 12] lengthy, good-topped gelding: modest form in bumpers: sold 1,400 gns Doncaster October Sales. *R. F. Fisher*

HARD N SHARP 7 ch.g. Rakaposhi King – Hardwick Sun (Dieu Soleil) [2006/7 h92, **h–** F90: 20mᵖᵘ May 5] workmanlike gelding: modest novice hurdler: should stay beyond 2½m: acts on soft and good to firm ground: tried tongue tied. *Evan Williams*

HARDWICK 8 br.g. Oscar (IRE) – Paper Tigress (IRE) (King's Ride) [2006/7 16d* **c–** 16m² c17m Jun 19] point winner: fairly useful hurdler: won minor event at Ballinrobe in **h122** May: best effort when second to Chicago Vic in similar race at Listowel month later: lame on chasing debut: should stay beyond 2m: acts on good to firm and good to soft going. *Adrian Maguire, Ireland*

HARDYBUCK (IRE) 6 b.g. Saddlers' Hall (IRE) – Miss Beaufleur (IRE) (Good **c– x** Thyne (USA)) [2006/7 c76x, h–: 24m⁵ 17v* 16d⁴ 17d 17v⁴ 16s² 19g Mar 28] rather **h83 x** unfurnished gelding: poor handicap hurdler: won conditional jockeys event at Market Rasen in October: bled final outing: similiar form in maiden chases: should stay beyond 17f: acts on good to firm and heavy going: tried blinkered: often tongue tied: not a fluent jumper. *N. A. Twiston-Davies*

HARDY EUSTACE (IRE) 10 b.g. Archway (IRE) – Sterna Star (Corvaro (USA)) **h161** [2006/7 h162: 19d* 17s² 16d* 16d⁴ 16m³ Apr 27]

   The AIG Europe Champion Hurdle was promoted beforehand as 'possibly the best hurdle race ever run in Ireland.' All eight runners, except the juvenile Lounaos, had won at Grade 1 level but, if the star billing was justified, then it would have been for the two previous runnings, and other races as well. Hardy Eustace, Brave Inca and Macs Joy, who filled the first three places at Leopardstown in January, were meeting in the race for the third year in succession and it was the seventh time that the three had met in just over two years. The only time Hardy Eustace had finished in front of the other pair was in the Champion Hurdle at the 2005 Cheltenham Festival when Brave Inca came third (beaten by two necks) and Macs Joy fifth. In two meetings earlier that particular season Macs Joy, Brave Inca and Hardy Eustace had filled the first three places—in that order—in the December Festival Hurdle and the AIG Europe (separated by a short head and a head). The trio met three times in the 2005/6 season, Brave Inca winning from Macs Joy, with Hardy Eustace seventh, in the AIG Europe, before they finished first, second and third in the same order in the Champion Hurdle and Macs Joy then turned the tables on Brave Inca, with Hardy Eustace third, in the ACCBank Champion at Punchestown. Macs Joy and Brave Inca were meeting for the twelfth time in all in the latest AIG Champion, while Hardy Eustace went on to meet Brave Inca for an eighth time in the latest Champion Hurdle and Macs Joy for an eighth time in the latest ACCBank Champion Hurdle. Those last two races—won by Sublimity and Silent Oscar respectively—almost certainly signalled the end of an era that has provided some tremendous entertainment on both sides of the Irish Sea.

   Hardy Eustace won two Champion Hurdles at Cheltenham—he was defending his title when Brave Inca and Macs Joy were third and fifth in 2005—but his victory in the AIG Europe Champion Hurdle was his first in that race. Typically looking in good order beforehand, and with more familiar tactics readopted after being waited with when beaten by Detroit City in the International (formerly the

*Coral Ascot Hurdle—an impressive winning return by Hardy Eustace,
who isn't hard pressed to beat the stayers Mighty Man (centre) and Lough Derg (left)*

Bula) at Cheltenham, the 9/1-shot Hardy Eustace made all, jumping accurately, and battled on gamely to hold off the favourite Brave Inca by three lengths, with a race-rusty Macs Joy a further three behind in third, Lounaos a very good fourth, Christmas Hurdle winner Jazz Messenger fifth and second favourite Iktitaf last, a long way below the form of his second to Brave Inca in the December Festival Hurdle the time before. There was talk of Hardy Eustace taking in the Red Mills Trial at Gowran next, the race he had contested before each of his Champion Hurdle wins, but, in the end, he went to Cheltenham without another race. Hardy Eustace started second favourite behind Detroit City, whom he met on terms 4 lb better than in the International, but neither reached the first three. Hardy Eustace's fourth place, three lengths, a neck and the same behind Sublimity, Brave Inca and Afsoun, spoiled his record of never having been out of the first three at Cheltenham, his seven appearances also including a win in the Royal & SunAlliance Novices' Hurdle in 2003 and a second in the Cleeve Hurdle in the season he won his first Champion. Hardy Eustace's fourth appearance in the Champion Hurdle—he was the oldest in the line-up—was probably his last, connections announcing after his below-form third to Silent Oscar and Macs Joy in the ACCBank Champion Hurdle that he will be aimed at staying hurdles in the next season, an option taken with Brave Inca at Punchestown where he contested the Champion Stayers' Hurdle, running poorly.

Hardy Eustace has already shown himself fully effective at around two and a half miles, most recently when routing the opposition in the Coral Ascot Hurdle in November, fit from a recent spin on the Flat (behind Lounaos at the Curragh) and winning by eleven lengths and ten from Mighty Man (who gave him 8 lb) and Lough Derg, leading on the bit three out and always in complete control from that point. This race had been run for the two previous years at Windsor, while the Ascot course underwent extensive redevelopment, both to the stands and to the course itself, particularly to a strip of ground in the straight (the water jump in Swinley Bottom was also replaced by a plain fence). The return of jumping to Ascot had a mixed reception at first with criticism of the new surface—'a young soil structure only eighteen months old'—before the October meeting for which the going was good to firm, amid very testing conditions elsewhere in the country at that time.

AIG Europe Champion Hurdle, Leopardstown—the ten-year-old gains his first verdict over Brave Inca (centre) since the 2005 Champion Hurdle; another old rival Macs Joy (noseband) fills third

The HRA's senior inspector of courses Richard Linley agreed there was 'very little organic matter in the new surface and a tendency for the moisture not to be retained.' He pointed out that when the straight Flat track was put down in the 'forties, it wasn't raced on for six years. Ascot described the surface as 'good, safe summer jumping ground' and the fields for the October meeting, which staged very valuable handicaps over hurdles and fences, held up better than expected, fears that the going would be exceptionally firm proving unfounded. The ground may have been safe but there did appear to be some 'bedding-in' issues with the new surface as there were numerous races, particularly over hurdles, which saw the field finish far more strung out than seemed likely given the race times or official going description. In addition, there were plenty of occasions when those who'd raced prominently seemed at a distinct advantage. The healthy field sizes were undoubtedly aided by a big increase in prize money, which was a significant feature of jump racing at the 'new' Ascot, as was an initiative to increase the number of foreign runners—Hardy Eustace's Ascot Hurdle win played a big part in Dessie Hughes picking up the €25,000 prize for leading overseas trainer at the track in 2006/7. This so-called 'aggressive commercial attitude' did not please some other racecourses including Wetherby, whose Charlie Hall Chase faced competition on the same day from Ascot's United House Gold Cup (an open handicap worth over £10,000 more to the winner)—2005 Charlie Hall winner Ollie Magern ran in the Ascot race instead. Nearly £1.4m was on offer at Ascot's six jump meetings before the turn of the year, including another very valuable new handicap chase for the two-milers (sponsored by Carey Group) which boosted the Ascot Hurdle card. That meeting was preceded the day before by a deluge which, according to Ascot, would have resulted in the fixture being lost before the reconstruction work. As it was, no inspection was required and the going was good to soft, the course coming in for praise, in contrast to the widespread criticism of the watered ground the week before for Cheltenham's Open meeting, which Hughes described as 'a disgrace'. Ascot seems to accept that, once Christmas is over, jumping is dominated by the prospect of the Cheltenham Festival and Aintree. It points out also that Punchestown and the late-season fixture at Sandown, among others, make the end of the season too congested for an Ascot Festival in late-May to be considered (as suggested in the introduction to *Chasers & Hurdlers 2005/06*, along with a call to end the jumps season on the last Saturday in May). Ascot's view is that it is best to concentrate its quality jumps programmes on the period from October to February (not too close to Cheltenham), with the aim of helping to advance the general profile of jumping in the first part of the season. Whether Ascot might end up staging the King George VI Chase (which at present 'belongs' to Kempton, or to the group of which it is part) is an interesting question. Kempton is packed to the rafters at Christmas and Ascot could accommodate a much larger crowd. There would be controversy, but a mood for change might well be created if Ascot succeeds over the next few years in its ambition to attract new racegoers and make a real difference to jumping's autumn and winter programme.

Hardy Eustace (IRE) (b.g. 1997)	Archway (IRE) (ch 1988)	Thatching (b 1975)	Thatch
			Abella
		Rose of Jericho (b 1984)	Alleged
			Rose Red
	Sterna Star (b or br 1984)	Corvaro (b 1977)	Vaguely Noble
			Delmora
		Star Girl (b 1973)	Sovereign Gleam
			Sterna

The good-topped Hardy Eustace is by the sprinter Archway (whose sire Thatching was also a sprinter), but the now-deceased Archway was also a half-brother to 1992 Derby winner Dr Devious and has sired middle-distance winners on the Flat, making a name for himself in Australia. Hardy Eustace's dam Sterna Star, who is also dead, gained her only victory in a ladies race over a mile and a half, but she was out of a half-sister to the 1975 Eclipse and Prix de l'Arc winner Star Appeal. Sterna Star was also represented on the racecourse in the latest season by the fair chaser Ca Na Trona (by Accordion) who won two staying handicap chases for Charlie Mann before being sold for 23,000 guineas at the Doncaster May Sales.

Mr Laurence Byrne's "Hardy Eustace"

Another of her offspring, the €160,000-purchase Bill Cody (also by Accordion) showed some ability when fourth in a bumper at Killarney on his racecourse debut for the Hughes stable, while Hardy Eustace's half-sister Forgotten Star (by Don't Forget Me), a modest maiden who stayed a mile, was again represented by her first foal the bumper winner Star Award who was placed at up to two and three quarter miles in mares novice hurdles. Lack of stamina probably wasn't the explanation for Hardy Eustace's below-par performance on his only try at three miles so far (in the Sefton Novices' Hurdle three weeks after he had won the Royal & SunAlliance). He should get the trip and is likely to make up into a leading contender for the World Hurdle in the next season, probably after making further visits to Ascot in the meantime. The game and reliable Hardy Eustace, who is often a front runner, acts on heavy going (possibly not good to firm). He is usually blinkered or visored nowadays, equipped with the former in the AIG Europe Champion and the latter in the Ascot Hurdle (he was blinkered for both his Champion Hurdle wins). *D. T. Hughes, Ireland*

HARDY FELLA 9 b.g. Rakaposhi King – Swallowfield (Wattlefield) [2006/7 c20d c19m^pu c20f^6 c22m c20g Oct 7] winning pointer: once-raced over hurdles: poor maiden chaser: will stay 3m: tried blinkered. *John Long, Ireland*　**c77 h–**

HARISSA (IRE) 5 ch.m. King Luthier – Hollowfield Bug (IRE) (Magical Wonder (USA)) [2006/7 F74: F17d 17m^ur 16m^F 17g Jun 20] little impact in bumpers/over hurdles (let down by jumping). *J. W. Mullins*　**h– F–**

HARLEQUIN HUGO 4 b.g. Polar Prince (IRE) – Ecaterina (NZ) (March Legend (NZ)) [2006/7 F16v F17g Mar 24] workmanlike gelding: second foal: dam maiden in New Zealand: well held in maiden bumpers. *R. Ford*　**F–**

HARLOES COFFEE (IRE) 7 b.g. Shernazar – Beauchamp Grace (Ardross) [2006/7 F89d: F16s 17d 16d^2 21m^5 26m^pu 17s^pu Oct 25] bumper winner: poor maiden hurdler: often tongue tied: ungenuine: sold 2,200 gns Doncaster November Sales. *Ronald Thompson*　**h76 § F–**

HARLOV (FR) 12 ch.g. Garde Royale – Paulownia (FR) (Montevideo) [2006/7 c110§, h–: c28d^6 c25f* c25d^F c25s^ur c32v^5 c24g^3 c31s^pu Apr 27] well-made gelding: fair handicap chaser: won at Kelso in May: stays 4m: acts on any going: wears headgear: unreliable. *A. Parker*　**c108 § h–**

HARMONY BRIG (IRE) 8 ch.g. Accordion – Bridges Daughter (IRE) (Montelimar (USA)) [2006/7 h125+: c16s* c19d^5 c20v^pu c20m^4 Apr 21] strong, lengthy gelding: fairly useful hurdler: similar form in novice chases: made all in 4-runner event at Ayr in November, beating Percussionist by 3 lengths despite tending to jump right: off 3½ months, stiff task when fourth of 6 to Sir in Sir in Grade 2 event there: bred to stay beyond 2½m: acts on heavy going, seemingly on good to firm: looked ungenuine second/third starts: one to treat with caution. *N. G. Richards*　**c127 § h– §**

HARONI (IRE) 4 b.g. King Charlemagne (USA) – Gaia Bronswick (Brief Truce (USA)) [2006/7 16g* 16d* 16g^2 18s^6 16s^6 20m^4 Apr 28] fairly useful on Flat (stays 10.5f): similar standard over hurdles, won juveniles at Tramore (maiden) and Tralee in August: off 5 months, creditable fourth of 23 to Brave Right in conditional jockeys handicap at Punchestown final start: stays 2½m: acts on soft and good to firm going. *Ms F. M. Crowley, Ireland*　**h112**

HAROUM (USA) 4 ch.g. Diesis – Up Her Sleeve (USA) (Secreto (USA)) [2006/7 17m^5 17m^3 17g^4 16s^pu 16d 20m^4 Apr 9] smallish gelding: tailed off only start on Flat for Heather Dalton: poor form over hurdles, sold out of P. Haslam's stable 9,000 gns Doncaster October Sales after third start: likely to prove best around 2m: acts on good to firm ground: in cheekpieces 3 of last 4 outings. *B. Storey*　**h76**

HARPER'S PRIDE 7 b.g. Deploy – Lamees (USA) (Lomond (USA)) [2006/7 16v c24v^3 Feb 15] rather leggy ex-Irish gelding: modest hurdler: left Peter McCreery, breathing problem on chasing debut: should stay beyond 2m: acts on heavy ground. *Evan Williams*　**c– h–**

HARPOON HARRY (IRE) 10 ch.g. Alphabatim (USA) – Procastrian (IRE) (Lancastrian) [2006/7 21s^F Dec 3] lightly-raced gelding: maiden pointer: fair form on hurdling debut in 2003/4, let down by jumping only 2 outings after: dead. *K. C. Bailey*　**h–**

HARPS COUNSEL (IRE) 5 b.g. Leading Counsel (USA) – Up The Harps (IRE) (Lord Americo) [2006/7 F16d F16s^6 F16g Apr 23] first foal: dam unraced: best effort in maiden bumpers (modest form) on second start. *J. K. Magee, Ireland*　**F78**

HARPS HALL (IRE) 13 ch.g. Yashgan – Parsons Glen (IRE) (Glen Quaich) [2006/7 **h–**
h–: 26d⁵ May 17] workmanlike gelding: maiden pointer: no show over hurdles.
N. I. M. Rossiter

HARPURS GIRL 6 b.m. Overbury (IRE) – Kingy's Girl (Makbul) [2006/7 F71: 16s² **h58**
16s 17d 16s⁶ 17s 16v⁴ 19sᵖᵘ Mar 7] neat mare: bad hurdler: likely to stay 2½m: acts on
heavy going: in cheekpieces last 2 starts. *J. Mackie*

HARRIHAWKAN 9 b.g. Alflora (IRE) – Beatle Song (Song) [2006/7 c–: c20m⁶ **c68**
c21mᵖᵘ c20mᵘʳ c19m⁵ c16s⁴ c21dᵖᵘ Nov 30] rangy gelding: winning pointer: poor maiden
chaser, left Mrs T. Hill after second start: stays 23f: acts on soft and good to firm going.
A. King

HARRINGAY 7 b.m. Sir Harry Lewis (USA) – Tamergale (IRE) (Strong Gale) [2006/7 **c108**
h120: c21d² c20sᶠ c20d⁴ c22g³ Mar 24] lengthy, useful-looking mare: fairly useful **h–**
hurdler: fair form at best over fences: likely to stay 3m: acts on good to soft going: tongue
tied: held up, and has found little. *Miss H. C. Knight*

HARRIS BAY 8 b.g. Karinga Bay – Harristown Lady (Muscatite) [2006/7 c123, h–: **c134**
21m* c24d* c24dᵖᵘ c24vᵖᵘ Jan 6] rangy gelding: has reportedly had soft palate operation: **h97 +**
useful handicap chaser: further appreciable improvement when winning valuable event
at Ascot in November by 1½ lengths from Lou du Moulin Mas, very confidently ridden:
ran poorly both starts after: odds on, best effort over hurdles when winning novice
handicap at Towcester in October with something in hand despite jumping sloppily: stays
3m: acts on soft and good to firm ground: tongue tied: held up. *Miss H. C. Knight*

HARRISBURG 4 ch.g. Alhaarth (IRE) – Pennsylvania (USA) (Northjet) [2006/7 **F98 +**
F16v² Feb 24] well-made gelding: half-brother to several winners, including fairly useful
7f (at 2 yrs) to 1m winner East Liberty (by Halo) and French/Spanish winner up to 1½m
Toofman (by Lahib): dam, maiden who stayed 1¼m, daughter of high-class performer up
to 1½m Mrs Penny: encouraging debut when 5 lengths second to Evelith Echo in bumper
at Kempton, tying up in testing conditions after going clear. *Miss E. C. Lavelle*

HARRIVAL 7 ch.g. Hazaaf (USA) – Departure (Gorytus (USA)) [2006/7 h71: 19s⁵ **c–**
22v⁴ 22s⁵ 22v 22g⁶ c24mᵖᵘ Apr 14] medium-sized gelding: poor maiden hurdler: breath- **h70**
ing problem on chasing debut: barely stays 2¾m: acts on heavy going. *Miss M. Bragg*

HARROVIAN 10 b.g. Deploy – Homeoftheclassics (Tate Gallery (USA)) [2006/7 **c–**
c115, h95: c25vᵖᵘ c25d⁵ Dec 28] winning hurdler: fairly useful handicap chaser: off 9 **h–**
months, shaped as if in need of race 2 starts in 2006/7: will stay beyond 25f: acts on heavy
going: in cheekpieces/blinkers last 4 outings: not a straightforward ride (tends to go in
snatches). *Miss P. Robson*

HARROWMAN (IRE) 5 b.g. Zaffaran (USA) – Moon Storm (IRE) (Strong Gale) **F102**
[2006/7 F16g* F16d⁶ Dec 16] €27,000Y: rangy gelding: has scope: fourth foal: dam
unraced out of sister to high-class 2m to 3m hurdler Mole Board: favourite, looked good
prospect when winning bumper at Haydock on debut by ¾ length from Tazbar: tended to
hang left when disappointing in Grade 2 at Ascot following month: will stay beyond 2m:
tongue tied. *N. A. Twiston-Davies*

HARRYCAT (IRE) 6 b.g. Bahhare (USA) – Quiver Tree (Lion Cavern (USA)) **h117**
[2006/7 h100: 17m 20f* 22g² 22d² 21gᵖᵘ Oct 24] lengthy gelding: fairly useful handicap
hurdler: much improved when winning at Worcester in June and Stratford (by 9 lengths
from Peeyoutwo) in July: ran poorly final outing: stays 2¾m: acts on firm and good to
soft going: wears cheekpieces: races prominently. *C. P. Morlock*

HARRY COLLINS 9 ch.g. Sir Harry Lewis (USA) – Run Fast For Gold (Deep Run) **c87 x**
[2006/7 c108x, h–: 23s⁴ 20d² 25dᵖᵘ c20v³ c25sᵖᵘ 22v² Feb 28] workmanlike gelding: fair **h92**
chaser on his day: modest handicap hurdler: barely stays 25f: acts on heavy going: tried
tongue tied: usually let down by jumping over fences: has found little. *B. I. Case*

HARRYCONE LEWIS 9 b.g. Sir Harry Lewis (USA) – Rosie Cone (Celtic Cone) **c112 §**
[2006/7 c121, h118: 21g c24gᵘʳ c25v⁴ 24s⁶ c24s² c24gᵖᵘ Mar 24] leggy gelding: fair **h112 §**
handicap hurdler/chaser nowadays: stays 3¼m: acts on soft going, probably on good to
firm: tried in cheekpieces, effective blinkered or not: can take plenty of driving. *Mrs P. Sly*

HARRY FLASHMAN 6 ch.g. Minster Son – Youandi (Silver Season) [2006/7 h102, **h108**
F–: 16g* 20g² 20s² 20v 22g* Apr 15] leggy gelding: fair novice hurdler: won at Hexham
in May and Kelso (idled) in April: stays 2¾m: acts on soft going. *D. W. Whillans*

HARRY HENDERSON 6 b.g. North Col – Blazer's Baby (Norton Challenger) **h–**
[2006/7 F16m² 16fᶠ Aug 22] 1,800Y: first foal: dam poor 1¼m winner/maiden hurdler: **F86 ?**
no form in maiden points (ran out once): allowed to build clear lead when second in

bumper at Worcester: seemed set to drop away when fell 3 out in maiden there on hurdling debut. *M. Mullineaux*

HARRY HUSYAN (IRE) 11 b. or br.g. Husyan (USA) – Showphar (IRE) (Phardante (FR)) [2006/7 c20g* c23g³ c20m³ c22m³ c20g² c23d^{pu} c22s c24d^{pu} Dec 10] winning hurdler/pointer: modest handicap chaser: won at Clonmel in May: stays 3m: has form on soft going, best efforts under less testing conditions (acts on firm): blinkered once (ran out): usually tongue tied. *G. Keane, Ireland*   **c88 §** **h– §**

HARRY MAY 5 b.g. Lujain (USA) – Mrs May (Carlingford Castle) [2006/7 h–: 17d⁶ 16m Jul 12] little impact over hurdles. *C. L. Tizzard*   **h–**

HARRY POTTER (GER) 8 b.g. Platini (GER) – Heavenly Storm (USA) (Storm Bird (CAN)) [2006/7 c103, h103: c16f^{ur} c16g^{pu} c16m* c17g* c17m³ 18g* 16m⁵ c20g^F Oct 24] good-topped gelding: fairly useful hurdler/novice chaser: won over fences at Worcester (maiden) and Stratford (readily by 17 lengths) in July, and handicap hurdle at Fontwell in September: stays 2½m: acts on firm and good to soft going: tried in visor, has won with or without cheekpieces: has had tongue tied. *Evan Williams*   **c115** **h115**

HARRY'S DREAM 10 b.g. Alflora (IRE) – Cheryls Pet (IRE) (General Ironside) [2006/7 c122, h108: c24g* c24d⁵ c24d Dec 27] leggy, workmanlike gelding: fair hurdler: useful handicap chaser: improved further when winning quite valuable event at Kempton in October in good style by 7 lengths from See You Sometime: mistakes when below form next 2 starts: stays 3m: has form on soft going, best efforts under less testing conditions (acts on good to firm). *P. J. Hobbs*   **c132** **h–**

HARRY'S LANE 6 ch.g. Sir Harry Lewis (USA) – Moor Lady (Primitive Rising (USA)) [2006/7 16d³ Mar 26] 8,000 4-y-o: rather leggy gelding: first foal: dam, winning pointer, sister to fairly useful 3m chaser Moor Lane: well beaten in points: poor form when third to Spirit of New York in novice at Stratford on hurdling debut: bred to be suited by further than 2m. *B. I. Case*   **h80**

HARRY THE DEALER (IRE) 8 b.g. King Luthier – Ballygunaghan Babe (IRE) (Un Desperado (FR)) [2006/7 c20d⁵ c20s^F Dec 26] winning pointer: poor maiden chaser: stays 2½m: in cheekpieces in 2006/7: makes mistakes. *G. Keane, Ireland*   **c72 x**

HARRY WOOD (FR) 5 b.g. Cyborg (FR) – Madame Fifi (FR) (Mille Balles (FR)) [2006/7 F17s* F17v* Mar 18] second foal: dam winning 2m hurdler in France: fairly useful form when winning both starts in bumpers at Carlisle, beat Banoge by 9 lengths on second occasion. *D. McCain Jnr*   **F103 +**

HARU 5 b. or gr.m. Sir Harry Lewis (USA) – Ruby Vision (IRE) (Vision (USA)) [2006/7 F16d F17g Mar 24] third foal: half-sister to poor hurdler/modest chaser Classic Rock (by Classic Cliche), stays 3m: dam modest hurdler who stayed 3m: soundly beaten in bumpers. *Mrs L. C. Jewell*   **F–**

HASHID (IRE) 7 b.g. Darshaan – Alkaffeyeh (IRE) (Sadler's Wells (USA)) [2006/7 16g c16s² c24s^{pu} c24s^F Jan 13] useful-looking gelding: winning hurdler, off 20 months prior to return: fair form on completed outing over fences: stays 21f: acts on soft going: tried blinkered. *P. C. Ritchens*   **c106** **h–**

HAS SCORED (IRE) 9 b.g. Sadler's Wells (USA) – City Ex (Ardross) [2006/7 c88, h–: c27v^{pu} c32v^{pu} c26g^{pu} c20g⁴ Apr 23] sturdy gelding: handicap chaser: poor form only completed outing in 2006/7 (off over a year before reappearance): should stay beyond 25f: raced on good going or softer: in cheekpieces last 2 starts. *Paul Murphy*   **c83** **h–**

HASTY GOER (IRE) 5 b.g. Petorius – Agoer (Hadeer) [2006/7 F17m Sep 28] half-brother to 7f winner Snark (by Cape Cross), stays 1½m: dam modest 7f winner: well beaten in bumper on debut. *N. J. Hawke*   **F–**

HASTY PRINCE 9 ch.g. Halling (USA) – Sister Sophie (USA) (Effervescing (USA)) [2006/7 c–, h146: c16s⁵ c17d² 16d⁵ c16g² c16g² c16g Apr 12] leggy, sparely-made gelding: useful hurdler/chaser: good efforts in handicap chases in 2006/7 when runner-up, beaten 3 lengths by Andreas in 23-runner Grade 3 Grand Annual Chase at Cheltenham penultimate outing: out of depth in Grade 1 hurdle third start: best short of 3m: acts on soft and good to firm going: tried blinkered/tongue tied: usually held up. *Jonjo O'Neill*   **c144** **h132**

HATCH A PLAN (IRE) 6 b.g. Vettori (IRE) – Fast Chick (Henbit (USA)) [2006/7 h94: 16f² 16g⁵ 16d^F 16f⁴ Apr 5] angular gelding: fair handicap hurdler: best at 2m with emphasis on speed: acts on firm going. *Mouse Hamilton-Fairley*   **h101**

HATSNALL 9 b.g. Mtoto – Anna of Brunswick (Rainbow Quest (USA)) [2006/7 c–, h–: c19s^{pu} 23d^{pu} May 21] good-topped gelding: maiden hurdler/chaser: successful in point in January: stays 3m: acts on heavy and good to firm going. *Miss C. J. E. Caroe*   **c–** **h–**

HATTON HOUSE (IRE) 7 b.g. Dr Massini (IRE) – Chancy Gal (Al Sirat) [2006/7 c–
h89?, F–: 16s⁶ 21m⁵ 20m⁴ 17g⁵ c20d Oct 6] medium-sized gelding: poor novice hurdler: **h80**
not fluent on chasing debut: should have been suited by further than 17f: dead. *D. McCain
Jnr*

HAT TRICK MAN 6 gr.h. Daylami (IRE) – Silver Kristal (Kris) [2006/7 17g 17dᶠ **h71**
17g⁵ 16f Jul 19] little form over hurdles: raced mainly around 2m: tongue tied 4 of last 5
starts. *Evan Williams*

HAUNTED HOUSE 7 ch.g. Opera Ghost – My Home (Homing) [2006/7 h95, F–: 16s **c110**
c16d* c19sᶠ c16s³ c16g³ c19g³ Apr 11] sturdy gelding: maiden hurdler: fair handicap **h–**
chaser: won novice event at Ludlow in January: stays 19f: acts on heavy going: usually
held up. *H. D. Daly*

HAUTCLAN (FR) 8 b.g. Chef de Clan II (FR) – Haute Tension (FR) (Garde Royale) **c127**
[2006/7 c20s³ c24s⁵ c28s⁴ c29s⁶ c32s⁶ 23s 22d 22m* Mar 31] workmanlike gelding: **h132**
useful handicap hurdler: well backed, returned to best when winning at Uttoxeter in
March by 6 lengths from Itsmyboy, ridden much more positively than usual and eased
after last: fairly useful handicap chaser: probably stays 3½m: acts on soft and good to
firm going, probably on heavy: tried in cheekpieces/blinkers: signs of temperament.
Jonjo O'Neill

HAUT DE GAMME (FR) 12 ch.g. Morespeed – Chantalouette (FR) (Royal Charter **c112**
(FR)) [2006/7 c137, h127: 24d⁵ c26g c24s c20vᵖᵘ c20s⁴ c20v⁴ Mar 10] sturdy gelding: **h115**
one-time useful handicap chaser/fairly useful hurdler: below best in 2006/7: stays 27f:
raced mainly on going softer than good (acts on heavy). *Ferdy Murphy*

HAVENSTONE (IRE) 6 b. or br.g. Needle Gun (IRE) – Melodic Tune (IRE) (Roselier **h83 +**
(FR)) [2006/7 F16m⁴ F16m F17m⁵ F16m* 19s 17s⁵ 16v⁴ Feb 15] second foal: dam failed **F88**
to complete in 2 Irish points: won bumper at Ludlow in October: modest form over
hurdles: hard puller and possibly not straightforward, though may do better now qualified
for handicaps. *Evan Williams*

HAWADETH 12 ch.g. Machiavellian (USA) – Ghzaalh (USA) (Northern Dancer) **h114**
[2006/7 h124: 20f 18d* 18s⁴ 16m Apr 10] compact gelding: fair hurdler nowadays: won
claimer at Fontwell (easily) in November: stays 2½m, at least when emphasis is on speed:
acts on good to firm and heavy going: has worn blinkers, effective with or without
cheekpieces: sometimes races lazily. *V. R. A. Dartnall*

HAWICK 10 b.g. Toulon – Slave's Bangle (Prince Rheingold) [2006/7 20sᵖᵘ May 17] **h–**
placed in bumpers: well beaten on completed outing over hurdles: tried tongue tied.
D. W. Whillans

HAWK ARROW (IRE) 5 ch.g. In The Wings – Barbizou (FR) (Selkirk (USA)) **h–**
[2006/7 17s Dec 18] fair 11.6f winner at 3 yrs for H. Morrison, well held both starts on
Flat in 2006 for Miss S. West: no show in maiden on hurdling debut. *G. L. Moore*

HAWKES RUN 9 b.g. Hernando (FR) – Wise Speculation (USA) (Mr Prospector **h– §**
(USA)) [2006/7 21g 16s 19g 23dᵖᵘ Dec 4] close-coupled gelding: one-time fairly useful
handicap hurdler: no show in 2006/7 after lengthy lay-off: barely stayed 3m: acted on soft
and good to firm going: tried blinkered/in cheekpieces: ungenuine: dead. *A. G. Blackmore*

HAWK ROYAL (FR) 5 gr.g. Epervier Bleu – Altesse du Chenet (FR) (Katowice (FR)) **F–**
[2006/7 F16d Dec 29] compact gelding: fourth foal: half-brother to winning hurdler
around 2m Papajo (by Dreams To Reality): dam, successful on Flat up to around 1½m,
also won up to 19f over hurdles: tongue tied, not unduly knocked about when well held in
bumper on debut. *B. G. Powell*

HAWKSBURY HEIGHTS 5 ch.h. Nashwan (USA) – Gentle Dame (Kris) [2006/7 **h–**
h–: 22gᵘʳ 16gᵘʳ 20s⁵ 16gᵖᵘ Oct 21] sparely-made horse: no solid form over hurdles: tried
blinkered. *J. J. Lambe, Ireland*

HAWK'S LANDING (IRE) 10 gr.g. Peacock (FR) – Lady Cheyenne (Stanford) **c121 x**
[2006/7 c109x, h–: c24m³ c23m³ c21f⁶ c20d* c22s* c22g⁴ 19d 20s⁶ c20s⁵ c21g Mar 19] **h–**
well-made gelding: winning hurdler: fair useful handicap chaser: back near best when
winning at Carlisle and Towcester (beat Fill The Bunker by 1¾ lengths) in October: well
held last 4 starts: stays 25f: acts on heavy and good to firm going: tried in cheekpieces:
has been let down by jumping/found little. *Jonjo O'Neill*

HAWKWELL (IRE) 6 b.g. Topanoora – Royal Daisy (Crash Course) [2006/7 h87p: **h84 +**
20s² 16g 20sᵖᵘ Apr 27] some promise over hurdles, though had breathing problem second
outing: will stay beyond 2½m. *N. G. Richards*

Sporting Index Handicap Chase (Cross Country), Cheltenham—Heads Onthe Ground and Nina Carberry have the measure of subsequent Grand National winner Silver Birch

HAWRIDGE KING 5 b.g. Erhaab (USA) – Sadaka (USA) (Kingmambo (USA)) **h108**
[2006/7 h109: 17g³ 19d* 21d⁴ 19s Dec 7] fair and consistent maiden on Flat (stays 12.6f): fair novice hurdler: won at Taunton in October: stays 19f: raced on good going or softer: tried visored. *W. S. Kittow*

HAWRIDGE STAR (IRE) 5 b.g. Alzao (USA) – Serenity (Selkirk (USA)) [2006/7 **h115**
16d* 16g² 17s² 19v⁶ Jan 17] compact gelding: fair maiden on Flat (stays 13f): fairly useful form over hurdles: won maiden at Chepstow on debut in November readily by 6 lengths from Shannon Springs: good effort when 3 lengths second to Private Be at Exeter third outing: raced mainly around 2m: acts on soft ground. *W. S. Kittow*

HAWTHORN PRINCE (IRE) 12 ch.g. Black Monday – Goose Loose (Dual) **h88**
[2006/7 c–, h110: 24g Apr 21] winning pointer: fair handicap hurdler: off nearly 2 years before return: stays 27f: acts on soft and good to firm going: tried blinkered. *Mrs P. Sly*

HAXTON 7 b.g. Sadler's Way – Ember (Nicholas (USA)) [2006/7 21gᵖᵘ 16g 22m⁶ Apr **h–**
22] strong gelding: no form in novice hurdles, trained on return by D. Bridgwater. *Ms J. S. Doyle*

HAYLEY'S PEARL 8 b.m. Nomadic Way (USA) – Pacific Girl (IRE) (Emmson) **c–**
[2006/7 c–, h–: c16f⁴ c16m Mar 29] angular mare: fourth in novice chase at Ludlow, only **h–**
sign of ability. *Mrs P. Ford*

HAYSTACKS (IRE) 11 b.g. Contract Law (USA) – Florissa (FR) (Persepolis (FR)) **h– §**
[2006/7 h87§: 23g 22gᵖᵘ Nov 4] leggy gelding: handicap hurdler, no show in 2006/7: often visored/in cheekpieces: has carried head awkwardly/found little. *James Moffatt*

HAZARD AWAY 4 ch.g. Hazaaf (USA) – Departure (Gorytus (USA)) [2006/7 F17g Apr 27] third foal: dam, winning hurdler/pointer, stayed 25f: soundly beaten in bumper on debut. *Miss M. Bragg* — **F—**

HAZEAM 4 b.g. Hazaaf (USA) – Di's Dream (Buckley) [2006/7 F14g F12v F16v⁵ Jan 27] tall, good-topped gelding: first foal: dam no form in novice hurdles: well held in bumpers. *C. Roberts* — **F—**

HAZEL BANK LASS (IRE) 11 b.m. Insan (USA) – Bonecastle Queen (Fitzpatrick) [2006/7 c90, h–: c22m May 28] winning Irish pointer: form in chases only when second in novice handicap in 2005/6: tried blinkered. *Andrew Turnell* — **c— h—**

HAZELBURY 6 b.m. Overbury (IRE) – Mira Lady (Henbit (USA)) [2006/7 16d 17m⁴ 18s 17d Jan 10] 4,000 4-y-o, 2,000 5-y-o: rather unfurnished mare: half-sister to several winners, including 2m hurdlers Eric's Bett (by Chilibang) and Nuin-Tara (by Petoski): dam 7f winner in Germany: form (poor) over hurdles only on second start. *N. J. Hawke* — **h76**

HAZELDENE 5 ch.g. Dancing High – Gaelic Charm (IRE) (Deep Run) [2006/7 F16g⁴ F16m Apr 21] tall gelding: has scope: fourth foal: brother to fair 2½m hurdle winner Reel Charmer: dam lightly-raced novice hurdler: just over 4 lengths fourth to Tazbar at Wetherby, not settling but better effort in bumpers. *G. A. Charlton* — **F97**

HAZELJACK 12 b.g. Sula Bula – Hazelwain (Hard Fact) [2006/7 c106, h–: c24d⁶ c28dᶠ c23s c26v⁶ c28g⁴ Mar 18] tall gelding: modest handicap chaser: stays 3½m: acts on heavy going. *A. J. Whiting* — **c91 h—**

HAZY JUBILEE 5 ch.m. Hazaaf (USA) – Departure (Gorytus (USA)) [2006/7 16gᵖᵘ Nov 4] second foal: dam, winning hurdler/pointer, stayed 25f: tongue tied, no show in selling hurdle on debut. *J. P. L. Ewart* — **h—**

HAZZARD A GUESS 6 ch.m. Primitive Rising (USA) – Handy Venture (Nearly A Hand) [2006/7 h–, F77: 22m⁶ c23fᵖᵘ 19gᵖᵘ Jun 20] no form outside bumpers. *J. W. Mullins* — **c— h—**

HEAD HELD HIGH (IRE) 6 br.g. Zaffaran (USA) – Miss Hollygrove (IRE) (King's Ride) [2006/7 16v² 18s⁴ 19v² 20s* 24g 24mᵖᵘ Apr 9] sturdy gelding: second foal: dam unraced sister to useful chaser/top-class hurdler Mister Morose, stayed 3m: fair hurdler: won maiden at Down Royal in February: should stay 3m: acts on heavy ground. *Mrs J. Harrington, Ireland* — **h109**

HEADS ONTHE GROUND (IRE) 10 br.g. Be My Native (USA) – Strong Wings (Strong Gale) [2006/7 c24v² c31s³ c24v⁴ c24s* c31d* Mar 13] rangy gelding: useful chaser: left D. Hughes, won both starts in points in October: showed himself better than ever when beating Silver Birch in cross-country events at Punchestown (by 10 lengths) in February and Cheltenham (Sporting Index Handicap by 3½ lengths) in March: stays 31f: acts on heavy ground: tried blinkered/in cheekpieces. *Enda Bolger, Ireland* — **c138 + h—**

HEAD TO KERRY (IRE) 7 b.g. Eagle Eyed (USA) – The Poachers Lady (IRE) (Salmon Leap (USA)) [2006/7 21g⁶ Mar 23] modest form 2 starts over hurdles 2 years apart: tried tongue tied. *D. J. S. ffrench Davis* — **h92**

HEALY'S PUB (IRE) 11 b.g. Accordion – Valary (Roman Warrior) [2006/7 c20s* c20g³ c25g⁴ 24m Apr 26] workmanlike gelding: winning hurdler: fairly useful chaser: off 11 months, made all in maiden at Clonmel (winning by 9 lengths from Liscooney) in March: good effort when 13 lengths fourth to Reveillez in quite valuable handicap at Aintree: stays 25f: acts on heavy and good to firm going: tried in headgear (below form): sometimes let down by jumping. *Oliver McKiernan, Ireland* — **c123 h101**

HEAR ME OUT (IRE) 7 b.g. Rock Hopper – Kindly Princess (IRE) (Radical) [2006/7 16s⁴ Jan 24] €25,000 3-y-o: well-made gelding: third foal: dam unraced half-sister to useful staying chaser Ghia Gneuiagh: bumper winner: modest form in novice hurdles, left E. O'Grady and off 18 months prior to only outing in 2006/7 (considerably handled): stays 2½m: open to improvement. *Jonjo O'Neill* — **h95 p**

HEARTACHE 10 b.g. Jurado (USA) – Heresy (IRE) (Black Minstrel) [2006/7 c74, h–: c22sᵖᵘ c24sᵖᵘ c24vᵖᵘ c23d⁶ c24sᵖᵘ c24vᵖᵘ Jan 21] tall gelding: handicap chaser, no form in 2006/7: tried in cheekpieces, usually blinkered. *R. Mathew* — **c— h—**

HEAR THE ECHO (IRE) 6 b.g. Luso – Echo Creek (IRE) (Strong Gale) [2006/7 c20d* c24vᵖᵘ c17s² c21d* c17sᶠ c24vᶠ c20v³ c24d⁴ c20m Apr 8] good-topped gelding: fourth foal: half-brother to 3 winners, including fair hurdler/fairly useful chaser Melford (by Presenting), stays 3m: dam lightly-raced maiden hurdler: winning hurdler for D. Wachman in 2005/6: useful novice chaser: won 5-runner minor event at Clonmel in — **c132 h—**

November and Grade 2 Paddy Fitzpatrick Memorial Novices' Chase at Leopardstown (by 1½ lengths from Justpourit) in January: stays 3m: acts on soft going: usually front runner. *M. F. Morris, Ireland*

HEARTHSTEAD DREAM 6 ch.g. Dr Fong (USA) – Robin Lane (Tenby) [2006/7 **h109** 20s 16v* 17v⁵ Jan 27] fair on Flat, successful in October: fair handicap hurdler: improved to win at Fairyhouse in January: well-backed favourite, soon plenty to do at Cheltenham next time: stays 2½m: raced on ground softer than good (acts on heavy): tried blinkered. *A. J. Martin, Ireland*

HEARTHSTEAD WINGS 5 b.g. In The Wings – Inishdalla (IRE) (Green Desert **h96 §** (USA)) [2006/7 16s 16g³ 17m² Apr 17] sturdy gelding: useful on Flat (effective at 1½m to 2m), successful in 2006, left M. Johnston after final start: modest form when placed over hurdles: blinkered: temperamental. *P. J. Hobbs*

HEARTOFMIDLOTHIAN (IRE) 8 ch.g. Anshan – Random Wind (Random Shot) **c–** [2006/7 c25sᵖᵘ 20d 16s c25sᵖᵘ c23s c20dᶠ Mar 26] workmanlike gelding: modest form **h–** in bumpers: off 2 years, no form over hurdles/fences: in cheekpieces last 2 starts. *K. C. Bailey*

HEART OF WEST (IRE) 9 b.g. Broken Hearted – Fairtown Fair (IRE) (Jurado **c96** (USA)) [2006/7 c20gᵖᵘ c20d² c20m⁵ c16s² c16gᵘʳ c16mᵖᵘ Nov 5] dead-heated in maiden point in Ireland in 2005: modest form when runner-up in novice chases (often let down by jumping). *C. Grant*

HEART SPRINGS 7 b.m. Parthian Springs – Metannee (The Brianstan) [2006/7 16g⁴ **h93** 16sᶠ 17s⁶ 20s³ 26gᶠ 24d³ 22m³ Apr 28] lengthy, angular mare: closely related to winning 2m hurdler Belle Derriere (by Kylian): dam, winning hurdler, stayed 21f: fair on Flat (stays 2¼m), below form both starts in 2006: modest novice hurdler: stays 2¾m: acts on soft and good to firm going. *Dr J. R. J. Naylor*

HEARTSTOPPER (IRE) 10 b.g. Over The River (FR) – Miss Qogan (Tarqogan) **c95** [2006/7 c17d⁴ c21d* c20m⁵ c21g⁶ Aug 21] winning hurdler: modest chaser: much **h–** improved when winning handicap at Sedgefield in May: stays 3m: acts on firm and good to soft ground. *A. J. Martin, Ireland*

HEARTY DOVE 5 b.m. Overbury (IRE) – Coney Dove (Celtic Cone) [2006/7 F16s **h68** 21d 19d³ Feb 19] small, angular mare: sixth foal: half-sister to winning 2½m hurdler **F65** Scratch The Dove (by Henbit): dam, 21f hurdle winner, half-sister to Champion Hurdle winner Flakey Dove: poor form in bumper/over hurdles: should be suited by further than 19f. *A. E. Price*

HEATHCOTE 5 b.g. Unfuwain (USA) – Chere Amie (USA) (Mr Prospector **h135** (USA)) [2006/7 h113: 16m 16d³ 16s 19d 16v² 17v 16d* Feb 10]
Trainer Gary Moore might have enjoyed his most successful season in terms of total prize money won, but he wasn't at all happy that the number of races won by his yard fell short of its best figure. Moore's quote in the aftermath of Altilhar's victory in a juvenile handicap hurdle at Ascot at the end of March wasn't what might have been expected from a trainer who had just saddled a winner. 'It's been crap. I've won three big handicaps and I'll probably get to £500,000 in prize money, but I've only had thirty-five winners after sixty-three last season,' said Moore, whose tally had risen to forty-five by season's end. In truth, there were actually just the two major handicap wins, those of Verasi in the Lanzarote Hurdle at Kempton (Moore's third win in the race), worth over £25,000, and of Heathcote in the totesport Trophy Hurdle at Newbury in February, worth over £85,000. The former started at 20/1, while the latter was sent off at 50/1 for what looked a slightly substandard renewal of the most valuable handicap hurdle of the season, 100/1-shot Self Defense the only one of Heathcote's nineteen rivals at longer odds. As his odds suggested, Heathcote hardly looked to have sound claims of winning such a well-contested event. He was still without a victory in handicap company, although he had been placed a couple of times earlier in the season, and had been well beaten off the same mark at Cheltenham on his previous outing. Heathcote found the necessary improvement, however. Ridden by his trainer's son Jamie, the champion conditional back in 2003/4, Heathcote was waited with in a race less truly-run than might have been expected, plenty still in with a shout early in the straight as a result. Heathcote made up his ground smoothly to dispute the lead two out and took a narrow advantage soon afterwards before finding plenty under pressure to hold the strong challenge of Overstrand by a neck, becoming the longest-priced winner of a

totesport Trophy Hurdle (Handicap), Newbury—50/1-shot Heathcote narrowly holds off Overstrand (hooped sleeves); Pedrobob (centre) and Caracciola (second left) fill the minor placings

race first run in 1963. The form of the latest renewal worked out well, though Heathcote himself didn't get the chance to frank it in the latest season. He did make an appearance after the end of the British season, at Auteuil towards the end of May, when facing a very stiff in the twenty-one-furlong Prix La Barka and doing best of the overseas challengers in finishing a never-dangerous seventh over a trip he probably doesn't stay under testing conditions. Unraced as a two-year-old, Heathcote showed fair form at three, winning a mile-and-half maiden at Chepstow. Sold out of Charles Cyzer's stable for 15,000 guineas at that year's Newmarket Autumn Sales, he quickly showed an aptitude for hurdling in the 2005/6 season, beaten only once in four starts, his wins coming in juvenile events at Lingfield, Plumpton and Towcester. A close-coupled gelding who should stay beyond two miles, Heathcote acts on heavy going and was well below form on the only occasion he has raced on firmer than good over hurdles. *G. L. Moore*

HEATHER LAD 14 ch.g. Highlands – Ragged Rose (Scallywag) [2006/7 c94: c21s c20m³ c20m⁶ c20s² c22m² c20m⁵ c21f⁴ c21m⁵ c21m⁴ Aug 29] modest maiden chaser: probably stays 3¼m: acts on firm going. *C. Grant*   **c85**

HEATHERLEA SQUIRE (NZ) 9 b.g. His Royal Highness (NZ) – Misty Gleam (NZ) (Gleam Machine (USA)) [2006/7 c–§, h61§: 17g 16v⁶ May 23] little form over hurdles (ran out once): unseated second on chasing debut: sold 500 gns Doncaster May (2006) Sales. *D. J. Wintle*   **c– §**
h– §

HEATHERS GIRL 8 ch.m. Superlative – Kristis Girl (Ballacashtal (CAN)) [2006/7 h–: c17g c16m⁶ c16mᵇᵈ c16f⁶ Jul 19] no form over hurdles/fences. *R. Dickin*   **c–**
h–

HEATHYARDS FRIEND 8 b.g. Forest Wind (USA) – Heathyards Lady (USA) (Mining (USA)) [2006/7 19s 16f Jul 19] leggy gelding: poor hurdler, very lightly raced: tried tongue tied. *B. Forsey*   **h–**

HEATHYARDS JOY 6 ch.m. Komaite (USA) – Heathyards Lady (USA) (Mining (USA)) [2006/7 16m⁵ 16m³ 16d* 16f 17g Apr 11] half-sister to 2m hurdle winner Heathyards Friend (by Forest Wind): modest maiden on Flat (stays 10.2f): poor hurdler: won seller at Ludlow in November: breathing problem final start: likely to prove best at 2m with emphasis on speed. *R. Hollinshead*   **h74**

HEAVENLY BLUES (GER) 5 b.g. Kallisto (GER) – Heavenly Storm (USA) (Storm Bird (CAN)) [2006/7 16s³ 16v* 16v³ 16v* 16m² Apr 9] ex-German gelding: half-brother to fairly useful hurdler/chaser up to 2½m Harry Potter (by Platini): successful 4 times on Flat in 2006 for H-J. Koll: fairly useful novice hurdler: won large-field events at Naas (maiden) in February and Navan (landed odds by 2½ lengths from Miss Mason) in March: good 4 lengths second to Scotsirish in minor event at Fairyhouse: likely to prove best around 2m: acts on heavy and good to firm going. *T. M. Walsh, Ireland*   **h128**

HEAVENLY CHORUS 5 b.m. Key of Luck (USA) – Celestial Choir (Celestial Storm (USA)) [2006/7 F80: 17d⁵ 16s⁵ 16g 16v⁵ 19sᵖᵘ 20m* 20g⁶ Apr 16] close-coupled mare: **h82**

poor novice hurdler: won mares handicap at Southwell in March: stays 2½m: acts on good to firm going, probably on heavy. *K. G. Reveley*

HEAVENLY KING 9 b.g. Homo Sapien – Chapel Hill (IRE) (The Parson) [2006/7 c–, h–: 22m⁴ 20sᵖᵘ Jun 25] quite good-topped gelding: poor maiden hurdler: unseated early on chasing debut: stays 2¾m: acts on good to firm ground: usually blinkered/in cheek-pieces. *Tim Vaughan*   c–
h79

HEAVENLY PLEASURE (IRE) 8 b.m. Presenting – Galynn (IRE) (Strong Gale) [2006/7 h–: 20dᵖᵘ 21vᵖᵘ 21g* Mar 28] tall, good-topped mare: first form over hurdles (left J. Hetherton after first outing) when 33/1-winner of mares novice at Towcester in March: stays 21f: tried tongue tied. *Simon Earle*   h82

HEAVY SEAS 4 b.g. Foxhound (USA) – Brookhead Lady (Petong) [2006/7 16dᵖᵘ 17s 17g 16sᵖᵘ Nov 11] tall gelding: no form on Flat/in juvenile hurdles: tried in cheekpieces. *P. D. Niven*   h–

HEAVY WEATHER (IRE) 9 ch.g. Glacial Storm (USA) – Tinkers Lady (Sheer Grit) [2006/7 h98: c19d² 21s* 26s⁴ 24vᵖᵘ c20v² Mar 4] workmanlike gelding: winning pointer: fair handicap hurdler: won at Towcester in November: runner-up both starts in chases: likely to prove best at 3m+: raced on ground softer than good. *Miss Joanne Priest*   c87
h104

HECKLEYHIGHVOLTAGE 8 b.m. Dancing High – Heckley Spark (Electric) [2006/7 20gᵖᵘ 20sᵖᵘ Apr 25] fourth foal: sister to modest chaser Flaming Heck, stays 2½m, and bumper winner Heckley Clare Glen: dam lightly-raced maiden: more signs of temperament than ability over hurdles. *Mrs L. B. Normile*   h–

HEDCHESTER 6 b.g. Missed Flight – Lady Manello (Mandrake Major) [2006/7 F–: F16g 20s 16s 16s 20g⁶ Mar 27] sturdy gelding: no solid form in bumpers/over hurdles: will be suited by 3m. *Mrs A. Hamilton*   h–
F–

HEDGE FUND 10 b.g. Slip Anchor – Burnished (Formidable (USA)) [2006/7 16v c16g c22gᵖᵘ Jul 9] maiden hurdler: no form over fences: tried in cheekpieces/tongue tied: sold £1,600 Ascot August Sales. *D. W. Thompson*   c–
h–

HEDGEHUNTER (IRE) 11 b.g. Montelimar (USA) – Aberedw (IRE) (Caerwent) [2006/7 c167, h–: 22v⁵ 16d c36g Apr 14] useful-looking gelding: winning hurdler: top-class chaser: better than ever when placed behind War of Attrition in Cheltenham Gold Cup and Numbersixvalverde in Grand National (won race previous year) last 2 outings in 2005/6: interrupted preparation (jarred knee and off 4 months after reappearance) and only ninth of 40 behind Silver Birch in latest renewal of Grand National, tiring after 3 out: stays 4½m: unraced on firm going, acts on any other: has sweated: has taken strong hold: excellent jumper: genuine. *W. P. Mullins, Ireland*   c163 ?
h101

HEEBIE JEEBIE 5 b. or br.m. Overbury (IRE) – Avec Le Vent (IRE) (Strong Gale) [2006/7 F–: F16s⁵ F16d Feb 2] poor form in bumpers. *Mrs P. Robeson*   F73

HEEZ A DREAMER (IRE) 7 b.g. Naheez (USA) – Tuitestown (Orchestra) [2006/7 c20g² c22v* c21s³ c25v⁶ c22v* c25s³ c19v* c24g⁵ Mar 13] €13,000 3-y-o: useful-looking gelding: half-brother to fair 2m chaser Island Pride (by Shardari): dam lightly raced in bumpers: won maiden point in 2005: useful chaser: won maiden at Uttoxeter in November and novices at Fontwell (2-finisher event) in January and Exeter (beat Professor Jack by 13 lengths) in February: also ran well most other starts, including when 10 lengths fifth of 23 to Joes Edge in William Hill Trophy (Handicap) at Cheltenham: will stay beyond 25f: acts on heavy going: reliable. *Miss Venetia Williams*   c137

HEEZ A STEEL (IRE) 6 b.g. Naheez (USA) – Ari's Fashion (Aristocracy) [2006/7 F16s² F16v⁶ F16d⁶ 16dᶠ 16v² 21g 20g⁴ Apr 23] €16,000 4-y-o: lengthy, angular gelding: third foal: dam lightly-raced maiden: runner-up in bumper at Hexham on debut: best effort over hurdles (modest form) when second in maiden at same course: should be suited by 2½m+: acts on heavy going. *G. A. Charlton*   h89
F91

HEEZ KOOL (IRE) 5 b.g. Naheez (USA) – Eurolucy (IRE) (Shardari) [2006/7 16s 19gᵖᵘ Nov 17] £7,000 3-y-o: medium-sized gelding: first foal: dam unraced half-sister to fair chaser The Red One, stays 3m: no show in novice hurdles. *N. J. Gifford*   h–

HEHASALIFE (IRE) 10 b.g. Safety Catch (USA) – America River (IRE) (Lord Americo) [2006/7 c94, h–: c25mᵖᵘ c23mᵖᵘ c24m* c25fᵖᵘ c24m c23m⁴ Nov 13] tall, shallow-girthed gelding: modest handicap chaser: won maiden at Bangor in September, only form in 2006/7: stays 25f: acts on firm and soft going: usually blinkered, also tried in cheekpieces/tongue tied: inconsistent. *Heather Dalton*   c90 §
h– §

HEIDI III (FR) 12 b.g. Bayolidaan (FR) – Irlandaise (FR) (Or de Chine) [2006/7 c108§, h–: c30d⁶ May 27] close-coupled gelding: fair handicap chaser: stays 3½m: acts   c– §
h–

on good to firm and heavy going: wears headgear: races prominently: inconsistent. *Micky Hammond*

HEIR TO BE 8 b.g. Elmaamul (USA) – Princess Genista (Ile de Bourbon (USA)) [2006/7 h119: 21g³ 24d⁵ 24v 22v⁴ 21s³ 22d⁶ Mar 17] sturdy gelding: fairly useful handicap hurdler: creditable efforts most starts in 2006/7: stays 25f: acts on heavy going: in cheekpieces last 2 starts: tried tongue tied (ran badly). *Mrs L. Wadham* **h119**

HEISAMODEL (IRE) 9 b.g. Balla Cove – Liffeyside Lady (IRE) (Cataldi) [2006/7 c87: 22s⁵ 22m⁴ 22d 24g 22g Apr 7] good-topped gelding: prolific winning pointer: refused last both starts in hunters: poor form over hurdles: stays 2¾m: acts on good to firm ground: tried blinkered. *B. J. M. Ryall* **c–**
h83

HEISSE 7 b.g. Darshaan – Hedera (USA) (Woodman (USA)) [2006/7 h80: 19g³ 20m 19g 24d 17d² 21g³ 21g 20m Mar 29] modest maiden hurdler: stays 19f: acts on good to soft going: has had tongue tied: not one to rely on. *Ian Williams* **h87 d**

HELENS VISION 4 b.f. Alflora (IRE) – Kinlet Vision (IRE) (Vision (USA)) [2006/7 F14g² F14g² F16s* F16g* F17g⁴ Apr 13] leggy filly: half-sister to several winners, including fair 2m hurdler Brave Vision (by Clantime): dam, 2½m hurdle winner, also sprint winner at 2 yrs: useful bumper performer: second in 3-y-o events prior to winning at Stratford (by 17 lengths) in February and Newbury (made all again to beat Snap Tie by 3½ lengths in 22-runner event) in March: faded after helping to force pace when fourth to Turbo Linn in listed mares event at Aintree. *Miss H. Lewis* **F106**

HELEN WOOD 4 b.f. Lahib (USA) – Last Ambition (IRE) (Cadeaux Genereux) [2006/7 16g⁶ 18s 16v² 16s* 18s* 16v³ 16d 18g³ 16m² Apr 20] leggy filly: half-sister to modest winning 2m hurdler Coctail Lady (by Piccolo): modest on Flat (stays 1¼m), won seller in October (sold from M. Usher 12,000 gns): fairly useful juvenile hurdler: easily won handicaps at Leicester (amateurs) in January and Fontwell (beat Scarlet Mix by 4 lengths) in February: creditable second to River Alder in mares handicap at Ayr final outing: likely to prove best up to 2¼m: acts on soft and good to firm going. *D. E. Pipe* **h110**

HELLO BABY 7 b.g. Jumbo Hirt (USA) – Silver Flyer (Silver Season) [2006/7 h82: 24g² 24g⁵ 24g² c22s⁴ Nov 17] leggy gelding: modest handicap hurdler: similar form when fourth in novice handicap on chasing debut: stays 3m: acts on soft and good to firm going: tried in cheekpieces. *A. C. Whillans* **c86**
h86

HELL OF A TIME (IRE) 10 b.g. Phardante (FR) – Ticking Over (IRE) (Decent Fellow) [2006/7 h–: 22vˢᵘ Feb 25] workmanlike gelding: lightly raced and no form over hurdles. *Mrs N. S. Evans* **h–**

HELLO IT'S ME 4 b.ch.g. Deploy – Evening Charm (IRE) (Bering) [2006/7 h–: 17d 16g⁴ 20g 21s* 20s³ 21m 24s 26m* 24g⁵ Apr 21] workmanlike gelding: fair hurdler, left K. Morgan after first outing: won handicaps at Ludlow (amateur novice) in December and Hereford (conditional jockeys, idling) in March: stays 3¼m: acts on soft and good to firm going: in cheekpieces last 2 starts. *D. McCain Jnr* **h99**

HELLO NODDY 5 ch.g. Double Trigger (IRE) – Setter Country (Town And Country) [2006/7 F–: 16g 16g Apr 15] no form in bumpers/novice hurdles: sold 2,400 gns Doncaster May Sales. *B. Mactaggart* **h–**

HELLO YOU 5 b.g. Pharly (FR) – Mardessa (Ardross) [2006/7 F16m* Apr 25] eighth foal: brother to bumper winner Phardesse: dam 1¼m/11f winner: 40/1, successful debut when beating Truckers Delight by 3 lengths in bumper at Worcester. *A. M. Hales* **F100**

HELM (IRE) 6 b.g. Alhaarth (IRE) – Pipers Pool (IRE) (Mtoto) [2006/7 h104: 22v* 24s* 23sᵖᵘ Feb 17] useful-looking gelding: fairly useful hurdler: won handicaps at Folkestone in November and Taunton (much improved, held up in strongly-run race, beat Manawanui by 16 lengths) in December: stays 3m: acts on heavy going: tried in cheekpieces. *R. Rowe* **h118**

HELTORNIC (IRE) 7 ch.m. Zaffaran (USA) – Majestic Run (Deep Run) [2006/7 h111: c23d* c24v³ c24s² c29s c25s* c28s* c24gᶠ Mar 13] **c139**
h–

    With the obvious exception of the unique obstacles on the Grand National course at Aintree, no other track's fences had the individual nature of Haydock's steeplechase course which became a thing of the past when the final race was run over the traditional fences at the course's fixture in early-April. As well as being recognised as among the stiffest around, Haydock's fences differed from those at other tracks on account of their slight drop on landing, a characteristic which made the course as good a test as any outside Aintree itself for prospective Grand National horses. Indeed, Red Rum's final preparatory run for all five of his Grand

National attempts came at Haydock, which was also the venue for the last run of his career in 1978. The stirring duel between Silver Buck and Night Nurse for the Embassy Premier Chase Final at Haydock in 1979 must rank as one of the most exciting races ever for anyone who witnessed it, whilst steeplechasing notables such as L'Escargot, Bula, Pendil, Forgive'N Forget, One Man and Jodami are just some of the other famous names to have graced Haydock's chase course down the years. From now on, however, chases at Haydock will be run over portable fences (some of which were already in use in the back straight) on what was the hurdles track, which has a tighter configuration inside the old chase course, another aspect which will change the nature of the test the course has traditionally provided. Haydock is familiar with using portable obstacles, as French-style brush hurdles have been used for some of its hurdle races for a number of seasons.

Although recognised as one of the best jumping tracks in the whole country, not just in the North, Haydock's dedicated chase track and its jumps programmes during the winter are less of a crowd-puller than the course's summer Flat cards, particularly the Friday evening meetings. 'In the summer, we get a large Friday evening crowd watching relatively modest Flat racing and supping champagne, as compared with a small crowd in winter watching a relatively expensive programme of chasing,' was how Haydock's clerk of the course summed up the situation. As a result, Haydock is due to reduce its jumps fixtures from ten to eight, whilst expanding its Flat fixtures by seven to twenty-seven per year. The extra ground yielded up by the chase course will enable Haydock to stage its enlarged programme of Flat meetings whilst maintaining fresh ground. Racecourses have to make money, of course, and are fully entitled to take decisions that are in their best commercial interests, or the wider commercial interests of their group (Haydock is part of Jockey Club Racecourses), but things have reached a pretty pass when the drinking habits of racegoers carry more weight in shaping a course's fixture list than the quality and heritage of its steeplechase course. Incidentally, whether champagne is actually consumed in quite the same quantity as other alcoholic

Red Square Vodka Gold Cup Chase (Handicap), Haydock—
the mare Heltornic lands the final big race to be staged over Haydock's famous drop fences

beverages at Haydock on a Friday night in the summer is a matter for debate. Erstwhile regular racegoers might beg to differ!

Whilst several northern-based trainers and jockeys in particular voiced their horror at Haydock's decision, opposition was by no means so strong as it might have been, with support for Haydock coming from the Horseracing Regulatory Authority and the National Trainers' Federation among others. The NTF urged its members to take a positive view, mindful perhaps that Haydock had at least not followed the lead of Nottingham and Windsor, other courses which once staged racing under both codes but which dropped jumps racing altogether to concentrate entirely on a more remunerative Flat programme. Whether the support is quite so forthcoming from sponsors is less clear. The choice of Haydock as the venue for the Betfair-sponsored Lancashire Chase, relaunched in 2005 complete with its £1m bonus, presumably had much to do with the course's steeplechasing heritage, and nothing at all to do with the prospect of the best staying chasers around being asked to race over portable obstacles on a sharp track. Betfair announced it would be 'keeping a watching brief'.

The last big race run over Haydock's fences in their traditional form was the Red Square Vodka Gold Cup, a long-standing Grand National trial run in February. Several of the sixteen-strong field in a really competitive renewal went on to run in the National itself, notably Philson Run who finished fourth at Aintree. The winner Heltornic did not hold a Grand National entry, however, still being a novice and having only her sixth run over fences. She had won twice earlier in the season, proving rather fortunate to make a winning chasing debut at Worcester in October (when aided by Jeremy Cuddle Duck's antics in the latter stages) and then starting as the outsider of seven when winning the totepool Towton Novices' Chase at Wetherby a fortnight before Haydock. Avoiding the mistakes which had often been a feature of her previous starts, Heltornic was sent on soon after halfway at Wetherby and stayed on strongly to win by three and a half lengths from Miko de Beauchene. Between those wins, Heltornic was placed in a couple of novice handicaps at Newbury and had finished seventh, from 9 lb out of the handicap, in the valuable totesport.com Classic Chase at Warwick in January, though on that occasion she'd still been in touch with the leaders when stopped in her tracks by a blunder five out.

Returned to handicap company at Haydock (3 lb out of the weights this time despite a penalty for her Wetherby win), Heltornic proved well suited by the extended three-and-a-half-mile test. Leading early on the final circuit and surviving a mistake at the last ditch four out, she was well in control from the next. The other mare in the field, L'Aventure, the previous season's Welsh National winner, was the only one to make any inroads into Heltornic's lead after the last, Heltornic winning by a length and a quarter with the pair fifteen lengths clear of Mon Mome, runner-up in the latest Welsh National as well as the Classic Chase at Warwick. Fellow novice and joint-favourite Cloudy Lane seemed not to get home, while the other joint favourite The Outlier, along with the next two in the betting Kilbeggan Blade and Kelami, and top weight Sir Rembrandt, were all pulled up. On a mark effectively 12 lb higher, Heltornic was still in a narrow lead and yet to be asked for maximum effort when falling two out in the William Hill Trophy at Cheltenham on her only subsequent outing. Heltornic has been partnered in most of her races by Tom Scudamore for his grandfather Michael. Heltornic's win at Haydock was the first leg of a hat-trick in big handicap chases on successive Saturdays for the jockey, followed by Nil Desperandum in the Eider at Newcastle and then Madison du Berlais in the vccasino.com Gold Cup at Newbury.

Heltornic (IRE) (ch.m. 2000)	Zaffaran (USA) (b 1985)	Assert (b 1979)	Be My Guest
			Irish Bird
		Sweet Alliance (b 1974)	Sir Ivor
			Mrs Peterkin
	Majestic Run (b 1985)	Deep Run (ch 1966)	Pampered King
			Trial By Fire
		Brickeendown (br 1979)	Bargello
			Killala Bay

It's fair to say that Heltornic's sire and dam were well acquainted, as Majestic Run visited Zaffaran every year for nine seasons after being retired to stud in

1992. Heltornic, in 2000, was the result of what turned out to be their final mating (Zaffaran died the following year but Majestic Run has since had foals by other sires) and their earlier matches yielded three other winners, all of them mares as well. The tail-swishing Glenmoss Tara was best of the three, progressing from being a useful bumper performer into a fairly useful novice hurdler. Zaffaran Express and Zaffaran Run were fair winning hurdlers, the latter, trained in Ireland and one to treat with caution, also a winning pointer and successful in bumpers. None of Heltornic's sisters were tried over long distances, though the Nicky Richards-trained duo Glenmoss Tara and Zaffaran Express gave the impression they would have stayed three miles. Majestic Run was very lightly raced with Martin Pipe, though beat two other finishers to win a poor novice hurdle on hard ground at Exeter over two miles and a furlong when ridden by Peter Scudamore—who, of course, is Michael's son and Tom's father. Grandam Brickeendown was successful in a bumper and a two-mile maiden hurdle in Ireland. The workmanlike Heltornic's future no doubt lies at stud in due course. She stays at least three and a half miles and acts well on heavy going, though her prominent showing at Cheltenham suggests she's not dependent on testing conditions. Heltornic was no better than fair as a novice over hurdles and she became lazy, but switching to fences in the latest season seemed to wake her ideas up, as well as bringing about a good deal of improvement in her form. She races prominently and, especially if she brushes up her jumping, she should enjoy further success in staying handicaps, with the Welsh National appealing as a suitable target. The Chepstow showpiece has been good to the Scudamore family down the years, Michael winning the race in 1957 during his riding days, as did Peter four times in the mid-'eighties and early-'nineties. *M. Scudamore*

HELVETIO 5 b.g. Theatrical – Personal Love (USA) (Diesis) [2006/7 16g³ Mar 17] useful on Flat (stays 2m), placed several times in 2006, sold out of A. de Royer Dupre's stable 82,000 gns Newmarket Autumn Sales: favourite, 13 lengths third to Daldini in maiden at Wetherby on hurdling debut. *Micky Hammond*   **h93 +**

HEMINGTON 4 gr.g. Shahrastani (USA) – Race To The Rhythm (Deep Run) [2006/7 F16g⁵ Apr 7] tall, leggy gelding: fourth foal: dam poor staying novice hurdler: modest form when fifth to Checkerboard in bumper at Haydock on debut. *M. Scudamore*   **F84**

HENBECK LADY (IRE) 5 b.m. Chickawicka (IRE) – Landsbury Lass (IRE) (Phardante (FR)) [2006/7 F16s F16g⁶ F16v F16v⁴ 16v⁵ 17g 17g Apr 20] first foal: dam runner-up in bumper: little impact in bumpers/novice hurdles. *Miss L. C. Siddall*   **h—**   **F—**

HENCHMAN 4 b.g. Anabaa (USA) – Gay Heroine (Caerleon (USA)) [2006/7 17g³ 17v³ 16v Jan 4] fair maiden on Flat (stays 1¼m): easily best effort in juvenile maiden hurdles (modest form) on debut: tried in cheekpieces. *Lady Herries*   **h88**

HENDRE HOTSHOT 5 b.m. Exit To Nowhere (USA) – Mutual Decision (IRE) (Supreme Leader) [2006/7 17m² 16g² 22g* Apr 1] second foal: dam placed in bumper/point: fair form in mares novice hurdles: runner-up twice prior to winning at Newton Abbot by 3½ lengths from Pyleigh Lady: stays 2¾m: raced on good/good to firm going. *J. W. Mullins*   **h108**

HENNESSY (IRE) 6 b.g. Presenting – Steel Grey Lady (IRE) (Roselier (FR)) [2006/7 F109: 16dF 17s⁵ Dec 1] has scope: useful form in bumpers: still to be asked for effort when fell 3 out in maiden on hurdling debut: only fifth in novice month later. *Carl Llewellyn*   **h88**

HENRIANJAMES 12 b.g. Tina's Pet – Real Claire (Dreams To Reality (USA)) [2006/7 c89+, h–: c16g⁶ c16m⁵ 16f⁶ c16f⁵ Jul 16] strong gelding: maiden hurdler: modest handicap chaser nowadays: raced around 2m: acts on firm and good to soft going. *K. G. Reveley*   **c92**   **h84**

HENRY HAMMOND (IRE) 12 b.g. Rashar (USA) – El-Caller (Callernish) [2006/7 c20sᵖᵘ 24vᵖᵘ Mar 15] workmanlike gelding: winning hurdler/chaser in Ireland: second in match on completed start in points in 2006: stays 3m: unraced on firm ground, probably acts on any other: effective with/without tongue strap. *Mrs H. O. Graham*   **c—**   **h—**

HENRY HENBIT 12 b.g. Henbit (USA) – Turn Mill (Latest Model) [2006/7 h–: 16dᵖᵘ May 21] winning pointer: no show in novice hurdles. *Mrs A. E. Brooks*   **h—**

HENRY HILL (IRE) 5 b.g. Beccari (USA) – Distinctly Lillie (IRE) (Distinctly North (USA)) [2006/7 F16m Mar 25] first foal: dam poor and untrustworthy maiden: tailed off in bumper on debut. *M. J. Gingell*   **F—**

HENRY'S PRIDE (IRE) 7 ch.g. Old Vic – Hightown Girl (IRE) (Over The River (FR)) [2006/7 c105, h–: c24v^{pu} c25s^6 c26v* c20g^3 c28g^3 Apr 7] angular gelding: fair chaser: left F. Jordan after second outing: didn't need to be at best to win novice at Warwick in February: stays 3½m: acts on heavy going. *R. Lee* **c101 h–**

HERAKLES (GER) 6 b.g. Lagunas – Haraka (FR) (Kahyasi) [2006/7 h121+: 22f^{pu} May 9] compact gelding: fairly useful hurdler: reportedly lame only outing in 2006/7: should stay 2¾m: acts on soft going. *N. J. Henderson* **h–**

HERALD ANGEL (FR) 4 b.g. Priolo (USA) – Heavenly Music (USA) (Seattle Song (USA)) [2006/7 16g^6 16s^{ur} 16g^6 17d Nov 16] good-topped gelding: brother to French hurdle winner around 2m Heaven Forbid and half-brother to fairly useful French 2m hurdle winner Heavenly Wings (by Sadler's Wells): placed 3 times on Flat prior to winning 14.5f claimer at Clairefontaine (claimed from J-C. Rouget €22,250) in August: let down by jumping in juvenile hurdles. *Miss Venetia Williams* **h– x**

HERALDRY (IRE) 7 b.g. Mark of Esteem (IRE) – Sorb Apple (IRE) (Kris) [2006/7 F108: 24g^{pu} 23v* Dec 2] workmanlike gelding: useful bumper winner: much better effort in novice hurdles 7 months apart when winning 16-runner event at Wetherby in December by 4 lengths from Allistathebarrista: stays 23f: acts on heavy going: open to further improvement. *P. C. Haslam* **h124 p**

HERBIE (IRE) 5 b.g. Good Thyne (USA) – Hamshire Gale (IRE) (Strong Gale) [2006/7 F16g^2 Mar 17] 30,000 4-y-o: half-brother to fair 2½m hurdler Optimus Prime (by Anshan): dam, poor maiden hurdler, sister to useful hurdler up to 3m Strontium: encouraging debut when 2 lengths second to Tazbar in bumper at Wetherby. *J. Howard Johnson* **F102**

HERCULES MORSE (IRE) 11 b.g. Spanish Place (USA) – Pragownia (Pragmatic) [2006/7 c21g* c25v^2 c24v^3 Mar 3] twice-raced over hurdles: modest chaser: won novice hunter at Folkestone in May: stays 25f: acts on heavy ground. *D. M. Grissell* **c87 h–**

HERE COMES CHOOSEY (IRE) 11 b. or br.g. Good Thyne (USA) – Bridgetown Girl (Al Sirat) [2006/7 c21g^{pu} Apr 9] maiden hurdler: poor pointer: no show in novice hunter on chase debut: blinkered last 3 starts. *Mrs T. H. Hayward* **c– h–**

HERE COMES HARRY 11 ch.g. Sunley Builds – Coole Dolly Day (Arctic Lord) [2006/7 h76: c25g^2 c21m^{ur} c25d^{pu} c21g^{ur} c20m* c21m^3 c23m^{pu} c20m^5 Sep 17] winning hurdler: poor chaser: won handicap at Uttoxeter in July: stays 25f: acts on good to firm going: tried in cheekpieces: has bled from nose. *C. J. Down* **c76 h–**

HERECOMESTANLEY 8 b.g. Missed Flight – Moonspell (Batshoof) [2006/7 c92, h94: c26g^3 c24d^2 c21d^{pu} c20m^{ur} c22g^F c24g^2 c21d* c21v* c24d^2 c23d^2 c21d* c21v^{pu} 18v^5 21s^3 c21g^2 c30g^5 c26g^5 Apr 7] good-topped gelding: modest hurdler: fair handicap chaser: much improved in 2006/7, won at Fakenham and Uttoxeter (novice) in October and Fakenham again in December: stays 3m: acts on heavy and good to firm going: usually wears hood: often let down by jumping. *M. F. Harris* **c113 x h92**

HEREDITARY 5 ch.g. Hernando (FR) – Eversince (USA) (Foolish Pleasure (USA)) [2006/7 h80: 16d^4 18s* 20s^2 18s* 20s^3 20d Mar 17] leggy gelding: fair hurdler: in cheekpieces, thrived in 2006/7, winning handicaps at Fontwell in December and February: stays 2½m: raced on going softer than good. *Mrs L. C. Jewell* **h112**

HERE'S JOHNNY (IRE) 8 ch.g. Presenting – Treble Base (IRE) (Orchestra) [2006/7 h99, F111: 20s^8 16v^2 19d^8 20s^4 24g 24s* Apr 26] rather leggy, close-coupled gelding: useful novice hurdler: won at Uttoxeter in October, Exeter in December and Perth (forged clear to beat Major Oak by 21 lengths) in April: stiff task, ran well when 24 lengths seventh to Wichita Lineman in Grade 2 at Cheltenham: stays 3m: acts on heavy ground. *V. R. A. Dartnall* **h130**

HERE TO ETERNITY (IRE) 6 b.g. In The Wings – Amnesty Bay (Thatching) [2006/7 F16m^4 F18v 21g 16m^6 17m^3 16g^4 Apr 27] stocky gelding: third foal: half-brother to smart sprinter Peace Offering (by Victory Note): dam 1m winner: won maiden point in 2006: bought 6,000 gns Doncaster May Sales: poor form in bumpers/maiden hurdles: should be suited by further than 17f. *C. J. Down* **h80 F64**

HERIOT 6 b.g. Hamas (IRE) – Sure Victory (IRE) (Stalker) [2006/7 h–§: 22g 19g May 17] compact gelding: little form on Flat/over hurdles: tried in headgear: often tongue tied: ungenuine: sold £3,300 Ascot August Sales. *S. C. Burrough* **h– §**

HERMANO CORDOBES (IRE) 7 b.g. Un Desperado (FR) – Queens Tricks (Le Bavard (FR)) [2006/7 h89: 23m^2 19v^5 20d^5 23s^{pu} Oct 27] poor novice hurdler: stays 23f: acts on good to firm and good to soft ground. *Mrs J. R. Buckley* **h78**

HERNE BAY (IRE) 7 b.g. Hernando (FR) – Charita (IRE) (Lycius (USA)) [2006/7 **h109** h111: 22s 19d 22d* 22m^{pu} Mar 31] leggy gelding: fair handicap hurdler: form in 2006/7 only when winning at Stratford in March: stays 2¾m: acts on firm and good to soft ground. *R. S. Brookhouse*

HERNINSKI 4 b.f. Hernando (FR) – Empress Dagmar (Selkirk (USA)) [2006/7 17g **h59** 16d 16g^5 16v 17m^3 Apr 15] leggy, angular filly: modest on Flat at 2 yrs when trained by P. Haslam: little form since, including over hurdles. *M. C. Chapman*

HERO AGAIN (IRE) 7 b.g. Oscar (IRE) – The Brass Well (Carlingford Castle) **h110** [2006/7 21d* 22s^2 20f^{pu} Aug 22] ex-Irish gelding: fair hurdler: left R. O'Leary, improved form when winning maiden at Towcester in May, idling/carrying head awkwardly: bled final outing: probably stays 2¾m: raced mainly on going softer than good. *Jonjo O'Neill*

HERONS COVE (IRE) 8 b.g. Top of The World – Rathsallagh (Mart Lane) [2006/7 **c–** h–, F79: c25s^F Feb 27] second in bumper: no show otherwise (including in points). **h–** *B. D. Leavy*

HERON'S FLIGHT (IRE) 5 b. or br.g. Heron Island (IRE) – Beau's Trout (Beau **h123 +** Charmeur (FR)) [2006/7 F16s^2 F16s^5 16v* 16v* Mar 11] €22,000 3-y-o: fourth **F110** foal: half-brother to fair hurdler/fairly useful chaser Lord of The Flies (by Lord Americo), stayed 21f, and fair chaser Sierra Bay (by Castle Keep), stayed 2½m: dam unraced half-sister to useful staying chaser Gay Return: progressive form in bumpers, winning 25-runner maiden at Fairyhouse in December by neck from Tranquil Sea: likewise over hurdles, successful in maiden at Punchestown (beat Montana Bay 2½ lengths) in January and novice at Naas (by length from Earth Magic) in March: will stay at least 2½m: raced on going softer than good. *N. Meade, Ireland*

HEROS COLLONGES (FR) 12 b.g. Dom Alco (FR) – Carmen Collonges (FR) **c–** (Olmeto) [2006/7 c134, h94: c27s^{pu} c29s^{pu} c30s^{pu} c20s^{pu} c24g^{pu} Mar 29] tall, good- **h–** topped gelding: lightly raced over hurdles: useful chaser on his day: no form in 2006/7, left P. Nicholls after first outing: stays 25f: raced on good going or softer: tried visored: weak finisher. *Mrs N. Macauley*

HE'S A STAR 5 ch.g. Mark of Esteem (IRE) – Sahara Belle (USA) (Sanglamore **h–** (USA)) [2006/7 h87: 16g^5 Mar 16] close-coupled gelding: fair on Flat (stays 2m): modest form in juvenile hurdles for Gay Kelleway, well held only outing in 2006/7. *Mrs S. J. Humphrey*

HE'S HOT RIGHT NOW (NZ) 8 b.g. Pentire – Philadelphia Fox (NZ) (Dahar **c–** (USA)) [2006/7 c84d, h98d: c17g c16g^6 c16g^F May 14] sturdy gelding: winning hurdler/ **h–** maiden chaser, no form in 2006/7: raced around 2m: acts on good to soft going, probably on firm: wears headgear: tried tongue tied: sold 900 gns Doncaster March Sales. *R. C. Guest*

HE'S MY BROTHER (IRE) 5 ch.g. Lahib (USA) – Bobby's Dream (Reference **F–** Point) [2006/7 F16m F17m^{pu} Apr 17] 1,500 3-y-o: third foal: dam, staying maiden on Flat, once-raced over hurdles: no show in points/bumpers. *Mrs L. J. Young*

HE'S THE BIZ (FR) 8 b.g. Nikos – Irun (FR) (Son of Silver) [2006/7 c94x, h–: c26d^6 **c102** c23m* c23m c26d* c23m^2 c21s^6 c27f^4 c23m^6 Apr 15] good-topped gelding: winning **h–** hurdler: fair handicap chaser: jumped better in 2006/7, winning at Worcester in July and Newton Abbot in August: stays 3¼m: acts on good to firm and good to soft going, probably on soft: has flashed tail. *Nick Williams*

HE'S THE BOSS (IRE) 10 b.g. Supreme Leader – Attykee (IRE) (Le Moss) [2006/7 **c–** c22s^{pu} c20v^R Feb 24] workmanlike gelding: fairly useful over hurdles at one time: novice **h–** chaser, off 2 years prior to return: stays 21f: raced on good going or softer: tried blinkered. *R. H. Buckler*

HE'S THE GAFFER (IRE) 7 b.g. Oscar (IRE) – Miss Henrietta (IRE) (Step **c118** Together (USA)) [2006/7 c102, h86: c19g^5 c19d^3 c26s^2 c22s* c21g^F c22s^3 c21g* c21g^5 **h–** c16g^5 Apr 19] lengthy gelding: maiden hurdler: fairly useful handicap chaser: won at Fontwell (conditional jockeys) in December and Wincanton (beat Free Gift by 3½ lengths) in March: ran well when fifth to Stern at Ascot penultimate outing: stays 3¼m: acts on soft and good to firm going: blinkered. *R. H. Buckler*

HESTHERELAD (IRE) 8 b.g. Definite Article – Unbidden Melody (USA) **h–** (Chieftain) [2006/7 h75: 22m^4 17d^5 21m Aug 29] maiden hurdler: stays 2½m: tried in cheekpieces: tongue tied last 2 starts. *R. Johnson*

HEVER ROAD (IRE) 8 ch.g. Anshan – The Little Bag (True Song) [2006/7 c124§, **c104 §** h–§: c20m^{pu} c24d^{pu} c31d c25g^5 c24g^6 Apr 21] tall gelding: handicap chaser, well below **h– §**

best in 2006/7 (runner-up in point in February): stays 3¼m: best efforts on good/good to soft ground: often wears headgear: ungenuine. *D. Pearson*

HEVERSHAM (IRE) 6 b.g. Octagonal (NZ) – Saint Ann (USA) (Geiger Counter (USA)) [2006/7 h75: 20d 22f* 23d⁵ 22g⁵ 22m⁶ Jul 20] modest novice hurdler: won handicap at Kelso in May: stays 2¾m: acts on firm ground: wears cheekpieces/blinkers. *J. Hetherton*   **h89**

HEY BOY (IRE) 8 b.g. Courtship – Make Me An Island (Creative Plan (USA)) [2006/7 c97d, h–: c24dᵘʳ Nov 8] maiden hurdler/chaser, modest form at best: stays 21f. *Mrs S. J. Humphrey*   **c–** **h–**

HEY CHARLIE (IRE) 5 b.g. Mister Mat (FR) – Reynards Run (Kemal (FR)) [2006/7 F16v² Feb 27] €15,000 4-y-o: good-bodied gelding: sixth foal: dam unraced: encouraging debut when 6 lengths second to Massasoit in maiden bumper at Catterick. *N. G. Richards*   **F95**

HEYNEWBOY 7 ch.g. Keen – Clown Around (True Song) [2006/7 F86: F13m³ F17g⁴ Aug 26] third on second of 2 starts in points in 2006: fair form in bumpers. *J. W. Mullins*   **F83**

HEY YOU M'LADY 7 b.m. Sovereign Water (FR) – Sea Countess (Ercolano (USA)) [2006/7 h–, F–: 26dᵖᵘ May 17] no sign of ability. *J. Rudge*   **h–**

HIALEAH 6 ch.g. Bal Harbour – Tommys Dream (Le Bavard (FR)) [2006/7 c–, h86, F78: c17g 17m Sep 26] lengthy gelding: novice hurdler: no form over fences, sold out of M. Easterby's stable 2,200 gns Doncaster May Sales after first outing. *Robert Gray*   **c–** **h–**

HIAWATHA (IRE) 8 b.g. Danehill (USA) – Hi Bettina (Henbit (USA)) [2006/7 h–: 16m² 16g⁵ 16f³ 16m³ 16g 16g³ Apr 22] smallish gelding: modest on Flat (stays 1½m): modest maiden hurdler: raced around 2m: acts on firm going. *A. M. Hales*   **h92**

HIBERNIAN (IRE) 7 br.g. Supreme Leader – Tullahought (Jaazeiro (USA)) [2006/7 h114: 22g c16sᵖᵘ c16s² c21s³ c24g⁴* Mar 16] strong, rangy gelding: novice hurdler: fair chaser: won maiden at Fakenham in March: stays 3m: raced on good ground or softer (acts on soft): has often shaped as if having a physical problem. *O. Sherwood*   **c104** **h–**

HI BLUE 8 b.g. Weld – Winnie Lorraine (St Columbus) [2006/7 c–, h–, F–: c19sᵖᵘ c22dᵖᵘ c24gᵖᵘ c25f³ Apr 5] no sign of ability: left R. Dickin after second outing: tried blinkered. *J. W. Stevenson*   **c–** **h–**

HICKORY LANE 5 b.g. Slip Anchor – Popping On (Sonnen Gold) [2006/7 F16v⁴ Dec 11] ninth foal: half-brother to useful hurdler Just Nip (by Lord Bud), stayed 3m, and fair hurdler up to 27f Top On (by Dunbeath): dam won 2½m hurdle: shaped as if in need of experience when fourth to Berwick Law in bumper at Ayr on debut. *J. R. Turner*   **F70**

HI CLOY (IRE) 10 b.g. Be My Native (USA) – Thomastown Girl (Tekoah) [2006/7 c157, h–: 16s⁶ c20v⁵ c17v³ c20s² c24v³ c21g⁶ c20g⁵ c25gᵖᵘ Apr 25] well-made gelding: winning hurdler: smart chaser in 2006/7, best efforts when second to Forget The Past in slowly-run Grade 2 at Thurles and sixth to Taranis (FR) in Festival Trophy at Cheltenham: ran poorly in Grade 1s at Aintree and Punchestown last 2 outings: effective around 2m to 25f, at least when conditions aren't testing: raced on good going or softer (below form on heavy): usually held up: very sound jumper. *M. Hourigan, Ireland*   **c151** **h119 +**

HI DANCER 4 b.g. Medicean – Sea Music (Inchinor) [2006/7 17m² 16m* 17g³ 16d⁵ 17d³ 16s³ 17s* 16v² 16v* Mar 12] modest on Flat (stays 11f): fairly useful juvenile hurdler: won at Stratford in July, Hereford (conditional jockeys handicap) in December and Plumpton (claimer, easily landed odds) in March: raced around 2m: acts on good to firm and heavy ground: front runner/races prominently: consistent. *P. C. Haslam*   **h112**

HIDDENFORTUNE (IRE) 7 b. or br.g. Denel (FR) – Hidden Play (IRE) (Seclude (USA)) [2006/7 h–, F74: 20s 22d 16v c25vᵖᵘ c16s c16v⁵ c20v⁵ c16g⁴ c20sᵘʳ Apr 27] quite good-topped gelding: winning pointer: no form over hurdles: poor maiden chaser: should stay beyond 2m. *Miss Lucinda V. Russell*   **c67** **h–**

HIDDEN JEM (IRE) 7 b.g. Un Desperado (FR) – Melody Gayle VII (Damsire Unregistered) [2006/7 F16v F16d 24mᵖᵘ 24m⁶ Apr 15] €28,000 3-y-o: half-brother to fair hurdler/chaser The Full Monty (by Montelimar) and fairly useful hunter Chism (by Euphemism), both of whom stayed 25f: dam unraced: no form in bumpers (for Ms F. Crowley) or over hurdles. *Jonjo O'Neill*   **h–** **F–**

HIDDEN LEGEND (IRE) 6 b.g. Aahsaylad – Hidden Play (IRE) (Seclude (USA)) [2006/7 c20sᵖᵘ c25gᵖᵘ Apr 2] third foal: half-brother to winning pointers by Denel and Jamesmead: dam placed once over hurdles: no form in 2 bumpers for C. McBratney or in maiden hurdles, though did win maiden Irish point in February. *F. P. Murtagh*   **c–**

HIDDENSEE (USA) 5 b.g. Cozzene (USA) – Zarani Sidi Anna (USA) (Danzig (USA)) [2006/7 21g Mar 20] fairly useful but temperamental on Flat (should be suited by 2m+) in 2006, sold out of M. Johnston's stable 38,000 gns Newmarket July Sales: mistakes when well held in maiden on hurdling debut: should do better. *M. Wigham* **h72 p**

HIDDEN SMILE (USA) 10 b.m. Twilight Agenda (USA) – Smooth Edge (USA) (Meadowlake (USA)) [2006/7 h62: 19g⁶ 16m Jun 8] tall mare: little form over hurdles: tried in cheekpieces: often tongue tied. *John R. Upson* **h–**

HIDDEN TALENTS (IRE) 7 b.g. Arctic Lord – Cherry Avenue (King's Ride) [2006/7 21sᵖᵘ Mar 11] €42,000 4-y-o: half-brother to modest hurdler/chaser Cherry Tart (by Persian Mews), stayed 2½m: dam unraced, out of sister to Irish Grand National winner Colebridge: form over hurdles only when winning maiden at Limerick in 2005/6: left M. Morris and off 10½ months prior to only outing in 2006/7: stays 19f: acts on soft going. *Jonjo O'Neill* **h–**

HIDE THE EVIDENCE (IRE) 6 ch.g. Carroll House – Andarta (Ballymore) [2006/7 F16dᵖᵘ F16s F16m² 18d* 16s* 16g* 16v* 16d 16d 16m⁴ Apr 24] **h130 F94**

Hide The Evidence, who saw the racecourse just once before the latest season, when shaping with promise in a bumper at Tramore, experienced a busy time of things in 2006/7 and developed into a useful hurdler. The highlight of his campaign came when winning the Grade 1 Bar-One Racing Royal Bond Novices' Hurdle at Fairyhouse in December by six lengths from Clopf. The Royal Bond regularly proves a good guide to the best of the Irish novices and many considered that the highly-regarded Clopf, who was sent off at odds on, was the one most likely to take high rank among the season's novices. In a first-time tongue strap, however, Hide The Evidence took the rise in class in his stride, travelling smoothly throughout, ridden more patiently than previously, and was soon in control once shaken up. Those patient tactics were arguably significant as he was covered up for longer than several of his rivals in a race that was run in gale-force winds (the remainder of the card was abandoned). A further step up in class proved beyond him when, again tongue tied, he managed only seventh of eight (beaten around twenty lengths) behind Hardy Eustace in the AIG Europe Champion Hurdle at Leopardstown in January. Hide The Evidence had pulled extremely hard under restraint that day and also failed to settle during the early stages of the Supreme Novices' Hurdle at Cheltenham next time (for which he was 9/1 third choice), unable to hold his place as the race took shape from the fifth and managing only a lowly fifteenth behind Ebaziyan. Hide The Evidence appeared slightly light in condition at Cheltenham and, although not disgraced on form, again gave the impression a busy season had caught up with him when seven and a half lengths fourth to Clopf in the two-mile Champion Novices' Hurdle at Punchestown in April. The tongue strap was left off for those final two starts, incidentally.

Bar-One Racing Royal Bond Novices' Hurdle, Fairyhouse—
Hide The Evidence (noseband) benefits from patient tactics as he defeats Clopf in gale-force conditions

Mr Maynard Hamilton's "Hide The Evidence"

After showing fair form when runner-up in two of his four starts in bumpers (suspected to be lame when pulled up early at Down Royal on his first 2006/7 outing), Hide The Evidence had made a fine start to his hurdling career, winning a two-and-a-quarter-mile maiden at Downpatrick in August by a wide margin before following up in two-mile novices at Roscommon (beat Bobs Pride a length and three quarters) and Cork in the space of two weeks in October, for the last-named success making all under a shrewd ride by Ireland's champion conditional jockey Andrew Leigh, who has partnered Hide The Evidence on all his starts over hurdles.

Hide The Evidence (Ire) (ch.g. 2001)	Carroll House (ch 1985)	Lord Gayle (b 1965)	Sir Gaylord
			Sticky Case
		Tuna (ch 1969)	Silver Shark
			Vimelette
	Andarta (b 1980)	Ballymore (b 1969)	Ragusa
			Paddy's Sister
		Saintliness (gr 1975)	St Alphage
			Contrail

It would come as no surprise to see the unfurnished Hide The Evidence sent novice chasing in 2007/8, and he looks more than capable of making his mark in that sphere. His dam's eighth and final foal, Hide The Evidence is the third winning son produced by the maiden Flat performer Andarta. He is closely related to the Nigel Twiston-Davies-trained Knowhere (by Lord Americo), who showed useful form in winning both his starts in novice hurdles in 2004/5 and reached a similar level over fences in the first part of the latest season before rather losing his way. Knowhere stays at least twenty-one furlongs. Hide The Evidence is also a half-brother to the fair winning hurdler at around two and a half miles Pingo Hill (by Salt Dome). Hide The Evidence, who acts on heavy and good to firm going, has mostly been raced at around two miles, but he should stay two and a half, particularly if he learns to settle better. *Mrs J. Harrington, Ireland*

HIERS DE BROUAGE (FR) 12 b.g. Neustrien (FR) – Thalandrezienne (FR) (Le Correzien (FR)) [2006/7 c99, h–: c23d^{pu} c19m^4 c19v* c21g^{pu} c19d^2 Feb 2] tall, rangy gelding: modest handicap chaser: won at Chepstow in November for second successive year: barely stays 3m: acts on heavy and good to firm going: wears cheekpieces: usually tongue tied: has been let down by jumping/shaped as if amiss. *J. G. Portman* — c96 h–

HI FI 9 b.g. Homo Sapien – Baroness Orkzy (Baron Blakeney) [2006/7 c98, h98: 16g c24d^2 c24d^6 c27g^5 c25f^3 Apr 22] leggy gelding: winning hurdler: handicap chaser, on downgrade: best form up to 2½m: acts on soft ground: tried blinkered. *Ian Williams* — c84 h–

HIGGYS PRINCE 5 b.g. Prince Sabo – Themeda (Sure Blade (USA)) [2006/7 16m 20m^{pu} Aug 11] showed more temperament than ability on Flat for D. Flood: no show over hurdles. *R. Curtis* — h–

HIGH AMBITION 4 b.g. High Estate – So Ambitious (Teenoso (USA)) [2006/7 F14g^5 F14v Dec 2] angular gelding: second foal: dam unraced: better effort in 3-y-o bumpers when fifth at Warwick: fair form on Flat, successful over 7f in April. *P. W. D'Arcy* — F83

HIGHBAND 4 b.f. Band On The Run – Barkston Singer (Runnett) [2006/7 18s Dec 23] well held in maidens on Flat and juvenile on hurdling debut. *M. Madgwick* — h–

HIGH BOUNCE (USA) 7 ch.g. Trempolino (USA) – Top Hope (High Top) [2006/7 16s Jan 10] compact gelding: no sign of ability: tried tongue tied. *R. J. Hodges* — h–

HIGH CALIBRE (IRE) 6 b.g. Definite Article – Pidgeon Bay (IRE) (Perugino (USA)) [2006/7 F95+: F16s^3 F16s^5 17s^5 16v^5 17g c16d^6 c16s* c16g^3 c20f^2 Apr 5] lengthy, good-topped gelding: placed in bumpers: not unduly knocked about in novice hurdles: took well to chasing, winning novice handicaps at Folkestone and Catterick (fair form, beat Aviation by ½ length with something to spare) in January: stays 2½m: acts on firm and soft ground. *Jonjo O'Neill* — c108 h89 F91

HIGH CAROL (IRE) 5 ch.g. Presenting – Madam Chloe (Dalsaan) [2006/7 F16m^3 F16d Feb 17] 26,000 3-y-o, 36,000 4-y-o: rather unfurnished gelding: sixth foal: half-brother to fair hurdler Instan (by Insan), stayed 2¾m, and poor 2m hurdler Austocon (by Be My Native): dam unraced: easily better effort in bumpers when third to Gun Smith at Ludlow. *Andrew Turnell* — F85

HIGH CHIMES (IRE) 8 b.g. Naheez (USA) – Forward Gal (The Parson) [2006/7 c20v^3 c19s^F c16m^5 c24v* Mar 10] good-topped gelding: sixth foal: brother to fair hurdler around 2m Reisk Superman and half-brother to 2½m hurdle winner Sancta Miria (by Toulon): dam winning pointer/hunter chaser: won maiden Irish point in 2004: fairly useful form in chases: upped in trip, confirmed earlier promise when winning 2-finisher maiden at Chepstow by distance: stays 3m: acts on heavy going: remains open to improvement. *Evan Williams* — c123 p

HIGH CLASS PET 7 b.m. Petong – What A Pet (Mummy's Pet) [2006/7 h73: 17d^{pu} May 31] poor maiden hurdler: tried blinkered: ungenuine. *F. P. Murtagh* — h– §

HIGH COMMISSION 7 ch.g. Bob's Return (IRE) – Florencebray (Rymer) [2006/7 F16s^4 19s^6 16v^6 17s 20g Apr 11] good-topped gelding: third foal: dam poor pointer: fourth of 8 in bumper at Uttoxeter: little impact over hurdles: bred to be suited by 2½m+. *H. D. Daly* — h74 F73

HIGH COTTON (IRE) 12 gr.g. Ala Hounak – Planalife (Beau Charmeur (FR)) [2006/7 c115§, h–: c26s c32s^3 c33g^4 c30g^3 c32m Apr 21] strong gelding: fairly useful but irresolute maiden chaser (in frame 23 of 27 completed starts): suited by 3m+: acts on heavy going: blinkered once. *K. G. Reveley* — c113 § h–

HIGH COUNTRY (IRE) 7 b.g. Danehill (USA) – Dance Date (IRE) (Sadler's Wells (USA)) [2006/7 h95: 20m^3 22g 20f 21m* 21m^5 21d^6 20g 20g Apr 3] fair handicap hurdler: won at Sedgefield in August: well beaten most other starts in 2006/7: stays 21f: acts on good to firm going. *Micky Hammond* — h101

HIGH DELIGHT 7 b.g. Dancing High – Dunrowan (Dunbeath (USA)) [2006/7 F–: F16m 20g Dec 20] no impact in bumpers/novice hurdle: tongue tied on debut: takes strong hold. *W. Amos* — h– F–

HIGH DYKE 5 b.g. Mujahid (USA) – Gold Linnet (Nashwan (USA)) [2006/7 h–: 20g^{rtr} Sep 6] shaped like non-stayer in juvenile hurdles: left K. Ryan, refused to race only outing in 2006/7 (as he did last 3 starts on Flat): one to avoid. *Miss P. Robson* — h– §

HIGH EXPECTATIONS (IRE) 12 ch.g. Over The River (FR) – Andy's Fancy   c77
(IRE) (Andretti) [2006/7 c82: c25f³ c25g c25s⁴ c25v³ c25g² c25g⁶ Apr 15] workmanlike
gelding: winning pointer: modest maiden hunter: stays 25f: acts on heavy going.
J. S. Haldane

HIGH FIVE 7 ch.g. Dancing High – Political Diamond (Politico (USA)) [2006/7 c–,   c78 x
h–, F–: c24vᵖᵘ c25sꟳ c25s³ c32vᵘʳ c27m⁴ c27g³ Apr 23] runner-up on completed start   h–
in points: little form over hurdles/in chases (has been badly let down by jumping):
blinkered/in cheekpieces last 5 starts. *S. G. Waugh*

HIGH FREQUENCY (IRE) 6 ch.g. Grand Lodge (USA) – Freak Out (FR) (Bering)   h79
[2006/7 22m⁴ 22d⁵ 20s 23gᵖᵘ Apr 3] smallish, good-bodied gelding: modest up to 2m on
Flat, successful in May, claimed from T. D. Barron £6,000 following month: poor form
over hurdles: stays 2¾m: tried in cheekpieces. *A. Crook*

HIGH GEAR (IRE) 9 br.g. Accordion – Holly Grove Lass (Le Moss) [2006/7 c97§,   c104 §
h98§: 22g² 27m³ 27d² c23m³ 22m² 26g5 Oct 3] fair handicap hurdler/chaser, in frame 19   h105 §
of 21 completed starts: stays 27f: unraced on heavy ground, acts on any other: usually
wears headgear: consistent, but no easy ride. *Jonjo O'Neill*

HIGHGLEN (IRE) 8 b.g. Old Vic – Nil Faic (IRE) (King's Ride) [2006/7 c23s³ c20g²   c104 x
c22g⁴ Apr 10] useful-looking gelding: winning hurdler: left P. Fahy, fair form first 2 starts   h–
over fences: stays 23f: acts on soft going: none too fluent over fences. *P. Bowen*

HIGH HOPE (FR) 9 ch.g. Lomitas – Highness Lady (GER) (Cagliostro (GER))   h107
[2006/7 h107: 21s* 23v⁶ 21sᵖᵘ Mar 2] leggy gelding: on downgrade on Flat: fair hurdler:
won claimer at Plumpton in November: stays 21f: acts on soft ground: blinkered in
2006/7. *G. L. Moore*

HIGH JACK (IRE) 5 b.g. Supreme Leader – Pharisee (IRE) (Phardante (FR)) [2006/7   h81
17d 16v 16d² Mar 26] big, deep-girthed gelding: chasing type: brother to smart hunter
chaser Caught At Dawn, stays 4m, and half-brother to fairly useful 2½m chasers Kew
Jumper and Bible Lord (both by Mister Lord): dam unraced: first form over hurdles when
second to easy winner Spirit of New York in novice at Stratford: bred to be suited by
2½m+. *Andrew Turnell*

HIGHLAND BRIG 11 b.g. Homo Sapien – Birniebrig (New Brig) [2006/7 c79: c25g²   c79
May 13] leggy, lengthy gelding: poor chaser: will stay beyond 25f: acts on good to firm
and heavy going: tried in cheekpieces/tongue tied. *T. Butt*

HIGHLAND CHIEF (IRE) 7 b. or br.g. Taipan (IRE) – Catatonia (IRE) (Cataldi)   c82
[2006/7 c–, h98*, F95: c19s c18d³ c24s⁶ c24s⁵ c22s² c19g⁵ Mar 29] rangy gelding: h–
novice hurdler: poor maiden chaser: stays 3m: acts on soft going (form in bumper on
good to firm): in cheekpieces last 4 starts: has found little. *Miss H. C. Knight*

HIGHLAND GAMES (IRE) 7 b.g. Singspiel (IRE) – Highland Gift (IRE) (Gene-   h117
rous) (IRE)) [2006/7 h–: 17d⁴ 20m³ 19m² 24s⁴ 21v* 20v³ 24s* 24g⁴ 21f² Apr 5] quite
good-topped gelding: fairly useful hurdler, sold out of P. Webber's stable 16,000 gns
Doncaster October Sales after third start: much improved after, winning handicaps at
Sedgefield in January and Ludlow (by 2½ lengths from Xellance) in March: stays 3m:
acts on any ground: tried visored: usually tongue tied for previous stable. *Evan Williams*

HIGH LIFE 5 br.m. Kayf Tara – By Line (High Line) [2006/7 h86+: F16g⁵ F17v² 17s²   h105
21s³ 16s³ 16g² 17g* 17g³ Apr 20] compact mare: in frame in bumpers: fair hurdler: won   F87
mares maiden at Newton Abbot in April: should stay beyond 17f: raced on good going or
softer. *A. King*

HIGH MOON (USA) 11 b.g. Alleged (USA) – Eclipse de Lune (USA) (Shahrastani   c–
(USA)) [2006/7 24g c20m⁴ Apr 9] prolific winner over jumps in France: left P. Cottin, no   h–
show 2 starts in Britain: stays 23f: acts on heavy ground: has worn blinkers/cheekpieces.
Paul Murphy

HIGH MOOR 5 b.g. Vitus – Pyewacket (Belfort (FR)) [2006/7 F77: 23vᵖᵘ 16v 16g   h–
Mar 17] sturdy gelding: in frame in bumpers: off 8 months, no show in maiden hurdles:
tried in cheekpieces. *J. D. Bethell*

HIGH RANK 8 b.g. Emperor Jones (USA) – Hotel Street (USA) (Alleged (USA))   c84
[2006/7 c86, h–: c20gᶠ c19d⁵ c20m² c21mᵖᵘ c24g⁵ Apr 8] tall, close-coupled gelding: h–
maiden hurdler/chaser, poor form over fences in 2006/7: sold out of J. Mackie's stable
£5,000 Ascot August Sales before final outing: successful in point in March: stays 21f:
best effort on good to soft going: tried in cheekpieces: has had tongue tied. *Andrew
J. Martin*

HIGH SEASONS 4 b.g. Fantastic Light (USA) – El Hakma (Shareef Dancer (USA)) **h–**
[2006/7 16g 17d Nov 16] fair on Flat (stays 1¼m): not fluent when well beaten in juvenile
hurdles. *B. R. Millman*

HIGH STAND LAD 5 gr.g. Rock City – Snowys Pet (Petong) [2006/7 16s² 23sᵖᵘ **h90**
Feb 17] second foal: half-brother to 2½m chase winner Whatcanyasay (by Prince
Daniel): dam unraced: 100/1, 8 lengths second to Raining Horse in maiden hurdle at
Newcastle on debut: much stiffer task next time. *I. McMath*

HIGH TOBY 8 b.g. Dancing High – Henny Penny (Le Coq d'Or) [2006/7 21s⁶ 22dᵖᵘ **h–**
16v⁶ 16v⁶ 19d Mar 21] 5,000 5-y-o, £2,000 7-y-o: sturdy gelding: sixth foal: dam maiden
sister to good staying chasers Strands of Gold and Canny Danny: no form over hurdles.
R. H. York

HIGHTORI 7 ch.g. Topanoora – High 'b' (Gunner B) [2006/7 20g⁵ 20g³ Jun 1] €9,000 **h97 p**
4-y-o, 4,800 5-y-o: third foal: dam unraced daughter of useful staying chaser Highfrith:
shaped with promise in novice hurdles, still green when third to Mr Strachan at Wetherby:
looked capable of better, but not seen out again. *Mrs S. J. Smith*

HIGH WINDOW (IRE) 7 b.g. King's Theatre (IRE) – Kayradja (IRE) (Last Tycoon) **h–**
[2006/7 h–: 16g 16m 16mᵖᵘ Jul 2] tall gelding: no form over hurdles. *G. P. Kelly*

HIHO SILVER LINING 6 gr.m. Silver Patriarch (IRE) – By Line (High Line) **h86**
[2006/7 h–, F96: 16v⁶ 20v³ 19d³ Mar 21] rather leggy mare: modest novice hurdler: stays
2½m: acts on heavy going: sold 21,000 gns Doncaster May Sales. *W. J. Musson*

HI HUMPFREE 7 b.g. Thowra (FR) – White Flash (Sure Blade (USA)) [2006/7 h86: **h118**
24d* 22m* 22d⁴ 24gᵖᵘ 24g⁵ Apr 19] stocky gelding: fairly useful hurdler: much
improved in 2006/7, winning novice handicaps at Aintree in May and Stratford (beat
Longueville Manor easily by 4 lengths) in June: good fourth to Rushneeyriver in valuable
handicap at Newton Abbot: stays 3m: acts on good to firm and good to soft going:
blinkered last 7 starts: front runner. *Heather Dalton*

HILAL 5 gr.g. Linamix (FR) – Magnificent Star (USA) (Silver Hawk (USA)) [2006/7 **F–**
F16v Nov 26] good-topped gelding: brother to fairly useful 1¾m winner Patrixprial and
half-brother to winning hurdler/chaser Profiler (by Capote), stayed 2½m, and 2m hurdle
winner Sir Alfred (by Royal Academy): dam won Yorkshire Oaks: soon off bridle when
well held in bumper on debut. *C. R. Egerton*

HI LAURIE (IRE) 12 gr.m. Roselier (FR) – Oh June (Le Bavard (FR)) [2006/7 c97, **c–**
h95: 24gᵖᵘ 19d 27d³ 22gᵖᵘ 21sᵖᵘ 16s 24v⁶ 20vᵖᵘ 20v 17g⁴ 20g Apr 14] angular mare: **h83 d**
winning chaser/hurdler, little form in 2006/7: left M. Scudamore after fourth start: stays
3m: acts on any going: usually front runner. *Mrs P. Ford*

HILL CLOUD 5 gr.g. Cloudings (IRE) – Hill Farm Dancer (Gunner B) [2006/7 F16d⁵ **F87**
F17v⁵ Jan 11] first foal: dam 1½m winner: better effort in bumpers when fifth to
Appleaday at Ludlow on debut. *W. M. Brisbourne*

HILLCREST (NZ) 8 b.g. Danasinga (AUS) – Centafair (NZ) (Centaine (AUS)) **c106**
[2006/7 h96: 16g 21s³ 23v⁵ 20d 20g⁴ 24m* Apr 10] sturdy gelding: modest maiden **h98**
hurdler: better effort in handicap chases (fair form) when winning at Chepstow in April
by length from Lizzie Bathwick: stays 3m: acts on soft and good to firm going. *Ian
Williams*

HILL FORTS HENRY 9 ch.g. Karinga Bay – Maggie Tee (Lepanto (GER)) [2006/7 **c67 §**
c70§, h73§: 22m⁶ 22m⁴ c26g* Oct 30] poor handicap hurdler/chaser: won novice **h73 §**
handicap over fences at Plumpton in October: stays 3¼m: acts on firm and soft going:
tried visored/usually wears cheekpieces: has had tongue tied (including at Plumpton): has
refused twice, and one to treat with caution. *J. W. Mullins*

HILL FORTS TIMMY 7 b.g. Thowra (FR) – Queen of The Suir (IRE) (Carlingford **h109**
Castle) [2006/7 h106, F96: 19m⁴ 16d* 19m³ 19m 19d³ 24s⁴ 20v² 22dᵘʳ 20g⁴ 20gᵖᵘ
Apr 20] good-topped gelding: fair novice hurdler: won at Towcester in June: should stay
3m: acts on any going: consistent. *J. W. Mullins*

HILLRIDGE 4 ch.g. Fumo di Londra (IRE) – Josifina (Master Willie) [2006/7 F16g* **F90**
Mar 21] fourth foal: dam fair 2m hurdler: successful debut when beating Chevy To The
Levy a short head in bumper at Chepstow. *B. De Haan*

HILLS OF ARAN 5 b.g. Sadler's Wells (USA) – Danefair (Danehill (USA)) [2006/7 **h123**
16m⁴ 17g 19v³ 20s² 20s² 21v³ 20v⁵ 23s³ 21g 21g³ Mar 23] compact gelding: fairly useful
winner around 9f at 2 yrs, left A. O'Brien and well held on Flat in Britain in 2006: fairly
useful novice hurdler: best efforts when fifth to Wichita Lineman in Grade 2 at Chelten-

ham and mid-field in 28-runner Coral Cup (Handicap) at same course penultimate outing: stays 23f: unraced on firm going, acts on any other: has carried head awkwardly/found little. *W. K. Goldsworthy*

HILLS OF HOME (IRE) 6 b.g. Pasternak – Carrick Shannon (Green Shoon) [2006/7 F18m* Apr 26] 18,000 4-y-o: half-brother to several winners by Zaffaran, including fair staying hurdler/chaser Fournaught Alliance: dam once-raced half-sister to smart hurdler up to 2¾m Shannon Spray: impressive debut when winning bumper at Fontwell by 18 lengths from Bering de Lauriere: promising. *A. King*   **F110 +**

HILLTIME (IRE) 7 b.g. Danetime (IRE) – Ceannanas (IRE) (Magical Wonder (USA)) [2006/7 h110: 17m⁵ 17d 16m⁵ 21d 16g⁴ 16g⁵ 16g⁵ Apr 14] sturdy gelding: fairly useful handicap hurdler: left J. Quinn and off nearly a year, won at Market Rasen in June by neck from Tech Eagle: generally creditable efforts after, including when 3¾ lengths fifth of 22 to Kings Quay in valuable event at Aintree final outing: similar form when making successful chasing debut in novice at Uttoxeter in September by 1½ lengths from Cream Cracker: best around 2m with emphasis on speed: unraced on extremes of going: usually makes running/races prominently: reliable. *J. S. Wainwright*   **c116 h120**

HILL TRACK 13 b.g. Royal Match – Win Green Hill (National Trust) [2006/7 19dᵖᵘ Jun 14] good-topped gelding: lightly raced: winning hurdler: no form over fences: tried in cheekpieces/tongue strap. *A. M. Crow*   **c– h–**

HILL TRAIL 12 ch.g. Royal Match – Win Green Hill (National Trust) [2006/7 c19mᵖᵘ Apr 24] sturdy gelding: winning pointer: lightly raced and little form otherwise: tried tongue tied. *N. Thomas*   **c– h–**

HILLY GALE 7 b.g. Tamure (IRE) – Clodaigh Gale (Strong Gale) [2006/7 F16s² 21mᵖᵘ 25g* Apr 16] 68,000 4-y-o: half-brother to winning hurdler/fairly useful chaser Gumley Gale (by Greensmith), stays 4m, and winning staying chaser Hurricane Bay (by Karinga Bay): dam, placed once in bumpers, sister to useful chasers Full Strength and Wind Force: runner-up in bumper at Huntingdon: off 3 months and upped further in trip, much better effort over hurdles when winning maiden at Wetherby in April by 2½ lengths from Frankie Figg: clearly stays well: sold 42,000 gns Doncaster May Sales. *P. R. Webber*   **h99 F87**

HIMALAYAN TRAIL 8 b.g. Nomadic Way (USA) – Hindu Lady (Doon Lad) [2006/7 h–: 23v* c25s* c24v³ Feb 24] sturdy gelding: much better effort in novice hurdles when winning at Wetherby in May: off 7 months, better form when successful in maiden at Catterick on chase debut by 1¼ lengths from Nine de Sivola: disappointing in novice following month: stays 25f: acts on heavy going. *Mrs S. J. Smith*   **c113 h99 +**

HIP POCKET (IRE) 11 b.g. Ela-Mana-Mou – Ebony And Ivory (IRE) (Bob Back (USA)) [2006/7 c76, h–: c24g² Apr 21] close-coupled gelding: winning hurdler: fit from points, easily best effort in hunters when second to Red Brook Lad at Bangor: stays 3m: acts on soft and good to firm going: tried blinkered/in cheekpieces. *George Wilson*   **c102 h–**

HIPPODROME (IRE) 5 b.g. Montjeu (IRE) – Moon Diamond (Unfuwain (USA)) [2006/7 16g² 17d⁶ 16d 21v Nov 26] rather leggy gelding: useful on Flat (stays 1½m) at 3 yrs, sold out of A. O'Brien's stable 110,000 gns Newmarket Autumn Sales, below form (including in UAE) in 2006: best effort in novice hurdles when second to Massini's Maguire at Chepstow: blinkered: tried tongue tied: sent to Germany. *R. Simpson*   **h95**

HI RUDOLF 12 b.g. Ballet Royal (USA) – Hi Darlin' (Prince de Galles) [2006/7 c71x, h–: 17d⁵ Jun 12] small gelding: winning chaser/novice hurdler, often let down by jumping over fences: poor pointer nowadays. *H. J. Manners*   **c– x h–**

HIRVINE (FR) 9 ch.g. Snurge – Guadanella (FR) (Guadanini (FR)) [2006/7 c–, h–: 24m⁴ c26s⁶ c26sᵖᵘ 23v⁵ 25v 23s³ 23s² 24g 24gᵖᵘ Apr 19] good-topped gelding: fairly useful chaser: useful handicap hurdler, left P. Bowen after first outing: good efforts sixth/seventh starts, 1¾ lengths second of 20 to Millenium Royal at Haydock: let down by jumping/attitude after: should stay beyond 3¼m: acts on heavy going: usually wears headgear: often front runner: not a fluent jumper. *D. McCain Jnr*   **c125 x h134 x**

HISAR (IRE) 14 br.g. Doyoun – Himaya (IRE) (Mouktar) [2006/7 c–§, h–: c19mᵖᵘ Mar 29] leggy gelding: veteran jumper: tried blinkered: often tongue tied: unreliable. *Miss L. Rivers Bulkeley*   **c– § h–**

HIS NIBS (IRE) 10 b.g. Alflora (IRE) – Mrs Jennifer (River Knight (FR)) [2006/7 c–, h129: 24s³ 25dᵖᵘ 24dᵖᵘ 24g Mar 15] workmanlike gelding: refused first only outing over fences: useful handicap hurdler: left Miss Venetia Williams and off 9 months, good third   **c– h134**

to Desert Tommy at Chepstow: no show after, reportedly had hobday and tie-back operations prior to final outing: stays 25f: acts on heavy and good to firm going. *A. King*

HISTORIC APPEAL (USA) 4 b.g. Diesis – Karasavina (IRE) (Sadler's Wells (USA)) [2006/7 16g Apr 14] half-brother to fair hurdler around 2m Code Sign (by Gulch): fair maiden on Flat (should stay 1¼m), sold out of M. Channon's stable 7,000 gns Newmarket Autumn Sales: tailed off in novice on hurdling debut. *Ian Williams*   h–

HISTORY MASTER (IRE) 5 b.g. Dr Massini (IRE) – Native Emigrant (IRE) (Be My Native (USA)) [2006/7 F16s 22spu c24v³ Feb 23] good-topped gelding: first foal: dam, maiden hurdler, stayed 2½m: no show in bumper/maiden hurdle: left Heather Dalton, third in hunter at Warwick on chase debut: won point in April. *G. Costelloe*   c83 h– F–

HI TECH 8 b.g. Polar Falcon (USA) – Just Speculation (IRE) (Ahonoora) [2006/7 c16d⁶ 16s⁶ Mar 8] smallish, angular gelding: modest hurdler at best: off nearly 2 years, no show in 2006/7, including on chasing debut: effective around 2m to 3m: acts on soft and firm going: front runner. *Dr P. Pritchard*   c– h–

HIT THE SPOT 5 b.g. Kayf Tara – Suave Shot (Suave Dancer (USA)) [2006/7 F16s 16m Apr 25] €85,000 3-y-o: useful-looking gelding: has scope: first foal: dam once-raced half-sister to very smart hurdler/smart chaser up to 19f Grey Shot: well held in bumper/novice hurdle. *Jonjo O'Neill*   h– F–

HOBBS HILL 8 b.g. Alflora (IRE) – Rim of Pearl (Rymer) [2006/7 h110+: 16d² 17s* 16d Mar 13] tall, good sort: chasing type: bumper winner: useful form over hurdles, lightly raced: easily landed odds in novice at Folkestone (by 17 lengths from William Bonney) in January: looked ill at ease throughout when well beaten in Grade 1 novice at Cheltenham: stays 2¾m: raced on going softer than good. *C. R. Egerton*   h131

HOBBYCYR (FR) 12 b.g. Saint Cyrien (FR) – Sauteuse de Retz (FR) (Funny Hobby) [2006/7 c85, h–: c24d May 15] tall gelding: winning hurdler/chaser, well held only outing in 2006/7: stays 33f. *J. A. T. de Giles*   c– h–

HOCKENHEIM (FR) 6 b.g. Kadalko (FR) – L'Inka (FR) (R B Chesne) [2006/7 h104: 25s* 25s* 24spu Dec 9] big, leggy gelding: fairly useful novice hurdler: won at Carlisle in October (maiden, easily) and November, beat Ballyboley by 8 lengths (jumped left late on) in latter: presumably amiss in Grade 2 at Cheltenham: stays 25f: raced on good to soft/soft going. *J. Howard Johnson*   h118

HOGAN'S HEROES 4 b.g. Alhaarth (IRE) – Icicle (Polar Falcon (USA)) [2006/7 16gF 16d 16vpu Mar 3] quite attractive gelding: modest maiden on Flat (stays 1m) for G. Butler: well held completed start in juvenile hurdles: joined Eoin Doyle. *J. J. Lambe, Ireland*   h–

HOH NELSON 6 b.g. Halling (USA) – Birsay (Bustino) [2006/7 h89§: 16g⁶ 21dF 20g Apr 21] lengthy gelding: modest handicap hurdler: stays 3m: acts on firm and soft going: often wears headgear: ungenuine. *Mrs A. Price*   h– §

HOH VISS 7 b.g. Rudimentary (USA) – Now And Forever (IRE) (Kris) [2006/7 h126: c22v⁴ 22s* 25sF c24vpu c24s⁴ Mar 17] workmanlike gelding: fairly useful hurdler/novice chaser: won maiden over fences at Fontwell (by distance from Flintoff) in December: running well when falling 3 out in Grade 2 at Wetherby won by Heltornic next time: stays 2¾m: raced on going softer than good (acts on heavy). *C. J. Mann*   c119 + h–

HOLD THAT THOUGHT (IRE) 7 ch.g. Zaffaran (USA) – Tarasandy (IRE) (Arapahos (FR)) [2006/7 h–, F73: 17m 20g² 19g⁵ c19sF Jan 30] well-made gelding: easily best effort over hurdles when second to Vinando in maiden at Fontwell: jumped markedly left prior to falling heavily 4 out in maiden at Taunton on chasing debut: stays 2½m. *Miss H. C. Knight*   c– h98

HOLD THE BID (IRE) 7 b. or br.g. Luso – Killesk Castle (IRE) (Little Bighorn) [2006/7 h–: 23v² 20f 24g³ 25s³ 24v³ 25d⁵ c20vur c25s² c20gF c25g⁵ Apr 23] fair novice hurdler: generally let down by jumping over fences: stays 25f: acts on heavy going. *Mrs S. J. Smith*   c91 h101

HOLD THE LINE 6 b.g. Titus Livius (FR) – Multi-Sofft (Northern State (USA)) [2006/7 19dpu 21s⁶ Nov 29] stocky gelding: modest hurdler, off 2 years prior to return: probably stayed 21f: usually wore cheekpieces: dead. *W. G. M. Turner*   h93

HOLIDAY COCKTAIL 5 b.g. Mister Baileys – Bermuda Lily (Dunbeath (USA)) [2006/7 16v 16s 16d Jan 19] half-brother to 2 winning jumpers, including smart Sir Talbot (by Ardross), also fairly useful chaser who stayed 21f: fair on Flat (stays 1¼m), successful in seller in March: no form in maiden/novice hurdles. *J. J. Quinn*   h–

HOLLANDIA (IRE) 6 gr.g. Needle Gun (IRE) – Steel Mariner (Kambalda) [2006/7   **h–** h–, F84: 16g 19d Nov 16] unfurnished gelding: no form over hurdles: sold 5,000 gns Doncaster May Sales. *Miss H. C. Knight*

HOLLAND PARK (IRE) 10 gr.g. Roselier (FR) – Bluebell Avenue (Boreen Beag)   **c–** [2006/7 c–, h–: c25g4 24g4 Mar 24] workmanlike gelding: well beaten completed outing   **h–** over fences: useful handicap hurdler at best, off 15 months before return: suited by test of stamina: raced mainly on going softer than good. *Mrs S. D. Williams*

HOLLOWS MILL 11 b.g. Rudimentary (USA) – Strawberry Song (Final Straw)   **c102 x** [2006/7 c102, h77+: c17f3 c17g3 c16f4 c16d3 c20g3 c16g3 c16d2 c16v4 17s* c16g Apr 7]   **h93** workmanlike gelding: fair handicap chaser, below best after second outing: modest handicap hurdler: won at Carlisle (fifth course win) in February: stays 21f: acts on any going: has finished weakly: sketchy jumper. *F. P. Murtagh*

HOLLOWS MIST 9 b.g. Missed Flight – Joyfulness (FR) (Cure The Blues (USA))   **c77** [2006/7 c–, h–: c25g3 c25m 20dpu c16d c20g3 c20g c20s c17grtr Apr 2] leggy gelding: **h–** maiden hurdler/chaser, largely well held in 2006/7: blinkered, refused to race final outing: probably stays 25f: sometimes tongue tied. *F. P. Murtagh*

HOLLY TREE (IRE) 7 br.g. Accordion – Lime Tree (Bulldozer) [2006/7 F17m4   **h135** 16mbd 16mF 16d3 17d2 16g3 18v2 16s2 16s* 16v3 16v2 16v3 16v* 16s3 16v3 20v3 20d*   **F97** 16m2 Apr 24] sturdy gelding: fifth foal: half-brother to modest hurdler/chaser Lime Supreme (by Supreme Leader), stayed 2¼m: dam no form over hurdles: bumper winner: useful novice hurdler: won at Cork (maiden) in November and Limerick in January and April (by ¾ length from Larkwing): placed all other completed starts, badly hampered turning in and promoted to second in Champion Novices' Hurdle won by Clopf at Punchestown final one: stays 2½m: acts on good to firm and heavy ground: tough and consistent. *E. Sheehy, Ireland*

HOLLY WALK 6 ch.m. Dr Fong (USA) – Holly Blue (Bluebird (USA)) [2006/7 h62:   **c–** c23v5 c19fpu Apr 11] sturdy mare: maiden hurdler: won maiden point in February: no   **h–** show in hunter chases: best form at 2m: acts on soft and good to firm ground: often in cheekpieces/visor. *James Cole*

HOLLYWOOD LAW (IRE) 6 ch.g. Zaffaran (USA) – Whoareyoutoday (IRE)   **h116** (Strong Gale) [2006/7 F20m* F17m3 F20d5 20s2 20s* 20v3 20v5 Jan 7] seventh foal: **F93** brother to winning pointer: dam, lightly raced in points, out of half-sister to dam of top-class staying chaser Barton Bank: fair form in bumpers, won at Gowran in June: confirmed promise of hurdling debut when winning 20-runner maiden at Punchestown in November by 10 lengths from Judge Deed: better effort after when 13 lengths third of 6 to Aran Concerto in Grade 1 novice at Navan: will stay beyond 2½m: raced on soft/heavy going over hurdles (bumper win on good to firm). *W. P. Mullins, Ireland*

HOLY BUCK (IRE) 8 br.g. Religiously (USA) – Castleview Rose (Master Buck)   **c–** [2006/7 16m3 24f4 Jul 19] ex-Irish gelding: placed in maiden points in 2005: tongue tied,   **h89** no show on chasing debut: left M. Colfer, modest form in maiden hurdles. *Evan Williams*

HOLY JOE (FR) 10 b.g. Pharly (FR) – Niffy Nora (Mandalus) [2006/7 c124, h–: c23v*   **c119** c21g Apr 12] medium-sized gelding: fairly useful chaser: off 11 months, successful   **h–** hunter debut when beating Paddy For Paddy 2 lengths at Leicester in March: never-nearer seventh of 27 to Scots Grey in Fox Hunters' at Aintree: stays 3¼m: acts on heavy going: has worn blinkers, also tried in cheekpieces. *Miss Venetia Williams*

HOMEBRED STAR 6 ch.g. Safawan – Celtic Chimes (Celtic Cone) [2006/7 16vpu   **h–** Feb 16] modest at best on Flat (stays 9.5f): no form over hurdles. *G. P. Enright*

HOME BY MIDNIGHT 8 b.m. Midnight Legend – Home From The Hill (IRE)   **c78** (Jareer (USA)) [2006/7 c24dF c19m2 Apr 24] winning pointer: modest form when second in maiden on completed start in hunter chases. *Mrs L. Redman*

HOMELEIGH SUN 8 b.m. Minster Son – Riverain (Bustino) [2006/7 F–: 16dpu 18spu   **h–** 19gpu Apr 8] no form in bumper/over hurdles. *N. J. Gifford*

HOMELEIGHWILDCHILD 6 ro.m. Silver Patriarch (IRE) – Give It A Bash (IRE)   **F–** (Gianchi) [2006/7 F16g4 F14s F16g Apr 9] long-backed, angular mare: first foal: dam winning pointer: no show in bumpers. *G. R. Pewter*

HOMELIFE (IRE) 9 b.g. Persian Bold – Share The Vision (Vision (USA)) [2006/7 h–:   **h75** 17dpu 16g5 16g6 20m6 Jul 26] compact gelding: poor maiden hurdler. *Mrs J. A. Saunders*

At The Races Bobbyjo Chase, Fairyhouse—
Homer Wells outbattles Jack High (blinkers) to follow up his win in the Thyestes

HOMER WELLS (IRE) 9 b.g. Arctic Cider (USA) – Run And Shine (Deep Run) **c138**
[2006/7 c124, h–: c24s c24v^F c24v* c25v* c36g^{pu} Apr 14] lengthy, useful-looking geld- **h–**
ing: winning hurdler: useful chaser: back to best to win Ellen Construction Thyestes
Chase at Gowran (by 3½ lengths from Livingstonebramble) in January and Grade 2 At
The Races Bobbyjo Chase at Fairyhouse (beat Jack High by 2 lengths) in February:
always behind in Grand National at Aintree: should stay beyond 25f: acts on heavy going.
W. P. Mullins, Ireland

HONAN (IRE) 8 b.g. College Chapel – Medical Times (IRE) (Auction Ring (USA)) **c– §**
[2006/7 c102§, h100§: 16d 17m^{pu} Jun 8] leggy gelding: fair hurdler/chaser, no show 2 **h– §**
starts early in 2006/7: best around 2m: acts on any going: visored: hard ride: one to treat
with caution. *D. E. Pipe*

HONDALIA (IRE) 5 b.g. City Honours (USA) – Rodalia (IRE) (Ela-Mana-Mou) **F–**
[2006/7 F16g Mar 24] workmanlike gelding: second foal: dam lightly-raced maiden:
backward, well held in bumper on debut. *J. A. Geake*

HONDURAS (SWI) 6 gr.g. Daylami (IRE) – High Mare (FR) (Highest Honor (FR)) **h98**
[2006/7 18g^2 16g^6 Oct 14] useful on Flat (stays 1½m), successful twice in Norway at
3 yrs: favourite, much better effort in novice hurdles when second to The Bonus King at
Fontwell: looked reluctant next time. *G. L. Moore*

HONEST ABE (IRE) 6 b.g. Houmayoun (FR) – Blasgan (IRE) (Yashgan) [2006/7 **c–**
h79: c20g^F Nov 5] sturdy gelding: poor form over hurdles: off 7 months, under pressure **h–**
when fell 4 out in handicap on chasing debut: would have stayed 2½m+: dead.
B. N. Pollock

HONEST ENDEAVOUR 8 b.g. Alflora (IRE) – Isabeau (Law Society (USA)) **c110 +**
[2006/7 c91, h108: c21g^6 c24g^{pu} 16s^{pu} 16g 16g c16s^5 c24g c20g^5 c16s* c20m* c20m* **h97**
Apr 28] well-made gelding: winning hurdler: fair handicap chaser: thrived late in season,
winning at Hexham (novice) and Market Rasen (2, novice on second occasion), all in
April: stays 2½m: acts on soft and good to firm going: has worn cheekpieces: often makes
running: sold 20,000 gns Doncaster May Sales. *J. M. Jefferson*

HONEST YER HONOUR (IRE) 11 b.g. Witness Box (USA) – Castle Duchess **c–**
(Abednego) [2006/7 c111, h–: c20g^{pu} Feb 21] sturdy gelding: won novice at Aintree in **h–**
May 2005, only completed outing in hunters: stays 25f: acts on soft going: tried in
cheekpieces. *Mrs C. J. Robinson*

HONEYCOMBE 6 b.m. Relief Pitcher – Hanglands (Bustino) [2006/7 F16s F16d **F–**
F16s Mar 8] big mare: half-sister to several winners, including 21f hurdle winner
Touch 'N' Pass (by Dominion): dam lightly-raced maiden: no form in bumpers.
Mrs S. P. Stretton

HONEY'S GIFT 8 b.m. Terimon – Honeycroft (Crofter (USA)) [2006/7 h99: 21g **c–**
c16d^6 c20v^6 c24d^6 Jan 15] compact mare: modest handicap hurdler: off 8 months, well **h–**
beaten over fences: stays 23f: acts on heavy and good to firm going. *G. G. Margarson*

HONEYSTREET (IRE) 7 b.m. Woodborough (USA) – Ring of Kerry (IRE) (Kenmare (FR)) [2006/7 17gF Apr 7] poor form both starts over hurdles over 3 years apart. *D. Burchell*　h66

HONOR AND GLORY 7 br.g. Past Glories – Scalby Anna (Sir Mago) [2006/7 c68: c24d* c24vpu c19s5 c22spu c24mpu Apr 14] rangy gelding: poor chaser: won novice handicap at Lingfield in November: stays 3m: acts on good to soft going. *Nick Williams*　c75

HONORARY CITIZEN 5 b.g. Montjoy (USA) – Heart So Blue (Dilum (USA)) [2006/7 h–: 17g 16m Jun 8] no form over hurdles. *Evan Williams*　h–

HONOURABLE COLLINS (IRE) 7 br.g. Glacial Storm (USA) – Club Caribbean (Strong Gale) [2006/7 h–: c23mpu Apr 22] angular gelding: no form. *Mrs Tracey Barfoot-Saunt*　c–
h–

HONOURABLE SPIDER 8 b.g. Nomadic Way (USA) – Baroness Spider (Baron Blakeney) [2006/7 c26g* c25v* c26g Mar 16] 2,400 3-y-o, 11,000 5-y-o: strong gelding: second foal: half-brother to winning pointer by Past Glories: dam winning pointer: successful 6 times in points, including in January: useful form in hunter chases: won at Folkestone in May and February, beating Sonevafushi by 2 lengths in 4-runner event in latter: jumped poorly when well beaten in Foxhunter at Cheltenham: stays 3¼m: acts on heavy ground. *Mrs Suzy Bull*　c120

HONOUR GUARD (IRE) 6 br.g. Darnay – Capincur Lady (Over The River (FR)) [2006/7 20g 20d 24vpu 20vpu Jan 20] €36,000 4-y-o: angular, useful-looking gelding: half-brother to 3 winners, notably smart hurdler/chaser Lord Transcend (by Aristocracy), stayed 3¼m: dam 2m hurdle winner: no form over hurdles. *J. Howard Johnson*　h–

HONOUR'S DREAM (FR) 4 ch.c. Acatenango (GER) – The Last Dream (FR) (Arazi (USA)) [2006/7 16vF 16d 16v6 17v3 Feb 25] rangy colt: has scope: fairly useful on Flat (stays 1½m), sold out of R. Pritchard-Gordon's stable 40,000 gns Newmarket Autumn Sales: let down by jumping/attitude in juvenile hurdles. *T. R. George*　h69

HOOBER 6 b.g. Mind Games – Chlo-Jo (Belmez (USA)) [2006/7 F–: 20d 17s 16gpu Mar 29] big, workmanlike gelding: no show in bumpers (for J. Gallagher) and over hurdles. *Evan Williams*　h–

HOOF IT HARRY (IRE) 6 ch.g. City Honours (USA) – Miss Boots (IRE) (Brush Aside (USA)) [2006/7 F16g5 F16m5 Oct 28] €3,200 4-y-o: workmanlike gelding: first foal: dam pulled up in point: better effort in bumpers when fifth to Wizard of Odds at Ascot second outing. *P. Henderson*　F85

HOOKY'S HOPE 4 b.f. Endoli (USA) – Hooky's Treat (Dutch Treat) [2006/7 F17g Apr 23] second foal: dam winning pointer: well held in mares bumper on debut. *Mrs H. O. Graham*　F–

HOO LA BALOO (FR) 6 b.g. Unfuwain (USA) – Via Saleria (IRE) (Arazi (USA)) [2006/7 c140+, h–: c17d3 c19d3 c16s5 c19d3 c24g c24s* c19g c16f2 Apr 28] good-topped gelding: won all 3 starts in 4-y-o hurdles: useful chaser: didn't have to be anywhere near best to land odds in Grand Military Gold Cup at Sandown in March: several creditable efforts otherwise in 2006/7, including when 7 lengths second to Dempsey in Grade 2 event at same course: successful at 3m, best form up to 19f: acts on good and firm going: has run well when sweating: effective making running or ridden more patiently. *P. F. Nicholls*　c142
h–

HO PANG YAU 9 b. or br.g. Pivotal – La Cabrilla (Carwhite) [2006/7 c16gpu 16m 16m 17m Jun 30] close-coupled gelding: winning hurdler: no form in 2006/7, including when chasing debut: difficult ride: joined J. Goldie. *Mrs R. L. Elliot*　c–
h–

HOPEFUL CHANCE (IRE) 10 b.g. Machiavellian (USA) – Don't Rush (USA) (Alleged (USA)) [2006/7 23spu 20s5 16s 17d Dec 26] close-coupled gelding: maiden chaser/winning hurdler: off 2 years, no form in 2006/7: stays 2½m: acts on soft going: tried visored: often tongue tied. *J. R. Turner*　c–
h–

HOPESARISING 8 b.g. Primitive Rising (USA) – Super Brush (IRE) (Brush Aside (USA)) [2006/7 c20s2 c24s2 c21s6 24m4 Apr 25] big gelding: maiden hurdler: modest novice chaser: won point in January: stays 3m: acts on soft ground. *P. R. Johnson*　c88
h72

HOPE'S ETERNAL 4 ro.g. Highest Honor (FR) – Tennessee Moon (Darshaan) [2006/7 16dF Dec 29] good-topped gelding: well held on Flat, sold out of J. Dunlop's stable 3,500 gns Newmarket July Sales: blinkered, blundered first and fell next on hurdling debut. *C. L. Popham*　h–

HOPE SOUND (IRE) 7 b.g. Turtle Island (IRE) – Lucky Pick (Auction Ring (USA)) **c81**
[2006/7 c–, h95: c19s⁶ c24dᵘʳ Mar 21] sturdy gelding: winning hurdler/chaser, modest **h–**
at best: off 20 months before return: stays 3m: acts on heavy going: sometimes wears
headgear. *R. J. Rowsell*

HOP FAIR 8 ch.m. Gildoran – Haraka Sasa (Town And Country) [2006/7 h73: 19m³ **c–**
20g 19s 19m⁶ 21m⁴ c23dᵘʳ 24dᵖᵘ Nov 20] bumper winner: little form over hurdles: **h86 ?**
unseated first on chasing debut: tried in cheekpieces. *J. L. Spearing*

HOPKINS (IRE) 6 ch.g. Topanoora – Derryclare (Pollerton) [2006/7 F93: 20s² 20v² **h107**
20s² 20v⁵ Jan 20] strong, good sort: type to make a chaser: fair form in novice hurdles,
runner-up first 3 starts: will stay 3m: raced on soft/heavy ground. *H. D. Daly*

HOPS'S TROUBLE 6 b.g. Double Trigger (IRE) – Hops And Pops (Lighter) [2006/7 **F–**
F16v⁶ Jan 27] third foal: dam useful hurdler/chaser who stayed 2¾m: tailed off in
bumper: dead. *D. P. Keane*

HORCOTT BAY 7 b.m. Thowra (FR) – Armagnac Messenger (Pony Express) [2006/7 **c– §**
c91§, h–: 21s c20sᵘʳ Dec 7] workmanlike mare: maiden hurdler/chaser, no show in **h–**
2006/7: tried blinkered: ungenuine. *M. G. Rimell*

HORDAGO (IRE) 7 gr.g. Highest Honor (FR) – Mirmande (Kris) [2006/7 h126: c20g⁶ **c109 §**
c22v c20d 25d c21s c22v* c24d c28v⁴ c33g⁶ c22d² c30mᶠ Apr 27] big, leggy gelding: **h–**
fairly useful handicap hurdler: fair chaser: won handicap at Limerick in December: stays
33f: acts on heavy going: often wears cheekpieces, blinkered last 2 outings: temperamental. *Eric McNamara, Ireland*

HORIZON HILL (USA) 9 b.g. Distant View (USA) – Accadia Rocket (CAN) (Bold **c– §**
Ruckus (USA)) [2006/7 c73§, h–§: c23dᵖᵘ May 17] maiden hurdler/chaser: winning **h– §**
pointer: stays 23f: acts on firm and good to soft going: tried blinkered: not one to trust.
T. W. Boon

HOTEL HILAMAR (IRE) 6 b.g. Flemensfirth (USA) – Gypsy Lass (King's Ride) **h118 p**
[2006/7 F16s* 16d² 16v* Nov 18] €38,000 4-y-o: fourth foal: half-brother to winning **F104**
hurdler/chaser The Young Bishop (by By My Native), stays 2¾m: dam, winning hurdler/
chaser, stayed 2¾m: better effort in bumpers when winning at Roscommon in October
comfortably by 8 lengths from Powerberry: confirmed promise of hurdling debut when
winning 22-runner maiden at Punchestown by 3½ lengths from Dancing Hero: will stay
beyond 2m: presumably met with setback but should still improve further. *N. Meade,
Ireland*

HOT GIRL 9 b.m. State Diplomacy (USA) – Hundred Islands (Hotfoot) [2006/7 23g **h–**
16g May 13] plain mare: of no account: sold 1,000 gns Doncaster May (2006) Sales.
S. P. Griffiths

HOT LIPS PAGE (FR) 6 b.m. Hamas (IRE) – Salt Peanuts (IRE) (Salt Dome (USA)) **c–**
[2006/7 c–, h–: 16s³ 16d² 16d⁴ 21s² 23s⁵ 19s² 21d 16g⁴ 19m⁴ Apr 22] neat mare: modest **h98**
handicap hurdler: well beaten only outing over fences: effective around 2m to 21f: acts
on soft going. *J. R. Holt*

HOT 'N' HOLY 8 b.g. Supreme Leader – Clonmello (Le Bavard (FR)) [2006/7 h113, **c129**
F102+: c24g* c24v* c24s³ Dec 13] close-coupled gelding: has reportedly had breathing **h–**
operation: bumper/hurdle winner: successful also first 2 starts in novice chases, at Chepstow (mistakes and jumped right) in October and Newbury (handicap, beat Irish Raptor a
neck) in November: will stay good 3m: raced on good going or softer (acts on heavy):
sold 15,000 gns Doncaster May Sales. *P. F. Nicholls*

HOT PLUNGE 11 b.g. Bustino – Royal Seal (Privy Seal) [2006/7 c94§, h–: c16g* **c94 §**
May 24] good-topped gelding: fair pointer/hunter chaser: won at Folkestone (by 18 **h–**
lengths) in May: stays 21f: acts on soft and good to firm going: tried in cheekpieces: has
started slowly, and refused to race final start in 2005/6. *Miss Kelly Smith*

HOT PORT (IRE) 5 ch.g. Moscow Society (USA) – Kim Mews (IRE) (Persian Mews) **h113**
[2006/7 F16s F16s⁴ 19s⁴ 18s* 22d 21g Mar 14] angular gelding: second foal: dam, no **F78**
form over hurdles, out of sister to useful staying chaser Camelot Knight: fourth in
bumper: fair form over hurdles: won 20-runner maiden at Leopardstown in December:
much stiffer tasks over longer trips after. *Eric McNamara, Ireland*

HOT PRODUXION (USA) 8 ch.g. Tabasco Cat (USA) – Princess Harriet (USA) (Mt **c74 §**
Livermore (USA)) [2006/7 c97§, h–§: c24g⁴ Apr 27] compact gelding: maiden hurdler/ **h– §**
chaser: fair pointer nowadays: stays 21f: acts on soft and good to firm going: tried
visored/in cheekpieces/tongue tied: not a fluent jumper or an easy ride (tends to wander
under pressure). *P. S. Davies*

HOT TODDY (IRE) 12 b.g. Glacial Storm (USA) – Technical Merit (Gala Perform-   **c82**
ance) [2006/7 c95: c30m⁴ May 16] fairly useful pointer: winning hunter chaser: stays 25f:
acts on firm and soft going. *G. L. Landau*

HOT WELD 8 b.g. Weld – Deb's Ball (Glenstal (USA)) [2006/7 c133, h112:   **c141**
c24sᵖᵘ c24dᵖᵘ c25gᵖᵘ c24g⁶ c32m* c29f* Apr 28]   **h–**
    'A donkey on soft ground, but a good staying chaser on good ground' was
how Hot Weld's trainer Ferdy Murphy succinctly summed the gelding up. Hot
Weld would have been given short shrift in these pages as well if it hadn't been for
a remarkable last eight days of the season which transformed a dismal campaign
into one of the most successful enjoyed by any chaser in training. Hot Weld became
the first horse to win the Scottish Grand National and Sandown's big end-of-season
staying chase, run in recent seasons as the Betfred Gold Cup. The two big races are
just a week apart and only the National at Aintree was worth more than them among
the handicap chases run in the latest season.
    Ferdy Murphy made no secret of the fact that Hot Weld had the Scottish
National as his target all season. Hot Weld was given a light campaign beforehand,
but, even so, there was little indication of what was to come. A running-on sixth in
quite a valuable handicap at Carlisle was his first completion of the season, a
fortnight before the Scottish National, but, before that, he had been pulled up on
all three of his starts. The first two were in amateur handicaps at Cheltenham in the
autumn when partnered by Mr Richard Harding, the rider who had been in the
saddle for Hot Weld's biggest success up to that point in the National Hunt Chase at
Cheltenham the previous spring. Hot Weld gave the impression that he was amiss
on his second run back, and it was four months before he was seen out again, at
Wetherby. Although his stable in general was in fine form at the time, Hot Weld still
seemed out of sorts, soon struggling after an early mistake.
    The warmest April in Britain since records began in 1659, and one of the
driest, resulted in good to firm ground at Ayr and even firmer ground at Sandown,
conditions which were seemingly instrumental in Hot Weld returning to form. In
addition, Hot Weld was equipped with cheekpieces for the two races, the first
time he had worn headgear of any sort. Front-running tactics were also readopted
at Ayr where Hot Weld was given a particularly good ride by his 5-lb claimer
P. J. McDonald—the dual-purpose jockey enjoyed a memorable two days in Scotland, his other wins at the meeting on the Murphy-trained pair Three Mirrors and
Spring Breeze netting a total prize money haul (including Hot Weld) of £128,735.
Hot Weld was a 14/1-chance in a race for which his stable also supplied the
5/1 favourite Nine de Sivola, still a maiden over fences but runner-up in the Irish
National earlier in the month. Character Building, runner-up in the latest National

Coral Scottish Grand National Handicap Chase, Ayr—Hot Weld, in first-time cheekpieces,
also benefits from an enterprising ride by P. J. McDonald to beat stable-companion Nine de Sivola (right)
and Parsons Legacy (centre)

Betfred Gold Cup Chase (Handicap), Sandown—stable jockey Graham Lee is back on board as Hot Weld completes a notable double just seven days on; the blinkered Zabenz blunders away his chance at the last

Hunt Chase, in which Nine de Sivola had fallen three out when moving into contention, was second favourite at 6/1. Twenty-three horses contested the Scottish Grand National (under new sponsors Coral and run over half a furlong shorter than previously at four miles and a hundred and ten yards) but few of them ever got into contention. Hot Weld set a sound gallop and was sent into a clear lead early on the final circuit which only Nine de Sivola and Parsons Legacy, another of those towards the head of the betting, proved able to reduce. Parsons Legacy headed Hot Weld two out but Hot Weld rallied tenaciously and was back in front at the last, finding enough on the run-in to hold off the challenge of Nine de Sivola by half a length. Parsons Legacy was just over a length behind the Murphy-trained pair in third, with a break of fifteen lengths to the previous year's winner Run For Paddy in fourth, the remainder well beaten. It was Murphy's third Scottish National after saddling Paris Pike in 2000 and Joes Edge in 2005; in 2004, the stable's Irish National winner Granit d'Estruval fell at the last, just five days after winning at Fairyhouse, when upsides eventual winner Grey Abbey at Ayr.

Hot Weld had just a week to recover from his exertions before going on to the Betfred Gold Cup at Sandown. Perhaps more of a worry than the horse beforehand was the well-being of stable jockey Graham Lee, who had ridden Nine de Sivola at Ayr but took the ride on Hot Weld at Sandown. He had taken a crashing fall on the stable's novice Aces Four at Punchestown in the interim, though fears that he might have broken his arm proved unfounded. Hot Weld showed no signs of having had a hard race at Ayr, looking in outstanding condition in the paddock at Sandown. Even from 11 lb out of the weights, Hot Weld was effectively 3 lb well in against his revised BHB mark and started the 6/1 third favourite in a disappointing turnout of ten, the smallest field for ten years. Reveillez, the 9/4 favourite after winning a valuable handicap at Aintree, and 4/1 second-favourite Cornish Sett, who had been runner-up in the Racing Post Chase, were going into unknown territory so far as stamina was concerned, but a couple of others in the field, Jack High and Juveigneur, were thoroughly proven on that score, having finished first and second in the race two years earlier. Hot Weld again set out to make all but a mistake at the fifth saw him lose the lead to Zabenz for the remainder of the first circuit. Driven back in front passing the winning post with a circuit to go, Hot Weld led the rest of the way, with Zabenz and My Will his closest pursuers from then on. Reveillez had joined them by the Pond fence but, renewing his effort, Zabenz posed the biggest threat when only a length down at the last. However, a blunder sent Zabenz sprawling badly on landing and Hot Weld was left clear to beat Reveillez by three lengths, with top weight My Will, under his 7-lb claiming amateur, in third for the second year running, another six lengths behind. Jack High ran on to pass Zabenz for fourth.

The closest any Scottish National winner had previously come to following up in what was then the Whitbread Gold Cup was Androma, beaten a neck by By The Way at Sandown in 1985. Androma's trainer Jimmy FitzGerald had also finished second in the Whitbread as a jockey twenty years earlier on Brasher, who chased home Arkle two weeks after landing the Scottish National on the final day's racing ever staged at that race's initial home Bogside. Only seven days separated Young Ash Leaf's bold bid at the double in 1971, with the Scottish-trained mare losing out to fellow northern raider Titus Oates at Sandown after her Ayr win, whilst the amateur-ridden Proud Tarquin finished second within a week in 1974 at both Ayr (to Red Rum) and Sandown (controversially losing first place to The Dikler in the stewards' room). More recently, Four Trix was a creditable third at Sandown seven days on from his Ayr victory, whilst the the 2001 Scottish National runner-up Ad Hoc was successful in the Whitbread a week later.

Hot Weld (b.g. 1999)	Weld (ch 1986)	Kalaglow (gr 1978)	Kalamoun
			Rossitor
		Meliora (b 1976)	Crowned Prince
			Grecian Craft
	Deb's Ball (b 1986)	Glenstal (b 1980)	Northern Dancer
			Cloonlara
		De'b Old Fruit (b 1971)	Levmoss
			Currarevagh

Mr S. Hubbard Rodwell's "Hot Weld"

Hot Weld's sire Weld was also reportedly the subject of a rather unflattering description—'slow'—by his rider after his sole outing at two, but he made into a very smart stayer as a three-year-old when his wins included the Queen's Vase (in course-record time on firm ground), the Doncaster Cup and the Jockey Club Cup. Leg trouble prevented him from fulfilling the promise which suggested he had the makings of a Gold Cup winner. Weld has not made much of a name for himself at stud but he's probably had few better or tougher mares than Hot Weld's dam Deb's Ball. She was modest on the Flat, though she still won four races at around a mile and a half. Over hurdles, though, the Dudley Moffatt-trained Deb's Ball proved useful at up to around three miles, winning eleven more races, notably the 1993 West Yorkshire Hurdle at Wetherby (with subsequent Champion Hurdle winner Flakey Dove among her victims). She fell on her only outing over fences. Although effective on all types of ground, Deb's Ball had a good record on firm. Deb's Ball's other winners are essentially no better than platers over hurdles, both Ball Games (by Mind Games) and Deb's Son (by Minster Son) proving unreliable into the bargain. Only Millie (by Prince Daniel) won a weak maiden hurdle at Kelso (also on firm ground) at 100/1 very early in the latest season and, in common with the previous pair, is in training with Moffatt's son James. The Nigel Hawke-trained four-year-old Itstooearly (by Overbury) has shown a little ability in a couple of bumpers, whilst Deb's Ball produced just one more foal, a 2005 Karinga Bay filly, prior to her death in 2006. The grandam De'b Old Fruit was a mile and a half winner in Ireland and a daughter of Currarevagh, who was a half-sister to the 1950 Irish Derby winner Dark Warrior. Currarevagh has a number of notable descendants, including 2002 St Leger winner Bollin Eric and she is also the grandam of the dual Prix du Cadran winner El Badr and—perhaps part of the reason Hot Weld has ended up where he has—grandam too of Brandeston, a useful two-and-a-half-mile chaser Ferdy Murphy trained in the early-'nineties. Hot Weld was sold for 10,000 guineas at Doncaster as a yearling but Murphy had to go to 47,000 guineas to buy him as a four-year-old at the same venue after he had finished second for Tom Tate in a bumper at Carlisle on his debut. The sturdy Hot Weld raced only on good ground or softer early in his career as a hurdler, winning three times over the smaller obstacles, but the combination of fences, long distances and firmer conditions have certainly brought out the best in him since then. A sound jumper on the whole who can race handily, he looks a future Grand National candidate. *Ferdy Murphy*

HOT ZONE (IRE) 5 b.g. Bob Back (USA) – Trixskin (IRE) (Buckskin (FR)) [2006/7 F87: 16m⁶ 16g⁵ 17d³ 16s² Feb 1] fair form over hurdles: likely to stay 2½m: acts on soft ground. *Jonjo O'Neill* **h104**

HOULIHANS FREE (IRE) 8 b.g. Gothland (FR) – Yawa Prince (IRE) (Yawa) [2006/7 c89, h71+, F88: c20f⁴ Apr 5] fair pointer, won in April: lightly raced over hurdles/in chases: stays 19f: usually tongue tied. *Miss J. Paddock* **c73 h–**

HOUSE MARTIN 5 b.m. Spectrum (IRE) – Guignol (IRE) (Anita's Prince) [2006/7 h–: 17m⁴ 16m³ 16g² 16d³ 16d² 16sᵖᵘ Nov 19] modest maiden on Flat (stays 1¼m): poor maiden hurdler: likely to prove best at 2m with emphasis on speed: in cheekpieces/blinkers in 2006/7: ungenuine. *C. R. Dore* **h79 §**

HOWARD HOWARD 7 b.g. Pyramus (USA) – Now In Session (USA) (Diesis) [2006/7 c19m* Apr 24] fair pointer, won maiden in April: successful also in maiden hunter at Towcester on chase debut by 3 lengths from Home By Midnight. *S. Flook* **c95**

HOWARDS DREAM (IRE) 9 b.g. King's Theatre (IRE) – Keiko (Generous (IRE)) [2006/7 h–: 16s⁴ Sep 21] little form over hurdles: tongue tied. *D. A. Nolan* **h–**

HOWARDS ROCKET 6 ch.g. Opening Verse (USA) – Houston Heiress (USA) (Houston (USA)) [2006/7 16g 20m 16v⁶ Dec 19] lightly raced on Flat: no form over hurdles. *J. S. Goldie* **h–**

HOW ART THOU (IRE) 6 b.g. Russian Revival (USA) – Bounty (IRE) (Cataldi) [2006/7 h104, F79: 17dᵖᵘ 22gᵘʳ May 12] fair hurdler: stays 2½m: acts on good to soft ground. *S. Donohoe, Ireland* **h95**

HOWBOUTNO (IRE) 7 br.m. Presenting – Hilda Howard (IRE) (Tidaro (USA)) [2006/7 c20d 21s 26g² Apr 20] €15,000 3-y-o: third foal: half-sister to 2m hurdle winner Arran Mews (by Persian Mews): dam unraced: won maiden point in 2006: first form over **c– h93**

hurdles when second in handicap at Hereford: no show in maiden chases: stays 3¼m: tongue tied last 2 starts, also in cheekpieces final one. *Edward J. Kinirons, Ireland*

HOWDO CHRISTIE (IRE) 7 gr.m. Arzanni – Tibo Hine (Scorpio (FR)) [2006/7 16s 16mᵖᵘ Jun 11] half-sister to winning pointer by Zaffaran: dam never ran: no show in bumper/over hurdles. *C. A. McBratney, Ireland*   **h–**

HOWDY CLOUD 7 b.g. Thowra (FR) – Lehmans Lot (Oats) [2006/7 F17m⁴ Jun 14] half-brother to winning 2m hurdlers Miss Lehman (by Beveled) and Kilcreggan (by Landyap): dam, placed in bumper, half-sister to smart 1m/1¼m performer Mellottie: won maiden point in 2006: soundly beaten in bumper. *J. D. Frost*   **F–**

HOWLE HILL (IRE) 7 b.g. Ali-Royal (IRE) – Grandeur And Grace (USA) (Septieme Ciel (USA)) [2006/7 h139; c18m* c16g* Oct 30] leggy gelding: useful handicap hurdler: successful both starts over fences, in maiden at Fontwell (odds on) in May and novice at Warwick (fairly useful form, beat Nous Voila by 3 lengths) in October: effective at 2m to 2½m: acts on soft and good to firm going: has sweated: usually patiently ridden: consistent. *A. King*   **c129**
  h–

HOWRWENOW (IRE) 9 b.g. Commanche Run – Maythefifth (Hardboy) [2006/7 c118, h–: c23d⁵ c25d* c23v* c24s² Mar 10] good-topped gelding: winning hurdler: fairly useful chaser: won maiden at Hereford (easily) in December and handicap at Exeter (5 ran, beat Charlies Future by ½ length) in February: will stay beyond 3¼m: acts on good to firm and heavy going. *Miss H. C. Knight*   **c121**
  h–

HUBRIS 5 b.g. Josr Algarhoud (IRE) – Feather-In-Her-Cap (Primo Dominie) [2006/7 F17m Apr 28] half-brother to several winners, including Irish 1½m winner Flame of Sion (by Be My Chief): dam unraced half-sister to smart sprinter Governor General: pulled hard and tailed off in bumper on debut. *Mrs Caroline Bailey*   **F–**

HUCKSTER (ZIM) 8 b.g. Tilden – Cavallina (SAF) (Best By Test (USA)) [2006/7 h107x: c20g⁵ 19d 20g²² 22d 21d⁵ 22g Apr 27] close-coupled gelding: fair handicap hurdler: won at Bangor in September: stays 21f: acts on heavy going: tried blinkered (folded tamely): usually makes mistakes (did so when well held on chasing debut). *Miss Venetia Williams*   **c– x**
  h104 x

HUE AND CRY 6 br.g. Monsun (GER) – So Rarely (USA) (Arctic Tern (USA)) [2006/7 F81: 20gᶠ 17d 20g 24g 24dᵖᵘ Feb 14] good-bodied gelding: modest form in bumpers for N. Henderson: no form over hurdles: dead. *M. Smith*   **h–**

HUGO DE GREZ (IRE) 12 b.g. Useful (FR) – Piqua Des Gres (FR) (Waylay) [2006/7 c–, h–: c25d² c24s* c25v³ c25dᵖᵘ c25sᵖᵘ c26gᵖᵘ Apr 7] tall, close-coupled gelding: modest handicap chaser nowadays: first success for 4 years at Newcastle in November: ran poorly last 3 outings: stays 3½m: acts on heavy going: tried in cheekpieces: has had tongue tied: has won 6 times at Carlisle. *B. Storey*   **c90**
  h–

HUGO HACKENBUSH (IRE) 5 ch.g. Quws – Storm Queen (IRE) (Le Bavard (FR)) [2006/7 F16v 16sᵘʳ 15f Feb 8] €10,000 3-y-o, resold 30,000 3-y-o: rather unfurnished gelding: second foal: dam ran once in bumper: signs of ability only when unseating 2 out in novice at Wincanton on hurdling debut: sold 2,000 gns Doncaster May Sales. *Noel T. Chance*   **h83**
  F–

HUGO THE BOSS (IRE) 5 ch.g. Trans Island – Heartland (Northfields (USA)) [2006/7 h–: 16fᵖᵘ 16sᵖᵘ Oct 26] no form over hurdles: sold £700 Ascot December Sales. *S. T. Lewis*   **h–**

HUGO WOLF (IRE) 5 b.g. Mtoto – Instabene (Mossberry) [2006/7 F16v F16s 21s 21m* Apr 9] compact gelding: half-brother to winning pointer by Bob's Return: dam winning pointer: well held in bumpers: second start over hurdles, won maiden at Huntingdon easily by 8 lengths from Nannys Gift: stays 21f: acts on good to firm going. *A. King*   **h96 +**
  F78

HUGS DESTINY (IRE) 6 b.g. Victory Note (USA) – Embracing (Reference Point) [2006/7 h85: 17dᵘʳ 16m⁴ 16f 16m* 16m³ c17m⁶ 16g Apr 2] close-coupled gelding: modest on Flat (stays 1¾m), successful in July: modest hurdler: won maiden at Southwell in June: soundly beaten in maiden on chasing debut: raced around 2m: acts on firm and good to soft going: often tongue tied. *M. A. Barnes*   **c–**
  h90

HUIC HOLLOA (IRE) 11 b.g. Denel (FR) – Buckalgo (IRE) (Buckskin (FR)) [2006/7 c24fᵖᵘ Jul 19] lengthy gelding: little form over hurdles: won maiden point in 2006: went as if amiss on chasing debut. *Tim Vaughan*   **c–**
  h–

HUKA LODGE (IRE) 10 gr.g. Roselier (FR) – Derrella (Derrylin) [2006/7 c–, h117: c26v² 23v 23v* c33v⁶ c31sᵖᵘ Apr 27] well-made gelding: fairly useful handicap hurdler: **c110**
  h118

won at Haydock in January for second successive year by 4 lengths from Desert Tommy: fair handicap chaser: stays 3¼m: raced on going softer than good (acts on heavy): refused once in 2005/6: inconsistent. *Mrs K. Walton*

HUMID CLIMATE 7 ch.g. Desert King (IRE) – Pontoon (Zafonic (USA)) [2006/7 c93§, h–§: 16d^{pu} c16g^5 c19g^{pu} Apr 27] strong, good-bodied gelding: novice hurdler: poor handicap chaser: stays 2½m: acts on firm and good to soft going: refused to race once in 2005/6: ungenuine. *Mrs H. E. Rees*   c83 § h– §

HUM (IRE) 6 ch.m. Cadeaux Genereux – Ensorceleuse (FR) (Fabulous Dancer (USA)) [2006/7 h–: 17v^5 Jan 9] no form over hurdles: tried in cheekpieces. *Evan Williams*   h–

HUMOUROUS (IRE) 5 b.g. Darshaan – Amusing Time (IRE) (Sadler's Wells (USA)) [2006/7 16f^5 17d^4 17m^{ur} 16f 20g 24d^5 24m^2 25v^F 20s^{pu} 20g Apr 16] good-topped gelding: fairly useful 1m winner on Flat at 2 yrs, well held only start in 2005, sold out of Saeed bin Suroor's stable 14,000 gns Doncaster January (2006) Sales: modest novice hurdler: stays easy 3m: acts on good to firm going, seemingly not on soft/heavy: tried in cheekpieces. *B. Storey*   h85

HUNCHEON PADDY (IRE) 10 b.g. Bob's Return (IRE) – Waterland Lady (Strong Gale) [2006/7 c98: c23g^2 c20m^5 c20f^4 c20s Apr 25] workmanlike gelding: fair handicap chaser: in narrow lead when bad mistake last (eased considerably) at Perth final start: stays 3m: acts on soft and firm going. *I. R. Ferguson, Ireland*   c107 +

HUNTER PUDDING 7 b.m. Shambo – Pudding (Infantry) [2006/7 h68: c17m^4 Apr 9] poor form over hurdles: well beaten in points/selling handicap chase. *N. J. Hawke*   c– h–

HUNTERS RIDGE (IRE) 6 b.g. Saddlers' Hall (IRE) – Dandy Poll (Pollerton) [2006/7 F80: 16m 17g Jun 20] well held in bumper/over hurdles: sold 1,400 gns Doncaster November Sales. *O. Sherwood*   h–

HUNTERSWAY (IRE) 10 ch.g. Treasure Hunter – Dunmanway (Le Bavard (FR)) [2006/7 c20m^{pu} May 18] fair pointer: in cheekpieces, no show in hunter on chase debut. *Mrs A. Price*   c– h–

HUNTING HAZE 4 b.g. Foxhound (USA) – Second Affair (IRE) (Pursuit of Love) [2006/7 16m^F 20g Apr 3] fair maiden on Flat (stays 1½m): shaped better than result suggested on completed outing in juvenile hurdles, weakening: likely to prove best around 2m: should do better. *Miss S. E. Hall*   h82 p

HUNTING JEAN 4 b.f. Hunting Lion (IRE) – Gemma Jean (Derek H) [2006/7 F16s F16g 22g^{pu} Apr 15] eighth foal: dam never ran: no form in bumpers/novice hurdle. *C. R. Wilson*   h– F–

HUNTING LODGE (IRE) 6 ch.g. Grand Lodge (USA) – Vijaya (USA) (Lear Fan (USA)) [2006/7 h94: 22g^6 21g^3 22m^4 21m* 22g* 24m^3 22m^5 20g^2 20d^{pu} Dec 28] small gelding: fair hurdler: won maiden at Huntingdon and handicap at Newton Abbot in June: stays 3m: unraced on firm going, acts on any other: blinkered last 6 starts. *H. J. Manners*   h100

HUNTING YUPPIE (IRE) 10 ch.g. Treasure Hunter – Super Yuppie (Belfalas) [2006/7 c–, h–: c22s^{pu} c20d c24m Jan 29] robust gelding: winning hurdler: runner-up in maiden on chasing debut in 2004/5: lightly raced and no form since: stays 3m: acts on soft ground. *N. A. Twiston-Davies*   c– h–

HURLERS CROSS (IRE) 9 b.g. Jurado (USA) – Maid of Music (IRE) (Orchestra) [2006/7 c26g c24v^{ur} c26v^3 c28g^3 c24g^{bd} c26m^2 c26g^2 Apr 23] sturdy gelding: poor handicap chaser, off 20 months prior to return: left F. Jordan after second outing: stays 3½m: acts on good to firm and good to soft going: tried in headgear: sketchy jumper. *P. A. Blockley*   c80 x h–

HURRICANE BASIL (IRE) 5 gr.g. Good Thyne (USA) – Toureen Gale (IRE) (Strong Gale) [2006/7 F16g F16g F16x 19v^{pu} 20v^{pu} Mar 22] €62,000 3-y-o, 15,000 4-y-o: rather leggy gelding: third foal: dam, fairly useful hurdler/fair chaser, stayed 2½m: no show in bumpers/novice hurdles: tried tongue tied. *R. Shiels*   h– F–

HURRICANE COAST 8 b.g. Hurricane Sky (AUS) – Tread Carefully (Sharpo) [2006/7 h–: 16g May 14] lengthy, rather sparely-made gelding: fair on Flat (stays 9.5f): no solid form over hurdles: tried blinkered. *K. McAuliffe*   h–

HURRICANE FRANCIS 7 ch.g. Minster Son – Joe's Fancy (Apollo Eight) [2006/7 h–, F86: 23g 26d^{pu} Jun 4] third in bumper on debut: no form over hurdles: sold £550 Ascot December Sales. *T. D. Walford*   h– F–

HUSH NOW 5 gr.g. Real Quiet (USA) – Holy Nola (USA) (Silver Deputy (CAN)) [2006/7 F16f Jul 16] second foal: half-brother to US Grade 2 8.5f winner Preachinat-   F–

thebar (by Silver Charm): dam, winner in USA, sister to smart US 1m/9f performer Bare Necessities: breathing problem in bumper on debut. *F. P. Murtagh*

HUSH TIGER 6 br.g. Moshaajir (USA) – Just Hush (Kind of Hush) [2006/7 h86, F92: 16g^2 16g 20g 17v^4 18s* 20s^4 20v^5 16v^3 18s^2 18g^4 Apr 15] good-topped gelding: fair hurdler: won handicap at Kelso in November: best efforts in similar events last 2 outings: stays 2½m: acts on heavy going: has been let down by jumping. *R. Nixon*   **h110**

HUTCH 9 b.g. Rock Hopper – Polly's Teahouse (Shack (USA)) [2006/7 h–: 17d^{pu} c16g^{ur} c16v^4 c16g^{bd} c17g^6 c20g^2 c20s^6 Apr 27] lengthy gelding: winning hurdler, left Mrs L. Normile and off 8 months after first start: form (poor) over fences only on penultimate outing: stays 2½m: raced mainly on good ground or softer: sometimes blinkered/in cheekpieces. *P. Beaumont*   **c82** **h–**

HUW THE NEWS 8 b.g. Primo Dominie – Martha Stevens (USA) (Super Concorde (USA)) [2006/7 c–, h–: 17m^{pu} 19d c16d^5 Jul 23] good-topped gelding: little sign of ability: tried blinkered/in cheekpieces. *S. C. Burrough*   **c–** **h–**

HYLIA 8 ch.m. Sir Harry Lewis (USA) – Lady Stock (Crofter (USA)) [2006/7 h84: 20m^4 22m 24g* Jun 15] modest handicap hurdler: won 17-runner event at Uttoxeter in June: stays 3m: acts on good to soft and good to firm going: tried in cheekpieces: has had tongue tied. *Mrs P. Robeson*   **h87**

HYPARK (IRE) 8 br.m. Oscar (IRE) – La Ronde (Common Grounds) [2006/7 F–: 19s^{pu} Mar 12] more signs of temperament than ability: tried visored. *R. J. Price*   **h–**

I

IAMWHATIAM 5 b.g. Morpeth – Super Sarena (IRE) (Taufan (USA)) [2006/7 F16m 16d 17d Oct 31] sturdy gelding: second foal: dam maiden on Flat (stayed 1¾m) and over jumps: no show in bumper/over hurdles. *J. D. Frost*   **h–** **F–**

IASKOFYOU (IRE) 10 br.g. Jolly Jake (NZ) – Deep Bart (Deep Run) [2006/7 c22s c20d^5 c18g^{pu} c19g^{pu} c19m^{ur} Apr 10] ex-Irish gelding: winning chaser: poor form in 2006/7, left D. Fitzgerald after third outing: stays 2½m: acts on soft and good to firm ground. *A. J. Chamberlain*   **c78**

IBBERTON 7 b.g. Sovereign Water (FR) – Betty Hayes (Jimsun) [2006/7 20v^4 21v^5 20v 24v^3 22d Mar 20] fifth foal: dam fair staying hurdler/chaser: won maiden on first of 2 starts in points in 2005: poor novice hurdler: stays 3m. *R. H. Alner*   **h77**

IBERIAN LIGHT (USA) 4 b.g. Fantastic Light – Spain Lane (USA) (Seeking The Gold (USA)) [2006/7 16d 16f^4 16s^4 16m^3 16s Oct 26] modest maiden on Flat (stays 1½m), sold out of N. Callaghan's stable 13,000 gns Newmarket July Sales: modest juvenile hurdler: tried blinkered/tongue tied. *G. Elliott, Ireland*   **h84**

IBERUS (GER) 9 b.g. Monsun (GER) – Iberica (GER) (Green Dancer (USA)) [2006/7 h94: 17s^{pu} 20m 17v^{pu} 16d 24m^3 Apr 17] angular gelding: poor handicap hurdler nowadays: sold out of S. Gollings's stable 1,800 gns Doncaster August Sales after first outing: stays 3m: acts on soft and good to firm going: tried visored/in cheekpieces/tongue tied. *V. J. Hughes*   **h76**

ICE AND FIRE 8 b.g. Cadeaux Genereux – Tanz (IRE) (Sadler's Wells (USA)) [2006/7 c–, h77: 16g^{pu} 17d^{pu} Feb 19] medium-sized gelding: modest on Flat (stays 2m), successful 3 times on all-weather in 2006: maiden hurdler: little show both starts over fences: should stay beyond 2m: tried visored/blinkered/tongue tied. *J. T. Stimpson*   **c–** **h–**

ICE AND SODA (IRE) 7 b.g. Arctic Lord – Another Vodka (IRE) (Moscow Society (USA)) [2006/7 22v 16d 21s Dec 7] rather leggy gelding: dam unraced half-sister to useful staying jumpers Stray Shot and Over The Last: bumper winner: modest maiden hurdler: sold out of C. Swan's stable 22,000 gns Doncaster May Sales after first outing: should stay beyond 19f: raced on good ground or softer (acts on heavy). *B. G. Powell*   **h89**

ICEBERGE (IRE) 11 b.g. Glacial Storm (USA) – Laura Daisy (Buckskin (FR)) [2006/7 c102, h–x: c25m^5 24m^4 20m^5 Aug 11] lengthy gelding: modest hurdler: successful on first of 2 outings over fences: stays 3¼m: acts on heavy going, probably on good to firm: tried visored/in cheekpieces. *Ian Williams*   **c–** **h89**

ICE BUCKET (IRE) 7 ch.g. Glacial Storm (USA) – Tranbu (IRE) (Buckskin (FR)) [2006/7 h92, F–: c20s c19s* c21g^2 c22g^3 Apr 7] sturdy, lengthy gelding: lightly raced   **c108** **h–**

over hurdles: fair form in novice chases: won at Hereford in December: stays 2¾m: acts on soft going. *Miss H. C. Knight*

ICE CREAM (FR) 6 ch.m. Cyborg (FR) – Icone (FR) (Nikos) [2006/7 h–, F87: 16s² 19g⁵ 20gᵖᵘ 20s⁴ Jan 26] unfurnished mare: form (modest) when only on reappearance: should stay beyond 2m: raced on good ground or softer. *M. E. D. Francis*
    h87

ICE CRYSTAL 10 b.g. Slip Anchor – Crystal Fountain (Great Nephew) [2006/7 c–§, h104§: 24s c16d⁴ c29vᵖᵘ c24g³ 27g* c26g* Apr 1] leggy gelding: fair handicap hurdler: back to best to win at Sedgefield in March: modest chaser: won 5-runner novice at Newton Abbot (by 16 lengths) in April: thorough stayer: acts on heavy going: has worn headgear, including last 2 outings: tongue tied: none too genuine. *K. J. Burke*
    c99
    h111

ICE IMAGE (IRE) 5 b.g. Darnay – Ice Trix (IRE) (Glacial Storm (USA)) [2006/7 F16g⁴ F16g Apr 23] first foal: dam unraced: much better effort in bumpers when fourth to Abstinence at Wetherby. *G. A. Charlton*
    F92

ICE LAD (NZ) 8 br.g. Woodbury Lad (USA) – Ice Queen (NZ) (Dorchester (FR)) [2006/7 24dᵖᵘ 16sᵖᵘ Jan 24] workmanlike gelding: placed twice around 11f from 12 starts on Flat in New Zealand: no show in novice hurdles. *D. J. Wintle*
    h–

ICE MELTED (IRE) 6 ch.g. Old Vic – Warren Thyne (IRE) (Good Thyne (USA)) [2006/7 h93+, F–: 20gᵖᵘ 20g 16m c19s* c20s² c24v* c24v² c20d² c24sᵖᵘ Mar 17] sturdy gelding: novice hurdler: fairly useful handicap chaser: won at Towcester in October and Bangor (idled) in December: good second next 2 starts, beaten 3½ lengths by Character Building at Market Rasen on second occasion: stays 3m: acts on heavy going. *Jonjo O'Neill*
    c118
    h–

ICE SAINT 12 gr.g. Ballacashtal (CAN) – Sylvan Song (Song) [2006/7 c21dᵖᵘ c24mᵖᵘ Jun 8] good-topped gelding: winning hurdler: yet to complete over fences: should stay 3m: acts on heavy and good to firm going. *Mrs A. V. Roberts*
    c–
    h–

ICE TEA (IRE) 7 ch.g. Glacial Storm (USA) – Kakemona (Kambalda) [2006/7 F111: 19g⁶ 27s² 25s³ 24m³ 24g* 20g² 20g⁴ 24m² Apr 20] sturdy, good-bodied gelding: bumper winner for M. Rimell (trained on debut by Heather Dalton): fairly useful hurdler: won handicap at Newcastle in March by 1¾ lengths from Brooklyn Breeze with something in hand: good efforts in frame after, 17 lengths second of 4 to Otto des Pictons in novice handicap at Ayr final outing: stays 27f: acts on soft and good to firm going: blinkered last 5 outings. *D. McCain Jnr*
    h120

ICHI BEAU (IRE) 13 b.g. Convinced – May As Well (Kemal (FR)) [2006/7 c17g⁵ c17m* c16m² c16d² 18s⁵ c21v⁶ c16v* 16d⁶ Feb 3] sturdy, deep-bodied gelding: winning hurdler, sold out of A. Martin's stable 2,800 gns Doncaster October Sales before fifth start: fair handicap chaser: won at Killarney in July and Haydock in January: barely stays 2½m: acts on heavy and good to firm going: tried in cheekpieces: often tongue tied: effective held up or making running: bold jumper of fences, though inclined to make odd mistake. *Dr P. Pritchard*
    c110
    h–

ICY PROSPECT (IRE) 9 ch.g. Glacial Storm (USA) – Prospect Lady (IRE) (Boreen (FR)) [2006/7 c108, h–: c22gᵖᵘ c21f Sep 10] angular gelding: bumper/hurdle winner: won handicap on chasing debut in 2005/6: no impact since, including in points, left N. Twiston-Davies and off over 8 months before return: should stay beyond 21f: acts on good to soft going: tried in cheekpieces. *D. G. Bridgwater*
    c–
    h–

ICY RIVER (IRE) 10 ch.g. Over The River (FR) – Icy Lou (Bluerullah) [2006/7 c–, h–: c20sᵖᵘ May 21] strong, lengthy gelding: winning hurdler: no show in handicap chases: should have stayed 3m: acted on good to firm and good to soft going: dead. *K. G. Reveley*
    c–
    h–

IDARAH (USA) 4 gr. or ro.g. Aljabr (USA) – Fatina (Nashwan (USA)) [2006/7 16v² 16s* 16s² Apr 27] useful on Flat (barely stays 1½m), sold out of W. Haggas's stable 85,000 gns Newmarket Autumn Sales, and gelded: fairly useful form over hurdles: won juvenile at Hexham in April by 5 lengths from Folk Tune: upped in trip, better effort when 10 lengths second to Le Briar Soul in novice at Perth on handicap debut later in month: stays 2½m: raced on soft/heavy ground: looked none too keen on debut. *L. Lungo*
    h121

IDBURY (IRE) 9 b.g. Zaffaran (USA) – Delcarrow (Roi Guillaume (FR)) [2006/7 c–, h97?: 24mᵖᵘ Jul 12] strong, good-topped gelding: little impact over fences: modest hurdler: won novice handicap at Worcester in July: stays 3m: acts on good to firm going, probably on heavy. *V. J. Hughes*
    c–
    h97

IDEAL DU BOIS BEURY (FR) 11 b. or br.g. Useful (FR) – Pampa Star (FR) (Pampabird) [2006/7 c77§, h–: c16s⁵ c16d⁴ 22v Mar 3] sturdy, lengthy gelding: winning
    c70 §
    h– §

hurdler: poor maiden chaser: seems to stay 25f: probably acts on any going: tried visored: tends to get behind: not one to trust. *A. Robson*

IDIDNTHINKIDMAKEIT 7 b.g. Alflora (IRE) – Levantine Rose (Levanter) **h–** [2006/7 F16g 20f^{pu} Jun 3] 30,000 4-y-o: sixth foal: brother to fair hurdler up to 2½m **F72** Fragrant Rose and half-brother to fair hunter chaser Derryrose (by Derrylin): dam, winning hurdler, stayed 25f: mid-field in bumper (kicked at start): no show in maiden on hurdling debut following month. *P. R. Webber*

IDIOME (FR) 11 b.g. Djarvis (FR) – Asterie L'Ermitage (FR) (Hamster (FR)) [2006/7 **c102** c102, h110: c20s^2 c19s^4 c22s^4 c19d^5 Feb 2] leggy gelding: fair handicap hurdler/chaser, **h–** left Mrs L. Taylor and off over 6 months before second start: stays 21f: unraced on firm going, acts on any other: has bled from nose/had breathing problem. *P. C. Ritchens*

IDLE TALK (IRE) 8 br.g. Hubbly Bubbly (USA) – Belon Breeze (IRE) (Strong Gale) **c149** [2006/7 c150p, h–: c27d^2 c26s^6 c25v^{ur} c26g^{ur} c36g^{ur} c32m^{ur} Apr 21] strong gelding: **h–** winning hurdler: very smart chaser: good second to My Will in Grade 3 handicap at Cheltenham on return, best of those to race prominently: below form in Hennessy Cognac Gold Cup (Handicap) 2 weeks later: unseated all starts after, bought privately out of T. George's stable after first of them: stays 33f: acts on soft ground. *D. McCain Jnr*

IDOLE FIRST (IRE) 8 b.g. Flemensfirth (USA) – Sharon Doll (IRE) (Shahras- **c144** tani (USA)) [2006/7 c125x, h–: c20s* c21v^3 c22v^4 c21g* Mar 15] **h–**
　　　　　Handicaps at the Cheltenham Festival are among the most fiercely competi- tive races of the season and, for the majority of horses, success in such an event marks the high point of a career. Only a select band have managed to win more than one handicap at the Festival and Idole First joined their number in the latest season. Chu-Teh (1967 & 1968) and Glyde Court (1985 & 1986) both won the Fulke Walwyn Kim Muir Handicap Chase twice, Top Twenty (1958 & 1959) and Dulwich (1974 & 1976) were both dual winners of the Grand Annual. The National Hunt Handicap Chase (now the William Hill Trophy) has been won twice by Sentina (1957 & 1958) and Scot Lane (1982 & 1983) and dual winners of the Mildmay of Fleet are The Tsarevich (1985 & 1986) and Elfast (1992 & 1994). Interestingly only the evergreen Willie Wumpkins (also a Festival novice winner), who achieved three consecutive victories in the Coral Golden Hurdle from 1979 onwards, has won a handicap hurdle at the Festival more than once. The only six horses to have won two separate handicaps include Political Pop, who won the 1981 Mildmay of Flete and 1982 Kim Muir, and Flyer's Nap, who won the latter race in 1995 prior to landing the William Hill Trophy two years later. Irish raider Khan followed up his

Racing Post Plate (Handicap Chase), Cheltenham—a second Festival win for Idole First (No.14) and Alan O'Keeffe, who are chased over the last by Mariah Rollins (third) and the grey Reveillez (sixth)

1970 County Hurdle success by winning the Grand Annual the following season. Good Prospect won the Coral Golden Hurdle in 1976 before landing the Kim Muir four years later and the same period separated the victories of Blowing Wind in the 1998 County Hurdle and the 2002 Mildmay of Flete. Idole First became the sixth member of this group when winning the latest renewal of the Racing Post Plate (formerly the Mildmay of Flete), two years on from his 33/1 win in the Coral Cup.

The smallish, angular Idole First failed to convince with his jumping when switched to fences in 2005/6—managing just one win from five starts—and was notably disappointing when well held in the Jewson Novices' Handicap Chase at the Cheltenham Festival. In four handicap chases in the latest season, Idole First's jumping was generally much improved and he matched the useful form of which he was capable as a hurdler. The latest renewal of the Racing Post Plate was a very competitive twenty-three-runner event with Idole First one of the better-fancied contenders, starting at 12/1. He was well ridden by Alan O'Keeffe, who gets on well with him and has ridden him on all but one of his starts over jumps, including in the Coral Cup. Never far away in a race few managed to get into, Idole First led two out and quickened impressively from the last to beat another previous Festival handicap winner, the 2003 Grand Annual hero Palarshan, by four lengths. Still only an eight-year-old, Idole First should have a few more years in which to attempt to emulate Willie Wumpkins by winning a third handicap at Cheltenham—indeed, Willie Wumpkins left it until the age of eleven before starting his remarkable handicap winning spree.

Idole First has gone well fresh before and made a successful return from over nine months off when winning the twelve-runner intercasino.co.uk Handicap Chase at Kempton in January by two and a half lengths from Laskari. Two weeks later Idole First ran respectably when three and a half lengths third of ten to Whispered Secret in a Grade 3 handicap at Cheltenham, though it's debatable how useful a trial this proved to be for the Festival given that six fences were omitted due to the course's recurring problems with low winter win. Idole First looked ill at ease from a long way out when a remote fourth to Nozic at Uttoxeter next time, seemingly not having recovered from the exertions of his two previous outings, though the barely raceable conditions there were probably a factor, too.

Idole First (IRE) (b.g. 1999)	Flemensfirth (USA) (b 1992)	Alleged (b 1974)	Hoist The Flag
			Princess Pout
		Etheldreda (ch 1985)	Diesis
			Royal Bond
	Sharon Doll (IRE) (b 1991)	Shahrastani (ch 1983)	Nijinsky
			Shademah
		Ah Ya Zein (b 1983)	Artaius
			Come True

The pedigree of Idole First was covered in *Chasers & Hurdlers 2004/05* and there is little to add to what was stated there, although it's worth pointing out that his prolific sire, Flemensfirth, from whose first crop Idole First comes, has been enjoying considerable success. The likes of Tidal Bay, Black Harry, Imperial Commander and Ponmeoath are all at least useful performers of his who also figured fairly prominently at the latest Cheltenham Festival. Idole First has gained most of his wins at around two and a half miles but is effective at up to three miles. He has raced only on good ground or softer to date (acts on heavy). *Miss Venetia Williams*

IDRIS (GER) 6 ch.g. Generous (IRE) – Idraak (Kris) [2006/7 h111: c20g² c21d³ c18d² c20s* c22s⁴ c19dᵖᵘ c20m* Apr 27] sturdy gelding: winning hurdler: fairly useful chaser: won novice handicaps at Sandown in December and April, well backed when beating Art Virginia by 2½ lengths on latter occasion: stays 2½m: acts on heavy and good to firm going: races prominently: consistent. *G. L. Moore* **c120** **h—**

I FEEL FINE 4 ch.f. Minster Son – Jendorcet (Grey Ghost) [2006/7 F16s Mar 7] second foal: dam poor maiden hurdler: tailed off in bumper on debut. *D. W. Barker* **F—**

IFFY 6 b.g. Orpen (USA) – Hopesay (Warning) [2006/7 h99+: 16m* 17m³ 16m* 16m² 16g⁴ 16g* 16s³ 16g⁴ 16gᶠ Mar 23] close-coupled gelding: progressive hurdler in 2006/7: won novice at Worcester in June and handicaps at Stratford in August and Aintree (fairly useful form when beating Unjust Law by 1½ lengths) in October: good efforts in frame **h123**

next 2 starts: likely to prove best around 2m: acts on soft and good to firm going: patiently ridden. *R. Lee*

IF IN DOUBT 6 b.g. Zaffaran (USA) – Rodney's Sister (Leading Man) [2006/7 F16d[4] Dec 14] workmanlike gelding: half-brother to bumper winner Bala Pyjama (by Henbit): dam unraced half-sister to Triumph Hurdle winner Saxon Farm: fair form when fourth to Tot O'Whiskey in bumper at Catterick on debut. *A. Parker* **F88**

IFNI DU LUC (FR) 11 b. or br.m. Chamberlin (FR) – Acca du Luc (FR) (Djarvis (FR)) [2006/7 c20g[6] c20g[2] Apr 16] leggy mare: one-time useful chaser for N. Henderson: fit from points (successful in February), better effort in hunters in 2006/7 when runner-up at Wetherby: barely stays testing 3m: acts on heavy going: has run well when sweating. *D. McCain Jnr* **c90 h–**

IGLOO D'ESTRUVAL (FR) 11 br.g. Garde Royale – Jalousie (FR) (Blockhaus) [2006/7 c–x, h–: 26d c26d[4] 27d[pu] Aug 20] lengthy, useful-looking gelding: winning hurdler/chaser: lightly raced and modest form at best since 2004: stays 3¾m: acts on soft going: often visored: sketchy jumper of fences. *Mrs L. C. Taylor* **c89 x h–**

I HEAR THUNDER (IRE) 9 b.g. Montelimar (USA) – Carrigeen Gala (Strong Gale) [2006/7 c123, h–: c24g[2] c27s[3] c21g* Nov 19] lengthy gelding: fairly useful handicap chaser: won 20-runner Grand Sefton Chase at Aintree in November by 7 lengths from Shannon's Pride: effective around 2½m and stays 3½m: raced on good going or softer (acts on soft): genuine. *R. H. Buckler* **c128 h–**

IHURU 5 b.g. Atraf – E Sharp (USA) (Diesis) [2006/7 h–, F–: 16d 16m 16m[pu] Jul 4] leggy gelding: no form in bumper/over hurdles. *M. J. Gingell* **h–**

IKDAM MELODY (IRE) 11 b.g. Ikdam – Music Slipper (Orchestra) [2006/7 c94d, h–: c24v[pu] c27m[ur] c23m 24m Aug 4] sturdy gelding: winning hurdler/chaser: little show in 2006/7: stays 3¼m: acts on firm and soft going: tried visored, usually in cheekpieces. *Miss J. E. Foster* **c– h–**

IKEMBA (IRE) 10 b.g. Executive Perk – Ardglass Pride (Golden Love) [2006/7 c92, h–: 24v[4] 24s[2] 21v[2] 26s* 24v[5] Mar 10] rangy gelding: winning pointer: runner-up on completed start in hunter chases: poor hurdler: won handicap at Hereford in January: stays 3¼m: acts on heavy going: tongue tied last 4 starts: has been let down by jumping. *J. B. Groucott* **c– h83**

IKTITAF (IRE) 6 b.g. Alhaarth (IRE) – Istibshar (USA) (Mr Prospector (USA)) [2006/7 h145p: 18d* 16d* 16s* 16v[2] 16d 16d[F] 16m[6] Apr 27] **h162**

After the assassination of President Kennedy in 1963, a seemingly remarkable list of coincidences, numbering well into double figures, between that event and the assassination of President Lincoln ninety-eight years earlier soon appeared in the popular press and still get trotted out to this day. For example, Lincoln was elected to Congress in 1846, Kennedy in 1946; Lincoln was elected President in 1860, Kennedy in 1960; both were succeeded by southerners called Johnson; both were shot on a Friday, both were shot in the head and when with their wives; both assassins were known by three names—John Wilkes Booth and Lee Harvey Oswald—which comprised fifteen letters; Kennedy had a secretary called Lincoln who warned him not to go to Dallas, Lincoln had a secretary called Kennedy who warned him not to go to the theatre. Most of the coincidences are either superficial (apart from the year they were elected to Congress there is virtually no parallel between the two political careers until Lincoln and Kennedy became President), unsurprising (a presidential public appearance with the First Lady), logically likely (given their backgrounds and the political situation at the time, it would have been unlikely that Lincoln and Kennedy would have anything other than a southern running mate) or simply not a coincidence (boringly, Lincoln's secretary was actually called John George Nicolay!). Not so amazing after all.

Consider, also, the parallels between Iktitaf and Detroit City: both won twice at Grade 1 level in their novice season over hurdles; both won a race called the Cesarewitch before their reappearance over hurdles; both won their first three starts over hurdles in 2006/7, a haul which each included a race whose status had been considerably enhanced since the previous year; both subsequently disappointed in Grade 1 company; both wore a tongue strap on their final start; both have Mr Prospector as a grandsire; both their trainers have five letters in their surname. Iktitaf and Detroit City were also of similar merit in their first season over hurdles,

Maplewood Developments Morgiana Hurdle, Punchestown—
Iktitaf claims the scalps of Asian Maze and Brave Inca (out of shot)

rated 145p and 146p respectively in *Chasers & Hurdlers 2005/06*. The year-older
Iktitaf gained his Grade 1 wins as a novice in the Royal Bond at Fairyhouse and
the two-mile Champion Novices' at Punchestown, in which he beat the British
challenger Straw Bear. He didn't run at either of the major British Festivals
where Detroit City gained his successes. Both were prospective candidates for top
honours in open company.

The Irish Cesarewitch at the Curragh, like its Newmarket counterpart, has
long been an attractive target for trainers of jumpers—Vincent O'Brien won the
race back in the late-'forties with both Cottage Rake and Hatton's Grace, three-
times winners of the Cheltenham Gold Cup and Champion Hurdle respectively.
Iktitaf had been a fairly useful three-year-old for John Gosden, when raced at up to
a mile and a quarter, and took full advantage of a fairly lenient mark and the step up
to two miles to justify favouritism at the Curragh, as over hurdles being produced
late after travelling strongly held up. Good performance though it was, Iktitaf's
form on the Flat is still some 20 lb behind that of Detroit City in that sphere. Iktitaf
was already as short as 12/1 for the Champion Hurdle when he returned over jumps
at Punchestown ten days later. Long odds on in a four-runner listed event, Iktitaf
was nevertheless impressive and followed up in even easier fashion in the Anglo
Irish Bank Hurdle at Down Royal. This intermediate event was promoted to Grade
3 status for the first time and, given that Feathard Lady and Macs Joy (who beat
Brave Inca) had won the two previous runnings, there was some logic to the move.
Without Iktitaf, however, the latest renewal would have been poor indeed, as he
started at 7/1-on against three markedly inferior rivals. After that success, Iktitaf
was due to be stepped up to two and a half miles, in the Hatton's Grace Hurdle at
Fairyhouse. However, the indisposition of his stable-companion Harchibald meant
that Iktitaf stood in for him in the Maplewood Developments Morgiana Hurdle at
Punchestown, newly promoted to Grade 1 at the expense of what was formerly the
McManus Memorial at Tipperary at the start of October. The move made sense
from an Irish point of view, the Morgiana having a fine roll of honour since it has
been run at two miles (Limestone Lad three times, Moscow Flyer, Harchibald
and Brave Inca among the winners) but it means there are now two Grade 1
two-mile hurdles a week apart in Britain (the 'Fighting Fifth' at Newcastle) and
Ireland. Three weeks after the Morgiana is the even more valuable International

Hurdle (a race formerly known as the Bula which Cheltenham will presumably be pushing to have promoted to Grade 1 at some point). The concern must be that there will not be enough good horses to fill all three races. For the third race running, Iktitaf faced just three opponents, though his rivals in the Morgiana were a good deal tougher than those he'd encountered previously in 2006/7: the Champion Hurdle winner Brave Inca, the Aintree Hurdle winner Asian Maze and the Champion Chase victor Newmill. With the advantage of race fitness, Iktitaf started favourite and while Newmill, clearly, and Brave Inca, probably, were going to improve for the run, Asian Maze certainly didn't shape as if short of fitness. Iktitaf made pretty short work of her, cruising into the lead before the last and ridden out as he idled to score by a length and a quarter.

Iktitaf was quoted at 5/1 for the Champion Hurdle after the Morgiana, but that proved the highpoint of his season. Brave Inca, only third in the Morgiana, turned the tables in another four-runner race, the December Festival Hurdle at Leopardstown, Iktitaf much less well suited to a tactical race than he had been by a well-run one at Punchestown and unable to quicken after being awkward at the last, going down by a length and a quarter, with six lengths back to third-placed Silent Oscar. Iktitaf, who might have gone to Kempton instead of Leopardstown for the Christmas Hurdle (which his stable-companion Jazz Messenger won), was again doing duty for the still-absent Harchibald and did so once more in the AIG Europe Champion Hurdle back at Leopardstown in late-January. On this occasion, Iktitaf ran lamentably and gave further fuel to those critics who had rather harshly crabbed him for his finishing effort the time before, coming last of eight to Hardy Eustace (with Brave Inca second), virtually pulled up in the end and later reported to have a lung infection. After those defeats, Iktitaf drifted in the Champion Hurdle betting and when he lined up at Cheltenham he went off at 14/1, with Brave Inca 11/2 and another old rival Straw Bear 7/1. Detroit City, still in the ascendant, started 6/4 favourite. As it turned out, none of that quartet showed fully what they could do, but, of the four, Iktitaf offered most for the future. In a race run more to suit him than the Festival Hurdle, he was still travelling strongly close up when he fell three out, too far out to say where he would have finished, but leaving open the question about whether he might still prove to be as good a two-mile hurdler as there was around. Alas, Iktitaf's final appearance did nothing to advance that view. In his fifth successive Grade 1, the ACCBank Champion Hurdle at Punchestown, Iktitaf started second favourite to Cheltenham absentee Macs Joy, preferred by stable jockey Paul Carberry to both Sweet Wake and Harchibald, who was finally back in action. In another steadily-run affair, Iktitaf failed to settle and didn't quicken when ridden, possibly finding the ground firmer than ideal. He was far from the only leading contender to run below form in the Grade 1 events at Punchestown and, like some of the others, may be best forgiven his effort there.

			Northern Dancer
		Unfuwain	Height of Fashion
	Alhaarth (IRE)	(b 1985)	
	(b 1993)	Irish Valley	Irish River
Iktitaf (IRE)		(ch 1982)	Green Valley
(b.g. 2001)		Mr Prospector	Raise A Native
		(b 1970)	Gold Digger
	Istibshar (USA)		
	(br 1991)	Namaqua	Storm Bird
		(b 1985)	Courtly Dee

Iktitaf was rated just behind Detroit City in last year's Annual but figures just ahead of him this time. Both have the ability to make an impact at the top level in years to come, though it's safe to say both go into 2007/8 with plenty to prove. Of the pair, Iktitaf would appear to have more plausible explanations for his later flops and it's probably significant that Noel Meade announced in May that Iktitaf had been hobdayed following his campaign. He has worn a tongue strap since mid-2005/6. That there were parallels between Iktitaf and Detroit City is hardly surprising but, as can be seen, some of them are due solely to the absence of Harchibald. The presence of Mr Prospector in the pedigrees of Iktitaf and Detroit City isn't much of a surprise, either, given that both are Flat-bred. Detroit City is by the Mr Prospector stallion Kingmambo, whereas Iktitaf has Mr Prospector as his maternal grandsire. Iktitaf's dam Istibshar showed fair form at six and seven furlongs, winning a maiden over six. Iktitaf is one of five winners out of Istibshar,

Mrs P. Sloan's "Iktitaf"

the pick of the others his close relative Mostabshir (by Unfuwain), who was fairly useful at up to a mile and a half, and his half-sister Furaat (by Danehill), a fairly useful seven-furlong winner. Istibshar's latest foal to race Julatten, a sister to Iktitaf, showed very little in three runs on the Flat in 2006. Meanwhile, her 2005 Val Royal filly was bought for €28,000 by Liam Cashman's Glenview Stud as a yearling. The tall, useful-looking Iktitaf has raced mainly at around two miles over hurdles, though clearly connections have some hope that he will stay two and a half miles, given they were considering the Hatton's Grace. Iktitaf acts on heavy going, though he may prove best under less testing conditions. With question marks over Harchibald, and the 2006 Royal & SunAlliance Hurdle winner Nicanor surely likely to be sent over fences should he return, Iktitaf is likely to remain his stable's standard bearer in Grade 1 hurdles. Noel Meade, like Philip Hobbs, does indeed have five letters in his surname, but then Lincoln and Kennedy both have seven and that's hardly an amazing coincidence either. *N. Meade, Ireland*

IL'ATHOU (FR) 11 b.g. Lute Antique (FR) – Va Thou Line (FR) (El Badr) [2006/7   **c125** c130, h111: c20d³ c19s² c20v^{pu} 21s Jan 24] tall, lengthy gelding: winning hurdler: fairly   **h–** useful handicap chaser: creditable efforts first 2 starts in 2006/7, 2½ lengths second to Wain Mountain at Chepstow: barely stays 3m: acts on heavy going: tried in cheekpieces (ran badly): tends to get on toes and sometimes sweats: bold-jumping front runner. *S. E. H. Sherwood*

IL DE BOITRON (FR) 9 b.g. Sheyrann – Ilkiya (FR) (General Holme (USA))   **c103** [2006/7 c119, h–: c20v c24s c31d c34f^{pu} Apr 26] good-topped gelding: winning chaser,   **h–** races mainly in cross-country events nowadays: below best in 2006/7: stays 31f: acts on heavy ground: tried blinkered/in cheekpieces. *Thomas Gerard O'Leary, Ireland*

IL DUCE (IRE) 7 br.g. Anshan – Glory-Glory (IRE) (Buckskin (FR)) [2006/7 h138: **c138** c21s* c20d² c20d³ c23s* c24sᵖᵘ c20vᶠ c20v² c21g³ Apr 19] tall, angular gelding: useful **h–** hurdler: as good over fences: won novices at Uttoxeter in May and Taunton (beat Back For The Craic by 13 lengths) in December: back to form under less testing conditions when keeping-on 1½ lengths third to Ofarel d'Airy in novice handicap at Cheltenham final outing: stays 23f: has won on soft going, possibly best on good/good to soft: blinkered last 2 starts. *A. King*

ILE DE PARIS (FR) 8 b.g. Cadoudal (FR) – Sweet Beauty (FR) (Tip Moss (FR)) **c112** [2006/7 c112, h–: 22v⁴ 22s 20s² 24s³ 25v² c29v³ Feb 23] leggy gelding: fair handicap **h111** hurdler/chaser: probably stays 29f: acts on heavy ground: often in headgear nowadays. *R. Lee*

ILE FACILE (IRE) 6 b.g. Turtle Island (IRE) – Easy Pop (IRE) (Shernazar) [2006/7 **h–** h91: 16fᵖᵘ Apr 22] leggy gelding: fair on Flat (stays 1½m): modest form over hurdles, lightly raced: lame only outing in 2006/7: has raced freely. *B. De Haan*

ILE MAURICE (FR) 7 b.m. Dernier Empereur (USA) – Indesha (FR) (Top Ville) **h–** [2006/7 h120: 25sᶠ Oct 28] medium-sized mare: fairly useful hurdler: stayed 3m: acted on heavy ground: dead. *Ferdy Murphy*

IL EN REVE (FR) 9 b.g. Denham Red (FR) – Itaparica (FR) (Mistigri) [2006/7 c22m* **c124** Jun 5] lengthy gelding: winning hurdler: fairly useful handicap chaser: off 9 months, won **h–** at Listowel by 5 lengths from Seaforde: stays 3m: probably acts on any going: tried in cheekpieces, blinkered nowadays. *S. J. Treacy, Ireland*

ILEWIN ROSE 6 b.m. Alflora (IRE) – Bridepark Rose (IRE) (Kemal (FR)) [2006/7 **F–** F16s Dec 3] third foal: dam winning hurdler around 2½m: well held in bumper on debut. *G. Brown*

ILIKEHIMMAC (IRE) 8 ch.g. Denel (FR) – Culkeern (Master Buck) [2006/7 22d⁵ **c75** c20f⁴ c23m⁴ Aug 1] ex-Irish gelding: second on completed start in points: maiden **h69** hurdler: left G. Stewart, poor form in 2 chases. *Mrs S. J. Smith*

I'LL ASK O'JAY 6 b. or gr.m. Environment Friend – Creeping Jane (Rustingo) **h–** [2006/7 F16s F16m 18gᶠ 20g Sep 17] sixth foal: sister to a winning pointer and half-sister **F–** to 3m hurdle winner Ouh Jay (by Karinga Bay): dam fair pointer: no impact in bumpers/novice hurdles: tried in cheekpieces. *P. Bowen*

I'LL DO IT TODAY 6 b.g. Mtoto – Knayton Lass (Presidium) [2006/7 16g 16g 20d⁶ **h73** Jan 5] workmanlike gelding: fair on Flat (stays 2m), successful in April: poor maiden hurdler: likely to stay beyond 2½m: raced on good/good to soft ground. *J. M. Jefferson*

ILLICIT SPIRIT (IRE) 5 ch.g. Pistolet Bleu (IRE) – Hackler Poitin (IRE) (Little **h112** Bighorn) [2006/7 16d 16d 16s⁴ 16s² Mar 3] €15,000 3-y-o: well-made gelding: second foal: dam, bumper winner/fair hurdler who stayed 2½m, out of half-sister to Champion Hurdle winner For Auction: ran out in maiden Irish point in 2006: progressive form in novice hurdles, runner-up to Strawberry at Newbury on handicap debut: should stay 2½m: raced on good to soft/soft going: not straightforward. *C. R. Egerton*

ILLUMINATI 5 b.g. Inchinor – Selection Board (Welsh Pageant) [2006/7 h94: 19s⁴ **h75** Mar 12] angular gelding: modest form at best over hurdles, off a year prior to only outing in 2006/7: likely to prove best around 2m: raced on good to soft/soft ground. *L. Corcoran*

ILONGUE (FR) 6 b.m. Nononito (FR) – Marie de Geneve (FR) (Nishapour (FR)) **h–** [2006/7 h64: 21gᵖᵘ 19d 22f⁵ Apr 5] rather unfurnished mare: little form over hurdles. *R. Dickin*

ILOVETURTLE (IRE) 7 b.g. Turtle Island (IRE) – Gan Ainm (IRE) (Mujadil **c93** (USA)) [2006/7 c74x, h80: 16v c16s⁶ c25d* c16v* c24v⁶ c24v⁶ c23s⁵ c22d³ c20d⁴ c28g* **h–** Apr 7] lengthy gelding: maiden hurdler: modest handicap chaser: won at Market Rasen (novice) in December, Wetherby in January and Haydock in April: stays 3½m: acts on good to firm and heavy going: usually tongue tied. *M. C. Chapman*

IL PENSEROSO (IRE) 9 br.g. Norwich – Railstown Phairy (IRE) (Phardante (FR)) **c117** [2006/7 c75, h–: c16g² c17g⁴ 17m⁶ c18g* c16f* c17m* c16d* c17m* 16g* c22gᵖᵘ Sep **h107** 23] handicap hurdler/chaser, claimed from P. Blockley £5,000 third outing: successful next 6 starts, over fences at Market Rasen, Perth, Newton Abbot and Stratford (2), fairly useful form when beating Thedublinpublican easily by 8 lengths in 4-runner event at last-named on eighth outing: took advantage of much lower mark over hurdles in novice event at Uttoxeter month later, idling markedly: probably amiss final start: has won at 2½m, best form over shorter: probably acts on any going: usually wears cheekpieces. *Mrs A. M. Thorpe*

IL POTERE (IRE) 6 b.g. Luso – She's Aflyer (IRE) (Over The River (FR)) [2006/7 **h–** F18s³ F16d 22dᵖᵘ 21g⁵ Mar 26] €15,000 3-y-o: lengthy gelding: first foal: dam winning **F85** pointer: in frame in maiden Irish points in 2005: third in bumper at Plumpton: no form after, in novice hurdles last 2 starts. *B. G. Powell*

IMAGICA ROSE (IRE) 6 b. or br.m. Accordion – Whothatis (Creative Plan (USA)) **h–** [2006/7 F16v F16m 16gᵖᵘ 17dᵖᵘ Oct 25] €2,400 4-y-o: half-sister to winning hurdler/ **F–** chaser Avas Delight (by Ajraas), stays 2½m: dam lightly-raced half-sister to useful chaser up to 2¾m Moon Devil: no sign of ability. *Miss Lucinda V. Russell*

I'M A LEGEND 5 b.g. Midnight Legend – I'm Maggy (NZ) (Danseur Etoile (FR)) **h–** [2006/7 F16d 17s 20s 22vᵖᵘ 19d Mar 21] second foal: dam, fairly useful hurdler, stayed **F–** 21f: no show in bumper/over hurdles. *D. P. Keane*

IM A TANNER 6 b.g. I'm Supposin (IRE) – Galix (FR) (Sissoo) [2006/7 F–: 20s 16sᵖᵘ **h– x** 16vᵖᵘ Mar 3] no form in bumpers/over hurdles (mistakes). *Miss C. Dyson*

IM A WITNESS (IRE) 7 b.g. Witness Box (USA) – Welsh Sitara (IRE) (Welsh Term) **h105** [2006/7 22s 20s 25g² 26s² 24s 24m* Mar 25] good-topped gelding: first foal: dam point/ bumper winner: placed in bumpers: fair hurdler, left D. Kelly before return: easily landed odds in maiden at Southwell in March: stays 3¼m: acts on soft and good to firm going: tried in cheekpieces (ran poorly): often tongue tied. *P. Bowen*

IMAZULUTOO (IRE) 8 b.g. Marju (IRE) – Zapata (IRE) (Thatching) [2006/7 c87, **c–** h–: c16mᶠ c21mᵖᵘ Jul 16] good-topped ex-Irish gelding: one-time fairly useful hurdler **h–** for Mrs J. Harrington: modest form at best over fences: raced mainly around 2m: acts on heavy going. *Evan Williams*

IM BUSY 6 b.m. Busy Flight – What Chance (IRE) (Buckskin (FR)) [2006/7 F17d³ **h90** F16m³ 16d⁵ 17d⁴ Oct 31] 3,000 5-y-o: rather unfurnished mare: second foal: dam fair **F82** hunter chaser: third in bumpers: better effort in novice hurdles when fourth to Beau Michel at Exeter, though again finished weakly. *L. Corcoran*

I'M DELILAH 5 b.m. Overbury (IRE) – Gallants Delight (Idiot's Delight) [2006/7 **F109 p** F17g* Apr 19] rather unfurnished mare: second foal: half-sister to bumper winner Watch My Back (by Bob Back): dam, useful pointer/hunter, stayed 25f: won 18-runner mares bumper at Cheltenham on debut by 7 lengths from Worbarrow Bay with something to spare: promising. *N. G. Richards*

I'M FOR WAITING 11 ch.g. Democratic (USA) – Fausterlerie (Faustus (USA)) **c–** [2006/7 c–, h–: 20sᵖᵘ May 14] small gelding: winning hurdler/maiden chaser, little form **h–** since 2004/5: blinkered once. *John Allen*

I'M FREE 5 b.g. I'm Supposin (IRE) – Gaye Mercy (Petoski) [2006/7 F–: 21v³ 22sᵖᵘ **h–** Jan 4] lengthy, unfurnished gelding: no form in bumper/over hurdles. *D. E. Pipe*

I'M INNOCENT 6 b.g. Silver Patriarch (IRE) – Lady Confess (Backchat (USA)) **h–** [2006/7 16m Jul 2] well held in bumper/novice hurdle 15 months apart: poor maiden pointer. *P. J. Hobbs*

IMLAAK 5 ch.h. Giant's Causeway (USA) – Karen S (USA) (Kris S (USA)) [2006/7 **h–** h–: 17mᵖᵘ 17m⁵ 16d⁵ 16dᶠ 20gᵖᵘ Apr 23] little show over hurdles: sometimes tongue tied. *James Moffatt*

I'M LOVIN IT (IRE) 7 b.g. Supreme Leader – Sparky Mary (IRE) (Strong Gale) **c102** [2006/7 F88: 20v 20s⁵ 16s⁴ 17s* 16s 16sᵖᵘ c20g⁵ c20g² c22mᵘʳ Apr 24] lengthy gelding: **h99** modest hurdler: easily landed odds in seller at Taunton (sold from P. Nicholls 6,500 gns) in February: easily best effort over fences when second in handicap at Fontwell: should stay 2¾m: acts on soft ground, probably on good to firm: tried tongue tied. *M. A. Allen*

IMMINENT VICTORY 4 b.g. Benny The Dip (USA) – Brave Vanessa (USA) **h–** (Private Account (USA)) [2006/7 F13g² F13s F12vʳᵒ F14v³ 16gᵖᵘ Mar 17] eighth foal: **F82** half-brother to 1¼m winner Simiola (by Shaamit): dam, 6f winner who stayed 1m, sister to US Grade 2 winner around 1m Topicount: best effort in bumpers (modest form) when second at Towcester on debut: ducked wrong side of rail at start on third outing: no show in maiden on hurdling debut. *R. M. H. Cowell*

IM OVA ERE DAD (IRE) 4 b.g. Second Empire (IRE) – Eurolink Profile (Prince **h–** Sabo) [2006/7 16d Dec 4] fair on Flat (stays 1m), successful in January/February: not knocked about after blundering fourth in juvenile maiden on hurdling debut. *D. E. Cantillon*

I MOVE EARTH 10 b.m. Bandmaster (USA) – Lady of Milton (Old Jocus) [2006/7 **c–** c16mᵖᵘ Aug 2] lengthy mare: modest form in bumpers in 2001/2: no form outside points **h–** since: tried tongue tied. *M. S. Sweetland*

IMPACT CRUSHER (IRE) 7 b.g. Sri Pekan (USA) – Costume Drama (USA)   c–
(Alleged (USA)) [2006/7 20s^{ur} 18v 16v⁶ c20g^{ur} c25g^{pu} Apr 23] strong gelding: no form   h–
over jumps. *J. Wade*

IMPATIENCE 5 b.m. Kayf Tara – Clifton Girl (Van Der Linden (FR)) [2006/7 F17d   **F–**
Aug 21] second foal: dam poor maiden: no show in bumper on debut. *A. G. Juckes*

IMPECCABLE GUEST (IRE) 4 b.f. Orpen (USA) – Perfect Guest (What A Guest)   **h100**
[2006/7 16g* 16v* 16d³ Feb 14] smallish filly: half-sister to fairly useful hurdler Return
Again (by Top Ville) and winning hurdler Sharp Outlook (by Shernazar), both stayed
2½m: modest maiden on Flat (stays 1¾m): fair form in juvenile hurdles, successful at
Catterick in November and Wetherby (fortunate to beat April San by 3 lengths) in
December: likely to stay 2½m: acts on heavy ground. *P. C. Haslam*

IMPEK (FR) 11 b.g. Lute Antique (FR) – Attualita (FR) (Master Thatch) [2006/7   **c166**
c163, h–: c17d* Oct 31]   **h–**

    Twelve months after the death of Best Mate with a suspected heart attack in
the Haldon Gold Cup, the light blue and maroon striped colours of his owner were
carried to victory in the same race by Impek. It was owner Jim Lewis' fourth win in
the Exeter showpiece, following Best Mate in 2001 and the now-retired Edredon
Bleu in 2002 and 2003. Ill-luck struck Impek afterwards, however, and he was not
seen again, being intermittently lame and found to have a hairline fracture of the
cannon bone. Impek was being aimed at the King George VI Chase at Kempton, a
race in which the Lewis colours were also carried to victory by both of those
illustrious stable companions and in which Impek had finished a good third to
Kicking King in the most recent running (at Sandown). Impek had shown himself
better than ever in 2005/6, winning the Old Roan Chase at Aintree and the Peterborough Chase at Huntingdon (another race in which the Lewis colours have a
notable record).

    Carrying top weight, the 9/1-shot Impek won the William Hill Gold Cup (as
it was renamed in the latest season) at Exeter by nineteen lengths and eleven from
Ground Ball and Hoo La Baloo, giving a bold, front-running display under Tony
McCoy, jumping with typical fluency and still travelling strongly when his nearest

William Hill Gold Cup Chase (Limited Handicap), Exeter—
Impek emulates his illustrious stable-companions Best Mate and Edredon Bleu

pursuer Chilling Place unseated his rider four out after effectively being knocked over by Impek's riderless stable-companion Racing Demon (who was sent off favourite). Impek would probably have won anyway and looked sure to make a bold bid to win a second Peterborough Chase before injury intervened—Racing Demon stood in for him and recorded a seventh win (in nine years) for Henrietta Knight. There is a possibility that Impek may be entered in the 2008 Grand National—'if I can persuade the trainer,' says the owner. Henrietta Knight's record in the National is nothing to write home about. Her three-pronged attack in 2003 yielded just a last place out of fourteen finishers for outsider Southern Star, with the well-fancied pair Chives (pulled up early due to a burst blood vessel) and Maximize (fell nineteenth) failing to make an impact. She has had only three other runners in the Aintree marathon, namely What's The Crack in 1992 (thirteenth), Full of Oats in 1997 (fell first) and Southern Star again in 2004 (pulled up). When tried over the Aintree fences in the 2005 Topham Trophy, Impek fared well, finishing fifth under a big weight after leading at the last, whilst his record of twenty-six starts over fences without a fall (only once unseating his rider when hampered) should also help Lewis during those negotiations with Knight.

Impek (FR) (b.g. 1996)	Lute Antique (FR) (b 1985)	No Lute (b 1978)	Luthier Prudent Miss
		Sweet Annie (ch 1980)	Pharly Beronaire
	Attualita (FR) (b 1988)	Master Thatch (ch 1978)	Thatch Miss Sarah
		Gaouri (b 1972)	Pan Rieuse III

Impek's sire Lute Antique was one of the best four-year-old hurdlers of his generation in France and eventually made into a good chaser, while Impek's dam Attualita was also French and won twice at a mile and a quarter. Though well held on his only start on heavy, Impek is proven on ground ranging from good to firm to soft and is also versatile so far as distance is concerned, showing his form from two miles to three miles. He goes particularly well for Tony McCoy, who can boast two wins and two placed efforts at graded level from just four rides over fences on a gelding who'd previously proved difficult to win with since his novice campaign. *Miss H. C. Knight*

IMPERIAL AMBER 5 ch.m. Emperor Fountain – Bambolona (Bustino) [2006/7 F17v F17s Jan 30] 1,150 3-y-o: half-sister to several winners, including fairly useful chaser up to 2½m Scottish Bambi and fairly useful 2m hurdler Miss Haggis (both by Scottish Reel): dam 2-y-o 6f winner: well beaten in bumpers: fair form on second of 2 outings in maidens on Flat. *Karen George*   **F—**

IMPERIAL COMMANDER (IRE) 6 b.g. Flemensfirth (USA) – Ballinlovane (Le Moss) [2006/7 F16s* 21d⁴ 24s* 20s* 21g 24g³ Apr 13] €19,000 3-y-o: big, strong gelding: chasing type: fourth foal: half-brother to winning pointer by Alphabatim: dam winning pointer: won maiden Irish point on debut in 2005: successful also in bumper at Cheltenham in October in very good style: useful novice hurdler: again impressive when winning 18-runner event at Newcastle in January by 19 lengths from Jass: far from discredited in Grade 1 events at Cheltenham and Aintree last 2 starts, 22 lengths third to Chief Dan George at latter: stays 3m: acts on soft ground: ran as if amiss third outing. *N. A. Twiston-Davies*   **h135 F110**

IMPERIAL DREAM (IRE) 9 b.g. Roselier (FR) – Royal Nora (IRE) (Dromod Hill) [2006/7 c–, h–: c24d⁶ c22g³ c25s⁵ c25gᵖᵘ c25dᵖᵘ 24sᵖᵘ Apr 25] tall gelding: maiden hurdler: fair handicap chaser: ran poorly after second outing: should stay beyond 25f: raced on good going or softer: usually wears headgear: tried tongue tied: temperament under suspicion. *H. P. Hogarth*   **c101 h—**

IMPERIAL ROCKET (USA) 10 b. or br.g. Northern Flagship (USA) – Starsawhirl (USA) (Star de Naskra (USA)) [2006/7 c99, h100: c19mᵖᵘ 16m⁵ 17d⁵ Aug 7] strong, lengthy gelding: winning hurdler: maiden chaser: no show in 2006/7: acts on firm and good to soft going: has worn cheekpieces: tongue tied. *W. K. Goldsworthy*   **c— h—**

IMPERIAL ROYALE (IRE) 6 ch.g. Ali-Royal (IRE) – God Speed Her (Pas de Seul) [2006/7 h88: 16s 16s² 16g⁶ Jun 15] angular gelding: modest handicap hurdler: probably stays 19f: acts on heavy going. *P. L. Clinton*   **h88**

IMPERIAL SILVER 6 gr.g. Silver Patriarch (IRE) – Bambolona (Bustino) [2006/7 F17v F16s² Mar 8] 20,000 5-y-o: big, workmanlike gelding: half-brother to several winners, including fairly useful chaser up to 2½m Scottish Bambi and fairly useful 2m hurdler Miss Haggis (both by Scottish Reel): dam 2-y-o 6f winner: easily better effort in bumpers when second to Gansey in maiden at Wincanton. *K. Bishop* **F87**

IMPERIAL SUN (IRE) 8 b.g. Un Desperado (FR) – Ashley's Princess (IRE) (Lafontaine (USA)) [2006/7 c22g⁵ c21s c24vᵘʳ c24v* c24d⁶ Feb 17] tall gelding: fair hurdler/chaser: won maiden over fences at Punchestown in December: stays 3m: acts on heavy ground: tried visored (stiff task). *D. T. Hughes, Ireland* **c108 h–**

IMPERIOLI 5 b.g. Fraam – Jussoli (Don) [2006/7 h–: 26gᵖᵘ May 4] no form on Flat/over hurdles: sold £1,600 Ascot August Sales. *P. A. Blockley* **h–**

IMPERO 9 b.g. Emperor Jones (USA) – Fight Right (FR) (Crystal Glitters (USA)) [2006/7 h–: 21mᵖᵘ May 18] medium-sized gelding: maiden hurdler: usually visored/blinkered: tried tongue tied. *G. F. Bridgwater* **h–**

IMPORTANT BOY (ARG) 10 ch.g. Equalize (USA) – Important Girl (ARG) (Candy Stripes (USA)) [2006/7 h–§: 22m c23mᵖᵘ 24f Jul 19] compact gelding: maiden hurdler: no form since 2004, including on chasing debut: has been visored: usually tongue tied: ungenuine. *D. D. Scott* **c–§ h–§**

IMPORTANT BUSINESS (IRE) 4 ch.g. Mutamam – Opus One (Slip Anchor) [2006/7 F16g² Mar 19] €28,000 3-y-o, resold 32,000 3-y-o: seventh foal: half-brother to 3 winning hurdlers, including Golden Odyssey (by Barathea), around 2½m, and Sun King (by Zilzal), at up to 19f: dam, 1¾m winner, half-sister to high-class hurdler/smart chaser up to 2½m Squire Silk: 1¼ lengths second to I'msingingtheblues in maiden bumper at Wincanton on debut. *Mrs P. Robeson* **F92**

Our Friends In The North's "Imperial Commander"

IMPOSTOR (IRE) 4 b.g. In The Wings – Princess Caraboo (IRE) (Alzao (USA)) **h97**
[2006/7 16dᵣₒ 16vᵖᵘ 16g² 19d⁵ Mar 26] compact gelding: fairly useful maiden on Flat
(barely stays 1¾m), sold out of J. Fanshawe's stable 16,000 gns Newmarket Autumn
Sales: modest form over hurdles: stays 19f: blinkered last 3 starts: ran out on debut.
N. A. Twiston-Davies

IMPRESS 4 ch.g. Fantastic Light (USA) – Kissogram (Caerleon (USA)) [2006/7 16s⁶ **h99**
16s⁴ 16s 16s 20vᵖᵘ 19g² 20gᵖᵘ Apr 21] strong gelding: well beaten in 1½m maiden at
3 yrs, sold out of M. Johnston's stable 4,500 gns Doncaster May Sales, and gelded: easily
best effort over hurdles (fair form) when second in juvenile handicap at Newbury:
breathing problem final start: stays 19f: best effort on good ground: tried blinkered, in
cheekpieces last 2 outings. *D. McCain Jnr*

IMPS WAY 12 br.m. Nomadic Way (USA) – Dalton's Delight (Wonderful Surprise) **c111**
[2006/7 c116: c25m² c23g* c20g* Apr 16] leggy mare: useful hunter chaser, won readily
at Wetherby early and late in season: fit from points (successful in March), beat Ifni du
Luc by 3 lengths on latter occasion: best efforts short of 3m: acts on soft and good to firm
going: patiently ridden. *Mrs T. Corrigan-Clark*

I'MSINGINGTHEBLUES (IRE) 5 b.g. Pistolet Bleu (IRE) – Nova Rose (Ra Nova) **F97 +**
[2006/7 F16s³ F16g* Mar 19] second foal: dam, fairly useful hurdler up to 19f, out of
half-sister to dam of Grand National winner Numbersixvalverde: fairly useful form in
bumpers, won 16-runner maiden at Wincanton readily by 1¼ lengths from Important
Business. *P. F. Nicholls*

I'M SO LUCKY 5 b.g. Zilzal (USA) – City of Angels (Woodman (USA)) [2006/7 16d³ **h113**
16s² 17v² 16s* 16d 16gᵖᵘ Apr 14] leggy gelding: half-brother to fair/irresolute 2m hurdler
Angels Venture (by Unfuwain) and bumper winners by Pursuit of Love and Unfuwain:
useful on Flat (stays 1½m) for M. Johnston: fair hurdler: landed odds in novice at Ludlow
in March: stiff tasks next 2 starts: likely to prove best at 2m: acts on heavy going: tongue
tied last 3 outings: threw away winning opportunity when hanging right third start.
R. S. Brookhouse

IM SPARTACUS 5 b.g. Namaqualand (USA) – Captivating (IRE) (Wolfhound (USA)) **h117 +**
[2006/7 20s* 20s⁴ 16g* Apr 8] half-brother to winning 2m hurdler Antony Ebeneezer
(by Hurricane Sky): useful on Flat (stays 10.5f) at 3 yrs, left D. Flood after final outing
(reportedly became seriously ill after) and well below best in 2006 for D. Barker: made
good start over hurdles, winning novice at Southwell (easily) in December and handicap
at Towcester (beat Upright Ima by 6 lengths) in April: likely to prove best around 2m:
may do better still. *Evan Williams*

I'M SUPREME (IRE) 5 b.g. Supreme Leader – Imtheone (IRE) (Meneval (USA)) **h101 +**
[2006/7 F84: 17s 19s⁵ 20g² Apr 14] fair form in novice hurdles, much improved when
second to Inherent at Chepstow: will stay beyond 2½m. *P. J. Hobbs*

IMTIHAN (IRE) 8 ch.g. Unfuwain (USA) – Azyaa (Kris) [2006/7 h116: 20s³ 20v⁴ **c95**
19d³ 20g⁴ c16g⁵ c20m³ c23m⁶ Apr 25] compact gelding: fairly useful handicap hurdler: **h116**
modest form at best over fences: stays 2¾m: acts on heavy and good to firm going: tried
visored/tongue tied. *Mrs S. J. Smith*

IMTOUCHINGWOOD 6 b.m. Fleetwood (IRE) – Shanuke (IRE) (Contract Law **h–**
(USA)) [2006/7 h–: 19sᵖᵘ 20sᵖᵘ Dec 5] no sign of ability: tried visored. *L. A. Dace*

I'M WILLIE'S GIRL 11 br.m. Royal Fountain – Milton Lass (Scallywag) [2006/7 c–, **c61**
h–: c25v⁵ Mar 3] strong mare: winning pointer: well beaten completed outing in chases. **h–**
Miss J. Luton

I'M YOUR MAN 8 gr.g. Bigstone (IRE) – Snowgirl (IRE) (Mazaad) [2006/7 c–, h–: **c–**
16g² 16v* 16g⁴ 16m* 20f* 16s⁴ 22g² Jul 9] workmanlike gelding: no show in maiden **h105**
chases: fair handicap hurdler: much improved in 2006/7, won at Wetherby in May and
Perth (novice) and Hexham in June: stays 2½m: acts on any going. *Mrs E. Slack*

IN ACCORD 8 ch.g. Accordion – Henry's True Love (Random Shot) [2006/7 h120: **c117**
c22s⁴ c23s² c24s³ c24s² c24d c33sᵖᵘ Mar 17] tall, good-bodied gelding: fairly useful **h–**
hurdler/novice chaser: in frame first 4 starts over fences, 25 lengths second of 4 finishers
to Gungadu at Warwick on fourth occasion: possibly amiss final outing: stays 3¼m: acts
on heavy going. *H. D. Daly*

INAKI (FR) 10 b.g. Dounba (FR) – Incredule (FR) (Concertino (FR)) [2006/7 c92, h–: **c91**
c23v² c20g⁵ Mar 22] leggy, useful-looking gelding: modest chaser nowadays: stays 23f: **h–**
acts on heavy ground: effective blinkered/visored or not. *Miss E. Thompson*

INARO (IRE) 6 b.g. Bahhare (USA) – Doo Han (IRE) (Doulab (USA)) [2006/7 h119, **c108 +**
F101: c22s^{pu} c24s^{pu} c20d^5 c19s^F c20d^4 c24g* c24s^4 Apr 26] useful-looking gelding: fair **h–**
hurdler/novice chaser: won handicap at Ascot in March: stays 3m: acts on heavy going:
tried tongue tied. *Jonjo O'Neill*

INCANDESCENCE (IRE) 6 b.g. Insatiable (IRE) – Glowing Embers (Nebbiolo) **h– x**
[2006/7 h–, F–: 20d^{pu} 16g 22d^{pu} 19g Mar 28] angular gelding: no form in bumpers/over
hurdles (not fluent): blinkered in 2006/7. *Mrs P. Robeson*

INCAS (FR) 11 br.g. Video Rock (FR) – Amarante II (FR) (Brezzo (FR)) [2006/7 **c112**
c20d^{pu} 20f^{pu} 20f^2 20g^3 c20m^3 c21d* c20g* c24m^4 c21g^2 c22m^3 c20d^6 20s^5 c21g c16v^{pu} **h83**
c20s^3 c20s^2 Apr 25] sturdy gelding: maiden hurdler: fair handicap chaser, sold out of
A. Moore's stable 7,000 gns Doncaster May Sales after first outing: better than ever when
winning at Cartmel in August and Uttoxeter in September: probably stays 3m: acts on
heavy and good to firm going: tried in cheekpieces/tongue tied: waited with. *Miss
Lucinda V. Russell*

INCA TRAIL (IRE) 11 br.g. Un Desperado (FR) – Katday (FR) (Miller's Mate) **c132 §**
[2006/7 c139§, h–§: c24g^6 c20s^3 c26g^5 Nov 19] tall, good sort: useful chaser: stayed 31f, **h– §**
at least on cross-country course: acted on soft and good to firm going: blinkered: tried
tongue tied: weak finisher: dead. *D. McCain Jnr*

INCHCONNEL 6 b.g. Inchinor – Sharanella (Shareef Dancer (USA)) [2006/7 16m **h–**
24m^{pu} Jul 5] third in maiden on Flat at 2 yrs, only form. *D. Brace*

INCHDHUAIG (IRE) 4 ch.g. Inchinor – Be Thankfull (IRE) (Linamix (FR)) [2006/7 **h72**
16d 17s 16d 16s Dec 16] sparely-made maiden on Flat (stays 1¼m): poor
form in juvenile hurdles: tried tongue tied (jumped poorly). *P. C. Haslam*

INCH HIGH 9 ch.g. Inchinor – Harrken Heights (IRE) (Belmez (USA)) [2006/7 h–: **h89**
18v^5 16v^2 18s 16v* Mar 9] modest chaser (stays 1¼m), successful in May: modest
handicap hurdler: won novice event at Ayr in March: raced around 2m: acts on heavy
ground. *J. S. Goldie*

INCHING CLOSER 10 b.g. Inchinor – Maiyaasah (Kris) [2006/7 c–, h130d: 23f^4 **c–**
May 6] tall, good-topped gelding: winning chaser: fairly useful handicap hurdler: stays **h120**
27f: acts on soft going, probably on firm: tried blinkered: sold 20,000 gns Doncaster May
(2006) Sales, resold 2,500 gns Doncaster January Sales. *J. Howard Johnson*

INCHING WEST 5 ch.m. Inchinor – Key West (FR) (Highest Honor (FR)) [2006/7 **h68 ?**
F–: F14s 17g 17g^3 17g^6 Apr 27] lengthy mare: little form in bumpers/over hurdles. **F–**
C. J. Down

INCH OVER 6 b.g. Overbury (IRE) – Inch Maid (Le Moss) [2006/7 F–: F16m^6 c24s^{pu} **c–**
20g^5 21s 21d Jan 8] workmanlike gelding: poor maiden pointer: little impact in other **h91 ?**
events. *S. A. Brookshaw* **F74**

INCH PRIDE (IRE) 8 b.m. Beneficial – Stradbally Bay (Shackleton) [2006/7 h125: **c111 §**
c21s^2 c19m^3 c23m* c22g 24d c19s^2 c20s* 20v^6 c20v^2 Jan 25] leggy mare: fairly useful **h–**
hurdler, well held both starts in 2006/7: fair novice chaser: won at Stratford in June and
Huntingdon in December: should stay 3m: acts on soft and good to firm going: often
finishes weakly. *D. E. Pipe*

IN COMPLIANCE (IRE) 7 b.g. Old Vic – Lady Bellingham (IRE) (Montelimar **c152 p**
(USA)) [2006/7 c146, h–: c20s* c20v* c25g^3 Apr 25] **h–**

A season that had been going so well ended up a less-than-satisfactory one
for the Michael O'Brien stable which had just three wins in the last three months,
although it did at least enjoy a happy Easter thanks to the victories of hurdlers
De Valira in a Grade 2 novice and Essex in a listed race, both at Fairyhouse. Along
with the rest of the stable's chasers, the two highest-rated performers in the yard,
the Sean Mulryan-owned pair In Compliance and Forget The Past, failed to register
a single victory in this period. They had made significant contributions earlier
in the season, though, particularly In Compliance who was as low as 6/1 for the
Cheltenham Gold Cup after winning his first two starts. However, like many of his
stable-companions, In Compliance was seemingly under a cloud subsequently and
the Gold Cup was one of the races to go by without him as he reportedly failed
to please his trainer. It was April before In Compliance returned to action, in the
Punchestown Gold Cup run over twenty-five furlongs, a distance half a mile further
than In Compliance had tackled previously. In Compliance looked in good shape
and was a well-backed favourite, but he didn't last home (after taking a keen hold)

John Durkan Memorial Punchestown Chase—In Compliance (noseband) lowers the colours of Cheltenham Gold Cup winner War of Attrition; outsider Sher Beau (right) takes third

in finishing third behind British-trained challengers Neptune Collonges and Kings-cliff, drawing clear with that pair after five out, but coming under pressure three out and tiring when making a mistake at the last. Still only seven and relatively lightly raced, In Compliance may still fulfil earlier promise, particularly if his stable returns to the sort of form that saw it operate with a strike rate of at least 20% for three successive seasons earlier in the decade. Given his troubled preparation, In Compliance is probably worth another chance at around three miles despite that Punchestown capitulation.

In Compliance was racing at two miles when he first started out in 2004/5, winning a bumper and a maiden hurdle at that trip, although he also showed his form over two and a half miles as he quickly developed into a useful hurdler that season. Nor did it take long for In Compliance to show himself even better as a chaser in 2005/6, winning a maiden at Fairyhouse and a novice at Leopardstown on his first two runs over fences before being placed in Grade 1 events won by Justified at Fairyhouse and Accordion Etoile at Punchestown. The race chosen for In Compliance's return in the latest campaign was the Grade 3 Killultagh Properties Ltd Chase at Down Royal in November, for which he was one of four runners in a race that beforehand looked a match between him and another of the previous season's smart novices Wild Passion. In Compliance, a shade odds on, just had the edge in the betting, and there was also little between the pair at the end of the race itself, where they were separated by just three quarters of a length. In Compliance's superiority over a below-par rival was, however, far greater than that suggests. Despite sending his rider up his neck when overjumping five out, In Compliance was still on the bridle when taking the lead after the second last and he won with something in hand. Wild Passion was in opposition again when In Compliance was turned out at Punchestown five weeks later for the John Durkan Memorial Punchestown Chase, in which there were far tougher rivals among the six other runners. Three started at shorter odds than In Compliance, the Cheltenham Gold Cup winner War of Attrition sent off favourite, with Nickname and Justified next in the betting. It seemed a well-contested renewal beforehand, though only In Compliance and 40/1-shot Sher Beau, a no-more-than-useful performer who took third place, gave their true running. In Compliance won by two and a half lengths from War of Attrition (who'd also run below par when fifth in the same race twelve

450

months earlier). While In Compliance didn't achieve so much as first appeared in taking some notable scalps, there was still a lot to admire about a performance which underlined that he was very much on the upgrade. Once again he impressed with his jumping and, having gone to the front on the bridle after three out this time, he found extra under pressure when War of Attrition renewed his challenge.

In Compliance (IRE) (b.g. 2000)	Old Vic (b 1986)	Sadler's Wells (b 1981)	Northern Dancer Fairy Bridge
		Cockade (b 1973)	Derring-Do Camenae
	Lady Bellingham (IRE) (b 1994)	Montelimar (b 1981)	Alleged L'Extravagante
		Lovely Stranger (b 1982)	Le Bavard Vulvic

The well-made In Compliance, bought for €36,000 at the 2003 Derby Sale, is the first foal of the unraced Lady Bellingham. Her second foal, a full brother to In Compliance named One Cool Cookie, was already a winning pointer when he fetched 165,000 guineas at Doncaster almost two years later. The Charlie Swan-trained One Cool Cookie has just completed his first season over fences and has shown himself just as good as In Compliance was at the same stage, the last of his three wins coming when going one place better than his brother in the Powers Gold Cup at Fairyhouse. Significantly, One Cool Cookie also appeared not to stay when stepped up to twenty-five furlongs at Punchestown on his final start. Lady Bellingham produced fillies by Old Vic in 2005 and 2006, with the former sold for €46,000 as a yearling. Their grandam Lovely Stranger won at two miles over hurdles in Ireland, while the next dam Vulvic showed little on the racecourse but had a fair amount of success at stud, one of her winners the smart three-mile chaser Cavity Hunter. The consistent In Compliance, who hasn't been out of the first three since his debut, has raced only on good ground or softer and acts on heavy. *M. J. P. O'Brien, Ireland*

INCONEL (IRE) 7 ch.g. Mister Lord (USA) – Templebraden Silky (IRE) (Eurobus) [2006/7 F16m² Jul 26] €14,000 4-y-o: fourth foal: dam unraced: second of 5 in bumper at Worcester on debut: sold 1,000 gns Doncaster May Sales. *G. A. Swinbank*   **F87**

IN CONTRAST (IRE) 11 b. or br.g. Be My Native (USA) – Ballinamona Lady (IRE) (Le Bavard (FR)) [2006/7 c106x, h–: c20f^pu Jun 3] leggy gelding: smart hurdler in his prime: fair form at best over fences, not convincing with jumping: stays 21f: acts on good to firm and good to soft going: hangs left under pressure: held up and suited by truly-run race. *P. J. Hobbs*   **c– x h–**

INCORPORATION 8 b.g. In The Wings – Danishkada (Thatch (USA)) [2006/7 c?, h79: c17d* c16g² c18g c16m³ c20m⁵ c17m c16v² c20g Mar 22] thrice-raced over hurdles: modest handicap chaser: won novice event at Cartmel in May: should stay 2½m: unraced on firm going, acts on any other: in cheekpieces in 2006/7. *Mrs L. Williamson*   **c95 h–**

INDALO (IRE) 12 b.g. Lord Americo – Parson's Princess (The Parson) [2006/7 c121, h–: c25d^ur May 19] compact gelding: one-time useful handicap chaser, below best since 2004/5: stays 3m: acts on heavy and good to firm going: takes strong hold and usually races up with pace: sometimes let down by jumping. *Miss Venetia Williams*   **c– h–**

INDESTRUCTIBLE (FR) 8 b.g. Hero's Honor (USA) – Money Bag (FR) (Badayoun) [2006/7 c21m⁶ c22g⁵ c23d^pu c20s⁴ Feb 14] no sign of ability. *M. Appleby*   **c– h–**

INDIAN CHASE 10 b.g. Terimon – Icy Gunner (Gunner B) [2006/7 25d³ 23d³ Mar 21] lengthy gelding: failed to complete both starts over fences: first form (poor) over hurdles final outing: stays 23f: ungenuine. *Dr J. R. J. Naylor*   **c– § h70 §**

INDIAN DOCTOR 7 b.g. Dr Massini (IRE) – Icy Miss (Random Shot) [2006/7 F16g 17s 18g^pu Mar 18] €36,000 4-y-o: eighth foal: half-brother to several winners, including fairly useful chasers up to 25f Indian Gunner (by Gunner B) and Indian Chance (by Teenoso): dam, winning hurdler/chaser, stayed 3m: no show in bumper/over hurdles (breathing problem final start). *Dr J. R. J. Naylor*   **h– F–**

INDIAN GIRL 4 b.f. Erhaab (USA) – Natchez Trace (Commanche Run) [2006/7 17g Nov 5] modest maiden on Flat (appears to stay 2m): no show in juvenile on hurdling debut. *M. R. Channon*   **h–**

INDIAN GUNNER 14 b.g. Gunner B – Icy Miss (Random Shot) [2006/7 c106, h–: c24d⁴ c16d⁵ c19s⁶ Oct 22] tall, good-topped gelding: veteran chaser: stays 25f: acts on soft and good to firm going: has had tongue tied. *Dr J. R. J. Naylor* **c91** **h–**

INDIAN OPEN 6 b.g. Commanche Run – Golf World (Mandalus) [2006/7 F77: 26dᵖᵘ 22m⁶ 24fᵖᵘ Jun 21] no form over hurdles: sold £1,600 Ascot August Sales. *J. W. Mullins* **h–**

INDIAN PIPE DREAM (IRE) 5 br.h. Indian Danehill (IRE) – Build A Dream (USA) (Runaway Groom (CAN)) [2006/7 16d⁴ 17g² 20d⁴ 16d⁵ Feb 14] strong horse: useful on Flat (stays 2m), successful 4 times in 2005, sold out of J. Gosden's stable 58,000 gns Doncaster November (2005) Sales: off over 12 months, modest form in novice hurdles: should stay 2½m: raced on good/good to soft ground. *S. Gollings* **h97**

INDIAN RAIDER (IRE) 13 b.g. Commanche Run – Borecca (Boreen (FR)) [2006/7 c19m c23dᵖᵘ May 17] winning pointer: no form in hunter chases: tried in cheekpieces. *R. G. Chapman* **c–**

INDIAN SOLITAIRE (IRE) 8 b.g. Bigstone (IRE) – Terrama Sioux (Relkino) [2006/7 h83: 17g 20m Jun 28] leggy gelding: maiden hurdler: in cheekpieces 6 of last 7 starts: dead. *B. P. J. Baugh* **h–**

INDIAN STAR (GER) 9 b.g. Sternkoenig (IRE) – Indian Night (GER) (Windwurf (GER)) [2006/7 h100+: 17d 16s⁵ 16g 21s³ 16s 18g⁵ Apr 10] leggy gelding: modest hurdler: stays 21f: acts on soft going: tongue tied. *J. C. Tuck* **h97**

INDIAN STORM (IRE) 5 b.g. Ridgewood Ben – Brushes Bride (IRE) (Brush Aside (USA)) [2006/7 F17d* F16g³ F16g Feb 2] unfurnished gelding: first foal: dam well beaten in bumpers/points: fair form in bumpers, won at Sedgefield (by 12 lengths) in November. *G. M. Moore* **F91**

INDIAN WIND 5 ch.g. Chocolat de Meguro (USA) – Helm Wind (North Col) [2006/7 F–: 17m 20s 24fᵖᵘ 17m Aug 6] no form: tongue tied last 5 starts. *M. A. Barnes* **h–**

INDIAN WIZARD (IRE) 4 b.g. Indian Ridge – Ragtime Rumble (USA) (Dixieland Band (USA)) [2006/7 16g³ 16mᵖᵘ Sep 2] fair on Flat (stays 1m), successful in 2006 for P. Howling: no form in juvenile hurdles: tried tongue tied. *D. A. Rees* **h–**

INDIGO SKY (IRE) 6 gr.h. Adieu Au Roi (IRE) – Urban Sky (FR) (Groom Dancer (USA)) [2006/7 h–§: 20mᵖᵘ 20d³ 19s* 21s⁴ 19v⁴ 19g 18g⁵ 17m³ Apr 17] leggy horse: poor handicap hurdler: won conditional jockeys novice event at Exeter in December: stays 21f: acts on heavy and good to firm going. *B. G. Powell* **h81**

IN DISCUSSION (IRE) 9 b.g. King's Theatre (IRE) – Silius (Junius (USA)) [2006/7 c20g³ c20fᵖᵘ 20f⁴ 24m² c21d⁶ 22gᵖᵘ c20mᵖᵘ Sep 24] medium-sized gelding: fairly useful handicap chaser at best: easily best effort over hurdles (fair form) on fourth outing: temperamental displays last 2 starts: stays 3m: acts on firm and good to soft ground: tried in cheekpieces: formerly tongue tied: sold 2,200 gns Doncaster October Sales, pulled up in point. *Jonjo O'Neill* **c116 d** **h113 d**

IN DREAM'S (IRE) 5 b.g. Dr Fong (USA) – No Sugar Baby (FR) (Crystal Glitters (USA)) [2006/7 h87: 20d² 20g⁶ 20v⁵ 19s³ 25s² 25g 20v* 24s² Apr 25] small, close-coupled gelding: fairly useful hurdler, left M. Barnes prior to fourth start: improved form when winning novice at Newcastle in March by 25 lengths from Speedro: ran well when 8 lengths second to Mumbles Head in novice handicap at Perth following month: stays 25f: acts on heavy going: tongue tied for previous stable. *G. M. Moore* **h120**

INDUSTRIAL STAR (IRE) 6 ch.g. Singspiel (IRE) – Faribole (IRE) (Esprit du Nord (USA)) [2006/7 h113: 16d³ 16s² 16g⁴ 16gꟳ 18g⁵ Apr 15] tall gelding: modest on Flat (stays 2m), won in June: fair handicap hurdler: should be suited by further than 2m: acts on soft going, bumper winner on good to firm. *Micky Hammond* **h112**

INDY MOOD 8 ch.g. Endoli (USA) – Amanta (IRE) (Electric) [2006/7 h120: 23f 22g May 24] workmanlike gelding: fairly useful hurdler, lightly raced nowadays: stays 3m well: acts on heavy going. *Mrs H. O. Graham* **h113**

IN EXTRA TIME (IRE) 8 b. or br.g. Topanoora – Overtime (IRE) (Executive Perk) [2006/7 17d⁶ 16g 16s 16g c16s² c19sᵖᵘ c21dᵖᵘ Jan 16] tall gelding: third foal: brother to fairly useful hurdler/chaser Adarma, stayed 3m, and half-brother to fairly useful chaser Lost Time (by Glacial Storm), stays 23f: dam once-raced half-sister to smart hurdler/useful chaser up to 25f Time For A Run: never dangerous over hurdles: poor form completed outing over fences: should be suited by 2½m. *Jonjo O'Neill* **c81** **h–**

INFINI (FR) 11 gr.g. Le Nain Jaune (FR) – Contessina (FR) (Mistigri) [2006/7 c100x, h86: c30d^{pu} c20g^{F} 24m^{pu} Aug 4] tall, leggy gelding: fair hurdler/chaser at best: failed to complete in 2006/7: barely stays 3¼m: acts on any going: tried visored/in cheekpieces: sketchy jumper. *R. Ford*

c– x
h–

INGHWUNG 5 b.m. Kayf Tara – Mossy Fern (Le Moss) [2006/7 F14s^3 F17s^2 F16v^2 Feb 18] compact mare: half-sister to fairly useful hurdler up to 19f Samby (by Anshan) and modest hurdler Mossy Bay (by Phardante), stayed 3¼m: dam useful staying chaser: fair form when placed all 3 starts in mares bumpers. *O. Sherwood*

F90

INGLEBOROUGH LAD 5 b.h. Cloudings (IRE) – The Vixen (IRE) (Brush Aside (USA)) [2006/7 F17m F16m Jun 17] first foal: dam unraced: well beaten in bumpers: tongue tied. *M. A. Barnes*

F–

INGLEWOOD LAD (IRE) 5 gr.g. Environment Friend – Pretty Obvious (Pursuit of Love) [2006/7 20s^{pu} 20s^{pu} Feb 19] first foal: dam, fair hurdler who stayed 2½m, winner up to 2m on Flat: no show in novice hurdles. *I. McMath*

h–

INGLIS DREVER 8 b.g. In The Wings – Cormorant Creek (Gorytus (USA)) [2006/7 h162: 24s* 24v^2 24g* 24g^3 Apr 12]

h166

'Ingalls Dreever', as he should be pronounced, became only the fourth horse to win the stayers' championship at Cheltenham more than once, following Crimson Embers (1982 and 1986), Galmoy (1987 and 1988) and Baracouda (2002 and 2003). The race is known as the Ladbrokes World Hurdle nowadays and has a higher profile than its predecessor the Stayers' Hurdle, being the centrepiece of the third day of the Festival and carrying a first prize in the latest season of £149,027. One opportunity that has been missed so far, however, is to make the race a truer test and extend the trip to the Gold Cup distance of three and a quarter miles (the start would be in front of the stands, instead of in the back straight). The official distance of the World Hurdle is three miles since it was switched to the New Course in 1993—times suggest the trip has been even shorter on occasions—and the race provides much less of a test of stamina than it traditionally did, or than is ideal.

In both 2002 and 2003 the Stayers' Hurdle was arguably the race of the meeting, Baracouda beating Iris's Gift and Limestone Lad in 2003 in a race described in *Chasers & Hurdlers* as 'one of the most memorable horse-races of recent times.' Iris's Gift reversed placings with Baracouda in 2004 in another splendid renewal. Baracouda and Iris's Gift were the highest-rated hurdlers of their respective years, their performances at Cheltenham better than those achieved by the corresponding winners of the Champion Hurdle, Hors La Loi III, Rooster Booster and Hardy Eustace. The two-mile division has traditionally been stronger than the staying division but, in both 2001/2 and 2002/3, Timeform's three highest-rated hurdlers were all better known for their achievements in staying events (the formidable front runner Limestone Lad also recorded the best performance in a two-mile hurdle during the first season in question).

Neither Iris's Gift nor Limestone Lad was in the line-up for the first edition of the World Hurdle in 2005, though ten-year-old Baracouda was still around and he started a hot favourite to regain his crown. Baracouda went on to contest the World Hurdle as an eleven-year-old as well (he finished fifth), but his performance in the 2005 edition signalled that his best days were behind him. The unknown quantity Inglis Drever had never run beyond two miles, five furlongs—over which trip he had finished second in the Royal & SunAlliance Novices' Hurdle as a five-year-old—and had followed a campaign in his second season more in keeping with a potential Champion Hurdle contender, all four of his outings (successful twice) before Cheltenham at around two miles in recognized trials for that race. Baracouda looked like recording his third victory in the stayers' championship as the field turned into the straight but, when shaken up, he didn't quicken as expected and couldn't hold off Inglis Drever who responded to pressure to win by three lengths, twice the distance by which Iris's Gift had beaten Baracouda the previous year. Looking at the performance in the context of the race overall, however, Inglis Drever's form did not match that shown by Baracouda and Iris's Gift when winning the event. But Inglis Drever remained favourite to win the following year's World Hurdle until being sidelined with a tendon strain in his near-fore which caused him to miss the rest of the season after winning Wetherby's West Yorkshire Hurdle and then beating Baracouda again in the Long Distance Hurdle at Newbury,

vccasino.com Long Distance Hurdle, Newbury—
Tony Dobbin guides Inglis Drever (centre) to a repeat win, with Irish Wolf pushing him closest

before falling when well held in the Long Walk Hurdle, which was transferred to Chepstow, on what turned out to be his final appearance.

Inglis Drever's fall in the Long Walk and his close fourth, finishing strongly after being hemmed in, in the Mersey Novices' Hurdle two weeks after his Royal & SunAlliance second, were the only times he finished out of the first two in his first sixteen races over hurdles. Those included two in the latest season before being returned to Cheltenham for the World Hurdle. Both were muddling, tactical affairs, in the first of which Inglis Drever repeated his previous season's victory in the vccasino.com Long Distance Hurdle at Newbury, ridden out to hold off Irish Wolf (who received 8 lb) by a neck. However, Inglis Drever went down by four lengths to Blazing Bailey (also received 8 lb) in the Cleeve Hurdle at Cheltenham's late-January fixture, held up and not going quite so well as the winner from some way out but keeping on from the last. Inglis Drever's rider Paddy Brennan, partnering the horse for the first time (Tony Dobbin was on board at Newbury), thought he should have had Inglis Drever closer through the race, but Inglis Drever's defeat was overshadowed in any event by that of fifth-placed Black Jack Ketchum who was a well-beaten favourite. Black Jack Ketchum started favourite again in the World Hurdle, at 2/1, with the previous year's third Mighty Man second favourite at 100/30, Inglis Drever next at 5/1, and Blazing Bailey at 8/1 the only other runner at single-figure odds in a field of fourteen. Black Jack Ketchum's supporters knew their fate much earlier than in the Cleeve as he made a rare jumping error at the third and came down. Inglis Drever, who looked very well beforehand, raced lazily in the first part of the race and was well down the field at halfway. Brennan got to work in earnest on Inglis Drever much earlier than he had in the Cleeve and Inglis Drever responded really well down the hill. After leading before the home turn, he was ridden out to hold off Mighty Man by three quarters of a length. Blazing Bailey was travelling well when he made a mistake two out and still held every chance when making another one at the last, eventually finishing four lengths behind Mighty Man in third. Brennan's handling of Inglis Drever was praised as one of the rides of the Festival but he was not retained for a second year as stable jockey to Howard Johnson who has appointed Denis O'Regan, who was second jockey to Noel Meade in the latest season. Brennan will be riding for Nigel Twiston-Davies in 2007/8. Inglis Drever was partnered for the last time by Brennan in the Long Distance Hurdle at Aintree where Inglis Drever was off the bridle with a circuit to go and unable to threaten Mighty Man or Black Jack Ketchum in the straight, going down by thirteen lengths and nine, well below his Cheltenham form.

Still only eight, Inglis Drever is young enough to be a factor in the World Hurdle for several more years. Baracouda made his final appearance in the race at eleven, Crimson Embers and Galmoy were twelve. Baracouda's record of two wins and two seconds from five appearances is the best overall record in the Stayers' Hurdle and his record might well have been even more impressive had the Cheltenham Festival not been abandoned in 2001 because of the foot and mouth epidemic (he won the substitute race staged at Sandown). The victories of Crimson Embers came four years apart and, like Baracouda, he was also very unlucky not to end up a triple winner. His 1985 defeat by stable-companion Rose Ravine must rank as one of the most controversial races in the Festival's long history, particularly as it capped a very eventful afternoon at Prestbury Park—odds-on Browne's Gazette, ridden by Dermot Browne, had ruined his chance in the Champion Hurdle thirty-five minutes earlier by squandering ground in puzzling circumstances at the start. Perhaps the stewards were worn out from dissecting that incident as they baffled the racing world after deliberating on the Stayers' Hurdle, in which Crimson Embers went down by just a neck after being badly hampered by Rose Ravine (who was favourite) early on the run-in. The consensus among racegoers was that the interference, albeit accidental, had clearly cost Crimson

Ladbrokes World Hurdle, Cheltenham—a never-say-die effort by Paddy Brennan sees the 2005 title-holder regain his crown; Mighty Man (right) and Blazing Bailey (white face) both run on well

Embers the race and he seemed certain to be awarded the race under the Rules of Racing at the time. However, trainer Fulke Walwyn forbade jockey Stuart Shilston from objecting to the winner as both horses were in the same ownership, whilst the stewards, who held their own inquiry, astonishingly allowed the result to stand, deeming that the placings hadn't been affected. A sustained media furore followed, mainly centring on those wronged backers of Crimson Embers, and the Jockey Club's Disciplinary Committee took the unusual step of looking into the incident a couple of weeks later, ruling the Cheltenham stewards had been wrong not to award the race to Crimson Embers. Unfortunately, no appeal had been lodged against the findings of the local stewards and the Committee was powerless to alter the placings. Crimson Embers' sixth and final appearance in the Stayers' Hurdle coincided with Galmoy's first win in 1987, his fifth place that day matching the finishing position he'd achieved in 1984 (he also finished fourth in 1983). Galmoy made five appearances in the race, finishing runner-up the year after his second win.

Inglis Drever (b.g. 1999)	In The Wings (b 1986)	Sadler's Wells (b 1981)	Northern Dancer
			Fairy Bridge
		High Hawk (b 1980)	Shirley Heights
			Sunbittern
	Cormorant Creek (b 1987)	Gorytus (b 1980)	Nijinky
			Glad Rags
		Quarry Wood (b 1968)	Super Sam
			Phrygia

This is the fourth essay to appear in *Chasers & Hurdlers* on the sturdy, close-coupled Inglis Drever whose pedigree has been covered in detail in previous editions. He is by the now-deceased In The Wings out of the fair mile-and-a-quarter winner Cormorant Creek, a half-sister to the 1983 Champion Stakes winner Cormorant Wood and also to River Ceiriog, winner of the 1986 Supreme Novices' Hurdle. Cormorant Creek, who died in 1999, produced three other winning jumpers including Inglis Drever's full brother the fair staying hurdler Bodfari Creek; her two other successful hurdlers, the fair Far Removed (by Distant Relative) and the fairly useful Spartan Royale (by Shareef Dancer), were two-milers. Inglis Drever's grandam Quarry Wood was a sister to the useful staying hurdler Super Trojan and a half-sister to the smart two- to two-and-a-half-mile hurdler Cullen, who won the Great Metropolitan Handicap on the Flat. Another of Quarry Wood's half-sisters, Davett, bred the high-class staying chaser Young Hustler. Inglis Drever stays well, has been raced only on good going or softer (acts on heavy) during his jumping career and is effective held up or making the running. He tends to race lazily but is genuine and consistent (out of the first two only three times now in eighteen starts over hurdles). *J. Howard Johnson*

IN GOOD FAITH (USA) 6 b. or br.m. Dynaformer (USA) – Healing Hands (Zafonic (USA)) [2006/7 h76: 16g^{pu} May 2] poor maiden hurdler. *N. J. Henderson*   **h–**

INGRATITUDE (IRE) 4 ch.g. Inchinor – Merci (IRE) (Cadeaux Genereux) [2006/7 16d^4 16s^5 17g* 16m^2 Apr 25] lengthy, angular gelding: useful on Flat (stays 1m), successful in May, sold out of R. Beckett's stable 48,000 gns Newmarket Autumn Sales: fair form over hurdles: won novice at Newton Abbot in April by ¾ length from Mole's Chamber: carried head awkwardly when 1¾ lengths second of 25 to Phantom Lad in juvenile at Punchestown later in month: likely to prove suited by test of speed at 2m. *N. J. Henderson*   **h112**

INGRES 7 b.g. Sadler's Wells (USA) – Bloudan (USA) (Damascus (USA)) [2006/7 c–, h101: 20f 22g^6 24m^{pu} 22g^4 c23m^{pu} 22g^5 21f^3 22m^6 26g 25m 24d^6 22m^4 25d^3 22s^5 26s^6 24s 22s^5 22g^4 27m^2 Apr 26] useful-looking gelding: little aptitude for chasing: modest handicap hurdler: stays 27f: acts on heavy and good to firm going: usually wears headgear/tongue tied: ungenuine. *B. G. Powell*   **c– §**
h97 §

INHERENT (IRE) 5 ch.m. In The Wings – Serpentara (Kris) [2006/7 F90: 16d^2 16g* 20g* Apr 14] heavy-topped mare: bumper winner: fair form in novice hurdles: made all at Towcester (16 ran) in March and Chepstow in April, beating I'm Supreme a neck at latter: stays 2½m. *H. D. Daly*   **h101**

INHERIT (IRE) 5 b.g. Princely Heir (IRE) – Flora Wood (IRE) (Bob Back (USA)) [2006/7 17d^F Jun 14] modest maiden at best on Flat (should stay 7f) at 3 yrs: left R. Fahey, tailed off when fell last in novice on hurdling debut. *B. S. Rothwell*   **h–**

IN HIS DREAMS 7 b.g. Petoski – Topsy Bee (Be Friendly) [2006/7 F16s⁵ 19g⁴ 19s⁴ 22s Feb 3] 16,000 4-y-o: sturdy gelding: half-brother to fairly useful chaser Gottabe (by Gunner B), stayed 3¼m and 21f chase winner Oscar Wilde (by Arctic Lord): dam no worthwhile form over jumps: third on completed start in points in 2005: fifth in bumper: best effort over hurdles (modest form) when fourth in novice at Ascot: blinkered, reportedly finished distressed (claimed from P. Nicholls £6,000) in seller next time. *Miss Tor Sturgis* **h85 F72**

IN HOPE 4 b.f. Most Welcome – Frankie Fair (IRE) (Red Sunset) [2006/7 16g 16d⁴ 16s⁵ 16s 17d 24mᶠ Mar 31] small filly: half-sister to fair 2m hurdler Fair Spin (by Pivotal): poor maiden for several trainers on Flat (stays 7f), sold out D. Ivory's stable £1,000 Ascot October Sales: little impact over hurdles: in cheekpieces last 3 starts. *Mrs L. J. Young* **h–**

INISHCLARE (IRE) 6 br.g. Warcraft (USA) – Ivory Queen (Teenoso (USA)) [2006/7 F16s⁵ Sep 21] fourth foal: dam once-raced in bumpers: no show in points/bumper. *J. J. Lambe, Ireland* **F–**

INISHTURK (IRE) 8 b. or br.g. Glacial Storm (USA) – Judy Henry (Orchestra) [2006/7 h97: 20g⁵ 24d* 26sᵖᵘ c24s² c24gᵖᵘ Mar 28] lengthy gelding: fair hurdler: won handicap at Kempton in November: similar form on completed outing in handicap chases (let down by jumping/attitude next time): should stay beyond 3m: raced on good ground or softer (acts on soft). *A. King* **c104 h106**

INJUNEAR (IRE) 9 ch.g. Executive Perk – Chancy Gale (IRE) (Strong Gale) [2006/7 16sᵖᵘ 19m⁵ May 11] very lightly raced and poor form over hurdles, off 25 months and left T. McGovern before return. *G. L. Moore* **h78**

INKPEN 6 b.m. Overbury (IRE) – Nunsdream (Derrylin) [2006/7 F16s Nov 22] first foal: dam unraced: well held in bumper on debut. *W. M. Brisbourne* **F–**

INLAND RUN (IRE) 11 b.g. Insan (USA) – Anns Run (Deep Run) [2006/7 c89, h–: c24gᵖᵘ Jun 8] well-made gelding: winning hurdler: maiden chaser: stays 23f: acts on good to firm and good to soft going: inconsistent. *P. Grindey* **c– h–**

INMATE (IRE) 6 b.g. Needle Gun (IRE) – Highland Spirit (Scottish Reel) [2006/7 h–: 17dʳᵗʳ 21m Sep 26] lengthy gelding: no form in bumpers/over hurdles. *Mrs E. Slack* **h–**

IN MEDIA RES (FR) 6 b.g. Dushyantor (USA) – Colour Scheme (FR) (Perrault) [2006/7 h129: 17g Sep 8] compact gelding: fairly useful hurdler: no show only outing in 2006/7: stays 21f: acts on soft and good to firm, ran poorly on heavy. *N. J. Henderson* **h–**

INMOM (IRE) 6 b.m. Barathea (IRE) – Zakuska (Zafonic (USA)) [2006/7 h–: 16s May 14] no show in 2 starts over hurdles: tried tongue tied. *S. R. Bowring* **h–**

INN FOR THE DANCER 5 b.g. Groom Dancer (USA) – Lady Joyce (FR) (Galetto (FR)) [2006/7 h84: 16g 17m² 16g² 17d² 17s³ 16s³ 17d⁵ Mar 20] lengthy gelding: fair maiden handicap hurdler: raced around 2m: acts on soft and good to firm going. *J. C. Fox* **h100**

INN FROM THE COLD (IRE) 11 ch.g. Glacial Storm (USA) – Silver Apollo (General Ironside) [2006/7 h72+: 24g⁶ 18v³ 24v 20v 24s² Apr 25] strong gelding: poor handicap hurdler: stays 3m: acts on heavy ground: none too consistent. *L. Lungo* **h83**

INNISFREE (IRE) 9 ch.g. Presenting – Sweet Peach (IRE) (Glenstal (USA)) [2006/7 c91, h80: 20f c22m c25f⁵ c22d c27m⁵ c23dᶠ c31dᵇᵈ c24d⁴ c24d c28v³ c25s³ c32v² c28g³ Apr 15] smallish gelding: poor handicap chaser/maiden hurdler, sold out of J. Carr's stable 2,800 gns Doncaster November Sales after seventh start: stays 3½m: acts on any going: often in cheekpieces/blinkers: tried tongue tied. *Mrs H. O. Graham* **c82 h–**

INNOCENT REBEL (USA) 6 ch.g. Swain (IRE) – Cadeaux d'Amie (USA) (Lyphard (USA)) [2006/7 h94: c25dᵖᵘ c19f² c21g* Apr 27] lengthy, angular gelding: novice hurdler: successful both starts in points in 2006: best effort in hunter chases when winning novice at Newton Abbot by distance: stays 21f: acts on firm going, probably on soft. *C. Heard* **c100 h–**

IN NO HURRY (IRE) 6 b.g. Supreme Leader – South Quay Lady (Quayside) [2006/7 h77: 22g⁵ 17d⁵ 17m* Jun 30] workmanlike gelding: fair hurdler: improved form when easily winning novice handicap at Market Rasen in June: should stay beyond 17f: acts on good to firm going. *M. G. Quinlan* **h103**

INNOX (FR) 11 b.g. Lute Antique (FR) – Savane III (FR) (Quart de Vin (FR)) [2006/7 c149: c25sᶠ 20s⁶ c25s c29sᵖᵘ c21v c24g Mar 13] good-topped gelding: smart chaser, well below best in 2006/7: sixth in minor event on hurdling debut: stays 29f: acts on heavy ground: blinkered. *F. Doumen, France* **c123 h104**

IN ON THE ACT (IRE) 4 b.f. In The Wings – Mosquera (GER) (Acatenango (GER))   **h83**
[2006/7 16d³ 18s⁵ 18s⁵ 23d 21g^pu Apr 23] disappointing maiden on Flat: poor form over
hurdles: tried tongue tied: dead. *Jamie Poulton*

INSATIABLE LADY (IRE) 5 ch.m. Insatiable (IRE) – Ziggy Ace (Ovac (ITY))   **F—**
[2006/7 F16s F16v Feb 22] seventh foal: dam won point in Ireland: no show in bumpers.
B. S. Rothwell

INSPIRED FOREVER (IRE) 5 b.g. Luso – Forever Second (IRE) (Parliament)   **F—**
[2006/7 F16d F16v Jan 12] 23,000 4-y-o: tall gelding: third foal: dam unraced: well
beaten in bumpers. *P. R. Webber*

INSTIGATOR 4 b.g. Observatory (USA) – Imaginary (IRE) (Dancing Brave (USA))   **F85**
[2006/7 aF13g⁵ F16m Apr 8] 14,000 2-y-o: half-brother to smart 1½m to 2¼m winner
Rainbow High (by Rainbow Quest) and useful French 9f (at 2 yrs) to 11f winner Imagina-
tive (by Last Tycoon), also 21f winner over hurdles: dam, 1¼m winner, half-sister to
Lowther Stakes winner Kingscote: better effort in bumpers when fifth in 3-y-o polytrack
event on debut. *S. Donohoe, Ireland*

INSTRUCTOR 6 ch.g. Groom Dancer (USA) – Doctor's Glory (USA) (Elmaamul   **h101**
(USA)) [2006/7 16g³ 16g² 16g⁵ Dec 10] rather leggy gelding: closely related to fair
hurdler around 2m Dolzago (by Pursuit of Love): fairly useful on Flat (stays 1½m),
successful in July: fair form in novice hurdles: raced at 2m on good ground. *R. A. Fahey*

INSUBORDINATE 6 ch.g. Subordination (USA) – Manila Selection (USA) (Manila   **h—**
(USA)) [2006/7 h—: 16g Oct 19] no show in novice hurdles. *J. S. Goldie*

INSURGENT (IRE) 5 b.g. Fasliyev (USA) – Mountain Ash (Dominion) [2006/7 h81,   **c95 §**
F88: 16g 17m 18m² 16d⁶ c16d³ c16g⁴ c16s² c16s² c17v⁵ c20d⁴ c16s⁴ c17g⁸ c21g³ c20m²   **h91 §**
c20m² Apr 28] sturdy gelding: maiden hurdler: modest handicap chaser: won at Kelso in
April, left in lead last: stays 2½m: acts on soft and good to firm going: usually visored/in
cheekpieces: often let down by jumping/attitude. *R. C. Guest*

INTAVAC FLIGHT 7 b.g. Tamure (IRE) – Mossfield (Le Moss) [2006/7 h—: 19d^pu   **h—**
Dec 26] compact gelding: no sign of ability. *R. A. Fahey*

INTAVAC GIRL 4 b.f. Sinndar (IRE) – Messila Rose (Darshaan) [2006/7 16g⁶ 16s^F   **h—**
Nov 15] angular filly: no form on Flat/completed start in juvenile hurdles. *R. A. Fahey*

INTEGRATION 7 b.g. Piccolo – Discrimination (Efisio) [2006/7 19d⁶ Feb 19] small-   **h—**
ish, rather leggy gelding: modest maiden on Flat (stays 13f): well beaten both starts over
hurdles. *Miss M. E. Rowland*

INTENSE SUSPENSE (IRE) 4 ch.g. Bob's Return (IRE) – In Sin (IRE) (Insan   **h– p**
(USA)) [2006/7 F13v⁵ F17d⁶ 16v 16g⁵ 17m⁴ Apr 15] 13,500 3-y-o: leggy, unfurnished   **F77**
gelding: first foal: dam unraced: modest form in bumpers: well held in novice hurdles:
should do better, especially granted stiffer test of stamina. *M. W. Easterby*

INTERACTIVE (IRE) 4 b.g. King's Best (USA) – Forentia (Formidable (USA))   **F—**
[2006/7 aF16g^pu Mar 9] 3,500 3-y-o: fourth foal: half-brother to 2 winners on Flat,
including useful performer up to 1½m Tizzy May (by Highest Honor): dam, 2-y-o 5f
winner, half-sister to Prix Morny and Middle Park winner Bahamian Bounty: bolted
before and during race in bumper on debut: last in Flat maiden month later. *Andrew
Turnell*

INTERDIT (FR) 11 b. or br.g. Shafoun (FR) – Solaine (FR) (Pot d'Or (FR)) [2006/7   **c102**
c116, h—: c25f⁵ c24s⁴ May 18] leggy gelding: fairly useful handicap chaser at best: **h—**
successful 3 times in points in 2006/7: stays 4m: acts on any going: effective blinkered or
not, visored once (unseated): usually races prominently. *Mrs B. K. Thomson*

INTERNATIONALGUEST (IRE) 8 b.g. Petardia – Banco Solo (Distant Relative)   **h—**
[2006/7 h—: 17d 20m Mar 29] no form over hurdles or in points: tried tongue tied/in
cheekpieces. *D. J. Wintle*

INTERSKY EMERALD (IRE) 6 b.g. Luso – Green Formation (Green Desert   **h—**
(USA)) [2006/7 F83: 16g^pu May 13] fourth at Wetherby, only form in 4 bumpers in
2005/6: no show in novice on hurdling debut. *G. A. Swinbank*

INTERSKY FALCON 10 ch.g. Polar Falcon (USA) – I'll Try (Try My Best (USA))   **c118**
[2006/7 h151: c16g* c17g^pu Jul 5] leggy gelding: very smart hurdler at best, won 3   **h—**
Grade 1 events, including Christmas Hurdle at Kempton twice: best placing in Champion
Hurdle when third in 2004: won novice at Newton Abbot in May on completed start
over fences: stayed 2½m when conditions weren't testing: acted on firm and soft going:
blinkered: usually tongue tied: reportedly retired. *Jonjo O'Neill*

INTERSKY HIGH (USA) 5 b. or br.m. Royal Anthem (USA) – Worood (USA) **F84**
(Vaguely Noble) [2006/7 F16m³ Jun 17] 4,500 2-y-o: closely related to French winner up
to 15.5f Sixty And Steele (by Theatrical) and half-sister to several winners: dam French
1m to 1½m winner: favourite, third in bumper at Hexham on debut: sold 9,500 gns Doncaster October Sales. *G. A. Swinbank*

INTERSKY MUSIC (USA) 4 b.g. Victory Gallop (CAN) – Resounding Grace **h91**
(USA) (Thunder Gulch (USA)) [2006/7 16d^F 16s 16d Jan 8] leggy gelding: fair form
when sixth in 1m maiden on debut, sold out of P. Chapple-Hyam's stable 18,000 gns
Newmarket Autumn Sales: running to modest level when falling 3 out in juvenile at
Uttoxeter on hurdling debut: well held next 2 outings. *Jonjo O'Neill*

INTERSKY NATIVE (IRE) 11 ch.g. Be My Native (USA) – Creative Music (Crea- **c–**
tive Plan (USA)) [2006/7 c25g^{pu} Apr 23] well-made gelding: maiden hurdler: winning **h–**
pointer: no show in chases: stays 3m: acts on good to firm and good to soft going: tried in
cheekpieces (found little). *Mrs Sheena Walton*

IN THE FRAME (IRE) 8 b.g. Definite Article – Victorian Flower (Tate Gallery **c116**
(USA)) [2006/7 c117, h–: c20g c16m³ 20f⁶ c20d⁴ c20d^{ur} Nov 21] rather leggy gelding: **h–**
winning hurdler: fairly useful handicap chaser: stays 21f: acts on soft and good to firm
going: tried in cheekpieces (found little). *Evan Williams*

IN THE HAT (IRE) 11 br.g. Roselier (FR) – Cotton Gale (Strong Gale) [2006/7 h81: **h–**
22g 22m 27d^{ur} Aug 15] winning hurdler, no show in 2006/7: stays 3¼m: successful on
soft ground, probably more effective under less testing conditions (acts on good to firm).
J. R. Jenkins

IN THE HIGH GRASS (IRE) 6 b.g. In The Wings – Gale Warning (IRE) (Last **c131**
Tycoon) [2006/7 c17g c16s c17d² c16v* c17s³ c19s² c16v* c20s³ c17m⁴ c20g³ Apr 25] **h–**
15,000 2-y-o: seventh foal: half-brother to several winners, including useful 1½m/1¾m
winner Takwin (by Alzao): dam French 2-y-o 6f winner: winning hurdler: useful novice
chaser: won maiden at Thurles in November and handicap at Gowran (beat On The Net
by 5½ lengths) in March: best effort when 3¾ lengths third to Royal County Star in
handicap at Punchestown final start: effective at 2m to 2½m: acts on heavy ground,
probably on good to firm. *T. J. Taaffe, Ireland*

INTHEJUNGLE (IRE) 4 ch.g. Bob Back (USA) – Whizz (Salse (USA)) [2006/7 **F–**
F12v Jan 17] €70,000 3-y-o: rather leggy gelding: second foal: dam, fair maiden who
stayed 1½m, half-sister to smart hurdler/top-class chaser Tiutchev, stayed 25f: favourite,
well held in 4-y-o bumper at Newbury on debut. *T. Doumen, France*

IN THE LEAD (USA) 5 b. or br.m. Bahri (USA) – Air de Noblesse (USA) (Vaguely **h98**
Noble) [2006/7 16g³ 17g² 16m² Apr 25] fairly useful maiden up to 1¾m on Flat, sold out
of J. Dunlop's stable 30,000 gns Newmarket Autumn (2005) Sales: modest form when
placed 3 starts over hurdles: should stay beyond 2m. *P. J. Hobbs*

INTO THE SHADOWS 7 ch.m. Safawan – Shadows of Silver (Carwhite) [2006/7 **h129**
h122: 16f 16g⁴ 20g² 20v* 20g^{pu} Apr 12] angular mare: useful on Flat (stayed 1¾m): fairly
useful handicap hurdler: improved when upped in trip, winning at Wetherby in December
by 1½ lengths from stable-companion Totally Scottish: stayed 2½m: acted on heavy
going: dead. *K. G. Reveley*

INTREPID SAMSON 9 br.g. Terimon – Jasmin Path (Warpath) [2006/7 19v^{pu} 22s^{pu} **h–**
20d^{pu} Oct 20] brother to 1¼m winner Senor Eduardo: dam, irresolute winning hurdler,
stayed 2¾m: no show in novice hurdles. *N. J. Pomfret*

INVESTMENT AFFAIR (IRE) 7 b.g. Sesaro (USA) – Superb Investment (IRE) **h–**
(Hatim (USA)) [2006/7 16v Dec 30] tall hurdler: fair hurdler in 2004/5: off 2 years,
pulled too hard on return: raced around 2m: acts on soft going. *D. McCain Jnr*

INVESTMENT PEARL (IRE) 4 b.f. Desert Sun – Superb Investment (IRE) (Hatim **h–**
(USA)) [2006/7 16d 17s 16s Jan 24] sturdy filly: half-sister to fairly useful staying chaser
Cool Investment (by Prince of Birds) and fair 2m hurdlers Investment Affair (by Sesaro)
and Investment Force (by Imperial Frontier): fair maiden up to 1¼m on Flat for J. Oxx:
well held over hurdles: tried visored. *D. R. Gandolfo*

INVESTMENT WINGS (IRE) 5 b.g. In The Wings – Superb Investment (IRE) **h113 d**
(Hatim (USA)) [2006/7 h101x: 19s 24s³ 25g 24g^{pu} 20m³ 16f² Apr 5] tall, useful-looking
gelding: fair novice hurdler on his day, largely disappointing in 2006/7: stays 3m: acts on
soft going: usually in headgear/tongue tied: sketchy jumper. *D. E. Pipe*

IPAY ISAY (IRE) 5 gr.g. Bob Back (USA) – Zephyrelle (IRE) (Celio Rufo) [2006/7 **h83 +**
16v 16s 22s^{pu} 19v⁶ 20s Apr 1] €65,000 3-y-o: useful-looking gelding: fifth foal: brother

to bumper winner Boberelle: dam, fair form in bumpers, sister to useful 2m hurdler Winter Squall and half-sister to smart 2m hurdler Carobee: poor form in novice hurdles. *B. J. Curley*

IRILUT (FR) 11 br.g. Lute Antique (FR) – Patchourie (FR) (Taj Dewan) [2006/7 c106x: c23v* c23v⁴ Mar 9] close-coupled gelding: prolific winning pointer: fairly useful hunter: won maiden at Leicester in February readily by 14 lengths from Cash In Hand: stays 3¼m: acts on heavy and good to firm going: wears cheekpieces. *R. Waley-Cohen*   **c106**

IRIS BLEU (FR) 11 ch.g. Beyssac (FR) – Dear Blue (FR) (Cyborg (FR)) [2006/7 c145d, h–: c25f c25m⁴ c29s³ c29vᵖᵘ c24vᵖᵘ c24g Mar 24] stocky gelding: smart handicap chaser at his best, on downgrade: stays 29f: acts on heavy and good to firm going: tried blinkered: unreliable. *D. E. Pipe*   **c127 d** **h–**

IRIS DE BALME (FR) 7 ch.g. Phantom Breeze – Fleur d'Ecajeul (FR) (Cyborg (FR)) [2006/7 20s 18s c18d⁶ c17g³ c20g² c21s³ c23d³ c21s⁶ c25s² c26v² c23s⁶ Jan 31] third foal: half-brother to fairly useful French hurdler up to 2½m Jonquille de Balme (by Mansonnien): dam of little account: maiden hurdler/chaser, left J-L. Henry after eighth outing: stays 3¼m: acts on heavy going: has been blinkered. *S. Curran*   **c93** **h76**

IRISH BLESSING (USA) 10 b.g. Ghazi (USA) – Win For Leah (USA) (His Majesty (USA)) [2006/7 h81§: 22g 16v⁶ 19sᵖᵘ 16s 20gᵖᵘ Apr 14] smallish gelding: winning hurdler, no form in 2006/7: tried blinkered, usually wears cheekpieces: tongue tied: ungenuine. *F. Jordan*   **h– §**

IRISH CASTLE (IRE) 9 b.g. Mister Lord (USA) – Musicara (Black Minstrel) [2006/7 c24sᵖᵘ c24dᵘʳ c16v¹ c27mᵖᵘ Apr 9] big, heavy-topped gelding: no sign of ability: tried tongue tied. *R. Johnson*   **c– x**

IRISH GROUSE (IRE) 8 b.g. Anshan – Another Grouse (Pragmatic) [2006/7 c–, h64: c26g⁵ Oct 30] has reportedly had breathing operation: little form: tongue tied once. *N. B. King*   **c–** **h–**

IRISH GUARD 6 b.g. Infantry – Sharp Practice (Broadsword (USA)) [2006/7 F–: 16s² 19v* 24sᵖᵘ 19vᵖᵘ Feb 23] big, good-topped gelding: chasing type: fair form when winning maiden hurdle at Towcester (by 28 lengths) in May: off 8 months, ran poorly last 2 outings: should stay beyond 19f: acts on heavy going. *J. G. O'Neill*   **h105**

IRISH HAWK (GER) 5 ch.g. Platini (GER) – Irish Fritter (USA) (Irish River (FR)) [2006/7 h–: 16m Jul 12] sturdy gelding: no impact over hurdles. *M. F. Harris*   **h–**

IRISHKAWA BELLEVUE (FR) 9 b. or br.g. Irish Prospector (FR) – Strakawa (FR) (Sukawa (FR)) [2006/7 c81§, h116§: c25dᵖᵘ 24m c23dᵖᵘ 24s 25dᵖᵘ 24s 24v 24v Mar 10] smallish gelding: maiden chaser: one-time fairly useful handicap hurdler, no form in 2006/7: stays 3m: acts on soft and good to firm going: tried in cheekpieces, usually blinkered: ungenuine. *Jean-Rene Auvray*   **c– §** **h– §**

IRISH LEGEND (IRE) 7 b.g. Sadler's Wells (USA) – Wedding Bouquet (Kings Lake (USA)) [2006/7 h103: 22s c23s⁵ c19s³ Feb 26] smallish gelding: fair hurdler: off 14 months, seemed in need of run on return: well held over fences: stays 3m: acts on heavy going. *C. Roberts*   **c–** **h–**

IRISHMAN (IRE) 13 b.g. Bob Back (USA) – Future Tense (USA) (Pretense) [2006/7 c31gᵖᵘ May 24] lengthy, workmanlike gelding: winning chaser: runner-up in point in 2006: tried blinkered/in cheekpieces. *Mrs K. Erskine Crum*   **c–** **h–**

IRISH NATION (NZ) 8 b.g. Yamanin Vital (NZ) – Tripartite (NZ) (Tawfiq) [2006/7 24v² 18v* 20s c20v c17d c17vᶠ c16dᵘʳ c22dᵇᵈ c16d* Apr 3] successful over 1m and 10.5f on Flat in New Zealand: fair hurdler: won maiden at Wexford in October: much improved over fences (fairly useful form) when winning novice at Gowran by 29 lengths from Hurricane Carter, leading 4 out: effective at 2m to 3m: raced on going softer than good (acts on heavy). *N. Meade, Ireland*   **c126 +** **h113**

IRISH PROMISE (IRE) 7 b.g. Grand Plaisir (IRE) – Spanish Lover (IRE) (Ballad Rock) [2006/7 22gᵖᵘ Mar 19] first foal: dam unraced: no form in Irish points/novice hurdle (mistakes). *Miss M. Bragg*   **h–**

IRISH RAPTOR (IRE) 8 b. or br.g. Zaffaran (USA) – Brownskin (Buckskin (FR)) [2006/7 c–, h87: c21s³ c25s* c25sᵘʳ c24dᵘʳ c24v² c24s* c24s² c24v c24s* c24gᵘʳ c21g Apr 13] big, rangy gelding: novice hurdler: developed into useful chaser, winning handicaps at Wincanton in October, Newbury (another novice) in December and Sandown (never challenged, beat Mokum by 13 lengths) in February: not discredited when seventh to Dunbrody Millar in Topham Chase at Aintree final start, bad mistake 2 out: stays 25f: acts on heavy going: front runner: often jumps sketchily. *N. A. Twiston-Davies*   **c135** **h–**

IRISH TOTTY 8 b.m. Glacial Storm (USA) – Elver Season (Vital Season) [2006/7 h–: 22g[pu] c19s[F] 22d 19d 16f c16g[pu] Apr 20] tall, workmanlike mare: little impact over hurdles: yet to complete over fences: bred to be suited by 2½m+: acts on firm going: tongue tied last 2 starts. *C. J. Down* **c– h73**

IRISH WEDDING (IRE) 5 b.m. Bob Back (USA) – Pharney Fox (IRE) (Phardante (FR)) [2006/7 F14s[5] F17s[*] F16d aF16g[2] Mar 9] rather leggy, unfurnished mare: second foal: dam, modest form in Irish bumpers, half-sister to fairly useful hurdler Back To Ben Alder (by Bob Back), stays 2½m: fair form in bumpers (trained on debut by C. Tinkler), won mares maiden at Folkestone in January. *P. D. Cundell* **F94**

IRISH WHISPERS (IRE) 4 b.g. Marju (IRE) – Muneera (USA) (Green Dancer (USA)) [2006/7 18g[3] 18m[*] 16g[4] 16d[2] 18s 21m[2] 22f[2] Apr 22] fair maiden on Flat (stays 13f): fair juvenile hurdler: won at Fontwell in September: finished lame final outing: stays easy 21f: acts on good to firm and good to soft ground, probably unsuited by soft. *B. G. Powell* **h102**

IRISH WOLF (FR) 7 b.h. Loup Solitaire (USA) – Erins Run (USA) (Irish River (FR)) [2006/7 h111: 19m[*] 22d[3] 19g[3] 24d[*] 23d[2] 24s[2] 25d 24v 24g[5] 21m[2] Apr 21] smallish, sturdy horse: smart hurdler: vastly improved in 2006/7, winning handicaps at Market Rasen in August and Aintree in October: several good efforts after, including when neck second to Inglis Drever in Grade 2 at Newbury and 4¾ lengths fifth to Albertas Run in listed handicap at Aintree: stays 3m: acts on firm and soft going: wears cheekpieces: usually races prominently. *P. Bowen* **h148**

IRIS ROYAL (FR) 11 b.g. Garde Royale – Tchela (FR) (Le Nain Jaune (FR)) [2006/7 c121, h–: c21d[2] c24d[ur] Dec 16] smallish gelding: useful handicap chaser: off another 8 months, neck second to Herecomestanley at Fakenham: unseated third next time: stays 3m: acts on any going. *N. J. Henderson* **c132 h–**

The Hacking Partnership's "Irish Wolf"

IRIS'S FLYER 5 b.g. Terimon – Miss Shaw (Cruise Missile) [2006/7 F16m⁴ F16v 21d **h87** 17s³ 16m³ Apr 10] unfurnished gelding: third foal: dam poor novice chaser: fourth in **F84** bumper: modest form in maiden hurdles: should be suited by further than 17f. *Jonjo O'Neill*

IRIS'S GIFT 10 gr.g. Gunner B – Shirley's Gift (Scallywag) [2006/7 c147, h–: c25s⁵ **c132** c24d⁵ Nov 18] big, workmanlike gelding: top-notch hurdler in his prime, won 2004 **h–** Stayers' Hurdle at Cheltenham: reportedly suffered hairline fracture of cannon bone before going chasing, and useful form at best over fences: should have stayed beyond 25f: won on good to firm going, possibly best on softer than good (acted on heavy): seemed best on left-handed tracks: did idle, but was thoroughly genuine: has reportedly been retired. *Jonjo O'Neill*

IRIS'S PRINCE 8 ch.g. Gunner B – Colonial Princess (Roscoe Blake) [2006/7 c106d, **c104** h101d: c23g² c25g⁵ c23g⁴ c22mᵖᵘ c22s* c19g² c21g² Apr 1] big gelding: winning hurd- **h–** ler: fair chaser: left A. Crook and off 7 months, back to form when winning handicap at Fontwell in February: should stay beyond 3m: acts on soft and good to firm going: in cheekpieces/blinkers nowadays. *J. L. Flint*

IRON EXPRESS 11 b.g. Teenoso (USA) – Sylvia Beach (The Parson) [2006/7 c–§, h–: **c83 §** c31s³ Apr 26] sparely-made gelding: winning chaser: fair pointer/hunter nowadays: stays **h–** 4m: acts on heavy and good to firm going: tried blinkered, often in cheekpieces: hard ride: unreliable. *Miss A. Armitage*

IRON MAID 6 b.m. Shambo – Brass Castle (IRE) (Carlingford Castle) [2006/7 F71: **h100** 20g² 17d³ 20s⁴ 24s 21g² Mar 20] fair novice hurdler: should be suited by further than 21f: acts on good to soft ground, below form on soft. *O. Sherwood*

IRON MAN (FR) 6 ch.g. Video Rock (FR) – Key Figure (FR) (Fast Topaze (USA)) **c131** [2006/7 c118, h–: c16v² c22g⁶ c24dᵖᵘ c22s* c25d⁵ c19d⁵ c24v⁴ c25sᵘʳ c24g c24v c21g **h–** c21gᵘʳ c24s³ Apr 26] leggy, close-coupled gelding: useful handicap chaser, sold out of J. Howard Johnson's stable 70,000 gns Doncaster May Sales after first outing: improved to win at Market Rasen in November by 13 lengths from Classic Capers: creditable efforts next 3 outings: barely stays 25f: acts on heavy going: in cheekpieces 5 of last 6 outings: tried tongue tied: often races prominently. *P. Bowen*

IRONMAN MULDOON (IRE) 10 gr.g. Roselier (FR) – Darjoy (Darantus) [2006/7 **c–** c24sᵖᵘ Jan 24] sturdy gelding: made winning debut in novice hurdle in 2004/5: pulled **h–** up only 2 outings since, including on chasing debut: should stay beyond 2½m. *Mrs A. J. Bowlby*

IRONSIDE (IRE) 8 b.g. Mister Lord (USA) – The Helmet (IRE) (Riot Helmet) **c100 x** [2006/7 c92x, h–: c24d² c19sᵖᵘ c24s* c28s⁵ c23v² c25d c26v⁵ c24s³ 26m Mar 29] **h–** sturdy gelding: maiden hurdler: fair handicap chaser: won at Chepstow in December: stays 3¼m: acts on heavy going: usually blinkered: tried tongue tied: sketchy jumper: ungenuine. *C. L. Tizzard*

IRON WARRIOR (IRE) 7 b.g. Lear Fan (USA) – Robalana (Wild Again **c–** (USA)) [2006/7 h90: c20d⁶ c27sᵘʳ c27v³ c25d⁵ c28v⁶ c24v³ c22d c25s⁵ Apr 1] rather **h–** sparely-made gelding: maiden hurdler/chaser: seems to stay 27f: acts on heavy going: tried in cheekpieces/tongue tied. *G. M. Moore*

IROQUOIS WARRIOR (IRE) 6 b.g. Lord Americo – Auntie Honnie (IRE) **F88** (Radical) [2006/7 F16d⁵ F16d Dec 29] €24,000 4-y-o: rather unfurnished gelding: fourth foal: brother to useful hurdler/chaser Lord Henry, stays 19f, and half-brother to modest staying chaser Lost In Normandy (by Treasure Hunter): dam, unplaced in bumper, sister to useful staying hurdler/chaser Morgans Harbour and useful 2½m hurdler Red Curate: better effort in bumpers when fifth to Golden Child at Worcester. *R. T. Phillips*

ISABEL'S STAR (IRE) 5 b.m. Intikhab (USA) – Star Club (IRE) (Bluebird (USA)) **h–** [2006/7 F16s 19gᵖᵘ Nov 5] first foal: dam, 13f to 17f winner on Flat, won up to 3m over **F–** hurdles: no promise in mares bumper/selling maiden hurdle (in cheekpieces). *R. T. Phillips*

ISAM TOP (FR) 11 b.g. Siam (USA) – Miss Sic Top (FR) (Mister Sic Top (FR)) **c–** [2006/7 c–, h86: 18g 17v* 18s⁴ 17v⁵ 18sᵖᵘ 18s⁶ 18vᵖᵘ Mar 7] compact gelding: maiden **h86 d** chaser: modest handicap hurdler: won at Folkestone (conditional jockeys) in November: below form after: stays 2¼m: acts on any going: blinkered twice: tried tongue tied. *M. J. Hogan*

ISAN (IRE) 5 b.g. Insan (USA) – Legal Action (IRE) (Supreme Leader) [2006/7 16g **h84** 16v Feb 24] €52,000 3-y-o: rather unfurnished gelding: second foal: dam bumper winner: some promise in novice hurdle on debut: shaped as if amiss almost 4 months later: likely to stay beyond 2m. *J. Howard Johnson*

ISELLIDO (IRE) 8 b. or br.m. Good Thyne (USA) – Souled Out (IRE) (Noalto)   **c–**
[2006/7 c103, h92: c25f May 9] smallish mare: fair hurdler/chaser at best: soundly beaten   **h–**
only start in 2006/7: stays 25f: acts on heavy going: tried in eyeshields: often makes
running. *R. C. Guest*

ISHARRAM (IRE) 4 ch. or b.f. Muhtarram (USA) – Ishaam (Selkirk (USA)) [2006/7   **h–**
17m Aug 26] maiden on Flat, well beaten in 2006: no show in juvenile on hurdling debut.
A. Berry

ISHKA BAHA (IRE) 8 ch.m. Shernazar – Briongloid (Callernish) [2006/7 c78, h98:   **c95**
c16m² c20f 21s^F c16d² c16d⁴ c16m* c16g⁴ Apr 7] workmanlike mare: modest hurdler/   **h–**
chaser: won handicap over fences at Uttoxeter (by 18 lengths) in March: probably best
with emphasis on speed at 2m: races prominently. *T. R. George*

IS IT ME (USA) 4 ch.g. Sky Classic (CAN) – Thea (GER) (Surumu (GER)) [2006/7   **h131**
16g* 17m* 17f* 17s* 16m* 17g² 16d 16g^pu Apr 12] fair on Flat (stays 1½m), successful
in July: made excellent start to hurdling career, winning juveniles at Stratford (2), Bangor,
Sedgefield and Market Rasen with ease, all by early-September: poor efforts in graded
events last 2 outings (blinkered final one) 5 months apart: raced around 2m: acts on firm
and soft going: front runner: fluent jumper in main, though has shown tendency to go left.
P. A. Blockley

ISLAND FAITH (IRE) 10 b. or br.g. Turtle Island (IRE) – Keep The Faith (Furry   **c– §**
Glen) [2006/7 c134§, h–: c17s^pu c16v^pu Dec 12] strong, compact gelding: useful handicap   **h–**
chaser on his day, failed to complete last 4 outings: acts on heavy going, possibly
possibly unsuited by good to firm: usually weak finisher. *J. Howard Johnson*

ISLAND KEY (IRE) 5 b.g. Insan (USA) – Kilkinamurry Home (IRE) (Woods of   **F91**
Windsor (USA)) [2006/7 F16g F16g Apr 7] unfurnished gelding: first foal: dam unraced:
failed to complete in 2 maiden points in Ireland in 2006: first and better effort in bumpers
when seventh of 15 at Wetherby. *G. M. Moore*

ISLAND KING (IRE) 4 br.g. Turtle Island (IRE) – Love of Paris (Trojan Fen) [2006/7   **h–**
F14v F16s 16v^pu Feb 5] eighth foal: half-brother to winner up to 10.5f in Italy by   **F–**
Distinctly North: dam unraced: no impact in bumpers/maiden hurdle. *T. D. Walford*

ISLAND LIFE (IRE) 4 b.g. Turtle Island (IRE) – Life Support (IRE) (High Estate)   **h113 +**
[2006/7 16d 16d² 16s³ 16v* 16v³ 16v⁵ Feb 24] well-made gelding: third foal: half-
brother to fairly useful but untrustworthy 2m hurdler Pasteur (by Eagle Eyed) and fair
2m hurdler Tyndall (by Perugino): dam, fairly useful 7f and modest 2m hurdle winner,
half-sister to useful 2m chaser Life Saver: unseated leaving stalls only start on Flat: fairly
useful juvenile hurdler: won at Clonmel (maiden) and Leopardstown in December,
beating Jack Absolute easily both times: folded tamely in graded events final 2 outings:
raced at 2m on going softer than good (best form on heavy): blinkered after third start:
front runner. *N. Meade, Ireland*

ISLAND LIGHT (USA) 7 ch.g. Woodman (USA) – Isla Del Rey (USA) (Nureyev   **h101**
(USA)) [2006/7 h–: 21g* 16d⁴ Dec 21] left P. Wegmann, first form over hurdles when
easily winning novice event at Ludlow on handicap debut in October: stays 21f: raced on
good ground or softer: tried in cheekpieces. *Mrs A. M. Thorpe*

ISLAND OF MEMORIES (IRE) 7 ch.m. Beneficial – Coronea Sea Queen (IRE)   **c87 x**
(Bassompierre) [2006/7 h–: 16d* 16v* 16d³ 19d c16m^pu c16m² c18v³ c16s^ur c16d* c16v²   **h75**
c20s^F c16v^ur c16s^pu Feb 26] workmanlike mare: poor hurdler: won novice seller at
Towcester in May: modest novice chaser: won handicap at Uttoxeter in November:
largely let down by jumping/attitude after: should stay beyond 2m: acts on good to firm
and heavy going: tried in cheekpieces, usually blinkered: sketchy jumper of fences.
D. P. Keane

ISLANDS THORNS 8 b.g. Thowra (FR) – Holly Hatch (Sulaafah (USA)) [2006/7   **h–**
20m Jul 12] no show in bumpers/over hurdles, left R. Alner and off 27 months prior to
only start in 2006/7. *M. F. Harris*

ISLAND WARRIOR (IRE) 12 b.g. Warcraft (USA) – Only Flower (Warpath)   **c– x**
[2006/7 c–x, h71: 20m 20m 19m³ 21g Oct 19] workmanlike gelding: poor hurdler: **h65 x**
stays 2¾m: acts on firm going: tried in headgear: often tongue tied: sketchy jumper.
B. P. J. Baugh

ISLE DE MAURICE 5 b.g. Sinndar (IRE) – Circe's Isle (Be My Guest (USA))   **h113**
[2006/7 h79: 20g⁴ 22v⁶ 20s⁵ 25s* 22v* 24d³ 26g⁴ 24g² Apr 18] angular gelding: fair
hurdler: won handicaps at Plumpton (novice) and Fontwell in January: stays 25f: acts on
heavy ground: blinkered last 6 starts: difficult ride (often soon off bridle). *D. M. Grissell*

ISN'T THAT LUCKY   4 b.g. Alflora (IRE) – Blast Freeze (IRE) (Lafontaine (USA))   **F103**
[2006/7 F14s* F16g Mar 14] unfurnished gelding: third foal: half-brother to fairly useful
hurdler/useful novice chaser Wee Robbie (by Bob Back), stays 3m: dam useful hurdler
up to 2½m: favourite, created good impression when winning bumper at Fontwell on
debut by 4 lengths from Cracking Cliche: mid-field in Grade 1 at Cheltenham following
month, carried wide top of hill. *Jonjo O'Neill*

ISOTOP (FR)   11 b.g. Port Etienne (FR) – Clorane (FR) (Rahotep (FR)) [2006/7 c90,   **c93 §**
h–: c26m³ c21s* May 26] angular, close-coupled gelding: maiden hurdler: modest novice   **h– §**
chaser: won handicap at Stratford in May: stays 3m: acts on heavy ground: inconsistent.
John Allen

ISSAQUAH (IRE)   5 b.m. Supreme Leader – Our Sioux (IRE) (Jolly Jake (NZ))   **F97**
[2006/7 F16d* F16s F17m* F17m² Apr 28] fifth foal: sister to fair hurdler around 2m
Dewasentah: dam unraced half-sister to useful hurdler/chaser up to 25f Kings Measure:
fairly useful form in bumpers: won mares events at Hexham in November and Market
Rasen (by 2½ lengths from Kentucky Sky) in April. *J. M. Jefferson*

ISTANBUL (IRE)   8 b.g. Revoque (IRE) – Song of The Glens (Horage) [2006/7 20dᵖᵘ   **h–**
20d 16v 18s 21m⁵ Apr 9] leggy, angular gelding: maiden hurdler: best at 2m: tried
blinkered/in cheekpieces: difficult ride. *Miss A. M. Newton-Smith*

IS THERE MORE   6 br.m. Classic Cliche (IRE) – Larksmore (Royal Fountain)   **h–**
[2006/7 h–, F–: 20dᵖᵘ May 1] tall mare: no show in bumpers/over hurdles. *J. M. Jefferson*

ISTRON BAY   5 b.g. Petoski – Annie Buckers (IRE) (Yashgan) [2006/7 F16v Jan 25]   **F–**
strong, workmanlike gelding: first foal: fairly useful chaser, stayed 25f: failed to
settle when well beaten in bumper on debut. *A. King*

ITALIANO   8 b.g. Emperor Jones (USA) – Elka (USA) (Val de L'Orne (FR)) [2006/7   **c– x**
c100, h–: c20g⁶ 17d 20m⁶ Jun 3] well-made gelding: winning hurdler: maiden chaser, fair   **h89**
form at best: stays 2½m: acts on good going: tried in cheekpieces (ran well): often let down
by jumping over fences. *P. Beaumont*

ITCANBEDONE AGAIN (IRE)   8 b.g. Sri Pekan (USA) – Maradata (IRE)   **h–**
(Shardari) [2006/7 h–: 16mᵖᵘ Oct 12] modest on Flat (best around 1¼m): won novice
handicap in 2003/4, only form over hurdles. *Ian Williams*

IT HAPPENED OUT (IRE)   6 gr.g. Accordion – Miss Hawkins (Modern Dancer)   **c–**
[2006/7 F91: 20d⁶ 16m⁵ 16s⁶ c20vᵖᵘ 16s 20g⁶ 17g⁵ Apr 27] lengthy, unfurnished gelding: **h87**
modest maiden hurdler: no impact on chasing debut: should stay 2½m: acts on soft
ground: tried in cheekpieces: has raced freely. *J. W. Mullins*

IT MAY BE WAR   7 b.g. Tulwar – Ninth of May (Comedy Star (USA)) [2006/7 F16s   **F–**
Dec 7] lengthy, angular gelding: fourth foal: half-brother to untrustworthy winning
hurdler/chaser Maybeseven (by Baron Blakeney), stays 3¼m: dam maiden pointer:
soundly beaten in bumper on debut. *O. Brennan*

ITSABOY   7 b.g. Wizard King – French Project (IRE) (Project Manager) [2006/7 16s   **h77**
16m 16m 17m 16g 20g⁶ 20f* 20s 24g Oct 7] little form on Flat: poor handicap hurdler:
won at Clonmel in September: stays 2½m: acts on firm and good to soft ground: tried
blinkered. *John Long, Ireland*

ITS A CLASSIC   6 b.g. Classic Cliche (IRE) – McMahon's River (Over The River   **h88**
(FR)) [2006/7 h–, F–: 19m 16m 20m³ 22m³ 20m² 19g⁴ 21m⁴ Nov 9] modest hurdler: won
18-runner handicap at Ludlow in November: stays 2¾m: raced on good/good to firm
ground. *Mrs N. S. Evans*

ITSA LEGEND   8 b.g. Midnight Legend – Onawing Andaprayer (Energist) [2006/7   **h132**
19dᶠ 22s⁴ 24s⁴ 23s² 24g³ Mar 16] good-topped gelding: bumper winner: useful novice
hurdler, off over 2½ years before return: won at Taunton in January by 1½ lengths from
Leading Contender: further progress after, 15 lengths second to Chief Dan George in
Grade 2 at Haydock and 18 lengths third to Wichita Lineman in 20-runner Grade 2 Spa
Novices' Hurdle at Cheltenham: will stay beyond 3m: acts on soft going. *A. King*

ITSALLUPINTHEAIR   11 b.g. Lion Cavern (USA) – Flora Wood (IRE) (Bob Back   **c68**
(USA)) [2006/7 c–, h–: c25g⁶ c23vᵘʳ c24g Apr 27] tall gelding: fair pointer, successful   **h–**
twice in 2007: little form in chases (often let down by jumping). *Mrs A. Sloyan*

IT'S A ROLL OVER   5 b.g. Lir – Cheren Lady (Comedy Star (USA)) [2006/7 F16d   **F–**
F17v Nov 28] second foal: dam of little account: no promise in bumpers. *J. D. Frost*

IT'S A ROOFER (IRE)   7 b.g. Topanoora – Chelsea Belle (IRE) (Supreme Leader)   **h100**
[2006/7 h95: 16g⁴ 16m² 16m²ᵈ 17m³ 20g* 22m⁵ 17s⁴ 20s Apr 1] fair hurdler: easily

justified favouritism in maiden at Perth in August: should stay 2¾m: acts on good to firm going. *Mrs K. Walton*

IT'S BERTIE 7 b.g. Unfuwain (USA) – Legend of Aragon (Aragon) [2006/7 h96, F82: 16f⁴ 22m² 22m* c21m⁶ c23dᵖᵘ c16s* c16s⁵ c18d⁴ c22dᵖᵘ Feb 19] rather leggy gelding: has reportedly had breathing operation: modest novice hurdler/chaser: won maiden hurdle at Cartmel in August and handicap over fences at Carlisle in October: has won over 2¾m, best form over shorter: acts on soft and good to firm going. *Mrs S. J. Smith*   c95 h93

IT'S BLUE CHIP 6 b.g. Polar Falcon (USA) – Bellateena (Nomination) [2006/7 h–: 20v 24sᵖᵘ 23v³ 20v c20v² Mar 18] workmanlike gelding: modest handicap hurdler nowadays: in cheekpieces, similar form when second in handicap on chasing debut: barely stays testing 23f: raced on ground softer than good (acts on heavy): tried blinkered. *R. T. Phillips*   c92 h92

ITS CRUCIAL (IRE) 7 b.g. Beneficial – Balda Girl (IRE) (Mandalus) [2006/7 c–, h–: c20d c24s* c21gᵖᵘ Apr 19] compact gelding: winning hurdler: upped in trip, easily best effort over fences (fairly useful form) when winning handicap at Huntingdon in February by 29 lengths from Inishturk: lost all chance with blunder first at Cheltenham 2 months later: will stay beyond 3m: raced on good going or softer (acts on soft). *N. A. Twiston-Davies*   c122 h–

IT'S DEFINITE (IRE) 8 b.g. Definite Article – Taoveret (IRE) (Flash of Steel) [2006/7 c103§, h111§: c24m⁴ c25g³ c22s² c27v* c30s⁶ c27v⁴ Feb 20] sturdy gelding: winning hurdler: fair handicap chaser: won at Sedgefield (by 14 lengths) in January: stays 27f: acts on any going: wears cheekpieces: often let down by jumping/attitude. *P. Bowen*   c107 § h– §

ITSDOWNTOBEN 6 b.g. Karinga Bay – Martins Lottee (Martinmas) [2006/7 h–, F89: 17mᵘʳ Apr 28] compact gelding: in frame in bumpers: mistakes over hurdles: fifth in point in April: tried tongue tied. *D. McCain Jnr*   h– x

ITS GOTTA BE ALFIE (IRE) 12 ch.g. Zaffaran (USA) – Nimbi (Orchestra) [2006/7 c23s⁴ Mar 12] big gelding: maiden hurdler/chaser, lightly raced: often let down by jumping over fences. *Mike Hammond*   c– x h–

IT'S IN THE STARS 7 b.g. Teenoso (USA) – Sail By The Stars (Celtic Cone) [2006/7 h105: 19s² 21vᵖᵘ Jan 13] sturdy, lengthy gelding: bumper winner: encouraging efforts first 2 starts in novice hurdles: off 13 months, 8 lengths second to Sir Jimmy Shand at Newbury: possibly amiss in Grade 2 event next time: should be suited by 2½m+: raced on ground softer than good: difficult to train. *H. D. Daly*   h112

IT'S LIKE THAT (IRE) 7 b.g. Accordion – Hollygrove Cezanne (IRE) (King's Ride) [2006/7 c22v⁶ c25g² Apr 25] strong gelding: second foal: half-brother to fair hurdler Different Class (by Shardari), stays 2¾m: dam unraced sister to top-class 2m to 3m hurdler Mister Morose and half-sister to smart 2½m chaser Southolt: won point in January on debut: better effort in hunters when 3½ lengths second of 18 to Joe Blake in Champion Hunters' Chase at Punchestown, travelling strongly long way: sure to improve further and win races outside points. *Enda Bolger, Ireland*   c122 p

IT'S MISSY IMP 8 ch.m. Fearless Action (USA) – Swordella (Broadsword (USA)) [2006/7 c20s c23vF Feb 27] first foal: dam winning pointer: won maiden on first of 4 starts in points in 2004: little impact in hunters. *Andrew J. Martin*   c–

ITSMYBOY (IRE) 7 br.g. Frimaire – Hawkfield Lass (IRE) (The Parson) [2006/7 h128: 22g⁴ 20v⁵ 24d 22m² Mar 31] tall gelding: fairly useful handicap hurdler: not quite at best in 2006/7, 6 lengths second to easy winner Hautclan at Uttoxeter (tongue tied): stays 2¾m: acts on heavy and good to firm going: in cheekpieces 5 of last 6 starts: hasn't always looked straightforward. *D. E. Pipe*   h123

IT'S MY PARTY 6 b.g. Danzero (AUS) – Addicted To Love (Touching Wood (USA)) [2006/7 c78§, h91§, F96: c22sᵖᵘ 22s c26v³ c26vᵖᵘ c26m* c26gᵘʳ Apr 23] tall, lengthy gelding: maiden hurdler: poor handicap chaser: won novice event at Plumpton (by 14 lengths) in April: stays 3¼m: acts on good to firm and heavy going: wears headgear: temperamental. *W. G. M. Turner*   c83 § h– §

IT'S NO EASY (IRE) 6 b.g. Beneficial – Ballough Bui (IRE) (Supreme Leader) [2006/7 h–, F–: 16s⁵ 16gᵖᵘ Nov 4] useful-looking gelding: little sign of ability. *N. G. Richards*   h–

IT'S RUMOURED 7 ch.g. Fleetwood (IRE) – Etourdie (USA) (Arctic Tern (USA)) [2006/7 c93d, h–: c24d 24d 16v* 16s Mar 11] maiden chaser: modest handicap hurdler: fit from Flat, won conditional/amateur event at Plumpton in February, only form in   c– h94 §

2006/7: stays 23f: acts on heavy and good to firm going: has worn cheekpieces/blinkers, including last 3 starts. *Jean-Rene Auvray*

ITS TEESCOMPONENTS (IRE) 5 b.m. Saddlers' Hall (IRE) – Windswept Lady **F92**
(IRE) (Strong Gale) [2006/7 F16s² F16g F17g Apr 13] big, good-topped mare: sixth
foal: closely related to fairly useful hurdler Pass It On (by Accordion), stays 3m, and
half-sister to bumper/2½m hurdle winner Windswept Leader (by Supreme Leader): dam,
fair hurdler, stayed 21f: best effort in bumpers when second to Sound Accord at
Huntingdon on debut. *K. G. Reveley*

IT'S THE LIMIT (USA) 8 b.g. Boundary (USA) – Beside (USA) (Sportin' Life **h95**
(USA)) [2006/7 h101: 24s 18g⁴ 19d^pu 21f⁴ 20g⁴ 20g Apr 27] rather leggy gelding: modest
maiden hurdler: probably stays 2½m: acts on soft going, possibly unsuited by firm: tried
blinkered/visored: effective tongue tied or not. *W. K. Goldsworthy*

ITSTOOEARLY 4 br.f. Overbury (IRE) – Deb's Ball (Glenstal (USA)) [2006/7 F16v⁶ **F70**
F18g⁵ Mar 26] 10,000 3-y-o: small filly: half-sister to several winners, notably useful
staying chaser Hot Weld (by Weld): dam useful hurdler who stayed 25f: poor form in
bumpers: bred to stay well. *N. J. Hawke*

ITSUKATE 7 b.m. Makbul – Kilvarnet (Furry Glen) [2006/7 h–, F–: 19g^pu 16g Jun 15] **h–**
no sign of ability: tried tongue tied. *J. Rudge*

ITSUPTOHARRY (IRE) 8 b.g. Old Vic – Celtic Gale (Strong Gale) [2006/7 c122, **c114**
h–: c20s* May 20] tall gelding: fair chaser: back to form to win 5-runner handicap at **h–**
Bangor in May, only outing in 2006/7: stays 2½m: acts on heavy going. *D. McCain*

ITS WALLACE JNR 8 b.g. Bedford (USA) – Built In Heaven (Sunley Builds) **c–**
[2006/7 c113, h110: 24m² 27m⁶ Jan 11] leggy gelding: fairly useful handicap hurdler: **h117**
best effort when runner-up to Jockser at Exeter: won 2-runner novice chase at Warwick in
2005/6 despite jumping markedly right (fell next time): should stay beyond 3m: has won
on good to soft going, best under less testing conditions: tongue tied. *Miss S. West*

ITSY BITSY 5 b.m. Danzig Connection (USA) – Cos I Do (IRE) (Double Schwartz) **F–**
[2006/7 F83: F16s Feb 16] unfurnished mare: modest form at best in bumpers: tried
visored. *W. J. Musson*

IT TAKES TIME (IRE) 13 b.g. Montelimar (USA) – Dysart Lady (King's Ride) **c133**
[2006/7 c153, h–: c24d³ c21d³ c20s⁴ c24g c27f² Apr 5] angular gelding: useful chaser **h–**
nowadays: best effort in 2006/7 when short-headed by The Bandit in 6-runner handicap
at Wincanton: effective from 2½m to 27f: acts on any going: has run well when sweating:
has edged left under pressure/idled. *D. E. Pipe*

IT WOULD APPEAR (IRE) 8 b.g. Un Desperado (FR) – Toi-Dante (IRE) **h–**
(Phardante (FR)) [2006/7 h90, F95: 17m^pu Jun 30] third in bumper: regressive form in
novice hurdles: bred to stay beyond 2½m. *Jonjo O'Neill*

IVANA ILLYICH (IRE) 5 ch.m. Tipsy Creek (USA) – Tolstoya (Northfields (USA)) **h– §**
[2006/7 h72: 16g 20s 20v 19d 17m 22m Aug 26] close-coupled mare: winning hurdler,
no show in 2006/7: usually wears headgear: temperamental. *J. S. Wainwright*

IVANOPH (FR) 11 b.g. Roi de Rome (USA) – Veronique IV (FR) (Mont Basile (FR)) **c88 §**
[2006/7 c81§, h–: c19g^pu c20s^pu c19m c24g Apr 21] tall, sparely-made gelding: has **h–**
reportedly had breathing operation: winning hurdler/chaser, little impact outside points
since 2003/4: often finds little. *S. Flook*

IVANS RIDE (IRE) 4 b.g. Night Shift (USA) – Ride Bold (USA) (J O Tobin (USA)) **h85**
[2006/7 16s⁶ 16s⁴ Jan 10] compact gelding: half-brother to fairly useful hurdler around
2m Alrida (by Ali-Royal): maiden on Flat: much better effort in juvenile hurdles when
fourth to Raslan at Wincanton. *M. F. Harris*

IVEGILL 5 b.m. Overbury (IRE) – My Dawn (River God (USA)) [2006/7 F16s F16s **F–**
Apr 1] 5,000 4-y-o: second foal: dam winning pointer: well beaten in bumpers.
F. P. Murtagh

IVERAIN (FR) 11 b.g. Le Riverain (FR) – Ursala (FR) (Toujours Pret (USA)) [2006/7 **c–**
c102, h–: c25f^pu May 10] good-topped gelding: fair handicap chaser in 2005/6: lame on **h–**
return: stayed 25f: acted on good to soft and good to firm going: blinkered once on return:
dead. *Sir John Barlow Bt*

IVOIRE DE BEAULIEU (FR) 11 b.g. Port Etienne (FR) – Kashmonde (FR) (Kash- **c–**
neb (FR)) [2006/7 c128+, h107p: c31d c31s c31d Mar 13] rather leggy gelding: fairly **h–**
useful form when winning cross-country handicap at Cheltenham on British debut in

December 2005: landed odds in novice on hurdling debut later in month: well held in cross-country events in 2006/7: stays 31f: acts on heavy going. *Ferdy Murphy*

IVORSAGOODUN 8 b.m. Piccolo – Malibasta (Auction Ring (USA)) [2006/7 19s 19v⁵ 19v³ 20gᵖᵘ Apr 14] leggy mare: maiden hurdler: probably stays 3m: acts on good to firm going: tried visored: ungenuine. *N. G. Ayliffe* **h56 §**

IVORY FAIR (USA) 5 ch.g. Daylami (IRE) – Iviza (IRE) (Sadler's Wells (USA)) [2006/7 F17m F17m⁴ Apr 17] 3,800 2-y-o: fifth foal: half-brother to useful but temperamental 1¼m winner Dane (by Doyoun): dam, 2-y-o 7f winner and second in Ribblesdale: last in bumpers. *K. A. Morgan* **F—**

IWILLREMEMBERYOU (IRE) 7 b. or br.g. Lord Americo – Endless Patience (IRE) (Miner's Lamp) [2006/7 16s 16s 24v 24v⁴ 23v 25v* Feb 27] €42,000 4-y-o: good-bodied gelding: second foal: dam unraced half-sister to useful staying chaser Moorcroft Boy: won maiden point in 2006: much improved over hurdles when winning novice handicap at Catterick in February: stays 25f: raced on soft/heavy going: sold 22,000 gns Doncaster May Sales. *Oliver McKiernan, Ireland* **h99 +**

IZITA STAR 4 b.f. Lomitas – Shaanara (IRE) (Darshaan) [2006/7 F16s² F17g Apr 13] smallish, angular filly: first foal: dam 2-y-o 7f winner: modest form in mares bumpers. *Mrs A. L. M. King* **F80**

IZNOGOUD (FR) 11 br.g. Shafoun (FR) – Vancia (FR) (Top Dancer (FR)) [2006/7 c–, h–: c24d⁴ c24d⁵ c24d³ c24v⁵ c24g Mar 24] tall, leggy gelding: has a markedly round action: fairly useful handicap chaser nowadays: effective at 2½m to easy 29f: acts on good to firm and heavy going: visored twice (departed early both times). *D. E. Pipe* **c122 h—**

IZZYIZZENTY 8 b.g. Myfontaine – More To Life (Northern Tempest (USA)) [2006/7 h94: 21mᵖᵘ 24g⁵ c20g c20mᵖᵘ c24sᵖᵘ Feb 22] lengthy gelding: maiden pointer: modest novice hurdler at best: no form in chases, left J. M. Jefferson before final outing: stays 2¾m: acts on heavy going. *Miss Louise Todd* **c— h—**

IZZYKEEN 8 b.g. Keen – Washita (Valiyar) [2006/7 c103, h103: 24m 22d⁵ 24m⁶ 24g 21m³ c20s⁴ 21d⁴ Nov 7] smallish, angular gelding: modest hurdler/maiden chaser: stays 2¾m: acts on good to firm and good to soft going: races prominently: has suffered breathing problem. *Mrs S. J. Smith* **c82 + h95**

J

JABO (FR) 5 b.g. Epervier Bleu – Reine Zazou (FR) (Castle Guard) [2006/7 h–, F73: 16s 16d 21s 20v 19g Mar 28] lengthy gelding: no solid form over hurdles: sold 2,000 gns Doncaster May Sales. *N. A. Twiston-Davies* **h— F73:**

JAC AN REE (IRE) 11 b.g. Supreme Leader – Nic An Ree (IRE) (King's Ride) [2006/7 c78, h–: c26gᵖᵘ May 24] maiden hurdler: winning pointer: runner-up on completed start in novice hunter chases: stays 19f. *Mrs D. M. Grissell* **c— h—**

JACARADO (IRE) 9 b.g. Jurado (USA) – Lady Mearba (IRE) (Le Bavard (FR)) [2006/7 c77, h–: c20s⁵ c22v⁶ c22g⁴ c23mᵖᵘ c24s c20gᶠ c19s* c24d⁶ c16v² c20s⁵ c19vᵖᵘ c23vᵖᵘ Mar 9] good-topped gelding: poor handicap chaser: won at Towcester in December: stays 3m: acts on heavy going: visored: inconsistent. *R. Dickin* **c81 h—**

JACARANDA (IRE) 7 ch.g. Bahhare (USA) – Near Miracle (Be My Guest (USA)) [2006/7 16m² 16m* 19g⁴ 16m* 16m* 16f⁵ Sep 17] fair up to 1½m on Flat for Mrs A. King: fair novice hurdler: won maiden at Worcester in July and handicaps at Stratford (conditional jockeys) and Huntingdon (battled well to beat Tashkandi by 1½ lengths) in August: likely to prove best around 2m: raced on good going or firmer. *P. J. Hobbs* **h107**

JACK ABSOLUTE (IRE) 4 gr.g. Fantastic Light – Crepe Ginger (IRE) (Sadler's Wells (USA)) [2006/7 16v⁵ 16v² 16v² 16v* 20v 16d 16m Apr 25] tall, leggy gelding: fair maiden on Flat (seems to stay 1¾m), sold out of B. Meehan's stable 18,000 gns Newmarket July Sales: fairly useful juvenile hurdler: won maiden at Limerick in January: ran well when 14½ lengths seventh of 24 to Gaspara in listed 4-y-o handicap at Cheltenham penultimate outing: unable to recover from bad mistake final next time: should stay beyond 2m: acts on heavy ground. *John Joseph Murphy, Ireland* **h112**

JACK DURRANCE (IRE) 7 b.g. Polish Precedent (USA) – Atlantic Desire (IRE) (Ela-Mana-Mou) [2006/7 h79: 17g 17m 26dᵘʳ 27m³ 24g 22mᵖᵘ 27d⁵ Aug 21] smallish gelding: poor hurdler: stays 27f: acts on good to firm and good to soft going. *G. A. Ham* **h79**

JACK FULLER (IRE) 10 b.g. Be My Native (USA) – Jacks Sister (IRE) (Entitled) **c99 §** [2006/7 c98§, h–§: c18s² c20vᵖᵘ Jan 12] tall gelding: modest handicap chaser: stays 25f, **h– §** effective at much shorter: acts on soft and good to firm going: wears headgear: has found little, and not one to rely on. *P. Winkworth*

JACK HIGH (IRE) 12 br.g. Erdelistan (FR) – Lyntim (Fidel) [2006/7 c139, h134: **c136 §** 20s c25s c24v c24d⁴ c28s c25v² c36gᶠ c29f⁴ Apr 28] smallish, lengthy gelding: winning **h112** hurdler: useful chaser: creditable efforts in frame 3 of last 4 completed starts, 15 lengths fourth to Hot Weld in Betfred Gold Cup (Handicap) at Sandown final one: stays 29f: acts on any going: blinkered/visored last 6 outings: held up: not a fluent jumper (failed to reach halfway both starts in Grand National at Aintree): none too genuine (flashes tail under pressure). *T. M. Walsh, Ireland*

JACKIE BOY (IRE) 8 b.g. Lord Americo – Riverpauper (IRE) (Over The River (FR)) **c–** [2006/7 c–, h73: 22m⁴ 24g* 21d² 20m⁴ 26m* Aug 28] sturdy gelding: modest handicap **h88** hurdler: won at Exeter in May and Huntingdon in August: let down by jumping in handicap chases: stays 3¼m: acts on heavy and good to firm going. *N. A. Twiston-Davies*

JACKIE JARVIS (IRE) 10 b.m. Alphabatim (USA) – Miss Brantridge (Riboboy **c–** (USA)) [2006/7 c20mᵖᵘ Jun 3] fair pointer: winning hunter chaser, no show only outing in 2006/7: stays 21f: has been reluctant to line up. *J. S. Swindells*

JACK INGHAM (IRE) 7 b.g. Supreme Leader – Silent Run (Deep Run) [2006/7 **h115** F104: F16g⁴ 18v⁶ 18v³ 16v* 16mᶠ 16m Apr 25] quite good-topped gelding: bumper **F86** winner: progressive form in maiden hurdles, won at Gowran in December easily by 3 lengths from Brave Right: ran poorly in handicap at Punchestown final start: will be suited by 2½m+: acts on heavy ground. *E. J. O'Grady, Ireland*

Hanbury Syndicate's "Jack The Giant"

JACK LYNCH 11 ch.g. Lancastrian – Troublewithjack (Sulaafah (USA)) [2006/7 c–, h–: 24f c21m c21m* Aug 29] winning hurdler: first solid form over fences when winning novice handicap at Sedgefield in August: stays 3m: acts on heavy and good to firm going. *Ferdy Murphy*   **c80 h–**

JACK MARTIN (IRE) 10 ch.g. Erins Isle – Rolling Penny (IRE) (Le Moss) [2006/7 c111x, h109: c22v^R Nov 30] leggy gelding: winning hurdler: fair but error-prone handicap chaser: temperamental display only start in 2006/7: stays 3m: acts on heavy going: in cheekpieces last 3 outings. *S. Gollings*   **c – x h–**

JACK MILLER 9 b.g. Forzando – Norvi (Viking (USA)) [2006/7 c19m^F May 9] fourth in bumper in 2001/2 for R. Fahey: no show in points: tongue tied, fell in novice hunter chase debut. *M. Ranger*   **c–**

JACK OF SPADES (IRE) 11 b.g. Mister Lord (USA) – Dooney's Daughter (The Parson) [2006/7 c91, h–: c24g^pu c24m^pu c25m^pu Apr 28] good-topped gelding: no form over hurdles: winning chaser, off 22 months prior to no show in 2006/7: stays 3¼m: tried in cheekpieces. *R. Dickin*   **c– h–**

JACK ROLFE 5 b.g. Polish Precedent (USA) – Haboobti (Habitat) [2006/7 h101: 16d^3 May 21] good-topped gelding: fair performer on Flat (stays 1¾m), successful in March: best effort in 3 starts over hurdles when fourth in juvenile in 2005/6: raced at 2m on good to soft ground. *G. L. Moore*   **h76**

JACKS CRAIC (IRE) 8 b.g. Lord Americo – Boleree (IRE) (Mandalus) [2006/7 c142, h–: c17d^5 c17s^6 c16s^4 c17d^pu c16s^3 c16v^4 c17d^2 c16g c16g^pu Apr 12] good-topped gelding: useful handicap chaser: not at best in 2006/7, let down by jumping last 2 outings: best form around 2m: acts on heavy going. *J. L. Spearing*   **c131 h–**

JACKS JEWEL (IRE) 10 b.g. Welsh Term – September Daydream (IRE) (Phardante (FR)) [2006/7 c–x, h–: c22m 22g^pu 20m^5 Jun 6] poor novice hurdler/chaser: stays 21f: acts on soft and good to firm going: usually let down by jumping over fences. *C. J. Down*   **c– x h73**

JACK'S LAD (IRE) 8 ch.g. High Roller (IRE) – Captain's Covey (Captain James) [2006/7 h101: 16g c16s^6 c16d^4 c17s s16m^5 c16m^5 Apr 15] workmanlike gelding: fair hurdler at best: mistakes and little form over fences: best form around 2m. *Mrs S. M. Johnson*   **c – x h–**

JACKSON (FR) 10 b.g. Passing Sale (FR) – Tynia (FR) (Djarvis (FR)) [2006/7 c110, h121: 24m^pu May 9] sturdy gelding: fairly useful hurdler/fair maiden chaser: stays 3¼m: acts on heavy going (won weak event on good to firm): tried tongue tied: temperamental: sold 5,000 gns Doncaster May (2006) Sales, runner-up in points in 2007. *A. King*   **c– § h– §**

JACKSONS PIER (IRE) 7 b.g. Accordion – Uhuru (IRE) (Jurado (USA)) [2006/7 h–, F80: 26s 20v^3 c18v^3 Jan 17] good-topped gelding: winning Irish pointer: poor form over hurdles/on chasing debut: stays 2½m: acts on heavy ground: likely to do better over fences. *M. Scudamore*   **c84 p h82**

JACKSONVILLE (FR) 10 b.g. Petit Montmorency (USA) – Quinine Des Aulnes (FR) (Air du Nord (USA)) [2006/7 c98, h–: c25s^2 c25v^2 c21g^R Apr 12] sturdy gelding: fair hunter chaser/pointer, successful in January: should stay beyond 25f: acts on heavy going: wears headgear: tried tongue tied. *Miss Vicky Simpson*   **c98 h–**

JACK TAR (IRE) 5 b.g. Jolly Jake (NZ) – Pretty Furry (Furry Glen) [2006/7 F16g Nov 14] sturdy gelding: third foal: dam, won 2m hurdle in Ireland, half-sister to useful chaser up to 2½m Around The Horn: soundly beaten in bumper on debut. *J. Wade*   **F–**

JACK THE BLASTER 7 b.g. Alflora (IRE) – Marsden Rock (Tina's Pet) [2006/7 F87: 19s* 19d 20v^pu 24s^2 24s^3 Apr 26] well-made gelding: bumper winner: fair novice hurdler: won at Market Rasen in November: stays 3m: raced on ground softer than good: tried tongue tied: has found little. *J. Howard Johnson*   **h109**

JACK THE GIANT (IRE) 5 b.g. Giant's Causeway (USA) – State Crystal (IRE) (High Estate) [2006/7 h125: 16d^2 c16g* c16g* c16d* c16g^3 c16g^6 Apr 14] tall gelding: has scope: fairly useful hurdler: progressed into smart novice chaser, winning maiden at Sandown and 4-y-o event at Warwick (by 16 lengths, flashing tail) in November, and Grade 2 Stan James Wayward Lad Novices' Chase at Kempton (beat Twist Magic by 1¾ lengths) in December: ran well when 6 lengths third to My Way de Solzen in Arkle Trophy at Cheltenham: let down by jumping when well held in another Grade 1 at Aintree final outing: likely to stay beyond 17f: acts on good to soft going: takes strong hold. *N. J. Henderson*   **c146 h123**

JACK WEIGHELL 8 b.g. Accordion – Magic Bloom (Full of Hope) [2006/7 h–: c21m^pu c20g^4 c23g^4 c22d^pu c24g^pu Jul 21] good-topped gelding: no solid form over   **c – x h–**

hurdles/fences, not impressing with jumping/attitude over fences: tried in blinkers/cheekpieces/tongue tied. *J. M. Jefferson*

JACK WHITE 10 b.g. Teenoso (USA) – Frabjous Day (Broadsword (USA)) [2006/7 h–: 20d Nov 3] useful-looking gelding: little form over hurdles, lightly raced. *Mrs S. J. Smith* **h–**

JACOB RUISDAEL (IRE) 5 b.g. Supreme Leader – South Quay Lady (Quayside) [2006/7 F16g May 14] 20,000 3-y-o, resold 20,000 3-y-o: eighth foal: brother to 17f hurdle winner In No Hurry and half-brother to fairly useful chaser Jolly Side (by Jolly Jake), stays 2¾m: dam bumper/2m hurdle winner: well held in bumper on debut. *N. J. Henderson* **F–**

JACOPO (FR) 10 b.g. Grand Tresor (FR) – Qolombine (FR) (Damsire Unregistered) [2006/7 22v^pu Feb 28] workmanlike gelding: winning hurdler: off almost 4 years, no show in handicap on return: stays 3m: acts on soft and good to firm going. *Mrs L. C. Jewell* **h–**

JACQUEMART COLOMBE (FR) 10 gr.g. Royal Charter (FR) – Tanie (FR) (Kashmir Ring) [2006/7 c107: c25m^ur c20m³ May 18] sturdy gelding: one-time fairly useful chaser: third in hunter completed outing in 2006/7: stayed 3¼m: acted on soft going: tried in cheekpieces: dead. *Mrs S. E. Busby* **c76**

JADES BROOKE 4 b.f. Carisbrooke – Jaydeebee (Buckley) [2006/7 aF13g F14s F18v Mar 7] lengthy, unfurnished filly: fourth foal: half-sister to 2½m hurdle winner Jades Double (by Double Trigger): dam, lightly raced in bumpers, half-sister to Cheltenham Gold Cup winner Master Oats: no show in bumpers. *M. Madgwick* **F–**

JADES DOUBLE 6 b.m. Double Trigger (IRE) – Jaydeebee (Buckley) [2006/7 h86: 16g⁶ 21d⁵ 20s* 20s 20v⁶ 23d² Mar 21] rather leggy mare: modest hurdler: off 11 months before return: won maiden at Fontwell in December: stays 23f: raced on good ground or softer. *M. Madgwick* **h87**

J'ADORE (GER) 5 b.g. Chato (USA) – Josa (GER) (Northjet) [2006/7 h–: 18m 18m 20m^pu 20m Jul 5] little impact over hurdles: tried blinkered. *R. Curtis* **h–**

JAFFNA 5 b.m. Makbul – Pondicherry (USA) (Sir Wimborne (USA)) [2006/7 F16g F16s^pu F17g Mar 25] seventh foal: half-sister to several winners, including useful 1m/1¼m winner Teresa Balbi (by Master Willie): dam 7f winner: no form in bumpers: tried tongue tied. *R. T. Phillips* **F–**

JAHASH 9 ch.g. Hernando (FR) – Jalsun (Jalmood (USA)) [2006/7 26g 20g 20g^ur Apr 14] rather leggy gelding: fairly useful hurdler/chaser at best, off 3 years before return: effective at 2m to easy 3m: unraced on heavy going, acts on any other. *Simon Earle* **c–**
h97 d

JAKARI (FR) 10 b.g. Apeldoorn (FR) – Tartifume II (FR) (Mistigri) [2006/7 c130§, h–: c24g⁶ May 6] rather leggy gelding: useful handicap chaser, well held at Uttoxeter early in season: placed in points in 2007: stays 3m: acts on soft and good to firm going: races prominently: inconsistent. *H. D. Daly* **c– §**
h–

JALAMID (IRE) 5 b.g. Danehill (USA) – Vignelaure (IRE) (Royal Academy (USA)) [2006/7 16m Aug 28] useful 1m winner at 3 yrs, below best on Flat in 2006, sold out of J. Gosden's stable Newmarket July Sales: tongue tied, breathing problem on hurdling debut. *G. C. Bravery* **h–**

JALLASTEP (FR) 10 b.g. Boston Two Step (USA) – Balladine (FR) (Rivelago (FR)) [2006/7 c97, h74: c16s 20m c16m³ c19m⁵ c16f^pu 20g* c20m* c16s* c22m² c16v⁵ c17g c16s Apr 26] lengthy, workmanlike gelding: modest handicap hurdler: won selling event at Perth in August: fair handicap chaser: won at same track later in month and in September: lost form after next start: stays 2¾m: acts on good and good to firm going: in headgear. *J. S. Goldie* **c101**
h86

JALOUX D'ESTRUVAL (FR) 10 b.g. Kadalko (FR) – Pommette III (FR) (Trac) [2006/7 c–x, h110: 24v* c25s c24d⁴ c29s⁴ c28s c22v³ Jan 27] tall, good-topped gelding: fair handicap hurdler: won at Uttoxeter (by 23 lengths) in May, sold out of Mrs L. C. Taylor's stable 12,000 gns Doncaster Sales later in month: modest chaser nowadays: stays 3¼m: acts on heavy going: has worn net muzzle/hood: tried tongue tied: often let down by jumping over fences. *Dr P. Pritchard* **c95 x**
h115

JAMAARON 5 ch.g. Bachir (IRE) – Kentmere (FR) (Galetto (FR)) [2006/7 h84: 17m⁶ 17g³ 17s³ 16f⁵ 16m* 16d^pu 16m⁴ 17g Apr 27] modest hurdler: easily won seller at Stratford in August: left J. Spearing prior to final outing: raced around 2m: acts on good to firm going: has found little. *E. Haddock* **h93**

JAMADAST ROMA 5 b.m. Doubletour (USA) – Outfield (Monksfield) [2006/7 F–: F16g^F 19s 21v^5 16s^F 16v^{pu} 16g^5 Mar 20] leggy, close-coupled mare: little form in bumpers/over hurdles. *N. A. Twiston-Davies* **h79 F—**

JAMADIEL (IRE) 6 ch.g. Kadastrof (FR) – Petal Dust (IRE) (Convinced) [2006/7 c24s^F Mar 10] good-topped gelding: first foal: dam pulled up in 2 points: successful 4 times in points, including twice in 2007: keeping on in share of fifth when fell seventeenth in amateur event at Sandown on chase debut: joined P. Charnings. *Shay Slevin, Ireland* **c95 +**

JAMES BAY (IRE) 6 b.g. Bob Back (USA) – Slave Gale (IRE) (Strong Gale) [2006/7 F85: 20s^6 20m 16m^{pu} 20d 17m Apr 9] sixth in maiden on hurdling debut: no form after, sold out of N. Richards' stable 1,800 gns Doncaster January Sales prior to final outing: will stay 3m. *A. J. Lockwood* **h75**

JAMES CAIRD (IRE) 7 ch.g. Catrail (USA) – Polish Saga (Polish Patriot (USA)) [2006/7 16g Mar 20] useful at best on Flat (probably stays 11f), successful in July: hampered fourth when tenth of 17 in novice on hurdling debut: likely to prove best at easy 2m: should do better. *M. H. Tompkins* **h81 p**

JAMESDOUBLEYOU 4 b.g. Chaddleworth (IRE) – Paper Fair (Paper Cap) [2006/7 F16m^6 Apr 10] second foal: dam unraced: well held after racing keenly in bumper on debut. *K. M. Prendergast* **F—**

JAMES STREET (IRE) 4 b.g. Fruits of Love (USA) – Humble Mission (Shack (USA)) [2006/7 16v^5 16m^4 17g Apr 18] close-coupled gelding: fair on Flat (best at 7f/ 1m): modest form in juvenile hurdles. *J. R. Best* **h80**

JAMES VICTOR (IRE) 9 b.g. Be My Guest (USA) – Antakiya (IRE) (Ela-Mana-Mou) [2006/7 c96: c16d^3 c17m^4 c21f^F c16s^2 c18g c21d^5 c19s^{pu} 16s Jan 20] leggy gelding: modest handicap chaser: well beaten on hurdling debut (jumped big): barely stays 2½m: acts on firm going, probably on soft: tried blinkered (ran sour race): temperament under suspicion (threw race away fourth outing). *N. R. Mitchell* **c89 h—**

JAMIE'S GEM 4 ch.f. Bold Edge – Easter Baby (Derrylin) [2006/7 F14s^{pu} F16s^{pu} Feb 1] half-sister to 2m winner Kintbury (by Kylian): dam winning 2m hurdler: no show in bumpers, breathing problem second time. *M. Wigham* **F—**

JAMORIN DANCER 12 b.g. Charmer – Geryea (USA) (Desert Wine (USA)) [2006/7 c–§, h–§: 17m^{pu} c16f^6 c16g^{pu} Oct 19] sturdy gelding: maiden hurdler/winning chaser: no form since 2003/4: tried blinkered, usually wears cheekpieces: irresolute. *S. G. Chadwick* **c– § h– §**

JAM PACKED (IRE) 5 ch.g. Beneficial – Mad House (Kabour) [2006/7 F16s^3 22m^4 16f^2 17g^3 c16s* c17g^5 21s^2 22v^{pu} Jan 1] €45,000 3-y-o: half-brother to winning 2¾m chaser Shanty Town (by Buckskin): dam, of little account, out of half-sister to smart hurdler/chaser up to 19f Denys Adventure: better effort in bumpers (trained by C. Roche on debut) when third at Uttoxeter: modest novice hurdler: similar form over fences, won 3-finisher novice handicap at Towcester in October: stays 21f: acts on soft and firm ground. *Jonjo O'Neill* **c85 h91 F77**

JANBRE (IRE) 8 br.g. Zaffaran (USA) – Black Gayle (IRE) (Strong Gale) [2006/7 c25f^{pu} c25d^{ur} 27s^{pu} Dec 5] useful-looking gelding: maiden hurdler: no show in 2006/7, including in handicap chases: tried visored/tongue tied. *M. Scudamore* **c— h—**

JANE'S RUG RAT 8 gr.g. Rebelsway – Noble Roxy (Touch of Grey) [2006/7 F–: 16g^{pu} 24g^3 Nov 9] more signs of temperament than ability in bumpers/over hurdles: tried blinkered/tongue tied: sold £1,800 Ascot December Sales. *C. L. Popham* **h—**

JAOKA DU GORD (FR) 10 b.g. Concorde Jr (USA) – Theorie du Cochet (FR) (Franc Ryk) [2006/7 c107: c24v^{pu} c23d^{pu} c28g^4 c25m^{pu} Apr 28] good-topped gelding: fair handicap chaser at best: off 14 months, little encouragement in 2006/7: stays 25f: acts on soft going: has finished weakly. *P. R. Webber* **c81**

JAQUOUILLE (FR) 10 b.g. Rough Magic (FR) – Topeka (FR) (Italic) [2006/7 c24s^F c24d^5 24s^6 c33s^{pu} c25m Apr 26] big gelding: fair hurdler: fairly useful handicap chaser nowadays: best effort in 2006/7 when fifth to Point Barrow in valuable event at Leopardstown: stays 3m: acts on heavy and good to firm going: patiently ridden. *A. L. T. Moore, Ireland* **c118 h101**

JARDIN DE BEAULIEU (FR) 10 ch.g. Rough Magic (FR) – Emblem (FR) (Siberian Express (USA)) [2006/7 c90, h–: 24v^{pu} c20v^4 c24m^6 c26v^{pu} c21s^{pu} Mar 17] leggy gelding: lightly raced over hurdles: handicap chaser, very much on downgrade: stays 3m: acts on soft and good to firm going: sometimes wears headgear: tried tongue tied. *M. Mullineaux* **c79 § h—**

JARDIN DE VIENNE (FR) 5 gr.g. Highest Honor (FR) – Vaguely Money (USA) **h75 p**
(Vaguely Noble) [2006/7 16v Mar 3] fair on Flat (stays 1m), successful 4 times in French
Provinces for D. de Watrigant: shaped better than result suggested when seventh of 8
finishers in novice at Kempton on hurdling debut: likely to need emphasis on speed at
2m: open to improvement. *Noel T. Chance*

JAROD (FR) 9 b.g. Scribe (IRE) – Somnambula (IRE) (Petoski) [2006/7 c–, h–: c24gᵖᵘ **c–**
c25dᵖᵘ May 17] sturdy gelding: little impact over hurdles: no show over fences: tried **h–**
blinkered. *Mark Doyle*

JARRO (FR) 11 b.g. Pistolet Bleu (IRE) – Junta (FR) (Cariellor (FR)) [2006/7 c102, **c120**
h–: c16m⁴ c16d⁴ c16m³ c17d² c19g² c16sᶠ c17s* c16d⁵ c16d* Dec 21] workmanlike **h–**
gelding: fairly useful handicap chaser: won at Stratford in October and Ludlow (beat Four
Schools by 1¾ lengths) in December: barely stays 19f: acts on good to firm and heavy
going: free-going sort. *Miss Venetia Williams*

JASPER 8 gr.g. Environment Friend – Fisima (Efisio) [2006/7 F–: 20fᵖᵘ 24f 24fᵖᵘ Jul 19] **h–**
no form. *S. Lycett*

JASPER ROONEY 8 b.g. Riverwise (USA) – Miss Secret (El Conquistador) [2006/7 **c– x**
c–, h–: 22mᵖᵘ May 12] no sign of ability. *C. W. Mitchell* **h– x**

JASS 5 b.g. Robellino (USA) – Iota (Niniski (USA)) [2006/7 F100: F16d* F16v² 16s³ **h112**
20s² 20g Apr 12] sturdy gelding: useful form in bumpers, won at Kelso in October: **F115**
good second to Schiehallion at Newbury following month: easily best effort over hurdles
when second to easy winner Imperial Command in novice at Newcastle: stiff task next
time: stays 2½m: raced on good going or softer: room for improvement in jumping.
K. G. Reveley

JAUNTY 4 ch.g. Pivotal – Invincible (Slip Anchor) [2006/7 F13d³ F13g³ F14g 17s 20v⁴ **h87 ?**
Jan 11] 2,000 2-y-o: quite good-topped gelding: first foal: dam 11f winner: modest form **F79**
in 3-y-o bumpers: easily better effort over hurdles when fourth in novice at Hereford.
N. E. Berry

JAUNTY FLIGHT 5 b.m. Busy Flight – Jaunty June (Primitive Rising (USA)) **h89**
[2006/7 F–: 16vᵘʳ 17s² 16g⁴ Mar 21] modest form over hurdles: will be suited by 2½m+.
B. J. Eckley

JAUNTY JOURNEY 4 ch.g. Karinga Bay – Jaunty June (Primitive Rising (USA)) **F81**
[2006/7 F17s³ F16g⁵ F16g⁶ Apr 7] smallish gelding: third foal: half-brother to fairly useful hurdler/useful chaser Jaunty Times (by Luso), stays 25f: dam, modest hurdler, stayed
2¾m: modest form in bumpers: will stay further than 2m: sold 20,000 gns Doncaster May
Sales. *B. J. Eckley*

JAUNTY TIMES 7 b.g. Luso – Jaunty June (Primitive Rising (USA)) [2006/7 h120: **c132**
c20g⁶ c25s² c24d* c24s* c24d³ c33sᵖᵘ c25g Apr 13] strong gelding: winning hurdler: **h–**
useful novice chaser: won at Ascot (handicap) in December and Huntingdon in January,
further improvement when beating Only Vintage by short head at latter: creditable third
to Gungadu in Grade 2 Reynoldstown Novices' Chase at Ascot: should stay beyond 25f:
acts on heavy and good to firm going. *H. D. Daly*

JAYENAR 6 b.m. Kadeed (IRE) – Anzarna (Zambrano) [2006/7 F–: F16v 22dᵖᵘ 22gᵖᵘ **h–**
20vᵖᵘ 19sᵖᵘ 24vᵖᵘ Jan 17] no sign of ability: tried visored. *W. S. Coltherd* **F–**

JAYO (FR) 4 ch.g. Grape Tree Road – Joie de Nuit (USA) (Affirmed (USA)) [2006/7 **h121**
16vᵖᵘ 16vᶠ 16d Mar 13] fair 1½m winner on Flat: fairly useful juvenile hurdler:
won maiden at Limerick in December very easily: reportedly lame next time: let down by
jumping last 2 outings, blundering 2 out when eighth of 24 to Gaspara in listed 4-y-o
handicap at Cheltenham: likely to stay beyond 2m: raced on ground softer than good.
W. P. Mullins, Ireland

JAZZ CITY 7 br.g. Rock City – Hullo Mary Doll (Lidhame) [2006/7 F74: F16m² F17g⁴ **h101**
17s² 17s³ 16v³ 19dᶠ 16mᵖᵘ Apr 10] smallish, workmanlike gelding: in frame in bumpers: **F76**
fair novice hurdler: lost action final start: probably stays 19f: acts on soft going (bumper
form on good to firm). *Mrs D. Thomas*

JAZZ D'ESTRUVAL (FR) 10 gr.g. Bayolidaan (FR) – Caro d'Estruval (FR) (Car- **c–**
amo (FR)) [2006/7 c–, h136: 23d³ 20s³ Dec 16] strong, useful-looking gelding: useful **h139**
chaser/handicap hurdler, lightly raced: off another 11 months, good 7¼ lengths third to
Halcon Genelardais in well-contested hurdle at Haydock: stays 25f: acts on heavy going.
N. G. Richards

JAZZ MESSENGER (FR) 7 bl.g. Acatenango (GER) – In The Saltmine (FR) **h155**
(Damister (USA)) [2006/7 h137x: 16v³ 16v* 16d* 16d⁵ 20g Apr 14]

A remarkable third win for the Australian jumper Karasi in the Nakayama Grand Jump went virtually unnoticed in Britain. For the fourth year running there were no representatives from Britain or Ireland, nor even France which had supplied runners in 2004 and 2005. The Noel Meade-trained Jazz Messenger, winner of the Stan James Christmas Hurdle at Kempton, had been invited but connections opted for the same day's Aintree Hurdle instead, and, despite the keenness of his connections to run, the reigning Order of Merit winner Royal Shakespeare was not deemed a sufficiently good replacement. Given the vast amount of prize money on offer, it is a bit surprising that so few British- or Irish-trained runners have accepted the invitations, particularly as in the inaugural international running in 2000 The Outback Way picked up around £119,000 for finishing third, and Cenkos earned connections nearly £42,000 for fifth place in 2002. Karasi's three wins have netted well over £1.1m in prize money. If the name Karasi rings a bell it might be because the son of Kahyasi started his racing career in Britain, winning three times for Sir Michael Stoute as a three-year-old on the Flat in the colours of his breeder the Aga Khan. The timing of the race (mid-April) and some unfamiliar aspects (started from stalls, on a very tight figure-of-eight track with sharp climbs and descents on firm ground and over varied obstacles) may well be off-putting, but there are surely some of the better jumpers for which this test would be both suitable and rewarding, particularly given the advances in equine transport compared to years gone by.

Such resistance to international racing over jumps hasn't always been the case. The inaugural running of the Colonial Cup at Camden in South Carolina back in 1970, which was another invitation race with a lucrative first prize ($60,000), attracted no fewer than nine foreign-trained challengers, including that year's Cheltenham Gold Cup first two L'Escargot (who fared best of the overseas contingent in fourth) and French Tan, the then Australian-trained Crisp and the popular Scottish-trained mare Young Ash Leaf. Also in the field was a four-year-old home-trained challenger called Tingle Creek who, of course, went on to achieve fame on British soil later in his career, as did two early winners of the Colonial Cup, Inkslinger (won 1973 Champion and Cathcart Chases) and Soothsayer (runner-up in 1975 Cheltenham Gold Cup). There was at least one British- or Irish-trained runner in each of the first nine renewals of the Colonial Cup, a group which included arguably the best chaser of the 'seventies Captain Christy, who finished a close fourth in the same year (1975) as when runner-up in the Grand Steeple-Chase de Paris at Auteuil, ridden on both occasions by seven-times Irish champion Bobby Coonan (who died in March 2007). Other leading jumpers from this decade to contest the American race were Lanzarote (fourth in 1976) and Sea Pigeon (fell in 1977), but pride of place went to the Derek Kent-trained Grand Canyon, who won the race in both 1976 and 1978 under Ron Barry. Unfortunately, injury restricted

*Stan James Christmas Hurdle, Kempton—Jazz Messenger proves an able deputy
for stable-companion Iktitaf; the grey Noble Request chases him home*

R. S. T. Syndicate's "Jazz Messenger"

Grand Canyon's appearances on British soil—though he showed very smart form when winning the 1978 SGB Chase at Ascot in course record time—but his overseas exploits made him only the second British- or Irish-based jumper to pass the £100,000 mark in winning prize money (Red Rum was the first, Night Nurse the third). If Grand Canyon was around today, it's unlikely he'd be sent over to the Colonial Cup as that race has now lost much of its original stature, a fate which has also befallen the Breeders' Cup Steeplechase (won in 1990 and 1991 by the Toby Balding-trained Morley Street). The same doesn't apply to Auteuil's richly-endowed International Jumps Weekend, at least in terms of prize money, yet this two-day November meeting has attracted just four British- or Irish-trained runners since its inception in 2005. Admittedly this quartet is headed by the Newmarket-based Tidal Fury, whose enterprising connections were rewarded with a prize money haul of around £200,000 after a juvenile hurdle campaign on mainly French soil in 2005/6. Willie Mullins is also one of the few British- or Irish-based National Hunt trainers who have exploited the greater prize-money opportunities on offer in France in recent years—his father Paddy enjoyed notable success with Dawn Run there in the mid-'eighties— and it will be interesting to see if any of his colleagues follow suit over the coming seasons.

   Noel Meade's preferred April option for Jazz Messenger, the Aintree Hurdle, was worth £91,000 to the winner and carried prize money down to sixth place, but the seven-year-old gelding could manage only ninth of ten finishers. He had earned nothing on his previous start either, when fifth to Hardy Eustace in the AIG Europe Champion Hurdle at Leopardstown in January, though earlier he had more than paid his way, garnering around £75,000 for his exploits over jumps, as well as over £35,000 for two wins on the Flat in the autumn, including the October Handicap at Naas.

The Christmas Hurdle was the undoubted highlight of Jazz Messenger's season. He was at Kempton rather as an understudy, his stable-companion Iktitaf, who had been due to run at Kempton, doing duty in the Festival Hurdle at Leopardstown in place of the absent Harchibald. Jazz Messenger, though, did what every fictional understudy does and made the most of his chance in the spotlight, left in the lead after halfway and kept up to his work to defeat Noble Request by four lengths. It should be stated that everything fell Jazz Messenger's way, literally with the departure of Afsoun at the fifth, and also with the favourite Straw Bear running as if amiss and another major contender Desert Quest seemingly finding the ground against him. Jazz Messenger was an intended runner, along with his two stable companions, in the Champion Hurdle itself, but in the event only Iktitaf lined up. Jazz Messenger's form at Kempton is a little short of that which would have been required for him to reach a place at Cheltenham. He had started odds on for his first two starts of the season, 5/2-on when beaten into third, let down by his jumping, in a minor event at Listowel in September (before his runs on the Flat) but making no mistake in a four-runner listed event at Thurles in December.

Prior to joining Meade, Jazz Messenger had been trained on the Flat by Gerard Butler and Alain de Royer Dupre, landing a valuable mile-and-a-quarter handicap at the 2003 Derby meeting for the former. In his first season over hurdles, Jazz Messenger showed useful form, winning twice at Navan and finishing a close seventh to Noland in the Supreme Novices' at Cheltenham and third to Iktitaf in the two-mile Champion Novices' at Punchestown. The last-named proved a pretty good pointer to the top two-mile hurdles in 2006/7: Iktitaf won the Morgiana Hurdle, the runner-up Straw Bear landed the 'Fighting Fifth' and the Kingwell, whilst the fourth Sublimity won the Champion Hurdle itself.

Jazz Messenger (FR) (bl.g. 2000)	Acatenango (GER) (ch 1982)	Surumu (ch 1974)	Literat
			Surama
		Aggravate (b 1966)	Aggressor
			Raven Locks
	In The Saltmine (FR) (b 1992)	Damister (b 1982)	Mr Prospector
			Batucada
		Isabellina (gr 1984)	Pentathlon
			Isabellita

Jazz Messenger carries the (FR) suffix but is a product of mostly German breeding. His sire Acatenango, who died as the result of head injuries suffered in a paddock accident in 2005, was a leading sire in Germany for many years but has been responsible for several other incidental jumpers apart from Jazz Messenger, including the 2005 Supreme Novices' runner-up Wild Passion, whom Meade also trains, and the 2004 Supreme Novices' fourth Cardenas. Jazz Messenger's dam In The Saltmine was a listed winner over a mile in Germany. She has produced three other winners, including Iwanowo (by Chief's Crown), who won at around a mile in Germany before being placed over hurdles for Jonjo O'Neill, and She Took A Tree (by Sri Pekan), a winner from six furlongs to a mile in France. In The Saltmine is a half-sister to the dam of the useful French middle-distance filly Lady In Grey. Before Aintree, where he was beaten too far out to blame the trip, the rather leggy Jazz Messenger had raced at around two miles over hurdles and he would be by no means certain to stay two and a half. He has raced on good going or softer over hurdles (acts on heavy), though he won on good to firm going at three on the Flat (unraced on firmer than good since that year). All four of his hurdles wins have come under Niall 'Slippers' Madden, who now seems the gelding's regular partner. *N. Meade, Ireland*

JAZZ SCENE (IRE) 6 b.g. Danehill Dancer (IRE) – Dixie Jazz (Mtoto) [2006/7 17g² 16m* 17dF 16s Dec 2] sturdy gelding: fairly useful on Flat (stays 1¼m), sold out of M. Channon's stable 15,000 gns Newmarket Autumn Sales: fair form in novice hurdles: won easily at Worcester in July: let down by jumping next 2 starts 4 months apart: likely to prove best at 2m with emphasis on speed. *L. Corcoran*   **h100**

JBALLINGALL 8 b.g. Overbury (IRE) – Sister Delaney (Deep Run) [2006/7 c80, h–: 20s³ c27d* 16v³ Dec 19] lengthy gelding: poor handicap chaser/maiden hurdler: back to   **c79** **h71**

best to win at Sedgefield in November: stays 27f: acts on heavy going: tried in cheek-pieces, effective blinkered or not: races prominently. *I. McMath*

JEANANN'S FIRST 4 ch.f. Shahrastani (USA) – Jeanann (Primitive Rising (USA)) [2006/7 F16v F16v F16m Apr 24] leggy filly: first foal: dam little form: tailed off in bumpers. *G. J. Smith*   F–

JEAN LE POISSON (FR) 5 b.g. Villez (USA) – Baladinine (FR) (Bering) [2006/7 F102: F16g⁴ Mar 24] good-topped gelding: useful form in bumpers, won at Newbury on debut in March 2006: off 11 months, good 8¼ lengths fourth of 22 to Helens Vision in same race. *N. J. Henderson*   F106

JEEPERS CREEPERS 7 b.g. Wizard King – Dark Amber (Formidable (USA)) [2006/7 h–, F74: 17mᵖᵘ May 11] workmanlike gelding: third in bumper in October 2005, only form. *Mrs A. M. Thorpe*   h–

JEFERTITI (FR) 10 ch.g. Le Nain Jaune (FR) – Nefertiti (FR) (Tourangeau (FR)) [2006/7 c91, h–: c16f³ c20mᶠ c16s³ c16s* c16g* c16s⁶ c16s Apr 26] rangy, good sort: fair handicap chaser: won at Uttoxeter in October and Newcastle in November: stays 2½m: acts on good to firm and heavy going: free-going sort, usually makes running/races prominently. *Miss Lucinda V. Russell*   c105
h–

JEFFSLOTTERY 5 b.g. Rock City – Thieves Welcome (Most Welcome) [2006/7 h–: 16mᵖᵘ 18mᵖᵘ Aug 24] failed to complete 3 starts over hurdles, lame final one. *D. W. Lewis*   h–

JEMEZ (IRE) 6 b.g. Supreme Leader – Our Sioux (IRE) (Jolly Jake (NZ)) [2006/7 F16s² Nov 11] rangy gelding: has plenty of scope: fourth foal: brother to 2m hurdle winner Dewasentah and bumper winner Issaquah: dam unraced half-sister to useful hurdler/chaser up to 25f Kings Measure: encouraging second to Digital Media in bumper at Wetherby on debut: will be suited by further than 2m. *Mrs S. J. Smith*   F94

JENDALI LAD 6 b. or br.g. Jendali (USA) – Magic Lake (Primo Dominie) [2006/7 F–: F16v F17v 20g 16d 16dᵘʳ 17s 20g* Apr 9] first form when winning novice handicap hurdle at Fakenham in April: stays 2½m. *R. C. Guest*   h76
F–

JENISE (IRE) 4 b.f. Orpen (USA) – Griqualand (Connaught) [2006/7 17v⁵ 17d Mar 19] modest maiden on Flat (stays 7f): little impact in juvenile hurdles. *Mark Campion*   h–

JENNA STANNIS 5 ch.m. Wolfhound (USA) – Darling Splodge (Elegant Air) [2006/7 h–: 17d May 31] no form over hurdles: tried visored. *W. Storey*   h–

JERED (IRE) 5 ch.g. Presenting – La Noire (IRE) (Phardante (FR)) [2006/7 F16m* F16m⁶ Apr 26] stocky gelding: first foal: dam, poor form in bumpers/well beaten only start over hurdles, half-sister to smart chaser Strong Run, stayed 2½m: successful in bumper at Fairyhouse on debut by ¾ length from Cuchulains Son: 4 lengths sixth to Meadow Vale in 24-runner similar event at Punchestown 2 weeks later: will stay beyond 2m. *N. Meade, Ireland*   F108

JEREMY CUDDLE DUCK (IRE) 6 b.g. Supreme Leader – Shean Bracken (IRE) (Le Moss) [2006/7 h128, F102+: c23d⁴ c19sᶠ Jan 26] big, lengthy gelding: bumper winner: fairly useful hurdler: looked sure to win maiden at Worcester on chasing debut until hanging and jumping violently right latter stages: fell fatally next time: should have stayed 3m+: acted on soft going. *N. A. Twiston-Davies*   c119
h–

JERICHO III (FR) 10 b.g. Lute Antique (FR) – La Salamandre (FR) (Pot d'Or (FR)) [2006/7 c122, h–: c16g* c17d* c16g⁶ 16s* 16gˢᵘ Mar 16] leggy gelding: lightly raced over hurdles, improved form when making all to win handicap at Wincanton in March by 6 lengths from Raslan, jumping badly right last: useful handicap chaser: better than ever in 2006/7, won at Folkestone in November and Ascot (beat Cossack Dancer by neck) in December: not discredited when sixth to Dempsey in valuable event at Sandown: best around 2m: acts on heavy and good to firm going: wears headgear: tried tongue tied: free-going front runner. *Miss Venetia Williams*   c131
h118

JERINGA 8 b.g. Karinga Bay – Jervandha (Strong Gale) [2006/7 h95: 23sᵖᵘ 20s 27s⁴ c20s² c20g⁴ c25gᵖᵘ Apr 23] good-topped, close-coupled gelding: modest novice hurdler/chaser: stays 21f: raced on good ground or softer (acts on heavy): tried in cheekpieces/tongue tied. *J. Wade*   c90
h84

JERRY LEE (IRE) 4 b.g. Orpen (USA) – Vinicky (USA) (Kingmambo (USA)) [2006/7 16vᵇᵈ 16s 16g Mar 20] maiden on Flat, sent M. Weiss in Switzerland after final start at 3 yrs: little impact in novice hurdles. *F. Jordan*   h–

JERSEYMAN 5 b.g. Wace (USA) – Anna Mong Men (Man Among Men (IRE)) [2006/7 F16s F16g Mar 28] tall, useful-looking gelding: first foal: dam unraced: mid-field in bumpers. *Miss E. C. Lavelle*   F84 +

JESNIC (IRE) 7 b.g. Kahyasi – Fur Hat (Habitat) [2006/7 c–, h–: c23m^pu c23s^5 c24g^pu c24g^pu Apr 27] strong, stocky gelding: little sign of ability: tried visored/tongue tied. *R. Dickin*   **c–** **h–**

JESSIE MAY (IRE) 6 b.m. Supreme Leader – Polly Platinum (IRE) (Phardante (FR)) [2006/7 F?: F17d^3 16s 20g Dec 10] poor form in bumpers for P. Webber: no show over hurdles: sold 1,200 gns Doncaster January Sales. *Miss P. Robson*   **h–** **F72**

JETHRO TULL (IRE) 8 b.g. Witness Box (USA) – Country Project (IRE) (Project Manager) [2006/7 c–, h97: c25g^3 Nov 4] lengthy gelding: modest hurdler: similar form on second of 2 outings over fences (finished lame): stays 27f: raced on good ground or softer: tried in cheekpieces. *G. A. Harker*   **c87 +** **h–**

JETHRO WHEELER 4 b.g. Marju (IRE) – Panorama (Shirley Heights) [2006/7 F12v F14v^6 Jan 25] leggy gelding: fourth foal: half-brother to useful French 7.5f/1m winner Sociando (by Loup Sauvage): dam, ran 3 times, half-sister to useful performer up to 1¾m Secret Archive: well beaten in bumpers. *E. J. Creighton*   **F–**

JET MAGIC (IRE) 7 b.g. Semillon – Kerry Minstrel (Black Minstrel) [2006/7 22s^6 c23s^F c24v^pu c23s^3 26m^pu Mar 29] useful-looking gelding: maiden hurdler, looked none too keen final start: poor form only completion (jumped right) in chases, then sold out of J. Spearing's stable £10,000 Ascot February Sales: probably stays 23f: blinkered/visored last 2 outings. *J. G. M. O'Shea*   **c82** **h–**

JET PROPELLED (IRE) 6 b.g. Oscar (IRE) – Fahy Quay (Quayside) [2006/7 22d^5 20s^5 20s* 22d* 24v^5 Feb 24] €100,000 3-y-o: half-brother to several winners, including one-time useful chaser Be My Manager, stays 3m, and fairly useful hunter Teelin Bay (both by Be My Native): dam poor in bumpers: bumper winner: fairly useful hurdler: won maiden at Down Royal (improved form) in December and handicap at Leopardstown (by ¾ length from Virginia Preuil) in January: favourite, respectable fifth to The Halfway Bar in valuable novice handicap at Fairyhouse final start: stays 3m: acts on heavy ground. *C. F. Swan, Ireland*   **h115 +**

JEUNE LOUP 5 b.g. Loup Sauvage (USA) – Secret Waters (Pharly (FR)) [2006/7 h–: 16m 17m Jul 20] compact gelding: no aptitude for hurdling. *P. C. Haslam*   **h–**

JEWEL OF INDIA 8 ch.g. Bijou d'Inde – Low Hill (Rousillon (USA)) [2006/7 16d 16g^6 Nov 1] sparely-made gelding: modest on Flat (stays 1¼m) in 2006, successful in August: winning 2m hurdler: little impact in handicaps in 2006/7: tried in cheekpieces. *Mrs A. L. M. King*   **h78**

JEWEL SONG 9 b.g. Faustus (USA) – Trustino (Relkino) [2006/7 c21v^2 Feb 28] second foal: dam poor maiden hurdler: fair pointer: second in maiden hunter at Folkestone on chase debut. *M. G. Hazell*   **c88**

JIDIYA (IRE) 8 b.g. Lahib (USA) – Yaqatha (IRE) (Sadler's Wells (USA)) [2006/7 17s 20d^4 18v 24g Dec 20] lengthy, good-topped gelding: bumper winner: fair on Flat (stays 2m), successful twice as 6-y-o, well held in 2006, sold out of S. Gollings' stable 1,200 gns Doncaster May Sales: poor maiden hurdler: blinkered last 5 starts. *Mrs H. O. Graham*   **h75**

JIGSAW DANCER (IRE) 5 ch.g. Old Vic – Moonshee (IRE) (Le Moss) [2006/7 16d 16s^bd 17s^ur 17s^4 Feb 26] €20,000 3-y-o: workmanlike gelding: half-brother to modest staying hurdler Gold Flo (by Fourstars Allstar): dam bumper winner: no form over hurdles. *Andrew Turnell*   **h–**

JILLANORY 5 b.m. Riverhead (USA) – Very Ominous (Dominion) [2006/7 F–: F17s May 20] well beaten in bumpers. *C. W. Moore*   **F–**

JIM BOBS GIRL (IRE) 6 b.m. Flemensfirth (USA) – Sinfonietta (Foolish Pleasure (USA)) [2006/7 F74: F16s^6 16g 21s 21d^6 20g^4 24g^3 c23m^3 Apr 15] winning Irish pointer: poor form in bumpers: little impact in novice hurdles: seemingly easily best effort in chases when third to Super Lord in maiden at Bangor: stays 3m. *W. Jenks*   **c89 ?** **h–** **F74**

JIMBOREAL (FR) 4 b. or br.g. Jimble (FR) – Fleur Boreale (FR) (Sicyos (USA)) [2006/7 16s* 16d^2 18s^2 16d 16g Mar 31] lengthy, good-topped gelding: fifth foal: brother to French sprinter Jim de Fleur and half-brother to 2 winners in France, including 19f hurdle winner Mon Espoir (by Arctic Tern): dam 6f to 1m winner: placed twice around 1½m on Flat: fair juvenile hurdler: won at Enghien in November for Y. Fouin: stays 2¼m. *Miss H. C. Knight*   **h107**

JIM EDWARDS (IRE) 6 ch.g. Bob Back (USA) – G W Superstar (Rymer) [2006/7 24v^6 22s 22s^3 24s^4 Mar 1] well-made gelding: chasing type: half-brother to one-time useful chaser Desailly (by Teamster), best at 2¾m+: dam, winning chaser, suited by test of stamina: won maiden Irish point in 2006: poor form over hurdles. *P. J. Hobbs*   **h81**

JIM (FR) 10 b.g. Glaieul (USA) – Beautywal (FR) (Magwal) [2006/7 c153, h–: c16v² **c136** c17vᶠ c16s⁶ c20v³ c20v³ Mar 24] strong, lengthy gelding: winning hurdler: smart chaser **h–** at best, below that in 2006/7: best up to 21f: raced on good going or softer (acts on heavy): tried in cheekpieces/blinkers: usually front runner. *J. T. R. Dreaper, Ireland*

JIMIVY GUNNER (IRE) 5 gr.g. Needle Gun (IRE) – Misty Joy (General Ironside) **h–** [2006/7 F17v F16v⁴ 20d 20g Apr 27] €20,000 3-y-o: big gelding: half-brother to fair **F69** hurdler Two For Joy (by Mandalus), stayed 3m: dam, novice hurdler, half-sister to Grand National winner Royal Athlete: little impact in bumpers/novice hurdles. *D. McCain Jnr*

JIM LAD 7 b.g. Young Ern – Anne's Bank (IRE) (Burslem) [2006/7 c83§, h–§: c16sᵇᵈ **c76 §** c16d² c21d c20v⁶ c26s² c25v⁵ c26v⁵ c26m³ c24g⁴ Apr 27] sturdy gelding: poor **h– §** novice chaser: stays 3¼m: acts on soft and firm going: often wears headgear: unreliable. *J. W. Mullins*

JIMMY BEDNEY (IRE) 6 b.g. Simply Great (FR) – Double Token (Furry Glen) **h–** [2006/7 h92, F87: 16g 20g Apr 11] angular gelding: modest form on hurdling debut in 2005/6, little show since: tried blinkered. *S. G. Griffiths*

JIMMY BER (IRE) 5 b.g. Supreme Leader – Hail To You (USA) (Kirtling) [2006/7 **F85** F16d F16s⁶ Dec 26] €51,000 3-y-o: sturdy gelding: half-brother to several winners, including Champion Bumper winner/fairly useful hurdler Liberman (by Standiford), stays 3m: modest form in bumpers. *D. T. Hughes, Ireland*

JIMMY BOND 8 b.g. Primitive Rising (USA) – Miss Moneypenny (Silly Prices) **c110** [2006/7 c103, h–: c25sᶠ c23s² c23s² c20s⁵ c20v* c20v³ 24s² c20v³ c20g⁴ Apr 3] strong, good- **h93** topped gelding: maiden hurdler: fair handicap chaser: won at Wetherby in December: stays 25f: acts on heavy going: usually sound jumper. *Mrs K. Walton*

JIMMYS DUKY (IRE) 9 b.g. Duky – Harvey's Cream (IRE) (Mandalus) [2006/7 **c78** c66, h–: c20sᵖᵘ c17v³ c19dᶠ c20v³ c16s² c16g³ Apr 23] workmanlike gelding: poor maid- **h–** en handicap chaser: stays 3m: acts on heavy going: tried in cheekpieces. *D. M. Forster*

JIMMY TENNIS (FR) 10 b. or br.g. Video Rock (FR) – Via Tennise (FR) (Brezzo **c110 x** (FR)) [2006/7 c–x, h–: c25d* c25s⁴ c24dᵖᵘ Dec 21] leggy, lengthy gelding: fair handicap **h–** chaser: won at Folkestone in November: stays 25f: acts on heavy going: tried blinkered: often let down by jumping. *Miss Venetia Williams*

JIM THE GENT (IRE) 5 ch.g. Pistolet Bleu (IRE) – Waydante (IRE) (Phardante **h99 p** (FR)) [2006/7 F17m* F16f* 16g⁴ Apr 2] first foal: dam, modest chaser, stayed 2¾m: fair **F90** form when winning bumpers at Market Rasen in June and Perth in July: off 9 months, encouraging fourth to Young Albert in novice at Kelso: should improve. *A. M. Crow*

JIVER (IRE) 8 b.g. Flemensfirth (USA) – Choice Brush (IRE) (Brush Aside (USA)) **c–** [2006/7 c107, h113: 24m⁶ May 9] fair handicap hurdler/maiden chaser: should stay **h103** extreme distances: raced largely on good going or softer (acts on soft): visored last 5 starts: lazy: joined Mike Hammond. *M. Scudamore*

Cox's Cash & Carry Champion Hunters' Chase, Punchestown—veteran Joe Blake (right) finally lands a top hunter prize; he's chased home by (from right to left) It's Like That, Ned Kelly and Arctic Times

JOAACI (IRE) 7 b.g. Presenting – Miss Sarajevo (IRE) (Brush Aside (USA)) [2006/7 c149: c27d^{pu} 26s* 26v* 23s⁴ 24g c32m^{pu} Apr 21] tall, workmanlike gelding: smart handicap chaser at best, has failed to complete all 5 starts over fences since successful on 2005/6 return: fairly useful form in novice hurdles: won easily at Hereford in December and January (beat Elbow Lane by 6 lengths): signs of temperament in Grade 2 events next 2 outings: stays 27f: acts on heavy going: in cheekpieces over hurdles: tongue tied last 2 starts. *D. E. Pipe*   c– h125

JOAN'S GIRL (IRE) 7 b.m. Supreme Leader – Keshia (Buckskin (FR)) [2006/7 16s 20s⁴ 18g² 19g* 20v³ 16v⁵ 17s Feb 19] sturdy ex-Irish mare: half-sister to smart 2m hurdler Georges Girl (by Montelimar): dam middle-distance winner: bumper winner: fair handicap hurdler, left F. Flood and off over 5 months before third outing: won conditional jockeys event at Catterick in November: let down by attitude last 2 starts: stays 2½m: acts on heavy going. *N. G. Richards*   h112

JOBSWORTH (IRE) 7 ch.g. Good Thyne (USA) – Brown Willows (IRE) (Kemal (FR)) [2006/7 h–, F89: 17g^{pu} c16s c16d 17d⁶ 22d³ c24d^{pu} c24v^{pu} Jan 27] sparely-made gelding: poor novice hurdler: no show in handicap chases: should be well suited by 3m: in cheekpieces/visor (downed tools) last 3 outings. *Evan Williams*   c– h68

JOCKSER (IRE) 6 b.g. Desert Story (IRE) – Pupa Fiorini (ITY) (Indian Ridge) [2006/7 h111: 21f⁴ 24m* 27d* 24s² 25d² 24s 24g 24g⁶ Apr 14] small, close-coupled gelding: fairly useful handicap hurdler: won at Exeter and Stratford in May: good efforts when runner-up last 2 starts, beaten 8 lengths by Star de Mohaison in valuable event at Cheltenham on second occasion: not discredited when staying-on sixth to Albertas Run in listed event at Aintree: stays 27f: acts on any going. *J. W. Mullins*   h125

JODANTE (IRE) 10 ch.g. Phardante (FR) – Crashtown Lucy (Crash Course) [2006/7 c117, h–: c20g^{ur} 21m* 22f² 24d³ c24m c20f* 22d Aug 28] strong, lengthy gelding: good mover: fair hurdler: won novice handicap at Southwell in May: fairly useful handicap chaser: successful by 5 lengths from South Bronx at Bangor (reportedly finished sore) in July: stays 3m: acts on any going: tried in blinkers, usually wears cheekpieces: held up, and often set plenty to do. *R. C. Guest*   c118 h103

JOE 5 b.g. Kayf Tara – Sailors Joy (Handsome Sailor) [2006/7 F16d Dec 29] rather unfurnished gelding: fifth foal: dam never ran: backward and tongue tied, well beaten in bumper on debut. *A. E. Jessop*   F–

JOE BLAKE (IRE) 12 b.g. Jurado (USA) – I've No Idea (Nishapour (FR)) [2006/7 c121: c25g³ c25g* Apr 25] big, workmanlike gelding: useful hunter chaser, lightly raced: better for reappearance, won 18-runner Cox's Cash & Carry Champion Hunters' Chase at Punchestown in April by 3½ lengths from It's Like That: effective from 2½m to 3¼m: probably acts on any going: has found little. *I. R. Ferguson, Ireland*   c123

JOE BROWN 7 br.g. Overbury (IRE) – Miss Roscoe (Roscoe Blake) [2006/7 h102: c23d^F Oct 5] quite good-topped gelding: winning pointer: fair hurdler: off 8 months, in lead when fell 2 out in novice handicap at Worcester on chasing debut: stays 25f: raced on ground softer than good. *Heather Dalton*   c109 h–

JOE DEANE (IRE) 11 ch.g. Alphabatim (USA) – Craic Go Leor (Deep Run) [2006/7 c105§, h–: c21g⁶ c24m³ c19m* c21d^{ur} c23s Dec 29] strong, lengthy gelding: modest handicap chaser: off 5 months, won at Exeter in November: stays 3½m: acts on good to firm and heavy going: tried in cheekpieces: often ridden by conditional/amateur: ungenuine. *M. J. Coombe*   c97 § h–

JOE DRAPER 5 ch.g. Forzando – Shanghai Lil (Petong) [2006/7 F16m Sep 2] second foal: dam 6f to 1½m winner: well held in bumper and maiden on Flat. *P. D. Evans*   F–

JOE JO STAR 5 b.g. Piccolo – Zagreb Flyer (Old Vic) [2006/7 16d⁶ Mar 22] poor on Flat (stays 11.7f): caught eye when sixth in claimer at Ludlow on hurdling debut: likely to improve. *B. P. J. Baugh*   h76 p

JOE LIVELY (IRE) 8 b.g. Flemensfirth (USA) – Forest Gale (Strong Gale) [2006/7 c23f^{pu} Jun 21] €12,000 4-y-o: half-brother to several winners, including fair staying chaser Forest Fountain (by Royal Fountain): dam unraced: winning pointer: blinkered, no show in maiden on chasing debut. *Mrs H. L. Needham*   c–

JOE MALONE 8 br.g. Rashar (USA) – Bucktina (Buckskin (FR)) [2006/7 h75§: 16g⁶ 24d³ 19d⁵ 23d Jan 15] tall gelding: poor maiden handicap hurdler: stays 3m: acts on good to firm and good to soft going: untrustworthy. *Mrs A. E. Brooks*   h72 §

JOE MCHUGH (IRE) 8 ch.g. Topanoora – Run For Shelter (Strong Gale) [2006/7 c94, h–: c25g^{pu} May 4] strong, heavy-topped gelding: no form in novice hurdles: modest   c– h–

chaser: lame only outing in 2006/7: stays 3m: acts on heavy going: has bled from nose.
C. J. Mann

JOES EDGE (IRE) 10 b. or br.g. Supreme Leader – Right Dark (Buckskin (FR)) **c140**
[2006/7 c131, h–: c24m c26g c24g* c36g^pu Apr 14] **h–**
'We are always trying to set a puzzle that the punters find difficult to solve.
We've spent hours and hours on these races and we don't want people coming up
with the winner in thirty seconds. I'd rather see a 50/1-shot win by ten lengths than
a driving finish with several horses together at the line. We like results that make
people ask "how did that win?"'
        As puzzling statements go this would be hard to match, especially since
they are the words of the BHB's senior handicapper Phil Smith, spoken at the
launch for the weights for the handicaps at the Cheltenham Festival. If the words
were intended to come out as spoken, Smith would appear to view himself and his
team as akin to crossword compilers, chewing the pencil for hours before coming
up with some cryptic clue that has all the readers scratching their heads. However,
this badly misrepresents the role of the official handicapper who is responsible for
assessing horses on their merits to ensure an equal chance for all. A ten-length
winner could indicate that the handicapper had not done his job quite so well as
he might, so why such a result should give more satisfaction than a tight finish
is puzzling. Unfortunately, the remarks also seemed to suggest that the official
handicappers regard racing as a lottery, a sport in which results regularly make no
sense, which, given that they spend their professional lives trying to interpret form,
is strange indeed. Even worse, the remarks conveyed the impression that the aim
was to bamboozle punters to help in raising the levy contributions from bookmakers (which are based on profits and increase with longer-priced winners).
Smith, who cited Heathcote's recent 50/1 win in the totesport Trophy at Newbury
as having earned more than £103,000 for the Levy, went on to explain: 'As
handicappers we don't like to see favourites winning. Last year's ten Festival
handicaps produced one outright winning favourite. It is a knock-on benefit that
racing's income does well out of outsiders winning.' Unsurprisingly these comments caused plenty of raised eyebrows amongst the assembled press and
bookmaker representatives, whilst they drew criticism from high-profile trainers
such as Paul Nicholls and Nicky Henderson (who were both also present).
        Phil Smith's remarks rather let down his work and that of his colleagues,
who, by and large, do a first-rate job. The standard of handicapping over jumps
has never been higher, slippage (the product of so-called trainer-friendly handicapping) a fading memory and the number of handicap 'blots' surprisingly few. The
lenient treatment of Irish-trained runners, resulting from the different handicapping
methods employed in Ireland, is a much less frequent occurrence, now that the
BHB handicappers compile and allot their own marks to Irish-trained horses. A
measure of the progress can be taken from the winning margins for the handicaps at
the Cheltenham Festival itself. In the first year of the four-day Festival, the ten
handicaps averaged a winning distance of 3.8 lengths, with eight lengths (for the
Irish-trained Dabiroun in the inaugural Fred Winter) the widest margin. In 2006,
the mean was down to 3.025, despite Non So winning the Racing Post Plate by nine
lengths. In 2007, it had come down still further, to 2.28 per race (the median was
slightly higher in 2007 than 2006). No handicap was won by further than the five
lengths of Gaspara's Fred Winter and the meeting featured the three closest finishes
in handicaps of the last three years.
        Given his remarks, it was ironic that the first of Mr Smith's three races at
the Festival, the William Hill Trophy Handicap Chase, went the way of a 50/1-shot.
Mr Smith was presumably disappointed that the race was one of the closest Festival
finishes for many years, with just a short head and the same separating Joes Edge,
Juveigneur and Distant Thunder, though he would have had the consolation of both
placed horses being among the co-favourites. Joes Edge was the winner of the 2005
Scottish National, which he also won by a short head (from Cornish Rebel), but his
performances in the interim had offered encouragement only intermittently. He
had, though, often been highly tried and his two best efforts since the start of 2005/6
had come at Cheltenham, when fourth in a listed handicap at the December meeting
in 2005 and when thirteenth of eighteen finishers in the 2006 Cheltenham Gold

William Hill Trophy Handicap Chase, Cheltenham—50/1-shot Joes Edge is only third at the last but collars Juveigneur (white face) and Distant Thunder (noseband) in a grandstand finish

Cup. Joes Edge won the Scottish National off a BHB mark of 137 (including 5 lb out of the weights) and was racing off 142 in that Cheltenham handicap, so a mark of 130 in the William Hill was lenient if he could recapture his old form—he'd been receiving just 7 lb from Cornish Rebel at Ayr, yet the same rival was carrying 17 lb more than him in the William Hill. That, though, was far from certain, as Joes Edge had shown little in a valuable handicap at Ascot on his reappearance and had been off since finishing a never-dangerous eighth, wearing cheekpieces, in the Becher Chase at Aintree. Indeed, he was very much Ferdy Murphy's second string and, with stable jockey Graham Lee opting for sixth-placed New Alco (the other co-favourite), the ride went to one of the trainer's former employees Davy Russell. In a strong renewal of the William Hill (formerly the National Hunt Handicap), Joes Edge looked an unlikely winner three out, where Irish Raptor, just headed, departed, nor did a win for Joes Edge look any more likely when narrow leader Heltornic fell at the next. At that stage the advantage lay with Distant Thunder but, as he faltered close home, first Juveigneur then, in the last stride, Joes Edge went past. It was the closest finish at the Festival, at least amongst the first three, over the past fifty years. Big Strand came from an even more unpromising position than Joes Edge when winning the 1997 Coral Cup in another tight three-way finish, beating stable-companion Allegation and Castle Sweep by a short head and head respectively, whilst Spirit Leader had just a neck and short head to spare over Balapour and Through The Rye in the 2003 County Hurdle. The latter race has had several memorable bunched finishes down the years, including in 1994 (won by Dizzy) and 1982 (won by Path of Peace) when the first five home were covered by under a length and a half and just over two lengths respectively.

As a result of his win at Cheltenham, Joes Edge became an interesting contender for the Grand National, in which he had been seventh, weakening from the Melling Road, the previous year. With his mark only 4 lb higher than in the William Hill, and with the likelihood of firmer ground than in 2006 also in his favour, Joes Edge was backed down to co-favouritism but was never in contention and was pulled up lame before the twentieth.

Joes Edge's Cheltenham success made him the highest money-earner for his now-deceased sire Supreme Leader in 2006/7, ahead of the smart staying hurdler Flight Leader and the useful Irish chaser Euro Leader. Details of his family

481

Chemipetro Limited's "Joes Edge"

Joes Edge (IRE) (b. or br.g. 1997)	Supreme Leader (b 1982)	Bustino (b 1971)	Busted Ship Yard
		Princess Zena (b 1975)	Habitat Guiding Light
	Right Dark (b or br 1984)	Buckskin (b 1973)	Yelapa Bete A Bon Dieu
		Right Performance (b 1976)	Gala Performance Cherry Princess

appeared in *Chasers & Hurdlers 2004/05*. He remains the only winner produced by his once-raced dam Right Dark. His half-sister Eva's Edge (by Good Thyne) was well held in a bumper early in 2006 and produced what *Hunter Chasers & Point-To-Pointers* described as a 'deplorable display' on one of her two starts in points this year. That she is grammatically correct is about all that can be said in her favour. Right Dark produced one more foal, a 2003 filly by Beneficial, prior to her death in 2004. The well-made Joes Edge stays four miles and a furlong. He acts on soft going, though his two biggest wins have come on good and he is probably effective on good to firm. His wins at Ayr and Cheltenham owed much to his sound jumping, though he has looked less polished over the National fences. *Ferdy Murphy*

JOEY 5 b.m. Polar Prince (IRE) – Understudy (In The Wings) [2006/7 h–: 16f 16d² 16g 20m* 19g⁵ 20g⁵ 24d⁶ 21m Oct 12] modest novice hurdler: won conditional jockeys handicap at Worcester in July: stays 2½m: acts on good to firm going: usually wears cheekpieces: sold 1,000 gns Doncaster January Sales. *R. Hollinshead*   **h86**

JOEY TRIBBIANI (IRE) 10 b.g. Foxhound (USA) – Mardi Gras Belle (USA) (Masked Dancer (USA)) [2006/7 c118, h–: 20m⁵ c23g⁵ c22g Jul 22] leggy gelding: maiden hurdler: fair handicap chaser: probably best up to 23f: acts on soft and good to firm going: patiently ridden. *T. Keddy*   **c113**
h86

JOFI (IRE) 8 b.g. Shernazar – Giolla Donn (Giolla Mear) [2006/7 c–, h–: c20g^pu Apr 30] strong gelding: of no account: tried in cheekpieces: sold 800 gns Doncaster May (2006) Sales. *Miss Lucinda V. Russell*
c–
h–

JOG ON (IRE) 7 b.g. Kadeed (IRE) – Parsons Toi (The Parson) [2006/7 16s* 20s 16v 16s^4 16v* 16v* 16m^5 Apr 24] rangy gelding: second foal: dam maiden: in frame in bumpers: useful hurdler: won maiden at Wexford in May and handicaps at Thurles in February and Gowran (by 4 lengths from McGruders Cross) in March: improved again when 7½ lengths fifth to Clopf in Grade 1 novice at Punchestown: should stay beyond 2m: acts on good to firm and heavy going. *P. A. Fahy, Ireland*
h131

JOHN CHARLES (IRE) 5 b.g. Fraam – Norwegian Queen (IRE) (Affirmed (USA)) [2006/7 16f^4 16d^4 16g^5 19m^5 16d^4 16d 16f* 16m Apr 22] rather leggy gelding: fair form on Flat (should stay 1¼m), successful in early-2006 for D. Elsworth: fair hurdler: won novice at Uttoxeter in October and handicap at Wincanton in April: likely to prove best around 2m: acts on firm and good to soft going: tried in cheekpieces. *B. De Haan*
h105

JOHN DIAMOND (IRE) 6 b.g. Un Desperado (FR) – Lessons Lass (IRE) (Doyoun) [2006/7 h92+, F89: 16s^ur c20g* c18g^5 Nov 3] big, rangy gelding: modest form in novice hurdles: much better effort in handicap chases when winning novice event at Huntingdon in October: likely to stay beyond 2½m: raced on good ground or softer: has flashed tail under pressure. *Miss H. C. Knight*
c107
h–

JOHN FOLEY (IRE) 9 b.g. Petardia – Fast Bay (Bay Express) [2006/7 c69+, h–: c21m* c22d^pu c23m^pu c20g^pu c19m^6 Mar 29] sturdy gelding: maiden hurdler: modest chaser: won novice handicap at Wincanton in May: left D. P. Keane after third start: stays 21f: acts on good to firm going: tried in headgear: tongue tied. *Ms L. J. Willis*
c89
h–

JOHN FORBES 5 b.g. High Estate – Mavourneen (USA) (Dynaformer (USA)) [2006/7 h89: 16d^2 20v^2 16v^4 20s^3 20v 17v^4 16s* 17s^3 16g 16g Apr 14] sturdy gelding: fair hurdler: won novices at Sedgefield in February and Catterick in March: stays 2½m: acts on heavy going. *B. Ellison*
h112

JOHN JORROCKS (FR) 8 br.g. Chamberlin (FR) – Caryatide (FR) (Maiymad) [2006/7 h56: 18m c19s c20v^pu Feb 27] rangy gelding: bad maiden hurdler: no show over fences: tried visored/in cheekpieces. *J. C. Tuck*
c–
h–

JOHNNIE DILLINGER (IRE) 7 b. or br.g. Supreme Leader – Kilbrien Star (Goldhill) [2006/7 22s^4 16s* 20v^4 19s^5 21g^F Mar 14] €34,000 3-y-o: big, good sort: halfbrother to fair staying hurdler/temperamental winning chaser Mohera King (by King's Ride) and winning pointer by Cardinal Flower: dam winning pointer: in frame in bumpers: confirmed hurdling debut promise when winning 25-runner maiden at Fairyhouse in December by 3 lengths from Corrigeenroe: showing considerable improvement (useful form) when falling last in Grade 1 novice at Cheltenham won by Massini's Maguire, disputing sixth at time: should stay beyond 2½m: acts on heavy ground. *M. F. Morris, Ireland*
h140

JOHNNY ALLJAYS (IRE) 6 b.g. Victory Note (USA) – It's Academic (Royal Academy (USA)) [2006/7 20v^6 17d^5 16g^4 16m^2 16s^pu Oct 25] good-bodied gelding: modest stayer on Flat, successful twice at 4 yrs for P. Blockley: easily best effort over hurdles (modest form) when second to Pearl King in maiden at Huntingdon, tending to hang left: raced mainly around 2m: acts on good to firm going: tried in cheekpieces. *S. Lycett*
h91

JOHNNY BISSETT (IRE) 6 br.g. Oscar (IRE) – Millers Run (Deep Run) [2006/7 F16d* F16s^5 F16s* Dec 26] €19,000 3-y-o: half-brother to bumper/2m chase winner Abacus (by Be My Native): dam ran twice: fairly useful form in bumpers: won at Uttoxeter in November and Huntingdon (beat Space Mission by 6 lengths) in December: joined D. Arbuthnot. *C. Tinkler*
F99

JOHNNY ROCHE (IRE) 5 b.g. Oscar (IRE) – Ou La La (IRE) (Be My Native (USA)) [2006/7 F17v^6 22d^4 21s^4 23v^3 24d^3 Jan 19] €12,000 3-y-o: resold 20,000 3-y-o: fourth foal: half-brother to winning pointer by Invited: dam unraced: runner-up in maiden Irish point in 2006: sixth in bumper: modest form in frame over hurdles: stays 3m: raced on ground softer than good. *J. Howard Johnson*
h87
F83

JOHN RICH 11 b.g. Mesleh – South Lodge (Current Magic) [2006/7 c71§, h–§: 23g^pu Apr 30] lengthy gelding: poor handicap chaser: no form over hurdles: probably stays 25f: acts on firm going: usually in headgear/tongue tied: has run out/refused: not one to trust. *M. E. Sowersby*
c– §
h– §

JOHNSTON'S SWALLOW (IRE) 9 b.g. Commanche Run – Mirror of Flowers (Artaius (USA)) [2006/7 c17s^4 c18d^4 c20s^pu c24v^pu c24v^4 c26s^pu Jan 15] strong, rangy
c78 §
h–

gelding: winning 2m hurdler for M. J. P. O'Brien: off 18 months prior, disappointing over fences: blinkered last 2 starts, also tongue tied final one: temperamental. *Jonjo O'Neill*

JOHN STORM (IRE) 9 b.g. Glacial Storm (USA) – Johns Rose (IRE) (Euphemism) **h78 ?**
[2006/7 24f³ 20m⁶ 20g⁴ Jul 21] well beaten in Irish points prior to winning maiden in Britain in 2006: poor form over hurdles: stays 3m: tried tongue tied. *D. A. Rees*

JOHN THE GREEK (IRE) 11 b. or br.g. Aristocracy – Lucky Minstrel (IRE) (Black **c–**
Minstrel) [2006/7 c–, h–: 20m⁴ May 5] lengthy gelding: let down by jumping in chases: **h–**
winning hurdler, little show both starts since long lay-off: little impact in points in 2007:
often visored/blinkered. *A. M. Hales*

JOIZEL (FR) 10 b.g. Fill My Hopes (FR) – Anne de Boizel (FR) (Dhausli (FR)) **c104 §**
[2006/7 c87, h–: 22g⁵ 22d c17d⁶ c19s² c19s⁴ c23v⁶ 23s c21gᵖᵘ Apr 1] chunky gelding: **h–**
maiden hurdler: fair chaser: lame final outing: stays 23f: acts on soft going: tried blinkered in France: inconsistent. *V. G. Greenway*

JOKE CLUB 6 b.g. Inchinor – Kicka (Shirley Heights) [2006/7 F17v⁶ 19s 18s³ 16s⁵ **h85**
Jan 15] rather leggy gelding: runner-up in bumper for V. Dartnall in 2004/5, off almost 20 **F89**
months before return: modest form over hurdles: tongue tied last 2 starts. *B. G. Powell*

JOLIBOB (IRE) 5 b.g. Bob's Return (IRE) – Short of A Buck (IRE) (Buckskin (FR)) **h–**
[2006/7 F16s⁶ F16s 22sᵖᵘ 21g 20g⁶ Apr 14] €30,000 3-y-o: sturdy gelding: fourth foal: **F72**
half-brother to fair hurdler Russian Buck (by Moscow Society), stays 21f: dam lightly
raced over hurdles/in points: poor form in bumper on debut: little show over hurdles, left
M. Rimell after third outing. *R. Dickin*

JOLI CHRISTMAS 10 b.g. Joligeneration – Christmas Bash (Shaab) [2006/7 c–: **c81**
c19m⁶ c23d⁵ May 17] modest pointer, successful twice in 2007: maiden hunter chaser.
G. Chambers

JOLI CLASSICAL (IRE) 5 b.m. Classic Cliche (IRE) – Mesp (IRE) (Strong Gale) **h90**
[2006/7 h80: 16sᵖᵘ 18s* 16s 17d² 22s 17s⁶ 16v⁴ 19s² 24g Mar 25] workmanlike mare:
modest hurdler: won mares maiden at Fontwell in November: should be suited by further
than 19f: acts on soft and good to firm going: blinkered last 2 starts. *R. J. Hodges*

JOLLIE ABILOLA 4 gr.f. Shahrastani (USA) – Bonita Blakeney (Baron Blakeney) **F–**
[2006/7 F12s F16v F16m⁶ Apr 9] smallish, good-topped filly: second foal: half-sister to
fair hurdler Joshua's Bay (by Karinga Bay), stayed 23f: dam of little account: well beaten
in bumpers. *J. R. Jenkins*

JOLLY BOY 8 b.g. Franc Bleu Argent (USA) – Lady Charrecey (FR) (Fin Bon) **c103 §**
[2006/7 c94, h–: c19s* c16d⁶ c22s⁵ c19dᶠ c24s⁶ 16s³ 19d² Mar 21] good-topped gelding: **h72 §**
maiden hurdler: fair handicap chaser: won at Taunton in December: let down by attitude/
jumping after: stays 2½m: raced on good going or softer (acts on soft): blinkered: usually
races prominently: not one to trust: sold 18,000 gns Doncaster May Sales. *Miss Venetia
Williams*

JOLLY JOE (IRE) 10 b.g. Jolly Jake (NZ) – The Bread Robber (Mandalus) [2006/7 **c–**
c–, h–: c22gᵖᵘ c25g⁵ Apr 18] big, workmanlike gelding: winning pointer: no form over **h–**
hurdles/in chases. *S. T. Lewis*

JOMELAMIN 5 gr.m. Silver Patriarch (IRE) – Jomel Amou (IRE) (Ela-Mana-Mou) **h–**
[2006/7 F–: 18s⁶ 19s 16g⁶ Dec 26] little sign of ability. *R. J. Hodges*

JONANAUD 8 b.g. Ballet Royal (USA) – Margaret Modes (Thatching) [2006/7 c–, **c–**
h103: c23gᵖᵘ May 14] leggy gelding: fairly useful handicap hurdler at one time: no **h–**
solid form over fences: effective at 2m to 3m: acts on heavy going: tried blinkered.
H. J. Manners

JONDAWMAR 6 b.g. Commanche Run – Kamakaze Girl (Kampala) [2006/7 F16dᶠ **F90**
Oct 5] £3,700 4-y-o: seventh foal: dam 1m winner: in second when broke leg over 2f out
in bumper at Worcester on debut. *Mrs K. M. Sanderson*

JONNY'S KICK 7 b.g. Revoque (IRE) – Prudence (Grundy) [2006/7 c95, h–: c24s² **c106**
c24d* Jun 2] big, strong, lengthy gelding: novice hurdler: fair chaser: won handicap **h–**
at Towcester in June: should stay beyond 3m: acts on heavy going: tried blinkered.
T. D. Easterby

JONTYS'LASS 6 b.m. Tamure (IRE) – Gay Muse (Scorpio (FR)) [2006/7 h111, F87: **h100**
20s⁵ 21d 19vᵘʳ 24s 20s⁶ 19s⁴ Jan 24] lengthy, quite good-topped mare: fair handicap
hurdler: stays 23f: acts on heavy going (won bumper on good to firm). *A. Crook*

JORDANS SPARK 6 ch.g. Opening Verse (USA) – Ribot's Pearl (Indian Ridge) **h–**
[2006/7 h66: 16g Nov 4] modest on Flat (stays 1¼m), successful twice in 2006: little
promise over hurdles. *P. Monteith*

JORIS DE VONNAS (FR) 10 ch.g. Dear Doctor (FR) – Carine de Neuvy (FR) **c85**
(Shelley (FR)) [2006/7 c–, h–: c25d^{pu} 24v 23g^3 c24m* Apr 14] poor chaser/maiden **h85**
hurdler: won handicap at Chepstow in April: stays 3m: acts on heavy and good to firm
going: usually tongue tied. *K. M. Prendergast*

JOSEAR 5 b.g. Josr Algarhoud (IRE) – Real Popcorn (IRE) (Jareer (USA)) [2006/7 **h106**
h105: 17d^4 Mar 20] good-topped gelding: fair hurdler, off 12 months prior to only start in
2006/7: raced mainly around 2m: acts on heavy going: front runner/races prominently:
consistent. *C. J. Down*

JOSE BOVE 5 ch.g. So Factual (USA) – Dark Sirona (Pitskelly) [2006/7 h75: 16d 16s **h73**
16g^5 Apr 27] smallish gelding: little sign of ability. *R. Dickin*

JOSEPH BEUYS (IRE) 8 ch.g. Flemensfirth (USA) – Final Countdown (King's **c–**
Ride) [2006/7 c92, h77+, F71: c24s^{pu} c24g^5 Mar 14] lengthy gelding: maiden hurdler: **h–**
modest handicap chaser: should have stayed beyond 25f: raced on good ground or softer:
dead. *D. P. Keane*

JOSHUAS VISTA 4 gr.g. M'Bebe – Parodia (Glint of Gold) [2006/7 F12v F16d F16s **F–**
Mar 8] workmanlike gelding: second foal: dam ran once: no form in bumpers. *P. D. Evans*

JOSH YOU ARE 4 b.g. Josr Algarhoud (IRE) – Cibenze (Owington) [2006/7 16d^{pu} **h–**
Dec 4] modest on Flat (stays 2m), claimed from M. Wallace £6,000 in October, successful
in December/January: not knocked about after blundering fourth in juvenile maiden on
hurdling debut. *D. E. Cantillon*

JO'S SALE 6 b.g. Germany (USA) – Clonmeen Lodge (IRE) (Buckskin (FR)) **c–**
[2006/7 c–, h–: c16v^{pu} Jan 11] runner-up in maiden Irish point: little other form: dead. **h–**
Evan Williams

JOUEUR D'ESTRUVAL (FR) 10 gr.g. Perrault – Alrose (FR) (Kalyan (FR)) **c121**
[2006/7 c128, h125: 17s 20v^5 24d c24v^6 c25v^5 c16v 16m Apr 10] leggy, useful-looking **h116**
gelding: fairly useful hurdler/chaser, below best in 2006/7: effective at 2m to 25f: acts on
heavy going: often fails to impress with finishing effort: sold 18,000 gns Doncaster May
Sales. *W. P. Mullins, Ireland*

JOUR DE MEE (FR) 10 ch.g. Beyssac (FR) – Une de Mee (FR) (Sarpedon (FR)) **c–**
[2006/7 c80, h72: 20s May 14] good-topped gelding: poor hurdler/chaser: stays 2½m: **h–**
raced on going softer than good (acts on soft): tried blinkered/tongue tied. *G. J. Smith*

JOURNEY SOUTH (IRE) 7 b.g. Luso – Light Argument (IRE) (Tale Quale) [2006/7 **h–**
22d^{pu} Oct 21] second foal: half-brother to fair 17f chase winner In Technicolor and (by
Germany): dam, fair hunter chaser, half-sister to useful staying chaser Knight Oil and
useful hurdler up to 2¾m Vazon Bay: pulled up in 2 maiden Irish points in 2006: bought
2,000 gns Doncaster May Sales: no show in novice on hurdling debut: sold 1,500 gns
Doncaster January Sales. *M. Smith*

JOVE (IRE) 5 b.g. In The Wings – Propitious (IRE) (Doyoun) [2006/7 F16s aF16g **F–**
Mar 21] sixth foal: closely related to 2-y-o sprint winner in Italy by Barathea: dam Irish
1m winner: well beaten in bumpers. *R. Dickin*

JOYE DES ILES (FR) 10 b.g. Mont Basile (FR) – Titjana (FR) (Quart de Vin (FR)) **c79**
[2006/7 c21g^{pu} c21g^3 May 24] tall gelding: winning pointer: maiden chaser: stays 21f: **h–**
usually blinkered (not in 2006/7). *Anthony Ward-Thomas*

JOYFUL JACK (IRE) 8 b.g. Zaffaran (USA) – Joyful Rosanna (Kemal (FR)) [2006/7 **c–**
22d^6 20v c20s^F 20v c25v^3 c20v^{pu} Mar 22] sixth foal: brother to winning 2½m chaser **h77**
Ammieanne: dam unraced: successful 3 times in points, including once in 2006: poor
form over hurdles: let down by jumping in chases. *B. R. Hamilton, Ireland*

JOYRYDER 6 gr.g. Cloudings (IRE) – Knight Ryde (Broadsword (USA)) [2006/7 **h98 p**
F101: 20s^3 24v^2 Nov 23] big, lengthy gelding: has scope: bumper winner for M. Pitman:
placed in novice hurdles at Uttoxeter: should do better. *Carl Llewellyn*

JUBILANT NOTE (IRE) 5 b.g. Sadler's Wells (USA) – Hint of Humour (USA) **h120**
(Woodman (USA)) [2006/7 h117: 16f* 17f* 16d^5 16g* 16d^4 16g Apr 14] rather leggy
gelding: fairly useful hurdler: won maiden at Tipperary in June, novice at Bellewstown in
July and handicap at Listowel (beat Querido by 5½ lengths) in September: creditable
effort when mid-field in valuable handicap at Aintree final outing: raced around 2m:

acts on firm and soft going: blinkered in 2006/7: has had tongue tied: fluent jumper.
M. D. Murphy, Ireland

JUBILEE DREAM 5 b.g. Bluebird (USA) – Last Dream (IRE) (Alzao (USA)) [2006/7   **h83**
h81: 18m³ 24f² 24f Jul 19] poor maiden hurdler: stays 3m: acts on firm and soft going.
Mrs L. J. Mongan

JUDDA 6 b.g. Makbul – Pepeke (Mummy's Pet) [2006/7 16vᵖᵘ Dec 26] half-brother to   **h–**
fair chaser Castletown Count (by Then Again), stayed 25f: no form on Flat or on hurdling
debut. *R. F. Marvin*

JUDGE DEED (IRE) 6 b.g. Flemensfirth (USA) – Kouron (Pauper) [2006/7 F16s*   **h115**
20s² 18v⁴ 20v² 19v² 24v³ Mar 11] €25,000 4-y-o: sixth foal: half-brother to fairly useful   **F108**
2m hurdler Royal Destiny (by King's Ride): dam fair 2m hurdler: won bumper at
Fairyhouse in October on debut: in frame all 5 starts in maiden hurdles, best effort (fairly
useful form) on third one when 9 lengths second to Arrive Sir Clive at Leopardstown:
should stay beyond 2½m: raced on soft/heavy ground. *N. Meade, Ireland*

JUDGE'N'THOMAS 7 b.g. Sadler's Way – Stapleford Lady (Bairn (USA)) [2006/7   **h–**
h–, F–: 16f⁵ Aug 22] lengthy gelding: no solid form: tried in cheekpieces. *M. R. Bosley*

JUDGE REILLY (IRE) 10 b.g. Arctic Lord – Shanna Golden (IRE) (Le Bavard (FR))   **c66 x**
[2006/7 c23v⁶ Mar 9] ex-Irish gelding: second foal: half-brother to winning pointer by   **h–**
Homo Sapien: dam ran once in bumper: fair pointer: well held in other events: tried
visored. *P. J. Millington*

JUDGE ROY BEAN (IRE) 4 b.g. Sadler's Wells (USA) – Be My Hope (IRE) (Be   **F102**
My Native (USA)) [2006/7 F16s* F16g F16d⁶ Apr 1] sturdy gelding: sixth foal: brother
to fairly useful hurdler/useful chaser Bob Hall, stays 2½m, and very smart chaser
Cane Brake, stays 3½m: dam useful hurdler around 2m: fairly useful form in bumpers:
favourite, won at Punchestown on debut in February comfortably by 7 lengths from Red
Seven: much stiffer task when sixteenth in Grade 1 at Cheltenham following month.
E. J. O'Grady, Ireland

JUDY'S LAD 8 ch.g. Master Willie – Flexwing (Electric) [2006/7 h–, F–: 20f⁴   **h–**
19gᵖᵘ Jul 23] no sign of ability, including in points (twice ran out): tried blinkered.
Mrs H. R. J. Nelmes

JUDY THE DRINKER 8 b.m. Snurge – Mardessa (Ardross) [2006/7 h–§, F79§: 16v⁵   **h73**
16s⁴ 20m² Mar 25] poor novice hurdler: stays easy 2½m: acts on good to firm and heavy
going: tried visored/blinkered: has been hard ride. *H. D. Daly*

JUG OF PUNCH (IRE) 8 ch.g. In The Wings – Mysistra (FR) (Machiavellian (USA))   **h101 §**
[2006/7 h87§: 16d 20m³ 16f⁶ 19s⁴ 16m 26g* 26g⁴ 24s⁴ 26s² 24v⁴ 26s⁵ 24g⁶ 24gᵖᵘ
Apr 19] smallish gelding: fair handicap hurdler: won at Hereford in October: suited by
3m+ nowadays: acts on heavy and good to firm going: temperamental (takes plenty of
driving). *S. T. Lewis*

JULIUS CAESAR 7 b.g. Sadler's Wells (USA) – Stiletta (Dancing Brave (USA))   **c– x**
[2006/7 c122, h–: c24s c25vᵖᵘ 25v³ 23s⁶ 23sᵖᵘ 24g Mar 15] strong, compact gelding: **h122**
fairly useful handicap hurdler: creditable effort in 2006/7 only when third to Rowley Hill
at Warwick: won maiden on chasing debut in 2005/6, badly let down by jumping since:
stays 25f: acts on heavy ground: tongue tied third to fifth starts. *J. Howard Johnson*

JUMBO'S DREAM 16 b.g. Jumbo Hirt (USA) – Joyful Star (Rubor) [2006/7 c–, h–:   **c–**
c21d May 31] deep-girthed gelding: veteran chaser: tried blinkered, usually in cheek-   **h–**
pieces. *J. E. Dixon*

JUMEIRAH JANE 4 br.f. Kayf Tara – Ace Girl (Stanford) [2006/7 F16m³ F17m³   **F78**
Apr 15] seventh foal: half-sister to 1998 2-y-o 5f winner Sound's Ace (by Savahra
Sound): dam 1m winner: modest form in mares bumpers. *Mrs S. J. Smith*

JUMP JET (IRE) 5 ch.g. Beneficial – Cherry In A Hurry (IRE) (Be My Native (USA))   **h103 p**
[2006/7 F16d F18s⁵ 19d* Mar 26] sturdy, lengthy gelding: first foal: dam, winning   **F81**
pointer, out of half-sister to smart staying chaser Omerta: modest form in bumpers: off 4
months, successful hurdling debut when beating Winds And Dragons by ¾ length in a
maiden at Stratford: will be suited by 2½m+: likely to progress. *Carl Llewellyn*

JUMP TO IT 7 b.m. Minster Son – Half Asleep (Quiet Fling (USA)) [2006/7 F16f 16g⁵   **h69**
16g 20s Nov 25] lengthy mare: half-sister to 3 winners, notably useful chaser B The One   **F–**
(by Gunner B), stayed 2½m: dam, fair hurdler, best around 2½m: well held in bumper:
form (poor) in novice hurdles only when fifth at Hexham: sold 1,500 gns Doncaster
March Sales. *Mrs S. J. Smith*

JUNCTIONTWENTYFOUR 6 b.g. Gildoran – Layston Pinzal (Afzal) [2006/7 20v 19v 22d^F c23m Apr 15] lengthy, workmanlike gelding: third foal: half-brother to fairly useful pointer Bally Blue (by Roselier): dam placed in point: won both starts in points in 2006: little impact over hurdles/in handicap chase. *N. J. Hawke*   c–
h–

JUNGLE GINGOES (IRE) 7 b.g. Lord of Appeal – Whatt Ya Doin (IRE) (Duky) [2006/7 h–: 26m^pu 19m^pu Jul 17] no form over hurdles: tried blinkered: won point in April. *N. G. Ayliffe*   h–

JUNGLE JINKS (IRE) 12 b.g. Proud Panther (FR) – Three Ladies (Menelek) [2006/7 c116, h–: c25s c25s^3 c23s* c25v^3 c25v^3 c25v^pu c28s c25g^6 Mar 17] smallish, workmanlike gelding: fairly useful handicap chaser: has won 5 times at Wetherby, including in November by 2½ lengths from Jimmy Bond: stays 25f: acts on heavy going: often races prominently: inconsistent. *G. M. Moore*   c115
h–

JUNGLELAND (IRE) 5 b.g. Flemensfirth (USA) – Lady Chauffer (IRE) (Good Thyne (USA)) [2006/7 F16v 16v^3 20d* Mar 17] €20,000 3-y-o: strong gelding: second foal: dam unraced, out of sister to high-class 2m chaser I'm A Driver: weak late after racing freely in bumper: second start in novice hurdles, won 18-runner event at Uttoxeter in March by 7 lengths from Tanners Court: stays 2½m: open to further improvement. *D. McCain Jnr*   h109 p
F–

JUNIOR 4 ch.g. Singspiel (IRE) – For More (FR) (Sanglamore (USA)) [2006/7 16v^2 16m^2 16s^5 16d^6 Mar 13] strong, lengthy gelding: dam, fairly useful French hurdler, half-sister to useful but unreliable hurdlers/chasers Sonevafushi and Celtic Son, both stays at least 3m: fairly useful on Flat (stays 2m), successful in April: useful form in juvenile hurdles: runner-up first 2 starts, behind Pauillac at Sandown and Punjabi at Ludlow: blinkered, best effort when sixth of 24 to Gaspara in Fred Winter Novices' Handicap at Cheltenham: will be suited by 2½m: acts on heavy and good to firm going: not yet a fluent jumper. *B. J. Meehan*   h125

JUNIOR FONTAINE (FR) 10 b.g. Silver Rainbow – Blanche Fontaine (FR) (Oakland (FR)) [2006/7 c125d, h–: c20g^2 Mar 27] workmanlike ex-Irish gelding: fairly useful chaser at best, runner-up in hunter at Sedgefield on March: stays 2¾m: acts on any going: tried blinkered. *David M. Easterby*   c98 +
h–

JUNKANOO 11 ch.g. Generous (IRE) – Lupescu (Dixieland Band (USA)) [2006/7 19s* 23s^3 20v^2 20v^2 24d 20v 20s Apr 26] tall, workmanlike gelding: fairly useful hurdler: won claimer at Market Rasen in November by ¾ length from Pro Dancer: ran poorly in handicaps last 3 outings: stays 3¼m: raced mainly on going softer than good (acts on heavy): usually ridden prominently: none too reliable. *K. G. Reveley*   h119

JUPITER JO 11 b.g. Jupiter Island – Marejo (Creetown) [2006/7 c76: c17d^6 c20s^4 c21m^4 c24m^pu c25g^pu Apr 23] sturdy gelding: winning pointer: poor maiden chaser, left J. Walton after fourth outing: stays 21f: acts on soft and firm going. *D. Forsyth*   c72

JUPITER'S FANCY 12 ch.m. Jupiter Island – Joe's Fancy (Apollo Eight) [2006/7 c89, h–: c25m* c26d^5 c20m^3 c25s^5 c25g^pu Apr 15] big, strong mare: winning pointer, including in 2007: fair hunter chaser: won at Hexham in May: stays 25f: acts on good to firm and good to soft going: tried in cheekpieces: none too reliable. *M. V. Coglan*   c89
h–

JUPON VERT (FR) 10 b.g. Lights Out (FR) – Danse Verte (FR) (Brezzo (FR)) [2006/7 c94, h–: c17m^5 c17v^6 c16m c16g^4 c16s^2 c16g c16d* c17d^5 c16g^6 c16g^3 c16f^3 Apr 22] leggy gelding: modest handicap chaser: ridden by A. McCoy, won at Folkestone in January: stays easy 3m, effective at much shorter: acts on any going: formerly tongue tied: effective held up or making running. *R. J. Hodges*   c99
h–

JUPSALA (FR) 10 ch.g. Video Rock (FR) – Belle d'Avril V (FR) (Quart de Vin (FR)) [2006/7 c68, h–: c20s^6 c24d^6 c24s^4 20g c27m^2 c27g^F Apr 23] smallish gelding: winning pointer: no show over hurdles: bad maiden chaser: stays 27f: usually in headgear: tongue tied last 2 starts. *J. W. F. Aynsley*   c58
h–

JURADO EXPRESS (IRE) 11 b.g. Jurado (USA) – Express Film (Ashmore (FR)) [2006/7 c118, h–: c16s^5 c16d* c16v^2 Dec 2] workmanlike gelding: fairly useful handicap chaser: better for reappearance, won 5-runner event at Wincanton in November by 10 lengths from Kawagino: good second of 6 to Coat of Honour at Wetherby following month: raced mainly around 2m: acts on heavy and good to firm going: has found little. *Miss Venetia Williams*   c126
h–

JURALAN (IRE) 12 b.g. Jurado (USA) – Boylan (Buckskin (FR)) [2006/7 c21g May 3] tall, good sort: winning hurdler: fairly useful chaser at best: no show in hunter only start in 2006/7: stays 21f: raced mainly on good going or softer. *P. H. Hogarth*   c–
h–

JURANCON II (FR) 10 b.g. Scooter Bleu (IRE) – Volniste (FR) (Olmeto) [2006/7 c25s³ c25s⁶ c25vᵖᵘ c25vᵖᵘ Mar 9] tall, leggy gelding: smart handicap chaser in 2003/4: little impact since, left M. Pipe and off nearly 2 years before return: stays 4m: acts on good to firm and heavy going: tried visored. *P. Monteith*   **c–**
h–

JUST A FLUKE (IRE) 6 b.g. Darshaan – Star Profile (IRE) (Sadler's Wells (USA)) [2006/7 16g⁴ 16m Jul 11] fair at best on Flat (stays 1¼m), well beaten both outings in 2006: poor form when fourth in maiden hurdle: tongue tied. *M. R. Bosley*   **h81**

JUSTAHARF 6 b.m. Primitive Rising (USA) – Grand Queen (Grand Conde (FR)) [2006/7 F17m F17d F17s⁴ F16g 19sᵖᵘ Jan 1] strong, lengthy mare: sister to fair hurdler/ useful chaser Harfdecent, stayed 25f, and fairly useful hurdler Brave Rebellion, stays 2½m: dam bad Flat maiden: little impact in bumpers/novice hurdle. *K. G. Reveley*   **h–**
F–

JUST A MAN 9 b.g. Primitive Rising (USA) – Pretty Tactfull (State Diplomacy (USA)) [2006/7 c–: c23gᵖᵘ May 11] modest pointer: in cheekpieces, no show in hunter chases. *Richard Mason*   **c–**

JUST ASK 7 ch.m. Busy Flight – Last Shower (Town And Country) [2006/7 h–, F–: 26gᵖᵘ 20m 21d Oct 30] lengthy mare: no form in bumpers/over hurdles: blinkered last 2 starts. *N. R. Mitchell*   **h–**

JUST A SPLASH (IRE) 7 ch.g. Synefos (USA) – Guitane Lady (IRE) (Commanche Run) [2006/7 c105, h95: c19s² c19sF c26d⁴ c24s³ c23dᵖᵘ c26g³ Mar 24] rangy, useful-looking gelding: modest hurdler/novice chaser: stays 3¼m when conditions aren't testing: acts on soft going, probably on heavy: tried in cheekpieces. *N. J. Gifford*   **c96**
h–

JUST A THOUGHT (IRE) 4 b.g. Orpen (USA) – Gold Fly (IRE) (Be My Guest (USA)) [2006/7 F12v² F16d² F16g Mar 14] 6,000 3-y-o: lengthy gelding: fifth foal: half-brother to fairly useful 5f to 7f winner Marshman (by College Chapel) and winner in Italy by Foxhound: dam unraced: useful form in bumpers: runner-up at Newbury first 2 starts, length behind Crocodile Rock in Grade 2 event on second occasion: well held in Grade 1 at Cheltenham. *H. J. L. Dunlop*   **F109**

JUST A TOUCH 11 ch.g. Rakaposhi King – Minim (Rymer) [2006/7 c97, h–: c16g⁶ Mar 20] workmanlike gelding: modest handicap chaser: off 11 months, well held only start in 2006/7: probably best around 2m: acts on any going. *P. Winkworth*   **c–**
h–

JUST BETH 11 ch.m. Carlingford Castle – One For The Road (Warpath) [2006/7 h119: 25dᵖᵘ 20g⁶ 20s⁶ 24s* 24v* 24g 24g⁵ 24g Apr 14] angular mare: fairly useful handicap hurdler: successful at Bangor in December and Cheltenham (outbattled Ladalko to win by ½ length) in January: rare poor effort final start: stays 25f: acts on heavy and good to firm going: tried blinkered: can take plenty of driving: tough and consistent. *G. Fierro*   **h120**

JUST BEWARE 5 b.m. Makbul – Bewails (IRE) (Caerleon (USA)) [2006/7 h74: 18m 20m⁴ 20m⁴ 18g³ 16m 16d³ 18s⁶ 16v⁴ 17v⁴ 16v 18g⁵ 18mᵘʳ Apr 26] sturdy mare: poor maiden hurdler: best around 2m: acts on good to firm and heavy ground: tried blinkered, formerly wore cheekpieces. *Miss Z. C. Davison*   **h74**

JUST BUDDY 6 b.g. Chaddleworth (IRE) – Roscoe's Gemma (Roscoe Blake) [2006/7 h–: 16sᵖᵘ 16sᵘʳ 20fᵖᵘ Jun 3] no show over hurdles. *R. Dickin*   **h–**

JUST DIFFERENT (IRE) 10 ch.g. Be My Native (USA) – Just For A Laugh (Idiot's Delight) [2006/7 c97, h–: c16mᵖᵘ c21sᵖᵘ c16gᵖᵘ c25fᵖᵘ Apr 5] maiden hurdler: winning chaser: no show in 2006/7, sold out of P. Murphy's stable £3,100 Ascot June Sales after first start: raced mainly around 2m on good ground or firmer (has run poorly on soft): has worn cheekpieces/blinkers. *James Young*   **c– x**
h–

JUST FILLY (IRE) 6 ch.m. Woodborough (USA) – Good Aim (IRE) (Priolo (USA)) [2006/7 h–: 16m⁵ 16m 16f 17mᵖᵘ Aug 6] no form over hurdles. *Miss C. J. E. Caroe*   **h–**

JUST FOR FUN (IRE) 9 b.g. Kahyasi – Copper Breeze (IRE) (Strong Gale) [2006/7 c–x, h–: c25mᵘʳ May 6] smallish gelding: winning hurdler: let down by jumping most starts in chases: modest pointer: stays 27f: acts on good to firm and heavy going: usually in cheekpieces/blinkers nowadays. *K. Robson*   **c– x**
h–

JUST FOR MEN (IRE) 7 gr.g. Glacial Storm (USA) – Regents Ballerina (IRE) (Commanche Run) [2006/7 h81±: c24dR c23s³ Dec 1] winning Irish pointer: in frame over hurdles: modest form on completed outing in chases: improve. *P. F. Nicholls*   **c89**
h–

JUST FOR NOW (IRE) 8 b.g. Flemensfirth (USA) – Sara's Pinkie (IRE) (Roselier (FR)) [2006/7 h109: c22vᵖᵘ c22sF c22vᵖᵘ c24gᵖᵘ c25s⁵ Mar 8] workmanlike gelding: in frame in novice hurdles: blinkered, modest form first completed outing over fences: needs to improve jumping. *T. R. George*   **c88**
h–

JUST FREYA 6 b.m. Chaddleworth (IRE) – Country Kizzie (Ballacashtal (CAN)) **h–**
[2006/7 F–: 17s^{pu} 16m^{pu} 16g^{ro} 17d 16d 20g Nov 13] more signs of temperament than ability: tongue tied last 4 starts. *R. Dickin*

JUST GOOD FRIENDS (IRE) 10 b.g. Shalford (IRE) – Sinfonietta (Foolish **c–**
Pleasure (USA)) [2006/7 17m^6 16f 20g^4 22m^6 21m c25g^4 c25g^4 c25g^4 Apr 23] maiden **h–**
hurdler/pointer: no form in chases: tried blinkered/tongue tied. *A. M. Crow*

JUSTICE JONES 6 b.g. Emperor Jones (USA) – Rally For Justice (Dominion) **h–**
[2006/7 h–: 26g^{pu} 26d^4 21m 21s^{pu} 26s 19g^{pu} Mar 29] leggy, sparely-made gelding: no
form. *Mrs P. Ford*

JUSTIFIED (IRE) 8 b. or br.g. Leading Counsel (USA) – Monkeylane (Monksfield) **c152**
[2006/7 c152p, h–: c17d* c24s^3 c20v^{pu} c17v^2 c16g^5 c16m^2 Apr 24] angular gelding: **h–**
smart chaser: won 4-runner listed race at Limerick (easily, by 7 lengths from Tumbling
Dice) in October: bad mistake 4 out when well-held fifth behind Voy Por Ustedes in
Champion Chase at Cheltenham, then 1¼ lengths second to Mansony in Kerrygold
Champion Chase at Punchestown: effective at 2m to 2½m: acts on heavy and good to
firm going: often front runner: tends to jump left (though 9 of 10 wins on right-handed
tracks). *E. Sheehy, Ireland*

JUST IN DEBT (IRE) 11 b. or br.g. Montelimar (USA) – No Debt (Oats) [2006/7 **c129 §**
c132, h–: c25f^2 c24m^6 c24s^3 c26g^{pu} c21g c24f^4 Apr 27] useful-looking gelding: winning **h–**
hurdler: fairly useful handicap chaser: creditable placed efforts first/third starts, third to
Bothar Na in Kerry National at Listowel: stays 27f: acts on firm and soft going: effective
with/without headgear: usually sound jumper: weak finisher. *M. Todhunter*

JUSTINO 9 b.g. Bustino – Jupiter's Message (Jupiter Island) [2006/7 c–, h84: 20m^5 **c–**
21m^5 Oct 4] workmanlike gelding: poor novice hurdler: in rear when fell 5 out only **h69**
outing over fences: will stay 3m. *J. A. Geake*

JUST IN TIME 12 b.g. Night Shift (USA) – Future Past (USA) (Super Concorde **c– x**
(USA)) [2006/7 c–x, h116: 20s^{pu} Apr 26] leggy gelding: winning chaser, usually let **h–**
down by jumping: fairly useful handicap hurdler, no show only start in 2006/7 after long
lay-off: stays 3m: acts on soft and firm going. *James Clements, Ireland*

JUST JAFFA (IRE) 8 ch.g. Zaffaran (USA) – East Link (IRE) (Over The River (FR)) **h94**
[2006/7 F–: 17d^4 16s^3 19s^4 16d^4 20s^4 Apr 25] well held in bumper: modest maiden
hurdler: likely to stay beyond 2½m: raced on good to soft/soft going. *Miss Venetia
Williams*

JUST JASMIN 4 b.f. Wizard King – Rose Hill (Sabrehill (USA)) [2006/7 16d^{ur} Nov 1] **h–**
little sign of ability on Flat/in juvenile hurdle. *P. D. Evans*

JUST JIMBO 11 ch.g. Karinga Bay – Ruby Green VII (Damsire Unregistered) [2006/7 **c60**
c21m^5 c26d^3 Jun 12] tall, angular gelding: poor maiden hurdler/chaser: stays 3¼m: acts **h–**
on heavy going: has broken blood vessels. *B. J. M. Ryall*

JUST JOLLY (IRE) 12 b.g. Jolly Jake (NZ) – Bulgaden Gypsy (Ballinamona Boy) **c–**
[2006/7 c–, h–: c18v^{pu} c24s^{pu} Oct 11] good-topped gelding: winning handicap chaser up **h–**
to 3m, lightly raced and no form since 2004/5. *J. R. Cornwall*

JUST LIKE MAGIC (IRE) 7 b.g. Taipan (IRE) – Red Bush (Red Regent) [2006/7 **c–**
c24f^{pu} Jul 6] €7,500 3-y-o: ex-Irish gelding: second foal: dam bumper winner: won
maiden point in 2005: no form in bumpers (for J. Crowley)/novice chase. *Barry Potts,
Ireland*

JUST MUCKIN AROUND (IRE) 11 gr.g. Celio Rufo – Cousin Muck (IRE) **c87 §**
(Henbit (USA)) [2006/7 c94§, h–§: c21g^5 c18m* c22f^{pu} c20m^f c21m^4 c21g^3 c21f^4 c16g^4 **h– §**
c19m c19s^3 c18s c16s^3 c18g^2 c16g^3 Apr 20] lengthy gelding: modest handicap chaser:
won selling event at Fontwell in May: stays 2¾m: probably acts on any going: often
tongue tied: sometimes let down by jumping: inconsistent. *R. H. Buckler*

JUST OBSERVING 4 ch.g. Observatory (USA) – Just Speculation (IRE) (Ahonoora) **h88**
[2006/7 17v 16v^4 16s 16v 16g^6 Mar 20] half-brother to modest hurdler Hi Tech (by Polar
Falcon), stays 3m: fairly useful on Flat (stays 9.8f), sold out of E. Dunlop's stable 23,000
gns Newmarket July Sales: best effort over hurdles (modest form) on final outing: has
taken good hold: claimed £12,000 on Flat in April. *P. C. Haslam*

JUST PLAYFULL 5 b.g. Sure Blade (USA) – Miss Millie (Homeboy) [2006/7 F16s **h–**
F16d 20m^6 24m^5 Apr 15] first foal: dam pulled up in point and novice hurdle: well held **F78**
in bumpers/novice hurdles: tried tongue tied. *M. G. Rimell*

JUST POPPYTEE 5 br.m. Emperor Fountain – State Lady (IRE) (Strong Statement **h97**
(USA)) [2006/7 F67: 20g 21s 19s³ 21s* 24s⁵ Jan 30] modest novice hurdler: won mares
event at Plumpton in January: should stay 3m: acts on soft going. *R. H. Alner*

JUST POSH 5 b.m. Moshaajir (USA) – Split The Wind (Strong Gale) [2006/7 F17g **F—**
Apr 23] second foal: dam maiden pointer: well held in bumper on debut. *R. Nixon*

JUST POSIN 6 ch.m. I'm Supposin (IRE) – We're In The Money (Billion (USA)) **h—**
[2006/7 h–, F–: 16d 17vᵖᵘ Nov 30] leggy mare: no form in bumpers/over hurdles.
Mrs S. Lamyman

JUSTPOURIT (IRE) 8 b.g. Glacial Storm (USA) – Gale Choice (IRE) (Strong Gale) **c132 §**
ered) [2006/7 h132: c20s⁵ c16s² c16s² c21v* c21d² c21vᵘʳ c16v³ c24g c17m⁵ c21m Apr 27] **h— §**
lengthy gelding: useful hurdler: similar standard over fences: landed odds in maiden at
Fairyhouse in January: best efforts when second of 3 finishers to Hear The Echo in
Grade 2 novice at Leopardstown (looked to pull himself up after being left in front) and
eighth to Denman in Royal & SunAlliance Chase at Cheltenham, fifth/eighth outings:
stays 3m: acts on heavy ground: tried blinkered/in cheekpieces: tends to idle, sometimes
markedly. *D. T. Hughes, Ireland*

JUST REUBEN (IRE) 12 gr.g. Roselier (FR) – Sharp Mama VII (Damsire Unregist- **c73 §**
ered) [2006/7 c75: c18f c21gᵖᵘ c20m³ c20g c26d² c26m³ c25f* c26g² c16s⁵ c23s⁵ c26s⁵ **h— §**
24v⁵ c26m⁴ c26m⁴ Apr 26] leggy gelding: poor handicap chaser: won at Wincanton (by
22 lengths) in October: no show on hurdling debut: stays 3¼m: acts on any going: tried
blinkered/visored: unreliable. *R. H. Alner*

JUST ROMEO (IRE) 6 ch.g. Executive Perk – Stella Romana (Roman Warrior) **h—**
[2006/7 20fᵖᵘ Jun 3] €31,000 3-y-o, 8,000 4-y-o: half-brother to fairly useful hunter
Alpha Romana (by Alphabatim), stayed 21f: dam unraced half-sister to staying chasers
Androma (very smart) and Bigsun (useful): no show in maiden hurdle on debut. *R. Lee*

Mr Trevor Hemmings' "Juveigneur"

JUST RUBY 6 ch.m. Gunner B – First Crack (Scallywag) [2006/7 h–, F–: 16g⁵ Jun 8] no form. *F. Jordan*   **h–**

JUST SILVER 6 gr.g. Silver Patriarch (IRE) – Silver Mood (Jalmood (USA)) [2006/7 21v⁵ Mar 12] second foal: dam unraced: well beaten in novice hurdle on debut. *Miss Suzy Smith*   **h–**

JUST SMOKIE 5 gr.m. Cloudings (IRE) – Rakajack (Rakaposhi King) [2006/7 F16v F16v⁴ 17v⁵ 17g³ Mar 24] half-sister to winning hurdler/fair chaser Paxford Jack (by Alflora), stays 25f: dam unraced half-sister to dam of useful staying chaser You're Agoodun: poor form in bumpers: better effort in novice hurdles when third to Annie's Answer at Bangor: will stay beyond 17f: likely to do better. *D. McCain Jnr*   **h83 p F74**

JUST SMUDGE 5 b.g. Fraam – Flakey Dove (Oats) [2006/7 h87: F16d³ 21m² 22d⁴ 19g 20g Apr 11] unfurnished gelding: fair form in bumpers: disappointing after second to Air Force One in novice on hurdling debut: stays 21f. *A. E. Price*   **h99 F93**

JUST STANDEESE (IRE) 5 b.g. Shahrastani (USA) – Vaguely Deesse (USA) (Vaguely Noble) [2006/7 F18v F16g 20g⁵ Apr 27] half-brother to several winners, including fairly useful hurdler Corlande (by Teamster), stays 3m, and fair chaser up to 3m New Era (by Distinctly North): dam ran once: soundly beaten in bumpers/novice hurdle. *J. W. Mullins*   **h– F–**

JUST STUNNING (IRE) 5 ch.m. Presenting – Top Dresser (IRE) (Good Thyne (USA)) [2006/7 F16d⁶ F16s⁴ 20v⁶ 20s⁴ 24d⁵ Mar 22] workmanlike mare: third foal: half-sister to fair hurdler Top Cloud (by Cloudings), stays 27f: dam ran twice: fourth in bumper: poor form in mares novice hurdles: should prove suited by further than 2½m. *D. McCain Jnr*   **h75 F78**

JUST SUPERB 8 ch.g. Superlative – Just Greenwich (Chilibang) [2006/7 h97: 16g⁵ c16gF 16s c19sᵖᵘ 20vᵖᵘ 16g 16g 19g³ 20g⁴ 16m Apr 24] smallish gelding: modest handicap hurdler: let down by jumping over fences: best up to 2½m: acts on soft going: tried in cheekpieces/blinkers (ran in snatches): usually races prominently. *P. A. Pritchard*   **c– x h97 d**

JUST SUPPOSIN 5 b.g. I'm Supposin (IRE) – Devinette (IRE) (Be My Native) (USA)) [2006/7 F95: 19s 19s² 21g⁶ 16mᵖᵘ Apr 8] rather unfurnished gelding: runner-up in maiden bumper: modest form in novice hurdles: may prove best around 2m. *D. E. Pipe*   **h90**

JUSTTHEONEFORYOU 5 ch.g. Classic Cliche (IRE) – Cerise Bleue (FR) (Port Lyautey (FR)) [2006/7 F16g⁶ Jun 8] first foal: dam, 17f hurdle winner in France, half-sister to fairly useful 2m hurdler Dibea Times: sixth of 13 in bumper on debut. *J. M. Jefferson*   **F75**

JUST TOUCH WOOD 6 ch.g. Fraam – Versaillesprincess (Legend of France (USA)) [2006/7 h–, F–: 16mᵖᵘ Apr 8] sturdy gelding: no form in bumper/over hurdles. *J. J. Bridger*   **h–**

JUSTUPYOURSTREET (IRE) 11 b.g. Dolphin Street (FR) – Sure Flyer (IRE) (Sure Blade (USA)) [2006/7 c24g⁶ 22gᵖᵘ Apr 2] rather leggy gelding: one-time fair 2m hurdler: amiss both starts in 2006/7, including on chasing debut: tried tongue tied. *Miss L. Harrison*   **c– h–**

JUST WAZ (USA) 5 ch.g. Woodman (USA) – Just Tops (USA) (Topsider (USA)) [2006/7 16s⁵ 16s 17g⁵ 16g Mar 17] useful-looking gelding: modest on Flat (barely stays 2m): mid-division in novice/maiden hurdles. *R. M. Whitaker*   **h82**

JUSTWHATEVERULIKE (IRE) 6 b.g. Courtship – Rose of Summer (IRE) (Taufan (USA)) [2006/7 h–, F74: 20s 20sᵖᵘ 21v⁴ 16vᵖᵘ 24v³ Mar 15] poor maiden hurdler: stays 3m: acts on heavy going: tongue tied last 3 starts, also in cheekpieces last 2. *Miss S. E. Forster*   **h72**

JUVEIGNEUR (FR) 10 ch.g. Funny Baby (FR) – Azurea (FR) (On My Way (USA)) [2006/7 c143: 21d³ c26s² c29s³ 21v* c24g² c29mᵖᵘ c29f Apr 28] tall, close-coupled, good-topped gelding: smart handicap chaser: better than ever in 2006/7, placed in Hennessy Cognac Gold Cup at Newbury (4 lengths second to State of Play), Coral Welsh National at Chepstow (10 lengths third to Halcon Geneladais) and William Hill Trophy at Cheltenham (short-head second to Joes Edge): twice-raced in novice hurdles, fairly useful form when third to Massini's Maguire at Cheltenham: very easy task at Plumpton in February: stays 29f: acts on heavy going, below form on firmer than good last 2 outings: open to improvement over hurdles. *N. J. Henderson*   **c154 h118 p**

J'Y VOLE (FR) 4 ch.f. Mansonnien (FR) – J'Y Reste (FR) (Freedom Cry) [2006/7 17s* 18s 18s⁵ 18s² 16v* 16v² 17g⁵ Mar 16] tall, lengthy filly: second foal: dam won all 3 starts over hurdles up to 2¼m, out of half-sister to very smart French hurdler up to 25f   **h121**

Full of Ambition: unplaced both starts on Flat: fairly useful juvenile hurdler: won at Auteuil in October and, having been sold from T. Trapenard €100,000 after fourth outing, at Fairyhouse in February and Auteuil (Group 3 Gras Savoye Prix de Longchamp, by length from stable-companion Financial Reward) after end of British season: also ran well when 6 lengths second to Duty in Grade 3 at Fairyhouse and 23 lengths fifth to Katchit in Triumph Hurdle at Cheltenham: likely to prove better at 2½m than 2m: acts on heavy ground. *W. P. Mullins, Ireland*

K

KABALLERO (GER) 6 ch.g. Lomitas – Keniana (IRE) (Sharpo) [2006/7 17d⁴ 16g 16s Nov 25] compact ex-German gelding: successful 4 times up to around 9f on Flat: sixth in minor event at Rome on hurdling debut in 2005: left A. Wohler, modest form first 2 starts in Britain: likely to need sharp 2m. *S. Gollings* **h89**

KADAM (IRE) 7 b.g. Night Shift (USA) – Kadassa (IRE) (Shardari) [2006/7 c93§, h106§: c21g² c21mᵖᵘ May 12] big, lengthy gelding: fair handicap hurdler: modest form over fences: stays 2¾m: acts on good to soft ground: wears blinkers: tongue tied on debut: temperamental. *P. F. Nicholls* **c95 § h– §**

KADDASAN (IRE) 5 b.g. Indian Lodge (IRE) – Kadassa (IRE) (Shardari) [2006/7 F75: F17g³ F16g² 20d Oct 20] useful-looking gelding: placed in bumpers: tailed off in novice on hurdling debut. *D. E. Cantillon* **h– F87**

KADIA 4 ch.f. Arkadian Hero (USA) – Soba Up (Persian Heights) [2006/7 F14v Dec 2] big, long-backed filly: fifth foal: half-sister to useful performer up to 2m Saint Alebe (by Bishop of Cashel): dam fair performer on Flat who stayed 13.4f: well beaten in bumper: poor form on all-weather on Flat, won weak maiden in April. *P. T. Midgley* **F–**

KADOUN (IRE) 10 b.g. Doyoun – Kumta (IRE) (Priolo (USA)) [2006/7 c–x, h145: c20s³ 20v² 24d 24g Mar 15] leggy gelding: smart hurdler: below best in 2006/7, including when neck second to Studmaster in minor event at Punchestown: one-time useful chaser, let down by jumping/attitude over fences since 2003/4: stays 3m: acts on heavy going, probably on good to firm: has worn headgear. *M. J. P. O'Brien, Ireland* **c117 § h134**

KADOUNT (FR) 9 b.g. Our Account (USA) – Une de Lann (FR) (Spoleto) [2006/7 c138, h–: 17sᵖᵘ 19s 16d c22vᵖᵘ 24m⁴ Apr 20] strong, good-bodied gelding: useful hurdler/chaser at one time, disappointing since 2004/5, left A. King before reappearance: stays 21f: acts on heavy going: tried in headgear. *L. Lungo* **c– h109**

KAHUNA (IRE) 10 b.g. Mister Lord (USA) – My Baloo (On Your Mark) [2006/7 c125, h–: c17mˢᵘ c17f² c17g* c16s* c17v* c16v⁵ c16g 16d⁴ c16m Apr 24] tall, angular gelding: useful chaser: won minor event at Ballinrobe in August and handicaps at Listowel in September and Galway (best effort, beat Cane Brake 4 lengths) in October: fairly useful hurdler, fourth to Wishwillow Lord in minor event at Limerick penultimate start: best around 2m: acts on heavy and good to firm going: tried in cheekpieces/blinkers: usually front runner: has hinted at temperament. *E. Sheehy, Ireland* **c133 h117**

KAHYSERA 6 b.m. Kahyasi – Recipe (Bustino) [2006/7 F76: 16g³ 20mᵖᵘ 16mᵖᵘ 16mᵖᵘ 17m 20g 16v⁵ Nov 23] lengthy mare: form (poor) over hurdles only on debut, left Mrs S. Smith after third start: tried tongue tied. *F. Jordan* **h77**

KAI KURI (IRE) 6 br.m. Carroll House – Lucy's Light (IRE) (Miner's Lamp) [2006/7 F16m² F17m³ F16m 16d⁵ 16g Nov 2] second foal: dam unraced: placed in bumpers: better effort in selling hurdles when fifth at Stratford (gambled on): well beaten in maidens on Flat. *P. W. Hiatt* **h64 F82**

KAKY (FR) 5 b.g. Kabool – Lady Juliette (FR) (Baillamont (USA)) [2006/7 17s c17s* 17fᵖᵘ 20vᵖᵘ 20gᵖᵘ Mar 17] ex-French gelding: third foal: half-brother to winning hurdler/chaser around 2m Monsieur Plume and 7f to 11.5f winner Plume Blanche (both by Apeldoorn): dam 1¼m winner: maiden hurdler: won 4-y-o claiming chase at Auteuil (claimed from P. Costes €10,200) in June: no form in Britain: has worn blinkers/cheekpieces. *M. Todhunter* **c79 h–**

KAL 4 b.f. Kalanisi (IRE) – Towaahi (IRE) (Caerleon (USA)) [2006/7 17m 17d 22f⁴ 24m⁶ 21g⁴ Apr 23] half-sister to fairly useful but temperamental hurdler/winning chaser Kristoffersen (by Kris), stays 21f: no form in maidens on Flat for Jean-Rene Auvray or over hurdles, sold out of Mrs L. Young's stable £1,000 Ascot August Sales after debut: tongue tied last 2 outings. *M. B. Shears* **h–**

KALADIN 4 b.g. Kalanisi (IRE) – Minstrel's Gift (The Minstrel (CAN)) [2006/7 16m^ur **h80** 17d^F Aug 21] modest maiden on Flat (stayed 11.6f): failed to complete both starts in juvenile hurdles, held in second when falling fatally 2 out in maiden won by Mambo Sun at Newton Abbot. *G. L. Moore*

KALAMAZOO (IRE) 6 b.g. Flemensfirth (USA) – Cheryls Pet (IRE) (General **h–** Ironside) [2006/7 F84: 16s 24s^4 16s 22g 19m Apr 17] strong gelding: modest form in bumpers: little show over hurdles, visored final outing: bred to be suited by 2½m+. *Nick Williams*

KALANI STAR (IRE) 7 b.g. Ashkalani (IRE) – Bellissi (IRE) (Bluebird (USA)) **h–** [2006/7 16m^pu Nov 9] half-brother to fair 2m hurdler Pure Mischief (by Alhaarth): poor on Flat (stays 8.6f): tongue tied, no show both starts over hurdles, left I. McInnes after debut. *Miss M. E. Rowland*

KALANTERA (IRE) 4 b.g. Kalanisi (IRE) – Tintera (IRE) (King's Theatre (IRE)) **h83** [2006/7 17g^3 16g^4 17s^pu Dec 18] strong gelding: fair maiden on Flat (stays 13.8f), sold out of A. Balding's stable £7,500 Ascot July Sales: modest form over hurdles, lame final outing. *C. L. Popham*

KALATIME (IRE) 4 b. or br.f. Kalanisi (IRE) – Dream Time (Rainbow Quest (USA)) **h70** [2006/7 16g 16g^4 16d^5 17s 16m^3 Apr 9] unfurnished filly: fair maiden on Flat (stays 11.6f), claimed from A. Balding £6,000 in October: poor form over hurdles: raced around 2m. *M. F. Harris*

KALAWOUN (FR) 5 b.g. Highest Honor (FR) – Kalajana (USA) (Green Dancer **h–** (USA)) [2006/7 h89: 26g May 4] good-topped gelding: form over hurdles only when third in juvenile in 2005/6: wore headgear last 2 starts. *Ferdy Murphy*

KALCA MOME (FR) 9 b.g. En Calcat (FR) – Belle Mome (FR) (Grand Tresor (FR)) **c141** [2006/7 c136, h–: c17s^4 c16s* c19d^2 c16g c19v^2 c20s c19g^6 Mar 31] leggy gelding: **h–** winning hurdler: useful handicap chaser: won at Cheltenham in December by 2 lengths from Bohemian Spirit: creditable efforts next and fifth outings: effective from 2m to 2½m: acts on heavy and good to firm going: sometimes gets behind. *P. J. Hobbs*

KALDERON (GER) 7 br.g. Big Shuffle (USA) – Kreuzdame (GER) (Acatenango **h137** (GER)) [2006/7 h108: 16s* 16s* 16d 16s^4 16d^6 20m^2 Apr 27] leggy gelding: smart on Flat (stays 1½m), won listed race in September: useful novice hurdler: won at Listowel (maiden) in September and Tipperary (Grade 3 Kevin McManus Bookmaker Joe Mac Novices' Hurdle, beat Mill House Girl easily by 5 lengths) in October: good efforts in Grade 1 events at Cheltenham (sixth of 22 to Ebaziyan in Supreme Novices') and Punchestown (5 lengths second to Glencove Marina) last 2 starts: stays 2½m: acts on soft and good to firm ground. *T. Hogan, Ireland*

KALDOUAS (FR) 6 bl. or br.g. Kaldou Star – Popie d'Ecorcei (FR) (Balsamo (FR)) **c122** [2006/7 h106+, F91: c21m^F c20s^F c20d^3 c21s* Jan 20] useful-looking gelding: winning **h–** hurdler: fairly useful form over fences (fell first 2 starts): won novice at Wincanton by short head from Mandingo Chief, idling markedly after leading 2 out: stays 2¾m: acts on soft and good to firm ground: tongue tied on chasing debut. *P. F. Nicholls*

KALIC D'ALM (FR) 9 b.g. Passing Sale – Bekaa II (FR) (Djarvis (FR)) [2006/7 **c92** h73: c17d^3 c17g^F c17s^F c16s^4 c17v c16s c16v c20v^3 c16s^pu c20g Apr 7] tall gelding: **h–** maiden hurdler: modest novice chaser: stays 2½m: acts on heavy going, probably on good to firm. *W. S. Coltherd*

KALIN DE THAIX (FR) 9 ch.g. Agent Bleu (FR) – Une Amie (FR) (Prove It Baby **h–** (USA)) [2006/7 20d Oct 18] sturdy gelding: no form in 2 starts over hurdles more than 2½ years apart, or in points. *P. F. Nicholls*

KALMO BAY (FR) 4 b.g. Alamo Bay (USA) – Kermesse (USA) (Irish River (FR)) **h93** [2006/7 15d^6 17s^pu 18v* 16v^pu 16v 20m^4 Mar 25] quite good-topped gelding: twice-raced on Flat: won 3-y-o claimer at Auteuil (claimed from T. Trapenard €18,500) in November: only poor form over hurdles in Britain: edgy sort (has worn earplugs in preliminaries). *Ferdy Murphy*

KALOU (GER) 9 b.g. Law Society (USA) – Kompetenz (IRE) (Be My Guest (USA)) **c92** [2006/7 c107, h–§: c16m^6 c18g^6 c16m^4 Apr 21] good-topped gelding: winning hurdler: **h–** fair handicap chaser at best: sold out of C. Grant's stable 1,800 gns Doncaster October Sales after second outing: stays easy 2½m: acts on good to firm and good to soft going, probably on soft: tried in cheekpieces: has finished weakly. *J. K. Magee, Ireland*

KALUSH 6 b.g. Makbul – The Lady Vanishes (Robin Des Pins (USA)) [2006/7 16m^pu **h–** 20s^pu 16s^pu Nov 22] disappointing maiden on Flat: no show over hurdles. *Miss A. Stokell*

KAMANDA LAUGH 6 ch.g. Most Welcome – Kamada (USA) (Blushing Groom **h82 +**
(FR)) [2006/7 16g 16d⁵ Dec 28] half-brother to useful hurdler Doctor Goddard (by
Niniski), stayed 2½m: useful on Flat (stays 1¼m): poor form in novice/maiden hurdles:
likely to need sharp 2m. *K. A. Ryan*

KAMES PARK (IRE) 5 b.g. Desert Sun – Persian Sally (IRE) (Persian Bold) [2006/7 **h–**
16gᵘʳ Dec 30] useful on Flat (stays 1¾m), successful twice in March: took strong hold
and unseated third after jinking left in novice on hurdling debut. *I. Semple*

KANAD 5 b.g. Bold Edge – Multi-Softt (Northern State (USA)) [2006/7 16s⁵ 17d² 20d⁴ **h117**
16m* 17v² 16sᵖᵘ 16m* Apr 25] good-topped gelding: half-brother to modest 2m hurdler
Hold The Line (by Titus Livius): fairly useful up to 11f on Flat (tried blinkered), sold out
of E. Dunlop's stable 25,000 gns Newmarket Autumn (2005) Sales: fairly useful hurdler:
reportedly had breathing operation after second start: won handicap at Ludlow (by 3
lengths from Sasso) in January and novice at Worcester (by neck from In The Lead) in
April: may prove best around 2m: acts on good to soft and good to firm ground: has had
tongue tied, including at Worcester (also in cheekpieces). *C. J. Mann*

KANDJAR D'ALLIER (FR) 9 gr.g. Royal Charter (FR) – Miss Akarad (FR) **c133**
(Akarad (FR)) [2006/7 c141, h108: c20d c24s* c28s c36gᶠ Apr 14] leggy gelding: fair **h–**
hurdler: useful handicap chaser: won quite valuable event at Haydock in December by ½
length from Wild Cane Ridge, patiently ridden: stays 3m: acts on heavy going: has been
let down by jumping (fell first Canal Turn in Grand National). *A. King*

KANDORA 5 b.m. El Conquistador – Rakanda (Rakaposhi King) [2006/7 F17d³ F16g **h–**
18s⁵ 16g 22d Feb 1] workmanlike mare: first foal: dam unraced: better effort in bumpers **F76**
when third to easy winner Rudinero at Hereford: never dangerous in 3 mares events over
hurdles. *J. W. Mullins*

KANEKT LADY (IRE) 6 b.m. Old Vic – Tulach A' Tsolais (IRE) (Strong Gale) **h–**
[2006/7 22d 20m 20v Mar 2] first foal: dam little form: fifth in bumper on debut: well
beaten over hurdles, left Michael McElhone before final start. *Lindsay Woods, Ireland*

KANPAI (IRE) 5 br.g. Trans Island – David's Star (Welsh Saint) [2006/7 h101: **h130**
20f³ 16m* 16m* 16g* 19d* 20g* 20s* 20d* 21d⁶ Dec 29]
　　　　There was a six-month period during the latest season when novice hurdler
Kanpai was carrying all before him, notching up seven straight wins over jumps
and also successful on the Flat in a National Hunt jockeys handicap over two miles
at Goodwood. To say he was a much improved performer is an understatement. A
modest maiden on the Flat at three, Kanpai showed himself marginally better when
first switched to hurdling but was still without a win after six attempts when he
lined up for a four-year-old novice hurdle at Worcester in June. In cheekpieces, as
on his previous start, Kanpai managed to justify favouritism in a modest contest but
was all out to do so. Wins number two, another novice at Worcester in June, and
three, a handicap at Southwell in July, soon followed, Kanpai now in a visor which
he was to wear on all his subsequent starts. However, it wasn't until he was returned
to further than two miles that Kanpai really began to show what he was capable of.
Stretching his run to five in novice events at Newton Abbot in August and Huntingdon in October, in the latter giving Tony McCoy (on board for six of the gelding's
wins) his 2,500th domestic victory, Kanpai was then stepped up in class. In the
Grade 2 Ballymore Ontario Tower Novices' Hurdle (Persian War) at Chepstow
later in October, Kanpai's impressive set of form figures seemed to count for little
so far as punters were concerned, the betting dominated by odds-on French import
Granit Jack and Massini's Maguire, with Kanpai a 12/1-shot. In a race where the
two market leaders were way below their best, Kanpai came out on top once again.
Even though the race took less winning than had seemed likely, Kanpai, conceding
weight all round, still showed himself useful in winning by twelve lengths from
Massini's Maguire, taking it up entering the straight and galloping on strongly,
having the race sewn up between the last two flights. No further improvement was
required from Kanpai to make it seven wins at Haydock in November, though he
did have to work very hard to land the odds. Kanpai made a couple of mistakes back
over brush-type obstacles, notably four out, and McCoy had to be at his strongest to
get him home by half a length from Mr Strachan. That Kanpai's exertions had
finally begun to catch up with him seemed a plausible explanation for his
disappointing run in the Challow Hurdle at Newbury at the end of December, when
he was last of six finishers behind the McCoy-ridden Wichita Lineman. It was

Ballymore Ontario Tower Novices' Hurdle (Persian War), Chepstow—
Kanpai (Tony McCoy) records the sixth of his seven wins

subsequently announced, however, that Kanpai would be on the easy list for a while after injuring his near-fore tendon. A good-bodied gelding who acts on heavy and good to firm going, Kanpai is likely to stay beyond two and a half miles and should be back in action in the next season. *J. G. M. O'Shea*

KANSAS FEATHER (IRE) 4 b.f. Darnay – Kissimmee Bay (IRE) (Brief Truce (USA)) [2006/7 17d^{pu} Nov 21] second foal: dam sprint maiden: no show in juvenile hurdle/maidens on Flat. *B. S. Rothwell* **h–**

KAPAROLO (USA) 8 ch.g. El Prado (IRE) – Parliament House (USA) (General Assembly (USA)) [2006/7 h–: 21g 21d^{pu} 17m^5 17m 16d^6 21m 17s^{ur} 17m Apr 15] strong gelding: one-time fair hurdler, little form since 2004/5. *John A. Harris* **h–**

KAPPELHOFF (IRE) 10 b.g. Mukaddamah (USA) – Miss Penguin (General Assembly (USA)) [2006/7 c66, h–: c24m Oct 4] leggy gelding: poor chaser: stays 25f: acts on soft going: blinkered/visored nowadays: has been let down by jumping. *Mrs L. Richards* **c– x**
h–

495

European Breeders' Fund Mares' Only 'National Hunt' Novices' Hurdle Final (Limited Handicap), Newbury—Karello Bay lands her second valuable mares' prize

KARADIN (FR) 13 b.g. Akarad (FR) – In River (FR) (In Fijar (USA)) [2006/7 c26m³ c23m c26dᶠ c26d⁴ Aug 7] workmanlike gelding: winning hurdler/chaser: trained on reappearance by Mrs Mandy Hand: probably stayed 3¼m: acted on firm and soft going: dead. *D. C. Turner* **c91 h–**

KARA DOOT 6 b.m. Bijou d'Inde – Meghdoot (Celestial Storm (USA)) [2006/7 16dᶠ 16sᵖᵘ 16g 17m⁵ Apr 28] well held in maiden on Flat at 3 yrs for H. Collingridge: no form over hurdles. *M. J. Gingell* **h–**

KARAKORUM HIGHWAY 6 b.g. Rakaposhi King – Garvenish (Balinger) [2006/7 F16d F16m⁵ 16m 16f 16f 16d 20f³ 16s⁵ 16m* Oct 12] half-brother to modest hurdler Algarve (by Alflora), stays 25f: dam, novice hurdler/chaser, half-sister to smart 2½m chaser Wayward King: modest form on last of 3 starts in bumpers: improved effort over hurdles when winning seller at Ludlow: stays 2½m: acts on firm going: has been blinkered, including last 3 outings. *Adrian McGuinness, Ireland* **h82 F81**

KARAKUM 8 b.g. Mtoto – Magongo (Be My Chief (USA)) [2006/7 c95, h–: 16g 16m c16dᵖᵘ c17g³ c16f² c17m⁴ c16fᶠ Aug 22] maiden hurdler: modest and error-prone novice chaser: stayed 2½m: acted on firm going: often made running: dead. *A. J. Chamberlain* **c89 x h–**

KARANJA 8 b.g. Karinga Bay – Proverbial Rose (Proverb) [2006/7 h126: 25d⁴ 24d* Nov 24] rangy, useful-looking gelding: chasing type: useful hurdler: in cheekpieces, improved effort when winning 21-runner handicap at Newbury by ¾ length from Oscar Park: should stay 3¼m: unraced on firm going, acts on any other: tried tongue tied (has finished weakly). *V. R. A. Dartnall* **h138**

KARANTAKA (IRE) 7 b.g. Warcraft (USA) – Lone Run (Kemal (FR)) [2006/7 c21gᵖᵘ Apr 27] poor pointer: no show in novice hunter. *Mrs K. M. Sanderson* **c–**

KARATHAENA (IRE) 7 b.m. Barathea (IRE) – Dabtara (IRE) (Kahyasi) [2006/7 h107: 19g⁴ 22s⁶ 19g* 16v³ 16v⁵ 19s³ 16v² 24d⁵ Mar 19] workmanlike mare: fair handicap hurdler: won at Market Rasen in December: at least respectable efforts all starts after (including in cheekpieces): stays 3m: raced on good going or softer (acts on heavy): tried tongue tied: normally patiently ridden. *M. E. Sowersby* **h109**

496

KARELLO BAY 6 b.m. Kahyasi – Caramello (Supreme Leader) [2006/7 F106: 18s³ **h133**
22d* 21v³ 21g* 21g⁵ Apr 19] rather leggy, useful-looking mare: useful hurdler: successful in mares novices at Wincanton (easily landed odds) in February and Newbury in March, best effort when beating Miss Mitch readily by 3 lengths in EBF Mares' Only NH Novices' Hurdle Final (Limited Handicap) at latter: stays 2¾m: raced on good ground or softer (bumper winner on heavy): tongue tied last 2 starts. *N. J. Henderson*

KARINGA KREAM 7 b.g. Karinga Bay – Cream By Post (Torus) [2006/7 17d³ 17d³ 16m⁴ **h92**
17vᵖᵘ 16s Jan 20] good-topped gelding: fifth foal: half-brother to 3 winners, including fair hurdler/chaser Cream Cracker (by Sir Harry Lewis), stays 2½m, and 2m chase winner Post It (by Thowra): dam, winning hurdler (probably stayed 2¾m)/fair pointer, out of half-sister to useful hurdler/chaser up to 25f Gallaher: modest form first 2 starts in novice hurdles: will stay 2½m: acts on good to firm and good to soft going, well below form on softer. *R. H. Alner*

KARINGA LEAP 10 ch.g. Karinga Bay – Church Leap (Pollerton) [2006/7 c24gᵖᵘ **c–**
May 5] modest pointer, runner-up completed start in 2006: showed nothing in hunter. *P. Cornforth*

KARINGA MAGIC 4 b.g. Karinga Bay – Foxgrove (Kinglet) [2006/7 F16g F16m **F–**
Apr 25] 10,000 3-y-o: good-topped gelding: fourth foal: half-brother to fairly useful hurdler/useful chaser Private Be (by Gunner B), stays 2½m: dam winning staying chaser: soundly beaten in bumpers. *Mrs Norma Pook*

KARO DE VINDECY (FR) 7 b.g. Mollicone Junior (FR) – Preves du Forez (FR) **c92**
(Quart de Vin (FR)) [2006/7 c92, h–: c16g² c16m⁵ c18g⁴ c16m⁴ c21f⁵ c21d³ c21m² **h–**
c20gᵖᵘ c16s⁵ Apr 26] leggy gelding: modest handicap chaser: effective at 2m to 21f: acts on firm and good to soft going: formerly tongue tied. *Micky Hammond*

KAROO 9 b.g. Karinga Bay – Cupids Bower (Owen Dudley) [2006/7 h–: 22m⁵ 19s⁵ **c87**
c19s⁴ c16g⁴ c16m* c19gᵖᵘ Apr 11] sturdy gelding: maiden hurdler: improved effort over **h–**
fences when winning novice handicap at Hereford in March: stays 2¾m, effective at much shorter: acts on soft and good to firm going: jumps left: headstrong. *K. Bishop*

KARRNAK 5 b.g. Hernando (FR) – Maiden Aunt (IRE) (Distant Relative) [2006/7 h71: **h–**
16m 16mᵖᵘ Jul 16] poor maiden over hurdles (stays 1½m): tried in cheekpieces/blinkers/tongue tied. *Miss J. Feilden*

KARSHAAN (FR) 4 b.g. Kahyasi – Mon Petitnamour (IRE) (Darshaan) [2006/7 18s **h92**
16v⁴ 17s⁴ 20v⁵ 19gᵖᵘ 23g³ Apr 9] smallish gelding: fair maiden on Flat (stays 2m): modest novice hurdler: will be suited by 3m+: acts on heavy ground. *P. Winkworth*

KARYON (IRE) 7 b.m. Presidium – Stealthy (Kind of Hush) [2006/7 c–, h–: 16g⁶ 16d **c–**
16s⁴ 16sᵖᵘ 17m⁶ Apr 15] smallish, workmanlike mare: bad hurdler: made all in selling **h59**
handicap at Catterick in January: no show out outing over fences: form only at 2m: acts on soft going: tried in cheekpieces/blinkers. *Miss Kate Milligan*

KASBAH BLISS (FR) 5 b.g. Kahyasi – Marital Bliss (FR) (Double Bed (FR)) [2006/7 **h154**
h145: 18s* 18s³ 19s* 20s³ 22d⁴ 24g⁵ 19s³ Apr 28] lengthy, angular gelding: smart hurdler: successful in 4-y-o events at Auteuil (listed) and October (Group 3 Prix Pierre de Lassus, by 2 lengths from Shinco du Berlais): best efforts when 2¾ lengths fourth of 16 to Taranis (FR) in valuable handicap at Sandown and 16¾ lengths fifth to Inglis Drever in World Hurdle at Cheltenham: stays 3m: acts on heavy going. *F. Doumen, France*

KASTHARI (IRE) 8 gr.g. Vettori (IRE) – Karliyka (IRE) (Last Tycoon) [2006/7 c130, **c–**
h–: c24gᵖᵘ c21gᶠ Apr 13] tall gelding: smart stayer on Flat: useful hurdler/chaser at best, **h–**
mostly let down by jumping/gone as if amiss since second start over fences in 2005/6: stays 2¾m: acts on soft and good to firm going: joined J. Bethell. *J. Howard Johnson*

KATCHIT (IRE) 4 b.g. Kalanisi (IRE) – Miracle (Ezzoud (IRE)) [2006/7 17g* **h151**
16g* 16s² 16d* 17s* 17v* 17g* 16g* Apr 12]
'Has little strength or scope but should go on all the same, as the run was quite encouraging.' As a first report goes, it is a little better than 'Can't act. Can't sing.' Balding. Can dance a little', reputedly the verdict on an early Fred Astaire screen test. Even so, Katchit's career has exceeded anything that could have been envisaged from *Timeform Perspective*'s view of his debut as a two-year-old. Although he won only once on the Flat, he proved a model of toughness and consistency in recording no fewer than sixteen runs in little over a year. When his attention was switched to hurdling, Katchit soon made up for his shortage of victories. He was beaten just once in eight starts, when conceding 8 lb to a smart

Wragge & Co Juvenile Hurdle (Finesse), Cheltenham—
the favourite Katchit (right) is pushed close by French raider Good Bye Simon (grey)

Flat performer and going down by a length and a half, whilst his haul included two wins apiece at both Grade 1 and Grade 2 level. He followed Detroit City in completing the Triumph/Anniversary Hurdle double and ended the season the top-rated juvenile hurdler from another above-average crop. Katchit's toughness, enthusiasm and excellent hurdling technique made him very hard to beat and will continue to stand him in good stead. His lack of stature continued to be held against him but proved no handicap to his progress. There is no reason why he should not go on to make his mark in good open company in 2007/8.

Katchit's Flat victory came on his fourteenth and final start for Mick Channon, in a mile-and-a-quarter handicap at Salisbury in June. Transferred to Alan King principally for hurdling, he ran twice on the polytrack at Kempton in August, finishing second on the first occasion. In all on the Flat, he was never worse than sixth and ran poorly only once, on his only outing on fibresand. Katchit took on the odds-on Is It Me, already successful five times over hurdles, at Market Rasen on his hurdling debut in September. Is It Me had looked well above average for an early-season juvenile, so when Katchit beat him in very impressive fashion by nine lengths, there was a tendency to think that the runner-up (who was conceding 8 lb) was not at his best, even though the time for the race compared very favourably with others on the card. That wasn't the last time Katchit was underestimated, nor the last that a strong clue to his true merit was found in the time of the race. Katchit was odds on for his next start, at Chepstow two weeks later when he defeated French import Chaninbar from the Paul Nicholls' yard. The margin was only a length and a half and *Timeform Perspective* suggested Katchit might be hard pressed to confirm his superiority were the pair to meet again. When this happened, three weeks later at Wetherby in the Wensleydale Hurdle, Chaninbar was only fourth, a good deal further behind Katchit, despite meeting him on terms marginally better than at Chepstow. The Wensleydale, though, was the race in which Katchit met with defeat, by the hurdling debutant Degas Art, a listed race winner at Newmarket on the Flat a month previously. Although Katchit's admirable qualities were again there for all to see, it was the winner who was the subject of most Triumph Hurdle speculation afterwards. When Katchit landed the Grade 2 Ryman

498

The Stationer Juvenile Novices' Hurdle at Cheltenham's Open meeting by a neck from Freeze The Flame, his performance was viewed as boosting the Triumph claims of Degas Art as much as Katchit's own. The expectation was that several possessed of more size and scope would come along to supplant Katchit as the winter progressed. Katchit was returned to Cheltenham the following month, for a valuable non-graded event at the newly-styled International meeting. Tritonix, a useful Flat performer in France who had won both starts over hurdles since joining Philip Hobbs, was narrowly favourite but Katchit saw him off in style, producing his best performance to that point in defeating outsider Ned Ludd by eight lengths, with Tritonix third. It took this performance for Katchit's merit to be fully recognised and he was promoted to favouritism for the Triumph afterwards.

The Adonis at Kempton was mentioned as Katchit's likely target after a short break but he returned to action a month sooner, in the Grade 2 Wragge & Co-sponsored Finesse Juvenile Hurdle at Cheltenham at the end of January. On going that was barely raceable, Katchit faced the strongest field assembled to that point of the season for a juvenile hurdle. Good Bye Simon, who had won the Grade 1 Finale Hurdle at Chepstow from Ned Ludd, as well as a trio of French imports who had been impressive in lesser company, Pauillac, Pancake and Predateur, were in the line-up. Katchit saw them off in game fashion, beating Good Bye Simon a length and three quarters, the time again a particularly good one. Katchit was shortened a good deal for the Triumph but his position at the head of the market was challenged the very next day, when the Irish mare Lounaos finished a good fourth in the AIG Europe Champion Hurdle behind Hardy Eustace.

Lounaos started favourite ahead of Katchit in a representative field of twenty-three for the JCB Triumph Hurdle, for which few of the better four-year-olds were missing from the line-up—Fred Winter winner Gaspara being the notable exception. The field was stronger, in Flat terms, than the Supreme Novices', with sixteen of the twenty-two that had raced on the Flat (not counting Pauillac, who had won the French equivalent of a bumper) showing fairly useful form or better. Four, including Lounaos, had been classed as smart, the three others including Degas

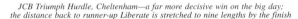

JCB Triumph Hurdle, Cheltenham—a far more decisive win on the big day;
the distance back to runner-up Liberate is stretched to nine lengths by the finish

Art, who went off at 7/1 after two victories in small fields since Wetherby, and 8/1-chance Mountain, who had run in three classics and won his only previous start over hurdles. Useful Flat performer Duty, a Grade 3 hurdles winner in Ireland, was at 9/1 (Katchit and Duty had met before, nearly eleven months previously, when fourth and second respectively in what turned out a rather good Windsor maiden, the winner Red Rocks terminating any hurdling prospects of his own by winning the Breeders' Cup Turf later in the year). Punjabi, wide margin winner of the Adonis Hurdle, was also at 9/1, with the useful Flat performer and promising hurdler Liberate next at 12/1. Nearly all those named were better than Katchit on the Flat and there was some prospect that less testing ground than for his earlier Cheltenham wins might make things harder for him. In the event Katchit proved well suited by the greater emphasis on speed, routing his field and winning by nine lengths from Liberate, with 33/1-chance Mobaasher and Punjabi completing the frame. Degas Art, facing more rivals than in three previous races combined, and Mountain were let down by lack of experience over hurdles, while neither Lounaos nor Duty gave their running. The time comparison with the concluding County Hurdle provides independent confirmation that this was an above-average Triumph Hurdle and, in Katchit, it had an outstanding winner. Indeed, Katchit's winning margin was the third biggest in the Triumph's history since it became a level-weights event at the Festival in 1973, one which has been bettered only by Oh So Risky in 1991 (twelve lengths) and Scolardy in 2002 (eleven lengths). The latter was beset by training problems after Cheltenham, failing to win from just three more starts, but Oh So Risky's subsequent career should please Katchit's connections as he developed into a top-class hurdler who finished a close second in the Champion Hurdle in both 1992 and 1994.

Katchit's final outing of the season came in the John Smith's Anniversary Hurdle at Aintree. Both Mobaasher and Punjabi reopposed, along with Degas Art, as well as old rivals Tritonix and Is It Me. Katchit wasn't quite so spectacular in victory as he had been at Cheltenham, but he left the impression he had something to spare in beating Punjabi by four lengths with Degas Art, improving considerably on his Cheltenham effort, eight lengths away in third and the rest well strung out. The Triumph/Anniversary double has been made easier to achieve since penalties were dropped in the latter race, but Katchit would have won even under the old conditions. Katchit is the highest-rated juvenile hurdler in *Chasers & Hurdlers* since Jair du Cochet in the 2000/1 season. Jair du Cochet was denied the chance to run in the Triumph because of the foot and mouth outbreak but his performance in winning the Finesse that season by a distance was, in our view, the best by a hurdler of his age since this series of Annuals started in 1975/76. All told, Katchit is the ninth leading juvenile to end the season with a rating above 150, though he is the

John Smith's Anniversary 4-Y-O Hurdle, Aintree—win number seven
of an exemplary campaign for Katchit who is again too good for Triumph fourth Punjabi;
Katchit's early-season Wetherby conqueror Degas Art (noseband) is third

first of that group to have won the Triumph Hurdle. Four were beaten at Cheltenham, Valmony (157 in 1975/6), who had won five of his first seven races but was well below his best at Cheltenham; Aldino (154 in 1986/7), who finished sixth but then won the Glenlivet, now the Anniversary, Hurdle at Aintree; Staunch Friend (151p in 1991/2), who was pulled up when favourite for the Triumph but later put up the best performance of the season in winning by a wide margin at Punchestown; and Escartefigue (159 in 1995/6), fourth behind Paddy's Return at Cheltenham before putting up a very smart performance when runner-up to Alderbrook in the Scottish Champion Hurdle. The remaining trio didn't take part in the Triumph, namely Out of The Gloom (151 in 1984/5), winner of the twenty-one-furlong novice at Aintree, Dark Raven (153p in 1985/6), unbeaten in four starts and winner of the Glenlivet, and Hors La Loi III (162p in 1998/9), who ran in and won the Supreme Novices' instead. Much has been made of the subsequent exploits of the 2006 Triumph Hurdle field and there must be a good chance that Katchit and his contemporaries will make a similar impact in 2007/8, but the Triumph Hurdle in which Aldino was sixth was a pretty strong one too. Apart from Aldino, winner subsequently of several significant hurdle races (including the 1989 Scottish Champion) and a Grand Annual Chase, the field included the winners of notable races in 1987/8 such as the Christmas Hurdle (Osric), Imperial Cup (Sprowston Boy), Nottingham's City Trial Hurdle (Nos Na Gaoithe), County Hurdle (Cashew King) and Welsh Champion and Swinton Hurdles (Past Glories). Past Glories, later third in a Champion Hurdle, Osric, High Knowl and Grabel, a prolific winner whose biggest success came in the Duelling Grounds International in Kentucky, were all at least very smart hurdlers. The winner Alone Success, High Knowl, Cashew King and Nos Na Gaoithe were all useful or better over fences as well as hurdles.

Of the eight previous leading juveniles with ratings above 150, only Hors La Loi III went on to win a Champion Hurdle. The best of Valmony had already been seen before the Triumph and his only subsequent win came in a Fakenham novice chase, while Dark Raven met with a setback after winning his only start in his second season. Escartefigue and Jair du Cochet principally made their mark over longer distances and over fences, both showing top-class form in that sphere. Out of The Gloom won a 'Fighting Fifth' but gained his other hurdling successes over further, notably in the Long Walk Hurdle. Aldino and Dark Raven apart, Staunch Friend was the only other in the list who was purely and simply a two-mile hurdler. He was in-and-out after his initial campaign, and made little impact in two Champion Hurdles, though won a Scottish Champion Hurdle and a Bula Hurdle.

			Doyoun	Mill Reef
		Kalanisi (IRE)	(br 1985)	Dumka
		(b 1996)	Kalamba	Green Dancer
Katchit (IRE)			(b 1991)	Kareena
(b.g. 2003)			Ezzoud	Last Tycoon
		Miracle	(b 1989)	Royal Sister II
		(gr 1996)	Madiyla	Darshaan
			(gr 1987)	Manntika

Katchit is yet another good jumper stemming from the Aga Khan's studs. Both his sire Kalanisi and grandam Madiyla were bred there. Katchit is one of three winning hurdlers so far from Kalanisi's first crop, the others including European Dream, who finished third in the Wensleydale and was successful in the Spring Mile on his return to the Flat in March. Kalanisi was a top-class middle-distance colt who was involved in some tremendous battles, the winning margin in all his races at four never more than half a length. He went down by a head to Giant's Causeway in both the Eclipse and International and beat Montjeu narrowly in the Champion Stakes before winning the Breeders' Cup Turf. He was tough and consistent and there is every chance he will make an impact as a sire of hurdlers. Katchit's family has enjoyed quite a bit of success on the Flat and over jumps. Madiyla has produced two above-average Flat fillies in the consistent Lethals Lady, who failed by just two heads to win the 2001 Poule d'Essai des Pouliches, and the useful mile-and-a-quarter performer Giving. Miracle, Katchit's dam, was a winner over a mile in France and in the States. Katchit is her first foal, her second Prince Erik (by Indian Ridge) cost 135,000 guineas as a yearling and is in training with

Dermot Weld, winning a mile-and-a-quarter maiden at Leopardstown in May prior to finishing sixth in the Irish Derby. Madiyla, who won a mile-and-a-half maiden on the Flat from two starts and was well held in a juvenile hurdle, produced three winning jumpers, the pointer Mogul, the bumper and maiden hurdle winner Found Gold, and Silver City, a novice hurdle winner who also won on the Flat. Her latest foal, Burn The Breeze, is a two-year-old in training with Henry Cecil. The third dam Manntika, who was herself a mile-and-a-quarter winner, is the dam of the prolific staying hurdler Premier Princess. Manntika also produced two above-average performers on the Flat by Kalanisi's sire Doyoun, namely the runaway 1993 National Stakes winner Manntari, and Fast Track, who went downhill after finishing third in the Glasgow Stakes on his second start. There isn't a lot of stamina in Katchit's pedigree and he may well prove best at around two miles, far from typical for a Triumph Hurdle winner incidentally—though his trainer's previous winner of the race, Penzance, had a similar profile. Katchit has raced on good going or softer over hurdles and acts on heavy, though his best form is on good and he was effective on good to firm on the Flat. *A. King*

KATE OF THE WEST (IRE) 7 ch.m. Oscar Schindler (IRE) – Honey View (IRE) (Forties Field (FR)) [2006/7 F16s 24s^{ro} c21g^{pu} Jun 4] sixth foal: dam unraced: no form in various events (ran out after third in novice hurdle). *B. W. Duke* c– h– F–

KATE'S GIFT 6 b.g. Supreme Leader – Ardentinny (Ardross) [2006/7 F99: F16d^2 Dec 14] unfurnished gelding: fairly useful form in bumpers: off 20 months, 10 lengths second to Tot O'Whiskey at Catterick: bred to stay 3m. *P. R. Webber* F99

502

KATESS (IRE) 4 b.f. Spectrum (IRE) – Esclava (USA) (Nureyev (USA)) [2006/7 **F89**
aF13g³ F12v⁴ F16s⁵ F16m* F17g⁶ Apr 13] unfurnished filly: half-sister to fairly useful
hurdler/chaser up to 21f Croix de Guerre (by Highest Honor) and fair hurdler/fairly useful
chaser up to 23f Sento (by Persian Bold), both unreliable: dam, third at 1¼m in France,
out of Prix de Diane winner Escaline: fair form in bumpers: won mares event at Uttoxeter
in March by 6 lengths from Thebelloftheball: ran well when sixth of 20 to Turbo Linn in
listed race at Aintree. *A. King*

KATHLEENS PRIDE (IRE) 7 b.g. Broken Hearted – Cyprus Hill (IRE) (Bulldozer) **h99**
[2006/7 16v⁴ 17s⁴ 22v³ 22d² Mar 20] useful-looking gelding: will make a chaser: second
foal: half-brother to 2¾m hurdle winner Tuatha de Danann (by Corrouge): dam well held
in bumper: runner-up on completed start in points in 2006: modest form in frame all 4
starts over hurdles, jumped better when 5 lengths second to Otantique in novice handicap
at Exeter, making most: will stay 3m. *T. R. George*

KATIES HERO 9 b.g. Pontevecchio Notte – Kindly Lady (Kind of Hush) [2006/7 **c–**
c23dᵖᵘ May 17] novice hurdler: winning pointer: no show in hunter chase: tried **h–**
blinkered. *Mrs Pauline Geering*

KATIES TUITOR 4 b.g. Kayf Tara – Penny Gold (IRE) (Millfontaine) [2006/7 16f² **h124**
16g* 16d* 16g 16m⁴ Apr 26] good-topped gelding: fair form on Flat (should be suited by
1¼m/1½m): successful at 2 yrs: fairly useful juvenile hurdler: won at Kempton (by 20
lengths from Urban Tiger) in October and Sandown (set good pace when beating Irish
Whispers 4 lengths) in November: 17 lengths fourth to Punjabi in Champion 4-Y-O
Hurdle at Punchestown: will stay beyond 2m. *B. W. Duke*

KAUSSE DE THAIX (FR) 9 ch.g. Iris Noir (FR) – Etoile de Thaix (FR) (Lute Anti- **c111 d**
que (FR)) [2006/7 c111: c25g⁶ c24d* c22vᴿ c23v⁵ c24gᵖᵘ c24g⁵ c31s³ Apr 27] lengthy,
useful-looking gelding: fair chaser: won handicap at Fakenham in May: sold out of
O. Sherwood's stable 26,000 gns Doncaster May Sales: well below best after: stays 3½m:
acts on soft going: tried blinkered/in cheekpieces/tongue tied. *H. P. Hogarth*

KAUTO STAR (FR) 7 b.g. Village Star (FR) – Kauto Relka (FR) (Port Etienne **c184 +**
(FR)) [2006/7 c166+, h–: c20s* c24d* c16s* c24d* c24d* c26g* Mar 16] **h–**
　　　　Kauto Star's legacy will be defined over the years to come, provided he
keeps clear of the illnesses and injuries that so often seem to blight the career of
a top steeplechaser. Whether or not history eventually affords Kauto Star a place
among jumping's icons, he has already made a major impact on the sport. His
Timeform rating is the joint highest (with Moscow Flyer) achieved by a jumper
since Desert Orchid, and has been bettered only by Arkle (212), Flyingbolt (210),
Mill House (191), Desert Orchid (187) and Dunkirk (186) in the now-extensive
period since the end of the Second World War. Those pre-war 'giants' Easter Hero
and Golden Miller earned Timeform equivalent ratings, compiled by Randall and
Morris for *A Century of Champions*, of 190 and 188 respectively.
　　　　Desert Orchid, the greatest jumper since the era of Arkle and his contemporaries, died peacefully at the age of twenty-seven at the stables (now at Newmarket)
of his trainer David Elsworth in November. The very tough and durable Desert
Orchid produced so many meritorious performances—he won thirty-four races in
a career spanning ten seasons—that it came as something of a surprise when his
hard-fought victory in the 1989 Cheltenham Gold Cup was voted 'the greatest race
of all time' in a *Racing Post* poll in 2005. The voters were convinced by Desert
Orchid's battling victory under foul conditions, the meeting given the go-ahead
only after a midday inspection when snow was followed by hours of rain. On form,
Desert Orchid gave no better than an around-average Gold Cup-winning performance. He was also successful four times in the King George VI Chase, a race with
just as good a record over the years for identifying the season's best staying chaser.
However, Desert Orchid did not earn his lofty Timeform rating in either the Gold
Cup or the King George, but with his performances in major handicaps including
victories in the Whitbread under 11-11, the Irish Grand National under 12-0 and a
brilliant effort carrying 12-3 (including a penalty) in the Racing Post Chase.
　　　　Versatility was a hallmark of Desert Orchid's career. He was unbeaten in
five races in the build-up to his Cheltenham Gold Cup victory, a straightforward
win over two miles five furlongs at Wincanton on his reappearance preceding an
all-the-way victory at Sandown in the Tingle Creek Chase, which was then a
handicap (Desert Orchid conceded between 18 lb and 28 lb to four rivals). An easy

victory in the King George (his second) on Boxing Day, achieved with a spectacular display of jumping, was followed by another major two-mile handicap, the Victor Chandler at Ascot, where Desert Orchid won by a head from the admirably consistent Panto Prince, a very smart chaser who received 22 lb. Further emphasising his versatility, Desert Orchid completed his Cheltenham Gold Cup preparation over an extended three miles in the Gainsborough Chase at Sandown, another handicap, in which he held off the Mackeson and A. F. Budge Gold Cup winner Pegwell Bay, who received 18 lb. Desert Orchid returned to the most emotional reception of his career after winning the Cheltenham Gold Cup with a tremendous rally, after making most to forge ahead again on the run-in for a length-and-a-half victory over 25/1-shot Yahoo. Only four of the thirteen runners, who included two previous winners The Thinker and Charter Party, completed the course without mishap, the conditions having a shattering effect on some.

Desert Orchid made a name for himself beyond the normal boundaries of the sport. Television had much to do with establishing his enormous popularity, the fact that he was a grey, coupled with his flamboyant front-running, bold-jumping style, creating a spectacular image for the camera. But it was evident after his death, from the prominence given by the media to his Gold Cup victory, that, for general sports enthusiasts, Cheltenham Gold Cup winners (along with Grand National winners) are still virtually the be-all and end-all for a jumper. Kauto Star's achievements in the latest season were remarkable but, even after four top-class performances on his first four starts including a victory in the King George VI Chase, it seemed inevitable that his campaign would be judged in the wider context by his performance in the Cheltenham Gold Cup in March. His short, ante-post odds for the Gold Cup—by which time his record for the season was five wins from five starts—were fully justified on form. Kauto Star was barely off the bridle when conceding weight all round and winning the Grade 2 Old Roan Chase over two and a half miles at Aintree by twenty-one lengths on his reappearance, and he had seventeen lengths to spare over Beef Or Salmon when winning the Lancashire Chase on his second start. Having shown at Haydock that he stayed three miles,

bonusprint.com Old Roan Chase (Limited Handicap), Aintree—
Kauto Star leaps to the top of the chasing tree with a highly impressive weight-carrying performance

Kauto Star was dropped back to two when producing another tip-top performance to beat the previous season's Arkle winner (and subsequent Champion Chase winner) Voy Por Ustedes by seven lengths in the Tingle Creek. Kauto Star's King George win came by eight lengths from Exotic Dancer who, coincidentally, had emulated Pegwell Bay in winning Cheltenham's two traditional big pre-Christmas handicaps, run in the latest season as the Paddy Power Gold Cup and the boylesports.com Gold Cup.

Until Best Mate and Kicking King also achieved it, Desert Orchid was the only horse to complete the King George/Gold Cup double in the same season since Arkle (Desert Orchid encountered vastly different conditions in the two races, the going at Kempton good to firm). The Gold Cup is run over two and a half furlongs further than the King George and over a stiffer course, placing more of a premium on stamina even under normal conditions. Just over a week before the latest Festival, the Cheltenham going was 'heavy, soft in places', with a further period of wet weather in prospect. Soft ground Festivals are much rarer than they used to be, but it looked at that time as though the latest Gold Cup was going to call for markedly different qualities in Kauto Star to those that had been required at Kempton. In the event, the weather relented and the ground dried out, the times indicating that the going on Gold Cup day was good, though the clerk of the course returned it good to soft. The reaction to Kauto Star's final race before the Gold Cup, the AON Chase at Newbury, in which he scrambled home by a neck from L'Ami in a muddling race, focussed on another concern, the fears expressed in some quarters about Kauto Star's jumping. Kauto Star made a bad mistake at the final fence in the AON, and had also made two when winning the King George, any of which could have resulted in his coming down at one of Cheltenham's downhill fences. He had fallen on his only previous start at Cheltenham, when a hot favourite for the Queen Mother Champion Chase on his final 2005/6 outing. That said, there seemed a danger that the attention given to Kauto Star's jumping was overshadowing his achievements. In truth, his supporters had little more to worry about in the Gold Cup than supporters of any of the other runners. Two of his main rivals, Exotic Dancer and Lexus Chase winner The Listener, also had at least one fall on their record in their last six runs.

The hallmark of the King George/Gold Cup doubles achieved by Best Mate and Kicking King had been accurate jumping and a turn of foot and, except for clipping the last, Kauto Star jumped well at Cheltenham, putting his stamp on the race most impressively when pulled out off the home turn after a muddling pace resulted in over a third of the field still being in contention turning in. Because of the steady gallop, Kauto Star and runner-up Exotic Dancer were not able to show their true superiority over the others on the day and, strictly on form, Kauto Star's Gold Cup performance wasn't that of even an average winner. Rather like Desert Orchid, though, Kauto Star still earned more attention from the general sporting public for his Gold Cup win than for any of his five other victories during the season. News of Desert Orchid's death made the front pages as well as the racing pages, and featured on television and radio news bulletins. Racing's popularity, however, is arguably not so strong nowadays as it was in Desert Orchid's heyday and probably only Best Mate has consistently earned wider recognition outside the narrow confines of the sport since. Kauto Star's Gold Cup win failed to make front-page headlines, with most of the coverage on the back pages and in the racing sections, concentrating on how much his victory had cost the bookmakers (estimates ranging widely from £5m up to £20m). The stories also covered Kauto Star's landing the £1m bonus offered by Lancashire Chase sponsors Betfair if the winner went on to success in the King George (or the Lexus) and the Gold Cup. An article in the news pages of *The Guardian* summed up Kauto Star's situation with the words 'he still has the chance to capture the public's imagination.' Another two Gold Cups ought to do it!

Best Mate and Kauto Star are among only five horses who have gone unbeaten through a Cheltenham Gold Cup-winning season since Arkle did so in 1965/6. The others were the twelve-year-old What A Myth in 1968/9 (two easy wins in hunter chases) and two seven-year-olds, Midnight Court in 1977/8 and Little Owl in 1980/1. Like Kauto Star, Midnight Court and Little Owl both enjoyed fairly busy campaigns, though neither ran in the King George VI Chase—consid-

*Betfair Chase (Lancashire), Haydock—the £1m bonus is on;
the step up in trip poses no problem as Kauto Star runs out a seventeen-length winner
from Beef Or Salmon (cheekpieces), L'Ami and Ollie Magern (centre)*

ered too soon—on the way to the Gold Cup. Both earned rave write-ups in *Chasers & Hurdlers*—'enthusiasm is not easily restrained when a Midnight Court arrives on the scene'/'Little Owl's prospects seem almost boundless'—but neither was the same again, misfortune dogging their careers afterwards. Kauto Star's career has already been interrupted by injury, a mishap in a three-runner novice chase at Exeter as a five-year-old—his near miss after being remounted made the national TV news—resulting in a small fracture to his near-hind which ruled him out of that season's Arkle for which he was ante-post favourite. Kauto Star returned the next season to win the Tingle Creek on only his fourth outing over fences—putting up the best two-mile performance seen during the campaign—but he made only three appearances in all, taking a heavy fall at the third in the Queen Mother Champion Chase on the last of them. Two falls in five steeplechases was a record that undermined the confidence of some in Kauto Star's future but, still only six, there seemed every prospect that, with more experience, he would establish himself as a tip-top chaser.

Kauto Star's trainer Paul Nicholls said at the start of the latest season that he had two main aims for Kauto Star: win the Tingle Creek again and run him more often ('he desperately needs more experience'). Nicholls felt that Kauto Star had been 'much too fresh' before Cheltenham, which had contributed to his fall. He had been unable to run again because he 'came back bruised all over'. Interestingly, Kauto Star was started off over two and a half miles in the latest season, connections evidently feeling that racing him over further than two might put less pressure on his jumping. As he had only won twice over fences, Kauto Star would have been qualified for one of the graduation chases—a subject discussed in the essay on Turpin Green—but he made his comeback in the bonusprint.com Old Roan Chase, a limited handicap at Aintree towards the end of October. Conceding weight all round, Kauto Star jumped well and drew clear effortlessly after the third last. A twenty-one-length beating of his generally reliable stable-companion Armaturk, who paid the winner a big compliment when just touched off in a good-quality handicap at Cheltenham less than three weeks later, represented outstanding form, on paper better than any effort recorded in Britain or Ireland the previous season.

Kauto Star shot to the head of the ante-post betting for the King George VI Chase, despite never having raced beyond two and a half miles. Some bookmakers also introduced Kauto Star into the Cheltenham Gold Cup market—at around 10/1—though he was still as short as 5/2 favourite for the Queen Mother Champion Chase at the time.

Another tilt at the Champion Chase soon began to appear unlikely, judged by statements emanating from connections. 'The Ryanair [2m5f] could be the race for him at Cheltenham this year,' his trainer announced the week after the Old Roan. But first things first. Kauto Star was to be tried over three miles in the Betfair-sponsored Lancashire Chase at Haydock in November, provided the going did not become too testing in the meantime. The second running of this new Grade 1 attracted a top-class field, including the first two in the race the previous year, Kingscliff and Beef Or Salmon (fresh from beating the Gold Cup winner War of Attrition in the Champion Chase at Down Royal), and French-trained L'Ami, who had reached the frame in both the King George and the Gold Cup the previous season. Kauto Star's trainer said that the £1m bonus on offer from the sponsors had not been a factor in choosing the race. 'Before someone reminded me, it had slipped my mind, but if he wins we'll be thinking about it . . . the horse comes first, though, and money isn't our priority . . . at this stage we simply want to find out if he is going to stay.' Nicholls need not have worried on that score. Kauto Star started a hot favourite and gave an exhilarating performance, never putting a foot wrong and travelling really well before quickening clear in the home straight. Kauto Star won in breathtaking style, looking like a horse who hadn't really started to race in earnest as he annihilated the field, barely off the bridle at any stage and still full of running at the line. Beef Or Salmon wasn't at his best, not jumping fluently, and got up for second only after the last, finishing seventeen lengths adrift of the winner, with L'Ami a length further away in third. Kingscliff dropped himself out at halfway and trailed in last of six.

The Betfair took so little out of Kauto Star that, despite initial reports that he would wait for the King George VI Chase, he reappeared a fortnight later in the William Hill-Tingle Creek Chase at Sandown. 'We won't be thinking about Tingle Creek Chases now, it's the King George and the Gold Cup,' the trainer had said straight after the Lancashire Chase. Owner Clive Smith's boldness and openness made a refreshing change, though it landed him in an awkward spot later in the season when he seemed to suggest that Kauto Star's much-publicised jumping errors late on in some of his races might have been due partly to his regular jockey Ruby Walsh's supposed tendency to get over-excited when the winning post is in sight. 'I just hope Ruby is cool in the Gold Cup,' he told guests of Betfair at a

William Hill-Tingle Creek Chase, Sandown—a return to the minimum trip yields a second successive win in this race, with subsequent Champion Chase winner Voy Por Ustedes no match for Kauto Star

Cheltenham preview. Smith was the driving force behind the change of plan to run Kauto Star in the Tingle Creek, a move backed by Walsh, with the trainer agreeing that 'it made sense because the horse has been in the form of his life since Haydock.' With bookmakers offering only 7/2 about Kauto Star going on to land the King George/Gold Cup double, he pulverised the opposition in the Tingle Creek, his jumping again very accurate in the main. Quickening clear into the straight, odds-on Kauto Star won with a lot in hand by seven lengths and the same from Voy Por Ustedes and Oneway (the previous year's third, beaten half as far again this time).

With the season less than half over, Kauto Star had recorded the best performances at two miles, two and a half, and three, versatility that was almost on a par with that shown by Desert Orchid who was Timeform's top-rated chaser at both two and three miles three years in succession from 1988/9 onwards (he was the best staying chaser five years in a row—his stamina stretching to win a Whitbread and an Irish National—and was elected jumping's Horse of the Year on a record four occasions). The outstanding Pendil was also champion at two and three miles in the 1972/3 season when he was unbeaten in five races, including the forerunners of both the Tingle Creek and Game Spirit Chases, namely the Benson & Hedges Chase and the Newbury Spring Chase respectively (easily beating that year's Champion Chase winner Inklslinger and Tingle Creek himself in the latter), before going down by a short head to The Dikler (whom he had beaten by five lengths in that winter's King George) in the Gold Cup. Legendary Irish mare Dawn Run is also worth a mention as, just six weeks after her historic Cheltenham Gold Cup success in 1986, she defeated that season's Champion Chase winner Buck House (at level weights) in a specially-arranged match over two miles at the Punchestown Festival.

Desert Orchid's life-sized statue at Kempton was unveiled while he was still racing and his ashes were buried under a headstone near the statue a few days before a ceremony was held to commemorate him at Kempton's Christmas fixture. It coincided with the first running of a new Grade 2 event, the Desert Orchid Chase over two miles, which has replaced the Castleford Chase in the National Hunt pattern (the latter race is now a 0-145 handicap still staged at Wetherby's Christmas fixture). With no Kauto Star to worry about, Voy Por Ustedes won the Desert Orchid from Oneway, with third going to the previous season's Maghull Chase winner Foreman (whom Kauto Star had slaughtered on his British debut). Kauto Star ran the previous day in the Stan James King George VI Chase, a race which he dominated in every sense. Not since the days of Desert Orchid had one horse hogged the headlines so much in the build-up to the race. Again odds on, Kauto Star faced eight rivals, including the highest-rated novice chaser of 2005/6 Monet's Garden who had won three times that season and just been touched off by Voy Por Ustedes (who received 5 lb) in the Arkle. Monet's Garden started second favourite

Stan James King George VI Chase, Kempton—the second leg of the Betfair Million;
Kauto Star already has the measure of Exotic Dancer (right) and Racing Demon two out

AON Chase, Newbury—a late scare, but L'Ami is unable to take advantage in a muddling race

at Kempton, ahead of Racing Demon, winner of the Peterborough Chase at Huntingdon on the same day Kauto Star had won at Haydock. Exotic Dancer was the only other runner to start at single-figure odds. Monet's Garden took the eye jumping boldly in front from the third, while Kauto Star was waited with, on the outside of the field in a handy position. Monet's Garden was soon beaten when challenged from the fourth last, which Kauto Star ploughed through, remarkably without losing any ground. Taking the lead at the next, Kauto Star was firmly in control from early in the home straight, only to make an even worse mistake at the last where he was clear and completely fluffed his jump. Without the mistakes, Kauto Star would have won by further than the eight lengths he finished ahead of Exotic Dancer, who made an equally bad mistake himself two out. Racing Demon came third, repeating his Peterborough Chase form, a length and a quarter behind Exotic Dancer and twenty lengths in front of fourth-placed Monkerhostin who had run Kicking King to a neck in the race twelve months earlier when it was run at Sandown. Kempton's redevelopment, centred around the installation of a polytrack Flat circuit, also involved some realignment of the bends on the jumps course (the water jump has been removed) and the repositioning of fences in the home straight.

Kauto Star's performance in the King George VI Chase may not have quite matched the expectations held for it, but he remained as short as 6/4 for the Cheltenham Gold Cup afterwards. 'We'll ride him differently, drop him in as we did at Haydock where he put in his best round of jumping without a doubt,' said Nicholls. Kempton's fences—rebuilt after the all-weather track was installed—clearly complied with Horseracing Regulatory Authority specifications, but Cheltenham had the potential to provide a stiffer examination of Kauto Star's jumping ability, with its undulations and sometimes-tricky downhill fences. Kicking King had blundered at the last in the 2004 King George at Kempton, though, before going on to success in the Cheltenham Gold Cup and the media reaction to Kauto Star's mistakes at Kempton, and to a last-fence blunder in the AON Chase at Newbury in February, seemed to be overdone. Kauto Star was let down a little after Christmas and his trainer reported before Newbury that he had 'left plenty to work on'. Starting at 9/2-on, Kauto Star made fairly heavy weather of conceding 10 lb to L'Ami in an event which effectively turned into a sprint from three out, responding gamely on the run-in after his howler to prevail by a neck.

Kauto Star was sent off at 5/4 favourite in the eighteen-runner totesport Cheltenham Gold Cup, the longest odds for any of his six races in the latest season (he had been odds on for all his races since the Lancashire Chase). Illustrating the difficulty of getting leading Gold Cup hopes to Cheltenham, neither of the two previous winners Kicking King or War of Attrition made the line-up. Kicking King suffered a recurrence of the tendon injury before Christmas that had kept him off the course after winning the previous season's King George and War of Attrition was sidelined after returning from exercise with heat in a leg thirteen days before the Gold Cup. War of Attrition's injury came close on the heels of the defection of another leading Irish contender, In Compliance, who had beaten War of Attrition in the Punchestown Chase in December, but was 'not firing' in his Gold Cup preparation. Exotic Dancer started second favourite at 9/2, with the Newbury Hennessy winner State of Play next at 8/1, followed by The Listener at 14/1, L'Ami, Beef Or Salmon and My Will at 16/1, the improving Irish handicapper Cane Brake (from Kicking King's stable) at 20/1, and 25/1 bar. The introduction of a minimum BHB rating of 130 for runners in Cheltenham's top races did not stop French-trained rank outsiders Sybellius d'Artaix and Marble Garden—both owned by Fergus Wilson whose so-called 'vanity' runners Astonville and Turnium had been withdrawn by the stewards in 2006—from taking their place in the Gold Cup line-up after running earlier at the meeting in the Queen Mother Champion Chase and Champion Hurdle respectively.

Kauto Star's rivals put his jumping and stamina under considerably less pressure than anticipated, the gallop much steadier than usual for a championship event. The patiently-ridden Kauto Star jumped well, except for a solitary mistake at the last (nothing like so serious as those at Kempton and Newbury). He made it look easy, quickening decisively to lead at the second last after Walsh manoeuvred him wide to get a clear run off the home turn. Held in briefly by Kauto Star and then done no favours by a loose horse, Exotic Dancer never looked like eating into Kauto Star's advantage, going down by two and a half lengths, with 40/1-shot Turpin Green, showing improved form in first-time blinkers, the same distance away in third, five lengths clear of fourth-placed Monkerhostin, last seen in the King George. Cane Brake, State of Play and L'Ami came next, with the previous year's third Forget The Past back in tenth, a place in front of The Listener. The fact that Marble Garden was still in touch when falling six out was an indication of how steadily the field had gone, as was the unusually large number still making up the leading group turning into the home straight. 'Once he was settled, I never had any

totesport Cheltenham Gold Cup Chase—plenty still in contention after a steady pace as the grey Neptune Collonges leads into the straight; the big two Kauto Star (left) and Exotic Dancer (cheekpieces, tracking the riderless Idle Talk) are beginning to make their moves

. . . the Million is landed despite another last-fence mistake;
Exotic Dancer (right) finishes a clear second, ahead of the blinkered Turpin Green (left)

worries . . . Paul Nicholls and his team had him spot-on and the only question was when to press the button,' said Walsh after a copybook ride in which Kauto Star never left the inside until brought to make his challenge. Kauto Star was Walsh's first Cheltenham Gold Cup winner, and the second for his trainer Paul Nicholls who won in 1999 with See More Business. Nicholls couldn't disguise his relief afterwards. 'Before the race, I kept hearing this rubbish, knocking him. He has become a public horse and all people seemed to do was pick holes in him. I found it hard to take. OK, he's had a few scares, but he's never looked like falling and is unbeaten all season. We always believed in him and he's been awesome, different class.' Old habits die hard, however, and the reports of the Gold Cup still talked about Kauto Star's 'fallibility', of his having a 'kink', of making his 'trademark blunder at the final fence'. My Way de Solzen in the Arkle and Voy Por Ustedes (who'd unseated on his Cheltenham prep run) in the Queen Mother Champion Chase both made mistakes in the closing stages on the way to their championship victories, but there was no comparable media focus on those much more serious errors.

Desert Orchid appeared once more in the 1988/9 season after winning the Gold Cup, spoiling his record with an uncharacteristic fall in the Martell Cup at Aintree. The 1995 Cheltenham Gold Cup winner Master Oaks also had an unblemished record in his Gold Cup-winning season up to Cheltenham but he was beaten afterwards in the Grand National, managing only seventh when running as though not fully recovered from his exertions at Cheltenham. Kauto Star did not run again after the Gold Cup. His success in the Cheltenham Gold Cup took his seasonal earnings to £607,263, a record in one season for a jumper trained in Britain and Ireland. His connections also collected 'The Betfair Million', the biggest bonus ever won in jumping. Bonuses are becoming a well-used marketing tool for sponsors—another betting exchange, WBX, offered £1m for a hurdler winning the WBX-sponsored 'Fighting Fifth', the Christmas Hurdle and the Champion—and Kauto Star was not the only horse chasing one at the Festival. Detroit City, favourite for the Champion Hurdle, would have landed an additional £200,000 offered by Boylesports if he had added the championship to his success in the International (formerly the Bula) over the course in December. Gaspara earned a £75,000 bonus from Imperial Cup sponsors Sunderlands for adding a race at the Festival to her success at Sandown (a bonus landed twice before by the Pipe stable, with Olympian in 1993 and Blowing Wind in 1998). Paddy Power linked a sponsored bumper at

Naas with success in the Champion Bumper and Plumpton racecourse put up £50,000 for any first-season chaser who went on to Festival success after winning at the Sussex course—Voy Por Ustedes scooped the latter bonus (then £25,000) in 2005/6. Kauto Star had a virtually unassailable lead in the Racing UK Order of Merit even before he won the Gold Cup. In its third year, the points-based Order of Merit had an amended prize structure with prizes for first (£200,000), second (£75,000) and third (£25,000) replacing the previous prizes for top hurdler, top chaser and overall winner. The Old Roan Chase was the first of sixty-five selected important races counting towards the Order of Merit which concluded on the last day of the season with the Celebration Chase and Betfred Gold Cup at Sandown, where Kauto Star was paraded before the first race as his connections collected their prizes. The programme for Kauto Star in the 2007/8 season was outlined as: the Lancashire Chase (sponsors Betfair having announced the bonus will be offered again), the Tingle Creek, the King George, the two-mile Game Spirit (rather than the same day's AON) and the Gold Cup. Jumping's followers everywhere will be keeping their fingers crossed.

Kauto Star (FR) (b.g. 2000)	Village Star (FR) (ch 1983)	Moulin (ch 1976)	Mill Reef / High Fidelyty
		Glitter (br 1976)	Reliance / Glistening
	Kauto Relka (FR) (b 1993)	Port Etienne (b 1983)	Mill Reef / Sierra Morena
		Kautorette (br 1981)	Kautokeino / Verdurette

    The angular Kauto Star began life in France. He was not raced on the Flat but was one of the best juvenile hurdlers of his year, coming to the attention of

Mr Clive D. Smith's "Kauto Star"

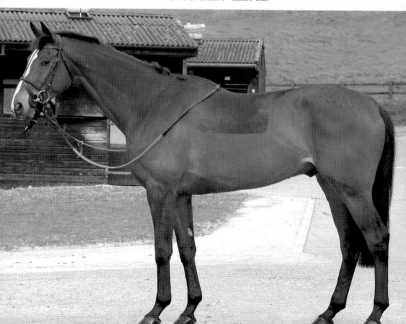

present connections for whom he was bought out of Serge Foucher's stable privately as a four-year-old for a reported €400,000. Indeed, Foucher held Kauto Star in such high esteem that he quickly dubbed him 'L'Extraterrestre', a sporting nickname of particular significance in France as it was also regularly used to describe the 'other-worldly' talents of popular Spanish cycling champion Miguel Indurain, a five-times Tour de France winner in the early-'nineties. Kauto Star's sire and dam are both French, his sire Village Star a late-developer who won the Grand Prix de Saint-Cloud as a five-year-old, and his dam the unraced Kauto Relka. The latter is a half-sister to Kauto Ray, a winner over hurdles and fences (the listed Prix James Hennessy Chase, for four-year-olds, at Auteuil). Kauto Ray is the only other 'black type' winner in recent generations of Kauto Star's family, further details of which can be found in earlier Annuals. Two of Kauto Star's younger siblings, three-year-old Kauto Relko and yearling Kauto Stone (both by With The Flow) appeared in the catalogue for the Brightwells National Hunt Sales held at Cheltenham in April. The former was withdrawn and the latter (who also appeared in the catalogue for the Tattersalls Ireland February National Hunt Sale) was led out unsold at £90,000. Kauto Relka's only other winner so far, apart from Kauto Star, is the mare Kauto Lumen Dei (by Useful), a nine-furlong winner on the Flat and at around two miles over both hurdles and fences. Kauto Star, who wears a tongue strap, is effective at two miles to three and a quarter and acts on soft going (unraced on firmer than good). Kauto Star is essentially a fine jumper, his habit of making the odd mistake only a slight weakness in his make-up, whilst his tendency to drift left off the bridle also isn't a major issue. One final point. Most commentators pronounce the first half of his name 'Kay-toe', the pronunciation used by his trainer, though linguists maintain that the name is Norse and should be pronounced 'Cow-toe'. Then again, there is 'Kor-toe' (as in auto), which his owner has used, and 'Koe-toe' which was reportedly the pronunciation adopted by staff at his original stable in France. *P. F. Nicholls*

KAVATCHA (FR) 4 gr.g. Nikos – Kaleigh's Jovite (USA) (St Jovite (USA)) [2006/7 F17s* F16d⁶ 20gᵘʳ Apr 11] smallish gelding: first foal: dam fairly useful hurdler up to around 2½m in France: fair form in bumpers, won at Taunton in January by ¾ length from She's A Player: favourite, badly hampered and unseated first in maiden on hurdling debut. *D. E. Pipe*   **h– p**
F94

KAVI (IRE) 7 ch.g. Perugino (USA) – Premier Leap (IRE) (Salmon Leap (USA)) [2006/7 c94, h–: 24g³ 24m³ Apr 15] neat gelding: fair on Flat (stays 2m): likewise over hurdles: modest form both starts over fences (let down by jumping latter stages): stays easy 3m: raced on good/good to firm going: tried blinkered. *Simon Earle*   **c–**
h102

KAWACATOOSE (IRE) 5 b.g. Imperial Ballet (IRE) – Cree's Figurine (Creetown) [2006/7 17mᵖᵘ 16mᶠ Oct 4] well held in maidens on Flat for G. Bravery: failed to complete in 2 novice hurdles, broke leg at Towcester. *Ferdy Murphy*   **h–**

KAWAGINO (IRE) 7 b.g. Perugino (USA) – Sharakawa (IRE) (Darshaan) [2006/7 c112x, h146: 16g² c17d⁴ c16d² 18s⁶ 16d 16d⁵ 17g⁴ 20g⁵ Apr 14] sturdy gelding: smart hurdler: good efforts last 3 starts, in Champion Hurdle and County Hurdle (Handicap) at Cheltenham in space of 4 days, and in Aintree Hurdle when fifth to Al Eile: not a fluent jumper and just fair form over fences: stays 2½m: acts on heavy going (unseated only start on firmer than good). *J. W. Mullins*   **c106 x**
h148

KAYCEECEE (IRE) 6 b.g. Mister Mat (FR) – Maid of Glenduragh (IRE) (Ya Zaman (USA)) [2006/7 h115, F–: c16s⁴ c22v⁶ c16s⁵ c16v² c16v³ c18s³ c18sᵘʳ c17g⁵ Mar 24] tall, useful-looking gelding: fair hurdler: modest novice chaser, often let down by jumping: should stay beyond 17f: acts on heavy going. *H. D. Daly*   **c99**
h–

KAYF KEEL 4 gr.f. Kayf Tara – Royal Keel (Long Leave) [2006/7 F13d² F13g Nov 2] first foal: dam unraced half-sister to high-class 2m hurdler Relkeel: better effort in 3-y-o bumpers when 5 lengths second to Big Secret at Exeter: will stay 2m. *R. T. Phillips*   **F74**

KAYTASH 8 b.m. Silverdale Knight – Lady Swift (Jalmood (USA)) [2006/7 20mᵘʳ 17m Apr 15] very lightly raced and little sign of ability. *K. W. Hogg, Isle of Man*   **h–**

KAZAL (FR) 6 ch.g. Villez (USA) – Moody Cloud (FR) (Cyborg (FR)) [2006/7 24v* 20v* 22v* 20v* 20d* 20v* 20v* Mar 8]   **h143 +**

    Those who tend to concentrate on British racing may not be acquainted with Kazal, but that probably won't be the case for much longer. Kazal developed into a smart novice hurdler in the latest season and, with plenty of size about him, appeals as one who could prove capable of better still in the years to come. Along with Lounaos he was one of two prominent first-season hurdlers for Eoin Griffin but, unlike that filly, his season went from strength to strength. That Kazal didn't take on the leading staying novices at one of the Festivals is something of a disappointment, seeing that he won six of his seven starts, and marked himself out as a thoroughly likeable individual.

Kazal made a winning start to his hurdling career in a three-mile novices' event at Wexford in October and was pitched straight into Grade 1 company at Navan seven weeks later, over a four-furlong shorter trip. A 33/1-shot, he improved on the form of his debut success, but was no threat behind Aran Concerto, finishing fourteen and a half lengths fourth of six. Kazal then enjoyed five wins on the bounce, ending the campaign rated just 1 lb behind Aran Concerto, highlighting that things would have been much closer had the pair met again later in the campaign. A decisive win in the Grade 3 ladbrokes.com Dorans Pride Novices' Hurdle at Limerick over Christmas was followed by a Grade 2 success at Naas just ten days later by a length and three quarters from Earth Magic, where Kazal's fighting qualities were in evidence for the first time. Kazal's next three wins further confirmed him as a tough and genuine performer who finds plenty under pressure. Firstly, in the Grade 3 Toshiba Copier Novices' Hurdle at Leopardstown, on the only occasion he has encountered ground other than heavy, Kazal rallied splendidly to beat Aitmatov (received 5 lb) by a head, allowed to keep the race despite carrying the runner-up to the right. The Grade 2 paddypower.com Johnstown Novices' Hurdle at Naas in February saw further improvement as Kazal led or disputed matters for most of the way before battling on to beat Callherwhatulike by a length and a quarter, the pair clear. With the decision made to bypass the Spa Hurdle, Kazal instead took in the Grade 2 Michael Purcell Memorial Novices' Hurdle at Thurles less than a week before the Cheltenham Festival where he did not have to repeat the best of his form to land the odds by three lengths from Chomba Womba, headed three out before once more battling back in typically game fashion. Underfoot conditions were considered unsuitable at both the Aintree and Punchestown Festivals and Kazal wasn't seen out again.

paddypower.com Johnston Novices' Hurdle, Naas—
a typically gritty display from the prolific Kazal (right) sees off the mare Callherwhatulike

Mr Joseph Comerford's "Kazal"

		Lyphard's Wish	Lyphard
	Villez (USA)	(b 1976)	Sally's Wish
	(ch 1992)	Valhalla	New Chapter
Kazal (FR)		(ch 1974)	Varig
(ch.g. 2001)		Cyborg	Arctic Tern
	Moody Cloud (FR)	(ch 1982)	Cadair
	(ch 1990)	Chattannooga Choo	In The Mood
		(ch 1981)	Folie Furieuse

The big, good-topped Kazal, who was third to The Luder in a maiden point in April 2005, will make a chaser and he will probably be competing in novice chases next season. The second foal of Moody Cloud, a winner at around two miles over both hurdles and fences in France and placed in some good races for four-year-olds over fences at Auteuil. Kazal has an unraced brother and three as-yet unraced half-brothers. His sire, Villez, has enjoyed success with several French exports, most notably Voy Por Ustedes and Le Duc. Kazal stays three miles and acts on good to soft going and goes particularly well on heavy going. *Eoin Griffin, Ireland*

KEALSHORE BOY 4 br.g. Overbury (IRE) – Rippling Brook (Phardante (FR)) **F120** [2006/7 F16v* F16v* Feb 24] good-topped gelding: first foal: dam unraced, out of half-sister to useful staying chaser Southern Star: successful in bumpers at Kelso in January and Newcastle (beat Of Course by head, pair clear) in February: improved again when 1½ lengths second to Theatrical Moment in valuable event at Aintree after end of season: will be suited by further than 2m: sold 290,000 gns Doncaster May Sales to join J. Howard Johnson. *G. M. Moore*

KEALSHORE LAD 6 b.g. Supreme Leader – Our Aisling (Blakeney) [2006/7 F105: **h112**
20d* 25s⁵ 20s⁵ 20s² 24v² Mar 10] useful-looking gelding: fair novice hurdler: won at
Bangor in October: good efforts when runner-up in handicaps last 2 starts, travelled best
long way when beaten 5 lengths by Climax at Ayr second occasion: may prove best short
of 3m when conditions are testing: raced on going softer than good (acts on heavy).
D. McCain Jnr

KEDGEREE 5 b.g. Fleetwood (IRE) – Coh Sho No (Old Vic) [2006/7 F94: F16d³ 16v⁶ **h90 p**
16s³ 17g⁵ Mar 24] workmanlike gelding: fair form both starts in bumpers: yet to run to **F92**
same level over hurdles, but remains open to improvement granted greater emphasis on
stamina. *H. D. Daly*

KEEL (IRE) 4 b.g. Carrowkeel (IRE) – First Degree (Sabrehill (USA)) [2006/7 16d **h96**
16g⁶ 16s 16dᵖᵘ Nov 11] fairly useful on Flat (stays 1¼m), successful twice in 2006, sold
out of J. Osborne's stable 38,000 gns Newmarket July Sales: easily best effort in juvenile
hurdles when sixth at Gowran. *Anthony Mullins, Ireland*

KEELUNG (USA) 6 b.g. Lear Fan (USA) – Miss Universal (IRE) (Lycius (USA)) **h86**
[2006/7 16mᵖᵘ 16s³ 16g 16s⁶ Oct 27] compact gelding: fairly useful 1¼m winner in 2004
for M. Jarvis, seemed to go wrong way temperamentally later that year (tried in cheekpieces): modest form over hurdles (fell first on debut for P. Hobbs): tongue tied final
outing (possibly amiss). *R. Ford*

KEEN AND EASY 7 b.m. Keen – Mildame (Milford) [2006/7 F17s 20m Jun 13] half- **h–**
sister to 2 winning chasers by Primitive Rising, including at 3m Just Adam: dam lightly **F–**
raced: ran out in maiden point: well held in mares bumper/maiden hurdle. *Miss J. S. Davis*

KEENAN'S FUTURE (IRE) 6 ch.g. Safety Catch (USA) – The Singer (IRE) (Acco- **c102**
rdion) [2006/7 h113, F102: c22sᵇᵈ c20g³ c19drᵒ c23m* Apr 22] tall gelding: successful **h–**
both completed starts over hurdles: first form over fences (ran out third outing) when
winning maiden at Stratford easily by length from Chicago Bulls: stays 23f: acts on heavy
and good to firm going. *Ian Williams*

KEENOATS 6 b.m. Keen – Aintree Oats (Oats) [2006/7 F17s F16d Feb 2] fourth foal: **F–**
half-sister to fair pointer/hunter chaser Tooley Park (by Homo Sapien), effective at 2m to
3m: dam winning pointer: well beaten in bumpers: headstrong. *J. W. Mullins*

KEEN WARRIOR 7 gr.g. Keen – Briden (Minster Son) [2006/7 h86, F80: 16s⁶ 16d² **h108**
16d 19v² 19d⁴ 16v³ 20v* Feb 17] tall gelding: fair hurdler: improved form when winning
handicap at Uttoxeter by 8 lengths from Speedro: will stay 2¾m: raced on good going or
softer (acts on heavy). *Mrs S. Lamyman*

KEEPASHARPLOOKOUT (IRE) 5 b.g. Rossini (USA) – Zoyce (Zilzal (USA)) **h77 §**
[2006/7 h79§: 20gᵖᵘ 17s⁴ 17d⁵ 16gᵖᵘ 17m 24m Jul 12] small gelding: poor maiden
hurdler: stays 19f: tried in cheekpieces/eyeshields/tongue strap: one to treat with caution
(virtually refused to race sixth 2005/6 outing). *C. W. Moore*

KEEPATEM (IRE) 11 ch.g. Be My Native (USA) – Ariannrun (Deep Run) [2006/7 **c124**
c26sᵖᵘ c25s³ c25v⁴ c22v² c32v² c33s⁵ Mar 17] rather leggy gelding: winning hurdler: **h–**
fairly useful handicap chaser: left M. Morris prior to reappearance: back near best when
runner-up at Uttoxeter and Kelso, travelled strongly long way when beaten 1¼ lengths by
Bellaney Jewel in Scottish Borders National at latter: stays 4m: raced on good going or
softer (acts on heavy). *Jonjo O'Neill*

KEEPERS MEAD (IRE) 9 ch.g. Aahsaylad – Runaway Pilot (Cheval) [2006/7 c81+, **c–**
h113: 26m c23m⁴ 25d Nov 18] useful-looking gelding: fair handicap hurdler, lame final **h–**
outing: not fluent both starts over fences: stays 3¼m: acts on heavy going: temperament
under suspicion (has looked awkward under pressure). *R. H. Alner*

KEEPITSECRET (IRE) 6 b.g. Topanoora – Try Your Case (Proverb) [2006/7 F17g* **c– p**
F16m⁴ 16s 17s 16d c16sᵖᵘ Feb 26] €70,000 4-y-o: well-made gelding: half-brother to **h– p**
several winners, including fairly useful chaser up to 3m Native Man (by Be My Native): **F94**
dam, winning pointer, half-sister to dam of One Man: won bumper at Hereford on debut
in October easily by 2½ lengths from Check Up: well held in novice hurdles in 3-week
period, but left impression capable of better: folded tamely on chasing debut: will be
suited by further than 17f. *Jonjo O'Neill*

KEEP SMILING (IRE) 11 b.g. Broken Hearted – Laugh Away (Furry Glen) [2006/7 **c– x**
c–x, h–: c24sᵖᵘ 18vᵖᵘ c24dᵖᵘ c25sᶠ Apr 1] tall, rather sparely-made gelding: maiden **h–**
hurdler: winning chaser, no form since 2004/5: stays 2¾m: acts on good to soft going:
wore cheekpieces last 3 starts: poor jumper. *Mrs C. J. Kerr*

KEEP THE DAY JOB 8 b.m. Thowra (FR) – Mitsubishi Colour (Cut Above) [2006/7 **h–**
21vᵖᵘ 22sᵖᵘ Jan 16] close-coupled mare: bad pointer: pulled up both starts over hurdles:
tried blinkered. *F. E. Sutherland*

KEEPTHEDREAMALIVE 9 gr.g. Roselier (FR) – Nicklup (Netherkelly) [2006/7 **c103 x**
c114, h123: c24gᵖᵘ c20g² c17d³ Oct 31] rather leggy gelding: fairly useful handicap **h–**
hurdler on his day: fair maiden chaser: should stay 3m: probably acts on any going: often
let down by jumping over fences. *R. H. Buckler*

KEIRAN (IRE) 13 b.g. Be My Native (USA) – Myra Gaye (Buckskin (FR)) [2006/7 **c–**
24sᵖᵘ Dec 8] sturdy gelding: fairly useful handicap chaser: winning hurdler: off 2 years, **h–**
dropped away quickly 3 out in handicap at Southwell: stays at least 25f: acts on good to
firm and heavy going: successful blinkered or not. *H. P. Hogarth*

KELAMI (FR) 9 b.g. Lute Antique (FR) – Voltige de Nievre (FR) (Brezzo (FR)) **c140**
[2006/7 20s* c25s c21s³ c24d c24g² c28sᵖᵘ c21s² c36gᵖᵘ Apr 14] tall gelding: lightly **h?**
raced over hurdles, successful at Compiegne in October: useful chaser: showed himself
as good as ever when ¾-length second of 18 to idling Rambling Minster in valuable
handicap at Sandown fifth outing: lost touch from second Canal Turn in Grand National
at Aintree final start: stays 29f: raced on good going or softer (acts on heavy): tried
blinkered: has had tongue tied: sound jumper. *F. Doumen, France*

KELANTAN 10 b.g. Kris – Surf Bird (Shareef Dancer (USA)) [2006/7 c106, h–: c24sᵖᵘ **c–**
Dec 1] tall gelding: won completed outing over hurdles: fair handicap chaser: off 13 **h–**
months, soon pulled up and dismounted in 4-runner race at Sandown: stays 25f: acts on
soft going: effective with or without cheekpieces. *K. C. Bailey*

KELLBURY 5 b.g. Overbury (IRE) – Kellamba (Netherkelly) [2006/7 H87: 20s² 16s⁵ **h91**
20s⁶ Jan 31] strong gelding: clear second to Pass It On in novice at Leicester on hurdling
debut: disappointing both starts after: likely to stay beyond 2½m: raced on good to soft/
soft ground. *H. D. Daly*

KELLY (SAF) 10 b.g. Ethique (ARG) – Dancing Flower (SAF) (Dancing Champ **c117**
(USA)) [2006/7 c117+, h–: c23sᶠ Dec 1] strong gelding: winning hurdler: unbeaten in 3 **h–**
completed starts over fences: off 18 months, every chance when fell 3 out in handicap
won by Abragante at Taunton: stays easy 3m: acts on soft and good to firm going: room
for improvement in jumping, but may still do better over fences. *Miss Venetia Williams*

KELLYS FABLE 7 b.g. Thowra (FR) – Kellys Special (Netherkelly) [2006/7 c–, h–: **c–**
c21mᵖᵘ c19dᵘʳ c21gᵖᵘ Jun 20] tall gelding: no solid form over hurdles/in chases: tried in **h–**
cheekpieces/tongue tied: sold £3,000 Ascot August Sales, won maiden point in April.
J. W. Mullins

KELNIK GLORY 11 b.g. Nalchik (USA) – Areal (IRE) (Roselier (FR)) [2006/7 24f* **h96**
22m³ 22m³ Aug 3] placed both completed starts in points in 2006: modest hurdler: won
weak maiden at Worcester in June: better form both outings after: stays 3m: acts on any
going: tried visored/blinkered. *Mrs S. M. Johnson*

KELREV (FR) 9 ch.g. Video Rock (FR) – Bellile II (FR) (Brezzo (FR)) [2006/7 c137§, **c118 §**
h–: c20d c20s⁴ c16s⁶ 19d² 19s c20s c21gᵖᵘ Mar 15] leggy, angular gelding: fairly useful **h120 §**
hurdler, ¾-length second to Lord of Beauty in handicap at Ascot fourth outing: useful
handicap chaser, below best in 2006/7: stays 21f: has won on heavy going, best form
under less testing conditions. *Miss Venetia Williams*

KELTECH LEADER (IRE) 8 b.g. Supreme Leader – Alice O'Malley (The Parson) **h99**
[2006/7 21d² Oct 30] €54,000 4-y-o: fourth foal: half-brother to fair/ungenuine staying
hurdler Reasonable Reserve (by Fourstars Allstar) and bumper/17f chase winner Intacta
Print (by Glacial Storm): dam unraced half-sister to smart staying chasers Chives and
McKelvey. 16/1 from 7/1, 2 lengths second to Toemac in novice hurdle at Plumpton on
belated debut: presumably hard to train. *R. H. Alner*

KELTIC BARD 10 b.g. Emperor Jones (USA) – Broughton Singer (IRE) (Common **c121**
Grounds) [2006/7 c133, h–: c25mᵖᵘ c26s c25s⁵ c20sᵖᵘ Jan 13] good-topped gelding: **h–**
smart novice chaser in 2003/4: very lightly raced since (suffered stress fracture to near-
fore cannon bone after only outing in 2005/6 and little encouragement on return): stays
2½m: acts on soft going: tried in cheekpieces/visor. *C. J. Mann*

KELTIC LORD 11 b.g. Arctic Lord – Scarlet Dymond (Rymer) [2006/7 c111, h85: **c95 x**
c25m⁵ c23m⁵ c24mᶠ 24m⁴ c23g³ c21fᶠ 24d c21f³ c24mᵖᵘ Oct 12] sparely-made gelding: **h83**
lightly raced over hurdles: handicap chaser, only modest form and often let down by
jumping in 2006/7: walked over in point in April: stays 3¼m: acts on firm going: tongue
tied once. *P. W. Hiatt*

KELTIC MOON (IRE) 6 b.g. Posidonas – Birthday Honours (IRE) (Florida Son) **F74**
[2006/7 F17v⁴ Feb 13] lengthy gelding: first foal: dam unraced sister to useful 2½m

chaser Kurakka: well-held fourth of 6 to King Jack in bumper at Folkestone on debut. *N. J. Gifford*

KELTIC ROCK 8 ch.g. Bigstone (IRE) – Sibley (Northfields (USA)) [2006/7 19g* Nov 5] tall gelding: fair hurdler: off 20 months, didn't need to be at best to win novice at Market Rasen by 8 lengths from Mr Shambles, making all (reportedly suffered over-reach): stays 2¾m: raced on good going or softer (acts on soft). *J. A. Geake*   **h94**

KELV 6 gr.g. Karinga Bay – Pendle Princess (Broxted) [2006/7 F83: 16s 16d 16g 20g* 20g^{pu} Apr 27] good-topped gelding: bumper winner: form (modest) over hurdles only when winning 18-runner event at Hereford in April on handicap debut by 7 lengths from Oeil d'Estruval: stays 2½m. *J. A. B. Old*   **h96**

KEMPLEY GREEN (IRE) 4 b.g. Revoque (IRE) – Alaroos (IRE) (Persian Bold) [2006/7 F13d F13g^5 16gf 17g^2 Apr 20] half-brother to useful 1997 2-y-o 6f winner Arawak Cay (by Common Grounds) and Persian Conquest (by Don't Forget Me): dam unraced: better effort in 3-y-o bumpers when fifth to Kid Charlemagne at Towcester: modest form in frame in 2 novice hurdles, 1¼ lengths second to Sabre Hongrois at Hereford. *M. Scudamore*   **h97 +** **F77**

KEMPSKI 7 b.g. Petoski – Little Katrina (Little Buskins) [2006/7 c–, h86: 20s^{pu} 17s^5 17v^3 22s^2 22v^6 20v* 20v* 20s^3 22v^6 20s^4 20v^4 21v^{pu} 22g^3 20s Apr 26] workmanlike gelding: fair handicap hurdler: won twice at Ayr in December: behind when refused sixth only outing over fences: stays 2¾m: raced on good going or softer (acts on heavy): tried in cheekpieces, usually wears blinkers: often front runner. *R. Nixon*   **c–** **h101**

KEN'S DREAM 8 b.g. Bin Ajwaad (IRE) – Shoag (USA) (Affirmed (USA)) [2006/7 h117: 16f^F 16m* 17d* Jul 22] workmanlike gelding: fairly useful hurdler: won novices at Uttoxeter and Market Rasen in July, better effort when beating Wiggy Smith 5 lengths at latter: likely to stay 2½m: acts on soft and good to firm ground. *Mrs L. Wadham*   **h121**

KENTFORD LADY 6 b.m. Emperor Fountain – Kentford Duchess (Jupiter Island) [2006/7 h75: 17d 24g^{pu} Jul 21] tall, close-coupled mare: novice hurdler, poor form at best: stays 21f. *R. Ford*   **h–**

KENTFORD MIST 4 gr.f. Silver Patriarch (IRE) – Kentford Duchess (Jupiter Island) [2006/7 F12s F16d^5 F16g Mar 29] good-topped filly: third foal: dam unraced half-sister to useful 2½m/3m chaser The Land Agent: poor form in bumpers, though has shaped as if capable of better. *J. W. Mullins*   **F75 +**

KENTUCKY BANKES 5 b.g. Bluegrass Prince (IRE) – Countess Bankes (Son Pardo) [2006/7 17m Jun 8] of little account at 2 yrs for W. Turner: tailed off on hurdling debut. *N. G. Ayliffe*   **h–**

KENTUCKY BLUE (IRE) 7 b.g. Revoque (IRE) – Delta Town (USA) (Sanglamore (USA)) [2006/7 h120: c16v^2 c16d^3 c19s^5 c16v^3 c16g^2 Apr 7] smallish, sturdy gelding: fairly useful handicap hurdler: fair maiden chaser: stays 19f: acts on heavy and good to firm going: has worn headgear (has looked less than straightforward). *T. D. Easterby*   **c106** **h–**

KEN'TUCKY (FR) 9 b.g. Video Rock (FR) – La Salamandre (FR) (Pot d'Or (FR)) [2006/7 c122, h–: c25m^{pu} May 18] leggy gelding: winning hurdler: fairly useful chaser: stayed 3¼m: acted on good to soft going: dead. *A. King*   **c–** **h–**

KENTUCKY SKY 5 gr.m. Cloudings (IRE) – Dawn Gait (Fearless Action (USA)) [2006/7 F17m^2 Apr 15] 5,000 4-y-o: third foal: dam unraced, out of half-sister to Champion Hurdle winner Royal Gait: 2½ lengths second to Issaquah in mares bumper at Market Rasen on debut, running on strongly from well back. *Mrs L. Wadham*   **F86**

KENWYN 5 b.g. Efisio – Vilany (Never So Bold) [2006/7 17g 17d^6 16s 19v 19s 16f 17g Apr 27] compact gelding: modest maiden on Flat (probably stays 1m) at 3 yrs for S. Earle: looks to have stamina limitations over hurdles. *K. Bishop*   **h69**

KENZO III (FR) 9 ch.g. Agent Bleu (FR) – Kelinda (FR) (Pot d'Or (FR)) [2006/7 c19d* c20s^{pu} c24g^3 c25g^2 Apr 18] tall, angular gelding: lightly raced: useful form over fences: off 20 months, won handicap at Hereford in December by length from Kalca Mome: better efforts when placed in similar events last 2 outings, ½-length second to Alexanderthegreat at Cheltenham: stays 25f: acts on good to soft going: front runner/races prominently. *N. J. Henderson*   **c131**

KERCABELLEC (FR) 9 b. or br.g. Useful (FR) – Marie de Geneve (FR) (Nishapour (FR)) [2006/7 c94, h–: c16s^4 c21d^3 c21s^4 c16d^4 c16g^5 c24m^{pu} c21d^{ro} c20s^4 c20g* c20d^{ur} c24v^5 c20v c16v^4 c16s^5 c20v* c20s* c22d* c21g^5 Apr 9] lengthy gelding: winning hurdler: fair handicap chaser: won at Market Rasen (3) and Leicester in 2006/7: stays 2¾m: acts on good to firm and heavy going: tried tongue tied: headstrong (ran out seventh start). *J. R. Cornwall*   **c103** **h–**

KERRYHEAD WINDFARM (IRE) 9 br.g. Bob Back (USA) – Kerryhead Girl **c132 x**
(IRE) (Be My Native (USA)) [2006/7 c124x, h152?: 21s c21d³ c24s² c24v c28s c29m **h–**
Apr 9] tall, good-topped gelding: winning hurdler, appeared to excel himself when
second to Asian Maze in Champion Stayers' Hurdle at Punchestown final start in 2005/6:
useful chaser: best effort when 4 lengths second to Cane Brake in Troytown Handicap at
Navan: well held in Irish National final outing: stays 3m: acts on heavy going: held up:
usually makes mistakes. *M. Hourigan, Ireland*

KERRY LADS (IRE) 12 ch.g. Mister Lord (USA) – Minstrel Top (Black Minstrel) **c128**
[2006/7 c127x, h–: c26s⁵ c25v² c25v* c22v³ c25g³ c24sᵖᵘ Apr 26] workmanlike gelding: **h–**
fairly useful handicap chaser: won 5-runner event at Wetherby (third course success) in
January by ½ length from Sharp Jack: creditable efforts other starts in 2006/7 prior to
final one: stays 33f: acts on heavy and good to firm going: wears cheekpieces: usually
races prominently. *Miss Lucinda V. Russell*

KERRY'S BLADE (IRE) 5 ch.g. Daggers Drawn (USA) – Treasure (IRE) (Treasure **c100**
Kay) [2006/7 h98: 16s c16f⁴ c21m* c20gᶠ c16g Oct 7] tall gelding: modest hurdler: fair **h–**
form when winning handicap chase at Sedgefield in September: well beaten both other
completed starts over fences: stays 21f: acts on good to firm and good to soft going: has
worn blinkers/cheekpieces: joined Micky Hammond. *P. C. Haslam*

KERSTINO TWO 10 b.g. Cruise Missile – Cresswell (Push On) [2006/7 c91: c21g³ **c131**
c21g² c24g* c24g* c23g* c24d² c26s² c24v* Jan 6] tall gelding: useful chaser: left Mrs
Caroline Keevil after second start: much improved after, winning handicaps at Ludlow
(amateur event) in October, Huntingdon and Taunton in November and Sandown (by 3
lengths from Preacher Boy) in January: reportedly broke leg on gallops in early-March:
stayed 3¼m: acted on good to firm and heavy going: usually raced prominently.
C. E. Longsdon

KESTICK 12 b.g. Roscoe Blake – Hop The Twig (Full of Hope) [2006/7 c97: c21g **c89**
May 3] sturdy gelding: winning pointer/hunter chaser: fairly useful at best: probably stays
3¼m: acts on good to firm going. *Mrs R. Kennen*

KESTLE MILL (IRE) 11 ch.g. Be My Guest (USA) – Tatisha (Habitat) [2006/7 c–, **c–**
h–: c24m Jun 8] workmanlike gelding: won maiden point in 2004: little show in other **h–**
events: tried tongue tied. *B. G. Powell*

KESWICK (IRE) 7 b. or br.g. Taipan (IRE) – Tigrinium Splenden (Buckley) [2006/7 **c–**
h101: 19dᶠ 22sᵖᵘ c19dᶠ c19vᵖᵘ 22dᵖᵘ 19m Apr 17] rangy gelding: modest novice hurdler: **h96 d**
won at Towcester in June: sold out of N. Henderson's stable 14,000 gns Doncaster August
Sales: no form after, let down by jumping over fences: should stay beyond 19f: tried in
cheekpieces. *Mrs S. Gardner*

KETTYSJAMES (IRE) 9 ch.g. Over The River (FR) – Friendly Sea (Callernish) **c82**
[2006/7 c82: c26dᵖᵘ 21v c24s c20s³ c21vᵖᵘ c26dᵇᵈ c23s² c25mᶠ c22mᵖᵘ Apr 15] win- **h–**
ning pointer: poor maiden chaser: stays 25f: acts on soft going: has worn cheekpieces.
J. G. Carr, Ireland

KETY STAR (FR) 9 b.g. Bojador (FR) – Danystar (FR) (Alycos (FR)) [2006/7 c–, h–: **c112**
c20m⁵ c16m* c20m⁵ c17m³ c16d⁴ c20g² c24dᵖᵘ c21d c16g Mar 28] leggy gelding: **h–**
maiden hurdler: fair handicap chaser: won at Uttoxeter in July: effective from 2m to
2½m: acts on good to firm and good to soft going: often let down by jumping over fences:
inconsistent. *Miss Venetia Williams*

KEW GREEN (USA) 9 b. or br.g. Brocco (USA) – Jump With Joy (USA) (Linkage **h71 p**
(USA)) [2006/7 16g⁵ Mar 16] smart on Flat (stays 10.5f), successful in April: favourite,
around 26 lengths fifth to Peacock in conditional jockeys maiden at Fakenham on
hurdling debut: likely to need sharp 2m: should be better for experience. *P. R. Webber*

KEY IN 6 ch.m. Unfuwain (USA) – Fleet Key (Afleet (CAN)) [2006/7 h67: 16s Dec 8] **h–**
smallish, angular mare: little form over hurdles: tried visored: usually tongue tied.
I. W. McInnes

KEYNEEMA 5 b.g. Kayf Tara – Nothings Forever (Oats) [2006/7 F–: F17d⁶ 16d Oct 5] **h–**
well beaten in bumpers/maiden hurdle. *Karen George* **F–**

KEY PARTNERS (IRE) 6 b.g. Key of Luck (USA) – Teacher Preacher (IRE) (Taufan **h–**
(USA)) [2006/7 16s 16g Apr 14] fair on Flat (stays 1½m): well held in novice hurdles,
taking strong hold. *B. D. Leavy*

KEY PHIL (FR) 9 ch.g. Beyssac (FR) – Rivolie (FR) (Mistigri) [2006/7 c126+, h–: **c127**
c20g* c25m³ c20v² 20d* c24g⁵ Oct 14] good-topped gelding: fairly useful handicap **h111**
chaser: successful at Huntingdon (by 16 lengths from Navarone) in May: first start over

KEY

hurdles in Britain, won novice at Worcester in September by 10 lengths from Grand Slam Hero: probably stays 3m: acts on heavy going: not a fluent jumper. *D. J. Wintle*

KEY TIME (IRE) 5 b.g. Darshaan – Kasota (IRE) (Alzao (USA)) [2006/7 20g² 20g* 20m* Feb 4] smallish gelding: useful on Flat (stays 21f), successful 5 times in 2006 for Sir Mark Prescott: easily made all in novice hurdles at Musselburgh in December and February (beat Bob's Dream 6 lengths): will stay 3m: room for improvement in jumping, but still likely to go on to better things. *J. Howard Johnson*   **h123 p**

KEY TO CAIUS (IRE) 4 b.g. Shinko Forest (IRE) – Alpine Lady (IRE) (Tirol) [2006/7 F14s F16d Jan 19] fourth foal: half-brother to useful winner up to 7f Silver Wraith (by Danehill Dancer) and 5f (at 2 yrs) and 7f winner Lady Piste (by Ali-Royal): dam tailed off both starts: well beaten in bumpers. *R. F. Fisher*   **F—**

KHACHATURIAN (IRE) 4 b.g. Spectrum (IRE) – On Air (FR) (Chief Singer) [2006/7 16v² 16s⁵ 17g^F 17g⁵ 20g Apr 12] tall gelding: dam winning hurdler: fairly useful on Flat (stays 1¾m), successful in July, sold out of T. Stack's stable 45,000 gns Newmarket Autumn Sales: modest form over hurdles (has been let down by jumping): should stay beyond 17f: front runner. *D. McCain Jnr*   **h97**

KHADIJA 6 ch.m. Kadastrof (FR) – Dark Sirona (Pitskelly) [2006/7 h–, F62: 26d² 19m^pu 21s⁵ 24s⁵ 20d 24v^pu 24d² 22g⁶ Apr 27] rather unfurnished mare: poor novice hurdler: stays 3¼m: acts on soft ground. *R. Dickin*   **h83**

KHARAK (FR) 8 gr.g. Danehill (USA) – Khariyda (FR) (Shakapour) [2006/7 c98, h95: 24d⁵ 22v c16v^pu c16g⁴ c20g Apr 7] good-bodied gelding: maiden chaser/winning hurdler, below best in 2006/7: stays 3m: acts on any going: tried in cheekpieces/visor: sold 1,600 gns Doncaster May Sales. *Mrs S. C. Bradburne*   **c85 h90**

KHARALINE (IRE) 5 b.m. Spectrum (IRE) – Kharaliya (FR) (Doyoun) [2006/7 16g 17g^pu Apr 7] half-sister to fair 2m hurdler Wilfred (by Desert King) and modest 2m hurdler/chaser Adecco (by Eagle Eyed): no form since debut at 2 yrs, including over hurdles. *Mrs Tracey Barfoot-Saunt*   **h—**

KHASAB (IRE) 6 br.g. Supreme Leader – Tower Princess (IRE) (King's Ride) [2006/7 17s* 17d 20s² Apr 26] €26,000 3-y-o: third foal: dam unraced out of half-sister to smart staying chasers Calling Brave and Ottowa: won maiden hurdle at Hereford on debut in January by 3 lengths from stable-companion President Royal: upped in trip, fairly useful form when ½-length second to Sharp Reply in handicap at Perth: will stay beyond 2½m: open to further improvement. *P. J. Hobbs*   **h117 p**

Pontin's Holidays Newton Novices' Hurdle, Haydock—owner Trevor Hemmings recoups his sponsorship money with Kicks For Free (centre); the blundering Self Respect (left) fills second

KHAYSAR (IRE) 9 b.g. Pennekamp (USA) – Khaytada (IRE) (Doyoun) [2006/7 h–: **h94** 21g 18m² 22m⁴ 20m Jun 8] smallish, sturdy gelding: modest handicap hurdler: stays 2¾m: acts on soft and good to firm going. *N. B. King*

KHAZAR (FR) 4 b.c. Anabaa (USA) – Khalisa (IRE) (Persian Bold) [2006/7 16d⁶ 17s⁶ **h95** 17v⁴ Feb 13] leggy colt: fairly useful on Flat (stays 10.5f), successful twice from 4 starts in 2006, sold out of A. de Royer Dupre's stable €320,000 Goffs Arc Sale: modest form over hurdles: likely to prove best at 2m under less testing conditions. *T. Doumen, France*

KHETAAB (IRE) 5 b.g. Alhaarth (IRE) – Liberi Versi (IRE) (Last Tycoon) [2006/7 **h–** 16d Dec 28] modest maiden on Flat (stays 1m) for E. Alston: bled on hurdling debut. *D. McCain Jnr*

KHETAAM (IRE) 9 b.g. Machiavellian (USA) – Ghassak (IRE) (Persian Bold) **c121 §** [2006/7 h130: c16s² c16s⁴ c17dF c17s³ c18v* c17v³ c17m⁶ c21mᵖᵘ Apr 27] lengthy **h–** gelding: useful hurdler: fairly useful novice chaser: 14 lengths third to Schindlers Hunt in Grade 1 at Leopardstown: didn't have to repeat that form to win maiden at Gowran in February: lame final outing: stays 2½m: acts on heavy and good to firm going: tried in blinkers, including in 2006/7: unreliable. *N. Meade, Ireland*

KHUDABAD (IRE) 6 ch.g. Ashkalani (IRE) – Kozana (Kris) [2006/7 19v 23v 16s 20v **h93** 20g⁴ 16m Apr 8] €6,000 3-y-o: angular gelding: half-brother to winning staying hurdler Khazari (by Shahrastani): dam French 1m and 1¼m winner, third in Arc: bumper winner: modest novice hurdler: stays 2½m: acts on firm and soft ground: fifth in minor event on Flat debut in April. *Frederick John Bowles, Ireland*

KHUMBU 5 b.g. Zaffaran (USA) – Kirov Royale (Rambo Dancer (CAN)) [2006/7 **F77** F16v⁵ F16v Jan 12] 13,500 3-y-o, resold 34,000 3-y-o: quite good-topped gelding: second foal: dam lightly-raced maiden on Flat/over hurdles: better effort in bumpers when fifth to Lodge Lane at Uttoxeter. *R. T. Phillips*

KIA KAHA 5 b.g. Sir Harry Lewis (USA) – Not Enough (Balinger) [2006/7 F16m* **F106** F16d³ Dec 16] 31,000 3-y-o: useful-looking gelding: half-brother to several winners, notably smart chaser Missed That (by Overbury), stayed 21f: dam novice selling hurdler: useful form in bumpers: won at Wincanton on debut by 2 lengths from Mutual Respect: 8½ lengths third to Seven Is My Number at Ascot following month. *Jonjo O'Neill*

KIAMA 5 b.m. Dansili – Catriona (Bustino) [2006/7 16g 16g⁶ 22g 26g Apr 20] poor **h74 ?** maiden on Flat (stays 2m), left M. Johnston after 2007 reappearance: little form in 4 starts over hurdles. *B. G. Powell*

KICKAHEAD (USA) 5 b.g. Danzig (USA) – Krissante (USA) (Kris) [2006/7 h91: **h116** 16g 16s* 17sᵖᵘ 16d⁴ 16g* Feb 21] sturdy gelding: fairly useful hurdler: won handicaps at Warwick in December and Ludlow (further improvement, found plenty for pressure to beat Ouninpohja a short head) in February: raced around 2m on good going or softer (acts on soft). *Ian Williams*

KICK AND PRANCE 4 ch.g. Groom Dancer (USA) – Unerring (Unfuwain (USA)) **h98** [2006/7 16d² 16s⁵ 18s⁴ 18v* 16s 19g⁴ Mar 24] lengthy, shallow-girthed gelding: modest on Flat (stays 1½m), successful in October: fair juvenile hurdler: won novice handicap at Fontwell in January: stays 19f: acts on heavy going: wore cheekpieces last 2 starts: tongue tied: races prominently. *J. A. Geake*

KICKING BEAR (IRE) 9 b.g. Little Bighorn – Rongo (IRE) (Tumble Gold) [2006/7 **h–** h–: 22mᵖᵘ 17fᵖᵘ 22mᵖᵘ Aug 26] rangy gelding: point winner: no form over hurdles: wears cheekpieces nowadays. *J. K. Hunter*

KICKS FOR FREE (IRE) 6 b.g. Flemensfirth (USA) – Keep The Change (IRE) **h132** (Castle Keep) [2006/7 F119: 16m* 16d* 17s² 16d³ 16d 20g Apr 12] smallish, close-coupled gelding: useful novice hurdler: easily landed odds at Wincanton and Haydock (listed race by 6 lengths from Self Respect) in November: better form at Cheltenham next (second to Tidal Bay) and fifth outings, but generally failed to see races out (bled fourth start): bred to stay beyond 2m: acts on soft and good to firm going: tongue tied last 2 outings. *P. F. Nicholls*

KID CHARLEMAGNE (IRE) 4 b.g. King Charlemagne (USA) – Albertville (GER) **F108** (Top Ville) [2006/7 F13g* F14v* Jan 25] sixth foal: half-brother to several winners in Germany, including useful performer up to 11f Alpacco (by Desert King): dam maiden: successful both starts in bumpers, at Towcester in November and Fontwell in January, impressive when beating Ouragan Lagrange by 8 lengths in 7-runner event at latter. *Carl Llewellyn*

KIDITHOU (FR) 9 b.g. Royal Charter (FR) – De Thou (FR) (Trebrook (FR)) [2006/7 c86x, h102d: c26s^{ur} c21d^6 24g^3 c26s 24m 25d 25d^F 22g* 20g^2 24m^{ur} Apr 20] workmanlike gelding: fair handicap hurdler: back to best in spring, winning at Kelso and Fakenham, and second to Wot Way Chief at Wetherby: capable of similar form over fences, but often let down by jumping: stays 27f: acts on heavy going: wore cheekpieces once, blinkered nowadays. *R. C. Guest* **c– x h108**

KIDS INHERITANCE (IRE) 9 b.g. Presenting – Princess Tino (IRE) (Rontino) [2006/7 c107, h–: 20m^6 20g^4 c21g^6 c22m* c20d c22g^2 c25s 22v c22s c20v^6 c20g Apr 3] good-topped gelding: modest hurdler: fairly useful handicap chaser: won at Kelso (by 8 lengths from Jallastep) in October: lost form after sixth outing: stays 2¾m, at least when emphasis is on speed: acts on heavy and good to firm going: jumped poorly only try in cheekpieces. *J. M. Jefferson* **c117 h93**

KID'Z'PLAY (IRE) 11 b.g. Rudimentary (USA) – Saka Saka (Camden Town) [2006/7 c124, h–: c24m c20f^{pu} Jul 6] sturdy gelding: fairly useful hurdler/chaser: no form in 2 starts early in 2006/7: stays 2½m: acts on good to firm and heavy going: front runner. *J. S. Goldie* **c– h–**

KIFTSGATE 10 ch.g. Kris – Blush Rambler (IRE) (Blushing Groom (FR)) [2006/7 c84, h–: c24s^5 c24d^4 c24s^{pu} c24s^{pu} Dec 26] leggy gelding: very lightly raced and poor form over hurdles/fences: stays 3m: blinkered final outing. *Mrs P. Robeson* **c84 h–**

KIKOS (FR) 5 ch.g. Nikos – Balgarde (FR) (Garde Royale) [2006/7 F17s Jan 26] first foal: dam maiden on Flat/over hurdles in France: well held in bumper on debut. *A. King* **F–**

KILBEGGAN BLADE 8 b.g. Sure Blade (USA) – Moheli (Ardross) [2006/7 c23m^2 c23s* c23m^3 c25g^4 c24d* c28v* c28s* c28s^{pu} c32v^4 c25g^4 Apr 18] tall, rather leggy gelding: brother to winning staying hurdlers Esters Boy and At The Double and half-brother to another by Henbit: dam, modest hurdler up to 2¾m, out of smart staying hurdler Mayotte: modest form over hurdles for M. Hourigan: won completed start in points in 2006: later progressed into fairly useful chaser, winning maiden at Worcester in May, novice at Uttoxeter and handicap at Market Rasen in November and handicap at Haydock (beat Truckers Tavern by 9 lengths) in December: ran poorly 2 of last 3 outings: stays 3½m: acts on heavy going. *T. R. George* **c128 h–**

KILBREADY BOY (IRE) 12 b.g. Beau Sher – Ginger Dee (Le Moss) [2006/7 c24s^F Dec 2] rangy gelding: very lightly raced: useful hunter chaser at best: off 20 months, fell heavily fourth in handicap at Chepstow: stays 25f: acts on heavy going. *Mrs L. J. Young* **c–**

KILBREENA (IRE) 7 b.g. Carroll House – Simply Lucky (IRE) (Simply Great (FR)) [2006/7 18g^5 16m c24g* Apr 27] sturdy ex-Irish gelding: modest novice hurdler: left D. Broad, successful twice in points prior to easily winning novice hunter at Chepstow on chasing debut: stays 3m: acts on heavy ground: tried tongue tied. *R. Scrine* **c99 + h85**

KILBURN BUST 4 ch.g. Shahrastani (USA) – Barton Bust (Bustino) [2006/7 F16g Apr 23] first foal: dam unraced: raced freely when well held in maiden bumper on debut. *G. A. Harker* **F–**

KILCARTY (IRE) 7 b. or br.g. Oscar Schindler (IRE) – Maggie's Beauty (IRE) (Seclude (USA)) [2006/7 c23d c23d c25v^{pu} Jan 1] €29,000 4-y-o: third foal: dam unraced half-sister to useful chaser around 2½m Multum In Parvo: runner-up in maiden Irish point in 2006: bought 12,500 gns Doncaster May Sales: no form in chases. *N. J. Hawke* **c–**

KILCASKIN GOLD (IRE) 12 ch.g. Ore – Maypole Gayle (Strong Gale) [2006/7 c82: c31s^{pu} Apr 26] modest pointer/hunter chaser: should stay beyond 25f: acts on heavy going: tried blinkered: takes plenty of driving. *R. A. Ross* **c–**

KILDEE LASS 8 gr.m. Morpeth – Pigeon Loft (IRE) (Bellypha) [2006/7 c–, h96: 16d* 16d^3 16s^4 16g^5 19g^4 Mar 27] leggy, angular mare: modest hurdler: won seller at Leicester in December: claimed from J. Frost £6,000 next time: well held only outing over fences: stays 19f: acts on soft and good to firm going. *A. W. Carroll* **c– h86**

KILGOWAN (IRE) 8 b.g. Accordion – Gaiety Lass (Le Moss) [2006/7 h112: 16d^F 20g^{pu} 20d^{pu} Dec 6] sturdy gelding: fair handicap hurdler: failed to complete all 3 starts in 2006/7: stays 21f: acts on soft going. *Ian Williams* **h–**

KILINDINI 6 gr.g. Silver Patriarch (IRE) – Newlands Corner (Forzando) [2006/7 c–, h108: c23m^{pu} 24m^3 22m 19m^3 Oct 14] fair hurdler: jumped poorly both starts over fences: stays 3m: acts on firm going: front runner/races prominently. *Miss E. C. Lavelle* **c– h108**

KILLAGHY CASTLE (IRE) 7 b.g. Topanoora – One Eyed Lucy (IRE) (Miner's Lamp) [2006/7 h131p: c17d* c18s^2 c16s* c25g^{pu} Apr 13] tall, good sort: useful hurdler: **c134 h–**

jumped soundly when successful 2 of first 3 starts over fences, in maiden at Newbury (by 1½ lengths from Briareus) in November and 3-runner novice at Sandown (simple task) in March: upped in trip, ran poorly in Grade 2 novice at Aintree: should stay 3m: raced on good going or softer. *N. J. Gifford*

KILLARD POINT (IRE) 8 b.g. Old Vic – Chic And Elite (Deep Run) [2006/7 c80: c20m² 21g² 21s² 22d⁴ 20d⁶ 19s⁴ 24g Feb 21] rather leggy gelding: winning pointer: in frame twice from 3 starts in hunter chases: fair maiden hurdler: first past post in novice at Warwick second outing but demoted after hanging left into Ordre de Bataille: should stay beyond 2¾m: acts on soft going, probably on good to firm. *Mrs Caroline Bailey*
  c87
  h102

KILL DEVIL HILL (IRE) 7 b.g. Carroll House – Home In The Glen (Furry Glen) [2006/7 c136, h–: c20v² c16vᵖᵘ c21g c29mᵖᵘ Apr 9] strong gelding: smart chaser: short-head second of 4 to Sir OJ in Grade 2 at Clonmel on reappearance: well held in valuable handicap at Cheltenham only completed start after: should stay beyond 21f: acts on heavy ground. *Paul Nolan, Ireland*
  c146
  h–

KILLER CAT (FR) 6 b.g. Lost World (IRE) – Heat Storm (USA) (Storm Cat (USA)) [2006/7 h91d: 16d⁵ 19g 20f 20sᶠ c21g Apr 27] sturdy gelding: maiden hurdler: won maiden point in December: well beaten completed outing in novice hunters: stays 19f: acts on good to firm and good to soft going: often wears headgear/tongue strap. *G. F. Edwards*
  c–
  h78

KILLER JIM 5 ch.g. Killer Instinct – Sister Jim (Oats) [2006/7 F13m Mar 29] second foal: dam, no sign of ability, half-sister to smart staying hurdler Jimbalou and useful 2m hurdler Jimsintime: looked badly in need of experience in maiden bumper on debut. *W. Davies*
  F–

KILLING JOKE 7 b.g. Double Trigger (IRE) – Fleeting Vision (IRE) (Vision (USA)) [2006/7 h–: 16s 17vᵖᵘ Jan 9] no form over hurdles. *J. J. Lambe, Ireland*
  h–

KILLING ME SOFTLY 6 b.g. Kingsinger (IRE) – Slims Lady (Theatrical Charmer) [2006/7 h117: c20sᵖᵘ c20v³ c16v⁴ c19vʳᵒ c20s c20v⁵ 22d Mar 17] lengthy gelding: fairly useful handicap hurdler, well beaten final outing: not fluent and no form over fences: stays 2½m: best efforts on soft/heavy going: wears headgear. *J. Gallagher*
  c–
  h–

KILLONE MOONLIGHT (IRE) 8 b.m. Moonax (IRE) – Killone Brae (King's Ride) [2006/7 c91?, h109: 21s 21m 24g⁵ 24g⁴ Apr 21] lengthy mare: winning pointer: well held completed outing in chases: modest handicap hurdler: stays 25f: acts on good to soft going: tail swisher. *D. R. Stoddart*
  c–
  h92

KILLULTAGH STAR (IRE) 7 b.g. Oscar Schindler (IRE) – Rostrevor Lady (Kemal (FR)) [2006/7 18s 17s⁵ 16v³ Mar 12] half-brother to several winners, notably useful hurdler/chaser up to 2½m Killultagh Storm (by Mandalus): dam, winning hurdler/chaser, stayed 3m: poor form 3 starts over hurdles, not knocked about when third of 7 to Enlightenment in novice at Plumpton: will be suited by 2½m+: raced on soft/heavy ground. *Noel T. Chance*
  h72 +

KILLY LASS (IRE) 11 b.m. Buckskin (FR) – Nataf (Whistling Deer) [2006/7 c71: 27mᵖᵘ Jun 8] ex-Irish mare: winning pointer: poor maiden chaser: pulled up and dismounted after second on hurdling debut: stays 3m: acts on firm and good to soft ground. *B. J. Llewellyn*
  c–
  h–

KILMACKILLOGE 8 b.g. Lancastrian – Garjun (IRE) (Orchestra) [2006/7 h103: c17g* c19s⁴ c16gᵖᵘ Apr 7] fair hurdler: off 7½ months, beat Terlan by 17 lengths in novice at Kelso in November on chasing debut: disappointing after, bled final outing: likely to prove best around 2m: raced on good going or softer. *M. Todhunter*
  c118
  h–

KILPEDDER (IRE) 6 b.g. Taipan (IRE) – Ladydale (IRE) (Aristocracy) [2006/7 F16d* 16v 19v² 20v² Mar 19] second foal: dam unraced: improved effort in bumpers when winning at Limerick in December by 15 lengths from My Old Piano: best form in maiden hurdles when second to An Fear Doiteain at same course penultimate start: should stay beyond 2½m: front runner. *Paul Nolan, Ireland*
  h100
  F107

KILROSSANTY (IRE) 8 b. or br.g. Accordion – Baby Clair (Gulf Pearl) [2006/7 h70: 19v⁶ 16s⁶ 17d³ 17g³ Apr 1] lengthy, workmanlike gelding: poor maiden hurdler: raced mainly around 2m: tongue tied last 2 outings: headstrong. *R. Flint*
  h78

KILTIMONEY (IRE) 7 gr.g. Kasmayo – Rosie's Midge (General Ironside) [2006/7 F18d⁵ c20d³ c17vᵖᵘ c23s⁴ c20sᵖᵘ c24d c20vᶠ c19g Mar 29] half-brother to bumper winner Tomies Wood (by Husyan): dam winning 2m chaser: runner-up once from 6 starts in
  c–
  F81

maiden Irish points: bought 6,500 gns Doncaster May Sales: fifth in bumper at Plumpton: no form in chases. *N. R. Mitchell*

KILTY STORM (IRE) 8 b.g. Glacial Storm (USA) – Hogan's Cherry (General Ironside) [2006/7 h122: 21g c20g c22v³ c27v* c24v⁵ c23s³ Feb 14] good-topped gelding: fairly useful handicap hurdler: similar standard over fences, landed odds in maiden at Sedgefield in December: better form when third, including in handicap at Leicester final outing: stays 27f: acts on heavy going: tongue tied nowadays: has found little/gone as if amiss. *D. E. Pipe*   **c119 h112**

KIMBERLITE KING (IRE) 5 b.g. Good Thyne (USA) – Daraheen Diamond (IRE) (Husyan (USA)) [2006/7 F16v* Mar 3] €26,000 3-y-o: third foal: dam unraced half-sister to fairly useful hurdler Daraheen Chief, stayed 2½m: won 9-runner bumper at Navan on debut by 4 lengths from Woodbine Willie: should progress. *Colm A. Murphy, Ireland*   **F106 p**

KIM FONTENAIL (FR) 7 b.m. Kaldounevees (FR) – Fontanalia (FR) (Rex Magna (FR)) [2006/7 c–, h–: 20d⁴ 20d 23d⁶ Nov 8] angular mare: fair hurdler/chaser at one time: lightly raced and below best since 2004: stays 2¾m: raced on good going or softer (acts on soft). *N. J. Hawke*   **c– h89**

KIMI (IRE) 6 b.g. Presenting – Hatherley (Deep Run) [2006/7 F98: 21s⁶ Oct 25] good-topped gelding: placed all 4 starts in bumpers, showing fairly useful form: lost shoe when well beaten in novice at Cheltenham on hurdling debut: should stay 21f: should do better over hurdles. *Noel T. Chance*   **h– p**

KIMONO ROYAL (FR) 9 b. or br.g. Garde Royale – Alizane (FR) (Mourtazam) [2006/7 c93, h97: 24d^pu 19m⁶ 16s 19g 19v^pu Jan 21] tall, useful-looking gelding: modest maiden hurdler/chaser: left A. King, no form in 2006/7: stays 3m: acts on firm and good to soft ground. *P. Kelsall*   **c– h–**

KINALLEN 7 b.g. Environment Friend – Creeping Jane (Rustingo) [2006/7 F–: 22m^pu Apr 22] won maiden point in 2006, only sign of ability. *A. J. Whiting*   **h–**

KINBURN (IRE) 8 gr.g. Roselier (FR) – Leadaro (IRE) (Supreme Leader) [2006/7 c130p, h–: c20s² c32s² c29s^pu c29s⁴ 21v^pu Mar 9] good-topped gelding: winning hurdler: seemed to go amiss when well backed in handicap final outing: useful handicap chaser: good efforts when runner-up at Wetherby and Hexham in autumn: stays 4m: acts on heavy and good to firm going: front runner/races prominently: not a fluent jumper. *J. Howard Johnson*   **c138 x h–**

KINCAID 4 ch.g. Dr Fong (USA) – Peacock Alley (IRE) (Salse (USA)) [2006/7 16m 17d^pu Nov 21] no form on Flat or in juvenile hurdles. *D. W. Thompson*   **h–**

KIND SIR 11 b.g. Generous (IRE) – Noble Conquest (USA) (Vaguely Noble) [2006/7 c107d, h87: c20s^pu c20m⁶ c20s³ c23m⁵ c16g^pu Sep 6] good-topped gelding: maiden hurdler: handicap chaser, on the downgrade: stays 2¾m: acts on good to firm and heavy going: blinkered twice: usually front runner. *A. W. Carroll*   **c74 h–**

KINETIC POWER (IRE) 4 gr.g. Alhaarth (IRE) – Nichodoula (Doulab (USA)) [2006/7 16s 16v 16d 17v² 19g⁶ 17g Apr 18] angular gelding: modest maiden on Flat (stays 1¼m), sold out of D. Elsworth's stable £2,400 Ascot August Sales: modest juvenile hurdler: raced mainly around 2m. *N. J. Hawke*   **h85**

KING AMBER 6 b.g. Wizard King – Dark Amber (Formidable (USA)) [2006/7 h–, F–: 24f^ur Sep 29] leggy gelding: failed to complete in 2 starts over hurdles a year apart. *A. Crook*   **h– F–**

KING AR AGHAIDH (IRE) 6 b.g. King's Theatre (IRE) – Shuil Ar Aghaidh (The Parson) [2006/7 F17s⁶ Nov 14] lengthy gelding: sixth foal: half-brother to fair hurdler/fairly useful chaser Bob Ar Aghaidh (by Bob Back), stays 3½m, bumper winner Top Ar Aghaidh (by Topanoora) and 2m hurdle winner Rith Ar Aghaidh (by Phardante): dam, very smart staying hurdler, half-sister to useful staying jumper Rawhide: favourite, looked in need of experience when sixth to Wise Men Say in bumper at Folkestone on debut. *C. Tinkler*   **F77**

KING BARRY (FR) 8 b.g. Cadoudal (FR) – Leonie Des Champs (FR) (Crystal Palace (FR)) [2006/7 c119+: 22g⁴ c24m* 20g² c24d c24d Dec 27] rather leggy gelding: fairly useful handicap chaser: won valuable event at Perth in June by 5 lengths from Undeniable: disappointing last 2 starts: easily better effort over hurdles when 1¼ lengths second to Nevertika in novice at Haydock: stays 25f: acts on good to firm and good to soft going. *Miss P. Robson*   **c126 h116**

KING BEE (IRE) 10 b.g. Supreme Leader – Honey Come Back (Master Owen) [2006/7 c116, h–: c24g6 c26gF c29s³ c24v³ c24v* Feb 22] sturdy gelding: fairly useful   **c116 h–**

handicap chaser: favourite, back near best when winning 3-finisher event at Haydock (for second year running) in February by 5 lengths from Strong Resolve, idling run-in: stays 3m: acts on heavy going: has finished weakly: sold 16,000 gns Doncaster May Sales. *H. D. Daly*

KING CAINE (IRE) 5 b.g. King's Theatre (IRE) – Kadarassa (IRE) (Warning) **F91**
[2006/7 F16g² F17s Jan 30] €30,000 3-y-o, resold 20,000 3-y-o: second foal: half-brother to 7f/1m winner in Italy by Revoque: dam, third over 1m in France, half-sister to smart 2m chaser Kadarann: better effort in bumpers when 7 lengths second to West Ridge at Wincanton. *P. F. Nicholls*

KING COAL (IRE) 8 b. or br.g. Anshan – Lucky Trout (Beau Charmeur (FR)) [2006/7 **c113**
c105, h–: c19s² c19g⁴ c23d* c25g c21g Mar 30] big, strong gelding: fair handicap chaser: **h–**
won at Leicester in December: should stay 3m: acts on soft going. *R. Rowe*

KING CYRUS (IRE) 5 br.g. Anshan – Miss Eurolink (Touching Wood (USA)) **h100 +**
[2006/7 F88: F16g³ F16s 19d⁶ 16d⁵ 21d⁵ Jan 8] rather unfurnished gelding: fair form **F88**
in bumpers: likewise over hurdles, and may do better, especially now qualified for handicaps. *Evan Williams*

KING DANIEL 6 br.g. Prince Daniel (USA) – Panic Button (IRE) (Simply Great (FR)) **h104**
[2006/7 F82: F16f⁴ F16f⁴ 20d⁵ 17v² 19g* 19s² 16d³ Jan 19] workmanlike gelding: **F87**
bumper winner: fair hurdler: won maiden at Catterick in November by 9 lengths from Amhairghin: creditable efforts when placed in novices after: has won at 19f, likely to prove best at shorter when conditions are testing: probably acts on any going. *Mrs E. Slack*

KINGDOM OF DREAMS (IRE) 5 b.g. Sadler's Wells (USA) – Regal Portrait **h82**
(IRE) (Royal Academy (USA)) [2006/7 16s 16d⁴ 16s 17d 16gᵖᵘ Apr 16] close-coupled gelding: fairly useful up to 1½m on Flat at 3 yrs for Sir Michael Stoute, in-and-out form in 2006 and sold out of J. Noseda's stable 10,000 gns Doncaster August Sales: poor form over hurdles: raced around 2m: tongue tied final outing. *J. Mackie*

KING EIDER 8 b. or br.g. Mtoto – Hen Harrier (Polar Falcon (USA)) [2006/7 c112, h–: **c76**
c25m³ Apr 15] smallish gelding: fairly useful handicap hurdler at one time: winning **h–**
chasing debut in maiden at Sedgefield in August 2005: left B. Ellison, let down by jumping latter stages when third to Vital Spark in hunter at Market Rasen 20 months later: will probably prove effective around 3m: acts on firm and good to soft going. *D. J. Kemp*

KINGER ROCKS (IRE) 6 b.m. Desert King (IRE) – Ramich John (Kampala) **h122**
[2006/7 16s² 16m Aug 3] sister to 2m hurdle winner Rock Angel and half-sister to fairly useful hurdler John Magical (by Magical Strike), stayed 2½m: bumper winner: fairly useful on Flat (stays 1¾m), won 2 listed events in 2006: progressive hurdler, won 2 novices in 2005/6: improved again when second in minor event at Punchestown and seventh in Galway Hurdle: raced at 2m over hurdles: unraced on firm going, acts on any other. *D. K. Weld, Ireland*

KING FAZ (IRE) 4 b.g. Fasliyev (USA) – White Satin (IRE) (Fairy King (USA)) **h–**
[2006/7 17s Aug 19] maiden on Flat, well beaten in 2006: most unlikely to make a hurdler: sold £400 Ascot August Sales. *P. A. Blockley*

KING GABRIEL (IRE) 5 b.g. Desert King (IRE) – Broken Spirit (IRE) (Slip Anchor) **h84**
[2006/7 h101p: 17d 16s Jan 10] rather leggy gelding: modest maiden on Flat (should stay 1½m): fair form when third in novice at Worcester on hurdling debut: twice well held under more testing conditions. *Andrew Turnell*

KING HARALD (IRE) 9 b.g. King's Ride – Cuilin Bui (IRE) (Kemal (FR)) [2006/7 **c–**
c127, h–: c24d⁵ c24g c24g Mar 24] close-coupled gelding: useful chaser at one time: off **h–**
13 months (reportedly fractured cannon bone), little impact in 2006/7 (stiff task on reappearance): stays 25f: acts on soft and good to firm going: front runner/races prominently. *M. Bradstock*

KING JACK 5 b.g. Classic Cliche (IRE) – Hack On (Good Thyne (USA)) [2006/7 **F111**
F17v* F16s⁴ Mar 3] 13,000 4-y-o: lengthy, rather unfurnished gelding: first foal: dam, poor novice hurdler, half-sister to fairly useful 2m hurdler/chaser Captain Khedive: useful form in bumpers: won 6-runner event at Folkestone in February by 5 lengths from My Friend Sandy: better effort when 2¼ lengths fourth of 21 to Diamond Harry at Newbury. *R. T. Phillips*

KING JOHNS CASTLE (IRE) 8 gr.g. Flemensfirth (USA) – Caislain Darai (IRE) **c132**
(Fujiwara) [2006/7 c17s* c20vᵖᵘ c21dᵘʳ c17s² c16v² c20mᵖᵘ Apr 8] strong, workmanlike **h–**
gelding: third foal: half-brother to winning pointer by Be My Native: dam no form in points/bumper: point/bumper winner: fairly useful hurdler: better over fences: won

maiden at Navan very easily in November: let down by jumping next 2 starts, and still not always fluent when 2 lengths second to Schindlers Hunt in Grade 1 novice at Leopardstown next time: reportedly bled final outing: stays 2¾m: acts on heavy going. *A. L. T. Moore, Ireland*

KING KILLONE (IRE) 7 b.g. Moonax (IRE) – Killone Brae (King's Ride) [2006/7   **c138** c125, h–: c26s⁴ c25s* c24s³ c25v Dec 26] tall gelding: useful chaser: further improve-   **h–** ment when winning handicap at Wetherby in November by 6 lengths from Silver Knight: easily better effort after when third to Neptune Collonges in valuable similar event at Newcastle: thorough stayer: raced on ground softer than good (acts on heavy). *H. P. Hogarth*

KINGKOHLER (IRE) 8 b.g. King's Theatre (IRE) – Legit (IRE) (Runnett) [2006/7   **c96** h109: c16d² c16m⁴ c16v³ Feb 27] fair handicap hurdler: modest form all 3 starts over   **h–** fences: will prove best around 2m: acts on good to firm and heavy going: has raced freely: carries head high but is consistent. *K. A. Morgan*

KING LOK (NZ) 5 b.g. Generous (IRE) – American Express (NZ) (Dahar (USA))   **F–** [2006/7 F16v⁵ Feb 5] New Zealand-bred gelding: 7/2 from 6/1 but green, fifth of 6 in maiden bumper at Hexham on debut. *C. E. Longsdon*

KING LOUIS (FR) 6 b.g. Nikos – Rotina (FR) (Crystal Glitters (USA)) [2006/7 h106,   **h109** F73+: 19dᵖᵘ 17v⁴ 17v⁵ 21sᵖᵘ 19g³ Mar 30] rangy, useful-looking gelding: fair novice hurdler: stays 19f: acts on heavy going (form in bumpers on good to firm). *R. Rowe*

KING MAK 5 b.g. Makbul – Miss Nova (Ra Nova) [2006/7 F16v⁵ F16s 20s 16v* 17g⁶   **h94** 20s Apr 27] 6,000 3-y-o: compact gelding: first foal: dam won 2½m hurdle: well beaten   **F–** in bumpers: modest form over hurdles: 100/1, won novice at Newcastle (made all to beat Lambrini Legend by 9 lengths) in March: should stay beyond 2m: acts on heavy ground. *P. Beaumont*

KING NEPTUNE 6 b.g. Rakaposhi King – Owena Deep (Deep Run) [2006/7 F16d⁴   **F91 p** Dec 21] half-brother to 2 winners over hurdles, including modest Karolena Bay (by Karinga Bay), stayed 3¼m: dam, winning hurdler around 2m, half-sister to smart chaser Chief Ironside, best around 2½m: green, 11 lengths fourth to Appleaday in bumper at Ludlow on debut: likely to improve. *Miss H. C. Knight*

KING OF CHAV'S (IRE) 4 ch.g. Beckett (IRE) – La Paola (IRE) (Common   **h–** Grounds) [2006/7 17mᵖᵘ Apr 15] little form on Flat: no show in juvenile on hurdling debut. *A. Bailey*

KING OF CONFUSION (IRE) 8 br.g. Topanoora – Rich Desire (Grey Desire)   **c110** [2006/7 h122: c23d² c20vᵘʳ c24v⁴ Feb 24] tall gelding: fairly useful hurdler: remote   **h–** second of 4 finishers to Hard Act To Follow in maiden at Wetherby on chasing debut: reportedly had breathing operation after, and went as if amiss on completed start on return: stays 3¼m: raced on going softer than good (acts on heavy). *Ferdy Murphy*

KING OF GOTHLAND (IRE) 8 gr.g. Gothland (FR) – Rose Deer (Whistling Deer)   **c101** [2006/7 c102, h–: c29s⁵ c24s* c24v⁴ c24s⁴ c28g Apr 7] tall gelding: fair handicap chaser: **h–** fortunate to win at Huntingdon in December: below form otherwise in 2006/7: should stay beyond 3m: acts on soft going: wore cheekpieces once. *K. C. Bailey*

KING OF SCOTS 6 ch.g. Halling (USA) – Ink Pot (USA) (Green Dancer (USA))   **h–** [2006/7 h–: 21sᵖᵘ May 8] no sign of ability: tried in cheekpieces. *R. J. Price*

KING OF SLANE 6 b.g. Prince Daniel (USA) – Singing Slane (Cree Song) [2006/7   **F–** F–: F16v⁶ Jan 28] well held in bumpers 9 months apart. *G. A. Swinbank*

KING OF THE ARCTIC (IRE) 9 b.g. Arctic Lord – Ye Little Daisy (Prince   **c115** Tenderfoot (USA)) [2006/7 c93, h–: c16s* 16d c16s³ c16v⁴ c20d³ c16v² c20s³ Apr 25]   **h–** winning hurdler: fair handicap chaser: won at Perth in May: creditable efforts last 2 outings, though found less than seemed likely: effective at 2m to 2½m: yet to race on firm going, acts on any other. *J. Wade*

KING OF THE JUNGLE (IRE) 6 ch.g. Accordion – What It Takes (IRE) (Tale   **F95 §** Quale) [2006/7 F16d F16g* F16g Apr 7] €38,000 3-y-o: has scope: fifth foal: dam unraced half-sister to useful staying hurdler Nancy Myles: made most when winning bumper at Huntingdon in March by 1¼ lengths from Lord Appellare, looking reluctant when initially challenged: again blinkered, appeared to down tools once headed next time: one to be wary of. *Carl Llewellyn*

KING OF THE MOUNTN (IRE) 6 b.g. Saddlers' Hall (IRE) – Deep Dollar (Deep   **F–** Run) [2006/7 F16m Jun 17] €15,000 4-y-o: half-brother to several winners, including fair hurdler/chaser up to 2½m Another Dollar (by Supreme Leader): dam, unraced, out of half-sister to high-class chaser Fifty Dollars More: well held in bumper on debut. *Miss T. Jackson*

KING ON THE RUN (IRE) 14 b.g. King's Ride – Fly Run (Deep Run) [2006/7 c–, h–: c25d^{ur} c28s^{pu} c23g^{pu} Jul 5] rangy gelding: one-time useful chaser: lightly raced nowadays, and has failed to complete last 4 outings: stays 3m: acts on good to firm and heavy going: wore cheekpieces final start. *Miss Venetia Williams*

c–
h–

KING REVO (IRE) 7 b.g. Revoque (IRE) – Tycoon Aly (IRE) (Last Tycoon) [2006/7 c16s^3 c16v^5 c16d^2 c16v* c21g^{pu} c20g^5 Apr 14] tall, useful-looking gelding: traces of stringhalt: useful handicap hurdler: missed 2005/6: fairly useful form over fences: landed odds in maiden at Hexham in February: best effort of season when fifth to Private Be in conditional/amateur novice handicap at Aintree final outing: effective at 2m to 21f: raced on good going or softer (acts on heavy): has jumped none too fluently over fences. *P. C. Haslam*

c119
h–

KINGS ADVOCATE (IRE) 7 b.g. Saddlers' Hall (IRE) – Definitely Maybe (IRE) (Brush Aside (USA)) [2006/7 h120: 23v^3 c20d^5 c20s* c20d^2 c16s^3 c21g^6 c29m^6 Apr 9] lengthy gelding: fairly useful hurdler: useful chaser: won amateur maiden at Limerick in November: better form all starts after, on last 2 sixth in handicaps at Cheltenham (listed novice event won by L'Antartique) and Fairyhouse (to Butler's Cabin in Irish National): stays 29f: acts on heavy and good to firm going. *T. J. Taaffe, Ireland*

c132
h120

KING'S BOUNTY 11 b.g. Le Moss – Fit For A King (Royalty) [2006/7 c104, h–: c22s^3 c20d c22g c22s^{pu} c25d^{pu} Dec 28] rangy gelding: fair handicap chaser: out of sorts in 2006/7, looking reluctant: stays 3½m: acts on good to firm and heavy going: blinkered. *T. D. Easterby*

c– §
h–

KINGS BROOK 7 br.g. Alderbrook – Kins Token (Relkino) [2006/7 c112§, h–§: c16g^2 c16m^2 c16m^4 c16d^2 c20m* c21d* c22g* c24m c20g^6 Apr 14] leggy gelding: maiden hurdler: fairly useful chaser: much improved in first half of 2006/7, winning maiden at

c125
h–

Mr Tony Gale's "Kings Brook"

Worcester and handicap at Newton Abbot in August and handicap at Market Rasen (beating Spectrometer 1¾ lengths) in September: stays 2¾m: acts on good to firm and good to soft going: has finished weakly, and suited by exaggerated waiting tactics. *Nick Williams*

KINGSBURY (IRE) 8 b.g. Norwich – Glen Na Mban (IRE) (Phardante (FR)) [2006/7 16g⁵ 16g 17v 18v 19d² 16v 17s² 16gᶠ Mar 17] good-bodied gelding: first foal: dam, well held in bumper, out of sister to top-class staying chaser Righthand Man: fair maiden hurdler: likely to be suited by 2½m+: raced on good ground or softer. *Ferdy Murphy*   **h102**

KINGSCLIFF (IRE) 10 b.g. Toulon – Pixies Glen (Furry Glen) [2006/7 c173§: c25s⁴ c24d⁶ c26g c25g² Apr 25] big, rangy gelding: top-class chaser at one time: largely disappointing these days, though ran best race since 2005 when 3½ lengths second to Neptune Collonges in Punchestown Guinness Gold Cup final outing, leading until after 5 out: stays 3¼m: best form on good/good to soft going: tried visored: unreliable. *R. H. Alner*   **c158 §**

KING'S COLLEGE (USA) 4 b.c. Stravinsky (USA) – Talent Quest (IRE) (Rainbow Quest (USA)) [2006/7 17mᵖᵘ Jun 30] little form on Flat: jumped poorly on hurdling debut. *G. L. Moore*   **h–**

KINGSCOURT LAD (IRE) 9 b.g. Norwich – Mrs Minella (Deep Run) [2006/7 h73: 20s² 24dᵖᵘ 16m⁶ 16m² 16f² 16f² 20m⁴ 16g 19g Oct 15] useful-looking gelding: poor maiden hurdler: claimed £6,000 only start for M. Sheppard on reappearance: stays 2¾m: acts on soft and firm going: tongue tied. *C. T. Pogson*   **h81**

KING'S CREST 9 b.g. Deploy – Classic Beauty (IRE) (Fairy King (USA)) [2006/7 17m* Jul 20] smallish, sturdy gelding: fair form over hurdles: fit from Flat, won maiden at Cartmel in July: best form around 2m: acted on heavy and good to firm going: dead. *J. J. Quinn*   **h106**

KING'S ENVOY (USA) 8 b.g. Royal Academy (USA) – Island of Silver (USA) (Forty Niner (USA)) [2006/7 h76: 20vᵖᵘ 22m⁴ 24g 20sᵖᵘ 22d 24vᵖᵘ 20m⁴ Feb 4] leggy gelding: poor novice hurdler: stays 2¾m: acts on good to firm and good to soft going: not one to rely on. *Mrs J. C. McGregor*   **h70 §**

KINGS GLEN (IRE) 11 b.g. King's Ride – Lady of Aherlow (Le Bavard (FR)) [2006/7 c111, h–: 22v 16d c26gᴿ c24vᵇᵈ 20v c28s c28vᵖᵘ c30m* Apr 27] rangy gelding: winning hurdler: fair handicap chaser: back to form when winning amateur event at Punchestown (third course success) in April: stays 3¾m: acts on heavy and good to firm going. *Thomas Carberry, Ireland*   **c113 h85**

KING SHAADI 7 b.g. Wizard King – Prim Ajwaad (Bin Ajwaad (IRE)) [2006/7 F–: F17d 20sᵖᵘ Jun 25] of little account. *C. A. Mulhall*   **h– F–**

KING'S HEAD (IRE) 4 b.g. King's Best (USA) – Ustka (Lomond (USA)) [2006/7 17g² Mar 25] useful up to 1½m on Flat, successful in May, sold out of M. Jarvis' stable 130,000 gns Newmarket Autumn Sales, and gelded: 12 lengths second to Artadi in juvenile maiden at Taunton on hurdling debut: sure to improve. *G. L. Moore*   **h97 p**

KING'S HILL (IRE) 5 b.g. Nazar (IRE) – Yashvaro (IRE) (Yashgan) [2006/7 F19m* Apr 7] fourth foal: dam unraced: fell in point: won 22-runner bumper at Cork by neck from Criaire Nouveau, responding well: open to improvement. *Mrs J. Harrington, Ireland*   **F98 p**

KINGSHOLM 5 ch.g. Selkirk (USA) – Putuna (Generous (IRE)) [2006/7 16s 17v Jan 8] smallish gelding: fairly useful on Flat (stays 1¼m), successful twice in 2006: doubtful stayer over hurdles. *Jonjo O'Neill*   **h–**

KING'S MINSTREL (IRE) 6 b.g. Cape Cross (IRE) – Muwasim (USA) (Meadowlake (USA)) [2006/7 16d 16g 16g Apr 23] tall gelding: modest maiden on Flat (stays 1½m), missed 2006: well beaten over hurdles. *R. Rowe*   **h–**

KING'S MOUNTAIN (USA) 7 b.g. King of Kings (IRE) – Statistic (USA) (Mr Prospector (USA)) [2006/7 h–: 24f Jul 19] little show over hurdles/in points: tried in cheekpieces/visor. *C. P. Morlock*   **h–**

KINGS ORCHARD (IRE) 10 ch.g. Castle Keep – Orchardstown Lady (Le Moss) [2006/7 c25d² c20m* c25f* c25d² Sep 8] medium-sized gelding: winning hurdler: fairly useful handicap chaser: won twice at Kilbeggan in June: further improvement when second to Deep Return there: stays 25f: unraced on heavy going, acts on any other: usually blinkered, effective when not. *Philip Fenton, Ireland*   **c128 h–**

Mrs Marie Taylor's "Kings Quay"

KING'S PROTECTOR 7 b.g. Hector Protector (USA) – Doliouchka (Saumarez) **c–** [2006/7 c–, h97: 16m⁵ May 6] rather leggy gelding: maiden hurdler: let down by jumping **h–** only outing over fences: stays 2½m: acts on soft and good to firm going: failed to settle in blinkers only start in 2006/7. *Micky Hammond*

KINGS QUAY 5 b.h. Montjeu (IRE) – Glen Rosie (IRE) (Mujtahid (USA)) [2006/7 **h127** 17s* 16f* 16m³ 16d 16m² 16d⁶ 16g* Apr 14] sturdy horse: useful on Flat (best at 1m/1¼m): fairly useful hurdler: won maiden at Market Rasen in August, novice at Plumpton (easily) in September and valuable 22-runner John Smith's Extra Smooth Handicap at Aintree in April, jumping better than most starts in between and quickening ahead from last despite edging left when beating Diego Cao a length in last-named: likely to prove best at 2m with emphasis on speed: tongue tied last 2 starts. *J. J. Quinn*

KING'S REVENGE 4 br.g. Wizard King – Retaliator (Rudimentary (USA)) [2006/7 **h123** 16s² 16v* 17s² 16s² 16d 16g* 17g² Apr 18] angular gelding: fairly useful up to 1½m on Flat (tried blinkered), successful twice in 2006, sold out of T. Easterby's stable 17,500 gns Newmarket Autumn Sales: fairly useful juvenile hurdler: won at Lingfield (maiden) in January and Towcester (long odds on) in April: also runner-up 4 times, beaten ¾ length by Laustra Bad at Cheltenham final start: should stay beyond 17f: acts on heavy going. *A. King*

KINGS SIGNAL (USA) 9 b.g. Red Ransom (USA) – Star of Albion (Ajdal (USA)) **h119** [2006/7 h109: 16s² 17v² 16dᶠ 16v⁴ 16d⁴ Feb 1] good-topped gelding: fairly useful form over hurdles, lightly raced: running best race when falling last in handicap won by

Princelet at Kempton: finished lame final outing: raced around 2m: acts on heavy ground. *M. J. Hogan*

KING'S SILVER (IRE) 6 b.g. King of Kings (IRE) – Almi Ad (USA) (Silver Hawk (USA)) [2006/7 F–: F16m³ Jul 26] rather leggy gelding: poor form in bumpers. *N. I. M. Rossiter* **F72**

KINGS SQUARE 7 b.g. Bal Harbour – Prime Property (IRE) (Tirol) [2006/7 c–§, h80§: c25gᵖᵘ 24mᵖᵘ 24m⁵ 26mᵖᵘ Aug 28] rather leggy gelding: poor hurdler: hasn't completed in 4 starts over fences: stays 3m: acts on good to soft going: tried blinkered: tongue tied last 2 starts: unreliable. *M. W. Easterby* **c– §** **h75 §**

KING'S THOUGHT 8 b.h. King's Theatre (IRE) – Lora's Guest (Be My Guest (USA)) [2006/7 h–: 16s³ 16v⁴ 16gᶠ Mar 14] good-topped horse: fairly useful on Flat (stayed 1¼m) as 7-y-o: modest form over hurdles: dead. *S. Gollings* **h92**

KINGSTON-BANKER 11 b.g. Teamster – Happy Manda (Mandamus) [2006/7 c86, h–: c26m⁴ May 5] sturdy gelding: fairly useful hunter chaser at best: won 3 times in points in February/March: will stay beyond 3¼m: acts on any going. *R. H. Alner* **c86** **h–**

KING'S TRAVEL (FR) 11 gr.g. Balleroy (USA) – Travel Free (Be My Guest (USA)) [2006/7 c–, h–: c21sᵖᵘ c19mᵖᵘ Mar 29] tall, angular gelding: winning hurdler/chaser around 2m, no longer of any account: tried visored. *Brian Robinson* **c–** **h–**

KING TRITON (IRE) 10 br.g. Mister Lord (USA) – Deepwater Woman (The Parson) [2006/7 c95?, h–: 25v* 19bᵈ Mar 21] modest hurdler, lightly raced: left L. Wells and off 14 months, made all in 4-runner handicap at Plumpton: behind when brought down fifth in similar event 9 days later: similar form on first of 3 starts over fences: thorough stayer: acts on heavy going: blinkered in 2006/7. *Jim Best* **c–** **h96**

KINKEEL (IRE) 8 b.g. Hubbly Bubbly (USA) – Bubbly Beau (Beau Charmeur (FR)) [2006/7 c70, h–: c21m⁴ c17dᵖᵘ c20m⁴ c19mᵖᵘ c20mᵖᵘ 16d c16v² c16d² c16s⁵ c16v c16s³ c20d² c17m² c16g³ Apr 20] workmanlike gelding: maiden hurdler: poor novice chaser: stays 2½m: acts on any going: often blinkered: tried tongue tied. *A. W. Carroll* **c70** **h–**

KINSFORD COWBOY 6 ch.g. Double Trigger (IRE) – Kinsford Rose (Roselier (FR)) [2006/7 F16m² F17g F17g⁴ Oct 15] first foal: dam, dual bumper winner/poor novice hurdler, stayed 2¾m: modest form in bumpers: will be suited by 2½m+. *Nick Williams* **F82**

KIORA BAY 10 b.g. Karinga Bay – Equasion (IRE) (Cyrano de Bergerac) [2006/7 c–: c20d* c25g⁴ c24g⁵ Apr 21] rangy gelding: fair hunter chaser: won novice at Aintree in May: stays 25f: raced mainly on good/good to soft going. *T. S. Sharpe* **c96** **h–**

KIPSIGIS (IRE) 6 b.g. Octagonal (NZ) – Kisumu (Damister (USA)) [2006/7 h120p: 22s² 23v 22sᵖᵘ Feb 17] good-topped gelding: fairly useful hurdler: most disappointing last 2 starts: should stay beyond 2¾m: raced on going softer than good (acts on heavy). *Lady Herries* **h116**

KIRBY'S VIC (IRE) 7 b.g. Old Vic – Just Affable (IRE) (Phardante (FR)) [2006/7 c–, h–: c16d c20g⁴ c16sᵘʳ Nov 19] fourth in handicap chase at Market Rasen, only solid form: stays 2½m: blinkered last 2 outings. *N. A. Twiston-Davies* **c69** **h–**

KIRKHAMMERTON (IRE) 5 ch.g. Grand Lodge (USA) – Nawara (Welsh Pageant) [2006/7 h–: 17d⁶ Jul 22] modest up to easy 1¾m on all-weather on Flat (usually wears headgear): tailed off on completed start over hurdles: visored on debut. *Mrs S. J. Smith* **h–**

KIRKISTOWN LASS (IRE) 7 b.m. Beneficial – Merry Tone (IRE) (Merrymount) [2006/7 F17m⁴ F16m F18m Jul 13] second foal: dam unraced: well held in bumpers: will be suited by 2½m+. *J. K. Magee, Ireland* **F–**

KIRKSTALL 5 b.h. Selkirk (USA) – Stiletta (Dancing Brave (USA)) [2006/7 F16g Apr 3] 42,000 3-y-o: half-brother to fairly useful 2m hurdler Articulation (by Machiavellian) and fairly useful hurdler/chaser Julius Caesar (by Sadler's Wells), stays 25f: dam unraced sister to Derby winner Commander In Chief and half-sister to Warning, Deploy and Dushyantor: tongue tied, found nothing when seventh to Abstinence in bumper at Wetherby on debut, having been on bridle 2f out. *C. F. Swan, Ireland* **F79**

KISSINTHEPEACH (IRE) 6 b.m. Witness Box (USA) – Balinloop (IRE) (Balinger) [2006/7 F–: F16f⁶ F16d⁵ 20s 20g 20v⁵ 20m 23gʳᵒ 16g Apr 23] smallish mare: poor form in bumpers/over hurdles: likely to stay beyond 2½m (ran out only try over further). *Mrs K. Walton* **h63** **F74**

KISSLAIN DES GALAS (FR) 10 b.g. Lute Antique (FR) – Miss Zedd (FR) (Zeddaan) [2006/7 c21v⁵ c32mᵖᵘ c26gᶠ Nov 19] rather leggy gelding: 13f winner on Flat: successful 6 times over jumps in France (fairly useful form), including 4 over fences in 2005/6 for F. Danloux: didn't see race out only completed outing in Britain (tongue tied after): stays 21f: acts on soft going. *D. E. Pipe* — **c111 h–**

KISS THE GIRLS (IRE) 8 ch.g. Roselier (FR) – Cheeney's Gift (Quayside) [2006/7 h66: 26dᵖᵘ May 17] angular gelding: little form: tried visored: sold 2,000 gns Doncaster May Sales. *Jennie Candlish* — **h–**

KIT CARSON (IRE) 7 b.g. Dr Massini (IRE) – Roses Niece (IRE) (Jeu de Paille (FR)) [2006/7 20s c17s* c16m² c17m² c16m* 17m³ c16g² c16g c18g³ Apr 25] good-bodied gelding: fair hurdler: better over fences, won maiden at Clonmel in May and 4-runner minor event at Roscommon in August: ran well in novice at Punchestown (11¾ lengths third to Pacolet) final outing: stays 2¼m: acts on good to firm and heavy going. *C. F. Swan, Ireland* — **c119 h107**

KITLEY HASSLE 5 b.g. Morpeth – Celtic Land (Landyap (USA)) [2006/7 F16d F16v Nov 22] first foal: dam, poor maiden hurdler, stayed 27f: mid-field at best in bumpers at Chepstow. *J. D. Frost* — **F77**

KITSKI (FR) 9 b.g. Perrault – Macyrienne (FR) (Saint Cyrien (FR)) [2006/7 c114x, h–§: c20d³ c20s³ c28v² c25d* c24v⁴ c28s⁶ c24g³ c20m³ Apr 15] sturdy gelding: winning hurdler (usually looked ungenuine): fairly useful chaser: won handicap at Market Rasen in December by 8 lengths from Pass Me By, jumping more fluently than usual: stays 3½m: acts on heavy going: blinkered once in bumpers: raced mostly on right-handed tracks. *Ferdy Murphy* — **c118 x h– §**

KITTY WONG (IRE) 5 b.m. Supreme Leader – Parson River (IRE) (Over The River (FR)) [2006/7 F14s³ F17s³ F16d Feb 2] fifth foal: dam placed in point: won mares maiden Irish point in 2006: placed in mares bumpers at Fontwell and Folkestone: possibly amiss final outing. *T. R. George* — **F90**

KIVOTOS (USA) 9 gr.g. Trempolino (USA) – Authorized Staff (USA) (Relaunch (USA)) [2006/7 h–: 24m⁴ c20m* c20f³ c24g* c23fᵖᵘ Sep 10] leggy gelding: fairly useful handicap hurdler, off nearly 2 years before only outing in 2005/6: fair form over fences, winning maiden (fortunate) in June and novice (went in snatches) in August, both at Southwell: probably amiss final outing: stays 3m: probably acts on any going. *D. E. Pipe* — **c113 h117**

KIWIJIMBO (IRE) 7 b.g. Germany (USA) – Final Touch (IRE) (Orchestra) [2006/7 h78+, F–: 16v* 16g² May 24] fair form over hurdles: much improved early in 2006/7, easily winning handicap at Perth: raced around 2m: acts on heavy going. *A. C. Whillans* — **h103**

KIWI RIVERMAN 7 b.g. Alderbrook – Kiwi Velocity (NZ) (Veloso (NZ)) [2006/7 h–: c21mᵖᵘ c23fᵖᵘ Jun 21] useful-looking gelding: no form. *C. L. Tizzard* — **c– h–**

KNAPP BRIDGE BOY 7 b.g. Wimbleball – Toll Bridge (New Member) [2006/7 F77: 17g Apr 1] signs of ability only on last of 3 outings in bumpers. *J. R. Payne* — **h–**

KNIFE EDGE (USA) 12 b. or br.g. Kris S (USA) – My Turbulent Miss (USA) (My Dad George (USA)) [2006/7 c122, h–: c26v* c28v* c25v³ c26g c24g⁴ Apr 21] tall gelding: useful hunter chaser nowadays: successful at Uttoxeter and Stratford (Pertemps Cup Champion Hunters' Chase, by 3 lengths from Vinnie Boy) in May: stays 3½m: acts on heavy and good to firm going: tried blinkered, now wears cheekpieces. *Jonjo O'Neill* — **c112 h–**

KNIGHT LEGEND (IRE) 8 b.g. Flying Legend (USA) – Well Trucked (IRE) (Dry Dock) [2006/7 h130, F?: c16g³ c20dᶠ c20s² c20s² c19d² c20v* c21vᵘʳ c20vᶠ c21g c25m² Apr 24] lengthy gelding: useful hurdler: often let down by jumping but at least as good over fences: won maiden at Punchestown in January easily by 19 lengths from Offshore Account: creditable second of 5 finishers to same horse in Grade 1 Champion Novices' Chase at Punchestown final start: stays 25f: acts on heavy and good to firm going. *Mrs J. Harrington, Ireland* — **c140 x h–**

KNIGHTON LAD (IRE) 7 b.g. Supreme Leader – Tarqueen (IRE) (King's Ride) [2006/7 h106: 24v* 24v² Mar 3] well-made gelding: fairly useful handicap hurdler: improved efforts after nearly a year off, winning conditional jockeys event at Newbury (by length from Seeador) in January and second to Ballyshan at Kempton: stays 3¼m: raced on good going or softer (acts on heavy): successful only outing in visor. *A. King* — **h116**

KNIGHTSBRIDGE HILL (IRE) 5 b.g. Raise A Grand (IRE) – Desert Gem (Green Desert (USA)) [2006/7 h96: 16m⁴ 16g⁴ 22d³ 21sᵖᵘ 21f⁵ 20gᶠ Apr 27] good-topped gelding: fair maiden hurdler: left A. King after fourth outing (blinkered): stays 2¾m: acts — **h101**

on good to firm and good to soft going: tongue tied final start (running well when falling). *M. Sheppard*

KNIGHTSBRIDGE KING 11 ch.g. Michelozzo (USA) – Shahdjat (IRE) (Vayrann) [2006/7 h–: 21m⁶ May 5] rather sparely-made gelding: modest winning hurdler, lightly raced and below form since 2004/5: stays 25f: acts on soft and good to firm going: has worn headgear: sold 1,500 gns Doncaster August Sales. *John Allen* **h–**

KNIGHT'S EMPEROR (IRE) 10 b.g. Grand Lodge (USA) – So Kind (Kind of Hush) [2006/7 c98x, h–: 17g 21m² 16g 19g³ c18g⁵ 19m³ Jul 17] good-topped gelding: winning hurdler/chaser, poor form in 2006/7: stays 19f: acts on firm and soft going: in cheekpieces last 3 starts: usually let down by jumping over fences. *J. L. Spearing* **c80 x** **h84**

KNIGHTSWOOD (IRE) 6 b.g. Simply Great (FR) – Brymar Lass (IRE) (Homo Sapien) [2006/7 F17g⁷ᵘ Apr 27] €17,000 4-y-o: first foal: dam, winning pointer, out of half-sister to dams of top-class staying chasers Grey Abbey and The Grey Monk: no promise in bumper on debut. *B. G. Powell* **F–**

KNOCKARA LUCK (IRE) 6 ch.m. Simply Great (FR) – Bonne Atthenagh (IRE) (Rontino) [2006/7 F102: 20f⁴ 20s² 20d² 21g Mar 24] sturdy mare: fairly useful in mares bumpers: not fluent and modest form at best over hurdles: stays 2½m: sold 20,000 gns Doncaster May Sales. *N. G. Richards* **h94**

KNOCK DAVRON (IRE) 8 ch.g. Beneficial – Chestnut Shoon (Green Shoon) [2006/7 c–: c20v⁵ c20s³ c16g c20m⁵ c16gᵖᵘ Apr 23] lengthy gelding: poor form in chases: will prove best at 2½m+: in cheekpieces final outing. *W. Storey* **c79 ?**

KNOCKER JOCK (FR) 7 b.g. Medaaly – Glorieuse Shadows (FR) (Le Glorieux) [2006/7 h–, F–: 16g⁵ 18m 16mᶠ 16d⁴ 16s 16g 21m³ Apr 9] rather leggy gelding: modest maiden hurdler: stays 21f: acts on good to firm and good to soft ground. *R. Rowe* **h84**

KNOCKHOLT 11 b.g. Be My Chief (USA) – Saffron Crocus (Shareef Dancer (USA)) [2006/7 20f Jun 17] novice hurdler: modest pointer, placed numerous times: stays 3m: acts on good to firm and good to soft going: tried visored. *W. T. Reed* **h–**

KNOCK LORD (IRE) 10 b.g. Mister Lord (USA) – Sister Duke (Bonne Noel) [2006/7 c26m² May 5] fifth foal: dam bumper winner: winning pointer, lightly raced: 10 lengths second of 3 finishers to Steppes of Gold in maiden at Southwell on chasing debut. *R. Ford* **c97**

KNOCKNABOOLY (IRE) 8 ch.g. John French – Valiyist (IRE) (Valiyar) [2006/7 F16s⁵ F16v⁴ 22vᶠ 16v* Feb 21] strong, good sort: useful form in bumpers in 2003/4: off over 2½ years before reappearance (reportedly due to leg trouble): won maiden at Punchestown on completed outing over hurdles, always handy and beating Kilcrea Asla 8 lengths: will stay 2½m: likely to improve if remaining sound. *W. P. Mullins, Ireland* **h111 p** **r98**

KNOTTY ASH GIRL (IRE) 8 ch.m. Ashkalani (IRE) – Camisha (IRE) (Shernazar) [2006/7 h–: 16m* 16m³ Jun 11] modest form over hurdles, won mares selling handicap at Worcester in May: raced mainly at 2m: acts on good to firm going. *D. J. Wintle* **h87**

KNOWHERE (IRE) 9 b.g. Lord Americo – Andarta (Ballymore) [2006/7 c–, h–: c20s* c20d* c20dᶠ c19d² c21s² c24d³ c21v c24g c36gᵘʳ Apr 14] big, well-made gelding: successful both starts over hurdles, including in Grade 2: useful chaser: easily won novices at Perth in September and Bangor in October: best efforts when runner-up in valuable handicaps at Ascot and Cheltenham (beaten 1½ lengths by Exotic Dancer in boylesports.com Gold Cup): lost his form after: should stay 3m: raced on good going or softer (acts on heavy). *N. A. Twiston-Davies* **c143** **h–**

KNOWLEDGE BOX (IRE) 7 br.g. Accordion – Bone of Contention (IRE) (Buckskin (FR)) [2006/7 19s³ 22d 19s² 20v 24g⁵ Apr 13] €9,000 3-y-o: lengthy, angular gelding: first foal: dam unraced half-sister to fair chasers Mutual Agreement (stayed 27f) and Mutual Trust (stayed 25f): won maiden point in 2006: fair maiden hurdler: out of depth at Aintree final outing: should stay beyond 2½m. *John Joseph Murphy, Ireland* **h104**

KNOW THE ROPES (IRE) 7 b.g. Muroto – Bobs My Uncle (Deep Run) [2006/7 c22m² c25f c25gᵖᵘ c25g³ Apr 23] €37,000 4-y-o: half-brother to fair hurdler/fairly useful chaser Putsometnby (by Phardante), stayed 4m, and winning pointer by Roselier: dam unraced: won maiden point in 2006: best effort in chases when second in 4-runner conditional jockeys handicap at Cork: left Enda Bolger after next outing: stays 2¾m: tried in cheekpieces. *J. Burke* **c97 d**

KOCK DE LA VESVRE (FR) 9 b.g. Sassanian (USA) – Csardas (FR) (Maiymad) [2006/7 c130, h–: c24d³ c25s² c24s⁴ c24sᵖᵘ Apr 26] leggy, lengthy gelding: fairly useful handicap chaser, off 17 months before reappearance: stays 25f: acts on any going: tried **c123** **h–**

blinkered in France: tongue tied third outing: sometimes finishes weakly. *Miss Venetia Williams*

KOFI 5 br.g. Emperor Fountain – La Vie En Primrose (Henbit (USA)) [2006/7 h–: 19s² 22v² 22d Mar 20] novice hurdler, easily best effort when second to Mark The Book in maiden at Exeter second outing: stays 2¾m: raced on going softer than good. *Karen George* **h99**

KOKO DANCER 4 b.f. Komaite (USA) – Flamebird (IRE) (Mukaddamah (USA)) [2006/7 F16s Mar 1] first foal: dam poor form completed start over hurdles: offered nothing in bumper on debut. *C. G. Cox* **F–**

KOKOSCHKA (IRE) 5 b.g. Oscar (IRE) – Sibley (Northfields (USA)) [2006/7 F97: F16g⁴ Apr 7] big, strong gelding: fair form when fourth in bumpers a year apart, beaten 19 lengths by Marleybow at Haydock on second occasion, looking ungainly when first under pressure: will be suited by 2½m+. *C. R. Egerton* **F94**

KOLN STARS (IRE) 9 b.g. Fourstars Allstar (USA) – Fraulein Koln (IRE) (Mandalus) [2006/7 h91d: 20d⁶ 20m 20m⁴ 16m³ 17dᵖᵘ 22g⁶ Sep 17] compact gelding: poor handicap hurdler: stays 2¾m: best form on good going or firmer (acts on firm): often races prominently. *Jennie Candlish* **h78**

KOMOTO 6 b.g. Mtoto – Imperial Scholar (IRE) (Royal Academy (USA)) [2006/7 c–, h–: c20dᶠ 17d 16f 24f 22m⁵ 24m² 24g 24s² 25s³ 24s³ c20d 24d⁵ Feb 14] modest maiden hurdler: let down by jumping over fences: stays 25f: acts on soft and good to firm going: wore cheekpieces after fourth outing. *Liam Lennon, Ireland* **c– h?**

KONIGSBOTE (GER) 5 b.g. Monsun (GER) – Karenina (GER) (Second Set (IRE)) [2006/7 16s⁶ Jan 10] good-topped gelding: useful maiden on Flat in Germany, placed on 5 occasions up to 11f, left P. Rau after final start in August: well-backed favourite but tongue tied, around 15 lengths sixth of 17 to Le Burf in maiden at Wincanton on hurdling debut, left with plenty to do and no extra after last: should do better. *P. F. Nicholls* **h87 p**

KONKER 12 ch.g. Selkirk (USA) – Helens Dreamgirl (Caerleon (USA)) [2006/7 c–, h–: c16vᵖᵘ c16g⁶ Oct 30] small, strong gelding: fairly useful 2m hurdler at best, no form for long time, mainly over fences. *J. R. Cornwall* **c– h–**

KONTINENT (GER) 5 ch.h. Benny The Dip (USA) – Kapitol (GER) (Winged Love (IRE)) [2006/7 16d* 16d² Nov 11] successful twice on Flat, including over 11f on all-weather at Ghlin in August: easy to back, won maiden at Stratford on hurdling debut by 4 lengths from Cottingham: not fluent but better form (fairly useful) when 2 lengths second of 4 finishers to Roll Along in novice at Uttoxeter following month, making most. *C. von der Recke, Germany* **h120**

KOPOOSHA (IRE) 9 b.m. Montelimar (USA) – Stiritup (IRE) (Mandalus) [2006/7 c16dᵖᵘ c18s⁶ c20s⁵ c16s⁵ c17v⁵ Jan 27] good-topped mare: second foal: dam, twice-raced in bumpers, half-sister to very smart staying chaser Belmont King: poor maiden hurdler/chaser: stays 2½m: wears headgear nowadays: often tongue tied. *A. L. T. Moore, Ireland* **c69 h–**

KORELO (FR) 9 b.g. Cadoudal (FR) – Lora du Charmil (FR) (Panoramic) [2006/7 c133, h151: 23d 24s 29sᵖᵘ 20s⁵ Feb 18] workmanlike gelding: formerly smart hurdler/useful chaser: no form in 2006/7, left D. Pipe after third start: stays 33f: acts on heavy and good to firm going: poor efforts in visor/cheekpieces: often let down by jumping over fences. *S. Gollings* **c– x h–**

KOSMOS BLEU (FR) 9 ch.g. Franc Bleu Argent (USA) – Fee du Lac (FR) (Cimon) [2006/7 c107, h–: c21g* c22m⁸ c26gᵖᵘ c21d⁵ c21mᵘʳ c20d² c19d c19s² Jan 30] tall gelding: has reportedly had breathing operation: fairly useful handicap chaser: won at Wincanton and Fontwell (beat Balladeer by 11 lengths) in May: stays 2¾m: acts on firm and soft going: tongue tied once. *R. H. Alner* **c120 h–**

KOSSIES MATE 8 b.m. Cosmonaut – Pola Star (IRE) (Un Desperado (FR)) [2006/7 h–, F–: 16g 17m³ 17d³ Aug 19] leggy mare: poor form over hurdles. *P. W. Hiatt* **h61**

KOUMBA (FR) 9 b.g. Luchiroverte (IRE) – Agenore (FR) (Le Riverain (FR)) [2006/7 c116, h94: 24g⁴ 24s⁶ 24v³ c24sᵖᵘ c24sᵘʳ c27g c21g c24m Apr 10] angular gelding: modest handicap hurdler: fairly useful chaser, below best in 2006/7: stays 3¼m: acts on heavy and good to firm going: tried in cheekpieces/visor: often let down by jumping over fences. *Evan Williams* **c99 h92**

KOUROSH (IRE) 7 b.g. Anshan – Pit Runner (Deep Run) [2006/7 h86?: 22mᵖᵘ 21g⁵ 21s 20mᵖᵘ Apr 25] poor on balance of form over hurdles: tongue tied last 3 outings. *C. P. Morlock* **h71**

KOVA HALL (IRE) 5 ch.g. Halling (USA) – My Micheline (Lion Cavern (USA)) **h–**
[2006/7 h–: 16v 16g 16s Feb 16] tall gelding: fairly useful at best on Flat (stays 1¼m),
sold out of B. Powell's stable 9,000 gns Newmarket Autumn Sales: no form over hurdles:
tried tongue tied/visored: sold 3,800 gns Doncaster March Sales. *M. F. Harris*

KRACK DE L'ISLE (FR) 9 b.g. Kadalko (FR) – Ceres de L'Isle (FR) (Bad Conduct **c–**
(USA)) [2006/7 24s^{pu} 20v^{pu} 23v^{pu} 22v^{pu} Jan 28] lengthy gelding: lightly-raced winning **h–**
hurdler, no form since 2003/4: fell first only outing over fences: stays 2¾m: acts on heavy
going: blinkered final start. *A. C. Whillans*

KRASIVI'S BOY (USA) 5 b. or br.g. Swain (IRE) – Krasivi (USA) (Nijinsky (CAN)) **h88**
[2006/7 h81: 16m^6 18d^3 16d 16v^6 16m^2 16g^3 Apr 23] rather leggy gelding: modest on
Flat (stays easy 2m), won in February: modest maiden hurdler: stays 2¼m: acts on good
to soft and good to firm going: blinkered last 5 outings (has looked less than straightforward). *G. L. Moore*

KRAZY KANGROO (IRE) 6 b. or br.m. Broken Hearted – Balda Grove (IRE) **F–**
(Kambalda) [2006/7 F16v Feb 27] €5,000 3-y-o: leggy mare: first foal: dam unraced
half-sister to useful hurdler/fairly useful chaser The Widget Man, stayed 3¼m: seventh of
15 in maiden bumper at Catterick on debut. *Miss J. E. Foster*

KRISMAS CRACKER 6 b.g. Kris – Magic Slipper (Habitat) [2006/7 h95: 16g^2 21s^2 **h105**
24s^{pu} Dec 30] good-topped gelding: fair novice hurdler: stayed 21f: acted on soft going:
tongue tied once: dead. *N. J. Henderson*

KRISTIANSAND 7 b.g. Halling (USA) – Zonda (Fabulous Dancer (USA)) [2006/7 **c–**
17d* 16g^3 16d^2 c17v^F 16g 16d^3 c17v^4 16g 16s^6 Apr 26] angular gelding: modest on **h95**
Flat (stays 15f) nowadays: likewise over hurdles: won maiden at Cartmel in August: very
stiff task completed outing over fences: raced around 2m: acts on good to soft ground.
P. Monteith

KRISTOFFERSEN 7 ch.g. Kris – Towaahi (IRE) (Caerleon (USA)) [2006/7 h109§: **c– §**
21f* c20g* c23m^{pu} c20g^{pu} 16g^6 Nov 2] compact gelding: fair handicap hurdler: won at **h114 §**
Ludlow (best effort, by neck from Cannon Fire) on first day of season: successful chasing
debut in maiden at Uttoxeter 3 months later: took little interest 3 starts after: stays 21f:
acts on soft and firm going: tried in cheekpieces: temperamental. *Ian Williams*

KUNG HEI FAT CHOI (IRE) 12 b.g. Roselier (FR) – Gallant Blade (Fine Blade **c80 x**
(USA)) [2006/7 c80x, h–: c20s^4 c25v^{pu} 24v^{pu} c25v^{ur} c29v^3 c21v^3 c25s^4 Apr 1] lightly **h–**
raced over hurdles: poor handicap chaser: stays 25f: acts on heavy going: usually makes
mistakes. *J. S. Goldie*

KYATHOS (GER) 6 br.g. Dashing Blade – Kajaana (Esclavo (FR)) [2006/7 h–: 16g **h–**
16s 16g 16d^{pu} 19s^5 16d Dec 28] good-bodied gelding: no form over hurdles: tried
blinkered/visored. *M. F. Harris*

KYBER 6 ch.g. First Trump – Mahbob Dancer (FR) (Groom Dancer (USA)) [2006/7 **h94**
h80: 20d 20m* 24d^F Feb 14] workmanlike gelding: modest hurdler: won handicap at
Musselburgh: still travelling well when falling ninth in similar event there 10 days later:
stays 3m: acts on good to firm and good to soft going: successful on Flat in April.
J. S. Goldie

KYLEMORE CASTLE (IRE) 8 b.g. Mukaddamah (USA) – L'Americaine (USA) **h–**
(Verbatim (USA)) [2006/7 17g Apr 27] ex-Irish gelding: poor maiden hurdler: left
A. Slattery and tongue tied, well beaten in handicap after near 2-year absence: raced
mainly around 2m: acts on soft and good to firm going: blinkered once. *D. J. Wintle*

KYLE OF LOCHALSH 7 gr.g. Vettori (IRE) – Shaieef (IRE) (Shareef Dancer **h77**
(USA)) [2006/7 h77: 16s 16m^5 18m^4 16g 17m^4 Apr 9] smallish, leggy gelding: modest
on Flat, successful in June/August: poor maiden hurdler: left J. Goldie after fourth outing:
stays 2½m: acts on good to firm going: tried tongue tied/in headgear. *Miss Lucinda
V. Russell*

KYLIEMOSS 6 b.m. Riverwise (USA) – Kalamoss (Kalaglow) [2006/7 F–: F17d **h– §**
17m^{rtr} Aug 2] no form in bumpers: refused to race on hurdling debut. *N. R. Mitchell* **F–**

KYMANDJEN (IRE) 10 b.g. Un Desperado (FR) – Marble Miller (IRE) (Mister Lord **c116 +**
(USA)) [2006/7 c132, h–: c24v 20v^3 Feb 24] angular gelding: lightly raced over hurdles, **h106**
third to Quintero in handicap at Fairyhouse: useful chaser: off 9 months, shaped as if in
need of run behind Homer Wells in valuable handicap at Gowran on reappearance: stays
29f: acts on good to firm and heavy going: wore cheekpieces in 2006/7: often front
runner: genuine. *Paul Nolan, Ireland*

KYNANCE COVE 8 b.g. Karinga Bay – Excelled (IRE) (Treasure Kay) [2006/7 h56: 22mF 20mpu 20f Jul 19] compact gelding: poor maiden hurdler, no form in early-2006/7: stays 21f: acts on good to firm going: tongue tied last 4 starts. *C. P. Morlock* h–

KYNO (IRE) 6 b.g. Accordion – Kelly Gales (IRE) (Strong Gale) [2006/7 c89, h102: 24d6 20m2 24m Jul 5] lengthy gelding: fair handicap hurdler: modest form on first of 2 outings over fences: stays 25f: acts on firm and soft going: tongue tied nowadays. *M. G. Quinlan* c– h101

KYPER DISCO (FR) 9 b.g. Epervier Bleu – Disconea (FR) (Bayolidaan (FR)) [2006/7 c99§, h–: c19d3 c21v4 c21g6 c19mpu c20g5 c19m3 Apr 24] well-made gelding: maiden hurdler/chaser: sold out of N. Henderson's stable 11,000 gns Doncaster August Sales after reappearance: stays 2½m: acts on good to firm and heavy going: wore cheekpieces last 2 starts: often tongue tied: weak finisher. *P. H. Hogarth* c84 § h–

KYRANO (FR) 5 ch.g. Grand Tresor (FR) – Deception (FR) (Tropular) [2006/7 F16s F18v5 F16mpu Apr 15] 25,000 3-y-o: fifth foal: half-brother to 3 winners, including smart 1m to 1¼m winner Commercante and 2m hurdle winner Deflation (both by Marchand de Sable): dam French maiden: no form in bumpers. *M. Bradstock* F–

L

LA BANDIDO (IRE) 7 br.m. Un Desperado (FR) – Matter of Course (IRE) (Glacial Storm (USA)) [2006/7 19d c20m2 c21g3 c24g* c24m Sep 8] ex-Irish mare: winning pointer: maiden hurdler for Daniel O'Connell: modest form in chases: won maiden at Southwell in July: stays 3m: acts on good to firm and heavy ground: tried in cheekpieces. *Evan Williams* c88 h–

LABELTHOU (FR) 8 b.m. Saint Preuil (FR) – Suzy de Thou (FR) (Toujours Pret (USA)) [2006/7 h82+: 18s8 c17s5 21s8 20s8 24s2 21v8 23s8 24g Mar 15] c102 P h142 +

It was a good season for fillies and mares in both Britain and Ireland and over both hurdles and fences. Amaretto Rose, Cailin Alainn, Celestial Wave, Gaspara, Gemini Lucy, Heltornic, Labelthou, Lounaos, Refinement and United all won races of note which weren't confined to their own sex, while the likes of

Ballymore Properties Leamington Novices' Hurdle, Warwick—
Labelthou's remarkable season continues as she defeats the juvenile Zilcash (right)

GDM Partnership's "Labelthou"

American Jennie, Asian Maze, Gazza's Girl, L'Aventure, Liberthine and Material World were other mares who showed at least useful form in important races.

Labelthou proved one of the best staying novices over hurdles of either sex, the latest season her second spell in Britain and considerably more successful than her first. Making her British debut in December 2003, she was placed in two of her first three starts in novice hurdles on these shores, but showed no better than fair form and was absent for the best part of two years after her second outing in Britain, changing stables in the interim from Frank Jordan to Lucy Wadham. Off the course for another six months after her third run, she reappeared in France with her original trainer Guy Cherel. On her first start back at Auteuil, Labelthou belatedly lost her maiden tag in a twenty-runner contest over hurdles, beating Maurice (another import to Britain later in the season) with Kamillo, a former Grand Steeple-Chase de Paris runner-up, and Sybellius d'Artaix, another who was to run in Britain later in the season, among those down the field. Labelthou then made her chasing debut against some fairly useful rivals at the same track a month later, finishing fifth, before being sent back across the Channel again, this time to Emma Lavelle's yard.

Labelthou's starts in Britain had all been at two miles and her runs at Auteuil over not much further. She began her latest campaign in Britain stepped up in trip for a mares novices hurdle at Towcester in November. She evidently relished the test at this stamina-sapping track, making all and pulling a distance clear of her rivals with ease. Mares-only contests invariably lack strength in depth, this one no exception, but Labelthou proved more than good enough to hold her own in open Grade 2 company, giving another display of strong galloping and accurate jumping when stepped up in class in the Winter Novices' Hurdle at Sandown, drawing right away from odds-on Granit Jack to win by twenty-two lengths. Turned out again quickly, Labelthou proved no match for another above-average novice, Flight Leader, in the Bristol Novices' Hurdle at Cheltenham, but she beat the remainder convincingly and saw out the three-mile trip well, sticking to her task when headed. Labelthou returned to winning ways in another Grade 2, the Ballymore Properties Leamington Novices' Hurdle at Warwick, not having to run to her to best to account for the juvenile Zilcash by a length and three quarters, the pair well clear. The Casino 36 Stockport Rendlesham Hurdle at Haydock in February should have presented a stiffer challenge for Labelthou outside novice company, but she proved a ready winner of a contest which failed to attract any of the leading stayers. Leading throughout as usual, Labelthou had her five rivals well strung out at the finish, winning by eight lengths from Afrad, with second favourite Material World another fourteen back in third on a rare off-day. The Spa Hurdle against fellow novices looked an easier option for Labelthou than the World Hurdle at the Cheltenham Festival, though she ended up contesting the latter. With the ground nowhere near so testing as it had been for Labelthou's earlier races, conditions which she clearly handled very well, she would possibly not even have run up to her best in the novice event in any case. As it turned out, the Spa would have provided the stiffer test of stamina the way the races were run and Labelthou managed only eighth of the thirteen finishers in the World Hurdle, racing in second until after halfway but unable to hold her place from three out.

			Dom Pasquini	Rheffic
Labelthou (FR) (b.m. 1999)	Saint Preuil (FR) (gr 1991)		(gr 1980)	Boursonne
		Montecha	Montevideo II
		(br 1972)	Chasseresse
	Suzy de Thou (FR) (b 1984)	Toujours Pret	Val de Loir
		(b 1969)	Dundee III
		Kaky	Mercure
		(b 1976)	Loyola II

Labelthou's sire Saint Preuil, a useful winner in France over hurdles at three and over fences at four, is best known in Britain as the sire of My Will and Crystal d'Ainay. The best horse in Labelthou's French saddlebred (selle francais) family is Otage du Perche, whose eleven wins over jumps in France included the 1986 Grand Steeple-Chase de Paris, which he won from the following year's King George winner Nupsala. Otage du Perche was out of a half-sister to Labelthou's unraced grandam Kaky. Labelthou's dam, Suzy de Thou, was raced almost exclusively in non-thoroughbred races on the Flat, winning two such events at Vichy over ten and eleven furlongs. She has bred two other winners in France besides Labelthou, Helathou (by Video Rock) and New Fate (by Blushing Flame), both successful at around a mile and a half on the Flat and the latter also a winning chaser (for Cherel) at seventeen furlongs and third in a listed chase for four-year-olds at Auteuil. Labelthou will have to find a fair bit more improvement to trouble the leading stayers over hurdles, but the creation of an improved series of mares-only pattern races over hurdles for the 2007/8 season could provide an ideal opportunity or two for her, while a switch back to fences is obviously also an option. Labelthou is almost certainly capable of improving a good deal upon her only outing over fences so far at Auteuil. If she can translate her particularly nimble hurdling style to the larger obstacles, she ought to do well. The compact Labelthou stays three miles and her best efforts have come on soft or heavy ground. *Miss E. C. Lavelle*

LA BONNE VIE 5 ch.g. Magic Ring (IRE) – Perfect Answer (Keen) [2006/7 F–: F17g 20s 16g^{ur} Feb 21] workmanlike gelding: no sign of ability. *C. Roberts*   **h–** **F–**

LABOREC (IRE) 4 gr.g. Oscar (IRE) – Bere Science (IRE) (Roselier (FR)) [2006/7 F16g* Apr 23] 20,000 3-y-o, resold 55,000 3-y-o: third foal: dam ran twice in bumpers: 11/10-on, created good impression when winning maiden bumper at Hexham on debut by 8 lengths from Ormus: promising. *J. Howard Johnson*   **F110 p**

LACDOUDAL (FR) 8 gr.g. Cadoudal (FR) – Belfaster (FR) (Royal Charter (FR)) [2006/7 c159, h137: c27d^6 c24d^4 c21v^4 c24v^3 c24g c25g^3 Apr 13] smallish, angular   **c150** **h–**

gelding: useful handicap hurdler: smart chaser: below best in handicaps in 2006/7, one of better efforts when 9½ lengths third to Reveillez in quite valuable event at Aintree final outing: stays 29f when conditions aren't testing: acts on heavy and good to firm going: usually sound jumper (mistakes second/third starts): genuine. *P. J. Hobbs*

LACKEN (IRE) 7 b.g. Supreme Leader – Sapphire Eile (Mujtahid (USA)) [2006/7 26dᵖᵘ May 17] €21,000 4-y-o: second foal: dam, unraced, out of half-sister to Istabraq: visored/tongue tied, no show in selling hurdle on debut. *Evan Williams*   **h–**

LA CONCHA (IRE) 6 b.g. Kahyasi – Trojan Crown (IRE) (Trojan Fen) [2006/7 h91: c19s⁴ c25sꟳ 23d⁵ 23g⁵ 27mⁿ Apr 26] compact gelding: maiden hurdler, below form in 2006/7: well held completed outing over fences: should stay 3m: acts on good to firm ground. *M. J. McGrath*   **c– h72**

LACONICOS (IRE) 5 ch.g. Foxhound (USA) – Thermopylae (Tenby) [2006/7 h83: 16d⁵ 16mꟳ 16m 21m 19d⁴ 20s 17d 17d 23gᵖᵘ Apr 3] leggy gelding: maiden hurdler, little form in 2006/7. *W. B. Stone*   **h70**

LADALKO (FR) 8 b.g. Kadalko (FR) – Debandade (FR) (Le Pontet (FR)) [2006/7 c143, h–: c25mꟳ c29sꟳ 24v² c29s* c33sᵖᵘ Mar 17] tall, useful-looking gelding: useful hurdler, ½-length second to Just Beth in handicap at Cheltenham: smart handicap chaser: better than ever when winning totesport.com Classic Chase (Handicap) at Warwick in January by 4 lengths from Mon Mome: reportedly ruptured artery next time: stays 33f: acts on heavy and good to firm going: usually held up: often makes mistakes over fences: has found little but is consistent. *P. F. Nicholls*   **c148 x h132**

totesport.com Classic Chase (Handicap), Warwick—
Ladalko (noseband) overhauls long-time leader Naunton Brook (who fades into third) at the last

LA DAME BRUNE (FR) 5 b.m. Mansonnien (FR) – Madame Extra (FR) (Sir Brink **h113 +**
(FR)) [2006/7 F79: 20s* 21v* 24s⁵ Mar 3] lengthy, rather unfurnished mare: fair form
when winning first 2 starts over hurdles, mares novices at Huntingdon (by 19 lengths)
and Warwick (by length from Wyldello) in December: disappointing next time: should
stay at least 2¾m: acts on heavy going. *N. J. Henderson*

LADIES FROM LEEDS 8 b.m. Primitive Rising (USA) – Keldholme (Derek H) **c–**
[2006/7 c–, h73: c25gᵖᵘ 25dᵖᵘ 24mᵖᵘ Mar 25] leggy mare: maiden hurdler: pulled up both **h–**
starts over fences: stays 25f: usually wears headgear nowadays. *A. Crook*

LADINO (FR) 7 bl.g. Acatenango (GER) – Lauderdale (GER) (Nebos (GER)) [2006/7 **h116**
h99: 16g⁶ 17m² 19d² 20m* 22m* 22d 24m² 22m⁴ 25g⁵ 21g Nov 7] rather leggy gelding: fairly useful hurdler: won maiden and novice (beat Cava Bien easily by 11 lengths)
at Uttoxeter in July: sold out of P. Hobbs's stable 18,000 gns Doncaster October Sales,
below form both starts after: stays 3m: acts on good to firm and good to soft going.
Miss S. West

LA DOLFINA 7 b.m. Pennekamp (USA) – Icecapped (Caerleon (USA)) [2006/7 h88: **h115**
16m* 17m³ 16m* 16m² Aug 24] leggy mare: fairly useful hurdler: much improved
early in 2006/7, winning novice events at Ludlow (handicap) in May and Uttoxeter and
Bangor (both with plenty in hand) in July: good second to Ellerslie Tom in similar race at
Stratford: raced around 2m: acts on good to firm going. *P. J. Hobbs*

LADRO VOLANTE (IRE) 5 b. or br.g. Benny The Dip (USA) – Genoa (Zafonic **F–**
(USA)) [2006/7 F–: F16m Sep 10] little show in 2 bumpers: dead. *D. J. Wintle*

LADY ALDERBROOK (IRE) 7 b.m. Alderbrook – Madame President (IRE) (Sup- **h–**
reme Leader) [2006/7 h82: 22m May 11] leggy, angular mare: maiden hurdler: stays
2½m: acts on heavy going. *C. J. Down*

LADY BARONETTE 10 b.m. Baron Blakeney – Rueful Lady (Streetfighter) [2006/7 **c67 x**
c–x: c24g⁴ c23mᵘʳ Apr 22] modest pointer, successful in March: little form in hunter
chases, often let down by jumping. *Ian Howe*

LADY BERNIE (IRE) 6 b.m. Supreme Leader – Noon Hunting (Green Shoon) **F99**
[2006/7 F16v* F16g Mar 29] half-sister to several winners, including fairly useful
hurdler/chaser Lordberniebouffant (by Denel), stayed 2½m: dam, unraced, half-sister to
dams of top-class staying chasers Grey Abbey and The Grey Monk: won mares bumper
at Towcester on debut by 9 lengths from Inghwung: only ninth of 16 under less testing
conditions there following month. *P. R. Webber*

LADY BLING BLING 6 b.m. Midnight Legend – Slipmatic (Pragmatic) [2006/7 **h86**
F93: 21v⁵ 16sᵖᵘ 20vᵖᵘ Feb 28] leggy mare: bumper winner: modest form when fifth to
Mountain Approach in mares novice at Newbury on hurdling debut: went as if amiss both
starts after. *P. J. Jones*

LADY CHATELAINE (IRE) 5 b.m. Supreme Leader – Lady Lock (IRE) (Executive **F77**
Perk) [2006/7 F16d F16v³ F16g Apr 7] €21,000 4-y-o: unfurnished mare: second foal:
half-sister to point winner/fair hurdler Prideoftheyankees (by Good Thyne), stays 2¾m:
dam unraced, out of half-sister to dam of Gaye Chance and Gaye Brief: modest form at
best in bumpers: will be suited by further than 2m. *Mrs S. C. Bradburne*

LADY GARLANDHAYES 5 b.m. Hatim (USA) – Blackdown Beauty (Deltic **F–**
(USA)) [2006/7 F17s F16m Jul 12] first foal: dam unraced: soundly beaten in bumpers.
D. E. Pipe

LADY HOWE 7 br.m. Lord Americo – Howcleuch (Buckskin (FR)) [2006/7 F17s F16g **h–**
F16d 24sᵖᵘ 22g⁵ Apr 15] 20,000 4-y-o: leggy mare: third foal: half-sister to useful **F–**
hurdler/chaser Rambling Minster (by Minster Son), stays 25f, and fair hurdler/fairly
useful chaser Lord Rodney (by Hatim), stayed 3m: dam fair staying chaser: no form in
bumpers (left Mrs J. K. Oliver after second start): no solid form in novice hurdles: needs
to learn to settle. *B. Storey*

LADY JOSH 4 b.f. Josr Algarhoud (IRE) – Dee-Lady (Deploy) [2006/7 16v 16s 17s⁶ **h–**
17d Mar 20] workmanlike filly: little form on Flat: well held over hurdles: wore
cheekpieces last 2 starts. *C. L. Tizzard*

LADY KORRIANDA 6 ch.m. Dr Fong (USA) – Prima Verde (Leading Counsel **h–**
(USA)) [2006/7 16d 22s⁴ 16v⁵ Feb 12] angular mare: half-sister to poor hurdler Envious
(by Hernando), stays 21f: poor maiden on Flat: mistakes and no form over hurdles, left
B. Johnson before final outing. *R. Curtis*

LADY LAMBRINI 7 b.m. Overbury (IRE) – Miss Lambrini (Henbit (USA)) [2006/7   c–
c73, h–: c20s⁶ c27gᵖᵘ Apr 23] leggy mare: winning pointer: maiden chaser: stays 3¼m: h–
acts on soft going. *Mrs L. Williamson*

LADY LOCHINVER (IRE) 4 ch.f. Raise A Grand (IRE) – Opening Day (Day Is   h–
Done) [2006/7 17d 16sᵖᵘ Nov 22] modest maiden on Flat (probably stays 9f): no form in
2 juvenile hurdles. *Micky Hammond*

LADY L'ORELEI 10 b.m. Baron Blakeney – Vi's Delight (New Member) [2006/7   c–
c23f 22g⁶ c20mᵖᵘ c26dᵖᵘ c21m³ 26m Sep 24] modest pointer, won in 2006: little show   h–
over hurdles/in chases: tongue tied last 2 starts. *R. H. York*

LADY LUCINDA 6 b.m. Muhtarram (USA) – Lady Phyl (Northiam (USA)) [2006/7   h–
16d Oct 22] no sign of ability on Flat/hurdling debut. *J. R. Holt*

LADY MARANZI 8 b.m. Teenoso (USA) – Maranzi (Jimmy Reppin) [2006/7 h93:   h94
24v⁴ 20s 20d 19v* 17g* Mar 24] leggy mare: modest hurdler: won selling handicap at
Taunton and mares claimer at Bangor in March: should stay beyond 19f: acts well on soft/
heavy going. *Mrs D. A. Hamer*

LADY MISPRINT 11 ch.m. Classic – Miss Primrose (Primitive Rising (USA))   c–
[2006/7 c–, h–: c24dᵖᵘ May 15] tall, leggy mare: winning hurdler/pointer (refused last 2   h–
starts): failed to complete both outings in chases: stays 23f. *Mrs Rebecca Jordan*

LADY OF SCARVAGH (IRE) 8 b.m. Zaffaran (USA) – Dim Drums (Proverb)   c120 x
[2006/7 24g* 27d⁴ c23m* c24g³ c24sᶠ 22m⁶ 25d c25gᶠ c24s* c24gᵘʳ c22gᵖᵘ Mar 24]   h108
leggy, workmanlike mare: fair hurdler: off 13 months, won mares handicap at Worcester
in May: error-prone chaser, though won maiden at Worcester in August and novice
handicap at Kempton in January: 50/1, apparently much improved when beating Bengo
18 lengths at latter, jumping much better than usual: bled final outing: stays 3m: acts on
soft and good to firm going: none too consistent. *M. Scudamore*

LADY PAST TIMES 7 b.m. Tragic Role (USA) – Just A Gem (Superlative) [2006/7   h–
h–: 20d⁶ May 19] small mare: poor hurdler: no form since 2004/5: stays 2½m: acts on
soft going: tried blinkered. *D. W. Whillans*

LADY RACQUET (IRE) 8 b.m. Glacial Storm (USA) – Kindly Light (IRE) (Sup-   c101
reme Leader) [2006/7 h109: c20s² c20g³ Mar 18] angular mare: fair hurdler: off nearly 2   h–
years, similar form both starts over fences: stays 2¾m: acts on soft and good to firm
going. *Mrs A. J. Bowlby*

LADY ROANIA (IRE) 7 b.m. Saddlers' Hall (IRE) – Ahead of My Time (IRE)   h85
(Royal Fountain) [2006/7 F71: F18m² F16g³ F16m* 18sˢᵘ 21d⁴ Dec 21] fair form in   F86
bumpers (left S. Burrough and off 10 months after debut): left clear 1f out when winning
at Ludlow in November: 8½ lengths fourth to Tambourine Davis in mares novice at
Ludlow on completed outing over hurdles: will stay 3m. *P. Bowen*

LADY ROCKET (IRE) 4 b.f. Rock Hopper – Accountancy Lady (Capitano) [2006/7   h63
F16s F16d F17d 16g⁵ Apr 8] smallish filly: second foal: dam, fairly useful hurdler, stayed   F–
3¼m: well held in bumpers/juvenile hurdle. *R. C. Guest*

LADY ROISIN (IRE) 5 b.m. Luso – Curracloe Rose (IRE) (Roselier (FR)) [2006/7   h68
F16s 16s 16g⁶ 16d⁶ 20g Apr 9] smallish mare: first foal: dam, well beaten over hurdles,   F–
sister to fairly useful staying hurdler/chaser Absolutly Equiname: well held in mares
bumper: poor form over hurdles: should be suited by 2½m+. *Mrs L. Wadham*

LADY SAMBURY 5 b.m. Overbury (IRE) – Skiddaw Samba (Viking (USA)) [2006/7   F69
F16v⁶ F16s Apr 1] compact mare: fourth foal: dam poor 2m hurdler: never dangerous in
bumpers. *J. R. Weymes*

LADY SPEAKER 6 b.m. Saddlers' Hall (IRE) – Stormy Gal (IRE) (Strong Gale)   c–
[2006/7 h86, F86: 19g 19d c25d⁶ c25sᵖᵘ Mar 7] big, workmanlike mare: maiden   h–
hurdler: no form in 2006/7, including over fences: should be suited by further than 2m.
T. D. Easterby

LADY STEPH (IRE) 4 br.f. Lord Americo – Garden Fair (IRE) (Brush Aside (USA))   h–
[2006/7 F14s F14v 19g 22dᵖᵘ 20vᵘʳ 20sᵖᵘ Mar 13] good-bodied filly: fifth foal: dam un-   F–
raced half-sister to useful but temperamental staying chaser Sister Stephanie: little sign
of ability. *E. W. Tuer*

LADY SUFFRAGETTE (IRE) 4 b.f. Mull of Kintyre (USA) – Miss Senate (IRE)   h73
(Alzao (USA)) [2006/7 16v² 16g³ 16m² Apr 24] modest maiden on Flat (stays 1½m):
poor form over hurdles: raced at 2m. *John Berry*

LADY SYNTHIA 4 b.f. Mull of Kintyre (USA) – Yo-Cando (IRE) (Cyrano de Berge- **h–**
rac) [2006/7 16g⁴ 16g^{su} Nov 1] compact filly: fair form on Flat at 2 yrs, last in handicaps
in 2006 for B. Palling: well held completed outing in juvenile hurdles. *Tim Vaughan*

LADY WILDE (IRE) 7 b.m. Oscar (IRE) – Lady Swinford (Ardross) [2006/7 F90: **h79**
16g^F 21v^F 19s⁴ 22g^{pu} Mar 31] good-topped mare: fair form in bumpers: not given hard
race (carried head high) only completed outing over hurdles: will stay 3m: sold 12,000
gns Doncaster May Sales. *Noel T. Chance*

LADY WURZEL 8 b.m. Dilum (USA) – Fly The Wind (Windjammer (USA)) [2006/7 **c–**
c–, h–: c23m^{pu} May 9] won maiden point in 2005, has shown little otherwise: tried **h–**
visored. *J. G. Cann*

LAERTES 6 gr.g. Theatrical Charmer – Handmaiden (Shardari) [2006/7 h113, F77: **c109**
c22s³ c25v* c24v^{pu} 23s* 22d⁵ Mar 17] leggy, angular gelding: fairly useful hurdler: some **h128**
improvement when winning handicap at Wetherby (beat Supreme's Legacy by 5 lengths)
in February: has failed to impress with jumping over fences, including when winning
4-runner novice at Hexham in December, off bridle long way out: will stay beyond 25f:
acts on heavy going: of suspect temperament. *C. Grant*

LAERTES CAUSE 5 ch.g. Giant's Causeway (USA) – La Virginia (GER) (Surumu **F83**
(GER)) [2006/7 F16m² F13m* F16m F16m Sep 10] half-brother to several winners,
including high-class French hurdler Laveron, stayed 25f, and Deutsches Derby winner
Lavirco (both by Konigsstuhl): dam German 1¼m winner, from outstanding German
family: modest form in bumpers: left A. Wohler, won at Hereford in June, only start for
M. Harris: saddle slipped/finished lame next 2 starts. *John Allen*

LAETITIA (IRE) 7 b.m. Priolo (USA) – Licimba (GER) (Konigsstuhl (GER)) [2006/7 **c146**
h125p, F101: 16v³ c22v* c24d² Apr 1] sturdy mare: progressive hurdler: useful form **h144**
when 10½ lengths third to Newmill in Grade 2 at Gowran on reappearance, making up
plenty of ground in straight: already as good over fences, winning Grade 3 mares novice
at Limerick (by 15 lengths from Sabina Park) on chasing debut in March: neck second to
Offshore Account in another Grade 3 at same course next time, losing momentum last
and reportedly lame: will stay beyond 3m: acts on heavy going: held up. *Charles Byrnes,
Ireland*

LAGAN LEGEND 6 gr.m. Midnight Legend – Piecemeal (Baron Blakeney) [2006/7 **c–**
h–, F69: 22g 19d⁶ 22v⁶ c22s^F 22g² 26g³ Apr 20] poor maiden hurdler: fell first on chasing **h69**
debut: stays 3¼m: blinkered last 3 starts: tried tongue tied. *Dr J. R. J. Naylor*

LAGO 9 b.g. Maelstrom Lake – Jugendliebe (IRE) (Persian Bold) [2006/7 h82: 20d⁴ **c77**
20s⁴ c24s^F 21v² 20v² c22v³ c21s⁵ Mar 17] compact gelding: modest hurdler, left James **h87**
Moffatt after first outing: poor form over fences: stays 2¾m: acts on heavy going: has
worn visor/cheekpieces: usually tongue tied. *R. Lee*

LAGO D'ORO 7 b.m. Slip Anchor – Salala (Connaught) [2006/7 c81+, h92, F83: c24s⁵ **c–**
c24d⁶ c26s^{pu} c21v⁵ c20v³ Jan 25] workmanlike mare: winning hurdler/maiden chaser: no **h–**
show in 2006/7: probably stays 2½m. *Dr P. Pritchard*

LAGOSTA (SAF) 7 ch.g. Fort Wood (USA) – Rose Wine (Chilibang) [2006/7 h–: **c–**
c16s⁶ Jan 24] workmanlike gelding: poor maiden hurdler: off 21 months, no show on **h–**
chasing debut: best around 2m: acts on good to firm and good to soft going: has been
blinkered. *G. M. Moore*

LA GRANDE VILLEZ (FR) 5 b.m. Villez (USA) – Grande Sultane (FR) (Garde **c–**
Royale) [2006/7 17s 17s³ 18d c17s^F 18d⁶ 18s³ 17s³ 18s* 16d^{pu} 16s⁵ 22f² 16m* Apr 24] **h104**
smallish, angular mare: fourth foal: half-sister to fairly useful hurdler/useful chaser
Grand Cyborg (by Cyborg), stays 2¾m: dam placed over hurdles/fences around 2m in
France: 12.5f winner on Flat: fell on chasing debut: fair novice hurdler: left M. Rolland,
won mares events at Fontwell (maiden) in November and Towcester (easily) in April:
stays 2¾m: acts on firm and soft going. *A. King*

LA GRIFFE (IRE) 11 b.g. Un Desperado (FR) – Brigette's Secret (Good Thyne **c91**
(USA)) [2006/7 c91, h–: c16g c23s² c21g^{pu} 24m^F 20g^F 20g Apr 14] ex-Irish gelding, **h–**
lightly raced: maiden hurdler: winning pointer: modest form in chases: left Tim Vaughan
before final outing: stays 23f: tried in cheekpieces (fell): tongue tied. *D. A. Rees*

LAHARNA 8 b.g. Overbury (IRE) – Royal Celt (Celtic Cone) [2006/7 h89: c23m^{pu} **c92**
c21d³ c20m^{pu} Apr 8] leggy, close-coupled gelding: winning Irish pointer: modest novice **h–**
hurdler: similar form completed outing (tongue tied) in handicap chases: stays 21f: acts
on soft going. *Miss E. C. Lavelle*

LAHIB THE FIFTH (IRE) 7 br.g. Lahib (USA) – Bob's Girl (IRE) (Bob Back (USA)) [2006/7 h100, F100: 20m⁴ 16m* 16g² c16g³ c20m⁴ Oct 12] progressive hurdler: successful on 3 of 5 starts, including in handicap at Worcester (by 2½ lengths from Dyneburg) in July: further improvement (fairly useful form) when 1¼ lengths second to Supply And Fix in similar event at Perth: none too fluent both starts over fences: should stay 2½m: raced on good going or firmer (bumper win on firm): should still do better over fences. *N. G. Richards*
c95 p
h117

LAHINCH LAD (IRE) 7 ch.g. Bigstone (IRE) – Classic Coral (USA) (Seattle Dancer (USA)) [2006/7 c95, h86: c25m* May 12] modest handicap hurdler/chaser: won over fences at Wincanton in May, only start in 2006/7: should prove effective at 3¼m: acts on firm and good to soft going. *B. G. Powell*
c95
h–

LAKE GUNNER 7 b.m. Gunner B – By The Lake (Tyrant (USA)) [2006/7 F17m⁵ F17s⁵ F17s 16g 16g 19g Apr 8] 3,000 5-y-o: half-sister to fair chaser Jokers Charm (by Idiot's Delight), best up to 21f, and modest hurdler Southend Scallywag (by Tina's Pet), stayed 2½m: dam poor staying maiden: well beaten in bumpers (wore eyeshields)/over hurdles. *R. C. Guest*
h–
F–

LAKE IMPERIAL (IRE) 6 b.g. Imperial Ballet (IRE) – Lakes of Killarney (IRE) (Ahonoora) [2006/7 h68: 16d 16g² 16gᵖᵘ 16m⁴ 19g² c20s³ c20sᶠ Dec 7] close-coupled gelding: modest maiden hurdler, left Heather Dalton after fourth outing: stamina seemingly stretched both starts in novice handicap chases: likely to prove best short of 2½m: acts on soft and good to firm going: in cheekpieces 2 of last 3 starts, also tongue tied final one. *Evan Williams*
c86
h90

LAKE MERCED (IRE) 7 b.g. Charente River (IRE) – Mitsubishi Art (Cure The Blues (USA)) [2006/7 c104, h98: c20mᵖᵘ c24gᶠ c23mᵖᵘ c22g⁵ c21f 20gᵖᵘ Sep 17] sturdy gelding: winning hurdler/chaser, no form in 2006/7: tried in cheekpieces/blinkers: temperamental. *Jonjo O'Neill*
c– §
h– §

LAKE SUPRIMA (IRE) 4 b.f. Primo Valentino (IRE) – Sulaka (Owington) [2006/7 16dᵖᵘ Nov 30] maiden on Flat, sold out of R. Whitaker's stable £2,400 Ascot August Sales: no show in juvenile on hurdling debut. *Miss C. J. E. Caroe*
h–

LAKIL PRINCESS (IRE) 6 gr.m. Bering – Russian Rebel (Machiavellian (USA)) [2006/7 c120, h120: c16s³ c20vᶠ 16v³ c16s² c16v⁶ c16m Apr 22] sparely-made mare: fairly useful hurdler/chaser: creditable efforts over fences at Naas fourth/fifth starts, 17 lengths third to Nickname in handicap (Grade 2 event): will probably prove best around 2m: acts on heavy going: front runner. *Paul Nolan, Ireland*
c120
h106

LA LAMBERTINE (FR) 6 b.m. Glaieul (USA) – Mesoraca (IRE) (Assert) [2006/7 h101§: 20d 24s Oct 27] leggy mare: winning hurdler: claimed from M. Pipe, no show in 2006/7: usually in headgear: ungenuine. *D. Brace*
h– §

LAMANVER HOMERUN 5 b.m. Relief Pitcher – Bizimki (Ardross) [2006/7 F16m⁴ F17s³ 16s³ 16g 19v² 22d⁵ Feb 1] has scope: second foal: dam poor form in bumpers: won bumper at Newton Abbot in June: best effort over hurdles (modest form) when second to Gaspara in mares novice at Taunton: stays 19f: acts on heavy ground. *P. F. Nicholls*
h92
F78

LA MARETTE 9 ch.m. Karinga Bay – Persistent Gunner (Gunner B) [2006/7 c–, h85: 20d 17d 21sᵖᵘ 22v* 22s³ 24v³ 25v³ 20s³ 22s⁶ 21s⁴ 21g⁵ Mar 20] sturdy mare: modest handicap hurdler, left John Allen after first outing: won at Uttoxeter in November: tailed off when refused on chasing debut: stays 25f: raced mainly on soft/heavy going nowadays: tried in cheekpieces (laboured effort ninth start): tongue tied after third outing. *M. Sheppard*
c–
h90

LAMBRIGGAN LAD 5 b.g. Mazurek – Alfs Classic (FR) (Sanglamore (USA)) [2006/7 20d 16mᵖᵘ Oct 12] first foal: dam poor juvenile hurdler: no promise over hurdles: tongue tied. *D. E. Pipe*
h–

LAMBRINI BIANCO (IRE) 9 br.g. Roselier (FR) – Darjoy (Darantus) [2006/7 c78, h–: c26d² c26g* c26d² c24m² c26d* c26d³ c27m Aug 29] leggy gelding: modest handicap chaser: won at Southwell in June and Newton Abbot in July: stays 29f: acts on soft and good to firm going: wears cheekpieces/blinkers: reliable. *Mrs L. Williamson*
c90
h–

LAMBRINI LEGEND (IRE) 5 br.g. Bob's Return (IRE) – Spur of The Moment (Montelimar (USA)) [2006/7 F–: F16d* F16v* 20s⁴ 20s⁴ 19d³ 16v⁴ 16v² Mar 6] strong, compact gelding: successful both completed starts in bumpers, at Towcester (maiden) and Wetherby in May: modest maiden hurdler: likely to stay 3m: raced on ground softer than good. *M. W. Easterby*
h91
F97

LAMBRINI MIST 9 gr.g. Terimon – Miss Fern (Cruise Missile) [2006/7 c–, h–: c21s **c62**
c23m^{pu} c24g^3 c20g^4 c21m^{ur} c22m* c20m^4 c25g^5 c20m* c21s^6 Jan 2] good-topped **h–**
gelding: poor handicap chaser: won at Kelso (novice event) in October and Leicester
(fortunate) in November: stays 25f: acts on good to firm and good to soft going (possibly
not on soft): wears headgear: tongue tied nowadays: sometimes let down by jumping.
Mrs L. Williamson

L'AMI (FR) 8 ch.g. Lute Antique (FR) – Voltige de Nievre (FR) (Brezzo (FR)) [2006/7 **c157**
c161, h–: 20s^5 c24d^3 c24v^4 c24d^2 c26g c36g Apr 14] tall, good-topped gelding: maiden **h111**
hurdler: very smart chaser: creditable efforts in 2006/7 when placed in graded events
won by Kauto Star at Haydock and Newbury, well ridden in muddling affair at latter: not
discredited when seventh behind same horse in Cheltenham Gold Cup: in cheekpieces,
well held in Grand National at Aintree, tiring and mistakes from second Becher's: should
stay beyond 27f: unraced on firm going, acts on any other: sound jumper: consistent.
F. Doumen, France

LAMPION DU BOST (FR) 8 b.g. Mont Basile (FR) – Ballerine du Bost (FR) (Fast **c106**
(FR)) [2006/7 c–, h83: 24s^4 22d^6 c20d^4 c20d^2 c21g^6 c25v^6 c24s^2 c22s^4 c25v^{pu} Mar 9] **h81**
good-topped gelding: maiden hurdler: fair handicap chaser: distressed final start: should
stay beyond 3m: acts on heavy ground: sound jumper. *A. Parker*

LANAKEN (IRE) 7 b.g. Capolago – Farriersfriend (IRE) (Tidaro (USA)) [2006/7 c98, **c82**
h88: c22m 20m c20m c25d c24g c21s^{pu} Oct 1] leggy gelding: winning handicap chaser: modest **h–**
handicap chaser, below form in 2006/7: stays 2¾m: acts on good to firm going: usually
blinkered: often front runner/races prominently: sold 6,000 gns Doncaster October Sales.
P. J. Rothwell, Ireland

LANCE TOI (FR) 8 br.g. Lampon (FR) – Devant Spring (FR) (Spring To Mind (USA)) **c–**
[2006/7 c–, h–: c20d^5 May 19] maiden hurdler/chaser: modest pointer: stays 2½m: acts **h–**
on soft and good to firm going: tried blinkered. *G. D. Hanmer*

LANCIER D'ESTRUVAL (FR) 8 ch.g. Epervier Bleu – Pommette III (FR) (Trac) **h77 §**
[2006/7 h72: 22m 25g* 21d^5 27s Nov 26] rather leggy gelding: poor handicap hurdler:
dead-heated in novice event at Plumpton in May: stays 25f: acts on good to soft going:
visored last 2 starts: tried tongue tied: moody. *Mrs H. J. Cobb*

LAND OF LIGHT 4 ch.g. Fantastic Light (USA) – Russian Snows (IRE) (Sadler's **h99**
Wells (USA)) [2006/7 h88: 18m^3 Sep 21] fair form on Flat (may prove better at 1½m than
1¾m), sold out of Saeed bin Suroor's stable £6,000 Ascot April Sales: blundered last 2
when third to Irish Whispers in juvenile at Fontwell on hurdling debut. *G. L. Moore*

LAND SUN'S LEGACY (IRE) 6 b.g. Red Sunset – Almost A Lady (IRE) (Entitled) **h–**
[2006/7 h63: 22m^{pu} Aug 26] leggy, close-coupled gelding: little show over hurdles: wears
cheekpieces. *J. S. Wainwright*

LANE MARSHAL 5 gr.g. Danzig Connection (USA) – Evening Falls (Beveled **h–**
(USA)) [2006/7 h76: 23d^{pu} 18m 16d Oct 22] leggy gelding: maiden hurdler: successful
twice in points in 2007. *Mrs S. J. Humphrey*

LANGDON LANE 6 b.m. Overbury (IRE) – Snowdon Lily (Town And Country) **h75**
[2006/7 h75: 20m^2 22m^5 26g^{pu} Apr 20] unfurnished mare: poor novice hurdler: left
P. Webber and off another 8 months before final outing: stays 2½m. *C. Tinkler*

LANHEL (FR) 8 ch.g. Boston Two Step (USA) – Umbrella (FR) (Down The River **h–**
(FR)) [2006/7 h–: 16s^{pu} Sep 20] workmanlike gelding: no form over hurdles: difficult
ride. *J. Wade*

LANKAWI 5 ch.g. Unfuwain (USA) – Zarma (FR) (Machiavellian (USA)) [2006/7 h99: **c126 +**
22g^2 21d c20v* c16v* c20m* c25g^2 c24s^2 Apr 25] tall, workmanlike gelding: fair **h111**
hurdler: developed into fairly useful novice chaser, winning at Sedgefield (maiden) in
February and Hexham and Southwell (made virtually all to land odds in 2-finisher event
by ½ length from Pay Attention) in March: ran well when second last 2 starts, beaten 3½
lengths by Caribou at Perth final one: stays 25f: acts on good to firm and heavy going:
may do better yet. *P. Bowen*

LANMIRE TOWER (IRE) 13 b.g. Celio Rufo – Lanigans Tower (The Parson) **c– §**
[2006/7 c87§, h–§: c22s^{pu} c23g^5 c22m^4 c25m^{pu} Aug 6] workmanlike gelding: winning **h– §**
hurdler/handicap chaser: no show in 2006/7: usually in headgear: temperamental (has
refused to race/ran out once). *S. Gollings*

LANNIGANS LOCK 6 b.g. Overbury (IRE) – Lacounsel (FR) (Leading Counsel **h86**
(USA)) [2006/7 h89: 20g 22v^3 22v^6 23d Mar 21] small gelding: modest maiden hurdler:
stays 2¾m: acts on heavy ground: has bled. *R. Rowe*

LANOS (POL) 9 ch.g. Special Power – Lubeka (POL) (Milione (FR)) [2006/7 h71: **h65**
16f⁴ 16f³ 16m Jul 27] smallish, angular gelding: poor maiden hurdler: raced around 2m:
acts on soft and firm going: tried in headgear: often tongue tied. *W. Davies*

LANSDOWNE PRINCESS 5 b.m. Cloudings (IRE) – Premier Princess (Hard **c–**
Fought) [2006/7 h–, F–: 19sᵖᵘ 22v c21f⁴ c22m⁵ Apr 26] lengthy mare: little form. **h–**
G. A. Ham

L'ANTARTIQUE (FR) 7 b.g. Cyborg (FR) – Moomaw (Akarad (FR)) [2006/7 **c140**
h122: c20d⁴ c22v² c20v² c20v* c22vᶠ c25v² c21g* c20gᵘʳ Apr 14] **h–**
 The competitiveness of races at the Cheltenham Festival means that even
stables with any number of leading fancies can leave the meeting empty-handed.
The trainer with the best record at the meeting, Nicky Henderson, for example,
drew a blank (from a team of twenty-three) at the latest Festival despite fielding
eight runners who started at shorter than 10/1, three of them favourites or co-
favourites. Ferdy Murphy's record of long-priced winners at Cheltenham in the last
two seasons is therefore remarkable. In 2006, the stable's 33/1-shots You're Special
and Hot Weld were successful in the Fulke Walwyn Kim Muir Challenge Cup and
the National Hunt Chase respectively, while twelve months later Joes Edge's
last-stride victory at 50/1 in the William Hill Trophy was followed by L'Antartique
winning the Jewson Novices' Handicap Chase at 20/1. It was the stable's third
Festival double, Murphy having first struck with another outside Stop The Waller,
whose last-gasp win (at 16/1) in the Fulke Walwyn Kim Muir was followed up by
Paddy's Return taking the Triumph Hurdle at 10/1. Two years later, French Holly
was a much more predictable winner of the Royal & SunAlliance Novices' Hurdle
when justifying favouritism at 2/1. In addition Murphy has saddled no fewer than
seven horses to be placed at the Festival at odds of 20/1 or more, including Truckers
Tavern's second at 33/1 to Best Mate in the 2003 Cheltenham Gold Cup. Incidentally, novice chasers Another Promise and Aces Four (subsequently successful at
Punchestown and Aintree respectively) were other horses from the yard to run
better at the latest Festival than their long odds might have suggested.
 It may turn out that L'Antartique's win at Cheltenham proves to flatter him
to some degree, as he came from well off the pace in a well-run race. That theory
couldn't be put to the test as L'Antartique was bumped and unseated his jockey
early on in the novices' handicap for amateur and conditional jockeys at Aintree on
Grand National day on his only subsequent start. However, the Jewson runner-
up Bob Hall had also come from well off the pace at Cheltenham and went on to
confirm his improvement there when second in the same race at Aintree. What isn't
in dispute is that L'Antartique ran his best race yet over fences at Cheltenham.
Despite the nineteen-runner field, the betting market made it a two-horse race
between top weight New Little Bric, 7/2 favourite after his win in the Scilly Isles
Novices' Chase at Sandown, and the Tony McCoy-ridden and J. P. McManus-
owned King Revo, a useful hurdler who had opened his account over fences at
Hexham the time before. L'Antartique was among a dozen in the field sent off at
16/1 or longer. Dropped out early on and not entirely fluent, L'Antartique had only
a few tailed-off rivals behind him at the top of the hill. But he made good ground

*Jewson Novices' Handicap Chase, Cheltenham—another Festival winner for Ferdy Murphy
as L'Antartique holds off Bob Hall (left) and Wee Robbie (centre)*

Mrs A. N. Durkan's "L'Antartique"

from then on, having to be switched wide for a clear run going to the third last but getting a smooth passage when manoeuvred back towards the inner rounding the home turn. Produced to lead from Wee Robbie going to the final fence, L'Antartique was kept going up the hill to win by two lengths from Bob Hall, with Wee Robbie another two and half lengths back in third and Rasharrow completing the frame. Both the market leaders were disappointing.

The Jewson, L'Antartique's first handicap, represented a very different test from his previous races over fences, most of which had been novice events in small fields run on heavy ground. His only win had come when landing the odds in work-manlike fashion against three rivals in a maiden at Bangor just before Christmas. L'Antartique finished second on three other occasions against some good novices though, going down by a short head to Heez A Dreamer at Uttoxeter and then being the only other one to get round when beaten by Royal Rosa at Wetherby. L'Antartique wasn't discredited against Dom d'Orgeval when stepped up in trip at Hexham on his last start before Cheltenham. His best chance of adding to his Bangor win had come when odds on for quite a valuable contest at Kelso in January when he had fallen still going strongly. L'Antartique's season had begun where it ended, at Aintree, where he finished fourth on his chasing debut behind Turko, when finishing a place behind another future Cheltenham Festival handicap winner in Cloudy Lane.

L'Antartique began his career in Ireland with Tony Mullins, and, while he won his first two starts in bumpers, he was less than straightforward in his early days. However, on only his second start over hurdles he finished second, albeit a remote one, to Hardy Eustace in the Red Mills Trial Hurdle at Gowran just before the latter's second Champion Hurdle win. Still a novice over hurdles in his first season in Britain with Ferdy Murphy in 2004/5, L'Antartique won twice before a knock (sustained when only fourth in the River Don Hurdle) prevented him taking his chance at Cheltenham that season. L'Antartique carries the royal blue, white hooped sleeves and pink cap of Mary Durkan, colours made famous by the outstanding Irish mare Anaglogs Daughter, whose many wins included the 1980 Arkle Trophy. Ferdy Murphy started out in Ireland as private trainer to the Durkan family and his association with that trailblazing mare even included partnering her to win at Chepstow just four days after she'd won the Arkle Trophy at Cheltenham.

L'Antartique (FR) (b.g. 2000)	Cyborg (FR) (ch 1982)	Arctic Tern (ch 1973)	Sea Bird II / Bubbling Beauty
		Cadair (b 1970)	Sadair / Blarney Castle
	Moomaw (b 1989)	Akarad (b or br 1978)	Labus / Licata
		Syzygy (b 1984)	Kenmare / Orbit

The leggy L'Antartique was sold for €74,000 as an unraced three-year-old at the Derby Sale. He is by Cyborg, one of the French sires with the highest profile in Britain in the last dozen years or so thanks largely to Festival winners Cyborgo, Cyfor Malta, Fondmort and Hors La Loi III. Cyborg is also the sire of the two other winners out of L'Antartique's dam Moomaw. The Jonjo O'Neill-trained Fier Normand, a fairly useful winning hurdler, wasn't seen out after making a successful chasing debut at Ludlow in the autumn, while their elder brother Cyborg de Sou is also a fairly useful hurdler and fair chaser at up to twenty-one furlongs. The dam Moomaw won on the Flat in France at a mile and a quarter and twice at up to two and a half miles over hurdles there. A couple of Moomaw's half-brothers won over jumps in the States and she is a half-sister to the listed-winning dam of Understood, who wasn't far behind the best jumpers in the States, finishing fourth in the Breeders' Cup Chase in 2005. L'Antartique's grandam Syzygy won at seven furlongs (at two) to a mile and a quarter in France. L'Antartique stays twenty-five furlongs and has raced only on good ground or softer so far; he acts on heavy. *Ferdy Murphy*

LAOUEN (FR) 9 br.g. Funny Baby (FR) – Olive Noire (FR) (Cadoudal (FR)) [2006/7 20s* 20g⁵ Apr 12] leggy gelding: useful hurdler: successful 6 of 8 starts, off 4 years prior to winning handicap at Hexham in April, not extended to beat Surricate by 16 lengths: favourite, below that form when fifth in similar listed event at Aintree 11 days later: stays 2½m: acts on soft and good to firm going (won bumper on heavy). *L. Lungo* **h131**

LAPPEENRANTA (IRE) 6 b.g. Presenting – Millies Luck (Al Sirat) [2006/7 F102: 19d³ Nov 8] fairly useful form when runner-up in bumper: off 7 months, shaped quite well when third to Nightfly in novice at Lingfield on hurdling debut: should improve, particularly over further. *V. R. A. Dartnall* **h102 p**

L'APPRENTI SORCIER (FR) 4 b.g. Phantom Breeze – Flower of Dream (FR) (Mansonnien (FR)) [2006/7 F17g Mar 24] fifth foal: dam won 2¼m hurdle in France: well held in maiden bumper on debut. *S. Curran* **F–**

LA PROFESSORESSA (IRE) 6 b.m. Cadeaux Genereux – Fellwah (IRE) (Sadler's Wells (USA)) [2006/7 h75: 16mᵖᵘ Oct 4] leggy mare: maiden hurdler, little form since 2004/5: tried tongue tied: sold £600 Ascot December Sales. *R. Curtis* **h–**

LARA'S GIRL 5 b.m. Tipsy Creek (USA) – Joe's Dancer (Shareef Dancer (USA)) [2006/7 h–: 16f 16mᵖᵘ 17m Jun 19] no form over hurdles: blinkered final outing: sold £500 Ascot February Sales. *K. G. Wingrove* **h–**

LARKWING (IRE) 6 b.h. Ela-Mana-Mou – The Dawn Trader (USA) (Naskra (USA)) [2006/7 16v³ 21s* 20d² 20g⁴ Apr 12] leggy horse: useful up to 18.7f on Flat (has hinted at temperament), sold out of G. Wragg's stable 40,000 gns Newmarket Autumn Sales: won maiden hurdle at Limerick in February by 4½ lengths from Ballycullen Boy: fairly useful form both starts after, 23½ lengths fourth to Tidal Bay in Grade 2 novice at Aintree, looking none too keen under pressure: will stay beyond 21f: raced on good going or softer. *Eric McNamara, Ireland* **h125**

LASCAR DE FERBET (FR) 8 br.g. Sleeping Car (FR) – Belle de Ferbet (FR) (Brezzo (FR)) [2006/7 c87, h–: c16d* 16g c16gᵘʳ Nov 24] leggy gelding: maiden hurdler: modest handicap chaser: won 5-runner conditional jockeys event at Worcester in **c93 h–**

LAU

October: probably best around 2m: acts on any going: tried tongue tied: has looked weak finisher. *R. Ford*

LASKARI (FR) 8 b.g. Great Palm (USA) – Hatzarie (FR) (Cyborg (FR)) [2006/7 c23dpu c20d³ c20s² c20spu Feb 9] tall, workmanlike gelding: modest form in novice hurdles: fairly useful handicap chaser, left Mrs L. Taylor and off 19 months prior to return: jumped much better than previous 2 starts when second to Idole First at Kempton, though carried head bit awkwardly under pressure: should stay beyond 2½m: acts on heavy and good to firm going: tongue tied last 2 starts. *P. R. Webber* — c121 h–

LA SOURCE A GOLD (IRE) 8 br.g. Octagonal (NZ) – Coral Sound (IRE) (Glow (USA)) [2006/7 c–: c20dpu c20vpu c16gpu Apr 23] no form over fences, left Nick Williams before second outing: tried tongue tied. *P. C. Haslam* — c–

LAST PIONEER (IRE) 5 b.g. New Frontier (IRE) – Toordillon (IRE) (Contract Law (USA)) [2006/7 16d 17v 17s Mar 11] fair maiden on Flat (stays 1½m), sold out of T. Tate's stable 10,000 gns Doncaster October Sales: poor form in novice hurdles: got loose to post on debut. *R. Ford* — h77

LATE CLAIM (USA) 7 ch.g. King of Kings (IRE) – Irish Flare (USA) (Irish River (FR)) [2006/7 h–: 22m⁶ 24g Jun 15] good-topped gelding: fair juvenile hurdler in 2003/4: lightly raced and little form in handicaps since: visored once. *R. T. Phillips* — h79

LATIMER'S PLACE 11 b.g. Teenoso (USA) – Pennethorne Place (Deep Run) [2006/7 c124, h–: c24g* c26sF c26s* c24v⁵ c24gpu c24g⁶ c21g³ Apr 13] sturdy gelding: useful handicap chaser: left J. Geake, better than ever when winning at Sandown (3 ran) in November and Newbury (impressive, beat Kerstino Two by 16 lengths) in December: respectable effort over inadequate trip when 8½ lengths third of 29 to Dunbrody Millar in Topham Chase at Aintree, blunder 4 out before finishing best of all: stays 3¼m: raced on good ground or softer (acts on soft): usually races prominently. *N. J. Gifford* — c139 h–

LATIN QUEEN (IRE) 7 b. or br.m. Desert Prince (IRE) – Atlantic Dream (USA) (Muscovite (USA)) [2006/7 c104, h101: c21m³ Jul 16] smallish mare: fair hurdler/chaser: stayed 19f: probably acted on any going: dead. *J. D. Frost* — c– h–

LATZOD'ALM (FR) 8 b.g. Passing Sale (FR) – Enea d'Alm (FR) (Djarvis (FR)) [2006/7 c25g* c25sF Mar 1] maiden hurdler: fair chaser: won hunter at Cheltenham in May for J. Groucott: stays 25f: raced on good ground or softer (acts on soft): tried blinkered. *Ms L. J. Willis* — c102 h–

LAUDERDALE 11 b.g. Sula Bula – Miss Tullulah (Hubble Bubble) [2006/7 c20v c20s⁵ c16v⁶ c20v⁴ c20s⁵ c25s⁶ c25v⁴ c20v⁵ Mar 18] good-topped gelding: handicap chaser, on downgrade: stays 3m: acts on heavy going. *Miss Lucinda V. Russell* — c89 d h–

LAUNCESTON 5 ch.m. Sula Bula – Lady Grenville (Aragon) [2006/7 F16s F14g² 18s³ 16g Dec 26] first foal: dam, sprint maiden, ran once over hurdles: poor form when runner-up in mares bumper: well held over hurdles. *Miss H. C. Knight* — h– F74

LAUNDE (IRE) 8 b.g. Norwich – Carbia's Last (Palm Track) [2006/7 c122: c16s* c16d* c16v⁵ c17d⁶ c20gpu Mar 24] workmanlike gelding: fairly useful handicap chaser, lightly raced: won at Aintree in October and Haydock (beat Lord Rodney by 1¾ lengths) in November: stays 19f: acts on heavy going: often front runner: jumps soundly in main. *B. N. Pollock* — c129

LAURELDEAN (IRE) 9 b.g. Shernazar – Power Run (Deep Run) [2006/7 16g c18vur c17v c17s⁵ 17v c16v* c17vpu c16m³ Apr 24] good-topped gelding: fairly useful handicap hurdler/chaser: won over fences at Fairyhouse in February by 3 lengths from Grangehill Dancer: should stay beyond 2¼m: acts on heavy and good to firm ground: usually patiently ridden: unreliable. *Michael Cunningham, Ireland* — c121 § h– §

LAURIER DE COTTE (FR) 8 b.g. Kadalko (FR) – Rafale de Cotte (FR) (Italic (FR)) [2006/7 c25vpu Feb 13] ex-French gelding: fifth foal: brother to winning chaser around 2¾m Minuit de Cotte and half-brother to winning hurdler/one-time useful chaser Esprit de Cotte (by Lute Antique), stays 25f: dam winner around 11f: twice-raced over jumps in Provinces in 2003, runner-up in 21f chase at La-Roche-Posay on second occasion: left G. Macaire, successful in point in Britain in 2006. *Miss Olivia Maylam* — c– h–

LAURIER D'ESTRUVAL (FR) 8 ch.g. Ragmar (FR) – Grive d'Estruval (FR) (Quart de Vin (FR)) [2006/7 c–, h–: c19spu c20dpu 20vpu c19s Mar 12] strong gelding: maiden hurdler: fair 2m chaser in 2004/5: lightly raced and no form since: tried blinkered/tongue tied. *S. E. H. Sherwood* — c– h–

547

Mrs Sarah Ling's "Laustra Bad"

LAUSTRA BAD (FR) 4 b.g. Astarabad (USA) – Love Crazy (FR) (Loup Solitaire   **c114**
(USA)) [2006/7 16d^2 17d* 18s^3 18s^4 c17s^4 c17s^{pu} c17s* c17s^4 16d^2 16d* 16d^3 17g*   **h130**
Apr 18] quite good-topped gelding: first foal: dam unraced: 11.5f winner on Flat: won
juvenile hurdle at Clairefontaine in August and 3-y-o chase at Enghien in November: sold
from T. Trapenard €75,000 after eighth start: useful form over hurdles in Britain, winning
at Chepstow (novice) in February and Cheltenham (beat King's Revenge by ¾ length,
pair clear) in April: also ran very well when 5¼ lengths third of 24 to Gaspara in Fred
Winter Juvenile Handicap at last-named: will stay 2½m: raced on good going or softer: in
cheekpieces last 2 outings. *D. E. Pipe*

LAVENOAK LAD 7 b.g. Cloudings (IRE) – Halona (Pollerton) [2006/7 h70: 22m^{pu} **c86**
22s^{pu} 20d 22v c19s c19s^6 c20v^4 c22s^4 c23v^F c23s* Mar 12] lengthy gelding: maiden   **h–**
hurdler: modest chaser: won minor event at Taunton in March: stays 23f: acts on soft
going: has worn cheekpieces: ran out final 2005/6 outing. *P. R. Rodford*

L'AVENTURE (FR) 8 b. or br.m. Cyborg (FR) – Amphitrite (FR) (Lazer (FR))   **c138 §**
[2006/7 c138§, h–§: 24s^6 c29s c29s c28s^2 c31d^{pu} c33s^4 c32m Apr 21] leggy, angular   **h123 §**
mare: fairly useful handicap hurdler: useful handicap chaser: best effort in 2006/7 when
1¼ lengths second to Heltornic in valuable event at Haydock in February: typically got
behind when fourth to Baron Windrush in Midlands Grand National at Uttoxeter (in
frame in race for third consecutive year): stays 33f: acts on heavy and good to firm going:
often blinkered: tongue tied: not a fluent jumper of fences: usually soon off bridle.
P. F. Nicholls

LAWAAHEB (IRE) 6 b.g. Alhaarth (IRE) – Ajayib (USA) (Riverman (USA)) [2006/7   **c91**
h83: 16g^4 16s c20m^3 c20m^{pu} c18g^6 c16f^3 16f^2 c20m^3 Sep 17] workmanlike gelding: **h87**
modest hurdler/maiden chaser: stays 2½m: acts on firm and good to soft going:
has worn visor/cheekpieces. *M. J. Gingell*

LAWGIVER (IRE) 6 b.g. Definite Article – Marylou Whitney (USA) (Fappiano   **c89 §**
(USA)) [2006/7 h99: c21g^4 c20f 20f 17d^2 19g 16g^5 16g Apr 16] smallish gelding: modest   **h98 §**

handicap hurdler, sold out of T. Fitzgerald's stable 8,500 gns Doncaster October Sales after fourth outing: much better effort over fences when fourth in novice handicap at Uttoxeter: likely to prove best up to 2½m: acts on firm and good to soft ground: has carried head high: inconsistent. *Mrs Marjorie Fife*

LAWOOD (IRE) 7 gr.g. Charnwood Forest (IRE) – La Susiane (Persepolis (FR)) [2006/7 16m c20f⁶ 21d 17s⁵ 24s c20vᵖᵘ Jan 25] good-bodied gelding: one-time fairly useful on Flat (stays 1½m), well held in 2006, left L. Grassick before final start: little impact over hurdles/fences: tried visored/in cheekpieces/tongue tied. *M. Scudamore*   **c–** **h–**

LAWYER DES ORMEAUX (FR) 8 ch.g. Sky Lawyer (FR) – Chaouia (FR) (Armos) [2006/7 c–, h110+: 26g* c23d³ c23s³ c26d² c25vᶠ c24m² Apr 10] leggy gelding: fairly useful handicap hurdler: off 13 months, won at Huntingdon (by 3½ lengths from Deo Gratias) in October: fair novice chaser, placed all 4 completed starts but makes mistakes: stays 3¼m: acts on soft and good to firm going. *P. Bowen*   **c110 x** **h120**

LAY DOWN THE LAW 6 b.m. Bob's Return (IRE) – Storming Lady (Strong Gale) [2006/7 22vᵖᵘ Jan 2] lengthy, angular mare: second foal: dam won 21f hunter chase: no show in novice hurdle on debut. *Miss A. M. Newton-Smith*   **h–**

LAZERITO (IRE) 9 b.g. Shernazar – Nemova (IRE) (Cataldi) [2006/7 h–: c18s³ Dec 13] lengthy, workmanlike gelding: lightly raced: bumper/hurdle winner: off another 8 months, fair form when third in handicap at Newbury (mistakes) on chasing debut, only outing in 2006/7: best short of 3m: acts on heavy going. *Miss Venetia Williams*   **c114** **h–**

LAZY BUT LIVELY (IRE) 11 br.g. Supreme Leader – Oriel Dream (Oats) [2006/7 c116d, h110d: 24d c26s³ c32s⁴ c24v⁴ c27s⁴ 23vᵖᵘ 24d 27gᵖᵘ Mar 27] sturdy gelding: handicap hurdler/chaser, modest nowadays: stays 4m: probably best on going softer than good: often let down by jumping/attitude. *R. F. Fisher*   **c95 x** **h87**

LAZY LENA (IRE) 8 b.m. Oscar (IRE) – Magnum Gale (IRE) (King's Ride) [2006/7 h72: 20g² 24g 20d 21v⁵ 23d⁶ 20v 21g⁶ 26g 22m² Apr 28] small mare: poor handicap hurdler: stays 3m: acts on firm and soft going: has taken little interest. *Miss L. C. Siddall*   **h71**

LEAC AN SCAIL (IRE) 6 b.g. Lord Americo – Swings'n'things (USA) (Shernazar) [2006/7 F16m* 21m 20dᵖᵘ 16v⁵ 21mᵖᵘ Apr 9] rather leggy gelding: fourth foal: dam, 2½m hurdle winner, successful over 1¼m on Flat: won bumper at Worcester on debut in July: sold out of T. George's stable 44,000 gns Doncaster August Sales: form over hurdles (breathing problem on debut) only on penultimate outing: sold 10,000 gns Doncaster May Sales. *K. C. Bailey*   **h88** **F94**

LEADAWAY 8 b.g. Supreme Leader – Annicombe Run (Deep Run) [2006/7 h73+: 20d* 20g⁵ 20f² 22m³ 22v⁵ Dec 12] leggy gelding: modest handicap hurdler: won at Sedgefield in May: sold out of Miss P. Robson's stable 5,200 gns Doncaster October Sales prior to final outing: will stay 3m: acts on firm and good to soft going, probably on soft. *D. M. Grissell*   **h88**

LEADING ATTRACTION (IRE) 6 b.g. Mister Mat (FR) – Cerise de Totes (FR) (Champ Libre (FR)) [2006/7 22d* Nov 16] sixth foal: half-brother to modest hurdler/chaser up to 3m Hussard (by Concorde Jr) and French cross-country chaser Isidora Bleue (by Fill My Hopes): dam unraced: won maiden Irish point on debut in 2006: bought 45,000 gns Doncaster May Sales: created good impression when winning 16-runner novice at Wincanton on hurdling debut by ¾ length from Flight Leader: will stay 3m: presumably met with setback, but remains likely to improve. *P. F. Nicholls*   **h121 p**

LEADING AUTHORITY (IRE) 6 br.g. Supreme Leader – Bonnie Thynes (IRE) (Good Thyne (USA)) [2006/7 F94: F16d⁴ 16s⁶ 22v² 19v* 21v⁶ 24v² Mar 10] rangy, good sort: bumper winner: fairly useful novice hurdler: landed odds at Exeter in January by neck from Melba Toast (pair clear): upped in trip, good second to impressive Mark The Book at Chepstow final outing: stays 3m: raced on ground softer than good (acts on heavy): takes plenty of driving. *C. L. Tizzard*   **h116** **F105**

LEADING CONTENDER (IRE) 6 b.g. Supreme Leader – Flair Dante (IRE) (Phardante (FR)) [2006/7 F114: 20d² 20d² 20v* 22g³ 24s² 25v⁴ 22d 24gᶠ Apr 19] rather unfurnished gelding: bumper winner: fairly useful novice hurdler: won at Chepstow (by short head from Carnival Town) in November: good placed efforts next 2 starts, 1½ lengths second to Itsa Legend at Taunton on second occasion: stays 3m: acts on heavy going: tried blinkered. *P. J. Hobbs*   **h120**

LEADING GOSSIP (IRE) 11 b.g. Leading Counsel (USA) – Fair Gossip (IRE) (Le Bavard (FR)) [2006/7 c21s May 29] angular ex-Irish gelding: once-raced over hurdles: winning pointer: maiden chaser: stays 3m: acts on heavy ground: tried tongue tied. *P. Jones*   **c–** **h–**

*skybet.com Rowland Meyrick Handicap Chase, Wetherby—
a big Boxing Day prize for Leading Man and Graham Lee*

LEADING MAN (IRE) 7 b.g. Old Vic – Cudder Or Shudder (IRE) (The Parson) **c130**
[2006/7 c126, h–: c26s c24s c25v* c24v⁴ c28s⁶ c24sᵖᵘ Apr 26] strong, workmanlike **h–**
gelding: winning hurdler: useful handicap chaser: won Grade 3 skybet.com Rowland
Meyrick Handicap Chase at Wetherby in December by 8 lengths from Sir Rembrandt:
went with little zest last 2 outings: probably stays 3½m: raced on going softer than good
(acts on heavy). *Ferdy Murphy*

LEADING RUN (IRE) 8 b.g. Supreme Leader – Arctic Run (Deep Run) [2006/7 **h118**
F123: 20d* 19s² 16v² 18v² 24g 20m⁴ Apr 8] sturdy gelding: will make a chaser: smart
bumper performer: fairly useful novice hurdler: won maiden at Punchestown in October:
runner-up next 3 starts, beaten 3 lengths by easy winner Aran Concerto in 3-finisher
Grade 1 at Leopardstown on third occasion: stays 2½m: acts on heavy and good to firm
going: not a fluent jumper. *N. Meade, Ireland*

LEAD ON (IRE) 6 b.g. Supreme Leader – Dressed In Style (IRE) (Meneval (USA)) **h127 p**
[2006/7 16sᶠ 17s* 16g² 17g* Apr 19] 21,000 2-y-o: good-topped gelding: second foal:
dam sixth in bumper on only start: made promising start over hurdles (would have won
on debut but for falling last), winning novices at Taunton in January and Cheltenham
(landed odds by 3 lengths from Nobelix in 4-runner event) in April: also ran well when
neck second of 18 to Special Envoy in similar event at Newbury: likely to be suited by
further than 2m: useful prospect, likely to win more races. *P. J. Hobbs*

LEA GREEN 6 b.m. Missed Flight – Houselope Brook (Meadowbrook) [2006/7 F16f **h–**
F17s 17vᵖᵘ Dec 12] first foal: dam winning pointer: no show in bumpers/maiden hurdle. **F–**
W. Storey

LEAMINGTON LAD (IRE) 4 gr.g. Beckett (IRE) – Nicea (IRE) (Dominion) **h100**
[2006/7 17g⁴ 16d² 16v² 16s³ 17v⁶ Feb 25] fair on Flat (stays 11.6f), won twice in 2006:
fair juvenile hurdler: raced around 2m: acts on heavy going: tried tongue tied: raced freely
last 2 starts. *J. A. Geake*

LEARNING THE BLUES (FR) 4 ch.g. Trempolino (USA) – Cure The Blues (IRE) **h104 p**
(Phardante (FR)) [2006/7 17s⁶ 16s³ 16v⁵ 20m* Mar 31] useful-looking gelding: half-
brother to fairly useful hurdler/chaser up to 19f Change Partner (by Turtle Island) and
winning hurdler/chaser around 2m Georgia On My Mind (by Belmez): maiden on
Flat: fair form over hurdles, sold out of J-P. Gallorini's stable €85,000 Goffs (France)
November Sale after debut: improved when making all in maiden at Uttoxeter: stays
2½m: best form on good to firm going: capable of better again. *D. E. Pipe*

LEASE 9 ch.g. Lycius (USA) – Risanda (Kris) [2006/7 24fᵘʳ c22d³ c25d 16f³ 21g c24s **c97**
Feb 4] angular gelding: modest chaser/hurdler: stays 2¾m: acts on firm and good to soft **h89**
going: tried blinkered, usually wears cheekpieces. *J. G. Carr, Ireland*

550

LEASE BACK (FR) 8 b.g. Sleeping Car (FR) – Salse Pareille (FR) (Perouges (FR)) [2006/7 c–, h114: 22s^{pu} 23s^4 22g Mar 19] winning chaser: fair hurdler on his day: stays 3m: acts on soft going: has had breathing problem. *L. Wells* **c– h100**

LEASE LEND 4 ch.g. Zilzal (USA) – Moogie (Young Generation) [2006/7 F14v* F13v* F16g^3 Mar 17] rather leggy, workmanlike gelding: half-brother to several winners, including fairly useful 7f winner Catwalk (by Shirley Heights): dam, 2-y-o 6f winner, later best at 9f: smart form in bumpers: won at Wetherby in December and Haydock (6 ran, beat Evelith Echo a head) in January: best effort when 4 lengths third to Theatrical Moment in valuable event at Aintree after end of season. *T. D. Easterby* **F117**

L'EAU DU NIL (FR) 6 b.g. Kadounor (FR) – Lamakara (FR) (Akarad (FR)) [2006/7 c–, h101: 20f^2 19m^3 22d^F Mar 26] fourth only start over fences: maiden hurdler, fair form at best, sold out of P. Hobbs's stable 11,000 gns Doncaster October Sales before final outing: stays 2½m: acts on soft going. *K. C. Bailey* **c– h96 d**

LEAVEITTOROG 5 b.g. Millkom – Fooling With Fire (Idiot's Delight) [2006/7 F16g Apr 23] fourth foal: dam, bumper winner, out of half-sister to top-class 2m hurdler/smart chaser Prideaux Boy: failed to complete in 4 points: blinkered, well beaten in maiden bumper. *Mrs L. Williamson* **F—**

LE BEAU BAI (FR) 4 b.g. Cadoudal (FR) – Dame Blonde (FR) (Pampabird) [2006/7 F16s* F17v* F16g Mar 14] €28,000 2-y-o: compact gelding: fourth foal: brother to bumper/hurdle winner Bumper, stays 2¾m: dam, won 2m hurdle, also successful up to around 11f on Flat: fairly useful form in bumpers: won at Towcester (beat Three Guesses by 3½ lengths, idled) and Exeter (very simple task) in February: well held in Grade 1 at Cheltenham. *D. E. Pipe* **F96**

LE BRIAR SOUL (IRE) 7 b.g. Luso – El Moss (IRE) (Le Moss) [2006/7 h101, F95: 20v^3 22s^{pu} 20s* Apr 27] good-topped gelding: fairly useful novice hurdler: off 5 months (trained second start only by Mrs A. Bowlby), improved from when winning handicap at Perth in April by 10 lengths from Idarah: likely to stay 3m: raced on going softer than good: jumping has lacked fluency. *V. R. A. Dartnall* **h120 +**

LE BURF (FR) 6 b.g. Lute Antique (FR) – Fripperie (FR) (Bojador (FR)) [2006/7 h87: 21s^4 20d^6 16s* 16s^2 16d Mar 13] rather unfurnished gelding: progressive hurdler: won maiden at Wincanton in January by 10 lengths from The Venetian: ran well next 2 starts, though possibly flattered when mid-field in Supreme Novices' Hurdle at Cheltenham (kept on from well back): likely to prove best around 2m: acts on soft going. *G. R. I. Smyly* **h121 ?**

LE CORVEE (IRE) 5 b.g. Rossini (USA) – Elupa (IRE) (Mtoto) [2006/7 h112: 16g 16v^5 17s 16d 16s Mar 11] good-topped gelding: has reportedly been hobbayed: fair juvenile hurdler for A. King: little impact in handicaps in 2006/7: raced around 2m: acts on good to soft going: tried visored. *A. W. Carroll* **h83**

LE DUC (FR) 8 b.g. Villez (USA) – Beberova (FR) (Synefos (USA)) [2006/7 c137, h–: 24s c26g c31s^4 c31d^3 c36g^{ur} c32m^{pu} Apr 21] tall, good-topped gelding: impresses in appearance: has reportedly had breathing operation: winning hurdler: useful handicap chaser: placed twice over National fences at Aintree, though not so fluent 2 starts there in 2006/7, unseated first Becher's in Grand National: respectable efforts in cross-country events at Cheltenham third/fourth outings, third to Heads Onthe Ground in Sporting Index Handicap: stays 31f: acts on heavy and good to firm going: tried blinkered: irresolute. *P. F. Nicholls* **c132 § h– §**

LEE GAP FAIR (IRE) 6 b.g. Bob Back (USA) – Trumpster's Gale (IRE) (Strong Gale) [2006/7 20v^5 16v^6 Dec 11] third foal: dam unraced half-sister to useful 2½m hurdler/staying chaser Bell Staffboy: poor form on first of 2 starts in novice hurdles. *M. Todhunter* **h75**

LEES'S LAD 7 b.g. Lyphento (USA) – Hi Duchess (Carwhite) [2006/7 16g^{pu} Apr 14] second foal: dam behind in 3 races over hurdles: no show in novice hurdle on debut. *M. B. Shears* **h–**

LE FLEUR BLEU 5 b.m. Pistolet Bleu (IRE) – Norstock (Norwick (USA)) [2006/7 F16m^5 F16g^{pu} Oct 30] fifth foal: half-sister to fair 2m hurdler Accumulus (by Cloudings) and fair chaser Stocks 'N Shares (by Jupiter Island), stayed 2½m: dam, prolific winning hurdler/fair chaser, effective at 2m to 3¼m: modest form in bumper on debut: lame next time. *C. J. Mann* **F78**

LE FOREZIEN (FR) 8 b.g. Gunboat Diplomacy (FR) – Diane du Forez (FR) (Quart de Vin (FR)) [2006/7 c–, h90: 26g^2 24f^{pu} c19s^5 c23s^4 Dec 18] modest handicap hurdler: winning chaser in France, poor form final outing in 2006/7: stays 3m: acts on soft going: tongue tied nowadays. *C. J. Gray* **c81 h90**

LEFT HAND DRIVE 4 b.g. Erhaab (USA) – Eyelet (IRE) (Satco (FR)) [2006/7 17d² **h96 §**
17m 17g* 18gᵖᵘ 16d* 17s 16s 20m² Mar 29] compact gelding: closely related to fairly
useful hurdler/winning chaser Openide (by Key of Luck), stays 3m, and half-brother to
bumper winner Oscars Vision (by Oscar Schindler): modest form on Flat (stays 11f):
fair juvenile hurdler: won at Newton Abbot in August and Plumpton in October: stays
2½m: acts on good to firm and good to soft going: blinkered/tongue tied: temperamental.
B. W. Duke

LEGACY (JPN) 7 b.g. Carnegie (IRE) – Idraak (Kris) [2006/7 17gᵖᵘ May 16] half- **h–**
brother to fair hurdler/fairly useful chaser Idris (by Generous), stays 2½m: modest on Flat
(stays 1¼m), successful in January 2006: no show on hurdling debut. *P. D. Evans*

LEGAL CALL 4 b.g. Easycall – Legal Sound (Legal Eagle) [2006/7 16f Sep 17] half- **h–**
brother to winning 2m hurdler Legatee (by Risk Me) and winning pointer by Mystiko:
poor maiden on Flat (stays 1m) for M. Appleby: tongue tied, lost all chance when
hampered first in juvenile on hurdling debut. *M. B. Shears*

LEGAL GLORY (IRE) 7 b.g. Bob Back (USA) – Native Shore (IRE) (Be My Native **c105**
(USA)) [2006/7 F85: F17d 24m² 22g³ 20f⁴ 24m⁴ c23d* c24gᵖᵘ Oct 7] bumper winner: **h108**
fair novice hurdler: won at Worcester in August: similar form when winning maiden there **F–**
on chasing debut: let down by jumping following month: stays 3m: acts on firm and good
to soft going. *B. G. Powell*

LEGAL JOY 5 ch.g. Double Trigger (IRE) – Raglan Lady (Carlingford Castle) [2006/7 **h–**
F16g F17d² 21s Dec 5] third foal: brother to 2¾m hurdle winner Penteli: dam poor novice **F79**
hurdler: better effort in bumpers when runner-up at Sedgefield: well beaten in novice on
hurdling debut. *F. P. Murtagh*

LEGALLY FAST (USA) 5 b.g. Deputy Minister (CAN) – Earthly Angel (USA) **h112**
(Crafty Prospector (USA)) [2006/7 h112: 22m 21s² 22s* 22s⁶ 21d Dec 26] tall, angular,
close-coupled gelding: fair hurdler, left S. Burrough after first outing: back to best to win
handicap at Market Rasen in November: stays 2¾m: acts on soft going: tried in blinkers.
P. Bowen

LEGAL WARNING 6 b.g. Contract Law (USA) – Carrie's Risk (Risk Me (FR)) **F–**
[2006/7 F–: F17g Aug 26] tailed off in bumpers 15 months apart. *C. J. Down*

LEGENDS LASS 5 b.m. Midnight Legend – Forgiving (Jellaby) [2006/7 F16m F16m **F–**
Apr 25] half-sister to winning 2m hurdler Moor Hall Lady (by Rambo Dancer): dam
modest 2m hurdler: little impact in bumpers. *D. J. Wintle*

LEIGHTON BUZZARD 5 b.g. Cyrano de Bergerac – Winsome Wooster (Primo **h77**
Dominie) [2006/7 16d³ 16d 20d 16g 16g⁴ 17m⁴ Apr 15] fair on Flat (seems to stay easy
1¾m), won handicap in June for Mrs A. Duffield: poor maiden hurdler: raced mainly
around 2m: unraced on extremes of going: tried in cheekpieces/blinkers. *N. B. King*

LE JAGUAR (FR) 7 b.g. Freeland (FR) – Fee La Maline (FR) (Maalem (FR)) [2006/7 **c119**
c118, h–: c24s³ c24d⁶ c31s c25g² c25s³ c27f³ Apr 5] tall, close-coupled gelding: has **h–**
reportedly had breathing operation: fairly useful handicap chaser: stays 31f: acts on heavy
going: effective blinkered or not: tongue tied. *P. F. Nicholls*

LE JOYEUX (FR) 8 br.g. Video Rock (FR) – Agra (FR) (Brezzo (FR)) [2006/7 24g **c–**
24m 22d³ 24g² 24d c18d⁵ Dec 26] strong gelding: modest novice hurdler: no solid form **h92**
over fences: stays 3m: acts on good to firm and good to soft going: visored final outing,
usually wears cheekpieces: has had tongue tied. *B. I. Case*

LE LAYON (FR) 11 b.g. Panoramic – Fleurette d'Anjou (FR) (Djarvis (FR)) [2006/7 **c–**
c20d³ c20s⁴ c20s⁵ c21s* c22d³ 16s³ c23gᵖᵘ 19g c20s³ c26v⁵ c20s Apr 22] winning **h–**
hurdler: successful 6 times over fences, including at Dieppe in July: left B. Jollivet after
fifth start, well held in 2 handicaps in Britain: stays 2¾m: acts on heavy going: usually
wears blinkers. *Mrs Savinja Braem, Belgium*

LE MARRON 4 ch.f. Rambling Bear – Stone Madness (Yukon Eric (CAN)) [2006/7 **F–**
F14s Feb 4] sixth foal: dam poor hurdler: no show in bumper on debut. *Miss
Z. C. Davison*

LE MILLENAIRE (FR) 8 b. or br.g. Ragmar (FR) – Ezaia (FR) (Iron Duke (FR)) **c–**
[2006/7 c–, h94: 22f⁶ 19g² 19d 20s⁴ 22s³ 24mᵖᵘ Apr 15] good-topped gelding: winning **h91**
pointer: no show only outing in chase: modest handicap hurdler, sold out of S. Shirley-
Beavan's stable 5,000 gns Doncaster May Sales and off 7 months prior to second start:
stays 2¾m: acts on soft and firm going: tried blinkered/tongue tied. *Miss Suzy Smith*

LEMON TREE 7 ch.m. Weldnaas (USA) – Go Gipsy (Move Off) [2006/7 F62+: **h–**
F16m⁵ 19g² 24f 20m 19m⁶ Aug 24] modest form in bumpers: mistakes and no form over **F76**
hurdles: sold 500 gns Doncaster October Sales. *N. M. Babbage*

intercasino.co.uk Molyneux Novices' Chase, Aintree—
an all-the-way win for chasing debutant Lennon and Paddy Brennan

LENNON (IRE) 7 b. or br.g. Beneficial – Stradbally Bay (Shackleton) [2006/7 h122: **c139**
c16g* c16g* c16d* c16g c16g⁴ 16s* Apr 25] tall gelding: useful hurdler: ridden far more **h133**
patiently than usual when winning at Perth in April (for second year running) by 5 lengths
from Charlotte Vale, idling and jinking left run-in: similar standard as novice chaser: won
at Aintree in October (listed event) and November (easily) and Catterick (simple task) in
December: good 10½ lengths fourth of 6 to Twist Magic in Grade 1 at Aintree: should
stay 2½m: acts on soft ground (bumper winner on good to firm): usually front runner.
J. Howard Johnson

LENNY 7 ch.g. Afzal – Sail On Lady (New Member) [2006/7 c20g c25s³ c25s c24v⁴ **c101 x**
c23s⁴ c26v² c23v* c19gF Mar 28] rather leggy, close-coupled gelding: fourth foal: half-
brother to winning pointer by Dragon Palace: dam of no account: successful twice from 4
starts in points in 2006: fair chaser: made all in 3-finisher maiden at Leicester in March,

553

winning by 25 lengths from Thatlldoya: stays 3¼m: raced mainly on soft/heavy ground: often let down by jumping. *Mrs Caroline Bailey*

LENNY THE BLADE 6 b.g. Master Willie – Limelight (Old Vic) [2006/7 17s 16s 16v **h68** 20g Apr 11] first foal: dam, fair hurdler, stayed 3m: poor form over hurdles: likely to prove suited by further than 2m. *R. T. Phillips*

LEO MCGARRY (IRE) 4 ch.g. Fantastic Light (USA) – Lilissa (IRE) (Doyoun) **h112** [2006/7 16d 22s² 20d³ 22s* 22s* 22m³ 24g⁵ Apr 18] lengthy gelding: fair on Flat (stays 17f), successful twice in 2006, sold out of S. C. Williams' stable 31,000 gns Doncaster November Sales: fairly useful juvenile hurdler: won maiden at Stratford and novice at Fontwell in February: probably stays 3m: acts on soft and good to firm going: wore cheekpieces final outing. *N. B. King*

LEONARDO'S FRIEND 4 b.g. Polish Precedent (USA) – Glider (IRE) (Silver Kite **h86** (USA)) [2006/7 18s⁴ 16v⁶ 16s 17g Apr 27] lengthy gelding: fairly useful on Flat (stays 11f) at 3 yrs in Germany for A. Trybuhl, well held in Britain in 2007: modest form over hurdles: stays 2¼m: tried tongue tied. *B. G. Powell*

LEONIA'S ROSE (IRE) 8 gr.m. Roselier (FR) – Sanafaa (Wolverlife) [2006/7 h66+: **h–** 20s⁵ 21dᵖᵘ 25s 20d Nov 21] ex-Irish mare: little form over hurdles: tried in cheekpieces. *Miss Lucinda V. Russell*

LEONIDOVICH 6 b.g. Pasternak – Steady Woman (IRE) (Aristocracy) [2006/7 F17m **F–** Jun 7] first foal: dam winning pointer: refused in point on debut in 2006: well beaten in bumper. *W. Storey*

LEOPOLD (SLO) 6 b.g. Solarstern (FR) – Lucera (GER) (Orofino (GER)) [2006/7 **c90** h97: c16m⁵ 18m³ c21g⁴ c20g³ c17m⁴ c23gᵂᵈⁱˢ c24g⁵ c26d⁴ Aug 20] leggy gelding: **h?** modest hurdler: third in Svenskt Champion Hurdle at Stromsholm second start: easily best effort over fences when winning handicap at Stratford (subsequently disqualified due to prohibited substance) in July: effective at 2m to 23f: acts on soft and firm going: tried visored. *M. F. Harris*

LEO'S LUCKYMAN (USA) 8 b. or br.g. Woodman (USA) – Leo's Lucky Lady **h–** (USA) (Seattle Slew (USA)) [2006/7 h96: 16gᵖᵘ May 4] workmanlike gelding: form over hurdles (modest) only on second outing in 2005/6: has had breathing problem. *R. S. Brookhouse*

LEO'S LUCKY STAR (USA) 5 b.g. Forestry (USA) – Leo's Lucky Lady (USA) **h–** (Seattle Slew (USA)) [2006/7 h103p: 16dᶠ 16sᶠ Nov 25] useful on Flat at one time: fell all 3 starts over hurdles, close second when departing 2 out in juvenile on debut in 2005/6: likely to prove best with emphasis on speed at 2m. *R. S. Brookhouse*

LE PASSING (FR) 8 b.g. Passing Sale (FR) – Petite Serenade (FR) (Trac) [2006/7 **c112** c147, h–: c20s* c21s* c22v⁴ c21gᶠ Apr 12] good-topped gelding: smart chaser at best: fit **h–** from points, easily landed odds in hunters at Fontwell and Fakenham in February: let down by jumping over National fences at Aintree, including in Fox Hunters' on final outing: stays 21f: acts on heavy and good to firm going: effective blinkered or not: weak finisher. *P. F. Nicholls*

LEPRECHAUN'S MAITE 5 b.g. Komaite (USA) – Leprechaun Lady (Royal Blend) **h80** [2006/7 h–: 16m 17m 18m³ 20vᵖᵘ 16d⁶ 24d⁴ Jan 19] close-coupled gelding: twice-raced on Flat: poor maiden hurdler, sold out of B. Pollock's stable 800 gns Doncaster November Sales after second outing: stays easy 3m: acts on heavy going: tried visored. *W. G. Young*

LERIDA 5 ch.g. Groom Dancer (USA) – Catalonia (IRE) (Catrail (USA)) [2006/7 h93: **c–** 18f 16m 16g⁴ 18g 16g 16d⁵ 20m⁶ 22g c16gᶠ Apr 23] leggy, close-coupled gelding: poor **h84** hurdler: fell first on chasing debut: stays 2½m: acts on good to firm going. *Miss Lucinda V. Russell*

LE ROCHELAIS (FR) 8 ch.g. Goldneyev (USA) – Olympiade de Brion (FR) (Night **c115** And Day) [2006/7 c105+, h95: c22v⁵ c16s⁴ c20vᶠ c21s² c19s* c21sᵖᵘ Mar 8] workman- **h–** like gelding: maiden hurdler: fairly useful chaser: won handicap at Hereford in February by 2½ lengths from Elegant Clutter: lame next time: needs further than 2m and stays 2¾m: raced on going softer than good (acts on heavy). *R. H. Alner*

LE ROUGE FATAL (FR) 5 ch.g. Bateau Rouge – Fatal Attraction (FR) (Gorytus **c92** (USA)) [2006/7 c18d⁵ c17s² c20sᶠ c17s⁶ 17d* 17v⁴ 16vᵖᵘ 16g Apr 16] ex-French geld- **h92** ing: third foal: half-brother to 1¾m hurdle winner Elfe de La Foret (by Cosmopolitan): dam 1¼m winner: modest hurdler/chaser: left L. Metais €21,100, won novice hurdle at Sedgefield on British debut in October: raced mainly around 2m: acts on heavy ground: has been blinkered. *M. Todhunter*

LE ROYAL (FR) 8 b.g. Garde Royale – Caucasie (FR) (Djarvis (FR)) [2006/7 c95x, h105: 24dᵖᵘ c25g² c25s² c17v⁴ 24d 20g⁶ Apr 7] leggy gelding: winning hurdler, no form in handicaps in 2006/7: modest novice chaser: probably stays 3¼m: acts on heavy going: tried tongue tied: has been let down by jumping over fences. *K. G. Reveley* **c94 h–**

LES BAUX BELLE (IRE) 7 b.m. Supreme Leader – Sister Stephanie (IRE) (Phardante (FR)) [2006/7 F90: F17v 16vᵖᵘ Jan 27] second in bumper on debut in 2005/6: no show in mares novice on hurdling debut: stoutly bred. *D. J. Wintle* **h– F–**

LESCER'S LAD 10 b.g. Perpendicular – Grange Gracie (Oats) [2006/7 c–x, h84?: 26gᵖᵘ 16m 16d 20g 20d⁴ c16s⁴ c19s² c21s* c21d* 26g³ 16g⁵ c25g⁴ Apr 11] tall, lengthy gelding: modest chaser/maiden hurdler: won 2 handicaps (first for amateurs) over fences at Folkestone in January: stays easy 3¼m: acts on soft going: tried tongue tied. *Mrs A. M. Woodrow* **c85 h89**

LESDREAM 10 b.g. Morpeth – Lesbet (Hotfoot) [2006/7 c102, h–: c19sᵖᵘ 20v* 18g² Mar 18] sturdy gelding: fair hurdler: won seller at Uttoxeter in January: similar form only once in 5 starts over fences: stays 3m: acts on heavy going. *J. D. Frost* **c– h104**

LE SEYCHELLOIS (FR) 7 ch.g. Mansonnien (FR) – Adjirah (FR) (Sicyos (USA)) [2006/7 c132d, h–: c21d⁵ c24d c20s² c21s³ c20f⁵ Apr 5] rather leggy gelding: has reportedly had breathing operation: fairly useful handicap chaser: best effort in 2006/7 when 1¼ lengths second to Milan Deux Mille at Kempton: stays 2½m: acts on heavy going: tried blinkered/tongue tied: sometimes let down by jumping: not one to rely on: sold 10,500 gns Doncaster May Sales. *P. F. Nicholls* **c123 § h–**

LESLEY COTTAGE 5 gr.m. Shambo – Bucklands Cottage (Roaring Riva) [2006/7 21vᵖᵘ 25s 24vᵖᵘ c26gᵖᵘ Apr 7] angular mare: first foal: dam fair pointer: no show in novice hurdles/handicap chase. *W. Amos* **c– h–**

LESLINGTAYLOR (IRE) 5 b.g. Orpen (USA) – Rite of Spring (Niniski (USA)) [2006/7 17g* 16g* 16v⁶ 16g² 16m Apr 10] rangy gelding: fairly useful on Flat (stays **h121**

Mrs Marie Taylor's "Leslingtaylor"

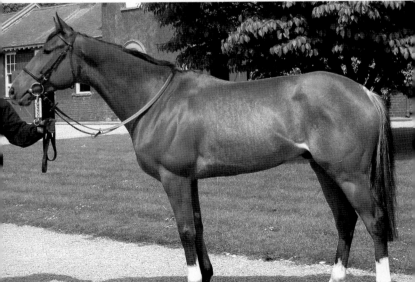

1¾m), won 3 times in 2006: successful on 3 of 5 starts over hurdles, in novices at Market Rasen and Musselburgh (fairly useful form, beat Crocodile Dundee by 1¾ lengths) in December and Newcastle (comfortably landed odds) in March: not discredited when mid-field in valuable handicap at Fairyhouse final outing: raced around 2m: ran poorly on heavy going: fluent jumper. *J. J. Quinn*

LESPRIDE 9 b.g. Morpeth – Lesbet (Hotfoot) [2006/7 19g⁶ 17mᵖᵘ Jun 14] sturdy gelding: no form: tried blinkered. *J. D. Frost* — **h–**

LESTER LEAPS IN (USA) 4 b. or br.g. Red Ransom (USA) – Rose Aurora (USA) (Majestic Light (USA)) [2006/7 16v² 16g⁸ 17g Apr 18] compact gelding: fair on Flat (stays 10.2f), successful in June, sold out of R. Hannon's stable 42,000 gns Newmarket Autumn Sales: fair form in juvenile hurdles: won 5-runner event at Plumpton in March: finished lame next time: likely to prove best around 2m. *N. J. Henderson* — **h104**

LETALUS (GER) 6 b.g. Tannenkonig (IRE) – Lerida (GER) (Lagunas) [2006/7 16g Mar 24] lengthy gelding: successful 8 times from 1m to 9f on Flat, including 5 in 2006, leaving U. Stoltefuss after winning at Neuss in November: took good hold when well held in novice on hurdling debut: likely to do better. *Carl Llewellyn* — **h78 p**

LET GO (GER) 4 b.c. Big Shuffle (USA) – Lady From Lucca (Inchinor) [2006/7 a16g² 16m 16v* 17s Mar 28] fair on Flat, successful 3 times up to 7.5f in 2006: well held in juvenile hurdle in Britain: won minor event at Neuss in March. *M. Hofer, Germany* — **h?**

LETHEM AIR 9 ch.g. Aragon – Llanddona (Royal Palace) [2006/7 c–, h97: 16g³ 16g c16g c16v⁴ c21v³ c20v² c20d⁶ c20s⁶ c17v³ c20v² Mar 22] big, lengthy gelding: fair hurdler: easily best effort over fences when second in handicap at Ayr sixth outing: stays 2½m: acts on good to firm and heavy going: usually wears headgear: signs of temperament. *T. Butt* — **c111 h100**

LETHEM PRESENT (IRE) 7 ch.m. Presenting – Present Tense (Proverb) [2006/7 h–, F–: c25m³ c24sᵖᵘ c20mᵖᵘ c20f c22vᵖᵘ c20d⁶ c24d* c24d⁴ c25s² c25vᵖᵘ c24g⁵ c20g⁶ Apr 2] no form over hurdles: poor chaser: won amateur handicap at Musselburgh in December: stays 25f: acts on soft going, seemingly not on heavy. *T. Butt* — **c84 h–**

LET IT BURN (FR) 5 b.g. Officiel (FR) – Fleur de Normandie (FR) (Chaparral (FR)) [2006/7 F14s 17g Mar 24] leggy, unfurnished gelding: half-brother to several winning hurdlers in France: dam placed up to 1¾m on Flat in France: well beaten in maiden bumper/novice hurdle. *D. E. Pipe* — **h– F–**

LETITIA'S LOSS (IRE) 9 ch.m. Zaffaran (USA) – Satin Sheen (Abednego) [2006/7 c–p, h100: 24s 21sᵖᵘ 23d* 25d⁴ 24d⁵ 21s⁴ 20g Mar 21] plain mare: fair handicap hurdler: sold out of N. Richards' stable 7,000 gns Doncaster May Sales after first start: jumped better when winning at Fakenham (by 19 lengths) in December: fell only outing over fences: stays 27f: acts on heavy going. *Mrs A. E. Brooks* — **c– h108**

LE TOSCAN (FR) 7 br.g. Double Bed (FR) – La Toscanella (FR) (Riverton (FR)) [2006/7 F104: 20d⁴ 19s* 20v* 20v⁵ 24v Feb 24] good-topped gelding: bumper winner: fairly useful novice hurdler: won at Naas in October and Clonmel (comfortably by 5½ lengths from Well Run) in November: below form in Grade 1 at Navan and valuable handicap at Fairyhouse last 2 starts: should stay 3m: acts on heavy going. *M. J. P. O'Brien, Ireland* — **h124**

LET'S BE SUBTLE (IRE) 8 b.m. Oscar (IRE) – Raven Night (IRE) (Mandalus) [2006/7 c–, h–: 22d⁵ c25fᵖᵘ Sep 29] runner-up on completed start in Irish points in 2005: no solid form over hurdles/in chases: tongue tied. *W. Amos* — **c– h–**

LET'S FLY (FR) 12 b.g. Rose Laurel – Harpyes (FR) (Quart de Vin (FR)) [2006/7 c108d, h–: c21g c23v² May 27] good-topped gelding: winning hurdler/chaser: prolific in points nowadays, successful 5 times between January and April: stays 3m: acts on heavy ground. *Ross Oliver* — **c91 h–**

LETS GO DUTCH 11 b.m. Nicholas Bill – Dutch Majesty (Homing) [2006/7 c90, h–: c24vᵖᵘ 24v c25g³ c26g* Apr 23] workmanlike mare: winning hurdler: modest handicap chaser: back to form to win at Plumpton in April: best at 3m+: acts on heavy going: tried tongue tied. *K. Bishop* — **c86 h–**

LETSPLAY (IRE) 7 ch.g. Accordion – Pennine Sue (IRE) (Pennine Walk) [2006/7 h73, F77: 22m 20m⁶ Jul 25] smallish gelding: well beaten over hurdles: won point in April: tried blinkered/tongue tied. *K. J. Burke* — **h–**

LET'S ROCK 9 b.g. Rock City – Sizzling Sista (Sizzling Melody) [2006/7 c73?, h–: c19d⁶ c16mᵘʳ c20dᵖᵘ c17g⁴ Apr 21] maiden chaser, no show in 2006/7: tried in cheekpieces. *Mrs A. Price* — **c– h–**

LETS ROLL 6 b.g. Tamure (IRE) – Miss Petronella (Petoski) [2006/7 16g² 16g⁴ **h101 p**
Dec 30] half-brother to fair hurdler Lord Nellsson (by Arctic Lord), stays 2¾m: useful on
Flat (stays 14.8f), successful in September: fair form when in frame in novice hurdles at
Musselburgh: will be suited by stiffer test of stamina. *C. W. Thornton*

LETS TRY AGAIN (IRE) 10 b.g. Barathea (IRE) – Intricacy (Formidable (USA)) **h– §**
[2006/7 h79: 22m 19spu 19mpu Aug 24] winning hurdler, no form in 2006/7: untrustworthy. *R. A. Farrant*

LETTERMAN (IRE) 7 br.g. Presenting – Papoose (IRE) (Little Bighorn) [2006/7 **c120**
h128: 17s⁴ c16s⁵ c22g* c24d⁴ c20dF c20v² c21m Apr 27] close-coupled gelding: fairly **h117**
useful hurdler/chaser: won maiden over fences at Thurles in November by 1¾ lengths
from Back To Bid: in frame in Grade 2 novices next 2 completed starts, 1¼ lengths
second to Benefit Night at Naas: should stay 3m: raced mainly on good going or softer
(acts on heavy). *E. J. O'Grady, Ireland*

LEVALLOIS (IRE) 11 b.g. Trempolino (USA) – Broken Wave (Bustino) [2006/7 **c98 §**
c87§, h–: c23m c26d² c26vF c24s⁴ c24v² c26spu c26s⁴ c24v³ c26v⁶ c24gpu c25mpu **h–**
Mar 29] smallish gelding: modest handicap chaser: no show last 3 starts: acts 3½m: acts
on heavy going: usually blinkered: ungenuine. *C. L. Tizzard*

LEVITSKI 6 br.g. Vettori (IRE) – Leisure (FR) (Fast Topaze (USA)) [2006/7 16s³ 16s⁵ **h102**
16d² Nov 19] smart on Flat (stays 1½m), successful at 4 yrs in France for Y. de Nicolay:
fair novice hurdler, left N. Madden after first start: raced mainly at 2m: tongue tied last 2
outings. *Jonjo O'Neill*

LE VOLFONI (FR) 6 b.g. Sicyos (USA) – Brume (FR) (Courtroom (FR)) [2006/7 **c146**
c142, h129: c21v³ c21v⁶ c21g⁴ c21g⁶ Apr 13] small, close-coupled gelding: winning **h–**
hurdler: smart chaser: changed hands 210,000 gns Doncaster May Sales and reportedly
had surgery after sinus infection in autumn: ran creditably in handicaps at Cheltenham
first 3 starts, 5¼ lengths fourth of 23 to Idole First in Racing Post Plate: far from fluent in
Topham at Aintree next time: stays 21f: acts on heavy ground. *P. F. Nicholls*

LEWIS ISLAND (IRE) 8 b.g. Turtle Island (IRE) – Phyllode (Pharly (FR)) [2006/7 **c– §**
c119§, h110§: c20mF c17d⁵ c20vpu 18g⁶ 19gur 16m⁵ Apr 27] well-made gelding: **h82 §**
fairly useful hurdler/chaser at best: generally well below form in 2006/7, claimed from
G. L. Moore £6,000 fourth outing: stays 2½m: acts on good to firm and heavy going: tried
tongue tied: often reluctant to start, and not one to rely on. *K. J. Burke*

LEWIS LLOYD (IRE) 4 b.g. Indian Lodge (IRE) – Sandy Fitzgerald (IRE) (Last **h–**
Tycoon) [2006/7 17gpu Aug 26] half-brother to fair 2m hurdler Corporate Express (by Sri
Pekan): dam unraced, half-sister to fairly useful 2m hurdler Creux Noir: modest on Flat
(stays 9.3f), successful in August: no show in juvenile on hurdling debut. *I. A. Wood*

LEWIS'S WORLD 4 br. or gr.g. Overbury (IRE) – Brenig (Horage) [2006/7 F16g Apr **F–**
7] €32,000 3-y-o: close-coupled gelding: brother to a winning pointer and half-brother to
fair hurdler/chaser Afon Alwen (by Henbit), stayed 25f: dam maiden half-sister to
Champion Hurdle winner Kribensis: well held in bumper on debut. *Mrs S. J. Smith*

LEYLAND COMET (IRE) 9 b. or br.g. Roselier (FR) – Firey Comet (IRE) (Buck- **c–**
skin (FR)) [2006/7 c25fpu c24dpu Oct 15] maiden hurdler: modest form when successful **h–**
only completed outing over fences: no show in points in 2007: should stay 4m: acts on
heavy going. *S. B. Clark*

LEY PREACHER (IRE) 6 b.g. High Roller (IRE) – Chapel Field (IRE) (Sayaarr **h74**
(USA)) [2006/7 h62²: 21m⁴ Aug 29] third in maiden Irish point on debut: poor form over
hurdles. *G. M. Moore*

LIAKOURA (GER) 5 b.g. Royal Academy (USA) – Lady Member (FR) (Saint **h107**
Estephe (FR)) [2006/7 16g³ 17s⁵ 16m* 16mF Apr 22] one-time useful performer on Flat
(stayed 1¼m), below best in 2006 for Mrs A. Perrett: fair form over hurdles: won maiden
at Plumpton in April: likely to have proved best with emphasis on speed around 2m: acted
on good to firm going: tried tongue tied: dead. *N. J. Gifford*

LIAMELISS 5 ch.m. Dr Fong (USA) – Ivory Palm (USA) (Sir Ivor (USA)) [2006/7 **h–**
16m 19d⁶ 16m Apr 24] half-sister to modest chaser Tommy Carson (by Last Tycoon),
stays 3¼m, and fair 2m hurdle winner The Budgee (by Muhtarram): modest maiden on
Flat (stays 1½m) at 3 yrs, well held in 2006: no form in novice hurdles. *M. A. Allen*

LIAM MELLOWS (IRE) 7 b.g. Anshan – Sea Skin (Buckskin (FR)) [2006/7 F16d **c–**
c17vpu c16vF Mar 19] lengthy, rather sparely-made gelding: half-brother to useful hurdler **F–**
Hard To Start (by Supreme Leader), stayed 3m: dam won 3m hurdle: no show in listed
bumper/maiden chases. *John Joseph Murphy, Ireland*

LIBERATE 4 ch.g. Lomitas – Eversince (USA) (Foolish Pleasure (USA)) [2006/7 **h142**
17d* 16d* 16d² 17g² 20g⁵ Apr 12]

Although he was unable to notch a third Triumph Hurdle victory in four
years, Philip Hobbs once again unearthed a smart juvenile in Liberate. In chasing
home Katchit at Cheltenham, Liberate was following in the hoofprints of several
stablemates in showing improved form over obstacles after racing on the Flat. Back
in 1994/5 the modest Flat performer Greenback compiled a remarkably successful
juvenile campaign, his eight wins including the Adonis Hurdle at Kempton. French
imports Lord Brex and Noble Request also went on to greater things over hurdles,
the former winning the Anniversary Hurdle at Aintree in 2000. Made In Japan was
fairly useful on the Flat before progressing well over hurdles, though his Triumph
Hurdle success was achieved at 20/1. After showing just fair form on the Flat, Fair
Along became a much more accomplished jumper, joining Hobbs after two bloodless victories for John Flint before going on to finish runner-up to his high-class
stablemate Detroit City in the Triumph Hurdle. Detroit City and Fair Along are
proof that Hobbs's prowess with such horses extends beyond their juvenile seasons,
which obviously bodes well for Liberate's prospects.

The improvement that Liberate showed through his juvenile season may not
have been of a similar magnitude to that he showed through his Flat career, but that
is hardly a mark against Hobbs, who acquired him after a typically astute three-
year-old handicap campaign yielded four victories at up to two miles for Sir Mark
Prescott. Liberate took well to jumping, beating Zilcash by fourteen lengths and
twelve lengths at Hereford and Wincanton respectively on his first two starts. A
good second behind Poquelin at Kempton, trying to concede 10 lb, marked Liberate

Mrs D. L. Whateley's "Liberate"

down as a leading Triumph Hurdle candidate. Sent off at 12/1 at Cheltenham, he easily turned around the form with his Kempton conqueror, showing improved form and just lacking the speed of Katchit from the home turn, finishing nine lengths adrift of that rival. Liberate was stepped up to two and a half miles and was sent off favourite for the Mersey Novices' Hurdle at Aintree, only to be let down by his jumping and finish a disappointing fifth behind Tidal Bay.

Liberate (ch.g. 2003)	Lomitas (ch 1988)	Niniski (b 1976)	Nijinsky
			Virginia Hills
		La Colorada (ch 1981)	Surumu
			La Dorada
	Eversince (USA) (b 1983)	Foolish Pleasure (b 1972)	What A Pleasure
			Fool-Me-Not
		Eternity (ch 1977)	Luthier
			El Mina

Bought by Sir Mark Prescott as a yearling for 52,000 guineas, Liberate was amongst the most expensive of Lomitas' progeny sold in 2004. He is a close relation of the remarkably tough (raced in thirteen countries), high-class German campaigner Caitano (by Niniski). Liberate is not the first of his siblings to run over obstacles. His half-brother Hereditary (by Hernando), who also started off on the Flat with Sir Mark Prescott, developed into a fair performer over hurdles, including when third in a Grade 2 event at Fontwell in the latest season. The tall, useful-looking Liberate has raced on good ground or softer to date over hurdles and should prove well suited by two and a half miles and beyond. Despite his disappointing effort at Aintree, Liberate's earlier form and physique very much suggest that he is a smart staying hurdle prospect for 2007/8. *P. J. Hobbs*

LIBERIA (FR) 8 b.g. Kadalko (FR) – Unica IV (FR) (Quart de Vin (FR)) [2006/7 c85, h–: 22d^{pu} Mar 20] leggy gelding: let down by jumping in maiden chases: maiden hurdler: left N. Henderson and off almost a year, no show only outing in 2006/7. *Mrs A. M. Thorpe*   **c–**
h–

LIBERMAN (IRE) 9 b.g. Standiford (USA) – Hail To You (USA) (Kirtling) [2006/7 h126: 24s^{pu} 24g^{pu} c23m^4 Apr 15] sturdy gelding: formerly fairly useful handicap hurdler: sold out of M. Pipe's stable and off 6 months, no impact in 2006/7 (bled on second start), including on chasing debut: stays 3m: acts on soft going, simple task when successful on good to firm: not a fluent jumper. *R. Curtis*   **c–**
h–

LIBERTHINE (FR) 8 b.m. Chamberlin (FR) – Libertina (FR) (Balsamo (FR)) [2006/7 c139, h–: c25s^4 24d c24g c36g^5 Apr 14] angular mare: winning hurdler in France: useful handicap chaser: won Topham Chase at Aintree in 2005/6: reportedly failed to get in foal to Poliglote during summer: creditable fourth to D'Argent in listed event at Cheltenham on return: sweating, respectable 22 lengths fifth of 40 to Silver Birch in Grand National at Aintree (third completion over fences), fading from 2 out: best form up to 29f: acts on soft and good to firm going: sound jumper in main: ridden by Mr S. Waley-Cohen (sometimes at overweight). *N. J. Henderson*   **c139**
h–

LIBERTY BEN (IRE) 7 b.g. Beneficial – Silver Fairy (IRE) (Lancastrian) [2006/7 h96: c20s^2 c20s* c24v^6 c24s^{pu} c21f^2 Apr 5] useful-looking gelding: maiden hurdler: fair novice chaser: won handicap at Wetherby in November: should stay beyond 2½m: acts on soft going, probably on firm. *R. H. Alner*   **c100**
h–

LIBERTY RUN (IRE) 5 ch.g. Grand Lodge (USA) – Bathe In Light (USA) (Sunshine Forever (USA)) [2006/7 h–: 18m^{pu} 16g^{pu} Nov 7] lengthy gelding: modest and inconsistent on turf on Flat (stays 1½m), successful in September: no form over hurdles. *Mouse Hamilton-Fairley*   **h–**

LIBERTY SEEKER (FR) 8 ch.g. Machiavellian (USA) – Samara (IRE) (Polish Patriot (USA)) [2006/7 c–, h118+: 16f c20f^6 Jul 6] good-topped gelding: fairly useful chaser/handicap hurdler: best effort over fences when sixth to Ball O Malt in quite valuable handicap at Perth: stays 2½m when emphasis is on speed: acts on firm and good to soft going: sold 18,000 gns Newmarket July Sales. *G. A. Swinbank*   **c124**
h118

LIFE ESTATES 7 b.g. Mark of Esteem (IRE) – Chepstow Vale (USA) (Key To The Mint (USA)) [2006/7 h–: 17m 16g^F Jun 1] in frame in points: little form over hurdles. *J. D. Frost*   **h63**

LIFE PEER 4 b.g. Mark of Esteem (IRE) – Sadaka (USA) (Kingmambo (USA)) [2006/7 16m^4 Jul 16] half-brother to fairly useful hurdler Hawridge King (by Erhaab),   **h75**

stays 19f: modest maiden on Flat (stayed 1½m): fourth in juvenile on hurdling debut: dead. *J. G. Portman*

LIFES A FLYER (IRE) 11 gr.g. Roselier (FR) – Your Life (Le Bavard (FR)) [2006/7 **c105 d**
c24m⁴ c22m² c21g⁴ c22g c24gᵖᵘ c24v³ c22d c20g Apr 16] winning hurdler: fair chaser: **h–**
sold out of Mrs J. Harrington's stable 5,400 gns Doncaster October Sales, well held last 3
starts: stays 3m: acts on firm and soft ground. *N. Wilson*

LIGHTENING FIRE (IRE) 5 b.g. Woodborough (USA) – Glowlamp (IRE) (Glow **h63 §**
(USA)) [2006/7 h–§: 16sᶠ 16g⁶ 19g⁴ 16m 20f Jul 19] poor maiden hurdler: likely to prove
best around 2m: wears cheekpieces/blinkers: refused first on debut. *B. J. Llewellyn*

LIGHTENING FLIGHT 6 b.g. Missed Flight – Paperback Writer (Efisio) [2006/7 **h–**
F16v 20gᵘʳ Apr 23] first foal: dam little form over hurdles: tailed off in bumper on debut: **F–**
unseated when trying to run out second in novice hurdle. *B. Storey*

LIGHTNING STAR (USA) 12 b.g. El Gran Senor (USA) – Cuz's Star (USA) **c– §**
(Galaxy Libra) [2006/7 c–, h91: 18dᵖᵘ 17v Dec 12] angular gelding: no show only start **h– §**
over fences: winning hurdler: off 18 months and left G. L. Moore, no show in 2006/7:
blinkered: ungenuine. *M. R. Hoad*

LIGHTNING STRIKE (GER) 4 ch.g. Danehill Dancer (IRE) – La Capilla (Machia- **h126 p**
vellian (USA)) [2006/7 20s² 17g 16g⁵ Apr 12] angular gelding: useful performer on Flat
(should stay beyond 2m), successful on 3 occasions in 2006: sold out of T. Mills's stable
200,000 gns Newmarket Autumn Sales, and gelded: promising start over hurdles, behind
Katchit in Grade 1 juveniles at Cheltenham (ninth of 23) and Aintree last 2 outings: open
to improvement, particularly at 2½m+, and sure to win races over hurdles. *Miss Venetia
Williams*

LIGHT ON THE BROOM (IRE) 11 b.g. Aristocracy – Montevelle (IRE) (Mont- **c121 +**
elimar (USA)) [2006/7 c121, h–: c20d⁴ c22m⁵ c22g c20d² c19v² c20g² c24s⁴ Nov 4] **h–**
winning hurdler: fairly useful chaser: creditable efforts when runner-up fourth to sixth
starts: stays 3m: acts on good to firm and heavy going: usually tongue tied. *G. Stack,
Ireland*

LIKE A BEE (IRE) 9 b.g. Montelimar (USA) – Dasdilemma (IRE) (Furry Glen) **c107**
[2006/7 c23d³ c23v⁴ c35v³ c29s² Mar 11] angular gelding: winning hurdler: fair handicap **h–**
chaser, left C. Roche before return: stays 3¾m: raced on going softer than good (acts on
heavy): tried in cheekpieces/blinkers. *Jonjo O'Neill*

LIKE A LORD (IRE) 9 b. or br.g. Arctic Lord – Likashot (Celtic Cone) [2006/7 h109: **h104**
24g² Apr 21] angular gelding: fair hurdler: off 16 months prior to only outing in 2006/7:
stays 3m: best efforts on good going. *Mrs S. J. Smith*

LIKE THE BUZZ (IRE) 9 b.m. Lord Americo – Crash Course Katie (IRE) (Crash **c–**
Course) [2006/7 24g⁴ 27d³ Aug 15] winning pointer: let down by jumping only outing in **h61**
chase: poor novice hurdler: stays 27f: tried in cheekpieces. *D. A. Rees*

LIKE TO GO 6 b.g. Meadowbrook – Never Been VII (Damsire Unregistered) [2006/7 **F–**
F16s May 20] first foal: dam unraced: well held in bumper/on completed start in points.
P. S. McEntee

LIK WOOD POWER (NZ) 10 b.g. Bigstone (IRE) – Lady Paloma (USA) (Clever **c–**
Trick (USA)) [2006/7 c112, h–: c20g⁵ c20s³ c25mᵖᵘ c19gᵘʳ c24g c20m⁴ Nov 13] useful- **h–**
looking gelding: maiden hurdler/winning chaser, no form in handicap chases in 2006/7:
joined J. Spearing. *D. J. Wintle*

LILAC 8 ch.m. Alhijaz – Fairfield's Breeze (Buckskin (FR)) [2006/7 h86: 24g 19m² **h100**
16g* 20m² 20m⁴ 22m³ Jul 27] smallish mare: fair handicap hurdler: won mares event at
Uttoxeter in June: stays 2½m: acts on soft and good to firm going: tried in cheekpieces.
Evan Williams

LILAC WINE 4 ch.f. Dancing Spree (USA) – Stay With Me Baby (Nicholas Bill) **F69**
[2006/7 F13d⁴ F13g F14s³ F12s Dec 13] leggy filly: second foal: dam 1m winner: poor
form in 3-y-o bumpers. *D. J. S. ffrench Davis*

LILLEBROR (GER) 9 b.g. Top Waltz (FR) – Lady Soliciti (GER) (Solicitor (FR)) **h–**
[2006/7 18g Sep 3] close-coupled gelding: form over hurdles (modest) only when easily
landing gamble in novice handicap in 2004/5: possibly unsuited by soft/heavy going.
B. J. Curley

LILLIE LOU 4 b.f. Tomba – Tread Carefully (Sharpo) [2006/7 16g Mar 14] dam, **h65**
maiden who stayed 1m, half-sister to Champion Hurdle winner Royal Gait: well held in
maidens on Flat: sold out of T. Easterby's stable 1,500 gns Doncaster August Sales:
seventh of 18 in mares maiden on hurdling debut. *R. Fielder*

LI LO BOSH (IRE) 5 b.g. Dr Devious (IRE) – Academic Miss (IRE) (College Chapel) **F80**
[2006/7 F16d F16g F16g³ Apr 8] workmanlike gelding: first foal: dam unraced: modest
form in bumpers. *A. W. Carroll*

LIL'RASCAL (IRE) 5 b.g. Oscar (IRE) – Mara Hill (IRE) (Dromod Hill) [2006/7 **F83**
F16g Mar 14] €5,800 3-y-o: fourth foal: dam placed in bumper: ninth of 14 in bumper on
debut. *Heather Dalton*

LIL'S LEGACY 4 b.g. Kayf Tara – Waff's Folly (Handsome Sailor) [2006/7 aF16g **F75**
F12g F18m⁶ Apr 26] unfurnished gelding: first foal: dam 6f winner: little impact in
bumpers. *D. J. S. ffrench Davis*

LILY TARA 5 b.m. Kayf Tara – Apprila (Bustino) [2006/7 F85: 22m³ 20s 16s⁴ Feb 15] **h79**
small, workmanlike mare: runner-up in bumper: poor form in novice hurdles: likely to
stay 3m. *A. M. Crow*

LIMERICK BOY (GER) 9 b.g. Alwuhush (USA) – Limoges (GER) (Konigsstuhl **c140**
(GER)) [2006/7 c144, h–: 20s 21g c22v* c24v⁶ c25gᵖᵘ Apr 13] leggy, close-coupled **h–**
gelding: one-time smart hurdler, well held in handicaps first 2 starts in 2006/7: useful
handicap chaser: back to form when winning 5-runner minor event at Haydock in
December by 16 lengths from Royal Emperor: stays 3m when emphasis is on speed: acts
on heavy and to firm going: sometimes let down by jumping. *Miss Venetia Williams*

LIMESTONE BOY (IRE) 5 b. or br.g. Beneficial – Limestone Lady (IRE) (Boreen **h–**
(FR)) [2006/7 F16v F17s⁶ 21gᵖᵘ Mar 20] first foal: dam unraced half-sister to fairly useful **F–**
hurdler You Sir, stays 2½m, out of sister to top-class hurdler Limestone Lad: no promise
in bumpers/maiden hurdle (not fluent). *J. G. M. O'Shea*

LIMITED EDITION (IRE) 9 b.g. Parthian Springs – Rosemount Rose (Ashmore **c135 +**
(FR)) [2006/7 c18vᵖᵘ c20s* c20v* c21gꟳ Mar 15] rangy gelding: winning hurdler: off **h–**
almost 2 years and left M. Pitman prior to return: useful form when successful both
completed starts over fences, in maiden and handicap (beat Fast Forward a distance, left
further clear last) at Kempton in February: still travelling smoothly when fell 4 out in
Jewson Novices' Handicap at Cheltenham won by L'Antartique: stays 2½m: acts on
heavy going. *Carl Llewellyn*

LINAGRAM 6 ch.m. Classic Cliche (IRE) – At Long Last (John French) [2006/7 F16f² **F78**
F16g⁴ F17v³ Dec 12] half-sister to fairly useful but temperamental hurdler/chaser up to
2¾m Gunnerblong and modest but unreliable 2m hurdler Gunner Sid (both by Gunner
B), and winning 2¾m Irish hurdler Seminole Chief (by Weld): dam unraced: modest form
in frame in bumpers. *G. A. Swinbank*

LINCOLN LEADER (IRE) 9 br.m. Supreme Leader – Tokay Lady (Furry Glen) **c–**
[2006/7 c–: c26dᵘʳ Jun 12] ex-Irish mare: lightly raced: winning Irish pointer: no form in
chases. *Evan Williams*

LINCOLN'S INN (IRE) 5 b.g. Old Vic – Eurodawn (IRE) (Orchestra) [2006/7 F94: **h104**
F16m⁴ 16s⁶ 19s² 21g* 20s⁴ Apr 27] medium-sized gelding: in frame in bumpers: fair **F90**
form over hurdles: won 18-runner maiden at Warwick in March: bred to stay beyond 21f:
acts on soft ground. *P. J. Hobbs*

LINDAMARIE (IRE) 6 b.m. Luso – Rookery Lady (IRE) (Callernish) [2006/7 F–: **h–**
21m⁶ 25g² Oct 30] no solid form in bumpers/novice hurdles: tried in cheekpieces: sold
1,600 gns Doncaster January Sales. *Heather Dalton*

LINDBERGH LAW (USA) 7 b.g. Red Ransom (USA) – Not So Shy (USA) (Crafty **h78**
Prospector (USA)) [2006/7 h92, F99: 20s⁵ May 20] dual bumper winner for G. A. Swinbank: modest form at best in novice hurdles: won point in April: stays 2½m: tried in
cheekpieces. *Heather Dalton*

LINDEN BOY (IRE) 8 gr.g. Van Der Linden (FR) – Gwan Ya Boya (Godswalk **h86**
(USA)) [2006/7 19d⁴ 16m² 17d Oct 17] third foal: dam placed over hurdles: modest form
over hurdles: stays 19f: joined J. O'Shea. *Jane Southcombe*

LINDOP 7 ch.g. Nashwan (USA) – Footlight Fantasy (USA) (Nureyev (USA)) [2006/7 **h119 p**
16s⁵ 16d³ 16d* Mar 21] won 1m maiden at 3 yrs for J. Toller, only start on Flat:
progressive over hurdles, fairly useful from when winning maiden at Lingfield readily by
13 lengths from Edgbriar: capable of better still. *R. H. Alner*

LINDSAY (FR) 8 b.g. Chamberlin (FR) – Oliday (FR) (Djarvis (FR)) [2006/7 c110, h–: **c110**
c20fꟳ c17m³ c20g³ c16g⁴ c16g⁴ Apr 19] good-topped gelding: fair chaser: stays 2½m: **h–**
acts on soft and good to firm going: consistent. *H. D. Daly*

LINDSEYFIELD LODGE (IRE) 6 br.g. Presenting – Missusan (IRE) (King's Ride) **h80**
[2006/7 F16m* F17g² F17m² 16s⁵ Apr 27] €15,500 3-y-o: first foal: dam unraced: fairly **F97**
useful form in bumpers, won at Hexham in June: left G. A. Swinbank and off 9 months,
only fifth in maiden on hurdling debut. *N. G. Richards*

LINE BALL (IRE) 6 b.g. Good Thyne (USA) – Navaro (IRE) (Be My Native (USA)) **h122**
[2006/7 h106p, F102: 16s* 18s* 16g² Sep 4] bumper winner: fairly useful hurdler: won
maiden at Punchestown and minor event at Wexford in May: good second of 6 to Davenport Democrat in novice at Roscommon: will stay 2½m: acts on soft going. *C. Roche,
Ireland*

LINNET (GER) 5 b.m. Dr Fong (USA) – Lauderdale (GER) (Nebos (GER)) [2006/7 **h107**
h105: 16g⁵ 16d⁶ 22d⁴ 20s² 22s 22m⁵ 21g Apr 19] good-topped mare: fair handicap
hurdler: below form last 3 starts: stays 2¾m: acts on soft going: tried visored/in cheekpieces. *Ian Williams*

LION'S DOMANE 10 b.g. Lion Cavern (USA) – Vilany (Never So Bold) [2006/7 **h77**
h–: 20s 17mᶠ 16f⁶ 17m 17d² 16s⁴ Sep 20] poor maiden hurdler: free-going front runner.
K. W. Hogg, Isle of Man

LIQUID LOVER (IRE) 5 b.g. Night Shift (USA) – New Tycoon (IRE) (Last Tycoon) **h–**
[2006/7 16s 16d 20mᵖᵘ Mar 31] modest maiden at best on Flat (stays 1½m): no impact
over hurdles. *W. M. Brisbourne*

LIQUID LUNCH 6 b.g. Posidonas – Domitor's Lass (Domitor (USA)) [2006/7 F16m³ **h101**
F19d³ F16s F18v³ 18s 20s³ Feb 7] fourth foal: dam poor and untrustworthy novice **F92**
hurdler: won maiden point in 2006: fair form when third in bumpers: much better effort
in maiden hurdles when third at Down Royal: stays 2½m. *B. R. Hamilton, Ireland*

LISNAGAR HIDE (IRE) 11 b. or br.g. Buckskin (FR) – Princess Isle (Deep Run) **c–**
[2006/7 c21g⁶ May 24] ex-Irish gelding: winning pointer: maiden chaser: tried in cheek-
pieces/blinkered. *N. W. Padfield*

LISRONA (IRE) 6 ch.m. Presenting – Milltown Lady (Deep Run) [2006/7 F16m **h–**
F17g⁶ 16s 19v 17g Apr 7] rather unfurnished mare: half-sister to 2m chase winner Deel **F–**
Time (by Gildoran): dam maiden: well held in bumpers (for R. Phillips)/over hurdles.
M. Keighley

LISSARA (IRE) 9 b.g. Glacial Storm (USA) – Bonnies Glory (General Ironside) **h94**
[2006/7 16d 17v⁶ 18s² 20d⁵ 24v⁵ 22s⁴ Mar 8] big, well-made gelding: fifth in Grade 2
bumper in 2004/5: modest novice hurdler: should be suited by further than 2½m: raced
on ground softer than good: sold 3,000 gns Doncaster May Sales. *Noel T. Chance*

LISTEN SON (IRE) 5 b.g. Desert Sun – Hear Me (Simply Great (FR)) [2006/7 F17s **h–**
F17s 17vᵖᵘ 17g Apr 1] 800 3-y-o: half-brother to several winners, including 1¾m winner **F–**
Danus Rex (by Roi Danzig): dam Irish 7f and 9f winner: no promise in bumpers/over
hurdles: tried tongue tied. *N. G. Ayliffe*

LISTENTOTHEMUSIC (IRE) 4 b.g. Distant Music (USA) – Moet (IRE) (Mac's **h–**
Imp (USA)) [2006/7 16sᵖᵘ 16g 16v Oct 29] third foal: half-brother to fairly useful 1½m
winner Champagne Shadow (by Kahyasi): dam 6f winner: no form in juvenile hurdles.
G. Elliott, Ireland

LIT ET MIXE (FR) 4 gr.g. Linamix (FR) – Lit (IRE) (Danehill (USA)) [2006/7 16vᵇᵈ **h101**
16s⁴ 17d Mar 19] leggy gelding: won 1¼m maiden in Provinces at 3 yrs for J-C. Rouget,
well held in handicaps on Flat in Britain: much better effort on completed outings in
juvenile hurdles (brought down first on debut) when fourth to Signs of Love at Newbury.
Noel T. Chance

LITTLE ALF 5 ch.g. Alflora (IRE) – Nuns Little One (Celtic Cone) [2006/7 F17s F16s **F–**
F14g F17m³ Apr 17] rather unfurnished gelding: fifth foal: dam, poor novice hurdler,
stayed 2¾m: no solid form in bumpers: blinkered final outing. *B. G. Powell*

LITTLE BIG HORSE (IRE) 11 b.g. Little Bighorn – Little Gort (Roselier (FR)) **c127**
[2006/7 c132, h–: 20m c25v⁴ 24vᵖᵘ c20v* c24g Mar 14] leggy gelding: maiden hurdler: **h–**
fairly useful handicap chaser: won at Newcastle in February by 1¼ lengths from Green
Ideal, rallying: well held in Kim Muir at Cheltenham following month: stays 25f: acts on
good to firm and heavy going: often races prominently: none too reliable. *Mrs S. J. Smith*

LITTLE BOB 8 ch.g. Zilzal (USA) – Hunters of Brora (IRE) (Sharpo) [2006/7 16s³ **h96**
17v⁶ 16v⁴ 16v² 16g³ 16s³ Apr 26] fair on Flat (stays 1¼m): modest novice hurdler:
will prove best around 2m: raced mainly on soft/heavy going: blinkered last 3 starts.
J. D. Bethull

Country Gentlemen's Association Chase (Limited Handicap), Wincanton—a winning British debut for the ill-fated Little Brick who proves too strong for top weight My Will (right)

LITTLE BRICK (FR) 8 ch.g. Bricassar (USA) – Doulina (FR) (Dastaan (FR)) [2006/7 c25s* c24g^pu Mar 13] leggy, narrow ex-French gelding: 12.5f winner on Flat: lightly raced over hurdles: progressive chaser, won 2 handicaps at Auteuil in first half of 2005/6 for E. Pilet: odds on, returned from 16-month absence to win 5-runner listed Country Gentleman's Association Chase (Limited Handicap) at Wincanton in February by 3½ lengths from My Will (pair clear): broke shoulder when blundered 4 out in William Hill Trophy at Cheltenham: stayed 25f: raced on good going or softer (acted on soft): dead. *D. E. Pipe*
  c152
  h–

LITTLE COMPTON LAD 5 ch.g. Pivotal – Fleur Rouge (Pharly (FR)) [2006/7 F16g F16m Jun 11] brother to smart performer up to 1m Red Carpet and half-brother to several winners, including fairly useful hurdler Red Valerian (by Robellino), stayed 21f: dam 2-y-o 6f winner: tailed off in bumpers. *R. Fielder*
  F–

LITTLE ENGLANDER 7 b.g. Piccolo – Anna Karietta (Precocious) [2006/7 17m May 9] modest on Flat (stays 1¼m), well beaten only start in 2005: no show in maiden on hurdling debut. *L. Corcoran*
  h–

LITTLE FLORA 11 ch.m. Alflora (IRE) – Sister's Choice (Lepanto (GER)) [2006/7 c94, h–: c17f c16d^pu c22g c20s^pu Nov 15] good-topped mare: modest handicap chaser, no form in 2006/7: stays 21f: acts on any going: often front runner. *S. J. Marshall*
  c–
  h–

LITTLE GIRL 9 b.m. Homo Sapien – Dancing Returns (Bali Dancer) [2006/7 24d^pu 20m Apr 15] maiden pointer: no show in mares novice hurdles: tried in cheekpieces. *R. E. Peacock*
  h–

LITTLE HERMAN (IRE) 11 b.g. Mandalus – Kilbricken Bay (Salluceva) [2006/7 c–, h–: c31gᵖᵘ May 24] well-made gelding: winning chaser: fairly useful pointer in 2006: tried blinkered/in cheekpieces: dead. *Mrs Alison Hickman*   **c–** **h–**

LITTLE JIMBOB 6 b.g. Desert Story (IRE) – Artistic Licence (High Top) [2006/7 17m* 16d 16d Nov 11] leggy gelding: half-brother to fairly useful hurdler The Names Bond (by Tragic Role), stays 3m: fairly useful on Flat (stays 9.8f): won novice at Sedgefield on hurdling debut in September: well beaten in handicaps after: likely to prove best around 2m with emphasis on speed. *R. A. Fahey*   **h103**

LITTLE LAURITA 5 b.m. Overbury (IRE) – Laura Lye (IRE) (Carlingford Castle) [2006/7 F–: F13m 17d² 20g⁵ Sep 30] mid-field in bumpers: poor form over hurdles, lame final outing: stays 2½m. *B. De Haan*   **h79** **F63**

LITTLE LU (IRE) 5 b.m. Danehill Dancer (IRE) – Tales of Wisdom (Rousillon (USA)) [2006/7 F16m* F17m* Jul 25] sixth foal: half-sister to winning hurdler/chaser Tales of Bounty (by Ela-Mana-Mou), stayed 3m, and 1½m winners by Eagle Eyed and Arcane: dam 1½m winner: plenty in hand when landing odds in bumpers at Uttoxeter and Bangor (beat Scholar King by 2 lengths in 6-runner race) in July: seemed likely to prove capable of better, but not seen out again. *G. A. Swinbank*   **F97 p**

LITTLE MISS FLUTE 7 br.m. Busy Flight – Travel Bye (Miller's Mate) [2006/7 F14g 20v⁶ 19d 20dᶠ 17m Apr 17] third foal: half-sister to 7f winner Radar O'Reilly (by Almoojid): dam modest maiden: won maiden point in 2006: no form in bumper/novice hurdles. *J. D. Frost*   **h–** **F–**

LITTLE MOON MAN 5 b.g. Contract Law (USA) – Mamoola Moon (Kasakov) [2006/7 F16v Dec 15] smallish, leggy gelding: first foal: dam unraced: tailed off in bumper on debut. *J. M. Saville*   **F–**

LITTLE PADDY (IRE) 6 b.g. Flemensfirth (USA) – Minor Tantrum (IRE) (Executive Perk) [2006/7 F99: F16g 16sᵖᵘ 16g 16d Jan 5] smallish, workmanlike gelding: little impact since debut in bumper, mainly over hurdles. *Mrs K. Walton*   **h–** **F72**

LITTLE ROCKER (IRE) 6 b.g. Rock Hopper – One Back (IRE) (Meneval (USA)) [2006/7 F88: 16v* 20s 20v³ 16vᵖᵘ 24g Mar 24] smallish, good-topped gelding: fairly useful novice hurdler: won at Uttoxeter in November by ¾ length from Here's Johnny: ran creditably when third to Classic Fiddle at Hereford, no show next 2 outings: stays 2½m: acts on heavy going: tried blinkered. *Carl Llewellyn*   **h115**

LITTLE RORT (IRE) 8 b.g. Ali-Royal (IRE) – Florinda (CAN) (Vice Regent (CAN)) [2006/7 h80: 17g 19gᵖᵘ 17g⁵ 24d² 19s³ 26s 24s* 24vᵖᵘ 21sᵖᵘ 19gᵖᵘ 20g⁵ Apr 14] sturdy gelding: modest handicap hurdler: won selling event at Taunton in December: stays 3m, effective over shorter: unraced on firm going, acts on any other: formerly tongue tied: often makes running/races prominently: not one to rely on. *S. T. Lewis*   **h86 §**

LITTLE SAID 7 ch.g. Rakaposhi King – Royal Chitchat (Le Bavard (FR)) [2006/7 20v⁵ 19g⁶ 22d⁵ 20g³ Mar 17] strong, lengthy gelding: seventh foal: brother to a winning pointer: dam unraced half-sister to useful staying hurdler/chaser Papo Kharisma from fair jumping family: won maiden Irish point in 2006: poor form in novice hurdles: better form when third of 5 in novice at Wetherby on chasing debut, though none too fluent: should stay beyond 2½m. *P. Beaumont*   **c95 ?** **h81**

LITTLE SALTEE (IRE) 7 ch.g. Anshan – Shuil Na Mhuire (IRE) (Roselier (FR)) [2006/7 h–: c24dᶠ 20dᵖᵘ Nov 11] bumper winner: no show over hurdles: fell fourth on chasing debut. *J. A. B. Old*   **c–** **h–**

LITTLE SAXTEAD (IRE) 7 ch.g. Anshan – Snape (IRE) (Strong Gale) [2006/7 h–: c24dᵇᵈ Oct 15] lengthy gelding: no sign of ability: left J. Supple, brought down first only start in 2006/7. *Ferdy Murphy*   **c–** **h–**

LITTLE SHILLING (IRE) 5 ch.g. Bob's Return (IRE) – Minouette (IRE) (Beau Sher) [2006/7 F16v F16s⁵ 16v 20s 19sᵖᵘ Mar 11] €6,000 4-y-o: rather unfurnished gelding: second foal: dam unraced half-sister to dam of smart hurdler Powerstation, stays 3m: never dangerous in bumpers/novice hurdles. *B. N. Pollock*   **h–** **F71**

LITTLE SIOUX (IRE) 7 b.m. Little Bighorn – Our Dorcet (Condorcet (FR)) [2006/7 F–: F17s⁵ 17d 16d 16g 20dᶠ 27vᵖᵘ Jan 28] no solid form in bumpers/over hurdles. *L. Lungo*   **h–** **F–**

LITTLESTAR (FR) 6 b.g. Robellino (USA) – Green Charter (Green Desert (USA)) [2006/7 17d 24g Jul 21] close-coupled gelding: maiden on Flat, very lightly raced since 2004: no form over hurdles. *B. D. Leavy*   **h–**

LITTLE SWALLOW 6 b.m. Bal Harbour – Alhargah (Be My Guest (USA)) [2006/7 F–
F17m Apr 28] half-sister to several winners, notably fairly useful hurdler Swift Swallow
(by Missed Flight), stayed 2½m: dam poor maiden: always behind in bumper on debut.
O. Brennan

LITTLE TASK 9 b.g. Environment Friend – Lucky Thing (Green Desert (USA)) c–
[2006/7 c–, h93: 16g⁶ 23v³ 21d⁵ 20m 24f 24m* 20d⁴ 22d⁵ 24g Sep 6] small gelding: h91
modest handicap hurdler: won conditional jockeys event at Bangor in August: stays 3m:
acts on any going: tried visored/in cheekpieces: held up. *J. S. Wainwright*

LITTLE TOBIAS (IRE) 8 ch.g. Millkom – Barbara Frietchie (IRE) (Try My Best c–
(USA)) [2006/7 h83§: 22m⁴ 18m 22d 20f⁴ 20m⁴ c26dF Aug 15] poor hurdler on balance: h72 §
fell fatally on chasing debut: stayed 2¾m: acted on firm going: tried visored/blinkered:
unreliable. *D. D. Scott*

LITTLETON ALDOR (IRE) 7 b.g. Pennekamp (USA) – Belle Etoile (FR) (Lead h–
On Time (USA)) [2006/7 16dᵖᵘ Jun 2] ex-Irish gelding: third foal: half-brother to 2m
hurdle winner Moorlaw (by Mtoto): dam French 7.5f winner: no form in bumpers (for
T. Walsh) or novice hurdle: headstrong: poor form on Flat. *P. R. Rodford*

LITTLE TRETHEW 8 ch.m. Presidium – Sister Claire (Quayside) [2006/7 20mᵖᵘ c–
c18d⁵ c20d c20sᵖᵘ Dec 5] no sign of ability. *R. C. Harper* h–

LITTLE VANTAGE 8 br.g. Mutamarrid – Shermago (Humdoleila) [2006/7 h–, F–: h81
16g⁴ 17d⁴ 17d Jun 14] poor form in novice hurdles: bad completion record in points:
should stay beyond 2m. *A. M. Crow*

LITTLE VENUS (IRE) 7 b.m. Moscow Society (USA) – Irene Good-Night (IRE) c78
(Shernazar) [2006/7 h100, F82: 16d* c16dF 20sᵖᵘ 21g 24d⁶ Mar 22] strong, sturdy mare: h94
fair form at best over hurdles, won mares novice at Towcester in October: no show last
3 starts: held when fell 2 out in novice on chasing debut: should be suited by further
than 19f: raced on good going or softer: tried blinkered: temperament under suspicion.
H. D. Daly

LITTLE VILLAIN (IRE) 9 b.g. Old Vic – Party Woman (IRE) (Sexton Blake) c76
[2006/7 h54: 19m c20m⁶ c21v² c24d⁵ c22v c23s c24v⁵ c22s² c24d c21v² c23s 20v² h72
Mar 10] leggy gelding: poor maiden hurdler/chaser: stays 3m: acts on heavy going: tried
blinkered/in cheekpieces. *T. Wall*

LITTLE WISHES 4 b.f. Most Welcome – Zac's Desire (Swing Easy (USA)) [2006/7 h–
16sᵖᵘ Oct 27] smallish, workmanlike filly: little show in maidens on Flat or in juvenile on
hurdling debut. *S. Parr*

LITTLE WORD 8 b.m. Rakaposhi King – Preacher's Gem (The Parson) [2006/7 h65, c57
F–: 26gᵖᵘ c23fᵖᵘ c23d⁴ c26v³ c25dᵖᵘ c24vᵘʳ c24dᵖᵘ c24dᵖᵘ Feb 2] winning pointer: bad h–
maiden hurdler/chaser: tried in cheekpieces. *P. D. Williams*

LIT UP (IRE) 4 ch.g. Fantastic Light (USA) – High Spirited (Shirley Heights) [2006/7 F87
F12v F16g F17mᵘ Apr 17] close-coupled gelding: half-brother to several winners, including 2m hurdle winner Rainbow Dash (by Rainbow Quest) and smart middle-distance
performers Legend Maker (by Sadler's Wells) and Amfortas (by Caerleon): dam 1¾m/
2m winner: fair form in bumpers: all out to land odds in 5-runner event at Exeter.
H. D. Daly

LITZINSKY 9 b.g. Muhtarram (USA) – Boulevard Girl (Nicholas Bill) [2006/7 h–: h–
24sF 25vᵖᵘ 19v Jan 21] well-made gelding: winning hurdler, no form since 2004/5: tried
in cheekpieces/tongue tied. *Mrs L. J. Young*

LIVELY DESSERT (IRE) 14 b.g. Be My Native (USA) – Liffey Travel (Le Bavard c–
(FR)) [2006/7 c25g May 24] lengthy gelding: winning chaser: poor pointer nowadays: h–
tried in headgear. *Miss C. Frater*

LIVERPOOL ECHO (FR) 7 b.g. Poliglote – Miss Echo (Chief Singer) [2006/7 c112, c126
h–: c20g⁴ c24d⁶ c19d c24s⁵ c24s⁵ c23d² c25g⁶ Apr 18] stocky gelding: fairly useful h–
handicap chaser: dropped long way in weights prior to winning at Stratford in March:
stays 25f: acts on soft and good to firm going: tried visored: tongue tied last 2 outings.
Mrs K. Waldron

LIVERPOOL (GER) 5 b.g. Platini (GER) – Lerida (GER) (Lagunas) [2006/7 F17d⁴ h–
F16m⁴ 16s 19g 16v 23vᵖᵘ Jan 3] sturdy gelding: sixth foal: closely related/half-brother to F77
3 winners on Flat in Germany: dam unraced: fourth in bumpers: no form over hurdles.
M. W. Easterby

LIVE THE LIFE (IRE) 5 ch.m. Good Thyne (USA) – Living A Dream (IRE) **h–**
(Heavenly Manna) [2006/7 F16v 22s^{pu} 22d Feb 1] €5,000 3-y-o: plain mare: first foal: **F–**
dam unraced, out of half-sister to dam of high-class chaser up to 2½m Function Dream:
no form in bumper/over hurdles. *J. G. Portman*

LIVIA (IRE) 6 b.m. Titus Livius (FR) – Passing Beauty (Green Desert (USA)) [2006/7 **h74**
16m^5 Jul 4] first form (poor) over hurdles when fifth in seller, only outing in 2006/7: tried
tongue tied/blinkered. *R. Flint*

LIVINGONAKNIFEDGE (IRE) 8 b. or br.g. Classic Memory – Duhallow Fiveo **c109 x**
(Black Minstrel) [2006/7 h114, F91: c16g^3 c20v^F c16m^6 c20s^5 20v* 16s 24g^{bd} Apr 14] **h122**
leggy, good-topped gelding: fairly useful handicap hurdler: won at Bangor in March by
16 lengths from Speed Venture: weakening when brought down 3 out in listed event at
Aintree: let down by jumping over fences (fair form on debut): stays 2½m: acts on heavy
going. *Ian Williams*

LIVINGSTONEBRAMBLE (IRE) 11 b.g. Supreme Leader – Killiney Side (Gene- **c135**
ral Ironside) [2006/7 c134, h–: c22s^3 18s^5 c19d 20v^4 18v^4 24v^2 c24v^2 20v^5 c21g c36g^{ur} **h113**
c20g Apr 25] compact gelding: winning hurdler: useful handicap chaser: good second of
16 to Homer Wells in valuable event at Gowran seventh start: below best after: effective
at 2m to 3m: acts on heavy going: usually held up. *W. P. Mullins, Ireland*

LIZ'S DREAM 7 b.g. Alflora (IRE) – Spicey Cut (Cut Above) [2006/7 16v^4 16v^4 24s^{pu} **h69**
24s^6 Apr 26] big, strong gelding: fifth foal: half-brother to fair staying hurdler Solway
Minstrel (by Jumbo Hirt) and modest hurdler/chaser Solway Breeze (by King's Ride),
stayed 3¼m: dam unraced, out of half-sister to smart 3m hurdler Maelkar: form (poor)
over hurdles only on debut: bred to be suited by further than 2m: breathing problem third
outing. *Miss L. Harrison*

LIZZIE BATHWICK (IRE) 8 b.m. Glacial Storm (USA) – Protrial (Proverb) **c104**
[2006/7 c98, h91: 24s c23g^4 c21d^4 c19s^3 c20s^2 c23v^{pu} c22g c24m^2 Apr 10] well-made **h–**
mare: winning hurdler: fair handicap chaser: stays 3m: acts on good to firm and heavy
ground: in cheekpieces/blinkers last 5 starts. *J. G. Portman*

LLAMADAS 5 b.g. Josr Algarhoud (IRE) – Primulette (Mummy's Pet) [2006/7 h83+: **h–**
19d Oct 26] compact gelding: fairly useful but inconsistent on all-weather on Flat (stays
easy 2m), fair on turf: poor form over hurdles. *C. Roberts*

LLYNFI 6 b.m. Wizard King – Tapua Taranata (IRE) (Mandalus) [2006/7 16g Mar 21] **h–**
£1,250 4-y-o: half-sister to winning 3m chaser Co Optimist and winning 2m hurdler
Gentle Beau (both by Homo Sapien): dam unraced: well beaten in maiden point/novice
hurdle. *S. A. Jones*

LOADED DICE (IRE) 6 b.g. Desert King (IRE) – Le Ciel (IRE) (Law Society (USA)) **h84**
[2006/7 20g^2 20s 27s^3 27v Feb 20] €36,000 3-y-o: big, strong, lengthy gelding: chasing
type: second foal: half-brother to 7.5f winner in Germany by Night Shift: dam, fairly
useful on Flat, won 2¼m hurdle: won maiden Irish point in 2006: bought 70,000 gns Doncaster May Sales: modest form over hurdles: likely to prove best short of 27f. *J. Howard
Johnson*

LOADED GUN 7 ch.g. Highest Honor (FR) – Woodwardia (USA) (El Gran Senor **h–**
(USA)) [2006/7 h–: 17d^6 16f^F 16g Nov 4] modest on Flat (stays 1½m): no solid form over
hurdles. *W. Storey*

LOBLITE LEADER (IRE) 10 b.g. Tirol – Cyrano Beauty (IRE) (Cyrano de Berge- **h94**
rac) [2006/7 17d^F 16g^{pu} Sep 17] good-topped gelding: lightly-raced maiden hurdler,
running well when falling last on return from 2-year absence: stays 19f: raced on good/
good to soft going. *G. A. Swinbank*

LOCHANEE (IRE) 7 br.g. Anshan – Sassy Sally (IRE) (Callernish) [2006/7 c–, h–: **c–**
16d c24v^{pu} c16g^{ur} Feb 2] no form: sold out of Mrs L. Jewell's stable £1,700 Ascot June **h–**
Sales before reappearance. *F. Kirby*

LOCH OSCAIG 7 b.g. Sir Harry Lewis (USA) – Paddys Cherub (Then Again) [2006/7 **h86**
25g^{pu} 19g 20g 16v^4 20m^2 Apr 25] strong gelding: second foal: dam no form on Flat:
fourth in point in 2005: first solid form over hurdles when second to easy winner Miss
Rideamight in handicap at Worcester. *R. D. E. Woodhouse*

LOCH TORRIDON 8 b.g. Syrtos – Loch Scavaig (IRE) (The Parson) [2006/7 c–, h–: **c–**
16g^{pu} c17d^{pu} May 27] lengthy gelding: of little account: tried tongue tied/in headgear. **h–**
James Moffatt

LOCKERLEY MAN 4 b.g. Man Among Men (IRE) – Branston Lucy (Prince Sabo) **F73**
[2006/7 F13d F14s⁶ F12v Jan 17] workmanlike gelding: first foal: dam modest 5f winner:
poor form in bumpers: fifth in maiden on Flat in April. *W. S. Kittow*

LOCKSMITH 7 gr.g. Linamix (FR) – Zenith (Shirley Heights) [2006/7 c138, h–: c17d⁴ **c133**
c16d⁶ c17s 16g 16m 16d³ c22v² 16g² c16g³ c20m² Apr 20] angular gelding: useful **h134**
handicap hurdler/chaser: left D. Pipe after third start: back somewhere near best later in
season, placed over hurdles at Newcastle (1½ lengths second to Double Vodka) and over
fences at Aintree (third to Bambi de L'Orme in Grade 3) and Ayr last 3 starts: stays 2¾m:
acts on heavy and good to firm going: takes strong hold, and usually races prominently.
P. Monteith

LOCKSTOCKANDBARREL (IRE) 8 b.g. Needle Gun (IRE) – Quill Project **h–**
(IRE) (Project Manager) [2006/7 F91: 20v⁶ 17v 16v³ Mar 10] bumper winner: off another
year, well held in heavy-ground novice hurdles: bumper form on good/good to firm
going: tongue tied. *R. Shiels*

LOCKSTOCK (IRE) 9 b.g. Inchinor – Risalah (Marju (IRE)) [2006/7 16sᵖᵘ Mar 8] **h–**
compact gelding: fair on Flat (stays 9.5f, usually wears headgear), successful in September: no show in maiden on hurdling debut. *M. S. Saunders*

LOCKSTONE LAD (USA) 4 gr.g. Mazel Trick (USA) – Humble (USA) (Valiant **h–**
Nature (USA)) [2006/7 17gᵘʳ 24f⁶ Apr 5] tailed off in 5f maiden at 2 yrs: well held
completed outing over hurdles. *Miss J. S. Davis*

LODESTAR (IRE) 10 br.g. Good Thyne (USA) – Let's Compromise (No Argument) **c69**
[2006/7 c108, h–: c25s⁵ c25g⁴ Apr 15] tall gelding: winning hurdler: fair chaser at best, **h–**
well beaten in hunters in 2006/7 (placed in points in between): stays 3½m: acts on good
to firm and good to soft going: blinkered 6 of last 7 starts, also tongue tied final one.
Mrs J. M. Walton

LODGE LANE (IRE) 6 b.g. Norwich – Garrenroe (Le Moss) [2006/7 F16v* F16v* **F111**
F16g Mar 14] rather unfurnished gelding: half-brother to several winners, including
fair staying hurdler Glacial Moss (by Glacial Storm) and prolific point winner/winning
hunter chaser Persian Hero (by Persian Mews), stays 3¼m: dam unraced, half-sister to
high-class hunter Eliogarty: useful form in bumpers: won at Uttoxeter in December and
January, by 6 lengths from Or d'Oudaries on latter occasion: tenth of 24 to Cork All
Star in Champion Bumper at Cheltenham, disputing lead when hanging badly right into
straight: will be suited by further than 2m. *V. R. A. Dartnall*

LODGICIAN (IRE) 5 b.h. Grand Lodge (USA) – Dundel (IRE) (Machiavellian **h106**
(USA)) [2006/7 h95: 20g² 17m* Sep 26] lengthy, useful-looking horse: fair on Flat (stays
2¼m), successful in July: best effort over hurdles when second to Arctic Echo in maiden
at Hexham: made most when landing odds in novice at Sedgefield 4 months later: will
stay beyond 2½m. *J. J. Quinn*

LOFTY LEADER (IRE) 8 b.g. Norwich – Slaney Jazz (Orchestra) [2006/7 h97§: **c91**
17sᵖᵘ c16g⁵ c17g⁴ c16s² Apr 26] modest hurdler/maiden chaser: raced mainly around 2m: **h– §**
acts on soft and good to firm going: tried in cheekpieces: has looked none too resolute
over hurdles. *Mrs H. O. Graham*

LOGGER RHYTHM (USA) 7 b.g. Woodman (USA) – Formidable Dancer (USA) **c–**
(Danzig (USA)) [2006/7 c–, h–: c25dᵖᵘ c19m Sep 28] modest maiden on Flat (stays 2m): **h–**
no form over hurdles in chases, left R. Dickin after first outing: tongue tied next time:
won maiden point in February. *Dr J. R. J. Naylor*

LOGIES LASS 8 b.m. Nomadic Way (USA) – Random Select (Random Shot) [2006/7 **h–**
h–, F–: 17d⁶ 20s 20vᵖᵘ Mar 10] smallish mare: no form. *J. S. Smith*

LOG ON INTERSKY (IRE) 11 ch.g. Insan (USA) – Arctic Mo (IRE) (Mandalus) **c96**
[2006/7 c115, h–: c17m c17m⁵ c21f⁵ c21g⁵ c21m⁴ c24d² c24gᵖᵘ c21gᵘʳ c20dᵖᵘ c22s Feb **h–**
15] lengthy gelding: has reportedly had wind operation: handicap chaser, deteriorated
further in 2006/7: stays 3m: acts on firm and soft going: tried in cheekpieces: formerly
tongue tied: usually makes running. *J. R. Cornwall*

L'OISEAU (FR) 8 br.g. Video Rock (FR) – Roseraie (FR) (Quart de Vin (FR)) [2006/7 **c104**
c110, h88: 19d c16dᶠ c19d⁵ c16g c19g⁴ Apr 27] leggy gelding: winning hurdler: fair **h–**
handicap chaser: below form in 2006/7 except when falling second outing: best form
around 2m with emphasis on speed: acts on good to firm and good to soft ground.
J. G. Portman

LOITA HILLS (IRE) 7 b.g. Norwich – Gleann Oisin (IRE) (Le Bavard (FR)) [2006/7 **c–**
h95: c17m⁶ 17s⁵ 16g* Apr 27] good-topped gelding: fair form over hurdles, improved **h101 +**

when winning maiden at Chepstow by 3½ lengths from Bauhaus on return from 4-month absence: seemingly amiss on chasing debut: stays 19f: acts on good to soft going: has found little. *P. J. Hobbs*

LOITOKITOK 5 b.g. Piccolo – Bonita Bee (King of Spain) [2006/7 h–: 19m⁵ Sep 28] no form on Flat or over hurdles. *P. D. Cundell* — h–

LOJO 5 ch.m. Pivotal – Myhat (Factual (USA)) [2006/7 h–: 16g 16g⁶ 16m 16m 20g⁵ 18m* c19m³ c16d⁴ Nov 26] angular mare: poor hurdler: won selling handicap at Fontwell in September: similar form on first of 2 outings over fences, left Miss S. West in between: stays 19f: acts on soft and good to firm going: sold £1,600 Ascot February Sales. *J. K. Price* — c72 h72

LOLA'S KISS 5 b.m. Riverhead (USA) – Susy Wells (IRE) (Masad (IRE)) [2006/7 F16d 16s 17s 16v⁶ Jan 27] first foal: dam no form over hurdles: well beaten in bumper/over hurdles. *D. McCain Jnr* — h– F–

LONE RIDER (IRE) 6 b.g. Anshan – Reen-O-Foil (IRE) (Strong Gale) [2006/7 h–, F79: c26g^pu Jun 4] useful-looking gelding: no form over hurdles or on chasing debut: should be suited by much further than 2m. *Jonjo O'Neill* — c– h–

LONE SOLDIER (FR) 11 ch.g. Songlines (FR) – Caring Society (Caerleon (USA)) [2006/7 c–, h92§: 19d^pu Jun 14] compact gelding: winning chaser: modest handicap hurdler: stays easy 19f: acts on firm and soft going: formerly tongue tied: has found little. *S. B. Clark* — c– § h– §

LONESOME BOATMAN (IRE) 7 b.g. Old Vic – Midnight Miss (NZ) (Princes Gate) [2006/7 F16s c19s⁴ c19v⁶ c22s⁶ Feb 1] €70,000 3-y-o: half-brother to fair hurdler Megsie Here (by Bob's Return), stayed 2¾m: dam, winning hurdler, stayed 25f: won maiden Irish point in 2004: no solid form in bumper/maiden chases. *A. J. Whitehead* — c– F–

LONESOME DAY (IRE) 7 b.g. Saddlers' Hall (IRE) – Lonely Teardrop (IRE) (Spanish Place (USA)) [2006/7 24v³ 20g c24s² c28d⁵ c24v³ c31s⁶ c17d⁵ c25v^F c24s c28v^pu c24f* Apr 27] sturdy gelding: maiden hurdler: fair chaser: first win in cross-country event at Punchestown in April: probably stays 31f: acts on any going: sometimes wears cheekpieces. *Enda Bolger, Ireland* — c115 ? h87

LONESOME MAN (IRE) 11 ch.g. Broken Hearted – Carn-Na-Ros (Royal Trip) [2006/7 c103, h–: c21m^ur 21d 20m 20m c16d⁵ c20g^ur c20v c19s c19m⁴ Apr 10] medium-sized gelding: maiden hurdler: poor chaser nowadays: sold out of Tim Vaughan's stable £2,800 Ascot August Sales after fourth outing: stays 21f: tried tongue tied: front runner. *Mrs L. J. Young* — c72 h–

LONGBOW WARRIOR 5 b.g. Tout Ensemble – D'Nial (Pragmatic) [2006/7 F17v⁶ F16s 18g Mar 18] workmanlike gelding: second foal: dam maiden pointer: mid-division in maiden bumpers: well held in novice hurdle. *J. D. Frost* — h– F77

LONGDALE 9 b.g. Primitive Rising (USA) – Gunnerdale (Gunner B) [2006/7 c105, h90: c16v⁶ c16g⁶ Apr 7] tall, lengthy gelding: winning hurdler: fair chaser, below best both starts in 2006/7: should stay beyond 2m: acts on any going: tried in cheekpieces: has hinted at temperament. *M. Todhunter* — c88 h–

LONG GONE 4 b.f. Mtoto – Absentee (Slip Anchor) [2006/7 F14g F14v F16m⁵ F16g Apr 9] leggy, close-coupled filly: second foal: dam, temperamental 1¾m winner, half-sister to very smart stayer Weld: poor form in bumpers. *John A. Harris* — F67

LONGING FOR CINDY (USA) 5 ch.m. Belong To Me (USA) – I C Cindy (USA) (Gallapiat (USA)) [2006/7 16m^pu Jun 11] poor maiden on Flat (stays 9.7f): no show in seller on hurdling debut. *W. M. Brisbourne* — h–

LONG NIGHT 8 b.g. Alflora (IRE) – Twice A Night (Oats) [2006/7 h–: c23d⁷ c28s^pu c25d^pu Feb 1] lengthy gelding: successful 4 times in points, including in 2007: also won 5-runner event at Exeter much earlier in season, only form in hunter chases. *Mrs M. J. McGuinness* — c101 h–

LONG ROAD (USA) 6 b.g. Diesis – Tuviah (USA) (Eastern Echo (USA)) [2006/7 h85+: 16g* c16s³ 17m⁴ 17m⁴ Jun 19] modest hurdler: won handicap at Wincanton in May: none too fluent when third to Schoolhouse Walk in novice handicap at Towcester on chasing debut: may prove best at 2m: acts on good to firm going: blinkered last 2 starts (found little). *Jonjo O'Neill* — c85 h97

LONGSHANKS 10 b.g. Broadsword (USA) – Brass Castle (IRE) (Carlingford Castle) [2006/7 c–, h–: c22v³ c36g Apr 14] workmanlike gelding: useful handicap chaser, lightly raced nowadays: won at Newbury in November by 11 lengths from Schuh Shine: off — c135 h–

another 4½ months, completed for third time over National fences at Aintree when well-held seventh to Silver Birch in Grand National, weakening on run to 2 out (suffered interrupted preparation): should stay beyond 3m: raced on good going or softer (acts on heavy): sound jumper. *K. C. Bailey*

LONGSTONE BOY (IRE) 15 br.g. Mazaad – Inger-Lea (Record Run) [2006/7 c100: c21g² c16g² c16m⁵ Jul 17] good-bodied gelding: veteran chaser: left E. Clough after first outing: won points in March/April: stays 3m: acts on firm and good to soft going: consistent. *D. A. Rees*   **c98**

LONGSTONE LADY (IRE) 10 b.m. Mister Lord (USA) – Monamandy (IRE) (Mandalus) [2006/7 c–, h80: 17m 16m² c21m⁴ c21m* 19vᵖᵘ 17g* Apr 1] modest hurdler/ chaser: well backed, won over fences (minor event) in August and hurdles (selling handicap) in April, both at Newton Abbot: stays 2¾m: acts on soft and good to firm going, below form 3 starts on heavy. *J. D. Frost*   **c87 h90**

LONGSTONE LASS 7 b.m. Wizard King – Kamaress (Kampala) [2006/7 c–, h99: 16d c20sᵖᵘ 24s⁶ c27v⁴ 23gᵖᵘ Apr 3] maiden chaser: modest hurdler: no form in 2006/7: stays 27f: acts on heavy going: has been visored: tried tongue tied: free-going front runner (has bolted to post). *Miss Tracy Waggott*   **c– h–**

LONGSTONE LOCH (IRE) 10 b.g. Executive Perk – Lyre-Na-Gcloc (Le Moss) [2006/7 c85x, h–: 21m³ May 5] lengthy gelding: modest form over hurdles/fences (generally let down by jumping): stays 21f: blinkered last 2 starts. *C. C. Bealby*   **c– x h85**

LONGUEVILLE MANOR (FR) 6 b.g. Tel Quel (FR) – Longueville (FR) (Turgeon (USA)) [2006/7 h99: c21mᶠ 22m² 20m² 22m² 20s² 22s² 24v² 20d⁴ 25v³ 22d⁴ 24g* Apr 21] workmanlike gelding: fairly useful hurdler: in frame all 11 completed starts in Britain prior to winning handicap at Bangor in April readily by 6 lengths from Like A Lord: none too fluent but still prominent when fell 2 out in handicap at Newton Abbot on chasing debut: stays 25f: unraced on firm ground, acts on any other: usually in cheekpieces/blinkers in 2006/7 (wasn't at Bangor): tends to find little. *Jonjo O'Neill*   **c111 h121**

LOOKER 4 b.f. Barathea (IRE) – Last Look (Rainbow Quest (USA)) [2006/7 17v Jan 27] sturdy filly: fair on Flat (stays 1¼m), successful in September (claimed from R. Beckett £10,000): tailed off in Grade 2 juvenile at Cheltenham on hurdling debut. *J. Gallagher*   **h–**

LOOKING FORWARD 11 b.g. Primitive Rising (USA) – Gilzie Bank (New Brig) [2006/7 c–: c20g Apr 23] good-topped gelding: one-time modest handicap chaser, lightly raced and no form since 2003/4: stays 21f. *Mrs S. A. Watt*   **c–**

LOOKING GREAT (USA) 5 b.g. Gulch (USA) – Shoofha (IRE) (Bluebird (USA)) [2006/7 h92: 19mᵖᵘ Aug 3] angular gelding: modest form at best over hurdles. *R. F. Johnson Houghton*   **h–**

LOOK OF EAGLES 5 b.m. Fraam – Dreamtime Quest (Blakeney) [2006/7 16g 18g⁴ Apr 10] half-sister to fair staying chaser Courage Under Fire (by Risk Me) and fair hurdler up to 19f Interdream (by Interrex): fair handicapper up to 1m on Flat for P. Cole: better effort in mares novice hurdles when 15¾ lengths fourth to Strawberry at Fontwell: likely to prove best at 2m. *C. J. Mann*   **h86**

LOOKS THE BUSINESS (IRE) 6 b.g. Marju (IRE) – Business Centre (IRE) (Digamist (USA)) [2006/7 h97: 16g³ 18m² 19m⁴ 16fᵖᵘ Oct 5] fair on Flat (stays 1½m), successful in July: modest handicap hurdler: raced mainly around 2m: acts on soft and firm going: often tongue tied. *W. G. M. Turner*   **h98**

LOOSE MORALS (IRE) 6 b.m. Luso – Lacken Star (IRE) (Be My Native (USA)) [2006/7 h76, F–: c25g³ c26sᵖᵘ c26m³ Apr 8] good-topped mare: poor maiden hurdler: let down by jumping both completed outings over fences: stays 25f: sold 3,800 gns Doncaster May Sales. *Miss E. C. Lavelle*   **c81 x h–**

L'ORAGE LADY (IRE) 9 ch.m. Glacial Storm (USA) – Commanche Glen (IRE) (Commanche Run) [2006/7 h90: 26dᵖᵘ Jun 4] modest handicap hurdler, very lightly raced nowadays: stays 3¼m: acts on firm going: tried in cheekpieces: sold 2,600 gns Doncaster January Sales. *Heather Dalton*   **h–**

LORD ADONIS (IRE) 4 b.g. Galileo (IRE) – Flaming June (USA) (Storm Bird (CAN)) [2006/7 16g² 16d³ 17s⁴ 16sᵘʳ 16v⁶ 17g Mar 16] leggy gelding: well held on Flat: generally highly tried in juvenile hurdles (possibly flattered when fourth to Katchit at Cheltenham): wore cheekpieces/blinkers last 2 outings. *K. J. Burke*   **h107 ?**

LORD ANNER (IRE) 8 br.g. Mister Lord (USA) – Anner Lodge (IRE) (Capitano) [2006/7 c112: c25g⁵ May 2] fair chaser: stays 3½m: raced on good/good to soft going: **c108**

blinkered last 4 starts, also tongue tied last 3: often makes mistakes: sold 10,000 gns Doncaster May Sales, failed to complete in points in 2007. *P. F. Nicholls*

LORD APPELLARE (IRE) 6 ch.g. Lord of Appeal – Rainbow Alliance (IRE) (Golden Love) [2006/7 F16s³ F16s⁵ F16g² Mar 14] rather unfurnished eye-catching gelding: sixth foal: half-brother to 19f chase winner Regal Bandit (by Un Desperado): dam winning pointer: best effort in bumpers when 1¼ lengths second to King of The Jungle at Huntingdon. *R. Rowe*   **F94**

LORD ASHFORDLY 7 ch.g. Alflora (IRE) – Zanditu (Presidium) [2006/7 F17g² F17d 20mᵖᵘ 20g 20g Apr 27] second foal: brother to winning pointer: dam unraced half-sister to useful staying hurdler Haile Derring: won maiden on completed start in points in 2006: modest form on first of 2 starts in bumpers: no show over hurdles. *J. G. M. O'Shea*   **h– F78**

LORD BASKERVILLE 6 b.g. Wolfhound (USA) – My Dear Watson (Chilibang) [2006/7 h84: 20g⁵ 16m² 16s* 17m* 16m* 16mᶠ 17d 16vᵒ 16g 16d 16g⁶ Apr 7] sturdy gelding: fairly useful hurdler: claimed from W. Storey £6,000 second outing: much improved after, winning handicap at Stratford in May and novices at Sedgefield and Stratford (by 3½ lengths from Traprain) in June: best effort when seventh to Tycoon Hall in valuable handicap at Market Rasen seventh start: likely to prove best around 2m: acts on good to firm and heavy going: usually races prominently. *C. T. Pogson*   **h121**

LORD BATHWICK (IRE) 6 b.g. Mister Lord (USA) – Belmount Star (IRE) (Good Thyne (USA)) [2006/7 F16s 25gᵖᵘ 21g 21s Dec 3] €25,000 3-y-o: lengthy, good-topped gelding: half-brother to 2½m hurdle winner Bell Star (by Roselier) and winning hurdler/chaser Double Bogey Blues (by Celio Rufo), stayed 3¼m: dam unraced out of half-sister to Wayward Lad: no form in bumper or over hurdles: wore cheekpieces final start. *B. G. Powell*   **h– F–**

LORD BEAU (IRE) 11 b.g. Beau Sher – Bonny Joe (Derring Rose) [2006/7 c106: c26gᵖᵘ Mar 16] lengthy gelding: fairly useful hunter chaser: off nearly 2 years, prominent when going amiss after 6 out in Foxhunter at Cheltenham: stays 3½m: acts on heavy going. *A. Bateman*   **c–**

LORD BROADWAY (IRE) 11 b.g. Shardari – Country Course (IRE) (Crash Course) [2006/7 c97, h–: c24d⁵ c22sᵖᵘ c24v⁶ c24vᵖᵘ Jan 21] very tall, angular gelding: modest handicap chaser, generally out of form in 2006/7 (blinkered final outing): stays 3½m: unraced on firm going, acts on any other: tried visored. *N. M. Babbage*   **c88 h–**

LORD BUSH (IRE) 11 b. or br.g. Lord Americo – Run of Luck (Lucky Brief) [2006/7 c20m* c28sᵖᵘ May 26] ex-Irish gelding: poor hurdler/chaser for H. de Bromhead: successful 5 times in points in Britain, including in 2007: improved form when winning novice hunter at Huntingdon much earlier in season: stays 3m: probably acts on any going: sold 6,000 gns Doncaster November Sales. *Mrs Edward Crow*   **c91 h–**

LORD CODE (IRE) 9 b.g. Arctic Lord – Tax Code (Workboy) [2006/7 c19mᵖᵘ May 9] tall gelding: novice hurdler: winning pointer, including in 2007: no show in 2 chases. *Mrs A. Fox-Pitt*   **c– h–**

LORD COLLINGWOOD (IRE) 6 ch.g. Accordion – Cracker Dawn (IRE) (Executive Perk) [2006/7 h91+, F90: 23v³ 25sᶠ 23s⁵ 25g⁴ 20g² Apr 16] tall, leggy, lengthy gelding: fair maiden hurdler: stays 23f: acts on heavy ground: has found little. *Micky Hammond*   **h100**

LORD DAVID (IRE) 7 b.g. Mister Lord (USA) – Ms Mellini (Duky) [2006/7 F16m c23mᵖᵘ c23d Nov 17] 7,000 4-y-o: seventh foal: dam unraced half-sister to dam of very smart hurdler up to 21f Monsignor (by Mister Lord): runner-up in maiden point in 2005: tongue tied, no show in bumper/2 chases. *A. J. Honeyball*   **c– F–**

LORD DUNDANIEL (IRE) 10 b. or br.g. Arctic Lord – Killoskehan Queen (Bustineto) [2006/7 c107, h–: c20f³ c24d³ c20m² c21fᵖᵘ Jul 19] smallish gelding: winning hurdler: fair handicap chaser: barely stays 3m: acts on soft and good to firm going: in cheekpieces/visor last 6 outings: front runner: has finished weakly. *B. De Haan*   **c107 h–**

LORD EURO (IRE) 10 b.g. Lord Americo – Orchards Beauty (IRE) (Miner's Lamp) [2006/7 c79: c26g³ May 24] winning pointer: modest hunter chaser: stays 3¼m. *Mrs D. M. Grissell*   **c79**

LORD GEE (IRE) 6 gr.g. Topanoora – Forever Bubbles (IRE) (Roselier (FR)) [2006/7 F88: 21d⁴ 19g² 22d⁵ 20v³ Feb 13] workmanlike gelding: modest form over hurdles: stays 2¾m. *O. Sherwood*   **h99**

Mrs Karola Vann's "Lord Henry"

LORD GUNNERSLAKE (IRE) 7 ch.g. Flying Spur (AUS) – Cry In The Dark (Godswalk (USA)) [2006/7 c84, h–: c16g⁶ c20m⁵ c16s⁵ c18s c20mᵘʳ c20mᵖᵘ c23m⁵ Apr 22] sturdy gelding: winning hurdler: maiden chaser, no form in 2006/7: probably stays 23f: acts on soft going: has worn headgear. *Miss C. J. E. Caroe* — **c–** **h–**

LORD HECCLES (IRE) 8 b.g. Supreme Leader – Parsons Law (The Parson) [2006/7 c17d⁴ Dec 15] well-made gelding: modest form on second of 3 outings in novice hurdles: off 22 months, finished lame when fourth to Charlton Kings in novice handicap at Ascot on chasing debut: stays 21f: raced on good going or softer. *G. L. Moore* — **c81** **h–**

LORD HENRY (IRE) 8 b.g. Lord Americo – Auntie Honnie (IRE) (Radical) [2006/7 h122+: 17g* c19m* 17g c17g* Mar 30] lengthy, quite good-topped gelding: useful hurdler: improved form when winning handicap at Bangor in May by 3 lengths from Unjust Law: off 9 months, well held in County Hurdle at Cheltenham: successful both starts over fences, in maiden at Hereford (by 20 lengths) in June and novice at Ascot (again made virtually all when beating Royal Shakespeare easily by 7 lengths in 5-runner event, despite jumping slightly left) in March: stays easy 19f: acts on good to firm and good to soft going: free-going sort: capable of better still over fences. *P. J. Hobbs* — **c144 p** **h134**

LORD HOPEFUL (IRE) 6 b.g. Lord Americo – Hidden Agenda (Abednego) [2006/7 h–, F82: 19v⁵ 22d Mar 20] poor form over hurdles. *C. P. Morlock* — **h79**

LORDINGTON LAD 7 br.g. Terimon – Fit For Firing (FR) (In Fijar (USA)) [2006/7 c–, h–, F83: 18g 21g³ c24d c16dᶠ c16sᵖᵘ Dec 12] leggy gelding: form (poor) over hurdles — **c– x** **h80**

only when third in handicap at Ludlow: let down by jumping over fences: should be suited by 3m. *B. G. Powell*

LORD JAY JAY (IRE) 7 b.g. Lord of Appeal – Mesena (Pals Passage) [2006/7 h89: c21m⁶ c23g⁴ c17m³ c20m² c18m² c23f² c18m* c24g² Oct 7] good-bodied gelding: maiden hurdler: left Miss H. Knight, much better over fences, straightforward task in maiden at Fontwell in September, though attempted to run out seventh: stays 3m: acts on firm and good to soft going: wore cheekpieces after reappearance: front runner. *Evan Williams*   c114 h–

LORD KERNOW (IRE) 7 b.g. Lord Americo – Bramble Ridge (IRE) (Remainder Man) [2006/7 F85: 22d Feb 1] workmanlike gelding: fair form in bumpers (virtually ran off course once): always behind on hurdling debut: dead *C. J. Down*   h–

LORD KILLESHANRA (IRE) 8 br.g. Mister Lord (USA) – Killeshandra Lass (IRE) (King's Ride) [2006/7 c137, h–: c24s⁴ c24s⁵ c25s⁵ c24g⁵ Feb 3] tall, lengthy gelding: maiden hurdler: useful novice chaser in 2005/6: yet to recapture that form: will be suited by further than 25f: raced on good going or softer (acts on heavy). *C. L. Tizzard*   c125 + h–

LORD KILPATRICK (IRE) 13 ch.g. Mister Lord (USA) – Running Frau (Deep Run) [2006/7 c83: c24s Mar 10] lengthy, workmanlike gelding: winning pointer: lightly-raced maiden chaser: stays 3m: acts on soft going. *J. D. Frost*   c–

LORD LEONARDO (IRE) 7 b.g. Norwich – Sue's A Lady (Le Moss) [2006/7 h–, F79: 22s⁵ᵖᵘ 22v⁶ Jan 2] sturdy gelding: no form over hurdles: in cheekpieces final outing (looked none too genuine). *L. Wells*   h– §

LORD LIEUTENANT (FR) 4 gr.g. Kaldounevees (FR) – Lady Lieutenant (IRE) (General Holme (USA)) [2006/7 17s 21g Mar 20] fourth foal: dam 9f/11f winner in France: well beaten only outing on Flat for D. Sepulchre and over hurdles. *N. J. Hawke*   h–

LORD LINGTON (FR) 8 b.g. Bulington (FR) – Tosca de Bussy (FR) (Le Riverain (FR)) [2006/7 c107§, h107§: 17d³ 16g⁴ c16g⁵ 17s 16d⁶ 16s³ 17s⁵ 16gᵘʳ Mar 28] rather leggy gelding: fair handicap hurdler: similar form at best over fences (has been let down by jumping): will stay beyond 17f: acts on heavy going: tried blinkered: ungenuine. *D. J. Wintle*   c101 § h112 §

LORD MAYOR 6 b.g. Machiavellian (USA) – Misleading Lady (Warning) [2006/7 19dᶠ 17s 20m⁵ 17g⁵ Apr 11] close-coupled gelding: useful on Flat (stays 1¼m) at 4 yrs for Sir Michael Stoute, has deteriorated considerably and claimed from R. Cowell £6,000 final start in 2006: poor form over hurdles. *B. N. Pollock*   h73

LORD MORLEY (IRE) 7 br.g. Lord Americo – Minature Miss (Move Off) [2006/7 F82: F16m May 6] modest form on first of 2 outings in bumpers: bred to stay well. *Karen McLintock*   F71

LORD MUSGRAVE (IRE) 8 b.g. Lord Americo – Raisin Turf (IRE) (Phardante (FR)) [2006/7 h–, F–: 22m 25g⁵ 24g⁶ 27d⁵ 22mᵖᵘ Aug 24] of little account: sold £1,700 Ascot December Sales. *L. Wells*   h–

LORD NELLERIE (FR) 8 b.g. Panoramic – Epsom Nellerie (FR) (Carmont (FR)) [2006/7 c108: c19g* May 4] ex-French gelding: useful hunter chaser: won at Hereford in May on second completed outing in Britain by 30 lengths from Nominate: stays 2½m: acts on good to firm and good to soft going. *B. G. Powell*   c120

LORD NELLSSON 11 b.g. Arctic Lord – Miss Petronella (Petoski) [2006/7 c–, h100: 20d⁴ 24d c23m³ Apr 25] compact gelding: maiden chaser: fair handicap hurdler: stays 3m: acts on soft and firm going: tried in cheekpieces: races prominently. *Andrew Turnell*   c86 h104

LORD 'N' MASTER (IRE) 11 b.g. Lord Americo – Miss Good Night (Buckskin (FR)) [2006/7 c110, h–: c24s⁶ c24g⁴ c24g⁴ c24mᵖᵘ c26g⁵ Apr 23] useful-looking gelding: fair handicap chaser at one time: off 19 months, well below best in 2006/7: stays 3¼m: acts on soft and good to firm going: usually makes mistakes. *R. Rowe*   c74 x h–

LORD NORMAN (IRE) 6 b.g. Norwich – Sue's A Lady (Le Moss) [2006/7 F89: F18v³ 22d⁶ Jan 30] stocky gelding: fair form on first of 3 outings in bumpers: well beaten in novice on hurdling debut. *L. Wells*   h– F68

LORD OF ADVENTURE (IRE) 5 b.g. Inzar (USA) – Highly Fashionable (IRE) (Polish Precedent (USA)) [2006/7 h98§: 18s⁶ 21s 24sᵖᵘ 22s³ 22s² 20s 18g⁵ c20m⁵ Apr 9] smallish, sturdy gelding: modest maiden hurdler: soundly beaten in maiden on chasing debut: stays 2¾m: acts on soft going: wears headgear: unreliable. *Mrs L. C. Jewell*   c– § h86 §

LORD OF BEAUTY (FR) 7 ch.g. Medaaly – Arctic Beauty (USA) (Arctic Tern (USA)) [2006/7 19d* 19s 20s⁴ 22d Mar 17] leggy, angular gelding: fairly useful hurdler: fit from Flat, best effort when winning handicap at Ascot in December by ¾ length from Kelrev: well below form after: stays 2½m: raced on good going or softer. *Noel T. Chance* **h124**

LORD OF ILLUSION (IRE) 10 b.g. Mister Lord (USA) – Jellaride (IRE) (King's Ride) [2006/7 c141, h–: 24d c24g c21g Apr 13] tall gelding: winning hurdler: useful chaser at one time, no form since early-2006: should stay beyond 3¼m: successful on soft going, best efforts under less testing conditions: tongue tied final outing: usually front runner. *T. R. George* **c–** **h–**

LORD OF METHLEY 8 gr.g. Zilzal (USA) – Paradise Waters (Celestial Storm (USA)) [2006/7 h73: 16m⁶ 19d⁵ 17d⁴ 16g⁵ 20m⁵ Jul 26] poor maiden hurdler: stays 2½m: visored final outing: tongue tied since debut. *S. Lycett* **h77**

LORDOFOUROWN (IRE) 9 b.g. Mister Lord (USA) – Twinkling (Star Appeal) [2006/7 c125, h–: c28d⁴ c24s⁴ c29s³ c29s⁴ c33vᵖᵘ Feb 24] angular, workmanlike gelding: maiden hurdler: useful handicap chaser: in frame all 4 completed starts in 2006/7, in Welsh National final occasion: would have stayed beyond 29f: acted on soft going: wore cheekpieces last 3 starts: dead. *S. Donohoe, Ireland* **c132** **h–**

LORD OF THE BRIDGE (IRE) 5 br.g. Mister Lord (USA) – Costly Alyse (Al Sirat) [2006/7 21g Mar 23] €22,000 3-y-o: big, lengthy gelding: ninth foal: dam unraced: tailed off in maiden hurdle on debut. *K. C. Bailey* **h–**

LORD OF THE HILL (IRE) 12 b.g. Dromod Hill – Telegram Mear (Giolla Mear) [2006/7 c100, h–: c20gᶠ c16m² c20m c16mᵖᵘ c16mᵖᵘ c19mᵖᵘ Sep 28] tall gelding: no form over hurdles: fair chaser, largely let down by jumping in 2006/7: stays 2½m: acts on good to firm going, possibly unsuited by softer than good: tried in cheekpieces: formerly tongue tied: headstrong front runner. *G. Brown* **c96 x** **h–**

LORD OF THE ROAD 8 b.g. Gildoran – Ethels Course (Crash Course) [2006/7 24d c24d² c27g² Mar 25] well-made gelding: winning pointer: novice hurdler, off 19 months before reappearance: fair form when runner-up both outings in chases: stays 27f: acts on soft going: tongue tied in 2006/7: sold 11,000 gns Doncaster May Sales. *P. F. Nicholls* **c110** **h–**

LORD ON THE RUN (IRE) 8 b.g. Lord Americo – Polar Crash (Crash Course) [2006/7 c116, h84: c20gᶠ 20g² 20m* 18g 20g⁶ 24s⁵ 18s³ 20gᵘʳ Apr 7] good-topped gelding: fairly useful chaser: fair handicap hurdler: won at Hexham in June: probably stays 3m: acts on soft and good to firm going: in cheekpieces last 2 outings. *P. C. Haslam* **c–** **h102**

LORD OSCAR (IRE) 8 b.g. Oscar (IRE) – Americo Rose (IRE) (Lord Americo) [2006/7 c98, h89+: c23m⁴ c16dᵖᵘ 17s⁵ Jun 27] tall gelding: winning pointer: modest novice hurdler/chaser, looked thoroughly temperamental in 2006/7: stays 2½m: acts on soft going: tongue tied last 4 outings: headstrong: one to avoid. *D. E. Pipe* **c82 §** **h– §**

LORD RODNEY (IRE) 8 b.g. Hatim (USA) – Howcleuch (Buckskin (FR)) [2006/7 c115, h–: 20g⁶ c16d² c20s³ c19s³ c24v² c21gᵇᵈ Apr 13] well-made gelding: fair hurdler/fairly useful chaser: stayed 3m: acted on heavy going: tried in cheekpieces (below form): sometimes let down by jumping over fences: dead. *P. Beaumont* **c115 x** **h101**

LORD ROSSKIT (IRE) 7 b. or br.g. Lord Americo – Redstone Lady (IRE) (Buckskin (FR)) [2006/7 h90: 20fᵘʳ 20mᵘʳ 17m* 16m³ 20s* 21v⁶ 20v 20g Apr 7] tall gelding: modest hurdler: won novice events at Cartmel (handicap) in July and Wetherby in October: should stay 2¾m: acts on any going. *G. M. Moore* **h99**

LORD RYEFORD (IRE) 7 br.g. Arctic Lord – Killoskehan Queen (Bustineto) [2006/7 h90, F81: c20s² c20dᵖᵘ c19d⁴ Feb 2] workmanlike gelding: modest hurdler: similar form on completed outings over fences: stays 2½m: raced mainly on good to soft going: tongue tied once. *T. R. George* **c96** **h–**

LORD SAAR (IRE) 8 b. or br.g. Arctic Lord – Lucycello (Monksfield) [2006/7 c20sᵖᵘ 22vᵖᵘ c20vᶠ 24v⁴ 27vᵖᵘ c20sᵖᵘ Apr 27] winning pointer: novice hurdler/chaser, poor form only completed outing in 2006/7: probably stays 3m: acts on any going: in cheekpieces last 3 starts. *A. C. Whillans* **c–** **h70**

LORD SAM (IRE) 11 b. or br.g. Supreme Leader – Russian Gale (IRE) (Strong Gale) [2006/7 c147x, h140: 23f² 25sᵖᵘ 22g* 22d c24g 24g Apr 14] stocky gelding: smart handicap hurdler: won at Wincanton in December by ¾ length from Lyes Green: mistakes when well held in listed event at Aintree final outing: similar form at best over fences **c– x** **h147**

(generally let down by jumping): should stay beyond 3m: acts on firm and soft going (unraced on heavy): wears cheekpieces nowadays. *V. R. A. Dartnall*

LORD SAMPOSIN 6 b.g. I'm Supposin (IRE) – Skiddaw Samba (Viking (USA)) F– [2006/7 F16g Apr 7] big, workmanlike gelding: third foal: dam poor 2m hurdler: tongue tied, tailed off in bumper on debut. *M. A. Barnes*

LORDS BRIDGE 6 b.g. Rakaposhi King – The Secret Seven (Balidar) [2006/7 F16m c– F17d c20m^F Apr 15] first foal: dam winning 2m chaser: no sign of ability in 2 bumpers/ F– novice chase: sold out of J. Cresswell's stable 700 gns Doncaster January Sales after debut. *M. E. Sowersby*

LORDSBRIDGE (USA) 5 b.g. Lord Avie (USA) – Victorian Style (Nashwan (USA)) c– [2006/7 h93p: 17s^5 c19s^pu 20g^3 Apr 27] modest form over hurdles, improved when third h97 in handicap at Chepstow (caught eye several times previously when with D. P. Keane): tongue tied, no show in handicap on chasing debut: stays 2½m: held up. *Andrew Turnell*

LORD SEAMUS 12 b.g. Arctic Lord – Erica Superba (Langton Heath) [2006/7 c99d, c83 h–: c25g^5 c24d^3 c23m^6 Jul 12] compact gelding: fair handicap chaser at one time, has h– deteriorated: won points in March/April: stays 4m: acts on firm and soft going: tried in cheekpieces. *K. C. Bailey*

LORD WHO (IRE) 10 b.g. Mister Lord (USA) – Le Bavellen (Le Bavard (FR)) c102 x [2006/7 c–, h112: c25v^* c25g^6 c31s^2 Apr 26] lengthy, angular gelding: fair hurdler/fairly h– useful chaser at best: left P. Hobbs and fit from points (successful), beat only other finisher a distance in hunter at Ayr in March: stays 31f: acts on heavy going: often let down by jumping. *J. P. G. Hamilton*

LORD YOUKY (FR) 13 b.g. Cadoudal (FR) – Lady Corteira (FR) (Carvin II) [2006/7 c– c–, h–: c21g^pu May 16] useful-looking gelding: veteran chaser: stays 25f: acts on firm and h– good to soft going. *Miss J. Hughes*

LORIENT EXPRESS (FR) 8 b.g. Sleeping Car (FR) – Envie de Chalamont (FR) c112 + (Pamponi (FR)) [2006/7 c124, h101p: c16s^4 c16g^3 c16s^5 16g^3 16g^2 c20m^6 Apr 22] tall, h106 angular gelding: fair handicap hurdler: fairly useful handicap chaser, not at best in 2006/7: best around 2m: has won on soft ground, best form under less testing conditions. *Miss Venetia Williams*

LORIKO D'AIRY (FR) 8 b.g. Oblat (FR) – Ursali d'Airy (FR) (Marasali) [2006/7 c– c–, h82: 16s^pu 16g^pu Mar 14] good-topped gelding: winning chaser: maiden hurdler, no h– form in 2 starts after 18-month absence: raced mainly around 2m on good going or softer: races freely. *Miss C. Dyson*

LORNA DUNE 5 b.m. Desert Story (IRE) – Autumn Affair (Lugana Beach) [2006/7 h– h78: 21v 16s^5 Feb 3] close-coupled mare: form (poor) over hurdles only when fourth in juvenile in 2005/6: tried in cheekpieces. *M. Scudamore*

LORRELINI (IRE) 6 ch.h. Among Men (USA) – Well Able (IRE) (Lahib (USA)) c70 [2006/7 h–: 21m^bd 22s^pu 16v^5 16g c16v c20v^3 c18g^6 c24g Mar 28] strong, lengthy horse: h77 poor novice hurdler/chaser: best short of 3m: acts on heavy going. *R. H. Alner*

LOS ANGEL EASE (USA) 5 b.g. Diesis – Kitza (IRE) (Danehill (USA)) [2006/7 F– F16d Dec 14] 1,000,000Y, 7,000 3-y-o: sturdy, heavy-bodied gelding: type to carry condition: second foal: half-brother to smart 7f/1m winner Fort Dignity (by Seeking The Gold): dam, runner-up in Irish 1000 Guineas and Irish Oaks, half-sister to smart sprinter Marouble: well held in bumper on debut: sold 1,200 gns Doncaster March Sales. *G. A. Swinbank*

LOSCAR (FR) 8 b.g. General Holme (USA) – Unika II (FR) (Rolling Bowl (FR)) c76 + [2006/7 h–: 20d^3 25s^6 16v^F 24s^pu c16v c20v^* Mar 15] poor maiden hurdler: much more h65 fluent than on chasing debut when easily winning handicap at Hexham: stays 2½m: raced on going softer than good (acts on heavy). *A. C. Whillans*

LOSE THE ATTITUDE (IRE) 7 br.g. Alphabatim (USA) – Legal Minstrel (IRE) h88 (Legal Circles (USA)) [2006/7 F16d^6 24v^3 20s^4 26s^pu Dec 26] €4,200 4-y-o: second foal: F81 dam unraced: won maiden Irish point in 2006: bought 10,000 gns Doncaster May Sales: sixth in bumper: modest form over hurdles: should prove suited by further than 3m. *T. R. George*

LOSING GRIP (IRE) 8 b. or br.m. Presenting – Executive Wonder (IRE) (Executive c– Perk) [2006/7 h88: 16s 17d^* 17m c16m^5 20m^5 c20g^pu Aug 14] poor hurdler: won seller h83 at Cartmel (mares novice) in May: no form in 2 chases: should stay beyond 17f: acts on soft going. *Mrs S. J. Smith*

LOS SUENOS (IRE) 6 br.g. Supreme Leader – Stormy Miss (IRE) (Glacial Storm (USA)) [2006/7 h–: 24v 22m Nov 7] no form over hurdles. *Nick Williams* h–

LOST DIRECTION 12 b.m. Heading North – Precis (Pitpan) [2006/7 16m 19g[pu] Jul 23] no sign of ability: left O. Carter after first outing. *C. J. Down* c– h–

LOST IN NORMANDY (IRE) 10 b.g. Treasure Hunter – Auntie Honnie (IRE) (Radical) [2006/7 c90, h–: c25d[pu] c20d c20g[5] c24v[pu] c24d[2] c20v c20v[4] Mar 9] lengthy gelding: handicap chaser, little form in 2006/7: stays 3¼m: acts on heavy and good to firm going: usually blinkered. *Mrs L. Williamson* c68 h–

LOST IN THE SNOW (IRE) 9 b. or br.g. Arctic Lord – Where Am I (Kambalda) [2006/7 c78, h–: c20m[5] c23m[4] c20m[2] c23m[6] c20f[ur] Sep 3] winning pointer: well held over hurdles: poor novice chaser, usually let down by jumping: stays 23f: raced on good going or firmer. *M. Sheppard* c78 x h–

LOST PROPERTY (IRE) 9 b.g. Phardante (FR) – Icy Rock (Boreen (FR)) [2006/7 c24f[pu] c20s[pu] 22g c17s[F] c20d[pu] 24s[4] 16s Apr 27] placed in Irish points in 2006: bought 8,000 gns Doncaster May Sales: no form over hurdles/in chases: has worn cheekpieces. *Mrs C. J. Kerr* c– x h–

LOST SOLDIER FOUR 4 b.g. In The Wings – Donya (Mill Reef (USA)) [2006/7 aF16g[4] Mar 9] 4,000 3-y-o: closely related to 2 winners by Barathea, notably smart stayer Lost Soldier Three, and half-brother to several winners, including fair 2m hurdler Wamdha (by Thatching): dam twice-raced half-sister to Rothman's International winner French Glory, out of Prix de Diane winner Dunette: unraced on Flat for L. Cumani: nearest finish when around 2 lengths fourth to Wisteria Lane in bumper at Lingfield on debut. *K. A. Morgan* F87 +

LOST TIME (IRE) 10 b.g. Glacial Storm (USA) – Overtime (IRE) (Executive Perk) [2006/7 c122, h111: 22v c24v[pu] c24d[pu] c20s[2] c21g[F] Apr 13] tall gelding: fair hurdler: fairly useful chaser: form in 2006/7 only when second to Dantes Reef in 5-runner minor event at Clonmel: fell heavily Chair in Topham Chase at Aintree: stays 23f: raced largely on going softer than good (acts on heavy): tried in cheekpieces. *C. Roche, Ireland* c122 h–

LOTHIAN FALCON 8 b.g. Relief Pitcher – Lothian Rose (Roscoe Blake) [2006/7 c108, h99: c25f[*] 25d[2] 24s[2] 24g[*] 24s[2] Apr 26] workmanlike gelding: progressive hurdler/chaser: fairly useful form when winning handicaps over fences at Kelso in May and hurdles at Cheltenham (by length from Isle de Maurice) in April: good second to Dream Alliance in handicap chase at Perth final outing: stays 3¼m: acts on firm and soft going: genuine. *P. Maddison* c121 + h116 +

LOTHIAN RISING 9 ch.g. Primitive Rising (USA) – Lothian Lightning (Lighter) [2006/7 c24g[*] Apr 7] fair pointer, won twice in March: successful also in hunter at Carlisle on chasing debut by 2½ lengths from Forever Eyesofblue: will stay beyond 3m. *Mrs E. J. Reed* c95 +

L'OUDON (FR) 6 ch.g. Alamo Bay (USA) – Stella di Corte (FR) (Lightning (FR)) [2006/7 h123: 16g[5] 19s[2] 16h[3] c19s[3] 16d[2] Mar 22] tall, close-coupled gelding: fairly useful hurdler: claimed to join E. Haddock £10,000 when below form final outing: badly let down by jumping when remote third to Always Waining in maiden at Taunton on chasing debut: stays 21f: raced on good going or softer (acts on soft): blinkered last 4 starts: tongue tied nowadays: patiently ridden. *P. F. Nicholls* c94 h123

LOUDSPEAKER (USA) 7 b.g. Royal Academy (USA) – Proud Fact (USA) (Known Fact (USA)) [2006/7 c16s[pu] Sep 20] maiden on Flat: form over jumps only when winning handicap hurdle at Clonmel in June 2004: left P. Hassett and off almost 2 years, breathing problem on chasing debut: raced at 2m: acts on firm ground. *J. J. Lambe, Ireland* c– h–

LOU DU MOULIN MAS (FR) 8 b.g. Sassanian (USA) – Houf (FR) (Morespeed) [2006/7 c127, h–: 25g[*] c24d[2] c24d[*] c29s c24g c25g[pu] Apr 13] rather leggy gelding: reportedly had breathing operation prior to reappearance: improved effort over hurdles when winning novice at Cheltenham in October by 5 lengths from Smart Mover: useful handicap chaser: successful in amateur event at Newbury in November by ½ length from Kerstino Two: stays 27f: acts on soft and good to firm going: tried blinkered: tongue tied: usually races prominently: sound jumper: consistent. *P. F. Nicholls* c131 h116

LOUGHANELTEEN (IRE) 9 b.g. Satco (FR) – Ruths Rhapsody (IRE) (Creative Plan (USA)) [2006/7 16v[4] 16s c18d[ur] c17m 20m[pu] Apr 24] useful-looking gelding: has reportedly had breathing operation: fair hurdler/maiden chaser: out of form c– h109 after reappearance: raced mainly around 2m: acts on any going: tongue tied on debut. *P. J. Rothwell, Ireland*

LOUGH DERG (FR) 7 b.g. Apple Tree (FR) – Asturias (FR) (Pistolet Bleu (IRE)) [2006/7 c137, h–: 19d³ 25d² 24v⁴ 24g 24g⁴ Apr 12] rather sparely-made gelding: useful hurdler: best efforts in 2006/7 when placed first 2 starts, second to Mighty Man in muddling Long Walk Hurdle at Ascot: winning chaser, largely let down by jumping over fences: stays 25f: acts on soft and good to firm going: visored last 6 starts: usually races prominently. *D. E. Pipe* — **c– h140**

LOUGH HONEY (IRE) 8 b.m. Oscar (IRE) – Lough Ruby (IRE) (Strong Gale) [2006/7 20m⁶ 20g Sep 17] first foal: dam ran 3 times in bumpers: runner-up in maiden Irish point in 2006: soundly beaten in 2 novice hurdles. *Evan Williams* — **h–**

LOUGH RYNN (IRE) 9 b.g. Beneficial – Liffey Lady (Camden Town) [2006/7 c–, h–: c22dᵖᵘ c22mᵖᵘ c20gᶠ Aug 14] tall gelding: lightly raced over hurdles: disappointing maiden chaser: stays 3m: acts on soft going: blinkered last 2 starts: sold 5,200 gns Doncaster October Sales, third in points in March/April. *C. J. Mann* — **c– h–**

LOUISEANDMELSLOVE 5 ch.m. Fumo di Londra (IRE) – Lady Sabina (Bairn (USA)) [2006/7 F17m Jun 7] third foal: dam 1¼m winner: soundly beaten in bumper on debut. *J. R. Norton* — **F–**

LOULOU NIVERNAIS (FR) 8 b.g. Lights Out (FR) – Clemence (FR) (Vorias (USA)) [2006/7 c95, h–: c16m³ c16d² c16s³ c20v* c22v* c22d* c20v* c25gᶠ 20g² Apr 7] leggy gelding: winning hurdler: fair form when second to ready winner Eleazar in handicap at Haydock final start: useful handicap chaser: left M. Todhunter after first outing: vastly improved after, winning at Wetherby and Uttoxeter in January, Market Rasen in February and Newcastle (easily, by 26 lengths from Welcome To Unos) in March: travelling powerfully under restraint when falling heavily eleventh at Wetherby: stays 2¾m well: has won on good to firm going, best efforts on softer (acts on heavy): usually races prominently: consistent. *B. Ellison* — **c136 h101**

Mr W. Frewen's "Lough Derg"

LOUNAOS (FR) 4 b.f. Limnos (JPN) – Luanda (IRE) (Bigstone (IRE)) [2006/7   **h142 ?**
16s* 16s* 16d⁴ 17g 20m⁴ Apr 8]

When a horse seems to show markedly improved form, particularly when
stepped up in class, it can sometimes be difficult to gauge whether they have shown
genuine improvement or whether they've been flattered. The problem often arises
with juvenile or novice hurdlers running in open company, Lounaos a perfect
example in the latest season. Her fourth place in the AIG Europe Champion Hurdle
at Leopardstown in late-January—when chasing home that trio of modern-day Irish
hurdling stalwarts Hardy Eustace, Brave Inca and Macs Joy—looked a top-notch
performance for a juvenile, yet Lounaos was unplaced when a short-priced favourite on both subsequent starts, notably in the Triumph Hurdle at Cheltenham.
The Irish Champion has had its fair share of apparent 'out-of-the-ordinary' novice
performers down the years, none more so than in 1991 when the four-year-old
Nordic Surprise became the only juvenile winner in the race's history—he subsequently fluffed his lines when well fancied for both the Supreme Novices' (fourth)
and Triumph Hurdle (twenty-fourth) at that year's Cheltenham Festival. The novice
His Song could manage only second when hot favourite (in a field of thirty) for the
1998 Supreme Novices' on the back of his second to Istabraq in that season's Irish
Champion, whilst Clifdon Fog (another four-year-old) and Stage Affair are two
novices placed in the Leopardstown race who both failed to win subsequently over
hurdles. Hopefully the latter fate won't befall Lounaos despite her anti-climactic
end to the season. After all, Danoli was runner-up in the 1994 Irish Champion as a
novice and went on to become a top-class performer over both hurdles and fences.

A smart performer on the Flat, Lounaos was always more likely than most
to fare well once sent hurdling and she made a winning debut, landing the odds in a
juvenile maiden at Navan in November by three lengths from Sophist. A month
later Lounaos showed a deal of improvement to win the Grade 2 Durkan New
Homes Juvenile Hurdle at Leopardstown by three and a half lengths from Robin du
Bois, the pair clear, Lounaos merely given a few reminders to make sure after the
last. Whilst this represented fairly useful form, Lounaos appeared to progress even
more significantly in the face of a much stiffer task when finishing eight lengths
fourth of eight to Hardy Eustace in what appeared a strong renewal of the AIG
Europe Champion Hurdle. The pace quickened significantly after the third last and,
after travelling strongly held up, Lounaos wasn't beaten off until approaching the
last. The weight-for-age terms are overly generous in such races—Lounaos was
receiving 19 lb from her male elders—but, with that taken into consideration, she
still appeared to have improved by the same amount as between her first two races.
What is equally clear, however, is that Lounaos failed to give anything like her Irish

*Durkan New Homes Juvenile Hurdle, Leopardstown—smart Flat recruit Lounaos continues
her good start over hurdles with a smooth defeat of Robin du Bois (noseband)*

Champion running under different conditions at Cheltenham (despite her 7 lb fillies and mares allowance), nor did she even match the form of her success at Leopardstown in December. Sent off 7/2 favourite in the Triumph, Lounaos was unable to make any impression from two out after being close enough at the top of the hill, eventually finishing tenth of twenty-three behind Katchit, beaten around thirty lengths. Lounaos fared only a little better on her one subsequent outing when five lengths fourth to Grangeclare Lark in a Grade 3 mares novice event at Fairyhouse, although it is possible that the two-and-a-half-mile trip stretched her stamina that day.

		Hector Protector	Woodman
	Limnos (JPN)	(ch 1988)	Korveya
	(ch 1994)	Lingerie	Shirley Heights
Lounaos (FR)		(b 1988)	Northern Trick
(b.f. 2003)		Bigstone	Last Tycoon
	Luanda (IRE)	(b 1990)	Batave
	(b 1997)	Lexington Star	Sadler's Wells
		(b 1992)	Last Tango

The rather leggy, useful-looking Lounaos is by the very smart mile-and-a-half performer Limnos, a half-brother to the latest Oaks winner Light Shift. Whilst he was bred in Japan, Limnos did all his racing in France for the Niarchos family. Lounaos is the third foal of her unraced dam Luanda who, herself, is out of a lightly-raced maiden who finished fourth in a listed event at Evry on the last of her six Flat starts in France and is a half-sister to Grand Criterium winners Lost World and Fijar Tango, the latter also being high class at up to a mile and a half (beat dual Derby winner Kahyasi in the 1988 Prix Niel). Luanda has produced another winning hurdler, namely La Bay (by Alamo Bay), who won over seventeen furlongs in the

Mrs Martina Griffin's "Lounaos"

French Provinces during the latest season. Lounaos was placed on her three starts in France as a two-year-old and progressed into a smart Flat performer in 2006, putting up her best effort when beating Al Eile by three lengths in the Leopardstown November Handicap over two miles on her final outing of the season. She barely stays two and a half miles over hurdles and acts on soft ground. It is difficult to predict exactly what course Lounaos' career will take. Her Irish Turf Club mark at the end of the season was 135 which could look rather lenient if she proves capable of living up to her AIG Europe Champion form. *Eoin Griffin, Ireland*

LOUP BLEU (USA) 9 b.g. Nureyev (USA) – Louve Bleue (USA) (Irish River (FR)) [2006/7 c–, h81: 21g 16g⁵ May 21] novice hurdler, poor nowadays: lame only outing in chase: stays 2½m: acts on heavy going: tried visored: runner-up in point in January. *Mrs A. V. Roberts*
c–
h81

LOUP DU SAUBOUAS (FR) 4 b.g. Loup Solitaire (USA) – Minaudeuse (CAN) (The Minstrel (CAN)) [2006/7 16v* 16v³ 16s 16m 16m³ Apr 25] good-topped gelding: lightly raced on Flat, won 1½m event in French Provinces in 2006 for R. Gibson: fairly useful form in juvenile hurdles: won maiden at Thurles in November: best effort when 1¾ lengths third of 25 to Phantom Lad at Punchestown final outing: raced at 2m: acts on heavy and good to firm going. *N. Meade, Ireland*
h112

LOUSTIC DES ILES (FR) 8 ch.g. Chamberlin (FR) – Enchantee (FR) (Down The River (FR)) [2006/7 17m 20g 17v 17v⁵ Dec 12] poor form at best over hurdles: blinkered final outing: tried tongue tied. *Eoin Doyle, Ireland*
h–

LOVE ANGEL (USA) 5 b. or br.g. Woodman (USA) – Omnia (USA) (Green Dancer (USA)) [2006/7 h88: 18g⁴ 20m* 18g⁵ 19m² 18d* 16g 18g* 22f⁵ 20f Apr 28] close-coupled gelding: modest on Flat nowadays: fair handicap hurdler: won at Fontwell in September (conditional jockeys novice), November and April: probably stays 2¾m, at least when emphasis is on speed: acts on firm and good to soft going. *J. J. Bridger*
h106

LOVE BEAUTY (USA) 5 b.g. Seeking The Gold (USA) – Heavenly Rhythm (USA) (Septieme Ciel (USA)) [2006/7 h–: 17g 20m 24gᵖᵘ 16s⁵ 16s Jan 21] tall, quite good-topped gelding: maiden on Flat: no form over hurdles: left M. Harris after third outing: has worn headgear/tongue strap. *H. von der Recke, Germany*
h–

LOVE FROM RUSSIA 5 b.g. Xaar – Heart (Cadeaux Genereux) [2006/7 17dᵖᵘ 22dᵖᵘ 16g 16d Jan 5] little form on Flat, none over hurdles. *Mrs H. O. Graham*
h–

LOVE OF CLASSICS 7 b.g. Classic Cliche (IRE) – Ardent Love (IRE) (Ardross) [2006/7 h121§: c23d⁶ Oct 26] workmanlike gelding: fairly useful hurdler: well held in maiden on chasing debut: should stay 3m: raced on going softer than good: has worn headgear since debut: untrustworthy. *O. Sherwood*
c– §
h– §

LOVEOFTHEDARKSIDE 4 br.f. Beat All (USA) – Parlez Moi d'Amour (IRE) (Precocious) [2006/7 F14v 20vᵖᵘ 19gᵖᵘ Apr 8] lengthy, angular filly: second foal: dam modest 2m hurdle winner: no sign of ability: tried in cheekpieces. *P. T. Dalton*
h–
F–

LOVES TRAVELLING (IRE) 7 b.g. Blues Traveller (IRE) – Fast Love (IRE) (Second Set (IRE)) [2006/7 17d⁵ 19g⁴ Jul 9] fairly useful at best on Flat (stays 1½m): modest form both starts in novice hurdles: likely prove best around 2m with emphasis on speed. *N. Wilson*
h83 +

LOVE THAT BENNY (USA) 7 ch.g. Benny The Dip (USA) – Marie Loves Emma (USA) (Affirmed (USA)) [2006/7 h107: 22f² 22g² 24d c22v⁵ c20s⁵ c19s Jan 24] tall gelding: fairly useful hurdler: ran well when second in intermediate events at Kelso: modest form over fences, not convincing with jumping/attitude fourth/fifth starts: should stay 3m: acts on firm and soft going. *J. Wade*
c87 +
h116

LOVE THE HAT 6 br.m. Overbury (IRE) – Give Me Credit (Le Bavard (FR)) [2006/7 F16m² F17s aF16g Mar 9] eighth foal: half-sister to 2½m chase winner Everything's Rosy (by Ardross): dam unraced half-sister to useful staying hurdler/chaser Gola Cher: best effort in bumpers when second to Shiwawa at Stratford on debut. *Mrs Norma Pook*
F82

LOW CLOUD 7 b.g. Danehill (USA) – Raincloud (Rainbow Quest (USA)) [2006/7 c92, h90: 17s 17m³ Apr 9] close-coupled, angular gelding: fair handicap hurdler: modest form on chasing debut (let down by jumping other outing over fences): races freely, and suited by test of speed around 2m: ran well in cheekpieces final start. *J. J. Quinn*
c–
h107

LOW DELTA (IRE) 7 ch.g. Old Vic – La-Greine (Strong Gale) [2006/7 F16g 22s³ 20vᵇᵈ 24v² 22f⁴ Apr 22] medium-sized ex-Irish gelding: second foal: dam, fair Irish
h95
F76

chaser, stayed 3½m: mid-field at best in bumpers for I. Duncan: modest form when placed over hurdles: stays 3m. *P. F. Nicholls*

LOWE GO 7 b.g. First Trump – Hotel California (IRE) (Last Tycoon) [2006/7 c91, h91: c21s⁶ c23mᵖᵘ 26m 24g 24d c23sᶠ c23sᶠ 24v 22g 20g³ 19m³ Apr 17] angular gelding: maiden chaser: poor handicap hurdler: effective from 2m to 3m: acts on soft and good to firm going: tried blinkered. *Miss J. S. Davis* — c– h75

LOWICZ 5 b.m. Polish Precedent (USA) – Eldina (Distant Relative) [2006/7 16dᵖᵘ 17gᵖᵘ 16d Nov 20] poor maiden on Flat (stays 9f, has had numerous trainers): no form over hurdles. *J. A. Danahar* — h–

LOWLANDER 8 b.g. Fuji Kiseki (JPN) – Lake Valley (USA) (Mr Prospector (USA)) [2006/7 c25f⁴ c22m⁵ c20d* c21s⁵ c20g⁴ c19f³ Apr 11] angular gelding: winning hurdler: fair chaser: won handicap at Killarney in September: sold out of D. Weld's stable 22,000 gns Doncaster October Sales after next outing: stays 25f: acts on firm and good to soft ground: usually blinkered. *B. G. Powell* — c107 h–

LOW PARK 6 b.m. Endoli (USA) – City Lighter (Lighter) [2006/7 F16v 20vᵖᵘ Mar 6] fourth foal: dam, of little account, out of useful chaser up to 3m Another City: no show in bumper/novice hurdle. *W. Amos* — h– F–

LOW REACTOR (IRE) 6 b.g. Taipan (IRE) – Strong Opinion (Strong Gale) [2006/7 16d 17v⁵ 20s 25vᵖᵘ 20sᵖᵘ Apr 1] good-bodied gelding: eighth foal: half-brother to fair chasers Always Present (by Presenting), stayed 25f, and Farmer Grant (by Flemensfirth) probably stays 3¼m: dam unraced: form (modest) over hurdles only when fifth to Open de L'Isle in novice at Carlisle: should be suited by further than 17f. *N. G. Richards* — h85

LOWSHA GREEN 6 b.g. Foxhound (USA) – Super Times (Sayf El Arab (USA)) [2006/7 h–, F–: 16g⁵ 16s* 17m 17d⁴ 17s² 17v⁵ 16v³ c16d⁵ c16vᶠ Jan 27] good-topped gelding: modest hurdler: won novice at Hexham in June: last of 5 in falsely-run maiden at Newcastle completed outing over fences: would probably have stayed beyond 17f: acted on heavy ground: tongue tied once: dead. *R. Johnson* — c– h97

LUBINAS (IRE) 8 b.g. Grand Lodge (USA) – Liebesgirl (Konigsstuhl (GER)) [2006/7 c109, h–x: c21f⁶ c20mᵖᵘ c16d³ c19sᶠ Jan 1] workmanlike, lengthy gelding: fair handicap hurdler/chaser: effective at 2m to 2¾m: acted on good to firm and heavy going: not a fluent jumper: dead. *F. Jordan* — c108 h– x

LUBY (IRE) 9 b.g. Be My Native (USA) – Foxed (IRE) (Carlingford Castle) [2006/7 16m⁶ Jul 5] point winner: third in bumper: off 2 years, sixth in seller on hurdling debut: dead. *Eugene M. O'Sullivan, Ireland* — h73

LUCCOMBE BAY 7 b.m. Karinga Bay – Bay Lough (IRE) (Lancastrian) [2006/7 F75p: F18m⁶ F16s⁶ 20v 17sᶠ 16v⁶ 16v⁴ 19g Mar 25] poor form in bumpers/over hurdles: will be suited by 3m. *M. G. Rimell* — h69 F73

LUCENT (IRE) 6 b.g. Luso – Allenswood Girl (IRE) (Bulldozer) [2006/7 h70, F76: 16sᵖᵘ May 8] hinted at ability in bumper/on first of 3 outings over hurdles: sold £9,500 Ascot December Sales. *Miss H. C. Knight* — h–

LUCIFER BLEU (FR) 8 b.g. Kadalko (FR) – Figa Dancer (FR) (Bandinelli (FR)) [2006/7 c19s* c21s* c24v⁴ Feb 24] leggy gelding: winning hurdler: useful handicap chaser: off 2½ years, vastly improved when winning at Hereford in January and Wincanton (beating Black Hills 11 lengths, again making all and heavily eased) in February: back up in trip, tired after forcing good pace when fourth to Simon in Racing Post Chase (Handicap) at Kempton: best around 2½m: acts on good to firm and heavy going: free-going sort. *D. E. Pipe* — c142 h–

LUCIFER DU MONTCEAU (FR) 8 b.g. Video Rock (FR) – Une de Montceau (FR) (Vorias (USA)) [2006/7 22m² Jun 8] ex-Irish gelding: half-brother to winning chaser around 2½m Kiwi du Montceau (by Trebrook): dam winning chaser up to around 2¾m in France: winning pointer: no form in chases: left A. Moore, modest form when ½-length second to Complete Outsider in novice at Newton Abbot on hurdling debut. *M. B. Shears* — c– h92

LUCIFEROUS (USA) 5 ch.m. Devil's Bag (USA) – Vital Laser (USA) (Seeking The Gold (USA)) [2006/7 16f 16dᵖᵘ Oct 14] modest maiden on Flat (will prove best short of 1m): no form in 2 starts over hurdles, visored second time: sold £900 Ascot November Sales. *P. G. Murphy* — h–

LUCINDA LAMB 5 b.m. Kayf Tara – Caroline Lamb (Hotfoot) [2006/7 F79: F17s³ F16s² F16g³ Apr 3] fair form in bumpers, in frame all 4 starts: will be suited by further than 2m. *Miss S. E. Hall* — F90

LUCIUS RUFO (IRE) 5 b.h. Luso – Filli Rufo (IRE) (Celio Rufo) [2006/7 F16f F17d[4] **F72**
Nov 7] second foal: dam of little account: poor form in bumpers: will be suited by further.
J. Wade

LUCKEN HOWE 8 b.g. Keen – Gilston Lass (Majestic Streak) [2006/7 c–, h–: c22m[pu] **c–**
c20d[pu] Oct 6] of no account: tried tongue tied. *Mrs J. K. M. Oliver* **h–**

LUCKY ARTHUR (IRE) 6 ch.m. Grand Lodge (USA) – Soltura (IRE) (Sadler's **h68**
Wells (USA)) [2006/7 h78: 17m[3] 16f 17s[6] 20d[3] 21g[6] 20v[pu] Mar 6] poor maiden hurdler:
stays 2½m: acts on good to firm and good to soft going: tried in cheekpieces (well
beaten). *M. Todhunter*

LUCKY BAMBLUE (IRE) 4 b.g. Key of Luck (USA) – Bamboo (IRE) (Thatching) **h–**
[2006/7 16m 17d[6] Jul 22] no form on Flat or in juvenile hurdles. *P. C. Haslam*

LUCKY BROUGHTON 4 ch.f. Benny The Dip (USA) – Coy Debutante (IRE) **F80**
(Archway (IRE)) [2006/7 F12s F12g Mar 23] sparely-made filly: second foal: dam
maiden who stayed 10.5f: mid-division in bumpers at Newbury: dead. *W. J. Musson*

LUCKY BRUSH (IRE) 13 b.g. Brush Aside (USA) – Luck Daughter (Lucky Brief) **c–**
[2006/7 c20v[5] May 18] workmanlike gelding: winning pointer: maiden chaser: tried in
cheekpieces/visor. *N. W. Alexander*

LUCKYCHARM (FR) 8 ch.g. Villez (USA) – Hitifly (FR) (Murmure (FR)) [2006/7 **c63 x**
c71x, h–: c23m[6] c22d[3] c23m[6] c25d[2] c20g[ur] c20m[2] c25s[pu] Oct 11] lengthy, plain gelding: **h–**
poor maiden chaser: stays 25f: has worn headgear: sketchy jumper: sold 5,000 gns
Doncaster November Sales, failed to complete in points. *R. Dickin*

LUCKY DO (IRE) 10 b.g. Camden Town – Lane Baloo (Lucky Brief) [2006/7 c–, **c–**
h100: 16f 17m[2] 18m 17m[2] 16m 20f* 18d[3] 22s[5] 24s[3] 26s Dec 22] medium-sized gelding: **h97**
modest hurdler, left V. Hughes after second start: won handicap at Worcester in July: fell
2 starts over fences: stays 3m: acts on soft and firm going. *Mrs A. M. Thorpe*

LUCKY DUCK 10 ch.g. Minster Son – Petroc Concert (Tina's Pet) [2006/7 c95+, h–: **c115**
c17f[2] c17g* c20m[4] c20m c16d[2] 19s[6] c19g[3] 17s[5] Feb 19] medium-sized gelding: winning **h96**
hurdler: fairly useful handicap chaser: won at Kelso (by 3½ lengths from Gone Too Far)
in May: good third to Milan Deux Mille at Catterick: stays 2½m: acts on firm and soft
going: in cheekpieces last 2 starts: front runner/races prominently. *Mrs A. Hamilton*

LUCKY HEROINE (IRE) 5 ch.m. Lucky Guest – Heroine (Sadler's Wells (USA)) **F98**
[2006/7 F16g* F16d* F16m Apr 25] good-topped mare: second foal: sister to 1¼m
winner Heroism: dam unraced: won mares bumpers at Kilbeggan in September and
Punchestown (by neck from Grapevine Sally) in October: off 6 months, well beaten in
Grade 1 at Punchestown. *Miss S. Collins, Ireland*

LUCKYLOVER 4 b.c. Key of Luck (USA) – Hang Fire (Marju (IRE)) [2006/7 16d[2] **h94**
16d[4] Dec 4] fairly useful on Flat (stays 1¼m), successful in January and April:
better effort in juvenile hurdles when second to Altilhar at Fakenham: tongue tied.
M. G. Quinlan

LUCKY LUK (FR) 8 b.g. Lights Out (FR) – Citronelle II (FR) (Kedellic (FR)) [2006/7 **c99**
c80, h–: c24m* Oct 4] compact gelding: no form over hurdles: modest handicap chaser: **h–**
off 5 months, improved form when winning at Towcester (by 22 lengths) in October, only
start in 2006/7: stays 29f: unraced on extremes of going: tried tongue tied. *K. C. Bailey*

LUCKY MASTER (IRE) 15 b.g. Roselier (FR) – Golden Chestnut (Green Shoon) **c–**
[2006/7 c–, h–: c26m[R] May 11] sturdy gelding: veteran chaser, little form outside points **h–**
since 2002/3. *Miss G. Swan*

LUCKY NELLERIE (FR) 8 ch.g. Grand Tresor (FR) – British Nellerie (FR) (Le **c108**
Pontet (FR)) [2006/7 24m[2] 20s 25s[4] c24v[pu] c27s* c25v[2] c28v* c32v[F] c25g* c31s Apr 27] **h83**
smallish, leggy gelding: fourth foal: dam ran once on Flat in France: in frame in novice
hurdles: fair chaser: won maiden at Sedgefield in December, and handicap in January and
novice (all out in match) in April, both at Kelso: should stay 4m: acts on heavy going.
Ferdy Murphy

LUCKY PEARL 6 b.m. Jendali (USA) – Fardella (ITY) (Molvedo) [2006/7 F–: F16d **F–**
F13m F17m[4] Jun 30] little sign of ability in bumpers. *O. Brennan*

LUCKY PETE 10 b.g. Lyphento (USA) – Clare's Choice (Pragmatic) [2006/7 c–, h–: **c–**
c20v[pu] 19v c16s[F] Feb 1] leggy, quite good-topped gelding: winning handicap hurdler/ **h–**
chaser: no show in 2006/7: tried in cheekpieces. *P. J. Jones*

LUCKY THIRD TIME 5 b.m. Terimon – Zanditu (Presidium) [2006/7 F–: 21m[pu] **h–**
19d[pu] 16d Jan 15] smallish mare: no form in bumpers/novice hurdles. *M. Scudamore*

LUCOZADE 6 b.g. Sir Harry Lewis (USA) – Brioletta (Gunner B) [2006/7 F16s³ F16v F17s 16g 18g 16g 26g^pu Apr 11] plain, angular gelding: first foal: dam unraced: form only when third in bumper on debut for J. Spearing. *R. Dickin* **h–**
F86

LUCY FEFFELL (IRE) 6 b. or br.g. Norwich – September Daydream (IRE) (Phardante (FR)) [2006/7 F16f May 10] second foal: dam unraced: tailed off in bumper on debut: dead. *Miss J. E. Foster* **F–**

LUCY LAMPLIGHTER (IRE) 5 bl.m. Accordion – May Gale (IRE) (Strong Gale) [2006/7 F16s F16s F16s F16s 19v⁶ 16v 18v 18s^pu 24m 24s⁵ Apr 26] fourth foal: dam, fair winning hurdler, stayed 2½m: no form in bumpers: poor maiden hurdler. *Neill McCluskey, Ireland* **h81
F–**

LUDERE (IRE) 12 ch.g. Desse Zenny (USA) – White Jasmin (Jalmood (USA)) [2006/7 24s⁵ 19s c21m^pu Jul 17] angular gelding: winning hurdler: off 17 months, no show in 2006/7: has failed to complete in chases/points: tried blinkered/in cheekpieces/tongue tied: moody. *Miss J. S. Davis* **c– §
h– §**

LUGO ROCK (IRE) 7 b. or br.g. Luso – Rocher Lady (IRE) (Phardante (FR)) [2006/7 c23g^R Nov 30] sturdy gelding: no impact in bumper and maiden chase 19 months apart. *P. R. Webber* **c–**

LUJAIN ROSE 5 b.m. Lujain (USA) – Rose Chime (IRE) (Tirol) [2006/7 h–: 16m 16m⁶ 20v^pu Jan 27] no form over hurdles. *N. M. Babbage* **h–**

LUNAN BAY 4 b.f. Defacto (USA) – Tangalooma (Hotfoot) [2006/7 F16s Mar 7] half-sister to several winners on Flat, including 1m winner Time Temptress (by Timeless Times): dam 2m hurdle winner: well beaten in bumper on debut. *G. M. Moore* **F–**

LUNAR CRYSTAL (IRE) 9 b.g. Shirley Heights – Solar Crystal (IRE) (Alzao (USA)) [2006/7 h126: 16f c19d³ c16m³ c16m* 16g c18s⁵ c21s⁴ 16v c19s⁵ c19s² 16s 16d* 16f⁴ Apr 5] leggy gelding: fair hurdler nowadays: won claimer at Ludlow in March: landed odds in 3-runner novice at Newton Abbot in June, but lost his way over fences after: best around 2m: acts on any going: tried in headgear. *D. E. Pipe* **c116
h113**

LUNARDI (IRE) 9 b.g. Indian Ridge – Gold Tear (USA) (Tejano (USA)) [2006/7 c–, h–: c19s^pu c26g⁴ c20d⁴ c20g Aug 26] neat gelding: winning hurdler/maiden chaser, no form since 2003/4: tried visored/in cheekpieces/tongue tied. *D. L. Williams* **c–
h–**

LUNAR ECLIPSE 7 b.m. Dancing High – Pauper Moon (Pauper) [2006/7 F88: 16g 16s⁵ 16s 17d* 21v⁵ 21v Feb 26] compact mare: bumper winner: poor novice hurdler: won mares handicap at Exeter in December: likely to prove best around 2m: probably acts on heavy going, bumper form on firm. *Miss Venetia Williams* **h73**

LUNAR EXIT (IRE) 6 gr.g. Exit To Nowhere (USA) – Moon Magic (Polish Precedent (USA)) [2006/7 h88: 16m Jun 18] lengthy gelding: fair form in juvenile hurdles in 2004/5, very lightly raced and little enthusiasm since: should be suited by further than 2m. *Lady Herries* **h81 §**

LUNAR FOX 8 b.m. Roselier (FR) – Leinthall Fox (Deep Run) [2006/7 h–: 21v^pu Nov 26] small mare: has no tail: no sign of ability. *J. L. Needham* **h–**

LUNAR PROMISE (IRE) 5 b.g. Mujadil (USA) – Lunadine (FR) (Bering) [2006/7 16d May 19] fairly useful and lightly raced on Flat (stays 1¼m), successful in January: finished distressed after taking strong hold on hurdling debut: should prove capable of better. *Ian Williams* **h75 p**

LUNAR SOVEREIGN (USA) 8 b. or br.g. Cobra King (USA) – January Moon (CAN) (Apalachee (USA)) [2006/7 h90: 19g² 19m³ 16m⁶ Aug 24] strong gelding: modest form over hurdles: likely to prove best up to 19f: tried visored: tongue tied last 4 starts: finishes weakly. *D. E. Pipe* **h91**

LUNAR THYME 6 ch.m. Rakaposhi King – Four Thyme (Idiot's Delight) [2006/7 F16s 19v⁵ 22d⁶ 19v Feb 20] rather unfurnished mare: fourth foal: dam, well beaten in bumper, half-sister to Festival Bumper winner Mucklemeg: no solid form in mares bumper/novice hurdles. *Evan Williams* **h–
F–**

LUNCH WAS MY IDEA (IRE) 7 b. or br.g. Tawrrific (NZ) – Equity Law (IRE) (Gunner B) [2006/7 h76: 20m 22m 20m³ Aug 1] rangy gelding: poor maiden hurdler, sold out of P. Nicholls' stable £1,200 Ascot June Sales prior to return: stays 2½m: acts on soft and firm going: tried tongue tied: has shaped as if amiss more than once. *Mrs S. M. Johnson* **h81**

LUNERAY (FR) 8 b.m. Poplar Bluff – Casandre (FR) (Montorselli) [2006/7 c118, h–: c25m^pu c22g^pu c24s c24m^F c24s^pu Mar 1] rather leggy mare: fairly useful handicap chaser **c–
h–**

at best: no show in 2006/7, left P. Nicholls after first outing: stays 3m: acts on soft and good to firm going: tried in cheekpieces, often blinkered/tongue tied. *R. Ford*

LUPIN (FR) 8 b.g. Luchiroverte (IRE) – Amarante II (FR) (Brezzo (FR)) [2006/7 c–p, h108: c20g⁰ᵖᵘ 20m* 20m³ 20m 20g 19m⁴ 21g Oct 19] leggy gelding: modest hurdler: won claimer at Worcester in August: pulled up in maiden chases: stays 2½m: acts on soft and good to firm going: tried tongue tied: unreliable. *A. W. Carroll*   **c– §** **h91 §**

LURID AFFAIR (IRE) 6 b.m. Dr Massini (IRE) – Miss Good Night (Buckskin (FR)) [2006/7 h–: 19g⁶ 20m² 20m 22g² 22g⁰ᵖᵘ 20m Apr 25] angular mare: poor maiden hurdler: stays 2¾m: acts on good to firm going. *Mrs S. Gardner*   **h82**

LUSABAWN (IRE) 5 b.g. Luso – Meelabawn (Abednego) [2006/7 F16s⁶ F16g Mar 17] €16,000 3-y-o: half-brother to point/bumper winner River Nith (by Over The River): dam unraced half-sister to fairly useful staying hurdler/chaser Riska's River: well held in bumpers. *W. T. Reed*   **F–**

LUSAKA DE PEMBO (FR) 8 b.g. Funny Baby (FR) – Crackeline (FR) (Prince Melchior (FR)) [2006/7 c107, h–: c16g⁰ᵘʳ c20g² c16d⁴ c21g c19s c24d c16s² c18s⁶ c19g² c20m³ Apr 25] compact gelding: modest handicap chaser: stays 2½m: acts on soft and good to firm going: tried tongue tied: often let down by jumping: sold 16,000 gns Doncaster May Sales. *N. A. Twiston-Davies*   **c98** **h–**

LUSHPOOL (IRE) 9 b.m. Supreme Leader – Dawn Hunt (IRE) (Architect (USA)) [2006/7 16m Jun 11] angular mare: very lightly raced and little sign of ability. *Tim Vaughan*   **h–**

LUSTRE LAD 6 b.g. Overbury (IRE) – Welsh Lustre (IRE) (Mandalus) [2006/7 21d⁶ 19d 18sᵖᵘ Jan 4] rather unfurnished gelding: fourth foal: dam, winning hurdler/chaser, stayed 3¼m: poor form over hurdles: likely to stay beyond 21f: tried tongue tied. *A. J. Honeyball*   **h73**

LUTEA (IRE) 7 ch.g. Beneficial – Francie's Treble (Quayside) [2006/7 c81, h86: 16f c17m* 20m* 16g* Apr 2] leggy gelding: fair hurdler, left M. Pipe and off 11 months prior to return: won handicaps at Perth in August and Kelso in April: similar form when awarded maiden chase at Cartmel in July (forced to snatch up run-in): stays 2¾m, effective over shorter: acts on soft and good to firm going: free-going sort. *P. Monteith*   **c113** **h103**

LUTHELLO (FR) 8 b.g. Marchand de Sable (USA) – Haudello (FR) (Marignan (USA)) [2006/7 h96: 16g 16m May 6] leggy gelding: very lightly-raced maiden hurdler, no show in 2006/7: tried blinkered. *J. Howard Johnson*   **h–**

LUTIN COLLONGES (FR) 8 b.g. Ragmar (FR) – Ariane Collonges (FR) (Quart de Vin (FR)) [2006/7 c–: c18m⁴ c19d⁶ c22sᵖᵘ c26mᵖᵘ Apr 8] of no account. *M. J. Roberts*   **c–**

LUVINYOU 8 b.m. Tigani – My Cherrywell (Kirchner) [2006/7 25sᵖᵘ 20gᵘʳ 20gᵖᵘ Apr 3] strong, lengthy mare: first foal: dam 5f/6f winner: no sign of ability in novice hurdles: left L. James after debut. *M. E. Sowersby*   **h–**

LYES GREEN 6 gr.g. Bien Bien (USA) – Dissolve (Sharrood (USA)) [2006/7 h119: 21g⁶ 21d 24s² 22g² 22d⁵ 24g² 24g² Apr 14] smallish gelding: useful handicap hurdler: good efforts last 5 starts, second at Bangor (beaten neck by McKelvey) and Aintree (in cheekpieces, stuck to task well when beaten ½ length by Albertas Run in 21-runner listed event) final 2 occasions: stays 3m: raced on good going or softer (acts on heavy): often races prominently. *O. Sherwood*   **h133**

LYNNE'S GIFT 6 ch.m. Keen – Miss Mezzorelko (Ardar) [2006/7 F17m⁶ Jul 25] third foal: dam unraced: no sign of ability in bumper/maiden point. *B. S. Rothwell*   **F–**

LYNNIE'S VIC (IRE) 5 b.g. Old Vic – Crest of The Hill (Prince Regent (FR)) [2006/7 F16s 21m 22g Mar 19] €30,000 3-y-o: half-brother to winning pointers by Husyan and Supreme Leader: dam unraced, out of half-sister to very smart hurdler/useful staying chaser Henry Mann: seemingly much better effort in novice hurdles when seventh of 12 finishers at Wincanton, final start. *P. J. Hobbs*   **h97 ?** **F–**

LYNS HOPE 7 b.g. Awesome – Royal Resort (King of Spain) [2006/7 F16g F17g Oct 15] sixth foal: dam, 7f seller winner, stayed 1¼m: well beaten in bumpers. *D. Burchell*   **F–**

LYNS RESOLUTION 7 b.g. Awesome – Our Resolution (Caerleon (USA)) [2006/7 16dᵖᵘ 16gᵖᵘ 19gᵖᵘ Nov 5] good-topped gelding: fourth in maiden on Flat in 2004: no other form. *D. Burchell*   **h–**

LYON 7 ch.g. Pivotal – French Gift (Cadeaux Genereux) [2006/7 h81: 16d* 16v² 19m* 20m 22m 20mᵖᵘ c20dꟳ c20s³ c22v⁵ c24g c19g⁶ c19g* c19g* Apr 27] modest hurdler: **c103** **h93**

won sellers at Towcester (for O. Sherwood) in May and Hereford (sold from D. Wintle 5,400 gns) in June: better form over fences, blinkered when winning handicaps at Hereford (novice) and Chepstow in April: best short of 3m: acts on heavy and good to firm going. *T. Wall*

LYRICAL GIRL (USA) 6 b.m. Orpen (USA) – Lyric Theatre (USA) (Seeking The Gold (USA)) [2006/7 h–: 16f^{pu} 16g May 14] little impact over hurdles. *H. J. Manners*   **h–**

LYRICAL LILY 9 b.m. Alflora (IRE) – Music Interpreter (Kampala) [2006/7 h–: 25s^2 22v* Feb 13] leggy mare: poor hurdler, off 12 months prior to return: won handicap at Folkestone in February: stays 25f: acts on heavy going. *B. J. Llewellyn*   **h77**

LYRICIST'S DREAM 8 b.m. Dreams End – Lyricist (Averof) [2006/7 h68: 19g 17v^{pu} Nov 28] sparely-made mare: maiden hurdler: should stay beyond 2m: acts on firm and good to soft going. *R. L. Brown*   **h–**

LYSANDER (GER) 8 br.g. Monsun (GER) – Leoparda (GER) (Lagunas) [2006/7 h106: 20g^F 22g^4 c16g* c20s Oct 25] tall gelding: fair hurdler: won novice at Hexham on chasing debut in October: not fluent next time: stays 2½m: acts on soft and good to firm going. *M. F. Harris*   **c105 h104**

LYSTER (IRE) 8 b.g. Oscar (IRE) – Sea Skin (Buckskin (FR)) [2006/7 h84, F82: 24f^{pu} Jun 3] close-coupled gelding: poor maiden hurdler: stays 2½m: tried visored. *D. L. Williams*   **h–**

M

MA'AM (USA) 5 ch.m. Royal Anthem (USA) – Hide The Bride (USA) (Runaway Groom (CAN)) [2006/7 17g 22f^3 Apr 22] fairly useful at best on Flat (stays 1¼m), below form last 4 starts in 2006: little impact over hurdles. *I. A. Wood*   **h–**

MAAREES 6 b.m. Groom Dancer (USA) – Shemaleyah (Lomond (USA)) [2006/7 h–, F78: 16g^{pu} May 14] modest form in bumpers: little show over hurdles: in cheekpieces 3 of last 4 starts. *G. P. Enright*   **h–**

MABEL RILEY (IRE) 7 b.m. Revoque (IRE) – Mystic Dispute (IRE) (Magical Strike (USA)) [2006/7 16m 16g^4 16g^3 16f^2 16m^2 16f^5 Jul 19] sparely-made mare: poor maiden hurdler, claimed from C. Kellett £6,000 fifth start: best at 2m with emphasis on speed: reliable: dead. *B. N. Pollock*   **h81**

MA BURLS 7 b.m. Perpendicular – Isabeau (Law Society (USA)) [2006/7 F84: F18g 18g^{pu} Apr 10] neat mare: modest form in bumpers: no show in mares novice on hurdling debut. *K. F. Clutterbuck*   **h– F–**

MACARONI GOLD (IRE) 7 b.g. Rock Hopper – Strike It Rich (FR) (Rheingold) [2006/7 h–: 20f^5 16m Sep 24] well held 3 starts over hurdles. *Evan Williams*   **h–**

MACCHIATO 6 br.m. Inchinor – Tereyna (Terimon) [2006/7 h76: 20g^3 17d* 16s 19d^5 17s^6 16s^4 16v^3 16g^2 Apr 16] smallish, leggy mare: modest hurdler: won novice at Sedgefield in May: stays 2½m: acts on heavy going: often races prominently. *R. E. Barr*   **h94**

MAC FEDERAL (IRE) 5 b.g. In The Wings – Tocade (IRE) (Kenmare (FR)) [2006/7 h100: 16f^4 16g^3 17m* 21v* 16s 24g^5 24g Apr 14] leggy gelding: fairly useful hurdler, claimed from M. Quinlan £11,000 second start: progressed significantly to win handicaps at Hereford in June and Kempton (by 14 lengths) in February: also ran well when 23 lengths fifth to Wichita Lineman in Grade 2 Spa Novices' Hurdle at Cheltenham: stays 3m: acts on heavy and good to firm going. *Miss S. West*   **h127**

MACGYVER (NZ) 11 b.g. Jahafil – Corazon (NZ) (Pag-Asa (AUS)) [2006/7 c85d, h–: c16f^3 c18g Sep 3] medium-sized gelding: maiden hurdler: poor handicap chaser nowadays: best around 2m: acts on good to firm and good to soft going. *D. L. Williams*   **c63 h–**

MACHHAPUCHHARE 4 ch.g. Most Welcome – Spring Flyer (IRE) (Waajib) [2006/7 17s^4 16v Jan 4] half-brother to useful staying hurdler/fairly useful chaser Rover-etto (by Robellino) and fair staying hurdler Miss Tango (by Batshoof): modest maiden up to 11f on Flat (tried in cheekpieces) for W. M. Brisbourne: much better effort in maiden hurdles when fourth to South O'The Border at Taunton. *D. E. Pipe*   **h87**

MACHINE GUN RIO (IRE) 5 ch.m. Old Vic – Roses Red (IRE) (Exhibitioner) [2006/7 16s 20m 19g 23s^{pu} 20d^{pu} Nov 21] half-sister to 3 winners abroad: dam ran twice in Ireland: maiden on Flat, ran in Germany, Poland and Czech Republic at 3 yrs for M. Novakowski: no form over hurdles: tried in cheekpieces. *R. C. Guest*   **h–**

MACHO DANCER (IRE) 4 ch.f. Desert Prince (IRE) – Mynador (USA) (Forty **h–**
Niner (USA)) [2006/7 17g 16f[6] Oct 5] modest maiden on Flat (stays 1½m): well beaten
in juvenile hurdles: sold 1,900 gns Doncaster October Sales. *K. J. Burke*

MACLEAN 6 b.g. Machiavellian (USA) – Celtic Cross (Selkirk (USA)) [2006/7 h106§: **c90 §**
21g[5] 19s[ur] c18f[6] c20m[pu] c16s[2] c19s[3] Dec 29] tall, close-coupled gelding: fair hurdler on **h92 §**
his day: best effort in handicap chases (modest form) on penultimate outing: stays 2¼m:
acts on soft going: tried in cheekpieces, usually blinkered: ungenuine. *G. L. Moore*

MACMAR (FR) 7 b.g. Ragmar (FR) – Ex Des Sacart (FR) (Balsamo (FR)) [2006/7 **c–**
c108, h98: 22g[2] 19m[pu] 22d 24d[2] 22d 22s 24v[6] 21g[5] Mar 28] big, good-topped gelding: **h111**
winning chaser (sometimes let down by jumping): fair handicap hurdler: stays 3m: acts
on heavy going: tried blinkered/visored: has shaped as if amiss more than once.
R. H. Alner

MAC REAMOINN (IRE) 8 b.g. Corrouge (USA) – Allenswood Girl (IRE) (Bull- **c–**
dozer) [2006/7 c22s[4] c21s[pu] Jan 30] tall ex-Irish gelding: fourth foal: dam once-raced **h–**
sister to fairly useful chaser Inch Lady, who stayed 3m: little sign of ability: tried in
cheekpieces/blinkers: tongue tied in 2006/7: sold 1,400 gns Doncaster January Sales.
K. J. Burke

MACREATER 9 b.m. Mazaad – Gold Caste (USA) (Singh (USA)) [2006/7 h65: 16s[pu] **h72**
16d[4] 16f 19g 19d[3] 19s[2] 19g 16m* Apr 24] leggy mare: poor handicap hurdler: won
selling event at Towcester in April: probably stays 2½m: acts on soft and good to firm
ground: tried visored, usually in cheekpieces. *K. A. Morgan*

MACS BROOK 7 ch.g. Alderbrook – McMahon's River (Over The River (FR)) **F–**
[2006/7 F16m[5] Jul 2] second foal: half-brother to 21f hurdle winner Its A Classic (by
Classic Cliche): dam winning pointer: soundly beaten in bumper on debut. *Mrs
N. S. Evans*

MAC'S ELAN 7 b.g. Darshaan – Elabella (Ela-Mana-Mou) [2006/7 c–, h88: 16g **c–**
Nov 1] leggy gelding: maiden hurdler, modest form at best: no show on chasing debut: **h–**
raced mainly around 2m on good going or softer. *A. B. Coogan*

MACS FLAMINGO (IRE) 7 br.g. Rashar (USA) – Parkality (IRE) (Good Thyne **c128**
(USA)) [2006/7 c120, h–: c16s[2] c19d c24s[pu] c17s[ur] c19s[4] c20v[5] c20v[pu] Mar 24] rangy **h–**
gelding: winning hurdler: fairly useful chaser: best effort when 2½ lengths second to
Southern Vic in Grade 3 at Naas on return, though generally disappointing after: stays
2¾m: raced on good going or softer (acts on heavy): has shaped as if amiss more than
once. *P. A. Fahy, Ireland*

MACS JOY (IRE) 8 b.g. Religiously (USA) – Snob's Supreme (IRE) (Supreme **h156**
Leader) [2006/7 h166: 16d[3] 16v[2] 16m[2] Apr 27] smallish, strong gelding: high-class
hurdler, won ACC Bank Champion Hurdle at Punchestown in 2005/6: bit below best all 3
starts since, third to Hardy Eustace in AIG Europe Champion Hurdle at Leopardstown
and runner-up to Newmill in Grade 2 at Gowran and Silent Oscar in latest renewal of
Punchestown's Champion Hurdle: best short of 2½m: acts on good to firm and heavy
going: usually tracks pace: reliable. *Mrs J. Harrington, Ireland*

MACSTHEMAN (IRE) 7 b.g. Old Vic – Odstone Pear (Kemal (FR)) [2006/7 F16d[pu] **h–**
24v[pu] 24s Jan 30] fourth foal: dam winning 2¾m hurdler: pulled up in 2 maiden Irish **F–**
points: bought £1,000 Ascot February (2006) Sales: no show in bumper/over hurdles.
Mrs L. J. Young

MAC THREE (IRE) 8 b.g. Lord Americo – Le Nuit (Le Bavard (FR)) [2006/7 h123: **c125**
c22d[2] c20d[2] c21s* c20v c21d[3] c33g[F] c29m[pu] c21m[4] Apr 27] lengthy gelding: fairly **h–**
useful hurdler/chaser: won maiden over fences at Cork in November easily by 15 lengths
from Vedelle: blinkered, back to best when fourth to Alexander Taipan in valuable novice
handicap at Punchestown: should stay beyond 3m: acts on soft and good to firm going.
N. Meade, Ireland

MAD 6 br.m. Pursuit of Love – Emily-Mou (IRE) (Cadeaux Genereux) [2006/7 16g[4] 19d **h75**
Mar 26] modest on all-weather on Flat (stays 1¼m), mostly respectable efforts in 2006
for Ernst Oertel: poor form when fourth in mares maiden hurdle: likely to prove best
around 2m with emphasis on speed. *Mrs Caroline Bailey*

MADAM BLAZE 7 gr.m. Overbury (IRE) – Roslin (Roscoe Blake) [2006/7 16g[3] 16v[pu] **h78**
16g 22s[pu] Mar 8] smallish, angular mare: first foal: dam unraced: form (poor) over
hurdles only on debut. *M. Sheppard*

MADAM CAVERSFIELD 5 b.m. Pursuit of Love – Madam Alison (Puissance) **h90**
[2006/7 h84: 17g* 19d[2] 19m[6] Jun 4] smallish mare: modest hurdler: won novice handicap
at Hereford in May: stays 19f: acts on good to soft going: tried in cheekpieces (ran
poorly): sold £1,500 Ascot February Sales. *J. L. Flint*

MADAM CLICHE 5 b.m. Classic Cliche (IRE) – Mirador (Town And Country) [2006/7 F17s F16d^{pu} F18v^5 F16d^5 20m^2 Apr 15] rather unfurnished mare: third foal: half-sister to moody 19f chase winner Romney Marsh (by Glacial Storm): dam 2¼m winner on Flat/modest staying hurdler: little impact in bumpers (effectively ran out second outing): modest form when second to Picacho in mares maiden at Worcester on hurdling debut (swerved badly right after last): stays 2½m: should do better. *R. Curtis*   h95 p F– §

MADAME SYLVIA 4 gr.f. Silver Patriarch (IRE) – Lady Coldunell (Deploy) [2006/7 F12s F16g Apr 8] workmanlike filly: first foal: dam, winner up to 13f on Flat and fair 2m hurdler, half-sister to useful 2m hurdler Masamadas: no show in bumpers, left J. Pearce after debut. *P. S. McEntee*   F–

MADAM FLEET (IRE) 8 ch.m. Carroll House – Bucktan (Buckskin (FR)) [2006/7 h73, F–: 20d 22s 20v^{pu} 19g Mar 25] poor maiden hurdler: likely to stay 3m: acts on heavy ground: often tongue tied. *M. J. Coombe*   h72

MADAM HARRIET 5 b.m. Sir Harry Lewis (USA) – Norska (Northfields (USA)) [2006/7 F16s 19v^6 16d 16d 19v^2 24s^4 19s^4 20m^6 Mar 25] 8,000 3-y-o: tall, unfurnished mare: half-sister to several winners, including fairly useful hurdler/winning chaser Eponine (by Sharpo), stayed 21f: dam maiden who stayed 1¼m: well held in bumper: poor maiden hurdler: should be suited by 2½m+: acts on heavy going: needs to brush up jumping. *R. Dickin*   h81 F–

MADAM KILLESHANDRA 7 b.m. Jurado (USA) – Killeshandra Lass (IRE) (King's Ride) [2006/7 h–, F73: 16g 22d 24m 24g Dec 20] lengthy mare: no form since debut in bumper. *A. Parker*   h–

MADASAHATTER 7 b.g. Contract Law (USA) – Nordic Crown (IRE) (Nordico (USA)) [2006/7 F16s^{ro} F16g^5 Oct 3] second foal: dam modest maiden who stayed 2½m: showed more temperament than ability in bumpers (ran out on debut). *B. D. Leavy*   F– §

MADE IN FRANCE (FR) 7 b.g. Luchiroverte (IRE) – Birgonde (FR) (Quart de Vin (FR)) [2006/7 c–§, h92§: c20g c19f^4 Apr 11] leggy gelding: winning hurdler/ chaser: fair hunter nowadays: stays 2½m: probably acts on any going: wears cheekpieces/ visor: often front runner: carries head high, and not one to rely on. *Miss V. J. Price*   c87 § h– §

MADE IN JAPAN (JPN) 7 b.g. Barathea (IRE) – Darrery (Darshaan) [2006/7 c139, h–: 21g^4 24d 24s 17g 19s^5 16m^{pu} Apr 10] tall, useful-looking gelding: useful handicap chaser/fairly useful hurdler, left P. Hobbs before return: stays 21f: acts on soft going: effective with or without blinkers. *A. Bateman*   c– h128

MADE IN MONTOT (FR) 7 b.g. Video Rock (FR) – Deep Turple (FR) (Royal Charter (FR)) [2006/7 c116p, h–: c20g^2 c20s^F c17d^6 c17d^4 Mar 2] tall, useful-looking gelding: has reportedly had breathing operation: winning hurdler in France: useful chaser: best effort when 5 lengths second to Butler's Cabin in handicap at Cheltenham: found less than needed final outing: stays 2½m: raced on good going or softer: tongue tied last 5 starts: sold 15,000 gns Doncaster May Sales. *P. F. Nicholls*   c131 h–

MADEMOISELLE 5 b.m. Efisio – Shall We Dance (Rambo Dancer (CAN)) [2006/7 h–: 16g 16m^{pu} 16g 16d 16v^{ur} Dec 15] lengthy mare: modest on Flat (stays 1¼m), claimed £5,000 in January and successful in March for R. Harris: no show over hurdles. *R. Curtis*   h–

MAD FISH (IRE) 5 b.g. Flemensfirth (USA) – Lucky Trout (Beau Charmeur (FR)) [2006/7 F16v^2 F16g Mar 14] well-made gelding: eighth foal: half-brother to winning hurdler/fairly useful chaser Supreme Catch (by Supreme Leader), stays 3m and fair chaser King Coal (by Anshan), stays 23f: dam, winning pointer, sister to NH Chase winner Smooth Escort: won maiden point on debut: smart form in bumpers: odds on, 5 lengths second to Aranleigh in maiden at Fairyhouse, looking sure to win early in straight (reportedly gurgled): tongue tied and heavily backed, 6¾ lengths eighth of 24 to Cork All Star in Champion Bumper at Cheltenham 2 months later, again finding little after travelling strongly. *W. P. Mullins, Ireland*   F115

MADFORMAKEUP (IRE) 7 b.m. Luso – Hello Vera (IRE) (Cyrano de Bergerac) [2006/7 c24s^{pu} 20g 20m^4 22g Sep 15] €600 3-y-o: third foal: dam modest winning pointer: modest handicap hurdler: no show on chasing debut: stays 2½m: acts on good to firm going. *A. J. Martin, Ireland*   c– p h86

MADGE 5 b.m. Marju (IRE) – Aymara (Darshaan) [2006/7 h87: 16s^3 17d^6 17m 18m 24g Oct 7] angular mare: maiden hurdler, poor form in 2006/7: raced mainly around 2m: usually visored: temperamental. *W. Storey*   h73 §

MADGE CARROLL (IRE) 10 b.m. Hollow Hand – Spindle Tree (Laurence O) [2006/7 c24m^3 May 16] small, sturdy mare: winning hurdler/chaser: fairly useful pointer,   c97 h–

successful in February: third in ladies hunter much earlier in season: stays 25f: acts on soft and good to firm going. *Mrs D. Williams*

MADGIK DE BEAUMONT (FR) 7 b. or br.g. Sleeping Car (FR) – Matalie (FR) (Danoso) [2006/7 20d 20v Feb 17] close-coupled gelding: no form in bumper/over hurdles. *Ian Williams* — h–

MADHAVI 5 gr.m. Diktat – Grey Galava (Generous (IRE)) [2006/7 16s Nov 22] sturdy mare: half-sister to fairly useful 2m hurdler Millagros (by Pennekamp): fair but ungenuine up to 1½m on Flat, winner 3 times in 2006, sold out of R. Hannon's stable 29,000 gns Newmarket Autumn Sales: edgy, well held in novice on hurdling debut. *B. S. Rothwell* — h–

MADIBA 8 b.g. Emperor Jones (USA) – Priluki (Lycius (USA)) [2006/7 18g* 20g² 24s^pu 19g^F Mar 23] leggy gelding: fair on Flat (stays 2m), successful twice in 2006: fair hurdler: won handicap at Fontwell in September: should stay beyond 2½m: raced on good ground or softer (acts on heavy). *P. Howling* — h109

MADIRAN (IRE) 5 ch.g. Beneficial – Teach Na Finiuna (IRE) (Heavenly Manna) [2006/7 F16m Jan 29] first foal: dam winning pointer: well beaten in bumper on debut. *J. A. Geake* — F–

MADISON AVENUE (GER) 10 b.g. Mondrian (GER) – Madly Noble (GER) (Irish River (FR)) [2006/7 c–, h88: 18g 21s 17v³ 22v² 22s² 22s³ 22v⁵ 20v Mar 10] leggy gelding: poor hurdler: fell only outing in chase: stays 2¾m: acts on heavy and good to firm going: tried visored, usually blinkered: sometimes makes mistakes. *T. M. Jones* — c– h79

MADISON DE VONNAS (FR) 7 b.g. Epervier Bleu – Carine de Neuvy (FR) (Shelley (FR)) [2006/7 c99, h99: c17m⁴ c20f Jun 3] good-topped gelding: winning hurdler: modest maiden handicap chaser: best form around 2m: acts on soft going, probably on good to firm: tongue tied: sold 1,800 gns Doncaster August Sales, in frame in points. *Miss E. C. Lavelle* — c91 h–

MADISON DU BERLAIS (FR) 6 b.g. Indian River (FR) – Anais du Berlais (FR) (Dom Pasquini (FR)) [2006/7 c130+, h–: c17d c21s⁶ c19s⁴ c16s* c16v* c16g⁵ c16s³ c20s* c21g c21g³ Apr 18] close-coupled gelding: smart handicap chaser: won at Warwick — c150 h–

vccasino.com Gold Cup Handicap Chase, Newbury—a third successive big Saturday winner for jockey Tom Scudamore as Madison du Berlais (noseband) overhauls Nozic

Roger Stanley & Yvonne Reynolds II's "Madison du Berlais"

and Southwell in January and Newbury (beat Nozic a neck in Grade 3 vccasino.com Gold Cup) in March: creditable efforts in other graded events at Cheltenham last 2 starts, 5½ lengths third to Nycteos: stays 21f: acts on heavy and good to firm ground: blinkered once. *D. E. Pipe*

MAD MAX TOO 8 gr.g. Environment Friend – Marnworth (Funny Man) [2006/7 c–, h71: 23g^F Apr 30] lengthy gelding: little form over hurdles: has failed to complete in chases: third in point: has worn cheekpieces. *N. Wilson* — **c–** **h–**

MAD PROFESSOR (IRE) 4 b.g. Mull of Kintyre (USA) – Fancy Theory (USA) (Quest For Fame) [2006/7 16g^F 18g^6 16f^6 17m^5 Sep 28] maiden on Flat, well below best both starts for D. ffrench Davis in 2006: poor form in juvenile hurdles. *Tim Vaughan* — **h75**

MADROOS 4 ch.c. Medicean – Soolaimon (IRE) (Shareef Dancer (USA)) [2006/7 16s^5 16v 16v* 16v^4 16v^4 16d Mar 13] good-topped colt: fairly useful and consistent up to 1¾m on Flat, sold out of J. Dunlop's stable 60,000 gns Newmarket Autumn Sales: fairly useful juvenile hurdler: won maiden at Gowran (by 10 lengths from Duty) in January: creditable fourth next 2 starts, to Convincing in Grade 2 at Leopardstown on second occasion: jumped poorly final outing: raced at 2m on ground softer than good. *J. Culloty, Ireland* — **h112**

MAE MOSS 6 b.m. Cayman Kai (IRE) – Miss Brook (Meadowbrook) [2006/7 h72, F76: 20f 24f^{pu} 24d 20v^4 c20v^5 c27m^3 Apr 9] poor maiden hurdler: similar form in handicap chases (looked hard ride): probably stays 27f: acts on heavy and good to firm going: has worn cheekpieces/visor. *W. S. Coltherd* — **c61** **h61**

MA FURIE (FR) 7 gr.m. Balleroy (USA) – Furie de Carmont (FR) (Carmont (FR)) **c122 +**
[2006/7 c20g* c20s⁵ c20sᵖᵘ c19dᵘʳ c20g* Mar 22] good-topped mare: winning hurdler **h–**
(often shaped as if amiss/looked none too keen): fairly useful novice chaser: off 19
months, won 4-runner mares event at Fontwell in November and handicap at Ludlow
(by 6 lengths from Baodai) in March: stays 2½m: acts on soft going: tongue tied.
Miss H. C. Knight

MAGE D'ESTRUVAL (FR) 7 b.g. Sheyrann – Ivresse d'Estruval (FR) (Synefos **c116**
(USA)) [2006/7 c111: c26v⁵ c24v* Mar 4] useful-looking gelding: fairly useful chaser,
lightly raced: won handicap at Bangor in March by 9 lengths from Lord Rodney, forging
clear from last: should stay beyond 3m: acts on heavy ground: has shaped as if amiss.
H. D. Daly

MAGENKO (IRE) 10 ch.g. Forest Wind (USA) – Bebe Auction (IRE) (Auction Ring **c– §**
(USA)) [2006/7 c20v⁵ c27dᵖᵘ Nov 21] quite good-topped gelding: poor handicap hurdler: **h– §**
no show over fences: stays 3m: acts on good to firm and heavy going: tried blinkered:
ungenuine. *F. P. Murtagh*

MAGGIE MATHIAS (IRE) 6 b.m. Portrait Gallery (IRE) – The Marching Lady **F94**
(IRE) (Archway (IRE)) [2006/7 F96: F17g* F17v* F16s Mar 10] sturdy mare: fair form
in bumpers: won maiden at Taunton and mares event at Folkestone in November: bled
final outing. *B. G. Powell*

MAGGIES BROTHER 14 b.g. Brotherly (USA) – Sallisses (Pamroy) [2006/7 c93: **c–**
c25gᵖᵘ c29gᵖᵘ Mar 21] workmanlike gelding: hunter chaser, lightly raced: no form since
successful in May 2005. *R. Shail*

MAGICAL HARRY 7 b.g. Sir Harry Lewis (USA) – Magic (Sweet Revenge) [2006/7 **c93**
F92: c23s³ c19v⁴ c19v⁴ c22m² Apr 26] runner-up in bumper for P. Nicholls: modest form
in chases: stays 2¾m: best efforts on good/good to firm going. *A. J. Honeyball*

MAGICAL ISLAND 4 gr.g. Thowra (FR) – Alice's Mirror (Magic Mirror) [2006/7 **F89**
F17g⁴ F17g Apr 27] brother to fair 2m hurdle winner Demesne (stays 3m) and bumper
winner Magical Wonderland and half-brother to fair hurdler Magical Legend (by Midnight Legend), stays 2½m: dam modest and temperamental hurdler up to 2½m: much
better effort in bumpers when fourth at Taunton. *L. Corcoran*

MAGICAL KINGDOM 7 b.g. Petoski – Saxon Magic (Faustus (USA)) [2006/7 F16s **h–**
16dᵖᵘ Dec 28] no form in bumpers or selling hurdle. *J. A. Bennett*

MAGICAL LEGEND 6 gr.m. Midnight Legend – Alice's Mirror (Magic Mirror) **h114**
[2006/7 h112, F93: 19m² 20g⁴ 16g⁶ 17s³ 16d² 17s³ 16v² Jan 27] leggy mare: fair handicap
hurdler: effective at 2m to 2½m: acts on heavy and good to firm going: tried tongue tied:
not a fluent jumper: consistent. *L. Corcoran*

MAGICAL QUEST 7 b.g. Rainbow Quest (USA) – Apogee (Shirley Heights) [2006/7 **h107**
17d³ 16s² 17sꟳ 17s⁶ 20g 20g 20gᵖᵘ Apr 27] good-topped gelding: ran 3 times on Flat in
2004, fairly useful form when winning 1¾m maiden: sold out of Mrs A. Perrett's stable
30,000 gns later that year, and gelded: fair maiden hurdler, form deteriorated: tongue tied
final outing. *P. J. Hobbs*

MAGIC BENGIE 8 b.g. Magic Ring (IRE) – Zinzi (Song) [2006/7 c–, h–: 16d c19sᵘʳ **c–**
c20sᵖᵘ Jan 31] strong, lengthy gelding: won selling handicap hurdle in 2003/4, only form: **h–**
often tongue tied. *F. Kirby*

MAGIC BLADE (GER) 5 b.g. Dashing Blade – Magic Dawn (IRE) (Caerleon **F73**
(USA)) [2006/7 F16v³ May 25] second foal: half-brother to French winner up to 11.5f
Magic Kaldoun (by Kaldoun): dam unraced daughter of high-class middle-distance
performer Magic Night: poor form when third in bumper on debut: sold 6,500 gns
Doncaster May (2006) Sales. *T. P. Tate*

MAGIC BOX 9 b.g. Magic Ring (IRE) – Princess Poquito (Hard Fought) [2006/7 c69, **c84**
h–: c16m* c16g² c17gᵖᵘ c16fᵖᵘ Jul 16] angular gelding: winning hurdler: poor chaser: **h–**
won handicap at Hexham in May: best around 2m: acts on good to firm and good to soft
going (well below form on firm/soft): tongue tied last 5 starts.
A. M. Crow

MAGICIEN (FR) 11 b.g. Muroto – French Look (FR) (Green River (FR)) [2006/7 c84, **c79**
h–: c20m² c28vᵖᵘ c20g c20g Mar 12] fair pointer, successful twice in April: maiden **h–**
chaser: stays 3m: acts on good to firm going: tried tongue tied. *Steve Isaac*

MAGIC MERLIN 6 b.g. Magic Ring (IRE) – St James's Antigua (IRE) (Law Society **h81**
(USA)) [2006/7 h81: 16g 16m 16m 16m⁶ Jul 27] poor novice hurdler: raced around 2m
on good/good to firm going. *C. P. Morlock*

MAGIC OF SYDNEY (IRE) 11 b.g. Broken Hearted – Chat Her Up (Proverb) **c82 x**
[2006/7 c99x, h–: c24g5 c25d5 c24g3 Apr 8] sturdy gelding: lightly raced: modest **h–**
handicap chaser, below best in 2006/7: stays 25f: acts on good to soft going: often let
down by jumping. *R. Rowe*

MAGICO (NZ) 9 b.g. Casual Lies (USA) – Majica (NZ) (Star Way) [2006/7 c116, h94: **c–**
20g5 21s3 c20d c21spu Feb 17] lengthy, angular gelding: modest handicap hurdler: fairly **h95**
useful chaser, no show last 2 starts: stays 21f: acts on good to soft going, possibly unsuited by
firmer than good: blinkered. *Miss Venetia Williams*

MAGIC ROUTE (IRE) 10 b.g. Mr Confusion (IRE) – Another Chapter (Respect) **c86**
[2006/7 c21spu c21m3 c20g* c20g4 c21m c20g4 c20g c20g4 Apr 16] tall gelding: winning **h–**
pointer: modest chaser: won handicap at Southwell (by 15 lengths) in August: stays
21f: acts on good to firm ground: has worn cheekpieces: usually amateur ridden.
Miss T. Jackson

MAGIC SCORE 5 b.m. Shambo – Bewitch (Idiot's Delight) [2006/7 F16s2 Dec 7] **F91**
fourth foal: dam, second in bumper, half-sister to fairly useful hurdlers/chasers up to 3m
First Love and Shining Strand, out of half-sister to high-class staying chaser Spanish
Steps: favourite, 1½ lengths second to Owlesbury Dream in mares bumper at Ludlow on
debut. *N. J. Henderson*

MAGIC SKY (FR) 7 b.g. Simon du Desert (FR) – Kailasa (FR) (R B Chesne) [2006/7 **c140**
c127, h105: 19g3 20s* 16g 16d3 16v2 16s2 19s3 19d c17d* 16g3 c19g3 c16g5 Apr 12] **h120**
rather leggy gelding: fairly useful hurdler: easy winner of seller at Uttoxeter (sold from
P. Nicholls 11,500 gns) in October: several creditable efforts in handicaps after: useful
handicap chaser: won at Newbury in March by 11 lengths from Jacks Craic: good efforts
at Ascot and Aintree (Grade 3, never-nearer fifth to Bambi de L'Orme) last 2 starts: stays
19f: acts on heavy and good to firm going: tried visored/tongue tied. *M. F. Harris*

MAGNESIUM (USA) 7 ch.g. Kris S (USA) – Proflare (USA) (Mr Prospector (USA)) **c91**
[2006/7 c–, h105: c21s3 c19dpu 16d5 16g2 16s* c18s5 21dpu 16s3 19g 20f Apr 28] lengthy, **h113**
useful-looking gelding: fair hurdler: won handicap at Sandown in December: form
(modest) over fences only on sixth outing: best around 2m: acts on soft and good to firm
going, probably on heavy: tried in cheekpieces: tongue tied: seems suited by forcing
tactics: temperament under suspicion. *B. G. Powell*

MAGNETIC POLE 6 b.g. Machiavellian (USA) – Clear Attraction (USA) (Lear Fan **c86**
(USA)) [2006/7 h–: 21m3 20d c20v* c21s c19g2 c19g4 Apr 8] useful-looking gelding: **h83**
modest maiden hurdler: similar form when winning novice handicap at Bangor on
chasing debut in March: stays 21f: acts on heavy and good to firm ground: often tongue
tied, also in cheekpieces last 4 starts: sold 16,000 gns Doncaster May Sales. *B. I. Case*

MAGNIFICENT SEVEN (IRE) 8 ch.g. Un Desperado (FR) – Seven Hills (FR) **c–**
(Reform) [2006/7 c95, h–: 24m3 c24d6 24g* 24d3 c26gpu Apr 7] well-made gelding: **h97**
modest handicap hurdler/chaser: won over hurdles at Musselburgh in December: should
stay beyond 3m: acts on soft and good to firm going. *J. Howard Johnson*

MAGNIFICO 8 b.g. Mark of Esteem (IRE) – Blush Rambler (IRE) (Blushing Groom **h–**
(FR)) [2006/7 17d Nov 23] half-brother to 2½m hurdle winner Ponderon (by Hector
Protector): useful on Flat at 3 yrs, winning twice at 1m, but well held both starts at
4 yrs and left Sir Michael Stoute: little aptitude for hurdling in maiden at Taunton.
Mrs P. Robeson

MAGNIFICO (FR) 6 b.g. Solid Illusion (USA) – Born For Run (FR) (Pharly (FR)) **c–**
[2006/7 h124: c23dur 24vF 24s2 20s 24s2 24v5 25v 24g 16m6 Apr 10] leggy gelding: in **h129**
rear when unseated on chasing debut: fairly useful handicap hurdler: creditable efforts in
2006/7 only when second: stays 3m: acts on heavy going: visored/tongue tied last 2 starts:
none too reliable. *Mrs K. Waldron*

MAGNOLIA DRIVE (IRE) 8 gr.g. Roselier (FR) – Test Drive (Crash Course) **h–**
[2006/7 24g 20v Nov 12] sixth foal: half-brother to fair chaser/winning hurdler Cluain
Rua (by Be My Native) and fair hurdler Testify (by Montelimar), both of whom stay 3m:
dam lightly raced over hurdles: little form in maiden Irish points/novice hurdles. *Ferdy
Murphy*

MAG NUM (FR) 7 b.g. Kadalko (FR) – Attualita (FR) (Master Thatch) [2006/7 17sur **h99 p**
20v4 17g2 Mar 24] sixth foal: half-brother to winning hurdler/top-class chaser Impek (by
Lute Antique), effective at 2m to 3m: dam 9.5f/10.5f winner: much better effort on
completed starts over hurdles when second to Annie's Answer in novice at Bangor,
finishing strongly: likely to prove suited by further than 17f: remains capable of better.
Evan Williams

MAGNUM OPUS (IRE) 5 b.g. Sadler's Wells (USA) – Summer Breeze (Rainbow **h84**
Quest (USA)) [2006/7 16v⁶ 16d Dec 28] ex-French gelding: runner-up 3 times up to 12.5f
from 4 starts on Flat at 3 yrs: sold out of A. Fabre's stable 85,000 gns Newmarket Autumn
Sales, fair form at best in 2006: well held in novice/maiden hurdles: tongue tied on debut.
T. J. Pitt

MAGNUS VERITAS (IRE) 9 br.g. Jolly Jake (NZ) – Goldens Monkey (Monksfield) **c–**
[2006/7 c88: c26gᵖᵘ May 3] winning pointer: third in novice on completed start in
hunters: stays 3m. *Miss Gina Weare*

MAGO SANTHAI (IRE) 5 b.m. Revoque (IRE) – Caurselle (IRE) (Bob Back (USA)) **h108**
[2006/7 16v 16v 16v⁴ 16g⁸ 16g³ Apr 14] no form on Flat: fair novice hurdler, left
T. F. Lacy after second start: won mares event at Chepstow in March: raced at 2m on good
ground or softer. *A. W. Carroll*

MAGOT DE GRUGY (FR) 7 b.g. Tzar Rodney (FR) – Hirlish (FR) (Passing Sale **c86**
(FR)) [2006/7 h117: c20s⁶ c19d⁴ c20d³ c19v⁵ c19g⁵ c16m² Apr 14] compact gelding: **h–**
fairly useful hurdler: modest novice chaser: stays 2¾m: acts on heavy and good to firm
going: usually ridden prominently: tends to idle. *R. H. Alner*

MAGS AND BOB 6 gr.g. Environment Friend – Princess Semele (Imperial Fling **F–**
(USA)) [2006/7 F17d May 1] seventh foal: half-brother to fairly useful staying hurdler/
chaser Tara-Brogan (by Jupiter Island) and fair hurdler/chaser up to 21f Governor Daniel
(by Governor General): dam 11f winner on Flat/fair 2m hurdler: no sign of ability in
bumper/points. *R. C. Guest*

MAGS TWO 10 b.g. Jumbo Hirt (USA) – Welsh Diamond (High Top) [2006/7 h81: 16f **h85**
20s* 20f⁶ 22g⁴ 24d⁵ 20sᶠ Dec 5] close-coupled gelding: modest hurdler: won conditional
jockeys selling handicap at Hexham in June: sold out of I. McMath's stable 5,250 gns
Doncaster August Sales after next start: effective from 2½m to 3¾m: acts on soft and
good to firm going. *R. Ford*

MAGUIRE (GER) 6 ro.g. Medaaly – Mayada (USA) (The Minstrel (CAN)) [2006/7 **h79**
17m 16f⁶ 16d 16d⁵ 17vᶠ 16v 17v⁵ 19sᵖᵘ Mar 12] good-topped gelding: poor novice
hurdler: raced mainly around 2m: acts on good to soft going: usually tongue tied in
2006/7. *M. F. Harris*

MAHARAAT (USA) 6 b.g. Bahri (USA) – Siyadah (USA) (Mr Prospector (USA)) **h78**
[2006/7 h96: 24g Jul 31] good-topped gelding: modest hurdler: below form in handicap
after year off: stays 2¾m: acts on good to firm going: tried blinkered (went with little
zest)/tongue tied. *P. J. Hobbs*

MAHARBAL (FR) 7 b.g. Assessor (IRE) – Cynthia (FR) (Mont Basile (FR)) [2006/7 **h122**
21d* 17v 24dᵖᵘ Feb 10] good-topped gelding: fairly useful hurdler: off 2 years and
favourite, improved from when winning handicap at Kempton in December by 5 lengths
from Golden Bay: ran poorly both starts after: should stay beyond 21f: acts on soft and
good to firm going. *N. J. Henderson*

MAHOGANY BLAZE (FR) 5 b.g. Kahyasi – Mahogany River (Irish River (FR)) **h136**
[2006/7 h124, F94: 16g⁸ 20s⁶ 16d⁵ 16d 19d 21g 24g Apr 14] tall, unfurnished gelding:
chasing type: useful handicap hurdler: won quite valuable 4-y-o event at Chepstow in
October by 1½ lengths from Ameeq, off bridle from early stage: respectable efforts at
best in valuable races after: best form at 2m, should prove as effective over further: acts
on heavy and good to firm going: tried blinkered. *N. A. Twiston-Davies*

MAIDSTONE MONUMENT (IRE) 12 b.g. Jurado (USA) – Loreto Lady (Brave **c111**
Invader (USA)) [2006/7 c92, h–: c21m⁸ c22f² c20m* c23g* c21d⁵ 22g* 22mᵖᵘ Sep 10] **h96**
lengthy gelding: modest handicap hurdler/fair handicap chaser: better than ever in first
half of 2006/7, winning over fences at Newton Abbot in May and Stratford (twice,
awarded race second time) in July and over hurdles at Fontwell in September: lame final
outing: stays 3¼m, effective at shorter: acts on firm and good to soft going: blinkered
once: best on left-handed tracks: front runner. *Mrs A. M. Thorpe*

MAITRE LEVY (GER) 9 b.g. Monsun (GER) – Meerdunung (EG) (Tauchsport **c99**
(EG)) [2006/7 c–, h–: c25sᵖᵘ c21vᶠ c24gᶠ c25gᵘʳ Apr 2] maiden hurdler: winning pointer: **h–**
failed to complete all 5 starts in chases, running easily best race when falling 3 out in
hunter won by Scots Grey in penultimate one: should stay beyond 17f: acts on
soft going: has had tongue tied. *A. S. McPherson*

MAIZY MISSILE (IRE) 5 b.m. Executive Perk – Landsker Missile (Cruise Missile) **h– p**
[2006/7 F16s 16g Feb 21] second foal: half-sister to bumper/hurdle winner Reel Missile **F–**
(by Weld), stays 2½m: dam fairly useful hunter who stayed 21f: well held in bumper:

some encouragement when seventh to Viper in maiden at Ludlow on hurdling debut, not given hard time after travelling smoothly: should improve. *Mrs M. Evans*

MAJED (FR) 11 b.g. Fijar Tango (FR) – Full of Passion (USA) (Blushing Groom (FR)) [2006/7 c–§, h–§: c31s^{pu} Apr 26] compact gelding: one-time useful hurdler/fair chaser, no form outside points (won in March) since 2004/5: stays 3½m: acts on good to firm and heavy going: usually blinkered/visored: ungenuine. *Mrs Carolyn Innes*   c– § h– §

MAJESTIC CONCORDE (IRE) 4 b.g. Definite Article – Talina's Law (IRE) (Law Society (USA)) [2006/7 16v^3 16v^2 Jan 13] lengthy gelding: half-brother to fairly useful 2¼m/19f hurdle winner Queen Astrid (by Revoque) and 2m hurdle winner Mujalina (by Mujadil): dam fairly useful juvenile hurdler: twice successful at 1½m at 3 yrs on Flat, fairly useful form when second over 2m final start: placed in juvenile hurdles at Leopardstown and Punchestown, much better form when short-head second to Convincing in Grade 3 at latter, staying on well: will be suited by further than 2m: open to further improvement. *D. K. Weld, Ireland*   h117 p

MAJESTIC VISION 6 ch.g. Desert King (IRE) – Triste Oeil (USA) (Raise A Cup (USA)) [2006/7 19m^{pu} 17m* 16d* Aug 14] half-brother to modest 2m hurdler Secret Gift (by Cadeaux Genereux): modest maiden on Flat (stays 2m) in 2005, sold out of W. Swinburn's stable 4,000 gns Doncaster October Sales: successful both completed outings (saddle slipped on debut) over hurdles, in maiden at Newton Abbot and seller at Southwell (easily, sold 12,500 gns) in August: will stay beyond 17f. *L. Corcoran*   h106

MAJIMOURIEN (FR) 4 b.f. Majorien – Jolie Jim (FR) (Double Bed (FR)) [2006/7 17s 18s^F Dec 23] second foal: dam unraced sister to very smart 1m/1¼m performer Jim And Tonic: maiden on Flat: seventh in juvenile hurdle at Fontainebleau: well beaten when falling last at Fontwell. *F. Doumen, France*   h?

MAJOR BELLE (FR) 8 ch.m. Cyborg (FR) – Mistine Major (FR) (Major Petingo (FR)) [2006/7 c84x, h–: c21v c16s c20v^2 c22s^6 c20v^2 c25m* Apr 28] lengthy mare: winning hurdler: modest handicap chaser: won at Market Rasen on last day of season: stays 25f: acts on heavy and good to firm going: often makes mistakes. *John R. Upson*   c86 x h–

MAJOR BENEFIT (IRE) 10 b.g. Executive Perk – Merendas Sister (Pauper) [2006/7 c118: c28s^{pu} c23v^{rtr} Jan 1] strong, workmanlike gelding: fairly useful handicap chaser: out of sorts since 2005 (refused to race when blinkered final outing): stays 27f: raced almost exclusively on soft/heavy going: one to leave alone. *Mrs K. Waldron*   c– §

MAJOR BLADE (GER) 9 b.g. Dashing Blade – Misniniski (Niniski (USA)) [2006/7 h–: 17m^6 17d 17m^2 16f^4 c16d^4 c16g^3 c16s^F c16s^4 c16d^3 c16m^2 c20m^2 c20m^5 Apr 28] good-topped gelding: poor maiden hurdler/chaser: stays 2½m: acts on soft and good to firm going: usually blinkered/in cheekpieces/tongue tied in 2006/7. *Heather Dalton*   c84 h80

MAJOR BLUE 12 ch.g. Scallywag – Town Blues (Charlottown) [2006/7 c26v^{pu} c24d^5 c25d^{pu} 26s c24v^3 c21v^4 c26v^4 c26v^{pu} Mar 10] rangy gelding: winning hurdler/maiden chaser, no form in 2006/7 after lengthy absence: often wears cheekpieces nowadays. *J. G. M. O'Shea*   c– h–

MAJORCA 6 b.g. Green Desert (USA) – Majmu (USA) (Al Nasr (FR)) [2006/7 h99: 16g 16m^6 16s^4 c16g 16d^6 16g^F 16g 16g* 16g^3 Dec 30] tall gelding: fair handicap hurdler: left J. Howard Johnson after second outing: took advantage of drop in weights when winning at Musselburgh in December: well beaten in novice on chasing debut: probably best around 2m with emphasis on speed. *Ferdy Murphy*   c– h102

MAJOR CATCH (IRE) 8 b.g. Safety Catch (USA) – Inch Tape (Prince Hansel) [2006/7 h104: c22v^{ur} c24s^3 c22s^5 c20d^5 c20s^5 24g^4 c23m^{ur} c25m^4 Apr 28] strong, lengthy gelding: fair hurdler: modest novice chaser: stays 25f: acts on good to firm and heavy ground. *C. T. Pogson*   c94 h104

MAJOR COMET 5 b.g. Double Trigger (IRE) – Angela's Ashes (Common Grounds) [2006/7 F17m* F17s^{pu} Oct 22] compact, workmanlike gelding: first foal: dam unraced: won bumper at Market Rasen (beat Lindseyfield Lodge 5 lengths) on debut: broke down at Aintree 2 months later. *K. G. Reveley*   F102

MAJOR EURO (IRE) 10 b.g. Lord Americo – Gold Bank (Over The River (FR)) [2006/7 c112, h–: c20g^2 c20f^{pu} c20m^{pu} c20d^{pu} c20g^{pu} c16g c20d^{pu} 23s^{pu} 22d 20m^6 Apr 25] good-topped gelding: winning hurdler: fair handicap chaser: badly out of sorts after reappearance: stays 2½m: acts on soft and firm going: tried in cheekpieces. *S. J. Gilmore*   c115 d h–

MAJOR FAUX PAS (IRE) 5 b.g. Barathea (IRE) – Edwina (IRE) (Caerleon (USA)) **h81**
[2006/7 16d⁴ 17s 17s 16g 20gᵖᵘ Apr 9] sturdy gelding: fairly useful at best on Flat (stays
1¼m), sold out of J. Osborne's stable 18,000 gns Newmarket Autumn (2005) Sales: poor
form over hurdles: likely to prove best at 2m with emphasis on speed: tongue tied final
outing. *O. Sherwood*

MAJOR JON (IRE) 7 br.g. Shardari – Slyguff Lord (IRE) (Lord Americo) [2006/7 c–, **c–,**
h86, F84: c17mᶠ 20m c22mᵖᵘ 16fᶠ 16fᵖᵘ 16d 16g 16d³ 17v⁴ 16d² 16s 16s⁴ 19v⁵ 16m⁶ **h78**
Apr 9] workmanlike gelding: poor hurdler: no form over fences: sold out of W. Burke's
stable 5,500 gns Doncaster August Sales after third start: raced mainly around 2m: acts
on good to firm and heavy going: often blinkered. *Mrs T. J. Hill*

MAJOR LEAGUE (USA) 5 b.g. Magic Cat (USA) – Quick Grey (USA) (El Prado **h–**
(IRE)) [2006/7 h–: 16dᵖᵘ May 26] successful 3 times on Flat in USA, little impact in
handicaps in Britain: no show 2 outings over hurdles. *K. Bishop*

MAJOR MATT (IRE) 5 b.g. Mister Mat (FR) – By Golly (IRE) (Mandalus) [2006/7 **h78**
20v 19g 20g⁴ Apr 27] sturdy gelding: fifth foal: brother to bumper winner Ruairi: dam,
winning pointer, out of half-sister to useful chaser up to 25f Colonel In Chief: first form
over hurdles when around 30 lengths fourth to Ballamusic in novice at Chepstow, not
unduly punished after mistake 2 out: will be suited by 3m+. *D. E. Pipe*

MAJOR OAK (IRE) 6 b.g. Deploy – Mahaasin (Bellypha) [2006/7 h94, F91: 20d⁵ **h106**
24s³ 23v⁶ 19d* 20v² 20v⁴ 25g² 20g⁴ 24s² Apr 26] sturdy gelding: fair hurdler: won novice
at Market Rasen in December: stays 25f: raced on good going or softer (acts on heavy):
tried in cheekpieces, blinkered last 6 starts: hard ride but is consistent. *G. M. Moore*

MAJOR TITLE (IRE) 8 b.g. Brief Truce (USA) – Dariyba (IRE) (Kahyasi) [2006/7 **h99**
16g² 16s 16g² Dec 10] fairly useful on Flat (stays 1¼m): fair form when placed in
maiden/novice hurdles: likely to prove best at easy 2m. *M. J. Grassick, Ireland*

MAKANDY 8 b.g. Makbul – Derring Floss (Derring Rose) [2006/7 h75: 16s³ 17d³ 17d² **h85**
Mar 19] workmanlike gelding: poor maiden hurdler, placed several times (including in
sellers): best around 2m: acts on heavy going. *R. J. Armson*

MAKEABREAK (IRE) 8 ch.m. Anshan – Nilousha (Darshaan) [2006/7 h92: 19g² **h92**
19g² 20m* 20f⁵ Sep 29] lengthy, angular mare: modest hurdler: didn't need to be at best
to win mares maiden at Worcester in June: sold out of C. Mann's stable 10,000 gns
Doncaster August Sales: stays 21f: acts on soft and good to firm going, seemingly not on
heavy. *Miss J. E. Foster*

MAKE A MARK (IRE) 7 b.g. Victory Note (USA) – Election Special (Chief Singer) **h91**
[2006/7 F81: F16s⁴ F16d 16g 16d² 16m² 16g Apr 2] modest form in bumpers for Mrs **F–**
R. Elliot and over hurdles: raced at 2m: acts on good to firm and good to soft going.
W. Amos

MAKE IT A DOUBLE (IRE) 9 ch.g. Zaffaran (USA) – La Danse (Le Moss) [2006/7 **h–**
h91: 21s 24g Mar 30] strong gelding: modest winning hurdler, very lightly raced: never
dangerous in handicaps in 2006/7: stays 3m. *Noel T. Chance*

MAKE IT EASY (IRE) 11 b. or br.g. Alphabatim (USA) – Mammy's Friend (Miner's **c57**
Lamp) [2006/7 c66, h57: c25m⁵ c25d⁵ Aug 19] lightly-raced hurdler: poor handicap **h–**
chaser: stays 27f: acts on good to firm and good to soft going: has worn cheekpieces/
visor. *D. L. Williams*

MAKE MY HAY 8 b.g. Bluegrass Prince (IRE) – Shashi (IRE) (Shaadi (USA)) **h–**
[2006/7 h100: 16s 17m⁶ 16s 17vᵖᵘ Jan 2] small gelding: winning hurdler, no form in
2006/7: should stay 2½m: acts on heavy going: blinkered/visored nowadays.
J. Gallagher

MAKTU 5 ch.g. Bien Bien (USA) – Shalateeno (Teenoso (USA)) [2006/7 17g 20dᵘʳ **h105**
20v³ 17s⁴ 20v³ 20v² 22d⁵ Mar 26] tall, angular gelding: modest maiden on Flat: fair
novice hurdler: stays 2½m: acts on heavy going. *P. G. Murphy*

MALAGA BOY (IRE) 10 b.g. Nordic Brave – Ardglass Mist (Black Minstrel) **c102**
[2006/7 c100x, h100: c20s⁴ c19s* c23s⁵ c19vᵖᵘ Mar 10] good-topped gelding: fair hurd- **h–**
ler: similar form over fences, won handicap at Taunton in January: breathing problem
final outing: stays 2¾m: acts on heavy and good to firm going: has been let down by
jumping over fences. *C. L. Tizzard*

MALAKIYA (IRE) 4 b.g. Sadler's Wells (USA) – State Crystal (IRE) (High Estate) **h120**
[2006/7 16d 17s³ 16s* 16v* 18v⁶ 22m⁴ Apr 22] rather leggy gelding: half-brother to
fairly useful hurdler/smart chaser around 2m Jack The Giant (by Giant's Causeway):

fairly useful on Flat (stays 17f), successful in October, sold out of G. Butler's stable 42,000 gns Newmarket Autumn Sales: fairly useful juvenile hurdler: won at Stratford (maiden) and Plumpton (easily best effort, beat Signs of Love 2½ lengths) in February: looked ungenuine when beaten at odds on final outing: should be suited by further than 2m: acts on heavy going: temperament under suspicion. *Jonjo O'Neill*

MALAY 10 b.m. Karinga Bay – Malaia (IRE) (Commanche Run) [2006/7 h118: 19d⁵ 24m⁶ 21g 24s 20v⁴ 22vᵖᵘ Jan 25] leggy mare: unraced until 8 yrs: fair hurdler on balance: probably stays 3m: acts on soft and good to firm ground. *Mrs Norma Pook* **h110**

MALDOUN (IRE) 8 b.g. Kaldoun (FR) – Marzipan (IRE) (Green Desert (USA)) [2006/7 h–§: 24vᵖᵘ 20d 24dᵖᵘ 22vᵖᵘ c20g⁵ c21d* Mar 26] leggy gelding: winning hurdler: little show in 2006/7, well behind when left clear twelfth in maiden chase at Stratford: stays 2¾m: acts on soft going: often wears cheekpieces/visor: ungenuine. *Mrs Barbara Waring* **c?**
h– §

MALECH (IRE) 4 b.g. Bahhare (USA) – Choral Sundown (Night Shift (USA)) [2006/7 h82 p 16g Dec 30] fair on Flat (stays 8.3f), sold out of M. Bell's stable 11,000 gns Newmarket Autumn Sales: soon lot to do in juvenile at Musselburgh on hurdling debut: likely to do better. *K. G. Reveley* **h82 p**

MALETTON (FR) 7 b.g. Bulington (FR) – Reine Dougla (FR) (Faunus (FR)) [2006/7 h111: c24s³ c20d⁴ c25s* c24d* c25s* c19s² c24g Mar 14] leggy, lengthy gelding: winning hurdler: useful chaser: won maiden at Folkestone and handicaps at Fakenham and Wincanton (further improvement to beat Puntal by ¾ length in quite valuable event) within 3 weeks in January: mistakes when well held in valuable amateur handicap at Cheltenham final outing: stays 25f: raced mainly on going softer than good (acts on heavy): tried blinkered: races prominently. *Miss Venetia Williams* **c131**
h–

MALIBU (IRE) 6 b.g. Second Empire (IRE) – Tootle (Main Reef) [2006/7 h–: 17d 21mᵘʳ Apr 9] leggy gelding: modest on all-weather on Flat (stays 2m) nowadays: well held both completed outings in maiden hurdles. *M. Appleby* **h–**

Connaught Cup (Handicap Chase), Wincanton— Lord Killeshanra is an early casualty over Wincanton's stiff fences; Puntal (cheekpieces) emerges as the only one to make a race of it with hat-trick scorer Maletton (white cap)

MALJIMAR (IRE) 7 b.g. Un Desperado (FR) – Marble Miller (IRE) (Mister Lord **c119**
(USA)) [2006/7 h100: c24v^F c19d^2 c19s^3 c18s* c19d^3 Mar 20] useful-looking gelding: **h–**
winning hurdler: fairly useful form over fences: successful in novice handicap at
Newbury in March by 5 lengths from Officier de Reserve: would probably also have won
on chasing debut but for falling: likely to stay 3m: acts on heavy and good to firm going.
Nick Williams

MALKO DE BEAUMONT (FR) 7 b. or br.g. Gold And Steel (FR) – Givry (FR) **c93**
(Bayolidaan (FR)) [2006/7 c106, h96: c20s^pu 20g^4 20v^6 21s* 25g^5 21s^6 c23d^4 Mar 26] **h101**
good-topped gelding: fair hurdler: awarded handicap at Huntingdon in December: similar
form at best over fences: should stay 3m: raced on good going or softer. *K. C. Bailey*

MALMO BOY (IRE) 8 gr.g. Roselier (FR) – Charming Mo (IRE) (Callernish) **c96**
[2006/7 c25v^pu c26v* c24g* Mar 28] lengthy gelding: poor hurdler: off nearly 2 years **h–**
before reappearance: blinkered, successful both completed starts over fences, in handicaps at Plumpton and Towcester (made all to beat Dr Mann readily by 11 lengths) in
March: stays 3¼m: acts on heavy going: tongue tied in 2006/7. *Heather Dalton*

MALMOOS (USA) 4 ch.g. Gulch (USA) – Sedrah (USA) (Dixieland Band (USA)) **F78**
[2006/7 F14s^5 F17v^3 F17s Jan 30] 4,000 2-y-o: sturdy gelding: second foal: brother to
fair 2m hurdler Nesnaas: dam, 1½m winner, half-sister to Poule d'Essai des Pouliches
winner Ta Rib: modest form in bumpers. *B. G. Powell*

MALT DE VERGY (FR) 7 br.g. Sleeping Car (FR) – Intense (FR) (Roi de Rome **h88**
(USA)) [2006/7 h110, F103: 17d 16g^5 16g Apr 2] well-made gelding: dual bumper
winner: disappointing maiden hurdler: bred to stay beyond 2m. *L. Lungo*

MALTON 7 b.g. Bal Harbour – Elissa (Tap On Wood) [2006/7 F88: 20s 17d^5 16v^5 **h85**
Dec 6] workmanlike gelding: placed in point/bumper: form over hurdles only when fifth
in novice at Bangor second start. *M. W. Easterby*

MAMBO DES MOTTES (FR) 7 b.g. Useful (FR) – Julie Des Mottes (FR) (Puma **c126**
Des Mottes (FR)) [2006/7 c20s^4 c21s^2 c17d^ur c16v^ur c21s^2 c20s^4 c21g^4 c16g^pu Apr 7] **h–**
neat gelding: twice-raced over hurdles: fairly useful handicap chaser, missed 2005/6: best
efforts when runner-up at Cheltenham and Wincanton: stays 21f: raced on good going or
softer (acts on soft). *Miss Venetia Williams*

MAMBO (IRE) 9 b.g. Ashkalani (IRE) – Bold Tango (FR) (In Fijar (USA)) [2006/7 c–, **c–**
h–: 20g^5 17d^2 c21m^su 16g^4 c17g^ur Sep 17] tall, leggy gelding: fairly useful hurdler/chaser **h66**
at one time: only runner-up in selling hurdle (visored) in June: slipped up in Svenskt
Grand National at Stromsholm, final start for M. Harris: probably best around 2m: raced
mostly on good/good to soft going: has often run as if amiss. *D. Persson, Sweden*

MAMBO SUN 4 b.g. Superior Premium – The Manx Touch (IRE) (Petardia) [2006/7 **h102**
17d^2 17d* 18g^2 17g Sep 8] fair on Flat (stays 11f): similar standard in juvenile hurdles,
winning maiden at Newton Abbot in August by 27 lengths. *P. A. Blockley*

MAMIDEOS (IRE) 10 br.g. Good Thyne (USA) – Heavenly Artist (IRE) (Heavenly **c–**
Manna) [2006/7 c–, h–: c26s^5 May 14] lengthy, useful-looking gelding: fair handicap **h–**
chaser at best, very lightly raced since 2004/5: stays 3m: acts on soft going: usually
tongue tied. *T. R. George*

MAM RATAGAN 6 b.g. Mtoto – Nika Nesgoda (Suave Dancer (USA)) [2006/7 F97: **F85**
F16g^5 F16s Dec 3] lengthy gelding: won bumper at Warwick on debut in 2005/6: disappointing in similar events since: sold 1,000 gns Doncaster May Sales. *N. J. Henderson*

MANA-MOU BAY (IRE) 10 b.g. Ela-Mana-Mou – Summerhill (Habitat) [2006/7 **h83**
17d 16f 16f^2 Jul 16] lengthy gelding: fair 2m hurdler at best, very lightly raced since
2003: has worn cheekpieces: front runner/races prominently. *J. I. A. Charlton*

MANATHON (FR) 4 b.g. Marathon (USA) – Fleurissante (FR) (Legend of France **h–**
(USA)) [2006/7 16s 16s 17g Mar 25] angular gelding: won over 10.5f in French Provinces at 3 yrs, claimed from M. Roussel €25,600 after runner-up in October: well held
over hurdles. *A. E. Jones*

MANAWANUI 9 b.g. Karinga Bay – Kiwi Velocity (NZ) (Veloso (NZ)) [2006/7 c104§, **c– §**
h99§: c25m^pu 24d^pu 24s^3 24s^2 24s 24v 22g^pu Apr 7] sturdy gelding: fair hurdler/chaser **h102 §**
on his day, lame final outing: stays 3m: acts on soft going: effective visored or not:
unreliable. *R. H. Alner*

MANBOW (IRE) 9 b.g. Mandalus – Treble Base (IRE) (Orchestra) [2006/7 c111, h–: **c111**
c25g^2 c20d^3 c21g^F Nov 19] very tall gelding: fair handicap chaser: mistakes in rear and **h–**
fell heavily Canal Turn in Grand Sefton at Aintree: stays 25f: acts on soft and good to
firm going: has idled/carried head high: patiently ridden. *Micky Hammond*

MANCEBO (GER) 4 b.g. Acambaro (GER) – Marsixa (FR) (Linamix (FR)) [2006/7   **h73 ?** 17g Apr 1] placed 3 times up to 1½m from 5 starts on Flat in Germany in 2006, left A. Wohler after final one: never better than mid-division in steadily-run novice at Newton Abbot on hurdling debut. *R. Curtis*

MANDALAY BAY (IRE) 7 b.g. Humbel (USA) – Molly Bigley (IRE) (Lancastrian)   **h–** [2006/7 20g 20m 20s 16f 20sᵖᵘ Oct 11] first foal: dam maiden pointer: failed to complete in Irish points: no form over hurdles (tried blinkered): won point in April. *Mrs K. Walton*

MANDALAY LADY 5 gr.m. Environment Friend – Pretty Scarce (Handsome Sailor)   **F–** [2006/7 F16g Mar 28] 12,000 4-y-o: sturdy mare: fifth foal: half-sister to winning sprinters by Never So Bold and Wizard King: dam, little sign of ability, half-sister to smart bumper winner/chaser Missed That, stayed 21f: towards rear in bumper at Kempton on debut. *O. Sherwood*

MANDATUM 6 b.g. Mtoto – Reamur (Top Ville) [2006/7 17s 16v² 16v⁴ 16dᶠ Mar 17]   **h116** good-topped gelding: fairly useful and consistent handicapper up to 15f on Flat, sold out of L. Cumani's stable 55,000 gns Newmarket Autumn Sales: running easily best race over hurdles and beaten 5l when second on handicap debut at Uttoxeter when falling last: raced around 2m: may prove best away from soft/heavy going. *Jonjo O'Neill*

MANDINGO CHIEF (IRE) 8 b.g. Flying Spur (AUS) – Elizabethan Air (Elegant   **c121** Air) [2006/7 c92, h–: c22s⁵ c20mᶠ c20m* c20mᵘʳ c21f² c20d* c20g³ c24d⁶ c20sᵘʳ c20d²   **h–** c21s² c20mᶠ Apr 27] good-topped gelding: fairly useful chaser: sold out of R. Phillips' stable 17,000 gns Doncaster May Sales after first outing: much improved after, winning maiden at Southwell in July and handicap at Wetherby (beat New Alco 12 lengths) in October: good efforts later when runner-up at Leicester and Wincanton: possibly best up to 2¾m: acts on any going: tried tongue tied: often front runner. *B. G. Powell*

MANEKI NEKO (IRE) 5 b.g. Rudimentary (USA) – Ardbess (Balla Cove) [2006/7   **h100** h105: 16d² 18s⁵ Nov 17] good-topped gelding: fairly useful on Flat (stays 13.8f), successful twice in 2006 : fair novice hurdler, placed 5 of 7 starts: raced around 2m: acts on good to soft ground. *E. W. Tuer*

MANELE BAY 4 ch.f. Karinga Bay – Lacounsel (FR) (Leading Counsel (USA))   **F92** [2006/7 F12g³ Mar 23] sturdy filly: third foal: dam, lightly-raced maiden on Flat, half-sister to useful chaser (best around 2½m) Luzcadou: 2½ lengths third of 18 to Whiteoak in 4-y-o bumper at Newbury on debut. *R. Rowe*

MAN FROM HIGHWORTH 8 b.g. Ballet Royal (USA) – Cavisoir (Afzal) [2006/7   **c–** c85, h–: c16f c19vᵖᵘ Feb 25] sturdy gelding: one-time fairly useful hurdler: modest form   **h–** at best over fences: best at 2m: acts on soft going. *H. J. Manners*

MANGE TOUT (IRE) 8 br.g. Presenting – Nish Bar (Callernish) [2006/7 h–, F74:   **c108** 16d⁵ 16s³ c16v⁴ c16s³ c16g⁶ Mar 27] strong gelding: little impact in bumpers or novice   **h–** hurdles: fair form over fences: raced mainly at 2m on ground softer than good. *K. J. Burke*

MANHATTAN BOY (GER) 5 ch.g. Monsun (GER) – Manhattan Girl (USA) (Vice   **h124 +** Regent (CAN)) [2006/7 17d* 16v* 17s Dec 8] tall, leggy gelding: half-brother to modest 2m hurdle winner Montecorvino (by Acatenango): won 4 races up to around 1¼m on Flat in Germany, including 3 in 2006 for A. Trybuhl: successful first 2 starts over hurdles, in novice at Bangor (green) and conditional jockeys handicap at Newbury (fairly useful form, made all to beat Widely Accepted by 19 lengths) in November: finished distressed in handicap at Cheltenham following month. *P. J. Hobbs*

MANLY MONEY 9 b.g. Homo Sapien – Susie's Money (Seymour Hicks (FR))   **c100** [2006/7 c21mᵇᵈ c23d⁵ c23s Dec 18] lengthy gelding: winning hurdler: fair chaser: off 18   **h–** months and left P. Nicholls, close third when brought down 3 out in handicap won by Petitjean at Wincanton on reappearance: stays 2½m: acts on soft going, probably on good to firm. *A. J. Honeyball*

MANNERS (IRE) 9 b.g. Topanoora – Maneree (Mandalus) [2006/7 h122p: 16g 24sᵖᵘ   **h–** 21sᵖᵘ Jan 13] quite good-topped gelding: lightly raced: fairly useful hurdle winner, no form in handicaps in 2006/7: should stay beyond 2m: acts on heavy going (bumper form on good to firm): blinkered final outing. *Jonjo O'Neill*

MAN OF MINE 6 gr.g. Classic Cliche (IRE) – Dawn Spinner (Arctic Lord) [2006/7   **c73** h69, F85: c22sᶠ 19s⁶ c16d⁶ 19g 24m Apr 25] sturdy gelding: little form over hurdles/   **h–** fences: should stay 3m. *Heather Dalton*

MAN OF THE MOMENT 5 gr.g. Silver Patriarch (IRE) – Winnowing (IRE) (Strong   **h–** Gale) [2006/7 22s Feb 3] 20,000 3-y-o, resold £100,000 3-y-o: fourth foal: half-brother to useful hurdler/smart chaser Darkness (by Accordion), stays 25f: dam, winning hurdler who stayed 2½m, out of half-sister to top-class 2m to 25f hurdler Aonoch: well held in maiden hurdle on debut. *P. F. Nicholls*

MANOLO (FR) 7 b.g. Ragmar (FR) – Coriola (FR) (Brezzo (FR)) [2006/7 c–, h89: 17d² 17d Jun 12] modest maiden handicap hurdler: soundly beaten only outing over fences: likely to prove best around 2m: sold 1,500 gns Doncaster August Sales. *Heather Dalton*   **c–** **h89**

MANORAM (GER) 8 ch.g. Zinaad – Mayada (USA) (The Minstrel (CAN)) [2006/7 c92, h–: c16g c16m⁴ c18g c20m² c20m⁶ c17d⁴ Oct 14] smallish, sparely-made gelding: winning hurdler: modest handicap chaser: won 2 points in April: effective at 2m to 2½m: acts on soft and good to firm going: wears headgear: sometimes let down by jumping: reluctant to race third outing: unreliable. *Ian Williams*   **c91 §** **h–**

MANOR LAW (IRE) 5 b.g. Night Shift (USA) – Flush Rush (Zilzal (USA)) [2006/7 16s 16s 16v 17s Mar 12] fairly useful at best on Flat (stays 1m), successful twice in 2005: poor form over hurdles: likely to need emphasis on speed at 2m: tried tongue tied. *J. G. Carr, Ireland*   **h70**

MANORSON (IRE) 8 ch.g. Desert King (IRE) – Familiar (USA) (Diesis) [2006/7 h133: c16g² c17d² Oct 17] strong, compact gelding: useful handicap hurdler: fairly useful form when 7 lengths second of 6 to Natal at Exeter on completed outing in maiden chases: best with emphasis on speed around 2m: acts on good to soft going: fluent jumper of hurdles: races prominently. *O. Sherwood*   **c121** **h–**

MANOUBI 8 b.g. Doyoun – Manuetti (IRE) (Sadler's Wells (USA)) [2006/7 c82§, h97§: c21m² c16f² c20g* c20sᵖᵘ 19g 24g Dec 20] good-topped gelding: winning hurdler: fair chaser: won handicap at Hexham in October: stays 2½m: acts on firm and good to soft going (lost action on soft fourth start): has worn blinkers/cheekpieces: tried tongue tied: none too genuine. *M. Todhunter*   **c100** **h–**

MAN OVERBOARD 5 b.g. Overbury (IRE) – Dublin Ferry (Celtic Cone) [2006/7 F89: 16v³ 22vᵖᵘ 16m⁴ Apr 10] fourth in bumper for T. Tate: caught eye when not knocked about all 3 starts over hurdles: should stay beyond 2m: likely to do better, particularly now qualified for handicaps. *Evan Williams*   **h97 p**

MANQUE NEUF 8 b.g. Cadeaux Genereux – Flying Squaw (Be My Chief (USA)) [2006/7 h78: 24v 22v Feb 13] workmanlike gelding: poor handicap hurdler: off 14 months, no show in 2006/7: stays 25f: acts on soft and good to firm going: wears cheekpieces: not a fluent jumper: ran out once. *Mrs L. Richards*   **h–**

MAN RAY (USA) 6 b.g. Theatrical – Irtifa (Lahib (USA)) [2006/7 h108+: 17gᵖᵘ May 5] fair novice hurdler: off 5 months (looked reluctant and mounted on course), travelling comfortably when all but fell fifth only start in 2006/7: raced around 2m: acts on heavy going. *Jonjo O'Neill*   **h–**

MANSONN LEDA (FR) 4 b.f. Mansonnien (FR) – Oleada (IRE) (Tirol) [2006/7 F16m⁴ Mar 25] sixth foal: half-sister to winning hurdler/useful hunter chaser Cobreces (by Environment Friend), stays 25f, and 3 Flat winners in France: dam unraced: modest form when fourth in bumper on debut. *Ferdy Murphy*   **F77**

MANSONY (FR) 8 b.g. Mansonnien (FR) – Hairly (FR) (Air de Cour (USA)) [2006/7 c141, h125: c17s* c20v² c19v* c16m* Apr 24]   **c149** **h–**

The gamble involved in purchasing Mansony after he'd finished fourth in a juvenile maiden hurdle at Auteuil is one his connections will be delighted to have taken. Since joining his present yard, Mansony has won three races over hurdles and six over fences, his latest success coming in a Grade 1 Chase at Punchestown on his final outing in 2006/7, which took his earnings, win and place, to almost a quarter of a million pounds. Still only eight, Mansony should have plenty of opportunities to add substantially to that total, though it's unlikely he will get a better one at the highest level than that provided by the Kerrygold Champion Chase at Punchestown in April. With Nickname an absentee (as at the Cheltenham Festival) because of the ground and the previous year's winner Newmill, who started favourite, nowhere near his best, it was a substandard renewal and Mansony didn't need to improve to win it, even though his previous form had established him as just a smart chaser at best, albeit a consistent one. On what was his first outing on ground firmer than good, the normally front-running Mansony was dropped out last of seven as Newmill, Central House and Justified vied for the lead, the pace a good one. Mansony still had plenty to do four out, but he quickened well going to the

Kerrygold Champion Chase, Punchestown—Mansony (No.3) and Davy Russell swoop late to land a substandard renewal of this Grade 1; also pictured are runner-up Justified (No.2), fourth-placed River City (No.7) and below-par favourite Newmill

second last and took over from Justified after the last, going on to beat that horse by a length and a quarter, with 40/1-shot Steel Band (without a win now in his last twenty-two starts over fences) only a further three and a half lengths back in third.

The Champion Chase was Mansony's second Punchestown Festival victory, having landed a valuable listed handicap hurdle there two years earlier. His chasing career got under way the following winter, and it wasn't long before he was showing himself even better over fences than he was over hurdles, his three wins including one in the Grade 2 Flyingbolt Novices' Chase at Navan. He did turn in a couple of disappointing performances in 2005/6, though, most notably at Aintree on his sole appearance to date in Britain, Mansony reluctant to set off and seeming to sulk as he trailed throughout. There has been no suggestion of any temperament since, and Mansony, who was on his toes in the preliminaries at Aintree, clearly wasn't himself that day. In the latest campaign, Mansony had three races before Punchestown and won two of them, a handicap at Leopardstown in December and a minor event at Naas in March. He beat Our Ben (conceding 3 lb) by two lengths at Leopardstown, and landed the odds very easily at Naas (his third course win), in the latter jumping well, though typically out to his right. Mansony also ran well in between, when five lengths second to Watson Lake in the Red Mills Chase at Gowran. But for the abandonment of the Ascot fixture in January due to water-logging, Mansony would have contested the Victor Chandler Chase, for which he was one of the ante-post favourites. Clearly connections don't consider the travelling to have been responsible for his lacklustre display at Aintree, so there must be every chance that Mansony will be crossing the Irish Sea in the next season. Perhaps it will be for the Champion Chase at Cheltenham, for which Mansony received a quote of 20/1 immediately after Punchestown. In truth, he has plenty of improvement to make before he can be considered a leading contender for that race.

Mansony is by the Prix du Jockey Club fourth Mansonnien, also responsible in the latest season for the very smart chaser Taranis, and is the second foal of Hairly, a winning hurdler at around two miles in France. Mansony's year-younger half-sister Lyphairy (by Lyphard's Wish) won a couple of chases at around two miles in France as a three-year-old. Mansony is just as effective at two and a half miles as two miles and may well stay further. Significantly, he also held a Punchestown Festival entry in the Guinness Gold Cup, run over three miles and a furlong,

Mr Michael Mulholland's "Mansony"

Mansony (FR) (b.g. 1999)	Mansonnien (FR) (ch 1984)	Tip Moss (ch 1972)	Luthier Top Twig
		Association (ch 1977)	Margouillat La Soupe
	Hairly (FR) (br 1991)	Air de Cour (b 1982)	Vigors Amya
		Ulckey (br 1983)	Mad Captain Laquina

though understandably he was withdrawn from that race which took place the day after his Kerrygold Champion Chase triumph. A big, workmanlike gelding, Mansony acts on heavy and good to firm going. *A. L. T. Moore, Ireland*

MANX ROYAL (FR) 8 b.g. Cyborg (FR) – Badj II (FR) (Tadj (FR)) [2006/7 c107, h132: c21g² c24m⁶ c21mᶠ c22g* Mar 29] big, angular gelding: useful hurdler: fair chaser (has shaped as if amiss): off 8½ months, simple task in maiden at Towcester (idled) in March: should stay 3m: acts on good to soft and good to firm going, probably on firm: in cheekpieces last 5 starts: has worn net muzzle. *D. E. Pipe*
    c107
    h–

MAORI LEGEND 6 b.m. Midnight Legend – Hinemoa (IRE) (Mandalus) [2006/7 F–: 22s³ 20v 24s⁵ 22s c21dᶠ Mar 26] medium-sized mare: poor form over hurdles: let down by jumping on chasing debut: likely to prove suited by 3m+: raced on ground softer than good. *D. P. Keane*
    c–
    h81

MAPILUT DU MOULIN (FR) 7 b.g. Lute Antique (FR) – Api (FR) (El Badr) [2006/7 h66, F–: 26g⁴ 20s 20m 17m 19g² 17m⁴ 22d⁴ 19d⁴ 22m c16mᵖᵘ 21g² 17sᵘʳ 16g 19m² Apr 11] poor maiden hurdler: runner-up in point, saddle slipped early on chase debut: stays 2¾m: acts on good to firm and good to soft going: tried blinkered/tongue tied: claimed to join P. Butler £6,000 final outing. *R. J. Price*
    c–
    h85

MAPLEDURHAM (IRE) 5 ch.g. Grand Lodge (USA) – Gold Mist (Darshaan) **F72**
[2006/7 F17g⁵ Nov 5] 1,500 4-y-o: third foal: dam, 1¼m and 1¾m winner, sister to useful
hurdler up to 21f Clifdon Fog: poor form when fifth in bumper on debut. *R. J. Price*

MARAAKEZ 4 b.g. Kalanisi (IRE) – Questabelle (Rainbow Quest (USA)) [2006/7 17s **h–**
17g Mar 25] fair maiden on Flat (stays 11f), sold out of J. Gosden's stable 5,000 gns
Newmarket Autumn Sales: tailed off over hurdles. *N. J. Hawke*

MARADAN (IRE) 11 b.g. Shernazar – Marmana (USA) (Blushing Groom (FR)) **c–**
[2006/7 c–, h–: 24sᵖᵘ 16vᵖᵘ Dec 19] workmanlike gelding: fair hurdler at best: no form **h–**
for long time, including over fences. *Mrs J. C. McGregor*

MARADO (IRE) 6 ch.g. Un Desperado (FR) – Hi Marble (IRE) (Wylfa) [2006/7 **h–**
F16dᵖᵘ F16m⁵ F18m 21g 17sᵖᵘ 21gᵖᵘ Feb 21] €40,000 3-y-o: rangy, good sort: first foal: **F–**
dam, poor hurdler, stayed 25f: no solid form in bumpers/over hurdles, sold out of Miss
H. Knight's stable £2,400 Ascot December Sales before penultimate start. *S. T. Lewis*

MARALAN (IRE) 6 b.g. Priolo (USA) – Marilaya (IRE) (Shernazar) [2006/7 20s⁵ **h124**
16m³ 16m⁶ 17g⁶ 16s² 20s 16s⁴ 16d 18s 16d⁴ 16v² 16vᵛ 17g 16d³ 16m Apr 10] medium-
sized gelding: fairly useful hurdler: improved in 2006/7, winning handicap at Naas (by 4
lengths from Cadogan) in February: creditable efforts next 2 starts, 5 lengths third to
Wishwillow Lord in minor event at Limerick on second occasion: best around 2m: yet
to race on firm going, acts on any other: usually blinkered: held up. *Patrick O. Brady,
Ireland*

MARAUD 13 ch.g. Midyan (USA) – Peak Squaw (USA) (Icecapade (USA)) [2006/7 **h78**
20d⁵ 20s³ 17d 21m 17m 22g² 24d² 20dᵖᵘ 17mᶠ Apr 15] smallish gelding: poor handicap
hurdler: stayed 27f: acted on firm and soft going: tried blinkered/in cheekpieces: usually
front-runner: dead *R. Bastiman*

MARBLE GARDEN (USA) 6 b. or br.g. Royal Academy (USA) – Maria de La Luz **c125**
(Machiavellian (USA)) [2006/7 c20s c17s² c17s* c19s⁵ c20s³ c17s⁶ 16d c26gᶠ c24gᵖᵘ **h–**
Apr 7] small, angular gelding: first foal: dam useful 10.5f winner: maiden on Flat: fairly
useful hurdler/chaser: successful over fences at Auteuil in September: claimed from
A. Chaille-Chaille €26,600 sixth start, no form in Britain (left Richard Chotard before
final outing): stays 2½m: acts on soft ground: blinkered/tongue tied all starts in Britain.
Paul Murphy

MARBURY BOY 5 b.g. Classic Cliche (IRE) – Mulloch Brae (Sunyboy) [2006/7 **F84 p**
F16g⁴ Dec 26] €27,000 3-y-o: brother to cross-country chase winner Wonderkid and
half-brother to fairly useful staying hurdler Mini Moo Min (by Ardross): dam, winning
hurdler/fairly useful staying chaser, sister to useful staying chaser Bigsun and half-sister
to very smart staying chaser Androma: some promise when fourth to West Ridge in bumper at Wincanton on debut: will be suited by much greater test of stamina. *Noel T. Chance*

MARCEL (FR) 7 b.g. Bateau Rouge – Une Risette (FR) (Air du Nord (USA)) [2006/7 **c131**
c130, h–: c16gᶠ c20s* c20d⁴ c19v* c17d* c20s c16gᶠ c20m⁵ Apr 27] rather leggy **h–**
gelding: useful hurdler/chaser: raced only over fences in 2006/7, winning 2-finisher
events at Plumpton (maiden) in November and Taunton (novice handicap) in January, and
handicap at Ascot (beat Gentleman Jimmy by 3½ lengths) in February: stays 2½m: acts
on heavy and good to firm going: tried in cheekpieces: sometimes let down by jumping.
D. E. Pipe

MARC OF BRILLIANCE (USA) 4 ch.g. Sunday Silence (USA) – Rahcak (IRE) **h108**
(Generous (IRE)) [2006/7 16f* 16g² 16d⁴ 16v³ 16v³ 16g³ Mar 26] useful-looking
gelding: fair maiden (stays 1¼m) at 2 yrs, sold out of Saeed bin Suroor's stable 5,000 gns
Newmarket July (2006) Sales: fair juvenile hurdler: won at Plumpton in September: raced
at 2m: probably acts on any going: temperament under suspicion. *G. L. Moore*

MARCUS 6 gr.g. Silver Patriarch (IRE) – Loving Around (IRE) (Furry Glen) [2006/7 **h128 p**
F–p: 22d 22d 22d* Feb 1] well-made gelding: 50/1, much improved over hurdles (caught
eye first 2 starts) when winning novice at Wincanton in February by 6 lengths from
Trigger The Light: will stay 3m: raced on good to soft ground: open to further
improvement. *Miss E. C. Lavelle*

MARCUS DU BERLAIS (FR) 10 gr.g. Saint Preuil (FR) – Rosacotte (FR) (Rose **c104**
Laurel) [2006/7 c125, h–: c24v⁶ 20v⁴ c24d c24s⁵ c31d c29m Apr 9] good-topped gelding: **h109**
useful chaser/fairly useful hurdler at best, on downgrade: should stay beyond 29f: acts on
heavy going: tried in cheekpieces. *A. L. T. Moore, Ireland*

MARDEREIL (IRE) 10 ch.m. Moscow Society (USA) – Slap of The Stick (Weavers' **c–**
Hall) [2006/7 h–: c19m 20m⁴ 22m⁴ 20m⁶ 16mᵖᵘ 27d⁴ Aug 21] winning pointer: well held **h64**
on chase debut (for Miss S. Hayward): little form over hurdles. *N. J. Hawke*

MARDI ROBERTA (IRE) 5 b.m. Bob Back (USA) – Native Shore (IRE) (Be My Native (USA)) [2006/7 F93: F14g* F14s⁴ F14s⁴ 18g⁶ Apr 10] angular mare: fair form in mares bumpers: won at Fontwell in November: effort best ignored in mares novice on hurdling debut, bad mistake fourth and hampered 3 out (bled): sure to do better. *B. G. Powell*   **h– p**
F93

MARDONICDECLARE 6 b.g. Perpendicular – Daisy Girl (Main Reef) [2006/7 h–: 20fᶠ Jun 3] no promise over hurdles. *S. Lycett*   **h–**

MAREE HALL (IRE) 6 b.g. Saddlers' Hall (IRE) – My Sunny South (Strong Gale) [2006/7 20s⁵ 20s² 20v⁶ 16s⁵ 20d Feb 3] €8,000 3-y-o: sturdy ex-Irish gelding: half-brother to several winners over jumps, including fair hurdler/fairly useful chaser Cape Stormer (by Be My Native), stays 3m: dam maiden out of half-sister to dam of Jodami: won maiden point in 2005: modest novice hurdler, left W. Burke before penultimate outing: likely to stay beyond 2½m: acts on soft ground. *J. A. Geake*   **h97**

MARENAGHAN (IRE) 6 b.m. Needle Gun (IRE) – Ask Mama (Mummy's Pet) [2006/7 F17d Jun 14] €4,200 3-y-o: half-sister to several winners, including 2m chaser Music Please (by Music Boy): dam, 1¼m winner, half-sister to dam of very smart 2m chaser Young Snugfit: soundly beaten in bumper on debut. *Ian Williams*   **F–**

MAREOFLOT (IRE) 8 b. or br.m. Moscow Society (USA) – Mrs Pegasus (Bustomi) [2006/7 c17d³ c20m* c22m* c20m³ 24mᵘʳ c20d c22g c24g³ c25g² Oct 15] once-raced over hurdles: fair handicap chaser: successful at Punchestown and Cork in June: stays 25f: acts on good to firm ground: in cheekpieces last 2 starts. *Eric McNamara, Ireland*   **c101**
h–

MARFINCA (IRE) 6 b.g. Marju (IRE) – Hamsaat (IRE) (Sadler's Wells (USA)) [2006/7 c17s⁴ c16m⁵ c20f³ c16d² 16d⁴ 16g⁴ c16g⁴ c17g³ c16g* c16vᶠ c16g⁶ c17gᶠ Apr 21] sturdy gelding: fairly useful on Flat (stays 1¼m), successful in July: modest maiden hurdler: fair chaser: won maiden at Thurles in November: sold out of S. Treacy's stable 23,000 gns Doncaster Sales later in month, possibly amiss completed start in Britain: best at 2m: probably acts on any going: usually blinkered/tongue tied. *O. Sherwood*   **c101**
h98

MARFLEET 7 b.g. Prince Daniel (USA) – Gay Broad (Gay Fandango (USA)) [2006/7 F16s 16s⁵ 16fᵖᵘ 20f⁴ Jul 16] half-brother to 1989 12-y-o 6f winner Indian Chief (by Indian King) and winners in France and Hong Kong: dam 7f winner: no promise in bumper/novice hurdles. *R. Johnson*   **h–**
F–

MARGAM ABBEY (IRE) 5 gr.g. Silver Patriarch (IRE) – Coolvawn Lady (IRE) (Lancastrian) [2006/7 F17s Oct 22] good-topped gelding: second foal: dam modest staying chaser: always behind in bumper on debut. *D. Brace*   **F–**

MARGHUB (IRE) 8 b.g. Darshaan – Arctique Royale (Royal And Regal (USA)) [2006/7 h82: 16s⁴ 16d⁵ Nov 16] poor maiden over hurdles. *Miss C. Dyson*   **h82**

MARHABA MILLION (IRE) 5 gr.g. Modelliste (Machiavellian (USA)) [2006/7 h120: 20s⁶ 19s³ 19v² 20v³ 20g Apr 12] close-coupled gelding: fairly useful hurdler: mostly creditable efforts in 2006/7, though found little when ninth of 20 finishers to Two Miles West in listed handicap at Aintree: may prove best short of 2½m: acts on heavy going: tried in cheekpieces. *Eric McNamara, Ireland*   **h119**

MARIA BONITA (IRE) 6 b.m. Octagonal (NZ) – Nightitude (Night Shift (USA)) [2006/7 h66: 19v 16s⁵ 21g³ Mar 14] bad maiden hurdler: stays 2½m: acts on heavy and good to firm going. *C. N. Kellett*   **h52**

MARIAH ROLLINS (IRE) 9 b. or br.m. Over The River (FR) – Clonloo Lady (IRE) (Nearly A Nose (USA)) [2006/7 c137x, h–: c17s² c21v⁵ c21g³ Mar 15] lengthy mare: useful chaser, sold out of P. Fahy's stable 140,000 gns Doncaster August Sales before return: back to best when 5¼ lengths third of 23 to Idole First in Racing Post Plate (Handicap) at Cheltenham: stays 3m: unraced on firm going, acts on any other: often let down by jumping. *N. J. Henderson*   **c137 x**
h–

MARIAS DREAM (IRE) 5 b. or br.m. Desert Sun – Clifton Lass (IRE) (Up And At 'em) [2006/7 16d⁵ 16gᵖᵘ May 30] third foal: dam unraced: fair on Flat (stays 9f) in 2005 for E. Tyrrell: little form over hurdles. *John A. Quinn, Ireland*   **h78**

MARIDAY 6 br.g. Trifolio – Classic Hand (Some Hand) [2006/7 h84: c18mᶠ 20m c23f 16m² 19m⁵ 16m⁶ Apr 24] compact gelding: poor maiden hurdler: had several trainers in 2006/7, claimed £6,000 fourth outing, only one for Jim Best: no form over fences: form only around 2m: acts on good to firm going: tried blinkered/visored: signs of temperament. *D. E. Pipe*   **c– x**
h84

MARIGOLDS WAY 5 b.m. Nomadic Way (USA) – Miss Marigold (Norwick (USA)) [2006/7 F83: F16d⁵ F16s⁶ F17g⁵ 17g³ 18m⁵ Apr 26] lengthy mare: modest form in bumpers: better effort in mares maiden hurdles when third to High Life at Newton Abbot: should be suited by further than 17f. *R. J. Hodges*   **h84**
F83

MARINE GUNNER 6 b.g. Gunner B – Marina Bird (Julio Mariner) [2006/7 F17g F–
F17g F16m Apr 15] brother to bumper winner Bay Caster and half-brother to 3 winners,
including 19f hurdle winner Pearly Bay (by Karinga Bay): dam unraced: little impact in
bumpers: sold 800 gns Doncaster May Sales. *M. G. Rimell*

MARINE LIFE 5 b.g. Unfuwain (USA) – Aquamarine (Shardari) [2006/7 F101: 16m³ h107
16d* 16d^pu 16g^pu Mar 28] quite good-topped gelding: form (fair) over hurdles only when
winning maiden at Catterick in December: generally shaped as if amiss otherwise: raced
around 2m: visored last 3 starts, also tongue tied final one. *P. R. Webber*

MARINGO (FR) 7 b.g. Kadalko (FR) – Tacoma II (FR) (Quart de Vin (FR)) [2006/7 c–
23v 24s c25s⁶ c22v Feb 22] very big, workmanlike gelding: half-brother to several h–
winners in France, including fairly useful 2¼m chase winner Jaboun (by Silver Rainbow): dam unraced: won maiden on last of 3 starts in points in 2005: no form over
hurdles/in chases: tried blinkered: sold 3,600 gns Doncaster March Sales. *D. McCain Jnr*

MARINO GALE 6 ch.m. Commanche Run – Strong Attraction (Strong Gale) [2006/7 h–
20s 22s^pu 20v^pu Feb 13] 4,000 2-y-o: sturdy mare: fifth foal: dam, poor novice hurdler,
half-sister to fair chaser up to 21f Calon Lan: unseated in mares maiden Irish point: no
show in maiden hurdles: joined V. Dartnall. *L. A. Dace*

MARJINA 8 b.m. Classic Cliche (IRE) – Cavina (Ardross) [2006/7 h112: c20s³ c25s² c112
Jan 2] big, useful-looking mare: fair hurdler: off over a year, better effort over fences h–
(considerably handled on debut) when second to Maletton in maiden at Folkestone: stays
25f: raced on good going or softer. *Miss E. C. Lavelle*

MARKANDA (IRE) 7 b.g. Marju (IRE) – Shakanda (IRE) (Shernazar) [2006/7 20s c–
18v 20s^pu c16d c18d^pu c16g^pu Apr 20] maiden hurdler/chaser, no show in 2006/7: tried in h–
cheekpieces/tongue tied. *A. L. T. Moore, Ireland*

MARKED MAN (IRE) 11 b.g. Grand Plaisir (IRE) – Teazle (Quayside) [2006/7 c111 x
c130x, h–: c16s⁶ c16g⁵ c20s⁶ c24s c19s^bd c21g⁵ c23d⁵ Mar 26] good-topped gelding: fair h–
handicap chaser nowadays: stays 21f: acts on soft and good to firm going: often let down
by jumping. *R. Lee*

MARKET BANTER (IRE) 8 gr.g. Flemensfirth (USA) – Red City Rose (IRE) (Ros- c–
elier (FR)) [2006/7 20m^pu c20g^pu Jul 9] failed to complete in various events. *M. J. Gingell* h–

MARKINGTON 4 b.g. Medicean – Nemesia (Mill Reef (USA)) [2006/7 16g³ 18s³ h106
16g* 16v³ 16d 17m⁵ 20s⁵ Apr 26] close-coupled, good-bodied gelding: half-brother to 2
winning hurdlers by Mystiko, including Nemisto, stayed 2¾m: fairly useful on Flat (stays
11f), successful in July, sold out of J. Bethell's stable 25,000 gns Doncaster October
Sales: fair juvenile hurdler: won at Catterick in February: should stay 2½m: acts on heavy
going: wore cheekpieces after debut. *P. Bowen*

MARK THE BOOK (IRE) 6 b.g. Mister Lord (USA) – Boardroom Belle (IRE) h125 +
(Executive Perk) [2006/7 19s² 22v* 24v* 24g³ Mar 23] big, rangy gelding: will make a
chaser: fourth foal: half-brother to winning pointer by Fourstars Allstar: dam, once-raced,
out of half-sister to useful staying chaser On The Twist: won maiden Irish point in 2006:
fairly useful form in novice hurdles: won at Exeter (maiden) in February and Chepstow
(beat Leading Authority by 11 lengths) in March: possibly not recovered from those
exertions when well held at Newbury: stays 3m: acts on heavy going: may still do better.
P. J. Hobbs

MARLEYBOW (IRE) 4 br.g. Presenting – Gaye Artiste (IRE) (Commanche Run) F112
[2006/7 F16g* Apr 7] unfurnished gelding: second foal: dam unraced, out of half-sister
to top-class 2m to 3m hurdler Gaye Brief and very smart staying jumper Gaye Chance:
created good impression when winning 16-runner bumper at Haydock on debut by 5
lengths from Tropical Strait: will stay at least 2½m. *J. Howard Johnson*

MARLION (FR) 5 gr.g. Linamix (FR) – Marzipan (IRE) (Green Desert (USA)) h–
[2006/7 F68: 16s 16d Oct 30] lengthy, unfurnished gelding: poor form in bumper on
debut: no aptitude for hurdling: last on completed outings in points. *B. R. Johnson*

MARLOWE (IRE) 5 b.h. Sadler's Wells (USA) – Minnie Habit (Habitat) [2006/7 F68: F71
F16g² Jul 5] poor form in bumpers. *R. J. Hodges*

MARODIMA (FR) 4 b.g. Robin Des Pres (FR) – Balbeyssac (FR) (Beyssac (FR)) h120
[2006/7 16s² 16d* 16d³ 16s³ 20v⁴ 16d² 16v* 18v⁵ Mar 3] leggy gelding: first foal: dam
ran twice: fairly useful juvenile hurdler, left P. Journiac in France prior to return: landed
odds at Chepstow (easily) in November and Towcester (novice) in February: best at 2m:
raced on ground softer than good (acts on heavy): free-going sort (has gone early to post):
sold 145,000 gns Doncaster May Sales. *O. Sherwood*

MARQUE DEPOSEE (FR) 7 br.m. Cadoudal (FR) – Unextase (FR) (Quart de Vin (FR)) [2006/7 c–, h–: 16g 26s^F 22v^pu 17m 16m^pu Apr 24] of no account: tried tongue tied. *S. Lycett* **c– h–**

MARREL 9 b.g. Shareef Dancer (USA) – Upper Caen (High Top) [2006/7 h114: 21f^5 16g^6 c21s^2 20m^2 c21m* Jul 16] good-topped gelding: fair handicap hurdler: second start over fences, won novice at Stratford in July: stays 2¾m: acts on firm and good to soft going, probably on soft: usually visored. *D. Burchell* **c100 h114**

MARRONNIER (IRE) 4 ch.g. Vettori (IRE) – Reservation (IRE) (Common Grounds) [2006/7 17m^F 17d^5 18g^3 16d^3 19d 19s^2 22g Apr 7] fair maiden at best on Flat, well held in 2006, sold out of T. Easterby's stable 4,500 gns Doncaster May Sales: modest juvenile hurdler: stays 19f: acts on soft going: tried in cheekpieces. *N. J. Hawke* **h91**

MARSAM (IRE) 4 gr.g. Daylami (IRE) – Dancing Prize (IRE) (Sadler's Wells (USA)) [2006/7 16v^3 16v^F 16v^5 16v^5 16g^ur Apr 12] useful on Flat (stays 1¼m): fair juvenile hurdler, landed odds on debut: very stiff task final outing: raced at 2m, mainly on heavy ground. *John Joseph Murphy, Ireland* **h99**

MARSHALL HALL (IRE) 6 b.g. Saddlers' Hall (IRE) – Nocturnal Pleasure (IRE) (Supreme Leader) [2006/7 18m c24v^5 c20s^3 c24g^5 c20v^2 c16v* c16v* c16v* c16g^2 c16m Apr 14] €56,000 3-y-o: lengthy, useful-looking ex-Irish gelding: first foal: dam unraced half-sister to useful 2½m chaser Gnome's Tycoon: maiden hurdler: left A. Moore after first outing: progressed extremely well in handicap chases after, winning easily at Catterick in February and Ayr (2, novice first occasion, beat Brave Thought by 14 lengths on second) in March: best effort (useful form) when running-on 1½ lengths second to Bambi de L'Orme in Grade 3 event at Aintree penultimate start: best at 2m: acts on heavy going. *Ferdy Murphy* **c134 h–**

MARSH COURT 4 b.f. Overbury (IRE) – Lady Prunella (IRE) (Supreme Leader) [2006/7 F16m^2 F16s^4 F16g^3 Apr 9] third foal: half-sister to 2m chase winner Bollitree Bob (by Bob's Return): dam once-raced half-sister to useful staying chaser Latent Talent: modest form in frame in bumpers. *M. Scudamore* **F79**

MARSH FIRE 4 b.f. Overbury (IRE) – Sea Ice (Roscoe Blake) [2006/7 F12v F16m Apr 25] small filly: second foal: dam, poor form in bumpers, out of half-sister to Triumph Hurdle winner Saxon Farm: last in bumpers. *M. Scudamore* **F–**

MARSH RUN 8 b.m. Presenting – Madam Margeaux (IRE) (Ardross) [2006/7 c87+, h107: c20g^2 c20s^F c20s^ur c20d^3 16v 20s Jan 31] angular mare: fair handicap hurdler, well held last 2 starts: easily best effort over fences when second in handicap at Wetherby: stays 2½m: acts on soft ground (bumper winner on good to firm): tried blinkered. *M. W. Easterby* **c107 d h–**

MARS ROCK (FR) 7 b.g. Video Rock (FR) – Venus de Mirande (FR) (Carmont (FR)) [2006/7 h104p, F95: 21d 20d^pu Dec 6] rather leggy gelding: fair hurdler, probably amiss final outing: should stay beyond 2½m: raced on good to soft/soft going: has raced freely. *Miss Venetia Williams* **h93**

MARTHA'S KINSMAN (IRE) 8 b.g. Petoski – Martha's Daughter (Majestic Maharaj) [2006/7 c119p, h112: c24s^4 c24d c23d^3 c24m* c30g* c25g^5 Apr 18] sturdy gelding: winning hurdler: fairly useful handicap chaser: won at Ludlow (amateur) in January and Ascot (beat Garryvoe a length) in March: good 4½ lengths fifth to Alexanderthegreat at Cheltenham: stays 3¾m: acts on soft and good to firm going. *H. D. Daly* **c128 h–**

MARTIN OSSIE 10 b.g. Bonny Scot (IRE) – So We Know (Daring March) [2006/7 c96, h–: c24v^ur Feb 23] tall gelding: prolific winning pointer: modest chaser, often let down by jumping: stays 3m: tried in cheekpieces. *R. T. Baimbridge* **c– h–**

MARTON JUBILEE 5 gr.m. Paris House – Peep O Day (Domynsky) [2006/7 F–: 19g^ur Feb 2] no show in bumpers/novice hurdle: tried in cheekpieces. *A. D. Brown* **h–**

MARUFO (IRE) 5 b.g. Presenting – Bucks Cregg (IRE) (Buckskin (FR)) [2006/7 21s^F 20v^6 Jan 20] strong, short-backed gelding: fourth foal: dam, lightly raced in points, half-sister to useful 2m to 3m chaser Woodville Star: signs of ability over hurdles, smooth headway when fell 4 out in maiden at Warwick on debut: likely to do better. *Heather Dalton* **h– p**

MARVELLOUS DREAM (FR) 5 ch.m. Muhtathir – Abstraite (Groom Dancer (USA)) [2006/7 F16s^4 19s^4 21d^2 20v^5 24d^pu Mar 22] half-sister to fairly useful hurdler/chaser Nas Na Riogh (by King's Theatre), stayed 23f, and French hurdle winner up to 19f Bombardier Noir (by Turtle Island): dam 1¼m winner: fourth in mares bumper: modest form in novice hurdles, lame final start: should stay beyond 21f. *N. J. Henderson* **h92 F86**

MARY BUCK 5 b.m. Keen – Sharplaw (Mandalus) [2006/7 F16s^{pu} Mar 7] second foal: **F– §**
dam winning pointer: temperamental display in bumper on debut. *Cooper Wilson*

MARY CASEY 6 br.m. Accordion – Kosheen (IRE) (Supreme Leader) [2006/7 F–: **h74**
22d^3 24d^{ur} 20s^4 20m 20dp^u 25d^{pu} 16v^5 Jan 3] close-coupled, sparely-made mare: poor
novice hurdler: should stay 3m: tried in cheekpieces: sold 1,400 gns Doncaster January
Sales. *C. A. Mulhall*

MARY GRAY 5 gr.m. Mujahid (USA) – Ancestry (Persepolis (FR)) [2006/7 16d Oct 1] **h–**
half-sister to winning 2m hurdler/chaser Devilry (by Faustus): modest on Flat (stays
1¾m), sold out of M. Johnston's stable 15,000 gns Newmarket July Sales: well held in
novice on hurdling debut. *C. N. Kellett*

MARY MACS LAD (IRE) 8 b.g. Cois Na Tine (IRE) – Embustera (Sparkler) [2006/7 **c–**
c90, h83: 22d 20f^4 Jul 16] poor maiden handicap hurdler: runner-up in maiden on chasing **h83**
debut: stays 3¼m: acts on heavy ground: tried in cheekpieces, usually blinkered nowadays. *J. G. Carr, Ireland*

MARY PAT (IRE) 5 ch.m. Anshan – Cappuccino Girl (Broadsword (USA)) [2006/7 **F86**
F16d^2 Feb 14] €3,100 3-y-o: fourth foal: dam modest staying hurdler: won maiden point
in 2006: amateur ridden, 4 lengths second to Grangeclare Flight in mares bumper at
Musselburgh. *Bernard Jones, Ireland*

MARYSCROSS (IRE) 7 b.m. Presenting – Willowmere (IRE) (King's Ride) [2006/7 **h96**
h87p, F87: 23g^3 23m* 23d^2 May 21] big mare: winning pointer: modest form over
hurdles: easy task in novice at Fakenham in May: should stay 3¼m. *O. Brennan*

MARYS MOMENT 7 ch.m. Southern Music – Arley Gale (Scallywag) [2006/7 h–, **h–**
F–: 16m 16m 19gp^u Jul 23] tall, lengthy, angular mare: no sign of ability. *P. A. Pritchard*

MARZIBITS 10 b.m. Alflora (IRE) – Trigony Hill VII (Damsire Unregistered) [2006/7 **c–**
17mp^u 17fp^u 17mp^u c16sp^u Nov 6] no sign of ability (ran out in point on debut): tried **h–**
tongue tied. *M. A. Barnes*

MASAFI (IRE) 6 b.g. Desert King (IRE) – Mrs Fisher (IRE) (Salmon Leap (USA)) **h109**
[2006/7 h114: 16m 16g^6 16d 20f Apr 28] sturdy, well-made gelding: fair hurdler:
creditable effort in handicaps in 2006/7 only on second start: should stay beyond 2m: acts
on good to firm going: tongue tied last 2 starts: sketchy jumper. *J. Howard Johnson*

MASRA 4 b.g. Silver Patriarch (IRE) – Go Sally Go (IRE) (Elbio) [2006/7 F17d^2 F16s^2 **F95**
F16g^2 Apr 23] second foal: dam poor maiden: fairly useful form when runner-up in
bumpers, not looking keen under pressure. *G. A. Swinbank*

MASSASOIT (IRE) 5 br.g. Supreme Leader – Lady Margaretta (Rolfe (USA)) **F101 +**
[2006/7 F16v* F16v* Mar 22] good-topped gelding: first foal: dam, 2½m hurdle winner,
sister to high-class hurdler up to 3m Lady Rebecca: fairly useful form when successful
both starts in bumpers, at Catterick in February and Ayr (landed odds easily by 8 lengths
from Salveo) in March: will stay at least 2½m: sold £105,000 Cheltenham April Sales.
J. M. Jefferson

MASSIF CENTRALE 6 ch.g. Selkirk (USA) – Madame Dubois (Legend of France **h–**
(USA)) [2006/7 h94+: 16m Jun 18] useful at best on Flat: dam, 2½m hurdle winner,
tongue tied, well held completed outing in novice hurdles. *D. R. C. Elsworth*

MASSIMO (FR) 7 b.g. Gunboat Diplomacy (FR) – Gitane de L'Allier (FR) (Altayan) **h100**
[2006/7 19d^2 24d^2 Oct 5] well-made gelding: bumper winner for M. Pipe: fair form over
hurdles when runner-up in novice at Worcester final start: stays 3m. *B. J. M. Ryall*

MASSINI'S MAGUIRE (IRE) 6 b.g. Dr Massini (IRE) – Molly Maguire (IRE) **h147**
(Supreme Leader) [2006/7 h131, F100: 16g^8 20s^2 21d^4 24s^{ur} 21d^5 20v^3 21g* 24g^4
Apr 13]
    For the first time since the mare Gaelstrom triumphed in 1993, when it was
run under the Royal & SunAlliance banner, the Baring Bingham Novices' Hurdle,
as it is now registered, at Cheltenham in March was won by a second-season
novice, namely Massini's Maguire. That Gaelstrom should achieve so much in her
second season could hardly have been imagined given her performances in her
first—she made no fewer than seven appearances, one of those in a bumper, and
showed just modest form at best. Massini's Maguire, on the other hand, demonstrated early on that he was of well-above average ability. Successful in May 2005
on the second of his two outings in bumpers at Limerick, Massini's Maguire was
sold out of Mags Mullins' stable for 200,000 guineas (not 100,000 as recorded in
last year's Annual) at the Doncaster Sales later that month. He then showed useful

Gideon Kasler Novices' Hurdle, Cheltenham—a third success of the afternoon for Messrs Hobbs and Johnson as Massini's Maguire claims the notable scalp of Wichita Lineman (white face)

form when placed in novice hurdles on his first two starts for his new connections, finishing runner-up to Rimsky in the Grade 2 Persian War at Chepstow (below-par second to Kanpai in same race this October) and third to Black Jack Ketchum at Cheltenham. A bone growth above a knee resulted in Massini's Maguire having just one more outing that season, but he quickly made up for lost time on his return, landing the odds in a novice at Chepstow in October despite being unsuited by the drop to two miles.

Raced only over two and a half miles or more since Chepstow, Massini's Maguire put up his best performances before the Festival when contesting novice hurdles at Cheltenham in November and January. On the former occasion he won the Gideon Kasler Novices' Hurdle by half a length from Wichita Lineman, from whom he was receiving 3 lb, taking over at the sixth and keeping on willingly; on the latter he met Wichita Lineman at level weights and finished ten lengths behind him in third in the Classic Novices' Hurdle, the pair split by Tidal Bay. Massini's Maguire's limitations seemed to have been exposed, and as a consequence he was a 20/1-shot for the Ballymore Properties-sponsored Baring Bingham in March, a race

Ballymore Properties Novices' Hurdle (Baring Bingham), Cheltenham—
a second success at the course for 20/1-shot Massini's Maguire,
who is pressed two out by placed horses Tidal Bay (chevrons) and Catch Me (No.3)

Mr Alan Peterson's "Massini's Maguire"

not so strongly contested as it might have been with both Wichita Lineman and Flight Leader switched to the longer Spa Hurdle. Massini's Maguire still faced stiff opposition, though. Tidal Bay was one of his fourteen rivals, and others included Irish challenger Aran Concerto, successful in Grade 1 events on his two previous starts and favourite at 5/2, and Tolworth Hurdle winner Silverburn, second favourite at 7/2. With no-one else keen to make it, Richard Johnson was able to dictate the pace on Massini's Maguire, the majority of the field still bunched three out as a result. They had sorted themselves by the next, though, where Massini's Maguire lost the lead briefly to Catch Me, the pair pressed by Tidal Bay as Aran Concerto dropped away after stumbling. Soon back in front, Massini's Maguire edged right under pressure from the last but continued to find plenty and held on to win by a neck from Tidal Bay, with Catch Me a further length and a half back in third. Ironically, his performance was very reminiscent of the front-running Gaelstrom, who'd also rallied tenaciously when headed before the home turn at Cheltenham and lowered the colours of a better-fancied rival who'd beaten her earlier in 1992/3 (hot favourite Lord Relic had to settle for third). Gaelstrom narrowly failed to follow up in the three-mile Sefton Novices' at Aintree (when touched off by Cheltenham runner-up Cardinal Red), and Massini's Maguire also failed to complete that double in the latest season. The return to three miles at Aintree—he'd blundered and unseated his rider at the eighth at Cheltenham on his only previous attempt at the trip—seemed sure to suit Massini's Maguire, but this time he set an overly-strong pace (taken on by old rival Wichita Lineman a long way out) and had nothing left when headed three out, making a mistake at the next then hanging badly right. At the line he was a remote fourth behind Chief Dan George and out on his feet. Massini's Maguire will show his effectiveness at the trip in time, more than likely over fences which is where his future would appear to lie. Still not the most fluent jumper of hurdles, it's to be hoped the rather leggy, useful-looking Massini's Maguire proves more proficient as a chaser.

Massini's Maguire (IRE) (b.g. 2001)	Dr Massini (IRE) (b 1993)	Sadler's Wells (b 1981)	Northern Dancer Fairy Bridge
		Argon Laser (b 1983)	Bold Reason Special
	Molly Maguire (IRE) (b 1994)	Supreme Leader (b 1982)	Bustino Princess Zena
		Bright Note (b 1983)	Buckskin Holy Hills

A full-brother to the fair Irish hurdler Molly Massini, a winner over two and a half miles for Gerard Quirk, Massini's Maguire is the second foal of the unraced Molly Maguire and was bred by the aforementioned Quirk. Massini's Maguire's grandam Bright Note won four races over hurdles in Ireland for Quirk, showing fairly useful form at up to three miles, and has produced just one winner to date, Mrs Battle (also trained by Quirk) who was a fair winner at up to three miles over hurdles in that country. Molly Maguire, who is a non-thoroughbred, has produced two more foals since Massini's Maguire, a 2004 filly by Dr Massini (again) and a 2006 Imperial Ballet colt. Massini's Maguire has raced only on good ground or softer so far, and he probably acts on heavy. *P. J. Hobbs*

MASSINI SUNSET (IRE) 7 b.g. Dr Massini (IRE) – Burgundy Sunset (IRE)   h–
(Buckskin (FR)) [2006/7 19d^{pu} 19d⁵ 21d 20s⁵ 22s^{pu} 19s⁵ Feb 8] sturdy gelding: first foal: dam, ran once, out of sister to top-class 2m/2½m chaser Waterloo Boy: in frame in maiden Irish points in 2006: little form over hurdles. *N. R. Mitchell*

MASSIVE WAY (GR) 7 ch.h. Lai Lai (GR) – Alkmini (GR) (Guy Butters (GR))   h–
[2006/7 17d^{pu} 16g⁶ Apr 23] successful 6 times from 6f to 15f on Flat in Greece: little impact in maiden hurdles. *P. R. Chamings*

MASTER ALBERT (IRE) 9 b.g. Supreme Leader – Mullaun (Deep Run) [2006/7   c106
c20d³ c16s³ c20s⁶ c18s⁵ 20d 16v⁶ 16s Mar 3] well-made gelding: fairly useful hurdler   h–
at best, left D. Wachman before return: fair form over fences, generally let down by jumping/attitude: stays 2½m: raced on good ground or softer (acts on soft): tried blinkered (downed tools). *Jonjo O'Neill*

MASTER BELL 5 b.g. Bandmaster (USA) – Parklands Belle (Stanford) [2006/7 F17g³   h79
F17g⁶ F16v 17s 16d⁷ 20g Apr 11] strong gelding: half-brother to modest 2m hurdler Taw   F77
Park (by Inca Chief) and 6f winner Arab Gold (by Presidium): dam 1m winner: has shown a little ability in bumpers/over hurdles. *R. J. Hodges*

MASTER BILLYBOY (IRE) 9 b.g. Old Vic – Clonodfoy (Strong Gale) [2006/7   c– x
c100x, h–: c26g^{pu} Apr 19] leggy gelding: fair hurdler at best: left Mrs S. Williams, won   h–
point in March, but generally not fluent and little impact in chases: should be suited by 3m+: acts on soft and good to firm going, probably on heavy. *Mrs Sarah Faulks*

MASTER BREW 9 b.g. Homo Sapien – Edithmead (IRE) (Shardari) [2006/7 c–, h–:   c– §
22s^{ro} 24v^{pu} c24d c25g⁴ c20s⁴ c21s⁵ c20v^{pu} c22s c25v^{pu} Feb 28] angular gelding: of little   h– §
account: often in headgear: ungenuine. *Miss A. M. Newton-Smith*

MASTER BURY (FR) 6 gr.g. Overbury (IRE) – Kerry To Clare (Step Together (USA))   h–
[2006/7 F–: F17s F14v⁵ F16g⁶ 16v 16v⁶ 20g⁵ Mar 27] long-backed gelding: no solid form   F–
in bumpers/over hurdles. *Miss T. Jackson*

MASTER CLUB ROYAL 12 b.g. Teenoso (USA) – Miss Club Royal (Avocat)   c88
[2006/7 c24g⁴ c30m^F c24g^{pu} Apr 8] lengthy gelding: winning pointer: maiden chaser,   h–
clear when fell last in hunter at Huntingdon: stays 3¾m: acts on heavy and good to firm going: has worn visor, usually blinkered: tongue tied in 2006/7. *Mrs K. Baimbridge*

MASTER DARCY 5 b. or gr.g. Cloudings (IRE) – Swift Conveyance (IRE) (Strong   F81
Gale) [2006/7 F14s⁵ F16s Mar 3] 20,000 4-y-o: useful-looking gelding: has scope: sixth foal: half-brother to bumper winner Diamond Harry (by Sir Harry Lewis): dam, 2m hurdler, out of half-sister to dam of high-class staying chaser Drumlargan: better effort in bumpers when fifth in maiden at Fontwell, veering left final 1f. *Mrs L. J. Mongan*

MASTER D'OR (FR) 7 b.g. Cyborg (FR) – Une Pomme d'Or (FR) (Pot d'Or (FR))   c102
[2006/7 c106, h88+: c16s⁵ c16d⁴ c19v² c18s c20v³ Jan 7] leggy gelding: winning hurdler: h–
fair handicap chaser: stays 2¾m: raced on going softer than good (acts on heavy): held up: not a fluent jumper. *B. J. Llewellyn*

MASTER EDDY 7 b.g. Alflora (IRE) – Mistress Star (Soldier Rose) [2006/7 F88: 20v **h119** 20d² 20v 22s² 24g² 24s* 24g* Mar 23] tall, workmanlike gelding: will make a chaser: fairly useful novice hurdler: won twice at Newbury in March, beat Double Dizzy by 6 lengths on second occasion: will probably be suited by further than 3m: acts on soft going, runner-up in bumper on heavy: races prominently. *S. Lycett*

MASTER ELLIS (IRE) 8 b.g. Turtle Island (IRE) – Take No Chances (IRE) **h70** (Thatching) [2006/7 h–: 16v⁴ 20m Mar 29] workmanlike gelding: poor novice hurdler, lightly raced: probably stays 2½m: acts on good to firm and heavy going. *R. L. Brown*

MASTER HENRY (GER) 13 b.g. Mille Balles (FR) – Maribelle (GER) (Windwurf **c–** (GER)) [2006/7 c90, h–: c19g May 4] angular gelding: winning hurdler/chaser, well held **h–** in hunter early in 2006/7: raced mainly around 2m: acts on good to soft and good to firm going: usually free-going front runner (possibly needs to dominate). *Miss R. S. Reynolds*

MASTER JED (IRE) 10 br.g. Bob's Return (IRE) – Evan's Love (Master Owen) **c91** [2006/7 c16g³ c24s⁴ c22g⁵ Mar 28] workmanlike gelding: winning pointer: fair form in **h–** hunters: stays 2¾m. *Mrs Sarah Stafford*

MASTER JOCK 13 ch.g. Scottish Reel – Mistress Corrado (New Member) [2006/7 **c– x** c33g^pu May 3] workmanlike gelding: prolific winning pointer: little impact in hunters since 2003: tried tongue tied. *G. D. Hanmer*

MASTERJOE 5 b.g. Shambo – Littledrunkgirl (Carlingford Castle) [2006/7 F17v³ **F76 +** Mar 18] half-brother to winning pointers by Supreme Leader and Gildoran: dam, winning pointer, half-sister to dam of top-class 2m to 3m chaser One Man: green, well-held third to Harry Wood in bumper at Carlisle on debut. *Mrs K. Walton*

MASTER MAHOGANY 6 b.g. Bandmaster (USA) – Impropriety (Law Society **h122** (USA)) [2006/7 h106: 17d* 17s² 16s³ 16s⁴ 16s⁴ 16g² 17g^F Apr 1] angular gelding: fairly useful on Flat (stays 1¼m): fairly useful hurdler: won handicap at Exeter (by 6 lengths from Never So Blue) in December: in frame all 5 completed starts after, 3 lengths second of 17 to Tritonix in novice at Warwick penultimate outing: free-going sort, likely to prove best around 2m: acts on soft going: consistent. *R. J. Hodges*

MASTER NIMBUS 7 b.g. Cloudings (IRE) – Miss Charlie (Pharly (FR)) [2006/7 h92: **h98** 16g* 16m⁴ 16m^ur 16m⁴ 16m² Oct 1] leggy gelding: modest on Flat (stays 1¾m), successful in August: modest handicap hurdler: won ladies race at Wetherby in June: raced around 2m, needs good to firm going. *J. J. Quinn*

MASTER OF THE RACE 5 ch.g. Selkirk (USA) – Dust Dancer (Suave Dancer **h86** (USA)) [2006/7 16s 16g 16m³ Apr 8] good-topped gelding: fairly useful maiden up to 1¼m on Flat, sold out of Sir Michael Stoute's stable 24,000 gns Doncaster August Sales: easily best effort over hurdles (modest form) when third in maiden at Plumpton: likely to need sharp 2m. *Tom Dascombe*

MASTER OF THE WARD (IRE) 7 ch.g. King Persian – Sara Jane (IRE) (Brush **c–** Aside (USA)) [2006/7 h–: c21g c24g⁵ Jun 8] workmanlike gelding: well beaten over **h–** hurdles/in novice handicap chases: successful twice in points in 2007. *D. McCain Jnr*

MASTER OVERSEER (IRE) 4 b.g. Old Vic – Crogeen Lass (Strong Gale) [2006/7 **F115 p** F18v* Mar 7] €20,000 3-y-o, resold £56,000 3-y-o: well-made gelding: third foal: dam 21f chase winner: carrying condition, impressive debut when justifying favouritism in bumper at Fontwell by 23 lengths from Ouragan Lagrange: open to improvement, particularly granted similar test of stamina. *D. E. Pipe*

MASTER PAPA (IRE) 8 br.g. Key of Luck (USA) – Beguine (USA) (Green Dancer **c108** (USA)) [2006/7 c102, h–: c17g* c16s² c16m³ c20g³ c20s* c20d⁵ c20d⁶ c19g Feb 2] **h–** angular gelding: winning hurdler: fair handicap chaser: won at Bangor (novice) in May and Market Rasen in November: below best last 3 starts: effective at 2m to easy 3m: acts on good to firm and heavy going. *H. P. Hogarth*

MASTER REX 12 ch.g. Interrex (CAN) – Whose Lady (USA) (Master Willie) [2006/7 **c123** c128, h–: c17m² c16m⁵ Aug 2] lengthy gelding: winning hurdler: fairly useful handicap **h–** chaser: raced around 2m: unraced on heavy going, acts on any other: blinkered twice (raced freely): has refused to line up: sold 5,000 gns Doncaster August Sales. *B. De Haan*

MASTER SAM (IRE) 7 b.g. Supreme Leader – Basically (IRE) (Strong Gale) [2006/7 **h–** 20s^F 23v^pu 20g^pu Dec 20] strong, leggy gelding: third in bumper in 2004/5 for H. Daly: no show in novice hurdles: sold 1,200 gns Doncaster January Sales. *Ferdy Murphy*

MASTER SEBASTIAN 8 ch.g. Kasakov – Anchor Inn (Be My Guest (USA)) [2006/7 **c115** c111d, h–: c24s^pu c20d⁵ c21v⁶ c20s² c25s⁴ c20s⁴ c20v* c24s* c20s³ c32v⁶ c24s Apr 26] **h–** workmanlike gelding: fairly useful handicap chaser: won at Ayr and Newcastle (by 1½ lengths from Lampion du Bost) in January: stays 25f: acts on heavy going: genuine. *Miss Lucinda V. Russell*

MASTERS HOUSE (IRE) 4 b.g. Indian Lodge (IRE) – Aster Aweke (IRE) (Alzao (USA)) [2006/7 F14s Nov 29] 1,200 3-y-o: half-brother to fairly useful 2m hurdler Say What You See (by Charnwood Forest) and useful performer Another Bottle (by Cape Cross), stays 1¼m: dam 9f winner: well beaten in bumper on debut. *Mrs J. C. McGregor*   **F–**

MASTER SOMERVILLE 5 b.g. Alflora (IRE) – Lucy Glitters (Ardross) [2006/7 F94: 20g³ 20s 17s 21s Mar 2] smallish, workmanlike gelding: easily best effort over hurdles when third in novice at Haydock: will stay 3m. *H. D. Daly*   **h95**

MASTER TANNER 7 ch.g. Master Willie – Flaxen Tina (Beau Tudor) [2006/7 F–: 22spu Jan 10] lengthy gelding: no promise in bumpers/novice hurdle. *Miss C. Dyson*   **h–**

MASTER T (USA) 8 b.g. Trempolino (USA) – Our Little C (USA) (Marquetry (USA)) [2006/7 c103x, h–: c20g* c22f⁶ c20m c16d⁵ c20g* c20g⁴ c16g⁵ c20g⁵ Apr 10] neat gelding: fair handicap chaser: won at Plumpton in May and October: stays easy 2½m: acts on firm and soft going: tried in cheekpieces: often let down by jumping over fences. *G. L. Moore*   **c105 x** **h–**

MASTER WIZ 4 b.g. Wizard King – Mistress Corrado (New Member) [2006/7 F14s Dec 16] big, leggy gelding: half-brother to fair hunter chaser Master Jock (by Scottish Reel), stays 3m, and a winning pointer by Gunner B: dam maiden pointer: no promise in bumper on debut. *B. P. J. Baugh*   **F–**

MATCHO PIERJI (FR) 5 b.g. Cadoudal (FR) – La Brindille (FR) (Dom Pasquini (FR)) [2006/7 20v 16s² 17s c16g⁴ Feb 21] well-made gelding: second foal: brother to 17f chase winner Princesse Pierji: dam, 1½m winner, sister to smart French hurdler/chaser Saute Au Bois, stayed 23f: fair form over hurdles, left E. Leenders in France prior to return: similar form when fourth in handicap on chasing debut (not knocked about): likely to prove best around 2m for time being: acts on soft going: likely to do better over fences. *Jonjo O'Neill*   **c100 p** **h103**

MATERIALITY 5 ch.m. Karinga Bay – Material Girl (Busted) [2006/7 F17g F16s Nov 19] £42,000 3-y-o: sister to smart hurdler Material World, stays 3m: dam, fairly useful hunter chaser, stayed 2¾m: no show in bumpers. *Mrs K. Waldron*   **F–**

MATERIAL WORLD 9 b.m. Karinga Bay – Material Girl (Busted) [2006/7 h134: 24s* 23s³ 24g² Mar 15] sturdy mare: has only one eye (wears eyecover): smart hurdler: won handicap at Cheltenham (reportedly suffered overreach) in December: ran better still when ½-length second of 24 to Oscar Park in listed Pertemps Final (Handicap) at same   **h146**

Pertemps Handicap Hurdle (Qualifier), Cheltenham—
the one-eyed mare Material World shows her trademark battling qualities to overcome Freetown (stripes)

course: will stay beyond 25f: acts on soft and good to firm going: splendidly genuine and reliable. *Miss Suzy Smith*

MATINEE IDOL 4 ch.f. In The Wings – Bibliotheque (USA) (Woodman (USA)) [2006/7 17g 19d⁴ 17s Mar 11] small filly: closely-related to 2½m hurdle winner McQueen (by Barathea): maiden on Flat: poor form over hurdles: in cheekpieces last 2 starts. *Mrs S. Lamyman* **h75**

MATMATA DE TENDRON (FR) 7 gr.g. Badolato (USA) – Cora Des Tamarix (FR) (Iron Duke (FR)) [2006/7 c91, h91: c29s² c27d⁵ c27s* c25v² c24s⁵ c33v Feb 24] small, good-bodied gelding: maiden hurdler: modest handicap chaser: made all at Sedgefield in December: thorough stayer: acts on heavy going: in cheekpieces last 4 outings: tried tongue tied. *A. Crook* **c95 h–**

MATRIX (AUS) 10 b.g. Centaine (AUS) – Iced Lass (NZ) (Half Iced (USA)) [2006/7 c–, h–: c25g c26g⁵ c21g⁴ Apr 27] tall gelding: winning pointer: maiden hurdler/chaser: tried visored/tongue tied. *J. H. Berwick* **c– h–**

MATTHEW MUROTO (IRE) 8 b.g. Muroto – Glenmore Star (IRE) (Teofane) [2006/7 c110, h–: c21sᵘʳ c21v⁶ c23m⁴ c22s⁶ c18v² c19d⁶ c21s⁴ c21g c16f⁵ Apr 22] leggy, lengthy gelding: fair handicap chaser: in-and-out form in 2006/7: should stay 3m: acts on heavy and good to firm ground: tried blinkered/visored. *R. H. Alner* **c107 h–**

MATTHEW MY SON (IRE) 7 ch.g. Lake Coniston (IRE) – Mary Hinge (Dowsing (USA)) [2006/7 h–: 16mᵖᵘ May 6] little sign of ability. *F. P. Murtagh* **h–**

MATTIE STOKES 4 b.g. Largesse – Celtic H'Alo (Celtic Swing) [2006/7 F16g F16m Apr 24] first foal: dam 1m winner: little impact in bumpers. *John Berry* **F–**

MATTOCK RANGER (IRE) 7 b.g. Oscar (IRE) – Siberiansdaughter (IRE) (Strong Gale) [2006/7 h130, F102: c20s* c22v³ c24v⁴ c24vᵖᵘ c24v² c20mᵖᵘ Apr 8] strong, sturdy, good sort: bumper winner: useful form over hurdles: fairly useful chaser: won maiden at Punchestown (beat Knight Legend by 4 lengths) in October: creditable fourth to Cailin Alainn in Grade 1 novice at Leopardstown, but disappointing otherwise, shaping as if amiss more than once: stays 3m: acts on heavy going: usually races prominently. *N. Meade, Ireland* **c125 h–**

MATT THE THRASHER (IRE) 7 b.g. Courtship – Rose of Summer (IRE) (Taufan (USA)) [2006/7 20f 20m c16gᶠ c23d* c19g* c24d³ c21g³ c26g⁴ c25f* Apr 22] ex-Irish gelding: novice hurdler, sold out of F. Lacy's stable 7,000 gns Doncaster August Sales after second start: fair novice chaser: won maiden at Taunton in October and handicaps at Taunton again in November and Wincanton (3 ran) in April: stays easy 25f: acts on firm and good to soft going: tried blinkered, usually in cheekpieces. *Evan Williams* **c113 h–**

MAUNBY REVELLER 5 b.g. Benny The Dip (USA) – Aunt Tate (Tate Gallery (USA)) [2006/7 h80: 17fᵖᵘ Aug 11] close-coupled gelding: poor form in juvenile hurdles: tongue tied, took no interest only outing in 2006/7: in cheekpieces last 2 starts. *P. C. Haslam* **h–**

MAUNBY ROLLER (IRE) 8 b.g. Flying Spur (AUS) – Brown Foam (Horage) [2006/7 c–§, h–§: c21mᵖᵘ 16gᵖᵘ 19dᵖᵘ Dec 14] sturdy, good-topped gelding: winning hurdler, no form for long time, including over fences: usually in headgear: ungenuine. *K. A. Morgan* **c– § h– §**

MAURA'S LEGACY (IRE) 7 b.m. Zaffaran (IRE) – Sharp Fashion VII (Bustineto) [2006/7 h85, F84: 22d 25s⁶ 22s⁴ 22v³ 20s⁴ Feb 7] modest maiden hurdler: should stay at least 3m: raced on good going or softer (acts on heavy). *I. A. Duncan, Ireland* **h86**

MAURICE (FR) 7 ch.g. Video Rock (FR) – Beveland (FR) (Royal Charter (FR)) [2006/7 18s² c22s² 20d 20s 20v⁶ c20gᶠ c25g Apr 13] tall ex-French gelding: third foal: half-brother to winning jumpers up to 2¾m Ireland (by Kadalko) and Lettiland (by Ragmar): dam winning chaser around 2m: 1½m winner on Flat: maiden hurdler: left B. Secly, shaped as if amiss third to fifth starts: fairly useful chaser: tired after helping set good pace when eighth of 10 finishers to Reveillez in quite valuable handicap at Aintree final outing: stays 2¾m: raced on good ground or softer (acts on heavy): tongue tied last 3 outings. *D. McCain Jnr* **c128 h118**

MAXIMINUS 7 b.g. The West (USA) – Candarela (Damister (USA)) [2006/7 c–, h92: 22m⁵ c19g⁶ c21dᵖᵘ c20vᵖᵘ 22s c20d⁴ c26m⁶ Apr 26] tall, good-topped gelding: modest handicap hurdler, little show since 2005: no form over fences: stays 2¾m: acts on good to firm and good to soft going: tried visored: has hinted at temperament. *M. Madgwick* **c– x h–**

MAXIMIX 4 gr.g. Linamix (FR) – Time Will Show (FR) (Exit To Nowhere (USA)) [2006/7 16dᶠ 16d⁵ 16v⁵ Feb 12] fair on Flat (stays 1½m), successful in October, sold out **h92**

of B. Hills's stable 28,000 gns Newmarket Autumn Sales: modest form on first of 3 outings in juvenile hurdles, would have finished second but for falling last: nearly ran out after racing freely in clear lead final one: sold £8,400 Ascot February Sales. *G. L. Moore*

MAXIMIZE (IRE) 13 b.g. Mandalus – Lone Run (Kemal (FR)) [2006/7 c97§, h–§: c26g^{pu} c24d c29g^4 c23m Apr 22] strong gelding: maiden hurdler: fair pointer/hunter chaser nowadays: probably stays 33f: acts on any going: tried in cheekpieces/visor: usually sound jumper: temperamental. *D. M. Edwards* **c92 §** **h– §**

MAXIMOSS (IRE) 9 b.m. Glacial Storm (USA) – Gi Moss (Le Moss) [2006/7 21d^{pu} May 15] leggy mare: little show in bumpers/maiden hurdle. *J. A. Geake* **h–**

MAXIMUS (IRE) 12 br.g. Un Desperado (FR) – Fais Vite (USA) (Sharpen Up) [2006/7 c23m^2 Jul 12] hurdle/point winner: runner-up in handicap at Worcester on completed outing in chases, seemingly idling and headed close home: stays 23f: acts on soft and good to firm going: tried blinkered/tongue tied. *Mrs L. J. Young* **c86** **h–**

MAXIMUS MERIDUS 5 b.g. Mark of Esteem (IRE) – Lucie Edward (Puissance) [2006/7 F16d F14s^6 F16m Apr 15] rather leggy gelding: third foal: dam unraced sister to very smart 5f performer Mind Games: modest form in bumpers: tongue tied first 2 outings. *Mrs Norma Pook* **F78**

MAXXIUM (IRE) 6 b.g. Orpen (USA) – Florinda (CAN) (Vice Regent (CAN)) [2006/7 h124: 16m 17g* 16v^4 Sep 21] lengthy gelding: fairly useful handicap hurdler: back to best last 2 starts, winning at Tralee in August by length from Euro Leader and fourth to Sky To Sea at Listowel: raced around 2m: acts on heavy going, probably on good to firm: tongue tied. *M. Halford, Ireland* **h125**

MAYADEEN (IRE) 5 b.g. King's Best (USA) – Inaaq (Lammtarra (USA)) [2006/7 h75: 17m^6 20g 17m Sep 28] smallish, good-topped gelding: poor form over hurdles: tried tongue tied/in cheekpieces. *J. G. M. O'Shea* **h78**

MA YAHAB 6 ch.g. Dr Fong (USA) – Bay Shade (USA) (Sharpen Up) [2006/7 h107: 17g^2 16v^3 17v^3 16v^4 17d^2 20s^4 Apr 26] compact gelding: fair handicap hurdler: off 19 months, in frame all 6 starts in 2006/7: best around 2m: acts on good to firm and heavy going: blinkered final outing: consistent. *Miss Venetia Williams* **h114**

MAYBE A MALT (IRE) 5 b.m. Shernazar – Petite Deb (Cure The Blues (USA)) [2006/7 F14s^6 F14s^3 aF16g^5 F16g Mar 28] leggy mare: half-sister to fair chaser Sir Toby (by Strong Gale), stayed 21f, and fair 1m to 1½m winner Ashby Hill (by Executive Perk): dam, maiden stayer, half-sister to useful staying hurdler Deb's Ball, herself dam of useful staying chaser Hot Weld: modest form in bumpers. *R. Rowe* **F82**

MAYBELLINO (IRE) 5 b.m. Robellino (USA) – May Hills Legacy (IRE) (Be My Guest (USA)) [2006/7 F14s Dec 23] half-sister to modest hurdler/chaser Gargoyle Girl (by Be My Chief), stays 3m: dam 6f/1¼m winner: green, well held in bumper on debut. *Miss Venetia Williams* **F–**

MAYBESEVEN 13 gr.g. Baron Blakeney – Ninth of May (Comedy Star (USA)) [2006/7 c66§, h–: c25m^6 Aug 6] good-topped gelding: veteran jumper: stays 3¼m: acts on soft going, probably on good to firm: usually in headgear nowadays: unreliable. *R. Dickin* **c– §** **h–**

MAYNOOTH PRINCESS (IRE) 5 ch.m. Trans Island – Burren Breeze (IRE) (Mazaad) [2006/7 h–: 16s^6 17d^4 19g 17m 17s^3 16g c16s^{pu} 16s* c16d^{pu} 16v^2 Feb 27] big, workmanlike mare: poor hurdler: won seller at Southwell in December: stiff task both starts over fences: raced mainly around 2m: acts on heavy going: best efforts in cheekpieces: not straightforward (carries head awkwardly). *R. Johnson* **c–** **h72**

MAYOUN (IRE) 10 b.g. Houmayoun (FR) – Botswana (African Sky) [2006/7 c–, h103: c26m^{pu} c24g^2 c26s^5 c26s* c20s* c23d^F Dec 21] good-bodied gelding: fair hurdler: modest chaser: won handicaps at Plumpton (amateur event) in November and Fontwell (seller, sold from Evan Williams 6,000 gns) in December: running well when falling fatally next time: stayed 3¼m: acted on firm and soft going: usually wore headgear. *P. A. Blockley* **c91** **h–**

MAYYAS 7 b.g. Robellino (USA) – Amidst (Midyan (USA)) [2006/7 h94: 16s^5 17s 16s 16v^6 Feb 17] sturdy gelding: novice hurdler, little form in 2006/7: raced around 2m on good going or softer: tongue tied last 2 starts. *C. C. Bealby* **h–**

M'BOYO 5 gr.g. M'Bebe – Parodia (Glint of Gold) [2006/7 F16m^3 F16v F16m Jan 29] workmanlike gelding: first foal: dam ran once: form (poor) in bumpers only on debut: blinkered final outing. *P. D. Evans* **F75**

MCBAIN (USA) 8 br.g. Lear Fan (USA) – River City Moon (USA) (Riverman (USA)) **c107 +**
[2006/7 h134: c21m² c20mᶠ Jul 4] smallish, angular gelding: useful handicap hurdler: **h–**
running better race over fences when falling 2 out in maiden won by Mandingo Chief at
Southwell: stays 2¾m: acts on soft and good to firm going. *P. J. Hobbs*

MCKELVEY (IRE) 8 b.g. Anshan – Chatty Actress (Le Bavard (FR)) [2006/7 **c145**
c135, h–: c25f⁴ c32m* c27s c26g⁶ 24g* c36g² Apr 14] **h134**
 Welsh-born jockeys and trainers have won the Grand National in recent
times, among them the pairing of Carl Llewellyn and Nigel Twiston-Davies associated with Earth Summit in 1998 (Twiston-Davies also saddled the 2002 winner
Bindaree). However, no horse trained in Wales has won since Kirkland in 1905.
The Pembrokeshire-based McKelvey was possibly unlucky not to triumph in the
latest National, coming from well back and closing gradually on the winner Silver
Birch all the way to the line. McKelvey edged right from the elbow and was found
afterwards to have suffered a tendon injury which, coupled with the fact that he
was hampered at second Becher's and again crossing the Melling Road, made his
performance all the more meritorious. He was beaten only three quarters of a length
after jumping soundly (except for a minor error at the twenty-third) and he will be
one for the shortlist in 2008 provided he makes a full recovery in time.
 McKelvey is not a straightforward ride and sometimes looks hard work but
he went well at Aintree for the season's leading conditional Tom O'Brien (also
champion amateur in 2005/6), who rode forty-two of the Bowen stable's career-

Britannia Building Society English Summer National (Handicap Chase), Uttoxeter—
first-time cheekpieces and Tony McCoy do the trick on McKelvey;
also pictured is third-placed Dead-Eyed Dick

Mr N. Elliott's "McKelvey"

best seventy-four winners (though two late-season winners face likely disqualification after news in August that they had failed post-race tests) in the latest season at an impressive strike rate of 21%. O'Brien's boss Philip Hobbs supplied him with twenty-seven wins, his remaining thirty-eight—from a record seasonal total for a conditional of one hundred and seven—spread around twenty-one other trainers. Only Tony McCoy and Richard Johnson, both former champion conditionals, rode more winners in the latest season than twenty-year-old O'Brien whose father is head groom at Ballydoyle (Tom O'Brien is a nephew of Aidan). The seasonal record for a conditional was held by Joe Tizzard whose ninety-one winners in 1998/9 remains the best total of his career. Sixty-nine of Tizzard's winners that season were for Paul Nicholls but his subsequent reign as the stable's number-one was short-lived. O'Brien is keeping his feet on the ground—'I have been very lucky . . . You never know what next season is going to bring, it's easy to fall in a heap.' Racing records must always be kept in perspective, and O'Brien won't be a conditional in the next season, but he does look very much the type to hold his own 'among the big boys'.

McKelvey had already contested two 'Nationals' before his near-miss at Aintree. He ran in the Welsh National as a novice when he was among the market leaders after making a good start to his chasing career, only to be pulled up after racing lazily. McKelvey won the valuable Britannia Building Society English Summer National at Uttoxeter in July (ridden by McCoy who has won on him three times in four rides). McKelvey was tried in cheekpieces for the first time that day—and has worn them in all his races since—and responded to strong pressure to win by two lengths from the enigmatic Omni Cosmo Touch, in the process providing Bowen with his second win in this race in three years (Take The Stand won in 2004). McKelvey tackled the fences on the National course at Aintree in November when keeping on all too late in the Becher Chase (his rider Peter Buchanan was a late replacement for Tony Dobbin who was injured in the Grand Sefton earlier in the afternoon). McKelvey finished sixth behind Eurotrek but had a fair bit of running left in him and jumped well enough to suggest he would be well worth another try over the fences. That Becher run came after a change of heart from owner Noel Elliott, who'd been planning to sell the gelding at the Doncaster November Sales. After his encouraging Aintree showing, McKelvey was then put away for four months and confirmed his well-being with a victory, ridden by O'Brien for the first time, in a three-mile handicap hurdle (taking advantage of a much lower mark) at Bangor on his return in March. Hurdles will reportedly be on the agenda again in 2007/8 as Bowen, in issuing an upbeat bulletin on McKelvey's recovery from injury during the summer, stated that the gelding will be kept to the smaller obstacles until another tilt at the National next April in order to preserve his big-race handicap mark.

McKelvey (IRE) (b.g. 1999)	Anshan (ch 1987)	Persian Bold (br 1975)	Bold Lad
			Relkarunner
		Lady Zi (b 1980)	Manado
			Exbury Grace
	Chatty Actress (b 1981)	Le Bavard (ch 1971)	Devon
			Lueur Doree
		Southern Actress (b 1977)	Menelek
			Southern Slave

The useful-looking McKelvey has the pedigree, as well as the physique, of a chaser. His dam the unraced Chatty Actress has bred three other winners under Rules, all of whom stayed very well, most notably the very smart Chives who was placed twice in the Welsh National (including when third to Silver Birch in 2004) and ran in the 2003 Grand National (pulled up due to a broken blood vessel when amongst the favourites). McKelvey stays four and a half miles and acts on any going, though it's worth noting that Elliott reportedly switched the gelding to Bowen's yard (from Shane Donohoe) in early-2005 because of a lack of opportunities on 'good ground' in Ireland. He tends to race lazily and needs strong handling (won in blinkers early in his career and is best in cheekpieces nowadays). Incidentally, the Welsh connection isn't the only Grand National statistic McKelvey will have to overcome next April. The immortal Red Rum is the last National runner-up to go one better subsequently in the Aintree showpiece (his third National win in 1977 came after successive second places in 1975 and 1976), whilst 1975 winner L'Escargot (runner-up in 1974) is the only other horse to achieve the feat in the last fifty-three years. *P. Bowen*

MCMAHON'S BROOK 8 br.g. Alderbrook – McMahon's River (Over The River (FR)) [2006/7 h–: 22v^{pu} 24v^{pu} Mar 10] angular gelding: lightly raced and no sign of ability. *Mrs N. S. Evans*   h–

MCQUEEN (IRE) 7 ch.g. Barathea (IRE) – Bibliotheque (USA) (Woodman (USA)) [2006/7 h90: 20s^{pu} 20g 20g* 20f^2 22m^2 20g^3 19d 19m^6 Apr 28] angular gelding: modest hurdler: won conditional jockeys novice handicap at Uttoxeter (by distance) in July: ran poorly last 2 outings 6 months apart: stays 2½m: acts on firm and good to soft going. *B. D. Leavy*   h93

MCSNAPPY 10 ch.g. Risk Me (FR) – Nannie Annie (Persian Bold) [2006/7 c–, h–: c20g^5 c26d^{pu} c21s^F c26m^{pu} Jul 17] leggy gelding: maiden hurdler: winning chaser: no form in handicaps since 2003/4: stays 3m: acts on heavy going. *N. J. Hawke*   c– h–

MEADOW HAWK (USA) 7 b.g. Spinning World (USA) – Sophonisbe (Wollow) [2006/7 h96: 16m 22g^{pu} 16m^4 20g 19d 16d^{pu} 21m* Apr 9] leggy gelding: modest handicap hurdler at best: dropped steadily in weights before winning at Huntingdon in April: stays 21f: acts on soft and good to firm going: used to wear headgear. *A. W. Carroll*   h83

MEADOW VALE (IRE) 5 ch.g. Bob Back (USA) – Only Gossip (USA) (Trempolino (USA)) [2006/7 F18g* F16m* Apr 26] €18,000 3-y-o: lengthy, rather unfurnished gelding: closely related to smart hurdler/winning chaser Montalcino (by Robellino), stayed 21f, and half-brother to several winners, including 2½m hurdler Town Gossip (by Indian Ridge): dam French 1½m winner: unbeaten in 2 bumpers a week apart, winning at Tipperary (beat Devanha Dancer by 2 lengths) and Punchestown (useful form, by head from Arctic Tour in 24-runner event): promising. *P. A. Fahy, Ireland*   F109

MEANTIME (USA) 4 b.g. Point Given (USA) – Interim (Sadler's Wells (USA)) **h–**
[2006/7 16s 17g Nov 5] sturdy gelding: half-brother to fairly useful 2m hurdler Indemnity
(by Kris S): modest maiden on Flat (stays 11.5f): offered nothing in 2 juvenile hurdles:
tried in cheekpieces. *G. Prodromou*

MEDDLE 4 b.f. Diktat – Ingerence (FR) (Akarad (FR)) [2006/7 17g 16s^pu Oct 11] **h–**
half-sister to 2 winning hurdlers, including one-time fairly useful Mirant (by Danzig
Connection), stays 19f: no form on Flat or over hurdles. *J. Jay*

MEDIANOCHE (IRE) 7 b.g. Spanish Place (USA) – Midnights Daughter (IRE) **c–**
(Long Pond) [2006/7 20d^pu 21s^6 Dec 5] €62,000 3-y-o: second foal: half-brother to very **h–**
smart staying chaser One Knight (by Roselier): dam unraced half-sister to smart hurdler
up to 2¾m Shannon Spray and to dam of useful staying chaser Direct Access: won
maiden point in 2004: modest form over hurdles: easily best effort in chases when
winning maiden at Clonmel in 2005/6: sold out of M. Morris's stable 24,000 gns
Doncaster May Sales: no form in 2 starts in Britain: stays 2½m: acts on good to soft
ground. *R. Ford*

MEDICAL DEBENTURE (IRE) 7 b.g. Poliglote – Al Cairo (FR) (Vayrann) **h–**
[2006/7 F16g^2 F16m* F16f* F16g Aug 6] seventh foal: half-brother to 3 winners, **F102**
including fairly useful 1½m winner Marinnette (by Be My Guest): dam French 9f (at
2 yrs) to 12.5f winner: fairly useful in bumpers, won at Limerick and Tipperary in July:
sixth in novice at Punchestown on hurdling debut in late-2005/6: should improve over
hurdles. *M. Halford, Ireland*

MEDIC (IRE) 6 b.g. Dr Fong (USA) – Elupa (IRE) (Mtoto) [2006/7 F91: F16g **F70**
May 6] sturdy gelding: fair form in bumpers, well held at Uttoxeter in early-2006/7.
T. J. Fitzgerald

MEDISON (FR) 7 b. or br.g. Video Rock (FR) – Colombia III (FR) (Altayan) [2006/7 **c122 §**
c124+, h–: c16d^4 c19d^4 17s^pu Dec 8] tall, angular gelding: fairly useful hurdler/maiden **h– §**
chaser: should stay 2½m: acts on soft going: wore headgear last 2 starts: often let down
by jumping over fences: ungenuine. *D. E. Pipe*

MEDKHAN (IRE) 10 ch.g. Lahib (USA) – Safayn (USA) (Lyphard (USA)) [2006/7 **h–**
h–: 20s^pu May 20] leggy gelding: very lightly raced and little form over hurdles. *R. Jordan*

MEEHAN (IRE) 7 b. or br.g. Spectrum (IRE) – Seeds of Doubt (IRE) (Night Shift **c110**
(USA)) [2006/7 c101, h–: c23m* c23g^2 c23m^pu c24m* Oct 12] good-topped gelding: **h–**
maiden hurdler: fair chaser: won novice at Worcester in June and handicap at Ludlow in
October: stays 3m: acts on soft and good to firm going: has bled from nose (including
third outing). *Miss J. S. Davis*

MEERSBROOK (USA) 6 b.g. Kingmambo (USA) – Karakorum (IRE) (Fairy King **F98**
(USA)) [2006/7 F16v F17s^5 F16m^2 Apr 10] chunky gelding: second foal: closely related
to winner in USA by Smart Strike: dam 6f/7f winner: progressive form in bumpers, 7
lengths second to impressive The Tother One at Chepstow: tongue tied. *J. A. Geake*

MEET THE FAMILY (IRE) 7 b.m. Courtship – Instant Joy (IRE) (Accordion) **h95**
[2006/7 18m^F 20f^2 20g^6 20g^4 18d^pu 20d Nov 5] second foal: dam maiden sister to useful
chaser Laredo, stayed 21f: modest handicap hurdler: stays 2½m: probably acts on any
going. *F. J. Lacy, Ireland*

MEGA CHIC (FR) 7 b.g. Useful (FR) – Pampachic (FR) (Pampabird) [2006/7 18m^pu **h–**
19m^pu Jun 14] third foal: dam, 1½m winner/2m winning hurdler, half-sister to 3 winning
jumpers: twice-raced on Flat at 3 yrs in French Provinces for R. Passelande: no show over
hurdles. *J. C. Tuck*

MEGATON 6 ch.g. Nashwan (USA) – Pan Galactic (USA) (Lear Fan (USA)) [2006/7 **h115**
h100: 21g^3 19g* 22m^3 17m* 16s^2 22g* 22m* Aug 3] ex-French gelding: progressive
over hurdles, winning handicaps (first 2 novices) at Exeter in May, Hereford in June and
Stratford in July, and novice at Stratford (beat Longueville Manor 1½ lengths) in August:
stays 2¾m, at least when emphasis is on speed: acts on soft and good to firm going.
P. Bowen

MEGGIE'S BEAU (IRE) 11 ch.g. Good Thyne (USA) – Romantic Rose (IRE) **c110**
(Strong Gale) [2006/7 c104, h–: c26m^2 Oct 16] sturdy gelding: fair handicap chaser: stays **h–**
3¼m: unraced on firm going, acts on any other: blinkered last 2 outings in 2005/6. *Miss
Venetia Williams*

MEGGIES GAMBLE (IRE) 10 b.g. Zaffaran (USA) – Glaskerbeg Lady (IRE) **c–**
(Radical) [2006/7 c23g^pu May 14] tall gelding: fairly useful hurdler, very lightly raced: **h–**
off further 15 months, no encouragement in maiden on chasing debut, jumping reluct-

615

antly: stays 3m: raced on good going or softer (acts on heavy): front runner. *Miss Venetia Williams*

MEGGIE'S LAD (IRE) 10 b.g. Beau Sher – Kambaya (IRE) (Kambalda) [2006/7 c20f[5] Apr 5] rather sparely-made gelding: maiden hurdler: winning chaser: in frame in points in 2007: stays 25f: acts on soft ground: blinkered last 4 starts in 2004/5: free-going sort. *A. J. Mason*   c66 h–

MEILLEUR (NZ) 9 ch.g. Mellifont (USA) – Petite Cheval (NZ) (Engagement (USA)) [2006/7 h–: 22g[pu] May 2] very lightly raced, form only in bumper on debut: tried tongue tied. *A. J. Chamberlain*   h–

MELBA TOAST 6 b.g. Zaffaran (USA) – Ida Melba (Idiot's Delight) [2006/7 17d 20v 19v[2] 22d* Jan 30] big, rangy gelding: type to make a chaser: fourth foal: half-brother to useful chaser/winning hurdler Duncliffe (by Executive Perk), stays 3m: dam never ran: fair form in novice hurdles, winning at Folkestone by 14 lengths from Shardakhan: likely to be suited by 3m+: raced on going softer than good. *R. H. Alner*   h114

MEL IN BLUE (FR) 9 b.g. Pistolet Bleu (IRE) – Calligraphie (FR) (R B Chesne) [2006/7 c121, h112: c22s[6] 21s[5] c23m* Apr 22] tall, useful-looking gelding: fair hurdler, below form second outing: fairly useful chaser: successful hunter debut when beating Saint Romble easily by 10 lengths at Stratford: stays 23f: acts on soft and good to firm going. *R. Waley-Cohen*   c114 h97

MELOGRANO (IRE) 7 ch.g. Hector Protector (USA) – Just A Treat (IRE) (Glenstal (USA)) [2006/7 h–: 16g May 4] well beaten in maiden/novice hurdles. *Mark Campion*   h–

MELTONIAN 10 ch.g. Past Glories – Meltonby (Sayf El Arab (USA)) [2006/7 c88, h–: 16m[3] 16g[2] 16m 16m[2] 18g[6] Sep 3] compact gelding: modest hurdler/chaser on his day: best form up to 21f: acts on good to firm and good to soft going: visored once: sometimes let down by jumping over fences. *K. F. Clutterbuck*   c– h86

MEM O'REES 5 b.m. Alflora (IRE) – Vanina II (FR) (Italic (FR)) [2006/7 F16d[4] Feb 2] 100,000 3-y-o: sister to useful hurdler up to 2½m Bourbon Manhattan, and half-sister to top-class staying hurdler Mighty Man (by Sir Harry Lewis), stays 25f: dam, maiden, sister to very smart staying chaser Antonin: not given unduly hard time when 22 lengths fourth to Arctic Magic in mares bumper at Chepstow on debut: likely to improve. *Jonjo O'Neill*   F79 p

MEMORIES OF GOLD (IRE) 7 b.m. Carroll House – Sweet Harmony (IRE) (Altountash) [2006/7 c–, h–: 16m 20s[4] 20g[4] 22g[3] 24m[4] 24m[2] 26m Sep 24] tall mare: failed to complete all 3 starts over fences: poor maiden hurdler: stays 3m: acts on good to soft and good to firm going: tried in cheekpieces. *J. A. Danahar*   c– h82

MENAROW 7 br.m. Thowra (FR) – Menabilly (Sit In The Corner (USA)) [2006/7 F16f[4] F17g Oct 15] fifth foal: half-sister to winning pointer by Landyap: dam unraced: little show in bumpers/maiden point. *Mrs S. Gardner*   F–

MENDIP MAGIC 6 b.m. Classic Cliche (IRE) – Woodland Flower (Furry Glen) [2006/7 F17g F16s F18s Nov 29] sixth foal: half-sister to 3 fairly useful jumpers, including chaser Eljay's Boy (by Sir Harry Lewis), stays 2¾m: dam modest staying hurdler/chaser: never dangerous in bumpers. *J. C. Tuck*   F–

MENDO 7 b.g. Alderbrook – Ina's Farewell (Random Shot) [2006/7 F16d[2] 16v[4] 21s[5] 16v[2] 19s* 16g* Mar 30] good-topped gelding: useful form in bumpers: off 20 months, best effort when second to Crocodiles Rock at Newbury: fairly useful in novice hurdles, landed odds at Market Rasen (conditional jockeys event) and Ascot in March: best effort when 9 lengths second of 5 to Shatabdi in Grade 2 at Kempton: stays 21f: acts on heavy going. *Noel T. Chance*   h123 + F115

MENELAUS 6 b.g. Machiavellian (USA) – Mezzogiorno (Unfuwain (USA)) [2006/7 24f[2] 24m 24f c25g[5] 24d 19s 20v 19m[4] Apr 11] ex-Irish gelding: lightly raced on Flat: maiden hurdler: left Michael Cunningham before final outing: well beaten in maiden on chasing debut: stays 3m: acts on firm ground: tried in blinkers/cheekpieces. *K. A. Morgan*   c– h86

MENEMORE (IRE) 6 b.g. Presenting – Carmen (IRE) (Meneval (USA)) [2006/7 22d[pu] 18s Jan 4] good-topped gelding: second foal: half-brother to fair hurdler/winning pointer Buster Collins (by Alderbrook), stays 21f: dam once-raced sister to fairly useful staying jumper Menesonic: failed to complete in 2 points in 2006: no show both starts over hurdles. *R. H. Alner*   h–

MENEUR DE JEU (FR) 7 b.g. Sleeping Car (FR) – Tanie (FR) (Kashmir Ring) [2006/7 c–§, h96§: 20s 22g 26m[6] 22f[2] Apr 22] leggy gelding: winning chaser: modest   c– § h99 §

hurdler: stays 3m: acts on firm and soft going: visored/in cheekpieces 5 of last 6 outings, also tongue tied final one: irresolute. *D. E. Pipe*

MEN OF DESTINY (IRE) 6 b.g. Sadler's Wells (USA) – Caladira (IRE) (Darshaan) [2006/7 h99§, F76: 20g 21v²ᵈ 22sᵖᵘ 25v⁵ Dec 31] angular gelding: fair novice hurdler, let down by jumping/attitude last 2 starts: should stay 3m: acts on heavy going. *B. G. Powell* — **h108 §**

MENPHIS BEURY (FR) 7 b.g. Art Bleu – Pampa Star (FR) (Pampabird) [2006/7 c102, h–: c25gᵖᵘ May 4] sturdy gelding: maiden hurdler: fair handicap chaser: running creditably when going lame only outing in 2006/7: stays 3m: acts on any going: carries head high. *H. D. Daly* — **c102 h–**

MENSIO (IRE) 5 ch.g. Anshan – Rosie Fort (IRE) (Roselier (FR)) [2006/7 16s 18v 17v Feb 20] seventh foal: half-brother to winning pointer by Presenting: dam unraced half-sister to smart staying chaser Buckboard Bounce: well held in novice hurdles. *L. Lungo* — **h–**

MEPHISTO (IRE) 8 b.g. Machiavellian (USA) – Cunning (Bustino) [2006/7 23d Nov 18] close-coupled, quite good-topped gelding: smart hurdler in 2004/5, won Grade 2 novices at Haydock and Kelso: well beaten in valuable handicap at Haydock only outing since, travelling easily into contention before weakening 3 out: stays 23f, effective at much shorter: raced on good going or softer. *J. Howard Johnson* — **h–**

MERCARI 5 ch.m. Bahamian Bounty – Aonach Mor (Anabaa (USA)) [2006/7 h–: 16mᵖᵘ Nov 9] small, sparely-made mare: no form over hurdles, sold out of Mrs J. McGregor's stable 1,300 gns Doncaster August Sales. *J. W. Tudor* — **h–**

MERCHANT RED (USA) 4 b. or br.g. Red Ransom (USA) – Great Lady Slew (USA) (Seattle Slew (USA)) [2006/7 F16m Jan 29] 31,000 2-y-o: brother to smart winner up to 12.5f Slew The End and half-brother to 3 winners, including fair hurdler Pagan Magic (by Diesis), stays 2½m: dam, winner up to 1m in USA, out of half-sister to Breeders' Cup Distaff winner Lady's Secret: well held in bumper on debut. *P. R. Webber* — **F–**

MERCHANTS FRIEND (IRE) 12 b.g. Lord Americo – Buck Maid (Buckskin (FR)) [2006/7 c131x, h–: c24s³ c24gᵖᵘ Mar 24] good-topped gelding: useful handicap chaser on his day: stays 3½m well: raced mainly on good going or softer (acts on heavy): wears cheekpieces: often makes mistakes (including on reappearance). *C. J. Mann* — **c108 x h–**

MERCURIC 6 gr.g. Silver Patriarch (IRE) – Seymourswift (Seymour Hicks (FR)) [2006/7 20s⁵ 23vᵘʳ 24v c17v² c16s* c20v⁴ c24d³ Apr 1] lengthy, good-topped gelding: first foal: dam, winning hurdler/fair chaser, stayed 3¼m: fair hurdler: progressive novice chaser: won maiden at Thurles in February: best efforts (fairly useful form) in Grade 2 at Naas (fourth to Benefit Night) and Grade 3 at Limerick (third to Offshore Account): stays 3m: raced on going softer than good (acts on heavy). *Mrs J. Harrington, Ireland* — **c117 h107**

MERDEKA (IRE) 7 b.g. Luso – Gentle Reef (IRE) (Orange Reef) [2006/7 h133p: c20dF c21s² c22s* c24v⁵ c24v⁶ c25m⁵ Apr 24] rangy, useful-looking gelding: useful hurdler: fairly useful form over fences, winning maiden at Limerick in December by 2 lengths from Mouftari: well held last 3 starts, twice in graded events: should stay 3m: acts on soft going. *T. J. Taaffe, Ireland* — **c120 h–**

MERLIN'S MAGIC (FR) 5 gr.g. Marathon (USA) – Dompteuse (FR) (Dom Pasquini (FR)) [2006/7 F17v² F17s⁴ F16s Apr 27] 20,000 2-y-o, resold £4,200 2-y-o: second foal: dam, winning hurdler/chaser around 2m, half-sister to useful chaser Noisetine, stays 2¾m: fair form in frame first 2 starts in bumpers. *P. J. Hobbs* — **F88**

MERRYMAKER 7 b.g. Machiavellian (USA) – Wild Pavane (Dancing Brave (USA)) [2006/7 20g⁴ 20g* 20m³ 20sᵖᵘ Apr 1] fairly useful on Flat (stays 2m), successful in July, left W. M. Brisbourne after final start in 2006: fair form over hurdles, winning maiden at Musselburgh in December by 7 lengths from Amhairghin: breathing problem final outing. *N. G. Richards* — **h102**

MERRY PATH (IRE) 13 br.g. Alphabatim (USA) – Smokey Path (IRE) (Scallywag) [2006/7 c111, h–: c24m² May 16] sturdy gelding: one-time fairly useful chaser, second of 4 in hunter at Huntingdon early in 2006/7: won twice in points in April: stays 3¼m: acts on soft and good to firm going: tried blinkered/visored. *Evan Williams* — **c103 h–**

MERRY STORM (IRE) 8 b.g. Glacial Storm (USA) – Cap Reform (IRE) (Phardante (FR)) [2006/7 c96, h–: c28sᵖᵘ Oct 26] big, lengthy gelding: no show only start over hurdles: modest handicap chaser: breathing problem only outing in 2006/7: stays 25f: raced on good going or softer (acts on heavy): tongue tied last 3 starts. *Mrs K. Waldron* — **c– h–**

MERRYVALE MAN 10 b.g. Rudimentary (USA) – Salu (Ardross) [2006/7 h102: 16fᵖᵘ 16d* 17s⁴ May 21] leggy gelding: fair handicap hurdler: won at Towcester in May: — **h109**

finished lame next time: stays 2½m: acts on good to firm and heavy going: usually races prominently. *Miss Kariana Key*

MERTHYRMAWR 5 ch.g. Access Ski – Journo's Joy (First Footman) [2006/7 F16m F17d F16m 17g Oct 15] second foal: dam twice-raced in points: well beaten in bumpers/ novice hurdle: won maiden point in March. *Evan Williams*   **h–** **F–**

MESCALERA (GER) 6 b.m. Alkalde (GER) – Miskinissa (GER) (Esclavo (FR)) [2006/7 16m 21m⁵ 16d 16g 16d⁴ Nov 11] poor maiden on Flat (stays 8.5f): little form over hurdles: has pulled hard. *R. J. Price*   **h66**

METAL DETECTOR (IRE) 10 b.g. Treasure Hunter – Las-Cancellas (Monksfield) [2006/7 c104, h99: c25g² c25m⁴ c23mᵖᵘ c23dᵖᵘ c25s² c24g* Apr 8] good-topped gelding: winning hurdler: modest handicap chaser: won at Towcester in April: stays 25f: acts on soft and good to firm going: wears headgear: often finishes weakly/carries head awkwardly. *K. C. Bailey*   **c103 §** **h– §**

METHODICAL 5 b.m. Lujain (USA) – Simple Logic (Aragon) [2006/7 h90: 19d⁶ 19g⁵ 21s⁵ 21s² 23v⁴ 22sᵖᵘ 16g⁵ 20g Apr 27] short-backed mare: modest handicap hurdler: stays 23f: raced on good ground or softer (acts on heavy): has finished weakly. *B. G. Powell*   **h95**

MEXICAN BOB 4 b.g. Atraf – Eskimo Nel (IRE) (Shy Groom (USA)) [2006/7 17d Nov 16] brother to fairly useful 2m hurdler Mexican Pete: fair maiden up to 1¼m on Flat: tailed off in juvenile maiden on hurdling debut. *Heather Dalton*   **h–**

MEXICAN HONEYMOON 4 b.g. Hernando (FR) – Sweet Dreams (Selkirk (USA)) [2006/7 F14s⁵ Nov 26] 800 3-y-o: fourth foal: dam, 1m winner, out of smart performer up to 10.5f Ahohoney: fifth of 13 in 3-y-o bumper on debut. *D. A. Rees*   **F75**

MEXICAN (USA) 8 b.g. Pine Bluff (USA) – Cuando Quiere (USA) (Affirmed (USA)) [2006/7 c85§, h–§: c16vᵖᵘ c17m⁶ 16m Apr 7] rather leggy gelding: winning chaser/ lightly-raced maiden hurdler, no form in 2006/7, sold out of Micky Hammond's stable 1,600 gns Doncaster August Sales prior to final outing (tongue tied): raced around 2m: wears headgear: ungenuine. *Patrick Lacey, Ireland*   **c– §** **h– §**

MEY CLOUDS (IRE) 5 b.g. Cloudings (IRE) – Lady of Mey (IRE) (Executive Perk) [2006/7 F16s F16v² F16v² F16s Apr 27] good-topped gelding: first foal: dam unraced half-sister to useful hurdler/fairly useful chaser Tonoco, stayed 25f: fair form in bumpers, looking a stayer. *C. Grant*   **F90**

MEZEREON 7 b.m. Alzao (USA) – Blown-Over (Ron's Victory (USA)) [2006/7 h97: 16m² 16v⁶ 17m³ 16f⁶ 16g c16f c16mᶠ c16s c16f Sep 29] strong, close-coupled mare: modest hurdler, claimed from D. Carroll £5,000 third outing: no form after, including over fences: raced around 2m: acts on firm and soft ground. *B. Storey*   **c–** **h87**

MIALYSSA 7 b.m. Rakaposhi King – Theme Arena (Tragic Role (USA)) [2006/7 h–, F68: 16f 16s³ 16g³ Mar 16] poor maiden hurdler: should stay beyond 2m: acts on soft going: tongue tied last 2 starts. *M. R. Bosley*   **h61**

MIA (POL) 6 b.m. Llandaff (USA) – Mykos-Dream (SWI) (Mykonos) [2006/7 16gᵖᵘ 16m Jun 11] successful 4 times on Flat (stays 1¼m) in Poland, well held in Britain in 2006: no show over hurdles. *John Allen*   **h–**

MIA'S GIRL 7 b.m. Fleetwood (IRE) – Green Seed (IRE) (Lead On Time (USA)) [2006/7 21g⁶ Mar 28] fourth foal: half-sister to several winners, including fairly useful 2m hurdler Take Flite (by Cadeaux Genereux) and fair hurdler up to 2½m Rare Coincidence (by Atraf): dam 2-y-o 6f winner: mistakes in novice hurdle on debut. *N. B. King*   **h69**

MIBLEU (FR) 7 b.g. Agent Bleu (FR) – Eauseille (FR) (Un Numide (FR)) [2006/7 19d c19sᶠ c16d³ c23vᵖᵘ Mar 1] medium-sized ex-French gelding: third foal: dam unraced: placed once around 1¾m from 3 starts on Flat: little show over jumps, left P. Cottin before return: has been blinkered. *R. H. Alner*   **c88 ?** **h–**

MIC AUBIN (FR) 4 b.g. Broadway Flyer (USA) – Patney (FR) (Hasty Tudor (USA)) [2006/7 F16g⁵ F16m Apr 24] £4,100 3-y-o: half-brother to several winners in France, including hurdler/chaser up to 21f Saratova (by Noblequest): dam 1m to 11f winner in France: fair form when fifth to Gypsy Scholar in bumper at Towcester on debut: hampered next time. *M. Keighley*   **F90**

MICHABO (IRE) 6 b.g. Robellino (USA) – Mole Creek (Unfuwain (USA)) [2006/7 19d 21d* 24g⁴ 21d 16s⁴ Apr 25] good-topped gelding: fairly useful on Flat (stays 1¾m), sold out of H. Morrison's stable 16,000 gns Newmarket Autumn Sales: modest novice hurdler: awarded win in maiden at Ludlow on technical grounds: stays 21f: tried tongue tied: has carried head awkwardly. *P. Bowen*   **h95**

MICHAEL MUCK 5 b.g. Overbury (IRE) – Country Choice (IRE) (Paean) [2006/7 **h124 +** F16d⁴ 20v* 16s² 20v 20v⁴ 22d* Mar 17] rather unfurnished gelding: third foal: half- **F90** brother to winning pointers by Alflora and Sovereign Water: dam winning pointer: won maiden Irish point in 2006: bought £61,000 Cheltenham April Sales: fourth in bumper: fairly useful hurdler: won novice at Chepstow in November and handicap at Uttoxeter (battled on well to beat Opera de Coeur by 1¼ lengths) in March: will be suited by 3m: raced on going softer than good (acts on heavy). *P. F. Nicholls*

MICHAELS DREAM (IRE) 8 b.g. Spectrum (IRE) – Stormswept (USA) (Storm **h109** Bird (CAN)) [2006/7 h106: 22s* 22d² 20m 22d³ 22mᵖᵘ 22g⁴ 23g³ 20s 27d⁴ 23v⁶ 19s 21s⁴ 20s⁵ Apr 1] compact gelding: fair handicap hurdler: won at Market Rasen in May: stays 27f: acts on firm and soft going: tried visored, usually blinkered. *N. Wilson*

MICHAELS JOY (IRE) 8 br.g. Presenting – Scarteen Lower (IRE) (Royal Fountain) **c75 +** [2006/7 c20vᶠ c25s³ c20s³ Apr 27] strong, workmanlike gelding: third on completed **h–** outing in novice hurdles: off over 2 years, poor form over fences (tended to jump right final start): probably stays 25f: raced on soft/heavy ground over jumps. *G. M. Moore*

MICHIGAN D'ISOP (FR) 7 b.g. Cadoudal (FR) – Julie du Berlais (FR) (Rose **h89** Laurel) [2006/7 h95p: 20d 19dᵘʳ Dec 21] useful-looking gelding: lightly raced, modest form at best over hurdles. *B. J. M. Ryall*

MICK DIVINE (IRE) 9 gr.g. Roselier (FR) – Brown Forest (Brave Invader (USA)) **c84 x** [2006/7 c89, h–: c25mᵘʳ c23m⁴ c26d³ c23mᵖᵘ c23d³ c19dᶠ Nov 1] leggy, angular gelding: **h–** winning hurdler: modest maiden chaser: let down by jumping/attitude in 2006/7, left C. Mann after third start: stayed 27f: acted on soft ground: tried in cheekpieces/blinkers: was sometimes tongue tied: dead. *J. D. Frost*

MICKEY CROKE 10 b.g. Alflora (IRE) – Praise The Lord (Lord Gayle (USA)) **c–** [2006/7 c–, h–: c25gᵖᵘ May 13] rangy, good sort: winning hurdler: no form over fences: **h–** should stay 3m: tried in cheekpieces. *M. Todhunter*

MICKEY GILROY (IRE) 9 ch.g. Orange Reef – Single Street Lady (Le Bavard **c–** (FR)) [2006/7 c23d⁶ 24f² Jul 6] won maiden point on debut in 2006: favourite, last of 6 in **h81** hunter on chase debut: poor form when second in maiden hurdle 2 months later. *S. Donohoe, Ireland*

MICKEY PEARCE (IRE) 5 b.g. Rossini (USA) – Lucky Coin (Hadeer) [2006/7 **h84** h80: 21s³ 24g⁵ 20vᶠ 21s⁶ 24v 20v 20v 20g² Apr 14] quite good-topped gelding: poor hurdler: won novice seller at Towcester in May: probably stays 3m: raced on good going or softer (acts on heavy): usually wears headgear. *J. G. M. O'Shea*

MICKLEDO 5 b.g. Perryston View – Ever So Lonely (Headin' Up) [2006/7 17m Jun 4] **h–** maiden on Flat: no show on hurdling debut. *A. Bailey*

MICK MURPHY (IRE) 10 b.g. Jurado (USA) – Lee Ford Lady (Kemal (FR)) **c–** [2006/7 c–, h75: 20m c19mᵖᵘ Jun 19] big, lengthy gelding: maiden chaser: poor **h–** handicap hurdler: stays 2¾m: acts on good to firm and good to soft going: tried in cheekpieces/tongue tied: sketchy jumper: sold £1,400 Ascot August Sales, resold £1,200 Ascot February Sales. *V. J. Hughes*

MICK THE MAN (IRE) 6 b.g. Saddlers' Hall (IRE) – Nuala's Pet (Buckskin **F117** (FR)) [2006/7 F16s* F16v² F20v³ F16s² F16m² F16m* Apr 25]

Mick The Man upstaged the principals from the Champion Bumper at Cheltenham when he landed the Paddy Power Champion INH Flat race at Punches- town in April. In doing so, he gained just his second win from six starts, having finished runner-up on all four outings after his debut, in the process giving his trainer Noel Meade a third win in four years in the Grade 1 event. It is to be hoped that Mick The Man, a rangy, good sort in appearance and every inch a jumping type, makes a better fist of things than either of Meade's two previous winners, Geill Sli (who was killed on his chasing debut in June after failing to win in nine starts over hurdles) and Leading Run (failed to win in five starts after a successful hurdling debut in October).

That Mick The Man was well regarded was clear from the start, as he was odds on when he made his debut at Navan in November, justifying his reputation with a very easy win. A fair proportion of the punters' winnings, however, must have been squandered on his subsequent defeats. He was odds on when beaten a short head by Shirley Caspar in a Grade 2 at Navan, even money when losing out to both Notre Pere (who received 7 lb) at Leopardstown and Raven's Run (who

Paddy Power Champion INH Flat, Punchestown—Nina Carberry and Noel Meade repeat their 2006 success as Mick The Man (noseband) gets the better of Woodbine Willie (second left) and Shirley Casper (diamond on cap); Cheltenham winner Cork All Star (rails) is only fifth

received 3 lb) at Naas, and 3/1 second favourite when going down by a length and a half to Sizing Africa (who received 1 lb) at Fairyhouse at Easter. That last performance was as good as Mick The Man had produced, though it still left his form some way short of that shown by the best of his opponents in the championship race. They looked to be Cork All Star, Sophocles and Shirley Caspar, who had all made the frame at Cheltenham. Having plenty of use made of him at Fairyhouse, Mick The Man didn't lead until a furlong out at Punchestown, ridden out to beat Woodbine Willie by two lengths with Shirley Caspar doing best of the Champion Bumper runners in third. Fifth-placed Cork All Star plainly ran below form. The runner-up had won just once from four previous starts and it is unlikely Mick The Man had to improve markedly on his Fairyhouse form to win as he did.

Mick The Man's success was a further boost for his sire Saddlers' Hall, whose purpose-bred jumpers running during the season also included the useful stayers Patsy Hall and Abragante. Mick The Man's dam Nuala's Pet won a bumper, a mares maiden hurdle and a mares beginners chase and produced one previous winner, Mark The Man (by Supreme Leader), a useful bumper performer who later won at two miles over hurdles and three miles over fences. Mark The Man proved fragile and didn't fulfil his potential as a jumper, but Nuala's Pet herself was pretty durable, as were her winning half-brothers Pantechnicon (a fairly useful two-mile chaser for Arthur Barrow) and Paddy's Pet who ran well over a hundred times between them. Mick The Man looks a chaser but presumably will start off over hurdles. He was ridden on all but his second start by leading Irish amateur Nina Carberry, who rode all bar three of her thirty Irish wins in 2006/7 in bumpers and was claiming a second successive win in the Punchestown race herself. *N. Meade, Ireland*

MICKWELL BAY 6 b.g. Bal Harbour – Katie's Kitty (Noble Patriarch) [2006/7 c19m⁴ Nov 5] second foal: brother to modest performer Westcourt Dream, stays 1¼m: dam poor maiden who stayed 7f: won maiden point in 2006: well held in maiden on chase debut. *Mrs Caroline Bailey*   **c–**

MIDAS WAY 7 ch.g. Halling (USA) – Arietta's Way (IRE) (Darshaan) [2006/7 h116p: 16s⁴ 16d³ 20d³ 21v⁵ 20f Apr 28] leggy, close-coupled gelding: useful on Flat (stays 2m): fairly useful handicap hurdler, well held last 2 outings: stays 2½m: acts on soft going: temperament under suspicion. *P. R. Chamings*   **h119**

MID DANCER (FR) 6 b.g. Midyan (USA) – Dancer Lady (FR) (Pink (FR)) [2006/7 c135p, h154: 18s⁴ 21s⁸ 25s⁸ c20s² c22v⁸ c22v⁸ 19s⁸ Apr 28] rather leggy, lengthy gelding: smart hurdler/chaser: unbeaten in 17 runs over jumps in France, successful 3   **c151 h154**

times at Auteuil after creditable second to Monet's Garden in minor event at Carlisle in October, then beat Lord Carmont by 15 lengths in Group 1 Gras Savoye Grand Steeple-Chase de Paris at Auteuil after end of British season, asserting in good style from 2 out: stays 29f: raced mainly on soft/heavy going: jumps right: very reliable. *A. Chaille-Chaille, France*

MIDDLEHAM PARK (IRE) 7 b.g. Revoque (IRE) – Snap Crackle Pop (IRE) (Statoblest) [2006/7 h103: 18g⁴ Apr 10] lengthy gelding: fair handicap hurdler: off 15 months, not unduly punished only start in 2006/7: stays 2¾m: best efforts on good going. *J. W. Mullins* **h91 +**

MIDDLETON DENE (IRE) 5 b.g. Oscar (IRE) – Sharonamar (IRE) (Merrymount) [2006/7 F16d³ F16g* 16v⁴ 20d³ Feb 14] €40,000 3-y-o: useful-looking gelding, un-furnished at present: fifth foal: dam unraced, out of half-sister to 2m hurdler/very smart 3m chaser Ivan King: fair form in bumpers, won maiden at Newcastle in November: better effort in novice hurdles when fourth to Crocodile Dundee at Kelso: should prove suited by 2½m+: remains likely to do better. *N. G. Richards* **h93 p** **F93**

MIDDLEWAY 11 b.g. Milieu – Galway Gal (Proverb) [2006/7 c72x, h–: c27m³ c24mᵖᵘ c27mᵖᵘ c25f² c25sᵖᵘ c27dᵖᵘ c27m⁶ Apr 9] workmanlike gelding: winning hurdler: poor handicap chaser: stays 27f: acts on firm and good to soft going: effective with or without cheekpieces: often let down by jumping over fences. *Miss Kate Milligan* **c77 x** **h–**

MIDNIGHT CHASE 5 b.g. Midnight Legend – Yamrah (Milford) [2006/7 16s* Apr 27] eighth foal: brother to fair chasers up to around 3m Barton May and Midnight Gold and half-brother to fairly useful 2m hurdler Capricorn Princess (by Nicholas Bill): dam successful up to 11.5f: successful in maiden hurdle at Perth on debut by 3 lengths from Platin Grounds (pair clear): will be suited by further than 2m: likely to improve. *D. P. Keane* **h100 p**

MIDNIGHT CREEK 9 b.g. Tragic Role (USA) – Greek Night Out (IRE) (Ela-Mana-Mou) [2006/7 h112§: 24m Jun 22] leggy gelding: fair handicap hurdler: stays 3m: acts on heavy going: tried in cheekpieces/visor: tongue tied once: irresolute. *A. Sadik* **h– §**

MIDNIGHT DIAMOND (IRE) 4 b.c. Alzao (USA) – Derena (FR) (Crystal Palace (FR)) [2006/7 16s⁵ 16d² 16s⁴ 17s⁶ 16v³ 17v* 19g³ Mar 24] close-coupled colt: thrice-raced in maidens on Flat: fair juvenile hurdler: won 6-runner maiden at Bangor (by 16 lengths) in March: stays 19f: raced on good ground or softer (acts on heavy): in cheekpieces last 5 starts. *Mrs L. Williamson* **h97**

MIDNIGHT GOLD 7 ch.g. Midnight Legend – Yamrah (Milford) [2006/7 h95: c21m* c22f⁴ c19m² c20f* Jul 25] medium-sized gelding: novice hurdler: fair form over fences: won novices at Southwell (handicap) in May and Bangor in July: stays 3m: acts on firm and good to soft going. *A. King* **c112** **h–**

MIDNIGHT GUNNER 13 b.g. Gunner B – Light Tonight (Lighter) [2006/7 c108§, h–: c26sᵖᵘ c27m² c24m³ c27m³ c26m⁴ c25s* c26g⁵ Oct 30] well-made gelding: modest handicap chaser: won at Wetherby in October: best at 3m+: acts on any going: tried tongue tied: hard ride. *A. E. Price* **c95** **h–**

MIDNIGHT MAGGIE 6 b.m. Midnight Legend – I'm Maggy (NZ) (Danseur Etoile (FR)) [2006/7 F16v F16v 20gᵖᵘ 21gᵖᵘ Apr 23] 650 4-y-o: workmanlike mare: first foal: dam, fairly useful hurdler, stayed 21f: no form in bumpers/novice hurdles. *M. A. Barnes* **h–** **F–**

MIDNIGHT MARINE 6 b.g. Midnight Legend – The Bizzo (Malaspina) [2006/7 F–: F14g⁶ F16d 20g Nov 3] first foal: dam, poor novice hurdler, stayed 3m: little impact in bumpers/maiden hurdle. *J. F. Panvert* **h–** **F–**

MIDNIGHT QUEEN 6 b.m. Midnight Legend – Panda Shandy (Nearly A Hand) [2006/7 22dᵖᵘ 22g⁵ Apr 1] compact mare: first foal: dam, fair pointer/hunter chaser, half-sister to useful hurdler/chaser up to 2¾m Hops And Pops: fifth to Hendre Hotshot at Newton Abbot on completed start in mares novice hurdles. *K. Bishop* **h87 ?**

MIDNIGHT SPIRIT 7 b.g. Midnight Legend – West-Hatch-Spirit (Forzando) [2006/7 h–: 16m Sep 3] plain gelding: no sign of ability. *F. E. Sutherland* **h–**

MIDNIGHT TRAVELLER 4 b.g. Daylami (IRE) – Swift Dispersal (Shareef Dancer (USA)) [2006/7 16v⁴ 16v⁴ 16v⁴ 16v⁴ 16v⁶ 16d⁵ 22m Apr 9] rather leggy gelding: fairly useful maiden on Flat (stays 1½m), sold out of L. Cumani's stable 40,000 gns Newmarket Autumn Sales: fairly useful juvenile hurdler: much improved when 8¾ lengths fifth of 24 **h117**

to Gaspara in Fred Winter Juvenile Novices' Handicap at Cheltenham: raced mainly at 2m: acts on good to soft ground. *Thomas Cooper, Ireland*

MID SUSSEX SPIRIT 8 b.g. Environment Friend – Ranyah (USA) (Our Native (USA)) [2006/7 h–: 16d 20m⁴ 20m² 20dᵖᵘ Nov 4] leggy gelding: poor novice hurdler: stayed 2½m: blinkered last 3 starts: dead. *G. L. Moore*   **h84**

MIGHT HE GO 8 b.g. Allazzaz – Watch Her Go (Beldale Flutter (USA)) [2006/7 24sᵖᵘ 20mᵖᵘ Jul 2] eighth foal: dam ran once at 2 yrs: no promise over hurdles. *B. D. Leavy*   **h–**

MIGHTY FELLA 5 gr.g. Cloudings (IRE) – Zany Lady (Arzanni) [2006/7 h84: 17m 20s 22mᵖᵘ Apr 28] strong, lengthy gelding: little form over hurdles. *Mrs E. Slack*   **h–**

MIGHTY FINE 13 gr.g. Arzanni – Kate Kimberley (Sparkler) [2006/7 c–, h94: 19g 16g⁶ 16d⁴ 17v⁶ 16s³ c16g² Apr 7] rangy gelding: fair handicap chaser: as good as ever when second to Nifty Roy at Carlisle: modest hurdler: won seller at Musselburgh in January: stays 21f: acts on any going: genuine. *Mrs E. Slack*   **c114 h95**

MIGHTY MAN (FR) 7 b.g. Sir Harry Lewis (USA) – Vanina II (FR) (Italic) [2006/7 h166: 19d² 25d* 24g² 24g* 24mᵖᵘ Apr 26]   **h172**

    A rupture of a superficial flexor tendon on the approach to the straight at Punchestown on his final start almost certainly ended prematurely the racing career of Mighty Man. There was some suggestion in May that, following stem cell treatment, he would perhaps be able to return but, even in the unlikely event of that coming true, it would be a long time before Mighty Man was seen in action again and it would be most unlikely that he would return as good as he was. In what continues to be a particularly fruitful period for staying hurdlers, Mighty Man achieved the highest Timeform rating in this division for the second successive season, when landing the John Smith's Liverpool (Long Distance) Hurdle for a second time at Aintree in April. Not only that, he is the highest rated hurdler over any distance in *Chasers & Hurdlers 2006/07*. In three seasons, Mighty Man won a bumper and seven of fourteen starts over hurdles and was twice placed in the World Hurdle. In terms of status, his win in the BGC Long Walk Hurdle at Ascot in December was his most notable, but it was at Aintree that he excelled, his victory in the Liverpool Hurdle his third successive win at the Grand National meeting, victory in the 2005 Top Novices' Hurdle preceding his two Liverpool

BGC Long Walk Hurdle, Ascot—Mighty Man lands the odds in a muddling affair from outsiders Lough Derg (star on cap) and Temoin (No.10); Blazing Bailey (white face) finishes a close fourth

John Smith's Liverpool Hurdle (Long Distance), Aintree—Mighty Man comprehensively overturns Cheltenham form for the second year running, with Inglis Drever (chevrons) only third behind well-beaten runner-up Black Jack Ketchum

Hurdle wins. Mighty Man was ideally suited by a good test of stamina and raced prior to Punchestown on good going or softer.

Mighty Man's latest victory in the Liverpool Hurdle was of a similar nature to his win twelve months previously. He went to Aintree after a defeat when well fancied for the World Hurdle at Cheltenham. In 2006, he started favourite at Cheltenham, only to finish third behind My Way de Solzen and Golden Cross, before comprehensively reversing places with the former at Aintree. In 2007, he was second favourite at Cheltenham but went down by three quarters of a length to Inglis Drever after the favourite Black Jack Ketchum had been an early faller. The trio met again at Aintree, in a field of six which also included the World Hurdle third Blazing Bailey and the outsiders Fire Dragon and Lough Derg. Black Jack Ketchum was favourite once more, narrowly from Mighty Man, with Inglis Drever only third choice in the market. Inglis Drever was generally regarded as being likely to be less effective on the track at Aintree, while Mighty Man had shown before that Aintree suited him at least as well, if not better than Cheltenham. Richard Johnson (who rode Mighty Man in all but one of his fifteen races) had received some criticism for his riding at Cheltenham and made more use of his mount than on that occasion, setting out to ensure a good test of stamina. With

MIG

Inglis Drever struggling to keep up from quite early in the race, a match developed in the straight between Mighty Man and Black Jack Ketchum. The latter was going equally as well approaching three out but Mighty Man responded stoutly and stayed on much the stronger after the next, going on to defeat Black Jack Ketchum by thirteen lengths, with Inglis Drever nine further back in third. The performance was the best of Mighty Man's career, with the more enterprising tactics clearly partly responsible.

Mighty Man is one of ten hurdlers rated above 170 in the *Chasers & Hurdlers* series that have raced in the last nine seasons and only two of them, Istabraq and Dato Star, were raced primarily at around two miles. Two of the eight others, Le Sauvignon and Mon Romain, earned their ratings from performances in France. The remainder are Limestone Lad (177), Baracouda and Deano's Beeno (both 175), Iris's Gift (172) and Le Coudray (171). Only two of those, Iris's Gift and Baracouda (twice), won the Stayers' Hurdle, as it then was. Like Mighty Man, both Limestone Lad and Le Coudray were runners-up in the race when not quite at their best, though Limestone Lad was third in the epic 2003 renewal, one of the great hurdle races of the modern era, in which Baracouda defeated Iris's Gift. Deano's Beeno finished sixth in that race but was never near his best in three attempts in the Stayers'.

The strong, good-bodied Mighty Man had long been felt likely to make an even better chaser than a hurdler, though whether that prediction would have

Mr E. R. Hanbury's "Mighty Man"

proved accurate may be doubted given the records of those in that elite group that did have a go at making the grade over fences. Limestone Lad, Le Coudray and Iris's Gift were similarly imposing physical types and all made the switch, but none with unalloyed success. Le Coudray (who was sidelined for three years prior to embarking on his chasing career) came closest to matching his hurdles form, showing high-class form when runner-up to both Best Mate and Florida Pearl in Grade 1 events at Leopardstown in 2003/4. Limestone Lad returned successfully to hurdling after an unconvincing novice chasing campaign, though it's worth pointing out that he ended up with a record of four wins (plus a placed effort in Grade 1 company) from just six starts over fences. Iris's Gift couldn't live up to the hopes held for him as a chaser and was retired following two runs in the autumn. Le Sauvignon dropped dead after finishing runner-up to Jair du Cochet in the 2002 Feltham on just his second start over fences. Deano's Beeno was a wide-margin winner of a Newbury novice chase on his sole outing over fences. Istabraq, Bara-couda, Dato Star and Mon Romain weren't risked over the larger obstacles.

Mighty Man had two runs at Ascot before Christmas. In the first, he was no match for Hardy Eustace over two and a half miles in the Ascot Hurdle, though, considering he was conceding the dual Champion Hurdle winner 8 lb, his wasn't a bad effort. In the following month's Long Walk Hurdle, Mighty Man started 11/8-on, with those closest to him in the market being the Rehearsal Chase winner Neptune Collonges (runner-up to My Way de Solzen in the 2005 renewal) and Blazing Bailey, who'd been no match for Black Jack Ketchum at Cheltenham the week previously. In the event it was the outsiders Lough Derg and Temoin who gave Mighty Man the most to do, Johnson needing to get very serious late on as the gelding scrambled home only by a length and a quarter from Lough Derg. Given that the latter failed to get within forty lengths of Mighty Man on their two subsequent meetings, it's safe to say that this Ascot Hurdle actually represented one of his lesser efforts. So far as the other Grade 1 staying hurdle in Britain is concerned, Mighty Man would surely have been ante-post favourite for the 2008 World Hurdle had injury not intervened. It is true he has won just once from five starts at Cheltenham, and Aintree seems to have shown him to better advantage, but his form in the latest World Hurdle was still the third best performance of his career and, with a ride of the type he got at Aintree, the result might have been different.

Mighty Man (FR) (b.g. 2000)	Sir Harry Lewis (USA) (b 1984)	Alleged (b 1974)	Hoist The Flag
			Princess Pout
		Sue Babe (b 1978)	Mr Prospector
			Sleek Dancer
	Vanina II (FR) (b 1987)	Italic (b 2003)	Carnaval
			Bagheira II
		Pin'hup (b 1981)	Signani
			Julie

Mighty Man's pedigree has been fully covered in previous editions of *Chasers & Hurdlers*. There are a couple of updates. His half-sister Mem O'Rees (by Alflora) shaped quite well when fourth in a Chepstow bumper on her debut for Jonjo O'Neill in February, having been bought by J. P. McManus for 100,000 guineas at the Doncaster May Sales in 2005. Meanwhile, Lucky Luk, who is out of a half-sister to Mighty Man's dam Vanina II, gained his first win when successful in a handicap chase at Towcester in October. Vanina II has yet to produce another foal since her 2005 Alflora colt, though a three-year-old gelding by that sire out of another of Vanina II's half-sisters, Grignette, made €50,000 at the 2007 Derby Sale. Mighty Man had a tendency to be worked up in the preliminaries, sometimes causing him to miss a parade, and he was tried with ear plugs to keep him calm. However, his temperament never got the better of him in a race, where he was never less than thoroughly genuine and reliable. He was mostly patiently ridden before the latest Liverpool Hurdle. His regrettable absence will make the top staying hurdles weaker in 2007/8. *H. D. Daly*

MIGHTY MATTERS (IRE) 8 b.g. Muroto – Hasaway (IRE) (Executive Perk) **c101** [2006/7 c106, h–: c24s^{pu} c21m^{pu} c25s^{ur} c24d^4 c25g^F c25d c20v^3 c24g Mar 29] tall, **h–** useful-looking gelding: fair handicap chaser: only creditable effort in 2006/7 on fourth start: shaped as if amiss last 3: stays 3m: acts on good to soft going. *T. R. George*

MIGHTY MESSENGER 7 b. or br.g. Awesome – Bold Dove (Never So Bold) **h–**
[2006/7 16d 16s^{pu} Jan 24] compact gelding: fourth foal: dam unraced: no show over
hurdles. *M. D. I. Usher*

MIGHTY MINSTER 10 ch.m. Minster Son – Mighty Fly (Comedy Star (USA)) **c– §**
[2006/7 26m^2 c16m^{pu} c19m^{ur} c26g^{pu} Nov 15] lengthy mare: maiden hurdler, largely out **h67 §**
of form since 2002/3: no show over fences: stays 3¼m: acts on good to firm and heavy
going: usually in cheekpieces: temperamental. *A. E. Jones*

MIGHTYMISSISSIPPI (IRE) 8 b. or br.g. Lord Americo – Travel On River (IRE) **h–**
(Over The River (FR)) [2006/7 22m^{pu} 21s^{pu} Oct 25] €17,000 3-y-o: big, good-topped
gelding: fifth foal: half-brother to 3m hurdle winner Insan Brook (by Insan): dam
unraced: runner-up on completed start in maiden Irish points in 2005: no show over
hurdles: sold £1,700 Ascot December Sales. *L. Corcoran*

MIGHTY MONTEFALCO 11 b.g. Mtoto – Glendera (Glenstal (USA)) [2006/7 **c–**
c107, h–: c25d^6 Mar 20] workmanlike gelding: has been freeze fired: one-time fairly **h–**
useful hurdler/chaser: prolific winning pointer, well held in hunter in March: stays 25f:
acts on good to firm and good to soft going: tried tongue tied: has been let down by
jumping. *Mrs A. De Lisle Wells*

MIGHTY MOOSE (IRE) 7 b.g. Mister Lord (USA) – Brief Pace (IRE) (Riot Helmet) **c101 +**
[2006/7 c–: c23d c25v^3 c20v* c23v^4 c19g* Mar 21] fair chaser: won handicaps at
Fontwell in January and Chepstow (novice) in March: should stay 3m: acts on heavy
going: tried tongue tied. *Nick Williams*

MIGHTYMULLER (IRE) 5 b.g. Montjeu (IRE) – Anazara (USA) (Trempolino **h–**
(USA)) [2006/7 h94, F–: 17d^5 Oct 7] leggy gelding: modest form at best over hurdles,
tailed off only start in 2006/7: stays 2¼m. *D. R. Gandolfo*

MIGIGI 7 b.m. Alflora (IRE) – Barton Bay (IRE) (Kambalda) [2006/7 h–, F69: 19m **h69**
22s^5 22v^2 Feb 28] rangy mare: poor form over hurdles: likely to be suited by 3m.
M. J. Roberts

MIGRATION 11 b.g. Rainbow Quest (USA) – Armeria (USA) (Northern Dancer) **c–**
[2006/7 c–, h–: 16s^3 Feb 3] tall, useful-looking gelding: one-time fairly useful hurdler, **h78**
little form since 2004: well held only outing over fences: stays 19f: acts on soft going:
tried in cheekpieces. *Mrs S. Lamyman*

MIGUELA 7 b.m. Petoski – Balula's Girl (Gildoran) [2006/7 F16s^5 16v^5 19s Mar 12] **h72**
first foal: dam unraced sister to fair chaser L'Orphelin, stayed 21f: poor form in bumper/ **F74**
over hurdles: should stay at least 2½m. *C. L. Tizzard*

MIGWELL (FR) 7 b.g. Assessor (IRE) – Uguette IV (FR) (Chamberlin (FR)) [2006/7 **c–**
c116, h–: 18s c20s 19s 21v* Feb 12] useful-looking gelding: fairly useful handicap **h119 +**
hurdler: trained by G. Cherel in France first 3 starts: back to best when winning at
Plumpton by 7 lengths from English Jim: ran to similar level when successful on chasing
debut, but no other form over fences: should stay 3m: raced on good going or softer (acts
on heavy): tried blinkered. *Miss E. C. Lavelle*

MIKADO 6 b.g. Sadler's Wells (USA) – Free At Last (Shirley Heights) [2006/7 h118: **h134**
24s 24d 24s^4 22d* 22g 22d 24g^2 Mar 30] smallish, sturdy gelding: useful handicap
hurdler: won 17-runner event at Ascot in December by 3 lengths from Nobel, making all
under good ride: best effort when second to Present Glory (pair clear) at same course:
stays 3m: acts on soft going: ran as if amiss fifth outing. *Jonjo O'Neill*

MIKADO MELODY (IRE) 8 b.g. Supreme Leader – Double Symphony (IRE) **c– §**
(Orchestra) [2006/7 h105: 16g^3 16s* 20g 16d 16v^6 c17v^{pu} 16s^5 Mar 3] smallish, sturdy **h110 §**
gelding: fair handicap hurdler, sold out of A. King's stable 14,000 gns Doncaster May
Sales after first outing: off 5 months, won at Wincanton in October: below form after, lost
all chance when nearly fell third on chasing debut: should stay beyond 2m: raced on good
going or softer (acts on soft): not one to trust. *J. G. Portman*

MIKASA (IRE) 7 b.g. Victory Note (USA) – Resiusa (ITY) (Niniski (USA)) [2006/7 **c81 §**
c81§, h–§: c20s^{pu} c26d^{pu} c21d^4 c20g Mar 27] maiden hurdler: poor chaser: sold out of **h– §**
R. Fisher's stable 8,500 gns Doncaster August Sales prior to final outing: stayed 21f:
acted on heavy going: tried in cheekpieces/blinkers: ungenuine: dead. *S. G. Waugh*

MIKE GOLDEN (IRE) 9 ch.g. Shardari – Dessie's Girl (IRE) (Orchestra) [2006/7 **c93**
c93: c25m^3 c28s^F May 26] winning pointer: fair form when placed in hunters: stays 25f.
R. W. J. Willcox

MIKE INDIA FIVE 5 ch.g. Busy Flight – Latin Beat (Puissance) [2006/7 F14v F16g **F—**
Mar 17] second foal: dam unraced: soundly beaten in bumpers: sold 600 gns Doncaster
May Sales. *S. P. Griffiths*

MIKE SIMMONS 11 b.g. Ballacashtal (CAN) – Lady Crusty (Golden Dipper) [2006/7 **h86**
h–: 16s² 20s⁶ 22mᵖᵘ Sep 10] small gelding: modest handicap hurdler: seems best up to
21f: acts on soft going: tried in cheekpieces: inconsistent. *L. P. Grassick*

MIKO DE BEAUCHENE (FR) 7 b.g. Nashamaa – Chipie d'Angron (FR) (Grand **c135**
Tresor (FR)) [2006/7 h120: c24s* c25vᵖᵘ c25s² c33gᵘʳ Mar 15] strong, good sort: fairly **h—**
useful hurdler: better still over fences: easy winner of maiden at Chepstow in October:
best effort when 3½ lengths second of 4 finishers to Heltornic in Grade 2 novice at
Wetherby: still travelling smoothly when unseating 3 out in National Hunt Chase
(Amateurs) at Cheltenham won by Butler's Cabin: likely to stay beyond 25f: acts on
heavy going, possibly not on good to firm. *R. H. Alner*

MILAN DEUX MILLE (FR) 5 b.g. Double Bed (FR) – Uberaba (FR) (Garde **c138**
Royale) [2006/7 h100, F98: c16g⁶ c24s c18v* c20v* c19g* c20s* c19v³ c21g c21g⁵ **h—**
Apr 13] tall gelding: thrice-raced over hurdles: progressed extremely well over fences,
winning handicaps at Newbury (by 14 lengths) and Warwick in January and Catterick and
Kempton (beat Le Seychellois by 1¼ lengths despite jumping markedly left in second
half of race) in February: ran creditably in quite valuable events last 3 starts, faring best
of those held up when fifth of 29 to Dunbrody Millar in Topham Chase at Aintree:
free-going sort, best short of 3m: acts on heavy going: likely to prove best on left-handed
courses. *D. E. Pipe*

MILAN KING (IRE) 14 b.g. King's Ride – Milan Moss (Le Moss) [2006/7 c–, h–§: **c—**
17f⁵ 17mᵖᵘ Aug 29] lengthy gelding: veteran hurdler: stays 21f: acts on any going: **h57 §**
blinkered twice (pulled up both times): unreliable. *A. J. Lockwood*

MILANSHAN (IRE) 7 b.m. Anshan – Milan Moss (Le Moss) [2006/7 h83?, F78: 22m **h—**
22mᵘʳ 27mᵖᵘ Aug 2] lengthy mare: little impact over hurdles: tried visored. *J. W. Mullins*

MILD FROST 7 gr.g. Shambo – Kellytino (Neltino) [2006/7 F17s Dec 23] £2,500 **F—**
5-y-o: first foal: dam very lightly raced in points: tailed off in bumper on debut. *S. Curran*

MILE HIGH CITY (IRE) 8 b.g. Welsh Term – Jenny's Star (IRE) (Torus) [2006/7 **c—**
c23gᵖᵘ May 11] workmanlike gelding: winning pointer: maiden chaser: sold out of
T. Walsh's stable 12,500 gns Doncaster May (2005) Sales: in cheekpieces, no show in
hunter early in 2006/7. *W. M. Burnell*

MILITAIRE (FR) 9 ch.g. Bering – Moon Review (USA) (Irish River (FR)) [2006/7 **c—**
c–, h–: c24m⁵ c26gᵖᵘ May 24] close-coupled gelding: winning hurdler/pointer: third in **h—**
hunter in 2004, only form in chases: has had tongue tied. *J. M. Turner*

MILITANT (FR) 7 b.g. Cyborg (FR) – Giuletta (FR) (Petit Montmorency (USA)) **c122 p**
[2006/7 16s 16v² 16s³ 16s* c17v* Mar 24] second foal: dam unraced half-sister to **h107**
Champion Hurdle winner Hors La Loi III and high-class staying chaser/hurdler Cyborgo:
runner-up in bumper: fair form over hurdles, won maiden at Down Royal in December by
1¼ lengths from Running Wild: promising chasing debut when winning novice at Navan
by 12 lengths from Glen Harley with plenty to spare: will stay beyond 17f: acts on heavy
going: useful chaser in the making. *J. T. R. Dreaper, Ireland*

MILK AND SULTANA 7 b.m. Millkom – Premier Princess (Hard Fought) [2006/7 **h—**
h65: 17sᵖᵘ Feb 8] modest up to 1½m on Flat, successful 3 times on all-weather in 2006:
seems to have stamina limitations over hurdles. *G. A. Ham*

MILLAGROS (IRE) 7 b.m. Pennekamp (USA) – Grey Galava (Generous (IRE)) **h115**
[2006/7 h109: 16m² 16g⁵ 16m⁶ 16d Feb 14] fair on Flat (stays 13f): fairly useful handicap
hurdler: has run at Musselburgh last 7 starts, best efforts when second (to Pilca) and sixth:
likely to prove best around 2m: acts on good to firm and good to soft going. *I. Semple*

MILLARDS LAD (IRE) 8 b.g. Flemensfirth (USA) – Toransha (Torus) [2006/7 22s⁶ **h69**
21g⁶ 16s Nov 25] €14,000 4-y-o: sturdy, good-bodied gelding: half-brother to fairly
useful 2½m hurdler Keevers (by Commanche Run): dam unraced half-sister to useful
2½m to 3¼m chaser Frazer Island, out of half-sister to high-class staying chaser
Drumlargan: unbeaten in 4 starts in points in 2006: poor form over hurdles: tongue tied
final start. *A. Bateman*

MILL BANK (IRE) 12 b.g. Millfontaine – Mossy Bank (IRE) (Le Moss) [2006/7 c92, **c98**
h63: c19m* c21f² c23f⁴ c20gᵖᵘ c20gᵖᵘ c20fᵖᵘ Apr 5] sturdy gelding: maiden hurdler: **h—**

modest chaser: won handicap at Hereford in June: no form last 3 starts, left Evan Williams after first of them: stays 3m: acts on firm and soft going: tried in cheekpieces/ blinkers: front runner. *Miss C. C. Jones*

MILLBROOK STAR (IRE) 4 b.g. Orpen (USA) – Lady Bodmin (IRE) (Law Society (USA)) [2006/7 17g⁶ 16d 16d Nov 14] small, sparely-made gelding: poor maiden on Flat (stays 1m): poor form in juvenile hurdles. *M. C. Chapman* **h71 ?**

MILLDALUS (IRE) 12 b. or br.g. Mandalus – Chancery Vision (Pauper) [2006/7 c21g^pu May 2] won maiden Irish point in 2001, runner-up both completed starts in Britain in 2006: no show in hunter chase. *Miss L. A. Blackford* **c–**

MILLENIUM MAG (FR) 7 b.g. Cyborg (FR) – Feat (FR) (Cadoudal (FR)) [2006/7 c22d^F c21d⁴ c22g c21d³ c21d c19s^F c18s³ c18v^pu c24g^pu Apr 21] once-raced on Flat/over hurdles: fair chaser, successful twice in Provinces: left E. Leenders and off 4½ months, no show in handicap on British debut: stays 23f: acts on soft ground: has worn blinkers. *F. Jordan* **c101 h–**

MILLENIUM ROYAL (FR) 7 ch.g. Mansonnien (FR) – Pink Champagne (FR) (Blue Courtier) [2006/7 h142: 20s⁵ 24s⁵ 23d 23s* 24g 21s^pu Apr 22] rather leggy gelding: very smart hurdler: improved form when winning 20-runner handicap at Haydock in February by 1¾ lengths from Hirvine, carrying head high: well held in valuable handicap at Cheltenham following month: stays 3m: best form on going softer than good: tried blinkered. *F. Doumen, France* **h155**

MILLENIUM WAY (IRE) 13 ch.g. Ikdam – Fine Drapes (Le Bavard (FR)) [2006/7 c108, h–: c24m² c26s⁴ c23m Apr 22] medium-sized gelding: fairly useful hunter chaser: successful 4 times in points in 2007: stays 3¼m: acts on any going: tried blinkered. *Mrs C. L. Taylor* **c100 h–**

MILLENNIUM ACCORD (IRE) 7 br.m. Accordion – Kissowen (Pitpan) [2006/7 22m³ Apr 17] ex-Irish mare: half-sister to 3 winners, including smart bumper winner Alexander Millenium (by Be My Native) and fair hurdler/fairly useful chaser Factor Ten (by Kemal), stayed 3m: dam unraced half-sister to smart 2½m and 3m chaser Kissane: third in bumper on debut: left Mrs H. Baird, failed to complete in 2 points in Britain: poor form over hurdles. *D. E. Pipe* **h66**

MILLENNIUM HALL 8 b.g. Saddlers' Hall (IRE) – Millazure (USA) (Dayjur (USA)) [2006/7 h97: 20s* 16m³ 16s^F 20g 16v^F Dec 11] short-backed gelding: modest on Flat (stayed 13f): fair hurdler: won maiden at Perth in September: stayed 2½m: acted on soft and good to firm going: dead. *Miss Lucinda V. Russell* **h100**

MILLERS JEWEL 4 b.f. Sly – Old Castle Liziann (The Dissident) [2006/7 F16s F16s Mar 1] first foal: dam unraced: well held in bumpers. *C. J. Price* **F–**

MILL HOUSE GIRL (IRE) 6 ch.m. Basanta (IRE) – Karalee (IRE) (Arokar (FR)) [2006/7 F16f⁶ 16f² 16d⁵ 18d^pu 16g⁴ 16s² 16d³ 16m^pu 16m⁵ Apr 20] good-topped mare: 7f winner on Flat: useful form in bumpers: fairly useful novice hurdler: won at Tipperary in September: better form when placed in graded events there and at Cheltenham (set strong pace when 3 lengths third to Moon Over Miami) next 2 outings: raced around 2m: acts on soft ground (bumper wins on good to firm). *S. Donohoe, Ireland* **h116 F93**

MILLICENT CROSS (IRE) 9 b.g. Executive Perk – Flynn's Girl (IRE) (Mandalus) [2006/7 h76+: 16g Sep 17] lightly-raced maiden hurdler, well held last 2 outings 10 months apart. *R. Ford* **h–**

MILLIES LAD 5 b.g. Whittingham (IRE) – Goodbye Millie (Sayf El Arab (USA)) [2006/7 F16g Apr 3] 2,500 5-y-o: second foal: dam 6f to 1¾m winner: tailed off in bumper on debut. *M. Smith* **F–**

MILLIESOME 9 b.m. Milieu – Some Shiela (Remainder Man) [2006/7 h–: 16f^pu Jul 6] modest form in bumpers: well held completed outing over hurdles. *J. I. A. Charlton* **h–**

MILLIE THE FILLY 4 b.f. Erhaab (USA) – Life Is Life (FR) (Mansonnien (FR)) [2006/7 F14s⁴ F14s F14v F16v⁴ 18s⁴ 16v 16v Mar 10] good-topped filly: first foal: dam 2m hurdle winner and smart stayer on Flat: poor form in bumpers/on hurdling debut: will be suited by 2½m. *P. Monteith* **h68 F68**

MILLIGAN (FR) 12 b.g. Exit To Nowhere (USA) – Madigan Mill (Mill Reef (USA)) [2006/7 c98?, h105?: c16f⁶ 21g 25s⁵ 25d 24s^F 20s⁵ 20v⁴ 16v 20v 20d⁴ Feb 2] close-coupled gelding: maiden chaser: fair hurdler nowadays: stays 2½m when emphasis is on speed: acts on soft and good to firm going, possibly not on heavy. *Dr P. Pritchard* **c– h100**

MILLITANT MAN 5 b.g. Kayf Tara – Ruby Laser (Bustino) [2006/7 F16v⁶ F16v Jan **F71**
25] rangy gelding: first foal: dam, modest and temperamental maiden on Flat, well held
both starts over hurdles: poor form in bumpers: bred to stay well. *S. E. H. Sherwood*

MILLJAZ 7 ch.m. Karinga Bay – Penhill Flame (Main Reef) [2006/7 F16m⁵ F16m **F—**
Jul 12] first live foal: dam winning pointer: won maiden point in 2006: little impact in
bumpers: sold 4,000 gns Doncaster August Sales. *M. R. Bosley*

MILTON DES BIEFFES (FR) 7 gr.g. Princeton (FR) – Rose Fuschia (FR) (Court- **c92**
room (FR)) [2006/7 c21m 26sᵖᵘ 19v* c16v* c16v* c16v⁴ c23vᵖᵘ c24s² c17g Mar 24] **h86**
angular ex-Irish gelding: first foal: dam unraced: won twice in Irish points in 2006:
modest ex-novice chaser, left Garvan Donnelly after first outing: won handicaps at Hereford
and Towcester (again idled) in January: similar form when winning novice handicap
hurdle at Warwick previous month: stays 3m: acts on heavy ground: in cheekpieces 3 of
last 4 starts (seemed to lose interest final one). *Mrs K. Waldron*

MILTON MOSS 8 ch.m. Le Moss – Milton Lass (Scallywag) [2006/7 20sᵖᵘ 20gᵖᵘ **h—**
Nov 10] angular mare: no show in various events. *W. S. Coltherd*

MILTON STAR (IRE) 8 ch.g. Mukaddamah (USA) – Bajan Girl (IRE) (Pips Pride) **h101**
[2006/7 16s² 16g³ Nov 7] sturdy gelding: fair maiden hurdler, left G. Lynch before return:
raced at 2m: acts on any going. *John A. Harris*

MINELLA SILVER (IRE) 14 gr.g. Roselier (FR) – Mrs Minella (Deep Run) [2006/7 **c97**
c108, h—: c16v³ Mar 9] workmanlike gelding: fair hunter chaser: stays 3m: acts on heavy **h—**
and good to firm going: usually front runner. *Ms L. J. Willis*

MINELLA TIPPERARY (IRE) 6 b.g. Saddlers' Hall (IRE) – Graigueheshia (IRE) **h119**
(Strong Gale) [2006/7 22s* 24d² 22s* 22s⁶ 24s* 24d² 24s² 24g⁶ Mar 30] useful-looking
gelding: second foal: dam unraced: unplaced in 2 bumpers, but successful twice in Irish
points in between: sold out of T. Horgan's stable £62,000 Cheltenham April (2006) Sales:
fairly useful novice hurdler: won at Uttoxeter in October and handicaps at Exeter in
November and Ascot (beat Lothian Falcon by ¾ length) in December: good efforts when
runner-up sixth/seventh (16 lengths behind Master Eddy at Newcastle) starts: will stay
beyond 3m: raced mainly on ground softer than good. *P. J. Hobbs*

MINGLING 10 b.g. Wolfhound (USA) – On The Tide (Slip Anchor) [2006/7 16g 16s⁵ **h90**
20g 17m⁵ Jun 30] sturdy gelding: modest novice hurdler, left C. Mann and off over 4
years prior to return: raced mainly around 2m. *A. King*

MINI MINSTER 5 b.m. Minster Son – Dreamago (Sir Mago) [2006/7 F16s F16s⁴ **F82**
F17g³ Apr 23] half-sister to fair hunter chaser Go Nomadic, stays 31f, and
winning pointer Nomadic Star (both by Nomadic Way): dam modest pointer: modest
form in mares bumpers: will be suited by stiffer test of stamina. *P. G. Atkinson*

MINIPERSE (FR) 7 ch.g. Lyphard's Wish (FR) – Lady Persane (FR) (Roi de Perse II) **c—**
[2006/7 c—, h—: 16d⁶ Sep 22] plain gelding: no solid form over hurdles/in novice chase. **h—**
G. R. I. Smyly

MINIVET 12 b.g. Midyan (USA) – Bronzewing (Beldale Flutter (USA)) [2006/7 c—, **c—**
h—: 16g 22d⁴ 19d⁶ 20sᵖᵘ 24fᵖᵘ 20g⁶ 20f Aug 11] close-coupled gelding: fair hurdler in **h—**
2004/5, no form since: tried visored/in cheekpieces. *R. Allan*

MINNIGAFF (IRE) 7 b.g. Supreme Leader – Across The Pond (IRE) (Over The River **c—**
(FR)) [2006/7 c—, h—: c20vᵖᵘ May 18] poor maiden pointer: no form in other events. **h—**
Mrs L. Williamson

MINOUCHKA (FR) 7 br.m. Bulington (FR) – Elbury (FR) (Royal Charter (FR)) **c94**
[2006/7 c77: c16f² c16mᵘʳ c16s³ c16g³ c20s³ Oct 25] leggy mare: modest novice chaser,
placed all 8 completed starts: successful both outings in points: stays 2½m: best efforts
on good going or softer. *S. H. Shirley-Beavan*

MINSTER ABBI 7 b.m. Minster Son – Elitist (Keren) [2006/7 h68: 24v⁵ 24v 19v* **h94**
20v³ 20v* Mar 18] tall, good-topped mare: modest handicap hurdler: won at Catterick
(ladies seller) in February and Carlisle (novice) in March: effective from 17f to 25f: acts
on heavy going: wears cheekpieces. *W. Storey*

MINSTER BLUE 9 b.m. Minster Son – Elitist (Keren) [2006/7 c—, h—: 22d May 29] **c—**
good-bodied mare: of little account: tried in cheekpieces. *F. P. Murtagh* **h—**

MINSTER LANE 7 ch.g. Minster Son – Coverdale Lane (Boreen (FR)) [2006/7 F—: **F—**
F17sᵖᵘ May 21] no sign of ability. *J. M. Saville*

MINSTER PARK 8 b.g. Minster Son – Go Gipsy (Move Off) [2006/7 h81, F–: 22m³ **h88** 24fᵖᵘ Jun 3] modest maiden hurdler: would probably have stayed 3m: acted on firm going: tongue tied last 4 starts: dead. *S. C. Burrough*

MINSTER SHADOW 8 b.g. Minster Son – Polar Belle (Arctic Lord) [2006/7 27d⁵ **h103** 27s³ 23v³ 22v² 20s³ 22v⁶ 25v⁵ Mar 18] tall gelding: fair handicap hurdler: thorough stayer: raced on ground softer than good (acts well on heavy): tried in cheekpieces. *C. Grant*

MINSTREL'S DOUBLE 6 ch.g. Jumbo Hirt (USA) – Hand On Heart (IRE) (Taufan **h–** (USA)) [2006/7 h–: 20d 20m 16f 20g Aug 1] little form, left F. Murtagh after first outing (visored). *M. A. Barnes*

MINTHARE (IRE) 4 br.g. Bahhare (USA) – Mintaka (IRE) (Fairy King (USA)) **h83** [2006/7 16s³ 16s⁵ Oct 11] fair maiden on Flat (stays 12.4f): better effort in juvenile hurdles when third at Perth: tongue tied next time: sold 8,000 gns Doncaster October Sales. *C. Grant*

MIOCHE D'ESTRUVAL (FR) 7 bl.g. Lute Antique (FR) – Charme d'Estruval (FR) **c– §** (Mistigri) [2006/7 c117§, h–§: c28sᵖᵘ May 26] angular gelding: winning hurdler: fairly **h– §** useful chaser, no show in handicap early in 2006/7: successful in point in April: stays 3¼m: acts on soft and good to firm going: has worn visor: often soon off bridle: unreliable. *D. E. Pipe*

MIRACLE BABY 5 b.m. Atraf – Musica (Primo Dominie) [2006/7 16dᵖᵘ 16g Nov 15] **h–** sturdy mare: poor maiden on Flat: no impact in novice hurdles. *A. J. Chamberlain*

MIRAGE PRINCE (IRE) 5 ch.g. Desert Prince (IRE) – Belle Bijou (Midyan (USA)) **h–** [2006/7 16f⁶ 16m⁵ 16m 16s 16fᵖᵘ Apr 5] has reportedly been tubed: maiden on Flat: little show over hurdles: tried tongue tied. *S. T. Lewis*

MIRANT 8 b.g. Danzig Connection (USA) – Ingerence (FR) (Akarad (FR)) [2006/7 **c– §** h108: 19s⁵ c16mᶠ 16gᶠ 17d 19d 19m⁴ 19m⁵ 19m² Oct 4] quite good-topped gelding: **h88 §** modest hurdler nowadays: beaten when falling on chasing debut: stays 19f: acts on good to firm and good to soft going: visored last 6 outings: temperamental. *D. E. Pipe*

MIRJAN (IRE) 11 b.g. Tenby – Mirana (IRE) (Ela-Mana-Mou) [2006/7 h133§: 16vᵖᵘ **h– §** Feb 24] angular gelding: useful stayer on Flat, successful in August: useful handicap hurdler, little impact only start in 2006/7: stays 23f, at least when emphasis is on speed: acts on heavy and good to firm going: usually wears headgear. *L. Lungo*

MISBEHAVIOUR 8 b.g. Tragic Role (USA) – Exotic Forest (Dominion) [2006/7 **h105 §** h108: 16s³ 16g 16g 16d⁵ 18s² 16v 17s 16v Feb 26] sparely-made gelding: fair handicap hurdler: beaten around 2m: acts on heavy going: has worn visor/cheekpieces: weak finisher: joined Jim Best. *G. L. Moore*

MISCHIEF MAN 5 b.g. Alflora (IRE) – Rascally (Scallywag) [2006/7 F17g* F16d⁶ **h–** 16d 16v⁵ 16s Mar 7] tall, good-bodied gelding: first foal: dam, fair hurdler, stayed 2¾m: **F95** fairly useful form in bumpers, won at Market Rasen on debut in September: well held in novice hurdles: tends to race freely. *M. W. Easterby*

MISCHIEF NIGHT 5 ch.g. Lake Coniston (IRE) – On Till Morning (IRE) (Never So **h–** Bold) [2006/7 24sᵖᵘ 17v 16d Dec 28] tall, good-topped gelding: modest maiden on Flat (stays 1½m) for M. Dods: little show in maiden hurdles. *J. J. Davies*

MISCHIEVOUS JOSH 4 br.g. Classic Cliche (IRE) – Celestial Ridge (IRE) (Indian **F–** Ridge) [2006/7 F16v F13m Mar 29] third foal: dam ran once: tailed off in bumpers. *D. W. Thompson*

MISLEAIN (IRE) 7 b.m. Un Desperado (FR) – Naar Chamali (Salmon Leap (USA)) **h71 §** [2006/7 F91: F16d F16m³ 16g 16v² 17v⁴ 20m Mar 25] angular mare: disappointing since **F76 §** third in bumper on debut: ungenuine (almost refused to race final start). *J. R. Turner*

MISS ACADEMY (FR) 6 ch.m. Video Rock (FR) – Mademoiselle Wo (FR) (Prince **h119** Wo (FR)) [2006/7 h116: 18fᵖᵘ 16s³ 16s 16vᵖᵘ Jan 27] leggy, close-coupled mare: fairly useful handicap hurdler: form in 2006/7 only when third to Daryal at Lingfield, enterprisingly ridden: raced around 2m: acts on heavy going. *D. E. Pipe*

MISS BABS (IRE) 6 b.m. Arctic Lord – Miss Ivy (IRE) (Le Bavard (FR)) [2006/7 **h–** 20mᶠ Apr 15] fourth foal: half-sister to winning hurdler Toulouse Express (by Toulon), stays 2½m, and winning pointer by Semillon: dam bumper winner: won maiden point in March: behind when fell last in mares maiden on hurdling debut. *G. Elliott, Ireland*

MISS BIDDY 12 ch.m. Sula Bula – Bickfield Approach (Dubassoff (USA)) [2006/7 c21g^pu Apr 27] winning pointer: no show in novice hurdle/hunter 4 years apart. *Miss Olivia Maylam*

c–
h–

MISS BUSTINO 5 b.m. Overbury (IRE) – Miniture Melody (IRE) (Kemal (FR)) [2006/7 F17s Jan 26] 4,500 4-y-o: third foal: dam, bad novice hurdler, placed in points: well beaten in bumper on debut. *D. J. Wintle*

F–

MISS CAMPANELLA 6 b.m. Bal Harbour – Tinkle (Petoski) [2006/7 F16f* Jul 6] fifth foal: dam ran once: modest form when winning bumper at Perth on debut by 3 lengths from Champagne Only, dictating. *W. S. Coltherd*

F78

MISS CEKA (IRE) 5 gr.m. Rudimentary (USA) – Party Woman (IRE) (Sexton Blake) [2006/7 F17s^4 Jan 24] €30,000Y: fifth foal: half-sister to fair hurdler Miss Mitch (by King's Theatre), stays 2½m: dam, fairly useful hurdler, stayed 2½m: fair form when fourth to Irish Wedding in mares maiden bumper at Folkestone on debut. *R. H. Alner*

F87

MISS CHAMPAGNE (IRE) 4 b.f. Tagula (IRE) – Champagne Lady (IRE) (Turtle Island (IRE)) [2006/7 16g^pu 16s 17g^pu Apr 23] modest on Flat (stays 8.6f), successful early in 2006 for M. Quinn: no show in juvenile hurdles. *A. Wilson*

h–

MISS CHIPPY (IRE) 7 ch.m. Mister Lord (USA) – My Alanna (Dalsaan) [2006/7 h–, F85: c20d^4 c26s^pu 22s^pu Feb 17] no solid form over jumps: sketchy jumper. *T. R. George*

c–
h–

MISS COSPECTOR 8 ch.m. Emperor Fountain – Gypsy Race (IRE) (Good Thyne (USA)) [2006/7 23g Oct 19] leggy, lengthy mare: modest hurdler: off 18 months, well held only start in 2006/7: stays 3m: acts on heavy going. *T. H. Caldwell*

h–

MISS DEFYING 5 b.m. Shambo – Doug (Risk Me (FR)) [2006/7 h–: 24s^pu Dec 18] compact mare: no sign of ability: tried visored. *R. Curtis*

h–

MISS DOMINO 6 b.m. Alderbrook – Mrs Moneypenny (Relkino) [2006/7 h–, F–: 19d^pu 16s Dec 6] good-topped mare: no sign of ability. *S. J. Gilmore*

h–

MISS FIRELIGHT 7 b.m. Sir Harry Lewis (USA) – Miss Firecracker (Relkino) [2006/7 F17d May 17] third foal: half-sister to winning pointer Impatient Lady (by Morpeth): dam, poor form in bumpers/novice hurdles, half-sister to top-class 2m hurdler/very smart chaser Prideaux Boy: last in bumper on debut. *J. D. Frost*

F–

MISS FLEUR 4 b.f. Bandmaster (USA) – Floral Park (Northern Park (USA)) [2006/7 F18v^4 aF16g Mar 9] first foal: dam no worthwhile form: well held in bumpers. *W. G. M. Turner*

F–

MISS FLOSSY (IRE) 6 ch.m. Bob Back (USA) – Moscow Money (IRE) (Moscow Society (USA)) [2006/7 h–: 20d 22s^pu 24s Dec 18] no form over hurdles: tried in cheekpieces. *Mrs S. D. Williams*

h–

MISS GRACE 7 ch.m. Atticus (USA) – Jetbeeah (IRE) (Lomond (USA)) [2006/7 h72+: 19g^pu May 16] poor form over hurdles, amiss only outing in 2006/7. *J. D. Frost*

h–

MISSION MAN 6 b.g. Revoque (IRE) – Opopmil (IRE) (Pips Pride) [2006/7 17s Mar 11] fairly useful on Flat (stays 1m) at one time, well below best in 2007 after 2½-year absence: well held in novice at Market Rasen on hurdling debut: dead. *M. G. Rimell*

h76

MISSION TO MARS 8 b.g. Muhtarram (USA) – Ideal Candidate (Celestial Storm (USA)) [2006/7 16s^pu 16d Dec 30] strong gelding: useful on Flat (stayed 1½m) at one time, well below best in 2007: no form in 2 novice hurdles: dead. *P. G. Murphy*

h–

MISSIS POTTS 6 b.m. Overbury (IRE) – Potter's Gale (IRE) (Strong Gale) [2006/7 F95: 20v^3 19v^2 16s* 21g^pu 16g* 19m* Apr 22] good-topped mare: comes from very good jumping family (dam half-sister to Denman amongst others): fairly useful hurdler: successful last 3 completed starts, in maiden at Wincanton in March, and novice at Chepstow and mares handicap at Stratford (further improvement when beating Sovietica by 7 lengths) in April: bred to be suited by further than 19f: acts on heavy and good to firm going. *P. J. Hobbs*

h121 +

MISS IVERLEY 5 b.m. Shambo – Blanche The Almond (Northern Park (USA)) [2006/7 h–: 16s^4 Jun 25] no form over hurdles. *J. M. Dun*

h–

MISS KILKEEL (IRE) 5 b.m. Religiously (USA) – Shakiyka (IRE) (Shardari) [2006/7 c92, h101: c16g 19f 16d 20s 20v^6 24s 24d^6 Jan 19] twice-raced over fences: winning hurdler, below best in 2006/7: stays 2½m: acts on firm and good to soft going. *Roy Wilson, Ireland*

c–
h87

MISS LEHMAN 9 ch.m. Beveled (USA) – Lehmans Lot (Oats) [2006/7 h88: 17m 19d[4] c16d[5] Aug 20] modest handicap hurdler, respectable effort second start: tailed off on chasing debut next time: probably stays 19f: acts on soft and good to firm going. *J. D. Frost*
   c–
   h81

MISS LIGHTNING 4 b.f. Mujahid (USA) – Salu (Ardross) [2006/7 F14v F16s Feb 3] good-topped filly: half-sister to fair hurdler Merryvale Man (by Rudimentary) and modest/untrustworthy hurdler Mister Moussac (by Kasakov), both of whom stay 2½m: dam successful up to 2m on Flat: showed nothing in 2 bumpers. *R. Bastiman*
   F–

MISS MATTIE ROSS 11 b.m. Milieu – Mother Machree (Bing II) [2006/7 c114, h–: c22m[pu] c25d[pu] c25s[6] Nov 17] medium-sized mare: fair handicap chaser, has lost her form: stays 25f: acts on heavy and good to firm going: usually front runner/races prominently. *S. J. Marshall*
   c–
   h–

MISS MEE (FR) 7 ch.m. Epervier Bleu – Une de Mee (FR) (Sarpedon (FR)) [2006/7 20m 20m[F] Jul 2] maiden on Flat, placed 4 times up to around 1¾m in French Provinces: well beaten in 5-y-o event there on chasing debut: left S. Foucher, also well held completed start over hurdles: dead. *Mrs L. Wadham*
   c–
   h–

MISS MERENDA 6 b.m. Sir Harry Lewis (USA) – Cool Merenda (IRE) (Glacial Storm (USA)) [2006/7 h84§: 22m[6] 23d 23g[4] 22m[pu] Apr 28] poor hurdler: little form in handicaps in 2006/7: stays 2¾m: acts on soft and good to firm going: tried in cheekpieces: temperamental. *J. F. Panvert*
   h74 §

MISS MIDNIGHT 6 b.m. Midnight Legend – Miss Marigold (Norwick (USA)) [2006/7 h87, F86: 19m May 9] angular mare: modest novice hurdler: stays 19f: acts on good to firm and good to soft ground: blinkered 4 of last 5 starts in 2005/6: often runs as if amiss. *R. J. Hodges*
   h– §

MISS MILLFIELD 6 b.m. Hatim (USA) – Miss Millbrook (Meadowbrook) [2006/7 h–, F–: 24f Jun 21] no show in bumpers/maiden hurdles: runner-up in maiden point in April. *V. J. Hughes*
   h–

MISS MITCH (IRE) 6 b. or br.m. King's Theatre (IRE) – Party Woman (IRE) (Sexton Blake) [2006/7 F83: 16d[4] 21d[6] 20s[F] 20s[*] 21g[2] Mar 24] tall, good-topped mare: useful form over hurdles: won mares events at Towcester (novice, easily) in October and Hereford (handicap) in January: further improvement when 3 lengths second of 18 to Karello Bay in listed mares novice handicap at Newbury: likely to stay 3m: raced on good ground or softer. *R. H. Alner*
   h130

MISS MOLLY BE RUDE (IRE) 5 b.m. Perugino (USA) – Ediyrna (IRE) (Doyoun) [2006/7 F16m F17m[3] F16g F17d 16g 20m Apr 15] fourth foal: half-sister to fair 2m hurdle winner Swift Spirit (by Lake Coniston) and modest hurdler Don't Ask Me (by Spectrum), stays 2¾m: dam unraced: no form in bumpers/maiden hurdles. *J. R. Norton*
   h–
   F–

MISS MORELLI (IRE) 6 b.m. Beneficial – That's Lucy (IRE) (Henbit (USA)) [2006/7 F16g[6] 20s 20d 16m[5] 20v[pu] 24s[pu] Apr 25] second foal: dam no form: in frame in mares maiden points in 2006: little form in bumpers/over hurdles. *I. R. Ferguson, Ireland*
   h70
   F74

MISS MUSCAT 7 b.m. Environment Friend – Fisima (Efisio) [2006/7 c78x, h–: 22d[4] c19m[pu] c20m[4] c23m[3] c24g[4] 27d[*] 26m[5] Aug 28] small, angular mare: poor handicap hurdler/chaser: won over hurdles at Newton Abbot in August: stays 27f: acts on good to soft and good to firm ground: held up: not always fluent over fences: joined C. Roberts. *S. Lycett*
   c81
   h76

MISS NOSEY 5 b.m. Danzero (AUS) – Miss Nosey Oats (Oats) [2006/7 h–: 20g[6] 16m[pu] Jun 17] little form in novice hurdles. *Mrs E. Slack*
   h–

MISS O'MURCHU 5 b.m. Overbury (IRE) – Gulsha (Glint of Gold) [2006/7 F14s F17s F16g[6] Apr 9] seventh foal: half-sister to fairly useful hurdler/chaser Gulshan (by Batshoof), stayed 3m: dam, fairly useful hurdler up to 2½m, half-sister to smart 2m hurdler/winning chaser Bold Boss: little impact in mares bumpers. *B. I. Case*
   F71

MISSOURI (USA) 4 b.g. Gulch (USA) – Coco (USA) (Storm Bird (CAN)) [2006/7 16s 18s 16v[5] 17g[6] 16m Apr 24] modest on Flat (stays 1½m), claimed from G. M. Moore £5,000 when successful in December: no solid form over hurdles. *W. G. M. Turner*
   h–

MISS PEBBLES (IRE) 7 ch.m. Lake Coniston (IRE) – Sea of Stone (USA) (Sanglamore (USA)) [2006/7 h103: 16g[5] 16d c16d[5] Nov 26] workmanlike mare: winning hurdler, below best in handicaps in 2006/7: jumped poorly on chasing debut: best around 2m: raced on good going or softer. *R. Dickin*
   c–
   h95

MISS PORTSIDE 4 b.f. Mull of Kintyre (USA) – Collision (Wolfhound (USA)) **F—**
[2006/7 F14s Dec 16] unfurnished filly: second foal: dam ran twice: tailed off in bumper
on debut. *J. C. Haynes*

MISS PROSS 7 b.m. Bob's Return (IRE) – Lucy Manette (Final Straw) [2006/7 c99, **c109**
h92: 17v² 16s⁴ c16s* 16v⁴ c16v³ 17s* 20g⁵ Apr 7] good-topped mare: fair handicap **h106**
hurdler/chaser: won over fences in December and over hurdles in March, both times at
Sedgefield: may prove best short of 2½m: raced on good going or softer (acts on heavy).
T. D. Walford

MISS RIDEAMIGHT 8 b.m. Overbury (IRE) – Nicolynn (Primitive Rising (USA)) **h105**
[2006/7 h—: 20d 19v² 16v⁵ 20v⁶ 20g* 20m* 22g* Apr 27] smallish, lengthy mare: fair
handicap hurdler: much improved after claimed from G. Brown £5,600 fourth outing,
winning at Chepstow (seller), Worcester (heavily eased) and Newton Abbot (beat
Commemoration Day a short head after again travelling strongly) within 2 weeks in
April: stays 2¾m: acts on heavy and good to firm going. *P. D. Evans*

MISS ROYELLO 10 b.m. Royal Fountain – Lady Manello (Mandrake Major) [2006/7 **c92**
c27mᵖᵘ c24m⁵ c26m⁴ c25s² Oct 27] modest handicap chaser, off 18 months before
reappearance: stays 27f: acts on heavy and good to firm going: usually races prominently.
Mrs A. Hamilton

MISS SALLYFIELD (IRE) 8 b.m. Mister Lord (USA) – Rose of Solway (Derring **c—**
Rose) [2006/7 c19v 16v 21v³ c24mᵖᵘ Mar 25] successful twice in points: not fluent and **h—**
no form over hurdles/in chases: tried blinkered. *R. Curtis*

MISS SHAKIRA (IRE) 9 b.m. Executive Perk – River Water (Over The River (FR)) **c107**
[2006/7 c101, h97: 20d³ 24s⁴ c20g² c21g c24s⁶ Mar 3] leggy mare: modest hurdler: fair **h90**
chaser: stays 3m: acts on heavy going: seems best ridden from front/prominently: has
hung/jumped right. *N. A. Twiston-Davies*

MISS SHRED EASY 7 ch.m. Gunner B – D C Flyer (Record Token) [2006/7 20v 19g **h73**
20d 16v⁵ 20g Apr 3] 3,600 5-y-o: big mare: third foal: dam, winning pointer, half-sister
to fairly useful staying hurdler/chaser Gunner Mac (by Gunner B): poor form over
hurdles: likely to prove best at 2½m+. *R. C. Guest*

MISS SKIPPY 8 b.m. Saddlers' Hall (IRE) – Katie Scarlett (Lochnager) [2006/7 h96: **h104**
20m² 20m² 22m³ 22g³ 22g³ Apr 27] angular mare: fair handicap hurdler: won at
Southwell in July: good efforts all starts: stays 2¾m: acts on good to firm ground,
seemingly not on soft/heavy: tried tongue tied. *A. G. Newcombe*

MISS WIZADORA 12 ch.m. Gildoran – Lizzie The Twig (Precipice Wood) [2006/7 **c—**
c76, h—: c21d² Oct 20] smallish, angular mare: poor handicap chaser, lightly raced: **h—**
should stay 3m: raced on good going or softer (acts on heavy): has been let down by
jumping. *Simon Earle*

MISS WOLF 7 b.m. Wolfhound (USA) – Jussoli (Don) [2006/7 F13m F17g⁶ F16m **F—**
Oct 12] half-sister to 3 winners, including 2½m hurdle winner Miss Ellie (by Elmaamul)
and fair hunter chaser Rooster (by Roi Danzig): dam Irish 7f (at 2 yrs) to 1¼m winner:
well beaten in bumpers and maidens on Flat. *G. H. Jones*

MISSYL (FR) 7 gr.g. Great Palm (USA) – Elite Dacadour (FR) (Sarpedon (FR)) **c99**
[2006/7 c78, h94: c18m² c20m² c20g³ c24g⁴ Nov 7] good-topped gelding: modest novice **h—**
hurdler/chaser: should have stayed beyond 2½m: acted on good to firm going: dead.
R. H. Alner

MISSY MOSCOW (IRE) 9 b.m. Moscow Society (USA) – Bright Shares (IRE) **c86**
(Mandalus) [2006/7 c—, h—: c21m⁵ 22mᵖᵘ c24m³ c23d² c23d² c23m⁴ c21dᵖᵘ c20s c22m* **h—**
Apr 24] leggy mare: maiden hurdler: modest chaser: won weak maiden at Towcester:
stays 3m: acts on good to firm and good to soft going: blinkered after reappearance.
H. J. Evans

MISSYOUMARY 7 b.m. Petrizzo – Muskerry Miss (IRE) (Bishop of Orange) [2006/7 **c—**
22d 24d⁵ 21sᵖᵘ c20gᵖᵘ Mar 18] no sign of ability. *H. J. Manners* **h—**

MIST AGAIN 4 ch.f. Double Trigger (IRE) – Idiot's Lady (Idiot's Delight) [2006/7 **F67**
F16s⁴ Mar 11] second foal: dam, fairly useful hurdler/chaser, suited by test of stamina:
green, 13¾ lengths fourth of 9 to Fiddle in mares bumper at Warwick on debut: will be
suited by further. *Mrs A. J. Bowlby*

MISTANOORA 8 b.g. Topanoora – Mistinguett (IRE) (Doyoun) [2006/7 h—: c21s⁴ **c—**
21g⁶ 23d 24s⁶ 24v 23s 24g⁴ 24g Apr 14] small, workmanlike gelding: jumped pond- **h130**
erously when well held only outing over fences: useful handicap hurdler on his day:

dropped in weights, 4½ lengths fourth of 24 to Oscar Park in listed Pertemps Final at Cheltenham: stays 25f: acts on any going: usually blinkered. *N. A. Twiston-Davies*

MISTER APPLE'S (FR) 7 ch.g. Video Rock (FR) – Doryane (FR) (Bayolidaan (FR)) [2006/7 c97, h–: c22v^{pu}c25s c20v^5 c22s^3 c24v^2 c24g^2 c24m^2 c25m^2 Apr 20] tall gelding: maiden hurdler: modest handicap chaser, placed last 5 starts: stays 25f: acts on heavy and good to firm going: wears headgear: none too resolute. *Ian Williams* **c96 h–**

MISTER BECKS (IRE) 4 b.g. Beckett (IRE) – Cappuchino (IRE) (Roi Danzig (USA)) [2006/7 16d 16g 16g Nov 29] tall, good-topped gelding: poor on Flat (stays 6f): unlikely to stay over hurdles. *M. C. Chapman* **h–**

MISTER BENEDICTINE 4 b.g. Mister Baileys – Cultural Role (Night Shift (USA)) [2006/7 16d* 16d 17d^2 17m^2 16m Apr 25] workmanlike gelding: half-brother to fairly useful 2m hurdler Dont Call Me Derek (by Sri Pekan): fairly useful on Flat (should stay 1m), sold out of W. Muir's stable 15,000 gns Newmarket Autumn Sales: successful hurdling debut in juvenile maiden at Plumpton in November: better form when second in juveniles won by River Logic at Market Rasen and Classic Dream at Hereford: likely to prove best around 2m with emphasis on speed. *B. W. Duke* **h111**

MISTER BIGTIME (IRE) 13 br.g. Roselier (FR) – Cnoc An Oir (Goldhill) [2006/7 c26s^3 c24g^2 Apr 27] well-made gelding: maiden chaser, fairly useful at one time: placed in hunters in 2006/7 (won point in between): stays 3¼m: acts on heavy going: tried in cheekpieces/blinkers: tongue tied last 3 starts. *Richard Mathias* **c84 h–**

MISTER CEE JAY (IRE) 5 b.g. Old Vic – Juggling Act (IRE) (Be My Native (USA)) [2006/7 F13m^6 21g 19v^F 16s 19g Mar 25] €7,200 3-y-o: unfurnished gelding: fifth foal: dam of no account on Flat: sixth in bumper at Hereford on debut: mid-division at best over hurdles, including in handicap. *Ian Williams* **h70 F77**

MISTER CHRISTIAN (IRE) 6 ch.g. Shernazar – Laurabeg (Laurence O) [2006/7 F81: F17s 20m Jul 12] modest form first 2 starts in bumpers: well held in novice on hurdling debut: bred to be suited by 2½m+. *W. K. Goldsworthy* **h– F64**

MISTER CLUB ROYAL 8 b.g. Alflora (IRE) – Miss Club Royal (Avocat) [2006/7 c96, h–: c21g^F c25d^4 c26g^{pu} Apr 19] good-topped gelding: fair hunter chaser: won point in March: stays 3¼m: acts on heavy going, probably on good to firm: tried blinkered/tongue tied. *Ms Emma Oliver* **c89 h–**

MISTER COMPLETELY (IRE) 6 b.g. Princely Heir (IRE) – Blue Goose (Belmez (USA)) [2006/7 h83: 22g 18m^4 20m^3 20m^5 Aug 24] modest on all-weather on Flat (stays 16.5f): poor novice hurdler: stays 2½m: acts on heavy and good to firm going: sold £6,400 Ascot August Sales, won on Flat in January for Ms J. Doyle. *Miss S. West* **h83**

MISTER EL BEE 7 b.g. El Conquistador – Sybillabee (Sula Bula) [2006/7 F16f F17m^6 22m Aug 26] sixth in bumper at Market Rasen, only sign of ability. *C. Grant* **h– F70**

MISTER ETEK 6 b.g. Defacto (USA) – Boulevard Girl (Nicholas Bill) [2006/7 F81: F16g^6 20s^6 Oct 11] tall gelding: modest form first 2 starts in bumpers: well held in novice on hurdling debut: sold 2,000 gns Doncaster November Sales. *T. D. Walford* **h– F74**

MISTER FIZZBOMB (IRE) 4 b.g. Lend A Hand – Crocus (IRE) (Mister Baileys) [2006/7 17g^5 16d^4 17s^4 16g Apr 16] lengthy gelding: modest on Flat (stays 1½m, has refused to enter stall), successful in June: best effort over hurdles when fourth to European Dream in juvenile at Wetherby second outing: raced around 2m on good going or softer: in cheekpieces last 3 outings. *J. S. Wainwright* **h84**

MISTER FLINT 9 b.g. Petoski – National Clover (National Trust) [2006/7 c125, h–: 16g Oct 24] workmanlike gelding: fairly useful chaser: winning hurdler, off 13 months before well held in handicap only outing in 2006/7: should stay beyond 2½m: acts on firm and soft going. *P. J. Hobbs* **c– h–**

MISTER FRIDAY (IRE) 10 b. or br.g. Mister Lord (USA) – Rebecca's Storm (IRE) (Strong Gale) [2006/7 c116, h–: c26g* c24m^{pu} Jun 22] leggy gelding: useful hunter chaser: third success at Cheltenham when beating No Retreat 9 lengths in May: stays 27f: unraced on firm going, acts on any other: visored: patiently ridden. *C. A. Mulhall* **c114 h–**

MISTER FROG (FR) 6 b.g. Dress Parade – Baronne de Meucon (FR) (Master Thatch) [2006/7 F100: F16g^6 Nov 10] heavy-topped gelding: better effort in bumpers a year apart when third at Sedgefield on debut: sold 3,000 gns Doncaster March Sales. *G. A. Swinbank* **F86**

MISTER HIGHT (FR) 5 bl.g. Take Risks (FR) – Miss High (FR) (Concorde Jr (USA)) [2006/7 h135: 19s 16d^4 16d* 16d^2 16d^5 21g^5 Mar 14] close-coupled gelding: **h147**

smart hurdler: won minor event at Limerick in December by 3½ lengths from Rindoon: good efforts in very valuable handicaps all 3 starts after, at Leopardstown (2½ lengths second to Spring The Que), Newbury (around 4 lengths fifth to Heathcote) and Cheltenham (fifth of 28 to Burntoakboy, running on strongly after left poorly placed): stays 21f: acts on soft and good to firm going. *W. P. Mullins, Ireland*

MISTER JUNGLE (FR) 5 b.g. Saint Cyrien (FR) – Fabuleuse Histoire (FR) (Fabulous Dancer (USA)) [2006/7 F85: 16s² 20s* 20gᵖᵘ Nov 2] unfurnished gelding: second start in novice hurdles, won at Wetherby in October by head from Rudaki: ran poorly next time: stays 2½m: acts on soft going. *Mrs S. C. Bradburne*   **h90**

MISTER KNIGHT (IRE) 8 ch.g. Mister Lord (USA) – Knights Bounty (IRE) (Henbit (USA)) [2006/7 F91: 22s⁴ 22s⁵ 24s³ 24g³ 24g Mar 25] tall, lengthy gelding: fifth on completed outing in maiden points: off further 14 months, progressive form first 4 starts over hurdles, third to Shannon Springs in maiden at Ludlow on last occasion: stays 3m: raced on good going or softer (acts on soft): usually waited with. *P. F. Nicholls*   **h112**

MISTERMAGICMAN (IRE) 7 gr.g. Daar Alzamaan (IRE) – Roseliers Girl (IRE) (Roselier (FR)) [2006/7 c16f⁵ c21mᶠ c17dᵘʳ c20d⁶ c20d⁴ c20dᵖᵘ c25sᵖᵘ Feb 27] leggy gelding: first foal: dam unraced: maiden pointer: modest form in chases, possibly flattered. *Miss Kate Milligan*   **c86 ?**

MISTER MAGNUM (IRE) 9 b.g. Be My Native (USA) – Miss Henrietta (IRE) (Step Together (USA)) [2006/7 c–, h–: c16m² c16s⁵ c22m⁴ c25g² c20d⁵ c16d c20v³ c24s⁴ c22v⁶ c21v⁵ c16v³ c16vᵖᵘ c16v⁴ c20v² c20g Apr 23] leggy, close-coupled gelding: poor maiden handicap chaser: lame final outing: probably stays 3m: acts on good to firm and heavy going: has worn cheekpieces: temperamental. *P. Monteith*   **c81 §**
h–

MISTER MAQ 4 b.g. Namaqualand (USA) – Nordico Princess (Nordico (USA)) [2006/7 16sᵖᵘ Sep 20] modest on Flat (stays 1¼m), successful in July: no show in juvenile on hurdling debut: sold 2,800 gns Doncaster October Sales, joined A. Crook. *M. Dods*   **h–**

MISTER MCGOLDRICK 10 b.g. Sabrehill (USA) – Anchor Inn (Be My Guest (USA)) [2006/7 c158, h146: c20s⁵ c17d⁴ c20s² c17v⁴ 16v⁴ c16g⁶ c19g c16f Apr 28] workmanlike gelding: smart hurdler/very smart chaser: out of sorts last 5 outings, left Mrs S. Smith after second of them: effective at 2m to 2½m: acts on good to firm and heavy going: effective held up or ridden prominently: bold jumper: free-going, enthusiastic sort: has won 7 of 8 starts at Wetherby. *Carl Llewellyn*   **c153**
h125

MISTER MOONAX (IRE) 7 ch.g. Moonax (IRE) – Edna Cottage (The Parson) [2006/7 F–: F18s 19v Jan 1] well beaten in bumpers/novice hurdle (tongue tied): sold 3,000 gns Doncaster May Sales. *M. G. Rimell*   **h–**
F—

MISTER MUSTARD (IRE) 10 b.g. Norwich – Monalma (IRE) (Montekin) [2006/7 c–, h113: 17gᶠ 17s 16dᵖᵘ 19s³ 17dᶠ 16m⁶ 17dᵖᵘ 20gᵖᵘ Apr 7] good-topped gelding: let down by jumping 2 of 3 starts over fences: fair handicap hurdler: stays 2½m: acts on soft and good to firm going (won bumper on heavy): unreliable. *Ian Williams*   **c–**
h109 §

MISTER PAN (IRE) 5 b.g. Taipan (IRE) – Forest Mist (Dalsaan) [2006/7 F16s⁵ F16v⁴ Mar 3] 15,000 3-y-o, resold 15,000 3-y-o: brother to fairly useful hurdler The Real Deal, stays 3m, and half-brother to 2½m hurdle winner Dicky's Rock (by Be My Native): dam winning 2m hurdler: failed to last home under testing conditions in bumpers at Wetherby (favourite, fifth to Cast Iron Casey) and Kempton (tended to hang left). *P. R. Webber*   **F73**

MISTER PETE (IRE) 4 b.g. Piccolo – Whistfilly (First Trump) [2006/7 17d⁶ 16gᵖᵘ Nov 29] sturdy, compact gelding: twice-raced on Flat, sold out of D. Barker's stable 700 gns Doncaster August Sales: little encouragement in 2 juvenile hurdles. *W. Storey*   **h–**

MISTER PINK 7 ch.g. Accordion – Place Stephanie (IRE) (Hatim (USA)) [2006/7 F–: F16m² F18m⁵ Oct 16] well-made gelding: best effort in bumpers when second of 8 to Satchelman at Worcester: bred to be suited by further than 2m: carries head awkwardly under pressure. *R. Rowe*   **F91**

MISTER POTTER 7 b.g. Classic Cliche (IRE) – Potter's Gale (IRE) (Strong Gale) [2006/7 F16s F16s² 20v* 20v² 20v* 20gᵖᵘ Apr 7] tall, lengthy gelding: chasing type: brother to fair staying hurdler Potts of Magic and half-brother to fairly useful hurdler Missis Potts (by Overbury), stays 2½m: dam, useful hurdler/fairly useful chaser up to 21f, half-sister to Denman and Silverburn: third in maiden Irish point in 2006: runner-up at Towcester on second of 2 starts in bumpers: fair form when winning novice hurdles at Haydock in January (by 14 lengths from Aitch Doubleyou) and February: soon detached under less testing conditions there final outing: will be suited by further than 2½m: acts well on heavy going. *R. Lee*   **h114**
F96

MISTER POUS (FR) 8 b.g. Kaid Pous (FR) – Epson Lady (FR) (Mendez (FR)) **c90**
[2006/7 17s* 20s 19s 18s c19s c20v[pu] 18s[5] 18v[2] 17s[3] 18s[4] Apr 13] leggy gelding: brother **h113**
to 3 winners in France, including hurdler/chaser up to 19f La Corbonaise: dam, 1½m
winner, successful around 2m over hurdles: 11f winner on Flat: successful also several
times over jumps, including in handicap hurdle at Auteuil in May: little impact in
2 handicap chases in Britain: stays 2½m: acts on heavy going: has had tongue tied.
F. Cottin, France

MISTER QUASIMODO 7 b.g. Busy Flight – Dubacilla (Dubassoff (USA)) [2006/7 **c131**
h133: c24s[pu] c23s[2] c19v* c21s[F] c19v[pu] 16g[F] Mar 23] tall gelding: useful hurdler: similar **h–**
form when second to Pole Star in maiden chase at Exeter in December: simple task in
similar event there following month: failed to complete 3 starts after: stays 23f: goes very
well on soft/heavy going. *C. L. Tizzard*

MISTER RIGHT (IRE) 6 ch.g. Barathea (IRE) – Broken Spirit (IRE) (Slip Anchor) **h93**
[2006/7 16g 16f[4] Apr 5] leggy gelding: fairly useful on Flat (stays 1¾m), successful in
June: best effort over hurdles when 5¼ lengths fourth to Moon Star in novice handicap at Wincanton: raced at 2m: acts on firm going (reportedly unsuited by heavy).
D. J. S. ffrench Davis

MISTER SHER (IRE) 8 b.g. Shernazar – Running River (IRE) (Riverhead (USA)) **c–**
[2006/7 c–, h–: 24s* 24v[pu] 25v 24d 22d Mar 20] strong, compact gelding: winning point- **h94**
er: easily best effort over hurdles when winning novice at Uttoxeter in May: stays 3m: let
down by jumping more than once (including only outing in chase). *Mrs L. J. Young*

MISTER TIBUS (FR) 6 b.g. Signe Divin (USA) – Ferlia (FR) (Noir Et Or) [2006/7 **c90**
F–: c19s[pu] c19s[pu] c21v[5] c23g[2] Mar 25] leggy, rather unfurnished gelding: first form when
½-length second of 5 to Craven in maiden chase at Taunton. *J. A. Geake*

MISTER TOP NOTCH (IRE) 8 b.g. Mister Lord (USA) – Turn A Coin (Prince Han- **c133**
sel) [2006/7 h124: 18v c17d[2] c19v[3] c21d[F] c21v* c20v[6] Feb 25] big, long-backed gelding: **h100**
fairly useful hurdler: useful novice chaser: won Grade 1 Dr P. J. Moriarty Novices' Chase
at Leopardstown in February by 7 lengths from Vic Venturi, left clear when Alexander
Taipan fell last: held up when below form in Grade 2 at Naas 2 weeks later: stays 3m: acts
on heavy going: usually races prominently. *D. E. Fitzgerald, Ireland*

MISTER TRICKSTER (IRE) 6 b.g. Woodborough (USA) – Tinos Island (IRE) **h77**
(Alzao (USA)) [2006/7 16g 17d 17s 16f[5] 17g[2] Apr 27] modest on Flat (stays 1m) at 3 yrs:
poor form over hurdles: takes good hold, and likely to prove best around 2m with
emphasis on speed. *R. Dickin*

MISTER WISEMAN 5 gr.g. Bal Harbour – Genie Spirit (Nishapour (FR)) [2006/7 **F–**
F16s Feb 3] 7,000 4-y-o: fifth foal: dam poor maiden hurdler: third in maiden point in
December: weakened quickly when well held in bumper at Stratford. *N. J. Hawke*

MISTER ZAFFARAN (IRE) 8 ch.g. Zaffaran (USA) – Best Served Cherry (IRE) **h–**
(Sheer Grit) [2006/7 h79?, F80: 20m[5] 26g[pu] Oct 15] placed in point/bumper: no solid
form over hurdles: tried tongue tied: dead. *Mrs N. S. Evans*

MISTIFIED (IRE) 6 b.g. Ali-Royal (IRE) – Lough N Uisce (IRE) (Boyne Valley) **c–**
[2006/7 h92: 22m[4] 19g[3] 24d 19d[4] 22s[5] c19s 20g[6] Apr 27] sturdy gelding: modest maiden **h94**
hurdler: below form after second outing (little impact in novice handicap on chasing
debut): stays 25f when conditions aren't testing, effective at much shorter: acts on soft
and good to firm going: blinkered once: tried tongue tied. *J. W. Mullins*

MISTRAL DE LA COUR (FR) 7 bl.g. Panoramic – Gracieuse Delacour (FR) (Port **c82 x**
Etienne (FR)) [2006/7 c113x, h–: 16g 17d[6] 16g c16s[pu] c16d[6] c20s[6] c16v c20m[2] c20m[3] **h–**
c20m[3] Apr 15] lengthy, useful-looking gelding: maiden hurdler: winning chaser, poor
nowadays: sold out of R. Ford's stable 5,500 gns Doncaster August Sales after third
outing: stays 2½m: acts on good to firm and heavy going: often wears headgear: makes
mistakes. *C. A. Mulhall*

MISTRESS KAYTEE 5 b.m. Kayf Tara – Mistress Corrado (New Member) [2006/7 **F–**
F17s[5] F16g Jun 8] half-sister to fair hunter chaser Master Jock (by Scottish Reel), stays
3m, and winning pointer by Gunner B: dam maiden pointer: well beaten in bumpers.
B. P. J. Baugh

MISTRESS NELL 7 b.m. Thethingaboutitis (USA) – Neladar (Ardar) [2006/7 h–: 24d **c93**
20d[pu] c24v[4] c26s[3] c24d[3] c23v[2] Feb 27] lengthy mare: no show over hurdles: modest form **h–**
over fences: stays 3¼m: acts on heavy going. *A. J. Lidderdale*

MISTRESS TO NO ONE 4 b.f. Exit To Nowhere (USA) – Frosty Mistress (Arctic **F84**
Lord) [2006/7 F12s[2] F12v aF16g[3] Mar 9] unfurnished filly: first foal: dam, modest

maiden hurdler, out of half-sister to top-class staying chaser Monsieur Le Cure: modest form in bumpers. *C. E. Longsdon*

MISTTORI BELLE 4 b.f. Vettori (IRE) – Misbelief (Shirley Heights) [2006/7 F16s⁴ 16g 17m⁵ 17g Apr 23] lengthy, unfurnished filly: half-sister to fair 2m hurdler/chaser Arresting (by Hector Protector): dam useful up to 14.6f on Flat: clear with winner entering straight when fourth to Turbo Linn in bumper at Catterick on debut: well beaten 3 starts over hurdles. *M. W. Easterby*   **h–**
F71

MISTY DANCER 8 gr.g. Vettori (IRE) – Light Fantastic (Deploy) [2006/7 c111, h–: c16g c16s* c17d⁴ c16g c19g* Mar 31] close-coupled gelding: winning hurdler: useful handicap chaser: won at Warwick (comfortably by 5 lengths from Jupon Vert) in December and Ascot (improved form, by 1¼ lengths from Bishop's Bridge in quite valuable event) in March: stays 19f: acts on soft and good to firm ground: tongue tied once. *Miss Venetia Williams*   **c132**
h–

MISTY FUTURE 9 b.g. Sanglamore (USA) – Star of The Future (USA) (El Gran Senor (USA)) [2006/7 c112, h–: 26d c23mᶠ c23g⁵ c24sᵘʳ c23m³ Sep 2] sturdy gelding: winning hurdler: fair handicap chaser: in frame in points in 2007: stays 3¼m: acts on firm and good to soft going: has worn blinkers, including last 4 starts: sometimes let down by jumping. *Miss Venetia Williams*   **c110**
h–

MISTY GEM (IRE) 6 b.m. General Monash (USA) – Jade's Gem (Sulaafah (USA)) [2006/7 16m 20m 18d 19dᶠ Oct 26] ex-Irish mare: second foal: dam lightly-raced maiden: little impact over hurdles: left Dermot Day after third outing: successful in points in February/March. *Evan Williams*   **h–**

MISTY'S EXPRESS (IRE) 9 b.m. Un Desperado (FR) – Misty's Wish (Furry Glen) [2006/7 c24g* c28sᵖᵘ c17v⁶ c22v⁶ Jan 1] twice-raced over hurdles: winning pointer: modest chaser: won hunter at Limerick in May: stays 3m. *Shane Joseph Kelly, Ireland*   **c90**
h–

MITEY PERK (IRE) 8 b.g. Executive Perk – More Dash (Strong Gale) [2006/7 h–: c17d⁵ c17sᵇᵈ c16v* c16vᵖᵘ Mar 2] won 2-finisher maiden chase at Ayr in December by distance: no form otherwise outside points: bled final outing. *Mrs A. F. Tullie*   **c?**
h–

MITH HILL 6 b.g. Daylami (IRE) – Delirious Moment (IRE) (Kris) [2006/7 h109: 16g 21d* 17s³ 23s 24g 21g⁵ Apr 18] angular gelding: fairly useful handicap hurdler: won at Cheltenham in November by neck from According To Pete: below best after next outing: should stay 3m: acts on soft ground. *Ian Williams*   **h117**

MITRASH 7 b.g. Darshaan – L'Ideale (USA) (Alysheba (USA)) [2006/7 16vᶠ 16v⁵ Mar 10] very lightly raced and no form. *D. McCain Jnr*   **h–**

MITRE PEAK (IRE) 5 b.g. Shernazar – Auction Piece (IRE) (Auction Ring (USA)) [2006/7 aF16g⁵ F16m² Apr 24] half-brother to bumper winner Aberdeenshire (by Looking For) and a winning pointer by Toulon: dam unraced: fair form in bumpers, 4 lengths second to The Package in maiden at Towcester. *K. J. Burke*   **F90**

MIXSTERTHETRIXSTER (USA) 11 b.g. Alleged (USA) – Parliament House (USA) (General Assembly (USA)) [2006/7 c133, h–: c20g* c20s² c20f⁴ c22vᵖᵘ 25v 25v Jan 25] tall, angular gelding: winning hurdler: fairly useful handicap chaser: won at Worcester in May by 6 lengths from Major Euro: well below form last 3 starts: stays 2¾m: acts on any going: effective making running or waited with. *Mrs Tracey Barfoot-Saunt*   **c126 d**
h–

MIZINKY 7 b.m. El Conquistador – Miss Pimpernel (Blakeney) [2006/7 h80: 19dᵖᵘ Mar 21] small, angular mare: poor hurdler: should stay 3m: acts on good to firm and good to soft going. *W. G. M. Turner*   **h–**

MIZNIX 7 b.m. Presenting – Lady's Island (IRE) (Over The River (FR)) [2006/7 F13s Dec 16] fourth foal: dam, poor novice chaser who stayed 3m, half-sister to useful 2½m to 3m hurdler Mr Red Banner: tailed off in bumper on debut. *Robert Gray*   **F–**

M'LORD 9 b.g. Mister Lord (USA) – Dishcloth (Fury Royal) [2006/7 h–: 19g* 20m Sep 3] workmanlike gelding: lightly raced: fair hurdler: best effort when winning novice handicap at Stratford in July, held up in strongly-run race: well beaten next time: should stay beyond 19f: raced mainly on good/good to soft going: tried tongue tied. *J. A. Geake*   **h105**

MNASON (FR) 7 gr.g. Simon du Desert (FR) – Mincing (FR) (Polyfoto) [2006/7 c–, h–: 19g 19v⁵ 26s 23dᶠ 20s c19g Apr 11] leggy gelding: fair hurdler at best, no form since 2004/5 (including over fences): visored once, in cheekpieces last 3 starts: one to avoid. *S. J. Gilmore*   **c– §**
h– §

Seasons Holidays' "Mobaasher"

MOBAASHER (USA) 4 ch.g. Rahy (USA) – Balistroika (USA) (Nijinsky (CAN)) **h140**
[2006/7 18s* 17g³ 16g⁶ Apr 12] big, good sort: on weak side at present: fairly useful on
Flat (stays 1½m), successful in September, sold out of Sir Michael Stoute's stable 55,000
gns Newmarket Autumn Sales: won juvenile at Fontwell on hurdling debut in February:
much better form (useful) when 10¾ lengths third of 19 finishers to Katchit in JCB
Triumph Hurdle at Cheltenham: not always fluent when only sixth to same horse in
another Grade 1 at Aintree. *C. J. Mann*

MOBANE FLYER 7 b.g. Groom Dancer (USA) – Enchant (Lion Cavern (USA)) **c–**
[2006/7 c16vᵖᵘ Mar 9] has reportedly had wind operation: modest on Flat (stays 10.3f) in **h–**
2006, sold out of R. Fahey's stable 1,000 gns Doncaster October Sales: no form over
jumps, including in points: tried tongue tied. *S. Flook*

MOBASHER (IRE) 8 b.g. Spectrum (IRE) – Danse Royale (IRE) (Caerleon (USA)) **c– §**
[2006/7 c88§, h105§: 20m c19sᵖᵘ Dec 29] leggy gelding: winning hurdler, little form **h– §**
since 2003/4: maiden chaser, usually let down by jumping: probably stays 3m: tried
blinkered/tongue tied: ungenuine. *P. Kelsall*

MOCHARAMOR (IRE) 9 b. or br.g. Distinctly North (USA) – Oso Sure (IRE) (Sure **c111**
Blade (USA)) [2006/7 c110, h110: c20d⁶ c24sᵖᵘ 23f² 24f³ c26m² c24g⁵ 24dᵖᵘ 16sᶠ Nov 1] **h114**
sturdy gelding: fair handicap hurdler/chaser: placed 3 times in 2006/7, including over
fences at Cartmel, caught on line after jockey stopped driving final few strides: stays
3¼m: acts on firm and soft ground: blinkered (ran creditably) once. *J. J. Lambe, Ireland*

638

MOCHO (IRE) 6 b.g. Accordion – Supreme Kellycarra (IRE) (Supreme Leader) **h98**
[2006/7 F92: 20d⁵ 21g³ 16sᶠ 20vᵖᵘ 19g Mar 30] good-topped gelding: modest form
over hurdles, ran poorly last 2 outings (left Ian Williams before final one): stays 21f.
J. L. Spearing

MODAFFAA 7 b.g. Darshaan – Irish Valley (USA) (Irish River (FR)) [2006/7 16m² **h87**
16m⁵ Aug 1] won bumper on debut in 2004: fairly useful on Flat (stays 1¾m): better
effort in maiden hurdles at Worcester when 9 lengths second to Jacaranda. *P. R. Webber*

MODARAB 5 b.g. Barathea (IRE) – Jathaabeh (Nashwan (USA)) [2006/7 F16v F17s **h–**
F16m 16g 16d Feb 14] 6,500 2-y-o: first foal: dam, 1m winner, out of half-sister to **F–**
high-class miler Cape Cross: well held in bumpers/over hurdles. *Mrs L. B. Normile*

MODEL SON (IRE) 9 b.g. Leading Counsel (USA) – Miss Mutley (Pitpan) [2006/7 **c126**
c135, h115: 24dᵖᵘ c27d⁴ c25s c24vᵖᵘ 24s⁶ Mar 11] workmanlike gelding: fair handicap **h108**
hurdler: useful chaser: shaped well when fourth to My Will in Grade 3 handicap at
Cheltenham, but let down by jumping next 2 outings (left F. Jordan after first of them):
should stay beyond 3½m: acts on heavy and good to firm going: usually front runner/
races prominently. *Mrs A. M. Thorpe*

MODICUM (USA) 5 b.g. Chester House (USA) – Wandesta (Nashwan (USA)) **h123**
[2006/7 F97: 16g⁶ 16g² 16d² 16m* 16g² Mar 30] good-topped gelding: fairly useful
hurdler: easily landed odds in maiden at Musselburgh in February: best effort when
½-length second to Mendo in novice at Ascot following month, drifting left when shaken
up after last: likely to prove best around 2m: acts on good to firm and good to soft going:
usually amateur ridden. *N. G. Richards*

MOFFIED (IRE) 7 b.g. Nashwan (USA) – Del Deya (IRE) (Caerleon (USA)) [2006/7 **c–**
h–: c17sᵘʳ c20dᵖᵘ Dec 10] no sign of ability. *J. Barclay* **h–**

MOHAWK STAR (IRE) 6 ch.g. Indian Ridge – Searching Star (Rainbow Quest **h105**
(USA)) [2006/7 h96: 18g³ 19d² 16s² 16d⁴ 16s² 16s Dec 2] fair handicap hurdler: stays
19f: acts on soft going: effective blinkered or not: has hinted at temperament: joined
P. Bowen. *I. A. Wood*

MOHAYER (IRE) 5 gr.g. Giant's Causeway (USA) – Karlafsha (Top Ville) [2006/7 **h121**
h–, F83: 17d³ 17d⁴ 16v² 17v* 16v* 16v³ 16v² 18v² 16g Apr 7] tall gelding: fairly useful
hurdler: won at Sedgefield (maiden, easily) and Haydock (novice, beat Westgate 5
lengths) in December: placed next 3 starts, best effort when head second to Wizard of Us
in handicap at Uttoxeter on second of them: raced around 2m: acts well on heavy going:
tough. *D. McCain Jnr*

MOKUM (FR) 6 b.g. Octagonal (NZ) – Back On Top (FR) (Double Bed (FR)) [2006/7 **c106**
c100, h85: c21sᶠ 21sᵖᵘ c20g⁴ c20d* c20s³ c24s² c23v³ c24g³ Mar 29] workmanlike geld- **h–**
ing: maiden hurdler: fair handicap chaser: won at Leicester in December: ran creditably
all starts after: stays 3m: raced on good going or softer (acts on heavy): tried blinkered/
visored: races lazily. *A. W. Carroll*

MOLE'S CHAMBER (IRE) 6 b.g. Saddlers' Hall (IRE) – Magic Gale (IRE) (Strong **h111 p**
Gale) [2006/7 F95: F16v⁴ 24s⁶ 17g² Apr 1] fair form on first of 2 outings in bumpers: **F73**
dropped back markedly in trip, much better effort in novice hurdles when ¾-length
second to Ingratitude at Newton Abbot, keeping on well despite wandering and bridle
between last 2: bred to stay beyond 17f: open to improvement. *V. R. A. Dartnall*

MOLLIES DOLLY (IRE) 9 ch.m. Over The River (FR) – Spring Trix (IRE) (Buck- **c–**
skin (FR)) [2006/7 20g c25g⁴ c25g⁶ c23sᵖᵘ Oct 1] winning pointer/hurdler: maiden **h–**
chaser, little show in 2006/7: stays 25f: acts on firm ground: front runner. *P. J. Rothwell,
Ireland*

MOLLIFY 7 ch.g. Rakaposhi King – Just Molly (Furry Glen) [2006/7 F17s Oct 6] third **F–**
foal: dam bad winning pointer: fell in maiden point: soundly beaten in bumper. *W. T. Reed*

MOLLYALICE 5 b.m. Slip Anchor – Cumbrian Rhapsody (Sharrood (USA)) [2006/7 **h–**
F66: F17s F16s 17g 19d 16v⁶ 16v Feb 27] unfurnished mare: no form in bumpers/novice **F–**
hurdles: blinkered final start. *T. D. Easterby*

MOLLYCARRSBREKFAST 12 b.g. Presidium – Imperial Flame (Imperial Lan- **c74 x**
tern) [2006/7 c71x, h–: c23m⁶ c25d* c23f² c20m⁵ c19d⁵ Oct 26] well held over hurdles: **h–**
poor handicap chaser: won at Market Rasen in August: stays 25f: acts on firm and good
to soft going: front runner: often let down by jumping. *K. Bishop*

MOLOSTIEP (FR) 7 b.g. Video Rock (FR) – Unetiepy (FR) (Marasali) [2006/7 **c–**
h102p, F97: c19s³ c21sᵖᵘ c23d⁵ Mar 20] tall gelding: point winner: successful also only **h–**

outing over hurdles: off a year, no form in chases: should stay beyond 19f. *Mrs Susan Nock*

MOMENT OF MADNESS (IRE) 9 ch.g. Treasure Hunter – Sip of Orange (Celtic Cone) [2006/7 c116, h–: c20g³ c20d² c19g⁶ c24s³ c24g³ c25gᵖᵘ Apr 3] big, lengthy gelding: fair handicap chaser: stays 3m when conditions aren't testing: raced on good going or softer (acts on soft): wore cheekpieces last 2 starts. *T. J. Fitzgerald*   **c105 h–**

MONASHEE GREY (IRE) 4 b.g. Monashee Mountain (USA) – Ex-Imager (Exhibitioner) [2006/7 17g² 16s² 17d⁴ 20g 20g Apr 3] angular gelding: poor maiden on Flat (will stay beyond 2m): runner-up first 2 starts in juvenile hurdles: sold out of R. Fahey's stable 22,000 gns Doncaster October Sales, well beaten all 3 outings after: should be suited by 2½m+. *P. Bowen*   **h86**

MONASH LAD (IRE) 5 ch.g. General Monash (USA) – Story Time (IRE) (Mansooj) [2006/7 h94: 16f³ 16m⁵ 19d 17v³ 17s 21gᵖᵘ 16f⁶ 24mᵖᵘ Apr 17] smallish, close-coupled gelding: fair up to 1½m on Flat, successful twice in July, sold from M. Tompkins 11,500 gns second occasion: poor novice hurdler: form only around 2m: tried in cheekpieces/ tongue tied. *Mrs K. Waldron*   **h77**

MONCADA WAY (IRE) 6 b. or br.g. Scribano – Na Moilltear (IRE) (Miner's Lamp) [2006/7 F16d Nov 4] €8,500 4-y-o: fourth foal: dam lightly raced in points: won maiden Irish point in 2006: bought 65,000 gns Doncaster May Sales: always towards rear in bumper at Sandown. *Noel T. Chance*   **F–**

MONCADOU (FR) 7 b.g. Cadoudal (FR) – Palencia (FR) (Taj Dewan) [2006/7 20s* c24s² c24s³ c21v⁴ c21g Mar 15] tall gelding: half-brother to 19f chase winner Iacacia (by Silver Rainbow): dam, winning chaser up to 21f, half-sister to top-class French chaser Ucello II: 12.5f winner on Flat: fairly useful form over fences: twice ran well when placed prior to winning 5-runner maiden at Folkestone in February by 3 lengths from Professor Jack: never a threat in valuable handicap at Cheltenham following month: similar standard over hurdles, won Group 3 handicap at Auteuil in May by ½ length from Marie d'Anjou: stays 3m: acts on heavy going: tongue tied. *T. Doumen, France*   **c127 h127**

MONDIAL JACK (FR) 8 ch.g. Apple Tree (FR) – Cackle (USA) (Crow (FR)) [2006/7 c101d, h114d: c19g³ May 4] leggy, lengthy gelding: winning hurdler: useful chaser at one time, now only fair pointer: stays easy 25f: acts on soft and good to firm going: usually wears visor/cheekpieces: sketchy jumper. *Mrs K. Waldron*   **c– x h–**

MONEAMON 8 b.g. Mon Tresor – De Valera (Faustus (USA)) [2006/7 h–: 20gᵖᵘ May 30] no form over hurdles: tried in cheekpieces. *R. Johnson*   **h–**

MONET'S GARDEN (IRE) 9 gr.g. Roselier (FR) – Royal Remainder (IRE) (Remainder Man) [2006/7 c156p, h–: c20s* c24d⁶ c19d* c21g⁴ c20g* Apr 13]   **c160 h–**

The highest-rated novice chaser of 2005/6 didn't progress quite so well as might have been expected in his second season over fences. Yet Monet's Garden still enjoyed a very successful campaign, winning three of his five starts including two Grade 1 events, his first successes at that level, his victories improving what was already an impressive-looking record. Successful on his only outing in bumpers, Monet's Garden has had eighteen races since, over hurdles and fences, and won eleven of them, his win-and-place prize money earnings now standing at over £380,000. And there should be plenty more opportunities for him to add substantially to that total. High-class over hurdles, Monet's Garden has proved himself just as good over fences, showing himself a fine jumper in the process; and he is also versatile as regards distance. For example, the Queen Mother Champion Chase over two miles and the Gold Cup over three and a quarter were both realistic targets for him at the Cheltenham Festival, as was the twenty-one-furlong Ryanair Chase (Festival Trophy) which connections eventually opted for.

The King George VI Chase at Kempton was Monet's Garden's first major target in the latest season, and he was warmed up for it in a five-runner intermediate event at Carlisle in late-October. Looking as though his first race for six months would do him good, Monet's Garden made all in landing the odds by two and a half lengths from the leading French chaser Mid Dancer (who is still unbeaten on home soil), after which Monet's Garden was promoted to favouritism for the Stan James King George with the race's sponsors. The King George was Monet's Garden's first race over fences over as far as three miles, and it seemed likely to show him in an even better light, given that he had put up his best performances over hurdles at that distance, notably when winning the 2005 Liverpool Hurdle. In the event, the trip

Commercial First Ascot Chase—northern raider Monet's Garden gets back on track with a convincing win from Thisthatandtother (hooped sleeves)

was irrelevant. Second favourite on the day behind Kauto Star, Monet's Garden turned in a rare disappointing display, jumping boldly in front from the third but folding dramatically once challenged after four out, dropping away to finish a remote sixth.

'Mystified' was the immediate post-race reaction of trainer Nicky Richards, who subsequently reported that his stable star was dehydrated upon his return to Cumbria. Apparently the gelding isn't a good 'boarder' so Richards adopted a new policy for the grey's next start, in the Commercial First Ascot Chase in February, and made the long journey South with Monet's Garden on the day of the race (the horsebox set off at 5am!) as opposed to the trainer's usual practice of travelling his southern raiders the day before. The nineteen-furlong Grade 1 event (to be run over twenty-one and a half in future) looked a good opportunity for Monet's Garden to get back on track and he was sent off the 11/10 favourite to account for six rivals whose best form fell a little short of his own. Ridden more patiently than usual as Irish challengers Central House and Fota Island took each other on up front, Monet's Garden was still travelling well when he deprived them of the lead four out and was soon well in command, needing only to be kept up to his work in the straight to win by eight lengths from Thisthatandtother. Unfortunately, the new travel arrangements didn't have the same result when Monet's Garden contested the Ryanair Chase on his next start (for which he started 7/4 favourite), though he was far from disgraced in finishing just over four lengths fourth to Taranis who was in receipt of 5 lb. It was still viewed as a disappointing effort, however, with jockey Tony Dobbin's pre-race fears that he'd have a job to settle the strong-travelling grey proving well wide of the mark—'I couldn't even lie up with them. He was never going to win at any stage.' Monet's Garden reportedly scoped badly afterwards and was found to have bled.

Monet's Garden took on Taranis again a month later, this time at level weights in the John Smith's Melling Chase over two and a half miles at Aintree. The six-runner field also included Crozan, in front when falling four out in the

John Smith's Melling Chase, Aintree—
the grey already has the measure of Well Chief (white face) and the blinkered Crozan two out

Festival Trophy, the 2006 Melling Chase winner Hi Cloy and two horses who had fallen in the Queen Mother Champion Chase on their previous start, Oneway two out when still in touch and Well Chief at the second. Well Chief, as in the Champion Chase, was the hot favourite, that despite tackling a distance beyond seventeen furlongs for the first time, with Monet's Garden and Taranis next in the betting. The race was run at a good pace, set by Crozan, Monet's Garden having the leader in his sights before moving smoothly past him after four out. Well Chief managed to get to within a couple of lengths or so of Monet's Garden two out, but he soon weakened as Monet's Garden kept up the gallop to score by three and a half lengths, Taranis taking second late on without ever threatening the winner (Well Chief was a further nine lengths away in third). It was Richards' biggest success to date and maintained his fine recent record at Aintree's three-day Grand National meeting— the stable has had four wins, plus six placed efforts at graded level, from just sixteen runners there over the past three years. Monet's Garden can boast a similarly impressive record at the Merseyside course (two wins and one second from three starts) and is likely to return there for his 2007/8 reappearance in the Old Roan Chase, a race Kauto Star won in the latest season. Richards is reportedly keen to have another crack at Kauto Star in the King George again at Kempton. Monet's Garden certainly deserves another chance to show what he can do at three miles over fences.

Monet's Garden (IRE) (gr.g. 1998)	Roselier (FR) (gr 1973)	Misti IV (br 1958)	Medium
			Mist
		Peace Rose (gr 1959)	Fastnet Rock
			La Paix
	Royal Remainder (IRE) (b 1991)	Remainder Man (ch 1975)	Connaught
			Honorine
		Beyond The Rainbow (b 1977)	Royal Palace
			Villa Marina

Monet's Garden, whose pedigree has been well documented in previous Annuals, is the first foal of the unraced Royal Remainder, a sister to a winning pointer and to the fairly useful Irish bumper winner One More Chance. Royal Remainder's second foal Another Henry (by Beneficial) is her only other to reach the racecourse so far, failing to show any ability in three runs in bumpers in Ireland.

Dr David Wesley Yates's "Monet's Garden"

Meanwhile, her 2006 filly by Norwich was bought back for €30,000 as a foal through the sale-ring in November. The strong, deep-girthed Monet's Garden is a genuine sort who usually races with plenty of zest. He has raced only on good ground or softer (acts on soft). *N. G. Richards*

MONETS MASTERPIECE (USA) 4 b.g. Quiet American (USA) – Math (USA) (Devil's Bag (USA)) [2006/7 16f⁴ 18g⁵ 16m² Apr 9] fair but ungenuine maiden on Flat (stays 13f): 4/1 from 7/1, best effort over hurdles when 2½ lengths second to Woolly Bully in juvenile at Plumpton, mistakes last 2 flights. *G. L. Moore*   **h93**

MONEY HILLS 5 b.g. Vettori (IRE) – Starfida (Soviet Star (USA)) [2006/7 20sᵖᵘ 16g Mar 16] angular gelding: maiden on Flat, tailed off only outing at 4 yrs: no show in 2 starts over hurdles: tried in cheekpieces. *Mrs C. A. Dunnett*   **h–**

MONEYLAWS (IRE) 6 b.m. Zaffaran (USA) – Winter Sunset (Celio Rufo) [2006/7 F16v F16s⁶ F16v⁶ Mar 6] €15,500 4-y-o: tall mare: third foal: sister to unreliable winning hurdler/chaser Elfkirk, stayed 2½m: dam, Irish maiden hurdler, half-sister to fairly useful chaser up to 2¾m Strong Paladin: well beaten in bumpers. *S. J. Marshall*   **F–**

MONEY LINE (IRE) 8 b.g. Roselier (FR) – Pharleng (IRE) (Phardante (FR)) [2006/7 c–, h97, F71: 17s⁵ 24d⁴ 21sᵘʳ 22s² 24s c22s* c19v* Feb 18] rather leggy gelding: fair handicap hurdler: successful both completed outings over fences, in novice (challenging when left clear 2 out) in December and handicap in February, both at Towcester: stays 3m: raced on going softer than good (acts on heavy): wore cheekpieces last 5 starts. *Jonjo O'Neill*   **c110 h102**

MONEY ORDER (IRE) 5 b.g. Supreme Leader – Dipper's Gift (IRE) (Salluceva) [2006/7 F16s* 19s³ 16d⁴ 21s* Mar 2] €52,000 3-y-o: rather unfurnished gelding: sixth foal: dam unraced half-sister to smart staying chaser Royal Dipper and very smart staying   **h119 p F103**

hurdler/useful chaser Henry Mann: won bumper at Towcester on debut in December by 7 lengths from Mister Potter: progressive over hurdles, winning novices at Newbury in February and March: upped in trip, fairly useful form when beating Super Nick a neck (pair clear) on latter occasion: will stay beyond 21f: raced on good to soft/soft ground: capable of better still. *B. G. Powell*

MONFILS MONFILS (USA) 5 b.g. Sahm (USA) – Sorpresa (USA) (Pleasant Tap (USA)) [2006/7 16s* 16s 17g⁴ Apr 1] rather leggy gelding: fairly useful on Flat (stays 11f) in France at 4 yrs, successful twice including at Maisons-Laffitte in July, sold out of Rodolphe Collet's stable €72,000 Goffs (France) November Sale: fair form in novice hurdles: won 17-runner event at Huntingdon on debut in January: raced around 2m. *N. J. Henderson*   **h101**

MONGER LANE 11 b.m. Karinga Bay – Grace Moore (Deep Run) [2006/7 c98§, h109§: c26s⁴ c22m⁵ c25mᵖᵘ c24sᵖᵘ c20sᵖᵘ c23vᵖᵘ 24g Apr 21] tall, good sort: winning hurdler: modest chaser: stays 23f: seems best on going softer than good: tried blinkered: ungenuine. *K. Bishop*   **c90 §** **h– §**

MONICA ROSE 6 b.m. Defacto (USA) – Keldholme (Derek H) [2006/7 F–: F17s³ F16sᵖᵘ Jan 31] tall, workmanlike mare: form (poor) in bumpers only when third at Carlisle. *A. Crook*   **F74**

MONIFIETH 7 b.m. Double Eclipse (IRE) – Parslin (The Parson) [2006/7 h–, F82: 24dᵖᵘ 24vᵖᵘ Jan 2] modest form in bumpers: little impact over hurdles. *D. W. Whillans*   **h–**

MONKERHOSTIN (FR) 10 b.g. Shining Steel – Ladoun (FR) (Kaldoun (FR)) [2006/7 c167, h–: c20g³ c24d⁴ c26g⁴ c36gᴿ c25g⁵ Apr 25] good-bodied gelding: top-class chaser: back somewhere near best when fourth behind Kauto Star in Cheltenham Gold Cup (five mistakes) in March: well-backed co-favourite, didn't take to fences at all in Grand National at Aintree (refused seventh): lacklustre effort final outing: stays 3¼m: acts on any going: tried in visor/cheekpieces: held up. *P. J. Hobbs*   **c157** **h–**

MONKEY MASSINI (IRE) 5 b.g. Dr Massini (IRE) – Madam's Monkey (Monks-field) [2006/7 F16v³ F16g Mar 28] €14,000 4-y-o: useful-looking gelding: has scope: sixth foal: dam, maiden hurdler, half-sister to useful hurdler Gravity Gate, stayed 2¾m: much better effort in bumpers when third to Evelith Echo at Kempton: will stay beyond 2m. *B. De Haan*   **F96**

MONKSTOWN ROAD 5 b.g. Makbul – Carolside (Music Maestro) [2006/7 16d² 17d 16m⁵ 17m 17g 16m⁵ 16g 16d 16s² c16sᵖᵘ c18s c20mᵖᵘ c16m Mar 31] half-brother to winning 2m hurdler Otto E Mezzo (by Persian Bold): one-time fair 7f winner on Flat: poor maiden hurdler/chaser, generally let down by jumping over fences: raced mainly around 2m: acts on good to firm going: tried in cheekpieces/tongue tied. *C. N. Kellett*   **c71 x** **h78**

MON MICHEL (IRE) 4 b.g. Montjeu (IRE) – Miniver (IRE) (Mujtahid (USA)) [2006/7 16sᶠ 16v⁵ 16s² 16v² 16g² Mar 31] lengthy gelding: useful on Flat (stays 1½m), successful twice in 2006, sold out of K. Prendergast's stable 120,000 gns Newmarket Autumn Sales: fairly useful juvenile hurdler: runner-up last 3 starts, beaten ½ length by stable-companion Altilhar at Ascot on handicap debut final one: raced at 2m on good ground or softer (acts on heavy). *G. L. Moore*   **h112**

MON MOME (FR) 7 b.g. Passing Sale (FR) – Etoile du Lion (FR) (New Target) [2006/7 c138, h–: c25d⁴ c29s² c29s² c24v⁴ c28s³ c24g⁴ Mar 13] leggy, close-coupled gelding: smart handicap chaser: in frame all 6 starts in 2006/7, runner-up in Coral Welsh National at Chepstow (beaten 4 lengths by Halcon Genelardais) and totesport.com Classic Chase at Warwick (4 lengths behind Ladalko): also ran creditably last 2 starts, sweating and mistake 6 out when 8 lengths fourth to Joes Edge in William Hill Trophy at Cheltenham final one: stays 29f: raced on good going or softer (acts on heavy): reliable. *Miss Venetia Williams*   **c145** **h–**

MON OISEAU (FR) 7 b.g. Port Lyautey (FR) – Amour d'Oiseau (FR) (Dirak Creio-min (FR)) [2006/7 c16d⁶ c22s² c21g Nov 19] good-bodied gelding: third foal: half-brother to winning chaser Go L'Oiseau (by Shafoun), stays 25f: dam never ran: 11f winner on Flat: no form over hurdles: fair handicap chaser: stays 25f: acts on firm and soft going. *A. L. T. Moore, Ireland*   **c106** **h–**

MONOLITH 9 b.g. Bigstone (IRE) – Ancara (Dancing Brave (USA)) [2006/7 h123: 21g* 23s 24g 21m³ Apr 21] compact, heavy-bodied gelding: useful handicap hurdler: won 19-runner event at Cheltenham in October by ½ length from Emotional Article: respectable effort when seventh to Oscar Park in listed event at same course third outing: stays 3m: acts on soft and good to firm going: patiently ridden. *L. Lungo*   **h133**

MONROE GOLD 7 ch.g. Pivotal – Golden Daring (IRE) (Night Shift (USA)) [2006/7   **c–**
h68: 16m c16g 16m 16m Aug 11] close-coupled gelding: maiden hurdler: no form in   **h–**
2006/7, including on chasing debut: tried tongue tied/in headgear. *Jennie Candlish*

MONROES RELATIVE (IRE) 5 b.g. Xaar – White Lavender (USA) (Mt Liver-   **h–**
more (USA)) [2006/7 16s^F 16v^{pu} 19d Dec 14] workmanlike gelding: no form on Flat in
Ireland or over hurdles. *R. Johnson*

MONSIEUR DELAGE 7 b.g. Overbury (IRE) – Sally Ho (Gildoran) [2006/7 h95:   **h99**
17m² 19s³ 22m⁶ Sep 10] good-topped gelding: modest maiden hurdler: should stay
beyond 19f: acts on soft and good to firm going: has shaped as if amiss more than once:
sold 2,300 gns Doncaster January Sales. *S. Gollings*

MONSIEUR (FR) 7 b.g. Cyborg (FR) – Quintessence III (FR) (El Condor (FR))   **h121**
[2006/7 20g⁴ 16s² 16g³ 16g* 19g⁶ 18m* 17d⁴ 16s* 18s 19g² 16g Mar 16] useful-looking
ex-Irish gelding: brother to high-class staying hurdler/chaser Cyborgo and high-class 2m
hurdler/useful chaser Hors La Loi III: dam, 9f winner, placed 3 times over jumps: fairly
useful hurdler: left N. Madden, much improved in 2006/7, winning handicaps at Stratford
in July, Kelso in October (both novice events) and Wetherby (most impressive, beat
Industrial Star by 15 lengths) in November: creditable second to Sir Boreas Hawk in
novice at Catterick penultimate start: stays 2½m: acts on soft and good to firm going:
tried in cheekpieces: front runner. *P. C. Haslam*

MONSIEUR GEORGES (FR) 7 b.g. Kadalko (FR) – Djoumi (FR) (Brezzo (FR))   **c79 x**
[2006/7 c77, h87d: 16s³ 19v⁵ 16d⁴ 26m 19g c19g⁴ c20v² c19s² c23s⁴ c20v^{pu} Mar 7] good-   **h78**
topped gelding: poor maiden hurdler/chaser: probably stays 3¼m: acts on good to firm
and heavy going: tried blinkered/in cheekpieces: makes mistakes over fences. *F. Jordan*

Mrs Vida Bingham's "Mon Mome"

MONSIEUR JACK (IRE) 7 b. or br.g. Supreme Leader – Marie's Pride (IRE) (Henbit (USA)) [2006/7 16vᵖᵘ 24mᵖᵘ Mar 31] third foal: half-brother to bumper/2m hurdle winner Native Churchtown (by Be My Native): dam, poor in bumpers and over hurdles, half-sister to dam of high-class hurdler/smart chaser Ned Kelly: no show in maiden hurdles. *Mrs D. A. Hamer* **h–**

MONSIEUR VILLEZ (FR) 5 b.g. Villez (USA) – Dame de Trefles (FR) (Antheus (USA)) [2006/7 c18s⁵ c17s c17s c17s c17s⁶ c20s* c17s³ 19v c23vᵖᵘ c21gᵖᵘ 19m⁶ Apr 11] €15,000 3-y-o: fifth foal: half-brother to 2¼m chase winner Trefle du Ganges (by Ganges) and winning hurdler up to 21f Dadjal du Bourg (by Ajdayt): dam won up to 1¾m on Flat: maiden hurdler: successful 3 times in claiming chases at Auteuil, including in 4-y-o event in October: claimed from T. Trapenard €10,500, no show in Britain last 4 outings: stays 2½m: raced largely on going softer than good: tried in cheekpieces. *G. A. Ham* **c92 h–**

MONSIGNORITA (IRE) 5 b.m. Classic Cliche (IRE) – Black Spring (IRE) (Mister Lord (USA)) [2006/7 F16v F16s⁵ Mar 11] strong, good-bodied mare: second foal: dam, poor maiden hurdler/chaser, sister to Champion Bumper winner/unbeaten hurdler Monsignor: never dangerous in bumpers. *Carl Llewellyn* **F64**

MONSIGNOR JACK (IRE) 6 ch.g. Aahsaylad – Take No Chances (IRE) (Thatching) [2006/7 20s 21g Nov 7] workmanlike gelding: third foal: dam Irish 5f (at 2 yrs) to 9f winner: no promise in novice hurdles: sold £800 Ascot December Sales. *P. J. Hobbs* **h–**

MONSTER JAWBREAKER (IRE) 8 b.g. Zafonic (USA) – Salvora (USA) (Spectacular Bid (USA)) [2006/7 17d 16s Oct 27] tall, strong gelding: soundly beaten in bumper (for W. M. Brisbourne) and over hurdles. *J. T. Stimpson* **h–**

MONTANA BAY (FR) 5 b.g. Pistolet Bleu (IRE) – Jonque (FR) (April Night (FR)) [2006/7 F16g³ F16s⁵ 16v³ 16v² 16s* 16v² 20m⁶ 16g⁵ Apr 27] €80,000 3-y-o: lengthy, good-topped gelding: first foal: dam unraced sister to fairly useful hurdler/smart chaser Ilare, stays 29f: better effort in bumpers when third at Limerick: fairly useful form over hurdles: won maiden at Punchestown (easily by 5½ lengths from Bad Bad Bad Day) in February: best effort when second to Wins Now in novice there next time: seems best short of 2½m: acts on heavy going, probably on good to firm: races prominently. *M. J. P. O'Brien, Ireland* **h121 F92**

MONTANA GOLD (IRE) 6 b.g. Bob Back (USA) – Tell A Tale (Le Bavard (FR)) [2006/7 F16s 22dᵘʳ 21s⁶ 24s³ Mar 3] €25,000 4-y-o: close-coupled, unfurnished gelding: sixth foal: half-brother to bumper winner/winning 2m hurdler She's Our Daisy (by Supreme Leader): dam winning Irish 2½m hurdler: well beaten in bumper: fair form in novice hurdles, not knocked about both completed outings: stays 3m: raced on good to soft/soft ground. *N. J. Henderson* **h105 + F–**

MONTANAH JET 5 b.g. Montjoy (USA) – Nashwanah (Nashwan (USA)) [2006/7 h–, F–: 16fᵖᵘ Apr 30] no sign of ability. *C. N. Kellett* **h–**

MONTARA (IRE) 8 b.g. Perugino (USA) – Tatra (Niniski (USA)) [2006/7 h–: 16f⁵ Jul 6] leggy gelding: modest on Flat (stays 11f): little show in novice hurdles: tried tongue tied. *Barry Potts, Ireland* **h–**

MONTE CARRIO 4 ch.g. Observatory (USA) – Kundalini (USA) (El Gran Senor (USA)) [2006/7 16s 17g 16d 16dᵖᵘ Dec 21] little sign of ability on Flat or in juvenile hurdles. *C. Drew* **h–**

MONTECORVINO (GER) 6 ch.g. Acatenango (GER) – Manhattan Girl (USA) (Vice Regent (CAN)) [2006/7 h96: c16s⁶ 25v⁴ 26sᵖᵘ 24vᵘʳ 26m³ Mar 29] tall, good-topped gelding: modest handicap hurdler: let down by jumping on chasing debut: stays 3¼m: unraced on firm going, acts on any other: tried visored/tongue tied, blinkered last 2 starts. *N. A. Twiston-Davies* **c– h85**

MONTEFORTE 9 b.g. Alflora (IRE) – Double Dutch (Nicholas Bill) [2006/7 c101, h–: c20s² c24sᵖᵘ c23v* c22g⁶ Mar 23] lengthy, good sort: lightly raced: bumper/hurdle winner: off another 4 months, much improved when winning handicap at Leicester in February by 1¾ lengths from Mistress Nell: seemingly amiss following month: will stay beyond 25f: acts on heavy ground: tongue tied last 2 starts: has jumped left. *J. A. B. Old* **c115 h–**

MONTE MAJOR (GER) 4 ch.g. Trempolino (USA) – Monbijou (GER) (Dashing Blade) [2006/7 16d 16s⁵ 17g Mar 25] leggy gelding: poor maiden on Flat (stays 2m) for D. Daly: easily best effort in juvenile hurdles on second outing. *Evan Williams* **h97**

MONTENDA 6 b.g. Classic Cliche (IRE) – Polly Leach (Pollerton) [2006/7 h–: 22s **c90** c19g c23m³ Apr 22] big gelding: little form over hurdles: seemingly much better effort **h–** over fences when third in maiden at Stratford. *Mrs S. Gardner*

MONTE ROSA (IRE) 8 b.m. Supreme Leader – Green Thorn (IRE) (Ovac (ITY)) **h–** [2006/7 h84: 22g May 24] won novice hurdle at Kelso in 2004/5, very lightly raced and little show since: sold 4,000 gns Doncaster May (2006) Sales. *N. G. Richards*

MONTESINO 8 b.g. Bishop of Cashel – Sutosky (Great Nephew) [2006/7 h86: 20mᵖᵘ **h–** May 5] good-bodied gelding: winning hurdler, largely out of form since 2004: has worn cheekpieces/visor: sold £2,200 Ascot June Sales, runner-up in point. *M. Madgwick*

MONTEVIDEO 7 b.g. Sadler's Wells (USA) – Montessori (Akarad (FR)) [2006/7 c–, **c–** h105: 22d² 24g* 22m² 24d 22m² 24d³ Nov 18] leggy, useful-looking gelding: fair **h109** hurdler: won handicap at Uttoxeter in September: generally let down by attitude after: fell only outing over fences: stays 3m: acts on good to firm and good to soft going: tried blinkered/in eyeshields/tongue tied. *Jonjo O'Neill*

MONTEYS CRYSTAL (IRE) 9 b.g. Montelimar (USA) – Kindly Lass (Wolver **h–** Hollow) [2006/7 25sᵖᵘ Oct 15] placed in Irish points in 2003: in cheekpieces, no show in maiden on hurdling debut. *S. G. Chadwick*

MONTGERMONT (FR) 7 b.g. Useful (FR) – Blowin'in The Wind (FR) (Saint **c–** Cyrien (FR)) [2006/7 c141+, h–: c26s Nov 25] tall, leggy gelding: novice hurdler: useful **h–** chaser: left Mrs L. Taylor and well-supported favourite, shaped as if amiss (reportedly suffered tendon injury) in Hennessy Cognac Gold Cup (Handicap) at Newbury, only outing in 2006/7: should stay beyond 3m: acts on soft going. *C. R. Egerton*

MONTICELLI (GER) 7 b.g. Pelder (IRE) – Marcelia (GER) (Priamos (GER)) **c–** [2006/7 c98, h120: 20g* Apr 14] good-topped gelding: fairly useful hurdler: left P. Hobbs **h128** and off 18 months, better than ever when winning handicap at Chepstow in April by ½ length from Templer: mistakes both outings over fences: stays 2½m: acts on soft and good to firm going. *Simon Earle*

MONTOSARI 8 ch.g. Persian Bold – Sartigila (Efisio) [2006/7 16gᵖᵘ Jul 5] strong **h–** gelding: fair on Flat (stays 2m), successful 3 times in 2006: no form over hurdles since second in maiden on debut in 2003/4. *P. Mitchell*

MONTRACHET BELLE 5 ch.m. Kadeed (IRE) – Swiss Hat (Hatim (USA)) [2006/7 **h–** 17m 17s⁶ Aug 19] little sign of ability in Flat/novice hurdles. *R. Johnson*

MONTREAL (FR) 10 b. or br.g. Chamberlin (FR) – Massada (FR) (Kashtan (FR)) **c– §** [2006/7 c106§, h–: c25f⁶ May 10] leggy gelding: one-time useful chaser, little sign of **h–** retaining ability in points in 2007: tried visored, often in cheekpieces: moody. *D. E. Pipe*

MONTU 10 ch.g. Gunner B – Promitto (Roaring Riva) [2006/7 c–, h–: c26mᶠ c23mᵖᵘ **c–** Jul 26] short-backed gelding: won 3m maiden on chasing debut in 2004/5, only form. **h–** *Karen George*

MONTY BE QUICK 11 ch.g. Mon Tresor – Spartiquick (Spartan General) [2006/7 **c–** c75, h–: 26g Apr 20] leggy gelding: maiden hurdler: won maiden chase in May 2005, no **h–** form since: stays 2½m: has had tongue tied. *J. M. Castle*

MONTYS ISLAND (IRE) 10 b.g. Montelimar (USA) – Sea Island (Windjammer **c–** (USA)) [2006/7 c72, h–: c21d⁴ 21m² 24f⁶ Jun 21] good-topped gelding: winning pointer: **h90** modest maiden chaser/hurdler: stays 3m: acts on good to firm going. *Evan Williams*

MONTY'S MOON (IRE) 5 b.g. Moonax (IRE) – Brett And Danny (IRE) (Yashgan) **F82** [2006/7 F16mᴬ Apr 10] second foal: dam lightly raced: modest form when fourth in bumper at Chepstow on debut. *Evan Williams*

MONTYS TAG (IRE) 14 b.g. Montelimar (USA) – Herbal Lady (Good Thyne **c97** (USA)) [2006/7 c104: c24m* c28vᵖᵘ c24g³ Apr 8] sturdy, lengthy gelding: fair hunter chaser: won at Fakenham in May: stays 3½m: acts on soft and good to firm going: tongue tied last 2 starts: sound jumper. *S. R. Andrews*

MONTYS TAN (IRE) 9 b.g. Montelimar (USA) – Tender Tan (Tanfirion) [2006/7 **c99** c16m c21g³ c20m³ c24g³ c26m² Aug 24] ex-Irish gelding: blinkered, well beaten in **h–** maiden hurdles for K. Riordan: successful in point in Britain in 2005: modest novice chaser: won handicap at Stratford in July: stays 3¼m: acts on good to firm going. *Evan Williams*

MONZON (FR) 7 b.g. Kadalko (FR) – Queenly (FR) (Pot d'Or (FR)) [2006/7 c97, **c–** h88: 22mᵖᵘ 22mᶠ c18s³ c18v⁵ c17v³ c20v³ c17g4 Mar 30] good-topped gelding: maiden **h–**

hurdler/chaser: little solid form for various trainers in Britain: stays 2¾m: acts on heavy going. *Miss Z. C. Davison*

MOON BEAR 6 b.g. Petoski – Culm Country (Town And Country) [2006/7 c21g² c–
Apr 27] second foal: dam, well beaten in bumpers, out of fairly useful staying chaser Culm Port: won maiden point in April: visored, remote second in novice hunter on chase debut. *Miss L. A. Blackford*

MOON CATCHER 6 b.m. Kahyasi – Moonlight Saunter (USA) (Woodman (USA)) **h113**
[2006/7 h101§: 20d* 19s* 20f* 24m³ Jun 28] angular mare: fair handicap hurdler: improved attitude in 2006/7, winning at Aintree (mares) and Stratford (amateurs) in May and Worcester in June: stays 3m: acts on any going: visored on debut: effective tongue tied or not. *D. Brace*

MOON CAT (IRE) 5 b.m. Desert Story (IRE) – Dilwara (IRE) (Lashkari) [2006/7 **F–**
F17v F16s Nov 22] half-sister to fairly useful performers Scottish Spice (by Selkirk), barely stays 1¼m, and The Bystander (by Bin Ajwaad), stays 1m: dam French 10.5f winner: well held in bumpers. *J. S. Wainwright*

MOON EMPEROR 10 b.g. Emperor Jones (USA) – Sir Hollow (USA) (Sir Ivor c–
(USA)) [2006/7 c–, h–: 16m Oct 4] close-coupled gelding: fair on Flat (stays 2m), **h– §**
successful in February: winning hurdler, took little interest last 2 starts: twice-raced over fences: should stay beyond 2m. *J. R. Jenkins*

MOONFLEET (IRE) 5 b.m. Entrepreneur – Lunasa (IRE) (Don't Forget Me) [2006/7 **c61**
h98: c17mur c16g² Apr 20] good-topped mare: fair juvenile hurdler in 2005/6: off over 17 **h–**
months, poor form on completed outing over fences: raced around 2m: acts on firm and good to soft going: tried visored. *M. F. Harris*

MOONLIGHT MISTRESS 5 b.m. Wizard King – Rasayel (USA) (Bering) [2006/7 **F–**
F16s Dec 7] third foal: half-sister to 1¼m winner Got To Be Cash (by Lake Coniston): dam, 1¼m to 1¾m winner, became unreliable: tailed off in bumper on debut. *D. McCain Jnr*

MOONLIGHT MUSIC (IRE) 4 ch.f. Rossini (USA) – Jarmar Moon (Unfuwain **h–**
(USA)) [2006/7 17s 16d 16g 16g Mar 14] half-sister to fair 2m hurdler/chaser Moon Glow (by Fayruz): fair maiden on Flat (stays 1½m) for E. O'Neill: well beaten over hurdles (bled final start). *K. C. Bailey*

MOONLIT HARBOUR 8 b.g. Bal Harbour – Nuit de Lune (FR) (Crystal Palace **c108 x**
(FR)) [2006/7 c97, h–: c20d⁵ c23d⁴ c24s³ c24gᶠ c24mᶠ c24d⁴ c22v* c25s³ c20s³ c24d⁵ **h–**
Jan 15] medium-sized gelding: fair chaser, sold out of F. Murphy's stable 11,000 gns Doncaster May Sales before second outing: won 4-runner handicap at Market Rasen in November: stays 25f: acts on heavy and good to firm going: not a fluent jumper. *M. F. Harris*

MOON MELODY (GER) 4 b.g. Montjeu (IRE) – Midnight Fever (IRE) (Sure Blade **h–**
(USA)) [2006/7 16d 17spu 17v⁵ 16s 19spu 17dpu Apr 15] close-coupled, good-bodied gelding: lightly raced and little form on Flat, sold out of M. Bell's stable 4,500 gns Newmarket July Sales: no solid form over hurdles: tried in cheekpieces. *M. E. Sowersby*

MOON MIST 9 gr.m. Accondy (IRE) – Lillies Brig (New Brig) [2006/7 c–, h78: c24dpu **c–**
24v⁴ c25vᶠ c28v c25vpu Mar 2] tall mare: maiden hurdler: winning chaser, no form in **h–**
2006/7: stays 3½m: raced on going softer than good (acts on heavy): tried tongue tied. *N. W. Alexander*

MOONOKI (IRE) 8 ch.g. Moonax (IRE) – Aoki (IRE) (Roselier (FR)) [2006/7 c28s² **c101**
c26gpu Mar 16] smallish gelding: fairly useful pointer: 4 lengths second to Coomakista in novice hunter at Stratford on chase debut: much stiffer task in Foxhunter at Cheltenham: stays 3½m: acts on soft ground. *B. Tulloch*

MOON OVER MIAMI (GER) 6 b.g. Dashing Blade – Miss Esther (GER) (Alkalde **h128**
(GER)) [2006/7 h113: 16g⁴ 16s* 16g² 16m² 16d² 16d* 16d² Dec 15] tall, leggy gelding: fairly useful novice hurdler: won at Wincanton and Uttoxeter in May and Cheltenham (beat War General a length in Grade 2 Anglo Irish Private Banking Novices' Hurdle) in November: good ½-length second to Tagula Blue in similar event at Ascot final outing: raced at 2m: acts on soft and good to firm going: has got on toes: takes strong hold, and usually waited with. *C. J. Mann*

MOONSHINE BAY (IRE) 13 b.g. Executive Perk – Sister of Slane (The Parson) c–
[2006/7 c21s⁴ Mar 8] compact gelding: fairly useful hurdler/chaser at best: runs mostly in **h99**
points nowadays, fourth at Wincanton on hunter debut: stays 2¾m: acts on heavy going, below best on good to firm: has refused/been reluctant to race. *H. W. Wheeler*

MOONSHINE BILL 8 ch.g. Master Willie – Monongelia (Welsh Pageant) [2006/7 **h–**
19d^{pu} 16g Apr 14] lengthy gelding: modest on Flat (stays 1½m), successful in September:
failed to settle both outings over hurdles. *P. W. Hiatt*

MOON SHOT 11 gr.g. Pistolet Bleu (IRE) – La Luna (USA) (Lyphard (USA)) [2006/7 **c–**
c–, h–: 16d^3 19v^{pu} 16d 17g Apr 1] winning hurdler, poor nowadays: little show in novice **h73**
chases: raced mainly around 2m: acts on good to soft and good to firm going: has had
tongue tied, also wore cheekpieces last 2 starts. *A. G. Juckes*

MOON STAR (GER) 6 b.g. Goofalik (USA) – Maria Magdalena (GER) (Alkalde **h112**
(GER)) [2006/7 16m^R 16s^{pu} 16v 16d^6 17s^2 16s^3 16s^F 16f* 16m* Apr 22] sturdy gelding:
successful 5 times from 6f to 1¼m on Flat in Italy/Switzerland: fair novice hurdler, left
F. Jordan after fourth start: progressed well after, winning handicaps at Wincanton and
Stratford in April: raced around 2m: acts on firm and soft going: temperamental display
on debut. *A. M. Hales*

MOORAMANA 8 ch.g. Alflora (IRE) – Petit Primitive (Primitive Rising (USA)) **c98**
[2006/7 c88, h88: c17g^2 c20g^2 c20m c20m^4 c20m* Aug 4] good-topped gelding: maiden **h–**
hurdler: modest novice chaser: in cheekpieces, won handicap at Bangor in August: at
least as effective at 2½m as shorter: acts on any going. *P. Beaumont*

MOORESINI (IRE) 7 b.g. Dr Massini (IRE) – Mooreshill (IRE) (Le Moss) [2006/7 **c86**
h86: c21s^4 19v^4 c22s^5 c25v^2 c26v^2 c24g^{pu} Mar 28] deep-girthed gelding: modest maiden **h86**
handicap hurdler/chaser: stays 3¼m: acts on heavy going: usually in cheekpieces/
blinkers: tried tongue tied. *N. J. Gifford*

MOORE'S LAW (USA) 9 b.g. Technology (USA) – Brass Needles (USA) (Twice **h126**
Worthy (USA)) [2006/7 17s* 16s^2 16v* 16d 16m Apr 25] leggy gelding: fairly useful
hurdler: back to best in 2006/7, won minor events at Tralee in October and Cork (beat
Drummer First impressively by 4½ lengths) in January: not discredited when tenth to
Heathcote in totesport Trophy at Newbury next time: probably stays 21f: acts on heavy
and good to firm going. *M. J. Grassick, Ireland*

MOORLAND MONARCH 9 b.g. Morpeth – Moorland Nell (Neltino) [2006/7 c78, **c–**
h81: c23m^6 May 9] maiden hurdler/chaser: runner-up in point: stays 2¾m: acts on soft **h–**
and firm going. *J. D. Frost*

MOORLANDS AGAIN 12 b.g. Then Again – Sandford Springs (USA) (Robellino **c105**
(USA)) [2006/7 c117, h112: 21g^5 c29s^5 c28s^3 c25v^3 c29v^4 Feb 23] good-topped gelding: **h98**
maiden hurdler: fairly useful handicap chaser, not at best in 2006/7: stays 4m: acts on
heavy going: tried in cheekpieces: tongue tied: tends to jump right: front runner.
M. Sheppard

MOORLANDS RETURN 8 b.g. Bob's Return (IRE) – Sandford Springs (USA) **h96 §**
(Robellino (USA)) [2006/7 h–: 22d^4 25v^2 24v^3 24v^{pu} 26g Mar 14] big, workmanlike
gelding: modest maiden handicap hurdler: stays 25f: acts on heavy ground: has worn
cheekpieces: often soon off bridle. *Mrs A. M. Thorpe*

MOORLAW (IRE) 6 b.g. Mtoto – Belle Etoile (FR) (Lead On Time (USA)) [2006/7 **c93 x**
c86, h–: 16f^5 17m 16f 16m* 16g* 17s^4 c16g^4 c16s^3 c17g^4 c16g^2 c16d^4 c16d^5 Jan 8] **h93**
angular gelding: modest hurdler/novice chaser: won 2 sellers over hurdles at Uttoxeter in
July: raced around 2m: acts on firm and soft going: blinkered once: has raced freely: tends
to make mistakes over fences. *D. McCain Jnr*

MOORS MYTH 6 b.g. Anabaa (USA) – West Devon (USA) (Gone West (USA)) **h–**
[2006/7 16g^{pu} May 4] fair at best on Flat (barely stays 1m), below form since 2005:
jumped badly on hurdling debut. *Mrs P. Robeson*

MOOR SPIRIT 10 b.g. Nomadic Way (USA) – Navos (Tyrnavos) [2006/7 c115, h–: **c–**
c25s c16d^5 c16s Dec 26] tall, good-topped gelding: initially progressed well over fences, **h–**
but has lost his way: effective at 2m to 3m: acts on soft and good to firm going: has worn
blinkers/cheekpieces. *P. Beaumont*

MORAL JUSTICE (IRE) 14 b.g. Lafontaine (USA) – Proven Right (IRE) (Kemal **c–**
(FR)) [2006/7 c68, h–: c20g c23m^4 Aug 24] good-topped gelding: veteran chaser: stays **h–**
25f: raced mainly on good going or firmer (acts on firm): tried visored/in cheekpieces:
usually races prominently. *S. J. Gilmore*

MORANDI (IRE) 9 b.g. Insan (USA) – Eliza Everett (IRE) (Meneval (USA)) [2006/7 **c71**
25s^{pu} 16s 16v^{pu} 20g^6 c24d^F c20g^2 c25g^{pu} Apr 23] IR 21,000 3-y-o, €80,000 4-y-o: second **h–**
foal: dam unraced: won maiden Irish point on debut in 2004: no show over hurdles: form
(poor) over fences only when second in handicap at Sedgefield: stays 2½m. *A. Parker*

MORE EQUITY 5 b.m. Classic Cliche (IRE) – Sillymore (Silly Prices) [2006/7 F–: F16v⁵ 16g 22g⁶ Apr 15] well held in bumpers: poor form in novice hurdles: will stay 3m. *Mrs A. F. Tullie*
h71
F–

MORE GOOD TIMES 5 b.g. Morpeth – Amiable Times (Good Times (ITY)) [2006/7 16d Mar 26] big gelding: first foal: dam unraced: well held in novice hurdle on debut. *J. D. Frost*
h–

MORE LIKELY 6 b.m. Shambo – Admire-A-More (Le Coq d'Or) [2006/7 h97, F77: c20d c20sᵖᵘ 22s 24m⁴ c22v* c22v* c24v² c22gᵖᵘ c25mᵖᵘ Apr 21] workmanlike mare: modest hurdler: fair novice chaser: improved when twice making all at Kelso (mares event on first occasion) in January: stays 3m: goes well on heavy going. *Mrs A. F. Tullie*
c113
h97

MORENITO (FR) 4 b.g. Nononito (FR) – Cohiba (FR) (Ti King (FR)) [2006/7 F17d⁴ F16m Apr 25] 12,500 3-y-o, resold 34,000 3-y-o: lengthy, unfurnished gelding: fifth foal: half-brother to modest hurdler/chaser Lancero (by Epervier Bleu), stayed 3½m: dam, winning hurdler/chaser around 2m in France, half-sister to Grand Steeple-Chase de Paris winner El Triunfo: better effort in bumpers when fourth to Threatical Moment at Market Rasen: will be suited by greater test of stamina. *Heather Dalton*
F87

MORE SHENNANIGANS 6 ch.g. Rock City – Blooming Spring (IRE) (Strong Gale) [2006/7 F16m F16v Dec 11] first foal: dam, poor hurdler, stayed 3m: no promise in bumpers. *Mrs J. C. McGregor*
F–

MORE TROUBLE (IRE) 6 b.g. Zaffaran (USA) – Athas Liath (IRE) (Roselier (FR)) [2006/7 F–: F16m² 21gᶠ 20g³ 22d 21m³ Apr 9] sturdy gelding: runner-up in bumper: modest form over hurdles: likely to stay 3m: acts on good to firm going: visored last 4 starts. *P. R. Webber*
h91
F87

MORGAN BE 7 b.g. Alderbrook – Vicie (Old Vic) [2006/7 h118: c20v⁵ c16v² c21v* c25v* c24s⁶ Apr 26] angular gelding: fairly useful hurdler/chaser: successful over fences in maiden in December and handicap (beat Strong Resolve by 3 lengths, idling) in March, both at Ayr: stays 25f: acts on heavy going: reliable. *Mrs K. Walton*
c120
h–

MORGAN THE MIGHTY (IRE) 5 b. or br.g. Presenting – Another Grouse (Pragmatic) [2006/7 F16s⁶ F16v⁶ Feb 17] 13,500 3-y-o: fourth foal: dam fairly useful staying chaser: no impact in bumpers. *N. A. Twiston-Davies*
F–

MORNING ROSES 5 b.m. Overbury (IRE) – Society News (Law Society (USA)) [2006/7 F79: F16d³ F16d⁴ Feb 14] fair form in bumpers: bred to be suited by further. *K. G. Reveley*
F85

MORSON BOY (USA) 7 b.g. Lear Fan (USA) – Esprit d'Escalier (USA) (Diesis) [2006/7 h96§: 19mᵖᵘ Oct 4] tall gelding: modest hurdler: off 16 months, no show only start in 2006/7: stays 2¾m: acts on good to firm and good to soft ground: tried blinkered/tongue tied: often runs as if amiss/finds little. *Mrs K. Waldron*
h– §

MORT DE RIRE (FR) 7 gr.g. Luchiroverte (IRE) – Fia Rosa (FR) (Royal Charter (FR)) [2006/7 c127, h–: c17s⁴ c24v c20v³ c20mᵖᵘ Apr 22] well-made gelding: fairly useful chaser at best, no form in 2006/7: stays 25f: acts on soft going. *R. H. Alner*
c–
h–

MORTIMERS CROSS 6 b.g. Cloudings (IRE) – Leinthall Doe (Oats) [2006/7 F16v³ F16v³ F17s⁶ Jan 26] close-coupled gelding: first foal: dam, poor maiden hurdler/chaser, half-sister to Grand National winner Red Marauder: modest form in bumpers. *J. L. Needham*
F84

MOSCOW COURT (IRE) 9 b.g. Moscow Society (USA) – Hogan Stand (Buckskin (FR)) [2006/7 c99x, h–: c25f⁴ c24d³ c28vᵘʳ c20g⁴ Mar 22] ex-Irish gelding: fair pointer/hunter chaser: stays 25f: probably acts on any going: tongue tied once: sketchy jumper. *Mrs David Plunkett*
c97 x
h–

MOSCOW GOLD (IRE) 10 ch.g. Moscow Society (USA) – Vesper Time (The Parson) [2006/7 c81, h–: c20dᵖᵘ c16vᵖᵘ Jan 11] big gelding: winning chaser, no show in 2 starts in 2006/7: tried blinkered/in cheekpieces: has had tongue tied. *A. E. Price*
c–
h–

MOSCOW LEADER (IRE) 9 ch.g. Moscow Society (USA) – Catrionas Castle (IRE) (Orchestra) [2006/7 c99, h–: c22sᵖᵘ c26gᵖᵘ c24v c24v³ c24s³ c24vᵖᵘ c28dᵖᵘ c21sᵖᵘ Jan 2] sturdy gelding: winning hurdler: modest handicap chaser, largely out of sorts in 2006/7: stays 3¼m: acts on any going: usually wears cheekpieces, also tongue tied last 2 starts. *B. N. Pollock*
c–
h–

MOSCOW'S RETURN (IRE) 10 ch.g. Moscow Society (USA) – Arkinfield (IRE) (Ovac (ITY)) [2006/7 c20m⁶ May 16] modest pointer, successful once in 2006: not fluent in novice hunter in chase debut. *Nick Kent*
c– x

MOSCOW WHISPER (IRE) 10 b.g. Moscow Society (USA) – Native Woodfire (IRE) (Mister Majestic) [2006/7 c110x, h110x: 26m³ 24m⁴ c23mᵖᵘ Jun 13] lengthy, angular gelding: winning chaser: fair handicap hurdler: stays 3¼m: acts on soft and good to firm going: usually let down by jumping (unseated in points). *P. J. Hobbs* **c– x h108 x**

MOSSBANK (IRE) 7 b.g. Kadeed (IRE) – Miromaid (Simply Great (FR)) [2006/7 h133: c24s* c20d² c20v⁵ c24vᶠ c24g c21mᵖᵘ Apr 27] rather leggy, useful-looking gelding: useful hurdler: similar standard over fences: easily won maiden at Clonmel in October: best effort when 13¼ lengths fifth to Cailin Alainn in Grade 1 at Fairyhouse: let down by jumping in similar company next 2 outings: stays 3m: acts on heavy going. *M. Hourigan, Ireland* **c133 h–**

MOSS BAWN (IRE) 11 b.g. Jurado (USA) – Boylan (Buckskin (FR)) [2006/7 c–, h–: c16m* c20g* c23m⁵ c19m* c25f⁵ Oct 5] workmanlike gelding: modest handicap chaser: left B. Storey, improved form when winning at Newton Abbot and Southwell in July, and Hereford (selling event) in September: stays 21f: acts on any going: usually in headgear. *Evan Williams* **c93 h–**

MOSSVILLE (FR) 6 b.m. Villez (USA) – Mosstraye (FR) (Tip Moss (FR)) [2006/7 22d* 21s² 21d⁴ 21g³ Apr 19] €14,000 3-y-o, £41,000 5-y-o: lengthy, angular mare: first foal: dam, French 17f winner on Flat and placed at 2¼m over hurdles, half-sister to useful hurdler up to 2½m Grand Match: well beaten only outing on Flat for B. Secly in France at 3 yrs: won maiden point in Britain in 2006: progressive novice hurdler: won at Wincanton on debut in October: fairly useful form when 9 lengths third of 18 to Silver Charmer in listed mares handicap at Cheltenham: will stay 3m: raced on good going or softer: tried tongue tied. *R. H. Buckler* **h117**

MOSSY GREEN (IRE) 13 b.g. Moscow Society (USA) – Green Ajo (Green Shoon) [2006/7 c146, h124: c22g² 22v* c22v² c20s³ c20v⁴ c19v³ c17m³ Apr 10] lengthy, workmanlike gelding: useful chaser/hurdler nowadays: successful in minor event over hurdles at Thurles (beat Pacolet by 2½ lengths, idling) in November: in frame over fences all other starts in 2006/7, best effort when 3 lengths third to Forget The Past in Grade 2 at same course fourth outing: stays 2¾m: raced mainly on good going or softer (acts on heavy): races prominently. *W. P. Mullins, Ireland* **c139 h134**

MOTIVE (FR) 6 ch.g. Machiavellian (USA) – Mistle Song (Nashwan (USA)) [2006/7 h118: 16g Apr 7] sturdy, lengthy gelding: fairly useful handicap hurdler: well held only outing in 2006/7: raced at 2m: acts on good to soft and good to firm going. *J. Howard Johnson* **h–**

MOTORWAY (IRE) 6 b.g. Night Shift (USA) – Tadkiyra (IRE) (Darshaan) [2006/7 h125: 16f 19g Mar 31] rather leggy gelding: fairly useful handicap hurdler: well held 2 starts in 2006/7 11 months apart: stays 2½m: acts on good to soft and good to firm going. *P. J. Hobbs* **h–**

MOUNTAIN APPROACH 5 b.m. Kayf Tara – Fortunes Course (IRE) (Crash Course) [2006/7 F89: F16g* 20d³ 21v* 21s 21g Mar 24] useful-looking mare: won bumper at Worcester in May: fair form over hurdles: won mares novice at Newbury in November: well beaten in handicaps after: stays 21f: acts on heavy going: tongue tied last 3 outings. *Jean-Rene Auvray* **h104 F95**

MOUNTAIN (IRE) 4 b.g. Montjeu (IRE) – Skidmore Girl (USA) (Vaguely Noble) [2006/7 16d* 17gᵖᵘ Mar 16] rather leggy ex-Irish gelding: smart on Flat (probably stays 1¾m), successful in September, left A. O'Brien and gelded after runner-up in St Simon Stakes: impressive hurdling debut in juvenile at Sandown (beat Counting House by length after not fluent last 2) in February: again travelled strongly long way in Triumph Hurdle at Cheltenham following month: still has plenty of potential as a hurdler. *Jonjo O'Neill* **h116 p**

MOUNTAIN MAYHEM (IRE) 9 br.g. Be My Native (USA) – Arctic Lucy (Lucifer (USA)) [2006/7 h70: 19ᵖᵘ c19dᵖᵘ Feb 2] workmanlike gelding: novice hurdler, very lightly raced: lame on chasing debut. *M. G. Rimell* **c– h–**

MOUNTAIN MIX 7 ch.g. Bigstone (IRE) – Cormorant Bay (Don't Forget Me) [2006/7 h–, F71: c22mᵖᵘ Oct 1] poor form in bumpers: no show over hurdles/in novice chase: tried blinkered. *Mrs L. B. Normile* **c– h–**

MOUNTAIN OF DREAMS 5 ch.g. Primitive Rising (USA) – Coraletta (Buckley) [2006/7 F–: F16g³ 24sᵖᵘ 26sᵖᵘ 21s 19d⁵ 22g Mar 18] big, workmanlike gelding: modest form in bumpers: no show over hurdles. *R. H. York* **h– F82**

MOUNTAIN OSCAR (IRE) 6 b.g. Oscar (IRE) – Mountain Beauty (IRE) (Executive Perk) [2006/7 F16s* F16s⁶ 16g² 20d Mar 17] half-brother to winning pointer by Be **h95 F92**

My Native: dam unraced half-sister to fairly useful hurdler up to 3m Latchford: overcame greenness to win bumper at Towcester in November: much better effort over hurdles when second to Viper in maiden at Ludlow: should stay 2½m. *T. R. George*

MOUNTAIN SINGER (IRE) 8 b.g. Carroll House – Mountain Grove (Paddy's h–
Stream) [2006/7 20f⁵ Jun 3] good-bodied gelding: winning pointer: little impact in other events. *M. S. Wilesmith*

MOUNT BENGER 7 ch.g. Selkirk (USA) – Vice Vixen (CAN) (Vice Regent (CAN)) h96
[2006/7 h77: 20s³ 16d⁶ 16f 16m² 16d² 17s* 17v* 16v⁴ 17s³ 20v Feb 16] quite good-topped gelding: modest handicap hurdler: ridden by R. Johnson, improved to win at Hereford (novice) in December and Folkestone in January: likely to prove best around 2m: acts on good to firm and heavy ground: wears cheekpieces. *Mouse Hamilton-Fairley*

MOUNT CLERIGO (IRE) 9 b.g. Supreme Leader – Fair Ava (IRE) (Strong Gale) c124
[2006/7 c133, h110+: c25vᶠ c29s c24v³ Jan 27] tall gelding: winning hurdler: useful over h–
fences, below form in 2006/7: stays 3m: acts well on heavy ground: sometimes let down by jumping. *V. R. A. Dartnall*

MOUNT COOK (FR) 7 b.g. Gold And Steel (FR) – Debandade (FR) (Le Pontet (FR)) c–
[2006/7 c23s⁵ c17sᵖᵘ Feb 3] fourth in juvenile hurdle: off nearly 3 years, again not h–
knocked about on chasing debut: bled 2 months later: clearly very difficult to train. *Heather Dalton*

MOUNT GEORGE (IRE) 9 b. or br.g. Greensmith – Baylands Sunshine (IRE) h– §
(Classic Secret (USA)) [2006/7 17g 16mʳᵗʳ 16fᵖᵘ Sep 17] ex-Irish gelding: poor winner up to 13f on Flat: maiden hurdler: has worn cheekpieces: usually tongue tied: refused to race penultimate start: one to leave alone. *Evan Williams*

MOUNTHENRY (IRE) 7 ch.g. Flemensfirth (USA) – Tudor Lady (Green Shoon) c122
[2006/7 h138: c20dᶠ c18d² c20d⁴ 20v³ 16v⁵ 20m⁵ Apr 9] lengthy, angular gelding: useful h137
hurdler: easily best effort in 2006/7 when third to Celestial Wave in Grade 2 at Navan: fairly useful form when 4 lengths second to Gemini Lucy in listed novice at Punchestown, first of 2 completed outings over fences: will stay 3m: acts on heavy going: tried in cheekpieces: effective held up/making running. *Charles Byrnes, Ireland*

MOUNTHOOLEY 11 ch.g. Karinga Bay – Gladys Emmanuel (Idiot's Delight) c72
[2006/7 c83, h81: c24s³ c25gᵖᵘ May 24] strong gelding: maiden hurdler/chaser: stays 3m: h–
acts on soft and good to firm going. *B. Mactaggart*

MOUNT LEITRIM (IRE) 8 gr.g. Ala Hounak – Monteleck (IRE) (Montelimar c–
(USA)) [2006/7 c22v c25mᶠ Mar 29] winning pointer: poor maiden chaser: left Michael Hourigan, fell on British debut: stays 3m: acts on heavy ground: blinkered/in cheekpieces last 3 starts. *P. Bowen*

MOUNT OSCAR (IRE) 8 b.g. Oscar (IRE) – Sweet Mount (IRE) (Mandalus) [2006/7 h–
16d Mar 21] first foal: dam lightly-raced half-sister to 2 winning hurdlers: won maiden Irish point in February: well held in maiden on hurdling debut. *R. Rowe*

MOUNT SANDEL (IRE) 6 b.g. Supreme Leader – Droichidin (Good Thyne (USA)) h116
[2006/7 F102: 16g³ 19v* 19s³ 16vᵖᵘ Jan 20] well-made gelding: bumper winner: fairly useful form over hurdles: easily landed odds in novice at Hereford in November: good third to Sir Jimmy Shand in similar event at Newbury next time, distressed final outing: will stay beyond 19f: acts on heavy ground. *O. Sherwood*

MOUNTSORREL (IRE) 8 b.g. Charnwood Forest (IRE) – Play The Queen (IRE) c49
(King of Clubs) [2006/7 c–, h–: c19sᵖᵘ c20v³ c18g c25m² c24mᵖᵘ Apr 14] winning h–
pointer: bad maiden chaser: stays 25f: tried tongue tied. *F. Jordan*

MOUSEEN (IRE) 4 ch.g. Alhaarth (IRE) – Marah (Machiavellian (USA)) [2006/7 h81
16v⁴ 17g⁵ 17g⁴ Apr 11] fair on Flat (stays 7.5f), successful in 2006 for P. Henley in Ireland: poor form over hurdles, sold out of R. Harris's stable 3,500 gns Doncaster March Sales after debut: will prove best at 2m. *R. J. Price*

MOUSESKI 13 b.g. Petoski – Worth Matravers (National Trust) [2006/7 c–, h114: c116
c21s* c20g* Mar 22] smallish gelding: winning hurdler: left P. Nicholls, won point in h–
January: successful also in hunters at Wincanton and Ludlow (15 ran, beat Go For Bust by ¾ length) in March: stays 3m: acts on heavy going. *R. Barber*

MOUS OF MEN (FR) 4 b.g. Lord of Men – Mousmee (FR) (Kaldounevees (FR)) h102
[2006/7 16s⁵ 16m⁵ 16s 18g² Mar 18] useful-looking gelding: second foal: dam placed over 11f on only start: successful once over 11.5f from 5 starts on Flat in France in 2006 for G. Cherel: best effort over hurdles (fair form) when short-head second (carried

left run-in) to Nicki Boy in handicap at Fontwell: stays 2¼m: tried tongue tied. *Miss H. C. Knight*

MOUSTIQUE DE L'ISLE (FR) 7 gr.g. Dom Alco (FR) – Gratiene de L'Isle (FR) (Altayan) [2006/7 c101, h104: c24d* c26s² c32s^F c25d 23v c33v⁴ c25g^pu Mar 17] leggy, plain gelding: winning hurdler: fairly useful handicap chaser: won at Bangor in October: ran very well when second of 16 to Twelve Paces at Carlisle later in month, but failed to repeat that form: stays 31f, at least when conditions aren't testing: acts on heavy going: blinkered/visored: ungenuine. *C. C. Bealby*
c117 §
h– §

MOVE OVER (IRE) 12 ch.g. Buckskin (FR) – Move Forward (Deep Run) [2006/7 c110d, h90: c24d⁶ c25d⁶ c21d⁶ May 31] lengthy gelding: winning handicap hurdler/chaser, no form in 2006/7: stays 25f: acts on heavy going: tried in cheekpieces. *R. C. Guest*
c–
h–

MOVING EARTH (IRE) 14 b.g. Brush Aside (USA) – Park Breeze (IRE) (Strong Gale) [2006/7 c117§, h89§: c24m² c21s⁴ c21s⁵ c21g Apr 12] lengthy gelding: winning hurdler: fair hunter chaser nowadays: stays 25f: acts on soft and firm going: has had tongue tied: has refused to race several times, and one to treat with caution. *C. E. Ward*
c97 §
h–

MOYNE PLEASURE (IRE) 9 b.g. Exit To Nowhere (USA) – Ilanga (IRE) (Common Grounds) [2006/7 h86+: 20d² 20s 21m* 19d 16s³ 20v* 20s 20s⁴ Apr 1] small gelding: modest handicap hurdler: won at Sedgefield (seller) in June and Hexham in February: stays 21f: acts on good to firm and heavy going: in cheekpieces final start. *R. Johnson*
h96

MR AITCH (IRE) 5 b.g. Soviet Star (USA) – Welsh Mist (Damister (USA)) [2006/7 16d 16g³ 16g² 19g 17s Dec 29] good-topped gelding: fairly useful on Flat (stays 1½m), successful twice in 2006: modest novice hurdler: likely to prove best around 2m with emphasis on speed: tongue tied. *R. T. Phillips*
h97

MR ALBANELLO (ARG) 8 b.g. Southern Halo (USA) – Heiress (USA) (Greinton) [2006/7 h67: 20m^pu 17s^pu Oct 25] rather leggy gelding: little form over hurdles: tried in cheekpieces. *Ferdy Murphy*
h–

MR ATTITUDE 7 ch.g. Respect – Leighten Lass (IRE) (Henbit (USA)) [2006/7 c–, h–: c16m⁵ 16g c25v^pu c16s^pu Dec 26] good-topped gelding: no form in various events, left W. S. Coltherd after second outing. *C. Grant*
c–
h–

MR BARNACLE (IRE) 6 br.g. Zaffaran (USA) – Going Native (IRE) (Be My Native (USA)) [2006/7 F16g⁴ Apr 7] €40,000 4-y-o: good sort: first foal: dam lightly-raced, out of sister to useful staying jumpers Open The Gate and Over The Last and useful hurdler/chaser up to 2½m Stray Shot: fair form when fourth to Checkerboard in bumper at Haydock on debut: likely to be suited by 2½m+. *N. G. Richards*
F86

MR BIGGLESWORTH (NZ) 9 ch.g. Honor Grades (USA) – Panza Anne (NZ) (Sound Reason (CAN)) [2006/7 c104, h102: 19d c16v⁴ c19g c16g² c16g^pu c17g Mar 24] lengthy gelding: winning hurdler: fair handicap chaser, left R. C. Guest and off 18 months prior to return: raced mainly around 2m: acts on heavy going: patiently ridden. *J. L. Spearing*
c101
h–

MR BILBO BAGGINS 4 ch.g. Magic Ring (IRE) – I'll Try (Try My Best (USA)) [2006/7 17g Nov 5] half-brother to several winners over jumps, notably very smart hurdler/winning chaser Intersky Falcon (by Polar Falcon), stayed 2½m: no form on Flat/in juvenile hurdle. *J. S. Moore*
h–

MR BOO (IRE) 8 b.g. Needle Gun (IRE) – Dasi (Bonne Noel) [2006/7 c130, h–: 21g² c19d c20s^pu c21g² c20m² Apr 27] good-topped gelding: fair hurdler: fairly useful handicap chaser: runner-up last 2 starts, beaten 4 lengths by Black Hills in 5-runner event at Sandown final one: stays 2¾m: acts on good to firm going. *G. L. Moore*
c128
h106

MR COONEY (IRE) 13 b.g. Van Der Linden (FR) – Green Orchid (Green Shoon) [2006/7 c–: c20v^ur c21s c26d^pu May 31] rangy gelding: winning pointer: no form in chases: tried in cheekpieces/blinkers. *James Clements, Ireland*
c–

MRDEEGEETHEGEEGEE (IRE) 5 b.g. Sadler's Wells (USA) – Department (USA) (Secretariat (USA)) [2006/7 F79: F16f² F16g F17v 16v^pu 16s 20d 16g Mar 17] tall, good-bodied gelding: modest form in bumpers: no solid form over hurdles: often tongue tied. *E. W. Tuer*
h–
F79

MR DINGLAWI (IRE) 6 b.g. Danehill Dancer (IRE) – Princess Leona (IRE) (Naiyli (IRE)) [2006/7 h–: c20s^F c17v^pu 20s⁴ 16v^pu Jan 6] good-topped gelding: fairly useful hurdler in 2004/5: below form after, failed to complete both outings over fences: stayed
c–
h105

2½m: acted on soft going, probably on good to firm: blinkered last 2 starts: dead. *D. M. Grissell*

MR DIP 7 b.g. Reprimand – Scottish Lady (Dunbeath (USA)) [2006/7 h67: 20f 24g⁵ 27d⁴ 22m⁴ Aug 24] poor maiden hurdler: probably stays 3m: acts on good to firm ground: sold £1,500 Ascot August Sales, won point in February. *L. A. Dace* **h67**

MR DOW JONES (IRE) 15 b.g. The Bart (USA) – Roseowen (Derring Rose) [2006/7 c–, h–: c28s² c25mᵖᵘ c26m⁶ c24v* c28s* c26s⁴ c29s* c26s⁴ c29s c32s³ c29v² Feb 23] medium-sized gelding: winning hurdler: fair handicap chaser: won at Chepstow and Stratford in October and Warwick in December: best up to 29f: best form on good going or softer (acts on heavy): tough. *W. K. Goldsworthy* **c113 h–**

MR DUFFY (IRE) 5 br.g. Presenting – Senorita Bonita (IRE) (Strong Gale) [2006/7 F16g 20s⁶ F16s 18s 16v⁵ 19g⁵ Mar 30] €48,000 3-y-o: lengthy gelding: first foal: dam, fair 2½m hurdle winner, half-sister to useful 3m chaser Saxophone: modest form in bumpers/maiden hurdles: likely to be suited by further than 2½m: raced on good ground or softer. *D. T. Hughes, Ireland* **h97 F77**

MR ED (IRE) 9 ch.g. In The Wings – Center Moriches (IRE) (Magical Wonder (USA)) [2006/7 c130p, h147: 25d 24dᶠ c23f² c24g³ Apr 21] tall, good-topped gelding: smart hurdler at best, well below form first 2 outings in 2006/7: fairly useful chaser: respectable efforts in handicaps last 2 starts: stays 3m: acts on firm and soft going: wears cheekpieces (tends to idle): patiently ridden. *P. Bowen* **c126 h–**

MR EX (ARG) 6 b.g. Numerous (USA) – Express Toss (ARG) (Egg Toss (USA)) [2006/7 h82, F89: 19g 16d² 20m 24d⁶ 16s² 17gᵖᵘ Apr 11] compact gelding: bumper winner: modest maiden hurdler: left G. A. Swinbank after second start, claimed from J. Howard Johnson £6,000 penultimate one: probably stays 2½m: acts on soft going: effective in cheekpieces or without: irresolute. *G. A. Harker* **h89 §**

MR EXCEL (IRE) 4 b.g. Orpen (USA) – Collected (IRE) (Taufan (USA)) [2006/7 16s Jan 13] tall, good sort: fairly useful on Flat (stays 2m), successful in November: left J. Osborne, well held in juvenile on hurdling debut: sold 8,000 gns Doncaster May Sales. *N. J. Henderson* **h–**

MR EYE POPPER (IRE) 8 b.g. Sadler's Wells (USA) – Tipperary Tartan (Rarity) [2006/7 h–: c22vᵖᵘ 19dᶠ 22sᵖᵘ 24m Mar 25] angular gelding: lightly raced and little sign of ability. *J. T. Stimpson* **c– h–**

MR FAST (ARG) 10 ch.g. Numerous (USA) – Speediness (ARG) (Etienne Gerard) [2006/7 h–: c16fᵖᵘ Apr 30] no show in maiden hurdle/novice chase: sold £900 Ascot June Sales. *J. Gallagher* **c– h–**

MR FLOPPY (IRE) 6 b.g. Un Desperado (FR) – Bright Future (IRE) (Satco (FR)) [2006/7 F16g 20dᵖᵘ 20s⁵ Apr 25] big gelding: third foal: brother to useful hurdler Very Optimistic, stayed 23f: dam unraced half-sister to fairly useful chaser Pennybridge, stayed 3m: seventh in bumper: poor form on completed start over hurdles, not knocked about: likely to do better. *Ferdy Murphy* **h71 p F78**

MR FLUFFY 10 br.g. Charmer – Hinton Bairn (Balinger) [2006/7 c122, h122: c23mᵖᵘ c22mᵘʳ c22g³ c24s* c22g c24g c24dᶠ Nov 17] leggy gelding: fairly useful handicap hurdler/chaser: won over fences at Bangor in August by length from Celtic Boy: well held in more competitive events next 2 starts: stays 3m: acts on soft and good to firm going. *A. W. Carroll* **c127 h–**

MR GUPPY (IRE) 6 b.g. Clerkenwell (USA) – Gene of The Glen (IRE) (Golden Act (USA)) [2006/7 F17v² F16d⁵ F16d³ 16vᵖᵘ Mar 9] 12,000 3-y-o: fourth foal: half-brother to 2½m bumper winner Camden Village (by Camden Town): dam unplaced in bumpers: fairly useful form in bumpers: favourite, little impact in maiden on hurdling debut: should do better. *L. Lungo* **h– p F97**

MR HAWKEYE (USA) 8 ch.g. Royal Academy (USA) – Port Plaisance (USA) (Woodman (USA)) [2006/7 c–, h–: c25m c16g⁴ c20m⁵ Jun 22] workmanlike gelding: novice chaser: fair pointer, won 3 times in 2007: tongue tied in 2006/7. *Mrs A. Hamilton* **c86 h–**

MR IRONMAN 6 b.g. Jendali (USA) – Carly-J (Cruise Missile) [2006/7 F78: 22g 20sᵖᵘ 20dᶠ 20g Nov 10] big, workmanlike gelding: no show over hurdles: joined N. Twiston-Davies. *R. C. Guest* **h–**

MR JAKE 14 b.g. Safawan – Miss Tealeaf (USA) (Lear Fan (USA)) [2006/7 c–, h–: c21g c25d c19m Sep 28] big, workmanlike gelding: winning hurdler/chaser, retains little ability. *H. E. Haynes* **c– h–**

MR JAWBREAKER (IRE) 8 b.g. Sadler's Wells (USA) – Abury (IRE) (Law Society (USA)) [2006/7 h–§, F89: 16v^{pu} 20g Apr 3] fair form in bumpers: well beaten sole completion over hurdles: temperamental. *J. T. Stimpson* — h– § F–

MR LAGGAN 12 b.g. Tina's Pet – Galway Gal (Proverb) [2006/7 c72, h–: c20g c22g^{pu} c21m c19d^5 c20s Jan 31] workmanlike gelding: poor handicap chaser, no form in 2006/7: stays 25f: acts on firm and soft going: blinkered once, sometimes wears cheekpieces. *Miss Kate Milligan* — c– h–

MR MAHDLO 13 b.g. Rakaposhi King – Fedelm (Celtic Cone) [2006/7 c–§, h–: c26v^5 May 20] leggy, workmanlike gelding: winning hunter chaser in 2005, no form in 3 starts since: should stay beyond 27f: acts on heavy going: blinkered once, effective with or without cheekpieces: has had tongue tied: inconsistent. *B. R. Woodhouse* — c– § h–

MR MAXIM 5 ch.g. Lake Coniston (IRE) – White Hare (Indian Ridge) [2006/7 h84: 18g 17m^3 21g^2 16s^4 16d^6 18s^5 c19s^F Dec 22] smallish, stocky gelding: modest maiden on Flat (stays 2m), claimed from R. Whitaker £6,000 in August: modest novice hurdler: similar form on chasing debut (fell last): stays 21f: acts on soft and good to firm ground: visored/blinkered last 6 starts: tried tongue tied. *L. Corcoran* — c94 h96

MR MAYFAIR (IRE) 5 ch.g. Entrepreneur – French Gift (Cadeaux Genereux) [2006/7 h–: 17m^5 17m 19s^{pu} Jun 27] no form over hurdles. *Miss L. Day* — h–

MR MCDELLON (IRE) 10 ch.g. Duky – Erin Brownie (Seclude (USA)) [2006/7 c–, h–: c24s^{pu} c23m^{pu} c24d^5 c25s^{pu} c20g^6 27m Apr 26] stocky gelding: no sign of ability: tried in cheekpieces. *J. F. Panvert* — c– x h–

MR MERLOT 5 ch.g. Alflora (IRE) – Eloquent Lawyer (Law Society (USA)) [2006/7 F16s F16m^3 Apr 25] 4,000 4-y-o: second foal: dam winning pointer: better effort in bumpers when third to Hello You at Worcester. *R. T. Phillips* — F88

MR MEYER (IRE) 10 b.g. Alphabatim (USA) – Parsons Alert (IRE) (The Parson) [2006/7 c–, h–: c16m^{pu} Jun 11] chunky gelding: winning hurdler/chaser, no form after 2004/5: stayed 2½m: acted on firm and soft going: usually blinkered: front runner: dead. *S. Donohoe, Ireland* — c– h–

MR MICKY (IRE) 9 b.g. Rudimentary (USA) – Top Berry (High Top) [2006/7 c–, h–: 27m^{pu} c16s^4 c20v^5 c19g^3 c21f^3 c24m Apr 14] workmanlike gelding: winning hurdler: poor maiden chaser: stays 21f. *M. B. Shears* — c69 h–

MR MIDAZ 8 ch.g. Danzig Connection (USA) – Marmy (Midyan (USA)) [2006/7 h99: 16d^3 May 19] sturdy gelding: fair handicap hurdler: stays easy 2½m: acts on heavy going. *D. W. Whillans* — h100

MR MINSTER MOSS 5 b.g. Minster Son – Ciara's Gale (IRE) (Strong Gale) [2006/7 F16g Apr 3] first foal: dam, little sign of ability, out of half-sister to smart staying chaser Buck Rogers: tailed off in bumper on debut. *S. T. Mason* — F–

MR NABORRO (IRE) 10 b.g. Hollow Hand – Grow Up (Kambalda) [2006/7 c25g^{pu} May 3] modest pointer, won in April: little impact in hunter on chase debut. *Graeme P. McPherson* — c–

MR POINTMENT (IRE) 8 b.g. Old Vic – Bettyhill (Ardross) [2006/7 h135: c20g* c21s^2 c24d^2 Feb 10] strong, good sort: useful hurdler: similar form over fences: won maiden at Bangor in November by 1¼ lengths from Heez A Dreamer: runner-up in novices after, beaten 1¾ lengths by Don't Push It at Cheltenham and a distance by Denman in 3-runner race at Newbury: should prove effective at 3m: raced on good going or softer (acts on soft): has joined P. Nicholls. *C. R. Egerton* — c140 h–

MR POSTMAN 6 ch.g. Private Despatch (USA) – Palm Lady (Palm Track) [2006/7 F71: 21m^{pu} 20s 20g Apr 11] little sign of ability. *G. J. Powell* — h–

MR PREACHER MAN 5 b.g. Sir Harry Lewis (USA) – Praise The Lord (Lord Gayle (USA)) [2006/7 20s^2 20v^4 18v 20s^3 24v^3 20s^2 Apr 25] workmanlike gelding: half-brother to several winners, including useful hurdler/chaser up to 2½m Whip Hand (by Bob Back): dam Irish maiden: fair novice hurdler: should stay beyond 2½m: raced on soft/ heavy going. *Miss Lucinda V. Russell* — h103

MR PRICKLE (IRE) 7 ch.g. Carroll House – Auntie Prickle Pin (IRE) (Sexton Blake) [2006/7 c106, h–: c16s* c16d^6 c16v^6 c17d c16s^{ur} Apr 26] leggy, quite good-topped gelding: maiden hurdler: fairly useful handicap chaser: won at Wetherby in November and Newcastle (beat Lucky Duck easily by 12 lengths) in January: effective at 2m to 2½m: raced on good going or softer (acts on heavy). *P. Beaumont* — c120 h–

MR PROTECTED 7 b.g. Thowra (FR) – Protected (FR) (Blakeney) [2006/7 F17s F—
Jun 27] fifth foal: dam unraced: well held in bumper on debut (unruly to post): failed to
complete in points. *J. D. Frost*

MRS BE (IRE) 11 ch.m. Be My Native (USA) – Kilbrack (Perspex) [2006/7 c112: **c92 §**
c26g⁴ c25m⁴ c28v⁵ May 27] lengthy mare: fair chaser, below best in hunters in 2006/7:
suited by good test of stamina: acts on soft going, easy task on good to firm: temperamental. *J. G. Cann*

MRS BRIDGE 5 gr.m. Environment Friend – Celtic Bridge (Celtic Cone) [2006/7 F17s **h— §**
F16d 17s 22g Apr 1] sixth foal: half-sister to ungenuine hurdler/chaser Over Bridge **F— §**
(by Overbury), stays 3m: dam, no form over hurdles, half-sister to fairly useful/temp-
eramental staying jumper Derring Bridge: soundly beaten in bumpers/over hurdles:
ungenuine. *Mrs S. M. Johnson*

MR SHAMBLES 6 ch.g. Karinga Bay – Urban Lily (Town And Country) [2006/7 F93: **h99**
F16s 17g² 19v* 16s² 19g² 22s 19v³ 19d⁶ 17v 20sᵖᵘ 22m³ Apr 15] rather leggy gelding: **F70**
runner-up in bumper: modest novice hurdler: won at Market Rasen in October: stays
2¾m: acts on good to firm and heavy going: blinkered/in cheekpieces 5 of last 6 starts.
S. Gollings

MRS HIGHAM (IRE) 6 ch.m. Pasternak – Crowther Homes (Neltino) [2006/7 h–, **h—**
F65: 16s⁴ May 28] little sign of ability in various events. *M. Scudamore*

MR SMITHERS JONES 7 br.g. Emperor Jones (USA) – Phylian (Glint of Gold) **c92**
[2006/7 h78: 21m c16v* Nov 28] little impact over hurdles: modest form when winning **h—**
4-runner novice handicap at Hereford on chasing debut: should stay 2½m: acts on heavy
ground. *Mrs S. M. Johnson*

MRS MONEYBAGS (IRE) 4 b.f. Exit To Nowhere (USA) – Christopherssister **h85**
(Timeless Times (USA)) [2006/7 17s⁵ 16m 16s² 16d 16g 19m Apr 22] small filly:
successful 3 times from 14 starts on Flat in Scandinavia, including twice over 1½m in
2006 for L. Kelp in Denmark: modest juvenile hurdler: raced mainly around 2m: in
cheekpieces last 2 starts. *M. Scudamore*

MR SNOWMAN 15 b.g. Lightning Dealer – Eventime (Hot Brandy) [2006/7 c23mᵖᵘ **c—**
Jul 12] smallish gelding: useful hunter chaser at best: lightly raced nowadays, won point
in February: stays 3¼m: acts on good to firm and heavy going. *Mrs T. J. Hill*

MRS O'MALLEY 7 b.m. Overbury (IRE) – Chapel Hill (IRE) (The Parson) [2006/7 **h78**
F75: 16s³ 21d 16v³ 16v 21g⁴ Mar 28] good-topped mare: poor novice hurdler: stays 21f:
raced on good going or softer (acts on heavy). *D. McCain Jnr*

MRS PHILIP 8 b.m. Puissance – Lightning Legacy (USA) (Super Concorde (USA)) **c—**
[2006/7 c–, h92: 24m 20m 21f⁴ Sep 17] modest handicap hurdler, below form in 2006/7: **h79**
well beaten only outing over fences: stays 2¾m: acts on firm and good to soft going:
blinkered last 2 starts. *P. J. Hobbs*

MR SPLODGE 13 b.g. Gildoran – Ethels Course (Crash Course) [2006/7 c108, h–: **c108**
c26mᵖᵘ c25m² c23m* c20dᵖᵘ c21s⁴ c25d⁶ c26v⁶ c24g⁶ Mar 29] lengthy, angular gelding: **h—**
fair handicap chaser: won at Leicester in November: below form after: stays 3¼m when
conditions aren't testing: unraced on firm going, acts on any other: has been let down by
jumping. *Mrs T. J. Hill*

MR STRACHAN (IRE) 6 b.g. Zaffaran (USA) – Call Girl (IRE) (Dromod Hill) **h128**
[2006/7 F95: 20gf² 20g* 20d² 20s³ 20v* 24g 20g Apr 7] strong gelding: fairly useful
novice hurdler: won at Wetherby in June and Uttoxeter (by a distance) in February: well
held back under less testing conditions last 2 starts (got loose before Grade 2 at Cheltenham on first occasion): should stay 3m: has won on good ground, best form on softer (acts
on heavy). *Mrs S. J. Smith*

MR STROWGER 6 b.g. Dancing Spree (USA) – Matoaka (Be My Chief (USA)) **h—**
[2006/7 h–: 16m⁶ 20mᵖᵘ Aug 11] no form over hurdles: tried in cheekpieces (saddle
slipped). *S. Curran*

MRS TWEEDY (IRE) 4 b.f. Publisher (USA) – Tullabards Leader (IRE) (Supreme **h—**
Leader) [2006/7 F17v 16g 16m Apr 10] third foal: dam unraced: soundly beaten in **F—**
bumper/over hurdles (mistakes). *Miss H. E. Roberts*

MRS WHITE (IRE) 7 b.m. Alflora (IRE) – Annicombe Run (Deep Run) [2006/7 F–: **F—**
F16s F17m Jun 4] little form in bumpers/points. *M. S. Wilesmith*

MR TAMBOURINE MAN (IRE) 6 b.g. Rainbow Quest (USA) – Girl From **h77**
Ipanema (Salse (USA)) [2006/7 h73: 16g⁶ 16m⁵ 17d* 16g 17m 16f Oct 5] poor handicap

hurdler: won at Newton Abbot in June: well held after: raced around 2m: acts on firm and good to soft going. *B. J. Llewellyn*

MR TEE PEE (IRE) 7 b.g. Norwich – Msadi Mhulu (IRE) (Kambalda) [2006/7 F–: F16g⁵ F13s 19s 16m Apr 25] big gelding: winning pointer: modest form in bumpers: little impact in novice hurdles 4 months apart. *R. D. E. Woodhouse*   **h–** **F79**

MR TWINS (ARG) 6 ch.g. Numerous (USA) – Twins Parade (ARG) (Parade Marshal (USA)) [2006/7 h81: 16g⁶ c16g⁵ c16m³ c20s³ c22mᶠ 20s⁶ 25d⁶ c24gᵖᵘ c24dᶠ c24d³ 24m c25s⁵ c25sᵖᵘ c20m² c20g* c25g⁴ c20m⁴ Apr 28] sturdy gelding: poor maiden hurdler: modest chaser: trained fourth/fifth starts by B. Storey: won maiden at Wetherby in April: stays easy 25f: acts on soft and good to firm going: tried in cheekpieces/blinkers: usually tongue tied. *M. A. Barnes*   **c85** **h81**

MR VESUVIUS (NZ) 7 ch.g. Pompeii Court (USA) – Snow Dance (NZ) (Tights (USA)) [2006/7 16s⁶ 16g⁵ 16g Apr 27] rangy gelding: won 1m maiden from 2 starts on Flat in New Zealand for P. Lock: easily best effort when fifth to Special Envoy in novice at Newbury: not given hard time once shuffled back home turn at Chepstow following month: tongue tied on debut: probably remains capable of better. *Miss Venetia Williams*   **h104 p**

MR WOODENTOP (IRE) 11 b.g. Roselier (FR) – Una's Polly (Pollerton) [2006/7 c113+, h–: 24vᵖᵘ c28d⁴ c28s³ 25v⁶ c24s⁵ Apr 26] leggy, close-coupled gelding: winning hurdler: fair chaser nowadays: stays 3½m: acts on heavy and good to firm going: tried visored: has idled/finished weakly. *Miss P. Robson*   **c112** **h96 +**

MR WOODS 5 b.g. Then Again – Lucky Lievre (Nomadic Way (USA)) [2006/7 F16s⁵ F17s² F17v⁵ Mar 18] tall, good-bodied gelding: first foal: dam well beaten in bumpers: easily best effort in bumpers when second to Harry Wood at Carlisle. *Mrs H. O. Graham*   **F91**

MS RAINBOW RUNNER 4 b.f. Josr Algarhoud (IRE) – Silk Law (IRE) (Barathea (IRE)) [2006/7 16gᵖᵘ Oct 14] modest on Flat (stays 1¼m): reportedly lame on hurdling debut. *P. Butler*   **h–**

MT DESERT 5 b.g. Rainbow Quest (USA) – Chief Bee (Chief's Crown (USA)) [2006/7 16f 18m³ 22m* 22m⁵ 20vᵖᵘ 19s 20g³ Mar 17] fairly useful on Flat (stays 13f) at 3 yrs: fair novice hurdler: easily landed odds at Cartmel in July: sold out of C. Mann's stable 10,000 gns Doncaster October Sales before fifth start: stays 2¾m: acts on firm going: has shaped as if stamina more than once. *E. W. Tuer*   **h105**

MTILLY 6 br.m. Mtoto – Corn Lily (Aragon) [2006/7 16m 16g⁶ 16g 20g⁵ 16v Dec 26] lengthy, rather leggy mare: half-sister to 2 winning hurdlers by Minster Son, including fairly useful Cathedral Belle (stayed 25f): dam fairly useful 2m hurdler: lightly raced on Flat: poor form in novice hurdles. *K. G. Reveley*   **h65**

MUCHO LOCO (IRE) 4 ch.g. Tagula (IRE) – Mousseux (IRE) (Jareer (USA)) [2006/7 18s 17s 16mᵖᵘ Apr 9] smallish, angular gelding: modest maiden on Flat (stays 8.3f) for J. Portman: no form over hurdles. *R. Curtis*   **h–**

MUCKLE FLUGGA (IRE) 8 ch.m. Karinga Bay – Dancing Dove (IRE) (Denel (FR)) [2006/7 h104: 20d⁴ 21m 20m Feb 4] fair handicap hurdler, lame final outing: stays 3m: acts on good to firm and heavy going. *N. G. Richards*   **h101**

MUCKSHIFTER 6 b.g. Topanoora – Melody Maid (Strong Gale) [2006/7 F–: 20m⁴ Mar 31] well beaten in bumper (for P. Blockley) and maiden hurdle (raced freely) a year apart. *Miss H. Lewis*   **h69**

MUGHAS (IRE) 8 b.g. Sadler's Wells (USA) – Quest of Passion (FR) (Saumarez) [2006/7 h149: 23fᵖᵘ May 6] good-topped gelding: smart handicap hurdler: ran as if amiss only outing in 2006/7: likely to stay beyond 3m: acts on good to firm and heavy going: visored last 2 outings. *A. King*   **h–**

MUHTENBAR 7 b.g. Muhtarram (USA) – Ardenbar (Ardross) [2006/7 c118, h–: c20g⁴ c20g² c16s² c20dᵖᵘ c16g³ Mar 22] big, good-topped gelding: winning hurdler: fairly useful maiden chaser, in frame all 8 completed outings: stays 2½m: acts on heavy going: front runner/races prominently: sound jumper: has tendency to bleed. *Miss H. C. Knight*   **c118** **h–**

MUJAZAF 5 b.g. Grand Lodge (USA) – Decision Maid (USA) (Diesis) [2006/7 h–: 16sᵖᵘ May 14] no show in 2 starts over hurdles: dead. *D. Burchell*   **h–**

MUJIMAC (IRE) 5 b.g. Mujadil (USA) – Cross Dall (IRE) (Blues Traveller (IRE)) [2006/7 16f 17g 16f 16g⁵ 16m⁶ 27dᵖᵘ Aug 15] modest maiden on Flat (stays 1½m), sold   **h–**

out of P. Blockley's stable £800 Ascot February Sales: no form over hurdles: often tongue tied: sold £1,100 Ascot August Sales. *G. F. Edwards*

MULLIGAN'S PRIDE (IRE) 6 b.g. Kahyasi – Babs Mulligan (IRE) (Le Bavard (FR)) [2006/7 h–, F83: 23g 25g⁴ 19s 25vᵖᵘ Feb 27] good-topped gelding: in frame in bumpers: modest on Flat (stays 2m): no form over hurdles, sold out of G. A. Swinbank's stable 5,000 gns Doncaster October Sales before third start: tried visored. *James Moffatt*   **h–**

MULL OF DUBAI 4 b.g. Mull of Kintyre (USA) – Enlisted (IRE) (Sadler's Wells (USA)) [2006/7 16d⁶ 16d⁴] fair on Flat (stays 1½m), successful 3 times in 2006: never dangerous in juvenile on hurdling debut: should do better. *J. S. Moore*   **h72 p**

MULLZIMA (IRE) 4 b.f. Mull of Kintyre (USA) – Habaza (IRE) (Shernazar) [2006/7 16g 16g⁵ 17dᵘʳ 16d⁴ 16s⁶ 16d Dec 21] poor maiden on Flat (stays 1m): left P. D. Evans, no form over hurdles: tried in cheekpieces. *M. A. Doyle*   **h–**

MULTEEN GUNNER 10 b.g. Homo Sapien – Sister Delaney (Deep Run) [2006/7 c88§, h–§; c20sᵘʳ Feb 4] winning pointer: maiden hurdler: modest chaser: stays 3m: acts on firm and good to soft ground: usually wears headgear. *Miss J. H. Jenner*   **c– §** **h– §**

MULTEEN RIVER (IRE) 11 b.g. Supreme Leader – Blackwater Mist (IRE) (King's Ride) [2006/7 c117x, h–; c26pu c23mᵖᵘ c21dᵘʳ Oct 14] tall, useful-looking gelding: fairly useful handicap chaser: creditable second to Goblin at Worcester, only completed start in 2006/7: stayed 21f: acted on soft and firm going: tried tongue tied: often let down by jumping. *Jonjo O'Neill*   **c117 x** **h–**

MULTI TALENTED (IRE) 11 b.g. Montelimar (USA) – Boro Glen (Furry Glen) [2006/7 c–§; c26gᵖᵘ Nov 15] tall gelding: one-time fair handicap chaser, has deteriorated considerably: suited by 3m+: acts on heavy going: usually blinkered, tried in cheekpieces: often looks hard ride, though has run well for amateur/conditional. *L. Wells*   **c– §**

MUMBLES HEAD (IRE) 6 ch.g. Flemensfirth (USA) – Extra Mile (Torus) [2006/7 F102: 22m* 24v² 22m⁶ 24g³ 24s* 27s* Apr 27] tall, good-topped gelding: will make a chaser: bumper winner: most progressive hurdler: won maiden at Stratford in September and 2 handicaps (first a novice event) within 3 days at Perth in April: useful form when beating Oscar The Boxer by 20 lengths in conditional jockeys event final outing: stays 27f: acts on good to firm and heavy going: has taken strong hold. *P. Bowen*   **h134**

MUNAAWESH (USA) 6 b.g. Bahri (USA) – Istikbal (USA) (Kingmambo (USA)) [2006/7 h74: 21m⁴ 17m² 20f* 17m⁵ 20f⁴ 22d² 20m⁵ Sep 3] modest handicap hurdler: won at Perth in July: stays 2¾m: acts on firm and soft going. *Mrs Marjorie Fife*   **h85**

MUNADIL 9 ch.g. Nashwan (USA) – Bintalshaati (Kris) [2006/7 c78, h76: c16m* c17gᵖᵘ c16fᵖᵘ 16mᵖᵘ 16mᵖᵘ Apr 9] maiden hurdler: easily best effort over fences when winning minor event at Worcester in May: largely let down by jumping/temperament after: raced around 2m: tongue tied: headstrong. *A. M. Hales*   **c86 d** **h–**

MUNGO JERRY (GER) 6 b.g. Tannenkonig (IRE) – Mostly Sure (IRE) (Sure Blade (USA)) [2006/7 h94: 21m⁵ 20f⁴ 16f 20gᵖᵘ Jul 21] 1½m winner on Flat: modest novice hurdler: stays easy 21f: probably acts on any going: tongue tied last 5 starts. *B. N. Pollock*   **h94**

MUNNINGS TOUCH (IRE) 7 b.g. Bob Back (USA) – Castle Mews (Persian Mews) [2006/7 F16d F16d F16v Jan 12] €31,000 4-y-o, resold 20,000 4-y-o: rather unfurnished gelding: first foal: dam, winning pointer, out of half-sister to very smart chaser Father Delaney: no better than mid-division in bumpers. *N. J. Henderson*   **F82**

MUNNY HILL 7 b.g. Golden Heights – More Laughter (Oats) [2006/7 h–: c23fᵖᵘ Sep 10] leggy gelding: little sign of ability. *M. Appleby*   **c–** **h–**

MUNTAMI (IRE) 6 gr.g. Daylami (IRE) – Bashashah (IRE) (Kris) [2006/7 h94: 24g 20g⁶ 20s 16s⁴ 16sᵖᵘ 18v 16g* Mar 20] workmanlike gelding: fair handicap hurdler: left S. Donohoe, won amateur event at Warwick in March: successful also twice on Flat after rejoining current stable: likely to prove best at 2m with emphasis on speed: tried blinkered. *John A. Harris*   **h106**

MURAQEB 7 ch.g. Grand Lodge (USA) – Oh So Well (IRE) (Sadler's Wells (USA)) [2006/7 h–: 22sᵖᵘ 20dᵖᵘ Apr 22] stocky gelding: no solid form over hurdles: tried in cheekpieces/tongue tied. *Mrs Barbara Waring*   **h–**

MURPHY (IRE) 5 b.g. Lord Americo – Kyle Cailin (Over The River (FR)) [2006/7 F16v F16g Apr 7] good-scoped gelding: has scope: brother to high-class chaser around 2m Dempsey and useful chaser up to 3m Puget Blue: dam, winning pointer, sister to fairly useful hunter Overheard: favourite, travelled well long way and not knocked about in bumper on debut: dropped out tamely in another 4 months later. *Carl Llewellyn*   **F–**

MURPHY'S MAGIC (IRE) 9 br.g. Hubbly Bubbly (USA) – Wishing Trout (Three   **c–**
Wishes) [2006/7 c82: c24g^{pu} Jun 8] sturdy gelding: winning pointer: poor form in chases:
usually in cheekpieces/blinkers. *Mrs T. J. Hill*

MURPHYS MILLION (IRE) 6 ch.g. Carroll House – Flashey Blond (Buckskin   **h89**
(FR)) [2006/7 F16s^5 F16v^4 19d* 19s^6 20s^{pu} Apr 27] €16,000 4-y-o: quite good-topped   **F84**
gelding: half-brother to several winners, including fairly useful Irish jumper Titian
Blonde (by Callernish), stayed 3m: dam unraced half-sister to Irish Grand National
winner Perris Valley: mid-field in bumpers: modest form over hurdles: won maiden at
Market Rasen in February: should be suited by 2½m+: raced on ground softer than good.
R. Ford

MURPHY'S NAILS (IRE) 10 b.g. Bob's Return (IRE) – Southern Run (Deep Run)   **c84**
[2006/7 c–, h90: c19g^4 16d^5 16m^6 c24g^{ur} Nov 1] strong, lengthy gelding: maiden hurdler,   **h70**
below best in 2006/7: poor form completed start over fences: stays 21f: acts on firm and
good to soft going: tried blinkered, usually wears cheekpieces. *K. C. Bailey*

MURPHY'S QUEST 11 ch.g. Sir Harry Lewis (USA) – Rondeau (Orchestra) [2006/7   **c–**
c–, h–: 24d^{pu} 22d^{pu} Dec 15] tall gelding: winning hurdler/maiden chaser: lightly raced   **h–**
and no form since 2004/5. *Lady Herries*

MUSALLY 10 ch.g. Muhtarram (USA) – Flourishing (IRE) (Trojan Fen) [2006/7 c–x,   **c– x**
h96: 21f^F 24m^2 20m^5 22g^5 20g^2 19m^3 21m^6 21g^4 21d^3 20g^3 Apr 14] angular gelding: **h102**
maiden chaser, usually let down by jumping: fair handicap hurdler: best up to 3m: acts on
good to soft going, raced mainly on firmer (acts on firm): tried blinkered/in cheekpieces.
W. Jenks

MUSICAL CHAIRS (IRE) 5 b.g. Musical Pursuit – Kings Pearl (IRE) (King's Ride)   **h–**
[2006/7 F16s F16s 18g Mar 18] useful-looking gelding: fifth foal: dam placed in points: **F–**
well held in bumpers/novice hurdle (bled): races freely. *Miss H. C. Knight*

MUSICAL CHORD (IRE) 8 ch.g. Accordion – Slieveglagh Queen (Proverb)   **c–**
[2006/7 h–, F89: c20d^{pu} c16v^2 c19s c20v^{pu} c27m^{pu} Apr 9] lengthy, good-topped gelding: **h–**
no form over jumps: tried in cheekpieces. *B. Storey*

MUSICAL GIFT 7 ch.g. Cadeaux Genereux – Kazoo (Shareef Dancer (USA)) [2006/7   **h–**
17g Sep 23] modest on Flat (stays easy 1¼m): well beaten in novice hurdles: sold £2,100
Ascot February Sales. *P. A. Blockley*

MUSIC TO MY EARS (IRE) 9 ch.g. Phardante (FR) – Evas Charm (Carlburg)   **c110**
[2006/7 c100, h–: c25m^2 c23m^2 c20m^3 c26d^{pu} c26g^5 c24g^3 Oct 19] workmanlike gelding: **h–**
fair handicap chaser: should stay beyond 25f: acts on any ground: has worn cheekpieces/
visor: tongue tied once (won). *Jonjo O'Neill*

MUSIMARO (FR) 9 b.g. Solid Illusion (USA) – Musimara (FR) (Margouillat (FR))   **c–**
[2006/7 c–, h–: 20m^5 17d^4 19g^2 16s Dec 3] sturdy gelding: modest handicap hurdler   **h90**
nowadays: trained on reappearance only by Mrs P. Ford: no show only outing over fences:
stays 2½m: acts on good to soft and good to firm going: tried blinkered, usually in
cheekpieces. *C. Nenadich*

MUSIQUE EN TETE (FR) 7 ch.g. Minds Music (USA) – Ula Bamberina (FR)   **F80**
(Mont Basile (FR)) [2006/7 F16m^2 Jun 11] third foal: dam cross-country chase winner up
to 25f: runner-up in maiden bumper won by Chosen at Stratford on debut: will be suited
by 2½m+. *A. W. Carroll*

MUSSEL BUOY (IRE) 11 b.g. Phardante (FR) – Windy Run (Deep Run) [2006/7   **c75**
c19m May 9] ex-Irish gelding: fair pointer, won once in 2006: litte impact in hunters.
M. J. Tuckey

MUST BE KEEN 8 b.g. Emperor Jones (USA) – As Mustard (Keen) [2006/7 F79:   **h–**
16d^{ur} 16g^6 17g 16d Dec 15] tall gelding: modest in bumpers and on Flat (successful in
January): no solid form over hurdles. *Ernst Oertel*

MUTUAL ATTRACTION (IRE) 7 b.m. Sesaro (USA) – Baby Caroline (Martin   **c–**
John) [2006/7 18g 20g 18g^6 c25g c25g 18v^3 20d 16g Apr 5] €2,000 3-y-o: half-sister to   **h65**
several winners on Flat, including 13f winner Parish Walk (by Pennine Walk): dam Irish
maiden who stayed 1½m: well held in maiden chases: poor maiden hurdler: best around
2m: raced on good going or softer (acts on heavy): tried in cheekpieces: often tongue tied
nowadays. *Patrick Mooney, Ireland*

MUTUAL RESPECT (IRE) 5 b.g. Moscow Society (USA) – Deepest Thoughts   **F104**
(IRE) (Supreme Leader) [2006/7 F16m^2 F16s* F16d^5 Feb 10] lengthy, useful-looking
gelding: first foal: dam unraced out of half-sister to dam of high-class staying chaser
Trabolgan: fairly useful form in bumpers: landed odds at Chepstow in December by 1¾

lengths from The Jazz Musician (pair clear): fifth to Crocodiles Rock in Grade 2 at Newbury: will be suited by 2¼m+. *P. F. Nicholls*

MVEZO 9 ch.g. Karinga Bay – Queen of The Celts (Celtic Cone) [2006/7 c–, h–: c24g^{pu} Apr 27] no form over hurdles: failed to complete in chases: successful twice in points in 2007: tried visored. *J. S. Hughes*   **c–** **h–**

MY BEAUTIFUL LOSER (IRE) 5 gr.m. Silver Patriarch (IRE) – Miss Diskin (IRE) (Sexton Blake) [2006/7 F16m⁶ Apr 25] £17,000 4-y-o: third foal: half-sister to fair hurdler Double Dizzy (by Double Trigger), stays 3m: dam, winning hurdler/fairly useful staying chaser: mid-field in bumper on debut: bred to be suited by further. *R. Dickin*   **F–**

MY BEST BUDDY 11 b.g. Vital Season – Trade Only (Andrea Mantegna) [2006/7 c97: c24d⁵ c16v² c22g² Mar 28] prolific winning pointer: fairly useful hunter chaser: stays 3m, effective at much shorter: acts on heavy going, probably on good to firm. *G. T. H. Bailey*   **c100**

MY BEST SECRET 8 ch.g. Secret Appeal – Mohibbah (USA) (Conquistador Cielo (USA)) [2006/7 F–: 16f 17d^{pu} May 31] third in bumper on debut: no aptitude for hurdling. *L. Lungo*   **h– x**

MY BIG SISTER 8 gr.m. Thethingaboutitis (USA) – My Concordia (Belfort (FR)) [2006/7 c–, h–: 16m May 6] lightly raced and no form: sold £2,400 Ascot June Sales. *J. W. Mullins*   **c–** **h–**

MY BOO 5 b.m. Sri Pekan (USA) – Malwiya (USA) (Shahrastani (USA)) [2006/7 20d^{pu} 16s^{pu} 21g^{pu} Feb 21] poor on Flat (stays 1½m), sold out of T. Keddy's stable 1,500 gns Newmarket July Sales, resold £1,000 Ascot October Sales: no show over hurdles. *R. C. Harper*   **h–**

MY CAROLE (IRE) 7 b.m. Needle Gun (IRE) – Moores Glen (IRE) (Furry Glen) [2006/7 F16s F16s 21v⁴ 20d⁵ Jan 15] €5,500 4-y-o: angular mare: eighth foal: dam unraced: well beaten in maiden Irish points: bought 1,200 gns Doncaster May Sales: mid-division in bumpers: some promise both starts over hurdles, travelled strongly long way when fifth to Sa Nau in maiden at Fakenham: likely to prove best around 2m: capable of better. *D. T. Turner*   **h86 p** **F70**

MYCENEAN PRINCE (USA) 4 b.g. Swain (IRE) – Nijinsky's Beauty (USA) (Nijinsky (CAN)) [2006/7 17m⁵ 17g 17g⁶ 16d⁵ 17g² Apr 23] poor maiden on Flat: blinkered, best effort in juvenile hurdles when second to Plemont Bay in maiden at Sedgefield. *R. C. Guest*   **h81**

MY CONDOR (IRE) 6 b.g. Beneficial – Margellen's Castle (IRE) (Castle Keep) [2006/7 F17m² 17d⁶ 16m² 19d 17v^{pu} 17m⁵ Apr 17] €36,000 4-y-o: second foal: dam sixth in bumper: fair form in bumpers (trained by W. J. Burke, reportedly swallowed tongue on debut): disappointing over hurdles, often shaping as if amiss: left P. Nicholls after second start. *D. McCain Jnr*   **h74** **F91**

MY FAVOURITE 5 b.m. Classic Cliche (IRE) – Joline (IRE) (Roselier (FR)) [2006/7 aF16g 21g^{pu} 21m^{pu} Apr 8] first foal: dam, little form over hurdles, sister to fairly useful staying chaser Mr Woodentop: no sign of ability. *M. J. Roberts*   **h–** **F–**

MY FINAL BID (IRE) 8 b.g. Supreme Leader – Mini Minor (IRE) (Black Minstrel) [2006/7 h115, F104: 22f May 9] runner-up all 3 starts in bumpers and first 2 over hurdles, fairly useful form twice: stays 3m: acts on heavy going (well beaten on firm). *Mrs A. C. Hamilton*   **h–**

MY FRIEND FRITZ 7 ch.g. Safawan – Little Scarlett (Mazilier (USA)) [2006/7 F16v Dec 31] strong gelding: poor form on first of 2 starts in bumpers over 2 years apart: third in claimer on Flat in January. *P. W. Hiatt*   **F–**

MY FRIEND PAUL 7 b.g. Bold Fox – Annie Bee (Rusticaro (FR)) [2006/7 F–: F17d Jun 4] tall, workmanlike gelding: soundly beaten in bumpers. *O. Brennan*   **F–**

MY FRIEND SANDY 6 ch.g. Anshan – Gaye Fame (Ardross) [2006/7 F17v² Feb 13] smallish gelding: fourth foal: half-brother to useful staying hurdler/Irish Grand National runner-up Oulart (by Sabrehill) and bumper winner Round The Horn (by Master Willie): dam, modest hurdler who stayed 3m, half-sister to smart staying chaser Simon, out of sister to very smart staying chaser Black Humour: favourite, 5 lengths second of 6 to King Jack in bumper at Fakenham. *J. A. B. Old*   **F98**

MY GOOD LORD (IRE) 8 br.g. Mister Lord (USA) – Glenstal Forest (IRE) (Glenstal (USA)) [2006/7 h92: 20d 20m^{pu} 22m⁴ 20g^{su} 21m² 21m* 20d² 20s⁴ 21d^{pu} 20g³ Apr 16] small gelding: modest hurdler: won conditional jockeys novice handicap at   **h95**

Sedgefield in September: will stay 3m: acts on soft and good to firm going: wore cheekpieces fourth to ninth starts. *G. M. Moore*

MY IMMORTAL 5 b.g. Monsun (GER) – Dame Kiri (FR) (Old Vic) [2006/7 h128: 16m* 16d 19d⁴ 22d 24f* 21g³ Apr 18] compact gelding: fairly useful hurdler: didn't need to be at best to win novices at Towcester in October and Ludlow in April: creditable efforts in very valuable handicaps second/third outings: stays 3m: acts on firm and good to soft going: makes running/races prominently. *D. E. Pipe* — **h124**

MY LADY LINK (FR) 8 bl.m. Sleeping Car (FR) – Cadoudaline (FR) (Cadoudal (FR)) [2006/7 c–, h95: 24s⁵ 22d² 20g* Apr 3] strong mare: winning chaser in France (often let down by jumping in Britain): fair handicap hurdler: won at Wetherby in April: stays 3m: acts on heavy going: tried blinkered. *Miss Venetia Williams* — **c–**, **h107**

MY LAST BEAN (IRE) 10 gr.g. Soviet Lad (USA) – Meanz Beanz (High Top) [2006/7 h109: 17s Dec 29] lengthy gelding: fair handicap hurdler: well beaten only outing in 2006/7: should stay at least 19f: acts on good to firm and good to soft ground. *M. R. Bosley* — **h–**

MY LEGAL EAGLE (IRE) 13 b.g. Law Society (USA) – Majestic Nurse (On Your Mark) [2006/7 h6g⁵ 16g^pu 17s^pu Dec 29] rather sparely-made gelding: modest on Flat: fair handicap hurdler, ran poorly last 2 outings: should stay 2½m: acts on soft and good to firm going. *E. G. Bevan* — **h100**

MYLO 9 gr.g. Faustus (USA) – Bellifontaine (FR) (Bellypha) [2006/7 c102§, h104§: 22m⁶ c20m² c22m^pu c21m* c21d c24m 22s 22d 23v² 22v³ 24v⁶ Feb 20] compact gelding: fair handicap hurdler: similar standard over fences, won maiden at Newton Abbot in July: stays 3m: acts on any going: sometimes wears headgear: irresolute. *Jonjo O'Neill* — **c103 §**, **h108 §**

MYLORD COLLONGES (FR) 7 bl.g. Video Rock (USA) – Diane Collonges (FR) (El Badr) [2006/7 h–: c20s c24d^F c25s⁴ Mar 8] lengthy, good-topped gelding: well held over hurdles: poor form over fences, though has shaped as if capable of better: may prove best short of 3m. *Mrs Susan Nock* — **c85**, **h–**

MY MATILDA 4 gr.f. Silver Patriarch (IRE) – Upton Lass (IRE) (Crash Course) [2006/7 F14g F13s 16s^pu 16m^pu 16m⁴ Apr 24] lengthy filly: third foal: dam poor maiden pointer: little form in bumpers and over hurdles. *Andrew Turnell* — **h60**, **F–**

MY MICHELLE 6 b.m. Ali-Royal (IRE) – April Magic (Magic Ring (IRE)) [2006/7 17d^pu 19s⁶ Dec 7] fair on Flat (stays 9.5f), successful in January/February: no form in 2 starts over hurdles. *B. Palling* — **h–**

MY MON AMOUR 6 b.m. Terimon – Roll Over Darling (Double Bed (FR)) [2006/7 h–, F–: 16d^pu 18s^F 16v^pu 16m^pu Apr 8] good-topped mare: no sign of ability. *C. J. Drewe* — **h–**

MY MUM MARY 4 b.f. Montjoy (USA) – Jeedamaya (Taufan (USA)) [2006/7 16m^pu Jul 16] seventh foal: half-sister to French 1m/1¼m winner Davids Diamond (by Sizzling Melody): dam maiden who stayed 1m: visored, jumped badly and soon detached in juvenile hurdle on debut. *B. R. Johnson* — **h–**

MY PETRA 4 b.f. Midnight Legend – Lac Marmot (FR) (Marju (IRE)) [2006/7 16g* 16g* 16d* 16d⁴ 17g 20g⁶ 16m³ Apr 20] workmanlike filly: fairly useful on Flat (stays 1½m): similar standard over hurdles: won juveniles at Haydock in October and Hunting-don (fillies) and Newbury in November: good efforts next and final starts: should stay beyond 2m: acts on good to firm and good to soft going (unraced on extremes): sold 75,000 gns Doncaster May Sales. *A. King* — **h121**

MY PORTFOLIO (IRE) 5 b.g. Montjeu (IRE) – Elaine's Honor (USA) (Chief's Crown (USA)) [2006/7 20s⁶ 20s⁶ 16s 20s Nov 4] lightly-raced maiden on Flat, sold out of R. Charlton's stable 10,000 gns Newmarket July (2005) Sales: poor form over hurdles. *J. J. Lambe, Ireland* — **h71**

MY RETREAT (USA) 10 b.g. Hermitage (USA) – My Jessica Ann (USA) (Native Rythm) [2006/7 h68: 22m³ 22m 19g⁵ 20f² 20g² 24m 22m⁴ 19m* 19g 22d⁵ 21m³ 20g⁶ 21g² Apr 23] close-coupled gelding: poor handicap hurdler: won conditional jockeys selling event at Exeter in October: probably stays 3m: acts on any going: blinkered once. *R. Fielder* — **h68**

MY ROCKET 4 b.f. Muthahb (IRE) – Tapper (IRE) (Elbio) [2006/7 F13d^pu F13g F14g Nov 15] sparely-made filly: first foal: dam unraced: no form in bumpers. *M. Appleby* — **F–**

MY ROSIE RIBBONS (IRE) 8 b.m. Roselier (FR) – Georgic (Tumble Gold) [2006/7 h91, F–: 22d^F 24m² Apr 15] lengthy mare: modest maiden hurdler: best effort — **h99**

when second to Natoumba in handicap at Worcester: stays 3m: acts on good to firm and heavy going: ran out on hurdling debut. *P. J. Hobbs*

MY SKIPPER (IRE) 6 b.g. Old Vic – Nil Faic (IRE) (King's Ride) [2006/7 h–: 20g 16d 17s Feb 26] useful-looking gelding: won bumper on debut in 2004/5: little impact in 4 starts in novice company over hurdles, though has shaped as if capable of better. *Miss H. C. Knight* **h82 p**

MYSON (IRE) 8 ch.g. Accordion – Ah Suzie (IRE) (King's Ride) [2006/7 c99, h80: 22m c20d² c16d³ Nov 22] tall gelding: lightly raced over hurdles: modest handicap chaser: left D. Feek after first outing: stays 21f: probably acts on heavy going: wore cheekpieces/blinkers 5 of last 6 starts: patiently ridden. *G. L. Moore* **c92 h77**

MYSTERI DANCER 9 b.g. Rudimentary (USA) – Mystery Ship (Decoy Boy) [2006/7 16g 16d⁶ Nov 19] lightly-raced winning hurdler: well beaten both starts in handicaps in 2006/7 after long lay-off: raced at 2m. *J. Joseph* **h–**

MYSTERY (GER) 9 br.g. Java Gold (USA) – My Secret (GER) (Secreto (USA)) [2006/7 h–: 17d⁶ Dec 26] compact gelding: lightly-raced winning hurdler: off 19 months and left T. George, sixth in selling handicap only outing in 2006/7: stays 2½m: raced on good going or softer: has had tongue tied, including last 3 starts. *Miss Joanne Priest* **h–**

MYSTICALLY 4 b.g. Diktat – Mystic Beauty (IRE) (Alzao (USA)) [2006/7 F14v⁵ F14s⁴ F16s 19m⁵ Apr 28] strong, lengthy gelding: third foal: closely related to 2¾m hurdle winner Mystic Forest (by Charnwood Forest), also 1m to 1¾m winner on Flat: dam unraced: modest form in bumpers: never a factor in novice on hurdling debut. *M. W. Easterby* **h74 F80**

Mountgrange Stud's "My Turn Now"

MYSTIC GLEN 8 b.m. Vettori (IRE) – Mystic Memory (Ela-Mana-Mou) [2006/7 c–, h64: 16f* 19s⁴ 16d⁴ c16g* c17v c19d³ c16d² Jan 15] poor hurdler: off over a year, won ladies handicap at Perth in July: similar form over fences, won handicap at Musselburgh in November: probably stays 21f: acts on firm and soft going: has worn cheekpieces. *P. D. Niven*   **c82 h75**

MYSTIC STEEL (IRE) 6 gr.m. Norwich – Miss McCormick (IRE) (Roselier (FR)) [2006/7 F18s 21s 20s Dec 7] leggy mare: half-sister to fair 21f hurdle winner Castle Richard (by Sexton Blake): dam lightly-raced hurdler: won mares maiden Irish point in 2006: form in bumpers only when third to Callherwhatyoulike in mares event at Gowran: sold out of P. J. Rothwell's stable 25,000 gns Doncaster May Sales and off 6 months, well held in mares novice hurdles. *Mrs P. Sly*   **h– F–**

MYSTIFIED (IRE) 4 b.g. Raise A Grand (IRE) – Sunrise (IRE) (Sri Pekan (USA)) [2006/7 17d³ 16m³ 19s⁴ 20g⁴ Mar 27] modest on Flat (stays 2m): seemingly best effort over hurdles when third to Stainley in juvenile at Musselburgh second start: wore cheekpieces final one. *R. F. Fisher*   **h80**

MY SWEET CAROLINE 7 b.m. Presidium – Balgownie (Prince Tenderfoot (USA)) [2006/7 F16f Sep 29] half-sister to winning pointer by Lochnager: dam 1¼m winner: in rear in bumper on debut: sold 1,600 gns Doncaster May Sales. *G. A. Harker*   **F–**

MYTHICAL KING (IRE) 10 b.g. Fairy King (USA) – Whatcombe (USA) (Alleged (USA)) [2006/7 c106x, h120: 20g 20s 19g² c20sF Nov 16] workmanlike gelding: fairly useful hurdler at best: blinkered and dropped markedly in class, second in conditional jockeys seller (claimed from R. Lee £6,000) at Hereford: usually let down by jumping over fences, close second and running best race when falling last in handicap won by Master Papa at Market Rasen: stays 3m: acts well on heavy going: patiently ridden: inconsistent. *R. M. Stronge*   **c112 x h99 +**

MYTHICAL SON (IRE) 7 gr.g. Son of Sharp Shot (IRE) – Royal Myth (USA) (Sir Ivor (USA)) [2006/7 24m⁵ 20g 21g c23d⁴ c28gᵖᵘ 25gᵖᵘ Apr 16] tall gelding: won maiden Irish point in 2005: no solid form over hurdles/in chases. *P. Grindey*   **c– h–**

MY TRUE ROMANCE (IRE) 6 b.m. Orpen (USA) – Mary's Way (GR) (Night Shift (USA)) [2006/7 17d³ 17mᵖᵘ 19m⁶ 16d 19d 16vF 20v⁵ 16v* 16v 16s⁶ 16s² 18s Mar 25] lightly raced on Flat: modest novice hurdler: won at Cartmel in May and, having left A. Sadik after third start, Tramore in January: best form around 2m: acts on heavy going: blinkered last 2 starts: tongue tied once in bumpers. *Shane Joseph Kelly, Ireland*   **h88**

MYTTON'S DREAM 5 br.m. Diktat – Courtisane (Persepolis (FR)) [2006/7 16dF Mar 22] modest at best on Flat (barely stays 1m): fell third on hurdling debut. *Miss Joanne Priest*   **h–**

MY TURN NOW (IRE) 5 ch.g. In The Wings – Wishful (IRE) (Irish River (FR)) [2006/7 F101: F16d² 16m* 16d* 16s* 17s* 16vF 20s* 21g⁶ 21g* Apr 18] smallish, close-coupled gelding: bumper winner, left E. Hales before reappearance: useful novice hurdler: justified favouritism at Ludlow and Kempton in November, Sandown and Taunton in December, Huntingdon in February and Cheltenham in April: ran well both starts in Grade 1 events, including when sixth to Massini's Maguire at Cheltenham: likely to stay beyond 21f: acts on heavy ground, has won on good to firm. *C. J. Mann*   **h138 F104**

MY WAY DE SOLZEN (FR) 7 b.g. Assessor (IRE) – Agathe de Solzen (FR) (Chamberlin (FR)) [2006/7 c–p, h164: 25s² c16d* c16s² c21v* c20v* c16g* Mar 13]   **c157 p h147 +**

For the first time in over half a century 'The Duke' was missing from the Cheltenham Festival. David Nicholson died at the age of sixty-seven in late-August 2006, just after *Chasers & Hurdlers 2005/06* had gone to print. Born into racing—his father Frenchie Nicholson was joint-champion jockey in 1944/5 and his mother hailed from a family (Holman) with very strong links to Cheltenham racecourse—he became a successful jump jockey himself (he rode Mill House to victory in the 1967 Whitbread), before turning his hand to training. Twice champion, he saddled Charter Party to win the 1988 Cheltenham Gold Cup, and won the 1993 King George VI Chase with Barton Bank and the Queen Mother Champion Chase twice in the 'nineties with Viking Flagship. He also enjoyed plenty of success with hurdlers, his best horses in this sphere including the top-class performer Broadsword, who was an early standard-bearer for the yard and made the frame twice in the Champion Hurdle.

The dogmatic Nicholson was a distinctive character and few in jumping had a neutral opinion about him—he could, at times, be forthright or insufferably arrogant, depending on your point of view—but, if he sacrificed diplomacy for straight talking on occasions, admonishments and disagreements were quickly forgotten. Indeed, a reflection of the latter was illustrated by the fact that more than eight hundred people attended a memorial service held for him at Stow-on-the-Wold in September. Many of that sizeable congregation had worked at some stage for Nicholson, who took particular pride in his mentoring of young jockeys, a role in which he espoused the traditional values of politeness, tidiness (lads who arrived with long hair soon learned to have it cut regularly) and punctuality. Such methods had clearly worked well for Frenchie Nicholson, who earned a reputation during the latter half of his training career as a master tutor of young jockeys, his most successful graduate being the eleven-times Flat champion Pat Eddery, whilst others included the classic-winning riders Walter Swinburn, Tony Murray and Paul Cook. If anything, 'The Duke' surpassed those achievements within the National Hunt ranks, as no fewer than five of the ten jump jockeys who have ridden a thousand-plus winners in Britain worked for him at some stage of their careers. In truth, Nicholson could take little credit in the case of Peter Niven (who left the yard after one unsuccessful year there as an amateur), but both Richard Dunwoody and Adrian Maguire spent most of their careers with him. In addition, the locally-born pair of Peter Scudamore and Richard Johnson spent their formative years with Nicholson before graduating to stable jockey. Robert Thornton isn't in the thousand club yet but he's another leading jockey to come through the ranks with Nicholson, becoming champion amateur in 1996/7 and leading conditional the following season, having joined the yard at the age of fourteen (he didn't have long hair in those days!). When My Way de Solzen won the World Hurdle at the Cheltenham Festival in 2006, Nicholson was able to boast that he had trained the jockey (Thornton), the horse's lad (David Barker) and the trainer. My Way de Solzen's trainer Alan King was assistant to Nicholson for over a decade. King took over briefly from his former boss at Jackdaws Castle in late-1999 before setting up at Barbury Castle in Wiltshire where Nicholson kept in touch by phone almost daily to offer advice and encouragement. He would have been particularly proud of King's achievements in the latest season when he finished in his highest position so far in the trainers' table, earning £1,543,850 in 1,2,3 prize money. Thornton himself

Aquanti Group 'Dipper' Novices' Chase, Cheltenham—
My Way de Solzen resumes winning ways with an emphatic victory over the grey Turko

bonusprint.com Novices' Chase, Haydock—another seventeen-length win completes his Arkle preparations

enjoyed his best-ever season, falling just one short of a maiden century, and is in good company in being better known by his nickname 'Chocolate'. Nicholson's father was rarely referred to by his real name Herbert once he'd been dubbed 'Little Frenchie' by fellow stable lads after returning from an apprenticeship in France during his early teens, whilst 'The Duke' picked up his moniker (also from stable staff) after reportedly returning from public school one holiday with a posher accent.

My Way de Solzen started the latest season over hurdles, though his trainer announced that he 'should be chasing before Christmas'. In need of the outing when beaten by Redemption in the West Yorkshire Hurdle at Wetherby, My Way de Solzen made his long-awaited debut over British fences (he had been pulled up on his chasing debut in France back in July 2004) in a beginners chase over two miles at Lingfield towards the end of November. He wasn't at all extended to win by fourteen lengths and, more importantly, his jumping was most assured. Turned out again ten days later at Sandown in the Henry VIII Novices' Chase, again over two miles, My Way de Solzen found the concession of a 9-lb age allowance to the four-year-old Fair Along beyond him on the day, going down by ten lengths. Fair Along remains the only horse to have beaten My Way de Solzen over fences in Britain so far (King believes the Henry VIII came too soon after Lingfield). Stepped up to around two and a half miles, My Way de Solzen didn't have to run anywhere near his best to get back to winning ways in a couple of Grade 2 events in January, the Aquanti Group 'Dipper' Novices' Chase at Cheltenham in January and the bonusprint.com Novices' Chase at Haydock, in both of which he landed the odds by seventeen lengths. My Way de Solzen's Cheltenham Festival target seemed, for a time, likely to be the Ryanair-sponsored Festival Trophy over two miles five furlongs. The trainer had ruled out the Royal & SunAlliance right at the start of the season because 'he doesn't need three miles and how often do the winners of that race go all the way subsequently?' David Nicholson would have had a view about the best target for My Way de Solzen, for whom connections—to general surprise—eventually chose the Irish Independent Arkle Trophy instead of the Festival Trophy. The decision prompted Michael Dickinson, when he bumped into King on the day of the race, to call him 'the biggest prat ever for going over two miles'. But King's judgement was vindicated as My Way de Solzen gave a flawless performance, jumping splendidly, to overturn earlier form with Fair Along

Irish Independent Arkle Challenge Trophy Chase, Cheltenham—all change two out as Twist Magic (left) and Don't Push It (white cap behind leaders) are about to fall; My Way de Solzen survives a blunder himself as he is just led by Jack The Giant, with eventual second Fair Along (right) just in view

and win by five lengths, the runner-up doing well to get up to deprive Jack The Giant of second after being one of the sufferers in a less-than-satisfactory start, in which some of the runners became excitable after a false start; Fair Along was also hampered by a faller at the second last. My Way de Solzen would have been pushed closer had Twist Magic and Don't Push It not come down two out when poised to challenge, Twist Magic at the winner's quarters and still on the bridle at the time. With My Way de Solzen retired for the season, Twist Magic went on to beat Fair Along by five lengths in the Maghull Chase at Aintree.

			Niniski	Nijinsky
My Way de Solzen (FR) (b.g. 2000)	Assessor (IRE) (b 1989)		(b 1976)	Virginia Hills
		Dingle Bay	Petingo
		(b 1976)	Border Bounty
	Agathe de Solzen (FR) (b 1988)	Chamberlin	Green Dancer
		(b 1978)	On The Wing
		Nathanaelle	Djarvis
		(b 1979)	Idaline

The stable's 2006 Arkle winner Voy Por Ustedes returned to win the latest edition of the Queen Mother Champion Chase, but it is unlikely that the versatile My Way de Solzen will follow a similar course. His trainer asked the assembled press after the Arkle 'The Queen Mother or the Gold Cup next year?', but My Way de Solzen is likely to prove ideally suited by further than two miles. He failed to do himself justice in the Supreme Novices' Hurdle when the emphasis was on speed at Cheltenham in 2005 and makes more appeal for the Gold Cup than for the Queen Mother Champion Chase and figures as joint-third choice at 8/1 (along with Exotic Dancer) with sponsors totesport in their ante-post list for the 2008 renewal of the former race, in which the Paul Nicholls-trained pair Kauto Star (2/1) and Denman (5/1) head the market. If Gold Cups were won in the paddock, the tall, strong My Way de Solzen would be a worthy favourite. He nearly always takes the eye of our racecourse representatives. My Way de Solzen arrived from France as a four-year-old as a twice-raced maiden and he has now won at a range of distances from two miles to three miles, and he will stay further. His sire Assessor and grandsire Niniski both won the Prix Royal-Oak (French St Leger), Assessor's other wins also

666

B Winfield, A Longman, J Wright & C Fenton's "My Way de Solzen"

including the Yorkshire Cup, the Doncaster Cup and the Prix du Cadran. Niniski's sire, the triple crown winner Nijinsky, also appears on the dam's side of My Way de Solzen's pedigree. He is the grandsire of Chamberlin, the sire of My Way de Solzen's non-thoroughbred dam Agathe de Solzen, who was successful twice on the Flat in non-thoroughbred races in France and in seven steeplechases at up to twenty-one furlongs. My Way de Solzen acts on heavy going and has yet to race on firmer than good. It bears repeating that he is a superb jumper of fences and, all in all, he looks a most exciting prospect. *A. King*

MY WEE WOMAN 8 ch.m. Alflora (IRE) – Just A Tipple (IRE) (Roselier (FR)) **h76 +** [2006/7 20d 20g Nov 2] rather leggy mare: no show in 2 bumpers in 2004/5 for Miss V. Scott: mid-division in maiden/novice hurdles. *Ferdy Murphy*

MY WILL (FR) 7 b.g. Saint Preuil (FR) – Gleep Will (FR) (Cadoudal (FR)) **c160** [2006/7 c155, h–: c27d* c25s³ c25s² c26g c25g² c29f³ Apr 28] **h–**

When placed in the Betfred Gold Cup (formerly known as the Whitbread Gold Cup) for the second successive season, My Will emulated the achievements of two grand campaigners from the 'eighties, Father Delaney and Ottery News. The duo finished second and third behind dual winner Diamond Edge at Sandown in 1981, twelve months on from Father Delaney also filling the runner-up spot (to

667

The Stewart Family's "My Will"

Royal Mail) in 1980. Meanwhile, Ottery News claimed her second placed effort when finishing one place higher as runner-up to the lightly-weighted Shady Deal in 1982 (Father Delaney was a close fifth). While those two were nine when achieving their second successive Whitbread placing, My Will matched their feat in the latest season at the age of just seven. Father Delaney retained his ability right through a fine career, gaining his final victory as a twelve-year-old. Ottery News flourished under the typically eccentric guidance of Oliver Carter, who'd upstaged the big yards when winning the Sandown showpiece back in 1976 with Otter Way. In addition to her Whitbread placings and a Horse and Hound Cup victory, Ottery News temporarily found herself in a new career as a broodmare, foaling a Sagaro filly in 1984. Never one to follow convention, Carter returned her to pointing subsequently at the age of twelve when a collision with a BMW while loose looked sure to force her into permanent retirement. However, undaunted, Carter returned her to action the following season, when she ran up a hat-trick of victories in ladies' points before returning to Sandown for one last hurrah, finishing fifth (at 100/1) to Plundering in the Whitbread.

Carter hit the headlines during the latest campaign when his one-time smart chaser Venn Ottery came to a sad end, the gelding pulled up injured and later put down after contesting the Game Spirit Chase at Newbury in controversial circumstances (sent off at 200/1). Paul Nicholls, who trained Venn Ottery for a brief (but very successful) period, was among the most vocal pre-race critics of the twelve-year-old's presence in the Grade 2 event, the gelding having gone twenty starts (including in three points) since his last success. The Nicholls-trained My Will also came into 2006/7 after a campaign without a win, but the similarities between him and his former stable companion end there. Whereas Venn Ottery was a headstrong sort who was best at two miles and often found little, My Will is an ultra-consistent performer who is versatile with regard to both the trip and ground. He impressed as having done well physically before his reappearance in the Grade 3 Servo Computer Services Trophy Handicap at Cheltenham and, jumping well, he duly recorded his first win since his novice campaign of 2004/5, knuckling down gamely to beat Idle Talk by half a length. My Will improved again to confirm himself a high-class chaser when beaten two short heads by D'Argent and New Alco over the same course next time, again impressing with a sure-footed round of jumping and an honest attitude. Further creditable placed efforts at Wincanton (behind the ill-fated Little Brick) and Aintree (no match for Exotic Dancer) sandwiched a below-form performance in the Cheltenham Gold Cup, where My Will jumped uncharacteristically poorly. A reflection of the steady progress My Will has made was the fact that his third in the latest Betfred Gold Cup (beaten nine lengths by Hot Weld) came off a mark 12 lb higher than when filling the same position (behind Lacdoudal) twelve months earlier. My Will's consistent campaign proved a lucrative one for connections as he accumulated £105,173 in total prize money (two-thirds of which came from his placed efforts). Only Cheltenham Festival winners Kauto Star, Taranis and Denman earned more for the stable on British soil in 2006/7.

My Will (FR) (b.g. 2000)	Saint Preuil (FR) (gr 1991)	Dom Pasquini (gr 1980)	Rheffic
			Boursonne
		Montecha (br 1972)	Montevideo II
			Chasseresse
	Gleep Will (FR) (b 1994)	Cadoudal (b or br 1979)	Green Dancer
			Come To Sea
		Lissia (b 1977)	Laniste
			Quenotte

As with many of the best French-bred steeplechasers, My Will is a French saddlebred (selle francais). His sire, Saint Preuil, was a useful winner in France over hurdles at three and at fences at four. While he has some way to go to match the stud record of another French-raced grey National Hunt stallion Roselier, Saint Preuil is doing well enough, his best offspring also including the Rendlesham Hurdle winners Crystal d'Ainay and Labelthou, plus the one-time useful staying chaser Marcus du Berlais (who was placed in the 2004 and 2005 Irish Nationals). The selle francais family of My Will has proved prolific, with his grandam and great grandam producing eight winners between them. His dam, Gleep Will, showed glimmers of ability in five starts on the Flat, twice finishing fifth up to thirteen furlongs. She is a half-sister to five winners, including Free Will, successful thirteen times over jumps in France and Italy. My Will is her first foal, and is the most accomplished so far, her 2001 filly, Ney Will (by Pistolet Bleu), a nineteenfurlong chase winner in France in 2005/6, being the only other to win so far. Her twice-raced five-year-old gelding Other Will (by Robin des Champs) was bought by Oliver Sherwood for only 7,000 guineas at the latest Doncaster May Sales, though her 2005 gelding by Dark Moondancer made €100,000 at Saint-Cloud six weeks later. The tall, strong My Will stays twenty-nine furlongs and acts on any going. He often impresses with his appearance, and should pay his way again in the staying handicap division in 2007/8. *P. F. Nicholls*

MY WORLD (FR) 7 b.m. Lost World (IRE) – Fortuna Jet (FR) (Highest Honor (FR)) [2006/7 c114, h–: c20s^2 c17d^4 c19s c17d^6 c19v^3 Mar 10] tall, good-topped mare: winning hurdler: fairly useful chaser: poor efforts last 3 outings: stays 2½m: raced on going softer than good (acts on heavy): tried blinkered in France: sound jumper. *R. H. Alner*   **c115 h–**

N

NABIR (FR) 7 gr.g. Linamix (FR) – Nabagha (FR) (Fabulous Dancer (USA)) [2006/7 h–§: c16g^3 c18g c20f^3 c16s* c18v* c16s^6 c16s^F c16s^{pu} Feb 9] angular gelding: maiden hurdler: modest chaser: won handicaps at Perth (novice) in September and Market Rasen in October: probably stays 2½m: probably acts on any going: tried tongue tied: none too genuine. *P. D. Niven*   **c92 § h–**

NACADOUR (FR) 6 b.g. Port Lyautey (FR) – Digit II (FR) (Hard Leaf (FR)) [2006/7 21d³ 17s³ 16v³ Feb 22] first foal: dam 13.5f winner: modest form over fences: sold from F. Danloux €78,000 and off 19 months, fair form over hurdles in Britain, beaten 7 lengths by Tyson in novice at Haydock final start, again running on strongly not knocked about: sure to prove capable of better, particularly now qualified for handicaps. *D. E. Pipe* **c–** **h99 p**

NACHO DES UNCHERES (FR) 6 b.g. Bulington (FR) – Radieuse Gamine (FR) (Chateau du Diable (FR)) [2006/7 F76?: 24s 26s Dec 22] signs of ability in bumpers: well beaten both outings over hurdles. *D. G. Bridgwater* **h–**

NADOVER (FR) 6 br.g. Cyborg (FR) – Djerissa (FR) (Highlanders (FR)) [2006/7 c110+, h–: c23d^pu c19s* c24v³ c24v^pu c24g^F Mar 14] close-coupled gelding: fair form over hurdles: useful handicap chaser: much improved when winning at Chepstow in December by ½ length from Nozic, making all: creditable third to Kerstino Two at Sandown: jumped with little fluency (went right) in valuable events last 2 starts (blinkered final one): stays 3m: raced on good ground or softer (acts on heavy). *C. J. Mann* **c132** **h–**

NAE BOTHER AT ALL (IRE) 6 b.g. Luso – I'll Say She Is (Ashmore (FR)) [2006/7 h99p: 16d² 21s Dec 5] modest form when runner-up in maiden hurdles at Kelso: should prove suited by 2½m+. *N. G. Richards* **h94**

NAGAM (FR) 6 b.g. Denham Red (FR) – Gamaytoise (FR) (Brezzo (FR)) [2006/7 h107d: 25g⁴ c23g^ur c25s³ c23d² c22s⁴ c23s^pu c23d* Mar 20] close-coupled gelding: disappointing maiden hurdler: modest chaser: in cheekpieces, won novice handicap at Exeter in March: stays 25f: acts on heavy going: tried visored (looked unenthusiastic). *A. Ennis* **c94** **h–**

NAHLASS 4 ch.f. Bluegrass Prince (IRE) – Nahla (Wassl) [2006/7 17d³ Aug 15] third foal: dam, bumper winner, half-sister to very smart hurdler/smart chaser Blowing Wind, best up to 25f: little form on Flat: remote last of 3 finishers in juvenile on hurdling debut. *Ms J. S. Doyle* **h–**

NAIAD DU MISSELOT (FR) 6 b.g. Dom Alco (FR) – Une Nuit (FR) (Le Pontet (FR)) [2006/7 17v³ 16v* 16s² Jan 31] neat gelding, unfurnished at present: fifth foal: dam of little account: fair form over hurdles: green on debut, then won novice at Wetherby in December by ¾ length from Bywell Beau, idling: will be suited by 2½m+: raced on soft/heavy going: remains open to improvement. *Ferdy Murphy* **h115 p**

NAILED ON 8 ch.g. Factual (USA) – Highlights (Phountzi (USA)) [2006/7 c75: c23m⁴ Apr 22] winning pointer: best effort in hunters when fourth to Mel In Blue at Stratford in April: stays 23f: jumps left. *Andrew J. Martin* **c90**

NAJA DE BILLERON (FR) 6 b.g. Video Rock (FR) – Valse de Billeron (FR) (Cupids Dew) [2006/7 h104: 19d^pu c19m^F 17s^pu Nov 17] leggy gelding: runner-up in 4-y-o hurdle at Auteuil: no form in Britain (fell first on chasing debut): visored last 2 outings: tongue tied nowadays. *D. E. Pipe* **c–** **h–**

NAJCA DE THAIX (FR) 6 b. or br.g. Marmato – Isca de Thaix (FR) (Cimon) [2006/7 c81, h99: 16d² 16d* 16m c16s^pu c20g^pu 16s^pu Dec 7] stocky gelding: novice chaser: modest hurdler: won handicap at Towcester in June: lost form again after: raced mainly around 2m on going softer than good: has worn blinkers, including at Towcester. *C. N. Allen* **c–** **h99**

NAKOMA (IRE) 5 b.m. Bahhare (USA) – Indian Imp (Indian Ridge) [2006/7 F16s⁵ F16d² Mar 22] 6,000 4-y-o: third foal: half-sister to fair 2m hurdler Telemachus (by Bishop of Cashel), also useful up to 1¼m on Flat: dam unraced half-sister to very smart 1½m/1¾m performer Mons: better effort in bumpers at Ludlow when 11 lengths second of 8 to Val du Ciron. *H. D. Daly* **F80**

NAMED AT DINNER 6 ch.g. Halling (USA) – Salanka (IRE) (Persian Heights) [2006/7 c–, h77: c16g c16s 20g 20s⁵ 24m² 20s⁴ 20d⁶ 20d* 24g⁶ 20s 24g c24d² 20v⁴ 20v^pu Mar 6] small gelding: poor handicap hurdler: won selling event at Hexham in November: no form over fences: stays 2½m: acts on good to firm and heavy going: usually wears headgear: often front runner: unreliable. *Miss Lucinda V. Russell* **c– §** **h77 §**

NAMROUD (USA) 8 b.g. Irish River (FR) – Top Line (FR) (Top Ville) [2006/7 16g³ 16s⁴ Nov 29] fair on Flat (stays 1m), claimed £8,000 in April: better effort in novice hurdles when third to Spear Thistle at Leicester: likely to prove best at 2m with emphasis on speed. *R. A. Fahey* **h94**

NANARD (FR) 6 br.g. Double Bed (FR) – Isabellita (FR) (Cyborg (FR)) [2006/7 F84: 16v⁴ 20v^F 16g 26g⁶ Apr 20] lengthy gelding: poor form over hurdles: tongue tied final outing. *D. E. Pipe* **h85**

NANNYS GIFT (IRE) 8 b.m. Presenting – Last Royal (Kambalda) [2006/7 h–, F74: **h72**
21m³ 16g 21m² Apr 9] compact mare: poor form in bumpers/maiden hurdles: stays 21f.
O. Brennan

NAPALM (IRE) 6 b.g. Warcraft (USA) – Cross My Palm (IRE) (King Luthier) [2006/7 **h–**
F–: F17g² 19g⁶ Nov 5] better effort in bumpers when 13 lengths second to Mischief Man **F79**
at Market Rasen: well beaten in novice there on hurdling debut. *C. C. Bealby*

NAPOLITAIN (FR) 6 b.g. Ajdayt (USA) – Domage II (FR) (Cyborg (FR)) [2006/7 **c137**
c129, h–: c24g⁴ c26sᵖᵘ c24gᶠ c25s⁴ c24g⁶ c32mᵖᵘ Apr 21] sturdy gelding: winning **h–**
hurdler: useful chaser: creditable efforts in handicaps in 2006/7 on first/fifth outings:
went lame final one: stays 25f: unraced on firm going, acts on any other. *P. F. Nicholls*

NARLEN (CZE) 5 ch.g. Rainbows For Life (CAN) – Neris (POL) (Dniepr (POL)) **h78**
[2006/7 h–: 16d² 16s 16v⁶ 16g 21g² Mar 26] tall gelding: poor maiden hurdler: stays 21f:
raced on good going or softer. *Mrs P. Townsley*

NARVAL D'AVELOT (FR) 6 b.g. Video Rock (FR) – Reine Des Planches (FR) **c–**
(Diaghilev) [2006/7 c91, h?: c18m³ c22fᵖᵘ c19mᵖᵘ c21mᵖᵘ c18g⁴ c20m⁴ c24d³ Oct 1] **h–**
ex-French gelding: once-raced over hurdles: maiden chaser, little form in Britain: tried in
headgear/tongue tied. *D. G. Bridgwater*

NAR VALLEY 6 b.g. Alflora (IRE) – Barton Bay (IRE) (Kambalda) [2006/7 F–: 20dᵖᵘ **h–**
Jan 15] close-coupled, good-topped gelding: no show in bumpers/maiden hurdle. *A. King*

NASRAWY 5 b.g. Grand Lodge (USA) – By Charter (Shirley Heights) [2006/7 F17m **F– §**
F16sʳᵗʳ F16s Nov 4] 8,000 3-y-o, resold 700 3-y-o: half-brother to numerous winners on
Flat, including smart performer up to 2m First Charter (by Polish Precedent): dam, 2-y-o
7f winner who seemed to stay 1½m, daughter of Time Charter: temperamental displays
in bumpers (refused to race second start). *J. J. Lambe, Ireland*

NATAL (FR) 6 b.g. Funny Baby (FR) – Donitille (FR) (Italic (FR)) [2006/7 h148: **c146**
c17d* c16d² c19s* c19d⁴ c20v* 24g c20m² Apr 21] **h137**

Cheltenham preview nights have become an annual ritual for many, their
popularity evident from the increasing number held all over Britain and Ireland in
the weeks before the Festival. In the latest season, Paul Nicholls found himself
musing about the World Hurdle whilst a panellist at one such event during the week
before the four-day meeting. After texting Natal's owners Monica and John
Hackett, Nicholls managed to convince them to stump up £12,500 to supplement
him for the race and interrupt his novice chasing campaign, during which he
had already proved himself a smart performer. *Chasers & Hurdlers 2005/06*
commented that the likely strength in depth of Nicholls' string—notably in the
novice chasing division—was such that Natal was likely to have a limited number
of opportunities in 2006/7, without taking on his better stablemates. However,
whilst Nicholls tends to have strong contenders for many of the top races, this has
not been so in the World Hurdle—he'd never even saddled a runner in the staying showpiece prior to Natal. The highlight of Natal's prolific novice hurdling
campaign in 2005/6 had been when defeating Blazing Bailey (who received 10 lb)
in the Grade 2 Mersey Novices' Hurdle at Aintree on his final start. Despite his
good start over fences, it was considered that the gelding's best chance of success at
the latest Festival would be to put him back over the smaller obstacles, particularly
as Blazing Bailey had since developed into a leading World Hurdle contender.
Looking very well and sent off a 16/1-shot (Blazing Bailey was half those odds),
Natal failed to run up to his best tackling three miles for the first time, finishing
a well-held seventh to Inglis Drever in the World Hurdle. Unfortunately for his
sporting owners, prize money went down only to sixth place.

Natal landed the odds on his chasing debut at Exeter in October by seven
lengths from Manorson, barely needing shaking up to assert in the straight. He was
again sent off at odds on at Cheltenham the following month but was beaten nine
lengths by chasing debutant Fair Along. Conceding the winner 12 lb, Natal's effort
was subsequently made to look better than it appeared at the time and he easily
resumed winning ways in a four-runner novice at Taunton in December. Back in
Grade 2 company at Ascot eight days later, and once again odds on, Natal was let
down by his jumping as he finished fourth of five to Briareus. On his return from a
ten-week absence, Natal returned to his best when, for the first time during 2006/7,
he faced one of his stablemates, conceding the year-younger Good Spirit 11 lb and

racingpost.co.uk Pendil Novices' Chase, Kempton—
Natal grinds out a victory over stable-companion Good Spirit (noseband) in very testing conditions

beating him by three lengths in another Grade 2 event, the racingpost.co.uk Pendil Novices' Chase at Kempton. The testing conditions made for a dour struggle in the closing stages, with the first two having looked likely to finish further clear of third-placed Ursis than they eventually did, both tiring from the turn for home. After the World Hurdle, Natal was put back over fences, finishing eleven lengths second of five finishers to Yes Sir in the Future Champions Novices' Chase at Ayr in April, not looking entirely comfortable after a mistake at the ninth and unable to get in a blow at the all-the-way winner, possibly finding the emphasis too much on speed. However, it was announced in August that Yes Sir had failed a dope test, so it seems likely Natal will be awarded a third win at Grade 2 level.

Natal (FR) (b.g. 2001)	Funny Baby (FR) (b 1988)	Baby Turk (b 1982)	Northern Baby Vieille Villa
		Funny Reef (b 1980)	Mill Reef Fancy's Child
	Donitille (FR) (b 1991)	Italic (b 1974)	Carnaval Bagheira II
		Verte Pomme (b 1985)	Pamponi Verveine IV

The leggy, quite good-topped Natal is capable of smart form over hurdles and fences, and still has some potential in the latter sphere. He is always likely to need the emphasis to be on stamina at around two and a half miles, and is well worth another try over further. Natal acts on good to firm and heavy going and has been tongue tied on all of his starts in Britain, whilst Nicholls is reportedly of the view he's best on a flat track. His pedigree was discussed in the last edition of *Chasers & Hurdlers* but it is worth adding that his four-year-old half-sister Paula (by Network) has now won twice at around eleven furlongs in the French Provinces. It is also interesting that Natal's sire, Funny Baby, has enjoyed considerable success from the few runners he has had in Britain, with the likes of Juveigneur and Laouen, as well as Natal. Of the seven horses to represent him in Britain and Ireland only Lusaka de Pembo has failed to win. *P. F. Nicholls*

NATHOS (GER) 10 b.g. Zaizoom (USA) – Nathania (GER) (Athenagoras (GER)) [2006/7 c–, h135: 20s³ 21g⁵ 16s 16d 20sᶠ 21s 22d⁶ 22s² 21g Mar 14] close-coupled gelding: winning chaser: useful handicap hurdler: stays 2¾m: raced on good going or softer (acts on heavy): usually waited with: sometimes finishes weakly. *C. J. Mann*   c–
h131

NATIAIN 8 ch.g. Danzig Connection (USA) – Fen Princess (IRE) (Trojan Fen) [2006/7 c101+, h–: c25m* c22v² c25g* c25g* Apr 15] good-topped gelding: pulled up in novice   c115
h–

hurdle: useful pointer/hunter chaser: successful at Hexham (maiden) early in season and twice at Kelso (idled when beating Anshan Spirit a length on second occasion) in April: stays 25f: acts on good to firm and heavy ground: free-going front runner. *Alistair M. Brown*

NATIONAL DIPLOMA (IRE) 7 b.g. Warcraft (USA) – Lady of Spain (Aragon) [2006/7 22d^{pu} 20d 24s Apr 26] €3,600 4-y-o: first foal: dam, modest maiden, half-sister to smart 1½m/1¾m performer/high-class hurdler up to 2½m Midnight Legend: won maiden Irish point in 2006: no form in novice/maiden hurdles. *D. P. Keane*   **h–**

NATIONAL HEALTH 4 b.g. Medicean – Precious (Danehill (USA)) [2006/7 F16v F16m Feb 4] 9,000 3-y-o: tall, good-topped gelding: first foal: dam, ran twice, out of half-sister to high-class miler Barathea: little show in bumpers, visored second outing. *P. D. Niven*   **F–**

NATIONAL TRUST 5 b.g. Sadler's Wells (USA) – National Treasure (Shirley Heights) [2006/7 19s⁶ 16s³ 19d³ 19d* Mar 26] sturdy gelding: useful on Flat (stays 1½m) at 3 yrs for Sir Michael Stoute, bought 20,000 gns Doncaster March (2006) Sales: fair form over hurdles: won maiden at Stratford by 1¾ lengths from Spirit of Man: stays 19f: raced on good to soft/soft ground. *Miss H. Lewis*   **h113 +**

NATION STATE 6 b.g. Sadler's Wells (USA) – Native Justice (Alleged (USA)) [2006/7 16d⁵ 16s³ 20s^{ur} 21s⁴ 19d² 21g 21g^{pu} Mar 28] useful-looking gelding: fairly useful handicap hurdler: in frame in valuable events at Sandown, Kempton and Ascot in 2006/7, keeping on well when beaten ¾-length second to Overstrand at last-named: reported to be coughing after running poorly final outing: will stay beyond 21f: raced on good ground or softer (acts on soft): usually wears headgear. *G. L. Moore*   **h126**

NATIVE AMERICAN 5 b.g. Indian Lodge (IRE) – Summer Siren (FR) (Saint Cyrien (FR)) [2006/7 16d 17s 16g 17m⁵ Apr 17] modest 1¼m winner on Flat: poor form over hurdles, finished lame on handicap debut: raced around 2m . *T. D. McCarthy*   **h83**

NATIVE CITY (IRE) 5 b.g. City Honours (USA) – Fourroads-Native (IRE) (Be My Native (USA)) [2006/7 F16d 19s 16s 17s c16v⁵ Feb 15] €15,000 3-y-o: third foal: dam lightly-raced Irish maiden: mid-division in bumper/maiden hurdles: again easy to back, fifth to All Sonsilver on chase/handicap debut at Chepstow, jumping deliberately in rear and not knocked about: will be suited by 2½m+. *Jonjo O'Neill*   **c73 +**
h80
F87

NATIVE COLL 7 ch.g. Primitive Rising (USA) – Harrietfield (Nicholas Bill) [2006/7 c–, h–, F–: 20v c25v^{pu} c20v 16v³ Mar 9] first sign of ability when third in novice handicap hurdle at Ayr. *N. W. Alexander*   **c–**
h61

NATIVE COMMANDER (IRE) 12 b.g. Be My Native (USA) – The Better Half (IRE) (Deep Run) [2006/7 c–, h83: 17m⁴ 17g³ 16s³ c18f³ c16d² c21d^F 18g⁵ c16d² c22s^{ur} c20v⁴ c17v³ 19g* c17m³ c18m* Apr 28] rangy gelding: poor hurdler: won handicap at Taunton in March: bit better over fences, successful in 5-runner selling handicap at Fontwell: stays easy 19f: acts on good to firm and heavy going: tried blinkered: usually patiently ridden, and finds little. *G. L. Moore*   **c91 §**
h83 §

NATIVE CORAL (IRE) 9 ch.g. Be My Native (USA) – Deep Coral (IRE) (Buckskin (FR)) [2006/7 c123, h–: c25g³ May 24] lengthy, angular gelding: winning hurdler: fairly useful form over fences, found little only outing in 2006/7: effective at 2½m to 3m: acts on good to firm and heavy going: jumps soundly. *N. G. Richards*   **c102**
h–

NATIVE CUNNING 9 b.g. Be My Native (USA) – Icy Miss (Random Shot) [2006/7 c–, h75: 27s⁵ c24v 26s⁶ c25v⁶ Feb 28] big, well-made gelding: poor hurdler/maiden chaser, no form in 2006/7: suited by 3m+: acts on soft ground: tried blinkered. *R. H. Buckler*   **c–**
h–

NATIVE DAISY (IRE) 12 b.m. Be My Native (USA) – Castleblagh (General Ironside) [2006/7 c98: 19m³ Apr 11] workmanlike mare: modest handicap chaser: left C. Down and off 19 months, shaped as if in need of outing when third in novice seller at Exeter on hurdling debut: stays 23f: acts on soft and good to firm going: tried in cheekpieces: front runner/races prominently. *J. G. M. O'Shea*   **c–**
h72 +

NATIVE EIRE (IRE) 13 b.g. Be My Native (USA) – Ballyline Dancer (Giolla Mear) [2006/7 c–, h–: c21d^F May 31] tall, angular gelding: winning hurdler/chaser, poor on balance: stayed 27f: acted on heavy going: dead. *N. Wilson*   **c–**
h–

NATIVE FOREST (IRE) 6 ch.g. Insan (USA) – Oak Lodge (IRE) (Roselier (FR)) [2006/7 h67, F–: 16g⁶ 20d⁶ Nov 12] good-topped gelding: upped in trip, best effort over hurdles when sixth to Once A Brownie in maiden at Fontwell: will be suited by further than 2½m: sold 2,200 gns Doncaster May Sales. *Miss H. C. Knight*   **h84**

NATIVE HEIGHTS (IRE) 9 b.g. Be My Native (USA) – Shirley's Dream (IRE)   c–
(Mister Majestic) [2006/7 c–, h–: c21d 19s^pu 17s^pu 21s Mar 13] strong, lengthy gelding: h–
winning hurdler/chaser: no form since 2004/5, left M. Todhunter after first start: successful with/without blinkers: tried tongue tied. *J. K. Hunter*

NATIVE IVY (IRE) 9 b.g. Be My Native (USA) – Outdoor Ivy (Deep Run) [2006/7   c–
c122, h–: c28s^pu c26g^pu Jun 8] leggy gelding: fairly useful handicap hurdler/chaser: h–
pulled up all 4 starts in first half of 2006, though runner-up in points since: stays 3½m:
raced on good going or softer (acts on soft): tried tongue tied. *C. Tinkler*

NATIVE JACK (IRE) 13 br.g. Be My Native (USA) – Dorrha Daisy (Buckskin (FR))   c119
[2006/7 c130, h–: 20s c31d^4 c26g^pu c24s^6 c31d Mar 13] tall, lengthy gelding: winning   h–
hurdler: fairly useful chaser, raced mostly in cross-country events nowadays: stays 31f:
raced on good going or softer (acts on heavy): wore cheekpieces once. *P. J. Rothwell,
Ireland*

NATIVE PERFORMANCE (IRE) 12 b.g. Be My Native (USA) – Noon Perform-   c96
ance (Strong Gale) [2006/7 c–, h–: c26m² c22f^ur Jun 6] tall, useful-looking gelding: h–
winning hurdler/chaser, has deteriorated: runner-up in point in April: stays easy 3m: acts
on firm and soft ground: tried blinkered, in cheekpieces/tongue strap last 3 outings.
N. J. Gifford

NATIVE ROYAL (IRE) 5 ch.m. Zaffaran (USA) – Native Sound (IRE) (Be My   F100
Native (USA)) [2006/7 F16d* F18v³ F16v⁵ F16v F16m* Apr 27] €3,400 3-y-o: first foal:
dam winning hurdler up to 3m in Ireland: fairly useful in bumpers, winning at Cork
(maiden) in November and Punchestown (beating Cloth Fair by 5 lengths) in April.
T. Hogan, Ireland

NATOUMBA (FR) 6 ch.g. Hawker's News (IRE) – Vanella (FR) (Quart de Vin (FR))   h98
[2006/7 F86p: 21s⁴ 26s 22s^pu 24m* Apr 15] modest form over hurdles: visored, much
improved when winning at Worcester on handicap debut by length from My Rosie
Ribbons: stays 3m: acts on good to firm ground. *H. D. Daly*

NATURAL (IRE) 10 b.g. Bigstone (IRE) – You Make Me Real (USA) (Give Me   c85 §
Strength (USA)) [2006/7 c85§, h–: c20v⁶ c26d c24g⁶ c31s^pu Apr 26] good-topped geld-   h–
ing: winning hurdler: modest hunter chaser on his day: won 2-finisher point in March:
stays 31f: unraced on firm going, acts on any other: tried in headgear: has had tongue tied:
unreliable. *Mrs J. Williamson*

NATURALLY INSPIRED (FR) 4 b.f. Ungaro (GER) – Teardrops Fall (FR) (Law   F–
Society (USA)) [2006/7 F17m Apr 15] 9,000 3-y-o: sixth foal: half-sister to 3 winning
hurdlers around 2m: dam placed up to around 1½m on Flat in France: well held in bumper
on debut. *Mrs S. Lamyman*

NAUGHTY DANDY (IRE) 14 gr.g. Celio Rufo – Annie Will Run (Deep Run)   c–
[2006/7 c21g May 24] workmanlike gelding: winning pointer: maiden hurdler/chaser: h–
tried tongue tied. *Mrs S. J. Hickman*

NAUGHTY DIESEL 4 b.g. Killer Instinct – Scottish Royal (IRE) (Night Shift (USA))   h–
[2006/7 F16d⁵ 16d 17m^pu Apr 15] fifth foal: half-brother to 6f winner Mouseman   F81
(by Young Ern) and 9f winner Northern Gold (by Goldmark): dam unraced, out of half-
sister to Dancing Brave and Jolypha: faded when fifth to Theatrical Moment in bumper
at Musselburgh: no form in 2 starts over hurdles, left B. Ellison after first of them.
R. Bastiman

NAUGHTYNELLY'S PET 8 b.g. Balnibarbi – Naughty Nessie (Celtic Cone)   h–
[2006/7 h–: 23g Apr 30] no form. *A. M. Crow*

NAUJELLA GIRL (IRE) 7 b.m. Un Desperado (FR) – Naujella (Malinowski (USA))   h77
[2006/7 20m³ 21g⁴ Apr 23] half-sister to fair hurdler/winning chaser Plumbob (by Bob
Back), stayed 3¼m: dam maiden on Flat: better effort in novice hurdles at Sedgefield
when 7½ lengths third to Tell Henry: signs of temperament next time. *G. A. Harker*

NAUNTON BROOK 8 b.g. Alderbrook – Give Me An Answer (True Song) [2006/7   c136
c122, h–: c24g c23d⁴ c32s* c25s* c29s⁵ c29s³ c28s c24g^pu c36g^pu Apr 14] big, lengthy   h–
gelding: winning hurdler: useful handicap chaser: won at Hexham (quite valuable event)
in November and Exeter (by 9 lengths from Kock de La Vesvre) in December: good third
to Ladalko in valuable race at Warwick, lost his form after (blinkered in Grand National
final outing): stays 4m: acts on heavy going: best efforts in tongue strap: front runner.
N. A. Twiston-Davies

NAUTIC (FR) 6 b.g. Apple Tree (FR) – Bella Dicta (FR) (Vayrann) [2006/7 h92: 19g   c76
16s c17d c23d^F c24s³ c20v^pu c19g c22g⁵ Mar 29] good-topped gelding: modest hurdler: h–
little form in 2006/7, mostly over fences: should stay beyond 2m. *R. Dickin*

NAVADO (USA) 8 b.g. Rainbow Quest (USA) – Miznah (IRE) (Sadler's Wells (USA)) **h114**
[2006/7 h115: 24v⁴ 20m* 24m³ Aug 1] angular gelding: fair handicap hurdler: won at
Worcester in June: stays 3m, at least when conditions aren't testing: acts on good to firm
and good to soft going: wore cheekpieces last 2 outings: has been difficult on way to post.
Jonjo O'Neill

NAVAL ATTACHE 5 b.g. Slip Anchor – Cayla (Tumble Wind) [2006/7 17dᵖᵘ 16gᶠ **h–**
Mar 20] modest maiden on Flat (stays 9.5f), claimed from B. Johnson £6,000 in July:
failed to complete both outings over hurdles, sold out of P. Blockley's stable 3,200 gns
Doncaster November Sales in between. *Mrs A. M. Thorpe*

NAVAL HERO (IRE) 4 b.g. Arkadian Hero (USA) – Isla Negra (IRE) (Last Tycoon) **h–**
[2006/7 16sᵖᵘ 16g⁶ Apr 8] no form on Flat/in juvenile hurdles. *Mrs L. Williamson*

NAVARONE 13 b.g. Gunner B – Anamasi (Idiot's Delight) [2006/7 c104, h–: c20g² **c93**
c20m³ c24gᵖᵘ Jul 31] tall gelding: modest handicap chaser: stays 3m: acts on good to **h–**
firm and good to soft going: effective tongue tied or not: bold-jumping front runner. *Ian
Williams*

NAVELINA 7 b.m. Presidium – Orange Imp (Kind of Hush) [2006/7 F81: F16g⁴ F16g **h–**
16s 16sᵖᵘ Mar 7] smallish, lengthy mare: modest form in bumpers: no show both starts **F81**
over hurdles. *T. J. Fitzgerald*

NAVY LARK 5 ch.g. Nashwan (USA) – Holly Blue (Bluebird (USA)) [2006/7 F84: **h–**
19m Sep 28] eighth in slowly-run bumper at Newbury on debut: tailed off in novice
hurdle. *D. E. Pipe*

NAWAADI 4 b.g. Intikhab (USA) – Elhilmeya (IRE) (Unfuwain (USA)) [2006/7 17s³ **h102**
17s* 19g Mar 24] well-made gelding: half-brother to smart bumper performer/very smart
1½m winner Alfie Flits (by Machiavellian): fairly useful maiden on Flat (stays 1¼m),
sold out of M. Tregoning's stable 32,000 gns Newmarket Autumn Sales: confirmed
promise of hurdling debut when winning novice at Taunton in January by 2 lengths from
Rashartic: tongue tied and sweating, breathing problem when well backed on handicap
debut next time. *P. J. Hobbs*

NAWAMEES (IRE) 9 b.g. Darshaan – Truly Generous (IRE) (Generous (IRE)) **c–**
[2006/7 c104, h–: 16f 18g⁴ 16g Apr 7] leggy gelding: fairly useful on Flat: similar **h122**
standard over hurdles, best effort in handicaps in 2006/7 when fourth to Wee Dinns at
Fontwell: fair form at best over fences (hasn't convinced with jumping): stays 2½m:
acts on good to firm and good to soft going: sometimes wears headgear nowadays.
G. L. Moore

NAWOW 7 b.g. Blushing Flame (USA) – Fair Test (Fair Season) [2006/7 c103, h–: **c96**
c21gᵘʳ 20d² 20g c20d Dec 28] compact gelding: fairly useful on Flat (stays easy 2m), **h102**
successful in December/January: fair hurdler/chaser: stays 21f: unraced on extremes of
going over jumps: held up. *P. D. Cundell*

NAXOX (FR) 6 ch.g. Cupidon (FR) – Frou Frou Lou (FR) (Groom Dancer (USA)) **h–**
[2006/7 16g 16v Jan 4] ex-French gelding: half-brother to winning chasers around 2¾m
Niangara (by Baby Turk) and Blue Chip (by Cadoudal): dam winning hurdler/chaser up
to 19f in France: successful twice up to 12.5f from 5 starts on Flat in France, including in
2006, left M. Postic after final one: shaped better than result when well held in novice at
Leicester on hurdling debut, still on bridle in lead 3 out: shaped as if amiss next time. *Miss
Venetia Williams*

NAYODABAYO (IRE) 7 b.g. Definite Article – Babushka (IRE) (Dance of Life **c131**
(USA)) [2006/7 c120, h–: c20f* 21m⁶ c20d² c20g* c20d c25dᵖᵘ 20g⁴ Apr 7] leggy **h104**
gelding: fair hurdler: useful handicap chaser: won at Ludlow on first day of season and
Sandown (4 ran, beat Stance 19 lengths) in November: stays 3m: acts on firm and good to
soft going: usually wears headgear (ran well without third outing): not a straightforward
ride. *Evan Williams*

NAZIMABAD (IRE) 8 b.g. Unfuwain (USA) – Naziriya (FR) (Darshaan) [2006/7 **c–**
c101, h–: 16m 20m⁶ 17mᶠ Jun 14] small, angular gelding: fair handicap chaser: poor **h75**
maiden hurdler: stayed 2½m, at least as effective around 2m: acted on firm and good to
soft going: tongue tied: front runner: dead. *Evan Williams*

NDITLIR 8 ch.m. Lir – Ndita (Be My Native (USA)) [2006/7 c23d² c28sᵖᵘ May 26] **c84**
winning pointer: seemingly modest form on completed start in hunter chases. *J. Heard*

NDOLA 8 b.g. Emperor Jones (USA) – Lykoa (Shirley Heights) [2006/7 h77: 17v 16s **h–**
Jan 31] workmanlike gelding: modest on Flat (stays 1½m): maiden hurdler, poor form at
best since debut: raced around 2m on good going or softer. *B. J. Curley*

NEAGH (FR) 6 b.g. Dress Parade – Carlie II (FR) (Highlanders (FR)) [2006/7 h–: 18m^{pu} 16s Dec 16] runner-up in novice on hurdling debut in 2004/5: lightly raced and no form since: ridden by Miss R. Davidson. *N. G. Richards*   **h–**

NEARDOWN BISHOP 5 b.g. Imperial Ballet (IRE) – Firedancer (Nashwan (USA)) [2006/7 h–: 16f^6 18m 18m^6 May 28] no solid form over hurdles. *M. Wigham*   **h–**

NEAR GERMANY (IRE) 7 b.g. Germany (USA) – Night Year (IRE) (Jareer (USA)) [2006/7 16v^{pu} 16v^{pu} 17s 16v^F Feb 26] workmanlike gelding: successful 3 times on Flat (stays 9f) in Germany for T. Gibson: no form over hurdles: tongue tied last 2 starts. *R. Curtis*   **h–**

NEARLY A BREEZE 7 b.m. Thowra (FR) – Nearly At Sea (Nearly A Hand) [2006/7 F–: 19s^5 17d^2 17g^F Apr 11] well held in bumpers: off 20 months, poor form over hurdles: stays 19f. *C. J. Down*   **h74**

NEATANDSWEET 5 b.m. Sir Harry Lewis (USA) – Easter Sunday (Afzal) [2006/7 F16m F17m^3 F17g^5 F16g 22g 22m^4 Apr 17] second foal: dam unraced: modest form in bumpers: little impact in novice hurdles. *C. J. Down*   **h–** **F76**

NEBRASKA CITY 6 b.g. Piccolo – Scarlet Veil (Tyrnavos) [2006/7 h–: 17m^6 16m^4 16g 16d^4 17v* 17d^6 c16g^2 c16g^2 Mar 27] neat gelding: poor hurdler: won selling handicaps at Catterick in December and Sedgefield (conditional jockeys) in January: much better form when runner-up in maiden chases: raced around 2m: acts on heavy going: races up with pace. *D. W. Thompson*   **c100** **h75**

NECKER (FR) 6 b.g. Useful (FR) – Babouche (FR) (Pure Flight (USA)) [2006/7 16g c16s^5 c19s^4 c16s^4 c16f^{ur} Apr 22] brother to cross-country chase winner Hispaniola and half-brother to winning hurdler/cross-country chase winner up to 2½m Issachar (by Chef de Clan): successful twice around 11f on Flat for J-M. Robin: thrice-raced over hurdles in France, runner-up twice in juvenile events at Vichy in early-2005/6: needed run on British debut: poor form over fences: raced mainly at 2m. *Ian Williams*   **c82** **h–**

NECTAR DE GUYE (FR) 6 ch.g. Dom Alco (FR) – Audacieuse de Guye (FR) (Olmeto) [2006/7 23g 24f^4 20d^6 c26s c27d^4 c25v^2 c27s^2 c27v^4 c25s c32v^{pu} c27g^{pu} Apr 23] rather leggy gelding: sixth foal: brother to 12.5f winner Marquise de Guye: dam unraced: twice-raced on Flat: left P. Peltier in France, no show over hurdles: modest maiden chaser, ran poorly last 3 outings: thorough stayer: acts on heavy going: blinkered/ in cheekpieces last 6 starts: sold 5,000 gns Doncaster May Sales. *Ferdy Murphy*   **c86** **h–**

NED KELLY (IRE) 11 ch.g. Be My Native (USA) – Silent Run (Deep Run) [2006/7 c147, h–: c26g^3 c21g^F c25g^3 Apr 25] big, strong gelding: one-time high-class hurdler/ smart chaser: successful both completed starts in points in 2007 prior to 15½ lengths third to Drombeag in Foxhunter at Cheltenham: fell tenth (Becher's) in Fox Hunters' at Aintree: barely stays 3¼m: acts on heavy and good to firm going: has found little. *E. J. O'Grady, Ireland*   **c126** **h–**

NED LUDD (IRE) 4 b.g. Montjeu (IRE) – Zanella (IRE) (Nordico (USA)) [2006/7 17s* 16g^2 17s^2 16s^2 16d^3 16d Mar 13] small, angular gelding: half-brother to poor/ temperamental hurdler Monsal Dale (by Desert King), stays 2¾m: fairly useful maiden on Flat (stays 2m), sold out of R. Hannon's stable 9,000 gns Newmarket Autumn Sales: fairly useful juvenile hurdler: won maiden at Folkestone in November: placed next 4 starts, on third occasion 4 lengths second to Good Bye Simon in Grade 1 Finale Hurdle at Chepstow: mistakes and met trouble when well held in listed handicap at Cheltenham: will stay beyond 2m: acts on good going: genuine. *J. G. Portman*   **h118**

NEEDLE PRICK (IRE) 6 b.g. Needle Gun (IRE) – Emerson Supreme (IRE) (Supreme Leader) [2006/7 F79: 16m 16g 16m^3 24d^3 24d* 26g 26s^4 24s^4 26g c24m Mar 25] leggy gelding: modest hurdler: won selling handicap at Worcester in October: often none too fluent, and let down by jumping on chasing debut: stays 3¼m: acts on soft going, probably on good to firm. *N. A. Twiston-Davies*   **c–** **h89**

NEEDWOOD SPIRIT 12 b.g. Rolfe (USA) – Needwood Nymph (Bold Owl) [2006/7 h68: 17s^4 16g 17s^5 20d^6 19s* 16v^6 19g 16s^6 19s^{ur} 24v Mar 15] close-coupled gelding: poor handicap hurdler: won selling event at Catterick in January: stays 3m, effective at shorter: acts on soft and good to heavy going: unreliable. *Mrs A. M. Naughton*   **h71 §**

NEE LEMON LEFT 5 b.m. Puissance – Via Dolorosa (Chaddleworth (IRE)) [2006/7 16s^{pu} Oct 26] tall mare: maiden on Flat, little form since placed early at 2 yrs: no show in seller on hurdling debut. *M. Mullineaux*   **h–**

NEGOCIANT (FR) 6 b.g. Roi de Rome (USA) – Quartaxie (FR) (Saumon (FR)) [2006/7 h81: 22s^{pu} Oct 26] tall, angular ex-French gelding: third in 4-y-o event at Auteuil for F. Cottin, only completion in 3 starts over hurdles. *R. M. Stronge*   **h–**

NEGUS DE BEAUMONT (FR) 6 b.g. Blushing Flame (USA) – Givry (FR) **h131**
(Bayolidaan (FR)) [2006/7 h81, F82: 25s³ 24g* 27d* 24s* 24v* 25s⁵ 26s* 24g⁶ Mar 16]
strong, heavy-bodied gelding: chasing type: left F. Jordan, much improved hurdler in
2006/7: won handicaps at Newcastle, Sedgefield and Ayr in November, Uttoxeter in
December and Hereford (useful form, by 13 lengths from Im A Witness) in February:
creditable never-nearer sixth to Wichita Lineman in Spa Novices' Hurdle at Cheltenham:
suited by thorough test of stamina: raced on good going or softer (acts on heavy): races
lazily. *Ferdy Murphy*

NEIDPATH CASTLE 8 b.g. Alflora (IRE) – Pennant Cottage (IRE) (Denel (FR)) **c–**
[2006/7 h82: 24v⁴ c20dᵖᵘ Oct 15] rangy gelding: bumper winner: maiden hurdler, modest **h80**
form at best: off 5 months, no show on chasing debut: possibly best short of 3m: raced on
ground softer than good (acts on heavy). *A. C. Whillans*

NELSON DU RONCERAY (FR) 6 b.g. Lute Antique (FR) – Trieste (FR) (Quart de **h114**
Vin (FR)) [2006/7 h99: 18v³ 22v 18s⁴ 16v* 16v* 16g⁵ Apr 2] leggy gelding: fair novice
hurdler: improved form when winning twice at Ayr in March: best at 2m: acts well on
heavy going. *P. Monteith*

NELSONS COLUMN (IRE) 4 b.g. Benny The Dip (USA) – Sahara Rose (Green **h102 p**
Desert (USA)) [2006/7 16g³ Oct 19] has only one eye: fairly useful up to 1½m on Flat
(usually makes running), won 3 handicaps in July/August: fair form when third to My
Petra in juvenile at Haydock on hurdling debut: should do better. *G. M. Moore*

NELSON'S SPICE (IRE) 6 b.g. Presenting – My Native Glen (IRE) (Be My Native **c108 +**
(USA)) [2006/7 F16g³ F16g* 20f³ 17m 16s⁵ c19g⁵ Mar 21] €26,000 3-y-o: second foal: **h92 +**
dam unraced half-sister to useful/unreliable chaser up to 3m Montana Glen: easily landed **F94**
odds in 5-runner bumper at Stratford in July: best effort over hurdles when third in
maiden at Uttoxeter: better form in novice handicap at Chepstow on chasing debut (in
share of second before blunder last): stays 2½m: acts on firm going. *Jonjo O'Neill*

NELTINA 11 gr.m. Neltino – Mimizan (IRE) (Pennine Walk) [2006/7 c116, h–: c22m⁴ **c117**
c16d* c21g c21d⁵ c17g³ c20m⁵ Apr 22] workmanlike mare: winning hurdler: fairly **h–**
useful handicap chaser: won at Towcester in June by 3 lengths from Borehill Joker: form
after only when third to Allumee at Newbury: stays 2¾m: acts on good to soft going
(bumper winner on good to firm): usually races prominently. *Mrs J. E. Scrase*

NEMETAN (FR) 6 ch.g. Port Lyautey (FR) – Annabelle Treveene (FR) (Spoleto) **c94**
[2006/7 h–x: 17m⁵ c19gᶠ c19s* c16d³ c16v³ c19g⁴ Apr 11] compact gelding: maiden **h74**
hurdler: modest novice chaser: jumped much better than usual when winning handicap at
Taunton in December: stays 19f: acts on heavy going. *R. H. Alner*

NENUPHAR COLLONGES (FR) 6 b.g. Video Rock (FR) – Diane Collonges (FR) **c132 +**
(El Badr) [2006/7 c17d⁶ c17s* c17g* c19v* c19dᶠ c23s² c24s* Mar 17] lengthy gelding: **h–**
fourth foal: brother to 1½m winner Mylord Collonges and half-brother to cross-country
chase winner up to 25f Karesse Collonges (by Kadalko): dam, successful on Flat up to
2m, out of half-sister to dam of high-class staying chaser Neptune Collonges: once-raced
over hurdles: useful novice chaser: won non-thoroughbred event at Dieppe in June (for
M. Rolland) and handicaps at Bangor and Hereford (2-finisher event) in November and
Uttoxeter (further improvement when beating Fast Forward by ¾ length) in March: will
stay beyond 3m: raced on good going or softer (acts on heavy): blinkered (tends to race
lazily): may do better still. *A. King*

NEOPHYTE (IRE) 8 gr.g. Broken Hearted – Dunmahon Lady (General Ironside) **c73**
[2006/7 c–, h–: 20gᵖᵘ c20g Mar 22] lengthy, angular gelding: little form: left M. Evans **h–**
after first outing: in frame in points: tried blinkered/tongue tied. *S. Turner*

NEPTUNE 11 b.g. Dolphin Street (FR) – Seal Indigo (IRE) (Glenstal (USA)) [2006/7 **h–**
h–: 16f 20mᵖᵘ Aug 1] lengthy gelding: winning hurdler, no form since 2002/3. *J. C. Fox*

NEPTUNE COLLONGES (FR) 6 gr.g. Dom Alco (FR) – Castille Collonges **c161**
(FR) (El Badr) [2006/7 c–, h155: c25s² c24s* 25d⁶ c25vᶠ c26g c25g* Apr 25] **h132**
     After having to spend his first season in Britain over hurdles, Neptune
Collonges got back to business over fences in the latest season, fulfilling the early
promise he had shown in France and making into a high-class chaser. Unbeaten in
his five completed starts over fences as a juvenile, four at Pau and a Group 3 contest
at Auteuil which he won by fifteen lengths, Neptune Collonges was ineligible for
novice chases in Britain, meaning he had to take on older and more experienced
rivals once switched back to the larger obstacles. With soft ground ruling out stable-
companion Star de Mohaison from the Charlie Hall Chase at Wetherby in October,

Punchestown Guinness Gold Cup—
Cheltenham also-rans Neptune Collonges and Kingscliff dominate throughout in driving rain

Neptune Collonges took his chance instead and, even in receipt of weight all round, he faced strong opposition on his British chasing debut, his first start over fences for nearly nineteen months. Backed down to 2/1 favourite, there was no shortage of confidence behind Neptune Collonges and, though he failed to justify his market position, he acquitted himself really well, jumping soundly in the main behind the leaders and keeping on gamely to be beaten seven lengths into second. Whilst finding Our Vic—on one of his going days—much too good for him, Neptune Collonges was followed in by Sir Rembrandt, Kingscliff, Iris's Gift and Take The Stand, his performance representing form at least the equal of that he had shown as a novice hurdler the previous season. Better was to come when a month later Neptune Collonges lined up under top weight for the wbx.com Rehearsal Chase at Newcastle (stable conditional Liam Heard took off a valuable 3 lb). Neptune Collonges had been given a BHB mark of 152, just a pound lower than stable-companion Cornish Rebel who headed the weights for the Hennessy Gold Cup at Newbury the same afternoon. Despite the clash with the Hennessy, the Rehearsal drew a competitive field but Neptune Collonges proved far superior to his ten rivals, more so than the bare result suggested. Leading outright from the seventh, he and the novice Another Promise (7 lb out of the weights) were out on their own for much of the straight, with Neptune Collonges winning by two lengths, King Killone staying on for third, half a length behind Another Promise.

In mid-season, Neptune Collonges suffered a couple of reverses. Firstly, he was returned to hurdling for the Long Walk at Ascot, a race in which he'd finished an excellent second to My Way de Solzen as a novice twelve months earlier (when the race had been rerouted to Chepstow). Starting second favourite for the latest edition, he could finish only sixth to odds-on Mighty Man, setting just a fair pace until entering the straight. Back over fences for the Cotswold Chase at Cheltenham, Neptune Collonges was a close third, but not going so well as either Exotic Dancer or Our Vic, when falling two out. Neptune Collonges had been purchased as a potential Cheltenham Gold Cup horse and had even been given an entry in the race as a five-year-old. He took his chance at the Festival but was very much his stable's third string behind Kauto Star and My Will in the Gold Cup, though whether he deserved to start at odds as long as 50/1 was another matter. Neptune Collonges ended up running creditably in a muddling contest, leading on the final circuit and still in front on the home turn, whilst his closest pursuers had to contend with a loose horse, before being brushed aside going to two out and eventually finishing little more than a dozen lengths behind Kauto Star in eighth (still fourth when hitting the last).

He may have had only a supporting role in his stable's successful Cheltenham Gold Cup challenge, but Neptune Collonges had the limelight to himself when making his final appearance of the season in the Punchestown Guinness Gold Cup. Starting at 8/1, he was joined in the field by other Cheltenham Gold Cup participants Monkerhostin (fourth, before refusing in the Grand National), Kingscliff (ninth) and Beef Or Salmon (last but one of the fourteen finishers at Cheltenham), the last-named seeking a second win in the race three years after his first. The well-supported 6/4 favourite was In Compliance, however, who had missed

Cheltenham with a setback but who had looked very much on the upgrade when winning the Punchestown Chase on his last run back in December. The four-strong British challenge in the field of ten was completed by Racing Demon, only fifth in the Festival Trophy at Cheltenham last time but second favourite on 4/1. Lacklustre efforts from some of his rivals undoubtedly helped to make Neptune Collonges' task that much easier. Few of the runners got into the race, but Neptune Collonges still showed some improvement, keeping up with the pace set by Kingscliff for a long way before taking over after the fifth last. Always going best from then on, Neptune Collonges was ridden out after the last to win by three and a half lengths from Kingscliff, with In Compliance beaten a further seven lengths in third after making a mistake at the last when tiring. Neptune Collonges was the only Nicholls-trained representative at this year's Punchestown Festival, but it wouldn't be a surprise if the stable became a more frequent visitor to the County Kildare course in the years to come—after all, Nicholls can now boast three winners from just seven runners at the Festival since taking out a licence, his Grade 1 double with Sporazene and Le Roi Miguel there in 2003 also supplemented by placed efforts from his two other runners at that year's meeting.

		Dom Pasquini	Rheffic
Neptune Collonges (FR) (gr.g. 2001)	Dom Alco (FR) (gr 1987)	(gr 1980)	Boursonne
		Alconaca	Nonoalco
		(ch 1978)	Vela
	Castille Collonges (FR) (br 1990)	El Badr	Weavers' Hall
		(b 1975)	Indian Maid
		Gitane Collonges	Vieux Chateau
		(br 1972)	Penelope

There are a couple of updates to Neptune Collonges' pedigree which was reviewed in detail in *Chasers & Hurdlers 2005/06*. His dam's next two foals are

Mr J. Hales' "Neptune Collonges"

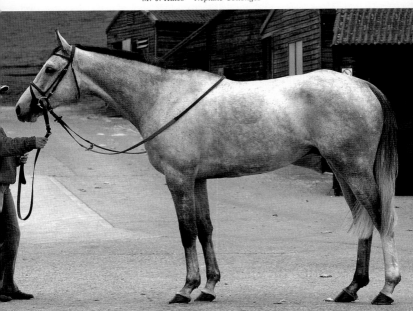

both now winners as well. Second foal Olmeto Collonges (by Brier Creek) won a two-mile novice hurdle at Uttoxeter for Henrietta Knight shortly after the start of the 2007/8 season, while their four-year-old half-sister Prouesse Collonges (by Apple Tree) won over fences (at around seventeen furlongs) at Enghien in the spring. The family could already boast a high-class chaser, before Neptune Collonges came along, in Baccarat Collonges (out of a sister to Neptune Collonges' dam) who won eleven races in France and was second in the Prix La Haye Jousselin. A neat gelding, Neptune Collonges may not have the size typical of a chaser, but he makes up for that with fluent jumping, often from the front. He will probably have to settle for third spot at best in his stable's pecking order of staying chasers behind Kauto Star and Denman for the foreseeable future. The fact that he was sent to Punchestown at the end of the latest season is an indication that the stable may have to cast its net a bit wider than usual in order to keep its best staying chasers apart as much as possible—'I could see him (Neptune Collonges) having a few trips to Ireland' commented Nicholls in the summer. One option that would be well worth taking up with Neptune Collonges is a return to Auteuil. A winner over fences at the track already, he's guaranteed to find suitable conditions there (he's yet to race on ground firmer than good), while the lack of high-class opponents and Neptune Collonges' eligibility for bonuses as a French-bred (on top of the good prize-money) are other incentives. The very valuable International Jumps Weekend staged at Auteuil in early-November appeals as a good target, though it appears the grey will be crossing the Irish Sea rather than the English Channel that weekend as the James Nicholson at Down Royal has been mooted as his first race of 2007/8. The Grand National could also be on the agenda later in the campaign. *P. F. Nicholls*

NEPTUNE D'ANZY (FR) 6 b.g. Lights Out (FR) – Dory (FR) (Italic (FR)) [2006/7 c111+, h–: 20s^{pu} Dec 16] ex-French gelding: maiden hurdler: off 10 months (reportedly had breathing operation), ran as if amiss only start in 2006/7: fair chaser, not given hard time sole outing over fences in Britain: stays 2¾m: acts on soft ground. *Jonjo O'Neill* c– h–

NEPTUNE JOLY (FR) 6 b.g. Chef de Clan II (FR) – Fortune Jolie (FR) (Un Numide (FR)) [2006/7 c105, h–: c20g^{pu} c22g^5 c16d^{pu} c20g c19g^{ur} 16s^6 17v* 16v^4 20m^2 16g^5 Apr 16] close-coupled gelding: fair handicap chaser, below form in 2006/7: modest novice hurdler: won at Sedgefield in February: needs good test at 2m and stays 2½m: unraced on firm going, acts on any other: sold 12,000 gns Doncaster May Sales. *Ferdy Murphy* c91 h94

NERONE (GER) 6 ro.g. Sternkoenig (IRE) – Nordwahl (GER) (Waajib) [2006/7 h103: 16v^3 16m^5 18s^2 17s^2 Dec 26] tall, useful-looking gelding: fair handicap chaser: likely to prove best at 2m: acts on soft and good to firm going, probably on heavy. *P. Monteith* h106

NERO WEST (FR) 6 ch.g. Pelder (IRE) – West River (USA) (Gone West (USA)) [2006/7 h98: 20v^{pu} 24g^{pu} 18s 20g^{pu} Mar 27] winning 2¾m hurdler: left Miss L. Bridges and off 9 months, no form in 2006/7: tried in cheekpieces: joined I. Semple. *Mrs L. B. Normile* h–

NESNAAS (USA) 6 ch.g. Gulch (USA) – Sedrah (USA) (Dixieland Band (USA)) [2006/7 h91: 16g^2 16d^5 c16f^2 16m^2 16f^3 16g* 16g^2 17g^4 Apr 11] medium-sized gelding: fair handicap hurdler: won at Ludlow in October: runner-up in maiden won by Fortune Point at Worcester on chasing debut (rider lost irons on flat): takes good hold, and likely to prove best with emphasis on speed at 2m: acts on firm going: tongue tied once: likely to improve over fences. *M. G. Rimell* c94 p h104

NETHERLEY (FR) 8 gr.g. Beyssac (FR) – Lessons In Love (FR) (Crystal Palace (FR)) [2006/7 21v* 21v* Mar 12] tall, useful-looking gelding: smart form in bumpers in 2004/5: off 2 years, easily landed odds in novice hurdles at Plumpton in December and March (fairly useful form, made all to beat Ruby Dante by 10 lengths): stays 21f: raced on going softer than good: remains open to improvement. *Miss Venetia Williams* h120 p

NETTLETON FLYER 6 b.g. Ajraas (USA) – Mybella Ann (Anfield) [2006/7 h–: 22m^F 16d^6 16m c21d^4 c22s^F Dec 26] of little account: tried blinkered/tongue tied. *Miss J. S. Davis* c– h–

NETWORK OSCAR (IRE) 6 b.g. Oscar (IRE) – Just Wonderful (IRE) (Prince Rupert (FR)) [2006/7 h90, F85: 20s 22v 16v 27v^5 Jan 28] small gelding: maiden hurdler, no show in 2006/7: tried blinkered. *M. W. Easterby* h–

NEURO (FR) 6 b.g. Passing Sale (FR) – El Serenade (FR) (Djarvis (FR)) [2006/7 c–, **c–** h–: c16g^{pu} c16m^{ur} c18g^{pu} Jul 9] no form: sold 4,000 gns Doncaster August Sales, remote **h–** third in maiden point. *Jedd O'Keeffe*

NEUTRINO 5 b.g. Mtoto – Fair Seas (General Assembly (USA)) [2006/7 h–: 16f* 20s^{F} **c88** 17s 16v c16s^{3} Apr 1] fairly useful on Flat (stays 1½m): form (modest) over hurdles only **h91** when winning novice at Hexham in September: ran to similar level when third in novice handicap at same course on chasing debut: best form at 2m: acts on soft and firm going. *P. C. Haslam*

NEUTRON (FR) 6 ch.g. Ragmar (FR) – Valentia (FR) (Brezzo (FR)) [2006/7 F82+: **h–** F16g^{2} 21v^{pu} 16d Jan 19] chasing type: fair form when second in bumper at Newcastle: **F91** little show in novice hurdles. *L. Lungo*

NEVADA RED 6 ch.g. Classic Cliche (IRE) – Sovereign Belle (Ardross) [2006/7 h94, **c106** F85: 24g^{3} 22d^{5} c23s^{4} c27s^{F} c24v^{4} c24d^{2} c27v* c25v^{2} c24g^{4} Apr 7] close-coupled, rather **h87** unfurnished gelding: maiden hurdler: fair novice chaser: improved to win handicap at Sedgefield (by 19 lengths) in February: stays well: acts on heavy going. *D. McCain Jnr*

NEVEESOU (FR) 6 gr.g. Kaldounevees (FR) – Tugend (GER) (Priamos (GER)) **c113 +** [2006/7 h126: 16s^{2} 17d^{2} 17d c20m^{3} 16s Nov 25] angular, quite good-topped gelding: **h125** fairly useful hurdler: downed tools final outing: favourite, mistakes latter stages when third to Royal Katidoki in maiden at Ludlow on chasing debut: stays 2½m: acts on soft and good to firm going: rejoined G. Cherel in France. *D. E. Pipe*

NEVEN 8 b.g. Casteddu – Rose Burton (Lucky Wednesday) [2006/7 h–: 17s^{6} 16g^{2} 16v **h70** 17m Apr 9] long-backed gelding: poor maiden hurdler: best at sharp 2m: acts on good to firm and good to soft going: tried in cheekpieces: usually tongue tied prior to 2006/7. *R. C. Guest*

NEVER AWOL (IRE) 10 ch.g. John French – Lark Lass (Le Bavard (FR)) [2006/7 **c76 §** c88§: c22g^{3} c24s^{6} c24v^{pu} c24s^{3} c24g^{pu} Mar 28] workmanlike gelding: modest handicap chaser, little form away from Towcester and below best in 2006/7: stays 3m: acts on soft and good to firm going: tried blinkered, usually in cheekpieces: ungenuine. *B. N. Pollock*

NEVER COMPROMISE (IRE) 12 br.g. Glacial Storm (USA) – Banderole (IRE) **c115** (Roselier (FR)) [2006/7 c115, h–: c24v* c24s^{3} c31d Mar 13] strong gelding: fairly useful **h–** chaser, runs in cross-country events nowadays: won at Punchestown in November by ½ length from Heads Onthe Ground: stays 3¼m (failed to stay 31f final outing): acts on heavy going: tried blinkered. *T. M. Walsh, Ireland*

NEVER RED (IRE) 4 ch.f. Flemensfirth (USA) – Latin Mistress (Scallywag) [2006/7 **F–** F16v F16g Mar 19] €15,000 3-y-o, resold 20,000 3-y-o: lengthy filly: fourth foal: half-sister to 2½m hurdle winner Wagga Wagga (by Desert Story): dam, bumper winner, out of smart staying hurdler Miss Nero: well held in bumpers. *N. J. Hawke*

NEVER SO BLUE (FR) 6 gr.g. April Night (FR) – Etiane Bleue (FR) (Reve Bleu **c– p** (FR)) [2006/7 h–: 17s^{3} 16d^{pu} 16g 17v^{2} 16v* 17d^{2} c19s 17v* 16v* 17v^{2} 16g Apr 14] leggy, **h114** close-coupled gelding: fair handicap hurdler: won at Uttoxeter (amateur/conditional novice) in December, and Sedgefield (conditional jockeys) and Plumpton (easily) in February: always behind on chasing debut (second run in 2 days): raced mainly around 2m: best form on heavy going: likely to do better over fences. *Miss Venetia Williams*

NEVERSTOPBELIEVING 7 b.m. Commanche Run – Flash 'n' Run (Record Run) **h–** [2006/7 F14s 16g^{pu} 18g^{pu} Apr 10] workmanlike mare: fourth foal: half-sister to winning **F–** 2m hurdler Cedar Broom (by Brush Aside): dam placed in points: no show in bumper/ novice hurdles. *Miss Z. C. Davison*

NEVERTIKA 6 b.g. Subotica (FR) – Griotte de Coddes (FR) (Silver Rainbow) **h122** [2006/7 F93: 20g* 20d^{2} 20v^{2disq} 20s^{3} 18v^{4} 20g^{3} Apr 7] unfurnished gelding: runner-up in bumpers: fairly useful novice hurdler: won at Haydock in November by 1¼ lengths from King Barry: good third of 16 to Or Jaune in handicap at same course final outing: stays 2½m: raced on good going or softer (acts on heavy). *Mrs K. Walton*

NEVILLE'S GIRL 4 gr.f. Turtle Island (IRE) – Swift Maiden (Sharrood (USA)) **F–** [2006/7 F12s F17s Feb 26] smallish filly: first foal: dam 1¼m winner: always behind in bumpers: tried in cheekpieces. *C. Roberts*

NEVSKY BRIDGE 5 b.m. Soviet Star (USA) – Pontressina (USA) (St Jovite (USA)) **h96** [2006/7 h102: 17v^{6} 16v^{6} 18g^{6} Apr 15] fair form at best over hurdles, well held in handicaps last 2 starts: likely to prove best around 2m. *M. Todhunter*

Mr D. McGowan And Mr S. Murphy's "New Alco"

NEW ALCO (FR) 6 b. or br.g. Dom Alco (FR) – Cabira Des Saccart (FR) (Quart de **c140** Vin (FR)) [2006/7 c128, h114p: c20d² c20d³ c25s² c21v² c24g⁶ c25g Apr 13] close- **h–** coupled, sparely-made gelding: winning hurdler (remains open to improvement): useful handicap chaser: largely good efforts in 2006/7, most at Cheltenham, ½-length second to Whispered Secret in Grade 3 event fourth outing: stays 25f: raced on good going or softer (acts on heavy). *Ferdy Murphy*

NEWBAY LADY 9 b.m. Terimon – Gospel (IRE) (Le Bavard (FR)) [2006/7 20d⁵ 25g* **c70** 20m⁵ c20s⁴ c20s⁴ c24s⁵ c16vᵖᵘ Jan 3] modest hurdler: left G. Stewart in Ireland prior to **h89** first outing: won maiden at Wetherby in June: little form over fences, possibly amiss last 2 starts: stays 25f: acts on soft going. *Mrs S. J. Smith*

NEWBAY PROP (IRE) 8 b.g. Good Thyne (USA) – Geray Lady (IRE) (Roselier **c125** (FR)) [2006/7 c16d c20v c29s* c24vᶠ 20v⁶ c33s³ c25mᵖᵘ Apr 26] strong gelding: **h98 p** winning pointer: fairly useful handicap chaser: won at Fairyhouse in December by short head from Camptect, despite bad mistake 4 out: good 12¼ lengths third of 18 to Baron Windrush in Midlands Grand National at Uttoxeter: modest form when sixth in minor event at Punchestown on hurdling debut (should do better): stays 33f: raced mainly on going softer than good. *A. J. Martin, Ireland*

NEW BIRD (GER) 12 b.g. Bluebird (USA) – Nouvelle Amour (GER) (Esclavo (FR)) **c86 §** [2006/7 c110§, h–: c16d⁶ c16m⁵ c17m⁶ Sep 2] tall gelding: handicap chaser, on down- **h–** grade: best around 2m: acts on heavy and good to firm going: blinkered last 2 starts: tried tongue tied: ungenuine. *Ian Williams*

NEW BLOOD (IRE) 4 b.g. Beckett (IRE) – Utmost (IRE) (Most Welcome) [2006/7 **h–** 16fᵘʳ 17sᵖᵘ 22sᵖᵘ Jan 16] leggy gelding: no form on Flat (for J. M. Bradley) or over hurdles. *Mrs L. P. Baker*

NEW DIAMOND 8 ch.g. Bijou d'Inde – Nannie Annie (Persian Bold) [2006/7 h–: 17g h–
16m 16m⁶ Jun 28] little impact over hurdles. *Mrs P. Ford*

NEW ENTIC (FR) 6 b.g. Ragmar (FR) – Entiqua Des Sacart (FR) (Lute Antique (FR)) c121 §
[2006/7 h127: c20g⁵ c21g⁵ c20s² c20d³ c20dᵖᵘ c20s⁴ c22d* c20d c22gᵖᵘ c20m⁵ Apr 27] h– §
well-made gelding: fairly useful hurdler/novice chaser: won handicap over fences at
Newbury in March by 1¾ lengths from Sha Bihan: stays 2¾m: acts on soft going: has
worn cheekpieces/blinkers: ungenuine. *G. L. Moore*

NEW FIELD (IRE) 9 b.g. Supreme Leader – Deep Steel (Deep Run) [2006/7 c122, c–
h–: 16s 16v⁴ 16d³ 16d 17g 16m² Apr 10] sturdy, lengthy gelding: fairly useful chaser/ h126
handicap hurdler: mainly in good form over hurdles after reappearance, under 5 lengths
seventh of 20 to Heathcote in very valuable event at Newbury fourth outing: stays 21f:
acts on heavy and good to firm going. *Thomas Mullins, Ireland*

NEWGATE GEM 6 b.m. Keen – Gemgem (Lochnager) [2006/7 F16d F17m Apr 15] F–
half-sister to winner in Greece by Timeless Times: dam 7f seller winner: soundly beaten
in bumpers. *Mark Campion*

NEWGATE SUDS 10 b.m. Kasakov – Newgate Bubbles (Hubbly Bubbly (USA)) h56
[2006/7 h–: 24s² 22s² 24g⁵ 27v⁶ Jan 28] strong mare: bad novice hurdler, lightly raced:
stays 3m: acts on soft going. *Mark Campion*

NEWICK PARK 12 gr.g. Chilibang – Quilpee Mai (Pee Mai) [2006/7 c86, h–: c19g c–
c21g May 24] good-topped gelding: winning chaser: blinkered, no show in hunters early h–
in 2006/7: has worn cheekpieces. *Mrs D. M. Grissell*

NEW LEADER (IRE) 10 b.g. Supreme Leader – Two Spots (Deep Run) [2006/7 c– §
c68§, h–: c20dᵖᵘ Nov 8] angular gelding: poor handicap chaser: stays 25f: acts on good to h–
firm and good to soft going: tried tongue tied: unreliable. *Mrs L. Richards*

NEW LITTLE BRIC (FR) 6 ch.g. Bricassar (USA) – Doulina (FR) (Dastaan c143
(FR)) [2006/7 c20d* c16s³ c19d* c20g* c21g Mar 15] h–
The generous bonus on offer to a novice or maiden chase winner at Plumpton who goes on to win a chase at the Cheltenham Festival that season was doubled
to £50,000 in the latest campaign, but, unlike in 2005/6 when connections of Voy
Por Ustedes benefited, the money went unclaimed. Four horses did attempt to
emulate Voy Por Ustedes, namely Fair Question in the National Hunt Chase—he
fell at the seventeenth when disputing the lead—and Desert Air and the stable-
companions New Little Bric and Phar Bleu in the Jewson Novices' Handicap. New
Little Bric, sent off the clear favourite, looked the most likely to succeed, and he did
come the closest of that trio to doing so, though his effort in finishing seventh
behind L'Antartique was somewhat disappointing considering how well he had
been progressing in non-handicaps. New Little Bric was unable to quicken after
being well placed turning in and was beaten just under twelve lengths in the end. A
lightly-raced six-year-old, New Little Bric may yet do better and his sound jumping
will stand him in good stead when he takes on more experienced chasers in the next
season.
New Little Bric had four races in France before joining his present yard
early in 2006, finishing runner-up over fifteen furlongs on the second of two starts
on the Flat, then unbeaten in a couple of runs over hurdles, both at Pau. He made his
chasing debut in a six-runner maiden at Plumpton in November when the ground
there wasn't too bad, unlike later in the season. The next seven fixtures staged at
Plumpton were run on soft or heavy going, with the majority of them very much in
the latter category—indeed, in common with a few other courses last winter, it was
surprising that at least one of those meetings (on December 11th) was allowed to go
ahead as runners had to splash their way round large waterlogged stretches of the
track. Such scenes provided a poor advert for racing but, unfortunately, worse was
to follow as this busy winter schedule took its toll when conditions began to dry
out. The ground was very patchy for the meeting there on Monday March 26th and
several horses broke down (two had to be put down as a result of their injuries),
while no fewer than seventeen horses were withdrawn from the last three races
because of concerns about the state of the going. New Little Bric's chasing debut
back in November hadn't been without incident, either, as second favourite
Schapiro suffered a fatal fall at the fifth and the third favourite Nonantais jumped to
the right throughout on his return from a long absence. As a result, New Little Bric

totesport.com Scilly Isles Novices' Chase, Sandown—a bold display from New Little Bric

was left with a simple task and drew clear on the bridle after three out to land the odds by thirteen lengths. In marked contrast to Plumpton, New Little Bric could hardly have faced a tougher test when he made his second appearance over fences just a couple of weeks later, in the Henry VIII Novices' Chase at Sandown. In finishing third behind Fair Along and My Way de Solzen, beaten fifteen lengths by the winner, he acquitted himself very well. After completing another very easy task in the meantime, winning a three-runner event at Exeter (when 7/1-on), New Little Bric was returned to Sandown in February for a Grade 1 event run over two and a half miles in which he faced much lesser opposition than in the Grade 2 Henry VIII Chase, run over two. The totesport.com Scilly Isles Novices' Chase rarely attracts more than a handful of runners, and for the third time in five years only four took part, New Little Bric opposed by the no-more-than-useful performers All Star, Aztec Warrior and Pretty Star. Starting at slight odds on, New Little Bric took up the running at the fourth and quickened away in the straight to win with plenty to spare by eight lengths from Aztec Warrior. New Little Bric jumped fluently apart from a blunder at the ninth, being particularly good at the last two fences after the pace had quickened.

New Little Bric (FR) (ch.g. 2001)	Bricassar (USA) (ch 1985)	Irish River (ch 1976)	Riverman
			Irish Star
		Lyrism (b 1979)	Lyphard
			Pass A Glance
	Doulina (FR) (ch 1991)	Dastaan (gr 1984)	Arctic Tern
			Denia
		Quianoa (b 1982)	Beaugency
			Drouchenka

The distance of the Jewson, twenty-one furlongs, is the longest New Little Bric has tackled to date, but that seems most unlikely to prove the limit of his stamina given that his full-brother Little Brick was successful over twenty-five furlongs on testing ground at Wincanton on his British debut in February. Sadly, Little Brick, a smart chaser, suffered a fatal injury himself at Cheltenham the following month when prominent in the Grand National betting. New Little Bric, the second foal of the unraced Doulina, is a good-topped gelding who usually takes the eye beforehand, and he very much impressed in appearance at Cheltenham. As with his brother, New Little Bric has raced only on good ground or softer and he acts on soft. *P. F. Nicholls*

NEW LODGE 4 b.g. Grand Lodge (USA) – New Abbey (Sadler's Wells (USA)) [2006/7 F16m³ F14d² F16s³ Apr 1] 22,000 3-y-o: third foal: dam, 1½m winner, sister to dam of smart French stayer Reefscape and half-sister to Irish Oaks winner Wemyss Bight: fair form when placed in bumpers. *N. G. Richards*   **F91**

NEW LODGE EXPRESS (IRE) 9 ch.g. Grand Lodge (USA) – Wakt (Akarad (FR)) [2006/7 c25gᵖᵘ May 3] ex-Irish gelding: fair pointer: no form in juvenile hurdles/hunter chase. *T. M. Stephenson*   **c–**   **h–**

NEWMILL (IRE) 9 br.g. Norwich – Lady Kas (Pollerton) [2006/7 c165p, h156: 16s⁴ c16sᶠ 16v* c16g⁴ c16m⁵ Apr 24]   **c151**   **h157**

The fall was as dramatic as the rise with Newmill the chaser. His performances in the three races he contested over fences in the latest campaign contrasted sharply with the three on his return to chasing in 2005/6, which had produced a hat-trick of wins including those in the Queen Mother Champion Chase and Kerrygold Champion Chase. Now rising ten, it seems unlikely that Newmill will reach such dizzy heights again, though he is no back number yet. His victory in a Grade 2 event over hurdles rescued what would otherwise have been a most disappointing season, and showed that he still retains plenty of ability.

Newmill contested both those championship events at Cheltenham and Punchestown again in 2006/7, his only other outing over fences during the season coming in the Tied Cottage Chase at Punchestown where he fell four out when still in contention. The Tied Cottage was run in thick fog and it was very difficult to gauge how Newmill had shaped until his departure but, tellingly, jockey Andrew McNamara reported 'I don't think we would have beaten the winner Nickname.' Newmill started second favourite for the latest renewal of the Queen Mother Champion Chase, having been a 16/1-shot when giving a bold-jumping, front-

Red Mills Trial Hurdle, Gowran Park—
a winning return to hurdles in an otherwise disappointing season for Newmill

running display in winning the 2006 edition by nine lengths from Fota Island. That victory over hurdles had given plenty of encouragement to those hoping he would be in the same sort of form on his return to Cheltenham—'I honestly believe he is even better this year,' said his trainer John Murphy—but that proved a vain hope. Unlike twelve months earlier, when he had had things very much his own way in front, Newmill was taken on for the lead by Ashley Brook, made a couple of mistakes, and dropped away from two out to finish nine lengths fourth behind Voy Por Ustedes. Despite this setback and the fact he'd missed Aintree after picking up a slight leg infection (he travelled over to Merseyside), Newmill was still sent off a short-priced favourite for the Champion at Punchestown, but he was even further below his best than at Cheltenham. Jumping into the lead at the sixth, Newmill was flat and not fluent at the fourth last and faded in the straight to finish fifth of seven behind Mansony. Newmill isn't always foot perfect but it was his jumping that kept him in contention for so long in the last-named race, which is surprising given the powerful display of galloping he'd shown when defeating the 2006 Champion Hurdle runner-up Macs Joy in the Red Mills Trial Hurdle at Gowran in February—there was even talk of Newmill himself going for the Champion Hurdle instead of the Queen Mother Champion Chase after that performance. Macs Joy started at long odds on for the Red Mills, his main rival in the five-runner field expected to be the 2005 Champion Hurdle runner-up Harchibald, but neither was at their best, unlike Newmill who reproduced the very smart form he'd shown over hurdles in 2005/6 when in the frame in a couple of races won by Brave Inca, incidentally finishing ahead of Macs Joy, at level weights, both times. Now in receipt of 8 lb, Newmill took full advantage of the concession, ensuring a truly-run race as he adopted his usual tactics, stepping up the tempo from early in the back straight. Macs Joy managed to get upsides turning for home, but then could do no more, whereas Newmill continued to run on strongly under just hands and heels and drew away again to win by eight lengths.

Newmill (IRE) (br.g. 1998)	Norwich (b 1987)	Top Ville (b 1976)	High Top / Sega Ville
		Dame Julian (br 1976)	Blakeney / March Spray
	Lady Kas (b 1984)	Pollerton (b 1974)	Rarity / Nilie
		Lady Dikler (b 1970)	Even Money / Coronation Day

Newmill's pedigree was dealt with in depth in *Chasers & Hurdlers 2005/06*, but there is an important addition to be made in respect to his full brother Mudslinger, who won a bumper at Clonmel early in 2007/8, that only his second start having been pulled up in a point on his debut. Their dam Lady Kas, a two-mile hurdle winner, is a daughter of an unraced half-sister to the 1973 Cheltenham Gold Cup and 1971 King George VI Chase winner The Dikler, as well as to the useful staying hurdler/chaser Kas. Lady Kas has produced two more foals by Newmill's sire Norwich since Mudslinger, a filly in 2004 and a colt in 2007. Her only other foal to report is a 2003 filly by Taipan who also has yet to be named. Newmill has won over as far as twenty-one furlongs, but he does most of his racing (and has put up his best performances) at two miles. A tall, good-topped gelding, he acts on heavy and good to firm going. *John Joseph Murphy, Ireland*

NEW MILL MOLL 4 b.f. Kayf Tara – Pretty Pride (IRE) (Doyoun) [2006/7 F16d2 F16s 17g Apr 1] angular filly: third foal: dam Italian maiden: runner-up in mares bumper at Chepstow on debut: well beaten after, failed to settle in novice hurdle. *D. Burchell*   **h–**
F85

NEW PERK (IRE) 9 b.g. Executive Perk – New Chello (IRE) (Orchestra) [2006/7 c104, h95: c24d4 c21d4 23d5 c24d2 23s* c27g* Mar 25] close-coupled gelding: modest handicap hurdler: won at Fakenham (sixth course win) in February: fair handicap chaser: left M. Gingell, further progress to beat Lord of The Road by ½ length at Taunton, idling: stays 27f: acts on firm and soft going: tried visored/tongue tied: game. *S. Curran*   **c105**
h94

NEW RACKHEATH (IRE) 4 b.g. Norwich – Bonne Sante (IRE) (Tremblant) [2006/7 F12g Mar 23] rather unfurnished gelding: third foal: dam unraced out of half-sister to smart French hurdler/chaser Boca Boca, stayed 25f: raced very freely when well held in 4-y-o bumper on debut. *C. J. Down*   **F–**

NEW REALM (USA) 5 b.g. Red Ransom (USA) – Mystery Rays (USA) (Nijinsky **h–**
(CAN)) [2006/7 16s 20v 16g^{pu} 16m^{pu} Apr 9] lengthy gelding: lightly-raced maiden on
Flat, trained at 3 yrs by H. Collingridge: no form over hurdles. *R. A. Farrant*

NEW'S FULL (FR) 6 b.m. Useful (FR) – Goldkara (FR) (Glint of Gold) [2006/7 **h–**
F–: 16g 20s Oct 15] big, rangy mare: little impact in bumpers/novice hurdles. *Ferdy*
Murphy

NEW SOURCE (IRE) 5 ch.m. Old Vic – Saucy Nun (IRE) (Orchestra) [2006/7 F16s **F–**
Mar 7] €9,000 4-y-o: first foal: dam poor handicap hurdler who stayed 27f: well held in mares
bumper on debut. *W. Amos*

NEW TEAM (FR) 6 ch.g. Green Tune (USA) – Fortuna Jet (USA) (Highest Honor (FR)) **h104**
[2006/7 h115+: 16s* 20s^{pu} 17s^5 21v^{pu} Feb 24] good-topped gelding: fair novice hurdler:
off 12 months, won maiden at Uttoxeter in October: ran as if amiss 2 of 3 starts (bled on
first one) after: should stay 2½m: acts on going softer than good. *R. H. Alner*

NEW TIME (IRE) 8 b.g. Topanoora – Fast Time (IRE) (Be My Native (USA)) [2006/7 **c101**
c–, h93: 20m^6 c23m^3 c23m^F Aug 3] good-topped gelding: modest hurdler: fair form over **h86**
fences: won handicap at Worcester in July: well in command when fell last in similar
event at Stratford: stays 23f: acts on firm ground. *Jonjo O'Neill*

NEWTON BRIDGE (IRE) 6 b.g. Among Men (USA) – Kaliningrad (IRE) (Red **c–**
Sunset) [2006/7 20s^2 16v 22s c17s c20d c16d c18m Apr 28] fourth foal: half-brother to **h90**
Italian winners by Treasure Kay and Darnay: dam unraced: runner-up on first of 2 outings
in points in 2005: modest form at best in maiden hurdles: no show over fences: stays
2½m: acts on soft going: tongue tied once (ran well). *G. Elliott, Ireland*

NEW WAVE 5 b.g. Woodman (USA) – Vanishing Point (USA) (Caller I D (USA)) **c79**
[2006/7 h–: 16g c16d^F c16m^3 c16m^{pu} Apr 9] smallish gelding: well beaten over hurdles: **h–**
poor form in novice chases: raced at 2m. *R. Lee*

NEW WISH (IRE) 7 b.g. Ali-Royal (IRE) – False Spring (IRE) (Petorius) [2006/7 h–: **h70**
16g 16f 16g^2 17m* 16f^{su} 17m^6 17m^5 17v^4 17s Oct 25] tall gelding: poor hurdler: won
selling handicap at Market Rasen in August: best around 2m with emphasis on speed: acts
on good to firm going. *S. B. Clark*

NEYSAUTEUR (FR) 6 ch.g. Beyssac (FR) – Belle Sauteuse (FR) (Le Nain Jaune **c124**
(FR)) [2006/7 c17g^2 c17g* c22v^2 c23d* c21v^3 c24d* c23d^4 c25g^3 c24s^3 c21g^{pu} Mar 19]
workmanlike gelding: third foal: dam maiden: once-raced on Flat: won minor event over
fences at Chalons in May: sold out of H. Billot's stable €24,000 Goffs (France) July Sale:
fairly useful handicap chaser in Britain: won easily at Exeter in October and Ascot
(novice) in November: stayed 25f: acted on heavy going: tried blinkered in France: dead.
C. E. Longsdon

NEZ ROUGE (FR) 6 gr.g. April Night (FR) – Gracieuse Des Bois (FR) (Panoramic) **F72**
[2006/7 F16v^5 F16m^5 Jun 28] €28,000 3-y-o, £20,000 4-y-o: first foal: dam 1½m winner:
poor form in maiden bumpers. *R. T. Phillips*

NGAURUHOE (IRE) 5 b.m. Desert Sun – Snowcap (IRE) (Snow Chief (USA)) **h–**
[2006/7 h81: 20m 16g^{pu} Jun 1] poor form at best over hurdles, lame final outing. *John*
Berry

NICE HORSE (FR) 6 ch.g. River Bay (USA) – Tchela (FR) (Le Nain Jaune (FR)) **c–**
[2006/7 h106: 19m* 21m^2 20g^4 26m^5 c21s^F Jun 27] leggy, close-coupled gelding: fair **h99 §**
hurdler: won maiden at Newton Abbot in May: fell ninth on chasing debut: stays 21f: acts
on soft and good to firm ground: in headgear in 2006/7: ungenuine. *D. E. Pipe*

NICE TRY (IRE) 8 b.g. Lord Americo – Lyntim (Fidel) [2006/7 c116, h98: c20d^5 c24g **c135**
c19s^3 c20v^{pu} c24s^4 c19v^2 c19v* c20g* Mar 24] close-coupled gelding: in frame in novice **h–**
hurdles: useful handicap chaser: jumped better than usual (raced prominently) and much
improved last 2 starts, winning at Chepstow (by distance) and Bangor (beat Brooklyn
Brownie by 5 lengths) in March: should stay beyond 2½m: raced on good going or softer
(acts on heavy). *Miss Venetia Williams*

NICHE MARKET (IRE) 6 b.g. Presenting – Juresse (IRE) (Jurado (USA)) [2006/7 **h–**
24d^{pu} Oct 5] €37,000 3-y-o: second foal: half-brother to bumper/25f chase winner Rock
On Tom (by Anshan): dam, won 2m hurdle, half-sister to smart staying chaser Strath
Royal: no show in novice hurdle on debut: won maiden point in January: sold £20,000
Cheltenham April Sales. *Mrs K. Waldron*

NICKI BOY (GER) 5 b.g. Dashing Blade – Nicely (GER) (Esclavo (FR)) [2006/7 **h109**
16g^6 16g^6 16d^6 16d^6 20d^6 18g* 16f^3 16m Apr 22] tall, workmanlike gelding: successful 3
times (all at 1¼m) on Flat in Germany for T. H. Hansen: fair novice hurdler: won

handicap at Fontwell in March: likely to prove best up to 2½m: acts on firm and good to soft going: in cheekpieces last 4 starts. *C. J. Mann*

NICKIT (IRE) 11 gr.g. Roselier (FR) – Run Trix (Deep Run) [2006/7 c72x, h–: c26m^{pu} May 11] quite good-topped gelding: winning pointer: maiden hurdler/chaser: stays 23f: acts on soft going: tried blinkered/visored: sketchy jumper of fences. *Mrs Susan Smith*

**c– x
h–**

NICKNAME (FR) 8 b.g. Lost World (IRE) – Newness (IRE) (Simply Great (FR)) [2006/7 c141, h–: c16s* c20v⁴ c17v* c17v* c16s* c16v* c20v* Mar 24]

**c164
h–**

Nickname's season would have had a different look to it if the Cheltenham Festival had come a week earlier—or the rains a week later. Few sets of connections would have been happier than Nickname's when the official going at Cheltenham was changed to heavy a week before the Festival. However, with conditions subsequently drying out all the time, Nickname, by then fourth in the betting, was withdrawn on the day from the Queen Mother Champion Chase. The ground had not been soft enough for him to contest the Arkle at the previous season's Festival either, and raced exclusively on ground right from his earliest days in France, there's no arguing that Nickname handles the mud supremely well. It doesn't look as though he'll be given the opportunity to prove himself on good ground or firmer, which is a pity, as it will considerably diminish his chances of clashing with Britain's top two-mile chasers, something which is yet to happen. But, as his trainer Martin Brassil explained, 'there are too many good races here [in Ireland] to risk horses like that on fast ground.' It is also worth pointing out that, ironically, these ground constraints have arguably resulted in Nickname being raced more often, rather than less, over the past two winters as connections realise the need to keep him busy, with the big spring meetings effectively likely to be out of the equation. 'There is no point in training him with the Champion Chase in mind as you don't normally get that sort of (soft) ground at the Festival,' Brassil said in March.

Paddy Power Dial-A-Bet Chase, Leopardstown—
Nickname gains the second of five verdicts over Central House (blinkered) in 2006/7

paddypower.com Newlands Chase, Naas—the novice Gemini Lucy (noseband) is already beaten off as Nickname goes on to the fifth of his six wins

The Irish graded-race programme offers plenty of opportunities for good two-mile chasers and, with the ground in his favour, Nickname pretty much swept the board in them through the winter, earning the equivalent of around £145,000 in win prize money in the process and proving a credit to his connections. In that context, missing Cheltenham (and Punchestown as well later in the spring) wasn't too much of a sacrifice. As a novice, Nickname had made a spectacular start to his chasing career with a couple of impressive wins at Leopardstown, though subsequent defeats, notably when a disappointing favourite for the Irish Arkle at the same course (he reportedly bled), put him some way behind the top novices at the end of his first season in Ireland. As a result, Nickname began his second as only fourth choice in the betting for the five-runner Navan Race Supporters Fortria Chase at Navan in November. With a change in the saddle—Conor O'Dwyer rode him as a novice but Niall 'Slippers' Madden and Ruby Walsh shared the rides in 2006/7—Nickname was ridden much more patiently than previously and set the tone for the season with the first of several victories over the joint favourites Central House and Watson Lake. On this occasion, Nickname received weight from those rivals and beat Central House by just three quarters of a length. There was daylight between them on all four subsequent meetings.

Next, though, came Nickname's only defeat of the season when he finished a well-held fourth to In Compliance in the Punchestown Chase over two and a half miles. The longer trip shouldn't have been his undoing and it may be more significant that Nickname was fitted with a tongue strap when taking on Central House again, this time at level weights, back over two miles in the Grade 1 Paddy Power Dial-A-Bet Chase at Leopardstown later in December. Central House was favourite to turn the tables in a race he had won two years earlier and should also have won in 2005 when his rider mistook the winning post. However, duelling for the lead in the heavy ground took its toll on the favourite, and Nickname came smoothly from off the pace to run out a fourteen-length winner from Central House, with the 2005 winner Hi Cloy third (badly hampered by the fall of the other pacesetter Jim two out) and Mister McGoldrick a well-held fourth. The latter, incidentally, was the only British-trained rival Nickname faced all season. Nickname was tongue tied for all bar one of his remaining starts.

If Central House had excuses at Leopardstown, he seemingly had none in the ladbrokes.com Normans Grove Chase at Fairyhouse almost a month later.

Mrs Claudia Jungo-Corpataux's "Nickname"

Nickname gained another impressive win, this time from Justified, storming clear after leading two out to win by fifteen lengths. Central House was a remote third, while the only other runner Watson Lake was remounted for fourth after falling when challenging three out, though he wouldn't have beaten Nickname had he stood up. Thus far, Nickname had yet to cross swords with Ireland's top two-mile chaser Newmill. Newmill had been an impressive winner of the Queen Mother Champion Chase and Punchestown's Kerrygold Champion Chase on his last two starts the previous spring, but had made his only appearance in the latest season over hurdles when last of four in the Morgiana at Punchestown. Nickname started odds on when they finally met in the Byrne Group plc Tied Cottage Chase at Punchestown in February when Newmill's fall four out spoiled any chance of seeing how they matched up. In truth, it was difficult to see how any of the eight runners fared in a race which was run in thick fog, but Nickname emerged from the gloom to win impressively from some by-now regular rivals, headed yet again by Central House seven lengths behind.

What would have been Nickname's final start before Cheltenham came in the paddypowerpoker.com Newlands Chase at Naas and, against a weaker field, Nickname gained a facile win over the useful novice mare Gemini Lucy (who received 10 lb). In what turned out to be his final race of the season, Nickname found further easy pickings in the Russell Restaurant An Uaimh Chase at Navan at the end of March. The trip was two and a half miles this time but his old rivals were back and Nickname brushed them aside easily under hands and heels, going clear to beat Central House by thirteen lengths, ahead of the enterprisingly-ridden Jim and an out-of-sorts Watson Lake. Good to firm ground for Punchestown's Kerry-gold Champion Chase ruled out Nickname on the day. Favourite Newmill was disappointing and Central House ran worse still. While Nickname hadn't met the winner Mansony in the course of the season, he had given much sounder beatings to Justified and Steel Band, the placed horses in the Kerrygold Champion, than Mansony did. Nickname looks set for another campaign similar to the one he had in the latest season. With his appearances dependent so much on the ground, his best chance of landing another Grade 1 contest looks to be at Leopardstown at Christmas again.

Nickname (FR) (b.g. 1999)	Lost World (IRE) (b 1991)	Last Tycoon (b 1983)	Try My Best Mill Princess
		Last Tango (br 1973)	Luthier La Bamba
	Newness (IRE) (b 1988)	Simply Great (b 1979)	Mill Reef Seneca
		Neomenie (b 1978)	Rheffic Nordenberg

It may not have been until the latest season that Nickname raised his profile, but he's no late developer. He was much the best of his generation as a juvenile hurdler in France when with Jean-Paul Gallorini and Timeform rated him 4 lb higher than the top four-year-old hurdler in Britain or Ireland that season, Sporazene. Among the leading hurdlers in France the following season, Nickname also finished a close fourth to Ireland's Rule Supreme in the 2004 Grande Course de Haies d'Auteuil. It was eighteen months before Nickname was seen out again, by which time he had joined Martin Brassil in Ireland. The smallish, strong, close-coupled Nickname was still an entire horse when he raced in France and *Chasers & Hurdlers* speculated at the time that, with his racing record backed up by a strong pedigree, a stallion career might have been awaiting him. That's no longer an option for the now-gelded Nickname, but his dam's stud record has only got better in the meantime. Newness had already produced several winning jumpers prior to Nickname, notably the Gallorini-trained pair N'Avoue Jamais (by Marignan) and Nom d'Une Pipe (by Linamix) who were also leading juvenile hurdlers in France. The latter proved smart over hurdles later in his career (also won over fences), while the filly N'Avoue Jamais has already made a successful start as a broodmare. Her first foal Nickelle won a listed race (over a mile and a quarter) at Longchamp in the spring after wins over both hurdles and fences. Since Nickname, Newness has produced the fillies New Destiny (by Highest Honor) and New Saga (by Sagamix), both useful winners on the Flat. New Saga excelled herself by finishing fifth in the 2005 Prix de Diane and, unusually for one who had run so well in a classic, was sent hurdling in the latest season, finishing placed on both her starts at Auteuil in the autumn. Newness won over both hurdles and fences, finishing third to Al Capone II in the top four-year-old chase, the Prix Maurice Gillois. Her half-brothers included Nile Prince, winner of France's most valuable handicap chase, the Prix du President de La Republique, and Nil Bleu, winner of the Group 3 Prix Berteux over fifteen furlongs on the Flat and another who was a good juvenile over hurdles. *Martin Brassil, Ireland*

NICK'S CHOICE 11 b.g. Sula Bula – Clare's Choice (Pragmatic) [2006/7 c–, h109: 16s^{pu} 20s^{pu} 24s^{pu} 20d⁵ 18s³ 17v³ 16s 20g⁴ 22m^{pu} 20g Apr 27] compact gelding: modest handicap hurdler nowadays, left M. Doyle after third start: effective at 2m to 2¾m: acts on heavy and good to firm going: tried blinkered/in cheekpieces: has bled (including only outing over fences). *P. D. Evans*   **c–**
h92

NICK THE JEWEL 12 b.g. Nicholas Bill – Bijou Georgie (Rhodomantade) [2006/7 c112, h–: c16m⁶ Jun 8] tall, angular gelding: lightly raced over hurdles: fair handicap chaser: bled only start in 2006/7: best around 2m: acts on soft and good to firm going: usually front runner. *Andrew Turnell*   **c–**
h–

NICKY TAM (IRE) 5 b. or br.g. Presenting – Wigmore (IRE) (Denel (FR)) [2006/7 F17s^{ro} F16v⁵ Mar 10] 50,000 4-y-o: second dam: lightly raced in points, half-sister to dam of high-class but unreliable chaser Turpin Green: modest form completed start (ran out debut) in bumpers. *Miss Lucinda V. Russell*   **F75**

NICODEMUS 13 br.g. St Ninian – Qurrat Al Ain (Wolver Hollow) [2006/7 c31g c24m^{pu} Sep 24] fair pointer: no form in chases. *J. R. Best*   **c–**
h–

NICO'S DREAM (IRE) 5 b.g. Old Vic – Magical Mist (IRE) (Be My Native (USA)) [2006/7 F–: F17s⁴ 20m 20v⁶ Jan 27] modest form when fourth in bumper: soundly beaten over hurdles, including in seller. *M. W. Easterby*   **h–**
F84

NICOZETTO (FR) 7 b.g. Nicolotte – Arcizette (FR) (Sarhoob (USA)) [2006/7 c–, h–: 17d c16m[5] c16g[6] c17m 21m[6] 20d* 20s[6] 25s[2] 20g 20v[pu] 16v 17s Feb 19] strong, lengthy gelding: no form over fences: modest novice hurdler: left N. Wilson after fourth outing: improved to win handicap at Carlisle in October: stays 25f: acts on soft going: tried tongue tied: none too reliable. *I. McMath* — **c–** **h93**

NICTOS DE BERSY (FR) 6 b.g. Useful (FR) – Tropulka God (FR) (Tropular) [2006/7 F96: 20d[6] 20v[3] 20s* 22d[pu] 20v[F] 24v[3] Mar 10] useful-looking gelding: in frame in bumpers: fair novice hurdler: won 16-runner event at Chepstow in December: stays 3m: raced on ground softer than good. *C. P. Morlock* — **h111**

NIEMBRO 7 b.g. Victory Note (USA) – Diabaig (Precocious) [2006/7 16g 21d[pu] Jun 4] winning hurdler, off 2 years before return: won point in March: seems to stay 19f: acts on good to firm going. *K. A. Morgan* — **h–**

NIETZSCHE (IRE) 6 b.h. Sadler's Wells (USA) – Wannabe (Shirley Heights) [2006/7 h73: 17s 16s 16g Dec 26] sturdy horse: poor form over hurdles: dead. *R. J. Hodges* — **h77**

NIFTY ROY 7 b.g. Royal Applause – Nifty Fifty (IRE) (Runnett) [2006/7 c105, h90: c20s 18v 24g c19s[6] c20v[4] c16v[4] c16g* c16g[3] Apr 19] angular gelding: winning hurdler: fair handicap chaser: back to best last 2 starts, winning at Carlisle in April: effective at 2m and stays at least 21f: acts on soft going: tried blinkered. *I. McMath* — **c106** **h71 +**

NIGELS DREAM (IRE) 8 b. or br.g. Turtle Island (IRE) – Black Orchid (IRE) (Persian Bold) [2006/7 c26g[4] May 24] winning pointer: fourth in novice hunter on chase debut (jumped left). *Miss Rachel Deakin* — **c62**

NIGHT CAP (IRE) 8 ch.g. Night Shift (USA) – Classic Design (Busted) [2006/7 h–: 16g May 14] no show over hurdles: sold £2,800 Ascot June Sales. *T. D. McCarthy* — **h–**

NIGHTFLY (IRE) 6 b.g. Fourstars Allstar (USA) – Except Alice (IRE) (Orchestra) [2006/7 F103: 19d* Nov 8] well-made gelding: won maiden bumper on debut in 2005/6 (highly tried next time) for M. Pitman: created good impression when justifying favouritism in novice at Lingfield on hurdling debut, not fully extended to beat Greenhill Bramble by 5 lengths: looked sure to improve but not seen out again. *Carl Llewellyn* — **h116 p**

NIGHT GROOVE (IRE) 4 b.g. Night Shift (USA) – Taysala (IRE) (Akarad (FR)) [2006/7 16g[6] Mar 16] half-brother to winning hurdler Full As A Rocket (by Foxhound), stays 2½m: modest on Flat (best form at 1m/1¼m): well held in maiden on hurdling debut. *N. P. Littmoden* — **h–**

NIGHT REVELLER (IRE) 4 b.f. Night Shift (USA) – Tir-An-Oir (IRE) (Law Society (USA)) [2006/7 16g[pu] 17v[6] 17d Mar 19] smallish filly: half-sister to useful hurdler Wee Dinns (by Marju), barely stays 21f: little sign of ability on Flat or in juvenile hurdles. *M. C. Chapman* — **h–**

NIGHT SAFE (IRE) 6 b.g. Safety Catch (USA) – Rock All Night (IRE) (Orchestra) [2006/7 F107: 24v* 25g[3] Oct 24] strong, heavy-topped gelding: bumper winner: fair form in novice hurdles: won at Market Rasen in October: again jumped none too fluently when third to Lou du Moulin Mar at Cheltenham later in month: stays 25f: acts on heavy going. *N. A. Twiston-Davies* — **h111**

NIGHT WARRIOR (IRE) 7 b.g. Alhaarth (IRE) – Miniver (IRE) (Mujtahid (USA)) [2006/7 h82: 16s 16m[6] c16m[3] 19d[5] 18d[2] 18d[3] Sep 27] lengthy gelding: modest maiden hurdler: similar form when third in novice handicap on chasing debut, final start for N. Littmoden: likely to prove best around 2m: tried blinkered. *Michael Mulvany, Ireland* — **c91** **h91**

NIGHTWATCHMAN (IRE) 8 b.g. Hector Protector (USA) – Nightlark (IRE) (Night Shift (USA)) [2006/7 h94: 20m 22g 24g Jul 31] maiden hurdler: no show in points: tongue tied 3 of last 4 starts. *S. B. Clark* — **h–**

NIGWELL FORBEES (IRE) 6 ch.g. Shernazar – Gender Gap (USA) (Shecky Greene (USA)) [2006/7 h–: 16v[6] 17d[3] May 31] well-made gelding: poor maiden hurdler, left J. Howard Johnson after first outing: probably stays 21f. *James Moffatt* — **h69**

NIKE WALKER (FR) 4 b.g. Bering – Albiatra (USA) (Dixieland Band (USA)) [2006/7 17m[4] 17m[4] 17d[F] 17d* 17v* 19s* Mar 2] close-coupled gelding: third foal: dam runner-up twice up to 1m on Flat: successful 6 times up to 10.5f on Flat in France, including in claimers at Saint-Cloud and Maisons-Laffitte (claimed from A. Junk €34,600) in 2006: fairly useful juvenile hurdler: off 6 months and tongue tied, much improved when easily winning handicaps at Market Rasen, Folkestone and Newbury (beat Dashing George by 7 lengths) within 11 days in February/March, last 2 conditional jockeys novice events: stays 19f: acts on heavy going: probably capable of better still. *D. E. Pipe* — **h112 p**

totesport.com Eider (Handicap Chase), Newcastle—the ill-fated Nil Desperandum is promoted to ante-post favouritism for the Grand National after a twelve-length victory over novice Nine de Sivola

NIKOLA (FR) 6 b.g. Roi de Rome (USA) – Envie de Chalamont (FR) (Pamponi (FR)) [2006/7 h117: c20s 20g 17s 16d* 17v 16g 16s 16g Apr 7] angular gelding: fairly useful handicap hurdler: won at Leicester in December by 1¾ lengths from Dhehdaah: generally well held otherwise in 2006/7, including on chasing debut: best at 2m: raced on good ground or softer: tried tongue tied (raced lazily final start). *N. A. Twiston-Davies* **c–** **h119**

NIKOLAIEV (FR) 6 b.g. Nikos – Faensa (FR) (Fabulous Dancer (USA)) [2006/7 h74: 16f⁵ 16m⁴ 16d 16m Oct 16] poor maiden hurdler: raced around 2m: tongue tied last 2 starts (took fierce hold). *N. J. Henderson* **h74**

NIL DESPERANDUM (IRE) 10 b.g. Un Desperado (FR) – Still Hoping (Kambalda) [2006/7 c143§, h–: c25m³ c26g⁴ c25s⁶ c25v⁴ c33v* c33sᵖᵘ Mar 17] useful-looking gelding: winning hurdler: very smart handicap chaser: left Ms F. Crowley after 2005/6: best effort when winning 16-runner totesport.com Eider Chase at Newcastle in March decisively by 12 lengths from Nine de Sivola: largely creditable efforts earlier in 2006/7, including when fourth to Eurotrek in Becher Chase at Aintree (completed all 4 starts over National fences, fourth to Numbersixvalverde in Grand National in 2005/6): broke down in valuable handicap at Uttoxeter: stayed 4½m: acted on good to firm and heavy going: tried in headgear: dead. *Miss Venetia Williams* **c159** **h–**

NILE MOON (IRE) 6 b.g. Simply Great (FR) – Reasonable Time (IRE) (Reasonable (FR)) [2006/7 h96, F–: 20dᵖᵘ c21vᶠ c25s² Mar 7] sturdy gelding: modest form on completed outing over hurdles/in novice hunter chases: stays 25f: won maiden point in April. *J. Howard Johnson* **c92** **h–**

NILS ANDERSON (FR) 6 b. or br.g. Franc Bleu Argent (USA) – Fee du Lac (FR) (Cimon) [2006/7 c20s³ 18sᵖᵘ c19sᵖᵘ c21dᶠ Mar 26] brother to fairly useful chaser Kosmos Bleu, stays 2¾m: 15f winner on Flat: maiden hurdler/chaser: left M. Blanchard-Jacquet and off 4 months, in share of lead when fell eleventh in chase at Stratford. *R. H. Alner* **c?** **h–**

NIMBY RUN (IRE) 9 ch.g. Commanche Run – Nimble Wind (Tumble Wind) [2006/7 16g⁴ 17m 16f 16g 16d⁵ 16d c16g³ c16g⁴ c16dᵘʳ c16s² c16s* c16g c17g³ c16m³ Mar 31] workmanlike gelding: maiden hurdler, left David O'Brien prior to sixth start: poor handicap chaser: won novice event at Kempton in February: stays 2½m: acts on firm and soft going: tried blinkered, in cheekpieces last 2 outings (looked none too keen). *Ian Williams* **c83** **h72**

The DPRP Sivola Partnership's "Nine de Sivola"

NINE DE SIVOLA (FR) 6 b.g. Video Rock (FR) – Quine de Chalamont (FR) (Do Do (FR)) [2006/7 c91p, h125: c23d⁵ c23s² c25d³ c25s⁴ c25s² c33v² c33gᶠ c29m² c32m² Apr 21] leggy gelding: fairly useful hurdler: useful maiden chaser: much improved over fences when runner-up in handicaps last 3 completed starts, in Eider Chase at Newcastle, Irish National (beaten length by Butler's Cabin) at Fairyhouse and Scottish National (beaten ½ length by stable-companion Hot Weld) at Ayr: still going well when falling 3 out in National Hunt Chase (Amateurs) at Cheltenham: stays 33f: acts on heavy and good to firm going. *Ferdy Murphy*   **c139 h–**

NINE O (IRE) 10 b. or br.g. Black Monday – Torrential Times (IRE) (Dromod Hill) [2006/7 24v³ 20s³ 21d⁵ c20v⁶ c20sᵘʳ c18d² Mar 29] medium-sized gelding: fair handicap hurdler/chaser: stays 3m: acts on heavy ground: tried in cheekpieces. *S. Braddish, Ireland*   **c110 h108**

NINETY NINE LOOKS (IRE) 5 ch.g. Old Vic – Oranrose (IRE) (Husyan (USA)) [2006/7 F16d F16s³ Feb 3] first foal: dam unraced, out of half-sister to Grand National winner Papillon: better effort in bumpers when third to Cast Iron Casey at Wetherby. *N. Wilson*   **F83**

NIPPY AYR 7 b.g. Distinctly North (USA) – Tees Gazette Girl (Kalaglow) [2006/7 F16v⁴ May 25] fourth foal: half-brother to winning pointer by Nomadic Way and winning hurdler up to 21f Time Marches On (by Timeless Times): dam 11f winner: tailed off in bumper on debut. *K. G. Reveley*   **F–**

NIPPY DES MOTTES (FR) 6 b.g. Useful (FR) – Julie Des Mottes (FR) (Puma Des Mottes (FR)) [2006/7 h130: c16g² c17g⁵ c16d² c16s* c16d³ c16f² c16g⁶ Apr 19] useful-looking gelding: useful hurdler: fairly useful chaser: won novice handicap at Wincanton in January by 2½ lengths from Sunley Shines: stays 19f: acts on any ground: tongue tied: has failed to impress with attitude, including when blinkered final start. *P. F. Nicholls*   **c123 h–**

NIRVANA DU BOURG (FR) 6 br.g. Cadoudal (FR) – Gnosca (FR) (Matahawk) [2006/7 c20s⁵ c22s* 18s⁴ 20s c22s⁶ c27s c22v⁴ 25v⁵ 24gᵖᵘ Mar 15] good-bodied ex-French gelding: second foal: half-brother to useful hurdler/winning chaser L'Interprete (by Poliglote): dam 11f winner: twice-raced on Flat: useful chaser: successful in Prix des Drays at Auteuil in June: ran well when fourth to Mid Dancer in Prix Georges Courtois   **c131 h120**

there in December: fairly useful hurdler: sold from T. Trapenard €160,000, shaped well under considerate handling when 7¼ lengths fifth to Rowley Hill in handicap at Warwick: ran as if amiss (looked in outstanding shape) in valuable similar event at Cheltenham 2 months later: stays 25f: raced on good going or softer (acts on heavy): has worn cheekpieces. *N. J. Henderson*

NIRVANA SWING (FR) 6 b.g. Chamberlin (FR) – Ukrainia II (FR) (Tadj (FR)) [2006/7 c111, h–: c25d² c24vᵖᵘ c24gᵖᵘ Mar 24] big gelding: maiden hurdler: fairly useful chaser: ran well when 2½ lengths second of 6 to Rosses Point in handicap at Wincanton: shaped as if amiss both starts after: stays 25f: acts on heavy going. *P. F. Nicholls*   c120 h–

NISBET 13 b.g. Lithgie-Brig – Drummond Lass (Peacock (FR)) [2006/7 c–, h–: c25g⁶ May 24] winning hunter chaser, no form since early-2004/5. *Miss M. Bremner*   c– h–

NITRAT (FR) 6 b.g. Brier Creek (USA) – Evane (FR) (Lute Antique (FR)) [2006/7 c21s* c21s c23s⁶ c29sᵖᵘ c24g⁶ c21v² c23sᵖᵘ Apr 22] angular gelding: second foal: half-brother to winning chaser up to around 2¾m Latex (by Lights Out): dam unraced sister to smart chaser Innox: twice-raced on Flat: maiden hurdler: fairly useful chaser: won 20-runner listed handicap at Auteuil in May: creditable efforts in handicaps fifth/sixth starts, sixth to Rambling Minster in valuable event at Sandown then 1½ lengths second to Grand Canal in listed event at Auteuil: stays 3m: raced on good going or softer: usually blinkered. *F. Doumen, France*   c124 h–

NIVER BAI (FR) 6 ch.g. River Bay (USA) – True Beauty (Sun Prince) [2006/7 F83: 16s³ 19d 16v² Jan 12] lengthy, unfurnished gelding: fair form in novice hurdles: should stay beyond 2m: raced on ground softer than good. *Miss H. C. Knight*   h107

NIZA D'ALM (FR) 6 b. or br.m. Passing Sale (FR) – Bekaa II (FR) (Djarvis (FR)) [2006/7 F–: F16f 16sᵘʳ 20gᵖᵘ 20mᵖᵘ Apr 9] sparely-made mare: no form (including on Flat), sold out of Miss Suzy Smith's stable 1,000 gns Doncaster August Sales after first outing. *A. Crook*   h– F–

NOBEL BLEU DE KERPAUL (FR) 6 b.g. Pistolet Bleu (IRE) – Gecika de Kerpaul (FR) (Sarpedon (FR)) [2006/7 h95: 22sᵖᵘ 21s 18s² 18g 18g Mar 18] tall, close-coupled gelding: modest handicap hurdler on his day: should stay beyond 2¼m: acts on soft going: blinkered last 3 starts. *P. Winkworth*   h94

NOBEL (FR) 6 gr.g. Dadarissime (FR) – Eire Dancer (FR) (Useful (FR)) [2006/7 h109: 18f² 22dᵘʳ 20m⁴ 20g³ 22d² 16v⁵ 24g⁵ c20g* Apr 23] good-topped gelding: fair handicap hurdler: readily landed odds in maiden at Sedgefield on chasing debut by 10 lengths from Bob Bites Back: bred to stay 3m: acts on firm and good to soft going. *N. G. Richards*   c107 h114

NOBELIX (IRE) 5 gr.g. Linamix (FR) – Nataliana (Surumu (GER)) [2006/7 16g* 16d* 16v 17g² Apr 19] smallish, sturdy gelding: fairly useful on Flat (stays 1¾m): fairly useful novice hurdler: landed odds at Kempton (easily) and Leicester (beat John Forbes by 1¼ lengths) in November: off 3 months, best effort when 3 lengths second of 4 to Lead On at Cheltenham, hanging left run-in: will stay beyond 2m: well held on heavy going. *J. R. Fanshawe*   h120

NOBILE (FR) 6 b.g. Kadalko (FR) – Elione (FR) (Video Rock (FR)) [2006/7 F78: c23vᵖᵘ Mar 1] off 10 months, lost action when jumping in maiden on chasing debut: sold 5,000 gns Doncaster May Sales. *M. Bradstock*   c–

NOBLE ACTION 8 ch.g. Mister Lord (USA) – Triggered (Gunner B) [2006/7 24v³ Oct 21] point/bumper winner: fair form in novice/maiden hurdles, left P. Nicholls and off almost 2 years between starts: stays 3m. *A. J. Honeyball*   h105

NOBLE BARON 11 gr.g. Karinga Bay – Grey Baroness (Baron Blakeney) [2006/7 c113x, h–: c24g⁴ c25dᵖᵘ 24dᵖᵘ Feb 10] workmanlike gelding: winning hurdler: fair chaser, below form since second outing in 2005/6: stays 25f: acts on soft going: tried in cheekpieces: usually tongue tied: often let down by jumping over fences. *C. G. Cox*   c85 x h–

NOBLE BEN (IRE) 5 ch.g. Beneficial – I'm Happy Now (IRE) (Torus) [2006/7 22s⁵ 16d² 24s⁴ Jan 30] third foal: half-brother to 21f hurdle winner Garranagree (by Beau Sher): dam winning pointer: back up markedly in trip, progressed further over hurdles when fourth to Itsa A Legend in novice at Taunton, not knocked about: capable of better again. *B. G. Powell*   h105 p

NOBLE BILY (FR) 6 b.g. Signe Divin (USA) – Vaillante Bily (FR) (The Quiet Man (FR)) [2006/7 h99: 19d² 21d 24s³ 22v³ c23s⁴ c19s⁶ 17s* c17m⁵ 17g⁵ Apr 27] rather leggy gelding: fair hurdler: didn't need to be anywhere near best to land odds in seller at Taunton in March: shaped better than result on 2 of 3 starts over fences: barely stays 3m: acts on heavy going, probably on good to firm: tried visored. *D. E. Pipe*   c101 h109

NOBLE BUCK (IRE) 11 b.g. Buckskin (FR) – Point The Finger (IRE) (Neshad (USA)) [2006/7 c89, h–: c24m^{pu} Jun 22] workmanlike gelding: modest chaser/winning hurdler: went as if amiss only outing in 2006/7: stays 31f: acts on any going: tried in cheekpieces. *Mrs L. J. Young*   c– h–

NOBLE CALLING (FR) 10 b.g. Caller I D (USA) – Specificity (USA) (Alleged (USA)) [2006/7 h101: 19d^3 22g^6 20g^3 19g 19g^4 22s^5 24s^{pu} 24v^{pu} Jan 8] leggy gelding: modest hurdler: should stay 3m: acts on heavy going: blinkered 6 of last 8 outings: ungenuine. *R. J. Hodges*   h92 §

NOBLE COLOURS 14 b.g. Distinctly North (USA) – Kentucky Tears (USA) (Cougar (CHI)) [2006/7 c–, h–: c20f^{pu} 20m^{pu} c20g c22g^5 c19m^5 Sep 28] small gelding: one-time fairly useful chaser, no longer of much account: has had tongue tied. *Mrs C. J. Ikin*   c– h–

NOBLE EDGE 4 ch.g. Bold Edge – Noble Soul (Sayf El Arab (USA)) [2006/7 17m 16g Nov 10] good-bodied gelding: fair on Flat (stays 1½m): poor form on second of 2 outings in juvenile hurdles, not fluent in steadily-run race: joined Karen McLintock. *Robert Gray*   h79

NOBLE HOUSE 10 ch.g. Gildoran – Trust To Luck (Mandamus) [2006/7 c70, h87: 20v^6 May 18] modest hurdler: not fluent and never dangerous only outing over fences: stays 21f: acts on good to soft going (ran poorly on heavy). *Mrs L. B. Normile*   c– h–

NOBLE RAIDER (IRE) 5 gr.g. Deploy – Smooth Princess (IRE) (Roi Danzig (USA)) [2006/7 F97: F17d^3 F16d^6 16s 16g* 20d^2 Dec 4] quite good-topped gelding: best effort in bumpers when fourth on debut in 2005/6 for T. Fitzgerald: second outing over hurdles, won novice at Warwick in November by 1½ lengths from Mr Aitch: better form when 6 lengths second to The Entomologist in similar event at Fakenham: stays 2½m: raced on good ground or softer. *Mrs P. Sly*   h106 F85

NOBLE REQUEST (FR) 6 gr.g. Highest Honor (FR) – Restless Mixa (IRE) (Lina-mix (FR)) [2006/7 h154+: 16m^4 16s^2 16d^2 Dec 26] tall, quite good-topped gelding: chasing type: smart hurdler: creditable efforts in 2006/7, runner-up to Straw Bear in 'Fighting Fifth' at Newcastle and Jazz Messenger in Christmas Hurdle at Kempton last 2 starts: raced around 2m: acts on good to firm and heavy going: patiently ridden nowadays: reliable. *P. J. Hobbs*   h152

NOBLE TIGER (IRE) 6 b.m. Tiger Hill (IRE) – Noble Conquest (USA) (Vaguely Noble) [2006/7 F16m 16s^{pu} Jun 25] no sign of ability: tried in eyeshields. *Mrs S. C. Bradburne*   h– F–

NOBODYS PERFECT (IRE) 7 br.m. Heron Island (IRE) – Likeness (Young Generation) [2006/7 h94: 20d* 17s^6 c16s c16d^{pu} 20d 20s* 17v^2 21s^2 17m Apr 9] leggy mare: fair hurdler: won maiden in May and conditional jockeys handicap (dead-heated with Cloudmor) in December, both at Sedgefield: no form in 2 starts over fences: should stay 3m: acts on good to firm and heavy going. *Ferdy Murphy*   c– h103

NOBODY TELLS ME (FR) 6 b. or br.g. Lute Antique (FR) – Becebege (FR) (Iron Duke (FR)) [2006/7 h123p: 25d^6 20s^3 c23s^2 c23v^{pu} 24g 22m^2 24m^4 Apr 17] rather leggy gelding: fair hurdler: similar form on completed outing over fences when 3½ lengths second to Rowlands Dream in maiden at Taunton: stays 3m: acts on good to firm and heavy going: visored last 2 starts: tried tongue tied: shapes as if having physical problems, and not one to trust. *D. E. Pipe*   c111 § h109 §

NOCATEE (IRE) 6 b.g. Vettori (IRE) – Rosy Sunset (IRE) (Red Sunset) [2006/7 c88§, h96§: c26m c21f 21m Sep 26] tall gelding: winning hurdler/chaser, has gone the wrong way temperamentally: in frame in points in 2007: stays 3m: acts on good to firm and heavy going: has worn cheekpieces/blinkers: tried tongue tied: one to leave alone. *P. C. Haslam*   c– § h– §

NOCIVO (FR) 6 b.g. Funny Baby (FR) – Esperance IV (FR) (Persifleur (USA)) [2006/7 h94p, F102: 16d 21m^3 16d^{ur} 17g* 16m^{pu} Apr 22] tall gelding: fair hurdler: improved form when winning handicap at Hereford in April: lame next time: may prove best around 2m. *H. D. Daly*   h114

NOCLOIX (FR) 6 b.g. Brier Creek (USA) – Belle Gambette (FR) (Quart de Vin (FR)) [2006/7 F–: F17d 17d^6 20m^6 16v^{pu} 20v^{pu} 24m c27g^{pu} Apr 23] little form, left R. Johnson after third outing. *J. M. Saville*   c– h– F–

NO COMMISSION (IRE) 5 b.g. General Monash (USA) – Price of Passion (Dolphin Street (FR)) [2006/7 h90: 17s^{pu} c21v^{ur} c20s^{pu} c20g^3 Apr 23] good-topped gelding: won 2m selling hurdle in 2005/6, only form over jumps. *R. F. Fisher*   c– h–

NO COMPLAINT (IRE) 7 b.g. Acting Brave – Carolin Lass (IRE) (Carlingford   h97
Castle) [2006/7 F16s⁶ 20s 16s 17s⁴ 25v⁴ 22g² Apr 7] workmanlike gelding: fourth foal: **F81**
half-brother to winning pointer by Shiel Hill: dam unraced: well held in maiden Irish
points in 2005: sixth in maiden at Uttoxeter: best effort over hurdles (modest form) when
second to Alderman Rose in novice handicap at Newton Abbot: seemed to find stamina
stretched over testing 25f time before. *T. R. George*

NOCTURNALLY 7 b.g. Octagonal (NZ) – Arletty (Rainbow Quest (USA)) [2006/7   h108
h101, F83: 21m³ 19s² May 27] fair effort over hurdles, best effort when second to Moon
Catcher in amateur handicap at Stratford: stays 21f: acts on soft and good to firm going.
V. R. A. Dartnall

NODDIES WAY 4 b.g. Nomadic Way (USA) – Sharway Lady (Shareef Dancer (USA))   h–
[2006/7 17m Mar 29] first foal: dam, winning hurdler, stayed 21f: fair maiden on Flat
(stays 21.6f): never dangerous in juvenile on hurdling debut: will be suited by much
further. *J. F. Panvert*

NODFORMS PAULA (IRE) 4 b.g. Rashar (USA) – Monamandy (IRE) (Mandalus)   **F111**
[2006/7 F16g² F16g* Apr 23] fifth foal: half-brother to winning hurdler/chaser Longstone Lady (by Mister Lord), stays 2¾m, and 2½m chase winner Cansalrun (by Anshan):
dam, winning pointer, out of half-sister to high-class staying chaser Simon Legree:
confirmed promise of debut when winning maiden bumper at Hexham easily by 17
lengths from Masra: likely to be suited by further over 2m. *Karen McLintock*

NODFORMS VICTORIA (IRE) 6 b.g. Arctic Lord – Webb Find (IRE) (Over The   h74
River (FR)) [2006/7 F–: F16g* F16g4 22dᵇᵈ 19g 22m² Apr 17] unfurnished gelding: fair   **F90**
form in bumpers, won at Hexham in October: sold out of Karen McLintock's stable
35,000 gns Doncaster November Sales: found little when 10 lengths second in poor
novice at Exeter, only form over hurdles. *P. J. Hobbs*

NODFORM WILLIAM 5 b.g. Prince Sabo – Periwinkle (FR) (Perrault) [2006/7 F97:   **F102**
F17s⁶ F16m* F16m³ Mar 25] lengthy gelding: fairly useful in bumpers: won maiden at
Musselburgh in November: when 9½ lengths third to Turbo Linn at
Southwell: likely to prove best at 2m with emphasis on speed. *Karen McLintock*

NO DIRECTIONS (IRE) 6 b.m. Norwich – Arctic Bead (IRE) (Le Moss) [2006/7   h76
F16s* 16d 17m⁷ Nov 7] €6,000 4-y-o: half-sister to fairly useful chaser Asparagus (by   **F90**
Roselier), stayed 29f: dam unraced: won mares bumper at Towcester on debut in May:
better effort in mares novice hurdles when third to Spinning Coin at Exeter: dead.
B. G. Powell

NOD'S STAR 6 ch.m. Starborough – Barsham (Be My Guest (USA)) [2006/7 h77:   h–
17dᵖᵘ Dec 21] modest on Flat (stays 16.5f), successful in January: poor maiden hurdler:
stays 2½m: acts on soft and good to firm ground: tongue tied. *Mrs L. C. Jewell*

NOD YA HEAD 11 ch.m. Minster Son – Little Mittens (Little Buskins) [2006/7 h76:   h69
23g⁴ 24m³ 23v³ 22d³ May 31] smallish mare: poor maiden hurdler: stays 25f: probably
acts on any going. *R. E. Barr*

NOEL'S PRIDE 11 b.g. Good Thyne (USA) – Kavali (Blakeney) [2006/7 c–, h–: c25g⁴   c74
c26g⁴ Jun 4] angular gelding: fairly useful hurdler at one time: poor maiden chaser: h–
winning pointer: stays 3m: acts on any going: tried in headgear/tongue tied. *C. C. Bealby*

NOEUD VERT (FR) 6 b.g. Kadalko (FR) – First Ball (FR) (Beyssac (FR)) [2006/7   h90
F16v² 22d⁵ 24s³ 22s⁵ 20v 20sᵖᵘ Apr 25] third foal: dam, ran once, out of sister to Sun   **F94**
Alliance Chase winner Rolling Ball: unseated in maiden point on debut: runner-up in
maiden hurdle at Uttoxeter only outing for D. McCain: modest form over hurdles, ran
poorly last 2 outings: stays 3m: raced on ground softer than good. *P. J. Hobbs*

NO FULL (FR) 6 b.g. Useful (FR) – Rosy Junior (FR) (Labus (FR)) [2006/7 c122+, h–:   c129
c20s²ᵈ c25s c19vᵖᵘ c20s³ c21g Mar 15] rather leggy gelding: maiden hurdler: fairly useful   h–
handicap chaser: creditable efforts in 2006/7 when placed at Newbury, disqualified due
to prohibited substance on first occasion, 8 lengths third to Madison du Berlais in Grade
3 event on second: best around 2½m: raced on good going or softer (acts on heavy): tried
in cheekpieces. *P. R. Webber*

NOGGLER 8 b.g. Primitive Rising (USA) – Sun Goddess (FR) (Deep Roots) [2006/7   c77
c–: c25m⁵ c22s³ May 21] fair pointer: prone to mistakes in hunter chases. *M. J. Brown*

NO GREATER LOVE (FR) 5 b.g. Take Risks (FR) – Desperate Virgin (BEL) (Chief   c77
Singer) [2006/7 16s³ 16s⁵ 16s c16m² Apr 9] good-topped ex-French gelding: fourth foal: h80
half-brother to smart 9f to 12.5f winner Rhythm Mad (by King's Theatre): dam 7.5f/1½m

697

winner: fair form on Flat (stays 1¾m), won maiden in January: poor form over hurdles/on chasing debut (pulled hard): raced at 2m over jumps. *Ian Williams*

NO GUARANTEES 7 b.g. Master Willie – Princess Hotpot (IRE) (King's Ride) [2006/7 h110: c20d² c24v² c24d² c24d⁴ c21sᶠ Jan 20] quite good-topped gelding: fair hurdler: fairly useful form over fences, runner-up first 3 starts, though jumping became a problem: stays 3m: raced on ground softer than good (acts on heavy): front runner. *N. A. Twiston-Davies*   c120 h–

NO HALF SESSION (IRE) 10 ch.g. Be My Native (USA) – Weekly Sessions (Buckskin (FR)) [2006/7 c–, h114+: c24sᵇᵈ c24d⁴ c24s c29s Dec 2] rangy gelding: fair hurdler: fairly useful chaser: ran well when around 5 lengths fourth to Pearly Jack in Munster National Handicap at Limerick: blinkered, below form last 2 outings: effective around 2½m to 25f: raced on good going or softer (acts on heavy): usually held up. *N. Meade, Ireland*   c124 h–

NOIR ET VERT (FR) 6 b.g. Silver Rainbow – Danse Verte (FR) (Brezzo (FR)) [2006/7 h107+: 23g⁵ 24m⁴ c27v² c24v³ c25g* c24g* c25m² Apr 26] leggy gelding: fair hurdler: won conditional jockeys handicap at Musselburgh in November: took well to fences after, winning maiden at Kelso and novice at Carlisle within 5 days in April, latter with something to spare by 2½ lengths from Windy Hills: further improvement when short-head second to American Jennie in valuable handicap at Punchestown, helping force pace and jumping well: stays 27f: unraced on firm ground, acts on any other. *Ferdy Murphy*   c128 + h110

NOISETINE (FR) 9 ch.m. Mansonnien (FR) – Notabilite (FR) (No Pass No Sale) [2006/7 c130, h–: c20g c20s⁶ c21g⁶ Apr 18] good-topped mare: useful handicap chaser at best: below form in 2006/7, off 6 months before final outing: stays 2¾m: has won on good going, best form under more testing conditions (acts on heavy): twice tongue tied: often makes running: inconsistent. *Miss Venetia Williams*   c119 h–

NO KIDDING 13 b.g. Teenoso (USA) – Vaigly Fine (Vaigly Great) [2006/7 c74x, h–: c16m c25mᵖᵘ c16g⁴ c20g⁴ c24d⁶ c27mᵖᵘ Apr 9] strong, lengthy gelding: poor handicap chaser: stays easy 3m: acts on firm and soft going: tried in cheekpieces: often let down by jumping. *G. A. Charlton*   c68 x h–

NOKIMOVER 13 ch.g. Scallywag – Town Blues (Charltown) [2006/7 c24g⁵ Apr 9] rather sparely-made gelding: winning hurdler/chaser: fair pointer nowadays, successful in January/February: stays 3¼m: acts on heavy going, probably on good to firm: has worn cheekpieces. *G. T. H. Bailey*   c– h–

NOLTON TOWN 4 ch.f. Karinga Bay – Out On The Town (Town And Country) [2006/7 F14g F14s Nov 26] small filly: first foal: dam winning pointer: well held in 3-y-o bumpers. *Tim Vaughan*   F–

NOLWENN (FR) 6 b.m. Lute Antique (FR) – Asterie L'Ermitage (FR) (Hamster (FR)) [2006/7 c18g⁴ c16m⁵ c17g⁴ 18sᶠ Feb 15] half-sister to several winners over jumps, including fair hurdler/chaser Idiome (by Djarvis), stays 21f: successful twice on Flat, including over 1½m in October (first start after leaving G. Macaire): maiden hurdler/chaser: left J-M. Robin, rear when fell sixth in handicap hurdle at Kelso: raced mainly around 2m. *S. H. Shirley-Beavan*   c? h–

NOMADIC BLAZE 10 b.g. Nomadic Way (USA) – Dreamago (Sir Mago) [2006/7 c87x, h–: c20sᵖᵘ c19d³ c16v⁵ c20v⁴ c20sᵘʳ c20gᵖᵘ Mar 27] leggy gelding: maiden jumper: should stay beyond 21f: acts on good to firm and heavy going: tried in cheekpieces: tongue tied last 4 starts: tends to make mistakes. *P. G. Atkinson*   c77 x h–

NOMADIC ICE 10 b.g. Nomadic Way (USA) – Icelolly (Idiot's Delight) [2006/7 c20gᶠ Mar 27] angular gelding: won maiden point in March: no form over hurdles/in chases. *Paul Williamson*   c– h–

NOMADIC MOUSE 7 b.g. Nomadic Way (USA) – Cornish Niece VII (Damsire Unregistered) [2006/7 F17g⁶ F17d Aug 21] first foal: dam unraced: poor form on first of 2 starts in bumpers. *Mrs S. Gardner*   F71

NOM DE GUERRE (IRE) 5 b.g. Presenting – Asklynn (IRE) (Beau Sher) [2006/7 F16m³ F16d⁴ F16s³ F16g⁵ Mar 24] €10,000 3-y-o: has scope: first foal: dam, fair hurdler, stayed 2½m: fair form in bumpers, 12½ lengths third to Forest Pennant in maiden at Kempton third start. *B. De Haan*   F94

NOMINATE (GER) 7 b.g. Desert King (IRE) – Northern Goddess (Night Shift (USA)) [2006/7 c88?, h–: c19g² c20m⁴ c21sᵖᵘ c20gᵖᵘ c19m⁵ c20f² c19mᵖᵘ Apr 24] pulled   c99 h–

up only outing over hurdles: fair hunter chaser: stays 2½m: raced mainly on good ground or firmer (acts on firm): has had tongue tied. *S. Flook*

NONA 4 ch.f. Halling (USA) – Zarma (FR) (Machiavellian (USA)) [2006/7 16m⁴ 22vᵖᵘ Feb 28] half-sister to fair hurdler/fairly useful chaser Lankawi (by Unfuwain), stays 25f: little impact on Flat: around 10 lengths fourth to Dubai Around in juvenile at Kelso on hurdling debut: sold out of Jedd O'Keeffe's stable 5,000 gns Doncaster October Sales: beaten long way out given totally different test next time. *S. Dow* **h84**

NONANTAIS (FR) 10 b.g. Nikos – Sanhia (FR) (Sanhedrin (USA)) [2006/7 c–, h127?: c20d² c22sᴿ c25s⁵ c25s⁴ c22s* c22d⁵ Feb 19] good-topped gelding: fairly useful handicap hurdler: fair chaser on balance, won maiden at Towcester in February by ½ length from Triple Mint: stays 25f: acts on heavy going: not a fluent jumper of fences, and seems best on right-handed tracks: not one to rely on. *M. Bradstock* **c103 §** **h–**

NONOTREALLY 6 b.g. Rakaposhi King – Wellwotdouthink (Rymer) [2006/7 h–, F–: 17dᵖᵘ Oct 6] little sign of ability. *B. Mactaggart* **h–**

NOPEKAN (IRE) 7 b.g. Sri Pekan (USA) – Giadamar (IRE) (Be My Guest (USA)) [2006/7 c102, h–: 17dᵖᵘ 16d³ Oct 14] rather leggy, close-coupled gelding: fairly useful hurdler at one time: dropped markedly in class, third in seller at Stratford: novice chaser, fair form at best: should stay beyond 2m: acts on firm and soft going: tongue tied once. *Mrs K. Waldron* **c–** **h83**

NO PICNIC (IRE) 9 ch.g. Be My Native (USA) – Emmagreen (Green Shoon) [2006/7 c94, h–: c25g⁴ c27m c24s² c24s³ c22g⁶ c25s³ c25v³ c25g c31s⁶ Apr 27] small, leggy gelding: winning hurdler: modest maiden chaser: should stay beyond 25f: acts on good to firm and heavy going: tried in cheekpieces. *Mrs S. C. Bradburne* **c91** **h–**

NOQUINA (FR) 6 ch.g. Epervier Bleu – Goquina (FR) (Beyssac (FR)) [2006/7 F16g Apr 3] first foal: dam, French maiden hurdler/chaser, half-sister to dam of useful French chaser up to 29f Lord Carmont: tailed off in bumper on debut. *Paul Murphy* **F–**

NORBORNE BANDIT (IRE) 6 b.g. Croco Rouge (IRE) – Saninka (IRE) (Doyoun) [2006/7 16g⁴ 17f² 16f² 16f² 16m* 16dᵖᵘ Nov 11] compact gelding: fair on Flat (stays 1½m): likewise over hurdles: won 4-runner novice at Tipperary in August: raced around 2m: acts on firm going (ran poorly on good to soft). *Adrian McGuinness, Ireland* **h101**

NO REFUGE (IRE) 7 ch.g. Hernando (FR) – Shamarra (FR) (Zayyani) [2006/7 h152x: 25s⁴ 19d⁴ 25d⁵ Dec 16] good-topped gelding: smart hurdler: not as best in 2006/7, moody effort when well-held fourth to Hardy Eustace in Grade 2 at Ascot second outing: stays 3m: raced on good going or softer (acts on soft): tried in visor/cheekpieces: has got on edge: not a fluent jumper. *J. Howard Johnson* **h139 x**

NO REGRETS (FR) 6 b.g. Nononito (FR) – Betty Royale (FR) (Royal Charter (FR)) [2006/7 21m⁶ Jan 29] good-topped gelding: bumper winner: off 22 months, travelled well long way and not given hard time when 20½ lengths sixth to Air Force One in novice at Ludlow on hurdling debut: should do better. *N. J. Henderson* **h92 p**

NO REMORSE 9 b.g. Alflora (IRE) – G'Ime A Buzz (Electric) [2006/7 17v Feb 20] winning pointer: well held both starts in novice hurdles, left R. Lee and off nearly 2 years in between. *R. Ford* **h–**

NO RETREAT (NZ) 14 b.g. Exattic (USA) – Lerwick (NZ) (Thoreau (USA)) [2006/7 c114, h–: c26g² c24s* c28v³ c25d⁶ c24v² c24v² c29g³ Mar 21] rangy gelding: useful hunter chaser: won at Bangor (for second successive year) in May: left J. Groucott after next outing: won point in April: stays 33f: acts on good to firm and heavy going: sound jumper: tough and reliable. *Ms L. J. Willis* **c114** **h–**

NO REWARD (IRE) 11 b.g. Persian Mews – Tara's Dream (Polar Jinks) [2006/7 c–: c25gᵖᵘ c21g⁴ c21g⁵ Mar 16] winning pointer: modest novice hunter chaser: stays 21f: tried tongue tied. *Mrs D. M. Grissell* **c76**

NORFOLK JIVE (USA) 4 b.g. Atticus (USA) – Derniere Danse (Gay Mecene (USA)) [2006/7 F16m 16s 17g 17gᵖᵘ Apr 23] angular gelding: half-brother to winning chaser Keen To The Last (by Keen), stayed 25f, and fairly useful performer up to 14.8f Kristina (by Kris): dam, French maiden, half-sister to smart French sprinter Divine Danse and very smart sprinter/miler Pursuit of Love: never dangerous in bumper at Ludlow: always behind in 3 starts over hurdles (none too fluent). *M. W. Easterby* **h–** **F71**

NORIOT (FR) 6 ch.g. Chef de Clan (FR) – Falka II (FR) (Mbaiki (FR)) [2006/7 F16v F16f⁶ F16m² F19m⁶ 21m³ 20m⁵ Nov 24] first foal: dam placed up to 2m on Flat in France: modest form in bumpers: better effort over hurdles when 11 lengths third to First Cry in maiden at Sedgefield: will stay 3m. *J. J. Lambe, Ireland* **h78** **F78**

NORMA HILL 6 b.m. Polar Prince (IRE) – Smartie Lee (Dominion) [2006/7 c111, h113: 16m 16f³ 16m⁶ Apr 20] leggy mare: fairly useful hurdler, off 12 months before reappearance: best effort in handicaps in 2006/7 when third of 5 to Tora Petcha at Ludlow: won maiden there on second of 2 outings over fences: raced around 2m: acts on soft and firm going: races up with pace. *R. Hollinshead*
c–
h121

NORMAN BECKETT 4 b.g. Beckett (IRE) – Classic Coral (USA) (Seattle Dancer (USA)) [2006/7 16g⁵ 17v⁶ 16m Apr 25] close-coupled gelding: half-brother to modest hurdler/chaser Lahinch Lad (by Bigstone), stays 25f: fair on Flat (stays 1½m), successful twice in 2006, claimed from I. Semple £12,000 on second occasion: best effort over hurdles when fifth to Impeccable Guest in juvenile at Catterick. *R. T. Phillips*
h101

NORMAN STANLEY 6 ch.g. Karinga Bay – Relatively Easy (Relkino) [2006/7 F18m⁴ F18s⁴ 19d 27v Jan 25] half-brother to 3 winners, including fair hurdler/modest chaser Easibrook Jane (by Alderbrook), stays 21f: dam, fair hurdler/chaser who stayed 3¼m, half-sister to useful 2m to 21f chaser Just Jasmine: fair form when fourth in bumpers at Plumpton: no show in 2 novice hurdles: bred to prove best at 2½m+. *C. L. Tizzard*
h–
F85

NORMINSTER 6 ch.g. Minster Son – Delightfool (Idiot's Delight) [2006/7 h72, F–: 18v⁴ 17s³ 18v c16s⁴ c16g c16s^ur Apr 27] good-topped gelding: poor maiden hurdler: similar form from second of 2 completed outings over fences: should be suited by 2½m+: acts on heavy going. *R. Nixon*
c78
h85

NOR'NOR'EAST (IRE) 9 b.g. Supreme Leader – Force Seven (Strong Gale) [2006/7 h128p: c23d² Oct 18] useful-looking gelding: lightly raced: progressive hurdler in 2005/6, winning 2 of 5 starts: 2½ lengths second to Heltornic in maiden at Worcester on chasing debut, jumping soundly until mistakes when hampered 4 out and 2 out (reportedly sustained leg injury): will stay 3m: raced on ground softer than good (acts on heavy): should improve over fences if recovering from injury. *Jonjo O'Neill*
c115 p
h–

NORSEMAN CATELINE (FR) 6 b.g. Poplar Bluff – Dame Jaune (FR) (Le Nain Jaune (FR)) [2006/7 16d⁵ c17d⁴ c16s² c16d² c16s^F c16d c16v^pu c16s^pu 19g Mar 25] lengthy gelding: novice hurdler: modest maiden chaser: would have won handicap at Wincanton fifth start but for falling 2 out: no form after: possibly best around 2m: raced mainly on good going or softer (acts on soft): visored once: free-going sort (has been early to post/very unruly at start). *M. Scudamore*
c86
h–

NORTELCO (IRE) 4 ch.g. Titus Livius (FR) – Irish Moss (USA) (Irish River (FR)) [2006/7 F14s⁵ F14v 16v^pu 16g 16g Apr 15] sturdy gelding: first foal: dam unraced: better effort in 3-y-o bumpers when fifth to Turbo Linn at Carlisle: no form over hurdles. *Micky Hammond*
h–
F78

NORTHAW LAD (IRE) 9 ch.g. Executive Perk – Black Tulip (Pals Passage) [2006/7 h106: 20m* 20v³ May 25] sturdy gelding: fair hurdler: easily won claimer at Fontwell (claimed from C. Tinkler £9,000) in May: stays 2½m: acts on good to firm and heavy going. *D. Carroll*
h97

NORTHERN ECHO 10 b.g. Pursuit of Love – Stop Press (USA) (Sharpen Up) [2006/7 c–§, h71§: c20d^pu c16g 24f^pu Jul 16] compact gelding: poor hurdler: no form over fences: stays 21f: acts on firm and good to soft going: wears headgear: has had tongue tied: ungenuine. *K. S. Thomas*
c– §
h– §

NORTHERN ENDEAVOUR 8 b.g. Alflora (IRE) – Northern Jinks (Piaffer (USA)) [2006/7 h–, F83: 24s^pu 22m⁵ 24m^pu c25s⁴ Dec 12] in frame in bumpers: no solid form in novice hurdles/handicap chase. *Simon Earle*
c–
h–

NORTHERN FLASH 13 b.g. Rambo Dancer (CAN) – Spinster (Grundy) [2006/7 c63, h61: c16s⁶ 17d³ c16m⁶ c16f³ c16m c18v⁵ 17s c16g⁶ c16g c16v^pu Jan 3] workmanlike gelding: poor chaser/maiden hurdler: best around 2m: acts on firm and soft going, below form on heavy: wears headgear: has had tongue tied. *J. C. Haynes*
c84 ?
h63

NORTHERN GAMBLE (IRE) 6 b.m. Synefos (USA) – Rose-Lee (IRE) (Cataldi) [2006/7 F16d F16g Oct 30] second foal: dam, lightly-raced maiden pointer, out of half-sister to useful 2m hurdler The Gatherer: no show in bumpers/maiden point. *J. G. M. O'Shea*
F–

NORTHERN LAD (IRE) 5 ch.g. Lord of Appeal – Deep Green (Deep Run) [2006/7 F16g³ Nov 2] smallish, good-bodied gelding: half-brother to several winners, including fairly useful hurdler Nickel Sun (by Phardante), stayed 2¾m, and fair staying chaser King's Whisper (by Rakaposhi King's Ride): dam lightly-raced maiden: looked green when 6¾ lengths third to Harrowman in bumper at Haydock on debut, keeping on well from rear despite hanging markedly: should improve for experience. *N. G. Richards*
F95 p

NORTHERN LINK (IRE) 8 b.g. Distinctly North (USA) – Miss Eurolink (Touching Wood (USA)) [2006/7 h78: 22m 20m* 20m* Jun 28] poor hurdler: won novice handicap at Fontwell in June: lame next time: stays 2½m: acts on good to firm going. *Miss Tor Sturgis* **h84**

NORTHERN MADRIK (FR) 6 b. or br.g. Useful (FR) – Belle Des Belles (FR) (Goldneyev (USA)) [2006/7 16d 17m 17g 22m^pu Oct 4] compact gelding: no form: tried tongue tied. *D. E. Pipe* **h–**

NORTHERN QUEST (IRE) 6 ch.g. Un Desperado (FR) – Strong Heather (IRE) (Strong Gale) [2006/7 h–, F–: 20d^6 16s^F 20s^pu 17s^3 16v^3 17d^5 17s Mar 13] lengthy, workmanlike gelding: poor maiden hurdler: best form around 2m: acts on heavy going. *H. P. Hogarth* **h68**

NORTHERN REVOQUE (IRE) 5 b.m. Revoque (IRE) – Delia (IRE) (Darshaan) [2006/7 20m^5 Apr 15] poor maiden at 2 yrs for A. Berry: well-held fifth in mares maiden at Worcester on hurdling debut, taking good hold. *J. P. L. Ewart* **h67**

NORTHERNSAIL (IRE) 5 b.g. Indian Lodge (IRE) – Folk Riviera (IRE) (Shareef Dancer (USA)) [2006/7 F17d F17s F16m^4 F16m^4 Apr 9] medium-sized gelding: first foal: dam 7.5f winner in Italy: poor form last 2 starts in bumpers, in cheekpieces final one. *Miss J. E. Foster* **F70**

NORTHERN SEREN 6 b.m. Bob's Return (IRE) – Northern Jinks (Piaffer (USA)) [2006/7 aF16g^ur F16g^4 F16g Apr 7] good-topped mare: fourth foal: dam, fair hurdler/fairly useful chaser, stayed 21f: best effort in bumpers (jinked and unseated rider at start on debut) when close fourth to King of The Jungle at Huntingdon: will be suited by 2½m+. *Simon Earle* **F86**

NORTHERN STARS (IRE) 6 b.g. Fourstars Allstar (USA) – Corun Girl (Apollo Eight) [2006/7 F–: F16g 20s^pu 25s^pu 20g 20m Apr 9] big, good-topped gelding: no form in bumpers/novice hurdles: tongue tied last 3 starts. *H. P. Hogarth* **h– F–**

NORTHERN VIC (IRE) 6 ch.g. Old Vic – Myra Gaye (Buckskin (FR)) [2006/7 F16g^4 F17s F16g 20d 24v 17g Mar 24] €70,000 4-y-o: strong gelding: half-brother to several winners, notably fairly useful hurdler/useful chaser Afistfullofdollars (by Be My Native), stays 3m: dam unraced out of half-sister to Gaye Brief and Gaye Chance: best effort in bumpers when fourth to Arctic Ghost at Uttoxeter: well held in novice hurdles: likely to prove best at 2½m+. *H. P. Hogarth* **h77 F79**

NORTH ISLAND (IRE) 5 b. or br.g. New Frontier (IRE) – Port-O-Call (Import) [2006/7 19g 16v 20g^6 21g^2 Apr 23] half-brother to useful hurdler Prince Ole (by Montelimar), stayed 3m, and fairly useful hurdler around 2m Home Port (by Digamist): dam of no account: easily best effort in novice hurdles when 1½ lengths second to That's Rhythm at Sedgefield, hanging left under pressure. *J. Howard Johnson* **h88**

NORTH LANDING (IRE) 7 b.g. Storm Bird (CAN) – Tirol Hope (IRE) (Tirol) [2006/7 h99: 20m* 16g 22d^5 21m^5 22m 20m^4 c20g^ur c21f^R 21m Aug 29] compact gelding: modest handicap hurdler: won at Hexham in May: lame final outing: failed to complete both starts over fences: stays 2½m: acts on soft going: tried in cheekpieces: unreliable. *R. C. Guest* **c– § h98 §**

NORTHORSOUTH (IRE) 5 b.g. Polar Prince (IRE) – What The Devil (Devil To Play) [2006/7 F16d Nov 11] first foal: dam poor form in bumpers/over hurdles: tailed off in bumper on debut. *C. W. Moore* **F–**

NORTH WALK (IRE) 4 b.g. Monashee Mountain (USA) – Celtic Link (IRE) (Toca Madera) [2006/7 16v 16m 17v^3 17m Mar 29] good-topped gelding: fairly useful on Flat (stays 8.6f), claimed from K. Ryan £12,000 in December: easily best effort over hurdles when 19½ lengths third to John Forbes in novice at Sedgefield: free-going sort. *Jennie Candlish* **h92**

NORTON SAPPHIRE 8 ch.m. Karinga Bay – Sea of Pearls (IRE) (King's Ride) [2006/7 h73+: 17s* 22s^2 17s^2 21v* 24s^3 22s* 22g^2 21g^6 Apr 19] smallish mare: fairly useful handicap hurdler: progressed markedly since leaving M. Gingell, winning at Exeter in November, Huntingdon (conditional jockeys) in January and Wincanton (beat Petit Lord a neck, pair clear) in February: at least respectable efforts last 2 starts, raced close up when sixth of 18 to Silver Charmer in well-run listed mares event at Cheltenham: stays 3m: acts on any going: tough and genuine. *V. R. A. Dartnall* **h117**

NORTONTHORPE LAD (IRE) 5 b.g. Charnwood Forest (IRE) – Tisima (FR) (Selkirk (USA)) [2006/7 F17v^4 F17s* F16s^4 19g 19g 16v^2 17d Mar 19] tall, good-bodied gelding: fourth foal: half-brother to 6f/1m winner Queen Charlotte (by Tagula): dam, **h75 F91**

lightly-raced maiden, likely to have proved best up to 1m: fair form in bumpers, won at Sedgefield in October: form over hurdles only when second to Top Dressing in novice at Newcastle. *M. W. Easterby*

NORWICH COUNTY (IRE) 8 br.g. Norwich – Ash Dame (IRE) (Strong Gale)   h–
[2006/7 16g 16d 16s Jan 20] big, rangy gelding: third foal: brother to fair hurdler/chaser Gaelic Flight, stays 3m, and half-brother to fair hurdler/fairly useful chaser up to 25f Mystic Lord (by Roselier): dam winning pointer: won maiden Irish point on debut in 2005: bought 28,000 gns Doncaster May (2005) Sales: well beaten in novice hurdles: bred to be suited by 2½m+. *J. A. B. Old*

NOSCAR (FR) 6 ch.g. Ragmar (FR) – Perle de Saisy (FR) (Italic (FR)) [2006/7 F–:   h–
F18g 19m^{pu} Jun 19] no show in bumpers/novice hurdle. *B. G. Powell*   F–

NO SHENANIGANS (IRE) 10 b.g. King's Ride – Melarka (Dara Monarch) [2006/7   c92
c21v^3 Mar 9] strong, good sort: bumper winner: fair form at best over fences, lightly raced: sold out of N. Henderson's stable 4,400 gns Doncaster May (2005) Sales: jumped right/ponderously throughout when last of 3 finishers on hunter debut at Ayr: stays 19f: acts on good to firm and good to soft going. *Jamie Alexander*

NO SIGNAL 5 b.g. Tragic Role (USA) – Run Lady Run (General Ironside) [2006/7   F75
F16m Apr 24] half-brother to winning pointer by Roselier: dam placed in points: ninth of 15 in maiden bumper at Towcester on debut. *J. Gallagher*

NOSLER (IRE) 5 ch.g. Anshan – Tricias Pride (IRE) (Broken Hearted) [2006/7 F16d^2 F106
Feb 1] rather unfurnished gelding: first foal: dam, fair hurdler who stayed 3m, half-sister to useful 2m hurdler Unarmed: length second of 17 to Bertie May in bumper at Wincanton on debut, leading over 2f out. *P. F. Nicholls*

NOSTRA (FR) 6 br.m. Limnos (JPN) – La Giudecca (FR) (R B Chesne) [2006/7 c97,   c–
h?: 16g May 14] leggy, angular mare: winning hurdler/chaser in France: little impact in 3   h–
starts in Britain: raced mainly around 2m: acts on heavy ground. *D. E. Pipe*

NOSTRINGSATTACHED (IRE) 6 b.g. Un Desperado (FR) – Site Mistress (IRE)   c– p
(Remainder Man) [2006/7 16g^6 16s 16d c19g^{ur} Apr 11] 25,000 4-y-o: useful-looking   h78 p
gelding: has scope: third foal: half-brother to 2½m hurdle winner Manesbil (by Fourstars Allstar): dam lightly-raced half-sister to useful staying chaser Streamstown: not knocked about all 3 starts in maiden hurdles: blundered and unseated seventh in novice handicap on chasing debut: will be suited by further than 2m: remains open to improvement. *Jonjo O'Neill*

NOT AMUSED (UAE) 7 ch.g. Indian Ridge – Amusing Time (IRE) (Sadler's Wells   c–
(USA)) [2006/7 h78: c20m^{pu} 20m^4 Aug 1] sturdy gelding: poor novice hurdler: no show   h78
in hunter on chasing debut (only start for R. Hodges): stays easy 2½m: acts on good to firm going: blinkered/visored last 6 starts: attitude under suspicion. *Ian Williams*

NOTANOTHERDONKEY (IRE) 7 b.g. Zaffaran (USA) – Sporting Talent (IRE)   c104
(Seymour Hicks (FR)) [2006/7 c96, h87: c20s* c23d^2 c24v^3 c28g^5 c24g Mar 30] tall,   h–
lengthy gelding: maiden hurdler: fair chaser: best effort when winning novice handicap at Cheltenham in October: ran poorly last 3 starts (bled final one): should stay 3m: acts on soft going (bumper form on good to firm). *M. Scudamore*

NOTAPROBLEM (IRE) 8 b.g. Oscar (IRE) – Smashed Free (IRE) (Carlingford   c85
Castle) [2006/7 h100: c16d c20s^6 c29s^3 c24s^F 25g^3 26g^6 26m^2 27s^6 Apr 27] sturdy geld-   h103
ing: fair handicap hurdler: best effort over fences when third to Celtic Flow in handicap at Wetherby: seems to stay 29f: unraced on firm going, acts on any other. *G. A. Harker*

NOT A TRACE (IRE) 8 b.g. Gothland (FR) – Copmenow (IRE) (Mandalus) [2006/7   c85
c88, h78: c24s^{pu} c20m c20m^5 c20g c16s^5 Apr 27] tall, close-coupled gelding: maiden   h–
hurdler: modest novice chaser: stays 3m: acts on soft and good to firm going, below form on heavy: visored/blinkered nowadays. *Mrs S. C. Bradburne*

NO TELLING (IRE) 5 b.g. Supreme Leader – Kissantell (IRE) (Broken Hearted)   F82 +
[2006/7 F17d^5 Feb 19] strong, good-topped gelding: second foal: dam once-raced half-sister to useful chaser Sam Vaughan, stayed 2½m: better for race, 28 lengths fifth to impressive Theatrical Moment in bumper at Market Rasen on debut. *B. N. Pollock*

NOT FOR DIAMONDS (IRE) 7 b.g. Arctic Lord – Black-Crash (Crash Course)   h94
[2006/7 h75, F95: 16m 17s 22d^3 22s^3 22s^6 26g* 26g^4 Apr 20] workmanlike gelding: modest hurdler: won conditional jockeys novice handicap at Hereford in April: stays 3¼m: acts on soft ground. *J. W. Mullins*

NOTIN HAPENED (IRE) 7 ch.g. Germany (USA) – Rathreigh More (IRE) (Long   c–
Pond) [2006/7 21g^{pu} 20v 24s^{pu} 24v^{pu} c19s^{pu} Mar 12] strong, workmanlike gelding: fifth   h–

foal: dam unraced: won maiden Irish point in 2006: no form over hurdles/on chasing debut. *A. E. Jones*

NOT LEFT YET (IRE) 6 b. or br.g. Old Vic – Dalus Dawn (Mandalus) [2006/7 h121: c20d* c33g^F Mar 15] tall, good-topped gelding: has scope: fairly useful handicap hurdler: favourite, won maiden at Carlisle in October on chasing debut by 6 lengths from No Guarantees: couple of mistakes but still travelling well when falling 3 out in National Hunt Chase (Amateurs) at Cheltenham won by Butler's Cabin 5 months later: stays 2¾m: acts on good to soft going: visored final 2005/6 outing: probably remains capable of better over fences. *D. E. Pipe* — **c125 p h–**

NOTRE CYBORG (FR) 6 ch.g. Cyborg (FR) – Cate Bleue (FR) (Katowice (FR)) [2006/7 F95: 17g^F 19g 16d^F 16m 20g³ Mar 27] leggy, close-coupled gelding: bumper winner for P. Nicholls: poor form over hurdles (has been let down by jumping). *D. McCain Jnr* — **h84 x**

NOTRE PERE (FR) 6 b.g. Kadalko (FR) – Gloria IV (FR) (Video Rock (FR)) [2006/7 F16s² F16v² F16v² F20v* 16v* 20v³ 23v³ Mar 24] big gelding: has scope: second foal: dam, unbeaten in 12 non-thoroughbred events up to 1½m on Flat in France, sister to useful 2m hurdler Osana: fairly useful in bumpers, runner-up 3 times prior to winning at Leopardstown in December by 1½ lengths from Mick The Man: favourite, successful in 28-runner maiden at Navan in February on hurdling debut, beating Guess easily by 10 lengths: better form when third in novices won by Kazal at Naas (Grade 2) and Tailor's Hall at Navan: will stay beyond 23f: raced on soft/heavy ground. *J. T. R. Dreaper, Ireland* — **h122 F102**

NOUGAT DE L'ISLE (FR) 6 b.g. Kadalko (FR) – Ceres de L'Isle (FR) (Bad Conduct (USA)) [2006/7 F91: F16d 20v⁵ 19d³ 22s² 22d⁴ 22g* Mar 19] tall gelding: fair form in bumpers: likewise in novice hurdles, winning steadily-run event at Wincanton by 5 lengths from Nudge And Nurdle, dictating: will stay 3m: acts on soft going: hasn't always convinced with attitude. *C. L. Tizzard* — **h113 F74**

NOUN DE LA THINTE (FR) 6 b.m. Oblat (FR) – Belis de La Thinte (FR) (Marasali) [2006/7 h95: 21d^{pu} May 15] ex-French mare: novice hurdler, form in Britain only when equal-second in mares event at Fontwell in 2005/6: should stay 2½m. *Miss Venetia Williams* — **h–**

NOUNOU 6 b.g. Starborough – Watheeqah (USA) (Topsider (USA)) [2006/7 16d⁴ 17d* 17g⁵ 20m⁴ 20g* 20d³ Oct 7] smallish gelding: fair hurdler, left D. Daly and off nearly a year before return: won maiden at Cartmel in May and novice at Uttoxeter in September: stays 2½m: acts on good to soft and good to firm going. *Miss J. E. Foster* — **h108**

NOUS VOILA (FR) 6 b.g. Video Rock (FR) – Ability (FR) (Olmeto) [2006/7 h137: c16g² Oct 30] smallish, close-coupled gelding: useful hurdler: encouraging chasing debut when 3 lengths second to Howle Hill in novice at Warwick: stays 2½m: acts on heavy going: looked sure to progress over fences but not seen out again. *D. E. Pipe* — **c120 p h–**

NOUVEAU MAIRE (FR) 6 b.g. Ragmar (FR) – Countess Fellow (FR) (Italic (FR)) [2006/7 18s 18s⁶ c20s^{pu} c20s³ c20s^{pu} c19s* c21v^{pu} c21s⁶ c21v^F c23s^{pu} Apr 22] workmanlike gelding: fifth foal: half-brother to 1½m winner Honoria (by Luchiroverte): dam unraced sister to The Fellow and Al Capone II: 17f winner on Flat: twice-raced over hurdles: fair chaser: won 5-y-o event at Enghien in December: stiff task when pulled up in novice handicap at Cheltenham following month: stays 21f: raced on soft/heavy going. *F. Doumen, France* — **c109 h97**

NOVACELLA (FR) 6 b.m. Beyssac (FR) – Une Risette (FR) (Air du Nord (USA)) [2006/7 h102: c20g³ c20g² c16d³ Nov 26] rather leggy mare: fair hurdler: has failed to convince with jumping and only modest form over fences: will stay beyond 21f: acts on soft and good to firm going. *R. H. Alner* — **c85 h–**

NOVEL IDEA (IRE) 9 ch.g. Phardante (FR) – Novelist (Quayside) [2006/7 c25g^{ur} May 24] workmanlike gelding: maiden hurdler: let down by jumping in chases: won point in April: tried blinkered. *R. Michael Smith* — **c– h–**

NOVESIA 6 ch.m. The West (USA) – Alvecote Lady (Touching Wood (USA)) [2006/7 F16s F14s 16g^{pu} Mar 21] workmanlike mare: half-sister to winning hurdler Tsunami and winning chaser Fight The Feeling (both by Beveled), both of whom stay 2½m: dam won 1½m seller: no sign of ability. *C. J. Drewe* — **h– F–**

NOVICIATE (IRE) 7 b.g. Bishop of Cashel – Red Salute (Soviet Star (USA)) [2006/7 h–: 16m 16f⁶ 16m^{pu} Jul 26] sturdy gelding: no form in bumpers/over hurdles. *Simon Earle* — **h–**

NO VISIBILITY (IRE) 12 b.g. Glacial Storm (USA) – Duhallow Lady (IRE) (Torus) [2006/7 c120, h–: c19s^{pu} c19s c16s³ c19s c22s⁴ Feb 18] big, useful-looking gelding: fairly useful handicap chaser, below form in 2006/7: stays 21f: acts on heavy and good to firm going: tried tongue tied. *R. H. Alner* **c104 h–**

NOWA HUTA (FR) 6 b.m. Passing Sale (FR) – Saperlipopette II (FR) (Prove It Baby (USA)) [2006/7 h84: 22d 16g 17m⁶ 16f^{pu} Jul 19] leggy mare: maiden hurdler: tried in cheekpieces. *Jedd O'Keeffe* **h–**

NOW AND AGAIN 8 b.g. Shaamit (IRE) – Sweet Allegiance (Alleging (USA)) [2006/7 h78: c21g^{pu} Apr 9] poor maiden hurdler: has failed to complete in points/hunter chase. *Mrs S. J. Stilgoe* **c– h–**

NO WAY BACK (IRE) 7 b.g. Eve's Error – Janeyway (Bulldozer) [2006/7 h111+: 24m^{pu} c23d³ c20g⁴ c19g³ c20m⁴ Apr 22] tall gelding: fair hurdler, much improved when successful in handicap final 2005/6 outing: similar form over fences: best form around 2½m: acts on firm ground: tried tongue tied: has found little. *Miss E. C. Lavelle* **c113 h–**

NOW LYN 5 b.g. Awesome – Reigning Royal (Tina's Pet) [2006/7 F17v F14s F13m 20g 22m^{pu} Apr 22] fourth foal: dam poor maiden hurdler around 2m: little impact in bumpers/over hurdles. *D. Burchell* **h– F–**

NOW THEN AUNTIE (IRE) 6 gr.m. Anshan – Tara's Lady (General Ironside) [2006/7 c–, h78, F71: c26d^{pu} c20m⁵ Jun 3] poor maiden hurdler: seemingly similar form on completed start over fences: tried in cheekpieces. *Mrs S. A. Watt* **c74 ? h–**

NOW THEN KATIE 5 b.m. Kayf Tara – Nativus (IRE) (Be My Native (USA)) [2006/7 F71: F16f 17d⁵ Oct 25] smallish, workmanlike mare: well held in bumpers/novice hurdle. *C. Grant* **h– F64**

NOW THEN SID 8 ch.g. Presidium – Callace (Royal Palace) [2006/7 c95, h–: c25f² c25m³ c20m² c20g⁵ c21f⁶ c27m² Aug 29] leggy, lightly-made gelding: modest handicap chaser: stays 27f: acts on firm and good to soft going: in cheekpieces last 2 starts. *Mrs S. A. Watt* **c95 h–**

NOZIC (FR) 6 b.g. Port Lyautey (FR) – Grizilh (FR) (Spoleto) [2006/7 c18g* c20s⁵ c20s* c19s² c21v² c19v* c22v* c20s² Mar 3] **c157 h–**

Once a horse starts improving by leaps and bounds, there's no telling where its development will end. Every season has its share of horses who rise significantly through the ranks before the handicapper finally gets their measure. Sometimes even those closest to an improving horse can be taken by surprise by its rate of progress. The ex-French six-year-old chaser Nozic came into that category in the latest season. He made his British debut in late-December, running in a handicap at Chepstow from a BHB mark of 125, but by the spring he was among his stable's top half-dozen chasers. On the day of his final start at Newbury in early-March, Nozic's progress was the subject of his trainer's highly informative Saturday column in the *Racing Post*. Nicholls remained unconvinced that he had improved by the amount his latest BHB mark, 153, implied. 'Nozic doesn't look like a 150-plus chaser to me,' stated the trainer. 'Check out his big-race entries at Cheltenham; he hasn't got any.'

Nozic had been put up 15 lb prior to Newbury, leading to his trainer calling for a limit on the amount a horse should be raised. 'Is it right to give these horses such an enormous increase in their rating?' asked Nicholls, whose gripe admittedly wasn't restricted solely to horses he trained. The trainer got his answer when Nozic went down only by a neck to Madison du Berlais in the valuable vccasino.com Gold Cup. The result suggested the BHB handicapper had him about right (Nozic actually ended up on 157 in the Anglo-Irish Jump Classifications). The handicapper's responsibility is to ensure competitive racing; treating wide-margin and/or easy winners with leniency simply because they are young horses isn't the way to achieve that. If the perception is that young horses are being 'over-handicapped', as Nicholls implied, it is simply because younger horses are more likely to be improving rapidly, and able to keep a step or two ahead of the handicapper for that much longer.

Nozic was beaten on his first two starts in Britain, finishing second to Nadover at Chepstow—when Madison du Berlais was fifteen lengths behind him in fourth off terms 12 lb worse than at Newbury—and then to Too Forward in a more valuable listed contest at Cheltenham just five days later. He went down by half a length at Chepstow, an effort which may have taken the edge off him for Cheltenham (where a bad mistake at the tenth also didn't help). It was a different story when Nozic returned from a six-week break for a £15,000 handicap back at Chepstow in February. Clearly travelling best some way out, Nozic was able to win, eased down, by twelve lengths from top weight Kalca Mome. Better still was to come just two days later under a penalty in exceptionally testing conditions at Uttoxeter. Despite more than £31,000 being on offer, the totesport.com Lord Gyllene Handicap Chase attracted a less competitive field (nine ran) than might have been expected for the money, the heavy ground presumably a factor in this. With main market rivals Idole First and Good Citizen failing to give their running, Nozic ran out an easy winner again in the style of a highly progressive chaser, going clear on the bridle three out. Not halted by a mistake there, he stretched ahead on the run-in to win by thirteen lengths from the eleven-year-old Keepatem. Sam Thomas had been on board at Chepstow, his double that day contributing to a career-best tally of seventy-three wins as he enjoyed a successful first season as second jockey to Ruby Walsh at the Nicholls stable. With Messrs Walsh and Thomas claimed elsewhere, former stable jockey Joe Tizzard stepped in at Uttoxeter to claim his only winner for Nicholls in 2006/7. Walsh was back in the plate at Newbury, where Nozic's second to Madison du Berlais represented more improvement (the first two finished eight lengths clear). Nozic may be able to progress a little more yet.

		Shirley Heights (b 1975)	Mill Reef
	Port Lyautey (FR) (b 1985)		Hardiemma
		Sierra Morena (ch 1973)	Canisbay
Nozic (FR) (b.g. 2001)			Saigon
		Spoleto (b 1978)	Nonoalco
	Grizilh (FR) (b 1994)		Antrona
		Azurea (b 1988)	On My Way
			Orpheline V

Nozic began his career in France with Guillaume Macaire and, whilst not showing anything out of the ordinary in his early days when kept largely to the

totesport.com Lord Gyllene Handicap Chase, Uttoxeter—
a second valuable prize within 48 hours for Nozic (No.2)

Provincial tracks, he established a remarkably consistent record which he has maintained so far in Britain, finishing out of the first two only once (from thirteen starts) in his career. He made a successful debut over hurdles as a four-year-old but was soon switched to fences, winning at Compiegne and Angers later that year. He won twice more over fences for Macaire in the autumn of the latest season, at Craon and then at Auteuil where he won a non-thoroughbred contest restricted to five-year-olds. Nozic's sire Port Lyautey was a smart French mile-and-a-half performer considered good enough to contest the Irish Derby, and a half-brother to a high-class filly at the same trip, Sierra Roberta, who was beaten a head in the 1989 Breeders' Cup Turf. Port Lyautey is also closely related to Barton's sire Port Etienne and a half-brother to Morespeed, the sire of Le Sauvignon, the top-class Grande Course de Haies winner whom Paul Nicholls trained in a brief and ill-fated novice chase campaign. Nozic is the first foal out of his dam Grizilh who was placed several times at up to around a mile and a half on the Flat in non-thoroughbred races but failed to win. Grandam Azurea was unraced and bred only three foals in total, but the two others are winners, much the better of them being Juveigneur who was better than ever in staying chases in the latest season, though his sole win of 2006/7 came in a Plumpton novice hurdle. The rather leggy Nozic is yet to race over as far as three miles but will stay that trip, and he acts on heavy ground. He was tongue tied for his last four starts. There may be more to come from Nozic in valuable handicaps, but, with his form verging on high class, he'll be worth his place in better company still. All being well, he surely won't be left out in the next season when Cheltenham Festival entries are being made. *P. F. Nicholls*

NUDGE AND NURDLE (IRE) 6 b.g. Shernazar – Firey Comet (IRE) (Buckskin (FR)) [2006/7 h73: 16d³ 21sˢᵘ 21g² 21v 24s 21s* 23s³ 22g² 24g⁶ Apr 18] tall, angular gelding: fair novice hurdler: won handicap at Kempton (by 19 lengths) in February: stays 3m: raced on good ground or softer. *N. A. Twiston-Davies*   **h114**

NUIT SOMBRE (IRE) 7 b.g. Night Shift (USA) – Belair Princess (USA) (Mr Prospector (USA)) [2006/7 c–, h104: 17mᵖᵘ c18m³ c16f⁴ c16m c16d⁵ Nov 1] compact gelding: fair hurdler at best, out of sorts since early-2005/6: best effort over fences (modest form) on second start: seems best around 2m: acts on good to firm and good to soft going, probably on soft: tried in cheekpieces: has hinted at temperament. *J. G. M. O'Shea*   **c91**
h–

NUITS ST GEORGE (IRE) 6 b.g. Zaffaran (USA) – Hollygrove Supreme (IRE) (Supreme Leader) [2006/7 20vᵖᵘ Jan 20] big, workmanlike gelding: first foal: dam, unraced half-sister to progressive hurdler Albertas Run, out of half-sister to top-class hurdler up to 3m Mister Morose: no show in novice hurdle on debut. *G. Brown*   **h–**

NUMBERSIXVALVERDE (IRE) 11 b.g. Broken Hearted – Queens Tricks (Le Bavard (FR)) [2006/7 c153, h118: 24v⁴ 24s c25v⁴ c36g⁶ Apr 14] lengthy gelding: fairly useful handicap hurdler, shaped with promise first 2 starts: smart handicap chaser: improved form when winning John Smith's Grand National at Aintree in 2005/6: insufficient emphasis on stamina and 3 mistakes when well-held sixth to Silver Birch in latest renewal of race: suited by thorough test of stamina: seems best on soft/heavy going: tried in cheekpieces/blinkers in 2004: held up: usually sound jumper. *Martin Brassil, Ireland*   **c134 +**
h111

NUMERO UN DE SOLZEN (FR) 6 b.g. Passing Sale (FR) – Tiffany's (FR) (Chamberlin (FR)) [2006/7 h106: c24s² c24d* c22s³ c32v³ c24v² Mar 18] good-topped gelding: winning hurdler: fairly useful chaser: presented with novice at Newcastle in January when Cloudy Lane blundered last: creditable third in handicaps at Kelso next 2 starts, beaten 5¼ lengths by Bellaney Jewel in valuable event on second occasion: stays 4m: raced on going softer than good (acts on heavy). *J. P. L. Ewart*   **c122**
h–

NUTCRACKER LAD (IRE) 9 ch.g. Duky – Allercashin Moon (IRE) (Callernish) [2006/7 20d⁶ Nov 14] small, sturdy gelding: winning hurdler, lightly raced and no form since 2003/4: has worn visor/cheekpieces. *Mrs A. V. Roberts*   **h–**

NUTLEY QUEEN (IRE) 8 b.m. Eagle Eyed (USA) – Secret Hideaway (USA) (Key To The Mint (USA)) [2006/7 h63: 17mᵖᵘ 16f⁶ 16mᵖᵘ Aug 3] compact mare: maiden hurdler, no show in 2006/7: usually tongue tied. *M. Appleby*   **h–**

NUZZLE 7 b.m. Salse (USA) – Lena (USA) (Woodman (USA)) [2006/7 h74: 16sᵖᵘ 16f⁵ 16m* 18g 18vᶠ Dec 3] poor hurdler: won conditional jockeys selling handicap at Uttoxeter in July: raced around 2m: acts on firm and soft going: sold 5,800 gns Doncaster January Sales. *N. G. Richards*   **h81**

Faucets For Mira Showers Silver Trophy Chase (Limited Handicap), Cheltenham—
Nycteos' jumping holds up better in this small field as he dictates throughout

NYBORG MADRIK (FR) 6 b.g. Cyborg (FR) – Little Blue (FR) (Reve Bleu (FR))   c–
[2006/7 24d c19s^F 16v^{pu} Jan 6] close-coupled ex-French gelding: won juvenile hurdle at   h–
Enghien in 2004/5: left G. Cherel, little impact in handicaps in Britain: placed 3
completed outings over fences, all at Auteuil: should stay beyond 2½m. *D. E. Pipe*

NYCTEOS (FR) 6 ch.g. Chamberlin (FR) – Cynthia (FR) (Mont Basile (FR)) [2006/7   c139
c130, h121: 21s^6 c21g c21g* Apr 18] tall, useful-looking gelding: fairly useful hurdler: h121
useful chaser: best effort when winning steadily-run Grade 2 Faucets For Mira Showers
Silver Trophy Chase (Limited Handicap) at Cheltenham in April by 3 lengths from Too
Forward, idling run-in: stays 21f: raced on good ground or softer: let down by jumping
second start. *P. F. Nicholls*

NYKEL (FR) 6 ch.g. Brier Creek (USA) – Une du Chatelier (FR) (Quart de Vin (FR))   c115
[2006/7 c100, h–: c25g* c25s^{pu} c24s^3 Mar 3] lengthy gelding: once-raced over hurdles: h–
fairly useful handicap chaser: off 8 months (reportedly hobdayed), much improved when
winning at Wincanton (by 3½ lengths from Le Jaguar) in December: stays 25f: acts on
soft going. *A. King*

NYRCHE (FR) 7 b.g. Medaaly – Thoiry (USA) (Sagace (FR)) [2006/7 c151, h–: c20s^4 c–
c16d c17d^{ur} Nov 18] leggy gelding: winning hurdler: smart chaser, well beaten completed   h–
starts in handicaps in 2006/7: best at 2m: has won on heavy going, better form under less
testing conditions (acts on good to firm): usually makes running: jumps well. *A. King*

O

OAKAPPLE DIAMOND (IRE) 4 b.f. Bob's Return (IRE) – Royal Nora (IRE)   F75
(Dromod Hill) [2006/7 F16d^5 F16m F17m Apr 15] €7,000 3-y-o: fifth foal: half-sister
to one-time fairly useful chaser Imperial Dream (by Roselier), stays 25f: dam unraced
half-sister to Cheltenham Gold Cup winner Imperial Call: form (modest) in mares
bumpers only on debut. *G. A. Harker*

OAKAPPLE EXPRESS 7 b.g. Alflora (IRE) – Royal Scarlet (Royal Fountain)   h–
[2006/7 F104: 25g^{pu} Apr 16] tall, close-coupled gelding: fairly useful form in bumpers:
off 14 months, possibly amiss on hurdling debut: should stay beyond 2m. *G. A. Harker*

OAKAPPLE PRINCESS (IRE) 6 b.m. Alderbrook – Timeless Rose (Bulldozer)   F–
[2006/7 F17d F16d Dec 14] €20,000 4-y-o: unfurnished mare: half-sister to winning

hurdler/fairly useful chaser Rose Perk (by Executive Perk), stayed 3m: dam unraced: well held in bumpers. *G. A. Harker*

OAKENDALE (IRE) 9 ch.g. Presenting – Quival (USA) (Val de L'Orne (FR)) [2006/7 20g⁵ 22mᵖᵘ Jul 20] successful both starts in points in Ireland in 2005: runner-up in minor event on first of 2 outings in chases: left M. Holden, poor form on hurdling debut: went amiss next time: stays 2¾m. *M. Todhunter* c– h84

OAKFIELD LEGEND 6 b.g. Midnight Legend – Kins Token (Relkino) [2006/7 h78, F–: c23g* c20mᵖᵘ c23m⁶ c20f⁴ c21g c23d² c25sF Oct 22] maiden hurdler: modest chaser: 33/1, won maiden at Worcester in May: stays 23f: acts on good to firm and good to soft going: free-going sort. *P. S. Payne* c91 h–

OAKLANDS LUIS 8 b.g. Primitive Rising (USA) – Bally Small (Sunyboy) [2006/7 c25s⁶ Mar 7] winning pointer: soundly beaten in novice hunter. *R. G. Russ* c–

OAKLANDS TED 9 b.g. Royal Fountain – Brig's Gazelle (Lord Nelson (FR)) [2006/7 c25m May 6] modest pointer: well beaten in maiden hunter. *R. G. Russ* c–

OASIS BANUS (IRE) 6 b.g. Shaamit (IRE) – Summit Else (El Conquistador) [2006/7 h64: 20s Sep 20] good-topped gelding: poor maiden hurdler: should be suited by 2½m+: has worn cheekpieces: sold 1,800 gns Doncaster October Sales, resold 900 gns Doncaster January Sales. *P. Monteith* h–

OASIS BLUE (IRE) 6 gr.g. Norwich – Mini Fashion (IRE) (Roselier (FR)) [2006/7 h69: 20sᵖᵘ Feb 16] rather leggy gelding: maiden hurdler, poor form at best: sold out of M. Pipe's stable 2,500 gns Doncaster May Sales: should be suited by 2½m+: sold 1,200 gns Doncaster March Sales. *Mrs A. M. Naughton* h–

OBAKI DE GRISSAY (FR) 5 b.g. Robin Des Pres (FR) – Topeka (FR) (Italic (FR)) [2006/7 F93: 20d⁵ 21v² 20v² 20v² 24v⁴ Mar 10] unfurnished gelding: third in bumper: fair maiden hurdler: probably stays 3m: acts on heavy ground. *H. D. Daly* h106

OBARA D'AVRIL (FR) 5 gr.m. April Night (FR) – Baraka de Thaix II (FR) (Olmeto) [2006/7 h–: 19s⁵ 16v 24sᵖᵘ 20v⁴ 17d⁵ Mar 19] rather leggy mare: poor form over hurdles. *Miss Kate Milligan* h71 +

OBELIX DE LONGECHAUX (FR) 5 ch.g. Bulington (FR) – Psyche II (FR) (Quart de Vin (FR)) [2006/7 c18d³ c19d² c19dᵘʳ c18s³ c18s* c21g³ c21sᵘʳ c19v³ c20d⁶ Mar 21] rather leggy gelding: fourth foal: half-brother to winning chasers Klef du Bonheur (by Lights Out) and Mystral (by Dom Alco), latter up to 3m: dam won up to 14.5f on Flat: runner-up twice around 11f on Flat: fair novice chaser, claimed €10,000 from P. Peltier in France second outing: won handicap at Newbury in December: stays 21f: raced on good ground or softer. *Noel T. Chance* c108

OBERON MOON (IRE) 6 gr.g. New Frontier (IRE) – Kemal's Princess (Kemal (FR)) [2006/7 F16m* Apr 10] €32,000 4-y-o: closely related to 2½m hurdle winner Polly's Joy (by Oscar) and half-brother to fair hurdler/fairly useful chaser Kemal's Council (by Leading Counsel), stayed 25f: dam unraced, out of half-sister to very smart 2m to 2½m hurdler Fane Ranger: 11/10-on and green, impressive winner of bumper at Chepstow on debut by 11 lengths from Brenin Cwmtudu: sure to improve. *P. F. Nicholls* F100 p

OBLIGEE DE SIVOLA (FR) 5 b.m. Video Rock (FR) – Quine de Chalamont (FR) (Do Do (FR)) [2006/7 17s 17s 24sᵖᵘ 16v 20s 25vᵖᵘ 3s Apr 25] rather leggy mare: sister to useful staying hurdler/maiden chaser Nine de Sivola and half-sister to 3 winners, including useful hurdler/smart chaser Graal de Chalamont (by Riverquest), stays 29f: dam winning chaser up to 2½m: once-raced on Flat: novice hurdler (left T. Trapenard after return), no form in Britain: should stay at least 3m. *Ferdy Murphy* h–

OBSTREPEROUS WAY 5 ch.g. Dr Fong (USA) – Fleet Key (Afleet (CAN)) [2006/7 h–: 20sᵖᵘ 20vᵖᵘ Dec 27] close-coupled gelding: no form over hurdles: tried in cheekpieces. *Miss Tracy Waggott* h–

OCARINA (FR) 5 b.g. Bulington (FR) – Alconea (FR) (Brezzo (FR)) [2006/7 16s⁵ 21v⁴ 18v⁴ 16v² 20vᵖᵘ 20sᵖᵘ Apr 1] 17,000 4-y-o: sixth foal: half-brother to 2 winners, including fair hurdler/fairly useful chaser up to 21f Kampala (by Video Rock): dam won twice over 11f in France: best effort over hurdles (modest form) when fourth in novice at Kelso: raced on soft/heavy ground. *J. P. L. Ewart* h88

OCARITO (GER) 6 b.g. Auenadler (GER) – Okkasion (Konigsstuhl (GER)) [2006/7 20dᵖᵘ 16m 16d 16g Nov 13] successful 5 times up to around 9f on Flat in Germany: left W. Hickst, no show over hurdles. *J. C. Tuck* h–

OCEAN DU MOULIN (FR) 5 b.g. Robin Des Champs (FR) – Hacienda du Moulin (FR) (Video Rock (FR)) [2006/7 F16s⁶ F16s² Feb 9] €16,000 3-y-o, resold 30,000 3-y-o: compact gelding: first foal: dam, won up to 1½m on Flat, half-sister to useful chaser up to 2½m Epsilon du Moulin: better effort in bumpers when 10 lengths second to Forest Pennant in maiden at Kempton: will be suited by 2¼m+. *P. F. Nicholls* **F96 +**

OCEAN FOU (FR) 5 b.g. Lute Antique (FR) – Vieille Folle (FR) (Carmont (FR)) [2006/7 F16d F16m Apr 9] leggy, lengthy gelding: third foal: half-brother to cross-country chase winner Histoire Folle (by Dress Parade): dam lightly-raced maiden chaser: well beaten in bumpers. *B. R. Summers* **F—**

OCEANOS DES OBEAUX (FR) 5 b.g. April Night (FR) – Gypsie d'Artois (FR) (Mistigri) [2006/7 17s² 16d³ 19v* 21s Feb 9] rather leggy gelding: second foal: half-brother to winning chaser up to 2¾m in France Nymphe des Obeaux (by Indian River): dam won at 12.5f and 13.5f in France: won 1½m event on Flat in France on debut in 2006 for N. Devilder: fairly useful form in novice hurdles: won at Newbury in January by 8 lengths from Apatura Dik: should be suited by further than 19f: raced on ground softer than good. *P. J. Hobbs* **h119**

OCEAN PRIDE (IRE) 4 b.g. Lend A Hand – Irish Understudy (ITY) (In The Wings) [2006/7 17s² 16s³ 17g⁶ 19g⁶ 17m⁴ Apr 17] small gelding: fairly useful on Flat (stays 13f), successful twice in 2006, claimed £10,000 from R. Hannon in December: modest juvenile hurdler: likely to prove best around 2m: ungenuine. *D. E. Pipe* **h90 §**

OCKLEY FLYER 8 b.g. Sir Harry Lewis (USA) – Bewails (IRE) (Caerleon (USA)) [2006/7 h81: 25g* 26d 26m* 27mᵖᵘ 23m⁵ Oct 4] tall gelding: modest novice hurdler: won at Plumpton (handicap, dead-heated) in May and Hereford (conditional jockeys) in June: mistakes when well beaten on chasing debut (lame): stays 27f: acts on good to firm ground: wears cheekpieces: tried tongue tied: has looked uncooperative. *Miss Z. C. Davison* **c—**
h87

OCO (FR) 5 ch.g. Phantom Breeze – Byrsa (FR) (Quart de Vin (FR)) [2006/7 16s³ 16s³ 16v² Feb 26] smallish, leggy gelding: fifth foal: dam ran twice on Flat: runner-up in 1½m event in May for E. Clayeux: fair form when placed in maiden hurdles (struck into final outing): should stay beyond 2m: raced on soft/heavy going. *A. King* **h106**

OCTOBER MIST (IRE) 13 gr.g. Roselier (FR) – Bonny Joe (Derring Rose) [2006/7 c—, h109: 20m Jun 22] stocky gelding: carries plenty of condition: winning chaser: fair handicap hurdler, badly hampered at Southwell in June: in frame in points in 2007: stays 23f: acts on soft/heavy going, possibly suited by less testing conditions nowadays: tried in cheekpieces/tongue tied. *K. G. Reveley* **c—**
h—

ODAL D'AIRY (FR) 5 b.g. Cadoubel (FR) – Dalina d'Airy (FR) (Marasali) [2006/7 16s⁴ 16d⁵ Mar 21] lengthy, good-topped gelding: fifth foal: half-brother to 3 winning jumpers in France, including 19f chase winner Kalishann d'Airy (by Sheyrann): dam 19f chase winner: third over 1½m on Flat: runner-up on completed start over fences at Pau: left J. Ortet, modest form in maiden hurdles in Britain. *P. J. Hobbs* **c—**
h92

ODDSMAKER (IRE) 6 b.g. Barathea (IRE) – Archipova (IRE) (Ela-Mana-Mou) [2006/7 h106: 16v⁵ Mar 22] leggy gelding: fair on Flat (stays 2m) in 2006: fair form over hurdles: raced too freely only outing in 2006/7: likely to prove best at 2m with emphasis on speed (raced only on soft/heavy going so far): tongue tied. *M. A. Barnes* **h—**

ODD SOCKS (IRE) 5 ch.g. Zaffaran (USA) – Mrs Marples (IRE) (Sexton Blake) [2006/7 F16v³ Mar 6] €85,000 4-y-o: second foal: dam unraced half-sister to top bumper performer Wither Or Which and to dam of top-class staying chaser Alexander Banquet: remote third of 7 in bumper at Newcastle on debut. *J. Howard Johnson* **F75**

OEDIPE (FR) 5 ch.g. Chamberlin (FR) – Massada (FR) (Kashtan (FR)) [2006/7 c17d* c17s² c20g² c18g² c20d* Dec 26] angular gelding: eighth foal: brother to one-time useful chaser Montreal, stays 3m, and half-brother to several other winners over jumps: dam winning chaser up to around 2½m: useful form over fences, successful at Dieppe in July: left G. Macaire, impressive when winning novice handicap at Kempton on British debut by 14 lengths from Black Hills: will stay beyond 2½m: raced on good ground or softer: looked sure to do better but not seen out again. *N. J. Henderson* **c135 p**

OEIL D'ESTRUVAL (FR) 5 b.g. Sheyrann – Image d'Estruval (FR) (Prince Melchior (FR)) [2006/7 19sᵘʳ 16s 20v 17v 22g 20g² Apr 11] small gelding: won around 1¾m from 4 starts on Flat in French Provinces in 2006 for J-M. Robin: first form over hurdles when runner-up in handicap at Hereford: stays 2½m: raced on good going or softer. *Ian Williams* **h83**

OENOLOGUE (FR) 5 b.g. Ragmar (FR) – Cabira Des Saccart (FR) (Quart de Vin — c–
(FR)) [2006/7 17s* 16s⁵ 19spu Nov 16] close-coupled gelding: sixth foal: half-brother to h99
3 winners, notably useful chaser New Alco (by Dom Alco), stays 25f, and fairly useful
chaser Jeu de Brook (by Trebrook), stays 3m: dam, twice-raced, out of sister to dam of
smart staying hurdler/chaser Tito L'Effronte: fell on chasing debut: won 4-y-o hurdle at
Auteuil in May: left F. Cottin, shaped as if amiss both starts in Britain: bred to stay beyond
17f: tried tongue tied: joined N. Madden. *Jonjo O'Neill*

OFAREL D'AIRY (FR) 5 b.g. Cadoubel (FR) – Farali d'Airy (FR) (Marasali) c137 +
[2006/7 16g² 16s² 16d⁵ c16s* c16s³ c21v² c21g* Apr 19] tall gelding: has scope: first h115
foal: dam won over fences around 2m in France: runner-up over 1½m on Flat at 3 yrs for
J. Ortet: fairly useful form over hurdles: soon much better over fences: won maiden at
Folkestone (easily landed odds) in January and novice handicap at Cheltenham in April:
further progress when beating Black Hills (briefly looked like hanging fire) at
latter: will stay beyond 21f: raced on good going or softer (acts on heavy): may do better
still over fences. *P. F. Nicholls*

OF COURSE (FR) 5 ch.g. Adnaan (IRE) – Intelectuelle (FR) (Montorselli) [2006/7 F96
F84: F16g³ F16v⁵ F16v² Feb 24] leggy, angular gelding: fairly useful form in bumpers:
head second to Kealshore Boy (pair clear) at Newcastle. *Miss Kate Milligan*

OFCOURSEHEKHAN (IRE) 9 b.g. Phardante (FR) – King's Gift (IRE) (King's c78
Ride) [2006/7 c–: c25g³ Apr 2] winning but temperamental pointer: in cheekpieces, third
in maiden hunter at Kelso: stays 25f. *Mrs N. C. Neill*

OFFEMONT (FR) 6 b. or br.g. Bulington (FR) – La Guyonniere (FR) (Silver Rain- c117
bow) [2006/7 c102, h–: c18s c22s c16s³ c16v² c16s² c16v* c16vpu c16s* Mar 10] rangy h–
gelding: maiden hurdler: fairly useful chaser, trained by S. Kalley in France first 2 starts
in 2006/7: improved form after fitted with blinkers, won handicaps at Warwick (5-runner
novice event) in January and Sandown (by ¾ length from Stan, idling) in March: lost
action in between: should stay 2½m: raced on good ground or softer (acts on heavy).
Noel T. Chance

OFFICIER DE RESERVE (FR) 5 br.g. Sleeping Car (FR) – Royaute (FR) (Signani c125
(FR)) [2006/7 c18dF c18g* 17v³ c19s* c19s* c18s² Mar 3] lengthy, angular gelding: h100
half-brother to winning hurdler/chaser Gotha (by Royal Charter), stays 23f: dam 1½m
winner: third in 4-y-o hurdle at Auteuil: fairly useful over fences, successful in 4-y-o
events at Bordeaux in October and December, and having left G. Macaire, novice at
Hereford (easily by 11 lengths from Lunar Crystal) in February: further improvement
when 5 lengths second of 6 to Maljimar in novice handicap at Newbury: stays 19f: acts
on soft ground. *P. F. Nicholls*

OFFSHORE ACCOUNT (IRE) 7 b.g. Oscar (IRE) – Park Breeze (IRE) (Strong c149
Gale) [2006/7 22d² 20d 24d 18v* 24v⁵ c20v² c21v* c20v* c24d* c25m* Apr 24] h106
    As a half-brother to The Listener, Distant Thunder and Fork Lightning, it
was always on the cards that steeplechasing would bring out the best in Offshore
Account. He was still a maiden over hurdles at the start of the latest season and had
been placed in bumpers as well prior to that, but he finally got his head in front at the
thirteenth attempt when winning a maiden hurdle at Gowran in December, almost
exactly two years after his racecourse debut. The booking of Ruby Walsh
and the application of cheekpieces for his handicap debut when favourite at
Clonmel the time before suggested that Offshore Account had been expected to get
off the mark one race sooner, but he had excuses on that occasion, being badly
hampered by a faller. After one more run over hurdles in handicap company at
Leopardstown, Offshore Account was switched to fences after the turn of the year
and immediately left his fair hurdling form well behind.
    Runner-up on his chasing debut at Punchestown, Offshore Account went
one better in a beginners chase at Fairyhouse in February, followed up in a novice
event at Naas in March and completed a hat-trick with a neck victory over the
favourite Laetitia in the Grade 3 Hugh McMahon Memorial Novices' Chase at
Limerick in April. Running at three miles over fences for the first time, Offshore
Account impressed throughout with his jumping at Limerick where a great leap at
the last effectively sealed victory after the runner-up (who reportedly finished
lame) had been steadied into it when seemingly set to take his measure. The final
fence proved even more pivotal in Offshore Account's final and most important
win of the season in the Ellier Developments Hanover Quay Champion Novices'

Chase at Punchestown. The Grade 1 was a new opportunity at the Punchestown Festival for staying novice chasers who were previously catered for at the meeting by a valuable handicap. It replaced a Grade 2 novice run over half a mile shorter which in turn became a handicap. The Champion Novices' Chase attracted a seven-runner field, the betting headed by Aintree's Mildmay Novices' Chase winner Aces Four at 6/4 and the Royal & SunAlliance Chase runner-up Snowy Morning on 9/4. Although improving, Offshore Account at 16/1 was his stable's second string behind One Cool Cookie, who had himself won a Grade 1 event earlier in the month when much improved in the Powers Gold Cup over two and a half miles at Fairyhouse and was the choice of David Casey (who'd ridden Offshore Account to all four previous wins). One Cool Cookie weakened over the longer trip at Punchestown and Snowy Morning proved disappointing, which left Offshore Account and Aces Four with the race between them as they drew clear from three out. Briefly looking to be going better than the favourite, after travelling well under a patient ride, Offshore Account was a couple of lengths adrift and probably held when Aces Four hardly rose at the last and took a crashing fall. That left Offshore Account clear to win by eleven lengths from the outsider Knight Legend, the horse who had prevented Offshore Account making a winning chasing debut at the course back in January. One Cool Cookie was a further two lengths behind in third, well clear of Snowy Morning and the other finisher Merdeka. It was the biggest win of the season for stand-in jockey Denis O'Regan, who was reportedly confident of success even before Aces Four's fall.

Offshore Account was one of three long-odds Grade 1 winners at the Punchestown Festival for his sire Oscar, followed by Refinement in the Champion Stayers' Hurdle and Silent Oscar in the ACCBank Champion Hurdle. Of Offshore Account's three noteworthy half-brothers mentioned above, The Listener (by Roselier) developed into a top-class chaser in the latest season, winning the Lexus Chase at Leopardstown. Highlight of the season for Distant Thunder (by Phardante) was his very close third in the William Hill Trophy at Cheltenham, a race won by

Ellier Developments Hanover Quay Champion Novices' Chase, Punchestown—
Offshore Account is left clear to complete a four-timer by Aces Four's crunching fall

Fork Lightning (also by Roselier) as a novice three years earlier. Fork Lightning was reportedly retired at the end of the latest season after a largely disappointing campaign, but, like Distant Thunder, he was a useful chaser at his best. The dam's fourteen-year-old son Moving Earth (by Brush Aside) was still active in the latest season in hunter chases, though has never possessed quite the same ability as his younger siblings, often proving temperamental (has refused to race several times). Offshore Account's year-younger brother Dooneys Gate has made a most promising start for Willie Mullins and he could easily prove well up to the family's high standards when eventually stepped up in trip and sent chasing. As it is, Dooneys Gate made a winning debut in a bumper early in the season and won the second of his two starts over hurdles. Their dam Park Breeze, like her own dam and grandam, was unraced and is a sister to Punchestown cross-country specialist Risk of Thunder. Offshore Account went through the Tattersalls (Ireland) sale-ring three times, ultimately joining Charlie Swan when bought by the trainer for €38,000 as a three-year-old at the Derby Sale.

Offshore Account (IRE) (b.g. 2000)			
	Oscar (IRE) (b 1994)	Sadler's Wells (b 1981)	Northern Dancer / Fairy Bridge
		Snow Day (b 1978)	Reliance II / Vindaria
	Park Breeze (IRE) (b or br 1988)	Strong Gale (br 1975)	Lord Gayle / Sterntau
		Park Delight (ch 1974)	Saint Denys / Lover's Delight

The lengthy Offshore Account will stay further than twenty-five furlongs, while his Punchestown win showed he acts on good to firm ground, having raced

Mr Brian Polly's "Offshore Account"

exclusively on going softer than good before that—his first three wins were on heavy ground. Offshore Account usually races prominently and his sound jumping, which has already paid dividends, will continue to be an asset. Offshore Account still has some way to go to make into a Cheltenham Gold Cup contender but, if he shows the sort of improvement The Listener did in his second season over fences, he could take advantage of the likely absence of sidelined Gold Cup winners Kicking King and War of Attrition in the top staying chases in Ireland. *C. F. Swan, Ireland*

OFF STAGE (IRE) 4 ch.f. Danehill Dancer (IRE) – Safe Exit (FR) (Exit To Nowhere (USA)) [2006/7 19v³ 16s⁶ 16g Mar 14] modest maiden on Flat (stays 7.5f) at 3 yrs for D. Wachman: poor form over hurdles: may prove best around 2m. *Carl Llewellyn*   **h70 +**

O'HANA (FR) 5 b.m. Nononito (FR) – Isati's (FR) (Chamberlin (FR)) [2006/7 F16v⁴ F16d* F17g⁵ F16m Apr 26] good-topped mare: first foal: dam second over 14.5f in France on only start: fair form in bumpers: won at Thurles in March. *W. P. Mullins, Ireland*   **F92**

OH BE THE HOKEY (IRE) 9 b.g. Be My Native (USA) – Lucky Perk (IRE) (Executive Perk) [2006/7 c20d³ c24s⁴ c20gᶠ Apr 25] tall gelding: winning hurdler: fairly useful handicap chaser: off 16 months, ran creditably when in frame behind Bothar Na in Denny Gold Medal at Tralee and Kerry National at Listowel: stays 3m: raced on good going or softer (acts on heavy): usually races handily. *C. F. Swan, Ireland*   **c120 h–**

OH DANNY BOY 6 b.g. Cadeaux Genereux – Final Shot (Dalsaan) [2006/7 16s 19d 16dᵖᵘ Mar 13] compact gelding: fair on Flat (stays 1¼m), sold out of Jane Chapple-Hyam's stable 4,000 gns Newmarket Autumn Sales: no show over hurdles (jumped badly second start). *M. C. Chapman*   **h–**

OH MISTER PINCEAU (FR) 5 bl.g. Cupidon (FR) – Altesse d'O (FR) (Tadj (FR)) [2006/7 h–: 17g May 4] tall, useful-looking gelding: well held over hurdles, including in seller: tried in cheekpieces/tongue tied: sold 8,000 gns Doncaster May (2006) Sales. *H. D. Daly*   **h–**

OH PICKLES (IRE) 5 b.g. Needle Gun (IRE) – Tartan Trouble (Warpath) [2006/7 F17s⁵ Feb 19] €38,000 4-y-o: seventh foal: dam, lightly raced in points, half-sister to dam of See More Business: green, modest form when fifth in bumper at Carlisle on debut. *J. Howard Johnson*   **F83**

OH SO HARDY 6 b. or br.m. Fleetwood (IRE) – Miss Hardy (Formidable (USA)) [2006/7 h73: 22m⁴ 22m⁵ 22gᵖᵘ Sep 17] maiden hurdler, form only on debut in 2005/6: tried blinkered: tongue tied. *M. A. Allen*   **h–**

OISEAU DE NUIT (FR) 5 b.g. Evening World (FR) – Idylle du Marais (FR) (Panoramic) [2006/7 F16d 17dᵖᵘ 20v⁵ 17s 17d² 16s Mar 3] good-topped gelding: chasing type: first foal: dam unplaced in 4 starts on Flat: well held in bumper: easily best effort over hurdles when runner-up in handicap at Market Rasen: tried tongue tied. *M. G. Rimell*   **h97 F74**

OKTIS MORILIOUS (IRE) 6 b.g. Octagonal (NZ) – Nottash (IRE) (Royal Academy (USA)) [2006/7 h–: 17g⁵ 16g 16f 16m 21g⁶ 19g 21m⁴ 24s⁵ 24s⁶ 16v 20m⁴ Mar 29] poor maiden hurdler: barely stays 3m: acts on soft and good to firm going: tongue tied last 7 starts. *J. A. Danahar*   **h80**

OLCHONS DEBUT (IRE) 9 ch.g. Denel (FR) – Buckskins Babe (IRE) (Buckskin (FR)) [2006/7 h–: 24sᵖᵘ May 20] failed to complete in maiden Irish points/novice hurdles. *Miss A. E. Broyd*   **h–**

OLD BEAN (IRE) 11 b.g. Eurobus – Princess Petara (IRE) (Petorius) [2006/7 c–, h–: 21mᵖᵘ May 5] leggy, angular gelding: won novice hurdle in January 2004: lightly raced and no form since, including on chasing debut (for O. Dukes): tried in cheekpieces. *P. T. Midgley*   **c– h–**

OLD BENNY 6 b.g. Saddlers' Hall (IRE) – Jack's The Girl (IRE) (Supreme Leader) [2006/7 F94: 20d⁵ 24s² 26s² 24v* 25s* Mar 11] sturdy gelding: fairly useful novice hurdler: won at Taunton (landed odds by 3 lengths from Low Delta) and Warwick (again idled markedly when beating Best Actor by head) in March: will stay beyond 3¼m: raced on ground softer than good: not straightforward (may benefit from headgear). *A. King*   **h118 +**

OLD FEATHERS (IRE) 10 b.g. Hernando (FR) – Undiscovered (Tap On Wood) [2006/7 h107x: 20s c20vᵖᵘ 20gᵖᵘ Apr 7] workmanlike gelding: fair handicap hurdler at best: left Jonjo O'Neill, no show in 2006/7, including on chasing debut: stays 3m: acts on   **c– x h– x**

good to firm and heavy going: usually blinkered/visored (has hinted at temperament): not a fluent jumper. *R. Ford*

OLD FLAME (IRE) 8 b.g. Oscar (IRE) – Flameing Run (Deep Run) [2006/7 c137, h–: c17v[6] 16s 17v[4] 16v[3] c16v[3] 16d[2] c17m[2] c20g Apr 25] sturdy, lengthy gelding: fairly useful handicap hurdler: creditable efforts when in frame in 2006/7, 5 lengths second of 16 to Wishwillow Lord in minor event at Limerick: useful handicap chaser: respectable 17 lengths second to Gemini Lucy in valuable event at Fairyhouse penultimate outing: stays 2½m: acts on heavy going, probably on good to firm: front runner. *Paul Nolan, Ireland* — **c128 h117**

OLD KILMINCHY (IRE) 11 b. or br.g. Cashel Court – Janeyway (Bulldozer) [2006/7 c21g[2] c24d[pu] c21g[4] c20s[5] Feb 16] lengthy ex-Irish gelding: winning hurdler/chaser: left M. Hourigan, successful 3 times in points in Britain in 2006: easily best effort in hunters when second at Cheltenham: should stay 3m: acts on heavy ground: tried in cheekpieces/blinkers. *Mrs C. M. Gorman* — **c100 h–**

OLD MARSH (IRE) 11 b.g. Grand Lodge (USA) – Lolly Dolly (Alleged (USA)) [2006/7 c129, h101+: c20s[5] c20g[5] Feb 21] strong gelding: winning hurdler: fairly useful chaser at best: off 18 months and left A. Carroll, only fifth in hunters in 2006/7 (for F. Brennan on return only): best around 2m: acts on soft and good to firm going: tried blinkered/tongue tied: prone to mistakes. *A. J. Chamberlain* — **c93 h–**

OLD NODDY (IRE) 7 ch.g. Duky – General Run (General Ironside) [2006/7 c25m[pu] c25s[4] c20s[4] c26g* c28g* Apr 15] won maiden point in 2006: modest chaser: improved form last 2 starts, winning handicaps at Carlisle and Kelso in April: stays well: in cheekpieces after debut. *J. W. F. Aynsley* — **c87**

OLDRIK (GER) 4 b.g. Tannenkonig (IRE) – Onestep (GER) (Konigsstuhl (GER)) [2006/7 16s[6] 16s 17s[2] 16g[3] Mar 31] close-coupled, rather unfurnished gelding: lightly raced on Flat when trained by Frau E. Schnakenberg, won 1m maiden at Bremen at 2 yrs: fair form over hurdles: raced around 2m: races freely. *P. J. Hobbs* — **h103**

OLD SCEW BALD (IRE) 7 b. or br.g. Glacial Storm (USA) – Leadaro (IRE) (Supreme Leader) [2006/7 c24v[2] Feb 10] lengthy, good-topped gelding: half-brother to useful chaser Kinburn (by Roselier), stayed well: dam unraced half-sister to very smart 2m hurdler Miller Hill: third in bumper: successful 2 of 3 starts in points, including in January: useful form when 11 lengths second to Whyso Mayo in hunter at Leopardstown on chase debut: will stay beyond 3m. *Denis Paul Murphy, Ireland* — **c122**

OLEOLAT (FR) 5 ch.g. Art Bleu – Contessina (FR) (Mistigri) [2006/7 16d 24v[6] 16v[5] 20v[5] 20s[pu] Apr 25] fifth foal: half-brother to fairly useful 2m hurdler Kimbambo (by Genevax Genie) and fair 2m to 3¼m hurdler/chaser Infini (by Le Nain Jaune): dam 1½m winner in France: no form over hurdles, left J. Ewart before final start: has had tongue tied. *W. Amos* — **h–**

OLIFAN D'OUDAIRIES(FR) 5 ch.g. Video Rock (FR) – Bouffonne (FR) (Shafoun (FR)) [2006/7 F16m[3] Jun 11] fourth foal: brother to winner around 1½m Mandarin d'Oudairi and half-brother to 21f chase winner Kid d'Oudairies (by Apple Tree): dam, 9.5f winner, half-sister to dam of one-time smart chaser Iznogoud: looked in need of experience when third to Dazzling Jim in maiden bumper at Stratford on debut: sold 17,000 gns Doncaster August Sales. *H. D. Daly* — **F72**

OLIMPO (FR) 6 ch.g. Starborough – Emily Allan (IRE) (Shirley Heights) [2006/7 h85: 16d[ur] 19v[F] 16v Jan 13] rather leggy, workmanlike gelding: fairly useful on Flat in 2006 (successful twice) for B. R. Millman: maiden hurdler, going best when falling heavily 3 out in handicap at Exeter: bled next time: likely to prove best around 2m: not a fluent jumper. *Nick Williams* — **h?**

OLIVAIR (IRE) 4 b.f. Daggers Drawn (USA) – Exhibit Air (IRE) (Exhibitioner) [2006/7 17m[ur] 17d[pu] 17s[pu] 16m[6] 17g 17v* 17d 17m Apr 15] maiden on Flat: form (poor) over hurdles only when winning juvenile maiden at Market Rasen in November: raced around 2m: acts on heavy going: blinkered last 3 outings. *M. E. Sowersby* — **h73**

OLIVAL (FR) 5 b.g. Le Balafre (FR) – Carvine d'Or (FR) (Pot d'Or (FR)) [2006/7 h95: c20s[6] c18s c20v[pu] Dec 30] tall gelding: modest hurdler: shaped better than result on chasing debut, disappointing next 2 starts: should stay 2½m: raced on going softer than good: tried in cheekpieces. *Jonjo O'Neill* — **c77 + h–**

OLIVERJOHN (IRE) 10 ch.g. Denel (FR) – Graeme's Gem (Pry) [2006/7 c99, h–: c16v[3] c16v[4] c16g Apr 7] lengthy gelding: modest handicap chaser, off 13 months before return: stays 21f: acts on heavy going: tried in cheekpieces/visor: front runner/races prominently. *Miss Lucinda V. Russell* — **c96 h–**

OLIVINO (GER) 6 ch.g. Second Set (IRE) – Osdemona (GER) (Solarstern (FR)) **h93**
[2006/7 18m⁵ 17m 16m⁴ 16f² 17m² 17d* Aug 15] successful 4 times on Flat (stays 16.5f)
in Germany, including twice in 2005 for H-J. Groschel, modest form in Britain: modest
hurdler, claimed from S. Dow £5,000 second start: easily landed odds in 5-runner maiden
at Newton Abbot in August: should stay beyond 17f: acts on firm and good to soft going
(unraced on softer). *B. J. Llewellyn*

OLLIE MAGERN 9 b.g. Alderbrook – Outfield (Monksfield) [2006/7 c162d, h–: **c156**
c24mᵘʳ c24d⁴ c24d Dec 26] smallish gelding: high-class chaser at best, won Charlie Hall **h–**
Chase at Wetherby on reappearance in 2005/6: largely disappointing since (has shaped as
if amiss more than once), though did run one of better races when 18¾ lengths fourth to
Kauto Star in Grade 1 at Haydock in November, headed only between last 2: stays 27f:
acts on firm and soft going: usually makes running. *N. A. Twiston-Davies*

OL' MAN RIVER (IRE) 7 b.g. Dr Massini (IRE) – Nearly Married (Nearly A Hand) **c77**
[2006/7 h83, F80: c24sᵖᵘ c23d² c31dᵖᵘ Nov 10] tall gelding: poor novice hurdler: similar **h–**
form on completed start over fences: should have stayed 3m+: raced on good going or
softer: wore cheekpieces/cheekpieces last 2 outings: dead. *C. E. Longsdon*

OLMETO COLLONGES (FR) 5 b. or br.g. Brier Creek (USA) – Castille Collonges **c95**
(FR) (El Badr) [2006/7 c17s² 19d⁵ Nov 8] second foal: half-brother to very smart hurdler/ **h88 p**
high-class chaser Neptune Collonges (by Dom Alco), stays 3¼m: dam maiden hurdler/
chaser: twice-raced over fences at Auteuil, runner-up to Onika d'Airy in 4-y-o event on
second occasion: left M. Rolland, 26 lengths fifth to Nightfly in novice at Lingfield on
hurdling debut: likely to be suited by further than 19f: should improve. *Miss H. C. Knight*

O'MALEY (FR) 5 b.g. Sleeping Car (FR) – Salse Pareille (FR) (Perouges (FR)) **c120 p**
[2006/7 c17d³ 21v⁶ Feb 24] tall, useful-looking gelding: brother to fair hurdler Lease **h–**
Back, stays 3m, and half-brother to 17f chase winner Babati (by Royal Charter): dam
maiden: fair form 2 starts over hurdles at Auteuil in 2005/6, winning 18-runner event in
March: left M. Lecoiffier, shaped as if in need of experience when 10½ lengths third of 6
to Killaghy Castle in maiden at Newbury on chasing debut: well beaten in handicap at
Kempton back over hurdles 3 months later: should improve over fences. *P. F. Nicholls*

OMAN GULF (USA) 6 b.g. Diesis – Dabaweyaa (Shareef Dancer (USA)) [2006/7 16g **h–**
Dec 10] fairly useful at best on Flat (stays 11f), sold out of J. Given's stable 12,500 gns
Doncaster October (2005) Sales, no form in 2006: soundly beaten in novice on hurdling
debut. *Micky Hammond*

OMIKRA (GER) 5 b.m. General Monash (USA) – Ost Tycoon (GER) (Last Tycoon) **h80**
[2006/7 16m⁴ 16g 16s 24d 20v 24vᵖᵘ Feb 18] maiden on Flat: poor form over hurdles.
Gerard Cully, Ireland

OMME ANTIQUE (FR) 5 b.g. Lute Antique (FR) – Saturbaine (FR) (Djarvis (FR)) **h85 +**
[2006/7 F16v F16s⁴ 19v 20g³ Apr 27] €14,000 3-y-o: lengthy, useful-looking gelding: **F85**
half-brother to several winners, including hurdler/chaser up to 23f Jupon Bleu (by
Passing Sale): dam won at 13f on Flat and up to 21f over fences in France: better efforts
in bumpers and over hurdles when in frame at Chepstow, beaten 22 lengths by Ballamusic
in novice on latter occasion. *Miss Venetia Williams*

OMMEGA (FR) 5 b.g. Ragmar (FR) – Cathou (FR) (Quart de Vin (FR)) [2006/7 18s² **c113**
c19s* c22s² c17s² c20s² Apr 6] third foal: dam placed over 1½m on Flat: 13.5f winner on **h103**
Flat: fair form over hurdles, first past post (demoted) in 4-y-o event at Enghien in
September: similar form over fences, won 4-y-o event at Fontainebleau in December:
runner-up all 3 starts after, beaten 1½ lengths by idling Classified at Fontwell next time:
stays 2¾m: raced only on soft ground. *F. Doumen, France*

OMNI COSMO TOUCH (USA) 11 b.g. Trempolino (USA) – Wooden Pudden **c128 §**
(USA) (Top Ville) [2006/7 20gᵇᵈ c25v* c26g* c32m² c20s³ c26s⁴ c29s c25sᵖᵘ c31d⁵ **h– §**
c29m c34f⁴ Apr 26] good-topped gelding: winning hurdler: fairly useful handicap chaser
when in the mood: won at Wetherby in May and Uttoxeter in June: good efforts next 3
starts, 13¾ lengths fourth to State of Play in Hennessy Cognac Gold Cup at Newbury: left
Mrs G. Smith, below best last 2 outings: stays 4m: acts on any going: blinkered once:
has often refused/been reluctant to race (including in cheekpieces final start): ungenuine.
Henry de Bromhead, Ireland

O'MUIRCHEARTAIGH (IRE) 7 b.g. Accordion – Brian's Delight (IRE) (Celio **c124 §**
Rufo) [2006/7 h134, F114: c20d³ c20s* c20vᵖᵘ c24vᶠ c24v² c21v⁵ c24vᵖᵘ c17m Apr 9] **h– §**
tall, rather leggy gelding: useful hurdler: made most when winning maiden chase at
Punchestown in November, but disappointing over fences after except when second to
Chelsea Harbour in Grade 2 novice at Naas: stays 3m: raced mainly on good ground or

softer: usually wears cheekpieces, laboured efforts in blinkers last 2 starts: ungenuine. *E. J. O'Grady, Ireland*

ON A DEAL 9 b.g. Teenoso (USA) – Gale Spring (IRE) (Strong Gale) [2006/7 27m Aug 2] long-backed gelding: maiden hurdler: won point in 2006: stays 2¾m: acts on soft and good to firm ground: tried blinkered: sold 700 gns Doncaster August Sales. *P. J. Hobbs*   **h–**

ONAROLL 7 ch.g. Fleetwood (IRE) – New Dawn (Rakaposhi King) [2006/7 F16g Nov 2] leggy gelding: well held in bumpers 21 months apart. *O. Brennan*   **F–**

ONCE A BROWNIE (IRE) 6 b.g. Oscar (IRE) – Chocolate Brownie (IRE) (Orchestra) [2006/7 F109: 22s² 20d* c20v² 20v^pu Feb 22] useful-looking gelding, unfurnished at present: useful bumper performer: best effort over hurdles when winning maiden at Fontwell in November by 5 lengths from Speed Winner: shaped as if amiss final outing (tongue tied): had run much better when 3 lengths second to Loulou Nivernais in handicap at Wetherby on chasing debut: should stay 3m: raced on ground softer than good (acts on heavy): has hung under pressure. *Jonjo O'Neill*   **c110 h105**

ONCE (FR) 7 gr.g. Hector Protector (USA) – Moon Magic (Polish Precedent (USA)) [2006/7 h75: 22m Jun 18] leggy gelding: poor form at best over hurdles. *M. G. Rimell*   **h–**

ONCE SEEN 7 b.g. Celtic Swing – Brief Glimpse (IRE) (Taufan (USA)) [2006/7 h102: 16g^F 20v 18s^pu Feb 4] close-coupled gelding: fair handicap hurdler: left O. Sherwood and off 17 months, close up when falling last at Warwick on reappearance: ran poorly both starts after: barely stays testing 2¾m: acts on soft and good to firm going: tried visored/blinkered: has carried head awkwardly. *C. P. Morlock*   **h97**

ONCLE BUL (FR) 5 b.g. Bulington (FR) – Galaxie (FR) (Useful (FR)) [2006/7 16d^pu 17s 17s Feb 8] second foal: dam 1¾m winner: successful once from 3 starts on Flat (all over 1½m) in France: sold out of T. Trapenard's stable €95,000 Goffs (France) July Sale: no form in novice/maiden hurdles. *R. H. Alner*   **h–**

ONE ACCORD 6 b.g. Accordion – Not So Prim (Primitive Rising (USA)) [2006/7 F16g F17d Jun 14] first foal: dam poor maiden pointer: soundly beaten in 2 bumpers. *Miss L. C. Siddall*   **F–**

ONE ALONE 6 b.m. Atraf – Songsheet (Dominion) [2006/7 h–: 20m⁵ May 28] poor form on hurdling debut: blinkered, no show in 3 starts since, lame only one in 2006/7. *Jean-Rene Auvray*   **h–**

ONE AND ONLY (GER) 6 ch.m. Kornado – On My Guest (IRE) (Be My Guest (USA)) [2006/7 h–: 17m⁶ 16f 22g^pu 22m^pu Jul 20] no form over hurdles. *D. W. Thompson*   **h–**

ONE COOL COOKIE (IRE) 6 ch.g. Old Vic – Lady Bellingham (IRE) (Montelimar (USA)) [2006/7 c22v* c20s³ c20d* c21d^pu c21v³ c20m* c25m³ Apr 24]   **c145 h–**
The sale of point-to-point winner One Cool Cookie mirrored the Coolmore/Sheikh Mohammed battles at the yearling sales, except there were more participants. With five separate bidders at Doncaster's 2005 May Sales willing to part with more than 100,000 guineas, it was Irish agent Mags O'Toole who emerged victorious at a record 165,000 guineas. After the sale, she initially reported that the

Powers Gold Cup, Fairyhouse—One Cool Cookie (left) goes one better than his brother In Compliance twelve months earlier with a defeat of Schindlers Hunt

Gigginstown House Stud's "One Cool Cookie"

horse was not for her biggest client, Ryanair chief executive Michael O'Leary, for whom she had, earlier that week, purchased a brother to Our Ben for 120,000 guineas. One Cool Cookie, however, turned out in the colours of O'Leary's Gigginstown House Stud. Never far from the limelight, O'Leary again hit the headlines in 2007. With Ryanair labelled the 'irresponsible face of capitalism' by climate change minister Ian Pearson, O'Leary struck back in typically no-nonsense style, alleging Pearson did 'not have a clue what he's talking about' and likening the attack to 'being savaged by a dead sheep.' (O'Leary arguably had the last laugh in that particular exchange given that Pearson was moved from his post in Gordon Brown's reshuffle in June). Those capitalist gains—which have amassed a fortune for O'Leary reported to be around £317m—have served him well in the sale-ring, his burgeoning Gigginstown House Stud team further bolstered by the sales-record 150,000-guinea purchase of a half-brother to Iris Bleu at Cheltenham's National Hunt Breeze-Up Sale (first held in 2004) in December 2006. The spending didn't stop there as O'Leary also splashed out 74,000 guineas (the sale's third-highest lot) to acquire a four-year-old gelding by Presenting, the sire of O'Leary's Cheltenham Gold Cup winner War of Attrition. From just three runners over jumps in Ireland during 2002/3, O'Leary's Gigginstown team has grown significantly and had forty-four in 2006/7. The growth has been matched by a commensurate climb up the owners' table in Ireland, seventeenth in 2003/4 becoming second in the past two seasons behind perpetual table-topper J. P. McManus.

One Cool Cookie still has some way to go to repay his purchase price, but he proved himself one of the best novice chasers in Ireland with victory in the Powers Gold Cup at Fairyhouse in April, travelling and jumping well in front before finding plenty to hold Schindlers Hunt by a length and a half, with a further nineteen lengths back to the remainder. The win provided Charlie Swan with his first success at Grade 1 level as a trainer, though only after O'Leary had prevailed in another exchange of views—Swan wanted to run One Cool Cookie in the following day's Irish Grand National, but O'Leary insisted upon the novice option. As previously mentioned, One Cool Cookie began his career in point-to-points, finishing third on his debut before winning a maiden at Dromoland by a distance. He started his career under Rules in hurdles in 2005/6, winning a maiden at Limerick before showing fair form to finish third in a Grade 2 event at Thurles. He has gone on to prove himself much better over fences, starting with a victory in a beginners chase at Listowel on his reappearance in September. Campaigned in graded races thereafter, he won a Grade 2 at Limerick in December but, despite again jumping well, One Cool Cookie was below form on his final outing, finishing thirteen lengths third to stable-companion Offshore Account in the three-miles-one-furlong Champion Novices' Chase at Punchestown, possibly failing to stay the longer trip (though his trainer wouldn't share that view).

One Cool Cookie (IRE) (ch.g. 2001)	Old Vic (b 1986)	Sadler's Wells (b 1981)	Northern Dancer
			Fairy Bridge
		Cockade (b 1973)	Derring-Do
			Camenae
	Lady Bellingham (IRE) (b 1994)	Montelimar (b 1981)	Alleged
			L'Extravagante
		Lovely Stranger (b 1982)	Le Bavard
			Vulvic

The second foal of his unraced dam Lady Bellingham, the good-topped One Cool Cookie's pedigree is dealt with in the essay on his full brother In Compliance. A front runner, One Cool Cookie isn't certain to stay much beyond two and three quarter miles, despite his trainer's optimism about the Irish National. One Cool Cookie acts on heavy and good to firm ground. He has a tendency to jump right—displaying it when third in the Dr P. J. Moriarty at Leopardstown on his fifth start—and may prove best kept to right-handed courses, a view also expressed by connections. *C. F. Swan, Ireland*

ONE CORNETTO (IRE) 8 b.g. Eurobus – Costenetta (IRE) (Runnett) [2006/7 c118, h–: c24m c18g c24s² c24m⁴ Apr 9] lengthy gelding: winning hurdler: fairly useful maiden chaser at best: little form in handicaps last 6 outings: stays 2¾m: acts on good to firm and heavy ground. *L. Wells* — **c96 h–**

ONE DREAM (FR) 5 b.m. Balleroy (USA) – Galene III (FR) (Bayolidaan (FR)) [2006/7 h–: 18sᵖᵘ 16gᵖᵘ 22fᵖᵘ Apr 5] no form over hurdles: tried tongue tied. *R. H. Alner* — **h–**

ONEFORBERTANDHENRY (IRE) 8 b.g. Rashar (USA) – Roi Vision (Roi Guillaume (FR)) [2006/7 c90, h–: c22d⁴ Jun 14] tall gelding: lightly raced and poor form over hurdles/fences: sold 4,500 gns Doncaster October Sales. *G. M. Moore* — **c– h–**

ONEFORSATURDAY (IRE) 5 ch.g. Presenting – Pennine Sue (IRE) (Pennine Walk) [2006/7 F16v F17g² Mar 24] 49,000 3-y-o: third foal: dam poor Irish maiden: much better effort in bumpers (trained on debut by Ms M. Mullins) when head second to Apache Brave in maiden at Bangor, going on strongly at finish. *G. A. Swinbank* — **F102**

ONEFOURFUN (IRE) 5 b.g. Taipan (IRE) – One For Millennium (IRE) (Husyan (USA)) [2006/7 F17d² F17v F16g⁶ 21m 21g² Mar 20] €14,500 3-y-o: first foal: dam, winning pointer, half-sister to prolific cross-country chaser Risk of Thunder and to dam of useful or better staying chasers Distant Thunder, Fork Lightning, Offshore Account and The Listener: modest form in bumpers: better effort over hurdles when 3½ lengths second to Lincoln's Inn at Warwick, carrying head high: stays 21f: takes strong hold. *C. E. Longsdon* — **h101 F83**

ONE GULP 4 b.f. Hernando (FR) – Elaine Tully (IRE) (Persian Bold) [2006/7 F16v* F16g F17g Apr 13] close-coupled filly: half-sister to several winners, including useful bumper performer Eye On The Ball (by Slip Anchor) and fair 2m hurdler Miami Explorer (by Pennekamp): dam fairly useful hurdler who should have stayed beyond 2¾m: impressive debut when winning mares bumper at Haydock in February by 14 lengths from Castlecrossings: similar form when ninth of 24 to Cork All Star in Grade 1 at Cheltenham: raced lazily when well held in listed event final start: will be suited by 2½m. *P. R. Webber* — **F105**

ONE KNIGHT (IRE) 11 ch.g. Roselier (FR) – Midnights Daughter (IRE) (Long   **c– x**
Pond) [2006/7 c154x, h–: 24d c29s Dec 27] tall gelding: winning hurdler: very smart   **h–**
chaser at best, won Royal & SunAlliance Chase at Cheltenham in 2002/3: lightly raced
and generally let down by jumping after, second when falling last in Welsh National in
2005: stayed 29f: acted on soft going: blinkered final start: usually made running:
reportedly retired. *P. J. Hobbs*

ONE MORE NATIVE (IRE) 10 ch.g. Be My Native (USA) – Romany Fortune   **c–**
(Sunyboy) [2006/7 c16vᵖᵘ Dec 15] angular gelding: very lightly raced and no form over   **h–**
hurdles/in chase: fourth only outing in points: tried tongue tied. *J. L. Needham*

ONE MORE STEP 6 b.g. Parthian Springs – Brush Belle (IRE) (Brush Aside (USA))   **h–**
[2006/7 F100: 17mᶠ May 9] smallish, well-made gelding: bumper winner: pulled hard
and fell fourth on hurdling debut: dead. *R. A. Farrant*

ONE NATION (IRE) 12 br.g. Be My Native (USA) – Diklers Run (Deep Run) [2006/7   **c–**
22s Dec 16] big, strong gelding: fairly useful hurdler/chaser: off 2 years, well beaten   **h–**
in handicap hurdles in 2006/7, soon clear on second occasion: should stay beyond 21f:
acts on heavy going. *R. S. Brookhouse*

ONEOFTHEMONGOES (IRE) 11 b.g. Ikdam – Miss Hganavak (Abednego)   **c–**
[2006/7 c20sᶠ Feb 14] little form over hurdles (tried in headgear): fair pointer, successful   **h–**
4 times in 2006: fell seventh in novice hunter on chasing debut: dead. *Miss B. J. Thomas*

ONE ROSE 4 b.f. Roi de Rome (USA) – Solo Rose (Roselier (FR)) [2006/7 F17g* Apr   **F94**
23] third foal: half-sister to fairly useful hurdler/useful chaser Ross River (by Over The
River), stays 25f: dam unraced, out of half-sister to Grand National winner Rubstic and
top-class staying chaser Kildimo: won mares bumper at Sedgefield on debut by 1¼
lengths from Sprinkler, not fully extended. *R. C. Guest*

ONE SNIFF (IRE) 8 b.g. Mister Lord (USA) – Deep Fern (Deep Run) [2006/7 h118p: **c127 p**
c25d* Nov 3] very lightly raced and presumably difficult to train, but won second of 2   **h–**
starts over hurdles (beaten by Denman first time) in 2005/6 and successful also in novice
at Hexham on chasing debut, beating The Reverend by 3 lengths: will stay beyond 25f:
raced only on good to soft going: remains likely to improve. *N. G. Richards*

ONE STEP CLOSER (IRE) 7 b.m. Broken Hearted – Toghermore Lass (Pry)   **c85**
[2006/7 F17v⁶ 22v c25s⁶ c21sᶠ c21v⁴ c26v³ c20d⁶ Mar 21] €4,000 4-y-o: sturdy mare: **h–**
fifth foal: half-sister to winning pointer by Supreme Leader: dam won 21f chase in Ireland: won maiden Irish point in 2006: well held in mares bumper/maiden hurdle: modest
maiden chaser: probably stays 3¼m: raced on going softer than good. *Mrs L. C. Jewell*

ONEWAY (IRE) 10 b.g. Bob's Return (IRE) – Rendezvous (Lorenzaccio) [2006/7   **c152**
c155, h–: c16d c16s³ c16d² c16g c16gᶠ c20g⁶ Apr 13] strong, workmanlike gelding: **h–**
smart chaser: creditable third to Kauto Star in last 2 renewals of Tingle Creek Trophy at
Sandown: well held in valuable handicap/Grade 1 event last 2 completed outings
(running creditably when falling 2 out in Queen Mother Champion Chase at Cheltenham
in between): effective at 2m to 2½m: raced mainly on good going or softer: blinkered last
2 starts: patiently ridden. *M. G. Rimell*

ONIZ TIPTOES (IRE) 6 ch.g. Russian Revival (USA) – Edionda (IRE) (Magical   **h109**
Strike (USA)) [2006/7 16s 17d 16m 17m⁶ 19s 17m* 16g² 18m⁵ 16d* 16mᵖᵘ Apr 22] fair
hurdler: missed 2005/6: won novice handicaps at Cartmel in August and Fakenham
(much improved) in November: best around 2m: acts on good to firm and good to soft
going: usually wears headgear. *J. S. Wainwright*

ON LES AURA (IRE) 8 b.g. Germany (USA) – Another Thurn (IRE) (Trimmingham)   **c–**
[2006/7 24s c26vᵖᵘ Dec 31] strong, heavy-topped gelding: novice hurdler: off over 2½   **h–**
years before reappearance: no show on chasing debut: stayed 2¾m: dead. *R. H. Alner*

ONLYBEGONEANHOUR 8 gr.g. Terimon – Phar Too Touchy (Mister Lord (USA))   **h–**
[2006/7 20d 20s 17d Oct 31] leggy, lengthy gelding: no form over hurdles: poor maiden
pointer: tongue tied in 2006/7. *D. Brace*

ONLY FOR SUE 8 ch.g. Pivotal – Barbary Court (Grundy) [2006/7 17s* 16s* Dec 2]   **h114 +**
modest at best on Flat (stays 1¾m), below form in 2006: took well to hurdling and won
both starts, novices at Exeter and Chepstow (beat Michael Muck by 6 lengths) 2 weeks
apart: may do better. *W. S. Kittow*

ONLY JUST BEGUN (IRE) 5 b.g. Rossini (USA) – Green Wings (General   **F81**
Assembly (USA)) [2006/7 F16g⁴ F16v⁵ F16m⁴ Apr 15] half-brother to several winners,
including fairly useful hurdler Entertainer (by Be My Guest), stayed 2¾m: dam Irish

1½m winner: best effort in bumpers (modest form) when 12 lengths fourth to Spud at Worcester final start. *Mrs L. Williamson*

ONLY MILLIE 6 b.m. Prince Daniel (USA) – Deb's Ball (Glenstal (USA)) [2006/7 h–, F–: 20d^{pu} 16f* 17m Aug 26] unfurnished mare: 100/1-winner of maiden hurdle at Kelso in May, only form: has had tongue tied. *James Moffatt*   **h73**

ONLY VINTAGE (USA) 7 b.g. Diesis – Wild Vintage (USA) (Alysheba (USA)) [2006/7 h134: c18d^3 c20d* c24s^2 c20s^{pu} c24s^{pu} Mar 17] lengthy gelding: useful handicap hurdler: similar form over fences: won maiden at Market Rasen in December, then short-head second of 4 to Jaunty Times in novice at Huntingdon: ran poorly in handicaps last 2 starts: stays 3m: raced on good ground or softer (acts on soft). *Miss H. C. Knight*   **c132 h–**

ONLY WORDS (USA) 10 ch.g. Shuailaan (USA) – Conversation Piece (USA) (Seeking The Gold (USA)) [2006/7 h78: 16g* 16v^2 16m^F 16f^2 20m^5 20f 16v^4 16v 20s 19s^2 17d 20g^5 Apr 3] workmanlike gelding: modest handicap hurdler: won amateur event at Wetherby on first day of season: stays 2½m: acts on any going: tried blinkered. *A. J. Lockwood*   **h87**

ONNIX (FR) 5 ch.g. Funny Baby (FR) – Elza III (FR) (Lazer (FR)) [2006/7 h111: 18s^2 16d^4 18v^{pu} 18s^3 19s^2 Mar 18] rather unfurnished gelding: fairly useful hurdler: best effort when fourth to Blazing Bailey in 6-runner 4-y-o handicap at Haydock: will stay 2½m: raced on ground softer than good. *F. Doumen, France*   **h125**

ONSLOW ROAD (IRE) 7 b.g. Un Desperado (FR) – Suelemar (IRE) (Montelimar (USA)) [2006/7 h–, F82: 20s^4 c26g^{pu} Jun 4] tall gelding: form (poor) over jumps only when fourth in handicap hurdle on reappearance. *Miss Venetia Williams*   **c– h69**

ON THE BENCH (IRE) 5 b.m. Leading Counsel (USA) – Glen Dieu (Furry Glen) [2006/7 F16s Nov 22] sister to 3m hurdle winner Glenbar and half-sister to 3 winners, including fairly useful but ungenuine hurdler/winning chaser Craven (by Accordion), stays 23f: dam, placed over hurdles/fences, half-sister to useful 2m to 3m chaser Bavard Dieu: tailed off in bumper on debut. *N. M. Babbage*   **F–**

ON THE FAIRWAY (IRE) 8 b.m. Danehill Dancer (IRE) – Asta Madera (IRE) (Toca Madera) [2006/7 h–: 16g^{pu} Nov 7] no form over hurdles: tried tongue tied. *Miss M. P. Bryant*   **h–**

ON THE FERRY 4 b.g. Kayf Tara – Shoptillyoudrop (Nishapour (FR)) [2006/7 F16m Apr 10] first foal: dam second at 1m on debut, only form: last in bumper on debut. *G. Brown*   **F–**

ON THE NET (IRE) 9 b.g. Torus – Petted Slave (Sandalay) [2006/7 c130, h116: c21d^4 c16g^2 20d^4 c24s^3 c20s* 17v^5 19v^3 c16v^2 c21g^F 20m^2 Apr 24] well-made gelding: useful handicap chaser/fairly useful handicap hurdler: won over fences at Limerick in December, left further clear at last: good efforts last 3 completed starts, ½-length second of 25 to Charlies First in valuable event over hurdles at Punchestown final one: stays 3m, effective at much shorter: acts on good to firm and heavy going: consistent. *Eoghan O'Grady, Ireland*   **c130 h120**

ON THE OUTSIDE (IRE) 8 ch.m. Anshan – Kate Fisher (IRE) (Over The River (FR)) [2006/7 c116, h–: c25m^{pu} c23m^3 c23g* 22m^4 c24g^{pu} Apr 21] winning hurdler: fairly useful handicap chaser: improved form when winning at Stratford in July by 4 lengths from Red Echo, making all: off 7½ months, ran poorly final outing: stays 3m: raced on good/good to firm ground over jumps: tongue tied. *S. E. H. Sherwood*   **c124 h93 +**

ON THE VERGE (IRE) 9 ch.g. Alphabatim (USA) – Come On Lis (Domynsky) [2006/7 24g^{pu} Jul 21] workmanlike gelding: maiden hurdler: left J. Jenkins and off 21 months, ran as if amiss only start in 2006/7: tried visored/blinkered: temperamental. *R. C. Guest*   **h– §**

ONWARD TO GLORY (USA) 7 b.g. Zabeel (NZ) – Landaria (FR) (Sadler's Wells (USA)) [2006/7 h100: 22g* 22g^5 20m^{pu} Jul 26] fair novice hurdler: easily best effort when winning at Wincanton in May by 3 lengths from Macmar: would also have won at Worcester in July but for breaking shoulder between last 2: stayed 2¾m: dead. *P. J. Hobbs*   **h115**

ONYORGARD (IRE) 5 b.g. Gulland – Gusserane Princess (Paddy's Stream) [2006/7 F16m^3 F17g^6 Apr 27] half-brother to several winners, including fairly useful hurdler/chaser Mr Pickpocket (by Roselier), stayed 3¼m, and to dam of high-class 2m chaser Dempsey: dam maiden: fair form in bumpers: will be suited by stiffer test of stamina. *R. H. Alner*   **F87**

ONYOURHEADBEIT (IRE) 9 b.g. Glacial Storm (USA) – Family Birthday (Sandalay) [2006/7 c102d, h–: c23s^2 c22s^3 c26v^{pu} c24g^{pu} Mar 21] good-topped gelding: **c96 d h–**

modest maiden chaser: below form last 3 outings: stays 3m: acts on heavy going: tried in cheekpieces: has found little. *K. C. Bailey*

ON Y VA (FR) 9 b.g. Goldneyev (USA) – Shakna (FR) (Le Nain Jaune (FR)) [2006/7 **c93 x** c106x, h113: 25m 20s c24s⁶ c23s⁶ Feb 14] leggy gelding: winning hurdler/chaser, **h–** generally let down by jumping over fences: stays 3m: unraced on firm going, probably acts on any other: in cheekpieces last 2 starts: tongue tied. *R. T. Phillips*

ONYX BRUERE (FR) 5 gr.g. Mansonnien (FR) – Hervine Bruere (FR) (Dom Pas- **h?** quini (FR)) [2006/7 17g* 16d Feb 10] leggy, angular gelding: first foal: dam successful 3 times up to around 2½m over fences in France: successful over 1½m on Flat: won 4-y-o event at Rochefort-sur-Loire on hurdling debut: left G. Macaire, not knocked about after blunder 2 out in novice at Newbury. *A. King*

ONYX D'ACE (FR) 5 b. or br.g. Simon du Desert (FR) – Diva de Chalamont (FR) **h80** (Balsamo (FR)) [2006/7 17sᵖᵘ 20m³ Apr 25] first foal: dam winning 3m cross-country chaser: in frame 5 times from 7 starts up to 15f on Flat in French Provinces for D. Limousy: poor form on completed outing in maiden hurdles. *A. King*

OODACHEE 8 b.g. Marju (IRE) – Lady Marguerrite (Blakeney) [2006/7 h135: c22d² **c131** c24d* c22g* c24s c21d² c24m⁵ c24d³ 20v³ c24g c29m c21m Apr 27] lengthy, angular **h118** gelding: useful hurdler/novice chaser: won first 3 starts over fences, maiden at Killarney and Grade 3 Hugh McMahon Memorial Chase at Limerick (by length from Vic Ville) in May, and novice at Galway in September: best effort when seventh of 29 to Butler's Cabin in Irish National at Fairyhouse penultimate outing: stays 29f: acts on firm and soft going: usually wears cheekpieces. *C. F. Swan, Ireland*

OOHOURBOO (IRE) 7 b.m. Old Vic – Tearaway Lady (IRE) (Tidaro (USA)) **h– §** [2006/7 h–§: 16v 21vᵖᵘ 16s Jan 31] tall, leggy mare: no form over hurdles (ran out on debut). *J. R. Holt*

OOPS (IRE) 8 b.g. In The Wings – Atsuko (IRE) (Mtoto) [2006/7 20dᵖᵘ 17d 19v⁵ 16v² **h91** 16v⁵ 16s³ 17s⁵ 16g⁴ 20g Apr 16] quite good-topped gelding: 2m winner on Flat: modest novice hurdler: best efforts around 2m: raced on good going or softer. *J. F. Coupland*

OPAL RIDGE 10 ch.g. Jupiter Island – The Beginning (Goldhill) [2006/7 c86: c21sᵖᵘ **c–** Mar 17] strong gelding: winning pointer: modest form at best in chases: probably stays 2¾m. *C. Roberts*

OPAL'S HELMSMAN (USA) 8 b.g. Helmsman (USA) – Opal's Notebook (USA) **h– §** (Notebook (USA)) [2006/7 h80§: 20dᵖᵘ May 1] maiden hurdler: won point in April: stays 3m: acts on good to firm and good to soft ground: tried in cheekpieces/visor/tongue tied: unreliable. *W. S. Coltherd*

OPARE (FR) 5 b.g. Agent Bleu (FR) – Fine Light (FR) (Sissoo) [2006/7 F–: 22s⁴ 24v⁵ **h75** 24s⁶ 20s Jan 24] lengthy, angular gelding: poor form over hurdles: lacks pace. *H. D. Daly*

OPEN DE L'ISLE (FR) 5 b. or br.g. Funny Baby (FR) – Gratiene de L'Isle (FR) **h111** (Altayan) [2006/7 F87: 20s 17v* 16v* 17v⁶ 20v⁵ 18v³ 20sᵖᵘ Apr 1] tall gelding: fair novice hurdler: won at Carlisle in November and Hexham in December: should stay 2½m: raced on soft/heavy going: free-going sort. *J. P. L. Ewart*

OPENDITCH (FR) 5 b.g. Video Rock (FR) – Enita (FR) (Brezzo (FR)) [2006/7 F17s* **h98 p** F16v³ 19g⁴ Mar 30] first foal: dam 10.5f winner in France: won maiden Irish point in **F108** September: impressive winner of bumper at Hereford in December, cruising clear to beat Rood Report by 18 lengths: disappointing next time: encouraging debut over hurdles when fourth to Shouldhavehadthat in maiden at Ascot, keeping on again not knocked about: will be suited by further than 19f: sure to improve over hurdles. *Miss H. C. Knight*

OPENIDE 6 b.g. Key of Luck (USA) – Eyelet (IRE) (Satco (FR)) [2006/7 h115§: 22d* **c129** 22d² c23f* c20s* c24s² c24d² c25sᵖᵘ c24g c25gᵖᵘ Apr 13] close-coupled gelding: fairly **h129** useful hurdler/novice chaser: won handicap hurdle (by 21 lengths from Harrycat) at Market Rasen in July, and over fences at Stratford in September and Tipperary (beat Rights of Man by 5 lengths in Grade 3 Kevin McManus Bookmaker Like-A-Butterfly Novices' Chase) in October: runner-up at Cheltenham behind Gungadu and Standin Obligation (flattered when beaten only length), but ran poorly last 3 outings: stays 3m: acts on heavy and good to firm going: tried visored/blinkered: has sometimes looked hard ride over hurdles. *B. W. Duke*

OPEN RANGE (IRE) 7 b.g. Saddlers' Hall (IRE) – L'Enfant Unique (IRE) (Phar- **h–** dante (FR)) [2006/7 h95: 18s 18g Mar 18] lengthy gelding: winning 2m hurdler: no form in Britain: tried in cheekpieces. *G. Wareham*

Pheasant Inn Novices' Chase, Newbury—
a second win at the track for Opera Mundi (No.4) who proves too strong for Private Be

OPEN SEASON (IRE) 7 b.g. Pierre – Poor Man's Rose (IRE) (Roselier (FR)) [2006/7 **h81**
19v⁴ Feb 23] €17,000 3-y-o: first foal: dam unraced, half-sister to fairly useful hurdler/
fair staying chaser Jet Boys: twice-raced in Irish points, third on completed start: poor
form when fourth in novice on hurdling debut. *Noel T. Chance*

OPERA DE COEUR (FR) 5 b.g. East of Heaven (IRE) – Eden de Coeur (FR) (Lam- **c110**
pon (FR)) [2006/7 h126p: c16g² c16vᵖᵘ c16d² c21s² 20vᵖᵘ 22d² 24g Apr 14] strong **h133**
gelding: useful hurdler: good second to Michael Muck in handicap at Uttoxeter: only fair
form when runner-up in novice chases, failing to convince with jumping (jockey banned
7 days for making insufficient effort on debut): stays 2¾m: raced on good going or softer.
H. D. Daly

OPERA KNIGHT 7 ch.g. In The Wings – Sans Escale (USA) (Diesis) [2006/7 h–: **h72**
16d⁶ 16g Nov 13] modest on Flat (stays 1½m), successful twice in 2006: poor form over
hurdles: tried in cheekpieces: sold 1,400 gns Doncaster January Sales. *A. W. Carroll*

OPERA MUNDI (FR) 5 b.g. Discover d'Auteuil (FR) – Gymnastique II (FR) (Aelan **c140 p**
Hapi (USA)) [2006/7 h111: c18s* c17v* c16s² c21g Mar 15] big, rather raw-boned **h–**
gelding: quickly showed himself a useful novice chaser, successful at Newbury in
November (handicap) and January (3 ran, beat Private Be by 4 lengths): also ran well when
¾-length second of 4 to Ursis (pair clear) in Grade 2 at Wincanton: favourite and in
outstanding shape, most disappointing in Racing Post Plate at Cheltenham: likely to prove
best at 2½m+: raced on good ground or softer (acts on heavy). *P. F. Nicholls*

OPERA WRITER (IRE) 4 b.g. Rossini (USA) – Miss Flite (IRE) (Law Society **h99**
(USA)) [2006/7 16g⁴ 16gᶠ 16g⁶ Nov 29] close-coupled gelding: half-brother to modest
hurdler Taranai (by Russian Revival), stays 2¾m: fair on Flat (stays 1½m), claimed from
J. Boyle £6,000 in September: fair form in juvenile hurdles: raced at 2m on good going.
R. Hollinshead

OPIO (FR) 5 b.g. Subotica (FR) – Alene (FR) (King Cyrus (USA)) [2006/7 F17m³ **h91**
F16m² F16g² F17sʳᵒ 16s⁶ 17d⁵ Nov 8] rangy gelding: second foal: dam of little account: **F91 §**
fair form in bumpers: better effort in novice hurdles when fifth at Bangor, pulling hard:
not straightforward (ran out final bumper outing). *M. W. Easterby*

OPIUM DES PICTONS (FR) 5 b.g. Grand Tresor (FR) – Ballaway (FR) (Djarvis **h–**
(FR)) [2006/7 h–: 17m 17m⁶ 18m Jun 6] little impact over hurdles: races freely.
D. E. Pipe

OPONCE (FR) 5 b.g. Varxi (FR) – Fraxinelle (FR) (Lou Piguet (FR)) [2006/7 17s 16d **h79** Nov 24] rather unfurnished gelding: dam unraced half-sister to very smart staying chaser Gingembre: looked in need of experience both starts over hurdles (for Mrs L. Taylor on debut). *Noel T. Chance*

OPPORTUNITY KNOCKS 7 gr.g. Wace (USA) – Madame Ruby (FR) (Homing) **c73** [2006/7 c69, h–: c24d^{pu} c20m* c20d^5 c21d c23s^{pu} c19m^5 22m Apr 28] tall gelding: **h–** winning hurdler: poor handicap chaser: won novice event at Plumpton in October: below form after: stays 2¾m: acts on soft and good to firm going: usually wears cheekpieces/blinkers. *N. J. Hawke*

OPTIC 5 b.m. Kayf Tara – Mid Day Chaser (IRE) (Homo Sapien) [2006/7 F17v F17s **F–** Jan 16] third foal: dam, bumper/2m hurdle winner, half-sister to fairly useful staying hurdler/chaser Lordberniebouffant: well held in mares bumpers: tried tongue tied. *P. R. Webber*

OPTIMISTIC ALFIE 7 b.g. Afzal – Threads (Bedford (USA)) [2006/7 h98d: c23g^3 **c84** c23m^F c25d^{pu} c24s c24s^3 c25s* c24g^5 Mar 29] lengthy gelding: maiden hurdler: poor **h–** chaser: took advantage of big drop in weights when winning handicap at Folkestone (by 17 lengths) in January: stays 25f: acts on soft ground: tried in cheekpieces/tongue tied, blinkered last 3 starts. *B. G. Powell*

OPTIMISTIC HARRY 8 b.g. Sir Harry Lewis (USA) – Miss Optimist (Relkino) **c–** [2006/7 c83, h–: 22d* 24m* Aug 22] close-coupled gelding: lightly raced: poor novice **h83** hurdler: off 10 months, won handicaps at Cartmel in May and Perth in August: similar form over fences: stays 3m: acts on soft and good to firm ground. *R. Ford*

OPTIMUM (IRE) 5 b.g. King's Best (USA) – Colour Dance (Rainbow Quest (USA)) **h93** [2006/7 h–: 16m* 16g^5 16d^{pu} 19g^4 21s^6 22d^6 24f^5 20g Apr 21] leggy, close-coupled gelding: fair on Flat (stays 1¾m), successful in July: modest hurdler: won handicap at Towcester in October: stays 19f: acts on good to firm going: blinkered last 2 starts. *J. T. Stimpson*

OPUS CAFE (FR) 5 b.g. Panoramic – Cafefleur (FR) (Le Correzien (FR)) [2006/7 21g **h92 p** 16d 19v^4 22s^3 Feb 3] sturdy gelding: fourth foal: dam placed on Flat/over fences (around 2m) in France: won maiden Irish point on debut in 2006: caught eye all 4 starts in novice/maiden hurdles, not knocked about: stays 2¾m: remains capable of better. *Miss E. C. Lavelle*

ORAN CLIMATE (IRE) 7 b.g. Oscar (IRE) – Approach The Dawn (IRE) (Orchestra) **c120** [2006/7 c22v^3 c20s^4 c20d^4 c21s^5 c17d* c16v^4 c20m 24m Apr 26] workmanlike gelding: **h105** fair hurdler: fairly useful novice chaser: won maiden at Leopardstown in January by 7 lengths from Ballytrim: good 11 lengths fourth to Young Desperado in Grade 2 at Navan next time: effective at 2m to 3m: acts on good to firm and heavy going: refused to race once in 2004/5. *John Paul Brennan, Ireland*

ORANGE STRAVINSKY 4 b.g. Stravinsky (USA) – Orange Sunset (IRE) (Roanoke **h–** (USA)) [2006/7 16g^6 17d Nov 21] fair maiden at 2 yrs, sold out of Sir Michael Stoute's stable 31,000 gns Doncaster November Sales, below best on Flat in 2006: no show over hurdles, including in seller. *P. C. Haslam*

ORANGE TOUCH (GER) 7 b.g. Lando (GER) – Orange Bowl (General Assembly **h87** (USA)) [2006/7 16s^5 16v^6 Feb 26] half-brother to fair 2m hurdler Eurotwist (by Viking): one-time smart performer on Flat (stays 1¾m), on downgrade: well held in novice/maiden hurdles at Plumpton. *Mrs A. J. Perrett*

ORANG OUTAN 5 b. or br.g. Baby Turk – Ellapampa (FR) (Pampabird) **c97** [2006/7 h93: 18g^3 c17s^4 c16s* 16v c19g 20s^6 c20m^3 Apr 20] sturdy gelding: modest **h97** maiden hurdler: similar form over fences: won maiden at Southwell in December: stays easy 2½m: acts on heavy and good to firm ground: usually tongue tied (rare poor effort when not). *J. P. L. Ewart*

OR APPLE'S (FR) 5 b.g. Ragmar (FR) – Entiqua Des Sacart (FR) (Lute Antique (FR)) **c99** [2006/7 c17g* c17d* c18v^{pu} c16v^5 c20g^5 c16g^3 c16f^4 Apr 22] smallish gelding: third foal: brother to fairly useful but ungenuine hurdler/chaser New Entic, stays 2¾m: dam, in frame over jumps around 2m in France, half-sister to fairly useful chaser up to 3m Koquelicot: once-raced on Flat: won both starts in chases in French Provinces, at Chatillon-sur-Chalaronne in September and Lyon Parilly in October: sold out of E. Clayeux's stable €48,000 Goffs (France) November Sale: modest form in handicaps in Britain: stays 2½m: tongue tied last 3 starts. *D. E. Pipe*

ORBIT O'GOLD (USA) 5 ch.g. Kingmambo (USA) – Lily O'Gold (USA) (Slew O' **h122** Gold (USA)) [2006/7 19d^2 16m^6 16s^3 18s* 16v* 16d 16s* 16d Mar 13] leggy gelding:

Mighty Macs Syndicate's "Orbit O'Gold"

fairly useful on Flat (probably stays 2m): fairly useful novice hurdler: won maiden at Downpatrick in November, minor event at Navan in December and Grade 2 Byrne Group plc Novices' Hurdle at Punchestown (50/1, much improved when making all to beat De Valira by 3 lengths) in February: stiff task, left behind 2 out in Supreme Novices' Hurdle at Cheltenham: will stay beyond 19f: acts on heavy going. *N. Meade, Ireland*

ORCADIAN 6 b.g. Kirkwall – Rosy Outlook (USA) (Trempolino (USA)) [2006/7 **h141** h122+: 16d² 16v⁵ 16d 16s* 16g⁶ Apr 14] lengthy, useful-looking gelding: smart but untrustworthy on Flat (stays 1¾m): useful handicap hurdler: improved form when winning at Newbury in March by 17 lengths from French Saulaie: creditable sixth of 22 to Kings Quay in listed contest at Aintree: raced around 2m on good ground or softer: races prominently: has been reluctant to post. *J. M. P. Eustace*

ORCHARD HOUSE (FR) 4 b.g. Medaaly – Louisa May (IRE) (Royal Abjar (USA)) **h–** [2006/7 16d 21g Mar 20] poor maiden on Flat: no show in maiden hurdles. *J. Jay*

OR DE GRUGY (FR) 5 b.g. April Night (FR) – Girlish (FR) (Passing Sale (FR)) **h92** [2006/7 20s 20s 20g⁶ 24g 20d² 20m² 16v² 20s² Apr 25] stocky gelding: second foal: dam never ran: successful twice from 5 starts up to 13.5f on Flat in French Provinces in 2006 for P. Cormier-Martin: modest novice hurdler: stays 2½m: acts on good to firm and heavy going. *Mrs S. C. Bradburne*

OR D'OUDAIRIES (FR) 5 b.g. April Night (FR) – Belle Truval (FR) (Rose Laurel) **F98** [2006/7 F16s³ F16v² Jan 27] close-coupled gelding: fifth foal: half-brother to 3 winners on Flat in France, including 13f winner Gamine d'Oudairies (by Passing Sale): dam unraced out of half-sister to dam of smart hurdler/chaser Barton, stayed 25f: better effort in bumpers (fairly useful form) when 6 lengths second to Lodge Lane at Uttoxeter. *M. W. Easterby*

ORDRE DE BATAILLE (FR) 5 gr.g. Ungaro (GER) – Hache de Guerre (FR) (Royal   **h118**
Charter (FR)) [2006/7 F94: 16s² 21g* 20v⁶ 20d 21d* 24g Apr 18] useful-looking gelding:
has scope: fairly useful hurdler: won novice at Warwick (awarded race after carried left
from last) in November and handicap at Ludlow (improved to beat Blaeberry by 1¾
lengths, pair clear) in March: may prove best short of 3m for time being: raced on good
ground or softer. *H. D. Daly*

ORGE D'ETE (FR) 5 gr.g. April Night (FR) – Fee Mousse (FR) (Sharken (FR))   **h120**
[2006/7 17s 16d⁶ 18d⁴ 16v² 19s* 16v* 22v³ 16d 16v Feb 10] rather leggy ex-French
gelding: placed twice from 4 starts on Flat: fairly useful novice hurdler: won at Limerick
(maiden) in November and Gowran (by 1½ lengths from Casey Jones) in December:
good 12 lengths third to Kazal in Grade 3 at Limerick: well held in handicap at Leopardstown final outing: stays 2¾m: acts on heavy going. *W. P. Mullins, Ireland*

ORIAK DES ORMEAUX (FR) 5 b.g. Sheyrann – Goode Des Ormeaux (FR) (Mis-   **h105**
tigri) [2006/7 17d* 17s⁴ 21gᵖᵘ Apr 18] rather leggy gelding: first foal: dam placed up to
19f over fences: successful around 1¾m on Flat in August: won 4-y-o event at Nantes on
hurdling debut in October: left Y. Fertillet, much better effort in novice hurdles in Britain
when fourth to Nawaadi at Taunton, carrying head high: presumably amiss 3 months later.
P. F. Nicholls

ORIGINAL FLY (FR) 5 b.g. Chef de Clan II (FR) – Ultim de Plaisance (FR) (Top   **c104**
Dancer (FR)) [2006/7 h102: c19g² c21d* c21sᵖᵘ c22v² c20s³ c16v² c17g² Apr 21] well-   **h–**
made gelding: fair novice hurdler: similar standard over fences: won conditional jockeys
handicap at Wincanton in November: left P. Nicholls after next start: should stay beyond
21f: raced on good going or softer (acts on heavy): usually blinkered: not straightforward.
D. McCain Jnr

ORIGINAL THOUGHT (IRE) 7 b.g. Entrepreneur – Troyanos (Troy) [2006/7   **c– p**
h113: 24s² c23gᶠ Nov 30] good-topped, close-coupled gelding: runner-up in Irish point: **h94 +**
fairly useful maiden hurdler: off 6 months, prominent when fell twelfth in maiden on
chasing debut: stays 3¼m: acts on soft and good to firm going: front runner/races prominently: consistent. *B. De Haan*

ORION DE LA FORME (FR) 5 ch.g. Golden Whip (FR) – Barre A Mine (FR)   **F–**
(King of Macedon) [2006/7 F16s May 20] third foal: half-brother to 9.5f winner Homere
du Plessis (by Alesso): dam 1½m winner: well held in bumper on debut. *D. G. Bridgwater*

ORION EXPRESS 6 b.g. Bahhare (USA) – Kaprisky (IRE) (Red Sunset) [2006/7 h77:   **h99**
19g² 19d⁶ 20m³ 16d 19d* 19g 19v⁶ 17g Apr 27] lengthy gelding: modest hurdler: left
M. Hill and improved in 2006/7, winning maiden at Newton Abbot (easily) in August and
conditional/amateur handicap at Taunton in October: stays 2½m: acts on good to soft and
good to firm going. *Mrs S. Gardner*

ORIONS ECLIPSE 6 b.m. Magic Ring (IRE) – Belle de Nuit (IRE) (Statoblest)   **h–**
[2006/7 h–, F–: 17v 16d Oct 22] of little account: tried tongue tied: sold 700 gns Doncaster November Sales. *M. J. Gingell*

ORION STAR (IRE) 5 ch.g. Fourstars Allstar (USA) – Rosies Sister (IRE) (Deep   **F78**
Run) [2006/7 F18g⁴ F18m Apr 26] €8,000 4-y-o: fifth foal: half-brother to fair hurdler
Chief Witness (by Witness Box), stayed 25f: dam, lightly raced in bumpers, half-sister to
fairly useful hurdler/chaser up to 2½m Bruton Street: modest form in bumpers: likely to
be suited by further than 2¼m. *J. W. Mullins*

ORISTANO (FR) 5 b.g. Smadoun (FR) ⸻ Quadrige du Marais (FR) (Le Pontet (FR))   **c–**
[2006/7 18s c18s c18g 16g 19d³ c16m⁴ Apr 9] strong gelding: sixth foal: dam, up to 11f on   **h80**
Flat, winner up to 25f over fences: poor form on balance over hurdles: left G. Cherel after
second outing: well beaten over fences: tried tongue tied. *M. F. Harris*

OR JAUNE (FR) 5 ch.g. Grand Tresor (FR) – Vancia (FR) (Top Dancer (FR)) [2006/7   **h117**
F97: F18g³ 19d 18s* 20d⁸ 20s³ 20s 20g* Apr 7] leggy gelding: bumper winner: pro-   **F92**
gressive over hurdles, winning maiden at Fontwell in January and novice handicaps at
Sandown in February and Haydock (fairly useful form, beat Sharp Reply by 1½ lengths,
despite hanging left) in April: will stay beyond 2½m: acts on soft going (bumper win on
good to firm). *G. L. Moore*

ORKI DES AIGLES (FR) 5 b.g. Le Balafre (FR) – Rose Des Aigles (FR) (Le Nain   **c96 +**
Jaune (FR)) [2006/7 h108d: 20s c25g* c28s² c28d² Dec 26] compact gelding: maiden   **h79**
hurdler: modest form in handicap chases: easily won novice event at Kelso in November:
stays well: acts on heavy going. *Ferdy Murphy*

ORLYHEART (FR) 4 b.c. Desert Style (IRE) – Blue Burgee (USA) (Lyphard's Wish   **h?**
(FR)) [2006/7 16s² 17d* 17v⁵ Feb 25] sixth foal: brother to a 1m winner in Italy and

half-brother to another Flat winner abroad by Fasliyev: dam 6f winner in France, later 8.5f winner in USA: placed once over 15f on Flat: twice-raced over hurdles at Pau, won 4-y-o claimer by distance in January (claimed from J-Y. Artu €20,000): failed to stay under very testing conditions in juvenile handicap on British debut: likely to need emphasis on speed around 2m. *R. H. Buckler*

ORMUS 4 b.g. Rambling Bear – Adar Jane (Ardar) [2006/7 F14s⁶ F16g² Apr 23] leggy gelding: fourth foal: dam unraced: better effort in bumpers 6 months apart when 8 lengths second to Laborec at Hexham. *C. R. Wilson*   **F97**

ORNAIS (FR) 5 b.g. Michel Georges – Imperia II (FR) (Beyssac (FR)) [2006/7 19d* 24v² 24g Mar 16] good-topped gelding: will make a chaser: first foal: dam, maiden, half-sister to fairly useful hurdler/useful chaser Napolitain, stays 25f: once-raced on Flat: fairly useful novice hurdler: left F. Cottin, won at Exeter in October by 27 lengths: creditable efforts next 2 outings, tenth of 20 to Wichita Lineman in Spa Novices' Hurdle at Cheltenham: stays 3m: raced on good going or softer (acts on heavy): tongue tied. *P. F. Nicholls*   **h124**

ORPEN WIDE (IRE) 5 b.g. Orpen (USA) – Melba (IRE) (Namaqualand (USA)) [2006/7 h107: 16f* 17d* 17m⁵ 17d⁴ 16m⁴ 16d² 16m* 16g² 16g* 16m* 16d⁴ 16d⁵ 16d 17v 16g^bd Mar 16] lengthy, angular gelding: fairly useful on Flat (stays 1m), won 3 times in 2006: fairly useful novice hurdler: won at Ludlow and Cartmel in first weeks of season, Stratford (handicap) in September, and Haydock and Ascot (by 5 lengths from Moon Over Miami) in October: likely to prove best around 2m: acts on firm and good to soft going, below form on softer: usually patiently ridden: tough and genuine. *M. C. Chapman*   **h126**

OR SING ABOUT (FR) 5 b.g. Le Balafre (FR) – Grande Folie (FR) (Highlanders (FR)) [2006/7 F91: F18g² F17m² 20g⁶ 19s 18s⁶ Jan 4] lengthy, workmanlike gelding: in frame in bumpers: poor form over hurdles. *J. W. Mullins*   **h80**
  F88

ORSUS (FR) 5 ch.g. Baloo du Camp (FR) – Belle de Bauregard (FR) (Quart de Vin (FR)) [2006/7 c17g^ur c18g* c17g² c17s* 19g* c18d² c18s⁶ c18s c23v^pu c21d c16d² c16g⁵ c19s² Mar 12] rangy gelding: second foal: dam ran once: once-raced on Flat: successful over fences at Cluny and Strasbourg in May and over hurdles at Wissembourg in June when trained by G-P. Levy: modest form in handicap chases in Britain: stays 19f: raced on good ground or softer. *H. J. L. Dunlop*   **c94**
  h?

ORTEGA (FR) 5 b.g. Useful (FR) – Madame Dabrovine (FR) (Vacarme (USA)) [2006/7 h93: 16m⁴ 20g^pu 19v⁴ 22v⁴ 20v³ 21s³ 21s⁵ Feb 9] leggy gelding: modest novice hurdler, sold out of P. Hobbs's stable 11,500 gns Doncaster May Sales after first outing: stays 21f: acts on heavy going. *C. E. Longsdon*   **h98**

ORTICA (FR) 5 b.g. Subotica (FR) – Volniste (FR) (Olmeto) [2006/7 F16m⁴ F17m⁴ 20d^ur 20g^pu 19v Feb 23] compact gelding: sixth foal: brother to fair staying hurdler/fairly useful staying chaser Red Echo and half-brother to 2 winners, notably smart staying chaser Jurancon II (by Scooter Bleu): dam 11f winner in France, later placed in cross-country chases: modest form in bumpers: well held completed outing over hurdles: dead. *D. G. Bridgwater*   **h–**
  F82

OSAKO D'AIRY (FR) 5 b.g. Cachet Noir (USA) – Esaka d'Airy (FR) (Marasali) [2006/7 c?, h106+: 16g³ 16s² c20m² Apr 15] tall, good-topped gelding: fair novice hurdler: winning chaser: off 6 months, similar form when runner-up in handicap at Market Rasen: stays 2½m: acts on soft and good to firm ground: tongue tied 3 of last 4 starts. *S. Gollings*   **c106**
  h99

OSANA (FR) 5 b.g. Video Rock (FR) – Voilette (FR) (Brezzo (FR)) [2006/7 16s* 16d² 20v⁴ 16s* 17g 16g² Apr 13] tall gelding, with scope: very much type to make a chaser: fifth foal: brother to leading non-thoroughbred Flat performer Gloria IV and half-brother to 2 winners, including fairly useful hurdler Krach (by Lute Antique), stayed 3m: dam winner up to 13f: successful twice over 1½m on Flat in 2006 for F. Doumen: useful hurdler: won novices at Plumpton (easily) in November and Wincanton (made all to beat Song of Songs by 6 lengths in good style) in February: ran creditably last 2 starts, in County Hurdle on handicap debut then 2½ lengths second to Blythe Knight in Grade 2 novice at Aintree: best around 2m: raced on good going or softer: strong-travelling sort, likely to do well over fences in 2007/8. *D. E. Pipe*   **h141 +**

OSCAR BUCK (IRE) 6 b.g. Oscar (IRE) – Rosey Buck (IRE) (Buckskin (FR)) [2006/7 F–: 22g³ May 2] well held in bumper: modest form when third to Onward To Glory in novice at Wincanton on hurdling debut: won maiden point in February: will stay 3m+. *V. R. A. Dartnall*   **h96**

OSCARDEAL (IRE) 8 b.g. Oscar (IRE) – Sleepy Bye Byes (IRE) (Supreme Leader) **c–**
[2006/7 h–: c16v^F c17s^{pu} 20d^5 20m* 20g Apr 7] workmanlike gelding: bumper winner: **h118**
best effort over hurdles (fairly useful form) when winning novice at Southwell in March
by 29 lengths from Santando: let down by jumping over fences: should stay beyond 2½m:
possibly best on good going or firmer: front runner. *C. T. Pogson*

OSCAR D'HYROME (FR) 5 gr.g. Myrakalu (FR) – Fluying (FR) (Luynes (USA)) **h98 §**
[2006/7 h97§: 22g^2 23v^{pu} 20s^{pu} Oct 11] leggy gelding: modest novice hurdler up to 2¾m
on his day, but most temperamental: one to leave alone. *C. Grant*

OSCAR INDIA (IRE) 8 b.g. Oscar (IRE) – Curry Lunch (Pry) [2006/7 c20d^2 c23s^3 **c117**
c24s^2 c26g^4 c25m^6 c25g Apr 25] medium-sized gelding: winning pointer: useful hunter
chaser: in frame first 4 starts in 2006/7, best effort when 17 lengths fourth to Drombeag in
Foxhunter at Cheltenham: will stay beyond 3¼m: acts on soft going, probably on good to
firm. *Henry de Bromhead, Ireland*

OSCAR IRELAND (IRE) 6 b. or br.g. Oscar (IRE) – Distinctly Scarlet (IRE) **c–**
(Import) [2006/7 16d c17d^{pu} 20g 16m Apr 25] good-topped gelding: second foal: dam **h–**
unraced: little sign of ability, left Henry de Bromhead after second outing. *Mrs S. J. Smith*

OSCAR JACK (FR) 6 b.g. Video Rock (FR) – Miss Noir Et Or (FR) (Noir Et Or) **c–**
[2006/7 c?, h–: 17g^3 16s^3 16v^3 Jan 13] lengthy, workmanlike ex-French gelding: maiden **h94**
chaser: modest novice hurdler: stays 19f: acts on heavy ground: has pulled hard. *Miss
Venetia Williams*

Mr Thomas Barr's "Osana"

Pertemps Final (Handicap Hurdle), Cheltenham—in fading light, Oscar Park holds off Material World (left), Adamant Approach (almost hidden) and Mistanoora (right)

OSCAR JEWEL (IRE) 7 b.m. Oscar (IRE) – Lady Letitia (Le Bavard (FR)) [2006/7 **h–** F16v 16g 20mᵖᵘ Apr 15] €5,500 4-y-o: leggy, close-coupled mare: half-sister to poor **F—** hurdler Whatashot (by Gunner B), stayed 27f, and winning pointers by Seymour Hicks and Gunner B: dam, winning Irish hurdler, half-sister to top-class chaser Wayward Lad: won mares maiden Irish point in 2006: bought 10,000 gns Doncaster May Sales: well held in bumper/completed start over hurdles: dead. *W. Jenks*

OSCAR PARK (IRE) 8 b.g. Oscar (IRE) – Parkavoureen (Deep Run) [2006/7 h133: **h147** 24d² 20sᶠ 22d 24g* Mar 15] leggy, angular gelding: smart handicap hurdler, left C. Tinkler after second start: tongue tied, better than ever when winning 24-runner listed Pertemps Final at Cheltenham in March by ½ length from Material World, battling well after going 3 lengths clear: stays 3m well: acts on soft going, possibly unsuited by good to firm: reliable. *D. W. P. Arbuthnot*

OSCAR PERFORMANCE (IRE) 12 gr.g. Roselier (FR) – Miss Iverk (Torus) **c–** [2006/7 c–, h–: c21g³ c26dᵖᵘ c20mᵖᵘ Jul 16] lengthy gelding: winning hurdler/maiden **h—** chaser, retains little ability: blinkered nowadays. *R. H. Buckler*

OSCAR'S ADVANCE (IRE) 8 b.g. Oscar (IRE) – Banna's Retreat (Vitiges (FR)) **c108** [2006/7 h118: c20g* c16s³ c20d⁵ c24sᵖᵘ 22d Mar 17] sturdy gelding: fairly useful **h96 +** hurdler: off 6 months and left C. Roche, shaped as if in need of run final outing: fair form over fences: easily won maiden at Tipperary in May: stays 3m: acts on heavy going. *Jonjo O'Neill*

OSCAR THE BOXER (IRE) 8 b.g. Oscar (IRE) – Here She Comes (Deep Run) **h95** [2006/7 h89: 20mᵖᵘ 20f⁵ 22m⁶ 24g⁴ 24m 18v⁶ 25d* 25g⁴ 27v² 25v 27s² Apr 27] lengthy, useful-looking gelding: modest handicap hurdler: won conditional jockeys event at Catterick in December: stays 27f: acts on any going. *J. M. Jefferson*

OSCATELLO (USA) 7 b. or br.g. Woodman (USA) – Galea Des Bois (FR) (Persian **h131** Bold) [2006/7 h129, F108: 24d 21d⁶ 21g⁴ 24g Apr 14] good-topped gelding: useful handicap hurdler: left Ian Williams and off nearly 3 months, good fourth of 28 to Burntoakboy in Coral Cup at Cheltenham: seems best short of 3m: raced on good going or softer (acts on heavy): reliable. *P. J. Hobbs*

OSHKOSH (IRE) 6 ch.g. Shernazar – Lucy Mews (IRE) (Persian Mews) [2006/7 **F96** F16s² F16v⁴ F16v⁴ Mar 6] 7,000 3-y-o: quite good-topped gelding: second foal: dam, maiden pointer, half-sister to useful staying chaser King Lucifer: 66/1, easily best effort in bumpers when 14 lengths second of 20 to Den of Iniquity at Warwick: will be suited by further than 2m. *K. C. Bailey*

728

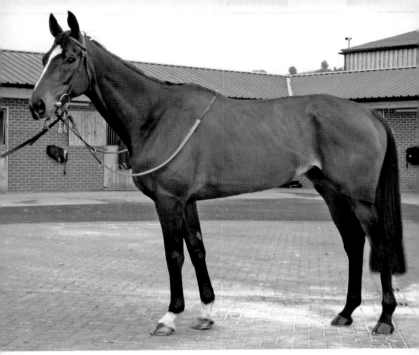

Mr George Ward's "Oscar Park"

OSLOT (FR) 5 b.g. Passing Sale (FR) – Une de Lann (FR) (Spoleto) [2006/7 17s* 16d² **h133 p**
16v³ 16g 20f* Apr 28] angular gelding: fifth foal: half-brother to one-time useful hurdler/
chaser Kadount (by Our Account), stays 21f, and to 3 middle-distance winners on Flat:
dam 13f winner: successful all 3 starts up to 13f on Flat in French Provinces at 4 yrs
for X-L. Le Stang: useful novice hurdler: won maiden at Taunton in December and
quite valuable handicap at Sandown (17 ran, improved to beat Chilling Place by 1¼

*Betfredcasino Handicap Hurdle, Sandown—the novice Oslot survives a mistake at the last
to beat Chilling Place (diamonds) in course record time*

lengths) in April: likely to stay beyond 2½m: acts on any going: open to further progress. *P. F. Nicholls*

O'SOGOOD (IRE) 5 b.g. Oscar (IRE) – Bula Supreme (IRE) (Supreme Leader) [2006/7 F17v F14v* Jan 13] €1,200 3-y-o, 7,500 4-y-o: first foal: dam unraced: much better effort in bumpers when winning at Wetherby in January by 11 lengths from Brave Brigadier: ridden by 10-lb claimer. *G. M. Moore* **F93**

OSPREY VIEW (IRE) 4 b.g. Observatory (USA) – Waffle On (Chief Singer) [2006/7 16d⁶ 16d 16g⁵ Apr 14] leggy ex-Irish gelding: trained by K. Prendergast, fair performer on Flat (stays 9f), blinkered when successful in September: off 3½ months, easily best effort over hurdles when fifth in novice at Chepstow. *N. A. Twiston-Davies* **h104**

OSSMANN (IRE) 7 b.g. Luso – Bit of A Chance (Lord Ha Ha) [2006/7 F16g⁶ 21v⁴ 20s⁵ 19s c24vᵖᵘ Jan 27] rangy gelding: chasing type: half-brother to 21f chase winner Lucky Sinna (by Insan) and 2m hurdle winner Movie Maid (by Be My Native): dam, fair 2½m hurdle winner, half-sister to smart staying hurdler Miss Nero: runner-up in maiden Irish point in 2006: bought 15,000 gns Doncaster May Sales: sixth in bumper: poor form over hurdles: pulled up on chasing debut. *T. R. George* **c–** **h79** **F79**

OSSMOSES (IRE) 10 gr.g. Roselier (FR) – Sugarstown (Sassafras (FR)) [2006/7 c146, h–: 23v⁴ c25v⁵ 20v² Mar 22] big gelding: lightly raced over hurdles, fairly useful form when neck second to Amstecos in novice at Ayr: smart handicap chaser: successful in Red Square Vodka Gold Cup at Haydock in 2005/6: respectable fifth to Leading Man in Grade 3 at Wetherby: reportedly strained tendon in build up to Grand National: stays 33f: raced on going softer than good (acts on heavy): front runner: sound jumper: game and reliable. *D. M. Forster* **c134 +** **h121**

OSTFANNI (IRE) 7 b.m. Spectrum (IRE) – Ostwahl (IRE) (Waajib) [2006/7 h119: 22f⁶ 22g* 24m⁴ 21g 20g² 24s 24g⁵ Mar 15] smallish mare: fair on Flat (stays 2m): fairly useful hurdler: won 2 minor events at Kelso in May: good efforts in handicaps 2 of last 3 starts, 8 lengths fifth of 24 to Oscar Park in Pertemps Final at Cheltenham (3 lb out of weights): stays 25f: has form on heavy going, best efforts under less testing conditions (acts on firm). *M. Todhunter* **h128**

OSTROGOTH (FR) 5 b.g. Ungaro (GER) – Holding (FR) (Useful (FR)) [2006/7 h108: 16s 16d Feb 1] sturdy gelding: fairly useful juvenile hurdler: off 10 months, well below form in 2006/7, too much use made of him on return: raced at 2m: tried tongue tied (raced freely). *N. J. Henderson* **h–**

OTANTIQUE (FR) 5 b.g. Lute Antique (FR) – Gracieuse Antique (FR) (Mont Basile (FR)) [2006/7 h88*, F83: 21d⁶ 18s⁶ 22d* Mar 20] leggy, useful-looking gelding: stepped up markedly on previous form over hurdles (caught eye more than once) when winning 17-runner novice event at Exeter on handicap debut in March by 5 lengths from Kathleens Pride: will stay beyond 2¾m: raced on going softer than good: open to further improvement. *Miss E. C. Lavelle* **h112 p**

OTARIE (FR) 5 b.m. Lute Antique (FR) – Birdie IV (FR) (Carmont (FR)) [2006/7 F16v F16v F16g² Apr 8] 15,000 4-y-o: tall mare: sixth foal: half-sister to cross-country chase winner Loup Sauvage (by Mollicone Junior) and 9f winner Merveille d'Un Soir (by Concorde Jr): dam ran once over hurdles: first form (poor) in bumpers when second to Aya at Towcester. *A. King* **F74**

OTIS B DRIFTWOOD 4 b.g. Tipsy Creek (USA) – Gi La High (Rich Charlie) [2006/7 16gᵘʳ Mar 20] poor on Flat (likely to prove best at 5f/6f), sold out of M. Quinn's stable 1,500 gns Newmarket July Sales: unseated fourth on hurdling debut: doubtful stayer. *Miss J. R. Tooth* **h–**

O'TOOLE (IRE) 8 b.g. Toulon – Legs Burke (IRE) (Buckskin (FR)) [2006/7 c110, h115+: 16g* c16m³ 17d⁶ 18gᵖᵘ 16g* 16d 17g Mar 16] lengthy gelding: fair chaser: fairly useful handicap hurdler: won at Worcester in May and Cheltenham (25/1, beat Figaro du Rocher by 7 lengths in conditional jockeys event) in October: well held after in 2 valuable events 4 months apart: should stay 2½m: has won on soft going, best efforts under less testing conditions (acts on good to firm): has carried head high. *P. J. Hobbs* **c110** **h124**

OTTO DES PICTONS (FR) 5 b.g. Grand Tresor (FR) – Sarawak (FR) (Djarvis (FR)) [2006/7 F17s⁵ 19s² 21v² 16s² 20s⁵ 24m* Apr 20] €24,000 3-y-o, resold 60,000 3-y-o: tall gelding: has scope: fifth foal: half-brother to winning 21f chaser Frisky (by Mill Pond) and 15f winner Ezera (by Chamberlin): dam unraced: shaped as if in need of run in bumper on debut: runner-up 3 of 4 starts over hurdles before showing marked improvement (useful form) to win 4-runner novice handicap at Ayr in April by 17 lengths from Ice Tea: stays 3m: has found little/carried head high. *P. F. Nicholls* **h130 +** **F91**

OUH JAY 9 ch.m. Karinga Bay – Creeping Jane (Rustingo) [2006/7 c19g⁵ c20d³ c20m² c16mᵖᵘ c16m⁶ c20g⁵ 24d* Mar 22] close-coupled mare: failed to complete in points: maiden chaser, little impact in handicaps fourth to sixth outings for P. Bowen: 66/1 and off over 7 months, much improved when winning mares novice at Ludlow on hurdling debut by 7 lengths from Khadija, allowed clear lead: stays 3m: acts on good to firm and good to soft going: front runner. *K. M. Prendergast* — **c76 h89**

OULAN BATOR (FR) 7 b.g. Astair (FR) – Scarieuse (FR) (Crackao (FR)) [2006/7 h62+: 16sᵖᵘ May 17] useful-looking gelding: little form over hurdles. *R. A. Fahey* — **h–**

OULART 8 ch.g. Sabrehill (USA) – Gaye Fame (Ardross) [2006/7 c126, h120: c20d⁶ c22gᵇᵈ c22ᵛᶠ c24ᵛᵖᵘ c24d 24s² 21g c29m Apr 9] lengthy gelding: useful handicap hurdler: good efforts sixth/seventh outings, length second to Contessa Messina at Punchestown and seventh of 28 to Burntoakboy in Coral Cup at Cheltenham: maiden chaser (runner-up in 2006 Irish Grand National at Fairyhouse), well held on completed starts in 2006/7: stays 29f: acts on heavy ground: effective with or without cheekpieces. *D. T. Hughes, Ireland* — **c102 h132**

OUMEYADE (FR) 5 b.g. Smadoun (FR) – Debandade (FR) (Le Pontet (FR)) [2006/7 16gᵖᵘ 19dᶠ 17s 16d Jan 8] compact gelding: fourth foal: half-brother to 3 winners, notably useful hurdler/smart chaser Ladalko (by Kadalko), stays 33f: dam winning hurdler/chaser up to around 2¾m in France: successful 3 times up to around 1½m on Flat: won 17f 4-y-o event over hurdles at Enghien: left G. Cherel, failed to see race out all 4 starts in Britain: tried tongue tied. *Miss H. C. Knight* — **h–**

OUNINPOHJA (IRE) 6 b.g. Imperial Ballet (IRE) – Daziyra (IRE) (Doyoun) [2006/7 17d* 17s³ 16g² 17g² 16g³ 16m² Apr 21] rather leggy gelding: half-brother to 2m hurdle winner Quasimodo (by Night Shift): smart on Flat (stays 1½m), successful 5 times at 4 yrs, placed all 7 starts in 2006 for G. A. Swinbank/I. Semple: useful novice hurdler: — **h141 §**

Mrs M. Findlay's "Ouninpohja"

landed odds in maiden at Taunton in November: placed all starts after, including when length second of 28 to Pedrobob in County Hurdle (Handicap) at Cheltenham and 4 lengths second of 8 to Emmpat in Scottish Champion Hurdle at Ayr (blinkered, ridden much more positively) fourth/final starts: likely to prove best in truly-run race around 2m: acts on good to firm and good to soft going: carries head high: ungenuine. *P. F. Nicholls*

OURAGAN DE PRAIRIE (FR) 5 ch.g. Brier Creek (USA) – Airelle de Prairie (FR) (El Badr) [2006/7 16s⁵ 24g⁴ Mar 23] compact gelding: fourth foal: half-brother to 17f chase winner Jason de Prairie (by Muguet d'Or): dam 2¼m chase winner: won 1½m event at Paray-Le-Monial in September: left M. Boudot, better effort in novice hurdles when fifth at Huntingdon. *N. A. Twiston-Davies* **h86**

OURAGAN LAGRANGE (FR) 5 b.g. Panoramic – Fannie de Lagrange (FR) (Torence (FR)) [2006/7 F14v² F18v² F18g³ Mar 26] €26,000 4-y-o: rangy, rather unfurnished gelding: first foal: dam maiden chaser in France: fair form when placed in bumpers. *G. L. Moore* **F92**

OUR BEN 8 ch.g. Presenting – Forest Pride (IRE) (Be My Native (USA)) [2006/7 c142, h–: c24v⁴ c17s² c18s⁸ 24v³ c24m⁴ c16m⁶ Apr 24] big, strong, good-topped gelding: useful hurdler/chaser: best effort in 2006/7 when 2 lengths second to Mansony in handicap at Leopardstown: easily landed odds in 5-runner listed chase at Cork in April: effective around 2m, should stay beyond 3m: acts on heavy going, probably on good to firm: jumps right. *W. P. Mullins, Ireland* **c140 h135**

OUR BILL 9 br.g. Alflora (IRE) – Flagg Flyer VII (Damsire Unregistered) [2006/7 c–: c24g^pu May 5] no show in points/hunter chases. *D. Pearson* **c–**

OUR FLOSSIE (IRE) 5 b.f. Midhish – Buckalgo (IRE) (Buckskin (FR)) [2006/7 F16s F16g F17d Mar 19] half-sister to winning pointer by Denel: dam unraced: well held in bumper and seller on Flat. *A. D. Brown* **F–**

OUR JASPER 7 gr.g. Tina's Pet – Dawn's Della (Scottish Reel) [2006/7 h101: 20d³ 20s^F 19g³ 19d* 19s* 20v³ 21g⁶ 20g Apr 12] tall gelding: fairly useful hurdler: left K. Reveley, improved in 2006/7, winning novice at Market Rasen in December and handicap at Catterick (beat Thunder Rock a neck, pair clear) in January: stays 2½m: acts on soft going. *D. McCain Jnr* **h116**

OUR JIM 5 ch.g. Sir Harry Lewis (USA) – Dawn's Della (Scottish Reel) [2006/7 F16m Oct 12] third foal: half-brother to fairly useful 19f hurdle winner Our Jasper (by Tina's Pet): dam poor maiden hurdler: favourite, well beaten in bumper on debut. *D. McCain Jnr* **F–**

OUR JOLLY SWAGMAN 12 b.g. Thowra (FR) – Queens Dowry (Dominion) [2006/7 c85d, h–: c21g^ur Apr 12] compact gelding: one-time fairly useful chaser, no longer of much account: wears headgear. *Mrs A. L. Tory* **c– h–**

OUR JOYCEY 6 b.m. Shernazar – Charisse Dancer (Dancing Dissident (USA)) [2006/7 h81, F79: 21m⁵ 20g* 24s 27v³ Feb 20] leggy mare: poor hurdler: off 6 months, won mares novice handicap at Leicester in November: stays 27f: acts on heavy going, respectable effort on good to firm. *Mrs K. Walton* **h84**

OUR KENNY 5 b.g. Overbury (IRE) – Auntie Alice (Uncle Pokey) [2006/7 F16g⁶ F16d 16g 16g^pu Dec 20] first foal: dam winning pointer: signs of ability only in bumper on debut. *C. W. Thornton* **h– F70**

OUR KEV (IRE) 11 b.g. Be My Native (USA) – Sunbath (Krayyan) [2006/7 c23f^pu Sep 3] tall gelding: won conditional jockeys handicap in 2003/4, only form in chases (very lightly raced since): stays 3m. *B. I. Case* **c– h–**

OUR LAWMAN 8 b.g. Shareef Dancer (USA) – Motoqua (Mtoto) [2006/7 c16d c20s^F 20d^pu Nov 3] no form over jumps. *Mrs S. J. Smith* **c– h–**

OUR MAN IN BANGKOK 7 b.g. Defacto (USA) – Ninety-Five (Superpower) [2006/7 c20d³ Mar 19] third foal: half-brother to 6f winner in USA by Most Welcome: dam 5f winner: third in maiden point (ran out on debut) in 2006: 9½ lengths third of 6 to Three Mirrors in maiden at Market Rasen on chasing debut. *T. J. Fitzgerald* **c79**

OUR MONTY (IRE) 4 b.g. Montjeu (IRE) – She's Our Mare (IRE) (Commanche Run) [2006/7 16d 16d³ 16s 16v 20g Apr 12] leggy gelding: fair maiden on Flat (stays 1½m) for J. Oxx: best effort over hurdles when around 2 lengths third to Boulavogue in 24-runner juvenile maiden at Punchestown: blinkered final outing (very stiff task). *K. F. O'Brien, Ireland* **h103**

OUR MR NAVIGATOR (IRE) 9 ch.g. Erins Isle – Latin Quarter (North Summit) c– x
[2006/7 c77: c26d^{pu} Nov 19] lightly-raced gelding: poor form only completed start in
chases: sketchy jumper. *N. R. Mitchell*

OUR PRIMA DONNA (IRE) 9 ch.m. Be My Native (USA) – Stage Debut (Decent c76
Fellow) [2006/7 c24g c23v^{ur} Mar 9] workmanlike mare: maiden hurdler/chaser, modest h–
form at best: probably stays 3m: raced on good going or softer: tongue tied in 2006/7.
B. N. Pollock

OUR SAMSON (IRE) 7 b.g. Old Vic – Strong Gale Pigeon (IRE) (Strong Gale) h91
[2006/7 21m 21g 22d^2 22v^2 Dec 12] small, close-coupled gelding: Irish point winner:
modest novice hurdler, off nearly 2 years before reappearance: stays 2¾m: acts on good
to soft going: in cheekpieces last 2 starts. *G. L. Moore*

OUR TEDDY (IRE) 7 ch.g. Grand Lodge (USA) – Lady Windley (Baillamont (USA)) h– p
[2006/7 18g^4 Sep 3] fairly useful on Flat (stays 1½m), successful 3 times in 2006:
well-held fourth to The Bonus King in novice at Fontwell on hurdling debut: should do
better. *P. A. Blockley*

OUR TEES COMPONENT (IRE) 6 b.m. Saddlers' Hall (IRE) – Shaiymara (IRE) F82
(Darshaan) [2006/7 F84p: F16v^4 F16g Mar 17] big, good-topped mare: modest form in
frame first 2 starts in bumpers 21 months apart: will be suited by 2½m+. *K. G. Reveley*

OUR TIME (IRE) 4 b.f. Danetime (IRE) – Tolomena (Tolomeo) [2006/7 16g 17g 16d^6 h74
17d^5 16d 17g^6 17g^F 17g^2 17g^3 Apr 27] angular filly: no form in maidens at 2 yrs (refused
to enter stall once): poor maiden hurdler: raced around 2m on good/good to soft ground.
H. S. Howe

OUR VIC (IRE) 9 b.g. Old Vic – Shabra Princess (Buckskin (FR)) [2006/7 c163, c168 §
h–: c25s* c25v^2 c21g^2 c25g^3 Apr 12] h–
  While a manager of a struggling football team might dread receiving a vote
of confidence from his chairman, a scenario which has so often led to the manager
being out of a job within weeks, there is surely no need for David Pipe to be alarmed
about losing some of the patronage of his principal owner. 'David Pipe continues
to train the vast majority of my horses and, as far as I'm concerned, that will not
change,' said David Johnson in June 2007, responding quickly to put an end to the
speculation which followed the announcement that he was to have a couple of
horses with Paul Nicholls in the 2007/8 season. Nicholls, of course, is the current
champion jumps trainer, having finally wrested the title from David Pipe's father
Martin in 2005/6, so it was only to be expected that such news would be regarded
by some as a loosening of Johnson's long-standing links with Pond House. The
horses concerned are the ex-French geldings Chapoturgeon and Marodima, the
latter bought for 145,000 guineas at the Doncaster May Sales after winning twice
over hurdles for Oliver Sherwood in the latest season, and, although Johnson owns
both in partnership, they will run in his colours. (It was announced in the summer
that an owner's prize money haul in the championship table would, from now on,
also include his or her share of any prizes won in a partnership).
  David Pipe was the leading trainer in terms of number of races won in
2006/7 (one hundred and thirty-four), his first season in charge. Yet Pipe-trained
runners carrying Johnson's familiar royal blue and emerald green silks didn't
occupy the winner's enclosure with their usual regularity during the second half of
2006/7—there were only ten winners after the turn of the year, including a near
two-month drought that took in both the Cheltenham and Aintree Festivals. Big-
race victories were noticeably thin on the ground, too, something which might have
added to speculation about the partnership. It had all looked much rosier in the first
half of the campaign, when Our Vic made an impressive return to
action in the bet365 Charlie Hall Chase at Wetherby in October. Our Vic had looked
potentially top class when starting off over fences in 2003/4, and he finally showed
himself to be just that at Wetherby. His career in between had contained at least as
many lows as highs, Our Vic's inconsistency partly down to his jumping which
let him down badly at times. However, he certainly got his act together in a good
renewal of the Charlie Hall, a Grade 2 event in which he and Kingscliff were set to
concede weight to each of the eight other runners. Apart from when giving a
lacklustre display in the Betfair Bowl at Aintree on his final start in 2004/5, Our Vic
had been raced only at around two and a half miles since winning the Reynoldstown

bet365 Charlie Hall Chase, Wetherby—
Timmy Murphy doesn't have to move a muscle as Our Vic makes an impressive return

and finishing third in the Royal & SunAlliance in his novice season. The step back up in to three miles and a furlong at Wetherby posed him no problems, even though the ground was testing and the pace good. Our Vic's jumping was impossible to fault as he travelled very well racing prominently. After taking the lead going to four out, he drew clear on the bridle to win by seven lengths from Neptune Collonges (who received 12 lb), his performance one of the best seen in this long-established contest. Our Vic's odds for the Cheltenham Gold Cup were cut to as low as 8/1 with one firm.

In the end, Our Vic didn't even make the Gold Cup line-up, once again the race now registered as the Festival Trophy his chosen engagement at the Cheltenham Festival, that target influenced to some extent by Our Vic's effort in the Cotswold Chase at Cheltenham on his only outing between Wetherby and the Cheltenham Festival. On ground even more testing than at Wetherby, Our Vic (who started favourite) finished eighteen lengths second to Exotic Dancer to whom he was conceding 4 lb, jumping well apart from a blunder when being strongly pressed two out, after which he weakened markedly, out on his feet at the line. Back over shorter in the Festival Trophy, Our Vic performed a great deal better than on his two previous appearances in the equivalent contest, and would probably have won but for being the worst affected of those hampered by the fall of Crozan four out. Our Vic had already lost his place by that stage, looking none too keen, but he rallied in the straight and finished strongly to take second, only a neck behind Taranis (who received 5 lb), coming out the best horse at the weights. That Our Vic was still as frustrating as ever was underlined on his only subsequent start, when he ran well below his best in a remote third of five behind Exotic Dancer in the Betfair Bowl at Aintree, already labouring by the fifteenth and tiring in the straight. Our Vic is still only nine and relatively lightly-raced—he seems best fresh—and there is a chance he could produce another display to match the one he put up in the Charlie Hall, though he certainly couldn't be backed with confidence to do so. He has been ridden in all his races over the past three seasons by Timmy Murphy who has again been retained to ride David Johnson's horses in 2007/8, though most of the others at Pond House will be partnered by newly-appointed stable jockey Tom Scudamore.

Our Vic (IRE) (b.g. 1998)	Old Vic (b 1986)	Sadler's Wells (b 1981)	Northern Dancer Fairy Bridge
		Cockade (b 1973)	Derring-Do Camenae
	Shabra Princess (b or br 1983)	Buckskin (b 1973)	Yelapa Bete A Bon Dieu
		Random View (b or br 1977)	Random Shot Rising View

Our Vic, whose pedigree has been well documented in previous Annuals, is the fourth foal of the maiden jumper Shabra Princess. The pick of her other produce is Our Vic's year-younger half-brother and stable-companion Commercial Flyer (by Carroll House), a useful staying hurdler/chaser who has become a rather frustrating performer himself in recent seasons. The latest foal out of Shabra Princess to reach the racecourse, Siegemaster (by Lord Americo), showed ability in bumpers and over hurdles in Ireland in the latest season. Shabra Princess has produced two more foals by Old Vic since, a 2003 filly (called Knockbounce View) and a 2005 colt. Her only other unraced foal to report is a 2002 Carroll House gelding called Commercial Vic. Our Vic, a tall, good-topped gelding, has raced only on good ground or softer and he acts on heavy. *D. E. Pipe*

OUTCLASS 5 b.m. Classic Cliche (IRE) – Winnetka Gal (IRE) (Phardante (FR)) [2006/7 F17s 20v^pu 16g^5 16m^6 Apr 24] lengthy mare: fourth foal: dam temperamental maiden: no form in bumper/over hurdles. *D. J. Wintle*   **h–** **F—**

OUTONHISOWN (IRE) 6 b.g. Moonax (IRE) – Twinkling (Star Appeal) [2006/7 F18s^2 F16s^5 F16v^3 20s^6 20g^5 Apr 11] half-brother to fair staying chaser/winning hurdler Oneofourown (by Varshan) and useful staying chaser Lordofourown (by Mister Lord): dam winning pointer: fair form when placed in bumpers: better effort over hurdles when 10½ lengths fifth to Valuta in maiden at Hereford: likely to be suited by stiffer test of stamina. *S. Donohoe, Ireland*   **h85** **F85**

OUTSIDE INVESTOR (IRE) 7 b. or br.g. Cadeaux Genereux – Desert Ease (IRE) (Green Desert (USA)) [2006/7 c–, h95: 20m^2 22d^3 22g^pu 20g Apr 27] workmanlike gelding: modest hurdler: well held both starts over fences: stays 2¾m: acts on firm and good to soft going: formerly often blinkered, wears cheekpieces nowadays. *P. R. Rodford*   **c–** **h95**

OUT THE BLACK (IRE) 9 b. or br.g. Presenting – Executive Wonder (IRE) (Executive Perk) [2006/7 c23d^su c22v^3 c25s^4 c24g^4 c24g* Apr 21] rather leggy gelding: useful handicap chaser: off nearly 2 years, would have won at Exeter but for idling markedly and slipping up near line: kept his form after and was successful at Bangor in April by ½ length from Bronzesmith: stays 3m: raced on good going or softer. *P. J. Hobbs*   **c130**

OUT TO LUNCH (IRE) 6 b.g. Accordion – Scent of A Rose (IRE) (Little Bighorn) [2006/7 F17s F16s^4 16v 18v 16v^6 20g 25g^pu Apr 16] strong, useful-looking gelding: first foal: dam unraced half-sister to fairly useful 2½m hurdler Symphony's Son: better effort in bumpers when fourth to Digital Media at Wetherby: little impact over hurdles, including in handicap: should be suited by 2½m+. *Mrs K. Walton*   **h–** **F79**

OUZBECK (FR) 5 b. or br.g. Denham Red (FR) – Volodia (FR) (Dhausli (FR)) [2006/7 16s^3 Feb 17] fifth foal: half-brother to winning cross-country chaser Grognard du Bosc (by Shafoun) and winner around 1¾m Keur Moussa (by Smadoun): dam in frame in cross-country chases: successful twice up to 15f from 5 starts on Flat in French Provinces at 4 yrs for F-X. Lefeuvre: shaped well when 13 lengths third to Osana in novice at Wincanton on hurdling debut: likely to improve for experience, and should win a similar event. *A. King*   **h121 p**

OVERAMOROUS 6 b.m. Overbury (IRE) – Random Romance (Eric) [2006/7 F80: F16v 20s^F 22s^6 19v 22s Mar 8] angular mare: fourth foal: little form since, including in handicap hurdle. *J. B. Groucott*   **h68** **F—**

OVERBRANCH 4 b. or br.f. Overbury (IRE) – Anabranch (Kind of Hush) [2006/7 F14v^6 F17g^4 Apr 23] useful-looking filly: first foal: dam fair hurdler/useful chaser up to 2½m: better effort in bumpers (modest form) when fourth to One Rose in mares event at Sedgefield. *J. M. Jefferson*   **F75**

OVER BRIDGE 9 b.g. Overbury (IRE) – Celtic Bridge (Celtic Cone) [2006/7 h84§: c23m^5 c25m^6 c21g^2 c21m^2 c21m^4 c23m^2 c23d^2 c25g^3 Oct 15] smallish, workmanlike gelding: poor hurdler: modest maiden chaser: stays 25f: acts on good to firm going: ungenuine. *Mrs S. M. Johnson*   **c87 §** **h– §**

OVERBRYN 7 b.g. Overbury (IRE) – Nero's Gem (Little Wolf) [2006/7 F16f 16d^pu May 15] second foal: dam, second in bumper/no form over hurdles, out of smart staying hurdler Miss Nero: no show in bumper/selling hurdle. *D. McCain*   **h–** **F—**

OVERBURY PEARL 4 b.f. Overbury (IRE) – Vi's Delight (New Member) [2006/7 F16s^6 F16s F17g 20m^6 Apr 25] half-sister to winning chaser Cool Song (by Michelozzo), stays 3¼m, and winning pointer by Baron Blakeney: dam won 3 races around 2½m over hurdles: well beaten in bumpers/maiden hurdle. *P. R. Johnson*   **h–** **F—**

OVERCLEAR 5 b.g. Overbury (IRE) – Callope (USA) (Recitation (USA)) [2006/7 **F95**
F17v³ F17s⁴ Jan 26] half-brother to fair hurdler/fairly useful chaser Arctic Chanter (by
Arctic Lord), stayed 25f: dam, modest novice hurdler, 1¾m winner on Flat: fair form in
frame in bumpers at Hereford, 12 lengths fourth to American Cricket on second occasion.
Mrs A. M. Thorpe

OVERDRAWN (IRE) 6 b.g. Daggers Drawn (USA) – In Denial (IRE) (Maelstrom **h80**
Lake) [2006/7 h–: 16g 16g³ 17d⁵ 20g Jun 8] leggy gelding: poor form over hurdles.
Mrs S. J. Smith

OVERFIELDS 7 b.g. Overbury (IRE) – Honey Day (Lucky Wednesday) [2006/7 F75: **c–**
17s 25g⁵ᵘ 21m 17vᵖᵘ 21dᵖᵘ c16sᵖᵘ 16vᵖᵘ Feb 18] leggy gelding: no form over hurdles/on **h–**
chasing debut, left S. R. Bowring after second outing: blinkered final one. *G. J. Smith*

OVERJOYED 6 b.m. Overbury (IRE) – Silk Touch (Lochnager) [2006/7 h–, F–: 19d⁶ **h69**
16v⁴ 20s⁶ 20s 22s 21gᵖᵘ Apr 23] sturdy mare: little form: blinkered final outing. *Miss Suzy
Smith*

OVERNIGHT 7 b.g. Overbury (IRE) – Misty Night (Grey Desire) [2006/7 h65, F78: **h–**
22dᵖᵘ May 27] leggy gelding: little form over hurdles/in points: signs of temperament.
Mrs A. C. Hamilton

OVERSERVED 8 b. or br.g. Supreme Leader – Divine Comedy (IRE) (Phardante **h113**
(FR)) [2006/7 h109: 24dᶠ 20v⁵ 20v* 22v 20s 20v⁵ 27s³ Apr 27] good-topped gelding: fair
handicap hurdler: won 5-runner event at Ayr in January: below form after: should stay
beyond 3m: raced on going softer than good (acts on heavy): visored/in cheekpieces last
6 starts (has run in snatches). *A. Parker*

OVERSIGHT 7 b.m. Overbury (IRE) – Silk Touch (Lochnager) [2006/7 c16s⁴ Jan 2] **c–**
sturdy mare: fifth foal: dam well held in bumper/points: no form in points/maiden chase
(in cheekpieces): sold 1,800 gns Doncaster May Sales. *Miss Suzy Smith*

OVERSTRAND (IRE) 8 b.g. In The Wings – Vaison La Romaine (Arctic Tern **h146**
(USA)) [2006/7 h119: 16f 16s* 16s* 16d 16v³ 16d² 19d* 24g 24gᶠ Apr 14]
Only a handful of horses each season earn the tailpiece 'a credit to connections' at the end of their Timeform comment, so for two horses from the same stable
to earn the accolade is some achievement. All the more so when those two horses
come from a yard which had just four individual runners all season, trained by a
permit-holder in his first season with a licence. Dr Richard Newland picked up both
Overstrand and Burntoakboy cheaply in the autumn and won valuable handicap
hurdles with both as the seemingly-exposed pair thrived in their new yard. The
nine-year-old Burntoakboy won the Coral Cup at Cheltenham—the trainer's first
runner at the Festival—while Overstrand won big prizes at Sandown and Ascot and

William Hill Handicap Hurdle, Sandown—
Overstrand repeats his 2003 win to maintain a tremendous start for his stable;
also pictured are runner-up Whispered Promises and fourth-placed Etoile Russe (stripes)

Betfair Handicap Hurdle, Ascot—
another valuable prize as Overstrand confirms Sandown placings with Nation State (blinkers)

went close to landing the season's richest handicap hurdle, the totesport Trophy at Newbury.

Overstrand had already been with several trainers before joining Dr Newland at Claines, near Worcester, looking at the time as though his best days were behind him. He started out as a fairly useful three-year-old on the Flat with Amanda Perrett, before enjoying what looked like being the most successful part of his career with Mary Reveley, for whom he became a useful hurdler. He had moved on to Martin Todhunter by the time he won a claimer at Perth in the summer of 2005 and joined Robert Gray for £15,000 following that win. Whilst still fairly useful and winning a handicap at Market Rasen early in 2006, Overstrand no longer seemed up to making an impact in more competitive affairs and, on his final start over hurdles before joining Dr Newland, he finished well beaten in the Swinton at Haydock very early in the season, starting at 66/1.

Out of sorts in the meantime on the Flat, Overstrand made his debut for his latest yard in a handicap hurdle at Leicester at the end of November and landed a gamble (backed down from 20/1 to 8/1) by nine lengths to give Dr Newland his first winner as a trainer. Turned out under a penalty six days later, Overstrand showed himself better than ever when following up in the William Hill Handicap Hurdle at Sandown at the same odds, again the subject of sustained support. Held up in the

737

seventeen-runner field, Overstand made smooth headway under his then 7-lb amateur Sam Jones (whose three wins for the yard accrued nearly £125,000 in prize money) to lead between the final two flights, winning by seven lengths from Whispered Promises, with Nation State faring best of four Gary Moore-trained runners in third. Overstrand had won the same race three years earlier for Mary Reveley—when beating Our Vic and Monkerhostin—and is the first horse to win this long-established valuable handicap more than once.

Overstrand finished well held off a higher mark in the Ladbroke Handicap Hurdle at Ascot (as had been the case in 2003/4) and then ran respectably outside handicap company when third behind Afsoun and The French Furze in the Champion Hurdle Trial at Haydock. But Overstrand was still not handicapped out of things, as he proved with career-best efforts just a week apart in February. In the twenty-runner totesport Trophy at Newbury, he found only 50/1-shot Heathcote too good, losing his position a little after halfway but getting right back into things from two out, eventually going down by a neck after the first two had pulled a couple of lengths clear from the last. Seven days later, Overstrand gained consolation in the Betfair Handicap Hurdle at Ascot over just short of two and a half miles, one of several valuable new races the course staged in its first jumps season after the track's refurbishment. Worth more than £50,000 to the winner, the race attracted a fourteen-strong field with Overstrand heading the weights. Always handy this time in a steadily-run race, Overstrand led two out and battled on well to hold Nation State by three quarters of a length. It was Overstrand's first start of the season at beyond two miles and, for his final two starts, he went into uncharted territory over three miles. He was beaten well before stamina became an issue when tailed off in the World Hurdle at Cheltenham (stiff task) and wasn't going well enough to suggest he would have been involved in the finish when falling heavily three out in a listed handicap at Aintree on Grand National day.

Overstrand (IRE) (b.g. 1999)	In The Wings (b 1986)	Sadler's Wells (b 1981)	Northern Dancer Fairy Bridge
		High Hawk (b 1980)	Shirley Heights Sunbittern
	Vaison La Romaine (ch 1982)	Arctic Tern (ch 1973)	Sea Bird II Bubbling Beauty
		Victory Tune (ch 1973)	Dr Fager Veda

The lengthy, angular Overstrand was bought by Dr Newland for 10,000 guineas at Doncaster in October and 'stood out like a flashing light' in the sales catalogue, according to his trainer. Overstrand's pedigree would have been secondary to his racing record by then, of course, as far as his trainer was concerned—'I like to focus on horses with a proven engine and experience, which for whatever reason have lost their way'—but his dam Vaison La Romaine has built a fine record at stud after an interesting racing career. Overstrand is one of ten winners out of his dam and much the best of the three to have been successful over jumps, the others being the winning hurdler Alosaili (by Kris) and winning chaser Classic Impact (by Generous), who were both raced mainly at around two miles. The dam's best winners on the Flat, La Strada and Vialli, were both by Niniski and made a name for themselves abroad. The filly La Strada was best of her sex in Spain at two and four and at stud has been responsible for the useful hurdler/chaser at up to two and three quarter miles Bow Strada and the fairly useful winning two-mile hurdler Valeureux. Vialli began his career in Germany where successful in a Group 2 over eleven furlongs before going on to Group 1 success in New Zealand, also finishing placed in the Queen Elizabeth II Cup in Hong Kong and the Cox Plate in Australia. Their dam, Vaison La Romaine, was trained by Henry Cecil for Daniel Wildenstein at two, finishing second in all three of her races and given the cautionary note 'one to have reservations about' by *Racehorses of 1984* after failing to build on a promising debut in the Sweet Solera Stakes. Sent to Patrick Biancone in France at three, she won a maiden at Saint-Cloud and showed useful form when fourth in the Prix Penelope behind Blue Tip, later the grandam of George Washington and Grandera. Vaison La Romaine made her final appearance when acting as pacemaker for Blue Tip in the 1985 Prix de Diane and was sold for 115,000 guineas at Newmarket at the end of that year. Grandam Victory Tune, a winner over eleven

Dr RDP & Mrs LJ Newland, CE Stedman's "Overstrand"

furlongs in France, was out of a half-sister to the 1962 Prix du Jockey Club winner Val de Loir and dual classic winner Valoris, who won the Oaks and Irish One Thousand Guineas in 1966.

Overstrand will have his work cut out to enjoy as successful a campaign again as he had in the latest season, but being effective at two to two and three quarter miles, and on heavy and good to firm ground, will give connections plenty of options. Overstrand has run well when sweating and has been tried in headgear by some of his former yards. As for his current trainer, who remains a part-time general practitioner, he took out a full licence at the end of the season but reportedly has no plans to expand his operation beyond having eight or ten horses in training. If the humans under Dr Newland's care are in the same rude health as his horses were in the latest season, he won't be kept too busy in his other profession. *Dr R. D. P. Newland*

OVER THE BLUES (IRE) 7 b.g. Bob Back (USA) – Fiona's Blue (Crash Course) [2006/7 h84+: c23d* c24v^{pu} c22s^{pu} 22v^2 c20m^{pu} Apr 28] maiden hurdler, easily best effort when second in handicap at Uttoxeter: off 12 months, won novice handicap at Worcester on chasing debut in October by 5 lengths from Oakfield Legend, despite   **c105 x**
h99

mistakes: let down by jumping all 3 outings over fences after: should stay 3m: acts on heavy going. *Jonjo O'Neill*

OVER THE CLIFF 4 b.f. Overbury (IRE) – Fringe Benefit (IRE) (Executive Perk) F—
[2006/7 F17v[6] Feb 13] unfurnished filly: third foal: sister to useful bumper winner/promising 19f hurdle winner Sir Boreas Hawk: dam poor 2m novice hurdler: last of 6 in bumper on debut. *Mrs Norma Pook*

OVER THE CLOUDS 6 gr.m. Cloudings (IRE) – Althrey Flame (IRE) (Torus) F—
[2006/7 F16s Oct 27] first foal: dam ran once: tailed off in bumper on debut. *F. Lloyd*

OVER THE CREEK 8 br.g. Over The River (FR) – Solo Girl (IRE) (Le Bavard (FR)) c118 +
[2006/7 c22s[ur] c24d[5] 24g Mar 15] tall, lengthy gelding: useful hurdler at best, out of depth h127
final start (in cheekpieces): off nearly 2 years, looked likely winner when unseating 3 out
in maiden at Towcester on chasing debut: jumped carefully when only
fifth of 7 to Gungadu in Grade 2 novice at Ascot: will stay beyond 3m: raced on good
ground or softer (acts on soft): patiently ridden. *D. E. Pipe*

OVER THE FLOW 5 br.m. Overbury (IRE) – Flow (Over The River (FR)) [2006/7 h95
F90: F17d 19s[2] 19v[3] 16v[2] 21g Mar 24] lengthy mare: easily best effort in bumpers when F—
second in 3-y-o event at Exeter on debut: modest form over hurdles, well held on
handicap debut: should stay beyond 19f: acts on heavy going. *R. H. Buckler*

OVER THE ODDS 5 b.m. Overbury (IRE) – Ashniader (IRE) (Buckskin (FR)) F—
[2006/7 F—: F17d May 1] well held in bumpers: tongue tied. *W. Storey*

OVER THE STORM (IRE) 10 b.g. Over The River (FR) – Naas (Ballymore) c92
[2006/7 c94+: c24g[4] c28s[3] c24s[3] c24s[6] c24m[pu] c28g[pu] Apr 7] workmanlike gelding:
modest handicap chaser: lame final outing: stays 3½m: raced mainly on good going or
softer (acts on soft): usually wears headgear nowadays: tried tongue tied. *H. P. Hogarth*

OVERTHROW 4 b.f. Overbury (IRE) – My Adventure (IRE) (Strong Gale) [2006/7 F86
F16g* Apr 9] sixth foal: half-sister to fairly useful hurdler Shanghide (by Supreme
Leader), stays 2½m, and winning pointer by Roselier: dam modest hurdler up to 25f: won
mares bumper at Fakenham on debut by 4 lengths from Storm Haven: will be suited by
2½m+. *R. D. E. Woodhouse*

OVERTHYME 5 b. or br.m. Overbury (IRE) – Four Thyme (Idiot's Delight) [2006/7 h—
16s[pu] 16d[pu] Oct 22] fifth foal: dam, well beaten in bumper, half-sister to Festival Bumper
winner Mucklemeg: in frame in juvenile hurdles in French Provinces for E. Danel: went
as if amiss both starts in Britain (tried tongue tied). *Evan Williams*

OVERTLY BLUE (FR) 5 b.g. Epervier Bleu – Ipsala (FR) (Quart de Vin (FR)) F79
[2006/7 F16g Mar 24] 25,000 4-y-o: useful-looking gelding: second foal: dam, placed up
to 13f, out of half-sister to top-class French chaser Ucello II: around 27 lengths eighth of
22 to Helens Vision in bumper at Newbury on debut, not impressing with head carriage
under pressure. *N. J. Henderson*

OVER TO JOE 7 br.g. Overbury (IRE) – Flo-Jo (DEN) (Pelton Lad) [2006/7 h–: c20s[pu] c—
c27s[ur] c27v[pu] 20v[5] 20v* 24s 19v[4] 20v[pu] Mar 6] good-topped gelding: won conditional h65
jockeys selling handicap hurdle at Newcastle in January, only form: wore cheekpieces/
blinkers last 5 starts. *C. Grant*

OVERTON LAD 6 gr.g. Overbury (IRE) – Safe Arrival (USA) (Shadeed (USA)) h—
[2006/7 F17d[4] F16d[4] F16g[3] F16v[6] F16s 25s[5] Mar 11] third foal: half-brother to 3¼m hurdle F84
winner Safe To Blush (by Blushing Flame): dam placed over hurdles and middle-distance
maiden on Flat: best effort in bumpers when third to Annie's Answer at Uttoxeter: upped
markedly in trip, well held in novice on hurdling debut. *P. A. Pritchard*

OVER TO YOU BERT 8 good-topped gelding: modest on Flat (stays easy 9.5f), successful in January h—
(awarded race) and March: no form over hurdles. *R. J. Hodges*

OWLESBURY DREAM (IRE) 5 b.m. Luso – Nancymar (IRE) (Montelimar F98
(USA)) [2006/7 F16s* F14s[2] F17g Apr 13] 5,000 4-y-o: useful-looking mare: first foal:
dam, of little account, sister to fairly useful chaser up to 3m Mistletoe: ran green when
winning mares bumper at Ludlow in December by 1½ lengths from Magic Score: much
better effort in similar events after when 14 lengths second to Princess Flame at Fontwell.
B. G. Powell

OWN LINE 8 b.g. Classic Cliche (IRE) – Cold Line (Exdirectory) [2006/7 h94: 20g h—
23s[pu] 23s[6] 20s 23g Apr 3] good-topped gelding: maiden hurdler, no form in 2006/7: stays
23f: acts on good to firm and good to soft going. *J. Hetherton*

OWN UP 5 b.g. Petoski – My Little Doxie (IRE) (Supreme Leader) [2006/7 F16m⁴ **F84** Apr 25] fifth foal: dam placed in bumpers: 16 lengths fourth to Hello You in bumper at Worcester on debut, veering left early in straight. *Mrs A. Barclay*

OXFORD DE LAGARDE (FR) 5 b.g. Sleeping Car (FR) – Gamine de Tanues (FR) **F85** (Fast (FR)) [2006/7 F16g F16mᵘʳ Apr 25] third foal: dam, placed up to 11f in France, ran twice over hurdles: 8/1 from 22/1, never a factor in bumper at Towcester on debut: whipped round and rider unseated start next time. *M. A. Peill*

OXYBAU (FR) 8 ch.g. Beaudelaire (USA) – Foxy (FR) (Moulin) [2006/7 h101: 19f⁴ **c–** 20g c16gᶠ c18d⁶ 19v c16v⁶ c16v⁵ c16g Apr 7] workmanlike gelding: fair hurdler at best: **h–** no form in 2006/7, including over fences: sold out of T. Taaffe's stable 7,000 gns Doncaster November Sales after fourth outing: stays 2½m. *N. G. Ayliffe*

OYEZ (IRE) 10 b.g. Jurado (USA) – Gleann Oisin (IRE) (Le Bavard (FR)) [2006/7 c–, **c93** h–: 16m² 16m⁶ 19f 17f* 17m⁶ 16f³ c16m⁴ 17f⁵ c20d c16g 18sᵖᵘ 18g Mar 18] maiden **h93** chaser: modest hurdler: won handicap at Bellewstown in July: left Michael Kelly before last 2 starts: stays 2½m: acts on firm and soft going: front runner. *Mrs H. R. J. Nelmes*

OYSTER PEARL (IRE) 8 ch.g. Karinga Bay – Latin Mistress (Scallywag) [2006/7 **h–** h87: 24f⁵ 20m 19g 22m⁴ Jul 27] maiden hurdler, no form in 2006/7: stays 21f. *M. F. Harris*

OYSTER POINT (IRE) 8 br.g. Corrouge (USA) – Ross Gale (Strong Gale) [2006/7 **h–** 20gᵖᵘ 24dᵖᵘ Jun 14] point winner in Ireland: no form over hurdles. *Mrs K. Walton*

OZYMANDIAS (FR) 5 b.g. Rajpoute (FR) – Delphes d'Or (Vorias (USA)) **c–** [2006/7 19d 18sᵖᵘ c18d⁶ c17sᵖᵘ 17s Jan 26] fourth foal: dam unraced: once-raced on Flat: **h–** no form over jumps: sold out of F. Doumen's stable €3,500 Goffs (France) November Sale before final start: has been blinkered. *B. R. Summers*

P

PABLO DU CHARMIL (FR) 6 ch.g. Lyphard's Wish (FR) – Pacifie du Charmil **c137 p** (FR) (Dom Pasquini (FR)) [2006/7 h128: c17m* c18s* c16v* c16g Mar 16] leggy geld- **h–** ing: fairly useful hurdler: took well to fences, winning maiden at Exeter and novice at Fontwell (beat Penzance by 6 lengths) in November and 3-runner novice at Warwick (9/2-on) in December: taken on for lead when well held in Grand Annual Chase (Handicap) at Cheltenham: raced around 2m: acts on heavy and good to firm going: blinkered once (well beaten): front runner: accurate jumper, and remains type to progress further over fences. *D. E. Pipe*

PACHA NOIR (IRE) 7 b. or br.g. Lord Americo – Brennan For Audits (IRE) (Creative **c–** Plan (USA)) [2006/7 c20s⁴ Feb 18] big, workmanlike gelding: second foal: dam, placed in bumpers, out of half-sister to very smart 2m chaser Uncle Ernie: won maiden Irish point in 2006: saddle slipped early (pulled hard) on chasing debut. *G. R. Pewter*

PACOLET (IRE) 8 b.g. Revoque (IRE) – Elupa (IRE) (Mtoto) [2006/7 20s² 20s² 20s³ **c135 p** 22v² 23vᵖᵘ 16v⁶ 20v c20m* c18g* Apr 25] workmanlike gelding: third foal: dam, fair **h124** maiden hurdler and 1½m and 2m winner on Flat, half-sister to smart 2m hurdler For Reg: fairly useful hurdler: good efforts first 4 outings, mostly in handicaps: promising start over fences, winning maiden at Cork and novice at Punchestown (beating Reisk Superman by 1¾ lengths) in April: stays 2½m: acts on any going: likely to improve further. *P. J. Flynn, Ireland*

PACON (GER) 14 b.g. Polar Falcon (USA) – Padang (GER) (Ile de Bourbon (USA)) **c–** [2006/7 c20d⁴ May 24] angular gelding: fair hurdler at best: winning pointer/twice-raced **h–** chaser: stays 2½m: tried blinkered/tongue tied. *W. Kinsey*

PADDY FITZ (IRE) 10 b. or br.g. Norwich – Queenlier (IRE) (Roselier (FR)) [2006/7 **c86** c22dᵖᵘ c20d c21g c24vᵖᵘ c20s⁵ c22d⁶ Apr 1] rather leggy gelding: winning hurdler: **h–** modest maiden chaser: stays 2¾m: acts on firm and soft going: wore cheekpieces last 2 outings. *P. J. Halley, Ireland*

PADDY FOR PADDY (IRE) 13 b.g. Mandalus – Lady Rerico (Pamroy) [2006/7 **c106** c115: c33gᵖᵘ c23v² c29g² Mar 21] useful hunter chaser: left G. Landau and off 10 months, respectable efforts when runner-up at Leicester and Chepstow: stays 33f: acts on heavy going: genuine. *Ms L. J. Willis*

PADDY GEORGE (IRE) 6 ch.g. Houmayoun (FR) – Pennine Way (IRE) (Waajib)   **F–**
[2006/7 F–: F16f Sep 29] well held in 2 bumpers 16 months apart. *A. J. Lockwood*

PADDY LIVE (FR) 4 b.g. Brier Creek (USA) – Iona Will (FR) (Kadalko (FR))   **F82**
[2006/7 F17s⁵ F16g⁵ Apr 7] first foal: dam unraced: modest form when fifth in bumpers
at Sedgefield and Haydock (rider unseated going to post). *M. A. Peill*

PADDYMCGINTYSGOAT (IRE) 4 b.g. Saddlers' Hall (IRE) – One More Dash   **F–**
(IRE) (Glacial Storm (USA)) [2006/7 F16s Apr 27] first foal: dam lightly raced in
bumpers: no show in bumper on debut. *Micky Hammond*

PADDYMCTUME 5 b.m. Overbury (IRE) – Esterelle (USA) (Trempolino (USA))   **h–**
[2006/7 F17g F16m 16d 16dᵘʳ 22sᵖᵘ 16g Mar 21] leggy, close-coupled mare: first foal: **F–**
dam modest winning hurdler up to 27f: no form in bumpers/over hurdles, left S. Curran
before final start. *H. J. Manners*

PADDYS PRINCESS 7 b.m. Regal Embers (IRE) – Kimmy's Princess (Prince Sabo)   **h–**
[2006/7 19vᵖᵘ Feb 20] pulled up in points/novice hurdle. *P. R. Rodford*

PADDY'S TERN 5 b.g. Fraam – Great Tern (Simply Great (FR)) [2006/7 h88: 20s³   **h107**
16vᶠ 16s* 16s⁴ Mar 3] small, angular gelding: fair form over hurdles: best effort when
winning handicap at Towcester in February readily by 9 lengths from Hot Zone: stays
2½m: probably acts on heavy going. *N. M. Babbage*

PADDY THE OPTIMIST (IRE) 11 b.g. Leading Counsel (USA) – Erne Duchess   **c90**
(IRE) (Duky) [2006/7 c91, h–: c25g⁴ c25d² c25m³ c26d* c25m² c23m⁶ Jul 5] sturdy   **h–**
gelding: modest handicap chaser: won at Newton Abbot in June: visored once, formerly blinkered. *D. Burchell*

PADDY THE PIPER (IRE) 10 b.g. Witness Box (USA) – Divine Dibs (Raise You   **c–**
Ten) [2006/7 c–, h131: 17d 17s⁶ 19g⁵ 24d³ Oct 22] quite good-topped gelding: one-time   **h115**
useful hurdler, not so good nowadays: landed odds in maiden chase in 2004/5, let down
by jumping (tended to go right) both other starts over fences: stays 3m: acts on soft and
good to firm going: wore visor/blinkers last 2 outings: tried tongue tied. *L. Lungo*

PADRE (IRE) 8 b.g. Mister Lord (USA) – Lee Valley Lady (IRE) (Boyne Valley)   **c–**
[2006/7 c92, h–: c16sᵖᵘ Feb 22] well-made gelding: very lightly raced: form only when   **h–**
third in 2½m novice chase in early-2005/6. *Carl Llewellyn*

PAGAN MAGIC (USA) 6 b.g. Diesis – Great Lady Slew (USA) (Seattle Slew (USA))   **h109**
[2006/7 20g* 20g⁴ 20s 16v 21d 20g² Apr 4] close-coupled gelding: fairly useful on Flat
(stays 1¾m): fair hurdler: won maiden at Sligo in August: stays 2½m: raced on good
ground (best efforts) or softer: visored fifth outing. *T. G. McCourt, Ireland*

PAGAN SKY (IRE) 8 ch.g. Inchinor – Rosy Sunset (IRE) (Red Sunset) [2006/7 h92:   **h103**
19m² May 9] fair form over hurdles: in cheekpieces, best effort when neck second to
Sultan Fontenaille in conditional jockeys novice handicap at Exeter: stays 19f. *Miss
Venetia Williams*

PAINTED SKY 4 ch.g. Rainbow Quest (USA) – Emplane (USA) (Irish River (FR))   **h72**
[2006/7 16v⁵ 16d 16g 17d Feb 19] rather leggy gelding: half-brother to fair hurdler/fairly
useful chaser around 2m Coach Lane (by Barathea): fairly useful maiden on Flat (stays
1½m), sold out of Mme C. Head-Maarek's stable 18,000 gns Newmarket Autumn Sales:
poor form over hurdles. *R. A. Fahey*

PAINTER MAN (FR) 5 b.g. Double Bed (FR) – Diana La Belle (FR) (Synefos (USA))   **h106**
[2006/7 F93+: 20f² 20v³ Nov 22] bumper winner: fair form when placed both starts over
hurdles, 7 lengths third to Leading Contender in novice at Chepstow. *D. E. Pipe*

PAINT THE LILY (IRE) 6 b.m. Barathea (IRE) – Chocolate Box (Most Welcome)   **h75**
[2006/7 17m 16m⁵ 17m 19s² 22d² 21m 20g 22g Apr 2] maiden on Flat: likewise over
hurdles, poor form at best: will stay 3m: acts on soft going: tried in cheekpieces: sold
3,800 gns Doncaster May Sales. *F. Watson*

PAK JACK (FR) 7 ch.g. Pitchounet (FR) – Miss Noir Et Or (FR) (Noir Et Or) [2006/7   **c126**
c122, h102: c20g c21g² Apr 12] lengthy gelding: maiden hurdler: fairly useful chaser: **h–**
trained by Jon Trice-Rolph on reappearance: back to best when ½-length second to Scots
Grey in 27-runner Fox Hunters' Chase at Aintree, going on travelling strongly 2 out but
worn down nearing line: stays 21f: raced on good going or softer: has found little.
R. Barber

PAKTOLOS (FR) 4 b.g. Dansili – Pithara (GR) (Never So Bold) [2006/7 16sᵖᵘ Dec 13]   **h– p**
good-topped gelding: useful on Flat (stays 13f), successful in September for C. Laffon-
Parias, and in Britain in March: easy to back, lost action on hurdling debut. *A. King*

PALACE WALK (FR) 5 b.g. Sinndar (IRE) – Page Bleue (Sadler's Wells (USA))   **c106**
[2006/7 h102: 18m⁵ 20f⁴ 20m⁵ c16f* Aug 11] leggy gelding: maiden on Flat: fair hurdler: **h104**
5/4 from 9/4, jumped soundly (tended to go right latter stages) when winning maiden at
Sedgefield on chasing debut by 3 lengths from General Alarm, not fully extended: stays
2½m: acts on firm going: front runner. *B. G. Powell*

PALAMEDES 8 b.g. Sadler's Wells (USA) – Kristal Bridge (Kris) [2006/7 h–: 22m   **h–**
24sᵖᵘ Dec 29] no form over hurdles: tried in cheekpieces/tongue tied. *B. J. Llewellyn*

PALARSHAN (FR) 9 b. or br.g. Darshaan – Palavera (Bikala) [2006/7 c21g²   **c138**
Mar 15] tall, good-topped gelding: winning hurdler: useful handicap chaser: off 2 years   **h–**
and in cheekpieces, showed himself just about as good as ever when 4 lengths second of
23 to Idole First in Racing Post Plate at Cheltenham, finishing strongly from long way
back: probably stays 3m: acts on soft and good to firm going. *H. D. Daly*

PALIETER (BEL) 8 gr. or ro.g. Zeami (IRE) – Just Lady (FR) (Seclusive (USA))   **c–**
[2006/7 22v 20vᵖᵘ 22g Apr 2] good-topped gelding: maiden hurdler, no form in Britain: **h–**
third in minor event at Moulins, only outing over fences. *E. J. Jamieson*

PALILA 5 b.m. Petoski – Mountain Lory (Ardross) [2006/7 F16m³ Nov 9] third foal: **F81**
dam unraced: tongue tied, 4½ lengths third of 6 to Lady Roania in bumper at Ludlow on
debut. *Mrs P. Robeson*

PALMERS PEAK (IRE) 8 b.g. Arctic Lord – Shahreza (Nishapour (FR)) [2006/7 c–:   **c100**
c25g⁴ May 3] fair pointer: ran well when fourth to Beauchamp Oracle at Cheltenham on
completed outing in hunter chases. *M. Keighley*

PALMERSTON PLACE (IRE) 7 b.g. Fourstars Allstar (USA) – Real Lace (Kam-   **h–**
pala) [2006/7 F–: 16d 16s 16s Apr 26] no form in bumper/over hurdles. *Miss Lucinda
V. Russell*

PALMRIDGE (GER) 7 b.g. Law Society (USA) – Pariana (USA) (Bering) [2006/7   **h83**
19d⁶ 19s* 21s³ 20s Dec 27] lengthy gelding: half-brother to useful hurdler Papini (by
Lomitas), stays 19f: 11.5f winner on Flat: twice-raced over hurdles in France, winning at
Lyon Parilly in November: never dangerous both outings in Britain, very stiff task on first
occasion. *T. Doumen, France*

PALOMAR (USA) 5 b. or br.g. Chester House (USA) – Ball Gown (USA) (Silver   **h95 p**
Hawk (USA)) [2006/7 16g 16g 16s⁴ Apr 26] smart on Flat (best around 1½m), left
R. Charlton after final start in 2006: best effort over hurdles when 6¾ lengths fourth to
South O'The Border in novice at Perth, still towards rear travelling well 4 out and not
given hard time: pulled too hard first 2 outings: now qualified for handicaps, and should
be capable of better. *N. G. Richards*

PALUA 10 b.g. Sri Pekan (USA) – Reticent Bride (IRE) (Shy Groom (USA)) [2006/7   **c131 §**
c135§, h–: c17v⁵ c16g⁴ c17m⁵ c16g² c16v c17dᵘʳ c16g Apr 19] lengthy gelding: useful   **h–**
handicap chaser: stays easy 3m, raced mainly over shorter (effective at 2m): acts on good
to firm and heavy going: tried visored: moody sort, best when able to dominate: not one
to rely on. *Miss E. C. Lavelle*

PAMS OAK 9 b.g. Afzal – Kins Token (Relkino) [2006/7 c–: c21d³ c20f³ c21f³ c21f*   **c104**
c22g* c20g³ c24d⁵ Oct 7] fair handicap chaser: won at Sedgefield and Market Rasen in
August: again jumped boldly up with pace when third to Incas at Uttoxeter next time:
should stay 3m: acts on firm and good to soft going. *Mrs S. J. Smith*

PANACHE DE THAIX (FR) 4 b.g. Subotica (FR) – Fanny de Longuenee (FR)   **h–**
(Grand Tresor (FR)) [2006/7 aF16g F16g 16g⁴ Apr 21] third foal: half-brother to 11.5f   **F–**
winner Odilon du Thaix (by Ragmar): dam lightly-raced sister to smart French staying
chaser Harmonie Tresor: well held in bumpers and juvenile hurdle (reluctant to race).
M. J. Gingell

PANAMA AT ONCE 7 ch.g. Commanche Run – Cherry Sip (Nearly A Hand) [2006/7   **c100**
F–: F17s⁵ 20g⁶ 20d⁶ 24s⁴ 20v⁶ 24v⁶ 27v⁵ c25g* Apr 23] angular gelding: better effort   **h72 +**
in bumpers when fifth at Market Rasen: poor novice hurdler: in cheekpieces, much   **F–**
improved form when winning novice handicap at Hexham on chasing debut by 28
lengths: stays 25f: raced on good going or softer: has finished weakly. *J. M. Saville*

PANAMA MERMAID (IRE) 6 b.m. Mister Mat (FR) – Drumquin Girl (IRE) (Brush   **h–**
Aside (USA)) [2006/7 F16d F16v 19d 16v 20vᵖᵘ 21g⁵ Apr 23] rather leggy mare: first   **F–**
foal: dam unraced: no form in bumpers/over hurdles: tried in cheekpieces/blinkers: has
had tongue tied. *J. M. Saville*

PAN

PANAMA THREE KNOTS 7 b.m. Primitive Rising (USA) – Emu (IRE) (Strong **c–**
Gale) [2006/7 F–: F17s 22d 20mᵘʳ c19m⁶ Apr 24] no form outside points (runner-up in **h–**
February): has worn cheekpieces. *J. M. Saville* **F–**

PANCAKE (FR) 4 ch.g. Cyborg (FR) – Six Fois Sept (FR) (Epervier Bleu) [2006/7 17s **h124**
18s⁶ 18s⁴ 16d² 16v* 17v⁵ 19v* 16d Mar 13] tall, plain gelding: third foal: half-brother to
15f hurdle winner Noceane (by Pistolet Bleu): dam winning hurdler/chaser around 2m
in France: fairly useful juvenile hurdler: left T. Trapenard, successful at Newbury in
December (beat Zilcash by 2 lengths) and January (easily in 4-runner race) and Warwick
(novice) in February: last of 24 in listed handicap at Cheltenham final start: likely to
stay beyond 19f: raced on ground softer than good (acts on heavy): usually front runner.
P. J. Hobbs

PANGBOURNE (FR) 6 b.g. Double Bed (FR) – Valgrija (FR) (Big John (FR)) **h100 p**
[2006/7 F114: 20d⁴ Oct 22] rangy gelding: useful bumper performer: beaten 24 lengths
when fourth to Wichita Lineman in novice at Aintree on hurdling debut, finding little
having dictated: should stay beyond 2m: has worn eyeshields and blinkers/visor since
debut: less than straightforward, but should still do better over hurdles. *A. King*

PANGERAN (USA) 15 b.g. Forty Niner (USA) – Smart Heiress (USA) (Vaguely **c– §**
Noble) [2006/7 c73§, h–: c24gᵖ* May 4] leggy gelding: poor handicap chaser: stays 27f: **h–**
acts on firm and soft going: has had tongue tied: not a fluent jumper: unreliable.
N. B. King

PANMURE (IRE) 11 b.g. Alphabatim (USA) – Serjitak (Saher) [2006/7 c92§, h–: c20f **c– §**
Jun 17] good-topped gelding: maiden hurdler: modest handicap chaser: lame only outing **h–**
in 2006/7: stays 2½m: best efforts on good going or firmer: tried blinkered/in
cheekpieces: has had tongue tied: unreliable. *P. D. Niven*

PANNOCHKA 4 b.f. Petoski – Alta (Arctic Lord) [2006/7 F13g F12s Dec 13] lengthy, **F–**
angular filly: first living foal: dam, fairly useful hurdler/fair maiden chaser, stayed 3m:
well held in bumpers. *P. W. Hiatt*

PANTALAIMON 6 b.g. Classic Cliche (IRE) – Threewaygirl (Orange Bay) [2006/7 **h106**
F99: 16g⁶ 19g³ 22d² 24s³ 21g⁴ Mar 23] lengthy, useful-looking gelding: fair form over
hurdles: should stay beyond 2¾m: acts on good to soft going (possibly unsuited by
softer). *H. D. Daly*

PAN THE MAN (IRE) 6 b.g. Muroto – Kilbally Quilty (IRE) (Montelimar (USA)) **c100**
[2006/7 h91, F93: c20g³ c22mᶠ c23m⁵ c23mᵖᵘ 20d 25v c19s³ c20g² c20m* Apr 8] sturdy, **h–**
good-bodied gelding: bumper winner: maiden hurdler: fair chaser: won handicap at
Plumpton (improved form) in April: bred to stay beyond 21f: acts on soft and good to
firm going. *J. W. Mullins*

PANTHERA LEO (IRE) 4 b.g. Beneficial – Katie Fairy (IRE) (Glacial Storm (USA)) **F92**
[2006/7 F16m* F16m Apr 24] €40,000 3-y-o: workmanlike gelding: first foal: dam,
bumper winner/fair staying hurdler, half-sister to fairly useful but moody staying chaser
Ebony Light: won bumper at Musselburgh on debut in February by 1¼ lengths from
Dundock: tenth of 22 to Gonebeyondrecall at Punchestown. *J. Howard Johnson*

PANTHERS RUN 7 b.g. Jendali (USA) – Dorado Beach (Lugana Beach) [2006/7 F–: **h93**
17s³ 16dᵘʳ 16m 16m⁴ 19m² 19s⁵ 20m 20s³ Apr 1] bumper winner: modest maiden
hurdler: sold out of Jonjo O'Neill's stable 5,000 gns Doncaster October Sales after
seventh outing: stays 2½m: acts on soft and good to firm going. *J. C. Haynes*

PANTHERUS (IRE) 4 b.g. Montjeu (IRE) – Panthere (GER) (Acatenango (GER)) **h93 +**
[2006/7 16s 17g⁴ 17m Apr 15] useful-looking gelding: thrice-raced on Flat in France in
2006, fourth over 1½m: left J. Hammond, best effort in juvenile hurdles when fourth to
French Opera in maiden at Taunton: jumped left next time. *Jonjo O'Neill*

PANZER (GER) 6 b.g. Vettori (IRE) – Prompt (Old Vic) [2006/7 h88: 20g* 22d² **h100**
May 31] lengthy gelding: fair hurdler: best effort when winning novice at Wetherby in
May by 1½ lengths from Bestofthebrownies: stays 2½m: possibly unsuited by soft going.
D. McCain

PAPARAAZI (IRE) 5 b.g. Victory Note (USA) – Raazi (My Generation) [2006/7 h90: **h–**
17v Nov 12] fair on Flat (barely stays 10.5f), claimed £8,000 in February: form (modest)
over hurdles only when runner-up in juvenile on debut: needs emphasis on speed at 2m:
tried visored. *R. A. Fahey*

PAPAWALDO (IRE) 8 ch.g. Presenting – Another Bless (Random Shot) [2006/7 h–: **c–**
20d 24gᵖᵘ c24dᵖᵘ Dec 30] leggy gelding: no sign of ability: has worn cheekpieces/ **h–**
blinkers. *R. C. Guest*

PAPEETE (GER) 6 b.m. Alzao (USA) – Prairie Vela (Persian Bold) [2006/7 16d* 16s³ 16g 18g² 22m⁴ Apr 26] fair on Flat (stays 2m), left Miss B. Sanders after final start in 2006: fair novice hurdler: won mares event at Lingfield in November by 1¼ lengths from Tambourine Davis: should stay 2½m: acts on good to soft going: tried tongue tied. *Mrs N. Smith* **h100**

PAPERCHASER 7 ch.g. Minster Son – Eye Bee Aitch (Move Off) [2006/7 h–: 24mᵖᵘ 21d³ 20f⁶ 24f⁶ 20m³ 22m² 20g⁶ 20vᵖᵘ 20m 21gᶠ Apr 23] rather leggy gelding: poor maiden hurdler: stays 2¾m: acts on firm going. *F. P. Murtagh* **h76**

PAPER DOLL 5 ch.m. Mister Baileys – Grand Coronet (Grand Lodge (USA)) [2006/7 16sᵖᵘ 16mᵖᵘ Jun 11] modest maiden on all-weather on Flat (should stay 1¼m): no show both starts over hurdles: tried in cheekpieces. *B. P. J. Baugh* **h–**

PAPERPROPHET 9 b.g. Glory of Dancer – Living Legend (ITY) (Archway (IRE)) [2006/7 h–§: 20m² 22g² 23s 24g 21mᵖᵘ Apr 21] leggy gelding: fairly useful handicap hurdler: form since 2004/5 only when second at Hexham and Kelso early in season: stays 25f: acts on soft and good to firm going: difficult ride, usually soon off bridle. *N. G. Richards* **h124 §**

PAPHIAN BAY 9 b.g. Karinga Bay – Bichette (Lidhame) [2006/7 c–, h–: c20d⁴ c23g² c24sᵖᵘ Dec 16] rangy gelding: lightly raced: winning hurdler: second to easy winner Standin Obligation in novice at Wetherby, only form over fences: should stay 3m+. *Ferdy Murphy* **c79 h–**

PAPILLON DE IENA (FR) 7 ch.g. Varese (FR) – Belle du Chesne (FR) (R B Chesne) [2006/7 c101, h117: c17m* c21s² c20gᵘʳ c16m 20m 19d⁶ 22g³ 19m⁵ 17d* 16v* 17v² c17v⁵ 16v⁶ c22vᵖᵘ 17s² 19s⁵ 18g 27m Apr 26] smallish, lengthy gelding: fair hurdler: won sellers at Hereford and Chepstow in November: claimed from D. Pipe £6,000 next time, below form after: fair form at best over fences, won handicap at Exeter in May: effective at 2m to 2¾m: acts on heavy and good to firm going: wears headgear nowadays: ungenuine. *M. A. Allen* **c108 § h103 §**

PAPINI (IRE) 6 ch.g. Lomitas – Pariana (USA) (Bering) [2006/7 h120: 16f 16g* 16v* 16d 17g Mar 16] well-made gelding: useful handicap hurdler: improved form when winning at Haydock in November and Sandown (beat Heathcote 5 lengths) in January: **h137**

ladbrokes.com Handicap Hurdle, Sandown—a second successive win for Papini, who copes well with the heavy conditions to beat Heathcote (No.5)

mid-field at best in valuable events after: stays 19f: acts on any ground: usually front runner/races prominently. *N. J. Henderson*

PAPSWOODMOSS 5 ch.m. Fleetwood (IRE) – Pab's Choice (Telsmoss) [2006/7 F68: F16g⁶ 17s 19d 22m^{pu} Apr 22] workmanlike mare: poor form in bumpers: no show in novice/maiden hurdles. *Mrs A. L. M. King* — h– F64

PAPUA 13 ch.g. Green Dancer (USA) – Fairy Tern (Mill Reef (USA)) [2006/7 c112§, h–: c19g May 4] quite good-topped gelding: fair chaser, successful 4 times at Uttoxeter: no show both outings in hunters: best around 2m: acts on firm and soft going: has been visored, usually blinkered: has had tongue tied: usually front runner: unreliable. *Geoffrey Deacon* — c– § h–

PARADI (FR) 4 b. or br.g. Video Rock (FR) – Gintonique (FR) (Royal Charter (FR)) [2006/7 16d* 16s⁵ 16v* Feb 16] fourth foal: brother to smart hurdler/fairly useful chaser Moulin Riche (stays 3m): dam, successful 4 times up to 1¾m on Flat, placed both starts over hurdles: trained by F. Doumen, successful both starts up to 15f on Flat at 3 yrs: fair form in juvenile hurdles: won at Leicester (by 2½ lengths from Leamington Lad) in November and Sandown (rallied to beat Lester Leaps In by neck) in February: will stay beyond 2m: acts on heavy going. *D. E. Pipe* — h110 +

PARADIGM INVESTOR (IRE) 4 b.g. Great Palm (USA) – Cruby Hill (IRE) (Prince Rupert) [2006/7 F16g F16g⁵ Apr 23] tall gelding: half-brother to useful bumper winner Berwick Law (by Snurge) and winner abroad by Simply Great: dam unraced: modest form on first (carried head high) of 2 starts in bumpers: tongue tied. *H. P. Hogarth* — F77

PARADISE EXPECTED 4 ch.f. North Briton – Phenomenon (Unfuwain (USA)) [2006/7 17v 16g 16v⁶ Feb 24] rather leggy filly: fair 1m winner on Flat (lightly raced), sold out of P. Chapple-Hyam's stable 4,000 gns Newmarket Autumn Sales: well beaten over hurdles. *C. Grant* — h–

PARADISE GARDEN (USA) 10 b.g. Septieme Ciel (USA) – Water Course (USA) (Irish River (FR)) [2006/7 h–: 16m 16f Jul 19] leggy gelding: no form over hurdles. *P. L. Clinton* — h–

PARADISE REGAINED (FR) 4 b.g. Lost World (IRE) – Bajabala (FR) (Nikos) [2006/7 F16s Mar 3] 30,000 3-y-o: unfurnished, short-backed gelding: second foal: dam unraced half-sister to useful French hurdler Elling, stayed 2½m: 8¾ lengths seventh of 21 to Diamond Harry in bumper at Newbury on debut. *A. King* — F98

PARADISE VALLEY 7 b.g. Groom Dancer (USA) – Rose de Reve (IRE) (Persian Heights) [2006/7 22s^{pu} 16m 19m^{pu} 17s⁵ 16v^{pu} 16g^{pu} Mar 26] modest on Flat (stayed 1¾m), sold out of Stef Liddiard's stable 4,000 gns Doncaster January (2006) Sales: no form over hurdles: often tongue tied: dead. *M. A. Trott* — h–

PARAKEET 6 ch.g. Silver Patriarch (IRE) – Mountain Lory (Ardross) [2006/7 F16s 24v^F Jan 21] second foal: dam unraced: well beaten in bumper: disputing lead when fell 3 out in novice at Towcester on hurdling debut. *Mrs P. Robeson* — h– F–

PARDINI (USA) 8 b.g. Quest For Fame – Noblissima (IRE) (Sadler's Wells (USA)) [2006/7 c93§, h–§: c25g c24s^{pu} c26v^{pu} c24d^{pu} c25d² c20v c24v³ c27s 21v c25s⁵ c25v⁴ c23v³ c26v⁴ c26v⁴ c23s^F c28g⁶ Mar 18] angular gelding: maiden hurdler: poor handicap chaser: stays 3¼m: acts on heavy going: often wears headgear: ungenuine: sold 5,500 gns Doncaster May Sales. *M. F. Harris* — c80 § h– §

PARDISHAR (IRE) 9 b.g. Kahyasi – Parapa (IRE) (Akarad (FR)) [2006/7 c115, h–: c16s⁴ c20s³ c17d³ c17g⁴ Mar 24] well-made gelding: winning hurdler: fair handicap chaser: stays 21f: acts on heavy and good to firm going: has worn cheekpieces: tongue tied once: not a straightforward ride. *G. L. Moore* — c108 h–

PARDON WHAT 11 b.g. Theatrical Charmer – Tree Poppy (Rolfe (USA)) [2006/7 c–x, h103x: 22s 22d 24s 20v⁵ 20v³ 22v³ 22g⁶ 22m⁴ 24m^{pu} Apr 15] leggy, lengthy gelding: winning chaser: modest handicap hurdler: stays 25f: acts on heavy and good to firm going: wears headgear: sketchy jumper: hard ride. *S. Lycett* — c– x h96 §

PARIS HEIGHTS 5 gr.g. Paris House – Petra Nova (First Trump) [2006/7 16s^{pu} 17g 17v^{pu} Feb 20] smallish, workmanlike gelding: modest on Flat (stays 1m), sold out of R. Whitaker's stable £5,600 Ascot August Sales: no show in maiden hurdles. *Mrs A. M. Thorpe* — h–

PARISH HOUSE (IRE) 7 b.g. Arzanni – Penny Gold (IRE) (Millfontaine) [2006/7 F82: 17g Sep 8] runner-up in bumper: mistakes when well beaten in novice on hurdling debut. *B. W. Duke* — h–

PARISH OAK 12 b.g. Rakaposhi King – Poppy's Pride (Uncle Pokey) [2006/7 c104§, **c99 §** h–§: c24g⁴ c24d^pu c21s^pu c20d⁴ c16v³ c16s³ c20s* c20v⁴ c19g² Apr 27] useful-looking **h– §** gelding: winning hurdler: modest handicap chaser, left Ian Williams and off 7 months after first outing: more consistent than usual in second half of season, winning at Leicester (has good record there) in February: stays 21f: acts on heavy going: tried tongue tied, not since early-2002/3: often runs as if amiss. *A. W. Carroll*

PARISIAN PLAYBOY 7 gr.g. Paris House – Exordium (Exorbitant) [2006/7 16g **h68** 16g^pu 16g 17v⁶ 16s^pu 16s 16g⁴ 16g* Apr 9] strong gelding: one-time modest 7f/1m winner on Flat, well held in 2006: best effort over hurdles when winning selling handicap at Fakenham in April: raced around 2m: tried in cheekpieces/tongue tied. *A. D. Brown*

PARISIENNE GALE (IRE) 8 b.m. Lapierre – Elegant Gale (IRE) (Strong Gale) **c116** [2006/7 c108, h103: 17d⁴ 21m* c20s* c24m^pu Jun 11] compact mare: fairly useful **h115** handicap hurdler/chaser: successful 8 of last 11 completed starts, including in hurdle at Huntingdon (beat Fox Point by 7 lengths in amateur event) and chase at Worcester (by 14 lengths from Mixsterthetrixster) in May: stays 21f: acts on good to firm and heavy going: tongue tied last 6 starts: makes running: a credit to connections. *R. Ford*

PARISI PRINCESS 6 ch.m. Shaddad (USA) – Crambella (IRE) (Red Sunset) [2006/7 **h–** h–: 16d Oct 22] poor maiden on Flat, left D. Williams after final start in 2006: no form over hurdles: tried tongue tied. *S. Curran*

PARK CITY 8 b.g. Slip Anchor – Cryptal (Persian Bold) [2006/7 h94: 20d⁶ 20d⁴ Nov 4] **h88** rather leggy gelding: modest handicap hurdler: stays 2½m: acts on heavy and good to firm going: none too consistent. *J. Joseph*

PARKING TICKET (IRE) 6 ch.m. Fourstars Allstar (USA) – Celia's Pet (IRE) **h77** (Kemal (FR)) [2006/7 20m³ 20f⁴ 17f⁴ 18d² 20f⁵ Sep 6] poor maiden hurdler: stays 2½m: acts on firm and good to soft going. *G. A. Kingston, Ireland*

PARKINSON (IRE) 6 br.g. Presenting – Be My Citizen (IRE) (Be My Native (USA)) **c121** [2006/7 c95, h–: 25s* 20s² 22s* 26s² c24s* c25d^ur c24s* c33s^pu Mar 17] close-coupled, **h98 +** unfurnished gelding: progressive handicap hurdler/chaser: successful over hurdles in amateur events at Carlisle (novice) in October and Exeter (beat Shirazi by ½ length) in December and over fences at Huntingdon in January and Ludlow (fairly useful form, by 5 lengths from Fill The Bunker) in March: should stay long distances: raced on ground softer than good (acts on heavy): wore cheekpieces/visor last 6 starts: not a fluent jumper of fences. *Jonjo O'Neill*

PARK LANE PRINCESS (IRE) 4 ch.f. King of Kings (IRE) – Heated Debate **h84** (USA) (Woodman (USA)) [2006/7 16g⁵ 17d⁵ 17d* 16v⁵ 16g² 16m* Apr 9] small, close-coupled filly: modest juvenile hurdler: won sellers at Taunton in November and Huntingdon (handicap, in cheekpieces) in April: raced around 2m: acts on good to firm and good to soft ground: tongue tied after debut. *D. E. Pipe*

PARK QUEST (IRE) 9 br.g. Jolly Jake (NZ) – Ann's Fort (Crash Course) [2006/7 **c–** c20d⁵ c19s³ c19v⁵ c22s^pu 24v^pu 21s^pu c20d⁵ c22m³ Apr 24] ex-Irish gelding: won maiden **h–** point in 2005: no solid form over hurdles/in chases. *Mrs C. J. Ikin*

PARRAIN (FR) 4 b.g. Brier Creek (USA) – Grenelle II (FR) (Quart de Vin (FR)) **h135** [2006/7 18s* 18s 18s³ 17v* 16d³ 16v² 17g^pu 18s Apr 13] lengthy gelding: second foal: dam 11f winner on Flat/19f winner over hurdles: third over 12.5f on Flat: smart juvenile hurdler: successful at Auteuil in September and Enghien (Group 3 Prix General de Saint-Didier, by 3 lengths from stable-companion Pommerol) in November: placed next 2 starts at Kempton, third to Poquelin then 19 lengths second to enterprisingly-ridden Punjabi in Grade 2 Adonis Hurdle: ran as if amiss in Triumph Hurdle at Cheltenham penultimate outing: will stay 2½m: acts on heavy ground. *F. Doumen, France*

PARSONS FANCY 9 ch.m. Alflora (IRE) – Preachers Popsy (The Parson) [2006/7 c–, **c–** h–: c23s⁵ c19d^pu c25s c24v^pu Jan 21] angular mare: won maiden point in 2006: no form **h–** in other events: usually tongue tied. *P. R. Rodford*

PARSONS LEGACY (IRE) 9 b.g. Leading Counsel (USA) – The Parson's Girl **c147** (IRE) (The Parson) [2006/7 c127, h–: c25m* c26s⁵ c26v⁴ c24g² c32m³ Apr 21] angular **h–** gelding: smart handicap chaser: won Badger Ales Trophy at Wincanton in November by 2½ lengths from Preacher Boy: improved form when 1¾ lengths third of 23 to Hot Weld

Mr R. A. S. Offer's "Parsons Legacy"

in Scottish Grand National at Ayr: stays 4m: won on soft going on chase debut, but much better under less testing conditions (acts on good to firm): often races prominently. *P. J. Hobbs*

PARTHIAN SHOT 7 b.m. Parthian Springs – Lavenham's Last (Rymer) [2006/7 h–, F81: 16m May 12] modest form in bumpers: well held over hurdles: headstrong. *R. T. Phillips* **h–**

PARTICIPATION 4 b.g. Dansili – Andaleeb (USA) (Lyphard (USA)) [2006/7 17g 17d 16s^{pu} 22s Feb 18] leggy, narrow gelding: fairly useful on Flat, won over 1¼m in July, claimed from M. Wallace £15,000 later in month: no form over hurdles: unlikely to stay 2¾m. *A. E. Jones* **h–**

PARTLY CLOUDY 6 b.g. Cloudings (IRE) – Old Betsy (Town And Country) [2006/7 F16g Apr 3] first foal: dam bad maiden jumper: well held in bumper on debut. *Mrs S. J. Smith* **F–**

PARTY GAMES (IRE) 10 b.g. King's Ride – Shady Miss (Mandamus) [2006/7 c107, h–: c25m^3 c24s^{pu} Feb 22] workmanlike gelding: winning hurdler: fair chaser: left G. L. Moore and off 9 months, no show final start: stays 25f: acts on good to firm and heavy going: has worn cheekpieces: sometimes let down by jumping over fences. *H. B. Hodge* **c112 h–**

PASAGAI (FR) 5 b.g. Panoramic – Saragay (FR) (Saratogan (USA)) [2006/7 c16v^3 c20d^3 Feb 19] has scope: first foal: dam winning hurdler/chaser around 2m: twice-raced over hurdles, won 4-y-o event at Bordeaux in 2005/6 for J-P. Totain: fair form over fences, including in handicap: stays 2½m. *C. C. Bealby* **c100 h–**

PASDELOU (FR) 4 ch.g. Network (GER) – First Ball (FR) (Beyssac (FR)) [2006/7 F16g Apr 7] 21,000 3-y-o: fifth foal: dam, ran once, out of sister to Sun Alliance Chase winner Rolling Ball: well held in bumper on debut. *D. McCain Jnr* **F–**

PASQUALINA MIA 4 b.f. Classic Cliche (IRE) – Anchor Express (Carlingford F–
Castle) [2006/7 F12s F12v F16v⁶ F16v Feb 22] leggy filly: third foal: half-sister to
winning pointer by Gunner B: dam, winning hunter, out of half-sister to Scottish Grand
National winner Cockle Strand: no show in bumpers. *G. Fierro*

PASSENGER OMAR (IRE) 9 b.g. Safety Catch (USA) – Princess Douglas (Bishop c104
of Orange) [2006/7 h108: c26v* c26vᴿ Feb 17] useful-looking gelding: lightly raced: h–
fair handicap hurdler: similar form over fences: off 9½ months, won 5-runner maiden at
Warwick in December: very tired when refusing last next time: stays 27f: acts on heavy
going: tongue tied: hard ride. *Noel T. Chance*

PASS GO 6 b.g. Kris – Celt Song (IRE) (Unfuwain (USA)) [2006/7 h–: 16vᵖᵘ 17m⁵ h75 §
16sᵖᵘ Sep 20] poor hurdler: raced around 2m: in cheekpieces last 2 starts: difficult ride:
sold 500 gns Doncaster November Sales. *J. J. Lambe, Ireland*

PASS IT ON (IRE) 8 br.g. Accordion – Windswept Lady (IRE) (Strong Gale) [2006/7 h123
h112p: 17d* 20sᶠ 20s* 20s⁴ 24s³ 24g³ Mar 24] workmanlike gelding: fairly useful
hurdler: didn't need to be at best to win novices at Carlisle in October and Leicester (beat
Kellbury by 3 lengths, idling) in November: in cheekpieces, good 4¼ lengths third of 16
to McKelvey in handicap at Bangor final outing: stays 3m: acts on heavy going. *Jonjo
O'Neill*

PASS ME A DIME 8 b.g. Past Glories – Hand Out (Spare A Dime) [2006/7 c121, c120 x
h92+: c17d* c17dᶠ c16s⁴ 20d2 24v⁴ 20gᵖᵘ Mar 21] rather leggy gelding: fairly useful h118 x
handicap hurdler/chaser: won chase at Exeter in November by ¾ length from Roofing
Spirit: stays 3m: acts on heavy going, probably on good to firm: tried in cheekpieces (fell
first): sketchy jumper. *C. L. Tizzard*

PASS ME BY 8 b.g. Balnibarbi – Errol Emerald (Dom Racine (FR)) [2006/7 c122, h–: c130
c25d² c29v* c24gᵖᵘ Feb 3] tall, angular gelding: winning hurdler: useful handicap chaser: h–
won skybet.com Sussex National at Plumpton in January by 1½ lengths from Zimbabwe
(FR), jumping markedly right latter stages: bled next time (blinkered): barely stays 4m:
acts on good to firm and heavy going: tried in cheekpieces, usually wears eyeshields.
Miss Suzy Smith

PASS THE CLASS (IRE) 7 b.g. Classic Cliche (IRE) – Passchendaele (IRE) h102
(Phardante (FR)) [2006/7 F91: F16v³ 20m* 20s³ 20d⁶ 17v 17s³ 20g² 24s Apr 25] lengthy F88
gelding: third in bumper: fair novice hurdler: won at Hexham in June: stays 2½m: acts on
soft and good to firm going. *Mrs S. J. Smith*

PASS WOOD (FR) 4 br.g. Sevres Rose (IRE) – Faveur d'Estruval (FR) (Castle Guard) F–
[2006/7 F16m F16gᵖᵘ Mar 28] unfurnished gelding: third foal: half-brother to 1½m/1¾m
winner Wonder Wood (by Phantom Breeze): dam unraced out of half-sister to smart
hurdler/chaser Barton, stayed 25f: more signs of temperament than ability in bumpers.
H. D. Daly

PAST ENTERTAINER (IRE) 6 b.g. Pasternak – Feodora (Songedor) [2006/7 20s⁶ c71
21g 21vᵖᵘ 16v³ 16vᵖᵘ c16v⁶ c24m Mar 25] compact gelding: half-brother to fair hurdler/ h77
chaser up to 3m Finewood (by Macmillion) and bumper winner Entertainment Park (by
Park Row): dam lightly raced over hurdles: little form over hurdles/in handicap chases.
R. Lee

PAST HERITAGE 8 b.g. Past Glories – Norman's Delight (IRE) (Idiot's Delight) c–
[2006/7 h72: 17m 16m⁴ 17gᵖᵘ c19sᵖᵘ Dec 29] medium-sized gelding: poor handicap h65
hurdler: no show on chasing debut: best form around 2m: tried in cheekpieces. *A. E. Jones*

PATAVIUM (IRE) 4 b.g. Titus Livius (FR) – Arcevia (IRE) (Archway (IRE)) [2006/7 h100
16gᵖᵘ 17v³ 19s⁶ 16v³ 16d* 19g 17m Apr 9] leggy gelding: modest maiden on Flat: fair
juvenile hurdler: improved form when winning handicap at Musselburgh in February:
free-going sort, likely to prove best at easy 2m. *E. W. Tuer*

PATCHES (IRE) 8 b. or br.g. Presenting – Ballykilleen (The Parson) [2006/7 c–, h–: c–
c26gᶠ Mar 16] well-made gelding: has reportedly had breathing operation: winning h–
hurdler/chaser, useful form at best: left P. Nicholls, won twice in points in 2007: not fluent
prior to falling ninth in Foxhunter at Cheltenham: should stay at least 3m: tongue tied
once. *R. Barber*

PAT COHAN (IRE) 7 b.m. Rock Hopper – Irish Hill Lass (Prominer) [2006/7 F16d⁴ h83
F20m F16s⁵ F16d⁶ 16s² 18v Dec 14] €3,200 4-y-o: half-sister to fairly useful staying F80
hurdler Hillson (by The Parson) and Irish bumper winner Sheisagale (by Strong Gale):
dam twice-raced pointer: modest form in bumpers: better effort over hurdles when second
in mares novice at Lingfield: should be suited by 2½m+. *S. Donohoe, Ireland*

Mr C. P. Byrne's "Patsy Hall"

PATMAN DU CHARMIL (FR) 5 b.g. Robin Des Pres (FR) – Pacifie du Charmil (FR) (Dom Pasquini (FR)) [2006/7 h124: c21s^{pu} c16g^4 c16d^4 c20s^2 c25d^{pu} c21v^6 c24g* c21g^{pu} c24s^{pu} Apr 25] tall, leggy gelding: fairly useful hurdler/chaser: best effort over fences when 4 lengths third (promoted) to Gallant Approach in handicap at Newbury: idled when winning 4-runner novice at Warwick in March: stays 3m: raced on good going or softer (acts on soft): tried tongue tied: has shaped as if amiss more than once. *N. A. Twiston-Davies*   **c116 h–**

PATOMA (IRE) 4 b.g. Vettori (IRE) – Heresheis (Free State) [2006/7 16g^5 16v^6 16s Mar 2] workmanlike gelding: fair form in all-weather maidens (will be suited by 1½m+) at 2 yrs: shaped with promise 3 starts in juvenile hurdles: likely to do better. *Miss E. C. Lavelle*   **h82 p**

PATRICKSNINETEENTH (IRE) 10 b.g. Mister Lord (USA) – Many Miracles (Le Moss) [2006/7 c134: c24g^{pu} c25g c20s* Apr 25] big, well-made gelding: one-time useful chaser, off 14 months (reportedly pulled muscles in back final 2005/6 outing) before return: easily best effort in 2006/7 when winning handicap at Perth in April by 1¾ lengths from Incas: needs good test around 2½m and stays 3m: raced on good going or softer. *P. R. Webber*   **c123**

PATRIXTOO (FR) 6 gr.g. Linamix (FR) – Maradadi (USA) (Shadeed (USA)) [2006/7 h–: 16m 16s^4 20g Apr 9] angular gelding: form (modest) since hurdling debut in 2004/5 only on second outing: should stay beyond 2m. *T. J. Fitzgerald*   **h95**

PATRONAGE 5 b.g. Royal Applause – Passionate Pursuit (Pursuit of Love) [2006/7 h90: 16g* 20m 16m Jul 12] angular gelding: modest hurdler: won 18-runner handicap at   **h95**

Uttoxeter in June: well held next 2 starts: may prove best around 2m: tried blinkered. *Jonjo O'Neill*

PATS LAST 5 b.g. Emarati (USA) – Bride's Answer (Anshan) [2006/7 F–: F16v Jan 25] lengthy gelding: tailed off in bumpers. *P. R. Rodford*

F–

PATSY BEE (IRE) 6 b.g. Saddlers' Hall (IRE) – Strong Profit (IRE) (Strong Gale) [2006/7 19g⁶ 22v 20v³ 19s⁴ 24d 20g Mar 21] €50,000 3-y-o: third foal: dam, unraced, out of sister to useful hurdler/chaser Belvederian: let down by jumping only outing over fences: fair hurdler on his day: largely disappointing in 2006/7, left E. O'Grady prior to final start: stays 2¾m: acts on heavy going. *Miss Tor Sturgis*

c–
h110 d

PATSY HALL (IRE) 7 b.g. Saddlers' Hall (IRE) – Clahada Rose (IRE) (Roselier (FR)) [2006/7 h129+: c20s c20d* c24dᶠ c25s* c24v² c24vᵘʳ c20v⁵ c24g c29mᵖᵘ Apr 9] strong, lengthy gelding: winning hurdler: useful novice chaser: won at Down Royal (maiden) in November and Cheltenham (beat Aces Four by 9 lengths, idled) in December: creditable second to Cailin Alainn (pair clear) in Grade 1 at Leopardstown: below form last 3 starts: should stay beyond 25f: acts on heavy going: usually held up. *Michael Cunningham, Ireland*

c142
h–

PATTON (FR) 4 b.g. Bonnet Rouge (FR) – Gesse Parade (FR) (Dress Parade) [2006/7 F16s Mar 3] €36,000 2-y-o, 15,000 3-y-o: fourth foal: half-brother to winning chaser up to 21f Nonita de Clerval (by Nononito), and 11.5f winner Otage de Brion (by Rajpoute): dam unraced half-sister to dam of top-class staying chaser First Gold: well held in bumper on debut. *A. King*

F–

PAUILLAC (FR) 4 b.g. Useful (FR) – Jolie Mome (FR) (Art Francais (USA)) [2006/7 17s³ 16s* 16v* 17v³ 17gᵖᵘ Mar 16] leggy, rather unfurnished gelding: half-brother to 2m hurdle winner Nurburgring (by Smadoun): 11f winner on Flat: useful juvenile hurdler: confirmed promise of debut (trained by G. Cherel) when winning at Newbury in December and Sandown in January, making all both times: good 4¼ lengths third to

h128 +

Mr D. A. Johnson's "Pauillac"

Katchit in Grade 2 at Cheltenham, racing freely: will stay beyond 17f: raced on soft/heavy ground prior to Triumph Hurdle final start (seemed amiss). *D. E. Pipe*

PAULO DANCER (FR) 6 b.g. Epaphos (GER) – Hora Dancer (FR) (Lashkari) [2006/7 h103: 21m* 21s* 21d⁵ 22d⁶ Feb 1] leggy, close-coupled gelding: fair hurdler: wide-margin winner of novices at Plumpton and Cheltenham (eased run-in) in October: below best last 2 outings: should stay beyond 21f: acts on soft and good to firm going. *P. F. Nicholls* **h114**

PAUL SUPERSTAR (FR) 5 gr.g. Kaldounevees (FR) – Lady Lieutenant (IRE) (General Holme (USA)) [2006/7 F–: F14g⁵ Sep 30] more signs of temperament than ability in bumpers. *N. J. Hawke* **F–**

PAUNTLEY GOFA 11 b.g. Afzal – Gotageton (Oats) [2006/7 c87x, h–: c18dᵖᵘ c19sᵖᵘ c16sᵖᵘ c16v⁶ c16g* Apr 20] tall gelding: winning hurdler: modest chaser: left R. Harper and off 3 months, first form in 2006/7 when winning handicap at Hereford in April: best around 2m: acts on good to soft and good to firm going: usually let down by jumping. *S. J. Gilmore* **c90 x** **h–**

PAVEY ARK (IRE) 9 b.g. King's Ride – Splendid Run (Deep Run) [2006/7 c76, h–: c16m⁶ c16g⁴ c21d⁵ c20dᵘʳ c16dᵖᵘ c19d c20g Apr 23] tall, lengthy gelding: poor handicap chaser: off 5 months, no show last 4 starts: should stay beyond 21f: acts on firm and soft going: visored/in cheekpieces. *James Moffatt* **c65** **h–**

PAWN BROKER 10 ch.g. Selkirk (USA) – Dime Bag (High Line) [2006/7 h100: 16vᵖᵘ Jan 13] sturdy gelding: maiden hurdler: raced around 2m on good going or softer: usually blinkered. *Miss J. R. Tooth* **h–**

PAY ATTENTION 6 b.m. Revoque (IRE) – Catch Me (Rudimentary (USA)) [2006/7 h125: c20v* c22v³ c20m² c20m* Apr 15] leggy, lengthy mare: fairly useful handicap hurdler: encouraging start over fences, winning novices at Wetherby in December and Market Rasen (by 16 lengths from eased Salhood) in April: ½-length second to Lankawi in 2-finisher novice at Southwell (would have won with better jump last): stays 21f: acts on good to firm and heavy going: sound jumper: reliable. *T. D. Easterby* **c116** **h–**

PAYMASTER (NZ) 12 ch.g. Norman Pentaquad (USA) – Tivy (NZ) (Noble Bijou (USA)) [2006/7 c16g⁴ May 3] good-topped gelding: winning hurdler: fair pointer: largely let down by jumping in chases: barely stays 21f: acts on good to firm going: sometimes tongue tied. *Mrs Jelly O'Brien* **c82** **h–**

PAYNESTOWN LAD (IRE) 11 b.g. Bravefoot – Athy Lady (Welsh Captain) [2006/7 16mᵖᵘ 16dᵖᵘ 16g 20d⁴ 20d* 21v⁴ 19v 22s⁴ 20s 21mᵖᵘ Apr 8] small, angular gelding: poor handicap hurdler: won selling event at Leicester in November: probably stays 2¾m: acts on soft and good to firm going. *Miss C. J. E. Caroe* **h61**

PAY ON (IRE) 4 ch.g. Danehill Dancer (IRE) – Richly Deserved (IRE) (Kings Lake (USA)) [2006/7 17v 16g 16v⁵ 18s⁵ 20v Mar 2] modest maiden on Flat (seems to stay 1¼m), sold out of W. Jarvis' stable 3,200 gns Doncaster August Sales: little form over hurdles. *A. C. Whillans* **h73 ?**

PAY OR PAY 5 b.g. Atraf – Petinata (Petong) [2006/7 F16v Feb 24] tall, workmanlike gelding: half-brother to 3 winners, including 7f winner Starlight (by King's Signet): dam ran twice: tailed off in bumper on debut. *P. S. McEntee* **F–**

PAZMO 5 b.g. Pasternak – Smoke (Rusticaro (FR)) [2006/7 F17d F16m Apr 9] tall, rather unfurnished gelding: seventh foal: half-brother to winning pointer by Petoski: dam, poor 2m novice hurdler, won over 1½m on Flat: soundly beaten in bumpers. *J. M. Jefferson* **F–**

PEACH GALETTE (USA) 5 b.m. Kris S (USA) – Souffle (Zafonic (USA)) [2006/7 F16s² May 8] half-sister to 19f hurdle winner Fordingbridge (by Diesis): dam, useful stayer on Flat, half-sister to very smart performer up to 1½m Grape Tree Road and smart stayers Red Route and Windsor Castle: fair form when ¾-length second to No Directions in mares bumper at Towcester on debut. *A. M. Balding* **F88**

PEACH OF A CITIZEN (IRE) 8 b.m. Anshan – Sweet Peach (IRE) (Glenstal (USA)) [2006/7 c75, h–: c20d c21m⁶ c24mᵖᵘ c23m⁵ c20f c20g c22s⁵ c25d³ c24dᶠ Jan 19] modest maiden handicap chaser, left E. O'Sullivan in Ireland before penultimate outing: stays 25f: acts on good to firm and good to soft going: tried in blinkers (went off too fast). *G. M. Moore* **c85** **h–**

PEACOCK (FR) 4 ch.g. Bulington (FR) – Algue Rouge (FR) (Perouges (FR)) [2006/7 17s 16s³ 16g* 20s⁶ Apr 26] useful-looking gelding: fourth foal: brother to fairly useful hurdler around 2m Monte Cinto: dam won cross-country chase: runner-up over 1½m on **h108**

Flat for T. Trapenard: fair form over hurdles: made all in conditional jockeys maiden at Fakenham in March: should stay beyond 2m: acts on soft ground. *N. A. Twiston-Davies*

PEAK SEASONS (IRE) 4 ch.g. Raise A Grand (IRE) – Teresian Girl (IRE) (Glenstal (USA)) [2006/7 16g⁶ 17gᵘʳ 17vᵘʳ 16d 19d 16g⁵ 17d 17d 17m² Apr 15] leggy, close-coupled gelding: poor form over hurdles: won 1¼m seller (sold from W. de Best-Turner 6,400 gns) in July: poor form over hurdles: likely to prove best around 2m: acts on good to firm ground: headstrong. *M. C. Chapman* **h82**

PEARCECROFT (IRE) 7 b.g. Grand Lodge (USA) – Tart (FR) (Warning) [2006/7 F16v 20mᵖᵘ Mar 31] no form in bumpers/maiden hurdle (jumped slowly). *P. A. Pritchard* **h–** **F–**

PEARL KING (IRE) 5 gr.g. Daylami (IRE) – Regal Opinion (USA) (Gone West (USA)) [2006/7 h98: 16m* 17g⁶ 16g² 16g³ c16m* c16g* c16f* c16m³ Apr 21] leggy gelding: fairly useful hurdler: landed odds in maiden at Huntingdon in August: successful first 3 starts over fences, in novices at Leicester (mistakes) in November and Ludlow (fairly useful form, beat Nippy des Mottes by 1½ lengths) in April, and handicap at Wincanton in between: again favourite, jumped poorly final outing: likely to prove best at 2m: raced on good ground or firmer (acts on firm). *P. J. Hobbs* **c125** **h119**

PEARLSFORTHEGIRLS 7 gr.m. Cloudings (IRE) – Rim of Pearl (Rymer) [2006/7 F16g 20m⁶ Apr 15] sixth foal: half-sister to useful bumper winners Posh Pearl (by Rakaposhi King) and Hobbs Hill (by Alflora), latter useful 17f hurdle winner: dam, poor maiden hurdler, half-sister to dam of top-class 2m chaser Pearlyman: well held in mares bumper (lame)/maiden hurdle. *Miss Suzy Smith* **h–** **F–**

PEARLY BAY 9 b.m. Karinga Bay – Marina Bird (Julio Mariner) [2006/7 h92: 19d⁶ 20m 20mᵖᵘ 17sᵖᵘ 16g Apr 23] lengthy mare: modest handicap hurdler, left M. Rimell and off 5½ months after third outing: stays 19f: acts on heavy ground: in cheekpieces 2 of last 3 starts: has bled from nose. *D. McCain Jnr* **h86**

PEARLY JACK 9 ch.g. Weld – Pearly Lady (Tycoon II) [2006/7 c123x, h111: c22g³ c24s² c24d* 20s* 20v³ Feb 21] rather leggy gelding: fairly useful hurdler/chaser: won Tote Munster National (Handicap) at Limerick (by 1½ lengths from Star Clipper) in October and handicap hurdle there in November: ran well when placed in Kerry National at Listowel previous outing for second successive year: stays 25f: raced on good going or softer (acts on heavy): effective held up or making running. *D. E. Fitzgerald, Ireland* **c127** **h121**

PEARLY STAR 6 b.g. Bob's Return (IRE) – Pearly-B (IRE) (Gunner B) [2006/7 h93, F–: 20d⁶ 22s* 20s* 21sᵖᵘ Mar 1] smallish gelding: fair handicap hurdler: improved form in 2006/7, winning at Fontwell in December (conditional jockeys) and January: lost action next time: will stay 3m: raced on good ground or softer: has worn visor/blinkers (including when successful). *Mrs A. E. Brooks* **h105**

PEARSON GLEN (IRE) 8 ch.g. Dolphin Street (FR) – Glendora (Glenstal (USA)) [2006/7 h87: 16g³ 17d⁴ 17d⁴ 17m 17m⁴ 16m² 17m² Sep 26] fair maiden hurdler: probably best at 2m: acts on good to firm going, probably on good to soft: usually wears cheekpieces/eyeshields: tried tongue tied. *James Moffatt* **h101**

PEBROCK (FR) 4 b.g. Video Rock (FR) – Envie de Chalamont (FR) (Pamponi (FR)) [2006/7 F16v* Jan 27] rather leggy, angular gelding: sixth foal: brother to 2½m chase winner Jockker and half-brother to 3 winners, including fair hurdler/fairly useful chaser around 2m Lorient Express (by Sleeping Car): dam unraced: joint favourite, won 4-y-o bumper at Southwell on debut by short head from Scale Bank (pair clear): sold 55,000 gns Doncaster May Sales. *N. A. Twiston-Davies* **F102**

PEDDARS WAY 8 b.g. Nomadic Way (USA) – Deep Selection (IRE) (Deep Run) [2006/7 h–: c23m³ c24sᵖᵘ c24dᵖᵘ Jan 8] leggy gelding: maiden hurdler: poor form only completed outing in handicap chases: stays 3m: acts on soft and good to firm going: tried visored/in cheekpieces. *R. Hollinshead* **c81** **h–**

PEDLARS SON 8 ch.g. Weld – The Pedlar (Riberetto) [2006/7 c20gᵖᵘ Mar 22] poor maiden pointer: troublesome at start, no show in hunter on chase debut. *G. C. Evans* **c–**

PEDLERS BRIDGE (IRE) 5 b.g. Moonax (IRE) – Lochda (Crash Course) [2006/7 F16d 16d 16s⁶ 20s Jan 31] lengthy gelding: has scope: half-brother to 3¼m chase winner Waders (by Good Thyne): dam, winning 2m hurdler, sister to fairly useful chaser Kittinger who stayed 3m: little form in bumper/over hurdles. *P. G. Murphy* **h–** **F74**

PEDLER'S PROFILES 7 br.g. Topanoora – La Vie En Primrose (Henbit (USA)) [2006/7 h65: 16g⁴ 16f* 16m² 16g² 17g Apr 7] selling hurdler: seemingly best effort when second at Worcester: won handicap at same course in June on previous start: raced mainly around 2m: acts on firm going. *Karen George* **h91 ?**

PEDROBOB (IRE) 9 ch.g. Pierre – Jazzelle (Roi Guillaume (FR)) [2006/7 h112p,   **h140**
F108: 16s* 21d 16v* 16d³ 17g* 16m Apr 10]

There are currently five Carberry siblings race-riding. Thomas, who rides
work for Noel Meade, is an amateur who has contested mainly bumpers. Paul is a
former dual Irish champion, a Grand National-winning jockey who holds a retainer
with Meade. Nina is the leading female rider (also based with Meade) and won
her second race at the Cheltenham Festival in the latest season on Heads Onthe
Ground in the cross country event. Eighteen-year-old Peter John had his first ride
on Hunterstown Queen in a bumper at Downpatrick in March. Philip crowned a
tremendously successful twelve months by following up his Champion Hurdle
success aboard Sublimity by winning the County Hurdle on Pedrobob three days
later. Were all five to compete in the same race, they would be matching the feat of
the Doyle brothers, Tony, Tommy, Jimmy, Joe and John junior, who are believed to
have ridden against each other in a race at the Curragh in April 1927. A more
realistic possibility, however, is for the Carberry clan to create some further history
in the Grand National—Paul, Philip and Nina were set to become the first three
siblings since 1889 to compete against each other in the Aintree showpiece only for
the last-named's mount, A New Story, to miss the cut from the latest renewal. They
were bidding to emulate another famous Irish racing family which dominated the
race towards the end of the nineteenth century. Between 1877 and 1892, the four
Beasley brothers—Tommy, Harry, Willie and Johnny—had thirty-four mounts
between them in the National, winning the race four times and finishing placed a
further eight times. The only year when all four took part (ironically without
success) was 1879, though Tommy Beasley had two of his brothers behind him
when recording a third National win (on Frigate) ten years later. Harry Beasley got
in on the act in 1891 when winning on Come Away, a horse he also trained, and
pursued a remarkably long career in the saddle—his final ride came aged eighty-
five, when he still made the weight at 9-7! Harry was the grandfather of Bobby
Beasley, who won most of National Hunt's big prizes (including the 1961 National
on Nicolaus Silver) during a more stop-start career and was a contemporary of
Tommy Carberry, who is the father of the aforementioned quintet and one of a
select number who have both ridden (L'Escargot) and trained (Bobbyjo) a Grand
National winner.

Pedrobob, who is trained by Anthony Mullins, a man also born into a racing
dynasty, came to racing relatively late. After winning three bumpers in early
2005/6, Pedrobob landed the odds in a maiden hurdle at Galway and ended that
campaign with two placings in novice events. Off for six months before his reappearance in October in the latest season, Pedrobob made a winning return when

*Vincent O'Brien County Handicap Hurdle, Cheltenham—a typically competitive renewal
of the 'getting-out' stakes; Irish raider Pedrobob (star on cap) is only seventh at the last,
as eventual runner-up Ouninpohja (hooped sleeves) challenges on the outer of eventual fifth Arcalis (grey)*

beating Beef Or Salmon—switched to hurdles in a prep race for Down Royal—by five lengths in an eleven-runner minor event at Fairyhouse. Pedrobob was next stepped up to two miles five furlongs in a competitive intermediate event at Cheltenham when making his handicap debut the following month. He was sent off 9/4 favourite in the sixteen-runner event but managed only seventh (beaten just over five lengths) to Mith Hill, staying on after the last. Pedrobob returned to winning ways in a minor event at Leopardstown's Christmas meeting before being returned to handicap company and putting up his two best performances, on the first occasion finishing two and a quarter lengths third to Heathcote in the totesport Trophy at Newbury, and then winning the Vincent O'Brien County Hurdle. As ever the County was a fiercely competitive event, for all that the presence of the previous year's winner Desert Quest under top weight meant eight of the twenty-eight runners were out of the weights. It was Philip Carberry's first ride on Pedrobob and he was rewarded for using more patient tactics than at Newbury. Indeed, the race for home began in earnest so far out in the County that there was an advantage to being patiently ridden, with plenty of those that were—as well as front-running Osana—in contention at the last. In a grandstand finish, in which at various stages on the run-in five horses held the advantage, 12/1-shot Pedrobob highlighted his enthusiasm for racing by staying on strongly to win by a length from the quirky novice Ouninpohja. Davy Russell was back on board for Pedrobob's final outing of the campaign, which came in another competitive handicap at Fairyhouse the following month. However, he ran poorly, seemingly amiss, never travelling and jumping with little fluency.

Pedrobob (IRE) (ch.g. 1998)	Pierre (b 1994)	Sadler's Wells (b 1981)	Northern Dancer / Fairy Bridge
		Reprocolor (ch 1976)	Jimmy Reppin / Blue Queen
	Jazzelle (ch 1986)	Roi Guillaume (b 1978)	Busted / Rescousse
		Disco Lady (ch 1976)	Herbager / Some Joy

The lengthy, angular Pedrobob is the second foal of the unraced Jazzelle. His six-year-old half-brother, Jasandy (by Shahanndeh), races for the same connections and was owner-ridden in two bumpers in the latest season, showing fair form. Pedrobob is from the first crop of the unraced Pierre, a brother to the fairly useful Flat stayer Lafitte The Pirate, and closely related to the 1994 Irish Champion Stakes winner Cezanne who subsequently became a fair hurdler after failing at stud. Pierre is also a half-brother to two leading Michael Stoute-trained fillies from the 'eighties, the 1985 One Thousand Guineas third Bella Colora and the 1986 Irish Oaks winner Colorspin, who have both done very well subsequently at stud—the latter is the dam of multiple Group 1 winners Opera House and Kayf Tara. Pierre's dam Reprocolor was a smart racemare herself, winning both the Lingfield Oaks Trial and Lancashire Oaks. Pierre's only other notable progeny to date is the smart staying hurdler/chaser Standin Obligation. Pedrobob is a genuine gelding who stays twenty-one furlongs and acts on heavy and good to firm going. He, too, was owner-ridden for each of his three successes in bumpers and also when in mid-field in a nineteen-runner maiden at Leopardstown on his Flat debut in June (for which he was sent off 11/8 favourite). *Anthony Mullins, Ireland*

PEDROS BRIEF (IRE) 9 b. or br.g. Leading Counsel (USA) – Pedros Pet (IRE) (Good Thyne (USA)) [2006/7 c90, h115: c19d^{pu} c21d^5 c19v^F Mar 10] lengthy, useful-looking gelding: winning pointer: fairly useful hurdle winner: maiden chaser, no form in 2006/7, left C. Tizzard after second start: will stay 3m: has shaped as if amiss more than once. *R. Lee* **c– h–**

PEE JAY'S DREAM 5 ch.g. Vettori (IRE) – Langtry Lady (Pas de Seul) [2006/7 16v^2 16s^8 20v^3 18s^8 16d^3 Mar 17] strong, close-coupled gelding: half-brother to fairly useful 2m hurdler Nowell House (by Polar Falcon): fair and consistent up to 2m on Flat: fair hurdler: won novice at Newcastle in December and handicap at Kelso in February: should stay 2½m: raced on going softer than good. *M. W. Easterby* **h114**

PEEPHOLE 4 ch.g. Pursuit of Love – Goodwood Lass (IRE) (Alzao (USA)) [2006/7 16m 17g 16m 17d 22v* 22d Mar 26] smallish gelding: half-brother to winning pointer by **h85**

Groom Dancer: fair at best on Flat (stays 1¼m), sold from P. Makin 4,500 gns after successful in 2006: upped in trip, easily best effort over hurdles (sold out of A. Bailey's stable 1,500 gns Doncaster November Sales after second outing) when winning novice at Fontwell in March: stays 2¾m: acts on heavy going: in cheekpieces last 4 outings. *Mrs A. M. Thorpe*

PEERLESS MOTION (IRE) 12 b.g. Caerleon (USA) – Final Figure (USA) (Super Concorde (USA)) [2006/7 h–: 16s³ c20d^F Mar 26] angular gelding: winning hurdler: fell fatally on chasing debut: raced mainly around 2m: acted on any going. *S. Lycett*
   c–
   h76

PEEYOUTWO 12 b.g. Golden Heights – Nyika (Town And Country) [2006/7 c106d, h–: 22g² 24m⁵ 19m^F Aug 2] winning pointer: maiden chaser: modest handicap hurdler: barely stays 3m: best efforts on good/good to firm going: tried in cheekpieces. *Mrs D. A. Hamer*
   c–
   h97

PEGGY'S BOY 5 b.g. Morpeth – Prudent Peggy (Kambalda) [2006/7 F17v 17s 19v 16d Mar 26] workmanlike gelding: second foal: dam, modest staying chaser, half-sister to fairly useful 2m hurdler Cotton Call: well held in bumper/novice hurdles: will be suited by 2½m+. *J. D. Frost*
   h79
   F–

PELO DU BIEF (FR) 4 b.g. Useful (FR) – Hopeful of Silver (FR) (Son of Silver) [2006/7 16v⁵ 16v 16v⁴ Mar 3] compact gelding: first foal: dam maiden: successful once over 11f from 5 starts on Flat at 3 yrs for C. Diard: progressive over hurdles, modest form in novice final outing: may do better again if jumping improves. *R. T. Phillips*
   h89

PENALTA 11 ch.g. Cosmonaut – Targuette (Targowice (USA)) [2006/7 16g^{pu} Jun 15] very lightly raced over hurdles: tried blinkered: little show in points. *W. M. Brisbourne*
   h–

PENALTY CLAUSE (IRE) 7 b.g. Namaqualand (USA) – Lady Be Lucky (IRE) (Taufan (USA)) [2006/7 c83d, h–: c18g* c31d^{pu} Nov 10] leggy gelding: winning hurdler: poor chaser: left Mrs L. Featherstone and dropped long way in weights, won handicap at Fontwell in September: out of depth next time: stays 2¾m: acts on good to firm and good to soft going: used to wear cheekpieces/visor: has had tongue tied. *P. Howling*
   c83
   h–

PENCIL HOUSE (IRE) 7 ch.g. Carroll House – Pencil (Crash Course) [2006/7 F–: F17s² 19d⁴ 20v 20g^{pu} Apr 16] strong, workmanlike gelding: runner-up in bumper at Aintree: modest form on hurdling debut: breathing problem final start: should stay beyond 19f. *D. McCain Jnr*
   h90
   F91

PENDRAGON (USA) 4 ch.g. Rahy (USA) – Turning Wheel (USA) (Seeking The Gold (USA)) [2006/7 F16m F16s Apr 27] €7,000 3-y-o: sturdy gelding: fourth foal: half-brother to 2 useful winners on Flat, including French performer up to 1¼m Imago Mundi (by Spinning World): dam useful 1¼m/11f winner: no show in bumpers. *Mrs L. B. Normile*
   F–

PENMARA 4 b.f. Mtoto – Pendulum (Pursuit of Love) [2006/7 16g^{pu} 16g 17g Apr 23] modest maiden on Flat (bred to stay 1½m), sold out of M. Tompkins' stable 3,000 gns Newmarket Autumn Sales: little show in juvenile hurdles (saddle slipped final outing). *Miss J. E. Foster*
   h–

PENNEYROSE BAY 8 ch.m. Karinga Bay – Pennethorne Place (Deep Run) [2006/7 c103, h130: c23f² c20g⁴ c21d³ c22g* Mar 24] lengthy mare: useful hurdler: fairly useful novice chaser, left J. Geake after first outing, trained next 2 by Miss A. Newton-Smith: easily best effort over fences when winning listed mares handicap at Newbury in March by 8 lengths from Chamoss Royale: should stay beyond 2¾m: acts on soft and good to firm going: front runner. *N. J. Gifford*
   c121 +
   h–

PENNYBID (IRE) 5 b.g. Benny The Dip (USA) – Stamatina (Warning) [2006/7 F–: 16g 20m 20g^{pu} Apr 23] big gelding: no form in bumper/novice hurdles: tried tongue tied. *C. R. Wilson*
   h–

PENNYFOURTHOUGHTS (IRE) 5 b.m. Almutawakel – Hirasah (IRE) (Lahib (USA)) [2006/7 16v 16v⁵ 16v* 16v³ 20v⁴ 16v^{pu} Mar 18] fairly useful up to 1¼m on Flat, refused to enter stall in late-September then left D. Gillespie: fair hurdler: won maiden at Naas in January: will prove best around 2m: acts on heavy going. *T. J. Arnold, Ireland*
   h101

PENNYHILL THYNE (IRE) 7 br.g. Good Thyne (USA) – Baylough Lady (IRE) (Lancastrian) [2006/7 c23g⁴ 20f² c22m^{pu} 22g* 21m^{pu} 24v⁶ 23s c20s Nov 19] half-brother to bumper winner Mr Lundy (by Ore) and a winning pointer by Commanche Run: dam unraced: winning pointer: poor hurdler: won handicap at Downpatrick in August: similar form on first of 3 outings in chases: stays 23f: acts on firm ground: effective with/without cheekpieces: tongue tied. *J. G. Carr, Ireland*
   c84
   h84

PENNY PARK (IRE) 8 ch.g. Flemensfirth (USA) – Penny Bride (IRE) (The Parson) [2006/7 h107+: c23d[pu] c24g[3] c24s[2] c24g[ur] c25g[4] Apr 18] lengthy gelding: winning Irish pointer: fair hurdler/novice chaser: stays 25f: acts on soft going: tried tongue tied: has hung left. *P. J. Hobbs* **c109 h–**

PENNY PICTURES (IRE) 8 b.g. Theatrical – Copper Creek (Habitat) [2006/7 c109p, h134: 21g 19g 24g[4] 20f[5] Apr 28] small gelding: useful handicap hurdler, off 11 months prior to return: back in form last 2 starts, 4½ lengths fifth to Oslot in quite valuable event at Sandown final one: fair form when fourth in maiden at Ludlow on chasing debut in 2005/6 (should do better): stays easy 3m: acts on soft and firm going. *D. E. Pipe* **c– h134**

PENNY'S CROWN 8 b.m. Reprimand – Two And Sixpence (USA) (Chief's Crown (USA)) [2006/7 h81§: 19d 21d 24d[d] 20d[d] 24s Dec 29] poor handicap hurdler: stays 3m: acts on soft and good to firm going: tried in headgear/tongue tied: unreliable. *G. A. Ham* **h74 §**

PENRIC 7 b.g. Marju (IRE) – Nafhaat (USA) (Roberto (USA)) [2006/7 h94: c19m[5] Nov 5] close-coupled gelding: modest hurdler: off a year, no show in maiden on chasing debut: stays 19f: acts on soft and good to firm going: tried blinkered. *J. K. Price* **c– h–**

PENTHOUSE MELODY 9 b.m. Seven Hearts – Pentameron (Heres) [2006/7 c–: c19m[4] c21g[4] c21g[pu] Apr 27] winning pointer: poor form on completed starts in chases. *Miss N. Stevens* **c77**

PENTHOUSE MINSTREL 13 b. or br.g. Seven Hearts – Pentameron (Heres) [2006/7 c106, h–: c23f[4] Jul 19] lengthy gelding: fair handicap chaser: off 8 months, well held only start in 2006/7: effective at 19f to 25f: acts on firm and good to soft going: often visored. *R. J. Hodges* **c– h–**

PENWELL HILL (USA) 8 b.g. Distant View (USA) – Avie's Jill (USA) (Lord Avie (USA)) [2006/7 17g[ur] Apr 11] one-time fairly useful performer on Flat (best at 7f to 8.5f), modest nowadays: weakening when unseated 2 out in novice seller on hurdling debut. *Miss M. E. Rowland* **h–**

PENZANCE 6 ch.g. Pennekamp (USA) – Kalinka (IRE) (Soviet Star (USA)) [2006/7 h147: c19d[*] c16g[2] c17d[2] c16d[3] c18s[2] 16m 16m[*] Apr 27] sturdy gelding: type to carry condition: useful hurdler: blinkered, well ridden from front when dead-heating with Arcalis in valuable minor event at Sandown in April: fairly useful chaser: landed odds in maiden at Hereford in May: placed all starts after, though looked rather laboured when 6 lengths second of 5 to Pablo du Charmil in novice at Fontwell fifth start: best around 2m: successful on soft going, best form under less testing conditions (acts on good to firm): has worn crossed noseband. *A. King* **c129 h139**

PEPITO COLLONGES (FR) 4 b.g. Brier Creek (USA) – Berceuse Collonges (FR) (Vorias (USA)) [2006/7 c17g[3] c17s[3] 16d 16g Mar 20] leggy, workmanlike gelding: fourth foal: dam won 3 times around 1½m on Flat: 1½m winner on Flat: third both starts over fences in Provinces for G-P. Levy: poor form over hurdles in Britain. *Mrs L. J. Mongan* **c? h80**

European Breeders' Fund/Thoroughbred Breeders' Association Mares' Only Novices' Chase Final (Handicap), Newbury—Penneyrose Bay lands the first running of this race at its new home, two years on from winning the equivalent event over hurdles

PEPPERSHOT 7 b.g. Vettori (IRE) – No Chili (Glint of Gold) [2006/7 h85d: c19m^F **c83** Apr 24] workmanlike gelding: maiden hurdler: won twice in points in 2007: staying on in **h–** third when fell last in maiden hunter on chase debut: stays 21f: acts on soft and good to firm going: tried in cheekpieces/blinkers: has had tongue tied. *P. York*

PEPPORONI PETE (IRE) 6 b.g. Un Desperado (FR) – Sister Shot (Celtic Cone) **h123** [2006/7 F115: 16g* 16d⁵ 19s 17g* 16g Apr 14] rather leggy, useful-looking gelding: bumper winner: fairly useful novice hurdler: won easily at Wincanton in October and Newton Abbot (beat Picacho by 7 lengths) in April: generally disappointing otherwise, finding little: should stay beyond 17f: all 3 wins on good ground: tongue tied last 2 starts: seems best fresh. *P. F. Nicholls*

PER AMORE (IRE) 9 ch.g. General Monash (USA) – Danny's Miracle (Superlative) **c75 §** [2006/7 c75, h–: c20g³ c16g³ c20m⁶ c20g^rtr c24d^pu 16g c20g^pu c24m³ c25m⁶ Apr 28] **h– §** medium-sized gelding: winning hurdler: poor handicap chaser: stays 21f: acts on any going: usually blinkered: increasingly reluctant to race nowadays, and one to leave alone. *D. Pearson*

PERANGE (FR) 11 ch.g. Perrault – La Mesange (FR) (Olmeto) [2006/7 c87, h–: **c82** c24m³ c20s⁴ Feb 4] close-coupled, workmanlike gelding: winning pointer: fair hunter **h–** chaser: stays 21f: acts on heavy and good to firm going. *Mrs D. M. Grissell*

PERCE ROCK 5 b.g. Dansili – Twilight Secret (Vaigly Great) [2006/7 F117: 16v* **h136** 16v² 16s Feb 4] strong gelding: smart form in bumpers: promising start over hurdles, easily landed odds in 20-runner maiden at Gowran in December: useful form when 4 lengths second of 7 to Silverburn in Grade 1 Tolworth Hurdle at Sandown: reportedly suffering from respiratory tract infection when disappointing final outing: raced at 2m: acts on heavy ground. *T. Stack, Ireland*

PERCIPIENT 9 b.g. Pennekamp (USA) – Annie Albright (USA) (Verbatim (USA)) **c– §** [2006/7 c76§, h80§: c17g c17g^pu Jun 4] useful-looking gelding: poor hurdler/maiden **h– §** chaser: best around 2m: acts on firm and soft going: blinkered/visored: not one to trust. *D. R. Gandolfo*

PERCUSSIONIST (IRE) 6 b.g. Sadler's Wells (USA) – Magnificent Style (USA) **c130** (Silver Hawk (USA)) [2006/7 h116: c16s* c16s² c17v² Mar 3] big, leggy gelding: very **h–** smart on Flat (stays 2m), won Yorkshire Cup in 2006: fairly useful hurdler: better over fences, won maiden at Wetherby in October by 19 lengths from Altay: creditable efforts when second in novices, beaten 3 lengths by Harmony Brig at Ayr and ½ length by Regal Heights at Kelso (jumped more convincingly): should be suited by further than 2m: raced on ground softer than good (acts on heavy): edgy type, often sweats. *J. Howard Johnson*

PERCY JAY (NZ) 8 ch.g. Rainbow Myth (NZ) – Zillah Grace (NZ) (Otehi Bay **h–** (AUS)) [2006/7 h–, F–: 16f^pu Apr 30] of little account: sold 600 gns Doncaster August Sales. *W. Jenks*

PERDIEM (IRE) 6 b.g. Executive Perk – Brass Band (IRE) (Orchestra) [2006/7 F16d **F–** Dec 21] €32,000 4-y-o: third foal: dam, modest novice hurdler who stayed 3m, half-sister to high-class staying chaser Run For Free: green, well held in bumper on debut. *N. J. Henderson*

PERFECT PUNCH 8 b.g. Reprimand – Aliuska (IRE) (Fijar Tango (FR)) [2006/7 **c85 x** c88, h–: c17f⁴ c17d⁴ c16m c21m⁶ c16v³ c20s^pu c16v² c16v⁵ c20g Apr 7] good-topped **h–** gelding: modest maiden handicap chaser: probably stays 21f: acts on any going: usually let down by jumping. *K. G. Reveley*

PERFECT STORM 8 b.g. Vettori (IRE) – Gorgeous Dancer (IRE) (Nordico (USA)) **h102** [2006/7 16g⁵ 17d⁶ 16m⁴ 16s Mar 3] smallish, sturdy gelding: fair novice hurdler, left M. Pipe and off 20 months before return: raced around 2m: acts on good to firm and good to soft going: tried tongue tied. *P. J. Hobbs*

PERKY PEAKS (IRE) 6 b. or br.g. Executive Perk – Knockea Hill (Buckskin (FR)) **h–** [2006/7 F81: 22d 16g 17v³ 16s 20v Mar 10] tall gelding: well held over hurdles, including in sellers. *N. A. Twiston-Davies*

PERRANPORTH LAD 4 b.g. Mazurek – Valmaranda (USA) (Sir Ivor (USA)) **h–** [2006/7 17g Apr 1] last in maiden at 2 yrs for Miss Victoria Roberts: tongue tied, soundly beaten in novice on hurdling debut. *D. E. Pipe*

PERSIAN CARPET 5 b.m. Desert Style (IRE) – Kuwah (IRE) (Be My Guest (USA)) **h78 ?** [2006/7 19g⁵ 16m⁵ 19g³ 20m⁵ Jul 25] half-sister to poor 17f hurdle winner Sunnyside Royale (by Ali-Royal): modest maiden on Flat (stays 1m): poor form over hurdles. *B. I. Case*

PERSIAN HERO (IRE) 11 ch.g. Persian Mews – Garrenroe (Le Moss) [2006/7 **c100** c30m⁶ c26s* c24gᶠ Apr 8] fairly useful pointer, successful 13 times, including in March: also won hunter chase at Warwick earlier in month: in front when fell last at Towcester: stays 3¼m: acts on soft ground. *G. T. H. Bailey*

PERSIAN NATIVE (IRE) 7 br.g. Anshan – Natina (IRE) (Be My Native (USA)) **h78** [2006/7 h93, F86: 16d⁵ 20g⁶ Sep 17] sturdy gelding: placed in bumper/maiden hurdle, poor form in 2006/7: should stay beyond 2m. *C. C. Bealby*

PERSIAN POINT 11 ch.g. Persian Bold – Kind Thoughts (Kashmir II) [2006/7 c94, **c91** h–: c17f³ c16d² c16d⁴ Nov 21] workmanlike gelding: maiden hurdler: modest chaser, **h–** lame final start: should stay beyond 21f: acts on any ground. *Miss S. E. Forster*

PERSIAN PRINCE (IRE) 7 br.g. Anshan – Real Decent (IRE) (Strong Gale) [2006/7 **h–** F86: 20d 20g 21s Dec 5] rangy gelding: third in bumper on debut: little show since. *J. Wade*

PERSONA (IRE) 5 b.m. Night Shift (USA) – Alonsa (IRE) (Trempolino (USA)) **h95** [2006/7 16v² 16s² 16g⁵ Mar 14] angular mare: fair maiden on Flat (stays 1½m): best effort in mares hurdles (modest form) when second to Annie's Answer in maiden at Huntingdon. *B. J. McMath*

PERSONAL ASSURANCE 10 b.g. Un Desperado (FR) – Steel Typhoon (General **c– x** Ironside) [2006/7 c113x, h–: 20v⁵ May 25] rangy gelding: winning hurdler: off 11 months **h–** and left Jonjo O'Neill, folded only start in 2006/7: fair but error-prone handicap chaser: probably stays 3¼m: unraced on firm going, acts on any other: blinkered/in cheekpieces last 3 outings: has been reluctant at start. *R. Ford*

PERTEMPS PROFILE 11 b.g. Petoski – Peristyle (Tolomeo) [2006/7 c21g⁴ May 2] **c– §** smallish, leggy gelding: winning chaser, lightly raced and no show since 2001/2: won **h– §** point in April: usually blinkered/visored. *Miss L. A. Blackford*

PERUVIAN BREEZE (IRE) 6 b.g. Foxhound – Quietly Impressive (IRE) **c–** (Taufan (USA)) [2006/7 h79: c19g May 4] poor maiden hurdler: always behind in novice **h–** handicap on chasing debut: stays 2¾m: acts on soft going: tried tongue tied. *Evan Williams*

PESSIMISTIC DICK 14 b.g. Derrylin – Tycoon Moon (Tycoon II) [2006/7 c90d, h–: **c–** c25mᵖᵘ Jun 3] sturdy gelding: winning chaser, failed to complete last 6 starts: tried **h–** blinkered. *Mrs J. C. McGregor*

PETERHOUSE 8 b.g. Persian Bold – Run With Pride (Mandrake Major) [2006/7 c–, **c–** h–: c20sᵖᵘ May 21] won handicap chase at Newcastle final start in 2004/5, only form. **h–** *Mrs E. Slack*

PETERS DELITE 5 b.g. Makbul – Steadfast Elite (IRE) (Glenstal (USA)) [2006/7 **h–** 16sᵖᵘ Oct 26] modest maiden on Flat (best form at 6f/7f): no show in seller on hurdling debut. *R. A. Fahey*

PETER'S IMP (IRE) 12 b.g. Imp Society (USA) – Catherine Clare (Sallust) [2006/7 **c–** c–, h89: 16g 22m⁵ 17d* Aug 28] small, good-bodied gelding: modest handicap hurdler: **h95** won selling event at Cartmel in August (fifth success at course and third in particular race): fell third only start over fences: effective at 17f to 2¾m: best efforts on good/good to soft going: tends to get behind. *A. Berry*

PETERS PRIDE 5 b.g. Silver Patriarch (IRE) – Manzanilla (Mango Express) [2006/7 **F100** F16s* F16v² Mar 2] second foal: dam runner-up in bumper only start: fairly useful form in bumpers: won 16-runner maiden at Catterick on debut in January by 9 lengths from Star Beat, eased: 8 lengths second of 8 to Quws Law at Ayr. *G. A. Swinbank*

PETERS STAR (IRE) 5 b.g. Fourstars Allstar (USA) – Supreme View (Supreme **F93** Leader) [2006/7 F16g³ Apr 7] €14,000 4-y-o: half-brother to modest staying hurdler/fair chaser Red Perk (by Executive Perk) and winning hunter chaser Shackleton (by Glacial Storm): dam unraced: fair form when third to Checkerboard in bumper at Haydock on debut: likely to be suited by 2½m+. *D. McCain Jnr*

PETER'S TWO FUN (FR) 10 b.g. Funambule (USA) – Spinner's Mate (FR) **c– §** (Miller's Mate) [2006/7 25v³ 25m⁵ 26g 22g Apr 27] leggy gelding: successful in point in **h– §** 2006: winning hurdler/maiden chaser, no form in 2006/7: has worn blinkers/visor: often front runner: not one to rely on. *J. H. Berwick*

PETERTHEKNOT (IRE) 9 ch.g. Beneficial – A Womans Heart (IRE) (Supreme **c114 +** Leader) [2006/7 c22m⁴ 19g⁵ 20s c16s⁴ c17v c33g c22d⁴ c25m c30m² Apr 27] good- **h109** topped gelding: one-time useful hurdler, better effort in 2006/7 in minor event second outing: fair maiden chaser: stays 3¾m: acts on heavy and good to firm going: wore cheekpieces fifth start: tends to finish weakly. *Thomas Cooper, Ireland*

PETITE MARGOT 8 b.m. Alderbrook – Outfield (Monksfield) [2006/7 25v c22v* c20s* c19v² c22g⁶ c25gᵖᵘ Apr 18] small mare: useful handicap hurdler at one time, off 22 months prior to reappearance: fair form when landing odds first 2 starts over fences, in mares maiden at Towcester in February and mares novice at Ludlow in March: no form in handicaps after, bled penultimate outing: will stay beyond 25f: acts on any going. *N. A. Twiston-Davies* **c111 h111**

PETITJEAN 7 ch.g. Garde Royale – Sainte Etoile (FR) (Saint Cyrien (FR)) [2006/7 h92, F90: c21m* c18s² c23d² c21s* c22g⁵ Mar 23] tall, good sort: modest form in maiden hurdles: much better over fences, winning handicaps at Wincanton in November and March, impressive when beating Supreme Catch by 13 lengths on latter occasion: let down by jumping final outing: stays 23f: acts on soft and good to firm ground. *P. J. Hobbs* **c125 h–**

PETIT LORD (FR) 5 ch.g. Lord of Men – Petite Majeste (FR) (Riverquest (FR)) [2006/7 17g³ 17s 17s 17s⁶ 22s² 22g³ 24m* Apr 20] useful-looking gelding: fourth foal: dam 11f winner: third over 11.5f on Flat: fair form over hurdles, sold out of F. Nicolle's stable €30,000 Goffs (France) July Sale after debut: landed odds in 5-runner handicap at Ayr readily by 3½ lengths from Russian Sky: had been much improved when placed in well-contested handicaps at Wincanton previous 2 starts: stays 3m: acts on soft and good to firm going. *P. F. Nicholls* **h115 +**

PETIT TURK (FR) 6 b.g. Baby Turk – Petite Mer (FR) (Tip Moss (FR)) [2006/7 F16v 16v⁵ 17s⁵ 16dᵖᵘ Mar 26] rangy gelding: sixth foal: half-brother to 15f hurdle winner Flamen Rock (by Nikos) and 17f chase winner Moldane (by Sicyos): dam, 6f winner on Flat, successful around 2m over hurdles in France: tailed off in bumper: poor form over hurdles: pulls hard, and has hung right. *Miss Venetia Williams* **h74 + F–**

PETOLINSKI 9 b.g. Petoski – Olnistar (FR) (Balsamo (FR)) [2006/7 c85, h–: c24s* c24d* c24dF Jun 2] winning hurdler: modest handicap chaser: all 3 wins at Towcester, last 2 in May: stayed 3m: acted on firm and soft going: wore cheekpieces: dead. *C. L. Popham* **c94 h–**

PETRICHAN (IRE) 4 b.g. Medicean – Numancia (IRE) (Alzao (USA)) [2006/7 16m 17s 17d 17v Nov 30] fair on Flat (stays 8.6f), successful twice early in 2006, sold out of K. Ryan's stable 3,800 gns Doncaster August Sales: no form in juvenile hurdles. *S. B. Clark* **h–**

PETROLERO (ARG) 8 gr.g. Perfect Parade (USA) – Louise (ARG) (Farnesio (ARG)) [2006/7 c–, h82: 17d 17m Jul 20] leggy gelding: maiden hurdler: well beaten only outing over fences: raced mainly around 2m: dead. *James Moffatt* **c– h–**

PETROUGE 11 b.g. Petoski – Red Spider (Red God) [2006/7 c21s May 29] fair pointer: no show in 2 hunters: has worn visor/cheekpieces: sold 2,200 gns Doncaster August Sales. *Ms W. Wild* **c– h–**

PETROVKA (IRE) 7 b.m. King's Theatre (IRE) – Adjacent (IRE) (Doulab (USA)) [2006/7 h73, F68: 16g² 16g 16vᵖᵘ 16g² 16m⁴ Apr 20] angular mare: modest novice hurdler: raced around 2m: best efforts on good going, possibly unsuited by soft/heavy. *S. Gollings* **h99**

PETRULA 8 ch.g. Tagula (IRE) – Bouffant (High Top) [2006/7 16f c16mᵖᵘ Aug 22] leggy, close-coupled gelding: fairly useful handicap hurdler at best, well beaten on reappearance: no show on chasing debut: stays 2½m: acts on heavy going, probably on good to firm: usually wears blinkers/cheekpieces. *K. A. Ryan* **c– h–**

PETWICK (IRE) 8 b. or br.g. Flemensfirth (USA) – Scottish Minnie (IRE) (Farhaan) [2006/7 h110: 22mᵖᵘ May 11] sturdy gelding: fair hurdler: poor efforts last 2 starts: stays 2½m: acts on heavy ground: temperament under suspicion. *A. King* **h–**

PEVENSEY (IRE) 5 b.g. Danehill (USA) – Champaka (IRE) (Caerleon (USA)) [2006/7 16s² 16d* 16d* 19dF Feb 17] smallish gelding: useful on Flat (stays 1½m), successful twice in 2006 for M. Buckley: promising start over hurdles, winning maiden at Catterick in December and novice at Musselburgh (readily landed odds by ¾ length from Modicum) in January: fell seventh in valuable handicap at Ascot: should stay beyond 2m: remains open to improvement. *J. J. Quinn* **h127 p**

PEVERIL PRIDE 9 b.g. Past Glories – Peveril Princess (Town And Country) [2006/7 c65§, h–§: c20m³ c24s² c24dF c26s* c24d² c26sᵖᵘ c23sᵖᵘ c25vᵖᵘ c24mᵖᵘ Apr 14] workmanlike gelding: poor handicap chaser: won at Fontwell in December: lost form after next outing: stays 3¼m: acts on soft going: tongue tied: sketchy jumper: temperamental (refused to race once). *J. A. Geake* **c80 § h– §**

PEWTER LIGHT (IRE) 10 gr.g. Roselier (FR) – Luminous Light (Cardinal Flower) [2006/7 c70§, h–§: c26vᵖᵘ Oct 21] sturdy gelding: poor handicap chaser: should stay beyond 25f: acts on soft going: tried in cheekpieces, usually wears blinkers nowadays: often races lazily. *B. J. M. Ryall*　　c– § h– §

PHAL 13 b.g. Derrylin – Royal Birthday (St Paddy) [2006/7 16dᵖᵘ 16dᵖᵘ Nov 19] rangy gelding: bumper winner: very lightly raced over hurdles, no show 2 starts after 5-year absence, in cheekpieces second one. *B. R. Johnson*　　h–

PHANTOM LAD (IRE) 4 b.g. Desert Prince (IRE) – Phantom Waters (Pharly (FR)) [2006/7 16s² 16v³ 16v* 16m³ 16m* Apr 25] compact gelding: fairly useful on Flat (probably stays 1½m), successful in September, left K. Prendergast after next start: fairly useful juvenile hurdler: won at Fairyhouse (11/4-on) in March and Punchestown in April, making much of running when beating Ingratitude 1¾ lengths in 25-runner event at latter: likely to stay beyond 2m: acts on heavy and good to firm going. *Mrs J. Harrington, Ireland*　　h115

PHAR AGAIN (IRE) 4 b.g. Beneficial – Phar From Men (IRE) (Phardante (FR)) [2006/7 F12g⁶ Mar 23] useful-looking gelding: brother to fairly useful hurdler Phar Out Phavorite, stayed 2½m, and a winning pointer: dam unraced: bit backward and green, 10¾ lengths sixth of 18 to Whiteoak in 4-y-o bumper at Newbury on debut: likely to do better for experience. *Miss E. C. Lavelle*　　F90 p

PHARANTO (IRE) 5 b.g. Dushyantor (USA) – Pharavo (IRE) (Phardante (FR)) [2006/7 F16g⁶ Apr 8] 12,500 4-y-o: second foal: dam winning pointer: won 2½m maiden point in March: in cheekpieces, 12¼ lengths sixth of 10 to Aya in bumper at Towcester. *C. C. Bealby*　　F72

PHARAOH PRINCE 6 b.g. Desert Prince (IRE) – Kinlochewe (Old Vic) [2006/7 16g⁴ Apr 23] modest on Flat (stays 1½m): 17½ lengths fourth of 9 to Classic Role in maiden at Plumpton on hurdling debut. *G. Prodromou*　　h76

PHAR BLEU (FR) 6 b.g. Agent Bleu (FR) – Guilt Less (FR) (Useful (FR)) [2006/7 h138: c17v* c16d² c20s² c16v³ c21g c22g³ c19f* Apr 11] tall, useful-looking gelding: has reportedly had breathing operation: useful handicap hurdler: generally disappointing over fences, though landed odds in 2-finisher novice at Plumpton (seemed just second best when left clear last) in January and 4-runner novice at Exeter (second start in 24 hrs) in April: stays 2¾m: acts on any going: blinkered fourth outing: usually tongue tied: usually waited with. *P. F. Nicholls*　　c112 h–

PHAR CITY (IRE) 10 b.g. Phardante (FR) – Aunty Dawn (IRE) (Strong Gale) [2006/7 c93x, h–: c26vᶠ c25g² Apr 20] strong, well-made gelding: maiden hurdler: modest chaser: successful 3 times in points in 2007, when also second to Cameron Bridge in hunter at Hereford: stays 25f: acts on soft and good to firm going: often let down by jumping. *R. H. Buckler*　　c94 x h–

PHARDESSA 6 b.m. Pharly (FR) – Mardessa (Ardross) [2006/7 F103: F17v 16s 16v⁶ 16g⁵ Mar 21] sturdy mare: 100/1-winner of bumper on debut for A. Crow: poor form over hurdles, though left impression capable of better, not fluent latter stages but not given hard time when fifth to Mago Santhai in mares novice at Chepstow: free-going sort, though bred to stay beyond 2m. *R. T. Phillips*　　h77 + F–

PHAREIGHT DEI (IRE) 9 b.g. Leading Counsel (USA) – Mullaghroe (Tarboosh (USA)) [2006/7 c–, h–: 21m³ 22s⁴ 25d³ 22v* c24s c25v* Feb 13] sturdy gelding: poor hurdler: won novice handicap at Exeter in January: similar form over fences when winning handicap at Folkestone: stays 25f: probably acts on any going: has looked none too keen, including at Folkestone. *Ian Williams*　　c77 h82

PHAR FROM FROSTY (IRE) 10 br.g. Phardante (FR) – Cold Evening (IRE) (Strong Gale) [2006/7 c97, h119: 24m⁵ 27d⁶ 24m Jun 22] lengthy, useful-looking gelding: fairly useful handicap hurdler: only modest form on 2 completed starts over fences: stays 27f: acts on firm and soft going: wore cheekpieces/tongue strap final start (folded tamely second successive time): front runner: one to treat with caution. *C. R. Egerton*　　c– § h116 §

PHARLY GREEN 5 ch.m. Pharly (FR) – Pastures Green (Monksfield) [2006/7 F–: F18gʳᵒ May 14] no show in bumpers (tailed off when running out on second occasion). *G. P. Enright*　　F–

PHARMISTICE (IRE) 16 b.g. Phardante (FR) – Lucylet (Kinglet) [2006/7 c92, h–: c25g May 24] sparely-made gelding: fair pointer/hunter chaser: stays 25f: acts on firm going. *Mrs N. C. Neill*　　c– h–

PHARNOON 11 b.g. Pharly (FR) – Mountain Willow (Doyoun) [2006/7 h–: c20d^{pu} **c–**
c20v^{pu} 24s^{pu} Apr 1] sturdy gelding: lightly raced and no sign of ability. *E. M. Caine*   **h–**

PHEONIX BELL (IRE) 7 ch.m. Eagle Eyed (USA) – Jealous One (USA) (Raise A   **h–**
Native) [2006/7 17d^{pu} 19m^{pu} 16g 17s Oct 4] maiden on Flat: poor hurdler: little show in
handicaps in 2006/7, left A. Sadik after third start: best form at 2m. *Shane Joseph Kelly,
Ireland*

PHILANTHROPIST 4 b.g. Fantastic Light (USA) – Someone Special (Habitat)   **h–**
[2006/7 16s 20s^6 19g 25m^4 Apr 9] good-topped gelding: half-brother to several at least
smart winners on Flat and to 3m hurdle winner Someone Brave (by Commanche Run):
dam, 7f winner who stayed 1m, half-sister to top-class miler Milligram: sold unraced out
of Saeed bin Suroor's stable 14,000 gns Doncaster May Sales: well held over hurdles,
including when well backed on handicap debut (visored). *Evan Williams*

PHILIP PIRRIP (IRE) 6 b.g. King's Theatre (IRE) – Ardrina (Ardross) [2006/7 F16v   **F–**
Jan 28] 14,000 4-y-o: first foal: dam fairly useful hurdler/fair chaser who stayed 3¾m:
well beaten in bumper on debut: sold 1,600 gns Doncaster May Sales. *G. A. Harker*

PHILOMENA 8 b.m. Bedford (USA) – Mandalay Miss (Mandalus) [2006/7 h92: 20d   **h–**
20g^{pu} Nov 3] bumper winner: successful also on hurdling debut, but no form in 3 starts
since (tried in cheekpieces/tongue tied): should stay beyond 2½m: sold £1,100 Ascot
December Sales. *V. R. A. Dartnall*

PHILSON RUN (IRE) 11 b.g. Un Desperado (FR) – Isis (Deep Run) [2006/7 c137:   **c137 +**
c28s c36g^4 Apr 14] strong gelding: useful handicap chaser, lightly raced: shaped much
better than result on reappearance, and ran close to best when 17 lengths fourth to Silver
Birch in Grand National at Aintree, twice hampered on second circuit but travelling well
until after 3 out: stays 4½m: acts on heavy going: waited with. *Nick Williams*

Gale Force One's "Philson Run"

PHILSON-WARRIOR (IRE) 10 b.g. Commanche Run – Madam's Well (Pitpan) c–
[2006/7 c21s[pu] Feb 16] maiden hurdler: winning chaser: modest pointer nowadays, won h–
in March: stays 3m: acts on soft ground: tongue tied last 2 starts. *Miss Katie Thory*

PHILTRE (IRE) 13 b.g. Phardante (FR) – Forest Gale (Strong Gale) [2006/7 c23m[pu] c–
Jun 13] tall, angular gelding: winning chaser: poor pointer nowadays: stays 3½m: acts on
good to firm going. *Mrs H. L. Needham*

PHOENIX EYE 6 b.g. Tragic Role (USA) – Eye Sight (Roscoe Blake) [2006/7 16d[5] h86
17m[6] 16g 20s[pu] 17s 17d 17d Mar 19] good-bodied gelding: half-brother to winning
hurdler/chaser Sailor A'Hoy, probably stays 3m, and winning 2m chaser The Roundsills
(both by Handsome Sailor): modest on Flat (stays 2m): best effort over hurdles when fifth
in novice at Aintree on debut. *M. Mullineaux*

PHOENIX HILL (IRE) 5 b.g. Montjeu (IRE) – Cielo Vodkamartini (USA) (Conquis- h–
tador Cielo (USA)) [2006/7 19d[6] 21v[pu] Mar 3] compact gelding: maiden on Flat (fair on
balance), sold out of J. Oxx's stable €38,000 Goffs February (2006) Sales: no encouragement in 2 novice hurdles. *D. R. Gandolfo*

PHONE TAPPING 6 b.g. Robellino (USA) – Miss Party Line (USA) (Phone Trick h–
(USA)) [2006/7 h–: 16s[pu] 20v[pu] Mar 2] no form in novice/maiden hurdles: tried
blinkered. *Mrs L. B. Normile*

PHOTOGENIQUE (FR) 4 b.f. Cyborg (FR) – Colombia (FR) (Le Riverain (FR)) h75
[2006/7 17m 20m[3] Apr 15] half-sister to middle-distance winners Mounir (by Epervier
Bleu) and Odile (by Smadoun): dam, 1½m winner on Flat, won around 2½m over fences:
fourth in claimer on second of 2 starts over 11f on Flat, sold out of M. Rolland's stable
€10,500 Goffs (France) November Sale: better effort over hurdles when 17 lengths third
to Picacho in mares maiden at Worcester (saddle slipped). *B. R. Summers*

PHOTOGRAPHER (USA) 9 b. or br.g. Mountain Cat (USA) – Clickety Click (USA) h82
(Sovereign Dancer (USA)) [2006/7 h97: 16s[6] 16g Mar 19] leggy gelding: modest maiden
hurdler at best, lightly raced: stays 2¼m: acts on soft and good to firm going: tongue tied
final outing (bled). *S. Lycett*

PHYSICAL FORCE 9 b.g. Casteddu – Kaiserlinde (GER) (Frontal) [2006/7 c–, h–: c80
c20d[4] c20m[4] Apr 9] workmanlike gelding: fair pointer: fourth in maidens on completed h–
starts in chases. *Mrs Marjorie Fife*

PIA JANE (IRE) 7 b.m. Beneficial – Modile (IRE) (Supreme Leader) [2006/7 F16s[6] h–
22g[pu] Mar 31] angular mare: third foal: dam, ran twice in Irish bumpers, half-sister to F86
smart chaser Fine Thyne, 29f: had run of race when sixth to Fiddling Again in
bumper at Fakenham: shaped as if amiss on hurdling debut. *P. R. Webber*

PIANO MAN 5 b.g. Atraf – Pinup (Risk Me (FR)) [2006/7 17m[5] Jun 8] fair maiden on h– p
Flat (stays 1¼m): fifth of 9 in novice at Newton Abbot on hurdling debut, taking keen
hold and not given hard time when left behind: should do better. *J. C. Fox*

PIANO PLAYER (IRE) 4 b.g. Mozart (IRE) – Got To Go (Shareef Dancer (USA)) h99
[2006/7 17v[5] 16v[F] Jan 25] fairly useful and consistent on Flat (stayed 1m), successful
3 times in 2006 for J. Osborne: found emphasis too much on stamina when 15½ lengths
fifth to Predateur in novice at Taunton on hurdling debut: fell fatally next time.
R. T. Phillips

PICACHO (IRE) 4 b.f. Sinndar (IRE) – Gentle Thoughts (Darshaan) [2006/7 17d[ur] h101 +
17g[2] 20m* Apr 15] fair on Flat (stays 2m), successful in August, sold out of J. Dunlop's
stable 25,000 gns Newmarket December Sales: fair form over hurdles: upped in trip,
landed odds in mares maiden at Worcester by 6 lengths from Madam Cliche: likely to stay
beyond 2½m. *P. J. Hobbs*

PICCOLOMINI 5 b.g. Diktat – La Dama Bonita (USA) (El Gran Senor (USA)) h75
[2006/7 20g[pu] 20d[F] 16v[4] 17v[4] 20s 16v[6] 17v 20v[pu] Mar 6] maiden on Flat, has deteriorated: poor novice hurdler, very stiff tasks in handicaps last 4 starts: wore cheekpieces
after debut. *E. W. Tuer*

PICK OF THE CROP 6 ch.g. Fraam – Fresh Fruit Daily (Reprimand) [2006/7 h78: h65
16m[6] 16m[6] Aug 28] poor 2m novice hurdler: tried blinkered/visored. *J. R. Jenkins*

PIC OF THE PADDOCK 6 b.m. Accordion – Galatasori Jane (IRE) (Mister Lord F78
(USA)) [2006/7 F13m[3] F17g Apr 19] rather unfurnished mare: second foal: dam fair
staying hurdler/chaser: better effort in bumpers when 3¼ lengths third to Regal Angel in
maiden at Hereford. *Nick Williams*

PICOT DE SAY 5 b.g. Largesse – Facsimile (Superlative) [2006/7 h100: 17g 16m[pu] 17s 19v[5] 16s[F] 16s[5] 16f[5] Apr 5] sparely-made gelding: fair handicap hurdler, largely below form in 2006/7: best around 2m: acts on soft going. *C. Roberts* **h100**

PICTS HILL 7 ch.g. Romany Rye – Nearly A Brook (Nearly A Hand) [2006/7 h–, F89: 22m[2] 22d[6] Dec 15] lengthy gelding: blinkered, best effort in 3 starts over hurdles when neck second to Sky Mack in novice at Wincanton, wayward under pressure: tongue tied when next seen 7 months later. *P. F. Nicholls* **h108**

PICTURE IN THE SKY (IRE) 6 ch.g. Portrait Gallery (IRE) – Little Bloom (Little Buskins) [2006/7 24g[6] Feb 21] half-brother to modest hurdler Pilkington (by Roselier), stayed 25f: dam lightly-raced maiden: won maiden Irish point in 2006: sixth to Shannon Springs in maiden hurdle at Ludlow, travelling well into contention only to tire: should do better. *Mrs Susan Nock* **h77 p**

PIE MARSH (IRE) 5 b.g. Anshan – Piepowder (In The Wings) [2006/7 F16d[5] 24d[pu] Oct 22] €7,000 3-y-o: fourth foal: half-brother to a winning pointer by Bob Back and an 11f/1½m winner in France by Kendor: dam maiden: no show in bumper/novice hurdle: poor maiden pointer. *C. C. Bealby* **h–** **F–**

PIEMONT (FR) 4 gr.g. April Night (FR) – Gazoute de Ferbet (FR) (Trebrook (FR)) [2006/7 F17s F16v F16m Mar 25] 12,000 3-y-o: first foal: dam, winning cross-country chaser, out of half-sister to smart chaser up to 2½m Ferbet Junior: well held in bumpers. *Ian Williams* **F–**

PIGEON ISLAND 4 gr.g. Daylami (IRE) – Morina (USA) (Lyphard (USA)) [2006/7 16d[5] 16d[4] 16d 16s[4] 19g[2] 20s[3] Apr 25] rather leggy gelding: fair maiden on Flat (stays 1¼m) for H. Candy: likewise over hurdles: stays 19f: best efforts on good/good to soft going: blinkered last 2 starts. *N. A. Twiston-Davies* **h108**

PIKESTAFF (USA) 9 ch.g. Diesis – Navarene (USA) (Known Fact (USA)) [2006/7 c–, h89: 22g May 24] small gelding: modest handicap hurdler, below form only outing in 2006/7: offered little both starts over fences: stays 27f: acts on firm and good to soft going: tongue tied. *M. A. Barnes* **c–** **h–**

PILCA (FR) 7 ch.g. Pistolet Bleu (IRE) – Caricoe (Baillamont (USA)) [2006/7 c–, h93d: 16m[3] 21m[2] 17d[2] 16m* 16m* 17s[2] 16d[4] 16v[6] 16m 16d Feb 14] small, leggy gelding: well held only outing over fences: fair hurdler: won conditional jockeys seller at Ludlow (sold from Mrs A. Thorpe 5,400 gns) and handicap at Musselburgh in November: good efforts in handicaps next 2 starts, including when fourth to Acambo in Ladbroke at Ascot: best around 2m: acts on soft and good to firm going (possibly not heavy): tried in blinkers/cheekpieces (including when successful): usually travels strongly. *D. Carroll* **c–** **h112**

PILLAGING PICT 12 ch.g. Primitive Rising (USA) – Carat Stick (Gold Rod) [2006/7 c–: c22v[3] c20v[2] c24g Apr 7] strong, lengthy gelding: winning chaser, modest form when placed in 2006/7: stays 2¾m: raced on good going or softer (acts on heavy). *J. B. Walton* **c97**

PILTOWN (IRE) 4 b.g. Namid – Mirwara (IRE) (Darshaan) [2006/7 16g[4] 16f* 16g[4] 16g[2] 16d[3] 16v* 16s[5] Dec 2] fairly useful maiden on Flat (stays 11f), won in July: similar standard in juvenile hurdles: successful at Clonmel (maiden) in September and Punchestown in November: raced at 2m: acts on any going. *Joseph Crowley, Ireland* **h110**

PIMBO LANE (IRE) 5 br.m. Bob's Return (IRE) – Wire To Wire (Welsh Saint) [2006/7 F16v F16d Feb 14] half-sister to 2m hurdle winner Wire Man (by Glenstal): dam maiden: well beaten in bumpers. *James Moffatt* **F–**

PIMBURY (IRE) 5 b.g. Pistolet Bleu (IRE) – Duchess of Kinsale (IRE) (Montelimar (USA)) [2006/7 16d[3] 16s[5] Jan 20] rather unfurnished gelding: first foal: dam unraced half-sister to high-class staying chaser Shotgun Willy and Welsh National winner Mini Sensation, out of very smart 2m/2½m hurdler Minorettes Girl: encouraging debut when 12½ lengths third to ready winner My Turn Now in novice hurdle at Kempton: unsuited by emphasis on speed in steadily-run event at Wincanton next time: will be suited by 2½m+: remains capable of better. *R. H. Alner* **h105 p**

PINCH ME SILVER 6 ch.m. Silver Patriarch (IRE) – Pinch (Ardross) [2006/7 F16m[3] F17m[4] F16s 20d[4] 20s[5] 22g 20s[pu] Apr 25] good-topped mare: fourth foal: dam, second over 1½m in France/poor novice hurdler in Britain, half-sister to useful hurdler/chaser up to 3m Heist: poor form in bumpers/over hurdles: will stay 3m. *P. Beaumont* **h63** **F66**

PINCH OF SALT (IRE) 4 b.g. Hussonet (USA) – Granita (CHI) (Roy (USA)) [2006/7 16d Dec 29] good-topped gelding: fairly useful maiden on Flat (likely to prove best short of 1½m): took strong hold when well held in juvenile at Newbury on hurdling debut. *A. M. Balding* **h–**

PINGPONG (FR) 4 b.g. Arnaqueur (USA) – Gardane (FR) (Video Rock (FR)) [2006/7   **F—**
F16g Apr 7] 8,000 3-y-o: first foal: dam won 3 times up to 13f on Flat in France: tailed off
in bumper on debut. *Mrs K. Walton*

PINK BAY 5 b.m. Forzando – Singer On The Roof (Chief Singer) [2006/7 16s⁴ 18gᵖᵘ   **h—**
Apr 10] modest handicapper on Flat (barely stays 1m) at 4 yrs, sold out of W. Kittow's
stable 2,200 gns Doncaster October Sales: no show in 2 selling hurdles. *K. F. Clutterbuck*

PINKERTON MILL 7 b.m. Rudimentary (USA) – Real Silver (Silly Season) [2006/7   **c—**
h81?: 17s⁵ 16s⁴ 17g² 16g⁶ 16d⁴ 16g³ 16d⁵ 20vᵖᵘ 17s⁴ c16sᶠ Feb 1] workmanlike mare: **h86**
bumper winner: modest maiden hurdler: fell fourth on chasing debut: raced mainly
around 2m on good going or softer. *J. T. Stimpson*

PINNACLE RIDGE 7 ch.g. Bob's Return (IRE) – Canal Street (Oats) [2006/7 h91:   **h—**
24g 22v Dec 3] tall, strong gelding: modest form at best over hurdles, well beaten in
handicaps in 2006/7 after 13-month absence: stays 25f: acts on heavy and good to firm
going. *Mrs K. Walton*

PINTAIL 7 b.g. Petoski – Tangara (Town Crier) [2006/7 h66: 25dᵖᵘ 22s⁶ 16vᵖᵘ Dec 15]   **h—**
lengthy gelding: second in selling handicap hurdle in 2005/6, only form. *Mrs P. Robeson*

PIPERS LEGEND 8 b.g. Midnight Legend – Pipers Reel (Palace Music (USA))   **h—**
[2006/7 h–: 16s⁴ 16v⁵ 16gᵖᵘ Jun 8] compact gelding: no solid form over hurdles: tried in
cheekpieces. *D. Burchell*

PIP MOSS 12 ch.g. Le Moss – My Aisling (John de Coombe) [2006/7 c–, h–: c26vᵖᵘ   **c68**
c24v³ c25s³ Dec 12] lengthy, workmanlike gelding: poor maiden hurdler/chaser, lightly   **h—**
raced: stays 3¼m: raced on going softer than good (acts on heavy): tongue tied in 2006/7.
J. A. B. Old

PIPPILONGSTOCKING 5 b.m. Makbul – Princess Ermyn (Shernazar) [2006/7 h–:   **h—**
20sᵖᵘ Dec 27] no show in 2 maidens on Flat or both starts over hurdles. *E. G. Bevan*

PIPPLING 5 b.g. Bandmaster (USA) – Sailors Moon (Indian Ridge) [2006/7 F16g⁴   **F80**
May 14] second foal: dam maiden who stayed 1m: 12¾ lengths fourth of 9 to Cheer Us
On in bumper at Worcester on debut. *C. J. Down*

PIPS ASSERTIVE WAY 6 ch.m. Nomadic Way (USA) – Return To Brighton (Then   **h76**
Again) [2006/7 h83?: 17d⁵ 17m⁶ 19g⁴ 20m 16g* 16m⁵ Aug 24] poor hurdler: made all
in novice seller at Stratford in July: best form at 2m: acts on good to firm going.
A. W. Carroll

PIPSSALIO (SPA) 10 b.g. Pips Pride – Tesalia (SPA) (Finissimo (SPA)) [2006/7 h112:   **c112**
c21s³ May 26] leggy gelding: fair hurdler: similar form when third in novice handicap at   **h—**
Stratford on chasing debut, none too fluent in rear before staying on strongly: stays 3m:
acts on soft going: has had tongue tied. *Jamie Poulton*

PIQUE DU JOUR (FR) 4 b.f. Turgeon (USA) – Wackie (USA) (Spectacular Bid   **h—**
(USA)) [2006/7 F16d⁵ F13m 20m Apr 9] rather leggy filly: fifth foal: half-sister to   **F—**
winning hurdler/chaser around 2m Pousky (by Kaid Pous): dam winning hurdler/chaser
up to 19f in France: well held in bumpers/novice hurdle. *D. W. Thompson*

PIRAEUS (NZ) 8 b.g. Beau Zam (NZ) – Gull Mundur (NZ) (Icelandic) [2006/7 h101:   **c– p**
22d 20s⁵ 24s² 25d* 23v⁵ c25v⁴ 20vᵖᵘ Feb 20] compact gelding: fair handicap hurdler: **h108**
won at Catterick in December: not given hard time when well-held fourth of 5 to Dom
d'Orgeval in novice at Hexham on chasing debut: stays 25f: raced on good ground or
softer (acts on soft): wore cheekpieces last 2 starts over hurdles: likely to do better over
fences. *R. Johnson*

PIRANDELLO DUE 13 b.g. Teenoso (USA) – Bay Girl (Persian Bold) [2006/7   **c– x**
c25vᵖᵘ c26vᵖᵘ Mar 12] sturdy gelding: winning pointer, little form otherwise: sketchy   **h—**
jumper. *Mrs Carol Stainer*

PIRANDELLO (IRE) 9 ch.g. Shalford (IRE) – Scenic Villa (Top Ville) [2006/7 c87,   **c—**
h108: c24dᴿ May 21] rather leggy gelding: fairly useful handicap hurdler at best: modest   **h—**
form completed outing over fences: probably best around 2m: acted on soft and good to
firm going: tried blinkered: dead. *K. C. Bailey*

PIRAN (IRE) 5 b.g. Orpen (USA) – Dancing At Lunasa (IRE) (Dancing Dissident   **c107**
(USA)) [2006/7 h120: c20m² c19m³ Oct 28] smallish gelding: fairly useful hurdler: fair   **h—**
form when placed in maiden chases, not convincing with jumping: stays 3m: acts on soft
and good to firm going: tried blinkered. *Evan Williams*

PIRATE FLAGSHIP (FR) 8 b.g. River Mist (USA) – Sacadu (Tyrant (USA))   **c120**
[2006/7 h130: c16g* c16g⁴ c16d² 16d 16d 20m⁴ Apr 20] big gelding: fairly useful   **h122**

handicap hurdler: similar form over fences, landed odds in maiden at Kempton in October on chasing debut: stays 2½m: acts on good to firm and good to soft going: tried tongue tied/blinkered (has looked hard ride): sold 21,000 gns Doncaster May Sales. *P. F. Nicholls*

PIRATE KING (IRE) 10 ch.g. Eurobus – Shakie Lady (Tug of War) [2006/7 c–, h–: c20mᵖᵘ May 16] rangy gelding: modest pointer: no form in other events. *H. Hill* — c–, h–

PISCATAQUA 5 b.g. Kayf Tara – Flitcham (Elegant Air) [2006/7 F16g⁴ F16d F16g⁵ Apr 3] tall gelding: has scope: sixth foal: half-brother to bumper winner Acushnet (by Ezzoud) and a winning sprinter by Prince Sabo: dam 13f earner: best effort in bumpers when 12 lengths fifth to Abstinence at Wetherby. *J. M. Jefferson* — F90

PISTOLET DOVE (IRE) 5 br.g. Pistolet Bleu (IRE) – Emerald Dove (Green Adventure (USA)) [2006/7 F16g Apr 7] lengthy gelding: has scope: third foal: dam, of little account, out of fairly useful hurdler up to 25f Nimble Dove: ninth of 17 in steadily-run bumper at Haydock on debut. *P. J. Hobbs* — F78

PITFUL TERCAH (FR) 4 b.g. Useful (FR) – Perle Des Mers (FR) (Spoleto) [2006/7 16g 16g Apr 8] useful-looking gelding: has scope: half-brother to 3 winners, including hurdler/chaser up to 21f Mercelo (by Ecossais): dam, placed around 1¾m, half-sister to Prix du Cadran winner Mercalle: won over 13f at 3 yrs: sold out of C. Le Guillard's stable €125,000 Goffs (France) July Sale: well held both starts over hurdles, though left impression capable of better. *N. J. Gifford* — h– p

PITSI KAHTOH 5 b.m. Petoski – Plectrum (Adonijah) [2006/7 h–: 16gᵘʳ 16mᵘʳ 17d⁴ Aug 19] poor maiden on Flat: no form over hurdles (let down by jumping). *P. W. Hiatt* — h– x

PIVOT OF JADE 4 b.g. Pivotal – Royal Jade (Last Tycoon) [2006/7 F14s⁵ Feb 4] half-brother to several winners up to 1m, including useful 6f winner Million Percent (by Ashkalani): dam, 7f winner, half-sister to smart sprinter Averti: 15 lengths fifth to Isn't That Lucky in bumper at Fontwell on debut, fading. *G. L. Moore* — F81

PLACE ABOVE (IRE) 11 b.g. Alphabatim (USA) – Lucky Pit (Pitpan) [2006/7 c92, h–: c28dᵖᵘ c26s² c23g² c24mᵖᵘ c27mᵖᵘ c31sᵘʳ Apr 26] workmanlike gelding: no form over hurdles: modest chaser: left E. Elliott after fifth outing, successful in point in March: stays 27f: acts on heavy going: tried blinkered: tends to make mistakes: unreliable. *Mrs Sarah L. Dent* — c92 §, h–

PLANET OF SOUND 5 b.g. Kayf Tara – Herald The Dawn (Dubassoff (USA)) [2006/7 F16g³ Apr 7] tall gelding: half-brother to several winners, including fairly useful hurdler/useful chaser From Dawn To Dusk (by Afzal), stays 2¾m, and fairly useful 2m hurdler Three Scholars (by Rakaposhi King): dam unraced: 18 lengths third to Marleybow in bumper at Haydock on debut, smooth progress and not given hard time once held. *P. J. Hobbs* — F95

PLANTAGANET (FR) 9 br.g. Cadoudal (FR) – Ever Young (FR) (Royal Charter (FR)) [2006/7 c83, h80: c17m³ c21gᵖᵘ Apr 1] useful-looking gelding: maiden hurdler/chaser: left Ian Williams after first outing: won point in April: stays 19f: acts on good to firm going. *G. Chambers* — c83, h–

PLANTERS PUNCH (IRE) 6 br.g. Cape Cross (IRE) – Jamaican Punch (IRE) (Shareef Dancer (USA)) [2006/7 h102: 17d² 16v⁴ 17s⁴ c16m³ 16vᵖᵘ 16g 17m Apr 9] compact gelding: fair on Flat (barely stays 15.8f): modest handicap hurdler, off 4 months and ran poorly last 3 outings: let down by jumping on chasing debut, continuing tailed off after refusing ninth: raced mainly around 2m: acts on heavy ground: tried in cheekpieces. *G. M. Moore* — c–, h98

PLATIN GROUNDS (GER) 5 ch.g. Waky Nao – Platin Queen (IRE) (Common Grounds) [2006/7 F17d* F17s³ 20s⁵ 16s² Apr 27] 3,000 3-y-o: second foal: half-brother to winner in Italy by Kornado: dam German 7f winner: fair form in bumpers, making all in maiden at Hereford (odds on) on debut in November: much better effort over hurdles when 3 lengths second to Midnight Chase in maiden at Perth. *N. A. Twiston-Davies* — h97, F91

PLAYER (FR) 4 ch.g. Apple Tree (FR) – Fleur Des Marais II (FR (Boyatino (FR)) [2006/7 16s⁴ 17v² 16v³ 16v⁵ Mar 3] workmanlike gelding: fifth foal: half-brother to winning chasers in France by Marmato and Blushing Flame: dam ran once on Flat: modest juvenile hurdler: likely to prove best around 2m: raced on soft/heavy ground. *J. Howard Johnson* — h82

PLAY IT AGAIN 7 b.g. Double Trigger (IRE) – Play For Time (Comedy Star (USA)) [2006/7 F62: 22s 21m Jan 29] strong, workmanlike gelding: poor form in bumper/novice hurdles. *Simon Earle* — h74

PLAY MASTER (IRE) 6 b.g. Second Empire (IRE) – Madam Waajib (IRE) (Waajib) **c90**
[2006/7 h–p: 16g 16m c16mᵖᵘ c16gᵖᵘ c16m⁴ c16gᶠ c16d⁴ c17mᵖᵘ Sep 2] novice hurdler/ **h94**
chaser, modest form on occasions: likely to prove best around 2m with emphasis on
speed. *C. Roberts*

PLAY THE BALL (USA) 5 ch.g. Boundary (USA) – Copper Play (USA) (Fast Play **h–**
(USA)) [2006/7 17dᵖᵘ 16d 16m Apr 8] fair on all-weather on Flat (stays 1m), sold out of
G. Butler's stable 6,000 gns Newmarket July Sales: no show in maiden hurdles.
J. J. Lambe, Ireland

PLEASANT 6 b.m. Topanoora – Devon Peasant (Deploy) [2006/7 16d⁶ Oct 1] fair **h80 +**
handicapper on Flat, left L. G. Cottrell after winning over 11.6f final start at 4 yrs: never a
threat when sixth to John Charles in steadily-run novice at Uttoxeter on hurdling debut.
D. P. Keane

PLEMONT BAY 4 b.g. Robellino (USA) – Jezyah (USA) (Chief's Crown (USA)) **h94 p**
[2006/7 18s⁶ 20m⁶ 17g* Apr 23] fair on Flat (stays 12.4f), successful in August, sold out
of M. Bell's stable 28,000 gns Newmarket Autumn Sales: in cheekpieces and well
backed, confirmed previous promise over hurdles when winning juvenile maiden at
Sedgefield by 3½ lengths from Mycenean Prince: probably capable of better again.
Charles Byrnes, Ireland

PLENTY CRIED WOLF 5 b.g. Wolfhound (USA) – Plentitude (FR) (Ela-Mana- **h96**
Mou) [2006/7 17v³ 16v⁴ 17g³ 16vᵖᵘ Jan 2] fair on Flat (stayed 1¾m): modest form over
hurdles, best effort when third to Open de L'Isle in novice at Carlisle on debut: dead.
R. A. Fahey

PLOUGH MAITE 4 b.g. Komaite (USA) – Plough Hill (North Briton) [2006/7 17m **h85 §**
16m 16m³ 18gᵖᵘ 21gᵖᵘ Oct 19] brother to modest 2m hurdler Plough Boy and bumper
winner Hartest Rose: poor maiden (stays 13.8f, refused to enter stall once) on Flat: best
effort over hurdles when third in juvenile at Huntingdon: reluctant to race/dropped out
quickly last 2 outings: one to treat with caution. *D. E. Cantillon*

PLUME D'OUDAIRIES (FR) 4 b.f. Grand Seigneur (FR) – Harmat (FR) (Marasali) **h86**
[2006/7 17s² 18s³ 16dᵖᵘ 17vᶠ 16g³ 17g⁵ Apr 7] lengthy, unfurnished filly: second
foal: dam unraced: runner-up both starts on Flat (1¼m/1½m) at Vichy for T. Trapenard:
modest form over hurdles, would probably have won maiden at Bangor but for falling 3
out: likely to prove best around 2m: free-going sort. *Miss H. C. Knight*

PLUM'TEE (FR) 12 b.g. Faucon Noir (FR) – Castaplume (FR) (Wildsun) [2006/7 **c121**
c22g* c23g* c25d* c31dˢᵘ c31s² Dec 8] angular gelding: prolific winner over fences in
French Provinces, including 13 times in cross-country events: off almost 3 years prior to
winning at Pompadour and Craon in August and Nancy in October: fairly useful former
when length second to Spot Thedifference in cross-country handicap at Cheltenham:
stays 31f: acts on heavy ground. *G. Macaire, France*

PLUMTREE LADD 4 br.g. Man Among Men (IRE) – My Poppet (Midyan (USA)) **F–**
[2006/7 F13s Dec 1] second foal: dam, of little account, half-sister to high-class sprinter
Kyllachy: tailed off in bumper on debut. *N. J. Hawke*

PLUTOCRAT 11 b.g. Polar Falcon (USA) – Choire Mhor (Dominion) [2006/7 c–, h–: **c94**
c23g² c21v² c21g* c21gᵖᵘ Apr 9] smallish, angular gelding: fairly useful handicap **h–**
hurdler at one time for L. Lungo: fair hunter chaser nowadays: won novice at Fakenham
in March: barely stays 3m: acts on good to firm and good to soft going, not at best on
softer: tried in cheekpieces: usually patiently ridden. *Mrs J. M. Hodgson*

POACHIN AGAIN (IRE) 10 b.g. Supreme Leader – Ariannrun (Deep Run) [2006/7 **c–**
c23g⁴ May 14] strong, stocky ex-Irish gelding: fairly useful hurdler at best: poor form **h–**
over fences, left A. Moore after final outing in 2005/6: should stay well beyond 2¼m:
acts on heavy going: sold 1,400 gns Doncaster May (2006) Sales. *N. J. Henderson*

POCKET ACES (IRE) 5 b.g. Dr Massini (IRE) – Mrs Mustard (IRE) (Le Johnstan) **F79**
[2006/7 F16g Mar 24] 12,000 3-y-o: medium-sized gelding: fourth foal: brother to
winning pointer Forget The Ref: dam maiden: second in maiden Irish point in 2006:
bought 16,000 gns Doncaster May Sales: ninth of 22 to Helens Vision in bumper at
Newbury, looking a stayer. *R. Rowe*

POCKET TOO 4 b.g. Fleetwood (IRE) – Pocket Venus (IRE) (King's Theatre (IRE)) **h97**
[2006/7 16g² 16d* 16d⁶ 21v 16s 19g 17g* Apr 27] workmanlike gelding: fair on Flat
(stays 2m), successful in January: similar standard over hurdles: won juvenile at Uttoxeter (by 21 lengths) in November and novice handicap at Newton Abbot in April: stays
21f: acts on heavy going: in cheekpieces last 2 starts. *M. Salaman*

POCKETWOOD 5 b.g. Fleetwood (IRE) – Pocket Venus (IRE) (King's Theatre (IRE)) [2006/7 h86: 16s^{pu} Dec 13] compact gelding: fairly useful on Flat (stays 1¾m): best effort over hurdles when second in juvenile at Plumpton in 2005/6. *Jean-Rene Auvray* **h–**

POEMS FOR LARA (IRE) 5 b.m. Shaamit (IRE) – Knockcairn Express (IRE) (Lafontaine (USA)) [2006/7 F16m^5 F16f^5 F16g F16s 20g^{pu} 16d^{pu} Jan 5] second foal: dam unraced: no form in bumpers (tongue tied) and over hurdles. *I. A. Duncan, Ireland* **h–** **F–**

POINT 10 b.g. Polish Precedent (USA) – Sixslip (USA) (Diesis) [2006/7 c94x, h94: c24g^3 c19s^{pu} c19s^{pu} 20v 16g^6 20g Apr 21] lengthy gelding: modest novice hurdler/chaser: stays 3m: acts on soft going: makes mistakes over fences. *W. Jenks* **c92 x** **h86**

POINT BARROW (IRE) 9 b.g. Arctic Lord – Credit Transfer (IRE) (Kemal (FR)) [2006/7 c135, h112: c22s^{pu} 22v 23v^4 c24v^{bd} c24d* c25v^3 22v^3 c36g^F 24m^2 Apr 26] tall, good-topped gelding: has reportedly had breathing operation: fairly useful hurdler: good second of 24 to Sonnyanjoe in handicap at Punchestown final start: useful handicap chaser: better than ever when winning Pierse Leopardstown Chase in January by ¾ length from A New Story: stayed on well when creditable third to Homer Wells in Grade 2 at Fairyhouse next time: co-favourite, fell first in Grand National at Aintree: will stay beyond 29f: unraced on firm going, acts on any other: tried tongue tied: held up. *Patrick Hughes, Ireland* **c142** **h128**

POINT ROUGE (FR) 4 b.g. Nashamaa – Delia Des Isles (FR) (Djarvis (FR)) [2006/7 16g^3 17d 25s 16s^4 Apr 1] lengthy, good-bodied gelding: second foal: dam maiden: runner-up over 11f on debut for G. Cherel: modest form in juvenile hurdles. *J. Howard Johnson* **h94**

POITIERS (FR) 8 b.g. Bering – Prusse (USA) (Ogygian (USA)) [2006/7 c21m^{pu} 18m^5 Jun 6] leggy gelding: one-time fair hurdler/novice chaser, has deteriorated considerably (failed to complete all 3 starts in points): stays 21f: acts on any going: usually visored. *D. E. Pipe* **c–** **h–**

POKER DE SIVOLA (FR) 4 b.g. Discover d'Auteuil (FR) – Legal Union (Law Society (USA)) [2006/7 16d^3 16s^5 16s* 19s^3 16g^4 20g* Apr 23] close-coupled gelding: half-brother to 3 winners, including 19f hurdle winner Le Marechal (by Arctic Tern): dam unraced: fairly useful hurdler, left T. Trapenard prior to reappearance: progressed very well last 4 outings, winning juvenile maiden at Hexham in November and novices at Catterick in January and Hexham (beating Dancer's Serenade 1½ lengths) in April: will stay beyond 2½m: raced on good ground or softer: likely to progress further. *Ferdy Murphy* **h120 p**

Pierse Leopardstown Handicap Chase—the previous season's Irish National winner Point Barrow (seams) takes the second last as he goes on to land another big handicap under a patient Timmy Murphy ride

POKER PAL (IRE) 10 b.g. Hollow Hand – Lady Dee (Kambalda) [2006/7 c20d³ c23m c22m³ c21m* Aug 8] useful-looking gelding: fair hurdler/chaser: won maiden over fences at Roscommon in August: stays 3m: acts on soft and good to firm going: usually tongue tied. *A. J. Martin, Ireland*   **c103 h–**

POKER QUEEN 5 b.m. Karinga Bay – Beamo (Oats) [2006/7 F14s² F16g Mar 19] third foal: dam unraced: better effort in bumpers when 3 lengths second to Debut in mares event at Fontwell. *C. J. Mann*   **F90**

POLAR GALE (IRE) 7 ch.g. Anshan – Ali-Kin (Strong Gale) [2006/7 c25m^pu c20d* 20s⁶ 20s⁶ 19d² 20d⁴ 25v 27g³ c27g^ur Apr 23] €8,200 3-y-o: quite good-topped gelding: sixth foal: dam, placed over hurdles, out of half-sister to very smart staying chaser Arctic Call: won all 3 starts in points in 2006: successful also in hunter at Sedgefield in May on completed outing in chases: modest novice hurdler: stays 27f: acts on good to soft ground (below best on softer). *J. Wade*   **c86 h93**

POLAR GUNNER 10 b.g. Gunner B – Polar Belle (Arctic Lord) [2006/7 c127, h116: 17g⁵ May 5] good-topped gelding: highly progressive hurdler/chaser in 2005/6, winning 5 handicaps in row: badly hampered latter stages (would have been below form even so) in handicap hurdle at Bangor in May, and not seen out again: best form around 2m: raced mainly on good going or softer (acts on heavy): tried tongue tied: often races prominently. *J. M. Jefferson*   **c– h–**

POLAR PASSION 5 b.m. Polar Prince (IRE) – Priorite (IRE) (Kenmare (FR)) [2006/7 h90: 16m^F Aug 24] small mare: modest juvenile hurdler in 2005/6: off 6 months, in rear when fell heavily 3 out in handicap at Stratford: raced around 2m: acts on good to firm going. *R. Hollinshead*   **h–**

POLAR SCOUT (IRE) 10 b.g. Arctic Lord – Baden (IRE) (Furry Glen) [2006/7 c–x, h101x: c21d³ c22s⁵ c20g^pu c24m^pu Apr 10] rather leggy gelding: fair handicap hurdler/chaser: off 18 months, regressive form over fences in 2006/7: best up to 2¾m: acts on any going: tongue tied: usually makes mistakes. *C. J. Mann*   **c95 x h– x**

POLAR SUMMIT (IRE) 11 b.g. Top of The World – Blackrath Beauty (Le Tricolore) [2006/7 c19m c20f^pu Apr 5] rangy gelding: maiden hurdler/chaser: modest pointer, won in 2006: tried blinkered. *Miss M. Bayliss*   **c79 x h–**

POLE STAR 9 b. or br.g. Polar Falcon (USA) – Ellie Ardensky (Slip Anchor) [2006/7 c–, h–: c23s* c21d² c21g^ur c25g^pu Apr 13] leggy, useful-looking gelding: useful hurdler at best: left J. Fanshawe, easily best effort over fences when winning maiden at Exeter in December by 5 lengths from Mister Quasimodo (pair clear), jumping much better than previously: finished lame next time: stays 23f: raced on good going or softer (acts on soft): in cheekpieces in 2006/7. *Evan Williams*   **c135 h–**

POLIGLOTTI (FR) 5 b.g. Poliglote – Loretta Gianni (FR) (Classic Account (USA)) [2006/7 16g 17g⁴ Nov 5] lengthy ex-French gelding: middle-distance maiden on Flat: left G. Henrot, twice-raced in maiden hurdles, much better effort when fourth at Hereford. *A. King*   **h95**

POLINAMIX (FR) 4 b.g. Loup Solitaire (USA) – Polynamia (FR) (Linamix (FR)) [2006/7 17s⁴ 18s 17v* 16v³ 17v⁴ 16v² 20d^F 21m* 22f* Apr 22] leggy, sparely-made gelding: second foal: dam successful 3 times up to 1½m on Flat: successful over 5.5f at 2 yrs, in frame 3 times in Provinces up to 10.5f in 2006: fairly useful hurdler, sold out of J-L. Pelletan's stable €42,000 Goffs (France) November Sale after second start: won juvenile at Sedgefield in December and novices at Plumpton and Wincanton (odds on, again poached clear early lead when beating Irish Whispers by wide margin) in April: stays 2¾m: acts on any going. *D. E. Pipe*   **h122**

POLISHED 8 ch.g. Danzig Connection (USA) – Glitter (FR) (Reliance II) [2006/7 c105, h104: c16v² 16d c16g Feb 21] leggy gelding: fair handicap hurdler/chaser: best around 2m: raced on good going or softer (acts on heavy): tried in cheekpieces, usually blinkered: waited with. *V. R. A. Dartnall*   **c102 h–**

POLISH LEGEND 8 b.g. Polish Precedent (USA) – Chita Rivera (Chief Singer) [2006/7 16g 16g^ur 19d 20s 17m 16f Sep 29] winning hurdler, no form in 2006/7: often blinkered: formerly tongue tied: ungenuine (has twice refused to race). *I. A. Brown*   **h§§**

POLITICAL CRUISE 9 b.g. Royal Fountain – Political Mill (Politico (USA)) [2006/7 c75, h75: c16m c16g^pu 20d 24s 24v* c20d c21v⁵ 24v 21v⁶ c20v⁶ 27v⁴ c25s c24v⁵ 24v c20v⁴ c25s* c26g Apr 7] small gelding: poor hurdler/chaser: won amateur handicaps at Hexham, over hurdles in December and fences (selling event) in April: stays 27f: acts on heavy going: blinkered once, in cheekpieces last 7 starts: sold 4,000 gns Doncaster May Sales. *R. Nixon*   **c76 h74**

POLITICAL DANCER 6 b.m. Dancing High – Political Diamond (Politico (USA)) [2006/7 F–: F16f F16f³ F16f 16sᵖᵘ 20g 16s 20g⁵ Apr 23] poor form when third in bumper (has shown signs of temperament): little impact over hurdles: usually tongue tied. *G. A. Charlton* **h– F72**

POLITICAL DISSENT 5 b.m. Commanche Run – Ranahinch (IRE) (Persian Mews) [2006/7 F16s F16s 19s 22mᵖᵘ Apr 22] unfurnished mare: first foal: dam, lightly-raced maiden, half-sister to useful hurdlers Red Curate and Morgans Harbour (also prolific staying chaser): no form in bumpers/over hurdles (lame final outing). *A. M. Hales* **h– F–**

POLITICAL PENDANT 6 br.m. Moshaajir (USA) – Political Mill (Politico (USA)) [2006/7 h81, F87: 18f³ 22g⁵ 16g 20v⁶ 16v 22v⁵ 21s* 20s 22g² Apr 15] workmanlike mare: poor hurdler: won handicap at Sedgefield in March: should stay beyond 21f: acts on firm and soft going: in cheekpieces/blinkers last 4 starts: not straightforward (led in at start last 2 outings). *R. Nixon* **h82**

POLITICAL SOX 13 br.g. Mirror Boy – Political Mill (Politico (USA)) [2006/7 c–, h101d: 24g³ 24s* 26d⁴ 24f 24g 20f 22d 24sᵖᵘ 24g⁵ 22d 24s⁴ Apr 25] compact gelding: modest handicap hurdler: won at Perth in May: below form after: placed in points: stays 27f: acts on any going: tried blinkered. *R. Nixon* **c– h89 d**

POLITKOVSKAYA 4 ch.f. Medicean – Soluce (Junius (USA)) [2006/7 16sᵘʳ Feb 3] half-sister to 2m hurdle winner Solo Sail (by Slip Anchor): no sign of ability on Flat: unseated fourth on hurdling debut. *T. H. Caldwell* **h–**

POLKA 12 b.g. Slip Anchor – Peace Dance (Bikala) [2006/7 c–, h–: c26d⁵ Jun 12] winning pointer: little impact over hurdles/in chases: tried tongue tied. *V. G. Greenway* **c– h–**

POLLOVER 6 b.m. Overbury (IRE) – Vale of Mowbray (Primitive Rising (USA)) [2006/7 22sᵖᵘ 16g 20mᵖᵘ Apr 15] 3,000 4-y-o: first foal: dam unraced half-sister to useful chaser up to 3¼m Gunner Welburn: no show in maiden point/over hurdles: tongue tied last 2 starts. *P. E. Cowley* **h–**

POLLY WHITEFOOT 8 b.m. Perpendicular – Cream O The Border (Meadowbrook) [2006/7 h87d: 18g⁵ 22v 20d³ 24m⁵ 20g² 22g⁵ 24sᵖᵘ Apr 25] good-topped mare: modest maiden hurdler: stays 2¾m: acts on good to soft going: tried tongue tied. *D. W. Whillans* **h85**

POLOBURY 5 b.m. Overbury (IRE) – Mazzelmo (Thethingaboutitis (USA)) [2006/7 F16m⁵ F16f⁵ F17s³ F16d 20v³ 23v⁵ 20s 22v Mar 3] 2,200 4-y-o: small mare: second foal: dam won up to 2¼m on Flat and over hurdles: signs of ability in bumpers/over hurdles. *Mrs H. O. Graham* **h89 ? F64**

POLONIUS 6 b.g. Great Dane (IRE) – Bridge Pool (First Trump) [2006/7 h–: 20mᵖᵘ Apr 25] no show in 2 starts over hurdles: tried in cheekpieces. *G. J. Smith* **h–**

POLYPHON (FR) 9 b.g. Murmure (FR) – Petite Folie (Salmon Leap (USA)) [2006/7 c115, h–: c17f May 9] maiden hurdler: fairly useful handicap chaser: shaped as if amiss only start in 2006/7: best at 2m: acts on heavy and good to firm going: often races prominently: sound jumper: none too resolute, but is consistent. *P. Monteith* **c– h–**

POMMEROL (FR) 4 b.g. Subotica (FR) – Irish Cofee (FR) (Video Rock (FR)) [2006/7 17s* 17v² 17s^F 16d⁴ c18s² c17s^F Mar 18] lengthy, quite good-topped gelding: first foal: dam 11f to 12.5f winner: runner-up over 11f on Flat: fairly useful form in juvenile hurdles: won at Enghien in November: still going well when fell heavily 2 out in race at Cheltenham won by Katchit: runner-up completed start in 4-y-o chases at Auteuil: raced around 2m on going softer than good (best form on soft/heavy): has had tongue tied. *F. Doumen, France* **c112 h120**

POMPEIUS MAGNUS (IRE) 5 b.g. Pistolet Bleu (IRE) – Shaiymara (IRE) (Darshaan) [2006/7 F16v* 16v² Dec 27] €27,000 3-y-o: big, good sort: has plenty of scope: third foal: dam unraced half-sister to smart hurdler around 2m Shawiya: won bumper at Navan on debut by 5½ lengths from Notre Pere: again shaped promisingly when 4 lengths second to Kendor Dine in 24-runner maiden hurdle at Leopardstown 18 days later: will stay beyond 2m: open to improvement. *N. Meade, Ireland* **h109 p F103**

PONCHATRAIN (IRE) 7 ch.g. Fourstars Allstar (USA) – Phardante Lilly (IRE) (Phardante (FR)) [2006/7 h87, F75: 21d³ 19d² 21s³ c20d⁶ c24s⁴ c16v⁴ 20g⁴ Apr 21] medium-sized gelding: modest maiden hurdler: similar form in novice handicap chases: stays 3m: acts on soft and good to firm going: tried tongue tied. *D. J. Wintle* **c88 h92**

PONMEOATH (IRE) 7 b.g. Flemensfirth (USA) – Cool N Calm (Arctic Lord) [2006/7 20v² 20d² 20s c20s^F c18v^F c22s³ c20v² c17s* c24g⁴ c24d⁵ c21m Apr 27] 8,500 3-y-o, 15,000 4-y-o: medium-sized gelding: second foal: dam, once-raced, out of half-sister to dam of Grand National winner Numbersixvalverde: winning hurdler: useful **c133 h122**

chaser: easy winner of maiden at Limerick in February: improved form when 3¼ lengths fourth of 24 to Cloudy Lane in Kim Muir Handicap Chase (Amateurs) at Cheltenham: stays 3m: raced mainly on good going or softer (acts on heavy). *Eric McNamara, Ireland*

PONTIUS 10 b.g. Terimon – Coole Pilate (Celtic Cone) [2006/7 c–x, h–: c25m^{pu} Jun 4] tall, leggy gelding: winning hurdler/chaser, has failed to complete all 4 starts in chases since 2003/4: successful twice in points in March: usually makes mistakes over fences. *N. A. Twiston-Davies*
c– x
h–

PONT NEUF (IRE) 7 b.m. Revoque (IRE) – Petite Maxine (Sharpo) [2006/7 h79: 16g^5 16d^5 Nov 11] leggy mare: poor maiden hurdler: raced mainly around 2m on ground softer than good (acts on heavy): tried in cheekpieces: often tongue tied. *A. Crook*
h62

POOR TACTIC'S (IRE) 11 b.g. Commanche Run – Hilary's Image (IRE) (Phardante (FR)) [2006/7 h81d: 24v^5 24f^5 24f* 24g^4 Aug 1] winning pointer: poor hurdler: won handicap at Perth in July: stays 3m: acts on any going. *J. J. Lambe, Ireland*
h82

POPCORN ROSIE 4 b.f. Diktat – Real Popcorn (IRE) (Jareer (USA)) [2006/7 aF16g^2 F17g Apr 19] 3,500 3-y-o: good-topped filly: sixth foal: half-sister to several winners, including fair 2m hurdle winner Josear (by Josr Algarhoud): dam 1½m winner: better effort in bumpers when second in polytrack event won easily by Aux Le Bahnn. *C. J. Down*
F84

POP (FR) 4 b.g. Cricket Ball (USA) – Senzi (FR) (Saint Cyrien (FR)) [2006/7 F12v^4 F16d^3 Mar 17] €20,000 2-y-o: angular gelding: third foal: half-brother to winning 2m hurdler Obelo (by Sheyrann): dam unraced: better effort in bumpers (fairly useful form) when 3¼ lengths fourth to Procas de Thaix in 4-y-o event at Newbury. *H. D. Daly*
F101

POP GUN 8 ch.g. Pharly (FR) – Angel Fire (Nashwan (USA)) [2006/7 h80: 16v^6 16d^4 24s^4 20v 16v^3 20v* 20g Apr 27] sturdy gelding: modest hurdler: won selling handicap at Chepstow in March: stays 2½m: acts on heavy going: tongue tied last 4 outings. *Mrs K. Waldron*
h88

POPPS PRINCESS 5 b.m. Silver Patriarch (IRE) – Bluebell. Miss (High Kicker (USA)) [2006/7 F16g^4 20g 19g Nov 5] fourth foal: dam 5f/1¼m winner: soundly beaten in bumper/over hurdles: sold £1,000 Ascot December Sales. *R. M. Stronge*
h–
F–

POPPY MAROON 9 b.m. Supreme Leader – Maries Party (The Parson) [2006/7 20s 26s^6 21s^4 25s^3 c24g^6 c24g* Mar 28] compact mare: winning pointer: poor form over hurdles: progressive in handicap chases, winning at Chepstow and Kempton (fair form) in March: stays 3m: front runner. *D. P. Keane*
c103
h73

POPPY SMITH 5 ch.m. Busy Flight – Alice Smith (Alias Smith (USA)) [2006/7 F69: F17g Apr 19] workmanlike mare: well held in mares bumpers 15 months apart. *B. J. Eckley*
F–

POPSLEEBOBROSS (IRE) 6 b.m. Revoque (IRE) – Flame of Sion (Be My Chief (USA)) [2006/7 h–, F–: 18s 24s 17g^4 Apr 7] fourth in selling hurdler, first sign of ability. *R. H. Buckler*
h66 ?

POQUELIN (FR) 4 bl.g. Lahint (USA) – Babolna (FR) (Tropular) [2006/7 16g^3 16d* 16v^3 17g^6 16m* Apr 21] tall, useful-looking ex-French gelding: has scope: half-brother to 17f hurdle winner Josee II (by Beaudelaire): useful on Flat (stays 10.5f) for F-X. de Chevigny: useful juvenile hurdler: won at Kempton in December and Ayr (landed odds by 7 lengths from English City) in April: also ran well when 23½ lengths sixth to Katchit in Triumph Hurdle at Cheltenham: raced around 2m: acts on good to firm and good to soft ground: takes good hold. *P. F. Nicholls*
h129

PORAK (IRE) 10 ch.g. Perugino (USA) – Gayla Orchestra (Lord Gayle (USA)) [2006/7 c–x, h95: 20d 16g^4 17d^6 16s 19v^4 Jan 8] close-coupled gelding: poor handicap hurdler nowadays: lightly raced over fences (let down by jumping): stays 2½m: acts on soft going: tried tongue tied. *W. Davies*
c– x
h81 §

PORTANT FELLA 8 b.g. Greensmith – Jubilata (USA) (The Minstrel (CAN)) [2006/7 c110, h115: 16m 16d* 17f* c16g* Sep 4] rather leggy gelding: fairly useful on Flat (stays 1¼m): similar standard over hurdles/fences: won minor event at Tralee and handicap at Bellewstown (by 2½ lengths from On The Other Hand) in August, both over hurdles, and handicap chase at Roscommon (beat Kit Carson comfortably by 7 lengths) in September: raced around 2m: acts on firm and good to soft going, probably on soft: effective in cheekpieces or without: tried tongue tied. *Ms Joanna Morgan, Ireland*
c122
h122

PORTAVADIE 8 b.g. Rakaposhi King – Woodland Flower (Furry Glen) [2006/7 c123, h121: c17m^{pu} 17d^3 17s^{pu} 19g 16d^5 17g^5 c19d^{pu} Dec 23] lengthy gelding: fairly useful handicap hurdler: good third of 17 to Tycoon Hall in valuable event at Market Rasen:
c–
h126

similar form at best over fences, though has failed to complete last 4 outings: bred to stay 2½m: acts on heavy going. *J. M. Jefferson*

PORT ERNE (IRE) 4 b.g. Stowaway – Little Nonnie (IRE) (Beneficial) [2006/7 F16g⁶ Apr 23] second foal: dam unraced: well held in maiden bumper on debut. *Ferdy Murphy* **F—**

PORTLAND BILL (IRE) 7 ch.g. Zaffaran (USA) – Donegal Moss (Le Moss) [2006/7 h101, F90: 22d* c23s^F 24s⁶ 22s* 22d³ 21v² Feb 24] good-topped gelding: fairly useful hurdler: successful at Wincanton in November (handicap) and December (beat Nougat de L'Isle by short head in novice): good efforts when placed last 2 starts, 14 lengths second to Mac Federal in handicap at Kempton: fell fourth on chasing debut: stays 2¾m: acts on heavy going. *R. H. Alner* **c– p / h119**

PORT NATAL (IRE) 9 b.g. Selkirk (USA) – Play Around (IRE) (Niniski (USA)) [2006/7 c–, h–: 16m May 6] no form over jumps: tried blinkered/in cheekpieces/tongue tied. *J. Wade* **c– / h—**

PORT OF MOGAN (IRE) 6 b.g. Lord Americo – Colleen Donn (Le Moss) [2006/7 24m^F 20m² 19m² 22s* 24v⁵ 16d^pu 22s^pu Jan 20] smallish, angular gelding: brother to useful hurdler Chief Dan George, stays 27f, and half-brother to several winners, notably very smart staying chaser Macgeorge (by Mandalus): dam unraced half-sister to top-class 2m hurdler Deep Idol: runner-up completed start in maiden Irish points in 2006: modest hurdler: claimed from M. Quinlan £6,000, won maiden at Stratford in October: no show in handicaps last 2 starts: stays 2¾m: acts on soft and good to firm going. *S. A. Brookshaw* **h90**

PORT TALBOT (IRE) 6 b.g. Pasternak – North End Lady (Faustus (USA)) [2006/7 F16g F18m⁵ Apr 26] lengthy gelding: second foal: dam bumper/17f hurdle winner: modest form in bumpers, weakening. *O. Sherwood* **F85**

PORTY FOX 6 b.g. Riverwise (USA) – Mildred Sophia (Crooner) [2006/7 F–: F17v^su F16s Nov 15] no form in bumpers. *M. A. Barnes* **F—**

POSH ACT 7 b.g. Rakaposhi King – Balancing Act (Balinger) [2006/7 h85: c19s^F Nov 19] stocky gelding: modest form in novice hurdles: off 8 months, weakening when fell heavily 2 out in minor event on chasing debut. *Miss H. C. Knight* **c– / h—**

POSH PENNY 5 b.m. Classic Cliche (IRE) – Myblackthorn (IRE) (Mandalus) [2006/7 F16s F16d 20g Apr 11] second foal: dam, fair chaser, stayed 2½m: well held in bumpers/maiden hurdle. *C. J. Down* **h— / F—**

POSH STICK 10 b.m. Rakaposhi King – Carat Stick (Gold Rod) [2006/7 c102, h94: c16s⁵ c20g c20d³ c20s² c20s c19d⁶ c20v^pu c22v⁴ c20v* Mar 18] smallish, angular mare: maiden hurdler: modest handicap chaser: dropped in weights, won at Carlisle in March: probably stays 2¾m: raced mainly on good going or softer (acts on heavy). *J. B. Walton* **c99 / h—**

POSITANO (IRE) 7 b.h. Polish Precedent (USA) – Shamaya (IRE) (Doyoun) [2006/7 h75: 16g^pu 16m 16g² 22m 17s⁴ 16m⁴ 17d³ 16m* c16d² 16g^pu Sep 6] modest hurdler: won selling handicap at Worcester (by 14 lengths) in August: similar form when runner-up in novice handicap on chasing debut: may prove best around 2m: acts on heavy and good to firm going: usually visored. *M. Scudamore* **c92 / h93**

POSSEXTOWN (IRE) 9 b.g. Lord Americo – Tasse du The (Over The River (FR)) [2006/7 c127: 22f³ 22g^pu 20m 24m* 24m* 24m³ 22m² c20g Oct 24] big, lengthy, good sort: fairly useful hurdler/chaser: won novice hurdles at Worcester in July and August (landed odds by 6 lengths from Ar An Shron, idling): good third to Waynesworld at same course next time: well held back over fences final outing: stays 3m: acts on soft and good to firm going: front runner/races prominently: reportedly bled third start. *N. G. Richards* **c– / h118**

POST IT 6 b.m. Thowra (FR) – Cream By Post (Torus) [2006/7 h89, F–: 17m³ 19g⁵ 19m c16g* Apr 20] bumper winner: modest maiden hurdler: poor form when successful on chasing debut in 5-runner maiden at Hereford: bred to stay 2½m+: blinkered last 2 starts: temperament under suspicion. *R. J. Hodges* **c66 + / h93 §**

POTOFFAIRIES (IRE) 12 ch.g. Montelimar (USA) – Ladycastle (Pitpan) [2006/7 c–, h–: c26g⁴ Apr 19] good-topped gelding: winning hurdler/maiden chaser: left Mrs S. Bramall and fit from points, fourth in hunter at Cheltenham: stays 3¼m: raced on good going or softer (acts on heavy): usually blinkered/in cheekpieces. *Mrs Krista Brown* **c87 / h—**

POTTS OF MAGIC 8 b.g. Classic Cliche (IRE) – Potter's Gale (IRE) (Strong Gale) [2006/7 h91: 24g^pu c23m^F c23m^pu 20m 24f* 24m* 27d³ 26g³ 24d⁴ 25d* Nov 18] fair handicap hurdler: won at Uttoxeter and Worcester in July and Ascot in November: let down by jumping both starts over fences: stays 27f: acts on soft and firm going (ran poorly on heavy): usually blinkered. *R. Lee* **c84 / h105**

POUR ELLIE (FR) 4 b.g. Cyborg (FR) – Quintessence III (FR) (El Condor (FR)) **F93**
[2006/7 F13s⁵ F17gˢᵘ F16m Apr 24] 63,000 3-y-o: brother to 3 winners, notably
high-class staying hurdler/chaser Cyborgo and high-class 2m hurdler Hors La Loi III:
dam, 9f winner, placed 3 times over jumps: running best race in bumpers when slipping
up 1½f out in maiden at Bangor. *P. R. Webber*

POUVOIR (FR) 4 gr.g. Verglas (IRE) – Policia (FR) (Policeman (FR)) [2006/7 16gᶠ **h124**
16g² 16s² 16s* 16d 16m³ Apr 21] tall, angular ex-French gelding: fifth foal: half-brother
to 2 winners including fairly useful 2¼m hurdle winner Poland Springs (by Kaldounevees): dam winning 21f chaser: won 1¼m handicap from 5 starts on Flat for F. Head:
fairly useful juvenile hurdler: won at Kempton (by 14 lengths from Prince Ary) in
January: finished weakly next 2 starts, albeit after giving chase to Gaspara when tenth
of 24 in listed handicap at Cheltenham: raced at 2m: acts on soft ground: room for
improvement in jumping. *A. King*

POWER AND DEMAND 10 b.g. Formidable (USA) – Mazurkanova (Song) [2006/7 **h–**
h63: 19d 17m⁶ 21m 16g Nov 29] good-topped gelding: maiden hurdler: tried in headgear/
tongue tied: has been reluctant to race. *C. W. Thornton*

POWERBERRY (IRE) 6 b.g. Shernazar – Bilberry (Nicholas Bill) [2006/7 F103: **h100**
F16s² F16s³ F16d* 20s⁵ 18v Dec 6] smallish gelding: fairly useful in bumpers, won at **F100**
Down Royal in November by 1½ lengths from First Author: better effort in maiden
hurdles when fifth to Hollywood Law at Punchestown: likely to stay beyond 2½m.
T. K. Geraghty, Ireland

POWER ELITE (IRE) 7 gr.g. Linamix (FR) – Hawas (Mujtahid (USA)) [2006/7 **c98 §**
h132§: c16s⁶ c17s 16s 16v⁶ 16d 19v⁵ 16m Apr 10] lengthy, well-made gelding: useful **h129 §**
hurdler: ran poorly last 3 starts: better effort over fences when sixth in novice at
Fairyhouse: raced mainly around 2m: acts on heavy going: tried blinkered: tongue tied
last 4 starts: temperamental. *N. Meade, Ireland*

POWER GLORY 5 b.g. Namaqualand (USA) – Belamcanda (Belmez (USA)) [2006/7 **c–**
h81: 16g⁵ 16d 16m 17mᶠ 16d⁴ 16fᵖᵘ Apr 9] maiden hurdler, little form in 2006/7: **h81 d**
left M. Gingell and fit from point, struggling when unseated 4 out in novice hunter on
chase debut. *B. Dowling*

POWER KING (IRE) 5 b.g. Supreme Leader – Quennie Mo Ghra (IRE) (Mandalus) [2006/7 **h–**
F17g 24mᵖᵘ Mar 31] half-brother to winning hurdler/chaser Scotch Corner (by **F–**
Jurado), stays 3m: dam poor maiden hurdler: well-backed favourite, finished lame in
bumper: again ran as if amiss on hurdling debut nearly 5 months later. *Miss H. Lewis*

Timeform Handicap Hurdle, Ascot—
Potts of Magic (blinkers) gains his third win of the campaign

POWERLOVE (FR) 6 b.m. Solon (GER) – Bywaldor (FR) (Magwal (FR)) [2006/7 **h94**
h94: 22f⁵ 24v² 22g 24m⁶ Nov 24] lengthy, angular mare: modest hurdler: stays 3m: acts
on any going: consistent. *Mrs S. C. Bradburne*

POWERSTATION (IRE) 7 b.g. Anshan – Mariaetta (IRE) (Mandalus) [2006/7 h136: **h153**
22v⁴ 16v³ 20s² 20v² 21g² 20m³ 24m² Apr 26] leggy, close-coupled gelding: smart
hurdler: improved efforts when second on 2 of last 3 starts, beaten 3 lengths by Burntoakboy in Coral Cup (Handicap) at Cheltenham and 2½ lengths by Refinement in Grade 1
Champion Stayers' Hurdle at Punchestown: stays 3m: acts on soft and good to firm going
(won bumper on heavy). *M. Phillips, Ireland*

POWER STRIKE (USA) 6 b.g. Coronado's Quest (USA) – Galega (Sure Blade **c72 §**
(USA)) [2006/7 h–: 20g⁶ c16g⁶ c16m⁴ c20mᵖᵘ c16f⁴ c20gᵖᵘ c16f 16f Sep 29] well **h– §**
beaten over hurdles: poor novice chaser: raced mainly around 2m: temperamental.
Mrs L. B. Normile

POYLE JOSH 7 b.g. Danzig Connection (USA) – Poyle Jezebelle (Sharpo) [2006/7 **h–**
16mᵖᵘ 16s Dec 7] half-brother to bumper winner Dark Character (by Reprimand): poor
and ungenuine maiden on Flat at 2 yrs for W. Turner, well beaten both starts in 2006: no
show over hurdles: tried blinkered. *F. E. Sutherland*

PRAGMATICA 6 b.m. Inchinor – Isabella Gonzaga (Rock Hopper) [2006/7 h–: 16m **h–**
Jun 11] no show in mares novice hurdles, including a seller. *R. M. H. Cowell*

PRAIRIE FIRE 7 b.g. Commanche Run – Light Your Fire (Bay Express) [2006/7 19sᵖᵘ **h–**
Dec 29] fifth in bumper on debut: no show in novice hurdle 2½ years later. *H. D. Daly*

PRAIRIE LAW (GER) 7 b.g. Law Society (USA) – Prairie Charm (IRE) (Thatching) **c– §**
[2006/7 c–§, h100§: 22gᵖᵘ 20g Mar 27] leggy gelding: winning hurdler: in cheekpieces, **h– §**
no show in 2006/7: unseated first only outing over fences: ungenuine. *B. N. Pollock*

PRAIRIE LORD (IRE) 7 b.g. Lord of Appeal – Johara (USA) (Exclusive Native **h70**
(USA)) [2006/7 19g Feb 2] €26,000 3-y-o, 3,000 6-y-o: half-brother to several Flat
winners, notably Gold Cup winner Ashal (by Touching Wood): dam won over 6f on debut
at 2 yrs: green, well held in novice hurdle on debut. *Mrs S. J. Smith*

PRAIRIE MINSTREL (USA) 13 b.g. Regal Intention (CAN) – Prairie Sky (CAN) **c74 §**
(Gone West (USA)) [2006/7 c82§, h–: c18v⁴ c20m² c18gᵖᵘ Mar 18] sturdy, close-coupled **h–**
gelding: poor handicap chaser: looked likely winner of 4-runner event at Leicester second
outing until rider took things too easy and headed post: broke down next time: stays 3m:
acts on any going: usually wears cheekpieces: untrustworthy. *R. Dickin*

PRAIRIE MOONLIGHT (GER) 7 b.m. Monsun (GER) – Prairie Princess (GER) **c96 p**
(Dashing Blade) [2006/7 h134*: 16d* 18s⁴ c16s⁵ 16g 18m Apr 25] tall mare: fair hurdler **h112 +**
nowadays: won mares race at Kilbeggan in September: well held in valuable handicap at
Aintree penultimate start: not knocked about when fifth in novice on chasing debut: best
at 2m: acts on good to soft going: capable of better over fences. *W. J. Burke, Ireland*

PRAYERFUL 8 b.m. Syrtos – Pure Formality (Forzando) [2006/7 c–, h88: 26dᶠ 20vᵖᵘ **c83**
19m c25mᵖᵘ c23m³ c22gᵖᵘ Jul 22] sturdy mare: winning hurdler: poor maiden chaser: **h–**
form in 2006/7 only on penultimate outing: stays 3¼m: acts on good to firm and heavy
going: has worn cheekpieces/visor: usually patiently ridden. *J. G. M. O'Shea*

PREACHER BOY 8 b.g. Classic Cliche (IRE) – Gospel (IRE) (Le Bavard (FR)) **c135**
[2006/7 c128: c25m² c26s³ c24v² c25s³ Feb 17] big, strong, lengthy gelding: useful
handicap chaser: good placed efforts first 3 starts in 2006/7, including when 13 lengths
third to State of Play in Hennessy Cognac Gold Cup at Newbury: stays 3¼m: acts on
good to firm and heavy going: improved jumper. *R. J. Hodges*

PRECIOUS BANE (IRE) 9 b.g. Bigstone (IRE) – Heavenward (USA) (Conquistador **c88**
Cielo (USA)) [2006/7 c111, h–: c32sᵖᵘ c26v⁶ c24v⁵ 21v c26v c22vᵖᵘ c23s c24s⁴ c26v² **h–**
c28g Mar 18] leggy, sparely-made gelding: maiden hurdler: fair handicap chaser at best,
has deteriorated: thorough stayer: acts on heavy going: tried in cheekpieces/blinkers.
J. B. Groucott

PRECIOUS LUCY (FR) 8 gr.m. Kadrou (FR) – Teardrops Fall (FR) (Law Society **c–**
(USA)) [2006/7 h–: 16gᵖᵘ 16s⁵ 20d 16g 17m⁵ 16m c17g⁴ c21m⁴ 18m Sep 21] winning **h71**
hurdler: little form in 2006/7, including over fences. *G. F. Bridgwater*

PRECIOUS MYSTERY (IRE) 7 ch.m. Titus Livius (FR) – Ascoli (Skyliner) **h100**
[2006/7 h109: 17s⁴ 21s 22dᵖᵘ Mar 26] leggy mare: fair handicap hurdler: left A. King
prior to final start: should stay beyond 21f: acts on heavy going: has been visored/
blinkered. *Mrs A. E. Brooks*

PRECISION PROFILE 5 b.m. Silver Patriarch (IRE) – La Brigantine (IRE) **F79**
(Montelimar (USA)) [2006/7 F16s⁴ May 20] second foal: dam, winning hurdler/fair 2m
chaser who became thoroughly temperamental, half-sister to one-time smart hurdler/
chaser up to 3m Fundamentalist: modest form when fourth in bumper at Worcester on
debut. *P. J. Hobbs*

PREDATEUR (FR) 4 b.g. Nikos – Fia Rosa (FR) (Royal Charter (FR)) [2006/7 16d³ **h127**
17v* 17v⁴ 16s⁴ Feb 17] rangy gelding: third foal: half-brother to fairly useful chaser Mort
de Rire (by Luchiroverte), stays 25f: dam won over fences around 2m: won 1¼m event at
Vichy on debut in August for T. Trapenard: useful juvenile hurdler: impressive winner of
novice at Taunton in January: failed to impress with finishing effort all 3 other starts,
including when fourth in Grade 2 at Cheltenham third outing: raced around 2m on going
softer than good (acts on heavy): temperament under suspicion. *P. F. Nicholls*

PREDATOR (GER) 6 b.g. Protektor (GER) – Polish Affair (IRE) (Polish Patriot **c129**
(USA)) [2006/7 c93, h–: 19d* c20m* c21d* c20g* c21m³ 24dᵖᵘ 19s⁴ 21d⁴ 19g* 20mᵖᵘ **h125**
Apr 24] close-coupled gelding: fairly useful handicap hurdler: won at Hereford in May
and Ascot (by 2½ lengths from Backbord) in March: similar form in novice chases:
successful first 3 starts, at Huntingdon (maiden) in August, Fakenham in October and
Huntingdon (beat Cream Cracker by 5 lengths) in November: stays 21f: acts on good to
firm and good to soft going: tried in cheekpieces: sold 20,000 gns Doncaster May Sales.
Jonjo O'Neill

PREDESTINE (FR) 7 ch.g. Signe Divin (USA) – Smyrna (FR) (Lightning (FR)) **c96**
[2006/7 c93, h–: c21v⁴ c24v⁴ c24v² c24v* c21v³ c25s³ Mar 8] tall gelding: winning **h–**
hurdler: modest handicap chaser: 5 lb out of weights, won 5-runner novice event at
Haydock in January, hanging left: should stay beyond 3m: raced on going softer than
good (acts on heavy): tongue tied 2 of last 3 starts, also in cheekpieces last 2: has been let
down by jumping over fences. *K. C. Bailey*

PREDICAMENT 8 br.g. Machiavellian (USA) – Quandary (USA) (Blushing Groom **c98 §**
(FR)) [2006/7 c101, h107: c16fᶠᵗʳ c19dᶠ c16m c20g² c21m³ c16g⁵ c21s⁵ c16g⁵ c20d⁶ **h– §**
c21s⁵ c21v⁴ Jan 1] leggy, angular gelding: fair hurdler/maiden chaser at best: sold out of
Jonjo O'Neill's stable 21,000 gns Doncaster May Sales after second outing: probably
stays 23f: acts on good and firm going: blinkered once (refused to race): tried tongue tied:
weak finisher: untrustworthy. *Dr P. Pritchard*

PREMIER DANE (IRE) 5 b.g. Indian Danehill (IRE) – Crystal Blue (IRE) (Bluebird **h139**
(USA)) [2006/7 h136: 18f* 17g³ 16d 16v 16m 17g³ 16m³ Apr 21] small, leggy gelding:
useful on Flat (stays 1½m): useful hurdler: easily landed odds in minor event at Kelso in
May: back in form when third in valuable handicaps last 2 starts, behind Pedrobob in
28-runner County Hurdle at Cheltenham and Emmpat in Scottish Champion Hurdle at
Ayr: raced around 2m: acts on firm and good to soft going (well held on heavy).
N. G. Richards

PREMIER ESTATE (IRE) 10 b.g. Satco (FR) – Kettleby (IRE) (Tale Quale) [2006/7 **c–**
c20s⁵ c22sᵖᵘ c25vᵖᵘ c26gᵖᵘ Mar 26] tall gelding: winning hurdler/chaser, no show in **h–**
2006/7 after lengthy absence: tried tongue tied. *R. Rowe*

PREMIER HOPE (IRE) 6 b.m. Second Empire (IRE) – Our Hope (Dancing Brave **h101 p**
(USA)) [2006/7 F71: 20g 21v 22dᵘʳ 19v 17m* Apr 17] fourth in bumper: much improved
over hurdles (fair form) when winning novice at Exeter on handicap debut by 10 lengths:
bred to stay beyond 17f: acts on good to firm going: likely to prove capable of better still.
Miss E. C. Lavelle

PREMIUM FIRST (IRE) 8 ch.g. Naheez (USA) – Regular Rose (IRE) (Regular **c94**
Guy) [2006/7 c94, h–: c25g⁵ May 3] lengthy gelding: bumper winner: modest form over **h–**
hurdles/in chases: successful 5 times in points in 2006: may prove best up to 25f.
A. G. Hobbs

PRESENCE OF MIND (IRE) 9 ch.g. Presenting – Blue Rose (IRE) (Good Thyne **c106**
(USA)) [2006/7 c109, h–: c25mᵖᵘ c23mᵈ c26dᵖᵘ c26m³ c26g² Sep 30] workmanlike **h–**
gelding: fair handicap chaser: probably stays 3½m: acts on good to firm and good to soft
going: effective visored or not: usually races prominently. *Miss E. C. Lavelle*

PRESENTABLE (IRE) 6 ch.g. Presenting – Crashrun (Crash Course) [2006/7 F16f⁵ **h78**
17d⁶ 19g⁶ 19s³ 27s⁵ 24g 25v⁶ 24v⁴ 23g Apr 3] €20,000 3-y-o, €18,000 4-y-o: lengthy **F80**
gelding: eighth foal: brother to winning hurdler/chaser around 2m Cumbrian Knight and
half-brother to fair hurdlers My Name's Not Bin (stayed 3m, by Good Thyne) and Clew

Bay Cove (2m winner, by Anshan): dam unraced: fifth in bumper: poor novice hurdler: stays 3m. *Grant Tuer*

PRESENTAL (IRE) 7 b.g. Presenting – Oriental Blaze (IRE) (Seamanship) [2006/7 F17d Nov 16] €22,000 3-y-o: second foal: dam winning pointer: runner-up completed start in points in 2005: soundly beaten in maiden bumper. *S. E. H. Sherwood* **F–**

PRESENTANDCORRECT (IRE) 6 ch.g. Presenting – Friston (IRE) (Roselier (FR)) [2006/7 F101: 16m² 16d⁶ 18g⁶ 16m⁴ Apr 22] rather unfurnished gelding: placed in bumpers: fair form over hurdles: landed odds in novice at Fontwell in March: stays 2¼m: acts on good to firm ground: has hung left under pressure. *P. J. Hobbs* **h111 +**

PRESENT BLEU (FR) 12 b.g. Epervier Bleu – Lointaine (USA) (Lyphard's Wish (FR)) [2006/7 c–, h–: c20gᵖᵘ c22f 19sᵖᵘ 19mᵖᵘ Jul 17] leggy gelding: useful hurdler/chaser in his prime, no longer of any account: has worn headgear/tongue strap. *D. E. Pipe* **c–** **h–**

PRESENTER (IRE) 7 ch.g. Cadeaux Genereux – Moviegoer (Pharly (FR)) [2006/7 h88x: 17g 20s² 20s³ May 28] sturdy gelding: poor maiden handicap hurdler: stays 2½m: acts on heavy going: tried blinkered: often let down by jumping: temperamental: sold £3,400 Ascot June Sales, no show in maiden points. *M. Sheppard* **h78 §**

PRESENT GLORY (IRE) 8 br.g. Presenting – Prudent Rose (IRE) (Strong Gale) [2006/7 h104: 24g* 24g³ Apr 19] lengthy gelding: will make a chaser: fairly useful hurdler: left C. Tinkler and off over 12 months, marked improvement when winning handicap at Ascot in March by 1¾ lengths from Mikado (pair clear): should stay beyond 3m: acts on soft going: tried to run out final 2005/6 outing. *D. W. P. Arbuthnot* **h119**

PRESENTING ALF (IRE) 7 b.g. Presenting – Hilary's Penny (Avocat) [2006/7 h73: 21m⁶ 20d⁴ 23s⁵ 19v* 16v 20v³ 25v c20g c20m* c20m² Apr 25] poor hurdler: won conditional jockeys handicap at Market Rasen in November: below form next 3 starts: similar form in handicap chases: won conditional jockeys event at Worcester in April: should be suited by further than 2½m: acts on good to firm and heavy ground. *Mrs S. J. Smith* **c82** **h84**

PRESENTING COPPER (IRE) 6 b.m. Presenting – Copper Supreme (IRE) (Supreme Leader) [2006/7 F18s* 19s⁵ 16g² Dec 26] first foal: dam fair hurdler/fairly useful chaser, stayed 21f: won Irish point on debut in 2006: won 20-runner mares point-to-point bumper at Tipperary in May for D. Coffey: better effort in mares novice hurdles when second to Apollo Lady at Wincanton: should prove suited by further than 2m. *P. J. Hobbs* **h94** **F85**

PRESENTING DIVA (IRE) 4 b.f. Presenting – Sue's A Lady (Le Moss) [2006/7 F18v⁶ F18g⁶ Mar 26] rather unfurnished filly: half-sister to several winners, notably one-time top-class staying chaser Sir Rembrandt (by Mandalus) and useful hurdler/fairly useful chaser Audacter (by Strong Gale), stayed 3m: dam bumper winner: never dangerous in bumpers. *L. Wells* **F–**

PRESENTING EDWARD 8 br.g. Presenting – Edwards Victoria (IRE) (Buckskin (FR)) [2006/7 22mᵖᵘ 22gᵖᵘ 21v⁴ 16vᵖᵘ Jan 17] fourth foal: dam unraced: no form over hurdles. *E. J. Jamieson* **h–**

PRESENTING EXPRESS (IRE) 8 b.g. Presenting – Glenbane Express (IRE) (Roselier (FR)) [2006/7 c119, h97+: 22m* c26m* c26mᵖᵘ c26sᵖᵘ c24d⁶ c30gᵖᵘ Mar 31] workmanlike gelding: lightly raced over hurdles, easily won novice handicap at Exeter: useful handicap chaser: readily landed odds at Plumpton later in October by 4 lengths from Meggie's Beau: below form after (bled final outing): stays 3¼m: acts on soft and good to firm going: still prone to mistakes over fences. *Miss E. C. Lavelle* **c130** **h105 +**

PRESENTING STAR (IRE) 6 b. or br.g. Presenting – Fair Ava (IRE) (Strong Gale) [2006/7 F16s 21s 21g Mar 20] lengthy, rather unfurnished gelding: half-brother to fairly useful hurdler/useful chaser Mount Clerigo (by Supreme Leader), stays 3m: dam unraced: mid-field in bumper: well beaten over hurdles. *Ian Williams* **h–** **F74**

PRESENTINGTHECASE (IRE) 9 b.g. Presenting – Let The Hare Run (IRE) (Tale Quale) [2006/7 c84, h–: c25g⁶ May 3] good-topped gelding: maiden chaser: modest pointer, won in April: tried blinkered. *Miss S. Mitchell* **c–** **h–**

PRESENT LOVE (IRE) 5 b.m. Presenting – Love You Madly (IRE) (Bob Back (USA)) [2006/7 F16v F17m⁵ F17m Apr 28] 15,000 4-y-o: leggy mare: fourth foal: dam, temperamental staying hurdler, sister to useful hurdler up to 3m Tarthooth: well beaten in bumpers: sold 7,000 gns Doncaster May Sales. *S. Gollings* **F–**

PRESENT M'LORD (IRE) 7 b.g. Presenting – The Red Side (IRE) (Brush Aside **c89**
(USA)) [2006/7 c21s² c23m³ c25s⁴ c25sᵖᵘ c20v³ c23s³ Mar 12] €20,000 4-y-o: first foal:
dam placed in bumpers/poor maiden hurdler: won maiden point in 2006: modest maiden
chaser: stays 25f: acts on good to firm and heavy going: sketchy jumper. *R. H. Alner*

PRESENT MOMENT (IRE) 9 b.g. Presenting – Springphar (IRE) (Phardante (FR)) **c–**
[2006/7 c–: c25s⁴ c21gᶠ c24g⁶ Apr 8] winning pointer: no form in other events: sold out
of Ruth Hayter's stable £2,100 Ascot June Sales prior to return. *P. J. Millington*

PRESENT ORIENTED (USA) 6 ch.g. Southern Halo (USA) – Shy Beauty (CAN) **h114**
(Great Gladiator (USA)) [2006/7 17s 17d³ 17d 17m 19g* 22m² 22m³ 22m* 22d* 20g
22g* 17v* 19m⁶ Oct 28] close-coupled gelding: lightly-raced maiden on Flat: fair hurdler: successful 5 times at Market Rasen in 2006/7, in novice events in July and August
and handicaps in August (conditional jockeys), September and October: stays 2¾m: acts
on good to firm and heavy going: front runner/races prominently. *M. C. Chapman*

PRESIDENT HILL (IRE) 9 b.g. Roselier (FR) – Bid For Fun (IRE) (Auction Ring **h–**
(USA)) [2006/7 20gᵖᵘ Apr 27] ex-Irish gelding: won maiden Irish point in 2005: bought
9,500 gns Doncaster May Sales: won twice in points in Britain in 2006: no show in 2
starts over hurdles. *M. Keighley*

PRESIDENT ROYAL (FR) 4 b.g. Video Rock (FR) – Etoile du Pontet (FR) (Le **h101**
Pontet (FR)) [2006/7 F13d F13s 18s⁶ 18s⁴ 17s² 17v* 17d⁵ Mar 19] useful-looking **F–**
gelding: fourth foal: dam, French 2¼m chase winner, sister to dam of useful staying
chaser Ladalko: twice-raced in bumpers: fair juvenile hurdler: made all in handicap at
Exeter in February: likely to stay beyond 2¼m: raced on going softer than good: keen
sort. *P. J. Hobbs*

PRESSMAN 4 b.g. Alflora (IRE) – Scoop (IRE) (Scenic) [2006/7 F16s Jan 24] strong, **F71**
workmanlike gelding: first foal: dam, 6f winner on Flat, modest 2m hurdler: seventh in
maiden bumper on debut. *Mrs S. A. Watt*

PRESTBURY KNIGHT 7 ch.g. Sir Harry Lewis (USA) – Lambrini (IRE) (Buckskin **c– x**
(FR)) [2006/7 h99: 22g³ 26d² 24m³ 21d⁶ c17d Dec 15] angular gelding: fair handicap **h111**
hurdler: jumped poorly when tailed off on chasing debut: stays 3¼m: acts on good to firm
and good to soft going: tongue tied in 2006. *N. A. Twiston-Davies*

PRESTON BROOK 10 b.g. Perpendicular – Tommys Dream (Le Bavard (FR)) **c–**
[2006/7 c26vᵖᵘ c21vᵘʳ Feb 20] sturdy gelding: winning hurdler: modest pointer, won in **h–**
February: generally let down by jumping in chases: stays 3m: raced on good going or
softer (acts on heavy). *Mrs C. A. Coward*

PRE TOKEN 6 b.g. Presidium – Pro-Token (Proverb) [2006/7 F17d F17g Mar 24] big **F87**
gelding: half-brother to useful hurdler up to 2½m Gods Token (by Gods Solution): dam
winning pointer: better effort in bumpers when seventh of 15 at Bangor, second start.
G. P. Kelly

PRETTY STAR (GER) 7 b.g. Lando (GER) – Pretty Ballerina (Sadler's Wells **c129**
(USA)) [2006/7 h132: c22s² c23s³ c24s* c20g⁴ c22g³ Mar 23] rather leggy gelding: **h–**
useful handicap hurdler: fairly useful novice chaser: won 4-runner maiden at Newbury in
December by 1½ lengths from Moncadou: good third of 7 to Always Waining in handicap
at Newbury final outing: stays 3m: raced on good going or softer over jumps (acts on
soft). *A. King*

PRIDE AND PASSION (IRE) 6 ch.g. Alderbrook – Shalgate (IRE) (Shalford (IRE)) **h–**
[2006/7 F16g 22vᵖᵘ 20g 20g 20g Apr 27] €16,000 3-y-o, £15,000 4-y-o: first foal: dam **F–**
unraced: no show in bumper/over hurdles, left E. Sheehy in Ireland after second start.
M. Scudamore

PRIDE OF FINEWOOD (IRE) 9 ch.g. Old Vic – Macamore Rose (Torus) [2006/7 **h–**
h89: 21m Sep 26] strong, lengthy gelding: modest maiden hurdler: stays 3m: raced
mainly on soft/heavy going. *E. W. Tuer*

PRIDE OF THE OAKS 7 b.m. Faustus (USA) – Annabel's Baby (IRE) (Alzao **c–**
(USA)) [2006/7 c22sᵖᵘ May 21] second in maiden point in 2006: no show in bumper/
hunter chase. *G. Sanderson*

PRIDEWOOD DOVE 8 b.m. Alderbrook – Flighty Dove (Cruise Missile) [2006/7 **c– §**
h–§: c26mᵖᵘ c19mᵖᵘ Jun 4] of no account and temperamental to boot. *R. J. Price* **h– §**

PRIESTESS (IRE) 11 b.m. Magical Wonder (USA) – Forest Treasure (USA) (Green **h–**
Forest (USA)) [2006/7 16gᵘʳ Jun 15] no sign of ability on Flat at 3 yrs for V. Soane:
unseated first on hurdling debut. *C. W. Moore*

PRIESTS BRIDGE (IRE) 11 ch.m. Mr Ditton – Paddys Gale (Strong Gale) [2006/7   c–
c21g^F Mar 19] sparely-made mare: fairly useful hurdler: off 3½ years, fell fatally second   h–
on chasing debut: stayed 3m: raced on good going or softer (acted on heavy): front runner.
N. A. Twiston-Davies

PRIMARY GOAL (IRE) 5 b.g. Rudimentary (USA) – Brooks Chariot (IRE)   c–
(Electric) [2006/7 16g 16g 19s^4 c16d^F Jan 8] €28,000 3-y-o: good-topped gelding: sixth   h89
foal: half-brother to winning pointers by Welsh Term and Jurado: dam unraced half-sister
to one-time smart hurdler/chaser Fundamentalist: modest form in novice hurdles: fell first
on chasing debut. *Jonjo O'Neill*

PRIME BERE (FR) 4 b.f. Epistolaire (IRE) – Hornblower Girl (Faraway Times   h97
(USA)) [2006/7 15s 15s^3 17s 17d^2 18g^4 18m^5 16s* 20v^4 18g^3 Apr 10] small filly: half-
sister to several winners, including smart hurdler/high-class chaser Matinee Lover (by
Double Bed), stayed 27f: dam unraced: once-raced on Flat: fair juvenile hurdler, sold out
of R. Chotard's stable €50,000 Goffs (France) July Sale after third start: heavily backed,
easily won conditional jockeys event at Kempton on handicap debut in February: stays
2½m: acts on heavy ground: tongue tied last 3 outings. *D. E. Pipe*

PRIME CONTENDER 5 b.g. Efisio – Gecko Rouge (Rousillon (USA)) [2006/7   h115 x
h115: 16d 16d^5 16s^5 Jan 13] sturdy gelding: fairly useful on Flat (stays 1½m), successful
twice in 2006: similar standard over hurdles: raced around 2m on going softer than good:
blinkered 2 of last 3 outings: not a fluent jumper. *G. L. Moore*

PRIMED UP (IRE) 5 b.g. Rainbow Quest (USA) – Cape Mist (USA) (Lure (USA))   h–
[2006/7 17s^{bd} 17s 16s 16g Mar 19] modest and inconsistent up to 11f on Flat, won seller
in May for G. L. Moore: no form over hurdles: tried blinkered. *R. M. Beckett*

PRIME GIFT (IRE) 6 b.g. Supreme Leader – Niamh's Dream (IRE) (Kambalda)   F–
[2006/7 F16v Dec 11] €65,000 4-y-o: second foal: half-brother to winning pointer by
Glacial Storm: dam, lightly raced in points, half-sister to very smart 3m chaser Sackville:
green, well beaten in bumper on debut. *C. Grant*

PRIME NUMBER (IRE) 5 gr.g. King's Best (USA) – Majinskaya (FR) (Marignan   h104
(USA)) [2006/7 16g^3 16d Dec 30] sturdy gelding: useful on Flat (stays 9f), successful 3
times in 2005, below best in 2006: left G. Butler, much better effort in novice hurdles
when third to Court Ruler at Ascot, hanging right under pressure. *J. Akehurst*

PRIME POWERED (IRE) 6 b.g. Barathea (IRE) – Caribbean Quest (Rainbow Quest   h–
(USA)) [2006/7 h80: 16d Feb 2] fairly useful on Flat (stays 1½m), successful 3 times in
2006 for G. L. Moore: little impact on 3 starts over hurdles. *R. M. Beckett*

PRIME PRESENT (IRE) 7 b.m. Presenting – Prime Thyne (IRE) (Good Thyne   h62
(USA)) [2006/7 F16v 17g^3 Mar 24] €3,000 3-y-o: smallish mare: second foal: half-sister   F–
to 2½m hurdle winner Keep'nitreal (by Anshan): dam ran once: well beaten in bumper:
in cheekpieces, poor form when third in mares claimer on hurdling debut. *A. Middleton*

PRIMITIVE ACADEMY 5 b.h. Primitive Rising (USA) – Royal Fontaine (IRE)   h98
(Royal Academy (USA)) [2006/7 F74+: 19v^5 17s^F 19d 16g^6 Apr 14] tall, leggy horse: fair
form on Flat (for H. Cecil) in 2006: modest form over hurdles: stays 19f: tried tongue
tied. *J. R. Holt*

PRIMITIVE POPPY 8 b.m. Primitive Rising (USA) – Lady Manello (Mandrake   h87 §
Major) [2006/7 h84: 24g* 20m Jun 3] modest hurdler: won handicap at Hexham in May:
stays 3m: acts on soft going: inconsistent. *Mrs A. Hamilton*

PRIMITIVE WAY 15 b.g. Primitive Rising (USA) – Potterway (Velvet Prince)   c81
[2006/7 c90: c25f^4 c25f^5 c28s^{pu} c24d^{pu} c24d^3 c25s^{pu} c26g^2 Apr 7] sturdy gelding:
poor handicap chaser nowadays: stays 31f: acts on any going: wears headgear. *Miss
S. E. Forster*

PRIMONDO (IRE) 5 b.g. Montjeu (IRE) – Tagiki (IRE) (Doyoun) [2006/7 16v^4 19g^3 h99
Apr 8] fair on Flat (stays 2m), successful in August, sold out of J. Fanshawe's stable
16,000 gns Newmarket Autumn Sales, well held in 2007: visored, better effort over
hurdles when third in maiden at Towcester. *A. W. Carroll*

PRIMROSE PARK 8 b.m. Thowra (FR) – Redgrave Rose (Tug of War) [2006/7 h–:   c87
c26m* May 5] well held in bumper/over hurdles: 33/1 and blinkered, won handicap at   h–
Fontwell on chasing debut in May: stays 3¼m: acts on good to firm going. *K. Bishop*

PRIMUS INTER PARES (IRE) 6 b.g. Sadler's Wells (USA) – Life At The Top   c101
(Habitat) [2006/7 17m^2 17d^2 17m^5 16g 16d^2 c16g^3 c16s* c16s^{pu} c17g^3 19m^3 Apr 28]   h105
useful at best on Flat (stays 1m), lightly raced since 2005: fair maiden hurdler: similar

form over fences: won maiden at Catterick in March: will prove best around 2m: acts on soft and good to firm going. *N. Wilson*

PRINCE ADJAL (IRE) 7 b.g. Desert Prince (IRE) – Adjalisa (IRE) (Darshaan) [2006/7 c99x, h95x: 22g³ 22s 24s 24vᵖᵘ 16v 17v³ 24v² 24s* 27s⁴ Apr 27] winning chaser: fair handicap hurdler: won amateur event at Perth (by 13 lengths) in April: stays 3m: acts on any going: tried in cheekpieces/eyeshields, not since mid-2005/6: takes strong hold: not a fluent jumper. *Miss S. E. Forster*   c– x
h100 x

PRINCE AMONG MEN 10 b.g. Robellino (USA) – Forelino (USA) (Trempolino (USA)) [2006/7 h96: 16m* 17m² 20m² 21m² 16g 16v⁵ 16m 20s 20m* Apr 20] angular gelding: fair hurdler: won seller at Hexham (didn't have to be near best) in May and 4-runner conditional jockeys handicap at Ayr in April: stays 21f: acts on any going, raced mainly on good or firmer nowadays: effective visored or not: has idled/found little. *N. G. Richards*   h111

PRINCE ARY 4 b.g. Desert Prince (IRE) – Aryaf (CAN) (Vice Regent (CAN)) [2006/7 16d 16d* 16s² 16g⁴ 16g² 16f² Apr 22] leggy gelding: fairly useful for B. Hills on Flat (stays 1¼m), successful in August: fairly useful juvenile hurdler: won maiden at Fakenham in December by 8 lengths from Doctor David: best effort when second to Missis Potts in novice at Chepstow fifth outing: likely to prove best at 2m: acts on soft going, probably on firm. *D. E. Pipe*   h118

PRINCE BERE (FR) 4 b.g. Epistolaire (IRE) – Known Alibi (USA) (Known Fact (USA)) [2006/7 17d³ 17s 17gᵘʳ 16m Apr 8] fifth foal: half-brother to 2 winners on Flat, including French 1½mile winner Olga Bere (by Broadway Flyer): dam unraced: maiden on Flat: modest form at best over hurdles, claimed from J. Bertran de Balanda €18,100 in April 2006: in cheekpieces/tongue tied, badly let down by jumping final start: raced around 2m: acts on heavy going. *D. E. Pipe*   h82 x

PRINCE BROC (FR) 4 gr.g. Madoun (FR) – Elseural (FR) (Seurat) [2006/7 16vᵖᵘ Jan 6] rather leggy, useful-looking gelding: fourth foal: dam third at 1¼m: third over 1½m on debut in September for C. Diard: took good hold when well held in juvenile on hurdling debut. *A. King*   h–

PRINCE DES NEIGES (FR) 4 b.g. Milford Track (IRE) – Miss Smith (FR) (Grand Lodge (USA)) [2006/7 17gᴿ Mar 25] fair on Flat (stays 10.5f), successful 3 times in 2006, including at Chantilly in August, left R. Pritchard-Gordon prior to well held on British debut: in cheekpieces, reluctant to race and refused first on hurdling debut: needs treating with caution. *Ian Williams*   h– §

PRINCE DUNDEE (FR) 12 ch.g. Ecossais (FR) – Princesse Normande (FR) (Belgio (FR)) [2006/7 c–§, h–§: 16d⁵ 26g⁵ 19v* Jan 8] angular gelding: maiden chaser: winning pointer: poor hurdler: in cheekpieces, won conditional jockeys selling handicap at Taunton in January: stays 21f: acts on any going: formerly blinkered/visored: has had tongue tied: sketchy jumper: ungenuine. *M. Keighley*   c– §
h65 §

PRINCE ICKARUS (IRE) 7 ch.g. Double Trigger (IRE) – Stripe (Bustino) [2006/7 F83: F17s Oct 15] smallish, angular gelding: form (modest) in bumpers only on debut in 2005/6 for Mrs S. Smith. *J. M. Saville*   F–

PRINCELET (IRE) 5 b.g. Desert Prince (IRE) – Soeur Ti (FR) (Kaldoun (FR)) [2006/7 h121+: 16d* 16s² 16gᵖᵘ Apr 14] angular gelding: has only one eye: fairly useful hurdler: won handicap at Kempton (beat Orcadian by ¾ length) in December: would have followed up but for stumbling last in similar event there following month: raced around 2m: acts on soft going: blinkered final outing: not a fluent jumper. *N. J. Henderson*   h125

PRINCE MANDALA (IRE) 10 bl.g. Mandalus – Lady Red (Red Regent) [2006/7 24f 22g⁵ 24m⁵ Aug 22] in frame in maiden Irish points: poor form over hurdles. *C. A. McBratney, Ireland*   h72

PRINCE OF ARAGON 11 b.g. Aragon – Queens Welcome (Northfields (USA)) [2006/7 c69, h–: 19g Mar 25] leggy gelding: winning hurdler/maiden chaser: little form since 2004/5: blinkered 3 of last 4 starts: tongue tied. *Miss Suzy Smith*   c–
h–

PRINCE OF PERSIA 7 b.g. Turtle Island (IRE) – Sianiski (Niniski (USA)) [2006/7 c–, h108: 16g⁵ c20d c19s³ c21dᶠ Mar 26] leggy, close-coupled gelding: fair handicap hurdler: easily best effort over fences on penultimate outing (usually makes mistakes): stays 2½m: acts on soft going, poor efforts on good to firm: usually wears cheekpieces. *R. S. Brookhouse*   c105 x
h–

PRINCE OF PLEASURE (IRE) 13 b.g. Spanish Place (USA) – Oronocco Gift **c115**
(Camden Town) [2006/7 c118, h–: c22s⁴ c16m* c17m² Aug 4] good-topped gelding: **h–**
winning hurdler: fairly useful handicap chaser: won at Perth in June by ½ length from
Clouding Over, making all: stays 2¾m, effective over shorter: probably acts on any
going: races prominently. *D. Broad, Ireland*

PRINCE OF SLANE 8 b.g. Prince Daniel (USA) – Singing Slane (Cree Song) [2006/7 **c103**
c117, h–: 24m c25dᵖᵘ c30sᶠ c32s c25g⁵ c25g³ c24g⁴ c32mᵖᵘ Apr 21] short-backed **h–**
gelding: novice hurdler: fair handicap chaser: stays 3¾m: acts on soft and good to firm
going. *G. A. Swinbank*

PRINCE OF TARA (IRE) 10 b.g. Prince of Birds (USA) – Fete Champetre (Welsh **c124**
Pageant) [2006/7 c123, h144?: 20sᵖᵘ c29s⁵ 20v⁵ 24v c24d 21v⁴ Feb 18] strong, **h123**
workmanlike gelding: useful hurdler at best, stiff tasks in 2006/7: fairly useful handicap
chaser: stays 29f: raced on good going or softer (acts on heavy): held up. *S. J. Mahon,*
Ireland

PRINCE OF THE WOOD (IRE) 7 ch.g. Woodborough (USA) – Ard Dauphine **h–**
(IRE) (Forest Wind (USA)) [2006/7 20g Sep 8] strong, close-coupled gelding: modest
hurdler: off 18 months, well held only start in 2006/7: stays 3m: acts on firm ground:
wore cheekpieces in 2004/5. *A. Bailey*

PRINCE PICASSO 4 b.g. Lomitas – Auspicious (Shirley Heights) [2006/7 16v 16s⁵ **h96**
16v* 16sᶠ Mar 2] smallish, angular gelding: fairly useful on Flat (stays 1¼m), successful
3 times in 2006: sold out of Sir Mark Prescott's stable 18,000 gns Newmarket Autumn
Sales: fair juvenile hurdler: won maiden at Fairyhouse in February: held when fell last at
Newbury: raced at 2m on soft/heavy ground. *Eric McNamara, Ireland*

PRINCESSE GREC (FR) 9 b.m. Grand Tresor (FR) – Perimele (FR) (Mon Fils) **c– x**
[2006/7 c90x, h89: 20m³ 19m* Jun 4] plain mare: modest handicap hurdler/chaser: won **h92**
mares handicap hurdle at Hereford in June: stays 3m: acts on soft and good to firm going:
visored last 3 starts: sketchy jumper of fences. *M. Scudamore*

PRINCESS FLAME (GER) 5 br.m. Tannenkonig (IRE) – Pacora (GER) (Lagunas) **F105 +**
[2006/7 F14s* F16s F17gᵇᵈ Apr 13] angular mare: sister/half-sister to several winners in
Germany, including useful performer up to 1½m Pacajas (by Acatenango): dam 9f to 11f
winner in Germany: useful form when winning mares bumper at Fontwell on debut in
January by 14 lengths from Owlesbury Dream: left A. Newcombe and favourite, soon
plenty to do in listed mares event at Sandown 2 months later: brought down over 5f out in
similar race at Aintree. *B. G. Powell*

PRINCESS OF AENEAS (IRE) 4 b.f. Beckett (IRE) – Romangoddess (IRE) (Rho- **h72**
man Rule (USA)) [2006/7 16g⁵ 16s³ 17d² 16d² 16d⁴ 19g Feb 2] smallish, close-coupled
filly: modest on Flat (stays 1½m), left I. Semple after successful in October: poor juvenile
hurdler: raced mainly around 2m on good ground or softer. *D. McCain Jnr*

PRINCESS OF SPURS (IRE) 5 ch.m. Clerkenwell (USA) – Well Wisher (Jupiter **F–**
Island) [2006/7 F17v⁵ Feb 13] unfurnished mare: third foal: dam unraced half-sister to
useful chaser Longshanks: well held in bumper on debut. *Miss Venetia Williams*

PRINCESS STEPHANIE 9 b.m. Shaab – Waterloo Princess (IRE) (Le Moss) **c–**
[2006/7 c–, h53: 16m⁴ 17d 16m⁶ 16g⁴ 16m 16s 16g* Mar 16] fell only outing over fences: **h80**
poor handicap hurdler: won selling event at Fakenham in March: raced mainly around
2m: tried visored/in cheekpieces. *M. J. Gingell*

PRINCESS TOTO 4 b.f. Mtoto – Flower Princess (Slip Anchor) [2006/7 17f² 17s⁵ **h79**
16s⁵ 17s⁵ 21g Feb 21] good-bodied filly: half-sister to fair 2m hurdler Beryllium (by
Tragic Role): modest form on Flat: poor juvenile hurdler: likely to prove best at 2m with
emphasis on speed: in cheekpieces last 3 starts. *P. C. Haslam*

PRINCE VECTOR 5 b.g. Vettori (IRE) – The In-Laws (IRE) (Be My Guest (USA)) **h106**
[2006/7 17g² 17d⁴ Nov 23] fairly useful on Flat (stays 1¾m), below form in 2007: fair
form in frame both starts over hurdles: sold 10,000 gns Doncaster May Sales. *A. King*

PRINCE ZAFONIC 4 ch.g. Zafonic (USA) – Kite Mark (Mark of Esteem (IRE)) **h89 +**
[2006/7 16s³ 17s⁶ Dec 9] big, workmanlike gelding: fair maiden on Flat (should stay
beyond 1m), left W. Jarvis before final start at 3 yrs: blinkered and stiff task, well-held
sixth to Katchit in juvenile hurdle at Cheltenham, running in snatches: sold to join Miss
Gay Kelleway 16,000 gns Newmarket February Sales. *M. W. Easterby*

PRINCIPAL WITNESS (IRE) 6 b.g. Definite Article – Double Eight (IRE) **h86 p**
(Common Grounds) [2006/7 16g⁴ 16f 19m⁶ Aug 3] half-brother to 2m hurdle winner Fiza
(by Revoque): fair on Flat (stays 1¾m), successful early in 2006 for T. Dascombe: caught

eye under tender handling first 2 starts in maiden hurdles: should still do better. *Evan Williams*

PRINCIPE AZZURRO (FR) 6 b.g. Pistolet Bleu (IRE) – Massalia (GER) (Leone (GER)) [2006/7 h112, F93: c16v* c16s^F c20d^2 c21s^{ur} c24v^2 c24s^5 c22g^{ur} Apr 7] close-coupled gelding: fairly useful hurdler/novice chaser: won over fences at Towcester in November by neck from Flintoff: creditable effort when runner-up, to Wiscalitus at Ludlow and Fast Forward at Chepstow: stays 3m: acts on heavy going. *H. D. Daly*   **c119 h–**

PRIOLAINE (FR) 4 br.f. Cadoudal (FR) – Biolaine (FR) (Iron Duke (FR)) [2006/7 F16d F16m^5 F16s Apr 1] 31,000 3-y-o: third foal: half-sister to 8.5f winner Melanie du Chenet (by Nikos): dam, winner up to 14.5f on Flat, also successful up to 21f over jumps: more signs of temperament than ability in bumpers: tried blinkered. *I. R. Ferguson, Ireland*   **F–**

PRIORITISATION (IRE) 8 b.g. Shernazar – No One Knows (IRE) (Kemal (FR)) [2006/7 c89: c23f^F Sep 10] fair pointer, won in March: form in chases only when third in hunter. *Mrs K. Waldron*   **c–**

PRIORS DALE 7 b.g. Lahib (USA) – Mathaayl (USA) (Shadeed (USA)) [2006/7 c130, h125: 16m c18d* c16d* c16d^6 c16d* 16g^5 c16g Apr 12] tall, useful-looking gelding: fairly useful handicap hurdler: fifth to Fleet Street in strongly-run race at Newbury, looking set to win 2 out before tiring: useful novice chaser: won at Fontwell (maiden) and Kempton in November and Wincanton (beat Flying Enterprise by 4 lengths in handicap) in March: ran poorly in Grade 3 handicap at Aintree final outing: likely to prove best around 2m: acts on heavy ground: often makes running. *Miss E. C. Lavelle*   **c136 h125**

Mrs L. Alexander's "Priors Dale"

John Smith's Novices' Handicap Chase (Conditional Jockeys and Amateur Riders), Aintree—
Private Be survives a mistake at the last to beat Bob Hall

PRIVATE BE 8 b.g. Gunner B – Foxgrove (Kinglet) [2006/7 h122: 17s* c17v² 16d **c137** c17v* c20g³ c20g* Apr 14] workmanlike gelding: fairly useful hurdler: off 11 months, **h123** won handicap at Exeter in December by 3 lengths from Hawridge Star: well beaten in totesport Trophy at Newbury third start: useful form over fences: won maiden at Bangor in March and conditional/amateur novice handicap at Aintree (improved to beat Bob Hall by 3 lengths, despite tending to wander under pressure and blundering last) in April: will stay beyond 2½m: raced on good ground or softer (acts on heavy): may prove best on left-handed tracks: pulls hard. *P. J. Hobbs*

PRIVATE BENJAMIN 7 gr.g. Ridgewood Ben – Jilly Woo (Environment Friend) **h–** [2006/7 h89: 20m⁶ 18m Jun 6] leggy gelding: winning hurdler, no show last 3 starts: tried blinkered. *M. R. Hoad*

PRIVATE GARCIA (IRE) 7 b.g. Erins Isle – Southern Song (Persian Bold) [2006/7 **h96** 20g³ 21sᵖᵘ 21gᵖᵘ Mar 26] point/bumper winner: off 16 months and left D. Murphy, modest form over hurdles, close third when going lame before last in novice at Plumpton final start: should stay beyond 2½m: tongue tied. *D. G. Bridgwater*

PRIVATE NOTE 7 b.g. Accordion – Lady Geneva (Royalty) [2006/7 F16v* Nov 22] **F93** fairly useful form in bumpers: off 22 months, improved effort when winning at Chepstow in November by 2 lengths from Rood Report: will be suited by 2½m+. *S. Pike*

PRIZE FIGHTER (IRE) 5 b.g. Desert Sun – Papal (Selkirk (USA)) [2006/7 h120: **h–** 16s⁵ Jan 1] big, useful-looking gelding: fairly useful juvenile hurdler: off 10 months and left Jonjo O'Neill, raced freely when well held in handicap only outing in 2006/7: likely to prove best 2m: raced on good ground or softer: joined H. Cecil. *D. Carroll*

PROCAS DE THAIX (FR) 4 ch.g. Ragmar (FR) – Isca de Thaix (FR) (Cimon) **F111** [2006/7 F12v* F16s² F16m Apr 26] 15,000 3-y-o: compact gelding: second foal: half-brother to fair 2m hurdler Najca de Thaix (by Marmato): dam unraced: useful form in bumpers: won 17-runner 4-y-o event at Newbury on debut in January by ¾ length from Just A Thought: favourite, ½-length second of 21 to Diamond Harry there next time. *N. J. Henderson*

PROCRASTINATE (IRE) 5 ch.g. Rossini (USA) – May Hinton (Main Reef) [2006/7 **h69** h–: 16g⁴ 16g 16v Dec 19] poor form over hurdles. *R. F. Fisher*

PRO DANCER (USA) 9 b. or br.h. Pleasant Tap (USA) – Shihama (USA) (Shadeed **c102** (USA)) [2006/7 c98, h108: 19s² 21s⁴ 19g² c20g⁴ Apr 10] fair hurdler/handicap chaser: **h104** stays 21f: acts on any going: tried blinkered, in cheekpieces last 6 starts. *P. Bowen*

PROF DE L'ISLE (FR) 4 b.g. Kadalko (FR) – Gratiene de L'Isle (FR) (Altayan) **F84 p** [2006/7 F12g Mar 23] 16,000 3-y-o: rather unfurnished gelding: fourth foal: half-brother

782

to fair staying hurdler/chaser Moustique de L'Isle (by Dom Alco) and fair 2m hurdler Open de L'Isle (by Funny Baby): dam placed up to around 1½m: ninth of 18 in 4-y-o bumper on debut: likely to improve. *H. D. Daly*

PROFESSOR HIGGINS (IRE) 4 ch.g. Flemensfirth (USA) – Shuil Iontach (IRE) (Oscar (IRE)) [2006/7 F16d² Apr 1] first foal: dam unraced half-sister to several winners, including fairly useful chaser Good Step (by Be My Native): won point in February: fairly useful form when length second to Caravino in bumper at Limerick: sold to join J. Howard Johnson 110,000 gns Doncaster May Sales. *David A. Kiely, Ireland* **F97**

PROFESSOR JACK (IRE) 7 ch.g. Lord of Appeal – Lady Ghislaine (FR) (Lydian (FR)) [2006/7 c22v^F c21v² c19v² Feb 25] lengthy gelding: fourth foal: half-brother to fair hurdler Reminiscer (by Coronado), stays 2½m: dam winning hurdler/fair chaser up to 21f: won maiden Irish point in 2006: fairly useful form in chases: every chance when fell 2 out at Fontwell, and runner-up both completed starts, on second occasion beaten 13 lengths by Heez A Dreamer in novice at Exeter: should stay beyond 21f: front runner. *Miss E. C. Lavelle* **c117**

PROFOWENS (IRE) 9 b.g. Welsh Term – Cutty Sark (Strong Gale) [2006/7 c106, h–: c28s^F c25g⁴ c28d^pu c30s^pu c27v³ c32v^pu c25g* c25m⁴ Apr 20] workmanlike gelding: fair handicap chaser: won at Wetherby (by 12 lengths) in April: stays 27f: acts on heavy going: blinkered/in cheekpieces nowadays: ungenuine. *P. Beaumont* **c104 §**
h–

PROGRAMME GIRL (IRE) 5 ch.m. Definite Article – Targhyb (IRE) (Unfuwain (USA)) [2006/7 F92: F17s* F16m² F16d² 17v² Dec 12] fairly useful in bumpers, won at Bangor in May: favourite, encouraging second in maiden won by Mohayer at Sedgefield on hurdling debut: sure to improve. *G. A. Swinbank* **h97 p**
F104

PROGRESSIVE (IRE) 9 ch.g. Be My Native (USA) – Move Forward (Deep Run) [2006/7 c–x, h–: 22s^pu 20f⁶ 20m⁵ 24f³ 27m Aug 12] bumper winner: modest handicap hurdler: lost confidence after early blunder only outing over fences: stays 3m: probably acts on any going: in eyeshields/blinkers last 2 starts: ungenuine. *Jonjo O'Neill* **c– x**
h94 §

PROJECT SUNSHINE (GER) 4 b. or br.g. Xaar – Prada (GER) (Lagunas) [2006/7 18g^ur 16m 16s^pu Nov 11] quite good-topped gelding: little form on Flat for J. Osborne: no show in juvenile hurdles: tried blinkered: sold 1,200 gns Doncaster November Sales. *O. Sherwood* **h–**

PROPER ARTICLE (IRE) 5 b.g. Definite Article – Feather 'n Lace (IRE) (Green Desert (USA)) [2006/7 h115: 20s^pu 16s 16v Nov 26] unfurnished gelding: fair at best on Flat (stays 1½m): fairly useful form in juvenile hurdles: no show in handicaps in 2006/7: sold out of D. Weld's stable 20,000 gns Doncaster October Sales after first outing (blinkered): raced mainly at 2m. *Miss J. E. Foster* **h–**

PROPRIETOR (UAE) 5 ch.g. Timber Country (USA) – Potentille (IRE) (Caerleon (USA)) [2006/7 F16m⁴ 17d Nov 8] first foal: dam, Irish 1½m winner, sister to Derby Italiano winner Mukhalif: poor form when fourth in bumper: again soon off bridle when soundly beaten in novice on hurdling debut: sold £700 Ascot December Sales. *D. McCain Jnr* **h–**
F68

PROPRIOCEPTION (IRE) 5 ch.m. Danehill Dancer (IRE) – Pepper And Salt (IRE) (Double Schwartz) [2006/7 h92§: 16d 19m* 20g 24s 20v^pu Jan 11] leggy, close-coupled mare: modest maiden on Flat: modest handicap hurdler, sold out of A. King's stable 3,200 gns Doncaster May Sales after first outing: won at Hereford in September: ran badly after: stays 19f: acts on good to firm and good to soft going: tried visored: ungenuine. *W. K. Goldsworthy* **h97 §**

PROTOCOL (IRE) 13 b.g. Taufan (USA) – Ukraine's Affair (USA) (The Minstrel (CAN)) [2006/7 h81: 22g 17v² 16d^bd Oct 20] compact gelding: poor handicap hurdler: stays 2½m: acts on heavy going: tried visored, usually wears cheekpieces: tongue tied. *Mrs S. Lamyman* **h74**

PROUD SCHOLAR (USA) 5 br. or b.m. Royal Academy (USA) – Proud Fact (USA) (Known Fact (USA)) [2006/7 17v 16s⁶ 16g 22f^pu Apr 5] sister to winning 2m hurdler Loudspeaker: modest maiden on Flat: no form over hurdles. *R. A. Kvisla* **h–**

PROUD TO PRESENT (IRE) 6 b.g. Presenting – Proud Polly (IRE) (Pollerton) [2006/7 22s 21g 22m³ Apr 22] tall gelding: brother to fair hurdler Ellerslie George, stays 25f, and half-brother to 2m hurdle winner Mr Batim (by Alphabatim): dam unraced: won maiden Irish point in 2006: third in novice at Stratford, first form over hurdles: will be suited by 3m: may be capable of better. *B. G. Powell* **h79 +**

PROVOCATIVE (FR) 9 b. or br.g. Useful (FR) – All Blue (FR) (Noir Et Or) [2006/7   **c109**
c132, h–: 24s^{pu} c20s^3 c21s^3 c20g* Mar 28] tall, quite good-topped gelding: winning   **h–**
hurdler: fairly useful hunter chaser nowadays: sold out of M. Todhunter's stable 19,000
gns Doncaster May Sales after first outing: won at Kempton in March by 9 lengths from
Spring Margot, left clear thirteenth: stays 2½m: raced mainly on good going or softer
(acts on heavy). *D. J. Harding-Jones*

PSEUDONYM (IRE) 5 ch.g. Daylami (IRE) – Stage Struck (IRE) (Sadler's Wells   **h116**
(USA)) [2006/7 h109: 16f 17m* 19d^4 22g Jul 5] leggy, lengthy gelding: has reportedly
had wind operation: fair on Flat (stays 15f), successful in June (disqualified after failing
dope test): fairly useful hurdler: won novice at Hereford (by 1¾ lengths from Brads
House) in June: laboured effort final start: stays 21f: acts on soft and firm going: tried
tongue tied. *M. F. Harris*

PSYCHIATRIST 6 ch.g. Dr Devious (IRE) – Zahwa (Cadeaux Genereux) [2006/7 16d   **h95 ?**
16v 16g4 16f^{pu} Apr 5] sturdy gelding: useful on Flat (barely stays 9f), left R. Hannon/off
10 months prior to below form last 3 starts: modest form at best over hurdles: likely to
prove best at easy 2m. *Miss J. R. Tooth*

PSYCHIC STAR 4 b.f. Diktat – Southern Psychic (USA) (Alwasmi (USA)) [2006/7   **h70**
16g 16d 18s^3 16v^5 17m Apr 15] fairly useful but none too resolute on Flat (stays 9.7f),
sold out of W. Swinburn's stable 8,000 gns Newmarket Autumn Sales: poor juvenile
hurdler. *Miss Lucinda V. Russell*

PSYCHO CAT 4 b.g. Hunting Lion (IRE) – Canadian Capers (Ballacashtal (CAN))   **h88 d**
[2006/7 17m* 17d^F 16m 17g^{pu} Apr 18] rather leggy gelding: fair 6f/7f winner at 2 yrs and
several good placed efforts in 2006, but became increasingly temperamental: fortunate
winner of juvenile at Newton Abbot on hurdling debut: no form in similar events after,
sold out of P. Blockley's stable £7,400 Ascot August Sales before third start. *S. T. Lewis*

PSYCHOMODO 5 b.g. Mark of Esteem (IRE) – En Vacances (IRE) (Old Vic) [2006/7   **h108**
F91: F16m^4 F17s^2 F16s^3 18s^2 20m^{pu} Mar 31] well-made gelding: fair form in frame in   **F93**
bumpers: much better effort in maiden hurdles when second to Benetwood at Fontwell:
reportedly lost a shoe next time: should stay 2½m: acts on soft ground. *B. G. Powell*

PUBLIC REACTION 9 b.g. Husyan (USA) – Corrie's Girl (Whistling Deer) [2006/7   **c138 x**
c128, h111: c20g c22s^5 c22g* c20v^{pu} c22v^3 c18s^2 c20s^4 c28s^{pu} Feb 4] winning hurdler: **h–**
useful chaser: won minor event at Thurles in November by 17 lengths from Mossy Green:
placed in latest events after: stays 2¾m: acts on heavy going: front runner: prone to
mistakes. *E. U. Hales, Ireland*

PUCKS COURT 10 b.g. Nomadic Way (USA) – Miss Puck (Tepukei) [2006/7 h65:   **c–**
c16m^{pu} 16d^6 c16g^{pu} Apr 23] lengthy gelding: maiden hurdler: no form in 2006/7, includ-   **h–**
ing over fences. *I. A. Brown*

PUKKA (IRE) 6 b.g. Sadler's Wells (USA) – Puce (Darshaan) [2006/7 17g^5 16g*   **h124 p**
Dec 20] useful on Flat (should stay 1¾m), sold out of L. Cumani's stable 50,000 gns
Newmarket Autumn (2005) Sales, and gelded: easily better effort over hurdles (raced
freely on debut) when winning maiden at Musselburgh decisively by 6 lengths from
Modicum: tongue tied: capable of better still. *C. R. Egerton*

PUKKA TIQUE 4 b.g. Groom Dancer (USA) – Surf Bird (Shareef Dancer (USA))   **h99**
[2006/7 17g* 17m 22m^2 Apr 22] half-brother to 3 winning jumpers, including fair chaser
Kelantan (by Kris), stays 25f: fair maiden on Flat (stays 1½m): fair form in juvenile
hurdles: won at Hereford in November: stays easy 2¾m: raced on good/good to firm
going: joined Miss J. Davis. *R. Hollinshead*

PULBOROUGH 4 b.f. Rakaposhi King – Miss Muire (Scallywag) [2006/7 F14s aF16g   **h–**
21m^6 Apr 8] fourth foal: dam winning pointer: well beaten in bumpers/novice hurdle.   **F–**
Mrs H. J. Cobb

PUMBOO (FR) 4 gr.g. Dadarissime (FR) – Contessina (FR) (Mistigri) [2006/7 F14v   **F–**
Dec 2] tall, close-coupled gelding: sixth foal: half-brother to fairly useful 2m hurdler
Kimbambo (by Genereux Genie) and fair 2m to 3¼m hurdler/chaser Infini (by Le Nain
Jaune): dam 1½m winner in France: well backed, well beaten in 3-y-o bumper on debut.
G. A. Harker

PUMPKIN PICKLE 6 b.m. Wace (USA) – Gypsy Crystal (USA) (Flying Saucer)   **h–**
[2006/7 h–, F73: 20m^6 22s^6 24f^{pu} Jul 19] little impact over hurdles. *P. R. Rodford*

PUNJABI 4 b.g. Komaite (USA) – Competa (Hernando (FR)) [2006/7 16m* 16v*   **h145**
17g^4 16g^2 16m* Apr 26]
    As the season progressed, it became increasingly apparent that Mick
Fitzgerald was having second thoughts about his decision to bring his riding career
to an end on Grand National day. Fitzgerald is clearly still enjoying his job despite

having reached veteran status (he will be thirty-seven in the next season) and will have been more than happy to have notched up sixty wins in Britain during the latest campaign, particularly as he then rounded it off in style with a victory in a Grade 1 event in Ireland. That was courtesy of Punjabi in the Ballymore Properties Champion Four Year Old Hurdle, the latest in a long line of big-race winners Fitzgerald has ridden for Nicky Henderson since they teamed up in the mid-'nineties. Punjabi is one of many Fitzgerald will be very much looking forward to partnering again in 2007/8, another being Punjabi's sidelined stablemate Trabolgan on whom Fitzgerald won both the Royal & SunAlliance Chase and Hennessy Cognac Gold Cup in 2005.

Punjabi joined Henderson after being bought for 42,000 guineas at the Newmarket Autumn Sales, his price reflecting the fairly useful form he had shown at around a mile as a three-year-old when trained by Geraldine Rees, for whom he was successful at Newcastle, Nottingham and Ayr. Given his distance requirements on the Flat, it appeared that a sharp two miles might be required to see Punjabi to best advantage over hurdles. He was started off in January under such conditions, in a juvenile event at Ludlow. With the good to firm ground placing even more emphasis on speed at the trip, Punjabi made a highly encouraging hurdling debut in upsetting the odds laid on Junior, jumping soundly, leading three out and beating the favourite comfortably by three and a half lengths. It was a very different test which faced Punjabi on his next start, at Kempton in late-February. The race was the Grade 2 Racing Post Adonis Juvenile Hurdle, in which he faced five rivals including two who were already useful winners, Parrain and Poquelin. More to the point, it took place on heavy going, on which Punjabi was unproven. Even if Punjabi acted on the ground, there had to be a doubt about his stamina under the conditions, though that was something which appeared not to trouble Fitzgerald who was seen to particularly good effect once the race got under way, the field having stood for around seventeen seconds after the tapes went up. Fitzgerald employed front-running tactics on Punjabi, soon establishing a twenty-length lead without overtaxing his mount, then kicking on again after three out. Continuing to jump fluently, Punjabi extended his lead in the straight, winning by nineteen lengths from Parrain. It was a tricky race to assess but, equally, it was clear that Punjabi's impressive performance wasn't solely down to good tactics.

Punjabi's three subsequent races were all Grade 1 events and he came across the season's leading juvenile in the first two of those. He ran to a similar level as he had at Kempton when fourth, almost seventeen lengths behind Katchit, over seventeen furlongs in the Triumph Hurdle at Cheltenham, travelling strongly

Ballymore Properties Champion Four Year Old Hurdle, Punchestown—Punjabi (No.8) becomes the seventh British-trained winner in ten years; Financial Reward fares best of the home-trained runners

up with the pace and leading briefly before weakening in the straight. Next time, faced with slightly less of a test of stamina and ridden more patiently, Punjabi reduced the deficit to four lengths in finishing an excellent second to Katchit in the Anniversary Hurdle at Aintree, recovering from a mistake three out to chase the winner between the last two flights but edging left under pressure and unable to make any further impression. With no Katchit to worry about, Punjabi looked to have a gilt-edged opportunity to go one better in the Champion Four Year Old Hurdle at Punchestown, a race Henderson and Fitzgerald had won back in 1999 with Katarino. The leading Irish-trained juveniles looked a fair way below the pick of their British counterparts, and Punjabi was sent off a short-priced favourite to account for nine of them. He did so without having to run anywhere near his Aintree form. Again patiently ridden, Punjabi made smooth progress to lead two out, where he wasn't fluent, looked likely to win decisively entering the straight, but needed riding out after the last as he idled and his only challenger Financial Reward rallied, only three quarters of a length separating the pair at the line.

		Nureyev	Northern Dancer
Punjabi (b.g. 2003)	Komaite (USA) (b 1983)	(b 1977)	Special
		Brown Berry (b 1960)	Mount Marcy
			Brown Baby
	Competa (b 1999)	Hernando (b 1990)	Niniski
			Whakilyric
		Mo Chos Chle (b 1994)	Indian Ridge
			Liebside Lass

Mr Raymond Tooth's "Punjabi"

Punjabi's sire Komaite, who died in 2003, is an influence for speed and the bulk of his success as a sire has come on the Flat. The dam Competa is an unraced daughter of Mo Chos Chle, the winner of a two-year-old maiden over a mile at Listowel on the second of her two starts. Punjabi is Competa's first foal. Her second is Punjabi's full-sister Kompete, a cheaply-bought filly who showed fairly useful form at two, winning over five furlongs. Two miles will prove Punjabi's optimum trip over hurdles and, while he has a fair amount of improvement to make if he is to trouble the best, there should be better to come. The sturdy Punjabi is a good sort physically, very much the type to train on. *N. J. Henderson*

PUNTAL (FR) 11 b.g. Bering – Saveur (Ardross) [2006/7 c–, h–: c25s⁵ c24d⁵ c25s² c24v c33pu c36g Apr 14] medium-sized gelding: useful chaser nowadays: stays easy 29f: acts on any going: visored once (downed tools), in cheekpieces last 4 starts: tongue tied: often front runner: unreliable. *D. E. Pipe* — **c135 §** / **h–**

PUR DE SIVOLA (FR) 4 b.g. Robin Des Champs (FR) – Gamine d'Ici (FR) (Cadoudal (FR)) [2006/7 17s c17s c17s⁵ c17s⁵ c17s³ 18s³ 19v* 20dpu Mar 17] good-topped gelding: third foal: half-brother to 19f hurdle winner Myborg de Sivola (by Cyborg): dam unraced: fair hurdler: second outing after being sold from T. Trapenard €125,000, won novice at Taunton in February: every chance when lost action next time: similar form in 3-y-o events over fences when trained in France: should stay 2½m: raced on going softer than good: remains likely to do better over hurdles. *A. King* — **c111** / **h108 p**

PURE BRIEF (IRE) 10 b.g. Brief Truce (USA) – Epure (Bellypha) [2006/7 c88, h73: c16g² c20g⁵ c20m⁵ c16m³ c17m⁵ c17d⁴ c16g⁵ c16d⁴ c16d⁵ Nov 11] angular gelding: winning hurdler: modest handicap chaser: best around 2m: acts on any going: wears headgear. *J. Mackie* — **c88** / **h–**

PURE GENIUS (IRE) 4 gr.f. Exit To Nowhere (USA) – Lady of Gortmerron (IRE) (Orchestra) [2006/7 F17g Apr 19] rather leggy filly: first foal: dam fairly useful but temperamental staying chaser: eighth of 18 in mares bumper on debut. *D. E. Pipe* — **F79**

PURE IMAGINATION (IRE) 6 ch.g. Royal Academy (USA) – Ivory Bride (Domynsky) [2006/7 16g Nov 15] tall, good-topped gelding: fair on Flat (stays 8.6f), successful in October: none too fluent when seventh in novice at Warwick on hurdling debut: likely to prove best at easy 2m. *J. M. Bradley* — **h77**

PURE PLEASURE (NZ) 8 gr.g. Casual Lies (USA) – Pure Glory (NZ) (First Norman (USA)) [2006/7 h87: 19g⁵ 20mro 19s⁵ c16m⁶ Sep 28] rather leggy gelding: poor novice hurdler: well held in handicap on chasing debut. *N. M. Babbage* — **c–** / **h73 +**

PURPLE MOON (IRE) 4 ch.g. Galileo (IRE) – Vanishing Prairie (USA) (Alysheba (USA)) [2006/7 16d* 16m² Feb 4] half-brother to 2m hurdle winner Vanishing Dancer (by Llandaff): useful on Flat, sold out of Sir Michael Stoute's stable 440,000 gns Newmarket Autumn Sales and gelded: 6/4-on, successful hurdling debut in novice at Musselburgh: far from fluent when 12 lengths second of 4 to Degas Art in juvenile there following month, also tending to hang left: needed to improve jumping if he was to progress, but has gone back to the Flat, joining L. Cumani and winning Ebor in August. *N. G. Richards* — **h120**

PURPLE PATCH 9 b.m. Afzal – My Purple Prose (Rymer) [2006/7 h100: 17s³ 16d 17d 16v* 21s² 20g² 21g Apr 19] small, leggy mare: fair handicap hurdler: made all in mares event at Warwick in February: stays 2¾m, effective at shorter: acts on heavy going. *C. L. Popham* — **h105**

PURPLE SHUFFLE (IRE) 9 b.g. Accordion – Penny Shuffle (IRE) (Decent Fellow) [2006/7 c20s c16s⁵ c22v* c24vpu c20m c21m⁵ Apr 27] lengthy gelding: second foal: dam lightly raced in bumpers: fair hurdler: better over fences, won Grade 3 novice at Punchestown (beat Vic Venturi by head) in November: creditable efforts last 2 starts, when seventh to One Cool Cookie in Grade 1 novice at Fairyhouse and fifth to Alexander Taipan in winnable novice handicap at Punchestown: barely stays 3m: acts on heavy and good to firm going: usually tongue tied. *P. A. Fahy, Ireland* — **c123** / **h–**

PURR 6 b.g. Pursuit of Love – Catawba (Mill Reef (USA)) [2006/7 h58: 22g 22m 23v⁵ 20mrtr 23d 16s⁵ 16s 19s⁶ 19d 16g 20gur 21g³ Apr 23] close-coupled gelding: bad maiden hurdler: wears cheekpieces: tongue tied on debut. *M. Wigham* — **h–**

PURSLOW 7 b.m. Petoski – Return To Romance (Trojan Fen) [2006/7 F16f Apr 30] fifth foal: dam, winner up to 1½m on Flat, modest hurdler up to 2¾m: always behind in bumper on debut. *T. Wall* — **F—**

PUSH THE PORT (IRE) 5 b. or br.g. Dushyantor (USA) – Port Queen (IRE) (Nasha- **h92**
maa) [2006/7 F85: 16s 16s⁴ 22d³ Jan 30] lengthy gelding: third in maiden bumper: modest form in novice hurdles: stays 2¾m: raced on ground softer than good.
N. J. Gifford

PUTITAWAYFORAYEAR (IRE) 5 ch.g. Old Vic – Badsworth Madam (Over The **h–**
River (FR)) [2006/7 16v Feb 15] ninth foal: half-brother to winning pointer by Roselier:
dam unraced half-sister to top-class 2m chaser Badsworth Boy: tailed off in maiden
hurdle on debut. *D. E. Pipe*

PUZZLE PALACE (IRE) 6 b.m. Fourstars Allstar (USA) – Brandy Hill Girl (Green **h–**
Shoon) [2006/7 F16g 16mᵖᵘ Apr 24] £2,400 4-y-o: sister to 3m chase winner Casalani **F–**
and half-sister to winning pointers by Executive Perk and King's Ride: dam unraced: no
show in various events. *R. M. Stronge*

PYLEIGH LADY 6 b.m. Zaffaran (USA) – Lady Callernish (Callernish) [2006/7 h92, **h115**
F72: 19d⁵ 16v² 24s² 20v² 19g* 22g² Apr 1] angular mare: fairly useful hurdler: left
S. Burrough, much improved in 2006/7, won conditional/amateur novice handicap at
Newbury in March by 2½ lengths from Pigeon Island: stays 3m: raced on good ground or
softer (acts on heavy): ridden by conditional/amateur in 2006/7: held up. *P. J. Hobbs*

PYRAMID 5 ch.g. Pivotal – Mary Cornwallis (Primo Dominie) [2006/7 16d⁶ Nov 11] **h–**
modest maiden on Flat (stays 1m), left A. Lidderdale after final outing in 2006: well held
in seller on hurdling debut: sold 1,200 gns Doncaster November Sales. *V. Smith*

Q

QDOS (IRE) 5 br.g. Presenting – Emma's Way (IRE) (Le Bavard (FR)) [2006/7 20s **h77**
25g⁶ Mar 17] €64,000 4-y-o: sixth foal: half-brother to 3m hurdle winner Aisjm (by
Anshan): dam, placed in bumper, half-sister to useful staying chaser Bitofamixup, from
good family: poor form on first of 2 starts in novice hurdles. *J. Howard Johnson*

QIAN SHAN (IRE) 6 ch.g. Anshan – Bay Cottage (IRE) (Quayside) [2006/7 F16s **h–**
F17v³ F16g 17g 17mᶠ Apr 17] €9,500 4-y-o, resold €15,000 4-y-o, resold €12,000 4-y-o: **F–**
second foal: dam bumper winner: no solid form in bumpers/over hurdles: tried tongue
tied. *Mrs S. Gardner*

QUAI DU ROI (IRE) 5 ch.g. Desert King (IRE) – Emly Express (IRE) (High Estate) **h110**
[2006/7 16f² 16d³ 16g* 16g³ 16dᶠ Nov 11] angular gelding: first foal: dam 11.5f winner:
fairly useful on Flat: fair hurdler: won handicap at Roscommon in August: well kept
when fell last in novice handicap at Cheltenham: likely to prove best at 2m with emphasis
on speed: joined K. Ryan, refused to race on Flat in April. *T. G. McCourt, Ireland*

QUAINTON HILLS 13 b.g. Gildoran – Spin Again (Royalty) [2006/7 c–x, h–: 19m **c– x**
19d⁶ 22d 19d⁵ 23g⁵ Apr 3] medium-sized gelding: winning chaser/maiden hurdler, little **h–**
form since 2003/4: tried tongue tied: sketchy jumper of fences. *D. R. Stoddart*

QUALIFY 4 b.g. Mark of Esteem (IRE) – Raneen Alwatar (Sadler's Wells (USA)) **h–**
[2006/7 16d Nov 24] close-coupled gelding: fair on Flat (stays 1¼m), sold out of
M. Channon's stable 16,000 gns Newmarket July Sales: soundly beaten in juvenile on
hurdling debut. *Miss S. West*

QUALITY CONTROL (IRE) 6 b.g. Tiraaz (USA) – Booking Note (IRE) (Brush **F84**
Aside (USA)) [2006/7 F16g⁴ Apr 23] first foal: dam ran twice: fourth to impressive
Nodforms Paula in maiden bumper at Hexham on debut: likely to be suited by further
than 2m. *Ferdy Murphy*

QUANTOCK VENTURE 7 b.g. Beau Venture (USA) – Eidolon (Rousillon (USA)) **h–**
[2006/7 16s 15pᵘ 24mᵖᵘ Apr 15] first foal: dam, of no account, half-sister to useful
hurdler/chaser Foundry Lane, stayed 2½m: no form over hurdles: tried tongue tied. *Miss
Sarah Robinson*

QUARRY BOY (IRE) 11 ch.g. Beau Sher – Kundalu (Never Return (USA)) [2006/7 **c–**
c20gᵖᵘ Mar 22] angular gelding: fair chaser/modest handicap hurdler: sold out of **h–**
E. Sheehy's stable 800 gns Doncaster May (2006) Sales and off 11 months, no show only
start in 2006/7: raced mainly on ground softer than good: often in
cheekpieces/blinkered. *Miss L. Day*

QUARRY ISLAND (IRE) 6 b.m. Turtle Island (IRE) – Last Quarry (Handsome **h71**
Sailor) [2006/7 h–: 20m³ 16gᵖᵘ Apr 23] tall mare: maiden hurdler: off 14 months, poor

form on return: shaped as if amiss 2 weeks later: stays easy 2½m: acts on soft and good to firm going. *M. Todhunter*

QUARRYMOUNT 6 b.g. Polar Falcon (USA) – Quilt (Terimon) [2006/7 c84, h93: c20m³ c21g⁶ 16m² 16d⁶ Oct 5] sturdy, useful-looking gelding: modest maiden hurdler/ chaser: twice successful in points in 2007: should stay beyond 2m: acts on good to firm and good to soft going: tongue tied in 2006/7. *J. A. B. Old*   **c83 h89**

QUARRY TOWN (IRE) 5 b.g. Pistolet Bleu (IRE) – Dano Doo (IRE) (Orchestra) [2006/7 F17s F17s² 17s³ 21g⁵ Mar 23] useful-looking gelding: second foal: dam unraced out of half-sister to Welsh National winner Charlie H: won maiden Irish point in 2006: easily better effort in bumpers (useful form) when short-headed by American Cricket in 16-runner event at Hereford: shaped with promise when not unduly punished over hurdles: likely to improve. *Miss H. C. Knight*   **h100 p F107**

QUARTANO (GER) 4 ch.g. Platini (GER) – Queen's Diamond (GER) (Konigsstuhl (GER)) [2006/7 F13s* F12v* F16d⁴ Feb 17] strong, good-bodied gelding: fourth foal: half-brother to 3 winners, including winning hurdler/chaser Quirino (by Lagunas), stays 19f: dam German maiden: useful form when successful first 2 starts in bumpers, in 3-y-o race at Exeter in December and listed 4-y-o event at Cheltenham (beat Sophocles by 7 lengths) in January: upped in trip, raced too freely next time. *Carl Llewellyn*   **F112**

QUARTERBACK (IRE) 6 b.g. Bob Back (USA) – Bawnanell (Viking (USA)) [2006/7 F16v⁶ F16v⁴ 22dᵖᵘ 19v⁵ 22g⁵ 22m* Apr 22] €17,000 3-y-o, €20,000 4-y-o, resold 26,000 4-y-o: close-coupled gelding: eighth foal: brother to fair hurdler Backcraft, stays 2½m, and 2¾m chase winner Bobbawn: dam Irish 5f/6f winner: fourth in bumper: modest form in novice hurdles: in cheekpieces, won at Stratford in April, idling: stays 2¾m: tongue tied after hurdling debut. *C. P. Morlock*   **h99 F82**

QUARTERGILL 6 b.g. I'm Supposin (IRE) – Nessfield (Tumble Wind) [2006/7 F16v⁵ Mar 22] sixth foal: half-brother to 3m hunter chase winner Brer Bear (by Perpendicular): dam, fair hurdler/winning chaser who stayed 3¼m: tailed off in bumper on debut. *A. M. Crow*   **F—**

QUARTER MASTERS (IRE) 8 b.g. Mujadil (USA) – Kentucky Wildcat (Be My Guest (USA)) [2006/7 c22s* May 21] lengthy gelding: winning hurdler: poor chaser: successful in 3-finisher hunter at Market Rasen in May: also won point in January: stays 2¾m: acts on soft going: tried in cheekpieces. *Nick Kent*   **c83 h—**

QUASIMODO (IRE) 5 b.g. Night Shift (USA) – Daziyra (IRE) (Doyoun) [2006/7 h100: 16sᵖᵘ 17s 16v 16m⁵ 20g³ 20gᵖᵘ Apr 14] small, sturdy gelding: modest handicap hurdler: lame final start: stays 2½m: acts on soft and good to firm going: sometimes let down by jumping/temperament. *A. W. Carroll*   **h95**

QUATRE HEURES (FR) 5 b.g. Vertical Speed (FR) – Macyrienne (FR) (Saint Cyrien (FR)) [2006/7 h136p: 19s 19s⁶ 16d 16d Feb 10] tall, leggy gelding: useful juvenile hurdler, won Grade 1 at Punchestown: below best in 2006/7: should stay beyond 2m: raced on good going or softer: usually waited with. *W. P. Mullins, Ireland*   **h126**

QUAY MEADOW (IRE) 5 b. or br.g. Alderbrook – Harp Song (Auction Ring (USA)) [2006/7 F16s F16s 25gᵖᵘ 24m⁶ Mar 25] 8,000 4-y-o: half-brother to 3 winners, including 19f bumper winner Rathure (by Executive Perk) and fair chaser up to 2½m Rathgibbon (by Phardante): dam 2-y-o 5f winner: no form in bumpers or over hurdles. *J. R. Norton*   **h— F—**

QUAZAR (IRE) 9 b.g. Inzar (USA) – Evictress (IRE) (Sharp Victor (USA)) [2006/7 c115, h—: c20mᵖᵘ c20g⁶ c21g³ c22g³ c24g 21g 21g 22s Dec 2] strong, compact gelding: fair handicap chaser nowadays: one-time smart hurdler, well held in handicaps last 3 outings: barely stays 3m: acts on any going: usually wears headgear: tongue tied: ungenuine. *Jonjo O'Neill*   **c108 § h— §**

QUEEN BOUDICCA 8 b.m. El Conquistador – Tinsel Rose (Porto Bello) [2006/7 19v⁶ 22d Feb 1] sturdy mare: poor maiden pointer: mistakes when well held in mares novice hurdles: tried blinkered. *B. R. Millman*   **h—**

QUEEN EXCALIBUR 8 ch.m. Sabrehill (USA) – Blue Room (Gorytus (USA)) [2006/7 c—, h81x: 20f c16f⁵ c20gᵖᵘ Aug 14] winning hurdler: no form over fences: makes mistakes. *C. Roberts*   **c— h— x**

QUEENIES GIRL 11 b.m. Primitive Rising (USA) – Riverboat Queen (Rapid River) [2006/7 c79: c20dᶠ May 24] winning pointer, including in March: modest form in hunters, in second when fell heavily 2 out at Sedgefield: stays 25f. *Paul Frank*   **c78**

QUEEN MUSA 5 b.m. Parthian Springs – Metannee (The Brianstan) [2006/7 F16s F14s⁶ Dec 23] sister to fair stayer Heart Springs and closely related to winning 2m hurdler   **F—**

Belle Derriere (by Kylian): dam, winning hurdler, stayed 21f: well held in bumpers. *Dr J. R. J. Naylor*

QUEEN OF DIAMONDS (IRE) 4 b.f. Fruits of Love (USA) – Royal Jubilee (IRE) (King's Theatre (IRE)) [2006/7 16v 16v⁵ 16vᶠ 16g⁶ Mar 17] leggy filly: modest maiden on Flat (stays 1½m), sold out of Mrs P. N. Dutfield's stable 5,400 gns Doncaster November Sales: little impact over hurdles. *Mrs K. Walton*   **h66**

QUEEN OF SONG 5 b.m. Singspiel (IRE) – Fascination Waltz (Shy Groom (USA)) [2006/7 19v⁵ 16v³ 16s Feb 22] leggy, close-coupled mare: well held in maidens on Flat: easily best effort over hurdles when third in mares novice at Plumpton: joined Jim Best. *G. L. Moore*   **h80**

QUEEN OF THE BEES (IRE) 6 ch.m. Bob Back (USA) – Queen of Bakla (FR) (Bikala) [2006/7 F16m F18vᵖᵘ Feb 12] second foal: dam, winning hurdler/chaser around 2m, also won up to 2m on Flat: no promise in bumpers. *C. R. Egerton*   **F–**

QUEENS DESTINY 4 b.f. First Trump – Eventuality (Petoski) [2006/7 16v⁵ 16g 17g Apr 18] smallish filly: started slowly only outing on Flat: well beaten over hurdles. *P. W. Hiatt*   **h–**

QUEEN TARA 5 b.m. Kayf Tara – Lucy Tufty (Vin St Benet) [2006/7 16d⁴ 16g⁶ 16m 19g 16s 17vᵘʳ 16s* 16sᵖᵘ 16gʳᵗʳ Apr 9] lengthy mare: lightly raced and little form on Flat: 66/1-winner of selling handicap at Fakenham in February: little other form over hurdles: bred to be suited by further than 2m: acts on soft going: in cheekpieces last 4 starts: refused to race final outing, and one to treat with caution. *Mrs C. A. Dunnett*   **h72 §**

QUEL FONTENAILLES (FR) 9 b.g. Tel Quel (FR) – Sissi Fontenailles (FR) (Pampabird) [2006/7 h–: 26g⁵ Apr 11] sturdy gelding: little form over hurdles. *L. A. Dace*   **h–**

QUEST ON AIR 8 b.g. Star Quest – Stormy Heights (Golden Heights) [2006/7 h73x: 16m⁶ May 10] not fluent and little form over hurdles: in headgear since debut. *J. R. Jenkins*   **h– x**

QUIBBLE 10 ch.g. Lammtarra (USA) – Bloudan (USA) (Damascus (USA)) [2006/7 c87, h–: 20d⁵ c20g⁶ c25g² c24g* c24s⁵ Feb 1] quite good-topped gelding: lightly raced: maiden hurdler: modest handicap chaser: won novice event at Musselburgh in December: stays 25f: acts on good to soft going: usually blinkered/in cheekpieces. *A. Bailey*   **c92 h–**

QUICK 7 b.g. Kahyasi – Prompt (Old Vic) [2006/7 c–, h132: 23f⁵ c23g² 25d 24s 24d 24g 22m* 24mᶠ Apr 17] leggy gelding: useful handicap hurdler at his best: largely disappointing since 2004/5, though won 5-runner event at Exeter in April by 1½ lengths from Nobody Tells Me: modest form on completed start over fences: suited by 2¾m+: acts on firm and soft going: usually visored: usually front runner/races prominently: unreliable. *D. E. Pipe*   **c89 § h124 §**

QUICK JUDGEMENT (IRE) 5 b.g. Norwich – Bit of A Diva (IRE) (Montelimar (USA)) [2006/7 F16m F16m Apr 24] €3,500 4-y-o: first foal: dam unraced: little impact in bumpers. *B. N. Pollock*   **F–**

QUID PRO QUO (FR) 8 b.g. Cadoudal (FR) – Luzenia (FR) (Armos) [2006/7 c112, h–: c22d³ c21g⁴ Mar 16] lengthy gelding: winning hurdler/pointer: maiden chaser, below best in hunters in 2006/7: stays 23f: acts on soft and good to firm going. *T. Hind*   **c82 h–**

QUINNTOWIN (IRE) 9 b.m. Old Vic – Door Rapper (IRE) (Mandalus) [2006/7 16v c20v c20s c21vᵖᵘ 20vᵖᵘ 20d Mar 17] winning pointer: maiden hurdler/chaser, no form since 2004: tried tongue tied. *S. Wilson, Ireland*   **c– h–**

QUINTA DE LOBO 6 ch.g. Karinga Bay – Miss Club Royal (Avocat) [2006/7 F16s 20g 24vᵖᵘ 24g⁴ Apr 21] good-topped gelding: eighth foal: half-brother to several winners, including winning hurdlers/staying chasers Another Club Royal and Bannister Lane (both by Overbury), latter fairly useful: dam fair staying hurdler/chaser: no show in bumper/novice hurdles. *D. McCain Jnr*   **h– F–**

QUINTESSENTIALLY (IRE) 5 ch.g. Bob's Return (IRE) – Four Moons (IRE) (Cardinal Flower) [2006/7 F18v² F16g Mar 24] €25,000 4-y-o: good-topped gelding: seventh foal: dam, lightly raced in bumpers, half-sister to high-class staying chaser Trabolgan: much better effort in bumpers when 8 lengths second to Choumakeur in maiden at Plumpton: will be suited by further than 2¼m. *Carl Llewellyn*   **F87**

QUIRINO (GER) 6 b.h. Lagunas – Queen's Diamond (GER) (Konigsstuhl (GER)) [2006/7 16s* c19v* 16v² c16g* Apr 1] 10.5f winner on Flat: successful twice over hurdles, including at Neuss: also won both starts over fences, maiden at Towcester (fairly useful form, by head from Esprit Saint) later in January and minor event at Mannheim in   **c116 p h?**

April: stays 19f: acts on heavy ground: open to improvement over fences. *C. von der Recke, Germany*

QUITEB'CHANCE (IRE) 6 ch.m. Aahsaylad – De-Veers Currie (IRE) (Glenstal (USA)) [2006/7 h–, F–: 16sᵖᵘ Jan 20] no sign of ability. *Miss J. S. Davis* **h–**

QUIZZLING (IRE) 9 b.g. Jurado (USA) – Monksville (Monksfield) [2006/7 c82, h–: c22m³ c20m c23m Jul 5] lengthy gelding: poor handicap chaser: stays 25f: acts on soft and good to firm going. *B. J. M. Ryall* **c75 h–**

QUORN MASTER 5 b.g. Bal Harbour – Queen of The Quorn (Governor General) [2006/7 F17m⁵ Jun 7] sixth foal: half-brother to fair 5f to 1¼m winner Tony Tie (by Ardkinglass) and 7f winner Diamond Olivia (by Beveled): dam 6f/7f winner: raced freely when held in bumper on debut. *M. W. Easterby* **F—**

QUOTABLE 6 b.m. Master Willie – General Comment (IRE) (Torus) [2006/7 h88, F85: 17g⁵ 16m* Jun 11] modest hurdler: won mares novice seller at Stratford (sold 8,500 gns) in June: raced mainly around 2m: acts on good to firm going (fourth in bumper on soft). *O. Sherwood* **h88**

QURLISS (IRE) 7 b.m. Synefos (USA) – Best Served Cherry (IRE) (Sheer Grit) [2006/7 16f 18g* 20s⁵ 18vᵖᵘ Apr 9] leggy mare: fourth foal: dam unraced: third in bumper: modest hurdler: won mares maiden at Downpatrick in August: stays 2½m: acts on soft and good to firm going: tried blinkered. *S. Donohoe, Ireland* **h99**

QUWS LAW (IRE) 5 b.g. Quws – Love For Lydia (IRE) (Law Society (USA)) [2006/7 F16v* F16m² Apr 21] workmanlike gelding: sixth foal: dam maiden: won maiden Irish point in November: useful form in bumpers: won at Ayr in March by 8 lengths from Peters Pride: neck second to Evelith Echo there following month, hanging left and tying up final 1f. *Miss Lucinda V. Russell* **F106**

R

RABBIT 6 b.m. Muhtarram (USA) – Ninia (USA) (Affirmed (USA)) [2006/7 h–: 16f⁶ 16m² 16g³ 17m⁴ 20m* 16g⁴ 17s² 20m* 22m* 20d² 24g⁴ 19m Apr 22] angular mare: modest handicap hurdler: claimed from Mrs A. King £5,000 fourth outing and improved after, winning at Uttoxeter (mares event) in July and Worcester and Stratford in September: stays 2¾m: acts on soft and good to firm going. *M. Sheppard* **h95**

RACING DEMON (IRE) 7 b.g. Old Vic – All Set (IRE) (Electric) [2006/7 c155+, h–: c17dᵘʳ c20g* c24d³ 21sᶠ c21g⁵ c25g⁴ Apr 25] **c166 h–**

Perversely, the season in which Racing Demon developed into the sort of horse he'd always promised to be was also the one in which the flaws in his racing character became most evident. Right from his early days as a novice hurdler, Racing Demon had stood out as one of the best young prospects around. His novice chasing season gave every encouragement that those hopes were well on the way to being fulfilled, and, stepped up to three miles for the first time in the latest season, Racing Demon duly put up a high-class performance to finish third to an outstanding winner of the King George in Kauto Star. Comparisons with Best Mate, bestowed on him in his early days in some quarters, were never going to be easy to live up to, especially after Racing Demon made a sparkling winning debut over fences at Exeter in November 2005 barely half an hour after the demise of the stable's triple Gold Cup winner. Racing Demon might have failed to add his name to those of Best Mate and the stable's Edredon Bleu as winners of the King George but, starting third favourite, Racing Demon put up a career-best effort, holding every chance into the straight but unable to quicken with Kauto Star and not staying on quite so well as runner-up Exotic Dancer, beaten just over nine lengths by the winner. Timmy Murphy, who had ridden Racing Demon to all three of his wins in novice chases, took the ride at Kempton, surprisingly the only time he partnered the horse all season. Murphy was perhaps a most apt partner, given his usual style of riding, for a horse who took his name from a variation of the card game patience. Indeed, Racing Demon's novice chase season had been shaped in no small measure by Murphy's availability to ride the horse. The Knight stable took a second retainer on Murphy in the latest season which, in theory, should have enabled him to maintain the partnership on a regular basis, but, with Murphy committed to his

totesport.com Peterborough Chase, Huntingdon—Racing Demon emulates stable-companions Edredon Bleu, Best Mate and Impek to maintain Henrietta Knight's outstanding record in this race

main employer David Johnson, Graham Lee rode Racing Demon in all his other races.

Though unable to land a third King George for the stable, Racing Demon had managed to enhance Henrietta Knight's excellent record in the Peterborough Chase at Huntingdon just over a month earlier. The trainer had won six of the last eight runnings with Edredon Bleu's four-timer between 1998 and 2001, Best Mate in 2002 and Impek in 2005. Racing Demon stood in for the last-named (side-lined through injury) and started joint favourite with Monkerhostin for the totesport.com-sponsored Peterborough against three rivals. His defeat of pacesetter Thisthatandtother (who received 5 lb) represented Racing Demon's best effort up until then. He jumped well in the main, clearly going best after three out and quickening well when asked to win going away by four lengths, with Monkerhostin another five lengths back in third.

Huntingdon and Kempton represented the highlights of Racing Demon's season, but, on balance, his campaign was something of a frustrating one. Not for the first time, Racing Demon showed a tendency to jump right to varying degrees. It was interesting to note that, left to his own devices, Racing Demon jumped markedly right when running loose, having parted company with Lee at the fourth, when favourite for the William Hill Gold Cup at Exeter on his reappearance. Henrietta Knight has always maintained that the tendency has been exaggerated, but Richard Johnson for one will take some convincing. He was booked for second place (behind Impek) at Exeter when the riderless Racing Demon suddenly veered sharply right across the fourth-last fence, cannoning into Johnson's mount Chilling Place in mid-air and effectively knocking the horse from underneath him.

Racing Demon jumped well in the main at Huntingdon and Kempton, though, hugging the rail in the King George to keep him straight, he still got close to the birch uprights of the fences on occasions. Ironically, there had been a Johnson-owned runner in the King George field—outsider Commercial Flyer—but Murphy had been released from his commitments for that race. The Knight team, however, clearly decided such generosity couldn't be relied upon for the season's remaining big races and, even though Murphy was available at the meeting, Lee was back in the saddle for the gelding's next start, which saw Racing Demon returned to the smaller obstacles in the Lanzarote Hurdle back at Kempton. Although carrying top weight, Racing Demon was potentially well in on his chasing form and was sent off the 2/1 favourite against sixteen rivals. 'He jumps very high and the idea is to try to bring his jumping down a bit,' explained Miss Knight, though that proved an unfortunate choice of words given that Racing Demon fell four out just as he was being asked for his effort. Going left-handed, Racing Demon failed to land a blow when a running-on fifth to Taranis back over fences in the Festival Trophy at Cheltenham next time, but, stepped back up in trip and back on a right-handed track, he was the shortest-priced of four British-trained challengers when second favourite for the Punchestown Gold Cup. With his stable rather struggling for form during the latter months of the campaign, Racing Demon failed to take the eye in appearance beforehand (in contrast to his two starts at Kempton where he'd looked very well) and was very edgy. In the race itself he again clouted the uprights of several fences and initially seemed likely to drop away before staying on again for fourth behind Neptune Collonges. Racing Demon had also become stirred up at the start before the Arkle at Cheltenham prior to his only defeat over fences that season and had been described in the past by his trainer as like a 'hyperactive school child'. Another of Racing Demon's idiosyncrasies is his unusually low head carriage, a trait that his trainer says he shares with some others in her yard by Old Vic.

Racing Demon (IRE) (b.g. 2000)	Old Vic (b 1986)	Sadler's Wells (b 1981)	Northern Dancer
			Fairy Bridge
		Cockade (b 1973)	Derring-Do
			Camenae
	All Set (IRE) (b 1992)	Electric (b 1979)	Blakeney
			Christiana
		Merry Lesa (b 1975)	Dalesa
			Rozeen

The useful-looking Racing Demon's pedigree has been covered in previous Annuals, the main points being that his dam is an unraced half-sister to the top-class chaser Merry Gale, while his great grandam Rozeen is also the third dam of Brave Inca. Racing Demon has certainly shown more ability than either of his dam's two other offspring to have raced. Alltheroses (by Roselier) was pulled up in an Irish point on her only outing, while Kilcash Demon (by Lord Americo) has been well beaten so far in bumpers and over hurdles in Ireland. Racing Demon stays three miles and has raced only on good ground or softer (yet to race on heavy). He still has questions to answer about his jumping, especially going left-handed, which, at the moment, makes it hard to envisage his winning any race at Cheltenham, still less emulating Best Mate in a Gold Cup. On the other hand, he is still young with only eight completed starts over fences under his belt, only two of them at around what might prove his optimum trip of three miles. The next season will be important in determining which way his career goes. *Miss H. C. Knight*

RADAR (IRE) 12 b.g. Petardia – Soignee (Night Shift (USA)) [2006/7 17s³ 17s* 17v* 16v Jan 12] angular gelding: winning chaser: fair handicap hurdler: back to best when winning twice at Carlisle in November: raced mainly around 2m: has won on firm going, races mainly on soft/heavy nowadays. *Miss S. E. Forster*   **c–** **h104**

RADAR LOVE 5 ch.m. Classic Cliche (IRE) – Goldenswift (IRE) (Meneval (USA)) [2006/7 F16d⁶ Feb 2] 30,000 4-y-o: third foal: half-sister to fairly useful hurdler Golden Bay (by Karinga Bay), stays 2¾m: dam, a fair hurdler/chaser, stayed 3m: not knocked about once held in mares bumper on debut: likely to require stiffer test of stamina. *P. R. Webber*   **F–**

RADBROOK HALL 8 b.g. Teenoso (USA) – Sarah's Venture (Averof) [2006/7 22m c21s⁵ c19m⁵ c20m⁵ Jul 11] big, workmanlike gelding: winning pointer: novice hurdler: form (poor) in chases only on final start: should prove suited by 2½m+. *J. W. Mullins*   **c75** **h–**

RADCLIFFE (IRE) 10 b.g. Supreme Leader – Marys Course (Crash Course) [2006/7 **c96**
c100, h–: c22s^{pu} c24d* c25s^5 c22s^4 c25s c24g^5 Feb 21] rather leggy gelding: modest **h–**
handicap chaser: won 5-runner event at Ludlow (by 16 lengths) in November: suited by
3m+: acts on soft going, below form all starts on firmer than good: races prominently.
Miss Venetia Williams

RADIGAN LANE 7 b.m. Wimbleball – Spirit Level (Sunley Builds) [2006/7 F–: **h–**
F17d^6 17m 16s 19s 22v^{pu} 19g 22g Apr 1] no form in bumpers/over hurdles. *J. R. Payne* **F–**

RADMORES REVENGE 4 b.g. Overbury (IRE) – Harvey's Sister (Le Moss) **F–**
[2006/7 F12g Mar 23] sturdy gelding: first foal: dam once-raced sister to useful hurdler/
winning chaser Moss Harvey, stayed 25f: green, well held in 4-y-o bumper on debut.
J. G. M. O'Shea

RADNOR LAD 7 ch.g. Double Trigger (IRE) – Gabibti (IRE) (Dara Monarch) [2006/7 **h87**
h74: 26g 24v^F 22s 26s* 22v^3 26s^4 24v^3 24s^6 Mar 1] lengthy gelding: modest handicap
hurdler: improved from when winning at Hereford in December: thorough stayer: raced
on good going or softer (acts on heavy). *Mrs S. M. Johnson*

RAFFAELLO (FR) 6 b.g. Roi de Rome (USA) – Lady Noa (FR) (No Pass No Sale) **c124 p**
[2006/7 h116: c19s^F Dec 27] ex-French gelding: fairly useful form both starts in novice **h–**
hurdles in Britain in 2005/6, winning at Wincanton: off 10 months and favourite, likely to
have won on chasing debut but for falling 3 out (jumped soundly otherwise) in maiden at
Chepstow, length ahead at time: reported in mid-January to have suffered tendon injury:
stays 2½m: should progress over fences provided he recovers. *P. F. Nicholls*

RAFFISH 5 ch.g. Atraf – Valadon (High Line) [2006/7 h73: 16m^4 16m^5 17d^2 16g Mar **h93**
20] leggy gelding: modest form over hurdles, seemingly best effort in steadily-run
handicap at Worcester second start: raced around 2m: acts on good to firm going: visored/
in cheekpieces last 3 outings. *M. Scudamore*

RAFTERYSHILL (IRE) 8 b.g. Accordion – Cracker Dawn (IRE) (Executive Perk) **h–**
[2006/7 19m^{pu} Aug 3] fourth foal: dam, unraced, out of National Hunt Chase winner
Hazy Dawn: poor pointer, often failed to complete: bled on hurdling debut: dead.
W. K. Goldsworthy

RAGADOR 6 b.g. El Conquistador – Ragsi (Amerian (USA)) [2006/7 F16s F17v^4 **F70**
Dec 12] big gelding: brother to fair chaser Ragamuff, stayed 3¼m, and half-brother to
winning pointers by Sulaafah and Teamster: dam maiden pointer: poor form in bumpers,
shaping like a stayer. *Mrs S. J. Smith*

RAGDALE HALL (USA) 10 b.g. Bien Bien (USA) – Gift of Dance (USA) (Trem- **c–**
polino (USA)) [2006/7 16m^5 20m^4 20g* 20g^{pu} Sep 17] medium-sized gelding: fair **h114**
handicap hurdler: off 16 months before reappearance: won at Uttoxeter in September by
neck from Aldiruos, one of first off bridle: lightly-raced winning chaser: stayed plays
2¾m: acts on firm and good to soft going: tried blinkered/tongue tied, not since 2002/3:
held up. *J. Joseph*

RAG WEEK (IRE) 10 b.g. Roselier (FR) – Lady Rag (Ragapan) [2006/7 c–, h–: 26s^{pu} **c–**
c28g c26m^5 c26m^{pu} Apr 26] maiden hurdler/winning chaser: lightly raced and no form **h–**
(including in points) since early-2004/5. *A. J. Whiting*

RAHY'S CROWN (USA) 4 b.g. Rahy (USA) – Inca Princess (USA) (Big Spruce **h–**
(USA)) [2006/7 18g^5 Sep 3] fair on Flat (stays 1½m), successful twice in 2006, sold out of
R. Hannon's stable 25,000 gns Newmarket July Sales: well beaten in juvenile on hurdling
debut. *G. L. Moore*

RAICHU (IRE) 6 ch.m. Definite Article – Sindabezi (IRE) (Magical Strike (USA)) **h104**
[2006/7 F16d* F16f 16g* 17s^4 17g^4 Sep 8] second foal: dam, dual bumper winner/ **F92**
successful twice over hurdles up to 2¼m, half-sister to useful 2½m hurdler Northern
Slope: won bumper at Down Royal in May: left D. Gillespie, successful also in mares
novice at Uttoxeter on hurdling debut in July, soon clear: disappointing both starts after,
tongue tied final one (found little). *D. E. Pipe*

RAIDER OF THE EAST (IRE) 5 b.g. Darshaan – Convenience (IRE) (Ela-Mana- **F75**
Mou) [2006/7 F84: F16d F16d Jan 5] good-bodied gelding: modest form on first of 3
outings in bumpers, off 12 months after. *K. A. Morgan*

RAINBOW LORD (IRE) 7 b.g. Lord of Appeal – Rainbow Alliance (IRE) (Golden **h–**
Love) [2006/7 F83: 20s Oct 11] placed on completed start in Irish points: sixth in bumper:
well held in novice on hurdling debut: should be suited by 2½m+. *C. C. Bealby*

RAINBOWS AGLITTER 10 ch.g. Rainbows For Life (CAN) – Chalet Waldegg **c92**
(Monsanto (FR)) [2006/7 c–, h111: c20g^4 c20f^5 Jun 3] angular gelding: fair handicap **h–**

hurdler: winning chaser, modest form at best since 2003: stays 21f: acts on soft and good to firm going: edgy sort: held up: has found little. *D. R. Gandolfo*

RAINBOW'S CLASSIC 4 b.g. Muhtarram (USA) – Legend of Aragon (Aragon) **h–** [2006/7 17s 16g 16v^{pu} Jan 21] smallish, close-coupled gelding: half-brother to winning hurdler/chaser It's Bertie (by Unfuwain), stays 2¾m: fair maiden at best on Flat (barely stays testing 9f): no form over hurdles, sold out of K. Ryan's stable 5,400 gns Doncaster November Sales after second outing: races freely. *P. Beaumont*

RAINBOW TREE 7 b.g. Rainbows For Life (CAN) – Little Twig (IRE) (Good Thyne **c107** (USA)) [2006/7 c–, h96: c21g c27g* c25m^5 Apr 28] leggy gelding: novice hurdler: fit **h–** from points (successful twice), first form in chases when winning novice handicap at Sedgefield in April by 27 lengths: tended to jump right again and tired after forcing strong pace 5 days later: stays 27f: acts on soft going, probably on good to firm: blinkered 6 of last 8 starts. *C. C. Bealby*

RAINHA 10 b.m. Alflora (IRE) – Political Prospect (Politico (USA)) [2006/7 c–, h–: **c–** c21s^3 c24d^5 Oct 15] won both starts in points in 2004: no other form over jumps. **h–** *A. C. Whillans*

RAINING HORSE (FR) 5 b.g. Rainbow Reef – Gabatine (FR) (Garde Royale) **h98** [2006/7 20g^{pu} 16s^3 16v 16s* 18s 20g^6 Mar 17] fourth foal: half-brother to 1½m winner Lady Malika (by Volochine): dam unraced half-sister to useful French hurdler/chaser Florid River, stayed 23f: modest form over hurdles, winning maiden at Newcastle in January: well held in handicaps after: best form at 2m on soft ground: in cheekpieces after debut: tried tongue tied. *J. P. L. Ewart*

RAISBY REBEL 7 ch.g. Milieu – Ragged Rose (Scallywag) [2006/7 F17s Oct 15] **F–** seventh foal: half-brother to winning pointer by Highlands: dam failed to complete in 4 points: no sign of ability in points/bumper. *C. Grant*

RAISEAPEARL 12 b. or br.g. Pocketed (USA) – Little Anthem (True Song) [2006/7 **c78** c97d, h–: c25f^6 c26v^3 May 20] modest hunter chaser nowadays: stays 3¼m: acts on heavy **h–** ground. *Patrick Thompson*

RAISE YOUR GAME (IRE) 6 b.g. Saddlers' Hall (IRE) – Roscrea Travel (IRE) **h98 p** (Boreen (FR)) [2006/7 20s^2 Dec 8] €50,000 3-y-o: first foal: dam, fair hurdler/winning pointer who stayed 3m, out of half-sister to dam of one-time high-class chaser Truckers Tavern: shaped with promise despite mistakes when 3 lengths second to Im Spartacus in novice hurdle at Southwell on debut: will stay beyond 2½m: should improve. *Jonjo O'Neill*

RAJAM 9 b.g. Sadler's Wells (USA) – Rafif (USA) (Riverman (USA)) [2006/7 h112: **c95 +** c16d^6 c16s c16d^6 Dec 28] sturdy gelding: fair hurdler: fit from Flat, never dangerous in **h–** novice/maiden chases: raced mainly around 2m, solely on good ground or softer (acts on soft): tried visored, wore cheekpieces for all 3 wins over hurdles. *G. A. Harker*

RAJAYOGA 6 ch.g. Kris – Optimistic (Reprimand) [2006/7 h116: 17g^6 18g Sep 30] **h103** progressive hurdler early in 2005/6, winning 3 times: fit from Flat, below best in handicaps in 2006/7: stays 2½m: raced on good going or firmer (acts on firm). *M. H. Tompkins*

RAJEH (IRE) 4 b.g. Key of Luck (USA) – Saramacca (IRE) (Kahyasi) [2006/7 16s 16g **h83 p** Mar 20] rather leggy gelding: fairly useful on Flat (stays 1½m), successful in August, sold out of K. Prendergast's stable 70,000 gns Newmarket Autumn Sales: some promise both starts over hurdles, left with lot to do and not given hard time on second when seventh to Tritonix in novice at Warwick (banned for 40 days under non-triers rule): capable of better. *J. L. Spearing*

RAKALACKEY 9 br.g. Rakaposhi King – Celtic Slave (Celtic Cone) [2006/7 c95, h–: **c106** c24m^3 c24g* c24d^4 c24g^5 Mar 30] medium-sized gelding: winning hurdler: fair chaser: **h–** hasn't convinced with jumping or attitude, but did win novice handicap at Kempton in November: will stay beyond 3m: best form on good going: in cheekpieces last 2 outings. *H. D. Daly*

RAKI ROSE 5 b.g. Rakaposhi King – Fortria Rosie Dawn (Derring Rose) [2006/7 h–, **h87** F–: 21d^5 19d^6 22d 26s^5 24v^2 25s^{pu} Jan 15] modest novice hurdler: stays 3¼m: raced on going softer than good (acts on heavy): tongue tied third start (ran moody race). *M. Scudamore*

RAMBLEES HOLLY 9 ch.g. Alfie Dickins – Lucky Holly (General David) [2006/7 **c–** c–, h97: 24g^6 22s^4 20m^5 21m 21m^{pu} Sep 26] angular gelding: modest handicap hurdler, **h86** below best since early-2005/6: soon detached only outing over fences: best at 2½m/2¾m: acts on firm and soft going. *R. S. Wood*

Agfa Diamond Handicap Chase, Sandown—northern raider Rambling Minster (white face)
gets the better of Kelami (right), Briery Fox (spots) and Tikram (No.3)

RAMBLE ON TERRY (IRE) 9 b. or br.m. Jurado (USA) – Rambling Ivy (Manda- **h–**
lus) [2006/7 20m 20f⁵ 20fᵖᵘ Jul 6] ex-Irish mare: little show over hurdles, left H. Finigan
after second start. *F. Jestin*

RAMBLING MINSTER 9 b.g. Minster Son – Howcleuch (Buckskin (FR)) [2006/7 **c129**
c108P, h129: c20s⁴ c25v² c24g* c24g c32mᵖᵘ Apr 21] rather leggy gelding: fairly useful **h–**
handicap hurdler/chaser: won Agfa Diamond Chase at Sandown in February by ¾ length
from Kelami, idling markedly: should also have won at Kelso on second outing, plenty to
do and finishing strongly: little impact in valuable events last 2 starts: better around 3m
than shorter: acts on heavy going: usually patiently ridden. *K. G. Reveley*

RAMIREZ (IRE) 9 ch.g. Royal Abjar (USA) – Flooding (USA) (Irish River (FR)) **c–**
[2006/7 c106: c28s⁴ c22v⁶ c23vᵘʳ c22g Mar 28] strong gelding: fairly useful hunter chaser
at best, out of sorts in 2007: stays 25f: raced on good ground or softer. *Nick Kent*

RAMSDEN BOY (IRE) 6 b.g. Saddlers' Hall (IRE) – Double Glazed (IRE) (Glacial **h113**
Storm (USA)) [2006/7 20s⁵ 16v* 18s* Mar 25] €18,000 3-y-o: first foal: dam unraced
daughter of very smart hurdler/winning chaser up to 3m Double Wrapped: won maiden
point in 2006: progressive over hurdles, winning maiden (by 18 lengths) at Ayr and minor
event at Downpatrick (by 4½ lengths from Cool Running) in March: likely to be suited
by 2¾m+: acts on heavy going. *Roy Wilson, Ireland*

RANDOLF (IRE) 5 br.g. Good Thyne (USA) – Lester's Perk (IRE) (Executive Perk) **F82**
[2006/7 F16v² F16g Mar 24] useful-looking gelding: second foal: dam ran once over
hurdles: better effort in bumpers when 23 lengths second to Starting Point in 7-runner
event at Newcastle. *G. A. Charlton*

RANDOM NATIVE (IRE) 9 br.g. Be My Native (USA) – Random Wind (Random **h105**
Shot) [2006/7 h–: 20g* 20m⁴ Jul 2] rather leggy gelding: bumper winner: lightly raced
over hurdles, reportedly had breathing operation prior to easily winning novice handicap
at Hexham in May: found little next time: stays 2½m: best form on good ground.
N. G. Richards

RANDOM QUEST 9 b.g. Rainbow Quest (USA) – Anne Bonny (Ajdal (USA)) **h89 §**
[2006/7 h101§: 17m* 20mᶠ May 28] tall, workmanlike gelding: modest hurdler: won seller at Newton Abbot in May: should have stayed at least 2½m: acted on heavy and good
to firm going: wore headgear 5 of last 6 outings: unenthusiastic: dead. *B. J. Llewellyn*

796

RANDWICK ROAR (IRE) 8 b.g. Lord Americo – Le Bavellen (Le Bavard (FR)) **c115** [2006/7 c20s² c20m² c20d⁵ Nov 21] tall ex-Irish gelding: winning hurdler: fairly useful **h–** chaser: won maiden at Limerick in 2005/6: runner-up in minor events at Killarney and Listowel, final 2 starts for P. Doyle: stays 3m: acts on good to firm and heavy ground: consistent. *G. L. Moore*

RANELAGH GRAY (IRE) 10 gr.g. Roselier (FR) – Bea Marie (IRE) (King's Ride) **c107** [2006/7 c96, h105: c20g⁵ c24d² c23s* c28s⁶ Dec 16] rather leggy gelding: fair hurdler: **h–** similar standard over fences, won 5-runner handicap at Exeter in December: stays 4m: acts on soft going: front runner/races prominently. *Miss Venetia Williams*

RANSBORO (IRE) 8 br.g. Needle Gun (IRE) – Moylena (Bustomi) [2006/7 c122, **c127** h110: c22s* c20s³ 20v⁴ c22s^pu Feb 15] lengthy gelding: fair hurdler: fairly useful **h103** handicap chaser: won at Killarney (by ½ length from Strong Project) in May: sold out of C. Swan's stable 140,000 gns Doncaster Sales later in month: effective at 19f to 25f: acted on heavy going: raced prominently: dead. *N. G. Richards*

RAPALLO (IRE) 6 b.g. Luso – Sheeba Queen (Crozier) [2006/7 F84: 22d⁵ 24d⁵ **h89** Nov 18] tall gelding: third in bumper on debut: first and better effort in novice hurdles when fifth to Mossville at Wincanton. *Carl Llewellyn*

RAPIDE PLAISIR (IRE) 9 b.g. Grand Plaisir (IRE) – Royal Well (Royal Vulcan) **c116** [2006/7 c16f* c16g² Apr 19] rather leggy ex-Irish gelding: winning hurdler: fairly useful **h–** chaser: sold out of A. Moore's stable 8,000 gns Doncaster November (2005) Sales and off 6½ months, won novice at Ludlow on first day of season by 14 lengths from Minouchka: off another 12 months, better form when ½-length second to Glengarra in handicap at Cheltenham, forcing strong pace and 5 lengths clear at last: stays 2½m: best form on good going or firmer (acts on firm): front runner. *R. Lee*

RAPSCALLION (GER) 8 b.g. Robellino (USA) – Rosy Outlook (USA) (Trempolino **h85** (USA)) [2006/7 h99: 20f³ 17g⁵ 16s^pu 16s³ 16s⁶ 16g Mar 19] workmanlike gelding: modest maiden hurdler: stays easy 2½m: acts on firm and soft going: tried in visor/ cheekpieces/tongue tied. *Heather Dalton*

RARE COINCIDENCE 6 ch.g. Atraf – Green Seed (IRE) (Lead On Time (USA)) **c– x** [2006/7 h107: 20g⁴ 20g* 20s 20v⁴ c21v^ur c22s^F 22v Jan 28] close-coupled gelding: **h112** fair on Flat (stays 2m), successful in April: fair handicap hurdler: won at Uttoxeter in September: badly let down by jumping both starts over fences: stays 2½m: raced on good going or softer (acts on heavy): wears cheekpieces: usually front runner/races prominently: genuine. *R. F. Fisher*

RAREGEM 9 b.g. Syrtos – Ruby's Vision (Balinger) [2006/7 c117: c23v^pu Mar 1] **c– x** useful hunter chaser: sometimes let down by jumping, including only outing (odds on) in 2006/7: stays 3¼m: acts on good to firm and heavy going. *M. Biddick*

RARE GOLD (IRE) 7 br.g. Beneficial – Tara's Pride (IRE) (Montelimar (USA)) **c–** [2006/7 h104: c16g⁶ c24s^F c19v^pu c23s^ur 22g^pu Mar 19] poor/hurdle winner: seemed to **h–** lose confidence over fences after first 2 starts: should stay beyond 21f. *R. H. Alner*

RARE OUZEL (IRE) 11 b.g. Be My Native (USA) – Ring Ouzel (Deep Run) [2006/7 **c104** c30d⁴ 16v c22v⁶ c24v^pu c25v^pu 24v Feb 25] useful-looking gelding: fair handicap **h–** hurdler/off 6 months and below form after first outing: stays 4m: raced on good going or softer (acts on heavy): blinkered 3 of last 4 starts: tongue tied once: held up. *A. J. Martin, Ireland*

RARE SOCIETY (IRE) 9 b.g. Deep Society – Rare Glen (Glen Quaich) [2006/7 **c112** c102: 24g* c20m⁶ c24m c24m c23m* c23m⁴ c27m* 24f² Sep 29] rather leggy, lengthy **h100** gelding: fair hurdler/chaser: won maiden over hurdles at Hexham in May and over fences at Worcester in July, and handicap chase at Sedgefield in August: stays 27f: acts on soft and firm going. *Mrs S. J. Smith*

RASHARROW (IRE) 8 ch.g. Rashar (USA) – Fleeting Arrow (IRE) (Commanche **c132** Run) [2006/7 h131: c20g^pu c17s* c16d⁴ c16s² c21g⁴ c20m⁵ Apr 21] lengthy, useful- **h–** looking gelding: useful hurdler: similar standard over fences, easily landed odds in maiden at Kelso in November: creditable fourth 2 of next 3 outings, raced prominently when beaten 8½ lengths by L'Antartique in listed novice event at Cheltenham on handicap debut: stays 21f: acts on soft and good to firm going: has been bandaged behind. *L. Lungo*

RASHARTIC (IRE) 5 ch.g. Rashar (USA) – Gothic Ash (IRE) (Yashgan) [2006/7 **h99 p** F89: F17s 17s² 19d³ Feb 19] tall, good-topped gelding: has scope: better effort in **F–** bumpers when third at Perth on debut: placed both starts over hurdles, 2 lengths second to

Nawaadi in novice at Taunton: should be suited by further than 17f: remains capable of better. *Heather Dalton*

RASH DECISION (IRE) 12 b.g. Rashar (USA) – Lady Nethertown (Windjammer (USA)) [2006/7 c78, h–: 16d Jan 5] rangy gelding: winning hurdler: fair chaser at best: lightly raced and little form since 2001/2. *P. D. Niven*   **c–** **h–**

RASHIDA 5 b.m. King's Best (USA) – Nimble Lady (AUS) (Fairy King (USA)) [2006/7 h–: 16g 16d⁶ 16m 20d⁵ 19s² 23d⁵ 21g Feb 21] poor novice hurdler: probably stays 2½m: wears cheekpieces: tried tongue tied. *M. Appleby*   **h61**

RASH INVESTOR (IRE) 5 b.g. Rashar (USA) – Miss Pecksniff (IRE) (Orchestra) [2006/7 F16g Apr 23] 5,100 4-y-o: third foal: dam maiden: well beaten in bumper on debut. *H. P. Hogarth*   **F–**

RASH LEADER (IRE) 8 ch.g. Rashar (USA) – Leader Lady (IRE) (Supreme Leader) [2006/7 F–: 20g Nov 10] strong gelding: well beaten in bumper/maiden hurdle (distressed). *L. Lungo*   **h–**

RASH MOMENT (FR) 8 b.g. Rudimentary (USA) – Ashura (FR) (No Pass No Sale) [2006/7 c99d, h87: c25gᵖᵘ c16v⁵ c16m⁵ c23m⁵ c21m² c23m* c26d⁴ c23m* c23m⁴ c21g* c24mᶠ c24g⁵ c20g³ c23mᵖᵘ Apr 15] close-coupled gelding: winning hurdler: modest handicap chaser: won at Stratford in August (twice, novice event on first occasion) and Uttoxeter in September: below form after 5-month absence last 2 starts: should stay at least 3m: acts on good to soft and good to firm going: often wears headgear, also tongue tied last 2 outings. *Mrs K. Waldron*   **c96** **h–**

RASH PROMISE (IRE) 5 b.g. Rashar (USA) – Twilight Katie (Stubbs Gazette) [2006/7 16sᵖᵘ 16s 16v Mar 6] unfurnished gelding: brother to 2½m hurdle winner Here Comes Sally: dam Irish bumper winner: no show over hurdles. *J. R. Turner*   **h–**

RASH TALK (IRE) 5 br.g. Rashar (USA) – Talk Tonight (IRE) (Executive Perk) [2006/7 16s 16s 16sᵖᵘ 21gᵖᵘ Mar 14] €9,500 3-y-o, resold 13,000 3-y-o: tall gelding: chasing type: second foal: dam unraced: headstrong, and no form over hurdles: tongue tied. *D. P. Keane*   **h–**

RASLAN 4 b.g. Lomitas – Rosia (IRE) (Mr Prospector (USA)) [2006/7 18s² 18s* 16s* 16s² 21g 24g² Apr 21] smallish gelding: fairly useful on Flat (stays 2m), successful twice in July, sold out of M. Johnston's stable 45,000 gns Newmarket Sales later in month, and gelded: useful juvenile hurdler: won at Fontwell in December and Wincanton (by 5 lengths from Time Out with bit to spare) in January: good second 2 of last 3 starts, upped further in trip when beaten neck by Spirit of New York in 5-runner novice at Bangor final one: stays 3m: acts on soft ground: tried in cheekpieces (very stiff task). *D. E. Pipe*   **h132**

RASTAQUOUERE (FR) 7 b.g. Sheyrann – Rayonnante (FR) (Saint Cyrien (FR)) [2006/7 20fᵖᵘ 17fᵖᵘ Aug 11] no sign of ability: sold out of A. Moore's stable 1,500 gns Doncaster May Sales prior to return. *J. M. Saville*   **c–** **h–**

RATHCANNON BEAUTY 5 b.m. Muhtarram (USA) – Bint Alhabib (Nashwan (USA)) [2006/7 h–: 18g 16g⁵ Mar 26] small mare: no sign of ability. *Mrs L. P. Baker*   **h–**

RATHGAR BEAU (IRE) 11 b. or br.g. Beau Sher – Salerina (Orchestra) [2006/7 c147+, h–: c20gᵖᵘ Oct 7] useful-looking gelding: winning hurdler: very smart chaser: gained first Grade 1 win when beating below-par Moscow Flyer a short head in Kerrygold Champion Chase at Punchestown in April 2005: successful also in 4 Grade 2 events in previous 6 months: reportedly retired with recurrence of tendon injury after only outing in 2006/7: stayed 21f: raced mainly on going softer than good (acted on heavy): blinkered twice: held up: consistent and a credit to connections. *E. Sheehy, Ireland*   **c–** **h–**

RATHLIN ISLAND 9 b.g. Carroll House – Mermaid Bay (Jupiter Island) [2006/7 h83: 22m 22gᶜᵒ 19d⁵ c20mᵖᵘ c24g³ c23d⁴ Oct 11] maiden hurdler: no form in 2006/7, including over fences: usually wears blinkers/cheekpieces nowadays, also tongue tied final outing. *K. J. Burke*   **c–** **h–**

RATHOWEN (IRE) 8 b.g. Good Thyne (USA) – Owenageera (IRE) (Riot Helmet) [2006/7 h118, F–: c20v Nov 12] tall, good-topped gelding: fairly useful hurdler: mistakes and never dangerous in novice on chasing debut: likely to stay beyond 3m: acts on heavy going. *J. I. A. Charlton*   **c–** **h–**

RAUL SAHARA 5 br.g. Makbul – Sheraton Heights (Deploy) [2006/7 16m⁴ 17g Oct 15] modest maiden on Flat (stays 9.5f): fourth to Kanpai at Worcester on first of 2 starts in novice hurdles. *J. W. Unett*   **h72**

RAVEN HALL LADY (IRE) 6 b.m. Saddlers' Hall (IRE) – Dunraven Lady (Raka- **h72** poshi King) [2006/7 F–: F16v 17g⁵ Mar 24] unfurnished mare: well held in bumpers over **F—** a year apart (for M. Rimell on debut): poor form in mares claimer on hurdling debut: tried blinkered. *D. McCain Jnr*

RAVENSCAR 9 b.g. Thethingaboutitis (USA) – Outcrop (Oats) [2006/7 c–, h–: c23mᵖᵘ **c80** c20m⁶ Apr 28] workmanlike gelding: maiden hurdler: fair chaser at best: off 18 months, **h—** below form in handicaps in 2006/7: stays 3m: acts on heavy and good to firm going. *C. T. Pogson*

RAVENS FLIGHT (IRE) 6 br.g. I'm Supposin (IRE) – Cloncoose (IRE) (Remainder **h—** Man) [2006/7 F–: F16g F16m 20d 25g⁵ 21d 26sᵖᵘ 24mᵖᵘ Mar 25] big, lengthy gelding: no **F—** form in bumpers/over hurdles: tongue tied since debut. *S. A. Brookshaw*

RAVEN'S RUN (IRE) 5 b.g. Sea Raven (IRE) – Sandy Run (IRE) (Deep Run) [2006/7 **F113** F16v* F16v⁵ F16s* F16g Mar 14] sixth living foal: half-brother to winning Irish pointer by Phardante: dam unraced half-sister to dam of one-time useful chaser up to 3m Another Raleigh: won maiden on second of 2 starts in Irish points: useful form in bumpers: won at Gowran (maiden) in December and Naas (made all to beat Mick The Man by 8 lengths) in February: well held under less testing conditions in Champion Bumper at Cheltenham final start: likely to be suited by further than 2m. *Michael Cunningham, Ireland*

RAVENSTONE LAD (IRE) 5 br.g. Presenting – Brown Gillette (Callernish) [2006/7 **F—** F–: F16d Oct 18] unfurnished gelding: well beaten in bumpers. *Mrs P. Robeson*

RAWCLIFFE BAY 5 ch.g. Karinga Bay – Pedrosa (IRE) (Petardia) [2006/7 F16s **F—** F18v⁶ F16g Mar 19] third foal: dam unraced: last in bumpers. *W. G. M. Turner*

RAY BOY (IRE) 8 b. or br.g. Oscar (IRE) – Cappagale (IRE) (Strong Gale) [2006/7 **h138** h123: 22s⁵ 19m* Apr 8] lengthy gelding: useful hurdler, lightly raced: off 5 months, improved form when winning handicap at Cork by length from Charlies First: stays 2¾m: acts on soft and good to firm going. *P. C. O'Connor, Ireland*

RAYDAN (IRE) 5 b.g. Danehill (USA) – Rayseka (IRE) (Dancing Brave (USA)) **h92** [2006/7 16v⁴ 16s⁴ 16d⁶ 16s 17d Mar 20] sturdy gelding: half-brother to useful hurdler/ winning chaser Rayshan (by Darshaan), stays 2¾m: dam, smart middle-distance winner, half-sister to dam of smart French hurdler Tiger Groom and useful hurdler up to 2½m Rifawan: modest maiden hurdler (stays 13f) for J. Oxx: soundly beaten in handicaps last 2 starts: should stay beyond 2m: tongue tied final outing. *D. R. Gandolfo*

RAYGALE 10 b.g. Superpower – Little Missile (Ile de Bourbon (USA)) [2006/7 17dᵖᵘ **h67** 20g⁵ 21m⁶ Jun 7] sturdy gelding: poor form over hurdles, off 2 years before return. *Mrs K. Walton*

RAY MOND 6 b.g. Midnight Legend – Kinsale Florale (IRE) (Supreme Leader) **c—** [2006/7 h–, F–: c21dᵘʳ c20g c24dᵖᵘ Nov 14] sturdy gelding: of no account. *M. J. Gingell* **h—**

RAYSHAN (IRE) 7 b.g. Darshaan – Rayseka (IRE) (Dancing Brave (USA)) [2006/7 **c110 p** h136: 21s 16v² 21g c16g* Apr 7] leggy gelding: useful handicap hurdler: best effort in **h127** 2006/7 when 4 lengths second to Through The Rye at Newcastle: favourite, won maiden at Carlisle on chasing debut by 4 lengths from Kentucky Blue: barely stays 2¾m: acts on heavy going: likely to improve over fences. *N. G. Richards*

RAZZAMATAZZ 9 b.g. Alhijaz – Salvezza (IRE) (Superpower) [2006/7 c94, h–: **c90** c19s³ c22s³ c19g⁴ c20m⁵ Apr 28] lightly raced: winning hurdler: modest novice chaser: **h—** stays 3m: acts on soft and good to firm going. *R. Dickin*

R'CAM (IRE) 5 b. or br.g. Glacial Storm (USA) – Beann Ard (IRE) (Mandalus) **F95** [2006/7 F16d² F17v³ Jan 1] €22,000 3-y-o: strong, good-topped gelding: fourth foal: dam unraced sister to smart chaser Macgeorge, stayed 3¼m: better effort in bumpers (fairly useful form) when 1½ lengths second to Golden Child at Ascot: raced freely next time. *Carl Llewellyn*

REACH FOR THE TOP (IRE) 6 br.g. Topanoora – Burren Gale (IRE) (Strong **c124** Gale) [2006/7 h100, F94: c20g⁴ c23g² c24s⁵ c21s* c21gᵖᵘ Mar 19] lengthy, useful- **h—** looking gelding: maiden hurdler: fairly useful chaser: didn't need to be at best to land odds in maiden at Folkestone in January by 14 lengths from Le Rochelais: ran poorly 2 months later: should stay 3m: raced on good going or softer. *Miss H. C. Knight*

REACHING OUT (IRE) 5 b.g. Desert Prince (IRE) – Alwiyda (USA) (Trempolino **h99** (USA)) [2006/7 h103: 17m² 16g⁵ 16s⁴ 16gᵇᵈ Mar 16] compact gelding: fair on Flat (stays easy 1½m), successful in December: modest hurdler: raced around 2m: acts on soft and good to firm going: blinkered in 2006/7. *N. P. Littmoden*

READ ALL ABOUT IT (IRE) 7 b.g. Luso – Forty One (IRE) (Over The River (FR)) **c79**
[2006/7 c20s c20d5 c20mᵖᵘ c20g⁴ c23d⁵ c25mᵖᵘ Apr 28] €27,000 3-y-o: fifth foal: dam **h–**
fair 2m hurdle winner: no form in maiden hurdles: poor maiden handicap chaser: left
R. O'Leary and off 7 months, last down by jumping on British debut: stays 23f: acts on
heavy ground: has worn cheekpieces/blinkers. *Jonjo O'Neill*

READY RESPONSE (IRE) 5 gr.g. Gothland (FR) – Ballygrangans Lady (IRE) **h89 +**
(Insan (USA)) [2006/7 F16g⁵ 22sᶠ 20m* Apr 25] €8,500 3-y-o: first foal: dam unplaced **F–**
in points: won maiden Irish point in 2006: bought 21,000 gns Doncaster May Sales: well
held in bumper for R. Farrant: modest form on completed outing in maiden hurdles when
winning at Worcester in April, despite edging right: stays 2½m. *L. Corcoran*

REAL CHIEF (IRE) 9 b.g. Caerleon (USA) – Greek Air (IRE) (Ela-Mana-Mou) **h74**
[2006/7 h72: 17d* 16g 17d 17d 16gᵖᵘ Mar 16] leggy gelding: modest form on Flat
(probably stays 1½m): poor handicap hurdler: won selling event at Cartmel in May: no
show last 4 starts, in cheekpieces final one (saddle slipped): should stay beyond 17f: acts
on good to soft going. *Miss M. E. Rowland*

REAL DEFINITION 8 br.g. Highest Honor (FR) – Segovia (Groom Dancer (USA)) **c58**
[2006/7 c–, h–: c16d⁴ c24d⁵ c21dᵖᵘ 22vᵖᵘ Dec 12] good-topped gelding: bumper winner: **h–**
bad maiden hurdler/chaser: tried blinkered/tongue tied. *M. G. Rimell*

REAL EMPIRE (IRE) 6 b.m. Second Empire (IRE) – Real Guest (IRE) (Be My **h76**
Guest (USA)) [2006/7 16v 21m⁵ Nov 9] fair on Flat (stays 13f), successful twice in 2006:
poor form in 2 starts over hurdles. *T. G. McCourt, Ireland*

REASONABLY SURE (IRE) 7 b.g. Presenting – No Reason (Kemal (FR)) [2006/7 **c91**
c100, h90: c20v⁴ c20vᵖᵘ c24v⁵ c20s⁴ c20s² c20g³ c23g⁴ Apr 16] well-made gelding: **h–**
maiden hurdler: winning pointer: modest novice chaser: stays 3m: raced on good ground
or softer (acts on heavy): usually blinkered. *M. W. Easterby*

REBEL ARMY (IRE) 8 ch.g. Mister Lord (USA) – Mandasari (Mandalus) [2006/7 **c88**
c88: c20d⁴ c24s³ c27s² c24gᵖᵘ c24g⁶ Apr 21] lengthy gelding: fair pointer/hunter chaser:
stays 27f: raced on good going or softer. *Mrs C. J. Robinson*

REBEL LAD (IRE) 8 ch.g. Flemensfirth (USA) – Chancy Gale (IRE) (Strong Gale) **c–**
[2006/7 c26vᵖᵘ May 20] modest pointer, successful twice in 2006: no show in hunter on
chase debut. *Mrs C. J. Robinson*

REBELLE 8 b. or br.g. Reprimand – Blushing Belle (Local Suitor (USA)) [2006/7 **c94**
h100+: 24g c23d³ c19m³ c26gᶠ 27s³ c24dˢᵘ 24v* 26mᶠ Mar 29] quite good-topped geld- **h96**
ing: modest handicap hurdler: won at Hexham in March: similar form on second of 2
completed outings over fences (makes mistakes): stays 3m: acts on heavy and good to
firm going: blinkered (slipped up) once, usually wears cheekpieces. *P. Bowen*

REBELLING (IRE) 4 ch.g. Peintre Celebre (USA) – El Divino (IRE) (Halling (USA)) **h74 §**
[2006/7 17s 17g⁶ 16f 16sᵖᵘ 16s⁵ 19v 21g⁴ 21m⁴ Apr 8] leggy gelding: modest maiden on
Flat (stays 1½m), sold out of F. J. Houghton's stable 7,000 gns Newmarket July Sales:
poor juvenile hurdler: stays 21f: tried blinkered/visored/tongue tied: ungenuine: sold
2,600 gns Doncaster May Sales. *M. F. Harris*

REBEL MELODY (IRE) 6 b.g. Houmayoun (FR) – Queenford Melody (IRE) **h88 p**
(Orchestra) [2006/7 25g² Oct 30] sixth foal: dam unraced half-sister to useful staying
hurdler Rebel Song: won maiden Irish point in 2006: bought 17,000 gns Doncaster
August Sales: well-backed favourite, clear length second to Good Book in novice at
Warwick on hurdling debut, mistakes last 2: will be suited by thorough test of stamina:
looked likely to improve but not seen out again. *C. J. Mann*

REBEL RAIDER (IRE) 8 b.g. Mujadil (USA) – Emily's Pride (Shirley Heights) **h106**
[2006/7 h102: 16d² 16s⁵ 19d⁵ 16v* 16g⁴ 16m⁶ Apr 22] rather leggy gelding: fair handicap
hurdler: won 18-runner novice event at Huntingdon in January: raced mainly around 2m:
acts on good to firm and heavy going. *B. N. Pollock*

REBEL RHYTHM 8 b.g. Robellino (USA) – Celt Song (IRE) (Unfuwain (USA)) **c–**
[2006/7 c125, h–: 23f⁶ May 6] big, good-bodied gelding: has reportedly had wind **h–**
operation: useful hurdler at best, well held only outing in 2006/7: fairly useful chaser:
stays 25f: raced mainly on good going or softer (acts on heavy). *Mrs S. J. Smith*

REBEL ROCK (IRE) 5 b.g. Rock Hopper – Penstal Lady (IRE) (Glenstal (USA)) **F–**
[2006/7 F16s Mar 8] €15,000 4-y-o: well-made gelding: first foal: dam winning pointer:
looked in need of experience in maiden bumper on debut. *D. P. Keane*

REBOND (FR) 5 ch.g. Trempolino (USA) – Lattaquie (FR) (Fast Topaze (USA)) **c92**
[2006/7 18s⁶ 19s 18v 20dᵖᵘ 18s c17s³ Apr 18] tall gelding: brother to smart hurdler/very **h89**

smart chaser Bounce Back, stayed 29f: 15f winner on Flat: modest novice hurdler: no show in novice handicap at Sandown fourth start: similar form when third at Enghien on chasing debut: has worn blinkers. *F. Doumen, France*

RECENT EDITION (IRE) 9 b.g. Roselier (FR) – Hi Millie (Decent Fellow) [2006/7 c95: c24d⁴ c26s⁶ c27s⁶ c28vᵖᵘ c32v⁴ Mar 15] lengthy, good-topped gelding: modest handicap chaser, below form in 2006/7: thorough stayer: acts on heavy going: usually wears cheekpieces/blinkers: lazy. *J. Wade*   **c77 §**

RECKLESS VENTURE (IRE) 6 ch.g. Carroll House – Satin Talker (Le Bavard (FR)) [2006/7 20v 16v 16v³ 16v³ Mar 9] €21,000 4-y-o: unfurnished gelding: third foal: dam, winning pointer, half-sister to dam of Champion Hurdle winner Brave Inca: poor form over hurdles: bred to be suited by further than 2m: raced on heavy going. *Miss Lucinda V. Russell*   **h75**

RECOUNT (FR) 7 b.g. Sillery (USA) – Dear Countess (FR) (Fabulous Dancer (USA)) [2006/7 h104: 16m³ 17g* Jun 20] fair form over hurdles: landed odds with plenty in hand in maiden at Newton Abbot in June: raced around 2m on good/good to firm going: has carried head awkwardly: sold only 800 gns Doncaster May Sales. *C. J. Mann*   **h106**

RECTORY (IRE) 8 b.g. Presenting – Billys Pet (Le Moss) [2006/7 h85: 20s Jan 31] workmanlike gelding: lightly raced: modest form on second of 3 starts in novice hurdles: stays 2½m. *J. J. Quinn*   **h–**

RED ACRES (IRE) 7 ch.g. Eve's Error – Lady Sirat (Al Sirat) [2006/7 16f² 18m F16m⁴ F16m⁴ 16d⁴ 16g⁴ 16s c17m⁴ Apr 8] good-topped ex-Irish gelding: half-brother to winning pointer by Good Thyne: dam bumper winner/winning pointer: in frame in bumpers: modest maiden hurdler, left Ms Caroline Hutchinson before penultimate start: poor in novice on chasing debut (tongue tied): raced around 2m: acts on firm going. *B. De Haan*   **c82 h96 F99**

RED ALERT MAN (IRE) 11 ch.g. Sharp Charter – Tukurua (Noalto) [2006/7 c61, h–: c24v⁵ May 23] workmanlike gelding: poor handicap chaser: stays 3¼m: acts on heavy going: tried in cheekpieces, usually blinkered. *Mrs L. Williamson*   **c– h–**

RED ALF 8 ch.g. Alflora (IRE) – Red Dust (Saxon Farm) [2006/7 h–: 21dᵖᵘ May 15] no sign of ability. *Miss J. Wormall*   **h–**

RED BELLS 6 b.g. Magic Ring (IRE) – Redgrave Devil (Tug of War) [2006/7 F84: F16m⁴ F17d* Aug 21] fair form in bumpers: won at Newton Abbot in August: joined P. Hobbs. *D. J. Wintle*   **F92**

RED BIRR (IRE) 6 b.g. Bahhare (USA) – Cappella (IRE) (College Chapel) [2006/7 16d Dec 26] compact gelding: fairly useful on Flat (stays 1¼m), successful in February: tailed off in novice on hurdling debut. *P. R. Webber*   **h–**

RED BROOK LAD 12 ch.g. Nomadic Way (USA) – Silently Yours (USA) (Silent Screen (USA)) [2006/7 c119, h–: c21g* c25m² c25d⁵ c20g² c24g² c20f³ c24g* Apr 21] leggy gelding: useful hunter chaser: won at Wincanton in May and Bangor (didn't need to be at best to beat Hip Pocket by 1¼ lengths) in April: creditable second to easy winner Scots Grey at Newbury fifth start: effective around 2½m to 25f: acts on firm and good to soft going: tried blinkered over hurdles: usually held up: genuine and reliable. *C. St V. Fox*   **c118 h–**

RED BULLET 5 ch.h. Hatim (USA) – Enchanted Goddess (Enchantment) [2006/7 16m Jul 26] tailed off in maiden on Flat at 3 yrs: well held in novice on hurdling debut. *A. G. Newcombe*   **h–**

RED CANYON (IRE) 10 b.g. Zieten (USA) – Bayazida (Bustino) [2006/7 c–, h93: 16m 19d Aug 7] sturdy gelding: winning hurdler, has lost his form: let down by jumping only outing over fences: stays 3m: wears headgear. *C. L. Tizzard*   **c– h–**

RED CEDAR (USA) 7 ch.g. Woodman (USA) – Jewell Ridge (USA) (Melyno) [2006/7 h–: 17d³ 17d³ 17s 17vᵖᵘ Feb 20] small, leggy gelding: poor maiden hurdler, lightly raced: raced around 2m: tried tongue tied. *J. Wade*   **h79**

RED DAHLIA 10 b.m. Alflora (IRE) – Redgrave Devil (Tug of War) [2006/7 c–, h90: 19g³ Jul 23] rather sparely-made mare: modest hurdler: stays 21f when emphasis is on speed: acts on any going. *Carl Llewellyn*   **c– h91**

RED DAWN (IRE) 8 ch.g. Presenting – West Tour (Deep Run) [2006/7 h–: c21vᵖᵘ Feb 20] tall, good sort: no show in various events. *J. M. Saville*   **c– h–**

RED DESSERT 6 ch.m. Blue Ocean (USA) – Merry Marigold (Sonnen Gold) [2006/7 F16m Jun 11] fifth foal: dam fair 1¼m winner: no show in maiden bumper on debut. *B. R. Millman*   **F–**

John Smith's Hurdle (West Yorkshire), Wetherby—
the enigmatic Redemption lowers the colours of My Way de Solzen despite fluffing the last

RED ECHO (FR) 6 b.g. Subotica (FR) – Volniste (FR) (Olmeto) [2006/7 h105p: 22g² c23m* c23g² c24s⁵ c24sᶠ c32sᵖᵘ Nov 15] tall, useful-looking gelding: fair hurdler: fairly useful handicap chaser: won at Worcester in June by 3½ lengths from Music To My Ears: ran well when second to On The Outside at Stratford 3 weeks later, but let down by jumping/ran as if amiss last 3 starts: should stay beyond 23f: acts on good to firm going. *D. E. Pipe*   **c116 h107**

REDEMPTION 12 b.g. Sanglamore (USA) – Ypha (USA) (Lyphard (USA)) [2006/7 c135x, h139§: 25s* 25dᵖᵘ 24s⁴ 25d 24v c22vᵖᵘ 21g Mar 14] workmanlike gelding: useful hurdler/chaser: won John Smith's Hurdle (West Yorkshire) at Wetherby in October by 6 lengths from My Way de Solzen: form after (including over fences) only when fourth of 5 to Inglis Drever in another Grade 2 at Newbury: stays 25f: acts on heavy and good to firm going: blinkered once (went in snatches): tried tongue tied: usually finds little: often let down by jumping over fences. *N. A. Twiston-Davies*   **c– x h144 §**

RED FLYER (IRE) 8 br.g. Catrail (USA) – Marostica (ITY) (Stone) [2006/7 c89, h–: 21m 20v⁴ 21d⁶ Jun 4] leggy, quite good-topped gelding: modest hurdler/chaser, below form early in 2006/7: effective at 2m to 2¾m: acts on heavy and good to firm going: sold 1,400 gns Doncaster January Sales. *Ronald Thompson*   **c– h79**

RED GEORGIE (IRE) 9 ch.g. Old Vic – Do We Know (Derrylin) [2006/7 c117d, h–: c26sᵖᵘ c25gᶠ Dec 26] big, strong, workmanlike gelding: fairly useful hurdler: similar form when successful on chasing debut in 2005/6, very disappointing since: should stay beyond 3m: raced on good going or softer: usually front runner. *N. A. Twiston-Davies*   **c– h–**

REDGES HOPE (IRE) 6 br.m. Little Bighorn – Sujani (IRE) (Mazaad) [2006/7 F18v c20m⁶ Apr 9] good-bodied mare: first foal: dam of little account: no show in various events. *S. Donohoe, Ireland*   **c– F–**

RED GRANITE 7 gr.g. Rock City – Cherry Side (General Ironside) [2006/7 h82, F88: c21dᵖᵘ c20s⁶ Dec 5] compact gelding: poor form over hurdles: no show in handicap chases: tried visored. *K. C. Bailey*   **c– h–**

REDHOT FILLYPEPPER 8 b.m. Lancastrian – Millennium Classic (Proverb) [2006/7 21vᵖᵘ 16vᵖᵘ 16vᵖᵘ Feb 5] seventh foal: half-sister to fair chaser Sean Connors (by   **h–**

Executive Perk), stayed 21f, and winning pointer by Yashgan: dam winning 2½m chaser: no show over hurdles: tongue tied. *Robert Gray*

REDHOUSE CHEVALIER 8 b.g. Pursuit of Love – Trampolo (USA) (Trempolino (USA)) [2006/7 c–, h–: c26g² c25dᵖᵘ c24gᵖᵘ Apr 27] little form in chases: left B. Powell after second outing, won maiden point in March: blinkered last 6 outings: has been reluctant to race. *Luke Price*
c70 ?
h–

RED HUSSAR 5 ch.g. Muhtarram (USA) – Miss Bussell (Sabrehill (USA)) [2006/7 17s 16vᵖᵘ Feb 17] of little account. *R. J. Price*
h–

REDI (ITY) 6 b.g. Danehill Dancer (IRE) – Rossella (Shareef Dancer (USA)) [2006/7 h110: c18sᵖᵘ 24sᵖᵘ 16dᵖᵘ Feb 1] angular gelding: fair handicap hurdler at best: sold out of A. Balding's stable, no form in 2006/7, including on chasing debut: should have stayed beyond 2m: raced on good going or softer (acted on heavy): tried in cheekpieces: usually tongue tied: ungenuine: dead. *C. L. Tizzard*
c– §
h– §

REDLYNCH SPIRIT (IRE) 7 b.g. Executive Perk – Gently Ridden (IRE) (King's Ride) [2006/7 h71, F–: 22d 16g⁵ 16v 16v Feb 12] rather leggy, close-coupled gelding: poor maiden hurdler: sketchy jumper. *C. L. Tizzard*
h65

RED MAN (IRE) 10 ch.g. Toulon – Jamie's Lady (Ashmore (FR)) [2006/7 c110x, h101: c20d* 17d c20m* Jun 11] lengthy gelding: fair chaser/handicap hurdler: won novices over fences at Sedgefield (eased, by 14 lengths) in May and Perth (handicap) in June: stays 2¾m when emphasis on speed: acts on any going: wears cheekpieces: sold only 500 gns Doncaster May Sales. *Mrs E. Slack*
c114
h–

RED MAN RAY (IRE) 7 ch.g. Aahsaylad – Whakapohane (Kampala) [2006/7 F16v⁶ 21d 22d⁵ 25v⁶ c18s³ Mar 11] rangy gelding: half-brother to 3 winning jumpers, notably fairly useful 2m hurdler/chaser Sublime Fellow (by Phardante): dam unraced: well held in 2 maiden Irish points in 2005: mid-field in bumper: best effort over hurdles when fifth in novice at Folkestone: poor form third in handicap on chasing debut: stays 2¾m. *T. R. George*
c78 +
h87
F69

RED MINSTER 10 b.g. Minster Son – Minty Muncher (Idiot's Delight) [2006/7 c24dᵖᵘ c27d³ c20d⁵ c27dᵖᵘ Nov 21] sturdy, lengthy gelding: winning chaser, lightly raced and little form since 2002/3: usually in cheekpieces: tried tongue tied. *R. Shiels*
c–
h–

RED MOOR (IRE) 7 gr.g. Eagle Eyed (USA) – Faakirah (Dragonara Palace (USA)) [2006/7 h110: 17s* 16sᵖᵘ 17g⁵ 16d 19d⁴ 17s³ 16d⁵ Jan 8] fair handicap hurdler: won at Bangor in May: stays easy 19f: acts on firm and soft going: tried in cheekpieces (ran poorly). *Mrs D. A. Hamer*
h112

REDNECK GIRL (IRE) 8 b.m. Oscar (IRE) – Flamewood (Touching Wood (USA)) [2006/7 h–: 20d⁵ c26sᵖᵘ Jan 15] no form outside points: tried in cheekpieces. *A. E. Jones*
c–
h–

RED O'DONNELL (IRE) 4 ch.g. Presenting – Madam Chloe (Dalsaan) [2006/7 F16g Apr 3] seventh foal: half-brother to fair hurdler Instan (by Insan), stays 2¾m, and 2¼m hurdle winner Austocon (by Be My Native): dam unraced: well held in bumper at Wetherby on debut (raced alone in straight). *D. McCain Jnr*
F–

RED PERK (IRE) 10 b.g. Executive Perk – Supreme View (Supreme Leader) [2006/7 c94, h95: c25g* 24gᶠ May 13] workmanlike gelding: winning hurdler: fair handicap chaser: won at Wetherby on first day of season: thorough stayer: acted on any going: wore cheekpieces: usually raced prominently: dead. *R. C. Guest*
c102
h–

RED POKER 7 ch.g. Alflora (IRE) – Scarlet Ember (Nearly A Hand) [2006/7 h84+, F104: 16sᵖᵘ c25sᵖᵘ c25gᶠ Apr 2] bumper winner: little impact in novice hurdles/maiden chases: dead. *G. A. Harker*
c–
h–

RED RAMPAGE 12 b.g. King's Ride – Mighty Fly (Comedy Star (USA)) [2006/7 c98d, h–: c33gᵖᵘ May 3] good-topped gelding: winning chaser: no show in hunters in 2006: tried visored, usually blinkered/tongue tied. *P. H. Hogarth*
c–
h–

RED RATTLE (IRE) 5 ch.g. Old Vic – Only Her Way (IRE) (Jurado (USA)) [2006/7 F80: F16s² F16s⁴ Nov 19] good-topped gelding: modest form in bumpers: will be suited by 2½m+. *Miss H. C. Knight*
F82

RED ROCKS BOURREE 6 b.g. Parthian Springs – Granny Nix (Zambrano) [2006/7 F17g Jul 23] £1,200 4-y-o: second foal: dam unraced: soundly beaten in bumper on debut: sold £400 Ascot December Sales. *R. H. York*
F–

RED SCALLY 7 b.g. Alflora (IRE) – Southend Scallywag (Tina's Pet) [2006/7 h92: F16m³ F16v⁴ F17d² 22m⁵ 22m⁴ 17g* 20s* 20s* 21v* 23v 25g 20s³ 24s³ Apr 25] lengthy, angular gelding: placed in bumpers: fairly useful hurdler: won novice at Bangor
h116
F92

in September, handicaps at Carlisle (novice) in October and Hexham in November and novice at Towcester (idled) later in November: good efforts when third in novice handicaps last 2 starts, behind Albertas Run in valuable event at Sandown on first occasion: stays 3m: acts on heavy going: has raced lazily. *R. C. Guest*

RED SEA RAVEN 4 b.f. Sea Raven (IRE) – Little Twig (IRE) (Good Thyne (USA)) **F—**
[2006/7 F16m F16g Apr 9] fifth foal: half-sister to 19f hurdle winner Fourboystoy (by Roselier) and 27f chase winner Rainbow Tree (by Rainbows For Life): dam poor form in bumpers: behind in mares bumpers. *B. N. Pollock*

REDSKIN RAIDER (IRE) 11 b.g. Commanche Run – Sheltered (IRE) (Strong Gale) **c—**
[2006/7 c78, h–: c19m^{pu} Mar 29] lengthy gelding: winning chaser: fair pointer nowadays, **h—**
little impact in hunters: stays 25f: best on good/good to firm going. *Miss S. Sharratt*

RED SOCIALITE (IRE) 10 ch.g. Moscow Society (USA) – Dees Darling (IRE) **c– x**
(King Persian) [2006/7 c–x, h–: 21g^{pu} May 4] tall, angular gelding: winning hurdler, bled **h—**
only start in 2006/7: maiden chaser, failed to complete all 4 outings since debut: stays 21f. *D. R. Gandolfo*

RED SOCIETY (IRE) 9 ch.g. Moscow Society (USA) – Allendara (IRE) (Phardante **c91**
(FR)) [2006/7 19d 19g^{ur} 19d c19s^6 19m^4 Apr 17] angular gelding: fair handicap hurdler/ **h101**
chaser: off 18 months, below form in 2006/7 until final outing: stays 23f: acts on firm and soft going: tried in cheekpieces, usually blinkered. *P. J. Hobbs*

REDSPIN (IRE) 7 ch.g. Spectrum (IRE) – Trendy Indian (IRE) (Indian Ridge) [2006/7 **h—**
h97: 22g May 16] angular gelding: poor on Flat nowadays: modest hurdler: off 6 months, well held only outing in 2006/7: stays 3m: acts on firm going: has looked tricky ride. *J. S. Moore*

RED SQUARE EXPRESS 5 b.g. Kayf Tara – Formal Affair (Rousillon (USA)) **h97**
[2006/7 F89: F17v^6 19g^F 19g^2 17s^6 24f^4 Apr 5] rangy gelding: third in bumper: **F—**
modest form over hurdles: stays 3m: acts on firm ground: has twice shaped as if amiss. *M. W. Easterby*

RED SQUARE LAD (IRE) 11 ch.g. Toulon – Tempestuous Girl (Tumble Wind) **c—**
[2006/7 c–, h–: c20s^{pu} c22v^{pu} c20v^5 Mar 9] strong, lengthy gelding: winning pointer/ **h—**
hunter chaser, very lightly raced: no show in handicaps in 2006/7: wore cheekpieces/ tongue strap final outing (bled). *Mrs L. Williamson*

RED SQUARE LADY (IRE) 9 b.m. Moscow Society (USA) – Arctic Scale (IRE) **h132**
(Strong Gale) [2006/7 23f* 16f* 16m 18s^F 22m^4 Apr 9] lengthy mare: maiden on Flat: useful hurdler: won minor event at Navan in June and Grade 3 Kevin McManus Book-maker Grimes Hurdle at Tipperary (by 1½ lengths from Callow Lake) in July: ran creditably in competitive handicaps completed starts after, 7¼ lengths fourth to Supreme Being at Fairyhouse: effective at 2m to 3m: all wins on good ground or firmer (acts on firm): usually makes running. *M. Phillips, Ireland*

RED SQUARE RUN 5 gr.g. Commanche Run – Absolutley Foxed (Absalom) [2006/7 **h—**
h–, F–: 16g 20g 20s May 17] no sign of ability: dead. *M. W. Easterby*

RED SUN 10 b.g. Foxhound (USA) – Superetta (Superlative) [2006/7 h–: c20g^4 c16f^5 **c90**
20g^{pu} 17m* c20g Oct 7] small, leggy gelding: modest hurdler nowadays: won claimer at **h93**
Sedgefield (claimed from J. Mackie £6,000) in September: similar form on first of 3 outings over fences: stays 19f: acts on soft and firm going: often tongue tied. *R. C. Guest*

RED WHARF BAY 5 b.g. Ashkalani (IRE) – Forest Heights (Slip Anchor) [2006/7 **F83**
F16g^5 Dec 26] fourth foal: half-brother to 2002 2-y-o 5f winner Forest Rail (by Catrail): dam fairly useful 1½m winner: modest form when fifth in bumper on debut: sold 1,400 gns Doncaster May Sales. *P. R. Webber*

REDWORTH BOY (IRE) 7 b.g. Zaffaran (USA) – Blue Rinse (Bluerullah) [2006/7 **c—**
20g c24s^{pu} c25g^5 c20g^{pu} Apr 16] big gelding: half-brother to smart staying chaser Blue **h—**
Charm (by Duky): dam maiden: little show in novice hurdle/over fences: tried tongue tied. *D. M. Forster*

REEL CHARMER 7 b.m. Dancing High – Gaelic Charm (IRE) (Deep Run) [2006/7 **h114**
F90: F17s^2 F16m^2 20d* 20s* 20s^2 21g^{pu} Mar 24] deep-topped mare: in frame in bumpers: **F88**
fair form in novice hurdles: won at Hexham (idled) and Newcastle (by 13 lengths) in November: likely to stay 3m: acts on soft and good to firm ground. *G. A. Charlton*

REEL DANCER 10 b.g. Minshaanshu Amad (USA) – Sister Rosarii (USA) (Proper- **c—**
antes (USA)) [2006/7 c26g^{pu} Apr 19] sturdy gelding: winning chaser for N. Henderson: **h—**
fair pointer nowadays: stays 3¼m: acts on good to firm and good to soft going. *Mrs J. Marles*

REELINGA 8 b.m. Karinga Bay – Reeling (Relkino) [2006/7 h75: 22d^{pu} 19d^{pu} 19s^{bd} 24s³ 19v² c16s⁵ 17d⁵ 20m⁵ Mar 29] poor maiden hurdler: well held on chasing debut: probably stays 3m: unraced on firm going, acts on any other: inconsistent. *G. A. Ham* **c– §** **h69 §**

REEL MISSILE 8 b.g. Weld – Landsker Missile (Cruise Missile) [2006/7 c115+, h–: 22g^{pu} Jul 5] tall, lengthy, angular gelding: fairly useful form over fences: winning hurdler, possibly amiss only start in 2006/7: stays 2½m: acts on soft and good to firm going: races prominently. *C. T. Pogson* **c–** **h–**

REEM TWO 6 b.m. Mtoto – Jamrat Samya (IRE) (Sadler's Wells (USA)) [2006/7 h102: 24m³ 20g³ 24d² 24s 21m⁵ 24g 21g Apr 19] smallish mare: fair handicap hurdler: stays 3m: acts on firm and good to soft ground: tried in cheekpieces (lost action): not a straightforward ride. *D. McCain Jnr* **h106**

REENGAROGA RAINBOW (IRE) 7 b.m. Freddie's Star – Pike Review (Dawn Review) [2006/7 21g^R 18m^{pu} Apr 26] fourth foal: half-sister to 2½m hurdle winner Magalina (by Norwich) and fairly useful chaser Pancho's Tango (by Arapahos), stayed 3m: dam unraced: looked far from keen both outings over hurdles (behind when refused 2 out on debut). *P. R. Webber* **h– §**

REESHAN (IRE) 5 b.g. Green Desert (USA) – Romoosh (Formidable (USA)) [2006/7 F17m Jun 7] fifth foal: half-brother to 1m winner Ramzain (by Alzao) and 6.5f winner in France by Royal Applause: dam 1¼m winner out of half-sister to high-class hurdler Mysilv: soundly beaten in bumper on debut. *J. J. Lambe, Ireland* **F–**

REFINEMENT (IRE) 8 b.m. Oscar (IRE) – Maneree (Mandalus) [2006/7 h143: 24s 22m³ 24s⁴ 24d[*] 20v³ 22d^{pu} 20s² 24g 24g³ 24m[*] Apr 26] **h150**
Refinement added a second Grade 1 victory at the Punchestown Festival
—following her triumph in the Champion INH Flat in 2005—when she pulled off something of a surprise in the Dunboyne Castle Hotel & Spa Champion Stayers' Hurdle. The race was rightly billed as a clash between the two-mile and three-mile hurdling divisions, with 2006 Champion Hurdle winner Brave Inca (also runner-up in the latest renewal at Cheltenham) taking on leading stayer Mighty Man over the

*Dunboyne Castle Hotel & Spa Champion Stayers' Hurdle, Punchestown—
Refinement (white face) adds to her bumper win here in 2005 with victory over
Powerstation (hooped sleeves), United and Essex (noseband)*

longer trip. Unfortunately the latter (who was sent off favourite) broke down badly and Brave Inca ran a very poor race, which left 16/1-shot Refinement to pick up the pieces. Patiently ridden by Tony McCoy, she stayed on strongest to win by two and a half lengths from Powerstation, with a further three lengths back to fellow British-trained mare United, who had beaten Refinement on all three previous meetings in 2006/7 (albeit receiving weight each time). Refinement had already vindicated the decision of connections to delay her retirement to the paddocks by having another good season, completing a relatively simple task to win a mares handicap at Kempton in December (in which four of her five rivals had to race from out of the handicap) and finishing in the money on a further five starts. In truth, however, she did rather go off the boil after that Kempton win (let down by jumping twice) before bouncing back with a career-best effort when third to stable-companion Albertas Run in the listed three-mile handicap hurdle on Grand National day at Aintree (a race she had won twelve months previously). Retirement looked likely in the immediate aftermath of her latest Punchestown triumph, but over the summer the decision was made that Refinement will return in 2007/8, a decision coinciding with the announcement of an upgraded and expanded programme of mares only events (discussed in the essay on United). They include a new £100,000 mares conditions event over an extended two and a half miles at the Cheltenham Festival, a race almost tailor-made for a top-form Refinement.

		Sadler's Wells (b 1981)	Northern Dancer
Refinement (IRE) (b.m. 1999)	Oscar (IRE) (b 1994)		Fairy Bridge
		Snow Day (b 1978)	Reliance II
			Vindaria
	Maneree (b 1987)	Mandalus (b 1974)	Mandamus
			Laminate
		Damberee (ch 1975)	Deep Run
			Star O'Meath

The pedigree of the smallish, lengthy Refinement has been covered in depth in previous editions of *Chasers & Hurdlers*. She stays three miles and is unraced on firm ground, but probably acts on any other. Her first win in 2006/7 was achieved in both blinkers and a tongue strap, but at Punchestown she proved that she is equally effective without either device. There look to be several above-average performers around to contest the lucrative new series of mares races, but it will be a surprise if Refinement fails to pay her way again in 2007/8. *Jonjo O'Neill*

REFLECTED GLORY (IRE) 8 b.g. Flemensfirth (USA) – Clashdermot Lass (Cardinal Flower) [2006/7 c129, h–: c24s* Mar 10] tall gelding: winning hurdler: useful chaser: off a year, not fluent at times when winning 5-runner handicap at Sandown by 3½ lengths from Howrwenow, left with every chance last: will be suited by 3¼m+: raced on ground softer than good (acts on heavy): sold 21,000 gns Doncaster May Sales. *P. F. Nicholls*   **c132 h–**

REFLECTOR (IRE) 6 b.g. Alderbrook – Four Moons (IRE) (Cardinal Flower) [2006/7 h93p, F77: 16s³ 16d 16d 16v Jan 12] useful-looking gelding: modest novice hurdler: likely to be suited by 2½m+: raced on good going or softer. *Miss H. C. Knight*   **h90**

REFLEX BLUE 10 b.g. Ezzoud (IRE) – Briggsmaid (Elegant Air) [2006/7 c74§, h73§: 24m c21m* c24m⁶ c20s c21v⁵ c19m³ c24g Apr 27] sturdy gelding: winning hurdler: poor chaser: won maiden at Stratford in September: stays 21f: acts on firm and soft going: usually visored: temperamental. *R. J. Price*   **c74 § h– §**

REGAL ANGEL 4 ch.f. Roi de Rome (USA) – Dominion's Dream (Dominion) [2006/7 F13m* Mar 29] fifth foal: dam, modest hurdler who stayed 2½m, 7f winner on Flat: green, won maiden bumper at Hereford on debut by 2½ lengths from First Blue, tending to hang left: should improve. *Jean-Rene Auvray*   **F86 p**

REGAL FANTASY (IRE) 7 b.m. King's Theatre (IRE) – Threesome (USA) (Seattle Dancer (USA)) [2006/7 h–: 16g 20s 24v^{pu} 17v Jan 2] good-topped mare: no form over hurdles: tried tongue tied. *P. A. Blockley*   **h–**

REGAL FUTURE 5 b.m. Regal Embers (IRE) – In The Future (IRE) (Phardante (FR)) [2006/7 F–: F16m^{pu} F16d Mar 22] no show in bumpers, left R. Dickin after first outing. *M. Keighley*   **F–**

REGAL HEIGHTS (IRE) 6 b.g. Grand Plaisir (IRE) – Regal Hostess (King's Ride) **c133**
[2006/7 h123: c16s³ c16d⁵ c20v² c16d* c20v² c16s* c17v* c20m⁴ Apr 8] good-topped **h–**
gelding: fairly useful hurdler: useful chaser: won maiden at Newcastle in January, handicap at Haydock in February and novice at Kelso (by ½ length from Percussionist) in
March: respectable fourth to One Cool Cookie in Grade 1 novice at Fairyhouse: stays
2½m: acts on good to firm and heavy going: jumps well: usually races prominently.
D. McCain Jnr

REGAL RIVER (IRE) 10 b.g. Over The River (FR) – My Friend Fashion (Laurence **c–**
O) [2006/7 c61, h–: c25d⁵ c24sᵖᵘ 25vᵖᵘ c24g⁶ Mar 28] close-coupled gelding: winning **h–**
hurdler/chaser, no form in 2006/7. *John R. Upson*

REGAL SETTING (IRE) 6 br.g. King's Theatre (IRE) – Cartier Bijoux (Ahonoora) **h112**
[2006/7 h–: 17d 18f² 16dᵖᵘ Oct 21] leggy, useful-looking gelding: fair handicap hurdler:
will stay beyond 2¼m: acts on firm and good to soft going: tried in cheekpieces/tongue
tied: has run as if amiss more than once. *J. Howard Johnson*

REGAL SUNSET (IRE) 4 b.g. Desert Prince (IRE) – Sunsetter (USA) (Diesis) **h90 p**
[2006/7 16d³ Nov 14] fair maiden on Flat (stays 9.4f), sold out of W. Swinburn's stable
9,000 gns Newmarket Autumn Sales: modest form when third in juvenile at Fakenham
on hurdling debut: should do better, especially with even more emphasis on speed.
D. E. Cantillon

REGAL TERM (IRE) 9 b.g. Welsh Term – Regal Hostess (King's Ride) [2006/7 **c98 x**
c110, h100: c20sᵖᵘ 24d³ c22gᶠ c22vᵖᵘ c21sᵖᵘ c20d 19v⁶ c20s⁵ 19g c21g Mar 30] lengthy **h86**
gelding: maiden hurdler: modest chaser: stays 2½m: raced on good going or softer: tried
visored: usually let down by jumping over fences. *R. Dickin*

REGAL VISION (IRE) 10 b.g. Emperor Jones (USA) – Shining Eyes (USA) (Mr **c– §**
Prospector (USA)) [2006/7 c82, h73: c25gᵖᵘ 27m⁵ c23dᵘʳ Oct 26] leggy gelding: poor **h64 §**
handicap hurdler/chaser: stays 25f: acts on firm going, probably on soft: tried blinkered,
not since early-2004/5: ungenuine (has refused/been reluctant to race). *Miss C. Dyson*

REGENTS WALK (IRE) 9 b.g. Phardante (FR) – Raw Courage (IRE) (The Parson) **c100**
[2006/7 h–: c20s² c20gᵖᵘ Nov 18] sturdy gelding: lightly raced: winning hurdler: runner- **h–**
up in maiden at Stratford on chasing debut: possibly amiss (jumped left) following
month: should stay beyond 2½m: acts on soft and good to firm ground. *B. De Haan*

REHEARSAL 6 b.g. Singspiel (IRE) – Daralaka (IRE) (The Minstrel (CAN)) [2006/7 **c112**
h112: 16m⁵ 16d⁵ c16m* c20f⁶ Apr 5] leggy gelding: useful on Flat (probably stays 2m): **h107**
fair handicap hurdler: much better effort over fences when winning maiden at Ludlow in
January by 11 lengths from Craven: best around 2m: acts on good to firm and good to soft
going: not a fluent jumper of hurdles. *L. Lungo*

REIDWIL (FR) 4 b.g. Bonnet Rouge (FR) – Reine du Mont (FR) (Tip Moss (FR)) **h97**
[2006/7 16s⁶ 16v⁵ 16v² 18sᵘʳ 16vᵖᵘ Feb 22] €30,000 3-y-o: unfurnished gelding: second
foal: dam, 7f winner in France, failed to complete only outing over hurdles: fair juvenile
hurdler: raced around 2m on soft/heavy ground. *D. E. Pipe*

REISK SUPERMAN (IRE) 9 b.g. Naheez (USA) – Forward Gal (The Parson) **c121**
[2006/7 18f* 18g⁵ c16s⁴ c20d⁶ c16v⁶ c17s c17m² c16m c18g² Apr 25] €16,000 4-y-o: **h110**
workmanlike gelding: fifth foal: brother to fairly useful 3m chase winner High Chimes
and half-brother to 2½m hurdle winner Sancta Miria (by Toulon): dam winning pointer/
hunter chaser: fair hurdler: won minor event at Fairyhouse in June: fairly useful maiden
chaser: good efforts when runner-up in handicap at same course (beaten neck by Kranji)
and novice at Punchestown (second start in 24 hrs, 1¾ lengths behind Pacolet): stays
2¼m: acts on firm and soft going: has worn cheekpieces/blinkers: held up. *A. J. Martin,
Ireland*

REIVERS MOON 8 b. or br.m. Midnight Legend – Here Comes Tibby (Royal Foun- **c–**
tain) [2006/7 c109, h–: 22g³ c20f⁶ Jun 3] smallish, leggy mare: fair hurdler/handicap **h108**
chaser: effective at 2m to 3m: acts on firm and soft going: often races prominently.
W. Amos

RELATIVE HERO (IRE) 7 ch.g. Entrepreneur – Aunty (FR) (Riverman (USA)) **h86**
[2006/7 h75: 20g³ 19d² 20d² 20s³ 20v 22s⁴ 22d Mar 20] small gelding: modest
maiden hurdler, sold out of Miss S. Wilton's stable £3,400 Ascot August Sales after
second outing: stays 2¾m: acts on soft going, probably on firm: tried visored, usually in
cheekpieces. *Mrs T. J. Hill*

RELIX (FR) 7 gr.g. Linamix (FR) – Resleona (Caerleon (USA)) [2006/7 h100: 18f⁴ 16g **h94**
Apr 16] leggy gelding: modest hurdler: went as if amiss last 2 outings: stays 3m: acts on
any going: often tongue tied. *A. M. Crow*

REMAINDER 4 ch.g. Mark of Esteem (IRE) – Stay Behind (Elmaamul (USA)) [2006/7 F14s F14s 20d 20g^F 20m^6 Apr 9] 1,600 2-y-o: medium-sized gelding: first foal: dam, 1¼m winner, out of half-sister to Rainbow Quest: well held all completed outings, though has left impression may still do better over hurdles around 2m. *I. McMath* **h– p / F–**

REMEMBERING 7 b.g. Regal Embers (IRE) – Hip Joint (Brotherly (USA)) [2006/7 17s^pu 16g^pu Mar 20] second foal: dam maiden pointer: no sign of ability: tongue tied. *Mike Hammond* **h–**

REMEMBER RAMON (USA) 4 ch.g. Diesis – Future Act (USA) (Known Fact (USA)) [2006/7 16d^6 17g^4 Mar 25] useful on Flat (stays 1½m) for M. Wallace, successful twice in 2006: fair form in juvenile hurdles: needs to improve jumping, but remains capable of better. *P. J. Hobbs* **h99 p**

REMIS VELISQUE 4 ch.f. Fraam – Charming Tina (IRE) (Indian Ridge) [2006/7 F14g F14s Jan 4] lengthy, unfurnished filly: first foal: dam no sign of ability: well held in bumpers and on Flat. *B. G. Powell* **F67**

RENEE LARD (IRE) 4 ch.f. Titus Livius (FR) – Miss Body (IRE) (Hamas (IRE)) [2006/7 17m^F Aug 26] no sign of ability on Flat or on hurdling debut. *A. Berry* **h–**

RENEGE THE JOKER 4 b.g. Alflora (IRE) – Bunty (Presidium) [2006/7 F16v Jan 27] small gelding: first foal: dam, winner around 1m, half-sister to smart chaser Bold Investor, stayed 3m: well beaten in 4-y-o bumper on debut. *Mrs C. A. Dunnett* **F–**

RENVYLE (IRE) 9 b. or br.g. Satco (FR) – Kara's Dream (IRE) (Bulldozer) [2006/7 c92§, h98§: c20f c22g^5 c26m^3 c24g^2 c21d^2 c26m^5 c20g^3 c20g c24g* c23m^pu c24s^pu Nov 25] close-coupled gelding: winning hurdler: modest handicap chaser: won at Newcastle in November: stays 3¼m: acts on good to firm and heavy going: wears headgear: held up: often let down by jumping/temperament. *R. C. Guest* **c90 § / h– §**

REPLY TO MOSCOW (IRE) 5 ch.g. Moscow Society (USA) – Mail Road Lady (IRE) (Henbit (USA)) [2006/7 22d^5 16v Mar 10] €18,000 3-y-o: third foal: dam placed in points: runner-up in maiden Irish point in 2006: bought £40,000 Cheltenham April Sales: no form over hurdles, left M. Appleby and off over 9 months after debut: dead. *Mrs J. Harrington, Ireland* **h–**

RESEDA (IRE) 10 b.g. Rock Hopper – Sweet Mignonette (Tina's Pet) [2006/7 c–, h–: c23g^4 c20g^5 c23g^5 c25m 20s^6 c24f^3 c25m^pu Aug 6] useful-looking gelding: bumper winner: novice hurdler: poor maiden chaser: stayed 25f: blinkered last 2 starts: tongue tied: dead. *M. A. Barnes* **c83 / h75**

RESERVOIR (IRE) 6 b.g. Green Desert (USA) – Spout (Salse (USA)) [2006/7 h97§: 18m 20f Jun 21] stocky gelding: regressive hurdler: best around 2m: acts on soft and good to firm going: tried blinkered/in cheekpieces: ungenuine. *J. Joseph* **h83 §**

RESONANCE 6 b.m. Slip Anchor – Music In My Life (IRE) (Law Society (USA)) [2006/7 h88: 19g 16m^6 19m^5 19m^3 16d^4 17d^2 24s^6 Dec 18] lengthy mare: poor maiden hurdler, claimed from N. Twiston-Davies £6,000 third start: stays 19f: acts on firm and good to soft going: blinkered last 4 starts: tongue tied once: prone to mistakes. *S. Lycett* **h83**

betfair.com Handicap Chase, Aintree—the grey Reveillez wins impressively

RESPLENDENT STAR (IRE)   10 b.g. Northern Baby (CAN) – Whitethroat (Artaius (USA)) [2006/7 c111, h104: c16g⁴ 17d c20mᵖᵘ c17g² c20m⁴ c16m⁴ c20mᵖᵘ c21gᵘʳ c21g³ Apr 9] winning hurdler: modest novice chaser, sold out of Mrs L. Wadham's stable 11,000 gns Doncaster October Sales after seventh outing: best form up to 2½m: acts on firm and good to soft going: usually visored/blinkered: prone to mistakes over fences. *N. M. Bloom*   **c96 x** **h87**

RESSOURCE (FR)   8 b.g. Broadway Flyer (USA) – Rayonne (Sadler's Wells (USA)) [2006/7 h85§: 21g² 18m 17d⁵ Jun 12] leggy gelding: poor handicap hurdler: stays 21f: acts on heavy and good to firm going: blinkered: ungenuine. *G. L. Moore*   **h84 §**

RESTORATION (FR)   5 gr.g. Zafonic (USA) – Restless Mixa (IRE) (Linamix (FR)) [2006/7 h110: 17f² 16g⁴ 16g² 16g 16s⁵ 16m⁴ 16m⁶ Apr 24] well-made gelding: type to make a chaser: fairly useful hurdler: won maiden at Kilbeggan and handicap at Tralee in August: off 6 months, ran well when under 2 lengths fourth to De Valira in Grade 2 novice at Fairyhouse: raced around 2m: acts on soft and good to firm ground. *N. Meade, Ireland*   **h120**

RETURNED UN PAID (IRE)   10 b.g. Actinium (FR) – Claregalway Lass (Ardross) [2006/7 c–, h–: c25m⁶ 26m 24m 24m⁶ Jul 12] workmanlike gelding: poor chaser/maiden hurdler: stays 3¼m: acts on good to firm and heavy going: tried blinkered. *Mrs L. Williamson*   **c–** **h71**

RETURN HOME   8 b.g. Bob's Return (IRE) – Welgenco (Welsh Saint) [2006/7 h100: c16m* c16m² c20m² c16g³ c16d⁴ c20d² Nov 20] sturdy gelding: fair hurdler/novice chaser: won over fences at Sedgefield in June: stays 2½m: acts on soft and good to firm going: tried blinkered (raced freely)/tongue tied. *J. S. Smith*   **c100** **h–**

RETURN TICKET   8 br.g. Bob's Return (IRE) – Mrs Jennifer (River Knight (FR)) [2006/7 h100, F84: 24s 22m⁶ 22s 20v² 20v⁴ 20s* 20v⁴ 20g 27sᵖᵘ Apr 27] good-topped gelding: modest handicap hurdler: won at Newcastle in January: no show after: stays 3m: acts on heavy going. *Miss Lucinda V. Russell*   **h99**

REVE EN BLEU (FR)   5 gr.g. Saint Preuil (FR) – Reverie Bleue (FR) (Reve Bleu (FR)) [2006/7 17v³ 22s³ Feb 18] 12,000 2-y-o: useful-looking gelding: second foal: dam twice-raced half-sister to very smart French chaser Indien Bleu: won maiden Irish point in 2006: modest form when third in novice hurdles 3 months apart, squeezed and slipped badly home turn in race won by Leo McGarry at Fontwell on second occasion: likely to stay 3m. *P. F. Nicholls*   **h99**

REVEILLEZ   8 gr.g. First Trump – Amalancher (USA) (Alleged (USA)) [2006/7 c147, h–: c19dᶠ c21s c21g⁶ c25g* c29f² Apr 28] tall, leggy gelding: winning hurdler: smart handicap chaser: best effort when winning betfair.com Handicap Chase at Aintree in April by 7 lengths from Lankawi: again favourite, 3 lengths second to Hot Weld in Betfred Gold Cup at Sandown 15 days later, again travelling strongly long way (reportedly lost hind shoe): barely stays 29f: unraced on heavy going, acts on any other: tongue tied last 3 starts: sometimes ridden. *J. R. Fanshawe*   **c154** **h–**

REVELINO (IRE)   8 b.g. Revoque (IRE) – Forelino (USA) (Trempolino (USA)) [2006/7 22m Apr 22] useful-looking gelding: maiden hurdler: stays 19f: best form on good/soft to firm going: tried in cheekpieces: ungenuine. *Mrs N. S. Evans*   **h– §**

REVERSE SWING   10 b.m. Charmer – Milly Kelly (Murrayfield) [2006/7 c92, h72: 20m⁵ c26d³ c26d⁶ Jun 12] good-topped mare: modest handicap chaser: poor hurdler: stays 3m: acts on firm and heavy going: effective tongue tied or not: often makes running: sold 8,500 gns Doncaster August Sales. *Heather Dalton*   **c64 +** **h72**

REXMEHEAD (IRE)   6 b.g. Fort Morgan (USA) – Moon Rose (IRE) (Imperial Frontier (USA)) [2006/7 F13s F16d 16vᵖᵘ 20g Apr 15] €9,000 3-y-o: good-topped gelding: first foal: dam, fair maiden, stayed 9f: no show in bumpers/over hurdles. *A. Wilson*   **h–** **F–**

REYNARDS RETURN (IRE)   4 b.g. Humbel (USA) – She's No Tourist (IRE) (Doubletour (USA)) [2006/7 F17g Apr 27] 26,000 3-y-o: fourth foal: brother to bumper winner She's Humble and half-brother to bumper/19f hurdle winner Don And Gerry (by Vestris Abu): dam of little account: tailed off in bumper on debut. *J. A. T. de Giles*   **F–**

RHAPSODY IN BLOOM   6 b.g. Botanic (USA) – Jazzy Refrain (IRE) (Jareer (USA)) [2006/7 F–: F18m 21dᵖᵘ Oct 30] no form in bumpers/novice hurdle. *L. Wells*   **h–** **F–**

RHETORICAL   6 b.g. Unfuwain (USA) – Miswaki Belle (USA) (Miswaki (USA)) [2006/7 h76: 22m 22m 20m 26mᵖᵘ Jun 19] workmanlike gelding: maiden hurdler, no form in 2006/7: has worn cheekpieces/visor/tongue strap. *P. Butler*   **h–**

RHETORIC (IRE)   8 b.g. Desert King (IRE) – Squaw Talk (USA) (Gulch (USA)) [2006/7 c–, h–: c19gᵖᵘ 19g⁶ 16m 19g⁶ 19m³ 17s⁵ 17m 16d 17d³ 21m⁶ c16d⁵ Dec 21] angular gelding: poor maiden hurdler, left Miss Sarah-Jayne Davies after first outing: **c– §** **h66 §**

little impact in chases: stays easy 21f: acts on firm and good to soft going: tried tongue tied: temperamental (has been reluctant to race). *G. H. Jones*

RHINESTONE COWBOY (IRE) 11 b.g. Be My Native (USA) – Monumental Gesture (Head For Heights) [2006/7 20s^{pu} 23s⁵ 24g Mar 15] medium-sized, well-made gelding: top-class hurdler at best: won Aintree Hurdle and Champion Stayers' Hurdle at Punchestown in April 2004: off over 2½ years (leg trouble), smart form in handicaps in 2006/7 (reportedly suffered from colic after return), never-dangerous ninth of 24 to Oscar Park in Pertemps Final at Cheltenham: stays 3m: raced on good going or softer (acts on soft): held up: usually ridden by Mr J. P. Magnier. *Jonjo O'Neill*   **h145**

RHUBY RIVER (IRE) 5 b.m. Bahhare (USA) – Westside Flyer (Risk Me (FR)) [2006/7 16d^{pu} 16m⁴ 16d 16g 17g⁶ Apr 11] little form on Flat: bad novice hurdler: raced around 2m. *R. Dickin*   **h57**

RHUNA RED 8 ch.m. Good Thyne (USA) – Oh Dear (Paico) [2006/7 h76?: 20g^{pu} May 30] little form in novice hurdles (lame only start in 2006/7): tried tongue tied. *J. R. Bewley*   **h–**

RHYMNEY BITTER BOY 7 b.g. Alderbrook – Delta Rose (Swing Easy (USA)) [2006/7 16d^{pu} 24f^{pu} Apr 5] leggy gelding: ninth foal: dam poor novice selling hurdler: no show in novice hurdles. *D. Burchell*   **h–**

RHYTHM KING 12 b.g. Rakaposhi King – Minim (Rymer) [2006/7 c113, h–: c25g⁵ May 3] lengthy gelding: prolific winning pointer: fairly useful hunter chaser: stays 21f: raced on good going or softer: often let down by jumping. *G. C. Maundrell*   **c– x**
h–

RICARDO'S CHANCE 8 b.g. Alflora (IRE) – Jims Sister (Welsh Captain) [2006/7 20m* 24m* Apr 25] modest hurdler: left O. O'Neill and off 2 years, much improved when successful both starts in 2006/7, in novices at Hereford (well backed, seller) in March and Worcester (conditional jockeys handicap) in April: stays 3m: acts on good to firm going. *S. Lycett*   **h97 +**

RICCARTON 14 b.g. Nomination – Legendary Dancer (Shareef Dancer (USA)) [2006/7 c65, h–: 17m^{ur} c16s³ c16m c16d⁴ Jul 23] leggy gelding: veteran hurdler/maiden chaser: tried tongue tied. *D. C. Turner*   **c–**
h–

RICH ALBI 5 b.g. Mind Games – Bollin Sophie (Efisio) [2006/7 16g^{ur} 17m^{pu} Aug 2] sprint maiden on Flat: failed to complete over hurdles. *N. A. Dunger*   **h–**

RICHARDS CLAIRE (IRE) 6 b.m. Darazari (IRE) – Loquacious (IRE) (Distinctly North (USA)) [2006/7 16m 16m 16m 16m 17f 16v Dec 11] placed in bumpers: little form on Flat/over hurdles: left Colm Murphy prior to final outing (tongue tied): raced around 2m. *D. P. Keane*   **h75**

RICHARD'S SUNDANCE (IRE) 5 b.g. Saddlers' Hall (IRE) – Celestial Rose (IRE) (Roselier (FR)) [2006/7 F16v⁵ F17v^{ro} F17s⁶ F16g⁵ Mar 28] 20,000 3-y-o: unfurnished gelding: fourth foal: half-brother to 2¾m hurdle winner Jay Lo (by Glacial Storm): dam unraced: fair form in bumpers (ran out early second start): tried blinkered. *Mrs S. D. Williams*   **F86**

RICHEY DUNNE (IRE) 7 b.g. Fourstars Allstar (USA) – Woodville Time (IRE) (Lancastrian) [2006/7 F16g⁴ F20m Jul 27] fourth foal: half-brother to winning Irish pointer/hunter chaser Risky Deal (by Supreme Leader): dam thrice-raced maiden pointer: in frame both completed starts in maiden Irish points in 2005: well held in bumpers: likely to need good test of stamina. *Dermot Day, Ireland*   **F–**

RICH NOMAD 5 b.m. Nomadic Way (USA) – Weareagrandmother (Prince Tenderfoot (USA)) [2006/7 F16v 17s 19s Mar 12] small mare: seventh foal: half-sister to modest hurdler/fair chaser Alfy Rich (by Alflora), stays 25f, and fair hurdler Granny Rich (by Ardross), stayed 2½m: dam, winning hurdler, successful up to 12.5f on Flat: well held in bumper/maiden hurdles. *N. E. Berry*   **h–**
F–

RICH SONG (IRE) 9 b.g. Treasure Hunter – Sonnet Lady (Down The Hatch) [2006/7 c65, h–: 20g 21d^{pu} c20f⁵ c22m* c22g^F c21m c24g^{pu} c20s^{pu} c16m⁴ c20m^{pu} c16m⁶ Apr 24] angular gelding: maiden hurdler: little form over fences except when winning novice handicap at Market Rasen (by 14 lengths) in June: left Mrs S. Smith after sixth start: stays 2¾m: acts on good to firm going: sometimes let down by jumping. *M. Sheppard*   **c86**
h–

RICKETY BRIDGE (IRE) 4 ch.g. Elnadim (USA) – Kriva (Reference Point) [2006/7 aF13g⁶ Nov 22] half-brother to 3 winners, including useful performer up to 2m in Sweden Peruginos Flyer (by Perugino) and fairly useful 1¼m winner Shrivar (by Sri Pekan): dam 17f winner: left with plenty to do when sixth to Turbo Linn in 3-y-o bumper at Lingfield: successful on Flat debut in April. *P. R. Chamings*   **F81**

RICKY B 11 b.g. Rakaposhi King – Fililode (Mossberry) [2006/7 24s[5] c24v[pu] Mar 4] fair pointer, successful twice in April: no form in other events. *R. J. Hewitt* **c–** **h–**

RIDERS REVENGE (IRE) 9 b.g. Norwich – Paico Ana (Paico) [2006/7 c–, h–: c16s[3] c24v[pu] c19s 16v[bd] 16s 20g Apr 21] strong, compact gelding: maiden hurdler: little form since 2004/5, including over fences: tried tongue tied. *Miss Venetia Williams* **c–** **h–**

RIDGELINE 4 ch.g. Rainbow Quest (USA) – Bina Ridge (Indian Ridge) [2006/7 F14s[3] F16s Jan 24] smallish gelding: second foal: half-brother to French 11f/13f winner Prithee (by Barathea): dam, 9f winner from 2 starts, half-sister to winner up to 1¼m Bal Harbour and 1½m winner Bequeath, both smart: better effort in bumpers when third to easy winner Turbo Linn in 3-y-o event at Carlisle: tongue tied. *M. W. Easterby* **F81**

RIDGEWAY (IRE) 12 b.g. Indian Ridge – Regal Promise (Pitskelly) [2006/7 c23g[pu] May 11] lengthy gelding: winning chaser, lightly raced nowadays (including in points): in cheekpieces/blinkers last 5 outings. *P. Foster* **c–** **h–**

RIDJIT (FR) 7 b.g. Exit To Nowhere (USA) – Ridja Princess (FR) (Crystal Glitters (USA)) [2006/7 h92: 21s[4] c22s[F] 22v 16g[bd] c20m[4] Apr 9] sturdy gelding: maiden hurdler: well beaten completed outing over fences: tried tongue tied: sold 2,500 gns Doncaster May Sales. *N. J. Gifford* **c–** **h–**

RIFLEMAN (IRE) 7 ch.g. Starborough – En Garde (USA) (Irish River (FR)) [2006/7 c99§, h104§: c20m[4] c20g[6] c21f 20g[6] Apr 23] sparely-made gelding: maiden hurdler: modest chaser: stays 3m: acts on soft and good to firm going: has worn headgear: tongue tied: ungenuine. *D. W. Thompson* **c95 §** **h75 §**

RIGADOON (IRE) 11 b.g. Be My Chief (USA) – Loucoum (FR) (Iron Duke (FR)) [2006/7 c–§, h–: c24m[4] May 16] big, close-coupled gelding: winning chaser: last on completed outing in hunters: usually blinkered/in cheekpieces: untrustworthy. *Mrs J. L. Haley* **c– §** **h–**

RIGHTFUL RULER 5 b.g. Montjoy (USA) – Lady of The Realm (Prince Daniel (USA)) [2006/7 h–: 20s[3] 16f[3] 17s[4] 16g 16g Apr 15] modest novice hurdler: stays 2½m: acts on firm and good to soft going. *M. Todhunter* **h94**

RIGHT MIRACLE (IRE) 7 b.g. Right Win (IRE) – Murphy's Lady (IRE) (Over The River (FR)) [2006/7 20f 22s[bd] 22d 19g[pu] Mar 23] sturdy gelding: half-brother to fairly useful chaser Willie John Daly (by Mister Lord), stays 29f: dam winning pointer: in frame once from 3 starts in Irish points in 2006: left Michael Cronin, running easily best race over hurdles when brought down last (likely to have finished second) in maiden at Fontwell. *Miss H. C. Knight* **h94**

RIGHTONTIME (IRE) 11 b.g. Namaqualand (USA) – Come In (Be My Guest (USA)) [2006/7 21s[pu] 20g[2] 16s[2] 24s Dec 29] bumper winner: maiden hurdler, poor nowadays, left C. Roche before return: stays 3m: acts on soft ground (won bumper on firm): in cheekpieces last 2 starts. *D. J. Wintle* **h78**

RIGHT TO REASON (IRE) 11 b.m. Mac's Imp (USA) – Ellaline (Corvaro (USA)) [2006/7 19g[pu] May 4] only completion in points, won maiden in 2006: no show in mares novice on hurdling debut. *D. A. Rees* **h–**

RIGHTWAY STAR (IRE) 4 b.g. Stowaway – Decent Shower (Decent Fellow) [2006/7 F16d[2] Mar 17] 21,000 3-y-o: tall gelding: half-brother to fairly useful hurdler/chaser around 2m Stormy Lord and fair chaser Gayles And Showers (both by Lord Americo), stayed 3m: dam Irish bumper winner: green, neck second to Bertie May (pair clear) in bumper at Uttoxeter on debut. *D. McCain Jnr* **F105**

RILEYS DREAM 8 b.m. Rudimentary (USA) – Dorazine (Kalaglow) [2006/7 16f 16m Jun 11] poor performer on Flat (stays 7f), tailed off only outing in 2006: little impact over hurdles. *C. J. Price* **h–**

RI NA REALTA (IRE) 12 b.g. King's Ride – Realteen (Deep Run) [2006/7 c90, h–: c21g[2] c26g[F] c23f[3] c23d[5] c20m[ur] Oct 16] modest maiden chaser: no form in 2006/7 after first outing: should be suited by further than 21f: acts on heavy going: tried in cheekpieces. *J. W. Mullins* **c92** **h–**

RINDOON (IRE) 5 b.g. Beneficial – Upton Lodge (IRE) (Clearly Bust) [2006/7 F16g[6] F16g[2] 16d[2] 16s* 16s* 16d 16m[3] Apr 24] rather unfurnished gelding: first foal: dam unraced: runner-up in 4-y-o bumper: useful novice hurdler: won easily at Thurles (maiden) in January and Limerick (made all again despite couple of mistakes to beat Monoceros by 4 lengths) in February: improved further when 1¼ lengths second (demoted after hampering rival) to Clopf in Grade 1 Champion Novices' Hurdle at Punchestown: raced at 2m: acts on on soft and good to firm going. *E. Sheehy, Ireland* **h136** **F93**

RINGAROOMA 5 b.m. Erhaab (USA) – Tatouma (USA) (The Minstrel (CAN)) **h–**
[2006/7 16m 16m Jul 11] modest on Flat (stays 1¼m): well beaten in selling hurdles.
C. N. Allen

RINGAROSES 6 b.g. Karinga Bay – Rose Ravine (Deep Run) [2006/7 F106: 21g* **h136 p**
19d* Dec 16] good sort: has plenty of scope: successful twice in bumpers in 2005/6 (sixth
in Grade 2 final start): made good start over hurdles, winning novices at Kempton (easily)
in November and Ascot (useful form, beat Breathing Fire by 3½ lengths) in December:
will stay beyond 21f: looked sure to improve further, but reportedly suffered setback and
not seen out again. *Miss H. C. Knight*

RING BACK (IRE) 6 ch.m. Bob Back (USA) – Ardrom (Ardross) [2006/7 F101: 16g² **h108**
20s⁶ 21s² 16s* 21g Apr 19] sturdy mare: bumper winner: best effort over hurdles (fair
form) when winning mares maiden at Towcester (by 13 lengths) in February: stays 21f:
raced on good going or softer. *B. I. Case*

RINGO CODY (IRE) 6 b.g. Dushyantor (USA) – Just A Second (Jimsun) [2006/7 **h–**
F89: 20g Sep 30] third in bumper (blinkered): well beaten in novice on hurdling debut:
bred to stay at least 2½m. *D. R. Gandolfo*

RINGO (IRE) 7 b.g. Norwich – Fairly Lively (IRE) (Remainder Man) [2006/7 16s **h–**
Apr 27] failed to complete in 2 points in 2006: no show in maiden on hurdling debut.
S. G. Waugh

RING THE BOSS (IRE) 6 b.g. Kahyasi – Fortune's Girl (Ardross) [2006/7 h100p, **h125 p**
F75: 22s⁴ 21s 16s* 19v* 20g* Mar 17] tall gelding: fairly useful hurdler: left R. Woodhouse, unbeaten and improved good deal further last 3 starts, winning handicap in
January and novice in February, both at Catterick, and handicap at Wetherby (by
1¾ lengths from Camden George) in March: will stay 3m: raced on good ground or
softer (acts on heavy): capable of better yet: sold 100,000 gns Doncaster May Sales.
G. A. Swinbank

RINNWOOD LASS (IRE) 6 b.m. Courtship – Classic Difference (IRE) (Classic **h84**
Secret (USA)) [2006/7 21v⁶ 16s⁵ Apr 26] second foal: dam unraced: better effort in
novice hurdles when fifth to South O'The Border at Perth. *D. P. Keane*

RINROE (IRE) 5 b.g. Broken Hearted – Annie Log (Tap On Wood) [2006/7 F16s² **F108**
F16v³ F16v* Jan 7] €18,000 3-y-o: half-brother to bumper winner Port Jeff (by
Shernazar) and a winning pointer by Tremblant: dam unraced daughter of top-class
chaser Anaglogs Daughter: useful form in bumpers, won 18-runner maiden at Naas by 4
lengths from Bootlegger. *N. Meade, Ireland*

RINTY (NZ) 5 ch.g. Istidaad (USA) – Nearco Gold (NZ) (Virginia Privateer (USA)) **h87**
[2006/7 16s⁶ 17s 16sᵖᵘ Feb 17] lightly raced on Flat, including in New Zealand: modest
form over hurdles. *C. G. Cox*

RIO BRAVO (IRE) 7 b.g. Supreme Leader – Aiguille (IRE) (Lancastrian) [2006/7 21d **h95 p**
16s⁴ Dec 13] rangy, useful-looking gelding: will make a chaser: first foal: dam, fair hunter
chaser who stayed 3m, half-sister to Over The Deel and Smarty, both placed in Grand
National: successful 3 times in Irish points, including twice in 2006: much better effort
over hurdles when 16 lengths fourth to Climate Change in maiden at Newbury, again not
knocked about: should prove suited by 2¼m+: likely to improve again. *C. R. Egerton*

RIODAN (IRE) 5 ch.m. Desert King (IRE) – Spirit of The Nile (FR) (Generous (IRE)) **F91**
[2006/7 F94: F17d* May 1] tall mare: fair form in bumpers, won at Sedgefield in May:
similar standard on Flat, successful following month. *J. J. Quinn*

RIO DE JANEIRO (IRE) 6 b.g. Sadler's Wells (USA) – Alleged Devotion (USA) **h121**
(Alleged (USA)) [2006/7 h–: 16g³ 16d⁴ 16m³ 16v⁵ 19s* 16d Feb 10] sturdy gelding:
fairly useful hurdler: won at Stratford in May (novice) and February (handicap, beat
Absolut Power by 1¼ lengths): also ran well when fifth of 7 to Silverburn in Grade 1
Tolworth Hurdle at Sandown: stays 19f: acts on good to firm and heavy ground. *Miss
E. C. Lavelle*

RIPALONG LAD (IRE) 6 b.g. Zaffaran (USA) – King's Concubine (King's Ride) **F83**
[2006/7 F16sᵖᵘ Apr 10] first foal: dam, little sign of ability, granddaughter of Cheltenham
Gold Cup winner Glencaraig Lady: 12 lengths third to Oberon Moon in bumper at
Chepstow on debut: likely to be suited by stiffer test of stamina. *P. Bowen*

RISETOTHEOCCASION (IRE) 11 b.g. Glacial Storm (USA) – Cute Play (Sallu- **c84**
ceva) [2006/7 c23g³ 20s 24sᵖᵘ 22v 20v 27sᶠ Apr 27] fair handicap hurdler at best, no **h–**
show in 2006/7: poor maiden chaser: stays 27f: acts on heavy going: tried in cheekpieces.
C. A. McBratney, Ireland

RISING ACCOUNT 7 ch.g. Primitive Rising (USA) – Indian Cruise (Cruise Missile) **h93 ?**
[2006/7 22g Mar 19] 15,000 4-y-o: fourth foal: half-brother to fair chaser Bengal Bullet
(by Infantry), stays 3¼m: dam, winning chaser, stayed 2¾m: placed both completed starts
in maiden points in 2005: ninth of 12 finishers in novice on hurdling debut, possibly
flattered. A. J. Honeyball

RISING GENERATION (FR) 10 ch.g. Risen Star (USA) – Queen's Victory (FR) **c–**
(Carmarthen (FR)) [2006/7 c–, h123: 18f⁶ 16m Oct 1] tall gelding: fairly useful handicap **h109**
hurdler at best, below form last 4 outings: stays 19f: acts on good to firm and heavy going.
N. G. Richards

RISING TEMPEST 6 gr.m. Primitive Rising (USA) – Stormswift (Neltino) [2006/7 **h71**
h73, F85: 20m⁴ 22d⁴ 20f³ 17s 21m Nov 9] small, angular mare: bumper winner: poor
maiden hurdler: stays 2½m. J. M. Saville

RISINGTON 9 b.g. Afzal – Barton Rise (Raise You Ten) [2006/7 c71: c17g⁴ May 5] **c66**
winning pointer: poor maiden chaser: should be suited by further than 2m. Miss Venetia
Williams

RISK ACCESSOR (IRE) 12 b.g. Commanche Run – Bellatollah (Bellman (FR)) **c117**
[2006/7 c140§, h–: c25d³ c23v³ c21g Apr 13] tall gelding: useful chaser at best: third in **h–**
hunters first 2 outings in 2006/7, then lost all chance at start in Topham Chase at Aintree:
stays 3m: acts on good to firm and heavy going: tried in cheekpieces: often tongue tied in
past: bold jumper, prone to odd bad mistake: often finishes weakly. Jonjo O'Neill

RISK CHALLENGE (USA) 5 ch.g. Mt Livermore (USA) – Substance (USA) **h84**
(Diesis) [2006/7 F101: F16m² 16s 16g Apr 14] sturdy, workmanlike gelding: fairly useful **F96**
bumper winner: well held in novice hurdles: races freely. C. J. Price

RISK REVERSAL 7 b.g. Taipan (IRE) – Something Green (Green Shoon) **c102**
[2006/7 c21g⁴ c21d^pu Nov 30] 7,500F: strong gelding: fifth foal: dam unraced: successful
on last of 6 starts in maiden Irish points: bought £30,000 Cheltenham April Sales: not
knocked about when remote fourth of 5 to Aztec Warrior in novice at Folkestone on chase
debut: lame later in month. B. De Haan

RISK RUNNER (IRE) 4 b.g. Mull of Kintyre (USA) – Fizzygig (Efisio) [2006/7 16s² **h102**
16s* 17s⁵ 16v² 16d 17g⁶ Apr 18] close-coupled gelding: fairly useful but none too
consistent on Flat (stays 11.6f): fair juvenile hurdler: won at Warwick in December: raced
around 2m on good going or softer: visored/blinkered. A. King

RISKY RHYTHM 8 b.g. Primitive Rising (USA) – Heatheridge (IRE) (Carlingford **h82**
Castle) [2006/7 20g 24g 23v⁴ 25g² 20s⁵ Jun 25] second foal: dam of little account: poor
form over hurdles: will prove best at 3m+. R. Johnson

RISKY WAY 11 b.g. Risk Me (FR) – Hot Sunday Sport (Star Appeal) [2006/7 c91, h–: **c84**
c20m⁵ c16s^pu c16f^F c25g^pu Oct 7] leggy, close-coupled gelding: modest handicap chaser, **h–**
below best in 2006/7: best up to easy 2½m: acts on any going: visored twice, has won
with/without cheekpieces. W. S. Coltherd

RIVAL BIDDER 10 ch.g. Arzanni – Beltalong (Belfort (FR)) [2006/7 c–, h96: c21m³ **c99**
23g 24g⁴ c25g* c25d² Dec 14] close-coupled gelding: modest handicap hurdler/chaser: **h89**
back to best when winning over fences at Catterick in November: stays 25f, at least when
conditions aren't testing: acts on good to firm and good to soft going. Mrs S. J. Smith

RIVER ALDER 9 b.m. Alderbrook – River Pearl (Oats) [2006/7 h118: 22g⁵ c20m² **c83 p**
16m* Apr 20] big, strong mare: winning pointer: fairly useful hurdler, lightly raced: off **h117**
11 months, won mares handicap at Ayr in April by 2½ lengths from Helen Wood: had
been neck second to Field Roller in novice at Hexham on chasing debut: effective at 2m
to 2¾m: acts on soft and good to firm going: should do better over fences. J. M. Dun

RIVER AMORA (IRE) 12 b.g. Willie Joe (IRE) – That's Amora (Paddy's Stream) **c85 x**
[2006/7 c76x, h–: c18m³ c18f⁵ c18d* c18g³ c20m^pu Apr 8] stocky gelding: maiden **h–**
hurdler: modest handicap chaser: won at Fontwell in November: stays 21f: acts on any
going: tried visored, wears cheekpieces nowadays: tongue tied once: sketchy jumper.
Jim Best

RIVER BAILIFF (IRE) 11 ch.g. Over The River (FR) – Rath Caola (Neltino) [2006/7 **c88**
c80: c16g c21g* c20m³ c21m² c26d⁵ c22g² c20m⁶ Sep 21] sturdy gelding: modest chaser:
won maiden hunter at Folkestone in May, final outing for S. Garrott: stays 2¾m: acts on
firm going: tried in blinkers/cheekpieces. T. D. McCarthy

RIVERBANK RAINBOW 6 b.m. Overbury (IRE) – Riverbank Rose (Lighter) **F78**
[2006/7 F16d² F16s⁵ Apr 1] first foal: dam, fair hurdler, stayed 27f: modest form in
bumpers at Hexham 5 months apart. R. Ford

RIVER CITY (IRE) 10 b.g. Norwich – Shuil Na Lee (IRE) (Phardante (FR)) [2006/7 c153, h–: 16m³ c16d⁴ c19d³ c16g³ c16m⁴ c16f⁵ Apr 28] rangy gelding: fairly useful hurdler: smart chaser: good third, nearest finish and beaten 6½ lengths by Voy Por Ustedes, in Queen Mother Champion Chase at Cheltenham: below form both outings after 4 days apart: should stay 2½m: acts on any going. *Noel T. Chance* **c153 h120**

RIVER DANTE (IRE) 10 ch.g. Phardante (FR) – Astral River (Over The River (FR)) [2006/7 c94: c16g⁵ c20mᵖᵘ c20fᶠᵒ c21g Apr 12] big, lengthy gelding: fair hunter chaser: stays 21f: raced mainly on good going or firmer: tongue tied. *Miss L. A. Blackford* **c91**

RIVER GYPSY 6 b.g. In The Wings – River Erne (USA) (Irish River (FR)) [2006/7 16d 19v⁴ 16d 19d⁵ Mar 26] good-bodied gelding: regressive maiden (should stay 1¾m) on Flat: poor form in novice hurdles: likely to stay 2½m. *J. D. Frost* **h72**

RIVER HEIGHTS (IRE) 6 b. or br.g. Kotashaan (FR) – Mrs Cullen (Over The River (FR)) [2006/7 F91: F16d May 15] much better effort in bumpers when runner-up at Font-well on debut: sold 7,800 gns Doncaster May (2006) Sales, placed in points. *C. Tinkler* **F70**

RIVER INDUS 7 b.g. Rakaposhi King – Flow (Over The River (FR)) [2006/7 c–, h86: c23mᵖᵘ 22m³ c23sᵖᵘ c22s³ c24v² c23v⁵ c24g² 24m² Apr 15] rangy gelding: modest maiden hurdler/chaser: stays 3m: acts on heavy and good to firm going: prone to mistakes over fences. *R. H. Buckler* **c97 x h86**

RIVER LOGIC (IRE) 4 b.g. Fasliyev (USA) – Grey Again (Unfuwain (USA)) [2006/7 16d⁶ 17d* 16g⁴ 16s* 16v 17d* 16g 16g Apr 12] good-topped gelding: fair on Flat (stays 11f), successful 3 times in 2006: fairly useful juvenile hurdler: won at Sedgefield in November, Newcastle (handicap) in December and Market Rasen (beat Mister Benedictine by ¾ length in 16-runner event) in March: raced around 2m on good ground or softer (acts on soft). *A. D. Brown* **h116**

RIVER MERE 13 b.g. River God (USA) – Rupert's Daughter (Rupert Bear) [2006/7 c–, h–: c20gᵘʳ 24sᵖᵘ c21gᵖᵘ c17f⁴ c20sᶠ c24m c24sᵖᵘ Oct 11] workmanlike gelding: winning hurdler/chaser, retains only a little ability: barely stays 3m: acts on firm and good to soft going, probably not on softer: tried in cheekpieces. *Mrs P. A. Rigby* **c61 h–**

RIVER MIST (IRE) 8 ch.m. Over The River (FR) – Minature Miss (Move Off) [2006/7 c93p, h105: 22fᵖᵘ May 9] fair handicap hurdler: seemingly amiss only outing in 2006/7: soon plenty to do after mistake second only start over fences: stays 25f: raced mainly on good/good to soft going. *Karen McLintock* **c– h–**

RIVER OF DIAMONDS 6 b.g. Muhtarram (USA) – City Gambler (Rock City) [2006/7 20g⁵ 16s⁶ 19g 16vᵖᵘ Nov 23] good-topped gelding: modest at best on Flat (stays 11.5f), won seller in 2005 for Rae Guest: no form over hurdles: in cheekpieces last 2 starts: headstrong. *J. G. M. O'Shea* **h–**

RIVER OF LIGHT (IRE) 7 b.g. Flemensfirth (USA) – Stillbyherself (IRE) (Le Bavard (FR)) [2006/7 c95, h85: c20v c24v c28s Dec 16] lengthy gelding: mid-field at best in novice hurdles: form (modest) in handicap chases only when winning at Chepstow in 2005/6: should stay 3½m: raced on going softer than good (acts on heavy): tried in cheekpieces. *D. P. Keane* **c– h–**

RIVER QUOILE 11 b.g. Terimon – Carrikins (Buckskin (FR)) [2006/7 c80x, h–: c21gᵖᵘ c21g* c23fᵖᵘ c25g⁵ Oct 15] workmanlike gelding: poor handicap chaser: won at Newton Abbot in August, only form in 2006/7: stays 25f: acts on firm and good to soft going: tried blinkered: often let down by jumping. *R. H. Alner* **c71 x h–**

RIVER RIDE (IRE) 13 b.g. King's Ride – Over The Village (IRE) (Over The River (FR)) [2006/7 c20sᵘʳ Jun 25] very lightly raced and little sign of ability. *D. W. Thompson* **c– h–**

RIVER RIPPLES (IRE) 8 ch.g. Over The River (FR) – Aelia Paetina (Buckskin (FR)) [2006/7 h101, F93: c20sᵇᵈ c19g³ c23sᵖᵘ 21s* 21dᶠ 22d³ 24g Apr 18] good-topped gelding: winning Irish pointer: fair handicap hurdler: won novice event at Ludlow in March: third of 7 to What'sonyourmind completed start in handicap chases: stays 2¾m: acts on heavy going: tried tongue tied. *T. R. George* **c93 h101**

RIVER ROMANCE 4 b.f. River Falls – Future Romance (Distant Relative) [2006/7 F17g Apr 23] half-sister to 9.5f to 2m winner Regency Red (by Dolphin Street): dam unraced: tailed off in mares bumper on debut. *Mrs H. O. Graham* **F–**

RIVER SPIRIT (IRE) 6 b. or br.g. Rashar (USA) – River Rose (IRE) (Roselier (FR)) [2006/7 F17m 22mᵖᵘ Aug 24] first foal: dam winning pointer: won twice in Irish points in 2006: no show in bumper/novice hurdle. *K. J. Burke* **h– F–**

RIVER TIGRIS (IRE) 5 b.m. Dr Devious (IRE) – La Riveraine (USA) (Riverman (USA)) [2006/7 F90: 19d⁴ 17m⁶ 14d⁴ c20sᵖᵘ 22d 24s² 24sᵖᵘ Feb 8] leggy mare: winning pointer: seventh in listed bumper for O. Sherwood: easily best effort over hurdles (modest form) when runner-up in mares maiden at Taunton: no show on chase debut: stays 3m: tongue tied last 4 starts, also blinkered last 2. *D. E. Pipe* c– h90

RIVER TOP (IRE) 8 b.g. Norwich – River Swell (IRE) (Over The River (FR)) [2006/7 16dᵖᵘ Oct 5] third foal: brother to fairly useful hurdler/chaser Bishop's Bridge, stays 2½m, and half-brother to 2¼m hurdle winner Marcus William (by Roselier): dam unraced, out of half-sister to smart staying hurdler Gillan Cove: well beaten in Irish point in 2004: no show in maiden on hurdling debut. *Andrew Turnell* h–

RIVER TRAPPER (IRE) 8 b.g. Over The River (FR) – Mousa (Callernish) [2006/7 c106, h–: c20d Dec 21] rangy gelding: lightly raced: bumper winner: maiden hurdler/chaser: bred to stay 3m: raced on good ground or softer: sold 1,900 gns Doncaster May Sales. *Miss H. C. Knight* c– h–

RIVERTREE (IRE) 6 ch.g. Entrepreneur – French River (Bering) [2006/7 h79: 16sᵖᵘ May 14] little form over hurdles. *D. P. Keane* h–

RIVERWELD 5 ch.g. Weldnaas (USA) – Riverain (Bustino) [2006/7 16s Dec 8] modest maiden at 2 yrs for G. M. Moore, well held only 2 outings on Flat since: soundly beaten in maiden on hurdling debut. *J. R. Holt* h–

ROADWORTHY (IRE) 10 b.m. Lord Americo – Henry Woman (IRE) (Mandalus) [2006/7 c–, h60: 20s 20f⁶ 16g⁶ 20d² 24g³ 23s⁴ 24v⁵ 19d 16v* 24vᵖᵘ 17vᵖᵘ 24d Feb 14] smallish, workmanlike mare: well beaten completed outing in chases: poor hurdler: won conditional jockeys handicap at Ayr in December: effective at testing 2m to 3m: acts on heavy going: temperament under suspicion. *W. G. Young* c– h74

ROARING THUNDER 4 b.g. Thowra (FR) – Sweet On Willie (USA) (Master Willie) [2006/7 17sᵖᵘ 17g Apr 7] half-brother to 17f hurdle winner Mounts Bay (by Karinga Bay): dam winning pointer: no show in selling hurdles. *J. D. Frost* h–

ROARINGWATER (IRE) 8 b.g. Roselier (FR) – Supreme Cherry (Buckskin (FR)) [2006/7 c88, h–: 20m 20g² 23g⁴ 22v² 20v c20vᵖᵘ Jan 7] rather leggy gelding: modest novice hurdler: similar form over fences only on debut in 2005/6: stays 2¾m: acts on heavy going: blinkered last 3 starts: temperamental. *R. T. Phillips* c– § h96 §

ROBBER (IRE) 10 ch.g. Un Desperado (FR) – Christy's Girl (IRE) (Buckskin (FR)) [2006/7 c92, h–: c25m³ c30m⁵ May 16] leggy gelding: modest chaser: left P. Bowen and fit from points (successful), much better effort in hunters in 2006/7 when third at Hexham: thorough stayer: unraced on firm going, acts on any other: tried blinkered/in cheekpieces. *R. Morley* c94 h–

ROBBIE CAN CAN 8 b.g. Robellino (USA) – Can Can Lady (Anshan) [2006/7 h71+: 16m² 16d* Oct 22] leggy, close-coupled gelding: fair on Flat (stays 2¼m), successful in July: fair handicap hurdler: won amateur event at Towcester in October: should be suited by further than 2m: acts on good to firm and heavy going. *A. W. Carroll* h100

ROBBIE DYE 5 ch.g. Minster Son – Youandi (Silver Season) [2006/7 F16v³ F16s² Jan 31] rather leggy, lengthy gelding: third foal: brother to bumper winner/fair hurdler Harry Flashman, stays 2¾m: dam, winning 2m hurdler, out of half-sister to smart 2½m to 3m chaser Bishop's Pawn: better effort in bumpers (fair form) when short-headed by Breakwater House at Newcastle. *D. W. Whillans* F88

ROBBIE WILL 6 b.g. Robellino (USA) – Life's Too Short (IRE) (Astronef) [2006/7 h–: 19s 18m Sep 21] rather leggy gelding: no form over hurdles. *F. Jordan* h–

ROBBO 13 b.g. Robellino (USA) – Basha (USA) (Chief's Crown (USA)) [2006/7 c121§, h114§: c30d⁵ c32m Jul 2] strong, close-coupled gelding: veteran jumper: stays 33f: acts on heavy going: effective with or without headgear: ungenuine. *K. G. Reveley* c110 § h– §

ROBERT THE BRUCE 12 ch.g. Distinct Native – Kawarau Queen (Taufan (USA)) [2006/7 h105: 20v³ May 18] good-topped gelding: fair handicap hurdler, very lightly raced: stays 2½m: acts on heavy and good to firm going: clearly difficult to train. *L. Lungo* h98

ROBERTY BOB (IRE) 12 ch.g. Bob Back (USA) – Inesdela (Wolver Hollow) [2006/7 c25sᵖᵘ Mar 1] good-topped gelding: fairly useful handicap chaser at one time: left H. Daly and fit from points, no show in hunter at Ludlow: suited by 3m+: raced mainly on going softer than good (acts on heavy): often makes mistakes: lazy. *Mrs Sarah Stafford* c– § h–

ROBESON 5 br.g. Primo Dominie – Montserrat (Aragon) [2006/7 h81: 20d Oct 20] **h–**
poor form on first of 2 outings over hurdles: likely to prove best at 2m with emphasis on
speed: sold 6,200 gns Newmarket Autumn Sales. *D. M. Simcock*

ROBIN DE LA FOLIE (FR) 5 b.g. Robin Des Pres (FR) – Cazeres (FR) (Goodland **F–**
(FR)) [2006/7 F16v Mar 10] 33,000 4-y-o: sixth foal: half-brother to winning hurdler/
chaser up to 3m Good Boy (by Cadoudal) and 2½m hurdle winner Bleu Fonce (by
Epervier Bleu): dam won around 1½m: tailed off in bumper on debut. *James Moffatt*

ROBIN DE LA GARDE (FR) 6 bl. or br.g. Garde Royale – Relayeuse (FR) (Iron **c–**
Duke (FR)) [2006/7 c20d c20g 20s c20g^{pu} Apr 23] €145,000 3-y-o: ex-French gelding: **h–**
seventh foal: brother to useful hurdler around 2m Robin des Champs and half-brother to
3 winners, including useful hurdler/chaser around 2m Robin des Pres (by Cadoudal): dam
winning 2m hurdler: little sign of ability, left M. Rolland after first outing, trained next 2
by Evan Williams: tried tongue tied: sold 3,000 gns Doncaster May Sales. *M. Todhunter*

ROBIN DU BOIS (FR) 4 b.g. Robin Des Champs (FR) – Rouge Amour (FR) **h125**
(Cadoudal (FR)) [2006/7 15s² 15s* 16s² 16v 16m^F 16m⁶ Apr 26] rather leggy gelding:
second foal: dam placed in 15f hurdle: once-raced on Flat: useful juvenile hurdler: won at
Auteuil in June: left T. Trapenard and off over 6 months, good 3½ lengths second to
Lounaos in Grade 2 at Leopardstown: travelling strongly in front when falling 2 out in
minor event won by Bahrain Storm at Fairyhouse: will stay beyond 2m: acts on soft and
good to firm going. *A. J. Martin, Ireland*

ROBIN DU MOUTIER (FR) 5 ch.g. Robin Des Champs (FR) – Lucile (FR) (Royal **F–**
Charter (FR)) [2006/7 F16m Jul 27] third foal: dam unraced half-sister to useful French
hurdler Banville: well beaten in bumper on debut. *R. T. Phillips*

ROBINZAL 5 b.g. Zilzal (USA) – Sulitelma (USA) (The Minstrel (CAN)) [2006/7 16d² **h109**
16m³ 16m⁶ 16f* 16m³ 17g⁴ Oct 15] fair on Flat (should stay 1¼m), successful twice at
3 yrs, sold out of T. Easterby's stable 10,500 gns Newmarket Autumn (2005) Sales: fair
hurdler: won maiden at Worcester in August: raced around 2m: acts on firm and good to
soft going: tongue tied last 3 starts: waited with, and usually travels strongly. *C. J. Mann*

ROB THE FIVE (IRE) 10 b.g. Supreme Leader – Derravarragh Lady (IRE) (Radical) **c103 §**
[2006/7 c103§, h–: c21g c20g³ c21d* c20g² c20f⁵ Jun 21] ex-Irish gelding: fair handicap **h–**
chaser: won at Fakenham in May: stays 21f: acts on soft ground: tried in cheekpieces:
tongue tied last 4 starts: ungenuine: sold 4,000 gns Doncaster November Sales.
P. C. Haslam

ROBY DE CIMBRE (FR) 4 gr.g. Myrakalu (FR) – Belle de Liziere (FR) (Bojador **h112 p**
(FR)) [2006/7 16s³ 18d* 17g⁴ 16g⁴ 17g⁴ Apr 18] leggy gelding: third foal: half-brother to
1½m winner Ploeskob de Cimbre (by Art Francais): dam placed up to around 1¾m on
Flat: placed around 1½m on Flat: fairly useful juvenile hurdler: twice-raced at Cagnes-
sur-Mer for L. Viel, winning in December: encouraging fourth all 3 starts in Britain, not
unduly knocked about when beaten 17¼ lengths by Laustra Bad at Cheltenham final one:
likely to stay beyond 2¼m: remains open to improvement. *P. F. Nicholls*

ROCCA'S BOY (IRE) 5 b.g. Spectrum (IRE) – Quiet Counsel (IRE) (Law Society **h75**
(USA)) [2006/7 F86: F17d³ 16g⁵ Apr 23] fair bumper winner: 18 lengths fifth to Classic **F86**
Role in maiden at Plumpton on hurdling debut: sold 6,000 gns Doncaster May Sales.
M. Wigham

ROCK DIPLOMAT (IRE) 7 b.g. Oscar (IRE) – Pre-Let (IRE) (Supreme Leader) **c–**
[2006/7 19v³ 23v⁴ 19s³ 24v² 24v* 24m⁴ Apr 28] second foal: dam lightly raced: won **h116 +**
point in maiden: eighth in maiden hunter at Cork on chasing debut: fairly useful hurdler:
in cheekpieces, won maiden at Naas in March by 18 lengths from Druids Cross: thorough
stayer: acts on heavy going. *Michael Cunningham, Ireland*

ROCKET (IRE) 6 ch.g. Cadeaux Genereux – Prends Ca (IRE) (Reprimand) [2006/7 **h–**
16m^{pu} Sep 3] of no account on Flat nowadays: no show on hurdling debut. *H. J. Manners*

ROCK HAVEN (IRE) 5 b.g. Danehill Dancer (IRE) – Mahabba (USA) (Elocutionist **h–**
(USA)) [2006/7 16s^{pu} May 14] half-brother to winning hurdler in Italy by Mujtahid:
modest on Flat (stays 11f), successful on August: soon in trouble when pace increased in
novice on hurdling debut: sold 1,800 gns Doncaster January Sales. *J. Mackie*

ROCKING ROBIN 7 b.m. Rakaposhi King – Rockmount Rose (Proverb) [2006/7 20g **h–**
Apr 27] £850 4-y-o: fifth foal: dam, modest chaser, stayed 3m: won maiden point in 2006:
soundly beaten in novice on hurdling debut. *S. A. Jones*

ROCKNEST ISLAND (IRE) 4 b.f. Bahhare (USA) – Margin Call (IRE) (Tirol) **h–**
[2006/7 16g^{ur} 16g 16g 20v Mar 2] ex-Irish filly: second foal: dam, fair maiden, stayed

1½m: fair on Flat (stays 2m), successful in April: little impact in juvenile hurdles, left G. Lyons after debut. *P. D. Niven*

ROCKPILER 5 b.g. Halling (USA) – Emma Peel (Emarati (USA)) [2006/7 h–: 17v^{pu} 16d Dec 28] no form over hurdles. *D. W. Thompson*   **h–**

ROCK STAR APPEAL 6 b.g. Rock City – Turkish Star (Star Appeal) [2006/7 F16d Dec 29] rather leggy gelding: fourth foal: dam modest novice hurdler/chaser who stayed 2½m: well beaten in bumper on debut. *R. H. Alner*   **F–**

ROCK STREET (IRE) 6 b.g. Darazari (IRE) – Longueville (IRE) (Montelimar (USA)) [2006/7 F16s³ F16v^{rtr} F16d⁴ F16v* F16m Apr 25] €7,000 3-y-o: well-made gelding: first foal: dam unraced half-sister to smart bumper performer Forty Licks: fairly useful form in bumpers: won at Punchestown in January by ½ length from Mrs Hardy: tenth of 19 to Mick The Man in Grade 1 there next time: refused to race second start, and one to be wary of. *Robert Tyner, Ireland*   **F102 §**

ROCKWITHACAVEMAN (IRE) 5 b.g. Old Vic – Carrig Conn (IRE) (Torus) [2006/7 17s 19s^{pu} 17s 22g^{pu} Mar 18] fourth foal: brother to winning pointer: dam winning pointer: no form over hurdles: tried in cheekpieces. *D. E. Pipe*   **h–**

ROCK WREN 4 ch.g. Shahrastani (USA) – Wren Warbler (Relkino) [2006/7 F17m⁴ Apr 28] second foal: dam, winning hurdler/fair chaser, stayed 25f: 10½ lengths fourth to Georgian King in bumper at Market Rasen on debut. *Mrs P. Robeson*   **F85**

ROCKYS GIRL 5 b.m. Piccolo – Lady Rockstar (Rock Hopper) [2006/7 h76§: 17m 16v⁴ 17d⁴ 19v³ 24s* 24s³ 24v* 24g⁶ Mar 25] small mare: modest hurdler, claimed from P. Radford £6,000 second start: upped in trip, much improved when winning handicaps at Taunton in January (amateur event) and February: stays 3m: acts on heavy going: tried blinkered: often jumps sketchily/looks hard ride. *Mrs A. M. Thorpe*   **h96**

ROC TREDUDON (FR) 7 b.g. Double Bed (FR) – La Belle Polonaise (Bold Lad (IRE)) [2006/7 F16s³ 16v² 18v⁵ 20s 16v Mar 9] €25,000 3-y-o: brother/half-brother to several winners, including useful hurdler/chaser up to 21f Raikabag Junction: dam middle-distance maiden: some promise in bumper/novice hurdles: likely to prove best at 2m. *L. Lungo*   **h72 +**
  F66 +

RODALKO (FR) 9 b.g. Kadalko (FR) – Darling Rose (FR) (Rose Laurel) [2006/7 c126, h–: 26d⁴ Jun 4] good-topped gelding: lightly raced: modest hurdler: fairly useful chaser, off nearly 2 years prior to 2005/6: stays 3m: raced mainly on good to firm going over fences, won on good to soft over hurdles: races prominently. *O. Sherwood*   **c–**
  h85

RODD TO RICHES 9 br.g. Manhal – Lovely Lilly (Arrasas (USA)) [2006/7 h–: 18m^{pu} Jun 6] little impact over hurdles, including in sellers. *Jamie Poulton*   **h–**

RO ERIDANI 7 b.m. Binary Star (USA) – Hat Hill (Roan Rocket) [2006/7 h–: 17m⁵ 16m³ 24m⁶ 17m⁶ Aug 29] no solid form over hurdles: tongue tied last 2 starts. *Miss S. E. Forster*   **h–**

ROESHAN (IRE) 8 b.m. Anshan – Roseocean (IRE) (Roselier (FR)) [2006/7 16s⁵ 20m 16f⁴ 16f^{pu} Jul 19] ex-Irish mare: little form in bumpers/over hurdles: placed in points in Britain in 2005: tongue tied. *D. A. Rees*   **h75 ?**

ROGUES GALLERY (IRE) 7 b.g. Luso – Sarah May (IRE) (Camden Town) [2006/7 h93: c25s^{pu} c16v³ c24v² c24v^{F} Mar 6] sturdy gelding: fair hurdler: off over 18 months, form (modest) over fences only when runner-up in maiden: stayed 3m: acted on heavy going (won bumper on firm): dead. *J. Howard Johnson*   **c99**
  h–

ROJABAA 8 b.g. Anabaa (USA) – Slava (USA) (Diesis) [2006/7 h108: 20g^{bd} 17v^{su} 17d⁵ 16g 20g⁶ 19v² 17s 20v 19s^{F} Feb 3] small gelding: modest handicap hurdler: stays 2½m: acts on any going: blinkered/tongue tied once in 2003/4. *B. D. Leavy*   **h95**

ROLE ON (IRE) 5 gr.g. Bob's Return (IRE) – Banderole (IRE) (Roselier (FR)) [2006/7 F17v³ 18v* 20s⁴ Feb 19] 25,000 3-y-o: half-brother to 3 winners, including fairly useful hurdler around 2m Hegarty (by Topanoora) and smart hunter chaser Never Compromise (by Glacial Storm), stays 3¼m: dam unraced half-sister to useful hurdler up to 25f Sip of Orange: promising third to impressive Skippers Brig in bumper at Carlisle: fair form in novice hurdles: won at Kelso in January by 7 lengths from Cavers Glen: upped in trip, travelled best long way at Carlisle following month: remains likely to do better. *N. G. Richards*   **h107 p**
  F102

ROLFES DELIGHT 15 b.g. Rolfe (USA) – Idiot's Run (Idiot's Delight) [2006/7 c93§, h–: c25f⁴ Oct 5] workmanlike gelding: modest handicap chaser: stays 25f: acts on firm going: tried tongue tied: inconsistent. *A. E. Jones*   **c– §**
  h–

ROLL ALONG (IRE) 7 b.g. Carroll House – Callmartel (IRE) (Montelimar (USA)) **h121**
[2006/7 F112+: 16s* 16d* 21d³ 20g Apr 12] good-topped, useful-looking gelding:
unbeaten in 3 bumpers: fairly useful hurdler: won maiden at Cheltenham (by 1½ lengths
from Ofarel d'Airy) in October and novice at Uttoxeter (hung left under pressure and
made hard work of landing odds) in November: failed to progress further, 26 lengths third
to Wichita Lineman in Grade 1 Challow Hurdle at Newbury: should stay 2½m: raced on
good going or softer. *Carl Llewellyn*

ROLL EM OVER 4 b.f. Tamure (IRE) – Miss Petronella (Petoski) [2006/7 F16m **F–**
Mar 31] sister to Flat stayers Danzatrice and Lets Roll, latter useful, and half-sister to fair
hurdler Lord Nellsson (by Arctic Lord), stays 2¾m: dam unraced: well beaten in bumper
on debut. *C. W. Thornton*

ROLLING RIVER (IRE) 10 b.g. Over The River (FR) – Paddy's Dancer (Paddy's **c–**
Stream) [2006/7 c21m c21mᵖᵘ Aug 29] workmanlike gelding: winning pointer: maiden **h–**
chaser, failed to complete last 3 starts. *J. Wade*

ROLONS ADVICE 6 ch.g. Weldnaas (USA) – Clova (Move Off) [2006/7 F16m **c–**
c20mᵖᵘ 21mᶠ 19dᵖᵘ Feb 19] 8,000 4-y-o: leggy gelding: second foal: half-brother to **h–**
winning pointer by Minster Son: dam unraced sister to fairly useful hurdler Linlathen, **F–**
stayed 3m: little sign of ability: left V. Smith prior to hurdling debut. *B. N. Pollock*

ROMAN ARK 9 gr.g. Terimon – Larksmore (Royal Fountain) [2006/7 c128, h–: c20s⁵ **c139**
c16d³ c20d* c20v* c21v⁴ c21g c20g Apr 25] long-backed, workmanlike gelding: **h–**
winning hurdler: useful handicap chaser: improved in 2006/7, winning at Market Rasen
in December and Haydock (beat Wain Mountain by 14 lengths) in January: creditable 5¼
lengths fourth to Whispered Secret in Grade 3 event at Cheltenham: stays 21f: acts well
on heavy going. *J. M. Jefferson*

ROMAN ARMY (IRE) 5 b.g. Trans Island – Contravene (IRE) (Contract Law **h–**
(USA)) [2006/7 16m 16m 16m 16v 17v⁶ Feb 20] modest maiden on Flat (stays 1¾m):
little form over hurdles, sold out of David Marnane's stable 4,600 gns Doncaster
November Sales before final outing (wore cheekpieces). *James Moffatt*

ROMANOV RAMBLER (IRE) 7 b.g. Moscow Society (USA) – Roses Lady (IRE) **c81 ?**
(Buckley) [2006/7 h–, c–: 24mᵖᵘ 20s 20d⁵ 25sᵖᵘ 24g c20d⁵ c24s² c24dᶠ c25sᵖᵘ Feb 15] **h69**
novice hurdler/chaser, little form prior to 4 lengths second to Sports Express in novice
chase at Musselburgh: stays 3m: acts on soft going: tongue tied last 7 starts, also in
cheekpieces last 5. *Mrs S. C. Bradburne*

ROMAN RAMPAGE 12 b.g. Perpendicular – Roman Moor (Owen Anthony) [2006/7 **c85**
c99, h82: c24d5 c32sᵖᵘ c26vᵖᵘ c26s⁴ 22v* 24v 24g c21g⁴ Apr 9] medium-sized gelding: **h82**
poor handicap hurdler: won seller at Folkestone (for second successive year) in January,
idling: modest chaser: form in 2006/7 only on fourth start: stays 3½m: acts on heavy
going: wears headgear. *Miss Z. C. Davison*

ROMANY DREAM 9 b.m. Nomadic Way (USA) – Half Asleep (Quiet Fling (USA)) **c97 §**
[2006/7 c100, h80: c17m² c18f c20mᵖᵘ c16d⁶ c19d⁶ c20m³ c20g³ Apr 10] leggy mare: **h–**
maiden hurdler: modest handicap chaser: stays 21f: acts on soft and firm going: tried in
cheekpieces, usually blinkered: races prominently: has been reluctant to race: none too
reliable. *R. Dickin*

ROMANY PRINCE 8 b.g. Robellino (USA) – Vicki Romara (Old Vic) [2006/7 h122: **h126**
19d 16s* 16s 19g Mar 31] rather leggy gelding: fairly useful handicap hurdler: off 7
months and 40/1, better than ever when winning at Kempton in January by neck from
Princelet: well held 2 starts after: effective at 2m to 3m: acts on soft and good to firm
ground. *S. Gollings*

ROMEK (IRE) 7 ch.g. Presenting – Coco Point (IRE) (Good Thyne (USA)) [2006/7 **c123**
24m c23dᶠ c20g³ c22vᶠ c22gᶠ c23s* c24v² c24vᵖᵘ c24v³ c24v⁴ c24v³ c24m³ Apr 7] **h90**
lengthy, angular gelding: first foal: dam fourth both starts over hurdles: won maiden point
in 2006: mid-field in maiden on hurdling debut: fairly useful novice chaser: won maiden
at Downpatrick in November by 4½ lengths from Lovely Present: good second to Back
In Front in minor event at Thurles, generally below form after: will stay beyond 3m: acts
on heavy ground: front runner. *Mrs J. Harrington, Ireland*

ROMERS COMMON 7 b.g. Rakaposhi King – Phar Better Off (IRE) (Phardante **h–**
(FR)) [2006/7 19v 24s 22s Feb 3] 6,500 4-y-o: second foal: dam well held in bumper:
well held over hurdles. *C. E. Longsdon*

ROMILLY'S BOY (IRE) 7 b.g. King Persian – Camp Bay (IRE) (Classic Secret **h–**
(USA)) [2006/7 22d 18mᶠ 20v 24v Mar 9] no form, including in points: left William
Patton after first outing. *C. A. McBratney, Ireland*

ROMMEL 10 ch.g. Baron Blakeney – Sizzling Sun (Sunyboy) [2006/7 c19g May 4] c–
lengthy gelding: winning pointer, placed all 4 completed starts in 2006: tailed off in h–
hunter on chase debut. *Mrs L. Redman*

ROMNEY MARSH 6 br.m. Glacial Storm (USA) – Mirador (Town And Country) c93 ?
[2006/7 F83: 16g 16g^{pu} 19s 16v^{pu} 21v^{pu} c19g* c20m^F Apr 15] medium-sized mare: no h–
form over hurdles: 33/1-winner of handicap on chasing debut at Towcester in March,
taking little interest in rear much of way: let down by jumping following month: stays
19f: temperament under suspicion. *R. Curtis*

ROMPING HOME (IRE) 4 b.f. Rock Hopper – Euro Joy (IRE) (Eurobus) [2006/7 F94
F16s^5 Mar 3] 3,000 3-y-o: lengthy filly: second foal: dam unraced half-sister to smart
but thoroughly ungenuine chaser up to 3m Pimberley Place: 5¾ lengths fifth of 21 to
Diamond Harry in bumper at Newbury on debut. *N. J. Henderson*

RONALDO 4 b.g. Tomba – Satiric (IRE) (Doyoun) [2006/7 16f 18g^{pu} Sep 30] modest h–
maiden on Flat (stays 1m), sold out of W. Muir's stable £900 Ascot June Sales: little show
in juvenile hurdles. *A. M. Hales*

RONELLA 4 ch.f. Jumbo Hirt (USA) – Palmahalm (Mandrake Major) [2006/7 F16d F– §
F16d F16s^{pu} Mar 7] half-sister to winning pointer by Minster Son: dam, winning pointer/
hunter chaser who stayed 25f, out of half-sister to high-class 2m hurdler/smart chaser
Nohalmdun: no show in bumpers (all but refused to race final start). *G. M. Moore*

RONSARD (IRE) 5 b.g. Spectrum (IRE) – Touche-A-Tout (IRE) (Royal Academy h–
(USA)) [2006/7 17s Jan 26] fair on Flat (stays 1¼m), has had various trainers: tailed off
in maiden on hurdling debut. *J. C. Tuck*

ROOBIHOO (IRE) 8 b.g. Norwich – Griffinstown Lady (Over The River (FR)) c104
[2006/7 h114: c25f^2 c20d^4 c20v^{pu} c25s^3 c24v^3 c25g^{ur} c25g^2 Apr 15] rangy gelding: fair h–
handicap hurdler: patchy form over fences: stays 25f: acts on heavy going: tongue tied.
C. Grant

ROOD REPORT 7 ch.g. Gunner B – Quiet Dawn (Lighter) [2006/7 F–: F16v^2 F17s^2 h–
20v^{pu} 20v^{pu} Feb 15] fair form when second in bumpers: let down by jumping/failed to F91
settle in novice hurdles: should stay beyond 17f. *A. King*

ROOFING SPIRIT (IRE) 9 b.g. Beneficial – Vulcash (IRE) (Callernish) [2006/7 c114
c111, h–: c16d* c17d^2 c17s^5 c16g c16g^3 Mar 28] rangy gelding: fair handicap chaser: h–
won at Chepstow in November: effective at 2m to 23f: raced on good going or softer:
blinkered nowadays: has flashed tail under pressure. *D. P. Keane*

ROOKERY LAD 9 b.g. Makbul – Wayzgoose (USA) (Diesis) [2006/7 c97, h–: c20g* c126
c16g* c20v* c17m* c20f 16m^5 Aug 24] workmanlike gelding: maiden hurdler: fairly h85
useful handicap chaser: vastly improved in 2006/7, winning at Wetherby in April and
May (2) and Stratford (beat Master Rex by 5 lengths) in June: effective at 2m, barely
stays 3m: acts on any going: sound jumper: reliable. *C. N. Kellett*

ROOSTER'S REUNION (IRE) 8 gr.g. Presenting – Court Town (Camden Town) c115
[2006/7 c113, h–: c16m^2 c16f* c16g^3 c16g c16f^{pu} Apr 22] useful-looking gelding: h–
winning hurdler: fairly useful handicap chaser: won at Worcester (5 ran, by neck from
Alroyal) in August: off 3 months, ran poorly last 2 starts: raced mainly around 2m: best
form on good going or firmer: usually held up. *D. R. Gandolfo*

ROSADARE (IRE) 9 b.g. Roselier (FR) – Mosephine (IRE) (The Parson) [2006/7 h74
h67: 23v* May 25] placed in points: poor hurdler: won amateur handicap at Wetherby in
May: stayed 23f: acted on heavy going: dead. *Mrs K. Waldron*

ROSA FINA 5 b.m. Luso – Baroness Rose (Roselier (FR)) [2006/7 F17m^4 Apr 15] F78
2,500 4-y-o: second foal: dam unraced: 11¾ lengths fourth to Issaquah in mares bumper
at Market Rasen on debut. *T. D. Walford*

ROSAKER (USA) 10 b.g. Pleasant Tap (USA) – Rose Crescent (USA) (Nijinsky h152
(CAN)) [2006/7 h148: 20s* 20v^2 24v^4 24v^5 21v^2 20m^4 Apr 9] leggy, rather sparely-made
gelding: smart hurdler on his day: off over 10 months, won Grade 2 Philips Electronics
Lismullen Hurdle at Navan (for second time) in November by 6 lengths from Emotional
Moment: good ¾-length second of 5 to Brave Inca in Grade 1 at Fairyhouse, making
most: not at best after: effective at 2½m to 3m: acts on heavy and good to firm going: goes
well fresh. *N. Meade, Ireland*

ROSALYONS (IRE) 13 gr.g. Roselier (FR) – Coffee Shop (Bargello) [2006/7 c–§, h–: c– §
22d^{pu} 24s^{pu} 27v 20v Mar 2] leggy gelding: has stringhalt: maiden chaser (often let down h–
by jumping)/winning hurdler: no form in 2006/7: tried blinkered/in cheekpieces.
Mrs H. O. Graham

ROSARIAN (IRE) 10 b.g. Fourstars Allstar (USA) – Only A Rose (Glint of Gold) **c118**
[2006/7 h120: 26m² 27dᵖᵘ 27dᵘ c24dᵘʳ c23s⁴ c22v² c30g⁴ c31s² Apr 27] angular gelding: **h120**
fairly useful handicap hurdler: good second to Enhancer at Southwell: progressive
form over fences, 3½ lengths second to Back In Business in handicap at Perth final start:
stays 31f: unraced on firm going, acts on any other: wears visor/cheekpieces nowadays.
V. R. A. Dartnall

ROSCHAL (IRE) 9 gr.g. Roselier (FR) – Sunday World (USA) (Solford (USA)) **c–**
[2006/7 c104d, h90: 22f May 9] rather leggy gelding: fair handicap chaser: maiden **h–**
hurdler: stays 3m: acts on heavy going (bumper form on good to firm): blinkered once, in
cheekpieces last 3 starts: signs of temperament. *Miss Lucinda V. Russell*

ROSDARI (IRE) 10 b.g. Shardari – Tullahought (Jaazeiro (USA)) [2006/7 c20fᵖᵘ c20g **c–**
c21mᵖᵘ Aug 29] maiden pointer: little impact over hurdles/in chases: has worn headgear: **h–**
tongue tied. *J. M. Saville*

ROSEBANK (IRE) 5 b.m. Heron Island (IRE) – Molls Rose (IRE) (Coquelin (USA)) **F–**
[2006/7 F16v F14d F16v F16m Apr 21] workmanlike mare: fourth foal: dam unraced:
tailed off in bumpers. *W. G. Young*

ROSECLIFF 5 b.g. Montjeu (IRE) – Dance Clear (IRE) (Marju (IRE)) [2006/7 h120: **h113**
20g⁴ 16s 21d⁵ 25v⁶ 25g⁶ 22s⁶ 20g Mar 21] good-topped gelding: fair handicap hurdler:
below form last 3 starts: seems to stay 25f: acts on heavy going: often visored/tongue tied
in 2006/7: sometimes let down by jumping/attitude. *Heather Dalton*

ROSEDALE GARDENS 7 b.g. Fleetwood (IRE) – Freddie's Recall (Warrshan **h–**
(USA)) [2006/7 h–, F74: 16g Apr 30] good-topped gelding: poor form in bumpers: no
show over hurdles. *M. W. Easterby*

ROSEMARY'S FANCY 6 b.m. Oscar (IRE) – Fancy Nancy (IRE) (Buckskin (FR)) **h–**
[2006/7 F–: 16s 16d Dec 6] no sign of ability. *C. N. Kellett*

ROSEMAUVE (FR) 7 b.g. Cyborg (FR) – Sweet Jaune (FR) (Le Nain Jaune (FR)) **c§§**
[2006/7 c–§, h127§: c23g² c23fᵖᵘ 22gᵖᵘ Jul 5] leggy gelding: useful handicap hurdler at **h§§**
best: maiden chaser: stays 3¼m: acts on heavy and good to firm going: blinkered: most
ungenuine: sold 4,000 gns Doncaster August Sales. *D. E. Pipe*

ROSENBLATT (GER) 5 b.g. Dashing Blade – Roseraie (GER) (Nebos (GER)) **h–**
[2006/7 h90+: 19mᵖᵘ Aug 3] ex-German gelding: modest form on hurdling debut: lost
shoe only subsequent outing. *J. C. Tuck*

ROSE OF THE SHIRES (IRE) 4 b.f. Oscar (IRE) – Wilton Leader (IRE) (Supreme **F85**
Leader) [2006/7 F16g F17g Apr 19] second foal: dam unraced: modest form in bumpers:
dead. *K. G. Reveley*

ROSEVILLE (IRE) 7 b.m. Beneficial – Knockhouse Rose (IRE) (Roselier (FR)) **h–**
[2006/7 h–: 26gᵖᵘ 19v Nov 28] little form. *S. T. Lewis*

ROSEVINA (IRE) 7 b.m. Saint Preuil (FR) – Galvina (FR) (Northern Fashion (USA)) **h–**
[2006/7 F17s 19s 17g Apr 20] first foal: dam, placed around 1¼m, half-sister to top-class **F–**
chaser up to 21f Fadalko: well held in bumper/over hurdles. *J. G. M. O'Shea*

ROSIE ALL OVER 5 br.m. Overbury (IRE) – Hallo Rosie (IRE) (Mister Lord (USA)) **F80**
[2006/7 F16s³ F17g Apr 13] sturdy mare: third foal: dam unraced half-sister to fair
hurdler up to 3m Well Then Now Then: better effort in bumpers when third to Fiddle at
Warwick. *D. McCain Jnr*

ROSIE BEAR 4 b.f. Saddlers' Hall (IRE) – Minerstown (IRE) (Miner's Lamp) [2006/7 **F70**
F17g⁶ Apr 23] half-sister to fairly useful hurdler/chaser Ernest William (by Phardante),
stays 2¾m: dam unraced: showed need of experience when sixth to One Rose in mares
bumper at Sedgefield on debut. *Paul Murphy*

ROSIELLA 5 b.m. Tagula (IRE) – Queen of Silk (IRE) (Brief Truce (USA)) [2006/7 **c–**
16f 16s⁵ 16d 17d 16g⁶ 16d⁶ 18m⁵ 16f⁵ c18m⁵ c16m⁶ c19d⁶ Oct 26] poor on Flat nowadays **h–**
(best at 5f/6f), well held since leaving M. Blanshard in early-2006: no form over jumps:
tongue tied last 7 starts: sold 1,000 gns Doncaster November Sales. *M. Appleby*

ROSIE REDMAN (IRE) 10 gr.m. Roselier (FR) – Carbia's Last (Palm Track) **c–**
[2006/7 c121, h–: c25v⁴ c24sᵖᵘ c22s⁵ c32vᵖᵘ Mar 3] leggy mare: fairly useful handicap **h–**
chaser: out of sorts in 2006/7: stays 3½m: raced mainly on good going or softer: races
prominently. *J. R. Turner*

ROSIES GIFT 7 b.m. Safawan – Rinca (Unfuwain (USA)) [2006/7 F16m⁵ Jun 11] **F–**
£900 5-y-o: third foal: dam twice-raced half-sister to useful hurdler/chaser Ei Ei, stayed
21f: well beaten in maiden bumper on debut. *O. Brennan*

ROSITA BAY 6 b.m. Hernando (FR) – Lemon's Mill (USA) (Roberto (USA)) [2006/7 **h106** F96: 19g³ 21mᵖᵘ 21d* 19s* 19d⁵ 25g 21gᵖᵘ Mar 26] leggy, close-coupled mare: dual bumper winner: fair hurdler: won at Plumpton (novice) in November and Taunton (handicap) in December: stays 21f: acts well on soft going: has shaped as if amiss more than once (lame final outing, cheekpieces). *O. Sherwood*

ROSSCLARE (IRE) 7 b.g. Warcraft (USA) – Ivory Queen (Teenoso (USA)) [2006/7 **h95** h95, F87: 16f² 20gᵖᵘ Aug 1] placed in bumpers: modest maiden hurdler: seemingly amiss final outing: should stay beyond 2m. *J. J. Lambe, Ireland*

ROSS COMM 11 gr.g. Minster Son – Yemaail (IRE) (Shaadi (USA)) [2006/7 c140, **c128** h92: 20d³ c20s⁴ c26sᵖᵘ c24s⁶ c25v c24g c20gᵘʳ c32m⁵ Apr 21] angular gelding: fair **h100** hurdler: fairly useful handicap chaser: not discredited last 2 completed outings, fifth of 23 to Hot Weld in Scottish Grand National at Ayr: effective at testing 2½m, seemingly stays 4m: acts on any going: usually sound jumper. *Mrs S. J. Smith*

ROSSES POINT (IRE) 8 b.g. Roselier (FR) – Ballon Bombshell (IRE) (Supreme **c115** Leader) [2006/7 c98, h103: c25d* c25s* c24vᶠ⁶ 24v⁴ c24sᵖᵘ Apr 26] leggy gelding: **h82 +** winning hurdler: fairly useful handicap chaser: easily won 6-runner event at Wincanton (despite several mistakes) in November and Ludlow in December: let down by jumping both subsequent starts: stays 25f: raced on good going or softer (acts on soft): has worn cheekpieces, including when successful. *Evan Williams*

ROSS GO LAD (IRE) 10 b. or br.g. Convinced – Heather-Can (Cantab) [2006/7 **c–** c25dᵖᵘ Mar 20] winning pointer in Ireland: bought 900 gns Doncaster August Sales: no show in hunter on chase debut. *Mrs C. Hussey*

ROSSIN GOLD (IRE) 5 b.g. Rossini (USA) – Sacred Heart (IRE) (Catrail (USA)) **h106** [2006/7 h89: 17d* 16m 16f² 16g⁴ 16m⁴ 20s³ 17s* 18g⁶ 16v⁴ 16g³ Apr 15] close-coupled gelding: fair hurdler: won conditional jockeys handicaps at Cartmel in May and Carlisle in October: best short of 2½m: acts on firm and soft going, ran poorly only start on heavy (after 4 months off). *P. Monteith*

ROSS LEADER 10 b.g. Supreme Leader – Emmagreen (Green Shoon) [2006/7 **c–** c23vᵇᵈ Feb 20] workmanlike gelding: modest chaser: off 22 months, brought down tenth only start in 2006/7: stays 3m: clearly difficult to train. *Mrs Susan Nock*

ROSS RIVER 11 gr.g. Over The River (FR) – Solo Rose (Roselier (FR)) [2006/7 c132, **c141** h132: c18v* c21s 16d 21g c29mᵖᵘ 20m Apr 24] lengthy, useful-looking gelding: fairly **h123** useful hurdler: not discredited when tenth to Burntoakboy in Coral Cup at Cheltenham: useful handicap chaser: won at Punchestown (quickened readily to beat The Penitent Man by 1¾ lengths) in November: effective at 2¼m when conditions are testing and stays 25f: acts on heavy ground, ran poorly on good to firm: waited with. *A. J. Martin, Ireland*

ROSS'S ROSES (IRE) 4 b.f. Glacial Storm (USA) – Indian Legend (IRE) (Phardante **h–** (FR)) [2006/7 F16d⁶ F16s⁶ 20gᵖᵘ Apr 23] third foal: dam, poor novice hurdler who stayed **F74** 2½m, half-sister to top-class chaser Strong Promise: poor form in mares bumpers: raced too freely on hurdling debut: bred to be suited by 2½m+: sold 8,000 gns Doncaster May Sales. *J. Howard Johnson*

ROSTHWAITE (IRE) 4 b.f. Desert Style (IRE) – Thirlmere (Cadeaux Genereux) **h–** [2006/7 16g Nov 29] angular filly: fair on Flat at 2 yrs, left E. McMahon and well below form in 2006: jumped poorly on hurdling debut: sold 2,800 gns Doncaster January Sales. *Ronald Thompson*

ROSY ANNE 5 b.m. Paris House – Common Rock (IRE) (Common Grounds) [2006/7 **F–** F16sᵖᵘ F13s F16d Feb 14] tall, sparely-made mare: second foal: dam won 7f seller at 2 yrs: little impact in bumpers/on Flat debut: sold 1,200 gns Doncaster May Sales. *J. R. Turner*

ROTHBURY 7 b.g. Overbury (IRE) – The Distaff Spy (Seymour Hicks (FR)) [2006/7 **h123** h96, F98: 17s² 20fᶠ⁴ 23s* 20g* 21dᵖᵘ Dec 29] leggy gelding: fairly useful hurdler: off over 4 months, improved form when winning novice handicaps at Wetherby (conditional jockeys event) in October and Aintree (beat The Last Viking by 4 lengths in 20-runner race) in November: lame final outing: stays 23f: acts on soft and firm going. *J. I. A. Charlton*

ROTHERAM (USA) 7 b.g. Dynaformer (USA) – Out of Taxes (USA) (Out of Place **h76** (USA)) [2006/7 h92: 26d³ May 17] regressive form over hurdles: in cheekpieces last 2 starts: dead. *Evan Williams*

ROUGE DE BEAUVOIR (FR) 4 ch.f. Discover d'Auteuil (FR) – Gomanta (Bus- **h79** tino) [2006/7 16s⁶ 16g⁵ 17v 16dᶠ Jan 19] second foal: dam Italian maiden: maiden hurdler: claimed from Y. Fouin €18,000, poor form in Britain, fell fatally at Musselburgh: raced around 2m on good ground or softer. *Miss Lucinda V. Russell*

ROUGE ET NOIR 9 b.g. Hernando (FR) – Bayrouge (IRE) (Gorytus (USA)) [2006/7 20f* 24gpu 16s6 17m 20d 16d 20m 20gF Mar 17] modest stayer on Flat, claimed from K. Reveley £10,000 in June: modest novice hurdler: won at Perth in July, allowed to build clear lead: no form after: stays 2½m: acts on firm going: tried tongue tied: front runner: irresolute. *P. Monteith* **h98 d**

ROUND THE BEND 15 b.g. Revolutionary (USA) – No Love (Bustiki) [2006/7 c–: c23mpu Apr 22] winning pointer: no form in hunter chases since 2002. *Miss Louise Allan* **c–**

ROURKE STAR 5 b.g. Presidium – Mirror Four Sport (Risk Me (FR)) [2006/7 F86: F14d Feb 14] angular gelding: fair form in bumpers: left S. R. Bowring, tailed off only start in 2006/7: tried blinkered. *B. Storey* **F–**

ROUSSEA (IRE) 9 ch.g. Boyne Valley – River Regent (Over The River (FR)) [2006/7 c–, h–: c24g Apr 21] angular gelding: winning Irish pointer: little impact over hurdles/in chases. *S. G. Griffiths* **c–**
h–

ROWAN CASTLE 11 ch.g. Broadsword (USA) – Brass Castle (IRE) (Carlingford Castle) [2006/7 c–, h–: c20d3 c20dpu c25d5 c24vpu 27g5 Mar 27] workmanlike gelding: maiden hurdler/chaser, no solid form: tried in cheekpieces. *Sir John Barlow Bt* **c–**
h–

ROWDY YEATS (IRE) 6 ch.g. Un Desperado (FR) – Summerhill Express (IRE) (Roselier (FR)) [2006/7 24d 20d 16d5 20s c16s4 c16g* c16g* c17g2 c16spu Apr 26] €30,000 3-y-o: lengthy gelding: third foal: dam, winning pointer, out of half-sister to dam of top-class chaser Dublin Flyer: won maiden on second of 2 starts in Irish points in 2006: poor form over hurdles: modest handicap chaser: won at Wincanton (novice) and Warwick on consecutive days in March: should stay 2½m: raced on good going or softer. *N. A. Twiston-Davies* **c99**
h82

ROWLANDS DREAM (IRE) 7 b.m. Accordion – Bettyhill (Ardross) [2006/7 h99, F95: c20s5 c25d2 c23s* c24g4 Mar 20] big mare: winning hurdler: fair form over fences: won maiden at Taunton in February: went as if not right next time: stays 25f: acts on heavy ground: races prominently. *R. H. Alner* **c107**
h–

ROWLEY HILL 9 b.g. Karinga Bay – Scarlet Dymond (Rymer) [2006/7 c108?, h–: 24s* 24s4 25v* 23s 24g Mar 15] strong, good-bodied gelding: fairly useful handicap hurdler: won at Chepstow in December and Warwick (beat The Last Cast by 3½ lengths, travelled more sweetly than usual) in January: well held last 2 outings: maiden chaser, usually let down by jumping: stays 3¼m: best form on soft/heavy going: blinkered last 3 starts. *A. King* **c–**
h128

ROYAL ARMS 5 b.g. Desert King (IRE) – Opus One (Slip Anchor) [2006/7 F17s4 Dec 23] sixth foal: half-brother to 3 winning hurdlers, including Golden Odyssey (by Barathea), at up to 2½m, and Sun King (by Zilzal), best around 2m: dam, 1¾m winner, half-sister to high-class hurdler/smart chaser up to 2½m Squire Silk: well-held fourth to impressive Opendicth in bumper at Hereford on debut. *Evan Williams* **F76**

ROYAL ATTRACTION 6 b.g. Mon Tresor – Star Gal (Starch Reduced) [2006/7 F–: F17g* F16f 17d* 19mF 16g Nov 15] unfurnished gelding: form in bumpers only when successful at Market Rasen in July: also won novice at Bangor in October on hurdling debut: well beaten completed outing after: not sure to stay much beyond 2m. *W. M. Brisbourne* **h102 ?**
F97

ROYAL AUCLAIR (FR) 10 ch.g. Garde Royale – Carmonera (FR) (Carmont (FR)) [2006/7 c157, h–: c24m6 c31d5 c21v c24d3 c31d6 c36gF Apr 14] good-topped gelding: has reportedly had breathing operation: very smart chaser: not at best in 2006/7, even when third of 6 to stable-companion Kauto Star in muddling Grade 2 at Newbury: fell ninth in Grand National at Aintree: stays 4½m: acts on heavy and good to firm going: tried blinkered: tongue tied: usually sound jumper. *P. F. Nicholls* **c142**
h–

ROYAL CHINA (IRE) 9 b.g. Aristocracy – Luan Causca (Pampapaul) [2006/7 c21m* c20g3 c23fF c20g2 c20mpu Apr 25] leggy gelding: winning novice hurdler: winning pointer: poor chaser: won handicap at Uttoxeter in July: sold out of Tim Vaughan's stable 20,000 gns Doncaster August Sales before next outing: stays 21f: acts on soft and good to firm going. *M. Mullineaux* **c83**
h–

ROYAL CLICHE 8 b.g. Classic Cliche (IRE) – Princess Hotpot (IRE) (King's Ride) [2006/7 h91: 20gF 22d 20g3 Apr 14] lengthy gelding: poor novice hurdler: should stay beyond 2½m: raced on good going or softer. *M. F. Harris* **h83**

ROYAL COUNTY STAR (IRE) 8 ch.g. Magical Wonder (USA) – Belladoon (IRE) (Phardante (FR)) [2006/7 c16d⁶ c16s⁶ c17v c17d c17v² c22m* c20g* Apr 25] fourth foal: dam unraced: won maiden point in 2004: fairly useful over hurdles, won twice in 2005/6: similar form over fences, won maiden at Fairyhouse (easily by 7 lengths from My Auld Man) and handicap at Punchestown (best effort, beat Carrigeen Kalmia by ¾ length) in April: stays 2¾m: acts on heavy and good to firm going: held up. *A. J. Martin, Ireland* — c126 p, h–

ROYAL CRYSTALCADOU (FR) 5 b.g. Cadoudal (FR) – Crystalza (FR) (Crystal Palace (FR)) [2006/7 F14v⁶ 20m⁵ Apr 25] brother to one-time useful hurdler Royal Paradise, stays 21f, and half-brother to several other winners, notably smart hurdlers up to 3m Royale Athenia and Royal Rosa (both by Garde Royale): dam maiden on Flat: well held in bumper: poor form when fifth to Ready Response in maiden at Worcester on hurdling debut. *P. R. Webber* — h73, F–

ROYALEETY (FR) 8 b.g. Garde Royale – La Grive (FR) (Pharly (FR)) [2006/7 c119, h–: c20g Oct 24] leggy gelding: fairly useful handicap hurdler/chaser: never dangerous in competitive events over fences last 2 starts 11 months apart: barely stays 2¾m when conditions are testing: raced on good going or softer (acts on heavy): tried tongue tied. *Ian Williams* — c–, h–

ROYAL EMPEROR (IRE) 11 gr.g. Roselier (FR) – Boreen Bro (Boreen (FR)) [2006/7 c157, h150: c25sᵖᵘ c27dᶠ 23d c24d c22v² Dec 30] workmanlike gelding: very smart chaser/smart hurdler at best, won Grade 2 Rendlesham Hurdle at Haydock in 2005/6: well below form in 2006/7: stays 33f: acts on heavy and good to firm going: often front runner: has been let down by jumping over fences. *Mrs S. J. Smith* — c127, h123

ROYAL FACTOR 7 ch.g. Factual (USA) – Royal Rigger (Reprimand) [2006/7 F–: F17s F17g⁵ 16sᵖᵘ 19d Dec 26] no form in bumpers/over hurdles. *C. Smith* — h–, F–

ROYAL FLIGHT 6 b.g. Royal Applause – Duende (High Top) [2006/7 17m 16fᵖᵘ Jun 21] poor maiden on Flat for D. Daly: no show in novice hurdles: tried in cheekpieces: dead. *L. Corcoran* — h–

ROYAL FLYNN 5 b.g. Royal Applause – Shamriyna (IRE) (Darshaan) [2006/7 16s³ 16d² 16v² Mar 2] fair on Flat (stays 1½m), successful twice in 2006: ran to similar level when placed over hurdles: seemed to find stamina stretched when 9 lengths second to Nelson du Ronceray at Ayr final start: likely to prove best at 2m with emphasis on speed: may still do better. *M. Dods* — h102 +

ROYAL FONTENAILLES (FR) 8 ch.g. Tel Quel (FR) – Sissi Fontenailles (FR) (Pampabird) [2006/7 16s 19dᵖᵘ c17d⁶ 16g Mar 19] lengthy gelding: disappointing maiden hurdler: blinkered, mistakes when well held on chasing debut. *R. H. Buckler* — c–, h84

ROYAL GAME 5 b.g. Vettori (IRE) – Ground Game (Gildoran) [2006/7 16f⁶ 17d⁵ 16gᶠ Nov 2] unfurnished gelding: poor maiden on Flat at 3 yrs, sold out of M. Bell's stable 3,000 gns Doncaster August (2005) Sales: poor form in novice hurdles. *M. Todhunter* — h75

ROYAL GLEN (IRE) 9 b.m. Royal Abjar (USA) – Sea Glen (IRE) (Glenstal (USA)) [2006/7 h94: 16m* 16m⁵ 16f⁴ 16f⁵ 16g c16mᵘʳ c16sᵖᵘ c16gᵖᵘ Oct 7] modest handicap hurdler: won at Hexham in June: has failed to complete over fences: raced around 2m: acts on firm and good to soft going. *W. S. Coltherd* — c–, h89

ROYAL HECTOR (GER) 8 b.g. Hector Protector (USA) – Rudolfina (CAN) (Pleasant Colony (USA)) [2006/7 c127, h–: c21s² c24g⁵ c21gᵘʳ Apr 12] good-topped gelding: has reportedly had wind operation: fairly useful hurdler/chaser at best: off a year and left Jonjo O'Neill, best effort in hunters in 2006/7 when ½-length second to Mouseski at Wincanton: might well have made frame but for unseating 7 out in Fox Hunters' at Aintree: stays 21f: acts on heavy and good to firm going: visored once: held up. *A. G. Hobbs* — c111, h–

ROYAL KATIDOKI (FR) 7 b.g. Rochesson (FR) – Miss Coco (FR) (Bay Comeau (FR)) [2006/7 c–, h–: c20m* c20g⁶ 19d 22d⁶ c21s³ 22g* Mar 19] leggy, angular gelding: fairly useful hurdler/chaser: won maiden over fences at Ludlow (33/1 and first outing after leaving N. Henderson, by 1¼ lengths from Piran) in October and handicap hurdle (back to best to beat Norton Sapphire by 3 lengths) in March: stays easy 2¾m: acts on soft and good to firm going: tongue tied: usually races prominently: sold 18,000 gns Doncaster May Sales. *C. E. Longsdon* — c115, h124

ROYAL KICKS (FR) 6 b.g. Garde Royale – Al Kicks (FR) (Al Nasr (FR)) [2006/7 20d⁴ Mar 17] smallish gelding: second foal: half-brother to 7.5f to 1¼m winner Montreuillois (by Raintrap): dam, French maiden, half-sister to useful hurdler/chaser Celtic Son, stays 25f, and useful staying chaser Sonevafushi: successful twice in Irish points, — h92 p including in January: some promise when 17¾ lengths fourth of 18 to Jungleland in novice at Uttoxeter on hurdling debut: likely to improve. *H. D. Daly*

ROYAL MASTER 5 b.g. Royal Applause – High Sevens (Master Willie) [2006/7 h95: 16d Oct 14] rather leggy gelding: maiden on Flat: modest hurdler: well held in handicap only start in 2006/7: raced around 2m: acts on good to firm going. *P. C. Haslam* **h–**

ROYAL MELBOURNE (IRE) 7 ch.g. Among Men (USA) – Calachuchi (Martinmas) [2006/7 16s⁵ 17v⁶ 20m² Mar 31] lengthy, good-topped gelding: half-brother to fairly useful hurdler/useful chaser Calatagan (by Danzig Connection), stays 2½m: fair on Flat (stays 1¾m): modest form over hurdles: stays 2½m: acts on soft and good to firm ground: sold 8,000 gns Doncaster May Sales. *Miss J. A. Camacho* **h87**

ROYAL MILLER (IRE) 7 b.g. Mister Lord (USA) – Rose Miller (Roselier (FR)) [2006/7 16s 16v^pu 20s^pu Apr 25] €7,000 4-y-o: sixth foal: half-brother to 2m hurdle winner Vicar Street (by The Parson): dam failed to complete in 7 Irish points: no form over hurdles: tongue tied last 2 starts. *N. W. Alexander* **h–**

ROYAL NIECE (IRE) 8 b.m. Rakaposhi King – Sister Stephanie (IRE) (Phardante (FR)) [2006/7 h82: 20d 26s 21v c24s³ 24v^pu Feb 18] angular mare: maiden hurdler, no form in 2006/7: poor form in novice handicap at Huntingdon on chasing debut, in rear most of way: thorough stayer: raced on good going or softer (acts on heavy): tried in cheekpieces: possibly not straightforward. *D. J. Wintle* **c82 h–**

ROYAL PARADISE (FR) 7 b.g. Cadoudal (FR) – Crystalza (FR) (Crystal Palace (FR)) [2006/7 h134?: c20g c20d^pu c17s² c17v² 21g 24g^pu Mar 30] lengthy, angular gelding: one-time useful hurdler, no show in handicaps: best effort in maiden chases (fairly useful form) when 11 lengths second of 4 to easy winner Private Be at Bangor fourth outing: stays 21f: raced on good ground or softer (acts on heavy): in headgear last 4 starts: often shapes as if amiss. *P. R. Webber* **c115 h–**

ROYAL PRODIGY (USA) 8 ch.g. Royal Academy (USA) – Prospector's Queen (USA) (Mr Prospector (USA)) [2006/7 h–§: 17g² 17m^pu Jun 8] modest handicap hurdler, lightly raced nowadays: stays 19f: acts on firm and soft going: has worn headgear: not one to trust. *R. J. Hodges* **h85 §**

ROYAL RHYTHM (IRE) 5 b.g. King's Best (USA) – Ragtime Rumble (USA) (Dixieland Band (USA)) [2006/7 16d² 16g⁶ 16d⁵ 16d² Apr 1] smallish, leggy gelding: fair form at best on Flat (stays 1m), well beaten last 5 starts: modest maiden hurdler: likely to prove best at 2m: raced on good/good to soft ground. *John Joseph Murphy, Ireland* **h99**

ROYAL ROSA (FR) 8 ch.g. Garde Royale – Crystalza (FR) (Crystal Palace (FR)) [2006/7 c20v² c20v* c22v³ c25s^pu c24g c24s^pu Apr 25] good-topped gelding: smart hurdler at best: useful novice chaser, off over 20 months before return: won 3-runner event at Wetherby in December by 9 lengths from L'Antartique: little impact after (lost action fourth start): stays 3m: raced on good ground or softer (acts on heavy): in cheekpieces last 2 outings. *J. Howard Johnson* **c132 h–**

ROYAL SAILOR (IRE) 5 b.g. Bahhare (USA) – Old Tradition (IRE) (Royal Academy (USA)) [2006/7 h–: 16s 16g⁶ 16m Apr 9] tall gelding: modest maiden on Flat (stays 2m): no form over hurdles. *J. Ryan* **h–**

ROYAL SCANDAL 11 br.g. Royal Fountain – Langton Lass (Nearly A Hand) [2006/7 c?, h–: c23v* c25d³ Mar 20] workmanlike gelding: fair pointer/hunter chaser: won at Taunton in March: stays 3m: acts on heavy going. *Mrs Susan Smith* **c94 h–**

ROYALS DARLING (GER) 5 ch.g. Kallisto (GER) – Royal Rivalry (USA) (Sir Ivor (USA)) [2006/7 h130: 21s² 22d 21g 21m⁵ Apr 21] big, good-topped gelding: type to make a chaser: useful handicap hurdler: improved form when length second to Verasi in valuable event at Kempton on return: disappointing after: should stay beyond 21f: acts on soft going: has worn headgear. *N. J. Henderson* **h139**

ROYAL SHAKESPEARE (FR) 8 b.g. King's Theatre (IRE) – Persian Walk (FR) (Persian Bold) [2006/7 h145: 16m³ c16d² c19d³ c16d³ c16s* c17g² c16g³ c16m² Apr 26] tall, useful-looking gelding: useful hurdler, third to Crow Wood in limited handicap at Wincanton on reappearance: similar standard over fences: won novice at Kempton in January by 10 lengths from Trouble At Bay: good efforts when placed in Grade 1 events last 2 starts, 9 lengths third of 6 to Twist Magic in Maghull Novices' Chase at Aintree and 3½ lengths second to Another Promise in Swordlestown Cup Novices' Chase at Punchestown: seems to stay 19f: has form on heavy going, probably ideally suited by less testing conditions (acts on good to firm): has run well when sweating: consistent. *S. Gollings* **c141 h141**

ROYAL SNOOPY (IRE) 14 b. or br.g. Royal Fountain – Lovely Snoopy (IRE) (Phardante (FR)) [2006/7 c99x, h–: c23g⁵ c22s² May 21] lengthy gelding: fair hunter chaser nowadays: stays 27f: acts on any going: blinkered: front runner: usually makes mistakes/jumps right. *R. Tate*   **c86 x h–**

ROYAL STARDUST 6 b.g. Cloudings (IRE) – Ivy Edith (Blakeney) [2006/7 h99§: 16gᶠ 19dᵖᵘ 16m² Jun 11] big gelding: bumper winner: modest maiden hurdler: stays 2½m: acts on soft and good to firm ground: in cheekpieces last 4 starts: moody. *G. L. Moore*   **h97 §**

ROYALTEA 6 ch.m. Desert King (IRE) – Come To Tea (IRE) (Be My Guest (USA)) [2006/7 h74: 16m³ 16g² 16f* Jun 17] sparely-made mare: modest hurdler: won mares novice at Hexham in June: best around 2m: acts on firm going. *R. Ford*   **h92**

ROYMILLON (GER) 13 b.g. Milesius (USA) – Royal Slope (USA) (His Majesty (USA)) [2006/7 c–§, h–§: 27m⁶ Jun 8] leggy gelding: winning hurdler: no form in chases: placed in points in 2006: tried blinkered/in cheekpieces: often gets behind. *Mrs S. Gardner*   **c– § h– §**

ROZNIC (FR) 9 b.g. Nikos – Rozamie (FR) (Azimut (FR)) [2006/7 c120, h–: c19d c20s⁵ c19d c21g³ c16g* c16g Apr 19] useful-looking gelding: fair handicap chaser: won at Kempton in March: effective at 2m to 2½m: raced on good going or softer. *P. Winkworth*   **c111 h–**

RUAIRI (IRE) 6 b.g. Mister Mat (FR) – By Golly (IRE) (Mandalus) [2006/7 F16v* Mar 3] €22,000 3-y-o: fourth foal: dam, winning pointer, out of half-sister to useful chaser up to 25f Colonel In Chief: brought down in Irish point in 2006: created good impression when winning maiden bumper at Kempton by 6 lengths from Withiel Lad. *Miss Suzy Smith*   **F104**

intercasino.co.uk Novices' Chase, Kempton—
the sole win of the season for the consistent Royal Shakespeare

Beards Jewellers Cup (Handicap Chase), Cheltenham—
Rubberdubber (left) gets the better of 2004 winner Armaturk

RUBBERDUBBER 7 b.g. Teenoso (USA) – True Clown (True Song) [2006/7 c138, h–: c16d* Nov 10] tall, useful-looking gelding: winning hurdler: useful chaser: successful 3 of 4 completed starts, including when beating Armaturk by 3 lengths in quite valuable handicap at Cheltenham only start in 2006/7: may prove best up to 2½m: acts on soft and good to firm going: possibly hasn't finished improving, provided all well. *C. R. Egerton* **c140 h–**

RUBY DANTE (IRE) 9 b.m. Ajraas (USA) – Phar Glen (IRE) (Phardante (FR)) [2006/7 c–: 21m⁴ 20v³ 21v² 21g Mar 24] winning pointer: let down by jumping only outing in chase: modest form in novice hurdles: stays 21f: acts on good to firm and heavy ground. *Mrs A. M. Thorpe* **c– h91**

RUBY GALE (IRE) 11 b.g. Lord Americo – Well Over (Over The River (FR)) [2006/7 c125§, h–§: c26s⁵ Feb 18] sturdy gelding: has reportedly had wind operation: fairly useful hurdler/maiden chaser at best, off 15 months prior to fifth of 6 in hunter at Fontwell: stays 2¾m: raced mainly on good/good to soft going: tried blinkered/tongue tied: ungenuine. *P. F. Nicholls* **c97 § h– §**

RUBY JOY 5 b.m. Overbury (IRE) – Safari Park (Absalom) [2006/7 F88: 16f² 16s⁵ 16f⁵ 16m 16g Oct 19] runner-up in bumper: poor maiden hurdler: raced around 2m: acts on firm going. *Mrs H. O. Graham* **h74**

RUBY REW (IRE) 5 b.m. Supreme Leader – Brown Willows (IRE) (Kemal (FR)) [2006/7 F16d Mar 17] 9,000 4-y-o: good-bodied mare: sixth foal: dam, placed in points, out of half-sister to high-class staying chaser Cahervillahow: 7/1 from 25/1 but green to post, well held in bumper on debut. *C. P. Morlock* **F–**

RUBY SUNRISE (IRE) 5 ch.m. Polish Precedent (USA) – Kinlochewe (Old Vic) [2006/7 16m Jul 2] poor maiden on Flat (stays 11f): tailed off in novice on hurdling debut. *B. P. J. Baugh* **h–**

RUBY VALENTINE (FR) 4 b.f. Kayf Tara – A Ma Valentine (FR) (Caerwent) [2006/7 17g Apr 18] rather sparely-made filly: third foal: half-sister to 13f winner Sweet Valentine (by Dernier Empereur): dam 9.5f/10.5f winner: in frame 5 times up to 10.5f on Flat in France, claimed from S. Wattel in November: lost all chance with blunder 3 out in juvenile at Cheltenham on hurdling debut. *A. J. Wilson* **h–**

RUCOLINO (IRE) 7 ch.g. Rock Hopper – Tasmania Star (Captain James) [2006/7 F16m F16v 17s 21s⁶ 21g c23m⁶ Apr 15] close-coupled gelding: half-brother to a winning pointer by Lashkari and modest hurdler/fair chaser Slingsby (by Heraldiste), stayed 2½m: dam won in Italy: little sign of ability: sold 1,000 gns Doncaster May Sales. *M. G. Rimell* **c– h– F–**

RUDAKI 5 ch.g. Opening Verse (USA) – Persian Fountain (IRE) (Persian Heights) **h90 ?**
[2006/7 17g³ 20s² 19g⁵ Nov 5] close-coupled gelding: half-brother to winning hurdler/
chaser Pertino (by Terimon), stayed 2½m: modest on Flat (stays 1¼m): seemingly ran to
similar level when placed in novice hurdles: stays 2½m. *M. E. Sowersby*

RUDE HEALTH 7 b.m. Rudimentary (USA) – Birsay (Bustino) [2006/7 h89: c20g³ **c80 x**
c19dᵖᵘ 22vᵖᵘ c19sᶠ c19sᵘʳ 20v⁵ 22s⁴ 21v 22s Mar 8] workmanlike mare: modest handicap **h–**
hurdler, little form in 2006/7, including over fences (usually let down by jumping): stays
2½m: acts on heavy going. *N. J. Hawke*

RUDINERO (IRE) 5 gr.g. Rudimentary (USA) – Cash Chase (IRE) (Sexton Blake) **h89 +**
[2006/7 F17d* 16s⁶ 20v Jan 11] unfurnished gelding: third foal: dam, fairly useful **F104**
hurdler, stayed 2½m: well-backed favourite, won bumper at Hereford on debut in May by
16 lengths from stable-companion Shropshire Girl: better effort over hurdles (modest
form) when sixth in maiden at Cheltenham. *Heather Dalton*

RUDIVALE (IRE) 5 ch.g. Rudimentary (USA) – Conjure Up (IRE) (Jurado (USA)) **h80**
[2006/7 F16m⁵ F16v⁵ 19s⁴ 16s Jan 10] €10,000 4-y-o: strong, lengthy gelding: first foal: **F90**
dam, winning pointer, half-sister to dam of smart staying chaser Fiddling The Facts: fifth
in bumpers: poor form over hurdles, taking good hold. *C. L. Tizzard*

RUDOLF RASSENDYLL (IRE) 12 b.g. Supreme Leader – Chantel Rouge (Boreen **c– x**
(FR)) [2006/7 c108x, h–x: c24sᵖᵘ May 8] workmanlike gelding: winning handicap **h– x**
hurdler/chaser, no form since 2005/6 reappearance: tried blinkered: often let down by
jumping. *Miss Venetia Williams*

RUFIUS (IRE) 14 b.g. Celio Rufo – In View Lass (Tepukei) [2006/7 c–§, h–§: 22m **c– §**
c26vᵖᵘ c26g⁴ c26gᵖᵘ Nov 15] workmanlike gelding: maiden hurdler/winning chaser: no **h– §**
form for long time, including in points: tried blinkered/tongue tied: ungenuine. *P. Kelsall*

RUGGTAH 6 gr.m. Daylami (IRE) – Raneen Alwatar (Sadler's Wells (USA)) [2006/7 **c74 x**
c90, h–: c24m³ c20s³ c25d⁴ c22v⁴ Feb 18] leggy mare: no show in novice hurdles: **h–**
successful twice in points in 2006: poor maiden chaser, usually let down by jumping:
wears blinkers. *C. C. Bealby*

RULE WATER (IRE) 7 b.g. Supreme Leader – Regal Spark (Royal Match) [2006/7 **h–**
22fᵖᵘ 21s 21vᵖᵘ Jan 2] half-brother to fairly useful hurdler/winning chaser Fountain
Page (by Be My Native), stayed 3m: dam bumper winner: no show over hurdles.
A. H. Mactaggart

RULING REEF 5 b.m. Diktat – Horseshoe Reef (Mill Reef (USA)) [2006/7 16g 16s **h90**
16s⁶ 16g⁶ 19v³ 20v² 21v² 21g⁶ Mar 20] leggy mare: half-sister to fair hurdler A Bit of Fun
(by Unfuwain), stays 2½m: modest on Flat (stays 1¾m): modest novice hurdler: stays
21f: acts on heavy going. *M. D. I. Usher*

RUMBLING BRIDGE 6 ch.g. Air Express (IRE) – Rushing River (USA) (Irish River **h–**
(FR)) [2006/7 h81: 22g May 2] leggy gelding: maiden hurdler, no form last 4 starts: tried
in cheekpieces/blinkers. *Miss J. S. Davis*

RUM CAKE (IRE) 6 b.g. Warcraft (USA) – Some Madam (Some Hand) [2006/7 F18d **F–**
Oct 30] €8,000 3-y-o: sixth foal: half-brother to 2 winning pointers by Mandalus: dam
bumper winner: soundly beaten in bumper on debut: successful all 3 completed starts in
points. *C. L. Popham*

RUM POINTER (IRE) 11 b.g. Turtle Island (IRE) – Osmunda (Mill Reef (USA)) **c95**
[2006/7 c95+, h96+: c24d⁵ Nov 24] small gelding: fairly useful hurdler/chaser at **h–**
one time, on downgrade: stays 3m: raced on good going or softer (acts on heavy).
R. H. Buckler

RUN ATIM 9 ch.g. Hatim (USA) – Run Pet Run (Deep Run) [2006/7 c–, h–: c20dᵖᵘ **c–**
c16s⁶ c20v Mar 18] lightly raced and no form over jumps. *Mrs L. B. Normile* **h–**

RUNAWAY BISHOP (USA) 12 b. or br.g. Lear Fan (USA) – Valid Linda (USA) **c91**
(Valid Appeal (USA)) [2006/7 c93, h79: c24s⁵ c24d³ c24v* c24d⁵ c24mᵖᵘ 26m c22v³ 16d **h70**
c22g⁶ c24s⁵ 19vᵖᵘ 16v c24s⁶ 19v c20v* c25s² Apr 1] lengthy gelding: maiden hurdler:
modest handicap chaser: won at Towcester (fourth course success) in May and Leicester
(amateur event) in March: effective at 19f (given good test) to 29f: acts on any going:
effective blinkered/visored or not: not a straightforward ride: tough. *J. R. Cornwall*

RUN DANI RUN (IRE) 6 b.m. Saddlers' Hall (IRE) – Georgic (Tumble Gold) **h–**
[2006/7 F–: F16f 16s 19v⁴ 17d 22mᵖᵘ 21f 19g Oct 15] of little account: tried blinkered. **F–**
B. W. Duke

RUN FOR HENRY 7 b.g. Gunner B – On Golden Pond (IRE) (Bluebird (USA)) **F–**
[2006/7 F16s Dec 26] 5,400 5-y-o: first foal: dam, poor/unreliable hurdler, stayed 21f:
always behind in bumper on debut. *Jim Best*

RUN FOR PADDY 11 b.g. Michelozzo (USA) – Deep Selection (IRE) (Deep Run) **c136**
[2006/7 c141, h–: c27s⁴ c27d³ c29s c29v⁵ c32m⁴ Apr 21] useful-looking chaser: useful **h–**
handicap chaser: won Scottish Grand National at Ayr in 2005/6: mainly respectable
efforts in 2006/7, 16¾ lengths fourth of 23 to Hot Weld in same race (tried in cheekpieces): stays 33f: acts on soft and good to firm going, unsuited by heavy. *Carl Llewellyn*

RUNNER BEAN 13 b. or br.g. Henbit (USA) – Bean Alainn (Candy Cane) [2006/7 **c90**
c106, h–: c20g³ c23mᵖᵘ c20mᵖᵘ Sep 24] lengthy gelding: fair handicap chaser at best (in **h–**
frame on all but 5 of 35 completed starts): stayed 2½m: acted on soft and firm going:
blinkered once (reportedly bled): dead. *R. Lee*

RUNNING HOT 9 b.g. Sunley Builds – Running Cool (Record Run) [2006/7 c31d **c82 x**
c21dꟻ c20v³ c20s² c20v⁵ c20v⁴ c20v* c20g⁴ Mar 26] good-topped gelding: poor handicap
chaser: made all in 4-runner novice event at Plumpton in March: stays 2½m: raced on
good ground or softer (acts on heavy): has got very much on toes: headstrong: often
makes mistakes. *N. J. Hawke*

RUNNING HOTTER 6 b.m. Wace (USA) – Running Cool (Record Run) [2006/7 F–: **F–**
F17v F16v Jan 25] angular, long-necked mare: no promise in bumpers. *N. J. Hawke*

RUNNING TIMES (USA) 10 b.g. Brocco (USA) – Concert Peace (USA) (Hold Your **c–**
Peace (USA)) [2006/7 c–, h–: c16gᵖᵘ 18mᵖᵘ Sep 21] workmanlike gelding: winning hurd- **h–**
ler: no form over fences, including in points: usually visored/blinkered. *H. J. Manners*

RUN ON THYNE (IRE) 11 b.m. Good Thyne (USA) – Run With Rosie (Deep Run) **c–**
[2006/7 c25m May 6] winning pointer: well beaten in maiden hunter on chase debut.
J. P. Elliot

RUNSHAN (IRE) 7 ch.g. Anshan – Whitebarn Run (Pollerton) [2006/7 c83, h88: **c81**
c25s⁵ Oct 22] lengthy gelding: largely poor form in novice hurdles/handicap chases. **h–**
D. G. Bridgwater

RUNTHATPASTMEAGAIN (IRE) 5 b.g. Accordion – Hollygrove Cezanne (IRE) **h110 p**
(King's Ride) [2006/7 19v³ 17s² Mar 11] rangy gelding: third foal: brother to a winning
pointer and half-brother to fair hurdler Different Class (by Shardari), stays 2¾m: dam
unraced sister to top-class 2m to 3m hurdler Mister Morose and half-sister to smart 2½m
chaser Southolt: shaped well when placed in novice hurdles behind Oceanos des Obeaux
at Newbury and Valiant Shadow at Market Rasen: likely to improve and win races. *Jonjo
O'Neill*

RUN TO THE KING (IRE) 9 b.g. Woods of Windsor (USA) – Miss Firion (Tan- **c69**
firion) [2006/7 c–, h–: c26m⁵ c23m³ c26gᵖᵘ c23m⁵ c23m⁵ c26m⁴ c24mᵖᵘ Oct 4] winning **h–**
Irish pointer: little form in chases: tried blinkered/in cheekpieces. *P. C. Ritchens*

RURAL REPRIMAND 8 br.g. Reprimand – Lady Gwenmore (Town And Country) **h–**
[2006/7 16m 17s 20s 22sᵖᵘ 25mᵖᵘ Apr 9] strong gelding: third foal: dam, maiden hurdler,
stayed 2¾m: no show over hurdles. *J. W. Mullins*

RUSHNEEYRIVER (IRE) 9 b.g. Supreme Leader – Liffey Travel (Le Bavard (FR)) **h123**
[2006/7 16g 19d 19dⁿ 19g⁴ 24m² 24m⁴ 24m⁴ 24m² 22dⁿ 21gꟻ 24s Dec 8] angular
ex-Irish gelding: fairly useful hurdler, left R. Burns before return: vastly improved once
fitted with cheekpieces, winning handicaps at Market Rasen (seller) and Newton Abbot
in June and, after claimed from D. Lewis £5,000, at Uttoxeter in July and Worcester and
Newton Abbot (beat Openide by ½ length, idling, in valuable totepool Summer Festival
Hurdle) in August: stays 3m: acts on firm and good to soft going: tried blinkered: tends to
idle, and seems best produced late. *Mrs A. M. Thorpe*

RUSINGA 9 gr.g. Homo Sapien – Royal Blaze (Scallywag) [2006/7 c21gᵖᵘ c20mᵖᵘ **c–**
c20g⁵ Jul 9] good-bodied gelding: no form, left Ms L. Stock after first outing: sold £1,600
Ascot December Sales. *Mrs L. C. Jewell*

RUSSIAN CONSORT (IRE) 5 ch.g. Groom Dancer (USA) – Ukraine Venture (Slip **h91**
Anchor) [2006/7 16s⁵ 16d 17sᵖᵘ Jan 30] rather leggy gelding: useful 7f/1m winner at
2 yrs, missed 2005 (reportedly injured tendon), respectable efforts in 2006: modest form
on first of 3 outings over hurdles. *A. King*

RUSSIAN LORD (IRE) 8 br.g. Topanoora – Russian Gale (IRE) (Strong Gale) **c–**
[2006/7 c88+, h–: c26g Jun 4] strong, good sort: no show in novice hurdles: modest **h–**
winner over fences: well held in handicap only start in 2006/7: stays 3¼m: acts on good
to firm going: in cheekpieces 4 of last 5 outings: signs of temperament. *V. R. A. Dartnall*

RUSSIAN SKY 8 gr.g. Endoli (USA) – Anzarna (Zambrano) [2006/7 c101, h110: c25f³ **c106 x** c25g² c20m² c24f² c24g² c26v⁴ c25s⁴ c25d⁶ c24dᵘʳ c24s³ 24m² Apr 20] close-coupled **h110** gelding: fair hurdler/novice chaser: stays 27f: acts on firm and soft going: front runner/ races prominently: often let down by jumping/attitude over fences. *Mrs H. O. Graham*

RUSSIAN TRIGGER 5 b.g. Double Trigger (IRE) – Cobusino (Bustino) [2006/7 17s⁵ **h109 p** 20s* Apr 25] half-brother to 3m hunter chase winner Union Man (by Teamster): dam poor maiden on Flat and over hurdles: confirmed debut promise when winning maiden hurdle at Perth in April by 6 lengths from Mr Preacher Man: will stay 3m: open to further improvement. *V. R. A. Dartnall*

RUSTARIX (FR) 6 b.g. Housamix (FR) – Star of Russia (FR) (Soviet Star (USA)) **c–** [2006/7 c98, h106: 19v* 21g² Apr 18] good-topped gelding: in frame over fences in **h125** France: fairly useful novice hurdler: off 15 months, won at Taunton in March by 3 lengths from Thirty Five Black: best effort when 9 lengths second to My Turn Now at Cheltenham: stays 21f: raced on good going or softer (acts on heavy). *A. King*

RUST EN VREDE 8 b.g. Royal Applause – Souveniers (Relko) [2006/7 h81: 17m⁴ **h92** 17g² 19g² 19s* 16m 16d³ 16dᵖᵘ 17g⁶ Apr 11] leggy gelding: modest handicap hurdler: improved in 2006/7, winning novice event at Market Rasen in August: stays 19f: acts on soft and good to firm going: tried visored: bled fifth start. *J. J. Quinn*

RUSTIC JOHN 7 ch.g. Afzal – Spartiquick (Spartan General) [2006/7 c21gᵖᵘ 20d **c70** c23d⁴ c20sᵖᵘ c21v⁴ c20v³ c19g c16m³ c20gᵘʳ Apr 23] lengthy gelding: winning pointer: **h–** little solid form in chases: well beaten only outing over hurdles. *H. J. Manners*

RUSTLER 5 b.g. Green Desert (USA) – Borgia (Machiavellian (USA)) [2006/7 h–p: **h101** 16g⁵ 16s⁴ 16m 16g⁵ Feb 21] workmanlike gelding: has had breathing operation: fair novice hurdler: raced at 2m: acts on soft going: tried blinkered. *N. J. Henderson*

RUSTY SLIPPER 7 b.m. Slip Anchor – Run For Russ (IRE) (Mujtahid (USA)) **h–** [2006/7 F16s 16vᵖᵘ Jan 7] plain, sparely-made mare: first foal: dam little form on Flat: no **F–** show in bumper/novice hurdle. *Miss D. Mountain*

RUTLEDGE RED (IRE) 11 gr.g. Roselier (FR) – Katebeaujolais (Politico (USA)) **c–** [2006/7 c21gᵖᵘ Apr 27] tall gelding: winning hurdler: maiden chaser: successful in point **h–** in April: stays 3m: acts on soft and good to firm going. *Dr S. G. F. Cave*

RYDAL PARK (IRE) 6 b.g. Saddlers' Hall (IRE) – Strong Grove (IRE) (Strong Gale) **h97** [2006/7 17s⁶ 19s 19v 22g³ Apr 7] sturdy gelding: third foal: half-brother to fair hurdler Ballygar Glin (by Fourstars Allstar), stayed 2½m: dam point/2¾m hurdle winner: best effort in novice hurdles (modest form) on handicap debut final start: will stay 3m: raced on good ground or softer. *Mrs S. D. Williams*

RYDERS STORM (USA) 8 b. or br.g. Dynaformer (USA) – Justicara (Rusticaro **c121** (FR)) [2006/7 c121, h–: c24m* May 10] workmanlike gelding: fairly useful chaser: **h–** looked more genuine than usual when winning last 3 starts, including novice at Fakenham (3 ran, beat Vingis Park by 15 lengths) in May: stays 3m: acts on heavy and good to firm going: tried visored/in cheekpieces: joined C. Llewellyn. *T. R. George*

RYE BROOK 10 b.g. Romany Rye – Nearly A Brook (Nearly A Hand) [2006/7 24m⁴ **c99** c21m² c21gᶠ Apr 27] workmanlike gelding: bumper winner: little impact over hurdles: **h83** better form in chases: left P. Nicholls, in second when falling 2 out in novice hunter at Newton Abbot: successful in points, including earlier in April: stays 21f: acts on good to firm going. *R. Barber*

RYHOPE CHIEF (IRE) 4 b.g. Indian Danehill (IRE) – Rachel Pringle (IRE) (Doulab **h75** (USA)) [2006/7 17f³ 17m² 16f 16s² 16s² 17v² 21sᵖᵘ 17s 16vᵖᵘ Feb 18] leggy, close-coupled gelding: poor maiden on Flat: poor juvenile hurdler, claimed from J. Quinn £6,000 fifth start: raced mainly around 2m: probably acts on any going: visored/in cheekpieces last 6 starts: sold £1,000 Ascot February Sales. *M. Sheppard*

RYMINSTER 8 ch.g. Minster Son – Shultan (IRE) (Rymer) [2006/7 c–, h–: c21fᵘʳ **c88** c27m⁶ c25f⁴ c27d² c25v* c25sᵛᵘ c25s⁴ c27m* Apr 9] lengthy gelding: modest handicap **h–** chaser: won at Kelso in January and Sedgefield in April: stays 27f: probably acts on any going: in cheekpieces last 3 starts. *J. Wade*

RYTHM N RHYME (IRE) 8 ch.g. Danehill Dancer (IRE) – Valley Heigh (IRE) **h65** (Head For Heights) [2006/7 16sᵖᵘ 17s 16g³ 16m 16m⁵ Jul 2] ex-Irish gelding: sixth in bumpers: poor maiden hurdler: little show in points: raced around 2m: tried tongue tied. *John A. Harris*

S

SAAFEND ROCKET (IRE) 9 b.g. Distinctly North (USA) – Simple Annie (Simply Great (FR)) [2006/7 c118, h–: c20f⁴ c16m⁵ 20f² 20m³ c23f⁵ c20g Sep 6] leggy, sparely-made gelding: fair handicap hurdler/chaser: best up to 23f: acts on firm and soft going: usually patiently ridden. *Mrs S. M. Johnson* — **c104 h103**

SABINA PARK (IRE) 8 b. or br.m. Arctic Lord – Lisglassick (IRE) (Euphemism) [2006/7 c22m⁵ c25g⁵ c22g³ c18d* c18d³ c22v* c20s² c22v² Mar 18] first foal: dam unraced: winning pointer: fairly useful chaser: much improved in 2006/7, won maiden at Downpatrick in September and handicap at Tralee in January: runner-up last 2 starts, in Grade 3 mares novice events at Thurles (beaten 4 lengths by Gazza's Girl) and Limerick (15 lengths behind Laetitia): stays 2¾m: acts on heavy ground: formerly quirky (refused to race once), but exuberant front runner nowadays. *Mrs D. A. Love, Ireland* — **c120**

SABREFLIGHT 7 ch.m. Sabrehill (USA) – Little Redwing (Be My Chief (USA)) [2006/7 h103, F96: 16v² 17s³ 16v 20gᵖᵘ Apr 7] big, workmanlike mare: fair hurdler: below form last 3 starts, left J. Howard Johnson before final one: stays 21f: raced on good going or softer (acts on heavy). *Carl Llewellyn* — **h100**

SABRE HONGROIS (FR) 4 b.g. Ungaro (GER) – L'Arme Au Poing (FR) (Comrade In Arms) [2006/7 F17v⁵ F16v 17v⁵ 17g² 17g* Apr 20] rather leggy gelding: fifth foal: half-brother to 11f/1½m winner La Cagnotte (by Kizitca): dam placed over hurdles around 2m: mid-field in bumpers: fair hurdler: won novice at Hereford in April by 1¼ lengths from Kempley Green: raced around 2m on good/heavy ground. *D. E. Pipe* — **h104 F79**

SABRE'S EDGE (IRE) 6 b.g. Sadler's Wells (USA) – Brave Kris (IRE) (Kris) [2006/7 16dᶠ Nov 16] very lightly raced on Flat, runner-up in maiden at 2 yrs for J. Gosden: no show over hurdles, left M. Hourigan in Ireland before only start in 2006/7 (pulled hard/jumped erratically). *K. Bishop* — **h–**

SABREUR 6 b.g. Thowra (FR) – Sleepline Princess (Royal Palace) [2006/7 h103, F88: 17g³ May 4] unfurnished gelding: fair maiden hurdler: will stay 2½m: acts on good to firm going, probably on soft. *Ian Williams* — **h103**

SABY (FR) 9 b. or br.g. Sassanian (USA) – Valy Flett (FR) (Pietru (FR)) [2006/7 c93, h72: c16m³ c17m² c21g⁵ c20m³ c21f⁶ Oct 5] tall gelding: maiden hurdler: modest handicap chaser: stays 21f, at least with emphasis on speed: probably acts on any going: joined L. Corcoran. *P. J. Hobbs* — **c87 h–**

SACHSENWALZER (GER) 9 ch.g. Top Waltz (FR) – Stairway To Heaven (GER) (Nebos (GER)) [2006/7 c102, h98: c17m⁵ c17v³ c17mᶠ Jun 11] modest hurdler/chaser: raced around 2m: acts on good to firm and good to soft going, possibly not on soft/heavy. *M. Appleby* — **c98 h–**

SACRIFICE 12 b.g. Arctic Lord – Kellyann (Jellaby) [2006/7 c99§: c20f³ c20m⁵ c23m c20s⁴ c21f Sep 10] sturdy gelding: modest handicap chaser: stays easy 3m: acts on firm and good to soft going: inconsistent. *K. Bishop* — **c95 §**

SADDLERS CLOTH (IRE) 7 b.m. Saddlers' Hall (IRE) – Strong Cloth (IRE) (Strong Gale) [2006/7 c100+, h–, F82: c20g⁶ 21d 21d³ 24s 21g² Mar 26] leggy, lengthy mare: modest chaser/novice hurdler, left J. Geake after first outing: probably stays 3m: acts on soft going. *N. J. Gifford* — **c– h97**

SADDLERS' CRUISER (IRE) 7 b.g. Saddlers' Hall (IRE) – Jerusalem Cruiser (IRE) (Electric) [2006/7 F17m⁴ F17g Oct 15] ex-Irish gelding: fourth foal: half-brother to fair hurdler/chaser Warrens Castle (by Fourstars Allstar), stays 21f: dam bumper winner: winning pointer: poor form in bumpers: tried tongue tied: sold £580 Ascot February Sales. *Mrs L. J. Young* — **F71**

SADDLERS EXPRESS 6 b.m. Saddlers' Hall (IRE) – Swift Conveyance (IRE) (Strong Gale) [2006/7 h–: 22mᶠ 17m 16d⁶ Oct 20] lengthy mare: little sign of ability. *M. F. Harris* — **h–**

SADDLERS' HARMONY (IRE) 6 b.g. Saddlers' Hall (IRE) – Sweet Mignonette (Tina's Pet) [2006/7 F81: F16v² May 25] leggy gelding: modest form in bumpers: sold 4,500 gns Doncaster August Sales, placed in points in April. *K. G. Reveley* — **F81**

SADDLERS LADY (IRE) 7 b.m. Saddlers' Hall (IRE) – Mirador (Town And Country) [2006/7 F–: F18g F16m⁶ F16m 19g⁴ 18g 16f 22m 19dᵖᵘ Oct 26] no form: tried visored: dead. *R. Curtis* — **h– F–**

SADDLER'S QUEST 10 b.g. Saddlers' Hall (IRE) – Seren Quest (Rainbow Quest (USA)) [2006/7 c76, h76: 17sᴾᵘ c20f⁵ c24s⁶ c19s⁴ c24sᶠ 20d Nov 30] angular gelding: maiden hurdler/chaser, little form in 2006/7: stays 2½m: acts on good to firm and heavy going: sometimes wears headgear: tongue tied last 3 starts: has bled from nose. *B. P. J. Baugh* **c69 h–**

SADDLERS' SON (IRE) 6 b.g. Saddlers' Hall (IRE) – Polleroo (IRE) (Pollerton) [2006/7 h85, F–: 16s 19s⁶ 21s c25sᶠ 24m⁶ Apr 25] medium-sized gelding: maiden hurdler, no solid form in 2006/7: held when fell 3 out on chasing debut: tried in cheekpieces: tongue tied last 4 starts. *Heather Dalton* **c– h–**

SADLER'S COVE (FR) 9 b.g. King's Theatre (IRE) – Mine d'Or (FR) (Posse (USA)) [2006/7 17dᵘʳ 16f⁵ 18m 16s⁴ 18s⁴ 20v⁵ 20g³ Apr 23] compact gelding: poor maiden hurdler: stays 2½m: in cheekpieces last 6 starts: usually tongue tied. *J. K. Magee, Ireland* **h82**

SADLER'S STAR (GER) 4 b.g. Alwuhush (USA) – Sadlerella (IRE) (King's Theatre (IRE)) [2006/7 16d Dec 29] tall, useful-looking gelding: fairly useful on Flat, successful once over 1¼m in Germany in 2006 for H. Groschel: raced freely when well held in juvenile on hurdling debut: should improve. *B. G. Powell* **h– p**

SAD MAD BAD (USA) 13 b.g. Sunny's Halo (CAN) – Quite Attractive (USA) (Well Decorated (USA)) [2006/7 c26vᵘʳ May 20] workmanlike gelding: veteran jumper: tried blinkered/visored. *David M. Easterby* **c– h–**

SAFAAH 4 b.g. Almushtarak (IRE) – Lawn Order (Efisio) [2006/7 17mᵖᵘ Jun 30] no form on Flat or in juvenile hurdle. *M. J. Gingell* **h–**

SAFARI 4 b.f. Namaqualand (USA) – Breakfast Creek (Hallgate) [2006/7 17sᴾᵘ 16s 16v 16g 16gᵖᵘ Apr 27] poor maiden up to 7f on Flat, sold out of R. Hodges' stable £1,000 Ascot October Sales: no form over hurdles. *F. E. Sutherland* **h–**

SAFARI ADVENTURES (IRE) 5 b.g. King's Theatre (IRE) – Persian Walk (FR) (Persian Bold) [2006/7 F101: 16v 17s 17v* 19v⁵ 16g Mar 29] good-topped gelding: bumper winner: fair novice hurdler: won at Folkestone in February: raced mainly around 2m on soft/heavy ground. *P. Winkworth* **h105**

SAFARI SUNSET (IRE) 5 b.g. Fayruz – Umlani (IRE) (Great Commotion (USA)) [2006/7 16s Jan 24] smallish gelding: fair on Flat (stays 7f): tailed off in novice on hurdling debut. *P. Winkworth* **h–**

SAFE SHOT 8 b.g. Salse (USA) – Optaria (Song) [2006/7 h–: 20g Aug 1] leggy gelding: maiden on Flat: little form over hurdles: wears cheekpieces. *Mrs J. C. McGregor* **h–**

SAFE TO BLUSH 9 gr.m. Blushing Flame (USA) – Safe Arrival (USA) (Shadeed (USA)) [2006/7 h72: 26g² 22m 24fᴾᵘ 22mᵖᵘ 20g⁵ 26g* 26g⁶ 26gᵖᵘ Apr 11] big mare: poor hurdler: won handicap at Hereford in November: stays 3¼m: acts on heavy going: tried blinkered/in cheekpieces/tongue tied. *P. A. Pritchard* **h68**

SAFFRON SUN 12 b.g. Landyap (USA) – Saffron Bun (Sit In The Corner (USA)) [2006/7 c17f, h–: c21vᶠ May 27] tall, workmanlike gelding: fairly useful handicap chaser: well beaten when fell fatally last at Stratford: stayed 25f: acted on firm and soft going. *J. D. Frost* **c– h–**

SAFIN (GER) 7 b.g. Pennekamp (USA) – Sankt Johanna (GER) (High Game) [2006/7 16d 16s⁵ 16g⁵ 16v 16v⁶ 16s Feb 22] close-coupled gelding: useful at one time on Flat (stays 11f) in Germany, has deteriorated considerably: poor novice hurdler, left Frau C. Bosckai after debut: raced at 2m on good ground or softer. *P. Jordan* **h82**

SAHARA KNIGHT 7 b.m. Petoski – Lady Rosemount (Morston (FR)) [2006/7 F16m Sep 2] third foal: dam well held in bumpers: tailed off in bumper on debut. *S. T. Lewis* **F–**

SAHARA PRINCE (IRE) 7 b.g. Desert King (IRE) – Chehana (Posse (USA)) [2006/7 16d⁴ 17m* Apr 17] one-time fairly useful performer on Flat (best at 6f/7f), modest nowadays: modest form over hurdles: won maiden at Exeter in April: likely to prove best around 2m. *K. A. Morgan* **h94**

SAHARA'S DREAM 4 b.f. Alphabatim (USA) – Just The Ticket (IRE) (Jolly Jake (NZ)) [2006/7 F16s F17m Apr 15] second foal: dam of little account: well held in mares bumpers. *G. H. Jones* **F–**

SAHF LONDON 4 b.g. Vettori (IRE) – Lumiere d'Espoir (FR) (Saumarez) [2006/7 16d² 16v⁵ 17v 16g⁴ Mar 16] medium-sized gelding: modest on Flat (stays 1½m), successful in January: modest form over hurdles: raced around 2m on good ground or softer (acts on heavy). *G. L. Moore* **h90**

SAIF SAREEA 7 b.g. Atraf – Slipperose (Persepolis (FR)) [2006/7 h119: 16f³ 16m⁵ **h128**
16g³ 16g 16d 18g* Apr 15] smallish, sturdy gelding: fairly useful on Flat (stays 1½m):
fairly useful handicap hurdler, sold out of R. Fahey's stable 50,000 gns Doncaster May
Sales after first outing: best effort when winning at Kelso in April by 9 lengths from
Circassian, dictating: stays 2¼m: acts on firm and good to soft going, not at best on
softer: fluent jumper: takes good hold, effective making running or held up: genuine.
N. G. Richards

SAILOR A'HOY 11 b.g. Handsome Sailor – Eye Sight (Roscoe Blake) [2006/7 c91, **c83 §**
h–: 21m c28v⁴ c28spu c27vpu c22d³ c24vpu c22d⁵ c25m⁴ c27m⁵ Apr 9] workmanlike **h– §**
gelding: winning hurdler: poor handicap chaser: stays 3½m: acts on heavy and good to
firm going: usually wears headgear: ungenuine. *M. Mullineaux*

SAILOR'S SOVEREIGN 6 b.g. Sovereign Water (FR) – Tirley Pop Eye (Cruise **F–**
Missile) [2006/7 F16g Apr 7] third foal: half-brother to winning pointer by Michelozzo:
dam unraced half-sister to useful hurdler/chaser up to 33f (Scottish Grand National
winner) Run For Paddy: never dangerous in bumper on debut. *J. S. Smith*

SAINT GODEGRAND (FR) 5 gr.g. Saint Preuil (FR) – Sa Majeste (FR) (Garde **c106**
Royale) [2006/7 c18dpu 17g* 17g² c17v* c19s³ c19v³ c24vF 16d⁵ 21m⁴ 20spu Apr 27] **h90**
compact gelding: fifth foal: half-brother to middle-distance winners in France by Courtroom and Homme de Loi: dam lightly raced on Flat: winning hurdler/chaser in France,
including over hurdles at Les Sables-d'Olonne in August and in 4-y-o chase at Enghien
in October: left A. Lacombe, in touch when falling heavily 4 out in novice chase at
Chepstow: modest form in novice hurdles next 2 starts: should stay beyond 21f: acts on
heavy and good to firm going. *M. F. Harris*

SAINT ROMBLE (FR) 10 b.g. Sassanian (USA) – Limatge (FR) (Trac) [2006/7 **c103**
c23v⁵ c23m² Apr 22] leggy gelding: successful 10 times in points, including twice in **h–**
2007: fair chaser: ran well when 10 lengths second to Mel In Blue in hunter at Stratford:
stays 23f: acts on heavy and good to firm going. *P. J. Hobbs*

SAINTSAIRE (FR) 8 b.g. Apeldoorn (FR) – Pro Wonder (FR) (The Wonder (FR)) **c131**
[2006/7 c128, h–: c17s* c16g⁶ c20m⁵ Apr 20] leggy, useful-looking gelding: useful **h–**
handicap chaser: reportedly had breathing operation and off 7 months, won at Newbury
in November by 1¾ lengths from Bambi de L'Orme: creditable sixth of 23 to Andreas in
Grade 3 Grand Annual Chase at Cheltenham: stays 21f: acts on soft going: tried
blinkered. *P. F. Nicholls*

SAJOMI RONA (IRE) 10 ch.g. Riberetto – Mauma Lady (IRE) (Le Moss) [2006/7 **c84**
c20d² c20m* Jun 3] sturdy gelding: fair pointer: improved chaser in 2006/7, won hunter **h–**
at Hexham in June: should stay beyond 2½m: acts on good to firm and good to soft going:
tried blinkered/visored/tongue tied. *Mrs G. Smith*

UK Hygiene Handicap Chase, Newbury—
Saintsaire beats the grey Bambi de L'Orme to make a winning start for new connections

SAKENOS (POL) 7 b.g. In Camera (IRE) – Sakaria (POL) (Rutilio Rufo (USA)) **c81**
[2006/7 h97: 16g⁴ 20m⁶ 16f* 17m* c18m⁴ c16g⁴ c16f Sep 3] fair novice hurdler: won at **h113**
Uttoxeter in June (maiden) and July and Market Rasen (by 4 lengths from Green Finger)
in August: let down by jumping all 3 starts over fences within 10-day period: possibly
best around 2m: acts on firm and good to soft going: effective tongue tied or not: races
prominently: sold 3,500 gns Doncaster October Sales. *P. J. Hobbs*

SALES FLOW 5 ch.m. Double Trigger (IRE) – New Dawn (Rakaposhi King) [2006/7 **h–**
h–, F–: 16d May 15] sturdy mare: no form in bumpers/over hurdles: fourth (promoted) in
maiden point in April. *M. W. Easterby*

SALESIN 4 ch.g. Lomitas – Elisita (ARG) (Ride The Rails (USA)) [2006/7 16s² 16v⁶ **h91**
16v³ Feb 23] useful on Flat (stays 1¾m), successful in May, sold out of L. Cumani's
stable 58,000 gns Newmarket Autumn Sales: best effort in juvenile hurdles when second
to Risk Runner at Warwick: jumped badly right and none too keen under pressure final
start: raced at 2m on soft/heavy ground. *Jonjo O'Neill*

SALHOOD 8 b.g. Capote (USA) – Princess Haifa (USA) (Mr Prospector (USA)) **c110**
[2006/7 c88, h94: c18g³ c16m² c20d* c20f² c22g² c20sᵖᵘ c16g³ c20d³ c16dᵖᵘ c20m² **h–**
c20mᵘʳ Apr 28] big, lengthy gelding: winning hurdler: fair novice chaser: jumped better
than often does when winning at Market Rasen in August: stays 2¾m: acts on soft and
firm going: tried tongue tied (bled). *S. Gollings*

SALIM 10 b.g. Salse (USA) – Moviegoer (Pharly (FR)) [2006/7 c–, h–: 19dᵖᵘ Aug 21] **c–**
angular gelding: maiden hurdler: no form over fences: tried tongue tied. *Miss J. S. Davis* **h–**

SALINAS (GER) 8 b.g. Macanal (USA) – Santa Ana (GER) (Acatenango (GER)) **c109**
[2006/7 c92, h–: c16dᶠ c16d³ c16s⁵ c16v³ c16v² Jan 20] good-topped gelding: winning **h–**
hurdler: fair handicap chaser: effective at 2m to easy 21f: acts on heavy and good to firm
going: tried visored: formerly front runner. *M. F. Harris*

SALINGER (USA) 5 b.g. Lear Fan (USA) – Sharp Flick (USA) (Sharpen Up) [2006/7 **h–**
h–: 16m⁶ Sep 24] close-coupled gelding: modest on Flat (stays 1¼m): thrice-raced
in novice company over hurdles, too free only outing in 2006/7: joined Mrs A. Thorpe.
Mrs L. J. Mongan

SALLIEMAK 9 b.m. Makbul – Glenbrook Fort (Fort Nayef) [2006/7 c–, h–: c23gᴿ **c–**
May 14] maiden hurdler: failed to complete both outings over fences: tongue tied last 3 **h–**
starts. *A. J. Wilson*

SALLY SCALLY 15 ch.m. Scallywag – Petite Cone (Celtic Cone) [2006/7 24mᵖᵘ **c–**
c26dᵖᵘ Aug 28] smallish mare: winning pointer: maiden hurdler/chaser, no form since **h–**
early-2004/5: blinkered once: weak finisher. *Miss T. Jackson*

SALMATIAN KNIGHT 7 b.g. Rakaposhi King – Farrah's Darling (IRE) (Supreme **c–**
Leader) [2006/7 F17v c25sᵖᵘ c20gᵖᵘ Apr 16] €3,800 4-y-o: first foal: dam, poor novice **F–**
hurdler, stayed 21f: third in maiden point in 2006: no show in bumper/maiden chases.
A. M. Crow

SALTANGO (GER) 8 br.g. Acatenango (GER) – Salde (GER) (Alkalde (GER)) **h126**
[2006/7 h132: 20s² Oct 21] leggy gelding: useful hurdler: creditable second to Taranis
(FR) in listed handicap at Chepstow, only outing in 2006/7: stays 2¾m: raced on good
going or softer (acts on heavy): consistent. *A. M. Hales*

SALT CELLAR (IRE) 8 b.g. Salse (USA) – Athene (IRE) (Rousillon (USA)) [2006/7 **c–**
c–, h–§: 26g³ 24d⁴ 24m⁶ 22m* Jul 16] medium-sized gelding: modest handicap hurdler: **h94**
won at Stratford in July: fell eighth only outing over fences: stays 3¼m: acts on good to
firm and good to soft going (below form on softer): has worn visor, in cheekpieces in
2006/7. *R. S. Brookhouse*

SALUT SAINT CLOUD 6 b.g. Primo Dominie – Tiriana (Common Grounds) **h119**
[2006/7 h120: 16f⁵ 20m 16d 20gᶠ 21v Feb 24] leggy gelding: fair hurdler (stays 2m),
successful in March: probably stays 21f: acts on soft and firm going: has worn
cheekpieces/blinkers 6 of last 7 outings. *G. L. Moore*

SALVAGE 12 b.g. Kahyasi – Storm Weaver (USA) (Storm Bird (CAN)) [2006/7 c–, h–: **c–**
c16sᵖᵘ May 17] angular gelding: modest handicap chaser at best, went as if amiss only **h–**
outing in 2006/7: stays 2½m: acts on heavy and good to firm going: tried tongue tied.
Mrs J. C. McGregor

SALVEO (IRE) 5 b.g. Saddlers' Hall (IRE) – Devil Worship (Yashgan) [2006/7 F16v² **F80**
F17m Apr 28] seventh foal: dam, successful over 1m on Flat/2m winner over hurdles,
half-sister to useful hurdler Don Valentino: better effort in bumpers when 8 lengths
second of 6 to ready winner Massasoit at Ayr. *R. D. E. Woodhouse*

SALYM (FR) 6 ch.g. Limnos (JPN) – Tina's Crest (FR) (Ocean Falls) [2006/7 20g³ 22s **h86**
Feb 17] fairly useful up to 12.5f on Flat in France, modest form in Britain: modest novice
hurdler, left B. Secly before reappearance: stays 2½m: acts on heavy going: has worn
blinkers. *D. J. S. ffrench Davis*

SAM ADAMSON 12 br.g. Domitor (USA) – Sardine (Saritamer (USA)) [2006/7 c–, **c70**
h–: c20f^pu c21m^pu c21g^pu c23f* c24s^pu c23g³ Nov 9] sturdy gelding: poor handicap chas- **h–**
er nowadays: dropped markedly in weights prior to winning at Worcester in September:
stays 23f: best form on good going or firmer (acts on firm): tongue tied. *J. W. Mullins*

SAMARINDA (USA) 4 ch.g. Rahy (USA) – Munnaya (USA) (Nijinsky (CAN)) **h–**
[2006/7 16d 16d^pu Dec 4] half-brother to fairly useful hurdler Beseiged (by Cadeaux
Genereux), stays 19f: fairly useful on Flat (stays 1¼m), sold out of E. Dunlop's stable
20,000 gns Newmarket July Sales, successful in December/March: no show in juvenile
hurdles. *Mrs P. Sly*

SAMEROUS (IRE) 4 b.f. Shinko Forest (IRE) – Samriah (IRE) (Wassl) [2006/7 F12g **F–**
Mar 23] leggy, close-coupled filly: half-sister to several winners, including 19f hurdle
winner Cedar Master (by Soviet Lad), also winner up to 2m on Flat: dam unraced: well
held in 4-y-o bumper on debut. *N. J. Gifford*

SAM MCCOOMBE (IRE) 6 b.g. Roseberry Avenue (IRE) – Runaway Mary (IRE) **F91**
(Tidaro (USA)) [2006/7 F16g⁶ F16g F16m* Apr 9] 4,000 4-y-o: lengthy gelding: first
foal: dam, ran once in point, half-sister to dam of Our Vic: didn't need to repeat form
of first 2 starts in bumpers to win at Huntingdon by 1¼ lengths from Generous Star.
O. Brennan

SAMMY SPIDERMAN 4 b.g. Karinga Bay – Thorterdykes Lass (IRE) (Zaffaran **F86**
(USA)) [2006/7 F17s⁴ Feb 19] second foal: dam, poor novice hurdler who stayed 3m,
sister to useful staying chaser Heltornic and fairly useful 2½m hurdle winner Glenmoss
Tara: 10¾ lengths fourth to Harry Wood in bumper at Carlisle on debut. *A. C. Whillans*

SAMSBRO (IRE) 6 b. or br.g. Saddlers' Hall (IRE) – Russian Gale (IRE) (Strong **h–**
Gale) [2006/7 F16s 16s Apr 26] strong, compact gelding: sixth foal: half-brother to smart **F82**
hurdler/chaser Lord Sam (by Supreme Leader), stays 3m, and winning 3¼m chaser
Russian Lord (by Topanoora): dam won 3m chase in Ireland: seventh of 13 in bumper on
debut: well held in novice hurdle: likely to be suited by 2½m+. *V. R. A. Dartnall*

SAMS LAD (IRE) 6 b.g. Saddlers' Hall (IRE) – Cellatica (USA) (Sir Ivor (USA)) **c81**
[2006/7 h–, F95: 17m² 16f² 16f² 20m³ 19f 20g c25g² Sep 15] modest maiden hurdler: runner- **h87**
up in maiden at Kilbeggan on chasing debut: stays 25f: acts on firm going (runner-up in
bumper on soft). *S. Donohoe, Ireland*

SAMSON DES GALAS (FR) 9 b. or br.g. Agent Bleu (FR) – Sarema (FR) (Primo **h63 §**
Dominie) [2006/7 h61§: 17d² 19d 20g^pu 17f 17d⁵ 19v^pu 19v^pu 20g^pu Apr 16] good-topped
gelding: poor maiden hurdler: no form after reappearance, left Robert Gray after fifth
start: stays 2¾m: acts on soft going: tried in cheekpieces/tongue tied: ungenuine.
L. R. James

SAMS PARTY (IRE) 6 b.m. Beneficial – Dont Look Back (IRE) (Satco (FR)) [2006/7 **F–**
F17v Nov 12] first foal: dam unraced, out of sister to useful 2m hurdler Hidebound: well
beaten on completed start in points and in bumper. *J. S. Wainwright*

SAMUEL WILDERSPIN 15 b.g. Henbit (USA) – Littoral (Crash Course) [2006/7 **c– §**
c89, h–: c25d^pu May 17] rangy gelding: veteran chaser: stays 33f: acts on heavy going, **h–**
possibly not on good to firm: formerly tongue tied: has broken blood vessels/looked
unwilling. *Miss Kerry Lee*

SAN ANTONIO 7 b.g. Efisio – Winnebago (Kris) [2006/7 17d* 16s⁶ 16s Dec 7] **h96**
good-topped gelding: fairly useful on Flat (stays 1m) nowadays: modest hurdler: won
handicap at Bangor in November: likely to prove best around 2m: acts on good to soft
ground: blinkered in 2006/7: inconsistent. *Mrs P. Sly*

SA NAU 4 b.g. Generous (IRE) – Trellis Bay (Sadler's Wells (USA)) [2006/7 16g³ 16d⁴ **h108**
18s² 20d* 19s⁵ 20g⁵ Apr 3] half-brother to fair hurdler Water Taxi (by Zafonic), stays
2½m: fair stayer on Flat, successful twice in 2006: fair juvenile hurdler: won maiden at
Fakenham in January by 1¼ lengths from Wise Owl: well below form after: stays 2½m:
raced on good going or softer. *T. Keddy*

SANDALPHON (USA) 4 b.g. King Cugat (USA) – Noumea (USA) (Plugged Nickle **F–**
(USA)) [2006/7 F12v F16s Feb 9] angular gelding: fifth living foal: half-brother to 3
winners abroad: dam 1m/8.5f winner in USA: well held in bumpers and maiden on Flat.
J. A. Geake

SAN DENG 5 gr.g. Averti (IRE) – Miss Mirror (Magic Mirror) [2006/7 16g³ 16g³ 16g⁵ **h98**
Apr 15] half-brother to modest chaser Constant Husband (by Le Solaret), stayed 2½m:
fair on Flat (stays 1½m), sold out of W. Muir's stable 34,000 gns Newmarket Autumn
Sales, and gelded: modest form when third at Musselburgh first 2 starts over hurdles.
Micky Hammond

SANDMARTIN (IRE) 7 b.g. Alflora (IRE) – Quarry Machine (Laurence O) [2006/7 **c– §**
h94§: c24dᵖᵘ May 15] lengthy gelding: modest hurdler: stays 2¾m: acts on soft going: **h– §**
blinkered last 4 starts: usually let down by jumping/temperament, including on chasing
debut: sold 3,800 gns Doncaster May Sales, won point in January. *P. J. Hobbs*

SAND REPEAL (IRE) 5 b.g. Revoque (IRE) – Columbian Sand (IRE) (Salmon Leap **h–**
(USA)) [2006/7 16sᵘʳ Jan 24] angular gelding: half-brother to fair hurdler/chaser Tarn
Ridge (by Victory Note) and temperamental hurdler Peterson's Cay (by Grand Lodge),
both of whom stay 2½m: fair on Flat (stays 2m), successful 3 times in 2006: unseated
second on hurdling debut. *Miss J. Feilden*

SANDS RISING 10 b.g. Primitive Rising (USA) – Celtic Sands (Celtic Cone) [2006/7 **c105**
c101, h77+: 17s c16g⁴ c16d³ c20s* c16s c19s² c19g c20s* c22v⁵ c20v⁴ Mar 18] lengthy **h–**
gelding: winning hurdler: fair handicap chaser: won at Sedgefield in December and
Carlisle in February: stays 3m: raced on good going or softer (acts on heavy): wore cheekpieces after second outing: tongue tied: patiently ridden. *R. Johnson*

SANDY GOLD (IRE) 9 ch.g. Carroll House – Autumn Vixen (IRE) (Trigon) [2006/7 **c69**
c93?: c20d³ c21g⁵ c20mᵖᵘ c21fᵖᵘ c21m c21m⁵ c22m² c25s⁵ c21v⁶ c21v⁶ Feb 20] big,
well-made gelding: point winner, including in March: poor maiden chaser: trained largely
by Miss J. Foster: stays 2¾m: acts on soft and good to firm going: visored/blinkered last
4 starts. *P. Foster*

SANDYMAC (IRE) 7 b.m. Oscar (IRE) – Molly Owen (IRE) (Kambalda) [2006/7 **h102**
22v⁵ 20v⁵ 21v⁴ 18m* Apr 26] third foal: half-sister to a winning pointer by Alphabatim:
dam, winning pointer, out of half-sister to useful staying chaser Pilot Officer: won maiden
point in 2005: fair form over hurdles: left Thomas Carver in Ireland and well backed, won
mares maiden at Fontwell by 3 lengths from Cyd Charisse: should stay at least 2½m.
G. L. Moore

SANDY'S LEGEND (USA) 5 ch.g. Tale of The Cat (USA) – Avasand (USA) (Avatar **h101**
(USA)) [2006/7 20g⁵ 17g⁶ 16g² 16d Nov 11] compact gelding: modest maiden on Flat
(stays 2m): fair form over hurdles, 2½ lengths second to Bleak House in maiden at
Aintree: should prove suited by 2½m+: wears cheekpieces. *Mrs L. Williamson*

SANDYWELL GEORGE 12 ch.g. Zambrano – Farmcote Air (True Song) [2006/7 **c– §**
c–, h83d: c23mᵖᵘ c23gᵖᵘ 20m 24d 26g 20d 24d 26s Dec 23] good-topped gelding: **h– §**
winning hurdler/maiden chaser, no form for long time: usually wears visor/cheekpieces
nowadays: tongue tied: ungenuine. *L. P. Grassick*

SAN FRANCISCO 13 b.g. Aragon – Sirene Bleu Marine (USA) (Secreto (USA)) **c77**
[2006/7 c86, h–: c23g⁴ c25g³ c26d May 31] tall gelding: modest hunter chaser: successful **h–**
in point in March: stays 3¼m: acts on heavy going: effective tongue tied or not. *Miss*
Freya Hartley

SANGATTE (IRE) 9 b.g. Un Desperado (FR) – Mad House (Kabour) [2006/7 20gᵖᵘ **h–**
May 5] rangy gelding: lightly raced and little sign of ability: tried tongue tied. *D. McCain*

SANGENESIUS (IRE) 7 gr.g. Petong – Just Deserts (Alhijaz) [2006/7 c17g 16f 24msᵘ **c–**
16s³ 16s⁴ 18d² 16s 16s Nov 1] modest handicap hurdler, left Patrick Mooney after **h91**
third outing: soundly beaten completed start over fences: best form around 2m: acts on
soft and good to firm ground: has worn blinkers/cheekpieces: usually tongue tied.
Patrick O. Brady, Ireland

SAN HERNANDO 7 b.g. Hernando (FR) – Sandrella (IRE) (Darshaan) [2006/7 h110: **h97**
26g³ 26g⁶ Oct 3] fair on Flat (stays 2m), lightly raced nowadays: fair form at best over
hurdles: should stay beyond 2¾m: acts on soft and good to firm going: visored last 3
starts. *Miss E. C. Lavelle*

SAN LUCA (IRE) 7 ch.g. Flemensfirth (USA) – Sandy Ash (IRE) (Boreen (FR)) **h–**
[2006/7 F17v 24vᵖᵘ 20d Mar 17] €10,000 4-y-o: tall gelding: fourth foal: half-brother to **F–**
fairly useful chaser Ashstorm (by Glacial Storm): dam unraced: no form in
bumper/novice hurdles, left D. P. Keane after second outing. *J. B. Groucott*

SAN MALO (IRE) 10 b.g. Toulon – Laurel Escort (Mandalus) [2006/7 c25sᵖᵘ Jan 2] **c–**
big gelding: failed to complete in points/maiden chase. *Miss A. M. Newton-Smith*

SAN MARCO (IRE) 9 b.g. Brief Truce (USA) – Nuit Des Temps (Sadler's Wells (USA)) [2006/7 16m 19d⁶ 27mᵖᵘ c19m c21g² c23m² 20g Apr 11] winning hurdler, off nearly 2 years and no form in handicaps in 2006/7: poor form over fences: stays 3m: probably acts on any going: wears cheekpieces/blinkers: temperamental. *M. Sheppard*   **c83 §** / **h– §**

SAN PEIRE (FR) 10 b.g. Cyborg (FR) – Shakapoura (FR) (Shakapour) [2006/7 c–, h102: 27d³ 27s⁴ 21v³ 20v³ 25vᵖᵘ Mar 18] fair handicap hurdler: effective at testing 2½m to 27f: raced on good going or softer (acts on heavy): tried in cheekpieces/visor: all 4 wins at Sedgefield (including only outing over fences): temperamental. *J. Howard Johnson*   **c–** / **h99 §**

SANSEL 4 b.f. Well Beloved – Abbisluckystar (IRE) (Soughaan (USA)) [2006/7 16f 16mᵘʳ 18gᵖᵘ Sep 30] no form on Flat and in juvenile hurdles. *J. Ryan*   **h–**

SANTANDO 7 b.g. Hernando (FR) – Santarem (USA) (El Gran Senor (USA)) [2006/7 19v⁶ 19d⁴ 16v* 16s* 19s 21g 20m² 22m³ Apr 11] compact gelding: fair on Flat (stays 1¾m) in 2006, successful in October, sold out of C. Brittain's stable 11,000 gns Newmarket Autumn Sales: fair novice hurdler: won twice at Plumpton (dead-heated with Thunder Rock first time) in January: should prove as effective beyond 2m: acts on heavy going: has worn cheekpieces/blinkers: temperamental. *P. Bowen*   **h113 §**

SANTA'S SON (IRE) 7 ch.g. Basanta (IRE) – Rivers Town Rosie (IRE) (Roselier (FR)) [2006/7 20v² 24d 24m⁴ 24m⁵ Apr 26] smallish gelding: fairly useful handicap hurdler: progressed further in 2006/7, good fifth of 24 to Sonnyanjoe at Punchestown final start: stays 3m: acts on heavy and good to firm ground: usually tongue tied nowadays: often front runner. *J. F. O'Shea, Ireland*   **h125**

SANTO SUBITO (IRE) 6 b.g. Presenting – Shinora (IRE) (Black Minstrel) [2006/7 18m Jun 6] 14,500 4-y-o: second foal: dam, poor maiden in Ireland, half-sister to top-class 2m/2½m hurdler Mighty Mogul: well held in novice hurdle on debut. *R. M. Stronge*   **h–**

SAORSIE 9 b.g. Emperor Jones (USA) – Exclusive Lottery (Presidium) [2006/7 c82§, h91§: 16m 17d⁴ c16f⁵ c20f Sep 3] leggy gelding: modest handicap hurdler: poor form in chases: won 2-finisher point in April: best around 2m: acts on soft and good to firm going: tried in headgear: held up: inconsistent. *J. C. Fox*   **c82 §** / **h88 §**

SAPHIRE NIGHT 6 b.m. Sir Harry Lewis (USA) – Tyrilda (FR) (Saint Cyrien (FR)) [2006/7 16v* 21g³ Mar 28] first foal: dam unraced: winning debut in novice selling hurdle at Uttoxeter (sold from D. McCain Jnr 10,500 gns) in February: 11/8-on, mistakes last 2 when 4½ lengths third of 7 finishers in mares novice at Towcester: should stay 21f. *T. R. George*   **h96**

SARAHS QUAY (IRE) 8 b.m. Witness Box (USA) – Artistic Quay (IRE) (Quayside) [2006/7 c108, h100: 21s⁵ 20sʳʳ Dec 16] workmanlike mare: fair chaser/novice hurdler: should stay beyond 21f: acts well on heavy going: tried blinkered, best efforts in cheekpieces: front runner/races prominently: temperamental (refused to race final start). *K. J. Burke*   **c– §** / **h– §**

SARATOGANE (FR) 5 b.m. Saratoga Springs (CAN) – Asturias (FR) (Pistolet Bleu (IRE)) [2006/7 F100: 17m⁵ 19d⁵ 19s* 19v* 24v 21g⁴ 22g* 24g Apr 18] leggy, close-coupled mare: fair hurdler: won mares novices at Exeter in December, Lingfield in January and Ascot (best effort when beating Fountain Crumble 8 lengths) in March: should stay 3m: acts on heavy going: visored last 2 starts: not a fluent jumper: has looked difficult ride. *D. E. Pipe*   **h110**

SARGASSO SEA 10 gr.g. Greensmith – Sea Spice (Precipice Wood) [2006/7 c102x, h104: c20s⁴ c20s² Feb 16] strong gelding: fair chaser/maiden hurdler: left J. Old after first outing: won point in March: stays 21f: raced on good going or softer: has been let down by jumping. *Mrs Alison Hickman*   **c112** / **h–**

SARIN 9 b.g. Deploy – Secretilla (USA) (Secreto (USA)) [2006/7 h90: 19d* 19d⁵ 16d⁴ c16v² c19sᵘʳ Feb 26] fair form over hurdles: impressive winner of novice handicap at Hereford in November: encouraging chasing debut when neck second to Brave Villa in novice handicap at Taunton: badly hampered and unseated seventh when favourite for handicap at Hereford 6 days later: stays 19f: raced on good ground or softer (acts on heavy): remains open to improvement over fences. *Miss Venetia Williams*   **c108 p** / **h108**

SARROCOCCA (IRE) 8 b.g. Supreme Leader – What's The Story (Homeboy) [2006/7 20s Oct 27] good-bodied gelding: half-brother to bumper winner Emerald Prince (by Executive Perk): dam unraced half-sister to Grand National runner-up Romany King: sixth in bumper on debut: sold out of N. Meade's stable 5,500 gns Doncaster May Sales: offered little in novice hurdle: placed in points in 2007. *C. P. Morlock*   **h–**

SASHENKA 5 b.m. Silver Patriarch (IRE) – Annie Kelly (Oats) [2006/7 F16s⁵ F17d* F17g³ 19s^pu 16g^ur 18g⁶ Mar 18] fourth foal: dam modest 2m hurdler/chaser: fair form in bumpers, won at Market Rasen in June: jumped better than previously over hurdles when sixth in novice at Fontwell. *J. L. Spearing* **h72 F92**

SASSO 5 b.g. Efisio – Sioux (Kris) [2006/7 h106: 16g 21s⁶ 16m² 16g³ 20f Apr 28] sturdy, good-bodied gelding: fairly useful handicap hurdler: best efforts when placed at Ludlow and Haydock: best around 2m: acts on soft and good to firm going: tried tongue tied. *Jonjo O'Neill* **h116**

SATCHELMAN (IRE) 7 ch.g. Presenting – Whipper Snapper (Menelek) [2006/7 F16m* 20s⁴ 22m Sep 10] €6,000 4-y-o: half-brother to 3 winners, including smart chaser Dun Belle, stayed 3m, and winning 3m hurdler Dunbell Boy (both by Over The River): dam bumper winner: won 8-runner bumper at Worcester in June on debut: not knocked about after travelling smoothly long way in maiden hurdle at Bangor: lame next time: bred to be suited by 3m+. *T. R. George* **h– F92**

SATCHMO (IRE) 15 b.g. Satco (FR) – Taradale (Torus) [2006/7 c103: c21g c21g⁵ May 24] big gelding: impresses in appearance: veteran chaser, useful at his best: effective at 2½m to 25f: acts on firm and soft going: races prominently: bold jumper. *Mrs D. M. Grissell* **c89**

SATCO'S DECEPTION (IRE) 10 br.g. Satco (FR) – Deceptive Response (Furry Glen) [2006/7 c22s^F c22s c18s c24g⁴ c26m* c26m² Apr 26] winning pointer: once-raced over hurdles: modest handicap chaser, left Paul Stafford in Ireland after third start: won at Plumpton in April: stays 3¼m: acts on soft and good to firm going: tried blinkered/in cheekpieces. *E. J. Creighton* **c87 h–**

SATIN STARLIGHT 5 b.m. I'm Supposin (IRE) – Taciturn (USA) (Tasso (USA)) [2006/7 F17v F14s 18m Apr 26] half-sister to winner in Czech Republic by Law Society: dam bad maiden: well beaten in mares bumpers/maiden hurdle. *R. Rowe* **h– F–**

SATINTHESLIP (IRE) 6 b.m. Idris (IRE) – Gauloise Bleue (USA) (Lyphard's Wish (FR)) [2006/7 F16m⁶ F16m⁶ F17m⁶ Sep 28] half-sister to 2 winners by Treasure Kay, including fairly useful 1995 2-y-o 7f winner Fag End: dam, twice-raced, half-sister to top-class French miler Gravelines: poor form in bumpers: well beaten both starts on Flat. *Mrs P. Ford* **F69**

SAUCY NIGHT 11 ch.g. Anshan – Kiss In The Dark (Starry Night (USA)) [2006/7 c–, h80: 20s⁵ 22m² c21s* c24d^pu c21s^ur c21g^4 c24m c21g⁴ Apr 1] stocky gelding: poor hurdler: fair handicap chaser: won at Uttoxeter in October: let down by jumping next 3 starts: stays 2¾m: acts on soft going, probably on good to firm: often makes running. *Simon Earle* **c105 h81**

SAUNDERS ROAD (IRE) 6 b.g. King's Theatre (IRE) – Shaunies Lady (IRE) (Don't Forget Me) [2006/7 F–: 17d 16v 16v 16s^F 17v* c17g Mar 24] well-made gelding: fair hurdler: much improved when winning conditional jockeys handicap at Taunton in March despite hanging left, jumping more fluently: soon behind in handicap on chasing debut: raced around 2m: acts on heavy going: not straightforward. *P. J. Hobbs* **c– h102**

SAVANNAH RIVER (IRE) 6 b.m. Desert King (IRE) – Hayward (Indian Ridge) [2006/7 h69: 16g 23s^pu c24s^pu c25s^rtr 24v^rtr Mar 15] leggy mare: maiden hurdler: refused to race both outings after pulled up on chasing debut: sometimes wears cheekpieces: tried tongue tied: one to avoid. *Miss Kate Milligan* **c§§ h§§**

SAVOY CHAPEL 5 br.g. Xaar – Royal Gift (Cadeaux Genereux) [2006/7 16g 17g Apr 11] modest on all-weather on Flat (stays 1m) nowadays, lightly raced on turf: no show in maiden (for D. Carroll) and seller over hurdles. *A. W. Carroll* **h–**

SAWPIT SUNSET 6 br.m. Classic Cliche (IRE) – Moonlight Air (Bold Owl) [2006/7 F77: F16d⁴ 17s 18s 22s⁶ 26m⁴ 22g Apr 7] leggy mare: twice-raced in bumpers: poor maiden hurdler: stays 3¼m: acts on soft and good to firm going. *J. L. Spearing* **h74 F77**

SAXON LEADER (IRE) 5 b.g. Supreme Leader – Bronica (IRE) (Waajib) [2006/7 F83: F16d 16d 16v 20v 22g Mar 18] rather unfurnished gelding: third in bumper on debut for T. Tate: no form since. *D. O. Stephens* **h– F–**

SAXON MILL 12 ch.g. Saxon Farm – Djellaba (Decoy Boy) [2006/7 c74, h–: c17g May 5] workmanlike gelding: maiden hurdler: little form since 2002/3, including over fences. *T. J. Fitzgerald* **c– h–**

SAXON MIST 8 b.g. Slip Anchor – Ruby Venture (Ballad Rock) [2006/7 h–: 22m^pu Sep 10] strong, close-coupled gelding: bumper winner: no form over hurdles. *Cooper Wilson* **h–**

SAXON STAR (IRE) 4 b.g. Vettori (IRE) – Thicket (Wolfhound (USA)) [2006/7 16s   **h–**
17g^{pu} 17g^{pu} Apr 27] leggy gelding: poor maiden on Flat (stays 7f): sold out of M. Usher's
stable £3,300 Ascot August Sales, resold £2,400 Ascot December Sales: no show over
hurdles: tried in cheekpieces. *L. Corcoran*

SAYAGO (GER) 5 b.g. Seattle Dancer (GER) – Sweet Virtue (USA) (Halo (USA)) [2006/7   **h–**
16g Apr 14] half-brother to San Suru (by Surumu), prolific winning hurdler in Germany:
successful 3 times around 9f on Flat in Germany, including at Leipzig and Magdeburg in
2006: left A. Wohler, reluctant at start and soon plenty to do in novice on hurdling debut.
C. J. Mann

SCALE BANK (IRE) 4 b.g. Indian Danehill (IRE) – Cory Everson (IRE) (Brief Truce   **F102**
(USA)) [2006/7 F16v^2 Jan 27] strong, sturdy gelding: second foal: dam unraced: joint
favourite, beaten short head by Pebrock (pair clear) in 4-y-o bumper at Southwell on
debut. *G. A. Swinbank*

SCALLOWAY (IRE) 7 b.g. Marju (IRE) – Zany (Junius (USA)) [2006/7 c122, h93:   **c129**
20m^6 c16m* c16f^3 Aug 22] angular gelding: winning hurdler: fairly useful chaser: imp-   **h94 +**
roved form when winning handicap at Newton Abbot in August by 10 lengths from
Rooster's Reunion: creditable third of 4 finishers to same rival in similar event at
Worcester later in month: best around 2m: raced mainly on good going or firmer (acts on
firm): takes good hold. *Carl Llewellyn*

SCALLYWELD 9 ch.g. Weld – Scally Jenks (Scallywag) [2006/7 c24g c26v^4 May 20]   **c77**
modest pointer: much better effort in hunters when 24 lengths fourth to Knife Edge at
Uttoxeter. *G. C. Evans*

SCAMP 8 b.m. Selkirk (USA) – Cut And Run (Slip Anchor) [2006/7 h73§: 20v^{pu} 21m^{pu} **h– §**
Jun 7] leggy mare: maiden hurdler: runner-up in point in February: often in cheekpieces/
blinkers: unreliable. *R. Shiels*

SCANIA CLASSIC 6 gr.g. Thethingaboutitis (USA) – Gifted Gale (Aird Point)   **c–**
[2006/7 h–: 20s^{pu} c16s^{pu} c16s^{ur} c16g^6 Apr 20] sparely-made gelding: no sign of ability: **h–**
tried tongue tied. *M. Scudamore*

SCARAMOUCHE 7 b.g. Busy Flight – Laura Lye (IRE) (Carlingford Castle) [2006/7   **h106 +**
h98: 20s^5 19s^5 20v^4 Feb 16] lengthy gelding: off 3 months and tongue tied, improved
effort over hurdles (fair form) when winning novice handicap at Sandown in February:
stays 2½m: raced on going softer than good (acts on heavy). *B. De Haan*

SCARECROW (IRE) 6 b.g. Presenting – Rossacrowe Gale (IRE) (Strong Gale)   **h–**
[2006/7 F82: 22d 20v^{pu} 20g 25g^6 Apr 16] modest form in bumpers for Mrs P. Sly: little
impact over hurdles. *B. Storey*

SCARFACE 10 ch.g. Hernando (FR) – Scarlatine (IRE) (Alzao (USA)) [2006/7 h72:   **h89**
22m* 22m^2 24s* 24f^4 24g 27d^2 Aug 21] modest hurdler: won handicaps at Fontwell and
Uttoxeter (conditional jockeys) in May: acts on soft and good to firm going: tried visored:
usually races prominently. *J. L. Spearing*

SCARLET BOY 8 gr.g. Arzanni – Scarlet Berry (Zambrano) [2006/7 c23g^{pu} c23s^{pu} **c–**
c19m^{pu} Jun 4] maiden point: no show in maiden chases: tried tongue tied. *R. J. Price*

SCARLET BUTTERFLY 6 b.m. Thethingaboutitis (USA) – Scarlet Berry (Zamb-   **F–**
rano) [2006/7 F16s^{pu} F17d Nov 16] second foal: dam fair pointer: no show in bumpers.
R. J. Price

SCARLET MIX (FR) 6 gr.g. Linamix (FR) – Scarlet Raider (USA) (Red Ransom   **c–**
(USA)) [2006/7 c–§, h82§: 16d^2 16g* 19g* 20s 18s^2 21s* 20g^5 Mar 21] lengthy gelding: **h107**
fair handicap hurdler: better attitude and back to best in 2006/7, winning at Warwick in
October, November and March: let down by jumping over fences: stays 21f:
acts on soft going: tried visored/blinkered. *Mrs A. M. Thorpe*

SCARRABUS (IRE) 6 b.g. Charnwood Forest (IRE) – Errazuriz (IRE) (Classic Music   **c–**
(USA)) [2006/7 c85, h84: 16g May 30] regressive maiden on Flat and over hurdles: **h–**
winning chaser, but has been let down by jumping: probably best up to 2½m: acts on firm
ground. *A. Crook*

SCARTHY LAD (IRE) 9 ch.g. Magical Wonder (USA) – Grangeclare Rose (IRE)   **c–**
(Gianchi) [2006/7 16s* Oct 1] tall, leggy, close-coupled gelding: useful chaser: similar   **h129 +**
standard over hurdles: off 17 months, won 5-runner Grade 2 Tipperary Hurdle by 5½
lengths from Maralan, only start in 2006/7: effective at 2m to 3m: raced on good going or
softer (acts on heavy): sometimes let down by jumping over fences. *Thomas Gerard
O'Leary, Ireland*

SCARVAGH DIAMOND (IRE) 6 b.m. Zaffaran (USA) – Bucks Slave (Buckskin
(FR)) [2006/7 F98: F16d⁴ 16v² 20v* 23sᵖᵘ 20s² Mar 13] leggy mare: bumper winner for
Mrs R. Elliot: fair form over hurdles: won mares novice at Haydock (by 17 lengths) in
January: should stay beyond 2½m: acts on heavy going: has got on toes (very stirred up
penultimate start). *N. G. Richards*   **h112**
F81 +

SCENIC STORM (IRE) 12 b.g. Scenic – Sit Elnaas (USA) (Sir Ivor (USA)) [2006/7
c91, h–: c25m² c25g² c25v⁴ c25g² Apr 2] well-made gelding: fair pointer/hunter chaser:
stays 25f: acts on soft and good to firm going: in cheekpieces last 2 starts. *Miss Lucinda
Broad*   **c95**
h–

SCHAPIRO (USA) 6 b.g. Nureyev (USA) – Konvincha (USA) (Cormorant (USA))
[2006/7 h124: c20g⁵ c20dᶠ Nov 19] compact gelding: fairly useful handicap hurdler:
similar form when fifth to Mr Pointment at Bangor on completed start in maiden chases:
fell fatally 11 days later: stayed 2½m: acted on good to firm going (well below form on
soft/heavy). *Jonjo O'Neill*   **c119**
h–

SCHEMER FAGAN (IRE) 7 ch.g. Nucleon (USA) – Less Hassle (IRE) (Strong
Gale) [2006/7 F83p: F17s 22d 19vᵖᵘ 24v⁴ 22gᵖᵘ Mar 18] workmanlike gelding: second in
bumper: little impact over hurdles (bled final outing). *P. Henderson*   **h–**
F—

SCHIEHALLION (IRE) 5 b.g. Pistolet Bleu (IRE) – Lessons Lass (IRE) (Doyoun)
[2006/7 F16v* F16d⁴ Dec 29] £37,000 4-y-o: useful-looking gelding: fourth foal: half-
brother to 19f hurdle winner My Pal Val (by Classic Cliche) and fair chaser John
Diamond (by Un Desperado), stays 2½m: dam, fairly useful hurdler, stayed 21f: useful
form when winning 18-runner bumper at Newbury on debut in November by 5 lengths
from Jass: odds on, only fourth to Crocodiles Rock there month later. *N. J. Henderson*   **F110**

SCHINDLERS HUNT (IRE) 7 ch.g. Oscar Schindler (IRE) – Snipe Hunt (IRE)
(Stalker) [2006/7 c18d⁵ c16s* c16s* c20v² c17s* c17s* c20vᶠ c20m² c16m⁵ Apr 26]   **c144**
h–
    A clerical error robbed Schindlers Hunt of the chance of competing in the
Arkle at the Cheltenham Festival in March, a race for which he was as short as 8/1
third favourite before it was discovered that his name wasn't among the entries in
January. In the event, he would have had to have shown marked improvement to
trouble My Way de Solzen, but, with the exception of that horse, who can be
expected to race over further in the future, Schindlers Hunt finished the season not
far off the best of the two-mile novice chasers. Schindlers Hunt showed fair form to

*Baileys Arkle Perpetual Challenge Cup Novices' Chase, Leopardstown—Schindlers Hunt (No.4) asserts
two out from the grey King Johns Castle and Hear The Echo (about to fall)*

Slaneyville Syndicate's "Schindlers Hunt"

win on his fourth start in bumpers and at the same stage over hurdles in 2005/6, but he had been sent off favourite for a valuable bumper on his racecourse debut and was highly tried on occasions over hurdles. Indeed, it was in listed company that Schindlers Hunt began his chasing career at Punchestown in October. He was, however, let down by his jumping and finished a distant fifth to Gemini Lucy, making a bad mistake five from home. Schindlers Hunt got off the mark over fences at the same course two weeks later, winning an eighteen-runner maiden by a neck from Rights of Man, with Sky's The Limit, a warm order on his own chasing debut, a further three and a half lengths back in third. Schindlers Hunt then showed significant improvement to run the mare Cailin Alainn to three quarters of a length in a Grade 1 event at Fairyhouse in December, emerging as the best horse at the weights. With Cailin Alainn taking in different races, Schindlers Hunt won twice in Grade 1 company at Leopardstown on his two next outings. At the Christmas meeting, he ran out a clear-cut winner of the Durkan New Homes Novices' Chase, the return to shorter proving no problem as he beat outsider Hear The Echo by ten lengths, putting himself forward as a serious Arkle contender in the process. The oversight which kept Schindlers Hunt out of the two-mile championship at the Festival had come to light by the time he landed the odds in the Baileys Arkle Perpetual Challenge Cup in late-January by two lengths from King Johns Castle, always seemingly in control from the second last, albeit needing firmish handling on the run-in as the runner-up rallied.

With Cheltenham off the agenda, Schindlers Hunt next appeared in a Grade 2 event at Naas in late-February. He was less than fluent and appeared held, three lengths behind all-the-way winner Benefit Night, when falling at the last. In the Powers Gold Cup at Fairyhouse in April, Schindlers Hunt returned to his best to finish a good second to One Cool Cookie, the pair well clear. In a competitive renewal of the Swordlestown Cup at Punchestown later in the month, Schindlers Hunt was again set to run creditably, and was still in with every chance alongside eventual winner Another Promise, when making a bad mistake two out, Roger Loughran losing his irons but managing to jump the last before dismounting on the run-in. Reminded by the stewards that there was prize money for fifth, Loughran returned and completed the course on Schindlers Hunt.

Schindlers Hunt (IRE) (ch.g. 2000)	Oscar Schindler (IRE) (ch 1992)	Royal Academy (b 1987)	Nijinsky
			Crimson Saint
		Saraday (ch 1980)	Northfields
			Etoile Gris
	Snipe Hunt (IRE) (ch 1988)	Stalker (b 1983)	Kala Shikari
			Tarvie
		Little Angle (ch 1971)	Gulf Pearl
			Lady Be Lucky

The strong, well-made Schindlers Hunt was sold for IR £7,600 as a yearling before fetching €28,000 as a four-year-old. With a Flat-oriented pedigree, he is the fourth foal of Snipe Hunt who was placed once as a two-year-old. Schindlers Hunt is a half-brother to Young Alex (by Midhish), a fairly useful winner at up to seven furlongs. Snipe Hunt's first foal, Native Snipe (by Be My Native), showed fair form from four starts in bumpers but was killed when falling at the last on his hurdling debut. Snipe Hunt's five-year-old Hunters Dream (by Rudimentary) finished tailed off on his bumper debut in the latest season. Meanwhile, her 2003 Bishop of Cashel gelding is to become a stable companion of Schindlers Hunt after trainer Dessie Hughes bought him for €42,000 at the latest Derby Sale in June. Snipe Hunt is a half-sister to eight winners, including Try Kola who, as a broodmare, has several classic winners in India among her descendants. Schindlers Hunt's sire Oscar Schindler was a game and genuine dual winner of the Irish St Leger, who also made the frame twice in the Prix de l'Arc de Triomphe. His oldest crop is seven, but he has enjoyed only limited success to date, with four individual National Hunt winners, three of those gaining just a bumper win. Schindlers Hunt is easily the best of his progeny seen on the racecourse to date. Schindlers Hunt, who often impresses in appearance and is usually patiently ridden, is unraced on firm going but acts on any other and stays two and a half miles. *D. T. Hughes, Ireland*

SCHINDLER'S LIST 7 b.g. Oscar Schindler (IRE) – Prepare (IRE) (Millfontaine) [2006/7 h–, F79: 22v^{pu} 22g^{pu} Apr 7] tall gelding: modest form in bumpers: little impact over hurdles: lame final start. *D. E. Pipe* **h78**

SCHINKEN OTTO (IRE) 6 ch.g. Shinko Forest (IRE) – Athassel Rose (IRE) (Reasonable (FR)) [2006/7 h88: 16g c17g^3 c16g* c16m^6 c16f^2 c16m* c16g* c16g* c16s^F c16d^6 c17s^3 c16d^3 c16g c16s Apr 26] workmanlike gelding: maiden hurdler: fair handicap chaser: won at Uttoxeter (3, novice on first occasion) and Southwell (novice) between June and September: likely to prove best at 2m: acts on firm and good to soft going, unsuited by soft/heavy: front runner: often jumps right. *J. M. Jefferson* **c105** **h–**

SCHOLAR KING 6 b.g. Rakaposhi King – Top Scholar (Derrylin) [2006/7 F17m^2 F17m Sep 28] first foal: dam poor form in bumpers: better effort in bumpers when 2 lengths second of 6 to Little Lu at Bangor: lost action next time: won point in April. *Evan Williams* **F81**

SCHOOL CLASS 7 b.m. Classic Cliche (IRE) – School Run (Deep Run) [2006/7 h–: 17s^{pu} 20v^{pu} 16g^{pu} 20m^6 Mar 29] little show in bumpers/over hurdles: blinkered/visored last 2 starts. *Mike Hammond* **h–**

SCHOOL FIELDS 6 gr.g. Paris of Troy – Beltalong (Belfort (FR)) [2006/7 F16s Oct 27] tall, unfurnished gelding: third foal: half-brother to modest hurdler/chaser Rival Bidder (by Arzanni), stays 25f: dam, winning 2m hurdler, successful up to 1½m on Flat: failed to complete in points: well held in bumper. *Heather Dalton* **F–**

SCHOOLHOUSE WALK 9 b.g. Mistertopogigo (IRE) – Restandbejoyful (Taka-chiho) [2006/7 c77, h–: c16s* c20s⁴ c16d³ c16f⁵ c20s⁵ c18gᶠ Jul 9] winning hurdler: poor chaser: won novice handicap at Towcester in May: stayed 2½m: acted on soft going, probably on firm: tried blinkered, visored last 4 outings: dead. *M. E. Sowersby*   **c77 h–**

SCHUH SHINE (IRE) 10 gr.g. Roselier (FR) – Naar Chamali (Salmon Leap (USA)) [2006/7 c129, h–: c22v² c24s⁴ 25v* 20v* 27v* c24s³ Feb 16] robust gelding: reportedly had breathing operation after final 2005/6 start: fairly useful handicap chaser/fair hurdler: won handicap hurdles at Warwick (conditional jockeys) in December and Hereford in January and novice at Fontwell (beat The Risky Viking by 1¾ lengths) later in January: jumped stickily when below best back over fences final start: stays 27f: raced on good going or softer (acts on heavy): front runner/races prominently: genuine. *Miss Venetia Williams*   **c126 h115**

SCHUMANN 6 b.g. Rainbow Quest (USA) – Dance Sequence (USA) (Mr Prospector (USA)) [2006/7 h91, F91: 21mᵖᵘ 20m Jun 28] tall gelding: bumper winner: novice hurdler, below form early in 2006/7: stays 21f: acts on good to soft going. *Carl Llewellyn*   **h–**

SCIPPIT 8 ch.g. Unfuwain (USA) – Scierpan (USA) (Sharpen Up) [2006/7 h63: 16mᵖᵘ 17m Jun 30] small, compact gelding: maiden hurdler, lightly raced and little form since 2004: tongue tied once: has finished weakly. *Miss Tracy Waggott*   **h–**

SCOLBOA ARCTIC (IRE) 7 b.m. Dr Massini (IRE) – Arctic Vista (Deep Run) [2006/7 h–, F–: 17s 17d⁴ 19d⁵ 17d⁶ c21mᵖᵘ 17v Oct 1] little sign of ability. *J. M. Saville*   **c– h–**

SCOLBOA MUSIC MAN (IRE) 6 b.g. Accordion – Fatal Hesitation (Torus) [2006/7 F16s⁶ Apr 27] half-brother to winning pointer by Yashgan: dam, fairly useful chaser who stayed 3m, half-sister to dam of Grand National winner Numbersixvalverde: won maiden point in March: well held in bumper at Perth. *I. R. Ferguson, Ireland*   **F70**

John Smith's Fox Hunters' Chase, Aintree—Scots Grey (right) just gets the better of Pak Jack

SCOLBOA RAINBOW (IRE) 9 b. or br.g. Supreme Leader – Peggy Bull (IRE) h–
(Kemal (FR)) [2006/7 20d[pu] Nov 3] bumper winner: no form over hurdles: should have
stayed at least 2½m: dead. *J. M. Saville*

SCONCED (USA) 12 ch.g. Affirmed (USA) – Quaff (USA) (Raise A Cup (USA)) c– §
[2006/7 c79§, h78§: c30d[pu] 20f 20s² 20g Aug 1] smallish gelding: poor chaser/maid- h75 §
en hurdler: stays 3m: probably acts on any going: blinkered/in cheekpieces: ungenuine.
R. C. Guest

SCOTCH CORNER (IRE) 9 b.g. Jurado (USA) – Quennie Mo Ghra (IRE) (Manda- c62 §
lus) [2006/7 c94§, h–: c20m c18g c20g[pu] c21s[pu] c20g[pu] c20f⁶ Apr 5] lengthy gelding: h– §
winning hurdler/chaser: little show in 2006/7, sold out of B. Pollock's stable 2,000 gns
Doncaster August Sales after second start: won point in April: tried blinkered/tongue
tied: ungenuine. *Miss Sarah Kent*

SCOTLAND YARD (UAE) 4 b.g. Jade Robbery (USA) – Aqraba (Polish Precedent h115
(USA)) [2006/7 16s[ur] 16d³ 16m⁴ 17v² 19g² Mar 30] compact gelding: half-brother to fair
2m hurdler Timber Scorpion (by Timber Country): fairly useful on Flat (should be
suited by 1¾m+), successful twice in 2006, sold out of M. Johnston's stable 62,000 gns
Newmarket July Sales: fairly useful juvenile hurdler: in frame all 4 starts after debut, 5
lengths second to Shouldhavehadthat in maiden at Ascot final one: likely to stay beyond
19f: acts on good to firm and good to soft ground, below form on heavy (tongue tied).
D. E. Pipe

SCOTMAIL LAD (IRE) 13 b.g. Ilium – Nicholas Ferry (Floriferous) [2006/7 c84, c84 x
h–: c16g⁵ c20s³ c21d³ c20d[pu] c19d⁴ c16v⁴ c20v³ c20s c20g⁶ Mar 27] leggy, work- h–
manlike gelding: poor handicap chaser: effective at 2m to 3m: raced on good going or
softer (acts on heavy): wears headgear (usually cheekpieces): often let down by jumping.
C. A. Mulhall

SCOTMAIL TOO (IRE) 6 b.g. Saddlers' Hall (IRE) – Kam Slave (Kambalda) h99
[2006/7 h106+: 20s⁴ 22s⁶ 20s 25g 20g⁶ 20g³ 22m⁵ Apr 28] quite good-topped gelding:
modest handicap hurdler: should stay beyond 2½m: acts on soft and good to firm going.
J. Howard Johnson

SCOTS BROOK TERROR 5 b.m. Terimon – Angie Marinie (Sabrehill (USA)) h–
[2006/7 F–: F17m F17v 17s[F] 16g[pu] Mar 21] close-coupled mare: more signs of tempera- F–
ment than ability in bumpers/over hurdles. *Mrs N. S. Evans*

SCOTS DRAGOON 5 gr.g. Silver Patriarch (IRE) – Misowni (Niniski (USA)) h77
[2006/7 F17d 16g 20s⁴ 16s Apr 27] good-bodied gelding: half-brother to several winners, F77
including fairly useful hurdler/useful chaser up to 3m Scots Grey (by Terimon): dam
unraced half-sister to very smart 1½m winner Bustomi: seventh in bumper on debut: poor
form over hurdles: likely to prove suited by 2½m+. *N. J. Henderson*

SCOTS GREY 12 gr.g. Terimon – Misowni (Niniski (USA)) [2006/7 c137, h–: c24s[F] c126
c24g* c21g* Apr 12] sturdy gelding: winning hurdler: useful chaser: successful in h–
hunters last 2 starts, in 13-runner race at Newbury (easily by 13 lengths from Red Brook
Lad) in March and in 27-runner John Smith's Fox Hunters' Chase at Aintree (battled on
really well to beat Pak Jak by ½ length) in April: successful at 3m, best form around 2½m:
acts on any going: usually races prominently: has gone well fresh. *N. J. Henderson*

SCOTSIRISH (IRE) 6 b.g. Zaffaran (USA) – Serjitak (Saher) [2006/7 16v⁶ 16d³ 21g h134
16m* Apr 9] sturdy, lengthy gelding: half-brother to modest 2m hurdle winner Dan The
Liberator (by Anshan) and modest/unreliable chaser Panmure (by Alphabatim), stays
2½m: dam, winning hurdler, sister to Scottish Champion Hurdle winner Sayparee:
won Irish point on debut in 2005: fourth in maiden over hurdles, off nearly
11 months before first outing: won maiden at Leopardstown in January and minor event
at Fairyhouse (beat Heavenly Blues by 4 lengths) in April: also ran well when eighth
of 14 finishers behind Massini's Maguire in Grade 1 Baring Bingham Novices' Hurdle
at Cheltenham in between: stays 21f: acts on good to firm and good to soft going.
W. P. Mullins, Ireland

SCOTTS COURT 7 b.g. Case Law – Pennine Star (IRE) (Pennine Walk) [2006/7 h–, h–
F97: 16m[pu] May 6] sturdy gelding: bumper winner: shaped as if amiss both starts over
hurdles. *N. Tinkler*

SCOTT'S MILL 5 ch.g. Unfuwain (USA) – Mill On The Floss (Mill Reef (USA)) h–
[2006/7 20v Jan 20] lengthy gelding: closely related to fairly useful hurdler/chaser

Bosham Mill (by Nashwan), stays 33f: lightly raced and little form on Flat: sold out of M. Johnston's stable 14,000 gns Doncaster May Sales: soundly beaten in novice on hurdling debut. *Mrs S. J. Smith*

SCRAPPIE (IRE) 7 b.g. Fourstars Allstar (USA) – Clonyn (Wolverlife) [2006/7 F17v⁵ F16v² 20s⁵ 20s⁵ 20v³ 20v⁴ Mar 22] €10,000 3-y-o: close-coupled, sparely-made gelding: half-brother to fairly useful chaser Garrylough (by Monksfield), stayed 25f: dam, poor form in bumpers and maiden hurdles in Ireland, half-sister to useful Irish jumper Toranfield: runner-up in bumper: modest form over hurdles: failed to impress with attitude final start: will be suited by 3m: raced on soft/heavy going. *Miss Lucinda V. Russell* **h96 f91**

SCRATCH THE DOVE 10 ch.m. Henbit (USA) – Coney Dove (Celtic Cone) [2006/7 c81, h–: c21gᵖᵘ 20m Jul 11] sturdy mare: winning hurdler/maiden chaser, no show early in 2006/7: tried blinkered/in cheekpieces. *A. E. Price* **c– h–**

SCREEN TEST 5 b.m. Danzero (AUS) – Audition (Machiavellian (USA)) [2006/7 h92: 17m Jun 19] good-topped mare: maiden on Flat: modest hurdler: stays 2¼m: acts on soft and good to firm going: temperamental: sold £3,300 Ascot July Sales. *B. G. Powell* **h– §**

SCRIBANO EILE (IRE) 6 b.g. Scribano – Ean Eile (IRE) (Callernish) [2006/7 F110: 24s* 20sᵖᵘ 21d 24sᵖᵘ Apr 25] rangy gelding: chasing type: point/bumper winner: also promising start over hurdles when successful in novice at Perth in September: failed to progress: stays 3m: raced on going softer than good. *N. A. Twiston-Davies* **h100 +**

SCULASTIC 4 b.g. Galileo (IRE) – Mutual Consent (IRE) (Reference Point) [2006/7 16g³ 18s 16s² 16g* Apr 15] fairly useful maiden on Flat (will stay 1½m), sold out of L. Cumani's stable 80,000 gns Newmarket Autumn Sales: fair form over hurdles: won novice at Kelso in April: raced mainly at 2m: has found little. *J. Howard Johnson* **h103**

SCURRA 8 b.g. Spectrum (IRE) – Tamnia (Green Desert (USA)) [2006/7 16vᵖᵘ Dec 3] poor on Flat (stays 2m) nowadays: no show over hurdles. *A. C. Whillans* **h–**

SCURRY DANCER (FR) 11 b.g. Snurge – Fijar Dance (FR) (In Fijar (USA)) [2006/7 17mᵖᵘ Apr 9] lengthy gelding: winning hurdler/maiden chaser, lightly raced and no form since 2001/2: tried in cheekpieces. *S. G. Chadwick* **c– h–**

SCUTCH MILL (IRE) 5 ch.g. Alhaarth (IRE) – Bumble (Rainbow Quest (USA)) [2006/7 16d³ 16s Jan 31] small gelding: fair on Flat (stays 11f), successful twice in December, then left Karen George: 9 lengths third to Purple Moon in novice at Musselburgh on hurdling debut: hampered and jockey lost iron next time: tongue tied. *P. C. Haslam* **h85**

SCUZME (IRE) 4 br.g. Xaar – Decatur (Deploy) [2006/7 16d⁵ 18sᵖᵘ Dec 5] modest on Flat (stays easy 2m), successful in May for B. Ellison: no show in juvenile hurdles. *Miss S. West* **h–**

SEA CADET 5 gr.g. Slip Anchor – Stormy Gal (IRE) (Strong Gale) [2006/7 F78: 16d 20s 23vᵖᵘ 20v⁶ 19s³ 20g⁵ 23g* 24sᵖᵘ Apr 25] close-coupled, good-topped gelding: poor hurdler: won ladies handicap at Wetherby in April: stays 23f: acts on soft going: blinkered last 5 starts. *T. D. Easterby* **h84**

SEA COVE 7 b.m. Terimon – Regal Pursuit (IRE) (Roi Danzig (USA)) [2006/7 19g² 19vᵖᵘ 17m² c16gᵖᵘ Apr 23] leggy mare: poor maiden hurdler: soon beaten after mistake ninth in handicap on chasing debut: stays 19f: acts on good to firm going. *G. A. Swinbank* **c– h70**

SEA DRIFTING 10 b.g. Slip Anchor – Theme (IRE) (Sadler's Wells (USA)) [2006/7 c–, h–: 24m⁵ Jul 4] good-topped gelding: winning hurdler/chaser, lightly raced and little form since 2002/3: tried in cheekpieces. *Miss M. E. Rowland* **c– h–**

SEA EAGLE (IRE) 5 b.g. Sea Raven (IRE) – Roseocean (IRE) (Roselier (FR)) [2006/7 F–: 17d⁵ 19s⁵ 22s⁴ 24v³ Feb 20] rather unfurnished gelding: best effort in novice hurdles (fair form) when third of 5 finishers at Taunton: stays 3m: raced on ground softer than good. *H. D. Daly* **h108**

SEA FERRY (IRE) 11 b.g. Ilium – Nicholas Ferry (Floriferous) [2006/7 c102, h–: c24m³ c28vᵖᵘ May 27] good-topped gelding: fairly useful hunter chaser at best: should stay beyond 25f: acts on heavy going: tried in cheekpieces/visor. *C. C. Bealby* **c93 h–**

SEAFIELD BOGIE (IRE) 6 b.g. Darazari (IRE) – Lucky House (Pollerton) [2006/7 21m* 24d* 22s³ 24s⁶ c24s⁴ c24m c16g³ c20s⁴ c19g* c19g* c20m³ c20m⁴ Apr 27] good-topped gelding: won maiden Irish point in 2006: fair hurdler/chaser: won novice hurdles at Ludlow and Market Rasen early in season, and novice chases at Towcester in March **c113 h104**

and April (handicap, by 28 lengths): effective at 2m to 3m: acts on soft and good to firm going. *T. R. George*

SEAFIRE LAD (IRE) 6 b.g. Portrait Gallery (IRE) – Act The Fool (IRE) (Always **h79** Fair (USA)) [2006/7 h84: 20d³ 19vF 16s⁴ 17d* 16v 16s² 20g⁶ Mar 27] poor hurdler: won selling handicap at Market Rasen in December: stays 2½m: acts on soft and good to firm going: usually in cheekpieces nowadays, also often tongue tied in 2006/7. *R. Johnson*

SEAGULL EILE (IRE) 8 b.m. Oscar (IRE) – Precious Juno (IRE) (Good Thyne **c92** (USA)) [2006/7 20m³ 16f 20m 20m 19fᵖᵘ 19g c18d³ c20g⁴ Oct 19] modest handicap **h97** hurdler: better effort in maiden chases when 20 lengths third to Sabina Park at Down-patrick: stays 2½m: probably acts on any going: usually blinkered: tried tongue tied. *K. F. O'Brien, Ireland*

SEAHAM CLADDERS (IRE) 4 ch.g. Tagula (IRE) – Limerick Princess (IRE) **F–** (Polish Patriot (USA)) [2006/7 F14vᵖᵘ Dec 2] sixth foal: half-brother to several winners, including modest/unreliable hurdler Boing Boing (by King's Theatre), stays 2½m: dam 5f (at 2 yrs) and 6f winner: tongue tied, no show in 3-y-o bumper on debut. *N. Wilson*

SEA HAVEN 8 b.m. Sea Raven (IRE) – Another Delight (Politico (USA)) [2006/7 23g **h–** 24gᵘʳ 25gᵖᵘ Jun 1] first foal: dam, raced only at 10 yrs, of no account in points: no show in maiden hurdles/points. *P. Beaumont*

SEA LAUGHTER (IRE) 9 gr.m. Presenting – Bruna Rosa (Roselier (FR)) [2006/7 **h86** h–: 20s² 24v² 27v 21vᵖᵘ Mar 9] big mare: modest maiden handicap hurdler: stays 3m: acts on heavy going. *J. N. R. Billinge*

SEA MAP 5 ch.g. Fraam – Shehana (USA) (The Minstrel (CAN)) [2006/7 h94: 16g⁴ **c–** 16m² 20f² 22m³ 22m² c24sᵖᵘ Dec 7] close-coupled gelding: fair on Flat (stays 2m), **h104** claimed £12,000 in January: fair novice hurdler, in frame all 7 starts: let down by jumping on chasing debut: stays easy 2¾m: acts on firm and good to soft ground. *D. E. Cantillon*

SEA MORE BIRDS 6 b.g. Sea Raven (IRE) – See More Flowers (Seymour Hicks **F85** (FR)) [2006/7 F17g Apr 27] first foal: dam unraced: in cheekpieces, seventh of 15 in bumper at Newton Abbot on debut. *C. J. Down*

SEANIETHESMUGGLER (IRE) 9 b.g. Balla Cove – Sharp Shauna (Sayyaf) **c–** [2006/7 c101, h–: c22dᵖᵘ c20mᵖᵘ c18gᵖᵘ Jul 22] sturdy gelding: winning hurdler/chaser, **h–** no show in 2006/7: in cheekpieces/blinkers of last 6 outings: sold 3,000 gns Doncaster August Sales. *S. Gollings*

SEAN OG (IRE) 5 gr.g. Definite Article – Miss Goodbody (Castle Keep) [2006/7 16g **h80** 16s 16s² 16s Feb 16] angular gelding: fair maiden at best on Flat (stays 13f), well beaten in Britain: form over hurdles (left Richard Brabazon after first outing) only when second in novice claimer: tongue tied last 2 starts. *E. J. Creighton*

SEAPLACE (IRE) 6 b.g. Saddlers' Hall (IRE) – Mrs Hill (Strong Gale) [2006/7 F17d⁵ **h–** 21s 20g 20s Jan 5] €45,000 3-y-o: half-brother to poor/temperamental hurdler/chaser **F71** Sissinghurst Storm (by Good Thyne), stays 3¼m, and fair chaser Wap (by Be My Guest), stayed 3m: dam unraced half-sister to useful staying jumpers Sommelier and Bective Road: fifth in bumper: last in novice hurdles: sold 2,000 gns Doncaster May Sales. *Ferdy Murphy*

SEA SENOR 5 b.g. Sea Freedom – Portonia (Ascertain (USA)) [2006/7 F79: F16m² **h98** F17s 16d⁴ 16s⁵ 20d⁶ Mar 17] big, lengthy gelding, unfurnished at present: runner-up in **F88** bumper: best effort in novice hurdles (modest form) when fourth to Pevensey at Mussel-burgh: bred to stay at least 2½m. *M. W. Easterby*

SEA SNIPE 10 b.m. King Luthier – Seal Marine (Harwell) [2006/7 c23v⁴ Mar 1] fairly **c–** useful pointer, unbeaten in 2007: well held completed start in hunters. *Mrs R. Kennen*

SEA THE LIGHT 7 b.g. Blue Ocean (USA) – Lamper's Light (Idiot's Delight) **h115** [2006/7 h115: 16g* 16sᵖᵘ Dec 7] compact gelding: fairly useful hurdler: won handicap at Leicester in November by 1½ lengths from Flamand: possibly amiss following month: stays 19f: raced on good ground or softer (acts on soft): has hung left. *A. King*

SEA TRADER 7 b.g. El Conquistador – Little Sail (Little Wolf) [2006/7 F16v⁴ F16g **h–** 17d⁵ 20d 20v Mar 2] 4,200 4-y-o, 8,000 5-y-o: fourth foal: dam, dual bumper winner, **F68** half-sister to very smart 2m chaser Sea Merchant: signs of ability in bumpers: no form over hurdles. *S. H. Shirley-Beavan*

SEATTLE ROBBER 5 b.g. Robellino (USA) – Seattle Ribbon (USA) (Seattle Dancer **h88** (USA)) [2006/7 17s³ 17g⁵ 16g³ 19s Dec 1] fair on Flat (probably stays 1½m), successful twice in 2006: modest on balance of form over hurdles, claimed from P. Blockley £8,000 third outing (cheekpieces): likely to prove best around 2m. *Evan Williams*

SEA VENTURE (IRE) 5 b.g. Sea Raven (IRE) – Good Highlights (IRE) (Good Thyne (USA)) [2006/7 F16g³ F16v⁶ F16g Apr 3] 3,000 4-y-o: tall gelding: first foal: dam unraced: modest form in bumpers. *C. W. Thornton* **F78**

SEAVIEW LASS (IRE) 7 ch.m. Beneficial – Chestnut Shoon (Green Shoon) [2006/7 20sᵖᵘ Mar 13] €3,500 4-y-o: second foal: sister to winning Irish pointer: dam winning pointer: maiden hurdler: no show in novice on hurdling debut. *W. Storey* **h–**

SEA WALL 5 b.g. Giant's Causeway (USA) – Spout (Salse (USA)) [2006/7 h104: c20mᵖᵘ 21m* 21g Nov 7] lengthy, good-topped gelding: fair form over hurdles: won handicap at Ludlow in October: off 5 months, never dangerous in novice handicap on chasing debut: stays easy 21f: raced on good/good to firm going. *Jonjo O'Neill* **c–** **h109**

SEA YOU MADAME 8 b.m. Sea Raven (IRE) – Mildame (Milford) [2006/7 19v 16d 19v⁴ 17s² 19g³ Mar 25] poor novice hurdler, off 2½ years before first outing: will stay beyond 19f. *C. J. Down* **h73**

SEBAAQ (USA) 4 ch.g. Rahy (USA) – Malibu Karen (USA) (Seeking The Gold (USA)) [2006/7 17g⁶ 16d 17g 17vᵖᵘ Nov 30] temperamental maiden on Flat, sold out of M. Tregoning's stable 2,500 gns Newmarket July Sales: little impact in juvenile hurdles: in cheekpieces last 2 starts. *M. E. Sowersby* **h–**

SECAM (POL) 8 gr.g. Alywar (USA) – Scytia (POL) (Euro Star) [2006/7 17vᵖᵘ 16v⁴ 21sᵖᵘ 16g⁴ᵈ Mar 26] stocky gelding: modest on Flat (stays 1m): winning hurdler in Poland: no form in Britain: blinkered/in cheekpieces. *Mrs P. Townsley* **h–**

SECRETARY GENERAL (IRE) 6 b.g. Fasliyev (USA) – Katie McLain (USA) (Java Gold (USA)) [2006/7 16d⁴ 16d Oct 14] fairly useful on Flat (stays 1½m), successful in May/June: better effort in maiden hurdles when around 20 lengths fourth to Enlightenment at Worcester: sold 13,000 gns Newmarket Autumn Sales. *P. F. I. Cole* **h94 +**

SECRET DIVIN (FR) 7 b.g. Signe Divin (USA) – Lady Darling (Darshaan) [2006/7 h–: 16s² 16s⁶ May 27] modest novice hurdler: best around 2m: raced on good going or softer: tried visored. *Mrs D. A. Hamer* **h88**

SECRET DRINKER (IRE) 11 b.g. Husyan (USA) – Try Le Reste (IRE) (Le Moss) [2006/7 c–, h–: c25gᵖᵘ c24d c25sᵖᵘ Feb 15] useful-looking gelding: winning hurdler/chaser, lightly raced and no form since 2004/5: usually in cheekpieces/blinkers: temperamental. *N. P. McCormack* **c– §** **h– §**

SECRET GLEN (IRE) 8 b.g. Un Desperado (FR) – Bornacurra Ella (Bargello) [2006/7 16m c24g Apr 27] maiden hurdler, left Paul Nolan after first outing: won maiden point in April: always behind in novice hunter on chase debut: tried in cheekpieces. *R. Butterworth* **c–** **h–**

SECRET JEWEL (FR) 7 b.m. Hernando (FR) – Opalette (Sharrood (USA)) [2006/7 h–: 19mᵖᵘ 20s Oct 11] rather leggy mare: no form over hurdles. *Miss C. J. E. Caroe* **h–**

SECRET PACT (IRE) 5 br.g. Lend A Hand – Schust Madame (IRE) (Second Set (IRE)) [2006/7 h101: 19g* 21v 21d 22sᵖᵘ Jan 20] leggy gelding: modest novice hurdler: won at Market Rasen in November, tending to edge left: no show in handicaps after: stays 2½m: raced on good ground or softer (acts on heavy): tried blinkered. *A. M. Hales* **h88**

SECRET PLOY 7 b.g. Deploy – By Line (High Line) [2006/7 24s² 24s* 24g 24gᵖᵘ Apr 13] quite attractive gelding: fairly useful novice hurdler, off 21 months before return: won at Kempton (beat Barbers Shop by ½ length, idling) in January: stays 3m: raced on good going or softer (acts on soft): tried blinkered: ungenuine. *H. Morrison* **h124 §**

SECRET RUBY (IRE) 7 b.g. Grand Plaisir (IRE) – Brave Ruby (Proverb) [2006/7 24s⁴ 23v⁵ May 25] ex-Irish gelding: half-brother to modest chaser Up The Pub (by Carroll House), stays 3¼m: dam winning pointer: well beaten in bumper for F. Cunningham: won maiden Irish point in 2005: better effort in novice hurdles when 6½ lengths fourth to Mister Shen at Uttoxeter: folded tamely 11 days later. *T. R. George* **h89**

SECRET'S OUT 11 b.g. Polish Precedent (USA) – Secret Obsession (USA) (Secretariat (USA)) [2006/7 h89: 16m⁶ 16g 16m⁶ 16m³ 16g 17m³ 16g³ 16m² 16dᶠ Nov 20] leggy gelding: long-standing modest maiden hurdler, in frame 26 times, would have won seller at Ludlow (cheekpieces) final outing but for falling heavily last: best around 2m: acts on good to soft and good to firm going: effective visored or not: edgy type, takes good hold. *F. Lloyd* **h89**

SECRET SQUIRREL (IRE) 6 ch.g. Mister Lord (USA) – Crosschild (IRE) (Buckskin (FR)) [2006/7 16g 16m⁶ 16g 20v³ 19g* 21d³ 21d* Dec 26] workmanlike gelding: fair handicap hurdler: won at Hereford (conditional jockeys novice) in October and Limerick in December: will stay beyond 21f: acts on heavy going. *Eric McNamara, Ireland*   **h100**

SECRET TALK 4 b.f. Classic Cliche (IRE) – Strumpet (Tragic Role (USA)) [2006/7 F16v F16v F16s Apr 1] unfurnished filly: first foal: dam, 5f/1m winner on Flat, poor novice hurdler: well held in bumpers. *B. Storey*   **F–**

SECRET TRAVEL 7 b.m. Thowra (FR) – Travel Secret (Blakeney) [2006/7 F17d⁵ 22mᵖᵘ 19m²ᵖᵘ 17m 19s⁴ 24s⁶ 19v⁶ Jan 8] fourth foal: half-sister to winner up to 1¼m in Italy by Presidium: dam unraced: no form in maiden bumper/over hurdles: tried blinkered. *J. D. Frost*   **h– F–**

SECURED (IRE) 7 b.g. Safety Catch (USA) – Monalma (IRE) (Montekin) [2006/7 h111, F75: 21g c20d³ c20d⁵ c23dᶠ 21s⁵ 21d⁶ Mar 22] fair hurdler at best: 21 lengths third to Fourty Acers in maiden at Ludlow on chasing debut: badly let down by jumping next 2 starts: stays 21f: raced on good going or softer. *Ian Williams*   **c95 x h99**

SEEADOR 8 b.g. El Conquistador – Shepani (New Member) [2006/7 c–, h105: 26g* c24dᵖᵘ 26s³ 24v² 24g 24g Apr 18] workmanlike gelding: fair hurdler: easily won maiden at Hereford in May: no form in maiden chases: stays 3¼m: raced on good going or softer (acts on heavy): often races prominently. *J. W. Mullins*   **c– h108**

SEEJAY 7 b.m. Bahamian Bounty – Grand Splendour (Shirley Heights) [2006/7 h–: 16d Aug 14] no show in selling hurdles. *B. R. Johnson*   **h–**

SEEKING FAME (IRE) 5 ch.m. Glacial Storm (USA) – Seeking Gold (IRE) (Lancastrian) [2006/7 16vᵖᵘ 20vᵖᵘ 20sᵖᵘ Apr 25] third foal: dam modest staying chaser: no form over hurdles. *N. W. Alexander*   **h–**

SEEKING SHELTER (IRE) 8 b.m. Glacial Storm (USA) – Seeking Gold (IRE) (Lancastrian) [2006/7 c–, h68: 16v c22vᵖᵘ Jan 12] lengthy mare: little form over hurdles: has failed to complete over fences. *N. W. Alexander*   **c– h–**

SEEKING STRAIGHT (IRE) 4 b.g. Rainbow Quest (USA) – Alignment (IRE) (Alzao (USA)) [2006/7 16v 16v⁶ 20sᵖᵘ Apr 25] unfurnished gelding: half-brother to fairly useful hurdler around 2m Front Rank (by Sadler's Wells): once-raced on Flat, sold out of Sir Michael Stoute's stable 16,000 gns Newmarket July Sales: signs of only a little ability over hurdles. *Miss Lucinda V. Russell*   **h78**

SEEMARYE 5 ch.m. Romany Rye – Shepani (New Member) [2006/7 F16g F16d 22gᵖᵘ Apr 1] rather unfurnished mare: eighth foal: half-sister to useful hurdler/chaser See You Sometime (by Sharp Deal), stays 3¼m, fair staying hurdler Seeador (by El Conquistador) and bumper winner Seem of Gold (by Gold Dust): dam, maiden Irish pointer, half-sister to Rendlesham Hurdle winner See Enough: little impact in bumpers/mares novice hurdle. *J. W. Mullins*   **h– F75**

SEE ME FLY 5 b.m. Alflora (IRE) – See Me Shine (Lighter) [2006/7 F16d F17v⁴ 19s 22g Apr 1] first foal: dam winning pointer: well held in bumpers/over hurdles. *Mrs S. M. Johnson*   **h– F–**

SEEMMA 7 b.m. Romany Rye – Shepani (New Member) [2006/7 h83: 16g 22s⁶ 24s⁵ 19g⁶ 26gᵖᵘ Apr 11] lengthy mare: third in mares novice on hurdling debut early in 2005/6, little form since. *K. Bishop*   **h73**

SEE MORE JOCK 9 b.g. Seymour Hicks (FR) – Metafan (Last Fandango) [2006/7 h80: 22s 22v⁵ Mar 7] sturdy gelding: refused both starts in maiden points: maiden hurdler, well held in 2006/7. *Dr J. R. J. Naylor*   **h–**

SEE MY SOUL (IRE) 5 b.m. Mister Mat (FR) – Kawarau Queen (Taufan (USA)) [2006/7 F–: F17d Nov 16] well held in maiden bumpers. *T. Wall*   **F–**

SEE THE VIEW (IRE) 6 b. or br.h. New Frontier (IRE) – French View (IRE) (Toulon) [2006/7 F17d⁴ 18g⁶ Sep 3] €11,000 4-y-o: first foal: dam unraced half-sister to fairly useful chaser Theatre Knight, stays 33f: runner-up in maiden Irish point in 2006: bought 5,500 gns Doncaster May Sales: fourth in bumper: well beaten in novice on hurdling debut. *B. G. Powell*   **h– F78**

SEEYAAJ 7 b.g. Darshaan – Subya (Night Shift (USA)) [2006/7 c99, h–: c17f⁶ May 9] good-topped, close-coupled gelding: winning hurdler: modest chaser: no show only start in 2006/7: stays 2½m: probably acts on any going: tongue tied. *Miss Lucinda V. Russell*   **c– h–**

United House Gold Cup Handicap, Ascot—the riderless Ollie Magern
has been See You Sometime's only close pursuer from an early stage

SEE YOU SOMETIME 12 b.g. Sharp Deal – Shepani (New Member) [2006/7 c134, h–: c24g² c24g² c24m* c17d⁵ c24d Dec 16] medium-sized gelding: useful handicap chaser: as good as ever when winning valuable event at Ascot in October by 7 lengths from Zabenz: respectable fifth to Demi Beau there following month: needs good test at 2m, and stays 3¼m: acts on soft and good to firm going: front runner/races prominently: genuine. *J. W. Mullins* **c144 h–**

SEE YOU THERE (IRE) 8 br.g. Religiously (USA) – Bye For Now (Abednego) [2006/7 c115x, h–: c20d⁴ c25dF c25s* c25vᵖᵘ c24dᵖᵘ c28s* c24v* Mar 18] tall gelding: fairly useful chaser: won handicaps at Hexham (novice) in November and Carlisle in February and novice at Carlisle again (beat Numero Un de Solzen by 10 lengths) in March: stays 3½m: raced on going softer than good (acts on heavy): often makes mistakes. *Miss Lucinda V. Russell* **c122 x h–**

SEHOYA (IRE) 5 b. or br.m. Second Empire (IRE) – Blue Jazz (IRE) (Bluebird (USA)) [2006/7 16v 17m² 16g Apr 23] sturdy mare: modest on Flat (stays 1¼m), successful at 3 yrs, well beaten 3 starts in Britain: form over hurdles (left E. Doyle in Ireland prior to return) only when second in novice handicap at Sedgefield. *R. C. Guest* **h88**

SEISMIC SHIFT (IRE) 5 b.g. Taipan (IRE) – Castlefreke (IRE) (Good Thyne **h95 p** (USA)) [2006/7 F16d* F16d³ F16d³ 18g² Mar 18] sturdy gelding: first foal: dam, poor **F104** maiden hurdler, half-sister to fairly useful staying chaser Lord Jack: fairly useful form in bumpers, decisive winner of maiden at Ludlow in November: 1¾ lengths second to Presentandcorrect in novice at Fontwell on hurdling debut, not clear run after 3 out: will stay 2½m: likely to improve. *Miss H. C. Knight*

SEIZE 5 gr.g. Silver Patriarch (IRE) – Sleepline Princess (Royal Palace) [2006/7 F78+: **h98** 16g⁴ 17s⁵ 16s³ 19d 16m³ Apr 22] lengthy, good-topped gelding: modest novice hurdler: stays 19f. *Ian Williams*

SELECTION BOX (IRE) 6 b.g. Witness Box (USA) – Challenging Times (IRE) **h87** (Kemal (FR)) [2006/7 16v⁵ 16s³ Apr 25] £14,000 4-y-o: first foal: dam lightly raced in points: failed to complete in 4 maiden points: much better effort in maiden hurdles when 17 lengths third of 4 finishers to Brickies Mate at Perth. *C. A. McBratney, Ireland*

SELF DEFENSE 10 b.g. Warning – Dansara (Dancing Brave (USA)) [2006/7 h147: **h139** 16g* 19d⁵ 16d⁶ 16d 20g 16m⁴ Apr 27] sturdy gelding: useful hurdler nowadays: won 4-runner minor races at Kempton in October by 1½ lengths from Kawagino: little impact in stronger races after: should prove as effective at 2½m as 2m: unraced on firm going, acts on any other: held up. *Miss E. C. Lavelle*

SELF DISCIPLINE 5 b.g. Dansili – Cosh (USA) (A P Indy (USA)) [2006/7 20gᵖᵘ 20d **h–** Nov 3] lightly raced and no form on Flat, sold out of B. Hills's stable 5,500 gns Doncaster August (2005) Sales: no show over hurdles. *Mrs L. B. Normile*

SELF RESPECT (USA) 5 b.g. Lear Fan (USA) – Cap of Dignity (Shirley Heights) **h120** [2006/7 16d² 16g* 16d² 16sᵖᵘ 17g³ 19m* Apr 28] tall, good-topped gelding: fairly useful on Flat (stays 1¾m): fairly useful novice hurdler: won at Kempton (listed event, by 7 lengths from Moon Over Miami) in October and Market Rasen (easily landed odds) in April: failed to convince with attitude in between, jumped markedly right when 7 lengths third of 4 to Lead On at Cheltenham: stays 19f: may prove best on right-handed tracks. *A. King*

SEMI PRECIOUS (IRE) 9 ch.g. Semillon – Precious Petra (Bing II) [2006/7 c84, **c76** h–: c16s* Oct 22] plain gelding: winning hurdler: poor handicap chaser: blinkered, very **h–** fortunate winner of 3-finisher event at Wincanton in October (clear leader fell 2 out, runner-up idled): should stay 2½m: raced on going softer than good: not a fluent jumper. *D. P. Keane*

SENDANI (FR) 4 b.g. Grand Lodge (USA) – Sendana (FR) (Darshaan) [2006/7 16gᵖᵘ **h– p** Apr 12] rather leggy, useful-looking gelding: has reportedly had breathing operation: half-brother to several winners, notably high-class 1m/1¼m performer Sendawar (by Priolo) and useful but lightly-raced 2m hurdler Senanjar (by Kahyasi): dam unraced: useful form on Flat (stays 9.5f), successful twice from 5 starts at 3 yrs: sold out of A. de Royer Dupre's stable €170,000 Goffs Arc Sale: not persevered with after bad mistake first in Grade 1 juvenile at Aintree on hurdling debut: should do better. *P. F. Nicholls*

SENEGAL TIGER (IRE) 7 b.g. Anshan – Magic Beans (IRE) (Supreme Leader) **h–** [2006/7 26dᵖᵘ May 17] €4,400 4-y-o: fourth foal: dam unraced half-sister to fairly useful staying hurdler/chaser Menebuck: in frame in points: no show in maiden on hurdling debut. *Evan Williams*

SENIOR WHIM 5 b.g. Lahib (USA) – Euphorie (GER) (Feenpark (GER)) [2006/7 **c89** 16g 17s 20d c21dᵘʳ c20m* c16m⁴ Apr 24] modest form at best on Flat (stays 1½m): well **h–** held in novice hurdles: modest form over fences: easily won weak maiden at Plumpton in April: stays 2½m: acts on good to firm ground. *P. R. Webber*

SENORA SNOOPY (IRE) 6 b.m. Un Desperado (FR) – Lovely Snoopy (IRE) **h98** (Phardante (FR)) [2006/7 F96: 16s 21s² 20v² Jan 6] tall, useful-looking mare: has scope: bumper winner: modest form when runner-up in novice hurdles: stays 21f: acts on heavy going. *Ferdy Murphy*

SENOR EDUARDO 10 gr.g. Terimon – Jasmin Path (Warpath) [2006/7 h74: 18mᵖᵘ **h–** 25sᶠ Oct 29] workmanlike gelding: maiden hurdler, failed to complete last 3 starts. *Mrs H. O. Graham*

SENORITA RUMBALITA 6 b.m. Alflora (IRE) – Lavenham's Last (Rymer) **c115** [2006/7 h124: 16f c16g³ c21d* c21s⁶ Dec 9] useful-looking mare: fairly useful hurdler: **h–** easily best effort over fences when winning 5-runner mares novice at Wincanton in November by 12 lengths from Harringay: stayed easy 21f: acted on soft going (well held on firm): in foal to Presenting. *A. King*

SENOR SEDONA 8 b.g. Royal Vulcan – Star Shell (Queen's Hussar) [2006/7 c107, h–: 21g Apr 18] tall, useful-looking gelding: fairly useful hurdler at best: off 17 months, lame only start in 2006/7: highly tried and let down by jumping over fences: should stay beyond 2¾m: acts on soft going: tends to swish tail under pressure. *N. J. Gifford*   **c–** **h–**

SENSIBLE LASS (IRE) 11 b.m. Lord Americo – Rock of Sence (Swan's Rock) [2006/7 16d⁴ 16dᵖᵘ 16d 20g 16s⁴ 17d Nov 8] modest maiden hurdler: raced mainly around 2m, solely on good ground or softer: usually front runner. *M. A. Joyce, Ireland*   **h85**

SENTIERO ROSSO (USA) 5 b.g. Intidab (USA) – Kheyrah (USA) (Dayjur (USA)) [2006/7 16g⁵ Dec 30] fair on Flat (stays 1m, has looked reluctant), successful twice in 2006: tongue tied, tailed off in novice on hurdling debut. *B. Ellison*   **h–**

SENTO (IRE) 9 ch.g. Persian Bold – Esclava (USA) (Nureyev (USA)) [2006/7 c110, h–: c22mᵖᵘ c26gᵖᵘ c21d* c21g c21d* c20g⁵ c24gᵖᵘ Nov 8] good-topped gelding: fairly useful handicap chaser: won at Newton Abbot in August and Stratford (beat Dickensbury Lad by 7 lengths) in October: should stay at least 3m: acts on good to firm and good to soft going: has run as if amiss more than once. *A. King*   **c122** **h–**

SENTRY DUTY (FR) 5 b.h. Kahyasi – Standing Around (FR) (Garde Royale) [2006/7 16g⁴ Mar 24] rather leggy ex-French horse: useful on Flat (stays 15f), successful 6 times, including twice in 2006, left E. Libaud after final start: encouraging 13 lengths fourth of 18 to Special Envoy in novice at Newbury on hurdling debut: likely to be suited by further than 2m: open to improvement. *N. J. Henderson*   **h117 p**

SEPTEMBER MOON 9 b.m. Bustino – Lunabelle (Idiot's Delight) [2006/7 h96; c23fF c23m² c23f* c21gF c24fʳᵒ c24g⁴ c25m³ c23dᵖᵘ Oct 26] angular mare: modest chaser/handicap hurdler: won maiden chase at Worcester in June: stays 3¼m: acts on firm going: tried in cheekpieces (ran poorly): temperamental (ran out fifth start). *Evan Williams*   **c99 §** **h– §**

SERAPH 7 ch.g. Vettori (IRE) – Dahlawise (IRE) (Caerleon (USA)) [2006/7 c–, h76: 16gᵖᵘ 16g³ 21m⁶ 16mᵖᵘ Apr 24] rather leggy gelding: poor maiden hurdler, sold out of O. Brennan's stable 3,200 gns Doncaster October Sales before return: no show only outing over fences: stays 2½m: acts on soft going: tried in cheekpieces/blinkers: ungenuine. *Jim Best*   **c– §** **h66 §**

SERAPHIN (FR) 4 b.g. Muhtathir – Lirfa (USA) (Lear Fan (USA)) [2006/7 F14s Oct 29] sturdy gelding: half-brother to fairly useful hurdler/chaser Lirfox (by Foxhound), stayed 19f: dam unraced: seventh to Turbo Linn in 3-y-o bumper at Carlisle on debut. *G. A. Harker*   **F76**

SERBELLONI 7 b.g. Spectrum (IRE) – Rose Vibert (Caerleon (USA)) [2006/7 h100: c18mF c16g² c19m² c20m² c20mF Jun 28] winning hurdler: fair form first 2 completed starts over fences: stayed 19f: acted on soft and good to firm going: dead. *Evan Williams*   **c109** **h–**

SERENGETI SUNSET (IRE) 6 b.m. Luso – Crotty's Bridge (IRE) (Beau Sher) [2006/7 21vᵖᵘ Dec 31] €5,000 4-y-o: big, strong mare: chasing type: third foal: dam, winning pointer, sister to useful 2m chaser Town Crier: won mares maiden Irish point in 2006: dropped away in mares novice on hurdling debut. *S. E. H. Sherwood*   **h–**

SERGHEYEV 4 b.g. King's Best (USA) – Schezerade (USA) (Tom Rolfe) [2006/7 F16d* F16g Mar 14] useful-looking gelding: half-brother to several winners, including useful French hurdler up to 3m Sunspot (by Peintre Celebre) and smart Flat stayer Philanthrop (by Machiavellian): dam, 10.5f/1½m winner in France, closely related to top-class 1½m performer April Run: unraced on Flat for J. Osborne: won 4-y-o bumper at Leopardstown in January on debut easily by 2 lengths from Castlecrossings: left E. Hales, took keen hold and weakened quickly in Grade 1 at Cheltenham. *D. E. Pipe*   **F99**

SERIBASE (FR) 5 b.g. Dear Doctor (FR) – Reine de Thou (FR) (Roi de Rome (USA)) [2006/7 17s⁶ 16d 16s³ 16g³ 16s⁵ Apr 25] good-topped gelding: first foal: dam won over hurdles around 2m: fair hurdler: won 4-y-o event at Enghien in 2005/6 for P. Peltier: placed twice in handicaps in Britain: raced around 2m on good ground or softer (acts on soft): has found little. *P. J. Hobbs*   **h113**

SERPENTINE ROCK 7 ch.g. Hernando (FR) – Serpentara (Kris) [2006/7 c119, h114: c16s⁴ c19sF Dec 27] tall, lengthy gelding: fair hurdler: fairly useful chaser, not discredited on reappearance: probably best around 2m: acts on heavy going: sold only 1,500 gns Doncaster January Sales. *P. J. Hobbs*   **c112** **h–**

SERVE TIME 5 ch.g. Benny The Dip (USA) – Once Upon A Time (Teenoso (USA)) [2006/7 F16g* 16m* 16d² 16g Aug 29] half-brother to 3 winners, including smart performer up to 1½m Arabian Story (by Sharrood): dam, 8.5f and 1½m winner, half-sister   **h110 p** **F99**

SEX

to useful 2m hurdler Insular: won bumper at Sligo in June on debut: successful also in maiden hurdle at Ballinrobe following month: better form when length second to Summer Soul (pair clear) in novice at Galway: will stay 2½m: acts on good to firm and good to soft going: remains open to improvement. *N. F. Glynn, Ireland*

SESAME RAMBLER (IRE) 8 gr.g. Roselier (FR) – Sesame Cracker (Derrylin)   **c91**
[2006/7 h110: c21m* Jun 8] fair handicap hurdler: fortunate to win 3-finisher maiden   **h–**
at Newton Abbot on chasing debut, left clear last: stays 2¾m: best efforts on soft/heavy going: seemed likely to improve over fences, but presumably met with setback. *G. L. Moore*

SESSAY MILLER 10 b.g. Primitive Rising (USA) – Old Mill Lady (Royal Goblin)   **c78**
[2006/7 c21s² May 29] fair pointer, successful twice in 2006: 4 lengths second to Solway Sunset in maiden hunter at Cartmel on chasing debut: will stay 3m. *Oliver J. Turner*

SET BARABBAS FREE 8 b.h. Bishop of Cashel – Salanka (IRE) (Persian Heights)   **h76**
[2006/7 17m³ Jun 30] ex-Irish horse: modest at one time on Flat (stays 1m): left Joseph Quinn, first form over hurdles when third in selling handicap at Market Rasen, blundering 2 out. *R. Johnson*

SETITALIGHT (IRE) 6 b.g. Grand Plaisir (IRE) – Friendly Spirit (Nicholas Bill)   **h–**
[2006/7 16v⁵ 20s 16v Feb 5] €10,000 4-y-o: tall, strong gelding: second foal: dam, lightly raced in points, out of sister to useful chaser up to 21f Dis Train: pulled up both outings in Irish points in 2006: well held 3 starts over hurdles. *R. C. Guest*

SETT ASIDE 9 b.g. Set Adrift – Fields of Fortune (Anfield) [2006/7 c82, h–: c25g²   **c60**
c21d⁵ c20v⁵ c21d⁴ c18g c20m² c20g² Apr 23] workmanlike gelding: poor novice chaser: **h–**
probably stays 25f: acts on good to firm and heavy going: often wears cheekpieces. *Mrs L. C. Jewell*

SEVENEIGHTSIX (IRE) 7 ch.m. Old Vic – Necochea (Julio Mariner) [2006/7 c67+,   **c–**
h76: 20dᵖᵘ 20v Feb 17] good-topped mare: poor hurdler: lame only outing over fences: **h–**
possibly best short of 25f: usually wears blinkers/cheekpieces: temperament under suspicion. *D. J. Wintle*

SEVEN IS LUCKY (IRE) 5 b.g. Old Vic – Green Legend (IRE) (Montekin) [2006/7   **h90 p**
17s 19s 16s⁶ Jan 20] angular, good-topped gelding: half-brother to fairly useful hurdler Sully Shuffles (by Broken Hearted), stayed 27f, and 2½m hurdle winner Green Magical (by Magical Strike): dam unraced: modest form in novice hurdles, not given hard time last 2 starts: bred to be suited by 2½m+: type to do better, especially now qualified for handicaps. *D. E. Pipe*

SEVEN IS MY NUMBER (IRE) 5 b.g. Pistolet Bleu (IRE) – Waterloo Ball (IRE)   **F112**
(Where To Dance (USA)) [2006/7 F16d* F16d Feb 10] rather unfurnished gelding: fifth foal: half-brother to modest chaser Pure Platinum (by Roselier), stays 3¼m, and bumper winner City Deep (by Taipan): dam, fair hurdler/chaser who stayed 25f, out of half-sister to useful hurdler/chaser up to 25f Boyneside: useful form when winning bumper at Ascot on debut by 3½ lengths from Earth Planet: well held in Grade 2 at Newbury 2 months later. *D. E. Pipe*

SEVENMINUTESILENCE 5 ch.m. Master Willie – Kingky's Cottage (Kinglet)   **F74**
[2006/7 F16f³ Sep 29] fifth foal: sister to a winning pointer: dam unraced, out of half-sister to very smart staying chaser Tied Cottage: 11 lengths third to Shiwawa in bumper at Hexham on debut, nearest finish. *C. Grant*

SEVEN SKY (FR) 4 b.g. Septieme Ciel (USA) – Nuit de Crystal (FR) (Crystal Glitters   **h74**
(USA)) [2006/7 16d 16g Apr 27] brother/half-brother to winners on Flat in France: dam winning hurdler around 2m: 10.5f winner on Flat (stays 15f) at 3 yrs in France for S. Wattel: mid-division in maiden hurdles. *Carl Llewellyn*

SEVENTH SENSE 6 b.m. Pasternak – Sister Seven (IRE) (Henbit (USA)) [2006/7   **h80**
F75: F16g 20d 20v³ 16gᵖᵘ 20m⁵ 22gᵖᵘ Apr 21] leggy mare: well beaten in bumpers: form   **F–**
(poor) over hurdles only on third outing (bled next time). *G. A. Charlton*

SEX KITTEN 9 ch.m. Riverwise (USA) – Cut Above The Rest (Indiaro) [2006/7 19g³   **h–**
24f⁵ Jun 21] sixth foal: sister to fair staying hurdler/chaser Kittenkat: dam second in points: maiden pointer: well held both starts over hurdles. *L. Corcoran*

SEXY REXY (IRE) 6 b.g. Mister Lord (USA) – Cab On Time (IRE) (Alphabatim   **h103 p**
(USA)) [2006/7 F92: 16m² Oct 4] tall gelding: fair form in bumpers: off 6 months, encouraging hurdling debut when 5 lengths second to easy winner My Immortal in novice at Towcester, mistakes and nearest finish: will be suited by further than 2m: seemed sure to improve but not seen out again. *N. A. Twiston-Davies*

851

SEYMAR LAD (IRE) 7 b.g. Oscar (IRE) – Far And Deep (IRE) (Phardante (FR)) **c87**
[2006/7 h103: c20v⁴ c20d⁵ c16sʳ c20v⁶ c20v³ c17g⁶ c23g³ Apr 16] rangy gelding: fair **h–**
hurdler: modest and in-and-out form over fences (has been let down by jumping/attitude):
stays 23f: raced on good ground or softer (acts on heavy): tried blinkered/in cheekpieces:
sold 8,000 gns Doncaster May Sales. *P. Beaumont*

SEYMOUR WELD 7 ch.g. Weld – Seymour News (Seymour Hicks (FR)) [2006/7 **h85**
F77: F17s⁶ 20g³ 20m* 16g* 24d⁶ 20d 16s³ Oct 26] tall gelding: modest form in bumpers: **F78**
similar standard over hurdles, won sellers at Worcester in August and Uttoxeter in
September: stays 2½m: acts on soft and good to firm ground. *C. T. Pogson*

SGT PEPPER (IRE) 6 b.g. Fasliyev (USA) – Amandine (IRE) (Darshaan) [2006/7 **h–**
h97+: 18g 19m Oct 4] sturdy gelding: modest form at best over hurdles: ran poorly both
outings in 2006/7, in cheekpieces and claimed £6,000 second time. *O. Sherwood*

SHAABAN (IRE) 6 b.g. Woodman (USA) – Ashbilya (USA) (Nureyev (USA)) [2006/7 **h–**
h–: 24fᵖᵘ 16m 22m Sep 2] no form over hurdles: usually wears headgear. *R. J. Price*

SHA BIHAN (FR) 6 b.g. Villez (USA) – Shadrou (FR) (Kadrou (FR)) [2006/7 h–: 23g² **c115**
24s c22s* c24s⁵ c22d² c23d³ c25m³ Apr 20] workmanlike gelding: has reportedly had **h104**
breathing operations: fair hurdler: better form over fences, won handicap at Fontwell in
January by ¾ length from Dun An Doras: stays 23f: acts on soft going. *A. King*

SHADED (IRE) 13 b.g. Night Shift (USA) – Sarsaparilla (FR) (Shirley Heights) **c–**
[2006/7 19dᵖᵘ 19vᵖᵘ 17gᵖᵘ Apr 1] good-topped gelding: winning hurdler, no longer of any **h–**
account. *D. J. Minty*

SHADY ANNE 9 ch.m. Derrylin – Juno Away (Strong Gale) [2006/7 c–, h93: 16d 16g **c–**
16dᵖᵘ 20s⁶ 21mᶠ 20s 18v⁴ 22g* 21g⁵ 20g Apr 21] smallish mare: twice-raced over **h83**
fences: poor hurdler nowadays: won conditional jockeys handicap at Fontwell in March:
effective at 2m to 3m: acts on heavy going: wears cheekpieces. *F. Jordan*

SHADY HOLLOW (IRE) 6 b.g. Mister Lord (USA) – Suir Venture (Roselier (FR)) **h–**
[2006/7 20gᵖᵘ 24vᵖᵘ Jan 17] €36,000 3-y-o: half-brother to winning 2m hurdler Pateley
(by Cataldi) and 2¾m chase winner Oh Highly Likely (by Glacial Storm): dam, fairly
useful hurdler up to 3m, out of half-sister to smart 3m chaser Johnny Setaside: no show in
2 starts over hurdles: sold 2,400 gns Doncaster May Sales. *Ferdy Murphy*

SHADY MAN 9 b.g. Shaamit (IRE) – Miss Hardy (Formidable (USA)) [2006/7 h–: 17d **h–**
20sᵖᵘ Jun 25] chunky gelding: winning hurdler, no form since 2003/4. *J. K. Hunter*

SHADY MERLIN (IRE) 9 b.g. Shardari – Merillion (Touch Paper) [2006/7 c16g **c76**
c23m⁶ 17d c20g³ c18g³ 18m⁴ c19m⁴ 17s⁵ c20g² 19v c19d⁴ c18d 19s³ 17v³ c20gᵖᵘ 17m **h65**
Apr 15] known as Royal Cruise when winning maiden point in 2004: poor maiden
hurdler/chaser, sold out of R. York's stable 2,800 gns Doncaster October Sales after
seventh start: stays 2½m: acts on good to firm and good to soft going, below best on
softer: blinkered/visored 3 of last 4 outings: sold 2,600 gns Doncaster May Sales.
M. E. Sowersby

SHAHEER (IRE) 5 b.g. Shahrastani (USA) – Atmospheric Blues (IRE) (Double **h–**
Schwartz) [2006/7 16f 16dᵖᵘ 19m Jun 4] modest on Flat (stays 1½m), successful in
February: showed nothing over hurdles, including in sellers. *J. Gallagher*

SHAHNAMEH (IRE) 5 ch.g. Anshan – Novelist (Quayside) [2006/7 F16f F16v **F–**
Nov 26] €15,000 3-y-o, resold £23,000 3-y-o: rather unfurnished gelding: half-brother to
winning 3m chaser The Writer (by Royal Fountain) and winning 2¾m chaser Alexander
Fourball (by Phardante): dam unraced half-sister to dam of very smart hurdler/high-class
staying chaser Rule Supreme: soundly beaten in bumpers (tongue tied/breathing problem
second outing). *P. R. Webber*

SHAKA'S PEARL 7 ch.g. Infantry – Zulu Pearl (Sula Bula) [2006/7 h100: c16s² c18s **c97**
c19s³ c28g² Mar 18] angular gelding: fair hurdler: modest form when placed 3 of 4 starts **h–**
over fences: stays 3½m: raced on good going or softer (acts on soft). *N. J. Gifford*

SHAKERATTLEANDROLL (IRE) 6 b.g. Dr Fong (USA) – Speedybird (IRE) **h–**
(Danehill (USA)) [2006/7 F88: 20g 22dᵖᵘ 16g Nov 7] bumper winner/1¼m winner on
Flat: no form since 2005, including over hurdles. *Mrs L. Richards*

SHAKE THE SPEAR (IRE) 4 b.g. Lear Spear (USA) – Milladella (FR) (Nureyev **h–**
(USA)) [2006/7 16sᵘʳ 16v 16v Jan 25] leggy gelding: lightly raced on Flat: last on completed starts in juvenile hurdles. *Miss J. R. Tooth*

SHAKWAA 8 ch.m. Lion Cavern (USA) – Shadha (USA) (Devil's Bag (USA)) [2006/7 **c–** c–x, h82d: 16g 20s^{pu} 19d^{pu} 16m 17m^{pu} Mar 14] tall mare: maiden hurdler: no form for **h–** long time (let down by jumping over fences): tried tongue tied. *E. A. Elliott*

SHALATI PRINCESS 6 b.m. Bluegrass Prince (IRE) – Shalati (FR) (High Line) **h71** [2006/7 h81: 17s⁶ 19v 16v³ 17s⁴ Mar 12] leggy mare: poor maiden hurdler: claimed £6,000 final start: will stay 2½m: unraced on firm ground, acts on any other. *D. Burchell*

SHAMAN 10 b.g. Fraam – Magic Maggie (Beveled (USA)) [2006/7 h92: 16g* 18m³ **h90** 18m* 17m 19m² 16s³ 19s³ 16d² 16s⁶ 17v Mar 1] compact gelding: modest hurdler: won claimer at Plumpton and seller at Fontwell early in 2006/7 for G. L. Moore: trained sixth to ninth outings by D. Carroll: stays 19f: acts on good to firm and heavy going. *J. K. Price*

SHAMBAR (IRE) 8 ro.g. Linamix (FR) – Shamawna (IRE) (Darshaan) [2006/7 16d **h108** 17s⁵ 17s² Feb 8] lengthy gelding: half-brother to one-time useful chaser Shamawan (by Kris), stayed 21f: lightly-raced maiden on Flat: fair form over hurdles, 2½ lengths second to Cantabilly in maiden at Taunton, though again didn't look easy ride. *Miss E. C. Lavelle*

SHAMROCK BAY 5 b.m. Celtic Swing – Kabayil (Dancing Brave (USA)) [2006/7 **h91** h–: 17m⁵ 19s^F 20m⁵ 17d* Mar 19] modest form over hurdles, best effort when winning handicap at Market Rasen: should stay beyond 17f: acts on good to soft ground. *C. R. Dore*

SHAMSAN (IRE) 10 ch.g. Night Shift (USA) – Awayil (USA) (Woodman (USA)) **c–** [2006/7 c–, h90: 20f⁵ 20m² Aug 11] small, sturdy gelding: successful over hurdles (6 **h80** times)/fences, poor form in 2006/7: stays easy 21f: acts on firm and good to soft going: has worn blinkers/cheekpieces: often tongue tied: has idled and usually held up. *J. Joseph*

SHAMWARI FIRE (IRE) 7 ch.g. Idris (IRE) – Bobby's Dream (Reference Point) **h79** [2006/7 h–: 17m³ 16s 20d^{pu} 16g Nov 29] good-bodied gelding: poor and unreliable on Flat (stays 1¼m) nowadays: form over hurdles only when third in steadily-run novice at Sedgefield. *I. W. McInnes*

SHANAGOLDEN JUAN (IRE) 4 ch.g. King Charlemagne (USA) – Ida Lupino **h–** (IRE) (Statoblest) [2006/7 16d Nov 30] close-coupled gelding: no sign of ability in maiden on Flat or juvenile hurdle (tongue tied). *M. R. Bosley*

SHANAPOVA (IRE) 7 br.m. Anshan – Native Gale (USA) (Be My Native (USA)) **h67** [2006/7 F16s⁵ 21s 20v 16v⁵ Jan 17] signs of ability in bumpers/over hurdles. *Grant Tuer* **F–**

SHANDON STAR (IRE) 8 b.m. Priolo (USA) – Noble Choice (Dahar (USA)) **h120** [2006/7 16m² 22m⁵ Aug 5] second foal: half-sister to winning pointer by Dolphin Street: dam, fairly useful 2m hurdler, out of half-sister to Irish 1000 Guineas winner Nicer: bumper winner: fairly useful hurdler: won 3 times in 2005/6: successful also both starts on Flat in June/July: progressed further when 4-length second to Cuan Na Grai in Galway Hurdle (Handicap): ran creditably at same course 2 days later: effective at 2m to 3m: best form on good to firm/firm going. *W. P. Mullins, Ireland*

SHANEHILL (IRE) 5 b.g. Danehill – Shunaire (USA) (Woodman (USA)) **h–** [2006/7 F16g F16g^{ro} 17v^{pu} 16d 19v 17g 16f⁶ Apr 22] 9,000 3-y-o: fifth foal: half-brother **F74** to Irish 1¼m winner Smile From Heaven (by Rainbow Quest): dam Irish 6f winner: signs of ability in bumpers (trained by T. Walsh)/over hurdles, but has looked temperamental. *Evan Williams*

SHANGHIDE 6 br.g. Supreme Leader – My Adventure (IRE) (Strong Gale) [2006/7 **h118** 16s 20s⁴ 20v[*] 16v 16d 16g[*] 20m Apr 27] €32,000 3-y-o: well-made gelding: will make a chaser: fifth foal: half-brother to winning Irish pointer by Roselier: dam modest hurdler up to 25f: well held in bumper: fairly useful hurdler: won 22-runner maiden at Punchestown in December and novice at Gowran (much improved when beating Charlie Yardbird ¾ length) in April: out of depth final outing: will stay beyond 2½m: acts on heavy ground. *M. F. Morris, Ireland*

SHANKLY BOND (IRE) 5 ch.g. Danehill Dancer (IRE) – Fanellan (Try My Best **h99 p** (USA)) [2006/7 16s⁴ 20s 17s⁶ 16g² Mar 19] half-brother to fair hurdler The Indispensable (by College Chapel), stayed 21f: fair on Flat (stays 1½m) at 3 yrs for B. Smart: in cheekpieces, easily best effort over hurdles when 1¼ lengths second to Tytheknot in handicap at Wincanton: probably capable of better again. *Evan Williams*

SHANLYRE QUEST (IRE) 7 b.g. Eurobus – Manta Vision (IRE) (Golden Love) **h–** [2006/7 22s^{pu} Dec 23] fourth foal: dam unraced half-sister to Grand National winner Rough Quest: poor maiden Irish pointer: no show in maiden on hurdling debut. *Mrs S. Wall*

SHANNON CREEK 6 ch.m. Shahanndeh – Betsy Boop (Pauper) [2006/7 F16s F16g   **F–** F16s Apr 1] stocky mare: third foal: dam poor maiden jumper: tailed off in bumpers. *E. M. Caine*

SHANNON HOUSE 4 ch.g. Inchinor – Sulitelma (USA) (The Minstrel (CAN))   **h–** [2006/7 16g^{pu} Oct 14] half-brother to fair 2m hurdler Robinzal (by Zilzal): modest maiden on Flat (stays 1m): breathing problem on hurdling debut. *M. J. McGrath*

SHANNON LODGE (IRE) 9 gr.g. Aristocracy – Roseville Baroness (Sexton Blake)   **c76** [2006/7 24f^3 c23f^F c19m^6 Apr 10] won maiden in Ireland on debut in 2004, little show in   **h85** points since: bought £2,500 Ascot June Sales: first form over hurdles when third in maiden at Worcester: 3 lengths down and fading when falling heavily 4 out in novice there on chasing debut: stays 3m: acts on firm ground: tongue tied in 2006/7. *D. A. Rees*

SHANNONS BOY (IRE) 5 b.g. Anshan – Dusky Lady (Black Minstrel) [2006/7 20v^5 **h77** 20s 26v^3 24v^{pu} Mar 10] €16,000 3-y-o: half-brother to winning pointer by Commanche Run: dam, won 2½m chase, half-sister to smart chaser Lord Singapore, stayed 3¼m: poor form in novice hurdles, none too fluent: stays 3¼m. *Miss H. Lewis*

SHANNON'S PRIDE (IRE) 11 gr.g. Roselier – Spanish Flame (IRE) (Spanish   **c111** Place (USA)) [2006/7 c110, h–: c20g c20f c20g^2 c20d* c21g^2 c20s^4 c20v^5 c22s c22v^3 **h–** c24g^2 c21g^F c25m* Apr 20] lengthy gelding: winning hurdler: fair handicap chaser: won at Hexham (conditional jockeys) in November and Ayr (4-runner event) in April: placed in race for second successive year when runner-up to I Hear Thunder in Grand Sefton at Aintree fifth outing, and running well there again when falling in Topham: stays 3¼m: acts on heavy and good to firm going: wears cheekpieces: tried tongue tied. *R. C. Guest*

SHANNON SPRINGS (IRE) 5 b.g. Darshaan – Our Queen of Kings (Arazi (USA))   **h116** [2006/7 h111: 17d^2 16d^2 17s 16m^3 24g* 22g^4 24f^2 Apr 5] useful-looking gelding: fairly useful hurdler: won maiden at Ludlow in February by 2½ lengths from Master Eddy: unlucky when ½-length second to My Immortal in novice there final outing, sticking to task well despite slipped saddle: stays easy 3m: acts on firm and good to soft going, well below form on soft: free-going sort: type to do even better over fences than hurdles. *Andrew Turnell*

SHANTEEN LASS (IRE) 7 b.m. Shahanndeh – Margurites Pet (IRE) (Roselier (FR))   **c79** [2006/7 h77: c22v c24g^3 c31s^{pu} Apr 26] leggy mare: poor maiden hurdler: successful   **h–** twice in points in 2007: best effort in hunter chases when third to Lothian Rising at Carlisle: should stay beyond 3m: acts on heavy going. *M. V. Coglan*

SHANXI GIRL 4 br.f. Overbury (IRE) – Celtic Native (IRE) (Be My Native (USA))   **F93** [2006/7 F17g^3 Apr 19] medium-sized filly: first foal: dam, smart hurdler/fairly useful chaser who stayed 25f, out of half-sister to Grand National winner Red Marauder: carrying condition, 10½ lengths third of 18 to I'm Delilah in mares bumper at Cheltenham on debut. *P. J. Hobbs*

SHARAAB (USA) 6 b. or br.g. Erhaab (USA) – Ghashtah (USA) (Nijinsky (CAN))   **c99** [2006/7 h89: 17g^3 21m^3 c16g^4 c20m^4 c20m^F c20m* c16m^F 22f^2 20m Apr 25] modest   **h83** on Flat (stays 2m), successful in August: poor hurdler: better chaser, won handicap at Worcester in August: would have finished good second but for falling last in similar event at Huntingdon next time: stays 21f: raced mainly on good going or firmer (acts on firm): usually tongue tied. *D. E. Cantillon*

SHARA LIKE MAGIC 4 gr.f. Baryshnikov (AUS) – Total Tropix (Saddlers' Hall   **F–** (IRE)) [2006/7 F14g Nov 15] first foal: dam/unreliable maiden hurdler around 2m: well beaten in bumper on debut. *A. M. Crow*

SHARDAKHAN (IRE) 5 b.g. Dr Devious (IRE) – Sharamana (IRE) (Darshaan)   **h117** [2006/7 h78: 22s^{ro} 22v* 22d^2 20s^3 24v^3 Mar 3] workmanlike gelding: fairly useful novice hurdler: much improved when winning at Folkestone in January by 18 lengths from Supreme Huntress: ran well despite several mistakes when third of 5 to Ballyshan in handicap at Kempton final start: stays 3m: raced on ground softer than good (acts well on heavy). *G. L. Moore*

SHARDAM (IRE) 10 b.g. Shardari – Knockea Hill (Buckskin (FR)) [2006/7 c–, h–:   **c106** c25g c24s c24m^3 c24m* c24d^{pu} Nov 20] tall, leggy gelding: fair handicap chaser nowa-   **h–** days: plummeted in weights prior to winning 5-runner event at Ludlow in November, making virtually all: lame next time: should stay beyond 27f: acts on soft and good to firm going: tried tongue tied/blinkered. *N. A. Twiston-Davies*

SHARED ACCOUNT (IRE) 13 b.g. Supreme Leader – Ribble Rabble (Deep Run) **c97**
[2006/7 24m³ 19m* c23m² c23m³ 22g* 24s* 21g³ 23d 21s^pu Nov 29] sturdy gelding: **h103**
winning pointer: fair hurdler: won sellers at Newton Abbot in July and August and
handicap at Perth in September: much better effort in maiden chases at Worcester when
short-head second to Rare Society: stayed 25f: acted on good to firm and heavy going:
usually wore headgear in 2006/7: dead. *Evan Williams*

SHAREEF (FR) 10 b.g. Port Lyautey (FR) – Saralik (Salse (USA)) [2006/7 c102, h–: **c91**
c20g³ c23m^pu Apr 22] good-topped gelding: fairly useful maiden chaser at best, third at **h–**
Kempton on completed outing in hunters: stays 2¾m: acts on soft and good to firm going.
A. A. Wintle

SHARE MY DREAM (IRE) 8 b.m. Shernazar – Nature's Best (Nishapour (FR)) **h78**
[2006/7 20s³ 18g² 20g 16v² 16s⁴ 16v² 17v⁴ 17d* 19m⁵ Apr 11] ex-Irish mare: seventh
foal: half-sister to bumper winner Sunseara (by Montelimar): dam winning 2m hurdler:
poor hurdler, left P. Fenton before return: won novice seller at Exeter in March: best form
short of 2½m: acts on heavy going: often jumps none too fluently. *J. D. Frost*

SHARES (IRE) 7 b.g. Turtle Island (IRE) – Glendora (Glenstal (USA)) [2006/7 c111, **c110**
h104: c16v³ 16v⁶ 16v³ 16v c16v³ 18s c16v⁵ c16v⁴ 16v* c16s⁴ Apr 26] lengthy gelding: **h110**
fair handicap hurdler/chaser: won over hurdles at Ayr (by 16 lengths) in March: raced
around 2m on good going or softer (acts on heavy): patiently ridden: has been let down
by jumping over fences. *P. Monteith*

SHARKEYS DREAM (FR) 6 gr.g. Dom Alco (FR) – Dame Au Diamant (FR) **h93**
(Homme de Loi (IRE)) [2006/7 F16g 20s 20s⁶ 25s^ur 20v² 24v² 20s^pu Apr 25] small **F–**
gelding: first foal: dam ran once: well held in bumper: modest novice hurdler: should stay
beyond 3m: raced mainly on soft/heavy ground. *Ferdy Murphy*

SHARLOM (IRE) 10 br.g. Shardari – Sarahs Music (IRE) (Orchestra) [2006/7 c20m⁴ **c– x**
May 18] workmanlike gelding: maiden hurdler/chaser: winning pointer, including in **h–**
April: tried blinkered: makes mistakes over fences. *Miss T. McCurrich*

SHARP ACTION 5 b.m. Overbury (IRE) – Straight Touch (Touch of Grey) [2006/7 **h–**
F16v F18v⁴ 16s Feb 22] second foal: dam maiden pointer: little impact in bumpers/mares **F–**
maiden hurdle. *Mrs S. J. Humphrey*

SHARP BELLINE (IRE) 10 b.g. Robellino (USA) – Moon Watch (Night Shift **c113 §**
(USA)) [2006/7 c110§, h–§: 16s⁶ c23s⁴ c24s* c24v* c24v⁵ c32v^pu 24g⁵ c24g Apr 7] **h101 §**
small, close-coupled gelding: fair handicap hurdler/chaser: won over fences at Southwell
and Haydock in December: stays 3¼m: acts on any going: usually makes running:
temperamental. *Mrs S. J. Smith*

SHARP JACK (IRE) 9 b.g. Be My Native (USA) – Polly Sharp (Pollerton) [2006/7 **c110**
c116, h97: c24v^ur c25v² c24v⁶ c24v⁴ c20s Mar 11] useful-looking gelding: winning **h–**
hurdler: fair handicap chaser: stays 25f: raced on ground softer than good (acts on heavy):
takes strong hold. *R. T. Phillips*

SHARP RALLY (IRE) 6 ch.g. Night Shift (USA) – La Pointe (Sharpo) [2006/7 h–: **h–**
20m^pu 16m 16m⁴ 16f^pu 16d^F 16v 17v^pu 16m^pu Apr 9] good-topped gelding: little form
over hurdles: visored/in cheekpieces last 6 starts: usually tongue tied. *A. J. Wilson*

SHARP REPLY (USA) 5 b.g. Diesis – Questonia (Rainbow Quest (USA)) [2006/7 **h126**
20g* 16d* 20s⁵ 20g² 20s* Apr 26] smallish gelding: fairly useful on Flat (stays 1¾m),
sold out of R. Whitaker's stable 20,000 gns Doncaster October Sales: took well to hurdling, winning maiden in December and novice in February, both at Musselburgh, and
handicap at Perth (fairly useful form, beat Khasab by ½ length) in April: stays 2½m:
raced on good ground or softer (acts on soft). *Mrs S. C. Bradburne*

SHARP SPIRIT (IRE) 5 b.m. Brave Act – Saborinie (Prince Sabo) [2006/7 16s⁶ 19g **h–**
16f 20d^pu 20d^pu Nov 7] fourth foal: dam lightly-raced Irish maiden: maiden on Flat,
placed 3 times around 1m in Germany/Poland at 3 yrs for M. Novakowski: no form over
hurdles: tried in cheekpieces/tongue tied. *R. C. Guest*

SHARP TUNE (USA) 5 ch.g. Diesis – Moonflute (USA) (The Minstrel (CAN)) **h–**
[2006/7 17g Apr 7] no form on Flat: soundly beaten in seller on hurdling debut.
J. D. Frost

SHARP WORD (IRE) 8 br.g. Needle Gun (IRE) – Pas de Mot (Tender King) [2006/7 **h–**
20g^pu Apr 23] sixth in bumper for T. Tate: no show in novice hurdle nearly 4½ years later.
I. McMath

Anglo Irish Bank Novices' Hurdle (Dovecote), Kempton—
Shatabdi and Sam Waley-Cohen land a substandard renewal of this Grade 2

SHATABDI (IRE) 5 b. or br.m. Mtoto – Violet Express (FR) (Cadoudal (FR)) [2006/7 **h136**
17s 17v² 17s⁴ 17s² 16v* 16d^F 16v* 20g³ 16m Apr 21] small mare: first foal: dam fairly
useful hurdler/chaser up to 2½m: 1½m winner on Flat at 4 yrs: useful novice hurdler, left
J. Bertran de Balanda after fourth start: much improved after, won mares novice at
Kempton (by 29 lengths) and Grade 2 Anglo Irish Bank Novices' Hurdle (Dovecote) at
Kempton (beat Mendo easily by 9 lengths) in February: good third of 20 finishers to Two
Miles West in listed handicap at Aintree, left in front last: stays 2½m: acts on heavy going.
N. J. Henderson

SHAYDREAMBELIEVER 4 ch.g. Daggers Drawn (USA) – Aunt Sadie (Pursuit of **h92**
Love) [2006/7 17s* 17d³ Nov 7] half-brother to Irish bumper winner Chairmanforlife (by
Bob Back): fair on Flat (likely to prove best around 1m/1¼m): won juvenile hurdle at
Sedgefield in October by 3½ lengths from El Dee: below that form there 2 weeks later:
likely to prove best around 2m. *R. A. Fahey*

SHAYS LANE (IRE) 13 b.g. The Bart (USA) – Continuity Lass (Continuation) **c– §**
[2006/7 c–§, h–: c20g⁵ 20m Jun 3] rangy gelding: maiden hurdler/winning chaser: third **h–**
in point in March: often blinkered: ungenuine. *Ferdy Murphy*

SHAZAND (FR) 4 b.c. Daylami (IRE) – Shawara (IRE) (Barathea (IRE)) [2006/7 16v² **h109**
16v⁶ 16v⁶ 16d Mar 13] tall ex-French colt: useful up to 15f on Flat, successful in July,
sold out of A. de Royer Dupre's stable €130,000 Goffs Arc Sale: fair form in juvenile
hurdles: soon eased after mistake 2 out in listed 4-y-o handicap at Cheltenham final
outing: raced at 2m on going softer than good: reportedly lost shoe second start.
E. J. O'Grady, Ireland

SHEER GUTS (IRE) 8 b.g. Hamas (IRE) – Balakera (FR) (Lashkari) [2006/7 c–, **c86 §**
h91§: 20s⁶ c17d⁴ c16d^ur 19g 16v 16s^pu Feb 3] leggy gelding: winning hurdler, no show in **h– §**
2006/7: form over fences only on second start: stays 21f: acts on heavy and good to firm
going: usually in headgear/tongue tied: ungenuine. *Robert Gray*

SHEIKHMAN (IRE) 6 b.g. Sadler's Wells (USA) – Maria Isabella (USA) (Kris) **F94**
[2006/7 F16m² F16m⁶ F16g⁶ Mar 29] 12,000 3-y-o: first foal: dam, 1m winner who
stayed 1¼m, half-sister to Bosra Sham, Hector Protector and Shanghai: fair form in
bumpers, left Eoin Griffin prior to final start. *S. Kirk*

SHEKEL (IRE) 5 b.g. Shernazar – Last Hand (IRE) (Hollow Hand) [2006/7 F–: F16m(ur) Nov 9] looked quirky both starts in bumpers, hung badly left and rider unseated after saddle slipped second one. *Miss H. C. Knight* **F93 §**

SHELOMOH (IRE) 6 b.g. Zaffaran (USA) – Parson's Run (The Parson) [2006/7 F102: 16s(4) 19d 19v(3) 22g Apr 2] good-topped gelding: third in bumper on debut: easily best effort over hurdles (modest form) in novice at Catterick third outing: bred to stay well: acts on heavy ground. *D. M. Forster* **h90**

SHEM DYLAN (NZ) 8 ch.g. Stark South (USA) – Khozaderry (NZ) (Khozaam (USA)) [2006/7 h–: 17d(ur) Feb 19] strong gelding: no form over hurdles, off 15 months and left R. C. Guest before only start in 2006/7. *Miss Venetia Williams* **h–**

SHERAKING 6 b.g. Wizard King – Sheraton Girl (Mon Tresor) [2006/7 F16d F16v 20v(pu) Dec 15] lengthy, good-topped gelding: third foal: dam 7f winner: no form in bumpers/maiden hurdle. *M. Mullineaux* **h–** **F–**

SHER BEAU (IRE) 8 b.g. Beau Sher – Welsh Ana (IRE) (Welsh Term) [2006/7 c130, h–: c20v(3) c20v(3) c24v(bd) c20v(6) c25g(6) Apr 25] well-made gelding: winning hurdler: useful chaser: good third first 2 starts, beaten 3½ lengths by Sir Oj in Grade 2 at Clonmel and 11½ lengths by In Compliance in Grade 1 at Punchestown: let down by jumping next 2 outings: stays 3m: raced on good going or softer (acts on heavy). *Philip Fenton, Ireland* **c139 x** **h–**

SHERFIELD DON 6 b.g. Overbury (IRE) – Mindyerownbusiness (IRE (Roselier (FR)) [2006/7 F16d F17s Jan 30] £800 5-y-o: third foal: dam winning pointer: well beaten in bumpers: tried tongue tied. *Mrs H. R. J. Nelmes* **F–**

SHERGAEL (IRE) 6 b.g. Barathea (IRE) – Shergress (Siberian Express (USA)) [2006/7 h?: 17v(pu) 16v(pu) Feb 18] leggy gelding: maiden on Flat: no form over hurdles: sold £900 Ascot February Sales. *E. Haddock* **h–**

SHERGILL (IRE) 6 b. or br.g. Weld – Gaelic Holly (IRE) (Scenic) [2006/7 20g Apr 27] €7,000 4-y-o: first foal: dam unraced: not fluent when well held in novice hurdle on debut. *M. Appleby* **h–**

SHERIFF ROSCOE 7 b.g. Roscoe Blake – Silva Linda (Precipice Wood) [2006/7 h100: 22s(5) 20s(2) 22g 19m* 22m(2) Apr 26] stocky gelding: fair hurdler: readily won handicap at Exeter in April: stays 2¾m: acts on soft and good to firm going. *P. Winkworth* **h111**

SHERIFF'S DEPUTY 7 b.g. Atraf – Forest Fantasy (Rambo Dancer (CAN)) [2006/7 16d 16d(6) Dec 6] brother to fair hurdler/fairly useful chaser Goblin, stays 2¾m: fair on Flat (stays 10.5f), below form since 2005: well beaten over hurdles, including in seller: tried tongue tied. *C. N. Kellett* **h–**

SHERKIN ISLAND (IRE) 9 b.g. Shernazar – Tullerolli (IRE) (Barbarolli (USA)) [2006/7 c–, h94: 17s(5) c20v(6) c20v c18d(F) c16g(4) Apr 4] tall, useful-looking gelding: modest handicap chaser/hurdler, left Jonjo O'Neill after first outing: effective at 2m to 3m: raced on good going or softer (acts on heavy). *N. Madden, Ireland* **c95** **h–**

SHERMAN BAY 7 b.g. Alderbrook – Romantic Melody (Battle Hymn) [2006/7 F–: F17g Oct 15] no promise in bumpers 10 months apart. *G. F. Bridgwater* **F–**

SHERMAN'S NEESE (IRE) 6 br.m. Presenting – Pallastown Gale (IRE) (Strong Gale) [2006/7 F16m Jan 29] €7,000 4-y-o: fifth foal: half-sister to 2½m hurdle winner Terrappio (by Supreme Leader): dam, placed once over hurdles, out of half-sister to smart staying chaser Captain Dibble: green, soundly beaten in bumper on debut. *M. Keighley* **F–**

SHERNATRA (IRE) 8 b.g. Shernazar – Miss Nancy (Giolla Mear) [2006/7 h–: 21d(4) 16d(pu) 24s(5) 21s(pu) 19s(3) Mar 12] workmanlike gelding: modest hurdler on his day: stays 21f: raced mainly on going softer than good: tongue tied in 2006/7: has shaped as if amiss more than once. *J. A. B. Old* **h93**

SHERWOOD ROSE (IRE) 11 gr.m. Mandalus – Cronlier (Roselier (FR)) [2006/7 c96x, h–: c33g(pu) May 3] sturdy mare: maiden hurdler/chaser: winning pointer: stays 25f: tried in cheekpieces: sketchy jumper. *Mrs N. Field* **c– x** **h–**

SHERWOODS FOLLY 5 b.g. Classic Cliche (IRE) – Action de Balle (FR) (Cricket Ball (USA)) [2006/7 F90: 19s(2) 19s(2) 20s* 20s Mar 10] good-topped gelding: bumper winner: fair form over hurdles: won novice at Leicester in January by neck from Skippers Brig: will stay beyond 2½m: acts on soft/heavy going. *H. D. Daly* **h112**

SHE'S A GOER 7 b.m. Bluegrass Prince (IRE) – Bold Start Lady (Nicholas Bill) [2006/7 F16s(5) F16m F16m(6) F16s 24d(pu) 19g 21s(bd) 21v(pu) Nov 25] second foal: dam no sign of ability: mid-field at best in bumpers: no form over hurdles. *P. A. Pritchard* **h–** **F68**

SHE'S A PLAYER 6 b.m. Bandmaster (USA) – Fair Anne (All Fair) [2006/7 F17g³ **F88**
F16g³ F17s² F16vᵖᵘ Feb 18] second foal: dam unraced: fair form in bumpers: dead.
R. J. Hodges

SHE'S A RAINBOW (IRE) 7 b.m. Glacial Storm (USA) – Roselle (Derring Rose) **h–**
[2006/7 16g 22gᵖᵘ Apr 15] half-sister to 25f chase winner More Rush (by Lancastrian)
and bumper/2½m hurdle winner Torose (by Torus): dam ran 3 times: no show in novice
hurdles. *S. J. Marshall*

SHE'S BEAUTIFUL (IRE) 4 b.f. Darnay – Anck Su Namun (IRE) (Supreme **F71**
Leader) [2006/7 F16s⁶ F16m⁵ Mar 31] €9,000 3-y-o: first foal: dam unraced sister to fair
hurdler/fairly useful chaser Mullacash, stays 29f: poor form on second of 2 outings in
bumpers. *Jonjo O'Neill*

SHE'S HUMBLE (IRE) 5 ch.m. Humbel (USA) – She's No Tourist (IRE) (Double- **h–**
tour (USA)) [2006/7 F98: 16sᵖᵘ 18s⁴ 16g 18s⁶ Feb 4] tall mare: bumper winner: no form
over hurdles, left P. D. Evans after first outing. *Mrs L. C. Jewell*

SHE'S OUR DAISY (IRE) 7 b.m. Supreme Leader – Tell A Tale (Le Bavard (FR)) **h105**
[2006/7 h–, F–: 16f* 16g⁴ 17d* 17s⁶ 16d 16f 18m Apr 25] tall mare: fair hurdler: much
improved in 2006/7, won novices at Wincanton (handicap) and Taunton in October: best
efforts around 2m: acts on firm and good to soft going (bumper winner on soft): often
tongue tied: free-going front runner. *R. H. Buckler*

SHE'S OUR NATIVE (IRE) 9 b.m. Be My Native (USA) – More Dash (IRE) **c106**
(Strong Gale) [2006/7 c94+, h121: 22m⁵ c20d* c24d² 21s c19s Jan 30] small, lengthy **h116**
mare: fairly useful hurdler: fair handicap chaser: jumped more fluently than usual when
winning at Ludlow in November: bled final start: possibly best short of 2¾m when conditions are testing: acts on heavy going, probably on good to firm: tried visored/blinkered.
Evan Williams

SHE'S SUPERSONIC (IRE) 7 ch.m. Accordion – Clasical Influence (Monksfield) **h112**
[2006/7 16g 16v* 17s³ 16v 16v 19m⁶ Apr 8] half-sister to useful hurdler/chaser To Your
Honour (by Buckskin), stayed 21f: bumper winner: fair on Flat (stays 2m), successful
twice in 2006: fair handicap hurdler: won at Clonmel in November: best effort when 8
lengths third to Border Castle at Cheltenham: should stay beyond 2m: acts on heavy
ground: tried tongue tied. *A. J. Martin, Ireland*

SHE'S THE LADY 7 b.m. Unfuwain (USA) – City of Angels (Woodman (USA)) **h– p**
[2006/7 F92: 16d Mar 26] leggy mare: bumper winner: off a year and on toes, possibly
needed outing on hurdling debut. *R. S. Brookhouse*

SHETANGOSWELL (IRE) 5 b. or br.m. Clerkenwell (USA) – Two To Tango (IRE) **h–**
(Anshan) [2006/7 F16s 22mᵖᵘ Jan 24] second foal: dam, fair hurdler, stayed 3m: no **F–**
promise in bumper/novice hurdle. *Miss M. E. Rowland*

SHE WAS A BARGIN (IRE) 5 b.m. Foxhound (USA) – Viking Dream (IRE) (Vision **F–**
(USA)) [2006/7 F13m Mar 29] €1,000 4-y-o: third foal: dam, winning 2m hurdler,
half-sister to fairly useful 2m hurdler/chaser Feel The Pride: well held in maiden bumper
on debut. *Mrs N. S. Evans*

SHIFTY OVER 5 b.m. Overbury (IRE) – Shafayif (Ela-Mana-Mou) [2006/7 F17g **h–**
21sᶠ 16g Mar 21] fifth foal: half-sister to 2 winners by Ballet Royal, including fair **F–**
hurdler/chaser Rakassa, stayed 3m: dam winning/untrustworthy 2m selling hurdler: little
show in bumper/mares novice hurdles, left S. Curran before final start. *H. J. Manners*

SHINGLE STREET (IRE) 5 b.g. Bahhare (USA) – Sandystones (Selkirk (USA)) **h98 §**
[2006/7 h96d: 16f² 18g⁴ 16f⁴ 16d* 16s* 18dᵖᵘ 16v 17v⁶ 23sᵖᵘ 21m⁴ 22f* 27m Apr 26]
lengthy, good-bodied gelding: regressive maiden on Flat: modest hurdler: won 2 sellers
at Stratford in October (sold from I. Wood 5,200 gns first occasion) and 4-runner handicap at Wincanton in April: stays easy 2¾m: acts on soft and firm ground: effective with
or without blinkers/visor: often tongue tied: temperamental. *M. F. Harris*

SHINING JOY (IRE) 8 gr.g. Be Happy (NZ) – Sexton Gleam (Sexton Blake) [2006/7 **c–**
19mᵖᵘ 24m³ 24f² 24g² 24vᵖᵘ 23v c24sᵖᵘ Jan 24] lengthy, angular gelding: modest novice **h94**
hurdler: no show on chase debut: will stay beyond 3m: acts on firm going, seemingly
unsuited by soft/heavy. *M. Scudamore*

SHINJIRU (USA) 7 b.g. Broad Brush (USA) – Kalwada (USA) (Roberto (USA)) **c–**
[2006/7 h–, F70: 24d c16g⁶ Oct 30] sturdy gelding: poor form in bumpers: no form over **h–**
hurdles/in novice chase. *P. A. Blockley*

SHINKOSAN (IRE) 4 b.g. Shinko Forest (IRE) – Dashing Rocksville (Rock City) **F78**
[2006/7 F14g F14v F16s⁵ F16m⁶ Mar 25] 1,600 2-y-o: good-topped gelding: fourth foal:
dam 2-y-o 6f/7f winner: modest form in bumpers. *G. M. Moore*

SHIP'S HILL (IRE) 6 b.g. Oscar (IRE) – Ballykea (IRE) (Montelimar (USA)) **h117 p**
[2006/7 F98: F16d* 16v³ 16d* Jan 15] angular gelding: fairly useful form in bumpers, **F104**
won at Fakenham in October: confirmed promise of hurdling debut when easily winning
novice at Fakenham in January by 21 lengths from Noble Ben: will stay beyond 2m: open
to further improvement. *N. J. Henderson*

SHIRAZI 9 b.g. Mtoto – Al Shadeedah (USA) (Nureyev (USA)) [2006/7 h99: 20mᵖᵘ **h97**
18d⁴ 19dᵖᵘ 22s² 23v 24s³ 24g 24g Apr 21] sturdy gelding: modest handicap hurdler:
stays 3m: acts on soft and good to firm going: sometimes tongue tied: inconsistent.
D. R. Gandolfo

SHIRLEY CASPER (IRE) 6 b.m. Presenting – Glen Empress (IRE) (Lancastrian) **F114**
[2006/7 F16s* F16v* F16g⁴ F16m³ Apr 25] rather unfurnished mare: second foal: dam,
modest winning hurdler who stayed 2¾m, half-sister to useful staying chaser Bishops
Island: successful on completed start in mares maiden points in 2006: useful bumper
performer: won at Fairyhouse (easily) and Navan (all out to beat Mick The Man a short
head in Grade 2) in December: best effort when 3 lengths fourth to Cork All Star in
Champion Bumper at Cheltenham: will be suited by further than 2m. *Philip Fenton,
Ireland*

SHIWAWA 5 b.g. Halling (USA) – I Will Lead (USA) (Seattle Slew (USA)) [2006/7 **F106 p**
F16m* F16m* F16f* Sep 29] fifth foal: half-brother to useful 1¼m winner Stay Behind
(by Elmaamul) and 1½m winner Innovation (by Salse): dam unraced half-sister to Rainbow Quest: landed odds all 3 starts in bumpers, at Worcester in August and Stratford and
Hexham (useful form, stayed on strongly to beat Linagram by 6 lengths) in September:
capable of better still. *G. A. Swinbank*

SHOBROOKE MILL 14 ch.g. Shaab – Jubilee Leigh (Hubble Bubble) [2006/7 c82x: **c82 x**
c19m⁵ May 9] winning pointer: maiden hunter chaser: stays 3¼m: acts on good to firm
going: often let down by jumping. *Mrs S. Prouse*

SHOOT OUT 4 b.g. Killer Instinct – Icy (Mind Games) [2006/7 F16m Feb 4] first **F–**
foal: dam poor sprint maiden: well held after taking keen hold in bumper on debut.
C. W. Thornton

SHOOTTHEMESSENGER 7 b.g. Needle Gun (IRE) – More Chat (Torenaga) **F86**
[2006/7 F16g³ F16s F16d⁴ F16g Dec 10] half-brother to fair 2½m hurdler Atitandall (by
Warcraft) and fair staying chasers Chatterbuck and Party Animal (both by Buckskin):
dam placed in bumper: fair form in bumpers. *T. Hogan, Ireland*

SHOREACRES (IRE) 4 b.g. Turtle Island (IRE) – Call Me Dara (IRE) (Arapahos **F89**
(FR)) [2006/7 F12g Mar 23] €40,000 3-y-o: angular gelding: first foal: dam, fairly useful
chaser, stayed 3m: 11¾ lengths seventh of 18 to Whiteoak in 4-y-o bumper at Newbury
on debut. *B. G. Powell*

SHORTBREAD 5 ch.g. Selkirk (USA) – Breadcrumb (Final Straw) [2006/7 20g Dec **h–**
10] maiden on Flat, sold out of M. Salaman's stable £2,600 Ascot August Sales: tongue
tied, tailed off in maiden on hurdling debut. *D. W. Thompson*

SHORTGATE LANE (IRE) 6 b.g. Needle Gun (IRE) – Two-Penny Rice (Reformed **F–**
Character) [2006/7 F17g Jul 23] ninth foal: half-brother to winning hurdler/chaser Copper Coin (by Mandalus), stays 3m: dam maiden half-sister to smart 2m hurdler Carobee:
soundly beaten in maiden bumper on debut. *Jim Best*

SHOUDAWOUDACOUDA (IRE) 6 b. or br.g. Oscar (IRE) – Madame Champvert **h93**
(IRE) (Cardinal Flower) [2006/7 F16v 20v 20v³ 18g³ 21f Apr 5] smallish, sturdy gelding: **F–**
sixth foal: dam ran once: runner-up in bumper: modest form over hurdles, left T. Horgan
after second outing: stays 2½m: acts on heavy ground: has worn cheekpieces. *P. Bowen*

SHOULDHAVEHADTHAT (IRE) 5 b.g. Definite Article – Keep The Pace (IRE) **h120 p**
(Shardari) [2006/7 F100: F16s² F16d³ 17s⁴ 19g* Mar 30] leggy, useful-looking gelding: **F98**
placed in bumpers: fairly useful form over hurdles: favourite, won maiden at Ascot in
March by 5 lengths from Scotland Yard: stays 19f: raced on good ground or softer:
remains open to improvement. *N. J. Henderson*

SHOULTON (IRE) 10 br.g. Aristocracy – Jay Joy (Double-U-Jay) [2006/7 c69, h–: **c–**
c24sᵖᵘ c24sᵖᵘ c24sᵖᵘ Jan 24] workmanlike gelding: maiden chaser, little form since **h–**
2003/4: tried in cheekpieces. *G. H. Yardley*

SHOURNAGH VALLEY (IRE) 7 b.g. Boyne Valley – Aingeal (Fordham (USA)) **h–**
[2006/7 22vᵖᵘ 16v 17s Feb 8] winning pointer: little impact over hurdles: tried blinkered.
Ruaidhri Tierney, Ireland

SHOW ME THE RIVER 8 b.g. Flemensfirth (USA) – Quare Dream's (IRE) (Strong **c112**
Gale) [2006/7 c110, h83: c16g³ 16s² c20dᵖᵘ c16vᵖᵘ c20mᵖᵘ Apr 15] useful-looking **h–**
gelding: maiden hurdler: fair handicap chaser: shaped as if amiss last 3 outings (bled on
first one): stays 21f: raced mainly on good going or softer (acts on heavy). *Ferdy Murphy*

SHOW NO FEAR 6 b.g. Groom Dancer (USA) – La Piaf (FR) (Fabulous Dancer **c–**
(USA)) [2006/7 h–: 20m⁵ c20m 21m⁴ 16d 20d 20s 16s Jan 24] sturdy gelding: winning **h88 d**
hurdler, on downgrade: soundly beaten on chasing debut: probably stays 21f: acts on
good to soft going, probably on good to firm: tried visored/tongue tied. *G. M. Moore*

SHOW OF HANDS (IRE) 7 b.g. Zaffaran (USA) – New Technique (FR) (Formid- **h–**
able (USA)) [2006/7 F86: 17gᵖᵘ Nov 5] sturdy gelding: fair form in bumpers: off 17
months, no show in maiden on hurdling debut. *J. G. M. O'Shea*

SHOWTIME ANNIE 6 b.m. Wizard King – Rebel County (IRE) (Maelstrom Lake) **h74**
[2006/7 h83: 17d 20m⁵ Mar 25] sturdy mare: poor maiden hurdler: probably stays 2½m.
A. Bailey

SHOWTIME FAYE 5 b.m. Overbury (IRE) – Rebel County (IRE) (Maelstrom Lake) **h–**
[2006/7 h–: 17g 20gᵖᵘ May 5] no form over hurdles: tried in cheekpieces/blinkers.
A. Bailey

SHRADEN EDITION 10 b.g. Tina's Pet – Star Edition (Leading Man) [2006/7 c33g⁵ **c90**
c20d² c24s⁴ Feb 22] rangy gelding: winning pointer: fair maiden hunter chaser: stays 3m:
raced on good going or softer. *P. A. Jones*

SHREWD INVESTOR (IRE) 7 ch.g. Mister Lord (USA) – Mens Business (IRE) **h116**
(Buckskin (FR)) [2006/7 20v⁵ 24s* 20v⁴ 20v⁶ 25g* Mar 17] angular gelding: first foal:
dam unraced, out of half-sister to top-class 2m/2½m hurdler Large Action: won maiden
Irish point in 2006: fairly useful novice hurdler: won at Bangor (maiden) in December
and Wetherby in January and March (further improvement to beat Major Oak by 5
lengths, making all): stays 25f: acts on heavy going: races prominently. *H. P. Hogarth*

SHROPSHIRE GIRL 6 b.m. Cloudings (IRE) – Rosie O'Keeffe (IRE) (Royal Foun- **F81**
tain) [2006/7 F17d² F17m F17d⁴ Oct 7] half-sister to modest chaser General O'Keeffe
(by Alflora), stays 27f, and a winning pointer by Bob Back: dam unraced half-sister to
useful chaser up to 3m Highfrith: ran out in point in 2006: modest form in bumpers.
Heather Dalton

SHROPSHIRELASS 4 b.f. Beat All (USA) – Emma-Lyne (Emarati (USA)) [2006/7 **h87**
17s 19vᵖᵘ 16v 21g⁵ 16f* Apr 5] angular filly: modest maiden up to 1¼m on Flat:
improved effort over hurdles when winning seller at Ludlow in April: likely to prove best
at 2m: acts on firm ground: in cheekpieces last 2 starts. *Mrs Norma Pook*

SHUIL ARIS (IRE) 6 br.m. Anshan – Shuil Sionnach (IRE) (Mandalus) [2006/7 F109: **h124**
20s³ 16v⁴ 20m² 18m² Apr 25] tall mare: chasing type: bumper winner: fairly useful form
over hurdles when second to Grangeclare Lark in Grade 3 mares races at Fairyhouse
(novice) and Punchestown, beaten short head and 2½ lengths respectively: should stay
beyond 2½m: acts on good to firm going: sure to win races over jumps. *Paul Nolan,
Ireland*

SHULMIN 7 ch.m. Minster Son – Shultan (IRE) (Rymer) [2006/7 h–: 17f⁴ 21m⁵ c27d* **c65**
24g 24vᵖᵘ c27s⁵ Dec 26] sparely-made mare: no form over hurdles: won selling handicap **h–**
at Sedgefield in October on chasing debut: stays 27f: acts on good to soft ground. *J. Wade*

SIBERION (GER) 6 ro.g. Acambaro (GER) – Siberian's Image (Siberian Express **c133**
(USA)) [2006/7 17g⁵ 20g 20d² 20g² 18g* 20g² c20sᶠ c17v* c20vᵘʳ c17v⁵ c17m* c16m⁴ **h?**
Apr 26] smallish, angular gelding: half-brother to winning hurdler/chaser Siberius (by
Lomitas): successful 4 times over hurdles in Germany/Italy, including at Milan in
October: useful novice chaser: won at Plumpton in December and, having left C. von der
Recke, Fairyhouse (coasting home by 14 lengths from Django) in April: creditable fourth
to Another Promise in Grade 1 at Punchestown: best around 2m: acts on heavy and good
to firm going. *A. J. Martin, Ireland*

SIDNEY CHARLES (IRE) 5 br.g. Mister Baileys – Distant Music (Darshaan) **h77**
[2006/7 17v 16s 16d Mar 21] good-topped gelding: half-brother to poor hurdler Spectacular Hope (by Marju), stayed 19f: well beaten on Flat and in maiden hurdles. *J. A. B. Old*

SIEGFRIEDS NIGHT (IRE) 6 ch.g. Night Shift (USA) – Shelbiana (USA) (Chief- **c98 x**
tain) [2006/7 h103: 21f³ 22s⁵ 19d⁴ 24m* c20mᵖᵘ c20m² c20gᵖᵘ c24g³ c21mᵖᵘ Aug 26] **h117 ?**

smallish, plain gelding: fairly useful handicap hurdler: seemed to improve when winning at Southwell (beat Burren Moonshine 2½ lengths) in June: didn't take to chasing, making mistakes in general and looking reluctant final start: stays 3m: acts on soft and good to firm going: tongue tied. *M. C. Chapman*

SIGNATURE TUNE (IRE) 8 b.g. Gothland (FR) – Divine Affair (IRE) (The Parson) [2006/7 h94: 16g^pu 17s^4 19v^4 c16d^5 c22s^pu c20v^3 Mar 12] leggy gelding: modest handicap hurdler: similar form in handicap on chasing debut: jumped slowly in similar events next 2 outings: should stay beyond 17f: raced on good going or softer (acts on heavy): has bled from nose. *P. Winkworth*   **c84 h85**

SIGNOR ALBERTINI (IRE) 4 b.g. Bertolini (USA) – Snow Eagle (IRE) (Polar Falcon (USA)) [2006/7 16m Jul 16] little sign of ability on Flat/in juvenile hurdle. *P. C. Haslam*   **h–**

SIGNS OF LOVE (FR) 4 b.g. Poliglote – Severina (Darshaan) [2006/7 16v^3 16v^2 16s* Mar 2] useful-looking gelding: runner-up over 1¼m on last of 3 starts on Flat in French Provinces at 3 yrs for J-C. Rouget: fairly useful form in juvenile hurdles: won at Newbury in March by 8 lengths from Mon Michel: likely to be suited by further than 2m: raced on soft/heavy going. *Noel T. Chance*   **h111**

SILBERHORN EXPRESS 4 gr.g. Silver Patriarch (IRE) – Lotschberg Express (Rymer) [2006/7 F12v F16s^5 Mar 8] smallish, angular gelding: third foal: dam, fair hurdler, stayed 2¾m: better effort in bumpers (backward on debut) when fifth to Gansey in maiden at Wincanton: likely to be suited by further still. *D. R. Gandolfo*   **F80**

SILBER MOND 5 gr.g. Monsun (GER) – Salinova (FR) (Linamix (FR)) [2006/7 h86: 22m^5 May 28] best effort over hurdles (modest form) on only outing away from good to firm/firm going: will stay 3m. *Miss S. West*   **h79**

SILENCIO (IRE) 6 b.g. Sillery (USA) – Flabbergasted (IRE) (Sadler's Wells (USA)) [2006/7 h126: 17s 20g* 21g^3 Apr 18] sturdy gelding: fairly useful handicap hurdler: off 3 months, won at Chepstow in March by 2½ lengths from Purple Patch: good third to French Saulaie at Cheltenham: stays 21f: raced on good going or softer (acts on soft): has raced lazily. *A. King*   **h129**

SILENT AGE (IRE) 6 b.g. Danehill (USA) – Set Fair (USA) (Alleged (USA)) [2006/7 F81: F16g Jun 8] medium-sized gelding: modest form in bumpers: tried tongue tied: sold 500 gns Doncaster August Sales. *S. Gollings*   **F–**

SILENT BAY 8 b.g. Karinga Bay – Lady Rosanna (Kind of Hush) [2006/7 h96, h87: 24m* 22g c25s^5 Jan 1] rangy gelding: modest novice hurdler: won at Hexham in May: off 6 months, well held next 2 starts, including on chasing debut: should stay beyond 3m: acts on soft and good to firm ground. *J. Wade*   **c– h89**

SILENT CITY 7 ch.m. Karinga Bay – Gordons Girl (IRE) (Deep Run) [2006/7 F–: 22g 26d^pu May 17] lengthy mare: little sign of ability. *P. D. Williams*   **h–**

SILENT DREAM 9 b.g. Alflora (IRE) – Silent Surrender (Nearly A Hand) [2006/7 h90: 20m^3 22g^pu Sep 3] workmanlike gelding: modest form over hurdles, very lightly raced: should stay 3m. *Simon Earle*   **h92**

SILENT GUNNER 9 ch.g. Gunner B – Quiet Dawn (Lighter) [2006/7 c19v^F c26v^pu Feb 23] workmanlike gelding: modest form at best over fences: off 20 months, failed to complete in 2006/7 (bled final start): stays 3m: raced on going softer than good. *Andrew Turnell*   **c– h–**

SILENT OSCAR (IRE) 8 b.g. Oscar (IRE) – Silent Shot (Random Shot) [2006/7 h110p, F107: 16s^4 20s^4 18s^4 16v^3 16d 16m 16m* Apr 27]   **h157**
         There is no such thing in racing as a fluke—at least so far as students of form are concerned—there are just results that require interpretation. However, some require more interpretation than others. The Punchestown Festival, coming as it does at the very end of a long, and, for some, hard season, is more prone to such occurrences than most, but the latest Festival seemed to have more than its fair share. It wasn't so much that the results stretched the most sophisticated of form interpreters, more that nearly all the championship races fell short of the level expected, with at least one major contender in each running a long way below expectations. Ebaziyan, Newmill, Snowy Morning, Brave Inca and Iktitaf were among those whose running was too bad to be true, Cork All Star and In Compliance were favourites who failed to come up to scratch. Mansony, Neptune Collonges and Refinement were all successful at Grade 1 level, something of a

ACCBank Champion Hurdle, Punchestown—
outsider Silent Oscar upsets previous winner Macs Joy (noseband) and Hardy Eustace (out of shot)

surprise in each case given they appeared exposed as some way below top class. And then there was Silent Oscar.

Up against dual Champion Hurdle winner Hardy Eustace, Champion Hurdle runners-up Harchibald and Macs Joy, and Grade 1 Morgiana Hurdle winner Iktitaf, Silent Oscar started at 20/1 for the ACCBank Champion Hurdle, the subject of a gamble derived seemingly less by study of form than a visit to fabled astrologer Madam Osiris Gnomeclencher—'your lucky flower is cauli, as is your lucky dog'—and he was backed down from more than twice those odds. There was hardly anything in Silent Oscar's last five starts over hurdles prior to Punchestown that suggested he was remotely good enough to beat the four market leaders if they were anywhere near their best. He had started the same odds when fourth, receiving 8 lb, to the unreliable Rosaker in the Lismullen Hurdle; disappointed when joint-favourite for a six-runner minor event at Fairyhouse; had been sent off at 100/1 when third of four behind Brave Inca and Iktitaf in the December Festival Hurdle (beaten seven and a quarter lengths in a steadily-run contest); and hadn't made the first nine when racing off marks of 128 and 130 respectively in the Pierse (33/1) and Menolly Homes (25/1), two of Ireland's most competitive handicap hurdles. Silent Oscar had been useful in bumpers but had won just twice from ten starts over hurdles, a maiden at Clonmel (odds on) in 2005/6 and a minor event at Punchestown early in the latest season when still trained by Christy Donoghue. On balance, Silent Oscar looked no more than a fairly useful hurdler.

Silent Oscar had, it is true, beaten Macs Joy at level weights in a minor event over two miles on good to firm going on the Flat at the Curragh earlier in April but he was given an excellent ride that day, whereas the runner-up, regarded as using the race as a tuning-up exercise after missing Cheltenham, was left with plenty to do. Macs Joy was widely expected to reverse placings and started favourite at Punchestown to repeat his 2006 win in the race. The 2004 winner Hardy Eustace set the pace before Silent Oscar took over after halfway, gradually increasing the tempo up the hill but soon pressed by Macs Joy as Hardy Eustace was outpaced. There was nothing between Silent Oscar and Macs Joy as they came into the straight but, in a prolonged battle, Silent Oscar showed plenty of resolution and won by a neck with Hardy Eustace eight lengths back in third. On the face of it, Silent Oscar had shown much improved form but the presence in fourth of 66/1-shot Callow Lake suggests that Macs Joy and Hardy Eustace were both below form, as were Harchibald and Iktitaf who were well beaten in fifth and sixth places respectively. The time of the race compared poorly to the other two-mile hurdle on the card and how reliable the form turns out to be remains to be seen. Silent Oscar's success may well have owed much to the initiative of his rider Robbie Power who, ironically, rides regularly for Jessica Harrington, the trainer of both Macs Joy and Callow Lake. It was also a welcome big-race win for trainer Harry Rogers, who'd endured a miserable Flat campaign in 2006 which yielded just five wins from a string of sixty-six horses. Rogers, whose best moments as a journeyman jumps jockey had come through his association with 1986 Irish Champion Hurdle winner Herbert United, has actually enjoyed the bulk of his success on the Flat since taking out a training licence in the late-'nineties (Group 3-winning sprinter Moon Unit is his best performer). Indeed, Silent Oscar may well prove easier to place in that sphere than over hurdles given that he'll have to shoulder a Grade 1 penalty in lesser races in 2007/8. He was even considered a possible for the Gold Cup at Royal Ascot at one stage this summer.

Silent Oscar (IRE) (b.g. 1999)	Oscar (IRE) (b 1994)	Sadler's Wells (b 1981)	Northern Dancer Fairy Bridge
		Snow Day (b 1978)	Reliance II Vindaria
	Silent Shot (b or br 1982)	Random Shot (b 1967)	Pirate King Time And Chance
		Rosslea (br 1967)	Klairon Sayjune

Mr Patrick Convery's "Silent Oscar"

Silent Oscar, who is rather leggy in appearance, is the sixth foal out of the unraced Silent Shot and has more ability than her five other offspring to race put together. They have managed, all told, nineteen runs outside points and shown next to no ability. Ardlow and Rosey Buck, both by Buckskin, did manage to win a maiden point each, Ardlow on her only completed start in that sphere. Silent Shot herself is half-sister to a couple of above-average performers, Adanac, a temperamental winning hurdler/chaser who stayed three miles, and Reine Soleil, a useful five- to seven-furlong winner who was subsequently a very successful broodmare in Scandinavia. Silent Oscar has turned out something of a bargain at just the €13,500 he cost as a four-year-old store at the Goffs Land Rover Sale in 2004 (he had been led out unsold at barely half the price at Tattersalls (Ireland) August Sale the previous year). Silent Oscar didn't contest the 2004/5 Land Rover Bumper but won one of the bumpers at the Punchestown Festival that season. His trainer has described him as essentially a two-and-a-half-mile horse and Silent Oscar should certainly be at least as effective at that trip as at two miles. He acts on good to firm and heavy going. *Harry Rogers, Ireland*

SILENT SNIPE 14 ch.g. Jendali (USA) – Sasol (Bustino) [2006/7 c–, h–: c27m^{pu} Jun 7] leggy gelding: winning chaser: very lightly raced and no form since 2003/4: tried tongue tied. *Miss L. C. Siddall*   **c–** **h–**

SILISTRA 8 gr.g. Sadler's Wells (USA) – Dundel (IRE) (Machiavellian (USA)) [2006/7 h83§: 16d 16v 17v^6 16v^2 18v* 16g Mar 20] angular gelding: modest handicap hurdler: won conditional/amateur event at Fontwell in March, hanging right: stays 2½m: acts on heavy going: tried visored, usually in cheekpieces: has worn tongue strap: ungenuine. *Mrs L. C. Jewell*   **h86 §**

SILIVRI 5 gr.m. Silver Patriarch (IRE) – Riviere (Meadowbrook) [2006/7 F17d^5 F16v F17m^3 F17g 17d 20g Nov 10] good-bodied mare: first foal: dam bumper/3m hurdle winner: poor form in bumpers: well beaten over hurdles. *W. T. Reed*   **h–** **F67 ?**

SILK ROPE (IRE) 7 br.m. Presenting – Osiery Girl (IRE) (Phardante (FR)) [2006/7 F–: F17m^6 Jun 4] no form in maiden bumpers: tried tongue tied. *R. T. Phillips*   **F–**

SILK SCREEN (IRE) 7 b.g. Barathea (IRE) – Sun Screen (Caerleon (USA)) [2006/7 h122: 16g 16v^F 17s 16d 16m^{pu} Jan 29] good-topped gelding: fairly useful handicap hurdler at best: left W. Mullins, little impact in 2006/7: best form around 2m: acts on heavy going: sold £1,200 Ascot February Sales. *A. M. Hales*   **h103 d**

SILVER ACCORD (IRE) 4 b. or br.g. Accordion – Mazza (Mazilier (USA)) [2006/7 F16v^4 F17g^6 F16m^2 Apr 15] sturdy gelding: half-brother to 3 winners, including useful hurdler/chaser Claymore (by Broadsword), stayed 3m, and bumper/2m hurdle winner Poulakerry (by Shardari): dam, poor maiden on Flat, half-sister to top-class staying chaser Flashing Steel: fair form in maiden bumpers. *T. P. Tate*   **F92**

SILVER ADONIS (IRE) 6 gr.g. Portrait Gallery (IRE) – Fair Fontaine (IRE) (Lafontaine (USA)) [2006/7 F17m* F16g^2 F16g* 16g Sep 14] strong gelding: second foal: dam winning pointer: useful form in bumpers, won at Bellewstown (maiden, easily) in July and Roscommon in August: good second to Cork All Star at Galway in between: well beaten in novice on hurdling debut: should do better. *P. J. Rothwell, Ireland*   **h– p** **F106**

SILVER ALIDANTE 4 gr.f. Silver Patriarch (IRE) – Aubade (Henbit (USA)) [2006/7 F16g F17g Apr 23] 4,500 3-y-o: half-sister to 3 winners abroad: dam French 12.5f winner: well beaten in bumpers: tried tongue tied. *M. A. Barnes*   **F–**

SILVERBAR 5 gr.g. Silver Patriarch (IRE) – Ardenbar (Ardross) [2006/7 F17s 16v 21m 21s^4 Mar 2] strong gelding: chasing type: third foal: half-brother to 17f hurdle winner Muhtenbar (by Muhtarram): dam winning 21f chaser: well held in bumper: first form in novice hurdles when fourth of 7 to Money Order at Newbury: will stay 3m. *Miss H. C. Knight*   **h83** **F–**

SILVER BIRCH (IRE) 10 b.g. Clearly Bust – All Gone (Giolla Mear) [2006/7 c–, h106: c31s c24s^2 20v^4 c31d^2 c36g* Apr 14]   **c147** **h113**

Mention the Grand National and it is not long before the name of Foinavon comes up. Forty years have passed since that murky day when the blinkered 100/1-chance (444/1 on the Tote) won one of the most farcical runnings of the world's most famous race. That edition has become part of the rich folklore of the National and the commentary by the BBC's man at the twenty-third fence that day,

John Smith's Grand National Chase (Handicap), Aintree—
a delay to the start for the second year in succession as runners become caught in the tape

Michael O'Hehir, is one of the most oft-replayed sporting commentaries. 'They're turning now to the fence after Becher's and, as they do, the leader is Castle Falls with Rutherfords alongside . . . Rondetto has fallen, Princeful has fallen, Norther has fallen, Kirtle Lad has fallen and The Fossa has fallen . . . There's a right pile-up . . . Leedsy has climbed over the fence and left his jockey there . . . And now with all this mayhem Foinavon has gone off on his own . . . He's about fifty to one hundred yards in front of everything else.'

Amazingly, no horse or rider was seriously hurt in the incident after a loose horse, Popham Down, suddenly veered to the right, across the face of the fence, in front of the leaders. With horses falling, refusing, being baulked or simply being brought to a halt, and the ground strewn with fallen horses and jockeys, the scene was like a battlefield after a cavalry charge. Foinavon had been towards the rear but, steered to the wide outside, he managed to find a way through and scrambled over. 'At that stage, I had no idea whether anyone else had jumped the fence or not, and I was purely concerned about carrying on if I possibly could,' said Foinavon's jockey John Buckingham. The patiently-ridden favourite Honey End, whose jockey Josh Gifford went for the middle, eventually had to go back fifty yards to make a run before successfully negotiating the fence. Kirtle Lad, one of the first to get over at the second attempt, refused at the Canal Turn where Buckingham realised he was out on his own. 'I only had to give him one clip with my stick. That was after jumping the last where I thought Josh Gifford on Honey End and Terry Biddlecombe on Greek Scholar were getting a bit close,' said Buckingham.

Foinavon kept going to win by fifteen lengths and three lengths from Honey End and Red Alligator (who had taken several attempts to get over the twenty-third and went on to win the following year's race), with Greek Scholar fourth. Eighteen eventually completed but Foinavon was the only one to do so without stopping. He was one of four winners of the Grand National who have won the race in similar circumstances and been the only runners to get round without mishap. Glenside and Shaun Spadah did so on a sodden course in 1911 and 1921 respectively, as did another 100/1-shot Tipperary Tim in 1928 when at least half the runners were stopped at the first Canal Turn when one of the top weights Easter Hero fell back into the ditch that formed part of the fence at the time. But for the sure jumping of runner-up Smarty, Red Marauder would have been the only runner to complete without mishap in 2001.

The Grand National was Foinavon's sixteenth race of that campaign and he had failed to win beforehand, one of four placed efforts including a length-and-a-half second to Honey End (on similar terms to Aintree) at Devon & Exeter back in August. Foinavon had run twice in the fortnight before Aintree, coming last of six finishers, his rider breaking a leather, in the April Fools Handicap Chase at

Leicester the previous Saturday. Buckingham, who had ridden him once the previous season, became the sixth jockey to ride Foinavon in his Grand National-winning season after three others turned down the ride at Aintree. Buckingham, who said afterwards he would have ridden in the National for nothing, was unable to arrange any accommodation and slept the night on two armchairs pulled together at some digs near the racecourse he had used when a stable lad. Foinavon's trainer John Kempton was used to tilting at windmills and had partnered Foinavon in the King George VI Chase and the Cheltenham Gold Cup (500/1, tailed off last of seven finishers) earlier in the season.

Foinavon finished a remote fourth at Kempton in what turned out to be Arkle's final race (surprise winner Dormant, who caught the injured Arkle on the run-in, had been beaten a distance when runner-up to Arkle twelve months earlier). John Kempton, incidentally, could not have done the weight in the Natioinal and was not at Aintree, going instead to Worcester where he won the opening novice hurdle on another horse in his small Berkshire-based string, Three Dons, before watching the National on television. Foinavon's owner Cyril Watkins watched the race from home, the horse carrying his 'black with red and yellow braces' after Foinavon's other joint-owner had given him his share when unable to find anyone to buy it! Foinavon's change of colours, from the more familiar green silks of his previous joint-owner, were, incidentally, discovered by commentator Michael O'Hehir only as the jockeys were preparing to leave the weighing room. O'Hehir went over to Buckingham when he couldn't find the colours on the crayoned cards he had prepared. 'Without the chat, I'd have been completely lost when the drama unfolded. Wouldn't I have been in a mess?' he wrote later.

Foinavon's meeting with Arkle at Kempton was not his first acquaintances with that horse. The pair were former stable companions at Tom Dreaper's famous Greenogue stables near Dublin and shared the same owner in Anne, Duchess of Westminster, who named them after neighbouring mountains in the north-west corner of the Scottish Highlands. Foinavon (the Scottish mountain is actually spelt Foinaven) did manage three wins in the Arkle colours, including the Foxrock Cup at Leopardstown as a seven-year-old, a success that qualified him for the Grand National. In his earlier days, Foinavon accompanied the year-older Arkle twice to Cheltenham, finishing

The first—joint favourite Point Barrow crashes out

third in a novice hurdle when Arkle won at the 1962 Mackeson Gold Cup meeting and fifth in the Spa Hurdle (sent off second favourite) when Arkle won the Broadway Chase at the 1963 Festival. Pat Taaffe rode Foinavon on both of those occasions but, ironically, he cited a heavy fall at Baldoyle racecourse in 1965 (his final ride on the gelding) as an early insight into how Foinavon would cope with the unprecedented scenes of the 1967 National. 'We parted company in mid-air and, after I'd bounced, I looked round half expecting to see Foinavon in trouble. And there he was lying down—eating grass! Nothing ever worried him. Nothing ever scared him and I don't think I ever met a horse with less ambition,' Taaffe explained. Foinavon duly failed to win in eight races (placed once) in his first season trained in Britain—he'd been bought out of

Dreaper's stable for 2,000 guineas at the 1965 Doncaster October Sales—but he did go on to win again after the National, at Devon & Exeter and at Uttoxeter in the 1968/9 season (he had been brought down at the water when 66/1 to follow up in the 1968 National). The Consolation Handicap Chase at Uttoxeter on October 12th, 1968, bore some similarity to Foinavon's National triumph. After two of the six runners (including the short-priced favourite) had unseated their riders and another

First Canal Turn—2006 winner Numbersixvalverde (noseband) takes the fence safely as Knowhere (stars) and Kandjar d'Allier (grey) depart

had fallen, Foinavon came to the penultimate fence some way behind in third, only to be left clear to win unchallenged when the leader fell, carrying out the horse in second. Buckingham, who missed the ride in Foinavon's second National with a broken arm, won on him on both occasions he was successful in 1968/9 and was also in the plate when runner-up to old rival Honey End (and Gifford) at Plumpton in between those two wins. Buckingham was going well on another 100/1-shot Limeburner when falling two out (remounted) in the 1971 National won by Specify. His otherwise fairly modest career (he rode eighty-nine winners in total) in the saddle was ended by injury soon afterwards and he subsequently became a jockeys' valet. John Kempton, meanwhile, also handed in his training licence in the early-'seventies (his career total as a trainer was forty-six wins) due to his own retirement from the saddle.

The Grand National can make reputations, but it is certainly no respecter of them. Josh Gifford was on his way to a record-breaking championship season when suffering ill-fortune at Aintree on Honey End, who had changed hands on the morning of the race. Gifford missed out on National success in his career, as did other top-notch champions such as Stan Mellor, Terry Biddlecombe, Ron Barry, John Francome, Peter Scudamore and Jonjo O'Neill. The present champion Tony McCoy is still waiting for a Grand National win after twelve rides in the race, including on the consistent L'Ami and Clan Royal. L'Ami and Clan Royal, twice placed in the National, carried the colours of J. P. McManus, leading owner in both Britain and Ireland in the latest season but still looking for a Grand National winner (he won the Irish Grand National with Butler's Cabin in the latest season). Britain's champion trainer Paul Nicholls is another waiting for his day in the National. Since 1992, he has saddled thirty-seven runners and has had only one in the frame, the 2005 runner-up Royal Auclair. None of his ten runners in the last two Nationals has completed the course, including Royal Auclair, a first-fence faller in 2006 and a casualty at first Valentine's in the latest edition, the latter fall also ruining the chance of the stable's principal hope Eurotrek as he completely lost his place after being hampered badly.

The latest winner Silver Birch, who became the sixth Irish-trained horse successful in the National in the past nine years and the third in a row, had been with Nicholls until May when he was among a number from Manor Farm Stables sent to the sales to make way for the new intake of young horses. Silver Birch won a major Grand National, the Welsh version in 2004/5, when trained by Nicholls and had also shown an aptitude for the big, unusual fences on the National course when successful in that season's Becher Chase. Ante-post favourite for the 2005 National before injury intervened, Silver Birch was off the course for thirteen months,

The Chair—Ballycassidy (left) is in the van again, with another outsider Naunton Brook . . .

reportedly with a leg injury, before returning to action in the 2005/6 season with an encouraging fourth (a place behind fellow Aintree hopeful Clan Royal) in a handicap hurdle at Warwick. That season turned out to be a disappointing one, however, Silver Birch pulled up on two other starts before contesting the 2006 National in which he started at 40/1 and came down at the Chair—effectively bringing down another Nicholls-trained runner Heros Collonges! The decision to sell Silver Birch was taken on veterinary advice—the horse was diagnosed with a heart murmur—and he made 20,000 guineas at the Doncaster May Sales. It was always likely that Silver Birch would attract more interest from Ireland because winners of any steeplechase since June 2004, with a penalty value of £20,000 or more, were ineligible for British points in 2007. Silver Birch was bought by Brian Walsh, who had also paid a then world record for a jumps mare in training of £220,000 for Rhacophorus at the Cheltenham Sales a month before. Rhacophorus, who has so far failed to add to her Aintree mares bumper win in two outings in maiden hurdles, was sent to Paul Nolan in Ireland, while Silver Birch, bought as 'a fun horse for cross country races', was sent to a new young trainer Gordon Elliott, a former point-to-point rider who had ridden as an amateur in Britain when based with the Pipe stable and was running a yard largely for pointers. Like the owner, Elliott is in his twenties and was the youngest trainer with a runner in the latest Grand National. He had not trained a winner under Rules in his native country by the time of the National, though he had had three in Britain earlier in the season. Coincidentally, John Kempton (who was also in his late-twenties) ended his Grand National-winning season with a tally of just four wins.

Jason Maguire, offered the National ride on Silver Birch, chose to partner Idle Talk instead, the mount going to Robbie Power, a former European junior show jumping silver medallist before turning to race-riding. In common with John Buckingham and Foinavon, Power had ridden Silver Birch the once before, but he did have previous experience of the Grand National, having completed the course on Spot Thedifference (albeit a tailed-off eighteenth) two years earlier. His biggest wins before Silver Birch had come in 2003 when he won the Midlands

National at Uttoxeter on Intelligent and the Galway Plate on Nearly A Moose. Silver Birch was beaten in an open event at Westmeath point in November on his first outing after his change of stable, and having finished a close eighth in a cross-country race at Cheltenham the following month, Power rode him when second to Heads Onthe Ground over the banks at Punchestown in early-February, both those cross-country efforts giving an indication that Silver Birch might have retained most of his ability. Following that effort with a fair performance when fourth under a 7-lb claimer back over hurdles at the same course later in the month, Silver Birch then staked his claim as a plausible outsider for the National when a good second to Heads Onthe Ground (on terms 12 lb worse than at Punchestown) in the Cross Country Handicap Chase at the Cheltenham Festival.

The original owners of Silver Birch, Paul Barber and Des Nichols, are not alone in having sold a horse who went on to win the Grand National. The 1992 winner Party Politics was sold by his owner-breeder David Stoddart for a reported £80,000 shortly beforehand and carried the colours of Mrs Patricia Thompson whose family had purchased other experienced National candidates over the years in an attempt to win the race (some of whom ran in the colours of the Thompsons' Cheveley Park Stud). Three years earlier, Little Polveir won the National on his fourth appearance in the race. He had been in the lead and moving well when unseating his jockey five from home in the 1988 renewal. His owner Michael Shone sold him privately six weeks before the 1989 National, reportedly for £15,000, for the principal purpose of providing the new owner's son with a ride in the Grand Military Gold Cup at Sandown (in which he finished fourth before taking his chance at Aintree). Shone looked like getting another crack at the National in the latest season when his Nil Desperandum, who had finished sixth and fourth in the two previous editions, became one of the ante-post favourites after winning the Eider Chase at Newcastle. Sadly, Nil Desperandum had to be put down after shattering a pastern in the Midlands National at Uttoxeter, his last intended run before Aintree. Two other heavily-backed market leaders, the J. P. McManus-owned Far From Trouble and the David Pipe-trained French import Little Brick, failed to make it to Aintree either. Far From Trouble had to be put down following complications with a leg infection picked up after travelling over for the Chelten-

. . . but things aren't going so well for the fancied pair Billyvoddan (blinkers) and Joes Edge (checked sleeves); between them are the blundering Gallant Approach and Aintree veteran Clan Royal

*The nineteenth—Bewleys Berry leads over the big ditch
from Ballycassidy, Liberthine (No.29), Silver Birch (noseband), L'Ami (cheekpieces) and Sonevafushi*

ham Festival where Little Brick, backed to win £1m in the National before winning his first race in Britain at Wincanton, broke a shoulder in the William Hill Trophy.

After Nil Desperandum's death, Irish-trained Dun Doire, who won at Down Royal on the same day as the Midlands National, took over as Grand National favourite in most books, ahead of the last two National winners Numbersixvalverde and Hedgehunter. Still among the 'other prices on request' at this time was Silver Birch, whose trainer had two spells working for Dun Doire's trainer Tony Martin and, coincidentally, was renting his stables at Trim in County Meath from Barry Callaghan, who is the head of the syndicate that owns Dun Doire. Dun Doire drifted in the betting as the going dried out with Britain heading for its hottest April on record. Temperatures were consistently two or three degrees above average—often much more than that—and National day itself was like a day from high summer. The 2006 Irish National winner Point Barrow and the 2005 Scottish National winner Joes Edge vied for favouritism on the day, until a late plunge on the Cheltenham Gold Cup fourth Monkerhostin (from 20/1 in places) resulted in the trio starting 8/1 co-favourites. Top weight Hedgehunter, who had an interrupted preparation after jarring a knee, started at 9/1, having been in contention at the final fence in the last three Nationals (close third when falling in 2004 and runner-up in 2006). Next in the betting came the English Summer National winner McKelvey, who seemed likely to be suited by the drying conditions (the going had been on the firm side at Uttoxeter) and had run well over the National fences with a staying-on sixth behind Eurotrek (16/1 in the National) in the Becher Chase in November. Joes Edge, seventh in Numbersixvalverde's National, had finished eighth in the Becher, in which Dun Doire had fallen (when hampered) at the Chair.

Among others with form over the National fences were the Becher runner-up Bewleys Berry and the previous season's Topham winner Liberthine, ridden by her regular partner, amateur Sam Waley-Cohen, who applied for permission to ride under amended rules governing the minimum number of races an amateur must have won over jumps to take part in the National (effectively reduced from fifteen to ten, provided HRA dispensation is given). The veteran Clan Royal, with wins in the 2003 Topham and Becher Chases to go with his places in the National, was back again for a fourth tilt at the big race, while Ballycassidy, a faller when clear at second Valentine's the previous year, and Puntal, sixth to Numbersixvalverde, were, like Royal Auclair, running in their third National. Longshanks (another ride that Maguire turned down) had made the frame in the 2004 and 2005 renewals of the Topham—having missed the cut for the big race both times—and finally made the Grand National line-up after also losing out through injury in 2006 (he survived another injury scare with a stone bruise the week before the latest National). Among those having their first experience of the Grand National fences were the smart chasers Thisthatandtother, runner-up in the Ascot Chase, Billyvoddan, a close third in the Festival Trophy at Cheltenham, and the progressive Simon, winner of the Sky Bet Chase (formerly the Great Yorkshire) and Racing Post Chase on his last two outings. Simon ran in the colours of eighty-seven-year-old Mercy Rimell, widow of the late Fred Rimell, the only trainer with a record to match Ginger McCain's four National winners.

Not for the first time, the National start was an unsatisfactory scene. The stories about the anniversary of Foinavon's National failed to mention that that edition had begun rather ignominiously with the runners being despatched by flag after the starting gate failed. There was a false start—a 'breakaway' start as senior starter Peter Haynes preferred to call it—to the latest National, following the previous year when the field had had to be recalled when one of the runners got the tape in his mouth and the mechanism failed. The jockeys had been given the traditional weighing room briefing before the latest National about the dangers of a 'cavalry charge' to the first, but, as so often, over-eagerness got the better of some of them. There had been what looked like a breakdown of trust between the starter and the jockeys on the first two days of the Cheltenham Festival and some of the National jockeys seemed reluctant to follow instructions, especially after confusion about why the starter refused to let them go when the runners formed a reasonable line for the second attempt to get the field away. Unfortunately, the starter's assistants were still repairing the broken tape. With temperatures in the 'seventies, tempers became frayed and it took several more attempts before the starter—'I can't start you like that . . . Go back in line'—was finally happy. The field got away nearly ten minutes late. The stewards held an inquiry but decided to take no action, though the starter insisted afterwards that the blame lay with the jockeys. 'Basically the jockeys failed to obey instructions, there were several horses with their heads over the tape at the first attempt and the tape won't release properly if I haven't got clearance, so I didn't activate the button . . . before the second attempt, the runners were lovely and I instructed the riders to stop where they were, but what did they do? They kept coming forward until they got to the tape. I couldn't let them go because they would have run somebody over.' If Haynes had left it at that, the issue might have blown over but his additional remarks on the subject caused a stir on both sides of the Irish Sea, more of which can be found in the essay on Fair Along.

Irish-trained Cloudy Bays, one of those who had charged the tape initially, effectively lost all chance when left well behind once the race finally started and the general frustration felt by a section of the crowd was heightened when the main Irish hope Point Barrow departed at the first. The first fence has put paid to the chances of more National runners than any other on the first circuit in the last half century or so. A dozen went there in 1951, Nickel Coin's year, in which there was a shambolic start with some of the runners still milling around when the starter let them go, resulting in a scramble to the first as jockeys tried to make up lost ground.

Second Canal Turn—Denis O'Regan parts company with Ballycassidy as the leaders turn for Valentine's; 2005 winner Hedgehunter and McKelvey (right) are creeping into things

Second Valentine's—Silver Birch (noseband) chases Liberthine (No.29) and Slim Pickings as Simon (far side) crashes out

Ten went at the first in both 1952 and 1982, nine in 2002 and seven in both 1977 and 1995. Among other well-fancied National runners to come to grief at the first in the past forty years were Bassnet, second favourite in Foinavon's year, the favourite Gay Trip in 1971 when he was bidding for a second successive win, Aldaniti in 1982 when attempting to do the same (joint third favourite Three To One was also a first fence faller), Door Latch in 1986, the favourite Sacred Path in 1988, Double Thriller in 1999 and the Scottish National winner Paris Pike in 2002.

With Tikram also departing at the first, and Becher's claiming Livingstone-bramble, Jack High (who also failed to complete the first circuit the previous year), Le Duc and Zabenz (pulled up after a leather broke), thirty-four runners approached the smallest fence on the course which is now known as the 'Foinavon' fence. It has rarely had any influence on the National in the intervening years (though L'Escargot nearly unseated Tommy Carberry there on his way to victory in 1975) but it provided the second big shock of the latest National when Monkerhostin, already in rear, refused. Outsiders Kandjar d'Allier and Knowhere went at the Canal Turn, after which the leading group comprised Naunton Brook, Bewleys Berry, Ballycassidy, Longshanks, Liberthine, Royal Auclair, The Outlier, Soneva-fushi and Simon. Silver Birch had moved up by the time the field approached the main racecourse and was in third, behind Naunton Brook (who soon afterwards seemed to lose interest) and Ballycassidy, as twenty-nine survivors set out into the country for the second time. L'Ami, Hedgehunter and Slim Pickings had also made ground to be in touch with the leading group. With Billyvoddan pulled up before the nineteenth, struggling after being badly hampered at the Canal Turn, and Joes Edge pulled up reportedly lame before the twentieth (had been off the bridle a while), the race was already shaping up into a bad one for punters. Second Becher's claimed the leader Bewleys Berry, who was going with plenty of zest, and left Liberthine, Ballycassidy, L'Ami and Silver Birch leading the way. Ballycassidy lost his rider when baulked at the Canal Turn and Simon was going well up with the pace when falling at second Valentine's, having jumped soundly on the whole up to that point.

For the third year running, a sizeable group was still in fairly close touch crossing the Melling Road for the second time, with two fences left to jump on the main racecourse. Barely four lengths had covered the eleven still in with a chance in Hedgehunter's year, reminiscent of 1971 (Specify), 1978 (Lucius) and 1999 (Bobbyjo), and a group of six were clear at the second last in Numbersixvalverde's National. Ten were still in the hunt at the Melling Road in the latest National, Slim Pickings leading from Liberthine, Philson Run, Silver Birch, Thisthatandtother and McKelvey, with Hedgehunter and Longshanks a little further back, followed by L'Ami and Numbersixvalverde. By the second last, Silver Birch had moved into second behind Slim Pickings, with Liberthine, McKelvey and Philson Run next. Silver Birch was ridden to lead between the last two and went three lengths in front after Slim Pickings jumped the last stickily. Silver Birch had to be driven right out on the run-in, however, to hold off the strong-finishing McKelvey, who looked unlucky, coming from further back after being hampered at second Becher's and then checked by a loose horse (stable-companion Ballycassidy) crossing the Melling Road. McKelvey was still closing gradually on the winner as the line was reached, despite edging right from the elbow and subsequently found to have sustained a tendon injury.

Silver Birch held on by three quarters of a length, with the rallying Slim Pickings a length and a quarter behind McKelvey. The stewards found the Irish-based riders of Silver Birch and Slim Pickings guilty of breaching the guidelines on use of the whip. Power was suspended for four days for using his whip with excessive frequency and in the incorrect place, while Barry Geraghty on Slim Pickings was given three days for using the whip with excessive force. Both jockeys were able to defer their bans to ride at the Punchestown Festival, exploiting the loophole exempting cards with Grade 1 races. They fought out the finish to one such contest in the ACCBank Champion Hurdle, with Power (on Silent Oscar) again just getting the better of his higher-profile colleague (Geraghty rode Macs Joy). There was a gap of fifteen lengths in the National after Slim Pickings to fourth-placed Philson Run, who rose to the fences really well and was still travelling strongly crossing the Melling Road despite being hampered at second Becher's and again when Simon fell at Valentine's. Liberthine underlined how well she goes over the National course by finishing fifth, the highest placing by a mare since Dubacilla came fourth in 1995. In sixth, forty-three lengths behind the winner, was Numbersixvalverde, never really threatening off a BHB mark 11 lb higher than the previous year (Hedgehunter had been put up 12 lb the year after he won). The other finishers were Longshanks, Puntal, Hedgehunter, who tired as lack of peak fitness told after his interrupted preparation, L'Ami, Clan Royal, who was subsequently retired, and Gallant Approach. Twelve in all, the non-staying This-thatandtother pulled up before the last. Jason Maguire knew from an early stage he'd picked wrong from his choice of three mounts, Idle Talk uncharacteristically going with little zest in rear before unseating at the nineteenth.

The fourth last—Slim Pickings and Barry Geraghty lead the way,
chased by (from right to left) Silver Birch, Liberthine, Philson Run and the doubtful stayer Thisthatandtother

It was appropriate that a horse named Slim Pickings should be involved in the finish of the latest National. The starting prices of the first four—33/1, 12/1, 33/1 and 100/1—made the race a self-proclaimed 'bookies' benefit' for the off-course firms who estimate industry turnover for National day nowadays at £250m. 'Like Christmas came early,' said a spokesman for Hills. Had the BHB's senior handicapper Phil Smith not made the remarks about outsiders attributed to him (reproduced in the essay on Joes Edge), it might have been thought that there was little comfort for him in the Grand National result, given that none of the first five carried more than 10-8. Allowed discretion in framing the weights for jumping's most valuable race, Smith has—since 2001—treated the top weights *relatively* more favourably than they would have been away from Aintree. The original joint top weights in the latest edition, Exotic Dancer and Hedgehunter, for example, were leniently treated to the tune of 10 lb and 8 lb respectively, and others were let in lightly a little further down the weights. Mr Smith's controversial ambition that 'a horse with 11-0 or more' wins the National was presumably achieved with Hedge-hunter (11-1), the first to carry 11-0 or more to victory since Rhyme 'N' Reason in 1988. Horses have, however, consistently carried big weights into the frame in the National, most recently Suny Bay (runner-up under 12-0 in 1998), Whats Up Boys, Kingsmark, Monty's Pass, Royal Auclair (second under 11-10 to Hedgehunter) and Hedgehunter (second under 11-12 to Numbersixvalverde).

Frankly, it has always been hard to see any justification for treating the top-weighted horses leniently, the more so now it is having the effect of compressing the weights too much, with the bottom weights higher than the minimum permitted 10-0 in each of the last three years. The Grand National entries are also falling, down to 119 for the latest edition from 152 in 2005 as the perception becomes embedded that a horse needs to have a BHB assessment of over 130 to have a chance of running. The National is worth nearly £400,000 to the winner which should be incentive enough for connections of good horses, especially with the changes made to the National course since the late-'eighties, which have gradually made things easier for the likes of second-season chasers (such as McKelvey and Slim Pickings) and others with relatively limited experience. Hedgehunter won the National on his twelfth steeplechasing start and Numbersixvalverde on his

The last—a mistake by Slim Pickings hands the initiative to Silver Birch

The winning post—a brave rally by McKelvey (No.35) fails by three quarters of a length

eleventh. The National's safety record is also much better than it used to be, though there was an unfortunate casualty in the latest running when 100/1-shot Graphic Approach, who unseated his rider at second Becher's, then ran loose before collapsing with heat stress, crashing through the rails passing the elbow and colliding with three unsuspecting stewards. The horse was treated for the effects of the heat and concussion on the track, resulting in the following novice handicap chase being delayed for forty-five minutes (two runners were withdrawn after suffering adversely from the heat in the paddock) and the concluding bumper (due to be run on the hurdles course) eventually being cancelled in the interests of horse safety. The unseasonable heat was very much a factor in this series of incidents, which makes the delay to the Grand National start all the more unfortunate. Graphic Approach was successfully moved to the Royal Liverpool Veterinary College and hopes were high that he would make a full recovery. However, he developed pneumonia some time later and had to be humanely destroyed.

Calling off the bumper at the end of the Grand National card was one of the final acts at Aintree of managing director Charles Barnett who took up a new post at Ascot in May. Barnett's period at the helm was eventful—it included the void race of 1993 and the IRA bomb threat in 1997 that led to the high profile postponement and successful restaging of the race—but he certainly left Aintree in ruder health than he found it. He oversaw the £35m redevelopment that has taken place over the past two years, including two new grandstands and a new weighing room complex. The venue now fully matches the event, the only aim still unfulfilled being Barnett's desire to see the National prize fund reach £1m (it currently stands at £700,000), though that target is likely to be reached sooner rather than later. Barnett and the clerk of the course Andrew Tulloch have earned a justified reputation for producing 'the right ground' for the three-day National meeting (there are no plans to extend it to four days). The Aintree team produced splendid going with a carefully-planned watering programme that combatted a particularly dry spell for the time of year and contributed much to the spectacle of the three days. Barnett left Aintree with a call to 'protect and nurture the Grand National at all times . . . After all, the National was the reason why the racecourse was saved from closure. A total of 7.6m viewers tuned in to BBC TV's coverage of the latest National, the fall of 700,000 on the previous year widely predicted because of the warm weather. The audience share of 66.5% was, however, up from 64% and the Grand National re-run attracted 5.1m, nearly four times the audience that watched the Cheltenham Gold Cup live (1.3m). The National, incidentally, comfortably beat the FA Cup semi-final featuring Manchester United which followed on BBC TV afterwards (peak viewing figure 6.9m and audience share 43%). The BBC and

Aintree feel that the National would attract an even bigger audience if the current starting time of 4.15 was changed to 5.00—'a time that has become a key slot for live TV sport on a Saturday' according to the BBC. There was a change in pre-race coverage of the latest National when the traditional horse-by-horse view of the forty runners in the paddock was replaced with a more detailed look at a select number of runners. A BBC spokesperson said: 'There is never time to cover all of them properly.' The programme found time, however, to feature a 'People's Race' organised by the National sponsors John Smith's; a homegrown Liverpool poet; a style contest won by a David Beckham lookalike who went to school with Wayne Rooney's girlfriend; and the obligatory Sue Barker interview with now-retired Ginger McCain. And then there was the constant musical accompaniment, perhaps a precursor for the introduction of celebrity ice-dancing between races another year. Televised racing is a much different experience to the one in Foinavon's day!

Silver Birch (IRE) (b.g. 1997)	Clearly Bust (b 1980)	Busted (b 1963)	Crepello / Sans Le Sou
		Crystal Light (ch 1963)	Never Say Die / Chandelier
	All Gone (b 1981)	Giolla Mear (b 1965)	Hard Ridden / Iacobella
		Black Barret (b 1970)	Bargello / Black Grouse

Grand National horses come from a wide variety of backgrounds. The greatest Aintree horse of them all, Red Rum, was bred for the Flat and dead-heated

Mr Brian Walsh's "Silver Birch"

in a two-year-old seller over five furlongs at Aintree the day before Foinavon's National. Silver Birch is from a jumping background but his pedigree, dealt with fully in *Chasers & Hurdlers 2004/05*, is nothing to write home about and he went through the sale-ring for just IR 2,800 guineas as a yearling. His sire Clearly Bust, a son of Busted, was fairly useful at his best, successful three times at a mile and a half on the Flat and five times at around two miles over hurdles, but he was fortunate to get a chance at stud at all and was poorly patronised prior to his death in 1998. Silver Birch's dam All Gone ran three times in Irish bumpers without success and her only other winner is the Irish pointer Ride On Bye (by Kings Ride). Much the best horses produced by recent generations of the family before Silver Birch were Wither Or Which and Alexander Banquet, both winners of the Festival Bumper at Cheltenham, Alexander Banquet going on to make a name for himself over fences, winning the Hennessy Gold Cup at Leopardstown, though he failed to complete on both of his attempts in the Grand National. Silver Birch's grandam Black Barret was placed on the Flat and over hurdles and is the dam of three winners including a full sister to All Gone named Call Me Anna, a winning hurdler. Black Barret was a half-sister to the unraced Black-Crash, the dam of Wither Or Which and grandam of Alexander Banquet. Black-Crash also bred a fairly useful jumper in Total Confusion, who showed his form at up to three miles over hurdles and fences. Silver Birch's great grandam Black Grouse bred eight winners, most of them minor and the best of them probably the 1972 Tolworth Hurdle winner Black Plover. Silver Birch, a workmanlike gelding in appearance, stays four and a half miles well and is a sound jumper who put in an exhibition round in the National, a peck at Becher's second time around the only semblance of an error. Silver Birch will be considerably higher in the weights if he is returned to Aintree in 2008 but, if the ground turned out to be more testing, it would not adversely affect his chances as he has done most of his racing on going softer than good and goes well on heavy. Silver Birch has had his tongue tied down on five of his last six starts (he was reportedly due to undergo a breathing operation but he remained with Nicholls). Like Foinavon, he has been tried in blinkers, though that was on one of his rare spins over hurdles during his disappointing second half of 2005/6 and, overall, he's done little to suggest that headgear is required in his case. *G. Elliott, Ireland*

SILVER BOW 6 b.m. Silver Patriarch (IRE) – Isabeau (Law Society (USA)) [2006/7 **h86** h82, F83: 26g* 24g 20m² 26m³ 22g 22mᵖᵘ 25vᵖᵘ 26g 27g⁴ 22m⁴ Apr 28] close-coupled, good-topped mare: modest novice hurdler: won handicap at Huntingdon in May: stays 3¼m: best form on good/good to firm going. *J. M. Jefferson*

SILVERBURN (IRE) 6 b.g. Presenting – Polly Puttens (Pollerton) [2006/7 F98+: **h142** 20d² 16s* 16v* 21g⁴ 24g⁶ Apr 13]
   The careers of modest hurdler Miss Nosey Oats, ungenuine maiden chaser Rye Crossing and Ollar House, who was simply of no account, are reminders that being a full brother or a full sister to a good horse is no guarantee of being endowed with a similar level of ability. This trio are respectively the sister of Master Oats and the brothers of Cool Dawn and Looks Like Trouble, all of them winners of the Cheltenham Gold Cup. Best Mate's full brothers Cornish Rebel and Inca Trail have plenty of ability themselves but have proved nothing like so genuine or consistent as him. It might be tempting to believe that repeating the same mating between a given sire and dam will result in carbon copies but, more often than not, although the same genetic dice are being used, different numbers come up with each roll. Even some of the most successful jumping siblings could hardly be described as 'two peas in a pod'. Admittedly, the Champion Hurdle-winning brothers Morley Street and Granville Again had fairly similar profiles—they raced against each other six times (the score was 3-3!)—but it was a different story with the Rimell-trained brothers Gaye Chance and Gaye Brief or the French-bred pair Cyborgo and Hors La Loi III. In both instances the older brother gained his most notable win in the Stayers' Hurdle (Gaye Chance and Cyborgo) whilst the younger one landed the much shorter Champion Hurdle (Gaye Brief and Hors La Loi III). No doubt few references to Silverburn will be made in the media from now on without mentioning that he is the younger brother of stable companion Denman, with all the expectations that that entails. As individuals though, the two horses are quite

Anglo Irish Bank Tolworth Hurdle, Sandown—
Silverburn copes well with the testing conditions to beat Irish raider Perce Rock (right)

different physically. Whereas Denman is a big, strong, good sort who has always looked every inch a chaser, and looks like proving a top-class one at that, Silverburn is a leggy, close-coupled gelding, altogether less imposing than his year-older brother. Whilst lacking Denman's scope and, on looks at least, making less appeal as a future chaser, their trainer Paul Nicholls is in no doubt that Silverburn's future lies over fences and it would be foolish to bet against him making the grade.

Whilst the level of form shown by Silverburn in his novice hurdling campaign was a bit behind that shown by Denman the season before, he emulated his brother by winning a Grade 1 contest and being a leading contender for what was now the Ballymore Properties-sponsored Baring Bingham Novices' Hurdle at Cheltenham. Silverburn made a promising hurdling debut over two and a half miles at Aintree behind Wichita Lineman but was dropped back to two miles for his next two starts, winning both of them. Testing ground for both races made up for the shorter distance and placed the emphasis on stamina which was very much in Silverburn's favour. Firstly, he landed the odds in a novice event at Newbury on Hennessy Gold Cup day, looking a bit green once in front and needing plenty of assistance before knuckling down to beat second favourite Tagula Blue (subsequently a Grade 2 winner) by two lengths. In even more testing conditions, Silverburn met four other last-time-out winners in the seven-runner Grade 1 Anglo Irish Bank Tolworth Hurdle at Sandown in January. Silverburn proved easy to back in the face of strong support for the Irish-trained favourite Perce Rock, fourth in the previous season's Champion Bumper at Cheltenham, and Astarador, who had won both his races over hurdles in the North. My Turn Now, unbeaten in four runs over hurdles, and the 2005 Champion Bumper runner-up De Soto were also preferred in the betting to Silverburn who was sent off at 5/1. He belied that weakness in the market with a good staying performance in the conditions, seeing things out best of those in contention into the straight and leading two out. Perce Rock was four lengths back in second and Astarador another seven lengths away third, though My Turn Now would have almost certainly filled the runner-up spot if he hadn't taken a heavy fall at the final flight.

The totesport Trophy at Newbury was mooted as a possible next target— Silverburn was among the ante-post favourites for the country's most valuable handicap hurdle—but connections opted to wait instead for the Baring Bingham Novices' Hurdle at Cheltenham, where the extra five furlongs looked like being very much in Silverburn's favour. He started second favourite but, with conditions placing the emphasis on speed, he was unable to land a blow after coming under pressure at the top of the hill, finishing just over five lengths behind the winner

Massini's Maguire in fourth. Denman had met his only defeat in the same race (then the Royal & SunAlliance) the year before when second to Nicanor, he too essentially undone by conditions placing an emphasis on speed. The three miles of the Sefton Novices' Hurdle at Aintree therefore promised to suit Silverburn, all the more so given the strong pace that ensued, but he ran a flat race and dropped away after a mistake to finish tailed-off last of the six finishers.

		Mtoto		Busted
	Presenting	(b 1983)		Amazer
	(br 1992)	D'Azy		Persian Bold
Silverburn (IRE)		(b 1984)		Belle Viking
(b.g. 2001)		Pollerton		Rarity
	Polly Puttens	(b 1974)		Nilie
	(b 1982)	My Puttens		David Jack
		(b 1972)		Railstown

Silverburn was all set to begin his career, as Denman did, as a pointer with Adrian Maguire in Ireland but was bought by Paul Nicholls from Maguire before he had run, following Denman's win in the Challow Hurdle on New Year's Day in 2006. Maguire had been chosen as the brothers' original trainer as he had enjoyed plenty of success as a jockey on a couple of their dam's other winners Potter's Bay and Potter's Gale (both by Strong Gale). Both were useful performers for David Nicholson, the former better over fences (at up to three miles) and the latter over hurdles (at around two miles). The mare Potter's Gale has some way to go to match her own dam's stud record, but she's making a good start as her offspring Missis Potts, Mister Potter and Potts of Magic were all successful in the latest season for what is proving a burgeoning family. Silverburn's twenty-five-year-old dam Polly

Mr Paul Green's "Silverburn"

Puttens is still going strongly at stud herself and foaled a full sister to him and Denman in the spring—her fifteenth foal in total. All nine to reach the racecourse have been successful, with the lightly-raced Far Horizon (above average in bumpers and over hurdles) the best of those not already mentioned. Polly Puttens produced three foals in between Silverburn and that 2007 filly. The five-year-old Presenting mare Miss Denman has been sent straight to the paddocks (reportedly covered by Overbury in 2006) on the back of her brothers' exploits, and it wouldn't be a surprise if a similar path is chosen for her two younger half-sisters, a 2004 Witness Box filly and a 2005 Snurge filly. Polly Puttens was well held in a bumper and over hurdles in Ireland but she is a half-sister to the 1992 Galway Hurdle winner Natalies Fancy and the useful staying chaser Occold (another horse Maguire tasted success on). Silverburn may not be another Denman, but he won't need to be to enjoy a successful novice chase campaign in his own right, when three miles should prove to suit him very well. Like his brother, he has raced only on good ground or softer and clearly goes well on soft or heavy ground. According to their rider Ruby Walsh, Silverburn also shares Denman's tendency to be a bit idle once in front. *P. F. Nicholls*

SILVER BY NATURE 5 gr.g. Silver Patriarch (IRE) – Gale (Strong Gale) [2006/7 F16m⁴ F16s* Apr 27] tall gelding: third foal: dam unraced daughter of useful staying chaser Dalkey Sound: better effort in bumpers 6 days apart when winning at Perth by 3 lengths from Bold Policy (pair clear): will be suited by 2½m+: carried head high on debut. *Mrs L. B. Normile* **F104**

SILVER CHANCELOR (IRE) 6 gr.g. Taipan (IRE) – Abstemious (Absalom) [2006/7 h–: 23g⁶ c20d 23vᵖᵘ 17v⁵ c24dᵘʳ c16v⁴ c27vᵖᵘ 20g Mar 27] strong, good-bodied gelding: little sign of ability. *J. Howard Johnson* **c–** **h–**

SILVER CHARMER 8 b.m. Charmer – Sea Dart (Air Trooper) [2006/7 h120: 20fᵖᵘ 22gᶠ 19g⁴ 22d 21g⁴ 22m⁴ 20g⁴ 21g* Apr 19] angular mare: fairly useful handicap hurdler on her day: off 5 months, better than ever when winning listed mares event at Cheltenham (for second time) in April by 6 lengths from Christdalo: stays 2¾m with emphasis on speed: acts on good to firm and good to soft going: usually waited with. *H. S. Howe* **h129**

SILVER DAGGER 9 gr.g. Dr Devious (IRE) – La Belle Affair (USA) (Black Tie Affair) [2006/7 c71§, h71§: c20s* c17d³ c21d* c24g* c22d* c25sᵖᵘ c22g³ c24gᶠ c26d⁶ c22v⁴ c20d⁶ 20d c20s⁵ c24sᵖᵘ c20g⁵ c25m³ Apr 28] lengthy gelding: modest handicap chaser: transformed early in 2006/7, winning at Market Rasen (2), Cartmel and Uttoxeter in under a month: fell heavily eighth start, mainly laboured efforts after, including back over hurdles: stays 27f, effective at much shorter: acts on soft going, probably on good to firm: wears headgear (eyeshields in 2006/7): usually tongue tied: hard ride. *J. C. Haynes* **c97 §** **h– §**

SILVERDALES 5 b.g. Silver Patriarch (IRE) – Swallowfield (Wattlefield) [2006/7 F16m Jan 28] 8,000 3-y-o: sixth foal: half-brother to fair 2m hurdle winner Aerion (by Ardross): dam lightly raced: well beaten in maiden bumper on debut. *Miss Lucinda V. Russell* **F–**

SILVER DESTINY 6 gr.m. Cloudings (IRE) – Tibbi Blues (Cure The Blues (USA)) [2006/7 F16g Nov 10] smallish mare: fifth foal: dam won over 1m in France: always behind in maiden bumper on debut. *Ferdy Murphy* **F–**

SILVER DOLLARS (FR) 6 gr.g. Great Palm (USA) – Marie Olga (FR) (Dom Pasquini (FR)) [2006/7 h108, F–: 16m c16vᵖᵘ Feb 5] sturdy gelding: fair maiden hurdler: raced too freely on chasing debut: raced mainly around 2m: acts on good to soft ground: not straightforward. *J. Howard Johnson* **c– p** **h94**

SILVERETTA 6 gr.m. Terimon – Whirlwind Romance (IRE) (Strong Gale) [2006/7 F16g F16v F16g Apr 23] fourth foal: dam bad maiden hurdler: tailed off in bumpers. *Miss L. C. Siddall* **F–**

SILVER FEATHER (IRE) 5 gr.g. Silver Patriarch (IRE) – Merilena (IRE) (Roselier (FR)) [2006/7 F–: F16d 20g⁵ 24vᶠ Nov 23] good-topped gelding: little impact in bumpers: modest form when fifth to Ellerslie George in maiden at Newcastle on hurdling debut: 15 lengths down when fell 4 out in novice 2 weeks later: should stay beyond 2½m. *Ferdy Murphy* **h89** **F–**

SILVER GIFT 10 b.m. Rakaposhi King – Kellsboro Kate (Paddy's Stream) [2006/7 c–, h79§: 26mᵖᵘ 24g³ 26d³ 26d⁶ 24m 24mᵇᵈ Jul 11] leggy mare: poor handicap hurdler: stays **c–** **h72 §**

27f: ran respectably on soft going, all wins on good/good to firm: tried blinkered/in cheekpieces: held up: inconsistent. *G. Fierro*

SILVERGINO (IRE) 7 b.g. Perugino (USA) – Silvretta (IRE) (Tirol) [2006/7 c99, h–: c16m³ Apr 14] rather leggy gelding: fair handicap chaser at best: left Mrs Jeremy Young and off 20 months, not discredited only start in 2006/7: barely stays 2½m: acts on good to firm and good to soft going, below form on softer: free-going front runner: carries head high, though seems genuine. *Ian Williams* **c87 h–**

SILVERHAY 6 b.g. Inchinor – Moon Spin (Night Shift (USA)) [2006/7 17g³ 17s⁶ 16m⁴ Apr 8] fairly useful on Flat (stays 1½m), sold out of T. D. Barron's stable 23,000 gns Doncaster October Sales: best effort (modest form) in maiden hurdles on debut: in cheekpieces next 2 starts: room for improvement in jumping. *L. Corcoran* **h88**

SILVERIO (GER) 6 b.g. Laroche (GER) – Silvassa (IRE) (Darshaan) [2006/7 h77, F92: 22v⁴ 22s³ 21s Dec 26] poor handicap hurdler: stays 2¾m: acts on heavy going: tried in cheekpieces (ran poorly): none too reliable. *G. L. Moore* **h80 §**

SILVER ISLAND 6 ch.g. Silver Patriarch (IRE) – Island Maid (Forzando) [2006/7 h–: 17m 16f 16m² 16f* 16dF Sep 22] poor hurdler: easily best effort when winning conditional jockeys handicap at Worcester in August: likely to prove best over sharp 2m: acts on firm going: tried blinkered: tongue tied. *K. Bishop* **h84**

Yorkshire Bank Mares' Only Handicap Hurdle, Cheltenham—the patiently-ridden Silver Charmer makes it two wins from five attempts at this listed event as she overhauls Christdalo (white face)

SILVER JACK (IRE) 9 gr.g. Roselier (FR) – Consharon (IRE) (Strong Gale) [2006/7 **c124** c104, h–: c25s* c25d³ c22v* Mar 3] compact gelding: fairly useful handicap chaser: **h—** improved form in 2006/7, winning at Kelso in November and March (readily by 14 lengths from Locksmith): stays 25f: unraced on firm going, acts on any other: effective in cheekpieces or without: often makes running. *M. Todhunter*

SILVER JARO (FR) 4 ch.g. Muhtathir – John Quatz (FR) (Johann Quatz (FR)) **h111** [2006/7 17s³ 16v³ 16v* 16d 16m Apr 25] smallish, close-coupled ex-French gelding: second foal: dam 11f/1½m winner: successful twice up to 1½m from 5 starts on Flat in 2006 for F. Rohaut: fairly useful juvenile hurdler: won maiden at Warwick in January by 1¼ lengths from Stumped: well held next 2 starts, in listed handicap at Cheltenham on first occasion (blinkered): raced around 2m: acts on heavy going. *Jonjo O'Neill*

SILVER KNIGHT 9 gr.g. Simply Great (FR) – Hysteria (Prince Bee) [2006/7 c123, **c130** h–: c25d⁵ c20d c25s² c25v* c33v c25g² c25g Apr 13] tall, useful-looking gelding: useful **h—** handicap chaser: won at Wetherby in December by 22 lengths from Kerry Lads: best effort after when 2 lengths second to Undeniable at same course: should stay beyond 25f: acts on heavy going: blinkered (found little) once, in cheekpieces last 5 starts: has hung left/looked tricky ride: sound jumper. *T. D. Easterby*

SILVER PROVERB 5 gr.m. Silver Patriarch (IRE) – Proverbial Rose (Proverb) **F—** [2006/7 F16m Jun 28] 25,000 3-y-o: eighth foal: half-sister to 3 winners, including smart bumper performer/useful hurdler Karanja (by Karinga Bay), stays 3m, and fairly useful chaser Flinders Chase (by Terimon), stays 2½m: dam won 4 times in points: soundly beaten in maiden bumper on debut. *Mrs K. Waldron*

SILVER SAMUEL (NZ) 10 gr.g. Hula Town (NZ) – Offrande (NZ) (Decies) [2006/7 **c— x** c87, h–: c26gᵖᵘ c25sᶠ c22v⁴ c24gᵖᵘ Jan 8] big, lengthy gelding: winning hurdler/chaser, **h—** no show over fences in 2006/7: tried in cheekpieces/blinkers: tongue tied: often let down by jumping. *S. A. Brookshaw*

SILVER SEDGE (IRE) 8 gr.g. Aristocracy – Pollyfaster (Polyfoto) [2006/7 c110, **c113** h100: 17s⁶ c16g² c20s* c20s c16v⁴ 20g* c20g³ c20s⁶ Apr 25] rather leggy gelding: fair **h102** handicap chaser/hurdler: won over fences at Newcastle in November and hurdles there (second win in race) in March: stays 2½m: acts on heavy going. *Mrs A. Hamilton*

SILVER SEEKER (USA) 7 gr. or ro.g. Seeking The Gold (USA) – Zelanda (IRE) **h87** (Night Shift (USA)) [2006/7 h86: 24m² 19d⁶ 25d⁶ 27g 20g Apr 16] smallish gelding: modest handicap hurdler: sold out of A. Dickin's stable 3,800 gns Doncaster August Sales and off almost 9 months, form in 2006/7 only on return: stays 3m: acts on soft and good to firm going. *M. Todhunter*

SILVER SELINE 6 gr.m. Silver Patriarch (IRE) – Rive-Jumelle (IRE) (M Double M **h—** (USA)) [2006/7 h–, F–: 16sᵖᵘ May 8] no show in mares bumper/over hurdles. *B. N. Pollock*

SILVER SERG 6 b.g. Silver Patriarch (IRE) – Ranyah (USA) (Our Native (USA)) **h95** [2006/7 F83: F16s⁶ 21m⁵ 21d 24d 18s³ 19g³ 21g⁶ 21g² Apr 23] workmanlike gelding: **F80** third in bumper on debut: modest novice hurdler: stays 21f: acts on soft going, probably on good to firm. *Miss Suzy Smith*

SILVER SISTER 6 gr.m. Morpeth – Pigeon Loft (IRE) (Bellypha) [2006/7 F81: 17s⁶ **h111** 19s³ 17v* 22g³ Apr 1] runner-up in bumper: fair form over hurdles: improved when winning maiden at Taunton in February: will stay 3m: acts on heavy going. *J. D. Frost*

SILVER SNITCH (IRE) 7 gr.g. Supreme Leader – Banderole (IRE) (Roselier (FR)) **h115 p** [2006/7 F78: F17v⁴ 21s* Dec 5] better effort in bumpers when fourth to Skippers Brig at **F101** Carlisle: favourite and upped in trip, successful hurdling debut when beating Senora Snoopy by 2 lengths in novice at Sedgefield, despite blundering seventh and idling: will stay beyond 21f: likely to improve. *G. A. Swinbank*

SILVER SONG 5 gr.g. Silver Patriarch (IRE) – Singing The Blues (Bonny Scot (IRE)) **h85** [2006/7 17d⁶ 19d⁵ 22m⁵ 21s⁶ Dec 7] modest maiden on Flat (stays 2¼m) at 3 yrs for J. Dunlop: modest form over hurdles: probably stays 21f: tried blinkered/tongue tied. *P. F. Nicholls*

SILVER STEEL (FR) 4 b.g. Robin Des Pres (FR) – Oliver's Queen (FR) (King Cyrus **F81** (USA)) [2006/7 F16s⁴ Apr 27] €75,000 3-y-o: half-brother to 2 winning jumpers in France, notably smart hurdler/useful chaser Dukeen (by Iron Duke), stayed 2¾m: dam lightly-raced half-sister to smart French chaser Staff: favourite, 23 lengths fourth to Silver By Nature in bumper at Perth on debut: likely to be suited by further than 2m. *N. G. Richards*

SILVER STREAK (IRE) 13 gr.g. Roselier (FR) – Vulcash (IRE) (Callernish) [2006/7 c90, h–: c25m⁵ Apr 15] tall, good-topped gelding: winning chaser: fairly useful but untrustworthy pointer nowadays, won in February: tried blinkered (fell)/visored. *Milson Robinson* — c– h–

SILVERTOWN 12 b.g. Danehill (USA) – Docklands (USA) (Theatrical) [2006/7 16gᶠ Dec 30] sturdy, lengthy gelding: fairly useful on Flat (stays 2m), successful twice in 2006, pulled up in January: useful handicap hurdler: fell first at Musselburgh: stays 2½m: best on good going or firmer: often races up with pace. *L. Lungo* — h–

SILVERY HILL 6 gr.g. Silver Patriarch (IRE) – Nova Hill (Ra Nova) [2006/7 F16d F17m Jun 4] second foal: dam no sign of ability: no show in maiden bumpers/points. *P. A. Pritchard* — F–

SILVO (NZ) 8 gr.g. Lowell (USA) – Silvadella (NZ) (Silver Prospector (USA)) [2006/7 16m* 18m⁶ 16f 16m 16m³ Jul 16] won 1m maiden from 18 starts on Flat in New Zealand: also ran twice in maiden hurdles there: poor form in Britain, won seller at Fakenham in May: raced around 2m on good to firm/firm going: tried visored. *M. F. Harris* — h76

SIMIOLA 8 b.m. Shaamit (IRE) – Brave Vanessa (USA) (Private Account (USA)) [2006/7 c–, h–: c16f⁵ c16m c16f Aug 22] sturdy mare: little form over jumps. *S. T. Lewis* — c– h–

SIMLET 12 b.g. Forzando – Besito (Wassl) [2006/7 c–, h–: c24dᵇᵈ Oct 15] good-topped gelding: fair hurdler at best (won 7 times): maiden chaser: stayed 27f: acted on firm and soft going: sometimes wore cheekpieces/blinkers: often tongue tied: dead. *E. W. Tuer* — c– h–

SIMON 8 b.g. Overbury (IRE) – Gaye Memory (Buckskin (FR)) [2006/7 c130, h–: c24g⁵ c29s² c29s⁶ c24v* c24v* c36gᶠ Apr 14] — c146 h–

The Rimell name, synonymous with Aintree and the Grand National, looked like possibly making a sixth appearance on the winning roll of the world's most famous steeplechase as the leaders approached second Valentine's with six left to jump. Simon, a 20/1-shot owned and bred by the eighty-seven-year-old widow of Fred Rimell, Mercy, was travelling strongly up with the leaders and looked sure to play a part in the finish. Unfortunately, after jumping soundly on the

Sky Bet Chase (Handicap), Southwell—
Simon (Andrew Thornton) is clear in a poorly-contested renewal of this valuable event

Racing Post Chase (Handicap), Kempton—the same partnership triumphs in another unusually small field (five non-runners on the day); Cornish Sett (blinkers) and Lacdoudal (grey) fill the minor placings

whole up to that point, Simon came down. Still only eight, however, he looks very much the type to go well in the race another year. Fred Rimell's father Tom trained Forbra to win a Grand National (1932). Fred himself, whose training success was, in his words, 'very much a joint effort with Mercy', saddled four Grand National winners, namely E.S.B. (who won 'Devon Loch's National', the one in which no one remembers the winner) in 1956, Nicolaus Silver (the last grey to win) in 1961, Gay Trip in 1970 and Rag Trade (who beat Red Rum in the first season covered by *Chasers & Hurdlers*) in 1976. Mercy Rimell, who rode out every day and made all the entries in the heyday of Kinnersley stables, maintains that Gay Trip would have won two Nationals—he was second under a big weight, beaten only two lengths, two years after his win—'if Terry hadn't gone the long way, covering five miles instead of four and a half.' Terry Biddlecombe, stable jockey at Kinnersley, missed the ride on Gay Trip through injury the year he won. Mrs Rimell is fond of recalling Biddlecome as a 'playboy who enjoyed indulging himself, but had such an attractive personality . . . he rode so many great races for us.' 'Never a National though,' she always adds. Mrs Rimell was known for holding strong views on jockeys—and for not pulling punches with her criticism, even when it came to some of the successful Rimell stable jockeys down the years such as Bobby Beasley ('very temperamental'), Bill Smith ('I never got on with him ever—as a man or jockey') and Sam Morshead ('a bit wild . . . he wasn't one of our best jockeys by any means'). Given that, it might seem ironic that Simon was partnered in the Grand National by Andrew Thornton, a long-serving rider who has lost the ride on two Cheltenham Gold Cup hopes, Kingscliff and The Listener, in recent seasons, 'jocked off' by their respective owners. Thornton has won a Gold Cup on Cool Dawn and a King George on See More Business and Mrs Rimell admits to being 'a fan', though she reserves any hero-worship for Tony McCoy—'he's the best jockey I've seen in fifty years . . . his strength comes from his legs and lower body and he's most intelligent, his rides are always in the right place . . . it's a joy to watch him.'

Thornton struck up a good partnership with Simon as he progressed into a smart handicapper in his second season over fences. Formerly trained in Ireland by

Philip Fenton, for whom he won a point and a novice hurdle, Simon had won three of his seven starts as a novice chaser, including a handicap at Bangor (Thornton's first ride on the gelding), in his first season with John Spearing who now occupies the Kinnersley stables made famous by the Rimells. Thornton was reunited with the gelding at Sandown in December, on Simon's second start in the latest season, and, after finishing a good second there to Tana River, Simon started favourite for the Welsh National (a race Fred Rimell won four times). He managed only sixth and didn't jump so well as he can, but he shaped well enough to suggest he was going to continue to be of interest in valuable long-distance handicaps, particularly as he was 5 lb 'wrong' at Chepstow. Simon and Thornton won their next two races, the Sky Bet Chase at Southwell and the Racing Post Chase at Kempton. The Sky Bet was formerly known as the Great Yorkshire Chase and is another race Fred Rimell won four times, including with E.S.B. and Nicolaus Silver (both after their Aintree wins). The field of just ten runners for the latest Skybet was the joint-smallest since 1983, whilst the Racing Post wasn't a strong renewal either, with five non-runners on the day contributing to its smallest field since 1999. Nonetheless, Simon won the respective races by nine lengths and ten lengths (defying an 11-lb higher BHB mark at Kempton), his stamina coming into play as he galloped on resolutely on heavy going both times, in the process becoming the first to complete the double. The BHB handicapper put him up a further 9 lb for winning the Racing Post but he was able to contest the National off the same mark as at Kempton, as the National weights were already out and there are no penalties after the publication of the weights. Thornton, incidentally, was returning from over three weeks on the

Mrs Mercy Rimell's "Simon"

sidelines, when successful on Simon in the Racing Post Chase, after pulling muscles in a fall at Wincanton (initial fears suggested a broken leg).

		Caerleon	Nijinsky
	Overbury (IRE)	(b 1980)	Foreseer
	(br 1991)	Overcall	Bustino
Simon		(b 1984)	Melodramatic
(b.g. 1999)		Buckskin	Yelapa
	Gaye Memory	(b 1973)	Bete A Bon Dieu
	(ch 1983)	Artiste Gaye	Artist's Son
		(b 1961)	Goldlane

The good-topped Simon ('the spitting image of Gay Trip,' according to his
owner) looked in tremendous shape at Aintree, though he spoiled his appearance by
sweating as the protracted preliminaries wore on. He is from the family of Gaye
Brief who won the 1983 Champion Hurdle for Mercy Rimell when she took over
the licence at Kinnersley after the death of her husband following an accident on his
farm in the summer of 1981—Gaye Brief was the last horse he bought. Fred Rimell
was champion jockey four times (on one occasion sharing the title) and champion
trainer five times, on the last occasion in 1975/6 when he won the Gold Cup with
Royal Frolic, then adding Rag Trade's Grand National victory. Woodland Venture
also provided him with a Gold Cup winner and he twice won the Champion Hurdle
with Comedy of Errors. Mercy Rimell continued training until the end of the 1988/
9 season, when Gaye Brief was also retired. Gaye Brief's dam Artiste Gaye was an
outstanding broodmare, the Stayers' Hurdle winner and very smart chaser Gaye
Chance (a full brother to Gaye Brief) also among her many winning offspring. Gaye
Chance provided Fred Rimell with his last big-race win when landing the very
valuable Royal Doulton Hurdle (now the Swinton) at Haydock in 1981, a race his
half-brother Royal Gaye had won for the stable in its inaugural year of 1978.
Simon's dam Gaye Memory was Artiste Gaye's penultimate foal and she upheld
the family name by winning two bumpers before finishing runner-up on her only
outing over hurdles. Artiste Gaye's last foal was the very smart chaser Black
Humour, a full brother to Gaye Memory and, like most of Artiste Gaye's offspring,
a sound stayer—he departed at the Chair on his one attempt at the Grand National
(in 1994). More recently, a grandson of Artiste Gaye, the high-class Kingsmark,
has twice completed the National under big weights, his better effort coming when
fourth under 11-9 in 2002. Gaye Memory's career as a broodmare hasn't been
anywhere near so successful as that of her dam but she is also the dam of Taking
My Cut (by Classic Cliche), a fairly useful two-and-a-half-mile hurdle winner
(when ridden by McCoy) for Jonjo O'Neill in 2005/6, and Gaye Fame (by Ardross),
a modest winning hurdler in the mid-'nineties for Kim Bailey (a former assistant
trainer at the Rimell yard). Gaye Fame, incidentally, has followed the family tradition since retiring to the paddocks, her two winners to date including the 2005
Pertemps Final winner Oulart, who was also runner-up in the following year's Irish
National. The reliable Simon stays at least twenty-nine furlongs and will probably
get the Grand National trip. He has raced on good going or softer and acts on heavy.
He is normally a sound jumper. *J. L. Spearing*

SIMON'S HEIGHTS 6 b.g. Weldnaas (USA) – Star Thyme (Point North) [2006/7 h–: **h68**
16g Jun 15] poor maiden hurdler: raced mainly around 2m. *J. Mackie*

SIMOUN (IRE) 9 b.g. Monsun (GER) – Suivez (FR) (Fioravanti (USA)) [2006/7 c111? **c–**
, h–: 21m⁵ 21m³ 19m³ Jun 4] compact gelding: maiden chaser: winning hurdler, poor in **h81**
2006/7, claimed £5,000 final start: won point in January: stayed easy 21f: acted on soft
and good to firm going: formerly tongue tied: dead. *B. N. Pollock*

SIMPLE GLORY (IRE) 8 br.m. Simply Great (FR) – Cabin Glory (The Parson) **c– x**
[2006/7 c85, h85: c23mᵖᵘ 21s 25v 21m³ 21d⁴ 24g² 24m⁵ Apr 15] sturdy mare: winning **h92**
pointer: maiden chaser: modest handicap hurdler: stays 3m: acts on good to firm and good
to soft ground: tried blinkered: usually let down by jumping over fences. *R. Dickin*

SIMPLIFIED 4 b.f. Lend A Hand – Houston Heiress (USA) (Houston (USA)) [2006/7 **h79**
16m 16g³ 16m Apr 8] modest on Flat (stays 11f), successful in February: poor form in
maiden hurdles: raced at 2m on good/good to firm ground. *N. B. King*

SIMPLY DA BEST (IRE) 9 b.g. Lake Coniston (IRE) – Sakala (NZ) (Gold And Ivory (USA)) [2006/7 c–, h–: c20g^{pu} Apr 23] winning hurdler: no solid form since 2003/4, mostly over fences: usually in cheekpieces/blinkers: tongue tied once. *J. J. Lambe, Ireland* **c–**
h–

SIMPLY GIFTED 12 b.g. Simply Great (FR) – Souveniers (Relko) [2006/7 c–, h–: c19d Dec 23] well-made gelding: has reportedly had wind operation: one-time useful handicap chaser: lightly raced and no form since 2004/5: stays 4½m, raced mainly at much shorter: acts on heavy going, below best on good to firm: has worn blinkers/visor. *Jonjo O'Neill* **c–**
h–

SIMPLY HONEST (IRE) 12 ch.g. Simply Great (FR) – Susans Glory (Billion (USA)) [2006/7 16s^5 20m Apr 15] bumper winner/successful over 13f on Flat: maiden hurdler: stays 2½m. *Mrs A. Smith, Ireland* **h73**

SIMPLYIRRESISTIBLE (IRE) 7 b.m. Simply Great (FR) – Woolly (Giolla Mear) [2006/7 F–: 16g 21g 24f^{pu} Apr 5] no sign of ability. *S. T. Lewis* **h–**

SIMPLY MISS MOFFAT (IRE) 7 b.m. Simply Great (FR) – Susans Glory (Billion (USA)) [2006/7 F16s^{ur} May 8] sister to bumper winner Simply Honest, also successful over 13f on Flat: dam race once: looked reluctant going down then veered left and unseated rider at start in mares bumper on debut: one to avoid. *Mrs A. Smith, Ireland* **F– §**

SIMPLY ST LUCIA 5 b.m. Charnwood Forest (IRE) – Mubadara (IRE) (Lahib (USA)) [2006/7 h78: 17d^3 16s^5 16v^{pu} 16g^6 Apr 23] rather leggy mare: poor maiden hurdler: raced around 2m on good going or softer. *J. R. Weymes* **h76**

SIMPLY THE ONE (IRE) 10 ch.g. Simply Great (FR) – Lady Mearlane (Giolla Mear) [2006/7 c26v^6 c26s^{pu} Mar 11] close-coupled gelding: modest pointer, won in January: no form in chases: tried blinkered/visored. *Miss Jennifer Pidgeon* **c–**
h–

SINGHALONGTASVEER 5 b.g. Namaqualand (USA) – Felinwen (White Mill) [2006/7 h91: 16s^3 16m 20s 18g* 18s^6 20m 16g 20s^6 Apr 1] sturdy gelding: modest maiden up to 2m on Flat: modest handicap hurdler: won conditional jockeys event at Kelso in November: should stay beyond 2¼m: acts on soft going: wears cheekpieces/tongue strap: has looked difficult ride. *W. Storey* **h99 §**

SINGH ON SONG (IRE) 6 b.g. Luso – Shuil Amach (IRE) (Be My Native (USA)) [2006/7 F16v F18v* F16v^3 F16v* Jan 25] €64,000 3-y-o: first foal: dam unraced half-sister to useful staying chaser The Outlier: useful form in bumpers: won at Thurles (maiden) in November and Gowran (beat Arkendale by length) in January: will be suited by 2½m+. *Philip Fenton, Ireland* **F106**

SINGLE HANDED 5 b.m. Cloudings (IRE) – Hand Inn Glove (Alflora (IRE)) [2006/7 F64+: F17d^2 19d^4 17s^3 16s^4 21f^{pu} Apr 5] runner-up in bumper: modest form over hurdles: will prove suited by further than 17f: acts on soft ground, ran poorly on firm. *H. D. Daly* **h86**
F88

SINTOS 9 b. or br.g. Syrtos – Sindur (Rolfe (USA)) [2006/7 h–: 21g^3 22d 20s 24m^{pu} Apr 25] lengthy, workmanlike gelding: lightly-raced hurdler, easily best effort (modest form) on return: stays 21f. *Miss A. M. Newton-Smith* **h86**

SIOUXZANNAH 5 gr.m. Commanche Run – Baroness Blakeney (Blakeney) [2006/7 F16m^5 F16v Feb 22] smallish, strong mare: fourth foal: dam, well beaten in bumpers, sister to smart jumper Baron Blakeney: well held in bumpers. *A. E. Price* **F–**

SIR ALF 11 ch.g. Alflora (IRE) – D'Egliere (FR) (Port Etienne (FR)) [2006/7 c26d^{pu} May 31] good-topped gelding: fairly useful pointer, won 3 times in 2007 before end of April: won hunter chase in 2004/5, no show in 2 similar events since: stays 25f: tried tongue tied. *Miss Maria D. Myco* **c–**
h–

SIR ALFIE 4 b.g. My Best Valentine – Raghill Hannah (Buckskin (FR)) [2006/7 F18v Mar 7] sturdy gelding: fourth foal: dam unraced: well held in bumper on debut. *C. G. Cox* **F–**

SIR BATHWICK (IRE) 8 b.g. Oscar (IRE) – Karenda (Kambalda) [2006/7 h92: 21d^3 24s* 24s^5 24v^5 Jan 17] lengthy gelding: fair hurdler: won handicap at Southwell in December: stays 3m: acts on soft going: has carried head awkwardly. *B. G. Powell* **h105**

SIR BEN 6 b.g. Sir Harry Lewis (USA) – Jolejester (Relkino) [2006/7 F–: 16s^{pu} May 8] no show in bumper/novice hurdle. *A. Ennis* **h–**

SIR BOBBY 6 b.g. Kylian (USA) – Ishona (Selkirk (USA)) [2006/7 F14v 16g Mar 17] good-topped gelding: blinkered, modest form in bumper on debut: off over 2 years, well beaten in 2006/7, including on hurdling debut: sold 1,500 gns Doncaster March Sales. *M. Dods* **h–**
F–

European Breeders' Fund 'National Hunt' Novices' Hurdle (Qualifier), Catterick—
the season's leading amateur Tom Greenall steers Sir Boreas Hawk to an impressive hurdling debut win

SIR BOREAS HAWK 5 b.g. Overbury (IRE) – Fringe Benefit (IRE) (Executive Perk) **h129 p**
[2006/7 F95+: F16g² F16d* 19g* Feb 2] strong gelding: useful form in bumpers, **F109**
successful at Musselburgh in January: also very promising hurdling debut when winning
16-runner novice at Catterick by 14 lengths from Monsieur, leading on bridle 2 out:
seems sure to improve and win more races. *G. A. Swinbank*

SIR BRASTIAS 8 b.g. Shaamit (IRE) – Premier Night (Old Vic) [2006/7 h106: c16g* **c115 x**
c21sur 22d⁵ 20d³ c20d³ c24d⁵ c22g⁴ c24g⁵ Apr 21] useful chaser: won handicap at Worcester in May: mainly let down by jumping after: **h96**
probably stays 3m: acts on heavy going. *K. C. Bailey*

SIR BUMBLE (IRE) 7 b.g. Humbel (USA) – Adelinas Leader (IRE) (Supreme **h–**
Leader) [2006/7 24vᵖu 17s 20s 22sᵖu 23dᵖu Mar 21] €11,500 4-y-o: tall gelding: third
foal: half-brother to bumper winner Be My Adelina (by Be My Native): dam, maiden in
bumpers and points, half-sister to high-class 2m/2½m chaser Travado: no form over
hurdles. *D. P. Keane*

SIR COZZIE 4 b.g. Gorse – Last Night's Fun (IRE) (Law Society (USA)) [2006/7 F13d **F–**
F16m Apr 24] half-brother to 2 winners, notably bumper winner/3m hurdle winner
Corrib Eclipse (by Double Eclipse), also useful stayer on Flat: dam lightly raced in
Ireland: well beaten in bumpers. *W. J. Burke, Ireland*

SIR FREDERICK (IRE) 7 b.g. Insan (USA) – Promotor Fidei (Prominer) [2006/7 **c122**
h128: c22d⁴ c22v² c20s⁶ c20s² c21s* c24v⁵ c21dᵖu c20v⁴ c20g* Apr 5] strong, close- **h–**
coupled gelding: fairly useful hurdler: similar form over fences: won 22-runner maiden
at Fairyhouse in December and minor event at Clonmel (beat Arc En Ciel easily by 3½
lengths) in April: stays 3m: raced on good going or softer (acts on heavy): patiently
ridden. *W. J. Burke, Ireland*

SIR FROSTY 14 b.g. Arctic Lord – Snowy Autumn (Deep Run) [2006/7 c100: c25g⁶ **c101**
c30d* May 27] lengthy gelding: fair handicap chaser: won at Cartmel (for second year **h–**
running) in May: thorough stayer: acts on heavy going: has had tongue tied. *B. J. M. Ryall*

SIR GRENVILLE (IRE) 7 ch.g. Zaffaran (USA) – Whackers World (Whistling **h–**
Deer) [2006/7 19v^{pu} Feb 20] brother to bumper/2m hurdle winner Satoha and half-brother
to fair chaser Pettree (by King Persian), stayed 3¼m: dam 2m hurdle winner: failed to
complete in points in 2006 and novice hurdle. *V. R. A. Dartnall*

SIR HARRY COOL 4 b.g. Sir Harry Lewis (USA) – Cool Merenda (IRE) (Glacial **F80**
Storm (USA)) [2006/7 F16d F16g Mar 14] rather unfurnished gelding: second foal:
brother to temperamental 2¾m hurdle winner Miss Merenda: dam unraced: little impact
in bumpers. *B. G. Powell*

SIR HARRY ORMESHER 4 b.g. Sir Harry Lewis (USA) – Glamour Game (Nash- **F103**
wan (USA)) [2006/7 F12v^6 F16d* F16g Mar 14] leggy gelding: sixth foal: half-brother
to fair/temperamental hurdler De Tramuntana (by Alzao), stays 21f: dam, Irish 1¼m
winner, also successful at 2½m over hurdles: fairly useful form in bumpers: won at Ascot
in February by 3½ lengths from Busker Royal: worked up beforehand and pulled hard
when well held in Champion Bumper at Cheltenham following month: hung left on
debut. *C. J. Down*

SIR JIMMY SHAND (IRE) 6 b. or br.g. Accordion – Morganone (IRE) (Supreme **h137**
Leader) [2006/7 F108: 17v* 19s* 21d^2 24g 24s^{pu} Apr 26] tall, useful-looking gelding:
will make a chaser: dual bumper winner: useful novice hurdler: won easily at Folkestone
in November and Newbury (by 8 lengths from It's In The Stars) in December: further
improvement when 8 lengths second to Wichita Lineman in Grade 1 Challow Hurdle at
Newbury (wandered under pressure): went as if amiss last 2 starts: stays 21f: raced on
good ground or softer (acts on heavy). *N. J. Henderson*

Mr W. H. Pasonby's "Sir Jimmy Shand"

SIR LAUGHALOT 7 b.g. Alzao (USA) – Funny Hilarious (USA) (Sir Ivor (USA)) **h102**
[2006/7 16d⁴ 16d 18s^ur 18g⁵ 21m² Apr 9] close-coupled gelding: fair handicap hurdler:
stays 21f: acts on good to soft and good to firm ground: often held up. *Miss E. C. Lavelle*

SIR LEONARD (IRE) 6 b.g. Aahsaylad – Miss Paleface (Idiot's Delight) [2006/7 **F–**
F16g³ F16d Oct 20] third foal: brother to fair hurdler Cratloe Castle, stays 3m: dam,
winning pointer, sister to top-class hurdler/smart 2m chaser Prideaux Boy: 12 lengths
third of 5 to Grecian Groom in bumper at Huntingdon on debut: soundly beaten later in
month. *J. R. Jenkins*

SIRNANDO 5 b.g. Hernando (FR) – Rynechra (Blakeney) [2006/7 F16m* F14g² **F98**
F16m² F16d⁴ Nov 18] leggy, close-coupled gelding: brother to 2 winners, including fair
stayer Allez Mousson, closely related to smart 1m (at 2 yrs) to 14.6f (Park Hill) winner
Coigach (by Niniski), and half-brother to 3 winners, including smart 1¼m to 13f winner
Applecross (by Glint of Gold): dam 1½m winner: fairly useful form in bumpers: won at
Stratford in September by ¾ length from St Wilfrid: in frame all 3 starts after, sweating
and edgy prior to 4½ lengths fourth of 8 to Golden Child at Ascot: joined M. Salaman.
R. Simpson

SIR NIGHT (IRE) 7 b.g. Night Shift (USA) – Highly Respected (IRE) (High Estate) **c–**
[2006/7 h96: c16m⁶ c16f⁶ 16g⁴ 20g 16g² 16g² Dec 20] smallish gelding: fair handicap **h102**
hurdler: well held over fences: not sure to stay much beyond 17f: acts on good to firm and
good to soft going: usually races prominently. *Jedd O'Keeffe*

SIR NORMAN 12 b.g. Arctic Lord – Moy Ran Lady (Black Minstrel) [2006/7 17m^pu **c–**
c18m^ur May 28] tall gelding: maiden hurdler/winning chaser, no longer of any account: **h–**
tried in cheekpieces/blinkers: often tongue tied. *R. H. Buckler*

SIR OJ (IRE) 10 br.g. Be My Native (USA) – Fox Glen (Furry Glen) [2006/7 c142, h–: **c148**
c20g* c20v* Nov 16] close-coupled gelding: smart chaser: won Grade 2 National Lottery **h–**
Agent Champion Chase at Gowran (by 1½ lengths from Light On The Broom) in October
and Grade 2 Clonmel Oil Chase in November: beat Kill Devil Hill a short head in
4-runner event in latter, jumping markedly left but showing good attitude: stays 21f: raced
on good going or softer (acts on heavy): usually blinkered: sometimes let down by
jumping. *N. Meade, Ireland*

Clonmel Oil Chase—Sir OJ (noseband) pips Kill Devil Hill for his second win of a light campaign

SIRONI (IRE) 7 b. or br.g. Erins Isle – Nordic Cousin (IRE) (Nordico (USA)) [2006/7   **F72**
F18d⁶ Oct 30] €35,000 4-y-o: fourth foal: brother to bumper winner Marys Isle: dam
unraced: completed once from 5 starts in maiden Irish points: bought 9,000 gns Doncaster
May Sales: mid-field in bumper. *Mrs L. C. Jewell*

SIR OSCAR (IRE) 5 b.g. Oscar (IRE) – Same Token (Cheval) [2006/7 F16s⁵ F17v   **h–**
22sᵖᵘ Feb 3] compact gelding: sixth foal: dam unraced half-sister to smart staying chaser   **F74**
Envopak Token: signs of ability in bumper on debut: blinkered, jumped sloppily on
hurdling debut. *P. J. Hobbs*

SIR PETER (IRE) 5 ch.g. City Honours (USA) – Any Offers (Paddy's Stream)   **h69**
[2006/7 F16s⁶ 21d⁵ 22s Feb 3] €32,000 3-y-o: half-brother to fair hurdler/fairly useful   **F73**
chaser Malek (by Tremblant), stayed 4m, and bumper winner Pharaway Stream (by
Phardante): dam of little account: poor form in bumper/maiden hurdle: bled final start.
H. D. Daly

SIR QUIGLEY (IRE) 5 b.g. Pistolet Bleu (IRE) – Elect Her (Jumbo Hirt (USA))   **F–**
[2006/7 F16s F16m Nov 24] first foal: dam unraced, out of half-sister to dam of top-class
hurdlers Deano's Beeno and French Holly: well held in bumpers. *J. J. Lambe, Ireland*

SIR REMBRANDT (IRE) 11 b.g. Mandalus – Sue's A Lady (Le Moss) [2006/7   **c147 §**
c141, h–: c24g* c25s³ c27dᵖᵘ c25v² c29s c28sᵖᵘ c24gᵖᵘ c32m Apr 21] big, strong, lengthy   **h–**
gelding: smart chaser: won handicap at Uttoxeter in May by head from See You Sometime: creditable efforts at Wetherby when never-nearer 12 lengths third to Our Vic in
Charlie Hall Chase and 8 lengths second to Leading Man in Grade 3 handicap: no form
after: stays 29f: unraced on firm going, acts on any other: tried visored: looked unsuited
by right-handed track second 2004/5 outing: unreliable nowadays: joined V. Dartnall.
R. H. Alner

SIR RIQUE (FR) 4 b.g. Enrique – Fontaine Guerard (FR) (Homme de Loi (IRE))   **h96 p**
[2006/7 16dᶠ 16v 17g⁵ Apr 18] tall, useful-looking gelding: successful twice up to around
1½m in French Provinces at 3 yrs, sold out of R. Gibson's stable €46,000 Goffs November Sale: fair form in juvenile hurdles: not at all knocked about when fifth to Laustra Bad
at Cheltenham: probably capable of better. *P. J. Hobbs*

SIR ROCHESTER (IRE) 7 b.g. Nashamaa – Encalchoise (FR) (En Calcat (FR))   **h–**
[2006/7 20mᵖᵘ Apr 25] first foal: dam unraced: no show in maiden hurdle on debut.
S. Lycett

SIRROCO WIND 7 b.g. Oscar (IRE) – Gale (Strong Gale) [2006/7 h–: 20d 20vᵖᵘ   **h–**
20gᵖᵘ Apr 3] lightly raced and little sign of ability. *Mrs L. B. Normile*

SIR ROWLAND HILL (IRE) 8 b.g. Kahyasi – Zaila (IRE) (Darshaan) [2006/7 c–,   **c–**
h103: 24g⁶ 25g³ 20m⁴ Jun 11] sturdy gelding: fair maiden hurdler, well below form in   **h86 §**
2006/7: lacklustre efforts in novice chases: should stay beyond 3m: acts on good to soft
going: tried in cheekpieces/blinkers: unreliable. *Ferdy Murphy*

SIR WALTER (IRE) 14 b.g. The Bart (USA) – Glenbalda (Kambalda) [2006/7 c64,   **c–**
h90: 20f⁶ 16m c16f Aug 22] leggy gelding: veteran jumper: stays easy 2½m: acts on good   **h68**
to firm and heavy going: tried tongue tied, also in cheekpieces final outing: has found
little: often let down by jumping over fences. *Evan Williams*

SISSINGHURST STORM (IRE) 9 b. or br.m. Good Thyne (USA) – Mrs Hill   **c81 §**
(Strong Gale) [2006/7 c85, h69: c24s⁶ c25g³ c25m⁴ c25d⁴ c23f c24m⁴ Oct 4] workman-   **h–**
like mare: poor hurdler/handicap chaser: best at 3m+: acts on soft and good to firm going:
tried in cheekpieces (below form): temperamental: sold €36,000 Fairyhouse December
Sales. *R. Dickin*

SISTEMA 6 b.g. Danzero (AUS) – Shahdiza (USA) (Blushing Groom (FR)) [2006/7   **h–**
h89: 20d⁶ Dec 6] modest 17f hurdle winner: ran poorly only start in 2006/7: blinkered on
debut. *A. E. Price*

SISTER BURY 8 b.m. Overbury (IRE) – Chapel Hill (IRE) (The Parson) [2006/7 F–:   **h–**
25gᵖᵘ Oct 30] no sign of ability. *Mrs S. E. Handley*

SISTER GEE (IRE) 5 b.m. Desert Story (IRE) – My Gloria (IRE) (Saint Estephe   **h–**
(FR)) [2006/7 16sᵖᵘ Feb 22] smallish mare: poor maiden on Flat (best at 6f): mistakes and
no show on hurdling debut. *R. Hollinshead*

SISTER GRACE 7 b.m. Golden Heights – Black Spring (IRE) (Mister Lord (USA))   **c–**
[2006/7 h80: 25gᵖᵘ 16v⁴ 17v³ c21dᵖᵘ c24dᵖᵘ 21vᵖᵘ Feb 26] tall, useful-looking mare: poor   **h79**
handicap hurdler: no show in handicap chases: should be suited by further than 17f: raced
on good going or softer (acts on heavy): tried tongue tied. *N. J. Gifford*

SISTER LUCY (IRE) 6 ch.m. Old Vic – Pharlucy (IRE) (Phardante (FR)) [2006/7 F–: **F—** F16f⁶ May 10] soundly beaten in bumpers. *B. Storey*

SISTER O'MALLEY (IRE) 8 b. or br.m. Religiously (USA) – Arctic Laura (Le **h—** Bavard (FR)) [2006/7 21mᵖᵘ 24sᵖᵘ May 28] sturdy mare: little sign of ability: tried tongue tied. *J. R. Holt*

SITE SENTRY (IRE) 4 ch.c. Nashwan (USA) – Balwa (USA) (Danzig (USA)) **F79 ?** [2006/7 aF13g Nov 22] half-brother to several winners, including hurdler/chaser Laazim Afooz (by Mtoto), stays 27f: dam 5f (at 2 yrs) and 7f winner: seventh of 14 in 3-y-o bumper at Lingfield on debut, probably flattered. *M. F. Harris*

SITTING DUCK 8 b.g. Sir Harry Lewis (USA) – Fit For Firing (FR) (In Fijar (USA)) **c93** [2006/7 c87, h72: c24g⁶ c20d² c19sᵘʳ c20v* c20sᵖᵘ c19s⁵ Mar 12] lengthy gelding: **h—** maiden hurdler: modest handicap chaser: won at Huntingdon in January: probably stays 3m: acts on heavy going, probably on good to firm: front runner. *B. G. Powell*

SIYARAN (IRE) 6 ch.g. Grand Lodge (USA) – Sinndiya (IRE) (Pharly (FR)) [2006/7 **h—** h–: 21g May 4] leggy gelding: form over hurdles only when third in maiden in 2004/5: tongue tied last 2 starts. *D. R. Gandolfo*

SIZING AFRICA (IRE) 5 b.g. Bob's Return (IRE) – Brown Forest (Brave Invader **F119** (USA)) [2006/7 F16g* F16v³ F16m* Apr 8] useful-looking gelding: half-brother to several winners, including fair chaser Brown Buck (by Buckskin), stayed 21f: dam unraced: smart form in bumpers: won at Gowran in October and Fairyhouse (tongue tied, improved to beat Mick The Man by 1¼ lengths) in April: third to Schiehallion at Newbury in between. *Henry de Bromhead, Ireland*

SIZING EUROPE (IRE) 5 b.g. Pistolet Bleu (IRE) – Jennie Dun (IRE) (Mandalus) **h120** [2006/7 F16d⁵ F16s* 16d² 16v³ 16m⁵ 16g* Apr 27] tall, useful-looking gelding: half- **F110** brother to fairly useful hurdler The Spoonplayer (by Accordion), stays 2¾m: dam unraced: useful bumper winner, beating Rinroe 1¾ lengths at Naas in October: fairly useful form over hurdles: successful in maiden at Newbury (hung badly left run-in) in November and 24-runner novice at Punchestown (beat Big Zeb by 3½ lengths) in April: creditable efforts in Grade 2 novices in between: likely to prove best around 2m: acts on heavy and good to firm ground. *Henry de Bromhead, Ireland*

SKENFRITH 8 b.g. Atraf – Hobbs Choice (Superpower) [2006/7 c106, h–: 22vᵖᵘ **c—** c33vᵖᵘ c25vᵖᵘ c31sᵖᵘ Apr 27] small, compact gelding: fair handicap hurdler/chaser at **h—** best: no show in 2006/7: stays 27f: best efforts on soft/heavy going: tried in cheekpieces. *Miss S. E. Forster*

SKI DAZZLE (IRE) 6 b.g. Warcraft (USA) – Copperhurst (IRE) (Royal Vulcan) **h—** [2006/7 F17v⁵ F16s⁵ 19d 20mᵖᵘ Mar 25] €9,500 4-y-o: second foal: dam, winning **F72** hurdler/chaser who stayed 25f, out of sister to useful chaser up to 3m Bold Yeoman: fifth in bumpers: little impact in novice hurdles. *C. C. Bealby*

SKIDDAW JONES 7 b.g. Emperor Jones (USA) – Woodrising (Nomination) [2006/7 **h—** h90: 16g May 24] modest maiden hurdler: badly hampered fifth when well held only start **h—** in 2006/7: raced around 2m: acts on good to firm and good to soft going: tongue tied. *M. A. Barnes*

SKIDMARK 6 b.g. Pennekamp (USA) – Flourishing (IRE) (Trojan Fen) [2006/7 16g² **h87** 16m 16fᵖᵘ Jul 19] half-brother to modest hurdler up to 3m Musally (by Muhtarram): fairly useful at best on Flat (stays 1¼m), on downgrade: easily best effort over hurdles (modest form) on debut: seemed to go amiss final start. *Miss J. R. Tooth*

SKI JUMP (USA) 7 gr.g. El Prado (IRE) – Skiable (IRE) (Niniski (USA)) [2006/7 16g³ **h92 p** Mar 16] fairly useful on Flat (effective at 1½m to 2½m), successful in June: encouraging hurdling debut when 14¾ lengths third to Doctor David in conditional jockeys maiden at Fakenham: likely to be suited by further than 2m: open to improvement. *R. A. Fahey*

SKIMAGEE (IRE) 8 ch.m. Arctic Cider (USA) – Clonminch Lady (Le Bavard (FR)) **h—** [2006/7 20s⁶ 24sᵖᵘ Nov 29] winning pointer: no form over hurdles. *Michael McElhone, Ireland*

SKIP 'N' TUNE (IRE) 10 b.m. Mandalus – Molten (Ore) [2006/7 c–: c25m⁵ May 12] **c—** winning pointer: well beaten in hunter chases. *R. N. Miller*

SKIPPERHAM WELL 5 b.m. Wimbleball – Spirit Level (Sunley Builds) [2006/7 **F—** F16sᵖᵘ Mar 8] small mare: second foal: dam, poor hurdler, effective from 2m to 27f: no show in maiden bumper on debut. *J. R. Payne*

SKIPPERS BRIG (IRE) 6 b.g. Zaffaran (USA) – Mathewsrose (IRE) (Roselier (FR)) **h125**
[2006/7 F108: F17v* 20s^ur 20v* 20v* 20s^2 24g Mar 16] tall, good-topped gelding: chas- **F115**
ing type: useful bumper winner, beating Supremely Gifted easily by 10 lengths at Carlisle
in November: fairly useful novice hurdler: won at Ayr and Haydock (beat Nevertika by 8
lengths) in December: stiff task final outing: should stay 3m: acts on heavy ground: hung
left circuit out fifth start. *L. Lungo*

SKIPPING CHAPEL 6 ch.g. Minster Son – Harrietfield (Nicholas Bill) [2006/7 **F72 +**
F16v^5 Jan 28] third foal: half-brother to fair chaser Fearless Foursome (by Perpendicular), stayed 21f: dam unraced half-sister to fair chaser Solsgirth, stayed 25f: fifth to
Steady Tiger in maiden bumper at Kelso on debut, travelling strongly long way: likely to
do better. *N. W. Alexander*

SKISTORM 5 b.m. Petoski – Dai-Namic-Storm (IRE) (Glacial Storm (USA)) [2006/7 **h–**
F–: F17m F16g 22s^5 24s Dec 2] lengthy, angular mare: little impact in bumpers/maiden **F68**
hurdles. *D. A. Rees*

SKULLDUGGERY 6 b.g. Rakaposhi King – Orphan Annie (Gunner B) [2006/7 F17m **h–**
F17v F14v F16g 16v Mar 6] 3,100 4-y-o: second foal: dam unraced: no form in bumpers **F–**
(for R. Barr on debut)/novice hurdle. *C. Grant*

SKY BY NIGHT 6 b.m. Riverwise (USA) – Purbeck Polly (Pollerton) [2006/7 F–: **h–**
F14g 16g^pu Dec 26] neat mare: no form in bumpers/novice hurdle. *B. J. M. Ryall* **F–**

SKY MACK (IRE) 6 ch.g. Anshan – Ramona Style (IRE) (Duky) [2006/7 h100+, F91: **h110**
22m* 24m^pu 24g Apr 18] lengthy, unfurnished gelding: fair novice hurdler: won at
Wincanton in May: disappointing next 2 starts 9 months apart, leaving Evan Williams in
between: stays 2¾m: acts on good to firm and good to soft going. *Miss H. Lewis*

SKY'S THE LIMIT (FR) 6 gr.g. Medaaly – Highness Lady (GER) (Cagliostro **c120**
(GER)) [2006/7 h156: c16s^3 c16s^3 c17s^6 24m^2 24m Apr 26] close-coupled gelding: very **h127**
smart hurdler, well below best last 2 starts: just fairly useful form over fences: stays 21f:
acts on heavy going: usually wears headgear. *E. J. O'Grady, Ireland*

SKY TO SEA (FR) 9 b.g. Adieu Au Roi (IRE) – Urban Sky (FR) (Groom Dancer **h126**
(USA)) [2006/7 16d* 16v* 16v* 16s^5 Nov 12] compact gelding: fairly useful hurdler: left
Mrs A. O'Shea, much improved in 2006/7, winning maiden at Kilbeggan and handicaps
at Listowel later in September and Galway (by 2½ lengths from Lagudin) in October:
reportedly injured hind leg final outing: raced at 2m: acts on heavy going: tried blinkered.
R. Donohoe, Ireland

SKY WARRIOR (FR) 9 b.g. Warrshan (USA) – Sky Bibi (FR) (Sky Lawyer (FR)) **c106**
[2006/7 c124, h–: 20f 20m^3 24m^5 c21d c20m^4 c21s^pu c23s^3 c24m c21g^3 c21g^6 c20f^4 **h105**
c19g^3 Apr 27] medium-sized gelding: fair handicap hurdler/chaser: stays 3m: acts on soft
and firm going: tried in cheekpieces. *Evan Williams*

SLADE SUPREME (IRE) 5 b.m. Ridgewood Ben – Supremememories (IRE) (Sup- **F–**
reme Leader) [2006/7 F–: F16d Oct 18] no show in bumpers or points. *D. A. Rees*

SLALOM (IRE) 7 b.g. Royal Applause – Skisette (Malinowski (USA)) [2006/7 h93: **c92 x**
22s^pu c20m^F c20m^3 c20m^pu c20g^6 c20d^3 Aug 19] modest hurdler/maiden chaser: let down **h–**
by jumping/attitude last 3 starts: stays 2¾m: acts on firm going, below form on softer
than good: has worn cheekpieces/visor. *D. Burchell*

SLAVEDRIVER 6 ch.g. Karinga Bay – Gaygo Lady (Gay Fandango (USA)) [2006/7 **h–**
F17g^3 17s^F 16s^F 16s 17s Jan 26] workmanlike gelding: half-brother to 3 winners, includ- **F78**
ing 2m hurdle winner Thenameescapesme (by Alderbrook) and chase winner in Switzerland by Glenstal: dam 1m winner: third in bumper: no form over hurdles. *T. R. George*

SLAVONIC (USA) 6 ch.g. Royal Academy (USA) – Cyrillic (USA) (Irish River (FR)) **h–**
[2006/7 16f 17f^pu 16f^pu Sep 29] fair on Flat (stays 1¼m), successful twice in 2005 for
K. Ryan, tailed off both starts in 2006: no form over hurdles. *B. Storey*

SLEEPING NIGHT (FR) 11 b.g. Sleeping Car (FR) – Doll Night (FR) (Karkour **c–**
(FR)) [2006/7 c25v^F 24v^6 c24d^6 Feb 10] rather leggy gelding: winning hurdler: smart **h–**
chaser at best, won all 4 completed starts in 2004/5, including Christie's Foxhunter Chase
at Cheltenham: off 20 months, close up when falling heavily 4 out in handicap at
Wetherby: stiff task final outing: stays 3¼m: acts on heavy going: has high head carriage.
P. F. Nicholls

SLEEPLESS EYE 5 b.m. Supreme Leader – Blast Freeze (IRE) (Lafontaine (USA)) **h–**
[2006/7 16v^4 Nov 25] 37,000 3-y-o, 40,000 4-y-o: second foal: half-sister to fairly useful
hurdler/useful maiden chaser Wee Robbie (by Bob Back), stays 3m, and bumper winner

Isn't That Lucky (by Alflora): dam useful hurdler up to 2½m: tailed-off fourth of 5 finishers in mares novice hurdle on debut. *Jonjo O'Neill*

SLEW CHARM (FR) 5 b.g. Marathon (USA) – Slew Bay (FR) (Beaudelaire (USA)) [2006/7 h118: 16d² 16d² 19d^F 16g^pu 20f Apr 28] good-topped gelding: fairly useful handicap hurdler: good efforts first 2 starts, beaten 2 lengths by Blazing Bailey in 4-y-o event at Haydock on second occasion: disappointing last 2 outings: raced mainly around 2m on good going or softer: often tongue tied: has worn earplugs in preliminaries. *Noel T. Chance* **h127**

SLICK (FR) 6 br.g. Highest Honor (FR) – Seven Secrets (Ajdal (USA)) [2006/7 h–, F97: 16s 16d* 19d Nov 23] sturdy gelding: bumper winner: successful also in conditional/amateur novice handicap at Wincanton in November, but disappointing over hurdles otherwise: raced mainly at 2m on good to soft/soft going. *N. J. Henderson* **h92**

SLIGHT HICCUP 7 ch.m. Alderbrook – Very Ominous (Dominion) [2006/7 h–, F81: 21m^pu Nov 9] small, light-framed mare: no show over hurdles. *C. W. Moore* **h–**

SLIM PICKINGS (IRE) 8 b.g. Scribano – Adapan (Pitpan) [2006/7 c137, h–: c24d³ c20g³ c16s^pu c22g³ c24v^F c21g⁵ c36g³ Apr 14] rather leggy gelding: smart chaser, left Robert Tyner after fourth start: improved form when 2 lengths third to Silver Birch in Grand National at Aintree final start, leading from second Valentine's until meeting last 2 wrong, rallying: also ran well in valuable handicaps previous 2 outings, at Gowran (Thyestes Chase, likely to have been placed but for falling last) and Cheltenham (Racing Post Plate, fifth to Idole First despite mistakes): stays 4½m: raced on good going or softer (acts on heavy): tried in cheekpieces: travels strongly. *T. J. Taaffe, Ireland* **c148** **h–**

SLOW TO PART (IRE) 10 gr.g. Roselier (FR) – Comeragh Queen (The Parson) [2006/7 c25s^pu c21s² c22s² c24v^pu c25v c24g c28g⁶ c26m³ Apr 26] sturdy ex-Irish gelding: maiden hurdler: modest handicap chaser: below form last 5 starts, left Michael Cunningham before penultimate one: stays 3½m: acts on heavy ground: wears cheekpieces. *K. A. Morgan* **c91 d** **h–**

SMART AMBITION 6 b.g. Wolfhound (USA) – Gale (Strong Gale) [2006/7 F16f⁵ F16m 16g Apr 2] second foal: dam unraced daughter of useful staying chaser Dalkey Sound: little impact in bumpers/novice hurdle. *Mrs L. B. Normile* **h–** **F–**

SMART BOY PRINCE (IRE) 6 b.g. Princely Heir (FR) – Miss Mulaz (FR) (Luthier) [2006/7 h112: 22d^F 24f² 20s^pu Jan 31] leggy gelding: fair handicap hurdler: off 6 months, ran poorly final start: stays easy 3m: acts on firm and soft going: front runner/races prominently. *C. Smith* **h112**

SMART CAVALIER 8 b.g. Terimon – Smart Topsy (Oats) [2006/7 c109: c21g* c20m² Apr 22] good-topped gelding: fairly useful handicap chaser: off 12 months then improved form in April, winning at Newton Abbot in April by 1¾ lengths from Iris's Prince: 8 lengths second to East Tycoon at Stratford, tying up run-in: stays 21f: acts on soft and good to firm going: tongue tied. *P. F. Nicholls* **c119**

SMART GOLDEN BOY (IRE) 4 ch.g. Raise A Grand (IRE) – Stoneware (Bigstone (IRE)) [2006/7 16d 17s 18s⁶ Feb 4] maiden on Flat: well held in juvenile hurdles: tongue tied last 2 starts. *Mrs L. C. Jewell* **h–**

SMART MAN 5 gr.g. Silver Patriarch (IRE) – Run Tiger (IRE) (Commanche Run) [2006/7 h–: 20s 25s^pu 20s 16s^F 19s 17m Apr 9] tall gelding: no form in novice hurdles. *Mrs E. Slack* **h–**

SMART MINISTER 7 gr.g. Muhtarram (USA) – She's Smart (Absalom) [2006/7 16m³ 16m² 17m 16m² Aug 3] fair on Flat (best effort at 6f) at 4 yrs for J. Quinn: modest form over hurdles, left L. James after debut: likely to prove best at 2m with emphasis on speed: raced on good to firm going. *P. D. Niven* **h89**

SMART MOVER 8 b.g. Supreme Leader – Rachel C (IRE) (Phardante (FR)) [2006/7 h111: 22d² 25g² 21d^pu Dec 26] strong, compact gelding: fairly useful hurdler: best effort when 5 lengths second to Lou du Moulin Mas in novice at Cheltenham second start: stayed 25f: acted on soft and good to firm going: dead. *Miss H. C. Knight* **h120**

SMART (POL) 4 b.g. Professional (IRE) – Spisa (POL) (Animo (GER)) [2006/7 F16d Jan 19] Polish-bred gelding: tailed off in bumper on debut. *R. C. Guest* **F–**

SMART STREET 5 b.g. Silver Patriarch (IRE) – Smart Spirit (IRE) (Persian Bold) [2006/7 F–: F17m² F16m³ 17d⁴ 16d* 16s* 17s⁶ 16g² 16s² Apr 26] big, good-topped gelding: placed in bumpers: fair novice hurdler: won at Kelso in October (maiden) and November (beat To Tiger by 1¾ lengths): good efforts last 2 starts: raced mainly around **h114** **F87**

2m: acts on soft ground (bumper form on good to firm): front runner/races prominently. *K. G. Reveley*

SMART THINKER 6 gr.m. Silver Patriarch (IRE) – Smart Rhythm (True Song) [2006/7 20s 24v[pu] 27s[5] 27v 27v[su] c20s[5] c26g[5] Apr 7] angular mare: little form over hurdles/fences. *Ferdy Murphy* — **c74 h71**

SMART TIGER (GER) 5 b.g. Tiger Hill (IRE) – Smoke Signal (IRE) (College Chapel) [2006/7 h–: 19d[5] 17g[6] 20m[ur] 17m 17f[6] 19d[F] 20m[2] 22m[3] 19m* Apr 11] modest hurdler: off 6½ months, didn't need to be at best to win novice seller at Exeter in April: stays 2½m: acts on good to firm and good to soft going: in headgear since debut. *Evan Williams* — **h94**

SMART TOM (IRE) 6 b.g. Un Desperado (FR) – Paper Merchant (Hays) [2006/7 F17s[5] F13s* Dec 16] €11,000 3-y-o, £18,000 4-y-o, resold 26,000 4-y-o: tall, lengthy gelding: fifth foal: dam maiden: better effort in bumpers when winning at Haydock by 7 lengths from Alfabet Souk. *R. T. Phillips* — **F89**

SMARTYPANTS 9 b.g. Arms And The Man – Gold Tip (Billion (USA)) [2006/7 22m[pu] Aug 24] bad maiden pointer: no show on hurdling debut. *A. Ennis* — **h–**

SMEATHE'S RIDGE 9 b.g. Rakaposhi King – Mrs Barty (IRE) (King's Ride) [2006/7 c92, h77: c21v c24d[pu] c21d[2] c24d c20v[pu] Feb 27] good-topped gelding: maiden hurdler: modest handicap chaser: form in 2006/7 only on third start: should prove suited by 3m+: raced on good ground or softer (probably acts on heavy): tried in cheekpieces (mistakes). *J. A. B. Old* — **c92 h–**

SMEMI AN NADA 5 b.g. Selkirk (USA) – One Way Street (Habitat) [2006/7 h–: 16g[6] 18m 21m Nov 9] rather leggy gelding: signs of a little ability over hurdles. *P. Bowen* — **h78**

SMILEAFACT 7 b.g. So Factual (USA) – Smilingatstrangers (Macmillion) [2006/7 h79: 23g[pu] Apr 30] tall, angular gelding: maiden hurdler: in headgear last 5 starts: has worn off-side pricker. *Mrs Barbara Waring* — **h–**

SMILING APPLAUSE 8 b.g. Royal Applause – Smilingatstrangers (Macmillion) [2006/7 h73: 22m[pu] Apr 22] lightly raced: maiden hurdler: off 22 months, no show only start in 2006/7: tried visored. *Mrs Barbara Waring* — **h–**

SMILINGVALENTINE (IRE) 10 b.m. Supreme Leader – Cool Princess (Proverb) [2006/7 c–, h78: 21m* 19s[2] 20m[3] 24g[pu] Jul 21] winning Irish pointer: no show only start in chase: poor hurdler: won conditional jockeys seller at Ludlow in May: stays 2¾m: acts on heavy and good to firm going: tried blinkered (below form). *D. J. Wintle* — **c– h82**

SMITHS LANDING 10 b.g. Primitive Rising (USA) – Landing Power (Hill's Forecast) [2006/7 c125, h–: 17g c22g[4] Sep 23] medium-sized gelding: fairly useful chaser: creditable fourth to Kings Brook in valuable handicap at Market Rasen: similar form at best over hurdles, off 16 months before reappearance: stays 25f: acts on firm and soft going, below form only start on heavy: often races prominently. *Mrs S. J. Smith* — **c125 h108**

SMOKE TRAIL (IRE) 8 b.g. Zaffaran (USA) – Ardee Princess (Monksfield) [2006/7 h–, F–: 17m[4] 17m[2] 21s[pu] c17m[3] c16g[4] c16g[2] c17g[3] c16f* Apr 22] strong gelding: has stringhalt: maiden hurdler: fairly useful chaser: improved efforts last 2 starts, winning handicap at Wincanton in April by 4 lengths from Wages: best form around 2m (should stay further): acts on firm going, possibly unsuited by soft/heavy: often tongue tied. *R. H. Buckler* — **c116 h87**

SMOKEY MOUNTAIN (IRE) 6 b.g. Saddlers' Hall (IRE) – Coco Opera (IRE) (Lafontaine (USA)) [2006/7 h101, F87: 16m[4] 18m[4] 17d[4] 17m[4] c16m[4] c18g[4] c16d[3] c19g[pu] Nov 17] smallish gelding: fair hurdler/maiden chaser: likely to stay 2½m: acts on good to firm and good to soft going: joined J. Groucott. *D. P. Keane* — **c106 h101**

SMOKEY THE BEAR 5 ch.g. Fumo di Londra (IRE) – Noble Soul (Sayf El Arab (USA)) [2006/7 h85: 18m[6] May 5] modest form over hurdles: raced around 2m. *Miss S. West* — **h89**

SMOOTHLY DOES IT 6 b.g. Efisio – Exotic Forest (Dominion) [2006/7 h91: 16g[2] 17m[5] 17d[2] 16m[4] 16g[3] 16v* 16v* Jan 3] smallish, close-coupled gelding: fair on Flat (stays 1¼m): fair hurdler: claimed from Mrs A. Bowlby £6,000 fifth start: much improved when winning handicaps at Wetherby in December (easily) and January (favourite, beat The Hairy Lemon by 5 lengths): raced around 2m: acts on good to firm and heavy ground: takes keen hold, and patiently ridden: fluent jumper. *R. A. Fahey* — **h112**

SMOOTH MOVER 5 b.g. Mister Baileys – Dancing Heights (IRE) (High Estate) [2006/7 19d[pu] Mar 26] strong gelding: last in 1¼m maidens at 3 yrs for S. C. Williams: blinkered/tongue tied, always behind in maiden on hurdling debut. *A. Middleton* — **h–**

SNAKEBITE (IRE) 7 gr.g. Taipan (IRE) – Bee In The Rose (IRE) (Roselier (FR)) **c131**
[2006/7 h124: c20d⁴ c20v² c25s* c24v⁵ Jan 20] good-topped gelding: fairly useful **h–**
hurdler: good start over fences, in frame behind Denman in novices at Cheltenham and
Newbury (12 lengths second in Grade 2 event) prior to landing odds in maiden at
Folkestone in December: shaped better than result when 27½ lengths fifth of 9 to The
Outlier in valuable handicap at Haydock final start, travelling best long way and tiring
badly from last: may prove best short of 3m when conditions are testing: raced mainly on
going softer than good (acts on heavy): sound-jumping front runner. *Carl Llewellyn*

SNAKECHARM (IRE) 5 b.g. Taipan (IRE) – Sparkling Opera (Orchestra) [2006/7 **F88**
F14s² Feb 18] €24,000 3-y-o: rather unfurnished gelding: half-brother to several winners,
including fairly useful hurdler/fair chaser Ciara's Prince (by Good Thyne), stayed 3m:
dam unraced, out of half-sister to very smart 2m hurdler Miller Hill: best work at finish
when 1½ lengths second to easy winner Clay Hollister in bumper at Fontwell on debut.
J. A. B. Old

SNAKE RAVE (IRE) 5 b.g. Taipan (IRE) – Raveleen Rose (IRE) (Norwich) [2006/7 **c76 +**
20s⁴ 20s 23v 16d 24m⁶ 25v 27g⁶ c20g³ c20g^F Apr 23] sturdy gelding: first foal: dam **h92**
unraced, out of sister to top-class staying chaser The Grey Monk: little impact over
hurdles after debut: poor form when third of 4 finishers to Mr Twins in maiden at
Wetherby on completed start over fences: should stay 3m: acts on soft going. *J. Howard
Johnson*

SNAP TIE (IRE) 5 b.g. Pistolet Bleu (IRE) – Aries Girl (Valiyar) [2006/7 F16g* F16s² **F110**
F16d⁶ F16g² Mar 24] tall, unfurnished gelding: fourth foal: half-brother to bumper
winner Top Ram (by Topanoora); dam, useful hurdler around 2m, half-sister to useful 2m
hurdler Spokesman: won bumper at Limerick in May on debut by 3 lengths from
Daramas: left John Kiely, better form (useful) when runner-up in similar events at
Cheltenham and Newbury, beaten 3½ lengths by Helens Vision on return from 4½-month
break at latter. *P. J. Hobbs*

SNARGATE 7 b.g. Double Eclipse (IRE) – Loch Irish (IRE) (Lancastrian) [2006/7 F87: **h–**
F16d 20s^F 26v⁵ Jan 11] third in bumper on debut in early-2005/6, only form. **F–**
Mrs S. E. Handley

SNIPE 9 ch.g. Anshan – Flexwing (Electric) [2006/7 c96, h–: c24g⁴ c21g³ c20m⁶ c23f² **c89**
c23f⁵ c24m⁵ 21d c20m c23m* Apr 25] lengthy, angular gelding: winning hurdler: modest **h–**
chaser: left Ian Williams after sixth outing: won novice handicap at Worcester in April:
stays easy 3m: acts on firm and soft going: has found little. *J. B. Groucott*

SNIPE WALK (IRE) 5 ch.g. Great Palm (USA) – Tektouka (FR) (Always Fair (USA)) **h–**
[2006/7 F16g F16g F16s 16s 16v 16v 17g^pu Apr 11] first foal: dam maiden: no form: tried **F–**
tongue tied. *S. Donohoe, Ireland*

SNOB WELLS (IRE) 10 b.g. Sadler's Wells (USA) – Galitizine (USA) (Riverman **c–**
(USA)) [2006/7 19m⁶ 17d² 20m* 24g⁴ 20m⁵ c28s⁵ Oct 26] lengthy, useful-looking geld- **h92**
ing: winning chaser: modest hurdler: left N. Meade before reappearance: won conditional
jockeys seller at Huntingdon (sold from John Harris 8,000 gns) in August: stays 3m: acts
on good to firm and heavy going: has worn blinkers/cheekpieces: tongue tied: sometimes
let down by jumping over fences: has looked none too keen. *N. B. King*

SNOOPY LOOPY (IRE) 9 ch.g. Old Vic – Lovely Snoopy (IRE) (Phardante (FR)) **c–**
[2006/7 c101p, h–: c22s³ Nov 16] leggy gelding: lightly raced: one-time useful hurdler **h–**
for Miss V. Scott: better effort in maiden chases 16 months apart when second at Worcester in 2005/6 (reportedly finished sore): not fluent on return: stays 2½m: acts on heavy
going. *P. Bowen*

SNOOTY ESKIMO (IRE) 15 ch.g. Aristocracy – Over The Arctic (Over The River **c–**
(FR)) [2006/7 c89, h–: c20v^pu c20m Jun 3] workmanlike gelding: winning pointer: **h–**
maiden chaser: effective at 2m to 25f: acts on any going. *Mrs Marian Nicol*

SNOW PATROL 6 gr.g. Linamix (FR) – Overcast (IRE) (Caerleon (USA)) [2006/7 **h107**
16v* Feb 15] fair hurdler, formerly trained in France/Ireland: 11/8-on, made winning
return from 13 months off when beating Gunnasayso 5 lengths in maiden at Chepstow:
stays 19f: acts on heavy going. *P. J. Hobbs*

SNOW'S RIDE 7 gr.g. Hernando (FR) – Crodelle (IRE) (Formidable (USA)) [2006/7 **h–**
h104: 16g 20g^pu 20g^pu Apr 3] close-coupled gelding: fair hurdler at best: no form in
handicaps in 2006/7 (off 10 months before final outing): stays 21f: acts on good to firm
going, possibly not on heavy: tried in cheekpieces. *Micky Hammond*

SNOWTRE (IRE) 10 b.g. Glacial Storm (USA) – Forest Gale (Strong Gale) [2006/7 **h–**
26m⁶ Jun 14] winning pointer: in cheekpieces, last on hurdling debut. *Mrs H. L. Needham*

SNOW WOLF 6 ch.g. Wolfhound (USA) – Christmas Rose (Absalom) [2006/7 16g^{pu} **h–**
Sep 6] modest on Flat (effective at 5f/6f): unlikely to stay over hurdles. *J. M. Bradley*

SNOWY FORD (IRE) 10 b.g. Be My Native (USA) – Monalee Stream (Paddy's   **c– §**
Stream) [2006/7 c119§, h–§: c24d c26v^4 Dec 11] medium-sized gelding: winning hurd-   **h– §**
ler: fairly useful handicap chaser at best, no form since second outing in 2005/6: stays
3¼m: acts on heavy going: tried in blinkers (including when successful)/cheekpieces:
unreliable. *P. R. Webber*

SNOWY (IRE) 9 gr.g. Pierre – Snowy Gunner (Gunner B) [2006/7 c106, h–: c22m^5 **c111**
c26s c25g^6 c24d^5 c20d* c20v* Mar 10] good-topped gelding: winning hurdler: fair   **h–**
handicap chaser: tongue tied, back in form last 2 outings, winning at Musselburgh in
December and Ayr (4-runner race) in March: stays 25f: acts on any going. *G. A. Charlton*

SNOWY MORNING (IRE) 7 b.g. Moscow Society (USA) – Miss Perky (IRE)   **c148**
(Creative Plan (USA)) [2006/7 F16d^6 22v^2 24m* c20v* c19v^2 c20v* c24v* c24g^2 **h122**
c25m^4 Apr 24]   **F99**
    If there had been a jockeys' championship based on performances in
Britain and Ireland combined the winner in 2006/7 would have been Ruby Walsh.
Tony McCoy managed a combined total of 191 wins, with just seven from fifty-
three rides coming in Ireland, a surprisingly small number, given his retainer with
J. P. McManus—McCoy rode over half the owner's British winners, but just four of
fifty-seven gained by him in Ireland. Walsh, by contrast, managed a pretty similar
strike rate in both countries, seventy-three wins from 291 rides in Britain and 125
from 562 in Ireland, giving a combined total of 198 from 853 rides, seven wins
ahead of his great rival. Incidentally, that combined total looks set to rise to 200 as
two seconds for Walsh, both at Ayr late in the season, are due to be awarded races in
which the Peter Bowen-trained winners failed post-race tests. In Britain, Walsh
rides almost exclusively for Paul Nicholls, with all but five of his wins in 2006/7
coming for the champion trainer, four of the remainder for Irish yards. In Ireland,
Walsh's main supplier of rides is Willie Mullins, a third of his wins coming for that
yard, whilst Nicholls saddled only one runner on Irish soil in 2006/7 (Punchestown
Gold Cup winner Neptune Collonges!). Walsh's remaining Irish wins were shared
between thirty other trainers, which means he rode winners for exactly the same
number of trainers (thirty-two) as McCoy did on the way to his twelfth consecutive
British championship. McCoy and Walsh are often presented as chalk and cheese,
McCoy's greatest strength his will to win and power in the saddle, Walsh portrayed
as much more the polished horseman, a patient rider often seen oozing confidence
before producing his mount with a perfectly-timed challenge. Walsh's ride on
Ladalko to win at Warwick in the latest season was classic Walsh but, as he showed
when claiming a last-gasp win over the McCoy-ridden Straw Bear on board Noland
in the 2006 Supreme Novices', he can throw the kitchen sink to good effect when
required.
    Another good example of Walsh's strength in the saddle came on the
Mullins-trained Snowy Morning, in a novice chase at Gowran on Thyestes Chase
day in January. After being ridden along to go five lengths clear at the last, Snowy
Morning hung markedly left and needed firm driving to hold on all out by half a
length from Ponmeoath. That success was the fourth of five all told during the
season for Snowy Morning, whose campaign began with victory in a bumper at
Ballinrobe in May (when ridden by Walsh's sister Katie). He followed that with a
success on the second of two starts over hurdles, a three-mile maiden at Punchestown in June, then was off for six and a half months before making a winning start
over fences in a maiden at Navan. Snowy Morning was reported likely to be
stepped up next to Grade 1 level at the Leopardstown Christmas Festival but he
contested a novice at Naas instead, a tendency to wander and a trip short of two and
a half miles contributing to his defeat by outsider Baron de Feypo. Snowy Morning
got things back on track at Gowran and showed further improvement when returned
to Navan for the ladbrokes.com Ten Up Novices' Chase and a first attempt at three
miles over fences. Snowy Morning demonstrated abundant stamina on very testing
ground to defeat the useful mare Gazza's Girl by four lengths.
    Snowy Morning and Gazza's Girl met again in the Royal & SunAlliance
Chase at Cheltenham, and, even though he wasn't weighted to confirm placings,
Snowy Morning started much the shorter odds, sent off a 10/1 chance. Under Mick

Fitzgerald, Snowy Morning never looked likely to get to grips with the Walsh-ridden favourite Denman, who won by ten lengths, but Snowy Morning stayed on strongly to take second ahead of outsiders According To John and Aces Four, with Gazza's Girl fifth, just over five lengths behind. Snowy Morning was probably fortunate to finish in front of Aces Four, who wasn't helped by a bad stumble three out, and when the pair met again six weeks later at Punchestown Aces Four was favourite at 6/4 ahead of Snowy Morning at 9/4. Aces Four was in the lead when taking a crashing fall at the last but Snowy Morning wasn't the one to take advantage. He was a major disappointment, making little impression and beaten thirty-four lengths by the winner Offshore Account. As on his other appearances on right-handed tracks, he showed a distinct tendency to hang left (as he had when winning there over hurdles) and it may well be that he will prove ideally suited by left-handed courses.

The workmanlike Snowy Morning has a largely undistinguished pedigree. His unraced dam Miss Perky is a half-sister to the smart but ungenuine staying chaser Him of Praise, whose biggest victories came in the Mildmay Cazalet at Sandown and the Singer & Friedlander National Trial at Uttoxeter. He made the frame in the latter event three times and was also placed in two other noted National trials, the Greenalls at Haydock (twice) and the Becher Chase at Aintree, and it could well be that Snowy Morning also develops into a 'National' type rather than a serious contender for top conditions races. He will be suited by further than three miles and is likely to stay four miles or more. He has run his best race so far on good ground but also clearly handles heavy well, whilst his hurdles win came on good to firm.

Snowy Morning (IRE)	Moscow Society (USA)	Nijinsky	Northern Dancer
(b.g. 2000)	(ch 1985)	(b 1967)	Flaming Page
		Afifa	Dewan
		(ch 1974)	Hooplah
	Miss Perky (IRE)	Creative Plan	Sham
	(b 1989)	(b 1977)	Another Treat
		Tamed	Rusticaro
		(b 1983)	Viable

Snowy Morning has been through the sale-ring three times, as a foal, as a three-year-old, when he made €25,000 at the Derby Sale, and as a four-year-old, when he made 10,000 guineas at the Doncaster May Sales. He was due to return to the latter venue at five but, by that stage, he had made four appearances in points

Quayside Syndicate's "Snowy Morning"

in Ireland, winning on the last one after finishing runner-up three times, and was withdrawn from the sale. Snowy Morning made two further appearances in points early in 2006, winning on his completed start, before joining his present stable. Snowy Morning's success ensured that his three-year-old half-brother by Strategic Choice drew a bit more interest at the Derby Sale in June, making €30,000, sold to join Donald McCain. *W. P. Mullins, Ireland*

SOBERS (IRE) 6 b.g. Epervier Bleu – Falcon Crest (FR) (Cadoudal (FR)) [2006/7 **h126** h85p, F93: 17s* 17v* Dec 12] rangy, useful-looking gelding: left R. C. Guest and off 8 months, confirmed promise of eye-catching hurdling debut (jockey/horse banned under non-triers rule) when winning novices at Folkestone in November and December: again showed good attitude when beating Kings Signal by short head on latter occasion: reported in early-January to have suffered serious injury when schooling: raced around 2m, mainly on soft/heavy ground. *N. J. Gifford*

SO BRASH (IRE) 7 ch.g. Rashar (USA) – Oak Tavern Lady (Dublin Taxi) [2006/7 **c–** h93, F90: 17m⁵ 17m 20m* 20m* c16f⁶ 20g 19d 19g³ 22dᵖᵘ 17m⁶ 20gᵖᵘ Apr 27] sturdy **h92** gelding: modest novice hurdler: won twice at Worcester in July: largely below form after: never dangerous on chasing debut: stays 2½m: acts on soft and good to firm going. *P. C. Ritchens*

SOCARINEAU (FR) 9 b.g. Assessor (IRE) – Samya King (FR) (King of Macedon) **c–** [2006/7 c–, h72: 21mᵖᵘ 16g May 21] winning pointer: maiden hurdler/chaser: tried **h–** blinkered/in cheekpieces. *N. J. Pomfret*

SOCIETY BUCK (IRE) 10 b.g. Moscow Society (USA) – Bucks Grove (IRE) **c– §** (Buckskin (FR)) [2006/7 h100d: 26m 16d c21d² c23m⁵ c23mᵖᵘ Apr 25] smallish, lengthy **h– §** gelding: fair hurdler at best, has lost his way: no form over fences: should stay 3m: best efforts over hurdles on good going (won bumper on good to firm): tried in cheekpieces: one to leave alone. *John Allen*

SO CLOUDY 6 gr.m. Cloudings (IRE) – Sotattie (Teenoso (USA)) [2006/7 h71, F70: **h95** 16m⁶ 16g* 17m³ 16g³ 16f³ 17m² 16g² 17d³ 20d* 21s 17s⁶ 21fᵖᵘ Apr 5] modest novice hurdler: won at Hexham (amateur handicap) in May and Musselburgh (mares) in January (placed all 6 starts in between): stays 2½m: seems to act on firm and soft going: has raced freely (saddle slipped final outing): reliable. *D. McCain Jnr*

SODANTAY (IRE) 5 b.g. Accordion – Millennium Gift (IRE) (Balla Cove) [2006/7 **h–** F16v⁶ F16v⁴ 20sᵘʳ 16s Apr 27] €11,000 4-y-o: first foal: dam, no form in bumpers, out of **F70** half-sister to high-class hurdler/useful chaser Cockney Lad, best up to 2½m: poor form in bumpers: well held completed start in maiden hurdles. *A. C. Whillans*

SOEUR FONTENAIL (FR) 10 b.m. Turgeon (USA) – Fontanalia (FR) (Rex Magna **c103** (FR)) [2006/7 c106, h–: c20g⁴ Oct 30] big, lengthy mare: winning hurdler: fair handicap **h–** chaser on her day: stays 21f: acts on heavy going (no form on firmer than good): tried in cheekpieces: sound jumper: front runner/races prominently: often runs as if amiss. *N. J. Hawke*

SOFT SPOKEN (FR) 5 b.g. Turgeon (USA) – Miss Planette (FR) (Tip Moss (FR)) **h– p** [2006/7 F16d² F16f³ 16v Jan 7] fifth foal: half-brother to bumper winner The Weaver (by **F93** Villez): dam placed up to 21f over fences in France: best effort in bumpers when neck second to Raichu at Down Royal in May: off 6 months, well held in maiden on hurdling debut: should do better. *J. F. C. Maxwell, Ireland*

SOHO SQUARE 4 ch.g. Generous (IRE) – Stardance (USA) (Rahy (USA)) [2006/7 **h– x** 16m 17v 16v 16m Feb 4] fairly useful at best on Flat (stays 1½m), has hinted at temperament, sold out of M. Johnston's stable 23,000 gns Newmarket July Sales: badly let down by jumping over hurdles. *L. Lungo*

SOIXANTE (IRE) 4 b.g. Old Vic – Dantes Serenade (IRE) (Phardante (FR)) [2006/7 **F98** F16g² Mar 29] second foal: dam unraced: 2½ lengths second of 16 to Gypsy Scholar in bumper at Towcester on debut, eye-catching headway to lead briefly in straight. *Miss H. C. Knight*

SOLARIAS QUEST 5 b.g. Pursuit of Love – Persuasion (Batshoof) [2006/7 h–: 16sᵖᵘ **h–** Nov 25] strong, lengthy gelding: fairly useful on Flat at one time: amiss all 3 starts over hurdles: joined R. Lee. *A. King*

SOLARIUS (FR) 10 ch.g. Kris – Nouvelle Lune (FR) (Be My Guest (USA)) [2006/7 **c–** 23vᵖᵘ 22vᵖᵘ Jan 25] angular gelding: one-time useful hurdler/chaser in France: no show **h–** in handicaps in Britain, left M. Scudamore and off 22 months prior to reappearance: stays 2½m: acts on heavy ground: sold 4,000 gns Doncaster March Sales. *D. E. Pipe*

SOLAR SYSTEM (IRE) 10 b.g. Accordion – Fauvette (USA) (Youth (USA)) **c121**
[2006/7 c125, h–: c17v³ c26gᵘʳ Nov 19] lengthy gelding: fairly useful handicap chaser: **h–**
hampered and unseated sixth (Chair) in Becher Chase at Aintree: stays 29f, effective at
much shorter: acts on heavy going (unraced on firmer than good). *T. J. Taaffe, Ireland*

SOLDERSHIRE 10 b.g. Weld – Dishcloth (Fury Royal) [2006/7 c21g⁵ May 24] novice **c–**
hurdler: winning pointer: last in novice hunter on chasing debut: stays 2¾m: acts on good **h–**
to firm going: visored once. *James Etheridge*

SOLDIERS ROMANCE 4 b.g. Allied Forces (USA) – Still In Love (Emarati (USA)) **h–**
[2006/7 16dᵖᵘ 17sᵖᵘ Oct 25] angular gelding: modest form on Flat: no show in juvenile
hurdles. *T. D. Easterby*

SOLD ON (IRE) 5 b.g. Sea Raven (IRE) – Crashrun (Crash Course) [2006/7 F18s⁴ **h83**
F16s 24g⁵ F19v Mar 18] half-brother to winning hurdler/chaser around 2m Cumbrian **F–**
Knight (by Presenting) and fair hurdlers My Name's Not Bin (by Good Thyne), stayed
3m and Clew Bay Cove (by Anshan), 2m winner: dam unraced: no form in bumpers:
seemed suited by longer trip when 34 lengths fifth to Shannon Springs in maiden at
Ludlow on hurdling debut. *T. J. Arnold, Ireland*

SOLE AGENT (IRE) 5 b.g. Trans Island – Seattle Siren (USA) (Seattle Slew (USA)) **h109**
[2006/7 h102: 16g⁴ 16v⁴ 17s* 21s³ 20s 21v⁴ Feb 12] tall gelding: fair handicap hurdler:
won at Taunton in December: stays 21f: raced on good going or softer (acts on heavy): in
cheekpieces last 4 outings. *G. L. Moore*

SOLEIL D'HIVER 6 b.m. Bahamian Bounty – Catriona (Bustino) [2006/7 h–: 16d⁴ **h–**
25vᵖᵘ 16s 18vᵖᵘ 21m Apr 8] angular mare: winning hurdler, no form since 2004/5: tried
in headgear. *C. J. Drewe*

SOLEMN VOW 6 b.m. Zaffaran (USA) – Quick Quick Sloe (Scallywag) [2006/7 h–: **h–**
20g May 11] leggy mare: no form in bumpers/novice hurdles. *P. Maddison*

SOLENT SUNBEAM 7 b.m. Sovereign Water (FR) – Sail On Sunday (Sunyboy) **h–**
[2006/7 h–, F72: 20s Dec 7] good-topped mare: poor form in mares bumpers: soundly
beaten 2 starts over hurdles: bred to stay well beyond 2m. *K. C. Bailey*

SOLID AS A ROCK 7 b.g. Bijou d'Inde – Post Impressionist (IRE) (Ahonoora) **c97**
[2006/7 F98: F16s c26d⁵ c22s³ c23s⁵ c24s* Dec 26] point/bumper winner: first solid form **F87**
in chases when winning minor event at Towcester: stays 3m: raced on ground softer than
good (bumper win on heavy). *J. G. Cann*

SOLID SILVER 6 ch.g. Pharly (FR) – Shadows of Silver (Carwhite) [2006/7 F84+: **F94**
F16m* F16s² F16d⁵ Dec 14] lengthy, workmanlike gelding: fairly useful form in bumpers: stepped up on debut effort 3 months earlier when winning at Uttoxeter in July by ¾
length from Ksi Kuri. *K. G. Reveley*

SOLITARY PALM (IRE) 4 gr.g. Great Palm (USA) – Grande Solitaire (FR) (Loup **h107**
Solitaire (USA)) [2006/7 F14s 16v* 16v² 16s⁵ Apr 1] 20,000 3-y-o: lengthy, good-topped **F70**
gelding: first foal: dam unraced half-sister to useful French hurdler Grand Souvenir:
possibly needed run in bumper on debut: won juvenile maiden at Hexham in February on
first start over hurdles: better form (fair) when second to Soubriquet in juvenile at Kelso:
will be suited by further than 2m: tongue tied. *J. P. L. Ewart*

SOL RUN (FR) 4 b. or br.g. Solon (GER) – Run For Laborie (FR) (Lesotho (USA)) **h–**
[2006/7 F14s 16sᵖᵘ 18s⁶ 16v⁶ Mar 6] half-brother to fairly useful hurdler/chaser Baby **F–**
Baby Run (by Baby Turk), best around 2m: dam 9f winner: well beaten in bumper: little
show over hurdles: tongue tied last 2 starts. *J. P. L. Ewart*

SOLWAY BAY 5 b.g. Cloudings (IRE) – No Problem Jac (Safawan) [2006/7 F14d F16v **h–**
16g 16g 16s Apr 26] tall, unfurnished gelding: second foal: dam winning pointer: well **F–**
beaten in bumpers/novice hurdles. *Miss L. Harrison*

SOLWAY BEE 7 ch.m. Gunner B – Lady Mag (Silver Season) [2006/7 h80: 16s 25s **h83**
24v³ Mar 9] poor form over hurdles: stays 3m: acts on good going. *Miss L. Harrison*

SOLWAY CLOUD 7 b.m. Cloudings (IRE) – Oh Dear (Paico) [2006/7 h–: 16s 22d **h–**
May 29] no sign of ability. *Miss L. Harrison*

SOLWAY ED (IRE) 8 b.g. Mister Lord (USA) – Eds Luck (IRE) (Electric) [2006/7 h–: **h–**
24gᵖᵘ 20sᵖᵘ 22mᵖᵘ 25s 24vᵖᵘ Nov 23] of no account. *Miss L. Harrison*

SOLWAY FLO (IRE) 9 ch.m. Alflora (IRE) – Oh Dear (Paico) [2006/7 22mᵖᵘ 22m **c–**
c27g⁴ Apr 23] no form outside points (dead-heated in maiden in 2006): tried in cheek- **h–**
pieces. *Miss L. Harrison*

SOLWAY LARKIN (IRE) 9 b.m. Supreme Leader – In Any Case (IRE) (Torus) **h83**
[2006/7 h–: 24v^{pu} 22d^2 16g^4 16g^4 20f^4 22g^3 18m Oct 1] poor maiden hurdler: stays 2¾m:
acts on firm and good to soft going: effective in cheekpieces or without. *Miss L. Harrison*

SOLWAY MINSTREL 10 ch.g. Jumbo Hirt (USA) – Spicey Cut (Cut Above) [2006/7 **h95**
h80: 24s 26d* 27m^2 22v^3 24s^4 Nov 29] sturdy gelding: modest handicap hurdler: won
conditional jockeys event at Cartmel in May: thorough stayer: acts on any going:
effective in cheekpieces or without. *Miss L. Harrison*

SOLWAY SHELL 5 ch.m. Alflora (IRE) – Solway Moss (IRE) (Le Moss) [2006/7 **F–**
F16s Apr 27] seventh foal: dam unraced, half-sister to top-class staying chaser Docklands
Express: last in bumper on debut. *Miss L. Harrison*

SOLWAY STORM 6 bl.g. Cloudings (IRE) – Some Gale (Strong Gale) [2006/7 F16g^5 **F83**
Apr 23] half-brother to 3 winners, including fairly useful hurdler Long Room Lady (by
Brush Aside), stayed 2¾m, and 2½m hurdle winner Solway Gale (by Husyan): dam
unraced: 25 lengths fifth to Nodforms Paula in maiden bumper at Hexham on debut,
racing freely. *F. P. Murtagh*

SOLWAY SUNSET 8 br. or b.m. Primitive Rising (USA) – Just Jessica (State **c83**
Diplomacy (USA)) [2006/7 c81: c21s* 22d* c22m^6 c24s^3 22d^6 20d Nov 11] poor chaser: **h78**
won maiden hunter at Cartmel in May: similar form when following up in mares novice
at same course 3 months later on hurdling debut: possibly best short of 3m: acts on heavy
going: wore cheekpieces final outing. *Miss L. Harrison*

SOLWAY TRIGGER 5 b.g. Double Trigger (IRE) – Spicey Cut (Cut Above) [2006/7 **F–**
F17m^{pu} Aug 6] half-brother to modest staying hurdler Solway Minstrel (by Jumbo Hirt)
and winning hurdler/chaser Solway Breeze (by King's Ride): dam unraced, out of
half-sister to smart 3m hurdler Maelkar: soon outpaced in bumper on debut.
Miss L. Harrison

SOLWAY WILLY 6 ch.g. Bob's Return (IRE) – No Problem Jac (Safawan) [2006/7 **h–**
h–, F82: 16f^6 20s^{pu} May 17] fifth in bumper on debut for N. Richards, only form.
Miss L. Harrison

SOMEDO SOMEDONT 7 b.g. Sovereign Water (FR) – My Purple Prose (Rymer) **h94**
[2006/7 F95: 24f^3 25s^2 24v^3 Mar 15] winning pointer: runner-up in bumper for
P. Nicholls: modest form first 2 starts over hurdles, staying-on 6 lengths second to
Hockenheim in maiden at Carlisle: possibly needed run 5 months later: looks a thorough
stayer. *M. Todhunter*

SOME LEGEND (IRE) 7 b.g. Flying Legend (USA) – Albeit (Mandrake Major) **c118**
[2006/7 c24s^{ur} c17d* c18v^6 c24v c20v^5 c20g^F Apr 14] €13,000 3-y-o: lengthy gelding: **h–**
second foal: dam, 1m selling winner, lightly raced over hurdles: fair hurdler: fairly useful
novice chaser: easily won maiden at Clonmel in November: prominent when falling
heavily ninth in conditional/amateur handicap at Aintree final outing: effective at 2m to
21f: raced on good going or softer (acts on heavy). *E. J. O'Grady, Ireland*

SOME STORY (IRE) 11 b.g. Mandalus – April Lilly (Deep Run) [2006/7 24d Oct 5] **h–**
smallish gelding: poor maiden pointer: no form over hurdles. *Mrs N. Macauley*

SOMETHING CRISTAL (FR) 6 gr.g. Baby Turk – Something Fun (FR) (Rusticaro **h81 §**
(FR)) [2006/7 F72: 16s^{pu} 17s^6 19d Dec 26] strong, workmanlike gelding: poor form in
bumpers/over hurdles: tried blinkered: ungenuine. *M. Bradstock*

SOMETHING GOLD (FR) 7 gr.g. Baby Turk – Exiled (USA) (Iron Ruler (USA)) **h86**
[2006/7 h100: 24g^4 21s^5 22s^F 19d 19g Mar 23] good-topped gelding: bumper winner:
disappointing maiden hurdler: has worn blinkers. *M. Bradstock*

SOMETHING SILVER 6 gr.g. Silver Patriarch (IRE) – Phantom Singer (Relkino) **c– p**
[2006/7 h75: 20g^5 16v^3 c16v^{pu} c25v^{ur} c21v^{pu} 20v* 21v* 20v^3 Mar 22] fair hurdler: much **h108**
improved in spring, winning handicaps (conditional/amateur event first occasion) at Ayr,
second one by distance: failed to complete all 3 starts in handicap chases, twice shaping
as if amiss: will stay 3m: raced mainly on heavy ground: front runner: should still do
better over fences. *J. S. Goldie*

SOMETHING SIMPLE (IRE) 4 ch.g. Raise A Grand (IRE) – Baccara (IRE) (Sri **h–**
Pekan (USA)) [2006/7 16v 18s 17m Mar 29] ex-Irish gelding: fair maiden on Flat (stays
1¼m), left P. Henley prior to well beaten in Britain: no form in juvenile hurdles. *R. Ford*

SOMETHING WELLS (FR) 6 b.g. Dolpour – Linsky Ball (FR) (Cricket Ball **h107**
(USA)) [2006/7 h107: 22g^4 Mar 19] fair hurdler: off 15 months before only start in
2006/7: stays 2¾m: raced on good going or softer. *Miss Venetia Williams*

SOME TIMBERING (IRE) 8 b.g. Accordion – Hard Buns (IRE) (Mandalus) **c113**
[2006/7 c17d³ c16s* c17m⁵ c16v* c16s² c19sᵖᵘ c20vᵖᵘ Jan 6] sturdy, lengthy ex-Irish **h–**
gelding: winning hurdler: fair chaser: won minor event at Punchestown in May and
novice at Listowel (by 4 lengths from Anno Jubilo) in September: left E. Sheehy, no show
both starts in Britain: should stay beyond 19f: acts on heavy ground: in headgear last 6
outings. *M. Scudamore*

SOME TOUCH (IRE) 7 b.g. Scribano – Sarahs Touch (IRE) (Mandalus) [2006/7 **c113**
h112: c20g c20d* c16v* Jan 3] sturdy gelding: fair hurdler: similar form over fences: **h–**
won maiden at Musselburgh in December and 4-runner handicap at Wetherby in January:
will stay beyond 2½m: acts on heavy and good to firm going: front runner/races prominently. *J. Howard Johnson*

SOMEWHERE MY LOVE 6 br.m. Pursuit of Love – Grand Coronet (Grand Lodge **h–**
(USA)) [2006/7 h–: 16s 16s³ 16f 16vᵖᵘ Jan 27] little form over hurdles: tried in
cheekpieces: tongue tied in 2006/7. *K. G. Wingrove*

SOMEWIN (IRE) 7 b.m. Goldmark (USA) – Janet Oliphant (Red Sunset) [2006/7 h65, **h–**
F–: 19m Jun 4] leggy mare: poor handicap hurdler: off 10 months, well held only outing
in 2006/7: stays 21f: acts on firm going: usually in cheekpieces/visor. *Miss Joanne Priest*

SONEVAFUSHI (FR) 9 b.g. Ganges (USA) – For Kicks (FR) (Top Ville) [2006/7 **c123 §**
c139§, h–§: c24g⁵ c25d* c25v² c26g c36gᵖᵘ Apr 14] leggy, useful-looking gelding: useful **h– §**
hunter chaser nowadays: won at Wincanton in February by 1¼ lengths from Back Nine:
ninth to Drombeag in Foxhunter at Cheltenham, prominent until mistake 4 out: stays 27f:
acts on heavy and good to firm going: usually blinkered over hurdles (has been only once
over fences): good jumper: front runner/races prominently: reluctant to race third start:
unreliable. *Miss Venetia Williams*

SONG OF SONGS 5 b.g. Singspiel (IRE) – Thea (USA) (Marju (IRE)) [2006/7 16s² **h128 p**
Feb 17] half-brother to winning Irish 2m hurdler Dare To Dance (by Mtoto): fairly useful
1¼m winner on Flat at 3 yrs: shaped promisingly when 6 lengths second to Osana
in novice at Wincanton on hurdling debut, mistake 2 out: likely to prove best around
2m: presumably difficult to train, but likely to improve and win races over hurdles.
J. R. Fanshawe

SONG OF VALA 6 ch.g. Peintre Celebre (USA) – Yanka (USA) (Blushing John **h101**
(USA)) [2006/7 h96: 20g² 16g* 16m 17d 24fᵖᵘ Apr 5] sturdy gelding: fair form over
hurdles, won maiden at Plumpton in May: sold out of C. Mann's stable 14,000 gns
Doncaster October Sales after next outing, lame final one: likely to prove best around 2m:
tongue tied on debut. *Evan Williams*

SONIC ANTHEM (USA) 5 b.g. Royal Anthem (USA) – Whisperifyoudare (USA) **h97**
(Red Ransom (USA)) [2006/7 20m 16d⁶ 16d⁵ Mar 22] fair on Flat (stays 11f), successful
in March: easily best effort over hurdles (modest form) in claimer final start: likely to
prove best at 2m: headstrong. *P. C. Haslam*

SONNENGOLD (GER) 6 b.m. Java Gold (USA) – Standing Ovation (ITY) (Law **h96**
Society (USA)) [2006/7 h100: 24s⁶ 16d 16v² 19s⁶ Mar 11] leggy, workmanlike mare:
modest hurdler: should stay beyond 2m: raced on good going or softer (acts on heavy):
sometimes blinkered: none too reliable. *Mrs L. Wadham*

SONNTAG BLUE (IRE) 5 b.g. Bluebird (USA) – Laura Margaret (Persian Bold) **h76**
[2006/7 16d⁴ 16m 16g Nov 1] small, angular gelding: modest on Flat (stays 8.6f): form
(poor) in novice hurdles only on debut. *Miss J. Feilden*

SONNY PARKIN 5 b.g. Spinning World (USA) – No Miss Kris (USA) (Capote **h–**
(USA)) [2006/7 16sᵖᵘ Dec 8] fairly useful up to 1¼m on Flat (wears headgear), won in
August: looked less than keen on hurdling debut. *G. A. Huffer*

SONO 10 b.g. Robellino (USA) – Sweet Holland (USA) (Alydar (USA)) [2006/7 20g **c91**
22mᵖᵘ 24g² 24mᵖᵘ c20d³ 20g² Mar 27] leggy, close-coupled gelding: modest maiden **h92**
hurdler: similar form when third to Some Touch in maiden at Musselburgh on chasing
debut: stays 3m: probably acts on any going: tried in cheekpieces, visored 3 of last 4
starts. *P. D. Niven*

SON OF GREEK MYTH (USA) 6 b.g. Silver Hawk (USA) – Greek Myth (IRE) **c– §**
(Sadler's Wells (USA)) [2006/7 h98§: 20mᵘʳ 21f* 26g 25m³ 20g c25sᵖᵘ 21gᵘʳ 21mᵖᵘ **h90 §**
Apr 9] smallish, angular gelding: modest handicap hurdler: off 4 months, won at Plump-
ton in September: failed to complete last 3 starts, including on chasing debut: stays 3¼m:
acts on soft and firm going: usually wears blinkers, also tried in eyeshield: ungenuine.
G. L. Moore

SON OF OSCAR (IRE) 6 b.g. Oscar (IRE) – Mistress Kyteler (Sallust) [2006/7 19d   **h119**
16v* 16v² 16d 19v⁶ 16m Apr 10] fourth foal: dam placed once over hurdles: fairly useful
hurdler: won handicap at Cork in December by 1¾ lengths from Streetshavenoname: no
chance with Pedrobob when second in minor event at Leopardstown next time: stays 19f:
acts on heavy going. *Philip Fenton, Ireland*

SON OF SOPHIE 5 b.g. Band On The Run – Fair Enchantress (Enchantment) [2006/7   **h–**
h–: 16s⁶ 16dᵖᵘ 16vᵖᵘ 20d Nov 30] no form over hurdles: tried blinkered/in cheekpieces.
C. N. Kellett

SONOMA (IRE) 7 ch.m. Dr Devious (IRE) – Mazarine Blue (USA) (Chief's Crown   **h102**
(USA)) [2006/7 22g⁴ 19g* 19d³ 19g² 22mᵖᵘ 22m* 22d 19d⁴ Oct 26] one-time fair stayer
on Flat, below best when trained in 2005 by B. Rothwell: fair novice hurdler: won at
Newton Abbot (mares) in May and Fontwell in September: stays 2¾m, at least when
conditions aren't testing: acts on good to soft and good to firm going: usually races
prominently. *B. G. Powell*

SO NOW (IRE) 6 b.g. Heron Island (IRE) – Monty's Gayle (IRE) (Montelimar (USA))   **h97**
[2006/7 22d⁴ Oct 22] €15,000 4-y-o: first foal: dam unraced: won completed start in
maiden Irish points in 2006: tongue tied, 7¾ lengths fourth to Mossville in novice at
Wincanton on hurdling debut (none too fluent): likely to be suited by 3m+. *P. F. Nicholls*

SOOKY 7 ch.m. Double Trigger (IRE) – High Kabour (Kabour) [2006/7 F66: 19g May   **h–**
16] poor form in bumper: soundly beaten in novice on hurdling debut: should stay at least
2½m. *J. D. Frost*

SOOYOU SIR (IRE) 5 b. or br.g. Orpen (USA) – Naivement (IRE) (Doyoun) [2006/7   **h–**
20vᵖᵘ Feb 22] poor maiden on Flat, sold out of Mrs A. Duffield's stable 1,300 gns
Doncaster October (2005) Sales: no show in novice on hurdling debut. *Miss L. V. Davis*

SOPHIST (IRE) 4 b.g. Montjeu (IRE) – Cordon Bleu (USA) (D'Accord (USA))   **h119**
[2006/7 16v² 16s² 16s* 16v 16v⁴ 16v Feb 10] close-coupled gelding: lightly-raced maid-
en on Flat, sold out of J. Noseda's stable 7,000 gns Newmarket July Sales: fairly useful
juvenile hurdler: won at Fairyhouse (by 2½ lengths from Financial Reward) in December: well below best after: raced at 2m on soft/heavy going. *J. C. McConnell, Ireland*

SOPHOCLES 4 gr.g. In The Wings – Actoris (USA) (Diesis) [2006/7 F12v² F16v*   **F119**
F16g² F16m Apr 25] 5,000 3-y-o: lengthy gelding: fourth foal: half-brother to fairly
useful 7f winner Activity (by Pennekamp) and winner in Greece by Green Desert: dam
useful French 1m winner: smart form in bumpers: won maiden at Thurles in February in
good style: best effort when 1¼ lengths second of 24 to Cork All Star in Champion
Bumper at Cheltenham next time, staying on strongly despite hanging left: ridden by
Miss Pauline Ryan after debut. *James Leavy, Ireland*

SOPRANO (GER) 5 b.g. Sendawar (IRE) – Spirit Lake (GER) (Surumu (GER))   **h108**
[2006/7 17g³ 16d⁵ Dec 29] angular gelding: successful 3 times up to around 11f on Flat in
Germany in 2006: third in maiden at Rome on hurdling debut: fair form when fifth to Duc
de Regniere in novice at Newbury: joined Jonjo O'Neill. *M. Hofer, Germany*

SORT IT OUT (IRE) 10 br.g. Phardante (FR) – Call Girl (IRE) (Dromod Hill) [2006/7   **c–**
c–p, h88: c20d⁶ Nov 21] novice hurdler: runner-up in points: soundly beaten in chases 14   **h–**
months apart: stays 2½m: acts on firm ground: sold 1,000 gns Doncaster March Sales.
Ferdy Murphy

SOTELO 5 ch.h. Monsun (GER) – Seringa (GER) (Acatenango (GER)) [2006/7 16g   **h–**
17g⁴ Apr 19] compact horse: fairly useful on Flat, successful twice up to around 1¼m in
Germany, including at Cologne in June: left A. Wohler, well beaten in novice hurdles.
S. Gollings

SOTOVIK (IRE) 6 gr.g. Aahsaylad – Moenzi (IRE) (Paris House) [2006/7 h112: 25d   **h–**
Dec 14] good-topped gelding: fair hurdler: off 8 months, well beaten only start in 2006/7:
stays 3m: raced on going softer than good. *A. C. Whillans*

SOUBRIQUET (IRE) 4 b.g. Daylami (IRE) – Green Lucia (Green Dancer (USA))   **h104**
[2006/7 18gᵖᵘ 16g 18s² 16v* 16v² 16m⁴ Apr 21] lengthy, angular gelding: half-brother to
useful hurdler Ravenswood (by Warning), stayed 25f, and fair hurdler Kris Green (by
Kris), stayed 2½m: maiden on Flat (should be suited by 1½m+), sold out of T. Mills's
stable £2,000 Ascot October Sales: fair juvenile hurdler: improved form when winning at
Kelso in March: raced around 2m: acts on heavy going, probably on good to firm: tongue
tied after debut (looked reluctant): not fluent last 2 outings. *M. A. Barnes*

SOUK AL JABBA (IRE) 7 b.g. Oscar (IRE) – Knockananig (Pitpan) [2006/7 F19m 21g 25s^{pu} Mar 11] 18,000 4-y-o: half-brother to 2 winning chasers, including Irish Grand National runner-up Knock Knock (by Executive Perk): dam unraced half-sister to high-class 2m chaser I'm A Driver: no form in points: runner-up on bumper debut: left G. Keane and off 9 months, no show in novice hurdles (including seller): tried tongue tied: sold 1,500 gns Doncaster March Sales. *B. D. Leavy* **h–** **F–**

SOULARD (USA) 4 b.c. Arch (USA) – Bourbon Blues (USA) (Seeking The Gold (USA)) [2006/7 17g³ 16m² 17g Apr 18] good-topped colt: fair on Flat (stays 13.8f), successful in July, sold out of J. Noseda's stable 30,000 gns Newmarket Sales later in month: modest form over hurdles: raced around 2m: takes good hold. *J. L. Spearing* **h96**

SOUND ACCORD (IRE) 6 br.g. Accordion – Shuil Na Lee (IRE) (Phardante (FR)) [2006/7 F105p: F16d⁶ F16s* 19d² Feb 17] tall gelding: useful form in bumpers, successful at Huntingdon (wandered under pressure) in December: left C. Tinkler and still green, encouraging hurdling debut when 10 lengths second to Warlord in novice at Ascot: will be suited by 2½m+: sure to improve. *D. W. P. Arbuthnot* **h117 p** **F109**

SOUND AND VISION (IRE) 5 b.g. Fayruz – Lyrical Vision (IRE) (Vision (USA)) [2006/7 h77: 16f 17m⁶ 16g May 21] leggy gelding: poor maiden hurdler: raced around 2m: acts on firm and good to soft going. *J. K. Price* **h67**

SOUND OF CHEERS 10 br.g. Zilzal (USA) – Martha Stevens (USA) (Super Concorde (USA)) [2006/7 c106, h–: c16d⁵ c23d⁴ c24s² c19s⁵ c20v³ c19g⁵ c20s⁵ c22d^F c20g c20m⁵ c23g⁵ Apr 16] good-topped gelding: modest handicap chaser nowadays: well held last 4 completed outings: best form around 2½m: acts on heavy and good to firm going: tongue tied: sometimes finishes weakly. *F. Kirby* **c96** **h–**

SOUND SKIN (IRE) 9 gr.g. Sexton Blake – Ballinlassa (IRE) (Mandalus) [2006/7 h88: 21s³ 21v² 20m³ 20m 19g Jun 20] poor maiden hurdler: soundly beaten in points in 2007: best around 2½m: probably acts on any going: wears cheekpieces/visor. *A. Ennis* **h79**

SOUTH BANK (IRE) 5 b.g. Old Vic – Cluain-Ard (IRE) (Glacial Storm (USA)) [2006/7 F16d F16s⁶ 18g⁴ Mar 18] well-made gelding: first foal: dam, winning pointer, half-sister to useful hurdler/chaser Feathered Leader, effective at 2m to 29f: mid-field in bumpers: 6¼ lengths fourth to Presentandcorrect in novice at Fontwell on hurdling debut: will be suited by 2½m+: should improve. *Miss H. C. Knight* **h91 p** **F76**

SOUTH BRONX (IRE) 8 br.g. Anshan – Tender Tan (Tanfirion) [2006/7 c115, h–: c17f* c17g⁴ c20f⁴ c20f² 20m⁴ c16s² c20d⁶ 16g⁴ 16m 16d Feb 14] leggy gelding: fair hurdler/fairly useful handicap chaser: won over fences at Kelso in May by 3 lengths from Lucky Duck: several creditable efforts otherwise in 2006/7: stays 2¾m: acts on any going: tongue tied: consistent. *Mrs S. C. Bradburne* **c125** **h107**

SOUTHBURGH (IRE) 6 b.g. Spectrum (IRE) – College Night (IRE) (Night Shift (USA)) [2006/7 16g Mar 16] no form on Flat or on hurdling debut (raced freely). *Mrs C. A. Dunnett* **h–**

SOUTHERN BAZAAR (USA) 6 ch.g. Southern Halo (USA) – Sunday Bazaar (USA) (Nureyev (USA)) [2006/7 h63: 20g³ 16m* 17m 16m^{pu} 19s⁶ 17m 22m⁶ 16v⁴ 19v⁴ 19g* 17d⁴ 19s⁴ 24d⁶ 17m* 22m Apr 28] smallish gelding: poor handicap hurdler: won conditional jockeys selling events at Huntingdon (sold from M. Sowersby 6,400 gns) in June and Catterick in February and ladies seller at Market Rasen in April: stays 2½m: acts on good to firm and good to soft going, unsuited by soft/heavy: tried in cheekpieces. *M. C. Chapman* **h72**

SOUTHERN CLASSIC 7 b.g. Classic Cliche (IRE) – Southern Sky (Comedy Star (USA)) [2006/7 h69, F92?: 19s 27v⁶ 25m^{pu} Apr 19] strong gelding: poor form over hurdles, left R. Stronge after return: tried tongue tied: sold 2,000 gns Doncaster May Sales. *Miss E. C. Lavelle* **h72**

SOUTHERNCROSSPATCH 16 ch.g. Ra Nova – Southern Bird (Shiny Tenth) [2006/7 c–, h75: 24d Oct 5] strong, compact gelding: winning chaser/hurdler: well held last 4 starts: best at 3m+. *Mrs Barbara Waring* **c–** **h–**

SOUTHERNDOWN (IRE) 14 ch.g. Montelimar (USA) – Country Melody (IRE) (Orchestra) [2006/7 c82, h–: c26s³ c24m⁵ c26d³ c26d⁵ c24d² c26v² c24v* c24d² c26v³ c24m⁴ c24g Apr 27] sparely-made gelding: poor handicap chaser: won at Uttoxeter in November: stays 3¾m: acts on any ground: tried blinkered/visored: usually held up: consistent. *R. Lee* **c82** **h–**

SOUTHERN EXIT 4 b.f. Poliglote – Southern Sky (Comedy Star (USA)) [2006/7 F14v⁴ F16s³ Mar 7] big, useful-looking filly: half-sister to several winners, including 3 **F74**

over hurdles: dam 7f/1m winner: poor form in bumpers (carried head awkwardly second start): sold 21,000 gns Doncaster May Sales. *K. G. Reveley*

SOUTHERN TIDE (USA) 5 b.h. Southern Halo (USA) – My Own Lovely Lee (USA) (Bucksplasher (USA)) [2006/7 16f 17m Apr 17] poor on Flat (stays 1¼m) in 2006: left J. Pearce. little impact in novice/maiden hurdles. *L. A. Dace* **h–**

SOUTHERN VIC (IRE) 8 br. or b.g. Old Vic – Hug In A Fog (IRE) (Strong Gale) [2006/7 c141+, h–: c16s* c24s⁵ 20v² c24v⁵ c24vᶠ Jan 25] sturdy, good-topped gelding: useful hurdler: good 1½ lengths second to Celestial Wave in Grade 2 at Navan in December: smart chaser: won 5-runner Grade 3 Poplar Square Chase at Naas in October by 2½ lengths from Macs Flamingo: creditable fifth to Cane Brake in valuable handicap at Navan and The Listener in Grade 1 at Leopardstown: well held when falling last in valuable handicap at Gowran: needs good test around 2m, and will stay beyond 3m: raced on going softer than good (acts on heavy): reliable. *T. M. Walsh, Ireland* **c147 h140**

SOUTH HILL 4 b.f. Marju (IRE) – Briggsmaid (Elegant Air) [2006/7 16m 17g 17gᵖᵘ Apr 7] half-sister to poor/temperamental hurdler/chaser Reflex Blue (by Ezzoud), stays 21f: no form on Flat or over hurdles (reluctant to race final start). *R. J. Price* **h– §**

SOUTH O'THE BORDER 5 b.g. Wolfhound (USA) – Abbey's Gal (Efisio) [2006/7 17s* 17v³ 18s⁴ 16s* Apr 26] leggy gelding: fairly useful around 1¼m on Flat, successful in August, sold out of T. Mills's stable 36,000 gns Newmarket Autumn Sales: fair form over hurdles: won maiden at Taunton in December and novice at Perth in April: will prove best around 2m: races prominently: sweated/raced freely when below form third start. *Miss Venetia Williams* **h113**

SOUTH SANDS (IRE) 6 b.m. Shaamit (IRE) – Mariners Mirror (Julio Mariner) [2006/7 h–: 16d 19s 17s³ 17v² 26s 21v⁵ c19g³ c19g² c19gᵖᵘ Apr 27] big, angular mare: poor maiden hurdler: modest form when placed in handicap chases: may prove best up to 2½m. *M. Scudamore* **c88 h78**

SOU'WESTER 7 b.g. Fleetwood (IRE) – Mayfair (Green Desert (USA)) [2006/7 c–, h90: 16m² 16d² 17m* Jun 8] angular gelding: novice chaser: fair hurdler: back in trip and improved in 2006/7, won novice at Newton Abbot in June: best form around 2m: acts on heavy and good to firm going: tried tongue tied. *C. L. Tizzard* **c– h114**

SOVEREIGN KING 5 b. or br.g. Sovereign Water (FR) – Bedwyn Bridge (Over The River (FR)) [2006/7 F16m F16g Mar 19] workmanlike gelding: second foal: dam ran once in point: little impact in bumpers. *A. King* **F–**

SOVEREIGN'S JOY 6 b.g. Sovereign Water (FR) – Carmel's Joy (IRE) (Carlingford Castle) [2006/7 17s⁴ 20v⁴ 22s Feb 3] tall gelding: second foal: half-brother to modest chaser Trenance (by Alflora), stayed 3m: dam, winning hurdler/chaser, stayed 33f: modest form over hurdles: should prove suited by 2½m+: raced on soft/heavy ground. *T. R. George* **h97**

SOVEREIGN STATE (IRE) 10 b.g. Soviet Lad (USA) – Portree (Slip Anchor) [2006/7 h111: 20m⁴ c16gᵖᵘ 16s 22g 22m⁵ 24g⁵ 20fⁿ c21m⁶ c21mᵖᵘ 17s Oct 29] fair handicap hurdler at best, out of sorts in 2006/7: no form over fences: barely stays 2½m: acts on good to firm and good to soft going: usually wears headgear. *D. W. Thompson* **c– h98 d**

SOVIETICA (FR) 6 b.m. Subotica (FR) – Vieille Russie (Kenmare (FR)) [2006/7 F97: F17m* 17s⁴ 16gᶠ 19vᵖᵘ 21g 22f* 19m² Apr 22] leggy, close-coupled mare: successful twice in bumpers, including at Hereford in June: modest novice hurdler: won mares event at Wincanton in April: stays 2¾m: acts on firm going, ran poorly on heavy: keen-going sort. *S. Pike* **h98 F98**

SOVIET SCEPTRE (IRE) 6 ch.g. Soviet Star (USA) – Princess Sceptre (Cadeaux Genereux) [2006/7 19m² 17m² 16m³ 19mᶠ 20fᵖᵘ 16g⁵ Sep 6] modest 1¼m/1½m winner on Flat: modest hurdler: claimed from R. Phillips £6,000 third start: 16 lengths clear and still on bridle when falling last in conditional jockeys handicap at Newton Abbot: should stay beyond 19f: raced on good going or firmer: in cheekpieces/visor last 3 starts: tongue tied. *Evan Williams* **h98**

SOVIET SPIRIT 6 ch.m. Soviet Star (USA) – Kristina (Kris) [2006/7 17g 22mᵖᵘ Jul 17] modest maiden on Flat at 3 yrs: no show over hurdles. *D. C. Turner* **h–**

SOVIETTA (IRE) 6 b.m. Soviet Star (USA) – La Riveraine (USA) (Riverman (USA)) [2006/7 h–: 19v 16v⁵ Feb 26] leggy mare: modest on Flat (stays 13f): no solid form over hurdles. *A. G. Newcombe* **h–**

SO WISE SO YOUNG 6 br.g. Young Ern – Tendresse (IRE) (Tender King) [2006/7 h–, F80: 16s³ 16d⁴ 16s⁵ 16g⁴ Mar 30] sturdy gelding: fair novice hurdler, off 10 months **h102**

before improved in 2006/7: raced mainly around 2m on good to soft/soft ground. *R. H. Buckler*

SPACE COWBOY (IRE) 7 b.g. Anabaa (USA) – Lady Moranbon (USA) **h115** (Trempolino (USA)) [2006/7 h115: 16d 17m 17m* Jul 17] useful-looking gelding: has reportedly suffered back problems: fairly useful handicap hurdler: back to form when winning at Newton Abbot in July by ¾ length from Cream Cracker: best around 2m: acts on soft and good to firm going: usually blinkered/in cheekpieces. *G. L. Moore*

SPACE MISSION (IRE) 5 b.g. Kayf Tara – Jupiter's Message (Jupiter Island) **F85** [2006/7 F16v F16s² F16m Jan 29] well-made gelding: ninth foal: half-brother to smart hurdler/very smart chaser up to 3m Bellator (by Simply Great) and fair hurdler Lord Warford (by Bustino), stayed 2¾m: dam unraced: best effort in bumpers when 6 lengths second to Johnny Bissett at Huntingdon. *P. R. Webber*

SPACE STAR 7 b.g. Cosmonaut – Sophiesue (Balidar) [2006/7 c112, h–: c17m⁶ Jun 11] **c103** compact gelding: fair handicap hurdler: similar form over fences, off 11 months before **h–** only start in 2006/7: best around 2m: acts on good to soft and good to firm going: held up. *P. R. Webber*

SPANCHIL HILL 7 b.g. Sabrehill (USA) – War Shanty (Warrshan (USA)) [2006/7 **c84** h60: 22m 22m⁶ c23f⁵ c20g² c18g⁵ c24m² c25fˢᵘ c23d⁵ 24m⁴ Apr 17] bad maiden hurdler: **h59** better form over fences: stays 3m: acts on firm going: has finished weakly. *L. A. Dace*

SPANISH STORY 4 br.f. Vettori (IRE) – Spanish Heart (King of Spain) [2006/7 16v⁴ **h68** 16d⁵ Dec 21] poor maiden on Flat (stays 7f): little impact in juvenile hurdles. *J. G. Portman*

SPARE ME 4 b.g. Cloudings (IRE) – Spare Set (IRE) (Second Set (IRE)) [2006/7 F14v³ **h92** F14s² F13v⁴ 16v⁴ 17d⁴ 16s Apr 1] close-coupled gelding: first foal: dam, of little account, **F90** half-sister to winning stayer/jumper Snow Board: in frame in bumpers: modest form over hurdles: will be suited by further than 17f: raced on ground softer than good. *Mrs S. J. Smith*

SPARKBRIDGE (IRE) 4 b.g. Mull of Kintyre (USA) – Persian Velvet (IRE) **h–** (Distinctly North (USA)) [2006/7 17d 16sᵖᵘ 16m Nov 24] modest maiden on Flat (stays 9f): no show in juvenile hurdles: tried blinkered. *R. F. Fisher*

SPARKLING SABRINA 7 b.m. Classic Cliche (IRE) – Sparkling Yasmin (Derring **h–** Rose) [2006/7 h71: 24mᵇᵈ Jul 12] little form. *P. Bowen*

SPARKLING TAFF 8 b.g. Alderbrook – Sparkling Time (USA) (Olden Times) **c99** [2006/7 h86, F80: 20g⁴ 21d⁶ 23vᵖᵘ c16sᶠ c16s² c16g² c20m* Apr 20] compact gelding: **h86** modest maiden hurdler: fair form over fences: won 5-runner novice handicap at Ayr in April, idling: stays 2½m: acts on soft and good to firm ground. *Mrs S. J. Smith*

SPARKLINSPIRIT 8 b.g. Sovereign Water (FR) – Emilys Trust (National Trust) **h85** [2006/7 h93, F–: 21s 21m³ Nov 9] leggy gelding: modest novice hurdler: stays 2¾m: acts on good to firm and good to soft going. *J. L. Spearing*

SPARKY ROCKET 6 b.m. Overbury (IRE) – Viking Rocket (Viking (USA)) [2006/7 **h–** h–, F–: 20g 21vᵖᵘ Jan 2] little sign of ability. *B. Storey*

SPARTAN ENCORE 5 ch.g. Spartan Monarch – Debs Review (Grundy) [2006/7 F83: **h–** F16d F18d 19s 22v 19dᵖᵘ 17vᵘ Feb 28] poor form in bumpers: no show over hurdles. **F68** *Miss Suzy Smith*

SPA WELLS (IRE) 6 ch.g. Pasternak – La Tache (Namaqualand (USA)) [2006/7 h–, **h84** F77: 16d 17m 20f 17m² 18d⁴ 16g 18d* 16sᵇᵈ Oct 26] poor handicap hurdler: won at Downpatrick in September: likely to prove best around 2m: acts on good to firm and good to soft ground. *Barry Potts, Ireland*

SPEAR THISTLE 5 ch.g. Selkirk (USA) – Ardisia (USA) (Affirmed (USA)) [2006/7 **h107** h95: 16g* 16d⁵ 16d 20d 16g⁶ Mar 24] good-topped gelding: fairly useful on Flat (stays 2m): fair novice hurdler: won 19-runner event at Leicester in November: raced mainly around 2m (seemed not to stay 2½m): raced on good ground or softer (acts on heavy): in cheekpieces last 2 starts. *Mrs N. Smith*

SPECIAL AGENDA (IRE) 13 b.g. Torus – Easter Blade (IRE) (Fine Blade (USA)) **c– x** [2006/7 c–x, h–: c17s⁵ May 26] strong gelding: maiden hurdler: winning chaser: lightly **h–** raced and little form since 2003/4: tried in cheekpieces/blinkers/tongue strap: usually let down by jumping. *M. D. Jones*

Walters Plant Hire Ltd's "Special Envoy"

SPECIAL ENVOY (FR) 5 gr.g. Linamix (FR) – Pawnee Dancer (IRE) (Dancing **h142** Brave (USA)) [2006/7 17g³ 19d⁴ 22s* 17v⁶ 16d 16g* 20gᶠ Apr 12] angular gelding: useful on Flat (stays 1½m), successful twice in 2006, sold out of N. Clement's stable €230,000 Goffs Arc Sale: useful novice hurdler: won at Fontwell (maiden) in January and Newbury (18 ran, beat Lead On a neck) in March: would also have won 22-runner listed handicap at Aintree but for falling last when clear: stays 2¾m: raced on good ground or softer. *P. Bowen*

SPECIAL FLIGHT (IRE) 6 b.g. Topanoora – Swinging Sari (IRE) (Asir) [2006/7 **F67** F16m⁵ Jun 11] €14,500 3-y-o: fourth foal: dam, placed in points, half-sister to useful staying chaser Step On Eyre: shaped like a stayer when fifth of 10 in maiden bumper at Stratford on debut: sold 10,000 gns Doncaster August Sales. *Noel T. Chance*

SPECIAL ORDER (IRE) 4 b.g. Orpen (USA) – Siraka (FR) (Grand Lodge (USA)) **h89** [2006/7 F14sᶠ 16s² 17v⁵ 16v⁴ 16v⁶ 17g⁴ Apr 23] good-topped gelding: first foal: dam **F87** unraced: second when fell 1f out in 3-y-o bumper at Carlisle on debut: modest juvenile hurdler: below form last 3 starts: raced around 2m on good going or softer (acts on heavy): tongue tied last 2 outings. *J. Howard Johnson*

SPECIAL RATE (IRE) 10 br.g. Grand Plaisir (IRE) – Clerical Artist (IRE) (The **c–** Parson) [2006/7 c–, h114: 22g⁵ 24dᵖᵘ Feb 10] useful-looking gelding: one-time useful **h–** hurdler: off 22 months after final 2003/4 outing and little form since, including on chasing debut: stays 23f: acts on soft going (won bumper on good to firm). *A. King*

SPECTESTED (IRE) 6 ch.g. Spectrum (IRE) – Nisibis (In The Wings) [2006/7 h102: **c§§**
23s c26v^{rtr} c23v^4 c24s^{rtr} Mar 11] workmanlike gelding: fair hurdler at best, off a year **h§§**
before return: refused to race 2 of 3 starts in novice chases: visored/in cheekpieces last 2
outings: one to avoid. *A. W. Carroll*

SPECTROMETER 10 ch.g. Rainbow Quest (USA) – Selection Board (Welsh **c116**
Pageant) [2006/7 c118x, h129: c21d^4 17g c22g^2 Sep 23] leggy gelding: fairly useful **h–**
handicap hurdler/chaser: improved jumper of fences in 2006/7, and good second to Kings
Brook in valuable event at Market Rasen: stays 3m: acts on firm and soft going. *Ian
Williams*

SPECTRUM STAR 7 b.g. Spectrum (IRE) – Persia (IRE) (Persian Bold) [2006/7 c73, **c–**
h–: c25g^{pu} c20d^5 c27s^4 c20v^6 Jan 9] no form over hurdles: maiden chaser: stays 2½m. **h–**
F. P. Murtagh

SPECULAR (AUS) 11 b.g. Danehill (USA) – Spyglass (NZ) (Sir Sian (NZ)) [2006/7 **c–**
c113, h–: c17m 19g 16g Oct 3] smallish, strong gelding: useful hurdler/fair chaser at best: **h–**
little form in handicaps since 2005/6 return: stays 19f: acts on soft and good to firm going.
Jonjo O'Neill

SPEED KRIS (FR) 8 b.g. Belmez (USA) – Pandia (USA) (Affirmed (USA)) [2006/7 **c– §**
c–§, h101§: 24s^5 May 17] maiden chaser: modest handicap hurdler: probably stays 27f: **h83 §**
acts on any going: visored/in cheekpieces: ungenuine. *Mrs S. C. Bradburne*

SPEEDRO (IRE) 9 b.g. Glacial Storm (USA) – Sindys Gale (Strong Gale) [2006/7 **h104**
h82: 16d 18m^3 20v^F 20v^3 20v^2 20v^2 Mar 6] lightly raced: fair maiden hurdler: likely
winner when falling heavily 2 out in handicap at Ayr: will stay beyond 2½m: acts on
heavy going: tried in eyeshields: has started very slowly. *Miss Lucinda V. Russell*

SPEED UP (FR) 4 ch.g. Vertical Speed (FR) – Haiya (FR) (Saint Cyrien (FR)) [2006/7 **h94**
16g^3 16g^4 16s Dec 16] tall, leggy, close-coupled gelding: modest juvenile hurdler, left
T. Trapenard before return: raced around 2m: acts on soft ground. *Ferdy Murphy*

SPEED VENTURE 10 b.g. Owington – Jade Venture (Never So Bold) [2006/7 h105: **h99**
16d 16s^3 16g 19s^4 16s 16v^2 20v^6 16v* 20v^2 Mar 4] leggy gelding: modest handicap
hurdler: won at Haydock in February: stays 2½m: raced on good going or softer (acts on
heavy): visored/in cheekpieces: usually tongue tied: has found little. *J. Mackie*

SPEED WINNER (AUS) 8 b.g. Danehill (USA) – Think Twice (USA) (Alleged **h93**
(USA)) [2006/7 20d^2 20s^2 16d^4 21s^6 18g 16m^{pu} 22m^3 Apr 26] sturdy gelding: ran 47
times on Flat in Hong Kong, winning 3 times up to 11f: modest novice hurdler: stays
2¾m: acts on soft and good to firm going: tried blinkered. *G. L. Moore*

SPENCE APPEAL (IRE) 5 b.g. Nicolotte – It's All Academic (IRE) (Mazaad) **h–**
[2006/7 h82: 17v^6 Nov 28] poor form over hurdles, well held only start in 2006/7: raced
around 2m: acts on firm ground: room for improvement in jumping. *C. Roberts*

SPENDENT SPREE 4 b.f. Spendent – Posh Spice (Neshad (USA)) [2006/7 **h–**
F13d aF13g 18m^{su} Apr 26] first foal: dam, winning hurdler/maiden hunter chaser, stayed **F–**
3m: well held in 3-y-o bumpers: behind when slipped up in mares maiden on hurdling
debut. *A. Ennis*

SPEND EVEN 5 ch.m. Spendent – Easters Eve (Ginger Boy) [2006/7 F18m Oct 16] **F–**
second foal: dam maiden pointer: little impact in maiden bumper on debut. *Mrs
H. J. Cobb*

SPIDAM (FR) 5 b. or br.g. Moon Madness – Spinage (FR) (Village Star (FR)) [2006/7 **c113 §**
h118: c19v^2 c17v^2 c16v^2 c16s^2 Mar 12] big, lengthy gelding: winning hurdler: fair form **h– §**
over fences, runner-up all 4 starts: stays 19f: acts on heavy going: tongue tied last 3
outings, also blinkered final one: ungenuine. *P. F. Nicholls*

SPIDER BOY 10 b.g. Jupiter Island – Great Dilemma (Vaigly Great) [2006/7 c66, h67: **c70**
c26m^5 c20m^2 c20m^5 c20v^4 c22s^{pu} 23d^2 c20v^3 c24s^3 c21g^F Apr 9] workmanlike gelding: **h70**
poor maiden hurdler/chaser: stays 3¼m: acts on any going: wears cheekpieces/blinkers.
Miss Z. C. Davison

SPIERS PEACE (IRE) 8 b.g. Shernazar – Burling Moss (Le Moss) [2006/7 c31g^2 **c93**
c29g^{ur} Mar 21] 5,400 4-y-o: fifth foal: dam maiden pointer: fair pointer, successful in
April: neck second to Bright Approach at Folkestone on completed outing in hunter
chases: stays 31f: visored. *J. W. Dufosee*

SPIKE JONES (NZ) 9 b.g. Colonel Collins (USA) – Gloss (NZ) (Kaapstad (NZ)) **c98 x**
[2006/7 c–, h101: 16g c20s^{pu} c19s^{ur} c20v^4 c19d^3 c19s^4 c19s* c19g c19g^{pu} Apr 11] **h–**
medium-sized gelding: winning hurdler: modest chaser: won handicap at Taunton in

March: stays 19f: acts on heavy going (won bumper on good to firm): often let down by jumping over fences. *Mrs S. M. Johnson*

SPINAROUND 9 gr.g. Terimon – Re-Spin (Gildoran) [2006/7 c103, h–: c20g⁴ c16g² c16sᶠ Apr 26] workmanlike gelding: novice hurdler: fair handicap chaser: stays 2½m: acts on soft and good to firm going: visored last 5 starts: still room for improvement in jumping. *P. R. Webber* — **c105 h–**

SPINNING COIN 5 b.m. Mujahid (USA) – Cointosser (IRE) (Nordico (USA)) [2006/7 17m* 16s² 16f Apr 5] fairly useful on Flat (stays 1¾m), successful in September: fair form over hurdles: favourite, won mares novice at Exeter in November: raced around 2m: acts on soft and good to firm going: in cheekpieces final start: not a fluent jumper. *J. G. Portman* — **h104 x**

SPINNINGDALE 7 b.m. Afzal – Monsoon (Royal Palace) [2006/7 F16g 24sᵖᵘ Dec 18] sister to a winning pointer and half-sister to 2 winners by Master Willie, including fairly useful hurdler around 2m Wiggy Smith: dam winning staying hurdler/chaser: no form in mares bumper/maiden hurdle. *P. J. Jones* — **h– F–**

SPINOFSKI 12 b.g. Petoski – Spin Again (Royalty) [2006/7 c–§, h–: c22s⁴ c24gᵖᵘ Nov 7] angular gelding: winning chaser: left P. Webber, no form since 2004/5: tried in cheekpieces/blinkers/tongue strap: temperamental. *D. R. Stoddart* — **c– § h–**

SPIRIT CALLING (IRE) 6 br.g. Lord Americo – Satco Street (IRE) (Satco (FR)) [2006/7 19g⁴ 19d⁴ 16g³ 20g Mar 17] unfurnished gelding: first foal: dam unraced, sister to smart hurdler/very smart chaser Sackville, stayed 3m: form over hurdles: should stay 2½m. *M. Todhunter* — **h81**

SPIRIT GUIDE (FR) 5 b.g. Anabaa (USA) – Shining Molly (FR) (Shining Steel) [2006/7 16d 17d 20mᵖᵘ 19g 16f 16d 16g Nov 29] maiden on Flat, sold out of C. Head-Maarek's stable 18,000 gns Newmarket Autumn (2005) Sales, well beaten in 2006: no form over hurdles: dead. *R. C. Guest* — **h–**

SPIRIT OF MAN (IRE) 6 b.g. Saddlers' Hall (IRE) – Celestial Rose (IRE) (Roselier (FR)) [2006/7 F17s 22s 19d² Mar 26] €32,000 4-y-o: unfurnished gelding: third foal: half-brother to 2¾m hurdle winner Jay Lo (by Glacial Storm): dam unraced: mid-field in bumper: much better effort in maiden hurdles when 1¾ lengths second to National Trust at Stratford: bred to be suited by further than 19f: sold 46,000 gns Doncaster May Sales. *R. T. Phillips* — **h111 F70**

SPIRIT OF NEW YORK (IRE) 8 b.g. Topanoora – Fiona's Blue (Crash Course) [2006/7 c135p, F102: 16d* 24g* Apr 21] well-made gelding: very lightly raced: dual bumper winner: impressive winner of maiden at Stratford on first of 2 starts over fences: off nearly 16 months, successful also both outings in novice hurdles, at Stratford (easily) in March and Bangor (upped in trip, beat Raslan by neck in 5-runner event) in April: stays 3m: raced on good ground or softer: seemingly not easy to train but still has plenty of potential. *Jonjo O'Neill* — **c– h124 p**

SPIRITUAL DANCER (IRE) 12 b.g. King's Ride – Arctic Tartan (Deep Run) [2006/7 c–, h–: 20s⁴ 22m c19sᵘʳ c20vᵖᵘ Jan 25] deep-girthed gelding: has failed to complete over fences (trained third start only by Mrs A. Thorpe): maiden hurdler, little form since 2003/4: stays 25f: acts on heavy going: tried visored/blinkered: has worn near-side pricker. *M. A. Allen* — **c– h74**

SPIRITUAL SOCIETY (IRE) 7 b.g. Moscow Society (USA) – Sniggy (Belfort (FR)) [2006/7 c89, h101: c16g⁶ c16gᵖᵘ c16m⁴ c16g² c17g³ Apr 23] leggy gelding: winning hurdler: modest novice chaser: raced mainly around 2m: acts on heavy ground, probably on good to firm: tongue tied last 3 outings: free-going sort: prone to mistakes. *M. Scudamore* — **c94 h–**

SPITFIRE BOB (USA) 8 b.g. Mister Baileys – Gulf Cyclone (USA) (Sheikh Alba-dou) [2006/7 c–, h–: 22s⁵ 17g² 27s Nov 26] good-topped gelding: maiden hurdler: no show on chasing debut: tried blinkered/in cheekpieces. *S. C. Burrough* — **c– h–**

SPITFIRE SORTIE (IRE) 6 b.g. Sadler's Wells (USA) – Madame Est Sortie (FR) (Longleat (USA)) [2006/7 F101: F16g³ F17f⁶ Jul 7] close-coupled gelding: fairly useful form in bumpers: sold out of M. Easterby's stable 12,000 gns Doncaster May Sales, well held 2 months later: tried in blinkers. *S. J. Mahon, Ireland* — **F95**

SPIVITUS 6 br.g. Vitus – Split The Wind (Strong Gale) [2006/7 F17m⁶ F16f⁴ F16f² F17s⁴ 16d 22gᵖᵘ 20sᵖᵘ Apr 25] first foal: dam maiden pointer: in frame in bumpers: poor form over hurdles: stays 2¾m. *R. Nixon* — **h80 F80**

SPLASH AND DASH (IRE) 12 ch.g. Arcane (USA) – Quilty Rose (Buckskin (FR))   c–
[2006/7 c31g⁶ May 24] winning pointer/hunter chaser: stays 25f: acts on soft ground:
tried blinkered: not a fluent jumper. *Mrs S. J. Hickman*

SPORAZENE (IRE) 8 gr.g. Cozzene (USA) – Sporades (USA) (Vaguely Noble)   c153 x
[2006/7 c–, h143: c16g* c17s* c17d⁴ c16gᶠ Mar 16] tall, leggy, raw-boned gelding: h–
winning hurdler: smart chaser: won first 3 completed starts, including when making all in
4-runner minor events at Kempton in November and Exeter (beat Mariah Rollins by 21
lengths) in December: let down by jumping otherwise over fences, including when fourth
of 5 finishers to Well Chief in Grade 2 at Newbury: best around 2m: acts on soft and good
to firm going, probably on heavy. *P. F. Nicholls*

SPORTING CHANCE 15 ch.g. Ikdam – Tumbling Ego (Abednego) [2006/7 c82x,   c– x
h–: c21gᵖᵘ May 16] sturdy gelding: winning hunter chaser, but usually let down by   h–
jumping and little impact since 2004/5. *Mrs Jo Sleep*

SPORTING REBEL (IRE) 7 b.g. Zaffaran (USA) – High Church Annie (IRE)   h98 p
(Bustomi) [2006/7 17s 18s⁵ 16sᵘʳ Jan 10] sturdy gelding: third foal: dam lightly raced in
points: placed in maiden Irish points: better effort on completed starts over hurdles when
fifth to stable-companion Benetwood in maiden at Fontwell: will be suited by 2½m+:
raced on soft ground: likely to do better. *V. R. A. Dartnall*

SPORTS EXPRESS 9 ch.m. Then Again – Lady St Lawrence (USA) (Bering) [2006/7   c78
c84, h–: 20s 24s c20s⁵ c20g⁵ c20d² c24g c24s* c24dᵘʳ c25s Feb 15] lengthy, good-topped   h79
mare: maiden hurdler: poor novice chaser: won at Musselburgh in January: stays 3m: acts
on heavy going: usually in cheekpieces/visor: sold 900 gns Doncaster March Sales. *Miss
Lucinda V. Russell*

SPORTULA 6 b.m. Silver Patriarch (IRE) – Portent (Most Welcome) [2006/7 h84: 20fᶠ   c–
25s 18g 16vᵖᵘ 20vᵖᵘ 19vᵖᵘ c20mᵖᵘ c16gᵖᵘ Apr 23] leggy mare: maiden hurdler: no form   h–
in 2006/7, including over fences (bled final start): blinkered/in cheekpieces last 4 starts.
B. Storey

SPOTONCON 6 b.g. Contract Law (USA) – Emma Victoria (Dominion) [2006/7 F13m   h–
F16m F16m⁴ F17v 16gᵖᵘ 16g 16sᵖᵘ Dec 7] leggy gelding: first foal: dam won 17f   F–
claiming hurdle: of no account. *Mary Meek*

SPOT THEDIFFERENCE (IRE) 14 b.g. Lafontaine (USA) – Spotted Choice   c144
(IRE) (Callernish) [2006/7 c146, h–: 20s c31d⁴ c31s* c31d⁴ c34f* Apr 26] tall gelding: h–
maiden hurdler: smart cross-country chaser, successful 6 times at Cheltenham, in Sporting Index Chase for third occasion in November and handicap (beat Plum'tee by length)
in December, and La Touche Cup at Punchestown (beat Freneys Well by 4½ lengths) for
second time in April: creditable fourth to Heads Onthe Ground in Sporting Index
Handicap: thorough stayer: acts on any going: has run well in headgear (wore cheekpieces last 6 outings over fences): races lazily, and probably best with strong handling.
Enda Bolger, Ireland

SPOT THE LADY (IRE) 5 b.m. Gothland (FR) – Bayviewlady (IRE) (Castle Keep)   F–
[2006/7 F16v F17g Mar 25] third foal: dam lightly raced in bumpers: tailed off in
bumpers. *J. W. Mullins*

SPREEWALD (GER) 8 b.g. Dulcero (USA) – Spartina (USA) (Northern Baby   c–
(CAN)) [2006/7 17gᵖᵘ c18f 17m³ 16f⁶ Jun 21] rather leggy gelding: poor maiden hurdler/   h70
chaser, off 17 months prior to return: stays 21f: acts on firm and soft going: has worn
cheekpieces: tongue tied nowadays. *J. C. Tuck*

*Avon Ri Corporate & Leisure Resort Chase For The La Touche Cup, Punchestown—
the veteran Spot Thedifference (No.1) repeats his 2004 win; the same connections' Freneys Well (No.8)
shadows him throughout on his way to second place*

SPRINGAWAY 8 ch.g. Minster Son – Galway Gal (Proverb) [2006/7 h81: c20s⁵ c20g⁴ c24g² c20g⁴ Apr 7] leggy gelding: novice hurdler: well backed, easily best effort over fences (modest form) in novice handicap at Musselburgh third outing, looking likely winner until blundering last: stays 3m: acts on soft going, probably on good to firm. *Miss Kate Milligan*
    c88
    h–

SPRING BREEZE 6 ch.g. Dr Fong (USA) – Trading Aces (Be My Chief (USA)) [2006/7 h109: 21g 21d* c20d 20vᵖᵘ 23s 24m³ 21m* Apr 21] small, leggy gelding: fairly useful handicap hurdler: improved in 2006/7, winning at Sedgefield in November and Ayr (beat Irish Wolf by 4 lengths) in April: jumped none too fluently when well held in maiden on chasing debut: probably stays 3m: acts on good to soft and good to firm ground: often visored/blinkered, effective when not: has looked none too genuine (seemed to down tools fourth outing). *Ferdy Murphy*
    c–
    h123

SPRING BROOK (IRE) 8 b.g. Parthian Springs – Kemita (IRE) (Kemal (FR)) [2006/7 21dᵖᵘ c26dᶠ c21d⁴ c22s³ c20m³ c17g⁵ Apr 23] sturdy gelding: sixth foal: half-brother to winning pointers by Phardante and Mister Lord: dam unraced: pulled up most starts in Irish points, though did win maiden in 2006: bought 5,200 gns Doncaster August Sales: no form in novice hurdle/chases: usually in cheekpieces. *P. Butler*
    c–
    h–

SPRINGFIELD GUNNER 5 ch.g. Gunner B – Ledee (Le Bavard (FR)) [2006/7 F16g Apr 7] half-brother to useful hurdler Springfield Scally (by Scallywag), stayed 3¼m, and poor 2m hurdler Springfield Rhyme (by Idiot's Delight): dam unraced, half-sister to dam of Buck House: burly, well held in bumper on debut. *S. Gollings*
    F–

SPRING GROVE (IRE) 12 b.g. Mandalus – Lucy Lorraine (IRE) (Buckskin (FR)) [2006/7 c114, h–: c22d² c24g³ Mar 23] workmanlike gelding: winning chaser: left R. Alner, won point in January: better effort in hunters when 21 lengths third to Scots Grey at Newbury: best up to 3m: acts on heavy and good to firm going: has run well when sweating and on toes: races prominently. *A. D. Old*
    c104
    h–

SPRING LOVER (FR) 8 b.g. Fijar Tango (FR) – Kailasa (FR) (R B Chesne) [2006/7 c120, h–: c20g³ c20d⁴ c20v⁴ c24m³ c22d⁴ c24s³ c21g⁴ Mar 16] smallish gelding: maiden hurdler: fairly useful handicap chaser: stays 3m: unraced on firm ground, probably acts on any other: tried in cheekpieces/blinkers: inconsistent. *Miss Venetia Williams*
    c116
    h–

SPRING MARGOT (FR) 11 b.g. Kadalko (FR) – La Brunante (FR) (Chaparral (FR)) [2006/7 c132, h–: c21g⁴ c20v* c17s* c21s⁶ c20g² c20g³ Apr 16] tall, useful-looking gelding: fairly useful hunter chaser nowadays: won at Perth and Stratford (made all to beat Coole Glen by 24 lengths) in May: barely stays 3m: acts on good to firm and heavy going: consistent. *David M. Easterby*
    c105
    h–

SPRING THE QUE (IRE) 8 b.g. Parthian Springs – Que Tranquila (Dominion) [2006/7 20v² 16d* Jan 14] useful-looking gelding: half-brother to 3 winners, including fair 2m hurdler Euro Flyer (by Muharib): dam ran twice: useful handicap hurdler, lightly raced: off 18 months, highly encouraging second to View Mount Prince at Punchestown, and month later improved again to win 30-runner Pierse Hurdle at Leopardstown by 2½ lengths from Mister Hight: effective at 2m to 2½m: raced on good going or softer (acts on heavy). *Robert Tyner, Ireland*
    h139 +

Pierse Hurdle (Handicap), Leopardstown—7-lb claimer Philip Enright drives home
Spring The Que on the extended run-in to beat Mister Hight (centre) and New Field (right)

SPRING TIME GIRL 5 b.m. Timeless Times (USA) – Daira (Daring March) [2006/7 **h86** 16g 16g³ 20g^F Dec 30] modest on Flat (stays 1¼m): best effort over hurdles when third in maiden at Musselburgh. *B. Ellison*

SPRINGVIC (IRE) 7 b.g. Old Vic – Spring Beauty (IRE) (King's Ride) [2006/7 h93?: **h105** 20s^{pu} 16s* 16v⁵ 16v 16g 16s Apr 26] sturdy, workmanlike gelding: seemingly easily best effort over hurdles when winning novice at Wetherby in November: should stay 2½m: raced on good going or softer: takes keen hold: shaped as if amiss most starts in 2006/7. *G. M. Moore*

SPRINGWELL BEAU 5 ch.g. Then Again – Logani (Domynsky) [2006/7 F17d^{pu} **F–** F16v^{pu} Feb 24] unfurnished gelding: second foal: dam, no sign of ability, half-sister to useful staying chaser Ardent Scout: no show in bumpers. *D. W. Thompson*

SPRINGWOOD WHITE 13 gr.g. Sharkskin Suit (USA) – Kale Brig (New Brig) **c76** [2006/7 c–: c25f c20d³ c21s³ c20m⁶ Jun 3] modest pointer/hunter chaser: stays 25f: acts on soft and good to firm going: has worn cheekpieces: races prominently. *Mrs V. Park*

SPRINKLER 4 b.f. Emperor Fountain – Ryewater Dream (Touching Wood (USA)) **F93** [2006/7 F14g F17g² Apr 23] smallish filly: half-sister to several winners, including fair hurdler Dancing Hill (by Piccolo), stays 2½m, and fairly useful hurdler/chaser Touch Closer (by Inchinor), stays 25f: dam 11.7f winner: better effort in bumpers 6 months apart when 1¼ lengths second to One Rose in mares race at Sedgefield. *C. W. Thornton*

SPROSSER (IRE) 7 b.g. Alflora (IRE) – Dark Nightingale (Strong Gale) [2006/7 21s⁴ **h115** 21g⁴ Mar 20] big, rangy gelding: third foal: brother to modest hurdler/chaser One Five Eight, stays 3m: dam fair hurdler up to 2½m: won Irish point in 2005: 100/1, encouraging hurdling debut when 13 lengths fourth to Duc de Regniere in novice at Kempton: insufficient emphasis on stamina next time: will be suited by 3m+. *O. Sherwood*

SPUD 5 b.g. Spadoun (FR) – Parslin (The Parson) [2006/7 F16v² F16v³ F16m* Apr 15] **F99** 8,000 3-y-o: useful-looking gelding: half-brother to 2¾m hurdle winner Loch Nevis (by Roscoe Blake): dam unraced, out of half-sister to top-class staying chaser Brown Chamberlin: fairly useful form in bumpers: favourite, won maiden at Worcester by neck from Silver Accord: sold 95,000 gns Doncaster May Sales. *P. R. Webber*

SPUD ONE 10 b.g. Lord Americo – Red Dusk (Deep Run) [2006/7 c16g^{ur} May 3] **c?** lengthy, good-topped gelding: bumper winner/winning hurdler in 2002/3: well held in 2 **h–** points in 2006: badly hampered and unseated eleventh in hunter on chasing debut: raced around 2m: acts on firm and good to soft going: has taken little interest. *Miss S. Waugh*

SPURADICH (IRE) 7 b.g. Barathea (IRE) – Svanzega (USA) (Sharpen Up) [2006/7 **c99** h110: 16d³ 17s² c16g* c20g^{pu} c19d⁴ 21s^{pu} Dec 7] fair maiden hurdler, distressed final **h106** outing: won novice at Hereford in October on chasing debut: mistakes next 2 starts: likely to prove best around 2m: acts on firm and soft going. *Jonjo O'Neill*

SPY GAME (IRE) 7 b.g. Definite Article – Postie (Sharpo) [2006/7 16g Jun 15] leggy **h–** gelding: 1m winner at 3 yrs, lightly raced and little show on Flat since: maiden hurdler, fair form at best: sold out of D. Hughes's stable 9,000 gns Doncaster August (2005) Sales: raced mainly around 2m on good ground or softer: tried blinkered/visored. *Jennie Candlish*

SPY GUN (USA) 7 ch.g. Mt Livermore (USA) – Takeover Target (USA) (Nodouble **h–** (USA)) [2006/7 h–: 17s^{pu} 16d 16s 16m⁶ 16s⁵ Dec 7] modest and unreliable on Flat (stays 9.5f), raced mainly on all-weather: no form over hurdles, including in seller: headstrong. *T. Wall*

SQUANTUM (IRE) 10 b.g. Roselier (FR) – Coole Eile (IRE) (King's Ride) [2006/7 **c–** c–, h83: 26m^{pu} Mar 29] ex-Irish gelding: won first of 2 starts over fences: poor handicap **h–** hurdler: bled only outing in 2006/7: stays 3m: acts on soft and good to firm going: tried in cheekpieces/tongue tied. *Miss Joanne Priest*

SQUARE DEALER 6 b.g. Vettori (IRE) – Pussy Foot (Red Sunset) [2006/7 h–: 20s **h85** 20d 20d 20v² 20v 19v³ 17s² Mar 13] lengthy gelding: poor novice hurdler: probably best short of 2½m: raced on ground softer than good: visored/blinkered last 5 outings: has looked none too resolute. *J. R. Norton*

SQUARE MILE (IRE) 7 ch.g. Bob Back (USA) – Mother Imelda (IRE) (Phardante **c103** (FR)) [2006/7 h117: c24s^{pu} c20m^{pu} c23m* Apr 15] good-topped gelding: bumper/hurdle **h–** winner: first completed outing over fences when winning maiden at Worcester by ½ length from Alagon, jumping right in straight: stays 23f: acts on good to firm and good to soft ground: tried tongue tied. *Jonjo O'Neill*

SQUEAKER 6 br.m. Sovereign Water (FR) – Armagnac Messenger (Pony Express) **F–**
[2006/7 F–: F17d Oct 7] tailed off in 2 bumpers. *H. E. Haynes*

SQUIRES LANE (IRE) 8 b.g. Mister Lord (USA) – Perks Glory (IRE) (Executive **c–**
Perk) [2006/7 c109: c24vᵖᵘ Oct 21] tall gelding: fair chaser: ran poorly only outing in
2006/7: stays 3¼m: acts on heavy going. *Andrew Turnell*

SRIOLOGY (IRE) 6 b.g. Sri Pekan (USA) – Sinology (Rainbow Quest (USA)) **h86**
[2006/7 16v⁵ 18g² Apr 10] modest on Flat (should stay 1½m): best effort in 3 starts over
hurdles when second in seller at Fontwell (claimed £5,000): tried tongue tied. *M. R. Hoad*

STACK THE PACK (IRE) 10 ch.g. Good Thyne (USA) – Game Trix (Buckskin **c– x**
(FR)) [2006/7 c99, h–: c22dᵘʳ c24mᶠ c23mᵖᵘ Aug 11] lightly raced over hurdles: fair **h–**
chaser at best, usually let down by jumping (failed to complete all starts in 2006/7): stays
3m: acts on good to firm and good to soft going. *T. R. George*

STAGECOACH AMBER (USA) 5 b.g. Bright Launch (USA) – Clan Lake (USA) **F73**
(Navajo (USA)) [2006/7 F16d F16g Apr 23] 5,000 3-y-o: sturdy, lengthy gelding:
half-brother to numerous winners in USA/Brazil: dam won 7 races in USA: mid-field
both starts in bumpers. *Mrs S. J. Smith*

STAGECOACH DIAMOND 8 b.g. Classic Cliche (IRE) – Lyra (Blakeney) [2006/7 **c– p**
h117: 20g* c21s⁵ May 29] lengthy gelding: fairly useful hurdler: progressed further when **h125**
winning handicap at Uttoxeter in May by 10 lengths from Always Waining: odds on,
presumably amiss on chasing debut: should stay 3m: acts on soft and good to firm ground:
should prove capable of better over fences. *Mrs S. J. Smith*

STAGECOACH OPAL 6 b.g. Komaite (USA) – Rag Time Belle (Raga Navarro **h115**
(ITY)) [2006/7 h98p, F102: 22g³ 22d²² 20g 22v² 20v* 20v⁵ 24g³ 20s Apr 1] good-bodied
gelding: bumper winner: fairly useful hurdler: won novices at Cartmel (odds on) in May
and Wetherby (handicap, by length from Surricate) in December: ran poorly 2 of last 3
outings: stays 3m: acts on heavy going: hasn't convinced with attitude. *Mrs S. J. Smith*

ST AGNES FOUNTAIN 7 b.m. Thowra (FR) – Elmley Brook (Paddy's Stream) **h–**
[2006/7 F17g⁵ 24vᵖᵘ Oct 21] fifth foal: half-sister to 2 winning pointers: dam maiden **F75**
pointer: looked far from straightforward when fifth in bumper at Newton Abbot for
V. Dartnall, only sign of ability: wears cheekpieces. *Mrs S. D. Williams*

STAGNITE 7 ch.g. Compton Place – Superspring (Superlative) [2006/7 16m Oct 12] **h–**
modest on Flat (stays 7f, successful in July (for P. Blockley) and November: doubtful
stayer over hurdles (pulled very hard on debut): sold £2,200 Ascot February Sales. *Karen
George*

STAINLEY (IRE) 4 b.g. Elnadim (USA) – Fizz Up (Alzao (USA)) [2006/7 16m* 16g⁵ **h104**
16v* 18v 16gᵖᵘ 16sᵖᵘ Apr 25] smallish gelding: fair on Flat (stays 1¼m), sold out of
J. Bethell's stable 10,000 gns Doncaster October Sales: won juvenile hurdles at Musselburgh in November and Kelso in January: seemed to take little interest final outing: raced
around 2m: acts on heavy and good to firm going. *Mrs S. C. Bradburne*

STANBURY (USA) 5 ch.g. Zamindar (USA) – Staffin (Salse (USA)) [2006/7 16f⁶ **h88**
16mᵖᵘ Aug 11] runner-up on first of 2 starts on Flat, sold out of M. Channon's stable
2,800 gns Doncaster May (2005) Sales: modest form on completed outing over hurdles:
dead. *Mrs D. A. Hamer*

STANCE 8 b.g. Salse (USA) – De Stael (USA) (Nijinsky (CAN)) [2006/7 c127, h–: **c109 x**
c17m⁶ c20g² c16g⁴ Nov 14] sturdy, close-coupled gelding: useful hurdler: fairly useful **h–**
chaser, well below best in handicaps in 2006/7: best form around 2m: acts on firm and
good to soft going: effective with or without cheekpieces: has raced freely/made
mistakes. *G. L. Moore*

STANDANDBECOUNTED 6 ch.g. Fleetwood (IRE) – Sun Dante (IRE) (Phardante **h–**
(FR)) [2006/7 20sᵖᵘ 26sᵖᵘ Dec 26] fifth foal: half-brother to fair hurdler/fairly useful
chaser Alfie's Sun (by Alflora), stays 21f, and bumper winner Wolnai (by Cloudings):
dam unraced half-sister to useful hurdler/chaser up to 2½m Chauvinist, out of half-sister
to smart hurdler/useful chaser Forest Sun: won maiden point in 2006: no show in novice
hurdles. *O. Sherwood*

STAND EASY (IRE) 14 b.g. Buckskin (FR) – Geeaway (Gala Performance) [2006/7 **c– §**
c88§, h–§: c29g Mar 21] tall gelding: veteran chaser: stays 3¼m: acts on heavy and good **h– §**
to firm going: has worn cheekpieces: temperamental. *Miss Lisa Venables*

STANDIN OBLIGATION (IRE) 8 ch.g. Pierre – Clonroche Floods (Pauper) **c131**
[2006/7 h152+: c25f* c23g* c24d* c25s³ c24d³ c25gᵖᵘ Apr 13] good-topped gelding: **h–**
smart hurdler, successful 6 of 8 starts: jumped well in lead when landing odds in novices

first 3 outings in chases, at Kelso (3 ran) in May, Wetherby in June and Cheltenham (left clear 3 out when beating Openide a length with something in hand) in November: disappointing after, shaping as if amiss last 2 outings: will stay beyond 25f: acts on soft going, easy task on firm: joined P. Monteith. *D. E. Pipe*

STAN LEA MOORE 5 b.g. Josr Algarhoud (IRE) – Spriolo (Priolo (USA)) [2006/7 **F—** F17v Jan 11] fifth foal: dam well beaten only start: tailed off in bumper on debut. *N. A. Twiston-Davies*

STAN (NZ) 8 b.g. Super Imposing (NZ) – Take Care (NZ) (Wham (AUS)) [2006/7 **c130** c121p, h119: c22s³ c20dᵖᵘ c19s³ c16s² c17gᵘʳ c16g⁶ Apr 12] compact gelding: fairly **h—** useful hurdler: useful form over fences, left R. C. Guest and off 13 months before return: 6 lb out of weights, best effort when sixth to Bambi de L'Orme in Grade 3 handicap at Aintree final start, length up and still going well when blundering 2 out: probably best up to 2½m: acts on good to firm and heavy going: blinkered last 4 outings. *Miss Venetia Williams*

STANSTED (IRE) 6 b.g. Mister Mat (FR) – Blackwater Lady (IRE) (Torus) [2006/7 **h—** F—: 18g Mar 18] well held in bumper /novice hurdle nearly a year apart: sold 3,500 gns Doncaster May Sales. *M. J. McGrath*

STANTONS CHURCH 10 b.g. Homo Sapien – Valkyrie Reef (Miramar Reef) **c— §** [2006/7 c—§, h—§: c19g⁵ c20mᵖᵘ 16d 20dᵖᵘ c20d c20sᵖᵘ 26sᵖᵘ Jan 26] no longer of any **h— §** account and temperamental to boot: tried in cheekpieces. *Mrs P. Ford*

STANWAY 8 b.g. Presenting – Nicklup (Netherkelly) [2006/7 c—, h—: c19m c20gᵖᵘ **c—** c25gᵖᵘ Apr 20] close-coupled, workmanlike gelding: won on chasing debut in 2004/5, no **h—** form since: should be suited by 2½m+: tried blinkered. *Mrs Mary Hambro*

STAR ANGLER (IRE) 9 b.g. Supreme Leader – So Pink (IRE) (Deep Run) [2006/7 **c93** c96, h95: 16s c25s⁵ c21v* c19v⁴ c26v⁴ c19g Mar 21] useful-looking gelding: winning **h—** hurdler: modest chaser: won novice handicap at Uttoxeter in January: should stay beyond 21f: acts on heavy going: tried blinkered: tongue tied last 2 starts: none too reliable. *M. Sheppard*

STAR ANTIQUE (FR) 4 b.f. Lute Antique (FR) – Lady Start (FR) (Village Star (FR)) **c111** [2006/7 17sᵖᵘ 17g³ c17s³ c17g* c17s³ c17s⁴ 20gᵖᵘ 16m⁶ Apr 27] €11,000 2-y-o: tall, **h—** unfurnished filly: second foal: dam, winning hurdler/chaser in France up to 19f, half-sister to useful French chaser around 2½m Prince des Ifs: won 3-y-o hurdle at Pau in late-2005/6: fair chaser: won 3-y-o event at Nimes in October: left J. Ortet and tongue tied, little impact both starts over hurdles in Britain, in Grade 1 event on first occasion: raced mainly around 2m on good ground or softer: pulls hard. *K. J. Burke*

STAR AWARD (IRE) 6 b. or br.m. Oscar (IRE) – Forgotten Star (IRE) (Don't Forget **h94** Me) [2006/7 F91: 16gᵖᵘ 19d³ 21dᵖᵘ 22d² 21g 22f³ Apr 5] rather workmanlike mare: bumper winner for N. Henderson: modest novice hurdler: will stay 3m: acts on firm and good to soft ground: inconsistent. *Miss H. C. Knight*

STAR BEAT 4 b.g. Beat All (USA) – Autumn Leaf (Afzal) [2006/7 F13g⁶ F14v F16s² **F82** F17m Apr 28] rather leggy gelding: fifth foal: dam, little sign of ability, sister to useful staying chaser Billygoat Gruff: best effort in bumpers when 9 lengths second to Peters Pride in maiden at Catterick. *Mrs S. A. Watt*

STARBUCK 13 b.g. Brush Aside (USA) – Clonmello (Le Bavard (FR)) [2006/7 c76, **c—** h—: c25g⁵ Apr 2] tall gelding: winning pointer: poor maiden chaser: should stay beyond **h—** 25f: acts on firm and soft going: has worn cheekpieces. *Miss J. Fisher*

STARBURST DIAMOND (IRE) 5 ro.g. Old Vic – Camlin Rose (IRE) (Roselier **F—** (FR)) [2006/7 F16s Oct 25] good-topped gelding: second foal: dam unraced: well beaten in bumper on debut. *Miss H. C. Knight*

STAR CLIPPER 10 b.g. Kris – Anne Bonny (Ajdal (USA)) [2006/7 c126x, h—: c24d² **c128 x** c24s c24vᵖᵘ 22d 24s 20v 20v Mar 3] good sort: modest handicap hurdler: fairly useful **h96** handicap chaser: good second to Pearly Jack in Munster National at Limerick (won race previous year), but poor efforts behind Cane Brake next 2 starts: stays 3½m: acts on heavy going: tried tongue tied/blinkered in 2005/6: has found little: often makes mistakes. *N. Meade, Ireland*

STAR DE MOHAISON (FR) 6 b.g. Beyssac (FR) – Belle de Mohaison (FR) **c158 +** (Suvero (FR)) [2006/7 c146p, h—: 25d* c24s* Dec 1] **h142 +**
  Until injury intervened, Star de Mohaison did everything asked of him on the racecourse—winning both his starts—yet he still found himself slipping from

the head of the Manor Farm Stables' Cheltenham Gold Cup pecking order to no better than fourth by the end of the season. While both Kauto Star and Denman enjoyed full unbeaten campaigns and Neptune Collonges showed high-class form to win at Punchestown, Star de Mohaison suffered a tendon injury and was out for a large part of the season. Star de Mohaison's jumping had been impressive when winning the big staying novice chases at both Cheltenham and Aintree in 2005/6 and his reappearance was eagerly anticipated. Having sidestepped the Charlie Hall Chase due to ground concerns, he took advantage of a lower hurdles mark on his eventual reappearance in November. Star de Mohaison was sent off 6/4 favourite in a field of seventeen for the twenty-five-furlong Lombard Properties Handicap Hurdle at Cheltenham, a valuable listed event that has been dominated by the Pipe stable in recent years. Unsurprisingly, the David Pipe-trained Nobody Tells Me was Star de Mohaison's main rival in the betting, but, in truth, it proved an extremely one-sided affair—after racing with plenty of enthusiasm, Star de Mohaison went on two out and soon stretched clear to win by eight lengths from the consistent Jockser. He became ante-post favourite for the Hennessy Cognac Gold Cup in the wake of this success, but his owner thought better of running a five-year-old under 11-11, though trainer Paul Nicholls wanted to do so. In the fifty years of the Hennessy, only four five-year-olds had previously contested the three-and-a-quarter-mile event. Eudipe, who was the first to do so since Solray fell in 1959 (when the race was still held at Cheltenham), had been runner-up in the Royal & SunAlliance Chase the previous season and finished third to Suny Bay in 1997 (also runner-up in the 1998 renewal). Incidentally, Star de Mohaison's stable-companion Napolitain became the fifth five-year-old to contest this race when pulled up in the latest edition.

The John Smith's Future Stars Chase, an intermediate event at Sandown six days after the Hennessy, was chosen for Star de Mohaison's next outing. Just four

Lombard Properties Handicap Hurdle, Cheltenham—Star de Mohaison's much lower hurdles mark is exploited to claim a facile win in this valuable event; Jockser (noseband) takes second

John Smith's Future Stars Chase (Intermediate), Sandown—much closer this time as Star de Mohaison levels the score with tenderly-handled The Listener

runners contested what was a steadily-run affair, a completely different type of race to the one Star de Mohaison would have had at Newbury. Nevertheless, each of the quartet had contested the previous season's Royal & SunAlliance Chase, including the Cheltenham fourth Lord Killeshanra and fifth Zabenz, who both had a significant pull in the weights. However, the 2/1-on shot Star de Mohaison was pushed closest by Cheltenham faller The Listener, who had actually beaten the favourite twice earlier in 2005/6 and arguably would have done so again at Sandown under more vigorous handling (Andrew Thornton subsequently lost the ride). Whether slightly fortunate or not to extend his winning run to five, the Sandown performance still represented further improvement on Star de Mohaison's part—he won by a length and a quarter with a further twenty-six lengths back to third-placed Zabenz—and the subsequent exploits of The Listener only underlined as much. Sadly, twelve days on from this success, a scan revealed that Star de Mohaison had damaged his near-fore tendon. The prognosis for a successful return during the next season is thought to be very good.

		Paris Jour	Herbager
Star de Mohaison (FR) (b.g. 2001)	Beyssac (FR) (ch 1978)	(b 1962)	La Petite Hutte
		Dori	Nordiste
		(ch 1966)	Paraphernalia
	Belle de Mohaison (FR) (b 1987)	Suvero	Habitat
		(b 1977)	Heavenly Form
		Bella Linda	Prebois
		(b 1971)	Flee

The pedigree of the tall, leggy Star de Mohaison has been covered in detail in previous editions of *Chasers & Hurdlers* and there is nothing to add to what has been stated there. Given that Ogden's Exotic Dancer emerged as a leading Gold Cup contender in his absence, plus the strong competition within the Nicholls stable, it wouldn't be the biggest surprise if Star de Mohaison had his attentions turned to Aintree rather than Cheltenham—his notably fluent jumping could prove a real asset in the Grand National, a race neither Ogden nor Nicholls has yet won. Star de Mohaison races prominently, stays at least twenty-five furlongs and acts on soft and good to firm going (probably heavy). He has been tongue tied for his last five outings (all wins). *P. F. Nicholls*

STAR DOUBLE (ITY) 7 ch.g. Bob Back (USA) – Among The Stars (Pharly (FR)) [2006/7 h70p: 22s^pu 22d^4 17s^2 16v* 16s 21s c19g^ur Mar 28] strong, good-topped gelding: modest hurdler: won novice handicap at Warwick in January: below form next 2 starts: let down by jumping/attitude on chasing debut: effective at testing 2m to 2¾m: acts on heavy going: blinkered last 6 outings: temperament under suspicion. *N. A. Twiston-Davies*   c– h97

STAR FERN 6 br.g. Young Ern – Christening (IRE) (Lahib (USA)) [2006/7 20g^pu 20m^6 Apr 9] strong gelding: modest and unreliable on all-weather on Flat (stays 9.5f), little form on turf: left M. Attwater, little show in novice hurdles. *M. W. Easterby*   h–

STAR FEVER (IRE) 6 b.g. Saddlers' Hall (IRE) – Phenics Allstar (IRE) (Fourstars Allstar (USA)) [2006/7 h80, F79: 21m^3 24g^6 24d* c16v^3 c20g^6 c25g^3 Apr 23] modest hurdler: sold out of Miss H. Knight's stable 30,000 gns Doncaster May Sales after reappearance: won handicap at Musselburgh in January: similar form when placed over fences: stays 25f: acts on good to firm and heavy ground. *N. G. Richards*   c98 h90

STAR GALAXY (IRE) 7 b.g. Fourstars Allstar (USA) – Raven Night (IRE) (Mandalus) [2006/7 c–, h–: 22m c20s^2 c19s^5 c19s^pu c16v^4 c20v^6 c16v^4 c20v^F c25m^5 c16g^4 Apr 20] no form over hurdles: poor maiden chaser: claimed from Mrs Norma Pook £6,000 second start: stays 2½m: acts on soft ground: tried in cheekpieces. *M. A. Doyle*   c62 h–

STAR GLOW 13 b.g. Dunbeath (USA) – Betrothed (Aglojo) [2006/7 c26g^pu c22s^5 c24v* c21d^6 c25s^2 c25v^pu c26v^F Mar 12] angular gelding: maiden hurdler: winning pointer: modest chaser: 100/1, back to best when winning handicap at Lingfield in January: stays 3m: acts on heavy going: tried blinkered. *R. H. York*   c94 h–

STARLIGHT PROMISE (IRE) 6 br.m. Definite Article – Merry Twinkle (Martinmas) [2006/7 F16s^3 F17d 16g^ur 22d 17s^6 17g^pu Apr 7] 9,000 4-y-o: useful-looking mare: sister to 10.5f/1½m winner Ffiffiffer and half-sister to several winners, including fair hurdler/fairly useful chaser Smolensk (by Ela-Mana-Mou), stayed 2½m: dam ran twice in Ireland: third in mares bumper at Towcester on debut: no form after, mainly over hurdles: has had tongue tied. *V. R. A. Dartnall*   h– F88

STAR MEMBER (IRE) 8 b.g. Hernando (FR) – Constellation (IRE) (Kaldoun (FR)) [2006/7 h118: 17s^4 19g Sep 23] fairly useful hurdle winner, disappointing on second of 2 outings in handicaps in 2006/7: successful at 2¾m, better form over shorter: acts on soft ground. *Ian Williams*   h107

STARMIX 6 gr. or br.g. Linamix (FR) – Danlu (USA) (Danzig (USA)) [2006/7 h–: 17m Sep 26] small, leggy gelding: disappointing maiden on Flat: no form over hurdles: tried blinkered. *G. A. Harker*   h–

STARNEVEES (FR) 6 b.g. Kaldounevees (FR) – Stadia (FR) (Star Maite (FR)) [2006/7 16d 17s^4 Feb 8] angular gelding: dam winning chaser: fairly useful on Flat (stays 1¼m), sold out of L. Cumani's stable 9,000 gns Newmarket Autumn Sales: modest form over hurdles, 11 lengths fourth to Wise Owl in maiden at Taunton, poorly placed when pace increased: likely to improve. *C. J. Mann*   h88 p

STAR OF GERMANY (IRE) 7 b.g. Germany (USA) – Twinkle Bright (USA) (Star de Naskra (USA)) [2006/7 20m^pu 20g^3 20d^3 21s 21s^bd 20v^6 24v Feb 20] sturdy gelding: modest hurdler: stays 2½m: acts on good to soft going, below best on softer. *R. S. Brookhouse*   h90

STAR OF RAVEN 10 b.m. Sea Raven (IRE) – Lucy At The Minute (Silly Prices) [2006/7 c20s^4 c20g^2 Apr 23] winning hunter chaser: better effort in handicaps on return from lengthy absence when second to Gee Aker Malayo at Hexham: stays 25f: raced on good ground or softer (acts on soft): held up. *J. M. Saville*   c89

STAR OF THE DESERT (IRE) 4 b. or br.g. Desert Story (IRE) – Cindy's Star (IRE) (Dancing Dissident (USA)) [2006/7 16d 16m^6 16g^4 Mar 17] fair maiden on Flat (barely stays 1¼m), sold out of C. Cox's stable 18,000 gns Newmarket Autumn Sales: best effort over hurdles when fourth to Daldini in maiden at Wetherby. *Mrs K. Walton*   h84

STAROFTHEMORNING (IRE) 6 ch.m. Foxhound (USA) – Leggagh Lady (IRE) (Doubletour (USA)) [2006/7 16g^6 17s^3 16m^2 16d^4 16f^3 16d Nov 21] smallish mare: second foal: dam fairly useful 2m hurdler: poor maiden on Flat (stays 2m): likewise over hurdles, left P. Flynn prior to reappearance: raced around 2m: acts on firm and soft going: tried blinkered. *A. W. Carroll*   h74

STAROSKI 10 b.m. Petoski – Olnistar (FR) (Balsamo (FR)) [2006/7 h–: 16s 22d 22s Feb 17] lengthy mare: lightly raced: no form over hurdles. *Simon Earle*   h–

918

STAR PERFORMANCE (IRE) 12 ch.g. Insan (USA) – Leallen (Le Bavard (FR)) **c111**
[2006/7 c103, h86: 24d³ 24g⁵ 20s c31d² c21g⁵ c31dᵖᵘ c25m c34f³ Apr 26] workmanlike **h88**
gelding: modest maiden hurdler: fair chaser: best efforts in 2006/7 when placed behind
Spot Thedifference in cross-country events at Cheltenham and Punchestown: stays 4¼m:
acts on firm and soft going: often wears headgear: tried tongue tied. *Oliver McKiernan,
Ireland*

STAR PLAYER (IRE) 5 ch.g. Accordion – Folle Idee de Luz (FR) (Reve Bleu (FR)) **F88**
[2006/7 F16s³ F16v⁶ F16g⁶ Apr 3] unfurnished gelding: second foal: dam, maiden
hurdler/chaser, half-sister to useful chaser Luzcadou, best around 2½m: fair form in
bumpers. *C. Grant*

STARS DELIGHT (IRE) 10 ch.g. Fourstars Allstar (USA) – Celtic Cygnet (Celtic **h107**
Cone) [2006/7 h101: 18d⁵ 21s 24v* 22v⁴ 26g* Mar 14] compact gelding: fair handicap
hurdler: won at Taunton in January and Huntingdon in March: stays 3¼m: acts on any
going: in cheekpieces last 4 starts: not straightforward. *Jim Best*

STAR SHOT (IRE) 6 b.g. Cloudings (IRE) – B Final (Gunner B) [2006/7 h110p, F99: **h113**
16s² 19d⁴ 16s⁵ 16d 21d 16g⁵ 21g Mar 28] rather unfurnished gelding: fair handicap
hurdler: finished distressed final outing: should stay beyond 19f: raced on good ground or
softer (acts on soft). *P. R. Webber*

STARS IN HIS EYES 5 b.g. Wace (USA) – Madame Ruby (FR) (Homing) [2006/7 **h–**
16s 16d 22gᵇᵈ Mar 19] brother to 2½m chase winner Opportunity Knocks and half-
brother to winning hurdler/chaser Got News For You (by Positive Statement), stayed 3m:
dam, fair 17f hurdle winner, half-sister to fairly useful 2m hurdler Might Move: no form
in novice hurdles: dead. *N. J. Hawke*

STAR TIME (IRE) 8 b.g. Fourstars Allstar (USA) – Punctual (Lead On Time (USA)) **c– §**
[2006/7 c–§, h59§: 26g⁶ 26d⁵ 16v³ 24s* 27m² 24m 25s⁴ 27s² 27s⁶ 24v⁴ 24s⁶ Jan 31] **h75 §**
good-bodied gelding: poor hurdler: first win in conditional jockeys handicap at Uttoxeter
in May: no form in 2 starts over fences: stays 27f: acts on heavy and good to firm going:
usually visored, well held only start in cheekpieces: temperamental (takes plenty of
driving). *M. Scudamore*

STARTING POINT 5 br.g. Monashee Mountain (USA) – Louise Moillon (Mansingh **F104 p**
(USA)) [2006/7 F90: F16v⁴ F16v* Mar 6] tall gelding: fairly useful form in bumpers:
trained on reappearance only by R. Simpson: improved effort when winning 7-runner
event at Newcastle by 23 lengths from Randolf, pulling hard early, leading at halfway and
not extended to pull clear: capable of better again. *G. A. Swinbank*

STAR TROOPER (IRE) 11 b. or br.g. Brief Truce (USA) – Star Cream (Star Appeal) **c– §**
[2006/7 c–§, h72§: 18v 17v² 20v⁶ Mar 2] compact gelding: maiden chaser: poor handi- **h69 §**
cap hurdler: stays 2½m: acts on any going: tried blinkered, usually wears cheekpieces:
unreliable. *Miss S. E. Forster*

STAR WONDER 7 b.m. Syrtos – Galava (CAN) (Graustark) [2006/7 c–, h–: 16dᵖᵘ **c–**
Oct 1] of little account: tried blinkered. *G. R. I. Smyly* **h–**

STAR ZERO 6 b.g. Danzero (AUS) – Startino (Bustino) [2006/7 h82: 16g 16d⁵ 16v 18g **h72**
19g 24m Apr 25] tall gelding: poor novice hurdler: probably stays 19f. *John R. Upson*

STATE OF PLAY 7 b.g. Hernando (FR) – Kaprice (GER) (Windwurf (GER)) **c160**
[2006/7 c151, h107: c26s* c26g⁶ c25g⁴ Apr 12] **h–**

Racing's longest continuous commercial sponsorship, by cognac distrib-
utors James Hennessy & Co, celebrated its golden jubilee in the latest season. The
Hennessy Gold Cup (known as the Hennessy Cognac Gold Cup since 1971) has a
splendid history and, for most of its first fifty years, enjoyed a pre-eminent position
in the jumping calendar before Christmas. The winner of the inaugural Hennessy in
1957 was Mandarin, owned by Madame Killian Hennessy, a member of the
sponsoring family which had a long association with jumping in Britain. Mandarin
won a second Hennessy in 1961, when he went on to success in the same season's
Cheltenham Gold Cup and Grand Steeple-Chase de Paris. The early history of the
Hennessy, the first three editions of which were at Cheltenham, regularly featured
the top staying chasers. The reigning Cheltenham Gold Cup winner Linwell carried
12-2 into second place behind Mandarin in 1957, and that season's Gold Cup
winner the mare Kerstin went on to be beaten a short head by Taxidermist in the
1958 Hennessy under 11-9 (Mandarin, who came fifth, was top weight with 12-0).
Kerstin, incidentally, went on to win the 1959 Hennessy under 11-10.

After the Hennessy's move to Newbury, Mill House became the first reigning Gold Cup winner to win the Hennessy when carrying 12-0 to victory in the 1963 edition which staged the first meeting between Mill House and Arkle (third under 11-9). Arkle slipped on landing after overjumping at the last open ditch that day and he took his revenge on Mill House in the Cheltenham Gold Cup. Arkle won the Hennessy twice as the reigning Gold Cup winner, carrying 12-7 each time at Newbury (Mill House finished fourth under 12-4 on the first occasion which attracted a record crowd). Arkle ran in four successive Hennessys, a third victory under 12-7 narrowly foiled by rank outsider Stalbridge Colonist who received 35 lb. Stalbridge Colonist was beaten a head by three quarters of a length in the Cheltenham Gold Cup the following spring and also finished a close third in the next year's Gold Cup. He made the frame in the next two editions of the Hennessy as well, carrying 11-7 (beaten a head by Rondetto) and 12-4. What A Myth, receiving 33 lb from Arkle, was a length and a half behind him in third in Stalbridge Colonist's Hennessy and subsequently ran third in the 1967 Gold Cup, a race he won two years later. Other Gold Cup winners who went on to contest the Hennessy in the 'sixties and 'seventies under big weights were Woodland Venture (12-4), who ran in the Hennessy two seasons after winning the Gold Cup, L'Escargot (12-7) in 1971 and The Dikler (12-2), who ran in the 1974 Hennessy after winning the 1973 Gold Cup and finishing second at Cheltenham in 1974. The three last-named didn't make the frame in the Hennessy—Woodland Venture was pulled up, L'Escargot and The Dikler both finished sixth—and thirteen years elapsed after L'Escargot before another reigning Gold Cup winner lined up in the Hennessy. That was Burrough Hill Lad who put up a magnificent display to become the first horse to carry 12-0 or more to victory in the Hennessy since Mill House and Arkle. Only two others had won the race under top weight in the interim, Fighting Fit (joint top weight with 11-7 in 1979) and Diamond Edge (11-10 in 1981), the latter the seventh and last Hennessy winner saddled by Mandarin's trainer Fulke Walwyn. Burrough Hill Lad's performance at Newbury was the best seen in a steeplechase since Arkle's day and a major highlight in the Hennessy's illustrious story. After beating the then-dual King George winner Wayward Lad in the Charlie Hall Memorial at Wetherby (staged that season a fortnight after the Hennessy) and then winning the King George VI Chase itself, Burrough Hill Lad was odds on—before injury intervened—to become the first since L'Escargot to stage a repeat success in the Cheltenham Gold Cup.

Hennessy Cognac Gold Cup Chase (Handicap), Newbury—State of Play takes over at the final ditch; Juveigneur (white face) and Preacher Boy (right) chase him home

Garrison Savannah, who also carried 12-0 and was trained like Burrough Hill Lad by Jenny Pitman, is the only reigning Gold Cup winner since Burrough Hill Lad to contest the Hennessy (he was pulled up) as the race has faced increasing competition. The sponsors have been pushing up the value—the latest Hennessy had a first prize of £85,530—but the race has now lost its place as the most valuable event over fences in Britain before Christmas to the Betfair Chase, a Grade 1 weight-for-age race registered as the Lancashire Chase and staged the weekend before the Hennessy. Cheltenham's two big, traditional pre-Christmas handicaps, now known as the Paddy Power and the boylesports.com Gold Cup were worth £62,722 and £85,530 respectively to the winner in the latest season, while Ascot staged the seventeen-furlong Carey Group Handicap Chase (£74,364) on Betfair Chase weekend when Aintree had the Becher Chase (£57,020). The Grade 1 for the two-milers, the Tingle Creek at Sandown one week after the Hennessy was worth £79,828 to the winner in the latest season and attracted the Betfair winner Kauto Star. The Cheltenham Gold Cup winner War of Attrition met the Irish Hennessy Cognac Gold Cup winner Beef Or Salmon in early-November in the James Nicholson Wine Merchant Champion Chase at Down Royal (approximately £60,000), a weight-for-age race (now Grade 1) created in 1999. A little further afield, Auteuil's promotion of its International Jumps Weekend on that same weekend in early-November has highlighted another potentially lucrative target for some of the top staying chasers in Britain and Ireland (the latest edition of the Prix La Haye Jousselin had a first prize of £140,000). Although less valuable than these other races, the Rehearsal Chase (now staged at Newcastle on Hennessy weekend) is another counter attraction.

If the Hennessy no longer quite stands out as it once did, its tradition ensures that it remains one of the season's most prestigious races. Suny Bay is the Hennessy's most outstanding winner in recent times, carrying 11-8 to a thirteen-length victory in 1997 from the previous season's Gold Cup runner-up Barton Bank who shouldered top weight of 11-13. Suny Bay provided his rider Graham Bradley with a second Hennessy win, following that in 1982 on the previous season's Gold Cup runner-up Bregawn who put up a cracking performance under 11-10 (Night Nurse was top weight with 11-12) at Newbury and then went on to lead home the 'famous five' saddled by Michael Dickinson in that spring's Cheltenham Gold Cup— Captain John was runner-up in both races, incidentally, and received 10 lb from his stable companion at Newbury. Since Bregawn, Hennessy winners One Man and Teeton Mill—both of whom pulverised the opposition off a low weight at Newbury—have gone on to win major championship events, One Man successful in two King Georges and a Queen Mother Champion Chase and Teeton Mill winning the King George. Jodami finished second in the Hennessy (under 10-2) in his Cheltenham Gold Cup-winning season, while that year's Newbury third The Fellow (under 11-13) went on to land a second King George at Kempton prior to winning the following season's Cheltenham Gold Cup (from Jodami). In addition, an earlier Hennessy winner Brown Chamberlin (successful under 11-8) went on to finish second in the same season's King George and Gold Cup (behind Burrough Hill Lad). While Desert Orchid never ran in the Hennessy, another of racing's household names Red Rum contested it twice, going down by a short head under 11-4, following a nip-and-tuck duel in the straight with Red Candle, after the first of his Grand National wins, and finishing sixth under top weight of 11-9 two years later. Red Rum is one of eleven Aintree heroes who have contested the Hennessy as part of their Grand National-winning campaigns, the others being Kilmore (ninth), Corbiere (fifth), Hallo Dandy (pulled up), Maori Venture (third), Mr Frisk (third), Seagram (ninth), Party Politics (second), Rough Quest (second), Red Marauder (fifth) and Bindaree (fifth).

Many a Hennessy has been won by an improving young chaser. The 2005 winner Trabolgan, who became the first to win under top weight (11-12) since Burrough Hill Lad, had won the previous season's Royal & SunAlliance Chase but has sadly been sidelined since Newbury with a slow-to-heal tendon injury. Second-season chasers also filled the next five places in Trabolgan's Hennessy. The latest edition fell to a second-season chaser too, the up-and-coming State of Play who had won three of his first four starts over fences, rounding off his novice campaign with a runaway win from the subsequent Betfred Gold Cup winner Lacdoudal in the valuable betfair.com Handicap Chase at Aintree's Grand National meeting. The fiftieth Hennessy lacked a little in terms of quality, State of Play allotted 11-4, which was equivalent to a BHB mark of 145. There were only two other runners in the field of sixteen racing off a higher mark, the weights headed by the previous year's third Cornish Rebel (11-12) and the Mildmay Novices' Chase runner-up Turpin Green (11-10), who was carrying a 6-lb penalty for winning at Carlisle earlier in the month. Cornish Rebel was representing champion trainer Paul Nicholls, one of only three who have won the Hennessy both as a jockey and a trainer. Nicholls won successive editions on Broadheath and Playschool in the mid-'eighties and saddled the 2003 winner Strong Flow, the only novice to have won the Hennessy (though Be My Royal was first past the post in 2002 prior to losing the race on technical grounds). The others successful in both roles were Andy Turnell (rode April Seventh and trained Cogent) and Derek Ancil (trained and rode Knucklecracker). Another second-season chaser, the Reynoldstown winner Montgermont, who had changed stables over the summer, started 9/2 favourite, ahead of Turpin Green, the Paddy Power runner-up Vodka Bleu, Idle Talk (runner-up in the previous season's Royal & SunAlliance) and Cornish Rebel (whose stable had won three of the first four races on the card), the only runners to start at shorter than 10/1, the odds at which State of Play was sent off. Making his reappearance after being raised 17 lb by the handicapper for his Aintree win, the sound-jumping State of Play, well ridden by Paul Moloney, took the lead, going best, three out and ran on strongly to win by four lengths and nine from 12/1-shots Juveigneur and Preacher Boy. Idle Talk did best of the leading fancies, finishing sixth, a place ahead of Montgermont, while Cornish Rebel, Turpin Green and

Mr & Mrs William Rucker's "State of Play"

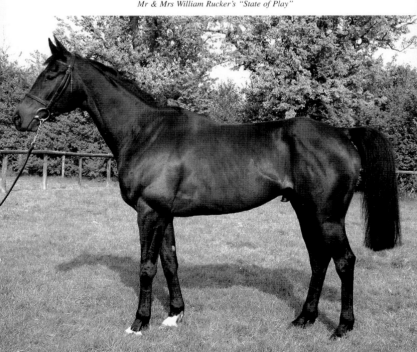

Vodka Bleu were among eight who failed to complete the course (all of them pulled up) in the testing conditions. State of Play joined an impressive list of chasers who have won the Hennessy as six-year-olds, a list headed by the first winner Mandarin who was followed by Taxidermist, Mill House, Spanish Steps (who contested four Hennessys), Bright Highway, Ghofar (who holds the time record for the race at 6m 28.29sec), One Man, Strong Flow and Celestial Gold. State of Play's Hennessy triumph was also the first by a horse trained in Wales, and the biggest success so far for his young trainer Evan Williams who is based in the Vale of Glamorgan. Williams bought State of Play, a fair novice hurdler who had yet to run over fences, out of Paul Webber's stable for 18,000 guineas at the Doncaster August Sales in 2005. It proved a very good day's shopping for Williams as, just seven lots earlier at the same sale, he bought Demi Beau for 10,000 guineas out of Charlie Mann's stable. Demi Beau won the Carey Group Handicap at Ascot a week before State of Play's Hennessy success.

State of Play was trained specifically for the Cheltenham Gold Cup after winning the Hennessy, connections having decided that 'a slog round Chepstow in the mud [Welsh National] would not be what the doctor prescribed at this stage of his career.' In fact, State of Play, for whom a Grand National entry was made, wasn't seen out between Newbury and Cheltenham, connections sidestepping a number of engagements saying they did not 'want the guts tearing out of him on soft ground before Cheltenham.' State of Play was sent off 8/1 third favourite for the Gold Cup, behind hot favourite Kauto Star and Exotic Dancer, who had filled the first two places in the King George VI Chase. State of Play was far from discredited but couldn't improve on his Hennessy form, managing just sixth at Cheltenham, over eleven lengths behind the winner Kauto Star. He didn't enjoy the clearest of passages late on at Cheltenham, though essentially held every chance. Along with the Gold Cup runner-up, third and twelfth—Exotic Dancer, Turpin Green and My Will—State of Play went on to contest the Betfair Bowl at Aintree four weeks later. State of Play didn't give his running, trailing in fourth of five behind Exotic Dancer, the field strung out at the finish. State of Play is still relatively lightly raced over fences and may improve again with another summer on his back. If he doesn't, he could prove hard to place.

			Niniski	Nijinsky
	Hernando (FR)		(b 1976)	Virginia Hills
	(b 1990)		Whakilyric	Miswaki
State of Play			(b 1984)	Lyrism
(b.g. 2000)			Windwurf	Kaiseradler
	Kaprice (GER)		(b 1972)	Wiesenweihe
	(b 1989)		Kama	Pentathlon
			(bl 1983)	Kaschira

State of Play isn't a top-class chaser on looks, being small and rather leggy, and isn't bred to be one either. His sire, the Prix du Jockey Club winner Hernando, has had success with some of his progeny who have found their way into jumping. They include Aintree Hurdle winner Sacundai, Royal & SunAlliance Novices' Hurdle winner No Refuge and Champion Bumper runner-up De Soto, though none of those possessed the size and scope usually associated with potential chasers (none of the trio has yet raced over fences). State of Play's dam Kaprice, an eleven-furlong winner in Germany, comes from a fairly ordinary German Flat family. Kaprice has bred a number of winners, including the six- and seven-furlong winner Ksara (by Most Welcome), the winner at up to a mile Komago (by Big Shuffle) and Kolmar (by Environment Friend), successful several times at up to a mile and a half in Germany. Grandam Kama was a half-sister to the dam of the useful Flat stayer Kaiser Wilhelm, winner of the Phil Bull Trophy at Pontefract and probably the most notable horse from the family before State of Play. State of Play stays three and a quarter miles and acts on soft and good to firm going. He has been tried visored, but not since joining his current yard early in the 2005/6 season. *Evan Williams*

STATE POWER (IRE) 9 b.g. Sadler's Wells (USA) – Lady Liberty (NZ) (Noble   **c–** Bijou (USA)) [2006/7 16s 16f 16f 18m Jul 13] modest hurdler at best: no form in 2006   **h–** after lengthy absence, including over fences: stays easy 2½m: acts on good to firm going: sometimes blinkered: tongue tied. *C. J. Cosgrave, Ireland*

STATUTE 5 b.g. Fasliyev (USA) – Unopposed (Sadler's Wells (USA)) [2006/7 22g 18v 16s 23d³ 23vᵖᵘ 20vᵖᵘ 20g Apr 19] maiden on Flat: poor maiden hurdler: stays 23f: acts on good to soft ground: tried blinkered/in cheekpieces: tongue tied. *Frederick John Bowles, Ireland* **h80**

STEADY TIGER (IRE) 5 b.g. Presenting – Mindyourown (IRE) (Town And Country) [2006/7 F16v* Jan 28] €70,000 3-y-o: eighth foal: brother to bumper winner Dans Pride and point winner Forresto: dam unraced, out of half-sister to smart hurdler/useful chaser Forest Sun: odds on, won maiden bumper at Kelso on debut by 4 lengths from Chestnut Charlie, leading on bridle turning in and green under pressure. *N. G. Richards* **F112 +**

STEAK N KIDNEY (USA) 4 br.g. Wild Again (USA) – Top Slipper (FR) (Top Ville) [2006/7 Feb 3] strong, workmanlike gelding: no show in Flat maiden/juvenile hurdle. *M. Wigham* **h–**

STEEL BAND 9 b.g. Kris – Quaver (USA) (The Minstrel (CAN)) [2006/7 c130?, h117: c20sᵘʳ c17m³ c22gᶠ c19v³ 16g⁵ 16s² c16s⁴ c16v³ c17v⁵ 17v c16s³ c16m³ Apr 24] workmanlike gelding: useful chaser: good efforts last 2 starts, third at Punchestown in Grade 2 won by Nickname and Grade 1 won by Mansony: fairly useful handicap hurdler: best around 2m: acts on heavy and good to firm going: tongue tied once (below form): held up. *Paul A. Roche, Ireland* **c144 h118**

STEEL MAN (IRE) 5 b.g. Anshan – One Edge (IRE) (Welsh Term) [2006/7 16gᵖᵘ 16g Apr 15] second foal: half-brother to bumper winner Bemo Two (by Saddlers' Hall): dam unraced half-sister to One Man: no promise in novice hurdles. *B. Mactaggart* **h–**

STEFAWI (IRE) 6 b.m. Taipan (IRE) – Our Alma (IRE) (Be My Native (USA)) [2006/7 20g 16g 17s 16d 24g Dec 20] first foal: dam maiden pointer: little form over hurdles: tried blinkered/tongue tied. *Miss Elizabeth Doyle, Ireland* **h73**

STEIG (IRE) 4 b.g. Xaar – Ring of Kerry (IRE) (Kenmare (FR)) [2006/7 16v 16s 16v⁴ 17m³ Apr 11] good-bodied gelding: fairly useful form on Flat (stays 1m): sold out of D. Wachman's stable 30,000 gns Newmarket Autumn Sales: modest form over hurdles: likely to prove best at 2m with emphasis on speed. *Carl Llewellyn* **h87**

STELLAR BRILLIANT 5 b. or br.m. Kris S (USA) – Subeen (Caerleon (USA)) [2006/7 16g 16dᶠ 16d Jan 5] tall, good-topped mare: twice-raced in maidens on Flat for Sir Michael Stoute at 3 yrs, winning 1¼m event (fairly useful form): failed to see race out all 3 starts over hurdles, including in seller. *P. C. Haslam* **h65**

STELLENBOSCH (USA) 4 b.g. Cape Town (USA) – New Account (USA) (Private Account (USA)) [2006/7 16d 16m³ 17d³ Mar 19] good-topped gelding: fair on Flat (stays 11.7f), once raced this season, sold out of J. Hills's stable 22,000 gns Newmarket Autumn Sales: best effort in juvenile hurdles when never-nearer third to Punjabi at Ludlow second start: likely to be suited by further than 2m. *C. J. Mann* **h113**

STEPASTRAY 10 gr.g. Alhijaz – Wandering Stranger (Petong) [2006/7 20g Apr 30] winning pointer: no form in 3 novice hurdles: sold £1,800 Ascot November Sales. *R. E. Barr* **h–**

STEP PERFECT (USA) 6 b.g. Royal Academy (USA) – Gossiping (USA) (Chati (USA)) [2006/7 h85: 20pᵖᵘ 21m 20s c24dᵖᵘ 19gᵖᵘ Feb 2] tall, angular gelding: maiden on Flat: likewise over hurdles, no form in 2006/7 (including on chasing debut): sold out of G. M. Moore's stable 3,500 gns Doncaster October Sales after second start: acts on soft going: tried in cheekpieces. *M. Mullineaux* **c– h–**

STEPPES OF GOLD (IRE) 10 b.g. Moscow Society (USA) – Trysting Place (He Loves Me) [2006/7 c121, h–: c26m* c23g³ c20m² c23f³ c20d² c20gᵖᵘ c24s⁴ Oct 25] tall, lengthy gelding: one-time useful hurdler: fair chaser: landed odds in maiden at Southwell in May: successful also in point in March: stays 3¼m: acts on any going: tried in cheekpieces/blinkers: irresolute. *Jonjo O'Neill* **c110 § h–**

STEP QUICK (IRE) 13 ch.g. All Haste (USA) – Little Steps (Step Together (USA)) [2006/7 c86x: c19g⁴ May 4] tall, angular gelding: winning chaser: fair pointer: stays 25f: acts on soft and firm going: tried in cheekpieces: makes mistakes. *Mrs S. E. Busby* **c73 x**

STERLING HEIGHTS (NZ) 8 br.g. Rainbow Myth (NZ) – Amrita (NZ) (Amyntor (FR)) [2006/7 h–: 24sᵖᵘ 19dᵖᵘ Jun 2] no show in 3 starts over hurdles, lame final one. *Mrs Tracey Barfoot-Saunt* **h–**

STERN (IRE) 8 b. or br.g. Executive Perk – Christian Lady (IRE) (Mandalus) [2006/7 h114: c20g² c22vᵖᵘ c21gᶠ c19d² c21g* Mar 30] sturdy gelding: lightly raced: winning hurdler: fairly useful form over fences: improved last 2 starts, winning handicap at Ascot **c120 p h–**

by 5 lengths from Mr Boo: stays 21f: acts on good to soft ground: prone to mistakes, but open to further progress over fences. *Miss E. C. Lavelle*

STEWARTS HOUSE (IRE) 5 b.g. Overbury (IRE) – Osocool (Teenoso (USA)) **F104** [2006/7 F16v² F16v² Mar 11] lengthy, good-topped gelding: second foal: half-brother to useful bumper winner Supreme Builder (by Supreme Leader): dam, in frame in bumpers, half-sister to useful hurdler/smart chaser Lyreen Wonder (by Derrylin): fairly useful form when runner-up in bumpers at Leopardstown (beaten 5 lengths by Tranquil Sky) and Naas, making running both times. *A. L. T. Moore, Ireland*

ST GEORGE'S DAY 7 gr.g. Sir Harry Lewis (USA) – Steel Typhoon (General Iron-**h78** side) [2006/7 F80: F16mp 16g 17v⁵ 16v 22v⁶ 20s Feb 22] lengthy gelding: has hinted at **F—** ability in bumpers/over hurdles, though well held in handicaps last 2 outings: should stay at least 2½m. *D. J. Wintle*

STICH UP LADY (IRE) 5 b. or br.m. Needle Gun (IRE) – Lady Laburnum (Carling- **F—** ford Castle) [2006/7 F16s F16m Apr 25] €10,000 3-y-o: seventh foal: half-sister to fair 21f hurdle winner Beare Necessities (by Presenting): dam lightly-raced half-sister to top-class 2m to 2½m chaser Waterloo Boy: soundly beaten in bumpers. *Mrs S. Gardner*

STICKY END 6 b.g. Endoli (USA) – Carat Stick (Gold Rod) [2006/7 h–, F77: 16g⁶ **h—** 17d⁵ May 24] signs of ability in bumpers/novice hurdles. *J. B. Walton*

STILL LEARNING (IRE) 6 b.m. Un Desperado (FR) – Sleepy Polly (Pollerton) **h—** [2006/7 19gp 17m Aug 6] ex-Irish mare: half-sister to 2½m hurdle winner Nellies Choice (by Shardari): dam unraced: no form over hurdles. *Mrs S. Lamyman*

STING (GER) 5 b.g. Turtle Island (IRE) – Simply Red (GER) (Dashing Blade) [2006/7 **F82** F16v⁴ Mar 10] first foal: dam German 1m winner: 23 lengths fourth of 8 to Berwick Law in bumper at Ayr on debut. *A. Parker*

STINKER (IRE) 5 gr.g. Shinko Forest (IRE) – Miss Mitchell (Sexton Blake) [2006/7 **F89** F16m⁴ Sep 2] €1,400 3-y-o: fifth foal: half-brother to winner in Italy by Petorius: dam, middle-distance stayer, sister to fairly useful staying chaser Miss Diskin: 8¾ lengths fourth to Sirnando in bumper at Stratford on debut. *N. A. Twiston-Davies*

ST MATTHEW (USA) 9 b.g. Lear Fan (USA) – Social Crown (USA) (Chief's Crown **c128** (USA)) [2006/7 c128, h142: 23d c25v³ 20s⁴ c20s* 23s⁶ c24g c20g⁶ c24sp Apr 26] stocky **h132** gelding: useful hurdler, off 11 months before reappearance: fairly useful handicap chaser: won 6-runner event at Wetherby in February by 1½ lengths from Coat of Honour: stays 3¼m: acts on heavy and good to firm going: sometimes let down by jumping: races prominently. *Mrs S. J. Smith*

STOCK EXCHANGE (IRE) 5 b.g. King's Best (USA) – Queen's Ransom (IRE) **h—** (Last Tycoon) [2006/7 h–: 16gp 16m Jun 13] no form in 3 starts over hurdles: tried tongue tied. *P. Bowen*

STOCKING ISLAND 6 ch.m. Desert King (IRE) – Rawya (USA) (Woodman (USA)) **h—** [2006/7 h85: 25g⁶ May 14] workmanlike mare: modest form over hurdles: stayed 19f: dead. *C. R. Egerton*

STOCKTON FLYER 6 b.g. I'm Supposin (IRE) – Orange Alert (Gildoran) [2006/7 **F85 ?** F–: F16s³ F16g Mar 29] workmanlike gelding: 9½ lengths third of 8 to Le Beau Bai at Towcester, only form in 3 bumpers. *Mrs D. A. Butler*

STOKESIES BOY 7 b.g. Key of Luck (USA) – Lesley's Fashion (Dominion) [2006/7 **h77** h–: 17g 16m⁶ 16m* 16g 17mp Sep 28] poor hurdler: won novice handicap at Uttoxeter in July: raced around 2m on good going or firmer. *C. Roberts*

STOLEN MOMENTS (FR) 6 gr.g. Villez (USA) – Brave Lola (FR) (Dom Pasquini **h98** (FR)) [2006/7 F104: 20s² 19d² 20s 20vp Feb 24] tall, good-topped gelding: bumper winner: runner-up in maiden/novice first 2 starts over hurdles, went as if amiss after: should be suited by further than 2½m. *P. D. Niven*

STOLEN SUMMER (IRE) 4 ch.g. Spectrum (IRE) – Touche-A-Tout (IRE) (Royal **h—** Academy (USA)) [2006/7 16sp 16gp Nov 29] rather leggy, lengthy gelding: 7f winner for T. Stack on reappearance at 3 yrs, disappointing since: no encouragement in juvenile hurdles. *B. S. Rothwell*

STONEFERRY 7 b.g. Hatim (USA) – Richards Kate (Fidel) [2006/7 F83: 20gp 17m **h—** 20gp Oct 7] good-bodied gelding: best effort in bumpers when fourth at Hexham on debut: no encouragement in 3 starts over hurdles: tried tongue tied. *R. Johnson*

STONERAKER (IRE) 6 b.g. Beneficial – Orchardstown Lady (Le Moss) [2006/7 **h112** 16d⁵ 20g⁶ F18g 16v 21s 20s³ 16v⁴ 16v* 16v* 16v* 16s Mar 10] workmanlike gelding: **F73**

chasing type: half-brother to bumper winner Kings Apple and fairly useful hurdler/chaser Kings Orchard, stays 25f, both by Castle Keep: dam unraced, half-sister to useful 2½m chase winner Haepenny Well: twice-raced in bumpers: fair hurdler: won handicaps at Cork in January and Fairyhouse and Navan in February: never in contention in Imperial Cup at Sandown final start: best form at 2m on heavy ground. *P. J. Rothwell, Ireland*

STONERAVINMAD 9 ch.g. Never So Bold – Premier Princess (Hard Fought) [2006/7 c–, h68: 26m^{pu} Sep 24] tall gelding: poor hurdler, lightly raced (lame only start in 2006/7): stays 25f: let down by jumping only outing over fences. *Mrs E. Slack*   c–
h–

STONERIGGS 6 gr.g. Silver Patriarch (IRE) – Maid To Match (Matching Pair) [2006/7 h71, F–: c16d^{pu} c20s^F 16s c27s^{pu} 19v^{ur} Feb 27] tall, lengthy gelding: signs of ability over hurdles: no form over fences, off 18 months before reappearance: sold 2,000 gns Doncaster May Sales. *Mrs E. Slack*   c–
h–

STONERIGGS MERC (IRE) 6 gr.g. Alderbrook – Betseale (IRE) (Step Together (USA)) [2006/7 c–p, h–, F83: c21d^4 17s^6 20s^4 Dec 26] lengthy gelding: poor form over hurdles/fences: stays 21f. *Mrs E. Slack*   c74
h70

STONERIGGS SILVER 6 gr.g. Silver Patriarch (IRE) – Carole's Crusader (Faustus (USA)) [2006/7 F–: F16g 16v^5 17v^{ro} 19v Feb 27] tall, lengthy gelding: probably flattered on hurdling debut, and little form otherwise: ungenuine. *Mrs E. Slack*   h– §
F72

STONEY DROVE (FR) 7 b.g. Exit To Nowhere (USA) – Miss Naelle (FR) (Al Nasr (FR)) [2006/7 h–, F91: 20v^6 19d c19s^5 c19g Mar 21] tall gelding: modest form over hurdles: went as if amiss both outings over fences: sold 6,200 gns Doncaster May Sales. *Miss H. C. Knight*   c–
h97

STONEYFORD BEN (IRE) 8 b.g. Beneficial – Rosie Rock (Swan's Rock) [2006/7 F72: 21d^{pu} 25g^5 17d^6 17m 17g^4 16m* c20m^4 c16d* c17m^2 c23f^F c22g^4 c16g^2 Oct 15] modest hurdler: won amateur handicap at Stratford in July: better form over fences, won novice handicap at Newton Abbot in August: stays 2½m: acts on good to firm and good to soft going (placed in bumper on soft): wears cheekpieces/tongue strap: sold 3,700 gns Doncaster January Sales. *S. Gollings*   c99
h86

STOOP TO CONQUER 7 b.g. Polar Falcon (USA) – Princess Genista (Ile de Bourbon (USA)) [2006/7 h102: 16s 16g* Mar 28] angular gelding: fairly useful on Flat in 2006 (successful in August) for J. Dunlop: fair form over hurdles: much better effort in handicaps in 2006/7 when winning conditional jockeys event at Kempton: probably stays 2¾m: raced on good ground or softer: tried tongue tied: usually makes mistakes. *A. W. Carroll*   h112 +

STOP THE PIGEON 9 gr.g. Norton Challenger – New Dawning (Deep Run) [2006/7 16s 16d 16d^4 16g 20g^6 Apr 9] sturdy gelding: no form in points/over hurdles: in cheekpieces last 3 starts. *N. J. Pomfret*   h–

STOPWATCH (IRE) 12 b.g. Lead On Time (USA) – Rose Bonbon (FR) (High Top) [2006/7 c57, h–: c21m^5 May 10] lengthy gelding: winning hurdler/maiden chaser: stays easy 21f: acts on soft and good to firm going: blinkered once (raced freely), often wears cheekpieces. *Mrs L. C. Jewell*   c–
h–

STORM CASTLE (IRE) 15 b.g. Carlingford Castle – Strong Rum (Strong Gale) [2006/7 c24m^{pu} May 16] sturdy gelding: veteran jumper, successful twice in points in 2006: stays 3¼m: acts on soft and firm going. *Miss J. Wickens*   c–
h–

STORM HAVEN 4 ch.f. Most Welcome – Blizzard (Petong) [2006/7 F14s F17d^5 F16g^2 Apr 9] half-sister to winner in Greece by Nicolotte: dam no form in bumpers, 4 lengths second to Overthrow at Fakenham. *Mrs L. Wadham*   F82

STORMINGMICHAELORI 4 b.g. Vettori (IRE) – Stormswept (USA) (Storm Bird (CAN)) [2006/7 16d 17s^5 16d 16s^3 Nov 22] half-brother to fair hurdler Michaels Dream (by Spectrum), stays 27f: poor maiden on Flat (stays 7f): poor form in juvenile hurdles. *N. Wilson*   h73

STORM OF APPLAUSE (IRE) 6 b.g. Accordion – Dolce Notte (IRE) (Strong Gale) [2006/7 h85: 16m May 18] modest form over hurdles: takes good hold, and may prove best around 2m. *P. J. Hobbs*   h85

STORMONT DAWN (IRE) 6 b.m. Glacial Storm (USA) – Andros Dawn (IRE) (Buckskin (FR)) [2006/7 F–: 16s 20s 16v^4 16v 16v 20g^{pu} Mar 17] workmanlike mare: no solid form: in cheekpieces final outing. *Mrs L. B. Normile*   h–

STORM PRINCE (IRE) 10 ch.g. Prince of Birds (USA) – Petersford Girl (IRE) (Taufan (USA)) [2006/7 20d^6 21s 22s^4 22s^{pu} 19v^2 22g^5 Mar 18] smallish gelding: poor   h83 handicap hurdler nowadays, off over 2 years before reappearance: stays 2¾m: acts on heavy and good to firm going: usually wears headgear: tongue tied once: front runner. *Miss T. Spearing*

STORM PROSPECT 4 b.g. Mujahid (USA) – Bajan Blue (Lycius (USA)) [2006/7   **h114** 16v* 16v² 16m⁴ 16d² 16m⁵ Apr 21] angular gelding: fair form on Flat (stays 13f), successful in September, sold out of C. Tinkler's stable 23,000 gns Doncaster October Sales: also fair form over hurdles, winning juvenile at Ayr in January by 15 lengths: easily best effort after when second to Wizard of Us in novice handicap at Uttoxeter fourth outing: raced at 2m: acts on heavy going, below form both starts on good to firm. *Miss Lucinda V. Russell*

STORM TALK (IRE) 8 b.m. Glacial Storm (USA) – Lotta Talk (IRE) (Le Moss)   **h–** [2006/7 19d⁵ 24v⁵ 21v⁴ Mar 12] sturdy mare: maiden pointer: well beaten in maiden/ novice hurdles. *Mrs A. M. Thorpe*

STORMY BAY (IRE) 6 b.g. Glacial Storm (USA) – Duffys Choice (IRE) (Yashgan)   **h86** [2006/7 h–, F83: 17s 16v^F 21s³ Mar 2] sturdy gelding: modest form over hurdles: will stay beyond 21f: raced on going softer than good. *D. R. C. Elsworth*

STORMY BEECH 11 b.g. Glacial Storm (USA) – Cheeny's Brig (New Brig) [2006/7   **c102** c–, h–: 16m 17s 17s* 16d⁴ c16d* c16s² c16s² c16d* c16d⁴ c16s⁵ c16v^ro 16v³ c16v³   **h79** Mar 22] angular gelding: poor handicap hurdler: won selling event at Sedgefield in October: much better over fences, making all in handicaps at same course in November and Catterick in December: barely stays 21f: acts on heavy going: usually wears headgear: tried tongue tied: free-going sort. *R. Johnson*

STORMYLAD 5 b.g. El Conquistador – Lady Magenta (Rolfe (USA)) [2006/7 F16s   **h–** F16v 24v⁵ 19s Feb 1] rather unfurnished gelding: seventh foal: half-brother to winning   **F–** pointer by Lyphento: dam, poor maiden on Flat, no form over hurdles: no form in bumpers/novice hurdles. *A. J. Whiting*

STORMY LORD (IRE) 11 br.g. Lord Americo – Decent Shower (Decent Fellow)   **c112** [2006/7 c–, h103: 18f³ 16v⁴ c16s³ Nov 29] tall gelding: fair handicap chaser/modest   **h98** handicap hurdler nowadays: best form around 2m: acts on any going: has tended to hang/ jump left: free-going front runner. *J. Wade*

STORMY SKYE (IRE) 11 b.g. Bluebird (USA) – Canna (Caerleon (USA)) [2006/7   **c95 §** c98§, h–§: c24d^pu c24d⁴ c26s² c26s² c24v³ c25s c24s⁵ c26v⁵ Mar 7] useful-looking   **h– §** gelding: modest handicap chaser: stays 3¼m: acts on heavy and good to firm going: wears blinkers: tried tongue tied: ungenuine. *G. L. Moore*

STORY ARMS 5 b.g. Kayf Tara – Young India (Indian King (USA)) [2006/7 h–: 16m   **h–** May 6] tailed off only completed outing over hurdles. *D. Burchell*

STORYMAKER 6 b.g. Midnight Legend – Amys Delight (Idiot's Delight) [2006/7   **h103** 20v 20v 21v⁵ 16v* 27v* 20v² 24s^pu Apr 25] smallish gelding: first foal: dam no sign of ability: won maiden point in 2006: fair hurdler: much improved once qualified for handicaps, winning easily at Newcastle and Kelso in January: much better form again when 8 lengths second to Bedlam Boy in novice event (9 lb out of weights) back at Newcastle: has won over 27f, may prove best at shorter: raced on soft/heavy going. *Miss S. E. Forster*

STOWAY (FR) 5 b.g. Broadway Flyer (USA) – Stowe (FR) (Garde Royale) [2006/7   **c105** 17s* c17s² c17v³ c20s^pu Feb 9] ex-French gelding: good sort: fourth foal: half-brother   **h?** to 1¼m/1½m winner French Hopper (by French Glory): dam unraced: fair hurdler: successful twice, including in minor event at Strasbourg in May: similar form when runner-up over fences at Auteuil: left G. Macaire and off 7 months, ran poorly both starts in Britain: should stay beyond 17f: acts on heavy ground. *A. King*

ST PANCRAS (IRE) 7 b.g. Danehill Dancer (IRE) – Lauretta Blue (IRE) (Bluebird   **h92** (USA)) [2006/7 16g³ 16d⁵ 17m* 17m 16d³ Aug 14] fairly useful on Flat (probably stays 1¼m) in 2004: modest hurdler: won novice at Sedgefield in June: likely to prove best around 2m with emphasis on speed. *C. C. Bealby*

ST PHILIPS GIRL 6 b.m. Executive Perk – Liddy's Choice (IRE) (Buckskin (FR))   **h–** [2006/7 F17d⁵ F17s F16m⁵ 20s⁵ 20s 20v 22d^pu Feb 19] medium-sized mare: third foal: **F71** half-sister to bumper winner Chosen (by Glacial Storm): dam unraced half-sister to 2 winning 3m chasers: poor form in bumpers: little show over hurdles: tried in cheekpieces. *M. Mullineaux*

ST PIRRAN (IRE) 12 b.g. Be My Native (USA) – Guess Twice (Deep Run) [2006/7   **c–** c–, h114d: 16d⁴ 19s⁵ 16d⁴ 16g 16g 16s³ Apr 25] tall gelding: one-time useful handicap   **h101**

chaser: fair handicap hurdler nowadays: best around 2m: acts on soft going: tried blinkered, usually wears cheekpieces nowadays: free-going sort, usually patiently ridden. *R. C. Guest*

STRADBROOK (IRE) 5 b.g. Midhish – Bowland Park (Nicholas Bill) [2006/7 F16s* F16v³ Jan 25] €3,500 3-y-o: third foal: dam poor form in bumpers: won 25-runner bumper at Punchestown on debut by 2 lengths from Windy Harbour: much better form when 1½ lengths third of 7 to Singh On Song in similar event at Gowran 3 months later: joined Jonjo O'Neill. *Joseph Crowley, Ireland* **F101 +**

STRAIGHT TALKER (IRE) 8 b.g. Warcraft (USA) – The Mighty Midge (Hard-green (USA)) [2006/7 c–, h–: 22mᵖᵘ May 11] form over hurdles only when runner-up in 2¾m novice handicap in 2004/5: fell only outing over fences: has worn visor/cheek-pieces. *H. S. Howe* **c–**
h–

STRANGELY BROWN (IRE) 6 b.g. Second Empire (IRE) – Damerela (IRE) (Alzao (USA)) [2006/7 h153: 25sᵘʳ 22s⁴ 20vᶠ 24v³ 24vᵖᵘ 24g⁶ 20g 16m Apr 27] smallish gelding: smart hurdler: not at best in 2006/7, though respectable efforts when third to Celestial Wave in Grade 2 at Leopardstown and sixth to Inglis Drever in World Hurdle at Cheltenham: stays 3m: acts on heavy going. *Eric McNamara, Ireland* **h143**

STRATHTAY 5 ch.m. Pivotal – Cressida (Polish Precedent (USA)) [2006/7 h88d: 16m 17m⁶ 20m⁵ 26m 24d Oct 5] close-coupled mare: winning hurdler for M. Pipe 8,000 gns: no form for present stable: often visored/blinkered: ungenuine. *M. Appleby* **h– §**

STRAVAIGIN 7 ch.m. Primitive Rising (USA) – Countryside First (Emperor Fountain) [2006/7 18v 20s c20s⁶ 24vʳᵒ 20g³ Mar 17] lengthy, workmanlike mare: second foal: dam unraced: first form (poor) over hurdles final start: well held on chasing debut: should stay 3m: ran out fourth start. *J. S. Goldie* **c–**
h84

STRAW BEAR (USA) 6 ch.g. Diesis – Highland Ceilidh (IRE) (Scottish Reel) [2006/7 h150p: 16s* 16d⁴ 16d² 16s* 16dᵖᵘ Mar 13] **h155**

While Kauto Star's owner Clive Smith pocketed the Betfair Million after his horse's successes in the Lancashire Chase, the King George VI Chase and the Cheltenham Gold Cup, J. P. McManus's prospects of doing the same for landing what was dubbed as the hurdling triple crown ended with Straw Bear's defeat in the Christmas Hurdle. Straw Bear was well below par there and again amiss in the Champion Hurdle itself, having won the first leg, the wbx.com 'Fighting Fifth' Hurdle at Newcastle in November. He also landed the odds in the Bathwick Tyres Kingwell Hurdle at Wincanton on his final run before Cheltenham, and, earlier in February, finished a good second to Detroit City in the Agfa UK Hurdle at Sandown. Straw Bear, who had been one of the leading novices of 2005/6, showed himself a very smart hurdler in the latest season but his best form fell a little way short of the standard required to make an impact in even a substandard Champion Hurdle and he will have to progress again if he is to make a bigger impact in 2007/8.

The launch of the million-pound bonus had, to some extent, a beneficial effect on the field for the 'Fighting Fifth', although there were no Irish-trained challengers after Harchibald and Macs Joy met with last-minute setbacks. Straw Bear might also have missed the race until rain eased the ground significantly the day before and he started evens favourite in a field of nine. Straw Bear had run well at all three major Festivals the previous spring and was unfortunate not to win the Supreme Novices' at Cheltenham, fluffing the last. He gained consolation in impressive fashion at Aintree before finishing second to Iktitaf at Punchestown, and fully justified his market position in the 'Fighting Fifth' on his return. Needing no more than shaking up to assert after two out, Straw Bear beat Noble Request by five lengths, with two former winners completing the frame, 66/1-chance The French Furze and the previous year's winner Arcalis. Straw Bear was helped by the poor performance of market rival Desert Quest, but the runner-up had been progressive the previous season and Straw Bear won as if there was a fair bit more to come. The French Furze, incidentally, was running in the 'Fighting Fifth' for the seventh successive season. He finished second on three occasions prior to winning in 2003, then took fifth in 2004 and third in 2005.

Although impressive at Newcastle, odds of as short as 11/2 for Straw Bear for the Champion Hurdle looked to overestimate his chances and he was also at shorter odds than his form entitled him to be when sent for the Christmas Hurdle at Kempton the following month. Straw Bear did not, though, show his true form, trailing in ten and three quarter lengths fourth behind Jazz Messenger, Noble Request and Desert Quest—three horses he had beaten at least once previously. A dirty scope after Kempton went some way to explaining that below-par effort and Straw Bear was reportedly not back in full training until the middle of January. However, he was sufficiently back on song by early-February to run Detroit City to a length and three quarters at Sandown. After travelling the better, he couldn't take advantage when his rival hit the last and, although Straw Bear had had a setback, there seemed little reason to expect placings to be reversed at Cheltenham. Two weeks later Straw Bear was out again in the Kingwell Hurdle at Wincanton where his main opponent in a field of five was Afsoun. Afsoun had fallen at the fifth when travelling strongly in the lead in the Christmas Hurdle and had since won the Haydock trial impressively, when beating The French Furze even more convincingly than Straw Bear had at Newcastle. Straw Bear was well supported at Wincanton and Afsoun weak in the market in a race in which the three opposing them had little obvious chance. The two market leaders dominated from some way out, though it was clear before the straight that Straw Bear had the edge on his main rival and he was not extended to beat Afsoun by seven lengths, albeit winning in a time that compared poorly with the novice event won by Osana earlier on the card. The runner-up was reported to be 'subdued' after the race, his performance clearly below par, and it's likely Straw Bear didn't need even to reproduce his 'Fighting Fifth' form.

Straw Bear and Afsoun met again in the Champion Hurdle. Straw Bear started fourth favourite at 7/1 and looked in good shape, but he dropped out of contention at the fifth and was pulled up at the next having burst a blood vessel badly—jockey Tony McCoy returned with blood on his breeches. Afsoun finished third to Sublimity, a horse Straw Bear had beaten twice as a novice. Straw Bear's performance was a particular disappointment for his trainer Nick Gifford who has not found it easy to make an impact since taking over from his father Josh. The

wbx.com 'Fighting Fifth' Hurdle, Newcastle—a convincing return by the favourite Straw Bear; 2005 winner Arcalis (grey) fades into fourth

stable managed just fourteen winners in 2006/7, the same tally as the previous season, and Straw Bear is very much the stable flagbearer. Hopefully, Straw Bear will be back in full health in 2007/8, when a campaign over fences is a possibility.

Straw Bear (USA) (ch.g. 2001)	Diesis (ch 1980)	Sharpen Up (ch 1969)	Atan Rocchetta
		Doubly Sure (b 1971)	Reliance II Soft Angels
	Highland Ceilidh (IRE) (b 1988)	Scottish Reel (ch 1982)	Northfields Dance All Night
		Savage Love (b 1983)	Wolver Hollow Camogie

Straw Bear is a strong, compact gelding and generally jumps hurdles well, though he is hardly bred for jumping. His dam Highland Ceilidh was useful at up to a mile and a half, placed twice in Group 3 company in Germany. She has produced six winners apart from Straw Bear, who himself was a useful winner at around a mile and a quarter for Sir Mark Prescott before being sent jumping. Highland Ceilidh's 2005 foal by Halling was bought back by her vendor for 38,000 guineas at the sales in October. Full details of the family were given in *Chasers & Hurdlers 2005/06*. Straw Bear is likely to stay beyond two miles and has raced on good going or softer. He acts particularly well on soft and is unlikely to be risked on firmer than good, given that he has a history of problems with his feet. *N. J. Gifford*

STRAWBERRY (IRE) 6 b.m. Beneficial – Ravaleen (IRE) (Executive Perk) [2006/7 F96: F16d 19d² 20s^pu 22d³ 16s* 21g 18g* 21g Apr 19] rather unfurnished mare: in frame in bumpers: fair novice hurdler: won at Newbury (handicap, by neck from Illicit Spirit) in March and Fontwell (mares event) in April: may prove best short of 2¾m: acts on soft going. *J. W. Mullins* **h114 F76**

STREAKY RASHER (IRE) 6 b.g. Denel (FR) – Ballywooden (IRE) (House of Cards) [2006/7 F18v^ro 19g Apr 8] smallish gelding: first foal: dam, no sign of ability, out of half-sister to smart 2m to 3m chaser Firions Law: more signs of temperament than ability in bumper/maiden hurdle. *P. Bowen* **h– F–**

STREETSHAVENONAME (IRE) 6 b.g. Old Vic – Glore River (IRE) (Broken Hearted) [2006/7 F107: 16s* 16v² 16d⁶ 19v 16m⁶ 20m^bd Apr 24] quite good-topped gelding: bumper winner: fairly useful form over hurdles: easily won maiden at Limerick in November: ran well in handicaps next 2 starts, sixth to Spring The Que in Pierse Hurdle at Leopardstown: stays 2¼m: acts on heavy going, probably on good to firm. *T. J. Taaffe, Ireland* **h118**

STRETCHING (IRE) 14 br.g. Contract Law (USA) – Mrs Mutton (Dancer's Image (USA)) [2006/7 20s May 20] close-coupled gelding: poor hurdler/novice chaser: fair pointer, very lightly raced nowadays: effective visored or not. *Miss Joanne Priest* **c– h–**

STRIDER 6 ch.g. Pivotal – Sahara Belle (USA) (Sanglamore (USA)) [2006/7 16v 17s 17v⁶ 16s Mar 3] small, angular gelding: fair on Flat (stays 1¼m) at 4 yrs, sold out of P. D. Evans' stable 3,200 gns Doncaster October (2005) Sales: no solid form over hurdles. *D. C. O'Brien* **h–**

STRIKE AN ARK (IRE) 6 b. or br.m. Shernazar – Me Little Mot (IRE) (Masterclass (USA)) [2006/7 16s 16d³ 16d² 18v 20d⁵ Jan 19] second foal: dam unraced, half-sister to smart chaser Don't Push It, stays 2½m: bumper winner: fair novice hurdler: best at 2m: acts on good to soft going (bumper win on soft). *A. Fleming, Ireland* **h102**

STRIKE BACK (IRE) 9 b.g. Bob Back (USA) – First Strike (IRE) (Magical Strike (USA)) [2006/7 c130x, h116: c16d⁵ c25d⁶ c19d⁵ c25v^F 21g⁶ Apr 18] angular gelding: winning hurdler: useful chaser at best: well below form in handicaps in 2006/7: stays 2½m: acts on heavy going: blinkered/in cheekpieces 6 of last 7 outings: often makes mistakes. *C. J. Mann* **c107 x h–**

STRING SERENADE (IRE) 6 b.m. Key of Luck (USA) – Bubbly Dancer (USA) (Crafty Prospector (USA)) [2006/7 16f⁶ Sep 17] modest on Flat (stays 11.5f): little form over hurdles: sold 500 gns Doncaster November Sales. *V. Smith* **h–**

STRIPE ME BLUE 5 b.g. Miner's Lamp – Slipmatic (Pragmatic) [2006/7 F94: F16d F16d² F17v* 19d^F 21s⁵ Mar 2] sturdy gelding: fairly useful form in bumpers, readily won maiden at Exeter in January: around 19 lengths fifth of 7 to Money Order at Newbury on completed start in novice hurdles: bred to stay at least 2½m, though has taken good hold. *P. J. Jones* **h83 F97**

STROLLING 10 br.g. Alflora (IRE) – Emmabella (True Song) [2006/7 c25g^{pu} May 3] c–
modest pointer, won in 2006: little impact in hunter on chase debut. *A. Hollingsworth*

STROLLING VAGABOND (IRE) 8 ch.g. Glacial Storm (USA) – Found Again c86
(IRE) (Black Minstrel) [2006/7 h74: c24s^F c24d^{pu} c24m^{pu} c26g^2 c26s^{pu} c26s* c26s* c23s h–
c26v* c28g* Mar 18] leggy gelding: winning hurdler: modest handicap chaser: won at
Fontwell in December, Plumpton (went in snatches) in January and Fontwell again twice
in March: thorough stayer: acts on heavy going: has looked wayward under pressure.
John R. Upson

STRONG APPROACH (IRE) 4 ch.g. Fruits of Love (USA) – Shragraddy Lass h–
(IRE) (Jareer (USA)) [2006/7 16m 16m 17v^{pu} Dec 12] fair maiden on Flat (stays 1m),
sold out of T. D. Barron's stable 4,500 gns Doncaster August Sales: no form in juvenile
hurdles. *S. B. Clark*

STRONG COFFEE 5 b.g. Classic Cliche (IRE) – Foehn Gale (IRE) (Strong Gale) F95
[2006/7 F17s^5 F16g^3 Mar 29] third foal: brother to fair chaser Superrollercoaster, stays
25f, and half-brother to modest/unreliable chaser Super Road Train (by Petoski), stays
3¼m: dam unraced: fairly useful maiden in bumpers, 7½ lengths third of 16 to Gypsy
Scholar at Towcester: will be suited by 2½m+. *O. Sherwood*

STRONG MAGIC (IRE) 15 br.g. Strong Gale – Baybush (Boreen (FR)) [2006/7 c93, c83 d
h–: c21s^{pu} c24d^2 c24g^3 c25d^2 c23d^3 c24s c24m c26v c24g c24m^5 Mar 25] workmanlike h–
gelding: poor handicap chaser: stays 25f: acts on soft and good to firm going, probably on
heavy. *J. R. Cornwall*

STRONG PROJECT (IRE) 11 ch.g. Project Manager – Hurricane Girl (IRE) c145
(Strong Gale) [2006/7 c142, h–: c22s^2 c19v^{ur} c24d c22s^4 22s* c16v^4 24v^6 Dec 28] work- h127
manlike gelding: fairly useful hurdler: won minor event at Thurles in October by head
from Wild Passion: stiff task when sixth to Celestial Wave in Grade 2 at Leopardstown:
smart chaser: good second to Ransboro in handicap at Killarney in May: below form
after: effective at 2¼m to 3m: unraced on firm going, acts on any other: often makes
mistakes over fences: usually front runner. *Sean O. O'Brien, Ireland*

STRONG RESOLVE (IRE) 11 gr.g. Roselier (FR) – Farmerette (Teofane) [2006/7 c118
c100, h103: c24s^2 c24g^4 c26v^3 c24s^5 c24v c24v^2 c25v^2 c24g^5 c32m Apr 21] leggy h–
gelding: winning hurdler: fairly useful handicap chaser: won at Haydock in October by
11 lengths from Russian Sky: generally respectable efforts after, seventh of 23 to Hot
Weld in Scottish Grand National at Ayr final outing: stays 4m: acts on heavy and good to
firm going: bold-jumping front runner: genuine. *Miss Lucinda V. Russell*

STRONG WILL 7 b.g. Primo Dominie – Reine de Thebes (FR) (Darshaan) [2006/7 c–
19v^{pu} c20d^{ur} Mar 19] good-topped gelding: modest maiden on Flat at 2/3 yrs for h–
C. Fairhurst: won maiden on completed start in points in 2005: no show in novice hurdle:
unseated tenth in maiden on chase debut. *J. R. Holt*

STROOM BANK (IRE) 7 b.g. Warcraft (USA) – All Alright (Alzao (USA)) [2006/7 c92
h86, F83: 21m^2 23d^4 21m^4 c16s^2 c20d^4 c19d^2 c16d^{ur} c16d^{pu} c20d^{pu} Mar 26] good-topped h93
gelding: modest novice hurdler/chaser: blinkered, failed to complete last 3 starts
(reportedly bled final one): stays 21f: acts on soft and good to firm going. *C. C. Bealby*

STRUCK SILVER 5 gr.m. Silver Patriarch (IRE) – Snowgirl (IRE) (Mazaad) [2006/7 F–
F16d Jan 19] sixth foal: half-sister to fair hurdler I'm Your Man (by Bigstone), stays
2½m: dam 5f/6f winner: tailed off in bumper on debut. *Mrs Dianne Sayer*

STRULE PEARL (IRE) 7 ch.m. Moscow Society (USA) – Waterloo Lady (Buckskin h–
(FR)) [2006/7 F16s 19g^{pu} Apr 8] third foal: dam winning hurdler: no show in bumper (for F–
P. McCreery in Ireland) or maiden hurdle. *Mrs A. E. Brooks*

STUDMASTER 7 ch.g. Snurge – Danlu (USA) (Danzig (USA)) [2006/7 h137: c16s^F c107 p
c17v^5 20s^5 20v* 19v^2 24v^2 Jan 25] useful hurdler: won minor event at Punchestown in h141
December by neck from Kadoun: runner-up both starts after, beaten 5 lengths by Celestial
Wave in Grade 3 at Gowran final outing: let down by jumping both starts over fences,
fifth of 7 to Vic Venturi in Grade 3 novice at Galway when completing: stays 3m: acts on
any going: likely to do better over fences if jumping improves. *Mrs J. Harrington, Ireland*

STUMPED 4 b.g. Bertolini (USA) – So Saucy (Teenoso (USA)) [2006/7 17g^5 17d^3 16s^4 h110
16v^2 16v* 16d Mar 13] sturdy gelding: half-brother to 2½m hurdle winner Saucy King
(by Amfortas): fair maiden on Flat (stays 1½m) for W. Haggas: fairly useful juvenile
hurdler: won maiden at Chepstow (beat Darusso by 8 lengths) in February: well held in
listed handicap at Cheltenham following month: raced around 2m: acts on heavy ground.
H. D. Daly

STURBURY 5 b.m. Topanoora – Carry Me (IRE) (Lafontaine (USA)) [2006/7 h87: **h90**
19m⁶ 20d⁶ 16f⁶ 16dᵖᵘ 16g⁶ 16g⁶ 16f² Apr 5] modest maiden hurdler: should stay 2½m:
acts on firm going: tried in cheekpieces (fell). *J. W. Mullins*

ST VALENTINE 5 br.g. Fraam – Birichino (Dilum (USA)) [2006/7 F16d F16m 19sᵖᵘ **h–**
Nov 16] lengthy gelding: second foal: dam unraced: no form in bumpers/novice hurdle. **F–**
M. C. Chapman

ST WILFRID 5 ch.g. Loup Sauvage (USA) – Fairy Flax (IRE) (Dancing Brave (USA)) **F97**
[2006/7 F16m² F16s* F16g⁴ F16d⁵ Dec 16] rather leggy gelding: half-brother to several
winners on Flat, including fairly useful Fairywings (by Kris), stayed 1¼m: dam 6f
winner: fairly useful form in bumpers: won at Uttoxeter in October by 1¾ lengths from
Farmer's Lad (pair clear): sold out of T. Walford's stable 80,000 gns Doncaster November
Sales before next outing. *J. Howard Johnson*

STYLISH DAVE (NZ) 13 bl.g. Stylish Century (AUS) – Calcutta (NZ) (My Friend **c–**
Paul (USA)) [2006/7 c26gᵖᵘ May 24] fair pointer, won 3 times in 2006: beaten circuit out
in hunter on chase debut. *Ms Lisa Stock*

STYLISH PRINCE 7 b.g. Polar Prince (IRE) – Simply Style (Bairn (USA)) [2006/7 **c–**
c–, h–: 16s c19mᵖᵘ 16mᵖᵘ Jul 4] lengthy, angular gelding: no form over jumps: tried **h–**
tongue tied. *R. Lee*

SUALDA (IRE) 8 b.g. Idris (IRE) – Winning Heart (Horage) [2006/7 16m* 16m³ 16g **h93**
Mar 28] fairly useful form (stays 2m), successful twice in 2006, claimed from R. Fahey
£15,000 in July: modest form over hurdles: won maiden at Worcester in September: raced
at 2m on good/good to firm going: joined P. D. Evans. *D. Carroll*

SUB ARTIC (IRE) 9 b.g. Arctic Lord – Suba (GER) (Limbo (GER)) [2006/7 20s 20s⁶ **h71**
21d Jan 8] €22,000 4-y-o: half-brother to several winners, including Irish bumper winner
Native Time (by Lanfranco): dam placed in Germany: runner-up on completed start in
maiden Irish points in 2004: poor form over hurdles. *S. E. H. Sherwood*

SUBLIMITY (FR) 7 b.g. Selkirk (USA) – Fig Tree Drive (USA) (Miswaki **h164**
(USA)) [2006/7 h138: 16v* 16d* Mar 13]
    The last hurrah of the undisputed golden age of hurdling came in the 1981
Champion Hurdle when victory went to Sea Pigeon, at the age of eleven. The
top hurdle races of the late-'seventies and early-'eighties had been dominated by Sea
Pigeon, Night Nurse, Monksfield and Bird's Nest—Night Nurse and Monksfield
the best and joint second-best hurdlers in Timeform's experience. Their rivalry
grew as they met time and again, and some of the closely-fought races between
them are among the most thrilling and memorable ever seen over hurdles. Twelve
months on from Sea Pigeon's second victory, it was decided that age had finally
caught up with him and he was retired on the eve of the Cheltenham Festival. In his
absence, the unconsidered For Auction landed the spoils in a field in which no
runner was older than seven. A quarter of a century later, the similar dominance of
a less lustrous quartet may well have come to an end with the victory of Sublimity
in the latest, Smurfit Kappa-sponsored running of the blue riband of hurdling. The
ten-year-old Hardy Eustace and nine-year-old Brave Inca, who between them had
won the race for the three previous years, were comprehensively outpointed by the
seven-year-old Sublimity, a smart Flat performer having just his sixth start over
hurdles.
    Sublimity was one of just ten who went to post at Cheltenham, the smallest
field since Sea Pigeon claimed his first Champion win (at the fourth attempt!) when
beating Monksfield and Bird's Nest in a nine-runner contest back in 1980. Both
Hardy Eustace and Brave Inca were well supported, sent off at 3/1 and 11/2 respectively, but the favourite at 6/4, and the most likely to break the dominance of the old
guard, was Detroit City, who was bidding for an eighth hurdles win in a row. The
'Fighting Fifth' and Kingwell Hurdle winner Straw Bear, no match for Detroit City
in the Agfa Hurdle at Sandown, was a 7/1 chance. The Noel Meade-trained Iktitaf
came next in the betting at 14/1. Between them the five at the top of the market had
won nearly all the top races in the build-up to Cheltenham and they also met each
other: Detroit City had defeated Hardy Eustace, on favourable terms admittedly, in
the boylesports.com International at Cheltenham, Hardy Eustace had beaten Brave
Inca in the AIG Europe at Leopardstown, while Brave Inca and Iktitaf, in the
Festival Hurdle and Morgiana respectively, had victories over one another. There

were inevitably absentees, most notably previous runners-up Harchibald and Macs Joy, the other half of the quartet. However, the Christmas Hurdle winner Jazz Messenger was the only winner of a major trial not in the line-up.

Sublimity, by contrast, had contested none of the major trials. This wasn't by design as illness had prevented his returning to action in the Festival Hurdle at Leopardstown at Christmas. Indeed, Sublimity had been rushed to veterinary hospital at Christmas with a temperature of 105.5F, trainer John Carr reporting that 'at one point the vet thought we might lose him.' He isn't the first Champion Hurdle winner to have experienced a brush with death just ten weeks before the big day. The screens were erected around the prostrate Beech Road for several minutes before he finally rose after a fall over fences in 1989. Sublimity's troubled preparation arguably proved a blessing in disguise given his good record when fresh. He duly showed his well-being on his eventual reappearance in a minor event at Navan. Seventeen went to post that day, but only one of the others had even won a race over hurdles and Sublimity had a very gentle reintroduction. Nevertheless, he won most impressively by twenty lengths, demonstrating that there were likely to be much better races in him. Afterwards, a choice between the Champion Hurdle and the County Hurdle (in which he was given 10-13, equivalent to a BHB mark of 148) was mooted, though it seems likely that connections were always intent on the bigger prize (his owner reportedly backed him at huge odds on the exchanges and he was matched at a high of 600/1 on Betfair). Sublimity was well supported as the ground dried in the week before Cheltenham, eventually sent off at 16/1.

For much of the way the Champion Hurdle was dominated by the older brigade, Hardy Eustace pressed by Brave Inca. Detroit City was bang there too but under pressure, while the riders of Sublimity and Iktitaf bided their time. Iktitaf was moving into contention when he fell three out. Sublimity, too, was beginning to make ground by now and, turning for home, he was clearly going best. Ridden to lead at the last and soon in command, Sublimity won by three lengths from Brave Inca with the Haydock Trial winner Afsoun staying on to deprive Hardy Eustace of third. Detroit City ran well below expectations, Straw Bear was pulled up amiss. It was by far the biggest win to date for Carr, a Maynooth farmer who has saddled

Smurfit Kappa Champion Hurdle Challenge Trophy, Cheltenham—
Philip Carberry bides his time on the strong-travelling Sublimity (noseband) behind former winners
Brave Inca and Hardy Eustace (visored); also pictured are the staying-on Afsoun.
outsider Kawagino (stripes) and disappointing favourite Detroit City (grey)

The last—the ante-post gamble is landed despite this final-flight error

fewer than forty winners since setting up his relatively small training operation. It proved a memorable day for owner Bill Hennessy, too, a businessman whose fortune is founded on a hearing aid business he named Bonavox—Bono, the lead singer of Irish rock band U2, takes his stage name from the firm's shop in Dublin.

Sublimity wasn't seen out again. He could conceivably have run under a penalty in the County Hurdle, in which he would obviously have looked very well in. Provisional plans to go for the Scottish Champion Hurdle came to nothing and, after being nominated as a likely runner in the ACCBank Champion Hurdle at Punchestown, the firmish ground ruled him out. Those that did run subsequently did little to frank the Champion Hurdle form. Neither Brave Inca, running over three miles, nor Hardy Eustace were near their best at Punchestown; Afsoun was only a respectable third in the Aintree Hurdle; Iktitaf ran poorly at Punchestown. By the end of the season the form of the Champion Hurdle looked worth rather less than it had at the time, though Sublimity's performance remains the best of the season at two miles over hurdles.

The 1982 winner For Auction returned to defend his title the following March and was sent off joint favourite but he could manage only third behind Gaye Brief. For Auction was followed home by the second and third from the previous year and was essentially an average winner of the race, Gaye Brief being one of the better ones between the 'golden age' and Istabraq. Whether Sublimity will prove better than an average winner remains to be seen. Unlike For Auction, who was in his third season over hurdles when he won the Champion, Sublimity is probably not yet fully exposed and he clearly had not done himself full justice as a novice. He won a maiden at Leopardstown on his debut before disappointing when stepped up in class on his next start (scoped abnormally). Lack of experience and trouble in running counted against him when he was a close fourth to Noland in the Supreme Novices' at Cheltenham before filling the same position in the two-mile Champion Novices' at Punchestown, behind Iktitaf, Straw Bear and Jazz Messenger. Any of that trio could yet be a threat to Sublimity's crown, though there is probably more prospect of Katchit, the outstanding leading juvenile of 2006/7, posing a bigger danger. At the time of writing, Sublimity is generally favourite for the 2008 Champion Hurdle, just ahead of Katchit.

That Sublimity had the potential to make an impact at a high level over hurdles was clear from his form on the Flat. He won the 2004 Doncaster Mile when with Sir Michael Stoute and gained a further listed success, in the mile-and-a-quarter Alleged Stakes in 2005, on his first outing after joining present connections. Sublimity finished last, however, on both subsequent starts that year and hasn't been seen on the Flat since beginning his hurdling career. After Cheltenham, there were plans to aim Sublimity at the Ebor but these were dropped in the summer and a return in listed or Group 3 company in the autumn, before he goes hurdling again, is said to be on the cards.

Sublimity (FR) (b.g. 2000)	Selkirk (USA) (ch 1988)	Sharpen Up (ch 1969)	Atan Rocchetta
		Annie Edge (ch 1980)	Nebbiolo Friendly Court
	Fig Tree Drive (USA) (b 1994)	Miswaki (ch 1978)	Mr Prospector Hopespringseternal
		Rose O'Riley (b 1981)	Nijinsky Rosetta Stone

Whether Sublimity would have the stamina required to last out a mile and three quarters on the Flat is in some doubt and he will probably prove best at around two miles over hurdles, in which sphere his turn of foot is likely to prove a most potent weapon. His sire Selkirk had a good season with his incidental jumpers, for, in addition to Sublimity, Blythe Knight won the Top Novices' Hurdle at Aintree, Convincing won a pair of graded juvenile events in Ireland and Whispered Secret landed a valuable Cheltenham handicap chase. Whispered Secret is unusual among Selkirk's jumpers in staying two and three quarter miles. His best hurdler before the latest season was the 2004 Imperial Cup winner Scorned. Although Sublimity carries the (FR) suffix—joining Sir Ken, Clair Soleil and Hors La Loi III in the group of French-bred Champion Hurdle winners—about the only thing French about him is the place of his birth, his dam Fig Tree Drive's family being all American. Fig Tree Drive showed fairly useful form in winning over six furlongs at

Mr W. Hennessy's "Sublimity"

Newbury on her only start and is out of a winning sister to the Hollywood Derby winner De La Rose and fellow US Grade 1 winner Upper Nile. Sublimity is Fig Tree Drive's second foal. The third Marbush (by Linamix) was of a similar standard to Sublimity on the Flat, smart at a mile to a mile and a quarter in Britain and the UAE. The fourth foal Estate (by Montjeu) was a disappointing maiden on the Flat for Dermot Weld but has shown fairly useful form over hurdles since joining Roger Brookhouse, winning twice in 2006/7. The sixth foal Ridge Rose (by Sadler's Wells) cost 270,000 guineas as a yearling and is in training with Luca Cumani, showing some promise as a three-year-old on her first three starts. The first foal Figlette (by Darshaan), also a filly, was sold unraced for 26,000 guineas at the Newmarket December Sales in 2002. Sublimity himself has twice been through the same Tattersalls ring: he made 210,000 guineas as a yearling and 32,000 guineas to join his current trainer at the end of his four-year-old campaign. Sublimity is a close-coupled gelding in appearance, not the most taking of individuals, and he didn't particularly impress in appearance at Cheltenham. On the Flat, he has been noted to sweat up. He has raced on good going or softer over hurdles, though is effective on good to firm (probably on firm) on the Flat. He has worn a tongue strap since his second Flat start. *J. G. Carr, Ireland*

SUBSIDISE (IRE) 4 br.g. Key of Luck (USA) – Haysong (IRE) (Ballad Rock) [2006/7 **h–**
17mᵖᵘ 16m⁵ 17s 16sᵖᵘ 16s⁵ 16vᵖᵘ Dec 19] strong gelding: brother to modest 2m hurdler Sauterelle: modest on all-weather on Flat (should stay 1¼m, usually wears headgear), sold out of J. Given's stable 7,500 gns Doncaster March (2006) Sales: no solid form over hurdles: has worn visor/cheekpieces. *F. P. Murtagh*

SUCH IS LIFE 6 ch.g. Sir Harry Lewis (USA) – Loch Na Keal (Weldnaas (USA)) **F–**
[2006/7 F16d F16m Apr 10] rather unfurnished gelding: first foal: dam, modest hurdler, stayed 2½m: tailed off in bumpers: sold 1,400 gns Doncaster May Sales. *Miss E. C. Lavelle*

SUDDEN APPROACH (IRE) 8 b.m. Topanoora – Sharp Approach (Crash Course) **h–**
[2006/7 22m Jun 18] ex-Irish mare: maiden hurdler: lightly raced and no form since 2004/5: left E. Hales, placed once from 4 starts in points in Britain in 2006. *C. P. Morlock*

SUDDEN IMPULSE 6 b.m. Silver Patriarch (IRE) – Sanshang (FR) (Astronef) **h– p**
[2006/7 16vᵖᵘ 16s 16s Mar 7] rather leggy mare: fair on Flat (stays 1½m), successful 3 times in 2006: some promise over hurdles: should do better now qualified for handicaps, particularly under less testing conditions. *A. D. Brown*

SUGAR MAN 6 b.g. Defacto (USA) – Samana Cay (Pharly (FR)) [2006/7 F17s Oct 15] **F–**
third foal: dam 2-y-o 7f seller winner: well beaten in bumper: dead. *P. T. Midgley*

SUIRE 4 b.f. Sovereign Water (FR) – Miss Wrensborough (Buckskin (FR)) [2006/7 **F–**
F16g Apr 9] half-sister to fair hurdler Fleurette (by Alflora), stays 21f: dam bumper winner/winning Irish pointer: green, well held in mares bumper on debut. *N. B. King*

SUITS ME 4 ch.g. Bertolini (USA) – Fancier Bit (Lion Cavern (USA)) [2006/7 16g **h79 p**
16g⁶ Feb 2] fair on Flat (stays 9f), sold out of J. Quinn's stable 17,000 gns Doncaster October Sales: poor form in juvenile hurdles, not knocked about when sixth at Markington at Catterick: likely to need emphasis on speed at 2m: should do better. *T. P. Tate*

SUIVEZ MOI (IRE) 5 ch.g. Daggers Drawn (USA) – Pamiers (Huntercombe) [2006/7 **h–**
h–: 16f Apr 30] tall gelding: soundly beaten over hurdles: tried tongue tied: dead. *M. F. Harris*

SUKEY TAWDRAY (IRE) 6 b. or br.g. Presenting – My Gonny (IRE) (Mandalus) **h–**
[2006/7 h–, F–: 16sᵖᵘ 17m 21m 17g⁴ Apr 27] unfurnished gelding: little sign of ability. *D. J. Wintle*

SULA'S LEGEND 6 ch.g. Midnight Legend – Sulapuff (Sula Bula) [2006/7 F82: 20s² **h101**
17v 17s 19v³ 19d³ 20g Apr 7] sturdy gelding: fourth in bumper: fair novice hurdler: stays 2½m: raced on good ground or softer. *D. P. Keane*

SULLIVAN'S CASCADE (IRE) 9 b.g. Spectrum (IRE) – Sombre Lady (Sharpen **c– x**
Up) [2006/7 h–: 17gᵖᵘ 16m c19mᵖᵘ Mar 29] close-coupled gelding: little form over **h–**
hurdles: left E. Bevan after second outing, failed to complete in points and hunter chase (jumped badly): tried tongue tied. *Miss I. H. Pickard*

SULTAN FONTENAILLE (FR) 5 b.h. Kaldounevees (FR) – Diane Fontenaille **h117**
(FR) (Tel Quel (FR)) [2006/7 h83: 19m* 20g* 19d² 20m* 22dᵖᵘ 22sᵖᵘ 21g 20g⁵ 22g⁴ Apr 27] compact horse: fairly useful handicap hurdler: progressive form in early-2006/7,

winning novice events at Exeter (conditional jockeys) in May and Uttoxeter in June and 14-runner race at Uttoxeter again in July: probably stays 2¾m: acts on good to firm and good to soft going: in cheekpieces last 2 starts: free-going sort. *N. J. Hawke*

SUMMER BOUNTY 11 b.g. Lugana Beach – Tender Moment (IRE) (Caerleon (USA)) [2006/7 16g^F Nov 2] close-coupled gelding: fair on Flat (stays 1½m): poor hurdler, running creditably when falling last in seller, only outing since 2003/4: stays 19f when emphasis is on speed: acts on firm and good to soft going. *F. Jordan* **h84**

SUMMEROFSIXTYNINE 4 b.c. Fruits of Love (USA) – Scurrilous (Sharpo) [2006/7 F12v F13m^5 Mar 29] leggy colt: third foal: dam, sprint maiden, half-sister to high-class French sprinter Ron's Victory: poor form in bumpers. *J. G. M. O'Shea* **F74**

SUMTOTOTAL 5 b.g. Mtoto – Garota de Ipanema (FR) (Al Nasr (FR)) [2006/7 F16m F16s F16s 20v 16s 24s Dec 23] leggy, lengthy gelding: second foal: dam, won around 1¼m in France, poor maiden hurdler: of no account: tried in cheekpieces. *Mrs K. Waldron* **h– F–**

SUNDARBOB (IRE) 5 bl.g. Bob Back (USA) – Villian (Kylian (USA)) [2006/7 F86: 17g 16m^5 20g^2 21s 16s Feb 22] close-coupled gelding: in frame in bumpers: modest form over hurdles: stays 2½m: acts on good to firm ground. *P. R. Webber* **h87**

SUNDAWN LADY 9 b.m. Faustus (USA) – Game Domino (Derring Rose) [2006/7 h78: 24g^ur 26m^6 24m^6 26m^3 26m* 26g Oct 15] medium-sized mare: poor handicap hurdler: won 20-runner event at Huntingdon in September: ran in snatches following month: stays 3¼m: acts on soft and good to firm going: blinkered. *C. P. Morlock* **h78**

SUNDAWN STAR 6 b.m. Sure Blade (USA) – Game Domino (Derring Rose) [2006/7 F–: F16m May 6] tailed off in bumpers. *C. P. Morlock* **F–**

SUNDAY CITY (JPN) 6 ch.g. Sunday Silence (USA) – Diamond City (USA) (Mr Prospector (USA)) [2006/7 h114: 18f^5 17s^ur 16m 21d 16d^3 16m^3 16g^3 16g^4 16g^2 16g^4 Apr 14] leggy gelding: fairly useful handicap hurdler, left P. Bowen after second start: good efforts in frame last 6 outings, 3 lengths fourth of 22 to Kings Quay in valuable event at Aintree final one: probably best up to 19f: acts on firm and soft going: in cheekpieces last 2 starts: usually races prominently. *D. McCain Jnr* **h125**

SUNGATES (IRE) 11 ch.g. Glacial Storm (USA) – Live It Up (Le Coq d'Or) [2006/7 c107?, h–: c25m* c24m* c23f^3 c26d^2 c24s^3 c25g* c24v^pu c24m^2 c28d^2 c24d^5 c32s^4 c24s^6 Mar 1] strong, lengthy gelding: winning hurdler: fair handicap chaser: won at Hereford in June, Southwell in July and Hereford again in October: stays 3½m: acts on soft and firm going: usually held up. *Evan Williams* **c110 h–**

SUN HILL 7 b.g. Robellino (USA) – Manhattan Sunset (USA) (El Gran Senor (USA)) [2006/7 h78: 22g^3 17m^2 16m 17g Apr 27] sturdy gelding: modest novice hurdler, left D. Burchell before final outing: stays 2¾m: acts on good to firm going. *L. Corcoran* **h86**

SUNISA (IRE) 6 b.m. Daggers Drawn (USA) – Winged Victory (IRE) (Dancing Brave (USA)) [2006/7 h93: 16g* 16g^6 16s* 16v^2 16g 16g Mar 23] angular mare: fairly useful on Flat (stays 1½m): fair handicap hurdler: improved in 2006/7, winning at Haydock in November and Huntingdon in December: raced around 2m on good going or softer (acts on heavy): tongue tied in 2005/6. *J. Mackie* **h110**

SUN KING 10 ch.g. Zilzal (USA) – Opus One (Slip Anchor) [2006/7 h108: 16m^3 16f* 17d^4 16g 16g 16s^6 Apr 25] close-coupled gelding: fair handicap hurdler: won at Perth (by short head from Gone Too Far) in July: off 6 months, below form last 2 starts: best efforts around 2m with emphasis on speed: tongue tied. *K. G. Reveley* **h112**

SUNLEY SHINES 7 ch.m. Komaite (USA) – Sunley Story (Reprimand) [2006/7 h109: c18s^pu c16v^2 c16s^2 c16m* Apr 14] lengthy, good-topped mare: fair hurdler: similar form over fences: long odds on when winning 4-runner maiden at Chepstow in April, overcoming bad mistakes 4 out and 2 out: stays 19f: acts on any going: races freely. *B. G. Powell* **c109 h–**

SUNLEY SONG 4 b.f. Fleetwood (IRE) – Sunley Sinner (Try My Best (USA)) [2006/7 16m* 16g^3 16g^bd 20g 17s 16m^5 Apr 9] leggy filly: well held on Flat: won juvenile at Huntingdon in September: regressive form after, possibly amiss final start: likely to prove best at 2m: acts on good to firm going. *B. G. Powell* **h80**

SUNNY BROOK 8 ch.m. Alderbrook – Merry Marigold (Sonnen Gold) [2006/7 21s^5 20v^3 20s^6 c20s^5 Feb 19] workmanlike mare: lightly raced over hurdles/fences, poor form on balance. *Mrs S. J. Smith* **c76 ? h88 ?**

SUNNY DISPOSITION (IRE) 4 b.c. Desert Sun – Madam Waajib (IRE) (Waajib) [2006/7 16g^pu Oct 14] little show on Flat: breathing problem on hurdling debut: sold £380 Ascot December Sales. *E. F. Vaughan* **h–**

SUNSET GIRL (IRE) 6 b.m. Corrouge (USA) – Encalchoise (FR) (En Calcat (FR)) **F—**
[2006/7 F16m Mar 31] second foal: dam unraced: tailed off in mares bumper on debut.
S. Lycett

SUNSET KING (USA) 7 b.g. King of Kings (IRE) – Sunset River (USA) (Northern **h—**
Flagship (USA)) [2006/7 h74: 17g Apr 7] small gelding: maiden hurdler: sold out of
R. Hodges' stable £3,300 Ascot June Sales. *W. J. Reed*

SUNSHAN 11 b.g. Anshan – Kyrenia Sunset (CYP) (Lucky Look (CYP)) [2006/7 c85: **c80**
c19m² c25f² c23d^F Oct 26] workmanlike gelding: poor handicap chaser: stayed 3m: acted
on firm going, probably on soft: tongue tied early in career: dead. *R. J. Hodges*

SUNSHINE KING (IRE) 5 b.g. King's Theatre (IRE) – Ilanga (IRE) (Common **F—**
Grounds) [2006/7 F16m^{pu} Jun 11] half-brother to 3 winners on Flat, including Moyne
Pleasure (by Exit To Nowhere), also modest winner up to 21f over hurdles: dam Irish 5f/
7f winner: broke leg in bumper on debut. *N. G. Richards*

SUNTINI (GER) 5 b.g. Platini (GER) – Sunita (GER) (Abary (GER)) [2006/7 17v^{pu} **h96**
19v 16v³ 16g³ Mar 28] 28,000 3-y-o: compact gelding: third foal: half-brother to German
9f winner Sunplayer (by Masterplayer) and German 1m winner Suta (by Lomitas): dam
German 6f to 1m winner: modest form in novice hurdles: likely to prove best at 2m with
emphasis on speed. *Miss E. C. Lavelle*

SUPA TRAMP 4 b.g. Kayf Tara – Shirley Superstar (Shirley Heights) [2006/7 17s³ **h87**
18s⁵ 17s 19s^{pu} Mar 2] good-topped gelding: lightly raced on Flat, sold out of
J. Fanshawe's stable 11,000 gns Newmarket July Sales: 19 lengths third to Ned Ludd in
juvenile maiden at Folkestone, only form over hurdles. *G. L. Moore*

SUPER BABY (FR) 5 b.g. Baby Turk – Norma Jane (FR) (Rahotep (FR)) [2006/7 h80: **c92**
16s³ 19d* 16v^{pu} c16g⁴ c16g Apr 7] sparely-made gelding: modest form over hurdles: **h98**
won 16-runner novice at Catterick in December: much better effort in maiden chases
when 8 lengths fourth to Andre Chenier at Sedgefield: bred to stay 3m: raced on good
going or softer. *J. P. L. Ewart*

SUPER CHILLED 4 b.g. Shambo – Drumkilly Lilly (IRE) (Executive Perk) [2006/7 **F—**
F17s Feb 19] fourth foal: half-brother to winning pointer by New Frontier: dam unraced:
well beaten in bumper on debut. *I. McMath*

SUPERCILIOUS (IRE) 5 b.g. Zafonic (USA) – Queen of Dance (IRE) (Sadler's **h—**
Wells (USA)) [2006/7 16s^{pu} Oct 28] lengthy gelding: fourth foal: half-brother to 3
winners on Flat, including Tawoos (by Rainbow Quest), useful up to 1½m: dam 7f
winner: fair form in 4-y-o hurdles, successful at Enghien in April: left X. Guigand, no
show in novice on British debut. *R. T. Phillips*

SUPER DOLPHIN 8 ch.g. Dolphin Street (FR) – Supergreen (Superlative) [2006/7 **c—**
c84, h—: c16d c16m⁶ c20d^{bd} c20g⁶ Dec 20] good-topped gelding: winning hurdler: **h—**
maiden chaser: off 10 months, no form in 2006/7: tried tongue tied. *R. Ford*

SUPERFLING 6 ch.g. Superpower – Jobiska (Dunbeath (USA)) [2006/7 h—: 20g^{pu} **h—**
Oct 3] no show in novice hurdles. *H. J. Manners*

SUPERFLY 5 b.g. Kayf Tara – Dawn Alarm (Warning) [2006/7 F16d⁴ F16d 16v^{pu} 17g^{pu} **h—**
Mar 24] 900 3-y-o: second foal: dam, lightly-raced maiden, half-sister to useful 2m **F83**
hurdler/chaser Swordplay: modest form in bumpers: no show in maiden/novice hurdles.
Mrs D. A. Hamer

SUPER FRANK (IRE) 4 b.g. Cape Cross (IRE) – Lady Joshua (IRE) (Royal Acad- **h—**
emy (USA)) [2006/7 16g^{pu} 16s^{pu} Dec 1] half-brother to rare 2m hurdler Lord Joshua (by
King's Theatre): fairly useful on all-weather on Flat (stays 1m), successful last 4 starts:
no show in juvenile hurdles, left G. Butler after first outing. *J. Akehurst*

SUPER JUDGE (IRE) 6 b.g. Saddlers' Hall (IRE) – Supreme Control (IRE) (Sup- **c99**
reme Leader) [2006/7 20g³ 20d 16g 19d 17s c24m⁴ c24g² c29g^{ur} c25g* c23m^F Apr 25] **h86**
useful-looking gelding: maiden hurdler, sold out of E. O'Grady's stable 20,000 gns
Doncaster May Sales after first outing: modest handicap chaser: won 5-runner event at
Hereford in April: stays 25f: acts on soft and good to firm going: in cheekpieces last 2
starts. *M. Sheppard*

SUPER LADY (IRE) 6 br.m. Mister Lord (USA) – Daisy's Dream (Paddy's Stream) **h—**
[2006/7 F17s 22d Feb 1] lengthy, rather unfurnished mare: fourth foal: sister to winning **F—**
hurdler/chaser Super Lord, stays 3¼m: dam placed in points: failed to complete in maid-
en Irish points in 2006: well held in mares maiden bumper/novice hurdle. *J. A. B. Old*

SUPER LORD (IRE) 9 br.g. Mister Lord (USA) – Daisy's Dream (Paddy's Stream) [2006/7 c114, h114: c25s³ c25dᵖᵘ c24g* Mar 24] good-topped gelding: fair form over hurdles/fences (usually makes mistakes): tongue tied, won 5-runner maiden chase at Bangor in March: stays 3¼m: acts on soft going. *J. A. B. Old*
**c104
h–**

SUPER MARTINA (IRE) 5 b.m. Flemensfirth (USA) – Runaway Tina (IRE) (Mandalus) [2006/7 F16g⁴ Mar 21] second foal: dam unraced half-sister to useful 2½m chaser King On The Run: favourite, just over 6 lengths fourth to Hillridge in bumper at Chepstow on debut. *Carl Llewellyn*
F76

SUPER NICK (IRE) 6 b.g. Supreme Leader – Nic An Ree (IRE) (King's Ride) [2006/7 F17v* F17s* 20s 21s² 24gᵖᵘ Apr 13] €25,000 4-y-o: lengthy, workmanlike gelding: fifth foal: brother to a winning pointer: dam, lightly raced over hurdles, sister to winning 2m chaser King of The Glen: successful both starts in bumpers, at Market Rasen and Aintree in October: very stiff task following month: should stay 3m: open to improvement. *N. A. Twiston-Davies*
**h109 p
F105**

SUPER NOMAD 12 b.g. Nomadic Way (USA) – Super Sue (Lochnager) [2006/7 c124§, h–: c19m c20mᵖᵘ Apr 22] strong gelding: fairly useful chaser at best: left M. Easterby and off 12 months, no show in hunter/handicap in 2006/7: effective at 2m to 2½m: acts on heavy and good to firm going: ran badly only outing in blinkers: tried tongue tied: sound jumper: tends not to go through with effort. *Lady Susan Brooke*
**c–
h–**

SUPER REVO 6 b.g. Revoque (IRE) – Kingdom Princess (Forzando) [2006/7 h80, F85: 22d⁵ 24g 22v³ 24vᵖᵘ 20g c20gᵖᵘ Apr 27] strong, lengthy gelding: poor maiden hurdler: no show in novice handicap on chasing debut: stays 2¾m: raced on good going or softer over jumps (acts on heavy): in cheekpieces 3 of last 4 starts. *Mrs K. Walton*
**c–
h69**

SUPER ROAD TRAIN 8 b.g. Petoski – Foehn Gale (IRE) (Strong Gale) [2006/7 c87§, h89§: c25m² c26d² Aug 28] bumper winner: maiden hurdler: modest handicap chaser, left O. Sherwood and off 8 months before return: stays 3¼m: acts on firm and good to soft going: has worn cheekpieces/blinkers: unreliable. *Mrs S. J. Smith*
**c98 §
h– §**

SUPERROLLERCOASTER 7 b.g. Classic Cliche (IRE) – Foehn Gale (IRE) (Strong Gale) [2006/7 c97§, h–§: c25s³ c25g* c25s* c25s² c22s* c22dᵖᵘ Mar 19] strong gelding: maiden hurdler: fair handicap chaser: successful at Folkestone in November/December and Fontwell in February: will stay beyond 25f: raced mainly on good going or softer (acts on soft): wears headgear: front runner/races prominently. *O. Sherwood*
**c101
h–**

SUPER SENSATION (GER) 6 b.g. Platini (GER) – Studford Girl (Midyan (USA)) [2006/7 16d⁶ 17s 16v³ Feb 26] good-topped gelding: successful on 3 occasions up to around 1¼m on Flat, including at Cologne in May: left C. von der Recke, thrice-raced over hurdles, best effort when 23 lengths third to stable-companion Wingman in maiden at Plumpton, not knocked about: capable of better, particularly now qualified for handicaps. *G. L. Moore*
h85 p

SUPERSHOT (IRE) 9 b.g. Son of Sharp Shot (IRE) – One To Two (IRE) (Astronef) [2006/7 h–: 16m³ 16d⁶ 16m⁵ 17m 19g⁶ c20dᶠ 19vᵖᵘ Dec 31] chunky gelding: poor novice hurdler: sold out of O. Brennan's stable 2,000 gns Doncaster October Sales after fourth start: fell ninth on chasing debut: stays 19f: acts on good to firm and good to soft going. *Miss L. V. Davis*
**c–
h72**

SUPPLY AND FIX (IRE) 9 b.g. Supreme Leader – Hannies Girl (IRE) (Invited (USA)) [2006/7 c–, h92: 17m 17f⁶ 16g* 18gᵇᵈ 16s² 16gʳᵒ 16s 20s 16m 16m 16m Apr 28] close-coupled gelding: third on completed start in hunter chases: fair handicap hurdler: won at Perth in August: largely below form after (ran out sixth start): best form up to 2½m: acts on firm and soft going, well below form on heavy: front runner. *J. J. Lambe, Ireland*
**c–
h105**

SUPREME BEING (IRE) 10 b.g. Supreme Leader – Parsonetta (The Parson) [2006/7 20v⁴ c17d⁷ c21s c20d⁶ c20d 20v⁴ 24d⁴ 24sᵘʳ 20v 22m* 20m Apr 24] well-made gelding: fairly useful handicap hurdler: better than ever when winning at Fairyhouse (beat Sizing Australia by ¾ length) in April: fair form over fences: won maiden at Ballinrobe in May: stays 3m: acts on good to firm and heavy going: wears blinkers/cheekpieces. *Michael Cunningham, Ireland*
**c109
h121**

SUPREME BREEZE (IRE) 12 b.g. Supreme Leader – Merry Breeze (Strong Gale) [2006/7 c115, h–: c28d⁵ 20s c32s⁶ c28sᵖᵘ c28d⁵ c30s c24s⁶ c28s⁵ c32v³ Mar 15] small, sturdy gelding: winning hurdler: fair handicap chaser: below form in 2006/7 after first outing: stays 4m: acts on heavy going: tried blinkered/in cheekpieces: has been let down by attitude/jumping. *Mrs S. J. Smith*
**c110 d
h–**

SUPREME BUILDER 6 b.g. Supreme Leader – Osocool (Teenoso (USA)) [2006/7 **F107**
F107: F16v⁵ F16s* Apr 1] tall, angular gelding: useful form in bumpers: landed odds
in maiden at Hexham in April by 1½ lengths from Masra, idling: will stay 2½m. *Ferdy
Murphy*

SUPREME CARA 7 b.m. Morpeth – Supreme Daughter (Supreme Leader) [2006/7 **h103**
F90: 21v³ 21v⁴ 20d³ 25v* Feb 23] rather leggy, lengthy mare: bumper winner: fair form
in novice hurdles: upped in trip, again none too fluent when winning at Warwick in
February by 1¼ lengths from Troglodyte: stays 25f: acts on heavy going. *C. J. Down*

SUPREME CATCH (IRE) 10 b.g. Supreme Leader – Lucky Trout (Beau Charmeur **c114**
(FR)) [2006/7 c115, h–: c22s³ c22g* c21sᵖᵘ c24g c22d² c21s² c21g Mar 30] workmanlike **h–**
gelding: fair handicap chaser: won at Market Rasen in November: creditable efforts
when runner-up after, to easy winners Loulou Nivernais at Market Rasen and Petitjean
at Wincanton: should stay beyond 3m: acts on heavy going: usually patiently ridden.
Miss H. C. Knight

SUPREME COPPER (IRE) 7 br.g. Supreme Leader – Black Wind (IRE) (Good **h98 p**
Thyne (USA)) [2006/7 h84p, F80: 17m⁶ 22d³ 24d⁴ 22v⁴ 21s² Feb 9] rangy gelding:
modest novice hurdler: stays 2¾m: acts on soft and good to firm going: has reportedly
had breathing problem: possibly still capable of better. *Miss E. C. Lavelle*

SUPREME DE PAILLE (IRE) 5 b.g. Supreme Leader – Wondermac (IRE) (Jeu de **F–**
Paille (FR)) [2006/7 F17s⁵ Dec 23] 23,000 4-y-o: third foal: half-brother to bumper/19f
hurdle winner An Fear Doiteain (by Saddlers' Hall): dam unraced half-sister to smart
chaser up to 3m Super Furrow: well held in bumper on debut. *A. Bateman*

SUPREME DEVELOPER (IRE) 10 b.g. Supreme Leader – Bettys The Boss (IRE) **c– x**
(Deep Run) [2006/7 c123x, h–: c20gᵖᵘ Oct 24] well-made gelding: fairly useful chaser: **h–**
went as if amiss only start in 2006/7: stays 3m: acts on soft and good to firm going: highly
tried only start in cheekpieces: usually let down by jumping. *Ferdy Murphy*

SUPREME GEM (IRE) 5 gr.m. Supreme Leader – Miss Henrietta (IRE) (Step **F81**
Together (USA)) [2006/7 F17g⁶ F17g Apr 19] has scope: sister to fairly useful chaser
Tollbrae, stays 2½m, and half-sister to fairly useful chaser He's The Gaffer (by Oscar),
stays 3¼m: dam lightly-raced hurdler: better effort in bumpers when sixth of 9 to Team
Chaser at Taunton. *Mrs S. M. Johnson*

SUPREME GLORY (IRE) 14 b.g. Supreme Leader – Pentlows (Sheer Grit) [2006/7 **c–**
c29g⁶ Mar 21] well-made gelding: one-time useful staying chaser: little impact since
2002/3, including in points: sound jumper. *Mrs S. J. Evans*

SUPREME HUNTRESS (IRE) 7 b.g. Supreme Leader – Luminous Girl (IRE) **h106**
(King's Ride) [2006/7 F16g⁵ 21d² 20s* 22v² 21v⁵ 21m⁴ Apr 21] €200,000 4-y-o: well- **F89**
made gelding: second foal: dam unraced, out of sister to high-class hurdler Mole Board:
fifth in bumper on debut: fair novice hurdler: won at Chepstow in December: stays 2¾m:
acts on heavy going: tends to finish weakly (reportedly bled fourth outing). *P. F. Nicholls*

SUPREME LEISURE (IRE) 10 b.g. Supreme Leader – Maid of Leisure (Le Moss) **c– x**
[2006/7 c–, h118: c20sᶠ c16s⁵ c23v³ c20vᶠ 20sᵘʳ Apr 1] rangy gelding: fairly useful hurd- **h–**
ler: mistakes and no form over fences, sold out of J. Howard Johnson's stable 15,000 gns
Doncaster October Sales before reappearance: should stay beyond 21f. *J. R. Cornwall*

SUPREME LOVER 8 b.g. Supreme Leader – Theme Arena (Tragic Role (USA)) **h86**
[2006/7 24m⁴ 24m Apr 15] sturdy gelding: modest form over hurdles, left Miss H. Knight
and off over 2 years before return: stays 3m. *C. E. Longsdon*

SUPREMELY GIFTED (IRE) 6 b.g. Supreme Leader – Some Gift (Avocat) [2006/7 **h96**
F79: F17v² 19g³ 20v² Dec 30] workmanlike gelding: better effort in bumpers when **F105**
second to impressive Skippers Brig at Carlisle: placed both starts over hurdles, beaten 28
lengths (promoted to second) by same rival in novice at Haydock second time: will be
suited by further than 2½m. *Mrs S. J. Smith*

SUPREMELY RED (IRE) 10 b.g. Supreme Leader – Her Name Was Lola (Pitskelly) **c66 §**
[2006/7 c23dᵖᵘ c19m c24s² c26gᵖᵘ c24vᶠ c24vᵖᵘ c24dᵖᵘ Jan 8] medium-sized gelding: **h– §**
winning hurdler: poor maiden chaser: stays 3m: acts on firm and soft going: has been
visored/blinkered: hard ride. *D. A. Rees*

SUPREMELY SMART (IRE) 7 b.g. Supreme Leader – Fair Lisselan (IRE) (Kemal **h–**
(FR)) [2006/7 h–, F–: 21d Nov 20] no form in bumper/over hurdles. *N. A. Twiston-Davies*

SUPREME MARQUE (IRE) 9 b.g. Supreme Leader – My Motif (IRE) (Glacial **c–**
Storm (USA)) [2006/7 22g 22mᵖᵘ 19dᵖᵘ 20g c23dᵘʳ 26g² 21sᵘʳ 26s 21d c16m c19s⁴ **h70**

Feb 26] second foal: dam unraced: won maiden Irish point in 2005: little form over hurdles/in chases, left P. Henderson after sixth outing. *Lady Susan Brooke*

SUPREME MELODY (IRE) 5 br.m. Supreme Leader – Strong Serenade (IRE) **F78**
(Strong Gale) [2006/7 F16v aF16g[6] F16m[3] Apr 15] rather unfurnished mare: sister to 3 winners, including useful hurdler/smart chaser Supreme Prince, stays 3m, and useful hurdler/fairly useful chaser Supreme Serenade, stays 2¾m, and half-sister to 3m hurdle winner That's The Story (by Montelimar): dam 2m hurdle winner: modest form in bumpers: likely to be suited by 2½m+. *P. J. Hobbs*

SUPREME NOVA 7 b.m. Supreme Leader – Qurrat Al Ain (Wolver Hollow) [2006/7 **F–**
F–: F17s May 20] no form in bumpers. *John Allen*

SUPREME PIPER (IRE) 9 b.g. Supreme Leader – Whistling Doe (Whistling Deer) **c–**
[2006/7 c–, h108: 24d[5] Nov 21] useful-looking gelding: handicap hurdler, on downgrade **h98**
since 2004: stays 25f: raced on good going or softer (acts on heavy). *Miss C. Dyson*

SUPREME PRINCE (IRE) 10 b.g. Supreme Leader – Strong Serenade (IRE) **c145**
(Strong Gale) [2006/7 c148, h–: 19d c20s[5] 21g[6] c20m[3] Apr 20] tall gelding: smart **h129**
handicap chaser: better effort in 2006/7 when 10¾ lengths third of 5 to Three Mirrors at Ayr, badly hampered 2 out: useful chaser: creditable sixth of 28 to Burntoakboy in Coral Cup (Handicap) at Cheltenham: effective at 2½m to 3m: has won on soft going, best form under less testing conditions (acts on good to firm): has had jumping problems, but generally more fluent nowadays. *P. J. Hobbs*

SUPREME PROSPECT 6 b.m. Supreme Leader – Dubai Dolly (IRE) (Law Society **h–**
(USA)) [2006/7 F–: F16d 16v[4] 16v 20s Feb 19] strong, workmanlike mare: well beaten **F–**
in bumpers and over hurdles. *R. Johnson*

SUPREME RETURN 8 b.g. Bob's Return (IRE) – Supreme Wonder (IRE) (Supreme **c93**
Leader) [2006/7 h88: 22g[5] c24g[2] Jun 8] tall gelding: modest novice hurdler: 14 lengths **h88**
second of 5 finishers to Silver Dagger in novice handicap at Uttoxeter on chasing debut: stays 3m: acts on good to firm going. *A. King*

SUPREME ROYAL (IRE) 5 b.g. Supreme Leader – View of The Hills (Croghan **h79**
Hill) [2006/7 F16d 19s 19v 22s[pu] Feb 3] €28,000 3-y-o: sturdy gelding: brother to 2 **F–**
winners, notably fairly useful hurdler/chaser Limerick Leader, stays 3m: dam unraced: little impact in bumper/over hurdles: bred to stay well. *P. J. Hobbs*

SUPREME'S LEGACY (IRE) 8 b.g. Supreme Leader – Lucylet (Kinglet) [2006/7 **c112**
h115, F107: c25s[2] c24s[3] c25s[3] c30s[pu] 23s[2] Feb 3] big, workmanlike gelding: fairly useful **h124**
hurdler: good 5 lengths second to Laertes in handicap at Wetherby: fair form over fences, leaving impression possibly capable of better: should stay beyond 25f: raced on good to soft/soft ground. *K. G. Reveley*

SUPREME TADGH (IRE) 10 b.g. Supreme Leader – Mariaetta (IRE) (Mandalus) **c105 x**
[2006/7 c103x, h–: c21v* c20s[2] c21s[pu] c19s[pu] c24v[F] c23s[6] c22d[6] Mar 19] sturdy gelding: **h–**
fair but error-prone handicap chaser: won at Uttoxeter in October: out of sorts after next outing: stays 2¾m: acts on heavy and good to firm going: claimer ridden. *J. A. Geake*

SUPREME TEAM (IRE) 4 b.g. Supreme Leader – La Gazelle (IRE) (Executive **h–**
Perk) [2006/7 F16v 21m[F] 20m[ur] Apr 25] lengthy, close-coupled gelding: second foal: dam, **F–**
poor maiden hurdler who stayed 3m, half-sister to top-class staying chaser Rough Quest: well held in bumper: failed to complete in maiden hurdles: bred to stay well. *B. I. Case*

SUPREME TRUCKER (IRE) 6 b.g. Supreme Leader – Cush Carrig (Brush **h–**
Aside (USA)) [2006/7 F16d F17v[5] 20s Jan 31] 15,000 4-y-o: first foal: dam unraced, out **F78**
of sister to smart 2½m to 3½m chaser Amtrak Express: well held in bumpers/novice hurdle (not fluent). *R. T. Phillips*

SUPRENDRE ESPERE 7 b.g. Espere d'Or – Celtic Dream (Celtic Cone) [2006/7 **c73**
h87, F89: 16g 16m 16s c19s[F] 19g[3] 21s c19s[pu] c20d[3] c20m[pu] Apr 28] lengthy gelding: **h92**
modest hurdler, left Jennie Candlish after first outing: little impact over fences: should stay 2½m: acts on heavy going, probably on good to firm: tried in cheekpieces: has run in snatches/made mistakes. *C. C. Bealby*

SUPSONIC 4 br.c. Marju (IRE) – Nicely (IRE) (Bustino) [2006/7 16d[ro] 16s* 16s[4] 16v[4] **h111**
16s[4] 16d Mar 13] tall, lengthy colt: second foal: dam, fairly useful on Flat, stayed 2m: won 15f claimer on Flat at Deauville (claimed from U. Suter €25,500): fairly useful juvenile hurdler: won at Sandown in December by 12 lengths from Pouvoir: raced at 2m on ground softer than good: has been blinkered: suspect temperament (ran out on debut). *P. J. Hobbs*

SUREFAST 12 ch.g. Nearly A Hand – Meldon Lady (Ballymoss) [2006/7 c91§, h–: c24s² c23v⁵ c26v⁶ c24d⁵ c26v⁵ c24g⁶ Mar 21] stocky gelding: modest handicap chaser: out of sorts after reappearance: stays 3¼m: acts on heavy going: unreliable. *P. R. Rodford* — **c90 §**
h–

SURE FLAME (IRE) 5 b.g. Needle Gun (IRE) – Gallic Flame (Cyrano de Bergerac) [2006/7 F16vᵘʳ F16v F16s Feb 1] €26,000 3-y-o: tall, close-coupled gelding: second foal: dam unraced, out of half-sister to top-class staying chaser Flashing Steel: no form in bumpers. *Mrs L. Wadham* — **F–**

SURELY TRULY (IRE) 4 b.f. Trans Island – Londubh (Tumble Wind) [2006/7 17mᵘʳ 16f⁵ 16d⁵ Nov 11] half-sister to Irish bumper winner Golden Thatch (by Goldmark): fairly useful at 2 yrs (successful twice at 6f), below form on Flat in 2006, left K. Burke £12,000 in July: no show on juvenile hurdles: in cheekpieces after debut. *A. E. Jones* — **h–**

SURFBOARD (IRE) 6 ch.g. Kris – Surfing (Grundy) [2006/7 h–, F83: 21s c16m⁴ c16d³ 24d³ c20v* c23v² c17g* Apr 23] compact gelding: maiden hurdler: fair novice chaser: won handicaps at Leicester in February and Plumpton in April: stays 3m, effective at much shorter: acts on good to firm and heavy going. *P. A. Blockley* — **c103**
h85 +

SURPRESA 7 b.m. Double Eclipse (IRE) – Let Me Finish (Chantro) [2006/7 F17d Oct 7] fourth foal: half-sister to winning hurdler/chaser Pink Harbour (by Rakaposhi King), stayed 21f: dam, tailed off in 2 bumpers, half-sister to fairly useful staying chaser River Sirene: green, well held in maiden bumper on debut. *D. McCain Jnr* — **F–**

SURRICATE (FR) 5 b.m. True Brave (USA) – Sweet Normania (FR) (Vincent) [2006/7 17s³ 16f² 16g² 20v³ 20v² 20v* 20s* 20s² Apr 1] half-sister to 2m winner Integrale (by Robore): dam unraced: once-raced on Flat/over fences: fair novice hurdler, claimed from D. Bressou €24,000 first outing: won mares events in January and March, both at Sedgefield: will stay beyond 2½m: probably acts on any going: reliable. *Ferdy Murphy* — **c–**
h112

SUSIEDIL (IRE) 6 b.m. Mujadil (USA) – Don't Take Me (IRE) (Don't Forget Me) [2006/7 16fᵖᵘ 16f⁵ 16f⁵ 20vᵖᵘ 20d 16v³ 16s⁶ Mar 7] modest and unreliable up to 1½m on Flat: poor maiden hurdler: best at 2m: in cheekpieces last 2 starts: has had tongue tied. *S. T. Mason* — **h63**

SUZABABE (IRE) 6 ch.m. Glacial Storm (USA) – Will I Or Wont I (IRE) (Black Minstrel) [2006/7 16s⁶ 20m⁵ Mar 31] third foal: dam, signs of ability in bumpers, sister to smart chaser up to 29f Amtrak Express: well held in maiden hurdles. *Charles Byrnes, Ireland* — **h–**

SWALLOW MAGIC (IRE) 9 b.g. Magic Ring (IRE) – Scylla (Rock City) [2006/7 c91, h–: c16gᵖᵘ c22dᵖᵘ c18g² c18g² c20g c20s⁴ c16m⁶ Mar 31] compact gelding: winning hurdler: modest handicap chaser: off 5 months, well held last 3 starts: stays 25f: best on good going or firmer (acts on firm): usually blinkered/visored nowadays: tried tongue tied: sold 2,000 gns Doncaster May Sales. *Ferdy Murphy* — **c95**
h–

SWALLOW SENORA (IRE) 5 b.m. Entrepreneur – Sangra (USA) (El Gran Senor (USA)) [2006/7 17s Mar 11] poor maiden on Flat (stays 7f): well beaten in novice on hurdling debut. *M. C. Chapman* — **h–**

SWANSEA BAY 11 b.g. Jurado (USA) – Slave's Bangle (Prince Rheingold) [2006/7 c120, h95: c24s⁴ c24g³ c25m⁵ c21g c26vᵖᵘ c21s⁵ c27gᵖᵘ Mar 25] lengthy gelding: winning hurdler: fairly useful handicap chaser: lost form after third outing: best at 3m+ on good going or firmer: sometimes wears headgear: tried tongue tied: has hinted at temperament more than once (refused to race final start in 2004/5). *Evan Williams* — **c121 d**
h–

SWAYTHE (USA) 6 b.m. Swain (IRE) – Caithness (USA) (Roberto (USA)) [2006/7 F93p: F16s² F16s* Mar 10] useful-looking mare: progressive in bumpers, off 15 months after debut: smart form when winning listed mares event at Sandown in March by 3½ lengths from Theatre Girl: will be suited by further than 2m. *P. R. Webber* — **F115**

SWEEPING STORM (IRE) 10 b.g. Glacial Storm (USA) – Sweeping Gold (Quayside) [2006/7 c21vᶠ Feb 20] modest pointer: fourth on completed start in hunter chases. *Mrs Elaine Smith* — **c–**
h–

SWEET DIVERSION (IRE) 8 b.g. Carroll House – Serocco Wind (Roi Guillaume (FR)) [2006/7 c140, h–: c32m⁴ c22g c21d c24g⁵ c24m³ c25mᵘʳ c25g³ c29fᵖᵘ Apr 28] sturdy gelding: has reportedly had breathing operation: useful handicap chaser: mainly respectable efforts in 2006/7, fourth to McKelvey in English Summer National at Uttoxeter: stays 4m: acts on soft and good to firm going: tongue tied. *P. F. Nicholls* — **c138**
h–

SWEET KILN (IRE) 8 b.m. Beneficial – Miss Pollerton (IRE) (Pollerton) [2006/7 16s⁵ 20d⁴ 20s⁶ 22v³ 20v⁴ 24v² 19v* 21v* 18v² 20m² Apr 9] lengthy mare: useful hurdler: — **h134**

landed odds in minor event at Naas in January and 5-runner Grade 3 McCabe Builders Boyne Hurdle at Navan (beat Rosaker by 8 lengths) in February: good 3 lengths second to Essex in listed race at Fairyhouse final outing: stays 3m: acts on good to firm and heavy going: usually front runner: reliable. *Michael J. Bowe, Ireland*

SWEET LORRAINE 5 b.m. Dashing Blade – Royal Future (IRE) (Royal Academy (USA)) [2006/7 16m^F Sep 3] modest maiden on Flat (should stay 1m) for T. Mills: well beaten when fell 2 out in maiden on hurdling debut. *M. Scudamore* **h–**

SWEET MATRIARCH 5 b.m. Silver Patriarch (IRE) – Pudding (Infantry) [2006/7 F17s 22v^3 Feb 28] third foal: dam winning pointer: in eyecover, little impact in mares bumper/novice hurdle. *B. I. Case* **h–**
F—

SWEET MEDICINE 5 ch.m. Dr Devious (IRE) – Crimley Crumb (Rainbow Quest (USA)) [2006/7 F80: 16g^2 18m^3 Apr 26] well-made mare: fourth in bumper: fair form at best on Flat: better effort in mares maiden hurdles when 2½ lengths second of 18 to Enforce at Huntingdon. *P. Howling* **h87**

SWEET MINUET 10 b.m. Minshaanshu Amad (USA) – Sweet N' Twenty (High Top) [2006/7 c78, h–: c18m^{pu} May 28] lengthy mare: winning hurdler: poor maiden chaser, lame only start in 2006/7: stays 3m: acts on any going: blinkered once. *M. Madgwick* **c–**
h–

SWEET WAKE (GER) 6 ch.g. Waky Nao – Sweet Royale (GER) (Garde Royale) [2006/7 h138: 16d 17g 16m 16m Apr 27] lengthy gelding: useful hurdler: off 4 months, back to form when 3 lengths seventh of 28 to Pedrobob in County Hurdle (Handicap) at Cheltenham second start: likely to prove best at 2m: acts on soft and good to firm going: tried tongue tied: tends to finish weakly. *N. Meade, Ireland* **h141**

SWIFT AND BOLD 5 b.g. Kayf Tara – Cede Nullis (Primitive Rising (USA)) [2006/7 F16d F14v F16m^6 19v^{pu} 17s Mar 11] smallish gelding: first foal: dam, fairly useful pointer/winning hunter, stayed 3m: little sign of ability. *P. Maddison* **h–**
F—

SWIFT HALF (IRE) 5 b.g. Bahhare (USA) – Brief Interval (IRE) (Brief Truce (USA)) [2006/7 F86: 16g^4 16d^6 17s^5 19g 20g^2 Apr 11] rather leggy gelding: modest novice hurdler: stays 2½m: best efforts on good ground (bumper winner on good to firm). *J. W. Mullins* **h95**

European Breeders' Fund/Doncaster Bloodstock Sales Mares' Only Standard Open National Hunt Flat Race Final, Sandown—Swaythe and William Kennedy have matters under control

SWIFT SAILOR 6 gr.g. Slip Anchor – New Wind (GER) (Windwurf (GER)) [2006/7 **h115**
16d 17m^pu 18m^6 16m 16m* 16s^bd 22d^5 21v^3 20s^3 22v^2 16s^3 16s^6 19g^3 Mar 31] good-
topped gelding: fairly useful handicap hurdler: won novice events at Plumpton in October
and Fontwell in November: further progress after, 3 lengths third to Predator at Ascot
final outing: stays 2¾m: acts on heavy and good to firm going: in cheekpieces last 8
starts: has looked quirky under pressure. *G. L. Moore*

SWIFTS HILL (IRE) 9 ch.g. Executive Perk – Tudor Lady (Green Shoon) [2006/7 **h–**
h101: 19g^5 Mar 29] sturdy gelding: fair hurdler: left T. George, off 17 months and in
cheekpieces, well held in seller only start in 2006/7: stays 3¼m: acts on firm ground.
B. J. Llewellyn

SWIFT SWALLOW 9 ch.g. Missed Flight – Alhargah (Be My Guest (USA)) [2006/7 **h–**
h126: 20m^F Jun 22] sturdy gelding: fairly useful handicap hurdler: fell fatally only start
in 2006/7: stayed 2½m: acted on good to firm and good to soft going. *O. Brennan*

SWIFT THYNE (IRE) 7 b. or br.g. Good Thyne (USA) – Firey Comet (IRE) (Buck- **c97**
skin (FR)) [2006/7 c21s^4 c25s* c33g^ur Mar 15] rangy gelding: fourth foal: half-brother to
27f chase winner Leyland Comet (by Roselier): dam unraced half-sister to fairly useful
chaser Joe White, stayed 25f: won maiden point in 2006: better effort on completed starts
in maiden chases when winning at Catterick in February by 8 lengths from Hold The Bid:
would have stayed beyond 25f: acted on soft ground: dead. *T. R. George*

SWING BILL (FR) 6 gr.g. Grey Risk (FR) – Melodie Royale (FR) (Garde Royale) **c110**
[2006/7 c17g^4 c17v^3 c16s^4 c16m^3 16g^2 20f Apr 28] rather leggy gelding: third foal: **h122**
half-brother to winning hurdler/chaser up to 2¾m Real Music (by Broadway Flyer): dam
5f to 1½m winner: runner-up over 17f on Flat: fairly useful hurdler, left G. Le Paysan
before return: good second to Fleet Street in handicap at Newbury: fair form over fences:
possibly best around 2m: acts on heavy going: tried in cheekpieces: tends to finish
weakly. *Miss H. C. Knight*

SWINGIT LAD 7 b.g. Alflora (IRE) – Promitto (Roaring Riva) [2006/7 F16g May 6] **F–**
€12,000 4-y-o: fifth foal: half-brother to 3m chase winner Montu (by Gunner B): dam,
poor maiden hurdler/pointer, half-sister to high-class hurdler up to 2¾m Swingit Gunner:
well held in bumper on debut. *C. Tinkler*

SWINGS 'N STRINGS (IRE) 9 ch.g. Accordion – Midsummer Blends (IRE) **c92**
(Duky) [2006/7 c22d^pu c27s c19v c23s^bd c19m* c24g* Apr 27] lengthy, workmanlike
ex-Irish gelding: modest handicap chaser: left G. Donnelly after first outing: won 2
selling events at Chepstow in April, left A. Moore in between: stays 3m: acts on soft and
good to firm ground: tried in cheekpieces/blinkers: often tongue tied. *M. Sheppard*

SWORD OF DAMASCUS (IRE) 5 b.g. Darshaan – Damascene (IRE) (Scenic) **h90 p**
[2006/7 F107: 20d^6 Oct 22] good-topped gelding: useful bumper performer: none too
fluent when well-held sixth to Wichita Lineman in novice hurdle at Aintree: looked likely
to do better but not seen out again. *D. McCain Jnr*

SYBARITE CHIEF (IRE) 5 b.g. Sinndar (IRE) – Fancy Wrap (Kris) [2006/7 F89: **h98**
17d^4 17v 17v^6 20d* 16v Jan 12] good-topped gelding: modest novice hurdler: upped in
trip, improved form when winning at Musselburgh on handicap debut in January: will
probably be suited by further than 2½m: acts on good to firm and good to soft going (well
held on heavy). *R. A. Fahey*

SYBELLIUS D'ARTAIX (FR) 7 b.g. Sassanian (USA) – Kadisha (FR) (Always Fair **c127**
(USA)) [2006/7 c22s^F 18s^6 c29s c22s^4 c22s^4 c22s c27s 18v^2 c16g c26g c32m^pu Apr 21] **h112**
leggy gelding: second foal: dam maiden: fair maiden hurdler, claimed from J-P. Gallorini
€26,000 eighth outing: fairly useful chaser: tongue tied, very highly tried in Britain (left
Richard Chotard before final start): stays 27f: raced mainly on good going or softer: has
worn cheekpieces. *Paul Murphy*

SYDNEY GREENSTREET (GER) 6 b.g. Acatenango (GER) – Spartina (USA) **h–**
(Northern Baby (CAN)) [2006/7 F95: 22g^pu 22d^6 May 31] fair form in bumpers: left
C. Egerton, no show in novice hurdles (bled on return). *R. Ford*

SYDNEY (IRE) 7 b.g. Saddlers' Hall (IRE) – Magic Gale (IRE) (Strong Gale) [2006/7 **h110 p**
20v* Feb 13] well-made gelding: eighth in maiden bumper: left M. Pitman and off 22
months, promising hurdling debut when winning maiden at Folkestone by 1¼ lengths
from Teamgeist: likely to stay 3m: open to improvement. *Carl Llewellyn*

SYLPHIDE 12 b.m. Ballet Royal (USA) – Shafayif (Ela-Mana-Mou) [2006/7 c83, h–: **c–**
c24m^6 27m^pu Jun 11] sparely-made mare: winning hurdler/chaser: fair pointer: stays **h–**
3¼m: acts on soft and good to firm going: held up. *H. J. Manners*

SYMBIOSIS 6 b.m. Bien Bien (USA) – Sound Appeal (Robellino (USA)) [2006/7   **h92**
F16g² 21s⁴ 16d³ 19s³ 20m⁴ Mar 25] £6,800 3-y-o: angular mare: first foal: dam fairly   **F91**
useful hurdler around 2m: runner-up in mares bumper on debut: modest form over
hurdles, hung/jumped right final start: stays easy 2½m: races prominently: sold 7,500 gns
Doncaster May Sales. *N. A. Twiston-Davies*

SYMPHONIQUE (FR) 6 ch.m. Epervier Bleu – Septieme Symphonie (FR) (Top   **c–**
Ville) [2006/7 c117, h–: 16d 16dᵖᵘ Dec 27] good-topped mare: winning hurdler/chaser,   **h–**
no form in handicaps in Britain: raced mainly around 2m on going softer than good.
P. J. Hobbs

SYNCOPATED RHYTHM (IRE) 7 b.g. Synefos (USA) – Northern Elation (IRE)   **c81**
(Lancastrian) [2006/7 c71, h75: c24d* c26v⁶ c24d Nov 8] rangy gelding: poor hurdler/   **h–**
chaser: won 3-finisher conditional jockeys handicap chase at Uttoxeter in October:
laboured efforts last 2 starts: stays 3m: raced on good going or softer. *N. A. Twiston-
Davies*

SYNISTERDEXTER 6 ch.g. Tina's Pet – Mossberry Fair (Mossberry) [2006/7 F17s   **F–**
Feb 26] 1,000 3-y-o: brother to winning hurdler/fair chaser around 2m Pegasus Bay and
half-brother to fair hurdler Weston Rock (by Double Eclipse), stayed 3m: dam fair 2m
hurdler: third on completed start in points in 2006: soundly beaten in bumper. *Evan
Williams*

SYNONYMY 4 b.g. Sinndar (IRE) – Peony (Lion Cavern (USA)) [2006/7 16s⁴ Dec 1]   **h–**
sturdy gelding: fair on Flat (stays 17f), successful in March: none too fluent when well
held in juvenile on hurdling debut. *M. Blanshard*

SYROCO (FR) 8 b.g. Homme de Loi (IRE) – La Pommeraie (FR) (Miller's Mate)   **c114**
[2006/7 c20d c16g* c16g* c16g³ c16s³ c16g⁴ c16gᵘʳ c16m² Apr 14] smallish, sturdy gelding: **h–**
maiden hurdler: fair handicap chaser: sold out of A. Moore's stable 5,000 gns Doncaster
May Sales and off nearly 6 months, won at Warwick in October: raced mainly around 2m:
acts on good to firm and heavy going: tried tongue tied: front runner/races prominently:
needs to brush up his jumping. *M. Sheppard*

SZEROKI BOR (POL) 8 b.g. In Camera (IRE) – Szuana (POL) (Five Star Camp   **h–**
(USA)) [2006/7 h–: 21g May 4] formerly fair hurdler: very lightly raced and no form
since 2004. *Carl Llewellyn*

T

TABARAN (FR) 4 ch.g. Polish Precedent (USA) – Tabariya (IRE) (Doyoun) [2006/7   **h94**
17s³ 17s 17s⁴ 16d⁵ 17s³ 20s 18vᵖᵘ Jan 25] sturdy ex-French gelding: second foal:
half-brother to 10.5f to 14.5f winner Tabarana (by Cape Cross): dam 1m winner: maiden
on Flat: modest juvenile hurdler, claimed from Mme L. Audon €13,600 first outing: raced
mainly around 2m on ground softer than good. *Noel T. Chance*

TABI 5 b.g. Kayf Tara – Bit of A Citizen (IRE) (Henbit (USA)) [2006/7 F16g May 14]   **F–**
first foal: dam half pointer: tailed off in bumper on debut. *C. R. Dore*

TABORA 5 b.m. Monsun (GER) – Thyatira (FR) (Bakharoff (USA)) [2006/7 17s² 17s²   **c101 p**
16v* 19sF 16v* c20v* Jan 25] tall, useful-looking mare: second foal: half-sister to fair   **h101 +**
hurdler Theocritus (by Trempolino), stays 19f: dam unraced half-sister to useful 2m to
21f hurdler Tryphaena: 10.5f winner in France at 3 yrs: placed twice from 3 starts over
hurdles in Provinces for M. Rulec: fair form when landing odds both completed starts in
mares novice hurdles in Britain (in contention when fell 3 out in between), at Towcester in
November and Wetherby (on toes, beat Misleain readily by 9 lengths) in January: 7/4-on,
successful also on chasing debut when beating Inch Pride by 11 lengths in 4-runner mares
novice at Warwick, despite mistakes: stays 2½m: raced on soft/heavy going: probably
capable of better: sold 25,000 gns Doncaster May Sales. *H. D. Daly*

TACITA 12 ch.m. Gunner B – Taco (High Season) [2006/7 c63, h–: c21m² c25dᵖᵘ c24m²   **c66**
c25dᵖᵘ Nov 16] lengthy mare: lightly raced: poor handicap chaser: stays 3m: acts on good   **h–**
to firm ground. *M. D. McMillan*

TACOLINO (FR) 13 ch.g. Royal Charter (FR) – Tamilda (FR) (Rose Laurel) [2006/7   **c88 §**
c102§, h–: c16gᵖᵘ c22s⁴ c23g⁶ c22g² c18g⁵ Jul 22] workmanlike gelding: veteran chaser: **h–**
stays 2¾m: acts on firm and good to soft going, probably on heavy: tried blinkered: has
had tongue tied: ungenuine: sold 4,400 gns Doncaster August Sales. *O. Brennan*

TADEUSZ MANDZIEJ (IRE) 7 b.g. Balla Cove – Princess Paula (Smoggy) [2006/7 F17s⁶ F16m 20g 17d 19v⁶ c20dᵖᵘ Mar 26] €18,000 4-y-o: rather leggy gelding: half-brother to several winners, including fairly useful chaser Scotmail Boy (by Over The River), stays 27f: dam lightly raced: mid-field in bumpers: little form in novice hurdles/ handicap chase. *P. J. Hobbs*   **c–** **h68** **F72**

TAGAR (FR) 10 b.g. Fijar Tango (FR) – Fight For Arfact (Salmon Leap (USA)) [2006/7 c90, h–: c16v* c16s⁴ c16d⁵ c20dᵖᵘ c20s c18s⁵ Mar 11] close-coupled gelding: maiden hurdler: modest handicap chaser: won at Uttoxeter in May: well below form after next outing: stays 2½m: acts on good to firm and heavy going: tried in cheekpieces: often let down by jumping: sold 1,500 gns Doncaster May Sales. *C. Grant*   **c89 x** **h–**

TAGULA BLUE (IRE) 7 b.g. Tagula (IRE) – Palace Blue (IRE) (Dara Monarch) [2006/7 h110: 18m³ 16s² 16d* Dec 15] good-bodied gelding: fairly useful novice hurdler: won at Fontwell (easily) in June and Ascot (beat Moon Over Miami by ½ length in Grade 2 Mitie Kennel Gate Novices' Hurdle) in December: also ran well when 2 lengths second to Silverburn at Newbury in between: likely to prove best around 2m: acts on soft and good to firm ground: tongue tied on debut. *Ian Williams*   **h126**

TAILI 6 b.m. Taipan (IRE) – Doubtfire (Jalmood (USA)) [2006/7 16v 20gᵖᵘ Dec 10] no form on Flat or over hurdles (ran out on debut). *D. A. Nolan*   **h–**

TAILOR'S HALL (IRE) 6 b.g. Saddlers' Hall (IRE) – Designer Lady (IRE) (Buckskin (FR)) [2006/7 F16v³ F20v⁵ 18v² 20v* 23v* Mar 24] unfurnished gelding: third foal: half-brother to fair hurdler Eternal Lady (by Supreme Leader), stays 2¾m: dam, poor in bumpers, out of half-sister to top-class 2m to 3m hurdler Gaye Brief and very smart staying jumper Gaye Chance: third in bumper: progressive over hurdles, won at Thurles (maiden) and Navan (useful form, beat Aitmatov by 5 lengths) in March: likely to be suited by 3m+: raced on heavy ground. *Mrs J. Harrington, Ireland*   **h133** **F79**

TAILS I WIN 8 b.g. Petoski – Spinayab (King of Spain) [2006/7 c82d, h–: c21m 16d c21d⁶ c20d⁴ c20d⁶ c20v c22s c24g c22gᵖᵘ Mar 29] lengthy, plain, sparely-made gelding: winning hurdler/maiden chaser, no longer of any account: tried visored/blinkered. *Miss C. J. E. Caroe*   **c–** **h–**

TAIPAN'S PROMISE (IRE) 5 b.g. Taipan (IRE) – She Is Promising (IRE) (Henbit (USA)) [2006/7 F16d F14s⁴ F16g F14g² Apr 10] £10,500 3-y-o, resold 4,200 3-y-o, 8,000 4-y-o: workmanlike gelding: first foal: dam unraced: modest form in bumpers. *R. H. Buckler*   **F82**

TAKE A MILE (IRE) 5 ch.g. Inchinor – Bu Hagab (IRE) (Royal Academy (USA)) [2006/7 h111: 16m⁶ 18g² 19d* 20g 20s* 21sᵖᵘ 24m⁵ Apr 17] small, angular gelding: fairly useful handicap hurdler: won at Stratford in October and Fontwell (by 3 lengths from Fenix) in December: no show last 2 starts: stays 2½m: acts on heavy going: held up. *B. G. Powell*   **h120**

TAKE IT THERE 5 ch.m. Cadeaux Genereux – Feel Free (IRE) (Generous (IRE)) [2006/7 16d Dec 29] angular mare: fair on Flat (stays 1m), successful in November: well-held seventh to Duc de Regniere in novice at Newbury on hurdling debut. *A. J. Lidderdale*   **h75 +**

TAKE THE OATH (IRE) 10 b.g. Big Sink Hope (USA) – Delgany Chimes (IRE) (Kafu) [2006/7 c79, h–: c19mᵖᵘ Jun 19] rangy gelding: poor handicap chaser: stays 21f: acts on soft and firm ground: tried blinkered/tongue tied. *D. R. Gandolfo*   **c–** **h–**

TAKE THE ODDS (IRE) 11 gr.g. Roselier (FR) – Skinana (Buckskin (FR)) [2006/7 c26s⁶ Mar 11] Irish point winner, no longer of much account. *Miss M. Palmer*   **c–** **h–**

TAKE THE STAND (IRE) 11 b.g. Witness Box (USA) – Denys Daughter (IRE) (Crash Course) [2006/7 c160x, h–: 25m* c25s⁶ c27dᵖᵘ c24d c25vᵖᵘ c33s Mar 17] leggy gelding: fairly useful handicap hurdler: won at Plumpton in October by head from Ballyhoo: high-class chaser at best (runner-up in 2005 Cheltenham Gold Cup), out of sorts in 2006/7: effective around 2½m to 4m: acts on heavy and good to firm going: in cheekpieces most starts in 2006/7: tends to make mistakes. *P. Bowen*   **c– x** **h120**

TAKE TIME 8 b.g. Teenoso – Fernessa (Roman Warrior) [2006/7 h79p: 22g Mar 19] lengthy gelding: signs of ability in novice hurdles 14 months apart. *M. G. Rimell*   **h–**

TAKOTNA (IRE) 5 b.m. Bering – Another Legend (USA) (Lyphard's Wish (FR)) [2006/7 F16s⁴ F16s Mar 3] 22,000 4-y-o: rather unfurnished mare: fifth foal: half-sister to 3 winners by Celtic Swing, including modest hurdler/chaser Celtic Legend (stays 3m): dam US Grade 2 9f winner: better effort in bumpers when 18¼ lengths fourth of 20 to Den of Iniquity at Warwick. *A. King*   **F84**

TAKSINA 8 b.m. Wace (USA) – Quago (New Member) [2006/7 c76, h–: c22m⁶ c16d* c19m⁶ c16s³ c22s⁵ c19s c18mᵖᵘ Apr 26] lengthy mare: poor handicap chaser: won at Worcester in October: effective at 2m to easy 3m: acts on soft going, probably on good to firm: tried tongue tied (ran well). *R. H. Buckler* **c73 h–**

TALARIVE (USA) 11 ch.g. Riverman (USA) – Estala (Be My Guest (USA)) [2006/7 h97§: 19m⁴ 22d³ 20g 24s⁶ 22gᵘʳ 24m⁵ 21s 20m 22g 22m⁶ Apr 28] smallish, sturdy gelding: modest hurdler: stays 2¾m: acts on heavy and good to firm going: wears cheekpieces: usually tongue tied: unreliable. *P. D. Niven* **h95 §**

TALBOT LAD 11 b.g. Weld – Greenacres Girl (Tycoon II) [2006/7 c–§, h–: c24d c24vᵖᵘ Dec 31] leggy gelding: maiden hurdler/winning chaser, lightly raced and no form since 2004/5: tongue tied. *S. A. Brookshaw* **c– § h–**

TALESOFRIVERBANK 4 b.f. Minster Son – The White Lion (Flying Tyke) [2006/7 F16v 16s⁶ 16s Apr 26] sister to winning pointers and half-sister to 3 winners, including fair hurdler/chaser Wynyard Knight (by Silly Prices), stayed 2½m: dam 1m/9f winner: well beaten in bumper: better effort over hurdles when sixth in slowly-run juvenile at Hexham. *A. C. Whillans* **h84 F–**

TALIKOS (FR) 6 b.g. Nikos – Talaya (FR) (Matahawk) [2006/7 h81: c16g⁴ c19g² c18s⁴ c24sᵖᵘ c21gᶠ c19g³ c19g⁵ Apr 11] compact gelding: maiden hurdler: fair novice chaser, disappointing after third outing: stays 19f: acts on soft going: sold 23,000 gns Doncaster May Sales. *Miss H. C. Knight* **c101 h–**

TALISKER ROCK (IRE) 7 gr.g. Tagula (IRE) – Hallatte (USA) (Trempolino (USA)) [2006/7 h–, F77: 16g Oct 19] sturdy gelding: form only in bumper on debut: tried tongue tied. *B. Storey* **h–**

TALLAHASSEE (IRE) 9 ch.g. Moscow Society (USA) – Kemperstrat (The Parson) [2006/7 h–: 24vᵖᵘ 21v c20vᵖᵘ c27mᵖᵘ Apr 9] strong gelding: no sign of ability. *James Moffatt* **c– h–**

TALLOW BAY (IRE) 12 b.g. Glacial Storm (USA) – Minimum Choice (IRE) (Miner's Lamp) [2006/7 c84, h–: c24sᵖᵘ c26v³ c24v⁶ c26sᵖᵘ c24dᵖᵘ c26v² c24vᵖᵘ c26gᵖᵘ Mar 26] sturdy gelding: poor handicap chaser: stays 3¼m: acts on heavy going, well below form on firm: tried blinkered/in cheekpieces: unreliable. *Mrs S. Wall* **c80 § h–**

TALLYHOBYE 4 b.g. Foxhound (USA) – Bebe de Cham (Tragic Role (USA)) [2006/7 17dᵖᵘ 17g Sep 8] half-brother to fair hurdler Cava Bien (by Bien Bien), stays 2¾m: modest on Flat (stayed 11f), successful in May (claimed from J. Weymes £5,000): little impact in juvenile hurdles (saddle slipped on debut): dead. *M. E. Sowersby* **h–**

TALPOUR (IRE) 7 ch.g. Ashkalani (IRE) – Talwara (USA) (Diesis) [2006/7 F78: F17m Jun 4] little form in bumpers: well held on Flat. *M. C. Chapman* **F–**

TAMARINBLEU (FR) 7 b.g. Epervier Bleu – Tamainia (FR) (Lashkari) [2006/7 c140, h–: c20d⁶ c21dᵖ c19gᵖᵘ c25g⁶ Apr 13] angular gelding: winning hurdler: useful chaser: won 6-runner minor event at Ascot in December by short head from Crozan: better effort after (lost action next start) when sixth to Reveillez in quite valuable handicap at Aintree, unable to land blow after mistakes: stays 25f: unraced on firm going, acts on any other: consistent. *D. E. Pipe* **c144 h–**

TAMBOURINE DAVIS (FR) 5 b.m. Cadoudal (FR) – Trumpet Davis (FR) (Rose Laurel) [2006/7 F96: 16d² 19d* 21d* 21gᵖᵘ Mar 24] tall, useful-looking mare: runner-up in bumpers: took well to hurdling, winning mares novices at Taunton in November and Ludlow in December: again favourite, ran as if amiss in listed event at Newbury on handicap debut: stays 21f: raced on good going or softer: sold 40,000 gns Doncaster May Sales. *N. J. Henderson* **h111**

TAMMANY (IRE) 5 ch.m. In The Wings – Tallahassee Spirit (THA) (Presidential (USA)) [2006/7 19d 16m 16f 16f³ 16g 20d³ Oct 20] lightly raced on Flat: poor novice hurdler: stays 2½m: acts on firm and good to soft going. *Eoin Doyle, Ireland* **h77**

TAMMY 4 b.f. Tamure (IRE) – Heather Honey (Insan (USA)) [2006/7 17g⁶ 16m 16d Oct 11] small filly: no form on Flat or in juvenile hurdles. *C. W. Thornton* **h–**

TAMREEN (IRE) 6 b.g. Bahhare (USA) – Na-Ayim (IRE) (Shirley Heights) [2006/7 h109: 17g⁴ 16g 16g 16d⁵ 16d 16g⁵ 18g⁶ Apr 10] good-topped gelding: fair handicap hurdler: stays 2¼m: raced on good ground or softer: tried in cheekpieces, usually blinkered: has had tongue tied: temperamental. *G. L. Moore* **h101 §**

williamhill.co.uk Marathon Chase (Handicap), Sandown—
Tana River (stripes) and Simon dominate in this long-distance affair

TANAGER 12 ch.g. Carlingford Castle – Tangara (Town Crier) [2006/7 c89§: c21g Apr 12] workmanlike gelding: fairly useful hunter chaser at best, below form in 3 starts since 2004/5: stays 3¼m: acts on heavy going: usually blinkered: unreliable. *Mrs K. Lawther*   **c– §**

TANA RIVER (IRE) 11 b.g. Over The River (FR) – Home In The Glen (Furry Glen) [2006/7 c125, h123: c27d* c29s* c29s[pu] 23s Feb 17] sturdy gelding: winning hurdler: useful handicap chaser: better than ever in 2006/7, winning at Wincanton (by 25 lengths from eased Xellance) in November and Sandown (beat Simon by 2 lengths in quite valuable event) in December, leading/disputing throughout each time: stays 29f: acts on heavy going: has shaped as if amiss more than once. *Miss E. C. Lavelle*   **c136 h–**

TANDORI 5 b.m. El Conquistador – Leatan (Leander) [2006/7 F14g 17s[su] 19v 17s[5] Mar 12] first foal: dam winning pointer: well held in bumper: signs of ability over hurdles. *J. D. Frost*   **h67 F–**

TANGO ROYAL (FR) 11 gr.g. Royal Charter (FR) – Nazia (FR) (Zino) [2006/7 c138d, h–: c20g c23m[4] c23g c21d[3] c24d[3] c24s* c24d[4] 21g[pu] Mar 28] lengthy gelding: winning hurdler: fairly useful handicap chaser: won at Newbury in December by ½ length from Irish Raptor: stays 3m: probably acts on any going: visored last 7 starts: tongue tied: usually held up: sketchy jumper. *D. E. Pipe*   **c129 x h–**

TANIKOS (FR) 8 b.g. Nikos – Tamana (USA) (Northern Baby (CAN)) [2006/7 c126, h118: c16g[pu] c20g[3] 17s c17d[3] c16g Mar 16] big, workmanlike gelding: winning hurdler: fairly useful handicap chaser: back to form when 6½ lengths third to Marcel at Ascot fourth outing: effective at 2m to 2½m: acts on soft going: none too reliable. *N. J. Henderson*   **c119 h–**

TANK BUSTER (FR) 7 b.g. Executive Perk – Macfarly (IRE) (Phardante (FR)) [2006/7 c–, h85?: c24s[2] c24s c24s c24d* c29g[3] c24g[2] Mar 29] good-topped gelding: well held in novice hurdles: modest chaser: won handicap at Ludlow in January: stays 29f: raced on good ground or softer (acts on soft). *Mrs E. Langley*   **c88 h–**

TANMEYA 6 gr.m. Linamix (FR) – Ta Awun (USA) (Housebuster (USA)) [2006/7 h–: 16v 16g 16m[pu] 16g[5] Jul 31] tall, lengthy mare: little show over hurdles: tried in eye-shields: sold 800 gns Doncaster August Sales, won maiden point in April. *R. C. Guest*   **h–**

948

TANNERS COURT 10 b.g. Framlington Court – True Nell (Neltino) [2006/7 16s² 17s **h108**
22s* 20s⁵ 20d² Mar 17] good-topped gelding: fair hurdler, off nearly 2 years before
reappearance: won maiden at Stratford in February: stays 2¾m: acts on soft going: free-
going sort, usually races prominently: trainer ridden: consistent. *Miss C. Dyson*

TANNERS DEN 7 br.g. Abzu – Equilibrium (Statoblest) [2006/7 16dᵖᵘ 16sᵖᵘ 16d **h–**
Mar 26] compact gelding: no sign of ability. *Miss C. Dyson*

TANNERS GROVE 6 b.g. Theatrical Charmer – Heldigvis (Hot Grove) [2006/7 h–, **h–**
F–: 16s⁶ May 20] no sign of ability: tried tongue tied. *Miss C. Dyson*

TANNING 5 b.m. Atraf – Gerundive (USA) (Twilight Agenda (USA)) [2006/7 16m⁶ **h85**
17m 19g⁶ 19g 24m⁵ 22m³ 21f⁶ 19mˣ 22d² 21g Nov 2] modest on Flat (stays 12.6f):
modest hurdler: won seller at Towcester in October: stays 2¾m: acts on good to firm and
good to soft ground: in cheekpieces last 7 starts. *M. Appleby*

TANTERARI (IRE) 9 b.g. Safety Catch (USA) – Cobblers Crest (IRE) (Step Together **c117 §**
(USA)) [2006/7 c109, h–: c26dᵖᵘ c26g* c27s* c26g c26s³ c24v c24s c24s⁴ c23d Mar 26] **h–**
rangy gelding: winning hurdler: fairly useful handicap chaser on his day: back to form
when winning at Fontwell (easily) in September, and followed up at Wincanton (beat
Tribal Venture by 1¼ lengths) 3 weeks later: out of sorts after: stays 27f: raced mainly on
good going or softer (acts on heavy): tongue tied nowadays: held up: not one to rely on.
D. E. Pipe

TANTIEN 5 b.m. Diktat – Tahilla (Moorestyle) [2006/7 16g 17gᵖᵘ Mar 24] poor maiden **h–**
on Flat (seems to stay 11f): no show over hurdles: tried blinkered. *T. Keddy*

TANZANITE DAWN 6 b.m. Gunner B – Quiet Dawn (Lighter) [2006/7 h–, F–: 17vˣ **h88**
19vˣ 22v⁴ Feb 13] sturdy mare: modest hurdler: left A. Turnell and off 10 months,
improved in 2006/7, winning handicaps at Folkestone (mares novice, by 18 lengths) and
Towcester (amateur event) in January: stays 2¾m: acts on heavy going. *Simon Earle*

TAP END 4 b.g. Slip Anchor – Tapas En Bal (FR) (Mille Balles (FR)) [2006/7 F14d³ **h– p**
F17d⁴ 17gᵖᵘ Apr 23] first foal: dam, French 7f/1m winner (including at 2 yrs), half-sister **F86**
to very smart performer up to 2m Give The Slip: in frame in bumpers: soon plenty to do
and not knocked about in juvenile maiden on hurdling debut: tried tongue tied: likely to
do better. *M. W. Easterby*

TARALINA 5 b.m. Kayf Tara – La Princesse (Le Bavard (FR)) [2006/7 F17g² F17g³ **F85 +**
Apr 27] 3,400 4-y-o: fifth foal: half-sister to winning pointer by Henbit: dam, fair hurdler
up to 2¾m, half-sister to Irish National winner Timbera: fair form when placed in
bumpers: still green, 4¾ lengths third to Covert Mission at Newton Abbot. *P. F. Nicholls*

TARANIS 4 b.g. Lomitas – Woodbeck (Terimon) [2006/7 17m³ Mar 29] modest maiden **h102 p**
on Flat (stays 1½m), sold out of Sir Mark Prescott's stable 30,000 gns Newmarket
Autumn Sales: 5½ lengths third to Classic Dream in juvenile at Hereford on hurdling
debut: likely to improve. *N. J. Henderson*

TARANIS (FR) 6 ch.g. Mansonnien (FR) – Vikosa (FR) (Nikos) [2006/7 c139p, **c159**
h–: 20s* c20dᶠ c21s³ 22d* c21g* c20g² Apr 13] **h140**
    Unbeaten in four completed starts over fences in 2005/6, Taranis enjoyed
an excellent second campaign in chases, showing very smart form in winning the
Grade 2 Festival Trophy, sponsored by Ryanair, at the Cheltenham Festival and
being placed in good company on both his other completed starts. He supplemented
those earnings with successes in two valuable handicap hurdles, the listed Blue
Square Silver Trophy at Chepstow and the Grade 3 Sandown Handicap. The latter
race, under the totescoop6 banner, gained wide publicity, through the success of
Agnes Haddock, a cleaner from Cheshire who won £688,620 for just a £2 stake
by picking the six Scoop6 winning horses the previous week and then plumping
for Taranis in what was the bonus race. Her success was the stuff of dreams for the
tabloids and the sponsors, who have been the subject of criticism, both for setting
the minimum stake as high as £2 and for the bet supposedly favouring big syndicates. Totesport reported in March that the number of '£2 players' contributing to
the pool had increased significantly in the wake of Haddock's success. Denman's
part-owner, the millionaire punter Harry Findlay, headed a syndicate that was
reported to have staked £180,000 when landing a total of £1.3m by winning the
Scoop6 and bonus in May, which works out at odds of a little over 7/1. Findlay and
associates also won £2m when landing the jackpot prize of rival pool bet Race O on
consecutive afternoons earlier that month.

totescoop6 Sandown Handicap Hurdle—
a second valuable hurdles win of the campaign for Taranis (checked sleeves),
who holds off the late challenge of Whispered Secret (No.14); top weight Kasbah Bliss (left) takes fourth

Taranis reappeared at Chepstow in October off what looked a favourable mark if he could reproduce anything like the improved form he'd shown when sent over fences the previous season (he appeared in a handicap chase on his next start off a BHB mark 27 lb higher). Taranis made the most of his opportunity at Chepstow, landing the odds by three lengths from Saltango after taking a while to get going on the extended run-in (final flight was omitted), and overcame a rise of 7 lb to win at Sandown three and a half months later. In a much more competitive affair than at Chepstow, Taranis prevailed in a steadily-run contest by half a length from the strong-finishing Whispered Secret, ironically the gelding who'd completed the sixth leg of Mrs Haddock's successful Scoop6 bet the previous weekend when winning the Ladbrokes Trophy Chase at Cheltenham. Taranis's successes over hurdles were not the first time his stable's horses had successfully mixed hurdling and chasing. Ad Hoc is probably the best example of a Paul Nicholls-trained staying chaser being freshened up by a spell of novice hurdling, while the top staying novice chaser of 2005/6 Star de Mohaison was successful on his return in the valuable listed staying handicap hurdle at the Cheltenham Open meeting.

Examples of good horses mixing chasing and hurdling in Britain were rare until recent times. The outstanding chaser Flyingbolt finished third in the 1966 Champion Hurdle the day after winning the Champion Chase, a feat considered as remarkable then for the switch in disciplines as it would be now for the demands made on the horse. Incidentally, that year's Champion Hurdle winner Salmon Spray had also mixed hurdling with chasing, the Bob Turnell-trained gelding having finished third to Flyingbolt in the Black & White Gold Cup at Ascot (over fences) earlier in the season. In the 'seventies, that globe-trotting money-spinner Grand Canyon mixed hurdles and fences with considerable success, whilst Gaye Chance switched from chasing (runner-up in that season's Hennessy Cognac Gold Cup) to hurdling to win the Rendlesham and Stayers' Hurdles in 1983/4. One of Gaye Chance's finest efforts as a novice chaser had come when runner-up to the more experienced Combs Ditch in the 1983 Lambert & Butler Premier Chase Final at Ascot, and the latter gelding's trainer David Elsworth also wasn't adverse to using the hurdles route when it came to preparing for the two premier chases of 1984/5. Combs Ditch won a handicap hurdle at Cheltenham just three weeks before pushing

Burrough Hill Lad to a short head in the King George VI Chase, whilst he was warmed up for the Cheltenham Gold Cup (where he was a disappointing favourite) with a fine second place over hurdles to Rose Ravine, who went on to succeed Gaye Chance on the Stayers' Hurdle roll of honour. Meanwhile, Taranis isn't the first horse who has won the Silver Trophy Hurdle at Chepstow prior to achieving even greater success over fences later in the season—2000 winner Young Spartacus went on to land both the Ladbrokes Trophy and the Racing Post Chase, whilst Lacdoudal's two subsequent chasing wins in 2005/6 included the Betfred Gold Cup.

It is fair to say that leading jumpers trained in France and Ireland have tended to straddle the two disciplines with more regularity, even excluding those recent Irish-trained Grand National candidates who have tended to be campaigned over hurdles to protect their handicap marks over fences. In 1978/9, the Mick O'Toole-trained Chinrullah broke off from a very successful novice chase campaign to land that season's Irish Sweeps Hurdle (veteran trainer Bunny Cox did the same with Atone fifteen years later). Chinrullah continued to mix hurdling and chasing the following season, finishing third under top weight in the Irish Sweeps prior to emulating Flyingbolt with two runs at the Cheltenham Festival, running out a wide-margin winner of the Champion Chase just twenty-four hours before finishing a respectable fifth in the Cheltenham Gold Cup. Unfortunately he was disqualified from both races on technical grounds, along with two other Irish-trained horses at that year's Festival (including Gold Cup winner Tied Cottage), prohibited substances traced to contaminated feed. More recently, the top-notch jumpers Dorans Pride and Rule Supreme have successfully combined the roles, whilst leading chasers such as Imperial Call and Beef Or Salmon (including last season) both performed with distinction back over hurdles. The 2006 Champion Chase winner Newmill gained his only success of the latest season in a Grade 2 hurdle, while the Willie Mullins-trained veterans Mossy Green and Adamant Approach mixed the two to good effect. The 'Three Musketeers'—the Francois Doumen-trained Ubu III, Ucello III and The Fellow—who dominated the French jumping scene in the early-'nineties were all campaigned regularly over both hurdles and fences. France's current jumping star Mid Dancer, unbeaten in seventeen races on home soil, defeated the 2006 Grand Steeple-Chase de Paris winner Princesse d'Anjou in a Grade 2 hurdle before winning the latest Grand Steeple-Chase in May.

Ryanair Chase (Festival Trophy), Cheltenham—a winning return to fences as Taranis hangs on from Our Vic (left) and Billyvoddan (blinkers) in a thriller

Mrs A. B. Yeoman & Mr C. R. Whittaker's "Taranis"

Winning two valuable handicap hurdles with Taranis was clearly excellent placing by his stable but his mark over fences looked a stiffish one. That view appeared to be confirmed when he ran in the big handicap chases before Christmas at Cheltenham. Taranis was well supported for the Paddy Power Gold Cup, sent off third favourite, and was still in contention when falling two out, though it's unlikely he'd have troubled the winner Exotic Dancer (who received 10 lb) had he completed. A month later, in the boylesports.com Gold Cup, he took third behind Exotic Dancer and Knowhere, meeting the winner at level weights this time.

The Festival Trophy attracted nine runners, the field a hotch-potch of those that might have run elsewhere and those that were chancing their luck in a higher grade (not exactly the right recipe for a race now promoted to championship status). Monet's Garden, impressive winner of the Ascot Chase the previous month, headed the market, but he faced stern opposition from the Charlie Hall winner Our Vic and the King George third Racing Demon (a faller when reverting to hurdles himself on his previous start). The last two were running in preference to contesting the Cheltenham Gold Cup, while Monet's Garden might well have been sent for the Champion Chase. Neither Hi Cloy nor 2005 winner Thisthatandtother had been at their very best in 2006/7 and several others in the field, including last-time handicap winners Too Forward and Billyvoddan, were stepping up in class. The race was shaped by the enigmatic outsider Crozan. Setting a good pace, he was still in front when falling four out, leaving Taranis with the advantage and hampering several,

952

including Our Vic and Billyvoddan, in the process. Taranis made the most of the opportunity, holding on by a neck and half a length from that pair in an exciting finish, the runner-up Our Vic giving him 5 lb, as was fourth-placed Monet's Garden. Taranis might have been a fortunate winner, and he couldn't confirm placings with Monet's Garden in the Melling Chase at Aintree, but he still ran creditably in finishing three and a half lengths second there (ahead of Well Chief). Nevertheless, he looked a bit lighter in appearance and his earlier exertions might have taken the edge off him. Taranis is young enough, at six, and there may be more to come from him in 2007/8, possibly over further than two miles five furlongs, the longest trip he has tackled so far over fences. Nicholls is reportedly keen to add him to the stable's already-strong roster for the 2008 Cheltenham Gold Cup.

		Tip Moss	Luthier
	Mansonnien (FR)	(ch 1972)	Top Twig
	(ch 1984)	Association	Margouillat
Taranis (FR)		(ch 1977)	La Soupe
(ch.g. 2001)		Nikos	Nonoalco
	Vikosa (FR)	(br 1981)	No No Nanette
	(ch 1996)	Vimosa	Armos
		(ch 1987)	Qualite de La Vie

The tall, useful-looking Taranis is a thoroughbred, by Mansonnien out of Vikosa, who won over fences at Dieppe and three times over hurdles at Auteuil as a three-year-old. He is her first foal. Vikosa is a half-sister to a winning hurdler (also by Mansonnien) and out of a half-sister to the prolific winning French hurdler/chaser Pantruche who gained his most notable win in the Prix Edmond Barrachin, a race in which Luzcadou, subsequently a useful chaser for Ferdy Murphy, finished third. However, this is mostly a Flat-oriented family. The grandam Vimosa was successful six times at up to a mile and a half on the Flat and was also placed over hurdles and fences. All told, ten of the third dam Qualite de La Vie's twelve foals won, nearly all of them on the Flat. Qualite de La Vie herself won three times at around a mile and three quarters on the Flat. Taranis will stay three miles. Taranis acts on soft going and unseated his rider during the early stages of his only start on firmer than good. He has been tongue tied since his reappearance in 2005/6. Like quite a few of his stable companions, he has reportedly had a breathing operation. *P. F. Nicholls*

TARA QUEEN 4 b.f. Kayf Tara – Kaydee Queen (IRE) (Bob's Return (IRE)) [2006/7 F12s F14s⁴ F16d³ Mar 22] €45,000 3-y-o: sturdy filly: first foal: dam unraced half-sister to useful chaser around 2m Queen of Spades, out of sister to very smart 3m chaser Garamycin: modest form in bumpers. *Carl Llewellyn* **F75**

TARAS KNIGHT (IRE) 5 b.g. Indian Danehill (IRE) – Queen of Art (IRE) (Royal Academy (USA)) [2006/7 F79: 17m⁴ 19g³ 17m^F 17m² 17g⁴ 16g* 16g 20d 16s Apr 26] useful-looking gelding: modest hurdler: won novice seller at Kelso (sold from J. Quinn 5,500 gns) in November: well held after: probably stays 19f: acts on good to firm going: usually tongue tied. *Miss Lucinda V. Russell* **h97**

TAR BRIDGE (IRE) 7 b.g. Arctic Cider (USA) – Amber Goer (Amber Rama (USA)) [2006/7 c25g⁴ c24g^F Apr 27] well beaten in Irish points prior to runner-up on British debut in February: let down by jumping in hunters. *W. K. Goldsworthy* **c–**

TARKESAR (IRE) 5 b.g. Desert Prince (IRE) – Tarwila (IRE) (In The Wings) [2006/7 16g 16d 16v 16d 16g² 17m³ 16f² Apr 22] rather leggy gelding: twice-raced on Flat at 3 yrs, won 9.5f maiden in June: sold out of J. Oxx's stable €28,000 Goffs October (2005) Sales: modest novice hurdler, left F. Jordan after third start: raced around 2m: acts on firm going: takes strong hold. *P. A. Blockley* **h89**

TARLAC (GER) 6 ch.g. Dashing Blade – Tintina (USA) (General Assembly (USA)) [2006/7 h124: 16d* 16d² 16d 17g Mar 16] close-coupled gelding: useful handicap hurdler: landed odds at Ascot in November with plenty in hand: further progress when 2 lengths second of 20 to Acambo in Ladbroke at same course month later: never dangerous in very valuable events last 2 starts: will prove best at 2m: has won on heavy going, probably best under less testing conditions (yet to race on firmer than good). *N. J. Henderson* **h134**

TAROTINO (FR) 5 b.g. Le Balafre (FR) – Zvetlana (Scorpio (FR)) [2006/7 17s⁴ 16s³ 20s⁴ 16s* 20s* 20s⁴ 20g Apr 7] leggy, useful-looking gelding: seventh foal: half-brother to 13.5f winner Le Clan Normand (by Chef de Clan): dam placed over hurdles/fences up **h123**

to 2½m: fairly useful novice hurdler, left Y. Fouin after debut: won at Wincanton in January and Fakenham (by 4 lengths from Apollo Lady) in February: good 6¾ lengths fourth of 16 to Albertas Run in valuable handicap at Sandown next time: stays 2½m: raced mainly on soft ground: sold 24,000 gns Doncaster May Sales. *N. J. Henderson*

TARTAN CLASSIC (IRE) 6 b.g. Classic Cliche (IRE) – Laboc (Rymer) [2006/7 h–: 23s³ 24g c27dᵖᵘ Nov 21] good-topped gelding: form (poor) over hurdles only on return: blinkered, no show in handicap on chasing debut: looks a thorough stayer. *J. Howard Johnson* **c–** **h68**

TARTAN SNOW 7 b.g. Valseur (USA) – Whitemoss Leader (IRE) (Supreme Leader) [2006/7 20sᵖᵘ 20s 20vᵖᵘ 16v³ Mar 22] sturdy gelding: first foal: dam lightly raced and little form over hurdles: no solid form over hurdles. *W. S. Coltherd* **h–**

TASHKANDI (IRE) 7 gr.g. Polish Precedent (USA) – Tashiriya (IRE) (Kenmare (FR)) [2006/7 h–: 17d* 16m² 20g 17v² 17s* 16d* 16d⁶ 16gᵘʳ 16g Apr 8] strong, lengthy gelding: smart at best on Flat (stays 1¼m), successful in June: much improved over hurdles in 2006/7, winning handicaps at Newton Abbot (novice, easily) in August and Market Rasen (lady riders) and Kempton (conditional jockeys novice) in November: likely to prove best around 2m: has won on soft going, likely to prove best under less testing conditions (acts on good to firm): tried visored, effective in cheekpieces or without: tongue tied once: has shaped as if amiss more than once. *P. Bowen* **h100**

TASMAN (IRE) 7 ch.g. Definite Article – Felin Special (Lyphard's Special (USA)) [2006/7 22m² 24v 22m⁵ 20m Apr 24] leggy, close-coupled gelding: maiden on Flat: useful hurdler, missed 2005/6: good second to Diego Garcia in handicap at Galway: left D. Weld and off 4 months, respectable fifth to Supreme Being in similar event at Fairyhouse: should stay 3m: acts on heavy and good to firm going. *Liam McAteer, Ireland* **h134**

TASTES LIKE MORE (IRE) 5 b.m. Close Conflict (USA) – Fly Your Kite (IRE) (Silver Kite (USA)) [2006/7 F17v⁵ 17s⁶ 20v⁴ 20v⁵ 25v c24g² c24gᶠ Apr 8] good-bodied mare: fourth foal: half-sister to winner in Italy by Portrait Gallery: dam, fair maiden, stayed 7f: won mares maiden Irish point in 2006: well held in bumper: poor form over hurdles/in chases: stays 3m: acts on heavy ground: tried blinkered. *D. McCain Jnr* **c84** **h76** **F62**

TA TA FOR NOW 10 b.g. Ezzoud (IRE) – Exit Laughing (Shaab) [2006/7 c91§, h–: c25f³ c25m⁴ c24m⁵ c24gᵘʳ c26d⁴ c24s⁶ c25g³ c26g Apr 7] lengthy gelding: winning hurdler: poor handicap chaser: stays 31f: acts on soft and firm going: tried blinkered/in cheekpieces: unreliable. *Mrs S. C. Bradburne* **c81 §** **h–**

TATE TIROL (IRE) 10 b.g. Tirol – Lovely Deise (IRE) (Tate Gallery (USA)) [2006/7 16gᵖᵘ Mar 20] big, workmanlike gelding: winning hurdler: runner-up only start in chase: lightly raced and no form in points nowadays. *S. J. Gilmore* **c–** **h–**

TAVALU (USA) 5 b.g. Kingmambo (USA) – Larrocha (IRE) (Sadler's Wells (USA)) [2006/7 18m⁴ 18m² 18m² 19d³ 21m³ Apr 8] fair maiden on Flat (stays 17f): modest novice hurdler: should stay beyond 2¼m: acts on good to firm going: blinkered fourth outing (lame). *G. L. Moore* **h98**

TAYMAN (IRE) 5 b. or br.g. Sinndar (IRE) – Sweet Emotion (IRE) (Bering) [2006/7 16d⁵ Feb 2] fair on Flat (stays 1½m), successful in August, sold out of G. Wragg's stable 20,000 gns Newmarket Autumn Sales: remote fifth of 16 to Laustra Bad in novice at Chepstow on hurdling debut, plenty to do and not knocked about: should improve. *C. J. Mann* **h77 p**

TAZBAR (IRE) 5 b.g. Tiraaz (USA) – Candy Bar (IRE) (Montelimar (USA)) [2006/7 F16m* F16g² F16g* F16g* Mar 17] good-bodied gelding: second foal: dam, poor over hurdles, half-sister to fairly useful 2m hurdler Instant Tan: looked very good prospect in bumpers, winning at Perth in June, Catterick (never off bridle) in November and Wetherby (useful form, beat Herbie by 2 lengths despite being caught in poor position) in March: unlucky when fast-finishing second to Harrowman at Haydock. *K. G. Reveley* **F114**

TCHERINA (IRE) 5 b.m. Danehill Dancer (IRE) – Forget Paris (IRE) (Broken Hearted) [2006/7 16d⁴ 16s⁴ 16s³ Mar 7] sturdy mare: fairly useful on Flat (stays 1½m): poor form in frame over hurdles: raced at 2m on good to soft/soft ground: should do better. *T. D. Easterby* **h82 p**

TEACH TO PREACH (USA) 4 ch.g. Pulpit (USA) – Chateaubaby (USA) (Nureyev (USA)) [2006/7 16d Dec 29] lengthy gelding: lightly raced on Flat, successful in 1m maiden in April, well held after, sold out of B. Hills's stable 15,000 gns Newmarket Autumn Sales: soundly beaten in juvenile on hurdling debut. *B. De Haan* **h–**

TEAM CAPTAIN 13 ch.g. Teamster – Silly Sausage (Silly Answer) [2006/7 c92§: c25d^{pu} c25m^5 c25m^5 Jun 19] angular gelding: modest handicap chaser on his day, little show since winning on 2005/6 reappearance: stays 3½m: acts on firm and good to soft going: tried in cheekpieces: inconsistent. *C. J. Down*   **c65 §**

TEAM CHASER (IRE) 6 b.g. Dr Massini (IRE) – New Chello (IRE) (Orchestra) [2006/7 F17s^2 F17g* Mar 25] €15,000 4-y-o: fourth foal: half-brother to modest hurdler/ fair chaser New Perk (by Executive Perk), stays 27f, and 2 winning pointers by Glacial Storm: dam unraced half-sister to fairly useful chaser up to 25f Phar From A Fiddle, out of half-sister to very smart 2m chaser Wolf of Badenoch: won maiden point in 2006: fairly useful form in bumpers: won at Taunton in March by 1¼ lengths from Taralina, making all: will be suited by 2½m+. *J. A. B. Old*   **F97**

TEAMGEIST (IRE) 6 b.g. Taipan (IRE) – Stage Debut (Decent Fellow) [2006/7 F16v^4 20v^2 Feb 13] €20,000 4-y-o: rangy gelding: half-brother to useful staying chaser Hati Roy (by Lafontaine) and fair winning 21f chaser Award (by Executive Perk): dam unraced half-sister to useful staying hurdler Mac Three: won maiden Irish point on debut in 2006: bought 40,000 gns Doncaster August Sales: shaped promisingly in bumper/ maiden hurdle, still green when 1¼ lengths second to Sydney in latter at Folkestone: will stay 3m: likely to improve. *C. J. Mann*   **h109 p**
F95

TEAM LEADER (IRE) 7 b.g. Supreme Leader – Lyshie Lashie (Mandalus) [2006/7 F90: 22s* 22d Dec 15] strong, lengthy gelding: chasing type: better effort in bumpers when fifth at Bangor: successful hurdling debut when beating Once A Brownie a neck in maiden at Stratford in October, hanging right run-in: mistakes and ran no sort of race in handicap 2 months later: likely to stay 3m: acts on soft ground. *N. A. Twiston-Davies*   **h100**

TEAM SECRET 6 b.m. Teamster – Silly Sausage (Silly Answer) [2006/7 F16g Mar 24] rather unfurnished mare: sister to winning chaser Team Captain, stays 3½m: dam poor 2m novice hurdler: well held in bumper on debut. *C. J. Down*   **F—**

TEAM TASSEL (IRE) 9 b.g. Be My Native (USA) – Alcmena's Last (Pauper) [2006/7 c113§, h–§: 22g^6 22m^4 Apr 11] tall gelding: winning hurdler/maiden chaser, has gone wrong way temperamentally: should stay 3m: acts on good to soft going: tried visored/in cheekpieces: tongue tied in 2006/7: one to avoid. *D. E. Pipe*   **c– §**
h– §

TEARS OF JADE (IRE) 6 b. or br.m. Presenting – Orient Nickel (IRE) (Executive Perk) [2006/7 F17d^6 F18v Dec 10] €4,500 4-y-o: second foal: dam unraced: poor form on first of 2 outings in bumpers. *E. U. Hales, Ireland*   **F70**

TECH EAGLE (IRE) 7 b.h. Eagle Eyed (USA) – Technik (GER) (Nebos (GER)) [2006/7 h115+: 17m^2 Jun 30] lengthy horse: fairly useful hurdler: good second to Hilltime in handicap at Market Rasen only start in 2006/7: stays 2¼m: acts on firm and soft going. *R. Curtis*   **h119**

TED MOSS 6 b.g. Supreme Leader – Carlingford Gale (IRE) (Carlingford Castle) [2006/7 17s 17s 16v^4 20s^4 25v^4 Mar 12] good-topped gelding: first foal: dam, fairly useful chaser, stayed 3¼m: poor novice hurdler: should stay beyond 2½m: raced on soft/ heavy ground. *T. R. George*   **h83**

TEE-JAY (IRE) 11 ch.g. Un Desperado (FR) – N T Nad (Welsh Pageant) [2006/7 c89, h–: c25m c25m^6 c22g^6 c26d^3 c25f^3 c25g* c25s^2 c25d^{pu} Oct 21] workmanlike gelding: winning hurdler: modest chaser: won minor event at Hexham (fifth course success, by 25 lengths) in October: stays 27f: acts on soft and good to firm going: in cheekpieces last 3 starts. *Micky Hammond*   **c89**
h–

TEEMING RAIN (IRE) 8 b.g. Supreme Leader – Lady Graduate (IRE) (Le Bavard (FR)) [2006/7 20s 24v c24d^3 c28s* c33v^{pu} Feb 24] strong, good-topped gelding: one-time useful hurdler, well held in handicap on return: fairly useful handicap chaser: won 16-runner event at Punchestown in February by ¾ length from Dublin Hunter: disappointing favourite for valuable event at Newcastle 20 days later (stopped quickly after 6 out): stays 3½m: raced on going softer than good (acts on heavy): usually patiently ridden. *C. F. Swan, Ireland*   **c121**
h–

TEENAGER 7 b.m. Young Ern – Washita (Valiyar) [2006/7 16s Oct 25] leggy mare: maiden hurdler, probably flattered when twice in frame: tried tongue tied. *P. Wegmann*   **h—**

TEENYBASH 5 b.m. Overbury (IRE) – Ayeknowso (Teenoso (USA)) [2006/7 F16d F17v 20s^{pu} Apr 25] first foal: dam poor staying novice hurdler: no form in bumpers/ maiden hurdle. *Mrs J. C. McGregor*   **h—**
F—

TEES COMPONENTS 12 b.g. Risk Me (FR) – Lady Warninglid (Ela-Mana-Mou) [2006/7 c–p, h135: 25s^3 23d^4 20s Dec 16] strong gelding: useful hurdler, has stood   **c—**
h134

little racing: creditable efforts first 2 starts, fourth to Halcon Genelardais in handicap at Haydock: detached by halfway there next time: unseated only outing over fences: stays 25f: acts on soft and good to firm going: tongue tied: patiently ridden: tends to edge left under pressure. *K. G. Reveley*

TEETON BABYSHAM 7 b.g. Shambo – Teeton Bubbley (Neltino) [2006/7 h121: c24s² Oct 21] winning pointer: fairly useful form when successful in maiden hurdle in 2005/6: off 6½ months, 9 lengths second of 3 finishers to Miko de Beauchene in maiden at Chepstow on chasing debut: will stay beyond 3m: acts on heavy going: tried tongue tied. *P. F. Nicholls* **c113 h–**

TEETON PRINCE 8 b.g. Shambo – Teeton Frolic (Sunley Builds) [2006/7 c21g⁴ Apr 9] modest pointer, successful twice in 2007: last of 4 finishers in novice hunter at Fakenham on chase debut. *Mrs Joan Tice* **c71**

TELEGONUS 4 b.g. Fantastic Light (USA) – Circe's Isle (Be My Guest (USA)) [2006/7 18gᵘʳ 16m⁵ 16g 17v Nov 30] half-brother to fairly useful hurdler Flint Knapper (by Kris), stayed 2½m, and fair hurdler Isle de Maurice (by Sinndar), stays 25f: lightly-raced maiden on Flat, sold out of G. Wragg's stable 20,000 gns Newmarket July Sales: no solid form in juvenile hurdles. *C. E. Longsdon* **h–**

TELEMOSS (IRE) 13 b.g. Montelimar (USA) – Shan's Moss (Le Moss) [2006/7 c118, h–: c20v³ c26gᵘʳ Mar 16] rangy, useful-looking gelding: winning hurdler: useful hunter chaser in 2006, off 10 months prior to unseating sixth in Foxhunter at Cheltenham: stays 3¼m: acts on good to firm and heavy going. *N. G. Richards* **c81 h–**

TELLEM NOTING (IRE) 10 b.g. Treasure Hunter – Imperial Butterfly (IRE) (Euphemism) [2006/7 c–§, h–§: c21g⁵ May 24] modest pointer: little form in chases: tried in cheekpieces/blinkers: has had tongue tied: has refused to race: sold £850 Ascot August Sales. *Mrs F. Marshall* **c– § h– §**

TELL HENRY (IRE) 7 ch.g. Broken Hearted – Valleymay (IRE) (King's Ride) [2006/7 h–, F95: 21m² 17d² 20g 16v* 20v² 20m* Apr 9] lengthy gelding: bumper winner: fair novice hurdler: easily landed odds at Ayr (maiden) in December and Sedgefield (made all) in April: stays 21f: acts on good to firm and heavy ground: free-going sort. *M. Todhunter* **h111**

TELLITLIKEITIS 6 b.g. Defacto (USA) – Chimes of Peace (Magic Ring (IRE)) [2006/7 F17g F16d F16m Nov 24] first foal: dam 1m winner: well beaten in bumpers and seller on Flat. *Miss Kariana Key* **F–**

TELL THE TREES 6 br.m. Tamure (IRE) – Bluebell Copse (Formidable (USA)) [2006/7 h104: 22m 17d May 26] small, sparely-made mare: fair handicap hurdler, well held in 2006/7: stays 27f: acts on good to firm and good to soft going (below form on soft/heavy): tried visored, in cheekpieces 3 of last 4 starts: not a fluent jumper: signs of temperament. *D. E. Pipe* **h–**

TEMOIN 7 b.g. Groom Dancer (USA) – Kowtow (USA) (Shadeed (USA)) [2006/7 h137: 24dᵖᵘ 25d³ 20v² 24g Mar 15] tall gelding: useful hurdler: good third to Mighty Man in muddling Grade 1 Long Walk Hurdle at Ascot: laboured performances after, blinkered when facing stiff task final start: stays 25f: acts on good to firm and heavy going: one to be wary of. *N. J. Henderson* **h139 §**

TEMPER LAD (USA) 12 b.g. Riverman (USA) – Dokki (USA) (Northern Dancer) [2006/7 h88: 24g² 27m c23m⁶ 22s 22s 16v* 24v Mar 10] neat gelding: modest handicap hurdler: off 2 months, back to form when winning selling event at Towcester in February: none too fluent when well held on chasing debut: effective over testing 2m and stays 27f: probably acts on any ground: tried blinkered: formerly often tongue tied. *J. D. Frost* **c– h87**

TEMPLARS (IRE) 5 ch.g. Moscow Society (USA) – Cool Carling (Carlingford Castle) [2006/7 F17sᵖᵘ Nov 14] lengthy gelding: fifth foal: dam winning pointer: won maiden Irish point in 2006: bought 12,500 gns Doncaster May Sales: no show in bumper: dead. *R. Rowe* **F–**

TEMPLE DOG (IRE) 11 ch.g. Un Desperado (FR) – Shower (Kings Lake (USA)) [2006/7 c24s³ c22d⁵ c23vᵖᵘ c25mᵖᵘ Apr 15] workmanlike gelding: fairly useful hurdler/ fair chaser at best, has become most temperamental: won point in January: left M. Loggin before final outing: has worn blinkers/cheekpieces: one to avoid. *J. R. Cornwall* **c86 § h– §**

TEMPLE GLEN 8 gr.g. Accondy (IRE) – Wish Me Well (Asir) [2006/7 c20m Jun 3] won maiden point in 2006: seventh of 10 finishers in hunter on chase debut. *Miss J. M. Hollands* **c69**

TEMPLE PLACE (IRE) 6 b.g. Sadler's Wells (USA) – Puzzled Look (USA) (Gulch (USA)) [2006/7 h112: 17s⁶ 16m⁶ 17s⁵ 17g 16g Apr 16] strong, angular gelding: winning hurdler: no form in handicaps in 2006/7: raced around 2m: acts on soft going: usually tongue tied: has looked awkward ride. *D. McCain Jnr*   h–

TEMPLER (IRE) 6 ch.g. Charmer – Ballinamona Lady (IRE) (Le Bavard (FR)) [2006/7 h96, F96: 17m² 17g² 16d* 17v⁴ 19g⁴ 20g² 20g² Apr 27] leggy gelding: fair hurdler: won handicap at Wincanton in November: ran well last 2 starts: stays 2½m: acts on good to firm and heavy going. *P. J. Hobbs*   h114

TEMPLET (USA) 7 b.g. Souvenir Copy (USA) – Two Step Trudy (USA) (Capote (USA)) [2006/7 h91: 16s 16m⁴ 20g* 24m⁵ 16m³ 20sᵖᵘ Sep 21] modest on Flat: likewise over hurdles: successful in sellers at Southwell in July, novice on second occasion: stays 2½m: acts on good to firm and heavy going: blinkered/visored since debut: has looked none too keen. *W. G. Harrison*   h91

TEMPLE WOOD 6 ch.g. Past Glories – Dreamago (Sir Mago) [2006/7 F17d F17s 24sᵖᵘ 21g⁶ Apr 23] fifth foal: half-brother to fair hunter chaser Go Nomadic, stays 31f, and winning pointer Nomadic Star (both by Nomadic Way): dam modest pointer: little impact in bumpers/novice hurdles. *P. G. Atkinson*   h– F–

TENACIOUS MELODY 11 b.g. Tina's Pet – High Run (HOL) (Runnymede) [2006/7 19gᵖᵘ 24sᵖᵘ Dec 2] workmanlike gelding: won maiden point in 2004: no form over hurdles. *H. W. Lavis*   h–

TENDERAL (FR) 8 gr.g. Turgeon (USA) – La Cancalaise (FR) (Dom Pasquini (FR)) [2006/7 c23s c21s² Mar 17] rather leggy gelding: third foal: half-brother to 2-y-o sprint winner by Grand Pavois: dam winning hurdler around 2m: maiden hurdler/chaser: claimed from M. Rolland €12,700 in 2004: absent over 2½ years, better effort over fences in Britain when ½-length second to Cetti's Warbler (pair clear) in handicap at Uttoxeter: stays 21f: raced on soft ground. *M. J. Wilkinson*   c85 h–

TENDER TANGLE 12 ch.g. Crested Lark – Red Tango (Legal Tender) [2006/7 c69, h–: c20m⁵ c19m⁵ Apr 24] tall gelding: poor form in hunter chases: won point in April: stays 2½m: acts on good to firm ground. *Miss S. A. Loggin*   c72 h–

TENDER TRAP (IRE) 9 b.g. Sadler's Wells (USA) – Shamiyda (USA) (Sir Ivor (USA)) [2006/7 16d 19d⁶ Feb 19] quite good-topped gelding: fairly useful on Flat (stays 2m), sold out of T. Mills's stable 6,000 gns Newmarket July Sales: well held in maiden hurdles (bled on debut): tried tongue tied. *Miss J. E. Foster*   h–

TENINI 4 ch.g. Bertolini (USA) – River Abouali (Bluebird (USA)) [2006/7 16m² 18gᵖᵘ 16sᵘʳ Dec 26] maiden on Flat, sold out of J. Osborne's stable 9,000 gns Doncaster March Sales: second in 5-runner juvenile at Bad Harzburg on hurdling debut: failed to complete next 2 starts, including at Fontwell. *C. von der Recke, Germany*   h–

TENKO 8 ch.m. Environment Friend – Taco (High Season) [2006/7 h–: c25dᵖᵘ c26gᶠ c26dᵖᵘ c25dᶠ Nov 16] small mare: signs of ability, though usually fails to complete. *M. D. McMillan*   c81 ? h–

TEN POUND POM 5 b.g. Gunner B – Dunsfold Dolly (Strong Gale) [2006/7 F18g² F16m³ Apr 24] second foal: dam, modest form in bumpers, out of useful staying hurdler Rositary: fair form in maiden bumpers, 4 lengths third to The Package at Towcester. *P. Winkworth*   F90

TEN PRESSED MEN (FR) 7 b.g. Video Rock (FR) – Recolte d'Estruval (FR) (Kouban (FR)) [2006/7 h91: 20sᵖᵘ May 20] good-topped gelding: third in bumpers: modest form at best over hurdles: should stay 2½m. *Jonjo O'Neill*   h–

TEO PERUGO (IRE) 8 b.g. Perugino (USA) – Teodosia (Ashmore (FR)) [2006/7 c17d* c17mˢᵘ c24m* c17m* c22g c20d⁵ c19v⁴ 19m 24m⁶ Apr 22] fair at best over hurdles: fairly useful chaser: won handicaps at Killarney in May and Tralee in June, and minor event at Killarney (beat Waltons Mountain by length) in July: stiff task next 2 starts: effective around 2m to 3m: acts on firm and good to soft going, not at best on softer. *Eugene M. O'Sullivan, Ireland*   c125 h94

TEORBAN (POL) 8 b.g. Don Corleone – Tabaka (POL) (Pyjama Hunt) [2006/7 h106: 24mᵖᵘ Apr 15] stocky gelding: fair on Flat (stays 17f): maiden hurdler: should stay 3m: acts on soft and good to firm going. *Mrs N. S. Evans*   h–

TEQUINHA 7 b.g. Petoski – Caipirinha (IRE) (Strong Gale) [2006/7 h–: 24gᵖᵘ Mar 23] failed to complete in points/novice hurdles. *C. P. Morlock*   h–

TERENZIUM (IRE) 5 b.g. Cape Cross (IRE) – Tatanka (ITY) (Luge) [2006/7 16d **h–**
Dec 28] modest on Flat (should stay 1¼m), sold out of L. Cumani's stable 9,000 gns
Newmarket Autumn Sales, and gelded: well beaten in maiden on hurdling debut. *Micky
Hammond*

TERIMAI 6 b.m. Terimon – Quilpee Mai (Pee Mai) [2006/7 F16m³ Apr 9] sturdy mare: **F66**
half-sister to several winners, including smart chaser Bengers Moor (by Town And
Country), stayed 3m, and one-time fair chaser Newick Park (by Chilibang), stays 21f:
dam, 11.5f winner on Flat, fourth only outing over hurdles: in need of experience
when 6¼ lengths third of 9 to Sam McCoombe in bumper at Huntingdon on debut.
J. G. M. O'Shea

TERLAN (GER) 9 b.g. Medicus (GER) – Taxodium (GER) (Blakeney) [2006/7 c17g² **c117**
c16v⁶ c16s* c16s⁴ c16v* c16s* Apr 26] leggy gelding: fair hurdler, missed 2005/6: took **h–**
well to chasing, winning novices at Newcastle (handicap) in December and Sedgefield in
January, and handicap at Perth (fairly useful form, beat Lofty Leader by 12 lengths) in
April: raced around 2m on good going or softer (acts on heavy). *P. Monteith*

TERRAGON 7 b.g. Gildoran – Taco (High Season) [2006/7 21m May 18] fifth **h–**
foal: dam, winning chaser, stayed 25f: jumped poorly in novice hurdle on debut.
M. D. McMillan

TERRAMARIQUE (IRE) 8 b.g. Namaqualand (USA) – Secret Ocean (Most Secret) **c102**
[2006/7 c71, h–: c22m* c24g³ 24g* 24m* c26m* c24m* 26g³ c24g³ c22m* Apr 26] fair **h98**
hurdler/chaser: left L. Lungo and much improved in 2006/7, winning handicap hurdles at
Uttoxeter in July and Worcester (amateur event) in August, handicap chases at Fontwell
in May and Plumpton and Huntingdon (novice) in September, and novice chase at
Fontwell (after 6-month absence) in April: stays 3¼m: best on good/good to firm going:
tried in cheekpieces, effective with or without visor. *N. J. Henderson*

TERRE DE JAVA (FR) 9 b.g. Cadoudal (FR) – Terre d'Argent (FR) (Count Ivor **c111**
(USA)) [2006/7 c118, h101: c17f⁵ c16s⁵ 20g Apr 7] strong, lengthy gelding: maiden **h–**
hurdler: fairly useful handicap chaser, respectable effort on return: stays 2½m: acts on
any going: tried tongue tied: has finished weakly. *Heather Dalton*

TERREROS 5 b.g. Dr Fong (USA) – Lypharita (FR) (Lightning (FR)) [2006/7 F16g **h86**
F16g 16d 18v⁶ 16v⁴ Feb 5] rather leggy gelding: half-brother to several winners, **F75**
including bumper winner Rasak (by Kris) and 2m selling hurdle winner Lixos (by Soviet
Star): dam won Prix de Diane: little impact in bumpers: best effort over hurdles (modest
form) when fourth in maiden at Hexham: raced around 2m. *F. P. Murtagh*

TERRIBLE TENANT 8 gr.g. Terimon – Rent Day (Town And Country) [2006/7 c91, **c101**
h–: c25d³ c25m² c19m² c16m* c21f² c19g⁴ c16m* c25d⁴ c21g⁵ Dec 26] good-topped **h–**
gelding: fair handicap chaser: won at Hereford in September and November: effective at
2m to 25f: acts on soft and firm going: front runner/races prominently: tough and
consistent. *J. W. Mullins*

TESSANOORA 6 b.m. Topanoora – Club Sandwich (Phardante (FR)) [2006/7 h119: **h118**
16g² 16v³ 19d Dec 30] useful-looking mare: has scope: fairly useful handicap hurdler:
should prove suited by further than 2m: raced on good going or softer. *N. J. Henderson*

TEST OF FRIENDSHIP 10 br.g. Roselier (FR) – Grease Pot (Gala Performance) **c95**
[2006/7 c80, h–: c26mᵖᵘ c25d* May 17] modest handicap chaser: won at Hereford in **h–**
May: stays 3¼m: acts on soft going. *Heather Dalton*

TETBURY (IRE) 6 b.g. Saddlers' Hall (IRE) – Rainbow Light (Deep Run) [2006/7 **h–**
24m Apr 15] 13,000 3-y-o: fourth foal: dam unraced, sister to dam of useful staying
chaser Dakyns Boy: green, well beaten in novice hurdle on debut. *M. Bradstock*

TETRAGON (IRE) 7 b.g. Octagonal (NZ) – Viva Verdi (IRE) (Green Desert (USA)) **c–**
[2006/7 17s² 16v² c20sᵖᵘ 18v⁶ 16pᵖᵘ Mar 26] compact gelding: fair on Flat (stays 1½m): **h70**
poor maiden hurdler: no show on chasing debut, final start for D. Carroll: raced mainly
around 2m: acts on heavy going: usually wore cheekpieces/blinkers prior to 2006/7: often
tongue tied. *A. M. Hales*

TETRODE (USA) 5 b.g. Quiet American (USA) – Mother Courage (Busted) [2006/7 **h–**
16g 16f⁵ 16f Apr 22] maiden on Flat: little show over hurdles. *M. F. Harris*

TEUTONIC (IRE) 6 b.m. Revoque (IRE) – Classic Ring (IRE) (Auction Ring (USA)) **h76 §**
[2006/7 h69§: 22d* 24m 27vᵖᵘ Jan 28] lengthy mare: modest maiden on Flat (stays 2m):
poor hurdler: won mares maiden at Cartmel in May: stays 2¾m: probably acts on heavy
going: has refused to race: ungenuine. *R. F. Fisher*

TEVERE (FR) 6 b.g. Turgeon (USA) – Silver River (FR) (Pampabird) [2006/7 16g* **c129** c20m* c22g⁶ c21d 16g* Apr 9] leggy ex-French gelding: successful 6 times over hurdles/ **h?** fences in France (claimed from R. Chotard €18,700 in November 2005): successful over hurdles in Jersey (for Ms V. Lucas) in May and on return there in April: fairly useful form when also winning handicap chase at Southwell (by 3½ lengths from Flight Command) in June: stays 2½m: acts on good to firm and heavy ground. *D. E. Pipe*

TEVIOT BRIG 6 b.g. Weldnaas (USA) – Here Comes Tibby (Royal Fountain) [2006/7 **h–** h–, F–: 16g 17d 16v⁵ Dec 19] well-made gelding: little impact in bumper/over hurdles. *L. Lungo*

TEVIOT LASS 5 b.m. Minster Son – Here Comes Tibby (Royal Fountain) [2006/7 **F–** F17s Oct 25] fifth foal: half-sister to fair hurdler/chaser Reivers Moon (by Midnight Legend), stays 3m: dam, poor hurdler/chaser, stayed 2¾m: no show in bumper on debut. *W. Amos*

TEXAS RANGER 9 b.g. Mtoto – Favorable Exchange (USA) (Exceller (USA)) **c90** [2006/7 c20sᵖᵘ c23m⁴ c20mᵖᵘ Aug 11] compact gelding: winning hurdler: fairly useful **h–** pointer, successful twice in April: fourth in maiden at Worcester on completed start in chases: should stay beyond 2½m: acts on good to firm going. *Miss J. E. Foster*

TEXAS TOM 6 b.g. Washington State (USA) – Rosemary Nalden (Great Commo- **h–** tion (USA)) [2006/7 F17s F17g 22gᵖᵘ Aug 26] second foal: brother to 1½m winner **F–** Peggy Lou: dam unraced: little impact in bumpers/selling hurdle (in cheekpieces). *B. J. Llewellyn*

TEXT 6 b.g. Atraf – Idle Chat (USA) (Assert) [2006/7 h99: 16gᶠ Sep 6] modest novice **h89** hurdler: fell fatally only start in 2006/7: raced around 2m: acted on good to firm ground. *L. Corcoran*

THAI HOE 7 b.g. Gunner B – Ballintava (Better By Far) [2006/7 20s 16s 16s 20g Apr 3] **h–** leggy gelding: third foal: dam thoroughly untrustworthy pointer: well held in novice hurdles. *Mrs S. J. Smith*

THAI VANGO (IRE) 6 b.g. Religiously (USA) – Danesway (Be My Native (USA)) **h91** [2006/7 F16s* F17s² 19d 26s⁴ 19s⁴ Mar 11] first foal: dam placed in Irish points: won **F87** maiden Irish point in 2006: successful also in bumper at Perth in September: modest form in novice hurdles: should prove suited by 2½m+: raced on good to soft/soft going. *N. A. Twiston-Davies*

THAMES (IRE) 9 b.g. Over The River (FR) – Aon Dochas (IRE) (Strong Gale) **c– p** [2006/7 c20d⁶ Dec 26] strong, lengthy gelding: fairly useful hurdler: off 21 months, well **h–** held in novice handicap on chasing debut: stays 3m: acts on soft going: should do better over fences, but clearly not easy to train. *N. J. Henderson*

THANKYOU MAAM 5 b.m. Bahamian Bounty – Barefoot Landing (USA) (Cozzene **F–** (USA)) [2006/7 F16d F16d Feb 14] third foal: dam poor novice hurdler: tailed off in bumpers. *A. Parker*

THATLLDOFORME 5 b.g. Dancing High – Bantel Bargain (Silly Prices) [2006/7 **h100** h–, F70: 22d⁶ 20g 16v² 20v² 22v* 21v³ Mar 9] rather leggy gelding: fair form over hurdles, making all in handicap at Kelso in March: stays 2¾m: raced on good ground or softer (acts on heavy). *A. C. Whillans*

THATLLDOYA 9 ch.g. Montelimar (USA) – Sevso (Jupiter Island) [2006/7 c83: **c83** c25m⁶ c30m² c31g⁵ c25s² c23v² c29g⁵ Mar 20] winning pointer: poor maiden chaser, left P. Grinrod after fourth start: stays 31f: acts on soft and good to firm going: amateur ridden. *Miss J. E. Foster*

THAT LOOK 4 b.g. Compton Admiral – Mudflap (Slip Anchor) [2006/7 17m* 16m² **h107** 17m⁴ 16f* Oct 5] modest maiden on Flat (seems to stay 2m): fair form in juvenile hurdles: won at Market Rasen in June and Wincanton (by neck from Katies Tuitor) in October: likely to stay beyond 2m: raced on good to firm/firm going. *D. E. Cantillon*

THAT MAN FOX 6 b.g. Sovereign Water (FR) – Oh No Rosie (Vital Season) [2006/7 **h98** h85, F77: 19vᵖᵘ 17g⁴ 26sᵖᵘ 16d³ 20g² 19m² Apr 28] modest novice hurdler, left M. Wigham after first outing: should stay beyond 2½m: acts on good to firm ground: blinkered last 3 starts: front runner/races prominently. *P. S. McEntee*

THATS CONFIDENTIAL (IRE) 5 b.g. Saddlers' Hall (IRE) – New Legislation **F93** (IRE) (Dominion Royale) [2006/7 F16v³ F16s⁴ F16g⁶ Mar 19] 16,000 3-y-o: rather leggy gelding: third foal: closely related to dual bumper/2m hurdle winner Keelaghan (by Accordion): dam, fair hurdler, stayed 2½m: fair form in bumpers, left C. Tinkler after debut: has rejoined D. Arbuthnot. *Miss H. C. Knight*

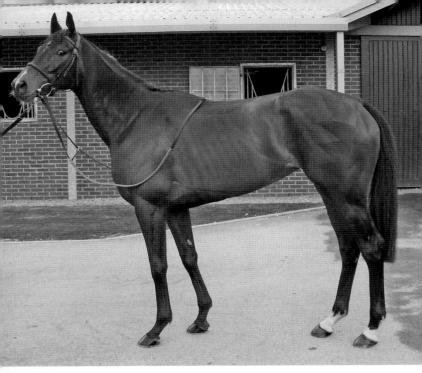

Let's Live Racing's "Theatre Girl"

THATS MORE LIKE IT (IRE) 8 ch.g. Accordion – What It Takes (IRE) (Tale **c76** Quale) [2006/7 c21v³ c16sᵘʳ Nov 19] big, strong gelding: third foal: dam unraced **h–** half-sister to useful staying hurdler Nancy Myles: poor form over hurdles/fences, left E. O'Grady before chasing debut: stayed 21f: dead. *Jonjo O'Neill*

THAT'S MY CHARLIE (NZ) 6 b.g. Magic of Sydney (AUS) – La Magnifique (NZ) **h81** (Kampala) [2006/7 F–: F17d² F16g² 16s 16m⁵ Apr 10] rather leggy, useful-looking **F87** gelding: runner-up in bumpers: left Jonjo O'Neill, better effort in maiden hurdles when fifth at Chepstow. *R. H. Alner*

THAT'S RACING 7 ch.g. Classic Cliche (IRE) – All On (Dunbeath (USA)) [2006/7 **h83 §** h74§: 16g 16d 16f 17g 17v⁶ 20d 17s* 16s² 17s⁴ Dec 23] workmanlike gelding: poor handicap hurdler: back to best when winning novice event at Sedgefield in December: stays 21f: acts on soft going: unreliable. *J. Hetherton*

THAT'S RHYTHM (FR) 7 b.g. Pistolet Bleu (IRE) – Madame Jean (FR) (Cricket **h103 p** Ball (USA)) [2006/7 h96p: 20g* 21g* Apr 23] leggy gelding: fair form over hurdles: off 15 months prior to winning at Sedgefield in March/April (beat North Island by 1½ lengths): stays 21f: acts on good to soft going: remains open to improvement. *M. Todhunter*

THE ABBOTS HABIT (IRE) 6 b.g. Taipan (IRE) – Thats Gospel (IRE) (Strong **h107** Gale) [2006/7 17d² 16s² 16v* 21v* Jan 2] €43,000 3-y-o: tall, useful-looking gelding: fifth foal: half-brother to bumper winner Golden Fantasy (by Shernazar): dam bumper winner: fair form in novice hurdles: landed odds at Ayr in December (by 25 lengths) and

January (very laboured effort when beating Dantor by short head): will probably stay 3m: raced on ground softer than good. *N. G. Richards*

THE APPRENTICE (IRE) 5 b.g. Shernazar – Kate Farly (IRE) (Phardante (FR)) [2006/7 F16v⁵ Feb 24] good sort: second foal: dam twice-raced in bumpers: met trouble and seemed in need of experience when 23½ lengths fifth to Evelith Echo in bumper at Kempton on debut: should do better. *V. R. A. Dartnall* **F82 p**

THE ASSOCIATE (IRE) 10 b. or br.g. Religiously (USA) – Stormy Trip (Strong Gale) [2006/7 c–: c24sᵖᵘ May 17] good-topped gelding: no form over fences. *Miss Lucinda V. Russell* **c–**

THEATRE BELLE 6 b.m. King's Theatre (IRE) – Cumbrian Rhapsody (Sharrood (USA)) [2006/7 h71: 16m May 6] close-coupled mare: poor novice hurdler: stays 19f: acts on good to firm and good to soft going. *Ms Deborah J. Evans* **h71**

THEATRE DIVA (IRE) 6 b.m. King's Theatre (IRE) – Rigobertha (IRE) (Nordico (USA)) [2006/7 17s* 16d² 16d 21d² 16s* 16d² 21m* Jan 29] medium-sized mare: fifth foal: half-sister to bumper winner Gollum (by Spectrum) and 2 winners on Flat: dam, fair 2-y-o 7f winner, half-sister to smart middle-distance filly Ballykett Nancy: fairly useful hurdler: left D. Hughes in Ireland, won maiden at Market Rasen in May and, having been sold out of K. Ryan's stable 18,000 gns Doncaster May Sales, mares handicaps at Ludlow in December and January (beat Chilly Milly easily by 3 lengths): stays 21f: seems to act on any going: tried blinkered: sold 21,000 gns Doncaster May Sales. *H. D. Daly* **h120**

THEATRE GIRL 4 b.f. King's Theatre (IRE) – Fortune's Girl (Ardross) [2006/7 F14g³ F14v* F16s³ F16s² F17g² Apr 13] useful-looking filly: half-sister to fairly useful hurdlers up to 2½m Diamond Sal (by Bob Back) and Ring The Boss (by Kahyasi): dam winning hurdler/chaser who stayed 27f: useful form in bumpers: won 4-y-o event at Wetherby in January: further improvement when runner-up in listed mares races at Sandown and Aintree, beaten 1¾ lengths by Turbo Linn at latter: will stay at least 2½m. *A. King* **F110**

THEATRE GROOM (USA) 8 ch.g. Theatrical – Model Bride (USA) (Blushing Groom (FR)) [2006/7 16mᶠ 16m³ 17m³ 20g² 20g⁵ 22d⁴ 19s Dec 7] sturdy gelding: bumper winner: modest novice hurdler: should have stayed beyond 2½m: acted on good to firm and good to soft going: successful on Flat in February: dead. *M. R. Bosley* **h92**

THEATRE KNIGHT (IRE) 9 b.g. Old Vic – Musical View (IRE) (Orchestra) [2006/7 c105, h–: c28d³ c26s* c21g³ c30s⁵ c25g⁴ c21g² Apr 13] rangy gelding: fairly useful handicap chaser: won at Carlisle in November by 1½ lengths from Willie The Fish: 20 lb out of weights, considerable improvement when 6 lengths second of 29 to Dunbrody Millar in Topham Chase at Aintree: stays 33f: raced on good going or softer. *J. Howard Johnson* **c128 h–**

THEATRE RIGHTS (IRE) 7 ch.g. Old Vic – Deep Perk (IRE) (Deep Run) [2006/7 h–, F–: 20vᵖᵘ 24vᵖᵘ 20vᵖᵘ 20vᵖᵘ Mar 22] no sign of ability. *J. S. Haldane* **h–**

THEATRE TINKA (IRE) 8 b.g. King's Theatre (IRE) – Orange Grouse (IRE) (Taufan (USA)) [2006/7 h100: 17s⁵ 20g⁵ 17gᶠ Jul 9] close-coupled gelding: modest handicap hurdler: fell fatally at Market Rasen: should have stayed beyond 17f: acted on soft going: tried in cheekpieces. *R. Hollinshead* **h87**

THEATRE (USA) 8 b.g. Theatrical – Fasta (USA) (Seattle Song (USA)) [2006/7 24d³ 23vᵖᵘ Jan 4] close-coupled gelding: fairly useful on Flat (stays 21f), successful in September: fairly useful hurdler: would have stayed beyond 3m: raced on good going or softer: jumped none too fluently: dead. *Jamie Poulton* **h119**

THEATRICAL MOMENT (USA) 4 b.g. Royal Anthem (USA) – Given Moment (USA) (Diesis) [2006/7 F16d* F17d* F17s* Mar 13] **F124**
Timeform has published ratings for National Hunt Flat races since the 1993/4 season and, so far, every horse that has topped the seasonal bumper ratings has gone on to win at least once over jumps. Not all of them have lived up to such encouraging early promise, of course, but the majority have turned out at least useful over hurdles and/or fences and some, such as Dato Star, Florida Pearl, Alexander Banquet and Rhinestone Cowboy, have gone all the way, developing into top-class jumpers. The main purpose of bumpers is to give later-maturing, more stoutly-bred jumping-bred horses some racing experience without coming up against the speedier and more precocious types they'd encounter in maidens on the Flat. However, not every horse that makes its racecourse debut in a bumper is

destined for a career over jumps. Collier Hill, whose record earnings for a British-trained gelding of more than £2.3 million have come largely from an international career, is the most successful example of a horse for whom a bumper win (in his case, at Catterick) presaged a career on the Flat rather than one over jumps.

Collier Hill did subsequently win a race over hurdles, though he failed to progress in that sphere whilst his Flat career went from strength to strength. He set something of a precedent for his stable as well. Alfie Flits showed smart form in bumpers for Alan Swinbank in 2005/6 before switching to the Flat and winning two listed races in 2006, his form not far behind that of Collier Hill. Two even better bumper performers from the same stable emerged in the latest season in Theatrical Moment and the filly Turbo Linn. Alfie Flits had been unbeaten in three races before starting favourite for the Grade 2 bumper at Aintree on Grand National day in which he finished a close fourth. A year on, Theatrical Moment took an identical record into the race, but, unlike Alfie Flits, he was able to justify favouritism at Aintree as well.

Theatrical Moment had to wait a bit longer than Alfie Flits to do so, however, as the John Smith's Champion Standard Open National Hunt Flat Race was postponed in unusual circumstances until Aintree's Friday evening meeting in May. Due to be run on the hurdles course as the last race on Grand National day as usual, the bumper was abandoned as Grand National faller Graphic Approach was still being treated on the course after collapsing. Fourteen runners contested the rescheduled event, half of whom had stood their ground from the original race. The prize money was virtually identical but the Grade 2 status of the race had been lost, meaning that multiple winners such as Theatrical Moment and second favourite

Elsa Crankshow & G. Allan II's "Theatrical Moment"

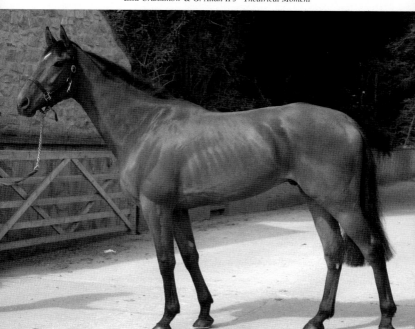

Tazbar had to carry a 7-lb penalty. Whilst Irish-trained horses had dominated the finish of the Champion Bumper at Cheltenham, there were none in the Aintree race. There was a domination of a different sort, however, as Theatrical Moment and the three who filled the frame behind him at Aintree were all trained in the North. As on his previous starts, Theatrical Moment impressed greatly with the way he travelled through the race, cruising to the front over two furlongs out before having to be ridden out by Tony Dobbin inside the final furlong as he tired slightly before holding another of the unbeaten runners Kealshore Boy by a length and a half. Lease Lend (a final ride for the retiring Russ Garritty) and Tazbar completed the frame. Theatrical Moment's stable companion Turbo Linn had gone to Aintree with four wins already under her belt and had made it five in a row in the listed mares' event, the last race on Friday. Turbo Linn was then switched to the Flat with conspicuous success, winning the Lancashire Oaks (staged at Newmarket) on her second start and following up in the listed Aphrodite Stakes at Newmarket later in July.

Theatrical Moment showed improved form at Aintree but had been impressive in his earlier wins, particularly the first two. He won both by eighteen lengths, at Musselburgh in January and Market Rasen a month later, though the winning margin could doubtless have been much wider both times if his rider had wished. Only four rivals took him on when he completed his hat-trick at Sedgefield in March, landing very short odds with plenty to spare by three lengths from the Market Rasen runner-up Auroras Encore.

'They stand around for five minutes at the start in these bumpers, and a lot of the runners are bred to win three-mile chases, so the mile-and-a-half horses can get away with it [the two-mile trip],' explained Alan Swinbank, 'and it makes sense to pick up a bit of prize-money while you're educating them.' This theory has been the basis for a lucrative sideline for Swinbank's Flat-oriented yard over the past couple of seasons, with its impressive haul of ten bumper wins (at a strike rate of 29%) in 2005/6 surpassed by an incredible nineteen wins (40%) during the latest campaign. The latter tally, of course, doesn't include Theatrical Moment's valuable Aintree win, which tipped the stable's total prize money earnings in bumpers for this period over the £100,000 barrier. Rather surprisingly, Swinbank has yet to saddle a runner in the Champion Bumper—Theatrical Moment reportedly sidestepped the Festival for Sedgefield due to his trainer's concerns about running a four-year-old in the Cheltenham race—but the Aintree prizes are always likely to look more appealing options given the largely Flat-bred types under his care.

Theatrical Moment (USA) (b.g. 2003)	Royal Anthem (USA) (b 1995)	Theatrical (b 1982)	Nureyev
			Tree of Knowledge
		In Neon (b 1982)	Ack Ack
			Shamara
	Given Moment (USA) (ch 1997)	Diesis (ch 1980)	Sharpen Up
			Doubly Sure
		Sunny Moment (b 1986)	Roberto
			Smile Even Though

Theatrical Moment is a tall gelding, still unfurnished, and certainly has the physique for a jumping career, though he's very much a Flat horse on pedigree. His sire Royal Anthem began his stud career in Kentucky after wins at the top level on both sides of the Atlantic, his best performance being an eight-length win in the 1999 Juddmonte International at York. He was also second to Daylami in the Breeders' Cup Turf later that season, but there is little demand for mile-and-a-half turf performers at stud in the States, even top-class ones, and in 2007 Royal Anthem moved to Ireland to begin a career as a jumps sire. Theatrical Moment was sold for just 13,000 dollars as a foal at Keeneland and joined the Swinbank stable for €20,000 at Tattersalls (Ireland) a year later. Theatrical Moment is his dam's third foal following two winners in the States, Conditional (by Gone West) and Thanks (also by Royal Anthem), the latter at eight and a half and nine furlongs. The dam Given Moment is an unraced sister to Duck Row who enjoyed a lengthy career as a smart mile/nine-furlong performer (for James Toller) in Britain. The family is American though. The grandam Sunny Moment won only a mile maiden there but she is a half-sister to the dam of the Secretariat Stakes winner Vaudeville and is out of a half-sister to another Grade 1 winner, Life Cycle, who was successful in the

Hollywood Invitational Turf Handicap. At one stage, it seemed that Theatrical Moment was destined for a Flat career too, with the Cesarewitch his reported target in the autumn, but it was reported in June that he had been sold privately (for an undisclosed sum) to join Tom Hogan in Ireland. *G. A. Swinbank*

THE BAILLIE (IRE) 8 b.g. Castle Keep – Regular Dolan (IRE) (Regular Guy)   **h–**
[2006/7 F79: 17m 20s^{pu} 17s^6 22m^{ur} 21m Sep 26] modest form in bumpers for C. Egerton: no show over hurdles: won maiden point in February: tried blinkered/in cheekpieces. *Miss J. E. Foster*

THE BAJAN BANDIT (IRE) 12 b.g. Commanche Run – Sunrise Highway VII   **c132 §**
(Damsire Unregistered) [2006/7 c143§, h138§: 23d c25v^F 20s^5 c26v^2 23s c24g^{ur} c24s^{pu} **h127 §**
Apr 26] sturdy gelding: useful hurdler/chaser, largely disappointing in 2006/7: stays 3¼m: acts on good to firm going, acts well on soft/heavy: effective with or without headgear: has been let down by jumping over fences: unreliable. *L. Lungo*

THE BANDIT (IRE) 10 b.g. Un Desperado (FR) – Sweet Friendship (Alleging   **c126**
(USA)) [2006/7 c134, h–: c24g^{pu} c24g c24g c27f* Apr 5] useful-looking gelding: win-   **h–**
ning hurdler: fairly useful handicap chaser: in cheekpieces, back to form when winning at Wincanton in April by short head from It Takes Time, in clear lead long way: stays 3¾m: acts on soft and firm going: tried in tongue strap (reportedly came off during race). *Miss E. C. Lavelle*

THE BAY BRIDGE (IRE) 8 b. or br.g. Over The River (FR) – Alamo Bay (Torenaga)   **h74 +**
[2006/7 h92+: 24f^4 24m Jul 5] lengthy, useful-looking gelding: novice hurdler, modest form at best: should stay 3m: acts on firm going: sold 6,500 gns Doncaster August Sales. *Miss E. C. Lavelle*

THE BEAMING BANDIT (IRE) 7 b.g. Shernazar – Celtic Smiles (IRE) (Nucleon   **h–**
(USA)) [2006/7 F–: F16d 19d^F Nov 8] well held in bumpers: badly hampered and fell   **F–**
fourth in novice on hurdling debut: sold 800 gns Doncaster May Sales. *M. G. Rimell*

THE BEDUTH NAVI 7 b.g. Forzando – Sweets (IRE) (Persian Heights) [2006/7 h–:   **h–**
21d^{pu} 19m^{pu} Jun 14] no form over hurdles. *D. G. Bridgwater*

THEBELLOFTHEBALL 4 ch.f. Classic Cliche (IRE) – Juste Belle (FR) (Manson-   **F79**
nien (FR)) [2006/7 F13s^3 F16v^3 F16s F16m^2 Mar 31] unfurnished filly: first foal: dam placed up to around 1½m on Flat in France: modest form in bumpers. *C. J. Down*

THE BIG CANADIAN (IRE) 6 b.g. Presenting – Glory-Glory (IRE) (Buckskin   **h105**
(FR)) [2006/7 F100: 16g 16m^3 16d^2 17v^3 20s 24f^3 Apr 5] lengthy gelding: has scope: bumper winner: fair novice hurdler: stays 3m: acts on any ground. *A. King*

THE BIG ORSE 5 b.g. Benny The Dip (USA) – Polar Queen (Polish Precedent (USA))   **F103**
[2006/7 F16g^3 Mar 24] big, lengthy gelding: half-brother to 2 winners, notably very smart middle-distance stayer Collier Hill (by Dr Devious), also successful in bumper/novice hurdle: dam 7f winner: never-nearer 4¼ lengths third of 22 to Helens Vision in bumper at Newbury on debut. *P. M. Phelan*

THE BIKER (IRE) 10 br.g. Arctic Lord – Glenravel (Lucifer (USA)) [2006/7 c100+,   **c111**
h–: c16v* c20s^5 c22g^4 c16s^{ur} c16v^F c16v^2 c20v^3 Jan 2] tall, workmanlike gelding: **h–**
winning hurdler: fair chaser: won 4-runner minor event at Perth in May: best short of 2¾m: acts on heavy going, probably on good to firm. *P. Monteith*

THE BLACK LION (IRE) 6 b.g. Un Desperado (FR) – Satrouse (IRE) (Satco (FR))   **F104**
[2006/7 F18m^2 F16d F16d^3 F16v^5 F16s* F16m^4 Apr 26] €20,000 3-y-o: good-topped gelding: third foal: dam unraced: fairly useful form in bumpers: won at Limerick in February: around 2½ lengths fourth to Meadow Vale in 24-runner event at Punchestown: reportedly lame second start. *Joseph Crowley, Ireland*

THE BONUS KING 7 b.g. Royal Applause – Selvi (Mummy's Pet) [2006/7 16f^4 16d* **h105**
16m^3 18g* 17d^6 Oct 7] fair on Flat (stays 1m), successful in April: fair novice hurdler: won at Southwell (easily) in August and Fontwell in September: stays 2¼m: acts on good to soft and good to firm ground. *J. Jay*

THE BOOBI (IRE) 6 b.m. Beneficial – Orogale (IRE) (Strong Gale) [2006/7 h72, F–:   **h–**
17d May 31] sparely-made mare: maiden hurdler, no show last 3 starts. *Miss M. E. Row-land*

THE BORDERER 4 ch.g. Definite Article – Far Clan (Clantime) [2006/7 F14s^6 F14v^4 **F74**
F17g Mar 24] first foal: dam unraced: poor form in bumpers. *M. W. Easterby*

THEBOYFROMBULAWAYO (IRE) 8 b. or br.g. Mister Lord (USA) – Lilly   **c107**
Bolero (Fearless Action (USA)) [2006/7 c20d^2 c24m^{pu} c20s^5 c25v^{pu} c24v^5 c28v^F c25v^2

c20d* c24v^{pu} c25m⁵ c25m Apr 28] second foal: dam unraced: won maiden point in 2005: fair chaser: won maiden at Down Royal in March: stays 25f: acts on heavy and good to firm going: tried blinkered. *C. A. McBratney, Ireland*

THE BROWN DOVE (IRE) 6 b.m. Saddlers' Hall (IRE) – Kamogue (Carlingford Castle) [2006/7 F20m 24m Jul 5] €5,000 4-y-o: third foal: dam, modest novice hurdler up to 2¾m, half-sister to useful staying hurdler Conquering Leader: placed twice from 7 starts in maiden Irish points in 2006: no show in bumper/novice hurdle: tried tongue tied. *Dermot Day, Ireland*
h–
F–

THE BUTTERWICK KID 14 ch.g. Interrex (CAN) – Ville Air (Town Crier) [2006/7 c102, h–§: c23g³ May 11] neat gelding: veteran chaser: effective at 2½m to 25f: acts on good to firm and heavy going: visored/blinkered: races prominently. *T. P. Tate*
c93
h– §

THE CASTILIAN (FR) 5 b.g. Enrique – Triciana (USA) (Afleet (CAN)) [2006/7 h97§: 22m⁵ 17m 16s⁵ 16f⁶ 16f⁴ Apr 22] small, leggy gelding: modest maiden hurdler: stays 2¾m: acts on firm and soft going (below form on heavy): visored/in cheekpieces: irresolute. *D. E. Pipe*
h91 §

THE CHEEKSTER 7 ch.g. Private Despatch (USA) – Sally's Dove (Celtic Cone) [2006/7 F17g F16d Nov 20] half-brother to winning hurdler Dove From Above, stayed 3¼m, and winning pointer (both by Henbit): dam winning 2m hurdler: well held in bumpers. *R. J. Price*
F–

THE CHEQUERED LADY 5 b.m. Benny The Dip (USA) – Hymne d'Amour (USA) (Dixieland Band (USA)) [2006/7 h86: 16g³ 18m 22m Jun 18] modest novice hurdler: stays 2¼m. *T. D. McCarthy*
h90

THE CITY KID (IRE) 4 b.f. Danetime (IRE) – Unfortunate (Komaite (USA)) [2006/7 16m 16d Nov 20] fair on Flat (stays 9.5f), claimed £8,000 after successful in March: no impact over hurdles: tried visored. *P. D. Evans*
h–

THE CLIENT (IRE) 6 b.g. Rakaposhi King – Woodram Delight (Idiot's Delight) [2006/7 F17s 19g c27s^{ur} c27v^{pu} 24s 24m³ Mar 25] €33,000 3-y-o: ninth foal: half-brother to fairly useful staying chaser Bank Avenue (by Homo Sapien): dam unraced half-sister to dual Scottish Grand National winner Androma and useful staying chaser Bigsun: runner-up on second of 2 starts in maiden Irish points in 2006: bought 8,000 gns Doncaster May Sales: first form otherwise when third in maiden hurdle at Southwell. *D. Pearson*
c–
h77 ?
F–

THE COMPOSER 5 b.g. Royal Applause – Superspring (Superlative) [2006/7 h105: 17s² 16d 17s Jan 30] lengthy gelding: fair on Flat (stays 1½m), successful in May: fair novice hurdler: raced around 2m on good ground or softer. *M. Blanshard*
h100

THE COOL GUY (IRE) 7 b.g. Zaffaran (USA) – Frostbite (Prince Tenderfoot (USA)) [2006/7 h136: c20v³ c24s^F Feb 16] tall gelding: useful bumper/hurdle winner: off 12 months, better effort over fences in 4-runner maiden at Fakenham, 4 lengths up and in control when falling last: stays 3m: raced on going softer than good: tends to hang left: should improve further over fences. *N. A. Twiston-Davies*
c118 p
h–

THE CORBY GLENN (IRE) 6 b.g. Broken Hearted – Always Proud (IRE) (Supreme Leader) [2006/7 h–, F89: 19d 16v 20s 20v^{pu} Mar 2] bumper winner: no show over hurdles. *Barry Potts, Ireland*
h–

THE CROOK (IRE) 7 b.m. Broken Hearted – Foxy-Lady (IRE) (Yashgan) [2006/7 16d⁵ 16f 17f 20m 16v⁴ 16g 16g³ Apr 16] in frame in bumpers: modest maiden hurdler, left M. Hourigan in Ireland and off 8 months before fifth start: best form at 2m: acts on soft going (bumper form on good to firm): tried in cheekpieces. *R. C. Guest*
h93

THE CUSTOS 6 b.g. Terimon – Carribean Sound (Good Times (ITY)) [2006/7 16s^{pu} 18v Jan 12] eleventh foal: dam, 7f winner, half-sister to fairly useful hurdler up to 3m Mariners Haven: no show in novice hurdles. *A. Parker*
h–

THE DARK LORD (IRE) 10 b.g. Lord Americo – Khalkeys Shoon (Green Shoon) [2006/7 c123x, h–: c24s^F c21g c25g^F Apr 18] lengthy gelding: one-time useful hurdler/fairly useful handicap chaser: let down by jumping over fences in 2006/7, headway when falling 4 out in race won by Alexanderthegreat at Cheltenham final outing: stays 25f: acts on good to firm and good to soft going: held up: makes mistakes. *Mrs L. Wadham*
c110 x
h–

THEDREAMSTILLALIVE (IRE) 7 ch.g. Houmayoun (FR) – State of Dream (IRE) (Carmelite House (USA)) [2006/7 c113p, h102: 24v⁵ c20v^{pu} c20v* c21g* Mar 19] sturdy gelding: winning hurdler, lightly raced and off a year before return: fairly useful form over fences: won novices at Leicester and Wincanton (beat Ice Bucket a length, again idling) in March: should stay 3m: raced on good going or softer (acts on heavy): tongue tied in 2006/7. *J. A. B. Old*
c115 +
h84 +

THEDUBLINPUBLICAN (IRE) 7 b.g. Beneficial – Ideal Woman (IRE) (King's Ride) [2006/7 h98: c21m^F c20g* c24d^4 c20m^5 c22m^4 c16g^2 c17m^2 20g^2 c21m^4 c19g^2 c20m^3 Apr 28] tall gelding: modest hurdler: fair chaser: won novice handicap at Wetherby in May: stays 2½m: acts on good to firm and good to soft going: races prominently. *C. C. Bealby* **c104 h98**

THE DUCKPOND (IRE) 10 ch.g. Bob's Return (IRE) – Miss Gosling (Prince Bee) [2006/7 c123p, h–: c24s^{pu} Mar 3] strong gelding: very lightly raced: winning hurdler/chaser (fairly useful form): off 15 months, slight advantage when pulled up 4 out in handicap only start in 2006/7: stays 3m: acts on heavy ground: clearly very hard to train. *J. A. B. Old* **c– h–**

THE DUKE'S SPEECH (IRE) 6 b.g. Saddlers' Hall (IRE) – Dannkalia (IRE) (Shernazar) [2006/7 h126p: c16s^6 c17s^3 c16d^{pu} 19s 16d 16g Apr 14] big, well-made gelding: fairly useful hurdler: just fair form over fences, not convincing with jumping: should stay beyond 2m: raced on good ground or softer (acts on soft). *T. P. Tate* **c105 h125**

THE EENS 15 b.g. Rakaposhi King – Snippet (Ragstone) [2006/7 c83, h–: c24s^5 May 20] rather leggy, close-coupled gelding: winning hurdler/chaser: fair pointer nowadays, successful 3 times in 2006: stays 27f: acts on heavy and good to firm going: tried in headgear. *D. McCain Jnr* **c– h–**

THE EGG MAN 5 b. or gr.g. Silver Patriarch (IRE) – The Dizzy Fox (Le Moss) [2006/7 F16m^{ur} Sep 10] first foal: dam runner-up in bumper: behind when unseated in bumper on debut. *Evan Williams* **F–**

THE ENTOMOLOGIST (IRE) 6 b.g. Saddlers' Hall (IRE) – Winter Ground (IRE) (Montelimar (USA)) [2006/7 F97: 20d* 18g^6 Mar 18] point/bumper winner: successful also on hurdling debut when beating Noble Raider by 6 lengths in novice at Fakenham in December: prominent long way in handicap over 3 months later: stays 2½m: acts on good to soft going. *C. R. Egerton* **h104**

THE FLYER (IRE) 10 b.g. Blues Traveller (IRE) – National Ballet (Shareef Dancer (USA)) [2006/7 h106§: 21m^2 20s^5 May 28] leggy gelding: fair hurdler, below best in 2006/7: stays 3m: acts on good to firm and heavy going: in cheekpieces last 4 starts: tongue tied: usually soon off bridle: sold £2,800 Ascot August Sales. *Miss S. J. Wilton* **h88 §**

THE FLYING PHENOM 4 gr.g. Paris House – Miss Flossa (FR) (Big John (FR)) [2006/7 F13s F17v 17s^4 Feb 8] brother to poor 2m hurdler Theflyingscottie and half-brother to 2 winners, including winning 2m hurdler/useful stayer The Flying Phantom (by Sharrood): dam French maiden: well held in bumpers: strong hold and saddle reportedly slipped when fourth to Cantabilly in maiden at Taunton on hurdling debut: tailed off in maiden on Flat. *J. D. Frost* **h81 F64**

THEFLYINGSCOTTIE 5 gr.g. Paris House – Miss Flossa (FR) (Big John (FR)) [2006/7 h69: 20g^6 16g^2 16g* 16g 16m Jul 27] workmanlike gelding: poor handicap hurdler: won selling event at Uttoxeter in June: best efforts at 2m on good going: visored last 4 starts. *B. N. Pollock* **h79**

THE FONZE (IRE) 6 br.g. Desert Sun – Ultimate Beat (USA) (Go And Go) [2006/7 16m^5 16s^{pu} Nov 4] fair on Flat (stays 1½m), successful twice in 2006: fairly useful handicap hurdler: further improvement when 5½ lengths fifth to Cuan Na Grai in Galway Hurdle, soon plenty to do and short of room: reportedly lame 3 months later: stays 19f: acts on heavy and good to firm going. *Eoin Doyle, Ireland* **h122**

THE FOUR PATS (IRE) 9 b.g. Satco (FR) – Ballinamona Thyne (IRE) (Good Thyne (USA)) [2006/7 18v 16v 20v c20g^3 19m Apr 7] winning pointer: poor maiden hurdler: better form when 7½ lengths third to Ma Furie in handicap at Ludlow on chasing debut: stays 2½m. *P. J. Rothwell, Ireland* **c92 h73**

THE FRENCH FURZE (IRE) 13 ch.g. Be My Guest (USA) – Exciting (Mill Reef (USA)) [2006/7 c–, h147: 16s^3 20v^3 16v^2 23s^4 Feb 17] leggy, close-coupled gelding: veteran hurdler, retains plenty of ability and enthusiasm: best efforts in 2006/7 when 6¼ lengths third to Straw Bear in 'Fighting Fifth' Hurdle at Newcastle (placed in race for sixth time, won in 2003) on reappearance and 9 lengths second to Afsoun in Champion Hurdle Trial at Haydock: still effective at 2m when conditions are testing and stays at least 21f: acts on heavy and good to firm going: tried blinkered, not since 1999/00: tough. *N. G. Richards* **c– h143**

THE FROSTY FERRET (IRE) 9 b.g. Zaffaran (USA) – Frostbite (Prince Tenderfoot (USA)) [2006/7 c84, h84: c25g May 13] big gelding: has stringhalt: poor maiden hurdler/chaser: stays 19f: acts on soft going: tried in cheekpieces: has finished weakly: sold 5,500 gns Doncaster May Sales. *J. M. Jefferson* **c– § h–**

THEFT 4 b.f. Silver Patriarch (IRE) – Piracy (Jupiter Island) [2006/7 F16s F16g* **F88 +**
Mar 28] 23,000 3-y-o: tall, rather unfurnished filly: third foal: dam unraced half-sister to
fairly useful chaser up to 25f Heist: better effort in bumpers when winning at Kempton in
March readily by 5 lengths from Easement: will stay beyond 2m. *N. J. Henderson*

THE GANGERMAN (IRE) 7 ch.g. Anshan – Ivy Lane (IRE) (Be My Native (USA)) **c– p**
[2006/7 h110: c24g^F Oct 7] leggy gelding: fair handicap hurdler: niggled but still every **h–**
chance when falling 5 out (not first mistake) in novice at Chepstow on chasing debut:
thorough stayer: acts on any going. *N. A. Twiston-Davies*

THE GAY GORDONS 6 b.g. Accordion – No Chili (Glint of Gold) [2006/7 F–: F16d **F–**
Jan 5] lengthy gelding: well held in bumpers 9 months apart, sold out of P. Webber's
stable after debut. *M. Smith*

THE GLEANER 5 b.g. Kayf Tara – Handmaiden (Shardari) [2006/7 F95: F17d⁶ 19d⁵ **h91**
20d² 20v^{pu} Mar 6] bumper winner: modest form in novice hurdles: stays 2½m: acts on **F78**
good to soft going. *M. W. Easterby*

THE GLEN 9 gr.g. Mtoto – Silver Singer (Pharly (FR)) [2006/7 c106, h–: c20g^{pu} c20f^{pu} **c–**
20m Jul 2] leggy gelding: fair hurdler/chaser at best: no form in handicaps early in **h–**
2006/7: stays 2¾m: acts on good to firm going. *R. Lee*

THE GLEN ROAD (IRE) 10 ch.g. Star Quest – Claret Mist (Furry Glen) [2006/7 c–, **c–**
h79: c19s^{pu} c20ff^{pu} Jun 3] winning pointer: runner-up in maiden in 2004/5, only comple- **h–**
tion in chases: poor form only start over hurdles. *A. W. Carroll*

THE GRANBY (IRE) 13 b.g. Insan (USA) – Elteetee (Paddy's Stream) [2006/7 c81+, **c92**
h–: c21g⁵ May 3] leggy gelding: winning hurdler/chaser, prone to mistakes in hunters: **h–**
fair pointer, won in February: stays 25f: acts on soft and good to firm going: in cheekpieces last 3 starts. *Mrs H. M. Kemp*

THE GRANDCHILD (IRE) 5 b.g. Moscow Society (USA) – Just Placed (IRE) **F77**
(Spanish Place (USA)) [2006/7 F16d⁴ F16g Apr 7] €23,000 3-y-o: third foal: dam lightly
raced in points: mid-field in bumpers, racing freely. *Ian Williams*

THE GREY BARON 10 gr.g. Baron Blakeney – Topsy Bee (Be Friendly) [2006/7 c–: **c85**
c26g² May 24] fair pointer, successful in April: first form in chases when 6 lengths second
to Honourable Spider in novice hunter at Folkestone: stays 3¼m: tried tongue tied.
A. Coveney

THE GREY MAN 6 gr.g. Muhtarram (USA) – Lavender Della (IRE) (Shernazar) **h100**
[2006/7 17g⁵ 17g* 17s 21d 17g^{pu} Apr 11] smallish, angular gelding: bumper winner: fair
on Flat, runner-up twice in 2m handicaps in 2006 for E. McMahon: fair hurdler: made all
in maiden at Taunton in November: should stay beyond 17f. *J. W. Mullins*

THE HAIRY LEMON 7 b.g. Eagle Eyed (USA) – Angie's Darling (Milford) [2006/7 **h111**
h112: 16v² 16s⁴ 16v⁴ Feb 26] quite good-topped gelding: fair handicap hurdler: best
around 2m: acts on heavy going: fluent jumper. *A. King*

THE HALFWAY BAR (IRE) 6 b.g. Leading Counsel (USA) – Le Sept (Le Bavard **h120**
(FR)) [2006/7 F20s² F20s³ 24v* 22v⁶ 24v* 23v⁴ Mar 24] fifth foal: dam winning pointer: **F89**
winning pointer: placed all 4 starts in bumpers: fairly useful hurdler: won maiden at
Gowran in December and novice handicap at Fairyhouse (18 ran, improved form when
beating Rock Diplomat by 10 lengths) in February: ran well when 17 lengths fourth to
Tailor's Hall in novice at Navan: stays 3m: raced on going softer than good. *Robert Tyner,
Ireland*

THE HARDY BOY 7 br.g. Overbury (IRE) – Miss Nero (Crozier) [2006/7 c–, h–: **c98**
c26g⁵ c21d^{ur} c20d* c21d⁴ c20v* c20s* c20v² c20d⁵ Mar 21] modest handi- **h–**
cap chaser: won at Lingfield in November and Plumpton in December and January (2,
novice event on second occasion): should stay beyond 2½m: raced on good ground or
softer (acts on heavy): tends to idle. *Miss A. M. Newton-Smith*

THE HEARTY JOKER (IRE) 12 b.g. Broken Hearted – Furryway (Furry Glen) **c– §**
[2006/7 c–§, h–§: 21s⁶ May 8] lengthy gelding: maiden hurdler: winning chaser: very **h– §**
lightly raced and no form since 2004: tried visored/blinkered: unreliable. *M. J. M. Evans*

THE HERO SULLIVAN (IRE) 6 b. or br.g. Muroto – You'll Never Know (IRE) (Un **c–**
Desperado (FR)) [2006/7 F–: 16g 20d³ 19d c16s⁶ 22m⁵ Apr 15] useful-looking gelding: **h94**
novice hurdler, easily best effort on second outing: well held on chasing debut: stays
2½m. *C. C. Bealby*

THE HOLLOW BOTTOM 6 b.g. Kadeed (IRE) – Leighten Lass (IRE) (Henbit **h101**
(USA)) [2006/7 F98: 20d⁵ 19g^{ur} 24s⁴ 21s^{pu} Mar 1] stocky gelding: bumper winner:

running best race over hurdles when blundering and unseating 2 out in novice at Ascot: stays 2½m: raced on good ground or softer. *N. A. Twiston-Davies*

THE HOLY BEE (IRE) 8 ch.g. Un Desperado (FR) – Ballycahan Girl (Bargello) [2006/7 c90, h–: c24g^{ur} c24d^{pu} c25m c22d^2 c23m^5 c22g* c23m^5 c24g^{pu} c26m^{pu} Apr 26] well-made gelding: maiden hurdler: modest chaser: won handicap at Market Rasen in July: stays 3m: acts on soft going: blinkered in 2006/7: tongue tied first outing (likely winner when unseating last): possibly not straightforward. *Mrs S. J. Humphrey*   **c100 d** **h–**

THE HONEST FIDDLER 4 b.g. Kayf Tara – Zihuatanejo (Efisio) [2006/7 F17v Mar 18] fifth foal: dam unraced: well held in bumper on debut. *A. Dickman*   **F–**

THE HOWARDIAN (IRE) 6 b.g. Zaffaran (USA) – Try Another Rose (IRE) (Roselier (FR)) [2006/7 22s^2 21g 19v 22s c23v^{pu} Jan 1] €34,000Y, €30,000 3-y-o, €20,000 4-y-o: tall, strong gelding: first foal: dam, unraced half-sister to useful 2m to 3m hurdler/chaser Tryfirion: runner-up in maiden point in 2006: bought £40,000 Cheltenham April Sales: second to Port of Mogan in maiden at Stratford on hurdling debut: no form after, blinkered on chase debut. *P. J. Hobbs*   **c–** **h90 d**

THE HUMBLE TRUCKER (IRE) 7 ch.g. Humbel (USA) – Rambling Rector (IRE) (The Parson) [2006/7 20d 16s 19d^6 Oct 31] €6,000 4-y-o: leggy gelding: fifth foal: dam unraced: no form in maiden Irish points/over hurdles. *D. Brace*   **h–**

THE IRON GIANT (IRE) 5 b.g. Giant's Causeway (USA) – Shalimar (IRE) (Indian Ridge) [2006/7 h92: 18m 17g 18g^6 16v Jan 12] unfurnished gelding: modest maiden on Flat (stays 1¾m): novice hurdler, no form in 2006/7. *B. G. Powell*   **h–**

THE JAZZ MUSICIAN (IRE) 5 b.g. Tiraaz (USA) – Royal Well (Royal Vulcan) [2006/7 F16d^2 F16s^2 Dec 27] €25,000 3-y-o, 31,000 4-y-o: half-brother to 3 winners, including fairly useful hurdler/useful chaser Royaltino (by Neltino), stayed 25f: dam unraced, half-sister to top-class chaser Teeton Mill: fairly useful form when runner-up in bumpers at Chepstow, beaten 1¾ lengths by Mutual Respect (pair clear) on second occasion. *C. L. Tizzard*   **F102**

THE JOKER (IRE) 9 ch.g. Montelimar (USA) – How Doudo (Oats) [2006/7 h107: 20m 16s 18s^4 16g^4 16d Jan 14] fair handicap hurdler: should be suited by 2½m+: has won on firm going, best efforts on good or softer: tongue tied last 4 starts. *J. K. Magee, Ireland*   **h101**

THE JOLLY SPOOFER (IRE) 5 b.g. Luso – Some News (IRE) (Be My Native (USA)) [2006/7 F16v Nov 26] sturdy gelding: fourth foal: brother to winning pointer: dam unraced half-sister to very smart staying chaser Belmont King: tailed off in bumper on debut. *Miss E. C. Lavelle*   **F–**

THE JOLLY TROLLEY (IRE) 6 b.g. Lord Americo – Princess Ross (Gleason (USA)) [2006/7 F16s^6 F16g 21g^{pu} Apr 23] €6,000 3-y-o: good-topped gelding: sixth live foal: dam unraced: poor form in bumpers: failed to settle and none too fluent in novice on hurdling debut. *A. Wilson*   **h–** **F74**

THE KING OF ANGELS (IRE) 5 b.g. Presenting – Vul Gale (Strong Gale) [2006/7 20g^2 24d^4 19g* 24s^{pu} 24g Apr 18] €46,000 3-y-o: good-topped gelding: half-brother to fairly useful chaser Carlingford Gale (by Carlingford Castle), stayed 3¼m, and fair hurdler/modest chaser Joint Agreement (by Good Thyne), stays 23f: dam unraced: fair novice hurdler: jumped better when winning at Ascot in November by 1¾ lengths from Lord Gee: should stay beyond 2½m: below best both starts on ground softer than good. *Jonjo O'Neill*   **h104**

THE KINGS FLING 11 b.g. Rakaposhi King – Poetic Light (Ardross) [2006/7 c102: c25g^3 May 3] fairly useful pointer/hunter, won point in April: stays 25f. *Miss E. Thompson*   **c102**

THE KOP END (IRE) 9 b.g. Topanoora – Shermaya (FR) (Shardari) [2006/7 c17s^{ur} 19g 16s 17s^{ur} 16v* 17v 16s Mar 10] big, heavy-bodied gelding: fair handicap hurdler, left C. Roche and off 21 months before return: back near best when winning at Haydock in December: let down by jumping both starts over fences: raced mainly around 2m on good going or softer: usually tongue tied. *Jonjo O'Neill*   **c–** **h114**

THE LANDLADY 6 b.m. Parthian Springs – Weldcome (Weld) [2006/7 F16g^5 Apr 9] £2,050 5-y-o: third foal: half-sister to winning pointer by Bob's Return: dam unraced half-sister to smart staying chaser High Edge Grey: around 16 lengths fifth to Overthrow in bumper at Fakenham on debut. *K. F. Clutterbuck*   **F72**

THE LANGER (IRE) 7 b.g. Saddlers' Hall (IRE) – Minigirls Niece (IRE) (Strong Gale) [2006/7 h67, F81: 24g^2 Nov 1] sturdy gelding: well held over hurdles, broke down only outing in 2006/7. *S. T. Lewis*   **h–**

THE LAST CAST 8 ch.g. Prince of Birds (USA) – Atan's Gem (USA) (Sharpen Up) [2006/7 c–, h–: c21vF c17m c23mF c26mpu 20gpu 24v3 25v2 25v5 24g Mar 15] workmanlike, angular gelding: fairly useful handicap hurdler/chaser, mostly let down by jumping over fences since 2004/5: seems to stay 25f: acts on heavy and good to firm going: tried in cheekpieces/blinkers: front runner/races prominently. *Evan Williams*   c128 h124

THE LAST HURRAH (IRE) 7 b.g. In The Wings – Last Exit (Dominion) [2006/7 17m* 16m3 16v2 16m4 16d Nov 12] rather leggy gelding: useful on Flat (stays 1¾m): developed into useful handicap hurdler once fitted with blinkers, winning at Kilbeggan in July: best effort when 3½ lengths behind to Sky To Sea at Listowel: ran poorly in valuable event at Cheltenham final start: raced around 2m: acts on good to firm and heavy going: blinkered last 7 outings. *Mrs J. Harrington, Ireland*   h131

THE LAST SABO 5 b.g. Prince Sabo – Classic Fan (USA) (Lear Fan (USA)) [2006/7 h–: 16f 20mpu May 28] no sign of ability. *M. Wigham*   h–

THE LAST TURN 5 b.m. Danzig Connection (USA) – Its My Turn (Palm Track) [2006/7 20gur Apr 23] half-sister to several winners, including fair hurdler up to 2½m Silverdale Lad (by Presidium) and modest staying hurdler Prince Nicholas (by Midyan): last all starts on Flat at 3 yrs for A. Berry: hampered and unseated second on hurdling debut. *I. McMath*   h–

THE LAST VIKING 7 b.g. Supreme Leader – Viking Rocket (Viking (USA)) [2006/7 h88, F81: 16d3 20g2 20s* 25d5 Dec 14] tall, close-coupled gelding: fair novice hurdler: won handicap at Ayr in November: lame following month: should be suited by further than 2½m: raced on good going or softer. *A. Parker*   h105

THE LAYING HEN (IRE) 7 ch.m. Anshan – Glacial Run (IRE) (Glacial Storm (USA)) [2006/7 h74, F–: c20d 22s c25mur Mar 29] maiden hurdler: no show in handicap chases: tried blinkered. *D. P. Keane*   c– h–

THE LISTENER (IRE) 8 gr.g. Roselier (FR) – Park Breeze (IRE) (Strong Gale) [2006/7 c150, h–: c24s2 c24v* c24v2 c26g Mar 16]   c168 h–

The owner pays the bills and, when it comes to it, calls the tune. The trainer may have day-to-day control, and a jockey may be the person the public associates with a particular horse, but the owner's wishes can override both. Andrew Thornton and Robert Alner know this only too well. The pair teamed up for Cheltenham Gold Cup glory in 1998 with Cool Dawn and Thornton has continued to take the bulk of rides for Alner ever since, though he has suffered the ignominy of losing out to less-experienced riders from the yard in a couple of recent high-profile incidents. After losing the plum ride on Kingscliff to Robert Walford at the beginning of 2005/6, on owner Arnie Sendell's insistence, Thornton found himself jocked off The Listener in the latest season with owner Ray Humphreys reportedly unhappy with the ride he gave the horse at Sandown on his reappearance. Stable conditional Daryl Jacob took the mount for the remainder of the campaign in which The Listener twice showed top-class form in Ireland. Irrespective of the criticism of his rider, the reappearance of The Listener in an intermediate event at Sandown in December was highly encouraging. The Listener had ended the previous season with two falls and the fact that he jumped well in the main at Sandown, except for a

Lexus Chase, Leopardstown—Daryl Jacob takes over on The Listener, who produces a top-class performance to defeat (from left to right) Beef Or Salmon, War of Attrition and L'Ami

Old Moss Farm's "The Listener"

mistake at a crucial stage three out, must, at least, have come as a relief. The Listener kept on strongly from the last but Thornton was quick to accept matters on the run-in, eventually going down by a length and a quarter to odds-on Star de Mohaison, the pair well clear of the two other runners.

In the Lexus Chase at Leopardstown later in the month, multiple Grade 1 winner Beef Or Salmon was favourite, with Cheltenham Gold Cup winner War of Attrition and L'Ami also at shorter odds than The Listener, the sole British challenger in the field of six. Jacob was unable to claim his 3-lb allowance because of the value of the race but that was never a factor as, under a much more forcing ride than at Sandown, The Listener never looked like being seriously threatened from two out after jumping boldly at the head of affairs, going on to win by eight lengths from Beef Or Salmon. Similar conditions prevailed when The Listener faced four rivals in the Hennessy Cognac Gold Cup back at Leopardstown in February. This time The Listener was odds on with Beef Or Salmon second favourite. As in the Lexus, The Listener soon took up the running, ridden to make it an even more thorough test, and he looked to have put a seal on matters when seven lengths clear of Beef Or Salmon at the last. However, the effort of forcing the pace in the conditions told as The Listener faltered on the run-in, Beef Or Salmon getting up close home. The performance nevertheless confirmed The Listener as a top-class chaser in testing conditions (he finished a distance clear of third-placed Hi Cloy). He gained revenge on Beef Or Salmon in the Cheltenham Gold Cup, but the contrasting conditions there didn't suit The Listener and he dropped away quickly on the final bend after not enjoying the clearest of passages (due mainly to a loose horse) coming down the hill, eventually finishing well held in eleventh. The Listener wasn't ridden so forcibly in what was a considerably larger field, but his jumping was still sound.

		Misti IV	Medium
	Roselier (FR)	(b 1958)	Mist
	(gr 1973)	Peace Rose	Fastnet Rock
The Listener (IRE)		(gr 1959)	La Paix
(gr.g. 1999)		Strong Gale	Lord Gayle
	Park Breeze (IRE)	(br 1975)	Sterntau
	(b or br 1988)	Park Delight	Saint Denys
		(ch 1974)	Lover's Delight

The strong, workmanlike The Listener is the type to carry condition. The Listener's dam Park Breeze has enjoyed a tremendously successful time of things as a broodmare, having produced six winners, including the useful handicap chaser Fork Lightning, a full brother to The Listener who was retired in the latest season. The Listener is also a half-brother to the progressive Irish staying chaser Offshore Account (by Oscar) and full details of this family can be found in that gelding's essay. Whereas Andrew Thornton lost out when Ray Humphreys chose to give the ride on The Listener to Daryl Jacob, both Thornton and Robert Alner suffered when Humphreys opted to move The Listener's half-brother Distant Thunder (by Phardante) to Noel Chance's yard for the latest season. Distant Thunder returned to his best when placed on two of his three starts for his new trainer, including a narrow defeat in the William Hill Trophy (a race Fork Lightning won in 2004). The Listener acts well on soft and heavy going and is unraced on firmer than good. He should stay beyond twenty-five furlongs. Despite falling twice in his novice season, The Listener is a bold and generally good jumper, something which should continue to stand him in good stead. *R. H. Alner*

THE LOCAL 7 b.g. Selkirk (USA) – Finger of Light (Green Desert (USA)) [2006/7 c116, h117: 16s 17s⁵ 16d 16s⁶ 16d³ 21v³ 16v³ 17d Mar 20] compact gelding: fair chaser/handicap hurdler: best around 2m: acts on heavy going: sometimes blinkered/in cheekpieces: usually front runner: lazy nowadays. *C. R. Egerton* c– h112

THE LOGICAL MAN (IRE) 6 b.g. Flemensfirth (USA) – Tudor Lady (Green Shoon) [2006/7 20v 16s 16d c25vᵖᵘ Feb 28] €60,000 4-y-o: has scope: brother to useful hurdler Mounthenry, stays 2½m, and half-brother to several winners, including fairly useful staying chaser/fair hurdler Satshoon (by Satco) and fairly useful hurdler/winning chaser Supreme Lady (by Supreme Leader), stayed 2¾m: dam ran once: no form in novice hurdles/handicap chase. *Jonjo O'Neill* c– h–

THE LONGFELLA 6 b.g. Petong – Miss Tri Colour (Shavian) [2006/7 F81: F17d 19d Dec 14] strong, rangy gelding: regressive form in bumpers: well held in novice on hurdling debut: may prove best at 2m. *G. M. Moore* h–

THE LUDER (IRE) 6 b.g. Naheez (USA) – Secret Sensation (IRE) (Classic Secret (USA)) [2006/7 h125: c24d* c23sᵘʳ c22s² c22d⁴ Mar 2] tall gelding: useful hurdler: fairly useful form over fences: landed odds in maiden at Kempton in November, idling: let down by jumping/attitude after: stays 3m: raced on ground softer than good: has worn blinkers, including when successful. *P. F. Nicholls* c117 § h– §

THE LUSO KID (IRE) 7 b.g. Luso – Sidhe Gaoth (Le Moss) [2006/7 20dᵖᵘ 18vᵖᵘ 20m Feb 4] €12,500 4-y-o: half-brother to modest hurdler Ar Nos Na Gaoithe (by Toulon), stays 21f, and to winning pointers by Rymer and Camden Town: dam winning Irish pointer: no form in novice hurdles. *J. Wade* h–

THEMANFROMCARLISLE 11 br.g. Jupiter Island – Country Mistress (Town And Country) [2006/7 c–, h–: c25g⁵ May 24] tall gelding: winning hurdler/chaser: fairly useful pointer, won in April: fifth at Kelso on hunter debut: probably stays 25f: acts on good to firm going, possibly not on softer than good. *Mrs S. H. Shirley-Beavan* c90 h–

THEMANFROMFRAAM 5 b.g. Fraam – Whey's Star (Bold Arrangement) [2006/7 F83: 17s 19s 17s 17s⁶ 20g⁵ Apr 11] rather unfurnished gelding: poor form over hurdles: stays 2½m. *Mrs S. M. Johnson* h75

THE MAN FROM SLATT (IRE) 6 b.g. Tiraaz (USA) – Miss Mutley (Pitpan) [2006/7 F16g F16m⁴ F18v³ F16m Apr 9] fourth foal: half-brother to useful staying chaser Model Son (by Leading Counsel): dam unraced: runner-up on completed start in maiden Irish points: modest form in bumpers. *W. P. Murphy, Ireland* F81

THE MASARETI KID (IRE) 10 b.g. Commanche Run – Little Crack (IRE) (Lancastrian) [2006/7 c–, h74: 23v⁴ 24s³ c25m² c20f⁴ c25s² c20f⁵ c20s⁶ c23fᵖᵘ c24m 22g c21s⁶ c23d⁶ Oct 14] workmanlike gelding: poor hurdler/chaser: left I. McMath after c79 § h64 §

sixth start, no form subsequently: stays 27f: acts on any going: usually in headgear: temperamental. *F. M. Barton*

THE MERRY MASON (IRE) 11 b.g. Roselier (FR) – Busters Lodge (Antwerp City) [2006/7 c111, h–: c24m^pu 24m c24s^pu c25s^5 c27v^5 c28g Apr 7] leggy, good-topped gelding: winning hurdler/chaser up to 3½m: largely disappointing since 2004/5: temperamental. *Mrs S. J. Smith*   c– § h– §

THE MIGHTY SPARROW (IRE) 14 b.g. Montelimar (USA) – Tamer's Belle (Tamerlane) [2006/7 c95x, h–: 20m c20g c16g^4 c16m^ur c19m^pu c16d^pu Oct 18] lengthy gelding: winning hurdler/chaser: no form in 2006/7: usually in cheekpieces/blinkers: often let down by jumping over fences. *A. E. Jones*   c– x h–

THE MINER 9 ch.g. Hatim (USA) – Glen Morvern (Carlingford Castle) [2006/7 c89x, h84: c20g^5 c20d^4 c20v^2 c20s^6 c24d^4 c25v^3 c20v^F c20s^2 c25s c20v^4 Mar 15] well-made gelding: maiden hurdler: modest handicap chaser: stays 25f: acts on heavy going: wears cheekpieces/visor: tongue tied after second outing: sketchy jumper. *Miss S. E. Forster*   c86 x h–

THE MOODY PYTHON 7 b.g. Perpendicular – Princess Ermyn (Shernazar) [2006/7 F16s Oct 25] good-topped gelding: second foal: dam, 11f/1½m winner, runner-up on completed start over hurdles: unseated in maiden point in 2006: well held in bumper. *M. Keighley*   F–

THE MURATTI 9 b.g. Alflora (IRE) – Grayrose Double (Celtic Cone) [2006/7 c–, h72: c21m^pu 27m Jun 8] workmanlike gelding: bumper winner: little form over jumps. *G. Brown*   c– h–

THE MYSTERY MAN (IRE) 8 ch.g. Roselier (FR) – Christys Best (IRE) (The Parson) [2006/7 c23g 22v^5 25s^3 Mar 11] no form: left Peter McCreery before second start. *Mrs Tracey Barfoot-Saunt*   c– h–

THENAMEESCAPESME 7 b.g. Alderbrook – Gaygo Lady (Gay Fandango (USA)) [2006/7 h93, F86: c21v^F c19d^pu 16s* 20v^4 16s 16v^4 Feb 17] sturdy gelding: modest hurdler: won novice claimer at Ludlow in December: badly let down by jumping in handicap chases: stays 21f: raced on going softer than good. *T. R. George*   c– x h85

THE NAMES BOND 9 b.g. Tragic Role (USA) – Artistic Licence (High Top) [2006/7 c97, h110: 18f^3 16g^2 20m* 22d^4 18s c24d^2 c20d^F Dec 30] close-coupled gelding: fair handicap hurdler/maiden chaser: won at Worcester in July: stays easy 3m: acts on soft and firm going. *N. G. Richards*   c105 h114

THE NEWSMAN (IRE) 15 b.g. Homo Sapien – Miller Fall's (Stubbs Gazette) [2006/7 c97, h–: c20g^pu c22g^3 c20m^pu Sep 21] tall gelding: winning hurdler: handicap chaser, form in long time only when winning at Plumpton in April 2006: stays 21f: probably acts on any going: tried blinkered: has won 6 times at Fontwell. *G. Wareham*   c– h–

THENFORD DUKE (IRE) 7 b.g. Dr Massini (IRE) – Ring-Em-All (Decent Fellow) [2006/7 16g 20s^6 Dec 5] €25,000 4-y-o: strong, lengthy gelding: half-brother to several winners, notably fairly useful hurdler Lisa's Storm (by Glacial Storm), stayed 2½m: dam unraced: fell in point in 2006: never dangerous 2 starts over hurdles: likely to prove better at 2½m than shorter. *D. J. Wintle*   h79

THENFORD FLYER (IRE) 7 b.g. Oscar (IRE) – Broadway Baby (Some Hand) [2006/7 F93?: F16m^2 F16m^3 F17g^2 16d^4 16s* 17s^3 21v^pu 17v^2 16v^5 Feb 17] good-bodied gelding: placed in bumpers: fair novice hurdler: won at Stratford in October: should be suited by further than 2m: acts on heavy going (bumper form on good to firm). *D. J. S. ffrench Davis*   h106 F92

THENFORD LORD (IRE) 6 b.g. Saddlers' Hall (IRE) – Laura's Native (IRE) (Be My Native (USA)) [2006/7 F87: 20s^pu 16v 20v^3 20g 25g^4 Apr 16] big, workmanlike gelding: poor novice hurdler: stays 25f: tried blinkered. *Mrs S. J. Smith*   h82

THENFORD SIR (IRE) 6 b.g. General Monash (USA) – Alpencrocus (IRE) (Waajib) [2006/7 F16m^6 20s^pu 16v^pu 16s^6 Apr 27] €8,000 3-y-o, 850 4-y-o: workmanlike gelding: half-brother to winning pointer by Darnay and winning sprinter in Italy by Forest Wind: dam ran once: won second of 2 starts in maiden points in 2006: little impact in bumper/over hurdles. *Miss S. E. Forster*   h77 F–

THENFORD SNIPE (IRE) 6 b.g. Clerkenwell (USA) – Peas (IRE) (Little Wolf) [2006/7 F16d F16s^2 20v^5 Feb 28] stocky gelding: third foal: closely related to useful bumper/2¼m hurdle winner Demarco (by Old Vic): dam unraced: won maiden Irish point in 2006: bought 36,000 gns Doncaster May Sales: fair form both starts in bumpers 2 days apart: well-held fifth to Gabier in maiden at Folkestone on hurdling debut: will be suited by 3m. *J. A. B. Old*   h– F87

THENFORD STAR (IRE) 6 b.m. Zaffaran (USA) – Limavady Lady (IRE) (Camden Town) [2006/7 h74+: 22d* 21s² 23d* 22s³ 26g⁴ Apr 11] lengthy, rather unfurnished mare: has had soft palate operation: modest hurdler: improved form in 2006/7, winning handicaps at Wincanton (novice) in November and Fakenham (led on line) in January: should stay 3m+: raced on good going or softer: tongue tied in 2005/6. *A. King* **h96**

THENFORD WOODCOCK (IRE) 6 b.g. Moonax (IRE) – American Flier (IRE) (Lord Americo) [2006/7 20mᵖᵘ Jul 26] second foal: dam, of little account, half-sister to smart hurdler/useful chaser Mr Percy, stayed 21f: fifth in bumper: sold out of E. O'Grady's stable 1,600 gns Doncaster May Sales: tongue tied, no show in novice on hurdling debut: sold £580 Ascot December Sales. *L. Corcoran* **h–**

THE NOMAD 11 b.g. Nomadic Way (USA) – Bubbling (Tremblant) [2006/7 c113, h–: c16s⁴ c16v³ c20v² c20vᵖᵘ c16v c20sᵖᵘ Apr 25] workmanlike gelding: fair handicap chaser: out of sorts last 3 starts: stays 21f: acts on heavy and good to firm going: races prominently. *M. W. Easterby* **c107 h–**

THEOCRITUS (GER) 6 b.g. Trempolino (USA) – Thyatira (FR) (Bakharoff (USA)) [2006/7 h107: c16d² c16d³ c20s⁵ c19vᶠ c19s³ Dec 22] lengthy, unfurnished gelding: fair hurdler: modest novice chaser: stays 19f: acts on soft and good to firm going. *Nick Williams* **c99 h–**

THEONEBEHIND (IRE) 7 b.g. Warcraft (USA) – Kelly's Bridge (Netherkelly) [2006/7 c25m c25g 24fᵖᵘ c16f c25d c16gᶠ Apr 23] well beaten in points in Ireland, successful in Britain in 2006: no form in chases/maiden hurdle: has worn headgear. *J. W. F. Aynsley* **c– h–**

THE OUTLIER (IRE) 9 gr.g. Roselier (FR) – Shuil A Cuig (Quayside) [2006/7 c110, h–: c20g⁴ c22v* c26sʳᵒ c24v² c24v* c28sᵖᵘ c33sᵖᵘ c36gᵘʳ Apr 14] rather leggy gelding: useful handicap chaser: improved further in 2006/7, winning at Towcester in November **c136 h–**

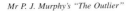

Mr P. J. Murphy's "The Outlier"

and Haydock (beat Turpin Green by 12 lengths in Grade 2 Peter Marsh Chase, staying on strongly after left ahead 4 out) in January: let down by jumping in other valuable events after: should stay 3½m+: acts on heavy going. *Miss Venetia Williams*

THE PACKAGE 4 br.g. Kayf Tara – Ardent Bride (Ardross) [2006/7 F16m* Apr 24] **F102 p** third foal: dam, showed little in bumper/novice hurdles, half-sister to useful 2m chaser Shamana: evens, created good impression when winning maiden bumper at Towcester on debut by 4 lengths from Mitre Peak: likely to improve. *D. E. Pipe*

THE PAINKILLER (IRE) 6 b.g. Erins Isle – Mariussa (IRE) (Fools Holme (USA)) **h109** [2006/7 24d³ 24v* 21s⁶ 22d³ Feb 19] €8,500 3-y-o: rangy gelding: chasing type: fifth foal: brother to a winning pointer and half-brother to 1¼m winner Russian Project (by Project Manager): dam unraced: won maiden point in 2006: bought 26,000 gns Doncaster May Sales: fair form over hurdles, winning novice at Uttoxeter in November: looks a thorough stayer: acts on heavy going. *C. C. Bealby*

THE PARTING GLASS (IRE) 5 b.g. Anshan – Ardfallon (IRE) (Supreme Leader) **F76** [2006/7 F16s F17s Jan 30] €21,000 3-y-o: seventh foal: half-brother to bumper/3m hurdle winner Golden Parachute (by Executive Perk): dam, fourth in bumper, half-sister to dams of useful chasers up to 3m Bells Life and Indian Tonic: mid-field in bumpers. *C. E. Longsdon*

THE PEN 5 ch.m. Lake Coniston (IRE) – Come To The Point (Pursuit of Love) [2006/7 **h–** h98: 16v 17v Feb 20] sparely-made mare: fair on Flat (stays 1½m), successful twice in 2006: no form over hurdles since juvenile at Wetherby on debut in 2005/6. *C. W. Fairhurst*

THE PENNYS DROPPED (IRE) 10 ch.g. Bob's Return (IRE) – Shuil Alainn **c–** (Levanter) [2006/7 c112, h–: c21sᵖᵘ Feb 16] sturdy gelding: fair chaser: off 19 months, **h–** badly let down by jumping in hunter only start in 2006/7: will stay beyond 3¼m: acts on good to soft and good to firm ground: tried visored/tongue tied: has bled from nose/had breathing problem: makes the odd mistake. *Jonjo O'Neill*

THE PIKER (IRE) 6 b.g. Darazari (IRE) – Top Step (IRE) (Step Together (USA)) **h–** [2006/7 h–, F–: 22sᵖᵘ Jan 16] tall gelding: no form: tried tongue tied. *B. G. Powell*

THE PIOUS PRINCE (IRE) 6 ch.g. Shahrastani (USA) – Ara Blend (IRE) (Persian **F103** Mews) [2006/7 F108p: F16d⁵ F16g* F16m⁶ Apr 21] sturdy gelding: fairly useful form in bumpers: won at Musselburgh in December by 1½ lengths from Dand Nee, making virtually all, despite hanging left: will stay beyond 2m. *L. Lungo*

THE POSER 6 b.g. I'm Supposin (IRE) – Fairy Ballerina (Fairy King (USA)) [2006/7 **c68** c25dᵖᵘ c20d c27s² c25s⁵ Feb 15] eighth foal: half-brother to useful hurdler Aspirant Dancer (by Marju), stayed 2¾m: dam Irish 2-y-o 7f winner: in frame both starts in maiden points in 2006: little form in chases. *J. Wade*

THE PREACHER 4 b.g. Namaqualand (USA) – Bustling Around (Bustino) [2006/7 **h80** 17s⁶ 17s² 17gᵖᵘ 16g³ 16sᶠ 17v Jan 27] lengthy gelding: modest maiden on Flat (stays 1½m), sold out of J. Wainwright's stable 4,600 gns Doncaster October Sales: modest juvenile hurdler: raced around 2m on good ground or softer. *K. J. Burke*

THE QUARRY MAN 9 b.g. Opera Ghost – Beauty's Imp (Impecunious) [2006/7 c–: **c70** c21g⁴ Apr 1] fair pointer, won twice in December: well held in novice on completed outing in hunters. *Miss E. Thompson*

THE RAILWAY MAN (IRE) 8 b.g. Shernazar – Sparky Sue (IRE) (Strong Gale) **c–** [2006/7 c144, h–: 19d* Nov 11] well-made gelding: fairly useful hurdler: didn't need to **h101 +** be at best to win 22-runner minor event at Naas in November by 5 lengths from Freemantle Doctor: smart novice chaser in 2005/6, won Grade 1 Dr P. J. Moriarty Novices' Chase at Leopardstown: stays 21f: acts on heavy going. *A. L. T. Moore, Ireland*

THEREALBAT (IRE) 13 ch.g. Rashar (USA) – Callmemeala (Callernish) [2006/7 **c–** c23mᵖᵘ Jul 12] ex-Irish gelding: maiden hurdler/chaser: winning pointer: tried blinkered/ **h–** tongue tied: sold £550 Ascot November Sales. *Mrs Tracey Barfoot-Saunt*

THE REAL DEAL (IRE) 6 b.g. Taipan (IRE) – Forest Mist (Dalsaan) [2006/7 h85: **h127 +** 16d² 16d 24s* 18s* 19d⁶ 20s Mar 10] well-made gelding: chasing type: progressed well over hurdles in 2006/7, winning handicap at Chepstow in December and novice at Fontwell (fairly useful form, beat Benetwood by 8 lengths) in February: good sixth to Overstrand in valuable handicap at Ascot: effective from 2¼m to 3m: raced on good to soft/soft ground. *Nick Williams*

THERE IS NO DOUBT (FR) 6 b.g. Mansonnien (FR) – Ma Chance (FR) (Dancehall **c–** (USA)) [2006/7 h96: c19vᶠ Nov 28] useful-looking gelding: dual bumper winner: modest **h–**

form at best over hurdles: left Miss L. Bridges and off 11 months, disputing lead when falling fatally 2 out in handicap at Hereford on chasing debut. *D. E. Pipe*

THE REPRESENTATIVE (IRE) 6 br.g. Presenting – Ticking Over (IRE) (Decent **F88 +** Fellow) [2006/7 F16s³ Apr 27] €32,000 4-y-o: fifth foal: half-brother to modest hurdler Westmorland (by Phardante), stays 3m, and winning pointer by Jolly Jake: dam ran once in point: 16 lengths third to Silver By Nature in bumper at Perth on debut, travelling smoothly close up. *N. J. Henderson*

THERESA (DEN) 5 b.m. Final Appearance (IRE) – Habibi (DEN) (Jammed Red **h70** (CAN)) [2006/7 19vᵖᵘ 17g 16m³ Apr 24] successful once (at 3 yrs over 1¼m) from 27 starts up to 1½m on Flat in Scandinavia: poor form over hurdles: tried tongue tied. *M. Scudamore*

THE REVEREND (IRE) 7 b. or br.g. Taipan (IRE) – Sounds Classical (IRE) (Over **c125** The River (FR)) [2006/7 h115p: c25d² c25s* c25v³ c20v² c20s⁴ c33g Mar 15] big, good- **h–** topped gelding: twice-raced over hurdles, won novice on debut in 2004/5: fairly useful chaser: won maiden at Wetherby in November by 10 lengths from Supreme's Legacy: below form after, shaping as if amiss final start: stays 25f: acts on soft going, possibly not on heavy. *J. Howard Johnson*

THE RIGHT PEOPLE (IRE) 7 ch.g. Deploy – Marlousion (IRE) (Montelimar **c–** (USA)) [2006/7 h82+: 20g³ 22d c24gᵘʳ 20d Jan 5] modest novice hurdler: unseated third **h91** on chasing debut: should stay beyond 2½m: raced on good ground or softer. *L. Lungo*

THE RING (IRE) 7 b.g. Definite Article – Renata's Ring (IRE) (Auction Ring (USA)) **h110** [2006/7 16s³ 20g 16v* 16s² 16v³ 16s² 16s² 16g Mar 17] good-topped gelding: fair hurdler: won maiden at Kelso in December: should stay 2½m: acts on heavy going. *K. G. Reveley*

THE RIP 6 ch.g. Definite Article – Polgwynne (Forzando) [2006/7 h80: 16dᶠ 16d 16sᵖᵘ **h–** Oct 26] good-topped gelding: maiden hurdler, no form in 2006/7: raced mainly at 2m: tried tongue tied. *R. M. Stronge*

Mrs Jane Williams' "The Real Deal"

THE RISING MOON (IRE) 8 br.g. Anshan – I'm So Happy (IRE) (Miner's Lamp) **c105 §**
[2006/7 c–x, h–: 16g⁴ 16s 19d³ 24m² 22g⁴ c20m⁶ c23f³ c26m⁶ c25mᵖᵘ Oct 4] good- **h110 §**
topped gelding: fair hurdler: form over fences only when third in handicap at Worcester:
stays 3m: acts on soft and good going: wore eyeshields last 7 starts: often let down by
jumping/attitude. *Jonjo O'Neill*

THE RISKY VIKING (IRE) 8 b.g. Supreme Leader – Queen's Flagship (IRE) **c–**
(Accordion) [2006/7 c26dᵖᵘ 24v² 26s⁴ 27v² 22s² 24v⁴ Feb 20] first foal: dam, won 2m **h104**
hurdle, sister to top-class 2m chaser Flagship Uberalles and half-sister to top-class 2m to
2½m chaser Viking Flagship: runner-up in maiden Irish point in 2006: bought 11,000 gns
Doncaster May Sales: let down by jumping (persistently went right) on chase debut: fair
novice hurdler: stays 27f: raced on ground softer than good. *Nick Williams*

THE RIVER JOKER (IRE) 11 ch.g. Over The River (FR) – Augustaeliza (IRE) **c64 §**
(Callernish) [2006/7 c80§, h–§: c24s³ c24s⁵ c24v⁵ 24v c24gᵖᵘ Mar 28] lengthy, angular **h– §**
gelding: winning hurdler: poor handicap chaser: thorough stayer: acts on heavy going:
ungenuine. *John R. Upson*

THE ROCKING DOCK (IRE) 6 gr.g. Dr Massini (IRE) – Ackle Backle (Furry **h108**
Glen) [2006/7 h95, F89: 16g⁸ 17s⁵ 16m⁸ 16m 19g⁴ 16g⁶ 20g Apr 7] workmanlike
gelding: fair novice hurdler: won at Wetherby (conditional jockeys) and Bangor in May
and Stratford in June: staus 19f: acts on soft and good to firm going. *D. McCain Jnr*

THE ROLLERSKATER (IRE) 7 b.g. High Roller (IRE) – Lashkari Rose (IRE) **c–**
(Lashkari) [2006/7 F–: 22mᵖᵘ 24sᵖᵘ c19vᵖᵘ c20g³ Apr 23] placed in maiden points in **h–**
2005: no form in other events, left Mrs A. Thorpe before third start: tongue tied in 2006/7.
K. Bishop

THE ROOKEN (IRE) 8 b.g. Fourstars Allstar (USA) – Be My Sweetheart (IRE) (Be **h–**
My Native (USA)) [2006/7 h–: 20g 16g 16s 24d 20vᵖᵘ Jan 17] smallish gelding: no form.
P. Spottiswood

THE ROYAL DUB (IRE) 9 b.g. Supreme Leader – Bettys The Boss (IRE) (Deep **c–**
Run) [2006/7 20v* 16d 20s* 24v² 22v⁴ Jan 1] winning pointer: fair handicap hurdler/ **h104**
maiden chaser: won at Perth in May and Fairyhouse in November: stays 3m: raced on
good going or softer (acts on heavy): tried blinkered. *A. J. Martin, Ireland*

THE SALTIRE TIGER 6 b.g. Busy Flight – Candlebright (Lighter) [2006/7 h–, F88: **h87**
20g 22m 20m⁶ 20m⁵ 16d⁶ 17m⁵ Apr 9] good-topped gelding: modest maiden hurdler:
stays 2½m: acts on good to firm and good to soft going. *Mrs L. B. Normile*

THE SAWYER (BEL) 7 ch.g. Fleetwood (IRE) – Green Land (BEL) (Hero's Honor **h120**
(USA)) [2006/7 h99, F99: 20d⁴ 24d⁴ 24s² 21v* 20v* 23s⁵ 20s 20g⁶ Apr 7] rangy gelding:
will make a chaser: fairly useful novice hurdler: won at Plumpton and Haydock (by 7
lengths from Mister Potter) in January: stays 3m: acts on heavy going (runner-up in
bumper on good to firm). *R. H. Buckler*

THESEUS (IRE) 11 b.g. Danehill (USA) – Graecia Magna (USA) (Private Account **c–**
(USA)) [2006/7 c16dᵘʳ c17g c16m⁶ Apr 14] useful-looking ex-Irish gelding: one-time **h–**
useful handicap chaser: left P. Hughes and off 15 months, no show in Britain in 2006/7:
best short of 2¾m: acts on firm and soft going: blinkered once. *Miss A. E. Broyd*

THE SHIRLEY HUNT 7 b.m. Rakaposhi King – Zalina (Tyrnavos) [2006/7 F80§: **F– §**
F16g⁵ Jul 5] neat mare: form in bumpers only on debut: refused to race next time. *Ian
Williams*

THE SHREWD COOKIE 4 b.g. Bertolini (USA) – Charlie Girl (Puissance) [2006/7 **F69**
F16d⁶ F13m Mar 29] third foal: closely related/half-brother to 2-y-o sprint winners by
Foxhound and Josr Algarhoud: dam 2-y-o 5f winner: shaped as if having stamina
limitations in bumpers: sold 1,500 gns Doncaster May Sales. *B. Ellison*

THE SHY MAN (IRE) 4 b.g. Grand Plaisir (IRE) – Black Betty (Furry Glen) [2006/7 **h82 +**
17v⁵ 19v⁴ Feb 27] €11,000 3-y-o: unfurnished gelding: eighth foal: dam unraced sister to
fairly useful staying hurdler Now Your Talkin: better effort in novice hurdles when 28
lengths fourth to Ring The Boss at Catterick, not given unduly hard time: should stay
2½m. *G. M. Moore*

THE SNEAKSTER (IRE) 9 b.m. Jurado (USA) – Royal Star (IRE) (Orchestra) **c75**
[2006/7 c–§, h–§: 19g⁴ 16m⁶ 20f⁵ 20m 17s⁶ 16m³ 20g 19m⁴ 21m³ 21g² 16g 21m² 21d³ **h86**
22d 21d⁵ c20s⁵ 24d⁴ c22g³ c20m³ Apr 28] rather leggy mare: modest maiden hurdler/
poor maiden chaser: stays 21f: acts on firm and good to soft going. *S. A. Brookshaw*

THE SNURGLAR (IRE) 5 b.g. Snurge – Burksie (IRE) (Supreme Leader) [2006/7 **F92**
F16d² F16v F16g³ Mar 28] 38,000 4-y-o: big, good-topped gelding: first foal: dam

976

unraced, out of sister to useful chaser up to 3m Edberg: fair form when placed in bumpers. *M. W. Easterby*

THE SOCIAL DRINKER 5 b.g. Tipsy Creek (USA) – Sanshang (FR) (Astronef) [2006/7 F14d F16g Apr 23] 2,500 4-y-o: second foal: half-brother to fair 1¼m/1½m winner Sudden Impulse (by Silver Patriarch): dam placed in Belgium at 2 yrs: tailed off in bumpers. *F. P. Murtagh*   **F–**

THE SPACER (IRE) 9 ch.g. Florida Son – Tacova's Gift (IRE) (Avocat) [2006/7 c24gF 20m³ 20m³ c23mF 27d* c23fF Sep 3] modest hurdler, sold out of M. Hourigan's stable 900 gns Doncaster October (2005) Sales: won seller at Newton Abbot in August: faller all 3 starts over fences: stays 27f: acts on firm and good to soft going. *Evan Williams*   **c– x** / **h87**

THE SPEAKER (FR) 6 b.g. Nikos – Ostenne (FR) (Rose Laurel) [2006/7 F16v F16v² 27v⁴ 25s⁴ Mar 11] 8,000 4-y-o: workmanlike gelding: third foal: half-brother to winning hurdler/chaser around 2m Stenborg (by Cyborg) and winning 2m chaser Stenbreeze (by Phantom Breeze): dam winning hurdler around 2m: runner-up in bumper at Warwick: let down by jumping/attitude in novice hurdles. *J. W. Mullins*   **h75** / **F97**

THE SPOONPLAYER (IRE) 8 b.g. Accordion – Jennie Dun (IRE) (Mandalus) [2006/7 h114, F80: 22d³ 20s⁵ 21d³ 16v³ 21g 17g 16m Apr 25] leggy gelding: fairly useful handicap hurdler: contested valuable 28-runner events at Cheltenham fifth/sixth outings, creditable effort when mid-field behind Burntoakboy on first occasion: stays 2¾m: acts on heavy ground: has run well when sweating. *Henry de Bromhead, Ireland*   **h122**

THE SPORTSMAN (FR) 4 ro.g. Fragrant Mix (IRE) – La Pulcinella (FR) (Bikala) [2006/7 F13s² F17s 16s 17g 17m⁶ Apr 17] rather leggy gelding: sixth foal: half-brother to several winners over jumps in France, including hurdler/chaser up to 2½m Beruchet (by Murmure): dam winning hurdler around 2m: runner-up in 3-y-o bumper on debut: not knocked about 3 starts in maiden hurdles: should do better, especially now qualified for handicaps. *D. E. Pipe*   **h– p** / **F98**

THE STAGGERY BOY (IRE) 11 b.g. Shalford (IRE) – Murroe Star (Glenstal (USA)) [2006/7 c94, h–: c16m⁴ Jul 11] sturdy gelding: modest handicap chaser: off 14 months before only start in 2006/7: stays 2¼m: acts on good to firm and heavy going: effective tongue tied or not. *M. R. Hoad*   **c94** / **h–**

THE STICKLER 8 ch.g. Weld – Bivadell (Bivouac) [2006/7 c19mᵖᵘ Apr 24] fair pointer, won in February: no form in other events. *Mrs Nicola Pollock*   **c–** / **h–**

THE TERMINATOR (FR) 5 b.g. Night Shift (USA) – Surmise (USA) (Alleged (USA)) [2006/7 16s 16f⁴ Apr 5] poor maiden on Flat (stays 8.6f): 7 lengths fourth in selling hurdle at Ludlow. *M. Mullineaux*   **h81**

THE TEUCHTER 8 b.g. First Trump – Barefoot Landing (USA) (Cozzene (USA)) [2006/7 h–§: 26g³ c25v⁴ 24s Dec 18] medium-sized gelding: poor maiden hurdler: well beaten on chasing debut: stays 3¼m: acts on soft going: tried blinkered, often in cheekpieces: ungenuine. *Mrs S. D. Williams*   **c– §** / **h71 §**

THE THUNDERER 8 gr.g. Terimon – By Line (High Line) [2006/7 16s 17v 16g Mar 19] lengthy gelding: bumper winner: little form over hurdles, left N. Henderson and off 21 months before return. *H. J. L. Dunlop*   **h–**

THE TINKERATER (IRE) 6 b.g. New Frontier (IRE) – Dozy Love (IRE) (Bulldozer) [2006/7 20m 24dᵘʳ 19g 23sᵖᵘ 20vF 23v⁶ c25sᵖᵘ Feb 27] €15,500 4-y-o: leggy gelding: half-brother to fair Irish chaser Martys Step (by Step Together), winner up to 25f: dam unraced: little sign of ability: tongue tied last 4 starts, also in cheekpieces last 2. *C. A. Mulhall*   **c–** / **h–**

THE TOKOLOSHE 5 ch.g. Zaha (CAN) – Hay Danzig (IRE) (Roi Danzig (USA)) [2006/7 F16s Nov 11] lengthy, good-topped gelding: first foal: dam unraced: tongue tied, tailed off in bumper on debut. *M. A. Barnes*   **F–**

THE TOTHER ONE (IRE) 6 b.g. Accordion – Baden (IRE) (Furry Glen) [2006/7 F16m* Apr 10] half-brother to high-class chaser Thisthatandtother (by Bob Back), stays 21f, and fair chaser Polar Scout (by Arctic Lord), stays 2¾m: dam, fairly useful hurdler, stayed 19f: favourite, impressive when winning bumper at Chepstow on debut by 7 lengths from Meersbrook: promising. *P. F. Nicholls*   **F105 p**

THE VENETIAN (IRE) 6 b.g. Presenting – Dashing March (Daring March) [2006/7 F16d² 17s 16s² 22g Mar 19] €16,000 3-y-o, 15,500 4-y-o: rangy, good sort: fifth foal: dam, poor novice hurdler around 2m, half-sister to very smart 2m hurdler Ra Nova: runner-up in bumper at Sandown on debut: modest form over hurdles: probably stays 2¾m. *V. R. A. Dartnall*   **h97** / **F94**

THE VERY MAN (IRE) 5 b.g. Flemensfirth (USA) – Christian Lady (IRE) (Mandalus) [2006/7 F16s* 16s² 18s² Dec 26] €15,500 3-y-o: fourth foal: half-brother to fair hurdler/fairly useful chaser Stern (by Executive Perk), stays 21f: dam unraced: won 21-runner bumper at Punchestown in November on debut by length from Heron's Flight: runner-up both starts in maiden hurdles, beaten 14 lengths by Aran Concerto at Navan and neck by Hot Port at Leopardstown: will stay 2½m: open to improvement. *Joseph Crowley, Ireland* **h105 p F111**

THE VILLAGER (IRE) 11 br.g. Zaffaran (USA) – Kitty Wren (Warpath) [2006/7 c111, h–: c21g⁴ c24m⁵ c24g Feb 21] workmanlike gelding: modest handicap chaser, left T. George and off 9 months before second outing: effective at 2½m to 27f: acts on heavy going (won bumper on good to firm): has had tongue tied, including last 4 starts: often let down by jumping: inconsistent. *Mike Hammond* **c98 § h–**

THE VINTAGE DANCER (IRE) 11 b.g. Riberetto – Strong Swimmer (IRE) (Black Minstrel) [2006/7 c84: c21m⁴ c24v³ c24g^F c22g³ c25m Aug 6] winning pointer: maiden chaser: stayed 3m: acted on heavy going, probably on good to firm: dead. *B. N. Pollock* **c71**

THE WANDERING MAN (IRE) 7 b.g. Beneficial – Whyme (Derring Rose) [2006/7 F16s* F18s* F16s Dec 2] third foal: half-brother to fair hurdler Sher Why Not (by Shernazar), stays 2½m: dam placed in points: useful form in bumpers, winning at Punchestown (by ½ length from Notre Pere) in May and Cork (odds on, beat Jennys Oscar by 2 lengths, eased) in November: disappointed next time and not seen out again. *Colm A. Murphy, Ireland* **F106**

THE WASHERWOMAN 7 b.m. Classic Cliche (IRE) – Olnistar (FR) (Balsamo (FR)) [2006/7 h80: 20d Jan 15] poor form on first of 2 outings over hurdles 13 months apart. *B. I. Case* **h–**

THE WEAVER (FR) 8 ch.g. Villez (USA) – Miss Planette (FR) (Tip Moss (FR)) [2006/7 h94: 22f 17vᵖᵘ 19g 24g 20g 16m⁴ 16vᵖᵘ 17mᵖᵘ 16g^F Apr 15] lengthy gelding: maiden hurdler: little form in 2006/7, sold out of L. Lungo's stable 8,000 gns Doncaster May Sales after reappearance: left B. Storey after fifth outing: barely stays 3m: acts on soft and good to firm going: tried in cheekpieces/blinkers: has had tongue tied: has found little. *M. A. Barnes* **h88 ?**

THE WEXFORD MAN (IRE) 7 br.g. Corrouge (USA) – Clonroche Windor (Paddy's Stream) [2006/7 24s⁶ 20s 16v c21vᵖᵘ Jan 27] fifth foal: half-brother to winning pointer by Rashar: dam lightly raced: won maiden Irish point in 2006: little show over hurdles/in novice handicap chase. *T. R. George* **c– h–**

THE WHISPERER (IRE) 6 b.g. Supreme Leader – Ring Mam (IRE) (King's Ride) [2006/7 22g* 24s³ 24v³ Jan 17] €26,000 4-y-o: workmanlike gelding: fourth foal: dam placed in points: won maiden Irish point in 2006: bought £115,000 Cheltenham April Sales: 7/4-on, impressive hurdling debut when winning novice at Kelso in November: fairly useful form when third to Flight Leader in Grade 2 novice at Cheltenham: disappointing final outing: stays 3m: acts on good ground: may still do better. *N. G. Richards* **h121 +**

THE WHISPERING OAK (IRE) 5 b.m. Silver Patriarch (IRE) – Celtic Remorse (Celtic Cone) [2006/7 F–: F16m 20mᵖᵘ 24mᵖᵘ 22m⁴ 24d Oct 5] little form: tongue tied last 2 starts. *P. S. Payne* **h66 F–**

THE WICKED WITCH 4 gr.f. Terimon – Welgenco (Welsh Saint) [2006/7 F14g⁴ Apr 10] half-sister to fair hurdler/chaser Return Home (by Bob's Return), stays 2½m, and bumper winners by Bob's Return and The Parson: dam, won up to 2¾m over jumps, also winning stayer on Flat: seemed in need of experience when 11½ lengths fourth to Blackthorn Boy in bumper at Fontwell on debut. *P. Winkworth* **F67 +**

THE WICKED WIZARD 4 br.g. Wizard King – Sallyoreally (IRE) (Common Grounds) [2006/7 F14v F14s Dec 16] small, heavy-bodied gelding: third foal: dam, modest maiden, probably stayed 1½m: no show in 3-y-o bumpers and sellers on Flat. *W. Storey* **F–**

THE WICKETKEEPER (IRE) 5 b.g. Double Bed (FR) – In Memoriam (IRE) (Buckskin (FR)) [2006/7 F–: F16d 17d⁴ 17g⁴ Apr 20] compact gelding: well held in bumpers: second and better effort in novice hurdles when fourth at Hereford. *M. Scudamore* **h85 F–**

THE WIFE'S SISTER (IRE) 6 b.m. Classic Cliche (IRE) – Hard Love (Rambo Dancer (CAN)) [2006/7 h80: 20g⁵ 26d* 20vᵖᵘ 27m⁴ 27dᵖᵘ Aug 15] leggy mare: poor hurdler: won seller at Hereford (left clear last) in May: stays 3¼m: raced mainly on good going or softer (acts on heavy): tried visored, usually blinkered: ungenuine. *Mrs K. Waldron* **h78 §**

THE WIZARD MUL 7 br.g. Wizard King – Longden Pride (Superpower) [2006/7 h–:   **h67**
16g⁶ 16vᶠ 19dᵖᵘ Dec 14] leggy gelding: little form over hurdles: tongue tied in 2006/7
(saddle slipped final start). *W. Storey*

THE WOODEN SPOON (IRE) 9 b.g. Old Vic – Amy's Gale (IRE) (Strong Gale)   **h74**
[2006/7 h95: 20s⁵ 20v⁴ Feb 13] rangy gelding: novice hurdler, modest form at best: will
stay beyond 3m: raced mainly on soft/heavy ground: joined Jim Best. *L. Wells*

THEXMOORLADY 7 b.m. Thowra (FR) – Alpine Song (True Song) [2006/7 20mᵖᵘ   **h–**
Apr 25] first foal: dam winning pointer: lost action in maiden hurdle on debut. *Miss
V. A. Stephens*

THEY ALL LAUGHED 4 ch.g. Zafonic (USA) – Royal Future (IRE) (Royal Acad-   **h–**
emy (USA)) [2006/7 16m 16m Oct 12] fair on Flat (stays 1¾m), successful in April: well
held in juvenile hurdles. *P. W. Hiatt*

THE YELLOW EARL (IRE) 7 b.g. Topanoora – Sweet Innocence (IRE) (King's   **c–**
Ride) [2006/7 h61: c17gᵖᵘ c21d c16f c16d⁵ c16sᵖᵘ Oct 29] big, strong gelding: little form.   **h–**
J. M. Jefferson

THEY GRABBED ME (IRE) 6 b. or br.m. Presenting – Royal Gale (Strong Gale)   **h–**
[2006/7 h68: 20g May 5] poor maiden hurdler: stays 3m: acts on firm and good to soft
going: tried visored/in cheekpieces: tongue tied last 5 outings. *M. C. Pipe*

THIEVERY 6 b.g. Terimon – Piracy (Jupiter Island) [2006/7 h–, F–: 26gᵖᵘ c19v⁵ c19s   **c70**
c16vᵖᵘ c16s⁶ c16s² c16m⁵ Mar 31] good-topped gelding: little form over hurdles: poor   **h–**
maiden handicap chaser: best at 2m: acts on soft going: in cheekpieces/blinkers last 5
outings. *H. D. Daly*

THIEVES'GLEN 9 b.g. Teenoso (USA) – Hollow Creek (Tarqogan) [2006/7 c102§,   **c85 §**
h96§: c20d⁶ c31sᶠ c19s⁴ c16v² c16s⁵ c19mᵘʳ c16g⁵ c24g Apr 27] good sort: maiden hurd-   **h– §**
ler: poor handicap chaser: left H. Morrison after sixth outing: effective at 2m to 25f: acts
on good to firm and heavy going: tried blinkered/tongue tied: free-going front runner:
irresolute. *Mrs K. Waldron*

THIMBLESFIRTH (IRE) 6 b.m. Flemensfirth (USA) – Miss Thimble (IRE) (Phar-   **h–**
dante (FR)) [2006/7 F16g³ 22sᵖᵘ 16d 16gᵇᵈ 16v⁵ 16d Dec 28] second foal: dam lightly   **F–**
raced in points: won mares maiden Irish point in 2006: bought 3,500 gns Doncaster May
Sales: distant third in maiden bumper: no form over hurdles: tried tongue tied: headstrong. *C. T. Pogson*

THINKING DOUBLE 9 br.g. Homo Sapien – Sheppie's Double (Scallywag) [2006/7   **h–**
16mʳᵒ 20mᵖᵘ 20f 16m 22m⁶ 22m⁵ 24dᵖᵘ Oct 5] of little account: tried blinkered. *Mrs
D. A. Butler*

THINK OF THE MONEY 7 b.m. Alderbrook – Pipers Reel (Palace Music (USA))   **h66**
[2006/7 F16m F16d⁶ 16d 19g 16v 16v³ 16s⁵ 17g Apr 1] sparely-made mare: third foal: **F–**
dam 1m winner: little form in bumpers/over hurdles. *D. Burchell*

THINK QUICK (IRE) 7 b.m. Goldmark (USA) – Crimson Ring (Persian Bold)   **h82**
[2006/7 h82: 24g 16g Jun 8] poor handicap hurdler: probably stays 2½m: acts on firm and
good to soft going, well beaten on heavy. *R. Hollinshead*

THIRTY FIVE BLACK (IRE) 6 b.g. Old Vic – Hi-Lo Piccolo (IRE) (Orchestra)   **h111**
[2006/7 17s* 21v³ 19v² Mar 1] €12,000 4-y-o: first foal: dam, showed little in bumpers/
over hurdles in Ireland, out of half-sister to useful staying chaser A N C Express: easily
won 18-runner novice hurdle at Exeter in December on debut by 1½ lengths from
Greenhill Bramble: didn't progress as expected: stays 19f: raced on soft/heavy ground.
D. E. Pipe

THIRTYTWO RED (IRE) 6 b.g. Revoque (IRE) – Trouville Lass (IRE) (Be My   **c–**
Native (USA)) [2006/7 c21gᵖᵘ Apr 1] second foal: half-brother to 13f winner Trouville
(by Mukaddamah): dam 2½m hurdle winner: fair pointer, successful in January: no show
in novice hunter on chase debut. *J. Apps*

THIS IS IT (IRE) 6 b.m. Saddlers' Hall (IRE) – Rub of The Court (IRE) (Law Society   **h70**
(USA)) [2006/7 h–, F79: 17f 18d⁵ 16m³ 16v 20v 16v Feb 3] poor maiden hurdler, left
T. McCourt after third outing: tongue tied last 3 starts. *L. McHugh, Ireland*

THISONEFORTHEGIRLS 8 gr.m. Silver Patriarch (IRE) – Bluebell Miss (High   **F–**
Kicker (USA)) [2006/7 F16d Nov 11] fifth foal: dam 5f/1¼m winner: tongue tied, well
beaten in bumper on debut: joined P. Bowen. *R. M. Stronge*

THISTHATANDTOTHER (IRE) 11 b.g. Bob Back (USA) – Baden (IRE) (Furry   **c151**
Glen) [2006/7 c164, h–: c20g² c21s⁵ c19d² c21g c36gᵖᵘ Apr 14] strong, useful-looking   **h–**

gelding: has reportedly been pin-fired: high-class chaser at best: smart form in 2006/7, runner-up to Racing Demon in Peterborough Chase at Huntingdon and Monet's Garden in Ascot Chase: stays 21f (travelled well long way in Grand National final start): acts on soft and good to firm going: reliable. *P. F. Nicholls*

THISTLE 6 ch.g. Selkirk (USA) – Ardisia (USA) (Affirmed (USA)) [2006/7 17m Apr 9] modest form in juvenile hurdles: well held in handicap only start in 2006/7: raced around 2m: acts on good to soft ground: tried tongue tied. *J. Howard Johnson*   **h80 +**

THIS WAY (IRE) 5 b.g. Exit To Nowhere (USA) – Hawthorn's Way (IRE) (Regular Guy) [2006/7 F16s F16v F16m Apr 15] tall gelding: third foal: dam poor maiden hurdler: mid-field in bumpers. *B. J. M. Ryall*   **F86**

THIS WAY THAT WAY 6 b.g. Dr Devious (IRE) – Ellway Dancer (IRE) (Mujadil (USA)) [2006/7 17d 20d⁶ 21d⁴ 16s 19g³ 21m⁴ Apr 9] smallish gelding: twice-raced on Flat: modest maiden hurdler: may prove best short of 2½m: acts on good to soft ground. *Ian Williams*   **h87**

THOMAND CHARGE (IRE) 8 ch.g. Zaffaran (USA) – Lexy Lady (IRE) (Strong Gale) [2006/7 c24sᶠ c23mᵘʳ Nov 7] second foal: dam, placed in bumper, out of half-sister to smart hurdler/useful chaser Gala's Image, stayed 25f: runner-up on completed start in maiden Irish points in 2005: bought 4,000 gns Doncaster August (2005) Sales: failed to complete in maiden chases. *Mrs L. J. Young*   **c–**

THOMAS A BECKETT (IRE) 4 b.g. Beckett (IRE) – Kenema (IRE) (Petardia) [2006/7 16vᵘʳ Mar 12] modest maiden on Flat (barely stays 1¼m): behind when unseated last in juvenile claimer on hurdling debut. *P. R. Chamings*   **h–**

THOMAS HARDY 4 ch.g. Fleetwood (IRE) – Miss Hardy (Formidable (USA)) [2006/7 F14s F18v F18gᵖᵘ Mar 26] half-brother to modest 2m hurdler Shady Man (by Shaamit): dam unraced: no form in bumpers (lame final start). *M. A. Allen*   **F–**

THOMPSONS WOOD (IRE) 9 b.g. Glacial Storm (USA) – Hot House Flower (Derring Rose) [2006/7 c24s* Feb 22] compact ex-Irish gelding: poor form over hurdles: sold out of S. Walsh's stable 5,500 gns Doncaster May (2005) Sales: fairly useful pointer, won twice in 2006: successful chase debut when beating Hopsarising by 3½ lengths in novice hunter at Huntingdon: stays 3m: raced on soft/heavy going. *Mrs Debby Ewing*   **c91 h–**

THORNFIELD CLO (IRE) 4 gr.f. Zafonic (USA) – Flounce (Unfuwain (USA)) [2006/7 16d⁴ Dec 21] modest on Flat (stays 9.7f), successful in June, left R. Hannon after final 3-y-o start: fourth in juvenile seller at Ludlow on hurdling debut: sold €9,000 Goffs February Sales. *Ms Joanna Morgan, Ireland*   **h64**

THORN OF THE ROSE (IRE) 6 gr.m. Terimon – Loch Scavaig (IRE) (The Parson) [2006/7 h76?, F65: 24m⁵ 22d² 26m⁵ 20s⁶ 20d 20v⁴ 16s³ 19sᵖᵘ Jan 1] rather leggy mare: poor maiden handicap hurdler: effective at 2m to 2¾m: acts on soft going: visored last 3 starts: signs of temperament. *James Moffatt*   **h70**

THORNTON BRIDGE 9 b.g. Presidium – Wire Lass (New Brig) [2006/7 c–, h68: 20gʳᵒ 21m Nov 9] form over hurdles only when winning 19f novice handicap in 2005/6, allowed to build clear lead: no show only start in chase: dead. *R. J. Hewitt*   **c– h–**

THORNTON WELCOME 4 ch.g. Most Welcome – Lindrick Lady (IRE) (Broken Hearted) [2006/7 16dᵖᵘ Oct 11] sparely-made gelding: no show in maiden on Flat or juvenile hurdle. *B. S. Rothwell*   **h–**

THORSGILL 9 ch.g. Denel (FR) – Italian Princess (IRE) (Strong Gale) [2006/7 c–, h–: c27sᵖᵘ c25g* Apr 23] workmanlike gelding: won point in January: first form in chases when making all in maiden hunter at Hexham: stays 25f: bled on reappearance. *P. Kirby*   **c96 + h–**

THOUTMOSIS (USA) 8 ch.g. Woodman (USA) – Toujours Elle (USA) (Lyphard (USA)) [2006/7 h110: 20gᵘʳ Jun 1] fair handicap hurdler: stays 3m: raced on good going or softer (acts on heavy): has been let down by jumping: runner-up on completed outing in points. *L. Lungo*   **h– x**

THREE COUNTIES (IRE) 6 b.h. Danehill (USA) – Royal Show (IRE) (Sadler's Wells (USA)) [2006/7 16s² 22gᵖᵘ May 12] compact horse: in frame in bumpers: well held on Flat: no show in novice hurdles: has carried head awkwardly. *N. I. M. Rossiter*   **h–**

THREE GUESSES (IRE) 6 b.g. Supreme Leader – Guess Twice (Deep Run) [2006/7 F87: F16d³ F16s² Feb 1] quite good-topped gelding: fairly useful form in bumpers: left M. Pitman and off 7 months, won at Chepstow in November by 1¼ lengths from The Jazz Musician: 3½ lengths second to Le Beau Bai at Towcester: will be well suited by further than 2m. *Carl Llewellyn*   **F104**

THREE LIONS 10 ch.g. Jupiter Island – Super Sol (Rolfe (USA)) [2006/7 c–, h104: 24m⁵ 24v² May 20] leggy gelding: modest handicap hurdler on balance: mistakes only start over fences: stays 3m: acts on soft and good to firm going, probably on heavy: tried in cheekpieces: has hinted at temperament. *R. S. Brookhouse*   c–
h92

THREE MILL (IRE) 10 ch.g. Hubbly Bubbly (USA) – Glen Fuel (IRE) (Meneval (USA)) [2006/7 c23gᵖᵘ c26d⁴ c24s c24f Apr 27] small gelding: winning pointer: little form otherwise: tried blinkered/in cheekpieces: tongue tied last 5 outings. *J. G. Carr, Ireland*   c–
h–

THREE MIRRORS 7 b.g. Cloudings (IRE) – Aliuska (IRE) (Fijar Tango (FR)) [2006/7 c21m² c20s² c22s² c20g² c20d* c20g* c16g³ c20m* Apr 20] tall ex-Irish gelding: winning hurdler: useful chaser: left A. Mullins prior to reappearance: progressed well late in season, winning maiden at Market Rasen in March and handicaps at Wetherby and Ayr (much improved when beating Locksmith by 9 lengths in 5-runner event) in April: stays 2¾m: acts on soft and good to firm going: has had tongue tied: has won when sweating. *Ferdy Murphy*   c131 +
h–

THREE SHIPS 6 ch.g. Dr Fong (USA) – River Lullaby (USA) (Riverman (USA)) [2006/7 h106: 16m 16g⁵ 16g³ 16s⁶ 16d⁶ 16g 17m³ Apr 28] small gelding: fair hurdler: raced around 2m: acts on firm going, probably on soft: headstrong. *Miss J. Feilden*   h104

THREE STEPS (IRE) 9 b.m. Torus – Joes Nightmare (Roi Guillaume (FR)) [2006/7 20gᵖᵘ Jul 21] ex-Irish mare: winning pointer: no form otherwise. *J. G. M. O'Shea*   c–
h–

THREE WELSHMEN 6 b.g. Muhtarram (USA) – Merch Rhyd-Y-Grug (Sabrehill (USA)) [2006/7 17m Jun 4] leggy, plain gelding: fair hurdle winner: fit from Flat, not knocked about once held only start in 2006/7: will prove best at 2m: acts on soft and good to firm going. *D. Burchell*   h90

THREEZEDZZ 9 ch.g. Emarati (USA) – Exotic Forest (Dominion) [2006/7 16d⁵ Oct 30] maiden hurdler: free-going sort, best at sharp 2m: tried tongue tied. *R. A. Harris*   h–

THROUGH THE RYE 11 ch.g. Sabrehill (USA) – Baharlilys (Green Dancer (USA)) [2006/7 c124, h–: 18f 16s⁵ 15s³ 16s* 16s 16v³ 23vᵖᵘ 16v⁴ 19s 16v* Feb 24] strong gelding: winning chaser: fairly useful handicap hurdler: won at Wetherby (by 16 lengths) in October and Newcastle (beat Rayshan by 4 lengths) in February: best around 2m: raced mainly on good going or softer (acts on heavy): tongue tied once: often front runner over hurdles: none too consistent. *Grant Tuer*   c–
h125

THUMBPRINT (IRE) 5 b.g. Aahsaylad – Tinerana Girl (IRE) (Executive Perk) [2006/7 20vᵖᵘ 19vᵖᵘ Mar 1] €9,000 3-y-o, £10,000 4-y-o: second foal: dam winning pointer, no show in novice hurdles. *C. J. Down*   h–

THUNDER CHILD 7 gr.g. Cloudings (IRE) – Double Dutch (Nicholas Bill) [2006/7 F–: F16s 17s 19v 22dᵖᵘ 22sᵖᵘ c23mᵖᵘ Apr 15] angular gelding: no sign of ability: sold out of John Allen's stable 7,500 gns Doncaster August Sales before return. *C. L. Popham*   c–
h–
F–

THUNDERCLAP 8 b. or br.g. Royal Applause – Gloriana (Formidable (USA)) [2006/7 17v 16d⁴ c16d c16s^F Jan 24] rather leggy gelding: poor maiden hurdler: well beaten completed start over fences: raced around 2m. *P. D. Niven*   c–
h70

THUNDER ROCK (IRE) 5 b.g. King's Best (USA) – Park Express (Ahonoora) [2006/7 16s⁶ 16v* 19s² 16gᵖᵘ 22m* Apr 26] quite good-topped gelding: half-brother to winning hurdler in France by Last Tycoon: useful on Flat (stays 1½m) for Sir Michael Stoute: fairly useful form over hurdles: won novices at Plumpton (dead-heated with Santando) in January and Fontwell (didn't need to be at best, wandered run-in) in April: stays 2¾m: blinkered fourth outing (ran poorly). *Jonjo O'Neill*   h118

THYNE SPIRIT (IRE) 8 ch.g. Good Thyne (USA) – Friston (IRE) (Roselier (FR)) [2006/7 c–, h–: 26g Nov 5] good-topped gelding: winning pointer: no solid form in other events. *S. T. Lewis*   c–
h–

THYNE SUPREME (IRE) 8 b.g. Good Thyne (USA) – Lisfuncheon Adage (Proverb) [2006/7 16d⁵ 16m 20f⁶ 21vᵖᵘ c16m c20m⁶ Apr 15] good-topped gelding: little show over hurdles/fences: signs of temperament. *M. G. Rimell*   c69
h–

TIANYI (IRE) 11 b.g. Mujadil (USA) – Skinity (Rarity) [2006/7 c67, h63: 17g 16m³ 19g 16m³ 20g² 16m⁵ 22m 22m 18m⁵ 19m⁴ Oct 4] angular gelding: poor hurdler, on lengthy losing run: little form over fences: stays easy 2½m: unraced on heavy going, acts on any other: blinkered/visored: often front runner: not one to trust. *M. Scudamore*   c– §
h67 §

TIAWANA (IRE) 11 b.g. Toulon – Tempo Rose (Crash Course) [2006/7 c24s^R Feb 16] ex-Irish gelding: one-time fair hurdler: no form over fences: tried blinkered/in cheek-pieces. *W. T. Reed*   c– h–

TICKATEAL 7 ch.g. Emperor Fountain – Mary Hand (IRE) (Hollow Hand) [2006/7 h95: 21d 24f⁵ 20f^F 21m 24g⁵ 26g⁴ 19g⁴ 24g³ 24d² 24d² Jan 19] leggy gelding: modest handicap hurdler: stays 27f: acts on good to firm and good to soft going. *R. D. E. Woodhouse*   h94

TICKET TO RIDE (FR) 9 ch.g. Pistolet Bleu (IRE) – Have A Drink (FR) (Hasty Tudor (USA)) [2006/7 c112, h?: c21v² c23g 20g c16d⁶ c16v⁵ c20s⁶ Mar 11] winning hurdler/chaser in France: badly out of sorts after first outing: stays 25f: acts on heavy ground: usually wears headgear: tongue tied. *A. J. Wilson*   c110 d h–

TICKFORD ABBEY 5 br.g. Emperor Fountain – Flash-By (Ilium) [2006/7 F86: F16s⁴ 16d^F Jan 15] leggy gelding: fair form in bumpers: fell first on hurdling debut. *Mrs F. Kehoe*   h– F88

TICKHILL TOM 7 ch.g. First Trump – Tender Loving Care (Final Straw) [2006/7 h–, F–: c20s Jun 25] big gelding: well beaten in various events. *C. W. Fairhurst*   c– h–

TIDAL BAY (IRE) 6 b.g. Flemensfirth (USA) – June's Bride (IRE) (Le Moss) [2006/7 F114: 20s* 20v* 17s* 20v² 21g² 20g* Apr 12]   h148

What price a dream? When considering the return Andrea and Graham Wylie are getting on their huge investment in bloodstock, emotional as well as financial factors must be considered. In jumping, it is unlikely that the sums paid for the most promising young horses nowadays can ever be recouped through prize money and, with no chance of a profit for stud on retirement, hefty losses are usually incurred. Graham Wylie acknowledges as much. 'For every pound I put in, I do not expect to get back a penny. I haven't done it as an investment. If I want to invest money, it goes into a business-and-property portfolio. I wouldn't say racing is a hobby, because I'm taking it far too seriously for that . . . but I am in it for the love of the sport.' Tidal Bay cost 300,000 guineas at the Doncaster May Sales in 2006 after finishing runner-up in two bumpers the previous season when trained by Alistair Charlton, notably when a neck second (at 66/1) to Pangbourne in the Grade 2 event at the Grand National meeting. In the latest season, Tidal Bay won four of his six outings over hurdles, showing himself to be a very smart prospect,

E.B.F./boylesports.com 'National Hunt' Novices' Hurdle (Qualifier), Cheltenham—
Tidal Bay (left) forges clear of favourite Kicks For Free

Citroen C4 Picasso Mersey Novices' Hurdle, Aintree—
a fourth win of the campaign as Tidal Bay is left clear by Wins Now's last-flight blunder

the type to do really well over fences. He won £79,692.50 in prize money and, in truth, his purchase may turn out to be one of the least costly made by the Wylies. He may well develop into a high-class performer in the seasons to come, unlike other high-profile acquisitions such as Acropolis, Balyan and Zeitgeist who have all failed to come close to justifying their big price tags. In addition, Wylie's fingers had been burnt before by a principal from the Aintree bumper as his 200,000-guinea outlay for 2004 winner Diamond Sal yielded just £16,188.73 in prize money from a fairly ordinary seven-race hurdling career (two wins), though being a mare she is one purchase that may yet pay her way at stud. On that subject, the Wylie brood-mare operation looks set for expansion judged on the acquisition of unbeaten hurdler Feathard Lady, in foal to Presenting and purchased for 270,000 guineas (a record for a jumps mare) at the Doncaster August Sales after her retirement because of injury.

Tidal Bay had no trouble landing the odds in novices at Wetherby in October and Carlisle in November on his first two starts over hurdles, winning with any amount in hand, before stepping up considerably in the far more competitive EBF/boylesports.com 'National Hunt' Novices' Hurdle at Cheltenham in December, a race won in recent years by the likes of Rhinestone Cowboy and Noland. Tidal Bay coped really well with the drop back in trip and beat the favourite Kicks For Free (third in that Aintree bumper) by six lengths, the pair pulling clear, Tidal Bay's performance showing him to be a smart novice, something confirmed in defeat back at the same course on his next two starts. Tidal Bay tended to carry his head awkwardly in the latter stages when six lengths second to Wichita Lineman in a Grade 2 event in late-January, while, in the Ballymore Properties-sponsored Baring Bingham Hurdle in March, his temperament might well have made the difference. Tidal Bay again displayed an awkward head carriage from two out and, despite closing at the line, finished a neck second to Massini's Maguire (who'd finished four lengths behind him in the January race). With Massini's Maguire taking on Wichita Lineman in the three-mile novice at Aintree—both were beaten by outsider Chief Dan George—Tidal Bay faced a considerably simpler task in the Citroen C4 Picasso Mersey Novices' Hurdle over two and a half miles the day before, a task made easier when his main market rival, the smart juvenile Liberate, ran well below his best. Tidal Bay was responding well to pressure when left clear at the last by the mistake of eventual runner-up Wins Now; Tidal Bay had eight lengths in hand of that horse at the line.

	Flemensfirth (USA) (b 1992)	Alleged (b 1974)	Hoist The Flag / Princess Pout
		Etheldreda (ch 1985)	Diesis / Royal Bond
Tidal Bay (IRE) (b.g. 2001)		Le Moss (ch 1975)	Le Levanstell / Feemoss
	June's Bride (IRE) (ch 1991)	Officer's Lady (ch 1986)	General Ironside / Mariamne

Tidal Bay, a brother to two winning pointers, is the fifth foal of the unraced June's Bride. Grandam Officer's Lady was also unraced but she is related to a couple of above-average staying jumpers, being a half-sister to the smart Irish chaser Buck Rogers and to the dam of smart hurdler Brewster. Third dam Mariamne, also unraced, was a daughter of the 1965 Irish Cesarewitch winner Agrippina, a mare who also won over hurdles. The sturdy, lengthy Tidal Bay will stay beyond two miles five furlongs and he acts on heavy going. His high head carriage—which arguably also cost him victory in the Aintree bumper—remains a slight concern, though sometimes the mannerism can be misleading. Sadler's Wells, for example, displayed an unusually high head carriage yet was a top-class, and notably tough, Group 1 performer who held his form admirably during a busy three-year-old campaign. Sadler's Wells has since become one of the greatest stallions of all time, whilst the fact plenty of his offspring have inherited his head carriage has, on the whole, not held them back. Tidal Bay is a son of Flemensfirth, not Sadler's Wells, but it is to be hoped the remark applies to him too as he remains a good prospect, one who looks sure to do well over fences. *J. Howard Johnson*

TIDAL FURY (IRE) 5 b.g. Night Shift (USA) – Tidal Reach (USA) (Kris S (USA)) [2006/7 h126: 19s 19s c16s* c19s⁴ c16s* c16g 18s⁴ Apr 6] close-coupled, quite good-topped gelding: has reportedly had breathing operation: fairly useful hurdler: useful chaser: won maiden at Carlisle (beat Akilak easily by 9 lengths) in November and novices at Haydock (beat Flying Enterprise by 7 lengths) in December and Southwell (simple task) in January: well held in Arkle at Cheltenham penultimate outing: best form at 2m: acts on heavy going: front runner/races prominently: has jumped left. *J. Jay*   **c134 h121**

TIDE SLIDER 4 b.g. Slip Anchor – Lyra (Blakeney) [2006/7 F17m Apr 28] 12,000 3-y-o: half-brother to several winners, notably fairly useful hurdler Stagecoach Diamond (by Classic Cliche), stays 21f: dam won 3 races in Belgium: never a factor in bumper on debut. *S. Gollings*   **F—**

TIDY (IRE) 7 b.g. Mujadil (USA) – Neat Shilling (IRE) (Bob Back (USA)) [2006/7 16s 16s 17v Dec 12] small, sturdy gelding: fair on Flat (stays 1¼m), successful in June: no form over hurdles. *Micky Hammond*   **h—**

TIE PIN (IRE) 7 b. or br.m. Taipan (IRE) – No Easy Way (IRE) (Mandalus) [2006/7 F16f Jul 6] third foal: dam unraced half-sister to fairly useful chaser On The Other Hand, stayed 27f: last in bumper on debut. *Barry Potts, Ireland*   **F—**

TIFFIN DEANO (IRE) 5 b.g. Mujadil (USA) – Xania (Mujtahid (USA)) [2006/7 h—: 16s³ 16m⁵ 20m² Aug 1] modest form over hurdles, faltering and headed close home in seller final outing: tried blinkered (soundly beaten). *H. J. Manners*   **h88**

TIFFIN JO (IRE) 4 b.f. Fruits of Love (USA) – Kick The Habit (Habitat) [2006/7 17s Aug 19] half-sister to fair hurdler Habitual (by Kahyasi), stays 3¼m: no sign of ability on Flat at 2 yrs/in juvenile hurdle. *P. C. Haslam*   **h—**

TIGER FROG (USA) 8 b.g. French Deputy (USA) – Woodyoubelieveit (USA) (Woodman (USA)) [2006/7 c—, h98: 16g³ May 11] lengthy gelding: winning chaser: fair handicap hurdler, ran well only outing in 2006/7: stays easy 2½m: acts on soft and firm going: tried in cheekpieces, blinkered nowadays: has had tongue tied. *J. Mackie*   **c— h101**

TIGERIFIC (IRE) 4 gr.f. Beneficial – Grey Mo (IRE) (Roselier (FR)) [2006/7 F17g **F69**
Apr 23] first foal: dam unraced half-sister to fair 2m hurdler Queens Consul: favourite,
only seventh of 14 in mares bumper at Sedgefield on debut. *J. Howard Johnson*

TIGER ISLAND (USA) 7 b.g. Grand Slam (USA) – Paris Wild Cat (USA) (Storm Cat **h–**
(USA)) [2006/7 h–: 16g^{pu} 16s^{pu} Jan 24] little form over hurdles: in cheekpieces last 3
starts: sold £1,250 Ascot February Sales. *A. E. Jones*

TIGER KING (GER) 6 b.g. Tiger Hill (IRE) – Tennessee Girl (GER) (Big Shuffle **h94**
(USA)) [2006/7 h92: 17d^6 16g^3 16m^3 Jun 11] lengthy gelding: modest novice hurdler:
stays 19f: acts on good to firm and good to soft going, seems unsuited by soft/heavy.
P. Monteith

TIGER TALK 11 ch.g. Sabrehill (USA) – Tebre (USA) (Sir Ivor (USA)) [2006/7 c64§, **c– §**
h77§: 20d c21m^6 c26d^6 20f Jul 6] angular gelding: poor handicap hurdler: little form over **h– §**
fences: stays easy 25f: acts on good to firm and heavy going: usually wears headgear:
tried tongue tied: ungenuine. *R. C. Guest*

TIGER TIPS LAD (IRE) 8 b.g. Zaffaran (USA) – Halens Match (IRE) (Matching **c87 d**
Pair) [2006/7 c103d, h–: 19s^4 17d 24s^{pu} c24g c24v^{ur} c24g^5 c24m^4 Apr 14] lengthy **h85**
gelding: winning hurdler/maiden chaser, on downgrade: stays easy 3m: acts on soft and
good to firm going: tried tongue tied/blinkered: sketchy jumper. *C. Roberts*

TIGHE CASTER 8 b.g. Makbul – Miss Fire (Gunner B) [2006/7 c118, h–: c20m* **c125**
c16g^5 c20d^{ur} c20s^5 c19d^6 c20f^3 c20s^5 Apr 25] good-topped gelding: winning hurdler: **h–**
fairly useful handicap chaser: left P. Webber, some improvement when winning at
Huntingdon in September by 5 lengths from Free Gift: largely below form after next
outing: stays easy 2½m: acts on firm and soft going: held up. *P. Bowen*

TIGHT CORNER (IRE) 8 b.g. Shardari – General Rain (General Ironside) [2006/7 **c–**
h–, F–: 20m^{pu} c20v^{pu} Dec 23] no form outside points: tried tongue tied: carries head **h–**
awkwardly. *Ian Williams*

TIGNASSE (FR) 6 b.m. Double Bed (FR) – Off Guard (FR) (Bakharoff (USA)) **h– §**
[2006/7 h91§: 17m May 11] modest hurdler: beaten mainly around 2m: acts on firm going:
tried blinkered/in cheekpieces: ungenuine. *Karen George*

TIHUI TWO (IRE) 7 b.m. Accordion – Maid of Glenduragh (IRE) (Ya Zaman (USA)) **c– §**
[2006/7 F103: 19m^{rtr} 16d 25g^{pu} 16s^5 c23m^{rtr} Apr 15] lengthy mare: bumper winner: little **h72 §**
form over hurdles: unseated rider twice, including on chasing debut: has been banned
from racing. *G. R. I. Smyly*

TIKRAM 10 ch.g. Lycius (USA) – Black Fighter (USA) (Secretariat (USA)) [2006/7 **c134 §**
c148, h–: c22g c21s^4 c24g^4 c21g c36g^{ur} c20m^3 Apr 27] tall, close-coupled gelding: useful **h–**
handicap chaser: left G. L. Moore after reappearance: best efforts in 2006/7 when fourth
in valuable events at Cheltenham and Sandown: unseated first in Grand National: stays
3m, effective at much shorter: acts on any going: has worn headgear: takes plenty of
driving. *A. King*

TILEN (IRE) 4 ch.g. Bluebird (USA) – New Sensitive (Wattlefield) [2006/7 16m **h–**
17m^{pu} Mar 29] 7f winner on Flat, little form since early-2006: no show in juvenile
hurdles, left V. Smith after debut. *S. Parr*

TILLA 7 b.m. Bin Ajwaad (IRE) – Tosca (Be My Guest (USA)) [2006/7 h–: 16m 16d **c–**
16m^4 17m^5 c21m^F 16m Aug 11] medium-sized mare: bad maiden hurdler: fell heavily on **h59**
chasing debut: wears headgear. *Mouse Hamilton-Fairley*

TILTILI (IRE) 4 ch.f. Spectrum (IRE) – Alexander Confranc (IRE) (Magical Wonder **h67 x**
(USA)) [2006/7 17d^2 16s^5 16s^5 Dec 8] modest maiden on Flat (seems to stay 2m):
runner-up in juvenile on hurdling debut, let down by jumping/attitude after. *P. C. Haslam*

TIMBERLAKE 5 b.m. Bluegrass Prince – Ambience Lady (Batshoof) [2006/7 **h–**
17g 19d Oct 31] first foal: dam bumper/2½m chase winner: maiden on Flat: never on
terms in novice hurdles. *Miss E. C. Lavelle*

TIMBUKTU 6 b.g. Efisio – Sirene Bleu Marine (USA) (Secreto (USA)) [2006/7 h84: **h85**
16g^2 16g^4 16g^3 16m^4 16f^3 Jun 17] modest novice hurdler: best around 2m: acts on firm
and soft going: tried in cheekpieces, blinkered in 2006/7: front runner. *B. Storey*

TIME FOR PERKS (IRE) 7 b.m. Executive Perk – Town of Trees (IRE) (Lancas- **c–**
trian) [2006/7 c22v^{ur} Feb 18] sister to fair hurdler/fairly useful chaser Time To Sell, stays
2¾m, and half-sister to winning 3m hurdler Carnival Buck (by Buckskin): dam unraced:
runner-up on completed start in maiden points in 2006: behind when unseating tenth in
mares maiden chase. *Evan Williams*

TIME FOR YOU 5 b.m. Vettori (IRE) – La Fija (USA) (Dixieland Band (USA)) **h–**
[2006/7 h79: 16g 16g⁴ 17g Apr 11] rather leggy mare: maiden hurdler, well beaten in
2006/7: raced around 2m: acts on soft and good to firm going. *J. M. Bradley*

TIME MARCHES ON 9 b.g. Timeless Times (USA) – Tees Gazette Girl (Kalaglow) **h106**
[2006/7 h94: 20m² 17s² 17s* 17v⁴ 22s⁵ 19g Nov 29] leggy gelding: fair handicap hurdler:
won at Carlisle in October: probably stays 2¾m: acts on heavy and good to firm going:
tried in cheekpieces/tongue tied, not since 2004/5: held up. *K. G. Reveley*

TIME OUT (IRE) 4 b.g. Alhaarth (IRE) – Waif (Groom Dancer (USA)) [2006/7 16d **h97**
16s² 16s⁶ Feb 3] compact gelding: lightly-raced maiden on Flat, sold out of A. Balding's
stable £13,000 Ascot July Sales: easily best effort in juvenile hurdles when second to
Raslan at Wincanton: raced at 2m on good to soft/soft ground. *Miss M. Bragg*

TIME TO REFLECT (IRE) 8 ch.g. Anshan – Castlemitchle (IRE) (Roselier (FR)) **c81 +**
[2006/7 c102, h–: c25g⁴ c24g^pu c26s^pu May 14] rather leggy gelding: has had breathing **h–**
operation: winning hurdler: fair handicap chaser: off 12 months, below best early in
2006/7 (presumably amiss final outing): stays 25f: acts on soft going (won bumper on
good to firm): tried visored/blinkered, usually wears cheekpieces: patiently ridden.
R. C. Guest

TIME TO REGRET 7 b.g. Presidium – Scoffera (Scottish Reel) [2006/7 16s^pu 16v^pu **h–**
Dec 15] tall, close-coupled gelding: fair maiden on Flat (stays 9.3f), successful 3 times in
January: little impact in 3 starts over hurdles. *I. W. McInnes*

TIMETORING 5 ch.g. Karinga Bay – Little Time (Arctic Lord) [2006/7 F16f⁵ F16m* **h–**
17g Oct 15] second foal: dam, fourth in bumper only start, out of useful 2m to 25f chaser **F84**
Olympian Princess, herself half-sister to smart staying chaser Bob Tisdall: won 5-runner
bumper at Ludlow in May: well beaten in novice on hurdling debut: will be suited by
2½m. *B. J. Eckley*

TIME TO ROAM (IRE) 7 br.g. Darshaan – Minstrels Folly (USA) (The Minstrel **h78**
(CAN)) [2006/7 h95: 16v⁵ 16v⁴ Mar 22] small, sparely-made gelding: modest handicap
hurdler: off 10 months, below form in 2006/7: barely stays 2½m: acts on heavy going,
probably on good to firm: wears headgear: carries head awkwardly. *Miss Lucinda
V. Russell*

TIME TO SELL (IRE) 8 b. or br.g. Executive Perk – Town of Trees (IRE) (Lan- **c123**
castrian) [2006/7 c20s^F 20v c16d⁵ 20s⁴ c16s² c22v⁴ c18v* 19v* 16s⁵ c20s* c19v⁴ c24v^pu **h108**
c20g³ 20m⁶ Apr 28] workmanlike gelding: half-brother to winning 3m hurdler Carnival
Buck (by Buckskin): dam unraced: fair hurdler: won handicap at Limerick in January:
fairly useful handicap chaser: won at Thurles in December and Limerick (conditional
jockeys) in February: improved further when 7 lengths third to Private Be in conditional/
amateur novice event at Aintree: stays 2¾m: acts on heavy ground. *Eugene M.
O'Sullivan, Ireland*

TIME TO SHINE 8 b.m. Pivotal – Sweet Jaffa (Never So Bold) [2006/7 c–, h121: **c116**
c19m* Oct 28] tall, leggy mare: fairly useful hurdler, lightly raced: similar form when **h–**
winning 4-runner maiden at Ascot (finished lame) on chasing debut in October, making
all to beat Enhancer by 4 lengths: stayed 2½m: acted on good to firm and heavy going:
reportedly retired. *Mrs L. J. Mongan*

TIMETWOGO 5 b.g. Double Trigger (IRE) – Golden Mile (IRE) (King's Ride) **F91**
[2006/7 F16v⁵ F17g⁵ Mar 24] 25,000 4-y-o: first foal: dam, poor novice hurdler who
stayed 2½m, out of sister to very smart staying chaser Deep Bramble: second and better
effort in bumpers when fifth to Apache Brave in maiden at Bangor: will be suited by
2½m+. *Mrs S. J. Smith*

TIMPO (FR) 4 ch.g. Baby Turk – Faensa (FR) (Fabulous Dancer (USA)) [2006/7 F16s⁶ **F101**
Mar 3] 15,000 3-y-o, resold 38,000 3-y-o: close-coupled gelding: fifth foal: half-brother
to 11f to 15f winner Doublon (by General Holme) and 17f hurdle winner Lamtar (by
Nikos): dam 1m winner: 5¾ lengths sixth of 21 to Diamond Harry in bumper at Newbury
on debut. *H. D. Daly*

TINARANA LORD (IRE) 10 br.g. Teamster – Tinerana League (IRE) (Gallic **c100**
League) [2006/7 c24d c22v⁵ c24v* Mar 4] long-backed gelding: second foal: dam **h–**
unraced: fell only outing over hurdles (blinkered): fair pointer, successful in January:
easily best effort in hunters when winning 4-runner event at Bangor in March by 1½
lengths from No Retreat: stays 3m: acts on heavy going. *G. D. Hanmer*

TINCHEL (IRE) 5 ch.g. Moonax (IRE) – Glenstal Forest (IRE) (Glenstal (USA)) **h91 p**
[2006/7 F16d F16d 18g⁵ Mar 18] long-backed gelding: second foal: half-brother to 21f **F–**
hurdle winner My Good Lord (by Mister Lord): dam maiden: well held in bumpers: 6¼

lengths fifth to Presentandcorrect in novice at Fontwell on hurdling debut: will stay at least 2½m: likely to improve. *N. J. Gifford*

TIN HEALY'S PASS 7 b.g. Puissance – Shaa Spin (Shaadi (USA)) [2006/7 c–, h–: 21m³ c16s³ c16d* c17v⁵ c24gᵖᵘ c20vᵖᵘ Jan 17] strong, lengthy gelding: poor hurdler/ chaser: won novice handicap chase at Hexham in November: possibly best around 2m: acts on soft ground: blinkered/visored last 5 starts, also tongue tied final one. *I. McMath*   **c73 h70**

TINIAN 9 b.g. Mtoto – Housefull (Habitat) [2006/7 h75: 16g⁶ 16s 17d⁶ 16g 17m⁴ 16m 16f³ 17fᵖᵘ Aug 11] poor maiden hurdler: raced around 2m: acts on firm going: has worn cheekpieces. *Miss Tracy Waggott*   **h74**

TINO (IRE) 11 ch.g. Torus – Delphic Thunder (Viking (USA)) [2006/7 c–§, h–: c26mᵖᵘ c21f c23d³ c24g² c26g⁵ c24sᵘʳ Dec 26] sturdy, lengthy gelding: maiden hurdler: poor handicap chaser: stays 3¼m: acts on firm and good to soft going: tried blinkered: often races prominently: has refused to race, and one to be wary of. *Andrew Turnell*   **c77 § h–**

TINOS LAD (IRE) 6 b.g. Un Desperado (FR) – Tinogloria (FR) (Al Nasr (FR)) [2006/7 F16s⁶ F16g Mar 14] strong gelding: first foal: dam 13f winner in France: modest form in bumpers, shaping as if possibly capable of better. *G. A. Harker*   **F81 +**

TIN SYMPHONY 9 ch.m. Opera Ghost – Bronze Age (Celtic Cone) [2006/7 19g⁵ c16gᵖᵘ Apr 7] medium-sized mare: fair maiden hurdler/chaser at best, very lightly raced nowadays: stays 19f: acts on soft going: temperamental (sometimes reluctant to race). *B. J. M. Ryall*   **c– § h– §**

TINTINHULL (IRE) 5 b.g. Presenting – Persian Avenue (IRE) (Persian Mews) [2006/7 F16d F16m⁶ Apr 10] has scope: second foal: dam unraced: mid-field in bumpers. *Mrs S. D. Williams*   **F81**

TINTO VERANO (IRE) 5 b. or br.m. Good Thyne (USA) – Sweet Roselier (IRE) (Roselier (FR)) [2006/7 F16d⁴ F16s⁶ F16v⁶ F16v⁵ Mar 6] close-coupled mare: sister to bumper winner Moonzie Laird: dam unraced, out of half-sister to useful staying jumpers Bective Road and Sommelier: modest form in bumpers. *Miss Lucinda V. Russell*   **F75**

TINVANE ROSE (IRE) 8 ch.m. Roselier (FR) – Grey's Delight (Decent Fellow) [2006/7 h70: 19m⁴ 26m⁴ 24g³ 24g Jul 31] poor maiden hurdler: stays 3¼m: acts on good to firm and heavy going: visored in 2006/7. *J. G. M. O'Shea*   **h70**

TIOGA GOLD (IRE) 8 b.g. Goldmark (USA) – Coffee Bean (Doulab (USA)) [2006/7 h74: 16g 21mᵖᵘ 21m Aug 29] modest on Flat (stays 1¾m), 125/1-winner in January: maiden hurdler, no show in 2006/7: tried in cheekpieces. *L. R. James*   **h–**

TIP AWAY (IRE) 9 b.g. Broken Hearted – Jesse Twist (IRE) (Sandalay) [2006/7 c24gᵖᵘ c26vᶠ Oct 21] maiden hurdler: won maiden point in 2006: failed to complete in chases: should stay 3m: tried in cheekpieces. *D. A. Rees*   **c– h–**

TIP ON (IRE) 5 b.g. Anshan – Hazy River (Over The River (FR)) [2006/7 F16s F16v 16d 16v⁵ 16v³ 24m³ 21g³ Apr 23] €48,000 3-y-o: half-brother to fair hurdler Supreme Quest (by Supreme Leader), stayed 27f: dam winning pointer: well held in bumpers: modest novice hurdler: stays 3m: unraced on firm going, acts on any other: tried tongue tied. *Charles Byrnes, Ireland*   **h86 F–**

TIPPERARY ALL STAR (FR) 7 b.g. Highest Honor (FR) – Moucha (FR) (Fabulous Dancer (USA)) [2006/7 16s* 16d* 16d 16d Mar 13] good-topped gelding: half-brother to fairly useful hurdler/chaser Tarasco (by Deploy), stayed 2½m, and French 17f chase winner by Saint Andrews: dual listed winner on Flat (stays 1½m): useful hurdler: much improved in 2006/7, easily winning handicaps at Punchestown and Cheltenham (beat Bonchester Bridge by 4 lengths in 20-runner novice event) in November: well held after in valuable handicap at Ascot and Grade 1 novice at Cheltenham: raced at 2m on good ground or softer (acts on soft). *M. Halford, Ireland*   **h131**

TIPP MID WEST (IRE) 5 b.m. Close Conflict (USA) – Delightful Choice (IRE) (Amoristic (USA)) [2006/7 20f 20m 22s c24v⁴ c24g⁵ 16g c16s⁴ Apr 27] half-sister to 25f chase winner Banraft (by Glacial Storm): dam winning pointer: once-raced on Flat: placed in points in 2006: signs of ability over hurdles/in chases (considerably handled), left A. McNamara after third outing: tried in cheekpieces. *R. Johnson*   **c– p h–**

TIPP TOP (IRE) 10 b.g. Brief Truce (USA) – Very Sophisticated (USA) (Affirmed (USA)) [2006/7 c84, h–: c19dᵖᵘ c20vᵖᵘ c24m⁶ c24gᵖᵘ Apr 8] tall gelding: handicap chaser, little impact in 2006/7: stays 3m: blinkered once: often tongue tied. *O. Brennan*   **c– h–**

TIPSY LAD 5 b.g. Tipsy Creek (USA) – Perfidy (FR) (Persian Bold) [2006/7 16vᵖᵘ Mar 3] fair at best on Flat (stays 7f), left D. ffrench Davis after final 4-y-o start: tongue tied, no show in novice on hurdling debut. *H. J. Manners*   **h–**

TIPTON RISE 11 b.m. Primitive Rising (USA) – Tipton Times (Sagaro) [2006/7 22g^{pu} Jul 23] first foal: dam, of little account, out of smart staying chaser Ottery News: no show in maiden hurdle on debut. *C. J. Down* **h–**

TIP TOP STYLE 4 b.g. Tipsy Creek (USA) – Eliza Jane (Mistertopogigo (IRE)) [2006/7 17d^{pu} Nov 7] modest maiden on Flat (stays 1m): tongue tied, raced freely in juvenile on hurdling debut. *J. Mackie* **h–**

TIRAILLEUR (IRE) 7 b.m. Eagle Eyed (USA) – Tiralle (IRE) (Tirol) [2006/7 16f 16g^2 17m* 18m^6 16d 21m^5 20d^2 17s^3 17v^6 16v^3 16g^4 19m^6 Apr 22] compact mare: poor handicap hurdler: won selling event at Sedgefield in August: stays easy 21f: acts on soft and good to firm going. *M. J. Gingell* **h81**

TIRLEY STORM 12 b.g. Tirley Gale – Random Select (Random Shot) [2006/7 c74x, h–: c21m^4 c21m Jul 27] rangy gelding: poor handicap chaser, below form since 2005/6 reappearance: stays 2¾m: acts on soft and good to firm going: usually let down by jumping. *J. S. Smith* **c– x** **h–**

TIROL LIVIT (IRE) 4 ch.g. Titus Livius (FR) – Orange Royale (IRE) (Exit To Nowhere (USA)) [2006/7 17d^5 16d^{co} 16s^3 16s 17v^4 20g 17m* Apr 28] close-coupled, good-bodied gelding: modest maiden on Flat (stays 1¼m): modest juvenile hurdler: won seller at Market Rasen in April: raced mainly around 2m: acts on soft and good to firm ground. *N. Wilson* **h86**

TISFREETDREAM (IRE) 6 b.g. Oscar (IRE) – Gayley Gale (IRE) (Strong Gale) [2006/7 F86: F16s 21g^6 21v^3 19s^{pu} 19s^{pu} 16s^2 16g^5 Apr 8] small gelding: unplaced in bumpers: modest novice hurdler: should stay beyond 2m: acts on soft ground. *P. A. Pritchard* **h89** **F–**

TISSEMAN (IRE) 5 ch.g. Bob Back (USA) – Native Sunset (IRE) (Be My Native (USA)) [2006/7 F16d^6 F18d* 18s^5 17s^3 19g^{ur} Mar 23] €35,000 3-y-o: unfurnished gelding: second foal: half-brother to winning pointer by Oscar: dam unraced, half-sister to very smart chaser Stormyfairweather, stayed 25f: won maiden bumper at Plumpton in October: modest form over hurdles: won maiden at Hereford in February by 5 lengths from Ashwell Lad: unseated fifth on handicap debut month later. *N. J. Henderson* **h97** **F97**

TITIAN FLAME (IRE) 7 ch.m. Titus Livius (FR) – Golden Choice (Midyan (USA)) [2006/7 h96§: 21f^{ur} 24g^4 24d^3 May 31] modest handicap hurdler: stays 3m: acts on good to firm and heavy going: usually wears cheekpieces: refused to race final 2005/6 outing, and one to be wary of. *D. Burchell* **h92 §**

TITUS MAXIMUS (IRE) 4 ch.g. Titus Livius (FR) – Haraabah (USA) (Topsider (USA)) [2006/7 16s 16d^{pu} Dec 21] 5f winner on Flat, sold out of G. Butler's stable £1,600 Ascot October Sales: no show in selling hurdles. *H. J. Manners* **h–**

TITUS ROCK (IRE) 5 b.m. Titus Livius (FR) – Cossack Princess (IRE) (Lomond (USA)) [2006/7 17d Nov 16] well held in 5f maiden on Flat and selling hurdle: sold £1,700 Ascot December Sales. *D. McCain Jnr* **h–**

TITUS SALT (USA) 6 ch.g. Gentlemen (ARG) – Farewell Partner (USA) (Northern Dancer) [2006/7 h74: 16g 16g May 11] leggy gelding: poor form over hurdles: dead. *Micky Hammond* **h–**

TITUS WONDER (IRE) 4 ch.f. Titus Livius (FR) – Morcote (IRE) (Magical Wonder (USA)) [2006/7 16g 16d^6 16d 16s Dec 13] smallish filly: modest on Flat (best at 5f/6f), sold out of P. Blockley's stable £3,000 Ascot August Sales: no form in juvenile hurdles. *J. W. Mullins* **h–**

TIZZY BLUE (IRE) 5 b.m. Oscar (IRE) – Satellite Dancer (IRE) (Satco (FR)) [2006/7 F16s^3 F17s^5 F16s^3 Mar 1] second foal: half-sister to winning pointer by Lord Americo: dam, lightly-raced hurdler, out of half-sister to top-class 2m chaser Rathgorman: modest form in bumpers. *Carl Llewellyn* **F82**

TOASTMASTER (IRE) 5 b.g. Oscar (IRE) – Melodic Tune (IRE) (Roselier (FR)) [2006/7 F16g Apr 7] €100,000 4-y-o: tall gelding: third foal: half-brother to bumper winner Havenstone (by Needle Gun): dam failed to complete in 2 Irish points: raced freely when eighth of 17 to Checkerboard in bumper at Haydock on debut. *Jonjo O'Neill* **F79**

TOBAR ISAUN (IRE) 8 ch.g. Semillon – Simply Sarah (Furry Glen) [2006/7 c22s^5 c20s^2 c25s^5 c20v^4 c24v^4 c22v^3 c25v* c28s^5 c20v^4 c33g^5 Mar 15] strong, work-manlike gelding: fair handicap chaser, left Martin Kinane after sixth start: much improved when successful at Fairyhouse (by 18 lengths) in January: several mistakes but ran creditably when fifth to Butler's Cabin in National Hunt Chase (Amateurs) at **c110** **h–**

Cheltenham final start: stays 33f: raced on good going or softer (acts on heavy): usually held up. *Paul A. Roche, Ireland*

TOBESURE (IRE) 13 b.g. Asir – Princess Citrus (IRE) (Auction Ring (USA)) [2006/7 c–x, h97: 22g⁶ 20m 22d⁴ 22s 21s⁶ 24v³ 22v⁴ 22v c20vᶠ Mar 15] sturdy gelding: winning chaser (sketchy jumper): modest handicap hurdler: stays 25f: acts on any going: tongue tied once. *G. A. Charlton*   **c– x c–x, h97: h91**

TOCANE (FR) 4 b.f. Phantom Breeze – Macyrienne (FR) (Saint Cyrien (FR)) [2006/7 F14s F17m Apr 15] €34,000 3-y-o: fifth foal: half-sister to 3 winners, notably useful 2m hurdler Quatre Heures (by Vertical Speed) and fairly useful chaser Kitski (by Perrault), stays 3½m: dam unraced: well held in bumpers. *Ferdy Murphy*   **F–**

TODLEA (IRE) 7 b.g. Desert Prince (IRE) – Imelda (USA) (Manila (USA)) [2006/7 16g⁴ 16vᵖᵘ Mar 3] has reportedly had wind operation: fair on Flat (stays 1¼m), successful twice in 2006: let down by jumping (went markedly left) in novice hurdles: likely to need sharp 2m: tongue tied. *Jean-Rene Auvray*   **h94 ?**

TOEMAC 8 b.g. Slip Anchor – Bobanlyn (IRE) (Dance of Life (USA)) [2006/7 h74: 21d* Oct 30] smallish gelding: dual bumper winner in 2003/4: only second outing over hurdles, won novice at Plumpton in October by 2 lengths from Keltech Leader: likely to stay beyond 21f: clearly difficult to train. *M. Bradstock*   **h107**

TOGA PARTY (IRE) 5 b.g. Turtle Island (IRE) – Fun Fashion (IRE) (Polish Patriot (USA)) [2006/7 F16v F18v 20mᶠ Apr 25] compact gelding: third foal: half-brother to 2002 2-y-o 5f winner Royal Fashion (by Ali-Royal): dam Irish maiden who stayed 1m: well held in maiden bumpers: narrow lead when wandering and falling heavily 4 out in maiden at Worcester on hurdling debut. *Miss S. West*   **h– F–**

TOJONESKI 8 b.g. Emperor Jones (USA) – Sampower Lady (Rock City) [2006/7 17g⁶ 20g 20mᵘʳ 19sᶠ 22m Apr 28] successful up to 13f on Flat, below form in 2006, left I. McInnes after final start: largely let down by jumping and little form over hurdles. *H. Alexander*   **h– x**

TOLEDO SUN 7 b.g. Zamindar (USA) – Shafir (IRE) (Shaadi (USA)) [2006/7 21d 20g Apr 11] maiden hurdler, tailed off both starts in 2006/7 after long lay-off: tried in cheekpieces. *S. Curran*   **h–**

TOM BELL (IRE) 7 b.g. King's Theatre (IRE) – Nordic Display (IRE) (Nordico (USA)) [2006/7 h106: 16d 17m³ 17m* c16dᶠ Jul 23] leggy gelding: fair handicap hurdler: won at Hereford in June: close up when falling sixth in maiden on chasing debut: best around 2m: acts on soft and good to firm going: tried in cheekpieces, effective visored or not. *J. G. M. O'Shea*   **c– h102**

TOMENOSO 9 b.g. Teenoso (USA) – Guarded Expression (Siberian Express (USA)) [2006/7 h110: 20v* 23v 20v⁶ 20s⁶ c20v⁶ Mar 18] lengthy gelding: fair handicap hurdler: off 14 months, won at Sedgefield in December: out of sorts after, including on chasing debut: stays 3m: acts on any going: usually front runner. *Mrs S. J. Smith*   **c– h111**

TOM FONTENAILLES (FR) 4 gr.g. Kaldounevees (FR) – Miss Fontenailles (FR) (Kautokeino (FR)) [2006/7 F14s Feb 4] brother to 2m winner Roger Fontenaille and half-brother to several winners, including 2m hurdler Master Fontenaille (by Comrade In Arms): dam maiden: never dangerous in bumper on debut. *N. J. Hawke*   **F–**

TOM FRUIT 10 b.g. Supreme Leader – Forever Mine (Phardante (FR)) [2006/7 c107, h–: 20s³ c20g² c25d⁵ c20v³ c20m⁶ Apr 15] tall, quite good-topped gelding: fair handicap hurdler/chaser: failed to see race out over fences last 3 outings: stays 25f: acts on heavy going. *T. D. Easterby*   **c105 h105**

TOMILLIELOU 6 br.g. I'm Supposin (IRE) – Belle Rose (IRE) (Roselier (FR)) [2006/7 F93: F17s³ 16s 17v 25s⁶ 19g⁵ 25v³ c25g² Apr 23] big gelding: has scope: third in bumper: modest novice hurdler: 28 lengths second to Panama At Once in novice handicap at Hexham on chasing debut: will stay 3½m: raced on good going or softer (acts on heavy). *G. A. Swinbank*   **c95 h98 F81**

TOMINTOUL 5 ch.g. Komaite (USA) – Bold Gayle (Never So Bold) [2006/7 F17v 16sᵖᵘ Nov 29] second foal: dam, maiden, likely to have proved best at 5f: no show in bumper/novice hurdle. *P. Monteith*   **h– F–**

TOMMY CARSON 12 b.g. Last Tycoon – Ivory Palm (USA) (Sir Ivor (USA)) [2006/7 c95, h–: c28s⁵ c25d³ c28d c25s⁵ c26v* c26g* c24m c26g⁴ Apr 23] compact gelding: modest handicap chaser, left Jamie Poulton after first outing: won at Plumpton in February (amateur event) and March (sixth course success): stays 3¼m: acts on good   **c90 § h–**

to firm and heavy going: has worn visor/blinkers, in latter last 5 outings: often makes running: lazy. *Miss Suzy Smith*

TOMMY SPAR 7 b.g. Silver Owl – Lady of Mine (Cruise Missile) [2006/7 c103, h92+: c23m^F c22m^2 c22f^3 c20m* c21s^{bd} c21f* c20m* c21s^4 Feb 17] winning hurdler: fairly useful handicap chaser: much improved in early-2006/7, won at Stratford in June, Uttoxeter in July and Market Rasen (beat Return Home by 6 lengths, despite reportedly finishing lame) in August: off over 6 months, tailed off final outing: stays 3m: acts on firm and good to soft going (possibly not on softer): tongue tied once. *P. Bowen* — **c123 h—**

TOM'N ED 6 b.g. Shaamit (IRE) – Manhunt (Posse (USA)) [2006/7 F–: 16gp^u Nov 13] lengthy, unfurnished gelding: no show in bumper and selling hurdle over 12 months apart. *D. R. Gandolfo* — **h—**

TOMS GONE GREY (IRE) 8 gr.g. Gothland (FR) – Cpv Lady (Le Moss) [2006/7 c21v^{pu} c19v^3 c23d^5 c21g^6 c20s^F c23v^{pu} c24m Apr 10] tall gelding: maiden hurdler: fairly useful handicap chaser in 2004/5: off 19 months, generally well below best since: stays 3m: acts on heavy going: tried visored: front runner/races prominently. *R. H. Alner* — **c102 h—**

TOM'S PRIZE 12 ch.g. Gunner B – Pandora's Prize (Royal Vulcan) [2006/7 c122, h–: c24v^4 c24gp^u Mar 23] plain gelding: one-time fairly useful hurdler/chaser: fourth to Tribal Run at Warwick on completed start in hunters: stays 3¼m: acts on any going: front runner: usually jumps soundly: game. *S. Joynes* — **c88 h—**

TOM'S TOYBOX 5 b.g. Classic Cliche (IRE) – Jobiska (Dunbeath (USA)) [2006/7 F71: F17s^2 F16g^5 16s^4 19d^3 25s^5 Jan 24] tall, lengthy gelding: has scope: runner-up in bumper: best effort in novice hurdles when 2½ lengths third to Super Baby at Catterick: should stay beyond 19f. *J. M. Jefferson* — **h92 F83**

TOM TOBACCO 10 b.g. Afzal – Monsoon (Royal Palace) [2006/7 h–: c23gp^u May 17] winning pointer: no form in other events: tried in cheekpieces/tongue strap. *A. S. T. Holdsworth* — **c— h—**

TOM TUG (NZ) 7 b.g. Flying Pegasus (IRE) – Flight Judge (AUS) (The Judge (AUS)) [2006/7 F80: F16m^3 F17m^4 F17g 17g 20d^4 16s 24d Nov 20] rather leggy gelding: modest form in bumpers: little show over hurdles: dead. *W. Jenks* — **h78 F77**

TON-CHEE 8 b.g. Vettori (IRE) – Najariya (Northfields (USA)) [2006/7 c99§, h95§: c16g^4 c16sp^u c16m^2 c16gp^u c17m c16s^6 c19d c16s^4 c16g* Mar 17] leggy gelding: modest handicap hurdler/chaser: won over fences at Newcastle in March: best around 2m: acts on good to firm and good to soft ground: tried tongue tied: has hung left under pressure: weak finisher. *F. P. Murtagh* — **c99 § h— §**

TONGARIRO CROSSING (IRE) 7 b.g. Old Vic – Miss Kertina (IRE) (Orchestra) [2006/7 F74: 24mp^u May 6] little sign of ability: tried tongue tied: sold 2,000 gns Doncaster May Sales. *W. T. Reed* — **h—**

TONI ALCALA 8 b.g. Ezzoud (IRE) – Etourdie (USA) (Arctic Tern (USA)) [2006/7 h96: 25s^3 Jan 1] modest stayer on Flat: novice hurdler: stays 27f: acts on heavy and good to firm going: tried in cheekpieces. *R. F. Fisher* — **h—**

TONIGHT (IRE) 5 b.g. Imperial Ballet (IRE) – No Tomorrow (IRE) (Night Shift (USA)) [2006/7 16g^6 17m^4 17s^5 16d^4 19g^5 21gp^u Nov 19] poor maiden on Flat: likewise over hurdles: stays 19f: sometimes tongue tied. *W. M. Brisbourne* — **h74**

TONY'S PRIDE 7 b.g. Alderbrook – Lucia Forte (Neltino) [2006/7 F–: 19d^3 Jun 2] no form in bumpers/novice hurdle: sold 7,500 gns Doncaster August Sales, in frame in maiden points. *P. T. Dalton* — **h—**

TOOFARBACK (IRE) 7 b.g. Mister Lord (USA) – Lady Pharina (IRE) (Phardante (FR)) [2006/7 h134, F102: c22v^3 c20s^3 c20v* c24v* c20v^3 c24dur 20m Apr 9] useful-looking gelding: useful hurdler, well beaten in listed race at Fairyhouse final outing: fairly useful novice chaser: won maiden at Punchestown in December by short head from Alexander Taipan, pair well clear: left with too much to do when 3½ lengths third to Snowy Morning at Gowran only completed start after: should stay at least 3m: acts on heavy going (below form on good to firm): poor jumper. *N. Meade, Ireland* — **c126 x h—**

TOO FORWARD (IRE) 11 ch.g. Toulon – One Back (IRE) (Meneval (USA)) [2006/7 c141, h–: c20s* c20d c21v* c21g c21g^2 Apr 18] tall, leggy gelding: smart handicap chaser: impressive winner of listed races at Wetherby in October and Cheltenham (nudged clear to beat Nozic) in January: good ¾-length second of 6 to idling Nycteos in Grade 2 at Cheltenham: has won over 25f, best form over shorter: acts on good to firm and heavy going. *Carl Llewellyn* — **c152 h—**

TOOKA 6 b.g. Sure Blade (USA) – Parsons Lass (IRE) (The Parson) [2006/7 F–: 16s³ **h93 ?**
19s⁵ 16v³ 19s⁶ Feb 1] leggy gelding: seemingly best effort over hurdles when never-
nearer third in novice at Towcester third outing: should prove suited by further than 2m:
raced on soft/heavy ground. *A. Middleton*

TOOLEY PARK 10 b.g. Homo Sapien – Aintree Oats (Oats) [2006/7 c25g³ c24d⁶ **c96**
c23v³ c16v* c22g⁴ c26gᵖᵘ Apr 19] prolific winning pointer: fair hunter chaser: won at
Leicester in March by neck from My Best Buddy: in cheekpieces, ran poorly at Cheltenham final outing: effective at 2m to 25f: acts on heavy ground. *G. J. Tarry*

TOO MUCH TALK (IRE) 7 b. or br.g. Luso – Credora Bay (Orange Bay) [2006/7 **c–**
c25sᵖᵘ c25gᶠ Apr 2] tall gelding: sixth foal: half-brother to winning pointer by Orchestra:
dam, poor maiden hurdler, half-sister to high-class hurdler/winning chaser King Credo:
won maiden point in 2006: failed to complete both starts in chases: tried visored.
I. R. Ferguson, Ireland

TOO POSH TO SHARE 9 b.m. Rakaposhi King – Two Shares (The Parson) [2006/7 **h76**
h62: 16m⁶ 16v³ 16g 16g² 20v⁵ 16vᵖᵘ 19gᵘʳ Mar 29] smallish, sturdy mare: poor maiden
hurdler: best at 2m: acts on heavy going: tongue tied. *D. J. Wintle*

TOOTHILL GUNNER 6 ch.g. Gunner B – Hazel Hill (Abednego) [2006/7 h–, F–: **h–**
24gᶠ 20g⁶ Sep 17] smallish gelding: no form in bumpers/novice hurdles: sold 800 gns
Doncaster January Sales. *J. K. Cresswell*

TOP ACHIEVER (IRE) 6 ch.g. Intikhab (USA) – Nancy Maloney (IRE) (Persian **h–**
Bold) [2006/7 h102d: 23g 16g 19g Nov 29] smallish, sturdy gelding: handicap hurdler,
no form since 2005/6 reappearance: raced mainly around 2m. *C. W. Moore*

Mr T. L. Gibson & Mr D. Mathias' "Too Forward"

TOPAMENDIP (IRE) 7 b.g. Topanoora – Bucks Cregg (IRE) (Buckskin (FR)) **h92 p**
[2006/7 F81: 22m⁵ 16g² Oct 22] sturdy gelding: third in bumper: much better effort in
novice hurdles when 19 lengths second to stable-companion Pepporoni Pete at Wincanton, not unduly knocked about: likely to improve further. *P. F. Nicholls*

TOPAZ LADY (IRE) 6 ch.m. Zaffaran (USA) – Miss Top (IRE) (Tremblant) [2006/7 **h82**
16v⁴ 20s 19v⁶ 24v⁵ Mar 15] €6,000 4-y-o: lengthy, workmanlike mare: third foal:
half-sister to fair hurdler Miss Toulon (by Toulon): stays 2½m: dam lightly raced: poor
form over hurdles: stays 3m: raced on soft/heavy ground. *N. G. Richards*

TOP CLOUD (IRE) 6 b.g. Cloudings (IRE) – Top Dresser (IRE) (Good Thyne (USA)) **h113**
[2006/7 F93: 22d⁴ 22g² 20g⁵ 27s* 27v* Feb 20] tall gelding: has scope: fair hurdler:
won novices at Kelso (conditional jockeys) in October and Sedgefield in December, and
handicap at Sedgefield again (further improvement) in February: stays 27f: raced on good
going or softer (acts on heavy). *Ferdy Murphy*

TOP DANCER (IRE) 7 ch.g. Danehill Dancer (IRE) – Shygate (Shy Groom (USA)) **c73**
[2006/7 22d 20v⁶ c17g⁴ Apr 23] leggy gelding: signs of ability in bumpers/over hurdles, **h—**
off 22 months before return: well-held fourth of 5 in novice handicap at Plumpton on
chasing debut, blundering last. *N. P. Littmoden*

TOP DOG (IRE) 8 b.g. Topanoora – Dun Oengus (IRE) (Strong Gale) [2006/7 c–, h–, **c—**
F–: c19d⁴ c20dᵖᵘ c25sᵖᵘ 27vᵖᵘ 19f⁴ Apr 11] little impact over jumps, sold out of **h—**
L. Wells's stable £1,400 Ascot February Sales before final outing. *Mrs L. J. Young*

TOP DRESSING (IRE) 6 br.g. Rashar (USA) – Ross Gale (Strong Gale) [2006/7 F87: **h92**
F17s⁴ 19g 16d⁴ 16v* 20m² Mar 12] lengthy, unfurnished gelding: in frame in bumpers: **F81**
modest form over hurdles: won novice at Newcastle (readily) in February: stays 2½m:
acts on good to firm and heavy going. *J. Howard Johnson*

TOP GALE (IRE) 8 b.m. Topanoora – Amy's Gale (IRE) (Strong Gale) [2006/7 c–x, **c66 x**
h–: c25dᵖᵘ c20m² c23mᵘʳ c25mᵖᵘ c21mᵖᵘ Sep 2] form in chases (often let down by **h—**
jumping) only when second in novice handicap at Uttoxeter: placed in points in 2007.
R. Dickin

TOP GUARD (IRE) 9 b.g. Topanoora – Garter Royale (IRE) (Garde Royale) [2006/7 **h—**
24dᵖᵘ 25gᵖᵘ Oct 30] winning pointer: no form in bumpers/over hurdles. *Mrs P. Ford*

TOPINAMBOUR (FR) 7 gr.g. Turgeon (USA) – La Deviniere (IRE) (Nashamaa) **c105**
[2006/7 c16g² c21m* c20s⁵ c20g c20s² c21v³ c16v⁴ Jan 3] smallish, sturdy ex-French **h—**
gelding: half-brother to 2 winners in France by Kaldounevees at 1m/1¼m: dam 6f/1m
winner: successful twice around 11f on Flat: fair hurdler/chaser: successful in 4-y-o
hurdles at Berck-sur-Mer and Nancy for J-P. Gallorini: off 20 months before return, won
maiden chase at Cartmel in August: stays 21f: acts on soft and good to firm going: tongue
tied after reappearance. *R. Ford*

TOP JARO (FR) 4 b.g. Marathon (USA) – Shahmy (USA) (Lear Fan (USA)) [2006/7 **h—**
16vᵖᵘ Jan 25] strong gelding: brother to modest hurdler Marathea, stayed 3m, and half-
brother to fairly useful hurdler Schampus (by Galetto), stayed 19f: fairly useful on Flat
(stays 1¼m), sold out of T. Tate's stable 20,000 gns Doncaster November Sales: no show
in juvenile maiden on hurdling debut: bolted and withdrawn 4 days later. *Jennie Candlish*

TOPLESS (IRE) 6 gr.m. Presenting – Tara The Grey (IRE) (Supreme Leader) [2006/7 **h96**
F86: 21s^F 18s³ 22s⁶ 24s* 26g Mar 14] modest novice hurdler: upped in trip, won mares
handicap at Taunton in February: stays 3¼m: acts on soft ground: tongue tied final outing.
D. P. Keane

TOP MAN TEE 5 gr.g. Vettori (IRE) – Etienne Lady (IRE) (Imperial Frontier (USA)) **h— x**
[2006/7 h–: 17mᵖᵘ 16v^F 16s Jan 23] smallish, leggy gelding: no form over hurdles, left
Evan Williams after reappearance: tried in cheekpieces: often tongue tied: poor jumper.
Michael E. O'Callaghan, Ireland

TOP OFFICIAL (IRE) 5 ch.g. Beneficial – Lobby Nes (IRE) (Lanfranco) [2006/7 **F72**
F16g⁵ F16g Apr 23] 6,000 3-y-o: third foal: brother to a winning pointer: dam unraced:
mid-field in bumpers. *Mrs K. Walton*

TOP RAM (IRE) 7 ch.g. Topanoora – Aries Girl (Valiyar) [2006/7 h85, F98: 16s³ 17s⁴ **h100**
Nov 14] strong, workmanlike gelding: bumper winner: best effort in 3 starts over hurdles
when length third to New Team in maiden at Uttoxeter. *J. A. B. Old*

TOP STYLE (IRE) 9 ch.g. Topanoora – Kept In Style (Castle Keep) [2006/7 h107: **h95 d**
16d³ 21d 19s⁵ 19g 23v 20v Jan 17] angular gelding: fair hurdler, little form since 2005:
best efforts around 2m: acts on soft going: tried visored, usually wears cheekpieces: sold
to join P. Clinton 1,800 gns Doncaster January Sales. *G. A. Harker*

TOP TENOR (IRE) 7 b.g. Sadler's Wells (USA) – Posta Vecchia (USA) (Rainbow **h71 ?**
Quest (USA)) [2006/7 h–: 17m⁴ 16fᵖᵘ Jun 17] little form over hurdles: joined W. Storey.
V. Thompson

TOP THE BILL (IRE) 7 b.g. Topanoora – Rio Star (IRE) (Riot Helmet) [2006/7 h–: **h92 §**
24gᵇᵈ 24g 24g² 24m 20d² 21m⁵ 20m 24g* Oct 7] close-coupled gelding: modest handicap
hurdler: won at Hexham in October: stays 3m: acts on good to firm and heavy going: has
taken little interest. *Mrs S. A. Watt*

TOP TREES 9 b.g. Charnwood Forest (IRE) – Low Line (High Line) [2006/7 h79§: **h98 §**
17m³ 17gʳᵗʳ 19g* 19d* 22d Aug 20] modest hurdler: improved form when winning minor
event at Newton Abbot in July, and followed up in handicap there next month: stays 19f:
acts on firm and good to soft going: tried in cheekpieces: temperamental (has twice
refused to race). *W. S. Kittow*

TOPWELL 6 b.g. Most Welcome – Miss Top Ville (FR) (Top Ville) [2006/7 h73, F105: **h93**
16m⁶ 16g 17d² 20g 19m³ 17m⁵ 20g⁴ 16g⁴ Sep 17] lengthy gelding: bumper winner:
modest maiden hurdler: best around 2m: acts on good to firm and good to soft going: in
cheekpieces/blinkers last 6 starts. *R. C. Guest*

TORA BORA (GER) 5 b.g. Winged Love (IRE) – Tower Bridge (GER) (Big Shuffle **c127**
(USA)) [2006/7 h119: c21s* c20g* c19d* c19s² 22g c21gᵖᵘ 24gᵖᵘ Mar 24] angular **h–**
gelding: winning hurdler: fairly useful novice chaser: successful first 3 starts, at Uttoxeter
(maiden) in October and Market Rasen and Exeter (handicap, by 2 lengths from Maljimar) in November: shaped as if amiss in listed event at Cheltenham penultimate outing:
stays 21f: raced on good going or softer (acts on heavy): successful with or without
blinkers/cheekpieces. *B. G. Powell*

TORAN ROAD (IRE) 8 ch.g. Hawkstone (IRE) – Mandablue (IRE) (Mandalus) **c85**
[2006/7 c22dᶠ c24s² c25mᶠ c24s³ 22m c24m³ 24s³ 24s⁴ Sep 21] winning **h82**
Irish pointer: poor maiden hurdler/chaser: stays 3m: acts on soft and good to firm ground:
tongue tied last 6 outings, also blinkered last 3. *G. Elliott, Ireland*

TORA PETCHA (IRE) 4 b.g. Bahhare (USA) – Magdalene (FR) (College Chapel) **h111 §**
[2006/7 16g² 17s² 16m² 17g³ 16m² 16g⁴ 16d* 16dᵖᵘ 16g 16f* 16m⁵ Apr 22] sturdy gelding: fairly useful juvenile hurdler: won handicaps at Ludlow in December and April (beat
Will The Till by neck in 5-runner event): raced around 2m: acts on firm and soft ground:
unreliable. *R. Hollinshead*

TORCHE (IRE) 9 b.g. Taos (IRE) – Orchette (IRE) (Orchestra) [2006/7 c120, h–: **c96 §**
c32s⁴ c28d⁶ c25v⁵ c24g³ Mar 21] strong gelding: modest handicap chaser nowadays: left **h–**
M. Scudamore and off 14 months before return: out-and-out stayer: acts on soft going:
visored: tongue tied final outing: not one to trust: sold 11,000 gns Doncaster May Sales.
Mike Hammond

TORKINKING (IRE) 8 b.g. Supreme Leader – Nicola's News (IRE) (Buckskin (FR)) **c110**
[2006/7 h126: 16s 16s 16v* 20v³ 16v* 16v 16v³ c16v² Mar 15] small, workmanlike **h134**
gelding: useful hurdler: successful in handicaps at Hexham in December and Wetherby
(beat Magic Sky by 10 lengths) in January: creditable third to Wizard of Us in similar
event at Uttoxeter penultimate outing: 1¼ lengths second to idling Lankawi in novice at
Hexham on chasing debut, ponderous at times: best around 2m on going softer than good
(acts on heavy): tongue tied: free-going front runner: genuine. *M. A. Barnes*

TORKSEY LOCK 5 b.g. Emperor Fountain – Liscannor Bay (IRE) (Executive Perk) **F—**
[2006/7 F17d F17m Apr 28] 8,000 4-y-o: tall gelding: fourth foal: dam little sign of
ability: well held in bumpers. *S. Gollings*

TORRID KENTAVR (USA) 10 b.g. Trempolino (USA) – Torrid Tango (USA) **c111 §**
(Green Dancer (USA)) [2006/7 c–, h–: 18g⁴ 17m⁵ 16s³ 16d 16v 16v c17m³ c16m² **h106 §**
Apr 24] compact gelding: fairly useful on Flat (stays 1½m): fair hurdler/handicap chaser
nowadays: best around 2m: acts on soft and good to firm going: free-going sort: temperamental. *J. J. Lambe, Ireland*

TORY ISLAND (IRE) 6 b.g. Oscar (IRE) – Blenheim Run (IRE) (Remainder Man) **h70**
[2006/7 F86: F16s 22d 16v 16s 16v 20gᵖᵘ Apr 11] third in bumper: poor maiden hurdler: **F68**
form only at 2m: acts on heavy ground: wore cheekpieces/tongue strap final outing.
S. Donohoe, Ireland

TORYT (POL) 8 b.g. Beaconsfield – Torana (POL) (Dixieland (POL)) [2006/7 16vᵖᵘ **h–**
20vᶠ Feb 28] successful 7 times up to 1½m on Flat in Poland: failed to complete both
starts over hurdles, in touch when fell 3 out in maiden at Folkestone. *Carl Llewellyn*

TOSCANINI (GER) 11 b.g. Goofalik (USA) – Tosca Stella (GER) (Surumu (GER)) c80 §
[2006/7 c79, h–: c19g⁶ c26m² c26vᶠ May 20] useful-looking gelding: hurdle/point h–
winner: modest maiden hunter chaser: stays 3¼m: acts on heavy and good to firm going:
difficult ride. *Mark Doyle*

TOSKYANNA 7 b.m. Contract Law (USA) – Bosky (Petoski) [2006/7 F14s Dec 23] F–
first foal: dam 7f winner: well beaten in mares bumper on debut. *Mary Meek*

TOSS THE CABER (IRE) 5 ch.g. Dr Devious (IRE) – Celtic Fling (Lion Cavern h113
(USA)) [2006/7 h110: 20m³ Sep 24] lengthy, leggy gelding: fair on Flat (stays 1¾m):
likewise over hurdles: tongue tied, good effort in handicap only start in 2006/7: stays
2½m: acts on firm and good to soft going. *K. G. Reveley*

TOSULA 4 b.f. Syrtos – Sulapuff (Sula Bula) [2006/7 16d⁴ 16d 18s Dec 5] sturdy filly: h–
third foal: dam unraced: well held in juvenile hurdles. *D. P. Keane*

TOTALLY SCOTTISH 11 b.g. Mtoto – Glenfinlass (Lomond (USA)) [2006/7 c–, c–
h114: 20v* 26d* 24m⁶ 20s² 22g² 20v² 24s⁵ 23v⁴ 24g c25gᵇᵈ Apr 2] rather sparely-made h121
gelding: fairly useful hurdler: won claimer at Wetherby in May and handicap at Southwell
(beat Prestbury Knight a length) in June: good efforts after when second in handicaps:
twice-raced in maiden chases, brought down fifth final outing: stays 3¼m: probably acts
on any going: wore blinkers/tongue strap on debut: usually held up. *K. G. Reveley*

TOTAL VICTORY (IRE) 4 br.g. Titus Livius (FR) – Snipe Victory (IRE) (Old Vic) h103
[2006/7 16g³ 16g* 16d* 16d 16s 16v Feb 15] workmanlike gelding: progressive on Flat,
won over 1¾m in September: fair juvenile hurdler: won at Aintree (by 3½ lengths from
Marc of Brilliance) in October and Cork in November: will stay beyond 2m: acts on good
to soft going: wears cheekpieces: tongue tied final outing (below form). *T. Hogan, Ireland*

TOTHEROADYOUVGONE 13 b.g. Carlingford Castle – Wild Rosie (Warpath) c107
[2006/7 c113, h88+: c23m² 24fᵖᵘ Jul 19] winning hurdler, went amiss final start: fair h–
handicap chaser: stays 3¼m: acts on firm and good to soft going: wears cheekpieces.
A. E. Jones

TO THE TOP 9 b.g. Petoski – Mrs Pepperpot (Kinglet) [2006/7 c–: c19m³ c21g² c20sᵖᵘ c94
c21v³ Feb 28] prolific winning pointer: fair hunter chaser: likely to stay beyond 21f: acts
on good to firm and heavy going: tried in cheekpieces (bled). *Alan Hill*

TO TIGER (GER) 6 b.g. Tiger Hill (IRE) – The Mood (GER) (Mondrian (GER)) h100
[2006/7 20s⁶ 16s² 16v 16s⁴ Dec 16] sturdy ex-German gelding: off over 12 months,
successful over 17f on Flat in September: best effort over hurdles (fair form) when
runner-up in novice at Kelso: should stay beyond 2m. *P. Monteith*

TOT O'WHISKEY 6 b.g. Saddlers' Hall (IRE) – Whatagale (Strong Gale) [2006/7 F111
F16s* F16d* F16g* F16g F16m Apr 25] €13,000 3-y-o: heavy-topped gelding: has
scope: sixth foal: dam, fair chaser, stayed 25f: useful form in bumpers: won at Hexham in
November and Catterick in December (by 10 lengths from Kate's Gift) and February:
mid-field in Grade 1 at Cheltenham next time, not knocked about after still plenty to do
5f out: laboured in similar contest following month: will stay at least 2½m. *J. M. Jefferson*

TOUCH CLOSER 10 b.g. Inchinor – Ryewater Dream (Touching Wood (USA)) c121 §
[2006/7 c118, h–: c24d* c29vᶠ c29s c24gᵖᵘ Apr 7] angular gelding: winning hurdler: h–
fairly useful handicap chaser: won at Ludlow in December by 5 lengths from She's Our
Native: should stay beyond 25f: acts on any going: in cheekpieces nowadays: hard ride:
sold 6,000 gns Doncaster May Sales. *P. Bowen*

TOUCH OF FATE 8 b.g. Sovereign Water (FR) – Coral Delight (Idiot's Delight) c–
[2006/7 c87+, h107: c25d⁶ Nov 27] good-topped gelding: fair hurdler: let down by h–
jumping both starts over fences a year apart: stays 25f: raced on good going or softer.
R. Rowe

TOUCH OF FLAME 8 b.g. Terimon – Flame O'Frensi (Tudor Flame) [2006/7 c25g² c97
c23d⁴ May 17] first foal: dam, winning hunter chaser, stayed 21f: fair pointer, won in
April: better effort in hunters when second to Latzod'alm at Cheltenham: stays 25f.
K. Cumings

TOUCH OF IRISH 5 b.g. Kayf Tara – Portland Row (IRE) (Zaffaran (USA)) [2006/7 F81
F16v⁴ Jan 28] first foal: dam winning pointer: favourite, 10¾ lengths fourth to Kealshore
Boy in maiden bumper at Kelso on debut. *G. A. Swinbank*

TOUCH OF IVORY (IRE) 4 b.f. Rossini (USA) – Windomen (IRE) (Forest Wind h90 §
(USA)) [2006/7 16s* 16g² 16g⁵ 16s⁶ 16v 16dᵖᵘ 16m³ 16d⁵ 16v 16g⁵ Apr 23] leggy filly:
fair on Flat (stays 1¼m), successful 3 times in 2006: modest juvenile hurdler: won at

Perth in September: didn't progress: raced at 2m: acts on soft going: usually in cheek-pieces/visor: ungenuine. *P. Monteith*

TOUCH THYME (IRE) 7 br.g. Pierre – Ringbeam (IRE) (Good Thyne (USA)) **F—**
[2006/7 F16d F16s F16v Dec 31] 1,600 5-y-o, resold 800 5-y-o: good-topped gelding: second foal: dam unraced: no form in bumpers, sold out of Mrs L. Young's stable £1,100 Ascot December Sales after debut: tried blinkered/tongue tied: resold £800 Ascot February Sales. *F. E. Sutherland*

TOUCH WOOD (IRE) 7 b.g. Son of Sharp Shot (IRE) – Lairin Liath (IRE) (Rising) **F—**
[2006/7 F16m Jul 5] €1,900 5-y-o: second foal: half-brother to winning Irish pointer by Supreme Leader: dam lightly-raced maiden pointer: failed to complete in 6 maiden points in 2006 (ran out 3 times): tailed off in bumper. *Mrs L. J. Young*

TOULOUSE EXPRESS (IRE) 8 b.g. Toulon – Miss Ivy (IRE) (Le Bavard (FR)) **c87**
[2006/7 h85: 16g 16s6 17s* 16m 16s5 c24fpu c20f4 c20g3 c20spu 20s4 c16s2 21s6 22v c16s3 **h101**
c19d2 c16s3 c16s6 17s 20v2 20s* 20s Apr 27] smallish gelding: fair handicap hurdler: won at Market Rasen in May and Hexham (idled) in April: modest novice chaser (has looked none too keen): stays 2½m: acts on heavy going: often wears headgear. *R. Johnson*

TOULOUSE (IRE) 10 b.g. Toulon – Neasham (Nishapour (FR)) [2006/7 c118, h—: **c121**
c17m* c16dpu c21gF Mar 19] rangy gelding: fairly useful handicap chaser: won at **h—**
Southwell in May by 5 lengths from Romany Dream, only completion in 2006/7: effective at 2m to 2½m: acts on soft and good to firm going: tongue tied 4 of last 5 outings. *R. H. Alner*

TOURNIQUET (IRE) 12 b.g. Torus – Treidlia (Mandalus) [2006/7 c26vpu c21spu **c—**
Feb 16] strong gelding: maiden hurdler: won 2-finisher novice in 2003 on chase debut: **h—**
failed to complete 3 starts outside points since, in hunters in 2006/7: stays 25f. *P. Senter*

TOUS CHEZ (IRE) 8 b.g. Carroll House – Sixfoursix (Balinger) [2006/7 h112, F97: **c106 p**
17g* 16vpu 16v5 16g6 c16g3 Apr 7] lengthy, workmanlike gelding: fair hurdler: well **h112**
backed, won handicap at Market Rasen in December: staying-on third to Rayshan in maiden at Carlisle on chasing debut: should stay 2½m: acts on heavy going: open to improvement over fences. *Mrs S. J. Smith*

TOUT LES SOUS 6 ch.g. Tout Ensemble – Suzie Sue (IRE) (Ore) [2006/7 h—: 21dpu **h—**
May 15] no show in maiden hurdles: resold £520 Ascot December Sales. *B. W. Duke*

TOWER HILL (IRE) 4 b.g. Grand Lodge (USA) – Champaka (IRE) (Caerleon **h82**
(USA)) [2006/7 16g4 16dpu Nov 19] half-brother to progressive hurdler Pevensey (by Danehill): fair form on Flat (stays 1¼m), sold out of M. Jarvis' stable 16,000 gns Doncaster May Sales: modest form in juvenile hurdles, lame second start. *Mrs L. C. Jewell*

TOWEROFCHARLEMAGNE (IRE) 4 ch.g. King Charlemagne (USA) – Nozet **h85 p**
(Nishapour (FR)) [2006/7 16g2 Apr 23] fair maiden on Flat (stays 8.3f), left Miss Gay Kelleway after final 3-y-o start: green, 5 lengths second of 4 to Cockatoo in juvenile at Plumpton on hurdling debut, not knocked about once headed: likely to prove best over easy 2m: should improve. *Miss E. C. Lavelle*

TOWNABRACK (IRE) 5 b.g. Oscar (IRE) – Marians Princess (IRE) (Alphabatim **F108 p**
(USA)) [2006/7 F16s* Dec 26] €25,000 3-y-o: first foal: dam unraced: favourite, won 21-runner bumper at Leopardstown on debut by ½ length from Whatuthink: likely to go on to better things. *N. Meade, Ireland*

TOWN CRIER (IRE) 12 br.g. Beau Sher – Ballymacarett (Menelek) [2006/7 c142, **c—**
h132: 16d 16gF Oct 21] tall gelding: useful hurdler/chaser: travelling well when falling **h98**
fatally 3 out in handicap hurdle at Aintree: should have stayed beyond 17f: successful on good to firm going, possibly suited by more testing conditions (acted on heavy). *Mrs S. J. Smith*

TOWNSVILLE (IRE) 5 b.g. Soviet Star (USA) – Valmarana (USA) (Danzig Connec- **h—**
tion (USA)) [2006/7 16d 17v5 Nov 28] maiden on Flat, sold out of E. O'Neill's stable £1,800 Ascot April Sales, resold £3,600 Ascot October Sales: well held in selling hurdles. *R. Lee*

TOY BOY (IRE) 9 b.g. Un Desperado (FR) – Too Sharp (True Song) [2006/7 c—, h—: **c—**
c22g6 Mar 28] lengthy gelding: little form over hurdles/in chases: in frame in points: tried **h—**
in cheekpieces. *Mrs S. S. Harbour*

TOY GUN (IRE) 5 b.g. Pistolet Bleu (IRE) – Di's Wag (Scallywag) [2006/7 20s 16s **h—**
21s 20vpu 17vF 20m5 Apr 9] tall gelding: eighth live foal: dam of little account: no form in novice hurdles. *J. Howard Johnson*

TRACKATTACK 5 ch.g. Atraf – Verbena (IRE) (Don't Forget Me) [2006/7 h79§: 17m⁵ 20m³ 19m⁶ c18dᶠ 20vᵖᵘ Dec 27] workmanlike gelding: poor maiden hurdler: sold out of P. Howling's stable £600 Ascot December Sales before final start: fell eighth on chasing debut: stays easy 2½m: acts on good to firm going, probably on soft: ungenuine. *M. Appleby*
c– §
h77 §

TRADE OFF (IRE) 9 b.g. Roselier (FR) – Lady Owenette (IRE) (Salluceva) [2006/7 c105, h–: c21g² c25m* c25d⁵ c25f² Apr 5] fairly useful pointer/hunter chaser: won at Wincanton in May by length from Red Brook Lad, making most: stays 3¼m: acts on firm and soft going: tried visored: races prominently. *Mrs S. Alner*
c108
h–

TRADE WAR (IRE) 6 b.g. Darazari (IRE) – Lynalo (IRE) (Bulldozer) [2006/7 F16m⁴ F17m* F16g F16m⁶ 16g⁵ 16s 16d Nov 2] €15,000 3-y-o: first foal: dam lightly raced: won maiden bumper at Bellewstown in July: poor form over hurdles: raced around 2m: often tongue tied: front runner/races prominently. *Philip Fenton, Ireland*
h76
F91

TRADING TROUBLE 10 b.g. Petoski – Marielou (FR) (Carwhite) [2006/7 c20s⁴ c21v⁴ c25vᶠ c25s* c23g* c20s* Apr 27] medium-sized gelding: winning hurdler: fair handicap chaser, left J. M. Jefferson and off over 3 years before return: back to best later in season, winning at Catterick in March and Wetherby and Perth (by 9 lengths from Great Jane, eased) in April): stays 25f: raced mainly on good ground or softer (acts on heavy). *J. Wade*
c112
h–

TRADINGUP (IRE) 8 b.g. Arctic Lord – Autumn Queen (Menelek) [2006/7 c89, h–: c25sᵖᵘ c24d³ c24v* c23s² c24vᵖᵘ c23v* c25s² c23d⁴ Mar 20] compact gelding: modest handicap chaser: won at Towcester (conditional jockeys) in November and Taunton in February: stays 25f: raced on going softer than good (acts on heavy): often let down by jumping. *Andrew Turnell*
c92 x
h–

TRAFALGAR MAN (IRE) 6 b. or br.g. Scribano – Call Over (Callernish) [2006/7 h–, F89: c19dᶠ c16vᶠ 16g³ 16g³ Apr 2] leggy gelding: modest form over hurdles: fell both outings in maiden chases: raced mainly at 2m. *Micky Hammond*
c–
h96

TRAGIC OHIO 8 b.g. Tragic Role (USA) – Kiniohio (FR) (Script Ohio (USA)) [2006/7 c–, h–: c16v⁶ c20v⁴ 16v Feb 17] tall, rather leggy gelding: successful first 2 starts over hurdles in 2004/5: lightly raced and has lost way since (including over fences), left P. Nicholls before return: should stay beyond 17f: acts on soft going. *D. McCain Jnr*
c88 +
h–

TRAGUMNA (IRE) 7 ch.g. Presenting – Billys Pet (Le Moss) [2006/7 20d 20d⁶ 24v⁶ 22d Dec 15] €24,000 3-y-o: stocky gelding: brother to fair but temperamental hurdler/chaser up to 2¾m Giorgio and half-brother to useful hurdler/chaser Ashwell Boy, stayed 25f, and fair hurdler up to 2½m Macaw-Bay (both by Strong Gale): dam unraced: unplaced in bumpers: modest novice hurdler, off 21 months before reappearance: stays 3m: raced on going softer than good (acts on heavy). *Mrs J. Harrington, Ireland*
h96

TRAMPOLINE KING (USA) 7 b.g. Trempolino (USA) – Bravalma (USA) (Danzig (USA)) [2006/7 16s 16m c17f⁵ 17fˢ c17m² c17m⁶ c16m c16d⁶ c16s⁵ c16d 17sᵖᵘ 16v⁵ 18g 16m Apr 22] sturdy gelding: maiden hurdler: fair novice chaser: sold out of E. O'Grady's stable €6,000 Fairyhouse November Sales, below form last 6 outings: raced mainly around 2m: acts on firm and soft going: has worn blinkers/cheekpieces: unreliable. *A. J. Whiting*
c102 §
h92 §

TRANOS (USA) 4 b.g. Bahri (USA) – Balancoire (USA) (Diesis) [2006/7 16g³ Mar 17] modest maiden on Flat (stays 1¼m), sold out of L. Cumani's stable 20,000 gns Newmarket Autumn Sales: around 3 lengths third to Leslingtaylor in novice at Newcastle on hurdling debut. *Micky Hammond*
h96

TRANQUIL SEA (IRE) 5 b.g. Sea Raven (IRE) – Silver Valley (IRE) (Henbit (USA)) [2006/7 F16v² F16v* F16m Apr 26] €10,000 3-y-o: unfurnished gelding: first foal: dam placed twice in points: won maiden point on debut: useful form in bumpers: won at Leopardstown in February by 5 lengths from Stewarts House: well held on totally different ground over 2 months later. *E. J. O'Grady, Ireland*
F109

TRANSIT 8 b.g. Lion Cavern (USA) – Black Fighter (USA) (Secretariat (USA)) [2006/7 c–, h105: 20g 17v³ c16gᵘʳ c16v* 16g⁵ c16d³ 16v c16v³ c20m³ Mar 31] rather leggy, close-coupled gelding: winning hurdler: fairly useful handicap chaser: won at Sedgefield in December by length from Bongo Fury: creditable efforts when third after: stays 2½m: acts on heavy and good to firm going: tried blinkered, usually in cheekpieces: tongue tied in 2006/7: held up: has looked less than keen. *B. Ellison*
c115
h98

TRAPRAIN (IRE) 5 b.g. Mark of Esteem (IRE) – Nassma (IRE) (Sadler's Wells (USA)) [2006/7 h119p: 17m² 16m² Jun 18] fairly useful hurdler: good second to Mac Federal in handicap at Hereford, upsides winner on bridle when blundering last: beaten at
h127

odds on in novice next time: likely to prove best around 2m with emphasis on speed: acts on good to firm ground. *P. J. Hobbs*

TRAVEL AGENT (IRE) 7 b.g. Shernazar – Brownskin (Buckskin (FR)) [2006/7 h114p: c23s⁴ 24v⁵ Mar 10] promising second in novice hurdle on debut in 2005/6: failed to progress, remote fourth of 5 finishers to Pole Star in maiden chase at Exeter on reappearance: sold only 2,500 gns Doncaster May Sales. *P. J. Hobbs*   **c101 h76**

TRAVELLING BAND (IRE) 9 b.g. Blues Traveller (IRE) – Kind of Cute (Prince Sabo) [2006/7 h–: 17s⁴ May 20] angular gelding: lightly-raced hurdler, fair at best: raced around 2m. *J. Mackie*   **h82**

TRAVELLING LIGHT (IRE) 5 b.g. Old Vic – Donaghmore Lady (IRE) (Orchestra) [2006/7 22d 20s 16s 16v 18v² Mar 7] close-coupled gelding: second foal: dam Irish bumper/2½m hurdle winner: easily best effort over hurdles (modest form) when ¾-length second to Silistra in conditional/amateur event at Fontwell on handicap debut: should stay 2½m: raced on going softer than good: open to further improvement. *D. E. Pipe*   **h86 p**

TRAVELLO (GER) 7 b.g. Bakharoff (USA) – Travista (GER) (Days At Sea (USA)) [2006/7 c20g c19s c17sᵖᵘ 16g² 16g* 17g c17mᵖᵘ c16g c18m⁴ Apr 26] good-bodied gelding: poor hurdler/chaser: won sellers at Chepstow (hurdles) in March and Plumpton (handicap chase) in April: raced mainly around 2m: acts on good to firm and good to soft going: tried blinkered: tongue tied last 3 starts. *M. F. Harris*   **c80 h84**

TRAVOLTA 4 b.g. Dansili – Generous Diana (Generous (IRE)) [2006/7 16d³ 17d³ Nov 23] modest maiden on Flat (stays 11.5f): not fluent when third in juvenile hurdles (second one a seller). *C. R. Egerton*   **h68**

TRAWBREAGA BAY 7 ch.g. Bijou d'Inde – Give Me A Day (Lucky Wednesday) [2006/7 F–: 17s 17dᵖᵘ 24d⁴ 24mᵖᵘ Jul 4] no form in bumper/over hurdles: tried in cheek-pieces/blinkers: sold 1,100 gns Doncaster August Sales. *P. Beaumont*   **h–**

TREACLE MOON 4 b.f. Kayf Tara – Monica's Story (Arzanni) [2006/7 F14v⁶ Dec 2] first foal: dam, fairly useful hurdler, stayed 21f: around 20 lengths sixth of 20 to Lease Lend in 3-y-o bumper at Wetherby on debut. *J. Howard Johnson*   **F70**

TREASULIER (IRE) 10 gr.g. Roselier (FR) – Flashy Treasure (Crash Course) [2006/7 c99: c25s⁴ c24d⁴ c24d² c23s³ c24v³ c25d³ c23v² c25s* c24g² c25f² Apr 22] rather leggy gelding: modest novice chaser: won (for first time) handicap at Wincanton in March: will stay beyond 3¼m: acts on any going: in cheekpieces last 8 starts: often makes running. *P. R. Rodford*   **c93**

TREASURY COUNSEL (IRE) 5 br.g. Leading Counsel (USA) – Dunacarney (Random Shot) [2006/7 F86: F16g² 19s* 20v³ 21g* 20f³ Apr 28] lengthy, unfurnished gelding: placed in bumpers: generally progressive over hurdles, won maiden at Hereford in December and handicap at Kempton (beat Corker by 3½ lengths) in March: favourite, 2½ lengths third to Oslot in quite valuable handicap at Sandown: will stay beyond 21f: acts on firm and soft going. *N. J. Henderson*   **h121 F92**

TREATAGUEST (IRE) 8 b. or br.g. Fumo di Londra (IRE) – Grecian Lady (IRE) (Be My Guest (USA)) [2006/7 24vᵖᵘ Oct 21] ex-Irish gelding: no form on Flat at 2/3 yrs for Ms F. Crowley: well beaten only completed start in points in 2005: no show in maiden on hurdling debut. *C. Roberts*   **h–**

TREAT EM MEAN 6 gr.g. Keen – Knowing (Lochnager) [2006/7 F16d Feb 10] rangy gelding: second foal: dam, winning pointer, half-sister to 2m chaser Byron Lamb and staying hurdler Lord Lamb, both useful: well held in Grade 2 bumper on debut. *Carl Llewellyn*   **F–**

TREATY FLYER (IRE) 6 ch.m. Anshan – Highways Daughter (IRE) (Phardante (FR)) [2006/7 h105, F80: 20d² 19d* 22d 22d⁵ 18g⁵ 19d 21d c20s² Dec 7] close-coupled mare: winning pointer: fair handicap hurdler: won at Market Rasen in June: encouraging 24 lengths second to Bold Fire in mares novice at Huntingdon on chasing debut, not knocked about: stays 2¾m: raced on good going or softer (acts on heavy): likely to improve over fences. *P. G. Murphy*   **c102 p h113**

TREBELLO 6 b.g. Robellino (USA) – Trempkate (USA) (Trempolino (USA)) [2006/7 h82: 22vᵖᵘ 21s*ᵈⁱˢ Dec 26] modest hurdler: blinkered, first past post in handicap at Huntingdon in December (subsequently disqualified for taking wrong course): stays 21f: raced on going softer than good (well held on heavy). *J. R. Boyle*   **h91 +**

TREBLE TROUBLE 11 b.g. Minster Son – Ferneyhill Lady (Menelek) [2006/7 c20dᵖᵘ May 19] good-topped gelding: winning pointer: little form otherwise: tried tongue tied. *P. J. Millington*   **c– h–**

TREGASTEL (FR) 12 b.g. Tel Quel (FR) – Myrtlewood (FR) (Home Guard (USA)) **c95 x**
[2006/7 c86x, h–: c24s³ c26d³ c26d* c24d⁶ c24d³ c28sᵘʳ c27vᵖᵘ c20v⁶ c25sᵖᵘ Apr 1] **h–**
good-topped gelding: winning hurdler: modest chaser: won handicap at Cartmel in
August: below form after: stays 3¼m: raced on good going or softer (acts on heavy): tried
in headgear: tongue let down by jumping over fences. *R. Ford*

TRES BIEN 5 b.g. Bien Bien (USA) – Zielana Gora (Polish Precedent (USA)) [2006/7 **h–**
F16f² F16m F16m⁶ 17s Dec 7] close-coupled gelding: second foal: dam no sign of ability: **F83**
modest form in bumpers: well held in novice hurdle and on Flat. *P. R. Webber*

TREW FLIGHT (USA) 5 b.g. Rahy (USA) – Magdala (IRE) (Sadler's Wells (USA)) **h63**
[2006/7 17d⁴ May 31] closely related to 3m hurdle winner Dalawan (by Nashwan):
modest maiden on Flat: fourth in maiden at Cartmel on hurdling debut, hanging right.
M. H. Tompkins

TRIBAL DANCER (IRE) 13 ch.g. Commanche Run – Cute Play (Salluceva) [2006/7 **c102 §**
c99§, h–: c24g⁵ c25m² May 18] leggy, close-coupled gelding: fair chaser: failed to **h–**
complete in points in 2007: stays 25f: acts on heavy and good to firm going: tried
blinkered: often makes running: not an easy ride (refused penultimate 2005/6 outing).
Miss Venetia Williams

TRIBAL RUN (IRE) 12 ch.g. Be My Native (USA) – Queen's Run (IRE) (Deep Run) **c103**
[2006/7 c–, h–: c24v* Feb 23] fairly useful novice chaser: off over a year, won at Warwick **h–**
in February by 1¼ lengths from No Retreat: stays 3¾m: acts on heavy going: tongue tied.
M. F. Loggin

TRIBAL VENTURE (FR) 9 gr.g. Dom Alco (FR) – Babacha (FR) (Latnahc (USA)) **c123 §**
[2006/7 c130, h–: c25f⁶ c28s⁴ c32m⁵ c26m⁵ c24g* c27s² c27d⁵ c29sᵖᵘ Dec 2] tall, angular **h–**
gelding: winning hurdler: fairly useful handicap chaser: reportedly had breathing operation prior to winning at Chepstow in October by 1½ lengths from I Hear Thunder: best at
3m+: acts on good to firm and heavy going: has been blinkered: tried tongue tied:
unreliable. *P. J. Hobbs*

TRICKSTEP 6 b.g. Imperial Ballet (IRE) – Trick of Ace (USA) (Clever Trick (USA)) **c–**
[2006/7 h81: 16m⁵ 20m 17d³ c19mᶠ Sep 28] small, close-coupled gelding: winning **h–**
selling hurdler, no form in 2006/7: fell fatally on chasing debut: tried in cheekpieces/
blinkers. *D. McCain Jnr*

TRICKY VENTURE 7 gr.g. Linamix (FR) – Ukraine Venture (Slip Anchor) [2006/7 **h–**
h75: 16f 16d⁴ Aug 14] leggy gelding: maiden hurdler: raced mainly at 2m: tried in
cheekpieces: carries head high: sold £1,800 Ascot August Sales. *Mrs L. C. Jewell*

TRIGGERNOMETRY 6 b.g. Double Trigger (IRE) – Dubacilla (Dubassoff (USA)) **h110**
[2006/7 F–: 22d² 22d³ 24s⁵ 22g³ 21gᵖᵘ Apr 18] lengthy, rather sparely-made gelding: fair
novice hurdler: placed 3 of 5 starts, lost action final one: will stay beyond 3m: raced on
good going or softer. *C. L. Tizzard*

TRIGGER THE LIGHT 6 ch.g. Double Trigger (IRE) – Lamper's Light (Idiot's **h127**
Delight) [2006/7 F90: 21s* 20v² 22d² 24v* 20s⁶ Mar 10] strong gelding: will make a
chaser: in frame in bumpers: fairly useful novice hurdler: won at Warwick (maiden) in
December and Taunton (by 3½ lengths from Ornais) in February: stiffish task, creditable
sixth of 16 to Albertas Run in valuable handicap at Sandown: stays 3m: raced on ground
softer than good. *A. King*

TRIPLE BLUFF 4 b.g. Medicean – Trinity Reef (Bustino) [2006/7 16s 17v⁴ 16s⁴ 17g **h78**
Mar 25] rather leggy colt: fair maiden on Flat (should stay 1½m), sold out of Mrs
A. Perrett's stable 17,000 gns Newmarket Autumn Sales: poor form in maiden hurdles:
raced around 2m. *N. J. Hawke*

TRIPLE MINT (IRE) 6 b.g. Flemensfirth (USA) – Bucktina (Buckskin (FR)) [2006/7 **c103**
h114, F84: c20v⁴ c24v⁴ c22s² Feb 1] tall, good-topped gelding: progressive over hurdles **h–**
in 2005/6: fair form over fences, ½-length second to Nonantais in maiden at Towcester:
will stay beyond 3m: raced on soft/heavy going: room for improvement in jumping over
fences. *D. McCain Jnr*

TRIPLE SEVEN (IRE) 5 b. or br.g. Rashar (USA) – Hill of Bargy (Over The River **h–**
(FR)) [2006/7 F16v F16d 24gᶠ Mar 23] €32,000 4-y-o: medium-sized gelding: half- **F74**
brother to winning Irish pointer by Lord Americo: dam winning 3m chaser in Ireland:
mid-field at best in bumpers: close up when falling seventh in novice on hurdling debut.
Miss H. Lewis

TRIP TO THE STARS (IRE) 7 b.m. Fourstars Allstar (USA) – Nora Dante (IRE) **c–**
(Phardante (FR)) [2006/7 h–: 22gᵖᵘ 22m⁴ 24f⁶ c26dᵖᵘ Jun 12] angular mare: little form **h–**

over hurdles: tongue tied, no show on chasing debut: won 2-finisher point in March. *D. P. Keane*

TRISONS STAR (IRE) 9 b.g. Roselier (FR) – Delkusha (Castle Keep) [2006/7 c100, h–: c25s³ c25sᵖᵘ c24sᵖᵘ c25vᵖᵘ c27v² c24v* c24g* c31sᵖᵘ Apr 27] rather leggy gelding: fairly useful hurdler at one time: fair chaser: successful in handicaps at Newcastle in March, up with pace throughout: stays 27f: acts on heavy going (won bumper on firm): has shaped as if amiss more than once. *Ferdy Murphy* **c104 h–**

TRITON 4 ch.g. Observatory (USA) – Questionable (Rainbow Quest (USA)) [2006/7 F16v⁴ Jan 27] 23,000 3-y-o: smallish, close-coupled gelding: fifth foal: half-brother to several winners, including chaser In Question, stayed 2½m: and bumper winner Debatable (both by Deploy): dam unraced: 13 lengths fourth to Pebrock in 4-y-o bumper at Southwell on debut, looking green. *N. G. Richards* **F84 +**

TRITONIX (IRE) 4 gr.c. Linamix (FR) – La Panthere (USA) (Pine Bluff (USA)) [2006/7 17d* 16g* 17s³ 16g* 16gᵖᵘ Apr 12] compact colt: useful on Flat (stays 1½m) for R. Chotard, successful twice, including at Deauville in August: useful juvenile hurdler: won at Bangor (maiden) and Huntingdon (by 15 lengths) in November and Warwick (novice, beat Master Mahogany readily by 3 lengths) in March: folded tamely third outing (reportedly had breathing operation after), went as if amiss in Grade 1 at Aintree final one: raced around 2m: tongue tied of last 4 starts. *P. J. Hobbs* **h130**

TRITONVILLE LODGE (IRE) 5 b.g. Grand Lodge (USA) – Olean (Sadler's Wells (USA)) [2006/7 h106+: 18m³ 20m² 22g 21g⁴ 24m* Apr 17] tall gelding: fairly useful hurdler: well backed, won handicap at Exeter in April by 6 lengths from College Ace: stays 3m: raced mainly on good/good to firm going. *Miss E. C. Lavelle* **h120**

TROCADENO (IRE) 5 b.g. Sea Raven (IRE) – Rose Runner (IRE) (Roselier (FR)) [2006/7 F14v F16s Apr 1] €18,000 3-y-o, 40,000 4-y-o: sixth foal: half-brother to bumper winner Billesey (by King's Ride): dam unraced: failed to see race out both starts in bumpers. *J. Howard Johnson* **F–**

TROGLODYTE 5 ch.g. Deploy – Wren Warbler (Relkino) [2006/7 F16d³ F16d⁶ 19s⁴ 21m⁵ 25v² 20s 24g³ Apr 21] angular gelding: first foal: dam, winning hurdler/fair chaser, stayed 25f: third in bumper: fair novice hurdler: will stay beyond 25f: acts on heavy going. *Mrs P. Robeson* **h110 F89**

TROLL (FR) 6 b.g. Cadoudal (FR) – Miss Dundee (FR) (Esprit du Nord (USA)) [2006/7 h98: 16g 17s* 16v⁴ 16v³ Mar 22] rangy, good-topped gelding: has scope: fair hurdler: won handicap at Sedgefield in December, making virtually all despite looking hard ride: stays easy 2½m: probably acts on heavy going. *L. Lungo* **h100**

TROMPETTE (USA) 5 b.m. Bahri (USA) – Bold Bold (IRE) (Sadler's Wells (USA)) [2006/7 h108: 16d³ 16d* 16vF 17g Mar 16] angular mare: progressed into useful handicap hurdler, winning at Ludlow in January easily by 5 lengths from Theatre Diva: every chance when falling 2 out in quite valuable mares event at Southwell, respectable effort in County Hurdle at Cheltenham final outing: likely to stay 2½m: raced on good ground or softer (acts on heavy). *N. J. Henderson* **h132**

TROODOS JET 6 b.g. Atraf – Costa Verde (King of Spain) [2006/7 h72: 16s 16g 17s* 17m⁵ 20sᵖᵘ Sep 21] leggy, lengthy gelding: poor handicap hurdler: won novice event at Bangor in August: raced mainly around 2m: acts on soft and good to firm going. *K. W. Hogg, Isle of Man* **h76**

TROOPER LEE (IRE) 5 b.g. Wizard King – Rubylee (Persian Bold) [2006/7 F70: 17s 17sᵖᵘ 17s Jan 30] little sign of ability: tried tongue tied. *Heather Dalton* **h–**

TROPICAL STRAIT (IRE) 4 b.g. Intikhab (USA) – Tropical Dance (USA) (Thorn Dance (USA)) [2006/7 F16g² Feb 3] lengthy gelding: half-brother to fairly useful 1m/9f winner Tropical Coral (by Pennekamp): dam fairly useful 5f/6f winner: 5 lengths second of 16 to Marleybow in bumper at Haydock on debut. *D. W. P. Arbuthnot* **F107**

TROTTERS BOTTOM 6 b.g. Mind Games – Fleeting Affair (Hotfoot) [2006/7 16f⁴ 16m⁵ 17g 16s⁵ 16m⁵ Nov 9] strong gelding: half-brother to several winners, including fairly useful hurdler Clandestine (by Saddlers' Hall), stayed 21f: fair but ungenuine sprinter on Flat (failed 2 stall tests), sold out of Andrew Reid's stable £6,000 Ascot October (2005) Sales, resold £1,500 Ascot June Sales: poor form over hurdles, looking to have stamina limitations. *Mrs S. M. Johnson* **h73**

TROUBLE AT BAY (IRE) 7 b.g. Slip Anchor – Fight Right (FR) (Crystal Glitters (USA)) [2006/7 20g c16d* c16s² c16d⁴ 16s³ 17g Mar 16] smallish, close-coupled gelding: fairly useful hurdler, off nearly 2 years before reappearance: 16 lengths third of 5 to **c127 h125**

Straw Bear in Grade 2 at Wincanton: similar form in novice chases: won at Hereford in December by 7 lengths from Opera de Coeur: laboured effort fourth start: stays 2½m: acts on soft and good to firm going: blinkered final outing: probably best in well-run race. *A. King*

TROVAIO (IRE) 10 b.g. Un Desperado (FR) – Hazy Fiddler (IRE) (Orchestra) [2006/7 c–, h–: c23g³ c26d* c26g³ c35s³ c22g^f Jul 9] poor handicap chaser: won at Cartmel in May: would have stayed beyond 3¼m: acted on soft going: tried in cheekpieces: dead. *Miss Lucinda V. Russell*   **c77 h–**

TROYSGREEN (IRE) 9 b.g. Warcraft (USA) – Moylena (Bustomi) [2006/7 c–§, h–§: c22d³ c21f^{pu} c20g^{ur} c20g⁶ c21m⁵ c22m^{pu} c25s⁶ c21d^{ur} Oct 20] little form, including in points: tried blinkered, usually wears cheekpieces: temperamental. *P. D. Niven*   **c70 § h– §**

TROYS RUN (IRE) 4 br.g. Cloudings (IRE) – Troja (Troy) [2006/7 F14s⁵ F16d⁴ 16v⁶ 20g 25g^{ur} Apr 16] half-brother to fair hurdler/modest chaser Snow Board (by Niniski), also winning stayer on Flat, and 19f hurdle winner Mistroy (by Damister): dam showed a little ability in France: fourth in bumper: running easily best race over hurdles when unseating last in maiden at Wetherby. *C. Grant*   **h92 F81**

TRUCKERS DELIGHT (IRE) 6 b.g. Darazari (IRE) – Windmill Star (IRE) (Orchestra) [2006/7 F16m* F16g² F16d F16m² Apr 25] rather unfurnished gelding: fourth foal: half-brother to ungenuine 23f hurdle winner Zaffran Lady (by Zaffaran): dam placed in point: won maiden Irish point on debut in 2005: useful form in bumpers: won at Stratford in September by 14 lengths from Sea Senor: runner-up at Chepstow and Worcester (3 lengths behind Hello You): owner ridden. *Jonjo O'Neill*   **F107**

TRUCKERS LADY (IRE) 8 b.m. Presenting – Classie Claire (IRE) (Phardante (FR)) [2006/7 25g³ Mar 17] successful 3 times in Irish points, including twice in 2007: let down by jumping in maiden chase/novice hurdle, pulled hard when third to Shrewd Investor at Wetherby in latter. *K. G. Reveley*   **c– h92**

TRUCKERS TAVERN (IRE) 12 ch.g. Phardante (FR) – Sweet Tulip (Beau Chapeau) [2006/7 c–, h119: c26s c24s⁶ c28s² c25v³ c24v³ c33v^F Feb 24] big, well-made gelding: winning hurdler: top-class chaser at best: second in Cheltenham Gold Cup in 2002/3, when also successful in Peter Marsh Chase at Haydock: still fairly useful in later stages of career: suited by 3m+: raced on good going or softer (acted on heavy): usually tongue tied: often let down by jumping over fences: dead. *Mrs S. J. Smith*   **c123 x h–**

TRUCKLE 5 b.g. Vettori (IRE) – Proud Titania (IRE) (Fairy King (USA)) [2006/7 h90: 17s^{pu} Dec 5] lengthy, sparely-made gelding: maiden hurdler: likely to prove best at 2m. *C. W. Fairhurst*   **h–**

TRUE DOVE 5 b.m. Kayf Tara – Pasja (IRE) (Posen (USA)) [2006/7 F87: F17g* F16d³ 16g Oct 22] fair form in bumpers: sold out of R. Fahey's stable 8,000 gns Doncaster May Sales: won maiden at Newton Abbot in July: always behind after mistake first in novice on hurdling debut. *C. L. Popham*   **h– F87**

TRUE GRIT (FR) 5 b.g. Goldneyev (USA) – Midweek Melody (Lucky Wednesday) [2006/7 F–: 19m⁶ May 11] soundly beaten in bumper/maiden hurdle. *L. Corcoran*   **h–**

TRUE NORTH (IRE) 12 b.g. Black Monday – Slip A Loop (The Parson) [2006/7 c–, h–: 24v^{pu} Dec 15] workmanlike gelding: fair hurdler in 2002/3: lightly raced and little form since (including over fences). *James Moffatt*   **c– h–**

TRUE STAR (IRE) 7 ch.g. Fourstars Allstar (USA) – Scouts Honour (IRE) (Electric) [2006/7 F79: F16g* F20f^{pu} 20s^{pu} Aug 19] better effort in bumpers when winning maiden at Uttoxeter in June: ran as if amiss in maiden hurdles. *Noel T. Chance*   **h– F90**

TRUE TANNER 9 b.g. Lyphento (USA) – True Nell (Neltino) [2006/7 16s 21v⁴ 21g^{pu} Mar 14] of no account: tried tongue tied. *Miss C. Dyson*   **h–**

TRUE TEMPER (IRE) 10 b.m. Roselier (FR) – Diamond Rock (Swan's Rock) [2006/7 c73, h74: c21m³ 22d³ 16m² 20f 20f 24f³ 24g³ c25g* c31s⁵ Apr 26] close-coupled mare: poor chaser/maiden hurdler: fit from points, won maiden at Kelso on hunter debut in April: stays 25f: acts on any going: tried blinkered/in cheekpieces/tongue tied. *A. M. Crow*   **c79 h76**

TRUE WEST (USA) 4 b.f. Gulch (USA) – True Life (USA) (El Gran Senor (USA)) [2006/7 17g^F Apr 11] maiden on Flat, left Miss Gay Kelleway after final outing: well held when falling last in novice seller on hurdling debut: dead. *N. B. King*   **h–**

TRULY FRUITFUL (IRE) 4 ch.g. Fruits of Love (USA) – Truly Flattering (Hard Fought) [2006/7 16d⁶ 16g⁶ 16v⁶ 19s⁵ Mar 7] lengthy, angular gelding: half-brother to   **h85**

fairly useful hurdler Truly Gold (by Goldmark), stays 3m: fair on Flat (stays 11f), demoted after first past post in July, sold out of K. Burke's stable 25,000 gns Newmarket Autumn Sales: modest form in juvenile hurdles: likely to prove best at 2m. *R. A. Fahey*

TRUMPED UP CHARGE 6 b. or br.g. First Trump – Bright-One (Electric) [2006/7 F17m⁵ 20gᵖᵘ Sep 6] €22,000 4-y-o: half-brother to fair hurdler/fairly useful chaser Albrighton (by Terimon), stayed 25f and 2¾m hurdle winner Mill-Dot (by Petoski): dam winning 2m hurdler: no impact in bumper/novice hurdle. *M. G. Rimell*   h–
F–

TRUMPINGTON 9 ch.m. First Trump – Brockton Flame (Emarati (USA)) [2006/7 21s 20m c23mᵖᵘ Jun 18] maiden hurdler: lightly raced and no form since 2002/3 (including on chasing debut): tried in cheekpieces. *D. G. Bridgwater*   c–
h–

TRUST FUND (IRE) 9 ch.g. Rashar (USA) – Tuney Blade (Fine Blade (USA)) [2006/7 c124x: c24g⁴ c24v³ Oct 21] rangy gelding: fair handicap chaser: thorough stayer: raced on good going or softer (acts on heavy): has been let down by jumping. *R. H. Alner*   c114

TRUSTING TOM 12 b.g. Teamster – Florista (Oats) [2006/7 c20s⁶ Feb 16] sturdy gelding: fair handicap chaser in 2003/4 for C. Bealby: runner-up in points: stays 3½m: acts on soft and good to firm going: has worn headgear. *Miss Jennifer Pidgeon*   c–

TRUST RULE 7 b.g. Selkirk (USA) – Hagwah (USA) (Dancing Brave (USA)) [2006/7 h89+: 17g⁶ 16s 16v⁶ Dec 27] compact gelding: novice hurdler: off 12 months, below best in 2006/7: tongue tied last 2 starts: sold 1,600 gns Doncaster May Sales. *M. W. Easterby*   h76

TRY 8 b.g. Rakaposhi King – Wonky (Hotfoot) [2006/7 F85?: 19m Apr 28] fourth in bumper: left A. Crow and off 18 months, tailed off in novice on hurdling debut. *J. Hetherton*   h–

TRY CATCH PADDY (IRE) 9 ch.g. Safety Catch (USA) – Blackwater Rose VII (Damsire Unregistered) [2006/7 c91, h102: c25s³ c25v² Mar 3] big, rather leggy gelding: winning hurdler: maiden chaser, better effort in hunters in 2006/7 when runner-up in novice at Kelso: stays 25f: acts on heavy going: tried in cheekpieces: often finds little. *Mrs A. F. Tullie*   c94 §
h–

TRY ME AND SEE 13 ch.g. Rock City – Al Raja (Kings Lake (USA)) [2006/7 c16mᵘʳ c16fᵖᵘ Aug 11] good-topped gelding: no form over jumps outside points: tried tongue tied. *A. M. Crow*   c–
h–

TSAR'S TWIST 8 b.g. Presidium – Kabs Twist (Kabour) [2006/7 c25f* c23d³ 24g* 27d² c23d⁴ 22d⁶ 24m⁵ c23m Apr 25] leggy, sparely-made gelding: modest hurdler: won novice handicap at Southwell in July: similar form over fences: fit from points (successful 5 times), won hunter at Ludlow on first day of season: stays 25f: acts on firm and good to soft going: tried blinkered: usually races prominently. *Mrs S. Gardner*   c95
h85

TUA (NZ) 8 br.g. Rainbow Myth (NZ) – Wayside Inn (NZ) (Long Row) [2006/7 20d 17s Nov 17] won once over 1m from 14 starts up to around 11f on Flat in New Zealand: soundly beaten over hurdles. *Andrew Turnell*   h–

TUAREG (IRE) 6 b.g. Ashkalani (IRE) – Shining Fire (Kalaglow) [2006/7 22m⁵ Apr 26] behind in 7f maidens at 2 yrs: won maiden point in 2006: tongue tied, jumped sketchily in novice on hurdling debut. *D. M. Grissell*   h–

TUATARA BAY (IRE) 7 b.g. Luso – Timely Reminder (IRE) (Phardante (FR)) [2006/7 F81: 16s 19d 19d⁶ 20m 20g Apr 3] sturdy, lengthy gelding: fourth in bumper: little impact over hurdles. *R. A. Fahey*   h–

TUBA (IRE) 12 b.g. Orchestra – Princess Paula (Smoggy) [2006/7 c92, h–: c19gᵖᵘ May 4] good-topped gelding: modest chaser: stays 3m: acts on firm and soft going: has had tongue tied. *S. A. Hughes*   c–
h–

TUDOR BUCK (IRE) 7 b. or br.g. Luso – Tudor Doe (IRE) (Buckskin (FR)) [2006/7 h91: c24gᵖᵘ Mar 28] tall gelding: lightly-raced maiden hurdler: off 15 months, little show in novice handicap on chasing debut. *R. Dickin*   c–
h–

TUDOR KING (IRE) 13 br.g. Orchestra – Jane Bond (Good Bond) [2006/7 c94, h–: c25mᵖᵘ c25m c23m c23m³ c26d⁶ c23fᵖᵘ c25f³ Oct 5] rather sparely-made gelding: winning hurdler/chaser, little form in 2006/7 (including in points). *Andrew Turnell*   c–
h–

TUDOR OAK (IRE) 5 b.g. Woods of Windsor (USA) – Tacheo (Tachypous) [2006/7 h–: 16m 16f⁶ 17m c16g³ c16s⁶ c16g⁵ Apr 23] leggy gelding: no solid form over jumps. *Mark Campion*   c–
h–

John Smith's Mares' Only Standard Open National Hunt Flat Race, Aintree—
Turbo Linn (noseband) becomes a rare five-time winner in bumpers as she defeats Theatre Girl

TUESDAY CLUB (IRE) 8 ch.g. Old Vic – Asfreeasthewind (IRE) (Moscow Society (USA)) [2006/7 h–: c19g^{pu} Mar 21] workmanlike gelding: no form in novice hurdles/ handicap chase: tried tongue tied. *J. A. B. Old* — c–, h–

TUESDAY'S CHILD 8 b.g. Un Desperado (FR) – Amazing Silks (Furry Glen) [2006/7 c93, h76: c20g^4 c16m^{pu} 20d^{pu} 17v 19g 20s c20m^6 c26m^6 Apr 9] maiden hurdler/ winning chaser: sold out of Miss H. Knight's stable 16,000 gns Doncaster May Sales after reappearance, no show after: tried in blinkers/cheekpieces. *Mrs S. J. Humphrey* — c74 d, h–

TUFTY HOPPER 10 b.g. Rock Hopper – Melancolia (Legend of France (USA)) [2006/7 c107, h–: c31s^{pu} Apr 26] sturdy gelding: fair hurdler/maiden chaser, lightly raced: successful twice in points in March: stays 27f: acts on heavy and good to firm going: carries head high. *D. R. Smailes* — c–, h–

TULCHAN GLEN 7 ch.g. Commanche Run – Glentanna Girl (Carlingford Castle) [2006/7 F16v^6 May 18] first foal: dam unraced: well held in bumper on debut. *Miss Lucinda V. Russell* — F–

TULKINGHORN 4 b.g. Kayf Tara – Miss Haversham (Salse (USA)) [2006/7 aF13g F16s F16g Mar 28] rather leggy gelding: half-brother to winning pointer by Bin Ajwaad: dam, maiden, stayed 1¼m: no form in bumpers. *C. A. Cyzer* — F–

TULLINISKY (IRE) 5 br.g. Marignan (USA) – Rosemead (IRE) (Fourstars Allstar (USA)) [2006/7 F16s 23v^{pu} Dec 2] smallish, leggy gelding: first foal: dam unraced daughter of half-sister to smart stayer Buckley: no show in bumper/novice hurdle. *J. R. Norton* — h–, F–

TULLYHAPPY LAD (IRE) 6 b.g. Shaamit (IRE) – Infinity (IRE) (Second Set (IRE)) [2006/7 h–, F78: 16s 16s 16s 18v^6 16d^6 16s Feb 7] poor maiden hurdler: raced around 2m: tongue tied in 2006/7. *I. A. Duncan, Ireland* — h68

TUMBLING DICE (IRE) 8 b.g. King's Theatre (IRE) – Eva Fay (IRE) (Fayruz) [2006/7 c141, h–: c17d^2 c20d c16v* c20s^5 c16s^5 c16v^4 Feb 25] lengthy gelding: winning hurdler: smart chaser: won Grade 2 O'Connell Logistics Hilly Way Chase at Cork in December by 10 lengths from Jim: below form in similar events after: effective at testing 2m to 3m: raced mainly on good going or softer (acts on heavy): often in cheekpieces nowadays: usually races handily: none too consistent. *T. J. Taaffe, Ireland* — c146, h–

TUNES OF GLORY (IRE) 11 b.g. Symboli Heights (FR) – Coxtown Queen (IRE) (Corvaro (USA)) [2006/7 c–, h82: 20g* May 5] good-topped gelding: modest hurdler: won selling handicap at Bangor in May: little show over fences since winning maiden on same course in 2004/5: stays 2½m: acts on firm going: in cheekpieces/blinkers last 3 starts: tongue tied once: sold £2,300 Ascot June Sales. *D. McCain* — c–, h98

TURAATH (IRE) 11 b.g. Sadler's Wells (USA) – Diamond Field (USA) (Mr Prospector (USA)) [2006/7 h107d: 21f 24v^{pu} 27m^{pu} 20s^6 25v Dec 31] stocky gelding: winning hurdler, no form since 2005/6 reappearance: has worn headgear (all wins without): tried tongue tied: unreliable. *A. J. Deakin* — h– §

TURBO (IRE) 8 b.g. Piccolo – By Arrangement (IRE) (Bold Arrangement) [2006/7 **h110 §** h114: 16d⁴ 16s⁴ 16s³ 16v⁴ 16d 16v⁶ 16v⁵ 20g⁴ 22m² Apr 15] close-coupled gelding: fair handicap hurdler: stays easy 2¾m: acts on any going: has worn cheekpieces/blinkers: tongue tied: held up, and often finds little. *M. W. Easterby*

TURBO LINN 4 b.f. Turbo Speed – Linns Heir (Leading Counsel (USA)) [2006/7 **F118** F14s* aF13g* F16s* F16m* F17g* Apr 13] leggy filly: second foal: dam bumper winner: unbeaten in 5 bumpers, winning at Carlisle in October and Lingfield in November (both 3-y-o events), Catterick (by 28 lengths) and Southwell in March, and Aintree (smart form when beating Theatre Girl in November by 1¾ lengths in 20-runner listed mares race) in April: created excellent impression on Flat afterwards, winning Lancashire Oaks and listed event at Newmarket. *G. A. Swinbank*

TURBO SHANDY 4 b.g. Piccolo – Carn Maire (Northern Prospect (USA)) [2006/7 **h77** F14g F14v 17d 16g Apr 2] rather leggy gelding: half-brother to several winners, **F–** including French 2m hurdle winner Frantic (by Fraam): dam 2-y-o 5f winner: well beaten in 3-y-o bumpers: signs of ability over hurdles. *C. Grant*

TURBULENT FLIGHT 6 b.m. Busy Flight – Pejawi (Strong Gale) [2006/7 F–: 16g **h–** 16f 16f⁵ 20m 20gᵖᵘ 24mᵖᵘ Aug 22] no form in bumpers/over hurdles. *Mrs L. B. Normile*

TURFINATOR 8 b.g. Alflora (IRE) – Mistress Star (Soldier Rose) [2006/7 24f³ 24f⁵ **h77** 24mᵖᵘ Sep 3] first foal: dam unraced: failed to complete in 3 points in 2006: poor form over hurdles: raced at 3m on good to firm/firm going: signs of temperament. *S. Lycett*

TURFTANZER (GER) 8 b.g. Lomitas – Tower Bridge (GER) (Big Shuffle (USA)) [2006/7 h–: 16g² 17d 17dᵘʳ 16sᵖᵘ 20gᵖᵘ 20gᵖᵘ 16g Apr 9] form over hurdles only when second in conditional jockeys novice at Wetherby: blinkered last 2 outings. *Lady Susan Watson*

Mr J. Nelson's "Turbo Linn"

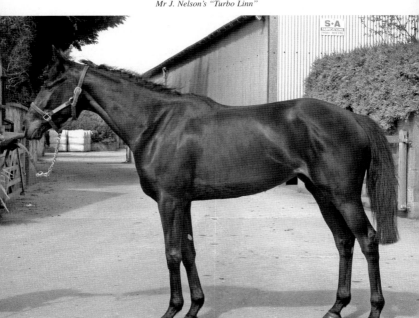

Digital Prints From bonusprint.com Novices' Chase, Aintree—a bold leap from Turko on the way to the first of three novice chase wins in 2006/7; also pictured is eventual third Cloudy Lane

TURGEONEV (FR) 12 gr.g. Turgeon (USA) – County Kerry (FR) (Comrade In Arms) [2006/7 c125d, h–: c17m[4] c20d[5] c20g[2] c19g[2] c16v[4] c20g[4] c19g[5] c16g* Apr 7] tall gelding: winning hurdler: useful handicap chaser: won at Haydock in April by 11 lengths from Glengarra: effective at 2m, barely stays 25f: acts on any going: tried blinkered: good jumper. *T. D. Easterby* **c131 h–**

TURKO (FR) 5 gr.g. Turgeon (USA) – Cambaria (FR) (Nice Havrais (USA)) [2006/7 h135: c20d* c21m* c21v[2] c20s* c24g c25g[pu] Apr 13] good-topped gelding: useful hurdler/novice chaser: won over fences at Aintree in October, Wincanton (Grade 2 totepool Rising Stars Novices' Chase, beat Boychuk by 3½ lengths) in November and Fontwell (by distance from Phar Bleu) in February: let down by jumping in graded events at Cheltenham and Aintree last 2 starts: stays 21f: acts on soft and good to firm ground: tongue tied. *P. F. Nicholls* **c137 h–**

TURNBERRY BAY (FR) 6 b.g. Phantom Breeze – Carmonera (FR) (Carmont (FR)) [2006/7 h109p, F85: 17d[2] 17s 21d[3] c22d[5] c24m[F] Apr 9] rather leggy gelding: novice hurdler, modest on balance: 12¾ lengths last of 5 in novice handicap at Newbury on completed outing over fences: bred to be suited by 2½m+: should do better over fences. *D. E. Pipe* **c97 p h93**

TURN CARD (IRE) 5 ch.g. Docksider (USA) – Poleaxe (Selkirk (USA)) [2006/7 22d[3] Aug 28] poor maiden on Flat: modest form over hurdles, left D. Gillespie before only start in 2006/7: may prove best over shorter than 2¾m. *J. J. Lambe, Ireland* **h92**

TURNER 6 gr.g. El Prado (IRE) – Gaily Royal (IRE) (Royal Academy (USA)) [2006/7 24g[ur] 24v[pu] 16g 24f Apr 5] modest and unreliable on Flat (stays 2m) in 2006, sold out of W. M. Brisbourne's stable 5,600 gns Doncaster October Sales: no show over hurdles. *J. B. Groucott* **h–**

TURN OF PHRASE (IRE) 8 b.g. Cadeaux Genereux – Token Gesture (IRE) (Alzao (USA)) [2006/7 c88§, h–§: 16g[3] 17v Nov 12] lengthy gelding: fair on Flat (stays 1¾m), won in September: modest handicap hurdler: lightly raced over fences: stays easy 21f: acts on soft and good to firm going (possibly not on heavy): often visored/blinkered: unreliable. *B. Ellison* **c– § h98 §**

TURNSTILE (IRE) 6 g.r.g. Linamix (FR) – Kissing Gate (USA) (Easy Goer (USA)) [2006/7 h113: c20s[3] c20d* c20g[2] c20g[5] c24s[pu] Apr 26] tall gelding: successful twice over hurdles in 2005/6: fairly useful chaser: won maiden at Sedgefield in November by length from Bougoure: best effort when 17¾ lengths fifth of 7 to Three Mirrors in handicap at **c117 h–**

Wetherby: stays 2½m: raced on good ground or softer: has shaped as if amiss more than once. *J. Howard Johnson*

TURN THE CORNER (IRE) 8 b.g. Bob Back (USA) – Tabu Lady (IRE) (Comman- c—
che Run) [2006/7 h79: 20f 16d 20d 20s c23s 22v c19v c25v c20s^{pu} Feb 7] maiden hurdler, h—
no show in 2006/7 (including over fences): tried in cheekpieces. *James Clements, Ireland*

TURPIN GREEN (IRE) 8 b.g. Presenting – Coolshamrock (IRE) (Buckskin c161 §
(FR)) [2006/7 c149p, h–: c20s* c26s^{pu} c24v² c26g³ c25g⁵ Apr 12] h—
    As in his first season over fences, Turpin Green's reappearance win at Carlisle proved to be the only success of his campaign. In 2005/6, he showed himself a smart novice after that debut over fences, and ran several good races in defeat. But his quirky nature, which became more apparent with time, contributed to a mixed bag of performances in the latest season. The highlight was his third behind Kauto Star in the Cheltenham Gold Cup but, on the other side of the coin, he produced a dismal effort when well fancied for the Hennessy Cognac Gold Cup at Newbury and a sour display against Gold Cup runner-up Exotic Dancer in the Betfair Bowl at Aintree. Aintree was the third meeting between Turpin Green and Exotic Dancer, who had first clashed in Turpin Green's race at Carlisle back in early-November. Just one other, the chasing debutant Turnstile, went to post and the race itself was farcical, the field standing still for twenty seconds before setting off, then crawling round. Turpin Green, at odds of 5/2-on, won by twenty-eight lengths from Exotic Dancer (who conceded 3 lb) with a distance back to Turnstile, but the form itself clearly couldn't be taken at face value, particularly as the runner-up was eased once second best.
    The race at Carlisle was the wbx.com Committed To National Hunt Racing Graduation Chase, and was one of six new weight-for-age races scheduled during the latest season. Designed to cater for above-average chasers who had had limited success (no more than two previous wins), they failed to attract more than a handful of runners and few of them made much appeal as betting media. The field sizes for the five other races were larger, but not by much—namely six, five and four (three times). Only one of these six graduation chases, a four-runner affair at Cheltenham in which there were 7/4 joint favourites and a 2/1-chance, saw a favourite start at longer than 11/8. While the Carlisle sponsors might have been committed to National Hunt racing, it remains to be seen how steadfast others within racing and betting will be with this particular concept. Five of the six races were staged at Jockey Club Racecourses tracks (as RHT is now known), with the other at Ascot. With payments to racecourses from bookmakers dependent on eight runners or more a race and on turnover, staging a graduation chase looks like becoming a costly exercise. The races are a good idea—champion trainer Paul Nicholls was a vocal supporter of them—but the programme is unlikely to be greatly expanded. There are plenty of signs showing the way the wind is blowing: more novice events turned into handicaps from ordinary novices, the replacement of hunter chases with more turnover-friendly races, the addition of bumpers to many summer jumping cards and the earliest ever start to the juvenile hurdle season in 2007/8 (not just due to the demands of the betting industry).
    To return to Turpin Green, he went to Newbury for the Hennessy with expectations high and well backed despite a 6-lb penalty for his Carlisle win, but he ran no sort of race and was pulled up soon after halfway. A second (under top weight) to The Outlier in a weak renewal of the Peter Marsh at Haydock in January got things partly back on track, and the fitting of blinkers in the Cheltenham Gold Cup saw Turpin Green back to his best. Backed at long odds, he travelled strongly held up and, though no match for the principals in the straight, came clear of the rest, five lengths behind the winner, despite the attentions of a loose horse (the same owner's Idle Talk) for much of the later stages. This lucrative third place at 40/1 added to Tony Dobbin's already fine record aboard outsiders in the Gold Cup, after previously finishing fourth (50/1) and second (66/1) on Go Ballistic in 1997 and 1999 respectively and second (25/1) and fifth (20/1) on Take The Stand in 2005 and 2006. However, if Cheltenham was a big step forward for Turpin Green, Aintree represented another backward step. Blinkered again, Turpin Green was under pressure at an early stage and trailed in last of the five runners, over forty lengths behind the winner. Dobbin reported that the race came too soon for Turpin Green,

Mr Trevor Hemmings' "Turpin Green"

but that makes an unconvincing fig-leaf. Together with his poor run at Newbury and a recalcitrant display in the previous season's Scilly Isles Novices' Chase at Sandown, in which he threw away certain victory by almost refusing at the last, Turpin Green's performance at Aintree, where he had run well the previous year after a five-day shorter gap between races, was another clear indication of his suspect temperament.

Turpin Green (IRE) (b.g. 1999)	Presenting (br 1992)	Mtoto (b 1983)	Busted / Amazer
		D'Azy (b 1984)	Persian Bold / Belle Viking
	Coolshamrock (IRE) (b 1992)	Buckskin (b 1973)	Yelapa / Bete A Bon Dieu
		Arctic Conditions (b 1978)	Lucifer / Arctic Brilliance

    Turpin Green would have looked well treated had he taken his chance in the Grand National, rather than the Betfair Bowl, and will presumably have that race on the agenda at some stage in the future given owner Trevor Hemmings' fondness for the world's most famous steeplechase. Turpin Green has the physique for the demands of the National course, being a big, good sort in appearance. He will stay beyond three and a quarter miles too. Quite how he would take to the course, though, is anybody's guess. He has yet to race on firm going but acts on any other. Turpin Green's pedigree was examined in detail in *Chasers & Hurdlers 2004/05*. He is the first foal of his dam Coolshamrock, who won a point but was pretty hopeless under Rules. Her second foal to race, Clover Green (by Turpin Green's sire Presenting), was bought for €90,000 as a three-year-old and showed little in two starts over hurdles for Ben Case in the latest season. Another relative, Nicky

Tam (by Presenting out of Coolshamrock's half-sister Wigmore), was a 50,000-guinea store purchase and showed modest form on his second start in bumpers for Lucinda Russell after running out on his debut. More successful has been another of Turpin Green's 'cousins' (out of an unraced half-sister to Coolshamrock). He won the Grade 2 bumper at Aintree in 2004/5 and, having shown himself a useful novice hurdler the following season, would have won on his second start over fences in 2006/7 but for falling at the last at Fakenham. Turpin Green's grandam Arctic Conditions was a useful hurdler and half-sister to the useful staying chaser Grange Brake, though he, like Turpin Green, was none too reliable. Whether Turpin Green can bounce back in 2007/8 is open to doubt and it may be that first time out is the likeliest time to catch him running to his best—he's made a winning reappearance in each of the three previous seasons. He certainly has something to prove, however. *N. G. Richards*

TURTHEN (FR) 6 ch.g. Turgeon (USA) – Majathen (FR) (Carmarthen (FR)) [2006/7 c120, h113: c24v⁶ c24gᵘʳ c24g c21gᵘʳ Apr 13] rather leggy gelding: winning hurdler: useful chaser: plenty on at weights in handicaps in 2006/7, best effort despite couple of mistakes when 9 lengths seventh of 24 to Cloudy Lane in Kim Muir at Cheltenham: in touch when unseating 6 out in Topham Chase at Aintree next time: stays 3m: raced on good going or softer (acts on heavy): tongue tied 4 of last 5 starts. *P. F. Nicholls* — c130 h–

TURTLE BAY 5 ch.m. Dr Fong (USA) – My Valentina (Royal Academy (USA)) [2006/7 h73: 16sᵖᵘ 16g⁵ 16f⁴ 16g⁴ 20d⁶ 17m Apr 9] close-coupled mare: poor novice hurdler: best around 2m: has suffered breathing problems. *B. Storey* — h77

TURTLE SOUP (IRE) 11 b.g. Turtle Island (IRE) – Lisa's Favourite (Gorytus (USA)) [2006/7 h141: 23fF 24s 21s⁵ 22d 19d⁵ 21g Mar 14] medium-sized gelding: useful handicap hurdler, not at best in 2006/7: stays 3m: best form on going softer than good (acts on heavy): often races prominently. *T. R. George* — h131

TUSCANY ROSE 4 ch.f. Medicean – Rosewood Belle (USA) (Woodman (USA)) [2006/7 16m 16g 16g⁵ Apr 15] modest on Flat (stays 13.8f), successful in seller in September, sold out of W. Muir's stable 10,000 gns Newmarket Autumn Sales: poor form over hurdles. *M. Todhunter* — h63

TWELVE PACES 6 b.g. Double Trigger (IRE) – Raise The Dawn (Rymer) [2006/7 h105, F90: c24s* c26s* c25s² c29sᵖᵘ c24sᵖᵘ Mar 17] sturdy gelding: bumper winner: novice hurdler: fairly useful handicap chaser: won twice at Carlisle in October: improved further when neck second to See You There in 2-finisher novice event at Hexham: ran poorly at Chepstow (Welsh National) and Uttoxeter (cheekpieces) last 2 starts: should stay beyond 3¼m: raced on good to soft/soft going over jumps. *D. E. Pipe* — c128 h–

TWENTI TWENTI (IRE) 6 ch.g. Topanoora – Ar Ais Aris (IRE) (Orchestra) [2006/7 F16f Apr 30] fourth foal: half-brother to 3m hurdle winner Umrigar Lord (by Lord Americo): dam lightly raced: well held in bumper on debut. *K. C. Bailey* — F–

TWENTY DEGREES 9 ch.g. Beveled (USA) – Sweet N' Twenty (High Top) [2006/7 c88§, h–§: c22m⁴ May 28] good-topped gelding: maiden hurdler: modest chaser: successful 4 times in points in 2007: stays 2½m: acts on heavy going: usually blinkered: temperamental. *G. L. Moore* — c83 § h– §

TWENTYTWOSILVER (IRE) 7 ro.g. Emarati (USA) – St Louis Lady (Absalom) [2006/7 c90, h78: c18f* c16m c17m³ c20m² c16mᵘʳ Nov 5] leggy gelding: maiden hurdler: modest chaser: won handicap at Fontwell in June: left D. Feek before final outing: barely stays 2½m: acts on firm and soft going. *L. Corcoran* — c94 h–

TWILL (IRE) 4 ch.g. Barathea (IRE) – Khafaya (Unfuwain (USA)) [2006/7 16g⁵ Mar 26] fairly useful but none too resolute on Flat (stays 2m) at 3 yrs, for H. Morrison, below form in 2007: last of 5 in juvenile on hurdling debut. *G. L. Moore* — h–

TWIST BOOKIE (IRE) 7 b. or br.g. Perugino (USA) – Twist Scarlett (GER) (Lagunas) [2006/7 h95: 16g⁶ c17dF c17s² c16m³ 16g⁴ 16g⁶ 16f* Apr 22] tall, angular gelding: modest on Flat in Britain, successful in December: fair handicap hurdler: won at Wincanton (conditional jockeys) in April: similar form over fences, would have won handicap at Stratford but for falling last: raced around 2m: acts on firm and soft going. *S. Lycett* — c100 h110

TWISTED LOGIC (IRE) 14 b.g. Tremblant – Logical View (Mandalus) [2006/7 c111, h–: c25g* c24d c26gᵖᵘ c26m⁴ c23d³ c23d⁵ c23s c27g⁴ c23f³ Apr 11] smallish, sturdy gelding: fair handicap chaser: won at Exeter (last 7 wins there) in May: mainly below form after: stays 3¾m: acts on firm and soft going: blinkered once: none too reliable. *R. H. Alner* — c102 d h–

TWIST MAGIC (FR) 5 b.g. Winged Love (IRE) – Twist Scarlett (GER) (Lagu-   **c154 p**
nas) [2006/7 h124: c16d* c16d² c16gᶠ c16g* Apr 14]   **h–**

        In the end, four- and five-year-old chasers became victims of their own success. In April, following a review, the British Horseracing Board announced a reduction in the weight allowances accorded to them which all but abolishes the concession they have long enjoyed. Too long, as regular readers will be aware. The subject is one returned to several times, including in the essays on Voy Por Ustedes in *Chasers & Hurdlers 2005/06* and on another five-year-old winner of the Arkle, Flagship Uberalles in the 1998/99 edition. As far back as 1994/95, the essay on the five-year-old Banjo remarked 'that Banjo met with defeat in the Sun Alliance did little to allay suspicion that the official allowance was too generous, and had been, largely unnoticed, for a very long time.' Banjo won three novice chases on British soil that season, including the Grade 1 Scilly Isles at Sandown and the Grade 2 Mumm Mildmay at Aintree, and his success prompted a review of the weight-for-age scale, though no changes were made to it until October 1999. After Flagship Uberalles became the second consecutive five-year-old winner of the Arkle earlier that year, the scale was revised but still allowed four- and five-year-olds too much, particularly over three miles where the scale was left unaltered. Since the 1991/92 season, the Timeform scale, based strictly on assessment of results, has allowed five-year-olds no weight concession and four-year-olds no more than 2 lb at any stage after July. The BHB's press release, announcing the revised scale, noted that four-year-old chasers had been enjoying a disproportionate degree of success in recent seasons 'particularly in the months of November and December', while the strike rate of five-year-old chasers in the 2005/6 season at just under 15% was above the average (11%), but not unacceptably so according to the BHB. Maybe it was no coincidence that the revision was announced little more than a year after the five-year-olds Voy Por Ustedes and Star de Mohaison had won the two principal

John Smith's Maghull Novices' Chase, Aintree—Arkle faller Twist Magic is in command two out;
Lennon (left) fades into fourth behind Fair Along and Royal Shakespeare (almost hidden)

novice chases of the season at the Cheltenham Festival, the Arkle and the Royal & SunAlliance Chase, the Arkle falling to a five-year-old for the fourth time in eight runnings.

The effective abolition of the weight allowance for five-year-old chasers brings the official scale more into line, not only with Timeform's treatment of the age group, but other countries' treatment of young chasers. For example, five-year-olds receive no weight concession in Japan's big international steeplechase, the Nakayama Grand Jump, run in the latest season over two miles five furlongs on the same day as the Grand National. France has no sliding weight-for-age scale for five-year-olds, but all five-year-old jumpers, hurdlers and chasers alike, receive a fixed two kilogram allowance from their elders throughout their five-year-old season to ease their graduation from racing almost exclusively against horses of their own age as three- and four-year-olds. France has been the source of the vast majority of the most successful five-year-olds to have profited from the weight allowance in Britain, showing little sign of the supposed immaturity that the allowance was supposed to offset, and indeed often having more experience than their British and Irish-bred elders. One of the trainers who has benefited most from the campaigning of four- and five-year-olds over fences is Paul Nicholls, who has won graded novice chases with young French imports including, in the last six years alone, Armaturk, Bal de Nuit, Exit To Wave, Hoo La Baloo, Le Roi Miguel, My Will, Napolitain, Star de Mohaison, Turko, Vol de Nuit and Whitenzo. The latest addition to that list was Twist Magic who may yet prove the best of all of them.

Despite a sizeable home reputation, Twist Magic had been no better than fairly useful as a juvenile hurdler, winning for Guillaume Macaire at Auteuil and for Nicholls at Wincanton on his second outing in Britain, though he had given the impression that all was not well with him on his last two starts over hurdles that season. There was clearly nothing ailing him when he made an impressive chasing debut on his reappearance at Fakenham in December. In a good race for the track, Twist Magic could hardly have made a better impression in beating the smart hurdler Royal Shakespeare by twenty-four lengths (albeit in receipt of 11 lb) without coming off the bridle, jumping fluently and going with great zest in front. Twist Magic was seen out only once more before the Arkle at Cheltenham and it was somewhat disappointing that he failed to confirm the promise of his Fakenham win when a length-and-a-quarter second to another four-year-old, Jack The Giant, in the Wayward Lad Novices' Chase at Kempton later in December, Royal Shakespeare finishing much closer behind him this time in third.

The Arkle presented a stiffer task for Twist Magic but he was looking all set to be concerned in the finish when falling two out, still on the bridle at the time and right on the quarters of the eventual winner My Way de Solzen. How exactly he would have fared against the winner was hard to say, but the John Smith's Maghull Novices' Chase at Aintree the following month was an opportunity to see how he measured up against the placed horses in the Arkle, fellow five-year-olds Fair Along and Jack The Giant, dual course-and-distance winner Lennon who had been seventh at Cheltenham, and Don't Push It who had also come down at the second-last in the Arkle when very much in contention. Outsider Royal Shakespeare made up the field of six. The Arkle fallers headed the betting in preference to the placed horses, with Twist Magic at 9/4 and Don't Push It at 11/4. With the emphasis on speed, Twist Magic ran out a decisive winner after a fine round of jumping, leading on the bridle after three out and keeping on strongly to beat Fair Along by five lengths (the same winning margin as My Way de Solzen's in the Arkle), with Royal Shakespeare four lengths back in third ahead of Lennon, while Don't Push It and Jack The Giant were both well beaten.

Although Twist Magic began his career in France and carries the (FR) suffix, he is to all intents and purposes German-bred. His sire Winged Love, the French-trained winner of the 1995 Irish Derby, began his stud career in Germany, though he now stands as a jumps sire in Northern Ireland. Twist Magic is his dam's fifth foal, with the first four all successful on the Flat in Germany. They include Twist Magic's full brother Twist Fire, who has also won at up to two and a half miles on the Flat in Belgium, and Twist Bookie (by Perugino) who was a fair winner over hurdles in Britain for Shaun Lycett in the latest season. Their dam

Barry Fulton Tony Hayward Michael Lynch's "Twist Magic"

Twist Scarlett won four times at up to a mile and a quarter in Germany but seemingly showed little aptitude for steeplechasing, finishing well beaten on her two completed starts in chases and falling on the two other occasions, though her half-sister Twist Pearl did win over fences in Germany. Grandam Twistqueen won at around nine furlongs and was a half-sister to the family's best Flat performer Twist King, a winner of three Group 3 races in Germany at up to eleven furlongs and fourth in the Deutsches Derby.

		In The Wings (b 1986)	Sadler's Wells
	Winged Love (IRE) (b 1992)		High Hawk
		J'Ai Deux Amours (b 1986)	Top Ville
Twist Magic (FR)			Pollenka
(b.g. 2002)		Lagunas (b 1981)	Ile de Bourbon
	Twist Scarlett (GER)		Liranga
	(b or br 1992)	Twistqueen (b 1982)	Athenagoras
			Twistlady

The tall, leggy Twist Magic is almost certainly capable of better still over fences after just four starts in chases and, still unfurnished, there's every chance he will improve physically too with another summer on his back. Notwithstanding his lapse in the Arkle, he is a fine jumper on the whole and looks sure to do well in the top two-mile chases. He acts on soft ground and is yet to race on ground firmer than good, though he looks unlikely to be inconvenienced by conditions which place an emphasis on speed. He was tongue tied once over hurdles, shaping as if amiss when a remote third under testing conditions in the Adonis Hurdle (staged that year at Sandown). It will be interesting to see how four- and five-year-old chasers fare from now on with a reduced or non-existent weight allowance. Trainers may take the view that there is less of an advantage to be had by running young horses early over fences, which could have an impact on the number of runners and the competitiveness of some novice chases. Those with a vested interest in supplying the top British yards with young French-bred horses may have mixed feelings about the loss of the allowance, too, but success on a level playing field for these imports will be a much better advertisement for them. Racing merit and aptitude for jumping fences play a much more important part in deciding the outcome of a novice chase than a horse's age. *P. F. Nicholls*

TWIST N TURN 7 b.m. Sir Harry Lewis (USA) – Gaye Gordon (Scottish Reel) [2006/7 c68, h59: 20g* 26m 20f Jul 19] rather leggy mare: poor hurdler/maiden chaser: won selling handicap at Wetherby on first day of season: probably stays 21f: acts on soft and good to firm going: tried blinkered: sold £2,000 Ascot February Sales. *D. McCain Jnr*
   c–
   h67

TWOFAN (USA) 6 b.g. Lear Fan (USA) – Double Wedge (USA) (Northern Baby (CAN)) [2006/7 h100: c22v c16s c20s c20m⁴ Mar 31] tall, angular gelding: fair hurdler: just poor form in maiden chases: stays 3m: probably acts on any going: has worn cheekpieces. *Charles Byrnes, Ireland*
   c68
   h–

TWO MILE OAK 5 b.g. Double Trigger (IRE) – Scarlet Dymond (Rymer) [2006/7 22dᵖᵘ 22vᵖᵘ Feb 25] stocky gelding: half-brother to several winners, notably fairly useful hurdler Rowley Hill (by Karinga Bay), stays 3¼m: dam won 17f chase: more signs of temperament than ability over hurdles. *Mrs S. D. Williams*
   h–

TWO MILES WEST (IRE) 6 b.g. Sadler's Wells (USA) – User Friendly (Slip Anchor) [2006/7 h131: 24s 25d⁵ 23d 22s 20g* Apr 12] rather leggy gelding: fairly useful hurdler: 25/1 and off 4 months, back to best when winning 22-runner listed handicap at Aintree in April by head from Gods Token after clear leader fell last: should stay beyond 2½m: acts on good to soft going: tried tongue tied. *Jonjo O'Neill*
   h129

TWO SHILLINGS 7 b. or br.m. Teenoso (USA) – Miss Muire (Scallywag) [2006/7 F82: 20mᵖᵘ Apr 15] better effort in bumpers when fourth on debut: lame on hurdling debut. *R. Curtis*
   h–

John Smith's Handicap Hurdle, Aintree—Special Envoy and Tom O'Brien crash out at the last with the race at their mercy; outsider Two Miles West (second right) is the chief beneficiary

totescoop6 Summer Hurdle (Handicap), Market Rasen—
the Bowen team work the oracle with Irish import Tycoon Hall (white face), who lands a shock win;
runner-up Wee Dinns still has ground to make up on Portavadie (noseband)

TWO STEPS TO GO (USA) 8 b.g. Rhythm (USA) – Lyonushka (CAN) (Private Account (USA)) [2006/7 h72: 16m 17m⁵ 17m 20f^pu 20g^pu 17f c17m^pu Aug 26] close-coupled gelding: winning hurdler, no form in 2006/7 (including on chasing debut): usually wears headgear: has had tongue tied. *B. Storey*   c– h–

TWO TONYS SHAM (IRE) 8 b.g. Fourstars Allstar (USA) – Millies Girl (IRE) (Millfontaine) [2006/7 22g 19s⁴ 24s^pu c19d⁵ c24s^pu Jan 5] rather leggy, close-coupled gelding: winning Irish pointer: third in novice on hurdling debut in 2004/5: off 2 years, little impact in 2006/7 (including over fences): has looked hard ride. *H. P. Hogarth*   c– § h– §

TWO T'THREE WEEKS 6 b.m. Silver Patriarch (IRE) – Misowni (Niniski (USA)) [2006/7 F–: F16m⁶ 17m 21s⁴ 24d^pu Mar 22] no form: tongue tied last 2 starts, also blinkered final one. *M. G. Rimell*   h– F–

TYCOON HALL (IRE) 7 ch.g. Halling (USA) – Tycooness (IRE) (Last Tycoon) [2006/7 17m 17d* Jul 22] rather leggy gelding: fairly useful hurdler: sold out of Mrs J. Harrington's stable 4,200 gns Doncaster May Sales before return: showed considerable improvement when winning valuable 17-runner handicap at Market Rasen in July by head from Wee Dinns: raced around 2m: acts on good to firm and heavy ground. *P. Bowen*   h127

TYHOLLAND (IRE) 8 br.g. Up And At 'em – Spanish Gypsy (IRE) (Reference Point) [2006/7 c20g⁵ Oct 7] leggy gelding: modest maiden hurdler, sold out of R. Osborne's stable 1,800 gns Doncaster October (2005) Sales: well held in handicap on chasing debut: stays 2¾m: acts on soft and good to firm going: tried in cheekpieces. *W. Amos*   c– h–

TYNEDALE (IRE) 8 b.g. Good Thyne (USA) – Book of Rules (IRE) (Phardante (FR)) [2006/7 h118: c24v⁴ c25v³ c25s^pu 27s^pu Apr 27] quite good-topped gelding: fairly useful handicap hurdler, took no interest final start: easily best effort over fences when 4 lengths third of 5 to Dom d'Orgeval in novice at Hexham: stays 25f: acts on heavy going (runner-up in bumper on good to firm): tried blinkered: lazy. *Mrs A. Hamilton*   c109 h–

TYRE HILL LILLY 10 br.m. Jupiter Island – The Howlet (New Brig) [2006/7 22m³ 24f^pu Jun 21] fair pointer, won 3 times in 2006: form in other events only when third of 9 in novice hurdle at Newton Abbot, possibly flattered: lame next time: tried tongue tied. *Mrs S. Gardner*   h82 ?

TYRONE TIM 6 b.g. Tamure (IRE) – Anatomic (Deerhound (USA)) [2006/7 F17g⁵ F16m 22g^pu Aug 26] third foal: brother to 17f hurdle winner Deer Dancer: dam ran twice: signs of ability in bumper on debut: virtually ran out in seller on hurdling debut. *Mrs S. Gardner*   h– F76

TYSON (SAF) 7 b.g. Silvino (USA) – Telle Belle (SAF) (Sledgehammer (NZ)) [2006/7 16v* 16d 16g Apr 13] robust gelding: smart on Flat (stays 1¼m), successful 7 times in South Africa (including in Group 1) prior to winning twice at Nad Al Sheba in early-2006 for M. de Kock: useful form in novice hurdles: won at Haydock in February on debut by   h130 p

1012

P. Beck D. Clarke L. Westwood M. Slack's "Tyson"

3½ lengths from Polinamix, despite blundering last: again took strong hold when ninth of 22 to Ebaziyan in Supreme Novices' Hurdle at Cheltenham following month, fading straight: jumped none too fluently when well held in Grade 2 at Aintree final start: probably remains capable of better granted emphasis on speed. *Miss Venetia Williams*

TYSOU (FR) 10 b.g. Ajdayt (USA) – Pretty Point (Crystal Glitters (USA)) [2006/7 c145, h–: c16d³ c17d⁶ c16sᵖᵘ c16g⁴ c16g c21g⁵ c16f³ Apr 28] smallish, angular gelding: useful chaser: creditable efforts in 2006/7 when in frame, stiffish task when third behind Dempsey in Grade 2 at Sandown final outing: best around 2m: acts on firm and good to soft going: usually sound jumper: usually held up. *N. J. Henderson*   **c140 h–**

TYSSAC (FR) 6 ch.g. Beyssac (FR) – Aktia (FR) (Lyphard's Special (USA)) [2006/7 c17gᶠ c18g* c20g* 19v* 19s* c18vᶠ 18s⁴ c19v* c18sᶠ c31dᵘʳ c24gᵖᵘ c20mᵖᵘ Mar 31] angular gelding: sixth foal: half-brother to 3 winners, including hurdler/chaser Art Stones (by Dark Stone), stayed 21f: dam ran twice: successful 6 times over jumps in French Provinces, including over fences at Craon in August, Ploermel in September and Angers in December, and over hurdles at Saint-Brieuc in October/November: left G. Macaire after fourth start, C. Le Galliard after ninth: failed to complete in handicap chases in Britain: stays 2½m: acts on heavy ground: has worn blinkers. *B. N. Pollock*   **c? h?**

TYTHEKNOT 6 b.g. Pursuit of Love – Bundled Up (USA) (Sharpen Up) [2006/7 h89: 17m³ 19dᵖᵘ 16g* 16m⁶ Apr 25] good-topped gelding: fair hurdler: off 5 months (reportedly hobdayed), won handicap at Wincanton in March: raced mainly around 2m: acts on good to firm and heavy going: tried in cheekpieces, blinkered in 2006/7. *O. Sherwood*   **h102**

TYUP POMPEY (IRE) 6 ch.g. Docksider (USA) – Cindy's Baby (Bairn (USA)) [2006/7 c74, h74: c19g⁶ 19m² 21g⁵ 21m 16d c16m c16g⁶ Mar 22] poor maiden hurdler/   **c– h76**

chaser, sold out of Miss J. Davis' stable £2,300 Ascot July Sales after reappearance: seems to stay 2¾m, at least with emphasis on speed: acts on firm ground. *Mrs A. Price*

U

UFFA FOX (IRE) 4 b.g. Bravefoot – Ocean Mist (IRE) (Crash Course) [2006/7 F16s Mar 3] 12,500 3-y-o: useful-looking gelding: seventh foal: half-brother to modest hurdler Atlantic Crossing (by Roselier), stays 2½m: dam unraced sister to smart staying chaser Captain Dibble: shaped as if in need of race and not knocked about when eighth of 21 to Diamond Harry in bumper at Newbury on debut. *B. De Haan* **F88**

UIG 6 ch.m. Bien Bien (USA) – Madam Zando (Forzando) [2006/7 16g 19d 17s[pu] Dec 7] smallish, lengthy mare: fairly useful 1¼m winner on Flat, below best in 2006: no form in novice hurdles. *H. S. Howe* **h–**

ULF THE UNWASHED (FR) 5 b.g. Kayf Tara – Shemaleyah (Lomond (USA)) [2006/7 F17m⁶ F17g⁶ F14g⁵ F18m Apr 26] half-brother to fair hurdler/chaser Kefaaf (by Lion Cavern), stays 2½m, and French 1¼m to 1¾m winner No Win No Deal (by Machiavellian): dam, 1¾m winner, half-sister to high-class 2m hurdler Kingsmill: well beaten in bumpers, sold out of S. Gollings' stable 1,800 gns Doncaster January Sales before third outing (in cheekpieces). *Miss Z. C. Davison* **F–**

ULTIMATE LIMIT 7 b.g. Bonny Scot (IRE) – Second Call (Kind of Hush) [2006/7 c96, h–: c24g³ c23d² c26g[pu] Oct 30] well-made gelding: modest handicap chaser: stays 25f: acts on firm and good to soft going. *A. Ennis* **c86 h–**

ULUSABA 11 b.g. Alflora (IRE) – Mighty Fly (Comedy Star (USA)) [2006/7 c–, h–: c27v[pu] c25g[pu] Apr 3] neat gelding: winning chaser: lightly raced and has failed to complete since 2004/5, left Ferdy Murphy before final outing: usually wears headgear: has had tongue tied: patiently ridden. *Paul Murphy* **c– h–**

UMBRELLA MAN (IRE) 11 ch.g. Insan (USA) – Askasilla (IRE) (Lucky Mickmooch) [2006/7 c127, h–: c20d* c24v[pu] c21g[pu] Apr 13] tall, rangy gelding: fairly useful handicap chaser: completed hat-trick when beating Kosmos Bleu by 1¾ lengths at Kempton in November: pulled up both starts after: stays 3m: acts on soft and good to firm going: takes good hold. *Miss E. C. Lavelle* **c129 h–**

UNALIENABLE RIGHT (USA) 10 b.g. Irish River (FR) – Freedom of Speech (USA) (Danzig (USA)) [2006/7 c20d[pu] c17f[F] 22d[pu] 16m⁴ 22m[pu] 17f Aug 11] successful 3 times over hurdles in USA: no form in Britain (including in novice chases): tried in cheekpieces: free-going sort. *James Moffatt* **c– h–**

UN AUTRE ESPERE 8 b.g. Golden Heights – Drummer's Dream (IRE) (Drumalis) [2006/7 c82, h78: 16s c16s 17d³ c16m² Mar 31] angular gelding: poor handicap hurdler/ maiden chaser: raced around 2m: acts on good to soft going: races prominently. *C. C. Bealby* **c65 + h79**

UNCLE ADA (IRE) 12 ch.g. Phardante (FR) – Park Belle (IRE) (Strong Gale) [2006/7 c–: c23g[F] c26d[pu] Jun 12] winning pointer: no form in chases: sometimes blinkered. *D. J. Minty* **c–**

UNCLE LIONEL 5 b.g. Sylvan Express – La Carlotta (Ela-Mana-Mou) [2006/7 F16v F16s F16m Apr 15] leggy gelding: half-brother to 2m selling hurdle winner Fastini Gold and a winning pointer (both by Weldnaas): dam unraced: well held in bumpers. *S. J. Gilmore* **F–**

UNCLE MAX (IRE) 7 b.g. Victory Note (USA) – Sunset Park (IRE) (Red Sunset) [2006/7 c95, h–: c20s* c22g⁴ 20m 22m⁵ c19g 16d 20d 16d⁶ c16d 23d[pu] Jan 15] leggy, close-coupled gelding: modest hurdler/fair handicap chaser: won over fences at Bangor (by 25 lengths) in August: no show last 6 starts: stays 2½m: acts on soft and good to firm going: tried in headgear/tongue tied: unreliable. *M. Scudamore* **c103 d h86 d**

UNCLE MICHAEL 6 b.g. Mon Tresor – De Valera (Faustus (USA)) [2006/7 F17v F16g Apr 23] sixth foal: half-brother to 2m hurdle winner Finbar's Law (by Contract Law): dam, poor maiden hurdler, stayed 3m: well held in bumpers. *R. Johnson* **F–**

UNCLE NEIL (IRE) 10 gr.g. Roselier (FR) – Bobs My Uncle (Deep Run) [2006/7 c–, h–: c20v⁴ c25g³ c31s[pu] Apr 27] fairly useful pointer: no show only start over hurdles: first solid form in chases when third of 5 finishers in maiden at Kelso: stays 25f: tried blinkered. *P. Monteith* **c84 h–**

UNCLE WALLACE 11 b.g. Neltino – Auntie Dot (Hallodri (ATA)) [2006/7 c110, h–: c16d c21s^{pu} Feb 17] lengthy, useful-looking gelding: fair handicap chaser: no show both outings in 2006/7, lame on second occasion: stays 21f: acts on soft going: none too consistent. *P. R. Webber*   c–
h–

UNDENIABLE 9 b.g. Unfuwain (USA) – Shefoog (Kefaah (USA)) [2006/7 c131, h–: c24g^{ur} c24m^2 c26v^{pu} c26g c24s c22v^5 c20v^5 c25g* c25g Apr 13] workmanlike gelding: useful handicap chaser: form after second outing only when winning at Wetherby in March by 2 lengths from Silver Knight: stays 25f: acts on soft and good to firm going: tongue tied once. *Mrs S. J. Smith*   c131
h–

UNDERWRITER (USA) 7 b.g. With Approval (CAN) – Night Risk (USA) (Wild Again (USA)) [2006/7 c121, h99: c24g^3 c24g^{pu} c20g^F Apr 25] good-topped gelding: winning hurdler: fairly useful handicap chaser: often let down by jumping, including all starts in 2006/7 (apart from reappearance): stays 25f: acts on soft and good to firm going, probably on heavy. *Ferdy Murphy*   c117 x
h–

UNDONE AGAIN (IRE) 8 b.m. Un Desperado (FR) – Ballinamona Thyne (IRE) (Good Thyne (USA)) [2006/7 c23g^{pu} c19d^{pu} Jun 2] ex-Irish mare: in frame in points: no show in maiden hurdle (for P. Rothwell)/chases. *Mrs Tracey Barfoot-Saunt*   c–
h–

UNEVEN LINE 11 b.m. Jurado (USA) – Altovise (Black Minstrel) [2006/7 c78x, h67: 21d^2 c27m^4 c20s* 22v^4 c27v^2 c20v^{pu} Mar 15] poor chaser/maiden hurdler: won mares handicap at Hexham in November: stays 27f: acts on heavy going: wears cheekpieces: has tongue tied: often let down by jumping. *Miss S. E. Forster*   c80 x
h73

UNEXPLORED (IRE) 7 b.g. Taipan (IRE) – White Lady Club (Callernish) [2006/7 h108: c25s^{ur} c20s^{pu} Mar 13] tall gelding: winning Irish pointer: fair form when second in novice on hurdling debut: has failed to complete all 5 starts since, including in maiden chases (unseated 2 out when length behind winner at Catterick). *J. Howard Johnson*   c?
h–

UNGARO (FR) 8 b.g. Epervier Bleu – Harpyes (FR) (Quart de Vin (FR)) [2006/7 h133: c17d* c20g* c24d* c24g^6 c25g^6 Apr 13]   c145
h–

When Keith Reveley took over the training licence from his mother Mary at Saltburn in 2004, he stated his intention that the stable would be less reticent than it had been in the past about running its horses in good races in the South. Ungaro has been one of the best examples of that bolder policy paying dividends. In his novice season over hurdles, Ungaro won the Grade 3 Sandown Handicap Hurdle (the stable won the Agfa Diamond Handicap Chase with Rambling Minster at the corresponding fixture in the latest season) and went away with an even bigger prize, the Grade 1 Feltham Novices' Chase at Kempton, on his next big southern trip.

Ungaro began his chasing career with wins on more familiar territory at Kelso and Huntingdon, the latter being one southern venue at which the Reveleys have long had a good record and where Ungaro had opened his account over hurdles the previous season. Looking to have learned plenty from his chasing debut at Kelso, Ungaro was stepped back up to a more suitable trip at Huntingdon in November and showed form on a par with his best efforts over hurdles, staying on well to beat the two other finishers convincingly. Whether he would have won if favourite Afrad had not fallen two out is open to debate, though given that rival's suspect attitude it's more than possible Ungaro would have won anyway. The Stan James-sponsored Feltham looked a far stiffer test, however, and Ungaro was made the outsider of the six-runner field at 14/1. The four-year-old filly Bold Fire, receiving a total of 20 lb from her older male rivals in age and sex allowances, shared favouritism with Yes Sir, unbeaten in seven starts over fences during the summer and tackling the Feltham instead of the King George VI (despite being gambled on for the latter race). Boychuk and the still-unbeaten According To John (in the same ownership as Ungaro) were others who had made promising starts over fences, while Knowhere could already boast smart form in handicaps. The joint favourites in particular proved disappointing, whilst Ungaro continued his progress with a much improved effort. Waited with as usual and clearly going best after four out, Ungaro overcame a couple of mistakes to lead three fences from home and ran on strongly for a ten-length win over Boychuk, with Knowhere five lengths back in third, According To John fourth, Yes Sir tailed off and Bold Fire pulled up.

Ungaro looked set for a prominent role in the big staying novice chases in the spring but finished only sixth in both the Royal & SunAlliance Chase at Cheltenham and the Mildmay Novices' Chase at Aintree, on both occasions unable

Stan James Feltham Novices' Chase, Kempton—
outsider of six Ungaro maintains his unbeaten start over fences in good style

to confirm placings with rivals from Kempton. Despite looking very well at Cheltenham after a break since Boxing Day, the 11/1-shot Ungaro was unable to make much impression when asked for his effort and this time it was third-placed According To John (66/1) who fared the better of Sir Robert Ogden's pair. At Aintree, a track which might have been expected to suit Ungaro better, he looked well again and started third favourite but was unable to sustain his effort and finished behind both Yes Sir and Boychuk. Under Mary Reveley, the Cheltenham Festival had rarely figured in the stable's running plans but Ungaro was making his second visit there following a good sixth in the Coral Cup the season before (the stable had three runners at the meeting in 2006/7).

Ungaro (FR) (b.g. 1999)	Epervier Bleu (b 1987)	Saint Cyrien (b 1980)	Luthier Sevres
		Equadif (b 1976)	Abdos Gracilla
	Harpyes (FR) (b 1987)	Quart de Vin (b 1972)	Devon Quartelette
		Halmahera (ch 1974)	Francois Saubaber Houlgate

Ungaro's year-younger full brother Blue Splash also enjoyed a good season in novice chases, showing useful form with Peter Bowen; the pair are by the top-class 1990 Arc runner-up Epervier Bleu. Their dam is also responsible for Harkosa (by Nikos), a fairly useful jumper at up to two and three quarter miles in France, and Let's Fly (by Rose Laurel), who was a fair hurdler in the Ogden colours when with Mrs Reveley and a prolific winner in points in the latest season. Their dam Harpyes was placed several times over fences in France at up to two and a half miles and grandam Halmahera (not to be confused with the triple Portland-winning sprinter of the same name) was a winner there over jumps. Third dam Houlgate's record was much more noteworthy (eighteen wins, fourteen of them over jumps) but she was put in the shade by the achievements of her half-sister Hyeres III and half-brother Haroue. Practically unknown in Britain, Hyeres III has almost legendary status in French jumping circles thanks to her three consecutive victories in the Grand Steeple-Chase de Paris (1964-1966), becoming the first of only two triple winners of France's most important chase. Haroue won the same race in 1968 and also finished runner-up twice. Harpyes is still producing at stud, though her latest three foals—a 2004 Nikos filly (named Harnikos), a 2005 Sleeping Car filly and a 2006 Kapgarde colt (named Garde Fou)—all made little impact at the sales during the past twelve months, the last-named failing to sell and the other two bought back by the vendor. The medium-sized, well-made Ungaro stays three miles and acts on heavy ground. He won a bumper on his debut on good to firm ground but hasn't encountered similar conditions since. *K. G. Reveley*

UNICORN REWARD (IRE) 7 b.g. Turtle Island (IRE) – Kingdom Pearl (Statoblest)   **h102**
[2006/7 17v 16d 17g² Apr 11] smallish, sturdy gelding: fair on Flat (stays 9f) in 2006, left D. Hughes after fourth outing: fair maiden hurdler: claimed from Mrs L. Jewell £6,000 second start: raced around 2m: below best on ground softer than good: tried in cheekpieces/visor/tongue strap. *A. King*

UNION DEUX (FR) 8 ch.g. Nikos – Sanhia (FR) (Sanhedrin (USA)) [2006/7 h–:   **h–**
25vᵖᵘ Mar 18] lengthy gelding: fair hurdler in 2004/5 when trained by Ferdy Murphy: pulled up only 2 outings since: should stay beyond 3m: raced mainly on going softer than good (acts on heavy). *Mrs S. J. Smith*

UNITED (GER) 6 b.m. Desert King (IRE) – Una Kasala (GER) (Law Society   **h145**
(USA)) [2006/7 h130: 16f 22m² 23d⁵ 20s* 20v* 20s* 24g⁴ 24m³ Apr 26]
    The Cheltenham Festival is to have an additional race in 2008. The executive has taken some persuading, but a Grade 2 race for mares and fillies, over two miles, four and a half furlongs, will be added to the Gold Cup day card. Named in honour of the late David Nicholson, who lobbied very hard for such a race to be part of the Festival programme, the race will be worth £100,000 and will be the culmination of a series that sees the number of 'black type' hurdle races for fillies and mares in the British programme increased from five to eleven. This will give the connections of such horses similar opportunities to those already provided for their Irish counterparts. Certainly, such races are an aid to breeders, for whom it will be easier to find a market for jumps-bred filly foals than formerly. Whether providing so many valuable opportunities for fillies and mares is worth the money and effort in terms of the spectacle provided is another matter, however, and the addition of yet another race to the Festival with the potential to draw runners from established championship events is a detrimental step, so far as Cheltenham is concerned. When the extension of the Cheltenham Festival to four days was originally proposed Timeform suggested a two-and-a-half-mile conditions hurdle, along the lines of the old Cathcart Chase, as an option likely to provide a race of suitable

totescoop6 Handicap Hurdle, Haydock—
United (left) battles back gamely to pip long-time leader Whispered Promises

Play Bingo At ladbrokes.com Mares' Only Handicap Hurdle, Sandown—heavy ground poses no problems for United as she holds off Chamoss Royale, whilst top weight Refinement blunders away her chance

quality without drawing too many runners from established races. Fillies and mares, of course, would still have been able to compete in such a contest with the aid of their sex allowance and surely that is preferable from a competition viewpoint. After all, if the Cheltenham Festival is to live up to its well-earned reputation as the Olympics of National Hunt racing then it should be aiming for the best performers in each category, whatever the sex, to race against each other. Had the proposed new mares race taken place in 2007, for example, it might well have taken away several leading contenders from established Grade 1 events at the Festival. Connections of Amaretto Rose (third) and Lounaos (unplaced), who started favourite for the Supreme Novices' and Triumph Hurdle respectively, could well have rerouted their charges to the mares race, whilst even those of Royal & SunAlliance Chase faller Cailin Alainn might have been lured by this lucrative option back over hurdles. The prospect of a conditions event for mares with a relatively small field would also have been an attractive option to the Pipe stable with its bonus-chasing juvenile Gaspara, who justified favouritism in the Fred Winter having had alternative novice options in the Baring Bingham and Triumph. The other main consequence of the new race will be to draw those slightly below the top class from championship races, thus reducing the size of fields for the top contests. Connections of Asian Maze, part of the smallest Champion Hurdle field for twenty-seven years anyway, and World Hurdle candidates United and Label-thou might well have found the option of the new race too hard to resist. Incidentally, although Gaspara was the only winner of her sex at the latest Cheltenham Festival, the fact a further seven fillies or mares made the frame (including three over fences) only strengthens the view that the 7-lb sex allowance is sufficient incentive for them to run at the meeting.

United, fourth in the World Hurdle, was one of that septet and took her chance at Cheltenham after a hat-trick of wins over around two and a half miles on soft or heavy going, quite valuable handicaps at Haydock and Sandown and the Grade 2 totesport.com National Spirit Hurdle at Fontwell. In truth, none of those races was particularly well contested—only six went to post in a mares-only race at

Sandown—and the field for the National Spirit was notably weak for the grade. Just five went to post, with the out-of-sorts Korelo and the fairly useful pair Hereditary and Lord of Beauty all starting at around 20/1. United went off at 7/4-on, with her only serious rival on form being Refinement. The pair had met twice already in 2006/7, including at Sandown (where Refinement had blundered away her chance at the last), and United was to come out on top again of the Jonjo O'Neill-trained mare (who admittedly was conceding weight each time). United was the only runner to show her form at Fontwell and ran out an easy winner by fourteen lengths. It proved a profitable weekend for the so-called 'fairer sex' as United's victory over Refinement was one of four wins at graded level by mares over the two days, the others being Labelthou in the Rendlesham Hurdle (another mare Material World was third), Heltornic in the Red Square Vodka Gold Cup and Sweet Kiln in the Boyne Hurdle.

Cheltenham, reportedly a likely option only if the ground were soft, provided a much sterner test for United and, in going down by just under fourteen lengths to Inglis Drever, she ran right up to her best, showing herself effective at the longer trip and demonstrating that soft ground wasn't required for her to show her form. She made her final start of the season in another Grade 1 three-mile hurdle, the Champion Stayers' at Punchestown, where she had every chance after the injury to Mighty Man but went down by five and a half lengths to her old rival Refinement. Punchestown had been the scene of United's biggest triumph, in the Grade 1 Champion Four Year Old Hurdle at the 2005 Festival. She was off after that until the following March's Imperial Cup at Sandown, in which she ran with credit. However, she failed to build on that effort in three subsequent runs that spring, including when pulled up in graded company at Auteuil, and struggled with her jumping. It wasn't until her return in the latest season, when stepped up in trip, that she finally showed her full ability. Clearly the additional races for mares will give connections greater options with her in 2007/8. Given she is smallish in stature and Flat bred, it seems unlikely that United will be sent over fences. She will have a new jockey following the unexpected retirement of regular rider Leighton Aspell in the summer, the popular thirty-one-year-old (who even had his own fan club!) deciding to hang up his boots with his career record standing at 422 wins in Britain and Ireland (including two on the Flat).

United (GER) (b.m. 2001)	Desert King (IRE) (b 1994)	Danehill (b 1986)	Danzig	
			Razyana	
		Sabaah (ch 1988)	Nureyev	
			Dish Dash	
	Una Kasala (GER) (b 1995)	Law Society (br 1982)	Alleged	
			Bold Bikini	
		Una Primola (ch 1979)	Prince Ippi	
			Unwetter	

United actually won on the Flat in Germany before joining Lucy Wadham and comes from a fairly good Flat family. Her dam Una Kasala was fairly useful and finished fourth in the local version of the One Thousand Guineas, while both grandam Una Primola and third dam Unwetter were also successful on the Flat, the last-named mare even managing a fourth place against the colts in the 1973 Deutsches Derby. Una Primola is a half-sister to Ustina, the dam of several useful or better performers, most notably the 1997 German St Leger winner Ungaro (not to be confused with the Feltham Novices' Chase winner of the same name). Despite connections' concerns, United acts on good to firm and heavy going, and wasn't disgraced on her only start on firm. She is genuine and reliable. *Mrs L. Wadham*

UNITED SPIRIT (IRE) 6 b.m. Fasliyev (USA) – Atlantic Desire (IRE) (Ela-Mana-Mou) [2006/7 h91: 16m 20m 17m⁴ c16gᵘʳ Sep 1] workmanlike mare: modest hurdler at best: sold out of Jedd O'Keeffe's stable 5,000 gns Doncaster August Sales, unseated 4 out in mares maiden on chasing debut: raced mainly around 2m: acts on good to firm going. *P. J. Rothwell, Ireland*   **c– h84**

UNJUST LAW (IRE) 6 b.g. Dushyantor (USA) – Go Tally-Ho (Gorytus (USA)) [2006/7 h116, F110: 17g² 16s⁴ 16g² 21d⁶ Nov 12] smallish, angular gelding: fairly useful handicap hurdler: generally ran well in 2006/7, second to Lord Henry and Iffy at Aintree: stays 21f: raced on good ground or softer (acts on soft). *N. J. Henderson*   **h125**

UNLEASH (USA) 8 ch.g. Benny The Dip (USA) – Lemhi Go (USA) (Lemhi Gold (USA)) [2006/7 c135, h–: 24m⁵ c24g³ Oct 14] leggy gelding: useful chaser/handicap   **c134 h130**

hurdler: creditable third to Harry's Dream in quite valuable handicap at Kempton: won point in April: stays 3m: acts on soft and good to firm going: has had jumping problems over fences. *P. J. Hobbs*

UNLIMITED 5 b.g. Bold Edge – Cabcharge Blue (Midyan (USA)) [2006/7 17g⁴ Nov 9] fair on Flat (stays 7f): raced freely when 16 lengths fourth of 7 to The Grey Man in maiden at Taunton on hurdling debut: will need sharp 2m. *R. Simpson* **h85**

UNMISTAKABLY (IRE) 10 gr.g. Roselier (FR) – Decent Debbie (Decent Fellow) [2006/7 c28vᵖᵘ May 27] good-topped gelding: winning hurdler/maiden chaser: useful pointer, won twice in 2006: tried blinkered: has gone in snatches/found little. *Evan Williams* **c– h– §**

UNOWATIMEEN (IRE) 7 b.g. Supreme Leader – Collinstown Queen (IRE) (King's Ride) [2006/7 F17v* 23v² 22d* Feb 19] €35,000 4-y-o: rangy gelding: first foal: dam unraced, out of half-sister to very smart chaser Father Delaney: third on completed start in Irish points in 2006: won maiden bumper at Sedgefield in December: also promising start over hurdles, winning novice at Market Rasen in February by 1¼ lengths from Barbers Shop: will stay 3m. *R. Ford* **h124 F100**

UNSIGNED (USA) 9 b. or br.g. Cozzene (USA) – Striata (USA) (Gone West (USA)) [2006/7 21m³ Nov 9] poor hurdler: left R. Buckler and off over 3 years before only start in 2006/7: stays 21f: raced on good to firm/firm going. *M. J. Coombe* **h79**

UNUSUAL SUSPECT 8 b.g. Syrtos – Sally Maxwell (Roscoe Blake) [2006/7 c–§, h94: c26mᵖᵘ May 5] good sort: modest handicap hurdler: no form over fences: stays 27f: acts on soft and good to firm going: usually blinkered: temperamental: sold £4,000 Ascot June Sales, placed in points. *G. L. Moore* **c– § h–**

UP ABOVE (IRE) 7 ch.g. Avarice – Amy Just (IRE) (Bustomi) [2006/7 h120, F95+: 20s c16d⁶ c17v c20d³ c20mᶠ Apr 9] lengthy, workmanlike gelding: fairly useful hurdler, well held on return: little impact over fences: stays 2½m: acts on good going: has worn cheekpieces, including when successful: front runner. *S. Donohoe, Ireland* **c88 h–**

UP AT MIDNIGHT 7 b.m. Midnight Legend – Uplift (Bustino) [2006/7 h96: 19d 21v³ Feb 26] compact mare: modest handicap hurdler: should stay beyond 21f: raced on good going or softer (acts on heavy). *R. Rowe* **h95**

UPHAM ATOM 4 b.g. Silver Patriarch (IRE) – Upham Lady (Bustino) [2006/7 F18v³ Feb 12] first foal: dam unraced: shaped like a stayer when 11 lengths third to Choumakeur in maiden bumper at Plumpton on debut. *B. G. Powell* **F81**

UPHAM LAD (IRE) 7 b.g. Relief Pitcher – Fussy Lady (Idiot's Delight) [2006/7 19dᵖᵘ 22d 21v⁴ Dec 11] workmanlike gelding: fourth foal: dam, winning hurdler, stayed 2¾m: no form in novice hurdles. *B. G. Powell* **h–**

UPIRLANDE (IRE) 7 b.g. Up And At 'em – Amiga Irlande (Whistling Deer) [2006/7 h–: 16m 17m 16f 20f 20g³ 22m 22gᵖᵘ Sep 17] no form over hurdles/in points: tried blinkered/in cheekpieces/tongue tied. *D. A. Rees* **h–**

UPRIGHT IMA 8 b.m. Perpendicular – Ima Delight (Idiot's Delight) [2006/7 h87: 16s⁴ 16g³ 16m 16d 17s³ 16g³ 16g²̇ Apr 8] lengthy, angular mare: modest handicap hurdler: best around 2m with emphasis on speed: reliable. *Mrs P. Sly* **h93**

UPSWING 10 b.g. Perpendicular – Moorfield Lady (Vicomte) [2006/7 c83, h81: c16g⁶ c20gᵘʳ c16g* c17dᵘʳ 16g⁴ c16m 17g c16gᵇᵈ c20m⁴ Aug 1] tall gelding: maiden hurdler: poor handicap chaser: won at Hexham in May: raced mainly around 2m: acts on soft and good to firm going: in cheekpieces last 2 starts: usually held up: poor jumper. *R. C. Guest* **c84 x h78 x**

UP THE GLEN (IRE) 13 b.g. Tale Quale – Etrenne (Happy New Year) [2006/7 c–, h–: c21gᵖᵘ May 3] angular gelding: winning chaser: lightly raced and no form since 2004/5. *Mrs Jackie Hunt* **c– h–**

UP THE PUB (IRE) 9 ch.g. Carroll House – Brave Ruby (Proverb) [2006/7 c84, h–: c21s⁵ c26v* c26g* c29sᵖᵘ c24s⁵ c24v⁴ c24d⁴ Feb 2] big, workmanlike gelding: modest handicap chaser: won at Chepstow and Warwick in October: stays 3¼m: acts on heavy going: has had tongue tied. *R. H. Alner* **c90 h–**

UPTON SILVER 8 gr.m. Arzanni – Spartan City (Dubassoff (USA)) [2006/7 24fᵖᵘ 19g Jul 5] no form in points/over hurdles. *M. Sheppard* **h–**

UPTOWN LAD (IRE) 8 b.g. Definite Article – Shoka (FR) (Kaldoun (FR)) [2006/7 c75, h100: c20d³ c20d² c16g May 30] compact gelding: fair hurdler/modest novice chaser: stays 2½m: acts on heavy going: tried in cheekpieces/blinkers: often tongue tied: usually held up. *R. Johnson* **c92 h–**

Bathwick Tyres Bridgwater HBLB Kingmaker Novices' Chase, Wincanton—a winning start for new connections by Ursis (noseband), who gets the better of a lengthy duel with Opera Mundi

URBAN DREAM (IRE) 6 ch.g. Foxhound (USA) – She's My Love (Most Welcome) [2006/7 h83: 21p^u 19m Jun 4] poor hurdler: no show last 4 starts: stays 19f: acts on soft and good to firm going: tried visored/in cheekpieces. *R. A. Farrant*　**h–**

URBAN FREEWAY (IRE) 8 b. or br.g. Dr Devious (IRE) – Coupe d'Hebe (Ile de Bourbon (USA)) [2006/7 20g^{pu} 24s^{pu} Nov 25] useful-looking gelding: 2m winner on Flat in 2002: very lightly raced over hurdles: tongue tied, no show in 2006/7: joined R. C. Guest. *Robert Gray*　**h–**

URBAN TIGER (GER) 4 b.g. Marju (IRE) – Ukraine Venture (Slip Anchor) [2006/7 16g^2 16g^3 16v^3 16g 17g Apr 27] close-coupled gelding: fairly useful on Flat (stays 11.6f), successful in June/August: fair form when 20 lengths second to Katies Tuitor in juvenile at Kempton on hurdling debut: failed to repeat that, twice shaping as if amiss, left A. King after second outing: raced around 2m. *Carl Llewellyn*　**h103 d**

URSIS (FR) 6 b.g. Trempolino (USA) – Bold Virgin (USA) (Sadler's Wells (USA)) [2006/7 h133: 20g c16d^3 c19s* c16s* c20v^3 c16g^4 c20m^5 c20g^{pu} Apr 25] smallish gelding: useful chaser: useful chaser: won maiden at Hereford in January and, having been sold out of Jonjo O'Neill's stable 50,000 gns Doncaster January Sales, Grade 2 Kingmaker Novices' Chase at Wincanton (beat Opera Mundi by ¾ length, pair clear) in February: good efforts in frame next 2 starts, mistake 4 out when 9½ lengths fourth to Andreas in Grade 3 Grand Annual Chase (Handicap) at Cheltenham: stays 2½m: acts on heavy going, below form on good to firm: races prominently. *S. Gollings*　**c140 h–**

URSUMMAN (IRE) 8 b.g. Leading Counsel (USA) – Canverb (Proverb) [2006/7 c125, h98+: 18m* c20f* c22g^4 Aug 2] useful handicap chaser: further progress when winning at Down Royal in June by 6 lengths from Bravery: creditable fourth of 22 to Far From Trouble in very valuable event at Galway: had run easily best race over hurdles when winning 21-runner handicap at Punchestown by 2½ lengths from Davenport Democrat: stays 3m, effective at much shorter: unraced on heavy going, acts on any other: usually tracks pace. *N. Madden, Ireland*　**c136 h122**

USHNU (USA) 4 ch.g. Giant's Causeway (USA) – Serape (USA) (Fappiano (USA)) [2006/7 F17v^4 F16m^4 F16g 16g^2 Apr 8] $875,000Y, 11,000 3-y-o: closely related to US Grade 3 8.5f/9f winner Batique (by Storm Cat) and half-brother to 2 minor winners in USA: dam US Grade 1 7f winner: modest form in bumpers: 13 lengths second to King's Revenge in juvenile at Towcester on hurdling debut: has shaped as though further will suit. *S. Curran*　**h86 F79**

V

VAGABONDO MAN (IRE) 6 b. or br.g. Kadastrof (FR) – Tacmahack (IRE) (Phardante (FR)) [2006/7 F16m^6 F16g^{pu} Apr 23] fifth foal: dam ran once in Irish point:　**F68**

won maiden point in 2006: little impact in bumpers 10 months apart: tried tongue tied. *J. W. F. Aynsley*

VAGUE IDEA 14 gr.g. Tout Ensemble – Roodle Doodle (Rugantino) [2006/7 c25m c26dᵖᵘ c21mᵘʳ Aug 2] winning chaser, no form outside points since 2003. *O. J. Carter*   c–
h–

VALANCE (IRE) 7 br.g. Bahhare (USA) – Glowlamp (IRE) (Glow (USA)) [2006/7 c105, h–: 16g 16m⁶ 24dᵖᵘ Nov 21] sturdy gelding: fairly useful on Flat (stays 2m), successful in August: fairly useful hurdler at best: tongue tied, not fluent when below form in handicaps in 2006/7: fortunate winner only outing over fences: should be at least as effective at 2½m as 2m: unraced on extremes of going: tried blinkered. *C. R. Egerton*   c–
h104

VALASSINI 7 b.m. Dr Massini (IRE) – Running Valley (Buckskin (FR)) [2006/7 F89: F16m Sep 2] runner-up in bumper on debut: tailed off year later. *J. L. Needham*   F–

VALDERRAMA 7 ch.g. Lahib (USA) – Silky Heights (IRE) (Head For Heights) [2006/7 h–, F–: 16gᵖᵘ c20dᵖᵘ c20dᵖᵘ Nov 21] workmanlike gelding: no sign of ability: tried tongue tied. *F. Kirby*   c–
h–

VAL DU CIRON (FR) 4 b.g. True Brave (USA) – Dix Huit Brumaire (FR) (General Assembly (USA)) [2006/7 F14dᵖᵘ Mar 22] fifth foal: half-brother to winning hurdler/fairly useful chaser Dix Villez (by Villez), stays 3m: dam unraced half-sister to smart 2m hurdler Mounamaix: 5/4-on, successful debut when beating Nakoma by 11 lengths (with plenty to spare) in bumper at Ludlow. *Miss H. C. Knight*   F101 +

VALENTINES LADY (IRE) 6 b.m. Zaffaran (USA) – Jessica One (IRE) (Supreme Leader) [2006/7 F16s* F16s⁵ F17g³ Apr 13] rather leggy, useful-looking mare: first foal: dam fairly useful hurdler up to 21f: fairly useful form in mares bumpers, green when winning 17-runner event at Wetherby in November on debut: 14¾ lengths third of 20 to Turbo Linn in listed race at Aintree: likely to be suited by further than 2m. *K. G. Reveley*   F98

VALENTINE SPAR 5 br. or bl.m. Rakaposhi King – Lady of Mine (Cruise Missile) [2006/7 F17g F16m Oct 12] third foal: half-sister to fairly useful chaser Tommy Spar (by Silver Owl), stays 3m: dam, winning chaser, stayed 23f: well beaten in bumpers: tried in cheekpieces. *Mrs D. A. Hamer*   F–

VALERUN (IRE) 11 b.g. Commanche Run – Glenreigh Moss (Le Moss) [2006/7 h79: 24g⁴ 24g 21d 20m⁴ 24fᵖᵘ Jul 16] lengthy, rather sparely-made gelding: poor handicap hurdler: stayed 3m: acted on firm going (won bumper on good to soft): usually wore headgear: dead. *R. C. Guest*   h75 §

VALFONIC 9 b.g. Zafonic (USA) – Valbra (Dancing Brave (USA)) [2006/7 16sᵖᵘ 17m 16f⁵ 17m 16mᵖᵘ Nov 9] winning hurdler, no form since 2002: left F. Jordan and off 2 years before return: tried visored/in cheekpieces: has had tongue tied: temperamental. *G. J. Smith*   h– §

VALIANT SHADOW (GER) 5 b.g. Winged Love (IRE) – Vangelis (Gorytus (USA)) [2006/7 19v⁴ 19d* 17s* Mar 11] strong, compact gelding: modest maiden on Flat (stays 1¼m), sold out of W. Jarvis' stable 7,000 gns Doncaster November Sales: fairly useful form over hurdles: won maiden in November and novice (18 ran, beat Runthatpastmeagain by 1½ lengths) in March, both at Market Rasen: stays 19f: raced on going softer than good. *Mrs A. M. Thorpe*   h118

VALJEAN (IRE) 11 b.g. Alzao (USA) – Escape Path (Wolver Hollow) [2006/7 c20gᵖᵘ c19m Mar 29] medium-sized gelding: fair pointer, won in April: no form otherwise: tried tongue tied. *Mrs Myfanwy Miles*   c–
h–

VALLEY HALL (IRE) 6 b.m. Saddlers' Hall (IRE) – Here She Comes (Deep Run) [2006/7 F86: 18s² 19vᵖᵘ 16v⁴ 17g Apr 7] runner-up in bumper: best effort in mares events over hurdles (modest form) when second to La Grande Villez in maiden at Fontwell: will be suited by 2½m+: acts on soft going. *C. J. Mann*   h86

VALLEYMORE (IRE) 11 br.g. Jolly Jake (NZ) – Glamorous Brush (IRE) (Brush Aside (USA)) [2006/7 c95§, h–: c23m³ May 6] lengthy gelding: modest maiden handicap chaser: stays 3½m: acts on soft going: tried blinkered/in cheekpieces: has had tongue tied: sold 5,200 gns Doncaster August Sales, fourth in point. *S. A. Brookshaw*   c72 §
h–

VALLEY RIDE (IRE) 7 b. or br.g. Glacial Storm (USA) – Royal Lucy (IRE) (King's Ride) [2006/7 h133: 21g⁵ 24s³ 24gᵖᵘ Apr 14] quite good-topped gelding: useful handicap hurdler: creditable third to Material World at Cheltenham: left C. Tinkler, beaten when hampered 3 out in listed event 4 months later: stays 25f: acts on soft and good to firm going: not straightforward. *D. W. P. Arbuthnot*   h135

VALLEY WARRIOR 10 b.g. Michelozzo (USA) – Mascara VII (Damsire Unregistered) [2006/7 c76, h–: c25g³ May 4] lengthy gelding: little impact over hurdles: poor handicap chaser: stays 25f: acts on good to soft and good to firm going: tried blinkered. *J. S. Smith* **c76**
h–

VALUABLE (IRE) 10 b.m. Jurado (USA) – Can't Afford It (IRE) (Glow (USA)) [2006/7 c73, h76: 16g 17d 16g c20s^pu 17f 17m c21m^pu c16f Sep 29] leggy mare: winning hurdler/maiden chaser, no form in 2006/7: tried in cheekpieces/tongue strap: held up: has found little. *R. Johnson* **c–**
h–

VALUTA (USA) 4 gr. or ro.c. Silver Charm (USA) – Misleadingmiss (USA) (Miswaki (USA)) [2006/7 17g 20g* Apr 11] fair maiden on Flat (stays 1½m): upped in trip, won maiden hurdle at Hereford in April by head from Swift Half, carried wide turning in: stays 2½m: tongue tied. *R. A. Kvisla* **h96**

VANDANTE (IRE) 11 b.g. Phardante (FR) – Vanessa's Princess (Laurence O) [2006/7 c82: c16m⁶ c21d² c21g* c20s^pu c21g⁴ c23f³ c24g^pu c25d⁴ Nov 16] sturdy gelding: modest chaser: made all in minor event at Newton Abbot in June: stays 3m: acts on firm and soft going: inconsistent. *R. Lee* **c86 §**

VANILLA DELIGHT (IRE) 4 b.f. Orpen (USA) – Fantastic Bid (USA) (Auction Ring (USA)) [2006/7 16g^su Nov 1] rather leggy filly: half-sister to fairly useful hurdler Formal Bid (by Dynaformer), stayed 2½m: fair on Flat (stays 1m): travelling well behind leaders when slipping up before 3 out in juvenile at Huntingdon on hurdling debut. *J. Howard Johnson* **h– p**

VANISHING DANCER (SWI) 10 ch.g. Llandaff (USA) – Vanishing Prairie (USA) (Alysheba (USA)) [2006/7 c19g^ur c23g⁴ c26g² c23m⁴ Apr 22] tall, leggy gelding: fair on Flat, successful twice in early-2007 for K. Burke: winning hurdler: modest handicap chaser: seems to stay 3¼m: acts on heavy and good to firm going: has had tongue tied, including all starts in 2006/7. *Mrs D. Thomas* **c86 ?**
h–

VAN NESS (IRE) 8 ch.g. Hubbly Bubbly (USA) – Brown Trout (IRE) (Beau Charmeur (FR)) [2006/7 c20s c22m* c24m c20m³ c21g Apr 12] tall gelding: maiden hurdler: modest chaser: won maiden at Tramore in June: sold out of M. Phillips' stable 16,000 gns Doncaster August Sales after fourth outing, successful in point in March: never dangerous in Fox Hunters' at Aintree: stays 25f: acts on heavy and good to firm ground: effective with or without cheekpieces. *Mrs Katie Baimbridge* **c99**
h–

VAQUERAS (FR) 4 b.g. Pennekamp (USA) – Las Americas (FR) (Linamix (FR)) [2006/7 16v⁵ 16v³ 16v⁵ 16v 16g⁵ Mar 31] lengthy gelding: has scope: successful over 1m/9f in France at 2 yrs for J. Bertran de Balanda: fair juvenile hurdler: likely to prove best given test of speed at 2m. *Mrs J. Harrington, Ireland* **h108**

VAUGHAN 6 b.g. Machiavellian (USA) – Labibeh (USA) (Lyphard (USA)) [2006/7 h115: 17m* 19m* 16m² c16g⁴ c16d³ c16s⁴ 16g⁶ 20g⁴ Apr 14] compact gelding: fair novice hurdler: won at Exeter (maiden) in May and Hereford in June: similar form in chases, 10 lengths third of 4 to Priors Dale in novice at Kempton: stays easy 2½m: acts on good to firm and good to soft ground: has found little: room for improvement in jumping over fences. *H. D. Daly* **c109**
h112

VA VAVOOM (IRE) 9 b.g. Supreme Leader – Shalom Joy (Kemal (FR)) [2006/7 c120, h98: c20g^ur c21g^F Apr 12] well-made gelding: maiden hurdler: fairly useful chaser at best: left N. Twiston-Davies, successful in point in March: hampered and failed to complete in hunters: probably best short of 3m: raced on good going or softer: blinkered once (ran poorly): tried tongue tied: often races prominently. *Mrs Fleur Hawes* **c–**
h–

VECCHIO SENSO (IRE) 5 b.g. Old Vic – Ravens Way (Niels) [2006/7 23v⁵ 23v⁴ 24v Jan 17] angular, good-topped gelding: fifth foal: dam unraced: best effort over hurdles (modest form) when fifth in novice at Wetherby on debut: stays 23f: raced on heavy going. *J. Howard Johnson* **h87**

VEDELLE (IRE) 8 b.g. Flemensfirth (USA) – Romitch (Le Bavard (FR)) [2006/7 c24s² c22v² c21s² c20v² c20s* c24d^pu Jan 14] fifth foal: dam third in point: point/bumper winner: twice-raced in maiden hurdles: fairly useful chaser: runner-up first 4 starts, beaten neck by Ballistraw in handicap at Punchestown on final occasion: didn't have to be at best to win maiden at Down Royal in December: stays 3m: raced on going softer than good. *Joseph Crowley, Ireland* **c117**
h–

VELOCISSIMA (IRE) 7 b.m. Heron Island (IRE) – Andonova (Prince Tenderfoot (USA)) [2006/7 17m⁵ 16f³ 17m Jul 20] ex-Irish mare: poor form over hurdles: raced around 2m on good going or firmer. *Ferdy Murphy* **h79**

VELVET BLU 5 gr.m. Environment Friend – Bit of A Bird (Henbit (USA)) [2006/7 F16s³ F16v F16v 24m⁴ 20mᵇᵈ Apr 25] lengthy mare: first foal: dam unraced: third in bumper: poor form completed outing over hurdles: may prove best short of 3m. *Mrs Pauline Adams* **h66 F76**

VELVET DOVE 8 b.m. Rakaposhi King – Careful Dove (So Careful) [2006/7 19d² 16g⁵ 21s⁶ 22g⁴ 26g² 24mʳᵗʳ Apr 25] rather leggy mare: fair pointer, won 3 times in 2006: modest novice hurdler: stays 3¼m: has refused to line up/race: temperamental. *Mrs Pauline Adams* **h88 §**

VELVET SKYE 7 gr.m. Terimon – Mermaid Bay (Jupiter Island) [2006/7 19g Apr 8] winning pointer, runner-up once from 4 starts in 2006: well held in maiden on hurdling debut. *Mrs Pauline Adams* **h–**

VELVET VALLEY (USA) 4 ch.g. Gone West (USA) – Velvet Morning (USA) (Broad Brush (USA)) [2006/7 16m Jan 29] fairly useful on Flat (stays 11f), sold out of Sir Michael Stoute's stable 12,000 gns Newmarket Autumn Sales, successful in March: jumped poorly when tailed off in juvenile on hurdling debut. *C. E. Longsdon* **h–**

VENALMAR 5 b.g. Kayf Tara – Elaine Tully (IRE) (Persian Bold) [2006/7 16s⁴ F16v² F16v* Mar 11] half-brother to several winners, including useful bumper performer Eye On The Ball (by Slip Anchor) and fair 2m hurdler Miami Explorer (by Pennekamp): dam fairly useful hurdler who should have stayed beyond 2¾m: encouraging start to career in maiden hurdle/bumpers, well backed when winning 14-runner event at Naas by 8 lengths from Stewarts House, closing smoothly from mid-field and pulling clear under pressure final 1f: will stay beyond 2m: sure to improve over hurdles. *M. F. Morris, Ireland* **h103 p F112**

VENICE ROAD (IRE) 6 ch.g. Halling (USA) – Croeso Cynnes (Most Welcome) [2006/7 16g 21vᵖᵘ 20v⁶ 16d 19s³ 19s* 19g⁵ Mar 28] leggy gelding: bumper winner: modest hurdler, off 21 months before return: won handicap at Taunton in March: likely to prove best at 2½m+: raced on good going or softer: in cheekpieces last 3 starts: hard ride. *Miss Venetia Williams* **h87**

VENN OTTERY 12 b.g. Access Ski – Tom's Comedy (Comedy Star (USA)) [2006/7 c–, h–: c21gᶠ 16m 19g c17dᵖᵘ Feb 10] rangy gelding: lightly raced over hurdles: developed into smart chaser in 2003/4 for P. Nicholls, largely well below form subsequently for variety of stables: headstrong, and was best at 2m on good going or firmer: often tongue tied: usually found little: dead. *Mrs S. Gardner* **c– h–**

VERASI 6 b.g. Kahyasi – Fair Verona (USA) (Alleged (USA)) [2006/7 h132: 16m 16d⁶ 20g⁵ 16s⁶ 16d 21s* 22d³ 21g 24g Apr 14] leggy gelding: useful handicap hurdler: won intercasino.co.uk Lanzarote Hurdle at Kempton in January by length from Royals Darling, despite hanging/carrying head awkwardly: well held in other valuable events last 2 starts: should stay 3m: best on going softer than good (acts on heavy): not straightforward, usually in cheekpieces/blinkers. *G. L. Moore* **h138**

VERCHENY 12 b.m. Petoski – Ekaytee (Levanter) [2006/7 19sᵖᵘ Jun 27] successful twice in points: blinkered, reluctant to race and pulled up after first in seller on hurdling debut. *Evan Williams* **h§§**

VERIFICATION 4 ch.g. Medicean – Viewfinder (USA) (Boundary (USA)) [2006/7 17d⁴ Nov 7] fair form on first of 3 starts on Flat at 2 yrs: last of 4 finishers in juvenile on hurdling debut, taking strong hold. *J. Howard Johnson* **h–**

VERSATILE 4 b.g. Vettori (IRE) – Direcvil (Top Ville) [2006/7 17sᵖᵘ Feb 8] in frame up to 10.5f in France for J-C. Rouget, little impact on Flat in Britain or on hurdling debut. *G. A. Ham* **h–**

VERSTONE (IRE) 5 b.m. Brave Act – Golden Charm (IRE) (Common Grounds) [2006/7 h79: 22d⁵ 17d² 20f 16m⁴ 17m⁴ 17m* 16g⁴ 20d⁵ 20sᵖᵘ 20gᶠ 16g³ Apr 23] leggy, angular mare: poor novice hurdler: won mares event at Sedgefield in August: probably stays 2¾m: acts on soft and good to firm going. *R. F. Fisher* **h83**

VERTIGO BLUE 4 b.g. Averti (IRE) – Soft Colours (Presidium) [2006/7 16s⁶ 16g 16v 18s 19vᵖᵘ Feb 27] poor maiden on Flat, sold out of C. Thornton's stable 1,400 gns Doncaster January (2006) Sales: no form over hurdles. *A. C. Whillans* **h–**

VERY COOL 5 b.g. Sir Harry Lewis (USA) – Laurel Diver (Celtic Cone) [2006/7 F16g 21g 20g³ Apr 11] half-brother to several winners, notably useful hurdler/fairly useful chaser Mr Cool (by Jupiter Island), stayed 25f: dam bumper winner: well beaten in bumper: much better effort in maiden hurdles when 4 lengths third to Valuta at Hereford. *D. E. Pipe* **h91 F–**

VERY SPECIAL ONE (IRE) 7 b.m. Supreme Leader – Bright News (Buckskin   **c–**
(FR)) [2006/7 c98, h88: 24g 19m³ 24m² 21m² 26g³ 26s* 21g³ 21gᵖᵘ Apr 19] workman-   **h122**
like mare: runner-up completed start in handicap chases: fairly useful novice hurdler:
won at Huntingdon in December by 16 lengths from Old Benny: ran well when 16 lengths
third of 18 to Karello Bay in listed mares handicap at Newbury 3 months later: lame final
outing: stays 3¼m: acts on soft and good to firm going: in cheekpieces/visor last 6 starts.
K. C. Bailey

VERY VERY NOBLE (IRE) 13 ch.g. Aristocracy – Hills Angel (IRE) (Salluceva)   **c102 §**
[2006/7 c–, h–: c24s² c20mʳᵗʳ c20sᵖᵘ c25dᵖᵘ c20vᵘʳ c20s c20v c25sᵘʳ c26gᵖᵘ Apr 7]   **h–**
lengthy gelding: once-raced over hurdles: fair handicap chaser: form in 2006/7 only on
first outing: stays 25f: usually tongue tied: front runner: temperamental (has refused to
race). *W. Storey*

VESTA FLAME 6 b.m. Vettori (IRE) – Ciel de Feu (USA) (Blushing John (USA))   **h61**
[2006/7 h–: 20g⁵ Nov 13] compact mare: little form: tried in cheekpieces. *Miss
L. V. Davis*

VEVERKA 6 b.m. King's Theatre (IRE) – Once Smitten (IRE) (Caerleon (USA))   **h97**
[2006/7 16mᵖᵘ 16f² 16m* 19mᵘʳ 16f⁴ 20m² 24d* 24d³ 21s² 22s⁴ 20d 22d⁶ 24m Apr 15]
angular mare: maiden on Flat: modest hurdler: won seller in July and handicap in September, both at Worcester: stays 3m: acts on firm and soft going. *J. C. Fox*

VIABLE 5 b.g. Vettori (IRE) – Danseuse Davis (FR) (Glow (USA)) [2006/7 h–: 16g   **h94**
16g⁵ 16d⁴ 16v⁵ Jan 4] tall, angular gelding: fair maiden on Flat (stays 1¼m): modest
novice hurdler: raced at 2m: acts on good to soft ground. *Mrs P. Sly*

VIAL DE KERDEC (FR) 4 b. or br.g. Poliglote – Love For Ever (FR) (Kaldoun (FR))   **h–**
[2006/7 17sᶠ 16v³ Jan 17] leggy, lengthy gelding: fourth foal: half-brother to winners on
Flat by Sillery and Green Tune: dam placed at 6f: successful once over 1¼m from 4 starts
on Flat in French Provinces at 3 yrs before sold from F. Rohaut €54,000: on toes, well-
held third of 4 in juvenile at Newbury on completed outing over hurdles. *M. Bradstock*

VIBE 6 gr.g. Danzero (AUS) – Courting (Pursuit of Love) [2006/7 h–: 16m³ Apr 25] tall   **h93**
gelding: modest on Flat (best at 6f to 1m): much better effort over hurdles (trained by
R. Price on debut in late-2005) when third to Kanad in novice at Worcester. *Evan
Williams*

VICARIO 6 gr.g. Vettori (IRE) – Arantxa (Sharpo) [2006/7 c103, h118: c24d c20s⁶ 20g   **c–**
20d² 20s* 23v⁴ 24g⁶ Apr 19] leggy gelding: winning chaser: fairly useful handicap   **h120**
hurdler: back to best when winning Jump/Flat jockeys event at Haydock (has won 3 of 5
starts there) in December by 7 lengths from Ile de Paris: barely stays testing 23f: acts on
heavy and good to firm going: tried blinkered. *D. McCain Jnr*

VICARS COURT (IRE) 7 b.g. Lord of Appeal – Lady Temba (Callernish) [2006/7   **F–**
F–: F16d May 15] good-topped gelding: well beaten in bumpers. *O. Brennan*

VICAR'S LAD 11 b.g. Terimon – Proverbial Rose (Proverb) [2006/7 c21g May 3] tall,   **c–**
leggy gelding: novice hurdler: fair pointer/hunter chaser: lightly raced since 2005: stays   **h–**
25f: acts on soft going. *Mrs Jelly O'Brien*

VICIANA 8 b.m. Sir Harry Lewis (USA) – Ludoviciana (Oats) [2006/7 c102p, h112:   **c–**
c23sᵖᵘ c18s c24sᶠ c24g Mar 14] good-topped mare: winning hurdler/chaser, no form in   **h–**
handicaps in 2006/7: stays 2½m. *Mrs L. Wadham*

VICIOUS PRINCE (IRE) 8 b.g. Sadler's Wells (USA) – Sunny Flower (FR) (Dom   **h82**
Racine (FR)) [2006/7 20s⁵ 24s⁵ 21v⁶ 24vᵖᵘ Mar 10] strong, lengthy gelding: fair on Flat
(stays 17.5f) as 6-y-o, well beaten in 2006: poor form over hurdles, left R. Whitaker after
debut. *Mrs J. C. McGregor*

VICITY 6 ch.m. Old Vic – Quiet City (True Song) [2006/7 17m May 17] small mare: **h–**
tailed off both outings over hurdles 19 months apart. *R. H. Alner*

VICKY BEE 8 b.m. Alflora (IRE) – Mighty Frolic (Oats) [2006/7 h93: 25dᵖᵘ 20sᵖᵘ 16g   **h80**
20m³ 20g³ Apr 9] good-topped mare: poor maiden hurdler: stays 2½m: acts on good to
firm going: usually tongue tied. *K. F. Clutterbuck*

VIC'S CHARM (IRE) 6 ch.g. Old Vic – Sapien Dame (IRE) (Homo Sapien) [2006/7   **F–**
F17d F16d Jan 5] €1,500 3-y-o, €1,000 5-y-o: first foal: dam unraced, out of half-sister
to useful chaser Lucisis: no form in bumpers (trained on debut by Robert Gray) and on
Flat. *D. Carroll*

VIC'S LAST CHANCE (IRE) 9 ch.g. Old Vic – Jemma's Gold (IRE) (Buckskin   **c91 +**
(FR)) [2006/7 c16v⁴ c21g² Mar 16] winning pointer, including in April: fair form in

hunter chases, 4 lengths second to Plutocrat in novice at Fakenham: will stay 3m: acts on heavy going. *Nick Kent*

VIC THE PILER (IRE) 8 ch.g. Old Vic – Strong Gale Pigeon (IRE) (Strong Gale) [2006/7 h115: c25m* c20m Jun 3] rather leggy gelding: fairly useful hurdler: odds on, won 4-runner minor event at Hexham on chasing debut in May by 4 lengths from Dolmur, idling: seemed unsuited by drop in trip month later: will stay beyond 25f: acts on good to firm and heavy going. *N. G. Richards* — **c111 h–**

VICTOR DALY (IRE) 6 b.g. Old Vic – Murphy's Lady (IRE) (Over The River (FR)) [2006/7 F89: 21m 20m³ 20g⁴ Apr 14] poor form over hurdles when third in maiden at Uttoxeter: will be suited by 3m+: type to do better. *Heather Dalton* — **h72 p**

VICTORIA'S BOY (IRE) 14 b.g. Denel (FR) – Cloghroe Lady (Hardboy) [2006/7 c90, h–: c26d⁶ May 31] strong gelding: fair pointer/hunter chaser: stays 3¼m: acts on soft and good to firm going: tried blinkered. *Ms W. Wild* — **c87 h–**

VICTORIAS GROOM (GER) 5 b. or br.g. Lavirco (GER) – Valda (RUS) (Dotsero (USA)) [2006/7 h116: c18sᵘʳ Dec 29] tall gelding: fairly useful hurdler: off 9 months, shaped well until unseating 5 out in novice at Newbury won by Fair Along on chasing debut: raced around 2m on ground softer than good. *Mrs L. Wadham* — **c– p h–**

VICTORS PRIZE (IRE) 5 b.m. Dr Devious (IRE) – Spoken Word (IRE) (Perugino (USA)) [2006/7 19vᵘʳ Jan 8] maiden on Flat: very slow first and unseated sixth in mares novice on hurdling debut. *S. Curran* — **h–**

VICTOR VICTORIOUS (IRE) 7 ch.g. Old Vic – Badsworth Madam (Over The River (FR)) [2006/7 c22m c24s⁶ c20d⁵ c23s c22gᵖᵘ 21m⁴ Apr 9] 3-y-o: work-manlike gelding: eighth foal: half-brother to winning pointer by Roselier: dam unraced half-sister to top-class 2m chaser Badsworth Boy: modest form over hurdles: similar form over fences only on third start: left E. O'Grady after next one: should stay beyond 2½m: acts on heavy going: tried blinkered/tongue tied. *G. Brown* — **c97 h–**

VICTORY GUNNER (IRE) 9 ch.g. Old Vic – Gunner B Sharp (Gunner B) [2006/7 c116, h–: c24vᵖᵘ c23d c24gᵖᵘ c24s⁴ c28d* c30s⁴ c29s³ c27g⁶ c25gᵖᵘ Apr 13] compact gelding: fair handicap chaser: dropped in weights, won at Market Rasen (for second successive season) in December: stays 33f: raced mainly on good going or softer (acts on heavy). *C. Roberts* — **c106 h–**

VICTRAM (IRE) 7 b.g. Victory Note (USA) – Lady Tristram (Miami Springs) [2006/7 h118: 16s* 16d³ 16d 16d⁶ Feb 10] leggy gelding: useful handicap hurdler: won at Down Royal in November by short head from Moore's Law: good efforts in valuable events 2 of 3 starts after, left with plenty to do when around 4 lengths sixth of 20 to Heathcote in totesport Trophy at Newbury: raced at 2m on going softer than good (acts on heavy): patiently ridden. *Adrian McGuinness, Ireland* — **h132 +**

VICTREE (IRE) 8 b.g. Old Vic – Boro Glen (Furry Glen) [2006/7 h–, F83: 21v² 22gᵘʳ 21m⁵ Apr 8] tall gelding: little impact over hurdles, including when second of 3 on return from 20-month absence. *L. Wells* — **h–**

VIC VENTURI (IRE) 7 ch.g. Old Vic – Carmen Lady (Torus) [2006/7 h136: c17v* c22v² c20v⁶ c21v² c21g⁵ c25mᵖᵘ Apr 24] sturdy, useful-looking gelding: useful hurdler/novice chaser: won Grade 3 over fences at Galway in October by length from Conna Castle: reportedly had breathing operation after third start and ran well next 2 outings, second to Mister Top Notch in Dr P. J. Moriarty Novices' Chase at Leopardstown and fifth to L'Antartique in Jewson Novices' Handicap at Cheltenham: badly let down by jumping next time: should be suited by 3m+: acts on heavy going: effective tongue tied or not. *Philip Fenton, Ireland* — **c132 h–**

VIE A DEUX (FR) 4 b.f. Jeune Homme (USA) – Callithea (Fools Holme (USA)) [2006/7 F16v Feb 27] 1,700 3-y-o: leggy, unfurnished filly: fifth foal: dam maiden: well beaten in maiden bumper on debut. *W. Storey* — **F–**

VIENNA PRINCE (USA) 4 b.g. Kingmambo (USA) – Valentine Waltz (IRE) (Be My Guest (USA)) [2006/7 16mᵖᵘ 16g 17s 22g Apr 7] thrice-raced up to 10.5f on Flat at 2/3 yrs in France for J. Pease: little impact over hurdles: tried visored/blinkered. *L. Corcoran* — **h–**

VIENNCHEE RUN 6 b.g. Commanche Run – Lucky Vienna (Lucky Wednesday) [2006/7 h–, F83?: 16gᵖᵘ 16g⁶ 17g Apr 20] unfurnished gelding: no solid form over hurdles. *K. F. Clutterbuck* — **h–**

VIEW MOUNT PRINCE (IRE) 6 b.g. Topanoora – Glacial Princess (IRE) (Glacial Storm (USA)) [2006/7 20v³ 20s* 20v* 16v* 16d 20v⁵ Feb 24] €21,000 4-y-o: tall geld- — **h117**

ing: has scope: first foal: dam, winning pointer, half-sister to smart 2m to 3m chaser Egypt Mill Prince: fairly useful hurdler: successful in first 3 handicaps, in large-field events at Navan in November and Punchestown and Leopardstown (novice, beat Dolphin Bay by 1½ lengths despite interference from loose horse) in December: effective at testing 2m to 2½m: raced on going softer than good (acts on heavy). *Patrick Hughes, Ireland*

VIGOUREUX (FR) 8 b.g. Villez (USA) – Rouge Folie (FR) (Agent Bleu (FR)) [2006/7 c95§, h–§: c20v³ c16s³ c22g⁵ c19vᵖᵘ 19g⁶ c16s⁴ Feb 14] angular gelding: winning hurdler: modest chaser on his day: probably stays 2½m: acts on good to firm and heavy going: tried blinkered, usually wears cheekpieces: unreliable. *S. Gollings*   **c95 §** **h– §**

VIKING SONG 7 b.g. Savahra Sound – Relikon (Relkino) [2006/7 c–, h–: c20d⁶ c20dᵖᵘ Oct 6] no form: tried in cheekpieces. *F. Kirby*   **c–** **h–**

VIKING WHARF 6 b.g. Alflora (IRE) – Pearlossa (Teenoso (USA)) [2006/7 F16s May 20] second foal: dam unraced: third on completed start in points in 2006: tailed off in bumper. *P. J. Hobbs*   **F–**

VILLA MARA (IRE) 7 b.g. Alflora (IRE) – Claudia Electric (IRE) (Electric) [2006/7 F–: 16m 22s 21m 20d³ 22vᵖᵘ c16gF Apr 23] good-topped gelding: bad maiden hurdler: left S. Kirk, fell first on chasing debut. *G. Brown*   **c–** **h56**

VINANDO 6 ch.h. Hernando (FR) – Sirena (GER) (Tejano (USA)) [2006/7 h112: 20g* 24gᵖᵘ Mar 16] leggy, close-coupled horse: useful on Flat (stays 2¾m): fair hurdler: won maiden at Fontwell in November: stiff task 4 months later: should stay beyond 2½m: usually blinkered: tongue tied 3 of 5 starts. *C. R. Egerton*   **h112**

VINCENT VEGAS 4 b.g. Foxhound (USA) – Annie's Song (Farfelu) [2006/7 16sᵖᵘ Oct 11] no form on Flat or in juvenile hurdle. *Mrs S. Lamyman*   **h–**

VINESTAR (IRE) 5 b.g. Fourstars Allstar (USA) – Regal Bloom (IRE) (Castle Keep) [2006/7 F16s F16v 19sᵖᵘ Feb 1] sturdy gelding: fourth foal: dam unraced out of half-sister to Grand National winner Rag Trade: no form in bumpers/novice hurdle. *M. B. Shears*   **h–** **F–**

VINGIS PARK (IRE) 9 b.g. Old Vic – Lady Glenbank (Tarboosh (USA)) [2006/7 c96+, h118§: c24m² 21d c19s⁴ c23s Dec 29] sturdy gelding: fairly useful hurdler, needed race second outing: fair chaser, tends to make mistakes: probably stays 3m: acts on good to firm and heavy going: tried in cheekpieces, usually blinkered: has had tongue tied: temperamental. *V. R. A. Dartnall*   **c100 §** **h– §**

VINMIX DE BESSY (FR) 6 gr.g. River Bay (USA) – Hesse (FR) (Linamix (FR)) [2006/7 h–: 16m 17s 16d c16sF c16g c17m* c17g² Apr 23] tall, good-topped gelding: winning hurdler: fair form over fences: jumped better than previously when easy winner of novice at Plumpton in April: likely to prove best around 2m: acts on soft and good to firm going: wore cheekpieces on chasing debut: takes good hold. *G. L. Moore*   **c112** **h–**

VINNIE BOY (IRE) 10 b. or br.g. Detroit Sam (FR) – Castle Ita (Midland Gayle) [2006/7 c106: c24d* c28v² c26s⁶ c26gᵖᵘ Apr 19] well-made gelding: winning pointer: fairly useful hunter chaser: won at Towcester in May and Cheltenham (back to form when beating Gallik Dawn by ½ length) in April: also ran well when second to Knife Edge in Champion Hunters' Chase at Stratford: will stay beyond 3¾m: acts on heavy and good to firm ground. *Mrs O. Bush*   **c110**

VINO VENUS 5 b.m. Tipsy Creek (USA) – Galaxy Glow (Kalaglow) [2006/7 h–: 16m 18d⁵ Nov 12] no form over hurdles. *Miss S. West*   **h–**

VINTAGE FABRIC (USA) 5 b.g. Royal Anthem (USA) – Sandalwood (USA) (El Gran Senor (USA)) [2006/7 F84: F17m³ F17s² 19d² 19g* 20d 18g Mar 18] placed all 4 starts in bumpers: modest form over hurdles: won 4-runner novice at Newton Abbot in August: may prove best up to 19f: acts on good to soft going. *N. J. Hawke*   **h89** **F85**

VINTAGE GOLD (USA) 6 b. or br.g. Lear Fan (USA) – Wild Vintage (USA) (Alysheba (USA)) [2006/7 17gᵖᵘ c16sᵖᵘ Oct 27] useful-looking gelding: half-brother to useful hurdler/chaser Only Vintage (by Diesis), stays 3m, and very smart Hong Kong performer up to 1¼m Bullish Luck (by Royal Academy): dam, French 1¼m winner: bumper winner: fair hurdler: left C. O'Brien, no show in handicap or maiden chase (distressed) in 2006/7: raced around 2m: acts on heavy going. *Jonjo O'Neill*   **c–** **h–**

VINTAGE TREASURE (IRE) 8 b.g. Norwich – Bann River (Over The River (FR)) [2006/7 c17v³ c17d* c19v⁵ c17s⁶ c16gᵖᵘ c17m c18g Apr 25] fairly useful novice chaser: won maiden at Limerick in December by 10 lengths from Mister Top Notch: not in same form after, sometimes shaping as if amiss: will stay 2½m: acts on heavy going: in cheekpieces 2 of last 3 starts. *Charles Byrnes, Ireland*   **c121** **h–**

VIP

VIPER 5 b.g. Polar Prince (IRE) – Maradata (IRE) (Shardari) [2006/7 F83: F16f⁶ 17s 16g* 16d Mar 26] big, workmanlike gelding: mid-field in bumpers: easily best effort over hurdles (modest form) when winning maiden at Ludlow in February: raced freely and jumped right month later: may prove best at easy 2m. *R. Hollinshead*   **h99** **F70**

VIRGOS BAMBINO (IRE) 10 ch.m. Perugino (USA) – Deep In September (IRE) (Common Grounds) [2006/7 c90: c16g⁶ c26mᶠ c23vᵖᵘ c19f⁵ Apr 11] fair pointer/hunter chaser, below best in 2006/7: should stay beyond 19f: acts on heavy going. *Miss V. J. Nicholls*   **c80**

VISCOUNT BANKES 9 ch.g. Clantime – Bee Dee Dancer (Ballacashtal (CAN)) [2006/7 c93, h–: c16gᶠ c20g* c19m² c20f* Apr 5] fairly useful hunter chaser: improved in 2006/7, won at Ludlow in February and April (by 1½ lengths from Nominate): stays easy 2½m: acts on soft and firm going: tried in cheekpieces: ran out once (looked possible winner). *Mrs Rosemary Gasson*   **c104** **h–**

VISCOUNT ROSSINI 5 b. or br.g. Rossini (USA) – Spain (Polar Falcon (USA)) [2006/7 16dᶠ 16g⁵ 16s³ 16s⁴ 16sᶠ 16d⁶ 16s* 17s* 20g⁶ Apr 20] poor maiden on Flat (stays 1¼m): modest novice hurdler: won claimer at Leicester in January and handicap at Taunton in March: raced mainly around 2m on good going or softer: has been let down by jumping. *A. W. Carroll*   **h89 x**

VISIBILITY (FR) 8 gr.g. Linamix (FR) – Visor (USA) (Mr Prospector (USA)) [2006/7 c–§, h111§: 19s 17d 24s 18g³ 19g* 16g³ 20g⁴ Apr 27] tall, leggy, angular gelding: winning chaser: fair hurdler: won ladies seller at Towcester in March: stays 2½m: acts on heavy and good to firm going: wears visor/cheekpieces: ungenuine. *D. E. Pipe*   **c– §** **h103 §**

VISION VICTORY (GER) 5 b.g. Dashing Blade – Val d'Isere (GER) (Surumu (GER)) [2006/7 h–: 24vᵖᵘ 16g Apr 15] no form over hurdles. *P. Spottiswood*   **h–**

VISTA VERDE 9 b.g. Alflora (IRE) – Legata (IRE) (Orchestra) [2006/7 c16gᶠ Apr 7] lengthy gelding: novice hurdler: winning chaser: off 2½ years, fell heavily fifth in handicap at Haydock: effective at 2m to 3m: acts on soft going. *A. King*   **c–** **h–**

VITAL SPARK 8 b.g. Primitive Rising (USA) – Enkindle (Relkino) [2006/7 c–, h–: c21v⁵ c20g⁵ c25m* Apr 15] tall, useful-looking gelding: modest form in hunter chases, won at Market Rasen in April: stays 25f: acts on good to firm ground (won bumper on good to soft). *J. M. Jefferson*   **c81** **h–**

VITELLI 7 b.g. Vettori (IRE) – Mourne Trix (Golden Love) [2006/7 19dᵖᵘ Jun 14] lengthy gelding: fairly useful hurdler in 2004/5 for G. A. Swinbank: off 20 months and tongue tied, no show on handicap debut: stays 2½m: acts on good to soft going. *A. L. Forbes*   **h–**

VIVANTE (IRE) 9 b.m. Toulon – Splendidly Gay (Lord Gayle (USA)) [2006/7 h88: 22g⁴ 26dᵖᵘ 19gᵖᵘ 24mᵖᵘ 26m 26g⁵ 20m⁵ Apr 25] smallish, lengthy mare: poor hurdler: stays 3¼m: acts on soft and good to firm going: tried blinkered, usually in cheekpieces/tongue strap. *A. J. Wilson*   **h83**

VODKA BLEU (FR) 8 b.g. Pistolet Bleu (IRE) – Viva Vodka (FR) (Crystal Glitters (USA)) [2006/7 c20d² c26sᵖᵘ c21v c19d⁴ c21g c21g Apr 13] leggy, rather sparely-made gelding: winning hurdler: useful chaser: off 2 years, as good as ever when 3 lengths second of 16 to Exotic Dancer in Grade 3 Paddy Power Gold Cup Chase (Handicap) at Cheltenham: little impact all 4 starts in similar company after, probably flattered when fourth in Ascot Chase: stays easy 3m: acts on good to firm and heavy going: tried visored: sound jumper. *D. E. Pipe*   **c137 +** **h–**

VOY POR USTEDES (FR) 6 b.g. Villez (USA) – Nuit d'Ecajeul (FR) (Matahawk) [2006/7 c152p, h–: c16s² c16d* c17dᵘʳ c16g* Mar 14]   **c163** **h–**

    With the previous year's Arkle Chase winner Chinrullah disqualified on technical grounds after running away with the 1980 Queen Mother Champion Chase, it wasn't until 1992 that this notable double was completed, a surprisingly long wait given that the Arkle had joined the Champion Chase (itself inaugurated only in 1959) on the Cheltenham Festival programme in 1969. The Tom Dreaper-trained trio of Fortria, Ben Stack and Flyingbolt had all won the Champion Chase after victory in the Arkle's forerunner, the Cotswold Chase, but Remittance Man in 1992 was the first horse to complete the double in its present form, since when it has become a fairly common occurrence, the feat achieved by Klairon Davis in 1996, Flagship Uberalles in 2002, Moscow Flyer in 2003 (the first of his two Champion Chase victories), Azertyuiop in 2004 and Voy Por Ustedes in the latest season. Flagship Uberalles was the only one not to manage it in consecutive years. In addition Travado, Nakir, Or Royal, Flagship Uberalles and Well Chief were all placed in the Champion Chase twelve months after their Arkle wins. The first five to do the Arkle-Champion Chase double all put up top-class performances when completing it, but Voy Por Ustedes didn't run to quite that level in winning what turned out to be an ordinary Champion Chase after the early departure of hot favourite Well Chief. However, it will be surprising if Voy Por Ustedes doesn't show top-class form one day, time being very much on his side. Inkslinger, in 1973, is the only other to have won a Champion Chase aged only six.

Voy Por Ustedes is also still relatively lightly raced over fences, six runs in his first season followed by just four in a second which was very much geared towards Cheltenham in March. It was December before he made his reappearance in the Tingle Creek Chase, for which Voy Por Ustedes would have been the centre of attention, and a hot favourite, but for a late about-turn by connections of Kauto Star. Kauto Star's appearance at Sandown on the way to the King George VI Chase changed the complexion of the Tingle Creek and he duly landed the odds impressively, though, to his credit, Voy Por Ustedes was the only one to make any sort of a race of it with the favourite. However, from two out Voy Por Ustedes was fighting a losing battle and his lack of a recent run began to tell as he faded late on, improving on his Arkle form even so in finishing seven lengths second. Voy Por Ustedes had no Kauto Star to contend with subsequently, with the latter returned to racing at three miles and more.

The next engagement for Voy Por Ustedes, like that for Kauto Star, was at Kempton's Christmas meeting, Voy Por Ustedes contesting the Desert Orchid Chase (Sponsored By Stan James), a new graded race for two-mile chasers which replaced the Castleford Chase at Wetherby (now run as a 0-145 handicap) in the jumps pattern. Voy Por Ustedes started at odds on up against four rivals, the pick of

Desert Orchid Chase (Sponsored By Stan James), Kempton—
early casualty Armaturk leaves Voy Por Ustedes in front but still plays his part in a muddling race

Seasons Holidays Queen Mother Champion Chase, Cheltenham—
Ashley Brook's bold bid ends with a fall as Voy Por Ustedes (left) sets sail for home
from Dempsey (spotted cap), River City (noseband) and 2006 winner Newmill

whom looked to be the 2006 Arkle third Foreman who had just come out on top when the pair had subsequently met in the Maghull Novices' Chase at Aintree. In a muddling race, with the pace steady following the departure of Armaturk at the third, Voy Por Ustedes easily turned the tables on Foreman, who suffered most from the attentions of the loose horse in the straight. Voy Por Ustedes, left in front at the third, made the rest of the running, soon recovering from a blunder at the eighth and quickening when Robert Thornton got serious with him in the straight, going on to win by five lengths from the Tingle Creek third Oneway, with Foreman a further length and a half back in third. It was a high-class performance from Voy Por Ustedes, one which resulted in his being promoted to favouritism for the Champion Chase. Thornton had seemed certain to miss the ride at Kempton after he was thought to have suffered a broken collar bone in a fall at Exeter just six days earlier. It transpired that it was damage to an old injury—he had broken his collar bone three times previously—but very painful all the same, and Thornton deserves plenty of credit for battling through it to take the mount on a horse whom he says isn't the easiest of rides. 'He does need knowing—he is gassy and volatile with a bit of temperament, though that isn't a bad thing.'

Whilst Thornton rightly earned all the plaudits at Kempton he endured a rare 'bad day at the office' on Voy Por Ustedes' next start, blaming himself for being unseated at the fifth in the Game Spirit Chase at Newbury in February. The race was won by Well Chief, the 2005 Champion Chase runner-up (and 2004 Arkle winner) making an impressive return from a long absence, and afterwards replacing Voy Por Ustedes at the head of the market for the 2007 renewal. On the day, Well Chief started at even-money, the 2006 winner Newmill second favourite at 4/1, with Voy Por Ustedes at 5/1 the only other at single-figure odds in a ten-runner field. The first two in the betting were both let down by their jumping, Well Chief falling at the second and Newmill making a couple of errors as he and Ashley Brook (2005 Arkle runner-up) helped force a good gallop. On this occasion, Thornton stuck fast as Voy Por Ustedes, who tracked the leaders, made a bad mistake at the second last which briefly looked as though it might cost him the race. The 20/1-shot Dempsey was sent for home at this point and Voy Por Ustedes was left with around three lengths to make up. To his credit, Voy Por Ustedes responded so well when asked for his effort that he managed to edge ahead of Dempsey at the last, where Ashley Brook, just a length or so behind them and rallying gamely, fell. Voy Por Ustedes gradually pulled away from Dempsey, a length and a half separating them at the line, with another five lengths back to River City who stayed on to take third place off Newmill. That was it for the season for Voy Por Ustedes, though the chances are he would have picked up another good prize had he been kept on the go, Dempsey easily winning Sandown's Celebration Chase without needing to run close to his Champion Chase form. Dempsey will no doubt be one of Voy Por Ustedes' chief rivals again in the top two-mile chases in 2007/8, though such as Well Chief and Nickname—not to mention Kauto Star if he goes for the Tingle Creek again—look a bigger threat, possibly along with Voy Por Ustedes' stable-companion My Way de Solzen. The last-named won the latest edition of the Arkle, but may well be campaigned over two and a half miles or more from now on.

		Lyphard's Wish	Lyphard
Voy Por Ustedes (FR) (b.g. 2001)	Villez (USA) (ch 1992)	(b 1976)	Sally's Wish
		Valhalla (ch 1974)	New Chapter
			Varig
	Nuit d'Ecajeul (FR) (b 1987)	Matahawk (b or br 1972)	Sea Hawk
			Carromata
		La Divette (b 1978)	Orvilliers
			Wild Girl

Voy Por Ustedes is the eighth foal of Nuit d'Ecajeul, who has produced three other winners. They are Le Pero (by Perrault), fairly useful over hurdles and fences in France at up to three miles, a winner on the Flat in Slovakia by Synefos, and En La Cruz (by Robin des Champs). The last-named, also owned by Sir Robert Ogden, was successful in four three-year-old events over jumps at Auteuil in 2006, two over hurdles at fifteen furlongs and two over fences at seventeen furlongs. Nuit d'Ecajeul is a half-sister to the 1992 Grande Course de Haies d'Auteuil runner-up Roi d'Ecajeul. Their dam La Divette gained her sole win in a two-and-three-quarter-mile chase at Auteuil. Voy Por Ustedes, a leggy, angular gelding, has raced

Sir Robert Ogden's "Voy Por Ustedes"

only on good ground or softer, and he acts on soft. A genuine sort who races with plenty of zest, he is notably consistent, the winner of seven of his nine completed starts over fences and a good second on the other occasions. *A. King*

VRISAKI (IRE) 6 b.g. Docksider (USA) – Kingdom Queen (IRE) (Night Shift (USA)) [2006/7 h77: 16g 16m⁵ 17m 17g 17m Aug 6] compact gelding: poor maiden hurdler: raced mainly around 2m: tried visored. *M. E. Sowersby*   **h72**

W

WADHAM HILL 5 b.m. Bandmaster (USA) – Sport of Fools (IRE) (Trojan Fen) [2006/7 F16m³ Jun 11] first foal: dam, modest hurdler, won twice at 17f: third to Chosen in maiden bumper at Stratford on debut. *W. J. Reed*   **F71**

WAGES 7 b.g. Lake Coniston (IRE) – Green Divot (Green Desert (USA)) [2006/7 c100, h77: 17m* 17m 17d* 18g² c16m² c16d² c16d² c16f² Apr 22] lengthy gelding: fair hurdler/handicap chaser: improved over hurdles in early-2006/7, winning sellers at Market Rasen in June (handicap) and August (first outing after leaving Evan Williams): left Mrs A. Thorpe before final start: raced around 2m: acts on firm and soft going: has worn cheekpieces: tried tongue tied: patiently ridden. *Tim Vaughan*   **c107 h100**

WAHCHI (IRE) 8 ch.g. Nashwan (USA) – Nafhaat (USA) (Roberto (USA)) [2006/7 17g Sep 23] half-brother to winning hurdler Penric (by Marju), stays 19f: 1m/1¼m winner on Flat, useful form at best: well held in novice on hurdling debut: dead. *M. W. Easterby*   **h–**

WAIMEA BAY 8 b.m. Karinga Bay – Smart In Sable (Roscoe Blake) [2006/7 c–, h–: 22m May 12] winning hurdler in 2004: no show in 2 starts over fences: tried blinkered. *D. P. Keane*   **c– h–**

WAINHILL LAD 11 b.g. Suluk (USA) – The-Adstone-Lodge (Royal Vulcan) [2006/7 c–: 19d⁵ 26mᵖᵘ Jun 14] no form in various events. *J. Gallagher*   **c– h–**

WAIN MOUNTAIN 11 b.g. Unfuwain (USA) – Mountain Memory (High Top) [2006/7 c125, h–: c19s* c19s⁶ c20v² c20s⁶ c19vᵖᵘ 22dᵖᵘ Mar 17] good-topped gelding: fairly useful handicap chaser: won at Chepstow in December: poor efforts last 3 starts, including back over hurdles (lost shoe): effective at testing 19f to 3¼m: acts on heavy going, possibly unsuited by good to firm: usually blinkered nowadays: tongue tied in 2006/7: none too genuine. *J. A. B. Old*   **c125 h–**

WAIT FOR THE CALL (IRE) 6 b.g. Dr Massini (IRE) – Castle Stream (Paddy's Stream) [2006/7 16vꟳ 27vᵖᵘ 16g⁵ Mar 16] good-topped gelding: half-brother to several winners, notably fairly useful hurdlers around 2½m Native Recruit and Native Shore (both by Be My Native), former also fairly useful chaser: dam unraced: of no account: left C. Swan prior to 2006/7: tried in cheekpieces/blinkers. *P. C. Haslam*   **h–**

WAKEUP SMILING (IRE) 9 b.g. Norwich – Blackmiller Lady (Bonne Noel) [2006/7 c102, h–: c18s⁴ Mar 3] rangy gelding: winning hurdler: fair maiden chaser: off 11 months, well held only start in 2006/7: barely stays 3m: acts on good to firm and good to soft going: visored once: has flashed tail. *Miss E. C. Lavelle*   **c– h–**

WAKING NED (IRE) 8 b.g. Supreme Leader – Kim's Choice (Le Bavard (FR)) [2006/7 c21v* c25v* c26gᵖᵘ c31s* Apr 26] strong ex-Irish gelding: winning hurdler: sold out of D. Hassett's stable 6,000 gns Doncaster May Sales, won point in January: fairly useful hunter chaser: won at Sedgefield in February, Kelso in March and Perth (beat Lord Who by 1¾ lengths) in April: stays 31f: acts on heavy ground: sometimes in cheekpieces: has had tongue tied. *P. Kirby*   **c106 h–**

WALCOT LAD (IRE) 11 b.g. Jurado (USA) – Butty Miss (Menelek) [2006/7 c116, h–: c22sᵖᵘ c24dᵖᵘ Jan 15] medium-sized gelding: fairly useful handicap chaser, won 4 times at Fontwell in 2005/6: off 9 months, let down by attitude in 2006/7: stays 3½m, effective over much shorter: acts on heavy and good to firm going: tried blinkered/visored, wears cheekpieces nowadays. *A. Ennis*   **c– h–**

WALDENSTROEM (GER) 4 gr.g. Silver Patriarch (IRE) – Weissglut (GER) (Lavirco (GER)) [2006/7 F12v³ Jan 17] has scope: first foal: dam unraced: 3¼ lengths third of 17 to Procas de Thaix in 4-y-o bumper at Newbury on debut, edging left. *Carl Llewellyn*   **F101**

WALDO'S DREAM 7 b.g. Dreams End – Landsker Pryde (Nearly A Hand) [2006/7   **h101**
F77: F16g⁶ F17m* F17m² 16g⁴ 19s 20d 16f 20g* Apr 21] won maiden bumper at Here-   **F90**
ford in June: fair hurdler: won handicap at Bangor in April: stays 2½m: probably acts on
firm going. *P. Bowen*

WALKIN AISY 7 b.g. Rudimentary (USA) – Lady Shipley (Shirley Heights) [2006/7   **c108 x**
h123: 16s³ c17s⁴ c16vᶠ c17dᶠ c18vᵘʳ c20v³ c22m Apr 8] fairly useful hurdler: creditable   **h120**
third to Silent Oscar in minor event at Punchestown: fair novice chaser, failed to complete
3 of 6 starts: stays 19f: raced mainly on going softer than good: needs to improve jumping
over fences. *D. T. Hughes, Ireland*

WALK IN THE GARDEN 5 br.m. Dr Fong (USA) – Woodland Garden (Godswalk   **F–**
(USA)) [2006/7 F16g F16m Jun 28] half-sister to several winners, including fair hurdler
Rock Garden (by Bigstone), stays 21f: dam unraced half-sister to useful 2½m to 3m
hurdler Mister Loot: tailed off in bumpers. *J. A. Danahar*

WALLY WONDER (IRE) 9 ch.g. Magical Wonder (USA) – Sally Gap (Sallust)   **c–**
[2006/7 c–, h97: 22s 19g 19d* 16d⁵ 16g⁴ 20m³ Apr 20] smallish gelding: fair handicap   **h100**
hurdler: won amateur event at Catterick in December: stays 21f: acts on firm and soft
going: tried visored, usually blinkered: usually front runner/races prominently. *Ferdy
Murphy*

WALSINGHAM (IRE) 9 b.g. Presenting – Let's Compromise (No Argument)   **c– p**
[2006/7 c–, h97: c19sᵖᵘ Dec 18] good-topped gelding: modest handicap hurdler: has   **h–**
failed to complete over fences, helped force overly-strong pace only start in 2006/7:
successful at 21f, best around 2m: acts on soft and good to firm going: blinkered once
(successful): takes good hold, usually races prominently: should do better over fences.
Evan Williams

WALTER GEE 7 ch.g. Dancing Spree (USA) – Star Flower (Star Appeal) [2006/7 22s   **h–**
20d 16g Mar 29] lengthy gelding: half-brother to 3 winners, including fairly useful 2m
hurdler Country Orchid (by Town And Country): dam, poor half-sister to very smart
stayer Duky: well beaten in novice hurdles: tried tongue tied. *Mrs F. Kehoe*

WALTER'S DESTINY 15 ch.g. White Prince (USA) – Tearful Sarah (Rugantino)   **c92 §**
[2006/7 c100§, h–: c25gᵖᵘ c25m⁴ c25d⁵ c25g⁵ c25d⁴ c27f⁶ Apr 5] lengthy gelding: **h–**
modest handicap chaser, raced only at Wincanton since 2004/5: probably stays 3¾m: acts
on good to firm and heavy going: lazy and unreliable. *C. W. Mitchell*

WALTHAM ABBEY 6 b.g. Relief Pitcher – Flash-By (Ilium) [2006/7 F16d⁴ F16s   **h100**
F16v⁴ 20s⁵ 21g³ 19g² Apr 8] fourth foal: half-brother to 2¾m hurdle winner Mighty   **F90**
Surprise (by Sure Blade) and 6f winner Flyover (by Presidium): dam unraced: fourth in
bumpers: fair form over hurdles: well backed when short-head second to Give Me A
Dime in maiden at Towcester, making most despite mistakes: stays 21f. *Mrs Caroline
Bailey*

WALTON WAY 7 b.g. Charmer – Needwood Poppy (Rolfe (USA)) [2006/7 h67, F–:   **h87**
16d* 16m 21sᵖᵘ 16d⁴ 19v³ 20sᵖᵘ 16s 21g* 22g³ 24m Apr 25] small, leggy gelding:
modest novice hurdler: won at Worcester (handicap) in September and Ludlow (seller) in
February: stays 2¾m: acts on good to soft going, possibly unsuited by softer: has been
blinkered, including last 3 starts. *P. W. Hiatt*

WALTZING ALONG (IRE) 9 b.g. Presenting – Clyduffe Fairy (Belfalas) [2006/7   **c–**
c79, h–: c16mᵖᵘ c21vᵖᵘ c20gᵘʳ Mar 27] lengthy gelding: maiden chaser: no form in   **h–**
2006/7 (including in points), sold out of L. Lungo's stable 2,000 gns Doncaster August
Sales after reappearance. *S. J. Robinson*

WANANGO (GER) 6 ch.g. Acatenango (GER) – Wanateluthspilgrim (USA) (Pilgrim)   **c121**
[2006/7 h130: c16s* c17s⁴ c17s⁴ Jan 28] tall, good-topped gelding: useful hurdler: won   **h–**
novice at Fairyhouse on chasing debut in November, recovering from mistake last to beat
Justpourit ¾ length with plenty to spare: let down by jumping when fourth in Grade 1
novices won by Schindlers Hunt at Leopardstown: should stay beyond 2m: raced on
going softer than good (acts on heavy). *T. Stack, Ireland*

WANDERING WAY 5 b.g. Nomadic Way (USA) – Lady Godiva (Keen) [2006/7   **F–**
F16m Mar 25] second foal: dam, 1m winner at 2 yrs, modest 2½m novice hurdler: well
held in bumper on debut. *B. N. Pollock*

WANTAGE ROAD (IRE) 5 br.g. Pistolet Bleu (IRE) – Glowing Lines (IRE) (Glow   **h78 p**
(USA)) [2006/7 F–p: 21g Mar 23] good-topped gelding: well beaten in bumper: mid-field
in maiden at Newbury on hurdling debut a year later, not given hard time: likely to do
better. *N. J. Henderson*

WAR AT SEA (IRE) 5 b.g. Bering – Naval Affair (IRE) (Last Tycoon) [2006/7 16m² **h94**
16m⁵ 16m Sep 24] fairly useful on Flat (stays 2m), successful in October (claimed to join
A. Carroll £12,000): 3½ lengths second to Jazz Scene in novice at Worcester on hurdling
debut, let down by jumping next 2 starts: possibly not straightforward (hung left on
debut): sold 10,000 gns Doncaster May Sales. *P. J. Hobbs*

WARDINGTON LAD 5 b.g. Yaheeb (USA) – Lavenham's Last (Rymer) [2006/7 **h–**
F16v* F16d 19s Feb 1] lengthy, well-made gelding: half-brother to several winners, **F97**
notably fairly useful hurdler/winning chaser up to 21f Senorita Rumbalita (by Alflora):
dam unraced half-sister to high-class staying chaser Cybrandian: won maiden bumper at
Uttoxeter in May: well held after, including in novice on hurdling debut. *B. I. Case*

WAR GENERAL 6 gr.g. Classic Cliche (IRE) – Absalom's Lady (Absalom) [2006/7 **h125**
16g* 20m³ 17m² 16s² 16d* 16d² Nov 10] 130,000 3-y-o: third foal: half-brother to useful
hurdler/smart chaser Bob Bob Bobbin (by Bob Back), stays 3¼m, and 2¾m hurdle
winner Big Business (by Slip Anchor): dam, very smart hurdler/winning chaser, stayed
3m: fairly useful hurdler: won maiden at Sligo in June and minor event at Naas in
October: good second to Moon Over Miami in Grade 2 novice at Cheltenham final start:
stayed 2½m: acted on good to firm and good to soft ground: dead. *T. J. Taaffe, Ireland*

WARJAN (FR) 10 b.g. Beaudelaire (USA) – Twilight Mood (USA) (Devil's Bag **c–**
(USA)) [2006/7 c20mᵖᵘ Jun 22] lengthy gelding: has had wind operation: fairly useful **h–**
handicap hurdler: off over 3 years, no show in maiden on chasing debut: raced mainly
around 2m: acts on heavy going. *R. T. Phillips*

WARLORD 6 b.g. Bob Back (USA) – Martomick (Montelimar (USA)) [2006/7 F92: **h126**
F16g² 19d³ 19d* 22gᶠ Mar 19] sturdy gelding: in frame in bumpers: confirmed promise **F92**
of hurdling debut when winning novice at Ascot by 10 lengths from Sound Accord: fell
fatally in similar event month later: would have stayed 3m: raced on good/good to soft
going on turf. *R. H. Buckler*

WARNE'S WAY (IRE) 4 ch.g. Spinning World (USA) – Kafayef (USA) (Secreto **h111**
(USA)) [2006/7 16d³ 18s* 16s³ 16v² 17v⁵ 16d Mar 13] compact gelding: fair form on
Flat, sold out of R. Hannon's stable 5,000 gns Newmarket July Sales: fairly useful
juvenile hurdler: won at Fontwell in December by 4 lengths from Raslan: ran well when
placed next 2 starts, in Grade 1 at Chepstow on first occasion: will stay 2½m: raced on
ground softer than good (acts on heavy): blinkered final outing (ran creditably): not a
fluent jumper. *B. G. Powell*

WARNINGCAMP (GER) 6 b.g. Lando (GER) – Wilette (GER) (Top Ville) [2006/7 **h126**
h123: 16d³ 16d* 19gᵘʳ 16gᵖᵘ Apr 14] compact gelding: fairly useful handicap hurdler,
lightly raced: won at Wincanton in February by 1¾ lengths from Basic Fact: let down by
jumping next 2 starts, still to be asked for maximum effort when unseating 2 out at Ascot:
raced mainly around 2m: acts on soft going. *Lady Herries*

WAR OF ATTRITION (IRE) 8 br.g. Presenting – Una Juna (IRE) (Good Thyne **c165**
(USA)) [2006/7 c169+, h–: c22s* c24s² c20v² c24v³ Dec 28] **h–**
    War of Attrition's bid to win a second successive Cheltenham Gold Cup
ended in early-March when heat in a leg ruled him out. He was generally second
favourite behind Kauto Star at the time, despite a record of just one win from four
starts in 2006/7, the outings all coming within a two-and-a-half-month period
before the turn of the year. War of Attrition's efforts suggested he retained all his
ability, though the form of his Gold Cup win, which looked slightly substandard at
the end of the 2005/6 season, if anything looked slightly worse at the end of the
latest season. As in 2006, War of Attrition was due to have his first race of 2007 in
the Gold Cup itself and, until his setback, trainer Mouse Morris was usually
reported to be pleased with his charge's progress. Had he made the line-up at
Cheltenham, however, War of Attrition would have needed to improve to trouble
the first two home, Kauto Star and Exotic Dancer.
    War of Attrition started his campaign in some style, landing the odds in
the Star 'Best For Racing' Chase, a listed event at Punchestown in October. He'd
beaten reigning Gold Cup winner Kicking King to land the race twelve months
earlier and, although the opposition wasn't anything like so strong this time around,
there was still plenty to like about the way War of Attrition gained a sixth win in
eight starts. He faced a much sterner test, again odds on, in the Grade 1 James
Nicholson Wine Merchant Champion Chase at Down Royal where he went down
by a neck to Beef Or Salmon, with hardly anything to find fault with in the

performance. War of Attrition had been regarded by Timeform, though somewhat controversially, as a little behind Beef Or Salmon, judged on their overall records and form, in 2005/6 and was collared by that rival near the finish at Down Royal. Two further defeats for War of Attrition at Grade 1 level followed and were less satisfactory, his performances both rated some way below his best. War of Attrition finished runner-up again when beaten two and a half lengths by the up-and-coming In Compliance in the John Durkan Memorial back at Punchestown. The form was held down by the presence in third of outsider Sher Beau, and War of Attrition himself was certainly laboured, jumping with less than his usual fluency (he'd also flopped in the same race in 2005). What turned out to be his final appearance of the season saw War of Attrition finish third of six behind The Listener and Beef Or Salmon in the Lexus Chase at Leopardstown, beaten eight and five lengths respectively. War of Attrition had been entered for the King George VI Chase at Kempton but his trainer was reportedly unwilling to take him to Britain at that stage of the season.

The ground was a ready excuse for War of Attrition's last two defeats. His first two runs came on soft ground, something he has shown he handles perfectly well, for all that his Gold Cup win came on good to firm. His last two outings were on heavy, and, though he had won the only previous time he had encountered such conditions (as a novice chaser), the impression was that such a surface might not suit him ideally. It could also be that a drop to two and a half miles wasn't in his favour against In Compliance. It was, though, surprising at the time that War of Attrition was actually shortened in the Gold Cup ante-post lists by some book-makers after his Punchestown defeat. His performance in the Lexus was generally discounted so far as his Gold Cup chances were concerned. After his setback in early-March, War of Attrition was given a ten-week course of stem-cell regeneration, though first reports suggest he may still have to miss 2007/8. The same fate befell his predecessor on the Gold Cup roll of honour, Kicking King, who was ruled out for the latest season after the recurrence of a tendon injury in December. He was last seen when winning the 2005 King George at Sandown and, at the time of writing, it is unclear whether he will be back in training for 2007/8 despite 'cautiously optimistic' noises from his connections. Also sidelined in 2006/7 was the 2006 Betfair Bowl winner Celestial Gold who missed his intended return in the Betfair at Haydock in November and was found to have heat in a leg in early-December.

Star 'Best For Racing' Chase, Punchestown—
War of Attrition on his way to a second successive win in the race

Celestial Gold had contested the 2006 Cheltenham Gold Cup but unseated his rider at the tenth. Eighteen of the twenty-two runners got round, though their subsequent achievements confirmed that the field had been more noticeable for quantity than quality. Just six of the finishers managed a win over fences in the latest season. Aside from War of Attrition and Beef Or Salmon (who plainly wasn't anywhere near his best in the 2006 Gold Cup), the other winners were the third Forget The Past, who won a Grade 2 at Thurles, the seventh Sir Rembrandt and thirteenth Joes Edge who won handicaps off BHB marks of 145 and 130 (William Hill Handicap) respectively and the sixteenth Cornish Rebel, who won a four-runner handicap during an otherwise disappointing campaign. Aside again from Beef Or Salmon and War of Attrition, the best performances by any of the field in 2006/7 were probably L'Ami's second to Kauto Star in the AON Chase and Kingscliff's second to Neptune Collonges in the Punchestown Gold Cup. The 2006 Cheltenham Gold Cup was anything but a vintage renewal.

War of Attrition (IRE) (br.g. 1999)	Presenting (br 1992)	Mtoto (b 1983)	Busted / Amazer
		D'Azy (b 1984)	Persian Bold / Belle Viking
	Una Juna (IRE) (b 1992)	Good Thyne (br 1977)	Herbager / Foreseer
		An Bothar Dubh (br 1986)	Strong Gale / Tullow Performance

War of Attrition's pedigree has been dealt with fully in previous Annuals. He remains his family's standard bearer, as his half-brother Mister Bloom (by Germany) has yet to manage so much as a place over hurdles (tried in cheekpieces) after nine starts. That is scant reward for the €66,000 he cost as a three-year-old and he was sold on for just 4,800 guineas, to join Yorkshire-based Harry Hogarth, at the latest Doncaster May Sales. Their latest sibling to come to auction, a gelded son of Saddlers' Hall, made €30,000 at the Derby Sale in June. The dam Una Juna had a colt by War of Attrition's sire Presenting in 2005 and he made €45,000 as a foal. *M. F. Morris, Ireland*

WARPATH (IRE) 6 b.g. Alderbrook – Blake's Fable (IRE) (Lafontaine (USA)) **h116**
[2006/7 16g 18m* 17m* 16s 19s³ 24spu 21s² 22g* Apr 7] lengthy gelding: third foal: dam, poor maiden hurdler, half-sister to fairly useful hurdler/chaser up to 3m Taelos: fairly useful hurdler, sold out of A. Mullins' stable 9,000 gns Doncaster May Sales after first outing: won novices at Fontwell in August and Exeter in October and handicap at Newton Abbot (best effort when beating Archduke Ferdinand by ½ length) in April: stays 2¾m: acts on soft and good to firm going. *Evan Williams*

WAR PENNANT 5 b.g. Selkirk (USA) – Bunting (Shaadi (USA)) [2006/7 16d 19m⁵ **h88 §**
16m³ 17d³ 20m⁶ Sep 21] fair 1½m winner at 3 yrs for M. Channon, well held only outing on Flat in 2006: modest novice hurdler: best around 2m: acts on good to soft and good to firm ground: blinkered last 2 outings: ungenuine. *G. L. Moore*

WARSAW PACT (IRE) 4 b.g. Polish Precedent (USA) – Always Friendly (High **h– p**
Line) [2006/7 16v Feb 16] brother to 2m hurdle winner Impartial: useful on Flat (stays 1¾m), successful 4 times in 2006, sold out of Sir Mark Prescott's stable 200,000 gns Newmarket Autumn Sales: joint favourite, jumped with little fluency when last of 7 in juvenile on hurdling debut (distressed): will prove capable of better. *P. J. Hobbs*

WAS EARLY ON (IRE) 6 gr.g. Bimsey (IRE) – Scotch Rose (IRE) (Roselier (FR)) **h–**
[2006/7 24gpu 20m Jun 3] first foal: dam winning pointer: no show over hurdles. *F. P. Murtagh*

WASHINGTON LAD (IRE) 7 ch.g. Beneficial – Kyle Lark (Miner's Lamp) [2006/7 **c122**
20vpu c17v² c18vF c22v* c24vpu c20m⁶ c21m³ Apr 27] lengthy gelding: fairly useful **h–**
hurdler, off 21 months before reappearance: similar form over fences: won maiden at Fairyhouse in February: best efforts last 2 starts, when sixth to One Cool Cookie in Grade 1 novice there and third to Alexander Taipan in valuable novice handicap at Punchestown: should stay 3m: acts on heavy and good to firm going. *P. A. Fahy, Ireland*

WASHINGTON PINK (IRE) 8 b.g. Tagula (IRE) – Little Red Rose (Precocious) **c– §**
[2006/7 c–, h70: 23v² c21vur c25v⁶ Mar 3] compact gelding: poor hurdler: no form in **h68 §**
chases: stays 3m: acts on heavy and good to firm going: has worn visor/cheekpieces: temperamental. *C. Grant*

WATCH MY BACK 6 b.g. Bob Back (USA) – Gallants Delight (Idiot's Delight) **F91**
[2006/7 F16f* May 10] 26,000 4-y-o: first foal: half-brother to bumper winner I'm
Delilah (by Overbury): dam, useful pointer/hunter chaser, stayed 25f: odds on, overcame
greenness to win 7-runner bumper at Kelso on debut by 6 lengths (with plenty to spare)
from Mrdeegeethegeegee. *N. G. Richards*

WATCH THE DOVE 10 b.g. Afzal – Spot The Dove (Riberetto) [2006/7 19d⁵ c22g⁴ **c92 x**
22f* 22s⁶ 20d c19m² c27d⁴ 21vᵖᵘ Feb 12] angular gelding: modest hurdler/chaser, off 2 **h92**
years before return: won handicap hurdle at Wincanton in October: stays 3¼m: acts on
any going: tried in cheekpieces/visor, usually blinkered (including for both wins)
nowadays: often front runner: not a fluent jumper. *C. L. Tizzard*

WATCH THE WIND 6 ch.m. High Kicker (USA) – Marejo (Creetown) [2006/7 F–: **h–**
16v 16s⁶ 16s⁶ 16v 16g Apr 23] no form in bumpers/over hurdles. *J. B. Walton*

WATERBERG (IRE) 12 b.g. Sadler's Wells (USA) – Pretoria (Habitat) [2006/7 **c– §**
c104§, h–: 26g c25g⁶ c26g⁶ c24vᵖᵘ Nov 25] smallish, workmanlike gelding: winning **h– §**
hurdler: one-time fairly useful handicap chaser, retains little ability: has worn blinkers:
sketchy jumper: unreliable. *M. A. Doyle*

WATERCRESS 7 b.m. Slip Anchor – Theme (IRE) (Sadler's Wells (USA)) [2006/7 **F–**
F75: F16d Dec 21] little form in bumpers: tongue tied since debut. *Miss M. E. Rowland*

WATERLOO SON (IRE) 7 b.g. Luso – Waterloo Sunset (Deep Run) [2006/7 h112: **c88 +**
24mᵖᵘ c19mᵘʳ c21d³ c20dᵖᵘ Jan 8] close-coupled gelding: fair hurdler: well-held third to **h–**
Flying Enterprise in maiden at Wincanton only completed outing over fences: stays easy
3m: acts on good to firm and good to soft going: sold 8,000 gns Doncaster May Sales.
H. D. Daly

WATERMILL (IRE) 4 b.g. Daylami (IRE) – Brogan's Well (IRE) (Caerleon (USA)) **F–**
[2006/7 aF13g F14s⁶ Nov 29] 3,500 3-y-o: fourth foal: half-brother to 3 middle-distance
winners on Flat: dam unraced: never dangerous in 3-y-o bumpers: well held on Flat.
D. W. Chapman

WATERMOUSE 7 b.g. Alhaarth (IRE) – Heavenly Waters (Celestial Storm (USA)) **h83**
[2006/7 h72: 20g² 26dᵖᵘ May 17] small gelding: poor hurdler: stays 2½m: raced on good
ground or softer. *R. Dickin*

WATER PISTOL 5 b.g. Double Trigger (IRE) – Water Flower (Environment Friend) **c– x**
[2006/7 h–: 23m³ 20m 22g⁴ 22m² 22m⁵ 19m⁴ 22m⁷ 22d⁷ 22gᵘʳ 26m⁵ 24v⁴ 20s 19g³ 21d **h76**
20d c16dᶠ c24sᵘʳ c18d⁶ 24vᵖᵘ 21v c23sᵖᵘ 19vᵖᵘ 20g⁴ 22m Apr 15] smallish gelding: poor
maiden hurdler: badly let down by jumping over fences: stays 3¼m: acts on good to firm
and heavy going: usually front runner. *M. C. Chapman*

WATERSHIP DOWN (IRE) 10 b.g. Dolphin Street (FR) – Persian Myth (Persian **c85**
Bold) [2006/7 c24g c23mᵖᵘ Apr 22] leggy gelding: lightly raced over hurdles: winning **h–**
chaser: fair pointer, won in April: stays 23f: acts on firm and good to soft going, possibly
not on heavy: in cheekpieces in 2006/7. *Miss C. L. Wills*

WATERSKI 6 b.g. Petoski – Celtic Waters (Celtic Cone) [2006/7 F16m Apr 21] big, **F–**
heavy-topped gelding: third foal: dam maiden staying hurdler/chaser: well held in
bumper on debut. *Mrs J. C. McGregor*

WATERSPRAY (AUS) 9 ch.g. Lake Coniston (IRE) – Forain (NZ) (Nassipour **c103**
(USA)) [2006/7 c–, h–: c16g³ c16m c17f* c17m c20g⁶ Oct 19] small, angular gelding: **h–**
winning hurdler: fair handicap chaser: won at Bangor in July, left clear last: ran badly
after: stays 19f: acts on firm and soft going: inconsistent. *Ian Williams*

WATER TAXI 6 ch.g. Zafonic (USA) – Trellis Bay (Sadler's Wells (USA)) [2006/7 **c108**
h110: 17d³ c16m³ c17d² c16g³ c16mᶠ c19sᶠ 20v⁶ c16g Mar 27] rather leggy gelding: fair **h106**
hurdler/novice chaser: no show last 4 starts, twice falling over fences: effective at 2m,
barely stays 25f: acts on soft going: tongue tied since debut. *Ferdy Murphy*

WATSON LAKE (IRE) 9 b.g. Be My Native (USA) – Magneeto (IRE) (Brush Aside **c150 §**
(USA)) [2006/7 c154, h–: c22s² c16s³ c20v⁶ c17v⁴ c16s⁴ c20v* c25vᵖᵘ c20v⁴ c25g Apr **h–**
25] tall, good sort: has reportedly had breathing operation: smart chaser: won Grade 2
Red Mills Chase at Gowran in February by 5 lengths from Mansony: below form after:
barely stays 25f: raced on good going or softer (acts on heavy): tried tongue tied: has won
held up and making running: has found little/shaped as if amiss. *N. Meade, Ireland*

WATTS WAY 4 ch.g. Rambling Bear – Dunmail Raise (Milieu) [2006/7 F16v F16v **F–**
Feb 24] 1,800 3-y-o: rather leggy gelding: second foal: dam no sign of ability: well held
in bumpers. *J. R. Bewley*

WAYNESWORLD (IRE) 9 b.g. Petoski – Mariners Mirror (Julio Mariner) [2006/7 **c111** c96, h86: c26g⁵ 24m³ 24g² c26d* c26d* c26m* 24m* c26g⁴ c28s⁴ c28d³ 24d⁶ c28sᵖᵘ **h105** Dec 16] small gelding: fair hurdler/handicap chaser: better than ever in 2006/7, winning over fences at Newton Abbot (2, conditional jockeys event on first occasion) and Font-well in August and novice hurdle at Worcester in September: ran poorly last 2 starts: stays 3¼m: acts on good to firm and good to soft going (no form on soft): tough. *M. Scudamore*

WAYWARD MELODY 7 b.m. Merdon Melody – Dubitable (Formidable (USA)) **c– §** [2006/7 c81§, h85§: 26d⁴ 24g⁵ 24m³ 27d* 24g⁶ 26g⁶ 24s³ 25vᵖᵘ Dec 31] good-topped **h85 §** mare: maiden chaser: modest handicap hurdler: sold out of G. L. Moore's stable £5,000 Ascot June Sales after first outing: won at Newton Abbot in August: stays 27f: acts on soft and good to firm going: usually wears headgear: ungenuine. *R. Flint*

WAZALINO 5 b.g. Wace (USA) – Voolino (Relkino) [2006/7 17d⁶ 16s⁵ Dec 1] **h98** good-topped gelding: fourth foal: dam third on first of 2 starts over hurdles: on toes, better effort in novice hurdles when fifth to My Turn Now at Sandown. *R. H. Alner*

WAZIRI (IRE) 6 b.g. Mtoto – Euphorie (GER) (Feenpark (GER)) [2006/7 h87: 16f² **h87 d** 17m³ 17d 19g 17d Aug 7] close-coupled gelding: modest maiden hurdler: left M. Sheppard, well beaten last 3 starts: best at 2m: acts on firm going, probably on good to soft: tried in cheekpieces/tongue strap. *A. S. T. Holdsworth*

WEBBSWOOD LAD (IRE) 6 b.g. Robellino (USA) – Poleaxe (Selkirk (USA)) **h100 ?** [2006/7 17s⁴ 17s⁵ 16gᵘʳ Mar 24] good-topped gelding: fair maiden on Flat (seems to stay 2m): 250/1, best effort in novice hurdles when 25 lengths fourth to De Soto at Taunton. *M. R. Bosley*

WEDNESDAY COUNTRY (IRE) 6 ch.g. Carroll House – Mettle Kettle (Cut **h84** Above) [2006/7 h–, F90: 16s 19v Feb 23] fifth in bumper: well held in novice hurdles: bred to stay well. *J. A. T. de Giles*

WEE ANTHONY (IRE) 8 gr.g. Roselier (FR) – Arctic Alice (Brave Invader (USA)) **c101** [2006/7 c–p, h109+, F85: 23d² c24sᵘʳ c24d* c32s³ c26v c22v² c20vᵖᵘ Mar 9] rather leggy **h109** gelding: fair hurdler/chaser: again well-backed favourite, first completion over fences when winning handicap at Lingfield in November: stayed 3m: raced on going softer than good (acted on heavy): in cheekpieces last 2 starts: lazy: dead. *Jonjo O'Neill*

WEE BERTIE (IRE) 5 b.g. Sea Raven (IRE) – Commanche Glen (IRE) (Commanche **h77** Run) [2006/7 F93: 16g 19v 16g 20sᵖᵘ Apr 27] bumper winner: little impact over hurdles: should be suited by further than 2m. *J. Howard Johnson*

WEE DANNY (IRE) 10 b.g. Mandalus – Bonne Bouche (Bonne Noel) [2006/7 h79: **c–** 22mᵖᵘ 24g 22m⁴ 27m* 24m⁴ 24d c23mᵖᵘ 26g Oct 15] workmanlike gelding: modest **h86** handicap hurdler: won at Newton Abbot in August: well below form after next outing, looking to hate experience of jumping fences: stays 27f: acts on firm and good to soft going: usually races prominently. *L. A. Dace*

WEE DINNS (IRE) 6 b.m. Marju (IRE) – Tir-An-Oir (IRE) (Law Society (USA)) **h132** [2006/7 h110: 18f* 16s⁶ 19d* 19g* 17d² 22d 18g* 16g² 21g² Nov 7] useful hurdler: progressed well in 2006/7, winning handicap at Kelso in May, novices at Newton Abbot in June and Stratford (mares) in July and handicap at Fontwell (best effort, by 1¼ lengths from Take A Mile) in September: creditable second to Glacial Sunset in handicap at Kempton final outing: barely stays 21f: acts on firm and good to soft going: doesn't always look straightforward, and probably suited by good pace and waiting tactics. *D. E. Pipe*

WEE FORBEES (IRE) 5 b.g. Shernazar – Gender Gap (USA) (Shecky Greene **h120** (USA)) [2006/7 20s⁵ 20g³ 25s* 20g* 24gᵖᵘ Apr 13] €20,000 3-y-o: rangy, unfurnished gelding: half-brother to winning pointer by Broken Hearted: dam won 4 races in North America: fairly useful novice hurdler: won at Catterick in January and Sedgefield (well backed, by 7 lengths from Escayola) in March, making all or most: stays 25f: acts on soft ground. *J. Howard Johnson*

WEE ROBBIE 7 b.g. Bob Back (USA) – Blast Freeze (IRE) (Lafontaine (USA)) **c138** [2006/7 h123+: c20gᵖᵘ c24d³ c24s⁴ c24d² c21g³ c29f Apr 28] rangy, good sort: winning **h–** hurdler: useful chaser: best efforts fourth/fifth starts, 4 lengths second to Gungadu in Reynoldstown Novices' Chase at Ascot and 4½ lengths third to L'Antartique in Jewson Novices' Handicap at Cheltenham: stays 3m: raced mainly on good going or softer (beaten long way out in Betfred Gold Cup on firm): sure to win races over fences. *N. J. Gifford*

WEET A HEAD (IRE) 6 b.g. Foxhound (USA) – Morale (Bluebird (USA)) [2006/7 **h91** h–: 17m⁴ 16d* 16s⁴ 16d Nov 11] sturdy gelding: on downgrade on Flat in 2006: modest hurdler: won seller at Uttoxeter in October: likely to prove best around 2m: acts on soft going: sold 1,800 gns Doncaster January Sales. *R. Hollinshead*

WEET AN HAUL 6 b.g. Danzero (AUS) – Island Ruler (Ile de Bourbon (USA)) [2006/7 h–: 17m 17mᵖᵘ Jun 19] no form over hurdles or in point: tried tongue tied. *T. Wall*   h–

WEET WATCHERS 7 b.g. Polar Prince (IRE) – Weet Ees Girl (IRE) (Common Grounds) [2006/7 h94?: 16m 16mᵖᵘ 21m 17d⁴ Nov 16] poor maiden hurdler: left T. Wall before third outing: raced mainly around 2m: acts on good to firm and good to soft going. *C. Nenadich*   h76

WEE WILLIAM 7 b.g. Bollin William – Our Amber (Kabour) [2006/7 c91: c21m² c25g* c25m* c24m² c24g⁴ Oct 19] lengthy gelding: fair chaser: won handicaps at Hexham in May and June: stays 25f: acts on good to firm going: tried in cheekpieces. *T. D. Walford*   c101

WE GOT HIM (IRE) 7 b.g. Taipan (IRE) – Falas Lass (Belfalas) [2006/7 22s 20d⁵ 20s⁴ 26s c23s³ 26sᵖᵘ c19f² c22m³ Apr 26] €20,000 3-y-o: half-brother to 2¾m hurdle winner Falas Lad (by Le Bavard) and bumper winner Supreme Lass (by Supreme Leader): dam unraced, half-sister to dam of top-class chaser Merry Gale: sixth on first of 2 starts in bumpers in 2004 for R. Tyner: runner-up in point in Britain in 2006: bought £6,000 Ascot June Sales: seemingly modest form over hurdles/in chases: probably stays 23f: probably acts on firm and soft going. *R. H. Buckler*   c87 ? h87 ?

WELCOME STRANGER 7 b.g. Most Welcome – Just Julia (Natroun (FR)) [2006/7 h116: 17m² Jun 8] fair form over hurdles, let down by jumping since winning on debut in 2005/6: likely to prove best around 2m. *G. L. Moore*   h110

WELCOME TO UNOS 10 ch.g. Exit To Nowhere (USA) – Royal Loft (Homing) [2006/7 c114, h111: 20v 20v c19s* 19s c19gᵘʳ c22s c20v⁶ c20v² c20s Mar 11] sturdy, close-coupled gelding: fair handicap hurdler/chaser: won over fences at Catterick in January: below form otherwise in 2006/7: stays 21f: acts on heavy and good to firm going: tried visored (has looked ungenuine). *K. G. Reveley*   c114 h98

WELL ACTUALLY (IRE) 7 b.g. Luso – Lake Garden Park (Comedy Star (USA)) [2006/7 h95: 22s 20v⁵ c22gᵖᵘ Mar 29] rangy, good sort: form over hurdles only on debut in 2005/6: blinkered, ran in snatches and folded tamely on chasing debut. *B. G. Powell*   c– h–

WELL BLESSED 4 b.f. Petoski – Danny Rhy (Rymer) [2006/7 F16s Mar 11] second foal: dam unraced: raced freely when well held in mares bumper on debut. *E. J. Creighton*   F—

WELL CHIEF (GER) 8 ch.g. Night Shift (USA) – Wellesiena (GER) (Scenic) [2006/7 c17d* c16gᶠ c20g³ Apr 13]   c167 + h–

The sight of Well Chief returning to action with a sparkling performance in the Game Spirit Chase at Newbury was one that must have cheered all true jumping supporters. He had been sidelined, after heat was found in a foreleg, since beating Azertyuiop in the Celebration Chase at Sandown on the last day of the 2004/5 season. That race had taken the score between Azertyuiop and Well Chief to 2-2, the pair of them both ending the season with a Timeform rating of 182. They had filled the places behind Moscow Flyer (Timeform 184) in the Tingle Creek (Azertyuiop runner-up) and the Queen Mother Champion Chase (Well Chief runner-up), and Azertyuiop had given Well Chief weight and a beating in the Game Spirit. The performances of Moscow Flyer, Azertyuiop and Well Chief contributed to a splendid 2004/5 season, their ratings ranked among the specialist two-milers of Timeform's experience only by the exuberant front-runner Dunkirk, whose short career included a facile twenty-length win in the Two-Mile Champion Chase in 1965, a fifteen-length victory over Mill House (at level weights) in the two-mile Frogmore Chase at Ascot and a win under 12-7 in the Mackeson Gold Cup (then run over two miles and a few yards). Well Chief is the last of the 'golden trio' of 2004/5 still in training. Moscow Flyer was retired at the end of an anti-climactic campaign in 2005/6, though he made a brief return in the latest season, winning a charity Flat race at the Punchestown Festival ridden by his trainer's daughter. Azertyuiop suffered a bad overreach when beaten by Well Chief in the Celebration Chase and, though the injury at first looked likely to keep him off the course for twelve months, he didn't make it back to the racecourse, his retirement on veterinary advice announced in September. Well Chief had time on his side—he was still only six when winning the Celebration Chase—and his winning return in the totepool Game Spirit in February provided a very strong indication that he was still

totepool Game Spirit Chase, Newbury—a sparkling comeback by Well Chief, who is far too good for Ashley Brook

a top-notch chaser. Jumping well and racing with plenty of zest, Well Chief moved into the lead on the bridle at the third last and soon quickened clear, allowed to coast home after the last but still winning by eleven lengths and eight from the favourite Ashley Brook and Armaturk. The Tingle Creek runner-up Voy Por Ustedes, who faced a stiff task conceding weight all round, unseated his rider at the fifth.

Well Chief looked a Cheltenham Festival banker in the Queen Mother Champion Chase and was backed down to evens, the shortest-priced favourite over the four days. The previous year's winner Newmill, Voy Por Ustedes and Ashley Brook were the only others to start at shorter than 20/1 in the Champion Chase. The normally sure-footed Well Chief, who had fallen only once before, got no further than the second, crumpling on landing after seemingly taking the fence cleanly. He was the fourth big name in as many years to have his chance ended before the race had begun in earnest. Kauto Star, all the rage for the previous year's Champion Chase, took a heavy fall at the third; the year before that, Azertyuiop lost any chance of victory with a bad mistake at the sixth (the water jump), though he kept on for third behind Moscow Flyer and Well Chief; and, in the 2003/4 season, odds-on Moscow Flyer unseated his rider after belting the fourth last.

Well Chief was given a chance to make amends in the Melling Chase over two and a half miles at Aintree a little over four weeks later, a race Moscow Flyer had gone on to win (for the first time) after his Cheltenham mishap. Well Chief started odds on but it was his first start beyond seventeen furlongs and he clearly found the extra distance beyond him, getting to within striking distance of Monet's Garden at the second last, only to tire and eventually finish third, beaten three and a half lengths and nine by Monet's Garden and the Festival Trophy winner Taranis. Interestingly, jockey Timmy Murphy reportedly felt that the favourite wouldn't have won even if the race had been over two miles. Whether or not his Aintree flop was solely down to stamina, it must be stressed that Well Chief's form in the Game Spirit—not to mention his old form—suggests he would have been a clear-cut winner of the Queen Mother Champion Chase had he given his running (his

Newbury victim Ashley Brook was still very much in contention when falling at the last at Cheltenham). Still only eight, Well Chief should have plenty more opportunities to restore his reputation and, all being well, looks set to start his next campaign by taking on the versatile Kauto Star in the Tingle Creek at Sandown in December. Kauto Star is the best chaser around, head and shoulders above the rest of the current crop of staying chasers, but he wouldn't have much in hand at two miles over a top-form Well Chief. The Tingle Creek already appeals as potentially one of the most mouth-watering races of 2007/8.

Well Chief (GER) (ch.g. 1999)	Night Shift (USA) (b 1980)	Northern Dancer (b 1961)	Nearctic Natalma
		Ciboulette (b 1961)	Chop Chop Windy Answer
	Wellesiena (GER) (b 1994)	Scenic (b 1986)	Sadler's Wells Idyllic
		Weltkrone (ch 1982)	Lord Udo Weltdame

Well Chief is angular in appearance and of no more than medium size—not an obvious chaser on looks. He was purchased privately off the Flat in Germany at the end of his three-year-old days after winning twice at around a mile and a quarter, one of the races a listed event (he also acquitted himself well in Group 3 company). Well Chief was bred for the Flat, by the Coolmore stallion Night Shift out of Wellesiena who didn't win but was placed in a listed trial for the Preis der Diana. Well Chief's great grandam Weltdame, a minor winner, was a daughter of Welt-wunder who was runner-up in the Preis der Diana. The 1999 Musidora and Nassau winner Zahrat Dubai was a great granddaughter of Weltwunder. Well Chief was one

Mr D. A. Johnson's "Well Chief"

of the best juvenile hurdlers around in his first season with the Pipe stable, just touched off in the Triumph Hurdle and third in the Anniversary Hurdle. Rather surprisingly, Well Chief is by no means the first above-average juvenile hurdler who has gone on to achieve even greater success as a specialist two-mile chaser—Badsworth Boy, Barnbrook Again, Sybillin, Viking Flagship, Flagship Uberalles, Azertyuiop, Nickname and Voy Por Ustedes also ended their debut campaign over hurdles ranked in the top fifteen of their age group by Timeform. Well Chief made an immediate impact over fences and emulated Flagship Uberalles by completing the Arkle/Maghull double at Cheltenham and Aintree as a five-year-old. Well Chief won his Arkle—a race also won by Moscow Flyer and Azertyuiop—from Kicking King who went on to win the Cheltenham Gold Cup the following season when Well Chief was second in the Queen Mother Champion Chase. Notwithstanding his fall in the latest edition of that race, Well Chief has a good record at Cheltenham. Apart from finishing first or second on his first three Festival appearances, he also put up an epic performance under 11-10, conceding lumps of weight all round, to win the 2005 Victor Chandler Chase (transferred from Ascot during that course's redevelopment). Well Chief has run six times in all at Cheltenham and should probably have won a handicap there on his reappearance in his second season over fences, when narrowly beaten by Armaturk after being left with plenty to do. Well Chief tends to race freely—which may have contributed to his fall in the latest Champion—and is ridden with restraint (raced prominently in his hurdling days). He is always likely to prove best at around two miles and acts on soft and firm going. Usually a sound jumper, he is game and reliable. *D. E. Pipe*

WELL DEFINED 4 b.f. Barathea (IRE) – Serene View (USA) (Distant View (USA))   **F—**
[2006/7 F16v F12g Mar 23] 3,500 3-y-o: good-topped filly: second foal: dam French 1m winner: soundly beaten in bumpers. *T. H. Caldwell*

WELL DISGUISED (IRE) 5 b.m. Beneficial – Executive Move (IRE) (Executive   **F86**
Perk) [2006/7 F73: F16v F16m² F16v⁴ Jan 17] best effort in bumpers when 5 lengths fourth to Flora May in mares event at Newcastle: will stay beyond 2m. *D. W. Whillans*

WELLINGTON HALL (GER) 9 b.g. Halling (USA) – Wells Whisper (FR) (Sad-   **h77**
ler's Wells (USA)) [2006/7 16g 16vᵖᵘ Jan 12] angular gelding: fairly useful on Flat (stays 1¾m), below form in 2007: lightly raced over hurdles, little form since debut: tried blinkered. *M. Wigham*

WELL MOUNTED (IRE) 6 b.g. Saddlers' Hall (IRE) – Granny Clark (IRE) (Welsh   **h119**
Term) [2006/7 16s³ 16d⁵ 16d⁶ 16v² Feb 10] big, strong gelding: second foal: half-brother to winning chaser What'sonyourmind (by Glacial Storm), stays 25f: dam unraced sister to Festival Bumper winner/useful hurdler up to 2½m Wither Or Which, and half-sister to dam of top-class staying chaser Alexander Banquet: runner-up on debut: fairly useful hurdler: improved form in handicaps in 2006/7, best efforts when fifth of 20 to Acambo at Ascot (Ladbroke) and head second to Farmer Brown at Leopardstown: raced around 2m on going softer than good (acted on heavy): dead. *A. L. T. Moore, Ireland*

WELL PRESENTED (IRE) 9 ch.g. Presenting – Casualty Madame (Buckskin (FR))   **c— x**
[2006/7 c126x, h—: c20sF c25vF c25dᵖᵘ 22v Jan 28] strong, workmanlike gelding: win-   **h—**
ning hurdler/chaser, no form in 2006/7: has had tongue tied: not a fluent jumper over fences. *M. W. Easterby*

WELL TUTORED (IRE) 8 b.g. Master Willie – Knockaverry (IRE) (Kemal (FR))   **c123 x**
[2006/7 c112x: c19d* c24v⁴ c24v³ c29m Apr 9] lengthy, angular gelding: fairly useful handicap chaser: won at Naas (easily by 4 lengths from Allez Petit Luis) in November: creditable efforts in valuable events after, ninth to Butler's Cabin in Irish National at Fairyhouse: stays 29f: acts on good to firm and heavy going: makes mistakes. *A. L. T. Moore, Ireland*

WELSH DANE 7 b.g. Chaddleworth (IRE) – Dane Rose (Full of Hope) [2006/7 h84:   **c87**
24f⁵ 26mᵖᵘ 24m c16f* c17mF Aug 3] sparely-made gelding: maiden hurdler, no form in   **h—**
2006/7: won novice handicap at Worcester in July on chasing debut: close third when falling 2 out 2 weeks later: stays 3¼m, effective at much shorter: acts on any going: effective in cheekpieces/visor or without. *M. Sheppard*

WELSH DREAM 10 b.g. Mtoto – Morgannwg (IRE) (Simply Great (FR)) [2006/7   **h97**
h95: 16g⁶ 21m 20m⁵ 21m³ 21m* 22d² 21d⁵ 20v⁵ 21v Jan 9] useful-looking gelding: modest handicap hurdler: won at Sedgefield in September: stays 2¾m: acts on good to firm and good to soft going, not at best on softer: amateur ridden. *Miss S. E. Forster*

WELSH GUARD (USA) 4 ch.g. Silver Hawk (USA) – Royal Devotion (USA) (His **F76**
Majesty (USA)) [2006/7 aF13g F12v F13m⁴ Mar 29] 7,500 3-y-o: close-coupled, good-
bodied gelding: half-brother to several winners on Flat in USA: dam won in USA: little
form in bumpers. *G. P. Enright*

WELSH MAIN 10 br.g. Zafonic (USA) – Welsh Daylight (Welsh Pageant) [2006/7 **c105**
c103, h–: 19d⁵ c19d² c24g⁶ Feb 21] sturdy gelding: fair handicap hurdler/chaser: should **h103**
stay beyond 19f: acts on good to firm and good to soft going. *Miss Tor Sturgis*

WELSH WHISPER 8 b.m. Overbury (IRE) – Grugiar (Red Sunset) [2006/7 16gᵖᵘ **h–**
Jul 31] poor on Flat (stays 9.5f): jumped poorly on hurdling debut. *S. A. Brookshaw*

WEMBURY POINT (IRE) 5 gr.g. Monashee Mountain (USA) – Lady Celina (FR) **c–**
(Crystal Palace) [2006/7 h112?: 22m 20f² 16f⁶ c21sᵖᵘ c20m⁵ c17dᵖᵘ Oct 17] rather **h105**
leggy gelding: winning hurdler, largely below form in handicaps: no show in maiden
chases: stays 2½m: acts on firm and good to soft going (ran poorly on soft/heavy):
sometimes blinkered: tried tongue tied. *B. G. Powell*

WENCESLAS (IRE) 7 b.g. Un Desperado (FR) – Lady of The West (IRE) (Mister **c–**
Lord (USA)) [2006/7 c98, h–: c23mᵖᵘ Apr 22] tall, good sort: winning hurdler: form **h–**
over fences only when winning 3-finisher novice at Fontwell in December 2005 for Miss
H. Knight: walked over in point in April: stays 2½m: acts on soft going. *M. G. Hazell*

WENDYS DYNAMO 10 b.g. Opera Ghost – Good Appeal (Star Appeal) [2006/7 c81: **c67**
c26s⁵ Mar 11] fair pointer, won twice in 2007: novice hunter chaser. *Mrs Y. Watson*

WENGER (FR) 7 b.g. Unfuwain (USA) – Molly Dance (FR) (Groom Dancer (USA)) **c105 §**
[2006/7 h98: 20s 21s⁵ c16s² c16v* c17v² c16gᵖᵘ c16m² Apr 24] tall, useful-looking **h– §**
gelding: winning hurdler: fair handicap chaser: won novice event at Taunton in March:
best around 2m: probably acts on any going: tried in cheekpieces, usually blinkered: has
worn tongue strap: temperamental: sold 10,000 gns Doncaster May Sales. *P. Winkworth*

WENLOCKS WONDER 6 b.g. I'm Supposin (IRE) – Idiots Money (Idiot's Delight) **c–**
[2006/7 h90, F–: c17gᵖᵘ 16s² 21d⁴ 20sᵖᵘ 16s 16vᵖᵘ 20gᵖᵘ Apr 21] rather leggy, unfurn- **h97**
ished gelding: novice hurdler, modest form on occasions: no show on chasing debut:
should stay beyond 2m: raced on good going or softer: tongue tied last 3 outings.
K. C. Bailey

WENRUS LADY 6 b.m. Overbury (IRE) – Persian Symphony (IRE) (Persian Heights) **h–**
[2006/7 F–: F17d F13m F17m 20mᵖᵘ Jul 25] little impact in bumpers or mares novice **F–**
hurdle: tongue tied in 2006/7. *K. J. Burke*

WENSLEY BLUE (IRE) 8 b.g. Blues Traveller (IRE) – Almasa (Faustus (USA)) **c70**
[2006/7 c25s⁴ c27dᵘʳ c27dᵖᵘ 24v c25s* 24v Mar 9] big, good-topped gelding: poor **h67**
hurdler/chaser: won handicap over fences at Kelso in February: stays 25f: raced on good
ground or softer: tried in cheekpieces. *W. Amos*

WENSLEYDALE STAR 4 b.g. Alzao (USA) – Janiceland (IRE) (Foxhound (USA)) **h73**
[2006/7 17dᶠ 17g⁴ 17g⁵ 16s 16sᵘʳ Nov 19] strong, workmanlike gelding: poor maiden on
Flat (stays 1½m), left T. D. Barron after final start at 3 yrs: poor juvenile hurdler: raced
around 2m on good going or softer: in cheekpieces/blinkers last 2 starts. *B. J. Llewellyn*

WENSLEYDALE WEB 5 b.m. Kayf Tara – Little Red Spider (Bustino) [2006/7 F82: **h–**
F17s 19gᵖᵘ 17g 19d 20vᵖᵘ Jan 9] workmanlike mare: runner-up in bumper on debut: no **F–**
form since, mainly over hurdles. *M. E. Sowersby*

WEST BAY MIST 6 b.m. Relief Pitcher – West Bay Breeze (Town And Country) **h–**
[2006/7 F–: 20mᵖᵘ Jun 13] no sign of ability: tried in cheekpieces. *Mrs H. R. J. Nelmes*

WESTENDER (FR) 11 b.g. In The Wings – Trude (GER) (Windwurf (GER)) [2006/7 **c– §**
c–§, h151§: 23f* May 6] tall, close-coupled gelding: smart hurdler: won handicap at **h152 §**
Haydock in May by short head from Lord Sam: runner-up on completed start over fences
(refused first next time): stays 3m: probably acts on any going: wears blinkers/cheek-
pieces: temperamental. *M. C. Pipe*

WEST END FINAL 4 b.g. Kayf Tara – Fine Fettle (Final Straw) [2006/7 F16g Apr 7] **F–**
good-topped gelding: eighth foal: dam unraced: soundly beaten in bumper on debut.
J. L. Spearing

WEST END KING (IRE) 5 b.g. Old Vic – Last Princess (Le Prince) [2006/7 F16v* **F108 p**
Jan 12] €29,000 3-y-o: useful-looking gelding: half-brother to several winners, notably
smart chaser Strath Royal (by Furry Glen), stayed 3½m: dam, 2m winner on Flat/2½m
chase winner, half-sister to high-class 2m to 2½m chaser Artifice: promising debut when

winning 18-runner maiden bumper at Huntingdon in January by 5 lengths from Atouch-betweenacara, taken very wide: good prospect. *Miss H. C. Knight*

WEST END WONDER (IRE) 8 b.g. Idris (IRE) – Miss Plum (Ardross) [2006/7 h113: c19g³ c20g⁴ c19mᶠ c16mᶠ 22m c21g³ Apr 27] sturdy gelding: fair hurdler: modest maiden chaser (often let down by jumping): left D. Burchell after fifth outing, last of 3 in point in April: will stay 3m: acts on good to firm going. *Miss V. J. Nicholls*   **c99 x h86 +**

WESTER LODGE (IRE) 5 ch.g. Fraam – Reamzafonic (Grand Lodge (USA)) [2006/7 20d 19d 16v⁶ Jan 4] leggy gelding: fair handicapper on Flat (should stay 1¾m): never dangerous in novice hurdles. *J. M. P. Eustace*   **h61 +**

WESTERNMOST 9 b.g. Most Welcome – Dakota Girl (Northern State (USA)) [2006/7 c80§, h89§: c24dᵖᵘ c20f c19m 20m⁶ c19s³ c19s² Dec 29] workmanlike gelding: modest hurdler: poor novice chaser: stays easy 21f: acts on heavy and good to firm going: tried in cheekpieces. *K. Bishop*   **c76 § h79 §**

WESTERN PRIDE 4 b.f. Classic Cliche (IRE) – Llanfihangel Lass (Gildoran) [2006/7 F12s Dec 13] tall, lengthy, unfurnished filly: third foal: dam unraced: well beaten in 3-y-o bumper on debut. *R. H. Buckler*   **F–**

WESTFIELD DANCER (IRE) 8 b.g. Danehill Dancer (IRE) – Morning Blush (IRE) (Glow (USA)) [2006/7 c16m² c16fᵖᵘ c16g³ c18g 18m³ 17g² 21g* Apr 23] ex-Irish gelding: modest maiden chaser/handicap hurdler: off over 5 months, improved form when winning selling event at Plumpton (by 25 lengths) in April: stays 21f: acts on firm ground: often in headgear. *Evan Williams*   **c90 h93**

WESTFIELD JOHN 12 ch.g. Little Wolf – Moonbreaker (Twilight Alley) [2006/7 c31gᵖᵘ May 24] big, workmanlike gelding: no show over hurdles: maiden chaser: successful in point in March: stays 3¼m: blinkered last 2 starts. *J. M. Turner*   **c– h–**

WESTGATE (IRE) 5 b.g. Saddlers' Hall (IRE) – Jasmin Path (Warpath) [2006/7 F–: F16d F17d⁵ 16gᵖᵘ 16g 19s 17g² 16v² 17s³ 19s³ 16d 19m⁴ Apr 28] big, lengthy gelding: chasing type: little impact in bumpers: modest maiden hurdler: stays 19f: acts on heavy going: temperamental. *S. Gollings*   **h95 § F75**

WESTGROVE BERRY (IRE) 7 br.m. Presenting – Mulberry (IRE) (Denel (FR)) [2006/7 F88: 16s⁵ 16s* 16s 16v² 16g* Apr 23] bumper winner: fair hurdler: won mares events at Leicester (novice, easily) in December and Hexham (handicap, beat Florazine by 10 lengths) in April: should stay at least 2½m: raced on good going or softer (acts on heavy). *N. G. Richards*   **h113**

WEST HIGHLAND WAY (IRE) 6 b.g. Foxhound (USA) – Gilding The Lily (IRE) (High Estate) [2006/7 16s 20g 20s 23gᵘʳ Apr 3] fairly useful on Flat (stays 1m) at 3 yrs for I. Semple, well held only 2 outings since: little show over hurdles: in cheekpieces final start. *Mrs H. O. Graham*   **h60**

WEST HILL (IRE) 6 b.g. Gone West (USA) – Altamura (USA) (El Gran Senor (USA)) [2006/7 h74: c17g³ c16d⁴ c16d c16dᵖᵘ Nov 16] good-topped gelding: poor hurdler/maiden chaser: raced around 2m: acted on soft and good to firm going: usually tongue tied: dead. *D. McCain Jnr*   **c78 h–**

WESTMEATH FLYER 12 b.g. Deploy – Re-Release (Baptism) [2006/7 c–, h111: 21m* c23s³ c20d* 26d c20f* c23gᵖᵘ Jul 23] sturdy gelding: fair hurdler: won seller at Southwell in May: similar form over fences: won maiden at Sedgefield later that month and novice at Perth in July: lame final start: stays 3m: acts on any going: wears cheekpieces nowadays. *P. A. Blockley*   **c111 h98 +**

WESTMERE 7 b.g. Alderbrook – Moonlight Air (Bold Owl) [2006/7 24g⁵ 24d³ 24vᵖᵘ 24dᵖᵘ Oct 22] modest form over hurdles: will stay beyond 3m: blinkered final start (looked temperamental). *J. L. Spearing*   **h85 §**

WESTMORLAND (IRE) 11 b.g. Phardante (FR) – Ticking Over (IRE) (Decent Fellow) [2006/7 c–, h–: 24g 24v² 24vᵖᵘ 27v 27v⁴ 22v 24v Mar 15] good-topped gelding: fell only outing over fences: poor handicap hurdler, left D. MacLeod and off 6 months after first start: should stay beyond 3m: acts on heavy going: in cheekpieces/visor last 3 starts. *James Moffatt*   **c– h82**

WEST RIDGE 6 ch.g. Ridgewood Ben – Western Ploy (Deploy) [2006/7 F95: F16d⁶ F16g* F16d⁶ 16gᵖᵘ Mar 30] quite good-topped gelding: fairly useful form in bumpers, won at Wincanton in December: suffered suspected fractured pelvis on hurdling debut. *B. G. Powell*   **h– F98**

WESTWOOD LIR 10 b.m. Lir – Brandy Season (High Season) [2006/7 22mᵖᵘ Jul 17] no show in points/mares novice hurdle. *Mrs S. Gardner*   **h–**

WHALEEF 9 b.g. Darshaan – Wilayif (USA) (Danzig (USA)) [2006/7 c99§, h–: c16g^{pu} 20m^{pu} 16m^3 19m^6 Jul 17] good-topped gelding: modest handicap chaser: winning hurdler, only poor form in 2006/7: raced mainly around 2m: acts on good to firm and good to soft going: effective in cheekpieces or not: often tongue tied: inconsistent. *B. J. Llewellyn*   **c– §**
h84 §

WHAT A BLAZE (IRE) 7 b.m. Oscar (IRE) – Imightn'imightn't (IRE) (Executive Perk) [2006/7 F–: F16d Nov 3] workmanlike mare: tailed off in bumpers. *Robert Gray*   **F–**

WHATABOUTYA (IRE) 6 br.g. Eve's Error – Tara's Tribe (Good Thyne (USA)) [2006/7 F18f* F17f^3 16d^F 20g^4 24m* 24m^6 Apr 26] €11,000 4-y-o: rather leggy gelding: fifth foal: brother to 27f hurdle winner Lord of The Track: dam modest 2½m hurdler: successful in bumper at Fairyhouse in June on debut: progressive over hurdles, winning maiden at Bellewstown in August: fairly useful form when sixth of 24 to Sonnyanjoe in handicap at Punchestown 8 months later: stays 3m: acts on firm ground. *N. Meade, Ireland*   **h115**
F98

WHAT A BUZZ 5 ch.g. Zaha (CAN) – G'Ime A Buzz (Electric) [2006/7 F16v^2 F16s^3 F16s^4 aF16g Mar 9] angular gelding: fifth foal: half-brother to 2-y-o 7f winner Cosmic Buzz (by Cosmonaut) and winning pointer by Alflora: dam, winning hurdler, stayed 2½m: fair form in bumpers, looking a stayer. *P. W. D'Arcy*   **F92**

WHATALOTWEGOT (IRE) 7 b.g. Saddlers' Hall (IRE) – Lady Claire (IRE) (Buckley) [2006/7 20s^4 24m 22g 24d^6 24s^{ur} 26s 22s^{pu} Feb 3] ex-Irish gelding: third foal: dam unraced: modest novice hurdler, left M. Morris after fifth start: stayed 3m: acted on soft going: tried in cheekpieces: dead. *D. J. Wintle*   **h92**

WHAT A MONDAY 9 b.g. Beveled (USA) – Raise Memories (Skyliner) [2006/7 h–: 20g^6 20d 23d^3 Nov 8] lengthy, angular gelding: bumper winner: modest novice hurdler: stays 23f: raced on good going or softer. *P. G. Murphy*   **h93**

WHAT A NATIVE (IRE) 11 b.g. Be My Native (USA) – Yukon Lil (Yankee Gold) [2006/7 c125, h–: 24s 23s^6 c24v c24d c33v^{pu} Feb 24] compact gelding: winning hurdler: fairly useful handicap chaser, little form since early-2006: stays 29f: raced on good going or softer (acts on heavy). *C. F. Swan, Ireland*   **c116**
h87

WHAT A SCIENTIST (IRE) 7 b.g. Karinga Bay – Half Irish (Carlingford Castle) [2006/7 20d^3 22d 24v* 20v* 24g Apr 18] €10,000 4-y-o: well-made gelding: will make a chaser: first foal: dam unraced, out of half-sister to Desert Orchid: won maiden Irish point in 2006: bought £25,000 Cheltenham April Sales: fair novice hurdler: won at Towcester in January and Chepstow (responded well to strong ride when beating Pyleigh Lady by ½ length) in February: looks a thorough stayer: acts well on heavy going. *T. R. George*   **h114**

WHATASHOCK 12 b.g. Never So Bold – Lady Electric (Electric) [2006/7 c93: c21g^3 c21g^{pu} May 16] medium-sized gelding: fair hunter chaser: stays 21f: acts on good to soft going: has folded tamely. *Mrs H. M. Tory*   **c89**

WHAT A VINTAGE (IRE) 7 ch.m. Un Desperado (FR) – The Vine Browne (IRE) (Torus) [2006/7 h108, F88: 21g^4 c24d^{pu} Dec 4] winning hurdler, fair form at best: travelling strongly in narrow lead when going wrong before 2 out in novice at Fakenham on chasing debut: should stay beyond 21f: raced on good ground or softer (bumper winner on heavy): likely to do better over fences if recovering from injury. *R. T. Phillips*   **c95 p**
h90

WHATCANISAY 8 b.g. Morpeth – Supreme Daughter (Supreme Leader) [2006/7 h–, F75: 19m^{pu} May 11] compact gelding: third in bumper: little impact over hurdles: won maiden point in March. *J. D. Frost*   **h–**

WHATCANYASAY 6 br.g. Prince Daniel (USA) – Snowys Pet (Petong) [2006/7 h–: 20g c22m^{pu} c16d^2 24v^{pu} 16v^4 c16v^{pu} c20g* c20g c27g^{pu} Apr 23] little form over hurdles: poor chaser: won handicap at Sedgefield in March: stays easy 2½m: usually in cheekpieces. *Mrs E. Slack*   **c78**
h57

WHAT DO'IN (IRE) 9 b. or br.g. Good Thyne (USA) – Della Wee (IRE) (Fidel) [2006/7 c20d^F c24g^{pu} 24v^5 20s^5 24s^5 24s^{pu} Apr 25] quite good-topped gelding: won amateur novice on hurdling debut in 2004/5: disappointing since (failed to complete both starts over fences), often failing to impress with attitude: needs treating with caution. *N. A. Twiston-Davies*   **c– §**
h84 §

WHAT'SONYOURMIND (IRE) 7 b.g. Glacial Storm (USA) – Granny Clark (IRE) (Welsh Term) [2006/7 h92: c19g* c22v^2 c24v^{pu} c19s^5 Dec 26] lengthy gelding: bumper winner: modest maiden hurdler: similar form over fences: won novice handicap at Towcester in November: stays 25f: raced on good going or softer (acts on heavy). *Jonjo O'Neill*   **c90**
h–

WHATS UP MAID 10 b.m. Emperor Fountain – Roman Maid (Roman Warrior) [2006/7 c–: c19m May 9] winning pointer: well held completed start in novice hunter chases. *Mrs Jo Sleep* **c69**

WHATUTHINK (IRE) 5 ch.g. Presenting – Glen's Encore (IRE) (Orchestra) [2006/7 F16s³ F16s² F19v* F16g Mar 14] rather unfurnished gelding: second foal: dam unraced sister to useful hurdler/fairly useful chaser Glens Music, stayed 2½m: useful form in bumpers: won maiden at Naas in January by 19 lengths from Oscar Supreme: mid-field in Grade 1 at Cheltenham (on toes, took good hold 2 months later): will stay at least 2½m. *Oliver McKiernan, Ireland* **F107**

WHEELAVIT (IRE) 4 b.g. Elnadim (USA) – Storm River (USA) (Riverman (USA)) [2006/7 16g 17g³ 16g³ Apr 27] fair on Flat (stays 1¼m), successful in July: modest form over hurdles. *B. G. Powell* **h89**

WHENALLELSEFAILS 6 b.g. Petoski – Miss Counsel (Leading Counsel (USA)) [2006/7 F16g Dec 26] second foal: dam unraced daughter of fairly useful staying chaser Culm Port: well held in bumper on debut. *C. J. Down* **F—**

WHEN YOUR READYLES (IRE) 7 b.g. Oscar (IRE) – Bellusis (Belfalas) [2006/7 h–: 20s 24s^{pu} Nov 25] sturdy, good-bodied gelding: little impact over hurdles: left M. Todhunter, lost confidence after blundering ninth in handicap on chasing debut. *F. P. Murtagh* **c—** **h—**

WHEREAREYOUNOW (IRE) 10 ch.g. Mister Lord (USA) – Angie's Delight (London Gazette) [2006/7 c–, h–: c26s⁶ c21s* c24s c22s* c20g⁵ Mar 24] workmanlike gelding: fairly useful handicap chaser nowadays: sold out of N. Twiston-Davies' stable 21,000 gns Doncaster May Sales after first outing: won conditional jockeys event at Cheltenham in December and amateur race at Kelso (by 1¼ lengths from Getinbybut-onlyjust) in February: effective at 2½m to 25f: very best efforts on going softer than good (acts on heavy): tried blinkered/tongue tied: sound jumper: usually races prominently. *B. G. Powell* **c122** **h—**

WHERE NOW (IRE) 11 b.g. Cataldi – Its A Honey (Raise You Ten) [2006/7 c21g³ Apr 12] tall gelding: prolific winner in points: fair chaser: creditable third of 27 to Scots Grey in Fox Hunters' at Aintree: stays 3m: acts on soft going: tried in blinkers/cheek-pieces. *John Queally, Ireland* **c108** **h—**

WHERE NOW MADAME 4 b.f. Exit To Nowhere (USA) – Hot 'n Saucy (El Conquistador) [2006/7 aF16g Mar 21] first foal: dam, fairly useful hurdler, stayed 21f: seventh to Aux Le Bahnn in bumper at Lingfield on debut. *J. C. Tuck* **F75**

WHERESBEN (IRE) 8 b.g. Flemensfirth (USA) – Chataka Blues (IRE) (Sexton Blake) [2006/7 20s² 22v² 20s 23v 19v³ 24s³ 20v* 19v* c20v⁵ 20m^{pu} Apr 24] stocky gelding: useful hurdler: won minor event at Punchestown in February and handicap at Naas (beat Camden Tanner a neck) in March: last of 5 finishers in Grade 3 at Navan on chasing debut: stays 3m: acts on heavy going: should do better over fences. *Seamus Fahey, Ireland* **c110 p** **h131**

WHERE'S DEXTER (IRE) 7 ch.g. Aahsaylad – De-Veers Currie (IRE) (Glenstal (USA)) [2006/7 22s^{pu} Feb 3] first foal: dam, 1¼m winner, half-sister to useful staying hurdler Loch Scavaig: no show in maiden hurdle on debut. *Miss J. S. Davis* **h—**

WHERES JOHNNY 6 gr.g. Touch of Grey – Lady Poly (Dunbeath (USA)) [2006/7 aF16g Mar 21] third foal: half-brother to 2m hurdle winner Blayney Dancer (by Contract Law): dam winner up to 2½m over hurdles: eighth of 13 in bumper on debut. *Jamie Poulton* **F79**

WHERE'S MY BABY (IRE) 5 b. or br.g. Good Thyne (USA) – Furry Dream (Furry Glen) [2006/7 F77: F16d³ F17g⁵ 21s^{pu} 21m 21s Feb 9] rather unfurnished gelding: placed in bumpers: never dangerous 3 starts over hurdles. *Jonjo O'Neill* **h74** **F79**

WHERE'S TRIGGER 7 ch.g. Aristocracy – Queens Connection (Bay Express) [2006/7 20g⁵ 16v 16s Mar 1] sixth in bumper: off nearly 2 years, well held over hurdles. *N. A. Twiston-Davies* **h—**

WHERE THERES SMOKE (IRE) 6 b.g. Executive Perk – Down The Garden (IRE) (Good Thyne (USA)) [2006/7 24m^{pu} May 6] sixth foal: dam unraced half-sister to useful staying chaser Darkorjon: dropped away after 2 out in novice hurdle at Hexham on debut. *J. Howard Johnson* **h—**

WHICH POCKET (IRE) 9 br.g. Norwich – Toran Pocket (Proverb) [2006/7 c86: c21g c20g* c22g² c21g⁴ c21g² Apr 27] lengthy gelding: winning pointer: fairly useful novice chaser: largely progressive in 2006/7, winning maiden at Fontwell in March by **c121**

3½ lengths from Highglen: best effort when fourth to Ofarel d'Airy in novice handicap at Cheltenham: should prove as effective at 3m as shorter: raced on good/good to firm going: tried visored. *B. G. Powell*

WHICH WAY NOW (IRE) 7 ch.g. Anshan – Pegus Gold (Strong Gale) [2006/7   **c101** c24g² May 5] fifth foal: half-brother to bumper winner Triple Rum (by Be My Native): dam placed in bumpers: fairly useful pointer: in frame in Ireland in 2005 prior to winning all 3 starts in Britain in 2006: 6 lengths second to Abbey Days in novice hunter at Bangor on chase debut: dead. *Mrs Edward Crow*

WHISKY IN THE JAR (IRE) 6 b.g. Right Win (IRE) – Princess Cellina (IRE) (Jolly   **c59** Jake (NZ)) [2006/7 h–: c21s⁶ c20m⁴ c20f^ur Jul 16] successful twice in points, including in   **h–** February: little show otherwise, left P. Grindrod after chase debut. *S. J. Marshall*

WHISPERED PROMISES (USA) 6 b.g. Real Quiet (USA) – Anna's Honor (USA)   **h141** (Alleged (USA)) [2006/7 h137: 16s⁶ 16s² 20s² 21s^pu 16d³ 17g 20g Apr 14] rather leggy, close-coupled gelding: useful hurdler: good efforts in 2006/7 when placed, second at Sandown (to Overstrand in William Hill Handicap) and Haydock and third in listed event won by Detroit City back at Sandown: stays 2½m: acts on soft going: races prominently. *R. S. Brookhouse*

WHISPERED SECRET (GER) 8 b.g. Selkirk (USA) – Wells Whisper (FR)   **c132** (Sadler's Wells (USA)) [2006/7 c135, h122: c21v⁴ c23m⁵ c23g c26m⁴ c17s³ c21v* 22d²   **h133** Feb 3] rather leggy gelding: useful handicap hurdler/chaser: landed gamble in Ladbrokes Trophy Chase at Cheltenham (all fences in straight omitted because of low sun) in January by ½ length from New Alco: best effort over hurdles when ½-length second of

Mr David Manasseh's "Whispered Secret"

16 to Taranis (FR) in valuable handicap at Sandown week later: stays 2¾m: unraced on firm ground, acts on any other. *D. E. Pipe*

WHISPERING HOLLY 8 b.g. Holly Buoy – Stuart's Gem (Meldrum) [2006/7 21m 21m 19g⁵ 24gᵖᵘ Nov 10] good-bodied gelding: maiden hurdler, no solid form in 2006/7: ungenuine. *R. S. Wood* **h– §**

WHISPERING MOOR 8 br.g. Terimon – Larksmore (Royal Fountain) [2006/7 24sᵖᵘ May 17] tall, good sort: awarded amateur handicap hurdle final in 2004/5: no show only start since: stays 3m: acts on heavy ground. *N. G. Richards* **h–**

WHIST DRIVE 7 ch.g. First Trump – Fine Quill (Unfuwain (USA)) [2006/7 21sᵖᵘ Dec 7] rather leggy gelding: fair hurdler: broke down halfway in handicap at Huntingdon: stays 23f: acts on soft going, probably on good to firm. *Mrs N. Smith* **h–**

WHISTLE BLOWING (IRE) 5 ch.g. Forzando – Philgwyn (Milford) [2006/7 h100: 20d³ 20g⁴ 16m⁴ 20m⁴ 17m² 17m² 22m³ Aug 26] workmanlike gelding: modest maiden hurdler, in frame all bar first of 12 starts, though below best in 2006/7 after first outing: stays 2½m: acts on good to firm and good to soft going: tried in cheekpieces. *D. McCain Jnr* **h98 d**

WHISTLING FRED 8 b.g. Overbury (IRE) – Megabucks (Buckskin (FR)) [2006/7 h89: 16g 19gᵖᵘ Mar 23] lengthy gelding: novice hurdler, lightly raced: raced mainly around 2m. *B. De Haan* **h–**

WHISTLING SONG 12 ch.m. True Song – Sancal (Whistlefield) [2006/7 c16m⁵ Jun 14] lightly raced and little form over fences. *R. Dickin* **c–**

WHITE DOVE (FR) 9 b.m. Beaudelaire (USA) – Hermine And Pearls (FR) (Shirley Heights) [2006/7 c–, h87: 24g May 14] winning chaser: modest handicap hurdler: stays easy 2½m: acts on soft and good to firm going: effective blinkered/visored or not. *Ian Williams* **c– h–**

WHITE GATE (IRE) 5 b.g. Bob Back (USA) – Mount Sackville (Whistling Deer) [2006/7 F16d⁴ F17v⁵ 22sᵖᵘ Dec 23] third foal: half-brother to fair hurdler Ballyjohnboy Lord (by Arctic Lord), stays 27f: dam maiden half-sister to very smart staying chaser/ smart hurdler Sackville: won maiden Irish point in 2006: fair form in bumpers: no show in maiden on hurdling debut: should be suited by 2½m+. *T. R. George* **h– F91**

WHITE LIGHTENING (IRE) 4 ch.g. Indian Ridge – Mille Miglia (IRE) (Caerleon (USA)) [2006/7 16g⁶ 16m⁴ 16v 16g Feb 2] compact gelding: lightly raced on Flat, best effort when second over 9f: raced from first 2 starts in juvenile hurdles: raced at 2m: acts on good to firm going. *J. Howard Johnson* **h87**

WHITENZO (FR) 11 b.g. Lesotho (USA) – Whitengy (FR) (Olantengy (FR)) [2006/7 c123, h–: c25d⁴ c24s² c25d* c25f* Apr 5] tall gelding: useful hunter chaser nowadays: easily won at Exeter in March and Wincanton (beat Trade Off by 20 lengths) in April: stays 29f: acts on any going: blinkered once (ran poorly): tongue tied. *P. F. Nicholls* **c117 + h–**

WHITEOAK (IRE) 4 b.f. Oscar (IRE) – Gayla Orchestra (Lord Gayle (USA)) [2006/7 F14v² F16v³ F12g* F17g Apr 13] €25,000 3-y-o: unfurnished filly: half-sister to useful hurdler Kinnescash (by Persian Heights), stayed 3m, and 2m hurdle winner Porak (by Perugino): dam Irish 2m winner: fairly useful form in bumpers: won 4-y-o event at Newbury in March by length from Fresh Air And Fun: hung left when well held in listed mares race at Aintree final start. *D. McCain Jnr* **F95**

WHITE ON BLACK (GER) 6 b.g. Lomitas – White On Red (GER) (Konigsstuhl (GER)) [2006/7 h107: 16s 16g⁶ Mar 16] smallish gelding: fair hurdler: raced around 2m on good going or softer. *G. L. Moore* **h106**

WHITE PARK BAY (IRE) 7 b.m. Blues Traveller (IRE) – Valiant Friend (USA) (Shahrastani (USA)) [2006/7 24mᵖᵘ 16m⁴ 17m 24gᵖᵘ 22vᵖᵘ c24v Jan 27] good-topped mare: maiden on Flat: no form over hurdles/in maiden chase: sold out of J. Magee's stable €3,000 Fairyhouse August Sales, won mares maiden point in October: tried tongue tied. *Leo J. Temple, Ireland* **c– h–**

WHITFORD DON (IRE) 9 b.g. Accordion – Whitford Breeze (Le Bavard (FR)) [2006/7 c117§, h–§: 27d⁵ c26gᵖᵘ c24dᵘʳ c26sᵖᵘ 20s 24s 24s 24v* 24v* c28gᶠ Apr 7] well-made gelding: fairly useful chaser at best: fair handicap hurdler, left A. Carroll after second outing and K. Burke after sixth: back to form when winning at Towcester in February, and followed up at Chepstow in March: stayed 3¼m: raced on good going or softer (acted on heavy): often wore headgear (also tried tongue tied) but not for final 2 victories: temperamental: dead. *Miss C. Dyson* **c– § h113 §**

WHITGIFT ROCK 6 b.g. Piccolo – Fly South (Polar Falcon (USA)) [2006/7 21m⁴ 16f³ Sep 17] fair on Flat (barely stays 1½m): better effort over hurdles when third in novice at Plumpton. *S. Dow* **h89**

WHO CARES WINS 11 ch.g. Kris – Anne Bonny (Ajdal (USA)) [2006/7 h79: 20m⁴ 20m² 22m² Sep 2] sparely-made gelding: modest hurdler: won point in April: stays 2¾m: acts on soft and good to firm going: wears cheekpieces/visor. *J. R. Jenkins* **h90**

WHO DARES (IRE) 9 b.g. Toulon – Rare Weed (Frigid Aire) [2006/7 c92, h–: c20f c20mᵖᵘ Apr 25] maiden hurdler/chaser: tried blinkered/in cheekpieces/tongue tied. *Jonjo O'Neill* **c– h–**

WHO ELSE KNEW (IRE) 7 b.g. Broken Hearted – Fosseleen (IRE) (Supreme Leader) [2006/7 c21g2 May 24] fair pointer, successful twice in 2007: favourite, short-head second to Hercules Morse in novice hunter at Folkestone on chase debut. *J. W. Dufosee* **c87**

WHOSETHATFOR (IRE) 7 b.g. Beneficial – Native Craft (IRE) (Be My Native (USA)) [2006/7 h98, F91: 20d⁴ 20v⁵ 21sᵖᵘ Mar 11] modest novice hurdler: struck into himself final outing: stays 2½m: raced on ground softer than good. *J. A. B. Old* **h98**

WHYSO MAYO (IRE) 10 b.g. Kasmayo – Why Cry (Pry) [2006/7 c125: c24s* c24v* c26g² c29m Apr 9] compact, good-bodied gelding: prolific winning pointer: smart hunter chaser, won Foxhunter at Cheltenham in 2005/6: successful at Thurles in January and Leopardstown in February: better than ever when ½-length second to Drombeag in latest renewal of Foxhunter, despite jumping far from fluently after blundering first: below form in Irish National at Fairyhouse on handicap debut: should stay beyond 3¼m: acts on heavy and good to firm ground: prone to errors. *Raymond Hurley, Ireland* **c131**

WHY THE BIG PAWS 9 ch.m. Minster Son – Springdale Hall (USA) (Bates Motel (USA)) [2006/7 c84+, h–: 24g c25v² c24mᶠ c24s⁴ c24d* c25s⁴ c25sᵖᵘ c25g Nov 29] lengthy, angular mare: maiden hurdler: fair handicap chaser: best effort when winning at Carlisle (by distance) in October: ran poorly last 2 outings: stays 25f: acts on good to firm and heavy going: in cheekpieces last 3 starts: usually races prominently. *R. C. Guest* **c111 h–**

WHY THE LONG FACE (NZ) 10 ch.g. Grosvenor (NZ) – My Charm (NZ) (My Friend Paul (USA)) [2006/7 c99x, h104: 16m⁵ May 6] leggy gelding: fair handicap hurdler/chaser on his day, often let down by jumping over fences: stays 21f: acts on heavy and good to firm going: usually wears headgear: has taken little interest: sold 500 gns Doncaster August Sales. *R. C. Guest* **c– x h91 §**

WICHITA BRAVE (IRE) 5 ch.m. Rudimentary (USA) – Monks Flight (Monksfield) [2006/7 F17mᵖᵘ Apr 15] £1,600 4-y-o, resold £1,800 4-y-o: fourth foal: half-sister to fairly useful hurdler around 2m Captain Dee Cee (by Dromod Hill): dam ran twice: bled in bumper on debut. *K. A. Morgan* **F–**

WICHITA LINEMAN (IRE) 6 b.g. King's Theatre (IRE) – Monumental Gesture (Head For Heights) [2006/7 F109+: 20d* 21d² 21d* 20v* 24g* 24g² Apr 13] **h152 p**
The average prize money per race (£132,000) at the latest Cheltenham Festival exceeded that for any other three-, four- or five-day fixture, Flat or jumping, in Britain and Ireland. The fundamental attraction of the immensely popular Festival—attendances of 55,903, 55,215, 55,023 and 65,921 over the four days (slightly down on 2006)—is that, traditionally, it has been the stage for jumping's prospective champions to meet. Timeform opposed the expansion from three days to four in 2005 because it seemed that the overall quality of the racing was unlikely to be maintained. From a purist's angle, there was simply no reason to add another day, though commercial arguments were always going to win the day. Cheltenham produced a review of the four-day format after the latest Festival, the third since the extra day was introduced. The report purported to show that extending the Festival had not compromised the quality of the event, the median BHB mark of the runners (of which there were around 100 extra) being maintained at the same level and, using similar criteria, the five new races all proving successful. Two of the new races—the Festival Trophy, which replaced the Cathcart, and the Spa Hurdle— have been promoted from Grade 2 to Grade 1 status from the next season after qualifying by virtue of the BHB marks allotted to their winners over the three years.
A better way of assessing the success or otherwise of the four-day format is to look at the competitiveness of the races. The Festival Trophy has been a qualified success and is a better race than the Cathcart (which was latterly restricted to

Ballymore Properties Challow Novices' Hurdle, Cheltenham—
Wichita Lineman (white face) stays on too strongly for Sir Jimmy Shand

novices and second-season chasers), but, as the essay on the latest winner Taranis points out, the race attracted something of a hotch-potch of runners that would either have been almost equally as well catered for by the Queen Mother Champion Chase or the Gold Cup, or by some of the handicaps at the meeting. The BHB assessments of its winners may technically qualify the Festival Trophy for Grade 1 status, but it isn't worthy of equal billing with the Champion Chase and the Gold Cup. Of the four new races added to the programme (the essay on United discusses the new mares hurdle to be added in 2008), the Fred Winter Juvenile Handicap Hurdle and the Jewson Novices' Handicap Chase have been good additions, having no seriously adverse effects on longer-established races at the meeting. The cross country chase was always a questionable addition and is the worst race at the Festival and a weak betting event. The fourth completely new race was the Spa Hurdle for novices over three miles which gave those needing further than two miles an alternative to the two-mile-five-furlong race now registered as the Baring Bingham (formerly the Royal & SunAlliance Novices' Hurdle). Unfortunately, the Spa provides an opportunity for the leading staying novice hurdlers to avoid each other, as in 2006 when Black Jack Ketchum was kept apart from Denman and Nicanor, and in 2007 when Wichita Lineman was sent for the longer race, leaving the finish of the Baring Bingham to be fought out by two horses who had filled the places behind him in the Classic Novices' Hurdle over the course in January. Both the Baring Bingham and the Spa have been well supported and competitive, but the prestige of the Baring Bingham has been affected and will suffer further when the Spa becomes a Grade 1.

The Baring Bingham—named after a former owner of Cheltenham race-course—more than served its purpose as a championship event in its days as the Royal & SunAlliance, as well as being a testing ground for future stars. The 2003 winner, for example, was Hardy Eustace who went on to win the next two Champion Hurdles, while those behind him included the next year's Irish Champion Hurdle winner Foreman and three others, Pizarro, Nil Desperandum and Hi Cloy, who were also successful in Grade 1 novice events over fences, as well as the next Betfred Gold Cup winner Puntal and the likes of Lord Sam, Sh Boom, Calling Brave and Mossy Green. Istabraq, by the way, won the race before taking three successive Champion Hurdles and his name might have been a better one to have given to the race when Royal & SunAlliance pulled out. If the Spa and the Baring Bingham are both to have Grade 1 status, there needs to be a clearer distinction between them. There is only three furlongs difference between them at present and the distance of the Spa needs extending beyond three miles or, if it is felt that such a move would make it too stiff a test for novices, it should remain as a Grade 2. The Spa, incidentally, is run over the same course and distance as the World Hurdle, which, as outlined in the essay on Inglis Drever, would also be more of a race for true stayers if it was run over an extended three and a quarter miles, the same distance as the Gold Cup. Extending the distance of the World Hurdle would create a clearer opening for the open conditions hurdle, along the lines of the Festival Trophy for chasers, suggested again in the essay on United.

An open conditions hurdle for four-year-olds and upwards, over two and a half miles or so, was among the new races suggested in a paper submitted by Timeform in October 2002 (as part of a wide consultation process undertaken by Cheltenham) in an attempt to suggest a programme that might minimize the inevitable watering down caused by the addition of a fourth day to the Festival. A valuable two-mile handicap for juveniles (the Fred Winter), a two-and-a-half-mile novice handicap chase (the Jewson) and a two-and-a-half-mile novice handicap hurdle were other races suggested in the paper, which also identified the need for an opportunity at the Festival for the seasoned, out-and-out staying handicap chasers who have no suitable Festival target at present. A very valuable open handicap chase over four miles—suggested as an alternative to the National Hunt Chase in its current form—is discussed in the essay on Butler's Cabin. Although both the William Hill Trophy and the Fulke Walwyn Kim Muir Challenge Cup were oversubscribed at the latest Festival, the two races cater for the same type of horses and are over the same distance. An amalgamation, first suggested in *Chasers &*

Ballymore Properties Novices' Hurdle (Classic), Cheltenham—another convincing display as he beats Tidal Bay (right), Massini's Maguire (partially hidden) and Osana (left)

Hurdlers 1996/97, might smooth the way for the proposed four-miler. Cheltenham's proposals for the 2008 Festival, incidentally, include moving the National Hunt Chase to the Wednesday, when it would be run on the Old Course, and staging the Fulke Walwyn Kim Muir on the Thursday. Thursday's programme, which has the World Hurdle as its centre piece, is the weakest of the four and swopping one amateurs race for another will do nothing to improve it, whereas the historical National Hunt Chase repackaged as one of the more important open handicaps of the season with huge betting appeal certainly would. And there is undoubtedly room for the two-and-a-half-mile open conditions hurdle—there were thirty-four eliminations from the latest Coral Cup, twenty-five from the County, sixteen from the Pertemps Final and a total of forty-two from the two juvenile hurdles, the Triumph (back to full strength with a maximum field of twenty-four) and the Fred Winter, not to mention five from the Spa.

For the first time in three runnings, the Spa Hurdle took more winning than its Grade 1 rival, the Baring Bingham carrying a first prize that was worth half as much again. Despite that, connections of the season's two highest-rated novice hurdlers at the time, Wichita Lineman and Flight Leader, opted for the Spa, decisions which detracted from the nominated championship event. Wichita Lineman had been successful on three of his four outings, improving on the useful form he had shown in bumpers in his first season, which had included two impressive successes (amateur ridden) at Newbury before managing only mid-division at the Cheltenham and Aintree Festivals. Wichita Lineman's campaign in novice hurdles began with a seven-length victory over Silverburn at Aintree in October and a narrow defeat, conceding 3 lb, by Massini's Maguire at the Cheltenham Open meeting in November. Wichita Lineman jumped soundly on both occasions and showed a good turn of foot after being waited with.

Stepped up to Grade 1 company in the Ballymore Properties Challow Hurdle at Newbury in late-December, Wichita Lineman got the better of a duel with the favourite Sir Jimmy Shand in the home straight, staying on stoutly after leading three out to win by eight lengths (Massini's Maguire back in fifth). The Challow is run over two miles five furlongs and Wichita Lineman gave the strong impression he would be even better suited by a longer trip, responding gamely after travelling less well than some five out. Wichita Lineman had one more race before the Festival (where the Spa was always his intended target). Returned to Cheltenham

Brit Insurance Novices' Hurdle (Spa), Cheltenham—
Wichita Lineman already has the measure of Black Harry when left clear by that rival's last-flight fall

Mr John P. McManus' "Wichita Lineman"

for the Grade 2 Classic Novices' Hurdle, sponsored by Ballymore Properties, on what is becoming known as 'Festival Trials day' at the end of January, Wichita Lineman won decisively in very testing condiitions. Briefly shaken up before two out, he quickened with Massini's Maguire and then stayed on well after leading into the home straight. Tidal Bay took second on the run-in but Wichita Lineman had six lengths to spare at the line, with Massini's Maguire four lengths further back in third.

By the time Wichita Lineman took his place in the twenty-strong field for the Brit Insurance-sponsored Spa Hurdle, his form had been franked by the performances of Massini's Maguire and Tidal Bay in the Baring Bingham, in which Silverburn came fourth. Wichita Lineman was all the rage for the Spa, starting a heavily-backed 11/8 favourite, with Flight Leader second favourite at 11/2 and Black Harry, Hairy Molly and Sir Jimmy Shand the only others at shorter than 20/1. Irish-trained Black Harry would have finished a clear second had he not fallen at the last where Wichita Lineman, typically responding well under pressure, was about a length up after drawing clear with Black Harry from two out. As expected, Wichita Lineman saw out the longer trip thoroughly and stayed on to win by twelve lengths and six from 25/1-shot Air Force One and 100/1-shot Itsalegend, neither ever looking like getting in a blow at the winner. Back in fourth was Flight Leader, who didn't run anywhere near his best under less testing conditions than he had previously encountered, while Hairy Molly came only eleventh and Sir Jimmy Shand last of the seventeen finishers, the pair of them fading after still being in contention at the second last.

Wichita Lineman and Massini's Maguire did meet again in the latest season, in the Grade 1 Sefton Novices' Hurdle over an extended three miles at Aintree (where Tidal Bay won the Grade 2 two-and-a-half-mile Mersey Novices' Hurdle). Wichita Lineman started at odds on and was the best horse in the race by some way, though that wasn't reflected in the result. The race developed into a no-holds-barred battle up front between Wichita Lineman and Massini's Maguire, the pair going at it hammer and tongs on the final circuit. The pace turned out to be much too strong for the good of either and Wichita Lineman tired badly in the closing stages, after seeing off Massini's Maguire three out. Ten lengths clear at the second last, Wichita Lineman was caught on the run-in by the Spa Hurdle eighth Chief Dan George (a 20/1-shot at Aintree). Wichita Lineman had nothing left and went down by four lengths, with Imperial Commander eighteen lengths behind in third and Massini's Maguire a further nine away in fourth.

		Sadler's Wells (b 1981)	Northern Dancer
Wichita Lineman (IRE) (b.g. 2001)	King's Theatre (IRE) (b 1991)		Fairy Bridge
		Regal Beauty (b or br 1981)	Princely Native
			Dennis Belle
	Monumental Gesture (b 1987)	Head For Heights (b 1981)	Shirley Heights
			Vivante
		Temporary Lull (ch 1980)	Super Concorde
			Magazine

The sturdy, good-bodied Wichita Lineman is a half-brother to the top-class hurdler Rhinestone Cowboy (by Be My Native)—both take their names from hit songs by country singer Glen Campbell—who won the Aintree Hurdle and the Champion Stayers' at Punchestown in 2004, as well as finishing third in the 2003 Champion Hurdle as a novice. Both Rhinestone Cowboy and Wichita Lineman were bred as potential jumpers, though the distaff side of the family contains notable winners on the Flat as well as over jumps. The dam Monumental Gesture won on the Flat and over hurdles (two miles) and is a half-sister to Rare Holiday, who was smart on the Flat and over hurdles (wins included the 1990 Triumph Hurdle), to Token Gesture, a smart seven-furlong and mile-and-a-half winner, and to Blazing Spectacle, a useful hurdler/chaser and middle-distance stayer. The grandam Temporary Lull was an unraced sister to Nell Gwyn winner Martha Stevens out of Coaching Club American Oaks winner Magazine who is closely related to the dam of the family's best-known jumper, the dual Queen Mother Champion Chase winner Barnbrook Again. Wichita Lineman, who stays three miles and acts on heavy going (won bumper on good to firm), is capable of better still and should do well again in the next season, whether kept to hurdling or—reportedly more likely—sent chasing. *Jonjo O'Neill*

WICHWAY NOW (IRE) 8 b.g. Norwich – Proverb's Way (Proverb) [2006/7 16s Jan 20] lengthy gelding: in frame in bumpers: fair form at best over hurdles, left Miss E. Lavelle and off over 2 years before only start in 2006/7: likely to stay 2½m. *A. King* — **h84**

WICKED LADY (UAE) 4 b.f. Jade Robbery (USA) – Kinsfolk (Distant Relative) [2006/7 16s^{ur} 16m^6 Apr 9] 800 3-y-o, resold 2,700 3-y-o: leggy filly: second foal: dam, ran once in Ireland, out of sister to multiple US Grade 1 winner Chief's Crown: signs of ability on Flat/hurdling debut. *B. R. Johnson* — **h—**

WICKED NICE FELLA 9 b.g. Warcraft (USA) – Down Town To-Night (Kambalda) [2006/7 c113, h100: 21g^{pu} c20d c22g^2 c20g^{pu} c21d^6 c24d^{pu} 23s^2 24d^3 27s^5 Apr 27] well-made gelding: fair handicap hurdler/chaser on his day: stays 3m: acts on soft and good to firm going: tried blinkered: unreliable. *C. C. Bealby* — **c106 §** / **h107 §**

WICKLOW WANDERER (IRE) 5 b. or br.m. Pasternak – Wicklow Way (IRE) (Pennine Walk) [2006/7 F16f F18f^6 F16g* F16s^3 16v 16s 19d Apr 1] first foal: dam, modest hurdler, stayed 3m: won bumper at Roscommon in September: poor form over hurdles: stays 19f. *Lindsay Woods, Ireland* — **h82** / **F87**

WIDELY ACCEPTED (IRE) 5 b.g. Mujadil (USA) – Costume Drama (USA) (Alleged (USA)) [2006/7 16v^2 17s 17d^{pu} Mar 20] fairly useful on Flat (stays 9f, refused to race final start at 2 yrs): fair hurdler: sold out of J. Crowley's stable 17,000 gns Doncaster May Sales: distressed final start: raced around 2m on good going or softer (acts on heavy): tongue tied in 2006/7. *Heather Dalton* — **h107**

WIGGY SMITH 8 ch.g. Master Willie – Monsoon (Royal Palace) [2006/7 h105: 16g^4 17d* 16f* 17d^2 19g 16g^2 16m^3 16s Nov 11] angular gelding: fair novice hurdler: easily landed odds at Market Rasen in June and Perth in July: best around 2m: acts on firm and good to soft going: sold 14,500 gns Doncaster November Sales. *O. Sherwood* — **h113**

WILD ABOUT HARRY 10 ch.g. Romany Rye – Shylyn (Hay Chas) [2006/7 c67, h–: c24s^5 Feb 16] workmanlike gelding: maiden hurdler/chaser. *M. I. Mason* — **c—** / **h—**

WILDBACH (IRE) 5 b.g. Law Society (USA) – Wurfspiel (GER) (Lomitas) [2006/7   **c?**
c18d a16g³ a18g* a16g* 24vᵖᵘ 20d 17g Apr 1] smallish, leggy gelding: successful over   **h?**
12.5f on Flat at 3 yrs in Germany: once-raced over fences: ran 3 times over hurdles at
Neuss, winning in January and February: left C. von der Recke, no form in novice hurdles
in Britain: tried in cheekpieces. *A. E. Jones*

WILD CANE RIDGE (IRE) 8 gr.g. Roselier (FR) – Shuil Na Lee (IRE) (Phardante   **c141**
(FR)) [2006/7 c133, h–: 20s² c20s* c24s² c24v⁶ c28s⁴ Feb 17] leggy, good-topped   **h135**
gelding: useful handicap hurdler/chaser: good second to Red Scally over hurdles at
Hexham on reappearance: landed odds in 4-runner chase at Ayr in November: ran well
when in frame in valuable events at Haydock after, ½-length second to Kandjar d'Allier
and 18¾ lengths fourth to Heltornic: stays 3½m: raced on going softer than good (acts
well on heavy): makes the odd mistake. *L. Lungo*

WILD CHIMES (IRE) 8 b.g. Oscar (IRE) – Jingle Bells (FR) (In The Mood (FR))   **c–**
[2006/7 c–, h107: 22g⁶ 19m⁵ 20mᵖᵘ 17sᵖᵘ Oct 15] workmanlike gelding: winning hurdler: **h–**
little show in handicaps in 2006/7: sometimes blinkered: tried tongue tied. *S. B. Clark*

WILDFIELD RUFO (IRE) 12 b.g. Celio Rufo – Jersey Girl (Hardboy) [2006/7   **c107 §**
c106§, h–: c30d³ c25sᵖᵘ c25gᵖᵘ Apr 2] rangy gelding: fair chaser on his day: stays 3¾m: **h–**
acts on heavy and good to firm going: effective in cheekpieces or without: unreliable.
Mrs K. Walton

WILD GOOSE 8 ch.m. Karinga Bay – Glenn's Slipper (Furry Glen) [2006/7 16f 16m⁶   **h–**
20dᵖᵘ Sep 22] half-sister to poor hurdler Miss Souter (by Sulaafah), stayed 3¼m: dam
2-y-o 7f winner: no form over hurdles: dead. *M. Sheppard*

WILD GROUND (IRE) 6 ch.m. Simply Great (FR) – Rapid Ground (Over The River   **c–**
(FR)) [2006/7 16s 17s 21v c20v⁴ c22s c25vᵖᵘ Feb 28] good-bodied mare: sixth foal: **h–**
half-sister to winning pointer by Lord Americo: dam, poor novice hurdler, sister to
Cheltenham Gold Cup winner Cool Ground: no form over hurdles/fences. *Mrs E. Langley*

WILD IS THE WIND (FR) 6 ch.g. Acatenango (GER) – Whirlwind (FR) (Leading   **c116**
Counsel (USA)) [2006/7 c101p, h123: c19s* c20s³ c23d² c26d³ c29s⁴ c26sᵘʳ c19d⁶ c21g*   **h–**
Apr 27] useful-looking gelding: fairly useful hurdler: similar standard over fences: won
at Towcester (maiden, by 23 lengths) in May and Newton Abbot (beat Which Pocket by 6
lengths in 4-runner novice) in April: probably stays 29f: acts on heavy going: tried in
cheekpieces/blinkers (ran poorly). *Jonjo O'Neill*

WILDLIFE 5 gr.m. Environment Friend – Rabdanna (Rabdan) [2006/7 F16s F16s   **F–**
Feb 9] small, close-coupled mare: fourth foal: dam lightly-raced half-sister to high-class
2m to 3m hurdler Floyd: tailed off in bumpers. *J. Gallagher*

WILD OATS 9 b.g. Primitive Rising (USA) – Miss Nosey Oats (Oats) [2006/7 c98, h–:   **c–**
c23gᵖᵘ c23dᵖᵘ c27dᵘʳ Nov 23] medium-sized gelding: winning hurdler/chaser, failed to   **h–**
complete in 2006/7 (jumped markedly left final start): stays 23f. *B. J. M. Ryall*

WILD PASSION (GER) 7 b.g. Acatenango (GER) – White On Red (GER) (Konigs-   **c134**
stuhl (GER)) [2006/7 c148, h–: 22s² c20s² Nov 4] tall, good-topped gelding: useful   **h127**
hurdler: head second to Strong Project in minor event at Thurles on reappearance: smart
chaser in 2005/6, fourth to Voy Por Ustedes in Arkle at Cheltenham: ¾-length second of
4 to easy winner In Compliance in Grade 3 at Down Royal: not seen out again: stays
2¾m: raced on good going or softer (acts on heavy): tried blinkered (below form).
N. Meade, Ireland

WILD POWER (GER) 9 br.g. Turtle Island (IRE) – White On Red (GER) (Konigs-   **c94 §**
stuhl (GER)) [2006/7 c99§, h–§: c16g⁵ c16m⁶ 16d c19s² c19s c16g² c16g⁶ c16m⁴ Apr 14]   **h– §**
stocky gelding: modest handicap chaser: stays 19f: acts on soft and good to firm going:
sometimes wears blinkers: tried tongue tied: not one to rely on. *Mrs H. R. J. Nelmes*

WILD TONTO (IRE) 4 b.g. Saddlers' Hall (IRE) – Shipping News (IRE) (Glacial   **h91**
Storm (USA)) [2006/7 F14g 17d⁶ 16dᵖᵘ 16s⁶ 16s⁶ 22s* Mar 8] neat gelding: third foal: **F83**
dam, bumper winner, half-sister to top-class 2m to 2½m chaser Waterloo Boy:
mid-division in 3-y-o bumper: modest hurdler: upped in trip, won handicap at Wincanton
in March: likely to stay 3m: acts on soft ground: has pulled hard/hung. *Miss H. Lewis*

WILFIE WILD 11 b.g. Nomadic Way (USA) – Wild Child (Grey Ghost) [2006/7 c91:   **c–**
c21g Apr 12] strong gelding: fair pointer/hunter chaser: stays 3¼m: raced on good going
or softer. *Mrs Lynne Ward*

WILHEWISPA 5 b.g. Winning Gallery – More To Life (Northern Tempest (USA))   **F73**
[2006/7 F17d⁵ F13m F16m Jul 5] brother to useful 6f to 1m performer Will He Wish: dam
no form over hurdles (refused to race once): mid-field at best in bumpers. *J. M. Jefferson*

WILJEN (IRE) 7 b. or br.m. Taipan (IRE) – Powleyvale (Roi Guillaume (FR)) [2006/7 **h–** F–: 20g 20g 23v 22m 21m^{pu} Aug 29] tall mare: of no account. *B. S. Rothwell*

WILLANDRICH (IRE) 5 b.g. Insan (USA) – Cool Mary (Beau Charmeur (FR)) **h–** [2006/7 16s^{pu} 17s 19s Mar 11] £21,000 4-y-o: useful-looking gelding: half-brother to winning hurdler/fairly useful chaser Croc An Oir (by Treasure Hunter), stays 3¼m: dam unraced: little impact in novice/maiden hurdles. *Ian Williams*

WILLHEBEMYGUY 8 b.g. Master Willie – Right You Be (Sunyboy) [2006/7 F–: 18g **h–** Mar 18] lengthy, angular gelding: no form in bumpers/novice hurdle. *Mrs H. R. J. Nelmes*

WILLIAM BONNEY (IRE) 7 b.g. Oscar (IRE) – Beaudel (Fidel) [2006/7 F96: **h119** 21d^{pu} 16d 17s³ 17v* 16v³ 17s² 16v* 20s Mar 10] good-topped gelding: chasing type: fairly useful novice hurdler, sold out of A. Mullins' stable 6,000 gns Doncaster May Sales before return: won at Cheltenham (handicap) in January and Sandown (by 2 lengths from Over The Flow) in February: creditable efforts when placed in between: should stay 2½m: acts on heavy going: has sweated/got on toes: takes good hold, and patiently ridden. *C. J. Mann*

WILLIAM BUTLER (IRE) 7 b.g. Safety Catch (USA) – Rosie Josie (Trombone) **c94** [2006/7 h82, F83: 20s^{pu} c20f^{pu} 17d⁶ c20d⁴ c16v² c16d c20v² c20v³ c21s³ c22v⁵ c17v⁴ **h88** Mar 4] tall, workmanlike gelding: maiden hurdler: modest novice chaser: effective at testing 2m and stays 3m: acts on heavy going. *S. A. Brookshaw*

WILLIAM JOHN 4 b.g. Foxhound (USA) – Classy Relation (Puissance) [2006/7 17v² **h96** 16g 16s Apr 1] fair on Flat (stays 1¼m), successful in August, left B. Ellison after final 3-y-o outing: best effort over hurdles when second in novice at Sedgefield: tongue tied 2 of 3 outings. *P. C. Haslam*

WILLIAM LIONHEART 13 b.g. Henbit (USA) – Come To Tea (IRE) (Be My Guest **c–** (USA)) [2006/7 c25g^F May 3] sturdy gelding: fair pointer: little show in other events: **h–** dead. *N. Cook*

WILLIAM'S WAY 5 b.g. Fraam – Silk Daisy (Barathea (IRE)) [2006/7 F72+: F16g **F74** Jun 8] took good hold when mid-field in bumpers: fairly useful handicapper on Flat (stays 1½m), successful in July/April. *I. A. Wood*

WILLIAM TELL (IRE) 5 b.g. Rossini (USA) – Livry (USA) (Lyphard (USA)) **h99** [2006/7 h93: 17d² 17d⁴ 17m^{pu} Sep 26] close-coupled gelding: fair on Flat (seems to stay easy 1¾m): modest form over hurdles: sold 1,500 gns Doncaster October Sales. *Micky Hammond*

WILLIAM THE BLOODY 6 b.g. Bob's Return (IRE) – Society News (Law Society **F–** (USA)) [2006/7 F16g F16v May 20] half-brother to several winners, including 3m chaser Native Society (by Be My Native): dam bumper winner: tailed off in bumpers. *P. T. Dalton*

WILLIE JOHN DALY (IRE) 10 b.g. Mister Lord (USA) – Murphy's Lady (IRE) **c–** (Over The River (FR)) [2006/7 c124, h–: c25s⁵ c29s^{pu} c29v⁵ Jan 7] leggy gelding: useful **h–** handicap chaser at best for P. Hobbs, no show in 2006/7: stays 29f: acts on heavy and good to firm going: tried blinkered. *G. P. Mcpherson*

WILLIE PEP (IRE) 6 b.g. Saddlers' Hall (IRE) – Favorable Exchange (USA) (Excel- **h94 p** ler (USA)) [2006/7 F102: F16d³ 20g⁴ Dec 20] workmanlike gelding: fairly useful bumper **F99** winner: not fluent and failed to see race out when fourth to Key Time in novice at Musselburgh on hurdling debut: should stay at least 2½m: should do better. *C. R. Egerton*

WILLIES WAY 7 ch.g. Nomadic Way (USA) – Willies Witch (Bandmaster (USA)) **c102** [2006/7 h96, F–: 26m⁶ 20m 20f⁵ 24s⁴ 19g⁵ c20d³ 25d³ Dec 14] lengthy gelding: fair han- **h102** dicap hurdler: similar form when 7 lengths third to Day of Claies in maiden at Sedgefield on chasing debut: stays 25f: acts on firm and good to soft going. *Mrs S. J. Smith*

WILLIE THE FISH (IRE) 10 b.g. King's Ride – Bricon Lady (Proverb) [2006/7 **c75** c16d c27d^F c26s² c27d^{pu} 25d² c27v⁵ 25s c26g⁴ Apr 7] big gelding: poor hurdler/handicap **h82** chaser: stays 3¼m: raced on good going or softer (acts on heavy): has been let down by jumping. *Mrs S. J. Smith*

WILLING WEASEL (IRE) 5 b.g. Rudimentary (USA) – Final Peace (IRE) (Satco **h–** (FR)) [2006/7 F16d 16s^{pu} 16s 19d^{pu} Mar 26] €34,000 3-y-o: workmanlike gelding: third **F81** foal: half-brother to winning pointer by Saddlers' Hall: dam unraced: mid-field in bumper: no form over hurdles: sold 2,500 gns Doncaster May Sales. *K. C. Bailey*

WILLOW HALL 6 b.g. Saddlers' Hall (IRE) – Willow Gale (Strong Gale) [2006/7 **F—**
F16g Mar 24] has scope: fourth foal: dam staying chaser: soundly beaten in bumper on
debut. *P. Butler*

WILL SHE SPIN 6 b.m. Master Willie – Spinayab (King of Spain) [2006/7 h62, F—: **h—**
21s 26dᵖᵘ May 17] selling hurdler. *J. W. Mullins*

WILLS WILDE (IRE) 8 b.g. Oscar (IRE) – Meadow Lane (IRE) (Over The River **c131**
(FR)) [2006/7 c123+, F86: c22gᶠ c20d⁴ c16g c16m* Apr 24] lengthy gelding: useful
chaser: fit from outing on Flat, further improvement when winning handicap at Punchestown in April for second successive year by neck from Torrid Kentavr, idling: stays 2½m:
acts on good to firm and good to soft ground. *P. A. Fahy, Ireland*

WILL THE TILL 5 b.g. Fraam – Prim Ajwaad (Bin Ajwaad (IRE)) [2006/7 16d⁶ 16s⁴ **h100**
17v 16f² Apr 5] rather leggy gelding: modest on Flat (stays 1m), left J. M. Bradley after
final start at 4 yrs: best effort over hurdles (fair form) when neck second of 5 to Tora
Patcha at Ludlow on handicap debut: raced around 2m: acts on firm ground. *Evan
Williams*

WILLY FURNLEY (IRE) 7 b.g. Synefos (USA) – Random Bay (Mandalus) [2006/7 **c—**
c16gᵖᵘ May 24] good-topped gelding: runner-up in bumper: successful only completed
outing in points in 2006: no show in hunter on chase debut. *Mrs Caroline Keevil*

WILLY (SWE) 5 ch.g. Heart of Oak (USA) – Kawa-Ib (IRE) (Nashwan (USA)) **h86**
[2006/7 16sᶠ 16g⁴ Nov 13] lengthy, good-topped gelding: successful 4 times on Flat
(stays 1½m, raced mainly on dirt) at Taby at 3 yrs, modest form in Britain: won maiden at
Taby on hurdling debut: fourth on completed start in selling hurdles in Britain: tongue
tied. *R. A. Kvisla*

WILLYWONT HE 8 b.g. Bollin William – Scalby Clipper (Sir Mago) [2006/7 20g³ **h79**
21m² 24g Oct 7] successful twice in points: poor form over hurdles: probably stays 21f:
acts on good ground. *P. T. Midgley*

WINANOSCAR (IRE) 8 b. or br.g. Oscar (IRE) – Not A Bid (IRE) (Buckskin (FR)) **h—**
[2006/7 20vᵘʳ 23sᵖᵘ Nov 22] second foal: dam lightly-raced half-sister to top-class
staying chaser Marlborough: won maiden Irish point in 2003, fifth on completed start in
Britain in 2006: no show over hurdles. *J. S. Wainwright*

WIN A ROSE (IRE) 8 b.m. Right Win (IRE) – Bettons Rose (Roselier (FR)) [2006/7 **h85**
22d² 24d* 22s³ 26s³ 24v⁶ 26s Jan 26] ex-Irish mare: half-sister to winning hurdler/fairly
useful staying chaser Celioso (by Celio Rufo): dam unraced half-sister to smart staying
chaser The Ellier: modest handicap hurdler, left Mrs O. Byrne before return: stays 3¼m:
acts on heavy going: usually races prominently. *P. Bowen*

WINDS AND DRAGONS (IRE) 7 b.g. Taipan (IRE) – Windy Bop (IRE) (Strong **h100**
Gale) [2006/7 F16d 18s⁴ 22s⁴ 20dᵘʳ 19d² Mar 26] €14,000 4-y-o: lengthy, good-topped **F74**
gelding: second foal: dam, lightly raced, half-sister to dam of high-class staying chaser
Lord Noelie: well held in bumper (for R. Phillips): best effort over hurdles (fair form)
when staying-on second to Jump Jet in maiden at Stratford: likely to prove best at 2½m+:
raced on good to soft/soft going: tongue tied 3 of last 4 starts. *Miss H. C. Knight*

WIND SHUFFLE (GER) 4 b.g. Big Shuffle (USA) – Wiesensturmerin (GER) (Lagu- **h—**
nas) [2006/7 17m Aug 4] thrice-raced on Flat, fair form when runner-up over 7f: well
beaten in juvenile on hurdling debut: sold 4,200 gns Doncaster October Sales. *T. P. Tate*

WINDSOR BOY (IRE) 10 b.g. Mtoto – Fragrant Belle (USA) (Al Nasr (FR)) [2006/7 **c—**
c128, h—: c24dᵖᵘ 21vᵖᵘ 16g 20f Apr 28] lengthy gelding: winning hurdler: fairly useful **h—**
handicap chaser: no form in 2006/7: stays 25f: acts on soft and good to firm going.
D. E. Pipe

WINDS SUPREME (IRE) 8 b.g. Supreme Leader – Richmond Breeze (Deep Run) **c—**
[2006/7 c—, h83: 16g⁵ 17s 17s³ 16v* 16s⁵ 17d³ 20v⁶ 20vᵖᵘ Mar 6] poor handicap hurdler: **h83**
won seller at Uttoxeter in November: no form in chases: stays 2½m: acts on heavy going:
tried in cheekpieces: usually tongue tied, effective when not. *Ferdy Murphy*

WINDYGATE (IRE) 7 b. or br.g. Supreme Leader – Moscow Maid (IRE) (Moscow **c—**
Society (USA)) [2006/7 h—, F—: 20s 20d 18vᵘʳ c21vᵖᵘ 27v³ Jan 28] sturdy gelding: poor **h75**
hurdler: won amateur handicap at Kelso in December: not over those exertions
on chasing debut: stays 27f: raced on going softer than good. *A. Parker*

WINDY HILLS 7 bl.g. Overbury (IRE) – Chinook's Daughter (IRE) (Strong Gale) **c114**
[2006/7 h104: 22s* c24sᵖᵘ c24g² c24g² Apr 7] well-made gelding: fairly useful hurdler: **h116**
won handicap at Kelso in November by length from Kempski: runner-up both completed

1057

outings over fences, better effort when beaten 2½ lengths by Noir Et Vert in novice at Carlisle (blinkered): stays 3m: raced on good going or softer (acts on soft). *N. G. Richards*

WINDY SPIRIT (IRE) 12 br.g. Religiously (USA) – Golden Gale (Strong Gale) [2006/7 c101, h91: 21m⁵ 27m* 24g c23m³ c26m² c24m⁶ 24vᵖᵘ 24s c27g c24m⁵ c24g⁵ Apr 27] angular gelding: modest hurdler/maiden chaser: won ladies selling handicap at Newton Abbot in June: stays 27f: acts on soft and firm going: tried blinkered/in cheek-pieces. *Evan Williams* — **c99 h99**

WINE RIVER (IRE) 8 b.g. Muroto – Croom River (IRE) (Over The River (FR)) [2006/7 h–, F–: 20sᵖᵘ Nov 11] lengthy, workmanlike gelding: no show in bumper/over hurdles. *John R. Upson* — **h–**

WINGED LADY (GER) 8 b.m. Winged Love (IRE) – Wonderful Lady (GER) (Surumu (GER)) [2006/7 19dᵖᵘ Aug 15] poor hurdler: no show in seller after 27-month absence: stays 21f. *A. G. Juckes* — **h–**

WINGMAN (IRE) 5 b.g. In The Wings – Precedence (IRE) (Polish Precedent (USA)) [2006/7 16dᵖᵘ 16s³ 17s² 16s² 16v* 16s Apr 25] half-brother to modest hurdler around 2m Charlie Tango (by Desert Prince): fairly useful on Flat (stays 1½m): fair hurdler: won maiden at Plumpton in February: raced around 2m on going softer than good (acts on heavy). *G. L. Moore* — **h109**

WINGS OF HOPE (IRE) 11 b.g. Treasure Hunter – She's Got Wings (Bulldozer) [2006/7 c89§, h–§: c16g c21g⁶ c16g³ c19m⁴ Mar 29] close-coupled, quite good-topped gelding: modest maiden hunter chaser: stays 3m: acts on any going: usually wears head-gear: irresolute. *James Richardson* — **c84 § h– §**

WIN IN GOLD 6 b.g. Pivotal – Sylvan Dancer (IRE) (Dancing Dissident (USA)) [2006/7 F16m⁶ Jul 2] 8,000 2-y-o: second foal: dam sprint maiden: well held in bumper (very green) and on Flat. *John A. Harris* — **F–**

WINNIE'S SPIRIT 6 ch.m. Commanche Run – Winnie The Witch (Leading Man) [2006/7 F16g Apr 8] fourth foal: dam, useful hurdler/fairly useful chaser, stayed 27f: soundly beaten in bumper on debut. *D. G. Bridgwater* — **F–**

WINNIE WILD 10 b.m. Primitive Rising (USA) – Wild Child (Grey Ghost) [2006/7 c–, h–: c20dᵖᵘ Dec 9] lengthy mare: won maiden point in 2006: no form in other events. *Miss T. Jackson* — **c– h–**

WINNING CONNECTION (IRE) 4 b.g. Beckett (IRE) – Schiranna (Seymour Hicks (FR)) [2006/7 17fᵖᵘ Aug 11] well beaten in maidens on Flat: soon tailed off in juvenile on hurdling debut: sold £700 Ascot August Sales, placed in points. *P. A. Blockley* — **h–**

WINSLEY 9 gr.g. Sula Bula – Dissolve (Sharrood (USA)) [2006/7 c115, h–: c24sᵘʳ c25g⁵ Apr 20] good-topped gelding: winning hurdler: fairly useful chaser at best: won point in February: should stay beyond 21f: acts on firm and soft going: tried in headgear: owner ridden (20 lb overweight on return) in 2006/7. *O. Sherwood* — **c– h–**

WINSLEY HILL 5 b.m. Midnight Legend – Hinemoa (IRE) (Mandalus) [2006/7 F16g⁵ Mar 14] third foal: dam, tailed off in bumpers, out of half-sister to Grand National winner Royal Athlete: around 4 lengths fifth to King of The Jungle in bumper at Huntingdon on debut. *D. P. Keane* — **F83**

WINSLOW BOY (USA) 6 b. or br.g. Expelled (USA) – Acusteal (USA) (Acaroid (USA)) [2006/7 h85: 20g⁴ Aug 1] small, close-coupled gelding: modest maiden hurdler: should stay beyond 2m. *P. Monteith* — **h–**

WINS NOW 6 ch.g. Croco Rouge (IRE) – Valdaia (Sadler's Wells (USA)) [2006/7 h101: 18s² 18v* 16s* 18v* 16v* 16d⁵ 20g² Apr 12] tall, useful-looking gelding: smart hurdler: left T. Doumen, much improved in 2006/7, won maiden at Navan in December, minor event at Cork in January and novice at Punchestown (by 2½ lengths from Montana Bay) in February: better form in defeat after, bad mistake last (upsides at time) when 8 lengths second to Tidal Bay in Grade 2 novice at Aintree: stays 2½m: raced on good going or softer (acts on heavy): tried tongue tied (ran as if amiss): held up. *N. Madden, Ireland* — **h145**

WIPE YOUR EYE 4 b.g. Magic Ring (IRE) – Rosella (Distant Relative) [2006/7 F14s* F14v⁴ Jan 25] strong, lengthy gelding: first foal: dam unraced, out of half-sister to dam of very smart hurdler Mantles Prince: favourite, won 3-y-o bumper at Newcastle in December by 1½ lengths from Spare Me, looking green in front: raced too freely when odds on month later. *B. G. Powell* — **F92**

WISCALITUS (GER) 8 b.g. Lead On Time (USA) – Wiscaria (GER) (Ashmore (FR)) **c124**
[2006/7 h113: 20g⁴ c16m* c17g² c17gᶠ c17m² c20g² c19g⁵ c20d* Jan 8] good-topped **h113**
gelding: fair hurdler: fairly useful novice chaser: won at Hereford (maiden) in June and
Ludlow (best effort when beating Principe Azzurro by 6 lengths) in January: stays 2½m
with emphasis on speed: acts on good to firm and good to soft going: sound jumper. *Miss
Venetia Williams*

WISE CHOICE 4 b.g. Green Desert (USA) – Ballykett Lady (USA) (Sir Ivor (USA)) **h97**
[2006/7 16m* 16s³ 17g⁴ 16s³ Feb 9] tall gelding: modest on Flat (stays 1¾m): fair form
in juvenile hurdles: won at Hereford in September: raced around 2m: acts on soft and
good to firm going: tried blinkered. *N. P. Littmoden*

WISE COUNSEL (IRE) 9 b. or br.g. Leading Counsel (USA) – Lilly's Way (Golden **c76**
Love) [2006/7 c24g³ c21d⁵ c24sᵖᵘ Sep 20] runner-up in maiden Irish points: poor
handicap chaser: sold out of T. Taaffe's stable 2,600 gns Doncaster May Sales before
reappearance: stays 25f: raced on good going or softer (acts on heavy): tried blinkered.
J. J. Lambe, Ireland

WISE MAN (IRE) 12 ch.g. Mister Lord (USA) – Ballinlonig Star (Black Minstrel) **c–**
[2006/7 c121d, h–: c24sᵖᵘ 20sᵖᵘ c31sᵖᵘ Apr 26] maiden hurdler: fairly useful chaser at **h–**
best: has deteriorated markedly, though successful 3 times in points in January/February:
tried visored/tongue tied. *N. W. Alexander*

WISE MEN SAY (IRE) 5 br.g. Grand Plaisir (IRE) – Queen Alda (Kambalda) [2006/7 **F94**
F18m³ F17s* F16d Feb 1] €19,000 4-y-o: sturdy gelding: half-brother to bumper winner
Old Trafford Queen (by John French): dam, winning hurdler/chaser, stayed 3m: fair form
in bumpers: won at Folkestone in November by ¾ length from Psychomodo (pair clear):
will be well suited by 2½m+. *C. L. Tizzard*

WISE OWL 5 b.g. Danehill (USA) – Mistle Thrush (USA) (Storm Bird (CAN)) [2006/7 **h116 +**
20d² 17s* 17v² 16m* Apr 10] fairly useful on Flat (stays 2m), successful early in 2006,
left J. Pearce after final start: fairly useful form over hurdles: successful in maiden at
Taunton (idled run-in) in February and on handicap debut at Chepstow (beat Adjami by
head) in April: stays 2½m: may be capable of better still. *D. E. Pipe*

WISE TALE 8 b.g. Nashwan (USA) – Wilayif (USA) (Danzig (USA)) [2006/7 h96: **c– §**
27mpu 19m² 24s³ 22gpu c20g c24d Dec 10] sturdy gelding: modest handicap hurdler: **h96 §**
well held over fences: stays 3m: acts on firm and soft going: visored: temperamental.
P. D. Niven

WISHIN AND HOPIN 6 b.g. Danzig Connection (USA) – Trina's Pet (Efisio) **h–**
[2006/7 h–: 20sᵖᵘ 16s 16v Feb 26] smallish, plain gelding: bumper winner: no form over
hurdles: tongue tied last 2 starts. *A. G. Newcombe*

WISHWILLOW LORD (IRE) 8 b.g. Lord Americo – The Mrs (Mandalus) [2006/7 **c97 p**
h126: 17s c17dᵘʳ c17v⁴ c16vᵘʳ 16dᶠ 16d* 16m 16m⁵ Apr 25] big, lengthy gelding: fairly **h125**
useful hurdler: back to best when winning minor event at Limerick in April by 5 lengths
from Old Flame: fourth at Clonmel on completed start in maiden chases (unseated other
2 tries over fences): should stay 2½m: acts on soft and good to firm going: front runner:
remains open to improvement over fences. *Leonard Whitmore, Ireland*

WISTERIA LANE (IRE) 4 b.g. In The Wings – Web of Intrigue (Machiavellian **F92**
(USA)) [2006/7 F13d⁵ aF16g* Mar 9] half-brother to two 1m winners on Flat, including
Dubonai (by Peintre Celebre), also winning hurdler around 2m: dam lightly-raced half-
sister to Yorkshire Oaks winner Catchascatchcan: won falsely-run bumper at Lingfield in
Marcy by ¾ length from Irish Wedding, always well placed. *Mrs A. L. M. King*

WISTON WIZO 11 b.g. Tigerwood – Official Lady (Official) [2006/7 c25d⁴ c23f⁶ **c72**
Jun 21] poor pointer, successful twice in 2005: poor form in chases, left Mrs B. Llewellyn
after first outing. *D. A. Rees*

WITCH POWER 6 b.m. Accondy (IRE) – Apprila (Bustino) [2006/7 h86, F–: 20g⁴ **h78**
16s 16m⁵ Jun 11] poor maiden hurdler: stays 2½m: best efforts on good/good to firm
going: tongue tied last 4 starts. *A. M. Crow*

WITCH WIND 7 b.g. Accondy (IRE) – Marie Zephyr (Treboro (USA)) [2006/7 h94: **h114**
17s 22g⁶ 20s³ 22v* 20s⁴ 22v* 23s⁵ 24s Mar 11] workmanlike gelding: fair hurdler:
improved in 2006/7, winning handicaps at Kelso in December (novice) and January:
should stay 3m: raced on good going or softer (acts on heavy): has bled from nose.
A. M. Crow

WITHIEL LAD 6 b.g. Thowra (FR) – Travel Myth (Bairn (USA)) [2006/7 F16v² 16m **h–**
Apr 10] half-brother to 2 winning sprinters by Presidium and and winning pointer by **F98**

Landyap: dam, ungenuine maiden, stayed 1¼m: 6 lengths second to Ruairi in maiden bumper at Kempton on debut: looked reluctant (not fluent) when soundly beaten in maiden hurdle month later. *D. E. Pipe*

WITHOUT A DOUBT 8 b.g. Singspiel (IRE) – El Rabab (USA) (Roberto (USA)) [2006/7 c133, h–: c19d⁶ c24vᶠ c24g⁵ c25gᵖᵘ Apr 13] good-topped gelding: winning hurdler: useful chaser: easily best effort in handicaps in 2006/7 when never-nearer fifth to Alderburn at Newbury: effective at 2m to 3m: acts on soft going, below form on good to firm. *Carl Llewellyn*   c132 h–

WITHOUT PRETENSE (USA) 9 b.g. St Jovite (USA) – Spark of Success (USA) (Topsider (USA)) [2006/7 h73: 16g³ 17g⁶ Jun 20] poor maiden hurdler: best around 2m: acted on good to soft going: dead. *N. G. Ayliffe*   h70

WITNESS RUN (IRE) 7 b.g. Witness Box (USA) – Early Run (Deep Run) [2006/7 h100: c21dᶠ c17d² c19d² c17gᵖᵘ Mar 24] tall gelding: winning pointer/hurdler: runner-up completed outings in chases, in handicaps at Ascot, better effort (fairly useful form) when beaten 2½ lengths by Fast Forward on second occasion: off 3 months, ran as if amiss final start: should stay 2½m: raced mainly on good to soft/soft going. *N. J. Gifford*   c121 h–

WITNESS TIME (IRE) 11 b.g. Witness Box (USA) – Lisnacoilla (Beau Chapeau) [2006/7 c103?, h110: c25gᵖᵘ May 4] strong, workmanlike gelding: fair handicap hurdler: has failed to complete 4 of 5 starts over fences (lame only one in 2006/7): suited by 3m+: acts on heavy and good to firm going: blinkered last 2 outings: races prominently. *B. J. Eckley*   c– h–

WIXFORD VENTURE 8 b.g. Presidium – Forgiving (Jellaby) [2006/7 16m 20sᵖᵘ 16m Sep 3] eighth foal: half-brother to winning 2m hurdler Moor Hall Lady (by Rambo Dancer): dam modest 2m hurdler: no form over hurdles: won point in April. *R. S. Brookhouse*   h–

WIZARD OF EDGE 7 b.g. Wizard King – Forever Shineing (Glint of Gold) [2006/7 c99, h–: c16d³ c18s⁶ c21g⁴ c23v³ c25d* c23s² Feb 8] workmanlike gelding: fair handicap chaser: won at Wincanton in February: stays 25f: raced on good going or softer (acts on heavy): effective blinkered or not: signs of temperament. *R. J. Hodges*   c105 h–

WIZARD OF ODDS 5 b.g. Wizard King – Chardon (IRE) (Camden Town) [2006/7 F16m* F16d Dec 16] rather unfurnished gelding: second foal: dam unraced: won bumper at Ascot in October on debut by neck from Sirnando: well held there 2 months later. *N. J. Gifford*   F94

WIZARD OF US 7 b.g. Wizard King – Sian's Girl (Mystiko (USA)) [2006/7 16v 16v* 16v⁴ 16v⁵ 16v* 16v³ 16d* Mar 17] leggy gelding: modest on Flat (stays 8.5f): fairly useful hurdler: successful in maiden in December and handicaps in February and March (beat Storm Prospect a neck in novice event, seemingly held when left in lead last), all at Uttoxeter: raced at 2m: acts on heavy going. *M. Mullineaux*   h122

WIZARD ROC 5 b.g. Wizard King – Rocky Revival (Roc Imp) [2006/7 F–: F16m F17g 19mᵘʳ 16sᵖᵘ Oct 26] tall gelding: no form. *J. G. M. O'Shea*   h– F–

WIZARD TIME 4 br.g. Wizard King – It'safact (So Factual (USA)) [2006/7 F14s F14s F16mʳᵒ Apr 10] sturdy gelding: first foal: dam 5f/6f winner: showed more temperament than ability in bumpers, ran out early final start (in cheekpieces). *P. D. Evans*   F– §

WIZZICAL LAD 7 ch.g. Selkirk (USA) – Entente Cordiale (USA) (Affirmed (USA)) [2006/7 h–: 20fᵖᵘ Jul 19] of no account: has worn cheekpieces/tongue strap. *B. N. Pollock*   h–

WOGAN 7 b.g. Presenting – Fall About (Comedy Star (USA)) [2006/7 h122: c20d⁵ c17d⁴ Nov 24] tall, good sort: fairly useful hurdle winner: better effort over fences when 15½ lengths fourth of 6 to Killaghy Castle in maiden at Newbury, though again finished weakly: stays 2½m: raced on good going or softer. *N. J. Henderson*   c119 h–

WOLDS DANCER 5 b.m. Fraam – Dancing Em (Rambo Dancer (CAN)) [2006/7 16g 16g 16s 16sᵖᵘ Dec 16] lengthy mare: modest maiden on Flat (stays 1¼m): no form over hurdles: tried blinkered. *T. D. Easterby*   h–

WOLDS WAY 5 b.g. Mujahid (USA) – Off Camera (Efisio) [2006/7 F98: 17s⁵ 17v³ 16v³ 16g⁵ Mar 17] big, workmanlike gelding: bumper winner: poor form over hurdles: tried blinkered (found little): temperament under suspicion. *T. D. Easterby*   h84

WONDERKID 7 b.g. Classic Cliche (IRE) – Mulloch Brae (Sunyboy) [2006/7 c16d⁶ c24v⁴ c31s⁵ c24s 20v c34fᵖᵘ Apr 26] lengthy, rather sparely-made gelding: fair chaser, raced mainly in cross-country events/hunters: travelling well when broke down after 7   c114 h88 +

out in La Touche Cup at Punchestown final start: not knocked about only outing over hurdles: stays 31f: acts on heavy ground. *A. J. Martin, Ireland*

WONDERSOBRIGHT (IRE) 8 br.g. Magical Wonder (USA) – Brightness (Elegant Air) [2006/7 c88, h76: c18m⁴ 16m⁵ 18m⁵ c18g^F c26m^pu 19m^pu 18g⁴ 17g⁴ 16v⁵ 17v⁶ 22v³ 22s⁵ 16v⁶ 21g⁵ 21m² 21g⁶ Apr 23] tall gelding: poor maiden hurdler/winning chaser, claimed from K. Burke £6,000 first outing: stays 2¾m: acts on good to firm and heavy going: has worn blinkers, usually in cheekpieces: tried tongue tied: often makes running: prone to mistakes. *P. Butler* **c75 h75**

WONDERWINDER (IRE) 5 b.g. Kayf Tara – Girlie Set (IRE) (Second Set (IRE)) [2006/7 F16v F16m Mar 25] first foal: dam, fairly useful 1m/9f winner on Flat, won at 2m over hurdles: well held in bumpers. *J. T. Stimpson* **F–**

WON MORE NIGHT 5 b.m. Kayf Tara – Wonderfall (FR) (The Wonder (FR)) [2006/7 F16s Feb 16] second foal: dam poor 2m hurdler: last in mares bumper on debut. *D. J. Wintle* **F–**

WOODBINE WILLIE (IRE) 6 b.g. Zaffaran (USA) – Good Foundation (IRE) (Buckskin (FR)) [2006/7 F107: F16v² F16m² Apr 25] useful-looking gelding: fell in maiden point: useful bumper performer: runner-up both starts in 2006/7, beaten 2 lengths by Mick The Man in 19-runner Grade 1 at Punchestown second time: will be suited by further than 2m. *Philip Fenton, Ireland* **F114**

WOODCOCK LASS (IRE) 7 b. or br.m. Grand Plaisir (IRE) – Cousin Rose (Track Spare) [2006/7 F16m F16m Jun 17] ninth foal: dam lightly-raced maiden: well held in bumpers: wears cheekpieces, also tongue tied second outing. *R. Johnson* **F–**

WOODENBRIDGE DREAM (IRE) 10 b.g. Good Thyne (USA) – Local Dream (Deep Run) [2006/7 c85, h–: c25d^pu c20f² c22g^pu c21f^pu Aug 11] sturdy gelding: modest handicap chaser, sold out of R. Lee's stable 1,200 gns Doncaster May Sales after first outing: stays 2½m: acts on soft and firm going: seems to need to dominate nowadays (has taken little interest). *Robert Gray* **c85 § h–**

WOODFORD CONSULT 5 b.m. Benny The Dip (USA) – Chicodove (In The Wings) [2006/7 h86§: 19v 21s 16v³ 16v⁵ 20v^pu Jan 27] lengthy mare: poor handicap hurdler: should stay beyond 2m: raced on ground softer than good: blinkered last 3 starts: unreliable. *M. W. Easterby* **h72 §**

WOODHOUSE (IRE) 8 b.g. Glacial Storm (USA) – Alices Run (Deep Run) [2006/7 20m² 16d 16s* 16s^pu 16v² 16d 16v⁶ c16v* c17g⁵ c17m c18g⁴ Apr 25] lengthy gelding: fairly useful handicap hurdler: won at Punchestown in November: good second to First Row at Leopardstown following month: successful in maiden at Gowran on chasing debut (beat Outlaw Princess by 1¾ lengths) in March: easily best effort after (mistakes next 2 starts) when fourth to Pacolet in novice at Punchestown: stays 2½m: acts on heavy and good to firm going. *Mrs J. Harrington, Ireland* **c112 h117**

WOODLAND PARK (USA) 9 b.g. Woodman (USA) – Yemanja (USA) (Alleged (USA)) [2006/7 c23f^pu Jun 21] good-topped gelding: modest hurdle winner: off 4 years, no show on chasing debut: stays 3¼m. *G. Haine* **c– h–**

WOODLANDS GEM (IRE) 5 b.m. Oscar (IRE) – Play It By Ear (IRE) (Be My Native (USA)) [2006/7 F16g^bd F16s⁶ F16s⁴ F16v⁵ 19g Apr 8] third foal: dam, lightly raced, out of half-sister to dam of very smart 2m to 3m chaser Opera Hat: little form in bumpers: well beaten in maiden on hurdling debut: tried in cheekpieces. *P. A. Pritchard* **h– F77**

WOODLANDS GENPOWER (IRE) 9 gr.g. Roselier (FR) – Cherished Princess (IRE) (Kemal (FR)) [2006/7 c104x, h110x: 27d³ c26s⁴ c25d³ c26v^pu c24g c28g Apr 7] quite good-topped gelding: fair hurdler: maiden chaser, out of sorts in 2006/7: thorough stayer: raced on good going or softer (acts on heavy): often in cheekpieces/blinkers nowadays: sketchy jumper: temperament under suspicion. *P. A. Pritchard* **c87 x h113 x**

WOODSTOCK EXPRESS 7 b.g. Alflora (IRE) – Young Tess (Teenoso (USA)) [2006/7 h–: 22d^pu Oct 17] lightly raced and little form over hurdles. *P. Bowen* **h–**

WOODSTOCK LASS (IRE) 8 b.m. Mister Lord (USA) – Alma's Choice (IRE) (Jeu de Paille (FR)) [2006/7 c17s^F c23s c27s³ c18s c24d* c20s³ c33g^ur c22m² c30m Apr 27] workmanlike mare: successful twice in points in 2006: modest chaser: made all in conditional jockeys handicap at Musselburgh in January: left Miss F. Slevin before penultimate outing: stays easy 3m: acts on soft and good to firm ground: wore cheekpieces/blinkers after second start: usually tongue tied. *Miss C. J. MacMahon, Ireland* **c91**

WOODVIEW (IRE) 8 ch.g. Flemensfirth (USA) – Marys Bard (Le Bavard (FR)) [2006/7 c88, h106: c27d^pu c25s^pu c27s³ c25v^pu c24v² Jan 21] lengthy, angular gelding: **c78 § h–**

fair maiden hurdler at best: poor novice chaser, usually let down by jumping/attitude: bought 10,000 gns Doncaster August Sales before return: suited by 3m+: acts on heavy going: often wears headgear: very reluctant to race penultimate start. *R. Ford*

WOODVILLE MANOR (IRE) 7 b.g. Bob Back (USA) – Woodville Star (IRE) (Phardante (FR)) [2006/7 20m⁴ Apr 25] second foal: dam, fairly useful hurdler/useful chaser, stayed 25f: won maiden Irish point in 2005: easy to back, 14¾ lengths fourth to Ready Response in maiden at Worcester on hurdling debut: likely to improve. *Jonjo O'Neill*   **h76 p**

WOODWISH (FR) 5 ch.g. Lyphard's Wish (FR) – Woodstock (FR) (Huntercombe) [2006/7 c18s² 16fᵖᵘ 22s⁴ c16s c16vᶠ c16s c20v⁵ c20m⁴ c20m Apr 28] smallish, leggy gelding: first foal: dam won 3 times up to 10.5f: maiden on Flat: maiden hurdler: modest chaser, won 4-y-o claimer at Auteuil in April 2006: claimed from Mme E. Holmey €11,000 following month: left Mrs K. Walton and off 3 months, form in Britain only on penultimate start: stays 2½m: acts on soft and good to firm going: tried in cheekpieces. *Miss J. E. Foster*   **c88 d** **h–**

WOODY VALENTINE (USA) 6 ch.g. Woodman (USA) – Mudslinger (USA) (El Gran Senor (USA)) [2006/7 h119: c20s 16g 16sᵖᵘ Apr 25] leggy, close-coupled gelding: fairly useful handicap hurdler at best: no show in 2006/7 (none too fluent on chasing debut): best form around 2m: acts on good to firm going: tried in cheekpieces: tends to get on toes. *Mrs Dianne Sayer*   **c–** **h–**

WOOLLY BULLY 4 b.g. Robellino (USA) – Belle Ile (USA) (Diesis) [2006/7 19gᵖᵘ 16m* Apr 9] small gelding: fairly useful on Flat (stays 1¼m), successful in October, left G. Huffer after final 3-y-o start: saddle slipped on hurdling debut, then won juvenile at Plumpton in April by 2½ lengths from Monets Masterpiece: likely to improve, especially if jumping does. *Evan Williams*   **h101 p**

WOOLSTONE BOY (USA) 6 ch.g. Will's Way (USA) – My Pleasure (USA) (Marfa (USA)) [2006/7 h70: 16dᵖᵘ 19vᵖᵘ 21mᶠ Apr 9] tall gelding: little form over hurdles: has worn cheekpieces: tried tongue tied. *A. M. Hales*   **h–**

WORBARROW BAY (IRE) 5 b.m. Zaffaran (USA) – Cribaline (FR) (Air de Cour (USA)) [2006/7 F17g² Apr 19] sturdy mare: third foal: dam, winning hurdler/chaser up to 21f in France, out of half-sister to Grand Steeple-Chase de Paris winner Chinco: staying-on 7 lengths second of 18 to I'm Delilah in mares bumper at Cheltenham on debut: likely to be suited by 2½m+. *R. H. Alner*   **F97**

WORD GETS AROUND (IRE) 9 b.g. King's Ride – Kate Fisher (IRE) (Over The River (FR)) [2006/7 c96, h91: 22g⁴ c20fᵖᵘ 24gᵖᵘ Aug 1] lengthy gelding: modest handicap hurdler/chaser: stays 2¾m: acts on good to firm going (won bumper on good to soft): has shaped as if amiss more than once: sold 500 gns Doncaster August Sales, no show in points. *L. Lungo*   **c–** **h94**

WORKING CLASS (IRE) 10 b.g. Denel (FR) – Air Supply (Fidel) [2006/7 20s 22sᵖᵘ 20v⁶ Dec 9] seventh foal: brother to 2½m hurdle winner Home I'll Be: dam, winning hurdler, stayed 2¾m: lightly raced and little form over hurdles. *H. Smyth, Ireland*   **h–**

WORKING GIRL 10 b.m. Morpeth – Workamiracle (Teamwork) [2006/7 19dᵖᵘ Aug 20] winning pointer: lightly-raced maiden hurdler. *J. D. Frost*   **h–**

WORKING LATE 5 b.g. Night Shift (USA) – All The Luck (USA) (Mr Prospector (USA)) [2006/7 19m² 20m 16m* 16f⁴ 18g 18f³ 16g* 19d 16gᵖᵘ 17gᵖᵘ Apr 11] little form on Flat: modest handicap hurdler: won at Wexford in July and Ballinrobe in August: left D. Hughes and off 6 months before penultimate start: stays 19f: acts on firm ground: tried in cheekpieces: usually tongue tied. *Mike Hammond*   **h86**

WORLABY DALE 11 b.g. Terimon – Restandbethankful (Random Shot) [2006/7 c91+, h–: 17d⁵ c24d⁴ c20sᵖᵘ c22s⁵ c20mᵖᵘ Apr 15] workmanlike gelding: maiden hurdler/chaser, little form in 2006/7: has worn cheekpieces. *Mrs S. Lamyman*   **c–** **h–**

WORLD REPORT (USA) 5 b. or br.g. Spinning World (USA) – Miss Woodchuck (USA) (Woodman (USA)) [2006/7 16m 17m Sep 26] fair maiden for R. Hannon at 2 yrs, no form on Flat since or over hurdles (left P. Hughes after first start). *Ferdy Murphy*   **h–**

WORLD VISION (IRE) 10 ch.g. Denel (FR) – Dusty Lane (IRE) (Electric) [2006/7 c118d, h–: c24gᵖᵘ c20g⁶ c24gᵘʳ c24d³ c20g² c20s² c28g⁵ Apr 15] big, leggy gelding: fair chaser nowadays, left F. Murphy after reappearance: stays 27f: acts on soft and firm going: usually wears cheekpieces. *B. Storey*   **c100** **h–**

WORTH ABBEY 5 b.g. Mujadil (USA) – Housefull (Habitat) [2006/7 18m 17s^{pu} 24m 16g Apr 27] modest at best on Flat (stays 8.6f), well beaten in 2006: no form over hurdles, left Mrs A. Roberts after debut. *J. A. Danahar*   **h–**

WORTH A GLANCE 6 b.g. Thowra (FR) – Henry's True Love (Random Shot) [2006/7 h78, F–: 22s^{pu} Oct 26] compact gelding: little impact in bumpers/maiden hurdles: bred to be suited by further than 2m: failed to complete in points. *H. D. Daly*   **h–**

WORTON BOY 6 ch.g. Manhal – Taffidale (Welsh Pageant) [2006/7 F17s F16d Mar 17] strong gelding: eighth foal: half-brother to point winner by Beveled: dam maiden who stayed 1½m: tailed off in bumpers. *B. L. Lay*   **F–**

WORTON LASS 5 b.m. Manhal – Rough Guess (IRE) (Believe It (USA)) [2006/7 F16m^{pu} Jun 11] half-sister to Italian 5f to 8.5f winner by Cyrano de Bergerac: dam placed at 5f at 2 yrs: no show in bumper on debut. *B. L. Lay*   **F–**

WOT ABOUT ME (IRE) 12 b.g. Jolly Jake (NZ) – Time Please (Welsh Saint) [2006/7 c–, h–: c20m^{pu} c20m^{pu} c16m^{pu} Jul 12] of little account. *Mrs C. J. Ikin*   **c–** **h–**

WOTASHAMBLES (IRE) 6 b.g. Shambo – Rent Day (Town And Country) [2006/7 h–, F96: 19v⁶ 18v^{pu} 20s* 22s⁵ 26g⁵ Apr 20] lengthy gelding: poor hurdler, off a year and left P. Webber before reappearance: won 19-runner handicap at Huntingdon in February: stays 3¼m: acts on soft going (placed in bumper on good to firm). *O. Sherwood*   **h82**

WOTCHALIKE (IRE) 5 ch.g. Spectrum (IRE) – Juno Madonna (IRE) (Sadler's Wells (USA)) [2006/7 h–: 17d* 16g⁴ 16g⁴ 19d 16d 20d 16f³ 20g⁵ Apr 20] sturdy gelding: fair handicapper on Flat (seems to stay easy 2m): fair novice hurdler: won at Exeter in October: below form last 5 starts: should stay beyond 17f: raced mainly on good/good to soft ground: tried visored/in cheekpieces: not a fluent jumper. *R. J. Price*   **h107 d**

WOT NO CASH 15 gr.g. Ballacashtal (CAN) – Madame Non (My Swanee) [2006/7 c–, h–: c18m² Apr 26] lengthy gelding: maiden hurdler/winning chaser: stayed 19f: dead. *R. C. Harper*   **c61** **h–**

WOT NO INDIANS 7 b.g. Commanche Run – Shafayif (Ela-Mana-Mou) [2006/7 21g^{pu} Mar 26] no form in bumpers/novice hurdle. *H. J. Manners*   **h–**

WOT WAY CHIEF 6 b.g. Defacto (USA) – Wych Willow (Hard Fought) [2006/7 h91, F–: 20g⁴ 20g² 24s⁴ 20s³ 19g* 20g 19d 20v⁶ 20g* 20s³ Apr 27] tall gelding: fair handicap hurdler: won at Market Rasen in November and Wetherby in April: stays 2½m: acts on soft going: has found little. *J. M. Jefferson*   **h110**

WOULD YOU BELIEVE 11 gr.g. Derrylin – Ramelton (Precipice Wood) [2006/7 c113: c25d^{ur} c24d² c24d² c24s⁶ c24s² c31s⁴ Apr 27] workmanlike gelding: fair handicap chaser: stays 3m: raced on good going or softer (acts on heavy): has shaped as if amiss more than once: prone to odd mistake. *P. J. Hobbs*   **c111**

WRAGS TO RICHES (IRE) 10 b.g. Tremblant – Clonea Lady (IRE) (Lord Ha Ha) [2006/7 c123, h103: 22m^{pu} c17v* c20f^{pu} 22m⁴ c21d^{pu} c21d⁶ c20d^{pu} 24g⁵ Mar 25] big, good-topped gelding: maiden hurdler, left J. Frost and off 4 months before final outing: fairly useful handicap chaser: back to best when winning at Stratford in May: poor efforts after: stays 21f: raced mainly on good going or softer (acts on heavy): tried blinkered. *C. J. Down*   **c127** **h107**

WRAPAROUND YOU (IRE) 10 b.g. Shernazar – Wraparound Sue (Touch Paper) [2006/7 c–, h–: c25m^{pu} c21v^{pu} c25g Apr 15] winning pointer: no form in hunter chases: tried tongue tied. *Norman Sanderson*   **c–** **h–**

WRAPITUP (IRE) 9 ch.g. Aristocracy – Lanesboro Lights (IRE) (Millfontaine) [2006/7 c101, h72: c23g^{pu} c20g^{ur} Mar 27] winning hurdler/chaser, retains little ability: tried in cheekpieces. *Mrs Joanne Brown*   **c–** **h–**

WREFORD LAKE 7 ch.g. Karinga Bay – Sporting Annie (Teamster) [2006/7 19v 17s³ 21g⁴ Feb 21] runner-up in maiden point in 2006: poor form over hurdles: stays 21f. *J. D. Frost*   **h67**

WRENLANE 6 ch.g. Fraam – Hi Hoh (IRE) (Fayruz) [2006/7 17d² 16m⁶ 17d³ 17f* 16s⁶ 16d³ 19g⁶ Nov 29] sturdy gelding: modest on Flat (stays 2m) in 2006: modest novice hurdler: fortunate winner at Sedgefield in August, left clear last: raced mainly around 2m: acts on firm and good to soft going. *J. J. Quinn*   **h95**

WUJOOD 5 b.g. Alzao (USA) – Rahayeb (Arazi (USA)) [2006/7 20m 16d 22s^{pu} 22s^{pu} Mar 8] neat gelding: fairly useful at best on Flat (stays 1¼m), just poor form in 2006, claimed from H. Morrison £6,000 in May: no form over hurdles. *A. E. Jones*   **h–**

WYLDELLO 6 b.m. Supreme Leader – Clonmello (Le Bavard (FR)) [2006/7 F104: 21v² 17s* 21s³ 21g⁵ Mar 24] good-topped mare: bumper winner: fairly useful over hurdles: easily landed odds in maiden at Hereford in January: better form after, fifth of 18 to Karello Bay in listed mares novice event at Newbury on handicap debut: likely to stay beyond 21f: raced on good ground or softer. *A. King*   **h122**

WYLE POST (IRE) 8 ch.g. Mister Lord (USA) – Daffydown Dolly (IRE) (The Parson) [2006/7 c79x, h89: 22mᵖᵘ Sep 10] winning Irish pointer: novice hurdler/chaser (usually let down by jumping): stays 3m: tried tongue tied. *Mrs K. Waldron*   **c– x** **h–**

WYN DIXIE (IRE) 8 b.g. Great Commotion (USA) – Duchess Affair (IRE) (Digamist (USA)) [2006/7 h95: 16f* c16g⁶ 16m 16d Jan 5] sparely-made gelding: modest hurdler: off a year, won seller at Hexham in September: sixth of 9 finishers in novice there on chasing debut: raced around 2m: acts on firm and soft going: races freely. *W. Amos*   **c77** **h96**

WYNYARD DANCER 13 b.m. Minster Son – The White Lion (Flying Tyke) [2006/7 c84x, h–: c20m 20g⁵ c25dᵖᵘ Aug 19] maiden hurdler: winning pointer/hunter chaser, no form in 2006/7: wears cheekpieces. *Miss T. Jackson*   **c– x** **h–**

X

XAAR BREEZE 4 b.f. Xaar – Dicentra (Rambo Dancer (CAN)) [2006/7 16dᵖᵘ Nov 14] modest maiden on Flat (stays 6f): in cheekpieces, no show in juvenile on hurdling debut: sold £400 Ascot December Sales. *Mrs P. Townsley*   **h–**

XAMBOROUGH (FR) 6 b.g. Starborough – Sudden Spirit (FR) (Esprit du Nord (USA)) [2006/7 h102: 16g⁵ May 11] leggy, angular gelding: novice hurdler, fair form at best: likely to prove best over easy 2m: raced on good going or softer. *B. G. Powell*   **h85**

XCENTRA 6 b.g. Docksider (USA) – Dicentra (Rambo Dancer (CAN)) [2006/7 h80, F84: 16mᵖᵘ May 12] tall, strong gelding: in frame in bumpers: poor form on completed outing over hurdles. *B. G. Powell*   **h–**

XELLANCE (IRE) 10 b.g. Be My Guest (USA) – Excellent Alibi (USA) (Exceller (USA)) [2006/7 c115, h127: c20f² c23g⁴ c20m⁶ c20g⁴ c20m³ c24gᵇᵈ c24m⁴ c24s² c22g³ c27d² c27d² c25s⁴ 16d 16m 22s 24s² 24s⁴ 22d⁴ 24g⁴ Apr 19] angular gelding: fair handicap hurdler/chaser, left P. Hobbs after fifth start: needs further than 2m nowadays and stays 27f: acts on firm and soft going: tried in cheekpieces: consistent. *Dr R. D. P. Newland*   **c113** **h107**

XILA FONTENAILLES (FR) 6 gr.m. Turgeon (USA) – Miss Fontenailles (FR) (Kautokeino (FR)) [2006/7 h89: 19d⁶ 21d 19g³ 19s⁴ 21g* 22g⁶ 20g Apr 27] good-bodied mare: modest handicap hurdler: won mares event at Warwick in March, despite wandering markedly/flashing tail: stays 21f: acts on soft ground: in cheekpieces 4 of last 5 starts (including for win). *N. J. Hawke*   **h93**

XLNT STEALTH 6 b.g. Contract Law (USA) – Dominion's Dream (Dominion) [2006/7 F16m⁴ F16f F16m 16v 17v 20mᶠ 20gᴿ Apr 23] third foal: half-brother to 13f bumper winner Regal Angel (by Roi de Rome): dam, modest hurdler who stayed 2½m, also 7f winner on Flat: no sign of ability: tongue tied last 2 starts. *J. M. Saville*   **h–** **F–**

Y

YABOYA (IRE) 8 b.g. King's Theatre (IRE) – Oh Jemima (Captain James) [2006/7 h127: c22s* c21sᶠ c20dᵖᵘ Dec 26] rangy gelding: fairly useful hurdler: odds on, successful chasing debut when beating Pretty Star by ¾ length in maiden at Market Rasen in November: failed to complete both starts after, disputing second when fell 4 out in conditional jockeys handicap at Cheltenham: stays 2¾m: raced on good going or softer (acts on soft). *P. J. Hobbs*   **c134** **h–**

YAIYNA TANGO (FR) 12 br.g. Fijar Tango (FR) – Yaiyna (FR) (Lashkari) [2006/7 h85: 20gᵖᵘ c18m⁶ c24dᶠ c16d⁶ c19d³ c16sᵖᵘ Nov 19] lightly-raced maiden hurdler/chaser, little form in 2006/7 (lame final start): tried in cheekpieces. *Miss L. Day*   **c64** **h–**

YAKAREEM (IRE) 11 b.g. Rainbows For Life (CAN) – Brandywell (Skyliner) [2006/7 c75, h–: c22g c20g² Jul 21] compact gelding: poor handicap chaser, very lightly   **c75** **h–**

raced in recent seasons: stays easy 3m: acts on firm and good to soft going: has had tongue tied, not since 2001/2. *G. F. Bridgwater*

YANKEEDOODLEDANDY (IRE) 6 b.g. Orpen (USA) – Laura Margaret (Persian Bold) [2006/7 h–: 18s² 22dᵖᵘ 19d Nov 18] strong, compact gelding: useful juvenile hurdler in 2004/5 for P. Haslam: form since only when second in minor event at Auteuil: stays 2¼m: raced on good going or softer (acts on soft). *C. Roberts* **h119**

YANKEE HOLIDAY (IRE) 7 b.g. Oscar (IRE) – Parloop (USA) (Buckley) [2006/7 h–, F–: 16v⁵ c16m³ c16f* c16g³ c20d³ c20g³ c17v³ c17g² Apr 2] maiden hurdler: modest handicap chaser: won at Hexham in September: stays easy 2½m: acts on firm and good to soft going, below best on softer: front runner/races prominently: takes good hold. *Mrs S. C. Bradburne* **c87 +** **h71**

YANN'S (FR) 11 b.g. Hellios (USA) – Listen Gyp (USA) (Advocator) [2006/7 c106§, h–: c23s² c23v⁵ Jan 8] lengthy, angular gelding: fair handicap chaser: stays 27f: acts on heavy going (possibly unsuited by good to firm): sound jumper: usually races prominently: unreliable. *R. T. Phillips* **c103 §** **h–**

YARDBIRD (IRE) 8 b.g. Moonax (IRE) – Princess Lizzie (IRE) (Homo Sapien) [2006/7 c126, h–: c24gᵖᵘ c24d² c24g c24g c25gᵖᵘ Apr 18] strong gelding: winning hurdler: fairly useful handicap chaser: creditable effort in 2006/7 only when length second to Alderburn at Kempton: should stay beyond 25f: unraced on extremes of going. *A. King* **c126** **h–**

YARRA MAGUIRE (IRE) 8 b.g. Shernazar – Balingale (Balinger) [2006/7 22g* 24mᶠ 23f³ 22m³ 22dᵖᵘ 20g* 24g² 20d³ c16d² c16s Nov 26] €42,000 4-y-o: seventh foal: brother to fairly useful hurdler/chaser Dizzy's Dream, stayed 2¾m and half-brother to 2 winners by Strong Gale, including fair chaser Heavy Hustler, stayed 3m: dam point/ bumper winner: bumper winner: fairly useful hurdler: won amateur event at Downpatrick (easily) in May and handicap at Kilbeggan (improved form, beat Bullhill Flyer by 1½ lengths, pair clear) in September: much better effort in maiden chases when second at Naas: stays 3m: acts on any going: remains open to improvement over fences. *N. Meade, Ireland* **c105 p** **h126**

YASHIN (IRE) 6 b.g. Soviet Star (USA) – My Mariam (Salse (USA)) [2006/7 16fʳᵒ 16mʳᵒ 16m⁶ 22m³ 20dᵖᵘ 22sᵖᵘ 21mᵖᵘ Nov 9] smallish, sturdy gelding: modest on Flat (stayed 11f), left P. Blockley after final start in 2006: poor form only 2 completed starts over hurdles (twice ran out): tried tongue tied: dead. *Mrs C. J. Ikin* **h77 §**

YASSAR (IRE) 12 b.g. Yashgan – Go Hunting (IRE) (Abednego) [2006/7 c89§, h–: c16v⁶ c19m c20g⁴ c22g c20s⁵ Dec 5] lengthy gelding: modest handicap chaser, below form in 2006/7: stays 3m: acts on soft and good to firm going: unreliable. *D. J. Wintle* **c75 §** **h–**

YEAH BUT NO BUT 6 b.g. Primitive Rising (USA) – Blakeney Sound (Blakeney) [2006/7 22s 22g Mar 19] 14,500 3-y-o: half-brother to useful hurdler Master Rastus and useful chaser Sounds Like Fun (both by Neltino), both of whom stayed 3m: dam unraced: won maiden point in 2006: possibly amiss on hurdling debut: badly hampered next time. *P. F. Nicholls* **h–**

YELLOW FLAG 4 b.g. Halling (USA) – Bunting (Shaadi (USA)) [2006/7 16s⁶ 17g 17s⁶ Nov 14] big, good-topped gelding: brother to smart 6f (at 2 yrs) and 1¼m (including in UAE) winner Parasol and half-brother to 3 winners, including smart 1m (at 2 yrs) and 1¼m winner Mot Juste (by Mtoto): dam, 1m (at 2 yrs)/1¼m winner, also third in Oaks d'Italia: third over 1½m at Clairefontaine on debut at 3 yrs: sold out of A. Fabre's stable 100,000 gns Newmarket July Sales: well held in juvenile hurdles. *Jonjo O'Neill* **h–**

YELLOW JERSEY 5 b.m. Mark of Esteem (IRE) – La Bicyclette (FR) (Midyan (USA)) [2006/7 F16v F17s F16d 17g⁵ 16f⁴ Apr 22] £500 3-y-o: small mare: first foal: dam unraced: well held in bumpers: tongue tied, signs of ability in novice hurdles. *S. C. Burrough* **h81** **F–**

YES MY LORD (IRE) 8 b.g. Mister Lord (USA) – Lady Shalom (IRE) (Aylesfield) [2006/7 c106+, h100+: c28s² c24dᶠ c24s⁴ c27g³ c26g² Apr 7] lengthy gelding: winning hurdler: fair handicap chaser: stays 3½m: raced on good ground or softer (acts on soft): in cheekpieces last 4 starts. *D. E. Pipe* **c114** **h–**

YES SIR (IRE) 8 b.g. Needle Gun (IRE) – Miss Pushover (Push On) [2006/7 c118, h147: c17f* c20s* c20m* c20s* c17g* c22g* c26d* c24d⁵ c21v⁵ c20v⁴ c25g⁴ c20m* Apr 28] **c148** **h–**
    Summer time, and the living was easy for Yes Sir. Between May and the end of August he ran up a sequence of seven wins over fences, justifying short-priced favouritism by very wide margins in most of them. In fact, taking his career as a

totesport.com Summer Plate (Handicap Chase), Market Rasen—the prolific novice Yes Sir completes a profitable day for Peter Bowen, who also saddled runner-up Ballycassidy

whole to the end of May 2007, Yes Sir has won no fewer than fourteen of his twenty starts in the months from March to August. His record in the six other months of the year stands at just two wins from seventeen races. It would be easy to jump to the conclusion that Yes Sir therefore needs conditions on the firm side, but he has won on all types of ground, heavy as well as firm. Generally speaking, jump racing in the summer is less competitive than at other times of the year, but by no means all of Yes Sir's successes have come in 'egg and spoon' contests. Having said that, there's little doubt that the combination of small fields and good ground or firmer is ideal for Yes Sir. A confirmed front runner, with a tendency to jump less than fluently on occasions, Yes Sir is best when allowed to do his own thing in front without his jumping coming under pressure, either from other rivals or from testing underfoot conditions.

Yes Sir was a smart hurdler, though even over the smaller obstacles his jumping was not always fluent. His early attempts over fences were disappointing and he ended his 2005/6 campaign with a fall at Catterick, still seeking a first win over fences after four attempts. Following a three-and-a-half-month break, Yes Sir returned in the summer to run up his sequence in chases. He did so on ground ranging from firm to soft and over distances from just over two miles to three and a quarter miles. He was sent all over the country to run up his seven-timer, starting off at Kelso and ending up at Newton Abbot, both novice chases. Along the way, he was also successful in novice company at Bangor, Stratford, Hexham (where he won by a distance) and Stratford again (where his rivals included the very smart hurdler Intersky Falcon) prior to seeing off seasoned handicappers at Market Rasen. He proved far too good for his rivals in those novice chases, but the £37,000 totesport.com Summer Plate at Market Rasen represented a somewhat sterner test. However, Yes Sir's mark over fences was still 23 lb lower than his last start in a handicap over hurdles and he made a mockery of it with another facile win, setting a sound gallop under Tony McCoy (also on board at Hexham) and always travelling strongly in front without being taken on for the lead. Typically awkward on occasions, Yes Sir made his worst mistake at the last fence, but was still able to coast home by six lengths from his stable-companion and former winner of the race Ballycassidy, Yes Sir completing a big-race double on the card for the stable which had been initiated by Tycoon Hall in the Summer Hurdle. Peter Bowen had completed the same double back in 1997 (with Stately Home and Kinnescash) and the Welsh trainer has won all of the main prizes available on the summer jumping schedule in recent years. McKelvey's win in the latest Summer National came two years after Take The Stand had landed the same race on the way to initiating a lucrative double for the stable at Newton Abbot later that summer, his win in the Lord Mildmay Memorial Chase followed up by stable-companion Mr Ed's victory in the Summer Festival Hurdle.

Bowen managed to maintain his impressive early-season form pretty much throughout 2006/7, ending the campaign with a career-best tally of seventy-four wins (though he's scheduled to lose two of those wins). Unfortunately, the same couldn't be said of his stable star. After completing his seven-timer at Newton

Ashleybank Investments Future Champion Novices' Chase, Ayr—Yes Sir claims an eighth win of the campaign, though is due to lose the race to runner-up Natal on technical grounds

Ms Y. M. Hill's "Yes Sir"

Abbot (a bloodless thirty-length victory back in novice company) in August, Yes Sir wasn't seen out again until December when he had the option of contesting the King George at Kempton but ran instead in the Feltham Novices' Chase on the same card, starting joint favourite. Yes Sir looked in good shape after his break, but performed a long way below form and returned tailed-off last of five finishers, his jumping not particularly to blame for his performance. He fared little better in two more starts during the winter, in a novice handicap at Cheltenham and the Pendil Novices' Chase back at Kempton.

The spring brought a revival in Yes Sir's form. He ran a much better race when belying odds of 25/1 to finish fourth behind Aces Four in the Mildmay Novices' Chase at Aintree. Jumping boldly in front (and better than he had done on heavy ground on his two previous outings) Yes Sir only lost second after the final fence and was conceding weight to the three who beat him. Yes Sir built on that with a career-best effort to register his eighth win of the season in the Ashleybank Investments Future Champion Novices' Chase at Ayr later in April. The joint favourites had both finished ahead of Yes Sir in his most recent races, Natal when winning the Pendil and Faasel when second at Aintree, but Yes Sir dealt them the same kind of beating he'd given to lesser rivals the previous summer. Going off strongly in front, he was given a breather at around halfway, and, whilst not foot-perfect himself, he exploited the jumping weaknesses in his rivals. Natal failed to land a blow eleven lengths behind the winner, while Faasel was fortunate to take third after Buena Vista had fallen three out. Yes Sir's stable-companion Always Waining was also successful later on the card, but both failed post-race tests which revealed the presence of tetramisole, a prohibited substance which seems likely to be traced to a worming treatment. Both are likely to lose the races involved. Yes Sir's jumping frailties were exposed a week after Ayr when he finished only seventh of eight in the Celebration Chase at Sandown, a much tougher assignment —outside novice company—as well as being over two miles. Yes Sir began the 2007/8 season where he'd begun the latest one, at Kelso, having little more than an exercise canter in accounting for two poor rivals in an intermediate chase in May. It was his fourth win at the course from as many starts.

			Sure Blade	Kris
Yes Sir (IRE)	Needle Gun (IRE)		(b 1983)	Double Lock
(b.g. 1999)	(b 1990)		Lucayan Princess	High Line
			(b 1983)	Gay France
			Push On	Pampered King
	Miss Pushover		(b 1970)	Crisper
	(b 1979)		Hopeful Bar	Bargello
			(br 1972)	Hopeful Queen

Yes Sir is the best horse sired so far by Needle Gun. Although Needle Gun's exploits were put in the shade somewhat by the international careers of a couple of younger half-brothers from the same stable in Luso (himself now a jumps sire) and the now-deceased Warrsan, Needle Gun was a smart middle-distance performer in his own right who was campaigned with typical boldness by Clive Brittain. For example, he finished second in the Derby Italiano and St James's Palace Stakes when still a maiden, and also contested the inaugural running of the Dubai World Cup. All three dams on the bottom line of Yes Sir's pedigree were unraced. As well as Yes Sir, his dam Miss Pushover has produced the modest chaser Heavenly Citizen (by Ovac), who was an out-and-out stayer, and a couple of winning pointers by Ovac and Warcraft. Miss Pushover was a half-sister to the useful chaser Bold Agent, winner of the 1986 Troytown Handicap Chase, runner-up in a Galway Plate and third in two Irish Grand Nationals. Yes Sir's great grandam Hopeful Queen was a half-sister to the 1955 Scottish National winner Bar Point. The lengthy Yes Sir has been hailed by his trainer as 'the best horse I've ever trained' and 'definitely better than Take The Stand.' That's high praise, given that Take The Stand was second in a Cheltenham Gold Cup. Yes Sir still has about a stone's improvement to find to be rated on a par with Take The Stand though. He's likely to find it harder to maintain his excellent wins-to-runs ratio from now on, his best chance of future success likely to be in conditions races with small fields which he can dominate. *P. Bowen*

YOGI (IRE) 11 ch.g. Glacial Storm (USA) – Good Performance VII (Damsire Unregistered) [2006/7 c87, h125§: 24d c25s⁴ c32s c26v³ Feb 23] smallish, leggy gelding: useful hurdler at best: on long losing run and generally out of sorts since 2004/5 (just modest form over fences), left T. Foley before return: stays 3m: acts on heavy going: tried in blinkers/cheekpieces: one to leave alone. *P. R. Webber*   **c93 §**   **h– §**

YORK RITE (AUS) 11 ch.g. Grand Lodge (USA) – Amazaan (NZ) (Zamazaan (FR)) [2006/7 c78x, h–: c26g⁶ c20s⁶ Feb 4] strong gelding: winning hurdler/maiden chaser: trained first start only by Ms Lisa Stock: won point in April: stays 3m: tried blinkered/visored, usually wears cheekpieces: has had tongue tied: makes mistakes. *Martin Page*   **c61 x**   **h–**

YOUAMAZEME 5 b.m. Kayf Tara – Janie-O (Hittite Glory) [2006/7 F16v F16g⁶ Apr 23] half-sister to bumper winner Danyerman (by Sylvan Express) and winning 3m hurdler Dunroyal Lad (by Primitive Rising): dam, winning 2m selling hurdler, best at 7f/1m on Flat: better effort in bumpers when sixth of 14 to Nodforms Paula in maiden at Hexham. *J. M. Jefferson*   **F75**

YOU BET (IRE) 7 b.g. Riberetto – Shoubad Melody (Jukebox) [2006/7 19dᵖᵘ 16s Mar 7] strong gelding: brother to 2¼m hurdle winner Bisley and half-brother to 2m winner Alshou (by Alzao): dam, winner up to 2m on Flat, also successful at 2m over hurdles: no show over hurdles. *Mrs S. J. Smith*   **h–**

YOU DO THE MATH (IRE) 7 b.g. Carroll House – Ballymave (IRE) (Jareer (USA)) [2006/7 h108: 20v⁴ 20s² c20v* c21g Apr 19] sturdy gelding: fair handicap hurdler: won   **c112**   **h114**

novice handicap at Plumpton in February on chasing debut by 1¾ lengths from The Hardy Boy: seemed to take little interest in similar event 2 months later: stays 2½m: raced on good going or softer (acts on heavy): temperament under suspicion: sold 22,000 gns Doncaster May Sales. *A. King*

YOULBESOLUCKY (IRE) 8 b.g. Accordion – Gaye Humour (IRE) (Montelimar (USA)) [2006/7 h116, F98: c23f² c20g* c24f* 21s⁴ c24d³ c25sᶠ Jan 20] leggy gelding: fairly useful hurdler: off 5 months, very stiff task fourth outing: fair novice chaser: won at Market Rasen (maiden) and Uttoxeter in July: stays 3m: probably acts on any going: in cheekpieces/blinkers 4 of last 5 starts. *Jonjo O'Neill*   **c111 h–**

YOULL DO FOR ME (IRE) 5 b.g. Beneficial – Eurocurrency (IRE) (Brush Aside (USA)) [2006/7 F16d 17s³ 20v* 20s⁴ 20s 20gᵖᵘ Apr 7] €44,000 3-y-o: useful-looking gelding: fourth foal: half-brother to fairly useful hurdler/useful chaser Aztec Warrior (by Taipan), stays 2¾m: dam unraced: mid-field in bumper: fair novice hurdler: won at Hereford in January: likely to stay beyond 2½m: raced on good going or softer (acts on heavy). *Jonjo O'Neill*   **h108 F79**

YOU ME AND THEBOYS 5 b.g. Overbury (IRE) – La Bella Villa (Relkino) [2006/7 F17d F16m F16g F14g³ Apr 10] 1,200 3-y-o: third foal: dam bumper winner: modest form in bumpers. *M. Appleby*   **F80**

YOUNG ALBERT (IRE) 6 br.g. Taipan (IRE) – Smooth Leader (IRE) (Supreme Leader) [2006/7 F104: 17d* 16s² 16g* 24s⁴ Apr 26] tall gelding: has scope: fairly useful bumper winner: fair form in novice hurdles: won at Sedgefield in October and Kelso in April: should stay at least 2½m: raced on good going or softer: probably remains capable of better. *N. G. Richards*   **h112 p**

YOUNG ALF 4 b.g. Balinbarbi – Sciacca (Dalsaan) [2006/7 F16g Apr 3] fifth foal: dam modest 2m hurdler: well held in bumper on debut. *James Moffatt*   **F–**

YOUNG BLADE 6 b.g. Cloudings (IRE) – Lady Shoco (Montekin) [2006/7 h–, F–: 20s 20sᵖᵘ Feb 20] rather unfurnished gelding: won maiden point in March: no form in other events: tried tongue tied. *M. V. Coglan*   **c– h–**

YOUNG BULL (IRE) 5 b.g. Lord of Appeal – Petaldante (IRE) (Phardante (FR)) [2006/7 F17s⁵ F17s⁵ F15s 16d 20g⁴ 20g⁴ Apr 16] smallish gelding: second foal: dam poor form over hurdles: fifth in bumpers: best effort over hurdles when fourth in novice at Wetherby final start, possibly flattered: likely to stay 3m. *C. A. Mulhall*   **h86 ? F–**

YOUNG CHEVALIER 10 b.g. Alflora (IRE) – Mrs Teasdale (Idiot's Delight) [2006/7 c91, h–: c16fᵖᵘ c17mᵖᵘ Sep 2] rangy gelding: winning 2m chaser, failed to complete 7 of last 8 starts. *J. R. Adam*   **c– h–**

YOUNG COLLIER 8 b.g. Vettori (IRE) – Cockatoo Island (High Top) [2006/7 c–, h–: c17d⁵ Mar 2] tall, useful-looking gelding: very lightly raced: fairly useful winner of first 2 starts over fences: off another year, set overly-strong pace only outing in 2006/7: should stay beyond 19f: raced on good ground or softer. *J. A. B. Old*   **c100 + h–**

YOUNG CUTHBERT 9 b.g. Homo Sapien – Deirdres Dream (The Parson) [2006/7 c24d⁶ 19g 23v⁶ c19s⁴ c25m³ Mar 29] ex-Irish gelding: one-time fair hurdler/maiden chaser: sold out of Mrs J. Harrington's stable 2,500 gns Doncaster August (2005) Sales: retains little ability: usually tongue tied. *Mrs S. E. Handley*   **c65 h–**

YOUNG DANCER (IRE) 9 b.g. Eurobus – Misquested (Lord Ha Ha) [2006/7 17d⁴ 20v* 20d⁴ 24v³ Feb 20] good-topped gelding: fair handicap hurdler, off 2 years prior to return: won at Uttoxeter in January: possibly best short of 3m when conditions are testing: raced on good going or softer (acts on heavy). *V. R. A. Dartnall*   **h110**

YOUNG DESPERADO (IRE) 9 ch.g. Un Desperado (FR) – Belclare Lass (IRE) (Deep Run) [2006/7 c16d* c17sᶠ c17s⁵ c16v* Feb 18] third foal: dam unraced: maiden hurdler: third in maiden point in 2005: useful novice chaser: won at Naas (maiden) in November and Navan (ridden more prominently when beating King Johns Castle by 3½ lengths in Grade 2 Kevin McManus Flyingbolt Novices' Chase) in February: stays 2½m: acts on heavy and good to firm going. *Robert Tyner, Ireland*   **c135 h–**

YOUNG DUDE (IRE) 8 b.g. Oscar (IRE) – Shuil Realt (IRE) (Jolly Jake (NZ)) [2006/7 h98: 22m 21m⁶ 19m³ 19g⁵ c24s c24s³ c24dᵖᵘ c20m⁶ Apr 25] angular gelding: modest hurdler (often let down by jumping): similar form first 2 starts in handicap chases: stays 3m: acts on heavy and good to firm going: tried blinkered/tongue tied: hard ride. *Jonjo O'Neill*   **c86 h91 x**

YOUNG EMMA 4 b.f. Vettori (IRE) – Just Warning (Warning) [2006/7 F14g Nov 1] angular filly: second foal: half-sister to smart middle-distance stayer Young Mick (by   **F–**

King's Theatre): dam, well beaten only start, half-sister to very smart 6f to 1m performer Young Ern: well held in 3-y-o bumper/maiden on Flat. *G. G. Margarson*

YOUNG ERIC 5 ch.g. Midnight Legend – Slippery Fin (Slip Anchor) [2006/7 F16s Mar 8] leggy, plain gelding: second foal: dam, placed on Flat (up to 1½m) and over hurdles, half-sister to useful French hurdler up to 19f Trait Union: always behind in maiden bumper on debut. *Mrs L. Richards* **F–**

YOUNG GARY 5 ch.g. Silver Patriarch (IRE) – Miss Michelle (Jalmood (USA)) [2006/7 aF16g² F16v 19s⁵ 20v 21g⁵ Mar 20] workmanlike gelding: second foal: dam won 2m hurdle: second of 4 in bumper on debut: modest form over hurdles: free-going sort. *A. E. Price* **h85 F83**

YOUNG GUNS (IRE) 6 b.g. Turtle Island (IRE) – Glorious Bid (IRE) (Horage) [2006/7 F83: F17m F13m⁴ 19g³ 17g 19s 20g Apr 11] runner-up in maiden Irish point: fourth in bumpers: poor form over hurdles: bled fifth outing. *J. G. M. O'Shea* **h69 F81**

YOUNG KATE 6 b.m. Desert King (IRE) – Stardyn (Star Appeal) [2006/7 16g Mar 14] modest on Flat (stays 1¼m), successful in early-2006 for J. R. Best: no aptitude for hurdling in mares maiden. *A. E. Price* **h–**

YOUNG LORCAN 11 ch.g. Bay Tern (USA) – Naughty Nessie (Celtic Cone) [2006/7 c112, h86: c21v⁴ 21s³ c19s⁵ 24v² c23v⁶ c22v⁶ 20vᵖᵘ Feb 17] rather leggy gelding: fair hurdler/handicap chaser, no form last 3 starts: acts on heavy and good to firm going: tried tongue tied: has refused to race. *Mrs K. Waldron* **c110 h100**

YOUNG OWEN 9 b.g. Balnibarbi – Polly Potter (Pollerton) [2006/7 c94§, h–§: c16m c20sᵖᵘ 16vᵖᵘ 18g⁴ 16g²* 17g⁴ Apr 1] rather leggy gelding: modest hurdler/chaser, left A. Juckes after second start: won selling handicap hurdle at Plumpton in March: stays 21f: acts on soft and good to firm going: tried in cheekpieces: often makes running: unreliable (has refused to race). *J. L. Spearing* **c– § h94 §**

YOUNG SCOTTON 7 b.g. Cadeaux Genereux – Broken Wave (Bustino) [2006/7 h–: 17d May 31] leggy gelding: useful bumper performer for K. Ryan: maiden on Flat: most disappointing over hurdles, often shaping as if amiss: tried in blinkers/cheekpieces. *J. Howard Johnson* **h–**

YOUNG SMOKEY (IRE) 6 gr.g. Cloudings (IRE) – Miss Aylesbury (IRE) (Le Moss) [2006/7 h–, F78: 20v 20s 20v⁵ c20v* c22vᵖᵘ c20m⁴ Apr 20] rangy gelding: little impact over hurdles: won handicap at Newcastle in January, only form over fences: should stay beyond 2½m: acts on heavy going: tried in cheekpieces. *P. Beaumont* **c88 h–**

YOUNG THRUSTER (IRE) 14 b.g. Over The River (FR) – Bit of Fashion (Master Owen) [2006/7 c33g² c24d² c28vᵖᵘ c24vᵖᵘ c24g² c25g³ Apr 20] lengthy, good sort: winning hurdler: fairly useful pointer/hunter chaser, second to Vinnie Boy at Towcester second start: below form after: stays 33f: acts on heavy and good to firm going: blinkered final outing: races prominently. *J. A. T. de Giles* **c109 d h–**

YOUNG TOT (IRE) 9 b.g. Torus – Lady-K (IRE) (Rock Chanteur) [2006/7 c–x, h94: c16m⁴ c19m c16f³ c16mˢᵘ 16m⁶ c16g² c16m² Nov 5] modest handicap hurdler: poor novice chaser: has form at 2½m, raced mainly over shorter: acts on firm and good to soft going: has worn headgear: front runner. *M. Sheppard* **c75 h84**

YOUNG VALENTINO 5 ch.g. Komaite (USA) – Caprice (Mystiko (USA)) [2006/7 17v Feb 20] 6f winner at 3 yrs, only form on Flat: soundly beaten in maiden on hurdling debut. *A. W. Carroll* **h–**

YOUNG WILL 8 b.g. Keen – Barkston Singer (Runnett) [2006/7 c21mᵖᵘ Sep 2] lengthy gelding: very lightly raced: placed in maiden points in 2006: third when pulled up lame between last 2 in maiden at Stratford on chase debut. *B. J. Llewellyn* **c60**

YOUNG YOZZA 5 b.g. Kayf Tara – Swift Messenger (Giolla Mear) [2006/7 17g Mar 24] half-brother to fairly useful staying chaser Hermes Harvest (by Oats): dam, winning hurdler/chaser, stayed well: 11¼ lengths seventh of 14 to Annie's Answer in novice hurdle at Bangor on debut: likely to do better, particularly over further. *M. Sheppard* **h87 p**

YOUR ADVANTAGE (IRE) 7 b.g. Septieme Ciel (USA) – Freedom Flame (Darshaan) [2006/7 c100, h–: c16d⁴ c16sF 16g c20s² c20v⁶ c17vF c20v⁵ Feb 24] good-topped gelding: winning hurdler: fair handicap chaser: off 12 months, form in 2006/7 only on fourth outing: stays 2½m: acts on soft and good to firm going: has worn blinkers/cheekpieces: tongue tied. *Miss Lucinda V. Russell* **c100 h83**

YOUR A GASSMAN (IRE) 9 b.g. King's Ride – Nish Bar (Callernish) [2006/7 c–, h–: c28dᵖᵘ 22g⁵ 20s c24v³ c32vᵖᵘ c28g⁴ Apr 15] tall, useful-looking gelding: winning **c106 § h99 §**

hurdler: useful novice chaser in 2004/5: form since only when last of 3 finishers in handicap at Haydock: stays 3¼m: raced on good going or softer: often blinkered nowadays: unreliable: sold 13,000 gns Doncaster May Sales. *Ferdy Murphy*

YOUR AMOUNT (IRE) 4 b.g. Beckett (IRE) – Sin Lucha (USA) (Northfields (USA)) [2006/7 16s⁴ 16v Jan 25] angular gelding: fair on Flat (stays easy 2m), successful in November: some promise when fourth to Pouvoir in juvenile at Kempton on hurdling debut: again not knocked about when well held later in month: likely to prove capable of better. *W. J. Musson* **h94 p**

YOU'RE AGOODUN 15 ch.g. Derrylin – Jennie Pat (Rymer) [2006/7 c30mᵖᵘ May 16] medium-sized gelding: useful handicap chaser at best: won point in 2005: always behind on hunter debut: stays 3½m: acts on heavy and good to firm going: used to wear blinkers, visored nowadays: often let down by jumping. *A. C. Kemp* **c– x h–**

YOURMAN (IRE) 7 b.g. Shernazar – Lantern Lover (Be My Native (USA)) [2006/7 h121: 21gᵖᵘ Nov 7] sparely-made gelding: fairly useful handicap hurdler: off 12 months, pulled up lame after first start only in 2006/7: stays 3m: acts on soft and firm going: usually held up: not straightforward. *D. E. Pipe* **h–**

YOURSOMETHINELSE (IRE) 6 b.m. Courtship – Iada (IRE) (Accordion) [2006/7 18f⁴ 22g* 20g⁴ 22d⁶ 20v Nov 16] third foal: dam 2½m hurdle winner: poor hurdler: won maiden at Downpatrick in August: stays 2¾m. *F. J. Lacy, Ireland* **h82**

YOU SIR (IRE) 7 b.g. Taipan (IRE) – Lime Lady (IRE) (Aristocracy) [2006/7 h112p, F103: 16s 16v³ 18s³ 18v² 19s* 20v² 24v 18v³ Mar 10] fairly useful hurdler: won minor event at Limerick in December by ¾ length from Gripit N Tipit: creditable efforts otherwise in 2006/7 when placed in similar events, third to Derravarra Eagle at Fairyhouse final start: stays 2½m: raced on going softer than good (acts on heavy): front runner: tough and genuine. *Michael J. Bowe, Ireland* **h120**

YOU'VEGOTMEROCKING (IRE) 7 b.g. Saddlers' Hall (IRE) – Stormy Miss (IRE) (Glacial Storm (USA)) [2006/7 20m c20f 16vᵖᵘ 20v³ 16g 26m⁵ 24m Apr 15] first foal: dam, modest hurdler, stayed 3m: fair hurdler at best: disappointing in 2006/7, left E. O'Grady after second outing, R. Ford after fourth: stays 2¾m: probably acts on heavy ground (bumper winner on good to firm): visored once, usually blinkered: often fails to impress with jumping/attitude (including on chasing debut). *Ian Williams* **c– § h83 §**

YUFO (IRE) 7 ch.g. Invited (USA) – Smart Lass (Martinmas) [2006/7 F90: 20d³ 19dᵘʳ 22s³ 21s⁴ Feb 9] sturdy gelding: runner-up in bumper: modest form over hurdles, off a year before return: stays 2¾m: acts on soft ground. *N. J. Gifford* **h98**

YUKON JACK 9 b.g. Tharqaam (IRE) – Spanish Mermaid (Julio Mariner) [2006/7 h–: 16m 16v May 23] no sign of ability. *N. J. Pomfret* **h–**

YVANOVITCH (FR) 9 b.g. Kaldounevees (FR) – County Kerry (FR) (Comrade In Arms) [2006/7 c–, h–: c20d⁵ c16vᵘʳ c16s³ c16gᵇᵈ c16vᵖᵘ c16mᵖᵘ Apr 24] big, strong gelding: modest handicap chaser, off 19 months before return: ran poorly after: brought down fourth start: stays 2½m: acts on heavy and good to firm going. *R. C. Guest* **c95 h–**

Z

ZABADOU 6 b.g. Abou Zouz (USA) – Strapped (Reprimand) [2006/7 h–: 20dᵖᵘ c20dᵘʳ c20dᵖᵘ 16g Nov 29] leggy gelding: of little account: tried in cheekpieces/blinkers. *F. Kirby* **c– h–**

ZA BEAU (IRE) 6 b.m. Beneficial – Shuil Na Gale (Strong Gale) [2006/7 16v⁶ 20v⁵ 16v³ Feb 5] €32,000 4-y-o: tall mare: closely related to 2 winners by Norwich, including one-time fairly useful (now ungenuine) hurdler El Viejo, stays 2¾m, and half-sister to 2 winners, including fair staying chaser Shuil Na Mhuire (by Roselier): dam unraced: poor form over hurdles. *J. S. Goldie* **h79**

ZABEEL PALACE 5 b.g. Grand Lodge (USA) – Applecross (Glint of Gold) [2006/7 17v 16d 16s 16s Feb 22] leggy gelding: fairly useful on Flat (best form at 1¼m), successful both starts in 2005, sold out of Saeed bin Suroor's stable 28,000 gns Newmarket Autumn Sales: never dangerous over hurdles: may yet do better. *B. J. Curley* **h– p**

ZABENZ (NZ) 10 b.g. Zabeel (NZ) – In The Country (NZ) (In The Purple (FR)) [2006/7 c142, h–: c24m² c24s³ c24d² c36gᵖᵘ c29f⁵ Apr 28] sturdy gelding: type to carry condition: smart handicap chaser: runner-up in valuable events at Ascot in 2006/7, and in **c145 h–**

process of putting up career-best effort when all but fell last in Betfred Gold Cup at Sandown final start: pulled up after first Becher's in Grand National at Aintree (broken leather): stays 29f: acts on firm and good to soft going: blinkered: usually sound jumper: front runner/races prominently. *P. J. Hobbs*

ZACATECAS (GER) 7 b.g. Grand Lodge (USA) – Zephyrine (IRE) (Highest Honor (FR)) [2006/7 h86: 16g 17m 26m^{pu} 24m c23f^{pu} Sep 3] maiden hurdler: no form in 2006/7, including on chasing debut (visored). *M. Scudamore*
c–
h–

ZACHAROVA (IRE) 4 b.g. Lil's Boy (USA) – Voronova (IRE) (Sadler's Wells (USA)) [2006/7 16s^{pu} 16v^6 16s^6 17s Jan 30] strong, good-bodied gelding: fairly useful on Flat (stays 1¼m), successful 3 times in 2006, sold out of J. Bolger's stable 31,000 gns Newmarket July Sales: modest form over hurdles: may do better with less emphasis on stamina: room for improvement in jumping. *Miss Venetia Williams*
h88

ZAFFAMORE (IRE) 11 ch.g. Zaffaran (USA) – Furmore (Furry Glen) [2006/7 c109, h–: c25g^4 c25m* c24m^{pu} c24g^2 Nov 7] strong gelding: fair handicap chaser: won at Ludlow (fourth course success) in May: stays 25f: acts on soft and good to firm going: well held both starts on left-handed tracks. *Miss H. C. Knight*
c109
h–

ZAFFARANI'S STAR 6 b.g. Zaffaran (USA) – Slipstream Star (Slip Anchor) [2006/7 F16g Mar 21] second foal: dam, fair maiden on Flat who stayed 9f, poor maiden hurdler: carried head awkwardly when last in bumper on debut. *Mike Hammond*
F–

ZAFFARELLA (IRE) 6 b.m. Zaffaran (USA) – Bay Gale (IRE) (Abednego) [2006/7 F17v^2 F16s^5 F16s^6 Mar 10] rather unfurnished mare: second foal: dam ran once: fair form in bumpers, sixth to Swaythe in listed mares event at Sandown: found little second start. *D. P. Keane*
F92

ZAFFARSSON (IRE) 6 ch.g. Zaffaran (USA) – Sheelin Bavard (Le Bavard (FR)) [2006/7 F–: 21g^{pu} Nov 15] close-coupled, good-topped gelding: type to carry condition: no show in bumpers/novice hurdle. *B. W. Duke*
h–

ZAFFAS MELODY (IRE) 7 ch.g. Zaffaran (USA) – Orchette (IRE) (Orchestra) [2006/7 24s^{pu} 21m^{pu} c24v^{pu} Mar 10] well-made gelding: in frame in bumpers: left M. Scudamore and off 19 months, no form over hurdles/in maiden chase: tried visored *Mike Hammond*
c–
h–

ZAFFEU 6 ch.g. Zafonic (USA) – Leaping Flame (USA) (Trempolino (USA)) [2006/7 16g^{pu} Nov 15] leggy gelding: has only one eye: modest on Flat (stays 2m), successful in November: no show in novice on hurdling debut (mistakes). *A. G. Juckes*
h–

ZAFFIE PARSON (IRE) 6 b.m. Zaffaran (USA) – Katie Parson (The Parson) [2006/7 h73+, F88: 21m^6 25s^{pu} 22d^3 25s 27d^2 27s* 27s^6 24s 22v 24v^6 24s Apr 25] quite good-topped mare: modest hurdler: won handicap at Sedgefield in December: below form after: stays 27f: acts on heavy going: in cheekpieces last 3 starts: tends to get on toes. *G. A. Harker*
h90

ZAFFIERA (IRE) 6 b.g. Zaffaran (USA) – Kiera's Gale (IRE) (Strong Gale) [2006/7 c–, h–: c25s^{ur} Mar 7] small, sturdy gelding: no form over hurdles/in chases: runner-up in point in April: tried tongue tied. *Paul Williamson*
c–
h–

ZAFFRAN GAIL (IRE) 6 ch.g. Zaffaran (USA) – Cara Gail (IRE) (Strong Gale) [2006/7 F16d 17v^{pu} Feb 20] €13,000 4-y-o: second foal: dam, poor maiden hurdler, half-sister to one-time fairly useful staying hurdler/chaser Young Thruster: no form in bumper/novice hurdle. *J. Wade*
h–
F–

ZAFFRAN LADY (IRE) 8 b.m. Zaffaran (USA) – Windmill Star (IRE) (Orchestra) [2006/7 c16s c24v^{pu} c20s^{pu} 24v 24v^{rtr} 22g c27m Apr 9] winning hurdler/maiden chaser: no form in 2006/7 (refused to race fifth start), left A. Moore after third outing: has worn cheekpieces/blinkers: tried tongue tied: needs treating with caution. *Ferdy Murphy*
c– §
h– §

ZAFFRE (IRE) 8 gr.m. Mtoto – Zeferina (IRE) (Sadler's Wells (USA)) [2006/7 h89: 16g^6 17s^{pu} Nov 14] big mare: modest hurdler: off 15 months, no form in handicaps in 2006/7: should stay beyond 2½m: acts on soft and good to firm going. *Miss Z. C. Davison*
h–

ZAGREUS (GER) 5 gr.g. Fasliyev (USA) – Zephyrine (IRE) (Highest Honor (FR)) [2006/7 h–: 16m^{pu} May 6] tall gelding: no form over hurdles. *F. E. Sutherland*
h–

ZAHARA JOY 4 ch.f. Cayman Kai (IRE) – Enjoy (IRE) (Mazaad) [2006/7 16m^6 17s^{pu} Oct 25] modest maiden on Flat at 2 yrs, well beaten in 2006: little impact in juvenile hurdles. *D. W. Thompson*
h–

ZAHRA'S PLACE 4 ch.f. Zaha (CAN) – La Piazza (IRE) (Polish Patriot (USA)) [2006/7 F14g^3 F14s* F16v^6 Feb 24] sturdy filly: second foal: dam 5f/6f winner: fair form
F90

in bumpers, won 3-y-o event at Fontwell in November by 5 lengths from Abutilon. *N. B. King*

ZAHUNDA (IRE) 8 b.m. Spectrum (IRE) – Gift of Glory (FR) (Niniski (USA)) [2006/7 h–: 20m Jun 13] leggy mare: little form over hurdles: tried visored. *M. J. Gingell*　　h–

ZAILANN (IRE) 5 b.g. Sinndar (IRE) – Zaila (IRE) (Darshaan) [2006/7 F17m³ 20m⁴ 16m⁵ 16fᵖᵘ 20gᵖᵘ Jul 31] half-brother to several winners, notably very smart hurdler Zaiyad (by Sadler's Wells), stays 3m: dam, French 10.5f and 11f winner, granddaughter of Petite Étoile: third in bumper: form (poor) over hurdles only when fifth in novice at Uttoxeter: tongue tied after debut, also visored final start. *D. E. Pipe*　　h80 F67

ZAIYAD (IRE) 6 b.g. Sadler's Wells (USA) – Zaila (IRE) (Darshaan) [2006/7 h140: 20s* 24s* 24s⁵ 18s 19v* Mar 31] smallish gelding: very smart hurdler: successful in 3 Group races at Auteuil in 2006/7, notably Group 1 Grand Prix d'Automne, beat Royale Athenia by 6 lengths) in November second start, and also won Group 1 Grande Course de Haies d'Auteuil (by 8 lengths from Mister Gyor) after end of British season: tongue tied, below form both starts in Britain, last of 5 behind Inglis Drever in Grade 2 at Newbury: stays 25f: raced on good to good or softer (acts on heavy): usually wears earplugs (reportedly not at Newbury). *A. Chaille-Chaille, France*　　h156

ZALDA 6 ch.m. Zilzal (USA) – Gold Luck (USA) (Slew O' Gold (USA)) [2006/7 h125: 19g* c20g* Sep 30] leggy mare: fairly useful handicap hurdler: won at Newton Abbot in July: again made all when beating Idris by 12 lengths in maiden at Fontwell on chasing debut 2 months later: stays 2½m: acts on good to soft and good to firm going. *P. J. Hobbs*　　c114 h120

ZANDEED (IRE) 9 b.g. Inchinor – Persian Song (Persian Bold) [2006/7 h–: 24mᵖᵘ 18dᵖᵘ Nov 12] no form over hurdles. *Miss L. Day*　　h–

ZANDO 5 b.g. Forzando – Rockin' Rosie (Song) [2006/7 h85: 19s⁶ 16s 16fᵖᵘ Apr 5] smallish gelding: winning selling hurdler: no form in 2006/7. *E. G. Bevan*　　h–

ZANZIBAR BOY 8 gr.g. Arzanni – Bampton Fair (Free Boy) [2006/7 h84+, F98: c23s⁴ c23d* c25d⁵ Feb 1] big, useful-looking gelding: modest form over hurdles/fences: won amateur handicap chase at Exeter in December: let down by jumping next time: stays 3m: acts on good to firm and good to soft going, probably on soft. *H. Morrison*　　c98 h–

ZARAKASH (IRE) 7 b.g. Darshaan – Zarannda (IRE) (Last Tycoon) [2006/7 h92: 22m² 16d⁵ 16v⁴ Dec 16] smallish gelding: modest handicap hurdler, left Jonjo O'Neill after reappearance: stays 2¾m, at least when emphasis is on speed: unraced on firm going, acts on any other: has taken strong hold. *N. Madden, Ireland*　　h96

ZARBEAU 5 ch.g. Zaha (CAN) – Isabeau (Law Society (USA)) [2006/7 F–: 20mᵖᵘ Jun 3] no form in bumpers/novice hurdle. *J. M. Jefferson*　　h–

ZARIYAN (FR) 4 b.c. Anabaa (USA) – Zarkana (IRE) (Doyoun) [2006/7 17s 16d 17s⁴ Mar 17] leggy, angular colt: useful on Flat (stays 9.5f), successful 3 times in 2006, sold out of A. de Royer Dupre's stable €290,000 Goffs Arc Sale: well held over hurdles, behind Katchit in juvenile at Cheltenham on debut (swished tail beforehand). *T. Doumen, France*　　h85

ZASTRA'S PRIDE 4 ch.f. Zaha (CAN) – Strath Kitten (Scottish Reel) [2006/7 17d⁶ Nov 23] little show on Flat for W. Turner: tongue tied, tailed off in juvenile seller on hurdling debut. *N. J. Dawe*　　h–

ZATOCHI (IRE) 5 b.g. Shernazar – Sarah's Smile (Callernish) [2006/7 F17m⁶ Apr 28] €13,500 3-y-o: ninth foal: half-brother to bumper winner Merry Music (by Good Thyne) and winning pointer by Mandalus: dam winning 2m hurdler: some late headway when sixth to Georgian King in bumper at Market Rasen on debut. *R. C. Guest*　　F66

ZEIS (IRE) 7 ch.g. Bahhare (USA) – Zoom Lens (IRE) (Caerleon (USA)) [2006/7 h84: 19gᵖᵘ 16mᵖᵘ Jul 2] maiden hurdler, no form last 4 starts: wore headgear in 2006/7: usually tongue tied. *Evan Williams*　　h–

ZEITGEIST (IRE) 6 b.g. Singspiel (IRE) – Diamond Quest (Rainbow Quest (USA)) [2006/7 h105: 16g 16v⁶ 20s 16v⁶ Mar 6] good-topped gelding: hurdle winner, little impact in handicaps in 2006/7: stays 21f: tried in visor (didn't impress with jumping or attitude)/tongue tied. *J. Howard Johnson*　　h92

ZELOSO 9 b.g. Alzao (USA) – Silk Petal (Petorius) [2006/7 h81§: 20g 22m* 20d³ Nov 14] leggy gelding: modest handicap hurdler: won conditional jockeys race at Fontwell in June: lame final start: stays 2¾m: acts on good to firm and heavy going: tried in cheekpieces/blinkers, usually visored: ungenuine. *M. F. Harris*　　h92 §

ZEN GARDEN 6 b.m. Alzao (USA) – Maze Garden (USA) (Riverman (USA)) [2006/7 F77: aF16g Mar 9] poor form in bumpers 21 months apart. *W. M. Brisbourne* — **F64**

ZEROBERTO (IRE) 7 ch.g. Definite Article – Blazing Soul (IRE) (Common Grounds) [2006/7 16m³ 16d* 20g* c16s⁵ Nov 19] fairly useful hurdler: won handicap at Galway in July and minor event at Roscommon (easily by 5 lengths from King Ali) in August: last of 5 finishers behind Blueberry Boy in Grade 2 novice at Punchestown on chasing debut: stays 2½m: acts on soft and good to firm going. *D. K. Weld, Ireland* — **c113 h121 +**

ZERO POINT 6 b.g. Danzero (AUS) – Uniform (Unfuwain (USA)) [2006/7 F17s F16vᵖᵘ F16g Apr 23] big gelding: first foal: dam, fairly useful 2m hurdler, also winner up to 2m on Flat: no form in bumpers. *A. Crook* — **F–**

ZHIVAGO'S PRINCESS (IRE) 5 b.m. Orpen (USA) – Collage (Ela-Mana-Mou) [2006/7 F83: F16s⁵ 16s⁶ 16mᵖᵘ 16mᵘʳ Jul 2] modest form in bumpers: little impact in novice hurdles: tried in cheekpieces. *P. T. Dalton* — **h– F83**

ZIBELINE (IRE) 10 b.g. Cadeaux Genereux – Zia (USA) (Shareef Dancer (USA)) [2006/7 c–, h113: c20s³ c19s⁴ Jan 24] leggy gelding: winning hurdler/maiden chaser, fair form over fences in 2006/7: stays 2½m: acts on soft going, probably on good to firm: usually wears headgear: tried tongue tied: sold 6,400 gns Doncaster May Sales. *B. Ellison* — **c108 h–**

ZILCASH 4 b.g. Mujahid (USA) – Empty Purse (Pennine Walk) [2006/7 17d² 16d² 16d² 21v² 20vᶠ 16d⁴ Mar 13] quite good-topped gelding: half-brother to 2 winning jumpers, notably fairly useful 2m hurdler/winning chaser Going For Broke (by Simply Great): fair up to 11.5f on Flat: useful hurdler: runner-up first 4 starts, beaten 1¾ lengths by Labelthou (pair well clear) in Grade 2 novice at Warwick on fourth occasion: top weight, good 8¼ lengths fourth of 24 to Gaspara in listed Fred Winter Juvenile Handicap at Cheltenham: stays 21f: acts on heavy going: has run well when sweating. *A. King* — **h139**

Mr David Bellamy & Mr Stephen Williams' "Zilcash"

ZILLA (FR) 6 ch.m. Gold Away (IRE) – Zarah (FR) (Zino) [2006/7 h51: 22m² 22dᵖᵘ   **h62**
20m Jul 4] poor maiden hurdler: saddle slipped second start: stays 2¾m. *D. P. Keane*

ZIMBABWE 7 b.g. Kahyasi – Zeferina (IRE) (Sadler's Wells (USA)) [2006/7 h–: 16d*   **h98**
22g 18g* Apr 10] sturdy gelding: fairly useful juvenile hurdler in 2003/4: off 13 months,
didn't need to be anywhere near best to win sellers at Leicester in December and Fontwell
in April: should stay beyond 2¼m: acts on soft and good to firm ground. *G. L. Moore*

ZIMBABWE (FR) 7 b.g. Turgeon (USA) – Razzamatazz (FR) (Always Fair (USA))   **c112**
[2006/7 c83, h–: c23m² c25mᵖᵘ c26g c23s* c26v* c23v* c29v² c23s* c23v⁵ Feb 25]   **h–**
sturdy gelding: fair handicap chaser: vastly improved in 2006/7, won at Exeter (novice)
and Plumpton in December, Exeter again in January and Leicester in February: stays
29f: acts on good to firm and heavy going: blinkered (below form) once, usually wears
cheekpieces: goes well for conditional Jay Harris. *N. J. Hawke*

ZINGING 8 b.g. Fraam – Hi Hoh (IRE) (Fayruz) [2006/7 18d⁴ 16gᵖᵘ Nov 17] compact   **h–**
gelding: modest and ungenuine on Flat (stays 1¼m), successful in May: no form over
hurdles. *J. J. Bridger*

ZION (IRE) 7 b.g. Dr Massini (IRE) – Lunulae (Tumble Wind) [2006/7 16m² 18gᵘʳ   **h89**
Sep 3] good-topped ex-Irish gelding: half-brother to several winners on Flat, including
fairly useful 7f winner Super Sonic Sonia (by Tirol): dam, fairly useful hurdler up to
2½m, half-sister to dam of Beef Or Salmon: fair form at best in bumpers: sold out of
J. Crowley's stable 4,500 gns Doncaster May Sales and off a year, 3½ lengths second to
Changing Gear in maiden hurdle at Worcester. *B. G. Powell*

ZIPALONG LAD (IRE) 7 b.g. Zaffaran (USA) – Rosy Posy (IRE) (Roselier (FR))   **h–**
[2006/7 h135: 21d 24dᵖᵘ Nov 24] good-topped gelding: useful hurdler at best: left
P. Bowen and off 7 months, no show in handicaps in 2006/7: would have stayed beyond
3m: acted on heavy ground: dead. *Miss H. Lewis*

ZIZOU (IRE) 4 b.g. Fantastic Light (USA) – Search Committee (USA) (Roberto   **h82**
(USA)) [2006/7 16fᵘʳ 18gᵖᵘ 16g⁶ 18s 16d 16mᵖ 16f⁵ Apr 22] maiden on Flat, has lost his
form: poor hurdler: won minor event at Plumpton in April: will prove best at sharp 2m:
acts on firm going. *J. J. Bridger*

ZONIC BOOM (FR) 7 ch.g. Zafonic (USA) – Rosi Zambotti (IRE) (Law Society   **h90**
(USA)) [2006/7 h90: 16m 17d⁴ 21mᵖ 19g⁵ 21s Dec 7] angular gelding: modest hurdler:
won maiden at Ludlow in November: stays easy 21f: acts on good to firm and good to soft
going: wore cheekpieces/tongue strap last 3 starts. *Heather Dalton*

ZUBROWSKO (FR) 6 b.g. Nikos – Tinozakia (FR) (General Holme (USA)) [2006/7   **h–**
h–: 17s 21d Jan 8] soundly beaten over hurdles. *J. A. Geake*

ZULETA 6 ch.m. Vettori (IRE) – Victoria (Old Vic) [2006/7 h73: 16d 16s³ 22d* Jun 12]   **h77**
poor hurdler: 100/1 and upped in trip, won at Newton Abbot in June on handicap debut,
soon off bridle: will stay 3m: acts on soft and good to firm going. *Mrs L. J. Young*

ZUMRAH (IRE) 6 b.g. Machiavellian (USA) – The Perfect Life (IRE) (Try My Best   **c–**
(USA)) [2006/7 h91, F96: 16m² 20fᵖᵘ c20m⁶ 16f⁵ 20f³ Jul 19] bumper winner: modest   **h99**
maiden hurdler: none too fluent when well beaten in novice handicap on chasing debut:
stays 2½m, at least when emphasis is on speed: raced on good to firm/firm going over
hurdles: has raced freely. *P. Bowen*

ZUM SEE (IRE) 8 ch.g. Perugino (USA) – Drew (IRE) (Double Schwartz) [2006/7   **c130 §**
c123, h–: c19v³ c16g* c16s⁴ c17v⁶ 18v c16g c17mᵖ c16m Apr 24] tall, well-made   **h–**
gelding: winning hurdler: useful handicap chaser: won at Cork (by 6 lengths from On The
Net) in October: creditable seventh of 23 to Andreas in Grade 3 Grand Annual Chase at
Cheltenham sixth outing: stays 19f: acts on heavy and good to firm going: often
blinkered: usually held up: tends to finish weakly. *N. Meade, Ireland*

ZUZU SUMMIT (IRE) 5 ch.m. Pasternak – Summit Else (El Conquistador) [2006/7   **h–**
F83: 19s 16m Apr 24] third in 3-y-o bumper on debut: no form since, left M. Scudamore
after first start over hurdles. *K. A. Morgan*

PROMISING HORSES

Selected British-trained horses in *Chasers & Hurdlers* thought capable of noteworthy improvement are listed under the trainers for whom they last ran.

R. H. ALNER
Lindop 7 ch.g h119p
Pimbury (IRE) 5 b.g h105p

D. W. P. ARBUTHNOT
Sound Accord (IRE) 6 br.g h117p F109

A. M. BALDING
Briareus 7 ch.g h— c146p

C. C. BEALBY
Extra Smooth 6 br.g h— c120p

P. BOWEN
Blue Splash (FR) 7 b.g h119 c135p

NOEL T. CHANCE
Aux Le Bahnn (IRE) 6 b.g F117p

H. D. DALY
Kedgeree 5 b.g h90p F92
Prof de L'Isle (FR) 4 b.g F84p
Royal Kicks (FR) 6 b.g h92p
Tabora 5 b.m h101+ c101p

V. R. A. DARTNALL
Lappeenranta (IRE) 6 b.g h102p
Mole's Chamber (IRE) 6 b.g h111p F73
Russian Trigger 5 b.g h109p
Sporting Rebel (IRE) 7 b.g h98p
The Apprentice (IRE) 5 b.g F82p

J. M. DUN
River Alder 9 b.m h117 c83p

C. R. EGERTON
Pukka (IRE) 6 b.g h124p
Rio Bravo (IRE) 7 b.g h95p
Willie Pep (IRE) 6 b.g h94p F99

J. M. P. EUSTACE
At The Money 4 b.g h108p

R. A. FAHEY
Ski Jump (USA) 7 gr.g h92p

J. R. FANSHAWE
Song of Songs 5 b.g h128p

N. J. GIFFORD
Give Me A Dime (IRE) 5 b.g h101p F85

P. C. HASLAM
Heraldry (IRE) 7 b.g h124p

N. J. HENDERSON
Classic Fiddle 5 ch.m h125p
French Opera 4 b.g h114p
Oedipe (FR) 5 ch.g c135p
Sentry Duty (FR) 5 b.h h117p
Ship's Hill (IRE) 6 b.g h117p F104
Taranis 4 b.g h102p

P. J. HOBBS
Eden Linty 6 b.m h111p
Gentle John (FR) 5 b.g h102p

Khasab (IRE) 6 br.g h117p
Lead On (IRE) 6 b.g h127p
Sir Rique (FR) 4 b.g h96p

J. HOWARD JOHNSON
Falpiase (IRE) 5 b.g h116p
Hard Act To Follow (IRE) 8 ch.g h— c128P
Key Time (IRE) 5 b.g h123p
Laborec (IRE) 4 gr.g F110p

D. P. KEANE
Midnight Chase 5 b.g h100p

A. KING
Ballamusic (IRE) 5 b.g h109p F87
Dragon Eye (IRE) 5 b.g F95p
My Way de Solzen (FR) 7 b.g h147+ c157p
Ouzbeck (FR) 5 b.g h121p
Pur de Sivola (FR) 4 b.g h108p c111

MISS H. C. KNIGHT
King Neptune 6 b.g F91p
Olmeto Collonges (FR) 5 b.g h88p c95
Openditch (FR) 5 b.g h98p F108
Quarry Town (IRE) 5 b.g h100p F107
Ringaroses 6 b.g h136p
Seismic Shift (IRE) 5 b.g h95p F104
West End King (IRE) 5 b.g F108p

MISS E. C. LAVELLE
Marcus 6 gr.g h128p
Opus Cafe (FR) 5 b.g h92p
Premier Hope (IRE) 6 b.m h101p
Stern (IRE) 8 b.g h— c120p
Supreme Copper (IRE) 7 br.g h98p

CARL LLEWELLYN
Carrick Oscar (IRE) 7 b.g h132p
Joyryder 6 gr.g h98p
Nightfly (IRE) 6 b.g h116p
Sydney (IRE) 7 b.g h110p

L. LUNGO
Berwick Law (IRE) 5 ch.g F111p

C. J. MANN
Air Force One (GER) 5 ch.h h137p
Rebel Melody (IRE) 6 b.g h88p
Teamgeist (IRE) 6 b.g h109p F95

D. MCCAIN JNR
Jungleland (IRE) 5 b.g h109p F—

G. L. MOORE
Gabier 4 b.c h116p

G. M. MOORE
Nelsons Column (IRE) 4 b.g h102p

J. S. MOORE
Mull of Dubai 4 b.g h72p

FERDY MURPHY
Aces Four (IRE) 8 ch.g h— c154p
Another Promise (IRE) 8 b.g h— c144p

Mr Floppy (IRE) 6 b.g h71p F78
Naiad du Misselot (FR) 6 b.g h115p
Poker de Sivola (FR) 4 b.g h120p

P. F. NICHOLLS
Another Bottle (IRE) 6 b.g h103p
Be Be King (IRE) 8 b.g h125+ c116p
Bold Policy (IRE) 4 b.g F101p
Denman (IRE) 7 ch.g h— c161p
Leading Attraction (IRE) 6 b.g h121p
Oberon Moon (IRE) 6 gr.g F100p
O'Maley (FR) 5 b.g h— c120p
Opera Mundi (FR) 5 b.g h— c140p
Oslot (FR) 5 b.g h133p
Raffaello (FR) 6 b.g h— c124p
Roby de Cimbre (FR) 4 gr.g h112p
The Tother One (IRE) 6 b.g F105p
Twist Magic (FR) 5 b.g h— c154p

JONJO O'NEILL
Albertas Run (IRE) 6 b.g h136p
Alternator (IRE) 5 ch.g h105p F102
Country Escape 4 b.g h91p
Fier Normand (FR) 8 b.g h— c109p
Matcho Pierji (FR) 5 b.g h103 c100p
Mountain (IRE) 4 b.g h116p
Nor'nor'east (IRE) 9 b.g h— c115p
Runthatpastmeagain (IRE) 5 b.g h110p
Spirit of New York (IRE) 8 b.g h124p c—
Wichita Lineman (IRE) 6 b.g h152p

D. E. PIPE
Abragante (IRE) 6 b.g h135+ c125p
Brave Broncho (IRE) 5 b.g h83p
Commander Vic (FR) 5 b.g h98p
El Bandindos (IRE) 6 b.g h93p
Gaspara (FR) 4 b.f h149+ c108p
Master Overseer (IRE) 4 b.g F115p
Nacadour (FR) 6 b.g h99p c—
Nike Walker (FR) 4 b.g h112p
Not Left Yet (IRE) 6 b.g h— c125p
Nous Voila (FR) 6 b.g h— c120p
Pablo du Charmil (FR) 6 ch.g h— c137p
Seven Is Lucky (IRE) 5 b.g h90p
The Package 4 br.g F102p
Travelling Light (IRE) 5 b.g h86p
Turnberry Bay (FR) 6 b.g h93 c97p

B. G. POWELL
Money Order (IRE) 5 b.g h119p F103

J. J. QUINN
Blythe Knight (IRE) 7 ch.g h144p
Pevensey (IRE) 5 b.g h127p

K. G. REVELEY
Bold Ransom (IRE) 5 b.g h73p F73
Hapeney (IRE) 4 b.f F86p

N. G. RICHARDS
Double Default (IRE) 6 ch.g h124p
Grangeclare Flight (IRE) 5 b.m F94p
Gunner Jack 6 b.g h114p
I'm Delilah 5 b.m F109p
Middleton Dene (IRE) 5 b.g h93p F93
One Sniff (IRE) 8 b.g h— c127p
Role On (IRE) 5 gr.g h107p F102
Young Albert (IRE) 6 br.g h112p

K. A. RYAN
Divine Gift 6 b.g h110p

MRS S. J. SMITH
Camden George (IRE) 6 b.g h117p F102
Tous Chez (IRE) 8 b.g h112 c106p

G. A. SWINBANK
Little Lu (IRE) 5 b.m F97p
Programme Girl (IRE) 5 ch.m h97p F104
Ring The Boss (IRE) 6 b.g h125p
Shiwawa 5 b.g F106p
Silver Snitch (IRE) 7 gr.g h115p F101
Sir Boreas Hawk 5 b.g h129p F109
Starting Point 5 br.g F104p

T. P. TATE
Suits Me 4 ch.g h79p

C. W. THORNTON
Lets Roll 6 b.g h101p

M. TODHUNTER
That's Rhythm (FR) 7 b.g h103p

M. H. TOMPKINS
Gee Dee Nen 4 b.g h83p

ANDREW TURNELL
Bible Lord (IRE) 6 ch.g h— c128p

N. A. TWISTON-DAVIES
Sexy Rexy (IRE) 6 b.g h103p
Super Nick (IRE) 6 b.g h109p F105
The Cool Guy (IRE) 7 b.g h— c118p

JOHN R. UPSON
Gritti Palace (IRE) 7 b.g h— c98p

MRS L. WADHAM
Desert Inferno (FR) 5 b.g h96p F94
Enforce (USA) 4 b.f h103p

P. R. WEBBER
Appleaday (IRE) 6 gr.g h98p F102
Edgbriar (FR) 5 b.g h102p F102

EVAN WILLIAMS
Corran Ard (IRE) 6 b.g h122p
Court Ruler 5 b.g h114p
Danehill Willy (IRE) 5 b.g h90p
High Chimes (IRE) 8 b.g c123p
Man Overboard 5 b.g h97p
Woolly Bully 4 b.g h101p

IAN WILLIAMS
Alagon (IRE) 7 b.g h— c91p

MISS VENETIA WILLIAMS
Lightning Strike (GER) 4 ch.g h126p
Mr Vesuvius (NZ) 7 ch.g h104p
Netherley (FR) 8 gr.g h120p
Sarin 9 b.g h108 c108p
Tyson (SAF) 7 b.g h130p

N. WILSON
Arctic Ghost 7 gr.g h97 c107p

SELECTED BIG RACES 2006/07

Prize money for racing abroad has been converted to £ sterling at the exchange rate current at the time of the race. The figures are correct to the nearest £.

HAYDOCK Saturday, May 6 FIRM

1 **Betfred Swinton Hcap Hdle (Gr 3) (1) (147) (4yo+)** £42,765   2m (8)

ACAMBO (GER) *MCPipe* 5-10-4[128] AndrewGlassonbury[7]	16/1	1
CALLOW LAKE (IRE) *MrsJHarrington,Ireland* 6-10-13[137] (b) ADLeigh[7]	15/2	1½ 2
SAIF SAREEA *RAFahey* 6-10-1[118] PadgeWhelan	8/1	6 3
EMMPAT (IRE) *CFSwan,Ireland* 8-10-2[119] RWalsh	7/1f	1¾ 4
Salut Saint Cloud *GLMoore* 5-10-3[120] (b) JimCrowley	16/1	¾ 5
Glimmer of Light (IRE) *SABrookshaw* 6-9-7[117] PhilKinsella[7]	22/1	1¾ 6
Papini (IRE) *NJHenderson* 5-10-6[123] AndrewTinkler	40/1	½ 7
Caracciola (GER) *NJHenderson* 9-11-4[135] MickFitzgerald	33/1	¾ 8
Into The Shadows *KGReveley* 6-10-1[118] RichardMcGrath	9/1	nk 9
Blazing Bailey *AKing* 4-11-12[147] RobertThornton	14/1	1 10
United (GER) *MrsLWadham* 5-11-6[137] LeightonAspell	25/1	¾ 11
Pseudonym (IRE) *MFHarris* 4-10-0[121] PJBrennan	50/1	nk 12
Liberty Seeker (FR) *GASwinbank* 7-10-8[125] MarkBradburne	18/1	½ 13
Lunar Crystal (IRE) *MCPipe* 8-10-12[129] TomScudamore	33/1	1½ 14
Overstrand (IRE) *RobertGray* 7-9-13[121] TomGreenway[5]	66/1	7 15
Senorita Rumbalita *AKing* 5-11-0[131] WayneHutchinson	14/1	20 16
Motorway (IRE) *PJHobbs* 5-10-10[127] RichardJohnson	10/1	8 17
Nawamees (IRE) *GLMoore* 8-10-13[130] (s) JamieMoore	33/1	9 18
Estepona *JHowardJohnson* 5-10-11[128] TonyDobbin	16/1	f
Ken's Dream *MrsLWadham* 7-10-0[117] TomDoyle	9/1	f
Merryvale Man *MissKarianaKey* 9-10-0[117] BenjaminHitchcott	200/1	pu

Mr D. A. Johnson 21ran 3m33.70

UTTOXETER Sunday, Jul 2 GOOD to FIRM

2 **Britannia Building Society English Summer National (Hcap Chase)**   4m110y (24)
(L) (1) 0-150(146) (5yo+) £45,072

MCKELVEY (IRE) *PBowen* 7-10-10[130] (s) APMcCoy	11/2	1
OMNI COSMO TOUCH (USA) *MrsSJSmith* 10-10-0[120] DavidO'Meara	15/2	2 2
DEAD-EYED DICK (IRE) *NickWilliams* 10-10-4[124] GLee	13/2	1¼ 3
Sweet Diversion (IRE) *PFNicholls* 7-11-8[142] (t) RWalsh	10/3f	2 4
Tribal Venture (FR) *PJHobbs* 8-10-1[121] (b) RichardJohnson	12/1	21 5
Galtee View (IRE) *EvanWilliams* 8-9-11[120] (s) TJO'Brien[3]	12/1	¾ 6
Gumley Gale *KBishop* 11-10-0[120] RJGreene	25/1	13 7
Robbo *KGReveley* 12-9-7[120] (b) JamesReveley[5]	33/1	dist 8
Ballycassidy (IRE) *PBowen* 10-11-12[146] JasonMaguire	14/1	ur
Kisslain Des Galas (FR) *DEPipe* 9-10-6[131] (t) AndrewGlassonbury[5]	66/1	pu
Calvic (IRE) *TRGeorge* 8-10-9[129] WayneHutchinson	12/1	pu
Dunbrody Millar (IRE) *PBowen* 8-10-6[126] JamieMoore	11/1	pu
Burwood Breeze (IRE) *TRGeorge* 8-10-0[120] PJBrennan	20/1	pu
Around Before (IRE) *JonjoO'Neill* 9-10-0[120] (s+t) SEDurack	33/1	pu
Charango Star *WKGoldsworthy* 8-9-9[120] TomMessenger[5]	40/1	pu

Mr N. Elliott 15ran 8m23.50

MARKET RASEN Saturday, Jul 22
Chase course: GOOD, Hurdles course: GOOD to SOFT

3 **totescoop6 Summer Hdle (Hcap) (2) 0-145(141) (4yo+)** £25,052   2m1f110y (8)

TYCOON HALL (IRE) *PBowen* 6-9-13[115] TJO'Brien[3]	33/1	1
WEE DINNS (IRE) *DEPipe* 5-10-7[120] TomScudamore	7/1	hd 2
PORTAVADIE *JMJefferson* 7-10-13[126] NoelFehily	50/1	1¼ 3
SUN KING *KGReveley* 9-9-7[113] (t) JamesReveley[7]	12/1	1¼ 4
Dune Raider (IRE) *TRGeorge* 5-10-6[119] JasonMaguire	13/2	2½ 5
O'Toole (IRE) *PJHobbs* 7-11-2[129] PJBrennan	33/1	½ 6
Lord Baskerville *CTPogson* 5-10-9[127] AdamPogson[5]	33/1	1½ 7
Neveesou (FR) *DEPipe* 5-11-5[132] TimmyMurphy	9/1	4 8
Crathorne (IRE) *MTodhunter* 6-10-12[125] GLee	9/1	1¾ 9
Double Vodka (IRE) *CGrant* 5-10-6[119] RichardMcGrath	12/1	1¾ 10
Hilltime (IRE) *JSWainwright* 6-10-1[121] MrRTierney[7]	12/1	2½ 11
Fair Along (GER) *PJHobbs* 4-11-12[141] RichardJohnson	8/1	3 12
Aleron (IRE) *JJQuinn* 8-11-1[128] (s) RussGarritty	20/1	½ 13
Albarino (IRE) *MScudamore* 7-10-5[118] RobertThornton	11/1	8 14
Paddy The Piper (IRE) *LLungo* 9-11-3[130] TonyDobbin	25/1	10 15

East Tycoon (IRE) *JonjoO'Neill* 7-11-0[127] (es) APMcCoy 6/1f 13 16
Ela Re *MrsSJSmith* 7-10-9[122] DavidO'Meara 16/1 4 17

Mrs Karen Bowen 17ran 4m09.50

4 **totesport.com Summer Plate (Hcap Chase) (L) (1)** 2¾m110y (14)
0-150(146) (5yo+) £37,063

	YES SIR (IRE) *PBowen* 7-10-10[130] APMcCoy	3/1f	1
2	BALLYCASSIDY (IRE) *PBowen* 10-11-12[146] JasonMaguire	20/1	6 2
	MR FLUFFY *AWCarroll* 9-10-0[125] TomMessenger[5]	50/1	1¼ 3
	Fool On The Hill *PJHobbs* 9-11-3[137] RichardJohnson	20/1	nk 4
	Bohemian Spirit (IRE) *NGRichards* 8-10-0[125] MissRDavidson[5]	14/1	1 5
	Tevere (FR) *DEPipe* 5-10-1[127] AndrewGlassonbury[5]	9/2	8 6
2	Sweet Diversion (IRE) *PFNicholls* 7-11-7[141] (t) RWalsh	4/1	3 7
	Joey Tribbiani (IRE) *TKeddy* 9-9-11[120] WTKennedy[3]	50/1	9 8
	Inch Pride (IRE) *DEPipe* 7-10-3[123] TimmyMurphy	17/2	1¼ 9
	Tikram *GLMoore* 9-9-11[145] (b+es) JamieMoore	20/1	5 10
	Celtic Boy (IRE) *PBowen* 8-11-5[139] ChristianWilliams	20/1	4 11
	Calatagan (IRE) *JMJefferson* 7-10-8[131] TJDreaper[3]	40/1	dist 12
	Full House (IRE) *PRWebber* 7-11-9[143] TomDoyle	15/2	pu
	Luneray (FR) *RFord* 7-10-0[120] (s+t) GLee	100/1	pu

Ms Y. M. Hill 14ran 5m32.61

GALWAY Wednesday, Aug 2 GOOD

5 **William Hill Plate (Hcap Chase) (Gr A) (148) (4yo+)** £83,425 2¾m (14)

	FAR FROM TROUBLE (IRE) *CRoche* 7-10-4[128] RLoughran	8/1	1
	ANSAR (IRE) *DKWeld* 10-11-10[148] RWalsh	4/1f	3½ 2
	DIX VILLEZ (FR) *PaulNolan* 7-9-10[120] PJBrennan	16/1	1¼ 3
	URSUMMAN (IRE) *NMadden* 7-10-9[133] NPMadden	9/1	nk 4
	Bothar Na (IRE) *WPMullins* 7-9-10[120] DJCondon	33/1	1¼ 5
	Mutakarrim *DKWeld* 9-10-2[126] (b) AndrewJMcNamara	16/1	nk 6
	Manjoe (IRE) *DWachman* 8-9-10[120] DJCasey	10/1	2½ 7
	Light On The Broom (IRE) *GStack* 10-9-10[120] (t) GCotter	33/1	12 8
	Montayral (IRE) *PatrickHughes* 9-9-10[120] PACarberry	100/1	2 9
	Always *NMeade* 7-11-0[138] (b) DNRussell	33/1	4½ 10
	Carlesimo (IRE) *NMeade* 8-10-0[124] DFO'Regan	20/1	16 11
	Teo Perugo (IRE) *EugeneMO'Sullivan* 7-9-13[130] MrRPMcLernon[7]	20/1	14 12
	Augherskea (IRE) *PatrickMartin* 7-10-3[127] RMPower	50/1	¾ 13
	Coast To Coast (IRE) *EJO'Grady* 7-10-0[124] (b+t) PWFlood	12/1	dist 14
	Banasan (IRE) *MJPO'Brien* 8-10-6[135] AELynch[5]	14/1	f
	Ball O Malt (IRE) *RAFahey,GB* 10-10-6[130] AnthonyRoss	16/1	f
	Steel Band *PaulARoche* 8-10-6[130] BJGeraghty	33/1	f
	Wills Wilde (IRE) *PAFahy* 7-9-12[125] APLane[3]	12/1	f
	Waltons Mountain (IRE) *AnthonyMullins* 8-9-13[123] RGeraghty	25/1	f
	More Rainbows (IRE) *NMeade* 6-9-10[120] TGMRyan	20/1	f
	Brutto Facie (IRE) *MrsJHarrington* 7-10-1[130] ADLeigh[5]	33/1	pu
	Domnul Admiral (IRE) *KJCondon* 8-9-10[120] JRBarry	33/1	pu

Mr John P. McManus 22ran 5m21.40

GALWAY Thursday, Aug 3 GOOD to FIRM

6 **Guinness Galway Hdle Hcap (137) (4yo+)** £83,082 2m (9)

	CUAN NA GRAI (IRE) *PaulNolan* 5-10-9[123] PWFlood	7/1	1
	SHANDON STAR (IRE) *WPMullins* 6-10-1[115] RWalsh	6/1f	4 2
	THE LAST HURRAH (IRE) *MrsJHarrington* 6-10-1[120] (b) ADLeigh[5]	10/1	½ 3
1	EMMPAT (IRE) *CFSwan* 8-10-3[117] NPMadden	12/1	hd 4
	The Fonze (IRE) *EoinDoyle* 5-10-5[119] GCotter	20/1	1 5
	Adamant Approach (IRE) *WPMullins* 12-11-2[137] RJKiely[7]	33/1	4½ 6
	Kinger Rocks (IRE) *DKWeld* 5-10-10[124] DFO'Regan	7/1	hd 7
	Crossbow Creek *MGRimell,GB* 8-11-6[134] GLee	25/1	½ 8
	Arc En Ciel (GER) *GerardCully* 6-10-11[125] DJCondon	25/1	¾ 9
	Red Square Lady (IRE) *MPhillips* 8-11-7[135] AndrewJMcNamara	20/1	1¼ 10
	Maxxium (IRE) *MHalford* 5-10-7[121] (t) TimmyMurphy	12/1	nk 11
	Chicago Vic (IRE) *EricMcNamara* 7-10-11[130] BCByrnes[5]	33/1	4 12
	Proud To Be Irish (IRE) *SO'Farrell* 7-10-10[120] MrJPO'Farrell[5]	12/1	1¼ 13
	Dbest (IRE) *MsJoannaMorgan* 6-10-5[119] (b) JPElliott	20/1	1¼ 14
	Portant Fella *MsJoannaMorgan* 7-10-6[120] (s) PACarberry	20/1	hd 15
	Breathing Fire *MrsJHarrington* 4-10-11[126] (s) RMPower	16/1	¾ 16
	Mirpour (IRE) *EoinGriffin* 7-9-13[120] TMolloy[7]	20/1	nk 17
	Barati (IRE) *MJPO'Brien* 5-10-5[124] (b) AELynch[5]	33/1	4½ 18
	Middlemarch (GER) *PAFahy* 5-10-5[119] DNRussell	12/1	1½ 19
1	Glimmer of Light (IRE) *SABrookshaw,GB* 6-10-1[115] SEDurack	50/1	pu

Mr John J. Brennan 20ran 3m37.70

NEWTON ABBOT Sunday, Aug 20   GOOD to SOFT

7   totepool Summer Festival Hcap Hdle (2) 0-140(136) (4yo+) £24,892   2¾m (8)

The first flight down the back was omitted

	RUSHNEYRIVER (IRE) *MrsAMThorpe* 8-10-8[118] (s) RobertThornton	8/1		1
	OPENIDE *BWDuke* 5-10-10[125] DarylJacob[5]	12/1	½	2
	IRISH WOLF (FR) *PBowen* 6-10-10[123] (s) TJO'Brien[3]	9/2	sh	3
	HI HUMPFREE *HeatherDalton* 6-10-2[115] (b) DougieCostello[3]	15/2	¾	4
	Treaty Flyer (IRE) *PGMurphy* 5-10-7[117] LeightonAspell	16/1	8	5
	Absolut Power (GER) *JAGeake* 5-10-8[118] (s) SEDurack.....................	20/1	6	6
	Ladino (FR) *PJHobbs* 6-10-10[120] RichardJohnson	4/1f	1¾	7
	Silver Charmer *HSHowe* 7-10-6[116] TimmyMurphy...............................	20/1	½	8
3	Crathorne (IRE) *MTodhunter* 6-11-1[125] GLee	16/1	4	9
3	Wee Dinns (IRE) *DEPipe* 5-11-1[125] TomScudamore	8/1	14	10
	Grave Doubts *KBishop* 10-10-13[123] (t) RJGreene..............................	40/1	20	11
	Top Trees *WSKittow* 8-10-0[110] PJBrennan...	25/1	hd	12
	Complete Outsider *NickWilliams* 8-10-10[120] WayneHutchinson................	12/1		ur
	Yankeedoodledandy (IRE) *CRoberts* 5-11-12[136] OllieMcPhail.....................	33/1		pu
	Sultan Fontenaille (FR) *NJHawke* 4-10-1[120] KeiranBurke[7]	16/1		pu
	Catchthebug (IRE) *JonjoO'Neill* 7-10-7[117] NoelFehily..........................	25/1		pu

Tristar 16ran 5m11.72

8   Lord Mildmay Memorial Hcap Chase (2) 0-145(139) (4yo+) £27,887   2m5f110y (16)

	KINGS BROOK *NickWilliams* 6-10-2[115] TimmyMurphy..........................	11/1		1
	GREEN FINGER *PBowen* 8-9-12[114] TJO'Brien[3]	6/1	1	2
	TANGO ROYAL (FR) *DEPipe* 10-10-11[124] (v+t) RJGreene......................	25/1	10	3
	Spectrometer *IanWilliams* 9-10-5[118] DavidDennis	14/1	7	4
	Maidstone Monument (IRE) *MrsAMThorpe* 11-10-1[114] SEDurack	10/1	8	5
	In Discussion (IRE) *JonjoO'Neill* 8-10-3[116] NoelFehily......................	8/1	18	6
4	Tevere (FR) *DEPipe* 5-10-13[131] AndrewGlassonbury[5]	8/1	5	7
4	Fool On The Hill *PJHobbs* 9-11-10[137] RichardJohnson	11/2f	3	8
4	Sweet Diversion (IRE) *PFNicholls* 7-11-7[139] (t) LiamHeard[5]	6/1	1¾	9
	Sky Warrior (FR) *EvanWilliams* 8-11-0[127] ChristianWilliams	40/1	sh	10
	Wrags To Riches (IRE) *JDFrost* 9-11-3[133] ChrisHonour[3].......................	33/1		pu
	Cameron Bridge (IRE) *PJHobbs* 10-11-3[130] PJBrennan	25/1		pu
	Bronzesmith *BJMRyall* 10-11-3[130] JoeTizzard	16/1		pu
2	Dead-Eyed Dick (IRE) *NickWilliams* 10-10-13[126] GLee	8/1		pu

Mr Tony Gale 14ran 5m16.69

LISTOWEL Wednesday, Sep 20   SOFT

9   Guinness Kerry National Hcap Chase (135) (4yo+) £61,064   3m (15)

What should have been the second last fence was omitted on the final two circuits due to a stricken horse

5	BOTHAR NA (IRE) *WPMullins* 7-10-13[127] RWalsh....................................	10/1		1
	PEARLY JACK *DEFitzgerald* 8-10-7[121] BJGeraghty	7/2f	2	2
	JUST IN DEBT (IRE) *MTodhunter,GB* 10-11-0[128] (s) MissNCarberry	25/1	5	3
	OH BE THE HOKEY (IRE) *CFSwan* 8-10-9[123] DJCasey	7/1	7	4
	Darby Wall (IRE) *EndaBolger* 8-10-6[120] RMPower...................................	20/1	4½	5
	Nonchalant (IRE) *MsFMCrowley* 8-9-12[112] TPTreacy............................	16/1	1	6
	Oodachee *CFSwan* 11-10-0[128] (s) DNRussell.....................................	9/1	1¾	7
	Loss of Faith (IRE) *MJPO'Brien* 8-10-1[122] RTDunne[7]...........................	25/1	12	8
	Monterey Bay (IRE) *MsFMCrowley* 10-10-10[124] (b) AndrewJMcNamara	8/1	19	9
5	Montayral (FR) *PatrickHughes* 9-10-2[116] PACarberry..............................	25/1	22	10
	Commonchero (IRE) *MJPO'Brien* 9-11-2[135] AELynch[5].............................	25/1		f
	One Four Shannon (IRE) *DJRyan* 9-10-9[123] TGMRyan............................	10/1		f
	Chetwind Music (IRE) *WilliamColemanO'Brien* 8-10-5[119] MDarcy.............	33/1		f
	No Half Session (IRE) *NMeade* 9-10-12[126] PCarberry	5/1		bd
	Billy Bonnie (IRE) *NMeade* 9-10-6[120] (b) DFO'Regan	16/1		pu
	Oscar's Advance (IRE) *CRoche* 7-10-5[119] RLoughran	14/1		pu
	Lotomore Lad (IRE) *DHassett* 8-9-11[111] (t) JRBarry............................	16/1		pu

Mrs Michael O'Dwyer 17ran 6m01.83

TIPPERARY Sunday, Oct 1   SOFT

10   Tipperary Hdle (Gr 2) (4yo+) £43,691   2m (9)

	SCARTHY LAD (IRE) *ThomasGerardO'Leary* 8-11-12 BJGeraghty	12/1		1
	MARALAN (IRE) *PatrickOBrady* 5-11-12 (b) JPElliott.............................	25/1	5½	2
	CEEAWAYHOME *JohnEKiely* 7-11-12 DNRussell.................................	10/1	1½	3
	Harchibald (FR) *NMeade* 7-11-12 PCarberry	4/9f	2	4
	Sweet Kiln (IRE) *JamesBowe* 7-11-7 RMPower	9/2	dist	5

Ballinascarthy Syndicate 5ran 3m55.06

LIMERICK Sunday, Oct 8   GOOD to SOFT

11   Tote Munster National Hcap Chase (Gr A) (147) (4yo+) £46,395   3m (16)

9	PEARLY JACK *DEFitzgerald* 8-9-10[120] NPMadden	3/1jf		1
	STAR CLIPPER *NMeade* 9-10-3[127] DJCondon	16/1	1½	2
5	DIX VILLEZ (FR) *PaulNolan* 7-9-10[123] RMMoran[3]	12/1	hd	3
9	No Half Session (IRE) *NMeade* 9-10-2[126] DFO'Regan	3/1jf	3½	4
9	Bothar Na (IRE) *WPMullins* 7-10-12[136] RWalsh	4/1	½	5
9	Loss of Faith (IRE) *MJPO'Brien* 8-9-9[122] AELynch[3]	10/1	23	6
	Strong Project (IRE) *SeanOO'Brien* 10-11-9[147] JMAllen	16/1	17	7
5	Domnul Admiral (IRE) *KJCondon* 8-9-10[120] PACarberry	20/1		ur
	Barrow Drive *AnthonyMullins* 10-11-2[140] (t) BJGeraghty	12/1		pu
9	Monterey Bay (IRE) *MsFMCrowley* 10-10-0[124] TGMRyan	14/1		pu
	Vic Ville (IRE) *MHourigan* 7-9-13[123] PJBrennan	12/1		pu

Mrs A. McCarthy 11ran 6m15.21

PUNCHESTOWN Thursday, Oct 19   SOFT

12   Star 'Best For Racing' Chase (L) (4yo+) £14,418   2¾m (15)

	WAR OF ATTRITION (IRE) *MFMorris* 7-11-12 CO'Dwyer	8/11f		1
	WATSON LAKE (IRE) *NMeade* 8-11-12 PCarberry	6/4	11	2
11	BARROW DRIVE *AnthonyMullins* 10-11-2 (t) BJGeraghty	25/1	17	3
11	Strong Project (IRE) *SeanOO'Brien* 10-11-12 JMAllen	25/1	4½	4
	Public Reaction *EUHales* 8-11-9 DNRussell	50/1	dist	5
	Point Barrow (IRE) *PatrickHughes* 8-11-12 PACarberry	25/1		pu

Gigginstown House Stud 6ran 6m04.95

CHEPSTOW Saturday, Oct 21   SOFT

13   Ballymore Ontario Tower Nov Hdle (Persian War) (Gr 2) (1) (4yo+) £17,106   2½m (11)

	KANPAI (IRE) *JGMO'Shea* 4-11-7 (v) APMcCoy	12/1		1
	MASSINI'S MAGUIRE (IRE) *PJHobbs* 5-11-4 RichardJohnson	10/3	12	2
	GRANIT JACK (FR) *PFNicholls* 4-11-0 RWalsh	4/7f	8	3
	Enlightenment (IRE) *EvanWilliams* 6-11-4 PaulMoloney	28/1	22	4
	Captain Marlon (IRE) *CLTizzard* 5-11-0 JoeTizzard	100/1	13	5
	Scribano Eile (IRE) *NATwiston-Davies* 5-11-4 TonyEvans	8/1		pu
	Fox 'n' Goose (IRE) *PCRitchens* 6-11-0 AndrewThornton	125/1		pu

Samurai Racing Syndicate 7ran 4m54.08

14   Blue Square Silver Trophy Hcap Hdle (L) (1) (147) (4yo+) £25,659   2½m (9)

The final flight was omitted due to false ground

	TARANIS (FR) *PFNicholls* 5-10-1[122] (t) RWalsh	4/5f		1
	SALTANGO (GER) *AMHales* 7-10-7[131] WTKennedy[3]	11/2	3	2
	NATHOS (GER) *CJMann* 9-10-6[137] KevinTobin[10]	14/1	2	3
	Brads House *JGMO'Shea* 4-10-0[121] DaveCrosse	10/1	1½	4
	Hasty Prince *JonjoO'Neill* 8-11-10[145] APMcCoy	10/1	6	5
	Mahogany Blaze (FR) *NATwiston-Davies* 4-11-4[139] TonyEvans	7/1	13	6
	Limerick Boy (GER) *MissVenetiaWilliams* 8-11-3[138] SamThomas	25/1	11	7
	Mythical King (IRE) *RLee* 9-10-0[121] TomDoyle	50/1	14	8
	Attorney General (IRE) *JABOld* 7-11-12[147] TimmyMurphy	25/1	15	9

Mrs A. B. Yeoman & Mr C. R. Whittaker 9ran 4m56.68

AINTREE Sunday, Oct 22   SOFT

15   bonusprint.com Old Roan Chase (Ltd Hcap) (Gr 2) (1) (167) (4yo+) £28,510   2½m (16)

	KAUTO STAR (FR) *PFNicholls* 6-11-10[167] (t) RWalsh	1/1f		1
	ARMATURK (FR) *PFNicholls* 9-11-1[158] JasonMaguire	13/2	21	2
	INCA TRAIL (IRE) *DMcCainJnr* 10-10-4[147] (b) GLee	12/1	8	3
	Nyrche (FR) *AKing* 6-10-10[153] RobertThornton	5/2	23	4
	Mister McGoldrick *MrsSJSmith* 9-11-3[160] DavidO'Meara	9/1	2	5

Mr Clive D. Smith 5ran 5m08.24

ASCOT Saturday, Oct 28   GOOD to FIRM

16   William Hill Hcap Hdle (2) (144) (4yo+) £49,576   2m (9)

	DESERT QUEST (IRE) *PFNicholls* 6-11-12[144] (b) RWalsh	2/1f		1
1	CARACCIOLA (GER) *NJHenderson* 9-11-2[134] MickFitzgerald	16/1	3	2
	ADOPTED HERO (IRE) *JHowardJohnson* 6-9-13[122] (v) BrianHughes[5]	20/1	11	3
6	The Last Hurrah (IRE) *MrsJHarrington,Ireland* 6-10-6[129] (b) ADLeigh[5]	10/3	5	4
	Amour Multiple (IRE) *SLycett* 7-10-6[124] KeithMercer	28/1	sh	5
	Valance (IRE) *CREgerton* 6-9-7[118] (t) SPJones[7]	22/1	2	6
3	East Tycoon (IRE) *JonjoO'Neill* 7-10-5[130] (es) JWFarrelly[7]	33/1	nk	7
	Priors Dale *MissECLavelle* 6-10-8[126] BarryFenton	25/1	1	8

Bureaucrat *PJHobbs* 4-10-13[131] RichardJohnson 8/1   1¾   9
Heathcote *GLMoore* 4-9-11[120] EamonDehdashti[5] 16/1   2   10
Masafi (IRE) *JHowardJohnson* 5-10-0[118] AlanDempsey 9/1   12   11
Verasi *GLMoore* 5-11-3[135] PhilipHide 16/1   1¼   12
Vinmix de Bessy (FR) *GLMoore* 5-10-0[118] JamieMoore 14/1   7   13
Almaydan *RLee* 8-11-1[133] TomDoyle 66/1   4   14
Front Rank (IRE) *MrsDianneSayer* 6-10-12[130] BrianHarding 25/1   5   15

Mrs M. Findlay 15ran 3m42.43

17   **United House Gold Cup Hcap Chase (2) (156) (4yo+)** £61,970   3m (20)

SEE YOU SOMETIME *JWMullins* 11-10-1[138] WayneKavanagh[7] 14/1   1
ZABENZ (NZ) *PJHobbs* 9-10-10[140] (b) RichardJohnson............................. 8/1   7   2
8   SWEET DIVERSION (IRE) *PFNicholls* 7-9-13[134] (t) LiamHeard[5]........... 8/1   1½   3
Bewleys Berry (IRE) *JHowardJohnson* 8-10-10[140] TonyDobbin 13/2   10   4
9   Oodachee *CFSwan,Ireland* 7-9-10[133] (s) DGHogan[7] 9/2jf   4   5
Royal Auclair (FR) *PFNicholls* 9-11-12[156] (t) RWalsh .... 10/1   ½   6
Joes Edge (IRE) *FerdyMurphy* 9-10-4[134] GLee 20/1   23   7
8   Kings Brook *NickWilliams* 6-10-2[132] PaulMoloney 8/1   2½   8
One Cornetto (IRE) *LWells* 7-10-0[130] JamieMoore 100/1   6   9
4   Ballycassidy (IRE) *PBowen* 10-11-2[146] JasonMaguire....................... 6/1   dist 10
Ollie Magern *NATwiston-Davies* 8-11-3[147] TonyEvans .... 9/2jf   ur

Mr J. A. G. Meaden 11ran 5m52.77

WETHERBY Saturday, Oct 28   SOFT

18   **John Smith's Hdle (West Yorkshire) (Gr 2) (1) (4yo+)** £22,808   3m1f (12)

REDEMPTION *NATwiston-Davies* 11-11-0 TimmyMurphy 12/1   1
MY WAY DE SOLZEN (FR) *AKing* 6-11-8 RobertThornton 4/9f   6   2
TEES COMPONENTS *KGReveley* 11-11-0 (t) DominicElsworth 17/2   6   3
No Refuge (IRE) *JHowardJohnson* 6-11-8 PJBrennan 4/1   3½   4
Milligan (FR) *DrPPritchard* 11-11-0 RJGreene 250/1   28   5
Carlys Quest *FerdyMurphy* 12-11-0 (b) TJDreaper........................... 33/1   21   6
Ile Maurice (FR) *FerdyMurphy* 6-10-7 PJMcDonald .... 33/1   f

Mr Michael Purtill 7ran 6m50.94

19   **bet365 Charlie Hall Chase (Gr 2) (1) (5yo+)** £51,318   3m1f (18)

OUR VIC *DEPipe* 8-11-10 TimmyMurphy 6/1   1
NEPTUNE COLLONGES (FR) *PFNicholls* 5-10-12 SamThomas 2/1f   7   2
SIR REMBRANDT (IRE) *RHAlner* 10-11-4 AndrewThornton................... 10/1   5   3
Kingscliff (IRE) *RHAlner* 9-11-10 RobertWalford 7/1   7   4
Iris's Gift *JonjoO'Neill* 9-11-3 DominicElsworth 8/1   11   5
Take The Stand (IRE) *PBowen* 10-11-0 (s) TJO'Brien 9/2   29   6
Church Island (IRE) *MHourigan,Ireland* 7-11-5 AJMcNamara .... 16/1   dist 7
Jungle Jinks (IRE) *GMMoore* 11-11-0 BarryKeniry 80/1   12   8
Jaloux d'Estruval (FR) *DrPPritchard* 9-11-0 RJGreene 150/1   26   9
Royal Emperor (IRE) *MrsSJSmith* 10-11-0 DavidO'Meara................. 8/1   pu

Mr D. A. Johnson 10ran 6m39.10

EXETER Tuesday, Oct 31   GOOD

20   **William Hill Gold Cup Chase (Ltd Hcap) (Haldon) (Gr 2) (1) (162)**   2m1f110y (12)
     (4yo+) £40,102

IMPEK (FR) *MissHCKnight* 10-11-10[162] APMcCoy 9/1   1
GROUND BALL (IRE) *CFSwan,Ireland* 9-9-11[142] DGHogan[7] 12/1   19   2
HOO LA BALOO (FR) *PFNicholls* 5-10-9[147] RWalsh 7/1   11   3
Locksmith *DEPipe* 6-10-4[142] TimmyMurphy .... 16/1   ½   4
Jacks Craic (IRE) *JLSpearing* 7-10-5[143] TonyEvans 25/1   27   5
Green Tango *HDDaly* 7-10-4[142] MarkBradburne .... 8/1   f
Racing Demon (IRE) *MissHCKnight* 6-11-6[158] GLee....................... 3/1f   ur
Dempsey (IRE) *CarlLlewellyn* 8-11-2[154] AndrewTinkler .... 5/1   ur
Chilling Place (IRE) *PJHobbs* 7-10-4[142] RichardJohnson .... 7/2   ur

Mr Jim Lewis 9ran 4m09.15

WINCANTON Saturday, Nov 4   GOOD to FIRM

21   **totepool Rising Stars Nov Chase (Gr 2) (1) (4yo+)** £23,693   2m5f (17)

TURKO (FR) *PFNicholls* 4-10-13 (t) RWalsh 4/7f   1
BOYCHUK (IRE) *PJHobbs* 5-11-10 RichardJohnson 6/1   3½   2
PREDATOR (GER) *JonjoO'Neill* 5-11-10 APMcCoy 5/1   21   3
Bowleaze (IRE) *RHAlner* 7-11-10 AndrewThornton .... 14/1   f
Aztec Warrior (IRE) *MissHCKnight* 5-11-6 TimmyMurphy .... 12/1   pu

The Stewart Family 5ran 5m06.59

22   **Badger Ales Trophy (Hcap Chase) (L) (1) 0-150(145) (4yo+)** £39,914 3m1f110y (21)

PARSONS LEGACY (IRE) *PJHobbs* 8-10-5[124] RichardJohnson 16/1		1
PREACHER BOY *RJHodges* 7-10-11[130] PJBrennan 14/1	2½	2
NIL DESPERANDUM (IRE) *MissVenetiaWilliams* 9-11-7[140]		6 3
TomScudamore 16/1		
Iris Bleu (FR) *DEPipe* 10-11-0[133] TimmyMurphy 9/2	5	4
Swansea Bay *EvanWilliams* 10-10-4[123] (b) PaulMoloney 12/1	1	5
4 Celtic Boy (IRE) *PBowen* 8-11-6[139] AndrewTinkler................................ 50/1	5	6
Ladalko (IRE) *PFNicholls* 7-11-4[140] DarylJacob³ 5/2f		f
Fork Lightning (IRE) *AKing* 10-11-1[134] RobertThornton 12/1		f
17 Sweet Diversion (IRE) *PFNicholls* 7-10-9[133] (t) LiamHeard⁵ 13/2		ur
17 Ballycassidy (IRE) *PBowen* 10-11-12[145] (s) JasonMaguire 40/1		pu
Keltic Bard *CJMann* 9-11-3[136] NoelFehily... 14/1		pu
Alderburn *HDDaly* 7-10-10[129] APMcCoy... 4/1		pu

Mr R. A. S. Offer 12ran 6m18.50

23   **£1 Million totetentofollow Elite Hdle (Ltd Hcap) (Gr 2) (1) (160) (4yo+)** £28,644   2m (7)

The flight after the stands was omitted due to the low trajectory of the sun

CROW WOOD *JJQuinn* 7-10-1[140] DougieCostello³ 9/2		1
16 DESERT QUEST (IRE) *PFNicholls* 6-11-10[160] (b) RWalsh 8/13f	½	2
ROYAL SHAKESPEARE (FR) *SGollings* 7-10-13[149] TomScudamore 12/1	4	3
Noble Request (FR) *PJHobbs* 5-11-9[159] RichardJohnson 11/2	½	4
Faasel (IRE) *NGRichards* 5-11-4[154] (b) BrianHarding 10/1	5	5
Flame Creek (IRE) *EJCreighton* 10-10-9[145] JasonMaguire 40/1		ur

Mrs Marie Taylor 6ran 3m32.01

DOWN ROYAL Saturday, Nov 4   SOFT

24   **James Nicholson Wine Merchant Champion Chase (Gr 1) (5yo+)** £56,376   3m (15)

BEEF OR SALMON (IRE) *MHourigan* 10-11-10 (s) AndrewJMcNamara... 11/4		1
12 WAR OF ATTRITION (IRE) *MFMorris* 7-11-10 CO'Dwyer 4/7f	nk	2
JUSTIFIED (IRE) *ESheehy* 7-11-10 PCarberry...................................... 5/1	13	3
5 Light On The Broom (IRE) *GStack* 10-11-10 (t) RMPower...................... 100/1	24	4
Another Rum (IRE) *IADuncan* 8-11-10 AnthonyRoss............................... 100/1	5	5
Cloudy Bays (IRE) *CharlesByrnes* 9-11-10 (s) DNRussell 33/1		f
11 Bothar Na (IRE) *WPMullins* 7-11-10 DJCondon 33/1		ur

Mr B. J. Craig 7ran 6m31.55

25   **Killultagh Properties Ltd Chase (Gr 3) (5yo+)** £21,846   2½m (14)

IN COMPLIANCE (IRE) *MJPO'Brien* 6-11-5 BJGeraghty 4/5f		1
WILD PASSION (GER) *NMeade* 6-11-2 PCarberry.................................... 6/5	¾	2
DESPERADO QUEEN (IRE) *LWDoran* 8-11-3 DNRussell 14/1	5½	3
Baron de Feypo (IRE) *PatrickOBrady* 8-10-12 JPElliott............................ 33/1	10	4

Mr S. Mulryan 4ran 5m34.80

AUTEUIL Saturday, Nov 4   SOFT

26   **Grand Prix d'Automne Hdle (Gr 1) (5yo+)** £96,644   3m (14)

ZAIYAD (IRE) *AChaille-Chaille,France* 5-10-3 CPieux 9/10f		1
ROYALE ATHENIA (FR) *BBarbier,France* 5-9-13 (b) CGombeau 7/2	6	2
LYCAON DE VAUZELLE (FR) *JBertrandeBalanda,France* 7-10-8		6 3
BChameraud 25/4		
Rock And Palm (FR) *CCardenne,France* 6-10-8 DGallagher 12/1	1	4
Millenium Royal (FR) *FDoumen,France* 6-10-8 ADuchene 11/1	1½	5
Musica Bella (FR) *FCottin,France* 6-10-3 PACarberry.............................. 26/1	2½	6
Lasecco (GER) *FBelmont,France* 7-10-8 JRicou 27/4	10	7

Mr S. Mulryan 7ran 5m56.00

AUTEUIL Sunday, Nov 5   SOFT

27   **Prix Maurice Gillois Chase (Gr 1) (4yo)** £105,705   2¾m (18)

OR NOIR DE SOMOZA (FR) *AChaille-Chaille,France* 4-10-6 CPieux..... 1/10f		1
SCARLET ROW (FR) *GMacaire,France* 4-10-1 BGicquel 13/1	3	2
FORZY ORIGNY (FR) *JBertrandeBalanda,France* 4-10-6 BChameraud ... 28/1	5	3
Olivia Des Bordes (FR) *FCottin,France* 4-10-1 PACarberry...................... 91/1	6	4
Orgeres (FR) *GCherel,France* 4-10-6 PMarsac...................................... 19/1	¾	5
Odeillo du Mathan (FR) *GCherel,France* 4-10-6 (b) CGombeau................. 46/1	2½	6
Gold Heart (FR) *GMacaire,France* 4-10-6 LSuzineau................................ 68/1	hd	7
Doumaja (FR) *GCherel,France* 4-10-6 EChazelle 77/1	1	8
Bravou (FR) *FCottin,France* 4-10-6 DGallagher 30/1	dist	9
Flower Des Champs (FR) *GMacaire,France* 4-10-1 JRicou........................ 31/4		ur

Mr S. Mulryan 10ran 5m30.83

28   **Prix La Haye Jousselin Chase (Gr 1) (5yo+)** £141,946   3m3f110y (22)

PRINCESSE D'ANJOU (FR) *FCottin,France* 5-9-13 PACarberry	13/2		1
LOUPING D'AINAY (FR) *FCottin,France* 7-10-8 DGallagher	22/1	5	2
LORD CARMONT (FR) *MmeIPacault,France* 7-10-8 SMassinot	35/4	4	3
Ne A Pron (FR) *MRolland,France* 5-10-3 JRicou	12/1	3	4
Cyrlight (FR) *AChaille-Chaille,France* 7-10-8 CPieux	3/10f	8	5
Hercule Noir (FR) *YFouin,France* 7-10-8 SDehez	17/1	1½	6
Saint Realise (FR) *MRolland,France* 9-10-8 (b) GAdam	63/1	3	7
Nirvana du Bourg (FR) *TTrapenard,France* 5-10-3 FBarrao	54/1	2	8
Sybellius d'Artaix (FR) *J-PGallorini,France* 6-10-8 JDucout	45/1	10	9

Mr J-P. Senechal 9ran 6m47.65

29   **Prix Cambaceres Hdle (Gr 1) (3yo)** £81,544   2¼m (11)

ROYAL HONOR (FR) *YFouin,France* 3-10-6 SDehez	12/1		1
GOOD BYE SIMON (FR) *TDoumen,France* 3-10-6 BDelo	11/1	½	2
PARRAIN (FR) *FDoumen,France* 3-10-6 ADuchene	15/2	4	3
Berryville (FR) *ACouetil,France* 3-10-6 JGuiheneuf	24/1	½	4
Fabulously (FR) *TTrapenard,France* 3-10-6 DGallagher	14/1	5	5
Haroni (IRE) *MsFMCrowley,Ireland* 3-10-6 PACarberry	13/1	¾	6
Mixmen (FR) *FNicolle,France* 3-10-6 OAuge	26/1	¾	7
Polinamix (FR) *J-LPelletan,France* 3-10-6 EPasteau	86/1	2	8
Brave d'Honneur (FR) *YLalleman,France* 3-10-1 NMilliere	25/1	1½	9
Boulavogue (IRE) *CFSwan,Ireland* 3-10-6 TGMRyan	16/1	6	10
Ecos de L'Orme (FR) *RCaget,France* 3-10-6 CGombeau	7/4f		11
Mundo (FR) *TDoumen,France* 3-10-6 CPieux	9/1		12
Mildon (FR) *J-LPelletan,France* 3-10-6 FEstrampes	23/4		13
City Note (FR) *TTrapenard,France* 3-10-6 AKondrat	80/1		14

Mrs M. O. Bryant 14ran 4m25.69

CHELTENHAM Friday, Nov 10   GOOD to SOFT (Old Course)

30   **Anglo Irish Private Banking Nov Hdle (Sharp) (Gr 2) (1) (4yo+)** £19,957   2m110y (8)

MOON OVER MIAMI (GER) *CJMann* 5-11-4 NoelFehily	16/1		1
WAR GENERAL *TJTaaffe,Ireland* 5-11-7 CO'Dwyer	16/1	1	2
MILL HOUSE GIRL (IRE) *SDonohoe,Ireland* 5-11-0 MickFitzgerald	20/1	2	3
Orpen Wide (IRE) *MCChapman* 4-11-7 RichardJohnson	9/1	1	4
Ofarel d'Airy (FR) *PFNicholls* 4-11-0 RWalsh	9/2	6	5
6 Cuan Na Grai (IRE) *PaulNolan,Ireland* 5-11-7 JCullen	7/4f	21	6
Kalderon (GER) *THogan,Ireland* 6-11-7 APMcCoy	2/1	2	7
Hippodrome (IRE) *RSimpson* 4-11-0 (b) JamesDavies	100/1	18	8
Jabo (IRE) *NATwiston-Davies* 4-11-0 TonyEvans	100/1	dist	9

Mrs A. E. Fulton & Mr M. T. Lynch 9ran 4m02.63

CHELTENHAM Saturday, Nov 11   GOOD to SOFT (Old Course)

31   **Ryman The Stationer Juv Nov Hdle (Gr 2) (1) (3yo)** £17,106   2m110y (8)

KATCHIT (IRE) *AKing* 3-11-6 RobertThornton	7/4f		1
FREEZE THE FLAME (GER) *CREgerton* 3-11-6 APMcCoy	3/1	nk	2
CHEVELEY FLYER *JPearce* 3-11-2 TimmyMurphy	20/1	11	3
Marc of Brilliance (USA) *GLMoore* 3-11-6 PhilipHide	20/1	5	4
Pigeon Island *NATwiston-Davies* 3-10-12 TonyEvans	40/1	1¼	5
Decree Nisi *LCorcoran* 3-10-12 JamieMoore	100/1	8	6
Total Victory (IRE) *THogan,Ireland* 3-11-6 (s) NoelFehily	6/1	hd	7
Prince Ary *DEPipe* 3-10-12 TomScudamore	7/1	8	8
Is It Me (USA) *PABlockley* 3-11-6 MarkBradburne	6/1	1¼	9
Keel (IRE) *AnthonyMullins,Ireland* 3-10-12 DenisO'Regan	66/1		pu

D S J P Syndicate 10ran 4m11.35

32   **Jim Brown Memorial Nov Chase (2) (5yo+)** £12,526   2½m110y (15)

DENMAN (IRE) *PFNicholls* 6-11-4 RWalsh	4/6f		1
DON'T PUSH IT (IRE) *JonjoO'Neill* 6-11-4 APMcCoy	10/3	¾	2
IL DUCE (IRE) *AKing* 6-11-4 RobertThornton	10/1	17	3
Snakebite (IRE) *CarlLlewellyn* 6-10-13 NoelFehily	10/1	¾	4
Wogan *NJHenderson* 6-10-13 MickFitzgerald	9/1	29	5
Predicament *DrPPritchard* 7-10-13 TJPhelan	200/1	11	6
Clearly Oscar *SeamusO'Farrell,Ireland* 7-10-13 MrJPO'Farrell	200/1		pu

Mrs M. Findlay & P. K. Barber 7ran 5m16.04

33   **Paddy Power Gold Cup Chase (Hcap) (Gr 3) (1) (149) (4yo+)** £62,722   2½m110y (15)

EXOTIC DANCER (FR) *JonjoO'Neill* 6-11-2[139] (s) APMcCoy	16/1		1
VODKA BLEU (FR) *DEPipe* 7-10-11[134] TimmyMurphy	4/1f	3	2
NEW ALCO (FR) *FerdyMurphy* 5-10-7[130] GLee	16/1	½	3

BUTLER'S CABIN (FR) *JonjoO'Neill* 6-9-7[123] JWFarrelly[7] 20/1   3½ 4
Graphic Approach (IRE) *CREgerton* 8-11-2[139] NoelFehily 14/1   2½ 5
Tamarinbleu (FR) *DEPipe* 6-11-10[147] TomScudamore .... 12/1   ¾ 6
Kandjar d'Allier (FR) *AKing* 8-10-13[136] RobertThornton 9/1   4 7
Nayodabayo (IRE) *EvanWilliams* 6-10-9[137] (b) NickWilliams[5] 50/1   12 8
Too Forward (IRE) *CarlLlewellyn* 10-11-10[147] TonyDobbin 12/1   7 9
4 Calatagan (IRE) *JMJefferson* 7-10-10[136] TJDreaper[3] 66/1   1½ 10
Tumbling Dice (IRE) *TJTaaffe,Ireland* 7-11-2[139] (s) NPMadden 14/1   3½ 11
Kelrev (FR) *MissVenetiaWilliams* 8-11-2[139] RichardJohnson 50/1   11 12
14 Taranis (FR) *PFNicholls* 5-11-12[149] (t) RWalsh .... 13/2   f
Knowhere (IRE) *NATwiston-Davies* 8-11-1[138] TonyEvans .... 17/2   f
Tighe Caster *PBowen* 7-10-6[129] TJO'Brien .... 40/1   ur
Copsale Lad *NJHenderson* 9-11-6[143] MickFitzgerald .... 5/1   pu

Sir Robert Ogden 16ran 5m20.26

34   **Lombard Properties Hcap Hdle (L) (1) (147) (4yo+)** £28,510   3m1f110y (13)

STAR DE MOHAISON (FR) *PFNicholls* 5-10-6[127] (t) RWalsh 6/4f   1
JOCKSER (IRE) *JWMullins* 5-10-0[126] WayneKavanagh[5] 14/1   8 2
CALUSA CHARLIE (IRE) *BGPowell* 7-9-7[121] SPJones[7] 20/1   3½ 3
KARANJA *VRADartnall* 7-10-8[129] NoelFehily 17/2   3 4
Two Miles West (IRE) *JonjoO'Neill* 5-10-11[132] APMcCoy 10/1   14 5
Nobody Tells Me (FR) *DEPipe* 5-10-1[122] TomScudamore 7/1   20 6
Hordago (IRE) *EricMcNamara,Ireland* 6-10-5[131] (s) BCByrnes[5] 16/1   10 7
Quick *DEPipe* 6-10-11[132] JamieMoore 40/1   21 8
18 Carlys Quest *FerdyMurphy* 12-11-2[140] (b) TJDreaper[3] .... 66/1   sh 9
Mr Ed (IRE) *PBowen* 8-11-10[145] (s) TJO'Brien 25/1   4 10
18 Milligan (FR) *DrPPritchard* 11-9-11[121] TJPhelan[3] 100/1   7 11
14 Attorney General (IRE) *JABOld* 7-11-12[147] JasonMaguire .... 33/1   pu
18 Redemption *NATwiston-Davies* 11-11-12[147] TimmyMurphy .... 15/2   pu
Brewster (IRE) *IanWilliams* 9-11-8[143] DavidDennis .... 20/1   pu
Hand Inn Hand *HDDaly* 10-11-2[137] MarkBradburne .... 33/1   pu
His Nibs (IRE) *AKing* 9-11-1[136] RobertThornton .... 12/1   pu
Just Beth *GFierro* 10-10-1[122] GerrySupple .... 66/1   pu

Sir Robert Ogden 17ran 6m37.37

35   **Servo Computer Services Trophy Hcap Chase (Gr 3) (1) (156) (4yo+)** £34,212   3m3f110y (21)

MY WILL (FR) *PFNicholls* 6-11-6[150] RWalsh 9/2cf   1
IDLE TALK (IRE) *TRGeorge* 7-11-0[144] JasonMaguire .... 9/2cf   ½ 2
RUN FOR PADDY *CarlLlewellyn* 10-10-9[139] NoelFehily 8/1   10 3
Model Son (IRE) *RJordan* 8-10-1[134] PCO'Neill[3] 25/1   6 4
2 Tribal Venture (FR) *PJHobbs* 8-10-0[130] TJO'Brien 10/1   5 5
Lacdoudal (FR) *PJHobbs* 7-11-12[156] RichardJohnson .... 7/1   ½ 6
19 Royal Emperor (IRE) *MrsSJSmith* 11-11-6[150] PadgeWhelan................... 25/1   f
19 Take The Stand (IRE) *PBowen* 10-11-11[155] (s) APMcCoy .... 16/1   pu
19 Sir Rembrandt (IRE) *RHAlner* 10-11-7[151] MickFitzgerald .... 8/1   pu
Joaaci (IRE) *DEPipe* 6-11-6[150] TimmyMurphy .... 9/2cf   pu
12 Barrow Drive *AnthonyMullins,Ireland* 10-10-12[142] (t) DenisO'Regan.......... 33/1   pu
Baron Windrush *NATwiston-Davies* 8-10-8[138] TomScudamore .... 20/1   pu

The Stewart Family 12ran 7m24.01

CHELTENHAM Sunday, Nov 12   GOOD to SOFT (Old Course)

36   **Independent Newspaper Nov Chase (November) (Gr 2) (1) (4yo+)** £25,780   2m (12)

3 FAIR ALONG (GER) *PJHobbs* 4-10-7 RichardJohnson 10/3   1
NATAL (FR) *PFNicholls* 5-11-5 (t) RWalsh 8/11f   9 2
PENZANCE *AKing* 5-11-5 RobertThornton 7/2   9 3
Patman du Charmil (FR) *NATwiston-Davies* 4-10-7 TonyEvans 25/1   9 4
Charlies Double *JRBest* 7-11-5 JoeTizzard.. 100/1   dist 5
1 Callow Lake (IRE) *MrsJHarrington,Ireland* 6-11-9 ADLeigh .... 14/1   ur

Mr Alan Peterson 6ran 4m05.45

37   **Greatwood Hcap Hdle (Gr 3) (1) (148) (4yo+)** £37,063   2m110y (8)

DETROIT CITY (USA) *PJHobbs* 4-11-12[148] (b) RichardJohnson 6/5f   1
AMEEQ (USA) *GLMoore* 4-10-3[125] RWalsh 8/1   14 2
CARAMAN (IRE) *JJQuinn* 8-10-2[127] DougieCostello[3] 50/1   3 3
3 Aleron (IRE) *JJQuinn* 8-10-13[135] (s) RussGarritty 33/1   2½ 4
14 Mahogany Blaze (FR) *NATwiston-Davies* 4-10-11[138] MrDEngland[5] 16/1   1 5
16 Verasi *GLMoore* 5-10-8[135] (s) EamonDehdashti[5] .... 20/1   ½ 6
3 O'Toole (IRE) *PJHobbs* 7-10-7[136] DarrenO'Dwyer[7] 14/1   6 7
Sweet Wake (GER) *NMeade,Ireland* 5-11-1[137] (t) DenisO'Regan .... 9/4   sh 8
16 The Last Hurrah (IRE) *MrsJHarrington,Ireland* 6-10-2[129] (b) ADLeigh[5] 12/1   8 9

Mr Terry Warner 9ran 4m01.85

38 **Gideon Kasler Nov Hdle (2) (4yo+)** £12,526   2m5f (10)

13	MASSINI'S MAGUIRE (IRE) *PJHobbs* 5-11-5 RichardJohnson	6/1	1
	WICHITA LINEMAN (IRE) *JonjoO'Neill* 5-11-8 APMcCoy	11/10f	½ 2
	JUVEIGNEUR (FR) *NJHenderson* 9-11-0 MickFitzgerald	20/1	6 3
	Imperial Commander (IRE) *NATwiston-Davies* 5-11-0 TonyEvans	11/4	2 4
	Paulo Dancer (FR) *PFNicholls* 5-11-8 RWalsh	11/2	24 5
	Miss Mitch (IRE) *RHAlner* 5-10-12 TimmyMurphy	25/1	dist 6
	Ackhurst (IRE) *GFEdwards* 7-11-0 MrDEdwards	200/1	4 7
	Blazing Batman *DrPPritchard* 13-11-0 DrPPritchard	150/1	6 8

Mr Alan Peterson 8ran 5m20.43

39 **Tiger Developments Open Bumper (Standard Open NHF)(L) (1)**   2m110y
    (4, 5 and 6yo) £8,553

CORK ALL STAR (IRE) *MrsJHarrington,Ireland* 4-11-7 RWalsh	7/2	1
AN ACCORDION (IRE) *DEPipe* 5-11-0 TomScudamore	16/1	4 2
BATTLECRY *NATwiston-Davies* 5-10-13 MrDEngland[5]	9/1	6 3
Leading Authority (IRE) *CLTizzard* 5-11-4 JoeTizzard	33/1	¾ 4
The Pious Prince (IRE) *LLungo* 5-11-4 TimmyMurphy	7/2	13 5
Snap Tie (IRE) *PJHobbs* 4-11-4 RichardJohnson	3/1f	1½ 6
Strawberry (IRE) *JWMullins* 5-10-2 WayneKavanagh[5]	20/1	4 7
Truckers Delight (IRE) *JonjoO'Neill* 5-10-11 MrBarryConnell[7]	7/1	sh 8
Double Eagle *DMcCainJnr* 4-11-4 JasonMaguire	25/1	6 9
Grecian Groom (IRE) *JonjoO'Neill* 4-11-7 APMcCoy	7/1	dist 10
Liam Mellows (IRE) *JohnJosephMurphy,Ireland* 6-10-7 EFPower[7]	50/1	dist 11

Mr Cathal M. Ryan 11ran 3m59.33

NAVAN Sunday, Nov 12   SOFT

40 **Philips Electronics Lismullen Hdle (Gr 2) (4yo+)** £21,700   2½m (11)

	ROSAKER (USA) *NMeade* 9-11-10 PCarberry	9/2	1
	EMOTIONAL MOMENT (IRE) *TJTaaffe* 9-11-10 BJGeraghty	10/1	6 2
	BROGELLA (IRE) *MsFMCrowley* 6-11-3 (b) JLCullen	15/2	2½ 3
	Silent Oscar (IRE) *HarryRogers* 7-11-2 RMPower	20/1	1 4
	Studmaster *MrsJHarrington* 6-11-5 TPTreacy	8/1	sh 5
10	Sweet Kiln (IRE) *JamesBowe* 7-11-3 DNRussell	10/1	2 6
	Al Eile (IRE) *JohnQueally* 6-11-12 CO'Dwyer	4/5f	17 7
25	Baron de Feypo (IRE) *PatrickOBrady* 8-11-8 JPElliott	40/1	22 8
	Turnium (FR) *MrsAMO'Shea* 11-11-5 AO'Shea	100/1	dist 9
	Prince of Tara (IRE) *SJMahon* 9-11-5 MrKBBowens	20/1	pu

High Street Ceathar Syndicate 10ran 5m07.81

41 **Navan Race Supporters Fortria Chase (Gr 2) (5yo+)** £26,040   2m (10)

	NICKNAME (FR) *MartinBrassil* 7-11-7 NPMadden	6/1	1
	CENTRAL HOUSE *DTHughes* 9-11-12 PWFlood	7/4jf	¾ 2
12	WATSON LAKE (IRE) *NMeade* 8-11-12 (t) PCarberry	7/4jf	6 3
5	Steel Band *PaulARoche* 8-11-4 DNRussell	33/1	2 4
	Fota Island (IRE) *MFMorris* 10-11-10 CO'Dwyer	4/1	5½ 5

Mrs Claudia Jungo-Corpataux 5ran 4m15.49

CLONMEL Thursday, Nov 16   HEAVY

42 **Clonmel Oil Chase (Gr 2) (5yo+)** £25,544   2½m (14)

	SIR OJ (IRE) *NMeade* 9-11-10 (b) PCarberry	11/8f	1
	KILL DEVIL HILL (IRE) *PaulNolan* 6-11-8 JLCullen	4/1	sh 2
	SHER BEAU (IRE) *PhilipFenton* 7-11-1 DNRussell	5/2	3½ 3
6	Adamant Approach (IRE) *WPMullins* 12-11-5 RWalsh	11/2	1 4

Mr Brian Keenan 4ran 5m27.90

ASCOT Friday, Nov 17   GOOD

43 **Allied Irish Bank (GB) Private Banking Hcap Chase (2) 0-145(137)**   3m (20)
    (4yo+) £31,315

	HARRIS BAY *MissHCKnight* 7-11-1[126] (t) TimmyMurphy	8/1	1
	LOU DU MOULIN MAS (FR) *PFNicholls* 7-10-13[124] (t) RWalsh	2/1f	1½ 2
8	TANGO ROYAL (FR) *DEPipe* 10-10-13[124] (v+t) RJGreene	16/1	2½ 3
	Iznogoud (FR) *DEPipe* 10-11-9[134] TomScudamore	33/1	29 4
	Harry's Dream *PJHobbs* 9-11-10[135] APMcCoy	3/1	2 5
	Liverpool Echo (FR) *MrsKWaldron* 6-11-5[130] RobertThornton	12/1	5 6
	King Barry (FR) *MissPRobson* 7-11-5[130] RichardMcGrath	11/2	3 7
	Florida Dream (IRE) *NATwiston-Davies* 7-10-7[118] (b) TonyEvans	11/1	3½ 8
4	Mr Fluffy *AWCarroll* 9-11-3[131] SJCraine[3]	50/1	f
22	Celtic Boy (IRE) *PBowen* 8-11-12[137] WayneHutchinson	28/1	pu
	Kety Star (FR) *MissVenetiaWilliams* 8-10-4[118] PCO'Neill[3]	33/1	pu

Mrs G. M. Sturges & H. Stephen Smith 11ran 6m17.30

ASCOT Saturday, Nov 18   GOOD to SOFT

44   **Amlin 1965 Chase (Limited Int Hcap) (Gr 2) (1) (146) (4yo+)**   2m3f (16)
£39,914

	CERIUM (FR) *PFNicholls* 5-11-8[144] SamThomas	12/1	1
33	KNOWHERE (IRE) *NATwiston-Davies* 8-10-11[138] MrDEngland[5]	4/1jf	3½ 2
20	HOO LA BALOO (FR) *PFNicholls* 5-11-5[146] LiamHeard[5]	20/1	8 3
	Medison (FR) *DEPipe* 6-10-6[128] (s) TimmyMurphy	6/1	11 4
	Billyvoddan (IRE) *HDDaly* 7-11-4[140] MarkBradburne	10/1	sh 5
	Without A Doubt *CarlLlewellyn* 7-10-12[134] PaulMoloney	10/1	4 6
	Mr Boo (IRE) *GLMoore* 7-10-7[129] JamieMoore	7/1	5 7
	Reveillez *JRFanshawe* 7-11-9[145] CO'Dwyer	11/2	f
20	Chilling Place (IRE) *PJHobbs* 7-11-3[139] RichardJohnson	4/1jf	f

B Fulton, T Hayward, S Fisher, L Brady 9ran 4m44.35

45   **Coral Ascot Hdle (Gr 2) (1) (4yo+)** £56,340   2m3f110y (11)

	HARDY EUSTACE (IRE) *DTHughes,Ireland* 9-11-0 (v) CO'Dwyer	11/8f	1
	MIGHTY MAN (FR) *HDDaly* 6-11-8 RichardJohnson	15/8	11 2
	LOUGH DERG (FR) *DEPipe* 6-11-0 (v) TomScudamore	16/1	10 3
18	No Refuge (IRE) *JHowardJohnson* 6-11-8 TimmyMurphy	8/1	9 4
	Self Defense *MissECLavelle* 9-11-4 MickFitzgerald	12/1	5 5
	Fire Dragon (IRE) *JonjoO'Neill* 5-11-8 (b) NoelFehily	9/1	8 6
7	Yankeedoodledandy (IRE) *CRoberts* 5-11-0 OllieMcPhail	100/1	dist 7

Mr Laurence Byrne 7ran 4m48.47

46   **Carey Group Hcap Chase (2) (156) (4yo+)** £74,364   2m1f (13)

	DEMI BEAU *EvanWilliams* 8-10-6[136] PaulMoloney	7/1	1
14	HASTY PRINCE *JonjoO'Neill* 8-10-3[133] NoelFehily	15/2	2 2
	ANDREAS (FR) *PFNicholls* 6-11-0[144] (t) SamThomas	11/2	2 3
15	Mister McGoldrick *MrsSJSmith* 9-11-12[156] DavidO'Meara	20/1	5 4
17	See You Sometime *JWMullins* 11-10-11[146] WayneKavanagh[5]	9/1	3½ 5
	Tysou (FR) *NJHenderson* 9-11-2[146] MickFitzgerald	5/1f	6 6
33	Calatagan (IRE) *JMJefferson* 7-10-2[135] TJDreaper[3]	20/1	nk 7
	Madison du Berlais (FR) *DEPipe* 5-10-5[135] TomScudamore	7/1	18 8
20	Green Tango *HDDaly* 7-10-12[142] RichardJohnson	6/1	ur
15	Nyrche (FR) *AKing* 6-11-8[152] JAMcCarthy	25/1	ur
	Contraband *DEPipe* 8-11-8[152] (v) TimmyMurphy	9/1	pu

Cunningham Racing 11ran 4m12.31

HAYDOCK Saturday, Nov 18   GOOD to SOFT

47   **Betfair Chase (Lancashire) (Gr 1) (1) (5yo+)** £114,040   3m (18)

15	KAUTO STAR (FR) *PFNicholls* 6-11-8 RWalsh	11/10f	1
24	BEEF OR SALMON (IRE) *MHourigan,Ireland* 10-11-8 (s) AJMcNamara	4/1	17 2
	L'AMI (FR) *FDoumen,France* 7-11-8 APMcCoy	7/2	1 3
17	Ollie Magern *NATwiston-Davies* 8-11-8 TonyEvans	25/1	¾ 4
19	Iris's Gift *JonjoO'Neill* 9-11-8 DominicElsworth	16/1	dist 5
19	Kingscliff (IRE) *RHAlner* 9-11-8 RobertWalford	7/1	dist 6

Mr Clive D. Smith 6ran 6m09.87

48   **Betfair Hcap Hdle (2) (157) (4yo+)** £62,630   2m7f110y (12)

	HALCON GENELARDAIS (FR) *AKing* 6-10-2[133] RobertThornton	5/1jf	1
7	IRISH WOLF (FR) *PBowen* 6-10-9[140] (s) APMcCoy	11/2	1¼ 2
	JAZZ D'ESTRUVAL (FR) *NGRichards* 9-10-9[140] TonyDobbin	6/1	6 3
18	TEES COMPONENTS *KGReveley* 11-10-6[137] (t) DominicElsworth	14/1	2½ 4
1	United (GER) *MrsLWadham* 5-10-3[134] LeightonAspell	12/1	3 5
	Be Be King (IRE) *PFNicholls* 7-10-3[134] RWalsh	5/1jf	4 6
34	Carlys Quest *FerdyMurphy* 12-9-13[135] PJMcDonald[5]	66/1	5 7
	Mistanoora *NATwiston-Davies* 7-10-11[142] (b) TonyEvans	18/1	3 8
	St Matthew (USA) *MrsSJSmith* 8-10-7[145] MichaelO'Connell[7]	33/1	6 9
35	Royal Emperor (IRE) *MrsSJSmith* 10-11-3[148] PadgeWhelan	25/1	5 10
	Korelo (FR) *DEPipe* 8-11-9[154] RJGreene	100/1	21 11
	Desert Tommy *EvanWilliams* 5-9-11[131] WTKennedy[3]	12/1	4 12
	Mephisto (IRE) *JHowardJohnson* 7-10-12[137] PJBrennan	9/1	21 13
26	Millenium Royal (FR) *FDoumen,France* 6-11-7[157] (b) ADuchene[5]	66/1	2 14
	The Bajan Bandit (IRE) *LLungo* 11-10-9[140] KeithMercer	66/1	7 15
34	Two Miles West (IRE) *JonjoO'Neill* 5-10-0[131] (t) BarryKeniry	20/1	8 16
	Brankley Boy *NJHenderson* 8-10-0[131] MarcusFoley	17/2	pu

Ian Payne & Kim Franklin 17ran 5m50.36

49   **totesport.com Peterborough Chase (Gr 2) (1) (5yo+) £43,268**   2½m110y (16)

20	RACING DEMON (IRE) *MissHCKnight* 6-11-5 GLee	13/8jf	1
	THISTHATANDTOTHER (IRE) *PFNicholls* 10-11-0 WayneHutchinson	4/1	4 2
	MONKERHOSTIN (FR) *PJHobbs* 9-11-6 TJO'Brien	13/8jf	5 3
20	Dempsey (IRE) *CarlLlewellyn* 8-11-4 AndrewTinkler	8/1	dist 4
4	Full House (IRE) *PRWebber* 7-11-4 TomDoyle	33/1	f

Mrs T. P. Radford 5ran 5m00.63

50   **totepool Grand Sefton Hcap Chase (3) 0-130(130) (4yo+)**   2m5f110y (Nat.) (18)
         £37,578

	I HEAR THUNDER (IRE) *RHBuckler* 8-11-2[123] DarylJacob[3]	12/1	1
	SHANNON'S PRIDE (IRE) *RCGuest* 10-10-6[110] (s) WarrenMarston	7/1jf	7 2
	THEATRE KNIGHT (IRE) *JHowardJohnson* 8-10-7[111] PJBrennan	10/1	3 3
	CASSIA HEIGHTS *SABrookshaw* 11-10-0[104] (s) SEDurack	16/1	1 4
	Star Performance (IRE) *OliverMcKiernan,Ireland* 11-10-1[108] (s) TGMRyan[3]	9/1	½ 5
	Lampion du Bost (FR) *AParker* 7-9-9[104] PhilKinsella[7]	20/1	2 6
22	Swansea Bay *EvanWilliams* 10-11-3[121] (s) PaulMoloney	12/1	3½ 7
	Mon Oiseau (FR) *ALTMoore,Ireland* 6-10-6[110] DNRussell	15/2	11 8
	Lusaka de Pembo (FR) *NATwiston-Davies* 7-9-11[104] SJCraine[3]	20/1	¾ 9
	Incas (FR) *MissLucindaVRussell* 10-10-9[113] PeterBuchanan	40/1	6 10
	Eskimo Pie (IRE) *CCBealby* 7-10-13[117] MarkBradburne	20/1	8 11
	Paddy Fitz (IRE) *PJHalley,Ireland* 9-10-3[107] BrianHarding	66/1	17 12
	Neltina *MrsJEScrase* 10-11-5[123] PACarberry	25/1	3 13
	Be My Better Half (IRE) *JonjoO'Neill* 11-11-5[123] APMcCoy	16/1	1 14
	Bob The Builder *NATwiston-Davies* 7-11-5[123] TonyEvans	10/1	4 15
	Hakim (NZ) *JLSpearing* 12-11-12[130] DominicElsworth	7/1jf	f
	Manbow (IRE) *MickyHammond* 8-10-5[109] GLee	14/1	f
	Glengarra (IRE) *DRGandolfo* 9-10-11[115] (t) TonyDobbin	25/1	ur
	Log On Intersky (IRE) *JRCornwall* 10-10-0[104] PadgeWhelan	66/1	ur
2	Burwood Breeze (IRE) *TRGeorge* 10-11-1[119] JasonMaguire	28/1	ur

Mr Nick Elliott 20ran 5m35.57

51   **totesport.com Becher Hcap Chase (L) (1) (147) (5yo+) £57,020**   3¼m (Nat.) (21)

	EUROTREK (IRE) *PFNicholls* 10-11-7[147] LiamHeard[5]	25/1	1
17	BEWLEYS BERRY (IRE) *JHowardJohnson* 8-11-3[138] PJBrennan	14/1	8 2
2	DUNBRODY MILLAR (IRE) *PBowen* 8-10-3[124] SEDurack	14/1	1 3
22	NIL DESPERANDUM (IRE) *MissVenetiaWilliams* 9-11-4[139] TomScudamore	8/1	½ 4
15	Inca Trail (IRE) *DMcCainJnr* 10-10-8[129] (b) JasonMaguire	10/1	8 5
2	McKelvey (IRE) *PBowen* 7-11-2[137] (s) PeterBuchanan	33/1	½ 6
	Le Duc (FR) *PFNicholls* 7-11-1[136] RobertThornton	14/1	1¾ 7
17	Joes Edge (IRE) *FerdyMurphy* 9-10-10[131] (s) KeithMercer	25/1	15 8
	Undeniable *MrsSJSmith* 8-10-13[134] DavidO'Meara	40/1	3½ 9
	Haut de Gamme (FR) *FerdyMurphy* 11-11-1[136] RichardMcGrath	14/1	dist 10
	Tanterari (FR) *DEPipe* 8-10-3[124] (t) TimmyMurphy	4/1f	dist 11
	Clan Royal (FR) *JonjoO'Neill* 11-11-8[143] APMcCoy	7/1	f
2	Dun Doire (IRE) *AJMartin,Ireland* 7-11-3[138] DNRussell	11/1	f
	Kisslain Des Galas (FR) *DEPipe* 9-9-13[125] (t) AndrewGlassonbury[5]	100/1	f
	King Bee (IRE) *HDDaly* 9-10-1[122] MarkBradburne	20/1	f
24	Another Rum (IRE) *IADuncan,Ireland* 8-10-10[131] AnthonyRoss	33/1	ur
	Forest Gunner *RFord* 12-10-13[134] MissNCarberry	25/1	ur
	Solar System (IRE) *TJTaaffe,Ireland* 9-10-9[130] MarcusFoley	25/1	ur
	Kings Glen (IRE) *ThomasCarberry,Ireland* 10-10-0[121] PACarberry	16/1	ref
	Native Jack (IRE) *PJRothwell,Ireland* 12-10-11[132] BrianHarding	40/1	pu
9	Just In Debt (IRE) *MTodhunter* 10-10-8[129] DominicElsworth	11/1	pu

Mr Paul Green 21ran 6m46.71

52   **Maplewood Developments Morgiana Hdle (Gr 1) (4yo+) £43,624**   2m (9)

	IKTITAF (IRE) *NMeade* 5-11-10 (t) PCarberry	5/4f	1
	ASIAN MAZE (IRE) *ThomasMullins* 7-11-5 RWalsh	7/2	1¼ 2
	BRAVE INCA (IRE) *ColmAMurphy* 8-11-10 BJGeraghty	7/4	7 3
	Newmill (IRE) *JohnJosephMurphy* 8-11-10 AndrewJMcNamara	11/1	dist 4

Mrs P. Sloan 4ran 4m07.20

53   **Unicoin Homes Nov Chase (Worcester) (Gr 2) (1) (5yo+) £19,957**   3m (18)

21	BOYCHUK (IRE) *PJHobbs* 5-11-5 RichardJohnson	7/2	1
	GUNGADU *PFNicholls* 6-11-9 SamThomas	4/9f	1½ 2

```
        WEE ROBBIE NJGifford 6-11-2 LeightonAspell........................................  14/1    24  3
        Letterman (IRE) EJO'Grady,Ireland 6-11-9 PWFlood ..................................  10/1    hd  4
        Roman Rampage MissZCDavison 11-11-2 (s) RobertLucey-Butler ............ 100/1   dist 5
        Mrs D. L. Whateley 5ran 5m59.36
```

NEWBURY Saturday, Nov 25   SOFT

54   vccasino.com Long Distance Hdle (Gr 2) (1) (4yo+) £22,808   3m110y (12)

```
        INGLIS DREVER JHowardJohnson 7-11-8 TonyDobbin.........................  15/8f     1
   48   IRISH WOLF (FR) PBowen 6-11-0 (s) TJO'Brien ...........................   7/2    nk  2
        DOM D'ORGEVAL (FR) NickWilliams 6-11-4 RWalsh..........................  11/2     5  3
   34   Redemption NATwiston-Davies 11-11-8 MrDEngland........................  16/1     6  4
   26   Zaiyad (IRE) AChaille-Chaille,France 5-11-8 (t) CO'Dwyer ..............   2/1     4  5
        Andrea & Graham Wylie 5ran 6m38.85
```

55   Hennessy Cognac Gold Cup Chase (Hcap) (Gr 3) (1) (153) (4yo+)   3¼m110y (21)
    £85,530

```
        STATE OF PLAY EvanWilliams 6-11-4¹⁴⁵ PaulMoloney .....................  10/1     1
   38   JUVEIGNEUR (FR) NJHenderson 9-11-1¹⁴² MickFitzgerald....................  12/1     4  2
   22   PREACHER BOY RJHodges 7-10-6¹³³ LeightonAspell.........................  12/1     9  3
    2   OMNI COSMO TOUCH (USA) MrsSJSmith 10-10-0¹²⁷ DavidO'Meara......  28/1    ¾  4
   22   Parsons Legacy (IRE) PJHobbs 8-10-5¹³² TJO'Brien .....................  25/1    15  5
   35   Idle Talk (IRE) TRGeorge 7-11-3¹⁴⁴ JasonMaguire .......................   8/1     1  6
        Montgermont (FR) CREgerton 6-11-2¹⁴³ RobertThornton.....................   9/2f   26  7
   22   Keltic Bard CJMann 9-10-9¹³⁶ (s) NoelFehily ...........................  33/1    10  8
        Cornish Rebel (IRE) PFNicholls 9-11-12¹⁵³ RWalsh.......................   8/1        pu
        Turpin Green (IRE) NGRichards 7-11-10¹⁵¹ TonyDobbin ...................   5/1        pu
        Ross Comm MrsSJSmith 10-11-0¹⁴¹ RMPower...............................  33/1        pu
        Ardaghey (IRE) NATwiston-Davies 7-10-9¹⁴¹ (t) MrDEngland⁵............  14/1        pu
   24   Bothar Na (IRE) WPMullins,Ireland 7-10-13¹⁴⁰ CO'Dwyer................  25/1        pu
        Napolitain (FR) PFNicholls 5-10-5¹³⁸ (b) PaddyMerrigan⁵ ..............  33/1        pu
        Presenting Express (IRE) MissECLavelle 7-10-10¹³⁷ BarryFenton ........  16/1        pu
   33   Vodka Bleu (FR) DEPipe 7-10-7¹³⁴ TimmyMurphy .........................  15/2        pu
        Mr & Mrs William Rucker 16ran 6m51.42
```

56   ladbrokes.com Hcap Chase (2) 0-145(143) (4yo+) £31,315   2½m (16)

```
        GALLANT APPROACH (IRE) CREgerton 7-11-1¹³² JAMcCarthy............  7/2jf     1
        NO FULL (FR) PRWebber 5-10-11¹²⁸ MickFitzgerald.......................   8/1    ½  2
   36   PATMAN DU CHARMIL (FR) NATwiston-Davies 4-9-0¹³⁰ MrDEngland⁵ ...  7/1    3½  3
   33   Butler's Cabin (IRE) JonjoO'Neill 6-10-8¹²⁵ NoelFehily.................  11/2    3½  4
   33   Kelrev (IRE) MissVenetiaWilliams 8-11-5¹³⁶ TimmyMurphy..............  14/1    14  5
   33   Tighe Caster PBowen 7-10-11¹²⁸ TJO'Brien..............................  16/1    11  6
        Claymore (IRE) OSherwood 10-11-6¹³⁷ LeightonAspell ..................   9/1        f
        Made In Montot (FR) PFNicholls 6-11-0¹³¹ (t) RWalsh..................  7/2jf       f
   34   Hand Inn Hand HDDaly 10-11-12¹⁴³ RobertThornton .....................  16/1        pu
        Big Rob (IRE) BGPowell 7-10-7¹³¹ SPJones⁷.............................  11/1        pu
        Byrne Bros (Formwork) Limited 10ran 5m17.27
```

57   Stan James Int Hdle (Ltd Hcap) (Gerry Feilden) (L) (1) 0-145(143)   2m110y (8)
    (4yo+) £17,106

```
        AFSOUN (FR) NJHenderson 4-11-10¹⁴³ MickFitzgerald.....................   5/2f     1
        CRAVEN (IRE) PFNicholls 6-10-4¹²³ RWalsh.............................  10/3     8  2
        IFFY RLee 5-10-4¹²³ RobertThornton....................................  12/1    2½  3
        Midas Way PRChamings 6-10-4¹²³ LeightonAspell........................   4/1     4  4
   16   Amour Multiple (IRE) SLycett 7-10-4¹²³ TJO'Brien......................  10/1    2½  5
        Whispered Promises (USA) RSBrookhouse 5-11-4¹³⁷ TomScudamore ...  14/1    hd  6
        Grasp GLMoore 4-10-4¹²³ (v) JamieMoore...............................  14/1     4  7
        Anemix (IRE) LCorcoran 5-9-13¹²³ HowieEphgrave⁵ ....................  10/1    23  8
    3   Neveesou (FR) DEPipe 5-10-13¹³² TimmyMurphy .........................  14/1    19  9
        Mr Trevor Hemmings 9ran 4m13.70
```

NEWCASTLE Saturday, Nov 25   SOFT

58   wbx.com Rehearsal Chase (Hcap) (L) (1) (152) (4yo+) £33,804   3m (18)

```
   19   NEPTUNE COLLONGES (FR) PFNicholls 5-11-9¹⁵² LiamHeard³ .............  10/3     1
        ANOTHER PROMISE (IRE) FerdyMurphy 7-10-0¹²⁵ GLee ..................  14/1     2  2
        KING KILLONE (IRE) HPHogarth 6-10-5¹³⁵ PhilKinsella⁵ .................   7/2    ½  3
        Bob Bob Bobbin CLTizzard 7-11-3¹⁴² JoeTizzard.........................  11/4f   ½  4
        Hautclan (FR) JonjoO'Neill 7-10-0¹²⁵ RichardMcGrath..................  12/1    sh  5
        Truckers Tavern (IRE) MrsSJSmith 11-10-0¹²⁵ (t) PadgeWhelan.........  33/1    10  6
        Leading Man (IRE) FerdyMurphy 6-10-3¹²⁸ KeithMercer...................  40/1     4  7
        Julius Caesar JHowardJohnson 6-10-5¹³⁰ PJBrennan .....................  40/1    11  8
        Direct Access (IRE) NGRichards 11-10-9¹³⁴ BrianHarding ..............  14/1     8  9
        A Glass In Thyne (IRE) BNPollock 8-10-1¹³³ MrAMerriam⁷.............   9/1    10 10
```

Fundamentalist (IRE) *NATwiston-Davies* 8-11-6[145] TonyEvans .... 12/1   dist 11
Mr J. Hales 11ran 6m05.01

59   **wbx.com 'Fighting Fifth' Hdle (Gr 1) (1) (4yo+)** £45,072   2m (9)
STRAW BEAR (USA) *NJGifford* 5-11-7 APMcCoy 1/1f   1
23   NOBLE REQUEST (FR) *PJHobbs* 5-11-7 RichardJohnson 9/2   5   2
THE FRENCH FURZE (IRE) *NGRichards* 12-11-7 BrianHarding 66/1   1¼ 3
Arcalis *JHowardJohnson* 6-11-7 PJBrennan .... 8/1   ¾   4
23   Faasel (IRE) *NGRichards* 5-11-7 (s) GLee 14/1   11 5
23   Crow Wood *JJQuinn* 7-11-7 RussGarritty 33/1   2½ 6
Torkinking (IRE) *MABarnes* 7-11-7 (t) RichardMcGrath 200/1   16 7
Charlotte Vale *MickyHammond* 5-11-0 BarryKeniry 250/1   8   8
23   Desert Quest (IRE) *PFNicholls* 6-11-7 (b) SamThomas 11/4   23 9
Mr John P. McManus 9ran 4m00.54

NEWBURY Sunday, Nov 26   HEAVY

60   **Stan James Berkshire Nov Chase (Gr 2) (1) (5yo+)** £19,957   2½m (14)
The second fence in the home straight was omitted due to the state of the ground
32   DENMAN (IRE) *PFNicholls* 6-11-7 SamThomas 2/11f   1
32   SNAKEBITE (IRE) *CarlLlewellyn* 6-11-0 NoelFehily 5/1   12 2
HIGH CHIMES (IRE) *EvanWilliams* 7-11-0 PaulMoloney .... 25/1   dist 3
36   Charlies Double *JRBest* 7-11-0 JasonMaguire .... 66/1   nk 4
Mrs M. Findlay & P. K. Barber 4ran 5m19.14

NAVAN Sunday, Nov 26   SOFT

61   **williamhill.ie Troytown Hcap Chase 0-150(147) (4yo+)** £37,230   3m (17)
CANE BRAKE (IRE) *TJTaaffe* 7-10-6[129] (s) BJGeraghty 10/1   1
KERRYHEAD WINDFARM (IRE) *MHourigan* 8-10-3[126]
     AndrewJMcNamara 9/1   4   2
ON THE NET (IRE) *EoghanO'Grady* 8-9-11[125] ADLeigh[5] 20/1   7   3
LORDOFOUROWN (IRE) *SDonohoe* 8-10-5[128] DNRussell .... 11/1   nk 4
Southern Vic *TMWalsh* 7-11-10[147] RWalsh .... 13/8f   hd 5
Ride The Storm (IRE) *EJO'Grady* 9-9-11[120] JRBarry 12/1   13 6
11   No Half Session (IRE) *NMeade* 9-10-4[127] (b) NPMadden 11/1   10 7
11   Star Clipper *NMeade* 9-10-7[130] PCarberry 10/1   22 8
Dublin Hunter (IRE) *DTHughes* 10-9-11[120] (b) PWFlood 25/1   1½ 9
Homer Wells (IRE) *WPMullins* 8-10-4[127] DJCondon 10/1   7 10
Rockspring Hero *JohnJWalsh* 10-9-7[119] RJMolloy[3] 14/1   16 11
Romaha (IRE) *TJArnold* 10-10-0[123] (s+t) JPElliott.......................... 33/1   27 12
Coljon (IRE) *PaulNolan* 8-10-4[127] (s) JLCullen 16/1   1¾ 13
Jaquouille (FR) *ALTMoore* 9-9-11[120] TGMRyan .... 14/1   f
Macs Flamingo (IRE) *PAFahy* 6-10-4[130] APLane[3] .... 33/1   pu
Anxious Moments (IRE) *ThomasO'Neill* 11-9-7[119] (s) AELynch[3] .... 33/1   pu
Mount Temple Two Racing Synd 16ran 6m39.40

SANDOWN Friday, Dec 1   SOFT

62   **Ballymore Properties Nov Hdle (Winter) (Gr 2) (1) (4yo+)** £15,966   2½m110y (9)
LABELTHOU (FR) *MissECLavelle* 7-11-0 BarryFenton 5/2   1
13   GRANIT JACK (FR) *PFNicholls* 4-11-0 RWalsh 4/7f   22 2
DUNCLIFFE *RHAlner* 9-11-7 AndrewThornton 14/1   21 3
Pass It On (IRE) *JonjoO'Neill* 7-11-7 NoelFehily 9/1   14 4
Chamacco (FR) *MFHarris* 6-11-7 MarkGrant 33/1   8   5
GDM Partnership 5ran 5m10.25

63   **John Smith's Future Stars Chase (Int) (2) (5yo+)** £15,658   3m110y (22)
34   STAR DE MOHAISON (FR) *PFNicholls* 5-11-10 (t) RWalsh 1/2f   1
THE LISTENER (IRE) *RHAlner* 7-11-10 AndrewThornton 7/2   1¼ 2
17   ZABENZ (NZ) *PJHobbs* 9-11-0 (b) TJO'Brien 5/1   26 3
Lord Killeshanra (IRE) *CLTizzard* 7-11-4 JoeTizzard 25/1   14 4
Sir Robert Ogden 4ran 6m25.83

SANDOWN Saturday, Dec 2   SOFT
The open ditch in front of the stands was omitted and the plain fence jumped instead in all chases

64   **Sodexho Prestige Henry VIII Nov Chase (Gr 2) (1) (4yo+)** £19,957   2m (13)
36   FAIR ALONG (GER) *PJHobbs* 4-10-13 RichardJohnson 2/1   1
18   MY WAY DE SOLZEN (FR) *AKing* 6-11-8 RobertThornton 4/7f   10 2
NEW LITTLE BRIC (FR) *PFNicholls* 5-11-8 RWalsh 9/1   5   3
60   Charlies Double *JRBest* 7-11-4 DaveCrosse .... 100/1   dist 4
Trampoline King (USA) *AJWhiting* 6-11-4 (s) SEDurack 100/1   28 5
Mr Alan Peterson 5ran 4m04.20

1091

65 **William Hill - Tingle Creek Chase (Gr 1) (1) (5yo+) £79,828**   2m (13)

47	KAUTO STAR (FR) *PFNicholls* 6-11-7 (t) RWalsh	4/9f		1
	VOY POR USTEDES (FR) *AKing* 5-11-7 RobertThornton	4/1	7	2
	ONEWAY (IRE) *MGRimell* 9-11-7 RichardJohnson	66/1	7	3
41	Central House *DTHughes,Ireland* 9-11-7 RLoughran	9/1	9	4
44	Hoo La Baloo (FR) *PFNicholls* 5-11-7 LiamHeard	66/1	6	5
41	Fota Island (IRE) *MFMorris,Ireland* 10-11-7 APMcCoy	18/1	5	6
49	Dempsey (IRE) *CarlLlewellyn* 8-11-7 AndrewTinkler	33/1		ur

Mr Clive D. Smith 7ran 4m02.17

66 **William Hill Hcap Hdle (L) (1) 0-140(140) (4yo+) £28,510**   2m110y (8)

1	OVERSTRAND (IRE) *DrRDPNewland* 7-10-5[126] SPJones[7]	8/1		1
57	WHISPERED PROMISES (USA) *RSBrookhouse* 5-11-7[135] AlanO'Keeffe	25/1	7	2
	NATION STATE *GLMoore* 5-10-3[117] (s) RWalsh	7/1	2	3
	ETOILE RUSSE (IRE) *PCHaslam* 4-9-9[114] (t) WayneKavanagh[5]	20/1	¾	4
	Star Shot (IRE) *PRWebber* 5-10-5[119] TomDoyle	16/1	7	5
37	Verasi *GLMoore* 5-11-6[134] (b) JamieMoore	11/2f	nk	6
16	Heathcote *GLMoore* 4-10-7[126] EamonDehdashti[5]	10/1	1	7
	Ellway Prospect *MGRimell* 6-10-3[117] RichardJohnson	12/1	3½	8
	Fenix (GER) *MrsLWadham* 7-11-3[131] (b) LeightonAspell	10/1	¾	9
	Rosecliff *HeatherDalton* 4-10-3[120] (v+t) DougieCostello[3]	33/1	¾	10
16	Caracciola (GER) *NJHenderson* 9-11-7[140] MrJSnowden[5]	25/1	½	11
	Elegant Clutter (IRE) *NATwiston-Davies* 8-9-9[114] MrDEngland[5]	12/1	3	12
	Guru *GLMoore* 8-10-8[122] APMcCoy	11/1	9	13
14	Nathos (GER) *CJMann* 9-11-0[138] KevinTobin[10]	25/1	1¾	14
	Miss Academy (IRE) *DEPipe* 5-10-10[124] TimmyMurphy	20/1	7	15
	Mohawk Star (IRE) *IAWood* 5-9-7[114] TMolloy[7]	33/1	19	16
	Self Respect (USA) *AKing* 4-11-0[128] RobertThornton	7/1		pu

Dr R. D. P. Newland 17ran 4m07.78

FAIRYHOUSE Sunday, Dec 3   HEAVY

The meeting was abandoned after 2 races due to gale-force winds

67 **Bar-One Racing Royal Bond Nov Hdle (Gr 1) (4yo+) £32,939**   2m (8)

The first flight in the back straight was omitted

	HIDE THE EVIDENCE (IRE) *MrsJHarrington* 5-11-12 (t) ADLeigh	10/1		1
	CLOPF (IRE) *EJO'Grady* 5-11-12 BJGeraghty	8/11f	6	2
	CLENI BOY (FR) *NMeade* 4-11-7 NPMadden	40/1	sh	3
	Bobs Pride (IRE) *DKWeld* 4-11-7 TimmyMurphy	16/1	15	4
	Blazing Sky (IRE) *FFMcGuinness* 6-11-7 PWFlood	4/1	1¾	5
	Askthemaster (IRE) *RobertTyner* 6-11-12 DNRussell	7/1	4	6
	Tango Jim (FR) *NMeade* 4-11-7 PCarberry	16/1	29	7
	Dancing Hero (IRE) *ThomasFoley* 5-11-12 CO'Dwyer	25/1	11	8
	Davenport Democrat (IRE) *WPMullins* 8-11-12 RWalsh	14/1	2½	9

Mr Maynard Hamilton 9ran 4m12.11

FAIRYHOUSE Wednesday, Dec 6   HEAVY

68 **Ballymore Properties Hatton's Grace Hdle (Gr 1) (4yo+) £43,624**   2½m (12)

52	BRAVE INCA (IRE) *ColmAMurphy* 8-11-12 APMcCoy	10/3		1
40	ROSAKER (USA) *NMeade* 9-11-12 PCarberry	10/1	¾	2
40	BROGELLA (IRE) *MsFMCrowley* 6-11-7 JLCullen	66/1	2	3
52	Asian Maze (IRE) *ThomasMullins* 7-11-7 RWalsh	4/7f	9	4
40	Al Eile (IRE) *JohnQueally* 6-11-12 TimmyMurphy	9/1	28	5

Novices Syndicate 5ran 5m22.77

69 **Ballymore Properties Drinmore Nov Chase (Gr 1) (5yo+) £43,624**   2½m (16)

	CAILIN ALAINN (IRE) *CharlesByrnes* 7-11-7 DNRussell	6/1		1
	SCHINDLERS HUNT (IRE) *DTHughes* 6-11-12 RWalsh	10/1	¾	2
	GAZZA'S GIRL (IRE) *MrsJHarrington* 6-11-7 ADLeigh	10/1	11	3
	Blueberry Boy (IRE) *PaulStafford* 7-11-12 AELynch	5/1	1¼	4
	Mossbank (IRE) *MHourigan* 6-11-12 CO'Dwyer	9/1	nk	5
	Vic Venturi (IRE) *PhilipFenton* 6-11-12 (t) AndrewJMcNamara	7/1	20	6
	Mac Three (IRE) *NMeade* 7-11-12 PCarberry	15/2	22	7
	Anothercoppercoast (IRE) *PaulARoche* 6-11-12 BJGeraghty	25/1	9	8
	King Johns Castle (IRE) *ALTMoore* 7-11-12 APMcCoy	3/1f		pu
	O'Muircheartaigh (IRE) *EJO'Grady* 6-11-12 (s) PWFlood	8/1		pu

Dewdrop Racing Syndicate 10ran 5m19.27

CHELTENHAM Friday, Dec 8   SOFT (New Course)

70   boylepoker.com Chase (Hcap) (L) (1) (156) (4yo+) £57,020 $\qquad$ 3m1f110y (21)

	D'ARGENT (IRE) *AKing* 9-10-5[135] RobertThornton	10/1	1
33	NEW ALCO (FR) *FerdyMurphy* 5-10-5[135] GLee	6/1jf	sh 2
35	MY WILL (FR) *PFNicholls* 6-11-12[156] RWalsh	6/1jf	sh 3
	Liberthine (FR) *NJHenderson* 7-10-4[141] MrSWaley-Cohen[7]	10/1	8 4
	Puntal (FR) *DEPipe* 10-10-4[134] (t) RichardJohnson	20/1	3 5
51	Nil Desperandum (IRE) *MissVenetiaWilliams* 9-10-9[139] TomScudamore	12/1	4 6
55	Cornish Rebel (IRE) *PFNicholls* 9-11-4[148] (b) SamThomas	20/1	1½ 7
56	No Full (FR) *PRWebber* 5-10-1[131] PJBrennan	9/1	12 8
19	Church Island (IRE) *MHourigan,Ireland* 7-10-11[141] AJMcNamara	16/1	7 9
	All In The Stars (IRE) *DPKeane* 8-10-11[141] NeilMulholland	33/1	8 10
55	Ardaghey (IRE) *NATwiston-Davies* 4-11-0[141] (t) TonyEvans	11/1	½ 11
	Jack High (IRE) *TMWalsh,Ireland* 11-10-11[141] DNRussell	40/1	1 12
	Innox (FR) *FDoumen,France* 7-10-11[151] (b) APMcCoy	11/1	8 13
35	Model Son (IRE) *FJordan* 8-10-0[133] PaddyMerrigan[3]	10/1	4 14
	Commercial Flyer (IRE) *DEPipe* 7-11-0[144] (t) TimmyMurphy	7/1	f

Mr Nigel Bunter 15ran 6m59.91

CHELTENHAM Saturday, Dec 9   SOFT (New Course)

71   boylepoker.com Juv Nov Hdle (2) (3yo) £12,526 $\qquad$ 2m1f (8)

31	KATCHIT (IRE) *AKing* 3-11-7 RobertThornton	7/4	1
	NED LUDD (IRE) *JGPortman* 3-11-3 RichardJohnson	33/1	8 2
	TRITONIX (IRE) *PJHobbs* 3-11-7 (t) APMcCoy	13/8f	6 3
	Lord Adonis (IRE) *KJBurke* 3-11-0 PaddyMerrigan	100/1	2½ 4
	Risk Runner (IRE) *AKing* 3-11-7 (b) WayneHutchinson	12/1	13 5
	Prince Zafonic (FR) *MWEasterby* 3-11-0 (b) MrTGreenall	66/1	6 6
31	Cheveley Flyer *JPearce* 3-11-3 TimmyMurphy	20/1	2 7
	Peacock (IRE) *NATwiston-Davies* 3-11-0 TonyEvans	25/1	½ 8
	Zariyan (FR) *TDoumen,France* 3-11-0 CO'Dwyer	14/1	2 9
	Ace Baby *KJBurke* 3-11-0 (t) BernieWharfe	200/1	15 10
	Jaunty *NEBerry* 3-11-0 SamThomas	150/1	1¼ 11
	Pommerol (FR) *FDoumen,France* 3-11-7 (t) ADuchene	7/1	f

D S J P Syndicate 12ran 4m19.11

72   Mears Group "Relkeel" Hdle (Gr 2) (1) (4yo+) £22,808 $\qquad$ 2m5f110y (10)

	BLACK JACK KETCHUM (IRE) *JonjoO'Neill* 7-11-7 APMcCoy	4/11f	1
1	BLAZING BAILEY *AKing* 4-11-1 RobertThornton	11/4	3 2
	PALMRIDGE (GER) *TDoumen,France* 6-11-1 CO'Dwyer	33/1	dist 3
	Youlbesolucky (IRE) *JonjoO'Neill* 7-10-12 NoelFehily	33/1	dist 4
	Sarahs Quay (IRE) *KJBurke* 7-10-5 (s) PaddyMerrigan	150/1	30 5

Mrs Gay Smith 5ran 5m37.58

73   boylesports.com Gold Cup (Hcap Chase) (Gr 3) (1) (157) (4yo+) £85,530 $\qquad$ 2m5f (17)

33	EXOTIC DANCER (FR) *JonjoO'Neill* 6-11-4[149] (s) TonyDobbin	8/1	1
44	KNOWHERE (IRE) *NATwiston-Davies* 8-10-11[142] TonyEvans	10/1	1½ 2
33	TARANIS (FR) *PFNicholls* 5-11-4[149] (t) RWalsh	3/1f	3½ 3
4	Tikram *AKing* 9-10-8[139] RobertThornton	14/1	5 4
49	Thisthatandtother (IRE) *PFNicholls* 10-11-9[157] LiamHeard[3]	12/1	½ 5
46	Madison du Berlais (FR) *DEPipe* 5-10-2[133] TomScudamore	22/1	7 6
	Ross River *AJMartin,Ireland* 10-11-1[146] DNRussell	11/2	9 7
44	Reveillez *JRFanshawe* 7-10-0[145] APMcCoy	5/1	13 8
44	Cerium (FR) *PFNicholls* 5-11-9[154] (t) SamThomas	14/1	4 9
56	Butler's Cabin (IRE) *JonjoO'Neill* 6-9-7[131] (s) JWFarrelly[7]	25/1	5 10
46	Contraband *DEPipe* 8-11-4[149] (s) RJGreene	50/1	dist 11
	Bannow Strand (IRE) *DEPipe* 6-10-5[136] TimmyMurphy	7/1	pu

Sir Robert Ogden 12ran 5m34.66

74   boylesports.com International (Hdle) (Gr 2) (1) (4yo+) £114,040 $\qquad$ 2m1f (8)

37	DETROIT CITY (USA) *PJHobbs* 4-11-4 (b) RichardJohnson	4/6f	1
45	HARDY EUSTACE (IRE) *DTHughes,Ireland* 9-11-8 (v) CO'Dwyer	6/4	1 2
59	CROW WOOD *JJQuinn* 7-11-4 APMcCoy	33/1	10 3
59	Arcalis *JHowardJohnson* 6-11-8 PJBrennan	16/1	1¼ 4

Mr Terry Warner 4ran 4m21.35

75   Brit Insurance Nov Hdle (Bristol) (Gr 2) (1) (4yo+) £19,957 $\qquad$ 3m (12)

	FLIGHT LEADER (IRE) *CLTizzard* 6-11-0 JoeTizzard	16/1	1
62	LABELTHOU (FR) *MissECLavelle* 7-11-0 BarryFenton	13/8f	9 2
	THE WHISPERER (IRE) *NGRichards* 5-11-4 TonyDobbin	13/2	17 3
	Christdalo (IRE) *DEPipe* 6-10-11 TimmyMurphy	7/2	4 4
	Air Force One (GER) *CJMann* 4-11-0 NoelFehily	50/1	6 5

1093

38	Imperial Commander (IRE) *NATwiston-Davies* 5-11-0 TonyEvans	10/1	27	6
38	Massini's Maguire (IRE) *PJHobbs* 5-11-7 RichardJohnson	4/1		ur
	Hockenheim (FR) *JHowardJohnson* 5-11-4 PJBrennan	16/1		pu

John and Heather Snook 8ran 6m11.56

PUNCHESTOWN Sunday, Dec 10   HEAVY

76   John Durkan Memorial Punchestown Chase (Gr 1) (5yo+) £43,624   2½m (14)

25	IN COMPLIANCE (IRE) *MJPO'Brien* 6-11-12 BJGeraghty	5/1		1
24	WAR OF ATTRITION (IRE) *MFMorris* 7-11-12 CO'Dwyer	2/1f	2½	2
42	SHER BEAU (IRE) *PhilipFenton* 7-11-12 PWFlood	40/1	9	3
41	Nickname (IRE) *MartinBrassil* 7-11-12 RWalsh	7/2	6	4
	Hi Cloy (IRE) *MHourigan* 9-11-12 AndrewJMcNamara	12/1	8	5
41	Watson Lake (IRE) *NMeade* 8-11-12 PCarberry	14/1	dist	6
24	Justified (IRE) *ESheehy* 7-11-12 APMcCoy	4/1		pu
12	Public Reaction *EUHales* 8-11-12 NPMadden	66/1		pu

Mr S. Mulryan 8ran 5m33.41

ASCOT Friday, Dec 15   GOOD to SOFT

77   Mitie Kennel Gate Nov Hdle (Gr 2) (1) (4yo+) £19,957   2m (9)

	TAGULA BLUE (IRE) *IanWilliams* 6-11-4 WayneHutchinson	8/1		1
30	MOON OVER MIAMI (GER) *CJMann* 5-11-7 NoelFehily	11/2	½	2
	CARLITOS *NATwiston-Davies* 4-11-0 TonyEvans	9/2	2½	3
	Albinus *AMBalding* 5-11-0 MarkBradburne	8/1	8	4
	Pepporoni Pete (IRE) *PFNicholls* 5-11-4 RWalsh	10/11f	¾	5
	Nicki Boy (GER) *CJMann* 4-11-0 DaveCrosse	100/1	4	6
30	Orpen Wide (IRE) *MCChapman* 4-11-7 DavidCullinane	20/1	11	7
	Court Ruler *EvanWilliams* 4-11-7 PaulMoloney	28/1	8	8
	Shambar (IRE) *MissECLavelle* 7-11-0 WayneKavanagh	100/1	13	9
	Must Be Keen *ErnstOertel* 7-11-0 ColinBolger	150/1	14	10

Boston R. S. Ian Bennett 10ran 3m49.88

78   Scanmoor Noel Nov Chase (Gr 2) (1) (4yo+) £22,536   2m3f (16)

	BRIAREUS *AMBalding* 6-11-5 MarkBradburne	7/2		1
	KNIGHT LEGEND (IRE) *MrsJHarrington,Ireland* 7-11-5 MickFitzgerald	12/1	3	2
23	ROYAL SHAKESPEARE (FR) *SGollings* 7-11-5 RobertThornton	16/1	sh	3
36	Natal (FR) *PFNicholls* 5-11-9 (t) RWalsh	8/13f	11	4
	Harmony Brig (IRE) *NGRichards* 7-11-9 TonyDobbin	8/1	dist	5

Miss E. J. Lambourne 5ran 4m47.54

ASCOT Saturday, Dec 16   GOOD to SOFT

79   BGC Silver Cup Hcap Chase (L) (1) (153) (4yo+) £39,438   3m (20)

44	BILLYVODDAN (IRE) *HDDaly* 7-10-12[139] (b) LeightonAspell	25/1		1
63	ZABENZ (NZ) *PJHobbs* 9-10-13[140] (b) BarryFenton	16/1	12	2
33	GRAPHIC APPROACH (IRE) *CREgerton* 8-10-12[139] PaulMoloney	15/2	2	3
35	LACDOUDAL (FR) *PJHobbs* 7-11-12[153] RichardJohnson	15/2	2	4
43	Iznogoud (FR) *DEPipe* 10-10-3[130] TomScudamore	33/1	6	5
70	Ardaghey (IRE) *NATwiston-Davies* 7-10-8[140] (t) MrDEngland[5]	33/1	½	6
	Cornish Sett (IRE) *PFNicholls* 7-11-6[147] (b) RWalsh	12/1	hd	7
46	See You Sometime *JWMullins* 11-11-0[146] WayneKavanagh[5]	12/1	5	8
	Kelami (FR) *FDoumen,France* 8-10-12[144] ADuchene[5]	18/1	nk	9
	Backbeat (IRE) *JHowardJohnson* 9-10-9[136] PJBrennan	25/1	12	10
35	Take The Stand (IRE) *PBowen* 10-11-12[153] (t) TJO'Brien	28/1	dist	11
48	Royal Emperor (IRE) *MrsSJSmith* 10-11-9[150] SEDurack	50/1	dist	12
	Iris Royal (FR) *NJHenderson* 10-10-8[135] DJCasey	16/1		ur
22	Fork Lightning (IRE) *AKing* 10-10-7[134] RobertThornton	12/1		ur
51	Clan Royal (FR) *JonjoO'Neill* 11-11-2[143] APMcCoy	25/1		pu
33	Copsale Lad *NJHenderson* 9-11-2[143] MickFitzgerald	6/1		pu
43	Harris Bay *MissHCKnight* 7-10-8[135] (t) TimmyMurphy	4/1f		pu
	Windsor Boy (IRE) *DEPipe* 9-9-12[130] AndrewGlassonbury[5]	16/1		pu

Mr Trevor Hemmings 18ran 6m10.20

80   Ladbroke (Hcap Hdle) (L) (1) 0-150(139) (4yo+) £84,510   2m (9)

1	ACAMBO (GER) *DEPipe* 5-11-9[136] TimmyMurphy	7/1		1
	TARLAC (GER) *NJHenderson* 5-11-3[130] APMcCoy	11/2	2	2
	VICTRAM (IRE) *AdrianMcGuinness,Ireland* 6-10-10[128] AELynch[5]	12/1	4	3
	PILCA (FR) *DCarroll* 6-9-9[113] WayneKavanagh[5]	14/1	½	4
	Well Mounted (IRE) *ALTMoore,Ireland* 5-10-6[119] DJCasey	5/1f	2½	5
	Chief Yeoman *MissVenetiaWilliams* 6-11-8[138] LiamTreadwell[3]	16/1	2½	6
	Pirate Flagship (FR) *PFNicholls* 7-11-1[128] RWalsh	20/1	½	7
	Kings Quay *JJQuinn* 4-10-1[117] DougieCostello[3]	9/1	¾	8
	Prime Contender *GLMoore* 4-10-7[120] (b) RichardJohnson	16/1	¾	9

Desert Air (JPN) *DEPipe* 7-11-11[138] (t) TomScudamore 33/1 2½ 10
37 Mahogany Blaze (FR) *NATwiston-Davies* 4-11-6[138] (b) MrDEngland[5] 50/1 2 11
Astronomic *JHowardJohnson* 6-11-7[134] PJBrennan 100/1 6 12
66 Star Shot (IRE) *PRWebber* 5-10-6[119] RobertThornton 18/1 4 13
66 Overstrand (IRE) *DrRDPNewland* 7-11-3[137] SPJones[7] 8/1 1 14
66 Nathos (GER) *CJMann* 9-11-0[137] KevinTobin[10] .... 100/1 sh 15
Premier Dane (IRE) *NGRichards* 4-11-5[139] PJBenson[7] 33/1 10 16
Tipperary All Star (FR) *MHalford,Ireland* 6-11-12[139] MickFitzgerald........... 7/1 16 17
Tamreen (IRE) *GLMoore* 5-9-9[113] (b) EamonDehdashti[5] 100/1 4 18
Symphonique (FR) *PJHobbs* 5-10-10[130] MrSWaley-Cohen[7] .... 66/1 hd 19
66 Verasi *GLMoore* 5-11-6[133] (b) JamieMoore.. 33/1 dist 20

Mr D. A. Johnson 20ran 3m52.31

81 BGC Long Walk Hdle (Gr 1) (1) (4yo+) £56,340   3m1f (14)
45 MIGHTY MAN (FR) *HDDaly* 6-11-7 RichardJohnson.............................. 8/11f   1
45 LOUGH DERG (FR) *DEPipe* 6-11-7 (v) TomScudamore 50/1 1¼ 2
TEMOIN *NJHenderson* 6-11-7 MickFitzgerald 33/1 1 3
72 Blazing Bailey *AKing* 4-11-7 RobertThornton 10/1 1¼ 4
45 No Refuge (IRE) *JHowardJohnson* 6-11-7 (s) PJBrennan 33/1 1¼ 5
58 Neptune Collonges (FR) *PFNicholls* 5-11-7 RWalsh 10/3 6 6
54 Irish Wolf (FR) *PBowen* 6-11-7 (s) TJO'Brien 14/1 23 7
54 Redemption *NATwiston-Davies* 11-11-7 MrDEngland 40/1 9 8
45 Fire Dragon (IRE) *JonjoO'Neill* 5-11-7 (b) APMcCoy............................... 14/1 dist 9

Mr E. R. Hanbury 9ran 6m13.16

HAYDOCK Saturday, Dec 16   SOFT

82 totescoop6 Hcap Hdle (2) (159) (3yo+) £19,518   2½m (9)
What should have been the second last was omitted due to a stricken jockey
48 UNITED (GER) *MrsLWadham* 5-10-1[134] JAMcCarthy 7/1   1
66 WHISPERED PROMISES (USA) *RSBrookhouse* 5-10-5[138] AlanO'Keeffe ... 8/1 ½ 2
48 JAZZ D'ESTRUVAL (FR) *NGRichards* 9-10-9[142] TonyDobbin 6/4f 15 3
48 St Matthew (USA) *MrsSJSmith* 8-10-12[145] DavidO'Meara 25/1 2 4
48 The Bajan Bandit (IRE) *LLungo* 11-10-7[140] KeithMercer .... 50/1 sh 5
34 Just Beth *GFierro* 10-10-8[133] DavidCullinane[7] 66/1 17 6
Magnifico (FR) *MrsKWaldron* 5-10-0[133] RJGreene 50/1 10 7
48 Tees Components *KGReveley* 11-9-11[137] (t) JamesReveley[7] .... 9/1 dist 8
Oscar Park (IRE) *CTinkler* 7-10-7[140] TomDoyle .... 7/2   f
Rhinestone Cowboy (IRE) *JonjoO'Neill* 10-11-12[159] MrJPMagnier .... 8/1 pu

Mr R. B. Holt 10ran 5m07.49

NAVAN Sunday, Dec 17   HEAVY

83 Giltspur Scientific Tara Hdle (Gr 2) (4yo+) £26,392   2½m (11)
CELESTIAL WAVE (IRE) *AdrianMaguire* 6-11-3 TimmyMurphy 10/3   1
61 SOUTHERN VIC (IRE) *TMWalsh* 7-11-5 RWalsh 5/2 1½ 2
MOUNTHENRY (IRE) *CharlesByrnes* 6-11-10 DNRussell........................ 9/4f 5½ 3
40 Sweet Kiln (IRE) *JamesBowe* 7-11-0 PCarberry 10/1 1¾ 4
40 Prince of Tara (IRE) *SJMahon* 9-11-5 BJGeraghty 25/1 24 5
40 Baron de Feypo (IRE) *PatrickOBrady* 7-11-2 JPElliott 66/1 19 6
68 Brogella (IRE) *MsFMCrowley* 6-11-3 (b) JLCullen .... 5/1 dist 7
Bawn Og (IRE) *AdrianSexton* 8-11-8 AndrewJMcNamara 25/1 3½ 8

Cahir Racing Syndicate 8ran 5m11.18

84 Barry & Sandra Kelly Memorial Nov Hdle (Gr 1) (4yo+) £43,919   2½m (11)
ARAN CONCERTO (IRE) *NMeade* 5-11-12 PCarberry 4/5f   1
FOOTY FACTS (IRE) *RobertTyner* 6-11-12 TimmyMurphy 15/8 7 2
HOLLYWOOD LAW (IRE) *WPMullins* 5-11-12 RWalsh 16/1 6 3
Kazal (FR) *EoinGriffin* 5-11-12 DNRussell 33/1 1½ 4
Le Toscan (FR) *MJPO'Brien* 6-11-12 BJGeraghty 7/1 20 5
Badgerlaw (FR) *MrsJHarrington* 6-11-12 RMPower 66/1 29 6

Mr John Corr 6ran 5m13.56

KEMPTON Tuesday, Dec 26   GOOD to SOFT

85 Stan James Feltham Nov Chase (Gr 1) (1) (4yo+) £40,102   3m (18)
UNGARO (FR) *KGReveley* 7-11-7 MickFitzgerald 14/1   1
53 BOYCHUK (IRE) *PJHobbs* 5-11-7 RichardJohnson 5/1 10 2
73 KNOWHERE (IRE) *NATwiston-Davies* 8-11-7 TonyEvans......................... 5/1 5 3
According To John (IRE) *NGRichards* 6-11-7 TonyDobbin 13/2 13 4
4 Yes Sir (IRE) *PBowen* 7-11-7 APMcCoy... 9/4jf dist 5
Bold Fire *PFNicholls* 4-10-2 RWalsh .... 9/4jf pu

Sir Robert Ogden 6ran 6m10.49

86   **Stan James Christmas Hdle (Gr 1) (1) (4yo+)** £57,020   2m (8)

	JAZZ MESSENGER (FR) *NMeade,Ireland* 6-11-7 NPMadden	10/1	1
59	NOBLE REQUEST (FR) *PJHobbs* 5-11-7 RichardJohnson	7/1	4 2
59	DESERT QUEST (FR) *PFNicholls* 6-11-7 (b) RWalsh	8/1	6 3
59	Straw Bear (USA) *NJGifford* 5-11-7 APMcCoy	4/6f	¾ 4
46	Hasty Prince *JonjoO'Neill* 8-11-7 TonyDobbin	40/1	24 5
45	Self Defense *MissECLavelle* 9-11-7 TimmyMurphy	25/1	13 6
57	Afsoun (FR) *NJHenderson* 4-11-7 MickFitzgerald	11/2	f

R.S.T. Syndicate 7ran 3m59.75

87   **Stan James King George VI Chase (Gr 1) (1) (4yo+)** £114,040   3m (18)

65	KAUTO STAR (FR) *PFNicholls* 6-11-10 (t) RWalsh	8/13f	1
73	EXOTIC DANCER (IRE) *JonjoO'Neill* 6-11-10 (t) APMcCoy	9/1	8 2
49	RACING DEMON (IRE) *MissHCKnight* 6-11-10 TimmyMurphy	7/1	1¼ 3
49	Monkerhostin (FR) *PJHobbs* 9-11-10 RichardJohnson	14/1	20 4
70	Puntal (FR) *DEPipe* 10-11-10 (t) NPMadden	100/1	9 5
	Monet's Garden (IRE) *NGRichards* 8-11-10 TonyDobbin	5/1	14 6
47	Ollie Magern *NATwiston-Davies* 8-11-10 TonyEvans	25/1	¾ 7
22	Ballycassidy (IRE) *PBowen* 10-11-10 NickWilliams	100/1	pu
70	Commercial Flyer (IRE) *DEPipe* 7-11-10 (t) TomScudamore	50/1	pu

Mr Clive D. Smith 9ran 6m05.73

WETHERBY Tuesday, Dec 26   HEAVY

88   **skybet.com Rowland Meyrick Hcap Chase (Gr 3) (1) (154) (4yo+)** £28,510   3m1f (18)

58	LEADING MAN (IRE) *FerdyMurphy* 6-10-0[128] GLee	9/1	1
35	SIR REMBRANDT (IRE) *RHAlner* 11-11-9[151] AndrewThornton	14/1	8 2
58	TRUCKERS TAVERN (IRE) *MrsSJSmith* 11-10-0[128] (t) PeterBuchanan	8/1	1 3
	Little Big Horse (IRE) *MrsSJSmith* 10-9-9[130] MichaelO'Connell[7]	40/1	nk 4
	Ossmoses (IRE) *DMForster* 9-10-12[140] RichardMcGrath	4/1	½ 5
	Heez A Dreamer (IRE) *MissVenetiaWilliams* 6-10-2[133] PCO'Neill[3]	8/1	10 6
55	King Killone (IRE) *HPHogarth* 6-10-3[136] PhilKinsella[5]	2/1f	½ 7
55	Ross Comm *MrsSJSmith* 10-10-7[135] DavidO'Meara	7/1	5 8
	Sleeping Night (FR) *PFNicholls* 10-11-7[154] MrCJSweeney[5]	8/1	f
58	Julius Caesar *JHowardJohnson* 6-10-0[128] PJBrennan	20/1	pu

Mrs C. McKeane 10ran 7m04.16

LEOPARDSTOWN Tuesday, Dec 26   SOFT

89   **Durkan New Homes Juv Hdle (Gr 2) (3yo)** £21,846   2m (8)

	LOUNAOS (FR) *EoinGriffin* 3-10-4 BJGeraghty	5/4f	1
	ROBIN DU BOIS (FR) *AJMartin* 3-10-9 DNRussell	10/1	3½ 2
	DEPUTY CONSORT (USA) *MJPO'Brien* 3-10-9 AELynch	6/1	14 3
	Financial Reward (IRE) *WPMullins* 3-10-9 DJCasey	13/2	¾ 4
	Celtic Warrior (IRE) *LiamRoche* 3-10-9 PWFlood	14/1	¾ 5
	Victoria Night (IRE) *MsFMCrowley* 3-10-4 BSCarey	20/1	nk 6
	Loup du Saubouas (FR) *NMeade* 3-10-9 PCarberry	14/1	8 7
31	Total Victory (IRE) *THogan* 3-10-9 (s) TPTreacy	12/1	4½ 8
	Apt To Run (USA) *MDMurphy* 3-10-9 (t) RMPower	40/1	3½ 9
	Settigano (IRE) *BrianNolan* 3-10-9 RLoughran	66/1	21 10
	Convincing *JohnJosephMurphy* 3-10-9 EFPower	14/1	1 11
	Rusty Red (IRE) *JosephCrowley* 3-10-12 JLCullen	16/1	5½ 12
	Dariak (FR) *SJMahon* 3-10-9 PACarberry	33/1	pu

Mrs Martina Griffin 13ran 4m06.93

90   **Durkan New Homes Nov Chase (Gr 1) (4yo+)** £43,624   2m1f (11)

69	SCHINDLERS HUNT (IRE) *DTHughes* 6-11-12 RLoughran	3/1	1
	HEAR THE ECHO (IRE) *MFMorris* 5-11-10 ADLeigh	50/1	10 2
69	BLUEBERRY BOY (IRE) *PaulStafford* 7-11-12 AELynch	4/1	1 3
	Wanango (GER) *TStack* 5-11-10 DJCasey	11/2	3½ 4
	Don't Be Bitin (IRE) *EoinGriffin* 5-11-10 DNRussell	12/1	sh 5
	Sky's The Limit (FR) *EJO'Grady* 5-11-10 (s) PWFlood	8/1	1½ 6
	Glenfinn Captain (IRE) *TJTaaffe* 7-11-12 BJGeraghty	11/4f	f
	Pom Flyer (FR) *FFlood* 6-11-12 KTColeman	33/1	f
	Young Desperado (IRE) *RobertTyner* 8-11-12 PACarberry	20/1	f

Slaneyville Syndicate 9ran 4m22.93

CHEPSTOW Wednesday, Dec 27   SOFT

91   **Coral Welsh National Hcap Chase (Gr 3) (1) (151) (4yo+)** £57,020 3m5f110y (22)

48	HALCON GENELARDAIS (FR) *AKing* 6-11-3[147] WayneHutchinson	7/1	1
	MON MOME (FR) *MissVenetiaWilliams* 6-10-3[136] LiamTreadwell[3]	14/1	4 2
55	JUVEIGNEUR (FR) *NJHenderson* 9-11-3[147] MickFitzgerald	11/1	6 3

61	LORDOFOUROWN (IRE) *SDonohoe,Ireland* 8-10-0[130] (s) PaulMoloney ...	11/1	4 4
	Naunton Brook *NATwiston-Davies* 7-9-10[131] (t) MrDEngland[5]	12/1	2 5
	Simon *JLSpearing* 7-10-2[132] AndrewThornton	11/2f	3 6
	L'Aventure (FR) *PFNicholls* 7-10-3[136] (b+t) LiamHeard[3]	6/1	nk 7
35	Run For Paddy *CarlLlewellyn* 10-10-9[139] NoelFehily	20/1	nk 8
43	Lou du Moulin Mas (FR) *PFNicholls* 7-10-2[132] (t) RWalsh	7/1	4 9
55	Omni Cosmo Touch (USA) *MrsSJSmith* 10-10-0[130] SEDurack	25/1	½ 10
	One Knight (IRE) *PJHobbs* 10-11-5[149] (t) JoeTizzard	25/1	dist 11
	Mount Clerigo (IRE) *VRADartnall* 8-9-9[130] JamesWhite[5]	16/1	1¼ 12
70	Innox (FR) *FDoumen,France* 10-11-7[151] (b) BarryKeniry	50/1	pu
70	All In The Stars (IRE) *DPKeane* 8-10-11[141] NeilMulholland	40/1	pu
	Kinburn (IRE) *JHowardJohnson* 7-10-7[137] TonyDobbin	8/1	pu
	Heros Collonges (FR) *MrsNMacauley* 11-9-12[133] TomMessenger[5]	100/1	pu
48	Korelo (FR) *DEPipe* 8-10-0[130] TomScudamore	40/1	pu
	Twelve Paces *DEPipe* 10-10-0[130] TimmyMurphy	12/1	pu

Ian Payne & Kim Franklin 18ran 7m40.90

92	**Coral Future Champion Finale Juv Hdle (Gr 1) (1) (3yo)** £28,510		2m110y (8)
29	GOOD BYE SIMON *TDoumen,France* 3-11-0 MickFitzgerald	9/4	1
71	NED LUDD (IRE) *JGPortman* 3-11-0 WayneHutchinson	7/1	4 2
	WARNE'S WAY (IRE) *BGPowell* 3-11-0 SPJones	13/2	6 3
	Supsonic *PJHobbs* 3-11-0 (b) JoeTizzard	16/1	½ 4
	Paradi (FR) *DEPipe* 3-11-0 TimmyMurphy	7/4f	10 5
	Darusso *JSMoore* 3-11-0 SEDurack	100/1	4 6
	In Hope *MrsLJYoung* 3-10-7 (s) ChrisHonour	100/1	dist 7
71	Ace Baby *KJBurke* 3-11-0 (t) RWalsh	50/1	18 8
	Philanthropist *EvanWilliams* 3-11-0 PaulMoloney	14/1	6 9
	Mon Michel (FR) *GLMoore* 3-11-0 JamieMoore	10/1	f
	The Preacher *KJBurke* 3-11-0 ColinBolger	100/1	f
71	Lord Adonis (IRE) *KJBurke* 3-11-0 PaddyMerrigan	18/1	ur

Mr J. Hayoz 12ran 4m03.16

KEMPTON Wednesday, Dec 27   GOOD to SOFT

93	**Stan James Wayward Lad Nov Chase (Gr 2) (1) (4yo+)** £18,246		2m (12)
	JACK THE GIANT (IRE) *NJHenderson* 4-10-13 AndrewTinkler	7/1	1
	TWIST MAGIC (FR) *PFNicholls* 4-10-13 SamThomas	11/8f	1¼ 2
78	ROYAL SHAKESPEARE (FR) *SGollings* 7-11-3 RichardJohnson	9/1	4 3
	Rasharrow (IRE) *LLungo* 7-11-7 KeithMercer	4/1	8 4
	Bob Hall (IRE) *JonjoO'Neill* 5-11-7 (t) APMcCoy	4/1	1¾ 5
16	Priors Dale *MissECLavelle* 6-11-9 BarryFenton	10/1	13 6

Hanbury Syndicate 6ran 3m54.49

94	**Desert Orchid Chase (Gr 2) (1) (Sponsored By Stan James) (5yo+)** £40,383		2m (12)
65	VOY POR USTEDES (FR) *AKing* 5-11-5 RobertThornton	4/6f	1
65	ONEWAY (IRE) *MGRimell* 9-11-0 RichardJohnson	10/1	5 2
	FOREMAN (GER) *TDoumen,France* 9-11-5 APMcCoy	5/2	1½ 3
	River City (IRE) *NoelTChance* 9-11-10 TomDoyle	25/1	10 4
15	Armaturk (FR) *PFNicholls* 9-11-6 SamThomas	11/1	ur

Sir Robert Ogden 5ran 3m55.16

LEOPARDSTOWN Wednesday, Dec 27   HEAVY

95	**Paddy Power Dial-A-Bet Chase (Gr 1) (5yo+)** £30,537		2m1f (11)
76	NICKNAME (FR) *MartinBrassil* 7-11-12 (t) NPMadden	5/2	1
65	CENTRAL HOUSE *DTHughes* 9-11-12 (b) RLoughran	6/4f	14 2
76	HI CLOY (IRE) *MHourigan* 9-11-12 AndrewJMcNamara	5/1	7 3
46	Mister McGoldrick *MrsSJSmith,GB* 9-11-12 DavidO'Meara	13/2	12 4
41	Steel Band *PaulARoche* 8-11-12 DNRussell	33/1	3 5
	Jim (FR) *JTRDreaper* 9-11-12 (s) AELynch	8/1	f

Mrs Claudia Jungo-Corpataux 6ran 4m29.77

96	**paddypower.com Future Champions Nov Hdle (Gr 2) (4yo+)** £21,846		2m (8)
	DE VALIRA (IRE) *MJPO'Brien* 4-10-13 AELynch	3/1	1
	CATCH ME (GER) *EJO'Grady* 4-10-13 BJGeraghty	1/1f	nk 2
	SIZING EUROPE (IRE) *HenrydeBromhead* 4-10-13 DFO'Regan	10/1	9 3
	Rare Bob (IRE) *DTHughes* 4-10-13 RLoughran	66/1	4 4
67	Cleni Boy (FR) *NMeade* 4-10-13 PCarberry	7/1	dist 5
	Mickataine (IRE) *MFMorris* 5-11-4 CO'Dwyer	33/1	2 6
	Turtle Dubh (IRE) *ESheehy* 5-11-4 MDarcy	7/1	4½ 7
	Derravarra Eagle (IRE) *MarkLeslieFagan* 6-11-4 RJMolloy	33/1	dist 8

Mr D. Mac A'Bhaird 8ran 4m21.80

97   **Paddy Power Chase (Hcap) (Gr B) 0-145(142) (5yo+)** £72,886   3m (17)

61	CANE BRAKE (IRE) *TJTaaffe* 7-11-3[142] (s) ABJoyce[7]	14/1	1
	BALLISTRAW (IRE) *MWHickey* 7-10-11[129] DFO'Regan	11/1	½ 2
	CHEEKY LADY (IRE) *ColmAMurphy* 9-9-10[114] JPElliott	50/1	2½ 3
	WELL TUTORED (IRE) *ALTMoore* 7-10-4[122] DNRussell	10/1	3 4
	A New Story (IRE) *MHourigan* 8-10-9[127] (s) AndrewJMcNamara	16/1	11 5
	Giolla An Bhaird (IRE) *MichaelFitzsimons* 9-9-9[106] AELynch[3]	33/1	nk 6
	What A Native (IRE) *CFSwan* 10-10-2[125] DGHogan[5]	25/1	nk 7
	Some Legend (IRE) *EJO'Grady* 6-9-13[117] PWFlood	16/1	3 8
	Camptect (IRE) *DEFitzgerald* 10-9-10[114] JMAllen	14/1	4½ 9
70	Jack High (IRE) *TMWalsh* 11-11-0[137] (b) MrRO'Sullivan[5]	50/1	12 10
	G V A Ireland (IRE) *FFlood* 8-10-13[131] CO'Dwyer	25/1	4 11
	Kickham (IRE) *EJO'Grady* 10-9-9[116] KTColeman[3]	33/1	7 12
	Teeming Rain (IRE) *CFSwan* 7-9-10[114] DJCasey	12/1	7 13
9	Lotomore Lad (IRE) *DHassett* 8-9-3[114] CDMaxwell[7]	66/1	18 14
	Liscannor Lad (IRE) *DTHughes* 8-9-12[116] (s) TGMRyan	20/1	5 15
61	Homer Wells (IRE) *WPMullins* 8-10-7[125] DJCondon	20/1	f
	Sound Witness (IRE) *RobertTyner* 8-9-10[121] PTEnright[7]	9/1	f
	Crossbarry Boy (IRE) *JohnJosephMurphy* 7-9-7[114] RJMolloy[3]	66/1	f
	Newbay Prop (IRE) *AJMartin* 7-9-7[114] RCColgan[3]	8/1	f
12	Point Barrow (IRE) *PatrickHughes* 8-11-4[136] BJGeraghty	20/1	bd
76	Sher Beau (IRE) *PhilipFenton* 7-11-3[135] NPMadden	6/1f	bd
51	Kings Glen (IRE) *ThomasCarberry* 10-9-10[114] PACarberry	33/1	bd
61	Ride The Storm (IRE) *EJO'Grady* 9-10-1[119] JRBarry	25/1	ur
	Brave Eagle (IRE) *PatrickGKelly* 11-9-7[114] ADLeigh[3]	25/1	ur
61	Star Clipper *NMeade* 9-10-12[130] PCarberry	33/1	pu
	Oulart *DTHughes* 7-10-9[127] RLoughran	20/1	pu
	Black Apalachi (IRE) *PJRothwell* 7-10-7[125] JLCullen	25/1	pu
	Lost Time (IRE) *CRoche* 9-10-5[123] RMPower	25/1	pu

Mount Temple Two Racing Synd 28ran 6m42.07

LEOPARDSTOWN Thursday, Dec 28   HEAVY

98   **Powers Whiskey Nov Chase (Gr 1) (5yo+)** £32,718   3m (17)

69	CAILIN ALAINN (IRE) *CharlesByrnes* 7-11-5 DNRussell	13/8f	1
	PATSY HALL (IRE) *MichaelCunningham* 6-11-10 RMPower	3/1	4½ 2
69	ANOTHERCOPPERCOAST (IRE) *PaulARoche* 6-11-10 RLoughran	50/1	16 3
	Mattock Ranger *NMeade* 6-11-10 PCarberry	7/1	¾ 4
	Sir Frederick *WJBurke* 6-11-10 TimmyMurphy	12/1	9 5
69	Mossbank (IRE) *MHourigan* 6-11-10 CO'Dwyer	14/1	f
69	O'Muircheartaigh (IRE) *EJO'Grady* 6-11-10 (s) PWFlood	16/1	f
	Toofarback (IRE) *NMeade* 6-11-10 NPMadden	12/1	f
69	Gazza's Girl (IRE) *MrsJHarrington* 6-11-5 ADLeigh	10/1	f
	Purple Shuffle (IRE) *PAFahy* 8-11-10 (t) BJGeraghty	25/1	pu
	Romek (IRE) *MrsJHarrington* 6-11-10 AndrewJMcNamara	25/1	pu

Dewdrop Racing Syndicate 11ran 6m45.45

99   **woodiesdiy.com Christmas Hdle (Gr 2) (4yo+)** £21,846   3m (12)

83	CELESTIAL WAVE (IRE) *AdrianMaguire* 6-11-3 TimmyMurphy	11/4	1
83	SWEET KILN (IRE) *JamesBowe* 7-10-12 DNRussell	14/1	10 2
	STRANGELY BROWN (IRE) *EricMcNamara* 5-11-10 RWalsh	13/2	2 3
68	Rosaker (USA) *NMeade* 9-11-8 PCarberry	2/1f	3 4
40	Emotional Moment (IRE) *TJTaaffe* 8-11-8 BJGeraghty	3/1	8 5
12	Strong Project (IRE) *SeanOO'Brien* 10-11-3 JMAllen	25/1	¾ 6
83	Prince of Tara (IRE) *SJMahon* 9-11-3 TGMRyan	100/1	3 7
	Bullhill Flyer (IRE) *SabrinaJoanHarty* 5-11-6 SJHassett	25/1	pu

Cahir Racing Syndicate 8ran 6m13.20

100   **Lexus Chase (Gr 1) (5yo+)** £65,436   3m (17)

63	THE LISTENER (IRE) *RHAlner,GB* 7-11-10 DarylJacob	7/1	1
47	BEEF OR SALMON (IRE) *MHourigan* 10-11-10 (s) AndrewJMcNamara	13/8f	8 2
76	WAR OF ATTRITION (IRE) *MFMorris* 7-11-10 CO'Dwyer	9/4	5 3
47	L'Ami (FR) *FDoumen,France* 7-11-10 APMcCoy	5/1	5½ 4
83	Southern Vic (IRE) *TMWalsh* 7-11-10 RWalsh	9/1	3 5
	Back In Front (IRE) *EJO'Grady* 9-11-10 PWFlood	28/1	dist 6

Old Moss Farm 6ran 6m45.15

NEWBURY Friday, Dec 29   GOOD to SOFT

101   **Ballymore Properties Challow Nov Hdle (Gr 1) (1) (4yo+)** £22,808   2m5f (11)

38	WICHITA LINEMAN (IRE) *JonjoO'Neill* 5-11-7 APMcCoy	11/4	1
	SIR JIMMY SHAND (IRE) *NJHenderson* 5-11-7 MickFitzgerald	2/1f	8 2
	ROLL ALONG (IRE) *CarlLlewellyn* 6-11-7 PaulMoloney	4/1	18 3

	Mossville (FR) *RHBuckler* 5-11-0 (t) WTKennedy	66/1	10 4
75	Massini's Maguire (IRE) *PJHobbs* 5-11-7 RichardJohnson	15/2	9 5
13	Kanpai (IRE) *JGMO'Shea* 4-11-7 (v) PCO'Neill	7/1	5 6
39	Battlecry *NATwiston-Davies* 5-11-7 TonyEvans	20/1	pu
	Rothbury *JIACharlton* 6-11-7 JanFaltejsek	28/1	pu

Mr John P. McManus 8ran 5m10.77

LEOPARDSTOWN Friday, Dec 29   HEAVY

102 **bewleyshotels.com December Festival Hdle (Gr 1) (4yo+) £43,624**   2m (8)

68	BRAVE INCA (IRE) *ColmAMurphy* 8-11-12 RWalsh	6/4	1
52	IKTITAF (IRE) *NMeade* 5-11-12 (t) PCarberry	4/6f	1¼ 2
40	SILENT OSCAR (IRE) *HarryRogers* 7-11-12 RMPower	100/1	6 3
68	Al Eile (IRE) *JohnQueally* 6-11-12 CO'Dwyer	14/1	4 4

Novices Syndicate 4ran 4m17.89

CHELTENHAM Monday, Jan 1   HEAVY (New Course)

103 **Aquanti Group 'Dipper' Nov Chase (Gr 2) (1) (5yo+) £19,957**   2m5f (17)

64	MY WAY DE SOLZEN (FR) *AKing* 7-11-4 RobertThornton	4/9f	1
21	TURKO (FR) *PFNicholls* 5-11-1 (t) RWalsh	2/1	17 2
	DALRIATH *MCChapman* 8-10-11 DavidCullinane	50/1	26 3
32	Predicament *DrPPritchard* 8-11-4 SEDurack	25/1	7 4
	Lago d'Oro *DrPPritchard* 7-10-11 JamesDavies	80/1	dist 5

B Winfield,A Longman,J Wright & C Fenton 5ran 5m46.69

104 **Unicoin Homes Chase (Hcap) (L) (1) (152) (5yo+) £22,808**   2m5f (17)

33	TOO FORWARD (IRE) *CarlLlewellyn* 11-11-4[144] TimmyMurphy	4/1	1
	NOZIC (FR) *PFNicholls* 6-9-12[127] (t) LiamHeard[3]	7/2	7 2
	LE VOLFONI (FR) *PFNicholls* 6-11-9[149] RWalsh	4/1	6 3
79	Lacdoudal (FR) *PJHobbs* 8-11-12[152] RichardJohnson	11/4f	14 4
	Mariah Rollins (IRE) *NJHenderson* 9-11-4[144] MickFitzgerald	5/1	24 5
	Ichi Beau (IRE) *DrPPritchard* 13-10-0[131] DrPPritchard[5]	100/1	25 6
37	Aleron (IRE) *JJQuinn* 9-9-11[126] (s) DougieCostello[3]	16/1	ur

Mr T. L. Gibson & Mr D. Mathias 7ran 5m47.01

SANDOWN Saturday, Jan 6   HEAVY

105 **Anglo Irish Bank Tolworth Hdle (Gr 1) (1) (4yo+) £25,659**   2m110y (8)

	SILVERBURN (IRE) *PFNicholls* 6-11-7 RWalsh	5/1	1
	PERCE ROCK *TStack,Ireland* 5-11-7 APMcCoy	2/1f	4 2
	ASTARADOR (FR) *JHowardJohnson* 5-11-7 PJBrennan	4/1	7 3
	De Soto *PRWebber* 6-11-7 (t) MickFitzgerald	9/2	1½ 4
	Rio de Janeiro (IRE) *MissECLavelle* 6-11-7 WayneKavanagh	100/1	7 5
3	Lord Baskerville *CTPogson* 6-11-7 AdamPogson	100/1	11 6
	My Turn Now (IRE) *CJMann* 5-11-7 NoelFehily	10/3	f

Mr Paul Green 7ran 4m12.16

106 **ladbrokes.com Hcap Hdle (2) 0-140(139) (4yo+) £31,315**   2m110y (8)

1	PAPINI (IRE) *NJHenderson* 6-11-3[130] MickFitzgerald	6/1	1
66	HEATHCOTE *GLMoore* 5-10-5[123] EamonDehdashti[5]	8/1	5 2
	MA YAHAB *MissVenetiaWilliams* 6-9-12[114] LiamTreadwell[3]	10/1	1¾ 3
	Kings Signal (USA) *MJHogan* 9-10-6[119] LeightonAspell	13/2	6 4
	Orcadian *JMPEustace* 6-11-3[130] MarkBradburne	9/2f	7 5
80	Pilca (IRE) *DCarroll* 7-10-1[114] BarryKeniry	11/2	18 6
	Misbehaviour *GLMoore* 8-10-0[113] JamieMoore	20/1	12 7
80	Premier Dane (IRE) *NGRichards* 5-11-12[139] BrianHarding	33/1	16 8
1	Lunar Crystal (IRE) *DEPipe* 9-11-0[127] (s) TomScudamore	14/1	6 9
	Tous Chez (IRE) *MrsSJSmith* 8-10-6[119] DavidO'Meara	15/2	pu
	Mr Dinglawi (IRE) *DMGrissell* 6-10-4[117] (b) JamesDavies	50/1	pu
	Nyborg Madrik (FR) *DEPipe* 6-10-4[117] TimmyMurphy	16/1	pu

Newbury Racehorse Owners Group 12ran 4m11.96

NAAS Sunday, Jan 7   HEAVY

107 **Woodlands Park 100 Slaney Nov Hdle (Gr 2) (5yo+) £25,512**   2½m (11)

84	KAZAL (FR) *EoinGriffin* 6-11-8 BJGeraghty	11/4	1
	EARTH MAGIC (IRE) *JamesBowe* 7-11-5 AndrewJMcNamara	12/1	1¾ 2
	CASEY JONES (IRE) *NMeade* 6-11-5 PCarberry	2/1f	4½ 3
	Treacle (IRE) *TJTaaffe* 6-11-5 NPMadden	8/1	9 4
84	Hollywood Law (IRE) *WPMullins* 6-11-5 RWalsh	9/4	1¼ 5
	Vale of Avocia (IRE) *MichaelCGriffin* 6-11-0 (s) DNRussell	100/1	19 6
	Duroob *PatrickOBrady* 5-11-1 JLCullen	100/1	dist 7
	The Pilot Son (IRE) *MartinPaulFitzgerald* 11-11-5 (b) JRBarry	100/1	dist 8

Mr J. Comerford 8ran 5m15.05

108   **intercasino.co.uk Lanzarote Hdle (Hcap) (2) (147) (4yo+)** £25,052   2m5f (10)

80	VERASI *GLMoore* 6-10-4[130] (b) EamonDehdashti[5]	20/1	1
	ROYALS DARLING (GER) *NJHenderson* 5-11-0[135] AndrewTinkler	25/1	1 2
	AFRAD (FR) *NJHenderson* 6-11-0[135] MickFitzgerald	9/1	¾ 3
66	NATION STATE *GLMoore* 6-10-0[121] (b) JamieMoore	14/1	2½ 4
	Turtle Soup (IRE) *TRGeorge* 11-11-0[140] RobertLucey-Butler[5]	40/1	11 5
	Daryal (IRE) *AKing* 6-10-6[127] WayneHutchinson	12/1	1 6
14	Brads House (IRE) *JGMO'Shea* 5-9-11[121] TomMalone[3]	16/1	¾ 7
	Rayshan (IRE) *NGRichards* 7-10-5[131] MissRDavidson[5]	14/1	5 8
80	Nathos (GER) *CJMann* 10-11-0[135] NoelFehily	16/1	22 9
	She's Our Native (IRE) *EvanWilliams* 9-10-4[125] PaulMoloney	25/1	dist 10
	Finger Onthe Pulse (IRE) *TJTaaffe,Ireland* 6-11-5[147] ABJoyce[7]	5/1	2½ 11
	Big Moment *MrsAJPerrett* 9-11-1[136] LeightonAspell	50/1	1½ 12
87	Racing Demon (IRE) *MissHCKnight* 7-11-11[146] GLee	2/1f	f
82	Whispered Promises (USA) *RSBrookhouse* 6-11-8[143] AlanO'Keeffe	9/1	pu
	Dalaram (IRE) *DJWintle* 7-10-13[134] (t) WarrenMarston	40/1	pu
	Take A Mile (IRE) *BGPowell* 5-9-13[125] SPJones[5]	20/1	pu
	Manners (IRE) *JonjoO'Neill* 9-10-0[121] (b) RichardJohnson	16/1	pu

F. Ledger J. Bateman 17ran 5m33.26

109   **Ballymore Properties Leamington Nov Hdle (Gr 2) (1) (4yo+)**   2m5f (9)
£22,808

The last flight before the home turn was omitted

75	LABELTHOU (FR) *MissECLavelle* 8-11-5 BarryFenton	8/13f	1
	ZILCASH *AKing* 4-10-7 RobertThornton	7/1	1¾ 2
	HILLS OF ARAN *WKGoldsworthy* 5-11-6 TJO'Brien	33/1	26 3
	Supreme Cara *CJDown* 7-10-13 ChrisHonour	20/1	23 4
	For All Mankind *CarlLlewellyn* 6-11-10 RWalsh	9/1	1¾ 5
39	Leading Authority (IRE) *CLTizzard* 6-11-10 JoeTizzard	14/1	15 6
	It's In The Stars *HDDaly* 7-11-6 MarkBradburne	7/1	pu

GDM Partnership 7ran 5m15.75

110   **totesport.com Classic Chase (Hcap) (Gr 3) (1) (151) (5yo+)** £39,914   3m5f (22)

22	LADALKO (FR) *PFNicholls* 8-11-1[140] RWalsh	9/2f	1
91	MON MOME (FR) *MissVenetiaWilliams* 7-11-1[140] SamThomas	5/1	4 2
91	NAUNTON BROOK *NATwiston-Davies* 8-10-5[135] (t) MrDEngland[5]	14/1	1 3
91	Kinburn (IRE) *JHowardJohnson* 8-10-12[137] PJBrennan	11/1	9 4
35	Baron Windrush *NATwiston-Davies* 9-10-4[129] TonyEvans	20/1	17 5
58	Hautclan (FR) *JonjoO'Neill* 8-10-0[125] (b) BrianHarding	10/1	hd 6
	Heltornic (IRE) *MScudamore* 7-9-7[125] JohnKington[7]	12/1	nk 7
91	L'Aventure (FR) *PFNicholls* 8-10-3[131] (b+t) LiamHeard[3]	6/1	11 8
	Touch Closer *PBowen* 10-10-0[125] (s) TJO'Brien	18/1	27 9
88	Sir Rembrandt (IRE) *RHAlner* 11-11-12[151] AndrewThornton	20/1	dist 10
	Mr Dow Jones (IRE) *WKGoldsworthy* 8-10-9[125] JamesWhite[5]	66/1	17 11
70	D'Argent (IRE) *AKing* 10-11-2[141] RobertThornton	5/1	pu
	Tana River (IRE) *MissECLavelle* 11-11-2[141] BarryFenton	12/1	pu

Mrs M. Findlay & P. K. Barber 13ran 7m41.62

111   **Pierse Leopardstown Hcap Chase (136) (5yo+)** £43,986   3m (17)

97	POINT BARROW (IRE) *PatrickHughes* 9-11-10[136] TimmyMurphy	14/1	1
97	A NEW STORY (IRE) *MHourigan* 9-11-1[127] (s) AndrewJMcNamara	9/1	¾ 2
97	TEEMING RAIN (IRE) *CFSwan* 8-9-6[109] DGHogan[5]	16/1	1 3
97	JACK HIGH (IRE) *TMWalsh* 12-11-7[133] (b) RWalsh	25/1	1¾ 4
61	Jaqouille (FR) *ALTMoore* 10-10-7[119] RMPower	14/1	hd 5
	American Jennie (IRE) *MichaelCullen* 9-10-13[125] BJGeraghty	9/1	½ 6
97	Black Apalachi (IRE) *PJRothwell* 8-10-12[124] JLCullen	25/1	3½ 7
97	G V A Ireland (IRE) *FFlood* 9-11-0[129] KTColeman[3]	20/1	sh 8
97	Sound Witness (IRE) *RobertTyner* 9-10-9[121] DNRussell	11/2f	23 9
99	Prince of Tara (IRE) *SJMahon* 10-11-1[127] DFO'Regan	33/1	4½ 10
34	Hordago (IRE) *EricMcNamara* 7-9-8[109] (s) BCByrnes[3]	13/2	12 11
	Golden Storm (IRE) *JosephCrowley* 10-10-8[120] JMAllen	50/1	4½ 12
	Marcus du Berlais (FR) *ALTMoore* 10-10-0[133] (s) SGCarey[7]	25/1	3 13
	Oulart *DTHughes* 8-11-0[126] (s) RLoughran	20/1	2 14
97	What A Native (IRE) *CFSwan* 12-10-12[124] PCarberry	12/1	3 15
	Julius (FR) *ALTMoore* 10-9-10[108] PACarberry	15/2	¾ 16
97	Liscannor Lad (IRE) *DTHughes* 9-10-3[115] PWFlood	20/1	f
97	Lost Time (IRE) *CRoche* 10-10-11[123] (s) APMcCoy	20/1	pu

Vedelle (IRE) *JosephCrowley* 8-10-5[117] TGMRyan .... 8/1   pu

Mrs P. Clune Hughes 19ran 6m41.09

112   **Pierse Hdle (Hcap) 0-145(130) (4yo+)** £53,142   2m (7)

What should have been the final flight was omitted due to a stricken horse

	SPRING THE QUE (IRE) *RobertTyner* 8-10-3[116] PTEnright[7]	16/1		1
	MISTER HIGHT (FR) *WPMullins* 5-11-10[130] DJCondon	20/1	2½	2
	NEW FIELD (IRE) *ThomasMullins* 9-10-7[113] APMcCoy	10/1	1¼	3
10	MARALAN (IRE) *PatrickOBrady* 6-10-1[110] (b) RJMolloy[3]	100/1	2½	4
	Jaamid *NMeade* 5-10-7[113] NPMadden	20/1	½	5
	Streetshavenoname (IRE) *TJTaaffe* 6-10-9[118] SMMcGovern[3]	14/1	1½	6
	Charlies First (IRE) *PeterCasey* 7-10-6[112] DFO'Regan	33/1	1	7
	Kendor Dine (FR) *EoinGriffin* 5-10-11[117] BJGeraghty	8/1cf	2½	8
	Quatre Heures (FR) *WPMullins* 5-11-10[130] RWalsh	12/1	nk	9
	Lenrey *ALTMoore* 7-11-0[120] (t) DNRussell	8/1cf	¾	10
102	Silent Oscar (IRE) *HarryRogers* 8-11-8[128] RMPower	33/1	¾	11
	First Row (IRE) *DTHughes* 5-10-11[117] RLoughran	25/1	¾	12
	Woodhouse (IRE) *MrsJHarrington* 8-10-6[112] TPTreacy	33/1	2½	13
	Dolphin Bay (IRE) *JamesGBurns* 7-9-11[110] ABZoyce[7]	14/1	sh	14
	Orge d'Ete (FR) *WPMullins* 5-10-8[121] CDMaxwell[7]	33/1	½	15
	Artist's Muse (IRE) *TMWalsh* 5-11-0[120] TGMRyan	33/1	½	16
80	Victram (IRE) *AdrianMcGuinness* 7-11-5[128] AELynch[3]	16/1	4	17
	Classic Croco (GER) *THogan* 6-10-0[113] (s+t) EFPower[7]	100/1	4½	18
	Orbit O'Gold (USA) *NMeade* 5-10-10[116] PCarberry	20/1	9	19
	View Mount Prince (IRE) *PatrickHughes* 6-10-11[117] TimmyMurphy	8/1cf	17	20
	Power Elite (IRE) *NMeade* 7-11-4[129] (b+t) EMButterly[5]	33/1	3½	21
	Cogans Lake (IRE) *KieranPurcell* 5-10-11[117] JMAllen	66/1	8	22
	Son of Oscar (IRE) *PhilipFenton* 6-11-10[120] JRBarry	25/1	2	23
73	Ross River *AJMartin* 11-11-4[124] AndrewJMcNamara	25/1	27	24
	The Last Stand *AnthonyMullins* 5-10-0[109] RMMoran[3]	100/1	18	25
	Wishwillow Lord (IRE) *LeonardWhitmore* 8-11-0[125] NJO'Shea[5]	66/1		f
6	Breathing Fire *MrsJHarrington* 5-10-10[119] (t) ADLeigh[3]	16/1		f
80	Well Mounted *ALTMoore* 6-10-8[114] PACarberry	10/1		f
83	Baron de Feypo (IRE) *PatrickOBrady* 9-10-9[122] RTDunne[7]	66/1		bd
	Escrea (IRE) *PaulNolan* 8-10-10[123] APCawley[7]	33/1		pu

Gaelforce Racing 30ran 3m56.68

HAYDOCK Saturday, Jan 20   HEAVY

What should have been the third fence in the back straight and the final flight in the home straight were omitted

113   **bonusprint.com Champion Hdle Trial (Gr 2) (1) (4yo+)** £28,510   2m (6)

86	AFSOUN (FR) *NJHenderson* 5-11-8 MickFitzgerald	11/8f		1
59	THE FRENCH FURZE (IRE) *NGRichards* 13-11-8 BrianHarding	14/1	9	2
80	OVERSTRAND (IRE) *DrRDPNewland* 8-11-8 GLee	14/1	12	3
95	Mister McGoldrick *MrsSJSmith* 10-11-4 DavidO'Meara	7/1	2	4
83	Mounthenry (IRE) *CharlesByrnes,Ireland* 7-11-8 (s) RobertThornton	4/1	9	5
74	Arcalis *JHowardJohnson* 7-11-12 (t) PJBrennan	8/1	¾	6
34	Milligan (FR) *DrPPritchard* 12-11-4 JodieMogford	200/1	7	7
59	Torkinking (IRE) *MABarnes* 8-11-4 (t) RichardMcGrath	7/1	6	8

Mr Trevor Hemmings 8ran 4m09.45

114   **Peter Marsh Chase (Ltd Hcap) (Gr 2) (1) (147) (5yo+)** £42,765   3m (16)

	THE OUTLIER (IRE) *MissVenetiaWilliams* 9-10-3[129] PCO'Neill[3]	8/1		1
55	TURPIN GREEN (IRE) *NGRichards* 8-11-10[147] TonyDobbin	11/2	12	2
88	TRUCKERS TAVERN (IRE) *MrsSJSmith* 12-10-4[127] (t) DavidO'Meara	14/1	2	3
88	Leading Man *FerdyMurphy* 7-11-0[137] GLee	6/1	11	4
60	Snakebite (IRE) *CarlLlewellyn* 7-10-4[127] NoelFehily	11/4f	2½	5
	Wild Cane Ridge (IRE) *LLungo* 8-11-8[145] KeithMercer	17/2	6	6
	Irish Raptor (IRE) *NATwiston-Davies* 8-10-4[127] TonyEvans	8/1	dist	7
	Strong Resolve (IRE) *MissLucindaVRussell* 11-10-4[127] PeterBuchanan	20/1	26	8
70	Model Son (IRE) *MrsAMThorpe* 9-10-4[127] RobertThornton	5/1		pu

Mr P. J. Murphy 9ran 6m44.21

115   **Anglo Irish Bank Nov Hdle (Rossington Main) (Gr 2) (1) (4yo+)** £17,106

	AMARETTO ROSE *NJHenderson* 6-11-1 MickFitzgerald	10/11f		1
105	ASTARADOR (FR) *JHowardJohnson* 5-11-11 PJBrennan	10/3	18	2
	MOHAYER (IRE) *DMcCainJnr* 5-11-8 SJCraine	12/1	10	3
	Mendo *NoelTChance* 7-11-4 TomDoyle	14/1	5	4
	Wizard of Us *MMullineaux* 7-11-4 AlanO'Keeffe	100/1	18	5
	Leslingtaylor (IRE) *JJQuinn* 5-11-11 GLee	15/2	dist	6

2m (6)

Nobelix (IRE) *JRFanshawe* 5-11-8 TonyDobbin 16/1   11 7
Mount Sandel (IRE) *OSherwood* 6-11-8 LeightonAspell............................... 20/1   pu

Weatherbys Racing Club 8ran 4m13.72

116   **bonusprint.com Nov Chase (Gr 2) (1) (5yo+)** £20,580   2½m (14)

103 MY WAY DE SOLZEN (FR) *AKing* 7-11-9 RobertThornton 1/6f   1
    REGAL HEIGHTS (IRE) *DMcCainJnr* 6-11-2 SJCraine 14/1   17 2
    THE COOL GUY (IRE) *NATwiston-Davies* 7-11-2 TonyEvans..................... 8/1   dist 3
    Curraheen Chief (IRE) *JLSpearing* 12-11-2 JamesDiment .... 100/1   pu

B Winfield,A Longman,J Wright & C Fenton 4ran 5m43.03

FAIRYHOUSE Sunday, Jan 21   HEAVY

117   **ladbrokes.com Normans Grove Chase (Gr 2) (5yo+)** £21,414   2m1f (13)

95 NICKNAME (FR) *MartinBrassil* 8-11-12 (t) RWalsh 1/1f   1
76 JUSTIFIED (IRE) *ESheehy* 8-11-12 CO'Dwyer 3/1   15 2
95 CENTRAL HOUSE *DTHughes* 10-11-10 (b) RLoughran 5/2   26 3
76 Watson Lake (IRE) *NMeade* 9-11-10 PCarberry .... 10/1   dist 4

Mrs Claudia Jungo-Corpataux 4ran 4m41.17

THURLES Tuesday, Jan 23   SOFT

118   **Maclochlainn Road Markings Ltd Kinloch Brae Chase (Gr 2)**   2½m (14)
    (6yo+) £21,275

    FORGET THE PAST *MJPO'Brien* 9-11-8 (t) AELynch 1/1f   1
95 HI CLOY (IRE) *MHourigan* 10-11-10 AndrewJMcNamara......................... 4/1   2 2
    MOSSY GREEN (IRE) *WPMullins* 13-11-3 RWalsh 8/1   1 3
76 Public Reaction *EUHales* 9-11-6 DNRussell... 10/1   13 4
33 Tumbling Dice (IRE) *TJTaaffe* 8-11-8 (s) BJGeraghty 9/2   5 5
    Nanny Nunny Nac (IRE) *JohnJosephMurphy* 7-11-3 EFPower .... 100/1   dist 6

Mr S. Mulryan 6ran 5m26.75

HUNTINGDON Wednesday, Jan 24   SOFT

119   **HBLB Lightning Nov Chase (Gr 2) (1) (5yo+)** £14,255   2m110y (9)

    The last fence before the winning post was omitted, as was the ditch in the back straight

58 ANOTHER PROMISE (IRE) *FerdyMurphy* 8-11-7 GLee.......................... 8/11f   1
93 RASHARROW (IRE) *LLungo* 8-11-3 KeithMercer.................................... 6/5   1 2
    MANGE TOUT (IRE) *KJBurke* 8-11-3 RJGreene...................................... 33/1   5 3
    Ballyrainey (IRE) *MrsLCJewell* 8-11-3 (s) OwynNelmes............................ 40/1   25 4
    Supreme Leisure (IRE) *JRCornwall* 10-11-3 JAMcCarthy............................ 33/1   26 5

Geoff Hubbard Racing 5ran 4m22.93

GOWRAN PARK Thursday, Jan 25   HEAVY

120   **Alo Duffin Memorial Galmoy Hdle (Gr 3) (5yo+)** £17,020   3m (13)

99 CELESTIAL WAVE (IRE) *AdrianMaguire* 7-11-3 CO'Dwyer 4/6f   1
40 STUDMASTER *MrsJHarrington* 7-11-6 TPTreacy.. 20/1   5 2
    OUR BEN *WPMullins* 8-11-0 RWalsh .... 5/1   nk 3
99 Emotional Moment (IRE) *TJTaaffe* 10-11-8 (s) BJGeraghty 12/1   4 4
99 Rosaker (USA) *NMeade* 10-11-8 DFO'Regan 15/2   12 5
    Emma Jane (IRE) *DPBerry* 7-10-12 AELynch[3] .... 33/1   dist 6
    You Sir (IRE) *JamesBowe* 7-11-3 DNRussell... 10/1   ½ 7
99 Strangely Brown (IRE) *EricMcNamara* 6-11-7 BCByrnes[3].......................... 14/1   pu

Cahir Racing Syndicate 8ran 6m40.11

121   **Ellen Construction Thyestes Hcap Chase (147) (5yo+)** £42,484   3m (16)

97 HOMER WELLS *WPMullins* 9-10-2[125] DJCondon............................. 16/1   1
    LIVINGSTONEBRAMBLE (IRE) *WPMullins* 11-10-10[133] DNRussell 14/1   3½ 2
97 WELL TUTORED (IRE) *ALTMoore* 8-10-1[124] PACarberry....................... 15/2   4 3
    KITSKI (FR) *FerdyMurphy,GB* 9-9-12[121] GLee 7/1   3 4
111 Black Apalachi (IRE) *PJRothwell* 8-9-8[124] (s) ShaneJackson[7] 14/1   1½ 5
    Joueur d'Estruval (FR) *WPMullins* 10-10-8[131] DJCasey 33/1   6 6
    Kymandjen (IRE) *PaulNolan* 10-10-7[130] (s) JLCullen................................. 33/1   4 7
61 Kerryhead Windfarm (IRE) *MHourigan* 9-10-12[135] AndrewJMcNamara 9/1   8 8
97 Camptect (IRE) *DEFitzgerald* 11-9-10[119] JRBarry 20/1   17 9
51 Another Rum (IRE) *IADuncan* 9-10-5[128] (b) ARoss.................................. 50/1   1½ 10
100 Southern Vic (IRE) *TMWalsh* 8-11-10[147] RWalsh .... 11/2f   f
    Slim Pickings (IRE) *TJTaaffe* 8-11-3[140] BJGeraghty .... 16/1   f
111 American Jennie (IRE) *MichaelCullen* 9-10-2[125] RLoughran .... 9/1   pu
    Mark The Man (IRE) *NMeade* 10-10-1[124] TGMRyan............................. 25/1   pu
111 Sound Witness (IRE) *RobertTyner* 9-9-12[121] NPMadden .... 12/1   pu
97 Cheeky Lady (IRE) *ColmAMurphy* 10-9-10[119] PWFlood .... 6/1   pu

Mrs M. McMahon 16ran 6m36.27

CHELTENHAM Saturday, Jan 27   HEAVY (New Course)

122   Ballymore Properties Nov Hdle (Classic) (Gr 2) (1) (4yo+) £17,106   2½m110y (10)

101	WICHITA LINEMAN (IRE) *JonjoO'Neill* 6-11-12 APMcCoy	1/1f		1
	TIDAL BAY (IRE) *JHowardJohnson* 6-11-12 PJBrennan	11/4	6	2
101	MASSINI'S MAGUIRE (IRE) *PJHobbs* 6-11-12 RichardJohnson	16/1	4	3
	Osana (FR) *DEPipe* 5-11-9 TomScudamore	11/1	1¼	4
109	Hills of Aran *WKGoldsworthy* 5-11-5 TimmyMurphy	80/1	sh	5
77	Carlitos *NATwiston-Davies* 5-11-5 TonyEvans	25/1	21	6
	Michael Muck *PFNicholls* 5-11-9 RWalsh	25/1	3	7
	Master Eddy *SLycett* 7-11-5 TJO'Brien	100/1	dist	8
109	Zilcash *AKing* 4-10-7 RobertThornton	7/1		f
	Don Castille (USA) *PRWebber* 5-11-5 JamesDavies	100/1		pu
	Lujain Rose *NMBabbage* 5-10-12 GerardTumelty	200/1		pu

Mr John P. McManus 11ran 5m16.38

123   Byrne Bros Cleeve Hdle (Gr 2) (1) (5yo+) £34,212   3m (12)

81	BLAZING BAILEY *AKing* 5-11-0 RobertThornton	14/1		1
54	INGLIS DREVER *JHowardJohnson* 8-11-8 PJBrennan	9/2	4	2
75	FLIGHT LEADER (IRE) *CLTizzard* 7-11-4 JoeTizzard	7/1	6	3
81	Lough Derg (FR) *DEPipe* 7-11-0 (v) TomScudamore	20/1	24	4
72	Black Jack Ketchum (IRE) *JonjoO'Neill* 8-11-8 APMcCoy	4/7f	1	5
88	Sleeping Night (FR) *PFNicholls* 11-11-0 RWalsh	33/1	15	6
81	Irish Wolf (FR) *PBowen* 7-11-0 (s) TJO'Brien	33/1	6	7
81	Redemption *NATwiston-Davies* 12-11-8 TonyEvans	66/1	5	8
81	Fire Dragon (IRE) *JonjoO'Neill* 6-11-8 (b) DominicElsworth	100/1		pu

Three Line Whip 9ran 6m25.29

124   Letheby & Christopher Chase (Cotswold) (Gr 2) (1) (5yo+) £57,288   3m1f110y (21)

87	EXOTIC DANCER (FR) *JonjoO'Neill* 7-11-6 (s) APMcCoy	6/1		1
19	OUR VIC (FR) *DEPipe* 9-11-10 TimmyMurphy	2/1f	18	2
91	HALCON GENELARDAIS (FR) *AKing* 7-11-6 RobertThornton	7/2	7	3
70	Nil Desperandum (IRE) *MissVenetiaWilliams* 10-11-0 TomScudamore	66/1	3½	4
58	Fundamentalist (IRE) *NATwiston-Davies* 9-11-0 TonyEvans	66/1	dist	5
81	Neptune Collonges (FR) *PFNicholls* 6-11-6 RWalsh	6/1		f
98	Cailin Alainn (IRE) *CharlesByrnes,Ireland* 8-10-13 DNRussell	9/2		f
55	Idle Talk (IRE) *TRGeorge* 8-11-2 RichardJohnson	12/1		ur
79	Take The Stand (IRE) *PBowen* 11-11-0 TJO'Brien	50/1		pu

Sir Robert Ogden 9ran 6m57.49

125   Wragge & Co Juv Nov Hdle (Finesse) (Gr 2) (1) (4yo) £17,106   2m1f (7)

What should have been the second last was omitted due to the state of the ground

71	KATCHIT (IRE) *AKing* 4-11-7 RobertThornton	2/1f		1
92	GOOD BYE SIMON (FR) *TDoumen,France* 4-11-7 MickFitzgerald	9/2	1¾	2
	PAUILLAC (FR) *DEPipe* 4-11-7 TimmyMurphy	3/1	2½	3
	Predateur (FR) *PFNicholls* 4-11-7 RWalsh	7/2	1	4
	Pancake (FR) *PJHobbs* 4-11-7 RichardJohnson	8/1	11	5
89	Celtic Warrior (IRE) *LiamRoche,Ireland* 4-11-4 PJBrennan	40/1	22	6
92	The Preacher *KJBurke* 4-11-0 PaddyMerrigan	100/1	dist	7
	Looker *JGallagher* 4-10-7 MattieBatchelor	100/1	dist	8

D S J P Syndicate 8ran 4m21.57

126   Ladbrokes Trophy Chase (Hcap) (Gr 3) (1) (150) (5yo+) £31,361   2m5f (9)

The four fences in the home straight were omitted due to the low sun

	WHISPERED SECRET (GER) *DEPipe* 8-10-3[127] RJGreene	8/1		1
70	NEW ALCO (FR) *FerdyMurphy* 6-11-1[139] GLee	4/1	½	2
	IDOLE FIRST (IRE) *MissVenetiaWilliams* 8-10-12[136] AlanO'Keeffe	6/1	3	3
	Roman Ark *JMJefferson* 9-11-2[143] FergusKing[3]	13/2	1¾	4
	Cousin Nicky *PJHobbs* 6-10-0[124] RichardJohnson	12/1	3	5
104	Le Volfoni (FR) *PFNicholls* 6-11-10[148] RWalsh	11/2	½	6
17	Royal Auclair (FR) *PFNicholls* 10-11-9[150] (t) LiamHeard[3]	33/1	15	7
85	Knowhere (IRE) *NATwiston-Davies* 9-11-10[148] TonyEvans	8/1	25	8
91	Innox (FR) *FDoumen,France* 11-11-8[146] (b) APMcCoy	20/1	16	9
55	Vodka Bleu (FR) *DEPipe* 8-11-12[140] TimmyMurphy	7/2f	dist	10

Mr David Manasseh 10ran 5m37.13

SOUTHWELL Saturday, Jan 27   HEAVY

127   Sky Bet Chase (Hcap) (L) (1) 0-145(142) (5yo+) £34,212   3m110y (19)

91	SIMON *JLSpearing* 8-11-2[132] AndrewThornton	7/1		1
79	ARDAGHEY (IRE) *NATwiston-Davies* 8-11-1[136] (t) MrDEngland[5]	12/1	9	2
91	MOUNT CLERIGO (IRE) *VRADartnall* 9-10-7[126] DarylJacob[3]	8/1	11	3
110	Mon Mome (FR) *MissVenetiaWilliams* 7-11-12[142] SamThomas	7/2	6	4

1103

	Sharp Belline (IRE) *MrsSJSmith* 10-9-9[118] MichaelO'Connell[7]	7/1	dist 5
	Rosses Point (IRE) *EvanWilliams* 8-10-4[120] PaulMoloney	5/2f	dist 6
	Ever Present (IRE) *NGRichards* 9-11-7[137] TonyDobbin	10/1	pu
	Nadover (FR) *CJMann* 6-11-4[134] NoelFehily	10/1	pu
	Umbrella Man (IRE) *MissECLavelle* 11-11-3[133] BarryFenton	25/1	pu
88	Little Big Horse (IRE) *MrsSJSmith* 11-10-13[129] SEDurack	14/1	pu

Mrs Mercy Rimell 10ran 6m40.65

LEOPARDSTOWN Sunday, Jan 28
Chase course: SOFT, Hurdles course: GOOD to SOFT

128 Baileys Arkle Perpetual Challenge Cup Nov Chase (Gr 1) (5yo+)   2m1f (11)
£33,987

90	SCHINDLERS HUNT (IRE) *DTHughes* 7-11-12 RLoughran	8/13f	1
69	KING JOHNS CASTLE (IRE) *ALTMoore* 8-11-12 APMcCoy	5/1	2 2
	KHETAAM (IRE) *NMeade* 9-11-12 NPMadden	14/1	12 3
90	Wanango (GER) *TStack* 6-11-12 DJCasey	20/1	nk 4
90	Young Desperado (IRE) *RobertTyner* 9-11-12 RWalsh	7/1	4 5
	Vintage Treasure (IRE) *CharlesByrnes* 8-11-12 DNRussell	12/1	10 6
90	Hear The Echo (IRE) *MFMorris* 6-11-12 CO'Dwyer	16/1	f

Slaneyville Syndicate 7ran 4m26.24

129 AIG Europe Champion Hdle (Gr 1) (4yo+) £65,359   2m (8)

74	HARDY EUSTACE (IRE) *DTHughes* 10-11-10 (b) CO'Dwyer	9/1	1
102	BRAVE INCA (IRE) *ColmAMurphy* 9-11-10 APMcCoy	11/8f	3 2
	MACS JOY (IRE) *MrsJHarrington* 8-11-10 BJGeraghty	10/1	3 3
89	Lounaos (FR) *EoinGriffin* 4-10-5 DNRussell	10/1	2 4
86	Jazz Messenger (FR) *NMeade* 7-11-10 NPMadden	12/1	2 5
68	Asian Maze (IRE) *ThomasMullins* 8-11-5 RWalsh	12/1	7 6
67	Hide The Evidence (IRE) *MrsJHarrington* 6-11-10 (t) ADLeigh	16/1	3½ 7
102	Iktitaf (IRE) *NMeade* 6-11-10 (t) TimmyMurphy	9/2	dist 8

Mr Laurence Byrne 8ran 3m59.68

SANDOWN Saturday, Feb 3   Chase course: GOOD, Hurdles course: GOOD to SOFT

130 Fraser Steele HBLB Hcap Chase (Gr 3) (1) (155) (5yo+) £28,510   2m (13)

65	DEMPSEY (IRE) *CarlLlewellyn* 9-11-10[153] TimmyMurphy	8/1	1
86	HASTY PRINCE *JonjoO'Neill* 9-10-7[136] APMcCoy	6/1	5 2
46	ANDREAS (FR) *PFNicholls* 7-11-1[144] (t) RWalsh	9/2f	1½ 3
46	Tysou (FR) *NJHenderson* 10-11-1[144] MickFitzgerald	12/1	6 4
73	Madison du Berlais (FR) *DEPipe* 6-11-4[147] TomScudamore	8/1	3½ 5
	Jericho III (FR) *MissVenetiaWilliams* 10-10-4[136] (b) PCO'Neill[3]	16/1	5 6
	Bambi de L'Orme (FR) *IanWilliams* 8-10-5[134] DominicElsworth	12/1	nk 7
	Kalca Mome (FR) *PJHobbs* 9-11-0[143] TJO'Brien	16/1	1½ 8
20	Ground Ball (IRE) *CFSwan,Ireland* 10-10-10[139] RichardMcGrath	25/1	7 9
94	Oneway (IRE) *MGRimell* 10-11-12[155] RobertThornton	11/1	22 10
44	Chilling Place (IRE) *PJHobbs* 8-10-13[142] RichardJohnson	5/1	30 11
4	Bohemian Spirit (IRE) *NGRichards* 9-10-2[136] MissRDavidson[5]	9/1	f

Mrs T. Brown 12ran 3m52.25

131 Agfa UK Hdle (L) (1) (5yo+) £17,106   2m110y (8)

74	DETROIT CITY (USA) *PJHobbs* 5-11-8 (b) RichardJohnson	1/3f	1
86	STRAW BEAR (USA) *NJGifford* 6-11-8 APMcCoy	7/2	1¾ 2
108	WHISPERED PROMISES (USA) *RSBrookhouse* 6-11-0 AlanO'Keeffe	66/1	6 3
73	Contraband *SGollings* 9-11-0 RWalsh	66/1	8 4
113	Arcalis *JHowardJohnson* 7-11-8 (t) MickFitzgerald	16/1	9 5
104	Ichi Beau (IRE) *DrPPritchard* 13-11-0 DrPPritchard	200/1	21 6

Mr Terry Warner 6ran 3m54.23

132 totesport.com Scilly Isles Nov Chase (Gr 1) (1) (5yo+) £28,510   2½m110y (15)

The pond fence was omitted due to the low trajectory of the sun

64	NEW LITTLE BRIC (FR) *PFNicholls* 6-11-6 RWalsh	10/11f	1
21	AZTEC WARRIOR (IRE) *MissHCKnight* 6-11-6 TimmyMurphy	7/2	8 2
	ALL STAR (GER) *NJHenderson* 7-11-6 MickFitzgerald	10/3	6 3
	Pretty Star (GER) *AKing* 7-11-6 RobertThornton	9/1	13 4

Mrs Kathy Stuart 4ran 5m10.64

133 totescoop6 Sandown Hcap Hdle (Gr 3) (1) (152) (4yo+) £28,510   2¾m (11)

73	TARANIS (FR) *PFNicholls* 6-10-3[129] (t) RWalsh	9/4f	1
126	WHISPERED SECRET (GER) *DEPipe* 8-10-1[127] RJGreene	12/1	½ 2
108	VERASI *GLMoore* 6-10-9[135] (b) JamieMoore	9/1	½ 3
	KASBAH BLISS (FR) *FDoumen,France* 5-11-9[152] ADuchene[3]	10/1	1¾ 4
	Lyes Green *OSherwood* 6-10-1[127] LeightonAspell	16/1	2 5
108	Nathos (GER) *CJMann* 10-9-10[132] KevinTobin[10]	33/1	½ 6

Golden Bay *MissSuzySmith* 8-9-11[126] ColinBolger[3] 22/1   2 7
Lord Sam (IRE) *VRADartnall* 11-11-6[151] (s) JamesWhite[5] 14/1   2½ 8
Mikado *JonjoO'Neill* 6-9-7[126] JWFarrelly[7] .... 50/1   ¾ 9
108 Turtle Soup (IRE) *TRGeorge* 11-10-6[137] WillieMcCarthy[5] .... 50/1   ¾ 10
Accordello (IRE) *KGReveley* 6-10-0[126] RichardMcGrath 15/2   4 11
Arrayou (FR) *OSherwood* 6-10-6[132] (v) WayneHutchinson .... 66/1   ¾ 12
82 Oscar Park (IRE) *DWParbuthnot* 8-11-0[140] TomScudamore .... 14/1   hd 13
Holland Park (IRE) *MrsSDWilliams* 10-10-8[134] JoeTizzard 100/1   17 14
108 Royals Darling (GER) *NJHenderson* 5-10-13[139] MickFitzgerald 4/1   7 15
Refinement (IRE) *JonjoO'Neill* 8-11-11[151] (t) APMcCoy .... 20/1   pu

Mrs A. B. Yeoman & Mr C. R. Whittaker 16ran 5m19.64

134   **Agfa Diamond Hcap Chase (2) 0-145(145) (5yo+)** £25,052   3m1f10y (18)

The pond fence and first fence in the home straight were omitted due to the low trajectory of the sun

RAMBLING MINSTER *KGReveley* 9-10-5[124] RichardMcGrath 15/2   1
79 KELAMI (FR) *FDoumen,France* 9-11-3[139] ADuchene[3] .... 25/1   ¾ 2
BRIERY FOX (IRE) *HDDaly* 9-11-1[134] MarkBradburne 40/1   6 3
73 TIKRAM *AKing* 10-11-5[138] APMcCoy .... 11/2f   ¾ 4
63 Lord Killeshanra (IRE) *CLTizzard* 8-11-0[133] JoeTizzard 25/1   5 5
Nitrat (FR) *FDoumen,France* 6-10-12[131] (b) JacquesRicou 66/1   3 6
Yardbird *AKing* 8-10-11[130] WayneHutchinson 7/1   1¼ 7
79 Fork Lightning (IRE) *AKing* 11-11-0[133] RobertThornton 12/1   1 8
65 Hoo La Baloo (FR) *PFNicholls* 6-11-9[145] LiamHeard[3] 20/1   6 9
Supreme Catch (IRE) *MissHCKnight* 10-10-3[127] TimmyMurphy 16/1   3½ 10
Flintoff (USA) *MissVenetiaWilliams* 6-10-13[135] (b) PCO'Neill[3] 7/1   1 11
43 Florida Dream (IRE) *NATwiston-Davies* 8-9-12[122] (b) MrDEngland[5] 12/1   7 12
Iron Man (FR) *PBowen* 6-11-0[133] (s) TJO'Brien 16/1   17 13
55 Napolitain (FR) *PFNicholls* 6-11-1[137] PaddyMerrigan[3] .... 33/1   f
Turthen (FR) *PFNicholls* 6-10-13[132] RWalsh .... 9/1   ur
Kasthari (IRE) *JHowardJohnson* 8-11-0[133] MickFitzgerald .... 33/1   pu
Latimer's Place *NJGifford* 11-10-13[132] SEDurack .... 14/1   pu
Pass Me By *MissSuzySmith* 8-10-7[129] (b) ColinBolger[3] .... 14/1   pu

The Lingdale Optimists 18ran 6m15.48

WETHERBY Saturday, Feb 3   SOFT

135   **Brit Insurance Nov Hdle (River Don) (Gr 2) (1) (4yo+)** £15,473   3m1f (12)

CHIEF DAN GEORGE (IRE) *JamesMoffatt* 7-11-9 (s) AlanDempsey 8/1   1
FASTAFFARAN (IRE) *IMcMath* 6-11-5 (s) MichaelMcAlister .... 16/1   hd 2
BRADLEY BOY (IRE) *CarlLlewellyn* 6-11-11 NoelFehily 5/2   7 3
Arctic Echo *GASwinbank* 8-11-9 DougieCostello 9/4f   15 4
Negus de Beaumont (FR) *FerdyMurphy* 7-11-9 GLee 6/1   1½ 5
All For Luck (IRE) *NGRichards* 6-11-5 TonyDobbin 4/1   2 6
Point Rouge (FR) *JHowardJohnson* 4-10-7 PJBrennan .... 50/1   dist 7

Mr Maurice W. Chapman 7ran 6m40.52

136   **totepool Towton Nov Chase (Gr 2) (1) (5yo+)** £17,408   3m1f (18)

110 HELTORNIC (IRE) *MScudamore* 7-11-1 GLee 14/1   1
88 MIKO DE BEAUCHENE (FR) *RHAlner* 7-11-4 RobertWalford 10/1   3½ 2
HEEZ A DREAMER (IRE) *MissVenetiaWilliams* 7-11-8 TonyDobbin 11/2   3 3
Blue Splash (IRE) *PBowen* 7-11-8 PeterBuchanan 5/1   1¾ 4
Hoh Viss *CJMann* 7-11-4 NoelFehily .... 15/8f   f
Royal Rosa (FR) *JHowardJohnson* 8-11-10 PJBrennan .... 7/2   pu
91 Omni Cosmo Touch (USA) *MrsSJSmith* 11-11-8 BrianHarding .... 12/1   pu

Mr Stephen W. Molloy 7ran 6m35.96

PUNCHESTOWN Sunday, Feb 4   SOFT

137   **Byrne Group plc Nov Hdle (Gr 2) (5yo+)** £23,556   2m (9)

112 ORBIT O'GOLD (USA) *NMeade* 5-10-13 NPMadden 50/1   1
96 DE VALIRA (IRE) *MJPO'Brien* 5-11-5 AELynch 6/4   3 2
HOLLY TREE (IRE) *ESheehy* 7-11-2 DNRussell .... 16/1   nk 3
30 Kalderon (GER) *THogan* 7-11-5 DJCasey .... 14/1   ¾ 4
Albanov (IRE) *MrsJHarrington* 7-11-2 BJGeraghty 25/1   3 5
112 Kendor Dine (FR) *EoinGriffin* 5-10-13 RWalsh 11/1   2½ 6
96 Turtle Dubh (IRE) *ESheehy* 6-11-2 RLoughran 33/1   10 7
105 Perce Rock *TStack* 5-11-2 APMcCoy 11/8f   3½ 8
Davorin (JPN) *RPBurns* 6-11-2 PWFlood 50/1   1½ 9
Dul Ar An Ol (IRE) *PHenley* 6-11-2 APCrowe 100/1   9 10
Academy Reward (IRE) *NMeade* 7-11-2 DFO'Regan .... 14/1   pu

Mighty Macs Syndicate 11ran 4m17.49

138 **Byrne Group plc Tied Cottage Chase (Gr 2) (5yo+)** £22,699   2m (11)

117	NICKNAME (FR) *MartinBrassil* 8-11-12 (t) RWalsh	9/10f			1
117	CENTRAL HOUSE (IRE) *DTHughes* 10-11-10 (t) RLoughran	12/1		7	2
95	STEEL BAND *PaulARoche* 9-11-4 DNRussell	100/1		1	3
117	Watson Lake (IRE) *NMeade* 9-11-10 DFO'Regan	8/1	1¼	4	
118	Tumbling Dice (IRE) *TJTaaffe* 8-11-10 (s) BJGeraghty	16/1		8	5
95	Jim (FR) *JTRDreaper* 10-11-4 AELynch	25/1		6	6
52	Newmill (IRE) *JohnJosephMurphy* 9-11-12 AndrewJMcNamara	3/1			f
	Tiger Cry (IRE) *ALTMoore* 9-11-4 DJCasey	33/1			pu

Mrs Claudia Jungo-Corpataux 8ran 4m17.00

139 **AON Chase (Gr 2) (1) (5yo+)** £28,510   3m (18)

87	KAUTO STAR (FR) *PFNicholls* 7-11-10 (t) RWalsh	2/9f			1
100	L'AMI (FR) *FDoumen,France* 8-11-0 APMcCoy	6/1	nk	2	
126	ROYAL AUCLAIR (FR) *PFNicholls* 10-11-6 (t) LiamHeard	40/1	14	3	
43	Tango Royal (FR) *DEPipe* 11-11-0 (v+t) RJGreene	40/1	13	4	
	King Harald (IRE) *MBradstock* 9-11-0 MattieBatchelor	33/1	4	5	
123	Sleeping Night (FR) *PFNicholls* 11-11-0 SamThomas	20/1	nk	6	

Mr Clive D. Smith 6ran 6m08.00

140 **totesport Trophy Hdle (Hcap) (Gr 3) (1) (146) (4yo+)** £85,530   2m110y (8)

106	HEATHCOTE *GLMoore* 5-10-6[126] JamieMoore	50/1			1
113	OVERSTRAND (IRE) *DrRDPNewland* 8-10-12[137] SPJones[5]	16/1	nk	2	
	PEDROBOB (IRE) *AnthonyMullins,Ireland* 9-10-13[133] NoelFehily	11/1	2	3	
66	CARACCIOLA (GER) *NJHenderson* 10-11-2[136] AndrewTinkler	33/1	¾	4	
112	Mister Hight (FR) *WPMullins,Ireland* 5-11-11[145] RobertThornton	20/1	1¼	5	
112	Victram (IRE) *AdrianMcGuinness,Ireland* 7-10-3[130] JWFarrelly[7]	14/1	hd	6	
112	New Field (IRE) *ThomasMullins,Ireland* 5-10-5[125] RMPower	16/1	½	7	
	Kawagino (IRE) *JWMullins* 7-11-1[140] WayneKavanagh[5]	50/1	nk	8	
106	Orcadian *JMPEustace* 6-10-9[129] MarkBradburne	16/1	1¾	9	
	Moore's Law (USA) *MJGrassick,Ireland* 9-10-8[128] DenisO'Regan	9/1	1¾	10	
86	Self Defense *MissECLavelle* 10-11-7[144] LiamTreadwell[3]	100/1	1¾	11	
	My Immortal *DEPipe* 5-10-7[127] RJGreene	20/1	nk	12	
106	Papini (IRE) *NJHenderson* 6-11-6[140] MickFitzgerald	15/2	¾	13	
80	Pirate Flagship (IRE) *PFNicholls* 8-10-7[127] (b) SamThomas	40/1	nk	14	
80	Tarlac (GER) *NJHenderson* 6-11-2[136] APMcCoy	9/2f	¾	15	
105	Rio de Janeiro (IRE) *MissECLavelle* 6-10-4[124] PJBrennan	25/1	24	16	
	Private Be *PJHobbs* 8-10-11[131] RichardJohnson	20/1	1½	17	
112	Quatre Heures (FR) *WPMullins,Ireland* 5-11-8[142] RWalsh	8/1	¾	18	
	Bongo Fury (FR) *DEPipe* 8-10-5[125] (v) TomScudamore	16/1	19	19	
80	Acambo (GER) *DEPipe* 6-11-12[146] TimmyMurphy	11/2			pu

B. Siddle & B. D. Haynes 20ran 3m58.89

141 **totepool Game Spirit Chase (Gr 2) (1) (5yo+)** £34,373   2m1f (13)

	WELL CHIEF (GER) *DEPipe* 8-11-0 TimmyMurphy	5/2			1
	ASHLEY BROOK (GER) *KBishop* 9-11-0 PJBrennan	9/4f	11	2	
94	ARMATURK (FR) *PFNicholls* 10-11-6 RWalsh	16/1	8	3	
	Sporazene (IRE) *PFNicholls* 8-11-6 SamThomas	9/1	1¼	4	
	Jupon Vert (FR) *RJHodges* 10-11-0 TomScudamore	200/1	22	5	
94	Voy Por Ustedes (FR) *AKing* 6-11-10 RobertThornton	5/1			ur
94	Foreman (GER) *TDoumen,France* 9-11-5 APMcCoy	9/2			pu
	Venn Ottery *MrsSGardner* 12-11-0 (t) AndrewGlassonbury	200/1			pu

Mr D. A. Johnson 8ran 4m07.20

142 **Tote Text Betting 60021 Standard Open NHF (Gr 2) (1) (4, 5 and 6yo)** £11,404   2m110y

	CROCODILES ROCK (IRE) *JonjoO'Neill* 5-11-7 APMcCoy	15/8jf			1
	JUST A THOUGHT (IRE) *HJLDunlop* 4-10-7 NoelFehily	20/1	1	2	
	EARTH PLANET (IRE) *PFNicholls* 5-11-7 SamThomas	16/1	9	3	
	Appleaday (IRE) *PRWebber* 6-11-7 RichardJohnson	28/1	5	4	
	Mutual Respect (IRE) *PFNicholls* 5-11-7 RWalsh	9/1	7	5	
	Definite Edge (IRE) *WJMusson* 5-11-3 LeightonAspell	100/1	16	6	
	Freddie The Third (IRE) *NATwiston-Davies* 5-11-7 TonyEvans	20/1	4	7	
	Greenbridge (IRE) *AKing* 5-11-7 RobertThornton	20/1	15	8	
	Treat Em Mean *CarlLlewellyn* 6-11-3 CarlLlewellyn	6/1	3½	9	
	Seven Is My Number (IRE) *DEPipe* 5-11-7 TimmyMurphy	15/8jf	1¼	10	

Mr Russell McAllister 10ran 4m00.13

143   Deloitte Nov Hdle (Gr 1) (5yo+) £42,763   2¼m (9)

84	ARAN CONCERTO (IRE) *NMeade* 6-11-10 PCarberry	4/6f		1
	LEADING RUN (IRE) *NMeade* 8-11-10 NPMadden	20/1	3	2
	ARRIVE SIR CLIVE (IRE) *PhilipFenton* 6-11-10 AndrewJMcNamara	6/1	3	3
96	Catch Me (GER) *EJO'Grady* 5-11-7 BJGeraghty	5/2		ur

Mr John Corr 4ran 5m03.11

144   Dr P.J. Moriarty Nov Chase (Gr 1) (5yo+) £47,039   2m5f (14)

	MISTER TOP NOTCH (IRE) *DEFitzgerald* 8-11-10 CO'Dwyer	14/1		1
69	VIC VENTURI (IRE) *PhilipFenton* 7-11-10 AndrewJMcNamara	8/1	7	2
	ONE COOL COOKIE (IRE) *CFSwan* 7-11-10 DJCasey	25/1	½	3
	Chelsea Harbour (IRE) *ThomasMullins* 7-11-10 DNRussell	4/1jf	1¾	4
98	O'Muircheartaigh (IRE) *EJO'Grady* 7-11-10 (s) PWFlood	10/1	9	5
98	Anothercoppercoast (IRE) *PaulARoche* 7-11-10 ADLeigh	16/1	½	6
	Alexander Taipan (IRE) *WPMullins* 7-11-10 DJCondon	9/2		f
	Justpourit (IRE) *DTHughes* 8-11-10 RLoughran	8/1		ur
78	Knight Legend (IRE) *MrsJHarrington* 8-11-10 BJGeraghty	4/1jf		ur
	Back To Bid (IRE) *NMeade* 7-11-10 PCarberry	8/1		pu

Mrs Marie Cronin 10ran 5m59.49

145   Hennessy Cognac Gold Cup (Gr 1) (5yo+) £74,013   3m (17)

100	BEEF OR SALMON (IRE) *MHourigan* 11-11-12 (b) AndrewJMcNamara	11/4		1
100	THE LISTENER (IRE) *RHAlner,GB* 8-11-12 DAJacob	9/10f	¾	2
118	HI CLOY (IRE) *MHourigan* 10-11-12 PCarberry	14/1	dist	3
118	Forget The Past *MJPO'Brien* 9-11-12 (t) AELynch	9/2	24	4
98	Patsy Hall (IRE) *MichaelCunningham* 7-11-12 DNRussell	20/1		ur

Mr B. J. Craig 5ran 6m42.02

146   Betfair Hcap Hdle (2) (141) (4yo+) £50,104   2m3f110y (11)

140	OVERSTRAND (IRE) *DrRDPNewland* 8-11-7[141] SPJones[5]	9/1		1
108	NATION STATE *GLMoore* 6-10-7[122] (b) JamieMoore	8/1	¾	2
	FLYING FALCON *MissVenetiaWilliams* 8-10-2[120] LiamTreadwell[3]	9/1	2	3
140	My Immortal *DEPipe* 5-10-10[125] RJGreene	12/1	4	4
133	Turtle Soup (IRE) *TRGeorge* 11-10-12[132] WillieMcCarthy[5]	16/1	4	5
	The Real Deal (IRE) *NickWilliams* 6-11-4[133] APMcCoy	9/2f	½	6
80	Mahogany Blaze (FR) *NATwiston-Davies* 5-11-8[137] CarlLlewellyn	25/1	1½	7
	Magic Sky (FR) *MFHarris* 7-10-4[124] (v) CharliePoste[5]	25/1	10	8
	Supreme Prince (IRE) *PJHobbs* 10-11-1[137] DarrenO'Dwyer[7]	25/1	3½	9
	Cool Roxy *AGBlackmore* 10-10-4[122] ChrisHonour[3]	50/1	nk	10
	French Saulaie (FR) *PJHobbs* 6-10-5[120] RichardJohnson	5/1	dist	11
	Cantgeton (IRE) *DEPipe* 7-10-8[123] TimmyMurphy	25/1	9	12
	Pevensey (FR) *JJQuinn* 5-10-13[131] DougieCostello[3]	7/1		f
	Slew Charm (FR) *NoelTChance* 5-10-12[127] (t) TomDoyle	9/1		f

Dr R. D. P. And Mrs L. J. Newland 14ran 4m55.09

147   John Smith's Reynoldstown Nov Chase (Gr 2) (1) (5yo+) £22,808   3m (20)

53	GUNGADU *PFNicholls* 7-11-10 RWalsh	4/7f		1
53	WEE ROBBIE *NJGifford* 7-11-4 LeightonAspell	33/1	4	2
	JAUNTY TIMES *HDDaly* 7-11-8 MarkBradburne	16/1	3½	3
85	According to John (IRE) *NGRichards* 7-11-8 TonyDobbin	7/1	5	4
	Over The Creek *DEPipe* 8-11-4 TimmyMurphy	7/2	7	5
	Imperial Sun (IRE) *DTHughes,Ireland* 8-11-8 (v) RLoughran	33/1	dist	6
	In Accord *HDDaly* 8-11-4 MrPCallaghan	33/1	13	7

Mrs M. Findlay & P. K. Barber 7ran 6m16.24

148   Commercial First Ascot Chase (Gr 1) (1) (5yo+) £84,675   2m3f (16)

87	MONET'S GARDEN (IRE) *NGRichards* 9-11-7 TonyDobbin	11/10f		1
73	THISTHATANDTOTHER (IRE) *PFNicholls* 11-11-7 RWalsh	4/1	8	2
94	RIVER CITY (IRE) *NoelTChance* 10-11-7 TomDoyle	20/1	3	3
126	Vodka Bleu (FR) *DEPipe* 8-11-7 TimmyMurphy	22/1	3	4
65	Fota Island (IRE) *MFMorris,Ireland* 11-11-7 APMcCoy	7/1	1½	5
138	Central House *DTHughes,Ireland* 10-11-7 (t) RLoughran	8/1	24	6
73	Cerium (FR) *PFNicholls* 6-11-7 RichardJohnson	13/2		pu

Mr David Wesley Yates 7ran 4m50.45

149   Casino 36 Stockport Rendlesham Hdle (Gr 2) (1) (4yo+) £22,808   2m7f110y (12)

109	LABELTHOU (FR) *MissECLavelle* 8-11-1 BarryFenton	5/4f		1
108	AFRAD (FR) *NJHenderson* 6-11-4 AndrewTinkler	13/2	8	2
	MATERIAL WORLD *MissSuzySmith* 9-10-11 (ec) ColinBolger	9/4	14	3

113	The French Furze (IRE) *NGRichards* 13-11-8 BrianHarding	12/1	7 4
	Witch Wind *AMCrow* 7-11-4 PJBrennan	25/1	11 5
82	St Matthew (USA) *MrsSJSmith* 9-11-4 PadgeWhelan	17/2	1¾ 6

GDM Partnership 6ran 6m05.16

150   **Red Square Vodka Gold Cup Chase (Hcap) (Gr 3) (1) (150) (5yo+)**   3½m110y (20) £71,275

The middle fence in the back straight was omitted

136	HELTORNIC (IRE) *MScudamore* 7-10-0[124] TomScudamore	12/1	1
110	L'AVENTURE (FR) *PFNicholls* 8-10-1[128] (t) PaddyMerrigan[3]	14/1	1¼ 2
127	MON MOME (FR) *MissVenetiaWilliams* 7-10-11[142] MrWBiddick[7]	12/1	15 3
114	WILD CANE RIDGE (IRE) *LLungo* 8-11-6[144] KeithMercer	25/1	2½ 4
70	Cornish Rebel (IRE) *PFNicholls* 10-11-7[148] (s) LiamHeard[3]	25/1	7 5
114	Leading Man (IRE) *FerdyMurphy* 7-10-12[136] GLee	16/1	2½ 6
111	G V A Ireland (IRE) *FFlood,Ireland* 9-10-7[131] NPMadden	10/1	2 7
	Philson Run (IRE) *NickWilliams* 11-10-13[137] PACarberry	33/1	3½ 8
51	Bewleys Berry (IRE) *JHowardJohnson* 9-11-1[139] PJBrennan	14/1	14 9
	Cloudy Lane *DMcCainJnr* 7-9-11[124] SJCraine[3]	11/2jf	dist 10
33	Kandjar d'Allier (FR) *AKing* 9-11-2[140] RobertThornton	16/1	1 11
110	Naunton Brook *NATwiston-Davies* 8-10-12[136] (t) TonyEvans	14/1	¾ 12
110	Sir Rembrandt (IRE) *RHAlner* 11-11-9[150] DarylJacob[3]	50/1	pu
134	Kelami (FR) *FDoumen,France* 9-11-1[139] JacquesRicou	8/1	pu
114	The Outlier (IRE) *MissVenetiaWilliams* 9-10-10[137] PCO'Neill[3]	11/2jf	pu
	Kilbeggan Blade *TRGeorge* 8-10-8[132] PaulMoloney	6/1	pu

Mr Stephen W. Molloy 16ran 7m32.19

151   **Brit Insurance Prestige Nov Hdle (Gr 2) (1) (4yo+)** £17,186   2m7f110y (12)

135	CHIEF DAN GEORGE (IRE) *JamesMoffatt* 7-11-11 (s) AlanDempsey	9/1	1
	ITSA LEGEND *AKing* 8-11-8 RobertThornton	10/1	15 2
122	HILLS OF ARAN *WKGoldsworthy* 5-11-4 GLee	15/2	5 3
35	Joaaci (IRE) *DEPipe* 7-11-8 (s) TomScudamore	6/4f	6 4
	The Sawyer (BEL) *RHBuckler* 7-11-11 DarylJacob	11/4	3 5
	High Stand Lad *IMcMath* 5-11-4 MichaelMcAlister	40/1	pu
	Scarvagh Diamond (IRE) *NGRichards* 6-11-1 BrianHarding	6/1	pu

Mr Maurice W. Chapman 7ran 6m18.18

UTTOXETER Saturday, Feb 17   HEAVY

152   **totesport.com Lord Gyllene Hcap Chase (2) (138) (5yo+)** £31,315   2¾m110y (14)

The first fence in the back straight was omitted due to the state of the ground

104	NOZIC (FR) *PFNicholls* 6-11-6[138] (t) JoeTizzard	11/4f	1
	KEEPATEM (IRE) *JonjoO'Neill* 11-10-0[118] BarryKeniry	11/1	13 2
	KERRY LADS (IRE) *MissLucindaVRussell* 12-11-0[132] (s) PeterBuchanan	11/2	9 3
126	Idole First (IRE) *MissVenetiaWilliams* 8-11-4[136] AlanO'Keeffe	9/2	10 4
51	Undeniable *MrsSJSmith* 9-11-3[128] MichaelO'Connell[7]	10/1	13 5
16	Almaydan *RLee* 9-11-0[132] (b) SEDurack	16/1	6 6
123	Redemption *NATwiston-Davies* 12-11-1[133] JasonMaguire	8/1	pu
	Good Citizen (IRE) *TRGeorge* 7-10-6[124] TJO'Brien	4/1	pu
	Foly Pleasant (FR) *MrsKWaldron* 13-9-11[120] (t) TomMalone[3]	33/1	pu

Mr S. Mcvie 9ran 6m21.04

WINCANTON Saturday, Feb 17   SOFT

153   **Bathwick Tyres Bridgwater HBLB Kingmaker Nov Chase (Gr 2) (1) (5yo+)** £17,106   2m (13)

	URSIS (FR) *SGollings* 6-11-3 DominicElsworth	7/2	1
	OPERA MUNDI (FR) *PFNicholls* 5-11-1 SamThomas	5/6f	¾ 2
80	DESERT AIR (JPN) *DEPipe* 8-11-3 (s+t) AndrewGlassonbury	4/1	26 3
132	All Star (GER) *NJHenderson* 7-11-10 MickFitzgerald	15/2	3 4

Mr P. J. Martin 4ran 4m02.83

154   **Bathwick Tyres Kingwell Hdle (Gr 2) (1) (4yo+)** £39,914   2m (7)

The first flight after the winning post was omitted due to the state of the ground

131	STRAW BEAR (USA) *NJGifford* 6-11-10 APMcCoy	8/11f	1
113	AFSOUN (FR) *NJHenderson* 5-11-10 MickFitzgerald	11/8	7 2
	TROUBLE AT BAY (IRE) *AKing* 7-11-2 WayneHutchinson	25/1	9 3
	Master Mahogany *RJHodges* 6-11-2 NoelFehily	66/1	2½ 4
131	Contraband *SGollings* 9-11-2 DominicElsworth	40/1	22 5

Mr John P. McManus 5ran 3m53.85

155 **Country Gentlemen's Association Chase (Ltd Hcap) (L) (1) (160)** 3m1f110y (21)
(5yo+) £28,845

	LITTLE BRICK (FR) *DEPipe* 8-10-7[143] APMcCoy	10/11f		1
70	MY WILL (FR) *PFNicholls* 7-11-10[160] RWalsh	5/2	3½	2
55	PREACHER BOY *RJHodges* 8-10-7[143] MickFitzgerald	9/2	dist	3
134	Napolitain (FR) *PFNicholls* 6-10-4[140] WayneHutchinson	16/1	7	4
	Bold Bishop (IRE) *JonjoO'Neill* 10-10-8[144] NoelFehily	20/1		pu

Mr Thomas Barr 5ran 6m44.84

GOWRAN PARK Saturday, Feb 17   HEAVY

156 **Red Mills Chase (Gr 2) (5yo+)** £21,700   2½m (14)

138	WATSON LAKE (IRE) *NMeade* 9-11-10 PCarberry	3/1		1
	MANSONY (FR) *ALTMoore* 8-11-10 DNRussell	4/1	5	2
138	JIM (FR) *JTRDreaper* 10-11-5 AELynch	10/1	12	3
118	Mossy Green (IRE) *WPMullins* 13-11-5 DJCasey	7/1	10	4
61	Macs Flamingo *PAFahy* 7-11-5 JLCullen	25/1	13	5
97	Sher Beau (IRE) *PhilipFenton* 8-11-5 AndrewJMcNamara	11/4f	17	6
144	Knight Legend (IRE) *MrsJHarrington* 8-11-5 BJGeraghty	11/2		f

Mr John Corr 7ran 5m21.30

157 **Red Mills Trial Hdle (Gr 2) (4yo+)** £26,040   2m (9)

138	NEWMILL (IRE) *JohnJosephMurphy* 9-11-3 AndrewJMcNamara	7/1		1
129	MACS JOY (IRE) *MrsJHarrington* 8-11-11 BJGeraghty	4/9f	8	2
	LAETITIA (IRE) *CharlesByrnes* 7-11-1 DNRussell	50/1	2½	3
	Conna Castle (IRE) *JamesJosephMangan* 8-11-6 DJCasey	20/1	11	4
10	Harchibald (FR) *NMeade* 8-11-11 PCarberry	4/1	1½	5

Mrs Mary T. Hayes 5ran 4m10.00

FONTWELL Sunday, Feb 18   SOFT

158 **totesport.com National Spirit Hdle (Gr 2) (1) (4yo+)** £22,536   2½m (10)

82	UNITED (GER) *MrsLWadham* 6-10-10 LeightonAspell	4/7f		1
133	REFINEMENT (IRE) *JonjoO'Neill* 8-11-0 (t) APMcCoy	2/1	14	2
	HEREDITARY *MrsLCJewell* 5-11-3 (s) SPJones	20/1	5	3
	Lord of Beauty (FR) *NoelTChance* 7-11-3 TomDoyle	22/1	11	4
91	Korelo (FR) *SGollings* 9-11-3 (s) RobertThornton	20/1	27	5

Mr R. B. Holt 5ran 4m55.09

NAVAN Sunday, Feb 18   HEAVY

159 **McCabe Builders Boyne Hdle (Gr 3) (5yo+)** £21,700   2m5f (11)

99	SWEET KILN (IRE) *JamesBowe* 8-10-11 DNRussell	8/13f		1
120	ROSAKER (USA) *NMeade* 10-11-10 PCarberry	3/1	8	2
120	EMOTIONAL MOMENT (IRE) *TJTaaffe* 10-11-10 (s) BJGeraghty	11/2	1¼	3
111	Prince of Tara (IRE) *SJMahon* 10-11-2 RWalsh	25/1	11	4
	Cashel Bay (USA) *LukeComer* 9-11-2 MJBolger	66/1	10	5

Mr James Bowe 5ran 5m43.55

160 **ladbrokes.com Ten Up Nov Chase (Gr 2) (5yo+)** £21,700   3m (17)

	SNOWY MORNING (IRE) *WPMullins* 7-11-5 RWalsh	10/3		1
98	GAZZA'S GIRL (IRE) *MrsJHarrington* 7-11-3 BJGeraghty	6/4f	4	2
	LOVELY PRESENT (IRE) *TKGeraghty* 8-11-0 RGeraghty	25/1	dist	3
98	Romek (IRE) *MrsJHarrington* 7-11-5 TPTreacy	25/1	18	4
	Theboyfrombulawayo (IRE) *CAMcBratney* 8-11-5 (b) PWFlood	66/1	dist	5
128	Hear The Echo (IRE) *MFMorris* 6-11-10 CO'Dwyer	9/2		f
98	Toofarback (IRE) *NMeade* 7-11-5 PCarberry	4/1		pu

Quayside Syndicate 7ran 6m49.49

KEMPTON Saturday, Feb 24   HEAVY

161 **racingpost.co.uk Pendil Nov Chase (Gr 2) (1) (5yo+)** £17,408   2½m110y (16)

78	NATAL (FR) *PFNicholls* 6-11-7 (t) RWalsh	5/2f		1
	GOOD SPIRIT (FR) *PFNicholls* 5-10-10 SamThomas	7/2	3	2
153	URSIS (FR) *SGollings* 6-11-10 RichardJohnson	9/2	4	3
85	Yes Sir (IRE) *PBowen* 8-11-10 TJO'Brien	9/1	dist	4
32	Il Duce (IRE) *AKing* 7-11-7 RobertThornton	15/2		f
	Dunsfold Duke *PWinkworth* 7-11-3 LeightonAspell	13/2		ref
	Classified (IRE) *DEPipe* 11-11-7 TimmyMurphy	10/1		pu

Mrs Monica Hackett 7ran 5m29.98

162 **Racing Post Chase (Hcap) (Gr 3) (1) (150) (5yo+)** £57,020   3m (18)

127	SIMON *JLSpearing* 8-11-5[143] AndrewThornton	11/2		1
79	CORNISH SETT (IRE) *PFNicholls* 8-11-7[145] (b) RWalsh	25/1	10	2
104	LACDOUDAL (FR) *PJHobbs* 8-11-12[150] RichardJohnson	8/1	½	3

Lucifer Bleu (FR) *DEPipe* 8-9-9[124] AndrewGlassonbury[5] 15/8f 2 4
79 Iznogoud (FR) *DEPipe* 11-10-1[125] RJGreene 16/1 13 5
14 Limerick Boy (GER) *MissVenetiaWilliams* 9-11-5[143] SamThomas 5/1 2½ 6
87 Puntal (FR) *DEPipe* 11-10-13[137] (s+t) APMcCoy 16/1 4 7
134 Iron Man (FR) *PBowen* 6-10-6[130] (s) TJO'Brien .... 12/1 dist 8
44 Without A Doubt *CarlLlewellyn* 8-10-9[133] PaulMoloney .... 20/1 f
Celtic Son (FR) *DEPipe* 8-11-5[143] (t) TimmyMurphy .... 8/1 pu

Mrs Mercy Rimell 10ran 6m42.38

163 **Racing Post Adonis Juv Nov Hdle (Gr 2) (1) (4yo) £14,825** 2m (8)

PUNJABI *NJHenderson* 4-11-2 MickFitzgerald 9/2 1
29 PARRAIN (FR) *FDoumen,France* 4-11-5 ADuchene 11/10f 19 2
POQUELIN (FR) *PFNicholls* 4-11-5 RWalsh 9/4 18 3
Gracechurch (IRE) *RJHodges* 4-11-2 RichardJohnson 14/1 19 4
92 Mon Michel (IRE) *GLMoore* 4-10-12 JamieMoore 14/1 19 5
92 Lord Adonis (IRE) *KJBurke* 4-10-12 (s) TimmyMurphy .... 33/1 dist 6

Mr Raymond Tooth 6ran 4m31.08

NEWCASTLE Saturday, Feb 24 HEAVY

164 **totesport.com Eider (Hcap Chase) (2) 0-150(138) (5yo+) £43,379** 4m1f (22)

The first fence in the home straight was omitted due to being damaged in an earlier race

124 NIL DESPERANDUM (IRE) *MissVenetiaWilliams* 10-11-12[138] 1
TomScudamore 6/1
NINE DE SIVOLA (IRE) *FerdyMurphy* 6-10-11[123] GLee 9/1 12 2
CHABRIMAL MINSTER *RFord* 10-9-10[113] TomGreenway[5] 16/1 11 3
MOUSTIQUE DE L'ISLE (FR) *CCBealby* 7-9-13[116] (b) TomMessenger[5].. 22/1 10 4
2 Calvic (IRE) *TRGeorge* 9-10-13[125] PJBrennan 16/1 5 5
Huka Lodge (IRE) *MrsKWalton* 10-10-3[115] RichardMcGrath 10/1 2½ 6
Devil's Run (IRE) *JWade* 11-10-8[120] PaddyAspell 20/1 7 7
Silver Knight *TDEasterby* 9-11-4[130] (s) RussGarritty 12/1 6 8
Matmata de Tendron (FR) *ACrook* 7-9-11[112] (s) DougieCostello[3] .... 25/1 dist 9
Cowboyboots (IRE) *LWells* 9-11-4[130] MattieBatchelor 20/1 5 10
114 Truckers Tavern (IRE) *MrsSJSmith* 12-11-0[126] (t) DavidO'Meara .... 11/1 f
91 Lordofourown (IRE) *SDonohoe,Ireland* 9-11-7[138] (s) LiamJFleming[5] .... 10/1 pu
111 Teeming Rain (IRE) *CFSwan,Ireland* 8-11-1[127] TonyDobbin .... 3/1f pu
111 What A Native (IRE) *CFSwan,Ireland* 11-10-13[125] TonyDobbin .... 25/1 pu
Datito (IRE) *MrsKWalton* 12-10-3[115] AlanDempsey .... 25/1 pu
Skenfrith *MissSEForster* 8-10-0[112] NeilMulholland .... 20/1 pu

Mr M. L. Shone 16ran 9m07.78

FAIRYHOUSE Saturday, Feb 24 HEAVY

165 **Aramark Winning Fair Juv Hdle (Gr 3) (4yo) £15,292** 2m (9)

DUTY (IRE) *KFO'Brien* 4-10-8 AELynch[3] 7/1 1
J'Y VOLE (FR) *WPMullins* 4-10-5 RJKiely[5] 6/1 6 2
89 FINANCIAL REWARD (IRE) *WPMullins* 4-11-1 (t) BJGeraghty 11/2 10 3
Miss Mason (IRE) *KFO'Brien* 4-9-13 (s) SWFlanagan[7] 33/1 3 4
Island Life (IRE) *NMeade* 4-11-1 (b) PCarberry 6/1 8 5
Crookhaven *JohnJosephMurphy* 4-10-6 DGHogan[5] 50/1 5 6
Yellow Ridge (IRE) *LukeComer* 4-10-11 MJBolger[7] .... 100/1 dist 7
89 Robin du Bois (FR) *AJMartin* 4-10-11 DNRussell 15/8f 12 8
Roundofapplause *ThomasMullins* 4-10-11 RMPower 66/1 11 9
House of Bourbon (IRE) *CFSwan* 4-10-11 DFO'Regan 20/1 21 10
Jayo (FR) *WPMullins* 4-10-11 DJCondon .... 5/1 f
Avelian (IRE) *SJMahon* 4-10-11 (t) MDarcy .... 50/1 pu
Alltap (USA) *PJRothwell* 4-9-13 ShaneJackson[7] .... 33/1 pu

Mr D. J. Sharkey 13ran 4m16.90

166 **At The Races Bobbyjo Chase (Gr 2) (5yo+) £21,846** 3m1f (20)

121 HOMER WELLS (IRE) *WPMullins* 9-11-3 DJCondon 9/2 1
111 JACK HIGH (IRE) *TMWalsh* 12-11-3 DNRussell 9/1 2 2
111 POINT BARROW (IRE) *PatrickHughes* 9-11-6 PACarberry 5/2f 1¾ 3
Numbersixvalverde (IRE) *MartinBrassil* 11-11-3 NPMadden 7/2 1 4
121 Joueur d'Estruval (FR) *WPMullins* 10-11-3 BJGeraghty .... 12/1 dist 5
Garvivonnian (IRE) *EdwardPMitchell* 12-11-3 MJFerris .... 20/1 f
156 Watson Lake (IRE) *NMeade* 9-11-8 PCarberry .... 9/2 pu

Mrs M. McMahon 7ran 7m14.11

NAAS Sunday, Feb 25 HEAVY

167 **paddypower.com Johnstown Nov Hdle (Gr 2) (4yo+) £21,846** 2½m (11)

107 KAZAL (IRE) *EoinGriffin* 6-11-10 BJGeraghty 5/2f 1
CALLHERWHATULIKE (IRE) *RobertTyner* 6-11-0 RWalsh 9/1 1¼ 2

NOTRE PERE (FR) *JTRDreaper* 6-11-5 AELynch 5/1 16 3
Chomba Womba (IRE) *MsMMullins* 6-11-0 MDarcy 12/1 5 4
137 Albanov (IRE) *MrsJHarrington* 7-11-5 RMPower 14/1 ½ 5
Gripit N Tipit (IRE) *CFSwan* 6-11-5 DJCasey 12/1 9 6
Out In Front (IRE) *OliverMcKiernan* 8-11-5 NPMadden 14/1 2½ 7
Bridge Run (IRE) *NMeade* 6-11-5 PCarberry 7/2 3 8
Offaly (IRE) *NMeade* 6-11-5 DFO'Regan 9/1 8 9
Jack Absolute (IRE) *JohnJosephMurphy* 4-10-5 AndrewJMcNamara 33/1 12 10

Mr J. Comerford 10ran 5m14.44

168 paddypowerpoker.com Newlands Chase (Gr 2) (5yo+) £26,215 2m (10)

138 NICKNAME (FR) *MartinBrassil* 8-11-12 RWalsh 1/4f 1
GEMINI LUCY (IRE) *MrsJHarrington* 7-11-2 ADLeigh 13/2 12 2
LAKIL PRINCESS (IRE) *PaulNolan* 6-10-13 RMMoran 20/1 5 3
138 Tumbling Dice (IRE) *TJTaaffe* 8-11-10 BJGeraghty 10/1 17 4
Lala Nova (IRE) *JohnJosephMurphy* 8-10-13 SGMcDermott 66/1 23 5

Mrs Claudia Jungo-Corpataux 5ran 4m31.02

NEWBURY Saturday, Mar 3 SOFT

169 vccasino.com Gold Cup Hcap Chase (Gr 3) (1) (153) (5yo+) £45,616 2½m (16)

130 MADISON DU BERLAIS (FR) *DEPipe* 6-11-5^{146} TomScudamore 12/1 1
152 NOZIC (FR) *PFNicholls* 6-11-12^{153} (t) RWalsh 7/2 nk 2
70 NO FULL (FR) *PRWebber* 6-10-5^{132} MickFitzgerald 7/1 8 3
It Takes Time (IRE) *DEPipe* 13-10-6^{136} TomMalone^{3} 28/1 11 4
146 Supreme Prince (IRE) *PJHobbs* 10-11-4^{145} RichardJohnson 10/1 ½ 5
124 Fundamentalist (IRE) *NATwiston-Davies* 9-11-3^{144} TonyEvans 20/1 1¾ 6
Marcel (FR) *DEPipe* 7-10-10^{137} TimmyMurphy 11/2 1¾ 7
Flying Enterprise (IRE) *MissVenetiaWilliams* 7-10-7^{134} SamThomas 11/4f 1½ 8
155 Bold Bishop (IRE) *JonjoO'Neill* 10-11-0^{141} NoelFehily 28/1 2½ 9
130 Kalca Mome (FR) *PJHobbs* 9-11-2^{143} AndrewThornton 12/1 20 10
56 Kelrev (FR) *MissVenetiaWilliams* 9-10-1^{131} PCO'Neill^{3} 14/1 dist 11

Roger Stanley & Yvonne Reynolds II 11ran 5m07.37

THURLES Thursday, Mar 8 HEAVY

170 Michael Purcell Memorial Nov Hdle (Gr 2) (5yo+) £32,990 2½m (11)

167 KAZAL (FR) *EoinGriffin* 6-11-8 BJGeraghty 5/6f 1
167 CHOMBA WOMBA (IRE) *MsMMullins* 6-10-12 TPTreacy 16/1 3 2
137 HOLLY TREE (IRE) *ESheehy* 7-11-3 RLoughran 10/1 nk 3
Druids Castle (IRE) *JosephCrowley* 6-11-3 DNRussell 11/2 3½ 4
107 Casey Jones (IRE) *NMeade* 6-11-3 DFO'Regan 10/1 16 5
Midnight Gift (IRE) *THogan* 7-10-12 (t) PACarberry 20/1 2 6
Knowledge Box (IRE) *JohnJosephMurphy* 7-11-3 EFPower 14/1 ½ 7
Abbeybraney (IRE) *JABerry* 6-11-3 CO'Dwyer 10/1 dist 8
167 Gripit N Tipit (IRE) *CFSwan* 6-11-3 DJCasey 16/1 1¼ 9
Nay (FR) *WPMullins* 6-11-3 RWalsh 7/1 4½ 10
137 Turtle Dubh (IRE) *ESheehy* 6-11-3 MDarcy 16/1 dist 11
Comfort Zone (IRE) *ThomasFoley* 6-11-3 NPMadden 50/1 pu
Wickford (IRE) *ColmAMurphy* 8-11-3 AndrewJMcNamara 16/1 pu

Mr J. Comerford 13ran 5m23.09

SANDOWN Saturday, Mar 10 SOFT

The first flight in the back straight was omitted in both races due to the state of the ground

171 European Breeders' Fund Sunderlands NH Nov Hcap Hdle Final (Gr 3) (1) (132) (4, 5, 6 and 7yo) £34,212 2½m110y (8)

ALBERTAS RUN (IRE) *JonjoO'Neill* 6-10-9^{115} APMcCoy 6/1 1
39 DOUBLE EAGLE *DMcCainJnr* 5-10-10^{116} JasonMaguire 33/1 4 2
RED SCALLY *RCGuest* 7-10-6^{112} WarrenMarston 50/1 2 3
TAROTINO (FR) *NJHenderson* 5-11-1^{121} MickFitzgerald 13/2 ¾ 4
Otto Des Pictons (FR) *PFNicholls* 5-10-6^{112} RWalsh 5/1f hd 5
Trigger The Light *AKing* 6-11-10^{130} RobertThornton 11/1 5 6
151 The Sawyer (BEL) *RHBuckler* 7-11-2^{125} WTKennedy^{3} 14/1 2 7
Or Jaune (FR) *GLMoore* 5-10-11^{117} WayneHutchinson 8/1 ¾ 8
William Bonney (IRE) *CJMann* 7-11-4^{124} NoelFehily 16/1 8 9
Cathedral Rock (IRE) *NJGifford* 5-10-11^{117} TimmyMurphy 12/1 7 10
Sherwoods Folly *HDDaly* 5-11-0^{120} RichardJohnson 14/1 3½ 11
Youll Do For Me (IRE) *JonjoO'Neill* 5-10-7^{113} TonyDobbin 20/1 1 12
Glinton *MrsPSly* 5-11-7^{130} RobertLucey-Butler^{3} 20/1 1¾ 13
146 The Real Deal (IRE) *NickWilliams* 6-11-9^{132} DarylJacob^{3} 10/1 4 14
Troglodyte *MrsPRobeson* 5-10-4^{115} SPJones^{5} 25/1 12 15
Mr Shambles *SGollings* 6-9-11^{106} PhilKinsella^{3} 66/1 pu

Mr Trevor Hemmings 16ran 5m02.44

172 Sunderlands Imperial Cup Hcap Hdle (L) (1) 0-150(132) (4yo+)   2m110y (7)
£34,212

	GASPARA (FR) *DEPipe* 4-10-5[126] APMcCoy	11/4f	1
146	FLYING FALCON *MissVenetiaWilliams* 8-10-10[123] SamThomas	9/1	6 2
	MAGNESIUM (USA) *BGPowell* 7-9-9[113] (t) SPJones[5]	33/1	½ 3
	DHEHDAAH *MrsPSly* 6-10-11[124] WarrenMarston	33/1	3½ 4
	Border Castle *MissVenetiaWilliams* 6-10-12[128] (b) LiamTreadwell[3]	16/1	1¼ 5
	Swift Sailor *GLMoore* 6-10-0[113] (s) WayneHutchinson	14/1	¾ 6
106	Lunar Crystal (IRE) *DEPipe* 9-10-4[120] TomMalone[3]	33/1	4 7
	Mac Federal (IRE) *MissSWest* 5-11-1[128] JamieGoldstein	16/1	2 8
	Livingonaknifedge (IRE) *IanWilliams* 8-10-8[124] PCO'Neill[3]	16/1	½ 9
	Stoneraker (IRE) *PJRothwell,Ireland* 6-9-8[114] ShaneJackson[7]	11/2	1¼ 10
	Forest Green (FR) *PFNicholls* 5-10-7[120] (t) RWalsh	10/1	¾ 11
	Loughanelteen (IRE) *PJRothwell,Ireland* 9-10-4[117] RichardJohnson	16/1	8 12
	Farmer Brown (IRE) *PatrickHughes,Ireland* 6-11-3[130] TimmyMurphy	9/2	nk 13
	Nikola (FR) *NATwiston-Davies* 6-10-7[120] TonyEvans	50/1	½ 14
	Romany Prince *SGollings* 8-11-0[132] AndrewGlassonbury[5]	50/1	16 15
	Boss Imperial (IRE) *MrsLWadham* 4-10-10[131] JAMcCarthy	33/1	½ 16
	The Kop End (IRE) *JonjoO'Neill* 9-10-7[120] (t) NoelFehily	66/1	3 17

Mr M. C. Pipe 17ran 4m05.25

CHELTENHAM Tuesday, Mar 13
Hurdles and Cross Country Course: GOOD to SOFT, Chase Course: GOOD (Old Course)

173 Anglo Irish Bank Supreme Nov Hdle (Gr 1) (1) (4yo+) £68,424   2m110y (8)

	EBAZIYAN (IRE) *WPMullins,Ireland* 6-11-7 DJCondon	40/1	1
62	GRANIT JACK (FR) *PFNicholls* 5-11-7 (t) RWalsh	15/2	3 2
115	AMARETTO ROSE *NJHenderson* 6-11-0 MickFitzgerald	2/1f	nk 3
105	De Soto *PRWebber* 6-11-7 (t) RichardJohnson	12/1	¾ 4
	Wins Now *NMadden,Ireland* 6-11-7 APMcCoy	10/1	¾ 5
137	Kalderon (GER) *THogan,Ireland* 7-11-7 DJCasey	20/1	3½ 6
	Special Envoy (FR) *PBowen* 5-11-7 TJO'Brien	125/1	2½ 7
	Kicks For Free (IRE) *PFNicholls* 6-11-7 (t) SamThomas	22/1	2½ 8
	Tyson (SAF) *MissVenetiaWilliams* 7-11-7 PCO'Neill	12/1	1¼ 9
137	De Valira (IRE) *MJPO'Brien,Ireland* 5-11-7 AJMcNamara	10/1	½ 10
	Cedrus Libani (IRE) *JHowardJohnson* 6-11-7 PJBrennan	80/1	6 11
	Le Burf (FR) *GRISmyly* 6-11-7 GerardTumelty	150/1	3 12
137	Orbit O'Gold (USA) *NMeade,Ireland* 5-11-7 NPMadden	20/1	sh 13
80	Tipperary All Star (FR) *MHalford,Ireland* 7-11-7 TimmyMurphy	16/1	½ 14
129	Hide The Evidence (IRE) *MrsJHarrington,Ireland* 6-11-7 ADLeigh	9/1	6 15
	I'm So Lucky *RSBrookhouse* 5-11-7 (t) AlanO'Keeffe	50/1	1 16
	Shanghide *MFMorris,Ireland* 6-11-7 CO'Dwyer	80/1	13 17
	Hobbs Hill *CREgerton* 8-11-7 RobertThornton	20/1	4 18
	She's Our Daisy (IRE) *RHBuckler* 7-11-0 (t) DarylJacob	100/1	3½ 19
	Rindoon (IRE) *ESheehy,Ireland* 5-11-7 MJDarcy	16/1	½ 20
	Classic Role *LWells* 8-11-7 LeightonAspell	125/1	23 21
	Oh Danny Boy *MCChapman* 6-11-7 DavidCullinane	250/1	pu

Mr Peter Garvey 22ran 3m56.10

174 Irish Independent Arkle Challenge Trophy Chase (Gr 1) (1) (5yo+)   2m (12)
£96,934

116	MY WAY DE SOLZEN (FR) *AKing* 7-11-7 RobertThornton	7/2	1
64	FAIR ALONG (GER) *PJHobbs* 5-11-2 RichardJohnson	10/3f	5 2
93	JACK THE GIANT (IRE) *NJHenderson* 5-11-2 MickFitzgerald	14/1	1 3
59	Faasel (IRE) *NGRichards* 6-11-7 (b) TonyDobbin	16/1	¾ 4
119	Another Promise (IRE) *FerdyMurphy* 8-11-7 GLee	25/1	6 5
	Buena Vista (IRE) *DEPipe* 6-11-7 (t) TimmyMurphy	9/1	20 6
	Lennon (IRE) *JHowardJohnson* 7-11-7 PJBrennan	20/1	3½ 7
161	Good Spirit (IRE) *PFNicholls* 5-11-2 SamThomas	20/1	12 8
	Tidal Fury (IRE) *JJay* 5-11-2 LeightonAspell	16/1	1¾ 9
168	Gemini Lucy (IRE) *MrsJHarrington,Ireland* 6-11-7 ADLeigh	20/1	10 10
32	Don't Push It (IRE) *JonjoO'Neill* 7-11-7 APMcCoy	4/1	f
93	Twist Magic (FR) *PFNicholls* 5-11-7 RWalsh	12/1	f
128	Vintage Treasure (IRE) *CharlesByrnes,Ireland* 8-11-7 (s) CO'Dwyer	100/1	pu

B Winfield,A Longman,J Wright & C Fenton 13ran 3m51.40

175 Smurfit Kappa Champion Hdle Challenge Trophy (Gr 1) (1) (4yo+)   2m110y (8)
£205,272

	SUBLIMITY (FR) *JGCarr,Ireland* 7-11-10 (t) PACarberry	16/1	1
129	BRAVE INCA (FR) *ColmAMurphy,Ireland* 9-11-10 RWalsh	11/2	3 2
154	AFSOUN (FR) *NJHenderson* 5-11-10 MickFitzgerald	28/1	nk 3
129	Hardy Eustace (IRE) *DTHughes,Ireland* 10-11-10 (v) CO'Dwyer	3/1	nk 4
140	Kawagino (IRE) *JWMullins* 7-11-10 WayneKavanagh	100/1	15 5

1112

131	Detroit City (USA) *PJHobbs* 5-11-10 (b) RichardJohnson	6/4f	hd 6
129	Asian Maze (IRE) *ThomasMullins,Ireland* 8-11-3 RMPower	20/1	¾ 7
	Marble Garden (USA) *RichardChotard,France* 6-11-10 (b+t) JamesDavies	250/1	dist 8
129	Iktitaf (IRE) *NMeade,Ireland* 6-11-10 (t) BJGeraghty	14/1	f
154	Straw Bear (IRE) *NJGifford* 6-11-10 APMcCoy	7/1	pu

Mr W. Hennessy 10ran 3m55.65

176   **William Hill Trophy Hcap Chase (Gr 3) (1) (150) (5yo+)** £48,467   3m110y (19)

51	JOES EDGE (IRE) *FerdyMurphy* 10-10-6[130] DNRussell	50/1	1
91	JUVEIGNEUR (FR) *NJHenderson* 10-11-9[147] MickFitzgerald	7/1cf	sh 2
	DISTANT THUNDER (IRE) *NoelTChance* 9-10-11[135] AJMcNamara	7/1cf	sh 3
150	MON MOME (FR) *MissVenetiaWilliams* 7-11-1[142] LiamTreadwell[3]	16/1	8 4
136	Heez A Dreamer (IRE) *MissVenetiaWilliams* 7-11-0[138] SamThomas	20/1	2 5
126	New Alco (FR) *FerdyMurphy* 6-11-4[142] GLee	7/1cf	sh 6
56	Gallant Approach (IRE) *CREgerton* 8-11-3[141] PJBrennan	20/1	7 7
88	Ross Comm *MrsSJSmith* 11-10-7[131] DavidO'Meara	50/1	sh 8
134	Rambling Minster *KGReveley* 9-10-8[132] RichardMcGrath	8/1	1 9
91	All In The Stars (IRE) *DPKeane* 9-10-8[132] (b) NeilMulholland	40/1	3½ 10
162	Lacdoudal (FR) *PJHobbs* 8-11-12[150] RichardJohnson	20/1	5 11
150	Cornish Rebel (IRE) *PFNicholls* 10-11-9[147] (b) RWalsh	20/1	¾ 12
149	St Matthew (USA) *MrsSJSmith* 9-10-3[134] TjadeCollier[7]	80/1	½ 13
126	Innox (FR) *FDoumen,France* 11-11-2[140] (b) APMcCoy	20/1	1 14
139	King Harald (IRE) *MBradstock* 9-10-7[131] MattieBatchelor	28/1	8 15
133	Lord Sam (IRE) *VRADartnall* 11-10-12[141] (v) JamesWhite[5]	33/1	5 16
87	Ballycassidy (IRE) *PBowen* 11-11-2[140] (s) TJO'Brien	50/1	dist 17
150	Heltornic (IRE) *MScudamore* 7-10-12[136] TomScudamore	14/1	f
114	Irish Raptor (IRE) *NATwiston-Davies* 8-11-0[138] TomScudamore	20/1	ur
155	Little Brick (FR) *DEPipe* 8-11-7[150] AndrewGlassonbury[5]	15/2	pu
150	Sir Rembrandt (IRE) *RHAlner* 11-11-8[146] AndrewThornton	40/1	pu
87	Commercial Flyer (IRE) *DEPipe* 8-11-6[144] (t) TimmyMurphy	16/1	pu
110	D'Argent (IRE) *AKing* 10-11-3[141] RobertThornton	25/1	pu

Chemipetro Limited 23ran 6m15.97

177   **Sporting Index Hcap Chase (Cross Country) (2) (150) (5yo+)** £28,184   3m7f (32)

	HEADS ONTHE GROUND (IRE) *EndaBolger,Ireland* 10-10-2[126] MissNCarberry	5/2f	1
	SILVER BIRCH (IRE) *GElliott,Ireland* 10-11-0[138] (t) JasonMaguire	14/1	3½ 2
51	LE DUC (FR) *PFNicholls* 8-10-10[134] SamThomas	8/1	12 3
	SPOT THEDIFFERENCE (IRE) *EndaBolger,Ireland* 14-11-12[150] (s) MrJTMcNamara	6/1	5 4
136	Omni Cosmo Touch (IRE) *MrsSJSmith* 11-10-1[125] DavidO'Meara	25/1	5 5
139	Royal Auclair (FR) *PFNicholls* 10-11-5[143] (t) JoeTizzard	10/1	11 6
134	Florida Dream (IRE) *NATwiston-Davies* 8-10-0[124] (b) TonyEvans	33/1	1 7
	Il de Boitron (FR) *ThomasGerardO'Leary,Ireland* 9-10-0[124] PACarberry	25/1	2 8
	Never Compromise (IRE) *TMWalsh,Ireland* 12-9-11[124] MsKWalsh[3]	12/1	10 9
111	Marcus du Berlais (FR) *ALTMoore,Ireland* 8-10-6[130] (s) DNRussell	20/1	19 10
51	Native Jack (IRE) *PJRothwell,Ireland* 13-10-12[136] JCullen	20/1	6 11
	Ivoire de Beaulieu (FR) *FerdyMurphy* 10-10-7[131] AlanO'Keeffe	14/1	14 12
	Hever Road (FR) *DPearson* 8-9-13[126] ChrisHonour[3]	100/1	17 13
	Tyssac (FR) *BNPollock* 6-9-11[126] TomMessenger[5]	66/1	ur
150	L'Aventure (FR) *PFNicholls* 8-10-7[134] (t) PaddyMerrigan[3]	10/1	pu
50	Star Performance (IRE) *OliverMcKiernan,Ireland* 12-10-2[129] (s) TGMRyan[3]	10/1	pu

Mr John P. McManus 16ran 8m43.71

178   **Fred Winter Juv Nov Hcap Hdle (L) (1) (140) (4yo)** £42,765   2m110y (8)

172	GASPARA (FR) *DEPipe* 4-10-11[130] AndrewGlassonbury[5]	9/2jf	1
	ALTILHAR (USA) *GLMoore* 4-10-8[122] (b) NoelFehily	12/1	5 2
	LAUSTRA BAD (FR) *DEPipe* 4-11-0[128] (s) TomScudamore	16/1	nk 3
122	ZILCASH *AKing* 4-11-7[140] GerardTumelty[5]	50/1	3 4
	Midnight Traveller *ThomasCooper,Ireland* 4-10-2[119] SGMcDermott[3]	66/1	½ 5
	Junior *BJMeehan* 4-10-12[127] (b) PaulMoloney	25/1	¾ 6
167	Jack Absolute (IRE) *JohnJosephMurphy,Ireland* 4-9-13[120] EFPower[7]	66/1	5 7
165	Jayo (FR) *WPMullins,Ireland* 4-10-12[126] RWalsh	9/1	1 8
125	Celtic Warrior (IRE) *LiamRoche,Ireland* 4-10-7[121] DenisO'Regan	100/1	¾ 9
	Pouvoir (FR) *AKing* 4-10-0[124] RobertThornton	9/2jf	1 10
89	Deputy Consort (USA) *MJPO'Brien,Ireland* 4-10-6[123] (t) AELynch[3]	25/1	¾ 11
92	Warne's Way (IRE) *BGPowell* 4-10-7[126] SPJones[5]	50/1	3½ 12
	King's Revenge *AKing* 4-10-11[125] WayneHutchinson	28/1	1 13
	Belord (GER) *EJO'Grady,Ireland* 4-10-7[121] (v) PWFlood	16/1	½ 14
71	Risk Runner (IRE) *AKing* 4-10-5[119] (b) JAMcCarthy	40/1	14 15

	Stumped *HDDaly* 4-10-6[120] MarkBradburne	33/1	5	16
163	Gracechurch (IRE) *RJHodges* 4-10-5[122] PaddyMerrigan[3]	66/1	2½	17
	Markington *PBowen* 4-10-6[120] (s) PJBrennan	50/1	2½	18
	Shazand (FR) *EJO'Grady,Ireland* 4-10-5[119] TimmyMurphy	16/1	nk	19
92	Ned Ludd (IRE) *JGPortman* 4-11-4[132] SamThomas	33/1	½	20
92	Supsonic *PJHobbs* 4-10-11[125] TJO'Brien	100/1	5	21
	Silver Jaro (FR) *JonjoO'Neill* 4-10-7[121] (b) APMcCoy	12/1	3	22
	Madroos *JCulloty,Ireland* 4-10-7[121] TomDoyle	12/1	1½	23
125	Pancake (FR) *PJHobbs* 4-11-4[132] RichardJohnson	9/1	4	24

Mr M. C. Pipe 24ran 3m57.01

CHELTENHAM Wednesday, Mar 14   GOOD (Old Course)

179   Ballymore Properties Nov Hdle (Baring Bingham) (Gr 1) (1) (4yo+)   2m5f (10)
£68,424

122	MASSINI'S MAGUIRE (IRE) *PJHobbs* 6-11-7 RichardJohnson	20/1		1
122	TIDAL BAY (IRE) *JHowardJohnson* 6-11-7 PJBrennan	10/1	nk	2
143	CATCH ME (GER) *EJO'Grady,Ireland* 5-11-7 BJGeraghty	7/1	1½	3
105	Silverburn (IRE) *PFNicholls* 6-11-7 RWalsh	7/2	3½	4
143	Aran Concerto (IRE) *NMeade,Ireland* 6-11-7 APMcCoy	5/2f	5	5
105	My Turn Now (IRE) *CJMann* 5-11-7 NoelFehily	15/2	sh	6
75	Imperial Commander (IRE) *NATwiston-Davies* 6-11-7 TonyEvans	25/1	3½	7
	Scotsirish (IRE) *WPMullins,Ireland* 6-11-7 DJCondon	12/1	5	8
101	Battlecry *NATwiston-Davies* 6-11-7 TomScudamore	100/1	3	9
	Foligold (FR) *MrsJHarrington,Ireland* 5-11-7 (v) TPTreacy	66/1	10	10
	Hot Port (IRE) *EricMcNamara,Ireland* 5-11-7 RMPower	150/1	6	11
	Raslan *DEPipe* 4-10-12 (s) TimmyMurphy	25/1	13	12
	Duc de Regniere (FR) *NJHenderson* 5-11-7 MickFitzgerald	9/1	14	13
	Santando *PBowen* 7-11-7 TJO'Brien	150/1	11	14
	Johnnie Dillinger (IRE) *MFMorris,Ireland* 7-11-7 DNRussell	100/1		f

Mr Alan Peterson 15ran 5m05.40

180   Royal & SunAlliance Chase (Gr 1) (1) (5yo+) £96,934   3m110y (19)

60	DENMAN (IRE) *PFNicholls* 7-11-4 RWalsh	6/5f		1
160	SNOWY MORNING (IRE) *WPMullins,Ireland* 7-11-4 MickFitzgerald	10/1	10	2
147	ACCORDING TO JOHN (IRE) *NGRichards* 7-11-4 TonyDobbin	66/1	3½	3
	Aces Four (IRE) *FerdyMurphy* 8-11-4 GLee	25/1	nk	4
160	Gazza's Girl (IRE) *MrsJHarrington,Ireland* 7-10-11 BJGeraghty	28/1	1½	5
85	Ungaro (FR) *KGReveley* 8-11-4 TimmyMurphy	11/1	4	6
103	Turko (FR) *PFNicholls* 5-10-8 (t) SamThomas	9/1	½	7
144	Justpourit (IRE) *DTHughes,Ireland* 8-11-4 (s) RLoughran	66/1	9	8
145	Patsy Hall (IRE) *MichaelCunningham,Ireland* 7-11-4 RMPower	20/1	1½	9
54	Dom d'Orgeval (FR) *DEPipe* 7-11-4 APMcCoy	8/1	2½	10
136	Royal Rosa (FR) *JHowardJohnson* 8-11-4 (v) PJBrennan	50/1	4	11
126	Knowhere (IRE) *NATwiston-Davies* 9-11-4 TonyEvans	28/1	nk	12
98	Mossbank (IRE) *MHourigan,Ireland* 7-11-4 AndrewJMcNamara	66/1	10	13
7	Openide *BWDuke* 6-11-4 NoelFehily	100/1	1¼	14
124	Cailin Alainn (IRE) *CharlesByrnes,Ireland* 8-10-11 DNRussell	13/2		f
144	Chelsea Harbour (IRE) *ThomasMullins,Ireland* 7-11-4 DJCasey	50/1		ur
	Eurochancer (IRE) *JGFox,Ireland* 8-11-4 RMPNally	100/1		pu

Mrs M. Findlay & P. K. Barber 17ran 6m06.88

181   Seasons Holidays Queen Mother Champion Chase (Gr 1) (1) (5yo+)   2m (12)
£176,762

141	VOY POR USTEDES (FR) *AKing* 6-11-10 RobertThornton	5/1		1
130	DEMPSEY (IRE) *CarlLlewellyn* 9-11-10 NoelFehily	20/1	1½	2
148	RIVER CITY (IRE) *NoelTChance* 10-11-10 TomDoyle	33/1	5	3
157	Newmill (IRE) *JohnJosephMurphy,Ireland* 9-11-10 AJMcNamara	4/1	2½	4
117	Justified (IRE) *ESheehy,Ireland* 8-11-10 APMcCoy	20/1	17	5
113	Mister McGoldrick *CarlLlewellyn* 10-11-10 PaulMoloney	33/1	1	6
28	Sybellius d'Artaix (FR) *RichardChotard,France* 7-11-10 (t) JamesDavies	150/1	22	7
141	Ashley Brook (IRE) *KBishop* 9-11-10 PJBrennan	10/1		f
130	Oneway (IRE) *MGRimell* 10-11-10 (b) RichardJohnson	50/1		f
141	Well Chief (GER) *DEPipe* 8-11-10 TimmyMurphy	1/1f		f

Sir Robert Ogden 10ran 3m53.88

182   Coral Cup (Hcap Hdle) (Gr 3) (1) (151) (5yo+) £45,616   2m5f (10)

	BURNTOAKBOY *DrRDPNewland* 9-9-12[128] SPJones[5]	10/1		1
	POWERSTATION (IRE) *MPhillips,Ireland* 7-11-0[139] DenisO'Regan	12/1	3	2
112	BARON de FEYPO (IRE) *PatrickOBrady,Ireland* 9-10-3[133] NO'Shea[5]	20/1	5	3
	OSCATELLO (USA) *PJHobbs* 7-10-8[133] RichardJohnson	8/1	1½	4
140	Mister Hight (FR) *WPMullins,Ireland* 5-11-6[145] RWalsh	8/1	1½	5
169	Supreme Prince (IRE) *PJHobbs* 10-10-9[134] TJO'Brien	66/1	1¼	6

111	Oulart *DTHughes,Ireland* 8-10-9[137] (s) RLoughran[3]	16/1	nk	7
	Dusky Lord *NJGifford* 8-10-5[130] BarryFenton	33/1	sh	8
	Dusky Warbler *GLMoore* 8-11-0[139] WayneHutchinson	33/1	½	9
112	Ross River *AJMartin,Ireland* 11-10-4[129] DNRussell	14/1	hd	10
133	Nathos (GER) *CJMann* 10-10-7[132] NoelFehily	33/1	hd	11
	The Spoonplayer (IRE) *HenrydeBromhead,Ireland* 8-10-1[129] AELynch[3]	20/1	¾	12
151	Hills of Aran *WKGoldsworthy* 5-10-5[130] GLee	33/1	½	13
146	Mahogany Blaze (FR) *NATwiston-Davies* 5-10-12[137] TomScudamore	40/1	½	14
108	Rayshan (IRE) *NGRichards* 7-10-2[132] MissRDavidson[5]	40/1	1¼	15
79	Copsale Lad *NJHenderson* 10-10-12[137] MarcusFoley	6/1f	¾	16
159	Emotional Moment (IRE) *TJTaaffe,Ireland* 10-11-5[151] (s+t) ABJoyce[7]	50/1	nk	17
133	Golden Bay *MissSuzySmith* 8-10-4[132] DarylJacob[3]	20/1	1	18
146	Nation State *GLMoore* 6-10-2[127] (b) PaulMoloney	12/1	nk	19
133	Royals Darling (GER) *NJHenderson* 5-11-0[139] AndrewTinkler	18/1	½	20
133	Verasi *GLMoore* 6-10-8[138] (b) EamonDehdashti[5]	16/1	1¼	21
	Royal Paradise (FR) *PRWebber* 7-10-8[133] (b) SamThomas	66/1	6	22
146	Turtle Soup (IRE) *TRGeorge* 11-10-1[131] WillieMcCarthy[5]	50/1	¾	23
	Dangerously Good *JHowardJohnson* 9-10-3[128] (b) TonyDobbin	50/1	10	24
152	Redemption *NATwiston-Davies* 12-11-8[147] TonyEvans	66/1	24	25
153	All Star (GER) *NJHenderson* 7-10-7[132] MickFitzgerald	11/1	2½	26
	Penny Pictures *DEPipe* 8-10-11[136] TimmyMurphy	33/1	9	27
108	Finger Onthe Pulse (IRE) *TJTaaffe,Ireland* 6-11-8[147] BJGeraghty	18/1	ur	

Dr R. D. P. And Mrs L. J. Newland 28ran 5m06.90

183 Fulke Walwyn Kim Muir Challenge Cup Hcap Chase (Amat) (2) 3m110y (19)
0-140(139) (5yo+) £33,011

150	CLOUDY LANE *DMcCainJnr* 7-10-11[124] MrRBurton	15/2f		1
55	PARSONS LEGACY (IRE) *PJHobbs* 9-11-3[130] MrDerekO'Connor	12/1	¾	2
121	CHEEKY LADY (IRE) *ColmAMurphy,Ireland* 10-10-7[123] MrRO'Sullivan[3]	20/1	2	3
	PONMEOATH (IRE) *EricMcNamara,Ireland* 7-11-1[131] MrJJDoyle[3]	16/1	½	4
9	Darby Wall (IRE) *EndaBolger,Ireland* 9-11-4[131] MissNCarberry	12/1	1½	5
155	Napolitain (FR) *PFNicholls* 6-11-3[137] MrNScholfield[7]	50/1	1¾	6
134	Turthen (FR) *PFNicholls* 6-11-5[132] (t) MrJSnowden	12/1	2½	7
91	Lou du Moulin Mas (FR) *PFNicholls* 8-11-5[132] (t) MrTGreenall	10/1	13	8
70	Liberthine (FR) *NJHenderson* 8-11-8[138] MrSWaley-Cohen[3]	9/1	nk	9
169	It Takes Time (IRE) *DEPipe* 13-11-6[136] MrDEdwards[3]	25/1	11	10
	Almost Broke *GBrown* 10-10-13[129] MissLHorner[3]	100/1	1¾	11
	Maletton (FR) *MissVenetiaWilliams* 7-11-2[134] MrWBiddick[5]	14/1	5	12
	Lord of Illusion (IRE) *TRGeorge* 10-11-6[138] MrSWByrne[5]	14/1	hd	13
17	Oodachee *CFSwan,Ireland* 8-11-4[131] (s) MrLPFlynn	16/1	6	14
134	Yardbird (IRE) *AKing* 8-11-1[128] MrKEPower	20/1	nk	15
	Direct Flight (IRE) *CREgerton* 9-11-1[128] (t) MrJJCodd	9/1	dist	16
127	Little Big Horse (IRE) *MrsSJSmith* 11-11-4[131] MrROHarding	40/1	14	17
127	Nadover (FR) *CJMann* 6-11-7[134] MrPCashman	33/1	f	
82	The Bajan Bandit (IRE) *LLungo* 12-11-7[139] (b) MrMJO'Hare[3]	66/1	ur	
	Lady of Scarvagh (IRE) *MScudamore* 8-10-9[125] MrJPMcKeown[3]	28/1	ur	
150	Naunton Brook *NATwiston-Davies* 8-11-6[136] (t) MrRMorgan[3]	33/1	pu	
	Patricksnineteenth (IRE) *PRWebber* 11-11-3[133] MrRHFowler[3]	16/1	pu	
	Alright Now M'Lad (IRE) *JonjoO'Neill* 7-11-5[132] MrJTMcNamara[3]	16/1	pu	
177	Tyssac (FR) *BNPollock* 6-10-6[126] MrAMerriam[7]	100/1	pu	

Mr Trevor Hemmings 24ran 6m14.12

184 Weatherbys Champion Bumper (Standard Open NHF) (Gr 1) (1) 2m110y
(4, 5 and 6yo) £28,510

39	CORK ALL STAR (IRE) *MrsJHarrington,Ireland* 5-11-5 BJGeraghty	11/2		1
	SOPHOCLES *JamesLeavy,Ireland* 4-10-11 MissPaulineRyan	40/1	1¼	2
	ARANLEIGH (IRE) *AnthonyMullins,Ireland* 5-11-5 APMcCoy	8/1	1½	3
	Shirley Casper (IRE) *PhilipFenton,Ireland* 6-10-12 AJMcNamara	25/1	nk	4
	Fiveforthree (IRE) *WPMullins,Ireland* 5-11-5 MsKWalsh	16/1	¾	5
142	Crocodiles Rock (IRE) *JonjoO'Neill* 5-11-5 FMBerry	20/1	1	6
	Cooldine (IRE) *WPMullins,Ireland* 5-11-5 DJCondon	50/1	1	7
	Mad Fish (IRE) *WPMullins,Ireland* 5-11-5 (t) RWalsh	4/1f	1	8
	One Gulp *PRWebber* 4-10-4 AndrewTinkler	16/1	5	9
	Lodge Lane (IRE) *VRADartnall* 6-11-5 JamesWhite	33/1	1½	10
	Tot O'Whiskey *JMJefferson* 6-11-5 FergusKing	10/1	1	11
	Isn't That Lucky *JonjoO'Neill* 4-10-11 MrAlanBerry	50/1	1¾	12
	Whatuthink (IRE) *OliverMcKiernan,Ireland* 5-11-5 MrRPQuinlan	25/1	2	13
	Raven's Run (IRE) *MichaelCunningham,Ireland* 5-11-5 DNRussell	20/1	hd	14
142	Just A Thought (IRE) *HJLDunlop* 4-10-11 NoelFehily	33/1	2½	15
	Judge Roy Bean (IRE) *EJO'Grady,Ireland* 4-10-11 MrJPMagnier	25/1	½	16
	Den of Iniquity *CarlLlewellyn* 6-11-5 CarlLlewellyn	7/1	1¼	17
	Berings Express (FR) *NClement,France* 4-10-11 TJO'Brien	16/1	¾	18
	Choumakeur (FR) *DEPipe* 5-11-5 TomScudamore	40/1	18	19

Le Beau Bai (FR) *DEPipe* 4-10-11 AndrewGlassonbury.............................. 100/1   7 20
Sergheyev *DEPipe* 4-10-11 TimmyMurphy 33/1   12 21
Sir Harry Ormesher *CJDown* 4-10-11 ChrisHonour 40/1   8 22
Fiddling Again *NJHenderson* 4-10-6 MickFitzgerald 18/1   11 23
Enquiring Mind (IRE) *EJO'Grady,Ireland* 5-11-5 JamieSpencer .... 8/1   pu

Mr Cathal M. Ryan 24ran 3m47.44

CHELTENHAM Thursday, Mar 15   GOOD (New Course)

185   **Jewson Nov Hcap Chase (L) (1) (146) (5yo+)** £45,616   2m5f (17)

	L'ANTARTIQUE (FR) *FerdyMurphy* 7-10-11[133] GLee	20/1	1
93	BOB HALL (IRE) *JonjoO'Neill* 6-10-9[131] (t) NoelFehily	10/1	2 2
147	WEE ROBBIE *NJGifford* 7-10-13[135] LeightonAspell	20/1	2½ 3
119	RASHARROW (IRE) *LLungo* 8-10-10[132] KeithMercer	14/1	4 4
144	Vic Venturi (IRE) *PhilipFenton,Ireland* 7-10-12[134] AJMcNamara	14/1	1¼ 5
	Kings Advocate (IRE) *TJTaaffe,Ireland* 7-10-12[134] BJGeraghty	9/1	1 6
132	New Little Bric (FR) *PFNicholls* 6-11-10[146] RWalsh	7/2f	1 7
	Milan Deux Mille (FR) *DEPipe* 5-10-13[144] TomMalone[3]	50/1	3½ 8
169	Flying Enterprise (IRE) *MissVenetiaWilliams* 7-10-9[134] LiamTreadwell[3]	16/1	3 9
	Dictum (GER) *MrsSusanNock* 9-10-12[134] TomScudamore	25/1	8 10
156	Knight Legend (IRE) *MrsJHarrington,Ireland* 8-11-3[139] RMPower	22/1	3½ 11
132	Aztec Warrior (IRE) *MissHCKnight* 6-11-1[137] DNRussell	20/1	8 12
	Phar Bleu (FR) *PFNicholls* 6-10-9[134] LiamHeard[3]	50/1	3 13
	Limited Edition (IRE) *CarlLlewellyn* 9-10-13[135] MickFitzgerald	10/1	f
80	Chief Yeoman *MissVenetiaWilliams* 7-10-9[134] SamThomas	16/1	f
	Pole Star *EvanWilliams* 9-11-1[137] (s) PaulMoloney	25/1	ur
153	Desert Air (JPN) *DEPipe* 8-10-9[136] (s+t) AndrewGlassonbury[5]	50/1	pu
	Tora Bora (GER) *BGPowell* 5-10-12[140] (s) TimmyMurphy	33/1	pu
	King Revo (IRE) *PCHaslam* 7-10-10[132] APMcCoy	5/1	pu

Mrs A. N. Durkan 19ran 5m10.62

186   **Ryanair Chase (Festival) (Gr 2) (1) (5yo+)** £99,785   2m5f (17)

133	TARANIS (FR) *PFNicholls* 6-11-0 (t) RWalsh	9/2	1
124	OUR VIC (IRE) *DEPipe* 9-11-5 TimmyMurphy	7/2	nk 2
79	BILLYVODDAN (IRE) *HDDaly* 8-11-0 (b) RichardJohnson	20/1	½ 3
148	Monet's Garden (IRE) *NGRichards* 9-11-5 TonyDobbin	7/4f	3½ 4
108	Racing Demon (IRE) *MissHCKnight* 7-11-3 GLee	6/1	¾ 5
145	Hi Cloy (IRE) *MHourigan,Ireland* 10-11-5 AJMcNamara	20/1	7 6
148	Thisthatandtother (IRE) *PFNicholls* 11-11-0 SamThomas	16/1	hd 7
104	Too Forward (IRE) *CarlLlewellyn* 11-11-0 PaulMoloney	16/1	28 8
	Crozan (FR) *NJHenderson* 7-11-0 (b) MickFitzgerald	20/1	f

Mrs A. B. Yeoman & Mr C. R. Whittaker 9ran 5m10.47

187   **Ladbrokes World Hdle (Gr 1) (1) (4yo+)** £149,027   3m (12)

123	INGLIS DREVER *JHowardJohnson* 8-11-10 PJBrennan	5/1	1
81	MIGHTY MAN (FR) *HDDaly* 7-11-10 RichardJohnson	10/3	¾ 2
123	BLAZING BAILEY *AKing* 5-11-10 RobertThornton	8/1	4 3
158	United (GER) *MrsLWadham* 6-11-3 LeightonAspell	22/1	9 4
133	Kasbah Bliss (FR) *FDoumen,France* 5-11-10 ADuchene	12/1	3 5
120	Strangely Brown (IRE) *EricMcNamara,Ireland* 6-11-10 DJCasey	50/1	8 6
161	Natal (FR) *PFNicholls* 6-11-10 (t) RWalsh	16/1	7 7
149	Labelthou (IRE) *MissECLavelle* 8-11-3 BarryFenton	20/1	2½ 8
123	Lough Derg (FR) *DEPipe* 7-11-10 (v) TomScudamore	40/1	9 9
147	Over The Creek *DEPipe* 8-11-10 (s) TimmyMurphy	100/1	¾ 10
123	Fire Dragon (FR) *JonjoO'Neill* 6-11-10 (b) NoelFehily	50/1	4 11
146	Overstrand (IRE) *DrRDPNewland* 8-11-10 SPJones	20/1	17 12
81	Temoin *NJHenderson* 7-11-10 (b) MickFitzgerald	25/1	dist 13
123	Black Jack Ketchum (IRE) *JonjoO'Neill* 8-11-10 APMcCoy	2/1f	f

Andrea & Graham Wylie 14ran 5m46.63

188   **Racing Post Plate (Hcap Chase) (Gr 3) (1) (155) (5yo+)** £57,020   2m5f (17)

152	IDOLE FIRST (IRE) *MissVenetiaWilliams* 8-10-7[136] AlanO'Keeffe	12/1	1
	PALARSHAN (FR) *HDDaly* 9-10-5[134] (s) RichardJohnson	28/1	4 2
104	MARIAH ROLLINS (IRE) *NJHenderson* 9-10-7[136] MickFitzgerald	20/1	1¼ 3
126	LE VOLFONI (FR) *PFNicholls* 6-11-2[145] JoeTizzard	16/1	hd 4
121	Slim Pickings (IRE) *TJTaaffe,Ireland* 8-10-11[140] BJGeraghty	33/1	¾ 5
73	Reveillez *JRFanshawe* 8-11-2[145] (t) NoelFehily	12/1	½ 6
169	Madison du Berlais (FR) *DEPipe* 6-11-9[152] TomScudamore	14/1	2½ 7
162	Iron Man (FR) *PBowen* 6-10-0[129] WayneHutchinson	50/1	3 8
50	Hakim (NZ) *JLSpearing* 13-10-0[129] SEDurack	100/1	nk 9
126	Roman Ark *JMJefferson* 9-11-0[143] FergusKing	33/1	1½ 10
148	Vodka Bleu (FR) *DEPipe* 8-10-13[142] TimmyMurphy	11/1	4 11
134	Tikram *AKing* 10-10-8[137] (b) RobertThornton	9/1	½ 12

141	Armaturk (FR) *PFNicholls* 10-11-12[155] SamThomas	50/1	½ 13
	Moncadou (FR) *TDoumen,France* 7-10-4[133] (t) APMcCoy	5/1	¾ 14
169	Bold Bishop (IRE) *JonjoO'Neill* 10-10-12[141] (s) RichardMcGrath	33/1	3 15
121	Livingstonebramble (IRE) *WPMullins,Ireland* 11-10-12[141] DJCondon	50/1	5 16
169	No Full (FR) *PRWebber* 6-10-2[131] AndrewTinkler	20/1	½ 17
42	Kill Devil Hill (IRE) *PaulNolan,Ireland* 7-11-3[146] JLCullen	20/1	hd 18
153	Opera Mundi (FR) *PFNicholls* 5-10-7[142] RWalsh	7/2f	9 19
	Nycteos (FR) *PFNicholls* 6-10-0[132] LiamHeard[3]	20/1	12 20
79	Graphic Approach (IRE) *CREgerton* 9-10-9[138] (b) PJBrennan	16/1	ur
169	Kelrev (FR) *MissVenetiaWilliams* 9-9-13[131] LiamTreadwell[3]	50/1	pu
56	Big Rob (IRE) *BGPowell* 8-10-1[130] LeightonAspell	33/1	pu

D and J Racing Ltd 23ran 5m11.44

189 NH Chase Challenge Cup (Amat Nov Chase) (2) (5yo+) £30,010   4m1f (27)

73	BUTLER'S CABIN (FR) *JonjoO'Neill* 7-12-0 (s) MrAlanBerry	33/1	1
	CHARACTER BUILDING (IRE) *JJQuinn* 7-12-0 MrDerekO'Connor	7/1	¾ 2
	COUNTESS TRIFALDI (IRE) *MPhillips,Ireland* 7-11-0 MrCJSweeney	100/1	10 3
	High Cotton (IRE) *KGReveley* 12-11-7 MrDThomas	50/1	8 4
	Tobar Isaun (IRE) *PaulARoche,Ireland* 8-11-1 MrDRoche	40/1	10 5
111	Hordago (IRE) *EricMcNamara,Ireland* 7-11-11 (s) MrBHassett	33/1	6 6
	Petertheknot (IRE) *ThomasCooper,Ireland* 9-11-7 MrMJO'Connor	66/1	2 7
	Ballytrim (IRE) *WPMullins,Ireland* 6-11-11 MrJJCodd	16/1	12 8
	Garde Champetre (FR) *JonjoO'Neill* 8-11-11 (s) MrJTMcNamara	12/1	2½ 9
	The Reverend (IRE) *JHowardJohnson* 7-11-11 MrMJO'Hare	33/1	dist 10
	Fair Question (IRE) *MissVenetiaWilliams* 9-12-0 MrWBiddick	12/1	f
147	Gungadu *PFNicholls* 7-12-0 MrJSnowden	2/1f	f
	Not Left Yet (IRE) *DEPipe* 6-11-11 MrDEdwards	16/1	f
	Swift Thyne (IRE) *TRGeorge* 7-11-11 MrSWByrne	40/1	ur
164	Nine de Sivola (FR) *FerdyMurphy* 6-11-7 MrROHarding	11/2	f
69	Mac Three (IRE) *NMeade,Ireland* 8-11-11 MissNCarberry	12/1	f
136	Miko de Beauchene (FR) *RHAlner* 7-11-11 MrMGMiller	11/1	ur
	Bengo (IRE) *BDeHaan* 7-11-7 MrFelixdeGiles	50/1	ur
	Woodstock Lass (IRE) *MissFSlevin,Ireland* 8-11-0 (s+t) MrDWCullen	100/1	ur

Mr John P. McManus 19ran 8m38.24

190 Pertemps Final (Hcap Hdle) (L) (1) (157) (5yo+) £39,914   3m (11)

What should have been the second last was omitted

133	OSCAR PARK (IRE) *DWPArbuthnot* 8-10-9[140] (t) TomDoyle	14/1	1
149	MATERIAL WORLD *MissSuzySmith* 9-10-9[143] (ec) ColinBolger[3]	14/1	½ 2
42	ADAMANT APPROACH (IRE) *WPMullins,Ireland* 13-10-13[151] MrPWMullins[7]	16/1	3½ 3
48	MISTANOORA *NATwiston-Davies* 8-10-0[131] (b) TonyEvans	33/1	½ 4
	Ostfanni (IRE) *MTodhunter* 7-10-0[131] GLee	28/1	3½ 5
48	Desert Tommy *EvanWilliams* 6-9-9[131] (v) SPJones[5]	40/1	3½ 6
	Monolith *LLungo* 9-10-4[135] KeithMercer	10/1	2½ 7
82	Just Beth *GFierro* 11-9-9[131] DerekLaverty[5]	20/1	2 8
82	Rhinestone Cowboy (IRE) *JonjoO'Neill* 11-11-9[157] MrJPMagnier[3]	12/1	1½ 9
34	Jockser (IRE) *JWMullins* 6-9-9[131] WayneKavanagh[5]	11/1	1¾ 10
82	Magnifico (FR) *MrsKWaldron* 6-9-11[133] (v+t) AndrewGlassonbury[5]	100/1	4 11
	Freetown (IRE) *LLungo* 11-10-3[134] (b) RWalsh	16/1	1 12
88	Julius Caesar *JHowardJohnson* 7-10-0[131] PJBrennan	100/1	2½ 13
34	Attorney General (IRE) *JABOld* 8-10-8[139] (s+t) JasonMaguire	9/1	1¾ 14
158	Refinement (IRE) *JonjoO'Neill* 8-10-13[149] (b) MrAlanBerry[5]	20/1	5 15
	Rowley Hill *AKing* 9-10-2[133] (b) RobertThornton	25/1	2½ 16
133	Arrayou (FR) *OSherwood* 6-10-1[132] (v) LeightonAspell	33/1	1¼ 17
	Kadoun (IRE) *MJPO'Brien,Ireland* 10-11-5[150] APMcCoy	13/2f	7 18
	The Last Cast *EvanWilliams* 8-9-9[131] (b) TomMessenger[5]	66/1	19 19
48	Millenium Royal (FR) *FDoumen,France* 7-11-9[157] ADuchene[3]	14/1	6 20
	Hirvine (FR) *DMcCainJnr* 9-10-5[136] (s) TonyDobbin	16/1	11 21
34	His Nibs (IRE) *AKing* 10-10-5[136] WayneHutchinson	33/1	29 22
24	Cloudy Bays (IRE) *CharlesByrnes,Ireland* 10-10-4[135] (s) DNRussell	14/1	f
28	Nirvana du Bourg (FR) *NJHenderson* 6-10-0[131] (s) MarcusFoley	8/1	pu

Mr George Ward 24ran 5m45.81

CHELTENHAM Friday, Mar 16   GOOD (New Course)

191 JCB Triumph Hdle (Gr 1) (1) (4yo) £68,424   2m1f (8)

125	KATCHIT (IRE) *AKing* 4-11-0 RobertThornton	11/2	1
	LIBERATE *PJHobbs* 4-11-0 RichardJohnson	12/1	9 2
	MOBAASHER (USA) *CJMann* 4-11-0 NoelFehily	33/1	1¾ 3
163	Punjabi *NJHenderson* 4-11-0 MickFitzgerald	9/1	6 4
165	J'Y Vole (FR) *WPMullins,Ireland* 4-10-7 DJCasey	33/1	6 5
163	Poquelin (FR) *PFNicholls* 4-11-0 SamThomas	50/1	¾ 6

1117

165	Crookhaven *JohnJosephMurphy,Ireland* 4-11-0 AJMcNamara	150/1	1¼	7
165	Financial Reward (IRE) *WPMullins,Ireland* 4-11-0 (s+t) RWalsh	33/1	nk	8
	Lightning Strike (GER) *MissVenetiaWilliams* 4-11-0 TomScudamore	25/1	2	9
129	Lounaos (IRE) *EoinGriffin,Ireland* 4-10-7 BJGeraghty	7/2f	2	10
	My Petra *AKing* 4-10-7 WayneHutchinson	50/1	1¼	11
	Degas Art (IRE) *JHowardJohnson* 4-11-0 PJBrennan	7/1	1	12
	Alqaab (USA) *NMeade,Ireland* 4-11-0 DenisO'Regan	18/1	nk	13
89	Convincing *JohnJosephMurphy,Ireland* 4-11-0 EFPower	33/1	1¼	14
31	Freeze The Flame (GER) *CREgerton* 4-11-0 GLee	25/1	18	15
163	Lord Adonis (IRE) *KJBurke* 4-11-0 (b) PaddyMerrigan	200/1	1	16
92	Darusso *JSMoore* 4-11-0 JamesDavies	200/1	1¼	17
	Counting House (IRE) *JABOld* 4-11-0 JasonMaguire	50/1	3	18
165	Duty (IRE) *KFO'Brien,Ireland* 4-11-0 NPMadden	9/1	dist	19
	Khachaturian (IRE) *DMcCainJnr* 4-11-0 SJCraine	150/1		f
	Mountain (IRE) *JonjoO'Neill* 4-11-0 APMcCoy	8/1		pu
163	Parrain (FR) *FDoumen,France* 4-11-0 ADuchene	33/1		pu
125	Pauillac (FR) *DEPipe* 4-11-0 TimmyMurphy	22/1		pu

D S J P Syndicate 23ran 3m54.53

192 **Brit Insurance Nov Hdle (Spa) (Gr 2) (1) (4yo+)** £45,616 3m (12)

122	WICHITA LINEMAN (IRE) *JonjoO'Neill* 6-11-7 APMcCoy	11/8f		1
75	AIR FORCE ONE (GER) *CJMann* 5-11-7 NoelFehily	25/1	12	2
151	ITSA LEGEND *AKing* 8-11-7 RobertThornton	100/1	6	3
123	Flight Leader (IRE) *CLTizzard* 7-11-7 JoeTizzard	11/2	2	4
172	Mac Federal (IRE) *MissSWest* 5-11-7 JamieGoldstein	100/1	3	5
135	Negus de Beaumont (FR) *FerdyMurphy* 6-11-7 GLee	40/1	½	6
	Here's Johnny (IRE) *VRADartnall* 8-11-7 MattieBatchelor	100/1	nk	7
151	Chief Dan George (IRE) *JamesMoffatt* 7-11-7 (s) AlanDempsey	20/1	2	8
151	Joaaci (IRE) *DEPipe* 7-11-7 (s+t) TimmyMurphy	66/1	nk	9
	Ornais (FR) *PFNicholls* 5-11-7 (t) SamThomas	50/1	1½	10
	Hairy Molly (IRE) *JosephCrowley,Ireland* 7-11-7 BJGeraghty	7/1	1¾	11
	Skippers Brig (IRE) *LLungo* 6-11-7 KeithMercer	66/1	11	12
	Secret Ploy *HMorrison* 7-11-7 (b) AndrewTinkler	28/1	4	13
143	Leading Run (IRE) *NMeade,Ireland* 6-11-7 NPMadden	25/1	8	14
	Head Held High (IRE) *MrsJHarrington,Ireland* 6-11-7 RMPower	40/1	18	15
	Mr Strachan (IRE) *MrsSJSmith* 6-11-7 MichaelO'Connell	40/1	3½	16
101	Sir Jimmy Shand (IRE) *JJHenderson* 6-11-7 MickFitzgerald	9/1	3½	17
	Black Harry (IRE) *WPMullins,Ireland* 7-11-7 RWalsh	13/2		f
	Celtic Major (IRE) *MissHLewis* 9-11-7 AndrewGlassonbury	100/1		pu
	Vinando *CREgerton* 6-11-7 (b+t) PJBrennan	50/1		pu

Mr John P. McManus 20ran 5m43.60

193 **totesport Cheltenham Gold Cup Chase (Gr 1) (1) (5yo+)** £242,335 3¼m110y (22)

139	KAUTO STAR (FR) *PFNicholls* 7-11-10 (t) RWalsh	5/4f		1
124	EXOTIC DANCER (FR) *JonjoO'Neill* 7-11-10 (t) APMcCoy	9/2	2½	2
114	TURPIN GREEN (IRE) *NGRichards* 8-11-10 (b) TonyDobbin	40/1	2½	3
87	Monkerhostin (FR) *PJHobbs* 10-11-10 RichardJohnson	25/1	5	4
97	Cane Brake (IRE) *TJTaaffe,Ireland* 8-11-10 (s) DJCasey	20/1	¾	5
55	State of Play *EvanWilliams* 7-11-10 PaulMoloney	8/1	½	6
139	L'Ami (FR) *FDoumen,France* 8-11-10 MickFitzgerald	16/1	1¼	7
124	Neptune Collonges (FR) *PFNicholls* 6-11-10 LiamHeard	50/1	sh	8
47	Kingscliff (IRE) *RHAlner* 10-11-10 RobertWalford	40/1	1½	9
145	Forget The Past *MJPO'Brien,Ireland* 9-11-10 (t) BJGeraghty	25/1	2½	10
145	The Listener (IRE) *RHAlner* 8-11-10 DarylJacob	14/1	2½	11
155	My Will (FR) *PFNicholls* 7-11-10 SamThomas	16/1	8	12
145	Beef Or Salmon (IRE) *MHourigan,Ireland* 11-11-10 (b) AJMcNamara	16/1	8	13
181	Sybellius d'Artaix (FR) *RichardChotard,France* 7-11-10 (t) JamesDavies	250/1	dist	14
175	Marble Garden (USA) *RichardChotard,France* 6-11-10 (b+t) JohnKington	250/1		f
124	Idle Talk (IRE) *DMcCainJnr* 8-11-10 JasonMaguire	50/1		ur
58	Bob Bob Bobbin *CLTizzard* 8-11-10 JoeTizzard	100/1		pu
124	Halcon Genelardais (FR) *AKing* 7-11-10 (b) RobertThornton	25/1		pu

Mr Clive D. Smith 18ran 6m40.93

194 **Christie's Foxhunt Chase Challenge Cup (2) (5yo+)** £24,008 3¼m110y (22)

	DROMBEAG (IRE) *JonjoO'Neill* 9-12-0 (s) MrJTMcNamara	20/1		1
	WHYSO MAYO (IRE) *RaymondHurley,Ireland* 10-12-0 MrDMurphy	2/1f	½	2
	NED KELLY (IRE) *EJO'Grady,Ireland* 11-12-0 MrKEPower	20/1	15	3
	Oscar India (IRE) *HenrydeBromhead,Ireland* 8-12-0 MrJEBurns	25/1	1½	4
	Bica (IRE) *RWaley-Cohen* 7-12-0 MrSWaley-Cohen	9/1	nk	5
	Arctic Times (IRE) *EugeneMO'Sullivan,Ireland* 11-12-0 (s) MrRPMcLernon	66/1	5	6
	Knife Edge (USA) *JonjoO'Neill* 12-12-0 (s) MrAlanBerry	25/1	2	7
	Cobreces *MrsLBorradaile* 9-12-0 MrJSnowden	25/1	11	8

1118

Sonevafushi (FR) *MissVenetiaWilliams* 9-12-0 MrTGreenall .... 16/1   nk 9
Climate Control (IRE) *JohnPaulBrennan,Ireland* 11-12-0 (t)   6 10
    MrColinMotherway 14/1
Carryonharry (IRE) *MissELeppard* 13-12-0 (s) MissCHaydon.................... 33/1   2 11
Big Zoomo (IRE) *SeanMcParlan,Ireland* 13-12-0 MrNMcParlan.............. 50/1   1¼ 12
Honourable Spider *MrsSuzyBull* 8-12-0 MrPBull 10/1   28 13
First Down Jets (IRE) *WJBurke,Ireland* 10-12-0 MrROHarding 14/1   5 14
Control Man (IRE) *MissGinaWeare* 9-12-0 (v) MrStuartRobinson 20/1   20 15
152   Foly Pleasant (IRE) *MrsKWaldron* 13-12-0 (t) MrFelixdeGiles.................... 80/1   f
      Gone To Lunch (IRE) *JScott* 7-12-0 MrNHarris .... 33/1   f
      Patches (IRE) *RBarber* 8-12-0 MissRAGreen .... 7/1   f
      Beauchamp Oracle *SFlook* 10-12-0 MrDMansell... 66/1   ur
      Telemoss (IRE) *NGRichards* 13-12-0 MissRDavidson .... 33/1   ur
      Christy Beamish (IRE) *PJones* 10-12-0 MrWHill.. 20/1   pu
      Lord Beau (IRE) *ABateman* 11-12-0 MrJETudor.. 66/1   pu
      Moonoki (IRE) *BTulloch* 8-12-0 MrPMason.. 100/1   pu
      Waking Ned (IRE) *PKirby* 8-12-0 (s) MrRTierney .... 33/1   pu
      Mr John P. McManus 24ran 6m46.54

195   **Johnny Henderson Grand Annual Chase Challenge Cup (Hcap)**   2m110y (14)
      (Gr 3) (1) (158) (5yo+) £48,467

130   ANDREAS (FR) *PFNicholls* 7-10-11[143] (t) RobertThornton 12/1   1
130   HASTY PRINCE *JonjoO'Neill* 9-10-5[137] APMcCoy 8/1   3 2
130   GROUND BALL (IRE) *CFSwan,Ireland* 10-10-5[137] DJCasey 33/1   4 3
161   URSIS (FR) *SGollings* 6-10-8[140] BJGeraghty 14/1   2½ 4
130   Bambi de L'Orme (FR) *IanWilliams* 8-10-0[132] GLee................................ 25/1   1¾ 5
      Saintsaire (FR) *PFNicholls* 8-10-2[134] RWalsh.. 5/2f   1½ 6
      Zum See (IRE) *NMeade,Ireland* 8-10-2[134] (b) NPMadden........................ 66/1   1¼ 7
130   Tysou (FR) *NJHenderson* 10-10-10[142] MickFitzgerald................................ 12/1   5 8
      Figaro du Rocher (FR) *DEPipe* 7-10-0[132] (t) RJGreene 100/1   1½ 9
      Coat of Honour (USA) *JHowardJohnson* 7-10-5[137] PJBrennan .... 28/1   nk 10
      Greenhope (IRE) *NJHenderson* 9-10-9[141] (t) AndrewTinkler................... 25/1   ¾ 11
      Misty Dancer *MissVenetiaWilliams* 8-9-11[132] LiamTreadwell[3] 50/1   6 12
      Tanikos (FR) *NJHenderson* 8-10-0[132] MarcusFoley 66/1   1 13
46   Calatagan (IRE) *JMJefferson* 8-10-7[142] TJDreaper[3].................................... 33/1   10 14
20   Jacks Craic (IRE) *JLSpearing* 8-10-3[135] TonyEvans................................. 12/1   2½ 15
      Pablo du Charmil (FR) *DEPipe* 6-10-10[142] TomScudamore....................... 6/1   sh 16
      Borora *RLee* 8-10-0[132] TomDoyle... 25/1   1 17
      Croix de Guerre (IRE) *PJHobbs* 7-10-0[132] (b) TJO'Brien......................... 50/1   2½ 18
      Kahuna (IRE) *ESheehy,Ireland* 10-10-6[138] MJDarcy............................... 40/1   6 19
9   Commonchero (IRE) *MJPO'Brien,Ireland* 10-10-1[136] AELynch[3] 100/1   1¼ 20
141   Sporazene (IRE) *PFNicholls* 8-11-12[158] SamThomas.............................. 20/1   f
      Carthalawn (IRE) *CharlesByrnes,Ireland* 6-9-9[132] DGHogan[5]................ 20/1   f
46   Demi Beau *EvanWilliams* 9-10-11[143] PaulMoloney .... 12/1   pu
      Mr Trevor Hemmings 23ran 3m56.93

196   **Vincent O'Brien County Hcap Hdle (Gr 3) (1) (161) (5yo+) £39,914**   2m1f (8)

140   PEDROBOB (IRE) *AnthonyMullins,Ireland* 9-10-0[135] PACarberry 12/1   1
      OUNINPOHJA (IRE) *PFNicholls* 6-10-0[135] RWalsh................................. 11/2   1 2
106   PREMIER DANE (IRE) *NGRichards* 5-10-0[135] BrianHarding .... 100/1   nk 3
175   KAWAGINO (IRE) *JWMullins* 7-10-0[140] WayneKavanagh[5] .... 20/1   ¾ 4
131   Arcalis *JHowardJohnson* 7-11-2[151] PJBrennan .... 16/1   hd 5
140   Caracciola (GER) *NJHenderson* 10-10-2[137] AndrewTinkler 16/1   1 6
37   Sweet Wake (GER) *NMeade,Ireland* 6-10-2[137] DenisO'Regan .... 12/1   sh 7
74   Crow Wood *JJQuinn* 8-10-9[144] GLee 33/1   1 8
36   Callow Lake (IRE) *MrsJHarrington,Ireland* 7-10-2[142] (b) ADLeigh[5] ...... 16/1   ¾ 9
122   Osana (FR) *DEPipe* 5-10-9[144] APMcCoy 11/2   2½ 10
      Trompette (USA) *NJHenderson* 5-10-0[135] TomDoyle.............................. 33/1   2 11
182   Baron de Feypo (IRE) *PatrickOBrady,Ireland* 9-10-0[135] NPMadden...... 40/1   1¼ 12
      Gods Token *MissVenetiaWilliams* 9-9-11[135] LiamTreadwell[3] 66/1   2½ 13
140   Tarlac (GER) *NJHenderson* 6-10-0[135] MarcusFoley .... 25/1   nk 14
112   Maralan (GER) *PatrickOBrady,Ireland* 6-9-9[135] RJMolloy[5]..................... 33/1   2½ 15
86   Desert Quest (IRE) *PFNicholls* 7-11-9[161] (b) LiamHeard[3].................... 20/1   sh 16
37   Ameeq (USA) *GLMoore* 5-9-9[135] SPJones[5]... 16/1   1 17
37   O'Toole (IRE) *PJHobbs* 8-9-8[136] DarrenO'Dwyer[7] 80/1   2½ 18
140   New Field (IRE) *ThomasMullins,Ireland* 9-10-0[135] DJCasey 25/1   1½ 19
      Made In Japan (JPN) *ABateman* 7-9-11[135] ColinBolger[3]......................... 50/1   1 20
      Lord Henry (IRE) *PJHobbs* 8-10-0[135] TJO'Brien 50/1   1¼ 21
154   Trouble At Bay (IRE) *AKing* 7-10-1[136] (b) RobertThornton 33/1   4 22
131   Whispered Promises (USA) *RSBrookhouse* 6-10-7[142] AlanO'Keeffe........... 25/1   ½ 23
      Cadogan (FR) *JTRDreaper,Ireland* 10-10-0[135] AELynch[3] 66/1   1½ 24
174   Fair Along (GER) *PJHobbs* 5-10-7[142] RichardJohnson 3/1f   8 25
23   Flame Creek (IRE) *EJCreighton* 11-10-10[145] MarkGrant 100/1   10 26

140 Papini (IRE) *NJHenderson* 6-10-6[141] MickFitzgerald.................................... 33/1   6 27
182 The Spoonplayer (IRE) *HenrydeBromhead,Ireland* 8-10-0[135] DJCondon ... 100/1   ½ 28

Mr Barry Connell 28ran 3m54.41

UTTOXETER Saturday, Mar 17   SOFT

197 John Smith's Midlands Grand National Chase (Hcap) (L) (1) (148)   4m1f110y (24)
(5yo+) £57,020

110	BARON WINDRUSH *NATwiston-Davies* 9-10-9[131] JasonMaguire	12/1	1
176	D'ARGENT (IRE) *AKing* 10-11-5[141] RobertThornton	40/1	12 2
97	NEWBAY PROP (IRE) *AJMartin,Ireland* 8-9-11[122] RobertColgan[3]...........	11/2jf	nk 3
177	L'AVENTURE (FR) *PFNicholls* 8-10-9[134] (b+t) PaddyMerrigan[3]	20/1	12 4
152	Keepatem (IRE) *JonjoO'Neill* 11-10-1[123] DJCasey...............................	9/1	3½ 5
	Even More (IRE) *RHAlner* 12-9-11[122] DarylJacob[3]	66/1	4 6
124	Take The Stand (IRE) *PBowen* 11-11-8[144] (s) TJO'Brien.......................	50/1	25 7
	Glen Warrior *JSSmith* 11-10-1[123] (s) PaulMoloney	66/1	f
110	Ladalko (FR) *PFNicholls* 8-11-12[148] RWalsh.....................................	13/2	pu
164	Nil Desperandum (IRE) *MissVenetiaWilliams* 10-11-11[147] TomScudamore	11/2jf	pu
150	The Outlier (IRE) *MissVenetiaWilliams* 9-11-11[137] SamThomas....................	20/1	pu
147	Jaunty Times *HDDaly* 7-11-0[136] MarkBradburne..................................	11/1	pu
162	Puntal (FR) *DEPipe* 11-10-13[135] (s+t) TimmyMurphy	33/1	pu
147	In Accord *HDDaly* 8-10-7[129] RichardJohnson	40/1	pu
150	G V A Ireland (IRE) *FFlood,Ireland* 9-10-7[129] MickFitzgerald..................	10/1	pu
	Garryvoe (IRE) *TRGeorge* 9-10-3[125] WayneHutchinson	14/1	pu
111	Jaquouille (FR) *ALTMoore,Ireland* 10-9-9[122] ADLeigh[5]	14/1	pu
	Parkinson (IRE) *JonjoO'Neill* 6-10-0[122] (s) RichardMcGrath	17/2	pu

The Double Octagon Partnership 18ran 9m01.19

NEWBURY Saturday, Mar 24   GOOD

198 European Breeders' Fund/Thoroughbred Breeders' Association   2¾m110y (17)
Mares' Only Nov Chase Final (Hcap) (L) (1) (131) (5yo+ m) £16,917

	PENNEYROSE BAY *NJGifford* 8-10-6[131] LeightonAspell	5/1	1
	CHAMOSS ROYALE (FR) *PFNicholls* 7-11-12[131] APMcCoy....................	11/2	8 2
	HARRINGAY *MissHCKnight* 7-10-12[117] (t) PaulMoloney	9/2f	24 3
85	Bold Fire *PFNicholls* 5-11-2[129] LiamHeard[3]	6/1	3 4
	Cloudless Dawn *PBeaumont* 7-11-1[120] RussGarritty.............................	13/2	13 5
	Petite Margot *NATwiston-Davies* 8-10-13[118] RichardJohnson..................	11/2	7 6
	Lizzie Bathwick (IRE) *JGPortman* 8-9-9[105] (b) GerardTumelty[5].............	25/1	5 7
183	Lady of Scarvagh (IRE) *MScudamore* 8-11-6[125] TomScudamore.............	16/1	pu
	More Likely *MrsAFTullie* 6-11-0[119] GLee...	15/2	pu

Sir Christopher Wates 9ran 5m32.93

199 European Breeders' Fund Mares' Only NH Nov Hdle Final (Ltd   2m5f (12)
Hcap) (L) (1) (122) (4yo+ f+m) £28,510

	KARELLO BAY *NJHenderson* 6-11-3[115] (t) MickFitzgerald........................	6/1	1
38	MISS MITCH (IRE) *RHAlner* 6-11-4[116] AndrewThornton	14/1	3 2
	VERY SPECIAL ONE (IRE) *KCBailey* 7-11-8[120] (v) APMcCoy.................	14/1	13 3
	BLACKBRIERY THYNE (IRE) *HDDaly* 8-10-10[108] MarkBradburne	25/1	1 4
	Wyldello *AKing* 6-11-10[122] RobertThornton	15/2	1 5
	Apollo Lady *AKing* 6-10-11[114] GerardTumelty[5].................................	10/1	9 6
	Ruby Dante (IRE) *MrsAMThorpe* 9-10-4[102] SEDurack	33/1	3½ 7
	Sovietica (FR) *SPike* 6-10-7[105] TomScudamore................................	33/1	1 8
	Bonchester Bridge *NJHenderson* 6-11-3[115] AndrewTinkler...................	16/1	3½ 9
	Knockara Luck (IRE) *NGRichards* 6-10-5[103] BrianHarding....................	10/1	6 10
39	Strawberry (IRE) *JWMullins* 6-10-10[113] WayneKavanagh[5]	16/1	1¼ 11
	Mountain Approach *Jean-ReneAuvray* 5-10-9[107] (t) NoelFehily	16/1	1¼ 12
	Over The Flow *RHBuckler* 5-10-4[105] DarylJacob[3]..............................	20/1	17 13
	Star Award (IRE) *MissHCKnight* 6-10-12[110] PaulMoloney	33/1	7 14
	Reel Charmer *GACharlton* 7-11-8[120] JanFaltejsek	33/1	pu
	Missis Potts *PJHobbs* 6-11-3[115] RichardJohnson	11/2	pu
	Back On Line (IRE) *MissVenetiaWilliams* 7-10-11[112] PCO'Neill[3]	33/1	pu
	Tambourine Davis (IRE) *NJHenderson* 5-10-10[108] OllieMcPhail..............	4/1f	pu

Turf Club 2006 18ran 4m53.66

NAVAN Saturday, Mar 24   HEAVY

200 Russell Restaurant An Uaimh Chase (Gr 3) (5yo+) £15,606   2½m (14)

168	NICKNAME (FR) *MartinBrassil* 8-11-12 (t) RWalsh	4/9f	1
148	CENTRAL HOUSE *DTHughes* 10-11-10 (t) RLoughran	11/1	13 2
156	JIM (FR) *JTRDreaper* 10-11-2 (b) AELynch[3].....................................	12/1	14 3
166	Watson Lake (IRE) *NMeade* 9-11-10 DFO'Regan	5/1	5½ 4
	Wheresben (IRE) *SeamusFahey* 8-10-9 MrJAFahey[7]	20/1	19 5
156	Macs Flamingo (IRE) *PAFahy* 7-11-5 BJGeraghty	33/1	pu

61   Romaha (IRE) *TJArnold* 11-11-2 (t) DJCasey.. 33/1   pu
      Mrs Claudia Jungo-Corpataux 7ran 5m52.43

      LIMERICK Sunday, Apr 1   GOOD to SOFT
201   Hugh McMahon Memorial Nov Chase (Gr 3) (5yo+) £15,395   3m (16)
         OFFSHORE ACCOUNT (IRE) *CFSwan* 7-11-5 DJCasey 9/2   1
  157   LAETITIA (IRE) *CharlesByrnes* 7-11-3 DNRussell.......................................   2/1f   nk 2
         MERCURIC *MrsJHarrington* 6-11-2 TPTreacy... 12/1   7 3
  160   Hear The Echo (IRE) *MFMorris* 6-11-10 CO'Dwyer...................................... 10/1   2 4
  183   Ponmeoath (IRE) *EricMcNamara* 7-11-2 RWalsh...   7/2   8 5
         Preists Leap (IRE) *ThomasGerardO'Leary* 7-11-2 JLCullen.......................   7/1   dist 6
         Ardlea Star (IRE) *PatrickOBrady* 9-10-8 NJO'Shea³ .... 20/1   dist 7
  160   Toofarback (IRE) *NMeade* 7-11-2 DFO'Regan ....   8/1   ur
      Mr Brian Polly 8ran 6m10.71

      FAIRYHOUSE Sunday, Apr 8   GOOD
202   Irish Stallion Farms European Breeders Fund (Mares) Nov Hdle   2½m (11)
      (Gr 3) (4yo+ f+m) £23,029
         GRANGECLARE LARK (IRE) *DTHughes* 6-11-3 RLoughran....................   7/1   1
         SHUIL ARIS (IRE) *PaulNolan* 6-10-11 JLCullen...   7/1   sh 2
  170   CHOMBA WOMBA (IRE) *MsMMullins* 6-11-3 TPTreacy............................   4/1   2½ 3
  191   Lounaos (FR) *EoinGriffin* 4-10-9 BJGeraghty 3/1f   2½ 4
  165   Miss Mason (IRE) *KFO'Brien* 4-10-1 (s) DJCasey 16/1   7 5
         Contessa Messina (IRE) *MFMorris* 7-11-0 ADLeigh 10/1   7 6
         La Marianne *JRHFowler* 7-10-11 (s) RGeraghty 16/1   7 7
   67   Blazing Sky (IRE) *FFMcGuinness* 7-11-0 PWFlood......................................   9/2   5½ 8
         Winning Counsel (IRE) *KFO'Brien* 5-10-10 (b) GTHutchinson 33/1   12 9
         Native Caroline (IRE) *MsMTCondon* 7-10-10 DJCondon 50/1   6 10
         Teffia Native (IRE) *DTHughes* 5-10-10 IJMcCarthy 40/1   1¾ 11
         Lough Cuan (IRE) *MrsJHarrington* 5-10-10 PACarberry 25/1   8 12
         Regal Force (IRE) *ThomasMullins* 8-10-11 RMPower............................... 50/1   4 13
         Gabrona (IRE) *HenrydeBromhead* 7-11-0 DFO'Regan............................... 20/1   pu
      Mr T. Hendy 14ran 4m43.74

203   Powers Gold Cup (Gr 1) (5yo+) £44,520   2½m (16)
  144   ONE COOL COOKIE (IRE) *CFSwan* 6-11-9 DJCasey 12/1   1
  128   SCHINDLERS HUNT (IRE) *DTHughes* 7-11-9 RLoughran.......................   5/2f   1½ 2
  144   ANOTHERCOPPERCOAST (IRE) *PaulARoche* 7-11-9 CO'Dwyer 33/1   19 3
  116   Regal Heights (IRE) *DMcCainJnr,GB* 6-11-9 GLee 11/2   1 4
  195   Ursis (FR) *SGollings,GB* 6-11-9 BJGeraghty 5/1   3 5
         Washington Lad (IRE) *PAFahy* 7-11-9 DFO'Regan.................................... 20/1   1½ 6
   98   Purple Shuffle (IRE) *PAFahy* 9-11-9 (s) RWalsh...................................... 16/1   ½ 7
         Hear The Echo (IRE) *MFMorris* 6-11-9 MDarcy 25/1   2½ 8
  201   Oran Climate (IRE) *JohnPaulBrennan* 7-11-9 JLCullen............................... 14/1   2½ 9
  128   King Johns Castle (IRE) *ALTMoore* 8-11-9 APMcCoy ....   4/1   pu
   98   Mattock Ranger (IRE) *NMeade* 7-11-9 PCarberry .... 16/1   pu
      Gigginstown House Stud 11ran 4m49.52

      FAIRYHOUSE Monday, Apr 9   GOOD to FIRM
204   Racing Post In Ireland Hdle (5yo+) £13,286   3m (13)
  190   ADAMANT APPROACH (IRE) *WPMullins* 13-11-10 RWalsh....................   7/4f   1
   90   SKY'S THE LIMIT (FR) *EJO'Grady* 6-11-10 (b) BJGeraghty 4/1   4½ 2
  193   FORGET THE PAST *MJPO'Brien* 9-11-1 (t) AELynch³ 3/1   10 3
         Santa's Son (IRE) *JFO'Shea* 7-11-1 (t) SGMcDermott³................................   8/1   hd 4
         Oriental Rock (GER) *SJMahon* 6-11-0 (t) TGMRyan................................. 33/1   4 5
         Druids Cross (IRE) *HenrydeBromhead* 6-11-0 DFO'Regan 25/1   1¼ 6
         Lucy Lamplighter (IRE) *NeillMcCluskey* 5-10-0 SWJackson⁷ 100/1   8 7
         Inch Sunset (IRE) *LeoJTemple* 6-10-9 (b) TonyDobbin.............................. 25/1   26 8
         Drumboy (IRE) *NeillMcCluskey* 6-10-7 MrAEKinirons⁷ 20/1   2½ 9
         Hey Bob (IRE) *JGMurphy* 6-11-0 PJScallan... 100/1   26 10
  192   Head Held High (IRE) *MrsJHarrington* 6-11-4 RMPower........................... 12/1   pu
         Gran Lady *MrsMaryWhelehan* 7-10-6 RJMolloy³ .... 150/1   pu
      Greenstar Syndicate 12ran 5m50.73

205   Powers Whiskey Irish Grand National Chase (Hcap) (159) (5yo+)   3m5f (23)
      £96,259
  189   BUTLER'S CABIN (FR) *JonjoO'Neill,GB* 7-10-4¹³⁵ (s) APMcCoy 14/1   1
  189   NINE DE SIVOLA (FR) *FerdyMurphy,GB* 6-10-0¹³¹ GLee 12/1   1 2
  121   AMERICAN JENNIE (IRE) *MichaelCullen* 9-10-0¹³¹ NPMadden............... 33/1   1¾ 3
   70   CHURCH ISLAND (IRE) *MHourigan* 8-10-4¹³⁵ AndrewJMcNamara......... 66/1   2 4
         Dantes Reef (IRE) *AJMartin* 11-9-11¹³¹ RCColgan³.................................. 33/1   ¾ 5

                                       1121

185	Kings Advocate (IRE) *TJTaaffe* 7-10-0[131] RWalsh	13/2f	½	6
183	Oodachee *CFSwan* 8-10-0[131] (s) DJCasey	33/1	nk	7
176	Distant Thunder (IRE) *NoelTChance,GB* 9-10-9[140] RichardJohnson	10/1	7	8
121	Well Tutored (IRE) *ALTMoore* 8-10-0[131] PACarberry	16/1	3	9
180	Chelsea Harbour (IRE) *ThomasMullins* 7-10-6[137] DNRussell	33/1	1	10
197	G V A Ireland (IRE) *FFlood* 9-9-7[131] SJHassett[7]	66/1	sh	11
180	Gazza's Girl (IRE) *MrsJHarrington* 7-9-12[132] ADLeigh[3]	16/1	14	12
194	Whyso Mayo (IRE) *RaymondHurley* 10-9-13[135] MrDMurphy[5]	10/1	3	13
121	Kerryhead Windfarm (IRE) *MHourigan* 9-10-1[132] DFO'Regan	33/1	4	14
177	Omni Cosmo Touch (USA) *HenrydeBromhead* 11-9-11[131] RMMoran[3]	66/1	5	15
182	Oulart *DTHughes* 8-9-7[131] CDMaxwell[7]	12/1	nk	16
177	Marcus du Berlais (IRE) *ALTMoore* 10-9-11[131] AELynch[3]	100/1	4½	17
183	Cheeky Lady (IRE) *ColmAMurphy* 10-9-7[131] SWFlanagan[7]	25/1		f
111	A New Story (IRE) *MHourigan* 9-10-0[131] (s) MissNCarberry	16/1		ur
183	Cloudy Lane *DMcCainJnr,GB* 7-10-0[131] TonyDobbin	11/1		ur
11	Dix Villez (FR) *PaulNolan* 8-10-0[131] PWFlood	16/1		bd
193	Cane Brake (IRE) *TJTaaffe* 8-11-7[159] ABJoyce[7]	20/1		pu
176	Juveigneur (FR) *NJHenderson,GB* 10-11-8[153] MickFitzgerald	9/1		pu
188	Kill Devil Hill (IRE) *PaulNolan* 7-11-0[145] JLCullen	66/1		pu
182	Ross River *AJMartin* 11-10-3[141] JWFarrelly[7]	33/1		pu
180	Patsy Hall (IRE) *MichaelCunningham* 7-10-6[137] RMPower	25/1		pu
176	All In The Stars (IRE) *DPKeane,GB* 9-10-0[131] NPMulholland	33/1		pu
189	Mac Three (IRE) *NMeade* 8-10-0[131] PCarberry	33/1		pu
9	One Four Shannon (IRE) *DJRyan* 10-10-0[131] (s) TGMRyan	66/1		pu

Mr John P. McManus 29ran 7m21.82

FAIRYHOUSE Tuesday, Apr 10   GOOD to FIRM

206 **Tattersalls Ireland Dan Moore Memorial Hcap Chase (156) (4yo+)**   2m1f (13)
£44,286

174	GEMINI LUCY (IRE) *MrsJHarrington* 7-10-0[135] ADLeigh[3]	5/2f		1
	OLD FLAME (IRE) *PaulNolan* 8-10-6[138] BJGeraghty	8/1	17	2
156	MOSSY GREEN (IRE) *WPMullins* 13-10-9[141] RWalsh	7/1	3	3
	In The High Grass (IRE) *TJTaaffe* 6-10-3[135] DJCasey	11/2	2½	4
200	Central House *DTHughes* 10-11-10[156] PWFlood	8/1	11	5
195	Zum See (IRE) *NMeade* 8-10-3[135] (b) NPMadden	10/1	½	6
	Say Again (IRE) *PaulNolan* 11-10-0[135] RMMoran[3]	16/1	10	7
	Accordion Etoile (IRE) *PaulNolan* 8-11-9[155] JLCullen	9/2		ur

Queens Prices Syndicate 8ran 4m00.96

207 **Dunboyne Castle Hotel & Spa Nov Hdle (Gr 2) (4yo+)** £26,571   2m (10)

173	DE VALIRA (IRE) *MJPO'Brien* 5-11-9 AELynch	3/1		1
30	CUAN GALA (IRE) *PaulNolan* 6-11-7 BJGeraghty	4/1	nk	2
	GLENCOVE MARINA (IRE) *WPMullins* 5-11-3 RWalsh	9/4f	1½	3
	Restoration (FR) *NMeade* 5-11-3 DNRussell	14/1	sh	4
96	Sizing Europe (IRE) *HenrydeBromhead* 5-11-3 DFO'Regan	4/1	3	5
96	Derravarra Eagle (IRE) *MarkLeslieFagan* 7-11-4 NPMadden	16/1	8	6
	Bad Day Bad Day *MrsJHarrington* 5-11-3 RMPower	20/1	8	7
	Danikhali (IRE) *PatrickOBrady* 5-11-3 NJO'Shea	50/1	dist	8

Mr D. Mac A'Bhaird 8ran 3m41.74

208 **Menolly Homes Hcap Hdle (140) (4yo+)** £57,483   2m (10)

6	EMMPAT (IRE) *CFSwan* 9-10-4[120] DJCasey	7/1		1
196	NEW FIELD (IRE) *ThomasMullins* 9-10-1[117] APCrowe	14/1	3	2
	MONOCEROS (IRE) *PJRothwell* 7-9-3[112] SWJackson[7]	16/1	1	3
112	JAAMID *NMeade* 5-9-12[114] NPMadden	12/1	4½	4
6	Dbest (IRE) *MsJoannaMorgan* 7-10-1[120] (b) RCColgan[3]	25/1	2½	5
112	Streetshavenoname (IRE) *TJTaaffe* 6-9-12[117] SMMcGovern[3]	20/1	hd	6
	Monty Mint (IRE) *ThomasFoley* 9-9-9[116] DFFlannery[5]	16/1	hd	7
196	Sweet Wake (GER) *NMeade* 6-11-7[137] BJGeraghty	5/1f	2½	8
112	Son of Oscar (IRE) *PhilipFenton* 6-10-3[119] PWFlood	25/1	2	9
112	Silent Oscar (IRE) *HarryRogers* 8-11-0[130] RMPower	25/1	hd	10
	Dreux (FR) *ThomasCooper* 5-10-0[119] (b) SGMcDermott[3]	50/1	½	11
115	Leslingtaylor (IRE) *JJQuinn,GB* 5-10-8[124] DougieCostello	14/1	hd	12
196	Callow Lake (IRE) *MrsJHarrington* 7-11-7[140] (b) ADLeigh[3]	20/1	sh	13
	Querido (USA) *EJO'Grady* 5-9-10[112] TGMRyan	33/1	3½	14
112	Wishwillow Lord (IRE) *LeonardWhitmore* 8-10-11[127] DFO'Regan	16/1	5	15
112	Power Elite (IRE) *NMeade* 7-10-10[126] (t) AndrewJMcNamara	33/1	2½	16
166	Joueur d'Estruval (FR) *WPMullins* 10-10-8[124] RWalsh	20/1	3	17
	Savitha (IRE) *PaulNolan* 7-9-10[115] RMMoran[3]	16/1	2	18
196	Pedrobob (IRE) *AnthonyMullins* 9-11-9[139] DNRussell	7/1	1¼	19
	Deutschland (USA) *WPMullins* 4-9-12[114] DJCondon	12/1	nk	20
	Rights of Man (IRE) *DEFitzgerald* 8-9-10[112] JRBarry	25/1	5½	21

1122

196	Maralan (IRE) *PatrickOBrady* 6-10-3[122] (b) NJO'Shea[3]	25/1	5½ 22	
172	Farmer Brown (IRE) *PatrickHughes* 6-10-7[123] MissNCarberry	16/1	f	

Mr Michael D. Mee 23ran 3m37.39

AINTREE Thursday, Apr 12　GOOD

209　John Smith's Liverpool Hdle (Long Distance) (1) (Gr 2) (4yo+)　3m110y (13)
£40,618

187	MIGHTY MAN (FR) *HDDaly* 7-11-10 RichardJohnson	15/8	1	
187	BLACK JACK KETCHUM (IRE) *JonjoO'Neill* 8-11-10 APMcCoy	7/4f	13 2	
187	INGLIS DREVER *JHowardJohnson* 8-11-10 PJBrennan	7/2	9 3	
187	Lough Derg (FR) *DEPipe* 7-11-2 (v) TomScudamore	33/1	24 4	
187	Blazing Bailey *AKing* 5-11-10 RobertThornton	9/1	f	
187	Fire Dragon (IRE) *JonjoO'Neill* 6-11-10 (b+t) NoelFehily	25/1	pu	

Mr E. R. Hanbury 6ran 6m10.12

210　Betfair Bowl Chase (Gr 2) (1) (5yo+) £85,530　3m1f (19)

193	EXOTIC DANCER (FR) *JonjoO'Neill* 7-11-12 (s) APMcCoy	6/4f	1	
193	MY WILL (FR) *PFNicholls* 7-11-8 RWalsh	10/1	13 2	
186	OUR VIC (FR) *DEPipe* 9-11-12 TimmyMurphy	5/1	12 3	
193	State of Play *EvanWilliams* 7-11-8 PaulMoloney	3/1	6 4	
193	Turpin Green (IRE) *NGRichards* 8-11-8 (b) TonyDobbin	9/2	10 5	

Sir Robert Ogden 5ran 6m22.22

211　John Smith's Anniversary 4-Y-O Nov Hdle (Gr 1) (1) (4yo) £74,126　2m110y (9)

191	KATCHIT (IRE) *AKing* 4-11-0 RobertThornton	1/1f	1	
191	PUNJABI *NJHenderson* 4-11-0 MickFitzgerald	6/1	4 2	
191	DEGAS ART (IRE) *JHowardJohnson* 4-11-0 PJBrennan	15/2	8 3	
	Grand Bleu (IRE) *FDoumen,France* 4-11-0 JacquesRicou	10/1	9 4	
191	Lightning Strike (GER) *MissVenetiaWilliams* 4-11-0 SamThomas	22/1	sh 5	
191	Mobaasher (USA) *CJMann* 4-11-0 NoelFehily	10/1	1¾ 6	
	River Logic (IRE) *ADBrown* 4-11-0 GLee	150/1	15 7	
	Doctor David *MrsCarolineBailey* 4-11-0 TomMessenger	66/1	5 8	
	Marsam (IRE) *JohnJosephMurphy,Ireland* 4-11-0 EFPower	100/1	ur	
31	Is It Me (USA) *PABlockley* 4-11-0 (b) MarkBradburne	33/1	pu	
	Sendani (FR) *PFNicholls* 4-11-0 RWalsh	33/1	pu	
71	Tritonix (IRE) *PJHobbs* 4-11-0 (t) APMcCoy	10/1	pu	

D S J P Syndicate 12ran 3m59.43

212　John Smith's Fox Hunt Chase (2) (6yo+) £21,007　2m5f110y (Nat.) (18)

	SCOTS GREY *NJHenderson* 12-12-0 MrRBurton	9/2	1	
	PAK JACK (FR) *RBarber* 7-12-0 MrROHarding	8/1	½ 2	
	WHERE NOW (IRE) *JohnQueally,Ireland* 11-12-0 MissNCarberry	16/1	21 3	
194	Arctic Times (IRE) *EugeneMO'Sullivan,Ireland* 11-12-0 (s) MrRPMcLernon	33/1	1½ 4	
	Ghadames (FR) *AKirtley* 13-12-0 MrPCallaghan	100/1	¾ 5	
194	Drombeag (IRE) *JonjoO'Neill* 9-12-0 MrJTMcNamara	6/1	9 6	
	Holy Joe (FR) *MissVenetiaWilliams* 10-12-0 MrOGreenall	14/1	4 7	
	Beachcomber Bay (IRE) *IJKeeling,Ireland* 12-12-0 MrJTKeeling	14/1	2 8	
	Van Ness (IRE) *MrsKatieBaimbridge* 8-12-0 MrTEdwards	66/1	¾ 9	
	Fable (USA) *GElliott,Ireland* 11-12-0 (t) MrJJCodd	66/1	15 10	
	Encore Cadoudal (FR) *MissTJackson* 9-12-0 MrTJackson	100/1	3½ 11	
	Eskimo Jack (IRE) *TRGeorge* 11-12-0 MrWLMorgan	33/1	2 12	
	Moving Earth (IRE) *CEWard* 14-12-0 MrCWard	100/1	¾ 13	
	Wilfie Wild *MrsLynneWard* 11-12-0 MrsLWard	100/1	4 14	
	Tanager *MrsKLawther* 12-12-0 MrRJBarrett	100/1	sh 15	
	Gangsters R Us (IRE) *AParker* 11-12-0 MrRMorgan	33/1	3½ 16	
	Algarve *NNevin,Ireland* 10-12-0 (s) MrMJO'Connor	100/1	6 17	
	River Dante (IRE) *MissLABlackford* 10-12-0 (t) MrJGuerriero	100/1	28 18	
	Alphazar (IRE) *WPMullins,Ireland* 12-12-0 MrEMullins	66/1	14 19	
	Benrajah (IRE) *PKirby* 10-12-0 MrRTierney	66/1	f	
	Cedar Chief *KTork* 10-12-0 (b) MrGGallagher	100/1	f	
	Le Passing (IRE) *PFNicholls* 8-12-0 (b) MrTGreenall	6/1	f	
194	Ned Kelly (IRE) *EJO'Grady,Ireland* 11-12-0 MrKEPower	4/1f	f	
	Va Vavoom (IRE) *MrsFleurHawes* 9-12-0 MrDKemp	33/1	f	
	Jacksonville (FR) *MissVickySimpson* 10-12-0 (s) MissVickySimpson	80/1	ref	
	Our Jolly Swagman *MrsALTory* 12-12-0 (b) MissETory	200/1	ur	
	Royal Hector (GER) *AGHobbs* 8-12-0 MrAWintle	25/1	ur	

Mr W. H. Ponsonby 27ran 5m29.90

213　John Smith's Red Rum Hcap Chase (Gr 3) (1) (154) (5yo+) £39,914　2m (12)

195	BAMBI DE L'ORME (FR) *IanWilliams* 8-10-2[130] DominicElsworth	13/2	1	
	MARSHALL HALL (IRE) *FerdyMurphy* 6-10-2[130] GLee	7/1	1½ 2	

20	LOCKSMITH *PMonteith* 7-10-2[130] WilsonRenwick	12/1	4	3
195	Greenhope (IRE) *NJHenderson* 9-10-12[140] (t) AndrewTinkler	25/1	1¼	4
146	Magic Sky (FR) *MFHarris* 7-10-6[139] CharliePoste[5]	16/1	1¾	5
	Stan (NZ) *MissVenetiaWilliams* 8-9-11[128] (b) LiamTreadwell[3]	33/1	nk	6
195	Hasty Prince *JonjoO'Neill* 9-11-1[143] APMcCoy	5/1f	8	7
	Kit Carson (IRE) *CFSwan,Ireland* 7-10-0[128] DJCasey	14/1	5	8
195	Demi Beau *EvanWilliams* 9-11-1[143] BJGeraghty	11/1	4	9
93	Priors Dale *MissECLavelle* 7-11-2[144] BarryFenton	25/1	18	10
195	Andreas (FR) *PFNicholls* 7-11-12[154] (t) RWalsh	11/2		f
169	Marcel (FR) *DEPipe* 7-10-9[137] (s) TimmyMurphy	16/1		f
	Alph *BRJohnson* 10-10-3[131] MattieBatchelor	66/1		f
6	Crossbow Creek *MGRimell* 9-11-11[153] RobertThornton	11/1		pu
195	Jacks Craic (IRE) *JLSpearing* 8-10-6[134] TonyEvans	9/1		pu

Mr & Mrs John Poynton 15ran 3m55.84

214   **Citroen C4 Picasso Mersey Nov Hdle (Gr 2) (1) (4yo+) £31,361**   2½m (11)

179	TIDAL BAY (IRE) *JHowardJohnson* 6-11-5 PJBrennan	9/4		1
173	WINS NOW *NMadden,Ireland* 6-11-3 APMcCoy	11/2	8	2
	BEDLAM BOY *NGRichards* 6-11-5 TonyDobbin	25/1	3½	3
	Larkwing (IRE) *EricMcNamara,Ireland* 6-11-3 DNRussell	7/1	12	4
191	Liberate *PJHobbs* 4-10-7 RichardJohnson	2/1f	1	5
191	My Petra *AKing* 4-10-3 RobertThornton	25/1	1½	6
	Double Obsession *AMBalding* 7-11-0 MarkBradburne	66/1	8	7
122	Carlitos *NATwiston-Davies* 5-11-3 TomScudamore	8/1	10	8
	Jass *KGReveley* 5-11-0 PhilKinsella	66/1	7	9
191	Khachaturian (IRE) *DMcCainJnr* 4-10-7 JasonMaguire	100/1	dist	10

Andrea & Graham Wylie 10ran 4m55.16

215   **John Smith's Hcap Hdle (L) (1) (144) (4yo+) £28,510**   2½m (11)

48	TWO MILES WEST (IRE) *JonjoO'Neill* 6-10-7[125] NoelFehily	25/1		1
196	GODS TOKEN *MissVenetiaWilliams* 9-10-9[130] LiamTreadwell[3]	33/1	hd	2
	SHATABDI (IRE) *NJHenderson* 5-10-7[132] MrSWaley-Cohen[7]	10/1	nk	3
	ICE TEA (IRE) *DMcCainJnr* 7-10-0[118] (b) GLee	16/1	2	4
	Laouen (FR) *LLungo* 9-10-1[119] BrianHarding	7/2f	2	5
140	Acambo (GER) *DEPipe* 6-11-12[144] TimmyMurphy	12/1	2	6
182	Burntoakboy *DrRDPNewland* 9-11-3[140] SPJones[5]	8/1	½	7
7	Absolut Power (GER) *JAGeake* 6-10-5[123] (s) RichardJohnson	25/1	4	8
	Marhaba Million (IRE) *EricMcNamara,Ireland* 5-10-8[126] APMcCoy	17/2	¾	9
172	Flying Falcon *MissVenetiaWilliams* 8-10-8[126] SamThomas	16/1	2½	10
140	Self Defense *MissECLavelle* 10-11-8[140] RobertThornton	25/1	8	11
173	Kicks For Free (IRE) *PFNicholls* 6-11-3[135] (t) DominicElsworth	7/1	2	12
157	Conna Castle (IRE) *JamesJosephMangan,Ireland* 8-11-10[142] DNRussell	33/1	8	13
185	Desert Air (JPN) *DEPipe* 8-11-3[135] (v+t) TimmyMurphy	66/1	4	14
	Our Jasper *DMcCainJnr* 7-9-9[118] GerardTumelty[5]	100/1	6	15
182	Dusky Warbler *GLMoore* 8-11-7[139] (s) JamieMoore	11/1	½	16
	Our Monty (IRE) *KFO'Brien,Ireland* 4-10-0[125] (b) GTHutchinson	100/1	½	17
	Gardasee (GER) *TPTate* 5-10-4[122] JasonMaguire	100/1	8	18
172	Forest Green (FR) *PFNicholls* 5-9-4[118] (t) HarrySkelton[10]	66/1	15	19
101	Roll Along (IRE) *CarlLlewellyn* 7-10-7[125] PaulMoloney	7/1	1	20
173	Special Envoy (FR) *PBowen* 5-11-1[133] TJO'Brien	20/1		f
1	Into The Shadows *KGReveley* 7-10-13[131] RichardMcGrath	50/1		pu

Mr John P. McManus 22ran 4m55.47

AINTREE Friday, Apr 13   GOOD

216   **John Smith's Mildmay Nov Chase (Gr 2) (1) (5yo+) £45,616**   3m1f (19)

180	ACES FOUR (IRE) *FerdyMurphy* 8-11-5 GLee	5/2f		1
174	FAASEL (IRE) *NGRichards* 6-11-2 (b) TonyDobbin	6/1	8	2
180	DOM D'ORGEVAL (FR) *DEPipe* 7-11-5 TomScudamore	16/1	½	3
161	Yes Sir (IRE) *PBowen* 8-11-9 TJO'Brien	25/1	6	4
85	Boychuk (IRE) *PJHobbs* 6-11-9 RichardJohnson	14/1	5	5
180	Ungaro (FR) *KGReveley* 8-11-9 MickFitzgerald	5/1	6	6
197	Jaunty Times *HDDaly* 7-11-5 MarkBradburne	40/1	dist	7
	Standin Obligation (IRE) *DEPipe* 8-11-7 TimmyMurphy	14/1		pu
	Killaghy Castle (IRE) *NJGifford* 7-11-5 LeightonAspell	8/1		pu
180	Turko (FR) *PFNicholls* 5-11-0 (t) RWalsh	4/1		pu

The DPRP Aces Partnership 10ran 6m23.05

217   **Citroen C6 Sefton Nov Hdle (Gr 1) (1) (4yo+) £54,169**   3m110y (13)

192	CHIEF DAN GEORGE (IRE) *JamesMoffatt* 7-11-4 (s) MickFitzgerald	20/1		1
192	WICHITA LINEMAN (IRE) *JonjoO'Neill* 6-11-4 APMcCoy	4/6f	4	2
179	IMPERIAL COMMANDER (IRE) *NATwiston-Davies* 6-11-4 TonyEvans	25/1	18	3
179	Massini's Maguire (IRE) *PJHobbs* 6-11-4 RichardJohnson	11/2	9	4

170	Knowledge Box (IRE) *JohnJosephMurphy,Ireland* 7-11-4 EFPower	100/1	24	5
179	Silverburn (IRE) *PFNicholls* 6-11-4 RWalsh	4/1	dist	6
179	Battlecry *NATwiston-Davies* 6-11-4 TomScudamore	100/1		pu
192	Secret Ploy *HMorrison* 7-11-4 AndrewTinkler	40/1		pu
	Super Nick (IRE) *NATwiston-Davies* 6-11-4 RobertThornton	50/1		pu
	Wee Forbees (IRE) *JHowardJohnson* 5-11-4 PJBrennan	16/1		pu

Mr Maurice W. Chapman 10ran 6m10.88

218   John Smith's Melling Chase (Gr 1) (1) (5yo+) £114,040   2½m (16)

186	MONET'S GARDEN (IRE) *NGRichards* 9-11-10 TonyDobbin	4/1		1
186	TARANIS (FR) *PFNicholls* 6-11-10 (t) RWalsh	5/1	3½	2
181	WELL CHIEF (GER) *DEPipe* 8-11-10 TimmyMurphy	4/5f	9	3
186	Crozan (FR) *NJHenderson* 7-11-10 (b) MickFitzgerald	14/1	8	4
186	Hi Cloy (IRE) *MHourigan,Ireland* 10-11-10 DNRussell	9/1	3	5
181	Oneway (IRE) *MGRimell* 10-11-10 (b) RichardJohnson	33/1	dist	6

Mr David Wesley Yates 6ran 5m00.84

219   John Smith's Topham Chase (Hcap) (2) (155) (5yo+) £62,630   2m5f110y (Nat.) (18)

51	DUNBRODY MILLAR (IRE) *PBowen* 9-10-0[129] JamieMoore	25/1		1
50	THEATRE KNIGHT (IRE) *JHowardJohnson* 9-10-0[129] WilsonRenwick	66/1	6	2
134	LATIMER'S PLACE *NJGifford* 11-10-1[130] LeightonAspell	25/1	2½	3
195	GROUND BALL (IRE) *CFSwan,Ireland* 10-10-10[139] APMcCoy	12/1	1¾	4
185	Milan Deux Mille (FR) *DEPipe* 5-10-9[142] TomScudamore	18/1	3	5
188	Le Volfoni (FR) *PFNicholls* 6-11-4[147] RWalsh	13/2f	hd	6
176	Irish Raptor (IRE) *NATwiston-Davies* 7-10-7[136] WayneHutchinson	8/1	5	7
51	Just In Debt (IRE) *MTodhunter* 11-10-0[129] (s) BrianHarding	40/1	¾	8
188	Hakim (NZ) *JLSpearing* 13-10-0[129] SEDurack	12/1	4	9
	Brooklyn Breeze (IRE) *LLungo* 10-10-7[136] GLee	15/2	1	10
	Risk Accessor (IRE) *JonjoO'Neill* 12-10-0[129] RichardMcGrath	25/1	1¾	11
188	Vodka Bleu (FR) *DEPipe* 8-10-1[140] DNRussell	14/1	4	12
	Flight Command *PBeaumont* 9-10-0[129] (s) TomSiddall	100/1	12	13
50	Cassia Heights *SABrookshaw* 12-9-11[129] (t) PhilKinsella[3]	100/1	dist	14
183	Lord of Illusion (IRE) *TRGeorge* 10-10-5[134] (t) DominicElsworth	14/1	dist	15
61	On The Net (IRE) *EoghanO'Grady,Ireland* 9-10-10[139] DJCasey	16/1		f
134	Kasthari (IRE) *JHowardJohnson* 8-10-0[129] PJBrennan	33/1		f
111	Lost Time (IRE) *CRoche,Ireland* 10-10-0[129] APCrowe	50/1		f
50	Shannon's Pride (IRE) *RCGuest* 11-9-7[129] (s) DavidCullinane[7]	50/1		f
188	Armaturk (FR) *PFNicholls* 10-11-12[155] SamThomas	33/1		bd
	Lord Rodney (IRE) *PBeaumont* 8-10-0[129] PeterBuchanan	80/1		bd
134	Briery Fox (IRE) *HDDaly* 9-10-5[134] MarkBradburne	8/1		ur
183	Turthen (FR) *PFNicholls* 6-10-1[133] (t) LiamHeard[3]	14/1		ur
188	Iron Man (FR) *PBowen* 6-10-0[129] (s) TJO'Brien	25/1		ur
183	Almost Broke *GBrown* 10-9-7[129] MissLHorner[7]	100/1		ur
	Espoir du Bocage (FR) *MScudamore* 12-9-7[129] JohnKington[7]	100/1		ur
127	Umbrella Man (IRE) *MissECLavelle* 11-10-2[131] BarryFenton	25/1		pu
56	Patman du Charmil (FR) *NATwiston-Davies* 5-10-0[133] PaulMoloney	33/1		pu
5	Always *JohnLong,Ireland* 8-10-2[136] (b) MJFerris[5]	100/1		rtr

Dundon Else Partnership 29ran 5m27.00

220   John Smith's Imagine Appeal Top Nov Hdle (Gr 2) (1) (4yo+) £31,361   2m110y (8)

	BLYTHE KNIGHT (IRE) *JJQuinn* 7-11-0 APMcCoy	14/1		1
196	OSANA (FR) *DEPipe* 5-11-0 TomScudamore	3/1	2½	2
196	OUNINPOHJA (IRE) *PFNicholls* 6-11-0 RWalsh	2/1f	5	3
	Bywell Beau (IRE) *GACharlton* 8-11-8 (t) JanFaltejsek	12/1	8	4
173	De Soto *PRWebber* 6-11-5 (t) RichardJohnson	7/2	10	5
	Crocodile Dundee (IRE) *JHowardJohnson* 6-11-5 PJBrennan	25/1	5	6
173	Tyson (SAF) *MissVenetiaWilliams* 7-11-0 PCO'Neill	7/1	7	7
	Enforce (USA) *MrsLWadham* 4-10-1 LeightonAspell	33/1	dist	8

Maxilead Limited 8ran 3m58.81

221   betfair.com Hcap Chase (2) (149) (5yo+) £31,315   3m1f (19)

188	REVEILLEZ *JRFanshawe* 8-11-8[145] (t) APMcCoy	9/2f		1
	LANKAWI *PBowen* 5-10-0[132] TJO'Brien	10/1	7	2
176	LACDOUDAL (FR) *PJHobbs* 8-11-12[149] RichardJohnson	8/1	2½	3
	HEALY'S PUB (IRE) *OliverMcKiernan,Ireland* 11-9-13[125] TGMRyan[3]	50/1	3½	4
182	Copsale Lad *NJHenderson* 10-11-6[143] MickFitzgerald	7/1	4	5
33	Tamarinbleu (FR) *DEPipe* 7-11-10[147] TomScudamore	33/1	1¾	6
176	New Alco (FR) *FerdyMurphy* 6-11-4[141] UGate	5/1	5	7
	Maurice (FR) *DMcCainJnr* 7-10-12[135] (t) JasonMaguire	50/1	3	8
152	Undeniable *MrsSJSmith* 9-10-4[127] DavidO'Meara	14/1	14	9
164	Silver Knight *TDEasterby* 9-10-10[133] (s) RussGarritty	22/1	12	10
162	Limerick Boy (GER) *MissVenetiaWilliams* 9-11-5[142] TonyDobbin	12/1		pu

	Green Belt Flyer (IRE) *MissVenetiaWilliams* 9-11-3[140] SamThomas	12/1	pu
169	Fundamentalist (IRE) *NATwiston-Davies* 9-11-3[140] (t) PJBrennan	25/1	pu
185	Pole Star *EvanWilliams* 9-11-0[137] (s) PaulMoloney	25/1	pu
180	Openide *BWDuke* 6-10-9[132] NoelFehily	50/1	pu
183	Lou du Moulin Mas (FR) *PFNicholls* 8-10-8[131] (t) RWalsh	9/1	pu
162	Without A Doubt *CarlLlewellyn* 8-10-6[129] LeightonAspell	14/1	pu
	Victory Gunner (IRE) *CRoberts* 9-10-0[126] LeeStephens[3]	100/1	pu

Mr John P. McManus 18ran 6m22.62

222 **John Smith's Mares' Only Standard Open NHF (L) (1) (4, 5 and** 2m1f
6yo f+m) £17,106

	TURBO LINN *GASwinbank* 4-11-4 TonyDobbin	5/2f	1
	THEATRE GIRL *AKing* 4-10-12 RobertThornton	10/1	1¾ 2
	VALENTINES LADY (IRE) *KGReveley* 6-11-1 PhilKinsella[3]	33/1	13 3
	Helens Vision *MissHLewis* 4-10-12 LiamTreadwell[3]	5/1	2 4
	O'Hana (FR) *WPMullins,Ireland* 5-10-11 MrPWMullins[7]	7/1	4 5
	Katess (IRE) *AKing* 4-10-12 WayneHutchinson	33/1	2½ 6
	Izita Star *MrsALMKing* 4-10-3 AdrianScholes[5]	80/1	5 7
	Drumderry (IRE) *WPMullins,Ireland* 5-11-7 RWalsh	7/1	1½ 8
	Diavoleria *MWEasterby* 4-10-12 MrTGreenall	100/1	12 9
	Haligreen (IRE) *JWMullins* 5-10-13 WayneKavanagh[5]	50/1	2 10
	Whiteoak (IRE) *DMcCainJnr* 4-10-12 JasonMaguire	25/1	1¾ 11
184	One Gulp *PRWebber* 4-10-12 AndrewTinkler	13/2	15 12
	Rosie All Over *DMcCainJnr* 5-10-7 PJBenson[7]	100/1	3 13
	Brook No Argument *JJQuinn* 5-11-4 GLee	40/1	½ 14
	Its Teescomponents (IRE) *KGReveley* 5-10-7 JamesReveley[7]	100/1	sh 15
	Dand Nee (USA) *GASwinbank* 5-11-4 TomDoyle	33/1	16 16
	Owlesbury Dream (IRE) *BGPowell* 5-10-13 CMStudd[5]	40/1	14 17
	Cracking Cliche *MissVenetiaWilliams* 5-11-0 SamThomas	50/1	f
	Princess Flame (GER) *BGPowell* 5-10-13 SPJones[5]	16/1	bd
184	Fiddling Again *NJHenderson* 4-11-1 MickFitzgerald	16/1	pu

Mr J. Nelson 20ran 4m04.77

AINTREE Saturday, Apr 14   GOOD

223 **John Smith's Extra Smooth Hcap Hdle (L) (1) (140) (4yo+)** £28,510   2m110y (9)

80	KINGS QUAY *JJQuinn* 5-10-2[119] (t) DougieCostello[3]	16/1	1
	DIEGO CAO (IRE) *NJGifford* 6-10-13[127] LeightonAspell	25/1	1 2
	DANCING LYRA *RAFahey* 6-9-11[114] PhilKinsella[3]	50/1	2 3
	SUNDAY CITY (JPN) *DMcCainJnr* 6-10-5[122] (s) TomGreenway[3]	40/1	sh 4
3	Hilltime (IRE) *JSWainwright* 7-9-11[118] MrRTierney[7]	100/1	¾ 5
140	Orcadian *JMPEustace* 6-11-12[140] MarkBradburne	14/1	¾ 6
	The Duke's Speech (IRE) *TPTate* 6-10-11[125] JasonMaguire	66/1	1¼ 7
	Forthright *AWCarroll* 6-10-4[118] WayneHutchinson	13/2f	2½ 8
	Oslot (FR) *PFNicholls* 5-11-1[129] RWalsh	18/1	2½ 9
	Never So Blue (FR) *MissVenetiaWilliams* 6-10-1[118] LiamTreadwell[3]	33/1	3½ 10
	Jubilant Note (IRE) *MDMurphy,Ireland* 5-10-13[127] (b) TimmyMurphy	14/1	sh 11
196	Ameeq (USA) *GLMoore* 5-10-12[126] JamieMoore	9/1	12 12
	Buster Hyvonen (IRE) *JRFanshawe* 5-10-11[125] TonyDobbin	12/1	1 13
77	Pepporoni Pete (IRE) *PFNicholls* 6-11-0[128] (t) RobertThornton	7/1	hd 14
	Prairie Moonlight (GER) *WJBurke,Ireland* 7-11-2[130] DNRussell	14/1	21 15
	John Forbes *BEllison* 5-10-6[120] GLee	100/1	10 16
112	Classic Croco (GER) *THogan,Ireland* 6-10-4[118] (b+t) DJCondon	66/1	28 17
146	Slew Charm (FR) *NoelTChance* 5-10-13[127] (t) TomDoyle	14/1	pu
	Warningcamp (GER) *LadyHerries* 6-10-13[127] MickFitzgerald	12/1	pu
	Princelet (IRE) *NJHenderson* 5-10-10[124] (b) APMcCoy	8/1	pu
173	I'm So Lucky *RSBrookhouse* 5-10-9[123] (t) AlanO'Keeffe	33/1	pu
	Thunder Rock (IRE) *JonjoO'Neill* 5-10-6[120] (b) NoelFehily	11/1	pu

Mrs Marie Taylor 22ran 3m57.01

224 **John Smith's Maghull Nov Chase (Gr 1) (1) (5yo+)** £71,275   2m (12)

174	TWIST MAGIC (FR) *PFNicholls* 5-11-1 RWalsh	9/4f	1
196	FAIR ALONG (GER) *PJHobbs* 5-11-1 RichardJohnson	7/2	5 2
93	ROYAL SHAKESPEARE (FR) *SGollings* 8-11-4 RobertThornton	20/1	4 3
174	Lennon (IRE) *JHowardJohnson* 7-11-4 PJBrennan	8/1	1½ 4
174	Don't Push It (IRE) *JonjoO'Neill* 7-11-4 APMcCoy	11/4	15 5
174	Jack The Giant (IRE) *NJHenderson* 5-11-1 MickFitzgerald	6/1	dist 6

Barry Fulton Tony Hayward Michael Lynch 6ran 3m54.15

225 **Baltika Beer Aintree Hdle (Gr 1) (1) (4yo+)** £91,232   2½m (12)

102	AL EILE (IRE) *JohnQueally,Ireland* 7-11-7 TimmyMurphy	12/1	1
178	GASPARA (FR) *DEPipe* 4-10-7 TomScudamore	11/1	1½ 2
175	AFSOUN (FR) *NJHenderson* 5-11-7 MickFitzgerald	13/2	3 3

1126

196	Arcalis *JHowardJohnson* 7-11-7 PJBrennan	11/1	2 4
196	Kawagino (IRE) *JWMullins* 7-11-7 WayneKavanagh	33/1	2 5
175	Asian Maze (IRE) *ThomasMullins,Ireland* 8-11-0 RWalsh	4/1	4 6
187	Strangely Brown (IRE) *EricMcNamara,Ireland* 6-11-7 DJCasey	10/1	7 7
196	Whispered Promises (USA) *RSBrookhouse* 6-11-7 AlanO'Keeffe	66/1	27 8
129	Jazz Messenger (FR) *NMeade,Ireland* 7-11-7 NPMadden	9/1	6 9
175	Detroit City (USA) *PJHobbs* 5-11-7 (t) RichardJohnson	7/4f	3 10
	Star Antique (FR) *KJBurke* 4-10-7 (t) DNRussell	100/1	pu

Mr M. A. Ryan 11ran 4m48.34

226	**John Smith's Extra Cold Hcap Hdle (L) (1) (150) (4yo+)** £28,510		3m110y (13)
171	ALBERTAS RUN (IRE) *JonjoO'Neill* 6-10-4[128] NoelFehily	9/2f	1
133	LYES GREEN *OSherwood* 6-10-6[130] (s) LeightonAspell	10/1	½ 2
190	REFINEMENT (IRE) *JonjoO'Neill* 8-11-10[148] (b) APMcCoy	9/1	1¼ 3
182	PENNY PICTURES (IRE) *DEPipe* 8-10-9[133] TomScudamore	40/1	2 4
123	Irish Wolf (FR) *PBowen* 7-11-11[149] (s) TJO'Brien	16/1	1 5
190	Jockser (IRE) *JWMullins* 6-10-0[129] WayneKavanagh[5]	25/1	9 6
182	Oscatello (USA) *PJHobbs* 7-10-11[135] RichardJohnson	13/2	1½ 7
190	Mistanoora *NATwiston-Davies* 8-10-13[137] (b) TonyEvans	20/1	1½ 8
182	Mahogany Blaze (FR) *NATwiston-Davies* 5-10-12[136] PJBrennan	40/1	1¼ 9
192	Mac Federal (IRE) *MissSWest* 5-10-6[130] JamieGoldstein	14/1	3½ 10
	Gidam Gidam (IRE) *JMackie* 5-10-7[134] (s) PhilKinsella[3]	10/1	1 11
135	Arctic Echo (IRE) *GASwinbank* 8-10-6[133] DougieCostello[3]	20/1	10 12
190	Just Beth *GFierro* 11-10-0[129] DerekLaverty[5]	66/1	9 13
	Opera de Coeur (FR) *HDDaly* 5-10-8[132] MarkBradburne	15/2	5 14
190	Freetown (IRE) *LLungo* 11-10-7[131] (b) BrianHarding	33/1	5 15
176	Lord Sam (IRE) *VRADartnall* 11-11-7[150] (s) JamesWhite[5]	33/1	3½ 16
182	Verasi *GLMoore* 6-11-0[118] (b) JamieMoore	25/1	14 17
187	Overstrand (IRE) *DrRDPNewland* 8-11-3[148] MrTWeston[7]	25/1	f
172	Livingonaknifedge (IRE) *IanWilliams* 8-10-6[130] WayneHutchinson	33/1	bd
	Valley Ride (IRE) *DWPArbuthnot* 7-10-12[136] TomDoyle	12/1	pu
135	Fastaffaran (IRE) *MissLucindaVRussell* 6-10-6[130] (t) PeterBuchanan	16/1	pu

Mr Trevor Hemmings 21ran 6m01.74

227	**John Smith's Grand National Chase (Hcap) (Gr 3) (1) 0-110(158) (6yo+)** £399,140		4½m (30)
177	SILVER BIRCH (IRE) *GElliott,Ireland* 10-10-6[138] (t) RMPower	33/1	1
51	MCKELVEY (IRE) *PBowen* 8-10-4[136] (s) TJO'Brien	12/1	¾ 2
188	SLIM PICKINGS (IRE) *TJTaaffe,Ireland* 8-10-8[140] BJGeraghty	33/1	1¼ 3
150	PHILSON RUN (IRE) *NickWilliams* 11-10-5[137] DarylJacob	100/1	15 4
183	Liberthine (FR) *NJHenderson* 8-10-6[138] MrSWaley-Cohen	40/1	5 5
166	Numbersixvalverde (IRE) *MartinBrassil,Ireland* 11-11-3[149] NPMadden	14/1	21 6
	Longshanks *KCBailey* 10-10-7[139] TonyDobbin	14/1	1¼ 7
197	Puntal (FR) *DEPipe* 11-10-5[137] (s+t) TomScudamore	80/1	13 8
	Hedgehunter (IRE) *WPMullins,Ireland* 11-11-12[158] RWalsh	9/1	1½ 9
193	L'Ami (FR) *FDoumen,France* 8-11-8[154] APMcCoy	14/1	dist 10
79	Clan Royal (FR) *JonjoO'Neill* 12-10-9[141] MrJTMcNamara	33/1	14 11
176	Gallant Approach (IRE) *CREgerton* 8-10-9[141] JAMcCarthy	33/1	2 12
166	Jack High (IRE) *TMWalsh,Ireland* 12-10-3[135] (b) RichardMcGrath	33/1	f
87	Royal Auclair (FR) *PFNicholls* 10-11-1[147] (t) JoeTizzard	33/1	f
166	Point Barrow (IRE) *PatrickHughes,Ireland* 9-10-12[144] PACarberry	8/1cf	f
162	Simon *JLSpearing* 8-10-11[143] AndrewThornton	20/1	f
150	Kandjar d'Allier (FR) *AKing* 9-10-8[140] RobertThornton	100/1	f
150	Bewleys Berry (IRE) *JHowardJohnson* 9-10-7[139] PJBrennan	22/1	f
190	Cloudy Bays (IRE) *CharlesByrnes,Ireland* 10-11-0[146] (s) AJMcNamara	100/1	ref
193	Monkerhostin (FR) *PJHobbs* 10-11-6[152] RichardJohnson	8/1cf	ref
193	Idle Talk (IRE) *DMcCainJnr* 8-11-2[148] JasonMaguire	20/1	ur
177	Le Duc (FR) *PFNicholls* 8-10-2[134] DominicElsworth	66/1	ur
180	Knowhere (IRE) *NATwiston-Davies* 9-10-13[145] TomDoyle	100/1	ur
176	Ballycassidy (IRE) *PBowen* 11-10-9[141] DenisO'Regan	33/1	ur
188	Livingstonebramble (IRE) *WPMullins,Ireland* 11-10-9[141] DNRussell	100/1	ur
188	Graphic Approach (IRE) *CREgerton* 9-10-6[138] PaulMoloney	100/1	ur
197	The Outlier (IRE) *MissVenetiaWilliams* 9-10-5[137] PCO'Neill	125/1	ur
188	Tikram *AKing* 10-10-5[137] WayneHutchinson	125/1	ur
55	Bothar Na (IRE) *WPMullins,Ireland* 8-10-6[138] DJCasey	20/1	pu
51	Eurotrek (IRE) *PFNicholls* 11-11-8[154] LiamHeard	16/1	pu
186	Thisthatandtother (IRE) *PFNicholls* 11-11-5[151] JamieMoore	50/1	pu
186	Billyvoddan (IRE) *HDDaly* 8-11-4[150] (b) LeightonAspell	16/1	pu
162	Celtic Son (FR) *DEPipe* 8-10-11[143] (t) TimmyMurphy	50/1	pu
51	Dun Doire (IRE) *AJMartin,Ireland* 8-10-8[140] PACarberry	20/1	pu
79	Zabenz (NZ) *PJHobbs* 10-10-8[140] (b) BarryFenton	66/1	pu
176	Joes Edge (IRE) *FerdyMurphy* 10-10-2[134] GLee	8/1cf	pu
166	Homer Wells (IRE) *WPMullins,Ireland* 9-10-6[138] DJCondon	33/1	pu

183	Naunton Brook *NATwiston-Davies* 8-10-4[136] (b+t) NoelFehily	125/1	pu
194	Sonevafushi (FR) *MissVenetiaWilliams* 9-10-3[135] MrTGreenall	150/1	pu
150	Kelami (FR) *FDoumen,France* 9-10-12[144] MickFitzgerald	33/1	pu

Mr Brian Walsh (Co. Kildare) 40ran 9m13.25

	228	**John Smith's Nov Hcap Chase (Cdtl Jocks And Amat) (2) (142)**	**2½m (16)**	
		(5yo+) £18,789		
140	PRIVATE BE *PJHobbs* 8-10-10[133] MrJGuerriero[7]	12/1		1
185	BOB HALL (IRE) *JonjoO'Neill* 6-11-7[137] (t) MrJTMcNamara	9/4f	3	2
	TIME TO SELL (IRE) *EugeneMO'Sullivan,Ireland* 8-10-2[125] MrRPMcLernon[7]	20/1	4	3
185	Chief Yeoman *MissVenetiaWilliams* 7-11-1[134] LiamTreadwell[3]	13/2	5	4
185	King Revo (IRE) *PCHaslam* 7-10-6[127] MrAlanBerry[5]	9/1	1½	5
17	Kings Brook *NickWilliams* 7-10-12[131] DarylJacob[3]	12/1	1½	6
	Bougoure (IRE) *MrsSJSmith* 8-10-1[124] TjadeCollier[7]	11/2	24	7
97	Some Legend (IRE) *EJO'Grady,Ireland* 7-10-6[127] MJFerris[5]	12/1		f
185	L'Antartique (FR) *FerdyMurphy* 7-11-9[142] TJDreaper[3]	7/2		ur
	Day of Claies (FR) *HPHogarth* 6-9-12[117] PhilKinsella[3]	8/1		pu

David and Daphne Walsh 10ran 4m58.73

The John Smith's Champion Standard Open NHF (Grade 2) had to be abandoned because an injured National runner was still being treated on the track. A replacement race was staged at Aintree's evening fixture on May 18th, and was won by Theatrical Moment from Kealshore Boy and Lease Lend.

CHELTENHAM Wednesday, Apr 18   GOOD (New Course)

	229	**Faucets For Mira Showers Silver Trophy Chase (Ltd Hcap) (Gr 2)**	**2m5f (17)**	
		(1) (151) (5yo+) £28,510		
188	NYCTEOS (FR) *PFNicholls* 6-10-4[131] RWalsh	10/3		1
186	TOO FORWARD (IRE) *CarlLlewellyn* 7-11-10[151] TimmyMurphy	11/2	3	2
188	MADISON DU BERLAIS (FR) *DEPipe* 6-11-10[151] TomScudamore	11/4f	2½	3
152	Almaydan *RLee* 9-10-4[131] (b) RobertThornton	4/1	hd	4
195	Tysou (FR) *NJHenderson* 10-10-13[140] MickFitzgerald	7/2	3	5
	Noisetine (FR) *MissVenetiaWilliams* 9-10-4[131] AlanO'Keeffe	14/1	9	6

The Stewart Family 6ran 5m09.13

AYR Saturday, Apr 21   GOOD to FIRM

	230	**Ashleybank Investments Future Champion Nov Chase (Gr 2) (1)**	**2½m (17)**	
		(5yo+) £25,780		
216	YES SIR (IRE) *PBowen* 8-11-10 TJO'Brien	5/1		1
187	NATAL (FR) *PFNicholls* 6-11-10 (t) RWalsh	9/4jf	11	2
216	FAASEL (IRE) *NGRichards* 6-11-3 (v) TonyDobbin	9/4jf	5	3
78	Harmony Brig (IRE) *NGRichards* 8-11-7 BrianHarding	40/1	7	4
185	Rasharrow (IRE) *LLungo* 8-11-3 KeithMercer	5/1	7	5
174	Buena Vista (IRE) *DEPipe* 6-11-10 (s) TomScudamore	13/2		f

Ms Y. M. Hill 6ran 4m45.88

	231	**Samsung Electronics Scottish Champion Hdle (Ltd Hcap) (Gr 2) (1)**	**2m (9)**	
		(151) (4yo+) £39,438		
208	EMMPAT (IRE) *CFSwan,Ireland* 9-10-7[134] DJCasey	10/3		1
220	OUNINPOHJA (IRE) *PFNicholls* 6-10-13[140] (b) RWalsh	3/1f	4	2
196	PREMIER DANE (IRE) *NGRichards* 5-10-12[139] TonyDobbin	7/2	1¼	3
178	Altilhar (USA) *GLMoore* 4-10-4[136] JamieMoore	11/2	2½	4
196	Caracciola (GER) *NJHenderson* 10-10-12[139] MickFitzgerald	6/1	5	5
104	Aleron (IRE) *JJQuinn* 9-10-4[134] (s) DougieCostello[3]	33/1	1	6
36	Penzance *AKing* 6-11-10[151] RobertThornton	14/1	2½	7
215	Shatabdi (IRE) *NJHenderson* 5-10-8[135] AndrewTinkler	16/1	1	8

M. D. Mee 8ran 3m43.35

	232	**Coral Scottish Grand National Hcap Chase (Gr 3) (1) (150) (5yo+)**	**4m110y (27)**	
		£96,934		
		HOT WELD *FerdyMurphy* 8-9-9[124] (s) PJMcDonald[5]	14/1		1
205	NINE DE SIVOLA (FR) *FerdyMurphy* 6-10-1[125] GLee	5/1f	½	2
183	PARSONS LEGACY (IRE) *PJHobbs* 9-10-10[134] RichardJohnson	8/1	1¼	3
91	RUN FOR PADDY *CarlLlewellyn* 11-10-10[134] (s) NoelFehily	12/1	15	4
176	Ross Comm *MrsSJSmith* 11-10-3[127] DavidO'Meara	20/1	6	5
227	Ballycassidy (IRE) *PBowen* 11-11-0[138] (s) TJO'Brien	20/1	9	6
114	Strong Resolve (IRE) *MissLucindaVRussell* 11-10-0[124] TomScudamore	50/1	2	7
	Catch The Perk (IRE) *MissLucindaVRussell* 10-10-0[124] (s) PeterBuchanan	66/1	10	8
189	High Cotton *KGReveley* 12-9-7[124] JamesReveley[7]	66/1	13	9
197	L'Aventure (FR) *PFNicholls* 8-10-6[133] (t) LiamHeard[3]	33/1	9	10
205	A New Story (IRE) *MHourigan,Ireland* 9-10-8[132] (s) AJMcNamara	33/1	½	11

121	Another Rum (IRE) *IADuncan,Ireland* 9-10-1[128] (b) RLoughran[3] 14/1	13	12
176	Sir Rembrandt (IRE) *RHAlner* 11-11-2[140] AndrewThornton 40/1	11	13
227	Idle Talk (IRE) *DMcCainJnr* 8-11-10[148] JasonMaguire 20/1		ur
	Classic Capers *JMJefferson* 8-10-6[130] (s) FergusKing 22/1		ur
192	Jooaci (IRE) *DEPipe* 7-11-12[150] (s+t) TimmyMurphy 40/1		pu
176	Cornish Rebel (IRE) *PFNicholls* 10-11-8[146] MickFitzgerald 33/1		pu
183	Napolitain (FR) *PFNicholls* 6-10-12[136] RWalsh 11/1		pu
189	Character Building (IRE) *JJQuinn* 7-10-7[134] DougieCostello[3] 6/1		pu
227	Le Duc (FR) *PFNicholls* 8-10-10[134] SamThomas 33/1		pu
176	Rambling Minster *KGReveley* 9-10-8[132] RichardMcGrath 8/1		pu
193	Sybellius d'Artaix (FR) *PaulMurphy* 7-9-8[125] (t) JohnKington[7] 150/1		pu
	Prince of Slane *GASwinbank* 8-9-11[124] PhilKinsella[3] 100/1		pu

Mr S. Hubbard Rodwell 23ran 7m53.65

PUNCHESTOWN Tuesday, Apr 24   GOOD to FIRM

233 vcbet.com Champion Nov Hdle (Gr 1) (5yo+) £46,395   2m (9)

Order as they passed the post

67	CLOPF (IRE) *EJO'Grady* 6-11-12 BJGeraghty 7/4f		1
173	RINDOON (IRE) *ESheehy* 5-11-11 MDarcy 25/1	1¼	2
170	HOLLY TREE (IRE) *ESheehy* 7-11-12 APMcCoy 20/1	nk	3
173	Hide The Evidence (IRE) *MrsJHarrington* 6-11-12 ADLeigh 8/1	6	4
	Jog On (IRE) *PAFahy* 7-11-12 DNRussell 66/1	hd	5
207	Restoration (FR) *NMeade* 5-11-12 PCarberry 25/1	15	6
220	Bywell Beau (IRE) *GACharlton,GB* 8-11-12 (t) JanFaltejsek 20/1	9	7
173	Ebaziyan (IRE) *WPMullins* 6-11-12 RWalsh 11/4	8	8
207	De Valira (IRE) *MJPO'Brien* 5-11-11 AELynch 9/2		ur

Mr Bernard Anthony Heffernan 9ran 3m45.76

234 Evening Herald Hcap Hdle 0-140(133) (4yo+) £33,214   2½m (12)

112	CHARLIES FIRST (IRE) *PeterCasey* 7-10-7[116] BJGeraghty....................... 14/1		1
219	ON THE NET (IRE) *EoghanO'Grady* 9-10-6[118] MJFerris[3] 20/1	½	2
	BAILY BREEZE (IRE) *MFMorris* 8-10-4[113] (b) PWFlood........................... 25/1	1	3
	SIGNIFICANT *MJPO'Brien* 5-9-12[110] AELynch[3] 16/1	1¼	4
	Streets of Gold (IRE) *CRoche* 5-10-2[114] (t) MPWalsh[3] 10/1	½	5
	Considine (USA) *EricMcNamara* 6-9-10[108] BCByrnes[3] 25/1	1	6
	Golden Empire (FR) *AndrewHeffernan* 6-10-8[117] BMCash 14/1	6	7
208	Dreux (FR) *ThomasCooper* 5-10-4[116] (b) SGMcDermott[3]........................ 66/1	1½	8
	Artiste Bay (IRE) *EoinGriffin* 5-10-2[118] (t) SWFlanagan[7] 25/1	3	9
	Supreme Being (IRE) *MichaelCunningham* 10-10-8[124] (b) SWJackson[7] ... 25/1	2½	10
205	Ross River *AJMartin* 11-10-13[122] RWalsh.. 14/1	13	11
	The Sliotar (IRE) *MFMorris* 6-10-0[112] ADLeigh[3] 14/1	1¼	12
	Emotional Article (IRE) *TJTaaffe* 7-11-0[123] NPMadden 10/1	2	13
167	Offaly (IRE) *NMeade* 6-10-12[121] PCarberry 33/1	4	14
208	Savitha (IRE) *PaulNolan* 7-10-1[113] RMMoran[3] 33/1	¾	15
	Fleet Street *NJHenderson,GB* 8-11-10[133] MickFitzgerald......................... 6/1f	sh	16
	Tasman (IRE) *LiamMcAteer* 7-11-0[130] DPFahy[7] 40/1	13	17
170	Gripit N Tipit (IRE) *CFSwan* 6-10-7[116] DJCasey 20/1		f
208	Streetshavenoname (IRE) *TJTaaffe* 6-10-7[116] DJCondon......................... 14/1		bd
200	Wheresben (GER) *SeamusFahey* 8-11-1[131] MrJAFahey[7] 25/1		pu
21	Predator (GER) *JonjoO'Neill,GB* 6-11-1[124] APMcCoy 10/1		pu
112	Lenrey *ALTMoore* 7-10-9[118] DNRussell 14/1		pu
	Bon Temps Rouler (FR) *ALTMoore* 8-10-5[114] PACarberry 16/1		pu
	Grapevine Sally (IRE) *EJO'Grady* 6-10-1[110] TGMRyan.......................... 20/1		pu
172	Loughanelteen (IRE) *PJRothwell* 9-10-3[112] DFO'Regan 50/1		pu

Mr Brendan Sweeney 25ran 4m59.56

235 Kerrygold Champion Chase (Gr 1) (5yo+) £84,531   2m (11)

156	MANSONY (FR) *ALTMoore* 8-11-12 DNRussell.. 13/2		1
181	JUSTIFIED (IRE) *ESheehy* 8-11-12 APMcCoy 9/2	1¼	2
138	STEEL BAND *PaulARoche* 9-11-12 DJCasey 40/1	3½	3
181	River City (IRE) *NoelTChance,GB* 10-11-12 TomDoyle 7/2	1¼	4
181	Newmill (IRE) *JohnJosephMurphy* 9-11-12 AndrewJMcNamara 13/8f	1¾	5
120	Our Ben *WPMullins* 8-11-12 RWalsh 8/1	2½	6
206	Central House *DTHughes* 10-11-12 (b+t) RLoughran 16/1	25	7

Mr Michael Mulholland 7ran 4m07.09

236 Ellier Developments Hanover Quay Champion Nov Chase (Gr 1)   3m1f (17)
(5yo+) £46,395

201	OFFSHORE ACCOUNT (IRE) *CFSwan* 7-11-10 DFO'Regan.................... 16/1		1
185	KNIGHT LEGEND (IRE) *MrsJHarrington* 8-11-10 BJGeraghty............... 25/1	11	2
203	ONE COOL COOKIE (IRE) *CFSwan* 6-11-10 DJCasey............................. 11/2	2	3
180	Snowy Morning (IRE) *WPMullins* 7-11-10 RWalsh................................... 9/4	21	4

Merdeka (IRE) *TJTaaffe* 7-11-10 DNRussell.................................. 16/1   22 5
216 Aces Four (IRE) *FerdyMurphy,GB* 8-11-10 GLee .... 6/4f   f
185 Vic Venturi (IRE) *PhilipFenton* 7-11-10 APMcCoy .... 9/1   pu

Mr Brian Polly 7ran 6m16.48

PUNCHESTOWN Wednesday, Apr 25
Chase course: GOOD, Hurdles course: GOOD to FIRM

237   **Bewleys Hotels Irish Stallion Farms European Breeders Fund**   2¼m (10)
      Mares Hdle (Gr 3) (4yo+ f+m) £31,000

202 GRANGECLARE LARK (IRE) *DTHughes* 6-11-5 RLoughran.................... 11/4   1
202 SHUIL ARIS (IRE) *PaulNolan* 6-10-10 RWalsh 6/4f   2½ 2
202 BLAZING SKY (IRE) *FFMcGuinness* 7-11-0 PWFlood .... 8/1   ½ 3
     Malachy's Attic (IRE) *MJPO'Brien* 7-10-10 TGMRyan 25/1   3 4
     Swift Post (IRE) *MJPO'Brien* 6-10-10 AELynch 25/1   1¾ 5
     Molly Massini (IRE) *GerardQuirk* 7-10-10 DJCasey 14/1   7 6
     Corrieann (IRE) *PMJDoyle* 6-10-10 MrJJDoyle .... 16/1   sh 7
170 Midnight Gift (IRE) *THogan* 7-10-10 DFO'Regan......................... 16/1   ¾ 8
223 Prairie Moonlight (GER) *WJBurke* 7-11-0 DNRussell 16/1   6 9
173 She's Our Daisy (IRE) *RHBuckler,GB* 7-11-0 DAJacob.................... 25/1   12 10
     Zamona (IRE) *MrsLouiseParkhill* 6-10-10 NPMadden 100/1   27 11
     Sorrentina (IRE) *WHarney* 6-10-10 RCColgan 40/1   17 12
     Media Queen (IRE) *DenisAhern* 6-10-10 (b+t) RMPower .... 50/1   pu

Mr T. Hendy 13ran 4m16.50

238   **Oberstown Developments Hcap Hdle 0-140(133) (4yo+)** £33,214   2m (9)

 67 BOBS PRIDE (IRE) *DKWeld* 5-11-1¹²⁴ RWalsh............................. 10/3f   1
     BIEN BRONZE *ALTMoore* 6-10-7¹¹⁶ DNRussell............................ 10/1   3 2
208 FARMER BROWN (IRE) *PatrickHughes* 6-11-1¹²⁴ RichardJohnson 7/1   1 3
     TOP THE CHARTS *AJMartin* 5-9-7¹⁰⁵ RCColgan³ 7/1   3 4
208 Wishwillow Lord (IRE) *LeonardWhitmore* 8-11-3¹²⁶ MDarcy.............. 40/1   1½ 5
208 Jaamid *NMeade* 5-10-5¹¹⁴ PCarberry 10/1   1¾ 6
     Strand Line (IRE) *PJRothwell* 7-9-3¹⁰⁵ SWJackson⁷ .... 33/1   ¾ 7
     Artistic Lad *MrsJHarrington* 7-9-11¹⁰⁹ ADLeigh³ 33/1   3½ 8
     Jawad (IRE) *MsJoannaMorgan* 6-10-5¹¹⁴ DJCasey 14/1   1¾ 9
208 Monty Mint (IRE) *ThomasFoley* 9-10-1¹¹⁵ DFFlannery⁵.................. 16/1   sh 10
112 First Row (IRE) *DTHughes* 5-10-7¹¹⁶ RLoughran 25/1   4 11
     Rathkenny (IRE) *WilliamColemanO'Brien* 8-9-6¹⁰⁸ PAGallagher⁷ 40/1   1¾ 12
     Silent Jo (JPN) *MJPO'Brien* 5-9-8¹⁰⁶ AELynch³ .... 10/1   ½ 13
140 Moore's Law (USA) *MJGrassick* 9-11-4¹²⁷ DFO'Regan................... 20/1   nk 14
196 The Spoonplayer (IRE) *HenrydeBromhead* 8-10-10¹¹⁹ BJGeraghty.......... 20/1   3 15
208 Dbest (IRE) *MsJoannaMorgan* 7-10-10¹¹⁹ (b) PWFlood 16/1   3 16
     Gunnison (IRE) *EoinGriffin* 6-9-4¹⁰⁶ (t) SWFlanagan⁷ 20/1   1¾ 17
208 Querido (USA) *EJO'Grady* 5-10-1¹¹⁰ TGMRyan .... 50/1   ½ 18
     Hurricane Alley (IRE) *AndrewLee* 6-10-3¹¹² NPMadden 50/1   10 19
234 Fleet Street *NJHenderson,GB* 8-11-10¹³³ MickFitzgerald............... 20/1   8 20
     Jack Ingham (IRE) *EJO'Grady* 7-10-6¹¹⁵ RMPower 20/1   25 21
     Stutter *JGCarr* 9-10-0¹⁰⁹ PACarberry .... 20/1   pu

Mr R. Blacoe 22ran 3m43.34

239   **Punchestown Guinness Gold Cup (Gr 1) (5yo+)** £102,041   3m1f (17)

193 NEPTUNE COLLONGES (FR) *PFNicholls,GB* 6-11-12 RWalsh.................. 8/1   1
193 KINGSCLIFF (IRE) *RHAlner,GB* 10-11-12 RobertWalford 16/1   3½ 2
 76 IN COMPLIANCE (IRE) *MJPO'Brien* 7-11-12 BJGeraghty 6/4f   7 3
186 Racing Demon (IRE) *MissHCKnight,GB* 7-11-12 GLee..................... 4/1   4 4
227 Monkerhostin (FR) *PJHobbs,GB* 10-11-12 RichardJohnson 15/2   4 5
156 Sher Beau (IRE) *PhilipFenton* 8-11-12 APMcCoy 25/1   8 6
200 Watson Lake (IRE) *NMeade* 9-11-12 PCarberry .... 25/1   sh 7
193 Beef Or Salmon (IRE) *MHourigan* 11-11-12 (b) AndrewJMcNamara......... 15/2   4½ 8
227 Cloudy Bays (IRE) *CharlesByrnes* 10-11-12 (s) DNRussell .... 66/1   dist 9
218 Hi Cloy (IRE) *MHourigan* 10-11-12 DFO'Regan .... 14/1   pu

Mr J. Hales 10ran 6m16.00

240   **Ulster Bank Hcap Chase 0-150(140) (5yo+)** £33,214   2½m (14)

     ROYAL COUNTY STAR (IRE) *AJMartin* 8-9-12¹¹⁷ RCColgan³................ 9/2f   1
     CARRIGEEN KALMIA (IRE) *RHLalor* 8-10-7¹³⁰ MissEALalor⁷ .... 20/1   ¾ 2
206 IN THE HIGH GRASS (IRE) *TJTaaffe* 6-10-7¹³⁰ ABJoyce⁷ 12/1   3 3
  5 CARLESIMO (IRE) *NMeade* 9-10-4¹²⁰ PCarberry 14/1   7 4
182 All Star (GER) *NJHenderson,GB* 7-11-0¹³⁰ MickFitzgerald.............. 10/1   1½ 5
     Phelans Fancy (IRE) *MJO'Connor* 9-9-10¹¹² NPMadden.................. 40/1   2½ 6
227 Livingstonebramble (IRE) *WPMullins* 11-11-9¹³⁹ RWalsh 14/1   5 7
188 Roman Ark *JMJefferson,GB* 9-11-10¹⁴⁰ FergusKing 14/1   2½ 8
     Curfew Tolls (IRE) *HenrydeBromhead* 11-9-7¹¹² AELynch³............... 33/1   28 9

206 Old Flame (IRE) *PaulNolan* 8-11-8[138] JLCullen..................................... 14/1 1 10
  9 Oh Be The Hokey (IRE) *CFSwan* 9-10-7[123] APMcCoy .... 15/2 f
       Underwriter (USA) *FerdyMurphy,GB* 7-9-12[117] PJMcDonald[3] .... 14/1 f
138 Tiger Cry (IRE) *ALTMoore* 9-11-9[139] DNRussell .... 6/1 pu
203 Ursis (FR) *SGollings,GB* 6-11-8[138] RichardJohnson .... 11/1 pu
       Dunguaire Lad (IRE) *PatrickHughes* 7-10-5[124] MFMooney[3]...................... 14/1 pu
       Amorini (IRE) *PJRothwell* 8-9-5[114] SWJackson[7]................................... 25/1 pu

Dunsany Racing Syndicate 16ran 5m05.40

241 **Paddy Power Champion I.N.H. Flat (Gr 1) (4, 5, 6 and 7yo m)**   2m
       £48,714

       MICK THE MAN (IRE) *NMeade* 6-12-0 MissNCarberry........................... 10/1   1
       WOODBINE WILLIE (IRE) *PhilipFenton* 6-12-0 MrKEPower................. 14/1   2 2
184 SHIRLEY CASPER (IRE) *PhilipFenton* 6-11-9 MrBTO'Connell 15/2   1¼ 3
       Cuchulains Son (IRE) *WPMullins* 5-11-13 MrPWMullins 33/1   1¼ 4
184 Cork All Star (IRE) *MrsJHarrington* 5-11-13 MrMFahey...................... 9/4f   nk 5
       King of The Titans (IRE) *BPGalvin* 4-11-6 MrRPMcNamara.............. 100/1   2 6
       Bootlegger (IRE) *ThomasMullins* 5-11-13 MrRO'Sullivan .... 16/1   ½ 7
       Giant Eagle (USA) *ThomasFoley* 5-11-13 MissAFoley .... 8/1   ½ 8
184 Sophocles *JamesLeavy* 4-11-6 MissPaulineRyan 13/2   1 9
       Rock Street (IRE) *RobertTyner* 6-12-0 MrDerekO'Connor 20/1   1½ 10
       Lady Bolino (IRE) *MichaelMulvany* 4-11-1 MrJTMcNamara............... 50/1   3 11
184 Coolnine (IRE) *WPMullins* 5-11-13 MsKWalsh.................................. 20/1   1¼ 12
184 Tot O'Whiskey *JMJefferson,GB* 6-12-0 MrOWilliams.......................... 12/1   ¾ 13
222 Drumderry (IRE) *WPMullins* 5-11-8 MrJJDoyle.................................. 33/1   nk 14
       Caravino (IRE) *EoinGriffin* 4-11-6 MrATDuff.................................... 20/1   3 15
       Lucky Heroine (IRE) *MissSCollins* 5-11-8 MrJPO'Farrell 20/1 18 16
       Azalea (IRE) *NMeade* 5-11-8 MrJPMcKeown 25/1 23 17
       Lucky Gun (IRE) *TJTaaffe* 5-11-13 MrJJCodd 100/1 19 18
       Castlekelly (IRE) *JamesMorrissey* 7-12-0 MrPCashman 100/1 2½ 19

Mr James Grace 19ran 3m43.20

PUNCHESTOWN Thursday, Apr 26   GOOD to FIRM

242 **Ballymore Properties Champion Four Year Old Hdle (Gr 1) (4yo)**   2m (9)
       £46,395

211 PUNJABI *NJHenderson,GB* 4-11-0 MAFitzgerald 6/4f   1
191 FINANCIAL REWARD (IRE) *WPMullins* 4-11-0 RWalsh .... 8/1   ¾ 2
       BAHRAIN STORM (IRE) *PJFlynn* 4-11-0 (b) DNRussell 5/1   8 3
       Katies Tuitor *BWDuke,GB* 4-11-0 NDFehily.................................... 9/1   8 4
191 Duty (IRE) *KFO'Brien* 4-11-0 APMcCoy 6/1   2½ 5
165 Robin du Bois (FR) *AJMartin* 4-11-0 PCarberry 7/1   4 6
178 Deputy Consort (USA) *MJPO'Brien* 4-11-0 AELynch......................... 33/1   1¾ 7
       Superjet (IRE) *MHalford* 4-10-9 EMButterly..................................... 25/1   1¼ 8
       Sicilian (IRE) *PatrickOBrady* 4-11-0 JLCullen.................................. 100/1   9 9
       Blackriver Boy *NiallMoran* 4-11-0 NPMadden................................. 100/1 16 10

Mr Raymond Tooth 10ran 3m43.84

243 **Swordlestown Cup Nov Chase (Gr 1) (5yo+)** £46,395   2m (11)

174 ANOTHER PROMISE (IRE) *FerdyMurphy,GB* 8-11-12 GLee 5/1   1
224 ROYAL SHAKESPEARE (FR) *SGollings,GB* 8-11-12 RJohnson 7/1   3½ 2
195 CARTHALAWN (IRE) *CharlesByrnes* 6-11-12 DNRussell...................... 20/1   3 3
       Siberion (IRE) *AJMartin* 6-11-12 RPMcNamara 8/1   4½ 4
203 Schindlers Hunt (IRE) *DTHughes* 7-11-12 RLoughran........................ 5/2   dist 5
 90 Blueberry Boy (IRE) *PaulStafford* 7-11-12 AELynch.......................... 10/1   f
206 Gemini Lucy (IRE) *MrsJHarrington* 7-11-7 ADLeigh............................ 9/4f   ur

Geoff Hubbard Racing 7ran 4m06.24

244 **Dunboyne Castle Hotel & Spa Champion Stayers' Hdle (Gr 1)**   3m (14)
       (4yo+) £84,354

226 REFINEMENT (IRE) *JonjoO'Neill,GB* 8-11-7 APMcCoy 16/1   1
182 POWERSTATION (IRE) *MPhillips* 7-11-12 DFO'Regan 20/1   2½ 2
187 UNITED (GER) *MrsLWadham,GB* 6-11-7 LAspell 16/1   3 3
       Essex (IRE) *MJPO'Brien* 7-11-12 AELynch.. 5/1   hd 4
204 Adamant Approach (IRE) *WPMullins* 13-11-12 MrPWMullins 12/1 11 5
175 Brave Inca (IRE) *ColmAMurphy* 9-11-12 RWalsh 3/1   2½ 6
204 Sky's The Limit (FR) *EJO'Grady* 6-11-12 (b) BJGeraghty.................... 20/1 16 7
       Kenilworth (USA) *PatrickOBrady* 8-11-12 JLCullen........................... 100/1 13 8
209 Mighty Man (FR) *HDDaly,GB* 7-11-12 RJohnson .... 5/4f   pu

Mr M. Tabor 9ran 5m50.34

245 **Barrack Homes Pat Taaffe Hcap Chase 0-145(136) (5yo+) £31,000**   3m1f (17)

205	AMERICAN JENNIE (IRE) *MichaelCullen* 9-11-7[136] NPMadden	12/1	1
	NOIR ET VERT (FR) *FerdyMurphy,GB* 6-10-11[126] GLee	7/2f	sh 2
	BEAUTIFUL VISION (IRE) *TJTaaffe* 7-9-12[113] (s) PACarberry	7/1	nk 3
	The Roney Man *PaulNolan* 7-9-10[111] JRBarry	12/1	2½ 4
	Aimees Mark (IRE) *FFlood* 11-9-8[112] ADLeigh[3]	16/1	3 5
	Dosco (IRE) *DTHughes* 8-10-8[123] RLoughran	12/1	2½ 6
197	Jaquouille (FR) *ALTMoore* 10-10-5[120] DFO'Regan	14/1	2 7
227	Bothar Na (IRE) *WPMullins* 8-11-7[136] (t) RWalsh	9/1	1¾ 8
205	Dix Villez (FR) *PaulNolan* 8-10-12[127] JLCullen	8/1	sh 9
97	Giolla An Bhaird (IRE) *MichaelFitzsimons* 10-9-11[115] (s) AELynch[3]	20/1	nk 10
97	Ride The Storm (IRE) *EJO'Grady* 10-10-1[116] PWFlood	16/1	3 11
	Deep Return (IRE) *NMeade* 10-10-0[115] PCarberry	12/1	16 12
197	Newbay Prop (IRE) *AJMartin* 8-9-12[116] RCColgan[3]	6/1	pu
	Sorry Al (IRE) *CFSwan* 7-10-0[115] DJCasey	20/1	pu

Mr L. Murray 14ran 6m16.70

PUNCHESTOWN Friday, Apr 27   GOOD to FIRM

246 **betfair.com Nov Hcap Chase (137) (5yo+) £46,395**   2m5f (15)

144	ALEXANDER TAIPAN (IRE) *WPMullins* 7-11-10[137] RWalsh	4/1f	1
203	ANOTHERCOPPERCOAST (IRE) *PaulARoche* 7-11-0[127] JRBarry	12/1	nk 2
203	WASHINGTON LAD (IRE) *PAFahy* 7-10-4[117] PWFlood	10/1	6 3
205	Mac Three (IRE) *NMeade* 8-10-12[125] DFO'Regan	20/1	5½ 4
203	Purple Shuffle (IRE) *PAFahy* 9-10-11[127] (t) APLane[3]	25/1	4 5
	Cool Running (IRE) *CRoche* 7-10-8[121] APMcCoy	7/1	1¾ 6
180	Justpourit (IRE) *DTHughes* 8-11-4[131] RLoughran	20/1	1¾ 7
201	Ponmeoath (IRE) *EricMcNamara* 7-10-12[128] BCByrnes[3]	9/1	2½ 8
205	Oodachee *CFSwan* 8-10-13[126] DJCasey	13/2	10 9
53	Letterman (IRE) *EJO'Grady* 7-11-1[128] BJGeraghty	13/2	17 10
168	Lala Nova (IRE) *JohnJosephMurphy* 8-10-0[116] RJMolloy[3]	66/1	3½ 11
180	Mossbank (IRE) *MHourigan* 7-11-1[128] CO'Dwyer	14/1	pu
128	Khetaam (IRE) *NMeade* 9-10-13[126] PCarberry	16/1	pu
	Anshire Tower (IRE) *SeamusNeville* 7-10-10[123] NPMadden	16/1	pu

Mr Noel O'Callaghan 14ran 5m29.10

247 **ACCBank Champion Hdle (Gr 1) (5yo+) £81,633**   2m (9)

208	SILENT OSCAR (IRE) *HarryRogers* 8-11-12 RMPower	20/1	1
157	MACS JOY (IRE) *MrsJHarrington* 8-11-12 BJGeraghty	7/4f	nk 2
175	HARDY EUSTACE (IRE) *DTHughes* 10-11-12 (b) CO'Dwyer	4/1	8 3
208	Callow Lake (IRE) *MrsJHarrington* 7-11-12 (b) ADLeigh	66/1	2 4
157	Harchibald (FR) *NMeade* 8-11-12 NPMadden	7/1	3 5
175	Iktitaf (IRE) *NMeade* 6-11-12 (t) PCarberry	9/4	sh 6
208	Sweet Wake (GER) *NMeade* 6-11-12 DFO'Regan	25/1	1¾ 7
225	Strangely Brown (IRE) *EricMcNamara* 6-11-12 RWalsh	25/1	13 8

Mr Patrick Convery 8ran 3m52.42

248 **Land Rover Champion Nov Hdle (Gr 1) (4yo+) £46,395**   2½m (12)

207	GLENCOVE MARINA (IRE) *WPMullins* 5-11-11 RWalsh	11/4jf	1
173	KALDERON (GER) *THogan* 7-11-12 DJCasey	10/1	5 2
	BREAKING SILENCE (IRE) *TJTaaffe* 6-11-12 RMPower	20/1	15 3
	Aitmatov (GER) *NMeade* 6-11-12 PCarberry	4/1	2½ 4
137	Davorin (JPN) *RPBurns* 6-11-12 DFO'Regan	20/1	20 5
	Optimus Prime (IRE) *WJBurke* 6-11-12 JRBarry	66/1	27 6
173	Shanghide *MFMorris* 6-11-12 CO'Dwyer	25/1	1 7
	Maxi (IRE) *MHourigan* 6-11-12 AndrewJMcNamara	66/1	¾ 8
179	Catch Me (GER) *EJO'Grady* 5-11-11 BJGeraghty	11/4jf	f
207	Cuan Na Grai (IRE) *PaulNolan* 6-11-12 APMcCoy	5/1	pu

Mr John J. Brennan 10ran 4m53.63

SANDOWN Saturday, Apr 28   FIRM

249 **Betfred Celebration Chase (Gr 2) (1) (5yo+) £57,020**   2m (13)

181	DEMPSEY (IRE) *CarlLlewellyn* 9-11-6 TimmyMurphy	5/4f	1
134	HOO LA BALOO (FR) *PFNicholls* 6-11-6 RWalsh	8/1	7 2
229	TYSOU (FR) *NJHenderson* 6-11-6 MickFitzgerald	16/1	1½ 3
213	Demi Beau *EvanWilliams* 9-11-6 ChristianWilliams	20/1	2½ 4
235	River City (IRE) *NoelTChance* 10-11-6 TomDoyle	13/2	1¼ 5
49	Full House (IRE) *PRWebber* 8-11-6 RichardJohnson	14/1	1¼ 6
230	Yes Sir (IRE) *PBowen* 8-11-6 TJO'Brien	7/2	1 7
181	Mister McGoldrick *CarlLlewellyn* 10-11-6 DominicElsworth	16/1	1½ 8

Mrs T. Brown 8ran 3m43.62

250 **Betfred Gold Cup Chase (Hcap) (Gr 3) (1) (161) (5yo+)** £91,232   3m5f110y (24)

232	HOT WELD *FerdyMurphy* 8-10-0[135] (s) GLee..	6/1	1
221	REVEILLEZ *JRFanshawe* 8-10-10[145] (t) APMcCoy..	9/4f	3 2
210	MY WILL (FR) *PFNicholls* 7-11-5[161] MrNScholfield[7].....................................	11/1	6 3
227	Jack High (IRE) *TMWalsh,Ireland* 12-10-0[135] (v) RichardMcGrath.............	20/1	6 4
227	Zabenz (NZ) *PJHobbs* 10-10-5[140] (b) RichardJohnson.................................	10/1	1¼ 5
162	Cornish Sett (IRE) *PFNicholls* 8-10-10[145] (b) RWalsh....................................	4/1	10 6
205	Juveigneur (FR) *NJHenderson* 10-11-5[154] MickFitzgerald.............................	12/1	nk 7
185	Wee Robbie *NJGifford* 7-10-4[139] LeightonAspell.......................................	13/2	dist 8
22	Sweet Diversion (IRE) *PFNicholls* 8-9-12[136] (t) LiamHeard[3].....................	12/1	pu
164	Cowboyboots (IRE) *LWells* 9-9-9[135] (b) SPJones[5]....................................	66/1	pu

Mr S. Hubbard Rodwell 10ran 7m11.03

AUTEUIL Sunday, May 27   SOFT

251 **Gras Savoye Cinema Prix Ferdinand Dufaure Chase (Gr 1) (4yo)**   2½m110y
£107,877

	REMEMBER ROSE (IRE) *J-PGallorini,France* 4-10-6 (s) CPieux..........	59/10	1
	MASTER MINDED (FR) *GMacaire,France* 4-10-6 RWalsh.......................	6/4f	8 2
29	MILDON (FR) *JOrtet,France* 4-10-6 PMarsac......................................	45/1	8 3
	Aviador (FR) *MRolland,France* 4-10-6 (b) GAdam...............................	9/1	8 4
	Parsou (FR) *YFouin,France* 4-10-6 SDehez..	49/1	10 5
	Mille Et Une (FR) *JBertrandeBalanda,France* 4-10-6 I1 BBenard...........	52/1	15 6
29	City Note (FR) *MRolland,France* 4-10-6 (b) RSchmidlin.......................	12/1	5 7
	Lucky du Berlais (FR) *JBertrandeBalanda,France* 4-10-6 BChameraud...	11/1	nk 8
	Limaranta (FR) *FCottin,France* 4-10-1 PACarberry...............................	6/1	20 9
	Pirak d'Airy (FR) *JOrtet,France* 4-10-6 DLesot.................................	64/1	f
	Simonet (FR) *AChaille-Chaille,France* 4-10-6 JRicou..........................	12/1	pu
29	Fabulously (FR) *RCollet,France* 4-10-6 CGombeau............................	22/1	pu

Mr Ernst Iten 12ran 5m10.00

252 **Gras Savoye Grand Steeple-Chase de Paris (Gr 1) (5yo+)** £246,575   3m5f

	MID DANCER (FR) *AChaille-Chaille,France* 6-10-8 CGombeau.........	15/2	1
28	LORD CARMONT (FR) *MmeIPacault,France* 8-10-8 SMassinot..............	5/1	15 2
	GOLDEN FLIGHT (FR) *GMacaire,France* 8-10-8 RWalsh.....................	15/1	dist 3
	Grand Canal (FR) *J-VToux,France* 11-10-8 RBonnet..........................	45/1	20 4
193	Marble Garden (USA) *RichardChotard,France* 6-10-8 ALecordier..........	117/1	20 5
28	Princesse d'Anjou (FR) *FCottin,France* 6-10-3 PACarberry.................	5/1	f
27	Or Noir de Somoza (FR) *AChaille-Chaille,France* 5-10-3 JRicou............	5/4f	f
	Norville du Bois (FR) *MmeEHolmey,France* 6-10-8 FDitta..................	33/1	pu
	Jerozin (FR) *FCottin,France* 6-10-8 DJHoward..............................	94/1	pu
	Sleeping Jack (FR) *JOrtet,France* 8-10-8 DLesot............................	64/1	pu
	Wisborough (FR) *JOrtet,France* 9-10-8 CPieux..............................	12/1	pu
	Kolorado (POL) *COlehla,CzechRepublic* 7-10-8 PaddyAspell.............	20/1	pu

Mr S. Mulryan 12ran 7m32.00

253 **Gras Savoye Hipcover Prix La Barka Hdle (Gr 2) (5yo+)** £53,938   2m5f110y

	SHINCO DU BERLAIS (FR) *RCollet,France* 5-10-1 CPieux....................	12/1	1
	MISTER GYOR (FR) *BBarbier,France* 7-10-3 CGombeau......................	17/1	1½ 2
	GRAY STEEL (FR) *JBertrandeBalanda,France* 5-10-1 BChameraud.........	14/1	8 3
	Monoalco (FR) *PPeltier,France* 7-10-6 DBerra................................	11/1	10 4
187	Kasbah Bliss (FR) *FDoumen,France* 5-10-1 ADuchene......................	8/1	10 5
	Cheler (FR) *BSecly,France* 8-10-3 SLeloup....................................	28/1	8 6
140	Heathcote *GLMoore,GB* 5-10-6 JamieMoore..................................	74/1	ns 7
248	Glencove Marina (IRE) *WPMullins,Ireland* 5-10-1 RWalsh.................	8/1	2 8
	Sonnyanjoe (IRE) *THogan,Ireland* 9-10-3 PACarberry......................	64/1	10 9
	Clear Riposte (IRE) *WPMullins,Ireland* 5-9-8 DGallagher.................	22/1	2½ 10
246	Alexander Taipan (IRE) *WPMullins,Ireland* 7-10-3 DJCasey..............	43/1	11
54	Zaiyad (FR) *AChaille-Chaille,France* 6-10-10 JRicou........................	5/4f	pu
	Water Dragon *CCardenne,France* 6-10-6 TMajorcryk........................	38/1	pu
	Icarro (FR) *J-PGallorini,France* 6-10-3 HGallorini..........................	32/1	pu
	Turgeoie Vireenne (FR) *DChevrollier,France* 5-9-8 JGuiheneuf...........	37/1	pu

Mr Robert Collet 15ran 5m26.00

AUTEUIL Saturday, Jun 16   SOFT

254 **Prix Alain du Breil - Course de Haies d'Ete des Quatre Ans Hdle**   2m3f110y (13)
(Gr 1) (4yo) £76,531

125	GOOD BYE SIMON (FR) *TDoumen,France* 4-10-6 BDelo....................	5/1	1
	BIG BUCK'S (FR) *RELecomte,France* 4-10-6 FBarrao.......................	21/1	2 2
	DROLE DE DRAME (FR) *RCaget,France* 4-10-1 DGallagher...............	33/1	2 3
	Gaelic Ocean (FR) *MRolland,France* 4-10-6 RSchmidlin..................	7/1	4 4
	Top of The Sky (FR) *SLoeuillet,France* 4-10-6 RO'Brien...............	40/1	2 5

242	Financial Reward (IRE) *WPMullins,Ireland* 4-10-6 RWalsh	5/1	ns 6
191	J'Y Vole (FR) *WPMullins,Ireland* 4-10-1 DJCasey	15/4f	2 7
	Dalina (FR) *ELeenders,France* 4-10-1 CSanterne	17/1	1½ 8
	Sing Faraway (FR) *AChaille-Chaille,France* 4-10-6 JRicou	11/1	8 9
251	Limaranta (FR) *FCottin,France* 4-10-1 (b) PACarberry	31/1	20 10
251	Mildon (FR) *JOrtet,France* 4-10-6 CPieux	8/1	pu

Mr J. Hayoz 11ran 4m55.85

255   **Grande Course de Haies d'Auteuil Hdle (Gr 1) (5yo+) £107,143**   3m1f110y (16)

253	ZAIYAD (FR) *AChaille-Chaille,France* 9/5f		1
253	MISTER GYOR (FR) *BBarbier,France* 7-10-8 CGombeau	7/1	8 2
253	MONOALCO (FR) *PPeltier,France* 7-10-8 DBerra	29/1	3 3
253	Shinco du Berlais (FR) *RCollet,France* 5-10-3 CPieux	19/4	2 4
	Risko (FR) *RichardChotard,France* 6-10-8 JDucout	15/1	½ 5
253	Kasbah Bliss (FR) *FDoumen,France* 5-10-3 ADuchene	31/4	5 6
253	Alexander Taipan (IRE) *WPMullins,Ireland* 7-10-8 RWalsh	28/1	5 7
	Alarm Call (FR) *JOrtet,France* 7-10-8 DLesot	27/4	3 8
253	Clear Riposte (IRE) *WPMullins,Ireland* 5-9-13 DJCasey	67/1	3 9
253	Cheler (FR) *BSecly,France* 8-10-8 SLeloup	49/1	8 10
	Liberty Rock (FR) *TDoumen,France* 8-10-8 BDelo	45/1	pu
26	Rock And Palm (FR) *MlleIGot,France* 7-10-8 DGallagher	24/1	pu
	Blue Calin (FR) *J-LGay,France* 6-10-8 SDehez	53/1	pu
	Le Prestigieux (FR) *J-LGuillochon,France* 10-10-8 (b) SZuliani	37/1	pu

Mr S. Mulryan 14ran 6m21.98

INDEX TO SELECTED BIG RACES

Baron de Feypo (IRE) c25[4], 40, 83[6], 112[bd], 182[3], 196
Baron Windrush c35[pu], c110[5], c197*
Barrow Drive c11[pu], c12[3], c35[pu]
Battlecry F39[3], 101[pu], 179, 217[pu]
Bawn Og (IRE) 83
Beachcomber Bay (IRE) c212
Beauchamp Oracle c194[ur]
Beautiful Vision (IRE) c245[3]
Be Be King (IRE) 48[6]
Bedlam Boy (IRE) 214[3]
Beef Or Salmon (IRE) c24*, c47[2], c100[2], c145*, c193, c239
Belord (GER) 178
Be My Better Half (IRE) c50
Bengo (IRE) c189[ur]
Benrajah (IRE) c212[F]
Berings Express (FR) F184
Berryville (FR) 29[4]
Bewleys Berry (IRE) c17[4], c51[2], c150, c227[F]
Bica (FR) c194[5]
Bien Bronze 238[2]
Big Buck's (FR) 254[2]
Big Moment 108
Big Rob (IRE) c56[pu], c188[pu]
Big Zoomo (IRE) c194
Billy Bonnie (IRE) c9[pu]
Billyvoddan (IRE) c445, c79*, c186[3], c227[pu]
Black Apalachi (IRE) c97[pu], c111, c121[5]
Blackbriery Thyne (IRE) 199[4]
Black Harry (IRE) 192[F]
Black Jack Ketchum (IRE) 72*, 123[5], 187[F], 209[2]
Blackriver Boy 242
Blazing Bailey 1, 72[2], 81[4], 123*, 187[3], 209[F]
Blazing Batman 38
Blazing Sky (IRE) 67[5], 202, 237[3]
Blueberry Boy (IRE) c69[4], c90[3], c243[F]
Blue Calin (FR) c255[pu]
Blue Splash (FR) c136[4]
Blythe Knight (IRE) 220*
Bob Bob Bobbin c58[4], c193[pu]
Bob Hall (IRE) c93[5], c185[2], c228[2]
Bobs Pride (IRE) 67[4], 238*
Bob The Builder c50
Bohemian Spirit (IRE) c45[5], c130[F]
Bold Bishop (IRE) c155[pu], c169, c188
Bold Fire c85[pu], c198[4]
Bonchester Bridge 199
Bongo Fury (IRE) 140
Bon Temps Rouler (FR) 234[pu]
Bootlegger (IRE) F241
Border Castle 172[5]
Borora c195
Boss Imperial (FR) 172
Bothar Na (IRE) c5[5], c9*, c11[5], c24[ur], c55[pu], c227[pu], c245
Bougoure (IRE) c228

Boulavogue (IRE) 29
Bowleaze (IRE) c21[F]
Boychuk (IRE) c21[2], c53*, c85[2], c216[5]
Bradley Boy 135[3]
Brads House (IRE) 14[4], 108
Brankley Boy 48[pu]
Brave d'Honneur (FR) 29
Brave Eagle (IRE) c97[ur]
Brave Inca (IRE) 52[3], 68*, 102*, 129[2], 175[2], 244[6]
Bravou (FR) c27
Breaking Silence (IRE) 248[3]
Breathing Fire 6, 112[F]
Brewster (IRE) 34[pu]
Briareus c78*
Bridge Run (IRE) 167
Briery Fox (IRE) c134[3], c219[ur]
Brogella (IRE) 40[3], 68[3], 83
Bronzesmith c8[pu]
Brooklyn Breeze (IRE) c219
Brook No Argument F222
Brutto Facie (IRE) c5[pu]
Buena Vista (IRE) c174[6], c230[F]
Bullhill Flyer (IRE) 99[pu]
Bureaucrat 16
Burntoakboy 182*, 215
Burwood Breeze (IRE) c2[pu], c50[ur]
Buster Hyvonen (IRE) 223
Butler's Cabin (FR) c33[4], c56[3], c73, c189*, c205*
Bywell Beau (IRE) 220[4], 233

Cadogan (FR) 196
Cailin Alainn (IRE) c69*, c98*, c124[F], c180[F]
Calatagan (IRE) c4, c33, c46, c195
Callherwhatulike (IRE) 167[2]
Callow Lane (IRE) 1[2], c36[ur], 196, 208, 247[4]
Calusa Charlie (IRE) 34[3]
Calvic (IRE) c2[pu], c164[5]
Cameron Bridge (IRE) c8[pu]
Camptect (IRE) c97, c121
Cane Brake (IRE) c61*, c97*, c193[5], c205[pu]
Cantgeton (IRE) 146
Captain Marlon (IRE) 13[5]
Caracciola (GER) 1, 16[2], 66, 140[4], 196[6], 231[5]
Caraman (IRE) 37[3]
Caravino (IRE) F241
Carlesimo (IRE) c5, c240[4]
Carlitos 77[3], 122[6], 214
Carlys Quest 18[6], 34, 48
Carrigeen Kalmia (IRE) c240[2]
Carryonharry (IRE) c194
Carthalawn (IRE) c195[F], c243[3]
Casey Jones (IRE) 107[3], 170[5]
Cashel Bay (USA) 159[5]
Cassia Heights c50[4], c219
Castlekelly (IRE) F241
Catch Me (GER) 96[2], 143[ur], 179[3], 248[F]
Catchthebug (IRE) 7[pu]
Catch The Perk (IRE) c232
Cathedral Rock (IRE) 171
Cedar Chief c212[F]
Cedrus Libani (IRE) 173

Ceeawayhome 10[3]
Celestial Wave (IRE) 83*, 99*, 120*
Celtic Boy (IRE) c4, c22[6], c43[pu]
Celtic Major (IRE) 192[pu]
Celtic Son (FR) c162[pu], c227[pu]
Celtic Warrior (IRE) 89[5], 125[6], 178
Central House (FR) c41[2], c65[4], c95[2], c117[3], c138[2], c148[6], c200[2], c206[5], c235
Cerium (FR) c44*, c73, c148[pu]
Chabrimal Minster c164[3]
Chamacco (FR) 62[5]
Chamoss Royale (FR) c198[2]
Character Building (IRE) c189[2], c232[pu]
Charango Star c2[pu]
Charlies Double c36[5], c60[4], c64[4]
Charlies First (IRE) 112, 234*
Charlotte Vale 59
Cheeky Lady (IRE) c97[3], c121[pu], c183[3], c205[F]
Cheler (FR) 253[6], 255
Chelsea Harbour (IRE) c144[4], c180[ur], c205
Chetwind Music (IRE) c9[F]
Cheveley Flyer 31[3], 71
Chicago Vic (IRE) 6
Chief Dan George (IRE) 135*, 151*, 192, 217*
Chief Yeoman 80[6], c185[F], c228[4]
Chilling Place (IRE) c20[ur], c44[F], c130
Chomba Womba (IRE) 167[4], 170[2], 202[3]
Choumakeur (FR) F184
Christdalo (IRE) 75[4]
Christy Beamish (IRE) c194[pu]
Church Island (IRE) c19, c70, c205[4]
City Note (FR) 29, c251
Clan Royal (FR) c51[F], c79[pu], c227
Classic Capers c232[ur]
Classic Croco (GER) 112, 223
Classic Role 173
Classified (IRE) c161[pu]
Claymore (IRE) c56[F]
Clearly Oscar (IRE) c32[pu]
Clear Riposte (IRE) 253, 255
Cleni Boy (IRE) 67[3], 96[5]
Climate Control (IRE) c194
Clopf (IRE) 67[2], 233*
Cloudless Dawn c198[5]
Cloudy Bays (IRE) c24[F], 190[F], c227[R], c239
Cloudy Lane c150, c183*, c205[ur]
Coast To Coast (IRE) c5
Coat of Honour (USA) c195
Cobreces c194
Cogans Lake (IRE) 112
Coljon (IRE) c61
Comfort Zone (IRE) 170[pu]
Commercial Flyer (IRE) c70[F], c87[pu], c176[pu]
Commonchero (IRE) c9[F], c195
Complete Outsider 7[ur]

1135

1139

ERRATA & ADDENDA

'Chasers & Hurdlers 1994/95'

The Fellow (FR) P721 line 5: In 1995, Ubu III became the <u>third</u> horse to win the Grand Steeple-Chase de Paris after winning the Grande Course de Haies d'Auteuil. The others were Blagueur II (won the two races in 1910/1911 respectively) and Loreto (1958/1963)

'Chasers & Hurdlers 2005/06'

Aleemdar (IRE) appeal not yet heard

Denman (IRE) P245 line 13: My Puttens is the <u>dam</u> of Natalies Fancy and Occold

Dubai Sunday (JPN) disqualified from last two starts in 2005/6 at a subsequent inquiry

Massini's Maguire (IRE) sold <u>2</u>00,000 guineas at Doncaster

TIMEFORM 'TOP HORSES IN FRANCE'

The musketeers ride again! In the early-'nineties, French jump racing was dominated by a trio of horses owned by the Marquesa de Moratalla and trained by Francois Doumen. The Fellow, Ubu III and Ucello II became known collectively as the 'three musketeers' and between them they won most of the major prizes in Paris, notably four editions of the Grand Steeple-Chase de Paris and two Grande Course de Haies. In addition, The Fellow's many visits to Britain, which included winning two King George VI Chases and (after a couple of near-misses) a Cheltenham Gold Cup, gave the trio a representative this side of the Channel and a name which British racegoers could identify with. Over a decade later, it is not a trio but a quartet of stable-companions in common ownership which is dominating French jump racing. **Cyrlight**, **Mid Dancer**, **Or Noir de Somoza** and **Zaiyad**, owned by Irish property developer Sean Mulryan (Ballymore Properties) and trained by Arnaud Chaille-Chaille, are well on their way to emulating the three musketeers. They cannot yet boast as great a record in the top contests at Auteuil, though a Grand Steeple-Chase and two Grande Course de Haies are already in the bag. None has yet shown form as good as any of the Doumen trio, and none has yet made much of an impression in Britain, but time is very much on their side—Cyrlight, the oldest of the four, is still only seven, Or Noir de Somoza the youngest just a five-year-old.

Before taking a look at their successes as individuals in the latest season, the statistics of their combined career records make remarkable reading. By the end of June 2007, the quartet had between them won 52 of their 66 starts in France over jumps (28 wins from 34 runs in steeplechases), with 33 of those successes coming in pattern races. Their combined career earnings to date come to more than €3.8 million (over £2.5 million) and have helped make Sean Mulryan champion jumps owner in France in 2005 (on win and place earnings) and runner-up in 2006 (when he was top by win-money only). Mulryan's colours—dark blue, yellow panel, checked cap—have also been carried with success over jumps in Ireland by the likes of Forget The Past and In Compliance, as well as to Group 1 success on the Flat in France with Linda's Lad. But it is his French jumpers who have led the way, the string put together from scratch as recently as 2004 starting with initial acquisition Cyrlight. He had had five runs for another owner with Chaille-Chaille's stable by then, while Mid Dancer and Or Noir de Somoza were both purchased after their respective debuts for other yards, the former privately and the latter for €135,000 at public auction. Zaiyad was another auction purchase (€140,000) after beginning his career on the Flat for the Aga Khan.

Cyrlight was out of action through injury for much of the latest season, putting the spotlight on his two younger stable-companions over fences instead after the turn of the year. Cyrlight returned over hurdles in the autumn with a win in the Prix de Compiegne

Gras Savoye Grand Steeple-Chase de Paris, Auteuil—Mid Dancer (right) remains unbeaten in France after seventeen starts, the 2006 Grande Course de Haies winner becoming only the fourth horse to boast wins in France's top hurdle race and steeplechase; a searching gallop in testing conditions set by eventual runner-up Lord Carmont results in only five finishers, previous year's winner Princesse d'Anjou (riderless horse) being one of the casualties

Prix Maurice Gillois, Auteuil—Or Noir de Somoza initiates a unique double,
winning the autumn's top chase for four-year-olds before following up in the equivalent event over hurdles,
the Prix Renaud du Vivier, a fortnight later

which bettered anything he had achieved previously over either hurdles or fences, and followed up on his return to fences in the Prix Heros XII. But Cyrlight met with only his second defeat in chases next time out in the Prix La Haye Jousselin, finishing only fifth and returning with a hairline fracture of his pelvis which ruled him out of a possible run in the King George at Kempton. Notwithstanding his injury, Cyrlight's defeat again raised questions about his stamina over distances beyond three miles following his capitulation in the Grand Steeple-Chase de Paris earlier in the year. In his comeback race in late-June, Cyrlight looked unlucky to lose his unblemished completion record when unseating in a listed event over hurdles.

Meanwhile, **Or Noir de Somoza** was maintaining his supremacy over his fellow four-year-old chasers during the autumn. A front-runner like Cyrlight, though less headstrong than that horse was as a youngster, Or Noir de Somoza emulated his older stable-companion by remaining unbeaten over fences as a four-year-old. He returned from the summer break to win the Prix Edmond Barrachin and Prix Orcada as a prelude to landing odds of 10/1-on in the Group 1 Prix Maurice Gillois. A fortnight later, Or Noir de Somoza completed an unprecedented double by landing the autumn's Group 1 prize for four-year-old hurdlers as well, the Prix Renaud du Vivier (Cyrlight had finished second when attempting the same feat two years earlier), effectively sealing him the Jumps Horse of The Year title in the process. Stiffer tasks against older rivals awaited Or Noir de Somoza in the spring but ridden with a bit more restraint, he won both the Prix Robert de Clermont-Tonnerre and Prix Murat to maintain his unbeaten record over fences going into the Grand Steeple-Chase de Paris. Sent off favourite, Or Noir de Somoza came to grief at the big water jump, the riviere des tribunes, on the first circuit, but his jumping is one of his chief assets, and all being well he'll have other chances to prove himself in the race in years to come. He subsequently met with his first defeat on completed starts over fences, below his best against a fresher rival, when just failing to give weight to **Lord Mirande** in the Prix des Drags three weeks later.

Mid Dancer also lined up for the Grand Steeple-Chase with an exemplary record behind him, at least in France where he had yet to be beaten in sixteen starts. Unlike Cyrlight and Or Noir de Somoza, Mid Dancer has raced in Britain, where he has met with his only two defeats. Last to finish in the 2006 Arkle at Cheltenham, he made his reappearance in the autumn in an intermediate chase at Carlisle and showed much more like his best form in running Monet's Garden to two and a half lengths. Back at Auteuil, he won the Prix Georges Courtois in December and the Prix Troytown in March before completing his preparation for the Grand Steeple-Chase with a win over hurdles in the Prix Leon Rambaud in April. Mid Dancer has switched successfully between hurdles and fences throughout his career, and he became only the fourth horse, and the first since one of the Marquesa de Moratalla's musketeers, Ubu, to win both a Grand Steeple-Chase de Paris and a Grande Course de Haies.

The latest Grand Steeple-Chase was a gruelling affair due to the combination of particularly wet conditions and an unrelenting pace set by the Prix Murat runner-up and confirmed front-runner **Lord Carmont**. With his rivals strung out with a circuit still to race, Lord Carmont made a bold bid to make all and had all bar Mid Dancer beaten in the back straight for the final time. Mid Dancer took the leader's measure between the last two obstacles to run out a fifteen-length winner, Lord Carmont improving on his third place in 2005 and finishing a distance clear of three others who completed in their own time, headed by the Ruby Walsh-ridden Golden Flight. For the record, the fairly useful handicapper **Grand Canal** and rank outsider Marble Garden (a faller in the Cheltenham Gold Cup) were the others to get round in a field of twelve. As well as Or Noir de Somoza, the other notable casualty of the race was the previous year's winner **Princesse d'Anjou** who unseated at the rail ditch and fence on the final circuit when in third place. She ran a game race though to get that far after a freak incident, having suffered what turned out to be a skull fracture resulting from being kicked in the head when landing on the heels of the leader at the water more than a circuit earlier. Runner-up in the Grande Course de Haies in 2006, Princesse d'Anjou was kept over hurdles for much of the season, finishing second in four more pattern races, including behind Cyrlight in the Prix de Compiegne and when beaten just a neck by Mid Dancer in the Leon Rambaud. Over fences, she became the first since Al Capone II in 1997 to win both the Grand Steeple-Chase de Paris and the Prix La Haye Jousselin in the same year when beating stable-companion **Louping d'Ainay** (who was given an entry for the latest Grand National) and Lord Carmont in the autumn. Giving weight away all round, Princesse d'Anjou ran another good race on her other start over fences when fourth to Or Noir de Somoza in the Prix Murat in April.

One of the few major chases at Auteuil which did not fall to either Princesse d'Anjou or one of the Mulryan trio of chasers was the Prix Ingre in May won by Pau-based **Wisborough** (pulled up in the Grand Steeple-Chase de Paris next time and a faller at the water in the Prix des Drags) from **Hercule Noir**. The runner-up had also been second to Cyrlight in the Prix Heros XII and nearly caused an upset in the Prix Troytown when running Mid Dancer to a short head. **Ne A Pron** was a close third in the Troytown and filled the same position behind Or Noir de Somoza in the Prix Murat, though collapsed and died after finishing last in the Prix Ingre. Front-running mare **Kario de Sormain** was another to run well in defeat in good company, finishing second to Mid Dancer in

Prix La Haye Jousselin, Auteuil—stable-companions Princesse d'Anjou and Louping d'Ainay take the first two places for trainer Francois Cottin and 2006 champion jumps owner Jean-Paul Senechal in the autumn's top chase; Irishmen Philip Carberry and Dean Gallagher are in the saddle

Grande Course de Haies d'Auteuil—a second consecutive win in France's 'Champion Hurdle'
for owner Sean Mulryan and trainer Arnaud Chaille-Chaille after Mid Dancer in 2006;
Zaiyad takes the last from placed horses Mister Gyor and Monoalco (noseband)

the Prix Georges Courtois and third behind Or Noir de Somoza in the Prix Robert de Clermont-Tonnerre. **Alarm Call** is yet to contest one of the big chases, but he'd be worth his place in one after winning a couple of Auteuil's major handicaps, the Prix Montgomery over fences in the autumn (from Louping d'Ainay and Ne A Pron) and the Grande Course de Haies de Printemps over hurdles in the spring. The Guillaume Macaire-trained **Moka de L'Isle** is seemingly hard to train but he has a good record and won both his starts at Auteuil in November, including a listed event from Kario de Sormain. At Enghien, veteran course specialist **Northerntown** failed in his attempt to win a fourth consecutive Grand Steeple-Chase at the track in the autumn when fifth to the previous year's runner-up **Cerilly**. That pair were beaten by an improving younger rival, **Moskitos d'Isigny**, in one of Enghien's principal chases in the spring, the Prix Romati, and that could be a sign of things to come at that track in the autumn.

Francois Doumen's chasers drew a blank on their visits to Britain in the latest season but **L'Ami** retained all his considerable ability, coming closest to beating Kauto Star in three encounters when running him to a neck (in receipt of 10 lb) in a muddling AON Chase at Newbury. Elder brother **Kelami** returned to form when second in the Agfa Diamond Handicap Chase at Sandown and also ran second to Or Noir de Somoza in the Robert de Clermont-Tonnerre at Auteuil the following month, though, along with L'Ami, he failed to figure in the Grand National. Thierry Doumen's **Foreman** was another to run well in defeat in Britain, finishing third in the Desert Orchid Chase at Kempton after warming up over hurdles with a second place in the Prix Leopold d'Orsetti at Enghien.

The fourth member of the Mulryan musketeers was **Zaiyad** and, as a Flat-bred son of Sadler's Wells, he is the only one of the four to have raced solely over hurdles. Like Mid Dancer, he has raced twice in Britain but disappointed both times, firstly in the 2006 Royal & SunAlliance Novices' Hurdle and again in the Long Distance Hurdle at Newbury in November. His disappointments haven't been confined to his runs abroad either, as he ran a couple of poor races at Auteuil as well, notably when pulled up in the Prix La Barka. But he won four other pattern races at Auteuil, taking the Prix Carmarthen before a Group 1 success in the Grand Prix d'Automne. He also beat Princesse d'Anjou in the Prix Hypothese in March and put his run in the La Barka behind him when winning the Grande Course de Haies d'Auteuil, making Sean Mulryan the first owner since the Marquesa de Moratalla in 1993 to win the Grand Steeple-Chase and Grande Course de Haies in the same year. Incidentally, in addition to his established stars, Mulryan looks to have a particularly promising three-year-old hurdler in Othermix (rated 124p) who has already won three times over hurdles at Auteuil and has the makings of a leading juvenile for 2007/8.

The places in the Grande Course de Haies went to seven-year-olds **Mister Gyor** and **Monoalco**, neither of whom had figured among the elite of Auteuil's hurdlers previously. However, they had both made the frame in the Prix La Barka beforehand (Mister Gyor runner-up in that race as well) and turned the tables on the La Barka winner **Shinco du Berlais** who finished fourth in the Grande Course de Haies. Zaiyad apart, the best 'full-time' French hurdlers, as opposed to those who mixed hurdling and chasing, were

Kasbah Bliss and **Millenium Royal**. Trained by the Doumens, junior and senior respectively, they ran their best races when contesting handicaps under big weights in Britain. Kasbah Bliss finished a good fourth in the Sandown Handicap Hurdle (giving 23 lb to Taranis) though possibly found his stamina stretched when a creditable fifth in the World Hurdle at Cheltenham and was below his best when sixth in the Grande Course de Haies. At Auteuil, he won the Prix Pierre de Lassus for four-year-olds in the autumn (from Shinco du Berlais and the subsequent Prix La Barka third **Gray Steel**) and ran his best race at the track in the spring behind Mid Dancer and Princesse d'Anjou in the Prix Leon Rambaud. Millenium Royal overcame a stiff-looking mark to win a Pertemps qualifier at Haydock before finishing well held in the Final of the series at Cheltenham. Earlier in the season, his best effort at Auteuil came when finishing fifth, attempting a second consecutive win, in the Grand Prix d'Automne. The placed horses from the Grand Prix d'Automne, **Royale Athenia** and **Lycaon de Vauzelle**, went on to finish first and second in the Prix Leon Olry-Roederer later in November, but Royale Athenia wasn't seen out again and Lycaon de Vauzelle was below form on his only appearance in the spring. The latter's last win came in the 2005 Grande Course de Haies but he has picked up plenty of place money since, finishing third in the 2006 renewal of the same race before being placed on all four of his starts in pattern races in the autumn.

Unusually for France, it was an Irish-bred gelding who led the way among the four-year-old chasers, at least among those who raced at Auteuil. **Remember Rose** gained his first big win over fences in the Prix Congress as a three-year-old in the autumn when beating Voy Por Ustedes' half-sister **En La Cruz** and another filly **Klassical Way**. However, it was not until much later in the season that he cemented his position among the best of his generation over fences. His best effort came in the Group 1 Prix Ferdinand Dufaure in May when he had his rivals well strung out in the testing conditions on the Grand Steeple-Chase card. He followed up giving weight away all round in the Prix La Periehole the following month. The Ferdinand Dufaure runner-up **Master Minded** started odds on after winning his two completed starts in chases at Auteuil, though he had come to grief in both previous attempts at pattern level. It was Master Minded's final start for Guillaume Macaire before joining Paul Nicholls, as he had been purchased by Kauto Star's owner Clive Smith beforehand, with Ruby Walsh taking the ride. Another of the better four-year-old chasers exported to Britain was the Prix Duc d'Anjou winner **Playing** who has joined Paul Webber. He beat two more subsequent pattern winners in the Duc d'Anjou (when left clear by Master Minded's last-flight fall, upsides at the time), with runner-up **Palibel d'Airy** going on to win the Prix Fleuret, and fifth-placed **Lucky du Berlais** making all for a long-odds win in the Prix Jean Stern. A notable absentee from the pattern races for four-year-old chasers was **Petit Robin**. He won both his starts over fences at Pau in the winter, in the second of them finishing clear with Playing and giving the runner-up 9 lb, suggesting he would have made his mark at Auteuil given the opportunity.

Gras Savoye Cinema Prix Ferdinand Dufaure, Auteuil—Remember Rose moves to the top of the four-year-old chasers' rankings with this Group 1 success in May; Ruby Walsh becomes acquainted with runner-up Master Minded ahead of the gelding's subsequent move to Paul Nicholls, as pace-setter Aviador fades into fourth

Prix Cambaceres, Auteuil—eventual winner Royal Honor (grey) disputes the lead in the early stages of the Group 1 for three-year-old hurdlers; placed horses Good Bye Simon (white cap, centre) and Parrain (second left) both ran well in Britain later in the winter

As in recent seasons, the French juvenile hurdlers lacked a clear leader, and for the most part took turns beating each other in the big events, though as usual this division had the most strands of form linking France and Britain. Timeform's idea of the best performance by a juvenile hurdler at Auteuil came from the front-running filly **Kruguyrova** who won the Prix Jacques d'Indy in March (from the subsequent Prix de Pepinvast winner **Gaelic Ocean**) in what proved to be her final start in France before joining Charlie Egerton. The juvenile with arguably the best overall record though was **Good Bye Simon** who won Grade/Group 1 contests in both Britain and France. He took the Finale Hurdle at Chepstow before finishing second to Katchit at Cheltenham in January, and beat several other pattern winners when taking the Prix Alain du Breil at Auteuil in June ahead of the surprise Prix Amadou winner **Big Buck's** and the filly **Drole de Drame**, who had completed a four-timer in the Prix Georges de Talhouet-Roy in the autumn. **Royal Honor** was an absentee from the Alain du Breil after disappointing in the Amadou beforehand, but he had put up some good efforts earlier in the season, notably when beating Good Bye Simon (got first run on that rival) and **Parrain** in the Group 1 Prix Cambaceres in the autumn. The Francois Doumen-trained Parrain went on to take the Prix General de Saint-Didier at Enghien (with Kruguyrova and Royal Honor among those he beat) before being placed twice at Kempton, including in the Adonis Hurdle. His stable-companion **Grand Bleu** fared even better in Britain, winning the Victor Ludorum at Haydock.

The dispersal sale of the stable of Thomas Trapenard, who ceased training at the end of 2006, attracted the interest of a number of British and Irish stables in December. Among the lots who joined British yards, Gaspara went on to have the most success, while another juvenile filly J'Y Vole, who joined Willie Mullins, was returned to France to win the Prix de Longchamp in May from stable-companion Financial Reward. Mullins, incidentally, was responsible for the majority of the total of a dozen Anglo-Irish runners on the Grand Steeple-Chase and Grande Course de Haies cards in May and June, meetings with a far more international flavour (there was also a Czech-trained runner in the Grand Steeple-Chase) than the International Jumps Weekend in November which again received a disappointingly lukewarm response from outside France, attracting just three runners from Ireland and none at all from Britain.

<table>
<tr><td>

Chasers (5yo+)
157	* L'Ami	8
155	* Foreman	9
151	Mid Dancer	6
149	Lord Mirande	8
148	Or Noir de Somoza	5
146	Cyrlight	7
143	Alarm Call	7
143p	Moka de L'Isle	7
141	Cerilly	10
141	Princesse d'Anjou (f)	6
141+	Louping d'Ainay	8
140	* Kelami	9
139	Lord Carmont	8
139	Moskitos d'Isigny	7
139	Ne A Pron	6
137	Kiko	6
136	Newman Des Plages	6
135x	Kario de Sormain (f)	9
134	L'As de Pembo	8
134	Wisborough	9
133	Hercule Noir	8
133+	Marie d'Anjou (f)	7
132	Dom Fontenail	8
132	Northerntown	11
131	Saint Realise	10
130	Nokara	6
130	Sphinx du Berlais	8
130	Super Bowl	6
130	Zarkali	6
129	Ombre d'Estruval (f)	5
129	Rock And Palm	7
128	Ben Veto	6
128	Gouidal Bihan	7
128	Mikador	7
128	Padisha Soy	5
128	Palapa (f)	6
128	Villez de Conde	8
127	Great Love	9
127	Ilare	11
127	Le Pero	9
127	* Moncadou	7
127	Nitrat	6
127	Norville du Bois	6
126	Doumaja	5
126	Lutin Ville	8
125	Grand Canal	11
125	Mendiant	7
125	Musica Bella (f)	7
124	Escort Boy	9
124	Mayev	7
124	Mon Milord	6
124	Objectif Special	5
124	Organiz	5

Hurdlers (5yo+)
157	Mid Dancer	6
156	Zaiyad	6
155	* Millenium Royal	7
154	* Kasbah Bliss	5
154+	Cyrlight	7
150	Lycaon de Vauzelle	8
148	Or Noir de Somoza	5
146	Mister Gyor	7

</td><td>

146	Rock And Palm	7
145	Royale Athenia (f)	6
143	Monoalco	7
143	Princesse d'Anjou (f)	6
142	Gray Steel	5
142	Phonidal	11
141	Card'son	5
141	Lina Drop (f)	5
141	Risko	6
141	Shinco du Berlais	5
139	Cerilly	10
138	Gold Magic	9
137	Alarm Call	7
136+	Grande Haya	8
135	Rocpistole	6
133	Malcom	8
131	Beringneyev	10
130	Tiger Blitz	7
130+	Foreman	9
129	Icarro	6
128	Cybergenic	9
128	Danaw	6
128	Empereur du Monde	8
128	Northerntown	11
128	Sphinx du Berlais	8
127	Espoir de Kerbarh	6
127	Onnix	5
127	Turgello	8
126	Water Dragon	6
125	Gouidal Bihan	7
125	Nouvea	6
125	Tinaki	7
124	Hairball	5
124	House Music	8
124	Magic Fabien	6
124	Nono des Ongrais	6
124	Royal Surabaya	5
124	Solon Abi	6
124	Trespass	9
123	Malikhan	5
123	Narock	6
123	Noble Kaid	5
123	Odeillo du Mathan	5
123	Poland Springs	6
123+	Oeil du Maitre	5

Chasers (4yo)
139p	Petit Robin
136	Remember Rose
132	En La Cruz (f)
129	Playing
126	Klassical Way (f)
125	Master Minded
125	Palibel d'Airy
125	Pasco d'Airy
124	Peldero
123	Lucky du Berlais
120	Mundo
119	Aviador
119	Fabulously
119	Perenny
118	Mildon
118	Roulez Cool
118	Si Grand

</td><td>

117	Mixmen
116	Berryville
116	Piraya
115	City Note
115	Limaranta (f)
114	Pepsyrock
114	Petit Wisky
113	Peplum
112	Pommerol
111	Count Your Change
111	Manadam
111	Mille Et Une (f)
111	Simonet
111	Vieux Villez
109	Nickelle (f)
109	Parsou
108	Colline de Clermon (f)
108	Pancho Villez
107	Cherue
107	Inoxe Royale (f)
107	Make Believe (f)
107	Pirak d'Airy
107	Polar Rochelais

Hurdlers (4yo)
137	Kruguyrova (f)
135	* Parrain
132	Good Bye Simon
132	Royal Honor
131p	* Grand Bleu
130	Big Buck's
129	Gaelic Ocean
126	Drole de Drame (f)
126	Pinn Up (f)
125	Prince des Bois
123	Rombaldi
123	Top of The Sky
123p	Shekira (f)
122	Mildon
122	Palmier
122	Sang Dolois
121	Dalina (f)
121	Fabulously
120	Consigliere
120	Ecos de L'Orme
120	Limaranta (f)
120	Parker
120	Peldero
120	Pommerol
120p	Gwanako
118	Si Grand
117	Berryville
117	Professeur
117	Sing Faraway
116	Danigan
116	Slim Pearl (f)
115	Cadouraki
115	Mahonia Royal
114	Sainte Nono (f)
112	Pensamor
111	Mongorno
111	Penn Da Benn

</td></tr>
</table>

NB Only horses trained in France appear in the above list. Those marked with an * achieved their best performance in GB or Ireland, otherwise ratings relate to performances in France between July 2006 and June 2007.

There is an essay in the main body of the book on Good Bye Simon.

INDEX TO PHOTOGRAPHS

PORTRAITS & SNAPSHOTS

RACE PHOTOGRAPHS

Brit Insurance Novices' Hurdle (Spa) (Cheltenham)	*Alec Russell*	1052
Byrne Bros Cleeve Hurdle (Cheltenham)	*George Selwyn*	129
Carey Group Handicap Chase (Ascot)	*Bill Selwyn*	246
Christie's Foxhunter Chase Challenge Cup (Cheltenham)	*Alec Russell*	280
Citroen C4 Picasso Mersey Novices' Hurdle (Aintree)	*Ed Byrne*	983
Citroen C6 Sefton Novices' Hurdle (Aintree)	*Ed Byrne*	198
Clonmel Oil Chase	*Caroline Norris*	890
Commercial First Ascot Chase	*John Crofts*	641
Connaught Cup (Handicap Chase) (Wincanton)	*Bill Selwyn*	594
Constant Security Wensleydale Juvenile Novices' Hurdle (Wetherby)	*Alec Russell*	245
Coral Ascot Hurdle	*John Crofts*	399
Coral Cup (Handicap Hurdle) (Cheltenham)	*John Crofts*	157
Coral Future Champion Finale Juvenile Hurdle (Chepstow)	*Ed Byrne*	375
Coral Scottish Grand National Handicap Chase (Ayr)	*Alec Russell*	429
Coral Welsh National (Handicap Chase) (Chepstow)	*Ed Byrne*	395
Country Gentlemen's Association Chase (Limited Handicap) (Wincanton)	*Bill Selwyn*	563
Cox's Cash & Carry Champion Hunters' Chase (Punchestown)	*Ed Byrne*	478
Deloitte Novices' Hurdle (Leopardstown)	*Caroline Norris*	75
Desert Orchid Chase (Sponsored By Stan James) (Kempton)	*Edward Whitaker/ Racing Post*	1029
Digital Prints From bonusprint.com Novices' Chase (Aintree)	*Ed Byrne*	1004
Dunboyne Castle Hotel & Spa Champion Stayers' Hurdle (Punchestown)	*Caroline Norris*	805
Dunboyne Castle Hotel & Spa Novices' Hurdle (Fairyhouse)	*Caroline Norris*	264
Durkan New Homes Juvenile Hurdle (Leopardstown)	*Peter Mooney*	577
E.B.F./boylesports.com 'National Hunt' Novices' Hurdle (Qualifier) (Cheltenham)	*Ed Byrne*	982
Ellier Developments Hanover Quay Champion Novices' Chase (Punchestown)	*Peter Mooney*	711
European Breeders' Fund/Doncaster Bloodstock Sales Mares' Only Standard Open National Hunt Flat Race Final (Sandown)	*George Selwyn*	943
European Breeders' Fund Mares' Only 'National Hunt' Novices' Hurdle Final (Limited Handicap) (Newbury)	*Bill Selwyn*	496
European Breeders' Fund 'National Hunt' Novices' Hurdle (Qualifier) (Catterick)	*Alec Russell*	888
European Breeders' Fund Sunderlands 'National Hunt' Novices' Handicap Hurdle Final (Sandown)	*George Selwyn*	45
European Breeders' Fund/Thoroughbred Breeders' Association Mares' Only Novices' Chase Final (Handicap) (Newbury)	*Bill Selwyn*	757
Faucets For Mira Showers Silver Trophy Chase (Limited Handicap) (Cheltenham)	*Ed Byrne*	707
Fraser Steele HBLB Handicap Chase (Sandown)	*John Crofts*	248
Fred Winter Juvenile Novices' Handicap Hurdle (Cheltenham)	*Alec Russell*	356
Fulke Walwyn Kim Muir Challenge Cup Handicap Chase (Amateur Riders) (Cheltenham)	*Caroline Norris*	210
Gideon Kasler Novices' Hurdle (Cheltenham)	*Bill Selwyn*	605
Giltspur Scientific Tara Hurdle (Navan)	*Caroline Norris*	185
Goffs Land Rover Bumper I.N.H. Flat (Punchestown)	*Bill Selwyn*	374
Greatwood Handicap Hurdle (Cheltenham)	*Ed Byrne*	260
Guinness Galway Hurdle (Handicap)	*Caroline Norris*	231
Hennessy Cognac Gold Cup (Leopardstown)	*Caroline Norris*	110
Hennessy Cognac Gold Cup Chase (Handicap) (Newbury)	*Ed Byrne*	920
Independent Newspaper Novices' Chase (November) (Cheltenham)	*Ed Byrne*	320
intercasino.co.uk Molyneux Novices' Chase (Aintree)	*Alec Russell*	553
intercasino.co.uk Novices' Chase (Kempton)	*Bill Selwyn*	825
Irish Independent Arkle Challenge Trophy Chase (Cheltenham)	*Ed Byrne*	666
Irish Stallions Farms European Breeders Fund (Mares) Novices' Hurdle (Fairyhouse)	*Peter Mooney*	381
James Nicholson Wine Merchant Champion Chase (Down Royal)	*Caroline Norris*	109
JCB Triumph Hurdle (Cheltenham)	*Peter Mooney*	499

Jersey Graduation Chase (Cheltenham)	*Ed Byrne*	223
Jewson Handicap Hurdle Race Final (Cheltenham)	*Ed Byrne*	266
Jewson Novices' Handicap Chase (Cheltenham)	*Alec Russell*	544
Jim Brown Memorial Novices' Chase (Cheltenham)	*John Crofts*	251
John Durkan Memorial Punchestown Chase	*Caroline Norris*	450
Johnny Henderson Grand Annual Chase Challenge Cup (Handicap) (Cheltenham)	*Peter Mooney*	66
John Smith's Anniversary 4-Y-O Hurdle (Aintree)	*Alec Russell*	500
John Smith's Extra Cold Handicap Hurdle (Aintree)	*Alec Russell*	46
John Smith's Fox Hunters' Chase (Aintree)	*Ed Byrne*	842
John Smith's Future Stars Chase (Intermediate) (Sandown)	*Bill Selwyn*	917
John Smith's Grand National Chase (Handicap) (Aintree)	*Bill Selwyn*	865
John Smith's Grand National Chase (Handicap) (Aintree)	*Liverpool Daily Post & Echo*	866
John Smith's Grand National Chase (Handicap) (Aintree)	*George Selwyn*	867
John Smith's Grand National Chase (Handicap) (Aintree)	*Alec Russell*	868
John Smith's Grand National Chase (Handicap) (Aintree)	*Liverpool Daily Post & Echo*	869
John Smith's Grand National Chase (Handicap) (Aintree)	*George Selwyn*	870
John Smith's Grand National Chase (Handicap) (Aintree)	*George Selwyn*	871
John Smith's Grand National Chase (Handicap) (Aintree)	*George Selwyn*	872
John Smith's Grand National Chase (Handicap) (Aintree)	*Ed Byrne*	873
John Smith's Grand National Chase (Handicap) (Aintree)	*Alec Russell*	874
John Smith's Grand National Chase (Handicap) (Aintree)	*George Selwyn*	875
John Smith's Handicap Hurdle (Aintree)	*Ed Byrne*	1011
John Smith's Hurdle (West Yorkshire) (Wetherby)	*Alec Russell*	802
John Smith's Imagine Appeal Top Novices' Hurdle (Aintree)	*George Selwyn*	133
John Smith's Liverpool Hurdle (Long Distance) (Aintree)	*Ed Byrne*	623
John Smith's Maghull Novices' Chase (Aintree)	*Bill Selwyn*	1008
John Smith's Mares' Only Standard Open National Hunt Flat Race (Aintree)	*Alec Russell*	1002
John Smith's Melling Chase (Aintree)	*Ed Byrne*	642
John Smith's Midlands Grand National Chase (Handicap) (Uttoxeter)	*Ed Byrne*	100
John Smith's Mildmay Novices' Chase (Aintree)	*Ed Byrne*	32
John Smith's Novices' Handicap Chase (Conditional Jockeys and Amateur Riders) (Aintree)	*Alec Russell*	782
John Smith's Red Rum Handicap Chase (Aintree)	*Alec Russell*	98
John Smith's Reynoldstown Novices' Chase (Ascot)	*Ed Byrne*	390
John Smith's Topham Chase (Handicap) (Aintree)	*Alec Russell*	287
Kerrygold Champion Chase (Punchestown)	*Bill Selwyn*	598
Ladbroke Handicap Hurdle (Ascot)	*George Selwyn*	30
ladbrokes.com Handicap Chase (Newbury)	*Ed Byrne*	352
ladbrokes.com Handicap Hurdle (Sandown)	*Ed Byrne*	745
ladbrokes.com Ten Up Novices' Chase (Navan)	*Caroline Norris*	898
Ladbrokes World Hurdle (Cheltenham)	*George Selwyn*	455
Land Rover Champion Novices' Hurdle (Punchestown)	*Peter Mooney*	367
Letheby And Christopher Chase (Cotswold) (Cheltenham)	*George Selwyn*	315
Lexus Chase (Leopardstown)	*Caroline Norris*	969
Lombard Properties Handicap Hurdle (Cheltenham)	*Ed Byrne*	916
Maplewood Developments Morgiana Hurdle (Punchestown)	*Peter Mooney*	440
Mears Group "Relkeel" Hurdle (Cheltenham)	*John Crofts*	125
Menolly Homes Handicap Hurdle (Fairyhouse)	*Peter Mooney*	302
National Hunt Chase Challenge Cup (Amateur Riders' Novices' Chase) (Cheltenham)	*Alec Russell*	160
Oberstown Developments Handicap Hurdle (Punchestown)	*Ed Byrne*	138
Paddy Power Champion INH Flat (Punchestown)	*Ed Byrne*	620
Paddy Power Chase (Handicap) (Leopardstown)	*Peter Mooney*	171
paddypower.com Johnston Novices' Hurdle (Naas)	*Caroline Norris*	514
paddypower.com Newlands Chase (Naas)	*Peter Mooney*	689
Paddy Power Dial-A-Bet Chase (Leopardstown)	*Peter Mooney*	688
Paddy Power Gold Cup Chase (Handicap) (Cheltenham)	*Bill Selwyn*	313

Pertemps Final (Handicap Hurdle) (Cheltenham)	*George Selwyn*	728
Pertemps Handicap Hurdle (Qualifier) (Cheltenham)	*Bill Selwyn*	609
Pheasant Inn Novices' Chase (Newbury)	*Bill Selwyn*	722
Pierse Hurdle (Handicap) (Leopardstown)	*Peter Mooney*	912
Pierse Leopardstown Handicap Chase	*Bill Selwyn*	768
Play Bingo At ladbrokes.com Mares' Only Handicap Hurdle (Sandown)	*George Selwyn*	1018
Pontin's Holidays Newton Novices' Hurdle (Haydock)	*Alec Russell*	520
Powers Gold Cup (Fairyhouse)	*Caroline Norris*	716
Powers Whiskey Irish Grand National Chase (Handicap) (Fairyhouse)	*Caroline Norris*	161
Powers Whiskey Novices' Chase (Leopardstown)	*Peter Mooney*	166
Prix Alain du Breil-Course de Haies d'Ete des Quatre Ans Hurdle (Auteuil)	*Ed Byrne*	376
Punchestown Guinness Gold Cup	*Ed Byrne*	678
Racing Post Chase (Handicap) (Kempton)	*John Crofts*	884
Racing Post In Ireland Hurdle (Fairyhouse)	*Peter Mooney*	36
Racing Post Plate (Handicap Chase) (Cheltenham)	*John Crofts*	437
racingpost.co.uk Pendil Novices' Chase (Kempton)	*Ed Byrne*	672
Red Mills Trial Hurdle (Gowran Park)	*Caroline Norris*	685
Red Square Vodka Gold Cup Chase (Handicap) (Haydock)	*Alan Wright*	412
Royal & SunAlliance Chase (Cheltenham)	*Ed Byrne*	253
Ryanair Chase (Festival Trophy) (Cheltenham)	*Peter Mooney*	951
Samsung Electronics Scottish Champion Hurdle (Limited Handicap) (Ayr)	*Alec Russell*	303
Seasons Holidays Queen Mother Champion Chase (Cheltenham)	*George Selwyn*	1030
Sky Bet Chase (Handicap) (Southwell)	*Alec Russell*	883
skybet.com Rowland Meyrick Handicap Chase (Wetherby)	*Alec Russell*	550
Sixty Years of Timeform Novices' Handicap Chase (Cheltenham)	*John Crofts*	340
Smurfit Kappa Champion Hurdle Challenge Trophy (Cheltenham)	*Ed Byrne*	933
Smurfit Kappa Champion Hurdle Challenge Trophy (Cheltenham)	*Ed Byrne*	934
Sodexho Prestige Henry VIII Novices' Chase (Sandown)	*Ed Byrne*	321
Sporting Index Handicap Chase (Cross Country) (Cheltenham)	*Caroline Norris*	406
Stan James Christmas Hurdle (Kempton)	*Ed Byrne*	473
Stan James Feltham Novices' Chase (Kempton)	*Ed Byrne*	1016
Stan James King George VI Chase (Kempton)	*Ed Byrne*	508
stanjamesuk.com Novices' Hurdle (Kempton)	*Ed Byrne*	258
Star 'Best For Racing' Chase (Punchestown)	*Bill Selwyn*	1035
Sunderlands Imperial Cup Handicap Hurdle (Sandown)	*Ed Byrne*	355
Swordlestown Cup Novices' Chase (Punchestown)	*Peter Mooney*	70
Timeform Handicap Hurdle (Ascot)	*John Crofts*	773
toteplacepot Novices' Chase (Newbury)	*Bill Selwyn*	252
totepool Game Spirit Chase (Newbury)	*Ed Byrne*	1040
totepool Premier Kelso Hurdle (Novices') (Kelso)	*Alec Russell*	164
totescoop6 Handicap Hurdle (Haydock)	*Alec Russell*	1017
totescoop6 Sandown Handicap Hurdle	*Bill Selwyn*	950
totescoop6 Summer Hurdle (Handicap) (Market Rasen)	*Alec Russell*	1012
totesport Cheltenham Gold Cup Chase	*Ed Byrne*	510
totesport Cheltenham Gold Cup Chase	*Caroline Norris*	511
totesport.com Becher Handicap Chase (Aintree)	*Ed Byrne*	310
totesport.com Classic Chase (Handicap) (Warwick)	*George Selwyn*	538
totesport.com Eider (Handicap Chase) (Newcastle)	*Alec Russell*	693
totesport.com Lord Gyllene Handicap Chase (Uttoxeter)	*Alan Wright*	705
totesport.com Peterborough Chase (Huntingdon)	*Peter Higby*	792
totesport.com Scilly Isles Novices' Chase (Sandown)	*Bill Selwyn*	684
totesport.com Summer Plate (Handicap Chase) (Market Rasen)	*Alec Russell*	1066
totesport Trophy Hurdle (Handicap) (Newbury)	*Ed Byrne*	409
UK Hygiene Handicap Chase (Newbury)	*Ed Byrne*	832
United House Gold Cup Handicap (Ascot)	*Bill Selwyn*	848
vcbet.com Champion Novices' Hurdle (Punchestown)	*Ed Byrne*	208
vccasino.com Gold Cup Handicap Chase (Newbury)	*Bill Selwyn*	587
vccasino.com Long Distance Hurdle (Newbury)	*Ed Byrne*	454

ADDITIONAL PHOTOGRAPHS

The following photographs appear in the Introduction:- The Betfair Million (facing Intro) top left taken by Ed Byrne, two other pictures by George Selwyn; Betfair Million presentation–Bill Selwyn; Hennessy Gold Cup–George Selwyn; Queen Mother Champion Chase–Ed Byrne; Betfred Gold Cup–John Crofts; Reg Griffin and J. P. McManus–George Selwyn; the Pipes and Gaspara–Bill Selwyn; Foinavon's National–London Express; last winner over Haydock's traditional fences–George Selwyn; Ruby Walsh and Tony McCoy in the Arkle–Bill Selwyn; Tom O'Brien–George Selwyn; Russ Garritty–Alec Russell.

Timeform Champions of 2006/7–picture of Kauto Star and Ruby Walsh by Caroline Norris

The following photographs appear in Timeform 'Top Horses In France':- Grand Steeple-Chase de Paris (by Bertrand); Prix Maurice Gillois, Prix La Haye Jousselin, Grande Course de Haies d'Auteuil, Prix Cambaceres (Ed Byrne); Prix Ferdinand Dufaure (Eamonn Byrne).

CHAMPIONS FROM THE 'CHASERS & HURDLERS' SERIES

Best Two-Mile Chaser

75/76	Lough Inagh	167	91/92	Remittance Man	173
76/77	Skymas	156	92/93	Katabatic	161 ?
77/78	Tingle Creek	154	93/94	Viking Flagship	166
78/79	Siberian Sun	151	94/95	Viking Flagship	169
79/80	I'm A Driver	163	95/96	Klairon Davis	177
80/81	Anaglogs Daughter	171	96/97	Martha's Son	177
81/82	Rathgorman	170	97/98	One Man	176
82/83	Badsworth Boy	179	98/99	Direct Route	166
83/84	Badsworth Boy	177	99/00	Flagship Uberalles	175
84/85	Bobsline	164 +	00/01	Flagship Uberalles	175
85/86	Dawn Run	167	01/02	Flagship Uberalles	170
86/87	Pearlyman	171	02/03	Moscow Flyer	170 p
87/88	Pearlyman	174	03/04	Moscow Flyer	183
88/89	Desert Orchid	182	04/05	Moscow Flyer	184 +
89/90	Desert Orchid	187	05/06	Kauto Star	166 +
90/91	Desert Orchid	178	06/07	Katuo Star	184 +

Best Staying Chaser

75/76	Captain Christy	182	91/92	Carvill's Hill	182
76/77	Bannow Rambler	163	92/93	Jodami	174 p
77/78	Midnight Court	164	93/94	The Fellow	171
78/79	Gay Spartan	166	94/95	Master Oats	183
79/80	Silver Buck	171	95/96	One Man	179
80/81	Little Owl	176	96/97	One Man	176
81/82	Silver Buck	175	97/98	Cool Dawn	173
82/83	Bregawn	177	98/99	Suny Bay	176
83/84	Burrough Hill Lad	175	99/00	See More Business	182
	Wayward Lad	175	00/01	First Gold	180
84/85	Burrough Hill Lad	184	01/02	Best Mate	173
85/86	Burrough Hill Lad	183		Florida Pearl	173
86/87	Desert Orchid	177	02/03	Best Mate	182
87/88	Desert Orchid	177	03/04	Best Mate	176 +
88/89	Desert Orchid	182	04/05	Kicking King	182
89/90	Desert Orchid	187	05/06	Beef Or Salmon	174 x
90/91	Desert Orchid	178	06/07	Kauto Star	184 +

Best Novice Chaser

75/76	Bannow Rambler	152 p	93/94	Monsieur Le Cure	156 p
76/77	Tree Tangle	159 §	94/95	Brief Gale	159
77/78	The Dealer	145	95/96	Mr Mulligan	154
78/79	Silver Buck	151	96/97	Strong Promise	171 +
79/80	Anaglogs Daughter	156	97/98	Escartefigue	171 p
80/81	Clayside	145	98/99	Nick Dundee	164 +
81/82	Brown Chamberlin	147 p	99/00	Gloria Victis	172
82/83	Righthand Man	150	00/01	Bacchanal	161 p
83/84	Bobsline	161 p		Shotgun Willy	161
84/85	Drumadowney	159	01/02	Moscow Flyer	159 p
85/86	Pearlyman	150	02/03	Beef Or Salmon	165 p
86/87	Kildimo	151 p	03/04	Strong Flow	156 p
87/88	Danish Flight	156 p	04/05	Ashley Brook	154 +
88/89	Carvill's Hill	169 p		Fundamentalist	154 p
89/90	Celtic Shot	152 p		Ollie Magern	154
90/91	Remittance Man	153 p	05/06	Monet's Garden	156 p
91/92	Miinnehoma	152 p	06/07	Denman	161 p
92/93	Sybillin	156			

Best Two-Mile Hurdler

75/76	Night Nurse	**178**	91/92	Granville Again	**165 p**
76/77	Night Nurse	**182**	92/93	Mighty Mogul	**170**
77/78	Monksfield	**177**	93/94	Danoli	**172 p**
78/79	Monksfield	**180**	94/95	Alderbrook	**174 p**
79/80	Sea Pigeon	**175**	95/96	Alderbrook	**174**
80/81	Sea Pigeon	**175**	96/97	Make A Stand	**165**
81/82	For Auction	**174**	97/98	Istabraq	**172 +**
82/83	Gaye Brief	**175**	98/99	Istabraq	**177 +**
83/84	Dawn Run	**173**	99/00	Istabraq	**180**
84/85	Browne's Gazette	**172**	00/01	Istabraq	**180**
85/86	See You Then	**173**	01/02	Limestone Lad	**167**
86/87	See You Then	**173**	02/03	Rooster Booster	**170**
87/88	Celtic Shot	**170**	03/04	Hardy Eustace	**167**
88/89	Beech Road	**172**	04/05	Hardy Eustace	**165**
89/90	Kribensis	**169**	05/06	Brave Inca	**167**
90/91	Morley Street	**174**	06/07	Sublimity	**164**

Best Staying Hurdler

75/76	Comedy of Errors	**170**	92/93	Sweet Duke	**161**
76/77	Night Nurse	**182**	93/94	Sweet Glow	**162**
77/78	Monksfield	**177**	94/95	Dorans Pride	**167**
78/79	Monksfield	**180**	95/96	Pleasure Shared	**163 p**
79/80	Pollardstown	**167**	96/97	Paddy's Return	**164**
80/81	Daring Run	**171 +**	97/98	Paddy's Return	**168**
81/82	Daring Run	**171**	98/99	Deano's Beeno	**165**
82/83	Gaye Brief	**175**		Princeful	**165**
83/84	Dawn Run	**173**	99/00	Limestone Lad	**177**
84/85	Bajan Sunshine	**162**	00/01	Le Sauvignon	**178**
85/86	Gaye Brief	**167**	01/02	Baracouda	**169 +**
86/87	Galmoy	**165**	02/03	Baracouda	**175**
87/88	Galmoy	**160**	03/04	Iris's Gift	**172**
88/89	Rustle	**169**	04/05	Inglis Drever	**162**
89/90	Trapper John	**159**	05/06	Mighty Man	**166**
90/91	King's Curate	**164**	06/07	Mighty Man	**172**
91/92	Nomadic Way	**162**			

Best Novice Hurdler

75/76	Grand Canyon	**159**	91/92	Royal Gait	**164 p**
76/77	Outpoint	**154**	92/93	Montelado	**150 P**
77/78	Golden Cygnet	**176**	93/94	Danoli	**172 p**
78/79	Venture To Cognac	**162**	94/95	Alderbrook	**174 p**
79/80	Slaney Idol	**143**	95/96	Pleasure Shared	**163 p**
80/81	Dunaree	**159**	96/97	Make A Stand	**165**
81/82	Angelo Salvini	**149**	97/98	French Holly	**151 P**
82/83	Dawn Run	**168**	98/99	Barton	**153 p**
83/84	Desert Orchid	**158**	99/00	Monsignor	**158 p**
84/85	Asir	**148 p**	00/01	Baracouda	**172**
85/86	River Ceiriog	**158 p**	01/02	Intersky Falcon	**152 p**
86/87	The West Awake	**153 p**	02/03	Iris's Gift	**172**
87/88	Carvill's Hill	**157 p**	03/04	Inglis Drever	**152**
88/89	Sondrio	**152 p**	04/05	Ambobo	**149 +**
	Wishlon	**152 +**	05/06	Black Jack Ketchum	**159 p**
89/90	Regal Ambition	**151**	06/07	Wichita Lineman	**152 p**
90/91	Ruling	**167**			

Best Juvenile Hurdler

Year	Horse	Rating	Year	Horse	Rating
75/76	Valmony	157	92/93	Shawiya	141 p
76/77	Meladon	149	93/94	Mysilv	144 p
77/78	Major Thompson	144	94/95	Kissair	143 p
78/79	Pollardstown	141	95/96	Escartefigue	159
79/80	Hill of Slane	144	96/97	Grimes	138 p
80/81	Broadsword	144	97/98	Deep Water	149 p
81/82	Shiny Copper	141	98/99	Hors La Loi III	162 p
82/83	Sabin du Loir	147 p	99/00	Grand Seigneur	148 p
83/84	Northern Game	142	00/01	Jair du Cochet	163
84/85	Out of The Gloom	151	01/02	Scolardy	147
85/86	Dark Raven	153 p	02/03	Nickname	142
86/87	Aldino	154	03/04	Maia Eria	143
87/88	Kribensis	143 p	04/05	Faasel	144 p
88/89	Royal Derbi	144		Penzance	144 p
89/90	Sybillin	138	05/06	Detroit City	146 p
90/91	Oh So Risky	149 p	06/07	Katchit	151
91/92	Staunch Friend	151 p			

Best National Hunt Flat Race Performer

Year	Horse	Rating	Year	Horse	Rating
93/94	Aries Girl	123	01/02	Pizarro	123
94/95	Dato Star	120		Rhinestone Cowboy	123
95/96	Wither Or Which	122	02/03	Rhinestone Cowboy	123
96/97	Florida Pearl	124	03/04	Secret Ploy	122
97/98	Alexander Banquet	126	04/05	Karanja	128
98/99	Monsignor	122	05/06	Leading Run	123
99/00	Quadco	129	06/07	Theatrical Moment	124
00/01	The Bajan Bandit	128			

Best Hunter Chaser

Year	Horse	Rating	Year	Horse	Rating
75/76	Otter Way	143	92/93	Double Silk	122 p
76/77	Under Way	124	93/94	Double Silk	130 p
77/78	Spartan Missile	133		Elegant Lord	130 p
78/79	Spartan Missile	133 +	94/95	Fantus	139 p
79/80	Rolls Rambler	132	95/96	Elegant Lord	138 p
80/81	Spartan Missile	169	96/97	Celtic Abbey	136 p
81/82	Compton Lad	142		Fantus	136
82/83	Eliogarty	147	97/98	Earthmover	140 p
83/84	Venture To Cognac	149	98/99	Castle Mane	148 p
84/85	Further Thought	141	99/00	Cavalero	142
85/86	Ah Whisht	148	00/01	Sheltering	136
86/87	Observe	146	01/02	Torduff Express	130
87/88	Certain Light	147	02/03	Kingscliff	137 P
88/89	Call Collect	142 p	03/04	Earthmover	133
89/90	Mystic Music	143	04/05	Sleeping Night	148
90/91	Mystic Music	143 ?	05/06	Katarino	133 +
91/92	Rushing Wild	127 p	06/07	Drombeag	131